THE

UNITED STATES

DICTIONARY

OF PLACES

THE
UNITED STATES
DICTIONARY
OF PLACES

FIRST EDITION

FIRST EDITION

Library of Congress Cataloging-in-Publication Data

The United States dictionary of places.

1. Names, Geographical--United States--Dictionaries.
2. United States--Administrative and political
divisions--Dictionaries. I. Somerset Publishers.
E155.U55 1988   917.3'03'21   87-32065
ISBN 0-403-09899-8

Copyright 1988 ©

SOMERSET PUBLISHERS, INC.
200 Park Ave. 303E.
New York, N.Y. 10017 U.S.A.

FOREWORD

In these days of accelerated personal mobility, populated places have taken on ever-increasing interest. Long existent national atlases provide basic locator and statistical data but lack human insights that have given these places their living qualities.

U.S. Dictionary of Places is an attempt to extend knowledge on as many populated places in the nation as is possible within the practical resource limits of a first-work. Along with statistical data allowing **USDP** to serve as a single-source reference, we believe it provides for the first time a "national place-name directory."

There are a number of sectional (usually state) geographical name directories on many areas, most of which are out of print. Very few libraries, including large university research libraries, have more than a few of these.

On the subject of place-name origins the following observations should be of interest:

> Robert Louis Stevenson is quoted as saying "There is no part of the world where nomenclature is so rich, poetical, humorous and picturesque as in the United States of America."

> H.L. Mencken says "No other country can match our geographical names for interest and variety."

The problem faced in the study of place-name origins has been cited by the Canadian geologist/author M. Ganong. "To find an origin for a place-name is usually easy, but to find the true origin is often difficult and sometimes impossible."

For the first edition of **U.S. Dictionary of Places** our editors have relied mainly on secondary sources for information although direct contact with knowledgeable agencies has supplemented this effort.

It is anticipated that in succeeding editions further efforts will be made with contemporaries for further verification and insights into existing material and as an aid to filling in data for entries that are incomplete.

Latest data sources were used in gathering mailing codes, geographical coordinates and elevations. Population figures are those supplied by the U.S. Census Bureau from the 1980 tabulation. Where figures are missing in any of these categories it is because the information was unavailable from the sources cited.

We have purposely not included telephone area codes because of the fluidity of this data. Also most users will have easy access to current data of this type.

U.S. Dictionary of Places has been limited mainly to <u>incorporated</u> places as indicated in U.S. Census Department data files. Some non-incorporated populated places are included when they already existed in our private files (used in publishing various of our other reference works; i.e., U.S. State Encyclopedia Series).

Inevitably there will be errors in a first-effort publication this complex although every effort has been made to avoid them. We welcome and encourage users of this publication to call errors to our attention and to make whatever suggestions they believe will be useful for later editions.

CONTENTS

•KEY TO ABBREVIATIONS/SYMBOLS
Pop. - Population based on 1980 U. S. Census Bureau reports or estimates from primary source.
CDP - Census Designated Place.
Elev. - Elevation in feet.
Lat. - Latitude   **Long.** - Longitude

•LOCATION NOTE
To find location of place in state draw two lines using Lat. figure on vertical side of map (in map section) and Long. figure along horizontal side. The point where lines intersect identifies the location.

•ZIP CODES
Larger cities have multiple zip code assignments. In these cases we list only the numbers that are common to the entire city, followed by + + symbols. (i.e. ALLENTOWN; Zip Code 181 + +;).

TABLE OF CONTENTS

ALABAMA

•**ABBEVILLE,** City; Henry County Seat; Pop. 3,155; Zip Code 36310; Lat. 31-33-28 N long. 085-14-56 W; Settled in the 1830's and named after the nearby Abbey Creek.

•**ADAMSVILLE,** City; Jefferson County; Pop. 2,498; Zip Code 35005; Lat. 33-35-55 N long. 086-57-07 W; Named after William B. Adams, a local citizen whose house became the railroad depot.

•**ADDISON,** Town; Winston County; Pop. 746; Zip Code 35540; Lat. 34-12-18 N long. 087-10-45 W; Originally Cobb's Store, the name was changed in honor of a local settler.

•**AKRON,** Town; Hale County; Pop. 604; Zip Code 35441; Elev. 130; Lat. 32-52-32 N long. 087-44-12 W; Founded in the 1880's and named for Akron, Ohio.

•**ALABASTER,** City; Shelby County; Pop. 7,079; Zip Code 35007; Lat. 33-12-04 N long. 086-47-16 W; Incorporated in the 1950's and named for calcite deposits (i.e. alabaster) found locally.

•**ALBERTVILLE,** City; Marshall County; Pop. 12,039; Zip Code 35950; Elev. 1063; Lat. 34-15-44 N long. 086-12-17 W; Settled in the 1850's and named for early settler Thomas Albert.

•**ALEXANDER CITY,** City; Pickens County; Pop. 3,207; Zip Code 35010; Elev. 707; Lat. 32-59-24 N long. 085-51-54 W; Founded in the early 1870's and named in honor of General Edward P. Alexander, President of the Savannah and Memphis Railroad.

•**ALEXANDER CITY,** City; Tallapoosa County; Pop. 13,807; Zip Code 35010; Lat. 32-59-24 N long. 085-51-54 W; Named in honor of General Edward P. Alexander, railroad president and one-time Confederate General.

•**ALLGOOD,** Town; Blount County; Pop. 387; Zip Code 35013; Elev. 788; Lat. 33-54-31 N long. 086-30-38 W; Settled in the early 1800's and named after postmaster, Dr. William B. Allgood.

•**ANDALUSIA,** City; Covington County Seat; Pop. 10,415; Zip Code 36420; Elev. 303; Lat. 31-17-00 N long. 086-27-06 W; Founded during the 1840's and named for a province in Spain.

•**ANDERSON,** Town; Lauderdale County; Pop. 405; Zip Code 35610; Lat. 34-50-06 N long. 087-16-01 W; The town is named for Anderson Creek, itself named for an early settler.

•**ANNISTON,** City; Calhoun County Seat; Pop. 29,523; Zip Code 36201; Elev. 710; Lat. 33-40-07 N long. 085-50-16 W; Alfred Tyler founded the Woodstock Iron Company here in the 1870's. The town is named for his wife Annie Scott Tyler.

•**ARAB,** City; Marshall County; Pop. 5,967; Zip Code 35016; Lat. 34-19-19 N long. 086-30-03 W; Founded around 1900 as Arad in honor of Postmaster Arad Thompson. Postal officials, however, confused the "D" for a "B", resulting in the town named of "Arab."

•**ARDMORE,** Town; Loimestone County; Pop. 1,096; Zip Code 35739; Established in 1913 and named Ardmore for uncertain reasons.

•**ARITON,** Town; Dale County; Pop. 844; Zip Code 36311; Lat. 31-35-52 N long. 085-43-14 W; In 1903 the towns of "Ariosto" and "Charleston" combined and took the name Ariton, a combination of the two previous names.

•**ARLEY,** Town; Winston County; Pop. 276; Zip Code 35541; Elev. 787; Lat. 34-04-44 N long. 087-12-55 W; Incorporated in 1898 and named for Robert Arley Gibson, the dead child of a popular minister.

•**ASHFORD,** Town; Houston County; Pop. 2,165; Zip Code 36312; Elev. 241; Lat. 31-10-53 N long. 085-15-28 W; Thomas Ashford was an early settler, the town is named after him.

•**ASHLAND,** Town; Clay County Seat; Pop. 2,052; Zip Code 36251; Elev. 1130; Lat. 33-16-05 N long. 085-49-54 W; The town is named after the famous Kentucky home of Henry Clay.

•**ASHVILLE,** Town; St. Clair County; Pop. 1,489; Zip Code 35953; Elev. 570; Lat. 33-42-54 N long. 086-23-49 W; Settled in 1818 and named for pioneer John Ashe.

•**ATHENS,** City; Limestone County Seat; Pop. 14,558; Zip Code 35611; Elev. 720; Lat. 34-48-20 N long. 086-58-22 W; Incorporated in 1819 and named for the famous Greek City.

•**ATMORE,** City; Escambia County; Pop. 8,789; Zip Code 36502; Elev. 205; Lat. 31-01-25 N long. 087-29-37 W; Founded in 1870 and named after Charles Atmore, an official of the L&N Railroad.

•**ATTALLA,** City; Etowah County; Pop. 7,737; Zip Code 35954; Elev. 550; Lat. 34-00-32 N long. 086-03-56 W; The town's name is a Cherokee Indian word meaning "mountain."

•**AUBURN,** City; Lee County; Pop. 28,471; Zip Code 36830; Elev. 709; Lat. 32-36-28 N long. 085-27-01 W; Settled in the 1830's and named after place found in the poetry of Oliver Goldsmith.

•**AUTAUGAVILLE,** Town; Autauga County; Pop. 843; Zip Code 36003; Lat. 32-25-59 N long. 086-39-17 W; The city is named after the Alibamo Indian village of "Atagi," a Creek word meaning "Border."

•**BAILEYTON,** Town; Cullman County; Pop. 396; Zip Code 35019; Elev. 973; Lat. 34-15-44 N long. 086-36-44 W; Established in 1870 and named in honor of an early settler, Robert Bailey.

•**BANKS,** Town; Pike County; Pop. 160; Zip Code 36005; Elev. 553; Lat. 31-48-57 N long. 085-50-34 W; Founded in 1890 and named for the local Banks family.

•**BAY MINETTE,** City; Baldwin County Seat; Pop. 7,455; Zip Code 36507; Lat. 30-53-38 N long. 087-46-38 W; The city is named after nearby Minette Bay, itself named for an early French explorer.

•**BAYOU LA BATRE,** City; Mobile County; Pop. 2,005; Zip Code 36509; Elev. 7; Lat. 30-24-36 N long. 088-16-34 W; Once the site of a French artillery battery, its name remembers that history.

•**BEAR CREEK,** Town; Marion County; Pop. 353; Zip Code 35543; Elev. 804; Lat. 34-16-36 N long. 087-42-14 W; Descriptively named for its location at the headwater of Big Bear Creek.

•**BEATRICE,** Town; Monroe County; Pop. 558; Zip Code 36425; Elev. 273; Lat. 31-44-46 N long. 087-12-44 W; Founded in 1900 and named for the daughter of a local railroad official.

•**BEAVERTON,** Town; Lamar County; Pop. 360; Zip Code 35544; Lat. 33-56-02 N long. 088-01-13 W; Descriptively named for its location on Beaver Creek.

•**BELK,** Town; Fayette County; Pop. 308; Zip Code 35545; Lat. 33-38-45 N long. 087-55-54 W; Originally "Mulberry Tank Junction," the town was renamed for a local family.

•**BERRY,** Town; Fayette County; Pop. 916; Zip Code 35546; Elev. 451; Lat. 33-39-36 N long. 087-36-03 W; Founded in 1883 and named in honor if its first settler, Thompson Berry.

ALABAMA

•**BESSEMER**, City; Jefferson County; Pop. 31,729; Zip Code 35020; Elev. 513; Lat. 33-24-40 N long. 086-53-52 W; Established in 1887 and named in honor of Sir Henry Bessemer, who invented the Bessemer process for producing steel.

•**BILLINGSLEY**, Town; Autauga County; Pop. 106; Zip Code 36006; Elev. 368; Lat. 32-39-27 N long. 086-43-02 W; Incorporated in 1901 and named local Revolutionary War Hero Clement Billingsley.

•**BIRMINGHAM**, City; Jefferson County; Pop. 284,413 , Zip Code 35200; Elev. 601; Lat. 33-31-33 N long. 086-48-30 W; Incorporated in 1871 and named after Birmingham, England.

•**BLACK**, Town; Geneva County; Pop. 156; Zip Code 36314; Elev. 220; Lat. 31-00-37 N long. 085-44-07 W; Settled in the late 1800's and named for the Black family.

•**BLOUNTSVILLE**, Town; Blount County; Pop. 1,509; Zip Code 35031; Elev. 714; Lat. 34-04-43 N long. 086-35-28 W; Founded in 1816 and named after Governor Willie Blount of Tennessee.

•**BLUE MOUNTAIN**, Town; Calhoun County; Pop. 284; Zip Code ; Settled in the 1830's and descriptively named for a nearby mountain.

•**BLUE SPRINGS**, Town; Barbour County; Pop. 112; Zip Code ; Established in the 1890's and named for a local mineral springs.

•**BOAZ**, City; Etowah & Marshall Counties; Pop. 7,151; Zip Code 35957; Elev. 1080; Lat. 34-10-16 N long. 086-09-19 W; Begun in the 1880's and given the name of a Biblical character.

•**BOLIGEE**, Town; Greene County; Pop. 164; Zip Code 35443; Elev. 124; Lat. 32-45-13 N long. 088-01-14 W; Boligee is a corruption of Choctow Indian word meaning "splashing water."

•**BON AIB**, Town; Dalladega County; Pop. 118; Zip Code 35032; Lat. 33-15-39 N long. 086-20-00 W; The origin of the town's name is uncertain.

•**BRANCHVILLE**, Town; St. Clair County; Pop. 365; Settled in 1819 and named for its location near a small "branch" stream.

•**BRANTLEY**, Town; Crenshaw County; Pop. 1,151; Zip Code 36009; Elev. 295; Lat. 30-38-49 N long. 088-09-08 W; Incorporated in 1895 and named for town promoter Thomas K. Brantley.

•**BRENT**, City; Bibb County; Pop. 2,862; Zip Code 35034; Elev. 240; Lat. 32-56-09 N long. 087-10-27 W; Founded in 1898 and named after surveyor Bent Armstrong.

•**BREWTON**, City; Escambia County Seat; Pop. 6,680; Zip Code 36426; Elev. 82; Lat. 31-05-23 N long. 087-03-59 W; Established before the Civil War and named for pioneer Edmund Brewton.

•**BRIDGEPORT**, City; Jackson County; Pop. 2,974; Zip Code 35740; Lat. 34-58-40 N long. 085-45-46 W; Settled in the 1830's and named in honor of town developer John Bridges.

•**BRIGHTON**, City; Jefferson County; Pop. 5,308; Zip Code ; Incorporated in 1901 and named after the English seaport town.

•**BRILLIANT**, Town; Marion County; Pop. 871; Zip Code 35548; Elev. 628; Lat. 34-01-24 N long. 087-45-50 W; Founded in 1898 and named after the Brilliant Coal Company.

•**BROOKSIDE**, Town; Jefferson County; Pop. 1,409; Zip Code 35036; Elev. 364; Lat. 33-38-15 N long. 086-55-03 W; Descriptively named for its location near a brook.

•**BROOKWOOD**, Town; Tuscaloosa County; Pop. 492; Zip Code 35444; Lat. 33-16-42 N long. 087-17-24 W; Originally "Horsehead," the name was changed to the descriptive Brookwood in 1890.

•**BRUNDIDGE**, City; Pike County; Pop. 3,213; Zip Code 36010; Lat. 31-43-16 N long. 085-48-58 W; Originally Collier, the name was later changed for a local settler.

•**BUTLER**, City; Choctaw County Seat; Pop. 1,882; Zip Code 36904; Elev. 172; Lat. 32-16-00 N long. 088-12-56 W; Founded in the 1840's and named for Mexican War hero Colonel Pierce Butler.

•**BYNUM**, (CDP); Calhoun County; Pop. 2,235; Zip Code 36253; Lat. 33-37-21 N long. 085-57-54 W; Bynum is named after an early local family.

•**CALERA**, Town; Shelby County; Pop. 2,035; Zip Code 35040; Elev. 497; Lat. 33-05-52 N long. 086-45-16 W; The site of a lime works, the town was given the Spanish named "Calera," or lime.

•**CAMDEN**, Town; Wilcox County Seat; Pop. 2,406; Zip Code 36726; Elev. 207; Lat. 31-59-42 N long. 087-18-03 W; Settled as Barboursville in the early 1830's, the name was changed after Camden, South Carolina.

•**CAMP HILL**, Town; Tallapoosa County; Pop. 1,628; Zip Code 36850; Elev. 684; Lat. 32-47-42 N long. 085-38-45 W; Descriptive name for a pioneer campsite.

•**CARBON HILL**, City; Walker County; Pop. 2,452; Zip Code 35549; Lat. 33-53-47 N long. 087-31-26 W; Founded as a coal mining town in the 1880's and named for that activity.

•**CARDIFF**, Town; Jefferson County; Pop. 140; Zip Code 35041; Elev. 357; Lat. 33-38-45 N long. 086-56-00 W; Named for Cardiff, Wales by 19th century coal miners.

•**CARROLLTON**, Town; Pickens County Seat; Pop. 1,104; Zip Code 35447; Lat. 33-15-37 N long. 088-05-49 W; Founded in the 1830's and named after Declaration of Independence signer Charles Carroll.

•**CARRVILLE**, Town; Tallapoosa County; Pop. 820; Zip Code ; Established in the 1890's and named after the first postmaster Jesse Carr.

•**CASTLEBERRY**, Town; Conecuh County; Pop. 847; Zip Code 36432; Elev. 164; Lat. 31-17-50 N long. 087-00-17 W; Settled in the 1830's and named after a local pioneer family whose home became a stage stop.

•**CEDAR BLUFF**, Town; Cherokee County; Pop. 1,129; Zip Code 35959; Elev. 602; Lat. 34-13-18 N long. 085-36-17 W; Descriptively named by its settlers in the early 1800's.

•**CENTRE**, City; Cherokee County Seat; Pop. 2,351; Zip Code 35042; Elev. 224; Lat. 32-56-31 N long. 087-07-57 W; The city is descriptively named after its location.

•**CENTREVILLE**, City; Bibb County Seat; Pop. 2,504; Zip Code 35042; Elev. 224; Lat. 32-56-31 N long. 087-07-57 W; The city is named for its location.

•**CHATOM**, Town; Washington County Seat; Pop. 1,122; Zip Code 36518; Lat. 31-28-05 N long. 088-15-47 W; Named after the ancestral home of President George Washington.

•**CHEROKEE**, Town; Colbert County; Pop. 1,589; Zip Code 35616; Lat. 34-45-36 N long. 087-58-21 W; The town is named for the Indians which once lived in the region.

•CHICKASAW, City; Mobile County; Pop. 7,402; The city is named after the Chickasaw Indians who once lived in the region.

•CHILDERSBURG, City; Talladega County; Pop. 5,084; Zip Code 35044; Elev. 419; Lat. 33-16-29 N long. 086-21-16 W; Settled in the 1850's and named for a pioneer, John Childers.

•CITRONELLE, City; Mobile County; Pop. 2,841; Zip Code 36522; Lat. 31-07-07 N long. 088-14-20 W; The city is named after a local type of grass.

•CLANTON, City; Chilton County Seat; Pop. 5,832; Zip Code 35045; Elev. 599; Lat. 32-50-45 N long. 086-38-17 W; The city is named in honor of Confederate General James H. Clanton.

•CLAYHATCHEE, Town; Dale County; Pop. 560; The town is descriptively named for its location near both Clay Bank Creek and the Choctawnotchee River.

•CLAYTON, Town; Barbour County Seat; Pop. 1,589; Zip Code 36016; Lat. 31-52-27 N long. 085-27-09 W; Begun in 1827 and named in honor of Judge Augustine Clayton.

•CLEVELAND, Town; Blount County; Pop. 487; Zip Code 35049; Elev. 535; Lat. 33-59-24 N long. 086-34-39 W; Named in honor of President Grover Cleveland.

•CLIO, Town; Barbour County; Pop. 1,224; Zip Code 36017; Elev. 611; Lat. 31-41-03 N long. 085-33-34 W; Clio was incorporated in 1892 and named after Clio, South Carolina.

•COFFEE SPRINGS, Town; Geneva County; Pop. 339; Zip Code 36318; Lat. 31-10-04 N long. 085-54-40 W; The town is named for nearby Coffee Creek.

•COFFEEVILLE, Town; Clarke County; Pop. 448; Zip Code 36524; Lat. 31-45-34 N long. 088-04-51 W; The town's name honors Indian fighter General John Coffee.

•COLLINSVILLE, Town; Cherokee & De Kalb Counties; Pop. 1,383; Zip Code 35961; Elev. 718; Lat. 34-14-26 N long. 085-50-41 W; The town is named for pioneer landowner Alfred Collins.

•COLUMBIA, Town; Houston County; Pop. 881; Zip Code 36319; Elev. 211; Lat. 31-21-14 N long. 085-08-32 W; Columbia was settled in the 1820's and named for Christopher Columbus.

•COLUMBIANA, City; Shelby County Seat; Pop. 2,655; Zip Code 35051; Elev. 524; Lat. 33-11-16 N long. 086-36-47 W; Established in the early 1820's and named for Christopher Gaustchi.

•COOSADA, Town; Elmore County; Pop. 980; Zip Code 36020; Lat. 32-29-54 N long. 086-19-50 W; Founded in 1818 and given an Indian village name, Koassati.

•COURTLAND, Town; Lawrence County; Pop. 456; Zip Code 35618; Elev. 564; Lat. 34-40-01 N long. 087-18-35 W; Incorporated in 1819 and named after the Federal Court.

•COWARTS, Town; Houston County; Pop. 418; Zip Code 36321; Elev. 327; Lat. 21-11-58 N long. 085-18-16 W; The town is named for a local family.

•CREOLA, Town; Mobile County; Pop. 1,652; Zip Code 36525; Lat. 30-53-40 N long. 088-02-54 W; Creola is named after pioneer Creole settlers.

•CROSSVILLE, Town; De Kalb County; Pop. 1,222; Zip Code 35962; Elev. 480; Lat. 34-17-18 N long. 085-59-22 W; Descriptively named for its location at two highway crossings.

•CUBA, Town; Sumter County; Pop. 486; Zip Code 36907; Elev. 234; Lat. 32-25-29 N long. 088-24-02 W; The town is named after the country Cuba.

•CULLMAN, City; Cullman County Seat; Pop. 13,084; Zip Code 35055; Elev. 799; Lat. 34-10-56 N long. 086-47-55 W; Incorporated in the 1870's and named in honor of Colonel Johann Cullman.

•DADEVILLE, City; Tallapoosa County Seat; Pop. 3,263; Zip Code 36853; Elev. 717; Lat. 32-49-41 N long. 085-45-11 W; Founded in the 1830's and named for Indian fighter Major Francis L. Dade.

•DALEVILLE, City; Dale County; Pop. 4,250; Zip Code 36322; Lat. 31-18-33 N long. 085-42-48 W; The city's name honors Creek Indian fighter Samuel Dale.

•DAPHNE, City; Baldwin County; Pop. 3,406; Zip Code 36526; Elev. 157; Lat. 30-35-57 N long. 087-54-04 W; A type of laurel shrub named Daphne grew in the area and gave the town its name.

•DAVISTON, Town; Tallapoosa County; Pop. 334; Zip Code 36256; Elev. 767; Lat. 33-01-30 N long. 085-37-48 W; Daviston is named for its first postmaster John O. Davis.

•DAYTON, Town; Marengo County; Pop. 113; Zip Code 36731; Elev. 249; Lat. 32-21-02 N long. 087-38-30 W; Settled in the 1820's and named for Dayton, Ohio.

•DECATUR, City; Morgan County Seat; Pop. 42,002, Zip Code 35601; Elev. 590; Lat. 34-33-15 N long. 086-58-52 W; Incorporated in 1826 and named for naval hero Stephen Decatur.

•DEMOPOLIS, City; Marengo County; Pop. 7,678; Zip Code 36732; Elev. 125; Lat. 32-30-41 N long. 087-50-58 W; Demopolis incorporated in 1821 and took a Greek name meaning "city of the people."

•DETROIT, Town; Lamar County; Pop. 326; Zip Code 35552; Lat. 34-01-39 N long. 088-10-13 W; The town is named after Detroit, Michigan.

•DORA, Town; Walker County; Pop. 2,327; Zip Code 35062; Elev. 387; Lat. 33-44-10 N long. 087-07-22 W; Founded in the 1880's and named after a local mineowner's wife.

•DOTHAN, City; Dale & Houston Counties; Houston County Seat; Pop. 48,750; Zip Code 36301; Elev. 326; Lat. 31-14-43 N long. 085-25-32 W; Named by its settlers after the Biblical city of Dothan.

•DOUBLE SPRINGS, Town; Winston County Seat; Pop. 1,057; Zip Code 35553; Lat. 34-08-45 N long. 087-24-08 W; Incorporated in 1943 and descriptively named for a local spring.

•DOUGLAS, Town; Marshall County; Pop. 116; Zip Code 35964; Elev. 940; Lat. 34-10-27 N long. 086-19-19 W; Pioneer Stephen Douglas donated land for the first school. The town is named in his honor.

•DOZIER, Town; Crenshaw County; Pop. 494; Zip Code 36028; Lat. 31-29-42 N long. 086-21-59 W; Settled in the 19th century and named for pioneer Daniel Dozier.

•DUTTON, Town; Jackson County; Pop. 276; Zip Code 35744; Lat. 34-36-24 N long. 085-54-48 W; M. M. Dutton was the first postmaster. The town is named for him.

•EAST BREWTON, City; Escambia County; Pop. 3,012; Descriptively named for its position near Brewton.

•ECLECTIC, Town; Elmore County; Pop. 1,124; Zip Code 36024; Elev. 577; Lat. 32-27-23 N long. 086-02-05 W; An adjective meaning "varied" given the town by its pioneers.

•EDWARDSVILLE, Town; Cleburne County; Pop. 207; Zip Code 36261; Elev. 193; Lat. 33-42-33 N long. 085-30-36 W; Settled in the 1830's and named for William Edwards, who donated land to the county.

•ELBA, City; Coffee County Seat; Pop. 4,355; Zip Code 36323; Lat. 31-25-00 N long. 086-04-18 W; Established in 1852 and named after the island on which Napoleon was exiled.

•ELBERTA, Town; Baldwin County; Pop. 491; Zip Code 36530; Lat. 30-24-52 N long. 087-35-48 W; Founded in 1903 and named for a nearby orchard of Elberta peaches.

•ELDRIDGE, Town; Walker County; Pop. 230; Zip Code 35554; Lat. 33-55-23 N long. 087-36-52 W; First settled in 1819 and named after innkeeper and State Representative Eldridge Mallard.

•ELKMONT, Town; Limestone County; Pop. 429; Zip Code 35620; Lat. 34-55-39 N long. 086-58-40 W; Settled in 1858 and named for the nearby Elk River.

•ENTERPRISE, City; Coffee & Dale Counties; Pop. 18,033; Zip Code 36330; Elev. 671; Lat. 31-18-34 N long. 085-48-34 W; Founded in 1881 and later named "Enterprise" by the town's hopeful residents.

•EPES, Town; Sumter County; Pop. 399; Zip Code 35460; Elev. 159; Lat. 32-41-38 N long. 088-07-27 W; Established in 1870 and named for Dr. John Epes who donated land to the railway.

•ETHELSVILLE, Town; Pickens County; Pop. 95; Zip Code 35461; Elev. 345; Lat. 33-24-38 N long. 088-13-03 W; The town is named for Ethel Hancock, a local resident.

•EUFAULA, City; Barbour County; Pop. 12,097; Zip Code 36027; Elev. 257; Lat. 31-52-46 N long. 085-09-03 W; Eufaula is the corruption of a Creek Indian town name, Yufala.

•EUTAW, City; Greene County Seat; Pop. 2,444; Zip Code 35462; Elev. 220; Lat. 32-50-16 N long. 087-52-51 W; Settled in 1820 and later named after General Nathaiel Green's Revolutionary War victory at Eutaw Springs, South Carolina.

•EVA, Town; Morgan County; Pop. 185; Zip Code 35621; Lat. 34-19-59 N long. 086-45-36 W; Eva is named for the wife of first postmaster Andrew J. Rooks.

•EVERGREEN, City; Conecuh County Seat; Pop. 4,171; Zip Code 36401; Elev. 367; Lat. 31-25-53 N long. 086-55-34 W; Settled in 1820 and named for the many evergreens in the area.

•EXCEL, Town; Monroe County; Pop. 385; Zip Code 36439; Elev. 409; Lat. 31-25-39 N long. 087-20-37 W; Established in 1884 and named by its incorporators for a hoped standard of excellence.

•FAIRFIELD, City; Jefferson County; Pop. 13,040; Zip Code 35064; Elev. 190; Lat. 33-27-44 N long. 086-56-04 W; Founded in 1910 and named after Fairfield, Connecticut.

•FAIRHOPE, City; Baldwin County; Pop. 7,286; Zip Code 36532; Elev. 122; Lat. 30-31-22 N long. 087-54-10 W; Begun in 1894 as an economic experiment, the town's name reflected its settler's hope.

•FAIRVIEW, Town; Cullman County; Pop. 450; Zip Code ; Fairview is descriptively named for its elevated views.

•FALKVILLE, Town; Morgan County; Pop. 1,310; Zip Code 35622; Elev. 611; Lat. 34-22-18 N long. 086-54-05 W; Incorporated in 1876 and named in honor of first postmaster Louis Falk.

•FAUNSDALE, Town; Marengo County; Pop. 174; Zip Code 36738; Elev. 208; Lat. 32-27-39 N long. 087-35-36 W; Founded as St. Michael's Parish, but later renamed after a local plantation.

•FAYETTE, City; Fayette County Seat; Pop. 5,287; Zip Code 35555; Elev. 360; Lat. 33-41-12 N long. 087-49-50 W; The city's name honors French-American Revolutionary War hero, the Marquis De LaFayette.

•FIVE POINTS, Town; Chambers County; Pop. 197; Zip Code 36855; Elev. 870; Lat. 33-01-04 N long. 085-20-43 W; Descriptively named for the intersection of five roads.

•FLOMATON, Town; Escambia County; Pop. 1,882; Zip Code 36441; Lat. 31-00-00 N long. 087-15-29 W; Originally Whiting, the present name is derivative of the Florida.

•FLORALA, City; Covington County; Pop. 2,165; Zip Code 36442; Lat. 31-00-21 N long. 086-19-26 W; Settled in 1875 and named by combining parts of the words Florida and Alabama.

•FLORENCE, City; Lauderdale County Seat; Pop. 37,029; Zip Code 35630; Elev. 541; Lat. 34-49-01 N long. 087-40-07 W; First established in 1818 and named for Florence, Italy.

•FOLEY, City; Baldwin County; Pop. 4,003; Zip Code 36535; Elev. 74; Lat. 30-24-18 N long. 087-40-56 W; Incorporated in 1915 and named for land company president John B. Foley.

•FORKLAND, Town; Greene County; Pop. 429; Zip Code 36740; Elev. 152; Lat. 32-38-55 N long. 087-52-58 W; So named for its location on the "fork" of the Tombigbee and Black Warrior Rivers.

•FORT DEPOSIT, Town; Lowndes County; Pop. 1,519; Zip Code 36032; Lat. 51-59-11 N long. 086-34-51 W; Founded in 1813 during the Indian Wars, and named as a "deposit" point for supplies.

•FORT MCCLELLAN, (CDP); Calhoun County; Pop. 7,605; Zip Code 36205; An early military post named for an army commander.

•FORT PAYNE, City; De Kalb County Seat; Pop. 11,485; Zip Code 35967; Elev. 899; Lat. 34-26-46 N long. 085-42-53 W; The city's name remembers an 1830's army commander who helped remove the Indians from the area.

•FORT RUCKER, (CDP); Dale County; Pop. 8,932; Zip Code 36362; Originally a military base named for a local commander.

•FRANKLIN, Town; Macon County; Pop. 133; Zip Code 36444; Elev. 220; Lat. 31-43-09 N long. 087-24-42 W; Settled in the early 1800's and named for Benjamin Franklin.

•FRISCO CITY, Town; Monroe County; Pop. 1,424; Zip Code 36445; Elev. 401; Lat. 31-26-11 N long. 087-24-19 W; Founded in 1888 and named after the Frisco Railroad.

•FRUITHURST, City; Cleburne County; Pop. 239; Zip Code 36262; Lat. 33-43-51 N long. 085-26-01 W; Founded by Alabama Fruit and Wine Grower Association and named after those local activities.

•FULTON, Town; Clarke County; Pop. 606; Zip Code 36446; Elev. 234; Lat. 31-47-14 N long. 087-43-27 W; Settled in the 1880's and named after the city of New York.

•FULTONDALE, City; Jefferson County; Pop. 6,217; Zip Code 35068; Lat. 33-36-31 N long. 086-48-29 W; Fulton Springs and Glendale were districts of the town, the town's name was created by combining them.

•FYFFE, Town; De Kalb County; Pop. 1,305; Zip Code 35971; Lat. 34-26-50 N long. 085-54-29 W; Incorporated in 1958 and named after a musical instrument.

•**GADSDEN,** City; Etowah County Seat; Pop. 47,565; Zip Code 35901; Elev. 554; Lat. 33-57-11 N long. 086-01-13 W; Founded as "Double Springs," but renamed to honor South Carolina Revolutionary War General, Christopher Gadsden.

•**GAINESVILLE,** Town; Sumter County; Pop. 207; Zip Code 35464; Elev. 131; Lat. 32-49-06 N long. 088-11-31 W; Established in 1832 and named after Indian agent George Gains.

•**GANTT,** Town; Covington County; Pop. 314; Zip Code 36038; Elev. 230; Lat. 32-29-31 N long. 087-42-40 W; Settled in 1879 and named for early postmaster I. F. Gantt.

•**GARDEN CITY,** Town; Cullman County; Pop. 655; Zip Code 35070; Elev. 496; Lat. 34-00-44 N long. 086-44-47 W; Founded in 1876 and named for the many gardens in the area.

•**GARDENDALE,** City; Jefferson County; Pop. 7,928; Zip Code 35071; Elev. 663; Lat. 33-39-18 N long. 086-48-32 W; Descriptively named by its settlers as a "garden spot."

•**GAYLESVILLE,** Town; Cherokee County; Pop. 192; Zip Code 35973; Elev. 586; Lat. 34-15-51 N long. 085-33-30 W; John Gayle was the sixth governor of Alabama. The town is named for him.

•**GENEVA,** City; Geneva County Seat; Pop. 4,866; Zip Code 36340; Elev. 105; Lat. 31-02-15 N long. 085-51-01 W; Incorporated in 1872 and named for Geneva, Switzerland.

•**GEORGIANA,** Town; Butler County; Pop. 1,993; Zip Code 36033; Elev. 293; Lat. 31-38-03 N long. 086-44-25 W; Settled in th 1820's and named for the daughter of the town's founder.

•**GERALDINE,** Town; De Kalb County; Pop. 911; Zip Code 35974; Elev. 1148; Lat. 34-20-59 N long. 086-00-03 W; The town is named after the wife of a settler.

•**GILBERTOWN,** Town; Choctaw County; Pop. 218; Zip Code 36908; Lat. 31-52-36 N long. 088-19-40 W; Named for a local citizen.

•**GLEN ALLEN,** Town; Fayette & Marion Counties; Pop. 312; Zip Code 35559; Lat. 33-53-47 N long. 087-44-35 W; Founded in 1889 and named by combining the last names of two railroad engineers.

•**GLENCOE,** City; Calhoun & Etowah Counties; Pop. 4,648; Zip Code 35905; Incorporated in 1939 and named for the city of Scotland.

•**GLENWOOD,** Town; Crenshaw County; Pop. 341; Zip Code 36034; Elev. 285; Lat. 31-40-03 N long. 086-10-14 W; Glenn was an early railroad engineer, the "wood" part of the name is descriptive.

•**GORDO,** Town; Pickens County; Pop. 2,112; Zip Code 35466; Elev. 274; Lat. 33-19-30 N long. 087-54-15 W; First settled in the 1850's and named for the American victory at Cerro Gordo during the Mexican-American War.

•**GORDON,** Town; Houston County; Pop. 362; Zip Code 36343; Elev. 166; Lat. 31-08-53 N long. 085-06-15 W; Settled in the 1830's and later named for Judge Dan Gordon.

•**GOSHEN,** Town; Pike County; Pop. 365; Zip Code 36035; Elev. 317; Lat. 31-43-22 N long. 086-07-16 W; Established prior to 1820 and given a Biblical name.

•**GRANT,** Town; Marshall County; Pop. 632; Zip Code 35747; Lat. 34-31-29 N long. 086-15-14 W; The town's name honors President Ulysses S. Grant.

•**GRAYSVILLE,** City; Jefferson County; Pop. 2,642; Zip Code 35073; Lat. 33-36-27 N long. 086-57-30 W; Founded as "Gintown," but renamed in 1896 for a local family.

•**GREENSBORO,** City; Hale County Seat; Pop. 3,248; Zip Code 36744; Elev. 290; Lat. 32-42-21 N long. 087-35-33 W; First settled in 1816 and named for Revolutionary hero Nathaniel Greene.

•**GREENVILLE,** City; Butler County Seat; Pop. 7,807; Zip Code 36037; Elev. 422; Lat. 31-49-34 N long. 086-37-38 W; Greenville began in 1819 as "Buttsville," but in 1871 the name was changed for Greenville, South Carolina.

•**GROVE HILL,** Town; Clarke County Seat; Pop. 1,912; Zip Code 36451; Lat. 31-42-02 N long. 087-46-15 W; Descriptively named for a local grove of trees on a hill.

•**GUIN,** Town; Marion County; Pop. 266; Zip Code 35563; Lat. 33-57-25 N long. 087-53-00 W; The town is named after pioneer settler J. M. Guin.

•**GULF SHORES,** Town; Baldwin County; Pop. 1,349; Zip Code 36542; Lat. 30-15-50 N long. 087-41-07 W; Located on the Gulf of Mexico and, hence, descriptively named.

•**GUNTERSVILLE,** City; Marshall County Seat; Pop. 7,041; Zip Code 35976; Elev. 800; Lat. 34-20-39 N long. 086-18-40 W; John Gunter arrived here in 1785, the town was later named in his memory.

•**GURLEY,** Town; Madison County; Pop. 735; Zip Code 35748; Elev. 644; Lat. 34-02-01 N long. 086-22-13 W; Settled in the 1830's and named for pioneer John Gurley.

•**HACKLEBURG,** Town; Marion County; Pop. 883; Zip Code 35564; Elev. 934; Lat. 34-16-26 N long. 087-50-12 W; Incorporated in 1909 and named for the many thorny vines in the area known as "hackles."

•**HALEYVILLE,** City; Winston County; Pop. 5,306; Zip Code 35565; Elev. 931; Lat. 34-13-44 N long. 087-37-15 W; Incorporated in 1889 and named after the first postmaster C. L. Haley.

•**HAMILTON,** City; Marion County Seat; Pop. 5,093; Zip Code 35570; Elev. 498; Lat. 34-08-15 N long. 087-59-11 W; Settled in 1818 and later named for Captain Albert Hamilton who donated land to the county in 1882.

•**HANCEVILLE,** City; Cullman County; Pop. 2,220; Zip Code 35077; Elev. 544; Lat. 34-03-41 N long. 086-45-35 W; First settled in 1855 and later named for Irish settler Hance Kinney.

•**HARPERSVILLE,** Town; Shelby County; Pop. 934; Zip Code 35078; Lat. 33-21-14 N long. 086-26-38 W; William Harper arrived here in the 1830's, the town is named for him.

•**HARTFORD,** City; Geneva County; Pop. 2,647; Zip Code 36344; Elev. 278; Lat. 31-06-11 N long. 085-41-30 W; Founded in 1894 and named for Hartford, Connecticut.

•**HARTSELLE,** City; Morgan County; Pop. 8,858; Zip Code 35640; Elev. 669; Lat. 34-26-32 N long. 086-56-32 W; Incorporated in 1875 and named for resident George Hartselle.

•**HAYDEN,** Town; Blount County; Pop. 268; Zip Code 35079; Elev. 570; Lat. 33-53-29 N long. 086-45-21 W; Originally Rockland, the name was changed in 1914 after a local army officer named Hayden.

•**HAYNEVILLE,** Town; Lowndes County Seat; Pop. 592; Zip Code 36040; Lat. 32-10-56 N long. 086-34-43 W; First settled in 1820 and named for South Carolina political leader Robert Hayne.

•**HAZEL GREEN,** "(CDP)",Cleburne County; Pop. 239; Zip Code 35750; Lat. 34-55-59 N long. 086-34-11 W; Incorporated in 1821 and descriptively named for the green hazel trees in the area.

•**HEATH,** Town; Covington County; Pop. 354; Settled in the 1850's and named for postmaster Kate Heath.

•**HEFLIN,** City; Cleburne County Seat; Pop. 3,014; Zip Code 36264; Elev. 977; Lat. 33-38-07 N long. 085-35-26 W; Heflin was settled in the 1880's and named for Dr. Wilson L. Heflin.

•**HELENA,** Town; Urban Part County; Pop. 2,114; Zip Code 35080; Lat. 33-12-48 N long. 086-49-30 W; Incorporated in 1877 and named for the wife of a surveying railroad engineer.

•**HENAGAR,** Town; De Kalb County; Pop. 1,188; Zip Code 35978; Lat. 34-37-30 N long. 085-45-18 W; Established in 1855 and named for an early settler.

•**HIGHLAND LAKE,** Town; Blount County; Pop. 210; Zip Code ; Descriptively named for a local lake.

•**HILLSBORO,** Town; Lawrence County; Pop. 278; Zip Code 35643; Elev. 598; Lat. 34-38-21 N long. 087-11-50 W; Founded as "Gilmer" in 1837 and renamed descriptively for its hilly terrain.

•**HOBSON CITY,** Town; Calhoun County; Pop. 1,268; Zip Code ; Begun in 1899 and named for Spanish War hero, Richard P. Hobson.

•**HODGES,** Town; Franklin County; Pop. 250; Zip Code 35571; Elev. 842; Lat. 34-19-43 N long. 087-55-37 W; Steve Hodges was a pioneer settler in the area. The town is named after him.

•**HOKES BLUFF,** Town; Etawah County; Pop. 3,216; Zip Code ; Daniel Hokes settled here in 1854. The town is named for him.

•**HOLLY POND,** Town; Cullman County; Pop. 493; Zip Code 5083; Elev. 849; Lat. 34-10-29 N long. 086-37-07 W; Incorporated in 1920 and named for a local pond.

•**HOLLYWOOD,** Town; Jackson County; Pop. 1,110; Zip Code 35752; Lat. 34-43-27 N long. 085-58-01 W; Descriptively named for the many holly bushes in the area.

•**HOMEWOOD,** City; Jefferson County; Pop. 21,412; Zip Code 35209; The city was established in a wooded area and so, descriptively named.

•**HOOVER,** City; Jefferson County; Pop. 19,792; Zip Code 35226; The city is named after insurance executive William Hoover.

•**HUEYTOWN,** City; Jefferson County; Pop. 13,309; Zip Code 35032; Named in honor of Captain John Huey who served in the Confederate Navy during the Civil War.

•**HUNTSVILLE,** City; Madison County Seat; Pop. 142,513; Zip Code 35800; Elev. 641; Lat. 34-43-31 N long. 086-35-32 W; Settled in 1805 and named for the first settler John Hunt.

•**HURTSBORO,** Town; Russell County; Pop. 752; Zip Code 36860; Lat. 32-14-20 N long. 085-24-30 W; Joel Hurt settled here in 1857. The town is named for him.

•**IDER,** Town; De Kalb County; Pop. 698; Zip Code 35981; Lat. 34-42-53 N long. 085-40-43 W; Established in 1877 and given a euphonious name by the first postmaster.

•**IRONDALE,** City; Jefferson County; Pop. 6,510; Founded as an ironworks during the Civil War, and named for that function.

•**JACKSON,** City; Clarke County; Pop. 6,073; Zip Code 36515; Elev. 227; Lat. 31-20-37 N long. 087-50-43 W; The city was founded in 1813 and named for General Andrew Jackson.

•**JACKSONVILLE,** City; Calhoun County; Pop. 9,735; Zip Code 36265; Elev. 672; Lat. 33-48-56 N long. 085-45-36 W; The city began as "Drayton" in 1822, but was later renamed to honor President Andrew Jackson.

•**JASPER,** City; Walker County Seat; Pop. 11,894; Zip Code 35501; Elev. 339; Named in honor of Revolutionary hero Sergeant Jasper of South Carolina.

•**JEMISON,** Town; Chilton County; Pop. 1,828; Zip Code 35085; Lat. 32-57-22 N long. 086-44-55 W; Founded in 1870 and named in honor of pioneer businessman Robert Jemison.

•**KANSAS,** Town; Walker County; Pop. 267; Zip Code 35573; Lat. 33-54-15 N long. 087-33-18 W; Settled in the 1870's and named after the state of Kansas.

•**KENNEDY,** Town; Lamar County; Pop. 604; Zip Code 35574; Lat. 33-35-08 N long. 087-58-57 W; Dr. W. H. Kennedy donated land to the railroad here in 1885. The town is named after him.

•**KILLEN,** Town; Lauderdale County; Pop. 747; Zip Code 35645; Elev. 614; Lat. 34-51-35 N long. 087-31-52 W; Established in 1900 and named for a pioneer family.

•**KIMBERLY,** Town; Jefferson County; Pop. 1,043; Zip Code 35091; Elev. 457; Lat. 33-46-10 N long. 086-48-30 W; Kimberly is named for the diamond mines of Kimberly, South Africa.

•**KINSTON,** Town; Coffee County; Pop. 604; Zip Code 36453; Elev. 275; Lat. 31-13-03 N long. 086-10-12 W; First settled in the late 1800's and named for a town in North Carolina.

•**LAFAYETTE,** City; Chambers County Seat; Pop. 3,647; Zip Code 36862; Elev. 849; Lat. 32-53-45 N long. 085-23-45 W; Named in honor of Revolutionary War hero, the Marquis De Lafayette.

•**LANETT,** City; Chambers County; Pop. 6,897; Zip Code 36863; Lat. 32-51-26 N long. 085-11-56 W; Layfayette Lanier and Theodore Bennett were early textile developers. The town is named for them.

•**LANGDALE,** (CDP); Chambers County; Pop. 2,034; Zip Code ; Founded in 1892 and named for Thomas Lang, a local businessman.

•**LEEDS,** City; Jefferson, Shelby & St. Clair Counties; Pop. 8,638; Zip Code 35094; Elev. 802; Lat. 33-32-31 N long. 086-31-46 W; Settled in the 1820's and later named after the English industrial city.

•**LEESBURG,** Town; Cherokee County; Pop. 116; Zip Code 35983; Elev. 584; Lat. 34-10-39 N long. 085-46-04 W; Founded in the 1830's and later named in honor of General Robert E. Lee.

•**LEIGHTON,** Town; Colbert County; Pop. 1,218; Zip Code 35646; Elev. 574; Lat. 34-42-07 N long. 087-33-52 W; The town is named for William Leigh, the first postmaster.

•**LESTER,** Town; Limestone County; Pop. 117; Zip Code 35647; Lat. 34-59-16 N long. 087-09-15 W; Named after a local settler.

•**LEXINGTON,** Town; Lauderdale County; Pop. 884; Zip Code 35648; Lat. 34-58-03 N long. 087-22-11 W; Settled in the 1830's and named after Lexington, Kentucky.

•**LINCOLN,** Town; Talladega County; Pop. 2,081; Zip Code 35096; Founded in 1850 and named in honor of Revolutionary War hero General Benjamin Lincoln.

•**LINDEN,** City; Marengo County Seat; Pop. 2,773; Zip Code 36748; Originally called Hohenlinden, the name was later shorted to Linden.

•LINEVILLE, Town; Clay County; Pop. 2,257; Zip Code 36266; Elev. 1057; Lat. 33-18-24 N long. 085-44-49 W; Descriptively named for its location between two counties.

•LISMAN, Town; Choctaw County; Pop. 638; Zip Code 36906· Elev. 158; Lat. 32-13-40 N long. 088-16-32 W; Railroad executive John Cochrane named the town after a New York investor-friend who lent him capital for the road's expansion.

•LITTLE SHAWMUT, (CDP); Chambers County; Pop. 2,793; Shawmut is an Indian word meaning "little Boston."

•LITTLEVILLE, Town; Colbert County; Pop. 1,262; Zip Code ; Settled in the 1890's and named for a pioneer Indian fighter.

•LIVINGSTON, City; Sumter County Seat; Pop. 3,187; Zip Code 35470; Elev. 149; Lat. 32-35-44 N long. 088-11-43 W; Founded in 1833 and named in honor of Secretary of State Edward Livingston.

•LOACHAPOKA, Town; Lee County; Pop. 335; Zip Code 36865; Elev. 687; Lat. 32-36-19 N long. 085-36-07 W; Established in the 1840's and given a Creek Indian name meaning "gathering place of the turtles."

•LOCKHART, Town; Covington County; Pop. 547; Zip Code 36455; Elev. 292; Lat. 31-00-33 N long. 086-21-06 W; Incorporated in 1931 and named for pioneer Aaron Lockhart.

•LOCUST FORK, Town; Blount County; Pop. 488; Zip Code 35097; Elev. 594; Lat. 33-54-28 N long. 086-36-58 W; Settled in 1819 and named for the locust fork of the Black Warrior River.

•LOUISVILLE, Town; Barbour County; Pop. 791; Zip Code 36048; Lat. 31-46-49 N long. 085-33-11 W; Incorporated in 1888 and named for an early pioneer.

•LOXLEY, Town; Baldwin County; Pop. 804; Zip Code 36551; Elev. 171; Lat. 30-37-17 N long. 087-45-07 W; The town is named after an early family who ran a lumber business.

•LUVERNE, City; Crenshaw County Seat; Pop. 2,639; Zip Code 36049; Elev. 366; Lat. 31-43-03 N long. 086-15-43 W; Incorporated in 1891 and named in the honor of a local pioneer's wife.

•LYNN, Town; Winston County; Pop. 554; Zip Code 35575; Elev. 722; Lat. 34-02-52 N long. 087-33-03 W; John Lynn was the direct descendant of a Revolutionary War veteran. The town is named for him.

•MADRID, Town; Houston County; Pop. 172; Zip Code 36320; The town is named for the city in Spain.

•MALVERN, Town; Geneva County; Pop. 558; Incorporated in 1904 and named after the Civil War battle of Malvern Hill.

•MAPLESVILLE, Town; Chilton County; Pop. 754; Zip Code 36750; Elev. 350; Lat. 32-47-15 N long. 086-52-27 W; Pioneer Billy Maples founded the town prior to 1850. It is named for him.

•MARGARET, Town; St. Clair County; Pop. 757; Zip Code 35112; Lat. 33-41-10 N long. 086-28-48 W; The town is named for the wife of a local coal company president.

•MARION, City; Perry County Seat; Pop. 4,467; Zip Code 36756; Elev. 376; Lat. 32-37-52 N long. 087-21-09 W; Marion's name honors Revolutionary War hero General Francis Marion.

•MAYTOWN, Town; Jefferson County; Pop. 538; Named for the wife of an early settler.

•MCINTOSH, Town; Washington County; Pop. 319; Zip Code 36553; Elev. 48; Lat. 31-16-02 N long. 088-01-53 W; Founded in 1800 and named after Captain William McIntosh.

•MENTONE, Town; De Kalb County; Pop. 476; Zip Code 35984; Elev. 1708; Lat. 31-55-44 N long. 088-27-31 W; Established in the 1880's and named for a famous French resort.

•MERIDIANVILLE, (CDP); Madison County; Pop. 1,403; Zip Code 35759; Lat. 34-51-03 N long. 086-34-20 W; Settled in the early 1800's and named for its location on a map meridian.

•MIDFIELD, City; Jefferson County; Pop. 6,536; Zip Code 35228; Descriptively named for its location between Birmingham and Bessemer.

•MIDLAND CITY, Town; Dale County; Pop. 1,903; Zip Code 36350; Elev. 376; Lat. 31-19-07 N long. 085-29-26 W; Named for its location between Montgomery and Thomasville.

•MIDWAY, Town; Bullock County; Pop. 593; Zip Code 36053; Lat. 32-04-38 N long. 085-31-12 W; The town is named for its location between two local spots.

•MILLBROOK, City; Elmore County; Pop. 3,101; Zip Code 36054; Elev. 199; Lat. 32-28-47 N long. 086-21-49 W; Descriptively named for a local gristmill on a nearby brook.

•MILLPORT, Town; Lamar County; Pop. 1,287; Zip Code 35576; Lat. 33-33-30 N long. 088-06-46 W; Founded in 1848 and named for the numerous water mills in the area.

•MILLRY, Town; Washington County; Pop. 956; Zip Code 36558; Lat. 31-37-55 N long. 088-20-08 W; Established in the early 1900's and named for Old Mill Creek.

•MOBILE, City; Mobile County Seat; Pop. 200,452; Zip Code 36600; Elev. 7; Lat. 30-40-55 N long. 088-06-19 W; An early French outpost named for the Mobile Indians.

•MONROEVILLE, City; Monroe County Seat; Pop. 5,674; Zip Code 36460; Elev. 418; Lat. 31-30-55 N long. 087-20-18 W; The city's name honors President James Monroe.

•MONTEVALLO, City; Shelby County; Pop. 3,965; Zip Code 35115; Lat. 33-04-31 N long. 086-50-39 W; Montevallo is an Italian name meaning "on a mound in the valley."

•MONTGOMERY, City; Montgomery County Seat; Pop. 178,157; Zip Code 36100; Elev. 287; Lat. 32-21-48 N long. 086-17-44 W; Settled in 1814 and named for Revolutionary War hero General Richard Montgomery.

•MOORESVILLE, Town; Limestone County; Pop. 58; Zip Code 35649; Lat. 34-37-33 N long. 086-52-43 W; Settled in 1808 and named for the Moore family.

•MORRIS, Town; Jefferson County; Pop. 623; Zip Code 35116; Elev. 414; The town is named after the Morris Mining Company.

•MOULTON, City; Lawrence County Seat; Pop. 3,197; Zip Code 35650; Elev. 650; Lat. 34-28-48 N long. 087-17-20 W; Incorporated in 1819 and named for an Indian fighter Michael Moulton.

•MOUNDVILLE, Town; Hale & Tuscaloosa Counties; Pop. 1,310; Zip Code 35474; Elev. 168; Lat. 33-00-16 N long. 087-38-51 W; Originally founded as Carthage, but later renamed for the many Indian mounds in the area.

•MOUNT VERNON, Town; Mobile County; Pop. 1,038; Zip Code 36560; Elev. 1297; Lat. 31-05-19 N long. 088-00-49 W; Founded in the early 1800's and named after George Washington's plantation.

•**MOUNTAIN BROOK,** City; Jefferson County; Pop. 19,718; Zip Code 35223; Incorporated in 1940 and named for Shades Creek which flows through the area.

•**MULGA,** Town; Jefferson County; Pop. 405; Zip Code 35118; Elev. 584; Lat. 33-32-37 N long. 086-59-09 W; The town's name is a corruption of a Creek Indian word meaning "all."

•**MUSCLE SHOALS,** City; Colbert County; Pop. 8,911; Zip Code 35662; Incorporated in 1923 and named after the Muscle Shoals.

•**MYRTLEWOOD,** Town; Marengo County; Pop. 252; Zip Code 36763; Elev. 221; Lat. 32-14-55 N long. 087-56-42 W; The town is named for the crepe myrtle growing nearby.

•**NAPIER FIELD,** Town; Dale County; Pop. 493; Zip Code 36301; Named after a local airbase, itself named for Major Edward Napier.

•**NAUVOO,** Town; Walker County; Pop. 259; Zip Code 35578; Elev. 562; Lat. 33-59-11 N long. 087-29-10 W; The town is named after Nauvoo, Illinois.

•**NEW BROCKTON,** Town; Coffee County; Pop. 1,392; Zip Code 36351; Lat. 31-23-12 N long. 085-55-33 W; Hugh Brock donated the land for the town, it is named for him.

•**NEW HOPE,** Town; Madison County; Pop. 1,546; Zip Code 35760; Elev. 369; Lat. 34-32-37 N long. 086-23-42 W; The town is named for a Methodist church in the area.

•**NEWBERN,** Town; Hale County; Pop. 307; Zip Code 36765; Lat. 32-35-30 N long. 087-31-29 W; Founded in the 1840's and named for Newberne, North Carolina.

•**NEWTON,** Town; Dale County; Pop. 1,540; Zip Code 36352; Elev. 261; Lat. 31-20-12 N long. 085-20-02 W; Incorporated in the 1840's and named for the prominent family.

•**NORTHPORT,** City; Tuscaloosa County; Pop. 14,291; Zip Code 35476; Lat. 33-13-57 N long. 087-35-42 W; Descriptively named for its location on the north bank of the Tuscaloosa River.

•**OAK HILL,** Town; Wilcox County; Pop. 63; Zip Code 36766; Lat. 31-55-11 N long. 087-05-28 W; First settled around 1846 and named for the area's numerous oak trees.

•**OAKMAN,** Town; Walker County; Pop. 770; Zip Code 35579; Elev. 327; Lat. 33-46-23 N long. 087-23-06 W; Settled in 1862 and named in honor of businessman W. G. Oakman.

•**ODENVILLE,** Town; St. Clair County; Pop. 724; Zip Code 35120; Lat. 33-40-18 N long. 086-24-51 W; Established in 1820's and named for a local family.

•**OHATCHEE,** Town; Calhoun County; Pop. 860; Zip Code 36271; Lat. 33-47-14 N long. 086-01-13 W; Ohatchee is a Creek Indian word meaning "upper creek."

•**ONEONTA,** City; Blount County Seat; Pop. 4,824; Zip Code 35121; Elev. 885; Lat. 33-54-58 N long. 086-26-44 W; Incorporated in 1891 and named after Oneonta, New York.

•**OPELIKA,** City; Lee County Seat; Pop. 21,896; Zip Code 36801; Elev. 822; Lat. 32-38-27 N long. 085-22-42 W; Settled in 1836 and given a Creek Indian word meaning "big swamp."

•**OPP,** City; Covington County; Pop. 7,204; Zip Code 36467; Elev. 335; Lat. 31-16-52 N long. 086-15-21 W; Founded in 1900 and named for lawyer Henry Opp.

•**ORRVILLE,** Town; Dallas County; Pop. 349; Zip Code 36767; Elev. 189; Lat. 32-18-40 N long. 087-16-53 W; First settled in the 1840's and named for original landowner James Franklin Orr.

•**OWENS CROSSROADS,** Town; Madison County; Pop. 804; Zip Code 35763; Elev. 581; Lat. 34-35-20 N long. 086-27-34 W; Settled prior to the Civil War and named for a prominent local family.

•**OZARK,** City; Dale County Seat; Pop. 13,188; Zip Code 36360; Elev. 409; Lat. 31-23-33 N long. 085-40-56 W; Settled before the Civil War and named for the Ozark Indians.

•**PAINT ROCK,** Town; Jackson County; Pop. 221; Zip Code 35764; Elev. 600; Lat. 34-46-35 N long. 086-19-35 W; Founded in 1835 and named for the nearby river.

•**PARRISH,** Town; Walker County; Pop. 1,583; Zip Code 35580; Elev. 333; Lat. 33-44-08 N long. 087-17-07 W; Incorporated in 1921 and named for 19th century industrialist Alfred Parrish.

•**PELHAM,** City; Shelby County; Pop. 6,759; Zip Code 35124; Elev. 119; Lat. 33-13-25 N long. 086-46-54 W; The city's name honors Confederate hero Major John Pelham.

•**PELL CITY,** City; St. Clair County Seat; Pop. 6,616; Zip Code 35125; Lat. 33-35-04 N long. 086-23-26 W; Founded in the early 1900's and named after founder and promoter George Pell.

•**PENNINGTON,** Town; Choctaw County; Pop. 355; Zip Code 36916; Elev. 106; Lat. 32-12-32 N long. 088-09-26 W; The town is named for a local family.

•**PETREY,** Town; Crenshaw County; Pop. 93; Zip Code 36062; Elev. 364; Lat. 31-51-01 N long. 086-12-31 W; Petrey is named for a turn-of-century resident George Petrey.

•**PHENIX CITY,** City; Lee & Russell Counties; Russell County Seat; Pop. 26,928; Zip Code 36867; Elev. 302; Lat. 32-28-12 N long. 085-00-45 W; Incorporated in 1883 and named for the old Phenix Mills.

•**PHIL CAMPBELL,** Town; Franklin County; Pop. 1,549; Zip Code 35581; Elev. 1025; Lat. 34-21-01 N long. 087-42-12 W; Named in honor of the chief engineer of the local railroad.

•**PICKENSVILLE,** Town; Pickens County; Pop. 132; Settled in 1817 and named for Revolutionary War hero General Andrew Pickens.

•**PIEDMONT,** City; Calhoun County; Pop. 5,544; Zip Code 36272; Lat. 33-55-41 N long. 085-36-39 W; Descriptively named for its location on the Piedmont Plateau.

•**PINCKARD,** Town; Dale County; Pop. 771; Zip Code 36371; Elev. 381; Lat. 31-19-03 N long. 085-32-27 W; Incorporated in 1909 and named in honor of schoolteacher J. O. Pinckard.

•**PINE APPLE,** Town; Wilcox County; Pop. 298; Zip Code 36768; Lat. 31-52-31 N long. 087-00-09 W; Named for an early apple cider mill located in a pine grove.

•**PINE HILL,** Town; Wilcox County; Pop. 510; Zip Code 36769; Lat. 31-57-30 N long. 087-34-52 W; Descriptively named for its location on a pine covered hill.

•**PISGAH,** Town; Jackson County; Pop. 699; Zip Code 35765; Lat. 34-40-52 N long. 085-50-39 W; The town was founded in the 1870's and given a Biblical name.

•**PLEASANT GROVE,** City; Jefferson County; Pop. 7,102; Zip Code 35127; Lat. 33-29-30 N long. 086-58-27 W; Founded in the early 1830's and given a descriptive name.

•**POINT CLEAR,** (CDP); Baldwin County; Pop. 1,812; Zip Code 36564; Lat. 30-28-30 N long. 087-55-08 W; Called "Punta Clara," of "Point Clear" by early Spanish settlers.

•**PRATTVILLE,** City; Autauga & Elmore Counties; Autauga County Seat; Pop. 18,647; Zip Code 36067; Lat. 32-27-49 N long. 086-27-29 W; Named after industrialist Daniel Pratt.

•**PRICEVILLE,** Town; Morgan County; Pop. 966; Incorporated in 1925 and named for pioneer Thomas Price.

•**PRICHARD,** City; Mobile County; Pop. 39,541; Zip Code 36610; Settler Cleveland Prichard bought the site in 1925, it is named for him.

•**PROVIDENCE,** Town; Marengo County; Pop. 363; Named "Need More" during a period of hard times, it was later renamed the more hopeful Providence.

•**RAGLAND,** Town; St. Clair County; Pop. 1,860; Zip Code 35131; Lat. 33-44-34 N long. 086-09-21 W; Settled in 1833 and later named for one of the principals in a local mining company.

•**RAINBOW CITY,** City; Etowah County; Pop. 6,299; Zip Code 35901; Incorporated in 1950 and given a euphonious name.

•**RAINSVILLE,** City; De Kalb County; Pop. 3,907; Zip Code 35986; Lat. 34-28-57 N long. 085-51-33 W; Incorporated in 1907 and named for local citizen Will Rains.

•**RANBURNE,** Town; Cleburne County; Pop. 417; Zip Code 36273; Lat. 33-31-36 N long. 085-21-21 W; Settled after the War of 1812 and named by combining the letters of Randolph County and Cleburne County.

•**RED BAY,** City; Franklin County; Pop. 3,232; Zip Code 35582; Elev. 623; Lat. 34-26-43 N long. 088-08-02 W; The city is named for the reddish bay flowers which grew in the area.

•**REFORM,** City; Pickens County; Pop. 2,245; Zip Code 35481; Lat. 33-22-43 N long. 088-00-57 W; Settled in the mid-1800's and named by a local preacher for the virtue of reform.

•**REPTON,** Town; Conecuh County; Pop. 313; Zip Code 36475; Elev. 352; Lat. 31-24-28 N long. 087-15-29 W; Named after an early pioneer.

•**RIDGEVILLE,** Town; Etowah County; Pop. 182; Founded in 1822 and later descriptively named for the local geography.

•**RIVER FALLS,** Town; Covington County; Pop. 669; Zip Code 36476; Lat. 31-21-07 N long. 086-34-28 W; Established in 1891 and descriptively named for a nearby waterfall on the Conecuh River.

•**RIVERSIDE,** Town; St. Clair County; Pop. 849; Zip Code 35135; Elev. 668; Lat. 33-36-45 N long. 086-12-26 W; Descriptively named for its location on the Coosa River.

•**ROANOKE,** City; Randolph County; Pop. 5,896; Zip Code 36274; Lat. 33-08-53 N long. 085-21-52 W; Settled in the 1830's and later named for the city of Virginia.

•**ROBERTSDALE,** City; Baldwin County; Pop. 2,306; Zip Code 36567; Lat. 30-33-53 N long. 087-42-28 W; Established in 1905 and named for Dr. B. F. Roberts, an official of the founding development company.

•**ROCKFORD,** Town; Coosa County Seat; Pop. 494; Zip Code 35136; Lat. 32-53-25 N long. 086-13-14 W; The town is descriptively named for a rocky ford on a nearby creek.

•**ROGERSVILLE,** Town; Lauderdale County; Pop. 1,224; Zip Code 35652; Lat. 34-50-00 N long. 087-19-37 W; A trader named Rogers lived here in the 1820's. The town is named for him.

•**ROOSEVELT CITY,** City; Bessemer County; Pop. 3,352; Zip Code 35020; The city's name honors President Theodore Roosevelt.

•**RUSSELLVILLE,** City; Franklin County Seat; Pop. 8,195; Zip Code 35653; Elev. 764; Lat. 34-30-17 N long. 087-43-46 W; Settled in the early 1800's and named in honor of Indian fighter Major William Russell.

•**RUTLEDGE,** Town; Crenshaw County; Pop. 496; Zip Code 36071; Lat. 31-43-55 N long. 086-18-36 W; Established prior to the Civil War and later named in honor of Confederate Captain Henry Rutledge.

•**SAMSON,** City; Geneva County; Pop. 2,402; Zip Code 36477; Elev. 205; Lat. 31-06-40 N long. 086-02-27 W; Originally named "Sampson," a postal spelling error led to the present name of "Samson."

•**SARALAND,** City; Mobile County; Pop. 9,833; Zip Code 36571; Lat. 30-48-41 N long. 088-05-21 W; In 1895 postmaster De Witt named the town after his wife.

•**SARDIS,** City; Etowah County; Pop. 883; Zip Code 36775; Elev. 584; Lat. 2-17-14 N long. 086-59-10 W; Founded in 1818 and named after the Biblical city.

•**SATSUMA,** City; Mobile County; Pop. 3,822; Zip Code 36572; Lat. 30-48-54 N long. 088-03-36 W; The city is named after a variety of orange tree.

•**SCOTTSBORO,** City; Jackson County Seat; Pop. 14,758; Zip Code 35768; Elev. 653; Lat. 34-39-24 N long. 086-01-25 W; Robert Scott owned the land around the town. It is named for him.

•**SECTION,** Town; Jackson County; Pop. 821; Zip Code 35771; Lat. 34-34-42 N long. 085-58-54 W; The town is named after the sixteenth section of the local land area, which was set aside by the Legislature for public schools.

•**SELMA,** City; Dallas County Seat; Pop. 26,684; Zip Code 36701; Elev. 139; Lat. 32-23-25 N long. 087-00-28 W; Settled in 1815 and named after the Civil War from McPherson's Ossian.

•**SHEFFIELD,** City; Colbert County; Pop. 11,903; Zip Code 35660; Elev. 502; Lat. 34-54-14 N long. 087-40-31 W; Named for the industrial city of England.

•**SILAS,** Town; Choctaw County; Pop. 343; Zip Code 36919; Lat. 31-46-12 N long. 088-20-01 W; Silas Shoemaker was an early resident, the town is named for him.

•**SILVERHILL,** Town; Baldwin County; Pop. 624; Zip Code 36576; Elev. 144; Lat. 30-32-56 N long. 087-45-04 W; Incorporated in 1926 and named for a pioneer.

•**SIPSEY,** Town; Walker County; Pop. 678; Zip Code 35584; Elev. 437; Lat. 33-49-36 N long. 087-07-28 W; Founded in 1912 and named for the Sipsey River.

•**SLOCOMB,** Town; Geneva County; Pop. 2,153; Zip Code 36349; Lat. 31-08-12 N long. 085-30-58 W; Incorporated in 1901 and named for a local businessman.

•**SOMERVILLE,** Town; Morgan County; Pop. 140; Zip Code 35670; Lat. 34-28-21 N long. 086-47-53 W; Named in honor of Lieutenant Robert Summerville killed during the War of 1812.

•**SPANISH FORT,** (CDP); Baldwin County; Pop. 3,415; Zip Code 36527; Founded by the Spanish as a military fort in 1780, the town retained the name.

•**SPRINGVILLE,** Town; st. Clair County; Pop. 1,476; Zip Code 35146; Elev. 726; Lat. 33-46-22 N long. 086-28-35 W; Settled in 1817 and named for the large spring near the town.

•**STEELE,** Town; St. Clair County; Pop. 795; Zip Code 35987; Elev. 582; Lat. 33-56-19 N long. 086-12-08 W; Incorporated in 1900 and named for pioneer J. Tolvier Steele.

•**STEVENSON,** City; Jackson County; Pop. 2,568; Zip Code 35772; Elev. 628; Lat. 34-52-36 N long. 085-49-45 W; Established in 1853 and named for Vernon Stevenson, a surveyor on the railroad.

•**SULLIGENT,** Town; Lamar County; Pop. 2,130; Zip Code 35586; Lat. 33-53-49 N long. 088-07-57 W; Founded in 1886 and named by combining the names of two railroad officials: Mr. Sullivan and Mr. Sargent.

•**SUMITON,** Town; Jefferson & Walker Counties; Pop. 2,815; Zip Code 35148; Elev. 522; Lat. 33-45-34 N long. 087-03-14 W; Descriptively named for its location among hills.

•**SUMMERDALE,** Town; Baldwin County; Pop. 546; Zip Code 36580; Elev. 112; Lat. 30-29-34 N long. 087-41-54 W; Eli Summers founded the town in 1904. It is named for him.

•**SWEET WATER,** Town; Marengo County; Pop. 253; Zip Code 36782; Lat. 32-05-43 N long. 087-51-38 W; Settled in 1838 and named after nearby Sweet Water Creek.

•**SYLACAUGA,** City; Talladega County; Pop. 12,708; Zip Code 35150; Elev. 600; Settled in 1814 and given a Creek Indian word meaning "buzzards roost."

•**SYLVANIA,** Town; De Kalb County; Pop. 1,156; Zip Code 35988; Elev. 1392; Lat. 34-33-48 N long. 085-48-41 W; The town is named for Sylvania, Georgia.

•**TALLADEGA,** City; Talladega County Seat; Pop. 19,128; Zip Code 35160; Elev. 555; Incorporated in 1835 and given a Creek Indian word meaning "border town."

•**TALLASSEE,** City; Elmore & Tallapoosa Counties; Pop. 4,763; Zip Code 36078; Elev. 395; Lat. 32-31-10 N long. 085-53-14 W; A Creek Indian word meaning "old town."

•**TARRANT CITY,** City; Jefferson County; Pop. 8,148; Zip Code 35217; Named for Dr. Felix Isram Tarrant.

•**THEODORE,** (CDP); Mobile County; Pop. 6,392; Zip Code 36582; Lat. 30-36-42 N long. 088-12-21 W; Established in 1880 and named after a local sawmill operator Theodore Hieronymous.

•**THOMASTON,** Town; Marengo County; Pop. 679; Zip Code 36783; Elev. 189; Lat. 31-16-21 N long. 088-15-00 W; The town is named for its founder Dr. C. B. Thomas.

•**THOMASVILLE,** City; Clarke County; Pop. 4,387; Zip Code 36784; Elev. 389; Lat. 31-15-52 N long. 088-20-36 W; Founded in 1887 and named for a railroad builder.

•**THORSBY,** Town; Chilton County; Pop. 1,422; Zip Code 35171; Named for an early settler.

•**TOWN CREEK,** Town; Lawrence County; Pop. 1,201; Zip Code 35672; Elev. 563; Lat. 34-40-54 N long. 087-24-21 W; Named after the local creek.

•**TOXEY,** Town; Choctaw County; Pop. 265; Zip Code 36921; Lat. 31-54-39 N long. 088-19-07 W; The town is named for an early settler.

•**TRINITY,** Town; Morgan County; Pop. 1,328; Zip Code 35673; Elev. 634; Lat. 34-35-19 N long. 087-05-31 W; The origin of the town's name is unsure.

•**TROY,** City; Pike County Seat; Pop. 12,945; Zip Code 36081; Elev. 543; Lat. 31-48-23 N long. 085-56-26 W; Troy is named after the ancient Homeric city.

•**TRUSSVILLE,** City; Jefferson County; Pop. 3,507; Zip Code 35173; Named after a pioneer settler.

•**TUSCALOOSA,** City; Tuscaloosa County Seat; Pop. 75,211; Zip Code 35401; Elev. 227; Lat. 33-11-56 N long. 087-31-56 W; The city has a Creek Indian name.

•**TUSCUMBIA,** City; Colbert County Seat; Pop. 9,137; Zip Code 35674; Elev. 470; Lat. 34-43-48 N long. 087-42-02 W; The Creek Indian word of uncertain origin.

•**TUSKEGEE,** City; Macon County Seat; Pop. 13,327; Zip Code 36083; Elev. 468; Lat. 32-25-31 N long. 085-41-58 W; Named after an old Creek Indian village.

•**UNION GROVE,** Town; Marshall County; Pop. 127; Zip Code 35175; Elev. 601; Given a descriptive name after a local grove of trees.

•**UNION SPRINGS,** City; Bullock County Seat; Pop. 4,431; Zip Code 36089; Elev. 528; Lat. 32-08-15 N long. 085-42-36 W; Named after a local springs.

•**UNIONTOWN,** City; Perry County; Pop. 2,112; Zip Code 36786; Lat. 32-27-02 N long. 087-30-46 W; A loose reference to the American union.

•**VALLEY HEAD,** Town; De Kalb County; Pop. 609; Zip Code 35989; Elev. 1029; Lat. 34-34-31 N long. 085-37-24 W; Descriptively named for its location.

•**VANCE,** Town; Tuscaloosa County; Pop. 254; Zip Code 35490; Elev. 516; Lat. 33-05-11 N long. 087-13-57 W; Named for an early settler.

•**VERNON,** City; Lamar County Seat; Pop. 2,609; Zip Code 35592; Elev. 304; Lat. 33-45-29 N long. 088-06-35 W; The city is named after a local pioneer family.

•**VESTAVIA HILLS,** City; Jefferson County; Pop. 15,722; Zip Code 35216; The city is named after a local geographic feature.

•**VINA,** Town; Franklin County; Pop. 346; Zip Code 35593; Elev. 723; Lat. 34-22-27 N long. 088-03-18 W; A Latin name given by early settlers.

•**VINCENT,** Town; St. Clair, Shelby & Talladega Counties; Pop. 1,652; Zip Code 35178; Elev. 446; Vincent is named for a pioneer settler.

•**VREDENBURGH,** Town; Monroe County; Pop. 433; Zip Code 36481; Lat. 31-53-29 N long. 087-19-20 W; The town is named for an early settler.

•**WADLEY,** Town; Randolph County; Pop. 532; Zip Code 36276; Elev. 690; Lat. 33-07-14 N long. 085-34-20 W; Named for a pioneer settler.

•**WATERLOO,** Town; Lauderdale County; Pop. 260; Zip Code 35677; Lat. 34-54-54 N long. 088-03-50 W; The town is named after the town in Iowa.

•**WAVERLY,** Town; Chambers & Lee Counties; Pop. 228; Zip Code 36879; Lat. 32-44-00 N long. 085-36-59 W; The city is named for the town in Massachusetts.

•**WEAVER,** Town; Calhoun County; Pop. 2,765; Zip Code 36277; Lat. 33-44-55 N long. 085-48-35 W; A pioneer settler named the town.

•**WEBB,** Town; Houston County; Pop. 448; Zip Code 36376; Lat. 31-15-47 N long. 085-16-25 W; Webb is named for an early landowner.

•**WEDOWEE,** Town; Randolph County Seat; Pop. 908; Zip Code 36278; Lat. 33-18-15 N long. 085-29-16 W; A Creek Indian word of uncertain origin.

•**WEST BLOCTON,** Town; Bibb County; Pop. 1,147; Zip Code 35184; Named for its location near Blocton.

•**WESTON,** Town; Marion County; Pop. 344; Zip Code 35185; Descriptively named for the town's geographic position.

•**WETUMPKA,** City; Elmore County Seat; Pop. 4,341; Zip Code 36092; Elev. 177; Lat. 32-31-13 N long. 086-12-12 W; A Creek Indian word, its meaning is unsure.

•**WILMER,** Town; Mobile County; Pop. 581; Zip Code 36587; Elev. 581; Lat. 30-43-51 N long. 088-27-44 W; Named for an early settler.

•**WILSONVILLE,** Town; Shelby County; Pop. 914; Zip Code 35186; Elev. 433; The town's name honors early settler Dr. Elisha Wilson.

•**WILTON,** Town; Shelby County; Pop. 642; Zip Code 35187; Founded in 1890 and named after Wilton, England.

•**WINFIELD,** City; Fayette & Marion Counties; Pop. 3,781; Zip Code 35594; Elev. 468; Lat. 33-55-13 N long. 087-48-01 W; Named in honor of General Winfield Scott.

•**WOODLAND,** Town; Randolph County; Pop. 192; Zip Code 36280; Lat. 33-21-59 N long. 085-23-54 W; Settled in 1837 and later descriptively named.

ALASKA

•AKHIOK, City; Kodiak Island Borough; Pop. 105; Zip Code 99615; Off the coast of south central Alaska. An Eskimo place name.

•AKIACHAK, City; Bethel Census Area; Pop. 438; Zip Code 99551; Lat. 60-54-30 N long. 161-25-45 W; West central Alaska. An Eskimo place name of uncertain meaning.

•AKIAK, City; Bethel Census Area; Pop. 198; Zip Code 99552; Lat. 60-55-00 N long. 161-13-00 W; West central Alaska. An Eskimo term meaing "crossing over place."

•AKUTAN, City; Aleutian Islands Census Area; Pop. 169; Zip Code 99553; Lat. 54-08-05 N long. 165-46-20 W; Located on a chain of islands that extend 1700 mi. from the Alaskan Peninsula. An Aleut Indian word meaning "a mistake."

•ALAKANUK, City; Wade Hampton Census Area; Pop. 522; Zip Code 99554; Lat. 62-41-20 N long. 164-37-00 W; West central Alaska. An Eskimo word meaning "wrong way."

•ALEKNAGIK, City; Dillingham Census Area; Pop. 154; Zip Code 99555; Lat. 59-17-00 N long. 158-36-00 W; Southwest central Alaska. A descriptive name meaning "dotted with tree covered islands."

•ALLAKAKET, City; Yukon-Koyukuk Census Area; Pop. 163; Zip Code 99720; Lat. 66-34-00 N long. 152-38-30 W; Central Alaska. Allkaket is an Indian word meaning "mouth of the Alatna River."

•AMBLER, City; Kobuk Census Area; Pop. 192; Zip Code 99786; Lat. 67-05-00 N long. 157-52-00 W; Northwestern Alaska. Named in honor of Dr. James Ambler, USN, who died while exploring the Arctic in 1881.

•ANAKTUVUK PASS, City; North Slope Borough; Pop. 203; Zip Code 99721; Lat. 68-08-00 N long. 151-45-00 W; northern Alaska. The city is named after the river, its name means "place where dung is found."

•ANCHORAGE, City; Anchorage Borough; Pop. 173,017; Zip Code 995+; Lat. 58-02-38 N long. 158-48-48 W; 470 mi. south of Fairbanks, a seaport City in southern Alaska. Descriptively named for the boat anchorage at the mouth of Ship Creek.

•ANDERSON, City; Yukon-Koyukuk Census Area; Pop. 517; Central Alaska. Arthur Anderson founded the town and named it after himself.

•ANGOON, City; Skagway-Yakutat-Angoon Census Area; Pop. 465; Zip Code 99820; Lat. 57-30-00 N long. 134-35-00 W; Southeastern Alaska. A Tlingit Indian name of uncertain meaning.

•ANIAK, City; Bethel Census Area; Pop. 341; Zip Code 99557; Lat. 61-34-08 N long. 159-23-40 W; West central Alaska. Named for the nearby river whose name is of uncertain origin.

•ANVIK, City; Yukon-Koyukuk Census Area; Pop. 517; Zip Code 99558; Lat. 62-39-15 N long. 160-12-30 W; Central Alaska. An Indian place name meaning "place of the Louse eggs."

•ATMAUTLUAK, City; Bethel Census Area; Pop. 219; Zip Code 99559; West central Alaska. An Indian name of unknown meaning.

•BARROW, City; North Slope Borough; Pop. 2,207; Zip Code 99723; Lat. 71-17-30 N long. 156-47-15 W; Located approx. 10 mi. south of Barrow Point, the most northerly point of Alaska. The city is named after Sir John Barrow, secretary of the British Admiralty, who supported Arctic exploration.

•BETHEL, City; Bethel Census Area; Pop. 3,576; Zip Code 99559; Lat. 60-48-56 N long. 162-42-41 W; Located near the mouth of the Kuskokwim River in western Alaska. Moravian missionaries gave the place the name Bethel, or "house of God" in 1885.

•BREVIG MISSION, City; Nome Census Area; Pop. 138; Zip Code 99785; Lat. 65-20-00 N long. 166-29-00 W; Northwestern Alaska. Named in honor of Presbyterian missionary T. L. Brevig.

•BUCKLAND, City; Kobuk Census Area; Pop. 177; Zip Code 99727; Lat. 65-59-00 N long. 161-08-00 W; Northwestern Alaska. Royal navy explorer Frederick Beechey named the river after a geology professor at Oxford University.

•CHEFORNAK, City; Bethel Census Area; Pop. 230; Zip Code 99561; Lat. 60-13-00 N long. 164-12-00 W; West central Alaska. An Eskimo word of uncertain meaning.

•CHEVAK, City; Wade Hampton Census Area; Pop. 466; Zip Code 99563; Lat. 61-31-40 N long. 165-35-00 W; West central Alaska. The town's name means "connecting slough."

•CHUATHBALUK, City; Bethel Census Area; Pop. 105; Zip Code 99557; West central Alaska. Chuathbaluk is an Eskimo term whose meaning is unsure.

•CLARK'S POINT, City; Dillingham Census Area; Pop. 79; Zip Code 99569; Lat. 58-49-45 N long. 158-33-15 W; Southwest central Alaska. Named in 1890 in honor of Professor Samuel F. Clark of Williams College.

•CORDOVA, City; Valdez-Cordova Census Area; Pop. 1,879; Zip Code 99574; Lat. 60-32-45 N long. 145-44-40 W; Coastal town on the southeastern corner of Prince William Sound in southeastern Alaska. Founded in 1906 and given the name. The original Spanish explorer Salvador Fidalgo christened the area in 1790.

•CRAIG, City; Prince of Wales-Outer Ketchikan Census Area; Pop. 527; Zip Code 99921; Lat. 55-28-30 N long. 133-09-00 W; Craig Miller was a local cannery owner. The town is named after him.

•DEERING, City; Kobuk Census Area; Pop. 150; Zip Code 99736; Lat. 66-04-00 N long. 162-42-00 W; Northwestern Alaska. The schooner Abbie Deering sailed the area's waters at the turn of the century. The town is named after that boat.

•DELTA JUNCTION, City; Southeast Fairbanks Census Area; Pop. 945; Zip Code 99737; Lat. 63-47-20 N long. 145-13-30 W; Central Alaska. Located on the Delta River at the junction of two highways, and hence descriptively named.

•DILLINGHAM, City; Dillingham Census Area; Pop. 1,563; Zip Code 99576; Lat. 59-23-58 N long. 158-38-00 W; Southwest central Alaska. Named in honor of Senator William Dillingham of Vermont who toured Alaska in 1903.

•DIOMEDE, City; Nome Census Area; Pop. 139; Northwestern Alaska. Russian explorer Vitus Bering named the Diomede Islands after Saint Diomede.

•EAGLE, City; Southeast Fairbanks Census Area; Pop. 110; Zip Code 99738; Lat. 64-47-00 N long. 141-12-00 W; Central Alaska. Settled in 1898 and descriptively named for the many American eagles nesting in the area.

•EEK, City; Bethel Census Area; Pop. 228; Zip Code 99578; Lat. 60-13-30 N long. 162-01-30 W; West central Alaska. A slight corruption of the Eskimo word EET which means "the two eyes."

•**EKWOK,** City; Dillingham Census Area; Pop. 77; Zip Code 99580; Lat. 59-22-00 N long. 157-30-00 W; Southwest central Alaska. An Eskimo word of uncertain meaning.

•**ELIM,** City; Nome Census Area; Pop. 139; Zip Code 99739; Lat. 64-37-00 N long. 162-15-00 W; Northwestern Alaska. The meaning of the village's name is unsure.

•**EMMONAK,** City; Wade Hampton Census Area; Pop. 567; Zip Code 99581; Lat. 62-45-00 N long. 164-30-00 W; West central Alaska. An Eskimo place name whose meaning is unclear.

•**FAIRBANKS,** City; Fairbanks North Star Borough; Pop. 22,645; Zip Code 99701; Lat. 64-50-32 N long. 147-46-32 W; Located at the junction of the Tanana and Chena Rivers in central Alaska. Founded in 1901 and named in honor of U.S. Senator Charles W. Fairbanks.

•**FORTUNA LEDGE,** City; Wade Hampton Census Area; Pop. 262; Zip Code 99585; Lat. 61-52-50 N long. 162-05-15 W; West central Alaska. Originally Marshall, it was renamed after the gold deposits found nearby.

•**FORT YUKON,** City; Yukon-Koyukuk Census Area; Pop. 619; Zip Code 99740; Lat. 66-39-00 N long. 143-43-00 W; Central Alaska. Descriptively named for its location on the Yukon River.

•**GALENA,** City; Yukon-Koyukuk Census Area; Pop. 765; Zip Code 99741; Lat. 64-44-00 N long. 156-56-00 W; Central Alaska. So named for the deposits of lead ore, or galena, mined in the vicinity.

•**GAMBELL,** City; Nome Census Area; Pop. 445; Zip Code 99742; Lat. 63-35-40 N long. 171-43-00 W; Northwestern Alaska. Named in honor of Presbyterian missionaries who lived here in the 1890's.

•**GOLOVIN,** City; Nome Census Area; Pop. 87; Zip Code 99762; Northwestern Alaska. A Russian brig, the Golovin, visited the area in 1821 and left its name on the nearby bay. The town is named after the bay.

•**GOODNEWS BAY,** City; Bethel Census Area; Pop. 168; Zip Code 99589; Lat. 59-06-53 N long. 161-35-12 W; West central Alaska. Translated from the Russian which referred to some good news that arived here in 1818. No one knows what it was, but the name stuck.

•**GRAYLING,** City; Yukon-Koyukuk Census Area; Pop. 209; Zip Code 99590; Lat. 62-57-00 N long. 160-03-00 W; Central Alaska. The town is named for the popular game fish found in Alaska's freshwater streams.

•**HAINES,** City; Haines Borough; Pop. 993; Zip Code 99827; Lat. 59-19-05 N long. 135-39-52 W; Southeastern Alaska. Settled in 1881 and named in honor of a Presbyterian official, Mrs. Francina Haines.

•**HOLY CROSS,** City; Yukon-Koyukuk Census Area; Pop. 241; Zip Code 99602; Lat. 62-12-00 N long. 159-46-00 W; Central Alaska. A Jesuit mission was founded here in 1886 with this title. The town took that name.

•**HOMER,** City; Kenai Peninsula Borough; Pop. 2,209; Zip Code 99603; Lat. 59-33-16 N long. 151-33-10 W; Southwest of Seward in southern Alaska. Founded in 1896 and named after gold prospector Homer Pennock.

•**HOONAH,** City; Skagway-Yakutat-Angoon Census Area; Pop. 680; Zip Code 99829; Lat. 58-06-30 N long. 135-26-30 W; Southeastern Alaska. A Tlingit Indian term meaning "cold lake."

•**HOOPER BAY,** City; Wade Hampton Census Area; Pop. 627; Zip Code 99604; Lat. 61-31-55 N long. 166-05-30 W; West central Alaska. The city is named after an American captain, Calvin Hooper.

•**HOUSTON,** City; Matanuska-Susitna Borough; Pop. 370; South central Alaska. Founded in 1917 and named in honor of U. S. Congressman, William C. Houston.

•**HUGHES,** City; Yukon-Koyukuk Census Area; Pop. 73; Zip Code 99745; Lat. 66-03-00 N long. 154-15-00 W; Central Alaska. Named in honor of circa 1910 New York Governor, Charles Evans Hughs.

•**HUSLIA,** City; Yukon-Koyukuk Census Area; Pop. 188; Zip Code 99746; Lat. 65-41-00 N long. 156-24-00 W; Central Alaska. Probably named for an early settler.

•**HYDABURG,** City; Prince of Wales- Outer Ketchikan Census Area; Pop. 298; Zip Code 99922; Lat. 55-12-20 N long. 132-49-28 W; Established in 1911 and named after the Haida Indians who settled the area after migrating from British Columbia.

•**JUNEAU,** City; Juneau Borough; Pop. 19,528; Zip Code 99801; Lat. 58-21-27 N long. 134-33-27 W; 90 mi. northeast of Sitka, located on the Gastineau Channel in southeastern Alaska. Juneau is the state capitol. Miner Joseph Juneau discovered gold here in 1880. The town is named in his honor.

•**KACHEMAK,** City; Kenai Peninsula Borough; Pop. 403; South central Alaska. An Aleut Indian word meaning "high cliff bay."

•**KAKE,** City; Wrangell-Petersburg Census Area; Pop. 555; Zip Code 99830; Lat. 56-58-30 N long. 133-55-30 W; Southeastern Alaska. The city is named after a once-warlike tribe of Tlingit Indians who lived in the area.

•**KAKTOVIK,** City; North Slope Borough; Pop. 165; Zip Code 99747; Lat. 70-08-00 N long. 143-38-00 W; Northern Alaska. An Eskimo Indian name meaning "place to fish."

•**KALTAG,** City; Yukon-Koyukuk Census Area; Pop. 247; Zip Code 99748; Lat. 64-20-00 N long. 158-43-00 W; Central Alaska. An Indian name referring to a species of salmon.

•**KASAAN,** City; Prince of Wales-Outer Ketchikan Census Area; Pop. 25; Southeastern Alaska. A Tlingits Indian word meaning "pretty village."

•**KENAI,** City; Kenai Peninsula Borough; Pop. 4,324; Zip Code 99611; South central Alaska. The city's name is an abbreviated version of Kenaiowkotana, a word meaning "non-Eskimo people."

•**KETCHIKAN,** City; Ketchikan Gateway Borough; Pop. 7,198; Zip Code 99901; Lat. 55-24-17 N long. 132-07-51 W; Southeastern Alaska on the southwestern coast of Revillagigedo Island. Ketchikan is a Tlingit Indian word meaning "eagle wing river."

•**KIANA,** City; Kobuk Census Area; Pop. 345; Zip Code 99749; Lat. 66-58-00 N long. 160-26-00 W; Northwestern Alaska. An Indian name which meaning is uncertain.

•**KING COVE,** City; Aleutian Islands Census Area; Pop. 460; Zip Code 99612; Lat. 55-04-15 N long. 162-10-30 W; Chain of islands extending 1700 mi. from the Alaskan Peninsula. Possibly named for an early settler.

•**KIVALINA,** City; Kobuk Census Area; Pop. 241; Zip Code 99750; Lat. 67-46-30 N long. 164-32-30 W; Northwestern Alaska. An Indian name whose meaning is unsure.

•**KLAWOCK,** City; Prince of Wales-Outer Ketchikan Census Area; Pop. 318; Zip Code 99925; Lat. 55-33-15 N long. 133-05-45 W; Southern Alaska. Klawock is a derivation of a Tlingit Indian village found here in the 1850's: Thlewhakh.

•**KOBUK,** City; Kobuk Census Area; Pop. 62; Zip Code 99751; Lat. 66-55-00 N long. 156-52-00 W; northwestern Alaska. An Eskimo word meaning "big river."

•**KODIAK,** City; Kodiak Island Borough; Pop. 4,756; Zip Code 99615; Lat. 57-20-48 N long. 153-09-58 W; Located in southern Alaska, on an island in the Gulf of Alaska, southeast of the Alaskan Peninsula. An Indian word meaning "island."

•**KOTLIK,** City; Wade Hampton Census Area; Pop. 293; Zip Code 99620; Lat. 63-02-00 N long. 163-33-00 W; West central Alaska. Kotlik is an Eskimo word meaning "breeches."

•**KOTZEBUE,** City; Kobuk Census Area; Pop. 2,054; Zip Code 99753; Lat. 66-53-46 N long. 163-01-10 W; Located at the tip of the Baldwin Peninsula in northwestern Alaska. The city is named after Russian explorer Otto von Kotzebue who sailed through this area in 1815.

•**KOYUK,** City; Nome Census Area; Pop. 188; Zip Code 99753; Lat. 64-56-00 N long. 161-09-00 W; Northwestern Alaska. An Indian word whose meaning has been lost.

•**KOYUKUK,** City; Yukon-Koyukuk Census Area; Pop. 98; Zip Code 99754; Lat. 64-50-00 N long. 157-42-00 W; Central Alaska. Koyukuk is an Indian word whose meaning has been forgotten.

•**KUPREANOF,** City; Wrangell- Petersburg Census Area; Pop. 47; Southeastern Alaska. The city's name honors Captain Ivan Kupreanof who served as governor of Russian American in 1835.

•**KWETHLUK,** City; Bethel Census Area; Pop. 454; Zip Code 99621; Lat. 60-49-00 N long. 161-26-00 W; West central Alaska. An Eskimo word meaning "bad river."

•**LARSEN BAY,** City; Kodiak Island Borough; Pop. 168; Zip Code 99624; Lat. 57-33-24 N long. 153-58-24 W; Off the coast of south central Alaska. Peter Larsen was a professionial hunter who worked in the area around 1900. The town is named after him.

•**LOWER KALSKAG,** City; Bethel Census Area; Pop. 246; Zip Code 99626; Lat. 61-30-50 N long. 160-21-30 W; West central Alaska. The origin of the town's name is uncertain.

•**MANOKOTAK,** City; Dillingham Census Area; Pop. 294; Zip Code 99628; Lat. 58-58-50 N long. 159-03-25 W; Southwest central Alaska. An Indian name whose meaning is unknown.

•**MCGRATH,** City; Yukon-Koyukuk Census Area;XSG; Pop. 355; Zip Code 99627; Lat. 62-57-30 N long. 155-35-30 W; Central Alaska. Peter McGrath was a fur trader and deputy marshall in the area in 1900. The town is named after him.

•**MEKORYUK,** City; Bethel Census Area; Pop. 160; Zip Code 99630; Lat. 60-23-00 N long. 166-11-00 W; West central Alaska. An Eskimo name of uncertain meaning.

•**MOUNTAIN VILLAGE**, City; Wade Hampton Census Area; Pop. 583; Zip Code 99623; Lat. 62-05-00 N long. 163-43-00 W; West central Alaska. Descriptively named for its location.

•**NAPAKIAK,** City; Bethel Census Area; Pop. 262; Zip Code 99634; Lat. 60-42-30 N long. 161-54-30 W; West central Alaska. An Eskimo name meaning "wood people."

•**NAPASKIAK,** City; Bethel Census Area; Pop. 244; Zip Code 99559; West central Alaska. Napaskiak is an Eskimo term meaning "wood people."

•**NENANA,** City; Yukon-Koyukuk Census Area; Pop. 470; Zip Code 99760; Lat. 64-25-00 N long. 149-15-00 W; Central Alaska. An Indian name meaning ... something "river."

•**NEWHALEN,** City; Dillingham Census Area; Pop. 87; Southwest central Alaska. The word is a corruption of the Eskimo Noghelingmute, or "people of the Noghelin River."

•**NEW STUYAHOK,** City; Dillingham Census Area; Pop. 331; Zip Code 99636; Lat. 59-29-00 N long. 157-20-00 W; Southwest central Alaska. Named after its former incarnation.

•**NEWTOK,** City; Bethel and Wade Hampton Census Areas; Pop. 131; Zip Code 99559; West central Alaska. An Indian word of uncertain origin.

•**NIGHTMUTE,** City; Bethel Census Area; Pop. 119; Zip Code 99690; West central Alaska. An Eskimo word with an unknown adjective attached to mute, or people.

•**NIKOLAI,** City; Yukon-Koyukuk Census Area; Pop. 91; Zip Code 99691; Lat. 52-56-23 N long. 168-51-35 W; Central Alaska. Named for an early Russian explorer.

•**NOME,** City; Nome Census Area; Pop. 2,301; Zip Code 99762; Lat. 64-57-20 N long. 165-48-35 W; 14 mi. west of Cape Nome and approx. 100 mi. east of the Bering Strait, on the south side of the Seward Peninsula in western Alaska. Originally Anvil City, the name comes from nearby Cape Nome.

•**NONDALTON,** City; Dillingham Census Area; Pop. 173; Zip Code 99640; Lat. 60-26-00 N long. 158-40-39 W; Southwest central Alaska. Nondalton is a Tanaina Indian word of uncertain meaning.

•**NOORVIK,** City; Kobuk Census Area; Pop. 492; Zip Code 99763; Lat. 66-50-00 N long. 161-03-00 W; Northwestern Alaska. Possibly a name given by early explorers.

•**NORTH POLE,** City; Fairbanks North Star Borough; Pop. 724; Zip Code 99705; Central Alaska. A promotional name given the town when it incorporated in 1953.

•**NUIQSUT,** City; North Slope Borough; Pop. 208; Zip Code 99723; Northern Alaska. An Eskimo word whose meaning is lost.

•**NULATO,** City; Yukon-Koyukuk Census Area; Pop. 350; Zip Code 99765; Lat. 64-43-00 N long. 158-06-00 W; Central Alaska. An Indian word meaning "place where the salmon come."

•**OLD HARBOR,** City; Kodiak Island Borough; Pop. 340; Zip Code 99643; Lat. 57-12-24 N long. 153-18-24 W; Located off the coast of south central Alaska. Descriptively named for its location as the first Russian settlement in Alaska.

•**OUZINKIE,** City; Kodiak Island Borough; Pop. 173; Zip Code 99644; Lat. 57-56-00 N long. 152-30-00 W; Located off the coast of south central Alaska. An English translation of the Russian term Uzen'kii, or "narrow," which referred to narrow strait where the city is located.

•**PALMER,** City; Matanuska-Susitna Borough; Pop. 2,141; Zip Code 99645; Lat. 61-35-43 N long. 149-20-02 W; 5 mi. northeast of Matanuska in southeastern Alaska. George Palmer was a local trader here in 1880. The town is named after him.

•**PELICAN**, City; Skagway-Yakutat-Angoon Census Area; Pop. 180; Zip Code 99832; Lat. 57-57-30 N long. 136-13-30 W; Southeastern Alaska. The town's founder owned a fishing boat named Pelican. The settlement took this name.

•**PETERSBURG**, City; Wrangell-Petersburg Census Area; Pop. 2,821; Zip Code 99833; Lat. 56-47-41 N long. 132-57-34 W; 35 mi. north, northwest of Wrangell in southeastern Alaska. Peter Buschmann founded a cannery here in 1897. The town is named after him.

•**PILOT STATION**, City; Wade Hampton Census Area; Pop. 325; Zip Code 99650; Lat. 61-56-20 N long. 162-52-30 W; West central Alaska. Descriptively named as a landmark by early riverboat pilots.

•**PLATINUM**, City; Bethel Census Area; Pop. 55; Zip Code 99651; Lat. 59-00-45 N long. 161-49-00 W; West central Alaska. Platinum was discovered here in 1927. The town was named for this discovery.

•**POINT HOPE**, City; North Slope Borough; Pop. 464; Zip Code 99766; Lat. 68-36-39 N long. 166-26-12 W; Northern Alaska. Royal navy captain Frederick Beechey named the nearby point for a friend, Sir William J. Hope.

•**PORT ALEXANDER**, City; Wrangell-Petersburg Census Area; Pop. 86; Zip Code 99836; Southeastern Alaska. Named in honor of Alexander A. Andreevich, governor of Russian America from 1799 to 1818.

•**PORT HEIDEN**, City; Dillingham Census Area; Pop. 92; Zip Code 99549; Southwest central Alaska. The city was named by Russian explorer Feodor Lutke after a Count Heiden.

•**PORT LIONS**, City; Kodiak Island Borough; Pop. 215; Zip Code 99550; Lat. 57-54-00 N long. 152-57-00 W; Located off the coast of south central Alaska. The Lions Club helped rebuild the former town of Afognak after it was destroyed in the 1964 earthquake. The grateful residents named it in their honor.

•**QUINHAGAK**, City; Bethel Census Area; Pop. 412; Zip Code 99655; Lat. 59-45-00 N long. 161-54-00 W; Southwest central Alaska. An Eskimo name which means "newly formed river."

•**RUBY**, City; Yukon-Koyukuk Census Area; Pop. 197; Zip Code 99768; Lat. 64-45-00 N long. 155-30-00 W; Central Alaska. The town is named after nearby Ruby Creek.

•**RUSSIAN MISSION** City; Wade Hampton Census Area; Pop. 169; Zip Code 99657; West central Alaska. Founded in 1837 and descriptively named as the site of a Russian Orthodox church.

•**ST. MARY'S**, City; Wade Hampton Census Area; Pop. 382; Zip Code 99658; Lat. 62-02-30 N long. 163-13-30 W; West central Alaska. Named after an early church.

•**ST. MICHAEL**, City; Nome Census Area; Pop. 239; Zip Code 99659; Lat. 63-29-00 N long. 162-02-00 W; Northwestern Alaska. Christened by Russian explorer Mikhail Tebenkov after his name saint in 1831.

•**ST. PAUL**, City; Aleutian Islands Census Area; Pop. 551; Zip Code 99660; Chain of islands extending from the Alaskan Peninsula. The city is named after biblical St. Paul.

•**SAND POINT**, City; Aleutian Islands Census Area; Pop. 625; Zip Code 99661; Lat. 55-17-22 N long. 160-31-27 W; Chain of islands extending 1700 mi. from the Alaskan Peninsula. Descriptively named for the low, flat, sandy spit nearby.

•**SAVOONGA**, City; Nome Census Area; Pop. 491; Zip Code 99769; Lat. 63-42-00 N long. 170-29-00 W; Northwestern Alaska. Savoonga is an Eskimo word of lost meaning.

•**SAXMAN**, City; Ketchikan Gateway Borough; Pop. 273; southeastern Alaska. Named in honor of schoolteacher Samuel Saxman who lived in the area in the 1880's.

•**SCAMMON BAY**, City; Wade Hampton Census Area; Pop. 250; Zip Code 99662; Lat. 61-50-45 N long. 165-35-00 W; west central Alaska. The city is named after Captain Charles Scammon who helped chart the area in 1865.

•**SELAWIK**, City; Kobuk Census Area; Pop. 361; Zip Code 99770; Lat. 66-36-00 N long. 160-00-00 W; northwestern Alaska. Selawik is an Eskimo word for a local species of fish.

•**SELDOVIA**, City; Kenai Peninsula Borough; Pop. 479; Zip Code 99663; Lat. 59-26-15 N long. 151-42-30 W; south central Alaska. The town's name is derived from a Russian word meaning "herring bay."

•**SEWARD**, City; Kenai Peninsula Borough; Pop. 1,843; Zip Code 99664; Lat. 60-07-02 N long. 149-26-19 W; south central Alaska. The city is named in honor of Secretary of State William Seward who led the effort to purchase Alaska from the Russians in 1867.

•**SHAGELUK**, City; Yukon-Koyukuk Census Area; Pop. 131; Zip Code 99665; Lat. 62-41-00 N long. 159-34-00 W; central Alaska. Shageluk is an Ingalik Indian name meaning "village of the dog people."

•**SHAKTOOLIK**, City; Nome Census Area; Pop. 164; Zip Code 99771; Lat. 64-20-00 N long. 161-09-00 W; northwestern Alaska. An Indian word of uncertain meaning.

•**SHELDON POINT**, City; Wade Hampton Census Area; Pop. 103; Zip Code 99666; west central Alaska. An early settler named Sheldon ran a salt mill nearby. The city is named after him.

•**SHISHMAREF**, City; Nome Census Area; Pop. 394; Zip Code 99772; Lat. 66-15-00 N long. 166-04-00 W; northwestern Alaska. The city is named for a nearby inlet, the inlet is named for a Russian officer who helped explore the region in 1816.

•**SHUNGNAK**, City; Kobuk Census Area; Pop. 202; Zip Code 99773; Lat. 66-52-00 N long. 157-09-00 W; Northwestern Alaska. An Eskimo term meaning "jade," and referring to the gemstones found in the vicinity.

•**SITKA**, City; Sitka Borough; Pop. 7,803; Zip Code 99835; Lat. 57-03-12 N long. 135-20-27 W; Located on the west coast of Baranof Island, 930 mi. north of Seattle, Washington, in southeastern Alaska. Sitka is a Tlingit Indian word meaning "by the sea."

•**SKAGWAY**, City; Skagway-Yakutat-Angoon Census Area; Pop. 768; Zip Code 99840; Lat. 59-27-30 N long. 135-18-45 W; Southeastern Alaska. The city's name is a descriptive Indian term meaning "end of the salt water," and referring to the town's location on an inlet.

•**SOLDOTNA**, City; Kenai Peninsula Borough; Pop. 2,320; Zip Code 99669; Lat. 60-29-00 N long. 151-03-00 W; South central Alaska. The city's name is derived from the Russian term for "soldier."

•**TANANA**, City; Yukon-Koyukuk Census Area; Pop. 388; Zip Code 99777; Lat. 65-10-00 N long. 152-04-00 W; Central Alaska. Located on the Tanana River, the term means "River Trail."

•**TELLER,** City; Nome Census Area; Pop. 212; Zip Code 99778; Lat. 65-16-00 N long. 166-22-00 W; Northwestern Alaska. Henry Teller was a U. S. Senator from Colorado in the 1870's. The town is named in his honor.

•**TENAKEE SPRINGS,** City; Skagway-Yakutat-Angoon Census Area; Pop. 138; Zip Code 99841; Lat. 57-46-50 N long. 135-13-00 W; Southeastern Alaska. Tenakee is an Indian word of uncertain meaning

•**TOGIAK,** City; Dillingham Census Area; Pop. 470; Zip Code 99678; Lat. 59-04-00 N long. 160-24-00 W; Southwest central Alaska. An Eskimo tribal name meaning "Togiaga people."

•**TOKSOOK BAY,** City; Bethel Census Area; Pop. 333; Zip Code 99637; West central Alaska. Toksook is an Indian term of uncertain meaning.

•**TUNUNAK,** City; Bethel Census Area; Pop. 298; Zip Code 99681; Lat. 60-37-00 N long. 165-15-00 W; West central Alaska. An Eskimo word meaning "reindeer."

•**UNALAKLEET,** City; Nome Census Area; Pop. 623; Zip Code 99684; Lat. 63-52-25 N long. 160-47-00 W; Northwestern Alaska. An Eskimo place name meaning "the southernmost one," and referring to its location just north of the river.

•**UNALASKA,** City; Aleutian Islands Census Area; Pop. 1,322; Zip Code 99685; Lat. 53-52-30 N long. 166-32-00 W; Chain of islands extending 1700 mi. from the Alaskan Peninsula. An Aleut Indian word meaning "this great land."

•**VALDEZ,** City; Valdez-Cordova Census Area; Pop. 3,079; Zip Code 99686; Lat. 61-07-00 N long. 146-16-00 W; Southern Alaska on the northeast shore of Prine William Sound. Spain's Minister of the Marine in 1791 organized the exploration of the area by Lt. Salvador Fidalgo. The Fiord and town are named in his honor.

•**WAINWRIGHT,** City; North Slope Borough; Pop. 405; Zip Code 99782; Lat. 70-38-15 N long. 160-01-45 W; Northern Alaska. British explorer Captain Frederick Beechey named the adjacent inlet in honor of expedition astronomer Lt. John Wainwright.

•**WALES,** City; Nome Census Area; Pop. 133; Zip Code 99783; Lat. 65-37-00 N long. 168-05-00 W; Northwestern Alaska. Captain Cook named the nearby cape after the Prince of Wales in 1778. The town later took its name from this designation.

•**WASILLA,** City; Matanusks-Susitna Borough; Pop. 1,559; Zip Code 99687; Lat. 61-33-30 N long. 149-43-29 W; south central Alaska. Founded in 1916 and named after a Knik Indian chief.

•**WHITE MOUNTAIN,** City; Nome Census Area; Pop. 125; Zip Code 99784; Lat. 64-41-00 N long. 163-24-00 W; northwestern Alaska. Named for the nearby mountain, white because of its limestone composition.

•**WHITTIER,** City; Valdez-Cordova Census Area; Pop. 198; Zip Code 99693; south central Alaska. Founded during World War II and named for poet John Greenleaf Whittier.

•**WRANGELL,** City; Wrangell-Petersburg Census Area; Pop. 2,184; Zip Code 99929; Lat. 56-28-00 N long. 132-22-40 W; located south of the mouth of the Stikine River, on the northern tip of Wrangell Island in southeastern Alaska, northeast of Prince of Wales Island. Baron Ferdinand Wrangell was governor of Russian America from 1830-1835. The town is named after him.

•**YAKUTAT,** City; Skagway-Yakutat-Angoon Census Area; Pop. 449; Zip Code 99689; Lat. 59-33-00 N long. 139-44-00 W; Southeastern Alaska. An Indian word meaning "ocean estuary."

ARIZONA

•**APACHE JUNCTION**, City; Pinal County; Pop. 9,935; Zip Code 85220; Lat. 33-24-55 N long. 111-33-58 W southern Arizona; Named for the Apache Trail which begins at the east end of the city.

•**AVONDALE**, City; Maricopa County; Pop. 8,134; Zip Code 85323; Lat. 33-26-00 N long. 112-20-50 W; W of Phoenix in SW central Arizona; Named for the nearby Avondale Ranch.

•**BENSON**, Town; Cochise County; Pop. 4,190; Zip Code 85602; Elev. 3581; Lat. 31-57-10 N long.110-17-48 W; 40m. SE of Tucson in SE Arizona; Founded in 1880 as the railroad town for Tombstone.

•**BISBEE**, City; Cochise County Seat; Pop. 7,154; Zip Code 85603; Elev. 5400; Lat. 31-25-14 N long. 109-54-08 W; 60m. E of Nogales in SE AZ.

•**BUCKEYE**, Town; Maricopa County; Pop. 3,434; Zip Code 85326; Elev. 1900; Lat. 33-22-17 N; long. 112-34-37 W; 30m. W of Phoenix in SW central Arizona; Early founders Thomas Newton Clanton and M. M. Jackson called this place Buckeye for their homestate of Ohio. When the post office was established, the town was named Sydney. So many people still used the name Buckeye however, that in 1931 the town was incorporated under that name.

•**CASA GRANDE**, City; Pinal County; Pop. 14,971; Zip Code 85222; Elev. 1395; Lat. 32-53-25 N; long. 111-43-42 W; 45m. SE of Phoenix in SW central Arizona; Named by the railroad after the nearby Casa Grande Indian ruins. In Spanish the words casa grande means "big house."

•**CHANDLER**, City; Maricopa County; Pop. 29,673; Zip Code 85224; Elev. 1213; Lat. 33-18-21; long. 111-45-37 W; 15m. SE of Phoenix in S Arizona; Named for Alexander John Chandler, who came to Arizona in 1887 as the territory's first veterinary surgeon.

•**CHINO VALLEY**, Town; Yavapai County; Pop. 2,858; Zip Code 86323; Elev. 4610; Lat. 34-44-38 N; long. 112-27-10 W; central Arizona; The Mexicans called the grama grass that grew in the valley "de china." When Amiel Whipple came to the valley in 1854 he called it Val de China or Chino for the Mexican name. In Spanish the word Chino means "curly hair." Since the grass had a curly appearance this may account for the origin of the name.

•**CLARKDALE**, Town; Yavapai County; Pop. 1,512; Zip Code 2568; Elev. 2568; Lat. 34-45-48; N; long. 112-03-30 W; central Arizona; A mining community named for William A. Clark, a Montana senator, who bought a mining interest and established a smelter there.

•**CLIFTON**, Town; Greenlee County Seat; Pop. 4,245; Zip Code 85533; Elev. 3460; Lat. 33-03-03 N; long. 109-18-05 W; 110m. NE of Tucson in NE Arizona; Situated in the midst of towering cliffs, this copper mining town was first called Cliff Town and later shortened to the present name.

•**COOLIDGE**, City; Pinal County; Pop. 6,851; Zip Code 85228; Elev. 1400; Lat. 32-58-41 N; long. 111-31-23 W; southern Arizona; The city was established and named when the Coolidge Dam was constructed nearby.

•**COTTONWOOD**, Town; Yavapai County; Pop. 4,550; Zip Code 86326; Elev. 3314; Lat. 34-43-41 N; long. 112-01-01 W; 15m SW Flagstaff in central Arizona; Named for a nearby circle of sixteen large cottonwood trees which have long since disappeared.

•**DOUGLAS**, City; Cochise County; Pop. 13,058; Zip Code 85607; Elev. 4004; Lat. 31-20-42 N; long. 109-32-16 W; on Mexican border in S Arizona; The place was first known as Black Water, for a dirty but much used water hole situated there. In 1901 a town was founded at that spot and named in honor of Dr. James Stewart Douglas.

•**DUNCAN**, Town; Greenlee County; Pop. 603; Zip Code 85534; Elev. 3642; Lat. 32-42-12 N; long. 109-03-07 W; SW Arizona; Named either for Duncan Smith, who sold his land to the Arizona Cooper Company at the coming of the railroad in 1883, or aftr the Duncan brothers, who settled here and were killed by Apaches around 1885.

•**EGGAR**, Town; Apache County; Pop. 2,791; Zip Code 85925; Lat. 34-06-40 N; long. 109-17-18 W; NE corner AZ.

•**EL MIRAGE**, Town; Maricopa County; Pop. 4,307; Zip Code 85335; Lat. 33-36-38 N; long. 112-19-16 W; 5m. NW of Phoenix in SW central Arizona; The origin of the town name is not known.

•**ELAY**, City; Pinal County; Pop. 6,240; Zip Code 85231; Elev. 1400; Lat. 32-45-24 N; long. 111-32-52 W; southern Arizona; Established around 1920 on a piece of land referred to as Eloy. City planners wanted to use the name cotton city but the post office rejected the name in favor of the traditionally used Eloy.

•**FLAGSTAFF**, City; Coconino County Seat; Pop. 34,641; Zip Code 86001; Elev. 910; 65m. NE of Prescott in N Arizona; There are varying stories as to the origin of the name. According to one account, either a scouting party or early settler F. F. McMillen spotted a lone pine on an open valley and stripped it of its branches in order to raise an American flag on the pole.

•**FLORENCE**, Town; Pinal County Seat; Pop. 3,391; Zip Code 85232; Elev. 1493; Lat. 33-01-33 N; long. 111-22-55 W; 50m. SE of Phoenix in S Arizona; In 1868 Gov. Richard McCormick named the town Florence, after his sister.

•**FREDONIA**, Town; Coconino County; Pop. 1.040; Zip Code 86022; Elev. 6752; Lat. 36-57-00 N; long. 112-31-29 W; northern Arizona; Founded by Mormons seeking freedom from prosecution for polygamy, and first named Hardscrabble. The name was later changed to Fredonia as a representative of their search for freedom.

•**GILA BEND**, Town; Maricopa County; Pop. 1,585; Zip Code 85337; Elev. 750; Lat. 32-56-57 N; long. 112-42-52 W; SW central Arizona; Named for its original location at a 90 degree bend in the Gila River. Early visitors called the place Big Bend, but this was gradually changed to Gila Bend.

•**GILBERT**, Town; Maricopa County; Pop. 5,717; Zip Code 85234; Lat. 33-21-00 N; long. 111-47-24 W; Named for Robert Gilbert who donated land on which the railroad station and town were located.

•**GLENDALE**, City; Maricopa County; Pop. 96,988; Zip Code 85301; Elev. 1150; Lat. 33-32-48 N; long. 112-11-11 W; 10m. NW of Phoenix in SW central Arizona; Established in 1892 by the New England Land Company. It is not known how the name Glendale was chosen for the town.

•**GLOBE**, City; Gila County Seat; Pop. 6,708; Zip Code 85501; Elev. 3509; Lat. 33-24-14 N; long. 110-47-47 W; 70m. E of Phoenix in E central Arizona; Named after the nearby Globe Mine. The origin of the name Globe may have come from silver prospectors who named the place for its immense size, or from a perfectly round boulder discovered in the area by cavalry men.

•**GOODYEAR**, Town; Maricopa County; Pop. 2,747; SW Arizona; Built on land purchased by the Goodyear Tire and Rubber Company to produce Egyptian cotton. The town, first called Egypt, after the cotton, was shortly after changed to Goodyear.

•GUADALUPE, Town; Maricopa County; Pop. 4,506; SW central Arizona; Established by Yaqui Indians who fled Mexico to avoid the persecution of Porfirio Diaz. The village was named for the virgin of Guadalupe, patron saint of Mexico.

•HAYDEN, Town; Gila and Pinal County; Pop. 1,205; Zip Code 85235; Elev. 8380; Lat. 33-00-12 N; long. 110-47-02 W; in E central Arizona; Named for Charles Hayden of Hayden, Stone and Company which operated mines in the area.

•HOLBROOK, City; Navajo County Seat; Pop. 5,785; Zip Code 86025; Elev. 5083; Lat. 34-54-33 N; long. 110-09-09 W; NE Arizona; Named in 1882 in honor of H. R. Holbrook when railroad staton was first established here.

•HUACHUCA CITY, Town; Cochise County; Pop. 1,661; Zip Code 85616; Lat. 31-37-21 N; long. 110-19-21 W; SE corner of Arizona; Called Huachuca, a name first used for a Pima Indian village at this place.

•JEROME, Town; Yavapai County; Pop. 420; Zip Code 86331; Elev. 5435; Lat. 34-44-28 N; long. 112-006-39 W; central Arizona; Jerome was a mining town which grew up around nearby copper mines. It is said, the copper in this area was mined by Indians as early as 1582.

•KEARNEY, Town; Pinal County; Pop. 2,646; Zip Code 85237; Lat. 33-03-17 N; long. 110-54-19 W; southern Arizona; Founded by the Kennecott Copper Company in 1958 and named after General Philip Kearny who explored the Gila River area from 1849-50.

•KINGMAN, City; Mohave County Seat; Pop. 9,257; Zip Code 86401; Elev. 3340; Lat. 35-12-06 N; long. 114-02-29 W; 65m. SE of Boulder Dam in NW Arizona; Named after Lewis Kingman, a railroad engineer who chose the locaton for the city in the 1880's.

•LAKE HAVASU CITY, City; Mohave County; Pop. 15,737; Zip Code 86403; Elev. 15909; Lat. 34-30-00 N; long. 114-20-00 W; NW corner of AZ.

•MAMMOTH, Town; Pinal County; Pop. 1,906; Zip Code 85618; Elev. 2399; Lat. 32-43-19 N; long. 110-38-32 W; southern Arizona; Named after the nearby Mammoth Mine. The site was the location for a stamp mill to work the gold ores from the mine. Later a town developed around the mill.

•MARANA, Town; Pima County; Pop. 1,674; Zip Code 85238; Elev. 1900; Lat. 32-27-21 N; long. 111-12-42 W; southern Arizona; The word marana is Spanish for "tangle" or "impassable because of briars and brambles." The town is located in a valley once noted for its thick growth of mesquite and other desert plants.

•MESA, City; Maricopa County; Pop. 152,453; Zip Code 85201; Elev. 244; Lat. 33-25-59 N; long. 111-49-56 W; 15m. E of Phoenix in SW AZ.

•MIAMI, Town; Gila County; Pop. 2,716; Zip Code 85539; Elev. 3411; Lat. 33-23-51 N; long. 110-52-11 W; E central Arizona; Located near the Mimi Mine and a custom mill, constructed by a group from Miami, Ohio who called the creek the Miami Wash, the town took its name from a blending of the two places.

•NOGALES, City; Santa Cruz County Seat; Pop. 15,683; Zip Code 85621; Lat. 31-20-38 N; long. 110-56-05 W; 60m. S of Tucson on the Mexican border. Named Nogales, the Spanish word for "walnuts" for two walnut trees at this spot, one on each side of the border.

•PAGE, City; Coconino County; Pop. 4,907; Zip Code 86036; Lat. 36-48-59 N; long. 111-38-17 W; N central Arizona; Named for John Chatfield Page, the Commissioner of Reclamation, 1937-43. The community began in 1957 as a home for construction workers for the Glen Canyon Dam.

•PARADISE VALLEY, Town; Maricopa County; Pop. 10,832; Zip Code ; SW central Arizona; When the promoters of the Rio Verde Canal Company first came to this valley in the spring of 1899, it was covered with flowers. This led to the name Paradise Valley.

•PARKER, Town; Yuma County; Pop. 2,542; Zip Code 85371; Elev. 2542; Lat. 34-08-42 N; long. 114-17-25 W; SW corner Arizona; Associated with the Colorado river Reservation. When a name was needed for the post office established here, the place was called Parker in honor of Gen. Eli Parker, Commissioner of Indian Affairs.

•PATAGONIA, Town; Santa Cruz County; Pop. 980; Zip Code 85624; Elev. 4057; Lat. 31-32-33 N; long. 110-44-44 W; southern Arizona; Although the name Rollen was proposed for the town by oil baron and rancher Rollen Richardson , the townspeople named it Patagonia after the nearby Patagonia Mountains.

•PAYSON, Town; Gila County; Pop. 5,068; Zip Code 85541; Elev. 4887; Lat. 34-14-09 N; long. 111-19-51 W; E central Arizona; Founded under the name Union Park in 1882, the people in the area continued to call the place Green Valley until the post office was established. Then the town was named in honor of Senator Louis Edward Payson.

•PEORIA, City; Maricopa County; Pop. 12,251; Zip Code 85345; Lat. 33-32-52 N; long. 112-13-19 W; SW central Arizona; Thought to have been named either by early settler Chauncey Clark, or by town planners D. S. Brown and J. B. Greenhut, all of whom came from Peoria, Illinois.

•PHOENIX, City; Maricopa County Seat; Pop. 764,911; Zip Code 85000; Lat. 33-29-43 N; long. 112-01-58 W; SW central AZ on the Salt River. Named by members of the Swilling Irrigation Canal Company who needed a specific address to speed the deliveruy of supplies. The name Phoenix was suggested because of the traces of an ancient civilization at the site. The new city, like the legendary Phoenix, would rise out of the ashes of the old.

•PIMA, Town; Graham County; Pop. 1,599; Zip Code 85535; Lat. 32-42-53 N long. 111-29-58 W; SE Arizona; Founded in 1879 by Mormons and named Smithville in honor of Mormon leader Jesse N. Smith. The town name was changed to Pima when the post office was established.

•PRESCOTT, City; Yavapai County; Pop. 20,055; Zip Code 8630l; Lat. 34-32-29 N long. 112-23-21W Elev.3542; 80m. NW of Phoenix in central Arizona; Established in 1864 and named for historian william Hickling Prescott who was noted for his books on the Azlees and Incas.

•PRESCOTT VALLEY, Town; Yavapai County; Pop. 2,284; Zip Code 86330; Lat. 34-35-04 N long. 111-34-20 W; central AZ.

•SAFFORD, City; Graham County Seat; Pop. 7,010; Zip Code 85546; Lat. 32-49-l2 N l09-42-3l W ; on Gila River in SE Arizona; Settled by farmers in 1874 and named for Gov. Anson Pacely Killen Safford, who had recently visited the valley.

•ST. JOHNS, City; Apache County Seat; Pop. 3,343; Zip Code 85936; Lat. 34-30-35 N long. 109-21-52W ; Elev. 5686; eastern Arizona; First known as El Vadito (little crossing) for its location at the crossing of the Little Colorado River. The name was later changed to San Juan (St. John) either for the first woman resident, Maria San Juan Baca de Padilla, or for the annual feast of San Juan on June 24.

•**SAN LUIS,** Town; Yuma County; Pop. 1,946; Zip Code 85349; Lat. 32-29-l3 N long. 114-47-00 W; SW corner of Arizona; Located on both sides of the United States/Mexico border. The source of the town name has not yet been ascentained.

•**SCOTTSDALE,** City; Maricopa County; Pop. 88,364; Zip Code 8525l; Lat. 33-29-26 N long. 111-55-59W ; eastern suburb of Phoenix in central Arizona; Named for Major Winfield Scott, an army chaplain and homesteader who first came to the area in 1881.

•**SHOW LOW,** City; Navajo County; Pop. 4,298; Zip Code 8590l; Lat. 34-l5-04 N long. 110-01-46 W; Elev. 6347; NE AZ.

•**SIERRA VISTA,** City; Cochise County; Pop. 25,968; Zip Code 856l3; Lat. 31-33-04 N long. 110-20-46 W; 50m. SE of Tucson in SE Arizona; First known as Garden Canyon, because the canyon at the edge of the community had produce gardens for nearby Fort Huachuca. In the late 1800's the name was changed to Fry, after Oliver Fry, a homesteader. Later, in 1955, the citizens petitioned to change the town name to Sierra Vista.

•**SNOWFLAKE,** Town; Navajo County; Pop. 3,510; Zip Code 85937; Lat. 34-30-40 N long. 110-04-49 W; NE Arizona; Named after William J. Flake, a rancher, and Erastus Snow who settled in the area in 1878.

•**SOMERTON,** Town; Yuma County; Pop. 5,761; Zip Code 85350; Lat. 32-35-53 N long. 114-42-59 W; SW corner of Arizona; The name for the town was suggested by Capt. A.D. Yocum, who reportedly named it after his hometown.

•**SOUTH TUCSON,** City; Pima County; Pop. 6,554; Zip Code ; southern Arizona; Named for nearby Sentinel Mountain. The Papago Indian name for the mountain was Chuk Shon. The Spanish corrupted the pronunciation to Tuqui son, or its current form, Tuscon.

•**SPRINGERVILLE,** Town; Apache County; Pop. 1,452; Zip Code 85938; Lat. 34-07-49 N long. 109-16-38 W; Elev. 69678; NE corner Arizona; Named after Harry Springer who opened a general store there in 1875. The place was first called Springer's Store. Later, when the name for the post office was chosen, it became "Springerville."

•**SUPERIOR,** Town; Pinal County; Pop. 4,600; Zip Code 86435; Lat. 35-l3-53 N long. 112-14-15 W; Elev. 3l95; southern Arizona; First known as Barnes. The town was laid out around 1910 and named for theArizona and Lake Superior Mining Company which operated silver mines in the area.

•**SURPRISE,** Town; Maricopa County; Pop. 3,723; Zip Code ; SW central Arizona; Named for a well sunk here which hit water at forty feet. Since most wells in the area had to go down one hundred to three hundred feet to find water, the discovery was a surprise.

•**TAYLOR,** Town; Navajo County; Pop. 1,915; Zip Code 85939; Lat. 34-28-22 N long. 110-05-18 W; NE corner of Arizona; Residents of this settlement originally wanted to call the town Walker, but since a post office named Walker already existed in Arizona, they called the town Taylor in honor of John Taylor, president of the Church of Latter-Day Saints.

•**TEMPE,** City; Maricopa County; Pop. 106,743; Zip Code 8528l; Lat. 33-25-0l N long. 111-59-30 W; 10m. NE of Phoenix in SW cen. Arizona; First known as Butte City, and later Hayden's Butte for its founder Charles Trumbull Hayden. The town was eventually named Tempe because of the similarity of the landscape to the Vale of Tempe in Greece.

•**THATCHER,** Town; Graham County; Pop. 3,374; Zip Code 85552; Lat. 32-50-26 N long. 109-45-11 W; SE Arizona; Settled by Mormons and named for the Mormon Apostle Moses Thatcher who visited the place in Christmas 1882.

•**TOLLESON,** City; Maricopa County; Pop. 4,433; Zip Code 85353; Lat. 33-27-02 N long. 112-15-31 W; SW cen. Arizona; Named for W. G.Tolleson in 1912.

•**TOMBSTONE,** City; Cochise County; Pop. 1,632; Zip Code 85638; Lat. 3l-4l-47 N long. 110-03-58 W; SE corner Arizona; Named by prospector Ed Schieffelin when he hit his first strike at this place in February 1870.

•**TUCSON,** City; Pima County Seat; Pop. 330,537; Zip Code 85700; Lat. 32-13-08 N long. 110-55-15 W; 105m. SE of Phoenix in S Arizona; Named for the nearby landmark known as Sentinel Mountain. The Papago Indian name for the mountain was Chuk Shon. The Spanish pronunciation changed the name to Tuqui Son, which eventaully became Tuscon.

•**WELTON,** Town; Yuma County; Pop. 911; Zip Code 85356; Lat. 32-40-20 N long. 114-08-17 W; SW corner of Arizona; Named for the Wells sunk here to supply water for trains coming through the region.

•**WICKENBURG,** Town; Maricopa County; Pop. 3,535; Zip Code 85358; Lat. 33-58-08 N long. 112-44-02 W; Elev. 2903; SW central Arizona; Named after Henry Wickenburg who fled Austria for selling coal instead of turning it over to the state. He came to Arizona in 1862 and built a ranch in the area that later became known by his name.

•**WILCOX,** City; Cochise County; Pop. 3,243; Zip Code 85643; Lat. 32-l5-02 N long. 109-49-40 W; northern Arizona; First called Maley after James H. Mahley, a rancher who gave right-of-way to the railraod over his lands. It is said that when the first train came through, Gen. Orlando B. Willcox, Commander of the Department of Arizona, was on board. He was given an ovation and the town name was probably changed in his honor.

•**WILLIAMS,** City; Coconino County; Pop. 2,266; Zip Code 86046; Lat. 35-l5-l0 N long. 112-11-14 W; northern Arizona; Named for its location at the base of Bill Williams Mountain.

•**WINKELMAN,** Town; Gila County; Pop. 1,060; Zip Code 85292; Lat. 32-59-2- N long. 110-46-03 W; E central Arizona; Named after Peter Winkelman who owned a ranch near here.

•**WINSLOW,** City; Navajo County; Pop. 7,291; Zip Code 86047; Lat. 35-0l-54 N long. 110-42-08 W; 60m. E of Flagstaff in in NE Arizona; First established as a terminal for the A & P Railroad. The city was either named for prospector Tom Winslow or for Gen. Edward Winslow, president of the associated St. Louis and San Francisco Railroad.

•**YOUNGTOWN,** Town; Maricopa County; Pop. 2,254; Zip Code 85363; Lat. 33-35-37 N long. 112-18-05 W; SW central Arizona; Established in 1955 as a retirement village and given the euphemistic name Youngtown.

•**YUMA,** City; Yuma County Seat; Pop. 42,433; Zip Code 85364; Lat. 32-43-56 N long. 114-34-44 W; SW corner of Arizona; The source of the name is not clear, but it may have come from the Indian title "yah-mayo" meaning "son of the captain." Early Spanish missionaries may have misunderstood its meaning and applied the name Yuma to the entire tribe.

ARKANSAS

ADONA, Town; Perry County; Pop. 230; Zip Code 72001; Elev. 371; Lat. 35-02-18 N long. 092-54-00 W; central Arkansas. The exact origin of Adona's name is uncertain.

•**ALICIA,** Town; Lawrence County; Pop. 246; Zip Code 72410; Elev. 254; NE Arkansas. Alicia is named after the wife of an early settler.

•**ALMA,** City; Crawford County; Pop. 2,755; Zip Code 72921; Elev. 430; NW Arkansas. Named after the Alma River in the Russian crimera.

•**ALMYRA,** Town; Arkansas County; Pop. 294; Zip Code 72003; Lat. 34-24-18 W long. 091-24-31 W; E Arkansas. The town is named after a pioneer's wife.

•**ALPENA,** Town; Boone County; Pop. 344; Zip Code 72611; Elev. 1,135 N Arkansas. Descriptively named for the town's mountainous geography.

•**ALTHEIMER,** City; Jefferson County; Pop. 1,231; Zip Code 72004; Lat. 36-17-33 N long. 093-17-36 W; SE central AR; Altheimer was an early settler. The town is named after him.

•**ALTUS,** City; Franklin County; Pop. 441; Zip Code 72821; Elev. 538; NW Arkansas. Latin for "highest." So named as the highest point on the rail line between Little Rock and Fort Smith.

•**AMAGON,** Town; Jackson County; Pop. 126; Zip Code 72005; Lat. 35-33-52 N long. 091-06-27 W; NE Arkansas. Amagon was a prominent settler.

•**AMITY,** City; Clark County; Pop. 859; Zip Code 71921; Elev. 140; Lat. 34-13-47 N long. 093-22-36 W; SW Arkansas. A descriptive name referring to an agreement reached in the town's early history.

•**ANTOINE,** Town; Pike County; Pop. 194; Zip Code 71922; Lat. 34-02-08 N long. 093-25-31 W; SW Arkansas. The personal name of a pioneer.

•**ARKADELPHIA,** City; Clark County Seat; Pop. 10,005; Zip Code 71923; Elev. 247; 30 m. S of Hot Springs in SW Arkansas. A compound of the word Arkansas and the Greek word adelphus, or "brother."

•**ARKANSAS CITY,** City; Desha County Seat; Pop. 668; Zip Code 71630; Elev. 140; SE Arkansas. The name of an early Indian tribe discovered by the French explorer Marquette and subsequently given to the area.

•**ASH FLAT,** Town; Sharp County; Pop. 524; Zip Code 72513; Elev. 670; Lat. N Arkansas. Named for the ash trees in the vicinity.

•**ASHDOWN,** City; Little River County Seat; Pop. 4,218; Zip Code 71822; Lat. 34-05-09 N long. 093-01-56 W; SW Arkansas. The surname of an early settler.

•**ATKINS,** City; Pope County; Pop. 3,002; Zip Code 72823; Elev. 357; NW central Arkansas. Atkins was an early settler in Arkansas.

•**AUBREY,** Town; Lee County; Pop. 267; Zip Code 72311; E Arkansas. Named for an early pioneer.

•**AUGUSTA,** City; Woodruff County Seat; Pop. 3,496; Zip Code 72006; Elev. 224 NE central Arkansas. Augusta is named after Augusta Hough, the niece of the town's founder.

•**AUSTIN,** Town; Lonoke County; Pop. 269; Zip Code 72007; Elev. 250 central Arkansas. The town's name recalls the city in Texas.

•**AVOCA,** Town; Benton County; Pop. 256; Zip Code 72711; Elev. 1358; Lat. 36-24-05 N long. 094-04-08 W; NW corner of Arkansas. Avoca is named after the town in Steuban County, New York.

•**BALD KNOB,** City; White County; Pop. 2,756; Zip Code 72010; Elev. 223 NE central Arkansas. A descriptive name for a local geographic feature.

•**BANKS,** Town; Bradley County; Pop. 216; Zip Code 71631; Elev. 231; Lat. 35-18-29 N long. 091-34-03 W; S Arkansas. The town's name honors a pioneer.

•**BARLING,** City; Sebastian County; Pop. 3,761; Zip Code 72923; W Arkansas. Barling is named for an early settler.

•**BASSETT,** Town; Mississippi County; Pop. 243; Zip Code 72313; Elev. 288 NE Arkansas. Named after an early lumberman.

•**BATESVILLE,** City; Independence County Seat; Pop. 8,263; Zip Code 72501; Elev. 266; NE central Arkansas. Named in honor of an early territorial judge James W. Bates.

•**BAUXITE,** Town; Saline County; Pop. 433; Zip Code 72011; Elev. 358; central Arkansas. Descriptively named for the nearby bauxite deposits.

•**BAY,** City; Craighead County; Pop. 1,605; Zip Code 72411; NE Arkansas. Descriptively named for its geography.

•**BEARDEN,** City; Ouachita County; Pop. 1,191; Zip Code 71720; Elev. 239; S Arkansas. Founded in 1882 and named after a prominent businessman.

•**BEEBE,** City; White County; Pop. 3,599; Zip Code 72012; Elev. 246; Lat. 35-04-21 N long. 091-53-02 W; NE central Arkansas. Beebe is named in honor of native son, oceangrapher William Beebe.

•**BEEDEVILLE,** Town; Jackson County; Pop. 183; Zip Code 72014; Lat. 35-25-43 N long. 091-06-15 W; NE Arkansas. The town's name remembers an early founder.

•**BELLEVILLE,** City; Yell County; Pop. 571; Zip Code 72824; Elev. 368 W central Arkansas. A French name meaning "good city."

•**BEN LOMOND,** Town; Sevier County; Pop. 155; Zip Code 71823; SW Arkansas. Named after the mountain in Scotland.

•**BENTON,** City; Saline County Seat; Pop. 17,437; Zip Code 72015; Elev. 416; Lat. 34-30-19 N long. 092-34-39 W; 20 m. SW of Little Rock in central Arkansas. Named for anti-slavery crusader Thomas Hart Benton, U. S. Senator from Missouri.

•**BENTONVILLE,** City; Benton County Seat; Pop. 8,756; Zip Code 72712; Elev. 1,305 N W corner of Arkansas. Founded in 1837 and named in honor of U.S. Senator Thomas Hart Benton.

•**BERGMAN,** Town; Boone County; Pop. 320; Zip Code 72615; Lat. 36-22-15 N long. 094-12-40 W; N Arkansas. Bergman was an early settler. The town is named after him.

•**BERRYVILLE,** City; Carroll County Seat; Pop. 2,966; Zip Code 72616; Elev. 1,256; NW Arkansas. Berry is the name of an early town founder.

•**BETHEL HEIGHTS,** Town; Benton County; Pop. 296; Zip Code ; NW corner of Arkansas. Bethel is a Biblical name, whereas heights is a descriptive name.

•BIGELOW, Town; Perry County; Pop. 373; Zip Code 72016; Elev. 297; Lat. 34-59-42 N long. 092-37-29 W; central Arkansas. The surname of a 19 century settler.

•BIG FLAT, Town; Baxter County; Pop. 150; Zip Code 72617; N Arkansas. Named for the local geography.

•BIGGERS, Town; Randolph County; Pop. 363; Zip Code 72413; Elev. 286; NE Arkansas. The town is named after a pioneer.

•BLACK OAK, Town; Craighead County; Pop. 309; Zip Code 72414; Elev. 233; NE Arkansas. Named for a landmark tree.

•BLACK ROCK, City; Lawrence County; Pop. 848; Zip Code 72415; Elev. 249; NE Arkansas. A prominent rock gave the town this name.

•BLEVINS, City; Hempstead County; Pop. 314; Zip Code 71825; Elev. 424; Lat. 33-52-00 N long. 093-34-37 W; SW Arkansas. Blevins is the surname of a pioneer.

•BLUE MOUNTAIN, Town; Logan County; Pop. 112; Zip Code 72826; Elev. 506; Lat. 33-06-01 N long. 093-39-21 W; W Arkansas. Descriptively named for a bluish haze around the mountain.

•BLUFF CITY, Town; Nevada County; Pop. 292; Zip Code 71722; Elev. 364; Lat. 33-43-08 N long. 093-08-01 W; SW Arkansas. The town is named for its position on a bluff.

•BLYTHEVILLE, City; Mississippi County Seat; Pop. 24,314; Zip Code 72315; 5 m. S of Missouri in NE Arkansas. The city is named for farmer Henry Blyth who settled here in the 1880's.

•BONO, Town; Craighead County; Pop. 967; Zip Code 72416; NE Arkansas. An Italian word meaning "good."

•BOONEVILLE, City; Logan County Seat; Pop. 3,718; Zip Code 72927; Elev. 511 W Arkansas. Named for Daniel Boone.

•BRADFORD, City; White County; Pop. 950; Zip Code 72020; Elev. 243 NE central Arkansas. The surname of an early settler.

•BRADLEY, City; Lafayette County; Pop. 790; Zip Code 71826; Elev. 259; SW Arkansas. Bradley's name honors early settler William L. Bradley.

•BRANCH, City; Franklin County; Pop. 353; Zip Code 72928; Lat. 35-18-27 N long. 093-56-59 W; NW Arkansas. The city is named for 19th century U. S. Senator John Branch.

•BRINKLEY, City; Monroe County; Pop. 4,909; Zip Code 72021; Elev. 204 E Arkansas. Named in honor of Memphis and Little Rock Railroad president R. C. Brinkley.

•BROOKLAND, Town; Craighead County; Pop. 840; Zip Code 72417; Lat. 34-48-05 N long. 091-08-48 W; NE Arkansas. Descriptively named for several nearby streams.

•BRYANT, City; Saline County; Pop. 2,682; Zip Code 72022; Lat. 34-35-56 N long. 092-29-31 W; central Arkansas. Named for a pioneer.

•BUCKNER, City; Lafayette County; Pop. 436; Zip Code 71827; Elev. 260; Lat. 33-21-33 N long. 093-26-13 W; SW Arkansas. The city is named after a 19th century settler.

•BULL SHOALS, City; Marion County; Pop. 1,312; Zip Code 72619; Lat. 36-22-58 N long. 092-34-57 W; N Arkansas. A shallow area in the White River named for the animal.

•BURDETTE, Town; Mississippi County; Pop. 328; Zip Code 72321; NE Arkansas. Burdette was the name of an early settler.

•CABOT, City; Lonoke County; Pop. 4,806; Zip Code 72023; Elev. 289; central Arkansas. Possibly named for early English explorer John Cabot.

•CADDO VALLEY, Town; Clark County; Pop. 388; Zip Code 71935; SW Arkansas. Caddo is the name of a group of Indian tribes with a common linguistic background who once lived in Arkansas.

•CALDWELL, Town; St. Francis County; Pop. 283; Zip Code 72322; Elev. 234; E Arkansas. Perhaps named for Matthew Caldwell, a Texas patriot during the 1836 War of Independence from Mexico.

•CALE, Town; Nevada County; Pop. 110; Zip Code 71828; Lat. 33-37-36 N long. 093-14-22 W; SW Arkansas. Cale is named for an early settler.

•CALICO ROCK, City; Izard County; Pop. 1,046; Zip Code 72519; Elev. 364; N Arkansas. The city is named for the large rock on the White River which forms part of the townscape.

•CALION, City; Union County; Pop. 638; Zip Code 71724; Elev. 93; S Arkansas. A combined name derived by taking part of the Union County name and part of the adjacent Calhoun County's name.

•CAMDEN, City; Ouachita County Seat; Pop. 15,356; Zip Code 71701; Elev. 198; 30 m. N of El Dorado in S Arkansas. Settled in the 1820's and named after Camden, New Jersey.

•CARAWAY, Town; Craighead County; Pop. 1,165; Zip Code 72419; NE Arkansas. The town's name remembers an early settler.

•CARLISLE, City; Lonoke County; Pop. 2,567; Zip Code 72024; Elev. 222; central Arkansas. Named after Carlisle, Pennsylvania, or Carlisle, Massachusetts.

•CARTHAGE, City; Dallas County; Pop. 568; Zip Code 71725; Lat. 34-04-26 N long. 092-33-24 W; S central Arkansas. The city takes its name from the famous ancient empire who fought a bitter war with Rome.

•CASH, Town; Craighead County; Pop. 285; Zip Code 72421; NE Arkansas. Named for an early settler.

•CAVE CITY, City; Independence & Sharp Counties; Pop. 1,634; Zip Code 72521; Elev. 659 NE central Arkansas. Descriptively named for the nearby caves.

•CAVE SPRINGS, City; Benton County; Pop. 429; Zip Code 72718; NW corner of Arkansas. Named for a spring found in a local cave.

•CENTERTON, City; Benton County; Pop. 425; Zip Code 72719; Lat. 36-21-37 N long. 094-17-06 W; NW corner of Arkansas. The town is named for its location in the county.

•CHARLESTON, City; Franklin County Seat; Pop. 1,748; Zip Code 72933; Lat. 35-17-54 N long. 094-02-21 W; NW Arkansas. Charleston is named after the famous port city in South Carolina.

•CHERRY VALLEY, City; Cross County; Pop. 729; Zip Code 72324; E Arkansas. Named after the local horticulture.

•CHESTER, Town; Crawford County; Pop. 139; Zip Code 72934; Lat. 35-40-40 N long. 094-10-08 W; NW Arkansas. The town is named after Chester, Pennsylvania.

ARKANSAS

•**CHIDESTER,** City; Ouachita County; Pop. 342; Zip Code 71726; Lat. 33-43-48 N long. 093-03-41 W; S Arkansas. The origin of the city's name is uncertain.

•**CLARENDON,** City; Monroe County Seat; Pop. 2,361; Zip Code 72029; Elev. 176 E Arkansas. The city is named for the town is South Carolina.

•**CLARKSVILLE,** City; Johnson County Seat; Pop. 5,237; Zip Code 72830; Elev. 370 NW Arkansas. Probably named for an early pioneer.

•**CLINTON,** City; Van Buren County Seat; Pop. 1,284; Zip Code 72031; Elev. 505; N central Arkansas. Named in honor of Erie Canal builder DeWitt Clinton.

•**COAL HILL,** City; Johnson County; Pop. 859; Zip Code 72832; Elev. 471; NW Arkansas. Descriptively named as a coal mining center.

•**CONCORD,** Town; Cleburne County; Pop. 234; Zip Code 72523; Elev. 1004; N central Arkansas. A euphonious and descriptive name given by the early settlers.

•**CONWAY,** City; Faulkner County Seat; Pop. 20,375; Zip Code 72032; Elev. 321; central Arkansas. The city is named for the prominent Conway family who produced two governors of Arkansas.

•**CORNING,** City; Clay County Seat; Pop. 3,650; Zip Code 72422; Elev. 291; NE corner of Arkansas. Named after Corning, New York.

•**COTTER,** City; Baxter County; Pop. 920; Zip Code 72626; Elev. 441; N Arkansas. Named for an early settler.

•**COTTON PLANT,** City; Woodruff County; Pop. 1,323; Zip Code 72036; Elev. 192; NE central Arkansas. Descriptively named for the local cotton production.

•**COVE,** Town; Polk County; Pop. 391; Zip Code 71937; Elev. 1,046; W Arkansas. The town is descriptively named for its geography.

•**COY,** Town; Lonoke County; Pop. 183; Zip Code 72037; Elev. 292; central Arkansas. The exact origin of the town's name is uncertain.

•**CRAWFORDSVILLE,** Town; Crittendon County; Pop. 685; Zip Code 72327; Elev. 227; E Arkansas. Named for a prominent early plantation owner.

•**CROSSETT,** City; Ashley County; Pop. 6,706; Zip Code 71635; Elev. 159; SE Arkansas. The city was founded and named after the Crossett Lumber Company.

•**CUSHMAN,** Town; Independence County; Pop. 556; Zip Code 72526; Elev. 712; NE central Arkansas. Cushman is named for an early settler.

•**DAMASCUS,** Town; Faulkner & Van Buren Counties; Pop. 307; Zip Code 72039; Lat. 35-21-51 N long. 092-24-24 W; central Arkansas. The town is named after the ancient Biblical city in Syria.

•**DANVILLE,** City; Yell County Seat; Pop. 1,698; Zip Code 72833; Elev. 387; W central Arkansas. Founded in 1841 and named for a pioneer.

•**DARDONELLE,** City; Yell County Seat; Pop. 3,621; Zip Code 72834; Elev. 325; W central Arkansas. Originally named Derdonnai after a French settler, this gradually became Dardonelle for its location on the Arkansas River, which resembled a similar spot in the straits below the Black Sea in Europe.

•**DATTO,** Town; Clay County; Pop. 112; Zip Code 72424; NE corner of Arkansas. Datto is named after an early settler.

•**DECATUR,** Town; Benton County; Pop. 1,013; Zip Code 72722; Elev. 1230; Lat. 36-20-08 N long. 094-27-33 W; NW corner of Arkansas. Named in honor of 1812 naval hero Stephen Decatur.

•**DELAPLAINE,** Town; Greene County; Pop. 161; Zip Code 72425; NE Arkansas. The surname of an early settler.

•**DELIGHT,** City; Pike County; Pop. 431; Zip Code 71940; Lat. 34-01-47 N long. 093-30-15 W; SW Arkansas. Named for the pioneers response to the area.

•**DELL,** Town; Mississippi County; Pop. 310; Zip Code 72426; NE Arkansas. Descriptively named for a local landform.

•**DE QUEEN,** City; Sevier County Seat; Pop. 4,594; Zip Code 71832; Elev. 432; SW Arkansas. Named for a Dutch railroad investor, De Geoijen; the name was anglicized to De Queen.

•**DERMOTT,** City; Prairie County Seat; Pop. 2,001; Zip Code 71638; Elev. 148; E central Arkansas. The McDermott family settled here in 1832. It is named after them.

•**DES ARC,** City; Prairie County Seat; Pop. 2,001; Zip Code 72040; Elev. 203; E central Arkansas. French for "at the curve," and referring to a bend in the White River.

•**DE VALLS BLUFF,** Town; Prairie County Seat; Pop. 738; Zip Code 72041; Elev. 192; E central Arkansas. A French word referring to the nearby bluffs.

•**DE WITT,** City; Arkansas County Seat; Pop. 3,928; Zip Code 72042; Elev. 189; E Arkansas. The town's name honors DeWitt Clinton, the builder of the Erie Canal.

•**DIAMOND CITY,** City; Boone County; Pop. 650; Zip Code 72644; N Arkansas. Descriptively named for the diamonds in the area.

•**DIAZ,** City; Jackson County Seat; Pop. 1,192; Zip Code 72043; Lat. 35-38-03 N long. 091-15-49 W; NE Arkansas. A Spanish surname - probably for an early settler.

•**DIERKS,** City; Howard County; Pop. 1,249; Zip Code 71833; Elev. 422; SW Arkansas. Dierks is the family name of a pioneer.

•**DOVER,** City; Pope County; Pop. 948; Zip Code 72837; Elev. 447; NW central AR. Named for the English city.

•**DUMAS,** City; Desha County; Pop. 6,091; Zip Code 71639; Elev. 166; 40 m. SE of Pine Bluff in SE Arkansas. A French surveyor had the town named after him.

•**DYER,** Town; Crawford County; Pop. 608; Zip Code 72935; Lat. 35-29-39 N long. 094-08-11 W; NW Arkansas. Named for a settler.

•**DYESS,** Town; Mississippi County; Pop. 446; Zip Code 72330; NE Arkansas. A family name of early pioneers.

•**EARLE,** City; Crittendon County; Pop. 3,517; Zip Code 72331; Elev. 217; E. Arkansas. Earle's name remembers a settler family.

•**ELKINS,** Town; Washington County; Pop. 579; Zip Code 72727; Elev. 1218; Lat. 36-00-09 N long. 094-00-37 W; NW Arkansas.

•**ELM SPRINGS,** Town; Washington County; Pop. 781; Zip Code 72728; Lat. 36-12-22 N long. 094-14-03 W; NW Arkansas.

•**EMERSON,** Town; Columbia County; Pop. 444; Zip Code 71740; Elev. 310; SW Arkansas.

•LONSDALE, Town; Garland County; Pop. 117; Zip Code 72087; Elev. 424; Lat. 34-32-33 N long. 092-48-32 W; W central Arkansas. The surname of a settler family.

•LOUANN, Town; Ouachita County; Pop. 282; Zip Code 71751; Lat. 33-23-26 N long. 092-47-23 W; S Arkansas. Named by an early settler for his wife.

•LOWELL, City; Benton County; Pop. 1,078; Zip Code 72745; Elev. 1343; Lat. NW corner of Arkansas. Lowell is named after the city in Massachusetts.

•LUXORA, Town; Mississippi County; Pop. 1,739; Zip Code 72358; Elev. 237; NE Arkansas. D. T. Waller founded the town in 1882. It is named after his daughter.

•LYNN, Town; Lawrence County; Pop. 345; Zip Code 72440; Elev. 354; NE Arkansas. The town is named for Lynn, Massachusetts.

•MADISON, City; St. Francis County; Pop. 1,227; Zip Code 72359; Elev. 209; E Arkansas. Named for President James Madison.

•MAGAZINE, City; Logan County; Pop. 799; Zip Code 72943; Elev. 456; Lat. 35-09-07 N long. 093-48-22 W; W Arkansas. The city is named from the French "magasin," or "storehouse."

•MAGNESS, Town; Independence County; Pop. 196; Elev. 267; Lat. 35-42-09 N long. 091-28-48 W; NE central Arkansas. The surname of a pioneer.

•MAGNOLIA, City; Columbia County Seat; Pop. 11,909; Zip Code 71753; Elev. 325; Lat. 33-16-13 N long. 093-14-07 W; 35 m. W of El Dorado in SW Arkansas. Descriptively named for the Magnolia tree which grows in the area.

•MALVERN, City; Hot Spring County Seat; Pop. 10,163; Zip Code 72104; Elev. 311; Lat. 34-22-33 N long. 092-48-50 W; 15 m. SE of Hot Springs in SW central Arkansas. Named after Malvern, Virginia.

•MAMMOTH SPRING, City; Fulton County; Pop. 1,158; Zip Code 72554; Lat. 36-29-39 N long. 091-3248 W; N Arkansas. Named for the large local spring.

•MANILA, City; Mississippi County; Pop. 2,553; Zip Code 72442; Elev. 245; NE Arkansas. Named after the Phillipine city.

•MANSFIELD, City; Scott County; Pop. 340; Zip Code 72944; Elev. 594 ; Lat. 35-03-47 N long. 094-14-55 W; W Arkansas. Mansfield is named after Mansfield, Massachusetts.

•MARIANNA, City; Lee County Seat; Pop. 6,220; Zip Code 2360; Elev. 227 E Arkansas. The city is named for Mary and An-, daughters of the woman who originally owned the townsite.

•ARION, City; Crittendon County Seat; Pop. 2,996; Zip Code 4; Elev. 225; E Arkansas. Marion is named in honor of eral Francis Marion, Revolutionary war hero.

•KED TREE, City; Poinsett County; Pop. 3,201; Zip Code Elev. 217 NE Arkansas. Descriptively named for a local

•ADUKE, City; Greene County; Pop. 1,168; Zip Code E Arkansas. Named for a pioneer.

•ALL, City; Searcy County Seat; Pop. 1,595; Zip Code 36-00-15 N long. 092-24-08 W; N Arkansas. Named at American Supreme Court Justice, John Marshall.

City; Phillips County; Pop. 1,724; Zip Code 72366; Arkansas. The surname of an early settler.

•MAYFLOWER, City; Faulkner County; Pop. 1,381; Zip Code 72106; Elev. 288; Lat. 34-57-10 N long. 092-25-29 W; central Arkansas. The city is named after the famous ship that brought the Pilgrim's to America.

•MAYNARD, Town; Randolph County; Pop. 381; Zip Code 72444; Elev. 381; NE Arkansas. The town is named after Maynard, Massachusetts.

•MCCASKILL, City; Hempstead County; Pop. 87; Zip Code 71847; Elev. 448; Lat. 33-55-00 N long. 093-38-27 W; SW Arkansas. Named for a Scottish settler.

•MCCRORY, City; Woodruff County; Pop. 1,942; Zip Code 72101; Lat. 35-15-39 N long. 091-11-52 W; NE central Arkansas. McCrory is named after a settler who came here from Scotland.

•MCDOUGAL, Town; Clay County; Pop. 239; Zip Code 72441; NE corner of Arkansas. McDougal is a Scottish name; it probably refers to an early settler in the area.

•MCGEHEE, City; Desha County; Pop. 5,671; Zip Code 71654; Elev. 149; Lat. 33-37-33 N long. 091-23-39 W; SE Arkansas. The town's name remembers an early arrival to the area.

•MCNEIL, City; Columbia County; Pop. 725; Zip Code 71752; Elev. 323 ; Lat. 33-20-52 N long. 093-12-22 W; SW Arkansas. McNeil was a pioneer in the area. The town is named after him.

•MCRAE, City; White County; Pop. 641; Zip Code 72101; NE central Arkansas. Named for an early settler.

•MELBOURNE, City; Izard County Seat; Pop. 1,619; Zip Code 72556; Elev. 604; Lat. 36-03-35 N long. 091-54-12 W; N Arkansas. Melbourne is named after the Australian city.

•MENA, City; Polk County Seat; Pop. 5,154; Zip Code 71953; Elev. 1,143; 70 m. W of Hot Springs in W. Arkansas. A Dutch railroad investor gave the town the shortened form of Wilhelmina.

•MENIFREE, Town; Conway County; Pop. 368; Zip Code 72107; Lat. 35-08-54 N long. 092-32-53; central Arkansas. The town is named after Menifee, Kentucky.

•MIDLAND, Town; Sebastian County; Pop. 286; Zip Code 72945; Lat. 35-05-32 N long. 094-21-13 W; W Arkansas. Descriptively named for its central location.

•MINERAL SPRINGS, City; Howard County; Pop. 936; Zip Code 71851; Lat. 33-52-42 N long. 093-55-15 W; SW Arkansas. The city is named after a nearby mineral springs.

•MINTURN, Town; Lawrence County; Pop. 169; Zip Code 72445; NE Arkansas. Probably named for a pioneer.

•MONETTE, City; Craighead County; Pop. 1,165; Zip Code 72447; NE Arkansas. Probably the name of a pioneer's wife or daughter.

•MONTICELLO, City; Drew County Seat; Pop. 8,259; Zip Code 71655; Elev. 298 ; Lat. 33-32-52 N long. 091-47-25 W; SE Arkansas. The city is named after Thomas Jefferson's famous Virginia home.

•MONTROSE, City; Ashley County; Pop. 641; Zip Code 71658; Lat. 33-17-42 N long. 091-30-17 W; SE Arkansas. Named after Montrose, Scotland.

•MORO, Town; Lee County; Pop. 327; Zip Code 72368; Lat. E Arkansas. The English spelling of a French personal name.

•MORRILTON, City; Conway County Seat; Pop. 7,355; Zip Code 72559; Elev. 389; Lat. 35-07-44 N long. 092-45-14 W; central Arkansas. The city is named after an early settler.

•EMMET, City; Hempstead & Nevada Counties; Pop. 475; Zip Code 71835; Elev. 310; Lat. 33-05-56 N long. 093-11-34 W; SW Arkansas.

•ENGLAND, City; Lonoke County; Pop. 3,081; Zip Code 72046; Lat. 34-32-31 N long. 091-52-36 W; central Arkansas. Named after America's mother country.

•ENOLA, Town; Faulkner County; Pop. 186; Zip Code 72047; Lat. 35-11-40 N long. 092-12-02 W; central Arkansas. Enola is named in honor of a settler's wife.

•EUDORA, City; Chicot County; Pop. 3,840; Zip Code 71640; Elev. 129; SE corner of Arkansas. Named after a female pioneer.

•EUREKA SPRINGS, City; Carroll County Seat; Pop. 1,989; Zip Code 72632; Elev. 1,463; NW Arkansas. A famous health spa, the name signifies "discovery" of a source of health.

•EVENING SHADE, Town; Sharp County Seat; Pop. 397; Zip Code 72532; Elev. 458; N Arkansas. Descriptively named for the light in the area at dusk.

•EVERTON, Town; Boone County; Pop. 134; Zip Code 72633; Elev. 856; Lat. 36-09-12 N long. 092-54-32 W; N Arkansas. Everton is named in honor of a pioneer.

•FARMINGTON, City; Washington County; Pop. 1,283; Zip Code 72730; Lat. 36-02-27 N long. 094-14-52 W; NW Arkansas. A descriptive name for the area's strong agriculture.

•FAYETTEVILLE, City; Washington County Seat; Pop. 36,604; Zip Code 72701; Elev. 1,427 ; Lat. 36-04-06 N long. 094-08-37 W; 50 m. N of Fort Smith in NW Arkansas. The city is named in honor of the Marquis De Lafayette who helped the American cause during the Revolutionary War.

•FIFTY-SIX, City; Stone County; Pop. 157; Zip Code 72533; N Arkansas. The town is named after the local "56" school district.

•FLIPPIN, City; Marion County; Pop. 1,072; Zip Code 72634; Elev. 650; Lat. 36-16-40 N long. 092-35-38 W; N Arkansas.

•FORDYCE, City; Dallas County Seat; Pop. 5,175; Zip Code 71742; S central Arkansas. Named for Samuel Fordyce who was a president of the St. Louis and Southwestern Railroad.

•FOREMAN, City; Little River County; Pop. 1,377; Zip Code 71836; Elev. 405; Lat. 33-43-11 N long. 094-23-48 W; SW Arkansas. A family name of a settler.

•FORREST CITY, City; St. Francis County Seat; Pop. 10,803; Elev. 510; Elev. 72335; Elev. 276 E Arkansas. Founded in 1867 and named in honor of Confederate General Nathan Bedford Forrest.

•FORT SMITH, City; Sebastian County Seat; Pop. 71,384; Zip Code 729+; Elev. 276; W Arkansas. Named in honor of General Thomas Smith who commanded frontier forces in the 19th century.

•FOUKE, City; Miller County; Pop. 614; Zip Code 71837; Lat. 33-15-35 N long. 093-53-05 W; SW corner of Arkansas. Fouke is a pioneer's name.

•FOUNTAIN HILL, Town; Ashley County; Pop. 352; Zip Code 71642; Elev. 196; Lat. 33-21-23 N 091-50-57 W; SE Arkansas. Descriptively named for a local hill.

•FRANKLIN, Town; Izard County; Pop. 253; Zip Code 72536; N Arkansas. Named in honor of Benjamin Franklin.

•FREDONIA (Biscoe), Town; Prairie County; Pop. 486; Zip Code 72017; E central Arkansas. A popular 19th century name for America.

•FRIENDSHIP, Town; Hot Spring County; Pop. 163; Zip Code 71962; Elev. 280; Lat. 34-13-33 N long. 093-00-01 W; SW central Arkansas. Named after the popular virtue.

•FULTON, City; Hempstead County; Pop. 326; Zip Code 71838; Elev. 269; Lat. 33-36-45 N long. 093-48-49 W; SW Arkansas. Fulton is named after the inventor of the steamboat Robert Fulton.

•GARFIELD, Town; Benton County; Pop. 187; Zip Code 72732; Elev. 1469; Lat. 36-28-01 N long. 093-58-16 W; NW corner of Arkansas. Named in honor of President James Garfield.

•GARLAND, Town; Miller County; Pop. 660; Zip Code 71839; Elev. 227; SW corner of Arkansas. Rufus Garland was the original landowner. The town is named after him.

•GARNER, Town; White County; Pop. 216; Zip Code 72052; Elev. 223; Lat. 35-08-21 N long. 091-40-34 W; NE central Arkansas. Named for a prominent settler.

•GASSVILLE, City; Baxter County; Pop. 859; Zip Code 72635; Lat. 36-16-51 N long. 092-29-45 W; N Arkansas. Gassville is named after a pioneer.

•GATEWAY, Town; Benton County; Pop. 75; Zip Code 72733; Lat. 36-29-14 N long. 093-56-09 W; NW corner of Arkansas. Descriptively named for its location as a portal to the Ozarks.

•GENTRY, City; Benton County; Pop. 1,468; Zip Code 72734; Lat. 36-15-45 N long. 094-25-03 W; NW corner of Arkansas. So named after the area's prosperous farmers.

•GILBERT, Town; Searcy County; Pop. 43; Zip Code 72636; Elev. 595; N Arkansas. The name of a prominent pioneer.

•GILLETT, City; Arkansas County; Pop. 927; Zip Code 72055; E Arkansas. Gillet is a personal name - probably for an early settler.

•GILLHAM, Town; Sevier County; Pop. 252; Zip Code 71841; SW Arkansas. Gillham is a personal name.

•GILMORE, Town; Crittendon County; Pop. 503; Zip Code 72339; E Arkansas. The town is named after a 19th century pioneer.

•GLENWOOD, Town; Pike County; Pop. 1,402; Zip Code 71943; Elev. 547; SW Arkansas. Descriptively named for its parklike forest area.

•GOSNELL, City; Mississippi County; Pop. 2,745; Zip Code ; NE Arkansas. Gosnell is named after an early settler.

•GOULD, City; Lincoln County; Pop. 1,671; Zip Code 71643; Elev. 167; SE Arkansas. Named after Jay Gould, Wall St. financier and railroad owner.

•GRADY, City; Lincoln County; Pop. 488; Zip Code 71644; Lat. 34-04-45 N long. 091-41-44 W; SE Arkansas. Named for a pioneer.

•GRANNIS, Town; Polk County; Pop. 349; Zip Code 71944; Elev. 927; Lat. 34-14-25 N long. 094-20-00 W; W Arkansas. Grannis's name remembers an early settler.

•GRAVETTE, City; Benton County; Pop. 1,218; Zip Code 72736; Lat. 36-25-12 N long. 094-27-08 W; NW corner of Arkansas. The city's name honors E. T. Gravette, a pioneer settler.

•**GREENBRIER,** City; Faulkner County; Pop. 1,423; Zip Code 72058; Lat. 35-14-09 N long. 092-23-09 W; central Arkansas. Named for the thorny vine, smilaz rotundifolia.

•**GREEN FORREST,** City; Carroll County; Pop. 1,609; Zip Code 72638; Elev. 1340; Lat. 36-20-04 N long. 093-25-59 W; NW Arkansas. Descriptively named for the original landcover.

•**GREENLAND,** Town; Washington County; Pop. 622; Zip Code 72737; Lat. 35-59-34 N long. 094-10-35 W; NW Arkansas. Named for the area's verdant covering.

•**GREENWAY,** Town; Clay County; Pop. 317; Zip Code 72430; NE corner of Arkansas. A descriptive name for the town's green surroundings.

•**GREENWOOD,** City; Sebastian County Seat; Pop. 3,317; Zip Code 72936; Elev. 409; Lat. 35-13-04 N long. 094-15-15 W; 18 W Arkansas. Set in a forested area, the town is descriptively named.

•**GREERS FERRY,** City; Cleburne County; Pop. 558; Zip Code 72067; N central Arkansas. Named for an early ferryman.

•**GRIFFITHVILLE,** Town; White County; Pop. 254; Zip Code 72060; Lat. 35-07-22 N long. 091-38-35 W; NE central Arkansas. The town is named for a pioneer farmer.

•**GRUBBS,** Town; Jackson County; Pop. 546; Zip Code 72431; Elev. 231; NE Arkansas. The surname of a settler family.

•**GUION,** Town; Izard County; Pop. 177; Zip Code 72540; N Arkansas. The town's name honors J. H. Guion, a Missouri Pacific Railroad conductor.

•**GURDON,** City; Clark County; Pop. 2,707; Zip Code 71743; Elev. 210; Lat. 33-55-15 N long. 093-09-02 W; 10 SW Arkansas. Gurdon is named after a pioneer settler.

•**GUY,** Town; Faulkner County; Pop. 209; Zip Code 72061; Elev. 685; Lat. 35-19-27 N long. 092-20-09 W; central Arkansas. Guy's name remembers an early landowner.

•**HACKETT,** City; Sebastian County; Pop. 505; Zip Code 72937; Elev. 536; Lat. 35-11-03 N long. 094-24-44 W; W Arkansas. A pioneer surname.

•**HAMBURG,** City; Ashley County Seat; Pop. 3,394; Zip Code 71646; Elev. 174; Lat. 33-13-37 N long. 091-48-01 W; SE Arkansas. Named after the great German city.

•**HAMPTON,** City; Calhoun County Seat; Pop. 1,627; Zip Code 71744; Elev. 202; Lat. 33-32-20 N long. 092-28-01 W; S Arkansas. Named after Hampton, England.

•**HARDY,** City; Sharp County Seat; Pop. 643; Zip Code 72542; Elev. 358; N Arkansas. The city is named for a railroad contractor on the Kansas City and Memphis Railroad.

•**HARRELL,** Town; Calhoun County Seat; Pop. 302; Zip Code 71745; Elev. 204; Lat. 33-30-36 N long. 092-23-54 W; S Arkansas. The town's name honors an early landowner.

•**HARRISBURG,** City; Poinsett County Seat; Pop. 1,921; Zip Code 72432; NE Arkansas. The city is named for town founder William C. Harris.

•**HARRISON,** City; Boone County Seat; Pop. 9,567; Zip Code 72601; Elev. 1182; Lat. 36-14-04 N long. 093-04-21 W; N Arkansas. Named in honor of U. S. President Benjamin Harrison.

•**HARTFORD,** City; Sebastian County; Pop. 613; Zip Code 72938; Lat. 35-01-23 N long. 094-22-53 W; W Arkansas. The city takes its name from Hartford, Connecticut.

•**HARTMAN,** Town; Johnson County; Pop. 517; Zip Code 72840; Elev. 366; Lat. 35-26-02 N long. 093-37-10 W; NW Arkansas. Named for a town founder.

•**HATFIELD,** Town; Polk County; Pop. 410; Zip Code 71945; Elev. 971 ; Lat. 34-29-12 N long. 094-22-44 W; W Arkansas. The surname of an early settler.

•**HAVANA,** City; Yell County; Pop. 352; Zip Code 72842; Elev. 377; Lat. 35-06-42 N long. 093-31-44 W; W central Arkansas. Named for the Cuban city.

•**HAYNES,** Town; Lee County; Pop. 359; Zip Code 72341; Elev. 222; Lat. 35-06-42 N long. 093-31-44 W; Arkansas. The surname of an early settler.

•**HAZEN,** City; Prairie County; Pop. 1,636; Zip Code 72064; Elev. 232; Lat. 34-47-11 N long. 091-34-27 W; E central Arkansas. Named in honor of U. S. Army General William Hazen.

•**HEBER SPRINGS,** City; Cleburne County Seat; Pop. 4,589; Zip Code 72543; Elev. 354; Lat. 36-19-32 N long. 093-58-09 W; N central Arkansas. The first name of the springs discoverer.

•**HECTOR,** Town; Pope County; Pop. 449; Zip Code 72843; Elev. 722; Lat. 35-27-50 N long. 092-58-29 W; NW central Arkansas. The Christian name of an early settler.

•**HELENA,** City; Phillips County Seat; Pop. 9,598; Zip Code 72342; Elev. 190; 90 m. ENE of Pine Bluff in E Arkansas. Named in honor of Helena Phillips, daughter of Sylvanus Phillips.

•**HERMITAGE,** Town; Bradley County; Pop. 378; Zip Code 71647; Lat. 33-26-56 N long. 092-10-25 W; S Arkansas. The town is named for Andrew Jackson's famous home in Nashville, Tenn.

•**HICKORY RIDGE,** City; Cross County; Pop. 478; Zip Code 72347; E Arkansas. Descriptively named for the geography and the vegetation.

•**HIGGINSON,** City; White County; Pop. 333; Zip Code 72068; Elev. 221; Lat. 35-11-47 N long. 091-42-46 W; N E central Arkansas. The surname of a pioneer settler.

•**HOLLY GROVE,** Town; Monroe County; Pop. 754; Zip Code 72069; E Arkansas. Descriptively named for the local holy shrubs.

•**HOPE,** City; Hempstead County Seat; Pop. 10,290; Zip Code 71801; Elev. 353 ; Lat. 33-41-49 N long. 093-34-51 W; 30 m. NE of Texarkana in SW Arkansas. Named after Hope Loughborough, the daughter of a local railroad director.

•**HORATIO,** City; Sevier County; Pop. 989; Zip Code 71842; Elev. 348; Lat. 33-56-41 N long. 094-21-19 W; SW Arkansas. The Christian name of an early settler.

•**HORSESHOE BEND,** City; Fulton, Izard & Sharp Counties; Pop. 1,909; Zip Code 72512; N Arkansas. Named for its shape.

•**HOT SPRINGS,** City; Garland County Seat; Pop. 35,166; Zip Code 71901; W central Arkansas. The city is named after the nearby warm springs.

•**HOUSTON,** Town; Perry County; Pop. 183; Zip Code 72070; Elev. 299; Lat. 35-02-05 N long. 092-41-48 W; central Arkansas. Named in honor of Texas patriot Sam Houston.

•**HOXIE,** City; Lawrence County; Pop. 2,961; Zip Code 72433; Elev. 271; NE Arkansas. The city is named after M. M. Hoxie, a Missouri Pacific Railroad official.

•**HUGHES,** City; St. Francis County; Pop. 1,919; Zip Code 72348; Elev. 205; E Arkansas. Named for an early settler.

•**HUMNOKE,** City; Lonoke County; Pop. 442; Zip Code 72070; Elev. 199; Lat. 34-32-31 N long. 091-45-27 W; central Probably the surname of a pioneer.

•**HUMPHREY,** Town; Arkansas & Jefferson Counties; Pop. 872; Zip Code 72073; Lat. 34-25-20 N long. 091-42-16 W; E Arkansas. The town's name honors Andrew Humphrey, Chief of the Army Corp of Engineers in the 1870's.

•**HUNTER,** Town; Woodruff County; Pop. 170; Zip Code 72074; Lat. 35-03-12 N long. 091-07-25 W; NE central Arkansas. Either named for an early settler, or descriptively named for the early pioneer's main occupation.

•**HUNTINGTON,** City; Sebastian County; Pop. 662; Zip Code 72940; Elev. 658; Lat. 35-04-52 N long. 094-15-49 W; W Arkansas. Named after an eastern city.

•**HUNTSVILLE,** City; Madison County Seat; Pop. 1,394; Zip Code 72740; Lat. 36-05-21 N long. 093-44-23 W; NW Arkansas. Named in honor of John Hunt, who founded Huntsville, Alabama.

•**HUTTING,** Town; Union County; Pop. 976; Zip Code 71747; Elev. 108; Lat. 33-02-15 N long. 092-10-58 W; S Arkansas. Huttig is named after an early settler.

•**IMBODEN,** Town; Lawrence County; Pop. 661; Zip Code 72434; Elev. 276; NE AT. The origin of the name is uncertain.

•**JACKSONPORT,** Town; Jackson County; Pop. 288; Zip Code 72075; Lat. 35-38-29 N long. 091-18-27 W; NE Arkansas. Named in honor of President Andrew Jackson.

•**JACKSONVILLE,** City; Pulaski County; Pop. 27,589; Zip Code 72076; Lat. 34-54-39 N long. 092-06-49 W; 15 m. NE of Little Rock in central Arkansas. The city's name honors Nicolas Jackson, the first postmaster.

•**JASPER,** City; Newton County Seat; Pop. 519; Zip Code 72641; Elev. 834; Lat. 36-00-20 N long. 093-11-15 W; NW Arkansas. Jasper's name honors Revolutinary War hero Sgt. William Jasper.

•**JEROME,** City; Drew County; Pop. 54; Zip Code 71650; SE Arkansas. Named for an early settler.

•**JOHNSON,** City; Washington County; Pop. 519; Zip Code 72741; NW Arkansas. The city is named for Benjamin Johnson, a jurist.

•**JOINER,** City; Mississippi County; Pop. 725; Zip Code 72350; NE Arkansas. The surname of an early pioneer.

•**JONESBORO,** City; Craighead County; Pop. 31,530; Zip Code 72401; NE Arkansas. Named in honor of state Senator William A. Jones.

•**JUDSONIA,** City; White County; Pop. 2,025; Zip Code 72081; Lat. 35-16-28 N long. 091-38-11 W; NE central Arkansas. The city's name remembers a prominent pioneer.

•**KEISER,** Town; Mississippi County; Pop. 962; Zip Code 72351; NE Arkansas. Named for the Keiser family, early settlers.

•**KENSETT,** City; White County; Pop. 1,751; Zip Code 72082; Elev. 229; Lat. 35-13-53 N long. 091-40-01 W; NE central Arkansas.

•**KEO,** Town; Lonoke County; Pop. 208; Zip Code 72083; Elev. 234; Lat. 34-35-59 N long. 092-00-44 W.

•**KINGSLAND,** City; Cleveland County; Pop. 320; Zip Code 71652; Elev. 214; Lat. 33-51-32 N long. 092-17-48 W; S Arkansas. The town's name remembers a pioneer landowner.

•**KNOBEL,** Town; Clay County; Pop. 503; Zip Code 72435; NE corner of Arkansas. Knobel is a pioneer's surname.

•**KNOXVILLE,** City; Johnson County; Pop. 264; Zip Code 72845; Elev. 191; Lat. 35-22-55 N long. 093-21-45 W; NW Arkansas. Named after Knoxville, Tennessee.

•**LAKE CITY,** Town; Craighead County Seat; Pop. 1,842; Zip Code 72437; NE Arkansas. Descriptively named for the nearby lake.

•**LAKEVIEW,** Town; Baxter County; Pop. 512; Zip Code 72642; Elev. 234; Lat. 36-20-37 N long. 092-28-35 W; N Arkansas. Named for the nearby lake.

•**LAKE VILLAGE,** City; Chicot County Seat; Pop. 3,088; Zip Code 71653; SE corner of Arkansas. Descriptively named for its position on a lake.

•**LAMAR,** City; Johnson County; Pop. 708; Zip Code 72846; Elev. 407; Lat. 35-26-20 N long. 093-23-25 W; NW Arkansas. Named in honor of a famous Texas statesman Mirabeau Lamar.

•**LAVACA,** City; Sebastian County; Pop. 1,092; Zip Code 72941; Lat. 35-20-19 N long. 094-10-33 W; W Arkansas. Derived from a French word meaning "cows" and referring, ironically, to buffalo.

•**LEACHVILLE,** City; Mississippi County; Pop. 1,882; Zip Code 72438; NE Arkansas. Named after a pioneer.

•**LEAD HILL,** Town; Boone County; Pop. 247; Zip Code 72644; Lat. 36-26-09 N long. 092-54-45 W; N Arkansas. Descriptively named for the hills lead bearing ore.

•**LEOLA,** Town; Grant County; Pop. 481; Zip Code 72084; Lat. 34-10-14 N long. 092-35-40 W; S central Arkansas. The town named after a female pioneer.

•**LEPANTO,** City; Pointsett County; Pop. 1,964; Zip Code NE Arkansas. The city is named after a famous nava which occurred in 1571.

•**LESLIE,** City; Searcy County; Pop. 501; Zip Code 975; Lat. 35-49-53 N long. 092-33-22 W; N Arkansas pioneer.

•**LETONA,** Town; White County; Pop. 231; Zip 35-21-46 N long. 091-49-34 W; NE central A name of an early female settler.

•**LEWISVILLE,** City; Lafayette County Sea 71845; Elev. 268; Lat. 33-22-22 N long. 0 sas. Lewis was a pioneer settler. The

•**LINCOLN,** City; Washington Cou 72744; Elev. 1502; Lat. 35-56-54 N l sas. Named in honor of Abraham

•**LITTLE ROCK,** City; Capital of Pop. 158,461; Zip Code 722 French explorers as the sma Arkansas River.

•**LOCKESBURG,** Town; Se Elev.436; Lat. 33-53-11 N town is named for a p

•**LONDON,** Town; P 35-19-57 N long. 09 the great English

•**LONOKE,** Cit 72086; Lat. 3 Named for c

•**MARVELL**
Elev. 210; E

•**MARSH**
72650; La
for the gr

•**MARN**
72443;

•**MA**
7236
featu

•MOUNTAINBURG, Town; Crawford County; Pop. 595; Zip Code 72946; NW Arkansas.

•MOUNTAIN HOME, City; Baxter County Seat; Pop. 7,447; Zip Code 72653; Elev. 820; Lat. 36-17-55 N long. 092-19-43 W; N Arkansas. Descriptively named for its topography.

•MOUNTAIN PINE, City; Garland County; Pop. 1,068; Zip Code 71956; Lat. 34-34-22 N long. 093-10-24 W; W central Arkansas. The city is descriptively named for the local vegetation.

•MOUNTAIN VIEW, City; Stone County Seat; Pop. 2,147; Zip Code 72560; Elev. 768; Lat. 35-52-00 N long. 092-06-56 W; N Arkansas. Named for its geography and the resulting view.

•MOUNT IDA, City; Montgomery County Seat; Pop. 1,023; Zip Code 71957; Elev. 663; W Arkansas.

•MULBERRY, City; Crawford County; Pop. 1,444; Zip Code 72947; Elev. 394; Lat. 35-30-43 N long. 094-04-52 W; NW Arkansas. The city is named after the Mulberry River.

•MURFREESBORO, City; Pike County Seat; Pop. 1,883; Zip Code 71958; Elev. 367; Lat. 34-03-43 N long. 093-41-36 W; SW Arkansas. Named in honor of Revolutionary War soldier Hardy Murfree.

•NASHVILLE, City; Howard County Seat; Pop. 4,554; Zip Code 71852; Elev. 383; Lat. 33-56-36 N long. 093-50-50 W; SW Arkansas. Named after Nashville, Tennessee.

•NEWARK, City; Independence County; Pop. 1,109; Zip Code 72562; Elev.239; Lat. 35-42-08 N long. 091-26-54 W; NE central Arkansas. The city is named after Newark, England.

•NEWPORT, City; Jackson County Seat; Pop. 8,339; Zip Code 72112; Elev. 227; Lat. 35-36-35 N long. 091-16-05 W; NE Arkansas. Descriptively named for the town's location on the White River.

•NORFORK, City; Baxter County; Pop. 399; Zip Code 72658; Lat. 36-12-17 N long. 092-16-47 W; N Arkansas. Norfork takes its name from Norfork, England.

•NORMAN, Town; Montgomery County; Pop. 539; Zip Code 71960; Lat. 34-27-19 N long. 093-40-44 W; W Arkansas. Named for an early settler.

•NORPHLET, City; Union County; Pop. 756; Zip Code 71759; Lat. 33-18-54 N long. 092-39-33 W; S Arkansas. The origin of the town's name is uncertain.

•NORTH LITTLE ROCK, City; Pulaski County; Pop. 64,419; Zip Code 72100; Elev. 291; Lat. 34-46-06 N long. 092-15-38 W; on Arkansas River in central Arkansas. Descriptively named for a geographical feature.

•OAK GROVE, Town; Carroll County; Pop. 265; Zip Code 72660; Lat. 36-27-22 N long. 093-26-10 W; NW Arkansas. Descriptively named for its oak trees.

•OAK GROVE HEIGHTS, Town; Greene County; Pop. 486; Zip Code 72660; NE Arkansas. Named for its geography and tree cover.

•ODEN, Town; Montgomery County; Pop. 186; Zip Code 71961; Elev. 761; Lat. 34-37-06 N long. 093-46-42 W; W Arkansas. Named after the mythological Norse god.

•OGDEN, Town; Little River County; Pop. 334; Zip Code 71853; SW Arkansas. Probably named after Ogden, Utah.

•OIL TROUGH, City; Independence County; Pop. 280; Zip Code 72564; Elev. 237; Lat. 35-37-48 N long. 091-27-33 W; NE central Arkansas. Descriptively named for local oil deposits.

•OKOLONA, Town; Clark County; Pop. 200; Zip Code 71962; Elev. 371; Lat. 34-00-05 N long. 093-20-21 W; SW Arkansas. A Choctaw Indian word referring to water.

•OLA, City; Yell County; Pop. 1,121; Zip Code 72853; Lat. 34-56-11 N long. 093-29-38 W; W central Arkansas. The origin of the town's name is uncertain.

•OMAHA, Town; Boone County; Pop. 191; Zip Code 72662; Elev. 1,354; Lat. 36-27-00 N long. 093-11-18 W; N Arkansas. The town is named after the Omaha Indians.

•OSCEOLA, City; Mississippi County Seat; Pop. 8,881; Zip Code 72370; Elev. 238; NE Arkansas. Osceola is named after the great Seminole Indian chief.

•OXFORD, Town; Izard County; Pop. 520; Zip Code 72565; Elev. 811; Lat. 36-13-23 N long. 091-55-35 W; N Arkansas. The town derives its name from Oxford, England.

•OZAN, City; Hempstead County; Pop. 111; Zip Code 71855; Elev. 382; Lat. 33-50-55 N long. 093-43-05 W; SW Arkansas. From the French "aux Arks," or "in the land of the Arkansas Indians."

•OZARK, City; Franklin County Seat; Pop. 3,597; Zip Code 72949; Elev. 397; Lat. 35-29-27 N long. 093-49-56 W; NW Arkansas. Derived from the French "aux Arks," or "in the Arkansas Indian country."

•PALESTINE, City; St. Francis County; Pop. 976; Zip Code 72372; E Arkansas. Named after Biblical Palestine.

•PANGBURN, City; White County; Pop. 673; Zip Code 72121; Elev. 335; Lat. 35-25-39 N long. 091-50-20 W; NE central Arkansas. Probably named for a pioneer settler.

•PARAGOULD, City; Greene County Seat; Pop. 15,214; Zip Code 72450; Elev. 295; 20 m. NE of Jonesboro in NE Arkansas. A combined name honoring railroad magnates John Paragould and Jay Gould.

•PARIS, City; Logan County Seat; Pop. 3,991; Zip Code 72855; Elev. 432; Lat. 35-17-41 N long. 093-43-20 W; W Arkansas. The city is named after the great French capital.

•PARKDALE, City; Ashley County; Pop. 471; Zip Code 71661; Lat. 33-07-07 N long. 091-32-46 W; SE Arkansas. Descriptive name for the area's parklike setting.

•PARKIN, City; Cross County; Pop. 2,035; Zip Code 72373; Elev. 223; E Arkansas. Parkin is named for a pioneer.

•PATTERSON, Town; Woodruff County; Pop. 567; Zip Code 72123; NE central Arkansas. Patterson is named for the original landowner.

•PEACH ORCHARD, Town; Clay County; Pop. 243; Zip Code 72453; NE corner of Arkansas. Descriptively named after the local horticulture.

•PEA RIDGE, City; Benton County; Pop. 1,488; Zip Code 72751; Elev. 158; Lat. 36-26-45 N long. 094-07-04 W; NW corner of Arkansas.

•PERRY, Town; Perry County; Pop. 254; Zip Code 72125; Elev. 335; Lat. 35-02-45 N long. 092-47-47 W; central Arkansas. Perry's name honors 1812 naval hero Oliver Hazard Perry.

•PERRYTOWN, City; Hempstead County; Pop. 282; Zip Code 71801; SW Arkansas. Named after Oliver Perry or a local settler.

•**PERRYVILLE,** City; Perry County Seat; Pop. 1,058; Zip Code 72126; Lat. 35-00-29 N long. 092-48-09 W; central Arkansas. Probably named after a pioneer.

•**PIGGOTT,** City; Clay County Seat; Pop. 3,762; Zip Code 72454; Elev. 303; NE corner of Arkansas. Piggott was an early settler in the area.

•**PINE BLUFF,** City; Jefferson County Seat; Pop. 56,576; Zip Code 71600; Elev. 230; Lat. 34-13-23 N long. 092-01-52 W; m. SE of Little Rock in SE central Arkansas. Named for its geography and tree cover.

•**PINEVILLE,** Town; Izard County; Pop. 163; Zip Code 72566; Elev. 697; Lat. 36-09-14 N long. 092-06-38 W; N Arkansas. Named for the predominant tree cover.

•**PLAINVIEW,** City; Yell County; Pop. 752; Zip Code 72857; Elev. 589; Lat. 34-59-28 N long. 093-17-42 W; W central Arkansas. Descriptively named by its settlers.

•**PLEASANT PLAINS,** Town; Independence County; Pop. 267; Zip Code 72568; Elev. 267; Lat. 35-33-00 N long. 091-37-30 W; NE central Arkansas. A descriptive and promotional name for the town.

•**PLUMERVILLE,** City; Conway County; Pop. 785; Zip Code 72127; Lat. 35-09-34 N long. 092-38-25 W; central Arkansas. Plumerville is named for an early settler.

•**POCOHONTAS,** City; Randolph County Seat; Pop. 5,995; Zip Code 72455; NE Arkansas. The town's name honors the famous Indian princess.

•**POLLARD,** Town; Clay County; Pop. 298; Zip Code 72456; NE corner of Arkansas. The town is named after a prominent pioneer.

•**PORTIA,** Town; Lawrence County; Pop. 480; Zip Code 72457; NE Arkansas. The name of a pioneer wife or daughter.

•**PORTLAND,** City; Ashley County; Pop. 701; Zip Code 71663; Lat. 33-14-12 N long. 091-30-31 W; SE Arkansas. The town's name is derived from Portland, England.

•**POTTSVILLE,** Town; Pope County; Pop. 564; Zip Code 72858; Lat. 35-15-04 N long. 093-02-50 W; NW central Arkansas. Named for an early settler.

•**POYEN,** Town; Grant County; Pop. 329; Zip Code 72128; Lat. 34-19-34 N long. 092-38-29 W; S central Arkansas.

•**PRAIRIE GROVE,** City; Washington County; Pop. 1,708; Zip Code 72753; Elev. 1165; Lat. 35-58-31 N long. 094-18-52 W; NW Arkansas. A descriptive name for the surrounding landscape.

•**PRATTSVILLE,** Town; Grant County; Pop. 317; Zip Code 72129; Elev. 301; Lat. 34-18-59 N long. 092-33-06 W; S central Arkansas. Possibly named for southern industrialist Daniel Pratt.

•**PRESCOTT,** City; Nevada County Seat; Pop. 4,103; Zip Code 71857; Elev. 320; Lat. 33-48-13 N long. 093-22-57 W; SW Arkansas. Prescott was a judge who served in the early pioneer days.

•**QUITMAN,** Town; Cleburne County; Pop. 556; Zip Code 72123; Elev. 582; Lat. 35-23-08 N long. 092-12-52 W; J.E. Quitman was a hero in the Mexican War. The town is named in his honor.

•**RATCLIFF,** City; Logan County; Pop. 197; Zip Code 72951; Lat. 35-18-23 N long. 093-52-27 W; Named for an early settler.

•**RAVENDEN,** Town; Lawrence County; Pop. 338; Zip Code 72459; A descriptive name for the birds found in the area.

•**READER,** Town; Nevada & Ouachita Counties; Pop. 127; Zip Code 71726; Reader is named after a well-known settler.

•**RECTOR,** City; Clay County; Pop. 2,336; Zip Code 72461; The city is named for a popular clergyman.

•**REDFIELD,** Town; Jefferson County; Pop. 745; Zip Code 72132; Lat. 34-26-40 N long. 092-10-57 W; Redfield took a name which describes the reddish color of the local soil.

•**REED,** Town; Desha County; Pop. 395; Zip Code 71670; Either a personal name or a reference to the growth of reeds.

•**REYNO,** Town; Randolph County; Pop. 521; Zip Code 72462; Probably a personal name.

•**RISON,** City; Cleveland County Seat; Pop. 1,325; Zip Code 71665; Lat. 33-57-37 N long. 092-11-24 W; Named after William R. Rison who settled in Arkansas after the Civil War.

•**ROE,** Town; Monroe County; Pop. 136; Zip Code 72134; Lat. 34-37-50 N long. 091-23-25 W; Either a personal name or a reference to fish eggs.

•**ROGERS,** City; Benton County; Pop. 17,429; Zip Code 71756; Elev.1371; Lat. 36-19-29 N long. 094-08-17 W; Rogers is named for an early settler.

•**ROSE BUD,** Town; White County; Pop. 202; Zip Code 72137; Elev. 632; Lat. 35-19-00 N long. 092-03-32 W; The town is named for the many wild roses in the area.

•**ROSSTON,** Town; Nevada County; Pop. 274; Zip Code 71858; Elev. 389; Lat. 33-33-36 N long. 093-24-22 W; Rosston's name honors a pioneer settler.

•**RUSSELL,** Town; White County; Pop. 232; Zip Code 72139; Elev. 234; Lat. 35-21-42 N long. 091-30-23 W; British doctor T.J. Russell lived here in the 1830's. The town is named after him.

•**RUSSELLVILLE,** City; Pope County Seat; Pop. 14,000; Zip Code 72801 ; Elev. 354; Lat. 35-16-39 N long. 093-09-18 W; Named after Dr. T.J. Russell.

•**SALEM,** City; Fulton County Seat; Pop. 1,424; Zip Code 72576; Lat. 36-15-59 N long. 091-46-48 W; A Hebrew word meaning "peace."

•**SCRANTON,** City; Logan County; Pop. 244; Zip Code 72863; Lat. 35-21-36 N long. 093-32-15 W; Named for Scranton, Pennsylvania.

•**SEARCY,** City; White County Seat; Pop. 13,612; Zip Code 72143; Elev. 264; Lat. 35-07-36 N long. 091-27-09 W; Named after Richard Searcy who was a lawyer and legislator in the early 1800's.

•**SEDGWICK,** Town; Lawrence County; Pop. 205; Zip Code 72465 The town's name honors Union General John Sedgwick who was killed during the Civil War.

•**SHERIDAN,** City; Grant County Seat; Pop. 3,042; Zip Code 72150; Elev. 279; Lat. 34-18-33 N long. 092-24-07 W; The city's name honors Civil War General Phil Sheridan.

•**SHERRILL,** Town; Jefferson County; Pop. 161; Zip Code 72152; Elev. 222; Lat. 34-22-57 N long. 091-57-00 W; Either a personal name of an early settler, or named for James Sherman who was vice-president under Taft.

•**SHERWOOD,** City; Pulaski County; Pop. 10,586; Zip Code 72116; Sherwood is named for an early settler.

•SHIRLEY, Town; Van Buren County; Pop. 354; Zip Code 72153; Elev. 542; Named after Shirley, Massachusetts.

•SIDNEY, Town; Sharp County; Pop. 270; Zip Code 72577; Elev. 610; Lat. 36-00-11 N long. 091-39-35 W; Sidney was an early settler.

•SILOAM SPRINGS, City; Benton County; Pop. 7,940; Zip Code 72761; Lat. 36-10-48 N long. 094-33-46 W; Named after the Biblical Siloam Springs where a blind man was healed.

•SMACKOVER, City; Union County; Pop. 2,453; Zip Code 71762; Lat. 33-21-49 N long. 092-43-34 W; From the French "chemin-couvert," or road-covered, possibly referring to a stream covered by branches.

•SPARKMAN, Town; Dallas County; Pop. 622; Zip Code 71763; Lat. 34-01-15 N long. 092-47-31 W; From a personal name of an early settler.

•SPRINGDALE, City; Benton & Washington Counties; Pop. 23,458; Zip Code 72157; Elev. 1329; Lat. 36-11-06N long. 094-08-34 W; A popular name given to generally rich lands of the area.

•STAMPS, City; Lafayette County; Pop. 2,859; Zip Code 71860; Lat. 33-21-40 N long. 093-29-49 W; Probably a personal name.

•STAR CITY, City; Lincoln County Seat; Pop. 2,066; Zip Code 71667; Elev. 274; Lat. 33-56-22 N long. 091-50-27 W; A euphonious name given by the town's settlers.

•STEPHENS, City; Ouachita County; Pop. 1,366; Zip Code 71764; Elev. 235; Lat. 33-24-42 N long. 093-04-05 W; A pioneer's personal name.

•STRAWBERRY, Town; Lawrence County; Pop. 280; Zip Code 72469; Elev. 327; Descriptively named for the local fruit grown nearby.

•STRONG, City; Union County; Pop. 785; Zip Code 71765; Lat. 33-06-22 N long. 092-21-37 W; A personal name of a settler.

•STUTTGART, City; Arkansas County Seat; Pop. 10,941; Zip Code 72160; Elev. 217; Lat. 34-29-07 N long. 091-33-10 W; Stuttgart is named after the city in Germany.

•SUBIACO, Town; Logan County; Pop. 744; Zip Code 72865; Elev. 468; Lat. 35-17-54 N long. 093-38-22 W; Named for a town in Italy which was the site of one of the first Benedictine monasteries.

•SUCCESS, Town; Clay County; Pop. 223; Zip Code 72470 ; A descriptive name applied by its founders to their town.

•SULPHUR ROCK, Town; Independence County; Pop. 316; Zip Code 72579; Lat. 35-45-15 N long. 091-29-59 W; Named for the nearby sulphur deposits.

•SULPHUR SPRINGS, City; Benton County; Pop. 496; Zip Code 72768 ; Lat. 36-29-00 N long. 094-27-41 W; A local springs contains the mineral sulphur. The town is named after this spring.

•SUMMIT, Town; Marion County; Pop. 506; Zip Code 72677; Lat. 36-14-58 N long. 092-41-26 W; A descriptive geographical name.

•SWIFTON, City; Jackson County; Pop. 859; Zip Code 72471; Named for an early pioneer.

•TAYLOR, City; Columbia County; Pop. 657; Zip Code 71861; Elev. 243; Lat. 33-06-06 N long. 093-27-36 W; Probably a personal name.

•TEXARKANA, City; Miller County Seat; Pop. 21,459; Zip Code 75501; A coined name for a town on the Texas-Arkansas border.

•THORNTON, Town; Calhoun County; Pop. 711; Zip Code 71766; Elev. 318; Lat. 33-46-30 N long. 092-28-55 W; Named after a pioneer settler.

•TILLAR, City; Desha & Drew Counties; Pop. 280; Zip Code 71670; Lat. 33-42-17 N long. 091-26-43 W; Either a personal name or descriptive of the local farming, or tilling.

•TONTITOWN, Town; Washington County; Pop. 571; Zip Code 72770; Lat. 36-10-19 N long. 094-13-38 W; Named for early French explorer Henri De Tonti.

•TRASKWOOD, Town; Saline County; Pop. 459; Zip Code 72167; Lat. 34-27-15 N long. 092-39-20 W; A personal name of a pioneer.

•TRUMANN, City; Poinsett County; Pop. 6,044; Zip Code 72472; Truman is named after an official of the St. Louis and San Francisco Railroad.

•TUCKERMAN, City; Jackson County; Pop. 2,078; Zip Code 72473; Elev. 248; Named for an early settler.

•TUPELO, Town; Jackson County; Pop. 248; Zip Code 72169; Lat. 35-23-27 N long. 091-13-39 W; A Creek Indian word meaning "swamp tree," and referring to trees of the nyssa genus.

•TYRONZA, Town; Poinsett County; Pop. 777; Zip Code 72386; Elev. 224; The origin of the town's name is uncertain.

•ULM, Town; Prairie County; Pop. 201; Zip Code 72170; Lat. 34-34-31 N long. 091-27-34 W; Ulm is named after the city in Germany.

•VALLEY SPRINGS, Town; Boone County; Pop. 190; Zip Code 72682; Lat. 36-09-20 N long. 092-59-56 W; A descriptive name for a local springs.

•VAN BUREN, City; Crawford County Seat; Pop. 2,020; Zip Code 72956; Elev. 443; Lat. 35-29-23 N long. 094-20-08 W; Named after President Martin Van Buren.

•VANDERVOORT, Town; Polk County; Pop. 98; Zip Code 71972; Elev. 1074 ; Lat. 34-22-52 N long. 094-21-53 W; A personal name of a Dutch settler.

•VICTORIA, Town; Mississippi County; Pop. 175; Zip Code 72370; Victoria is named in honor of 19th century empress, Queen Victoria.

•VILONIA, Town; Faulkner County; Pop. 736; Zip Code 72173; Lat. 35-04-59 N long. 092-12-50 W; Probably a personal name.

•VIOLA, Town; Fulton County; Pop. 362; Zip Code 72583; Lat. 36-24-05 N long. 091-59-30 W; The town is named after either the wife or daughter of a pioneer settler.

•WABBASEKA, City; Jefferson County; Pop. 428; Zip Code 72175; Lat. 34-21-37 N long. 091-47-28 W; The personal name of an Indian princess.

•WALDO, City; Columbia County; Pop. 1,685; Zip Code 71770; Lat. 33-21-07 N long. 093-17-39 W; Waldo is named after the city in Maine.

•WALDRON, City; Scott County Seat; Pop. 2,642; Zip Code 72958; Elev. 671; Lat. 34-54-27 N long. 094-23-23 W; A private name of a pioneer.

•WALNUT RIDGE, City; Lawrence County Seat; Pop. 4,152; Zip Code 72476 72476; Elev. 283; Descriptively named for the walnut trees on a nearby ridge.

•**WARD,** City; Lonoke County; Pop. 981; Zip Code 72176; Elev. 233; Lat. 35-01-52 N long. 091-57-08 W; Ward is named after a settler.

•**WARREN,** City; Bradley County Seat; Pop. 7,646; Zip Code 71671; Elev. 213; Lat. 33-36-43 N long. 092-004-05 W; The surname of a pioneer settler.

•**WATSON,** City; Desha County; Pop. 433; Zip Code 71674; Elev. 153; Lat. 33-50-29 N long. 091-15-42 W; The city's name honors an early landowner named Watson.

•**WEINER,** City; Poinsett County; Pop. 750; Zip Code 72479; Named for a 19th century farmer.

•**WELDON,** Town; Jackson County; Pop. 161; Zip Code 72177; Weldon is named after a pioneer.

•**WESTERN GROVE,** Town; Newton County; Pop. 378; Zip Code 72685; Descriptively named for a local groves' position.

•**WEST FORK,** City; Washington County; Pop. 1,526; Zip Code 72774; Elev. 1339; Lat. 35-55-28 N long. 094-11-05 W; A descriptive name of a local river.

•**WEST MEMPHIS,** City; Crittendon County; Pop. 28,138; Zip Code 72301; The city is named after Memphis, Tennessee.

•**WEST POINT,** Town; White County; Pop. 226; Zip Code 72178; Lat. 35-12-13 N long. 091-36-43 W; A geographically descriptive name.

•**WHELEN SPRINGS,** Town; Clark County; Pop. 156; Zip Code 71772; Lat. 33-50-09 N long. 093-07-34 W; The first settler gave his name to the local springs.

•**WHITE HALL,** City; Jefferson County; Pop. 2,214; Zip Code 71602; A descriptive name whose exact origins are uncertain.

•**WICKES,** Town; Polk County; Pop. 464; Zip Code 71973; Lat. 34-18-12 N long. 094-20-08 W; Wickes is named for an early settler.

•**WILLIFORD,** Town; Sharp County; Pop. 169; Zip Code 72482; Elev. 322; Named after a pioneer.

•**WILLISVILLE,** Town; Nevada County; Pop. 209; Zip Code 71864; Elev. 350; Lat. 33-30-59 N long. 093-17-58 W; Willisville's name honors the town's founder.

•**WILMOT,** City; Ashley County; Pop. 1,227; Zip Code 71676; Elev. 115; Lat. 33-03-21 N long. 091-34-20 W; Named for an original landowner.

•**WILSON,** Town; Mississippi County; Pop. 1,115; Zip Code 72395; A personal name.

•**WILTON,** Town; Little River County; Pop. 495; Zip Code 71865; Lat. 33-44-22 N long. 094-08-46 W; Named after the town in Connecticut.

•**WINCHESTER,** City; Drew County; Pop. 279; Zip Code 71677; Elev. 160; Lat. 33-46-26 N long. 091-28-33 W; Winchester is named after the famous English city.

•**WINSLOW,** Town; Washington County; Pop. 247; Zip Code 72959; Probably named for Edward Winslow, president of the St. Louis and San Francisco Railroad.

•**WINTHROP,** City; Little River County; Pop. 238; Zip Code 71866; Elev. 323; Lat. 33-49-51 N long. 094-21-08 W; The city takes its name from Winthrop, Massachusetts.

•**WOOSTER,** Town; Faulkner County; Pop. 398; Zip Code 72181; Elev. 314; Lat. 35-12-02 N long. 092-26-46 W; Named after Wooster, Massachusetts.

•**WYNNE,** City; Cross County; Pop. 7,805; Zip Code 72396; Wynne is named in honor of businessman and banker Jessie Wynne.

CALIFORNIA

•ABERDEEN, Village, Inyo County; Pop. Rural; Zip Code 93513; Elev. 3,314; Lat. 36-59-31 N long. 118-12-40 W; E. Central California; in the Inyo Mountains; 30 mi. S. of Bishop. Aberdeen was named by early settlers for the city in Scotland.

•ACTON, Town, Los Angeles County; Pop. 650; Zip code 93510. Lat. 34-28-12 N long. 118-11-45 W; A station of the Saugus-Mojave section of the Southern Pacific Railroad, built 1873-76.

•ADELANTO, City, San Bernardino County; Pop. 2,164; Zip Code 92301; Lat. 34-34-58 N long. 117-24-30 W; Founded 1917; 8 miles from the junction of US 66 with US 395. Name (Spanish) means "progress" or "advance."

•ADIN, City, Modoc County; Pop. 500; Zip Code 96006; Elev. 4,205; Lat. 41-11-38 N long. 120-56-39 W; In NE California, reached by US 299. Named by residents in 1870 for Adin McDowell, a native of Kentucky who had settled there in 1869.

•AFTON, Hamlet, Glenn County; Mail goes to Butte City, Zip Code 95920. Elev. 1408; Lat. 35-02-11 N long. 116-22-44 W; Rural.

•AGOURA, City, Los Angeles County; Pop. 380; Zip Code 91301; Lat. 34-08-35 N long. 118-44-13 W; Founded 1927; NW of Santa Monica Mountains. First known as Picture City.

•AGUANGA, Village, Riverside County, Pop. 50; Zip Code 92302; Elev. 1,940; Lat. 33-26-34 N long. 116-51-51 W; S. California. Aguanga is probably a Shoshonean Indian place name, first appearing in various spellings in 1850.

•AHWAHNEE, Town, Madera County; Pop. 600; Zip Code 93601; Elev. 2321; Lat. 37-21-56 N long. 119-43-31 W; in Yosemite National Park. Original name was probably something like Ahwahnachee, a Tokuts Indian word meaning "the people who inhabited the deep, grassy valley."

•ALAMEDA CITY, Alameda County; Pop. 63,852; Zip code 94501; Elev. 2,500; 5 mi. E. of San Francisco in W. California.

•ALAMO, Town; Contra Costa County; Pop. 4,500; Zip Code 94507; Elev. 250; Lat. 37-51-01 N long. 122-01-52 W; Founded 1852; 24 miles NE of San Francisco. Name (Spanish) means "poplar" or "cottonwood tree."

•ALBANY, City, Alameda County; Pop. 15,130; Zip Code 94706. Named Ocean View on incorporation in 1908. The next year renamed Albany after the New York birthplace of Frank J. Roberts, the California town's first mayor.

•ALBERHILL, Town, Riverside County; Pop. 45; Zip Code 92330. Name coined from Albers and Hill, owners of the land on which the town was built around 1890.

•ALBION, Town, Mendocino County; Pop. 350; Zip Code 95410; 4 miles from a junction with Cal. Highway 28. The ancient name for Britain was applied to a land grant at the mouth of the Albion River dated October 30, 1844, by William A. Richardson, captain of the port of San Francisco.

•ALDERPOINT, Town, Humboldt County; Pop. 300; Zip Code 95411. Named for the abundance of native white, red, and mountain alder trees.

•ALHAMBRA, City, Los Angeles County; Pop. 64,615; Zip Code 918+; Elev. 483; Residential city in SW California 5 miles ENE of Los Angeles. Name (Arabic) means "the red," an allusion to the color of the bricks used to construct the original Alhambra, a medieval fortress built in Granada by Moorish monarchs.

•ALLEGHANY, Village, Sierra County; Pop. 135; Zip Code 95910; Elev. 4,419; NE California. The town was named for the Alleghany Tunnel, begun here in 1853.

•ALMONTE, Town, Marin County; Pop. 3,200 (combined with Homestead Valley); Zip Code 94941. The old name, Mill Valley Junction, was changed in 1912 by the Southern Pacific Railroad at the request of residents, who wanted to avoid confusion with Mill Valley. The proximity of Muir Woods may have suggested the name (Spanish), which means "at the woods."

•ALPINE, Town, San Diego County; Pop. 1,900; Zip Code 92001. Mountain town established in 1883 by B. R. Arnold, a Connecticut importer of ivory for piano and organ keys. Name proposed by an early reident because the district resembled her native Switzerland.

•ALTA, Town, Placer County; Pop. 225; Zip Code 95701; Elev. 3,590; NE California. This town grew around a station of the Central Pacific Railroad, which named it for the San Francisco newspaper Alta California.

•ALTADENA, City, Los Angeles County; Pop. 42,380; Zip Code 91001; Elev. 1,240; Unincorporated urban community NE of Pasadena. Name (Spanish) derived from alta ("high") and the last part of Pasadena and applied to Altadena because of its location above Pasadena.

•AL TAHOE, Village, El Dorado County; Pop. (with South Lake Tahoe); Zip Code 95702; Elev. 6,225; NE California., This resort town above Lake Tahoe was known as Rowland's before 1912. It takes the Washoe Indian name meaning "big water."

•ALTA LOMA, Town, San Bernardino County; Pop. 6,100; Zip Code 91701. Name (Spanish) means "high hill."

•ALTAMONT, Village, Alameda County; No pop; Elev. 740; W. California. At the summit of Altamount Pass, Altamount was settled in 1868 when the Southern Pacific Railroad was built.

•ALTAVILLE, Town, Calaveras County; Pop. 1,710 (with Angels Camp); Zip Code 95221. An old mining camp variously known as Forks-of-the-Road, Low Divide, and Cherokee Flat, adopted its present name, Spanish and French for "high city," at a town meeting in 1857.

•ALTURAS, Town, Modoc County Seat; Pop. 3,025; Zip Code 96101; Elev. 4,366. Called Dorris Bridge (for Presley Dorris, who built a bridge across the Pit here) until 1876, when the legislature, up on petition, changed the name to the Spanish word meaning "heights."

•ALUM ROCK, City, Santa Clara County; Pop. 18,355; Zip Code 95127; Elev. 188. Named because of the striking monolith at its center, in the crevices of which alum dust can be found.

•ALVISO, Town, Santa Clara County; Pop. 400 (part of San Jose); Zip Code 95002; 4 miles from Milpitas on Cal. Highway 9; Founded in 1849. Named for Ignacio Alviso, who came from Spain as a child with the Anza expedition in 1776 and settled here in 1838.

•AMADOR CITY, City, Amador County; Pop. 156; Zip Code 95601; Elev. 1,100; NE California. The town was named for Jose Maria Amador, a Mexican soldier who established a mining settlement on the creek nearby in 1848.

•AMBOY, Town, San Bernardino County; Pop. 150; Zip Code 92304. Elev. 639; Lat. 34-33-28 N long. 115-44-37 W; Named by the Atlantic and Pacific Railroad in 1883, probably after one of the Amboys back East.

•ANAHEIM, City, Orange County; Pop. 221,847; Zip Code 928+; Elev. 160; Lat. 33-50-07 N long. 117-54-49 W; 16 miles east of Long Beach in SW California; Chapman Avenue is junction with US 101. Named after Santa Ana plus German suffix *heim* (home).

•ANDERSON, Town, Shasta County; Pop. 7,381; Zip Code 96007; Elev. 430; Lat. 40-26-54 N long. 122-17-48 W; Founded 1872; in northern California 10 miles south of Redding. Named for Elias Anderson, who granted right of way to the California and Oregon Railroad.

•ANDRADE, Town, Imperial County; Pop. 10; Zip Code 92283; Near Calexico. Named by the Imperial Land Co. for the Mexican general, Guillermo Andrade, who had sold the land to the California Development Co. in 1900 for colonization.

•ANGELS CAMP, Town, Calaveras County; Pop. 1,710; Zip Code 95222; Elev. 1,500; Lat. 38-04-37 N long. 120-33-08 W; Founded 1848; 6 miles from Vallicito on Cal. Highway 4. Named for George Angel, a member of Stevenson's Volunteers in the Mexican War, who started mining the creek in June 1848.

•ANGWIN, Town, Napa County; Pop. 2,690; Zip Code 94508; Lat. 38-34-33 N long. 122-26-56 W; Founded 1874. Named for Edwin Angwin, who operated a summer resort on his property, which was part of Rancho La Jota.

•ANTIOCH, City, Contra Costa County; Pop. 43,559; Zip Code 94509; Lat. 38-00-18 N long. 121-48-17 W; Founded 1849; western California. Known as Smith's Landing for the first settlers, twin brothers J. H. and W. W. Smith, until the inhabitants chose the name of the Biblical city in Syria at a picnic, July 4, 1851.

•APPLEGATE, Town, Placer County; Pop. 800; Zip Code 95703; Lat. 39-00-03 N long. 120-59-29 W; Founded 1870. Settled by Lisbon Applegate and was known as Bear River House.

•APTOS, Town, Santa Cruz County; Pop. 8,704; Zip Code 95003; Lat. 36-58-38 N long. 121-53-54 W; Founded 1831. Name is a Spanish rendering of an Indian word meaning "the meeting of two streams," referring to Valencia and Aptos creeks.

•ARBUCKLE, Town, Colusa County; Pop. 1,037; Zip Code 95912; Elev. 139; Lat. 39-01-03 N long. 122-03-24 W; N Central California. It was named by the Central Pacific railroad when it established a station here in 1875. T. R. Arbuckle had owned a ranch nearby since 1866.

•ARCADIA, City, Los Angeles County; Pop. 45,994; Zip Code 91006; Elev. 460; Lat. 34-08-23 N long. 118-02-04 W; Founded 1888. Named by Herman A. Unruh, of the San Gabriel Valley Railroad, for the district of the same name in Greece, a locale of rural simplicity.

•ARCATA, Town, Humboldt County; Pop. 12,338; Zip Code 95521; Elev. 33; Lat. 40-52-00 N long. 124-04-54 W; Founded 1850; NW California. Given its present name, of unknown Indian origin, when the original name, Uniontown, was confused with that of another settlement in El Dorado County.

•ARMONA, Town, Kings County; Pop. 1,392; Zip Code 93202; Elev. 236; Lat. 36-18-57 N long. 119-42-27 W; Central California. The village was begun as a rail stop on the Southern Pacific line in the 1890s.

•ARROWBEAR LAKE, Village, San Bernardino County; Pop. 200; Zip Code 92382; Elev. 6,080; Lat. 34-12-39 N long. 117-04-57 W; S California; 15 mi. N of San Bernardino. This resort town lies on the San Bernardino Mountains, on a lake between Lakes Arrowhead and Big Bear.

•ARROWHEAD HIGHLANDS, Town, San Bernardino County; Pop. 3,600 (with Crestline); Zip Code 92325; Lat. 34-13-48 N long. 117-15-43 W; Resort named after the arrow-shaped mark on nearby Arrowhead Peak (5,174 feet) created after the final uplift of the San Bernardino Range.

•ARROYO GRANDE, Town, San Luis Obispo County; Pop. 11,290; Zip Code 93420; Lat. 35-07-07 N long. 120-35-23 W; SW California. Name (Spanish) means "large watercourse" and dates from 1867-68 when a blacksmith shop and schoolhouse were built here.

•ARTESIA, City, Los Angeles County; Pop. 14,301; Zip Code 90701; Elev. 50, Lat. 33-51-57-N long. 118-04-56 W; NE of Long Beach. Named by the Artesia Co., which drilled artesian wells and established the town in the 1870s.

•ARVIN, Town, Kern County; Pop. 6,863; Zip Code 93203; Elev. 445; Lat. 35-12-33 N long. 118-49-39 W; Southern California, 16 miles SE of Bakersfield. Named for Arvin Richardson, first storekeeper in the colony, which was established in 1910.

•ASHLAND, City, Alameda County; Pop. 14,180; Zip Code 94541. Lat. 37-41-41 N long. 122-06-46 W; Named for the Oregon ash tree which was found growing there.

•ASILOMAR, Village, Monterey County; Pop. (with Pacific Grove); Zip Code 93950; W. California. This town was named for the Spanish words meaning "sea refuge."

•ASTI. Village, Sonoma County; Pop. 50; Zip Code 95413; Lat. 38-45-47 N long. 122-58-19 W; NW California. An Italian-Swiss colony was begun here in 1881 by a group from San Francisco as a commercial venture.

•ATASCADERO, Town, San Luis Obispo County; Pop. 15,930; Zip Code 93422; Lat. 35-29-22 N long. 120-40-11 W; Founded 1886. Name (Spanish) meaning "miry place," was derived from that of the provisional land grant dated December 21, 1839.

•ATHERTON, Town, San Mateo County; Pop. 7,797; Zip Code 94025; Elev. 50; Lat. 37-27-41 N long. 122-11-48 W; Suburb of Redwod City, 22 miles SE of San Francisco; Incorporated 1923. Named for Faxon D. Atherton, father-in-law of novelist Gertrude Atherton.

•ATWATER, City, Merced County; Pop. 17,530; Zip Code 95301; Lat. 34-06-59 N long. 118-15-20 W; NW of Merced. Founded in 1888 by the Merced Land and Fruit Co. and named for the property's owner, Marshall D. Atwater, a well-known wheat rancher.

•ATWOOD, Town, Orange County; Pop. including that of Placentia: 30,200; Zip Code 92601. Lat. 33-51-56 N long. 117-49-48 W; Named in 1920 for W. J. Atwood, purchasing agent for the Chanslor-Canfield-Midway Oil Co.

•AUBURN, Town, Placer County Seat; Pop. 7,540; Zip Code 95603; Elev. 1,297; Lat. 38-53-48 N long. 121-04-33 W; 36 miles NE of Sacramento; Seat of Placer County; founded as a gold-mining camp in 1848. Named for a city in New York State.

•AVALON, Town, Los Angeles County; Pop. 2,010; Zip Code 90704; Lat. 33-20-34 N long. 118-19-37 W; SW California, at eastern end of Santa Catalina Island. Named for the legendary elysium of King Arthur, a sort of Celtic paradise.

•AVENAL, City; Kings County; Pop. 4,137; Zip Code 93204; Lat. 36-00-15 N long. 120-07-41 W; SW central California.

•AVILA BEACH, Town, San Luis Obispo County; Pop. 400; Zip Code 93424. Elev. 20; Lat. 35-10-48 N long. 120-43-51 W; Unincorporated beach town named for Miguel Avila, grantee in 1839 of Rancho San Miguelito, on which the town was built in 1867.

•**AZUSA,** City, Los Angeles County; Pop. 29,380; Zip Code 91702; Elev. 612; Lat. 34-08-01 N long. 117-54-24 W; SW California, 18 miles ENE of Los Angeles. Settled 1887 as a citrus center on the Azusa Grant, for which it is named, at the foot of the San Gabriel Mountains. Name is a corruption of an Indian word, *azuncsabit,* meaning "skunk hill."

•**BADGER,** Town, Tulare County; Pop. 15; Zip Code 93603; Elev. 3030; Lat. 36-37-53 N long. 119-00-44 W; Founded 1892.

•**BAGBY,** Town, Mariposa County; Pop. Rural; Zip Code 95311; Elev. 1,000; Central California. Formerly Benton Mills, this little town was named for hotel-owner B. A. Bagby in 1897.

•**BAGDAD,** Town, San Bernardino County; Pop. 10; Zip Code 92304; Elev. 787; Lat. 34-34-58 N long. 115-52-29 W; Near US 66. Named after the city of Baghdad in Iraq in 1883 by the Southern Pacific Railroad when the original line (now the Santa Fe) was constructed; because it is in the desert.

•**BAIRD,** (obs.), Shasta County; No Pop.; N California; on the McCloud River near several Pleistocene caverns. Named when it was founded in 1879 for Spenser E. Baird, a federal fish commissioner.

•**BAKER,** Village, San Bernardino County; Pop. 500; Zip Code 92309; Elev. 923; Lat. 35-15-54 N long. 116-04-25 W; SE California, NE of Sada Lake. First known as Berry, for an old prospector, this town was renamed by the Tonopah and Tidewater Railway Company for its president, R. C. Baker.

•**BAKERSFIELD,** City, Kern County Seat; Pop. 105,611; Zip Code 933+; Elev. 406; Lat. 35-22-24 N long. 119-01-04 W; Southern California. Colonel Thomas Baker, who tried to develop a waterway from Kern Lake to San Francisco Bay in the early 1860s, had a corral here known as "Baker's field." In 1868 the name was applied to the city.

•**BALANCE ROCK,** Town, Tulare County; Pop. 10; Zip Code 93260; Lat. 35-48-22 N long. 118-39-04 W; the name, which refers to the huge rock which balances on another at the entrance to the resort, was applied by a Mrs. Shively in 1900.

•**BALBOA,** Subdivision, Orange County; Pop. (with Newport Beach); Zip Code 92661; Elev. 5; Lat. 33-35-13 N long. 117-54-00 W; S California. Named for the discoverer of the Pacific Ocean by a development company in 1905, Balboa is part of the City of Newport Beach.

•**BALDWIN PARK,** City, Los Angeles County; Pop. 50,554; Zip Code 91706; Elev. 374; Lat. 34-05-07 N long. 117-57-36; SE of Monrovia; Residential community in the San Gabriel Mts. Named in 1912 for E. J. "Lucky" Baldwin, a spectacular 1890s financier on whose former estate, Puente de San Gabriel, the city was built.

•**BANNER,** Location, San Diego County; Pop. Rural; Elev. 2755; Lat. 33-04-08 N long. 116-32-43 W; S California. This former mining town is now a camping and recreational site. It was established for gold mining in 1870.

•**BANNING,** City, Riverside County; Pop. 14,020; Zip Code 92220; Elev. 2,350; Lat. 33-55-32 N long. 116-52-32 W; SE California. This town was laid out in 1883 by Phineas Banning, a stagecoach operator, and transportation promoter in Southern California.

•**BARRETT LAKE,** Town, San Diego County; Zip Code 92017. Rural community on Cottonwood Creek shares a name with the lake created by the 1213-foot Barrett Dam completed in 1922. Settlement named in 1919 for the Barrett family, pioneers in this region in the 1870s.

•**BARTLE,** Village, Siskiyou County; No pop; Zip Code 96067; Elev. 3974; Lat. 41-15-28 N long. 121-49-12 W; N California. The town was originated as a station on the McCloud Logging Railroad in 1904 and named for Abraham and Jerome Bartle, who ran a resort and a cattle ranch in the area.

•**BARSTOW,** City, San Bernardino County; Pop. 17,690; Zip Code 92311; Elev. 2,170; Lat. 36-48-55 N long. 119-58-08 W; At foot of Calico Mts. Originally called Fishpond, then Waterman Junction (in honor of the governor, who owned a silver mine nearby). Named Barstow in 1886 by the Santa Fe Railroad for its president, William Barstow Strong.

•**BARTLETT,** Town, Inyo County; Pop. rural; No Zip Code. Lat. 36-28-36 N long. 118-01-48 W; Originally a health resort named for Green Bartlett, a native of Kentucky, who drove cattle across the plains to California in 1856.

•**BASSETT,** Town, Los Angeles County; Pop. 9,810 (with Avocado Heights); Zip Code 91746. Lat. 34-02-59 N long. 117-59-45 W; Site of hot springs near US 299.

•**BASS LAKE,** Town, Madera County; Pop. 300 (summer 3,000); Zip Code 93604. Elev. 3425; Lat. 37-19-12 N long. 120-31-45 W; Artificial lake behind a storage dam named in 1900 is town's principal asset.

•**BEAR VALLEY,** Town, Mariposa County; Pop. 25; Zip Code 95338; Elev. 2,100; Lat. 38-27-53 N long. 120-02-20 W; Central California. This was once Fremont's headquarters for his rich Mariposa mines. Ruins of his settlement, founded and named in 1848 are on the site.

•**BEAUMONT,** City, Riverside County; Pop. 6,818; Zip Code 92223; Lat. 33-55-46 N long. 116-58-35 W; S Central California. The region was opened to Anglo-Americans in 1853 by a herd of straying cattle. Dr. I. W. Smith, a Mormon, followed his strays from San Bernardino.

•**BECKWORTH,** Town, Plumas County; Pop. 120; Zip code 96129; Elev. 4,874; Lat. 39-49-13 N long. 120-22-40 W; Founded 1874. Once trade center of a lumbering area. Site of Beckworth Pass, named for James Beckworth, a Virginia-born mulatto hunter.

•**BEL AIR,** (See Beverly Hills).

•**BELDEN,** Village, Plumas County; Pop. 10; Zip Code 95915; Lat. 40-00-22 N long. 121-14-53 W; N California. Named for early settler and miner Robert Belden in 1909; Located near Oroville.

•**BELL,** City, Los Angeles County; Pop. 25,450; Zip Code 90201; Lat. 33-58-39 N long. 118-11-10 W; Residential city 5 miles south of LA; Founded 1898. Named for the founders of the town, A. and J. G. Bell. Incorporated 1927.

•**BELLFLOWER,** City; Los Angeles County; Pop. 53,441; Zip Code 90706; N of Long beach in S California.

•**BELL GARDENS,** City, Los Angeles County; Pop. 34,117; Zip Code 90201; Lat. 33-57-55 N long. 118-09-02 W; NW of Downey; Populated heavily by rural Westerners who arrived from the Dust Bowl during the 1930s. When the vegetable tracts developed by Japanese gardeners were subdivided in 1930, the area was named after nearby Bell, and in 1961 the town was incorporated.

•**BELLA VISTA,** Town, Shasta County; Zip Code 96008; Elev. 550; Lat. 40-38-27 N long. 122-13-53 W; Founded by the Shasta Lumber Co. in 1893. Name (Spanish) means "beautiful view."

•**BELMONT,** City, San Mateo County; Pop. 24,505; Zip Code 94002. Lat. 37-31-13 N long. 122-16-29 W; The name, a variation of the French for "beautiful mountain," was given by Steinburger and Beard because of the "symmetrically rounded eminence" nearby.

•**BELVEDERE,** Town Marin County; Pop. 2,401; Zip Code 94920; Elev. 313; Lat. 34-02-26 N long. 118-10-06 W; on San Francisco Bay. Founded in 1890 by the Belvedere Club of San Francisco on what was formerly known as Peninsular Island. Name is Italian for "beautiful view."

•**BEN LOMMOND,** Town, Santa Cruz County; Pop. 2,793; Zip Code 95005; in the Santa Cruz Mts. near Cal. Highway 9; Founded 1872. Named for the mountain in Scotland.

•**BENBOW,** Village, Humboldt County; Pop. 150; Zip Code 95440; Lat. 40-04-07 N long. 123-47-00 W; NW California. A resort hotel and summer homes make up this tiny community near the dammed Eel River. The Benbow family established this town.

•**BENICIA,** City, Solano County; Pop. 15,376; Zip Code 94510; Elev. 33; Lat. 38-02-58 N long. 122-09-27 W; W California; Near San Poolo Bay. Named Santa Francisca in honor of Vallejo's wife, the town did not become the leading city of bay. Vallejo and his associates renamed the town for his wife's second name, Benicia, when the citizens of Yerba Buena named the bay for San Francisco.

•**BENTON,** Town, Mono County; Pop. 65; Zip Code 93512; Elev. 5377; Lat. 37-49-09 N long. 118-28-32 W; Founded during the mining boom of 1865. Because it was in a silver-mining district, Benton may have been named for Senator Thomas H. Benton of Missouri, an advocate of metallic currency.

•**BERENDA,** Town, Madera County; Pop. 100; Zip Code 93637; Elev. 255; Lat. 37-02-25 N long. 120-09-09 W; Reached by US 99. A Southern Pacific Railroad station spanning the Fresno River is here. Name (Spanish) means "antelope."

•**BERKELEY,** City, Alameda County; Pop. 103,328; Zip Code 947+ zone; Elev. 216; Lat. 35-04-41 N long. 120-32-20 W; Residential and industrial city north of Oakland; Founded 1853; Incorporated 1909. Named in 1866 by Frederick Billings, a trustee of the University of California, for Bishop George Berkeley, who in 1728 wrote the famous line: "Westward the course of empire takes its way."

•**BETTERAVIA,** Town, Santa Barbara County; Pop. rural; Zip Code 93454; Elev. 185. Lat. 34-55-04 N long. 120-30-50 W; Name (French) means "beet" (*betterave*). Dominated by the Union Sugar refining plant which introduced the sugar-beet industry here in 1897.

•**BEVERLY HILLS,** City, Los Angeles County; Pop. 32,367; Zip Code 90213; Residential city, western suburb of LA, founded 1906. A newspaper account reporting that President Taft would spend a few days at Beverly Farms in Massachusetts suggested the name to Burton E. Green, president of the Rodeo Land and Water Co.

•**BIEBER,** Village, Lassen County; Pop. 300; Zip Code 96009; Elev. 4,169; Lat. 41-07-17 N long. 121-08-35 W; NE California. On the Pit River, Bieber was founded in 1877 by its first merchant and journalist, Nathan Bieber; it had been called Chalk Ford because of the numerous chalk deposits in the vicinity.

•**BIG BEAR CITY,** Town, San Bernardino County; Pop. 5,268; Zip Code 92315. Lat. 34-15-40 N long. 116-50-39 W; Center of resort area built around Big Bear Lake, an artificial 7-mile long reservoir created in 1884 by building the Old Bear Valley Dam in the San Bernardino Mts.

•**BIGGS,** Town Butte County; Pop. 1,413; Zip Code 95917. Lat. 38-56-48 N long. 119-58-03 W; A California and Oregon Railroad station named in 1870 for Major Marion Biggs, who was the first rancher to ship grain from here.

•**BIG OAK FLAT,** Village, Tuolumn County; Pop. 110; Zip Code 95305; Lat. 37-49-25 N long. 120-15-26 W; NE California. The town was founded as Savage Diggings by James Savage, who settled here with his five Indian wives and a retinue of servants in 1850. The present name was derived from an oak, 11 feet in diameter, that stood at the center of town until it was felled for the gold beneath its roots.

•**BIG PINE,** Town, Inyo County; Pop. 950; Zip Code 93513; Elev. 3,985; South of Bishop. Near the 28,000-acre Bristlecone Pine Forest of ancient, twisted trees, part of Inyo National Forest.

•**BIG SUR,** Town, Monterey County; Pop. 150; Zip Code 93920; Elev. 155; Lat. 36-16-13 N long. 121-48-23 W; About 10 miles along coast SE of Point Sur on Big Sur River. Named for El Rio Grande del Sur ("The Big River of the South"), once a rancho granted to Juan B. Alvarado in 1834.

•**BIOLA,** Town, Fresno County; Pop. 800; Zip Code 93606. Lat. 36-48-08 N long. 120-00-55 W; Name coined by William Kerchoff of Los Angeles from the initials of Bible Institute of Los Angeles when he established the town in 1912.

•**BIRD'S LANDING,** Town, Solano County; Pop. 40; Zip Code 94512; Elev. 58; Lat. 38-07-58 N long. 121-52-11 W; Formerly the shipping point of John Bird, a native of New York, who settled here in 1865 and who had a storage and commission business.

•**BISHOP,** Town, Inyo County; Pop. 3,333; Zip Code 93514; Elev. 4147; Lat. 37-21-4 9;lLong. 118-23-39 W; Eastern California in Owens river Valley 35 miles west of Nevada border; Elev. 4,147; Junction with US 6. Named for Samuel A. Bishop of Virginia, a cattleman who drove the first herd into Owens Valley in 1861.

•**BLACK POINT,** Town, Marin County; Pop. 275; Zip Code 94947. Lat. 38-40-46 N long. 123-25-38 W; Community at the mouth of the Petaluma River named for James Black, a Scottish sailor who arrived in 1832.

•**BLAIRSDEN,** Town, Plumas County; Pop. 100 (summer 500); Zip Code 96103; Elev. 4,500; Lat. 39-46-52 N long. 120-36-56 W; Junction Cal. Highway 9. Named around 1903 for the country home of James A. Blair, prominent in the early financing of the Western Pacific Railway.

•**BLOCKSBURG,** Town, Humboldt County; Pop. 40; Zip Code 95414. Elev. 1596; Lat. 40-16-34 N long. 123-38-07 W; Named for Benjamin Blockburger, an immigrant of 1853 and participant in Indian fights, who established a store here in 1872.

•**BLUE CANYON,** Town, Placer County; Pop. 10; Zip Code 95715. Lat. 39-15-26 N long. 120-42-36 W; Recieved its name from the blue smoke of the camps when extensive lumbering took place in the 1850s. May have been named originally for Old Jim Blue, who mined there in the 1850s.

•**BLUE JAY,** Town, San Bernardino County; Pop. 300 (2,000 summer); Zip Code 92317. Lat. 34-14-46 N long. 117-12-32 W; Named for the California jay bird.

•**BLUE LAKE,** Town, Humboldt County; Pop. 1,201; Zip Code 95525; Elev. 40; Lat. 40-52-59 N long. 123-58-58 W; 7 miles from a junction with US 101. Center of a farming and dairy area.

•**BLYTHE,** Town, Riverside County; Pop. 6,805; Zip Code 92225; Elev. 270; Lat. 33-36-37 N long. 114-35-44 W; SE California near the Colorado River in the Palo Verde Valley; Founded 1908. Named for Thomas H. Blythe of San Francisco, a promoter of irrigation in the 1870s.

•BODEGA, Town, Sonoma County; Pop. 100; Zip Code 94922; Lat. 38-20-43 N long. 122-58-22 W; Founded early 1850s. On the bay entered by the Spanish ship Sonorq on October 3, 1775, and named for her captain, Juan Francisco de La Bodega y Quadra.

•BODIE, Village; Mono County; Pop. (Rural); Lat. 38-12-44 N long. 119-00-40 W; At Nevada State line, E California. Gold was discovered in the area in 1852; The Mono Trail was blazed and W. S. Bodie found gold here in 1859.

•BOLINAS, Town, Marin County; Pop. 600; Zip Code 94924; Elev. 9; Lat. 37-54-34 N long. 122-41-07 W; NW Central California. First settler here was Gregorio Briones, owner of the 8,900 acre cattle domain of Baulinas Rancho.

•BONITA, Town, San Diego County; Pop. 2,300; Zip Code 92202. Elev. 206; Lat. 36-57-09 N long. 120-12-03 W; In 1884, Henry E. Cooper named his estate Bonita Ranch and the name was later applied to the post office. The Spanish word *bonita*, a diminutive of *buena*, means "pretty."

•BONSALL, Town, San Diego County; Pop 750; Zip Code 92003; Elev. 172. Lat. 33-17-20 N long. 117-13-29 W; A small trading center in a dairy and farming area named for James Bonsall, a native of Pennsylvania who set up a nursery here in the 1870s.

•BOONVILLE, Town, Mendocino County; Pop. 750; Zip Code 95415; Lat. 39-00-33 N long. 123-21-54 W; In the Anderson Valley; Founded as Kendall's City in 1864. Soon afterward, W. W. Boone bought the store of Levi and Straus and changed the name of the town to his own.

•BORON, Town, Kern County; Pop. 2,500; Zip Code 93516; Elev. 2460; Lat. 34-59-58 N long. 117-38-56 W; In Antelope Valley. Site of an borax mine. After the Pacific Coast Borax Co. moved from Death Valley to Amargo, the railway station and the post office took the name Boron, for the nonmetallic element in borax.

•BORREGO SPRINGS, Town, San Diego County; Pop. 900; Zip Code 92004; Elev. 590; Lat. 33-15-21 N long. 116-22-27 W; Residential community along the SW side of the Borrego Valley. Name (Spanish) means "sheep." Was an important watering place for the abundant bighorn sheep that once roamed the valley.

•BOULDER CREEK, Town, Santa Cruz County; Pop. 1,805 (4,000 summer); Zip Code 95006; Elev. 493; Lat. 37-07-34 N long. 122-07-16 W; In the Santa Cruz Mts. In the 1880's the lumber town Lorenzo took the name of the Boulder Creek post office, established in the 1870s.

•BOYES HOT SPRINGS, Town, and hot springs, Sonoma County; Pop. 3,558; Zip Code 95416; Elev. 129; Lat. 38-18-50 N long. 122-28-51 W; NW California. This resort community was developed by Captain H. E. Boyes, on a site used by Indians.

•BRADLEY, Town, Monterey County; Pop. 100; Zip Code 93426; Lat. 35-51-48 N long. 120-47-59 W; Founded 1886; Reached by US 101. Former Southern Pacific station named for the owner of the land, Bradley V. Sargent, state senator, 1887-89.

•BRAWLEY, City, Imperial County; Pop. 14,946; Zip Code 92227; Lat. 32-58-43 N long. 115-31-46 W; SE corner of California, in Imperial Valley south of Salton Sea; 115 feet below sea level; Founded 1902. Named for J. H. Braly of Los Angeles, who objected to the use of his name. Present spelling was then substituted by A. H. Heber, general manager of the Imperial Land Co., which laid out the town.

•BRAY, Town, Siskiyou County; Pop. 10; Zip Code 96066. Lat. 41-38-39 N long. 121-58-11 W; When the post office was established June 7, 1907, it was named after Bray Ranch, about one half mile from present settlement.

•BREA, City, Orange County; Pop. 27,913; Zip Code 91621; Elev. 349; Lat. 33-55-00 N long. 117-53-57 W; SW California, 22 miles NE of Long Beach; Reached by Imperial Highway. Named after a rancho called Canada de la Brea ("valley of pitch," or "bitumen") because of the asphalt beds here.

•BRENTWOOD, Town, Contra Costa County; Pop. 4,434; Zip Code 94513; Elev. 79; Lat. 37-55-55 N long. 121-41-41 W; 38 miles east of San Francisco; Founded 1878. Named after Brentwood in Essex, England, the ancestral home of John Marsh, who had owned Rancho Los Meganos on which the present town was built.

•BRICELAND, Town, Humboldt County; Pop. 75; Zip Code 95440; Lat. 40-06-29 N long. 123-53-56 W; Founded 1892. Named for John C. Briceland, a native of Virginia, who, around 1889, bought the ranch on which the present town was developed.

•BRIDGEPORT, Town, Mono County Seat; Pop. 500; Zip Code 93517; Elev. 6,473; Lat. 37-26-00 N long. 120-00-12 W; Settled in the late 1850s. Situated in a valley ringed by the Sierras and low, pinion-covered hills.

•BRISBANE, Town, San Mateo County; Pop. 2,969; Zip code 94005; Lat. 37-40-51 N long. 122-23-56 W; On San Francisco Bay 5 miles south of San Francisco; Promotor Arthur Annis, a native of Brisbane, Australia, changed the name in 1931 in honor of the well-known journalist Arthur Brisbane to avoid confusion with nearby Visitacion Valley.

•BRISTOL LAKE, Town, Orange County; Pop. included in Santa Ana; 156,601; Zip Code 92703; SW California, 20 miles east of Long Beach.

•BRODERICK, Town, Yolo County; Pop. 9,900; Zip Code 95605; Lat. 39-13-36 N long. 120-00-40 W; N Central California. Broderick was the seat of Yolo County for two brief periods (1851-57 and 1861-62) but lost the honor under stress of fire, flood and political storm.

•BROWNSVILLE, Town, Yuba County; Pop. 500; Zip Code 95919. Elev. 2235; Lat. 39-28-24 N long. 121-16-05 W; Named for I. E. Brown, who erected the first sawmill here in 1851.

•BRYN MAWR, Town, San Bernardino County; Pop. included with Loma Linda: 7,651; Zip Code 92318; Elev. 1202; Lat. 34-02-54 N long. 117-13-48 W; Founded 1895. Probably named after the town in Pennsylvania, which had been named after the town in Wales.

•BUCK'S LAKE, Town, Plumas county; Pop. 1,000; Zip Code 95971; Elev. 5,071; 9 miles from Spanish Peak. Named for Horace Bucklin, popularly known as "Buck," who settled here in 1850.

•BUELLTON, Town, Santa Barbara County; Pop. 1,402; Zip Code 93427; Elev. 361; Lat. 34-36-49 N long. 120-11-30 W; Post office named in 1916 by William Budd, the first postmaster, for Rufus T. Buell, a native of Vermont who settled here in 1874.

•BUENA PARK, City, Orange County; Pop. 64,165; Zip Code 90620; Elev. 74; Lat. 33-52-03 N long. 117-59-50 W; West of Anaheim; Founded 1887. Named Buena (Spanish for "good") in 1929.

•BURBANK, City, Los Angeles County; Pop. 84,625; Zip Code 915+; Elev. 598; Lat. 34-10-51 N long. 118-18-29 W; 10 miles NW of Los Angeles. Laid out in 1887 on the Providencia Rancho, and named for one of the subdividers, Dr. David Burbank, a Los Angeles dentist.

•BURLINGAME, City, San Mateo County; Pop. 26,173; Zip Code 94010; Lat. 37-35-03 N long. 122-21-54 W; Named in 1868 by

William C. Ralston for his friend, Anson C. Burlingame, then U.S. Minister to China.

•**BURNEY,** Town, Shasta County; Pop. 2,190; Zip Code 96013; Elev. 3973; Lat. 40-52-57 N long. 121-39-35 W; Named in memory of Samuel Burney, a trapper and immigrant guide of Scottish origin killed by Indians in the late 1850s.

•**BURREL,** Town, Fresno County; Pop. 75; Zip Code 93607; Lat. 36-29-18 N long. 119-59-03 W; Founded 1889. Named for Cuthbert Burrel, an immigrant of 1846 and one of the pioneers in stock raising in Fresno County, where he lived 1860-69.

•**BUTTE CITY,** Town, Glenn County; Pop. 200; Zip Code 95920; Lat. 39-27-53 N long. 121-59-20 W; Name (French) means "an isolated peak."

•**BUTTONWILLOW,** Town, Kern County; Pop. 1,193; Zip Code 93206; Elev. 269; Lat. 35-24-02 N long. 119-28-07 W; Founded 1895.Name is a California localism for the buttonbush, whose leaves resemble those of the willow.

•**BYRON,** Town, Contra Costa County; Pop. 685; Zip Code 94514; Elev. 25; Lat. 37-52-02 N long. 121-38-13 W; W. California. It was most likely named for one of the prominent Byron Families of the East Coast.

•**CABAZON,** Town, Riverside County; Pop. 598; Zip Code 92230; Elev. 1,791. Lat. 33-55-03 N long. 116-47-11 W; Laid out and named in 1884 after a Cahuilla Indian chief who had an unusually large head (Spanish = *cabezon*).

•**CADIZ LAKE,** Town, San Bernardino County; Pop. 50; Zip Code 92319. Elev. 791; Lat. 34-31-12 N long. 115-30-43 W; Named in 1883 by the Atlantic and Pacific Railroad after one of the towns of the same name in the eastern U.S.

•**CAJON JUNCTION,** Town, San Bernardino County; Pop. 30; Zip Code 92407; Elev. 4,301. Lat. 34-18-42 N long. 117-28-26 W; Derives its name from the Spanish word meaning "box."

•**CALAVERAS CITY;** Town, San Joaquin County; Pop. included with Stockton: 115,200; Zip Code 95204.

•**CALEXICO,** City, Imperial County; Pop. 14,412; Zip Code 92231; Elev. 2; Lat. 32-40-44 N long. 115-29-53 W; Founded 1908 on land owned by George Chaffey. International border town. Name coined by combining California and Mexico.

•**CALICO,** Village and amusement center, San Bernardino County; Pop. 20; Zip Code 92398; Lat. 35-37-58 N long. 119-12-20 W; S Central California. A ghost town perched high in the colorful Calico Mountains.

•**CALIENTE,** Town, Kern County; Pop. 65; Zip Code 93518; Lat. 35-17-28 N long. 118-37-37 W; Originally called Allen's Camp because a sheepowner named Allen had his camp here. Name (Spanish) means "warm" and refers to the hot springs in the canyon.

•**CALIFORNIA CITY,** City, Kern County; Pop. 2,743; Zip Code 93505; Lat. 35-07-33 N long. 117-59-06 W; Southern California.

•**CALIMESA,** Town, Riverside County; Pop. 2,400; Zip Code 92320; Lat. 34-00-14 N long. 117-03-40 W; Name a combination of California and *mesa,* Spanish word meaning "flat-topped hill."

•**CALIPATRIA,** City, Imperial county; Pop. 2,636; Zip Code 92233; Elev. 185; Lat. 33-07-32 N long. 115-30-48 W; SE California. This town, whose name takes that of the state and the Latin root meaning "fatherland," is an agricultural center.

•**CALISTOGA,** Town, Napa County; Pop. 3,879; Zip Code 94515; Elev. 362; Lat. 38-34-44 N long. 122-34-43 W; West central California, Residential and summer resort town founded by Samuel Brannan, who created its name by inadvertently combining the names of California and Saratoga, a famous spa in New York State.

•**CALLAHAN,** Town, Siskiyou County; Pop. 100; Zip Code 96014. Elev. 3123; Lat. 41-18-35 N long. 122-48-01 W; Named for M. B. Callahan, who built a cabin at the foot of Mt. Bolivar in 1851 and opened a hotel here in 1852.

•**CALPELLA,** Town, Mendocino County; Pop. 700; Zip Code 95418; Lat. 39-14-01 N long. 123-12-10 W; Named for Kalpela, the chief of a northern Pomo village. Possible Indian meaning: "mussel bearer," from *khal* ("mussel") and *pela* ("to carry").

•**CALPINE,** Town, Sierra County; Pop. 50; Zip Code 96124; Elev. 2,000; Lat. 39-39-59 N long. 120-26-19 W; NE California. In an agricultural area. Developed by a lumber company in 1919.

•**CALWA,** Town, Fresno County; Pop. 5,191; Zip Code 93725, Lat. 36-42-38 N long. 119-45-27 W; Named for initials of California Wine Assn.

•**CAMARILLO,** City, Ventura County; Pop. 37,732; Zip Code 93010; Lat. 34-12-59 N long. 119-02-12 W; SW California, 37 miles ESE of Santa Barbara; Named for Juan Camarillo, owner of Rancho Calleguas from 1859 until his death in 1880.

•**CAMBRIA,** Town, San Luis Obispo County; Pop. 1,716; Zip Code 93428. Elev. 65; Lat. 35-33-51 N long. 121-04-47 W; Called Slabtown when settled in the 1860s. A Welsh carpenter suggested the Roman name for his homeland.

•**CAMDEN,** Town, Fresno County; Pop. 50; Zip Code 93242. Elev. 234; Lat. 36-25-52 N long. 119-47-49 W

•**CAMINO,** Town, El Dorado County; Pop. 900; Zip Code 95709; Elev. 3,200; Lat. 38-44-18 N long. 120-40-26 W; Reached by US 101 which follows El Camino Real ("the public highway"), the route connecting various missions along the coast from San Diego to San Francisco.

•**CAMPBELL,** City, Santa Clara County; Pop. 27,067; Zip Code 95008; Western California, SW of San Jose; Founded 1885 by William Campbell, son of an immigrant who established a sawmill here in 1848 and a stage station in 1852.

•**CAMPO,** Town, San Diego County; Pop. 200; Zip Code 92006. Lat. 32-36-23 N long. 116-28-05 W; Name (Spanish) means "field" or "mining camp."

•**CAMPO SECO,** Village, Calaveras County; Pop. 45; Zip Code 95226; Elev. 700; Lat. 38-13-38 N long. 120-51-08 W; E California. Name is anglicized Spanish for "dry camp."

•**CAMPTONVILLE,** Town, Yuba County; Pop. 200; Zip Code 95922; Elev. 2,900. Lat. 39-27-07 N long. 121-02-51 W; Named in 1854 for Robert Campton, the town blacksmith.

•**CANBY,** Town, Modoc County; Pop. 450; Zip Code 96015. Elev. 4312; Lat. 41-26-38 N long. 120-52-09 W; Post office was named in 1880 for Gen. E. R. S. Canby, killed by Indians in the Modoc War of 1873.

•**CANTIL,** Town, Kern County; Pop. 80; Zip Code 93519. Elev. 2025; Lat. 35-18-32 N long. 117-58-03 W; Name (Spanish) means "steep rock." Built 1908-9 as a Nevada and California Railroad station.

•**CANYON,** Town, Contra Costa County; Pop. 200; Zip Code 94516; Founded 1910. Name is Spanish word for "pipe" or "cannon," used in Mexico to describe a narrow watercourse among the mountains. In California, it has come to mean a narrow valley, ravine, or gulch.

•**CAPISTRANO BEACH,** Town Orange County; Pop. 4,149; Zip Code 92624; Lat. 33-27-49 N long. 117-40-42 W; SW California, SE of Los Angeles; Spanish mission founded 1776. Shortened form of San Juan Capistrano. Named by Viceroy Bucareli (1775) for the fighting priest, St. Juan Capistrano (1385-1456), who took an heroic part in the first defense of Vienna against the Turks.

•**CAPITOLA,** City, Santa Cruz County; Pop. 9,095; Zip Code 95010; Lat. 36-58-31 N long. 121-57-08 W; W California. F. A. Hihn developed this resort village in 1876, calling it "camp capitola."

•**CARDIFF-BY-THE-SEA,** Town, San Diego County; Pop. 6,800; Zip Code 92007. Lat. 33-01-18 N long. 117-16-49W; Laid out in 1911 by J. Frank Cullen and named after the seaport in Wales.

•**CARLSBAD,** City, San Diego County; Pop. 35,490; Zip Code 92008; Lat. 33-09-29 N long. 117-20-59 W; NW of San Diego. Renamed in 1886 for Karlsbad in Bohemia by Gerhard Schutte because the mineral waters found in the two places are similar in composition.

•**CARMEL-BY-THE-SEA,** Town, Monterey County; Pop. 4,707; Zip code 93921; Lat. 36-33-18 N long. 121-55-06 W; Derives its name from that (Rio del Carmelo) given to its bay and river by Vizcaino in January 1603 because three Carmelite friars were with the expedition.

•**CARMEL POINT,** Town, Monterey County; Pop. 800 (summer 1,600); Zip Code 93921; On Pacific Ocean south of Monterey Bay.

•**CARMEL VALLEY,** Town, Monterey County; Pop. 3,026; Zip Code 93924; Lat. 36-28-47 N long. 121-43-53 W; East of Torrey Pines State Reserve.

•**CARPINTERIA,** Town, Santa Barbara County; Pop. 10,835; Zip Code 93013; Elev. 14; Lat. 34-23-56 N long. 119-31-03 W; Named "carpenter shop" by Father Crespi, a member of the Portola expedition (1769) because he found Indians building a canoe here and caulking it with local asphalt.

•**CARSON,** City, Los Angeles County; Pop. 81,221; Zip Code 907--; Lat. 33-49-53 N long. 118-16-52 W; SE of Los Angeles.

•**CASTIAS SPRINGS,** Town, Ventura County; Pop. 1,113; Zip Code 93001. Elev. 285; Lat. 34-22-17 N long. 119-18-20 W; The Arroyo de Las Casitas ("creek of the little houses") is recorded on a plat of the lands of ex-Mission San Buenaventura in 1864.

•**CASPAR,** Town, Mendocino County; Pop. 500; Zip Code 95420; Elev. 52; Lat. 39-21-49 N long. 123-48-53 W; NW California. Siegfried Caspar settled here in the late 1850s and in 1861 a sawmill was built on Caspar Creek. Jacob Green bought the town site in 1864 and named it for the early settler.

•**CASTAIC,** Town and Lake, Los Angeles County; Pop. 900; Zip Code 91310; Elev. 1,232; Lat. 34-29-20 N long. 118-37-19 W; S California. The name is derived from an Indian rancho called Castec in 1791 records. The name may be derived from a Chumash Indian word meaning "eyes."

•**CASTELLA** Town, Shasta County; Pop. 300; Zip Code 96017; Elev. 1,947; Lat. 41-08-19 N long. 122-19-00 W; Reached by U.S. 99. Name (Spanish) means "castles," inspired by the castle-like formation of the nearby granite pinnacles known as the Crags.

•**CASTRO VALLEY,** City, Alameda County; Pop. 42,800; Zip Code 94546; Lat. 37-41-39 N long. 122-05-07 W; Name commemorates Guillermo Castro, who became grantee of parts of the San Lorenzo and San Leandro lands on February 23, 1841.

•**CASTROVILLE,** Town, Monterey County; Pop. 3,235; Zip Code 95012; Elev. 23; Lat. 36-45-57 N long. 121-45-25 W. Central California. The town was founded in 1864 by Juan B. Castro on his father's rancho, which bore the name of Bolsa Nueva y Morro Coyo, or "new pocket and lame Moor," in reference to a lame black horse, or to the black soil.

•**CATHAY'S VALLEY,** Town, Mariposa County; Pop. 400; Zip Code 95306; Elev. 1321; Lat. 37-25-57 N long. 120-05-49 W; Named for James or Nathaniel Cathay, both residents.

•**CATHEDRAL CITY,** Village, Riverside County; Pop. 3,640; Zip Code 92234; Lat. 33-46-47 N long. 116-27-52 W; S Central California. This desert town, named for the church-like canyon nearby, has grown in recent years as a resort center-suburb of Palm Springs.

•**CAYUCOS,** Town, San Luis Obispo County; Pop. 1,772 (summer 5,000); Zip Code 93430; Lat. 35-26-34 N long. 120-53-28 W; Laid out and named in 1875 for a reference to a land grant of 1837 and 1842; Morro y Cayucos. Name derived from *cayuco* ("fishing canoe"), a Spanish rendering of the Eskimo kayak.

•**CAZADERP.** Village, Sonoma County; Pop. 300; Zip Code 95421; Elev. 117; Lat. 38-32-00 N long. 123-05-03 W; NW California. Named for the Spanish word meaning "hunting place."

•**CECILVILLE,** Town, Siskiyou county; Pop. 60; Zip Code 96027; Elev. 2,350. Lat. 41-08-28 N long. 123-08-20 W; A former Indian village on a narrow mountain road. Named for John Baker Sissel, who came to Shasta Valley sometime before 1849.

•**CEDARVILLE,** Town, Modoc County; Pop. 800; Zip Code 96104; Elev. 4,640; Lat. 41-31-45 N long. 120-10-20 W; Named by J. H. Bonner in 1867 after his home town in Ohio.

•**CENTERVILLE,** Town Alameda County; Pop. included in Fremont: 122,000; Zip Code 94536; Lat. 39-47-16 N long. 121-39-15 W A farm community on the site of one of the 4215 Indian shell mounds discovered around San Francisco Bay.

•**CENTRAL VALLEY,** Town, Shasta County; Pop. 2,361; Zip Code 96019; Lat. 40-40-50 N long. 122-22-12 W; When construction was begun on Shasta Dam, main unit of Central Valley Project, the two towns developed were simply called Central Valley and Project City.

•**CERES,** City, Stanislaus County; Pop. 13,281; Zip Code 95307; Elev. 88; Lat. 37-35-42 N long. 120-57-24 W; Central California. It was named for the Greek goddess of agriculture by early settler Elma Carter in 1874.

•**CERRO GORDO,** Village, Inyo County, No pop.; E. California; 15 mi. SE of Lone Pine; Elev. 9,127. The name is Spanish for "large hill."

•**CHEROKEE,** Village, Butte County; Pop. 25; Zip code 95965; Lat. 39-38-47 N long. 121-32-14 W; N Central California. This town was named for the Indian tribe, originally driven from their native lands in Georgia westward to the Great Plains, and eventually to California.

•**CHESTER,** Town, Plumas County; Pop. 1,531; Zip Code 96020; Elev. 4,531; Lat. 40-18-23 N long. 121-13-51 W; A lumber town named after Chester, Vermont, by Oscar Martin in the 1900s.

•**CHICAGO PARK,** Town, Nevada County; Pop. 200; Zip Code 95712. Name given by Paul Ulrich and a group of German settlers from Chicago, Illinois, in the 1880s.

•**CHICO,** City, Butte County; Pop. 26,601, Zip Code 95926; Lat. 39-43-43 N long. 121-50-11 W; northern California. Name (Spanish) means "little." Founded on ranchland once part of a land grant called Arroyo Chico ("little stream") bought in 1849 by John Bidwell.

•CHINO, City San Bernardino County; Pop. 40,165; Zip Code 91710; Elev. 720; Lat. 34-00-44 N long. 117-41-17 W; S Central California. Founded in 1887 when Richard Gird subdivided half of his 47,000 acre Rancho del Chino. Chino is a Spanish word used to describe persons of mixed blood.

•CHOLAME, Town, San Luis Obispo County; Pop. 15; Zip Code 93431; Elev. 1,157. Lat. 35-43-26 N long. 120-17-44 W; Name of a Salinan Indian rancheria mentioned in 1803 as Cholan and applied to the Cholam land grant in 1844.

•CHOWCHILLA, Town, Madera County; Pop. 5,122; Zip Code 93610. Elev. 240. Lat. 37-07-23 N long. 120-15-33 W; Name derived in the 1850s from Chauciles Indians.

•CHUALAR, Town, Monterey County; Pop. 600; Zip Code 93925. Lat. 36-34-14 N long. 121-31-03 W; Name (Spanish) means "pig weed."

•CHUBBUCK, Town, San Bernardino County; Pop. rural. Lat. 34-21-54 N long. 115-17-07 W; The station was named Kilbeck for an employee of the railroad. In 1937, the name was changed to Chubbuck for the owner and developer of local lime deposits.

•CHULA VISTA, Town, San San Diego County; Pop. 83,927; Zip Code 92012; Lat. 32-38-24 N long. 117-05-00 W; SW California, south of San Diego. Name derived in 1880 from chula, Mexican for "pretty" or "graceful," and vista, Spanish word meaning "view."

•CIMA, Town, San Bernardino County; Pop. 40; Zip Code 92323; Lat. 35-14-16 N long. 115-29-54 W; Founded 1907; Situated at the top of a pass between Kelso and Ivanpah in the Providence Mts. in the eastern Mojave. Name (Spanish) means "summit."

•CITRUS HEIGHTS, City, Sacramento County; Pop. 23,600; Zip Code 95610; Lat. 38-42-26 N long. 121-16-48 W.

•CLAREMONT, City, Los Angeles County; Pop. 30,950; Zip Code 91711; Lat. 32-47-50 N long. 117-11-30 W; SW California. Named in 1887 for Claremont, New Hampshire, home of a director of the development company.

•CLARKSBURG, Town, Yolo County; Pop. 400; Zip Code 95612. Elev. 14; Lat. 38-25-14 N long. 121-31-34 W; Named for Judge Clark, who settled here in 1849.

•CLAYTON, Town, Contra Costa County; Pop. 4,325; Zip Code 94511; Elev. 394; Lat. 37-56-28 N long. 121-56-05 W; Founded 1861. Named for Joel Clayton, who settled here in 1857.

•CLEAR CREEK, Town, Lassen County; Pop. 150; Zip Code 96137; Lat. 40-17-53 N long. 121-02-51 W; One of about 40 towns of same name in the mountainous sections of the state.

•CLEARLAKE HIGHLANDS, Town, Lake County; Pop. 2836; Zip Code 95422; Lat. 38-57-22 N long. 122-38-48 N.

•CLEARLAKE OAKS, Town, Lake County; Pop. 950; Zip Code 95423; Lat. 39-01-27 N long. 122-40-26 W; Near Clear Lake and Clear Lake Highlands.

•CLIFTON, Town, Los Angeles County; Pop. 1,750; Zip Code 90277; Lat. 33-49-39 N long. 118-22-44 W; 1 mile south of Redondo Beach.

•CLOVERDALE, Town, Sonoma County; Pop. 3,989; Zip Code 95425; Elev. 892; Lat. 40-28-25 N long. 122-28-29 W; Post office established August 15, 1857. Formerly known as Markleville, for R. B. Markle, former owner of the land.

•CLOVIS, City, Fresno County; Pop. 33,021; Zip Code 93612; Lat. 36-49-31 N long. 119-42-07 W; Named for Clovis Cole, through

whose land the Southern Pacific Railroad built a branch line in 1889.

•CLYDE, Town, Contra Costa County; Pop. 430; Zip Code 94520. Lat. 38-01-32 N long. 114-55-40 W; Name originated during WWI when the Clyde Shipyard was located here.

•COACHELLA, City, Riverside County; Pop. 9,129; Zip Code 92236; Elev. 71; Lat. 33-40-49 N long. 116-10-23 W; SE California, 80 miles NE of San Diego in the Coachella Valley. Name derived from Cahuilla (Indian) or perhaps as a corruption of the Spanish word conchilla ("shell") because of fossils found in the area.

•COALINGA, Town, Fresno County; Pop. 6,593; Zip Code 93210; Elev. 670; Lat. 36-08-23 N long. 120-21-33 W; Originally known as Coaling Station when the Southern Pacific Railroad built a branch line to tap its lignite deposits in 1888. Later given the more euphonious variant by a railway official.

•COARSEGOLD, Town, Madera County; Pop. 550; Zip Code 93614; Elev. 2206; Lat. 37-15-44 N long. 119-42-00 W; Name given in 1849 by Texas miners, probably because they found coarse gold nuggets here.

•COLEVILLE, Town, Mono County; Pop. 60 (summer 600); Zip Code 96107; Elev. 5,750; Lat. 38-33-49 N long. 119-30-22 W; Farm trading hamlet named for Cornelius Cole, Congressman 1863-67, U. S. Senator 1867-73.

•COLFAX, City, Placer County; Pop. 981; Zip Code 95713; Elev. 2,422; Lat. 39-06-03 N long. 120-57-08 W; NE California. Schuyler Colfax, Speaker of the U.S. House, visited California in 1865. The Central Pacific Railroad subsequently named the station here for him.

•COLLEGE HEIGHTS, Town, San Bernardino County; Pop. 150; Zip Code 91786; Lat. 34-06-24 N long. 117-41-18 W; Named in 1909 or 1910 by L. W. Campbell because of its proximity to Pomona College.

•COLMA, Town, San Mateo County; Pop. 395; Zip Code 94014; Lat. 37-40-37 N long. 122-27-28 W; Named Colma 1872. Various explanations are given for the name change: possibly a transfer name from Germany or Switzerland; the word for "moon" from the San Francisco dialect of Costanoan.

•COLOMA, Town, El Dorado County; Pop. 280; Zip Code 95613; Lat. 38-48-00 N long. 120-53-21 W; Near Placerville, 36 miles NE of Sacramento. Named after a Maidu Indian village.

•COLTON, City, San Bernardino County; Pop. 27,419; Zip Code 92324; Elev. 1,000; Lat. 34-04-26 N long. 117-18-46 W; S Central California.

•COLUMBIA, Village and State Park, Tuolumne County; Pop. 600; Zip Code 95310; Elev. 2,143; Lat. 38-02-11 N long. 120-24-01 W; E California.

•COLUSA. Town, Colusa County Seat; Pop. 4,075; Zip Code 95932; Elev. 61; Lat. 39-12-52 N long. 122-00-30 W; Name of a rancheria, Coru, mentioned in 1821 by Ordaz. First called Salmon Bend, then Colusi.

•COMMERCE, City, Los Angeles County; Pop. 10,509; Lat. 34-00-02 N long. 118-09-32 W; NW of Downey in SW California.

•COMPTON, City, Los Angeles County; Pop. 81,286; Zip Code 90220; Elev. 66; Lat. 33-53-45 N long. 118-13-09 W; The site of the Rancho San Pedro of the Dominguez family. Named in 1869 for Griffith D. Compton, founder of a Methodist temperance colony here.

•CONCORD, City, Contra Costa County; Pop. 103,255; Zip Code 94518; Elev. 65; Lat. 37-58-41 N long. 122-01-48 W; W California.

This farm shipping point is situated on the side of Rancho del Diablo (Devil's Ranch), granted to Salvio Pacheco in 1834.

•**CONEJO,** Town, Fresno County; Pop. 40; Zip Code 93662; Elev. 263; Lat. 36-31-06 N long. 119-43-05 W; Reached by US 101 and Cal. Highway 118. Name (Spanish) means "rabbit".

•**COPCO LAKE,** Town, Siskiyou County; Pop. 85; Zip Code 96044; Lat. 41-29-57 N long. 120-31-57 W; Name coined from California-Oregon Power Co. and applied to the post office in 1915 when the company's hydroelectric project was under construction.

•**CORCORAN,** Town, Kings County; Pop. 6,454; Zip Code 93212; Elev. 207; Lat. 36-05-53 N long. 119-33-34 W; SW central California. The town was named for a civil engineer of the Santa Fe Railroad.

•**CORNING,** City, Tehame County; Pop. 4,745; Zip Code 96021; Elev. 272; Lat. 39-55-40 N long. 122-10-41 W; N Central California. This town, surrounded by olive groves, was named for John Corning, an official of the Central Pacific Railroad.

•**CORONA,** City, Riverside County; Pop. 37,791; Zip Code 91720; Elev. 678; Lat. 33-52-31 N long. 117-33-56 W; S Central California. Formerly called South Riverside, Corona is a Latin word for "wreath" or "circle," and the Spanish use it to mean "crown."

•**CORONADO,** City, San Diego County; Pop. 16,859; Zip Code 92118; Lat. 32-41-09 N long. 117-10-56 W; Surveyed and named in 1602 after four Roman martyrs.

•**CORRALITOS,** Town, Santa Cruz County; Pop. 600; Zip Code 95076; Lat. 36-59-19 N long. 121-48-19 W; Name (Spanish), meaning "little corrals," was mentioned in 1807 and given to the land grant April 18, 1823.

•**CORTE MADERA,** City, Marin County: Pop. 8,074; Zip Code 94925; Elev. 27; Lat. 37-55-32 N long. 122-31-35 W; Name (Spanish for "place where lumber or timber is cut") applied to the Corte de Madera del Presidio land grant (1834) owned by John Reed because the sawmill he built here was the most important source of lumber for the Bay district.

•**COSTA MESA,** City, Orange County; Pop. 82,291; Zip Code 92626; Elev. 101; Lat. 33-38-28 N long. 117-55-04 W; When a subdivision was opened here in 1915, the present name, an Americanized combination of two Spanish words, *costa* ("coast") and *mesa* ("tableland"), was chosen as a result of a contest.

•**COTATI,** Town, Sonoma County; Pop. 3,475; Zip Code 94928; Lat. 38-19-37 N long. 122-42-22 W; Name of an Indian rancheria, Kotati, was applied in the present form to a land grant in 1844.

•**COTTONWOOD,** Town, Shasta County; Pop. 1,288; Zip Code 96022; Elev. 420; Lat. 40-23-09 N long. 122-16-47 W; Named for the widespread occurrence of the black and common (or Fremont) cottonwood tree, a deciduous variant of the poplar.

•**COULTERVILLE,** Town, Mariposa County; Pop. 180; Zip Code 95311; Elev. 1,683; Lat. 37-42-38 N long. 120-11-49 W; Reached by Cal. Highway 49. Named for George W. Coulter from Pennsylvania, who opened a store here in 1849 and later became one of the first commissioners of the Yosemite Valley grant.

•**COURTLAND,** Town, Sacramento County; Pop. 400; Zip Code 95615; Elev. 1398; Lat. 39-47-35 N long. 123-14-49 W; Named for Courtland Sims, son of the owner of the land on which a steamboat landing was built in the 1860s.

•**COVELO,** Town, Mendocino County; Pop. 950; Zip Code 95428; Elev. 546; Lat. 34-05-24 N long. 117-53-22 W; A quiet cowtown named in 1870 by Charles H. Eberle, probably not after a fortress in Switzerland, as the story goes, but after Covolo, the old Venetian fort in Tirol.

•**COVINA,** City, Los Angeles County; Pop. 33,751; Zip Code 91722; Lat. 38-14-26 N long. 119-59-28 W; SW California. Name (Spanish), meaning "place of vines," was applied to a subdivision of La Puente Rancho in the late 1880s.

•**COWAN HEIGHTS,** Town, Orange County; Pop. 2,100; Zip Code 92705; Elev. 113; Lat. 33-46-40 N long. 117-46-23 W.

•**COWELL,** Town, Contra Costa County; Pop. included with Concord: 91,800; Area Code 415; Zip Code 94520; Lat. 37-57-10 N long. 121-59-18 W; Named for Henry Cowell, of the Cowell Lime and Cement Co., who built the cement works here in 1908.

•**CRAFTON,** Town, San Bernardino County; Pop. included with Mentone: 2,400; Zip Code 92359; Elev. 1752; Lat. 34-03-47 N long. 117-07-15 W; Laid out and named in 1885 by the Crafton Land and Water Co. for Myron H. Crafts, the developer of a resort called Crafton Retreat (1887).

•**CRESCENT CITY,** Town, Del Norte County Seat; Pop. 3,099; Zip Code 95531; Elev. 44; Lat. 41-45-22 N long. 124-12-02 W; NW corner of California, on the coast. Named for the crescent-shaped bay.

•**CRESTLINE,** Town, San Bernardino County; Pop. 3,600 (summer 10,000); Zip code 92325; Elev. 5,000; Lat. 34-14-31 N long. 117-17-05 W; Name suggested by a Dr. Thompson when the post office was established in 1920.

•**CROCKETT** Town, Contra Costa County; Pop. 2,700; Zip Code 94525; Elev. 118; Lat. 38-03-09 N long. 122-12-43 W; On Carquinez Strait. Named in 1867 for Judge J. B. Crockett, of the California Supreme Court, who received 1,800 acres of land on which the town was laid out in 1881 as fee for settling a land case.

•**CROWLEY LAKE,** Town, Mono County; Pop. 100; Zip Code 93514; Lat. 39-24-33 N long. 123-25-28 W; Site of a 183,000-acre-feet reservoir created in 1935 by the construction of Long Valley Dam to supplement the water supply in the northern part of Owens Valley.

•**CUCAMONGA,** City, San Bernardino County; Pop. 19,484; Zip Code 91730; Elev. 1,110; Lat. 34-06-23 N long. 117-35-32 W; North of Guasti. Name, a Shoshonean Indian word meaning "sandy place," derives from the exploring expedition of Moraga in 1819.

•**CUDAHY,** City, Los Angeles County; Pop. 17,984; Zip Code 90201; Elev. 121; Lat. 33-57-38 N long. 118-11-04 W; 20 mi. SE of Los Angeles in SW California.

•**CULVER CITY,** City, Los Angeles County; Pop. 38,139; Zip Code 90230; Elev. 94; Lat. 34-01-16 N long. 118-23-44 W; SW of Los Angeles. Residential and industrial city named for Harry H. Culver, who came from Nebraska in 1914 and acquired and subdivided part of the Ballona land grant.

•**CUPERTINO,** City, Santa Clara County; Pop. 25,770; Zip Code 95014; Elev. 236; Lat. 37-19-23 N long. 122-01-52 W; Western California, Arroyo de San Jose Cupertino, named in honor of a seventeenth-century Italian saint, was mentioned by Anza and Font in 1776. The arroyo is now Stevens Creek, but the post office preserves the old name.

•**CUTLER,** Town, Tulare County; Pop. 2,503; Zip Code 93615; Lat. 36-31-24 N long. 119-17-09 W; Named by the Santa Fe Railroad in 1903 for John Cutler, a pioneer of the district and for many years a county judge.

•**CYPRESS,** City, Orange County; Pop. 40,391; Zip Code 90630; Elev. 36; Lat. 33-49-01 N long. 118-02-11 W; SW California, Named for preponderance of cypress, evergreen coniferous tree related to the pine.

•**DAGGETT,** Town, San Bernardino County; Pop. 650; Zip Code 92327; Elev. 2,003; Lat. 34-51-48 N long. 116-53-14 W; Named in 1882 by the Southern Pacific Railroad for John Daggett, lieutenant governor of California (1883-87).

•**DAILY CITY,** City, San Mateo County; Pop. 78,519; Zip Code 94014; Elev. 400; It was named for John Daly, a dairyman in the district since the 1850s.

•**DANA POINT,** Town, Orange County; Pop. 4,745; Zip Code 92629; Lat. 33-28-01 N long. 117-41-50 W; Headland between Laguna Beach and San Clemente named in 1884 by the Coast Survey for the exploit of Richard Henry Dana ("Two Years Before the Mast"), who swung over a cliff on halyards and dislodged some cowhides.

•**DANVILLE,** City, Contra Costa County; Pop. 7,000; Zip Code 94526; Elev. 368; Lat. 37-49-18 N long. 121-59-56 W; Named in 1867 for the hometown (Danville, Kentucky) of a relative of wheat farmer Daniel Inman, owner of the land, who settled here in 1858.

•**DARDANELLE,** Town, Tuolumne County; Pop. 500; Zip Code 95364; Elev. 5,775; Lat. 38-20-28 N long. 119-49-58 W; Lies at the base of the striking serrated mountain range. Mountains are so named because of the resemblance between the volcanic rock formations and the mountain castles which guarded the entrance to the Sea of Marmora in Turkey.

•**DAVENPORT,** Town, Santa Cruz County; Pop 300; Zip Code 95017; Lat. 37-00-42 N long. 122-11-27 W; Named around 1868 after the nearby whaling station, Davenport Landing, established by Capt. John P. Davenport in the 1850s.

•**DAVIS,** City, Yolo County; Pop. 36.640; Zip Code 95616; Elev. 50; Lat. 38-32-42 N long. 121-44-22 W; Named for Jerome C. Davis, a large landholder and rancher of the 1850s.

•**DAVIS CREEK,** Inyo County. Lat. 41-44-00 N long. 120-22-15 W; Named for David Davis, who came to the region around 1866, married Lizzie Wiles, an Indian woman, and raised cattle and potatoes for the mining camps.

•**DE LUZ,** Town, San Diego County; Pop. (with Camp Pendleton); Zip Code 92055; Elev. 146; Lat. 33-26-13 N long. 117-19-25 W; S California. It was named by Spanish-speaking neighbors of an English rancher named Luce.

•**DELANO,** City, Kern County; Pop. 16,491; Zip Code 93215; Elev. 316; Lat. 35-46-08 N long. 119-14-46 W; E Central California. Columbus Delano was U.S. Secretary of the Interior when the town was founded. It is named after him.

•**DELHI,** Town, Merced County; Pop. 2,063; Zip Code 95315; Lat. 37-25-56 N long. 120-46-39 W; Shown on Mining Bureau map of 1891. Modern town laid out in 1911. Named after historic city in India, famous for its gardens.

•**DEL LOMA,** Village, Trinity County; Pop. Rural; Zip Code 96010; Lat. 40-46-43 N long. 123-19-52 W; N California. It was supposedly named for a band of French Canadian trappers who left Oregon at the news of Reading's strike on the Trinity. "Del Loma" means "of the hill."

•**DEL MAR,** Town, San Diego County; Pop. 5,017; Zip Code 92014; Lat. 32-57-34 N long. 117-14-42 W; Founded in 1884 by Col. S. Taylor of Oklahoma. Name suggested by Bayard Taylor's poem, "The Fight of Paso del Mar."

•**DEL REY,** Town, Fresno County; Pop 900; Zip Code 93616; Lat. 36-39-33 N long. 119-35-34 W; Named in 1898, when the railroad reached the place, after the Rio del Rey ("river of the king") Ranch, site of the new station.

•**DEL REY OAKS,** City, Monterey County; Pop. 1,557; Zip Code 93940; Lat. 36-35-36 N long. 121-50-02 W; West, coastal California.

•**DEL ROSA,** Town, San Bernardino County; Pop. included with San Bernardino: 107,000; Zip Code 92404; Lat. 34-08-56 N long. 117-14-33 W; Post office and town bore the name Delrosa (possibly a family name) until 1905, when Zoeth S. Eldredge, a Spanish-language enthusiast, petitioned the Post Office Dept. for the change. The result is an incorrect combination of a feminine noun with a masculine article.

•**DENAIR,** Town, Stanislaus County; Pop. 1,128; Zip Code 95316; Lat. 37-31-35 N long. 120-47-45 W; Named by John Denair, a former superintendent of the Santa Fe division point at Needles, when he purchased the townsite in 1906.

•**DESERT CENTER,** Town, Riverside County; Pop. 100; Zip Code 92239; Elev. 906; Lat. 33-42-45 N long. 115-24-05 W.

•**DESERT HOT SPRINGS,** Town, Riverside County; Pop. 5,941 (winter 4,000); Zip Code 92240; Lat. 33-57-40 N long. 116-30-03 W.

•**DESCANSO** Town, San Diego County; Pop. 500; Zip Code 92016; Elev. 3396; Lat. 32-51-10 N long. 116-36-54 W; The Spanish word for "rest" or "respose" was applied to the post office February 16, 1877.

•**DEVORE,** Town, San Bernardino County; Pop. 670; Zip Code 92407; Elev. 2022; Lat. 34-12-59 N long. 117-24-02 W; Station named for John Devore, a landowner of the district, when the California Southern completed the railroad through Cajon Pass in 1885.

•**DI GIORGIO,** Town, Kern County; Pop. 250; Zip Code 93217; Lat. 35-15-10 N long. 118-51-02 W; Station named by the Southern Pacific Railroad in 1923 for an Italian immigrant, Joseph Di Giorgio, who was president of the Earl Fruit Co., the state's largest fruit-packing firm.

•**DIABLO,** Town, Contra Costa County; Pop. 500; Zip Code 94528; Lat. 37-50-06 N long. 121-57-25 W; Name (Spanish) means "Satan." Post Office established 1917.

•**DIAMOND BAR,** City, Los Angeles County; Pop. 10,576; Zip Code 91766; Lat. 34-01-43 N long. 117-48-34 W; Once Rancho Nogales in the Los Angeles Basin, now a planned city.

•**DIAMOND SPRINGS,** Town, Eldorado County; Pop. 900; Zip Code 95619; Elev. 1,778; Lat. 38-41-41 N long. 120-48-50 W; Discovery of pretty specimens of quartz crystals here in 1849 brought about the first large-scale rumor of the discovery of diamond fields.

•**DILLON BEACH,** Town, Marin County; Pop. 100 (summer 800); Zip Code 94929; Lat. 38-15-03 N Long. 122-57-51 W; Post office was established and named in 1923 for the Dillon family. George Dillon, a native of Ireland, had settled here before 1867.

•**DINUBA,** City, Tulare County; Pop. 9,907; Zip Code 93618; Elev. 328; Lat. 36-32-36 N long. 119-23-10 W; Probably a fanciful name applied by the construction engineer when the branch line was built in 1887-88.

•**DIXIELAND,** Village, Imperial County; Pop. Rural; Lat. 32-47-27 N long. 115-46-10 W; S California. Dixieland was established and named in 1909 in anticipation of a new high line canal west of the present town, which would have allowed cotton to be grown in the area.

•**DIXON,** Town, Solano County; Pop. 7,541; Zip Code 95620; Lat. 38-19-26 N long. 121-49-16 W; Central California, Elev. 67; Named in 1870 for Thomas Dickson, who gave 10 acres for the townsite. The present spelling was adopted by the Post Office Dept. through an error.

•**DOBBINS,** Town, Yuba County; Pop. 600; Zip Code 95935; Elev. 720; Lat. 39-22-18 N long. 121-12-18 W; Named for William M. and Mark D. Dobbins, brothers who settled at the creek in 1849.

•**DOMINGUEZ,** Town, Los Angeles County; Pop. included with Carson: 78,000; Zip Code 90810; Lat. 33-50-05 N long. 118-13-04 W; Place preserves the family name of the grantees of the vast San Pedro or Dominguez Rancho, granted first to Juan Jose Dominguez before November 20, 1784.

•**DORRIS,** Town, Siskiyou County; Pop. 836; Zip Code 96023; Elev. 4,240; Lat. 41-58-03 N long. 121-55-01 W; Named by the Southern Pacific Railroad in 1907 for Presley A. Dorris and his brother, Carlos J. Dorris, stock raisers in Little Shasta in the 1860s.

•**DOS PALOS,** Town, Merced County; Pop. 3,123; Zip Code 93620; Elev. 116; Lat. 33-55-29 N long. 120-37-32 W; The name (Spanish), meaning "two trees," was applied to the station when the Southern Pacific Railroad reached the place in 1889.

•**DOS RIOS,** Town, Mendocino County; Pop. 30; Zip Code 95429; Elev. 926; Lat. 39-43-01 N long. 123-21-08 W; Name (Spanish) means "two rivers" and refers to its position at the junction of two branches of the Eel River.

•**DOUGLAS CITY,** Town, Trinity County; Pop. 25; Zip Code 96024; Elev. 1,651; Lat. 40-39-08 N long. 122-56-37 W; Settled in early 1860s and named in memory of Stephen A. Douglas, the "Little Giant," who died in 1861.

•**DOWNEY,** City, Los Angeles County; Pop. 82,602; Zip Code 902--; Elev. 119; Lat. 33-56-24 N long. 118-07-54 W; SE of Los Angeles in SW California.

•**DOWNIEVILLE,** Town, Sierra County Seat; Pop. 500; Zip Code 95936; Elev. 2,899; Lat. 39-33-34 N long. 120-49-33 W; Named for "Mayor" William Downie, a Scot who mined gold at the forks of the Yuba River in 1849.

•**DOYLE,** Town, Lassen County; Pop. 300; Zip Code 96109; Elev. 4,267; Lat. 40-01-41 N long. 120-06-10 W; Named for John W. and Stephen A. Doyle, settlers in Long Valley since the 1860s.

•**DRYTOWN** Village, Amador County; Pop. 150; Zip Code 95699; Elev. 700; Lat. 38-26-28 N long. 120-51-12 W; E Central California. Gold and quartz mining was important along the Dry Creek here and in the surrounding gulches.

•**DUARTE,** City, Los Angeles County; Pop. 16,766; Zip Code 91010; Elev. 510; Lat. 34-08-22 N long. 117-58-35 W; Named for the original ranchero of the region, Andres Duarte, who settled on his Rancho Azusasin 1841.

•**DUBLIN,** City, Alameda County; Pop. 13,641; Zip Code 94566; Lat. 37-42-08 N long. 121-56-05 W; Post office, established here in the 1860s, called Dougherty's Station for James W. Dougherty of Tennessee. Dougherty called the southern part of the town Dublin because so many Irish lived there.

•**DUCOR,** Town, Tulare County; Pop. 200; Zip Code 93218; Elev. 545; Lat. 35-53-30 N long. 119-02-47 W; In 1899 the Southern Pacific Railroad station was given the abbreviated version of the former name, Dutch Corners, where the homesteads of four Germans joined.

•**DULZURA,** Town San Diego County; Pop. 20; Zip Code 92017; Elev. 1045; Lat. 32-38-39 N long. 116-46-50 W; Name (Spanish), meaning "sweetness," was applied because the honey industry was introduced into this region in 1869 by John S. Harbison.

•**DUME POINT,** Cape, Los Angeles County. Name given to the cape by Vancouver (1793) in honor of his host, Padre Francisco Dumetz of Mission San Buenaventura, but was misspelled in Vancouver's map and has never been corrected.

•**DUNCANS MILL,** Town, Sonoma County; Pop. 70; Zip Code 95430; Elev. 29; Lat. 38-27-14 N long. 123-03-14 W; Reached by US 101. Named for S. M. and A. Duncan, who built a mill here in 1860.

•**DUNLAP ACRES,** Town, San Bernardino County; Pop. 3,300; Zip Code 92399; Elev. 2,119; Lat. 34-01-52 N long. 117-06-24 W.

•**DUNSMUIR,** City, Siskiyou County; Pop. 2,253; Elev. 2,308; Zip Code 96025; Elev. 2289; Lat. 41-13-11 N long. 122-16-26 W; N California.

•**DURHAM,** Town, Butte County; Pop. 950; Reached by US 99. Named in 1880 for W. W. Dunham, a millowner and assemblyman from Butte County.

•**DUTCH FLAT,** Village, Placer County; Pop. 150; Zip Code 95714; Elev. 3,144; Lat. 39-12-22 N long. 119-23-23 W; N California. This small settlement played a large part in the history of the northern mines. Settled in 1851 by German miners, Joseph Doranback and his companions--"Dutchmen" to the other miners--it was soon crowded with thousands who flocked in to find gold.

•**EAGLELAKE,** Town Lassen County; Pop. 150; Zip Code 96130; Site NW of Susanville on the eastern edge of Lassen National Forest.

•**EAGLEVILLE,** Town, Modoc County; Pop. 70; Zip Code 96110; Lat. 41-18-59 N long. 120-06-53 W.

•**EARLIMART,** Town, Tulare County; Pop. 4,573; Zip Code 93919; Elev. 283; Lat. 35-53-03 N long. 119-16-17 W; Central California. Once a railroad stop known as Alila, Earlimart was renamed by promoters of agriculture in 1909.

•**EARP,** Town, San Bernardino county; Pop. 200; Zip Code 92242; Elev. 388; Lat. 34-09-53 N long. 114-18-01 W; Named in 1929 for Wyatt Earp, Arizona pioneer, peace officer, and miner who came to California in the 1860s. Station had been called Drennen since 1910.

•**EAST HIGHLANDS,** Town, San Bernardino County; Pop. 400; Zip Code 92329; Lat. 34-06-35 N long. 117-10-11 W.

•**EAST LOS ANGELES,** City, Los Angeles County; Pop. 101,000; Zip Code 90022; Elev. 280; Lat. 34-01-26 N long. 118-10-16 W; Unincorporated urban community east of the Los Angeles River, but still mainly within the city of L.A.

•**EAST PALO ALTO,** City San Mateo County; Pop. 18,099; Zip Code 94303; Elev. 21; Lat. 37-28-08 N long. 122-08-24 N; Unincorporated community has San Francisco Peninsula's largest Black population.

•**EASTON,** Town, Fresno County; Pop. 1,065; Zip Code 93706; Elev. 273; Lat. 36-39-01 N long. 119-47-23 W; First named Covell for A. T. Covell, resident manager of the Washington Irrigated Colony, founded in the 1870s. When post office was established in 1882, place was renamed for O. W. Easton, land agent of the colony.

•**EDGEMONT,** Town, Riverside County; Pop. 4,400; Zip Code 92508; Elev. 1537; Lat. 33-55-13 N long. 117-16-40 W.

•**EDGEWOOD,** Town, Siskiyou County; Pop. 150; Zip Code 96094; Elev. 2,953; Lat. 41-27-30 N long. 122-25-50 W; reached by US 99. Site chosen in 1851 as a stopping place by the first travelers on the California-Oregon Trail. first known as Butteville. In 1875, Joseph Cavanaugh changed the name to Edgewood, which he considered more appropriate for its situation at the edge of the forest bordering the Shasta Valley.

•**EDISON,** Town, Kern County; Pop. 350; Zip Code 93220; Reached by US 466; Elev. 564; Lat. 35-20-51 N long. 118-52-15 W; Named by Southern California Edison Co. when it built a sub-station here in 1905.

•**EDWARDS AIR FORCE BASE,** Military installation, Kern County; Pop. 10,331; Zip Code 93523; Lat. 34-55-34 N long. 117-56-03 W; Name of old Muroc Field changed to Edwards Air Force Base January 27, 1950, in memory of Capt. Glenn W. Edwards, who was fatally injured in the crash of an experimental YB-49 "Flying Wing."

•**EL CAJON,** City, San Diego County; Pop. 73,892; Zip Code 92020; Elev. 435; Lat. 32-47-41 N long. 116-57-42 W; SW California. This suburban extension of San Diego occupies part of the land of the old El Cajon Rancho, opened for settlement in 1869.

•**EL CENTRO,** City, Imperial County Seat; Pop. 23,996; Zip Code 92243; Lat. 32-47-31 N long. 115-33-44 W; Reached by US 80; Elev. 52 feet below sea level--the second largest town below sea level in the U.S.; Seat of Imperial County; SE corner of California, in Imperial Valley, 86 miles east of San Diego near the Mexican border; Settled 1906. Name (Spanish) refers to its position near the center of Imperial Valley. Previously called Cabarker for C. A. Barker, a friend of W. F. Holt, owner of the land on which town was developed.

•**EL CERRITO,** City, Contra Costa County; Pop. 22,731; Zip Code 94530; Elev. 66; Lat. 37-54-57 N long. 122-18-38 W; W Central California. The town was named for the Spanish "little hill."

•**EL DIOS,** Town, San Diego County; Pop. 450; Zip Code 92025; Lat. 33-04-22 N long. 117-07-06 W; Name is Spanish for "belonging to God."

•**EL GRANADA,** Town, San Mateo county; Pop. 1,473; Zip Code 94018; Lat. 37-30-10 N long. 122-28-06 W; Post Office named 1910. Some question regarding origin of name: if named after the Moorish castle in Spain, it does not need the article; if name chosen was the Spanish word for "pomegranate," the feminine article, *la,* should have been used.

•**EL MIRAGE LAKE,** Town, San Bernardino County; Pop. 200; Zip Code 92301; Lat. 36-10-40 N long. 119-01-03 W; Settled south of the lake of same name, which is west of Victorville. Named for the optical illusion frequently occurring in the desert, plus the Spanish indefinite article for good measure,

•**EL MODENA,** Village, Orange County; Pop. (with Orange); Zip Code 92667; Elev. 276; Lat. 33-47-16 N long. 117-48-31 W; SW California. Originally, the town was named Modena, for the old Italian city, but the Spanish El was added in 1890.

•**EL MONTE,** City, Contra Costa County; Pop 79,494; Zip Code 94521; Elev. 283; Lat. 34-04-07 N long. 118-01-36 W; SW California, 12 miles east of Los Angeles, SE of Pasadena. Settled in 1852 by squatters who believed there was a flaw in the title to the land. Name (Spanish), meaning "grove" or "thicket," refers to the dense growth of willows.

•**EL PORTAL,** Town, Mariposa County; Pop. 600; Zip Code 95318; Lat. 37-40-29 N long. 121-16-52 W; In 1907 the Yosemite Valley railroad gave the Spanish name to its terminus at the "gateway" to the park.

•**EL SEGUNDO,** City, Los Angeles County; Pop. 13,752; Zip Code 90245; Lat. 33-55-09 N long. 118-24-56 W; SW California, 14 miles SW of Los Angeles near Santa Monica Bay, just south of LA International Airport; Reached by US 101; Incorporated 1917. In 1911 named "the second" (Spanish) for Standard Oil's second refinery in the state, located here.

•**EL TIO,** Town, Ventura County; Pop. 6,173; Zip Code 93030 ; Elev. 80; SW California. Simon Cohn opened a general store here in 1875 and named it "New Jerusalem." The Post Office changed the name to the Spanish words for the river in 1895.

•**EL TORO,** Town, Orange County; Pop. 8,654; Zip Code 92630; Lat. 33-37-33 N long. 117-41-34 W; Reached by US 101; Elev. 144. Name (Spanish) means "bull."

•**EL VERANO,** Town, Sonoma County; Pop. 2,334; Zip code 95433; Elev. 107; Lat. 38-17-52 N long. 122-29-26 W; NW California. George Maxwell, early resident, named this town for the Spanish words meaning "the summer."

•**ELK CREEK,** Town, Glenn County; Pop. 300; Zip Code 95939; Lat. 39-36-19 N long. 122-32-17 W.

•**ELK GROVE,** Town, Sacramento County; Pop. 10,959; Zip Code 95624; Elev. 51; Lat. 38-24-32 N long. 121-22-14 W; N Central California. James Hall opened an inn here in 1850 and named it for the large animal found in the area.

•**ELIZABETH LAKE,** Town, Los Angeles County; Pop. 50; Zip Code 93550. Site of lake of same name, which was mentioned in 1853 in the Pacific Railroad "Reports" as Lake Elizabeth.

•**ELK,** Town, Mendocino County; Pop. 200; Zip Code 95432; Elev. 41; Lat. 36-45-01 N long. 119-29-31 W; Reached by Cal. Highway 1. Once a center for loading lumber brought inland by railroad. Also known as Greenwood.

•**ELSINORE,** (alt. LAKE ESLINORE), City, Riverside County; Pop. 5,982; Zip Code 92330; S California. This resort and retirement town lies on the northeastern shore of Lake Elsinore. Elsinore was named for the character in Shakespeare's Hamlet.

•**EMMERYVILLE,** City, Alameda County; Pop. 3,763; Zip Code 946 --; Lat. 37-49-53 N long. 122-17-03 W; W California on San Francisco Bay.

•**EMIGRANT GAP,** Town, Placer County; Zip Code 95715; Elev. 5,250; Lat. 39-17-49 N long. 120-40-18 W; Reached by US 40. Mountain notch on the western edge of Tahoe National Forest on the route from Donner Lake to Sacramento.

•**EMPIRE,** Town, Stanislaus County; Pop. 2,016; Zip Code 95319; Lat. 37-38-18 N long. 120-54-04 W; Founded as Empire City (probably named after New York, the "Empire City") in 1850, but shown on Gibbes' map (1852) as Empire. Although almost destroyed and deserted in 1852 and 1855, the place has survived with the name.

•**ENCINITAS,** Town, San Diego County; Pop. 6,300; Zip Code 92024; Elev. 85; Lat. 33-02-13 N long. 117-17-28 W; Reached by US 101; Settled in the 1880s. In 1769 the Portola expedition gave the name Canada de los Encinos ("valley of the little oaks") to the valley where the town is located.

•**ESCALON,** Town, San Joaquin County; Pop. 3,127; Zip Code 95320; Lat. 37-47-51 N long. 120-59-44 W; James W. Jones came upon the Spanish word meaning "step of a stair" in a book at the Stockton Public Library. Pleased with the sound of the word, he reserved it for the town which he laid out on his land with the coming of the railroad in 1895-96.

•**ESCONDIDO,** City, San Diego County; Pop. 62,480; Zip Code 92025; Elev. 684; Lat. 33-04-09 N long. 117-05-08 W; Reached by US 395; SW corner of California, 28 miles north of San Diego. In 1885 a syndicate of Los Angeles and San Diego businessmen bought 13,000 acres of the Rancho El Rincon del Diablo, laid out the town at the crossroads called Apex, and named it Escondido (Spanish for "hidden") after the creek.

•ESPARTO, Town, Yolo County; Pop. 1,088; Zip Code 95627; Elev. 191; Lat. 38-41-32 N long. 122-00-58 W; Name (Spanish) means "feather grass." The Vaca Valley Railroad (now Southern Pacific) reached the place in 1875 and called the station Esperanza ("hope"). When the post office was established in the 1880s, the name had to be changed because there was another Esperanza, in Tulare County.

•ESSEX, Town, San Bernardino County; Pop. 50; Zip Code 92332; Elev. 1,700; Lat. 34-44-01 N long. 115-14-39 W; Reached by US 66; In the NE Mojave Desert. Station had been called Edson by the Atlantic and Pacific Railroad in 1883. In 1906 the Santa Fe changed the name for operating convenience. According to local authorities, Essex was the name of a pioneer miner.

•ESTERO BAY, San Luis Obispo County. Large lagoon on the central coastline of the county whose interior portion is Morrow Bay. Name (Spanish), meaning "inlet" or "estuary," dates to the expedition of Costanso (1769).

•ETNA, Town Siskiyou County; Pop. 754; Zip Code 96027; Elev. 2929; Lat. 41-27-25 N long. 122-53-37 W; Reached by US 99. Original name, Rough and Ready--after a flour mill located here in the 1850s--was changed by statute in 1874 to that of its competitor, Etna.

•EUCALYPTUS HILLS, City, San Diego County; Pop. 15,300 (included with Lakeside); Zip Code 92040; Lat. 32-52-47 N long. 116-56-45 W.

•EUREKA, City, Humboldt County Seat; Pop. 24,500; Zip Code 95501; Elev. 44; Lat. 40-48-08 N long. 124-09-45 W; Reached by US 101; NW California, on Humboldt Bay 83 miles south of Oregon border; Port of entry. Name is Greek for "I have found it," the words attributed to James Ryan who surveyed the first town lots.

•EXETER, Town, Tulare County; Pop. 5,619; Zip Code 93221; Elev. 386; Lat. 36-17-46 N long. 119-08-28 W; South central California, 45 miles SE of Fresno. Founded in 1880 by D. W. Parkhurst for the Pacific Improvement Co. and named after his home city in England.

•FAIR OAKS, City, Sacramento County; Pop. 15,500; Zip Code 95628; Lat. 37-57-19 N long. 121-15-27 W; Name applied to the post office around 1895.

•FAIRFAX, City, Marin County; Pop. 7,391; Zip Code 94930; Elev. 120; Lat. 37-59-14 N long. 122-35-16 W; Western California, 15 miles NW of San Francisco. Named for Charles, Lord Fairfax, who went to California in the Gold Rush and settled in an elaborate home with his bride on site of present town, once part of Rancho Canada de Herrera.

•FAIRFIELD, City, Solano County Seat; Pop. 58,099; Zip Code 94533; Elev. 12; Lat. 38-14-58 N long. 122-02-20 W; Reached by US 40; Central California, 40 miles SW of Sacramento in the Vaca Valley; In 1859, Robert H. Waterman (1808-84), a famous clipper ship captain, lived here in a house he modeled after the prow of a ship. He gave land for a new city, which he named after Fairfield, Connecticut, his former home.

•FALLBROOK, City, San Diego County; Pop. 9,000; Zip Code 92028; Elev. 685; Lat. 33-22-35 N long. 117-15-01 W; Reached by US 395; In the San Diego Back Country, an area ideal for citrus growing. Named after Fallbrook, Pennsylvania, the former home of Charles V. Reche, who settled in the district in 1859 and became its first postmaster in 1878.

•FALL RIVER MILLS, Town, Shasta County; Pop. 600; Zip Code 96028; Elev. 3291; Lat. 41-00-17 N long. 121-16-14 W; Reached by US 299; At the junction of the Pit and Fall rivers. Named by Fremont in 1846 because of its falls and cascades.

•FAMOSA, (alt. FAMOSO), Village, Kern County; Pop. Rural; Elev. 422; Lat. 35-35-53 N long. 119-12-26 W; E Central California. Known as Poso until residents requested the Spanish name for "famous" around the turn of the century.

•FARMERSVILLE, Town, Tulare County; Pop. 5,544; Zip Code 93223; Elev. 360; Lat. 36-17-52 N long. 119-12-21 W; Post office established in 1870s.

•FARMINGTON, Town, San Joaquin County; Pop. 250; Zip Code 95230; Lat. 37-55-48 N long. 120-59-57 W; Settlement in the center of a rich farming area named in 1859 by W. B. Stamper.

•FEATHER FALLS, Town, Butte County; Pop. 560; Zip Code 95940; Lat. 39-35-36 N long. 121-15-19 W; Falls, 640 feet high, are in middle fork of Feather River, north central California. Town and falls named for Feather River, which Sutter said he named Rio de las Plumas ("river of feathers") in the 1840s because of the many feathers worn by the Indians of the area and the feathers scattered over the landscape.

•FELTON, Santa Cruz County; Pop. 4,564; Zip Code 95018; Elev. 286; Lat. 37-03-05 N long. 122-04-20 W; W California. George Treat, owner of the land in 1878, named the place for state assemblyman Charles Felton.

•FENNER, Town, San Bernardino County. Lat. 34-48-57 N long. 115-10-42 W; Sixth town in a line of alphabetically named Atlantic and Pacific Railroad stations between Amboy and the Arizona border.

•FERNBROOK, Town, San Diego County; Pop. 80; Zip Code 92065; Elev. 1,218; Lat. 32-58-05 N long 116-54-39 W Near Ramona.

•FERNDALE, Town, Humboldt County; Pop. 1,367; Zip Code 95536; Elev. 50; Lat. 40-34-35 N long. 124-15-46 W; An Eel Valley dairy village founded about 1870 and named because of the luxuriant growth of ferns in the valley.

•FILLMORE, City, Ventura County; Pop. 9,602; Zip Code 93015; Elev. 460; Reached by US 101; SW California, 43 miles WNW of Los Angeles at the mouth of Sespe Canyon. Named by the Southern Pacific Railroad in 1887 for J. A. Filmore, general superintendent of the company's Pacific system.

•FIREBAUGH, City, Fresno County; Pop. 3,740; Zip Code 93622; Elev. 151; Lat. 36-51-32 N long. 120-27-18 W South central California, 35 miles WNW of Fresno. In 1854, A. D. Fierbaugh established a trading post and a ferry across the San Joaquin river. Name misspelled as Firebaugh's Ferry as early as 1856; this version was used when the place became a station on the Gilroy-Sageland stage line in the 1860s.

•FLINN SPRINGS, Town, San Diego County; Pop. rural; Zip Code 92021; Elev. 1,300; Reached by US 99; Near El Cajon. Possibly named for W. E. Flinn, a native of North Carolina, who was a farmer at Ranchita in 1866.

•FLINTRIDGE, City, Los Angeles County; Pop. 21,038; Zip Codes 91011 and 91003; Lat. 34-11-11 N long 118-11-12 W; Incorporated with La Canada as La Canada-Flintridge. Named for Frank P. Flint, U. S. Senator from California, 1905-1911, when part of Rancho la Canada was subdivided in 1920.

•FLORIN, City, Sacramento County; Pop. 9,646; Zip Code 95828; Elev. 34; Lat. 38-29-46 N long. 121-24-28 W; Name given to the station by E. B. Crocker of the Central Pacific Railroad when the line was constructed in 1863-69. Possible derivations of the name: florin, a silver coin long used in Europe and still minted in England as a two-shilling piece; or the large number of flowers in the region.

•FLORISTON, Town, Nevada County; Pop. 100; Zip Code 96111; Lat. 39-23-41 N long 120-01-13 W; The post office was established here in 1891 and was named for flowers.

•FOLSOM, City, Sacramento County; Pop. 11,003; Zip Code 95630; Elev. 218; Lat. 38-40-41-N long. 121-10-30 W; N Central California. Black miners in 1849 dug for gold at this spot on the American River, and their camp was called Negro Bar. The camp, laid out on the Mexican rancho, Rio de los Americanos, on the Coloma Road, was granted to William A. Leidesdorff, U. S. vice-consul, October 8, 1844. After the death of Leidesdorff in 1848, Captain Joseph L. Folsom, assistant quartermaster of Stevenson's New York Volunteers, traveled to the West Indies to purchase the 35,000-acre estate on the American River from Leidesdorff's heirs.

•FONTANA, City, San Bernardino County; Pop. 37,109; Zip Code 92335; Elev. 1,232; Lat. 34-05-32 N long. 117-26-03 W; Reached by US 66; Southern California, west of San Bernardino. Once called Rosena, named in 1913 for the Fontana Development Co. Name may be Spanish word meaning "fountain," or name of a family.

•FORBESTOWN, Town, Butte County; Pop. 250; Zip code 95941; Elev. 2,800; Lat. 39-31-02 N long. 121-15-58 W; Reached by US 395. Named for Ben F. Forbes, a native of Wisconsin, who established a general store here in 1850.

•FORD CITY, Town, Kern County; Pop. 3,503; Zip Code 93268; Elev. 1,000; Lat. 35-09-16 N long. 119-27-19 W; Reached by US 399; Just east of Standard Oil's Camp 11C. In boom days of the field, town was an unnamed tent city. Named for its plethora of Model-T Fords.

•FOREST CITY, Village, Sierra County; Pop. 10; Zip Code 95910; NE California. Here in 1852, a company of sailors found gold. They called the thriving town Brownsville but the name was not good enough, and it was renamed for the agressive journalist, Mrs. Forest Mooney.

•FORESTHILL, Town Placer county; Pop. 900; Zip Code 95631; Elev. 325; Lat. 39-01-13 N long. 120-49-01 W; Settled in early 1850s and named for dense pine forest surrounding the place.

•FORESTVILLE, Town, Sonoma County; Pop. 950 (summer 1,500); Zip Code 95436; Lat. 38-28-25 N long. 122-53-21 W; At edge of timber country. Originally named Forrestville for its founder, A. J. Forrester. Present spelling generally used by end of 1880s.

•FORKS OF SALMON, Town, Siskiyou County; Pop. 50; Zip Code 96031; When post office was established in 1859, town was so named because of its location at the confluence of the north and south forks of the Salmon River.

•FORT BIDWELL, Town, Modoc County; Pop. 200; Zip Code 96112; Elev. 4,740; Lat. 41-51-38 N long. 120-09-01 W; Reached by US 395; In the Warren Mts. Named in 1865 for John Bidwell, a Congressman and general of the California militia who discoverd gold near the Feather River in 1848.

•FORT BRAGG, Town, Mendocino County; Pop. 5,019; Zip Code 95437; Elev. 60; Lat. 39-26-45 N long. 123 48-15 W; Western California Pacific coast, 96 miles south of Eureka; Reached by US 1; Founded 1885. Named after the military post established in 1857 by Lt. H. G. Gibson which was named in honor of Lt. Col. Braxton Bragg, Mexican War veteran and later a Confederate general.

•FORT DICK, Town, Del Norte County; Pop. 300; Zip Code 95538; Elev. 47; Lat. 41-52-05 N long. 124-08-52 W; Reached by US 101. Fort Dick Landing first mentioned in Civil War records. Fort was a log house built by citizens for defense against the Indians and probably named for a settler.

•FORT IRWIN, Town, San Bernardino County; Pop. 2,991; Zip Code 92311; Site of inactive Army Corps of Engineers base used by California National Guard, located near Barstow.

•FORT JONES, Town, Siskiyou County; Pop. 544; Zip Code 96032; Elev. 2,747; Lat. 41-36-28 N long. 122-50-21 W; N California. This town was known as Whellock, Scottsburg and Ottiewa before it was named for the U.S. Army outpost in 1858.

•FORT MACCARTHUR, Military installation, Zip Code 90731; Reached by US 101. U. S. Army defense post in San Diego, founded in 1914 and named for Gen. Arthur MacArthur.

•FORT ORD, City, Monterey County; Pop. (included with Seaside) 35,000; Area Code 408; Zip Code 93941; NE of Monterey. Founded as a camp in honor of Gen. E. O. C. Ord, became a fort in 1940.

•FORT YUMA INDIAN RESERVATION, Imperial County; Pop. 565; Zip Code 85344; Located in the Bard Valley, which is California's portion of the Yuma Valley on the upper delta of the Colorado River; Established 1884. Name (Indian) means "sons of the river" and is applied only to those Yuma Indians born on the banks of the Colorado River. Named after Fort Yuma, established in the middle of the Bard Valley in 1850.

•FORTUNA, City, Humboldt County; Pop. 7,591; Zip Code 95540; Lat. 40-35-54 N long. 124-09-22 W; NW California, 14 miles south of Eureka; Elev. 61; Reached by US 101. Settled in late 1870s. First called Springville, because of numerous nearby springs, and then Slide, for the landslide NW of town. Named Fortune (1870s) by a minister named Gardner, owner of the land, because he believed it an ideal place to live. Later changed the spelling, for sake of euphony.

•FOSTER CITY, City, San Mateo County; Pop. 23,287; Zip Code 94404; Lat. 37-33-31 N long. 122-16-12 W; San Francisco Bay Area's first preplanned "new town," established 1965 and named for T. Jack Foster, who deeded a large parcel of real estate to the county.

•FOUNTAIN VALLEY, City, Orange County; Pop. 55,080; Zip Code 92708; Elev. 28; Lat. 33-42-33 N long. 117-57-10 W; SW California, 28 miles SE of Los Angeles. Named after Artesian wells that once were located under the city.

•FOWLER, Town, Fresno County; Pop. 2,496; Zip Code 93625; Lat. 36-37-50 N long. 119-40-39 W; South central California, 10 miles SE of Fresno; Elev. 290; Reached by US 99. Named for Thomas Fowler, State Senator from Fresno, 1969-72 and 1877-78.

•FRAZIER PARK, Town, Kern County; Pop. 1,167; Zip Code 93225; Lat. 34-49-22 N long. 118-56-38 W; Named in 1926 by Harry McBain after Frazier Mt., itself named for the Frazier Mine on the south slope. A man named Frazier found a rock rich in gold ore while tracking down a wounded deer, and began his mining operation at that spot.

•FREEDOM, City, Santa Cruz County; Pop. 5,563; Zip Code 95019; Elev. 115; Lat. 36-56-07 N long. 121-45-19 W; Elev. 115; Reached by Cal. Highway 1. Known until prohibition as Whiskey Hill because of the unquenchable thirst of residents which was served by 11 saloons in 1852. In 1892 or 1893, an enterprising purveyor of alcoholic beverages had a huge sign put across the front of his place of business, sporting two American flags and the legend, "The Flag of Freedom," a name that stuck.

•**FREMONT,** City, Alameda County; Pop. 131,945; Zip Code 94536; Lat. 37-32-54 N long. 121-59-15 W; Western California, SSE of Oakland, Towns of Centerville, Niles, Irvington, Mission San Jose, and Warm Springs united to form this city (incorporated January 24, 1956). Named by the Incorporation Committee for John C. Fremont.

•**FRENCH CAMP,** Town, San Joaquin County; Pop. 500; Zip Code 95231; Elev. 15; Lat. 37-53-03 N long. 121-11-61 W; Reached by US 50. Southernmost regular camp site of Hudson Bay Co. trappers after La Framboise established headquarters here in 1832. Spanish Californians called it Campo de los Franceses, a name preserved in the land grant of January 13, 1844.

•**FRENCH CORRAL,** Village, Nevada County; Pop. Rural; Zip Code 95977; Elev. 522; Lat. 39-18-22 N long. 121-09-37 W; NE California. A French imigrant built a corral for his mules here in 1849; it is the oldest town in the San Juan Ridge. Several old buildings still stand.

•**FRENCH GULCH,** Village, Shasta County; Pop. 200; Zip Code 96033; Elev. 1355; Lat. 40-42-03-N long. 122-38-14 W; N California. A depot on the Shasta-Yreka Turnpike, is where the first mining is said to have been done here by a party of Frenchmen in 1849 or 1850.

•**FRESNO,** City, Fresno County Seat; Pop. 218,202; Zip Code 937+; Elev. 296; Lat. 36-44-52 N long. 119-46-17 W; 155 miles SE of San Francisco in San Joaquin Valley; Founded 1872, made county seat 1874, incorporated 1885. Spanish name for "ash" applied by the Central Pacific Railroad when it reached site of present city because the Oregon ash is native here.

•**FRIANT,** Town, Fresno County; Pop. 350; Zip Code 93626; Elev. 340; Lat. 36-59-16 N long. 119-42-39 W; Situated at the landing of the old Converse (later Jones) Ferry, established in 1852 by Charles Converse. Named Polasky (1891) when place became terminus of the Southern Pacific branch from Fresno, for Marcus Polasky, an agent of the railroad. In the early 1920s, town renamed for Thomas Friant of the White-Friant Lumber Co.

•**FULLERTON,** City, Orange County; Pop. 102,034; Zip code 92634; Elev. 161; Lat. 33-52-13 N long. 117-55-23 W; Reached by US 101; SW California, 17 miles NE of Long Beach. Founded in 1887 by the Wilshire brothers, George Amerigue and Edward, and named for George H. Fullerton, the Santa Fe "right of way" representative who arranged to route the railroad through the site.

•**FURNACE CREEK,** Settlement, Inyo County; Part of Death Valley National Monument; Pop. 30; Zip Code 92328; E California. This place, named for the intense heat of the region, was named by Dr. Darwin French in 1860.

•**GALT,** Town, Sacramento County; Pop. 5,514; Zip Code 95632; Elev. 47; Lat. 38-15-17 N long. 121-17-75 W; Reached by US 99. Named in 1869 by John McFarland, an early settler, after his former home in Ontario, Canada, which had been named for John Galt, the Scottish novelist.

•**GARBERVILLE,** Town, Humboldt County; Pop. 900; Zip Code 95440; Elev. 533; Lat. 40-06-01 N long. 123-47-38 W; Reached by US 101; In the redwood heartland (Eel River country); Post office established 1880. Named for Jacob C. Garber, a native of Virginia, who lived at Rohnerville in 1871 and soon after settled at the place that bears his name.

•**GARDENA,** City, Los Angeles County; Pop. 45,165; Zip Code 90247; Elev. 45; Lat. 33-53-18 N long. 118-18-29 W; Reached by US 6; Southern suburb of Los Angeles. Named in 1880 with the Spanish word for "garden."

•**GARDEN GROVE,** City, Orange County; Pop. 123,351; Zip Code 92640; Lat. 33-46-26 N long. 117-56-26 W; SW California, south of Anaheim in NW part of county. Once a farming settlement among citrus groves until the period after WWII when it boomed fantastically and developed mile after mile of tract housing.

•**GAREY,** Town, Santa Barbara County; Pop. rural; Zip Code 93454 ; Elev. 379; Lat. 34-53-19 N long. 120-18-50 W; Established in 1889 and named for Thomas A. Garey, who came to California in 1852 and settled first in Pomona Valley.

•**GARLOCK,** Town, Kern County; Pop. rural; Zip Code 93554; Lat. 35-24-09 N long. 117-47-21 W; Near Antelope Valley in the Mojave Desert. Old railroad station west of Randsburg named for Eugene Garlock, who set up the first stamp mill of the Randsburg Mining District in 1895 at the place called Cow Wells.

•**GASQUET,** Town, Del Norte county; Pop. 340; Zip Code 95543; Lat. 41-50-44 N long. 123-58-06 W; Named for the Gasquet family. Horace Gasquet, a native of France, came to Del Norte County before 1860 and had a ranch in Mountain township.

•**GAVIOTA,** Town, Santa Barbara County; Pop. rural; Zip Code 93017; Elev. 98; Lat. 34-28-18 N long. 120-12-50 W; Reached by US 101. Soldiers of the Portola expedition on August 24, 1769, named the place where they camped La Gaviota because they killed a seagull here.

•**GAZELLE,** Town, Siskiyou County; Pop. 125; Zip Code 96034; Elev. 2,953; Lat. 41-31-15 N long. 122-31-09 W; Reached by US 99. Post office named in 1874 for the small African antelope.

•**GEORGETOWN,** Town, El Dorado County; Pop. 900; Zip Code 95634; Lat. 38-54-25 N long. 120-50-15 W; NE California. At the northern end of the true Mother Lode, a group of Oregonians discovered gold in 1849. Growlersburg, as it was called in 1850 when George Phipps led a company of sailors here, was renamed in his honor two years later.

•**GERBER,** Town, Tehama County; Pop. 775; Zip Code 96035; Elev. 241; Lat. 40-03-23 N long. 122-08-57 W; Named in 1916 by the Southern Pacific Railroad for H. E. Gerber, of Sacramento, who sold the land to the railroad.

•**GEYSERVILLE,** Town, Sonoma County; Pop. 750; Zip Code 95441; Elev. 206; Lat. 38-42-28 N long. 122-54-05 W; Reached by US 101. Founded in 1851 by Elisha Ely, named to advertise nearby geysers.

•**GILROY,** City, Santa Clara County; Pop. 21,641; Zip Code 95020; Elev. 200; Lat. 37-00-21 N long. 121-13-40 W; Western California, 30 miles SE of San Jose in the lower Santa Clara Valley; Elev. 190; Junction with Cal. Highway 152; Reached by US 101. Named for John Gilroy, a Scots sailor, who arrived in California in 1814, settled in the Santa Clara Valley, and in 1833 came into possession of the land where city is located.

•**GLEN AVON HEIGHTS,** City, Riverside County; Pop. 5,759; Zip Code 92509; Lat. 34-00-42 N long. 117-29-02 W; Name, a combination of the word "glen" and another Celtic term meaning "river," chosen by L. V.W. Brown in 1909.

•**GLENDALE,** City, Los Angeles County; Pop. 139,060; Zip Code 912+; Elev. 573; Lat. 40-54-00-N long. 124-00-57 W; Reached by US 99; At the Coastal Plain entrance of the San Fernando Valley; SW California, 6 miles north of Los Angeles. Founded in 1880 on the Rancho San Rafael, the first Spanish land grant in California . First known as Riverdale, but name changed later because there was a Riverdale post office in Fresno County.

•**GLENDORA,** City, Los Angeles County; Pop. 38,654; Zip Code 91740; Elev. 776; Lat. 34-08-10 N long. 117-51-52 W; Reached by US 66; SW California, 22 miles ENE of Los Angeles. Name created in 1887 by a Chicago manufacturer, George Whitcomb, from the word "glen" and his wife's name, Ledora.

•GLENN, Town, Glenn County, Pop. 40; Zip Code 95943; Lat. 39-31-19 N long. 122-00-46 W; Named after Dr. Hugh J. Glenn, pioneer of 1849 and for many years the leading wheat grower in California, when the Southern Pacific Railroad branch from Colusa reached here in 1917.

•GLENVIEW, Town, San Diego County; Pop. 1,500; Zip Code 92021; Lat. 38-54-00 N long. 122-45-29 W; In El Cajon Valley. Apparently named for its scenic location.

•GOFFS, Town, San Bernardino County; Pop. rural; Zip Code 92332; Elev. 2,587; Lat. 34-55-09 N long. 115-03-43 W; Seventh in a line of alphabetically named Atlantic and Pacific Railroad stations between Amboy and the Arizona border.

•GOLD RUN, Town, Nevada County; Pop. 200; Zip Code 95717; Elev. 3,222; Lat. 39-10-51 N long. 120-51-17 W; NE California. Named for the creek nearby, this mining town was active in the 1860s and 70s.

•GOLETA, City, Santa Barbara County; Pop. 24,200; Zip Code 93017; Elev. 50; Lat. 34-26-09 N long. 119-49-36 W; Reached by US 101; Suburb of Santa Barbara, just to the west on the ocean. Developed on the land grant La Goleta, dated June 10, 1846, and named in 1875. Name (Spanish) means "schooner." It is not certain whether named because of the wreck of an American schooner in the estuary or because Capt. William G. Dana of Nipomo built a schooner here in 1829.

•GONZALES, Town, Monterey County; Pop. 2,891; Zip Code 93926; Elev. 127; Lat. 36-30-24 N long. 121-26-36 W; Reached by US 101. Railroad station named in 1873 either for Teodoro Gonzales because it was built on his extensive grant, Rincon de la Punta del Monte de la Soledad (1836), or for his sons, Alfredo and Mariano, who were prominently associated with the Monterey and Salinas Railroad.

•GORMAN, Town, Los Angeles County; Pop. 100; Zip Code 93243; Elev. 3,811; Lat. 34-47-46 N long. 118-51-06 W; S California. This town was named for Private Gorman of Fort Tejon who, on his discharge from service in 1864, was one of three soldiers to take up homesteads in this region.

•GOSHEN, Town, Tulare county; Pop. 1,324; Zip Code 93227; Lat. 36-21-04 N long. 19-25-09 W; Name, meaning "best of the land," was given to Jacob by Pharaoh in Egypt; it was applied to the town when the Southern Pacific Railroad reached here in 1872.

•GRAND TERRACE, City, San Bernardino County; Pop. 8,498; Zip Code 92324; Lat. 34-02-02 N long. 117-18-46 W; Southeastern California.

•GRANITEVILLE, Village, Nevada County; Pop. 5; Zip Code 95959; Elev. 4,900; Lat. 39-26-27 N long. 120-44-19 W; NE California. Named for the rock formations found in the mountains here.

•GRASS VALLEY, Town, Nevada County; Pop. 6,697; Zip Code 95945; Elev. 2,411; Lat. 39-13-09 N long. 121-03-36 W; Reached by Cal. Highway 49; Eastern California, 45 miles west of Lake Tahoe. Post office established in 1850 and called Centerville, then changed. Named after the valley, itself named Grass Valley in 1849 by immigrants who found plenty of forage for their half-starved cattle.

•GRATON, Town, Sonoma County; Pop. 900; Zip Code 95444; Lat. 38-26-11 N long. 122-52-07 W; Founded 1904 by James H. Gray and S. H. Brush of Santa Rosa and named for the former by abbreviating Graytown to Graton.

•GREENBRAE, Town, Marin County; Pop. 3,500; Zip Code 94904; Elev. 28; Lat. 37-56-55 N long. 122-31-25 W; Reached by US 101; Situated along Corte Madera Creek.

•GREENFIELD, Town, Monterey County; Pop. 4,181; Zip Code 93927; Elev. 287; Lat. 36-19-15 N long. 121-14-34 W; Reached by US 101; Western California, 32 miles SE of Salinas. Laid out on the Arroyo Seco Rancho by the California Home Extension Assn. (1902-5) and called Clarke City for John S. Clarke, one of its principal officers. Post Office Dept. declined to use the name and selected Greenfield in 1905, suggested by residents because of the surrounding alfalfa fields, which are green the year round.

•GREENVILLE, Town, Plumas County; Pop. 1,073; Zip Code 95947; Elev. 3,500; Lat. 40-08-23 N long. 120-57-00 W; Reached by Cal. Highway 89. A man named Green built a house here in the mid-1850s. Because his wife served meals to the miners, the house became known as Green's Hotel, and the settlement as Greenville.

•GREENWOOD, Village, El Dorado County; Pop. 75; Zip Code 95635; Lat. 38-53-48 N long. 120-54-42 ; Here the Greenwoods, a father and two sons, found gold and built their cabin in the spring of 1848.

•GRENADA, Town, Siskiyou County; Pop. 300; Zip Code 96038; Elev. 2,561; Lat. 41-38-50 N long. 122-31-08 W; Reached by US 99; Region originally known as Starve-Out because of its poor land. Town renamed after formation of irrigation district, possibly after Grenada County, Mississippi, known for its fertile soil.

•GRIDLEY, Town, Butte County; Pop. 3,982; Zip Code 95948; Elev. 91; Lat. 39-21-50 N long. 121-41-33 W; Northern California, 55 miles north of Sacramento; Named in 1870 by the Southern Pacific Railroad for George W. Gridley, owner of the land on which town is built.

•GRIMES, Town, Colusa County; Pop. 500; Zip Code 95950; Elev. 47; Lat. 39-04-28 N long. 121-53-34 W; Named around 1865 for Cleaton Grimes, who settled here in 1851.

•GROVELAND, Town, Tuolumne county; Pop. 300; Zip Code 95321; Elev. 2,846; Lat. 37-50-18 N long. 120-13-54 W; Reached by US 99. Name chosen in 1879 by residents to replace an earlier one, First Garrote, which had been applied in 1850 when miners hanged a thief here.

•GROVER CITY, City, San Luis Obispo County; Pop. 8,827; Zip Code 93433; Lat. 35-07-18 N long. 120-37-13 W; S of San Luis Obispo in Southwest, coastal California.

•GUADALUPE, Town, Santa Barbara County; Pop. 3,629; Zip Code 93434; Elev. 85; Lat. 34-58-18 N long. 120-34-15 W; Reached by Cal. Highway 1; SW California, 50 miles NW of Santa Barbara. Named for the Virgin of Guadalupe, patron saint of Mexico.

•GUALALA, Town, Mendocino County; Pop. 600; Zip Code 95445; Elev. 67; Lat. 38-45-57 N long. 123-31-37 W; Reached by Cal. Highway 1; At the mouth of Gualala river. There are several possible explanations for the name: anthropologists insist it is the Spanish rendering of the Pomo Indian word walali, "where the waters meet"; there was an Indian settlement at the site of modern Gualala called ghawalali, "water coming down place, rivermouth"; county histories and local tradition say name is the Spanish version of Walhalla, in Teutonic mythology the abode of heroes fallen in battle.

•GUASTI, Town, San Bernardino County; Pop. 100; Zip Code 91743; Lat. 32-50-56 N long. 116-33-23 W; SE California. Known as South Cucamonga when the railroad came through in the 1890s, this town's name was changed when the Italian immigrant Secundo Guasti moved there in 1902 and set out the first grape vines in this deserty area.

•GUERNEVILLE, Town Sonoma County; Pop. 900 (summer 5,000); Zip Code 95446; Elev. 56; Lat. 38-30-07 N long. 122-59-42 W; Reached by US 101; Settled 1860. Post Office established in

1870s and named for its founder, George E. Guerne, a native of Ohio, who built a saw-and-planing mill here in 1864.

•GUINDA, Town, Yolo County; Pop. 200; Zip Code 95637; Elev. 355; Lat. 38-49-45 N long. 122-11-34 W; Name (Spanish), meaning "cherry," was given to station by the Southern Pacific Railroad in early 1890s because an old cherry tree was then standing at the SE corner of the townsite.

•GUSTINE, Town, Merced County; Pop. 3,142; Zip Code 95322; Lat. 37-15-28 N long. 120-59-52 W; Laid out in the 1890s by Henry Miller, of Miller and Lux--California cattle barons--and named in memory of his daughter, Augustine, who had been thrown from a horse and killed.

•HALF DOME, Peak, NE California; In Yosemite National Park; Elev. 8,927; Named in 1851 by the Mariposa Battalion because of its flat, half-circular shape. Indians called it *Tissaack*.

•HALF MOON BAY, City, San Mateo County; Pop. 7,282; Zip Code 94019; Elev. 69; Lat. 37-27-49 N long. 122-25-39 W; Western California, on Half Moon Bay inlet; Elev. 10; Reached by Cal. Highway 1. Located on Rancho El Corral de Tierra ("the enclosure of earth"). Once called Spanish Town, post office was established in 1867 as Halfmoon Bay; spelling changed in 1960.

•HAMBURG, Town, Siskiyou County; Pop. 100; Zip Code 96045; Elev. 1,592; Lat. 41-46-59 N long. 123-03-33 W; Reached by US 99. Established as a mining camp in 1851 and named by Sigmund Simon after the seaport in Germany. Was also known as Hamburg Bar.

•HAMILTON CITY, Town, Glenn County; Pop. 800; Zip Code 95951; Lat. 30-44-34 N long. 122-00-45 W; Settled by a sugar company in 1906 and named for J. G. Hamilton, promoter of the town.

•HANFORD, City, Kings County Seat; Pop. 20,958; Zip Code 93230; Elev. 246; Lat. 36-19-39 N long. 119-38-41 W; Reached by US 99; SW central California, 30 miles south of Fresno, on western edge of Kaweah Delta; Settled 1871. Named in 1877 by the Central Pacific Railroad for its treasurer, James Hanford.

•HAPPY CAMP, Town, Siskiyou County; Pop. 800; Zip Code 96039; Elev. 1,087; Lat. 41-47-36 N long. 123-22-42 W; Reached by US 99; site of Ranger Station, the District Forest Supervisor's Headquarters. A number of stories are told about naming the old mining town in 1851. H. C. Chester, who interviewed Jack Titus (1882 or 1883), states that Titus named the camp because his partner, James Camp, upon arriving here, exclaimed: "This is the happiest day of my life!"

•HARBISON CANYON, Town, San Diego County; Pop. 2,300; Zip Code 92020; Lat. 32-49-13 N long. 116-49-45 W; Near El Cajon, west from Alpine. Named for an apiarist, John S. Harbison, who came to San Diego County in 1869 with a choice collection of 110 bee hives.

•HARMONY, Town, San Luis Obispo County; Pop. 5; Zip Code 93435; Elev. 175; Lat. 35-30-31 N long. 121-01-18 W; Reached by Cal. Highway 1; In Harmony Valley. Name applied to valley by settlers in 1860s. When post office was established in 1915, name was adopted at suggestion of Marius G. Salmina, of the Harmony Valley Creamery Assn.

•HAVASU LAKE, Town, San Bernardino County; Pop. 200 (winter 400); Zip Code 92363; Lat. 34-28-56 N long. 114-24-47 W; Site Havasu Lake in the eastern Mojave Desert between the Chemehuevi and Whipple Mts., SE of Needles. Artificial lake 45 miles long created in 1938 in the Colorado River by Parker Dam. Extends to and beyond the Arizona border. Given Mojave Indian word for "blue" in 1939 by John C. Page.

•HAVILAH, Village, Kern County; Pop. 20; Zip Code 93518; Lat. 35-31-04 N long. 118-31-04 W; Central California. It was named by Asbury Harpending in 1864 for the Biblical country.

•HAWAIIAN GARDENS, City, Los Angeles County; Pop. 10,548; Zip Code 90716; Elev. 29; Lat. 33-49-53 N long. 118-04-19 W; SW California, 19 miles SE of Los Angeles.

•HAWTHORNE, City, Los Angeles County; Pop. 56,447; Zip Code 90250; Elev. 69; Lat. 33-54-59 N long. 118-21-06 W; SW California, 12 miles SW of Los Angeles, Incorporated 1922. Residential suburb of LA named around 1906 for American novelist Nathaniel Hawthorne by Mrs. Laurine H. Woolwine, daughter of H. D. Harding, one of town's founders.

•HAYFIELD LAKE, Reservoir, Riverside County. Site of reservoir and pump lift of the Metropolitan Water District was humorously named because of thin growth of grass here used by cattlemen for pasturage.

•HAYWARD, City, Alameda County; Pop. 94,167; Zip Code 94541; Elev. 111; Lat. 37-40-08 N long. 122-04-47 W; Reached by US 50; Western California, 5 miles east of San Francisco Bay at the base of Walpert Ridge (western segment of Diablo-Mt. Hamilton Range). Named for William Hayward, a local hotel owner.

•HEALDSBURG, City, Sonoma County; Pop. 7,217; Zip Code 95448; Elev. 106; Lat. 38-36-38 N long. 122-52-05 W; Reached by US 101; Western California, 14 miles NNW of Santa Rosa; Founded 1852. Name applied to post office in 1857 to honor Harmon G. Heald, who had had a trading post here since 1846 and had built the town's first store in 1852.

•HEBER, Town, Imperial County; Pop. 950; Zip Code 92249; Elev. 9 feet below sea level; Lat. 32-43-51 N long. 115-31-44 W; Reached by US 99. Founded 1901 by Imperial Land Co. a few miles to the east and named Paringa. Renamed in 1903 for A. H. Heber, president of California Development Co.

•HELENDALE, Town, San Bernardino County; Pop. 50; Zip Code 92342; Elev. 2,430; Lat. 34-44-38 N long. 117-19-25 W; Reached by US 66. Santa Fe station originally called Point of Rocks was renamed Helen December 15, 1897, for daughter of A. G. Wells, vice president of the company. Name changed to Helendale September 22, 1918.

•HELM, Town, Fresno County; Pop. 150; Zip Code 93627; Elev. 185; Lat. 36-31-54 N long. 120-05-50 W; Named for William Helm, a Canadian who came to California in 1859, settled at Big Dry Creek in 1865, and for many years raised more sheep than anyone else in central California.

•HEMET, City, Riverside County; Pop. 23,211; Zip Code 92343; Elev. 1,596; Lat. 33-44-51 N long. 116-58-16 W; Reached by US 395; SE California, 31 miles SE of San Bernardino in the San Jacinto Basin west of San Bernardino National Forest; Founded 1898. Name may be the Luiseno Shoshonean Indian name for the valley nearby, or possibly derives from the Swedish word *hemmet,* meaning "in the home."

•HENSHAW LAKE, Reservoir, San Diego County. Created in 1924 and named for William G. Hanshaw, who owned that part of the old Warner's Ranch which is now flooded.

•HERCULES, Town, Contra Costa County; Pop. 5,963; Zip Code 94547; Elev. 8; Lat. 38-01-02 N long. 122-17-15 W; Reached by US 40; Overlooks San Pablo Bay. Named (1890s) for the Hercules Powder Co., established 1869 to manufacture dynamite for the mines.

•HERMOSA BEACH, City, Los Angeles County; Pop. 18,070; Zip Code 90254; Elev. 15; Lat. 33-51-44 N long. 118-23-55 W; Reached by Cal. Highways 20 and 29; SW California on Pacific Ocean 15 miles SSW of Los Angeles between Manhattan Beach and Redondo Beach. A residential subdivision laid out and named by the Hermosa Beach Land and Water Co. in 1901. Name (Spanish) means "beautiful."

•HERNDON, Town, Fresno County; Pop. 400; Zip Code 93706; Elev. 296; Lat. 36-50-12 N long. 119-54-59 W; Reached by US 99; In a fig-growing area. Sycamore station was renamed Herndon in 1895 for a relative of the promoter of a local irrigation project.

•HESPERIA, City, San Bernardino County; Pop. 5,700; Zip Code 92345; Elev. 3191; Lat. 34-25-35 N long. 117-18-00 W; In the upland west of Victor Valley. Station named in 1885 by the California Southern (Santa Fe) Railroad, possibly after Hesperia, Michigan. Greek and Roman poets used the word to mean "the western land."

•HIDDEN HILLS, City, Los Angeles County; Pop. 1,760; Lat. 34-09-37 N long.118-39-05 W; SW, coastal California.

•HIGHGROVE, Town, Riverside County; Pop. 2,900; Zip Code 92507; Elev. 949; Lat. 34-00-57 N long. 117-19-57 W; Reached by US 395; In a citrus growing area.

•HIGHLAND, City, San Bernardino County; Pop. 12,300; Zip Code 92346; Elev. 1,315; Lat. 34-07-42 N long. 117-12-28 W; Name applied to station when Santa Fe Railroad was built through the valley (1894-95). Actually in the lowlands; named after the narrow, fertile tableland several hundred feet above the valley nearby.

•HILLSBOROUGH, City, San Mateo County; Pop. 10,451; Zip Code 94010; Elev. 32; Lat. 37-34-27 N long. 122-22-42 W; Reached by US 101; Western California, 10 miles south of San Francisco, west of Burlingame, set in an oak woodland; Incorporated 1910. Elegant residential community founded by Henry T. Scott in 1910 and named after Hillsboro, New Hampshire, ancestral home of W. D. M. Howard, former owner of site.

•HILMAR, Town, Merced County; Pop. 900; Zip Code 95324; Lat. 37-24-31 N long. 120-50-50 W; Established in 1917 and named after the Hilmar Colony, which was founded as a colony of Swedes by Nels O. r Hilmar A. Carlson, a pioneer citizen.

•HILT, Town, Siskiyou County; Pop. 30; Zip Code 96044; Lat. 41-59-42 N long. 122-37-20 W; John Hilt came to Siskiyou County in 1855 and built a sawmill on Cottonwood Creek.

•HINKLEY, Town, San Bernardino County; Pop. 680; Zip Code 92347; Elev. 2,162; Lat. 34-56-05 N long. 117-11-54 W; Formerly spelled Hinckley. Named upon arrival of the railroad in 1882 by D. C. Henderson of Barstow for his son, Hinckley.

•HOBART MILLS, Village, Nevada County; Pop. 20; Zip Code 95734; Elev. 5,925; Lat. 39-24-02 N long. 120-10-58 W; NE California. This town has been a lumber center since 1897, when Walter Hobart opened a mill here. It was named for his company in 1900.

•HODGE, Town, San Bernardino County; Pop. 700; Zip Code 92311; Elev. 2,150; Lat. 34-48-56 N long. 117-11-33; Reached by US 466; Between Barstow and Oro Grande, near the Mojave River. At the suggestion of Arthur Brisbane, a well-known journalist (early 1900s) and owner of a ranch in the Mojave Desert, the Santa Fe Railroad changed name of its station in 1926 from Hicks to present name, for Gilbert and Robert Hodge of Buffalo, New York, owners of a ranch in the desert since 1912.

•HOLLISTER, City, San Benito County Seat; Pop. 11,488; Zip Code 95023; Elev. 91; Lat. 36-51-09 N long. 121-24-02 W; Named in 1868 by the San Justo Homestead Assn. of farmers for Col. W. Hollister, who had driven the first flock of sheep across the continent and acquired the San Justo grant on which the new town was established.

•HOLLYWOOD, Subdivision, Los Angeles County; Pop. (with Los Angeles); Zip Code 90028; Elev. 385; Lat. 34-05-54 N long. 118-19-33; S California. The present name dates from the boom of 1887 when Horace H. Wilcox opened a real estate subdivision, which his wife christened Hollywood.

•HOLTVILLE, Town, Imperial County; Pop. 4,399; Zip Code 92250; Elev. 10 feet below sea level; Lat. 32-48-40 N long. 115-22-46; Reached by US 80; 8 miles from El Centro. Established and named Holton in 1903 by W. F. Holt, president of Holton Power Co. and an organizer of the Imperial Valley irrigation project (1899).

•HONCUT, Town, Butte County; Pop. 270; Code 95965; Elev. 106; Lat. 39-19-45 N long. 121-31-58 W; Near Oroville. Name comes from Hoan' kut, a Maidu Indian village on the Yuba River. Applied to a land grant in 1844 and to the post office in 1867.

•HONDA, Town, Santa Barbara County; Pop. (included with Vandenburg AFB) 13,193; Zip Code 93437; Lat. 34-36-56 N long. 120-37-57 W; Name (Spanish) means "deep." Station named after the Canada Honda ("deep valley") Creek when last link of the Southern Pacific coast line between Surf and Ellwood was completed in 1900.

•HOOD, Village, Sacramento County; Pop. 350; Zip Code 95639; Elev. 7; Lat. 38-22-06 N long. 121-30-59 W; N California. Shipping center for a farming region along the Sacramento River; Named for William Hood, railroad engineer, in 1910.

•HOOPA, Town, Humboldt County; Pop. 600; Zip Code 95546; Lat. 41-03-02 N long. 123-40-24 W; Reached by US 99 and Cal. Highway 96;   Established in 1865, and named for the Hupa Indians of the Athabascan family.

•HOPLAND, Town, Mendocino County; Pop. 900; Zip Code 95449; Lat. 38-58-23 N long. 123-06-55 W; Founded 1850 and named Hopland in 1880 because Stephen Knowles' experiment of growing hops here proved successful.

•HORNBROOK, Town, Siskiyou County; Pop. 480; Zip Code 96044; Elev. 2,115; Lat. 41-54-37 N long. 122-33 17 W; Reached by US 99; Near Cottonwood Creek. Named in 1886 after the brook which ran through the property of David Horn.

•HORNITOS, Town, Mariposa County; Pop. 55; Zip Code 95325; Elev. 1,000; Lat. 37-30-08 N long. 120-14-14 W; Reached by Cal. Highway 49. Name (Spanish) is diminutive of horno, which means "bake oven" or "kiln."

•HUGHSON, Town, Stanislaus County; Pop. 2,943; Zip Code 95326; Elev. 2; Lat. 37-35-49 N long. 120-51-54 W; Laid out by Flack and Jacobson in 1907 and named for Hiram Hughson, owner of the land.

•HUNTINGTON BEACH, City, Orange County; Pop. 170,505; Zip Code 92646; Elev. 28; Lat. 33-39-37 N long. 117-59-54 W; SW California.

•HUNTINGTON PARK, City, Los Angeles County; Pop. 46,223; Zip Code 90255; Elev. 4; Lat. 33-58-54 N long. 118-13-27 W; 4 miles S of Los Angeles in SW California.

•HURON, Town, Fresno County; Pop. 2,768; Zip Code 93234; Elev. 368; Lat. 36-12-10 N long. 120-06-07 W; Name given by the French to a group of four Iroquoian tribes in Ontario. Applied by the Southern Pacific Railroad in 1877 to this station .

•**HYAMPOM,** Town, Trinity County; Pop. 50; Zip Code 96046; Elev. 1285; Lat. 40-37-03 N long. 123-27-05 W; Settled January 12, 1855. *Pom* means "land" or "place" in the Wintu Indian tongue, but the meaning of the specific part is unknown.

•**IDRIA,** Town, San Benito County; Pop. 5; Zip Code 95023; Lat. 36-25-01 N long. 120-40-24 W. Named after the New Idria quicksilver mine, which had been named in the 1850s after a famous mine on the Adriatic Sea.

•**IDYLLWILD,** Town, Riverside County; Pop. 900; Zip Code 92349; Elev. 5, 500; Lat. 33-44-24 N long. 116-43-05 W; Reached by US 395; Near San Jacinto Peak. Name, suggested by Mrs. Laura Rutledge to describe the timbered resort area, was accepted by the Post Office Dept. in 1899.

•**IGNACIO,** Town, Marin County; Pop. 2,600; Zip Code 94947; Elev. 24; Lat. 38-04-13 N long. 122-32-15 W; Near Novato. Named in 1840 for Ignacio Pacheco, a soldier who owned the land grant on which town was built.

•**IGO,** Town, Shasta County; Pop. 75; Zip Code 96047; Elev. 1,081; Lat. 40-30-20 N long. 122-32-26 W; Reached by US 99; Near Redding. Once called Piety Hill, post office was established as Igo in 1873. Could be an Indian name.

•**IMPERIAL,** Town, Imperial County; Pop. 3,451; Zip Code 92251; Elev. 65; Lat. 32-50-51 N long. 115-34-07 W; feet below sea level; Reached by US 99; Oldest town in Imperial Valley.

•**IMPERIAL BEACH,** City, San Diego County; Pop. 22,689; Zip Code 92032; Lat. 32-35-02 N long. 117-06-44 W; Reached by US 101; SW California, on San Diego Bay near Mexican border; Post office founded 1910.

•**INDEPENDENCE,** Town, Inyo County Seat; Pop. 950; Zip Code 93526; Elev. 3,920: Lat. 38-20-57 N long. 120-30-45 W; E California. Thomas Edwards laid out the town in 1866 and named it for a nearby army fort.

•**INDIO,** City, Riverside County; Pop. 21,611; Zip Code 92201; Elev. 14; Lat. 33-43-14 N long. 116-12-53 W; Founded 1876; 62 miles SE of San Bernardino; Reached by Cal. Highway 111, the Palm Springs Highway. Name (Spanish) refers to the large Indian population in early days when it was a construction camp for the Southern Pacific railroad.

•**INGLEWOOD,** City, Los Angeles County; Pop. 94,245; Zip Code 903+; Elev. 118; Lat. 33-57-42 N long. 118-21-08 W; Reached by US 101A; Residential and industrial city, SW California, Incorporated 1908. Named after the home town of its Canadian founder, Daniel Freeman.

•**INGOT,** Town, Shasta County; Pop. 25; Zip Code 96008; Elev. 2,000; Lat. 40-43-40 N long. 122-04-41 W; Reached by US 299; Mining town named about 1900 because of the foundry here in which metals are cast into convenient forms for shipping.

•**INVERNESS,** Town, Marin County; Pop. 600; Zip Code 94937; Lat. 38-06-04 N long. 122-51-21 W; sea level; Reached by Cal. Highway 1; On the west side of Tomales Bay. Summer resort town named in 1889 by a Scot named Thompson after his birthplace in Scotland, said to be similar in appearance and climate.

•**INYOKERN,** Town, Kern County; Pop. 800; Zip Code 93527; Elev. 2,442; Lat. 35-38-49 N long. 117-48-42 W; Reached by US 395; name adopted in 1913 by residents place is near boundary of Inyo and Kern counties.

•**IONE,** Town, Amador County; Pop. 2,207; Zip code 95640; Elev. 300; Lat. 38-21-10 N long. 120-55-54 W; Reached by Cal. Highway 49. Actual meaning and origin of name never established. Possi-

ble explanations: name applied 1848 by Thomas Brown for one of Bulwer-Lytton's heroines; named after Ione, Illinois; a variation of "I own."

•**IOWA HILL,** Village, Placer County; Pop. 35; Zip Code 95713; Elev. 3,200; Lat. 39-06-31 N long. 120-51-30 W; NE California. Settled and named by Iowa immigrants.

•**IRVINE,** City, Orange County; Pop. 62,134; Zip Code 92715; Elev. 30; Lat. 33-40-10 N long. 117-49-20 W; SW California. The town was named for James Irvine of San Francisco, who purchased the town's land.

•**IRVINGTON,** Town, Alameda County; Pop. (with Fremont); Zip Code 94538; Lat. 37-31-22 N long. 121-58-14 W. W California. It was known as "Washington Corners" in the 1870s. The name was changed in 1884 in honor of author Washington Irving.

•**IRWINDALE,** City, Los Angeles County; Pop. 1,030; Zip Code 91706; Elev. 467; Lat. 34-06-25 N long. 117-56-04 W; SW, coastal California.

•**ISLETON,** Town, Sacramento County; Pop. 914; Zip code 95641; Elev. 14; Lat. 38-09-43-N long. 121-36-38 W; Reached by Cal. Highway 24, part of the confluence of the Sacramento and San Joaquin rivers.

•**IVANHOE,** Town, Tulare County; Pop. 1,595; Zip Code 93235; Lat. 36-23-14 N long. 119-13-01 W. Named for Walter Scott's famous novel.

•**IVANPAH,** Town, San Bernardino County; Pop. 10; Zip Code 92366; Elev. 3,508; Lat. 35-20-26 N long. 115-18-35 W; Elev. 3508. Name is a Southern Piute word meaning "good water," applied to the terminal of the Santa Fe branch from Goffs in 1902.

•**JACKSON,** Town, Amador County Seat; Pop. 2,331; Zip Code 95642; Elev. 1,235; Lat. 38-20-56 N long. 120-46-23 W; Reached by Cal. Highway 49; Mining city in central California. When "Col." Alden M. Jackson, a lawyer from New England, opened an office in the camp and became generally liked for settling quarrels out of court, grateful miners named the place for him.

•**JACUMBA,** Town, San Diego County; Pop. 600; Zip Code 92034; Elev. 2,800; Lat. 32-37-03 N long. 116-11-20 W; Reached by US 80; A resort spa, 200 yards from the Mexican border; name is a Diegueno Indian word meaning "hut by the water."

•**JAMACHA,** Town, San Diego County; Pop. (included with Spring Valley) 34,700; Zip Code 92077; Elev. 367; Lat. 32-44-20 N long. 120-29-37 W; South of El Cajon. Scholars do not agree on meaning of name. Possible origins: Diegueno Indian word *hamacha*, "small wild squash," or words meaning "gourd" or "mock orange."

•**JAMESTOWN,** Town, Tuolumne County; Pop. 950; Zip Code 95327; Elev. 1,500; Lat. 37-57-12 N long. 120-25-18 W; SW of Sonora, reached by Cal. Highway 49; Founded 1848; Named by miners for founder, Col. George F. James, a San Francisco lawyer.

•**JAMUL,** Town, San Diego County; Pop. 700; Zip Code 92035; Elev. 993; Lat. 32-43-01 N long. 116-52-31 W; SE of Spring Valley. Name derived from Diegueno Indian word, *ha-mul*, for "foam" or "lather;" meaning has been declared "slimy water," or "place where antelope drink water."

•**JANESVILLE,** Town, Lassen County; Pop. 600; Zip Code 96114; Elev. 4,236; Lat. 40-17-48 N long. 120-31-23 W; Reached by US 395; post office named 1864 by L. N. Breed, the first postmaster, for Jane Bankhead, wife of the village blacksmith, and/or for Jane Hill, who was born here on May 17, 1862.

•JENNER, Town, Sonoma County; Pop. 175; Zip Code 95450; Lat. 38-26-59 N long. 123-06-52 W. Reached by Cal. Highway 1. Probably named for Elijah K. Jenner, a native of Vermont, or for his son, Charles, a native of Wisconsin; both lived in the county in the 1860s.

•JESMOND DENE, Town, San Diego County; Pop. 100; Zip Code 92025; Lat. 33-10-49 N long. 117-06-30 W; Near Escondido. Named in 1920s by a Scots subdivider after the public park in Newcastle-upon-Tyne in northern England.

•JOHANNESBURG, Town, Kern County; Pop. 300; Zip Code 93528; Elev. 3,536; Lat. 35-22-22 N long. 117-38-02 W; Reached by US 395. Former mining town named in 1897 by founders, Chauncey M. Depew and associates, after the famous mining center in the Transvaal, South Africa.

•JOHNSONDALE, Town, Tulare County; Pop. 200; Zip Code 93236; Elev. 4,720; Lat. 35-58-29 N long. 118-32-24 W; In the Southern Prongs, pine mill town named in 1938 by the Mt. Whitney Lumber Co. for Walter Johnson, one of its officials.

•JOSHUA TREE, Town, San Bernardino County; Pop. 1,300; Zip Code 92252; Elev. 2,728; Lat. 34-08-05 N long. 116-18-44 W; Named for desert tree, yucca breuifolia, called Joshua tree by the Mormons because it seemed to them to be a symbol of Joshua leading them to the Promised Land.

•JULIAN, Town, San Diego County; Pop. 500; Zip Code 92036; Elev. 4,129; Lat. 33-04-43 N long. 116-36-04 W; Reached by Cal. Highway 79; Gold Rush town laid out in 1870 by Drew Bailey and named for his cousin, Mike S. Julian, a mining recorder on whose government claim gold quartz had been discovered.

•JUNCTION CITY, Village, Trinity County; Pop. 175; Zip Code 96048; Elev. 1,407; Lat. 40-44-00 N long. 123-03-09 W; NW California. Descriptively named for the confluence of Canyon Creek and the Trinity River.

•KEDDIE, Town, Plumas County; Pop. 250; Zip Code 95952; Elev. 3,223; Lat. 40-00-54 N long. 120-57-36 W; Reached by Cal. Highway 24, named for Arthur W. Keddie, a Scotsman who came to California in 1863, surveyed Plumas County (1870-71 and 1874-77), and made the original survey for the Western Pacific route.

•KEELER, Town, Inyo County; Pop. 100; Zip Code 93530; Elev. 3,610; Lat. 36-29-14 N long. 117-52-23 W; Reached by US 395; Named by the Carson and Colorado Railroad in 1882 for J. M. Keeler, Forty-Niner, captain of an Owens Lake steamer and manager of the Inyo county Marble Quarry.

•KEENE, Town, Kern County; Pop. 300; Zip Code 93531; Lat. 35-13-25 N long. 118-33-41 W. Post office established February 13, 1879, and named for a member of the prominent Keene family.

•KELSEYVILLE, Town, Lake County; Pop. 900 (summer 2,700); Zip Code 95431; Elev. 1,500; Lat. 38-58-41 N long. 122-50-18 W; Reached by Cal. Highway 29; named Kelsey Town in memory of Andrew Kelsey, first settler in the county and a troublesome character who was killed in 1849 by the Indians in revenge for his mistreatment of them.

•KELSO, Town, San Bernardino County; Pop. 75; Zip Code 92351; Elev. 2,125; Lat. 35-00-45 N long. 115-39-10 W; Named for a railroad official (1906).

•KENSINGTON, City, Contra Costa County; Pop. 5,823; Zip Code 94707; Elev. 600; Lat. 37-54-38 N long. 122-16-45 W; Named after Kensington in England by Robert Bousefield when the track was opened in 1911.

•KENTFIELD, Town, Marin County; Pop. 2,500; Zip Code 94904; Elev. 12; Lat. 37-57-08 N long. 122-33-22 W; Named for Albert Emmett Kent, who established his home here in 1872 and called it Tamalpais.

•KERMAN, Town, Fresno County; Pop. 4,002; Zip Code 93630; Lat. 36-43-25 N long. 120-03-32 W; South central California, 14 miles west of Fresno. In 1906, when W. G. Kerckhoff and Jacob Mansar of Los Angeles established a colony of Germans and Scandanavians from the Middle West, the settlment and station were called Kerman, a name coined from the first three letters of each promoter's last name.

•KERNVILLE, Kern County; Pop. 1,660; Zip Code 92233; Elev. 2,569; Lat. 35-45-17 N long. 118-25-28 W; Central California. The town came to life as Whiskey Flat during the 1885 gold rush. When Whiskey Flat became a prosperous mining center in its own right it took its present name.

•KETTLEMAN CITY, Town, Kings County; Pop. 500; Zip code 93239; Elev. 234; Lat. 36-00-30 N long. 119-57-39 W; In the Kettleman Hills, part of the southern Coast Range, which adjoins the Tulare Lake Basin (Kings County) and is about 20 miles long and 5 miles wide. Named for David Kettleman, who came to California in 1849.

•KING CITY, Town, Monterey County; Pop. 5,495; Zip Code 93930; Elev. 338; Lat. 36-12-46 N long. 121-07-30 W; In the southern Salinas Valley, 90 miles SE of San Jose; Near Pinnacles National Monument. Market center named for C. H. King, who laid out the town on his Rancho San Lorenzo in 1886.

•KINGS BEACH, Town, Placer County; Pop. 2,000 (summer 7,000); Zip Code 95719; Lat. 39-14-16 N long. 120-01-32 W; Named by residents for Joe King in recognition of his gifts to the community.

•KINGSBURG, City, Fresno County; Pop. 5,115; Zip Code 93531; Elev. 297; Lat. 36-30-50 N long. 119-33-11 W; Central California.

•KLAMATH, Town, Del Norte County; Pop. 500; Zip Code 95548; Elev. 40; Lat. 41-31-36 N long. 124-02-14 W; Reached by US 101. Name derived from Tlamatl, the Chinook name for a sister tribe of the Modocs who called themselves Maklaks, "people."

•KNEELAND, Town, Humboldt County; Pop. 50; Zip Code 95549; Lat. 40-54-41 N long. 123-59-37 W. Post office established before 1880 and named after Kneeland's Prairie, a place which had been named for John A. Kneeland, a settler of the early 1850s.

•KNIGHTS LANDING, Town, Yolo County; Pop. 900; Zip Code 95645; Elev. 48; Lat. 38-47-59 N long. 121-43-02 W; Reached by Cal. Highway 24; 8 miles from a junction with US 99W at Woodland; Named to commemorate William Knight, of Indiana, who settled on the Sacramento in 1843.

•KOMANDORSKI VILLAGE, City, Alameda County; Pop. (included with Dublin) 13,641; Zip Code 94566; Lat. 37-42-58 N long. 121-54-28 W.

•KORBEL, Town, Humboldt County; Pop. 124; Zip Code 95550; Elev. 61; Lat. 40-52-14 N long. 123-57-26 W; Elev. 61. Known as North Fork when the Korbel brothers built their mill here in 1882. Post office established June 24, 1891, under name Korbel.

•KRAMER JUNCTION, Town, San Bernardino County; Pop. 40; Zip Code 93516; Elev. 2,482; Lat. 34-59-33 N long. 117-32-27 W; Near Boron; Reached by US 395. In 1882 the Southern Pacific Railroad gave the name to the junction ,possibly for Moritz Kramer, a German listed in the Great Register of 1879.

•KYBURZ, Town, El Dorado County; Pop. 100 (summer 400); Zip Code 95720; Elev. 4,700; Lat. 38-46-29 N long. 120-17-45 W;

Reached by US 50; Near Silver Fork of Truckee River. Post office established 1911 and named for the first postmaster, Albert Kyburz.

•**LA CANADA**, City, Los Angeles County; Pop. (included with Flintridge) 20,153; Zip Code 91011; Lat. 34-12-16 N long. 118-12-00 W; Unincorporated urban community NW of Pasadena; Name (Spanish), meaning "valley" or "glen."

•**LA CRESCENTA**, City, Los Angeles County; Pop. 14,900; Zip Code 91214; Elev. 1,600; Lat. 34-13-27 N long. 118-14-21 W; Settled early 1880s. Named by Dr. Benjamin Briggs for three crescent-shaped formations near his home.

•**LAFAYETTE**, City, Contra Costa County; Pop. 20,379; Zip code 94549; Elev. 295; Lat. 37-53-09 N long. 122-07-01W; Western California, 20 miles NE of San Francisco in the San Ramon Valley. Named in 1853 by Benjamin Shreve, owner of a store, for the French general who fought in the American War for Independence.

•**LAGUNA BEACH**, City, Orange County; Pop. 17,860; Zip Code 92651; Elev. 40; Lat. 33-32-32 N long. 117-46-56 W; Oceanside resort city 27 miles SE of Long Beach in a rugged coastal area. Name, Spanish word meaning "lake," derived from Laguna Canyon.

•**LA HABRA**, City, Orange County; Pop. 45,232; Zip Code 90631; Elev. 325; Lat. 33-55-55 N long. 117-56-43 W; Reached by US 101, 8 miles from Fullerton and 19 miles NE of Long Beach in SW California. Name is Spanish for "gorge" or "pass through the mountains."

•**LA HONDA**, Town, San Mateo County; Pop. (included with El Segundo) 15,620; Zip Code 90245; Elev. 403; Lat. 37-19-09 N long. 122-16-23 W; Reached by Cal. Highway 1; Post office established 1880. Name (Spanish) means "deep."

•**LA JOLLA**, Subdivision, San Diego County; Pop. (with San Diego); Zip Code 92037; Lat. 37-19-09 N long. 122-16-23 W; SW California. The name may be a corruption of *la joya*, or "the jewel," or of *la hoya*, or "the hollow."

•**LA MESA**, City, San Diego County; Pop. 50,342; Zip Code 92014; Lat. 32-46-04 N long. 117-01-20 W; SW corner of California, 8 miles NE of San Diego. Name is Spanish word for "table land."

•**LA MIRADA**, City, Los Angeles County; Pop. 40,986; Zip Code 90638; Elev. 181; Lat. 33-55-02 N long. 118-00-40 W; SW California, 17 miles SE of Los Angeles. Spanish name, meaning "glance" or "gaze," given to Santa Fe station when the line to San Diego was built in 1888.

•**LA PALMA**, City, Orange County; Pop. 15,663; Elev. 44; Lat. 33-50-47 N long 118-02-45 W; 18 miles SE of Los Angeles in SW California.

•**LA PORTE**, Town, Plumas County; Pop. 75 (summer 200); Zip Code 95981; Elev. 4,959; Lat. 39-40-56 N long. 120-58-59 W; Named 1857 after La Porte, Indiana, birthplace of Frank Everts, a local banker.

•**LA PRESA**, Town, San Diego County; Pop. (included with Spring Valley) 34,700; Zip code 92077; Elev. 351; Lat. 32-42-29 N long. 116-59-47 W.

•**LA PUENTE**, City, Los Angeles county; Pop. 30,882; Zip Code 917--; Lat. 34-01-12 N long. 117-56-55 W; NNE of Long Beach in SW California.

•**LAKE CITY**, Town, Modoc County; Pop. 125; Zip Code 96115; Elev. 4,559; Lat. 41-38-34 N long. 120-12-57 W; Post office established 1870s and named because it is situated between Up-per and Middle Alkali lakes (known locally as Surprise Valley lakes).

•**LAKE HUGHES**, Town, Los Angeles County; Pop. 600 (summer 900); Zip Code 93532; Lat. 34-40-37 N long. 118-26-40 W. Post office named 1925 after the lake nearby.

•**LAKEPORT**, Town, Lake County Seat; Pop. 3,675; Zip Code 95453; Elev. 1,350; Lat. 39-02-35 N long. 122-54-53 W; Reached by Cal. Highways 20 and 29. When community became the seat of newly created Lake County in 1861, town was named Lakeport because it is on the edge of Clear Lake.

•**LAKESIDE**, City, San Diego County; Pop. 15,300; Zip Code 92040; Lat. 32-51-26 N long. 116-55-17 W. Laid out on shore of Lake Lindo in 1886 by El Cajon Valley Co. and named after the lake.

•**LAKEVIEW**, Town, Riverside County; Pop. 500; Zip Code 92353; Elev. 374; Lat. 35-05-41 N long. 119-06-31 W; Post office established about 1895 and named because of the view of Lake Moreno, once called Brown's Lake (*moreno* = brown).

•**LAKEWOOD**, City, Los Angeles County; Pop. 74,654; Zip Code 90712; Lat. 33-51-13 N long. 118-07-59 W; SW coastal California, NE of Long Beach. Subdivision laid out in 1934 and named Lakewood Village because it is near Bouton Lake.

•**LAMONT**, City, Kern County; Pop. 7,007; Zip Code 93241; Lat. 35-15-35 N long. 118-54-48 W. Named by the MacFadden family, landholders, after their former home in Scotland.

•**LANARE**, Town, Fresno County; Pop. 150; Zip Code 93656; Lat. 36-25-50 N long. 119-55-48 W. Coined from name of L. A. Nares, chief promoter of the colonization project, and applied in 1911 when the Laton and Western Railway was built.

•**LANCASTER**, City, Los Angeles County; Pop. 48,027; Zip Code 93534; Lat. 34-41-53 N long. 118-08-09 W; Elev. 2,356; S Central California; In Mojave Desert. It was founded by settlers from Pennsylvania in 1877.

•**LARKSPUR**, City, Marin County; Pop. 11,064; Zip Code 94938; Elev. 43; Lat. 37-56-03 N long. 122-39-03 W; Western California, about 10 miles NW of San Francisco in the basin of Corte Madera Creek. Founded 1887 and named because blue larkspur grew profusely nearby.

•**LAS CRUCES**, Town, Santa Barbara County; Pop. 10; Zip Code 93017; Lat. 34-30-29 N long. 120-18-41 W; Near Gaviota. Name, Spanish for "the crosses," derived from a land grant, dated July 12, 1836.

•**LASSEN COUNTY**, NE California; Area 4,561 sq. miles; Pop. 21,661; Seat Susanville; Created from parts of Plumas and Shasta counties, and named April 1, 1964, by the legislature for noted Danish pioneer Peter Lassen.

•**LATHROP**, Town, San Joaquin County; Pop. 2,137; Zip Code 95330; Lat. 37-49-22 N long. 121-16-32 W. Laid out in 1887 and named by Leland Stanford for his brother-in-law, Charles Lathrop.

•**LA VERNE**, City, Los Angeles County; Pop. 23,508; Zip Code 91750; Elev. 1,050; Lat. 34-06-03 N long. 117-46-01 W; S California. It took the name of LaVerne College in 1916.

•**LAWNDALE**, Town, Sonoma County; Pop. rural; Zip Code 95452; Elev. 55; Lat. 33-53-14 N long. 118-21-0 6W; Near Kenwood; Elev. 113; Reached by US 101. Station of the Northwestern Pacific Railroad.

•**LAWS**, Town, Inyo County; Pop. rural; Zip Code 93514; Lat. 37-24-03 N long. 118-26-41 W. Near Bishop; Elev. 4,200; Reached by US 6. A railroad water stop named in 1883 for R. J. Laws, assistant superintendent of the Carson and Colorado Railroad.

•LAYTONVILLE, Town, Mendocino County; Pop. 900; Zip Code 95454; Elev. 1,600; Lat. 39-41-18 N long. 123-28-54 W; Reached by US 101; named for Frank B. Layton, who came to California from Nova Scotia, Canada, in 1867 and settled here in 1875.

•LE GRAND, Town, Merced County; Pop. 900; Zip Code 95333; Elev. 253; Lat. 37-13-43 N long. 120-14-50 W; Established 1896 Fe) and named for William Legrand Dickinson, a Stockton resident, who owned large tracts of land here.

•LEE VINING, Town, Mono County; Pop. 400; Zip Code 93541; Elev. 7,000; Lat. 37-57-27 N long. 119-07-15 W; Reached by US 395. Derives its name from nearby Leevining Canyon, named for Leroy Vining, of La Porte, Indiana, who came to California in search of gold in 1852.

•LEGGETT, Town, Mendocino County; Pop. 500; Zip Code 95455; Elev. 952; Lat. 39-51-57 N long. 123-42-47 W; Long known as Leggett Valley, for an earlier pioneer. Name abbreviated by Post Office Dept. when post office established here October 16, 1949.

•LEMON GROVE, City, San Diego County; Pop. 20,780; Zip Code 92045; Elev. 450; Lat. 32-44-33 N long. 117-01-50 W; Unincorporated residential community in southern California, east of San Diego. First named by the Allison brothers, who were convinced the area was perfect for lemon cultivation.

•LEMONCOVE, Town, Tulare County; Pop. 40; Zip Code 93244; Elev. 518; Lat. 36-22-58 N long. 119-01-25 W.

•LEMOORE, City, Kings County; Pop. 3,832; Zip Code 93245; Lat. 36-18-03 N long. 119-46-55 W; Central California. Dr. Lovern More moved here to found a settlement he called Latache for his ditch company. The town was later renamed for him.

•LEMOORE NAVAL AIR STATION, Military installation located at town of same name, Kings County; Pop. (town) 8,832; Zip Code 93245; Elev. 226; Reached by US 99; SW California. Agricultural town named for founder (1871), Dr. Lovern Lee Moore.

•LENNOX, City, Los Angeles County; Pop. 16,121; Zip Code 90304; Elev. 70; Lat. 33-56-17 N long. 118-21-06 W; SW California, SE of Santa Monica. Named before 1921 after Lenox, Massachusetts, the former home of a resident of the settlement.

•LENWOOD, Town, San Bernardino County; Pop. 3,834; Zip Code 92311; Elev. 2,229; Lat. 34-52-36 N long. 117-06-11 W; Reached by US 66; 5 miles from Barstow. Name coined from that of Ellen Woods, whose husband, Frank subdivided land.

•LEUCADIA, City, San Diego County; Pop. 6,500; Zip Code 92024; Lat. 33-04-05 N long. 117-18-09 W. Oceanside community founded in 1885 by English settlers who named it for the Ionian island on which Sappho supposedly died.

•LEWISTON, Town, Trinity County; Pop. 750; Zip Code 96052; Elev. 1,826; Lat. 40-42-27 N long. 122-48-23 W; Settled by B. F. Lewis in 1853.

•LIKELY, Town, Modoc County; Pop. 150; Zip Code 96116; Elev. 4,500; Lat. 41-13-50 N long. 120-30-11 W; Reached by US 395; present name acquired in 1878.

•LINCOLN, Town, Placer County; Pop. 4,132; Zip Code 95648; Elev. 163; Lat. 38-53-30 N long. 121-17-31 W; Reached by US 99E; 9 miles from Roseville, 25 miles north of Sacramento. Laid out at Auburn Ravine in 1859 by C. L. Wilson, and named for him November 4, 1861.

•LINCOLN ACRES, Town, San Diego County; Pop. 1,800; Zip Code 92047; Lat. 32-40-04 N long. 117-04-19 W. Probably named for Abraham Lincoln.

•LINDSAY, City, Tulare County; Pop. 6,924; Zip Code 93247; Elev. 383; Lat. 36-12-11 N long. 119-05-14 W; Reached by US 99; 52 miles SE of Fresno. Named by Capt. A. J. Hutchinson, founder (1888) of town, in honor of his wife, Nee Lindsay.

•LIVE OAK, City, Sutter County; Pop. 3,103; Zip Code 95953; Elev. 75; Lat. 38-29-03 N long. 121-04-23 W; N California. Named in 1874 for the native tree growing in the area.

•LIVE OAK SPRINGS, San Diego County; Pop. 75 (summer 225); Zip Code 92062; Lat. 32-41-26 N long. 116-20-01 W. Near Pine Valley. A small cabin resort in the mountains adjacent to Campo Indian Reservation, settled by Charles Hill in 1886.

•LIVERMORE, City, Alameda County; Pop. 48,349; Zip Code 94550; Elev. 458; Lat. 37-40-55 N long. 121-46-01 W; NW Central California. It was named for the English navigator Robert Livermore.

•LIVINGSTON, Town, Merced County; Pop. 5,326; Zip Code 95334; Elev. 131; Lat. 37-23-13 long. 120-43-21 W; Reached by US 99; Central California, named for explorer of central Africa, David Livingstone (minus the "e").

•LOCKEFORD, Town, San Joaquin County; Pop. 1,500; Zip Code 95237; Elev. 104; Lat. 38-09-49 N long. 121-08-56 W; Name first applied to ford which crossed the Mokelumne River on land of Dr. D. J. Locke.

•LODI, City, San Joaquin County; Pop. 35,221; Zip Code 95240; Elev. 51; Lat. 38-07-49 N long. 121-16-17; Named Lodi 1874. Possible sources of name: Napoleon's first spectacular victory, May 10, 1796, at Lodi, Italy; Lodi, a famous racehorse of 1870s.

•LODOGA, Town, Colusa County; Pop. 60; Zip Code 95979; Lat. 39-18-07 N long. 122-29-17 W; Perhaps named after large lake between Finland and Russia, or after Ladoga in Indiana or Wisconsin, or just for its pleasant sound.

•LOLETA, Town, Humboldt county; Pop. 800; Zip Code 95551; Elev. 50; Lat. 40-38-28 N long. 124-13-27 W ; Reached by US 101; said to be an Indian work of unknown origin.

•LOMA LINDA, City, San Bernardino County; Pop. 10,694; Zip Code 92354; Lat. 34-02-54 N long. 117-15-37 N; Name (Spanish) means "pretty hill."

•LOMITA, City, Los Angeles County; Pop. 17,191; Zip Code 90717; Lat. 33-47-32 N long. 118-18-51 W; SW California, SE of Torrance. Name is Mexican-Spanish diminutive of loma, which means "long, low hill."

•LOMPOC, City, Santa Barbara County; Pop. 26,267; Zip Code 93436; Elev. 104; Lat. 34-38-21 N long. 120-27-25 W; Reached by Cal. Highway 1; SW California; Near Pacific Ocean, 45 miles WNW of Santa Barbara; Name probably means "shell mound."

•LONE PINE, Town, Inyo County; Pop. 1,800; Zip Code 93545; Elev. 3,733; Lat. 36-36-22 N long. 118-03-43 W; a party camped here in 1860 ,and named the place for the tall pine which was a landmark for many years until it was undermined by the creek.

•LONG BEACH, Pop. 361,334. Elev. 29; Lat. 33-46-01 N long. 118-11-18 W; Located 20 miles south of Los Angeles; first known as Willmore City for W. E. Willmore who subdivided the area. After bankrupcy in 1888 the city was renamed Long Beach.

•LOOKOUT, Town, Modoc County; Pop. 200; Zip Code 96054; Elev. 4162; Lat. 41-12-29 N long. 121-09-15 W; Settlement named about 1860 after the hill above the town, on which, the story goes, the Pit River Indians had a lookout when the Modocs were on wife-stealing expeditions.

•**LOOMIS**, Town, Placer County; Pop. 1,108; Zip Code 95650; Elev. 399; Lat. 38-49-17 N long. 121-11-31 N; N California. The town was known as Pino and Pine before it was named for Jim Loomis, an agent for the Southern Pacific Railroad.

•**LOS ALAMITOS**, City, Orange County; Pop. 11,529; Zip Code 90720; Elev. 22; Lat. 33-48-11 N long. 118-04-18 N; SW California, 9 miles NE of Long Beach. Name is Spanish diminutive for "popular" or "cottonwood tree" (*alamos*).

•**LOS ALAMOS**, Town, Santa Barbara County; Pop. 600; Zip Code 93440; Elev. 575; Lat. 34-44-40 N long. 120-16-38 W; Name (Spanish) means "popular" or "cottonwood tree."

•**LOS ALTOS**, City, Santa Clara County; Pop. 25,769; Zip code 94022; Elev. 200; Lat. 33-47-38 N long. 118-07-28 W; Reached by US 101; SE of Palo Alto. Post office, established 1908, took Spanish name meaning "the heights," which the subdivider chose in 1907.

•**LOS ANGELES**, City, Los Angeles County Seat, Pop. 2,966,763; Elev. 330; Lat. 34-04-08 N long. 118-14-34 W; Founded in 1781 by monks of the San Gabriel mission. Early growth stimulated by the coming of the Sante Fe and South Pacific railroads. Complete name is *Our Lady Queen of the Angels de Porciuncula*, from the Spanish *El Pueblo de Nuestra Senora ls Reina de Los A ngeles de Porciuncula.*

•**LOS BANOS**, City, Merced County; Pop. 10,341; Zip Code 93635; Elev. 120; Lat. 37-03-30 N long. 120-50-56 W; Town known as Kreyenhagen's until post office was established at the store (1874) and named after Los Banos Creek ("creek of the baths").

•**LOS GATOS**, City, Santa Clara County; Pop. 26,593; Zip code 95030; Elev. 412; Lat. 37-13-36 N long. 121-58-25 W; Reached by US 101; At mouth of a forest-choked canyon within confines of former Rancho Rinconada de los Gatos ("little corner of the cats").

•**LOS MOLINOS**, Town, Tehama County; Pop. 900; Zip Code 96055; Elev. 220; Lat. 40-01-17 N long. 122-05-57 W; Reached by US 99E. Name (Spanish) means "the mills."

•**LOS NIETOS**, Town, Los Angeles County; Pop. 7,100; Zip Code 90606; Elev. 154; Lat. 33-58-06 N long. 118-04-11 W; SW California. This suburban development was originally an agricultural area named for Manuel Nieto, a local rancher, and his five sons.

•**LOST HILLS**, Town, Kern County; Pop. 200; Zip Code 93249; Elev. 300; Lat. 35-36-59 N long. 119-41-36 W; Took its name in 1910 from the Lost Hills, slight elevations which probably belong to the Kettleman Hills but look as if they were "lost."

•**LOWER LAKE**, Town, Lake County; Pop. 850; Elev. 1372; Lat. 38-54-38 N long. 122-36-33 W; Named for its proximity to Clear Lake.

•**LOYALTON**, Town, Sierra County; Pop. 1,030; Zip code 96118; Elev. 4,936; Lat. 39-40-35 N long. 120-14-24 W; Lumbering center named by Post Office Dept. in 1863 at suggestion of the first postmaster, who considered it expressive of the strong Union sentiment of the place.

•**LUCERNE**, Town, Lake County; Pop. 2,500; Zip Code 95458; Lat. 36-22-51 N long. 119-39-48 W; Its location on the shore of Clear Lake, which presumably resembled the Swiss lake, suggested the name for the hotel and post office established July 2, 1926.

•**LUCERNE VALLEY**, Town, San Bernardino County; Pop. 1,000 (summer 4,000); Zip Code 92356; Elev. 2,946; Lat. 34-26-38 N

long. 116-58-01 W; In an article written in April 1887, district was rechristened Lucerne Valley because of its resemblance to the Swiss one.

•**LUDLOW**, Town, San Bernardino County; Elev. 1,775; Lat. 34-43-16 N long. 116-09-33 W; Named in 1870s by the Central Pacific Railroad for William B. Ludlow, master car-repairer of the Western Division.

•**LYNWOOD**, City, Los Angeles County; Pop. 48,548; Zip Code 90262; Lat. 33-55-49 N long. 118-12-38 W; SW California, Name first applied to a dairy, for Lynn Wood Sessions, wife of the owner.

•**LYTTON**, Town, Sonoma county; Zip Code 95448; Elev. 185; Lat. 38-39-34 N long. 122-52-14 W; Near Healdsburg. Named for Captain Litton, who developed the place as a resort in 1875.

•**MACDOEL**, Town, Siskiyou county; Pop. 170; Zip Code 96058; Elev. 4,258; Lat. 41-49-37 N long. 122-00-15 W; When Southern Pacific Railroad extension from Weed to Klamath Falls was built in 1906, station was named for William MacDoel, owner of the land.

•**MADELINE**, Town, Lassen County; Pop. 40; Zip Code 96119; Elev. 5,314; Lat. 41-03-04 N long. 120-28-28 W; Name commemorates a little girl of same name, killed when a party of immigrants was attacked by Indians in the early 1850s.

•**MADERA**, City, Madera County Seat; Pop. 21,732; Zip code 93637; Elev. 272; Lat. 36-57-41 N long. 120-03-35 W; Name, Spanish for "wood" or "timber," given by California Lumber Co. to the lumber town at the terminus of the water flume connecting it to the railroad.

•**MAGALIA**, Town, Butte County; Pop. 350; Zip Code 95954; Lat. 39-48-44 N long. 121-34-28 W; In 1861, A. C. Buffum suggested the Latin word for "cottages" as a more suitable name, which was applied when post office transferred from Butte Mills November 14, 1861.

•**MALAGA**, Town, Fresno county; Pop. 800; Zip Code 93725; Elev. 293; Lat. 36-41-01 N long. 119-43-58 W; A wine center specializing in muscat grapes, a species imported from Malaga, Spain, in 1852. Post Office established 1885 and named for that city.

•**MALIBU**, City, Los Angeles County; Pop. 7,000; Zip Code 90265; Reached by US 101. Name is of Chumash Indian origin, from a rancheria called Umalibo and later part of 1805 grant, Rancho Topanga Malibu Sequil.

•**MAMMOTH LAKES**, Town, Mono County; Pop. 900 (summer 5,000); Zip Code 93546; Lat. 37-38-55 N long. 118-58-16 W; Takes its name from Mammoth City, a big boom town that flourished briefly after the organization of the Mammoth Lakes Recreation Area.

•**MANCHESTER**, Town, Mendocino County; Pop. 300; Zip Code 95459; Lat. 38-58-13 N long. 123-41-13 W; Post office established 1870s and probably named after one of the 35 Manchesters which already existed in the U.S.

•**MANHATTAN BEACH**, City, Los Angeles County; Pop. 31,542; Zip Code 90266; Elev. 46; Lat. 33-53-05 N long. 118-24-36 W; Named after Manhattan Island at the suggestion of Stewart Merrill, founder of the town.

•**MANTECA**, City, San Joaquin County; Pop. 24,925; Elev. 40; Lat. 37-47-51 N long. 121-12-54 W; In 1904 or 1905, the Southern Pacific Railroad named the station after a local creamery called Manteca, the Spanish word for "butter" or "lard."

•**MANTON**, Town, Tehama County; Pop. 150; Zip Code 96059;

Lat. 40-26-07 N long. 121-52-08 W; Named in 1892 by J. M. Meeder, probably after the town in Rhode Island.

•**MARCH AIR FORCE BASE**, Riverside County; Pop. 2,002; Zip code 92508; US. Established 1917 as a training school and named for Peyton C. March, Jr., son of the Chief of Staff, who lost his life in an airplane accident in San Antonio, Texas.

•**MARICOPA**, Town, Kern County; Pop. 946; Zip Code 93252; Elev. 854; Lat. 35-03-32 N long. 119-24-00 W; When the Southern Pacific Railroad built the extension from Sunset in 1904, the terminus was called Maricopa, apparently for the Indian tribe on the Gila River in Arizona.

•**MARINA**, City, Monterey County; Pop. 20,647; Zip Code 93933; Elev. 40; Lat. 364104N; Long. 1214804W; Name (Spanish) means "shore" or "coast." Suburb of Monterey.

•**MARIPOSA**, Town, Mariposa County Seat; Pop. 950; Zip Code 95338; Elev. 1,962; Lat. 37-29-06 N long. 119-57-55 W; Region was called Mariposas, Spanish for "butterflies," by a Spanish expedition in 1806, because the soldiers encountered multitudes of them.

•**MARTELL**, Village, Amador County; Pop. 200; Zip Code 95654; Elev. 1,490; Lat. 38-22-01 N long. 120-47-42 W; N California; Established in 1906 and named for the Louis Martell family.

•**MARTINEZ**, City, Contra Costa County Seat; Pop. 22,582; Zip Code 94553; Elev. 23; Lat. 38-01-10 N long. 122-07-59 W; Founded and named (1849) for Ignacio Martinez, commandant of the San Francisco Presidio (1822-27), on whose Rancho El Pinole the town was laid out.

•**MARYSVILLE**, City, Yuba County Seat; Pop. 9,898; Zip Code 95901; Elev. 63; Lat. 39-08-45 N long. 121-35-25 W; Town laid out by Charles Covillaud in 1849-50 and renamed for his wife, Mary, a survivor of the Donner party.

•**MAYWOOD**, City, Los Angeles County; Pop. 21,810; Zip Code 90270; Lat. 33-59-12 N long. 118-11-04 W.

•**McARTHUR**, Town, Shasta County; Pop. 400; Zip Code 96056; Elev. 3,342; Lat. 41-19-54 N long. 120-32-11 W; Named about 1896 by the John McArthur Co. for John McArthur, who settled in the Pit River Valley in 1869 and who owned most of the land in the district.

•**McCLOUD**, Town, Siskiyou county; Pop. 1,642; Zip Code 96057; Elev. 3,254; Lat. 41-15-21 N long. 122-08-18 W; Named for Alexander R. McLeod, leader of a Hudson's Bay Co. expedition that trapped in California, 1828-29.

•**McFARLAND**, Town, Kern County; Pop. 5,151; Zip Code 93250; Elev. 350; Lat. 34-40-41 N long. 119-13-42 W; Southern California, 23 miles north of Bakersfield. Chief cottonginning point in the state. Named in 1908 for J. B. McFarland, one of the town's founders.

•**McKINLEYVILLE**, Town, Humboldt County; Pop. 2,000; Zip Code 95521. Lat. 40-56-48 N long. 124-05-58 W; Settlement on US 101 named in honor of President McKinley after his assassination September 14, 1901. Had a post office from 1903 until 1921.

•**MENDOTA**, City, Fresno County; Pop. 5,038; Zip Code 93640; Lat. 36-45-13 N long. 120-22-50 W; South central California, 34 miles west of Fresno. Name given to station in 1895 when the Southern Pacific Railroad built the extension from Fresno in the Trough (north-south axis) of the San Joaquin Valley.

•**MENLO PARK**, City, San Mateo County; Pop. 25,673; Zip Code 94025; Elev. 63; Lat. 37-27-14 N long. 122-10-52 W; 23 miles SE of San Francisco; Settled 1861, incorporated 1930. In August 1854, D. J. Oliver and D. C. McGlynn, brothers-in-law, from Menlough, County Galway, Ireland, erected an arched gate at the joint entrance to their ranches with the inscription "Menlo Park" and the date. When the San Francisco and San Jose Railroad reached here (1863): it adopted the name for the station.

•**MERCED**, City, Merced County Seat; Pop. 36,499; Zip Code 95340; Elev. 170; Lat. 37-18-08 N long. 120-28-55 W; W Central California. This is the principal rail and motor gateway to Yosemite National Park. The name comes from that of a river, Nuestra Senora de la Merced, or "Our Lady of Mercy," given in 1806 by a Spanish expedition. The city grew rapidly after the railroad reached it in 1872.

•**MIDDLETOWN**, Town, Lake County; Pop. 900; Zip Code 95461; Elev. 1,300. Named in 1860s when it was the stage stop halfway between Lower Lake and Calistoga.

•**MIDWAY CITY**, Town, Orange County; Pop. 2,300; Zip Code 92655; Lat. 33-44-41 N long. 117-59-18 W; 23 miles from Yermo. Named because of its location exactly midway on Bolsa Avenue between Santa Ana and the Beach. Post office established 1930.

•**MILLBRAE**, City, San Mateo County; Pop. 20,058; Zip Code 94030; Elev. 8; Lat. 37-35-55 N long. 122-23-10 W; NW of San Mateo. Named applied to station (1860s) after the country place of Darius O. Mills, a leading banker and promoter of San Francisco and New York.

•**MILPITAS**, City, Santa Clara County; Pop. 37,820; Zip Code 95035; Elev. 13; Lat. 37-25-42 N long. 121-54-20 W; Near Penitencia Creek; Western California, south of Palo Alto. Name is Spanish for "little corn field." Founded in 1850s on the Milpitas land grant (1835), given to Maximo Martines.

•**MIRA LOMA**, Town, Riverside County; Pop. 8,707; Zip Code 91752, Elev. 787; Lat. 33-59-33 N long. 117-30-56 W; S Central California. The Charles Stern Winery opened here and named the settlement Wineville, but when the post office was begun in 1930, it was renamed for the Spanish words meaning "behold the sand."

•**MODESTO**, City; Stanislaus County; Pop. 76,500; Zip Code 953+; Elev. 86. Named by Central Pacific Railroad for San Francisco banker William C. Ralston, who declined the honor, an act that led to the present name, which is Spanish for "modest."

•**MOJAVE**, Town, Kern County; Pop. 2,573; Zip Code 93501; Elev. 2,751; Lat.35-03-09 N long. 118-10-23 W. Name derived from populous and warlike Yuman Indian tribe who once lived on the Colorado River where California, Arizona, and Nevada meet. Their word for "mountain" was *mac-ha-ves*.

•**MONTECITO**, City, Santa Barbara County; Pop. 7,500; Zip Code 93103; Elev. 250; Lat. 34-26-12 N long. 119-37-52 W; Reached by US 101; 6 miles from Carpinteria. Suburb of Santa Barbara, known for its elegant estates, fine gardens, country clubs, and golf courses. Suffered 2 severe fires in 1964 and 1977. Name (Spanish) means "little woods."

•**MONTEREY**, City; Monterey County; Pop. 28,700; Zip Code 93940; Elev. 40. Town developed around the presidio established by Portola in 1770, the first Spanish military post in California. Site of city discovered 1542 by Juan Cabrillo, rediscovered 1602 by Vizcaino.

•**MONTEREY PARK**, city, Los Angeles County; Pop. 54,338; Zip Code 91754; Lat. 34-03-45 N long. 118-07-19 W; 8 miles east of Los Angeles. Once a subdivision on the Repetto Ranch developed in 1906 and named Ramona Acres. At time of its incorporation, city was renamed after Monterey Pass to the west.

•**MONROVIA**, City, Los Angeles County; Pop. 30,531; Zip Code 91016; Elev. 560; Lat. 34-08-53 N long. 117-59-53 W; SW California, 14 miles ENE of Los Angeles; Incorporated 1887. Named for William N. Monroe, a railroad construction engineer, who, with his associates, laid out the town in 1886 on 60 acres of Ranchos Santa Anita and Azusa de Duarte.

•**MONTEBELLO**, City, Los Angeles County; Pop. 52,929; Zip Code 906√0; Elev. 600; Lat. 34-00-34 N long. 118-06-16 N; 8 miles ESE of Los Angeles; Incorporated 1920. In 1887 Harris Newmark purchased part of the Repetto Ranch and called the entire settlement Montebello (Italian for "beautiful mountain"), but the town itself was named Newmark. Name changed to Montebello October 16, 1920.

•**MORAGA**, City, Contra Costa; Pop. 15,014; Zip Code 94556; Lat. 37-50-06 N long. 122-07-43 W; Preserves the name of Joaquin Moraga, in 1835 co-grantee of the rancho on which station and its valley are situated. He was probably the son of the explorer and soldier, Gabriel Moraga. Post office established May 5, 1886, and re-established December 16, 1915, when the town was developed.

•**MORGAN HILL**, City, Santa Clara County; Pop. 8,500; Zip Code 95037; Lat. 37-07-50 N long. 121-39-12 W; Western California, 17 miles SE of San Jose. Named in 1892 for Morgan Hill, on whose ranch the settlement developed.

•**MOUNT BALDY**, Town, San Bernardino and Los Angeles counties; Pop. 300 (summer 700); Zip Code 959; Originally known as Camp Baldy, but on July 1, 1851, the name of the post office was changed upon petition of the residents.

•**MOUNT EDEN**, Town, Alameda County; Pop. (included with Hayward) 94,600; Zip Code 94557; Elev. 25; Lat. 37-38-10 N long. 122-05-56 W; Reached by US 50; 3 miles from the San Mateo-Hayward Bay Bridge across San Francisco Bay.

•**MOUNT HEBRON**, Town, Siskiyou County; Pop. 175; Zip Code 96058; Elev. 4,256; Lat. 41-47-14 N long. 122-00-11 W; Near Macdoel, Name is that of an ancient town in Palestine. Appears as Mt. Hebron on the Land Office map of 1891.

•**MOUNT SHASTA**, Town, Siskiyou County; Pop. 2,837; Zip Code 96067; Elev. 3,554; Lat. 41-18-36 N long. 122-18-34 W; Reached by US 99 and 99W; Founded 1850's; Located near base of Mt. Shasta (14,162 feet) between Klamath and Shasta National Parks, for which town is named.

•**MURPHYS**, Village, Calaveras County; Pop. 1,183; Zip Code 95247; Elev. 2,171; Lat. 38-08-15 N long. 120-27-31 W; NE California. Here the brothers Murphy, John and Daniel, were the first to discover gold in 1849.

•**MURRIETTA HOT SPRINGS**, Town, Riverside County; Pop. 50; Zip Code 92362; Elev. 1,309; Lat. 33-33-38 N long. 117-09-26 W; Reached by US 395. Post office established 1885 and named for John Murietta, ranch owner and for many years bookkeeper in the sheriff's office.

•**MUSCOY**, city, San Bernardino County; Pop. 7,200; Zip Code 92405; Elev. 1,385; Lat. 34-09-14 N long. 117-20-36 W.

•**NAPA**, City, Napa County Seat; Pop. 50,879; Zip Code 94558; Elev. 17; Lat. 38-17-50 N long. 122-17-04 W; N Central California. Napa was an old Indian tribe here.

•**NATIONAL CITY**, City, San Diego County; Pop. 48,772; Zip Code 92050; Elev. 25; Lat. 32-40-41 N long. 117-05-54 W; SW corner of California, on San Diego Bay, 5 miles south of San Diego. Named in 1868 after the Rancho de la Nacion, on which town was laid out.

•**NATOMA**, Village, Sacramento County; Pop. (Rural); Zip Code 95801; Elev. 162; Lat. 38-39-18 N long. 121-10-49 W; N Central California; Name is Indian for "eastern," or "upstream."

•**NEEDLES**, City, San Bernardino County; Pop. 4,120; Zip Code 92363; Elev. 488; Lat. 34-50-53 N long. 114-36-48 W; Reached by US 66; On the Colorado River in the Mojave Desert near Hoover Dam; Founded February 1883 as rail center for the Santa Fe on the Arizona side of Colorado River and named after nearby needlelike peaks.

•**NELSON**, Town, Butte County; Pop. 75; Zip Code 95958; Elev. 12; Lat. 39-33-08 N long. 121-45-52 W; Reached by US 99E; In the middle of a wheat-growing area. Established early 1870's as a station on the California and Oregon Railroad and named for A. D. Nelson and his sons, farmers in the district.

•**NEVADA CITY**, Town, Nevada County Seat; Pop. 2,431; Zip Code 95959; Lat. 34-00-51 N long. 121-00-54 W; Eastern California, 45 miles west of Lake Tahoe; Elev. 2,450; Reached by Cal. Highway 49. Name (Spanish) means "snow-covered" or "white as snow."

•**NEWARK**, City, Alameda County; Pop. 32,126; Zip Code 94560; Elev. 16; Lat. 37-31-47 N long. 122-02-21 W; SE of San Francisco in W California. The Southern Pacific named its station (1876) after the former New Jersey home of A. E. Davis and his brother.

•**NEWBERRY SPRINGS**, Town, San Bernardino County; Pop. 650; Zip Code 92365; Lat. 34-49-37 N long. 116-41-13 W; Southern Pacific station named 1883. In 1919 the Santa Fe changed the name to Water because for a long period the springs here supplied the railroad with all the water it needed. Name Newberry restored 1922.

•**NEWBURY PARK**, Subdivision, Ventura County; Pop. (with Thousand Oaks); Zip Code 91359; Elev. 700; Lat. 34-11-03 N long. 113-85-55 W; S. California. This growing residential town was once a stagecoach stop. Postmaster E. S. Newbury named it for himself in 1875.

•**NEWCASTLE**, Town, Placer County; Pop. 900; Zip Code 95658; Elev. 970; Lat. 38-12-27 N long. 121-07-56 W; Reached by US 40; 5 miles from Loomis. Station of Central Pacific Railroad named in 1864 after the old mining town nearby.

•**NEWMAN**, Town, Stanislaus County; Pop. 2,785; Zip Code 95360; Elev. 91; Lat. 37-18-50 N long. 121-01-11 W; 21 miles south of Modesto. Name applied to the Southern Pacific station in 1887 for Simon Newman, local merchant who donated the land for the right-of-way of the railroad.

•**NEWPORT BEACH**, City, Orange County; Pop. 63,475; Zip Code 92260; Lat. 33-37-08 N long. 117-55-41 W; Reached by US 101; 1 mile from Balboa on Pacific Ocean, 18 miles SE of Long Beach; Incorporated 1906. Residential and resort subdivision established February 16, 1904, and named by McFadden brothers of Delaware in 1873 after their steamer *Newport*.

•**NICE**, Town, Lake County; Pop. 700; Zip Code 95464; Lat. 39-07-24 N long. 122-50-50 W; Old name, Clear Lake Villas, changed to present one by citizens (1927 or 1928) because the general topography of the district was thought to resemble the Riviera landscape near Nice in France.

•**NICOLAUS**, Town, Sutter County; Pop. 200; Zip Code 95659; Elev. 34; Lat. 38-54-12 N long. 121-34-36 W; Reached by Cal. Highway 24. Named for Nicholaus Allgeier, a German who operated a ferry on the Feather River at time of the Gold Rush.

•**NILAND**, Town, Imperial County; Pop. 950; Zip Code 92257; Elev. 141; Lat. 33-14-24 N long. 115-31-05 W; 30 feet below sea level; Reached by US 99 and 99W; At northern end of Imperial

Valley. Name is contraction of "Nile land," selected 1916 by Imperial Farm Lands Assn. because of fertility of the irrigated region.

•**NILES**, Town, Alameda County; Pop. (with Fremont); Zip Code 94536; NW Central California. Known as Vallejo Mills in the 1850's. The Southern Pacific Railroad named this station in 1869 for state Supreme Court Judge Addison Niles.

•**NIPOMO**, Town, San Luis Obispo County; Pop. 3,642; Zip Code 93444; Elev. 330; Lat. 35-02-34 N long. 120-28-30 W; Reached by US 101. A Chumash Indian rancheria, Nipoma, recorded in 1799. The present spelling was used in name of land grant in 1837.

•**NORCO**, City, Riverside County; Pop. 21,126; Zip Code 91760; SE California, 45 miles west of Palm Springs. The name was coined from North Corona Land Co. by Rex B. Clark in 1922.

•**NORTH COLUMBIA**, Village, Nevada County; Pop. Rural; Zip Code 95959; Elev. 3018; Lat. 39-22-22 N long. 120-59-10 W; NE California; Located near the N Yuba River in old gold mining country. Named for a mining camp in the county.

•**NORTH SAN JUAN**, Village, Nevada County; Pop. 135; Zip Code 95960; Lat. 39-22-10 N long. 121-06-10 W; NE California. Christian Kentz, a Mexican War veteran, saw a resemblance to San Juan De Ulloa in Mexico in the hill where he discovered gold here in 1853, so he named it accordingly.

•**NORWALK**, City, Los Angeles County; Pop. 85,232; Zip Code 90650; Lat. 33-54-08 N long. 118-04-51 W; SE of Los Angeles. Settled by Atwood and Gilbert Sproul (1877) and named Corvallis, after their former home town in Oregon. Renamed after Norwalk, Connecticut, when the post office was established in 1879.

•**NOVATO**, City, Marin County; Pop. 43,916; Zip code 94947; Elev. 18; Lat. 38-06-27 N long. 122-34-07 W; Reached by US 101; north of San Francisco. The name is found in Canada de Novato mentioned in 1828, and in land grants of 1836 and 1839. Probably the Spanish name of a chief of Hookoeko Indians who converted to Christianity at Mission San Rafael.

•**NOYO**, Village, Mendocino County; Pop. 500; Zip Code 95437; Lat. 39-25-42 N long. 123-48-08 W; NW California. Noyo was the name given by the Pomo Indians to their village on this site.

•**NUBIEBER**, Town, Lassen County; Pop. 250; Zip Code 96068; Elev. 41,169; Lat. 41-05-45 N long. 121-10-55 W; Reached by US 6. A lumbering town called New Town when extensions of the Great Northern and the Western Pacific railroads met here in 1861. Renamed after pioneer town called Bieber in the same year when the post office was established.

•**NUEVO**, Town, Riverside County; Pop. 500; Zip Code 92367; Lat. 33-48-05 N long. 117-08-42 W; Name (Spanish) means "new." Post office named 1916.

•**OAK VIEW**, City, Ventura County; Pop. 4,872; Zip code 93022; Elev. 520; Lat. 34-24-00 N long. 119-17-57 W; Named 1925 at a public meeting because of the garden-like appearance of the oak groves.

•**OAKDALE**, City, Stanislaus County; Pop. 8,474; Zip Code 95361; Elev. 155; Lat. 37-46-00 N long. 120-50-46 W; Reached by US 99 and 99W. Established and named when the Copperopolis and Visalia Railroad Reached here in 1871.

•**OAKLAND**, City, Alameda County Seat; Pop. 339,288; Elev. 42; Lat. 37-48-16 N long. 122-16-11 W; Horace W. Carpentier acquired a townsite in the present downtown Oakland, imported a few "residents" from the redwoods, and in 1852 incorporated the Town of Oakland, with himself in the mayor's chair, the name he selected from the numerous snads of *encinas* (evergreen oaks) that dotted the landscape.

•**OAKVILLE**, Village, Napa County; Pop. 300; Zip Code 94562; Elev. 155; Lat. 38-26-13 N long. 122-24-04 W; N Central California. Named for the trees growing in the area when the railroad came through in the 1870's.

•**OCEANO**, Town, San Luis Obispo County; Pop. 4,478; Zip Code 83445; Elev. 47; Lat. 33-11-45 N long. 117-22-43 W; W California. South of Pismo Beach, the nearby beach has sand dunes which pile up to surprising heights.

•**OCEANSIDE**, City, San Diego County; Pop. 76,698; Zip Code 92054; Elev. 45; Lat. 37-05-20 N long. 119-19-00 W; Reached by US 101; SW corner of California, on Gulf of Santa Catalina 45 miles north of San Diego near San Luis Rey Valley; Incorporated 1888. Established and named 1883 by J. C. Hayes.

•**OCCIDENTAL**, Town, Sonoma County; Pop. 300; Zip Code 95465; Elev. 578; Lat. 38-24-27 N long. 122-56-50 W; Name first given to a Methodist church erected here in April 1876 on land given by M. C. Meeker, who then laid out the town. Railroad station called Howard until 1891, for William Howard, a settler of 1849.

•**OILDALE**, City, Kern County; Pop. 20,500; Zip Code 93308; Elev. 455; Lat. 35-25-11 N long. 119-01-13 W.

•**OJAI**, City, Ventura County; Pop. 6,816; Zip Code 93023; Elev. 746; Lat. 34-26-53 N long. 119-14-31 W; Reached by US 399; In Ojai Valley (SW California) of the Sierra Madre Range, 23 miles east of Santa Barbara. Name derived from a Chumash Indian word, *a'hwai*, meaning "moon," which was applied to a land grant in 1837.

•**OLANCHA**, Town, Inyo County; Pop. 260; Zip Code 93549; Elev. 3,648; Lat. 36-16-55 N long. 118-00-20 W; Reached by US 395. Established 1870 with the name of a tribe of either Shoshonean or Yokuts Indians.

•**OLEMA**, Village, Marin County; Pop. 80; Zip Code 94950; Elev. 67; Lat. 38-02-27 N long. 122-47-13 W; W California. Built along a creek by the same name, Olema was named for an Indian word meaning "coyote valley."

•**OLEUM**, Village, Contra Costa County; No Pop; Zip Code 94595; Lat. 38-02-41 N long. 122-14-50 W; W California; Named by the Union Oil Company for petroleum when it built a refinery here in 1912.

•**OLIVEHURST**, City, Yuba County; Pop. 8,100; Zip Code 95961; Lat. 39-05-44 N long. 121-33-04 W; South of Marysville in the Feather River Valley.

•**OMO RANCH**, Town, El Dorado County; Pop. 200; Zip Code 95684; Lat. 38-34-53 N long. 120-34-20 W; Named after Indian village at founding in 1891. Post office established 1892. Near Somerset.

•**O'NEALS**, Town, Madera County; Pop. 10; Zip Code 93645; Lat. 37-07-42 N long. 119-41-36 W; Post office, established October 4, 1887, took its name from Charles O'Neal's hotel.

•**ONO**, Town, Shasta County; Pop. 85; Zip Code 96001; Elev. 981; Lat. 40-28-31 N long. 122-37-01 W; Reached by US 99 and 99W; When post office was established 1883 at Eagle Creek, the settlers chose the name of the Biblical town (I Chron. 8:12) at the suggestion of the Rev. William S. Kidder.

•**ONTARIO**, City, San Bernardino County; Pop. 88,820; Zip Code 91761; Elev. 988; Lat. 34-03-48 N long. 117-39-00 W; S Central California. Founded by Canadians in 1882, Ontario was named for their home province.

•ONYX, Town, Kern County; Pop. 80; Zip Code 93255; Lat. 35-41-25 N long. 118-13-11 W; Known as Scodie's Store since 1860s. When post office was established 1890, the name Scodie was rejected because of its similarity to Scotia in Humboldt County.

•OPHIR, Village, Placer County; Pop. Rural; Zip Code 95064; Elev. 850; Lat. 38-53-28 N long. 121-07-21 W; NE California. The town's name was originally Spanish Corral, but exchanged it for the name of King Solomon's treasure trove.

•ORANGE, City, Orange County; Pop. 91,788; Zip Code 92667; Elev. 187; Lat. 33-47-16 N long. 117-51-08 W; Founded as Richland 1868, renamed 1875; Name chosen to accent the developing orange culture in the district.

•ORANGE COVE, Town, Fresno County; Pop. 4,026; Zip Code 93646; Elev. 425; Lat. 36-37-28 N long. 119-18-46 W; South central California, Situated in a "cove" in the Sierra foothills where citrus fruit thrives. Named (1913) after the Orosi Orange Lands Co.

•ORANGEVALE, City, Sacramento County; Pop. 16,493; Zip Code 95662; Elev. 237; Lat. 38-40-43 N long. 121-13-29 W.

•ORCUTT, Town, Santa Barbara County; Pop. 700; Zip Code 93454; Elev. 314; Lat. 34-51-55 N long. 120-26-06 W; Reached by Cal. Highway 1. Laid out by the Union Oil Co. (1903) and named for the company's geologist, W. W. Orcutt.

•ORICK, Town, Humboldt County; Pop. 900; Zip Code 95555; Elev. 34; Lat. 41-17-13 N long. 124-03-31 W; Reached by US 101. Name derived from that of the Bald Hill Indians, who were called Oruk by the Coast Indians.

•ORINDA, City, Contra Costa County; Pop. 18,700; Zip Code 94563; Lat. 37-52-38 N long. 122-10-43 W; NE of Oakland. Name transferred to the village from Orinda Park, the estate of Theodore Wagner, U.S. Surveyor General for California (1880).

•ORLAND, Town, Glenn County; Pop. 3,976; Zip Code 95963; Elev. 260; Lat. 39-44-51 N long. 122-11-43 W; Name given to commemorate the English birthplace of a settler.

•ORLEANS, Town, Humboldt County; Pop. 600; Zip Code 95556; Elev. 400; Lat. 41-18-06 N long. 123-32-24 W; Settled in 1850 and called New Orleans Bar, probably after the city in Louisiana.

•ORO GRANDE, Town, San Bernardino County Seat; Pop. 700; Zip Code 92368; Elev. 2,631; Lat. 34-33-55 N long. 117-20-00 W; Name goes back to that of a gold-mining camp. On May 1, 1925, name of the post office changed to Oro Grande, after the nearby mine.

•OROSI, Town, Tulare County; Pop. 2,757; Zip Code 93647; Elev. 373; Lat. 36-32-42 N long. 119-17-11 W; Name coined from oro, Spanish word for "gold," by Neal McCallan because the fields around were covered with golden poppies.

•OTTERBEIN, Town, Los Angeles County; Pop. (included with Rowland) 25,000; Zip Code 91745; Elev. 508; Lat. 33-59-15 N long. 117-53-02 W; In 1910 Bishop William M. Bell established a settlement for retired ministers of the Church of the United Brethren in Christ and named it in honor of the founder of the church, Philip W. Otterbein.

•OWENS LAKE, Inyo County. John C. Fremont named the lake in 1845 for Richard Owens, of Ohio, a member of his third expedition (1845-46), captain of Company A of the California Battalion, and his "Secretary of State."

•OXNARD, City, Ventura County; Pop. 108,195; Zip Code 93030; Elev. 52; Lat. 34-11-51 N long. 119-10-34 W; When the Southern Pacific branch from Ventura to Burbank was built in 1898-1900, the station was named for Henry T. Oxnard, who had established a beet-sugar refinery here in 1897.

•PACHECO, Town, Contra Costa County; Pop. 1,900; Zip Code 94553; Lat. 37-59-01 N long. 122-04-27 W; Named in 1858 for Salvio Pacheco, a native of Monterey and a former soldier who settled in 1844 on Rancho Monte del Diablo, granted to him in 1834.

•PACIFICA, City, San Mateo County, Pop. 36,866; Zip Code 94044; Elev. 76; Lat. 37-36-50 N long. 122-29-09 W; On Pacific coast south of San Francisco. Residential community created in 1957 when 9 communities incorported and chose the name, which alludes to their location along the ocean.

•PACIFIC GROVE, City, Monterey County; Pop. 15,755; Zip Code 93950; Elev. 120; Lat. 36-37-44 N long. 121-55-44 W; Western California, at south end of Monterey Bay; Founded 1874.

•PAICINES, Town, San Benito County; Pop. 100; Zip Code 95043; Lat. 36-43-44 N long. 121-16-39 W; Named after the Rancho Cienega de los Paicines, granted October 5, 1842, which derived its name from a Costanoan Indian Village called Paisi-n.

•PALA, Town, San Diego County; Pop. 250; Zip Code 92059; Lat. 33-21-55 N long. 117-04-33 W; May be a Luiseno Indian word meaning "water."

•PALERMO, Town, Butte County; Pop. 1,966; Zip Code 95968; Elev. 192; Lat. 39-26-08 N long. 121-32-13 W; Named 1887 after capital of Sicily because land and climate are suited for olive growing.

•PALMDALE, City, Los Angeles County; Pop. 12,277; Zip Code 93550; Elev. 2,659; SW California; Founded 1886 by German Lutherans and named for yucca palm, the Joshua Tree.

•PALM DESERT, City, Riverside County; Pop. 11,801; Zip Code 92260; Elev. 2,659; Lat. 34-34-46 N long. 118-06-56 W; On an alluvial fan near Palm Springs; Incorporated 1973.

•PALM SPRINGS, City, Riverside County; Pop. 32,271; Zip Code 92262; Elev. 466; Lat. 33-49-49 N long. 116-32-40 W; Originally named Palmetto Spring (1849) for the trees here; also called Big Palm Spring and Agua Caliente because of the hot springs.

•PALO ALTO, City, Santa Clara County; Pop. 55,225; Zip Code 943 zone; Elev. 23; Lat. 37-26-31 N long. 122-08-31 W; Named by Palau, a member of the Anza expedition (1774). Name (Spanish) means "tall trees," in reference to the redwoods nearby.

•PALOS VERDES ESTATES, City, Los Angeles County; Pop. 14,376; Zip Code 90274; Elev. 217; Lat. 33-48-02 N long. 118-23-21 W; Name of residential city derived from Canada de los Palos Verdes ("valley of green trees or timber").

•PALO VERDE, Town, Imperial County; Pop. 600; Zip Code 92266. Name derived from Spanish word for a small tree with bright green bark.

•PANORMA HEIGHTS. Town, Orange County; Pop. 1,800; Zip Code 92705; Lat. 33-46-40 N long. 117-47-50 W; Near Santa Ana.

•PARADISE, City, Butte County; Pop. 22,571; Zip Code 95969; Elev. 1,708; Lat. 39-44-47 N long. 121-38-10 W; founded 1879. Name spelled Paradice in 1900, Town could have been named after the Pair o' Dice Saloon or might be just a misspelling of present name.

•PARAMOUNT. City, Los Angeles County; Pop. 36,407; Zip Code 90723; Elev. 67; Lat. 33-53-22 N long. 809-32 W; Named for the movie company.

•**PARKFIELD**, Town, Monterey County; Pop. 30; Zip Code 93451; Lat. 35-53-59 N long. 120-25-54 W; Post Office Dept. rejected original name, Russelsville, in 1883. Postmaster Sittenfelt selected present name because of the surrounding natural oak park.

•**PARLIER**, City, Fresno County; Pop. 2,680; Zip Code 93648; Lat. 36-36-42 N long. 119-31-34 W; S Central California.

•**PASADENA**, City, Pop. 119,374; Elev. 865; Lat. 34-08-52 N long. 118-08-37 W; Pasadena lies in the foothills of the Sierra Madre Mountains.

•**PASKENTA**, Town, Tehama County; Pop. 200; Zip Code 96074; Lat. 39-53-05 N long. 122-32-41 W; Name derived from Central Wintun Indian word, *paskenti*, meaning "under the bank."

•**PASO ROBLES**, City, San Luis Obispo County; Pop. 7,168; Zip Code 93446; Elev. 721; Lat. 35-37-36 N long. 120-41-24 W; Founded 1886 with the name El Paso de Robles ("pass of oaks"). Name Paso de Robles applied to a land grant in 1844.

•**PATTERSON**, Town, Stanislaus County; Pop. 3,866; Zip Code 95363; Elev. 97; Lat. 37-28-18-N long. 121-07-43 W; 12 miles SW of Modesto. Laid out by a Fresno banker, Thomas W. Patterson in 1910 and named for his uncle, John D. Patterson, who purchased the land in 1864.

•**PEARBLOSSOM**, Town, Los Angeles County; Pop. 1,200; Zip Code 93553; Lat. 34-30-23 N long. 117-54-32 W; Named in 1924 by Guy C. Chase because it was then a center of pear orchards.

•**PEBBLE BEACH**, Town, Monterey County; Pop. 4,000; Zip Code 93953; Name developed locally because there is a beach with pebbles at this point, and was accepted by the Pacific Improvement Co. when it acquired the property in 1880.

•**PEDLEY**, Town, Riverside County; Pop. 4,300; Zip Code 92509; Lat. 33-58-31 N long. 117-28-30 W; Station named for Francis X. Pedley, at that time engaged in real estate promotion at Arlington.

•**PENRYN**, Village, Placer County; Pop. 320; Zip Code 95663; Elev. 619; Lat. 38-51-08 N long. 121-10-06 W; NE California. Griffith Griffith named this town for his birthplace of Penrhyn, Wales, Great Britain.

•**PERKINS**, Village, Sacramento County; Pop. (with Rosemount); Zip Code 95826; Elev. 48; Lat. 38-32-47 N long. 121-23-50 W; N Central California. The town was named for early settler and postmaster Thomas Perkins, a native of Massachusetts.

•**PERRIS**, Town, Riverside County; Pop. 6,740; Zip Code 92370; Elev. 1,457; Lat. 33-46-57 N long. 117-13-40 W; Laid out and named for Fred T. Perris, chief engineer of California Southern Railroad and one of the founders of the town.

•**PESCADERO**, Town, San Mateo County; Pop. 450; Zip Code 94060; Elev. 56; Lat. 37-15-18 N long. 122-22-49 W; In maritime Spanish, name is word used for "fishing place."

•**PETALUMA**, City, Sonoma County; Pop. 33,384; Zip Code 94952; Elev. 12; Lat. 38-13-57 N long. 122-38-08 W; Its Indian name means "beaUtiful view."

•**PETROLIA**, Town, Humboldt County; Pop. 50; Zip Code 95558; Lat. 40-19-32 N long. 124-17-09 W; First California oil deposits to be commercially exploited were found NE of the town by a U.S. Army officer in 1861.

•**PHILO**, Town, Mendocino County; Pop. 700; Zip Code 95466; Lat. 39-03-57 N long. 123-26-38 W; Named 1868 by Cornelius Prather: landowner and first postmaster, for his favorite female cousin, Philomena.

•**PICO RIVERA**, City, Los Angeles County; Pop. 53,459; Zip Code 90660; Elev. 161; Lat. 33-58-59 N long. 118-05-45 W; SE of Los Angeles in SW California.

•**PIEDMONT**, City, Alameda County; Pop. 10,498; Zip Code 94611; Lat. 37-49-28 N long. 122-13-50 W; Name, of French or Italian origin, means "at the foot of the mountain."

•**PIERCY**, Town, Mendocino County; Pop. 200; Zip Code 95467; Lat. 39-57-59 N long. 123-47-39 W; Name given to post office (1920) for Sam Piercy, the oldest white settler of the district.

•**PINEDALE**, Town, Fresno County; Pop. 2,300; Zip Code 93650; Lat. 36-50-84 N long. 119-47 20 W.

•**PINE GROVE**, Village, Amador County; Pop. 1,049; Zip Code 95665; Elev. 2,100; Lat. 38-24-47 N long. 120-39-28 W; E California. Name is descriptive of this mountain resort.

•**PINEHURST**, Town, Fresno County; Pop. 80 (summer 200); Zip Code 93641; Lat. 36-41-43 N long. 119-00-56 W; Near Miramonte.

•**PINE KNOT VILLAGE**, Village, San Bernardino County; Pop. (with Big Bear Lake); S California; In San Bernardino Mountain; Part of the Big Bear lakes resort community.

•**PINE VALLEY**, Village, San Diego County; Pop. 300; Zip Code 92062; Elev. 3,736; Lat. 32-49-17 N long. 116-31-42 W; S California; In Cleveland National Forest. This resort was settled in 1869 by Major William Emory.

•**PINOLE**, City, Contra Costa County; Pop. 14,253; Zip Code 94564; Elev. 21; 38-00-16 N long. 122-1 7-52 W; W California; Name is Indian for "parched grain."

•**PIRU**, Town, Ventura County; Pop. 990; Zip Code 93040; Elev. 692; Lat. 34-24-55 N long. 118-47-35 W; Name derived from Shoshonean Indian word, *pi-idhu-ku*, the name of a plant.

•**PISMO BEACH**, City, San Luis Obispo County; Pop. 5,364; Zip Code 93449; Elev. 33; Lat. 35-08-34 N long. 120-38-25 W; Anza camped near the site (1776), which was named with the Chumash Indian word meaning "tar."

•**PITTSBURG**, City, Contra Costa County; Pop. 33,034; Zip Code 94565; Lat. 38-01-41 N long. 121-53-01 W; named after the industrial city in Pennsylvania.

•**PIXLEY**, Town, Tulare County; Pop. 1,584; Zip Code 93256; Elev. 271; Lat. 35-58-07 N long. 119-17-27 W; Reached by US 99 and 99W. Named for Frank Pixley, founder and editor of the San Francisco Argonaut in 1880s.

•**PLACENTIA**, City, Orange County; Pop. 35,041; Zip Code 92670; Elev. 172 feet; Lat. 33-52-20 N long. 117-52-10 W; In June, 1879, Sarah Jane McFadden named the school "Placentia," which literally translated means "A Pleasant Place."

•**PLACERVILLE**, City, El Dorado County Seat; Pop. 6,739; Zip Code 95661; Elev. 1,866; Lat. 38-43-47 N long. 120-47-51 W; Reached by Cal. Highway 49; Named Placerville in 1850 because of the presence of rich placer holes.

•**PLANADA**, Town, Merced County; Pop. 2,406; Zip Code 95365; Lat. 37-17-27 N long. 120-19-03 W; Central California. Named for the Spanish word for "plain" after a contest among residents in 1911.

•**PLATINA**, Town, Shasta County; Pop. 100; Zip Code 96076. Post office established April 23, 1921, and named because it is in an area of platinum ore.

•**PLEASANT HILL**, City, Contra Cost County; Pop. 25,124; Zip Code 94523; Lat. 37-56-53 N long. 122-03-35W; Residential city NE of Oakland in the Intermont Basins.

•**PLEASANTON**, City, Alameda County; Pop. 35,160; Zip Code 94566; Elev. 352; Lat. 37-39-45 N long. 121-52-25 W; Named 1867 for Gen. Alfred Pleasonton by John W. Kottinger, an Austrian Pioneer of 1851.

•**PLYMOUTH**, Town, Amador County; Pop. 699; Zip Code 95669; Elev. 1,086; Lat. 38-28-55 N long. 120-50-37 W; Reached by Cal. Highway 49. Named after the nearby Plymouth Mines, active since the 1850s.

•**POLLOCK PINES**, Town, El Dorado County; Pop. 950; Zip Code 95776; Elev. 3,940; Lat. 38-45-41 N long. 120-35-08 W; Post office established 1935 and named for the grove of pines belonging to the first settlers.

•**POMONA**, City, Los Angeles County; Pop. 92,742; Zip Code 91766; Elev. 816; Lat. 34-03-19 N long. 117-45-05 W; Residential and commercial suburb of Los Angeles established and named in 1875 for Roman goddess of orchards and gardens and incorporated 1888.

•**PONDOSA**, Town, Siskiyou County; Pop. 100; Zip Code 96077; Lat. 41-11-58-N long. 121-41-16 W; Post office established 1926 and named for trade name of ponderosa pine.

•**POPE VALLEY**, Town, Napa County; Pop. 300; Zip Code 94567; Elev. 706; Lat. 38-36-55 N long. 122-25-36 W; Named for William Pope, a member of Pattie's party in 1828 and grantee of the Locaoallomi grant in 1841.

•**PORT COSTA**, Town, Contra Costa County; Pop. 300; Zip Code 94569; Lat. 38-02-47 N long. 122-10-56 W; Name applied to station of the Southern Pacific in 1878 because it was in Central Costa County and situated on the coast.

•**PORT HUENEME**, City, Ventura County; Pop. 17,803; Zip Code 93041; Elev. 12; Lat. 34-08-52 N long. 119-11-39 W; Seaport with a fine harbor bears name of a Chumash Indian village, given to it in 1856.

•**PORTERVILLE**, City, Tulare County; Pop. 19,707; Zip Code 93257; Elev. 459; Lat. 36-03-55 N long. 119-00-57 W; In 1859, Royal Porter Putnam operated a stage depot known as Porter's Station. In 1864, he laid out the town and named it Portersville.

•**PORTOLA**, Town, Plumas County; Pop. 1,885; Zip Code 96122; Elev. 4,834; Lat. 39-48-38 N long. 120-28-05 W; Post office established 1910 and named for Gaspar de Portola, leader of an expedition in 1769.

•**PORTOLA VALLEY**, City, San Mateo County; Pop. 3,939; Zip Code 94025; Lat. 37-23-03 N long. 122-14-03 W; Rural residential community, once a lumbering center, named for region's early explorer but pronounced in the American style.

•**POTTER VALLEY**, Town, Mendocino County; Pop. 200; Zip Code 95469; Elev. 945; Lat. 39-19-20 N long. 123-06-43 W; Named for first white settlers in the Chico region, William Potter and his brother, who arrived here in the early 1850s.

•**POWAY**, City, San Diego County; Pop. 15,000; Zip Code 92064; Lat. 32-57-46 N long. 117-02-06 W; Name derived from Paguay, mentioned as a rancho in 1828, a land grant in 1839, and an arroyo in 1841.

•**POZO**, Village, San Luis Obispo County; Pop. Rural; Zip Code 93453; Elev. 145; Lat. 35-18-13 N long. 120-22-32 W; W California. Name means "well" in Spanish.

•**PRINCETON**, Town, Colusa County; Pop. 500; Zip Code 95970; Lat. 39-24-12 N long. 122-00-32 W; Post office established 1858 and named at the suggestion of Dr. Almon Lull, a graduate of Princeton University.

•**PROBERTA**, Town, Tehama County; Pop. 250; Zip Code 96078; Elev. 245; Lat. 40-04-54 N long. 122-10-10 W; Name applied to Southern Pacific Railroad station in 1889 in honor of Edward Probert.

•**QUINCY**, Town, Plumas County Seat; Pop. 2,500; Zip Code 95971; Elev. 3,432; Lat. 39-56-13 N long. 120-56-46 W; Grew around hotel built by H. J. Bradley on his American Ranch (early 1850s) and named in 1854 for Bradley's home town in Illinois.

•**RACKERBY**, Town, Yuba County; Pop. 150; Zip Code 95972; Lat. 39-26-23 N long. 121-20-25 W; This is an old mining camp named for pioneer William Rackerby during the rush of '49.

•**RAMONA**, Town, San Diego County; Pop. 4,200; Zip Code 92065; Elev. 1,500; Lat. 38-32-51 N long. 121-24-28 W; Named for Helen Hunt Jackson's popular romance of 1884.

•**RANCHO CORDOVA**, City, Sacramento County; Pop. 35,400; Zip Code 95670; Elev. 77; Lat. 38-35-21 N long. 121-18-06 W; Urban community named 1955 after the Cordova Vineyards on the Rancho de los Americanos grant.

•**RANCHO MIRAGE**, City, Riverside County; Pop. 6,281; Zip Code 92270; Lat. 33-44-23 N long. 116-24-43 W; SE California.

•**RANCHO SANTA FE**, Town, San Diego County; Pop. 2,500; Zip Code 92067; Elev. 245; Lat. 33-01-13 N long. 117-12-07 W; In 1906, the Santa Fe Railroad purchased the San Dieguito Ranch for experimental planting of eucalyptus trees and gave it the present name.

•**RANDSBURG**, Town, Kern County; Pop. 600; Zip Code 93554; Elev. 3,523; Lat. 35-22-07 N long. 117-39-26 W; Central California. Park of the Rand Quadrangle, a productive mining district, this settlement was named for the gold mining district in the Transvaal, South Africa.

•**RAVENDALE**, Town, Lassen County; Pop. 30; Zip Code 96123; Elev. 5,299; Lat. 40-47-55 N long. 120-21-51 W; Reached by US 395; Post office established 1910.

•**RAYMOND**, Town, Madera County; Pop. 300; Zip Code 93653; Lat. 37-13-02 N long. 119-54-16 W; Named for Walter Raymond of the Raymond-Whitcomb Yosemite Tours, which started at this point.

•**RED BLUFF**, City, Tehama County Seat; Pop. 9,490; Zip Code 96080; Elev. 309; Lat. 40-10-43 N long. 122-14-l5 W; Known first as Leodocia, then as Covertsburg (1853). Laid out in 1854 and named Red Bluffs.

•**REDDING**, City, Shasta County Seat; Pop. 41,995; Zip Code 96001; Elev. 567; Lat. 40-35-12 N long. 122-23-26 W; Laid out in 1872 by B. B. Redding, a land agent for the Central Pacific Railroad.

•**REDLANDS**, City, San Bernardino county; Pop. 43,619; Zip Code 92373; Elev. 1,302; Lat. 34-01-54 N long. 117-12-28 W; Named for the colored soil on which are raised citrus fruits and other crops.

•**REDONDO BEACH**, City, Los Angeles County; Pop. 57,102; Zip Code 90277; Elev. 59; Lat. 33-50-57 N long. 118-23-15 W; Name derived from adjacent Rancho Sausal Redondo ("round willow grove").

•**REDWOOD CITY**, City, San Mateo County Seat; Pop. 54,965; Zip Code 94061; Elev. 15; Lat. 37-29-10 N long. 122-14-00 W; A lumber center and port named not so much because of the beautiful stands of redwoods once surrounding the site as for their commercial exploitation on a large scale.

•**REDWOOD TERRACE**, Town, San Mateo County; Pop. 50; Zip Code 94020; Lat. 37-18-53 N long. 122-17-38 W; Near La Honda.

59

•**REDWOOD VALLEY**, Town, Mendocino County; Pop. 500; Zip Code 95470; Elev. 708; Lat. 39-15-56 N long. 123-12-12 W.

•**REEDLEY**, City, Fresno County; Pop. 11,071; Zip Code 93654; Elev. 348; Lat. 36-35-47 N long. 119-26-58 W; Named for Thomas L. Reed, a veteran of Sherman's march to the sea, who in 1888 gave half of his holdings to the city.

•**REQUA**, Village, Del Norte County; Pop. 100; Zip Code 95548; Elev. 1; Lat. 41-32-49 N long. 124-03-55 W; E NW California. Requa is an Indian word meaning "mouth of the creek," and was the name of a tribe's village on this site.

•**RHEEM VALLEY**, Town, Contra Costa County; Pop. (included with Moraga) 11,327; Zip Code 94570; Lat. 37-51-36 N long. 122-07-22 W; Development on east slope of Mulholland Hill started by Donald L. Rheem.

•**RIALTO**, City, San Bernardino County; Pop. 35,615; Zip Code 92376; Elev. 1,205; Lat. 34-09-08 N long. 117-22-13 W; Founded and named by a group of Methodists from Halstead, Kansas, after the Rivus Altos, familiarly called Rialto--the Grand Canal of Venice.

•**RICE**, Town, San Bernardino County; Pop. 5; Zip Code 92280; Elev. 935; Lat. 34-05-01 N long. 114-50-56 W; Near Vidal. Santa Fe station named (before 1919) for Guy R. Rice, chief engineer of the California Southern Railroad.

•**RICHGROVE**, Town, Tulare County; Pop. 1,023; Zip Code 93261; Lat. 35-47-48 N long. 119-06-25 W; Developed and named in 1909 by S. R. Shoup and W. H. Wise of the Richgrove Development Co.

•**RICHMOND**, City, Contra Costa County; Pop. 74,676; Zip Code 948+; Elev. 55; Lat. 37-56-09 N long. 122-20-48 W; Name applied to the point by Coast Survey in 1852 and to the city in 1905.

•**RICHVALE**, Village, Butte County; Pop. 550; Zip Code 95974; Elev. 106; Lat. 39-29-38 N long. 121-44-37 W; N Central California. Samuel J. Nunn plotted and named the town in 1909, describing the character of the valley here.

•**RIO DELL**, Town, Humboldt County; Pop. 2,687; Zip Code 95562; Elev. 00126; Lat. 40-29-58 N long. 124-06-19 W; When post office was established in 1890, the name River Dell was suggested but was considered too similar to Riverdale. Rio, Spanish word for "river," then substituted.

•**RIO VISTA**, Town, Solano County; Pop. 3,142; Zip Code 94571; Elev. 22; Lat. 38-09-21 N long. 121-41-25 W; Founded 1857 by Col. N. H. Davis and called Brazos del Rio because it was near the three arms of the Sacramento River. Renamed in 1860.

•**RIPLEY**, Town, Riverside County; Pop. 500; Zip Code 92272; Elev. 248; Lat. 33-31-31 N long. 114-31-91 W; Terminus of Ripley branch of the Santa Fe named 1921 for E. P. Ripley, former president of the railroad.

•**RIPON**, Town, San Joaquin County; Pop. 3,509; Zip Code 95366; Elev. 62; Lat. 37-44-30 N long. 121-07-24 W; Named 1876 after Wisconsin home town of the first postmaster, Applias Crooks.

•**RIVERBANK**, Town, Stanislaus County; Pop. 5,695; Zip Code 95367; Lat. 37-44-10 N long. 120-56-04 W; In 1911, the Santa Fe Railroad established a new terminal and division point south of Burneyville named for its location on the Stanislaus River.

•**RIVERDALE**, Town, Fresno County; Pop. 1,722; Zip Code 93656; Lat. 36-25-52 N long. 119-51-31 W; When post office was established in 1875, the new name was chosen because of town's proximity to Kings River.

•**RIVERSIDE**, City, Riverside County Seat; Pop. 170,876; Zip Code 925+; Elev. 858; Lat. 33-71-21 N long. 117-23-43 W; Settled 1870s; Settlement began with the silk-making colony of Louis Prevost (1869), followed by a canal and township development with present name (1871).

•**ROAD'S END**, Town, Tulare County; Pop. 50; Zip Code 93238; Near Kernville. Post office named because it was at end of the road from Kernville.

•**ROBBINS**, Town, Sutter County; Pop. 450; Zip Code 95676; Elev. 18; Lat. 38-52-13 N long. 121-42-19 W; Named 1925 by Sutter Basin Co. for its president, George B. Robbins.

•**ROCKLIN**, Town Placer County; Pop. 7,344; Zip Code 95677; Elev. 248; Lat. 38-47-27 N Long. 121-14-05 W; Name suggested by nearby quarries, applied to station when the Central Pacific Railroad built the line from Sacramento to Newcastle in 1863-64.

•**RODEO**, City, Contra Costa County; Pop. 5,356; Zip Code 94572; Elev. 15; Lat. 38-01-59 N Long. 122-15-57 W; Name is Mexican-Spanish word meaning "a cattle round up."

•**ROHNERT PARK**, City, Sonoma County; Pop. 22,965; Zip Code 94928; Lat. 38-20-23 N Long. 122-42-00 W; W Central California; 5 mi. S of Santa Rosa. Named for the Waldo Rohnert Seed Farm located here.

•**ROHNERVILLE**, Town, Humboldt County; Pop. (included with Fortuna) 7,210; Zip Code 95540 Lat. 40-34-02 N Long. 124-08-04 W. Named for Henry Rohner, a Swiss who, with a man named Feigenbaum, opened a store here in 1859.

•**ROLINDA**, Town, Fresno County; Pop. 100; Zip Code 93705; Lat. 36-44-07 N Long. 119-57-39 W; Near Fresno.

•**ROLLING HILLS ESTATES**, City, Los Angeles County; Pop. 9,412; Zip Code 90274; Lat. 33-47-16 N Long. 118-21-26 W; 10 miles west of Long Beach.

•**ROMOLAND**, Town, Riverside County; Pop. 700; Zip Code 92380; Lat. 33-44-45 N Long. 117-10-27 W. Name Ramola chosen for new development by promoters about 1925. Post Office Dept. requested substitution of new name and spelling.

•**ROSAMOND**, Town, Kern county; Pop. 2,281; Zip Code 93560; Elev. 2310; Lat. 34-51-51 N Long. 118-09-45 W; Reached by US 6. Station named about 1888 for daughter of a Southern Pacific Railroad official.

•**ROSEMEAD**, City, Los Angeles County; Pop. 42,604; Zip Code 91770; Elev. 322; Lat. 34-04-50 N Long. 118-04-19 W; East of Alhambra near El Monte. Name originally applied (1870s) to the famous horse farm on Leonard J. Rose's Sunny Slope estate.

•**ROSEVILLE**, City, Placer County; Pop. 24,347; Zip Code 95678; Elev. 160; Lat. 38-45-08 N Long. 121-17-13 W; Name, applied to the station when the Central Pacific reached the Place (1864); was chosen by residents, at picnic, in honor of the most popular girl present.

•**ROSS**, Town, Marin County; Pop. 2,682; Zip Code 94957; Elev. 23; Lat. 37-57-45 N Long. 122-33-14 W; Named for James Ross, who acquired Rancho Punta de Quintin in 1859.

•**RUBIDOUX**, City, Riverside County; Pop. 12,400; Zip code 92509; Elev. 780; Lat. 33-59-46 N Long. 117-24-17 W; Name (misspelled) honors French pioneer Louis Robidoux who acquired a Part of Rancho Jurupa on which peak is located.

•**RUTHERFORD**, Town, Napa County; Pop. 450; Zip Code 94573; Elev. 183; Lat. 38-27-31 N Long. 122-25-17 W; NW California. It was named for early settler Thomas Rutherford.

•**RYDE**, Village, Sacramento County; Pop. 200; Zip Code 95680; Elev. 11; Lat. 38-14-19 N Long. 121-33-34 W; N Central California.

William Kesner laid out the town in 1892, and named it for the town on the Isle of Wight, England.

•**SACRAMENTO**, City, Sacramento County Seat and capital of California; Pop. 275,741; Zip Code 95813; Elev. 30 Lat. 38-34-54 N Long. 121-29-36 W; First settled by John A. Sutter in 1839 and incorporated as a town in 1848; Incorporated, city, in 1863; Named in honor of the Catholic sacrament by Jose Moraga, presidio commander of San Jose.

•**SALIDA**, Town, Stanislaus County; Pop. 1,456; Zip Code 95368; Elev. 70; Lat. 37-42-21 N Long. 121-05-02 W; Station named in 1870 by Southern Pacific Railroad with Spanish word meaning "departure."

•**SALINAS**, City, Monterey County Seat; Pop. 80,479; Zip Code 93901; Elev. 53; Lat. 36-40-40 N Long. 121-39-16 W; Name derived from the salt marshes at the mouth of the Salinas River.

•**SALTDALE**, Town, Kern County; Pop. 40; Zip Code 93519; Elev. 1927; Lat. 35-21-33 N Long. 117-53-12 W; Near Cantil. Named to describe peculiar taste of the water, which may come from presence of common salt or medicinal salts.

•**SALYER**, Town, Trinity County; Pop. 600; Zip Code 95563; Elev. 600; Lat. 40-53-25 N Long. 123-35-00 W; Post office established April 16, 1918, and named for Charles Marshall Salyer, a man prominent in mining.

•**SAMOA**, Town, Humboldt County; Pop. 600; Zip Code 95564; Elev. 97; Lat. 40-49-08 N Long. 124-11-07 W; Reached by US 101. Lumber town developed (1890s) by Samoa Land and Improvement Co. and named because the crisis in the Samoan Islands was emphasized in the newpapers and because Humboldt Bay was assumed to be similar to the harbor of Pago Pago.

•**SAN ANDREAS**, Town, Calaveras County Seat; Pop. 1,564; Zip Code 95249 1008; Elev. 1,008. Located on San Andreas Fault.

•**SAN ANSELMO**, Town, Marin County; Pop. 11,927; Zip Code 94960; Elev. 45; Lat. 37-58-29 N Long. 122-33-38 W; 14 miles NW of San Francisco in W California.

•**SAN ARDO**, Town, Monterey County; Pop. 350; Zip Code 93450; Elev. 459; Lat. 36-01-14 N Long. 120-54-15 W; Laid out (1886) when Southern Pacific Railroad reached by the place and was named San Bernardo by M. J. Brandenstein, buyer of the San Bernardo Rancho, June 16, 1841. Post Office Dept. objected to name because of possible confusion with San Bernardino, so Brandenstein created a new saint's name by lopping off "Bern."

•**SAN BERNARDINO**, City, San Bernardino County Seat; Pop. 118,057; Zip Code 924+; Elev. 1,049; Lat. 34-07-17 N Long. 117-18-08 W; Citrus-packing center named for St. Bernardino of Siena, Italy, a great Franciscan preacher of the fifteenth century.

•**SAN BRUNO**, City, San Mateo County; Pop. 35,417; Zip Code 94066 373750N1222436W; Elev. 50; Named after Richard Cunningham's San Bruno House (1862).

•**SAN BUENAVENTURA (VENTURA)**, City, Ventura County; Pop. 74,474; Zip Code 930--; 23 miles SE of Santa Barbara in SW California.

•**SAN CARLOS**, City, San Mateo County; Pop. 24,710; Zip Code 94070; Elev. 40; Lat. 37-29-47 N Long. 122-15-27 W; ; Name chosen because it was believed that the Portola expedition first saw San Francisco Bay on November 4, 1769, St. Charles' feast day, from the Hills behind the present town.

•**SAN CLEMENTE**, City, Orange County; Pop. 27,325; Zip Code 92672; Elev. 200; Lat. 33-25-37 N Long. 117-36-40 W; SW California. The town was founded in 1925 by a Los Angeles realtor and named it for Saint Clement, which is also the name of an island 60 miles northwest in the Pacific.

•**SAN DIEGO**, Pop. 875,504. Elev. 0-822. Lat. 32-45-5 N Long. 117-09-23 W. The oldest Spanish settlement in California, first visited in 1539 by Father Marcos and his followers. A mission was esttablished there in 1769 by Governor Portola with Franciscan friars and soldiers. he city was first called "Davis's Folly for William Heath Davis who first built there.

•**SAN DIMAS**, City, Los Angeles County; Pop. 24,014; Zip Code 91773; Elev. 952; Lat. 34-06-24 N Long. 117-48-21 W; 25 miles E of Los Angeles in SW California.

•**SAN FERNANDO**, City, Los Angeles County; Pop. 17,731; Zip Code 91340; Elev. 1061; Lat. 34-16-55 N 118-26-17 W; Mission established 1797, honored St. Ferdinand, King of Castile and Leon in the thirteenth century.

•**SAN FRANCISCO**, Pop. 678,974; Elev. 6-956; Lat. 37-46-30 N Long. 122-25-06 W; Settlement bega in 1776 when Don Juan Bautista de Anza erected shelters for some 200 colonists and Father Junipero Serra established a mission named San Francisco de Asis, later known as Mission Dolores.

•**SAN GABRIEL**, City, Los Angeles County; Pop. 30,072; Zip Code 91775; Elev. 430; Lat. 34-05-46 N Long. 118-06-18 W;

•**SAN GREGORIO**, Town, San Mateo County; Pop. 300; Zip Code 94074; Elev. 100; Lat. 37-I9-38 N long. I22-23-08 W; 3-Reached by Cal. Highway 1. Name of St. Gregory applied to a land grant dated April 16, 1839, and to the post office in the 1870s.

•**SAN JACINTO**, Town, Riverside County; Pop. 7,098; Zip Code 92383; Elev. 1,550; Lat. 33-47-02 N long. II6-57-28 W; n San Jacinto Viejo was a cattle ranch of Mission San Luis Rey in 1821. In the 1840s the name of St. Hyacinth (a Silesian-born Dominican) was applied to 3 land grants and in 1872 to the town.

•**SAN JOAQUIN**, Town, Fresno County; Pop. 1,930; Zip Code 93660. Lat. 36-36-24 N long. 120-11-17 W; Name of St. Joachim, father of the Virgin Mary, applied to river by Gabriel Moraga (1806). Town named for river.

•**SAN JOSE,** City; Santa Clara County Seat; Pop. 636,550; Elev. 100. Lat. 37-20-07 N long. 121-53-38 W; I2 San Jose was named for patron saint of California (Saint Joseph) with its name originally El Pueblo de Jan Jose de Guadalupe.

•**SAN JUAN BAUTISTA**, Town, San Benito County; Pop. 1,276; Zip Code 95045; Lat. 36-50-44 N long. 121-32-13 W; I2 Mission named 1797 for St. John the Baptist.

•**SAN JUAN CAPISTRANO**, City, Orange County; Pop. 18,959; Zip Code 92675; Elev. 103; Lat. 33-30-06 N long. II7-39-42 W; Reached by US 101; Named for St. John of Capistrano, a fourteenth-century Italian theologian.

•**SAN LEANDRO**, City, Alameda County; Pop. 63,952; Zip Code 94577; Elev. 45; Lat. 37-43-30 N long. I22-09-I8 W; Reached by US 50; 15 miles SE of Oakland; Incorporated 1872; Founded 1854 and named for a rancho owned by the Estudillo family.

•**SAN LORENZO**, Town, Alameda County; Pop. 23,200; Zip Code 94580; Elev. 35; Lat. 37-40-52 N long. I22-07- 24 W; W California. A suburban addition to San Leandro, this town is on the banks of San Leandro Creek.

•**SAN LUCAS**, Town, Monterey County; Pop. 100; Zip Code 93954; Elev. 408; Lat. 36-07-44 N long. 121-01-10 W; Reached by US 101; Founded 1886 and named after the San Lucas Rancho granted 1842 and named for St. Luke.

•**SAN LUIS OBISPO**, City, San Luis Obispo County Seat; Pop. 34,252; Zip Code 93401; Elev. 234. Lat. 35-16-58 N long. 120-39-31 W; I5-Lat Named in honor of St. Louis, Bishop of Toulouse, son of the King of Naples and Sicily.

•**SAN LUIS REY**, Town, San Diego County; Pop. (included with Oceanside) 56,000; Zip Code 92068; Site of a mission founded by Padre Lasuen on June 13, 1798, and named in honor of St. Louis, King of France.

•**SAN MARCOS**, City, San Diego; Pop. 17,479; Zip Code 92069; Elev. 570; Lat. 33-08-36 N long. 117-09-55 W; Il Valle San Marcos ("St. Mark's valley") mentioned in 1797 and used for a land grant, Vallecitos de San Marcos, in 1840. Applied to town 1887 by Santa Fe Railroad.

•**SAN MARINO**, City, Los Angeles County; Pop. 13,307; Zip Code 91108; Elev. 566; Lat. 34-07-17 N long. 118-06-20 W; Estate on site named by builder, James de Barth Shorb (1878), after his birthplace in Emmetsburg, Maryland.

•**SAN MARTIN**, Town, Santa Clara County; Pop. 1,392; Zip Code 95046; Elev. 287; Lat. 37-05-06 N long. 121-36-33 W; Named by James Murphy, son of Irish immigrant (1844) Martin Murphy who settled on the San Francisco de las Llagas grant, for his father's patron saint.

•**SAN MATEO**, City, San Mateo County; Pop. 77,561; Zip Code 944 zone; Elev. 28; Lat. 37-33-47 N long. I22-19-28 W; Reached by US 101; Site of an Arroyo de San Matheo recorded in 1776.

•**SAN MIGUEL**, Town, San Liuis Obispo County; Pop. 800; Zip Code 93451; Elev. 615; Lat. 35-45-09 N long. 120-41-43 W; Reached by US 101. Site of mission founded and named San Miguel Arcangel on July 25, 1797.

•**SAN PABLO**, City, Contra Costa County; Pop. 19,750; Zip Code 94806; Elev. 45; Lat. 37-57-44 N long. 122-20-40 W; Reached by US 40; North of Berkeley. Name, Spanish for "St. Paul," applied to point on shore of San Pablo Strait opposite San Pedro ("St. Peter").

•**SAN PASQUAL**, Town, San Diego County; Pop. rural; Zip Code 92025; Lat. 33-05-30 N long. II6-57-II W; Near Escondido; about 40 miles NE of San Diego. Site of a mission and land grant (1840s) named for St. Paschal, a sixteenth-century Franciscan.

•**SAN PEDRO**, Town, Los Angeles County; Pop. (included with Los Angeles) 2,750,000; Zip Code 90731; Lat. 33-44-09 N long. 118-17-29 W; Reached by US 101; Harbor of Los Angeles, 25 miles south of its downtown area. Discovered by Vizcaino November 16, 1602, feast day of the St. Peter martyred in Constaninople.

•**SAN RAFAEL**, City, Marin County Seat; Pop. 44,700; Zip Code 94901; Elev. 34; Lat. 37-58-25 N long. 122-31-48 W; Residential city 13 miles NW of San Francisco. Named for a mission founded as an asistencia of Mission Dolores on December 14, 1817, at the site called Nanaguani by the Indians.

•**SAN RAMON**, Town, Contra Costa County; Pop. 22,356; Zip Code 94583; Elev. 470; Lat. 37-46-48 N long. 121-58-37 W; W California. It was originally named Lynchville, and nicknamed Limerick, because most of the settlers were Irish. Sam Ramon came from the name of an early Spanish land grant in the area.

•**SAN SIMEON**, Town, San Luis Obispo County; Pop. 50; Zip Code 93452; Elev. 20; Lat. 37-16-08 N long. 121-58-28 W; W California.

•**SANGER**, City, Fresno County; Pop. 12,558; Zip Code 93657; Elev. 363; Lat. 36-42-29 N long. 119-33-18 W; R US 99. Station named for Joseph Sanger, Jr., official of the Pacific Improvement Co.

•**SANTA ANA**, City, Orange County Seat; Pop. 203,713; Zip Code 92711; Elev. 133; Lat. 33-44-44 N long. 117-52-01 W; Residential and commercial city, 20 miles east of Long Beach; Founded 1869; Incorporated July 18, 1769, and named for St. Anne, whose feast day is July 16.

•**SANTA BARBARA**, City, Santa Barbara County Seat; Pop. 74,542; Zip Code 931+; Elev. 42; Lat. 34-25-24 N long. 119-42-12 W; Seaside resort founded 1782 on the land called Yamnonalit by the Indians; Incorporated 1850.

•**SANTA CLARA**, City, Santa Clara County; Pop. 87,746; Zip Code 95050; Elev. 85; Lat. 37-20-51 N long. 121-15-63 W; Adjacent to San Jose (5 miles NW); Settled 1777 as Franciscan mission of Pour Clares; Incorporated 1852.

•**SANTA CRUZ**, City, Santa Cruz County Seat; Pop. 41,483; Zip Code 95060; Elev. 20; Lat. 36-58-27 N long. 122-01-47 W; At north end of Monterey Bay; Founded 1791; Incorporated 1876. Name (Spanish) means "holy cross."

•**SANTA FE SPRINGS**, City, Los Angeles County; Pop. 14,559; Zip Code 90670; Elev. 130; Lat. 33-56-50 N long. 118-05-04 W; (Spanish), meaning "holy faith," applied to mineral springs (1886) purchased by the Santa Fe from J. E. Fulton.

•**SANTA MARGARITA**, Town, San Luis Obispo; Pop. 800; Zip Code 93453; Lat. 35-23-24 N long. 120-36-29 W; In a valley named by the Portola expedition on July 20, 1769, because it was the feast day of Margaret of Antioch.

•**SANTA MARIA**, City, Santa Barbara County; Pop. 39,685; Zip Code 93454; Elev. 216; Lat. 34-57-11 N long. 120-26-05 W; 52 miles NW of Santa Barbara. Name applied in Spanish times and preserved through a land grant, also called Tepusquet, dated April 6, 1837.

•**SANTA MONICA**, City, Los Angeles County; Pop. 88,314; Zip Code 904+; Elev. 64; Lat. 34-01-10 N long. 118-29-25 W; On Santa Monica Bay 15 miles west of center of Los Angeles. Named by Portola expedition May 4, 1770, after the day's saint, the mother of St. Augustine.

•**SANTA PAULA**, City, Ventura County; Pop. 20,552; Zip Code 93060; Elev. 288. Lat. 34-21-15 N long. 119-03-30 W; Laid out and named 1872 on the Rancho Santa Paula, a noble Roman matron and disciple of St. Jerome.

•**SANTA RITA**, Town, Santa Barbara County; Pop. rural; Zip Code 93436. Lat. 36-43-26 N long. 121-39-18 W; Named because it is located on the Santa Rita land grant, dated April 10, 1839, and named for Santa Rita de Cassis, an Augustinian whose feast day is May 22.

•**SANTA ROSA**, City, Sonoma County Seat; Pop. 83,205; Zip Code 95401; Elev. 167; Lat. 38-26-26 N long. 122-42-48 W; 50 miles NNW of San Francisco. Settled 1868 by a missionary and named for an Indian girl he baptized.

•**SANTA SUSANA**, Town, Ventura County; Pop. (included with Simi Valley) 70,200; Zip Code 93063; Lat. 34-16-18 N long. 118-42-29 W; Named as early as 1804 for Roman virgin and martyr of third century.

•**SANTA VENETIA**, Town, Marin County; Pop. 4,000; Zip Code 94901; Lat. 37-59-55 N long. 122-31-27 W; Near San Rafael.

•**SANTA YNEZ**, Town, Santa Barbara County; Pop. 500; Zip Code 93460; Lat. 34-36-52 N long. 120-04-44 W; Used name of the mission (1804) founded to honor St. Agnes, one of the 4 great virgin martyrs of the early Roman Church.

•**SANTA YSABEL**, Town, San Diego County; Pop. 40; Zip Code 92070. Lat. 33-06-33 N long. 116-40-20 W; Name, honoring St. Elizabeth, Queen of Portugal, mentioned in records as early as 1818.

•**SANTEE**, City, San Diego; Pop. 31,900; Zip Code 92071; Elev. 369. Lat. 32-50-18 N long. 116-58-23 W; First known as Fanita, for Mrs. Fanita McCoon, then as Cowles, until residents voted new name for post office (established 1892) in 1902.

•**SAN YSIDRO**, Village, San Diego County; Pop. (with San Diego); Zip Code 92073; Lat. 32-33-07 N long. 117-02-32 W; S California. One of the principal points of entry into the U.S. from Mexico, this town was named after an early rancho in the area.

•**SARATOGA**, City, Santa Clara County; Pop. 29,261; Zip Code 95070; Elev. 455; Lat. 37-15-50 N long. 122-01-19 W; Located in Santa Cruz Mts. Name applied when post office established in 1867 because waters of nearby Pacific Congress Spring resemble those of Congress Spring at Saratoga, New York.

•**SATICOY**, Town, Ventura County; Pop. (included with Ventura) 64,800; ; Zip Code 93003; Lat. 34-16-59 N long. 119-08-56 W; Name derived from that of a Chumash Indian ranceria mentioned in a letter of May 20, 1826. Part of Santa Paula Saticoy land grant of 1834.

•**SAUGAS**, City, Los Angeles County; Pop. 7,700; Zip Code 91350; Lat. 34-24-41 N long. 118-32-21 W; Originally called Newhall, for Henry M. Newhall. Renamed 1879 after Newhall's birthplace in Massachusetts. Name means "outlet" in Algonkian Indian dialect.

•**SAUSALITO**, City, Marin County; Pop. 7,090; Zip Code 94965; Elev. 25; Lat. 37-51-33 N long. 122-29-03 W; Suburban residential city on San Francisco Bay. Name (Spanish) means "little willow grove." founded 1868 when Sausalito Land and Ferry Co. subdivided the land and established ferry service to San Francisco.

•**SCOTIA**, Town, Humboldt County; Pop. 950; Zip Code 95565; Lat. 40-28-57 N long. 124-05-59 W; Called Forestville when Pacific Lumber Co. built mill here in 1885. Renamed when post office was established July 9, 1888, because many millworkers were natives of Nova Scotia.

•**SCOTTS VALLEY**, City, Santa Cruz County; Pop. 6,891; Zip Code 95066; Lat. 37-03-04 N long. 122-00-49 W; Western, coastal California. Scott Valley was named for John Scott, who discovered gold at Scott's Bar.

•**SEAL BEACH**, City, Orange County; Pop. 25,975; Zip Code 90740; Elev. 10; Lat. 33-44-29 N long. 118-06-14 W; First called Bay City, given present name by Philip A. Stanton.

•**SEASIDE**, City, Monterey County; Pop. 36,567; Zip Code 93955; Elev. 20; Lat. 36-36-40 N long. 121-51-02 W; Laid out in 1888 by Dr.J. L. D. Roberts and named East Monterey. When Post Office Dept. rejected that name in 1890, Roberts chose the present one.

•**SEBASTOPOL**, Town, Sonoma County; Pop. 5,500; Zip code 95472; Lat. 39-21-46 N long. 121-07-12 W; 7 miles SW of Santa Rosa. Named about the time of the Anglo-French siege of the Russian port during the Crimean War (1854).

•**SEELEY**, Town, Imperial County; Pop. 950; Zip Code 92273; Elev. 42 feet below sea level; Lat. 32-47-35 N long. 115-41-25 W; New town started after destruction of Blue Lake by overflow of New River in 1905-07 and named for Henry Seeley, a pioneer in the development of Imperial Valley.

•**SELMA**, City, Fresno County; Pop. 10,942; Zip Code 93662; Elev. 308; Lat. 36-34-15 N long. 119-36-40 W; 15 miles SE of Fresno.

Established by Southern Pacific Railroad in 1880 and named for daughter of Max Gruenberg, at request of Leland Stanford.

•**SESPE**, Town, Ventura County; Pop. 350; Zip Code 93015; Lat. 34-24-00 N long. 118-56-58 W; The name, from Chumash Indian, is also applied to a creek, a gorge, hot springs, and oil fields.

•**SHAFTER**, City, Kern County; Pop. 7,010; Zip Code 93263; Lat. 35-30-02 N long. 119-16-15 W; 17 miles NW of Bakersfield in S California.

•**SHANDON**, Village, San Luis Obispo County; Pop. 400; Zip Code 93461; Elev. 1,040; Lat. 35-39-19 N long. 120-22-28 W; W California. Lying by the San Juan River, this town was named for one in a story appearing in Harper's magazine 1891.

•**SHASTA**, Town and Historic Park, Shasta County; Pop. 650; Zip Code 96087; Elev. 1,026; Lat. 40-35-58 N long. 122-29-27 W; N California. Named for the snow covered peak which dominates the landscape,itself named after the local Shasta Indians.

•**SHELL BEACH**, Town, San Luis Obispo County; Pop. (included with Pismo Beach) 4,043; Zip Code 93449; Lat. 35-09-19 N long. 120-40-17 W; Named for abundance of shells on shore nearby.

•**SHERIDAN**, Town, Placer County; Pop. 400; Zip Code 95681; Elev. 115; Lat. 38-58-47 N long. 121-22-28 W; Station of the Roseville-Marysville branch of the Central Pacific built after Civil War, named for Gen. Philip Sheridan.

•**SHINGLE SPRINGS**, Town, El Dorado County; Pop. 1,268; Zip Code 95682; Elev. 1,425; Lat. 38-39-57 N 120-55-30 W; NE California. The site of a shingle mill in 1849, it was also a stop for travel-worn gold seekers who wanted rest and refreshment at the springs west of town.

•**SHIVELY**, Town, Humnboldt County; Pop. 130; Zip Code 95565; Lat. 40-25-51 N long. 123-58-07 W; Near Scotia. Named for William R. Shively, a pioneer of Humboldt County who came to California from Ohio in 1852.

•**SHORE ACRES**, Town, Contra Costa County; Pop. 4,000; Zip Code 94565; Lat. 38-02-09 N long. 121-57-52 W; Near Pittsburg.

•**SHOSHONE**, Town, Inyo County; Pop. 200; Zip Code 92384; Elev. 1569; Lat. 35-58-23 n long. 116-16-13 W; Name of Indian tribe derived from *tso*, head," and *so'ni*, "tangles," referring to their headdress.

•**SIERRA CITY**, Town, Sierra County; Pop. 100; Zip Code 96125; Lat. 39-33-57 N long. 120-37-58 W; Spanish descriptive name for a mountain range applied here because of town's location in the northern part of Sierra Nevada.

•**SIERRA MADRE**, City, Los Angeles County; Pop. 10,837; Zip Code 91024; Elev. 840; Lat. 34-09-42 N long. 118-03-07; Name is Spanish for "mother range," given to town when Nathaniel C. Carter subdivided part of Rancho Santa Anita in 1881.

•**SIERRAVILLE**, Town, Sierra County; Pop. 300; Zip Code 96126; Elev. 4,950; Lat. 39-35-23 N long. 120-21-59 W; NE California. It lies in the Sierra Valley, where farming began in 1853.

•**SIGNAL HILL**, City, Los Angeles County; Pop. 5,734; Zip Code 90806; Elev. 100; Lat. 33-47-59 N long. 118-09-45 W; Once the rancho of John Temple and known then as Los Cerritos ("little hills"), renamed when it became the signal point of the coast survey (1889) just as its 300-foot eminence had once served the Indians and the Spanish as a beacon place.

•**SILVERADO**, Town, Orange County; Pop. 900; Zip Code 92676; Lat. 33-44-46 N 117-38-10 W; Name, coined in analogy to Eldorado, connating silver rather than gold, given to canyon where town is located in 1870s when silver was discovered here.

•SILVER LAKE, Town, Amador County; Pop 5 (summer 75); Zip Code 95642; Near Jackson.

•SKYFOREST, Town, San Bernardino County; Pop. 500 (summer 1,000); Zip Code 92385; Lat. 34-14-07 N long. 117-10-42 W; Founded 1928 and named because it is on top of a ridge more than a mile high, surrounded by a forest of pine, fir, cedar, and oak.

•SLEEPY HOLLOW, Town, Marin County; Pop. 2,100; Zip Code 94960; Lat. 33-56-52 N long. 117-46-40 W; Near San Anselmo.

•SLOAT, Town, Plumas County; Pop. 100; Zip Code 96103; Lat. 39-52-00 N long. 120-43-35 W; Near Cromberg. Western Pacific station named 1910 in honor of Commodore John Drake Sloat who, in July 1846, took possession of California for the United States.

•SMARTVILLE, Town Yuba County; Pop. 300; Zip Code 95977; Lat. 39-12-27 N long. 121-17-51 W; Named for James Smart, who built a hotel here in 1856. Post office established 1867 as Smartville.

•SMITHFLAT, (alt. SMITH'S FLAT), Village, El Dorado County; Pop. 400; Zip Code 95727; Elev. 2,200; Lat. 38-44-12 N long. 120-45-15 W; E California. Named for Jeb Smith, a pioneer, this was a rich mining camp of the 1850s.

•SMITH RIVER, Town, Del Norte County; Pop. 900; Zip Code 95567; Lat. 41-55-43 N long. 124-08-43 W; Named in honor of Jedediah Smith.

•SNELLING, Town, Merced County; Pop. 225; Zip Code 95369; Lat. 37-31-09 N long. 120-26-11 W; County seat 1855-72. Named for hotel built in 1851 and bought by Charles V. Snelling family, changing name of place to Snelling's Ranch.

•SODA SPRINGS, Town, Nevada County; Pop. 200; Zip Code 95728; Lat. 40-05-17 N long. 121-35-12 W; Developed by Mark Hopkins and Leland Stanford about 1870 and known as Hopkins Springs until the post office was established March 8, 1875.

•SOLEDAD, Town, Monterey County; Pop. 5,928; Zip Code 93960; Lat. 36-25-29 N long. 121-19-31 W; 35 miles SE of Monterey. Name (Spanish), meaning "solitude," applied by Portola expedition in 1769 because the name of an Indian they had met sounded like Soledad.

•SOMES BAR, Town, Siskiyou County; Pop. 150; Zip Code 95568; Near Orleans. Named for a gold miner, D. Maginnis. Post office established 1892.

•SONOMA, Town, Sonoma County; Pop. 6,054; Zip Code 95476; Lat. 38-17-31 N long. 122-27-25 W; 13 miles south of Santa Rosa. Name derived from the Wintun Indian word for "nose." First applied by Spaniards to an Indian chief with a big nose.

•SONORA, City, Tuolumne County Seat; Pop. 3,239; Zip Code 95370; Elev. 1,850; Lat. 37-59-03 N Long. 120-22-52 W; E California. In 1848 this was Sonorian Camp, settled natives of Sonora, Mexico.

•SOQUEL, City, Santa Cruz County; Pop. 5,795; Zip Code 95073; Lat. 36-59-17 N Long. 121-57-20 W; Name derived from that of a Shoshonean Indian village applied to land grant 1833. Post office established July 5, 1857.

•SOULSBYVILLE, Town, Tuolumne County; Pop. 300; Zip Code 95372; Elev. 3,000; Lat. 37-59-05 N Long. 120-15-46 W; E California. This mining town dates to 1856, and was named for the quartz mine built here by Benjamin Soulsby.

•SOUTH DOS PALOS, Town, Merced County; Pop. 700; Zip Code 93665; Elev. 115; Lat. 36-57-52 N Long. 120-39-08 W; Post office established 1907 and named after nearby Dos Palos.

•SOUTH EL MONTE, City, Los Angeles County; Pop. 16,623; Zip Code 91733; Lat. 34-03-07 N Long. 118-02-45 W; 10 miles SE of Los Angeles in SW California.

•SOUTH FONTANA, Town San Bernardino County; Pop. (included with Fontana) 23,900; Zip Code 92335; Elev. 1004; Lat. 34-03-46 N Long. 117-29-17 W.

•SOUTH LAGUNA, Town, Orange County; Pop. 2,566; Zip Code 92677; Lat. 33-30-02 N. Long. 117-44-32 W; Post office established 1933 and named Three Arches because of a picturesque rock formation. The name was changed to present one at request of residents in 1934.

•SOUTH LAKE TAHOE, El Dorado County; Pop. 20,681; Zip Code 95705; Elev. 6,260; Lat. 38-56-45 N Long. 119-58-13 W; NE California. Situated at the southern end of Lake Tahoe, this city has many resort facilities and housing districts.

•SOUTH PASADENA, City, Los Angeles County; Pop. 22,681; Zip Code 91030; Lat. 34-06-58 N Long. 118-08-58 W; 4 miles NE of Los Angeles in SW California.

•SOUTH SAN FRANCISCO, City, San Mateo County; Pop. 49,393; Zip Code 94080; Elev. 20; Lat. 37-39-17 N Long. 122-24-24 W; W California on San Francisco Bay. The settlement was first called Baden, but was incorported as the city of South San Francisco in 1908.

•SOUTHGATE, City, Los Angeles County; Pop. 66,784; Zip Code 90280; Elev. 115; Lat. 33-57-17 N Long. 118-12-40 W; Industrial city, 7 miles SSE of Los Angeles between Watts and Downey. Founded 1918 as a gardened entry area to the Cudahy Ranch on the old rancho of the Lugo family. Incorporated 1923.

•SPRING GARDEN, Village, Plumas County; Pop. 80; Zip Code 95971; Elev. 3,965; Lat. 39-53-42 N Long. 120-47-06 W; NE California; Summer resort.

•SPRING VALLEY, City, San Diego County; Pop. 34,700; Zip Code 92077; Elev. 500; Lat. 38-46-46 N Long. 120-31-36 W; Land originally part of a grant (1846) to the Arguello Family, later sold to Hubert H. Baneroft, famous California historian.

•SQUAW VALLEY, Town, Placer County; Pop. 600 (seasonal 4,000; Zip Code 95730; Elev. 6,240; Lat. 36-44-27 N Long. 119-14-44 W; In the Sierra Nevada on eastern slopes of Squaw Peak. Name dates back to early mining and lumbering activities and is an anglicized version of an Algonkian Indian word (eskwaw) meaning "woman."

•STANDISH, Town, Lassen County; Pop. 60; Zip Code 96128; Lat. 40-21-55 N Long. 120-25-16 W; Laid out 1897. In 1899, H. R. T. Coffin settled here and named it in honor of Miles Standish of the *Mayflower*.

•STANISLAU COUNTY, Central California; Established in 1854; Pop. 265,902; Lat. 38-08-18 N Long. 120-22-09 W; Covers 1,506 square miles; Seat, Modesto. Named for the river, which honored a Spanish-Indian leader named Estanislao. Later, Fremont used the Americanized version of this Saint's name.

•STANTON, City, Orange County; Pop. 21,144; Zip Code 90680; Elev. 60; Lat. 33-48-09 N Long. 117-59-32 W; SE of Anaheim. Named for its founder, Philip A. Stanton, Republican assemblyman from Los Angeles 1903-09. Post office established 1912.

•STEWART'S POINT, Town, Sonoma County; Pop. 80; Zip Code 95480; Elev. 109; Lat. 38-39-07 N Long. 123-23-53 W; Coast Survey charted the section 1875 and used this site as a secondary triangulation point. May be named for Lt. Col. C. S. Stewart of the Corps of Engineers, who in 1875 removed Noonday Rock from the Farallones.

•**STINSON BEACH**, Town, Marin County; Pop. 600; Zip Code 94971; Elev. 18; Lat. 37-54-02 N Long. 122-38-36 W; W California. This summer resort fronts a three mile white sand beach curving around Bolinas Bay. It was settled on land acquired by Nathan Stinson in 1871.

•**STIRLING CITY**, Town, Butte County; Pop. 375; Zip Code 95978; Elev. 3532; Lat. 39-54-28 N Long. 121-31-37 W; Named by J. F. Nash, superintendent of the Diamond Match Co., when it built a sawmill here in 1903 because he saw the firm name--Stirling Boiler Works--on the boilers ordered for the mill.

•**STOCKTON**, City, San Joaquin County Seat; Pop. 149,779; Zip Code 952--; Elev. 23; Lat. 37-57-28 N Long. 121-17-23 W; Central California; 50 mi. E of Oakland. Stockton was founded in 1847 by a German named Charles Weber who bought out his partner William Gulnac's interests in a 50,000 acre tract of land here for 60 dollars.

•**STONYFORD**, Town, Colusa County; Pop. 175; Zip Code 95979; Lat. 39-22-31 N Long. 122-32-35 W; Established by John L. Smith (1863) and called Smithville. In 1890, the Stony Creek Improvement Co. bought the town and moved it one-half mile to a new site called Stony Ford.

•**STRATFORD**, Town, Kings County; Pop. 800; Zip Code 93266; Lat. 36-11-22 N Long. 119-49-20 W; Laid out spring 1907 on the old Empre ranch and named Stratton for William Stratton, ranch's manager. Post Office Dept. rejected this name, and present one was substituted.

•**STRATHMORE**, Town, Tulare County; Pop. 1,221; Zip Code 93267; Elev. 402; Lat. 36-08-44 N Long. 119-03-35 W; A Scottish corporation, Balfour Guthrie Co., laid out town in 1908 and named it with Scottish word meaning "broad valley." Formerly called Roth Spur and Santos.

•**SUISUN CITY**, City, Solano County; Pop. 11,087; Zip Code 94585; Elev. 12; Lat. 38-14-18 N Long. 122-02-21 W; W California. Suisun was the name of an Indian tribe living near here.

•**SULTANA**, Town, Tulare County; Pop. 500; Zip Code 93666;Lat. 36-32-44 N Long. 119-20-21 W; Station called Alta when San Francisco and San Joaquin Valley Railroad reached here in 1898. Name given to post office (established 1900) for the Sultana grapes grown here at that time.

•**SUMMERLAND**, Town, Santa Barbara County; Pop. 800; Zip Code 93067; Lat. 34-25-17 N Long. 119-35-44 WLaid out in 1888 by H. L. Williams after the Santa Barbara-Ventura section of the Southern Pacific Railroad was built.

•**SUMMMIT**, Town, San Bernardino County; Pop. rural; Zip Code 92392; Elev. 4032; Lat. 35-07-40 N Long. 118-24-47 W; Near Victorville.

•**SUNCREST**, Town, San Diego County; Pop. 2,000; Zip Code 92021; Lat. 32-48-15 N Long. 116-51-49 W; NE of El Cajon. Once part of 360-acre Juanita Ranch owned by John McCutcheon, who sold the land in 1924 to Allen Hauser and Ray Coast. They developed a cabin resort community here in the 1930's.

•**SUNNYMEAD**, City, Riverside County; Pop. 6,708; Zip Code 92388; Lat. 33-56-24 N Long. 117-14-34 W; Sunnymead Orchard Tract laid out and named in 1913 for a Mr. Mead, one of original landowners.

•**SUNNYVALE**, City, Santa Clara County; Pop. 106,618; Zip Code 94086; Elev. 130; Lat. 37-22-08 N Long. 122-02-07 W; 8 miles WNW of San Jose. Settled 1849 by Martin Murphy, but named by real estate developer W. E. Crossman in 1900.

•**SUNOL**, Alameda County; Pop. 450; Zip Code 94586; Elev. 300; W California. In the 1840's the adobe ranch house of Antonio Sunol stood amid alders and sycamores near where the San Francisco water system's works now stands.

•**SURFSIDE**, Town, Orange County; Pop. (included with Seal Beach) 26,900; ; Zip Code 90743; Lat. 33-43-40 N Long. 118-04-53 W. Post office established April 5, 1953.

•**SUSANVILLE**, City, Lassen County Seat; Pop. 6,520; Zip Code 96130; Elev. 4,258; Lat. 40-24-59 N Long. 120-39-07 W; Known as Roop-town until 1857 for Isaac Roop, pioneer of the Honey Lake district, who then named town for his daughter.

•**SUTTER**, Town, Sutter County; Pop. 1,488; Zip Code 95982; Lat. 39-09-35- N Long. 121-44-52 W; Known as South Butte until the boom of the 1880's, when town was renamed for pioneer John A. Sutter, who built the fort which became the terminus of the emigrant trail from Missouri.

•**SUTTER CREEK**, Town, Amador County; Pop. 1,705; Zip Code 95685; Elev. 1,198; Lat. 38-23-35 N Long. 120-48-05 W. Named for nearby creek, which had been known locally by the name since Sutter had a mining camp here in 1849. Town founded 1854.

•**TAFT**, Kern County; Pop. 5,316; Zip Code 93268; Elev. 984; Lat. 35-08-33 N Long. 119-27-20 W; 28 miles SW of Bakersfield; Post office established 1909 and named for newly elected President William H. Taft.

•**TAJIGUAS**, Town, Santa Barbara County; Pop. rural; Lat. 34-28-00 N Long. 120-06-27 W. Name derived from that of a Chumash village which was itself named for *tayiyas*, the holly-leaved cherry.

•**TAMALPAIS VALLEY**, Town, Marin County; Pop. 4,800; Zip Code 94941; Elev. 36; Lat. 37-52-47 N 122-32-41 W; Near Mill Valley. Settlement at foot of Mt. Tamalpais. Known as Big Coyote until the post office was named for the mountain February 15, 1906. In 1908, Valley was added to the name.

•**TARZANA**, Subdivision, Los Angeles County; Pop. (with Los Angeles); Zip Code 91356; Elev. 930; Lat. 34-10-24 N Long. 118-33-11 W; SW California. The town grew around the estate of Edgar Rice Burroughs, who named it for his famous character of the jungle, Tarzan.

•**TAYLORSVILLE**, Town, Plumas County; Pop. 150; Zip Code 95983; Lat. 40-04-32 N Long. 120-50-19 W. Named for J. T. Taylor, who built the first barn, mill, and hotel here in 1852.

•**TECATE**, Town, San Diego County; Pop. 90; Zip Code 92080; Lat. 32-34-38 N Long. 116-37-36 W. Name used for a land grant of 1833 and for nearby mountain in 1855. Post office named after mountain in 1913. Two possible derivations of name: the common Mexican word, *tecatrs*, for a species of gourd; or the Mexican word *atecate*, which means "water in which the baker moistens her hands while making tortillas."

•**TECOPA**, Town, Inyo county; Pop. 200 (summer 700); Zip Code 92389; Elev. 1,329; Lat. 35-50-54 N Long. 116-13-32 W. Old mining camp named before 1892 by J. B. Osbourne for an old Paiute chief who later demanded $200 for the use of his name. Name is derived from *tecopet*, meaning "wildcat."

•**TEHACHAPI**, Town, Kern County; Pop. 4,126; Zip Code 93561; Elev. 3,973; 35-07-56 N 118-26-53 W. In 1876, the Southern Pacific built the railroad through the canyon of Cache Creek and named station with a derivation of a Yokuts Indian place name. Post office established between 1880 and 1892.

•**TEHAMA**, Town, Tehama County; Pop. 365; Zip Code 96090; Lat. 40-01-38 N Long. 122-07-20 W. Name may be derived from an Indian word or from the Mexican word *tejamanil*, "shingle."

•**TEMECULA**, Town, San Diego County; Pop. 1,783; Zip Code 92390; Elev. 1,006; Lat. 33-29-37 N Long. 117-08-51 W; S California. The name comes from that of a rancho of the late 1700's, and may be a Luiseno Indian name meaning "rising sun."

•**TEMPLE CITY**, City, Los Angeles County; Pop. 28,972; Zip Code 91780; Elev. 400; Lat. 34-06-26 N Long. 118-03-25 Named 1923 for Walter P. Temple, founder of town.

•**TEMPLETON**, Town, San Luis Obispo County; Pop. 750; Zip Code 93465; Lat. 35-32-59 N Long. 120-42-18 W. Laid out with coming of railroad in 1886 and called Crocker for Templeton Crocker of San Francisco.

•**TERMINOUS**, Town, San Joaquin County; Pop. rural; Zip Code 95240; Lat. 38-06-48 N Long. 121-29-40 W. Near Lodi. Established 1900 by John Dougherty and named because it was at the end of the road that ran into the Delta region.

•**THERMAL**, Town, Riverside County; Pop. 600; Zip Code 92274; Elev. 120 feet below sea level; Lat. 33-38-25 N Long. 116-08-19 W. Name applied to station before 1888 because of the extreme heat in the Salton Sea basin.

•**THORNTON**, Town, San Joaquin County; Pop. 800; Zip Code 95686; Elev. 11; Lat. 38-13-34 N Long. 121-25-25 W. A Scot, Arthur Thornton, established his New Hope Ranch here about 1855.

•**THOUSAND OAKS**, City, Ventura County; Pop. 77,797; Zip Code 91360; Elev. 800; Lat. 34-10-14 N Long. 118-50-12; 30 miles WNW of Los Angeles.

•**THREE ARCHES**, (alt. THREE ARCH BAY), Village, Orange County; Pop. (with South Laguna); Zip Code 92677; Lat. 33-29-27 N Long. 117-43-53 W; SW California. This closed, private community rests atop a cliff overlooking the small bay by the same name. Three large "arches" are formed on the northern point of the bay.

•**THREE RIVERS**, Town, Tulare County; Pop. 900; Zip Code 93271; Lat. 36-26-20 N Long. 118-54-13 W. Post office established 1878 and named because it is near junction of three forks of Kaweah River.

•**TIBURON**, City, Marin County; Pop. 6,685; Zip Code 94920; Elev. 90; Lat. 37-52-25 N Long. 120-37-03 W. Name comes from Punta de Tiburon ("shark's point"), mentioned in Jose Sanchez' diary of July 6, 1823.

•**TIPTON**, Town, Tulare County; Pop. 950; Zip Code 93272; Elev. 272; Lat. 36-03-34 N Long. 119-18-40 W. Name is that of an English town in Stafford County.

•**TORRANCE**, City, Los Angeles County; Pop. 131,497; Zip Code 905--; 15 mi. SSW of Los Angeles in SW California.

•**TRACY**, City, San Joaquin County; Pop. 18,423; Zip Code 95376; Elev. 43; Central California. The railroad named the place for an official named *Lathrop Tracy*.

•**TRANQUILITY**, Town, Fresno County; Pop. 600; Zip Code 93668. Applied to station by Southern Pacific when the Ingle-Harwick branch was built in 1912. Post office established 1912.

•**TRAVER**, Town, Tulare County; Pop. 400; Zip Code 93273. Founded 1884 and named for *Charles Traver* of Sacramento, who was interested in a land and canal development project here.

•**TRES PINOS**, Town, San Benito County; Pop. 200; Zip Code 95075. In 1873, the Southern Pacific gave name to terminal of the proposed Pacheco Pass route, appropriating it from a nearby settlement that had been named for its three pines.

•**TRIMMER**, Town, Fresno County; Pop. rural; Zip Code 93657; Near Sanger. Named in memory of *Morris Trimmer*, first settler and owner of the place.

•**TRONA**, Town, San Bernardino County; Pop. 1,500; Zip Code 93562; Elev. 1,660; Lat. 35-45-46 N long. 117-22-19 W; SE California. The town was founded on dry Searles Lake in 1916, and named for the mineral found there that is used in the manufacture of borax.

•**TRUCKEE**, Town, Nevada County; Pop. 1,392 (summer 2,500); Zip Code 95743; Elev. 5,820; Lat. 39-19-41 N long. 120-10-56 W; Named (1868) for nearby river and lake, themselves named for an Indian who piloted part of the *Stevens* party across the Sierra in 1844.

•**TULARE**, City, Tulare County; Pop. 22,475; Elev. 287; Zip Code 93274; Lat.36-12-28 N long. 119-20-47 W; 42 mi. SE of Fresno in S central California.

•**TULELAKE**, City, Siskiyou County; Pop. 783; Zip Code 96134; Lat. 36-12-28 N long. 119-20-47 W; NE corner of Siskiyou County in N California.

•**TUNITAS**, Town, San Mateo county; Pop. rural; Zip Code 94019; Near Half Moon Bay. Name is diminutive of *tuna*, the Spanish word for the fruit of the prickly pear cactus.

•**TUOLUMNE**, Town, Tuolumne County; Pop. 1,365; Zip Code 95379. Lat. 37-57-39 N long. 120-14-11 W; Station of the Sierra Railroad named Tuolumne (1899), a curruption of a Miwok Indian word, *talmalamne*, meaning "cluster of stone wigwams."

•**TURLOCK**, City, Stanislaus County; Pop. 26,291; Elev. 101; Zip Code 95380; Lat. 37-29-41 N long. 120-50-44 W; 38 mi. SE of Stockton in central California.

•**TUSTIN**, City, Orange County; Pop. 32,073; Elev. 122; Zip Code 92680; Lat. 33-44-45 N long. 117-49-31 W; 20 mi. E of Long Beach in SW California.

•**TUTTLETOWN**, Town, Tuolumne County; Pop. 60; Zip Code 95370; Lat. 37-59-30 N long. 120-27-31 W; NE California. This became a trade center and pack mule stop on the old Slumgullion Road, after Judge *A. H. Tuttle* built his log cabin here in August, 1843.

•**TWAIN**, Town, Plumas County; Pop. 120; Zip Code 95984. Lat. 40-01-08 N long. 121-01-58 W; Western Pacific station named 1907 in memory of *Mark Twain*.

•**UKIAH**, City, Mendocino County Seat; Pop. 12,035; Elev. 639; Zip Code 95482; Lat. 39-09-01 N long. 123-12-24 W; 54 mi. NNW of Santa Rosa in W California.

•**UNION CITY**, City, Alameda County; Pop. 39,406; Zip Code 94587; S of Oakland in W California.

•**UNIVERSAL CITY**, Subdivision, Los Angeles County; Pop. (with Los Angeles); Zip Code 91608; Lat. 34-08-20 N long. 118-21-09 W; S California. The town's first post office was opened the same time that the Universal Pictures Company established its first studio here in 1915.

•**UPLAND**, City, San Bernardino County; Pop. 47,647; Zip Code 91786; Lat. 34-05-51 N long. 117-38-51 W; 35 mi E of Los Angeles in SE California.

•**UPPER LAKE**, Town, Lake County; Pop. 700; Zip Code 95485; Elev. 1,343; Lat. 39-09-53 N long. 122-54-34 W; Post office established before 1867 and named Upper Clear Lake because of its nearness to the northern shore of Clear Lake.

•VACAVILLE, City, Solano County; Pop. 17,000; Zip Code 95688; Elev. 179; Lat. 38-21-24 N long. 121-59-12 W; Named for the *Vaca* family.

•VALLEJO, City, Solano County; Pop. 72,000; Zip Code 94590; Elev. 50; Lat. 38-06-15 N long. 122-15-20 W; founded (1850) by *Mariano Vallejo* on his rancho where the Napa River flows into San Pablo Bay.

•VALLEY CENTER, Town, San Diego county; Pop. 200; Zip Code 92082; Lat. 33-13-06 N long. 117-02-00 W; Named 1870s because of its location in the center of a valley.

•VALLEY FORD, Village, Sonoma County; Pop. 130; Zip Code 94972; Elev. 42; Lat. 38-19-05 N long. 122-55-23 W; NW California. It was named for the "valley ford" where an ancient Indian and Spanish trail crossed the Estero.

•VALYERMO, Village, Los Angeles County; Pop. 50; Zip Code 93563; Lat. 34-26-46 N long. 117-51-05 W; S central California; Resort village named for a Spanish ranch nearby; name means "desert valley."

•VANDENBURG AIR FORCE BASE, Military installation, Santa Barbara County; Pop. 13,193; Area 100,000 acres; Zip Code 93437; Near Lompoc. Created to test intercontinental ballistic missiles and to launch satellites. Was named in 1958 for *Gen. H. S. Vandenberg*, Chief of Staff, U.S. Air Force (1948-53).

•VENICE, Subdivision, Los Angeles County; Pop. (with Los Angeles); Zip Code 90291; Elev. 20; Lat. 38-36-20 N long. 123-00-25 W; SW California. An ocean-front pleasure town with an elaborate amusement section on the beach and pier. In the early 1900s Abbott Kinney, a middle-west manufacturer, set about creating a Venice on the tidal flats.

•VENTURA, City, Ventura County Seat; Pop. 74,800; Zip Code 93001; Elev. 50; Lat. 34-16-42 N long. 119-17-32 W; County seDeveloped in the 1860 and 1870s. Name an abbreviation of the name of the neighboring mission, San Buenaventura.

•VERDEMONT, Town, San Bernardino County; Pop. 150; Zip Code 92402; Lat. 34-11-36 N long. 117-21-51 W; Name coined from Spanish *verde* ("green") and *monte* ("mountain"), applied to the Santa Fe station after the line from Barstow to San Bernardino was built in 1883.

•VICTORVILLE, City, San Bernardino County; Pop. 14,220; Zip Code 92392; Elev. 2,715; Lat. 34-32-10 N long. 117-17-25 W; North of San Bernardino. Named Victor in 1885 for J. N. Victor, construction superintendent of California Southern Railroad (1881-88).

•VIDAL JUNCTION, Town, San Bernardino County; Pop. 50; Zip Code 92280; Lat. 34-11-19 N long. 114-34-24 W; Founded 1907 by Hansen Brownell and named for his son-in-law, named Vidal.

•VILLA PARK, City, Orange County; Pop. 7,137; Zip Code 92667; Lat. 33-48-52 N long. 117-48-44 W; Original name, Mountain View, changed to Villa Park when post office was established 1890.

•VINA, Town, Tehama County; Pop. 300; Zip Code 96092; Lat. 39-44-49 N long. 122-03-10 W; Name is Spanish for "vineyard." Listed in 1880 as a post office on Leland Stanford's once famous vineyard.

•VINE HILL, Town, Contra Costa County; Pop. 3,400; Zip Code 94553; Elev. 23; Lat. 38-00-31 N long. 122-05-42 W; Near Martinez. Named in reference to extensive local grape culture.

•VINTON, Town, Plumas County; Pop. 70; Zip Code 96135; Lat. 39-48-16 N long. 120-10-38 W; Name of the old post office, Sum-

mit, changed February 16, 1897, and renamed for Vinton Bowen, daughter of Henry Bowen of the Sierra Valleys Railway.

•VIOLA, Town, Shasta County; Pop. rural; Zip Code 96088; Lat. 40-31-05 N long. 121-40-36 W; Near Shingletown. Named by homesteader B. F. Loomis for his mother in 1888.

•VISALIA, City, Tulare County Seat; Pop. 49,729; Zip Code 93277; Elev. 331; Lat. 36-19-49 N long. 119-17-28 W; Largest city in county, founded (1852) by Nathaniel Vise, a frontiersman from Kentucky, where a town of the same name honored members of his family.

•VISTA, City, San Diego County; Pop. 35,834; Zip Code 92083; Elev. 331; Lat. 33-12-00 N long. 117-14-30 W; Name is Spanish for "view." Originally part of Buena Vista Rancho, a land grant (1845) to an Indian.

•VOLCANO, Village, Amador County; Pop. 100; Zip Code 95689; Elev. 2,053; Lat. 38-26-35 N long. 120-37-47 W; N California. Built in a crater-like hollow, this town was once one of the richest and most populous towns of the Mother Lode.

•VOLTA, Town, Merced County; Pop. 100; Zip Code 93635; Lat. 37-05-51 N long. 120-55-30 W; Near Los Banos. Name derived from that of the great Italian electrical inventor.

•WALNUT, City, Los Angeles County; Pop. 9,978; Zip Code 91789; Elev. 530; Lat. 38-22-50 N long. 121-14-35 W; 18 miles east of Los Angeles. Southern Pacific station called Leman until 1912, when present name was applied.

•WALNUT CREEK, City, Contra Costa County; Pop. 53,643; Zip Code 94598; Elev. 569; Lat. 34-01-13 N long. 117-51-52 W; Named after the creek when post office established 1860s. Name of creek is translation of its Spanish name, Arroyo de los Nogales ("creek of the walnuts").

•WALNUT GROVE, Town, Sacramento County; Pop. 900; Zip Code 95690; Lat. 37-54-23 N long. 121-30-38 W; Settled by wood-choppers as early as 1850, but present name not applied until early 1860s when post office was established.

•WARNER SPRINGS, Town, San Diego County; Pop. 30; Zip Code 92086; Elev. 3,132; Lat. 33-16-56 N long. 116-37-58 W; Named for Jonathan Trumbull Warner, who arrived in California in 1831.

•WASCO, City, Kern County; Pop. 9,613; Zip Code 93280; Elev. 333; Lat. 35-35-39 N long. 119-20-24 W; NW of Bakersfield. Name chosen by a settler, William Bonham, was that of his home county in Oregon.

•WASHINGTON, Town, Nevada County; Pop. 130; Zip Code 95986; Lat. 39-21-34 N long. 120-47-53 W; Old mining town.

•WATERFORD, Town, Stanislaus County; Pop. 2,683; Zip Code 95386; Lat. 37-38-29 N long. 120-45-34 W; Incorporated 1969. Name given to a much-used ford through Tuolumne river.

•WATSONVILLE, City, Santa Cruz County; Pop. 23,543; Zip Code 95076; Elev. 29; Lat. 36-54-37 N long. 121-45-21 W; Laid out in 1852 on a part of Rancho Bolsa del Pajaro by D. S. Gregory and Judge John H. Watson, owners of the land. Post office established 1854.

•WAUKENA, Town, Tulare County; Pop. 300; Zip Code 93282; Elev. 192; Lat. 36-08-19 N long. 119-30-31 W; Near Corcoran. Laid out by a development company in 1886.

•WAWONA, Town, Mariposa County; Pop. 150 (summer 1,500); Zip Code 95389; Elev. 4,012; Lat. 37-32-13 N long. 119-39-19 W; Part of Yosemite National Park. Founded (1857) by Galen Clark, discoverer of the Mariposa Grove. The Indian name, meaning "big tree," was applied by the Washburn brothers, who established a hotel here in 1875.

•WEAVERVILLE, Town, Trinity County Seat; Pop. 1,489; Zip Code 96093; Elev. 2,011; Lat. 40-43-52 N long. 122-56-27 W; Named (1850) for an early prospector of the gold mines in the area.

•WEED, City, Siskiyou County; Pop. 2,879; Zip Code 96094; Elev. 3,466; Lat. 41-25-22 N long. 122-23-06 W; N California. This lumbering town was named for Abner Weed, who founded a lumber company here at the turn of the century.

•WEIMAR, Town, Placer County; Pop. 900; Zip Code 9573; Lat. 39-28-39 N long. 121-02-55 W; Post office established 1886 and named in memory of "old Weimah," a colorful Chief of the Oleepas in the 1850s.

•WELDON, Town, Kern County; Pop. 100; Zip Code 93283; Elev. 2,653; Lat. 35-39-57 N long. 118-17-22 W; Named for William Weldon, a stockman of the 1850s.

•WEOTT, Town, Humboldt County; Pop. 450; Zip Code 95571; Elev. 338; Lat. 40-19-19 N long. 123-55-14 W; Name is Americanization of Wiyot, the Humboldt Bay Indians.

•WEST COVINA, City, Los Angeles County; Pop. 80,094; Zip Code 91790; Elev. 381; Lat. 34-04-07 N long. 117-56-17 W; Residential city in the San Gabriel Valley incorporated 1923.

•WEST END, Town, San Bernardino County; Pop. 100; Zip Code 93562; Lat. 37-47-07 N long. 122-26-45 W; Near Trona. Name changed in 1919 from Hanksite by F. M. ("Borax") Smith, president of the West End Consolidated Mining Co.

•WEST HOLLYWOOD, City, Los Angeles County; Pop. 34,000; Zip Code 90069; Elev. 287; Lat. 34-05-24 N long. 118-21-39 W; NE of Beverly Hills.

•WESTMINSTER, City, Orange County; Pop. 71,133; Zip Code 92683; Elev. 35; Lat. 33-45-33 N long. 118-00-21 W; SE of Long Beach. Named 1870s by Rev. L. P. Weber, who founded a colony here for people sympathetic with the ideals of the Presbyterian Church as laid down in the Westminster Assembly (1643-49).

•WESTMORELAND, Town, Imperial County; Pop. 1,590; Zip Code 92281; Elev. 159 feet below sea level; Lat. 33-02-14 N long. 115-37-14 W; Named 1910 to call attention to "more land to the west" in Irrigation District No. 8.

•WEST PITTSBURG, City, Contra Costa County; Pop. 5,969; Zip Code 94565; Elev. 50; Lat. 38-01-37 N long. 121-56-10 W.

•WEST POINT, Town, Calaveras County; Pop. 900; Zip Code 95255; Elev. 2,790; Lat. 38-23-57 N long. 120-31-35 W; Old mining town, called Indian Gulch in 1852 and West Point in 1854.

•WEST SACRAMENTO, City, Yolo County; Pop. 12,002; Zip Code 95691; Lat. 38-34-50 N long. 121-31-45 W.

•WESTPORT, Town, Mendocino County; Pop. 200; Zip Code 95488; Elev. 50; Lat. 39-38-09 N long. 123-46-55 W; NW California. First named Beal's Landing for Lloyd Beal, who arrived in 1864, the town was renamed Westport at the instigation of James T. Rogers, a native of Eastport, Maine.

•WESTWOOD, Town, Lassen County; Pop. 1,862; Zip Code 96137; Lat. 40-18-22 N long. 121-00-17 W.

•WHEATLAND, Town, Yuba County; Pop. 1,474; Zip Code 95692; Elev. 87; Lat. 39-00-36 N long. 121-25-19 W; When railroad was built from Scramento to Marysville (1867). name was applied to station because it was a wheat-growing district.

•WHEELER RIDGE, Town, Kern County; Pop. rural; Zip Code 9330; Elev. 964; Lat. 35-00-16 N long. 118-56-55 W; Near Mettler. Named for Lt. George M. Wheeler, in charge of the 1870s survey west of the 100th meridian.

•WHISKEYTOWN, Shasta County; Pop. 50; Zip Code 96095; Lat. 40-38-20 N long. 122-33-31 W; Named after the stream on which it is located.

•WHITE PINES, Town, Calaveras County; Pop. 150; Zip Code 95223; Lat. 38-15-58 N long. 120-20-23 W; Near Arnold. Post office established 1941 and named because of the presence of a species of white pine.

•WHITE WATER, Village, Riverside County; Pop. 100; Zip Code 92282; S Central California; Named for the milky appearance of the river flowing nearby.

•WHITTIER, City, Los Angeles County; Pop. 68,872; Zip Code 90605; Elev. 365; Lat. 33-58-45 N long. 118-01-55 W; Suburb of Los Angeles on its east. Founded (1881) by Quakers and named for the poet, *John Greenleaf Whittier.*

•WILDOMAR, Town, Riverside County; Pop. 400; Zip Code 92395; Lat. 33-35-52 N long. 117-16-40 W; Name coined 1883, when the old Ranch Laguna was subdivided, from names of the new owners: *William Collier* and *Donald* and *Margaret Graham.*

•WILLIAMS, Town, Colusa County; Pop. 1,655; Zip Code 95987; Elev. 801; Lat. 39-09-17 N long. 122-08-54 W; Named for *W. H. Williams,* who laid out town in 1876. Post office established 1880.

•WILLITS, Town, Mendocino County; Pop. 4,008; Zip Code 95490; Elev. 1,364; Lat. 39-24-35 N long. 123-21-16 W; Post office established late 1870s and named for *Hiram Willits,* who settled here in 1857.

•WILLOWS, Town, Glenn County Seat; Pop. 4,777; Zip Code 95988; Elev. 135; Lat. 39-31-28 N long. 122-11-33 W; Laid out in 1876 at a willow pond, the one watering place south of Stony Creek.

•WILMINGTON, Subdivision, Los Angeles County; Pop. (with Los Angeles); Zip Code 90744; Lat. 33-46-48 N long. 118-15-42 W; SW California.

•WILSEYVILLE, Town, Calaveras County; Pop. 500; Zip Code 95257; Lat. 38-22-45 N long. 120-30-49 W; Post office established September 16, 1947, and named for *Lawrence A. Wilsey,* an official of the American Forest Products Co.

•WILSONIA, Town, Tulare County; Pop. 5; Zip Code 93633; Lat. 36-44-06 N long. 118-57-20 W; In Kings Canyon National Park.

•WINCHESTER, Town, Riverside County; Pop. 300; Zip Code 92396; Elev. 1,474; Lat. 33-42-25 N long. 117-05-01 W; Named for one of owners of the land when it was subdivided in 1886.

•WINDSOR, Town, Sonoma County; Pop. 2,359; Zip Code 95492; Elev. 118; Lat. 38-32-50 N long. 122-48-55 W; Post office established August 31, 1855, and named at suggestion of Englishman *Hiram Lewis,* presumably after Windsor Castle.

•WINTER GARDENS, Town, San Diego County; Pop. (included with Lakeside) 15,300; Zip Code 92040; Lat. 32-49-52 N long. 116-55-57 W.

•WINTERS, City, Yolo County; Pop. 2,652; Zip Code 95694; Elev. 135; Lat. 38-31-30 N long. 121-58-11 W; N central California.

•**WINTON**, Town, Merced County; Pop. 3,393; Zip Code 95388; Lat. 37-23-22 N long. 120-36-44 W; New town called Winfield. Santa Fe Railroad station established 1911, and *N. D. Chamberlain* suggested the name Winton, for *Edgar Winton*, one of the surveryors who laid out the town.

•**WOODBRIDGE**, Town, San Joaquin County; Pop. 1,397; Zip Code 95258; Elev. 46; Lat. 38-09-15 N long. 121-18-01 W; First known as Woods' Ferry because *Jeremiah Woods* began operating a ferry across the river here in 1852. A bridge built in 1859, and name changed to present one.

•**WOODLAKE**, City, Tulare County; Pop. 5,375; Zip Code 93286; Lat. 38-09-08 N long. 121-14-32 W; 38 mi. SE of Fresno in S central California.

•**WOODLAND**, City, Yolo County Seat; Pop. 30,225; Zip Code 95695; Elev. 65; Lat. 36-24-49 N long. 119-05-52 W; N Central California. Woodland acquired its present name--suggested by the grove of huge oaks in which it stood--when the post office opened in 1859.

•**WOODLAND HILLS**, Subdivision, Los Angeles County; Pop. (with Los Angeles); Zip Code 91364; Lat. 34-10-06 N long. 118-36-18 W; SW California.

•**WOODSIDE**, Town, San Mateo county; Pop. 5,291; Zip Code 94062; Elev. 382; Lat. 37-25-48 N long. 122-15-10 W; Place named after a lumber camp as early as 1849. Post office established April 18, 1854.

•**WRIGHTWOOD**, Town, San Bernardino County; Pop. 950; Zip Code 92397; Elev. 5,931; Lat. 34-21-39 N long. 117-37-57 W; The old Circle C Ranch was made a residential community about 1924 and named for the subdivider, a Mr. Wright.

•**YOLO**, Town, Yolo County; Pop. 600; Zip Code 95697; Lat. 38-24-37 N long. 121-42-16 W; Post office established February 3, 1853. Formerly called Cacheville. Name may be a corruption of

the Indian word *yoloy*, meaning "a place abound with rushes," or may be derived from Yodoi, the name of a Patwin village at the site of Knights Landing.

•**YORBA LINDA**, City, Los Angeles County; Pop. 28,254; Zip Code 92686; Elev. 397; Lat. 33-53-19 N long. 117-48-44 W; A real estate name, combining those of two nearby places--Yorba and Olinda--commemorates name of one of the oldest pioneer families of southern California, the Yorbas.

•**YOUNTVILLE**, Town, Napa Valley; Pop. 2,893; Zip Code 94599; Elev. 97; Lat. 38-24-06 N long. 122-21-35 W; Named for George C. Yount of North Carolina, who came to California with the Wolfskill party in 1831 and in 1836, was grantee of Rancho Caymus, on which the town is situated.

•**YREKA**, City, Siskiyou County Seat; Pop. 5,916; Zip Code 96097; Elev. 2,625; Lat. 41-44-08 N long. 122-38-00 W; N California. The place was known as Thompson's Dry Diggins; then, when a town was laid out in May, as Shasta Butte City; and finally, in 1852, as Yreka, which is thought to be a corruption of Wai-ri-ka "mountain."

•**YUBA CITY**, City, Sutter County Seat, Pop. 18,736; Zip Code 95991; Elev. 70; Lat. 39-08-26 N long. 121-36-57 W; N California. One tale relates that Yuba is a corruption of Uva (grape), the name given the river in 1824 by Spanish explorers who found its banks overgrown with wild grapes; another, that a branch of the Maidu tribe in the neighborhood was called the Yu-ba.

•**YUCCA VALLEY**, Town, San Bernardino County; Pop. 4,300; Zip Code 92284; Elev. 3,279; Lat. 34-07-09 N long. 116-26-42 W; Yucca is another name for the Joshua Tree.

•**ZENIA**, Town, Trinity County; Pop. 10; Zip Code 95495; Elev. 2,969; Lat. 40-12-20 N long. 123-29-27 W; Name applied in 1900 by George Croyden, the first postmaster, for a girl of that name.

COLORADO

•**AGUILAR,** Town; Los Arimos County; Pop. 624; Zip Code 81020; Elev. 6,700; Lat. 37-23-43 N Long. 104-39-16 W; SE CO. Named for a prominent early pioneer of Southern Colorado, Jose Ramon Aguilar.

•**AKRON,** Town; Pop. Washington County Seat; Pop. 1,716; Zip Code; Elev. 4,661; Lat. 40-09-35 N Long. 103-13-11 W; The town takes its name from the home town of an early railroad official's wife, Akron, Ohio.

•**ALAMOSA,** City; Alamosa County Seat; Pop. 6,830; Zip Code 81101; Elev. 7,544; Lat. 37-28-08 N Long. 105-51-26 W; S Colorado. Founded by A.C. Hunt and given the Spanish name meaning "cottonwood."

•**ALMA,** Town; Park County; Pop. 132; Zip Code 80420; Elev. 10,353; Lat. 39-17-06 N Long. 106-03-33 W; central Colorado. The town is named after either the wife or the daughter of an early settler.

•**ANTONITO,** Town; Conejos County; Pop. 1,103; Zip Code 81120; Elev. 7,882; Lat. 37-04-39 N Long. 106-00-48 W; S Colorado. Named by railroad officials for the nearby San Antonio Mountains.

•**ARRIBA,** Town; Lincoln County; Pop. 236; Zip Code 80804; Lat. 39-17-22 N Long. 103-16-33 W; E Colorado. In Spanish the town's name means "above" and refers to the town's high altitude.

•**ARVADA,** City; Adams & Jefferson Counties; Pop. 84,576; Zip Code 800+; W of Denver in central Colorado. The city takes its name from early pioneer settler Hiram Arvada Hoskins.

•**ASPEN,** City; Pitkin County Seat; Pop. 3,678; Zip Code 81611; Elev. 7,907; Lat. 39-11-30 N Long. 106-49-30 W; W central Colorado. Early surveyor B. Clark Wheeler named the town for the many Aspen trees groves in the area.

•**AULT,** Town; Weld County; Pop. 1,056; Zip Code 80610; Elev. 4,939; Lat. 40-35-06 N Long. 104-44-12 W ; N Colorado. The town's name honors early grain merchant Alexander Ault.

•**AURORA,** City; Adams & Arapahoe Counties; Pop. 158,588; Zip Code 800+; Elev. 5,400; Lat. 39-42-31 N Long. 104-51-13 W; 5 m. E of Denver in NE central Colorado. Named by the town fathers, the word is Latin and means "dawn."

•**AVON,** Town; Eagle County; Pop. 640; Zip Code 81620; Elev. 7,465; Lat. 39-37-35 N Long. 106-31-26 W ; NW central Colorado. An early English settler named the town for England's famous Avon River.

•**BASALT,** Town; Eagle & Pitikin Counties; Pop. 529; Zip Code 81621; Elev. 6,600; Lat. 39-22-05 N Long. 107-01-50 W; NW central Colorado. The town is named after nearby Balsalt Peak.

•**BAYFIELD,** Town; La Plata County; Pop. 724; Zip Code 81122; Elev. 6,892; Lat. 37-13-37 N Long. 107-35-52 W; SW Colorado. The town's name honors W.A. Bay who first laid it out.

•**BENNETT,** Town; Adams County; Pop. 942; Zip Code 80102; Elev. 5,483; Lat. 39-45-40 N Long. 104-26-05 W ; NE central Colorado. Named in honor of H.P. Bennett, an early Denver postmaster.

•**BERTHOUD,** Town; Larimer County; Pop. 2,362; Zip Code 805+; Elev. 13; 5,240; Lat. 40-18-36 N Long. 105-05-16 W; N Colorado. The town's name recalls the chief engineer of the Colorado Central Railroad, Captain Edward Berthoud.

•**BETHUNE,** Town; Kit Carson County; Pop. 149; Zip Code 80805; Elev. 4,294; Lat. 39-18-26 N Long. 102-25-18 W; E Colorado. Founded during World War I, its name recalls a town in France.

•**BLACK HAWK,** Town; Gilpin County; Pop. 232; Zip Code 80422; Elev. 8,056; Lat. 39-48-47 N Long. 105-30-15 W; N central Colorado. The name given to the town by an early mining company, itself named after the famous Indian chief.

•**BLANCA,** Town; Costilla County; Pop. 252; Zip Code 81123; Elev. 7,870; Lat. 37-25-31 N Long. 105-31-03 W; S Colorado. The town is named for its location at the foot of Mt. Blanca.

•**BOONE,** Town; Pueblo County; Pop. 431; Zip Code 81025; Elev. 4,476; Lat. 38-14-35 N Long. 104-15-50 W ; SE central Colorado. A descendant of Daniel Boone gave the town its name.

•**BOULDER,** City; Boulder County Seat; Pop. 76,685; Zip Code 803+; Elev. 5,344; Lat. 40-00-23 N Long. 105-15-47 W; 25 m. NW of Denver in N central Colorado. Named after the profusion of boulders in the area.

•**BOW MAR,** Town; Arapahoe & Jefferson Counties; Pop. 930; NE central Colorado. The town is located between Bowles and Marston Lakes, hence its combined name.

•**BRANSON,** Town; Las Animas County; Pop. 73; Zip Code 81027; Elev. 6,299; Lat. 37-00-50 N Long. 103-52-18 W; SE Colorado. An early pioneer, Al Branson, gave the town its name.

•**BRECKENRIDGE,** Town; Summit County Seat; Pop. 818; Zip Code 80424; Elev. 9,602; Lat. 39-27-26 N Long. 106-02-40 W; central Colorado. The town is named after a Vice-President of the United States in the Civil War era.

•**BRIGHTON,** City; Adams & Weld Counties; Adams County Seat; Pop. 12,773; Zip Code 80601; Elev. 4,983; Lat. 39-56-56 N Long. 104-57-34 W; NE central Colorado. The wife of the original surveyor named it after her hometown in Massachusetts.

•**BROOMFIELD,** City; Adams, Boulder & Jefferson Counties; Pop. 20,730; Zip Code 80020; Elev. 5,400; Lat. 39-55-01 N Long. 105-05-56 W; NE central Colorado. Railroad officials gave the town its name for a nearby field of broom corn.

•**BRUSH,** City; Morgan County; Pop. 4,082; Zip Code 80723; Elev. 4,231; NE Colorado. An early cattleman, J.L. Brush, gave the town its name.

•**BUENA VISTA,** Town; Chaffee County; Pop. 2,075; Zip Code 81211; Elev. 7,955; Lat. 38-50-20 N Long. 106-08-01 W; central Colorado. A Spanish name meaning "good view."

•**BURLINGTON,** City; Kit Carson County Seat; Pop. 3,107; Zip Code 80807; Elev. 4,166; Lat. 39-18-46 N Long. 102-15-47 W; E Colorado. Original settlers from Burlington, Kansas recalled their prior home.

•**CALHAN,** Town; El Paso County; Pop. 541; Zip Code 80808; Elev. 6,558; Lat. 39-02-00 N Long. 104-18-30 W ; E central Colorado. Named for the contractor who built the local Chicago, Rock Island, and Pacific Railroad.

•**CAMPO,** Town; Baca County; Pop. 185; Zip Code 81029; Lat. 37-06-17 N Long. 102-34-11 W; SE corner of Colorado. A Spanish word meaning "field."

•**CANON CITY,** City; Fremont County Seat; Pop. 13,037; Zip Code 81212; Elev. 5,332; Lat. 38-25-48 N Long. 105-12-53 W; S central Colorado. Named after the nearby Grand Canyon of the Arkansas River.

•**CARBONDALE,** Town; Garfield County; Pop. 2,084; Zip Code 81623; Elev. 6,170; Lat. 39-24-10 N Long. 107-12-31 W; W Colorado. An original town father, John Mankin, named it for his home town in Pennsylvania.

•**CASTLE ROCK,** Town; Douglas County Seat; Pop. 3,921; Zip Code 80104; Elev. 6,000; Lat. 39-22-28 N Long. 104-51-40 W; central Colorado. Named by botantist, Dr. Edwin James, for a nearby castellated rock.

•**CEDAREDGE,** Town; Delta County; Pop. 1,184; Zip Code 81413; Elev. 6,264; Lat. 38-53-57 N Long. 107-55-23 W; W Colorado. Named after a nearby belt of cedar trees.

•**CENTER,** Town; Rio Grande & Saguache County; Pop. 1,630; Zip Code 81125; Elev 7,645; Lat. 37-44-41 N Long. 106-06-33 W; S Colorado. Named by early pioneers to designate the town's location in the center of the San Luis Valley.

•**CENTRAL CITY,** City; Gilpin County Seat; Pop. 329; Zip Code 80427; Elev. 8,496; Lat. 39-48-47 N Long. 105-31-23 W; N central Colorado. A trading town for surrounding mining camps, its central location suggested its name.

•**CHERAW,** Town; Otera County; Pop. 233; Zip Code 81030; Lat. 38-06-09 N Long. 103-29-52 W; SE Colorado. The Cheraw Indians left their name on a nearby lake and then the town.

•**CHERRY HILLS VILLAGE,** City; Arapahoe County; Pop. 5,127; NE central Colorado. The city is named for now vanished cherry orchards.

•**CHEYENNE WELLS,** Town; Cheyenne County Seat; Pop. 950; Zip Code 80810; Elev. 4,282; Lat. 38-49-04 N Long. 102-20-56 W; E Colorado. The town is the site of several wells and Cheyenne refers to the local Indians.

•**COAL CREEK,** Town; Fremont County; Pop. 190; Zip Code 81221; Lat. 38-21-37 N Long. 105-09-02 W; S central Colorado. The coal seams running alongside a nearby stream gave the town its name.

•**COKEDALE,** Town; Las Animas County; Pop. 90; Zip Code 81222; Elev. 6,350; Lat. 37-08-15 N Long. 104-37-10 W; SE Colorado. The town's refers to coke ovens used to process local coal.

•**COLLBRAN,** Town; Mesa County; Pop. 344; Zip Code 81624; Elev. 5,987; Lat. 39-14-09 N Long. 107-57-30 W ; W Colorado. The town's name remembers an early railroad man in the community.

•**COLORADO SPRINGS,** City; El Paso County Seat; Pop. 215,150; Zip Code 80900; Elev. 6,008; Lat. 38-50-53 N Long. 104-47-52 W; E central Colorado. Named for the numerous mineral springs in the area.

•**COMMERCE CITY,** City; Adams County; Pop. 16,234; Zip Code 80022; Lat. 39-48-39 N Long. 104-56-01 W; NE of Denver in NE central Colorado. Refering to the city's early industrial development.

•**CORTEZ,** City; Montezuma County Seat; Pop. 7,095; Zip Code 81321; Elev. 6,201; Lat. 37-20-58 N Long. 108-34-28 W; SW corner of Colorado. Named for the Spanish conqueror of Mexico.

•**CRAIG,** City; Moffat County Seat; Pop. 8,133; Zip Code 81625; Elev. 6,186; Lat. 40-31-04 N Long. 107-32-47 W; NW corner of CO, Rev. Bayard Craig, the town's developer, gave the city its name.

•**CRAWFORD,** Town; Delta County; Pop. 268; Zip Code 81415; Lat. 38-42-22 N Long. 107-36-30 W; W Colorado. Named for Geroge Crawford, former governor of Kansas.

•**CREEDE,** Town; Mineral County Seat; Pop. 610; Zip Code 81130; Elev. 8,838; Lat. 37-51-08 N Long. 106-55-34 W; S Colorado. A boom mining town developed after mineral discoveries by miner Nicolas Creede.

•**CRESTED BUTTE,** Town; Gunnison County; Pop. 959; Zip Code 81224; Elev. 8,908; Lat. 38-52-16 N Long. 106-58-51 W; W central Colorado. For a nearby mountain top which resembles a cock's comb.

•**CRESTONE,** Town; Saguache County; Pop. 54; Zip Code 81131; Elev. 7,500; Lat. 37-59-29 N Long. 105-42-13 W; S Colorado. A loose Spanish translation meaning "cock's comb."

•**CRIPPLE CREEK,** City; Teller County Seat; Pop. 655; Zip Code 80813; Elev. 9,508; Lat. 38-44-51 N Long. 105-10-43 W; central Colorado. Early cowboys gave the town its name for a cow crippled while crossing the creek.

•**CROOK,** Town; Logan County; Pop. 177; Zip Code 80726; Elev. 3,711; Lat. 40-51-22 N Long. 102-48-04 W ; NE Colorado. The Union Pacific Railroad named the town in honor of General George Crook.

•**CROWLEY,** Town; Crowley County; Pop. 192; Zip Code 81033; Elev. 4,347; Lat. 38-11-29 N Long. 103-51-22 W; E Colorado. Named after John Crowley, a local Colorado state senator.

•**DACONO,** Town; Weld County; Pop. 2,321; Zip Code 80514; Lat. 40-05-16 N Long. 104-56-47 W; N Colorado. Founding coal miner, C.L. Baum, named the town for his wife Daisy and her two friends Cora and Nona.

•**DE BEQUE,** Town; Mesa County; Pop. 279; Zip Code 81630; Elev. 4,954; Lat. 39-19-57 N Long. 108-13-00 W ; W Colorado. The town's name honors Dr. Wallace deBeque, a physician who settled in the area in 1883.

•**DEER TRAIL,** Town; Arapahoe County; Pop. 463; Zip Code 80105; Elev. 5,183; Lat. 39-35-13 N Long. 104-03-03 W; NE central Colorado. Frontiersman Oliver P. Wiggins named the town for a nearby deer trail.

•**DEL NORTE,** Town; Rio Grande County Seat; Pop. 1,709; Zip Code 81132; Elev. 7,778; Lat. 37-31-40 N Long. 106-21-05 W; S Colorado. Gold Miners shortened a Spanish name, Rio Grande del Norte, to Del Norte or "of the north."

•**DELTA,** City; Delta County Seat; Pop. 3,931; Zip Code 81416; Elev. 4,953; Lat. 38-44-13 N Long. 108-03-36 W; W Colorado. Named after its location on the delta of the uncompahgre river.

•**DENVER,** City; Denver County Seat; Pop. 491,396; Zip Code 802+; Elev. 5,280; Lat. 39-43-21 N Long. 104-58-39 W; On South Platte River in NE central Colorado. Kansas settlers named the city for their former governor, James W. Denver.

•**DILLON,** Town; Summit County; Pop. 337; Zip Code 80435; Elev. 8,600; Lat. 39-38-08 N Long. 106-03-34 W ; central Colorado. Gold miner Tom Dillion first discovered the area and later explorers named it in his honor.

•**DINOSAUR,** Town; Moffat County; Pop. 313; Zip Code 81610; Elev. 5,858; Lat. 40-14-21 N Long. 109-00-32 W; NW corner of Colorado. First called Artesia, the town's name refelcts its proximity to Dinosaur National Monument.

•**DOLORES,** Town; Montezuma County; Pop. 802; Zip Code 81323; Elev. 6,936;; SW corner of Colorado. Named for the Delores River that flows thru the town.

•**DOVE CREEK,** Town; Dolores County; Pop. 826; Zip Code 81324; Elev. 6,600; Lat. 37-45-56 N Long. 108-54-21 W; SW Colorado. Early pioneers named the area for the flocks of doves in the vicinity.

•**DURANGO,** City; La Plata County Seat; Pop. 11,426; Zip Code 81301; Elev. 6,523; Lat. 37-17-13 N Long. 107-52-18 W; 20 m. N of New Mexico border in SW Colorado. Former territorial governor, A.C. Hunt, named the city after the city in Mexico.

•**EADS,** Town; Kiowa County Seat; Pop. 878; Zip Code 81036; Elev. 4,213; Lat. 38-14-35 N Long. 104-15-50 W; E Colorado. The town's name honors noted engineer James B. Eads, who built the Eads Bridge across the Mississippi River at St. Louis.

•**EAGLE,** Town; Eagle County Seat; Pop. 801; Zip Code 81631; Elev. 6,600; Lat. 39-39-14 N Long. 106-49-48 W; NW central Colorado. Called Rio Aquilla by the railroad, early citizens changed it to Eagle after the nearby Eagle River.

•**EATON,** Town; Weld County; Pop. 1,932; Zip Code 80615; Elev. 4,839; Lat. 40-31-48 N Long. 104-42-50 W ; N Colorado. The town is named after Benjamin Eaton, fourth governor of Colorado.

•**EDDEY,** Town; Yuma County; Pop. 262; NE Colorado. Named for an early pioneer.

•**EDGEWATER,** City; Jefferson County; Pop. 5,714; Zip Code 80214; central Colorado. A descriptive name for the city's location on the shore of Sloan's Lake.

•**ELIZABETH,** Town; Elbert County; Pop. 789; Zip Code 80107 Elev. 6,448; Lat. 39-21-40 N Long. 104-36-10 W; E central Colorado. Governor John Evans named the town for his sister-in-law, Elizabeth Gray Kimbark Hubbard.

•**EMPIRE,** Town; Clear Creek County; Pop. 423; Zip Code 80438; Elev. 8,614; Lat. 39-45-39 N Long. 105-41-32 W; N central Colorado. The four original settlers named the town after the nickname for New York State.

•**ENGLEWOOD,** City; Arapahoe County; Pop. 30,021; Zip Code 801+; Elev. 5,369; Lat. 39-38-04 N Long. 104-58-55 W; NE central Colorado. An old English word meaning a "wooded nook," and named by incorporating citizens after a similarly named city in Illinois.

•**ERIE,** Town; Boulder & Weld Counties; Pop. 1,254; Zip Code 80516; Elev. 5,000; Lat. 40-03-01 N Long. 105-03-37 W ; N Colorado. The town was named by early miners for the mining town in Pennsylvania.

•**ESTES PARK,** Town; Larimer County; Pop. 2,703; Zip Code 80517; Elev. 7,522; Lat. 40-20-26 N Long. 105-34-20 W; N Colorado. Named for its first permanent settler, Joel Estes.

•**EVANS,** City; Weld County; Pop. 5,063; Zip Code 80620; Lat. 40-22-55 N Long. 104-42-02 W; N Colorado. The city is named for Colorado's second territorial governor, John Evans.

•**FAIRPLAY,** Town; Park County Seat; Pop. 421; Zip Code 80440; Elev. 7,040; Lat. 39-18-57 N Long. 105-53-35 W; Central Colorado. Named by early miners who discovered rich ore deposits after having been denied good locations in a nearby area.

•**FEDERAL HEIGHTS,** City; Adams County; Pop. 7,846; NE central Colorado. Named for the major north-south thoroughfare, Federal Boulevard, through western Denver.

•**FIRESTONE,** Town; Weld County; Pop. 1,204; Zip Code 80520; Lat. 40-06-58 N Long. 104-56-48 W; N Colorado. Founded by the Denslow Coal and Land Co. and named for original landowner, Jacob Firestone.

•**FLAGLER,** Town; Kit Carson County; Pop. 550; Zip Code 80815; Lat. 39-17-45 N Long. 103-03-48 W; E Colorado. Henry M. Fowler, a millionarie railraod man, extended the railroad through the area and gave the town his name.

•**FLEMING,** Town; Logan County; Pop. 388; Zip Code 80728; Elev. 4,240; Lat. 40-40-33 N Long. 102-50-19 W ; NE Colorado. H.B. Fleming, a representative of the Lincoln Land Co., gave the town his name when it was laid out in 1889.

•**FLORENCE,** City; Fremont County; Pop. 2,987; Zip Code 81226; Elev. 5,191; Lat. 38-23-06 N Long. 105-08-14 W; S central Colorado. Prominent town father and oil businessman, James McCandless, had the town named after his daughter, Florence.

•**FORT COLLINS,** City; Larimer County Seat; Pop. 64,632; Zip Code 805+; Elev. 5,003; Lat. 40-35-08 N Long. 105-06-07 W; N Colorado. Set up as an army base the city's name honors Colonel W. O. Collins, commander at Fort Laramie.

•**FORT LUPTON,** City; Weld County; Pop. 4,251; Zip Code 80621; Elev. 4,906; Lat. 40-05-16 N Long. 104-49-07 W; N Colorado. Lancaster Lupton, a former Army lieutenant, established a trading post in the area and gave it an army ring.

•**FORT MORGAN,** City; Morgan County Seat; Pop. 8,768; Zip Code 80701; Elev. 4,240; Lat. 40-15-47 N Long. 103-49-02 W; NE Colorado. The name honors civil war era colonel Christopher A. Morgan.

•**FOUNTAIN,** City; El Paso County; Pop. 8,324; Zip Code 80817; Elev. 5,546; Lat. 38-43-51 N Long. 104-44-12 W; E central Colorado. A descriptive name for the bubbling creek that flows through the city.

•**FOWLER,** Town; Otero County; Pop. 1,227; Zip Code 81039; Elev. 4,341; Lat. 38-07-45 N Long. 104-01-34 W ; SE Colorado. Named for Professor O.S. Fowler when the town was platted in 1887.

•**FRASER,** Town; Grand County; Pop. 470; Zip Code 80442; Elev. 8,574; Lat. 39-56-58 N Long. 105-49-33 W ; N Colorado. Named after the Fraser River that flows through the town.

•**FREDERICK,** Town; Weld County; Pop. 855; Zip Code 80530; Lat. 40-06-03 N Long. 104-56-48 W; N Colorado. The town gets its name from original landowner, Frederic A. Clark.

•**FRISCO,** Town; Summit County; Pop. 1,221; Zip Code 80443; Elev. 9.097; Lat. 39-34-44 N Long. 106-05-47 W; central Colorado. The first settler, H.A. Recen, named the town after San Francisco's nickname.

•**FRUITA,** Town; Mesa County; Pop. 2,810; Zip Code 81521; Elev. 4,512; Lat. 39-09-04 N Long. 108-43-43 W ; W Colorado. Ariculturalist William Pabot named the town to advertise the regions horticultural possibilities.

•**GARDEN CITY,** Town; Weld County; Pop. 85; N Colorado. Nearby Greeley, Colorado has the official slogan: "Garden city of the West." Early town fathers borrowed part of the description.

•**GENOA,** Town; Lincoln County; Pop. 165; Zip Code 80818; Elev. 5,594; Lat. 39-16-46 N Long. 103-30-05 W ; E Colorado. Named for Genoa, Italy.

•**GEORGETOWN,** Town; Clear Creek County Seat; Pop. 830; Zip Code 80444; Elev. 8,512; Lat. 39-43-09 N Long. 105-42-01 W; N central Colorado. Miners George and David Griffith discovered gold in the region and George left his name on the town.

•GILCREST, Town; Weld County; Pop. 1,025; Zip Code 80623; Elev. 4,751; Lat. 40-17-01 N Long. 104-47-05 W; N Colorado. Banker W.K. Gilcrest bought up large parts of the town and established a bank. He named the town to honor his father.

•GLENDALE, City; Arapahoe County; Pop. 2,496; Zip Code 802+; NE central Colorado. A suburb of Denver; the name was chosen for its pleasant sound.

•GLENWOOD SPRINGS, City; Garfield County Seat; Pop. 4,637; Zip Code 81601; Elev. 5,763; Lat. 39-32-31 N Long. 107-19-39 W; W Colorado. Named for Glenwood, Iowa, and recalling the town's mineral springs.

•GOLDEN, City; Jefferson County Seat; Pop. 12,237; Zip Code 80401; Elev. 5,674; Lat. 39-44-54 N Long. 105-10-37 W; central Colorado. An early settler, Thomas L. Golden, left his name on the city.

•GRANADA, Town; Prowers County; Pop. 557; Zip Code 81041; Elev. 3,484; Lat. 38-03-57 N Long. 102-18-21 W; SE Colorado. Named for the city and kingdom in Spain.

•GRANBY, Town; Grand County; Pop. 963; Zip Code 80446; Elev. 7,939; Lat. 40-05-20 N Long. 105-56-50 W ; N Colorado. Attorney Granby Hillyer helped found the town and left it his name.

•GRAND JUNCTION, City; Mesa County Seat; Pop. 28,144; Zip Code 81501; Elev. 4,597; Lat. 39-03-22 N Long. 108-32-43 W; W Colorado. Descriptively named for the nearby junction of the Gunnison and Grand Rivers.

•GRAND LAKE, Town; Grand County; Pop. 382; Zip Code 80447; Lat. 40-15-17 N Long. 105-49-50 W; N Colorado. A popular summer resort, the town is named for nearby Grand Lake, the largest natural freshwater lake in Colorado.

•GRAND VALLEY, Town; Garfield County; Pop. 338; Zip Code 81635; W Colorado. Named for the valley of the Grand (now Colorado) River.

•GREELEY, City; Weld County Seat; Pop. 53,006; Zip Code 80631 Elev. 4,664; Lat. 40-24-23 N Long. 104-42-07 W; N Colorado. The town's name honors famous newspaper editor Horace Greeley, who helped found the first settlement.

•GREEN MOUNTAIN FALLS, Town; El Paso & Teller Counties; Pop. 607; Zip Code 80819; Lat. 38-55-59 N Long. 105-02-08 W; E central Colorado. Named for a nearby waterfall on Green Mountain.

•GREENWOOD VILLAGE, City; Arapahoe County; Pop. 5,729; NE central Colorado. Although an urban area, named for its once wooded countryside.

•GROVER, Town; Weld County; Pop. 158; Zip Code 80729; Elev. 507; Lat. 40-52-12 N Long. 104-13-41 W; N Colorado. Pioneer settler, Mrs. Neal Donovan, gave the town her maiden name.

•GUNNISON, City; Gunnison County Seat; Pop. 5,785; Zip Code 81230; Elev. 7,703; Lat. 38-32-47 N Long. 106-55-23 W; W central Colorado. The city's name honors Captain J.W. Gunnison who explored the area in 1853.

•GYPSUM, Town; Eagle County; Pop. 743; Zip Code 81637; Elev. 6,320; Lat. 39-38-55 N Long. 106-56-59 W ; NW central Colorado. Descrptively name for the large gypsum deposits in the area.

•HARTMAN, Town; Prowers County; Pop. 122; Zip Code 81043; Lat. 38-07-03 N Long. 102-12-49 W; SE Colorado. Named by the Santa Fe Railroad for one of its former company superintendants.

•HASWELL, Town; Kiowa County; Pop. 126; Zip Code 81045; Lat. 38-27-10 N Long. 103-09-04 W; E Colorado. Named by railroad financier Jay Gould's daughter. The source of her choice is not known.

•HAXTUN, Town; Phillips County; Pop. 1,014; Zip Code 80731; Elev. 4,039; Lat. 40-38-19 N Long. 102-37-25 W; NE Colorado. Named for one of the contractors who helped build the Burlington railroad through this town in 1888.

•HAYDEN, Town; Routt County; Pop. 1,720; Zip Code 81639; Elev. 6,337; Lat. 40-29-37 N Long. 107-15-26 W ; NW Colorado. First settlers named the town in honor of Ferdinand Hayden, then head of the U.S. Geological Survey.

•HILLROSE, Town; Morgan County; Pop. 213; Zip Code 80733; Lat. 40-19-20 N Long. 103-31-29 W; NE Colorado. The Burlington Railroad settled the town and allowed original landowner Kate Emerson to select a name. She reversed her sister's name : Rose Hill.

•HOLLY, Town; Prowers County; Pop. 969; Zip Code 81047; Elev. 3,387; Lat. 38-03-10 N Long. 102-07-29 W ; SE Colorado. Named after pioneer rancher, Hiram Holly, who owned a large ranch in the area.

•HOLYOKE, Town; Phillips County Seat; Pop. 2,092; Zip Code 80734; Elev. 3,736; Lat. 40-34-44 N Long. 102-17-54 W; NE Colorado. The town is named for Holyoke, Massachusetts; itself named for Edward Holyoke, an early president of Harvard College.

•HOOPER, Town; Alamosa County; Pop. 71; Zip Code 81136; Lat. 37-46-18 N Long. 105-23-00 W; S Colorado. Renamed for Major S. Hooper, passenger agent for the Denver and Rio Grande Railroad.

•HOT SULPHUR SPRINGS, Town; Grand County Seat; Pop. 405; Zip Code 80451; Elev. 7,655; Lat. 40-04-32 N Long. 106-06-44 W; N Colorado. Named for the nearby hot springs.

•HOTCHKISS, Town; Delta County; Pop. 849; Zip Code 81419; Elev. 5,351; Lat. 38-48-01 N Long. 107-43-04 W; W Colorado. The town is named for Enos Hotchkiss, an early settler.

•HUDSON, Town; Weld County; Pop. 698; Zip Code 80642; Elev. 5,000; Lat. 40-04-33 N Long. 104-38-59 W ; N Colorado. Named by the Hudson Land Company which developed the town.

•HUGO, Town; Lincoln County Seat; Pop. 776; Zip Code 80821; Lat. 38-56-39 N Long. 103-16-13 W; E Colorado. Named either for pioneer Richard Hugo or French novelist Victor Hugo.

•IDAHO SPRINGS, City; Clear Creek County; Pop. 2,077; Zip Code 80452; Elev. 7,524; Lat. 39-44-37 N Long. 105-31-43 W; N central Colorado. A mining town founded in 1859, the city takes its name from the Indian word "idahi, which is given various meanings."

•IGNACIO, Town; La Plata County; Pop. 667; Zip Code 81137; Elev. 6,432; Lat. 37-06-58 N Long. 107-37-57 W; SW Colorado. The town's land was purchased from the Ute Indians and named in honor of one of their chiefs.

•ILIFF, Town; Logan County; Pop. 218; Zip Code 80736; Elev. 3,998; Lat. 40-45-32 N Long. 103-03-50 W ; NE Colorado. Early Colorado cattle king, John Iliff's ranch occupied the town site.

•JAMESTOWN, Town; Boulder County; Pop. 223; Zip Code 80455; Lat. 40-07-10 N Long. 105-23-52 W; N central Colorado. Known as Jimtown to early settlers, postal officials cleaned it up to Jamestown when setting up the post office.

•**JOHNSTOWN,** Town; Weld County; Pop. 1,535; Zip Code 80543
Lat. 40-20-07 N Long. 104-54-39 W; N Colorado. Harvey Parish founded the town and named it for his son John.

•**JULESBURG,** Town; Sedgwick County Seat; Pop. 1,528; Zip Code 80737; Elev. 3,477; Lat. 40-59-17 N Long. 102-15-30 W; NE corner of Colorado. Originally a stage stop at the ranch and trading post of Jules Beni--from which it takes its name.

•**KEENESBURG,** Town; Weld County; Pop. 541; Zip Code 80643; Elev. 4,958; Lat. 40-06-33 N Long. 104-31-25 W; N Colorado. Named after an early rancher, Mr.Keene, when the post office was set up in 1907.

•**KERSEY,** Town; Weld County; Pop. 913; Zip Code 80644; Lat. 40-23-31 N Long. 104-33-59 W; N Colorado. Union Pacific roadmaster John Painter named the town for his mother's maiden name in 1896.

•**KIM,** Town; Las Animas County; Pop. 100; Zip Code 81049; Elev. 5,680; Lat. 37-15-04 N Long. 103-21-18 W ; SE Colorado. Early settlers named the town after Kipling's famous boy hero, Kim.

•**KIOWA,** Town; Elbert County Seat; Pop. 206; Zip Code 80117; Lat. 39-20-57 N Long. 104-28-24 W; E central Colorado. Named for the Kiowa Indian Tribe.

•**KIT CARSON,** Town; Cheyenne County; Pop. 278; Zip Code 80825; Elev. 4,273; Lat. 38-45-53 N Long. 102-47-27 W; E Colorado. The town is named for the famous western scout and explorer.

•**KREMMLING,** Town; Grand County; Pop. 1,296; Zip Code 80459; Lat. 40-03-33 N Long. 106-23-31 W; N Colorado. The town began as a general merchandise storerun by Kare Kremmling, hence the name.

•**LA JARA,** Town; Conejos County; Pop. 858; Zip Code 81140; Elev. 7,602; Lat. 37-16-17 N Long. 105-57-46 W; S Colorado. A Spanish name used by the locals to refer to the brush undergrowth along the river banks.

•**LA JUNTA,** City; Otero County Seat; Pop. 8,338; Zip Code 81050; Elev. 4,100; Lat. 37-59-02 N Long. 103-31-27 W; SE Colorado. IN Spanish the town's name refers to the junction of the Santa Fe and Kansas Pacific railroads.

•**LA SALLE,** Town; Weld County; Pop. 1,929; Zip Code 80645; Elev. 4,676; Lat. 40-21-09 N Long. 104-42-17 W; N Colorado. The town's name honors the seventeenth century French explorer La Salle, who discovered the Mississippi River.

•**LA VETA,** Town; Huerfano County; Pop. 611; Zip Code 81055; Elev. 7,013; Lat. 37-29-47 N Long. 105-00-25 W; S Colorado. The Spanish word means "vein" and refers to the many dykes radiating from nearby West Spanish Mountain.

•**LAFAYETTE,** City; Boulder County; Pop. 8,985; Zip Code 80026; Elev. 5,236; Lat. 39-59-53 N Long. 105-06-30 W; N central Colorado. The original owner Lafayette Miller gave the town its name.

•**LAKE CITY,** Town Hinsdale County Seat; Pop. 206; 303,Zip Code 81235; Elev. 8,658; Lat. 38-04-14 N Long. 107-18-42 W; Named for Lake San Cristobal, one of the largest natural lakes in Colorado.

•**LAKEWOOD,** City; Jefferson County; Pop. 112,848; Zip Code 802+; Elev.; W of Denver in central Colorado. Originally an agricultural area with many orchards and small lakes, and so named for that character.

•**LAMAR,** City; Prowers County Seat; Pop. 7,713; Zip Code 81052 Elev. 3,622; Lat. 38-04-59 N Long. 102-36-39 W; SE Colorado. Named in honor of the Secretary of the Interior, L.C. Lamar, at the time of its establishment.

•**LARKSPUR,** Town; Douglas County; Pop. 141; Zip Code 80118; Lat. 39-13-45 N Long. 104-53-11 W; central Colorado. The town was named for the many Larkspur flowers on the surrounding hills.

•**LAS ANIMAS,** City; Bent County Seat; Pop. 2,818; Zip Code 81054; Elev. 3,893; Lat. 38-03-50 N Long. 103-12-46 W; SE Colorado. The city is named for the nearby Las Animas River.

•**LEADVILLE,** City; Lake County Seat; Pop. 3,879; Zip Code 80461; Elev. 10,152; Lat. 40-43-05 N Long. 106-54-48 W; central Colorado. So named because of the large amounts of lead-silver ores in the area.

•**LIMON,** Town; Lincoln County; Pop. 1,805; Zip Code 80828; Elev. 5,365; Lat. 39-15-58 N Long. 103-41-45 W; E Colorado. Originally camp for the Rock Island Railroad, it was called Limon's camp after the camp foreman.

•**LITTLETON,** City; Arapahoe & Douglas Counties; Arapahoe County Seat; Pop. 28,631; Zip Code 801+; Elev. 5,362; Lat. 39-36-33 N Long. 104-59-32 W; 10 m. S of Denver in NW central Colorado. The city was founded by civil engineer, Richard Little, who came to Colorado in 1860.

•**LOCHBUIE,** Town; Weld County; Pop. 895; N Colorado. One of the town's organizers commemorated an ancestor's home: the Lochbuie area on the Isle of Mull in Scotland.

•**LOG LANE VILLAGE,** Town; Morgan County; Pop. 709; NE Colorado. Established in the 1950s, originally every building in the town had to use logs in their construction-- thus the name.

•**LONGMONT,** City; Boulder County; Pop. 42,942; Zip Code 80501; Elev. 5,000; Lat. 40-10-43 N Long. 105-06-41 W; 30 m. N of Denver in N central Colorado. The city's name honors the famous engineer-explorer, Major Stephen H. Long.

•**LOUISVILLE,** City; Boulder County; Pop. 5,593; Zip Code 80027; Elev. 5,337; Lat. 39-57-55 N Long. 105-09-36 W; N central Colorado. An early settler, Louis Nawatny, discovered coal on his land,started a settlement, and gave it his first name.

•**LOVELAND,** City; Larimer County; Pop. 30,244; Zip Code 80537; Elev. 4,982; Lat. 40-24-20 N Long. 105-05-11 W; 10 m. S of Fort Collins in N Colorado. Named in honor of W.A. H. Loveland, a prominent Colorado railroad man and state politican.

•**LYONS,** Town; Boulder County; Pop. 1,137; Zip Code 80540; Elev. 5,375; Lat. 40-13-40 N Long. 105-16-44 W; N central Colorado. The town is named after Mrs. Carrie Lyons, a pioneer newspaper editor.

•**MAMASSA,** Town; Conejos County; Pop. 945; Zip Code 81141; Elev. 7,683; Lat. 37-10-18 N Long. 105-56-24 W; S Colorado. Settled by Mormon colonists and named for Manassa, eldest son of Joseph, of ancient Israel.

•**MANCOS,** Town; Montezuma County; Pop. 870; Zip Code 81328 Elev. 7,030; Lat. 37-21-03 N Long. 108-17-24 W; SW corner of Colorado. The town is named for the nearby Mancos River.

•**MEEKER,** Town; Rio Blanco County Seat; Pop. 2,356; Zip Code 81641; Elev. 6,239; Lat. 40-02-26 N Long. 107-54-44 W; S Colorado. The town's name remembers Indian agent Nathan Meeker, who was murdered by the Ute Indians in November 1879.

•**MERINO,** Town; Logan County; Pop. 255; Zip Code 80741; Elev. 4,035; Lat. 40-29-03 N Long. 103-21-24 W ; NE Colorado. Originally named Buffalo the town's name was changed in 1882 for the hugh flocks of merino sheep raised in the area.

•**MILLIKEN,** Town; Weld County; Pop. 1,506; Zip Code 80543; Elev. 4,760; Lat. 40-20-01 N Long. 104-51-30 W; N Colorado. Named in honor of John D. Milliken, prominent businessman and railroad president.

•**MINTURN,** Town; Eagle County; Pop. 1,060; Zip Code 81645; Elev. 7,825; Lat. 39-35-23 N Long. 106-25-59 W; NW central Colorado. Denver and Rio Grande railroad roadmaster, Thomas Minturn, gave the town its name.

•**MOFFAT,** Town; Saguache County; Pop. 105; Zip Code 81143; Elev. 7,561; Lat. 38-00-00 N Long. 105-54-26 W; S Colorado. When the Denver and Rio Grande railroad was built in the area, the towns founder named for the railroad's president, David Moffat.

•**MONTE VISTA,** City; Rio Grande County; Pop. 3,902; Zip Code 81144; Elev. 7,663; ENTER; Lat. 37-34-31 N Long. 106-07-12 W; S Colorado. Founded in 1886 the town's name is Spanish for "Mountain View."

•**MONTROSE,** City; Montrose County Seat; Pop. 8,722; Zip Code 81401; Elev. 5,806; Lat. 38-28-59 N Long. 107-52-05 W; W Colorado. Pioneer Joe Selie named the town for Sir Walter Scott's fictional Dutchess of Montrose.

•**MONUMENT,** Town; El Paso County; Pop. 690; Zip Code 80132; Elev. 6,961; Lat. 39-05-37 N Long. 104-52-56 W; E central Colorado. A Descriptive name for a large rock formation west to the town.

•**MORRISON,** Town; Jefferson County; Pop. 478; Zip Code 80465; Elev. 5,669; Lat. 39-40-00 N Long. 105-06-59 W; central Colorado. Early pioneer, Geroge Morrison, gave the town his name.

•**MOUNT CRESTED BUTTE,** Town; Gunnison County; Pop. 272; W central Colorado. Descriptively named for a nearby mountain that resembles a cox comb.

•**NATURITA,** Town; Montrose County; Pop. 819; Zip Code 81422; Elev. 5,431; Lat. 38-13-08 N Long. 108-33-14 W; W Colorado. Rockwood Blake, an early settler, gave the town its Spanish name which means "close to nature."

•**NEDERLAND,** Town; Boulder County; Pop. 1,212; Area Code Zip Code 80466; Elev. 8,233; Lat. 39-57-57 N Long. 105-31-12 W; N central Colorado. Dutch capitalists owned the nearby Caribou silver mines and gave the town its name in 1877. It means "lowland."

•**NEW CASTLE,** Town; Garfield County; Pop. 563; Zip Code 81647; Lat. 39-34-15 N Long. 107-31-58 W; W Colorado. After the discovery of large coal deposits the town was renamed after the famous English mining center, New Castle.

•**NORTHGLENN,** City; Adams County; Pop. 29,847; Zip Code 802+; NE central Colorado. A generic name chosen by the developers in the 1950s.

•**NORWOOD,** Town; San Miguel County; Pop. 478; Zip Code 81423; Elev. 7,006; Lat. 38-08-02 N Long. 108-17-20 W; SW Colorado. Named for a town in Missouri.

•**NUCLA,** Town; Montrose County; Pop. 1,027; Zip Code 81424; Elev. 7,000; Lat. 38-16-18 N Long. 108-32-15 W; W Colorado. A socialist experiment at its settlement, the town's name is a corruption of nucleus or center.

•**NUNN,** Town; Weld County; Pop. 295; Zip Code 80648; Elev. 5,185; Lat. 40-42-15 N Long. 104-47-04 W ; N Colorado. Named in honor of homesteader Tom Nunn, who prevented a serious train wreck by flagging a train after he discovered a burning bridge.

•**OAK CREEK,** Town; Routt County; Pop. 929; Zip Code 80467; Elev. 7,414; Lat. 40-16-23 N Long. 106-57-13 W; NW Colorado. Named by the Oak Creek Land and Mining Company after itself.

•**OLATHE,** Town; Montrose County; Pop. 1,262; Area Code Zip Code 81425; Elev. 5,356; Lat. 36-36-32 N Long. 107-58-48 W; W Colorado. Kansas settlers renamed the town for their former home in Kansas.

•**OLNEY SPRINGS,** Town; Crowley County; Pop. 253; Zip Code 81062; Lat. 38-09-57 N Long. 103-56-34 W; E Colorado. Named fro a Missouri and Pacific Railroad representative at the time the track was laid.

•**OPHIR,** Town; San Miguel County; Pop. 38; Zip Code 81426; Elev. 9,800; Lat. 37-51-54 N Long. 107-51-45 W; SW Colorado. Named after the Biblical mines of King Solomon.

•**ORCHARD CITY,** Town; Delta County; Pop. 1,914; Area Code Zip Code 80647; Lat. 40-19-50 N Long. 104-07-06 W; W Colorado. A descriptive name for the orchards surrounding the town.

•**ORDWAY,** Town; Crowley County Seat; Pop. 1,135; Zip Code 81063; Elev. 4,312; Lat. 38-13-00 N Long. 103-45-00 W; E Colorado. Named for the original settler and land company organizer, George Ordway.

•**OTIS,** Town; Washington County; Pop. 534; Zip Code 80743; Elev. 4,335; Lat. 40-08-43 N Long. 102-57-56 W; NE Colorado. Probably named for an official connected with the Chicago Burlington and Quincy Railroad which came through the area.

•**OURAY,** City; Ouray County Seat; Pop. 684; Zip Code 81427; Elev. 7,811; Lat. 38-00-48 N Long. 107-40-39 W; SW Colorado. Named in honor of the famous Ute chief.

•**OVID,** Town; Sedgwick County; Pop. 439; Zip Code 80744; Elev. 3,521; Lat. 40-57-30 N Long. 102-23-04 W ; NE corner of Colorado. Originally a railroad siding named Ovid aftrer a nearby resident bachelor. The town grew up and kept the name.

•**PAGOSA SPRINGS,** Town; Archuleta County Seat; Pop. 1,331; Zip Code 81147; Elev. 7,105; Lat. 37-12-28 N Long. 107-18-04 W; S Colorado. A Ute Indian word meaning "healing waters" and descriptive of the mineral springs at the site.

•**PALISADE,** Town; Mesa County; Pop. 1,551; Zip Code 81526; Elev. 4,739; Lat. 39-06-15 N Long. 108-21-21 W; W Colorado. Descriptiely named for the high perpendicular bluffs edging the valley to the north.

•**PALMER LAKE,** Town; El Paso County; Pop. 1,130; Zip Code 80133; Elev. 7,237; Lat. 39-07-00 N Long. 104-55-24 W; E central Colorado. The town is named for General William Palmer of Denver and Rio Grande Railroad fame.

•**PAOLI,** Town; Phillips County; Pop. 81; Zip Code 80746; Elev. 3,898; Lat. 40-36-25 N Long. 102-27-53 W ; NE Colorado. Named after the Pennsylvania town--itself named for the Italian general, Pasquale Paoli.

•**PAONIA,** Town; Delta County; Pop. 1,425; Zip Code 81428; Elev. 5,645; Lat. 38-52-00 N Long. 107-35-37 W ; W Colorado. Slightly altered by the U.S. Postoffice, it was originally Peony for the common flower--Genus Peaonia.

•**PEETZ,** Town; Logan County; Pop. 220; Zip Code 80747; Elev. 4,432; Lat. 40-57-40 N Long. 103-06-54 W ; NE Colorado. Renamed for Peter Peetz, a pioneer homesteader.

•**PIERCE,** Town; Weld County; Pop. 878; Zip Code 80650; Elev. 5,039; Lat. 40-38-07 N Long. 104-45-37 W ; N Colorado. The name honor General John Pierce, former surveyor general of Colorado, and president of the Denver Pacific Railroad.

•**PITKIN,** Town; Gunnison County; Pop. 59; Zip Code 81241; Elev. 9,241; Lat. 38-36-34 N Long. 106-30-33 W ; W central Colorado. First called Quartzville but later changed to Pitkin to honor Governor F.W. Pitkin.

•**PLATTEVILLE,** Town; Weld County; Pop. 1,662; Zip Code 80651; Elev. 4,820; Lat. 40-13-11 N Long. 104-49-43 W; N Colorado. Located on the east bank of the Platte River and named for the stream.

•**PONCHA SPRINGS,** Town; Chaffee County; Pop. 321; Zip Code 81242; Elev. 7,465; Lat. 38-30-49 N Long. 106-04-17 W; central Colorado. The town is named after nearby Poncha Pass and the areas famous mineral springs.

•**PRITCHETT,** Town; Baca County; Pop. 183; Zip Code 81064; Elev. 3,900; Lat. 37-19-54 N Long. 102-51-15 W ; SE corner of Colorado. A terminus for the Atchison, Topeka and Santa Fe Railway and named for one of the railroads directors Henry Pritchett.

•**PUEBLO,** City; Pueblo County Seat; Pop. 101,686; Zip Code 810+; Elev. 4,662; Lat. 38-16-46 N Long. 104-34-37 W; 40 mi. SSE of Colorado Springs in SE central C Known at first as Independence, the name was later changed to Pueblo, Spanish for "town."

•**RAMAH,** Town; El Paso County; Pop. 119; Zip Code 80832; Elev. 6,094; Lat. 39-06-59 N Long. 104-10-36 W ; E central Colorado. The origin of the town's name is not known.

•**RANGELY,** Town; Rio Blanco County; Pop. 2,113; Zip Code 81648; Elev. 5,261; Lat. 40-05-00 N Long. 108-47-26 W; NW Colorado. The original settler, D.B. Case, named the settlement for Rangely, Massachusetts.

•**RAYMER,** Town; Weld County; Pop. 80; N Colorado. The Lincoln Land C ompany named the town Raymer in honor of George Raymer, an assistant engineer on the Burlington and Missouri Railroad.

•**REDCLIFF,** Town; Eagle County; Pop. 409; Zip Code 81649; Elev. 8,598; Lat. 39-31-00 N Long. 106-22-27 W ; NW central Colorado. The town is named for the nearby quartzite cliffs.

•**RICO,** Town; Dolores County Seat; Pop. 76; Zip Code 81332; Elev. 8,827; Lat. 37-41-01 N Long. 108-01-59 W; SW Colorado. A rich silver district, the miners named the town the Spanish word for riches.

•**RIDGWAY,** Town; Ouray County; Pop. 369; Zip Code 81432; Elev. 6,988; Lat. 38-09-10 N Long. 107-45-24 W ; SW Colorado. Honoring R.M. Ridgeway, one time superintendant of the Denver and Rio Grande Railroad's Mountain division.

•**RIFLE,** City; Garfield County; Pop. 3,215; Zip Code 81650; Elev. 5,345; Lat. 39-31-59 N Long. 107-47-01 W; W Colorado. The local stream was dubbed rifle stream after a soldier in a surveying party found a lost gun on the stream bank. The town took the name.

•**ROCKVALE,** Town; Fremont County; Pop. 338; Zip Code 81244 Elev. 5,260; Lat. 38-22-09 N Long. 107-47-01 W; S central Colorado. Named for the town in Maryland.

•**ROCKY FORD,** City; Otero County; Pop. 4,804; Zip Code 81067; Elev. 4,250; Lat. 38-02-51 N Long. 103-42-39 W; SE Colorado. A descriptive name refering to a nearby ford of the Arkansas River.

•**ROMEO,** Town; Conejos County; Pop. 308; Zip Code 81148; Elev. 7,735; Lat. 37-10-18 N Long. 105-56-34 W ; S Colorado. Originally called Romero after an early settler, confusion with another town with that name led to its being changed to Romeo.

•**RYE,** Town; Pueblo County; Pop. 232; Zip Code 81069; Elev. 232; Lat. 37-54-48 N Long. 104-56-19 W; SE central Colorado. Originally called Table Mountain, the name was changed to describe the abundant grain surrounding the town.

•**SAGUACHE,** Town; Saguache County Seat; Pop. 656; Zip Code 81149; Elev. 7,694; Lat. 38-05-11 N Long. 106-08-32 W; S Colorado. A Ute Indian word meaning "Blue Earth," and refering to a nearby large spring in which blue clay was found.

•**SALIDA,** City; Chaffee County Seat; Pop. 4,870; Zip Code 81201; Elev. 7,050; Lat. 38-32-01 N Long. 105-59-38 W; central Colorado. A Spanish word meaning "exit," and given to the town in 1881.

•**SAN LUIS,** Town; Costilla County Seat; Pop. 842; Zip Code 81152; Elev. 7,965; Lat. 37-00-22 N Long. 105-32-22 W; S Colorado. Known as the oldest town in Colorado, San Luis is Spanish for St. Louis.

•**SANFORD,** Town; Conejos County; Pop. 687; Zip Code 81151; S Colorado. Started as a Mormon settlement, it was named for Silas Sanford Smith, first president of the San Luis stake.

•**SAWPIT,** Town; San Miguel County; Pop. 41; SW Colorado. A descriptive name for the town's early industry.

•**SEDGWICK,** Town; Sedgwick County; Pop. 258; Zip Code 80749; Elev. 3,500; Lat. 40-55-55 N Long. 102-31-13 W; NE corner of Colorado. Named in honor of Major General John Sedgwick, a Union officer killed in the Civil War.

•**SEIBERT,** Town; Kit Carson County; Pop. 180; Zip Code 80834; Lat. 39-18-05 N Long. 102-52-00 W; E Colorado. The town is named for Henry Seibert, an official of the Rock Island Railraod that came through the town in 1888.

•**SEVERANCE,** Town; Weld County; Pop. 102; Zip Code 80546; Lat. 40-31-44 N Long. 104-51-12 W; N Colorado. Named for Dave Severance who managed to sell 160 acres to a development company for $325.00 per acre, then an astronomical price.

•**SHERIDAN,** City; Arapahoe County; Pop. 5,377; NE central Colorado. The city's name honors General Phil Sheridan, Union War hero.

•**SHERIDAN LAKE,** Town; Kiowa County; Pop. 87; Zip Code 81071; Elev. 4,083; Lat. 38-27-55 N Long. 102-15-42 W; E Colorado. In honor of Civil War general Phillip Sheridan.

•**SILT,** Town; Garfield County; Pop. 923; Zip Code 81652; Elev. 4,452; Lat. 39-32-53 N Long. 107-39-13 W ; W Colorado. A descriptive name for the local soil type.

•**SILVER CLIFF,** Town; Custer County; Pop. 280; Zip Code 81249; Elev. 8,000; Lat. 38-08-03 N Long. 105-26-51 W; S central Colorado. Named for the low, black-stained cliff indicative of the rich silver deposits found nearby.

•**SILVER PLUME,** Town; Clear Creek County; Pop. 140; Zip Code 80476; Elev. 9,175; Lat. 39-41-50 N Long. 105-44-00 W; N central Colorado. Refering to the plume like streaks of silver in the local silver ores.

•**SILVERTHORNE,** Town; Summit County Seat; Pop. 989; Zip Code 80498; central Colorado. Named in honor of Marshall Silverton who ran a famous hotel in the town.

•**SILVERTON,** Town; San Juan County; Pop. 794; Zip Code 81433; Elev. 9,305; Lat. 37-48-36 N Long. 107-39-51 W; SW Colorado. First called Baker's Park, but later changed to Silverton to reflect the rich silver mining in the area.

•**SIMLA,** Town; Elbert County; Pop. 494; Zip Code 80835; Elev. 5,768; Lat. 39-08-27 N Long. 104-05-00 W ; E central Colorado. The town takes its name from an early railroad siding.

•**SNOWMASS VILLAGE,** Town; Pitkin County; Pop. 999; Zip Code 81615; Lat. 39-19-52 N Long. 106-59-02 W; W central Colorado. The town gets its name from the nearby Snowmass Creek.

•**SPRINGFIELD,** Town; Baca County Seat; Pop. 1,657; Zip Code 81073; Elev. 4,400; Lat. 37-24-21 N Long. 102-36-27 W; SE corner Colorado. The original landowner, Andrew Harrison, came from Springfield, Missouri and named the town for his former home.

•**STARKVILLE,** Town; Las Animas County; Pop. 127; Zip Code 81074; Elev. 6,500;; SE Colorado. Named in honor of H.G. Stark, who operated the first coal mine in the town.

•**STEAMBOAT SPRINGS,** City; Routt County Seat; Pop. 5,098; Zip Code 80477; Elev. 6,728; Lat. 40-29-32 N Long. 106-49-55 W; NW Colorado. An old springs, now destroyed, emitted a puffing sound that reminded the early settlers of the sound of the large river steamers.

•**STERLING,** City; Logan County Seat; Pop. 11,385; Zip Code 80751; Elev. 3,939; Lat. 40-37-35 N Long. 103-12-40 W; 40 mi. NE of Fort Morgan in NE Colorado. A railroad surveyor, David Leavitt, named his ranch after his old home town in Illinois. The city later took the name.

•**STRATTON,** Town; Kit Carson County; Pop. 705; Zip Code 80836; Elev. 4,404; Lat. 39-18-22 N Long. 102-36-03 W; E Colorado. In honor of Winfield Scott Stratton, a carpenter who became a mining magnate in the Cripple Creek Strikes.

•**SUGAR CITY,** Town; Crowley County; Pop. 306; Zip Code 81076; Elev. 4,325; Lat. 38-13-45 N Long. 103-39-20 W; E Colorado. A rich sugar beet area, the town was founded by employees of the National Sugar Company, who built a factory in the area.

•**SWINK,** Town; Otero County; Pop. 668; Zip Code 81077; Elev. 4,118; Lat. 38-00-42 N Long. 103-36-50 W ; SE Colorado. The old town is named after State Senator George Swink who farmed in the area besides being a politican.

•**TELLURIDE,** Town; San Miguel County Seat; Pop. 1,047; Zip Code 81435; Elev. 8,500; Lat. 37-56-24 N Long. 107-48-28 W; SW Colorado. Named for the gold-silver-tellurium deposits found in the local area.

•**THORNTON,** City; Adams County; Pop. 40,343; Zip Code 80229; N of Denver in NE central Colorado. A new town (1950s), it was named in honor of Colorado's Governor, Dan Thornton.

•**TIMNATH,** Town; Larimer County; Pop. 185; Zip Code 80547; Elev. 4,867; Lat. 40-32-00 N Long. 104-58-52 W; N Colorado. Named by a Presbyterian minister after an old testament city supposely visited by Samson.

•**TRINIDAD,** City; Las Animas County Seat; Pop. 9,663; Zip Code 81082; Lat. 37-06-39 N Long. 104-31-04 W; SE Colorado. Founded in 1859 and originally called "Santisima Trinidad" (most holy trinity), the name was shortened."

•**TWO BUTTES,** Town; Baca County; Pop. 84; Zip Code 81084; Lat. 37-33-43 N Long. 102-23-11 W; SE corner of Colorado. A descriptive name for two striking buttes near the town.

•**VAIL,** Town; Eagle County; Pop. 2,261; Zip Code 81657; Lat. 39-38-33 N Long. 106-23-02 W; NW central Colorado. Named for Colorado State Highway engineer Charles D. Vail of the 1930s era.

•**VICTOR,** City; Teller County; Pop. 265; Zip Code 80860; Elev. 9,695; Lat. 38-42-28 N Long. 105-08-19 W ; central Colorado. The city's name recalls the rich gold producing Victor Mine.

•**VILAS,** Town; Baca County; Pop. 118; Zip Code 81087; Lat. 37-22-26 N Long. 102-25-59 W; SE corner of Colorado. The town is named for William F. Vilas, Secretary of the Interior and Postmaster General in the 1880s.

•**VONA,** Town; Kit Carson County; Pop. 94; Zip Code 80861; Lat. 39-18-18 N Long. 102-44-24 W; E Colorado. An attorney, Pearl King promoted the town and gave it the name of his niece.

•**WALDEN,** Town; Jackson County Seat; Pop. 947; Zip Code 80480; Elev. 8,099; Lat. 40-33-42 N Long. 106-26-49 W; N Colorado. Named for one time postmaster Mark D. Walden.

•**WALSENBURG,** City; Huerfano County Seat; Pop. 3,945; Zip Code 81089; Elev. 6,182; Lat. 37-44-14 N Long. 105-17-22 W; S Colorado. Merchant Fred Walsen opened a general store and a town developed around his place. Named in his honor.

•**WALSH,** Town; Baca County; Pop. 884; Zip Code 81090; Lat. 37-23-12 N Long. 102-16-27 W; SE corner of Colorado. A retired railroad agent had the town named in his honor.

•**WARD,** Town; Boulder County; Pop. 129; Zip Code 80481; Elev. 9,250; Lat. 40-04-26 N Long. 105-31-06 W ; N central Colorado. In 1860 Calvin Ward discovered the gold-bearing "Ward Seam," and subsequent mining led to the town's development.

•**WELLINGTON,** Town; Larimer County; Pop. 1,215; Zip Code 80549; Elev. 5,000; Lat. 40-42-22 N Long. 105-00-31 W; N Colorado. As in many other Colorado towns, Wellington takes its name from a former railroad employee.

•**WESTCLIFFE,** Town; Custer County Seat; Pop. 324; Zip Code 81252; Elev. 7,800; Lat. 38-07-58 N Long. 105-28-13 W; S central Colorado. The town was renamed by Dr. W.A. Bell for his birthplace, Westcliff-on-the-Sea, England.

•**WESTMINSTER,** City; Adams & Jefferson Counties; Pop. 50,211; Zip Code 800+; Lat. 39-50-08 N Long. 105-01-14 W; NW of Denver in NE central Colorado. In 1891 Stanford White founded a Presbyterian College and named it Westminister. The town took the College's name.

•**WHEAT RIDGE,** City; Jefferson County; Pop. 30,293; Zip Code 80033; Lat. 39-46-13 N Long. 105-05-20 W; WNW of Denver in central Colorado. State Senator Henry Lee descriptively named the city for the rich wheat growing area surrounding it.

•**WIGGINS,** Town; Morgan County; Pop. 531; Zip Code 80654; Elev. 4,443; Lat. 40-13-42 N Long. 104-04-21 W ; NE Colorado. To honor Major Oliver P. Wiggens a Canadian employee of the Hudson Bay Company who accompanied Fremont on one of his expeditons.

•**WILEY,** Town; Prowers County; Pop. 425; Zip Code 81092; Lat. 38-09-22 N Long. 102-42-31 W; SE Colorado. The town is named for W.M. Wiley, one of the community's founders.

•**WILLIAMSBURG,** Town; Fremont County; Pop. 72; S central Colorado. After John Williams who founded the Williamsburg Mine in the early 1880s.

•**WINDSOR,** Town; Weld County; Pop. 4,277; Zip Code 80550; Lat. 40-28-47 N Long. 104-54-02 W; N Colorado. In honor of Methodist circut minister, the Rev. A.S. Windsor.

•**WINTER PARK,** Town; Grand County; Pop. 480; Zip Code 80482; Lat. 39-55-20 N Long. 105-45-58 W ; N Colorado. Originally called West Portal, the town's name was changed to publicize the superb winter sports in the area.

CONNECTICUT

•**ANDOVER,** Town; Tolland County; Pop. 2,144; Zip Code 06232; Elev. 380; Lat. 41-44-20 N Long. 072-22-43 W; N Connecticut.; Andover was named in 1747 either because its early settlers came from Andover, Massachusetts or because they came directly from the town of Andover, England.

•**ANSONIA,** City; New Haven County; Pop. 19,039; Zip Code 06401; Elev. 120; Lat. 41-20-35 N Long. 073-04-27 W; 10 m. WNW of New Haven in S Connecticut.; Named for Anson G. Phelps, senior partner of the firm of Phelps, Dodge & Co., which established the city.

•**ASHFORD,** Town; Windham County; Pop. 3,221; Zip Code 06278; Elev. 680; Lat. 41-51-49 N Long. 072-09-46 W; NE corner of Connecticut.; Most likely named after Ashford, Kent in October, 1710. The name may also have been inspired by the many ashtrees in the area.

•**AVON,** Town; Hartford County; Pop. 11,201; Zip Code 06001; Elev. 202; Lat. 41-48-35 N Long. 072-49-55 W; N Connecticut.; The town was officially named in 1830 for Stratford-upon-Avon, England, Shakespeare's birthplace.

•**BARKHAMSTED,** Town; Litchfield County; Pop. 2,935; NW corner of Connecticut.; Settled in the early 1700's and named Berkhamstead by the General Assembly from Berkhamstead, England. The name was subsequently spelled Barkhamstead to conform to its pronunciation.

•**BEACON FALLS,** Town; New Haven County; Pop. 3,995; Zip Code 06403; Elev. 200; Lat. 41-26-24 N Long. 073-03-18 W; S coastal Connecticut.; Named in 1856 for the falls in Beacon Brook. The brook took its name from nearby Beacon Hill.

•**BERLIN,** Town; Hartford County; Pop. 15,121; Zip Code 06037; Elev. 100; 10m. SSW of Hartford in central Connecticut.; First known as Great Swamp, Kensington, Worthington and Farmington Village. In 1785 the name was changed to Berlin, after Berlin, Prussia.

•**BETHANY,** Town; New Haven County; Pop. 4,330; ; Elev. 520; S coastal Connecticut.; A biblical name meaning "house of dates," Bethany was established as a parish in 1762.

•**BETHEL,** Town; Fairfield County; Pop. 16,004; Zip Code 06801; Elev. 400; Lat. 41-22-17 N Long. 073-24-35 W; SW corner coastal Connecticut.; Settled before 1700 and incorporated as a town in 1855. Either named for Bethel Barnum or for the Ecclesiastical Society of Bethel established in Danbury in 1758.

•**BETHLEHAM,** Town; Litchfield County; Pop. 2,573; Zip Code 06751; Elev. 861; Lat. 41-38-20 N Long. 073-12-35 W; NW corner of Connecticut.; Named in 1739 probably after Bethleham of Judea since the area nearby was then known as Judea. The town was known as Bethlem for many years due to an error in spelling.

•**BLOOMFIELD,** Town; Hartford County; Pop. 18,608; Zip Code 06002; Elev. 230; Lat. 41-49-09 N Long. 072-41-58 W; NNW of Hartford in N Connecticut.; Incorporated in 1835. The name probably came from a nearby orchard which was once settled by freeman William Blumfield or Bloomfield.

•**BOLTON,** Town; Tolland County; Pop. 3,951; Zip Code 06040; N Connecticut.; The origin of the name is uncertain. Possibly named for Bolton, England or for Charles Powlett, 2nd Duke of Bolton or another of the dukes in that line. Named by the General Assembly in October, 1720.

•**BOZRAH,** Town; New London County; Pop. 2,135; SE corner coastal Connecticut.; Named in 1786 or earlier for the ancient town in Syria. The place was known as Norwich Farms in the early 1700's.

•**BRANFORD,** Town; New Haven County; Pop. 23,363; Zip Code 06405; Lat. 41-16-36 N Long. 072-48-21 W; 5 m. ESE of New Haven in S Connecticut.; Branford takes its name from the town of Brentford, England. The Indian name for the place was Totoket.

•**BRIDGEPORT,** City; Fairfield County; Pop. 142,546; Zip Code 06600; Lat. 41-12-00 N Long. 073-08-08 W; 15 m. SW of New Haven in SW corner of Connecticut.; Incorporated in 1800 and named for the first drawbridge built over the Poquonock River.

•**BRIDGEWATER,** Town; Litchfield County; Pop. 1,563; Zip Code 06752; Elev. 580; Lat. 41-32-02 N Long. 073-22-07 W; NW corner of Connecticut.; Named in 1803 for a bridge across the Housatonic River. The town has been known by various names including: New Milford Neck, Shepaug Neck, or The Neck.

•**BRISTOL,** City; Hartford County; Pop. 57,370; Zip Code 06010; Elev. 240; Lat. 41-41-13 N Long. 072-55-45 W; 15 m. SW of Hartford in N Connecticut.; Selected by the General Assembly in 1785, the name probably came from the English city of Bristol.

•**BROOKFIELD,** Town; Fairfield County; Pop. 12,872; Zip Code 06804; Elev. 285; Lat. 41-28-56 N Long. 073-24-38 W; WSW of Waterbury in SW Connecticut.; Incorporated in 1788 and named in honor of Rev. Thomas Brooks, the town's first pastor. Prior to 1788 the region went by the names Quabaug, Whisconier, Pocono, Newbury and West Farms.

•**BROOKLYN,** Town; Windham County; Pop. 5,691; Zip Code 06234; Elev. 280; Lat. 41-47-13 N Long. 071-57-02 W; NE corner of Connecticut.; Named the Society of Brooklyn or Brookline, in 1752.

•**BURLINGTON,** Town; Hartford County; Pop. 5,660; Zip Code 06013; Elev. 700; N Connecticut.; Either named for Richard Boyle, 3rd Earl of Burlington or from the pronunciation of Bridlington, England. Incorporated in 1806. This place was earlier known as West Woods or West Briton.

•**CANAAN,** Town; Litchfield County; Pop. 1,002; Zip Code 06018; Elev. 580; Lat. 42-01-34 N Long. 073-19-46 W; NW corner of Connecticut.; The town was named Canaan after the "promised land" of the Israelites.

•**CANTERBURY,** Town; Windham County; Pop. 3,426; Zip Code 06331; Elev. 240; Lat. 41-41-53 N Long. 071-58-19 W; NE corner of Connecticut.; Named after the famous city in England.

•**CANTON,** Town; Hartford County; Pop. 7,635; Zip Code 06019; Elev. 347; Lat. 41-49-25 N Long. 072-53-52 W; N Connecticut.; Probably named after the city of Canton, China, due to a growing interest in trade with that country. Prior to 1806 the town was called Suffrage or West Simsbury.

•**CHAPLIN,** Town; Windham County; Pop. 1,793; Zip Code 06235; Lat. 41-47-43 N Long. 072-07-42 W; NE corner of Connecticut.; Named the Society of Chaplin in 1809 for Benjamin Chaplin, the first settler.

•**CHESHIRE,** Town; New Haven County; Pop. 21,788; Zip Code 06410; Elev. 250; Lat. 41-29-51 N Long. 072-54-17 W; S Connecticut.; The town was named after the county of Cheshire in England.

•**CHESTER,** Town; Middlesex County; Pop. 3,068; Zip Code 06412; Elev. 262; Lat. 41-24-01 N Long. 072-27-14 W; S coastal Connecticut.; Named around 1740 by Abraham Waterhouse for his ancestor's hometown of Chester, England.

•CLINTON, TOWN; Middlesex County; Pop. 11,195; Zip Code 06413; Lat. 41-16-43 N Long. 072-31-47 W; on Long Island Sound in S Connecticut.; Incorporated in 1838 and named either in honor of Gov. Dewitt Clinton of New York or after Clinton Abbey in England.

•COLCHESTER, Town; New London County; Pop. 7,761; Zip Code 06415; Elev. 425; Lat. 41-34-26 N Long. 072-19-44 W; SE Connecticut.; Named after the town of Colchester, England.

•COLEBROOK, Town; Litchfield County; Pop. 1,221; Zip Code 06021; Elev. 660; Lat. 41-59-24 N Long. 073-05-55 W; NW corner of Connecticut.; Named in May, 1732 for Colebrooke, England.

•COLUMBIA, Town; Tolland County; Pop. 3,386; Zip Code 06237; Elev. 500; Lat. 41-42-04 N Long. 072-18-25 W; N Connecticut.; Incorporated in 1804 and named Columbia, the poetic name for the U. S.

•CORNWALL, Town; Litchfield County; Pop. 1,288; Zip Code 06753; Elev. 110; Lat. 41-50-36 N Long. 073-19-50 W; NW corner of Connecticut.; In 1738 this town was named after the county of Cornwall, England.

•COVENTRY, Town; Tolland County; Pop. 8,895; Zip Code 06238; Lat. 41-47-54 N Long. 072-22-34 W; N Connecticut.; Named after the town of Coventry, England.

•CROMWELL, Town; Middlesex County; Pop. 10,265; Zip Code 06416; Elev. 40; Lat. 41-35-37 N Long. 072-38-59 W; S Connecticut.; Upon its incorporation in 1851, the town was called Cromwell in honor of Oliver Cromwell, of England. The name may also have come from the "Oliver Cromwell", of the first steamboats, constructed here in 1823.

•DANBURY, City; Fairfield County; Pop. 60,470; Zip Code 06810; Elev. 378; Lat. 41-24-04 N Long. 073-27-27 W; 20 m. NW of Bridgeport in SW Connecticut.; Incorporated in 1687 and named for Danbury, England. Early settlers wanted to call the town Swampfield or Swamfield.

•DARIEN, Town; Fairfield County; Pop. 18,892; Zip Code 06820; Elev. 60; Lat. 40-52-59 N Long. 073-08-10 W; on Long Island Sound in SW Connecticut.; As an early seaport and center for the shipping industry, Darien got its name because one of the wealthiest and most influential ship owners in the area made his fortune trading on the Isthmus of Panama, then known as Darien.

•DEEP RIVER, Town; Middlesex County; Pop. 3,994; Zip Code 06417; Elev. 60; Lat. 41-22-55 N Long. 072-25-57 W; S coastal Connecticut.; Originally part of the early town of Saybrook. Saybrook split into several towns leaving a small area with the name "Saybrook." Due to confusion between this and the village of Old Saybrook, the town was renamed Deep River in 1947, probably for a nearby stream.

•DERBY, City; New Haven County; Pop. 12,346; Zip Code 06418; Elev. 60; Lat. 41-19-00 N Long. 073-04-01 W; 10 m. W; of New Haven in S Connecticut.; Named after the town and county of Derby, England. The Indian name for this area was Paugasset or Paugasuck.

•DURHAM, Town; Middlesex County; Pop. 5,143; Zip Code 06422; Elev. 239; Lat. 41-29-04 N Long. 072-40-56 W; 5 m. S of Middletown in S Connecticut.; Named in 1704 for Durham, England, the original home of the family of Col. James Wadswworth, a prominent settler. The Indians called this place Coginchaug or Cockingchaug meaning "long swamp."

•EAST GRANBY, Town; Hartford County; Pop. 4,102; Zip Code 06026; Elev. 193; Lat. 41-27-16 N Long. 072-27-47 W; N Connecticut.; So named because it is on the east side of Granby.

•EAST HADDAM, Town; Middlesex County; Pop. 5,621; Zip Code 06423; Elev. 35; Lat. 41-35-03 N Long. 072-29-43 W; S Connecticut.; Located at Haddan on the eastern side of the Connecticut and Salmon Rivers. Incorporated in 1734.

•EAST HAMPTON, Town; Middlesex County; Pop. 8,572; Zip Code 06424; Elev. 412; S Connecticut.; Previously known as Chatham. The General Assembly changed the name to East Hampton in 1915. Early settlers to the area came from Eastham, Mass. East Hampton is presumed to be an adaptation of that name.

•EAST HARTFORD, Town; Hartford County; Pop. 52,536; Zip Code 06100; Elev. 1,225; N Connecticut.; First settled as part of Hartford, East Hartford was made a separate town in 1783. The Indian name for this place was Podunk.

•EAST HAVEN, Town; New Haven County; Pop. 25,028; Zip Code 06512; on Long Island Sound in S Connecticut.; Formerly known as the East Village of New Haven, this place was made a separate town in 1707.

•EAST LYME, Town; New London County; Pop. 13,870; Zip Code 06333; Lat. 41-22-01 N Long. 072-13-13 W; on Long Island Sound in SE Connecticut.; The eastern part of the town of Lyme.

•EASTON, Town; Fairfield County; Pop. 5,962; Zip Code 06425; 5 m. E of Bridgeport in SW Connecticut.; Incorporated in 1745 and named Easton, this being in the eastern part of Weston.

•EAST WINDSOR, Town; Hartford County; Pop. 8,925; Zip Code 06028; Lat. 41-55-41 N Long. 072-37-14 W; N CT on CT River; Named and incorporated in 1768, this town was the part of Windsor located east of the Connecticut River. Early known as Windsor Farms.

•EASTFORD, Town; Windham County; Pop. 1,028; Zip Code 06242; Lat. 41-54-07 N Long. 072-04-57 W; NE corner of Connecticut.; Formed in 1777 and named Eastford because it was the east parish of Ashford.

•ELLINGTON, Town; Tolland County; Pop. 9,711; Zip Code 06029; Lat. 41-54-15 N Long. 072-28-28 W; N Connecticut.; Either named for Ellington, England or because of the town's shape, with a long narrow strip projecting eastward. Originally known as the "Great Swamp" or "Marsh."

•ENFIELD, Town; Hartford County; Pop. 42,695; Zip Code 06082; Elev. 50; Lat. 40-54-32 N Long. 070-42-19 W; N CT, on Mass border; Named after Enfield, England, a suburb of London. An early name for the town was Freshwater.

•ESSEX, Town; Middlesex County; Pop. 5,078; Zip Code 06426; Lat. 41-21-47 N Long. 072-23-43 W; S Connecticut.; Originally part of the town of Saybrook. In 1820 this became a borough named for Essex, England.

•FAIRFIELD, Town; Fairfield County; Pop. 54,849; Zip Code 06430; Lat. 41-10-17 N Long. 073-15-16 W; on Long Island Sound in SW Connecticut.; Settled in 1639 and named by Roger Ludlow either for the surroundings, or for the Fairfield in Kent, England.

•FARMINGTON, Town; Hartford County; Pop. 16,407; Zip Code 06032; Lat. 41-43-26 N Long. 072-49-31 W; N Connecticut.; The origin of the name may have been descriptive or the town may have been named for Farmington, England. Before 1645 the place was known as Tunxes for the Tunxis Indians.

•FRANKLIN, Town; New London County; Pop. 1,592; SE corner coastal Connecticut.; Incorporated in 1786 and named in honor of Benjamin Franklin.

•GLASTONBURY, Town; Hartford County; Pop. 24,327; Zip Code 06033; Elev. 50; Lat. 41-41-23 N Long. 072-35-27 W; 5 m. SE of

Hartford in N Connecticut.; First called Naubuc, the town was renamed Glassenbury in 1692. The spelling was changed to Glastonbury by town vote in 1870.

•GOSHEN, Town; Litchfield County; Pop. 1,706; Zip Code 06756; Elev. 1,333; Lat. 41-49-54 N Long. 073-13-34 W; NW corner of Connecticut.; Laid out in 1722 and named New Bantam. The name was changed in 1737 to Goshen, a biblical name referring to the promised land.

•GRANBY, Town; Hartford County; Pop. 7,956; Zip Code 06035; Elev. 215; Lat. 41-57-14 N Long. 072-47-18 W; N Connecticut.; Named in 1786 for John Manners, Marquess of Granby and his son, Charles, 4th Duke of Rutland.

•GREENWICH, Town; Fairfield County; Pop. 59,578; Zip Code 06830; Lat. 41-02-26 N Long. 073-36-58 W; on Long Island Sound on NY border in SW Connecticut.; Named for Greenwich, England. Indians called this place Patuquapaen and Sicascock.

•GRISWOLD, Town; New London County; Pop. 8,967; SE corner of Connecticut.; Incorporated in 1815 and named in honor of Gov. Roger Griswold who died in office in 1812.

•GROTON, Town; New London County; Pop. 41,062; Zip Code 06340; Lat. 41-21-23 N Long. 072-02-42 W SE corner of Connecticut.; Named in the 1600's probably by settler Fitz John Winthrop whose family owned a country seat called Groton in Suffolk, England. The Indian name for the area was Poqouonnock.

•GUILFORD, Town; New Haven County; Pop. 17,375; Zip Code 06437; Lat. 41-23-29 N Long. 072-51-04 W; on Long Island Sound in S Connecticut.; Named by early settlers from Surrey for their hometown of Guilford, England.

•HADDAM, Town; Middlesex County; Pop. 6,383; Zip Code 06438; Elev. 89; Lat. 41-28-38 N Long. 072-30-54 W; S Connecticut.; The estates the first governor of Connecticut, John Haynes owned at Great Haddam, suggested the name for the town. Officially named in Oct. 1668 for Little Haddam, Hertfordshire, England.

•HAMDEN, Town; New Haven County; Pop. 51,071; Zip Code 06514; S Connecticut.; Named in 1786, either for John Hampden, an English patriot, or for Patrick J. Hampden.

•HAMPTON, Town; Windham County; Pop. 1,322; Zip Code 06247; Elev. 680; Lat. 41-47-07 N Long. 072-03-28 W; NE corner of Connecticut.; Named after the parish of Hampton in Middlesex County, England. The place was previously called: Canada, Kennedy and Windham Village.

•HARTFORD, City; Hartford County; Pop. 136,392; Zip Code 06100; Lat. 41-45-52 N Long. 072-41-26 W; 35 m. NNE of New Haven in N Connecticut.; In February 1636 the General Court named this town after Hartford, England, the birthplace of one of the ministers of the settlement.

•HARTLAND, Town; Hartford County; Pop. 1,416; N Connecticut.; The name is either a shortening of Hartford Land because it was owned by men from Hartford, or came from Hartland in Devon, England.

•HARWINTON, Town; Litchfield County; Pop. 4,889; Zip Code 06790; Elev. 860; NW corner of Connecticut.; Owned by proprietors from Hartford and Windsor, the name Harwinton is a combination of the first syllable of each word.

•HEBRON, Town; Tolland County; Pop. 5,453; Zip Code 06248; Elev. 542; Lat. 41-39-28 N Long. 072-22-07 W; 15 m. SE of Hartford in N Connecticut.; Named in 1707 for the biblical city of Hebron.

•KENT, Town; Litchfield County; Pop. 2,505; Zip Code 06757; Elev. 380; Lat. 41-43-29 N Long. 073-28-45 W; NW corner of Connecticut.; The town takes its name from the county of Kent, England. The early Indian name for this locality was Scatacook.

•KILLINGLY, Town; Windham County; Pop. 14,519; Elev. 300; NE corner of Connecticut.; Originally called Aspinock by the Indians. The town was named Killingly in 1708 after Killanslie, a manorial possession of the Saltonstall family.

•KILLINGWORTH, Town; Middlesex County; Pop. 3,976; Elev. 425; S coastal Connecticut.; Named in 1667 for the birthplace of pioneer Edward Griswold, in Kenilworth, England. The pronunciation varied and the name was finally set down by the town clerk in 1707 as Killingworth.

•LEBANON, Town; New London County; Pop. 4,762; Zip Code 06249; Elev. 414; Lat. 41-38-13 N Long. 072-12-53 W; SE corner coastal Connecticut.; Named Lebanon by Mr. Fitch because the landscape resembled the "Cedars of Lebanon." Early Indian names for the region include: Poque-Channug, Pomakuk and Poquedamseg.

•LEDYARD, Town; New London County; Pop. 13,735; Zip Code 06339; Elev. 190; 5 m. NE of New London in SE Connecticut.; Settled in 1653 as part of New London. The actual town of Ledyard was incorporated in 1836. It was named in honor of Col. William Ledyard and for his nephew John Ledyard.

•LISBON, Town; New London County; Pop. 3,279; Zip Code 06351; SE corner coastal Connecticut.; Once a part of Norwich, the town incorporated in 1786 and took its name from the fact that merchants Hezekiah and Jabez Perkins traded from Norwich with Lisbon, Portugal.

•LITCHFIELD, Town; Litchfield County; Pop. 7,605; Zip Code 06759; Elev. 1,086; Lat. 41-44-45 N Long. 073-11-20 W; NW corner of Connecticut.; Named after the cathedral city of Litchfield in Staffordshire, England. Before 1719 the Indians called the place Bantam. When the English arrived they called it New Bantam until the name was changed.

•LYME, Town; New London County; Pop. 1,822; SE corner coastal Connecticut.; Probably named after Lyme Regis in Dorsetshire, England. The name was given in 1667.

•MADISON, Town; New Haven County; Pop. 14,031; Zip Code 06443; Elev. 22; Lat. 41-16-42 N Long. 072-36-09 W; on Long Island Sound in SE Connecticut.; Named in 1826 in honor of President James Madison.

•MANCHESTER, Town; Hartford County; Pop. 49,761; Zip Code 06040; Elev. 140; Lat. 41-46-39 N Long. 072-31-17 W; N Connecticut.; First known as Five Mile Tract, later as the parish of Orford or Charlotte, Manchester was incorporated in 1823. Because the town had several silk and cotton manufacturers, it was named after Manchester, the English "Cotton City."

•MANSFIELD, Town; Tolland County; Pop. 20,634; Zip Code 06250; Lat. 41-49-32 N Long. 072-16-09 W; N Connecticut.; Either named for Major Moses Mansfield, a prominent landowner, or for Lord Mansfield, one of the original patentees. The Indian name for the place was Naubesatuck, from Nupees, meaning "land at the pond."

•MARLBOROUGH, Town; Hartford County; Pop. 4,746; Zip Code 06447; Elev. 540; N Connecticut.; Named in 1747, either for the Duke of Marlboro or the town of Marlborough, Mass.

•MERIDEN, City; New Haven County; Pop. 57,118; Zip Code 06450; Lat. 41-32-12 N Long. 072-48-02 W; 15 m. NE of New Haven in S Connecticut.; First called Merideen in an Indian deed of 1664. The city has variously been known as Moridan, Merredan and finally the present name, Meriden.

•MIDDLEBURY, Town; New Haven County; Pop. 5,995; Zip Code 06762; Elev. 700; Lat. 41-31-36 N Long. 073-07-27 W; S Connecticut.; Organized in 1790 and named for its location mid-way between Waterbury, Woodbury and Southbury.

•MIDDLEFIELD, Town; Middlesex County; Pop. 3,796; Zip Code 06455; Lat. 41-31-06 N Long. 072-42-48 W; S coastal Connecticut.; Named and organized in 1744 as Middlefield Parish of Middletown. Since it is not located at the middle of anything, it no doubt took its name from the parent town.

•MIDDLETOWN, City; Middlesex County; Pop. 39,040; Zip Code 06457; Lat. 41-33-15 N Long. 072-39-26 W; 15 m. S of Hartford in S Connecticut.; Formerly a plantation known as Mattabesick. In 1651 the General Court named the settlement Middletown, for its location halfway between Saybrook and towns Up-River.

•MILFORD, Town; New Haven County; Pop. 50,898; Zip Code 06460; Lat. 41-13-06 N Long. 073-03-19 W; S Connecticut.; Probably named for Milford Haven in Pembroke, Wales, however the town name may also have come from William Fowler's mill built here around 1640, or from Milford in Surrey, England.

•MONROE, Town; Fairfield County; Pop. 14,010; Zip Code 06468; Lat. 40-58-20 N Long. 072-37-10 W; SW Connecticut.; Incorporated in 1823 and named for President James Monroe. Early names for the place include: Flat Rock and Huntington.

•MONTVILLE, Town; New London County; Pop. 16,455; Zip Code 06353; Lat. 41-27-01 N Long. 072-07-58 W; SE Connecticut.; The name, which means "hill residence" was descriptive of the town's setting.

•MORRIS, Town; Litchfield County; Pop. 1,899; Zip Code 06763; Elev. 1099; Lat. 41-43-10 N Long. 073-14-37 W; NW corner Connecticut.; Named in honor of Major James Morris, a soldier in the Revolutionary War.

•NAUGATUCK, Town; New Haven County; Pop. 26,456; Zip Code 06770; Elev. 200; Lat. 41-29-35 N Long. 073-03-09 W; 5 m. S of Waterbury in S Connecticut.; Named for the Naugatuck River as early as the mid 1600's.

•NEW BRITAIN, City; Hartford County; Pop. 73,840; Zip Code 06000; Lat. 41-40-28 N Long. 072-47-07 W; 10 m. SW of Hartford in N Connecticut.; Laid out and named in 1754 by Col. Isaac Lee in honor of Great Britain.

•NEW CANAAN, Town; Fairfield County; Pop. 17,931; Zip Code 06840; Lat. 41-09-10 N Long. 073-29-55 W; SW Connecticut.; Organized in 1731 and named Canaan. The town later was incorporated under the name New Canaan to avoid confusion with another town called Canaan in the northwest part of the state.

•NEW FAIRFIELD, Town; Fairfield County; Pop. 11,260; Zip Code 06810; Elev. 700; 20 m. WSW of Waterbury in SW Connecticut.; Part of a 14 mile parcel of land granted to Fairfield in 1707, New Fairfield took its name from the parent city.

•NEW HARTFORD, Town; Litchfield County; Pop. 4,884; Zip Code 06057; Elev. 360; Lat. 41-52-58 N Long. 072-58-35 W; NW corner of Connecticut.; This place was originally part of the Western Lands allotted to Hartford. It was incorporated in 1738 and given the name New Hartford.

•NEW HAVEN, City; New Haven County; Pop. 126,109; Zip Code 06500; Lat. 41-18-42 N Long. 072-55-36 W; 35 m. SSW of Hartford in S Connecticut.; Settled by parties from Boston who called it a "new haven."

•NEW LONDON, City; New London County; Pop. 28,842; Zip Code 06320; Lat. 41-21-08 N Long. 072-06-14 W; 45 m. E of New Haven in SE Connecticut.; Named for the city of London, England. The Indian name for the place was Nameaug or Towawog and early settlers called it Pequot after the defeat of the Pequots in 1637.

•NEW MILFORD, Town; Litchfield County; Pop. 19,420; Zip Code 06776; Elev. 260; Lat. 41-34-37 N Long. 073-24-38 W; NW Connecticut.; Named in 1703 and organized by a land company from Milford.

•NEWINGTON, Town; Hartford County; Pop. 28,841; Zip Code 06111; Elev. 100; SW of Hartford in N Connecticut.

•NEWTOWN, Town; Fairfield County; Pop. 19,107; Zip Code 06470; Elev. 560; Lat. 41-24-45 N Long. 073-18-34 W; SW Connecticut.; First called Pootatuck and Quanneapagne by the Indians. In 1708 the settlement was incorporated and named New Town.

•NORFOLK, Town; Litchfield County; Pop. 2,156; Zip Code 06058; Elev. 1260; Lat. 41-59-24 N Long. 073-12-09 W; NW corner of Connecticut.; Named in 1738 after the county of Norfolk, England.

•NORTH BRANFORD, Town; New Haven County; Pop. 11,554; Zip Code 06471; Elev. 100; S central Connecticut.; Early known as North Farms. This town was first an Ecclesiastical Society and a part of Branford. In 1831 it became a separate town named after the parent city.

•NORTH CANAAN, Town; Litchfield County; Pop. 3,185; ; NW corner of Connecticut.; Named for its relation to Canaan, of which it originally formed a part city.

•NORTH HAVEN, Town; New Haven County; Pop. 22,080; Zip Code 06473; Elev. 41; Lat. 41-22-51 N Long. 071-54-17 W; S Connecticut.; Early known as East Farms, this later became the North East Ecclesiastical Society of New Haven. In 1786 it became a separate town and was named North Haven.

•NORTH STONINGTON, Town; New London County; Pop. 4,219; Zip Code 06359; SE corner coastal Connecticut.; Called Mashentuxet by the Indians. In 1724 it was named North Stonington for the North Society of Stonington. The village was also at one time known as Milltown.

•NORWALK, City; Fairfield County; Pop. 77,767; Zip Code 06800; Lat. 41-07-15 N Long. 073-25-53 W; on Long Island Sound in SW Connecticut.; So named because when it was purchased from the Indians, the boundary was to extend northward from the sea one day's walk. The name may also have been derived from the word nayang, meaning "point of land."

•NORWICH, City; New London County; Pop. 38,074; Zip Code 06360; Lat. 41-31-52 N Long. 072-04-48 W; SE Connecticut.; Named for the city of Norwich in England.

•OLD LYME, Town; New London County; Pop. 6,159; Zip Code 06371; Lat. 41-18-56 N Long. 072-20-01 W; SE Connecticut.; Formerly known as South Lyme, the name was changed to Old Lyme in 1857 as an imitation of Old Saybrook. The name Lyme probably came from Lyme Regis in Dorsetshire, England.

•OLD SAYBROOK, Town; Middlesex County; Pop. 9,287; Zip Code 06475; Lat. 41-16-53 N Long. 072-21-43 W; S coastal Connecticut.; Named for Lords Say and Brook.

•ORANGE, Town; New Haven County; Pop. 13,237; Zip Code 06477; Lat. 41-16-50 N Long. 073-01-35 W; S Connecticut.; Named for the Dutch, William IV, Prince of Orange.

•OXFORD, Town; New Haven County; Pop. 6,634; Zip Code 08483; Elev. 360; 10 m. W of New Haven in S Connecticut.; Probably named by John Twitchell who came from Oxford, Massachusetts. The Indians called this place Manchaug.

•**PLAINFIELD,** Town; Windham County; Pop. 12,774; Zip Code 06374; Elev. 203; Lat. 41-40-46 N Long. 071-55-18 W; NE Connecticut.; Named in 1699 by the governor. Since the site for the town was level in comparison to the surrounding country, it was named Plainfield.

•**PLAINVILLE,** Town; Hartford; Pop. 16,401; Zip Code 06062; Elev. 191; Lat. 41-40-19 N Long. 072-51-39 W; N Connecticut.; Known as Great Plain or the Great Plain of Farmington until 1829 when the name Plainville was selected. Named for its level topography.

•**PLYMOUTH,** Town; Litchfield County; Pop. 10,732; Elev. 700; Lat. 41-40-20 N Long. 073-03-14 W; N of Waterbury in NW Connecticut.; Henry Cook, the first settler, named this town Plymouth in 1795 because his great-grandfather had been one of the pilgrims at Plymouth, Massachusetts.

•**POMFRET,** Town; Windham County; Pop. 2,775; Zip Code 06258; Elev. 588; Lat. 41-53-44 N Long. 071-57-46 W; NE corner of Connecticut.; Named for the town of Pomfret in Yorkshire, England.

•**PORTLAND,** Town; Middlesex County; Pop. 8,383; Zip Code 06480; Elev. 220; Lat. 41-34-18 N Long. 072-38-27 W; NE of Middletown in S Connecticut.; Named Portland, probably because the stone in the quarries here resembled that in the sandstone quarries of Portland, England. This place was previously known by the names Wangunk and Chatham.

•**PRESTON,** Town; New London County; Pop. 4,644; Elev. 180; SE corner coastal Connecticut.; Named by Josiah Standish for Preston, England, the town where his father, Miles Standish, was born.

•**PROSPECT,** Town; New Haven County; Pop. 6,807; Zip Code 06712; 5 m. SE of Waterbury in S Connecticut.; Named for the view afforded by the town's elevation.

•**PUTNAM,** Town; Windham County; Pop. 8,580; Zip Code 06260; Elev. 400; Lat. 41-55-15 N Long. 071-54-30 W; 20 m. NE of Willimantic in NE Connecticut.; Named in honor of General Israel Putnam of Revolutionary War fame.

•**REDDING,** Town; Fairfield County; Pop. 7,272; Zip Code 06876; Elev. 705; Lat. 41-18-19 N Long. 073-22-53 W; SW Connecticut.; Established around 1717 and named Reading for Col. John Read the original patentee. Over time the pronunciation varied and the town was incorporated as Redding in 1767.

•**RIDGEFIELD,** Town; Fairfield County; Pop. 20,120; Zip Code 06877; Elev. 760; Lat. 41-16-58 N Long. 073-30-09 W; SW CT, on NY border; The Indians called this place Caudatowa, meaning high land". In 1709, the General Assembly selected the name Ridgefield for the town because of the high ridges in the area.

•**ROCKY HILL,** Town; Hartford County; Pop. 14,559; Zip Code 06067; Elev. 100; Lat. 41-39-53 N Long. 072-39-29 W; N Connecticut.; Named for Rocky or Shipman Hill, the most prominent physical feature of the area. Other names for the town included Lexington Parish and Stepney Parish.

•**ROXBURY,** Town; Litchfield County; Pop. 1,468; Zip Code 06783; Elev. 557; Lat. 41-44-48 N Long. 073-11-24 W; NW corner of Connecticut.; Early names for this area were Rucum or Rocum. The Indian name for this area was Shepaug or "the rocky river." The town was named Roxbury in 1743, probably the surrounding rocky area.

•**SALEM,** Town; New London County; Pop. 2,335; ; Elev. 362; SE corner coastal Connecticut.; Probably named by landowner Samuel Brown for his former home of Salem, Massachusetts.

•**SALISBURY,** Town; Litchfield County; Pop. 3,896; Zip Code 06068; Elev. 690; Lat. 41-59-06 N Long. 073-25-16 W; NW corner of Connecticut.; Named either for Salisbury, England or for a Mr. Salisbury who lived near the center of town.

•**SCOTLAND,** Town; Windham County; Pop. 1,072; Zip Code 06264; Elev. 240; Lat. 41-41-58 N Long. 072-04-56 W; NE corner of Connecticut.; Settled by Scotsman, Isaac Magoon around 1700 and named for his native country.

•**SEYMOUR,** Town; New Haven County; Pop. 13,434; Zip Code 06483; Elev. 160; Lat. 41-23-43 N Long. 073-04-27 W; N of Ansonia in S Connecticut.; Incorporated in 1850 and named for then Governor Thomas H. Seymour.

•**SHARON,** Town; Litchfield County; Pop. 2,623; Zip Code ; Elev. 714; Lat. 41-52-33 N Long. 073-28-49 W; NW corner of Connecticut.; First named New Sharon, after the fertile "plain" by the Mediterranean. It was incorporated in 1739 and simply called Sharon.

•**SHELTON,** City; Fairfield County; Pop. 31,314; Zip Code 06484; Elev. 120; Lat. 41-18-31 N Long. 073-07-33 W; SW Connecticut.; Known as Huntington before 1919 when the General Assembly changed the name to Shelton and probably named for Edward N. Shelton. The Indians called this area Quorum.

•**SHERMAN,** Town; Fairfield County; Pop. 2,281; Zip Code 06784; Elev. 500; Lat. 41-34-41 N Long. 073-29-58 W; SW corner coastal Connecticut.; Named in honor of Roger Sherman, signer of the Declaration of Independence.

•**SIMSBURY,** Town; Hartford County; Pop. 21,161; Zip Code 06070; Elev. 180; Lat. 41-52-07 N Long. 072-48-21 W; S of Granby in N Connecticut.; Known by the Indians as Massacoe. In 1670 the Assembly named this town Simsbury either for Simondsbury, England or in honor of "Sim" Wolcott.

•**SOMERS,** Town; Tolland County; Pop. 8,473; Zip Code 06071; Elev. 272; Lat. 41-59-20 N Long. 072-26-46 W; E of Enfield in N Connecticut.; Named in honor of Lord Somers.

•**SOUTH WINDSOR,** Town; Hartford County; Pop. 17,198; Zip Code 06074; Elev. 40; Lat. 41-49-25 N Long. 072-37-19 W; NE of Hartford in N Connecticut.; Called Nowashe by the Indians and Nowaas by the Dutch. Incorporated in 1845 and named for its parent city of Windsor. The town has also been called Wapping.

•**SOUTHBURY,** Town; New Haven County; Pop. 14,156; Zip Code 06488; Elev. 260; Lat. 41-28-53 N Long. 073-13-00 W; S Connecticut.; Southbury got its name in 1731 because it was the south part of Woodbury. The Indians called the locality Potatuck. It was also known early as South Purchase.

•**SOUTHINGTON,** Town; Hartford County; Pop. 36,879; Zip Code 06489; Lat. 41-28-35 N Long. 072-40-36 W; West of Berlin in S Connecticut.; Originally part of South Farmington, the word Southington is a contraction of that name.

•**SPRAGUE,** Town; New London County; Pop. 2,996; SE corner coastal Connecticut.; Named for William Sprague of Rhode Island who laid out the manufacturing center of town. Earlier known as the Hanover Society.

•**STAFFORD,** City; Tolland County; Pop. 9,268; Zip Code 06075; Elev. 591; Lat. 41-59-01 N Long. 072-17-20 W; NE of Sommers in N Connecticut.; Named for the county of Stafford, England.

•**STAMFORD,** City; Fairfield County; Pop. 102,453; Zip Code 06900; on Long Island Sound & NY border in SW Connecticut.;

Probably named for Stamford, England. An earlier name for the town was Rippowam.

•**STERLING,** Town; Windham County; Pop. 1,791; Zip Code 06377; Lat. 41-42-35 N Long. 071-49-50 W; NE corner of Connecticut.; Named after Dr. John Sterling, a resident of the town, who promised to donate a public library but failed to make good his promise.

•**STONINGTON,** Town; New London County; Pop. 16,220; Zip Code 06378; Lat. 41-21-16 N Long. 071-57-35 W; E of Groton in SE Connecticut.; Previously called Mistick, in 1666 the name was changed to Stonington for the many stones in the area.

•**STRATFORD,** Town; Fairfield County; Pop. 50,541; Zip Code 06497; E of Bridgeport in SW Connecticut.; An early English settler here named this town after his native city of Stratford-on-Avon, England.

•**SUFFIELD,** Town; Hartford County; Pop. 9,294; Zip Code 06078; Elev. 160; Lat. 41-58-58 N Long. 072-39-12 W; on Mass border in N Connecticut.; Originally called Southfield and situated in Massachusetts. Its name came from the fact that it was the southernmost town in that state. When the border changed, it became a part of Connecticut.

•**THOMASTON,** Town; Litchfield County; Pop. 6,276; Zip Code 06787; Elev. 393; Lat. 41-41-41 N Long. 073-06-39 W; NW Connecticut.; Named for the Thomas family, well-known manufacturers in this region.

•**THOMPSON,** Town; Windham County; Pop. 8,141; Zip Code 06277; Elev. 584; Lat. 41-57-27 N Long. 071-51-48 W; N of Putnam in NE Connecticut.; Named in 1728 in honor of its chief owner, Sir Robert Thompson.

•**TOLLAND,** Town; Tolland County; Pop. 9,694; Zip Code 06084; Lat. 41-52-23 N Long. 072-22-23 W; N Connecticut.; Incorporated in 1715 and named for the village of Tolland, England.

•**TORRINGTON,** Town; Litchfield County; Pop. 30,987; Zip Code 06790; Elev. 571; Lat. 41-48-35 N Long. 073-07-07 W; 20 m. NNW of Waterbury in NW Connecticut.; Named after the town of Torrington, England.

•**TRUMBULL,** Town; Fairfield County; Pop. 32,989; Zip Code 06611; N of Bridgeport in SW Connecticut.; Named in honor of Jonathan Trumbull, the second Connecticut governor of that name.

•**UNION,** Town; Tolland County; Pop. 546; Zip Code 06770; Elev. 980; N Connecticut.; Opened for settlement in 1727 under the name Union Lands or Union Right.

•**VERNON,** Town; Tolland County; Pop. 27,974; Zip Code 06066; NE of Manchester in N Connecticut.; Probably named for George Washington's home at Mount Vernon Virginia.

•**VOLUNTOWN,** Town; New London County; Pop. 1,637; Zip Code 06384; Elev. 260; Lat. 41-34-19 N Long. 071-52-12 W; SE corner in coastal Connecticut.; So named because most of the town was granted to the volunteers of the Narragansett War.

•**WALLINGFORD,** TOWN; NEW HAVEN County; Pop. 37,274; Zip Code 06492; Elev. 150; Lat. 41-27-52 N Long. 072-49-14 W; S OF Meriden IN S Connecticut.; The Indians called this place Coginchaug. When the first settlers came they called the area New Haven Village. This town was laid out in 1670 and named for Wallingford, England.

•**WARREN,** Town; Litchfield County; Pop. 1,027; Zip Code 06754; Elev. 1200; NW corner of Connecticut.; Named for Samuel Warren of Revolutionary War fame.

•**WASHINGTON,** Town; Litchfield County; Pop. 3,657; Zip Code 06794; Elev. 720; NW corner of Connecticut.; Like many towns in the U. S., this village was named in honor of George Washington.

•**WATERBURY,** City; New Haven County; Pop. 103,266; Zip Code 06700; Lat. 41-33-25 N Long. 073-02-27 W; 20 m. NNW of New Haven in S Connecticut.; Called Waterbury in 1686 for the many rivers, ponds, and swamps in the area. An early Indian name for this place was Mattatuck.

•**WATERFORD,** Town; New London County; Pop. 17,843; Zip Code 06385; Lat. 41-20-20 N Long. 072-08-38 W; SE Connecticut.; The name Waterford, was suggested by Isaac Rogers in 1801 because of the town's location on the sound and Niantic Cove.

•**WATERTOWN,** Town; Litchfield County; Pop. 19,489; Zip Code 06795; Elev. 600; Lat. 41-34-34 N Long. 073-05-40 W; NW of Waterbury in NW Connecticut.; Incorporated from Waterbury, in 1780, Watertown took its name from the parent city.

•**WEST HARTFORD,** Town; Hartford County; Pop. 61,301; Zip Code 06100; Elev. 100; W of Hartford in N Connecticut.; Organized in 1711 as the West Division Parish, or West Society of Hartford. Named West Hartford in 1806.

•**WEST HAVEN,** City; New Haven County; Pop. 53,184; Zip Code 06516; S CT, near New Haven.; Known for many years as the West Farms of New Haven.

•**WESTBROOK,** Town; Middlesex County; Pop. 5,216; Zip Code 06498; Lat. 41-16-39 N Long. 072-25-47 W; 5 m. W of mouth of CT River in S Connecticut.; Called Westbrook in 1810, a shortened version of its earlier name, the Saybrook West Ecclesiastical Society.

•**WESTON,** Town; Fairfield County; Pop. 8,284; Zip Code 06883; 10 m. WNW of Bridgeport in SW Connecticut.; First called Aspetuck by the Indians. Later named Weston because it was the western town or settlement of Fairfield.

•**WESTPORT,** Town; Hartford County; Pop. 61,301; Zip Code 06880; Lat. 41-08-05 N Long. 073-20-54 W; on Long Island Sound in SW Connecticut.; Once a part of the towns of Weston, Norwalk and Fairfield. Westport was so named because it was the western port for Fairfield.

•**WETHERSFIELD,** Town; Hartford County; Pop. 26,013; Zip Code 06109; S of Hartford in N Connecticut.; Named in 1637 for Wethersfield, England. An earlier name for the town was Watertown.

•**WILLIMANTIC,** City; Windham County; Pop. 14,652; Zip Code 06226; Elev. 260; Lat. 41-42-50 N Long. 072-12-47 W; NE Connecticut.; An Indian word meaning either "good lookout" or "Good cedar swamps."

•**WILLINTON,** Town; Tolland County; Pop. 4,694; N Connecticut.; Originally named Wellington for Wellington, England. The town was incorporated in 1727 under the name Willington.

•**WILTON,** Town; Fairfield County; Pop. 15,351; Zip Code 06897; N of Norfolk in SW Connecticut.; In 1726 the town was established as the Wilton Ecclesiastical Society. The name either came from the town of Wilton or Wilton Parish, England.

•**WINCHESTER,** Town; Litchfield County; Pop. 10,841; Zip Code 06094; N of Torrington in NW Connecticut.; Established as a town in 1771. The place was named in 1733 for Winchester, England.

•**WINDHAM,** Town; Windham County; Pop. 21,062; Zip Code 06280; Elev. 279; Lat. 41-41-55 N Long. 072-09-37 W; NE Connecticut.; Named for the town of Windham, England.

•**WINDSOR,** Town; Hartford County; Pop. 25,204; Zip Code 06095; Elev. 57; Lat. 41-50-32 N Long. 072-39-20 W; N of Hartford in N Connecticut.; First known as Dorchester. The name was changed to Windsor, after Windsor, England, by order of the General Court.

•**WINDSOR LOCKS,** Town; Hartford County; Pop. 12,190; Zip Code 06096; Elev. 80; Lat. 41-28-39 N Long. 071-51-48 W; S of Suffield in N Connecticut.; Once a part of Windsor, the name was proposed by Alfred Smith, President of the Enfield Falls Canal co. in anticipation of a manufacturing town located at the canal's lower locks.

•**WOLCOTT,** Town; New Haven County; Pop. 13,008; Zip Code 06716; NE of Waterbury in S Connecticut.; Named in honor of Frederick Wolcott.

•**WOODBRIDGE,** Town; New Haven County; Pop. 7,761; NW of New Haven in S Connecticut.; Named in 1784 for Rev. Benjamin Woodbridge, the town's first minister.

•**WOODBURY,** Town; Litchfield County; Pop. 6,942; Zip Code 06798; Elev. 350; Lat. 41-32-44 N Long. 073-12-24 W; NW Connecticut.; Established in 1674 and named for its wooded location. The Indian name for this place was Pomperaug.

•**WOODSTOCK,** Town; Windham County; Pop. 5,117; Zip Code 06281; Elev. 592; Lat. 41-56-54 N Long. 071-58-43 W; NW of Putnam in NE Connecticut.; Named for the town of Woodstock, England.

DELAWARE

•**ARDEN,** Village; New Castle County; Pop. 516; N Delaware. Originally known as Ardentown. The name may have come from the Forest of Arden, in Shakespeare's play As You Like It.

•**ARDENCRAFT,** Village; New Castle County; Pop. 267; N Delaware. Named for the nearby village of Arden.

•**ARDENTOWN,** Village; New Castle County; Pop. 1,194; N Delaware. A suburban development near Wilmington. The name was probably taken from the nearby village of Arden.

•**BELLEFONTE,** Village; New Castle County; Pop. 1,279 N Delaware. The name is probably of French origin, meaning "beautiful fountain."

•**BETHANY BEACH,** Town; Sussex County; Pop. 330; Zip Code 19930; Elev. 71; Lat. 38-32-25 N Long. 075-03-56 W; coastal Delaware. On the Atlantic coast. Bethany Beach was probably named for the village of Bethany in Palestine.

•**BETHEL,** Town; Sussex County; Pop. 197; Zip Code 19931; Elev. 40; Lat. 38-34-08 N Long. 075-37-15 W; coastal Delaware. The town may have been named for Bethel in Palestine.

•**BLADES,** Town; Sussex County; Pop. 664; coastal Delaware. Located on the left bank of the Nanticoke River just south of Seaford.

•**BOWERS,** Town; Kent County; Pop. 198; central Delaware. The name is a variant of Bowers Beach, also known as Reeds Landing.

•**BRIDGEVILLE,** Town; Sussex County; Pop. 1,238 ; Zip Code 19933; Elev. 47; Lat. 38-44-28 N Long. 075-36-10 W; S, coastal Delaware. Located north of Seaford. The town's name is a variation of Bridge Branch for the stream of that name that flows nearby.

•**CAMDEN,** Town; Kent County; Pop. 1,757; Zip Code 19934; Elev. 40; Lat. 39-06-47 N Long. 075-32-56 W; central Delaware. Known as Mifflin's Cross Roads in the 18th century. The name was later changed to Piccadilly and finally to Camden in the early 19th century.

•**CHESWOLD,** Town; Kent County; Pop. 269; Zip Code 19936; Elev. 44; Lat. 39-12-54 N Long. 075-35-12 W; central Delaware. First called Leipsic Station. The name was changed to Moorton in 1861, in honor of the postmaster, James S. Moore. It was renamed Cheswold in 1888 due to confusion between this town and the post office in Morton, Pa.

•**CLAYTON,** Town; Kent County; Pop. 1,216; Zip Code 19938; Elev. 43; Lat. 39-17-10 N Long. 075-37-57 W; central Delaware. Formerly known as Smyrna Station and Jimtown. The town was named Clayton in 1877 in honor of Senator John M. Clayton, a promoter of the Delaware Railroad.

•**DAGSBORO,** Town; Sussex County; Pop. 344; Zip Code 19939; Elev. 30; Lat. 38-32-55 N Long. 075-14-44 W; coastal Delaware. The place was known as Blackfoot in the 1750's. Later, the town was named for General John Dagworthy, a British officer in the French and Indian War. Also called Dagsbury and Dagsborough.

•**DELAWARE CITY,** City; New Castle County; Pop. 1,858 Zip Code 19706; Elev. 9; Lat. 39-34-30 N Long. 075-36-00 W; N Delaware. Named Newbold's Wharf by William L. Newbold. The city was later named Delaware after Thomas West, Lord de la Warr.

•**DELMAR,** Town; Sussex County;;Pop. 948; Zip Code 19940; Elev. 55; Lat. 38-27-18 N Long. 075-34-35 W; S, coastal Delaware. Founded in 1859 as the southern terminus of the Eastern Shore Railroad. Since the town was situated on the Delaware - Maryland border, its name was taken from the first three letters of each state.

•**DOVER,** City; Kent County Seat Pop. 23,512; Zip Code 19901; Elev. 36; Lat. 39-09-11 N Long. 075-31-19 W; 40 m. S of Wilmington in central Delaware. The capital of Delaware. Dover was named by William Penn in 1683.

•**ELLENDALE,** Town; Sussex County; Pop. 361; Zip Code 19941; Elev. 52; Lat. 38-48-25 N Long. 075-25-26 W; S, coastal Delaware. Named by Dr. John S. Prettyman for his wife, Ellen.

•**ELSMERE,** Town; New Castle County; Pop. 6,493 ; N Delaware. Situated at the junction of the Reading R.R. and the B & O R.R.

•**FARMINGTON,** Town; Kent County; Pop. 141; Zip Code 19942; Elev. 63; Lat. 38-51-53 N Long. 075-34-45 W; central Delaware. Located at the site of a railroad station, originally called Flatiron.

•**FELTON,** Town; Kent County; Pop. 547; Zip Code 19943; Lat. 39-00-12 N Long. 075-34-30 W; central Delaware. Known at one time as Felton Station.

•**FENWICK ISLAND,** Town; Sussex County; Pop. 114 ; Zip Code 19944; S, coastal Delaware. A peninsula that was formerly an island. This place has had various names including: Fenwicks Island, False Cape, Assawoman Beach, Phenix Island, Hinlopen Cape, and Hinloopen Cape.

•**FRANKFORD,** Town; Sussex County; Pop. 686; Zip Code 19945; Elev. 30; S, coastal Delaware. This town was once known as Gum's Store. As the place grew, the name was changed to Frankford.

•**FREDRICA,** Town; Kent County; Pop. 864; Zip Code 19946; Elev. 20; central Delaware. Also known as Indian Point, Johnnycake Landing and Frederica Landing. The name was eventually shortened to Frederica.

•**GEORGETOWN,** Town; Sussex County Seat Pop. 1,710 ; Zip Code 19947; Elev. 52; S, coastal Delaware. Named in honor of George Mitchell, who supervised the town's location. Georgetown was laid out in 1791 as the new county seat in place of Lewes.

•**HARRINGTON,** City; Kent County; Pop. 2,405; Zip Code 19952; Elev. 63; central Delaware. Originally called Clark's Corner. The name was changed to Harrington in 1859 to honor State Chancellor Samuel M. Harrington.

•**HARTLY,** Town; Kent County; Pop. 243; Zip Code 19953; Elev. 71; central Delaware. This town has had many names including: Arthurville, Arthursville, Butterpot, Butterpat, Davisville and the present name, Hartly.

•**HENLOPEN ACRES,** Town; Sussex County; Pop. 176 ; S, coastal Delaware. Henlopen Acres was probably named after a Dutch town or a prominent Netherlander.

•**HOUSTON,** Town; Kent County; Pop. 357; Zip Code 19954; Elev. 53; central Delaware. Named in 1854 in honor of Judge John W. Houston. The town was previously called Houston Station and Killens Crossroad.

•**KENTON,** Town; Kent County; Pop. 243; Zip Code 19955; Elev. 68; central Delaware. Known in the 18th century first as Lewis Cross Roads and later as Grogtown. The legislature changed the name to Kenton in 1806.

•**LAUREL,** Town; Sussex County; Pop. 3,052; Zip Code 19956; Elev. 29; S, coastal Delaware. Probably named for the nearby Laurel River which is now called Broad Creek.

•**LEIPSIC,** Town; Kent County; Pop. 228; central Delaware. Originally called Fast Landing. The town was named Leipsic in 1814 after the German city of the same name.

•**LEWES,** City; Sussex County; Pop. 2,197; Zip Code 19958; Elev. 18; S, coastal Delaware. Site of the first Dutch settlement in Delaware known as Zwaanendael, Valley of Swans. It takes its present name from a borough in Sussex County, England.

•**LITTLE CREEK,** Town; Kent County; Pop. 230; Zip Code 19961; Elev. 10; central Named for the nearby stream known as Little Creek. The town's present name is a shortened version of the original, Little Creek Landing. It was also known as Bayview.

•**MAGNOLIA,** Town; Kent County; Pop. 197; Zip Code 19962; Elev. 10; central Delaware. Originally known as White House. The name was eventually changed to Magnolia.

•**MIDDLETOWN,** Town; New Castle County; Pop. 2,946 ; Zip Code 19709; Elev. 66; Lat. 39-26-54 N Long. 075-42-46 W; N Delaware. Probably named for its central location.

•**MILFORD,** City; Kent & Sussex Counties; Pop. 5,356; Zip Code 19963; Elev. 21; central Delaware. Probably named after nearby Milford Mill Pond which is now known as Silver Lake.

•**MILSBORO,** Town; Sussex County; Pop. 1,233; Zip Code 19966; Elev. 26; S, coastal Delaware. This town has been known by several names including: Millsborough, Rock hole and Washington.

•**MILTON,** Town; Sussex County; Pop. 1,359; Zip Code 19968; Elev. 30; S. coastal Delaware. Known by a variety of names including: Clowes, Osbornes Landing, Conwells Leanding, Upper Landing, Head of Broadkiln, Broadkill and Sockumtown. The name Sockumtown applied to a neighborhood of Milton in the 19th century, and was probably named for the Sockum family, descendants of Isaac Sockum.

•**MILVILLE,** Town; Sussex County; Pop. 178; Zip Code 19967; Elev. 12; S, coastal Delaware. Located 3.5 miles west of Bethany Beach in Sussex County.

•**NEWARK,** City; New Castle County; Pop. 25,247 ; Zip Code 19700; Elev. 125; Lat. 39-38-02 N Long. 075-37-38 W; 10 m. WSW of Wilmington in N Delaware. Settled by Quaker, Valentine Hollingsworth and named New Worke. In 1688 he gave a small piece of this land for a meeting house and it became known as Newark.

•**NEW CASTLE,** City; New Castle County; Pop. 4907 ; Zip Code 19720; Elev. 19; Lat. 39-41-26 N Long. 075-34-22 W; N Delaware. Settled as an Indian village and named Tamakonck, possibly meaning "place of the beaver." Dutch settlers later called the place Santhoeck, or Sand Point. Under Swedish rule in 1654 the town was named Quinamkot and Fort Trefalldigheet (Fort Trinity). The name was subsequently changed to Niew Amstel by the Dutch and finally New Castle by the British.

•**NEWPORT,** Town; New Castle County; Pop. 1,167 ; Zip Code 19804; Elev. 20; N Delaware. Originally called Newport Ayre in 1735.

•**OCEAN VIEW,** Town; Sussex County; Pop. 495; Zip Code 19970; Elev. 14; S, coastal Delaware. Formerly known as Halls Store.

•**ODESSA,** Town; New Castle County; Pop. 384; Zip Code 19730; Elev. 50; Lat. 39-27-17 N Long. 075-39-18 W; N Delaware. Originally an Indian village called Appoquinini. In 1731 it was named Cantwell's Bridge, for Edmund Cantwell, the first sheriff and owner of a toll bridge over the Appoquinimink River. Renamed Odessa in 1855 for the Russian City.

•**REHOBOTH,** City; Sussex County; Pop. 1,730; Zip Code 19971; Elev. 16; S, coastal Delaware.

•**SEAFORD,** City; Sussex County; Pop. 5,256; Zip Code 19973; Elev. 29; 15 m. W of Georgetown in S, coastal Delaware. Founded in 1799 as Hooper's Landing. The town has also been known as Seford.

•**SELBYVILLE,** Town; Sussex County; Pop. 1,251; Zip Code 19975; Elev. 32; S, coastal Delaware. Named for Josiah Selby, the town's first postmaster.

•**SLAUGHTER BEACH,** Town; Sussex County; Pop. 121 ; S, coastal Delaware. A resort community named after nearby Slaughter Beach.

•**SMYRNA,** Town; Kent & New Castle Counties; Pop. 4,750; Zip Code 19977; Elev. 36; central Delaware. Formerly known as Duck Creek or Duck Creek Cross Roads. The town was renamed in 1806 for the Seaport in Turkey.

•**SOUTH BETHANY,** Town; Sussex County; Pop. 115 303; S, coastal Delaware. Named after nearby Bethany Beach, which probably took its name from the village in Palestine.

•**TOWNSEND,** Town; New Castle County; Pop. 386; Zip Code 19734; Elev. 64; Lat. 39-23-38 N Long. 075-41-27 W; N Delaware. Named in 1855 for Samuel Townsend, a local landowner. Prior to 1850 and the coming of the railroad, this was a black settlement known as Charleytown.

•**VIOLA,** Town; Kent County; Pop. 167; Zip Code 19979; Elev. 60; central Delaware. Built on a tract of land originally called Golden Thicket. Viola has also been known by the name Canterbury Station.

•**WILMINGTON,** City; New Castle County Seat Pop. 70,195; Zip Code 19800; Elev. 100; Lat. 39-48-05 N Long. 075-36-06 W; N Delaware. Site of the Swedish settlement Fort Christina in 1638. In the 1730's the English named the town, Willingtown, for local propertuy owner, Thomas Willing. In 1739 the name was changed to Wilmington in honor of Spenser Compton, Earl of Wilmington.

•**WOODSIDE,** Town; Kent County; Pop. 248; Zip Code 19980; central Delaware. Known as Fredonia until 1869 when the name was changed to Woodside. The place also went by the name Burnt House Crossroad at one time.

•**WYOMING,** Town; Kent County; Pop. 960; central Delaware. Early known as West Camden and Camden Station. Its present name was taken from the Wyoming Valley conference of Pennsylvania, home of the town's first minister. Wyoming is a Lenape name meaning "at the great flats."

DISTRICT OF COLUMBIA

•**WASHINGTON,** City; Pop. 638,333; Zip Code 20+++; Lat. 38-53-42 N long. 077-02-12 W; Named after George Washington, first President of the United States.

FLORIDA

•**ALACHUA**, City; Alachua County; Pop. 3,414; Zip Code 32615; Elev. 81; N Florida. An old map indicates that the Creek Indian settlement of Alachua occupied the approximate site of the present village in 1715.

•**ALTAMONTE SPRINGS**, City; Seminole County; Pop. 21,290; Zip Code 32701; 5 miles N of Orlando in Central Florida.

•**ANNA MARIA**, City and Island; Manatee County; Pop. 1,509; Zip Code 33501; W Florida, on Gulf of Mexico. Beach resort area.

•**APALACHICOLA**, City; Franklin County; Pop. 2,540; Zip Code 32320; Elev. 5; NW Florida. Indiam name for "people on the other side."

•**APOPKA**,City; Orange County; Pop. 5,908; Zip Code 32703; Elev. 145; 10 miles NNW of Orlando in Central Florida. Apopka (Ind., "potato eating place"), was settled in 1856 and until 1887 was called The Lodge, for a Masonic lodge building erected here by slaves shortly before the Civil War.

•**ARCADIA**, City; De Soto County; Pop. 6,047; Zip Code 33821; Elev. 57; Lat. 27-12-56 N long. 081-51-31 W; 45 miles ESE of Sarasota in SW central Florida.

•**ARCHER**, City; Alachua County; Pop. 1,159; Zip Code 32618; Elev. 88; Lat. 29-31-47 N long. 082-31-09 W; N Florida. Archer, founded in 1859 and originally called Deer Hammock, was renamed for Brigadier General James J. Archer of the Confederate army.

•**ATLANTIC BEACH**, City; Duval County; Pop. 7,893; Zip Code 32233; Elev. 13; Lat. 30-20-03 N long. 081-23-56 W; NE Florida.

•**AUBURN,** City; Androscoggin County; Pop. 23,128; Zip Code 04210; Lat. 44-05-33 N long. 070-14-09 W; 30 mi. N of Portland in SW Maine. Named either for Aubourn England or Goldsmith's poem, "Sweet Auburn.

•**AUBURNDALE**, City; Polk County; Pop. 6,515; Zip Code 33823; Elev. 169; Lat. 28-03-54 N long. 081-47-20 W; 10 miles E of Lakeland in central Florida.

•**AVON PARK**, City; Highlands County; Pop. 7,854; Zip Code 33825; Elev. 156; Lat. 27-35-44 N long. 081-30-23 W; 45 miles SE of Lakeland in S Florida. The town is named for Stratford-on-Avon in England.

•**BABSON PARK**, Polk County; Pop. est. 300; Zip Code 33827; Elev. 147; Lat. 27-49-54 N long. 081-31-21 W; Central Florida. Babson Park, once called Crooked Lake for the body of water on which it lies, was renamed by Roger Babson, business prognosticator, who in 1923 purchased most of the land within the town.

•**BALDWIN**, Town; Duval County; Pop. 1,521; Zip Code 32234; Elev. 86; Lat. 30-18-09 N long. 081-58-32 W; NE Florida. The town was renamed for Dr. A.S. Baldwin, through whose leadership a railroad was built between Jacksonville and Lake City in 1860.

•**BAL HARBOUR**, Village; Dade County; Pop. 2,657; Zip Code 33154; Lat. 25-53-29 N long. 080-07-38 W; SE Florida, N of Miami on Atlantic Ocean. Named for resort town in Maine.

•**BARTOW**, City; Polk County; Pop. 14,824; Zip Code 33830; Elev. 177; Lat. 27-53-46 N long. 081-50-36 W; 15 miles SSE of Lakeland in central Florida. The town was named in 1867 for General Francis Bartow of the Confederate army.

•**BASCOM**, Town; Jackson County; Pop. 134; Zip Code 32423; Lat. 30-55-40 N long. 085-07-07 W; NW Florida.

•**BAYARD**, Village, Duval County; Pop. Incl. with Jacksonville; NE Florida; Elev. 25; Lat. 30-08-36 N long. 081-30-47 W; 17 mi. S of Jacksonville. Bayard was named by Henry M. Flagler, builder of the Florida East Coast Railway, for his friend, Thomas F. Bayard, Ambassador to Great Britain (1893-97), the first American of that rank at the court of St. James's.

•**BELL**, Town; Gilchrist County; Pop. 214; Zip Code 32619; Elev. 70; Lat. 29-45-19 N long. 082-51-46 W; NW Florida.

•**BELLAIR**, Village; Pinellas County; Pop. 3673; Lat. 30-10-27 N long. 081-44-27 W; Elev. 42; W Florida; 3 mi. S of Clearwater; Residential suburb overlooking Clearwater Bay; Incorporated in 1925.

•**BELLEAIR BLUFFS**, City; Pinellas County; Pop. 2,510; Zip Code 33540; Elev. 42; Lat. 27-55-16 N long. 082-49-02 W; 20 miles W of Tampa in W Central Florida.

•**BELLE GLADE**, City; Palm Beach County; Pop. 14,480; Zip Code 33430; Elev. 20; Lat. 26-41-03 N long. 080-40-04 W; On SE shore of Lake Okeechobee in SE Florida.

•**BELLEVIEW**, City; Marion County; Pop. 1,816; Zip Code 32620; Elev. 82; Lat. 29-03-18 N long. 082-03-45 W; N central Florida.

•**BELLE ISLE**, Village, Orange County; Pop. 4,000; Elev. 97; Lat. 28-27-29 N long. 081-21-34 W; Central Florida; S suburb of Orlando.

•**BISCAYNE PARK**, Village, Dade County; Pop. 3,088; Lat. 25-52-56 N long. 080-10-51 W; SE Florida, 3 mi. N of Miami in a residential area.

•**BLOUNTSTOWN**, City; Calhoun County; Pop. 2,578; Zip Code 32424; Elev. 51; Lat. 30-26-36 N long. 085-02-43 W; 50 miles W of Tallahassee in NW Florida. Although not incorporated until 1925, the settlement was founded in 1823 and named for John Blount, Seminole Chief, a bitter opponent of the warring faction of the Creek, who for years kept settlers along the Georgia-Florida border in a state of constant alarm.

•**BOCA RATON**, City; Palm Beach County; Pop. 50,154; Zip Code 334+; Elev. 17; Lat. 26-21-30 N long. 080-05-00 W; 20 miles N of Fort Lauderdale in SE Florida. Boca Raton (Spanish rat's mouth), bears the name of an inlet just south of the community.

•**BONIFAY**, City; Holmes County; Pop. 2,510; Zip Code 32425; Elev. 120; Lat. 30-47-30 N long. 085-40-47 W; 85 miles ENE of Pensacola in NW Florida.

•**BOWLING GREEN**, City; Hardee County; Pop. 1,734; Zip Code 33834; Elev. 116; Lat. 27-38-17 N long. 081-49-27 W; Central Florida. Bowling Green was known as Utica until the late 1880s when farmers from Bowling Green, KY, purchased large holdings and settled in the district.

•**BOYNTON BEACH**, City; Palm Beach County; Pop. 34,341; Zip Code 334+; Lat. 26-31-30 N long. 080-04-00 W; SE Florida.

•**BRADENTON**, City; Manatee County; Pop. 29,579; Zip Code 335+; Elev. 2l; Lat. 27-29-55 N long. 082-34-30 W; 10 miles N of Sarasota in W Florida. Bradenton was named for Dr. Joseph Braden, who in 1854 built Braden Castle.

•**BRADENTON BEACH**, City; Manatee County; Pop. 1,599; Lat. 27-28-00 N long. 082-42-15 W; W Central Florida.

•BRANFORD, Town; Suwannee County; Pop. 626; Zip Code 32008; Lat. 29-57-32 N long. 082-55-42 W; N Florida.

•BRISTOL, City; Liberty County; Pop. 984; Zip Code 32321; Elev. 168; Lat. 30-25-55 N long. 084-58-33 W; NW Florida.

•BRONSON, Town; Levy County; Pop. 850; Zip Code 32621; Elev. 75; Lat. 29-26-51 N long. 082-38-33 W; NW Florida. The seat of Levy County, it was once called Chunky Pond, from the Indian word meaning dance. When incorporated in 1884, the town took its present name from an early settler.

•BROOKER, City; Bradford County; Pop. 428; Zip Code 32622; Lat. 29-53-19 N long. 082-19-58 W; NE Florida.

•BROOKSVILLE, City; Hernando County; Pop. 5,492; Zip Code 33512; Elev. 144; Lat. 28-33-18 N long. 082-23-17 W; 40 miles N of Tampa in W Florida. Brooksville, with wide oak-shaded streets leading to a white-columned red brick courthouse, was named for Preston Brooks, Congressman from South Carolina, who in 1859 struck Senator Charles Sumner on the floor of the Senate during a heated debate on secession.

•BUNNELL, City; Flagler County; Pop. 1,807; Zip Code 32010; Elev. 20; Lat. 29-27-57 N long. 081-15-29 W; NE Florida.

•BUSHNELL, City; Sumter County; Pop. 971; Zip Code 33513; Elev. 74; Lat. 28-39-53 N long. 082-06-47 W; Central Florida.

•CALLAHAN, Town; Nassau County; Pop. 866; Zip Code 32011; Lat. 30-33-43 N long. 081-49-51 W; NE Florida.

•CALLAWAY, City; Bay County; Pop. 7,020; Zip Code 32401; Lat. 30-09-10 N long. 085-34-12 W; NW Florida.

•CAMPBELLTON, Town; Jackson County; Pop. 329; Zip Code 32426; Lat. 30-56-57 N long. 085-24-08 W; NW Florida. Dating from the English occupation (1763-83), Campbellton has a grain elevator and lumber mill.

•CAPE CANAVERAL, City; Brevard County; Pop. 5,659; Zip Code 32920; Elev. 9; Lat. 28-24-20 N long. 080-36-18 W; 40 miles ESE of Orlando in E Florida.

•CAPE CORAL, City; Lee County; Pop. 31,884; Zip Code 33904; Lat. 26-33-45 N long. 081-56-59 W; SW Florida.

•CARRABELLE, City; Franklin County; Pop. 1,244; Zip Code 32322; Lat. 29-51-11 N long. 084-39-52 W; E of Apalachicola River in NW Florida.

•CARYVILLE, Town; Washington County; Pop. 629; Zip Code 32427; Elev. 58; Lat. 30-46-23 N long. 085-48-51 W; NW Florida.

•CASSELBERRY, City; Seminole County; Pop. 15,052; Zip Code 327+; Lat. 28-40-39 N long. 081-19-41 W; 10 miles NNE of Orlando in central Florida.

•CEDAR KEYS, City; Levy County; Pop. 698; Zip Code 32625; Elev. 13; Lat. 29-08-18 N long. 083-02-07 W; NW Florida.

•CENTER HILL, City; Sumter County; Pop. 740; Zip Code 33514; Elev. 91; Lat. 28-38-59 N long. 081-59-340 W; Central Florida.

•CENTURY, Town; Escambia County; Pop. 503; Zip Code 32535; Elev. 75; Lat. 30-58-23 N long. 087-15-50 W; NW Florida. Century, a mill town along the highway, commemorates in its name the establishment in January 1900 of the large sawmill around which the settlement grew.

•CHARLOTTE HARBOR, Village and Bay; Charlotte County; Pop. rural; Lat. 26-57-29 N long. 082-04-02 W; SW Florida. The name

Charlotte is probably a corruption of Carlos, one of the names used by the Spanish and French to denote the Calusa tribe which inhabited this section.

•CHATTAHOOCHEE, City; Gadsden County; Pop. 32324; Zip Code 32324; Lat. 30-42-18 N long. 084-50-35 W; NW of Tallahassee in NW Florida.

•CHIEFLAND, City; Levy County; Pop. 1,903; Zip Code 32626; Elev. 43; Lat. 29-30-13 N long. 082-52-19 W; NW Florida. Here a Creek chief and his tribesmen lived peaceably beside their white neighbors and engaged in farming.

•CHIPLEY, City; Washington County; Pop. 3,308; Zip Code 32428; Elev. 114; Lat. 30-46-54 N long. 085-32-19 W; 100 miles ENE of Pensacola in NW Florida. The town was originally known as Orange, but was renamed in honor of Colonel William D. Chipley, a railroad official.

•CHRISTMAS, Town; Orange County; Pop. rural; Zip Code 32709; Lat. 28-32-10 N long. 081-01-04 W; Central Florida, 20 miles E of Orlando.

•CLEARWATER, City; Pinellas County; Pop. 87,248; Zip Code 335+; Elev. 29; Lat. 27-57-56 N long. 082-48-01 W; 20 miles NW of St. Petersburg in W Florida.

•CLERMONT, City; Lake County; Pop. 5,404; Zip Code 32711; Elev. 105; Lat. 28-32-57 N long. 081-46-23 W. It was named for Clermont, France, the birthplace of A.F. Wrotnoski, one of its founders.

•CLEWISTON, City; Hendry County; Pop. 5,212; Zip Code 33440; Elev. 18; Lat. 26-45-14 N long. 080-56-02 W; S Florida. It was founded in 1921 as a construction camp during the building of the Moore Haven-Clewiston Railroad.

•COCOA, City; Brevard County; Pop. 16,021; Zip Code 32922; Elev. 26; Lat. 28-23-09 N long. 080-44-32 W; 40 miles SE of Orlando in E Florida. Incorporated in 1895 and named for the coco plum growing abundantly hereabouts.

•COCOA BEACH, City; Brevard County; Pop. 10,890; Zip Code 32931; Lat. 28-19-11 N long. 080-36-28 W; 45 miles ESE of Orlando in E Florida.

•COLEMAN, City; Sumter County; Pop. 1,028; Zip Code 33521; Lat. 28-47-58 N long. 082-04-13 W; Central Florida.

•COOPER CITY, City; Broward County; Pop. 10,106; Zip Code 33328; Lat. 26-03-25 N long. 080-16-19 W; SE Florida.

•CORAL GABLES, City; Dade County; Pop. 42,438; Zip Code 331+; Lat. 25-43-16 N long. 080-16-07 W; 5 miles SW of Miami in SE Florida; On Atlantic Ocean facing Key Biscayne.

•COTTONDALE, Town; Jackson County; Pop. 1,056; Zip Code 32431; Elev. 135; Lat. 30-47-49 N long. 085-22-36 W; NW Florida.

•CRAWFORDVILLE, Village; Wakulla County; Zip Code 32327; Lat. 30-10-33 N long. 084-22-31 W; NW Florida.

•CRESCENT CITY, City; Putnam County; Pop. 1,699; Elev. 53; Lat. 29-25-48 N long. 081-30-39 W; Zip Code 32012; NE Florida.

•CRESTVIEW, City; Okaloosa County; Pop. 7,591; Zip Code 32536; Elev. 233; Lat. 30-45-43 N long. 086-34-14 W; 50 miles ENE of Pensacola in NW Florida.

•CROSS CITY, Town; Dixie County; Pop. 2,119; Zip Code 32628; Elev. 53; Lat. 29-38-03 N long. 083-07-31 W; 50 miles W of Gainesville in NW Florida.

•CRYSTAL RIVER, City; Citrus County; Pop. 2,601; Zip Code 32629; Elev. 4; Lat. 28-54-08 N long. 082-35-34 W; W Florida.

•DADE CITY, City; Pasco County; Pop. 4,841; Zip Code 33525; Elev. 91; Lat. 28-21-52 N long. 082-11-46 W; 35 miles NE of Tampa in W Florida.

•DANIA, City; Broward County; Pop. 11,862; Zip Code 33004; Elev. 12; Lat. 26-03-07 N long. 080-08-39 W; 20 miles N of Miami in SE Florida. Danish families migrated here in 1896 and subsequently named the town.

•DAVENPORT, Town; Polk County; Pop. 1,508; Zip Code 33837; Elev. 136; Lat. 28-09-40 N long. 081-36-07 W; Central Florida.

•DAVIE, Town; Broward County; Pop. 20,548; Zip Code 33314; Elev. 26-03-52 N long. 080-13-56 W; SE Florida.

•DAYTONA BEACH, City; Volusia County; Pop. 53,608; Zip Code 320+; Elev. 7; Lat. 29-12-38 N long. 081-01-23 W; 90 miles SSE of Jacksonville in E Florida. Permanent settlement on the site of Daytona Beach began about 1870 when Mathias Day, of Mansfield, Ohio, bought a tract for $1,200, laid out the original plot of the town, and named the settlement Daytona.

•DAYTONA BEACH SHORES, City; Volusia County; Pop. 1,265; Zip Code 32016; Lat. 29-10-33 N long. 080-58-59 W; E Florida.

•DEERFIELD BEACH, City; Broward County; Pop. 31,468; Zip Code 33441; Elev. 15; Lat. 26-19-05 N long. 080-06-00 W; 40 miles NE of Miami in SE Florida. Deerfield Beach, was originally called Hillsborough, but adopted its present name about 1907 when deer were plentiful in the hammocks west of the town.

•DE FUNIAK SPRINGS, City; Walton County; Pop. 5,507; Zip Code 32433; Elev. 265; Lat. 30-43-17 N long. 086-06-56 W; 70 miles ENE of Pensacola in NW Florida. DeFuniak Springs was named for Colonel Fred DeFuniak, an official of the Louisville & Nashville Railroad.

•DE LAND, City; Volusia County; Pop. 13,764; Zip Code 32720; Elev. 27; Lat. 29-01-41 N long. 081-18-12 W; 20 miles WSW of Daytona Beach in E Florida. De Land was founded in 1876 by Henry A. DeLand, baking powder manufacturer, who planted water oaks 50 feet apart along prospective streets.

•DE LEON SPRINGS, Village; Volusia County; Pop. 1,135; Zip Code 32028; Lat. 29-07-09 N long. 081-21-06 W; E Florida. De Leon Springs is a quiet village known chiefly for the Ponce De Leon Springs.

•DELRAY BEACH, City; Palm Beach County; Pop. 34,006; Zip Code 334+; Lat. 26-27-40 N long. 080-04-23 W; 20 miles S of West Palm Beach in SE Florida.

•DRIFTON, Village; Jefferson County; Pop. rural; Lat. 30-29-430 N long. 083-52-46 W; N Florida.

•DUNDEE, Town; Polk County; Pop. 2,219; Zip Code 33838; Lat. 28-01-20 N long. 081-37-10 W; Central Florida.

•DUNEDIN, City; Pinellas County; Pop. 29,813; Zip Code 33528; Elev. 13; Lat. 28-01-10 N long. 082-46-19 W; 20 miles NW of St. Petersburg in W Florida. In 1878, with the establishment of a post office, it was given its present name by J.L. Douglas and James Somerville of Dunedin, Scotland.

•DUNNELLON, City; Marion County; Pop. 1,441; Zip Code 32630; Elev. 50; Lat. 29-02-56 N long. 082-27-40 W; N central Florida.

•EAGLE LAKE, City; Polk County; Pop. 1,659; Zip Code 33839; Elev. 172; Lat. 27-58-41 N long. 081-45-24 W; Central Florida.

•EATONVILLE, Town; Orange County; Pop. 2,029; Zip Code 32751; Lat. 28-36-52 N long. 081-22-51 W; Central Florida.

•EAU GALLIE, Village; Brevard County; Pop. rural; Zip Code 32951; Elev. 19; Lat. 28-07-44 N long. 080-37-50 W; E Central Florida. Eau Gallie, a name compounded of French and Indian words meaning rocky water, was christened by W.H. Gleason, who, shortly after the War between the States, was commissioned by the federal government to make a topographical and agricultural survey of Florida for the purpose of ascertaining whether it was suitable for black colonization.

•EBRO, Town; Washington County; Pop. 232; Zip Code 32437; Lat. 30-26-52 N long. 085-52-27 W; NW Florida.

•EDGEWATER, City; Volusia County; Pop. 6,693; Zip Code 32032; Elev. 6; Lat. 28-59-19 N long. 080-54-09 W; E Florida.

•ELLAVILLE, Village; Suwanee County; Pop. rural; Elev. 64; Lat. 30-58-29 N long. 085-22-36 W; NW Florida on the Suwannee River. The site of a large sawmill built by Governor George F. Drew in 1868, was named for Ella a servant in the governor's employ.

•ELLENTON, Village; Manatee County; Pop. 1,420; Zip Code 33532; Elev. 11; Lat. 27-31-17 N long. 082-31-40 W; W central Florida.

•ERIDU, Village; Taylor County; Pop. rural; Lat. 30-18-06 N long. 083-44-50 W; NW Florida. A wag with a classical bent gave this hamlet a name derived from Eridanus, mythological name of the River Po.

•ESTO, Town; Holmes County; Pop. 303; Zip Code 32425; Lat. 30-59-14 N long. 085-38-46 W; NW Florida.

•EUSTIS, City; Lake County; Pop. 9,494; Zip Code 32726; Elev. 71; Lat. 28-51-09 N long. 081-41-08 W; 30 miles NW of Orlando in central Florida. Known successively as Highlands and Pendryville, the town was later named for Lake Eustis, itself named about 1828 for General Abram Eustis, prominent in the Seminole War, whose forces had a skirmish with the Indians on the south shore of the lake.

•EVERGLADES CITY, City; Collier County; Pop. 346; Zip Code 33929; Elev. 3; Lat. 25-51-35 N long. 081-22-50 W; SW Florida.

•FALMOUTH, Village; Suwannee County; Pop. rural; Elev. 94; Lat. 30-21-46 N long. 083-07-53 W; N Florida; Near the Suwannee River. Falmouth, once known as Peacock, and renamed, accordt tradition, by Colonel Duval, a leading citizen and dog fancier, for his favorite pointer, Falmouth, killed on a hunting trip.

•FELLSMORE, City; Indian River County; Pop. 1,159; Zip Code 32948; Elev. 25; Lat. 27-46-03 N long. 080-36-06 W; E central Florida.

•FERNANDINA BEACH, City; Nassau County; Pop. 7,215; Zip Code 32034; Elev. 19; Lat. 30-40-10 N long. 081-27-46 W; 25 miles NE of Jacksonville in NE Florida.

•FLAGLER BEACH, City; Flagler County; Pop. 2,039; Zip Code 32036; Lat. 29-28-29 N long. 081-07-38 W; NE Florida.

•FLAMINGO, Village; Monroe County; Pop. rural; Zip Code 33030; Lat. 25-08-29 N long. 080-55-32 W; SE tip, Florida, in the Everglades National Park.

•FLOMATION, Village; Escambia County; Pop. 1,882; NW Florida; Once known as Pensacola Junction before 1884, straddles the state line.

•FLORAL CITY, Village; Citrus County; Pop. 950; Zip Code 32636; Elev. 57; Lat. 28-45-00 N long. 082-17-49 W; W Florida.

•**FLORENCE VILLA**, Village; Polk County; Pop. rural; Zip Code 33880; Elev. 149; Lat. 28-02-36 N long. 081-43-01 W; Central Florida; was founded by Dr. F.W. Inman, known as "the father of Florida co-operative marketing."

•**FLORIDA CITY**, City; Dade County; Pop. 5,394; Zip Code 33034; Elev. 9; Lat. 25-26-51 N long. 080-28-46 W; 25 miles SSW of Miami in SE Florida.

•**FORT LAUDERDALE**, City; Seat of Broward County; Pop. 154,035; Zip Code 333+; Elev. 10; Lat. 26-07-19 N long. 080-08-37 W; 25 miles N of Miami in SE Florida along the Atlantic Coast. It occupies the approximate site of a Seminole War fort constructed in 1838 and named for its commander, Major William Lauderdale.

•**FORT MEADE**, City; Polk County; Pop. 5,545; Zip Code 33841; Elev. 130; Lat. 27-45-07 N long. 081-48-07 W; 25 miles S of Lakeland in central Florida.

•**FORT MYERS**, City; Lee County; Pop. 36,624; Zip Code 339+; Elev. 9; Lat. 26-38-25 N long. 081-52-21 W; SW Florida.

•**FORT OGDEN**, Village; De Soto County; Pop. rural; Zip Code 33842; Elev. 37; Lat. 27-05-13 N long. 081-57-09 W; SW central Florida. Fort Ogden occupies the site of an Indian fort of the same name, built in 1841.

•**FORT PIERCE**, City; St. Lucie County; Elev. 24; Lat. 27-26-47 N long. 080-19-33 W; 30 miles NE of Lake Okeechobee in E Florida. Fort Pierce received its name from the fortification built here in 1838 as a link in a chain of east coast defenses against the Indians.

•**FORT WALTON BEACH**, City; Okaloosa County; Pop. 20,811; Zip Code 32548; Lat. 30-24-20 N long. 086-37-08 W; E of Pensacola in NW Florida. Fort Walton, a large summer resort on the site of a fort of the same name built during the Seminole War.

•**FORT WHITE**, Town; Columbia County; Pop. 242; Zip Code 32038; Elev. 72; Lat. 29-55-23 N long. 082-42-50 W; N Florida.

•**FREEPORT**, Town; Walton County; Pop. 667; Zip Code 32439; Lat. 30-29-53 N long. 086-08-10 W; NW Florida.

•**FROSTPROOF**, City; Polk County; Pop. 2,991; Zip Code 33843; Elev. 102; Lat. 27-44-44 N long. 081-31-51 W; 35 miles SE of Lakeland in central Florida.

•**FRUITLAND PARK**, City; Lake County; Pop. 2,483; Zip Code 32731; Elev. 113; Lat. 28-51-40 N long. 081-54-24 W; Central Florida. Fruitland Park was founded in 1876 by Major O.P. Rooks, and named for the Fruitland Nurseries of Augusta, Ga.

•**GAINESVILLE**, City; Alachua County; Pop. 72,270; Zip Code 326+; Elev. 185'; Lat. 29-39-05 N long. 082-19-30 W; 65 miles SW of Jacksonville in N Florida. A trading post established here in 1830, and was named Gainesville in 1853 for General Edmund P. Gaines, a Seminole War leader.

•**GIBSONTON**, Village; Hillsborough County; Pop. 2,500; Zip Code 33534; Lat. 27-51-12 N long. 082-22-58 W; W central Florida. Gibsonton, on the southern bank of the Alafia River, was named for the pioneer Gibson family.

•**GIFFORD**, Indian River County; Zip Code 32960; Elev. 19; Lat. 27-40-30 N long. 080-24-34 W; E central Florida. Gifford was named for F.Charles Gifford, credited with having selected the site for Vero Beach.

•**GLEN SAINT MARY**, Town; Baker County; Pop. 460; Zip Code 32040; Elev. 134; Lat. 30-16-32 N long. 082-09-39 W; NE Florida.

•**GONZALEZ**, Village; Escambia County; Pop. rural; Zip Code 32560; Lat. 30-34-53 N long. 087-17-29 W; NW Florida, along Hwy. 29, N of Pensacola. It was named for Don Manuel Gonzalez and was so recorded on a Florida map of 1828.

•**GOODNO**, Village; Hendry County; Pop. rural; Elev. 27; Lat. 26-46-06 N long. 081-18-43 W; S Florida. Goodno was named for E.E. Goodno, cattleman from Kansas, who did much to improve Florida beef stock by importing Brahma bulls from India in the 1860s.

•**GRACEVILLE**, City; Jackson County; Pop. 2,926; Zip Code 32440; Lat. 30-57-24 N long. 085-31-00 W; 20 miles NW of Marianne in NW Florida.

•**GRAND ISLAND**, Village; Lake County; Pop. rural; Zip Code 32735; Elev. 108; Lat. 28-52-56 N long. 081-43-45 W; Central Florida. Grand Island, settled in the late 1880s, was so named because it is almost encircled by Lakes Yale, Griffin, and Eustis.

•**GRAND RIDGE**, Town; Jackson County; Pop. 587; Zip Code 32442; Elev. 32; Lat. 30-42-44 N long. 085-01-13 W; NW Florida.

•**GREEN COVE SPRINGS**, City; Clay County; Pop. 4,163; Zip Code 32043; Elev. 28; Lat. 29-59-30 N long. 081-40-42 W; 25 miles S of Jacksonville in NE Florida. Green Cove Springs, seat of Clay County, is a resort centered around a spring that flows 3,000 gallons a minute, impounded to form a large swimming pool.

•**GREENSBORO**, Town; Gadsden County; Pop. 527; Zip Code 32330; Lat. 30-34-09 N long. 084-44-36 W; N Florida.

•**GREENVILLE**, Town; Madison County; Pop. 1,050; Zip Code 32331; Elev. 106; Lat. 30-28-09 N long. 083-37-49 W; N Florida. As the majority of the early settlers had migrated from the vicinity of Greenville, South Carolina, that name was selected.

•**GREENWOOD**, Town; Jackson County; Pop. 572; Zip Code 32443; Elev. 115; Lat. 30-52-12 N long. 085-09-43 W; NW Florida.

•**GRETNA**, Town; Gadsden County; Pop. 1,604; Zip Code 32332; Lat. 30-37-01 N long. 084-39-36 W; N Florida.

•**GROVELAND**, City; Lake County; Pop. 1,979; Zip Code 32736; Elev. 129; Lat. 28-33-28 N long. 081-51-05 W; Central Florida. Groveland was so named because of the extensive citrus farming in its region, was founded in the early 1900s as a naval-stores center and was first known as Taylorville.

•**GULF BREEZE**, City; Santa Rosa County; Pop. 5,457; Zip Code 32561; Lat. 30-21-25 N long. 087-09-50 W; 5 miles SE of Pensacola in NW Florida.

•**GULFPORT**, City; Pinellas County; Pop. 11,069; Zip Code 33737; Lat. 27-44-53 N long. 082-42-13 W; W Florida.

•**HAINES CITY**, City; Polk County; Pop. 10,578; Zip Code 33844; Elev. 166; Lat. 28-06-50 N long. 081-37-05 W; 20 miles E of Lakeland in central Florida. The name honors Henry Haines, South Florida Railroad official.

•**HALLANDALE**, City; Broward County; Pop. 36,772; Zip Code 33009; Lat. 25-58-51 N long. 080-08-55 W; 15 miles N of Miami in SE Florida.

•**HAMPTON**, City; Bradford County; Pop. 463; Zip Code 32044; Lat. 29-51-51 N long. 082-07-52 W; NE Florida.

•**HAMPTON SPRINGS**, Village and resort; Taylor County; Pop. 150; Elev. 27; Lat. 30-05-07 N long. 083-39-18 W; NW Florida. Old residents claim the springs were named by Joe Hampton, an early settler.

•**HASTINGS**, Town; St. Johns County; Pop. 615; Zip Code 32045; Elev. 10; Lat. 29-43-04 N long. 081-30-30 W; NE Florida.

•**HAVANA**, Town; Gadsden County; Pop. 2,932; Zip Code 32333; Lat. 30-37-25 N long. 084-24-53 W; N Florida. Havana is named for the Cuban capital.

•**HAWTHORNE**, City; Alachua County; Pop. 1,303; Zip Code 32640; Elev. 153; Lat. 29-35-30 N long. 082-05-15 W; N Florida; Incorporated in 1890, it was named for James M. Hawthorn, owner of the site.

•**HESPERIDES**, Village; Osceola County; Pop. rural; Elev. 118; Lat. 27-53-02 N long. 081-27-33 W; E central Florida. Hesperides, a small village surrounded by orange groves, was well named for the mythological Greek garden in which grew the precious "golden apples" sought by Hercules as one of his twelve labors.

•**HIALEAH**, City; Dade County; Pop. 143,627; Zip Code 330+; Lat. 25-51-26 N long. 080-16-42 W; 5 miles NW of Miami in SE Florida.

•**HICORIA**, Village; Highlands County; Pop. rural; Elev. 148; Lat. 27-09-04 N long. 081-21-11 W; S central Florida.

•**HIGHLAND BEACH**, Town; Palm Beach County; Pop. 2,009; Zip Code 33431; Lat. 26-23-57 N long. 080-03-57 W; SE Florida.

•**HIGH SPRINGS**, City; Alachua County; Pop. 2,350; Zip Code 32643; Elev. 75; Lat. 29-49-36 N long. 082-35-49 W; 20 miles NW of Gainesville in N Florida. High Springs, named for a hilltop spring, was established as a trading post in 1885.

•**HILLIARD**, Town; Nassau County; Pop. 1,882; Zip Code 32046; Lat. 30-41-27 N long. 081-55-03 W; NE Florida.

•**HOBE SOUND**, Village; Martin County; Pop. 20,593; Zip Code 33455; Elev. 24; Lat. 27-03-33 N long. 080-08-12 W; SE Florida, on Atlantic coast. Hobe Sound, bordered in places with Australian pines, appeared on maps under its present name as early as 1699. The name is probably a corruption of Jobe (Sp., Jupiter), although the Indians called it Hoe Sound.

•**HOLLY HILL**, City; Volusia County; Pop. 9,829; Zip Code 32017; Elev. 6; Lat. 29-14-36 N long. 081-02-16 W; 5 miles N of Daytona Beach in E Florida. Holly Hill, a suburb of Daytona Beach, named because of the holly trees that once grew here.

•**HOLLYWOOD**, City; Broward County; Pop. 116,832; Zip Code 330+; Elev. 11; Lat. 26-00-39 N long. 080-08-59 W; 20 miles N of Miami in SE Florida. It was founded in 1921 by Joseph W. Young and associates from California. It is a resort area and its main industry is electronic components.

•**HOLMES BEACH**, City; Manatee County; Pop. 4,013; Zip Code 33509; Lat. 27-29-50 N long. 082-42-33 W; 20 miles NW of Sarasota in W central Florida.

•**HOWEY IN THE HILLS**, Town; Lake County; Pop. 621; Zip Code 32737; Elev. 82; Lat. 28-43-00 N long. 081-46-25 W.

•**HYPOLOXO**, Town; Palm Beach County, Pop. 556; Elev. 12; Lat. 26-33-58 N long. 080-03-13 W; Settled 1873;

•**IMMOKALEE**, Village; Collier County; Pop. 3,764; Zip Code 33934; Lat. 26-25-06 N long. 081-25-03 W.

•**INDIALANTIC**, Town; Brevard County; Pop. 2,924; Zip Code 32903; Lat. 28-05-21 N long. 080-33-57 W; 20 miles ESE of Cocoa in E Florida.

•**INDIAN HARBOR BEACH**, City; Brevard County; Pop. 5,974; Zip Code 32937; Lat. 28-08-55 N long. 080-35-19 W; 10 miles ESE of Cocoa in E Florida.

•**INDIAN RIVER CITY**, City; Brevard County; Zip Code 32780; Lat. 28-33-34 N long. 080-47-58 W.

•**INDIAN RIVER SHORES**, Town; Indian River County; Pop. 1,247; Zip Code 32960; Lat. 27-42-59 N long. 080-23-04 W; E Central Florida.

•**INDIAN ROCKS BEACH**, City; Pinellas County; Pop. 3,680; Zip Code 33535; Lat. 27-52-30 N long. 082-51-05 W.

•**INGLIS**, Town; Levy County; Pop. 1,166; Zip Code 32649; Elev. 15; Lat. 29-01-48 N long. 082-40-08 W; NW Florida.

•**INTERCESSION CITY**, Village, Osceola County; Zip Code 33848; Lat. 28-15-44 N long. 081-30-29 W. Central Florida, was named Interocean City when platted in 1924, because it was midway between the Atlantic Ocean and the Gulf.

•**INTERLACHEN**, Town; Putnam County; Pop. 840; Zip Code 32048; Elev. 104; Lat. 29-37-25 N long. 081-53-26 W.

•**INVERNESS**, City; Citrus County; Pop. 3,965; Zip Code 32650; Elev. 50; Lat. 28-50-08 N long. 082-19-50 W. W Florida, on Lake Tsala Apopka, was named by an early settler for his home town in Scotland.

•**ISLAMORADA**, Village, Monroe County; Zip Code 33036; Lat. 24-55-26 N long. 080-37-41 W.

•**ISLAND GROVE**, Village, Alachua County; Zip Code 32654; Elev. 75; Lat. 29-27-12 N long. 082-06-24 W.

•**JACKSONVILLE**, City; Duval County; Pop. 541,274; Lat. 30-19-55 N long. 081-39-21 W. Named in honor of General Andrew Jackson, Territorial Governor.

•**JACKSONVILLE BEACH**, City; Duval County; Pop. 15,452; Zip Code 32250; Lat. 30-17-40 N long. 081-23-36 W; NE Florida.

•**JASPER**, City; Hamilton County; Pop. 2,040; Zip Code 32052; Lat. 30-31-05 N long. 082-56-54 W. 80 miles W of Jacksonville in N Florida, was established as a trading post in 1830 by families from South Carolina and Georgia, and named for Sergeant William Jasper, who had served with distinction in a South Carolina regiment during the Revolutionary War.

•**JAY**, Town, Santa Rosa County; Pop. 627; Zip Code 32565; Lat. 30-57-10 N long. 087-09-05 W; NW Florida.

•**JENNINGS**, Town; Hamilton County; Pop. 745; Zip Code 32053; Lat. 30-36-14 N long. 083-05-53 W. N. Florida. Was named for George Jennings, a northerner who is said to have come into this section on a raft by way of the Alapaha River in 1844.

•**JENSEN BEACH**, Martin County; Zip Code 33457; Lat. 27-15-15 N long. 080-13-48 W; SE Florida.

•**JULIETTE**, Marian County; Pop. rural; N Central Florida. The town wasw named, as was Romeo, for a local legend similar to that in the Shakespearean play; one of the lovers lived here and the other at what is now Romeo. The misspelling of the name was not intentional.

•**JUPITER**, Town; Palm Beach County; Pop. 9,388; Zip Code 33458; Elev. 8; Lat. 26-56-02 N long. 080-05-40 W.

•**KENNETH CITY**, Town; Pinellas County; Pop. 4,276; Zip Code 33709; W Florida.

•**KEY BISCAYNE**, Island and Town; Dade County; Pop. included with Miami; Zip Code 33149; Lat. 25-41-36 N long. 080-09-47 W, SE Florida, across Biscayne Bay from Coral Gobles on the Atlantic Ocean.

•**KEY COLONY BEACH**, City; Monroe County; Pop. 1,022; Zip Code 33051; Lat. 24-43-14 N long. 081-01-08 W; SW Florida.

•**KEY LARGO**, Island and Town; Monroe County; Pop. 2,866; Zip Code 33037.

•**KEYSTONE HEIGHTS**, City; Clay County; Pop. 1,058; Zip Code 32656, Elev. 136; Lat. 29-47-09 N long. 082-01-54 W; NE Florida, is the northern-most resort town of the lake region. Originally known as Brooklyn, the town was renamed in 1922 by J.J. Lawrence of Pennsylvania for the Keystone State.

•**KEY WEST**, City and Island; Monroe County; Pop. 17,903; Zip Code 33040, Lat. 24-33-19 N long. 081-46-58 W; SW Florida, named for its westerly location.

•**KISSIMMEE**, City; Osceola County; Pop. 15,331; Zip Code 32741; Lat. 28-17-30 N long. 081-24-28 W; 20 miles S of Orlando in central Florida.

•**KORONA**, Village, Flagler County; Pop. Rural; Elev. 31; Lat. 29-24-24 N long. 081-11-48 W; E Florida; 20 miles N of Daytona Beach. Was settled in 1912 by a group of Polish families from Chicago and vicinity.

•**LA BELLE**, City; Hendry County; Pop. 2,294; Zip Code 33935; Elev. 16; Lat. 26-45-41 N long. 081-26-19 W; in S. Florida was named by Captain Francis Asbury Hendry for his two daughters, Laura and Belle.

•**LA CROSSE**, Town, Alachua County; Pop. 174; Zip Code 32658; Elev. 46; Lat. 29-50-35 N long. 082-24-18 W; N Florida.

•**LADY LAKE**, Town; Lake County; Pop. 1,184; Zip Code 32659; Lat. 28-55-02 N long. 081-55-23 W; Central Florida.

•**LAKE BUTLER**, City, Union County; Pop. 1,828; Zip Code 32054, Lat. 30-01-21 N long. 082-20-23 W; NE Florida, was named for Colonel Robert Butler, who in behalf of the United States accepted East Florida from Spain at the time of its cession on July 10, 1821.

•**LAKE CITY**, City; Columbia County; Pop. 9,172; Zip Code 32055; Lat. 30-11-22 N long. 082-38-22 W; 45 miles NNW of Gainesville in N Florida.

•**LAKE HAMILTON**, Town; Polk County; Pop. 1,512; Zip Code 33851; Lat. 28-02-39 N long. 081-37-41 W.

•**LAKE HELEN**, City; Volusia County; Pop. 1,876; Zip Code 32744; Lat. 28-58-50 N long. 081-14-01 W; E Florida.

•**LAKE MARY**, City; Seminole County; Pop. 2,838; Zip Code 32746; Elev. 63; Lat. 28-45-31 N long. 081-19-05 W; Central Florida.

•**LAKE PARK**, Town; Plam Beach County; Pop. 6,374; Zip Code 334; Lat. 26-48-00 N long. 080-04-00 W: 5 miles N of Palm Beach in SE Florida.

•**LAKE PLACID**, Town, Highlands County; Pop. 955; Zip Code 33852; Elev. 136; Lat. 27-17-34 N long. 081-21-47 W; Central Florida. Its.name and that of a lake to the south were changed when the southern branch of Lake Placid Club of New York was established in the town.

•**LAKE WALES**, City; Polk County; Pop. 8,394; Zip Code 33853; Elev. 147; Lat. 27-54-04 N long. 081-35-10 W; 25 miles ESE of Lakeland in central Florida. The name of the lake and town as originally spelled Waels, for the Waels family who settled on the shore of the lake in the early 1900's; the spelling was changed when the town was platted in 1911.

•**LAKE WORTH**, City; Palm Beach County; Pop. 26,107; Zip Code 334+ zone; Elev. 21; Lat. 26-36-56 N long. 080-03-26 W; 5 miles S of West Palm Beach in SE Florida.

•**LAKELAND**, City; Polk County; Pop. 48,667; Zip Code 338+; Elev. 206; 30 miles E of Tampa in Central Florida. Is in the highland region of central Florida, with 14 natural lakes within or near its limits.

•**LAMONT**, Village, Jefferson County; Pop. Rural; Zip Code 32336; Lat. 30-22-37 N long. 083-48-47 W. N Florida, was originally called Lick Skillet, but in 1890 the villagers decided a more dignified name was needed. As Cornelius Lamont, Vice-president of the United States, had been a recent visitor, he was honored.

•**LANTANA**, Town; Palm Beach County; Pop. 7,959; Zip Code 334+; Elev. 10; Lat. 26-35-11 N long. 080-03-08 W; SE Florida.

•**LARGO**, City; Pinellas County; Pop. 60,827; Zip Code 335; Lat. 27-54-33 N long. 082-47-15 W; W central Florida.

•**LAUDERDALE-BY-THE-SEA**, Town; Broward County; Pop. 2,570; Zip Code 33308; Lat. 26-11-30 N long. 080-05-48 W; SE Florida; Suburb of Fort Lauderdale, on the beach N of town.

•**LAUREL HILL**, City; Okaloosa County; Pop. 609; Zip Code 32567; Elev. 289; Lat. 30-57-56 N long. 086-27-35 W; NW Florida.

•**LAWTEY**, City; Bradford County; Pop. 689; Zip Code 32058; Elev. 162; Lat. 30-02-38 N long. 082-04-19 W.

•**LEE**, Town; Madison County; Pop. 295; Zip Code 32059; Elev. 94; Lat. 30-25-10 N long. 083-18-02 W; N Florida.

•**LEESBURG**, City; Lake County; Pop. 13,164; Zip Code 32748; Elev. 98; Lat. 28-48-38 N long. 081-52-41 W; 40 miles WNW of Orlando in central Florida. Leesburg, the largest and oldest town in Lake County, founded in 1856 by the Lee family of New York, occupies an elevation between Lakes Griffin and Harris.

•**LEHIGH ACRES**, Village, Lee County; Pop. 5,000; Zip Code 33936; Lat. 26-37-30 N long. 081-37-30 W; SW Florida; on the edge of a vast swampland.

•**LIGHTHOUSE POINT**, City; Broward County; Pop. 11,420; Zip Code 33064; Lat. 26-16-31 N long. 080-05-15 W; NW Florida.

•**LIVE OAK**, City; Suwannee County; Pop. 6,408; Zip Code 32060; Elev. 102; Lat. 30-17-41 N long. 082-59-03 W; The naming of Live Oak preceded its founding. The old wagon road from the military post at Suwannee Springs to the Gulf passed a clear deep pond here under a huge live oak. Offering shade and an attractive camping ground, the spot became known as Live Oak.

•**LONGBOAT KEY**, Town and Island; Manatee & Sarasota Counties; Pop. 4,843; Zip Code 33548; Elev. 9; Lat. 27-24-44 N long. 082-39-33 W; 20 miles NW of Sarasota in W central Florida on Gulf coast.

•**LONGWOOD**, City; Seminole County; Pop. 9,902; Zip Code 32750; Lat. 30-27-38 N long. 086-35-19 W; 10 miles N of Orlando in Central Florida.

•**MACCLENNY**, Town; Baker County; Pop. 3,829; Zip Code 32063; Lat. 30-16-55 N long. 082-07-20 W; NE Florida.

•**MADEIRA BEACH**, City; Pinellas County; Pop. 4,494; Lat. 27-47-52 N long. 082-47-51 W; 5 miles W of St. Petersburgh in W central Florida.

•**MADISON**, City; Madison County; Pop. 3,423; Zip Code 32340; Lat. 30-28-09 N long. 083-24-47 W; 50 miles E of Tallahassee in N

Florida. First called Newton, Madison was settled in 1838 by planters from South Carolina, and named for President James Madison.

•**MAGNOLIA SPRINGS**, Village, Clay County; Pop. Rural; Lat. 30-00-42 N long. 081-41-44 W; N Central Florida; 25 miles SW of Jacksonville. Was established before the Civil War.

•**MAITLAND**, City; Orange County; Pop. 8,746; Zip Code 32751; Elev. 91; Lat. 28-37-39 N long. 081-21-48 W; 10 miles N of Orlando in central Florida. Was settled before the Civil War on the site of Fort Maitland, built in 1838, and named for Captain William S. Maitland of the U.S. army.

•**MALABAR**, Town; Brevard County; Pop. 1,092; Zip Code 32950; Elev. 25; Lat. 28-00-12 N long. 080-33-57 W; E central Florida. Is named for Cape Malabar on the African coast.

•**MALONE**, Town; Jackson County; Pop. 896; Zip Code 32445; Elev. 138; Lat. 30-57-27 N long. 085-09-44 W; NW Florida.

•**MANATEE**, Manatee County; Zip Code 33508; Lat. 27-29-46 N long. 082-32-23 W; W central Florida. The Indian name for the "sea cow."

•**MARATHON**, Village, Monroe County; Pop. 4,397; Zip Code 33050; Lat. 24-42-48 N long. 081-05-26 W; SW Florida.

•**MARGATE**, City; Broward County; Pop. 35,867; Lat. 26-14-39 N long. 080-12-24 W; SE Florida.

•**MARIANNA**, City; Jackson County; Pop. 6,974; Zip Code 32446; Elev. 117; Lat. 30-46-27 N long. 085-13-37 W; 60 miles WNW of Tallahassee in NW Florida. On the Chipola River, was founded in 1829 and named for Mary and Anna, daughters of a pioneer merchant.

•**MARY ESTHER**, Town; Okaloosa County; Pop. 3,520; Zip Code 32569; Lat. 30-24-35 N long. 086-39-47 W; 30 miles E of Pensacola in NW Florida.

•**MASARYKTOWN**, Hernando County; Zip Code 33512; Lat. 28-26-29 N long. 082-27-26 W; W Florida. Named for Thomas G. Masaryk, first President of Czechoslovakia.

•**MASCOTTE**, City; Lake County; Pop. 1,049; Zip Code 32753; Lat. 28-34-41 N long. 081-53-13 W; Central Florida.

•**MAYO**, Town; Lafayette County; Pop. 883; Zip Code 32066; Elev. 79; Lat. 30-03-10 N long. 083-10-30 W; NW Florida.

•**MCINTOSH**, Town; Marion County; Pop. 408; Zip Code 32664; Lat. 29-26-55 N long. 082-13-20 W; N central Florida.

•**MELBOURNE**, City; Brevard County; Pop. 45,986; Elev. 22; Lat. 28-04-43 N long. 080-36-10 W; 60 miles SE of Orlando in E Florida. Located on the Indian River, Melbourne was named by an Australian for his native city.

•**MELBOURNE BEACH**, Town; Brevard County; Pop. 2,648; Zip Code 32951; Elev. 12; Lat. 28-04-05 N long. 080-33-38 W; E central Florida, S of Melbourne.

•**MEXICO BEACH**, Town; Bay County; Pop. 625; Zip Code 32410; Lat. 29-56-52 N long. 085-25-05 W; NW Florida.

•**MIAMI**, City; Dade County; Pop. 335,718; Zip Code 335,718; Lat. 25-46-26 N long. 080-11-38 W; SE Florida; on the Atlantic Ocean. The name Miami is reputedly a variant of the Indian words, *maiha*, translated as "very large", and *mih*, "it is so". On Spanish maps of the early seventeenth century, an area adjacent to Miami is marked *Aymai* and *Mayami*.

•**MIAMI BEACH**, City; Dade County; Pop. 90,836; Zip Code 33139; Lat. 25-47-25 N long. 080-07-49 W; SE Florida; NE of City of Miami, on the Atlantic Ocean. Miami Beach is built on a series of islands one to three miles off the mainland with Biscayne Bay separating this city from Miami on the west, and the broad blue Atlantic stretching away eastward.

•**MIAMI SHORES**, Village, Dade County; Pop. 9,117; Lat. 25-51-46 N long. 080-11-35 W; 10 miles N of Miami SE Florida.

•**MIAMI SPRINGS**, City; Dade County; Pop. 12,202; Lat. 25-49-19 N long. 080-17-23 W; SE Florida; Suburb of Miami.

•**MICANOPY**, Town; Alachua County; Pop. 661; Zip Code 32667; Elev. 125; Lat. 29-30-16 N long. 082-16-48 W; N Florida. Powerful Seminole chiefs ruled this territory, among them Micanope, for whom the settlement was named.

•**MILTON**, City; Santa Rosa County; Pop. 7,126; Zip Code 32570; Lat. 30-37-56 N long. 087-02-23 W; 20 miles NE of Pensacola in SW Florida. Milton was founded on the Blackwater River as a trading post in 1825.

•**MINNEOLA**, City; Lake County; Pop. 843; Zip Code 32755; Lat. 28-34-27 N long. 081-44-47 W; Central Florida.

•**MIRAMAR**, City; Broward County; Pop. 32,651; Lat. 25-59-13 N long. 080-13-57 W; SE Florida.

•**MONTICELLO**, City; Jefferson County; Pop. 2,947; Zip Code 32344; Elev. 210; Lat. 30-32-42 N long. 083-52-13 W; 30 miles ENE of Tallahassee in N Florida. Named for Thomas Jefferson's famous home.

•**MONTVERDE**, Town; Lake County; Pop. 395; Zip Code 32756; Lat. 28-36-00 N long. 081-40-27 W; Central Florida.

•**MOORE HAVEN**, City; Glades County; Pop. 1,272; Zip Code 33471; Elev. 9; Lat. 26-49-58 N long. 081-05-36 W; S central Florida.

•**MOULTRIE**, Village; St. Johns County; Pop. Rural; Lat. 29-49-12 N long. 081-19-22 W; NE Florida, 6 miles S of San Augustine. Was named for John Moultrie, Lieutenant governor of Florida during the English occupation (1763-83), who lived near by in a large stone mansion on his plantation, Belle Vista.

•**MOUNT DORA**, City; Lake County; Pop. 5,742; Zip Code 32757; Lat. 28-48-08 N long. 081-38-41 W; Central Flroida.

•**MULBERRY**, City; Polk County; Pop. 2,939; Zip Code 33860; Lat. 27-53-42 N long. 081-58-25 W; 10 miles S of Lakeland in central Florida.

•**NAPLES**, City; Collier County; Pop. 17,598; Elev. 9; Lat. 26-08-30 N long. 081-47-42 W; 35 miles S of Fort Myers in SW Florida. Was named for the Italian city and planned as a winter resort as early as 1887.

•**NEPTUNE BEACH**, City; Duval County; Pop. 5,306; Zip Code 32233; Lat. 30-18-42 N long. 081-23-48 W; NE Florida.

•**NEWBERRY**, City; Alachua County; Pop. 1,674; Zip Code 32669; Elev. 83; Lat. 29-38-46 N long. 082-36-24 W; N Florida.

•**NEW SMYRNA BEACH**, City; Volusia County; Pop. 13,312; Zip Code 32069; Elev. 10; Lat. 29-01-32 N long. 080-55-38 W; 15 miles S of Daytona Beach in E Florida. Was formerly known as New Smyrna.

•**NICEVILLE**, City; Okaloosa County; Pop. 9,499; Zip Code 32578; Lat. 30-31-00 N long. 086-28-56 W; 40 miles ENE of Pensacola in NW Florida.

•NORTH FORT MYERS, Village; Lee County; Pop. 8,798; Zip Code 33903; Lat. 26-40-01 N long. 081-52-49 W; SW Florida; Suburb of Fort Myers, site of Edison Community College.

•NORTH MIAMI, City; Dade County; Pop. 42,221; Lat. 25-53-23 N long. 080-11-13 W; SE Florida.

•NORTH MIAMI BEACH, City; Dade County; Pop. 32,695; Zip Code 331+; Lat. 25-55-58 N long. 080-09-46 W; SE Florida.

•NORTH PALM BEACH, Village; Palm Beach County; Pop. 11,138; Zip Code 33408; Elev. 25; Lat. 26-49-02 N long. 080-04-56 W; 10 miles N of Palm Beach in SE Florida.

•NORTH PORT, City; Sarasota County; Pop. 6,183; Zip Code 33596; Lat. 27-03-00 N long. 082-15-00 W; W central Florida.

•OAK HILL, City; Volusia County; Pop. 926; Zip Code 32759; Lat. 30-14-46 N long. 081-45-05 W; E Florida.

•OAKLAND, City; Orange County; Pop. 631; Zip Code 32760; Lat. 28-33-17 N long. 081-38-00 W; Central Florida. Oakland occupies a wooded slope overlooking Lake Apopka. Giant oaks, for which the town was named, shade its quiet streets and shelter many large weathrbeaten frame houses erected in the early 1880s.

•OAKLAND PARK, City; Broward County; Pop. 20,280; Zip Code 333+; Lat. 26-10-19 N long. 080-07-56 W; SE Florida.

•OCALA, City; Marion County; Pop. 35,903; Zip Code 326+; Elev. 99; Lat. 29-11-13 N long. 082-08-25 W; 35 miles S of Gainesville in N cnetral Florida. Ocala, seat of Marion County, The town's name is a corruption of Ocali (Indian, "water's edge"), the name of a near-by Indian village through which DeSoto passed in 1539 on his march northward through Florida.

•OCOEE, City; Orange County; Pop. 7,746; Zip Code 32761; Elev. 156; Lat. 28-34-08 N long. 081-32-39 W; 10 miles W of Orlando in central Florida. Ocoee (Indian, "apricot vine place).

•OKAHUMPKA, Village; Lake County; Pop. Rural; Zip Code 32762; Lat. 28-44-51 N long. 081-53-46 W; Central Florida. Okahumpka (Indian "lonely or bitter water").

•OKEECHOBEE, City; Okeechobee County; Pop. 4,239; Zip Code 33472; Elev. 29; Lat. 27-14-37 N long. 080-49-48 W; SE central Florida. Named after the Indian word meaning "large water."

•OLDSMAR, City; Pinellas County; Pop. 2,496; Zip Code 33557; Lat. 28-02-02 N long. 082-39-55 W; W central Florida.

•OLD TOWN, Village, Dixie County; Pop. Rural; Zip Code 32680; Lat. 29-36-04 N long. 082-58-55 W; NW Florida.

•OLGA, Village, Lee County; Pop. Rural; Elev. 7; Lat. 26-43-07 N long. 081-42-45 W; E of Fort Myerson SW Florida.

•OPA-LOCKA, City; Dade County; Pop. 14,235; Zip Code 330+; Lat. 25-54-07 N long. 080-15-02 W; SE Florida.

•ORANGE CITY, City; Volusia County; Pop. 2,824; Zip Code 32763; Elev. 35; Lat. 28-56-55 N long. 081-17-56 W; E Florida. Founded in the 1870s by three families from Eau Claire, Wisconsin, attracted by the possibilities of citrus culture, was originally known as Wisconsin Settlement.

•ORANGE PARK, Town; Clay County; Pop. 8,776; Zip Code 32073; Lat. 30-09-57 N long. 081-42-24 W; NE Florida.

•ORLANDO, City; Orange County; Pop. 127,811; Zip Code 328+; Elev. 106; Lat. 28-32-17 N long. 081-22-46 W; 80 miles NE of Tampa in central Florida.

•ORMOND BEACH, City; Volusia County; Pop. 21,316; Zip Code 32074; Lat. 29-17-08 N long. 081-03-22 W; 10 miles N of Daytona Beach in E Florida. Originally called New Britain, the name was changed to Ormond in 1880 in honor of Captain James Ormond, a Scotsman from the Bahama Islands, who in 1815 settled a short distance to the north.

•OSPREY, Village; Sarasota County; Pop. 1,115; Zip Code 33559; Lat. 27-11-45 N long. 082-29-26 W; W central Florida. A fishing settlement on the Gulf, was named for the osprey, or fish hawk, a bird almost as large as an eagle, whose strong wings often carry it many miles to sea.

•OTTER CREEK, Town; Levy County; Pop. 167; Zip Code 32683; Elev. 39; Lat. 29-19-29 N long. 082-46-19 W; NW Florida. Obtained its name from the abundance of otter in the vicinity; otter were hunted here by Indians until the early 1850's, and later by trappers.

•OVIEDO, City; Seminole County; Pop. 3,070; Zip Code 32765; Elev. 48; Lat. 28-40-11 N long. 081-12-30 W; Central Florida.

•PAHOKEE, City; Palm Beach County; Pop. 4,771; Zip Code 33476; Lat. 26-49-11 N long. 080-39-56 W; SE Florida.

•PALATKA, City; Putnam County; Pop. 9,741; Zip Code 32077; Elev. 25; Lat. 29-38-54 N long. 081-38-16 W; 30 miles SW of St. Augustine in NE Florida. took its name from the Indian word *pilaklikaha* (crossing over).

•PALM BAY, City; Brevard County; Pop. 18,015; Zip Code 32905; Lat. 28-02-03 N long. 080-35-20 W; 25 miles SSE of Cocoa in E Florida.

•PALM BEACH, Town; Palm Beach County; Pop. 9,588; Zip Code 33480; Elev. 10; Lat. 26-42-19 N long. 080-02-12 W; SE Florida. The resort proper perhaps owes its existence to the wreck of a Spanish barque in 1878. The vessel's cargo of coconuts washed ashore and took root; early settlers gathered many nuts and planted them on their property, and in time the barren sand key was transformed into a patch of South Sea loveliness.

•PALMETTO, City; Manatee County; Pop. 8,451; Zip Code 33561; Elev. 9; Lat. 27-31-16 N long. 082-34-21 W; W Florida; On the north bank of the Manatee River.

•PALM HARBOR, Village; Pinellas County; Pop. 4,500; Zip Code 33563; Lat. 28-04-40 N long. 082-45-50 W; W central Florida.

•PANAMA CITY, City; Bay County; Pop. 33,100; Zip Code 324+; Lat. 30-09-31 N long. 085-39-37 W; NW Florida.

•PANAMA CITY BEACH, City; Bay County; Pop. 2,091; Zip Code 32407; Lat. 30-10-35 N long. 085-48-20 W; NW Florida.

•PANASOFFKEE, Village and Lake, Sumter County; Pop. Rural; Elev. 46; W Central Florida. Panasoffkee, (Indian, "deep valley"), is at the head of a lake of the same name.

•PARKER, City; Bay County; Pop. 4,283; Zip Code 32401; Lat. 30-07-51 N long. 085-36-12 W; NW Florida.

•PASS-A-GRILL BEACH, Beach; Pinellas County; Zip Code 33741; W Central Florida. The name is believed to have been coined by early smugglers, fishermen, or spongers, who landed to grill fish and beef on the shores of the pass at the southern end of the key.

•PAXTON, Town; Walton County; Pop. 659; Zip Code 32538; Lat. 30-58-53 N long. 086-18-27 W; NW Florida.

•PEMBROKE PINES, City; Broward County; Pop. 35,648; Zip Code 330+; Lat. 26-00-10 N long. 080-13-27 W; SE Florida.

•**PENNEY FARMS**, Town; Clay County; Pop. 630; Zip Code 32079; Lat. 29-58-46 N long. 081-48-38 W; NE Florida.

•**PENSACOLA**, City; Escambia County; Pop. 57,130; Zip Code 325+; Lat. 30-25-16 N long. 087-13-01 W; 10 miles E of Alabama border in NW Florida. Gradually the name Santa Maria was replaced by the present name, reputedly derived from the Indian *panshi*, meaning hair, and *okla*, meaning people, a name conferred upon natives of this region who wore their hair long. Some historiena, however, claim the settlement was named for the Spanish seaport Peniscola. Others say it derives from the Pansforlaya Indians who lived in the area.

•**PERRY**, City; Taylor County; Pop. 7,970; Zip Code 32347; Elev. 54; Lat. 30-07-02 N long. 083-34-55 W; 50 miles ESE of Tallahassee in N Florida.

•**PIERSON**, Town; Volusia County; Pop. 876; Zip Code 32080; Elev. 78; Lat. 29-14-21 N long. 081-27-57 W; E Florida.

•**PINELLAS PARK**, City; Pinellas County; Pop. 32,475; Lat. 27-50-33 N long. 082-41-59 W; N of St. Petersburg in W Central Florida.

•**PLANTATION**, City; Broward County; Pop. 48,464; Zip Code 333+; Lat. 26-07-38 N long. 080-14-00 W; 5 miles W of Fort Lauderdale in SE Florida.

•**PLANT CITY**, City; Hillsborough County; Pop. 19,055; Zip Code 33566; Elev. 137; Lat. 28-01-06 N long. 082-06-47 W; 20 miles E of Tampa in W central Florida. It was named for Henry B. Plant, who in 1884 had extended his South Florida Railroad into this section.

•**POLK CITY**, Town; Polk County; Pop. 567; Zip Code 33868; Elev. 173; Lat. 28-10-56 N long. 081-49-27 W; Central Florida.

•**POMONA PARK**, Town; Putnam County; Pop. 793; Zip Code 32081; Lat. 29-30-00 N long. 081-35-30 W; NE Florida.

•**POMPANO BEACH**, City; Broward County; Pop. 51,590; Lat. 26-14-15 N long. 080-07-30 W.

•**PONCE DE LEON**, Town; Holmes County; Pop. 454; Zip Code 32455; Lat. 30-43-22 N long. 085-56-15 W; NW Florida. Is the site of Ponce De Leon Springs, one of many "fountains of youth" named for the Spanish explorer.

•**PONTE VEDRA BEACH**, Village, St. Johns County; Pop. 1,000; Zip Code 32082; Lat. 30-14-22 N long. 081-23-09 W; NE Florida.

•**PORT CHARLOTTE**, Town; Charlotte County; Pop. 13,500; Zip Code 33952; Lat. 26-58-33 N long. 082-05-27 W; SW Florida; at mouth of Peace River, Charlotte Harbor. Name is derived by English settlers from the Spanish name Carlos. "Carlos" was a white man's corruption of Calusa, a local Indian tribe.

•**PORT ORANGE**, City; Volusia County; Pop. 18,338; Zip Code 32019; Elev. 12; Lat. 29-06-35 N long. 080-59-45 W; 5 miles SE of Daytona Beach inE Florida.

•**PORT RICHEY**, City; Pasco County; Pop. 2,154; Zip Code 33568; Elev. 11; Lat. 28-16-17 N long. 082-43-11 W; W central Florida.

•**PORT SAINT JOE**, City; Gulf County; Pop. 3,981; Zip Code 32456; Lat. 29-48-4 N long. 085-18-11 W; 275 miles SW of Tallahassee in NW Florida.

•**PORT SAINT LUCIE**, City; St. Lucie County; Pop. 14,751; Zip Code 33452; Lat. 27-17-37 N long. 080-21-02 W; E central Florida.

•**PUNTA GORDA**, City; Charlotte County; Pop. 6,485; Zip Code 339+; Elev. 61; Lat. 26-55-46 N long. 082-02-44 W; SW Florida.

•**PUNTA RASSA**, Village and Point, Lee County; Lat. 26-29-15 N long. 082-00-45 W; SW Florida; 20 miles SW of Fort Meyers; Elev. 7'. Punta Rassa (Sp., "flat point"), a fishing village, occupies the site of a military outpost established in 1837.

•**QUINCY**, City; Gadsden County; Pop. 8,252; Zip Code 32351; Elev. 187; Lat. 30-35-13 N long. 084-35-00 W; 20 miles WNW of Tallahassee in N Florida.

•**RAIFORD**, Town; Union County; Pop. 259; Zip Code 32083; Lat. 30-03-49 N long. 082-14-12 W; NE Florida.

•**REDDICK**, Town; Marion County; Pop. 628; Zip Code 32686; Lat. 29-21-59 N long. 082-11-51 W; N central Florida.

•**REDINGTON BEACH**, Town; Pinellas County; Pop. 1,676; Zip Code 33708; Lat. 27-48-30 N long. 082-48-41 W; W central; Florida.

•**RIVERVIEW**, Hillsborough County; Zip Code 33569; Lat. 30-24-21 N long. 081-41-15 W; W central Florida, on the bank of the Alafia River.

•**RIVIERA BEACH**, City; Palm Beach County; Pop. 25,571; Zip Code 33404; Elev. 11; Lat. 26-46-30 N long. 080-03-30 W; N of West Palm Beach in SE Florida.

•**ROCKLEDGE**, City; Brevard County; Pop. 11,735; Zip Code 32955; Lat. 28-21-02 N long. 080-43-32 W; 5 miles W of Cocoa in E central Florida.

•**RUBONIA**, Village; Manatee County; Pop. Rural; Zip Code 33561; Lat. 27-34-43 N long. 082-33-10 W; W central Florida.

•**RUSKIN**, Village, Hillsborough County; Pop. 2,414; Zip Code 33570; Lat. 27-43-14 N long. 082-26-00 W; W central Florida. At the mouth of the Little Manatee River, was founded in 1910 as a socialist colony by George M. Miller, Chicago lawyer and educator, and named for John Ruskin, English author and critic.

•**SAFETY HARBOR**, City; Pinellas County; Pop. 6,349; Zip Code 33572; Lat. 27-59-26 N long. 082-41-36 W; N of St. Petersburg in W central Florida; Resort.

•**SAINT AUGUSTINE**, City; St. Johns County; Pop. 11,807; Zip Code 32084; Lat. 29-53-40 N long. 081-18-53 W; 35 miles SE of Jacksonvile in NE Florida. This city is the oldest permanent white settlement in the United States. On September 8, 1565, Don Pedro Menendez de Aviles, Spanish admiral, took possession of the territory along the river and founded the settlement, naming it St. Augustine because he first sighted Florida on August 28.

•**SAINT AUGUSTINE BEACH**, City; St. Johns County; Pop. 1,275; Zip Code 32084; Lat. 29-51-01 N long. 081-15-56 W; NE Florida.

•**SAINT CLOUD**, City; Osceola County; Pop. 7,848; Zip Code 32769; Lat. 28-14-55 N long. 081-16-53 W; 25 miles S of Orlando in central Florida.

•**SAINT LEO**, Town; Pasco County; Pop. 914; Zip Code 33574; Lat. 28-20-13 N long. 082-15-31 W.

•**SAINT MARKS**, Town; Wakulla County; Pop. 277; Zip Code 32355; Lat. 30-09-39 N long. 084-12-23 W; NW Florida.

•**SAINT PETERSBURG**, City; Pinellas County; Pop. 233,532; Zip Code 337+; Elev. 44; Lat. 27-46-14 N long. 082-40-46 W; W central Florida, John C. Williams of Detroit, St. Petersburg's founder, acquired acreage in 1876 which became the nucleus of the city. He named it after the birthplace of a Russian business partner.

•**SAINT PETERSBURG BEACH**, City; Pinellas County; Pop. 9,195; Zip Code 337+; Lat. 27-43-30 N long. 082-44-29 W; W central Florida; Beach extension of the city of St. Petersburg.

•**SAN ANTONIA**, City; Pasco County; Pop. 531; Zip Code 33576; Lat. 28-20-09 N long. 082-16-29 W; W central Florida.

•**SANDERSON**, Village; Baker County; Pop. Rural; Zip Code 32087; Elev. 158; Lat. 30-15-07 N long. 082-16-23 W; Named in 1859 for an early settler.

•**SANFORD**, City; Seminole County; Pop. 20,721; Zip Code 32771; Elev. 31; Lat. 28-48-01 N long. 081-16-24 W; 20 miles NNE of Orlando in Central Florida.

•**SANIBEL**, City; Lee County; Pop. 3,343; Zip Code 33957; Lat. 26-26-55 N long. 082-01-21 W; SW Florida.

•**SAN MATEO**, Village; Putnam County; Pop. 900; Zip Code 32088; Elev. 69; Lat. 30-26-36 N long. 081-37-57 W; NE Florida.

•**SARASOTA**, City; Sarasota County; Pop. 48,800; Zip Code 335+; Elev. 18; Lat. 27-20-10 N long. 082-31-51 W; W central Florida; 40 miles S of St. Petersburg. The origin of Sarasota's name has been variously attributed to Spanish and Indian sources. It is possibly a corruption of the Spanish expression, *sarao sota*, meaning "place of dancing." The Elino de la Puente map of 1768 designated the site as Porte Sarasote, and a map issued by Laurie and Whittle in 1794 marks the site as Sara Zota, a separation of the word Sarazota that appeared on the Bernard Romans map of 1774, which designated the inlet as Boca Sarazota.

•**SATELLITE BEACH**, City; Brevard County; Pop. 9,149; Zip Code 32937; Lat. 28-10-33 N long. 080-35-25 W; 15 miles SSE of Cocoa in E Florida.

•**SATSUMA**, Putnam County; Zip Code 32089; Lat. 29-33-17 N long. 081-39-22 W; NE Florida. Named for the orange grown throughout north Florida, is a small trading center in a citrus and truck-growing area.

•**SEBASTIAN**, City; Indian River County; Pop. 2,835; Zip Code 32958; Elev. 21; Lat. 27-46-42 N long. 080-29-27 W; E central Florida. Sebastian, named for St. Sebastian, is a tourist settlement.

•**SEBRING**, City; Highlands County; Pop. 8,759; Zip Code 33870; Elev. 141; Lat. 27-29-43 N long 081-26-28 W; 50 miles SE of Lakeland in central Florida. Sebring is a "tailor-made" city, built according to plan. The townsite, on the eastern shore of Lake Jackson, was purchased by George Eugene Sebring (1859-1927), a pottery manufacturer of Sebring, Ohio, who planned a city on the pattern of the mythological Grecian city of Heliopolis (city of the Sun), with streets radiating from a central park representing the sun.

•**SEMINOLE**, City; Pinellas County; Pop. 4,548; Zip Code 33542; Lat. 30-28-44 N long. 086-24-36 W; W central Florida.

•**SEVILLE**, Village; Volusia County; Pop. 650; Zip Code 32090; Elev. 53; Lat. 29-19-00 N long. 081-29-34 W; E Florida. Named for the small Seville oranges that grow wild in the area.

•**SHALIMAR**, Town; Okaloosa County; Pop. 394; Zip Code 32579; Lat. 30-26-44 N long. 086-34-45 W; NW Florida.

•**SHAMROCK**, Village; Dixie County; Pop. Rural; Lat. 29-38-35 N long. 083-08-42 W; NW Florida.

•**SOPCHOPPY**, City; Wakulla County; Pop. 445; Zip Code 32358; Lat. 30-03-35 N long. 084-29-20 W; NW Florida.

•**SOUTH BAY**, City; Palm Beach County; Pop. 3,595; Zip Code 33493; Elev. 21; Lat. 26-39-49 N long. 080-42-59 W; SE Florida.

•**SOUTH DAYTONA**, City; Volusia County; Pop. 9,430; Zip Code 32021; Lat. 29-09-56 N long. 081-00-17 W; E Florida.

•**SOUTH MIAMI**, City; Dade County; Pop. 10,542; Zip Code 331+; Lat. 25-42-26 N long. 080-17-37 W; 10 miles SW of Miami in SE Florida.

•**SOUTH PASADENA**, City; Pinellas County; Pop. 4,201; Zip Code 33707; Lat. 27-45-17 N long. 082-44-16 W; W central Florida.

•**SPRINGFIELD**, City; Bay County; Pop. 7,073; Zip Code 32401; Lat. 30-09-11 N long. 085-36-41 W; E of Panama City in NW Florida.

•**STARKE**, City; Bradford County; Pop. 5,324; Zip Code 32091; Elev. 167; Lat. 29-56-38 N long. 082-06-36 W; NE Florida. Starke was named for Starke Perry, Florida's last ante-bellum governor (1857-61).

•**STUART**, City; Martin County; Pop. 9,282; Zip Code 33494; Lat. 27-11-50 N long. 080-15-11 W; 40 miles N of West Palm Beach in SE Florida.

•**SUMMERLAND KEY**, Village; Monroe County; Pop. Rural; Zip Code 33042; SW Florida; on a small island in the Florida Keys chain.

•**SUMTER**, City; Sumter County; Pop. 24,272; Zip Code 33585; Elev. 76; Central Florida. Sumter was named in the 1880s for General Thomas Sumter, a Revolutionary War officer.

•**SUN CITY**, Town; Hillsborough County; Pop. 2,143; Zip Code 33586; Lat. 27-40-41 N long. 082-28-44 W; W central Florida.

•**SUNRISE**, City; Broward County; Pop. 39,448; Zip Code 333+; Lat. 26-08-01 N long. 080-06-48 W; SW Florida.

•**SURFSIDE**, Town; Dade County; Pop. 2,957; Zip Code 33154; Lat. 25-52-41 N long. 080-07-33 W; 5 miles N of Miami Beach in SE Florida.

•**TAFT**, Town; Orange County; Pop. 1,183; Zip Code 32809; Elev. 97; Lat. 28-25-46 N long. 081-21-55 W; Central Florida. Was called Smithville prior to 1909, when it was renamed in honor of President William Howard Taft, who was inaugurated that year.

•**TALLAHASSEE**, City; Leon County; Pop. 80,759; Zip Code 323+; Elev. 216; Lat. 30-26-17 N long. 084-16-51 W; 25 miles N of Apalachee Bay in N Florida. The Indian meaning of Tallahassee is "Old Town," the name of the capital of the Apalachee Indians that was a flourishing settlement when De Soto and his men reached it in 1539.

•**TAMARAC**, City; Broward County; Pop. 28,206; Zip Code 333+; SE Florida.

•**TAMPA**, City; Hillsborough County; Pop. 268,709; Zip Code 336+; Elev. 15; Lat. 27-56-50 N long. 082-27-31 W; W central Florida; 25 miles NE of St. Petersburg. The meaning and origin of the word Tampa is uncertain, and it is not known when Espiritu Santo Bay, so christened by De Soto, first became known as Tampa Bay. Fontenado included Tampa in a list of Indian towns in 1580, and De Laet's map of 1625 apparently applied the name of an Indian village.

•**TAMPA SHORES**(Oldsmar), Village; Pinellas County; Pop. 2,600; Zip Code 336+; W Florida; On Old Tampa Bay, W of Tampa.

•**TARPON SPRINGS**, City; Pinellas County; Pop. 13,078; Zip Code 335+; Elev. 14; Lat. 28-08-45 N long. 082-45-25 W; 30 miles N of St. Petersburg in W central Florida. The town was founded in 1876 and named, it is said, because of a mistaken belief that tarpon spawned in Spring Bayou; but the fish seen splashing in the water here, as well as in the river and numerous lagoons, are mullet.

•**TAVARES**, City; Lake County; Pop. 4,079; Zip Code 32778; Lat. 28-48-14 N long. 081-43-33 W; 30 miles NW of Orlando in central Florida. Tavares was named in 1875 by its founder, Alexander St. Clair Abrams, for a Spanish ancestor.

•**TAVERNIER**, Village; Monroe County; Pop. 900; Zip Code 33070; Elev. 11; Lat. 25-00-40 N long. 080-30-55 W; SW Florida. Was named for the creek that winds past the southern end of Key Largo, said to have been a favorite hiding place of Tavernier, associate of Jean La Fitte, the pirate.

•**TEMPLE TERRACE**, City; Hillsborough County; Pop. 11,093; Zip Code 336+; Lat. 28-02-06 N long. 082-23-22 W; 10 miles NE of Tampa in W central Florida.

•**TEQUESTA**, Village; Palm Beach County; Pop. 3,589; Zip Code 33458; SE Florida.

•**TITUSVILLE**, City; Brevard County; Pop. 31,738; Zip Code 32780; Elev. 18; Lat. 28-36-43 N long. 080-48-28 W; 40 miles E of Orlando in E Florida. Titusville is a winter resort area and citrus center. The town was named for Colonel H.T. Titus, an early resident.

•**TREASURE ISLAND**, City; Pinellas County; Pop. 6,350; Zip Code 33740; Lat. 27-46-08 N long. 082-46-09 W; E Florida, near Largo, somewhere near here the Narvaez fleet is said to have anchored in 1528.

•**TRENTON**, City; Gilchrist; Pop. 1,124; Zip Code 32693; Elev. 56; Lat. 29-36-47 N long. 082-49-04 W; NW Florida.

•**UMATILLA**, City; Lake County; Pop. 1,848; Zip Code 32784; Elev. 98; Lat. 28-55-45 N long. 081-39-57 W; Central Florida.

•**UNION PARK**, Town; Orange County; Pop. 3,166; Zip Code 328+; Lat. 28-34-17 N long. 081-14-26 W; Central Florida.

•**VALPARAISO**, City; Okaloosa County; Pop. 6,129; Zip Code 32580; Lat. 30-29-48 N long. 086-29-19 W; NW Florida.

•**VENICE**, City; Sarasota County; Pop. 12,133; Zip Code 335+; Elev. 13; Lat. 27-05-58 N long. 082-27-16 W; 20 miles S of Sarasota in W central Florida.

•**VENUS**, Village; Highlands County; Pop. Rural; Zip Code 33960; Elev. 118; Lat. 27-04-01 N long. 081-21-25 W; central Florida. Was named for the Roman goddess of bloom and beauty, protectoress of gardens.

•**VERNON**, City; Washington County; Pop. 902; Zip Code 32462; Elev. 47; Lat. 30-37-22 N long. 085-42-44 W; NW Florida.

•**VERO BEACH**, City; Indian River County; Pop. 16,156; Zip Code 32960; Elev. 19; Lat. 27-38-18 N long. 080-23-51 W; 70 miles NNW of West Palm Beach in E Florida.

•**WABASSO**, Village; Indian River County; Pop. Incl. with Vero Beach; Zip Code 32970; Elev. 20; Lat. 27-44-53 N long. 080-26-11 W; E central Florida. The Guale Indians migrated to this section from Ossabaw Island, GA., and the name of the town is Ossabaw spelt backwards.

•**WALDO**, City; Alachua County; Pop. 965; Zip Code 32694; Elev. 157; Lat. 29-47-22 N long. 082-10-03 W; N Florida.

•**WALL SPRINGS**, Village; Pinellas County; Pop. Rural; W Florida; Lat. 28-06-04 N long. 082-46-19 W; S of Tarpon Springs on the Gulf Coast.

•**WARRINGTON**, Village; Escambia County; Pop. 15,850; Zip Code 32507; Lat. 30-23-02 N long. 087-16-30 W; NW Florida; S suburb of Pensacola.

•**WAUCHULA**, City; Hardee County; Pop. 3,004; Zip Code 33873; Elev. 107; Lat. 27-32-49 N long. 081-48-42 W; 40 miles S of Lakeland in central Florida. Wauchula (Indian "sandhill crane"), seat of Hardee County, like many other communities in the state, grew up around an early military post, Fort Hartsuff, built to protect settlers during the Seminole Wars.

•**WAUSAU**, Town; Washington County; Pop. 347; Zip Code 32463; Lat. 30-37-55 N long. 085-35-20 W; NW Florida.

•**WEBSTER**, City; Sumter County; Pop. 868; Zip Code 33597; Lat. 28-36-35 N long. 082-03-19 W; Central Florida.

•**WELAKA**, Town; Putnam County; Pop. 479; Zip Code 32093; Lat. 29-28-44 N long. 081-40-18 W; NE Florida.

•**WEST PALM BEACH**, City; Palm Beach County; Pop. 58,473; Zip Code 334+; Elev. 14; Lat. 26-42-54 N long. 080-03-13 W; 65 miles N of Miami in SE Florida.

•**WESTVILLE**, Town; Holmes County; Pop. 341; Zip Code 32464; Elev. 66; Lat. 30-46-28 N long. 085-51-06 W; NW Florida.

•**WEWAHITCHKA**, Town; Gulf County; Pop. 1,684; Zip Code 32465; Lat. 30-06-45 N long. 085-12-02 W; NW Florida. (Indian, "water eyes"), seat of Gulf County, is said to have been named for near-by twin lakes which, in the imagination of the Indians, resembled eyes.

•**WHITE CITY**, Village; St. Lucie County; Pop. Rural; Lat. 29-53-02 N long. 085-13-12 W; E Florida. Was settled shortly after 1893 by Danish immigrants fromn Chicago, who named their one street the Midway for the thoroughfare of that name at the fair, and called their little community White City, for Negroes were excluded.

•**WHITE SPRINGS**, Town; Hamilton County; Pop. 762; Zip Code 32096; Lat. 30-19-46 N long. 082-45-33 W; N Florida. Is built around medicinal springs.

•**WILDWOOD**, City; Sumter County; Pop. 2,663; Zip Code 32785; Lat. 28-51-54 N long. 082-02-21 W; Central Florida.

•**WILTON MANORS**, City; Broward County; Pop. 12,718; Zip Code 33305; Lat. 26-09-36 N long. 080-08-21 W; N of Fort Lauderdale in SE Florida.

•**WINDERMERE**, Town; Orange County; Pop. 1,303; Zip Code 32786; Lat. 28-29-43 N long. 081-32-06 W; Central Florida.

•**WINTER GARDEN**, City; Orange County; Pop. 6,673; Zip Code 32787; Elev. 126; Lat. 28-33-54 N long. 081-35-11 W; 10 miles W of Orlando in central Florida; Resort.

•**WINTER HAVEN**, City; Polk County; Pop. 21,133; Zip Code 33880; Elev. 175; Lat. 28-01-19 N long. 081-43-59 W; 15 miles E of Lakeland in central Florida.

•**WINTER PARK**, City; Orange County; Pop. 22,320; Zip Code 327+; Elev. 94; Lat. 28-35-59 N long. 081-20-22 W; NE of Orlando in central Florida. A suburb of Orlando, was built around Lakes Maitland, Osceola, Virginia, and Killarney. The town was founded as Lakeview in 1858, its name being changed to Osceola in 1870 and to Winter Park in 1881, when New Englanders laid out a new 600-acre townsite according to a city plan which has since been followed.

•**WINTER SPRINGS**, City; Seminole Conty; Pop. 10,393; Zip Code 32708; Elev. 49; Lat. 28-41-55 N long. 081-18-30 W; W Central Florida.

•**WORTHINGTON SPRINGS**, Town; Union County; Pop. 220; Zip Code 32697; Lat. 29-55-45 N long. 082-25-25 W; NE Florida.

•**YANKEETOWN**, Town; Levy County; Pop. 594; Zip Code 32698; Lat. 29-01-47 N long. 082-42-58 W; NW Florida.

•**YEEHAW**, Village, Osceola County; Pop. Rural; Lat. 27-42-00 N long. 080-54-16 W; E Florida; 33 miles W of Vero Beach.

•**YULEE**, Village; Nassau County; Pop. Rural; Zip Code 32097; Elev. 35; Lat. 30-37-54 N long. 081-36-24 W; NE Florida. Was named for David L. Yulee, U.S. Senator from Florida (1845-51; 1855-61). After election he had his name changed by act of the state legislature from David Levy to David Yulee.

•**ZEPHYRHILLS**, City; Pasco County; Pop. 5,795; Zip Code 33599; Elev. 88; Lat. 28-14-00 N long. 082-10-53 W; W central Florida.

•**ZOLFO SPRINGS**, Town; Hardee County; Pop. 1,234; Zip Code 33890; Elev. 64; Lat. 27-29-35 N long. 081-47-46 W; Central Florida.

GEORGIA

•**ABBEVILLE,** City; Wilcox County Seat; Pop. 985; Zip Code 31001; Elev. 259; Lat. 31-59-24 N long. 083-18-31 W; The city is named for either the Abbeville District of South Carolina or for the wife of David Fitzgerald who donated the land for the county seat.

•**ACWORTH,** City; Cobb County; Pop. 3,648; Zip Code 30101; Elev. 913; Lat. 34-03-58 N long. 084-40-21 W; Named in 1843 by Joseph Gregg for a New Hampshire town which was named for the English nobleman, Lord Acworth.

•**ADAIRSVILLE,** City; Bartow County; Pop. 1,739; Zip Code 30103; Elev. 714; Lat. 34-22-10 N long. 084-56-15 W; The city takes its name for the first settler - a Scottsman, Walter S. Adair.

•**ADEL,** City; Cook County Seat; Pop. 5,592; Zip Code 31620; Lat. 31-08-01 N long. 083-25-40 W; The first postmaster, Joel Parish, struck out the first and last four letters of Philadelphia to give the town its name in 1873.

•**ADRIAN,** City; Emanuel County; Pop. 376; Zip Code 31002; Elev. 286; Lat. 32-31-56 N long. 082-35-11 W; The city is believed to be named after an early settler.

•**AILEY,** Town; Montgomery County; Pop. 579; Zip Code 30401; Elev. 254; Lat. 32-12-04 N long. 082-31-08 W;

•**ALAMO,** City; Wheeler County Seat; Pop. 993; Zip Code 30411; Lat. 33-38-15 N long. 084-23-28 W; Incorporated in 1909 this city's name commemorates the famous mission in San Antonio, Texas.

•**ALAPAHA,** Town; Berrien County; Pop. 771; Zip Code 31622; Lat. 31-22-52 N long. 083-13-18 W; Named after the nearby Alapaha River, the word is thought to be Timicua Indian word meaning "Bear."

•**ALBANY,** City; Dougherty County Seat; Pop. 73,934; Zip Code 31700; Elev. 208; Lat. 31-34-42 N long. 084-09-33 W; Named for the capitol city of New York State.

•**ALLENHURST,** Town; Liberty County; Pop. 606; Zip Code 31301; Elev. 60; Lat. 31-47-05 N long. 081-36-14 W;

•**ALLENTOWN,** Town; Wilkinson County; Pop. 294; Zip Code 31003; Elev. 429; Lat. 24-25-26 N long. 062-25-37 W; Named for an early postmaster, J. W; Allen.

•**ALMA,** City; Bacon County Seat; Pop. 3,819; Zip Code 31510; Elev. 201; Lat. 31-32-27 N long. 082-27-48 W; Incorporated in 1906 and named for a traveling salesman's wife.

•**ALPHARETTA,** City; Fulton County; Pop. 3,128; Zip Code 30201; Elev. 1137; Lat. 34-04-25 N long. 084-17-47 W; The name is a variant of Alfarata, the fictional Indian girl of the 19th century song, The Blue Juniata.

•**ALSTON,** Town; Montgomery County; Pop. 111; Zip Code 30412; Lat. 32-04-52 N long. 082-28-38 W; The town is named after an early settler family.

•**ALTO,** Town; Banks County; Pop. 162; Zip Code 30510; Elev. 1394; Lat. 34-28-05 N long. 083-34-25 W; Named after the Italian word for high, and refering to the town's 1395 ft. elevation.

•**AMBROSE,** City; Coffee County; Pop. 360; Zip Code 31512; Elev. 306; Lat. 31-35-43 N long. 083-00-50 W.

•**AMERICUS,** City; Sumter County Seat; Pop. 16,120; Zip Code 31709; Lat. 32-04-20 N long. 084-13-37 W; The city was incorporated in 1832 and named after 16th century explorer Amerigo Vespucci.

•**ANDERSONVILLE,** Village; Sumter County; Pop. 267; Zip Code 31711; Elev. 895; Lat. 32-11-32 N long. 084-08-44 W; Made infamous by its Civil War prison, the town takes its name after the first settler.

•**ARABI,** Town; Crisp County; Pop. 376; Zip Code 31712; Lat. 31-49-45 N long. 083-44-28 W; A derivation from a family name of the early settlers.

•**ARAGON,** City; Polk County; Pop. 855; Zip Code 30104; Lat. 34-02-53 N long. 05-03-23 W; This city is named after the mineral aragonite, which has been mined in this region for use as a bleaching compound.

•**ARGYLE,** Town; Clinch County; Pop. 206; Zip Code 31623; Lat. 31-04-00 N long. 082-39-04 W; The name remembers Fort Argyle in Bryan County.

•**ARLINGTON,** City; Early County; Pop. 437; Zip Code 31713; Elev. 293; Lat. 31-26-04 N long. 084-43-33 W; The city's name recalls Robert E. Lee's estate in Virginia.

•**ARNOLDSVILLE,** City; Oglethorpe County; Pop. 187; Zip Code 30619; Elev. 778; Lat. 33-54-18 N long. 083-13-08 W; Named for Mr. Nat Arnold who was a large farmer in the county.

•**ASHBURN,** City; Turner County Seat; Pop. 4,766; Zip Code 31714; Lat. 31-42-44 N long. 083-39-15 W; The city is named after a Mr. Ashburn, an early settler.

•**ATHENS,** City; Clarke County Seat; Pop. 42,549; Zip Code 30601; Lat. 33-59-08 N long. 083-22-45 W; Named for the capitol of Greece.

•**ATLANTA,** City; Fulton County Seat; Pop. 387,739; Zip Code 303++; So named by Railroad Engineer, J. Edgar Thomson after the terminus of the Western and Atlantic Railroad.

•**ATTAPULGUS,** Town; Decatur County; Pop. 623; Zip Code 31715; Elev. 310; Lat. 30-45-01 N long. 084-28-50 W; Believed to be from the Greek Indian word for Dogwood Grove.

•**AUBURN,** Town; Barrow County; Pop. 692; Zip Code 30203; Lat. 34-00-30 N long. 083-49-12 W; The town is named after Oliver Goldsmith community in his poem "The Deserted Village."

•**AUGUSTA,** City; Richmond County Seat; Pop. 47,532; Zip Code 30900; Elev. 414; Lat. 33-28-06 N long. 081-59-33 W; Named by James Oglethorpe after Augusta, the Princess of Wales and mother of King George III.

•**AUSTELL,** City; Cobb County; Pop. 3,931; Zip Code 30001; Named for General Alfred Austell, a prominent early settler.

•**AVONDALE ESTATES,** City; DeKalb County; Pop. 1,313; Zip Code 30002; The city derives its name from the Avon River in England.

•**BACONTON,** City; Mitchell County; Pop. 763; Zip Code 31716; Lat. 31-22-31 N long. 084-09-49 W; Incorporated in 1903 the town was founded by Major Robert Bacon, a local lawyer and planter.

•**BAINBRIDGE,** City; Decatur County Seat; Pop. 10,553; Zip Code 31717; Lat. 30-54-23 N long. 084-34-08 W; The city's name honors U. S. Navy Captain William Beinbridge, Commander of "Old Ironsides.

•**BALDWIN,** Town; Habersham County; Pop. 755; Zip Code 30511; Named for Joseph A. Baldwin, an official of the Atlanta-Charlotte Railroad.

•**BALL GROUND,** City; Cherokee County; Pop. 640; Zip Code 30107; Elev. 1098; Lat. 34-20-19 N long. 084-22-30 W; The city's name recalls its former use by the Cherokee Indians as a site for their national pastime, the Ball-Plot.

•**BARNESVILLE,** City; Lamar County Seat; Pop. 4,887; Zip Code 30204; Lat. 33-03-09 N long. 084-09-53 W; Settled in 1826 the city is named for Gideon Barnes, who ran a tavern and operated a local stage line.

•**BARNEY,** Town; Brooks County; Pop. 146; Zip Code 31625 ; Elev. 239; Lat. 31-00-31 N long. 083-30-53 W; The railroad came into town in 1897, and the present name was adopted after a railroad equipment supplier, the Barney-Smith car Company of Ohio.

•**BARTOW,** Town; Jefferson County; Pop. 357; Zip Code 30413; Elev. 860; Lat. 32-52-49 N long. 082-28-36 W; The name honors General Francis S. Bartow, the first Confederate General to be killed in the Civil War.

•**BARWICK,** Town; Thomas County; Pop. 272; Zip Code 31720 ; Elev. 266; Lat. 30-53-34 N long. 083-44-29 W; The name is of unknown origin.

•**BAXLEY,** City; Appling County Seat; Pop. 3,586; Zip Code 31513; Lat. 31-46-39 N long. 082-21-01 W; The town is named for William Baxley, an early settler from North Carolina.

•**BENEVOLENCE,** Town; Randolph County; Pop. 138; Zip Code 31721; Lat. 31-52-55 N long. 084-44-08 W; Named for the Christian virtue.

•**BERLIN,** Town; Colquitt County; Pop. 538; Zip Code 31722; Lat. 31-04-06 N long. 083-37-16 W; This town was named for the great capitol city in Germany.

•**BETHLEHEM,** Town; Barrow County; Pop. 281; Zip Code 30620; Lat. 33-55-53 N long. 083-42-53 W; Founded in 1902, the name is derived from the nearby Bethlehem Methodist Church.

•**BISHOP,** Town; Oconee County; Pop. 172; Zip Code 30621 ; Elev. 782; Lat. 33-49-05 N long. 083-26-15 W; Incorporated in 1898 and named after W; H. Bishop, an original councilman.

•**BLACKSHEAR,** City; Pierce County Seat; Pop. 3,222; Zip Code 31516; Lat. 31-18-06 N long. 082-14-46 W; The city is named in honor of General David Blackshear who helped settle the area in the early nineteenth century.

•**BLAIRSVILLE,** City; Union County Seat; Pop. 530; Zip Code 30512; Lat. 34-52-31 N long. 083-57-36 W; The city takes it's name for Francis P. Blair, an associate of Andrew Jackson.

•**BLAKELY,** City; Early County Seat; Pop. 5,880; Zip Code 31723; Lat. 31-22-39 N long. 084-56-32 W; Incorporated in 1870, the city's name honors Captain Johnston Blakely, who was killed aboard the ship U.S.S. Wasp in the War of 1812.

•**BLOOMINGDALE,** City; Chatham County; Pop. 1,855; Zip Code 31302; Lat. 32-07-46 mN long. 081-17-54 W.

•**BLUE RIDGE,** City; Fannin County Seat; Pop. 1,376; Zip Code 30513; Lat. 34-51-44 N long. 084-19-27 W; Named for the Blue Ridge Mountains.

•**BREMEN,** City; Haralson County; Pop. 3,942; Zip Code 30110 ; Elev. 1424; Lat. 33-42-31 N long. 085-08-49 W; The city is named after the famous seaport in Germany.

•**BRINSON,** Town; Decatur County; Pop. 274; Zip Code 31725 ; Elev. 120; Lat. 30-58-47 N ong. 084-44-14 W; The town gets its name from its first master and postmaster, Simeon Brinson.

•**BRONWOOD,** Town; Terrell County; Pop. 524; Zip Code 31726 ; Elev. 367; Lat. 31-49-51 N long. 084-21-51 W.

•**BROOKLET,** Town; Bulloch County; Pop. 1,035; Zip Code 30415 ; Elev. 156; Lat. 32-22-53 N long. 081-39-40 W; So called for a nearby stream.

•**BROOKS,** Town; Fayette County; Pop. 199; Zip Code 30205; Lat. 33-17-29 N long. 084-27-33 W; Named for Wilort Brooks, an early settler who moved here in 1840.

•**BROXTON,** City; Coffee County; Pop. 1,117; Zip Code 31519; Lat. 31-37-34 N long. 082-53-15 W; Named after Henry Broxton, an early settler from South Caroline.

•**BRUNSWICK,** City; Glynn County Seat; Pop. 17,605; Zip Code 31520; Lat. 31-11-58 N long. 081-29-11 W; The city's name honors King George III who was of the House of Brunswick.

•**BUCHANAN,** City; Haralson County Seat; Pop. 1,019; Zip Code 30113 ; Elev. 1258; Lat. 33-48-05 N long. 085-11-22 W; Named for the fifteenth president of the United States.

•**BUCKHEAD,** Town; Morgan County; Pop. 219; Zip Code 30625; Lat. 33-34-00 N long. 083-21-47 W; Settled in 1838 by Henry Irby who killed a buck deer and nailed its head to a nearby tree thus giving the town it's name.

•**BUENA VISTA,** City; Marion County Seat; Pop. 1,544; Zip Code 31803 ; Elev. 657; Lat. 32-21-30 N long. 084-28-07 W; The city's name remembers General Zachary Torian's victory over Santa Ana at Buena Vista, Mexico in 1847.

•**BUFORD,** City; Gwinnett County; Pop. 6,688; Zip Code 30518; Established as a railroad town in 1868, it is named after president of the railroad, Colonel A. S.Buford.

•**BUTLER,** Town; Taylor County Seat; Pop. 1,959; Zip Code 31006 ; Elev. 628; Lat. 32-33-29 N long. 084-14-08 W; Incorporated in 1854 the town is named for General William Butler who was Commander of the U.S. Army in Mexico.

•**BYROMVILLE,** Town; Dooly County; Pop. 567; Zip Code 31007 ; Elev. 354; Lat. 32-12-10 N long. 083-54-24 W; Named for early settler, William H. Byrom who bought land here in 1852.

•**BYRON,** City; Peach County; Pop. 1,661; Zip Code 31008 ; Elev. 505; Lat. 32-39-28 N long. 083-45-14 W; The city is named for English author, George Noel Gordon, Lord Byron.

•**CADWELL,** Town; Laurens County; Pop. 353; Zip Code 31009 ; Lat. 32-20-17 N long. 083-02-39 W; The town is named for the husband of Mrs. Rebecca Cadwell, who donated the land for the town.

•**CAIRO,** City; Grady County Seat; Pop. 8,777; Zip Code 31728 ; Lat. 30-50-10 N long. 084-12-10 W; The city takes its name from the named Cairo, Illinois.

•**CALHOUN,** City; Gordon County Seat; Pop. 5,335; Zip Code 30701; Lat. 34-30-17 N long. 084-56-58 W; Incorporated in 1852, the town gets its name from Senator John C. Calhoun.

•**CAMILLA,** City; Mitchell County Seat; Pop. 5,414; Zip Code 31730; Lat. 31-14-00 N long. 084-12-32 W; The city is named for Camilla Mitchell, the daughter of Governor David Mitchell.

•**CANTON,** City; Cherokee County Seat; Pop. 3,601; Zip Code 30114; Lat. 34-14-27 N long. 084-28-52 W; Canton's name honors the great silk producing city in China.

•CARLTON, Town; Madison County; Pop. 291; Zip Code 30627; Lat. 34-02-43 N long. 083-02-02 W.

•CARNESVILLE, City; Franklin County Seat; Pop. 465; Zip Code 30521 ; Elev. 712; Lat. 34-22-10 N long. 083-14-06 W; Named for Judge and Congressman, Thomas Carnes.

•CARROLLTON, City; Carroll County Seat; Pop. 14,078; Zip Code 30117; Lat. 33-34-51 N long. 085-04-45 W; Founded in 1827, the town is named after Charles Carroll's colonial home on the Chesapeake.

•CARTERSVILLE, City; Bartow County Seat; Pop. 9,508; Zip Code 30120 ; Elev. 787; Lat. 34-10-07 Nlong. 084-47-55 W; the name honors Colonel Farish Carter who was one of Gerogia's wealthiest pre-war landowners.

•CAVE SPRING, City; Floyd County; Pop. 883; Zip Code 30124; Lat. 34-06-30 N long. 085-20-27 W; So named because of a spring that arises from a nearby cave.

•CEDARTOWN, City; Polk County Seat; Pop. 8,619; Zip Code 30125 ; Elev. 802; Lat. 34-00-44 N long. 085-15-16 W; The town's name refers to the numerous red cedars originally growing there.

•CHAMBLEE, City; De Kalb County; Pop. 7,137; Zip Code 30341; Named by the U. S. Postal authorities after one of the original petitioners for the post office.

•CHATSWORTH, City; Murray County Seat; Pop. 2,493; Zip Code 30705 ; Elev. 757; Lat. 34-46-03 N long. 084-47-50 W; Incorporated in 1906 the town is named after a railroad official.

•CHAUNCEY, Town; Dodge County; Pop. 350; Zip Code 31011; Elev. 300; Lat. 32-06-22 N long. 083-03-54 W; The town's name recalls Mr. Chauncey, who planned a church but died before it could be built.

•CHESTER, Town; Dodge County; Pop. 409; Zip Code 31012; Lat. 32-23-35 N long. 083-09-14 W; Founded about 1890 and named for Chester, New York.

•CHICKAMAUGA, City; Walker County; Pop. 2,232; Zip Code 30707; Elev. 119; Lat. 34-52-11 N long. 085-22-46 W; A Cherokee Indian word in turn derived from the Muskogean Indian "Tshiskamaga" which means "sluggish or dead water."

•CLARKESVILLE, City; Habersham County Seat; Pop. 1,348; Zip Code 30523; Lat. 34-40-14 N long. 083-27-22 W; The city's name honors General John C. Clark, Governor of Georgia from 1799 -1823.

•CLARKSTON, City; De Kalb County; Pop. 4,539; Zip Code 30021; Named for Colonel W. Clark, a prominent lawyer and railroad official.

•CLAXTON, City; Evans County Seat; Pop. 2,694; Zip Code 30414; Elev. 187; Lat. 32-09-05 N long. 081-58-20 W; Named for a popular actress of the time, Kate Claxton.

•CLAYTON, City; Rabun County Seat; Pop. 1,838; Zip Code 30525; Elev. 1925; Lat. 34-52-40 N long. 083-23-57 W; The city is named in honor of Judge Augustin J. Clayton, who presided over the first county court sessions.

•CLERMONT, Town; Hall County; Pop. 300; Zip Code 30527; Lat. 34-28-39 N long. 083-46-29 W; The town's name means "clear mountain."

•CLEVELAND, City; White County Seat; Pop. 1,578; Zip Code 30528; Elev. 1570; Lat. 34-35-54 N long. 083-45-44 W; It is believed the city's name honors Colonel Benjamin Cleveland, hero of the Revolutionary War.

•CLIMAX, Town; Decatur County; Pop. 407; Zip Code 31734; Lat. 30-52-36 N long. 084-25-53 W; Incorporated in 1905 the name refers to the mature order of plants and animals in the natural environment.

•COBBTOWN, City; Tattnall County; Pop. 494; Zip Code 30420; Lat. 32-16-51 N long. 082-08-22 W; Named for the Cobb family who were early settlers.

•COCHRAN, City; Bleckley County Seat; Pop. 5,121; Zip Code 31014; Elev. 342; Lat. 32-23-17 N long. 083-21-05 W; Settled in the 1850's the town's name recalls railroad president Arthur Cochran.

•COHUTTA, Town; Whitfield County; Pop. 407; Zip Code 30710; Lat. 34-57-29 N long. 084-57-23 W; A Cherokee Indian word meaning either "frog" or "a root supported by poles."

•COLBERT, City; Madison County; Pop. 498; Zip Code 30628; Lat. 34-01-14 N long. 083-11-46 W; Believed to be named after the great French foreign minister.

•COLEMAN, City; Randolph County; Pop. 164; Zip Code 31736; Elev. 385; Lat. 31-40-21 N long. 084-53-27 W; Probably named after an early settler.

•COLLEGE PARK, City; Fulton County; Pop. 21,143; Zip Code 30337; The city acquired the name in 1895 when Cox College moved to the town.

•COLLINS, City; Tattnall County; Pop. 639; Zip Code 30421; Elev. 235; Lat. 32-10-49 Nlong. 082-06-39 W; The city was incorporated in 1894 and named for a prominent citizen.

•COLQUITT, City; Miller County Seat; Pop. 2,065; Zip Code 31737; Lat. 31-08-17 N long. 084-42-32 W; The city is named for Attorney, Judge, and U. S. Senator from Georgia, Walter T. Colquitt.

•COLUMBUS, City; Muscogee County Seat; Pop. 169,441; Zip Code 31829; Lat. 32-28-37 N long. 084-56-49 W; The city's name honors Christopher Columbus.

•COMER, Town; Madison County; Pop. 930; Zip Code 30629; Elev. 17; Lat. 34-03-53 N long. 083-07-39 W; Named for the settler family of A. J. Comer.

•COMMERCE, City; Jackson County; Pop. 4,092; Zip Code 30529; Elev. 931; Lat. 34-12-16 N long. 083-27-18 W; A busy cotton trading center at one time, the name reflects the city's chief activity.

•CONCORD, Town; Pike County; Pop. 317; Zip Code 30206; Elev. 816; Lat. 33-05-33 N long. 084-26-13 W; So called after the Concord Primitive Baptist Church built nearby.

•CONYERS, City; Rockdale County Seat; Pop. 6,567; Zip Code 30207 ; Elev. 904; Lat. 33-40-38 N long. 084-00-12 W; Named for a local banker who helped bring the railroad to the town.

•COOLIDGE, City; Thomas County; Pop. 736; Zip Code 31738; Lat. 31-00-45 N long. 083-51-59 W; The town is named for the president of a local railroad.

•CORDELE, City; Crisp County Seat; Pop. 10,914; Zip Code 31015; Elev. 319; Lat. 31-57-53 N long. 083-46-54 W; The city is named after Miss Cordglia Hawkins, eldest daughter of the President of the Savannah and Montgomery Railroad.

•CORNELIA, City; Habersham County; Pop. 3,203; Zip Code 30531; Lat. 34-30-44 N long. 083-31-33 W; In the late 1880's Judge Pope Barron secured a railroad depot for the town. It was then named Cornelia in honor of his wife.

•**COVINGTON,** City; Newton County Seat; Pop. 10,586; Zip Code 30209; Lat. 33-40-10 N long. 083-51-30 W; The city's name honors General Leonard Covington, later a U. S. Congressman from Maryland.

•**CRAWFORD,** City; Oglethorpe County; Pop. 498; Zip Code 30630; Elev. 770; Lat. 33-53-09 N long. 083-09-28 W; Previously named Lexington Popot the city's name was changed to honor William H. Crawford.

•**CRAWFORDVILLE,** City; Taliaferro County Seat; Pop. 594; Zip Code 30631; Elev. 600; Lat. 33-33-24 N long. 082-53-44 W; Named in honor of William H. Crawford.

•**CULLODEN,** City; Monroe County; Pop. 281; Zip Code 31016; Lat. 32-51-48 N long. 084-05-38 W; The city's name commemorates the great English military victory in the 18th century.

•**CUMMING,** City; Forsyth County Seat; Pop. 2,094; Zip Code 30130; Lat. 34-13-34 N long. 084-11-40 W; Named for Colonel William Cumming of Augusta, a distinguished lawyer and editor.

•**CUSSETA,** City; Chattahoochee County Seat; Pop. 1,218; Zip Code 31805; Lat. 32-18-18 N long. 084-46-35 W; The town's name is derived from a Muskogean Indian word meaning "trading place."

•**CUTHBERT,** City; Randolph County Seat; Pop. 4,340; Zip Code 31740; Elev. 473; Lat. 31-46-13 N long. 084-47-39 W; Incorporated in 1831 and named in honor of Colonel John Cuthbert, Editor, Jurist, and U.S. Congressman.

•**DACULA,** City; Gwinnett County; Pop. 1,577; Zip Code 30211; Lat. 33-59-32 N long. 083-53-37 W; A name created by the city's first postmaster by using three letters from Atlanta and Decatur.

•**DAHLONEGA,** City; Lumpkin County Seat; Pop. 2,844; Zip Code 30533; Elev. 1454; Lat. 34-31-56 N long. 083-59-03 W; The center of a historic gold mining region, the city's name comes from a Cherokee Indian word meanig "Golden Color" on "Yellow Money."

•**DAISY,** City; Evans County; Pop. 174; Zip Code 30423; Elev. 177; Lat. 32-09-02 N long. 081-50-00 W; Named for the daughter of one of the first settlers, T.J. Edwards.

•**DARIEN,** City; Mcintosh County Seat; Pop. 1,731; Zip Code 31305; Lat. 31-22-12 N long. 081-25-38 W; The city is named after Ft. Darien, an early colonial outpost.

•**DAVISBORO,** City; Washington County; Pop. 433; Zip Code 31018; Lat. 32-56-30 N long. 082-38-10 W; Believed to be named about 1829 for the grandfather of an early settler, T.J. Davis.

•**DAWSON,** City; Terrell County Seat; Pop. 5,699; Zip Code 31742; Elev. 355; Lat. 31-46-27 N long. 084-26-26 W; Created in 1857 the city's name honors William C. Dawson, Lawyer, Soldier, and U. S. Senator.

•**DE SOTO,** Village; Sumter County; Pop. 248; Zip Code 31743; Lat. 31-57-13 N long. 084-03-44 W; This village is named for the famed Spanish explorer, Hernando De Soto, who crossed Georgia in the 1540's.

•**DEARING,** Town; McDuffie County; Pop. 539; Zip Code 30808; Elev. 469; Lat. 33-24-48 N long. 082-22-58 W; Formerly called Lombardy, the name was changed in 1893 to honor Mr. William Dearing, a Director of the Georgia Railroad.

•**DECATUR,** City; De Kalb County Seat; Pop. 18,404; Zip Code 30030; Named for Stephen Decatur, an ilustrious U. S. Navy Commodore.

•**DEMOREST,** City; Habersham County; Pop. 1,130; Zip Code 30535; Lat. 34-33-58 N long. 083-32-44 W; Founded in 1889 as a prohibition town and named for a leading provibition leader, W.J. Demorest.

•**DENTON,** City; Jeff Davis County; Pop. 286; Zip Code 31532; Elev. 259; Believed to be named for Samuel Denton who moved to Georgia around 1818.

•**DEXTER,** Town; Laurens County; Pop. 527; Zip Code 31019; Lat. 32-26-00 N long. 083-03-38 W.

•**DIXIE,** Town; Brooks County; Pop. 259; Zip Code 31629; Lat. 30-47-05 N long. 083-39-53 W; A name often used to refer to southern U. S. states, and perhaps refering the Mason-Dixon line that divided free and slave states.

•**DOERUN,** City; Colquitt County; Pop. 1,062; Zip Code 31744; Elev. 399; Lat. 31-19-21 N long. 083-55-05 W; So called because there was a deer run on the north side of town.

•**DONALSONVILLE,** City; Seminole County Seat; Pop. 3,320; Zip Code 31745; Lat. 31-02-30 Nlong. 084-52-39 W; Founded in 1897 and named after John E. Donaldson who owned the local sawmill.

•**DORAVILLE,** City; De Kalb County; Pop. 7,414; Zip Code 30340; Named for Dora Jack, whose father was an official of the Atlanta and Charlotte Air Line Railroad.

•**DOUGLAS,** City; Coffee County Seat; Pop. 10,980; Zip Code 31533; Elev. 259; Lat. 31-30-26 N long. 082-50-48 W; Established in 1858 and named in honor of Stephen A. Douglas.

•**DOUGLASVILLE,** City; Douglas County Seat; Pop. 7,641; Zip Code 30133; Elev. 1209; The city's name honors Congressman Stephen A. Douglas, who lost the presidency to Lincoln in 1860.

•**DU PONT,** Town; Clinch County; Pop. 267; Zip Code 31630; Elev. 182; Lat. 30-59-10 N long. 082-52-04 W; Incorporated in 1874 and honoring Captain DuPont who moved here with his family in 1858.

•**DUBLIN,** City; Laurens County Seat; Pop. 16,083; Zip Code 31021; Elev 228.; Lat. 32-32-30 N long. 082-53-32 W; An Irishman, Johnathan Sawyer, agreed to donate land for public buildings in 1812 if the town was called Dublin.

•**DUDLEY,** City; Laurens County; Pop. 425; Zip Code 31022; Lat. 32-32-30 N long. 083-04-26 W; Originally called Elsie, it's name was changed to honor U.S. Senator Dudley May Hughes.

•**DULUTH,** City; Gwinnett County; Pop. 2,956; Zip Code 30136; Lat. 33-59-37 N long. 084-09-48 W; Renamed in 1875 to commemorate a speech by Congressman, J. Proctor Knott who asked "Where in the world is Duluth?"

•**EAST DUBLIN,** Town; Laurens County; Pop. 2,916; Zip Code 31021; Named for the capital of Ireland.

•**EAST POINT,** City; Fulton County; Pop. 37,486; Zip Code 30344; So called as the Eastern terminus of the Atlanta and West Point Railroad.

•**EASTMAN,** City; Dodge County Seat; Pop. 5,330; Zip Code 31023; Elev. 362; Lat. 32-12-09 N long. 083-11-00 W; Named for William Eastman an early settler from New Hampshire.

•**EATONTON,** City; Putnam County Seat; Pop. 4,833; Zip Code 31024; Lat. 33-19-29 N long. 083-23-20 W; The city's name honors General William Eaton of Revolutionary war fame.

•EDISON, City; Galhoun County; Pop. 1,128; Zip Code 31746; Elev. 289; Lat. 31-33-29 Nlong. 084-41-56 W; Incorporated in 1902 and named in honor of the great inventor Thomas Edison.

•ELBERTON, City; Elbert County Seat; Pop. 5,686; Zip Code 30635; Lat. 34-08-11 N long. 082-49-35 W; Named for General Samuel Elbert who fought in the Revolutionary War and became Governor of Georgia in 1785.

•ELLAVILLE, City; Schley County Seat; Pop. 1,684; Zip Code 31806; Lat. 32-14-12 Nlong. 084-18-27 W; Laid out in 1859 and named for the oldest daughter of a leading citizen.

•ELLENTON, Town; Colquitt County; Pop. 277; Zip Code 31747; Lat. 31-10-31 N long. 083-35-05 W.

•ELLIJAY, City; Gilmer County Seat; Pop. 1,507; Zip Code 30540; Lat. 34-41-45 N long. 084-29-05 W; Either the name of a Cherokee Indian Chief or an Indian word meaning "place of green things".

•EMERSON, City; Bartow County; Pop. 1,110; Zip Code 30137; Elev. 170; Lat. 34-07-34 N long. 084-45-10 W; Incorporated in 1889 and named in honor of Georgia's Civil War Governor, Joseph Emerson Brown.

•ENIGMA, Town; Berrien County; Pop. 574; Zip Code 31749; Elev. 314; Lat. 31-24-31 N long. 083-19-48 W; Founded in 1906 - the derivation of the town's name is unknown.

•FAIRBURN, City; Fulton County; Pop. 3,466; Zip Code 30213; Elev. 1016; Lat. 33-35-14 Nlong. 084-33-46 W; The city is named after an English township in the county of York.

•FAIRMOUNT, City; Gordon County; Pop. 842; Zip Code 30139; Elev. 758; Lat. 34-26-11 N long. 084-41-51 W; Named by the first settlers for their original home in Fairmount, West Virginia.

•FAYETTEVILLE, City; Fayette County Seat; Pop. 2,715; Zip Code 30214; Elev. 937; Lat. 33-25-19 N long. 084-31-16 W; The city's name honors the Marquis De Lafayette who fought on the American side in the Revolutionary War.

•FITZGERALD, City; Benn Hill County Seat; Pop. 10,187; Zip Code 31750; Philander H. Fitzgerald, a Indiana newspaper publisher, settled the town in 1895 with a group of union veterans who had become tired of northern winters.

•FLOVILLA, City; Butts County; Pop. 458; Zip Code 30231; Lat. 33-14-40 N long. 083-55-09 W.

•FLOWERY BRANCH, Town; Hall County; Pop. 755; Zip Code 30542; Lat. 34-11-02 Nlong. 083-55-38 W; Named after the floral beauty of a nearby stream.

•FOLKSTON, City; Charlton County Seat; Pop. 2,243; Zip Code 31537; Elev. 81; Lat. 30-50-35 N long. 082-00-45 W; Named in honor of a prominent Folkston family.

•FOREST PARK, City; Clayton County; Pop. 18,782; Zip Code 30050; So named for the many park areas in the vicinity.

•FORSYTH, City; Monroe County Seat; Pop. 4,624; Zip Code 31029; Lat. 33-02-06 Nlong. 083-56-24 W; Named in honor of John Forsyth, famed Georgia diplomat and statesman.

•FORT GAINES, City; Clay County Seat; Pop. 1,260; Zip Code 31751; Lat. 31-37-12 N long. 085-03-14 W; A military fort and town erected in 1814 to check Seminole and Creek incursions into South Georgia. Named for General Edmund Gaines.

•FORT VALLEY, City; Peach County Seat; Pop. 9,000; Zip Code 31030; Lat. 32-33-12 N long. 083-53-22 W; Originally called Fox Valley, the name was misread as "Fort Valley" when being submitted as an application for a post office.

•FRANKLIN, City; Heard County Seat; Pop. 711; Zip Code 30217; Elev. 696; Lat. 33-21-1 N long. 085-04-04 W; The city's name honors Benjamin Franklin, U. S. Statesman, scientist, and writer.

•GAINESVILLE, City; Hall County Seat; Pop. 15,280; Zip Code 30501; Elev. 1249; Lat. 34-17-39 N long. 083-49-29 W; Named for General Edmund P. Gaines who served in the War of 1812.

•GARDEN CITY, City; Chatham County; Pop. 6,895; Zip Code 31408; Incorporated in 1939 as Industrial Gardens, the name was changed to Garden City in 1941.

•GENEVA, Town; Talbot County; Pop. 232; Zip Code 31810; Lat. 32-34-43 Nlong. 084-33-06 W; The town takes its name from the city in Switzerland.

•GEORGETOWN, Town; Quitman County Seat; Pop. 935; Zip Code 31754; Elev. 13; Lat. 31-52-57 N long. 085-06-37 W; Named after the town in the District of Columbia.

•GIBSON, City; Glascock County Seat; Pop. 730; Zip Code 30810; Lat. 33-06-31 N long. 082-36-28 W; Judge William Gibson donated $500 for the county's first public buildings and had the town named in his honor.

•GIRARD, Town; Burke County; Pop. 225; Zip Code 30426; Lat. 33-02-18 Nlong. 081-42-53 W.

•GLENNVILLE, City; Tattnall County; Pop. 4,144; Zip Code 30427; Lat. 31-56-12 Nlong. 081-55-30 W; Incorporated in 1905 and named for noted Minister and educator, Glenn Thompson.

•GLENWOOD, City; Wheeler County; Pop. 824; Zip Code 30428; Lat. 32-10-51 N long. 082-40-22 W; Believed to be a commendatory name.

•GOOD HOPE, Town; Walton County; Pop. 200; Zip Code 30641; Elev. 794; Lat. 33-47-06 N long. 083-36-32 W; Named to indicate early settler's hopes for the community.

•GORDON, Town; Wilkinson County; Pop. 2,768; Zip Code 31031; Lat. 32-53-50 N long. 083-18-57 W; A stop on the Central of Georgia Railroad, the town is named after the railroad's first president.

•GRANTVILLE, City; Coweta County; Pop. 1,110; Zip Code 30220; Lat. 33-14-01 N long. 084-50-01 W; Named for Chief Engineer of the Atlanta and West Point Railroad, Colonial L.P. Grant.

•GRAY, City; Jones County Seat; Pop. 2,145; Zip Code 31032; Elev. 603; Lat. 33-00-30 N long. 083-32-05 W; Named in honor of James Madison Grant, a leading financier of the Confederacy.

•GRAYSON, City; Gwinnett County; Pop. 464; Zip Code 30221; Elev. 1088; Lat. 33-53-38 N long. 083-57-27 W.

•GREENSBORO, City; Greene County Seat; Pop. 2,985; Zip Code 30642; Lat. 33-34-31 N long. 083-10-53 W; Named in honor of General Nathaniel Green, Revolutionary War hero.

•GREENVILLE, City; Meriwether County; Pop. 1,213; Zip Code 30222; Lat 33-03-40 N, long. 084-45-27 W. The city is named for Revolutionary War hero Nathaniel Green.

•GRIFFIN, City; Spalding County; Pop. 20,728; Zip Code 30223; Lat 33-14-42 N, long. 084-15-09 W. Founded in 1840 by Colonel Lewis Griffin and named in his honor.

•GROVETOWN, City; Columbia County; Pop. 3,384; Zip Code 30813; Lat 33-26-56 N, long. 082-11-43 W. Descriptively named for its healthy summer climate where the Coastal Plain and Piedmont Plateau meet in many groves of trees.

•GUYTON, City; Effingham County; Pop. 749; Zip Code 31312; Lat 32-18-48 N, long. 081-23-40 W. Named after a local settler.

•HAGAN, City; Evans County; Pop. 880; Zip Code 30429; Lat 32-09-26 N, long. 081-56-01 W. The town is named after the original landowner's wife: Susan Hagan.

•HAHIRA, City; Lowndes County; Pop. 1,534; Zip Code 31632; Elev. 225; Lat 30-59-21 N, long. 083-22-18 W. Incorporated in 1891 and named after a Biblical place.

•HAMILTON, City; Harris County Seat; Pop. 506; Zip Code 31811; Elev. 762; Lat 32-45-28 N, long. 084-52-27 W. The city's name honors South Carolina governor James Hamilton.

•HAMPTON, City; Henry County; Pop. 2,059; Zip Code 30228; Elev. 890; Lat 33-23-11 N, long. 084-17-06 W. The city is named in honor of Confederate General Wade Hampton.

•HARALSON, Town; Coweta and Meriwether Counties; Pop. 123; Zip Code 30229; Lat 33-13-26 N, long. 084-34-13 W. Named for army officer Hugh Haralson.

•HARLEM, City; Columbia County; Pop. 1,485; Zip Code 30814; Lat 33-24-58 N, long. 082-18-50 W. The city is named after Haarlem, Netherlands.

•HARRISON, Town; Washington County; Pop. 456; Zip Code 31035; Lat 32-49-36 N, long. 082-43-29 W. Green Harrison was a wealthy farmer here in the 1880's. The town is named after him.

•HARTWELL, City; Hart County Seat; Pop. 4,855; Zip Code 30643; Elev. 818; Lat 34-21-10 N, long. 082-55-42 W. Founded in 1856 and named in honor of Nancy Hart.

•HAWKINSVILLE, City; Pulaski County Seat; Pop. 4,372; Zip Code 31036; Lat 32-16-35 N, long. 083-27-42 W. Incorporated in the 1830's and named for U.S. Senator Benjamin Hawkins.

•HAZLEHURST, City; Jeff Davis County Seat; Pop. 4,249; Zip Code 31539; Elev. 253; Lat 31-52-04 N, long. 082-35-57 W. The town's name honors railroad civil engineer George Hazlehurst.

•HELEN, City; White County; Pop. 265; Zip Code 30545; Lat 34-42-00 N, long. 083-43-51 W. Named for the daughter of a local lumber businessman upon its founding in 1913.

•HELENA, Town; Telfair County; Pop. 1,390; Zip Code 31037; Elev. 248; Lat 32-04-27 N, long. 082-54-51 W. Incorporated in 1890 and given a popular feminine name.

•HEPHZIBAH, Town; Richmond County; Pop. 1,452; Zip Code 30815; Lat 33-18-47 N, long. 082-05-45 W. The town is named after the Hephzibah Baptist Association.

•HIAWASSEE, Town; Towns County Seat; Pop. 491; Zip Code 30546; Elev. 1980; Lat 34-56-56 N, long. 083-45-25 W. A Cherokee Indian word meaning "meadow."

•HILLTONIA, City; Screven County; Pop. 515; Zip Code 30467; Elev. 182; Lat 32-53-00 N, long. 081-39030 W. Named in honor of merchant Lee Hilton who lived here in the decades after the Civil War.

•HINESVILLE, City; Liberty County Seat; Pop. 11,309; Zip Code 31313; Lat 31-51-35 N, long. 081-35-26 W. Incorporated in 1916 and named in honor of Confederate soldier Charlton Hines.

•HIRAM, City; Paulding County; Pop. 1,030; Zip Code 30141; Lat 33-52-48 N, long. 084-45-26 W. The town is named after its first postmaster Hiram Baggett.

•HOBOKEN, City; Brantley County; Pop. 514; Zip Code 31542; Lat 31-10-56 N, long. 082-07-57 W. The town is named after the city in New Jersey.

•HOGANSVILLE, City; Troup County; Pop. 3,362; Zip Code 30230; Elev. 716; Lat 33-10-30 N, long. 084-52-25 W. Named for the original owner William Hogan.

•HOLLY SPRINGS, City; Cherokee County; Pop. 687; Zip Code 30142; Elev. 1100; Lat 34-10-28 N, long. 084-30-04 W. Descriptively named for a large spring near town with several holly trees around it.

•HOMER, Town; Banks County Seat; Pop. 734; Zip Code 30547; Lat 34-19-39 N, long. 083-30-04 W. Named for early settler Homer Jackson.

•HOMERVILLE, City; Clinch County Seat; Pop. 3,112; Zip Code 31634; Elev. 178; Lat 31-02-01 N, long. 082-44-47 W. Named after John Homer Mattox who settled here in the 1850's.

•HOSCHTON, City; Jackson County; Pop. 490; Zip Code 30548; Elev. 918; Lat 34-05-55 N, long. 083-45-40 W. Postmaster Russell Hosch ran a general store here. It is named after him.

•HULL, Town; Madison County; Pop. 188; Zip Code 30646; Lat 34-0-57 N, long. 083-17-40 W. Incorporated in 1905 and named after Reverend Hope Hull.

•IDEAL, Town; Macon County; Pop. 619; Zip Code 31041; Elev. 400; Lat 32-22-29 N, long. 084-11-16 W. Originally Joetown, railroad executives later named it "ideal" for its location.

•ILA, City; Madison County; Pop. 287; Zip Code 30647; Elev. 815; Lat 34-10-20 N, long. 083-17-32 W. Derived from a Choctaw Indian word meaning "dead."

•INDUSTRIAL CITY, City; Gordon, Murray and Whitfield Counties; Pop. 1,054; Zip Code 30336. Descriptively named for the city's industrial plants.

•IRON CITY, Town; Seminole County; Pop. 367; Zip Code 31759; Lat 31-00-49 N, long. 084-48-44 W. Located on an ore-carrying railroad line and named for this business.

•IRWINTON, Town; Wilkinson County Seat; Pop. 841; Zip Code 31042; Elev. 450; Lat 32-48-40 N, long. 083-10-23 W. Named after Georgia governor Jared Irwin.

•JACKSON, City; Butts County Seat; Pop. 4,133; Zip Code 30233; Lat 33-17-39 N, long. 083-57-40 W. The town's name commemorates Andrew Jackson's visit here in 1818.

•JACKSONVILLE, Town; Telfair County; Pop. 206; Zip Code 31544; Elev. 206; Lat 31-48-46 N, long. 082-58-41 W. Named in honor of President Andrew Jackson.

•JAKIN, Town; Early County; Pop. 194; Zip Code 31761; Elev. 148; Lat 31-05-20 N, long. 084-59-01W. Settled in 1817 and given a Biblically derived name.

•JASPER, City; Pickens County Seat; Pop. 1,556; Zip Code 30143; Elev. 1480; Lat 34-28-04 N, long. 084-25-40 W. Jasper is named in honor of Sergeant William Jasper, a Revolutionary War hero.

•JEFFERSON, City; Jackson County Seat; Pop. 1,820; Zip Code 30549; Lat 34-05-51 N, long. 083-34-06 W. Named in honor of Thomas Jefferson.

•JEFFERSONVILLE, City; Twiggs County Seat; Pop. 1,473; Zip Code 31044; Elev. 524; Lat 32-41-02 N, long. 083-20-25 W. The Jefferson family were pioneer developers of the county. The city is named in their honor.

•**JENKINSBURG**, Town; Butts County; Pop. 360; Zip Code 30234; Lat 33-19-41 N, long. 084-02-26 W. Incorporated in 1889 and named for a local settler.

•**JERSEY**, Town; Walton County; Pop. 201; Zip Code 30235; Lat 3-43-06 N, long. 083-48-03 W. Originally Centerville, the name was changed when a local planter imported a prize Jersey bull.

•**JESUP**, City; Wayne County Seat; Pop. 9,418; Zip Code 31545; Elev. 102; Lat 31-36-18 N, long. 081-52-59 W. Named in honor of an 1830's U.S. Army General.

•**JONESBORO**, City; Clayton County Seat; Pop. 4,132; Zip Code 30236; Lat 33-31-26 N, long. 084-21-23 W. Named for railroad civil engineer Captain Samuel Jones.

•**JUNCTION CITY**, Town; Talbot County; Pop. 254; Zip Code 31812; Elev. 678; Lat 32-36-09 N, long. 084-27-32 W. Descriptively named as the site of several railroad junctions.

•**KENNESAW**, City; Cobb County; Pop. 5,095; Zip Code 30144; Elev. 1092; Lat 34-01-37 N, long. 084-36-32 W. The town is named after an Indian chief who signed a treaty here with the whites in 1791.

•**KINGSLAND**, City; Camden County; Pop. 2,008; Zip Code 31548; Elev. 35; Lat 30-48-01 N, long. 081-41-25 W. Incorporated in 1908 and named for Mayor W.H. King.

•**KINGSTON**, City; Bartow County; Pop. 733; Zip Code 30145; Lat 34-14-04 N, long. 084-56-33 W. The town's name honors U.S. Senator John P. King.

•**KITE**, Town; Johnson County; Pop. 328; Zip Code 31049; Elev. 256; Lat 32-41-36 N, long. 082-31-00 W. Landowner Shaderick Kignt donated land for this town. The spelling was simplified to speed mail service.

•**LA FAYETTE**, City; Walker County Seat; Pop. 6,517; Zip Code 30728; Elev. 823; Lat 34-42-21 N, long. 085-21-57 W. Incorporated in 1885 and named in honor of Revolutionary War hero Marquis de La Fayette.

•**LA GRANGE**, City; Troup County Seat; Pop. 24,204; Zip Code 30240; Elev. 772; Lat 33-02-12 N, long. 085-02-02 W. Named after La Fayette's estate in France, i.e. La Grange.

•**LAKE PARK**, Town; Lowndes County; Pop. 448; Zip Code 31636; Lat 33-35-08 N, long. 084-20-33 W. Founded in 1890 and named for a nearby lake.

•**LAKELAND**, City; Lanier County Seat; Pop. 2,647; Zip Code 31635; Elev. 199; Lat 31-02-29 N, long. 083-04-18 W. Settled in the 1830's and named for its location near several large lakes.

•**LAVONIA**, City; Frankin County; Pop. 2,024; Zip Code 30553; Elev. 853; Lat 34-26-16 N, long. 083-06-26 W. The city is named in honor of Lavonia Jones, wife of railroad president John Henry Jones.

•**LAWRENCEVILLE**, City; Gwinnett County Seat; Pop. 8,928; Zip Code 30245; Elev. 1080; Lat 33-57-05 N, long. 083-59-19 W. The city's name honors Revolutionary War hero Captain James Lawrence.

•**LEARY**, City; Calhoun County; Pop. 783; Zip Code 31762; Lat 31-29-06 N, long. 084-30-40 W. Named for a pioneer settler.

•**LEESBURG**, City; Lee County Seat; Pop. 1,301; Zip Code 31763; Lat 31-44-02 N, long. 084-09-59 W. Leesburg is named after Revolutionary War General Richard Henry Lee.

•**LENOX**, Town; Cook County; Pop. 965; Zip Code 31637; Elev. 284; Lat 31-16-21 N, long. 083-27-48 W. Named for an early settler.

•**LESLIE**, Village; Sumter County; Pop. 470; Zip Code 31764; Elev. 344; Lat 31-57-13 N, long. 084-05-15 W. The town is named after a prominent pioneer family.

•**LEXINGTON**, City; Oglethorpe County Seat; Pop. 278; Zip Code 30648; Lat 33-52-18 N, long. 083-06-56 W. Incorporated in 1806 and named for the famous battle in the Revolution.

•**LILBURN**, City; Gwinnett County; Pop. 3,765; Zip Code 30247; Lat 33-53-17 N, long. 084-08-20 W. Founded in 1892 and given a name of uncertain origin.

•**LILLY**, Town; Dooly County; Pop. 202; Zip Code 31051; Lat 32-08-53 N, long. 083-52-33 W. The town was founded by the Lilly brothers in 1902. It is named after them.

•**LINCOLNTON**, City; Lincoln County Seat; Pop. 1,406; Zip Code 30817; Elev. 400; Lat 33-47-48 N, long. 082-28-38 W. Named in honor of Revolutionary War general Benjamin Lincoln.

•**LINDALE**, (CDP); Floyd County; Pop. 2,958; Zip Code 30147; Lat 34-11-05 N, long. 085-10-33 W. Named after an early pioneer family.

•**LITHIA SPRINGS**, (CDP); Douglas County; Pop. 9,145; Zip Code 30057; Elev. 1043; Lat 33-47-38 N, long. 084-39-38 W. Incorporated in 1918 and named for its location on a mineral rich spring.

•**LITHONIA**, City; DeKalb County; Pop. 2,637; Zip Code 30058; Elev. 939; Lat 33-42-44 N, long. 084-06-19 W. Settled in the 1830's and named for its underlying granite bedrock.

•**LOCUST GROVE**, City; Henry County; Pop. 1,479; Zip Code 30248; Lat 33-20-59 N, long. 084-06-35 W. Incorporated in 1893 and named for a grove or nearby locust trees.

•**LOGANVILLE**, City; Gwinnett and Walton Counties; Pop. 1,841; Zip Code 30249; Elev. 1003; Lat 33-50-35 N, long. 083-54-17 W. Shoemaker James Logan settled here in 1842. Forty-five years later they named the town in his honor.

•**LOUISVILLE**, City; Jefferson County Seat; Pop. 2,823; Zip Code 30434; Lat 32-59-52 N, long. 082-24-17 W. Icorporated in 1786 and named after King Louis 16th of France.

•**LOVEJOY**, Town; Clayton County; Pop. 205; Zip Code 30250; Elev. 953; Lat 33-26-17 N, long. 084-18-47 W. Incorporated in 1891 and given the euphonious name Lovejoy.

•**LUDOWICI**, City; Long County Seat; Pop. 1,286; Zip Code 31316; Lat 31-42-41 N, long. 081-44-46 W. The town's name honors German immigrant businessman William Ludowici who settled here in 1903.

•**LULA**, City; Banks and Hall Counties; Pop. 857; Zip Code 30554; Elev. 1304; Lat 34-23-27 N, long. 083-39-39 W. Established in 1876 and named by its founder after the daughter of a business associate.

•**LUMBER CITY**, City; Telfair County; Pop. 1,426; Zip Code 31549; Elev. 147; Lat 31-55-57 N, long. 082-40-56 W. Named for the lumber mill industry in the town.

•**LUMPKIN**, City; Stewart County Seat; Pop. 1,335; Zip Code 31815; Elev. 593; Lat 32-03-05 N, long. 084-47-42 W. Settled in 1830 and named after Wilson Lumpkin.

•**LUTHERSVILLE**, Town; Meriwether County; Pop. 597; Zip Code 30251; Elev. 931; Lat 33-11-16 N, long. 084-42-33 W. Probably named for an early settler.

•LYERLY, Town; Chattooga County; Pop. 482; Zip Code 30730; Lat 34-24-16 N, long. 085-24-19 W. Incorporated in 1891 and named after Charles Lyerly of Tennessee.

•LYONS, City; Toombs County Seat; Pop. 4,203; Zip Code 30436; Elev. 224; Lat 32-11-05 N, long. 082-17-24 W. Established in 1897 and named for a railroad promoter.

•MABLETON, (CDP); Cobb County; Pop. 25,111; Zip Code 30059; Lat 33-49-07 N, long. 084-34-57 W. Robert Mable settled here in 1843. The town is named after him.

•MACON, City; Bibb County Seat; Pop. 116,896; Zip Code 312+; Elev. 325. The first settlement here, established in 1821 was called Newtown. In 1823 the site was platted, after being ceded by the Creek Indians, and named Macon after Nathaniel Macon.

•MARIETTA, City; Cobb County Seat; Pop. 30,805; Zip Code 30007; Elev. 1128; Named either after the wife of Judge Thomas Cobb, for whom the county is named, or after the Ohio pioneer town of Marietta.

•MARSHALLVILLE, Town; Macon County; Pop. 1,540; Zip Code 31057; Lat. 32-27-22 N long. 083-56-33 W; Named after a beloved Methodist minister, Reverand John Marshall.

•MARTIN, Town; Stephens County; Pop. 305; Zip Code 30557; Elev. 90; Lat. 34-29-43 N long. 083-11-10 W; Incorporated in 1891 and named for an early revolutionary period governor of Georgia.

•MAYSVILLE, Town; Banks County; Pop. 368; Zip Code 30558; Lat. 34-14-51 Nlong. 083-33-34 W.

•MCCAYSVILLE, City; Fannin County; Pop. 1,219; Zip Code 30555; Elev. 1487; Lat 34-58-57 N, long. 084-22-11 W. The city is named after a prominent early settler.

•MEANSVILLE, City; Pike County; Pop. 303; Zip Code 30256; Lat. 33-02-48 N long. 084-18-00 W; Founded in 1913 and named for pioneer settler John Means.

•MEIGS, City; Thomas County; Pop. 1,167; Zip Code 31765; Elev.347; Lat. 31-04-39 N long. 084-05-25 W; The city's name honors Josiah Meigs, the first president of the University of Georgia.

•MENLO, Town; Chattooga County; Pop. 611; Zip Code 30731; Lat. 34-28-53 N long. 085-28-36 W; The town's name recalls Menlo Park, the workshop of inventor Thomas A. Edison.

•METTER, City; Candler County Seat; Pop. 3,531; Zip Code 30439; Elev. 200; Lat. 32-23-38 N long. 082-03-31 W; Established as a step on the Georgia Railroad, and said to have been named by a railroad official for his wife since he met her here.

•MIDVILLE, City; Burke County; Pop. 670; Zip Code 30441; Elev. 189; Lat. 32-34-11 N long. 082-15-24 W; Incorporated in 1877 and so called because it is halfway between Macon and Savannah.

•MIDWAY, City; Liberty County; Pop. 457; Zip Code 31320; Elev. 168; Lat. 31-48-19 N long. 081-25-40 W; Believed to been named for the Midway River in England.

•MILAN, Town; Telfair County; Pop. 478; Zip Code 31060; Elev. 282; Lat. 32-01-09 N long. 083-03-43 W; Founded in the 1890's and named for the large northern Italian city.

•MILLEDGEVILLE, City; Baldwin County Seat; Pop. 12,176; Zip Code 31062; John Milledge, a distinguished Georgia Governor, donated 633 acres to the University of Georgia in Athens. The city is named in his honor.

•MILLEN, City; Jenkins County Seat; Pop. 3,988; Zip Code 30442; Lat. 32-48-16 N long. 081-56-32 W; Settled in 1835, it was named Millen when the Central of Georgia Railroad came through to honor the railroad's superintendant.

•MILNER, City; Lamar County; Pop. 320; Zip Code 30257; Lat. 33-06-55 N long. 084-11-48 W; Settled about 1855 and named for Willis R. Milner who came from North Carolina.

•MITCHELL, Town; Glascock County; Pop. 214; Zip Code 30820; Elev. 539; Lat. 33-08-16 Nlong. 082-42-04 W; Established as a railroad town in 1886 and named for R. M. Mitchell, President of the Augusta Southern Railroad.

•MOLENA, City; Pike County; Pop. 379; Zip Code 30258; Elev. 772; Lat. 33-00-38 N long. 084-29-51 W; The name may come from the Spanish word "molina" meaning mill.

•MONROE, City; Walton County Seat; Pop. 8,854; Zip Code 30655; Lat. 33-48-21 Nlong. 083-45-34 W; Founded in 1821 and named in honor of President Monroe.

•MONTEZUMA, City; Macon County; Pop. 4,830; Zip Code 31063; Lat. 32-18-09 N long. 084-01-25 W; Named for the Aztec emperor by American soldiers returning from the Mexican War in the 1840's.

•MONTICELLO, City; Jasper County Seat; Pop. 2,382; Zip Code 31064; Elev.683; Lat. 33-18-14 Nlong. 083-41-05 W; Most of the original settlers were Virginians who honored the home of Thomas Jefferson near Charlottesville, Virginia.

•MORELAND, Town; Coweta County; Pop. 358; Zip Code 30259; Lat. 33-17-11 N long. 084-46-03 W; Changed from Puckett's Station in 1888 to honor Dr. John Moreland, the first doctor for the Atlanta and West Point Railroad.

•MORGAN, City; Calhoun County Seat; Pop. 364; Zip Code 31766; Elev. 247; Lat. 31-32-23 N long. 084-35-53 W; The city is believed named after the family of Hiram Morgan family.

•MORGANTON, Town; Fannin County; Pop. 263; Zip Code 30560; Elev. 1870; Lat. 34-52-25 Nlong. 084-14-43 W; Incorporated in 1856 and named for Morganton, North Carolina.

•MORROW, City; Clayton County; Pop. 3,791; Zip Code 30260; Lat. 33-35-54 Nlong. 084-20-19 W; The Rodford E. Morgon family owned most of the land and the local store and the city received their name.

•MOULTRIE, City; Colquitt County Seat; Pop. 15,708; Zip Code 31768; Lat. 31-10-34 Nlong. 083-47-42 W; Established in 1851 and named in honor of General William Moultrie, Revolutionary War hero and twice Governor of South Carolina.

•MOUNT AIRY, Town; Habersham County; Pop. 670; Zip Code 30563; Lat. 34-30-50 N long. 083-29-57 W; Founded in the 1870's and descriptively named for the climate of the locale with its abundant fresh air.

•MOUNT VERNON, City; Montgomery County Seat; Pop. 1,737; Zip Code 30445; Elev. 229; Lat. 32-10-46 Nlong. 082-35-39 W; Established in 1813 and named aftr Washington's home on the Potomac.

•MOUNT ZION, City; Carroll County; Pop. 445; Zip Code 30150; Lat. 33-38-02 N long. 085-11-03 W; Named after the Mt. Zion Methodist Church founded in 1843.

•MOUNTAIN CITY, Town; Rabun County; Pop. 701; Zip Code 30562; Elev. 2168; Lat. 34-54-58 N long. 083-23-11 W.

•**NAHUNTA,** City; Brantley County Seat; Pop. 951; Zip Code 31553; Elev. 65; Lat. 31-12-18 Nlong. 081-59-01 W; Incorporated in 1925 and believed to take its name from the Tuscarora Indian word meaning tall trees.

•**NASHVILLE,** City; Berrien County Seat; Pop. 4,831; Zip Code 31639; Lat. 31-12-23 N long. 083-14-56 W; Named in honor of General Francis Nash, a distinguished Revolutionary War soldier.

•**NAYLOR,** Town; Lowndes County; Pop. 228; Zip Code 31641; Lat. 30-54-26 Nlong. 083-04-43 W; Incorporated in 1906 and named for a railroad man, Captain Naylor.

•**NELSON,** City; Pickens County; Pop. 434; Zip Code 30151; Lat. 34-22-52 N long. 084-22-10 W; Named for John Nelson, a farmer and gunsmith, who was the original landowner.

•**NEWBORN,** Town; Newton County; Pop. 387; Zip Code 30262; Incorporated in 1894 and given the name after a stirring sermon by Evangelist Sam Jones who wished the town to born anew.

•**NEWINGTON,** Town; Screven County; Pop. 402; Zip Code 30446; Lat. 32-35-19 N long. 081-30-05 W.

•**NEWNAN,** City; Coweta County Seat; Pop. 11,449; Zip Code 30254; Lat. 33-26-25 Nlong. 084-43-49 W; Incorporated in 1823 and named for General Daniel Newnan who fought in the War of 1812 and later served as a Georgia state assemblyman.

•**NEWTON,** City; Baker County Seat; Pop. 711; Zip Code 31748; Lat. 31-21-20 N long. 084-27-56 W; The city's name honors Sergeant John Newton, a Revolutionary War hero.

•**NICHOLLS,** City; Coffee County; Pop. 1,114; Zip Code 31554; Elev. 186; Lat. 31-31-12 N long. 082-38-02 W; Founded in 1895 and named for Captain John Nicholls, Confederate States of America.

•**NICHOLSON,** Town; Jackson County; Pop. 491; Zip Code 30565; Lat. 34-06-43 N long. 083-25-49 W.

•**NORCROSS,** City; Gwinnett County; Pop. 3,317; Zip Code 30071; Elev. 1057; Lat. 33-56-23 N long. 084-12-24 W.

•**NORMAN PARK,** City; Colquitt County; Pop. 757; Zip Code 31771; Lat. 31-17-12 N long. 083-39-43 W; Named for J. B. Norman, who founded a college in the town.

•**NUNEZ,** Town; Emanuel County; Pop. 168; Zip Code 30448; Elev. 251; Lat. 32-29-30 N long. 082-20-55 W; Named for Dr. Samuel Nunez, a Jewish doctor, who was able to stop a contagious epidemic in eighteenth century Savannah.

•**OAKFIELD,** Town; Worth County; Pop. 113; Zip Code 31772; Lat. 31-46-39 N long. 083-58-17 W; A reference to the many oak trees in the area.

•**OAKMAN,** Town; Gordon County; Pop. 150; Zip Code 30732; Elev. 745; Lat. 34-33-55 N long. 084-42-29 W; Incorporated in 1939 and named for a local dealer in oak logs.

•**OAKWOOD,** Town; Hall County; Pop. 723; Zip Code 30566; Elev. 1149; Lat. 34-13-46 N long. 083-53-01 W; The town's name refers to a nearby oak woods.

•**OCHLOCKNEE,** Town; Thomas County; Pop. 627; Zip Code 31773; Lat. 30-58-30 N long. 084-03-20 W; Named for the river, it is an Indian word for "yellow water."

•**OCILLA,** City; Irwin County; Pop. 3,436; Zip Code 31774; Lat. 31-35-43 N long. 083-14-49 W; A variation of aucilla, the name of a Timicua Indian settlement.

•**OCONEE,** Town; Washington County; Pop. 306; Zip Code 31067; Lat. 32-51-08 N long. 082-57-27 W; Incorporated in 1876, it is named for the river, which in turn is named for an eighteenth century Indian tribe.

•**ODUM,** Town; Wayne County; Pop. 401; Zip Code 31555; Elev. 156; Lat. 31-39-57 N long. 082-01-33 W; Founded in 1907 and named for Mr. J. A. Odum, one of the original councilmen.

•**OGLETHORPE,** City; Macon County Seat; Pop. 1,305; Zip Code 31068; Lat. 32-17-39 N long. 084-03-39 W; Settled in 1840 and named in honor of General James Oglethorpe, founder of Georgia.

•**OMAHA,** City; Stewart County; Pop. 169; Zip Code 31821; Lat. 32-08-55 N long. 085-00-44 W; An old Indian name meaning against the wind.

•**OMEGA,** City; Colquitt County; Pop. 8; Zip Code 31775; Lat. 31-20-20 N long. 083-35-39 W; Established as a railroad town in 1889 and given the name for the last letter in the Greek alphabet, possibly signifying the end of the railline.

•**PEACHTREE CITY,** City; Fayette County; Pop. 6,429; Zip Code 30269; Incorporated in 1959 and named for Peachtree Creek, itself named from an old Cherokee Indian word meaning standing peachtree.

•**PEARSON,** City; Atkinson County Seat; Pop. 1,827; Zip Code 31642; Lat. 31-17-56 N long. 082-51-05 W; Named in honor of Benson Pearson, a wealthy and influential citizen of the early nineteenth century.

•**PELHAM,** City; Mitchell County; Pop. 4,306; Zip Code 31779; Elev. 365; Lat. 31-07-47 N long. 084-09-03 W; Named in 1868 to honor Major John Pelham of Alabama, a confederate artillery officer killed in action in 1863.

•**PEMBROKE,** City; Bryan County Seat; Pop. 1,400; Zip Code 31321; Lat. 32-08-28 N long. 081-37-24 W; Named for Pembroke Williams.

•**PENDERGRASS,** City; Jackson County; Pop. 302; Zip Code 30567; Elev. 866; Lat. 34-09-43 N long. 083-40-40 W; Incorporated in 1890 and named for Dr. J.B. Pendergrass, a prominent local physician.

•**PERRY,** City; Houston County Seat; Pop. 9,453; Zip Code 31069; Elev. 337; Lat. 32-27-25 N long. 083-44-00 W; Founded in 1823 the city's name honors Oliver Hazard Perry, naval hero of the War of 1812.

•**PINE LAKE,** City; De Kalb County; Pop. 901; Zip Code 30072; Lat. 33-47-27 N long. 084-12-21 W; With at least twelve species of pine in Georgia, many towns refer to this native tree.

•**PINE MOUNTAIN,** Town; Harris County; Pop. 984; Zip Code 31822; Lat. 32-53-14 N long. 084-49-47 W; A local pine covered mountain range gives the town its name.

•**PINEHURST,** City; Dooly County; Pop. 431; Zip Code 31070; Elev. 143; Lat. 32-11-43 N long. 083-45-45 W; Incorporated in 1895 and reflecting the predominance of pine forests in the area at the time.

•**PINEVIEW,** Town; Wilcox County; Pop. 564; Zip Code 31071; Elev. 280; Lat. 32-06-26 N long. 083-30-22 W; A descriptive name reflecting the widespread pine forests.

•**PITTS,** City; Wilcox County; Pop. 384; Zip Code 31072; Lat. 31-56-45 N long. 083-32-30 W. The city is named for an early settler H.H. Pitts.

•PLAINFIELD, Town; Dodge County; Pop. 128; Zip Code 31073; Lat. 32-17-13 N long. 083-06-41 W. Incorporated in 1912 and descriptively named.

•PLAINS, City; Sumter County; Pop. 651; Zip Code 31780; Elev. 499; Lat. 32-02-01 N long. 084-23-40 W. Originally called Plains of Dura from the Old Testament, the town gained fame in the 1970's as the home of U.S. President Jimmy Carter.

•PLAINVILLE, City; Gordon County; Pop. 281; Zip Code 30733; Lat. 34-24-22 N long. 085-02-22 W. The President of the local railroad, Captain E.G. Barney, named the city for his hometown, Plainville, Connecticut.

•POOLER, Town; Chatham County; Pop. 2,543; Zip Code 31322; Elev. Lat. 32-07-02 N long. 081-15-00 W; Founded in 1907 and believed named for Quentin Pooler.

•PORT WENTWORTH, City; Chatham County; Pop. 3,947; Zip Code 31407; Incorporated in 1957 but named for a prominent resident around 1918.

•PORTERDALE, Town; Newton County; Pop. 1,451; Zip Code 30270; Lat. 33-34-12 N long. 083-53-45 W; A well known milltown believed to be named for Oliver S. Porter, who purchased the mill from its original owner.

•POWDER SPRINGS, City; Cobb County; Pop. 3,381; Zip Code 30073; Lat. 33-51-39 N long. 084-40-38 W; At first called Gunpowder Springs, the name derives from the smell of sulphur in the water.

•PRESTON, City; Webster County Seat; Pop. 429; Zip Code 31824; Lat. 32-04-02 N long. 084-32-17 W; The name is thought to honor Senator William Preston, a leader in the Confederacy from South Carolina.

•PULASKI, Town; Candler County; Pop. 257; Zip Code 30451; Named for Count Casimir Pulaski, hero of the Revolutionary War, killed in action defending Savannah from the British.

•QUITMAN, City; Brooks County Seat; Pop. 5,188; Zip Code 30451; Elev. 211; Lat. 32-23-19 N long. 081-57-28 W; Incorporated in 1859.

•RANGER, Town; Gordon County; Pop. 171; Zip Code 30734; Lat. 34-30-00 N long. 084-42-35 W; Named for Ranger, North Carolina.

•RAY CITY, City; Berrien County; Pop. 658; Zip Code 31645; Originally Rays Mill when incorporated in 1909, the name was changed to Ray City in 1915.

•REBECCA, Town; Turner County; Pop. 272; Zip Code 31783 ; Elev. 351; Lat. 31-48-28 N long. 083-29-16 W; Named for Rebecca Clark, daughter of a prominent Turner County family, in 1904.

•REIDSVILLE, City; Tattnall County Seat; Pop. 2,296; Zip Code 30453 ; Elev. 207; Lat. 32-05-06 N long. 082-07-07 W; Founded in 1838 and named in honor of Robert Reid, a judge and territorial governor of Florida.

•RENTZ, Town; Laurens County; Pop. 337; Zip Code 31075; Elev. 310; Lat. 32-23-06 N long. 082-59-31 W; Named for E.P. Rentz, a local lumber merchant.

•REYNOLDS, Town; Taylor County; Pop. 1,298; Zip Code 31076; Elev. 429; Lat. 32-33-33 N long. 084-05-45 W; The town is named for L. C. Reynolds, Chief Engineer.

•RHINE, Town; Dodge County; Pop. 590; Zip Code 31077; Elev. 225; Lat. 31-59-17 N long. 083-12-08 W; Possibly named after the great river in Germany.

•RICEBORO, City; Liberty County; Pop. 216; Zip Code 31323; Lat. 31-44-09 N long. 081-25-55 W; The city's name stems from an early commercial activity in the rice trade.

•RICHLAND, City; Stewart County; Pop. 1,802; Zip Code 31825 ; Elev. 598; Lat. 32-05-16 N long. 084-39-41 W; Early settlers named the city after the Richland district in South Carolina.

•RICHMOND HILL, City; Bryan County; Pop. 1,177; Zip Code 31324; Lat. 31-57-04 N long. 081-18-37 W; Henry Ford developed a model community here and gave the city its name in 1925.

•RINCON, Town; Effingham County; Pop. 1,988; Zip Code 31326; Established in the 1890's the town has a Spanish name which means " corner."

•RINGGOLD, City; Catoosa County Seat; Pop. 1,821; Zip Code 31326; Lat. 32-17-48 N long. 081-14-05 W. The city's name honors Major Samuel Ringold, a hero of the Mexican War.

•RIVERDALE, City; Clayton County; Pop. 7,121; Zip Code 30274 ; Elev. 924; Lat. 33-34-23 N long. 084-24-57 W. Named for Spratin Rivers in 1908 when he gave land to the railroad.

•ROBERTA, City; Crawford County; Pop. 859; Zip Code 31078; The town is named for Roberta McCrary, daughter of Hiram McCrary who gave land for early settlement.

•ROCHELLE, City; Wilcox County; Pop. 1,626; Zip Code 31079; The city is named for the city in France.

•ROCKMART, City; Polk County; Pop. 3,645; Zip Code 30153; Slate deposits of great value are found nearby and hence the name Rockmart.

•ROME, City; Floyd County Seat; Pop. 29,654; Zip Code 30149 ; Elev. 605; Lat. 34-17-10 N long. 085-11-01 W. Founded in 1834 and named for the great city in Italy.

•ROOPVILLE, Town; Carroll County; Pop. 229; Zip Code 30170; Elev. 1253; Lat. 33-27-21 N long. 085-07-40 W. The town grew up around a granite quarry and was laid out by farmer John Roop.

•ROSSVILLE, City; Walker County; Pop. 3,749; Zip Code 30741; Lat. 34-56-35 N long. 085-17-33 W. Incorporated in 1905 but established earlier.

•ROSWELL, City; Fulton County; Pop. 23,337; Zip Code 30075; Lat. 34-01-28 N long. 084-20-39 W; The city was established by Roswell King and family in 1837.

•RUTLEDGE, City; Morgan County; Pop. 694; Zip Code 30663 ; Elev. 718; Lat. 33-37-43 N long. 083-36-33 W; The city's name derives from an early pioneer family, the Rutledges.

•SALE CITY, Town; Mitchell County; Pop. 336; Zip Code 31784; Elev. 377; Lat. 31-15-53 N long. 084-01-22 W; The town was founded in 1901 and named for T. D. Sale, a local real estate promoter.

•SANDERSVILLE, City; Washington County Seat; Pop. 6,137; Zip Code 31082 ; Elev. 446; Lat. 33-00-09 N long. 082-53-23 W. An early settlement founded in 1796 and named for local storekeeper M. Saunders.

•SARDIS, Town; Burke County; Pop. 1,180; Zip Code 30456; Elev. 234; Lat. 32-58-18 N long. 081-45-19 W; The town takes its name from the Sardis Baptist Church. Sardis is a ruined city in Asia Minor.

•SASSER, Town; Terrell County; Pop. 407; Zip Code 31785; Lat. 31-43-12 N long. 084-20-56 W; Incorporated in 1890 and named in honor of William Sasser.

•**SAVANNAH**, City; Chatham County Seat; Pop. 141,390; Zip Code 314+; Elev. 42. Founded by General James E. Oglethorpe who landed here in 1733. It was the seat of colonial government and capital of the commonwealth until 1786. The "Savannah," first steamboat to cross the Atlantic, sailed from here to Liverpool in 1819.

•**SCOTLAND**, City; Telflair County; Pop. 1996; Zip Code 31083; So named for the original Scotch settlers.

•**SCREVEN**, City; Wayne County; Pop. 872; Zip Code 31560; Lat. 31-29-05 N long. 082-00-59 W; Named for General James Screven, Revolutionary War hero.

•**SENOIA**, City; Coweta County; Pop. 900; Zip Code 30276; Elev. 863; Lat. 33-18-04 N long. 084-33-14 W; Settled in 1860 and named after an old Creek Indian chief.

•**SEVILLE**, Town; Wilcox County; Pop. 209; Zip Code 31084; Elev. 374; Lat. 31-57-43 N long. 083-35-55 W; Incorporated in 1890 and named for the famous city in Spain.

•**SHARPSBURG**, Town; Coweta County; Pop. 194; Zip Code 30277; Lat. 33-20-17 N long. 084-38-55 W; Settled in 1825 and named in honor of Judge Elias Sharp, one of the town's original commissioners.

•**SHELLMAN**, City; Randolph County; Pop. 1,254; Zip Code 31786; Lat. 31-45-15 N long. 084-36-51 W; The city's name honors W.F. Shellman who gave generously to a local academic institute.

•**SHILOH**, City; Harris County; Pop. 392; Zip Code 31826; Lat. 32-48-25 N long. 084-41-51 W. The city's name is biblical in origin and commemorates biblical Shiloh in Israel.

•**SILOAM**, Town; Greene County; Pop. 446; Zip Code 30665; Lat. 33-32-14 N long. 083-04-52 W. A biblical tunnel used by Hezekiah for the defense of Jerusalem.

•**SOCIAL CIRCLE**, City; Walton County; Pop. 2,591; Zip Code 30279; Lat. 33-39-25 N long. 083-43-05 W; Believed to have been a rest station on early westward migration where people could socialize. Hence the name.

•**SOPERTON**, City; Treutlen County Seat; Pop. 2,981; Zip Code 30457; Elev. 294; Lat. 32-22-48 N long. 082-35-45 W; Incorporated in 1902 and named for a construction engineer with the Macon, Dublin, and Savannah Railroad.

•**SPARKS**, Town; Cook County; Pop. 1,353; Zip Code 31647; Elev. 431; Lat. 31-09-59 N long. 083-26-16 W; Named in honor of a Mr. Sparks, Railroad Divison President for the Georgia Southern and Florida Railroad.

•**SPARTA**, City; Hancock County Seat; Pop. 1,754; Zip Code 31087; Elev. 660; Lat. 33-16-38 N long. 082-58-23 W; Established in 1795 and named for the famous classical Greek city.

•**SPRINGFIELD**, City; Effingham County Seat; Pop. 1,075; Zip Code 31329; Elev. 540; Lat. 32-22-21 N long. 081-18-26 W; Settled in 1799 and named for the plantation of General David Blockshear.

•**STAPLETON**, Town; Jefferson County; Pop. 388; Zip Code 30823; Elev. 440; Lat. 33-12-40 N long. 082-27-59 W; The town is named in honor of Colonel James Stapleton.

•**STATESBORO**, City; Bulloch County Seat; Pop. 14,866; Zip Code 30458; Elev. 258; Lat. 32-26-24 N long. 081-46-50 W; Founded in 1805 and named for the state of Georgia.

•**STATHAM**, City; Barrow County; Pop. 1,101; Zip Code 30666; Elev. 884; Lat. 33-57-55 N long. 083-35-57 W; The city's name honors Dr. Charles Statham, the former Chancellor of the University of Georgia.

•**STILLMORE**, Town; Emanuel County; Pop. 527; Zip Code 30464; Lat. 32-26-14 Nlong. 082-12-54 W; When the U. S. Post Office sent a list of names to the townspeople they indicated if none were acceptable they would send still more. So the last suggestion was used for the town and post offices.

•**STOCKBRIDGE**, City; Henry County; Pop. 2,103; Zip Code 30281; Elev. 799; Lat. 33-32-33 N long. 084-13-58 W; Settled in the 1820's and named for Thomas Stock, President of the Georgia Senate.

•**STONE MOUNTAIN**, City; De Kalb County; Pop. 4,867; Zip Code 30083 ; Elev. 1043; Lat. 33-48-22 N long. 084-10-14 W; The city has a descriptive name for the largest exposed granite rock in the world nearby.

•**SUMMERVILLE**, City; Chattooga County Seat; Pop. 4,878; Zip Code 30747; Lat. 34-28-47 N long. 085-20-50 W; Believed to be named for the beautiful environment in the city's mountain valley.

•**SUMNER**, Town; Worth County; Pop. 213; Zip Code 31789; Lat. 31-30-47 N long. 083-44-06 W; The town is named for John C. Sumner who owned the land of the original settlement.

•**SUNNY SIDE**, Village; Spalding County; Pop. 338; Zip Code 30284; Lat. 33-20-32 N long. 084-17-30 W; The village is descriptively named.

•**SURRENCY**, Town; Appling County; Pop. 368; Zip Code 31563; Lat. 31-43-17 N long. 082-11-50 W; Named for Millard Surrency, an early settler.

•**SUWANEE**, City; Gwinnett County; Pop. 1,026; Zip Code 31074; Elev. 1013; Lat. 34-03-08 N long. 084-04-24 W; The name of a former Cherokee Indian village. It may refer to the Suwanee Indians.

•**SWAINSBORO**, City; Emanuel County Seat; Pop. 7,602; Zip Code 30401; Elev.332; Lat. 32-31-17 N long. 082-19-19 W; Named for Colonel Stephen Swain, a state legislator.

•**SYCAMORE**, City; Turner County; Pop. 474; Zip Code 31790; Lat. 31-40-09 N long. 083-38-06 W; Founded in 1891 and named for the local sycamore trees.

•**SYLVANIA**, City; Sceven County Seat; Pop. 3,352; Zip Code 30467; Elev. 236; Lat. 32-48-59 N long. 081-38-49 W; Established in 1847 and given the latin name meaning "place in the woods."

•**SYLVESTER**, City; Worth County Seat; Pop. 5,860; Zip Code 31791; Elev. 426; Lat. 31-31-43 N long. 083-50-07 W; Either named for a pioneer family or the latin words for "four woods."

•**TALBOTTON**, City; Talbot County Seat; Pop. 1,140; Zip Code 31827; Lat. 32-40-39 N long. 084-32-17 W; The city is named for the county seat.

•**TALLAPOOSA**, City; Haralson County; Pop. 2,647; Zip Code 30176; Elev. 1134; Lat. 33-44-52 N long. 085-17-15 W; Named for the river, it is a Creek word meaning swift current.

•**TALLULAH FALLS**, Town; Habersham County; Pop. 90; Zip Code 30573; Lat. 34-43-58 N long. 083-23-14 W; A Cherokee Indian word given a variant of translations. The town was incorporated in 1885.

GEORGIA

•**TARRYTOWN,** Village; Montgomery County; Pop. 145; Zip Code 30470; Lat. 32-19-04 N long. 082-33-36 W; The village may be named for a early settler family.

•**TAYLORSVILLE,** Town; Bartow County; Pop. 222; Zip Code 30178; Incorporated as a town in 1916 and named for its original 1870's surveyor.

•**TEMPLE,** City; Carroll County; Pop. 1,520; Zip Code 30179; Lat. 33-44-16 Nlong. 085-02-02 W; Named for the civil engineer of the Georgia Pacific Railroad which reached the town in 1883.

•**TENNILLE,** City; Washington County; Pop. 1,709; Zip Code 31089; Elev. 466; Lat. 32-56-23 N long. 082-48-47 W; Named for one of several prominent citizens with the same last name. Either Colonel Robert Tennille, Benjamin Tennille, or Mr. Francis Tennille.

•**THOMASTON,** City; Upson County Seat; Pop. 9,682; Zip Code 30286; Elev. 76; Lat. 32-52-46 N long. 084-19-40 W; Established around 1825 and honoring General Jett Thomas, veteran of 1812 War, and builder of the state house in Milledgeville.

•**THOMASVILLE,** City; Thomas County Seat; Pop. 18,463; Zip Code 31792; Elev. 916; Lat. 30-50-217 N long. 03-58-45 W; The home of an annual rose festival, the town is named for General Jett Thomas.

•**THOMSON,** City; McDuffie County Seat; Pop. 7,001; Zip Code 30824; Elev. 532; Lat. 33-27-46 N long. 082-29-55 W; Once called Frogpond, the town was renamed in 1853 for J. Edgar Thomson, the civil engineer who survived the right-of-way for the Georgia railway.

•**TIFTON,** City; Tift County Seat; Pop. 13,749; Zip Code 31793; Elev. 357; Lat. 33-27-46 N long. 082-29-55 W; Called at first Lena, a sawmill worker renamed the city for his boss H. H. Tift.

•**TIGER,** Town; Rabun County; Pop. 299; Zip Code 30576; Lat. 34-50-49 N long. 083-26-02 W; Named for the Cherokee Chief, Tiger Tail.

•**TIGNALL,** Town; Wilkes County; Pop. 733; Zip Code 30668; Lat. 33-52-05 N long. 082-44-25 W.

•**TOCCOA,** City; Stephens County Seat; Pop. 9,104; Zip Code 30577; Lat. 34-34-31 N long. 083-19-34 W; Derived from the Cherokee word "Tagwahi" meaning "where the Catawbas lived."

•**TOOMSBORO,** Town; Wilkinson County; Pop. 673; Zip Code 31090; Elev. 236; Lat. 32-49-27 N long. 083-04-4 W; The town gets its name from Robert Toombs, a U. S. Congressman, and later general in the Confederacy.

•**TRENTON,** City; Dade County Seat; Pop. 1,636; Zip Code 30752; Lat. 34-52-22 N long. 085-30-30 W; First known as Salem, the name was changed to honor iron and coal developers from Trenton, New Jersey.

•**TRION,** Town; Chattooga County; Pop. 1,732; Zip Code 30753; Lat. 34-32-52 N long. 085-18-24 W; Named after the Trion Mills which was built by a "Trio" of founders.

•**TUNNEL HILL,** City; Whitfield County; Pop. 867; Zip Code 30755; Lat. 34-50-29 N long. 05-02-52 W; Descriptive of the nearby railroad tunnel which cuts through Chetoogeta Mountain.

•**TURIN,** Town; Coweta County; Pop. 260; Zip Code 30289; Elev. 903; Lat. 33-19-41 Nl ong. 084-38-05 W; Incorporated in 1890 and named for the Italian city.

•**TWIN CITY,** City; Emanuel County; Pop. 1,402; Zip Code 30471; Elev. 309; Lat. 32-34-50 N long. 082-09-24 W; A descriptive name adopted when the towns of Summit and Graymons were incorporated into one.

•**TY TY,** Town; Tift County; Pop. 618; Zip Code 31795; Lat. 31-28-24 N long. 083-39-01 W; Named for the many railroad ties cut and sold in this community.

•**TYBEE ISLAND,** City; Chatham County; Pop. 2,240; Zip Code 31328; Lat. 32-00-22 N long. 080-51-20 W; The site of the third lighthouse built in the United States, the city's name comes from the Ucnee Indian word for salt.

•**TYRONE,** Town; Fayette County; Pop. 1,038; Zip Code 30290; Elev. 993; Lat. 33-28-22 N long. 084-35-52 W; Named for the county in Ireland.

•**UNADILLA,** City; Dooly County; Pop. 1,566; Zip Code 31091; Lat. 32-15-40 N long. 083-44-05 W; An Iroquois Indian word that means "place of meeting."

•**UNION CITY,** City; Fulton County; Pop. 4,780; Zip Code 30291; Lat. 33-35-14 Nl ong. 084-33-46 W; Incorporated in 1908, the city is the meeting place of two railroads, hence the name.

•**UNION POINT,** City; Greene County; Pop. 1,750; Zip Code 30658; Elev. 685; Lat. 33-40-12 N long. 083-10-35 W; The name adopted when a railroad junction connecting two separate links of the Georgia Railroad met.

•**UVALDA,** Town; Montgomery County; Pop. 646; Zip Code 30473; Elev. 177; Lat. 32-02-09 N long. 082-30-31 W.

•**VALDOSTA,** City; Lowndes County Seat; Pop. 37,596; Zip Code 31601; Elev. 229; Lat. 30-51-02 N long. 083-15-18 W; Incorporated in 1860, the city's name comes from Italian and means "beautiful valley."

•**VARNELL,** City; Whitfield County; Pop. 288; Zip Code 30756; Elev. 809; Lat. 34-54-09 N long. 084-58-31 W; Named for M. P. Varnell, who was an early railroad agent here.

•**WACO,** City; Haralson County; Pop. 471; Zip Code 30182; Lat. 33-42-10 N long. 085-11-16 W; A Muskogean Indian word meaning heron.

•**WADLEY,** City; Jefferson County; Pop. 2,438; Zip Code 30477; Lat. 32-52-04 N long. 082-23-37 W; Incorporated in 1876, the town is named for William Morill Wadley, President of the Central of Georgia Railroad and prominent official of the Confederacy.

•**WALESKA,** City; Cherokee County; Pop. 450; Zip Code 30183; Lat. 34-19-05 N long. 084-33-12 W; the city is named after Warluskee, the daughter of a Cherokee Indian chief.

•**WALTHOURVILLE,** City; Liberty County; Pop. 905; Zip Code 31333; Lat. 31-47-10 N long. 081-36-00 W; Established in the early nineteenth century and named for a rich planter, Andrew Walthour.

•**WARM SPRINGS,** City; Meriwether County; Pop. 425; Zip Code 31830; Elev. 930; Lat. 32-54-11 N long. 084-43-30 W; Made famous as a health spa by Franklin D. Roosevelt, the name comes from the warm springs which generate 800 gallons of 87 degree F mineral water per minute.

•**WARNER ROBINS,** City; Houston County; Pop. 39,893; Zip Code 31028; Named for General Augustine Warner Robins, a pioneer officer of the U. S. Army Air Force.

110

•**WARRENTON,** City; Warren County Seat; Pop. 2,172; Zip Code 30828; Lat. 33-24-32 N long. 082-39-42 W; Named in honor of General Joseph Warren of Massachusetts who fell at the Battle of Bunker Hill.

•**WARWICK,** City; Worth County; Pop. 488; Zip Code 31796; Lat. 31-50-00 N long. 083-50-00 W; Named for Warwick, Rhode Island.

•**WASHINGTON,** City; Wilkes County Seat; Pop. 4,662; Zip Code 30673; Lat. 33-44-07 N long. 082-44-46 W; The first family to settle here had been neighbors of George Washington, and named the city in his honor.

•**WATKINSVILLE,** Town; Oconee County Seat; Pop. 1,240; Zip Code 30677; Lat. 33-52-13 N long. 083-27-21 W. The town is named for either Colonel Robert Watkins, a prominent attorney; or Major John Watkins, a Revolutionary War soldier.

•**WAVERLY HALL,** Town; Harris County; Pop. 913; Zip Code 31831; Lat. 32-40-57 N long. 084-44-10 W; The town takes its name from the historical novels of Sir Walter Scott.

•**WAYCROSS,** City; Ware County Seat; Pop. 19,371; Zip Code 31501; Lat. 31-13-40 N long. 082-21-52 W; Previously called by several names, the present name was chosen because of the many roads crossing here.

•**WAYNESBORO,** City; Burke County Seat; Pop. 5,760; Zip Code 30830; Lat. 33-05-34 N long. 082-01-04 W; Named for General Anthony Wayne, a famous Revolutionary War soldier who settled in Georgia after the war.

•**WEST POINT,** City; Harris County; Pop. 982; Zip Code 31833; Lat. 32-52-29 N long. 085-10-39 W.

•**WHIGHAM,** City; Grady County; Pop. 507; Zip Code 31797; Lat. 30-53-00 N long. 084-19-28 W; Named in 1880 for prominent merchant Robert Whigam.

•**WHITE,** Town; Bartow County; Pop. 501; Zip Code 30184; Elev. 840; Lat. 34-16-59 N long. 084-44-32 W; Named for the first postmaster and storeowner James A. White.

•**WHITE PLAINS,** Town; Greene County; Pop. 231; Zip Code 30678; Lat. 33-28-22 N long. 083-02-06 W; The town takes its name from the sandy white soil in the region.

•**WILLACOOCHEE,** Town; Atkinson County; Pop. 1,166; Zip Code 31650; Lat. 31-20-27 N long. 083-02-55 W; Named for the river and meaning in the Creek Indian language "little river."

•**WILLIAMSON,** Town; Pike County; Pop. 250; Zip Code 30292; Lat. 33-11-00 N long. 084-21-29 W; Formerly called Stearnsville, the town was renamed before the Civil War for Judge Isaac Williamson, prominent farmer, slave owner, and banker.

•**WINDER,** City; Barrow County Seat; Pop. 6,705; Zip Code 30680; Elev. 984; Lat. 33-59-11 N long. 083-42-34 W; Incorporated in 1893 and named for the President of the Seaboard Air Line, John N. Winder.

•**WINTERVILLE,** City; Clarke County; Pop. 621; Zip Code 30683; Elev.804; Lat. 33-57-55 Nlong. 083-16-54 W; Named for railroad agent John Winter in 1882.

•**WOODBINE,** City; Camden County Seat; Pop. 910; Zip Code 31569; Elev. 16; Lat. 30-57-47 N long. 081-43-22 W; Incorporated in 1908 and named for the common flower honeysuckle.

•**WOODBURY,** Town; Meriwether County; Pop. 1,738; Zip Code 30293; Lat. 32-57-31 N long. 084-36-37 W; A descriptive name for the wooded country nearby.

•**WOODLAND,** City; Talbot County; Pop. 664; Zip Code 31836; Lat. 32-47-10 N long. 084-33-43 W; Named in honor of C. S. Woods of Virginia who laid out the town.

•**WOODSTOCK,** City; Cherokee County; Pop. 2,699; Zip Code 30188; Lat. 34-06-03 N long. 084-31-07 W; A descriptive name for the original forest cover.

HAWAII

•AHUIMANU, Pop. 6,238; The town's name means "bird cluster."

•AIEA, Pop. 32,879; Zip Code 96701; Lat. 21-22-46 N long. 157-56-04 W; The town is named after a certain tree.

•BARBERS POINT HOUSING, Pop. 1,373; The town's name remembers Captain Henry Barber, who shipwrecked here in 1796.

•CAPTAIN COOK, Pop. 2,008; Zip Code 96704; Lat. 19-29-46 N long. 155-54-57 W; The town is named after the European discoverer of the Hawaiian Islands.

•EWA, Pop. 2,637; Ewa's name means "crooked."

•EWA BEACH, Pop. 14,369; Zip Code 96706; Lat. 21-20-31 N long. 158-01-41 W; The name of a beach between Pu'u-loa and One-ula Beach.

•HALEIWA, Pop. 2,412; Zip Code 96712; Lat. 21-35-55 N long. 158-05-04 W; The word means "house of frigate bird."

•HANAMAULU, Pop. 3,227; Hanamaulu means "tired" - as in walking.

•HANAPEPE, Pop. 1,417; Zip Code 96716; Lat. 21-54-57 N long. 159-35-27 W; The town's name means "crushed bay."

•HAUULA, Pop. 2,997; Zip Code 96717; Lat. 21-36-55 N long. 157-54-42 W; Hauula means "red hau tree."

•HEEIA, Pop. 5,432; Heeia is the name given by the goddess Haumea to her foster child.

•HICKAM HOUSING, Pop. 4,425; Named in honor of Air Force Colonel Horace Hickam.

•HILO, Pop. 35,269; Zip Code 96720; Elev. 38; Lat. 19-42-21 N long. 155-05-20 W; Possibly named for a Polynesian navigator.

•HOLUALOA, Pop. 1,243; Zip Code 96725; Elev. 1372; Lat. 19-37-13 N long. 155-57-06 W; The town's name means "long sled course."

•HONOKAA, Pop. 1,936; Zip Code 96727; Elev. 1114; Lat. 20-04-42 N long. 155-28-00 W; The name translates "rolling stones bay."

•HONOLULU, Pop. 365,048; Zip Code 968+; Elev. 18; Lat. 21-18-53 N long. 157-50-23 W; Honolulu is Hawaiian for "protected bay."

•IROQUOIS POINT, Pop. 3,915; Named for the Indians of New York state.

•KAHALUU, Pop. 2,925; The name means "diving place."

•KAHULUI, Pop. 12,978; Zip Code 96732; Lat. 20-53-01 N long. 156-28-24 W; Kahului means Qwinning."

•KAILUA, Hawaii County; Pop. 4,751; Zip Code 96734; Lat. 21-23-39 N long. 157-46-31 W; The name means "two currents."

•KAILUA, Honolulu County; Pop. 35,812; Kailua's name refers to two sea currents off of Hawaii.

•KALAHEO, Pop. 2,500; Zip Code 96741; Elev. 700; Lat. 21-55-53 N long. 159-31-39 W; Hawaiian for "proud day."

•KANEOHE, Pop. 29,919; Zip Code 96744; Lat. 21-24-36 N long. 157-48-23 W; Kaneohe means "bamboo husband."

•KAPAA, Pop. 4,467; Zip Code 96746; Lat. 22-04-27 N long. 159-20-00 W; Hawaiian for "solid rock."

•KAUNAKAKAI, Pop. 2,231; Zip Code 96748; Elev. 5; Lat. 21-05-37 N long. 157-01-24 W; The town's name means "beach landing."

•KEALAKEKUA, Pop. 1,033; Zip Code 96750; Lat. 19-31-14 N long. 155-55-22 W; Hawaiian for "pathway of a god."

•KEKAHA, Pop. 3,260; Zip Code 96752; Lat. 21-58-12 N long. 159-42-32 W; The town's name means "the place."

•KIHEI, Pop. 5,644; Zip Code 96753; Lat. 20-47-19 N long. 156-27-50 W; Kihei means "cape."

•KOLOA, Pop. 1,457; Zip Code 96756; Lat. 21-53-31 N long. 159-27-41 W; Koloa is named after a steep rock called Pali-o-koloa.

•LAHAINA, Pop. 6,095; Zip Code 967+; Lat. 20-56-35 N long. 156-40-09 W; Hawaiian for "cruel sun."

•LAIE, Pop. 4,643; Zip Code 96762; Lat. 21-38-38 N long. 157-55-48 W; Laie was a sacred princess of the Hawaiian pantheon.

•LANAI CITY, Pop. 2,092; Zip Code 96763; Elev. 1624; Lat. 20-49-48 N long. 156-55-21 W; Lanai means "day of conquest."

•LIHUE, Pop. 4,000; Zip Code 96715; Elev. 206; Lat. 21-59-49 N long. 159-21-28 W; Hawaiian for "cold chill."

•LOWER PAIA, Pop. 1,500; Paia is Hawaiian for "noisy."

•MAILI, Pop. 5,026; Maili means "pebbly."

•MAKAHA, Pop. 6,582; Makaha means "fierce."

•MAKAKILO CITY, Pop. 7,691; The town's name means "observing eyes."

•MAKAPU, Pop. 11,615; The city's name means "beginning of a hill."

•MAKAWOO, Pop. 2,900; Makawoo means "beginning of the forest."

•MAUNAWILI, Pop. 5,239; The town's name means "twisted mountain."

•MILILANI TOWN, Pop. 21,365; Mililani's name means "beloved place of chiefs."

•NAALEHU, Pop. 1,168; Zip Code 96772; Elev. 674; Lat. 19-03-55 N long. 155-35-14 W; The town's name means "volcanic ashes."

•NANAKULI, Pop. 8,185; The name means "look at the knee," and refers to a tatooed knee of a chief priest.

•NAPILI-HONOKOWAI, Pop. 2,446; The name refers to a particular set of cliffs.

•PAHALA, Pop. 1,619; Zip Code 96777; Lat. 19-12-13 N long. 155-28-56 W; Pahala means "cultivation by burning mulch."

•PAPAIKOU, Pop. 1,567; Zip Code 96781; Lat. 19-47-41 N long. 155-05-50 W; The town's name means "village in a grove."

•PEARL CITY, Pop. 42,575; Zip Code 96782; Lat. 21-23-54 N long. 157-57-59 W; Descriptively named for the pearls once found there.

•**PUKALANI,** Pop. 3,950; The town's name means "heavenly gate."

•**SCHOFIELD BARRACKS,** Pop. 18,851; Named in honor of Lt. General John Schofield, Secretary of War under President Andrew Johnson.

•**WAHIAWA,** Pop. 16,911; Zip Code 96786; Elev. 2413; Lat. 21-29-42 N long. 158-02-48 W; Wahiawa means "place of rough seas."

•**WAIALUA,** Pop. 4,051; Zip Code 96791; Lat. 21-34-53 N long. 158-06-29 W; The name means "water hole."

•**WAIANOE,** Pop. 7,941; Zip Code 96792; Lat. 21-26-07 N long. 158-10-31 W; The name means "mullet water."

•**WAILEA,** Pop. 1,124; Wailea means "water of the goddess Lea."

•**WAILUA,** Pop. 1,587; The town's name means "two waters."

•**WAILUKU,** Pop. 10,260; Zip Code 96793; Elev. 331; Lat. 20-53-44 N long. 156-30-27 W; The name means "water of destruction."

•**WAIMANALO,** Pop. 3,562; Zip Code 96795; Lat. 21-20-32 N long. 157-42-41 W; Waimanalo means "potable water."

•**WAIMANALO BEACH,** Pop. 4,161; The town's name means "potable water."

•**WAIMEA,** Hawaii County; Pop. 1,179; Zip Code 96796; Lat. 21-57-38 N long. 159-40-02 W; Waimea means "reddish water."

IDAHO

•ABERDEEN, City; Bingham County; Pop. 1,528; Zip Code 83210; Lat. 42-56-38 N long. 112-50-09 W; SE Idaho. Named for the city in Scotland.

•ACEQUIA, City; Minidoka County; Pop. 100; Zip Code 83310; S Idaho. The origin of the town's name is uncertain.

•ALBION, City; Cassia County; Pop. 286; Zip Code 83311; Lat. 42-24-40 N long. 113-34-52 W; S Idaho. The Latin name for England.

•AMERICAN FALLS, City; Power County Seat; Pop. 3,626; Zip Code 83211; Lat. 42-46-50 N long. 112-51-23 W; SE Idaho. The city is named after the falls.

•AMMON, City; Bonneville County; Pop. 4,669; SE Idaho. A Biblical name given by the early settlers.

•ARCO, City; Butte County Seat; Pop. 1,241; Zip Code 83213; Lat. 43-37-20 N long. 113-16-19 W; SE central Idaho. Named for Arco Smith, a stage operator.

•ARIMO, City; Pannock County; Pop. 338; Zip Code 83214; Lat. 42-33-37 N long. 112-10-13 W. The town is named after the Italian city.

•ASHTON, City; Fremont County; Pop. 1,218; Zip Code 83420; Lat. 44-03-52 N long. 111-22-11 W; E Idaho. Ashton was an early settler. The town is nameed for him.

•ATHOL, City; Kootenai County; Pop. 312; Zip Code 83801; Lat. 47-56-53 N long. 116-42-28 W. Athol is named for the city in Massachusetts.

•ATOMIC CITY, City; Bingham County; Pop. 34; Zip Code 83215; Lat. 43-26-43 N long. 112-48-47 W. A site of nuclear energy production and so descriptively named.

•BANCROFT, City; Caribou County; Pop. 505; Zip Code 83217; Lat. 42-43-00 N long. 111-52-56 W; SE Idaho. The city is named for a pioneer.

•BASALT, City; Bingham County; Pop. 414; Zip Code 83218; Lat. 43-19-03 N long. 112-10-47 W; SE Idaho. The city is named after local mineral deposits.

•BELLEVUE, City; Blaine County; Pop. 1,016; Zip Code 83313; Elev. 5190; Lat. 43-27-51 N long. 114-15-27 W; S central Idaho. A French word meaning "beautiful view."

•BLACKFOOT, City; Bingham County Seat; Pop. 10,065; Zip Code 83221; Lat. 43-11-18 N long. 112-20-35 W; 23 mi. N of Pocatello in SE Idaho. The city is named after the Indian tribe.

•BLISS, City; Gooding County; Pop. 208; Zip Code 83314; Elev. 3262; Lat. 42-55-27 N long. 114-56-58 W; S Idaho. A euphonious name given by the area's first settlers.

•BLOOMINGTON, City; County; Pop. 212; Zip Code 83223; Elev. 5969; Lat. 42-11-28 N long. 111-24-09 W; SE corner of Idaho. Named after the city in Indiana.

•BOISE CITY, City; Ada County Seat; Pop. 102,451; Zip Code 837--; Lat. 43-36-37 N long. 116-13-22 W; SW Idaho. Boise is a French word meaning "wooded area."

•BONNERS FERRY, City; Boundary County Seat; Pop. 1,906; Zip Code 83805; Lat. 48-41-27 N long. 116-19-04 W; N Idaho. Edwin Bonner was a ferry operator on the Kootenai River.

•BOVILL, City; Latah County; Pop. 289; Zip Code 83806; Lat. 46-51-29 N long. 116-23-32 W; NW Idaho. Named for an early settler.

•BUHL, City; Twin Falls County; Pop. 3,629; Zip Code 83316; Lat. 42-35-44 N long. 114-45-34 W; S Idaho. Frank Buhl helped found a large irrigation project in the area. The town is named in his honor.

•BURLEY, City; Cassia & Minidoka Counties; Cassia County Seat; Pop. 8,761; Zip Code 83318; 38 mi. E of Twin Falls in S Idaho. Burley's name recalls Union Pacific railroad official David Burley.

•BUTTE CITY, City; Butte County; Pop. 93; SE central Idaho. Descriptively named after the local geographic features.

•CALDWELL, City; Canyon County Seat; Pop. 17,699; Zip Code 83605; Lat. 43-39-36 N long. 116-40-58 W; 25 mi. W of Boise in SW Idaho. Caldwell was an early settler.

•CAMBRIDGE, City; Washington County; Pop. 428; Zip Code 83610; Lat. 44-34-26 N long. 116-40-22 W; W Idaho. Named after the city in Massachusetts.

•CASCADE, City; Valley County Seat; Pop. 945; Zip Code 83611; Lat. 44-30-51 N long. 116-02-38 W; W central Idaho. Descriptively named for the area's rushing waters.

•CASTLEFORD, City; Twin Falls County; Pop. 191; Zip Code 83321; Elev. 3866; Lat. 42-31-12 N long. 114-52-17 W; S Idaho. Named for a local rock formation resembling a castle.

•CHALLIS, City; Custer County Seat; Pop. 758; Zip Code 83226; Elev. 5288; Lat. 44-30-20 N long. 114-13-50 W; central Idaho. A. P. Challis founded the town. It is named for him.

•CHUBBUCK, City; Bannock County; Pop. 7,052; Zip Code 83201; SE Idaho. Earl Chubbuck was a train conductor. The town is named for him.

•CLARK FORK, City; Bonner County; Pop. 449; Zip Code 83811; Lat. 48-08-52 N long. 116-10-07 W; N Idaho. Named in honor of explorer George Rogers Clark.

•CLAYTON, City; Custer County; Pop. 43; Zip Code 83227; Lat. 44-15-48 N long. 114-23-38 W; central Idaho. Clayton is named after an early settler.

•CLIFTON, City; Franklin County; Pop. 208; Zip Code 83228; Lat. 42-11-17 N long. 112-00-15 W; SE Idaho. Descriptively named for cliffs in the area.

•COEUR D'ALENE, City; Kootenai County Seat; Pop. 20,054; Zip Code 83814; Elev. 2187; Lat. 47-41-52 N long. 116-46-59 W; 32 mi E of Spokane, WA in N Idaho. A French name for a Skitswish Indian tribe.

•COTTONWOOD, City; Idaho County; Pop. 941; Zip Code 83522; Lat. 46-03-03 N long. 116-21-15 W; N central Idaho. Named for the local cottonwood trees.

•COUNCIL, City; Adams County Seat; Pop. 917; Zip Code 83612; Lat. 44-43-45 N long. 116-26-18 W; W Idaho. The town is named after one of its early functions.

•CRAIGMONT, City; Lewis County; Pop. 617; Zip Code 83523; Lat. 46-14-29 N long. 116-28-29 W; W Idaho. Named for a prominent citizen.

•CULDESAC, City; Nez Perce County; Pop. 261; Zip Code 83524; Lat. 46-22-26 N long. 116-40-27 W; W Idaho. Descriptively named for the local topography.

•**DALTON GARDENS,** City; Kootenai County; Pop. 1,795; N Idaho. The city is named after an early pioneer.

•**DAYTON,** City; Franklin County; Pop. 368; Zip Code 83232; Elev. 4818; Lat. 42-06-36 N long. 111-59-11 W; SE Idaho. Dayton is named for Johnathon Dayton, Revolutionary War general.

•**DEARY,** City; Latah County; Pop. 539; Zip Code 83823; Lat. 46-48-09 N long. 116-33-05 W; NW Idaho. An endearing term used by early settlers that became the nameof the town.

•**DEDA,** City; Cassia County; Pop. 276; S Idaho. Probably named for a pioneer.

•**DIETRICH,** City; Lincoln County; Pop. 101; Zip Code 83324; S Idaho. Dietrich is named after a prominent landowner.

•**DONNELLY,** City; Valley County; Pop. 139; Zip Code 83615; Lat. 44-43-53 N long. 116-04-47 W; W central Idaho. Named for a pioneer.

•**DOWNEY,** City; Bannock County; Pop. 645; Zip Code 83234; Lat. 42-25-50 N long. 112-07-15 W; SE Idaho. The city is named for a pioneer family.

•**DRIGGS,** City; Teton County Seat; Pop. 727; Zip Code 83422; Elev. 6116; Lat. 43-43-29 N long. 111-06-13 W; E Idaho. The Driggs extended family composed a large part of the local Mormon settlement, an so gave their name to the town.

•**DUBOIS,** City; Clark County Seat; Pop. 413; Zip Code 83423; Elev. 5145; Lat. 44-10-19 N long. 112-13-57 W; E Idaho. Fred T. DuBois was U. S. Senator from Idaho in 1890. The town is named after him.

•**EAGLE,** City; Ada County; Pop. 2,620; Zip Code 83616; Lat. 43-51-31 N long. 116-18-57 W; SW Idaho. Descriptively named for the many eagles in the area.

•**EAST HOPE,** City; Bonner County; Pop. 258; N Idaho. Named for its relation to Hope.

•**EDEN,** City; Jerome County; Pop. 355; Zip Code 83325; Lat. 42-36-19 N long. 114-12-18 W; S Idaho. Given a Biblical name describing a perfect garden.

•**ELK RIVER,** City; Clearwater County; Pop. 265; Zip Code 83827; Lat. 46-46-58 N long. 116-10-50 W; NE Idaho. Once the site of large elk herds and so named.

•**EMMETT,** City; Gem County Seat; Pop. 4,605; Zip Code 83617; Lat. 43-52-24 N long. 116-29-51 W; SW Idaho. The city is named after Emmett Cahalan, a local settler.

•**FAIRFIELD,** City; Camas County Seat; Pop. 404; Zip Code 83327; Lat. 43-20-34 N long. 114-56-59 W; S central Idaho. Descriptively named asa beautiful place.

•**FERDINAND,** City; Idaho County; Pop. 144; Zip Code 83526; Lat. 46-09-11 N long. 116-23-31 W; 23 N central Idaho. Named after a local settler.

•**FILER,** City; Twin Falls County; Pop. 1,645; Zip Code 83328; Elev. 3756; Lat. 42-34-02 N long. 114-36-25 W; S Idaho. Named for a prominent citizen.

•**FIRTH,** City; Bingham County; Pop. 460; Zip Code 83236; Lat. 43-18-22 N long. 112-11-54 W; SE Idaho. A firth is a narrow inlet, and descriptively names the city.

•**GENESSE,** City; Latah County; Pop. 791; Zip Code 83832; Elev. 2675; Lat. 46-33-09 N long. 116-55-30 W; NW Idaho. Genesse is an Iroquoian Indian word meaning "beautiful valley."

•**GEORGETOWN,** City; Bear Lake County; Pop. 544; Zip Code 83239; Lat. 42-28-36 N long. 111-22-17 W; SE corner of Idaho. The city's name honors a local pioneer.

•**GLENNS FERRY,** City; Elmore County; Pop. 1,374; Zip Code 83623; Elev. 2560; Lat. 42-57-09 N long. 115-17-53 W; SW central Idaho. Named for an early ferryman.

•**GOODING,** City; Gooding County Seat; Pop. 2,949; Zip Code 83330; Elev. 3673; Lat. 42-56-19 N long. 114-42-47 W; S Idaho.

•**GRACE,** City; Caribou County; Pop. 1,216; Zip Code 83241; Lat. 42-34-40 N long. 111-43-45 W; SE Idaho. The town's name honors the wife of a pioneer.

•**GRAND VIEW,** City; Owyhee County; Pop. 366; Zip Code 83624; Elev. 2365; Lat. 42-59-18 N long. 116-05-28 W; SW corner of Idaho. Descriptively named for the view.

•**GRANGEVILLE,** City; Idaho County Seat; Pop. 3,666; Zip Code 83530; Lat. 45-55-29 N long. 116-07-24 W; N central Idaho. The city is named after the local Grange, a farmer's organization.

•**GREENLEAF,** City; Canyon County; Pop. 663; Zip Code 83626; Lat. 43-40-08 N long. 116-49-21 W; SW Idaho. Named for the local agriculture.

•**HAILEY,** City; Blaine County Seat; Pop. 2,109; Zip Code 83333; Lat. 43-31-09 N long. 114-18-49 W; S central Idaho. The city is named for landowner Bill Hailey.

•**HAMER,** City; Jefferson County; Pop. 93; Zip Code 83425; Elev. 4814; Lat. 43-55-38 N long. 112-12-19 W; E Idaho. Hamer was an early pioneer.

•**HANSEN,** City; Twin Falls County; Pop. 1,078; Zip Code 83334; Lat. 42-31-48 N long. 114-18-00 W; S Idaho. Named for an early citizen.

•**HARRISON,** City; Kootenai County; Pop. 260; Zip Code 83833; Lat. 47-27-23 N long. 116-47-09 W; N Idaho. Harrison is namedfor a 19th century landowner.

•**HAYDEN,** City; Kootenai County; Pop. 2,586; Zip Code 83835; N Idaho. Probably named in honor of geologist Ferdinand Hayden.

•**HAYDEN LAKE,** City; Kootenai County; Pop. 273; Zip Code 83835; Lat. 47-45-35 N long. 116-46-19 W; N Idaho. Named in honor of geologist Ferdinand Hayden.

•**HAZELTON,** City; Jerome County; Pop. 496; Zip Code 83335; Lat. 42-35-39 N long. 114-07-58 W; S Idaho. Hazelton is named after the wife of an early landowner.

•**HEYBURN,** City; Minidoka County; Pop. 2,889; Zip Code 83336; Lat. 42-33-28 N long. 113-45-30 W; S Idaho. Heyburn was a prominent resident, the town is named for him.

•**HOLLISTER,** City; Twin Falls County; Pop. 167; S Idaho. Hollister is named after an early landowner.

•**HOMEDALE,** City; Owyhee County; Pop. 2,078; Zip Code 83628; Lat. 43-37-15 N long. 116-56-10 W; SW corner of Idaho. Given a familiar name by its first settlers.

•**HOPE,** City; Bonner County; Pop. 106; Zip Code 83836; Lat. 48-15-16 N long. 116-18-17 W; N Idaho. The city's name expresses the aspirations of the location's settlers.

•**HORSESHOE BEND,** City; Boise County; Pop. 700; Zip Code 83629; Lat. 43-54-30 N long. 116-12-01 W; W central Idaho. The city is descriptively named for its shape.

•**HUETTER,** City; Kootenai County; Pop. 65; N Idaho. Huetter was an early resident.

•**IDAHO CITY,** City; Boise County Seat; Pop. 300; Zip Code 83631; Elev. 3906; Lat. 43-49-45 N long. 115-49-31 W; W central Idaho. Named after the state.

•**IDAHO FALLS,** City; Bonneville County Seat; Pop. 39,590; Zip Code 83401; Lat. 43-29-02 N long. 111-59-54 W; 50 mi. NNW of Pocatello in SE Idaho. Descriptively named for a local falls.

•**INKOM,** City; Bannock County; Pop. 830; Zip Code 83245; Lat. 42-47-40 N long. 112-15-02 W; SE Idaho. The meaning of the town's name is uncertain.

•**IONA,** City; Bonneville County; Pop. 1,072; Zip Code 83427; Lat. 43-31-45 N long. 111-55-45 W; SE Idaho. The city's name honors the wife of a settler.

•**IRWIN,** City; Bonneville County; Pop. 113; Zip Code 83428; Lat. 43-24-29 N long. 111-17-24 W; SE Idaho. Irwin was the family name of an early pioneer.

•**ISLAND PARK,** City; Fremont County; Pop. 154; Zip Code 83429; Lat. 44-31-22 N long. 111-19-59 W; E Idaho. Descriptively named for its topography.

•**JEROME,** City; Jerome County Seat; Pop. 6,891; Zip Code 83338; Lat. 42-43-26 N long. 114-31-06 W; 14 mi. N of Twin Falls in S Idaho. Jerome was a prominent settler.

•**JULIAETTA,** City; Latah County; Pop. 522; Zip Code 83535; Lat. 46-34-46 N long. 116-42-23 W; NW Idaho. Named for the wife of the original landowner.

•**KAMIAH,** City; Lewis County; Pop. 1,478; Zip Code 83536; Lat. 46-13-26 N long. 116-02-11 W; W Idaho. Kamiah is an Indian word of uncertain meaning.

•**KELLOGG,** City; Shoshone County; Pop. 3,417; Zip Code 83837; Lat. 47-32-19 N long. 116-07-35 W; NE Idaho. Noah Kellogg discovered a mine in the area. The town is named for him.

•**KENDRICK,** City; Latah County; Pop. 395; Zip Code 83537; Lat. 46-37-00 N long. 116-38-44 W; NW Idaho. Kendrick was an early settler.

•**KETCHUM,** City; Blaine County; Pop. 2,200; Zip Code 83340; Lat. 43-41-16 N long. 114-22-22 W; S central Idaho. Named for a prominent resident.

•**KIMBERLY,** City; Twin Falls County; Pop. 2,307; Zip Code 83341; Lat. 42-32-01 N long. 114-21-37 W; S Idaho. Kimberly is named after a local settler.

•**KOOSKIA,** City; Idaho County; Pop. 784; Zip Code 83539; Lat. 46-08-33 N long. 115-58-39 W; N central Idaho. Kooskia is an Indian word whose meaning is unsure.

•**KOOTENAI,** City; Bonner County; Pop. 280; Zip Code 83840; N Idaho. Named for the Kootenai Indians. The name means "water people."

•**KUNA,** City; Ada County; Pop. 1,767; Zip Code 83634; Lat. 43-29-22 N long. 116-25-08 W; SW Idaho. The origin of the town's name is uncertain.

•**LAPWAI,** City; Nez Perce County; Pop. 1,043; Zip Code 83540; Lat. 46-24-16 N long. 116-47-51 W; W Idaho. Lapwai is an Indian word of uncertain origin.

•**LAVA HOT SPRINGS,** City; Bannock County; Pop. 467; Zip Code 83246; Lat. 42-37-09 N long. 112-00-59 W; SE Idaho. The city and the hot springs are found on volcanic material.

•**LEADORE,** City; Lemhi County; Pop. 114; Zip Code 83464; Lat. 44-40-50 N long. 113-21-09 W; E central Idaho. Named for the metal mined in the area.

•**LEWISTON,** City; Nez Perce County Seat; Pop. 27,986; Zip Code 83501; Lat. 46-23-39 N long. 116-59-29 W; 95 mi. SSE of Spokane, WA in W Idaho. Named in honor of Meriwether Lewis, best known for the Louis and Clark expedition.

•**LEWISVILLE,** City; Jefferson County; Pop. 502; Zip Code 83431; Lat. 43-41-42 N long. 112-00-49 W; E Idaho. Lewisville is named for explorer Meriwether Lewis.

•**MACKAY,** City; Custer County; Pop. 541; Zip Code 83251; Lat. 43-54-43 N long. 113-36-50 W; central Idaho. Mackay was an early pioneer.

•**MALAD CITY,** City; Oneida County Seat; Pop. 1,915; Zip Code 83252; Lat. 42-10-51 N long. 112-14-28 W; S Idaho. Malad is French for "sick." The city is named after the Malad River.

•**MALTA,** City; Cassia County; Pop. 196; Zip Code 83342; Lat. 42-18-36 N long. 113-22-11 W; S Idaho; Malta is named after the famous island in the Mediterranean Sea.

•**MARSING,** City; Owyhee County; Pop. 786; Zip Code 83639; Lat. 43-32-46 N long. 116-48-22 W; SW corner of Idaho. Marsing was a pioneer settler.

•**MCCALL,** City; Valley County; Pop. 2,188; Zip Code 83638; Lat. 44-49-59 N long. 116-05-03 W; W central Idaho. The city is named for a prominent resident.

•**MCCAMMON,** City; Bannock County; Pop. 770; Zip Code 83250; Lat. 42-38-42 N long. 112-11-51 W; SE Idaho. Named for an early settler family.

•**MELBA,** City; Canyon County; Pop. 276; Zip Code 83641; Lat. 43-22-35 N long. 116-31-44 W; SW Idaho. Melba's name remembers the wife of a pioneer.

•**MENAN,** City; Jefferson County; Pop. 605; Zip Code 83434; Lat. 43-43-17 N long. 111-59-41 W; E Idaho. The city is named for an early resident.

•**MERIDIAN,** City; Ada County; Pop. 6,658; Zip Code 83642; Lat. 43-18-27 N long. 112-08-55 W; SW Idaho. Named for the town's location on the map grid.

•**MIDDLETON,** City; Canyon County; Pop. 1,901; Zip Code 83644; Elev. 2398; Lat. 43-42-24 N long. 116-37-26 W; SW Idaho. Descriptively named for the town's location.

•**MIDVALE,** City; Washington County; Pop. 205; Zip Code 83645; Lat. 44-28-22 N long. 116-43-45 W; W Idaho. So named for its location

•**MINIDOKA,** City; Minidoka County; Pop. 101; Zip Code 83343; Elev. 4286; Lat. 42-45-15 N long. 113-29-18 W; S Idaho. A Shoshoni Indian word meaning "broad expanse."

•**MONTPELIER,** City; Bear Lake County; Pop. 3,107; Zip Code 83254; Lat. 42-19-14 N long. 111-18-06 W; SE corner of Idaho.

•**MOORE,** City; Butte County; Pop. 210; Zip Code 83255; Lat. 43-48-49 N long. 113-24-52 W; SE central Idaho. Moore was an early settler.

•**MOSCOW,** City; Latah County Seat; Pop. 16,513; Zip Code 83843; Elev. 2583; Lat. 46-43-48 N long. 117-00-15 W; 25 mi. N of Lewiston in NW ID; on WA border. The city is named after the great Russian city.

•**MOUNTAIN HOME,** City; Elmore County Seat; Pop. 7,540; Zip Code 83647; Elev. 3143; Lat. 43-08-18 N long. 115-41-33 W; SW central Idaho. The city is descriptively named for the terrain.

•**MOYIE SPRINGS,** City; Boundary County; Pop. 386; Zip Code 83845; Lat. 48-43-38 N long. 116-11-19 W; N Idaho. Named after a local springs.

•**MUD LAKE,** City; Jefferson County; Pop. 243; E Idaho. Descriptively named for the lake's turbidity.

•**MULLAN,** City; Shoshone County; Pop. 1,269; Zip Code 83846; Elev. 3277; Lat. 47-28-13 N long. 115-47-47 W; NE Idaho. Named for a local landowner.

•**MURTAUGH,** City; Twin Falls County; Pop. 114; Zip Code 83344; Elev. 4082; Lat. 42-29-27 N long. 114-09-33 W; S Idaho. Murtaugh was an early settler. The town is named for him.

•**NAMPA,** City; Canyon County; Pop. 25,112; Zip Code 83651; Lat. 43-34-27 N long. 116-33-53 W; 18 mi. W of Boise in SW Idaho. Nampa was a Shoshoni Indian chief.

•**NEW MEADOWS,** City; Adams County; Pop. 576; Zip Code 83654; Elev. 3868; Lat. 44-58-11 N long. 116-17-19 W; W Idaho. A descriptive name given by the area's settlers.

•**NEW PLYMOUTH,** City; Payette County; Pop. 1,186; Zip Code 83655; Lat. 43-58-11 N long. 116-49-11 W; SW Idaho. The city is named for Plymouth, Massachusetts.

•**NEWDALE,** City; Fremont County; Pop. 329; Zip Code 83436; Lat. 43-53-10 N long. 111-36-05 W; E Idaho. A euphonious name meaning "new fields."

•**NEZPERCE,** City; Lewis County Seat; Pop. 517; Zip Code 83543; Lat. 46-14-06 N long. 116-14-35 W; W Idaho. The French name for the Chopunnish Indian tribe.

•**NOTUS,** City; Canyon County; Pop. 437; Zip Code 83656; Lat. 43-43-27 N long. 116-48-00 W; SW Idaho. The circumstances that led to the town being called "Notus" is uncertain.

•**OAKLEY,** City; Cassia County; Pop. 663; Zip Code 83346; Lat. 42-14-32 N long. 113-52-50 W; S Idaho. Named for the many oak trees in the area.

•**OLDTOWN,** City; Bonner County; Pop. 257; N Idaho. Descriptively named for its age.

•**ONAWAY,** City; Latah County; Pop. 254; NW Idaho. A stage stop that acquired the name "on-a-way."

•**OROFINO,** City; Clearwater County Seat; Pop. 3,711; Zip Code 83544; Lat. 46-28-58 N long. 116-15-28 W; NE Idaho. The town's name is Spanish for "fine ore," and refers to the gold mining in the area.

•**OSBURN,** City; Shoshone County; Pop. 2,220; Zip Code 83849; Lat. 47-30-18 N long. 115-59-49 W; NE Idaho. Osburn is named for an early settler.

•**OXFORD,** City; Franklin County; Pop. 65; SE Idaho. The city is named for the great university town in England.

•**PARIS,** City; Bear Lake County Seat; Pop. 707; Zip Code 83261; Elev. 5968; Lat. 42-13-44 N long. 111-23-51 W; SE corner of Idaho. Named after the French capital.

•**PARKER,** City; Fremont County; Pop. 262; Zip Code 83438; Lat. 43-57-32 N long. 111-45-21 W; E Idaho. The city is named after a local landowner.

•**PAYETTE,** City; Payette County Seat; Pop. 5,448; Zip Code 83661; Lat. 44-04-40 N long. 116-55-56 W; SW Idaho.

•**PECK,** City; Nez Perce County; Pop. 209; Zip Code 83545; Lat. 46-28-31 N long. 116-25-35 W; W Idaho.

•**PIERCE,** City; Clearwater County; Pop. 1,060; Zip Code 83546; Lat. 46-29-37 N long. 115-47-49 W; NE Idaho.

•**PINEHURST,** City; Shoshone County; Pop. 2,183; Zip Code 83850; Lat. 47-32-18 N long. 116-14-13 W; NE Idaho.

•**PLUMMER,** City; Benewah County; Pop. 634; Zip Code 83851; Elev. 2722; Lat. 47-20-52 N long. 116-49-58 W; NW Idaho.

•**POCATELLO,** City; Bannock County Seat; Pop. 46,340; Zip Code 83201; SE Idaho.

•**POST FALLS,** City; Kootenai County; Pop. 5,736; Zip Code 83854; Lat. 47-43-51 N long. 117-00-10 W; N Idaho.

•**POTLATCH,** City; Latah County; Pop. 819; Zip Code 83855; Lat. 46-55-30 N long. 116-53-35 W; NW Idaho.

•**PRESTON,** City; Franklin County Seat; Pop. 3,759; Zip Code 83263; Lat. 42-10-39 N long. 111-56-42 W; SE Idaho.

•**PRIEST RIVER,** City; Bonner County; Pop. 1,639; Zip Code 83856; Lat. 48-15-05 N long. 116-54-28 W; N Idaho.

•**RATHDRUM,** City; Kootenai County; Pop. 1,369; Zip Code 83858; Lat. 47-48-50 N long. 116-53-45 W; N Idaho.

•**REUBENS,** City; Lewis County; Pop. 87; Zip Code 83548; Lat. 46-19-13 N long. 116-32-27 W; W Idaho.

•**REXBURG,** City; Madison County Seat; Pop. 11,559; Zip Code 83440; Elev. 4865; Lat. 43-49-20 N long. 111-46-54 W; 25 mi. NE of Idaho Falls in E Idaho.

•**RICHFIELD,** City; Lincoln County; Pop. 357; Zip Code 83349; Lat. 43-03-04 N long. 114-09-17 W; S Idaho.

•**RIGBY,** City; Jefferson County Seat; Pop. 2,624; Zip Code 83442; Lat. 43-40-23 N long. 111-54-52 W; E Idaho.

•**RIGGINS,** City; Idaho County; Pop. 527; Zip Code 83549; Elev. 1800; Lat. 45-25-19 N long. 116-18-53 W; N central Idaho.

•**RIRIE,** City; Bonneville & Jefferson Counties; Pop. 555; Zip Code 83443; Lat. 43-38-15 N long. 111-44-31 W; SE Idaho.

•**ROBERTS,** City; Jefferson County; Pop. 466; Zip Code 83444; Lat. 43-43-23 N long. 112-07-42 W; E Idaho.

•**ROCKLAND,** City; Power County; Pop. 283; Zip Code 83271; Lat. 42-34-25 N long. 112-52-21 W; SE Idaho.

•**RUPERT,** City; Minidoka County Seat; Pop. 5,476; Zip Code 83350; Elev. 4158; Lat. 42-37-10 N long. 113-40-17 W; S Idaho.

•**ST. ANTHONY,** City; Fremont County Seat; Pop. 3,212; Zip Code 83445; Lat. 43-57-56 N long. 111-40-57 W; E Idaho.

•**ST. CHARLES,** City; Bear Lake County; Pop. 211; Zip Code 83272; Elev. 5944; Lat. 42-06-41 N long. 111-23-25 W; SE corner of Idaho.

•**ST. MARIES,** City; Benewah County Seat; Pop. 2,794; Zip Code 83861; Lat. 47-18-56 N long. 116-34-04 W; NW Idaho.

•**SALMON,** City; Lemhi County Seat; Pop. 3,308; Zip Code 83467; Lat. 45-10-41 N long. 113-53-36 W; E central Idaho.

•**SANDPOINT,** City; Bonner County Seat; Pop. 4,460; Zip Code 83864; Lat. 48-01-42 N long. 116-38-16 W; N Idaho.

•**SHELLEY,** City; Bingham County; Pop. 3,300; Zip Code 83274; Lat. 43-22-41 N long. 112-08-21 W; SE Idaho.

•**SHOSHONE,** City; Lincoln County Seat; Pop. 1,242; Zip Code 83352; Lat. 42-54-42 N long. 114-15-50 W; S Idaho.

•**SMELTERVILLE,** City; Shoshone County; Pop. 776; Zip Code 83868; Lat. 47-32-37 N long. 116-10-22 W; NE Idaho.

•**SODA SPRINGS,** City; Caribou County Seat; Pop. 4,051; Zip Code 83267; Lat. 42-39-25 N long. 111-35-35 W; SE Idaho.

•**SPENCER,** City; Clark County; Pop. 29; Zip Code 83446; Lat. 44-21-46 N long. 112-11-16 W; E Idaho.

•**SPIRIT LAKE,** City; Kootenai County; Pop. 834; Zip Code 83869; Lat. 47-57-57 N long. 116-51-31 W; N Idaho.

•**STANLEY,** City; Custer County; Pop. 99; Zip Code 83278; Lat. 44-12-58 N long. 114-56-13 W; Central Idaho.

•**STATE LINE,** City; Kootenai County; Pop. 26; N Idaho.

•**STITES,** City; Idaho County; Elev. 253; Zip Code 83552; Lat. 46-05-35 N long. 115-58-31 W; N central Idaho.

•**SUGAR CITY,** City; Madison County; Pop. 1,022; Zip Code 83448; Lat. 43-52-23 N long. 111-44-51 W; E Idaho.

•**SUN VALLEY,** City; Blaine County; Pop. 545; Zip Code 83353; Lat. 43-41-50 N long. 114-21-03 W; S central Idaho.

•**SWAN VALLEY,** City; Bonneville County; Pop. 135; Zip Code 83449; Elev. 5276; Lat. 43-26-33 N long. 111-18-28 W; SE Idaho.

•**TENSED,** City; Benewah County; Pop. 113; Zip Code 83870; Elev. 2557; Lat. 47-09-32 N long. 116-55-20 W; NW Idaho.

•**TETON,** City; Fremont County; Pop. 559; Zip Code 83451; Elev. 4949; Lat. 43-53-13 N long. 111-39-50 W; E Idaho.

•**TETONIA,** City; Teton County; Pop. 191; Zip Code 83452; Lat. 43-48-52 N long. 111-09-31 W; E Idaho.

•**TROY,** City; Latah County; Pop. 820; Zip Code 83871; Lat. 46-44-12 N long. 116-46-00 W; NW Idaho.

•**TWIN FALLS,** City; Twin Falls County Seat; Pop. 26,209; Zip Code 83301; Lat. 42-27-30 N long. 114-31-24 W; S Idaho.

•**UCON,** City; Bonneville County; Pop. 833; Zip Code 83454; Lat. 43-35-38 N long. 111-57-09 W; SE Idaho.

•**VICTOR,** City; Teton County; Pop. 323; Zip Code 83455; Lat. 43-36-13 N long. 111-06-36 W; E Idaho.

•**WALLACE,** City; Shoshone County Seat; Pop. 1,736; Zip Code 83873; Elev. 2744; Lat. 47-28-22 N long. 115-55-29 W; NE Idaho.

ILLINOIS

•**ABINGDON**, City, Knox County; Pop. 4,191; Zip Code 61410; W. Central Illinois; 10 miles S of Galesburg; Incorporated in 1857.

•**ADDISON**, Village, Du Page County; Pop. 28,228; Zip Code 61101; NE Illinois; W of Chicago; Named for the 18th century essayist, Joseph Addison.

•**ALBANY**, Village, Whiteside County; Pop. 1,035; Zip Code 61230; NW Illinois, On the Mississippi R. Named after Albany, New York.

•**ALBERS**, Village, Clinton County; Pop. 668; Zip Code 62215; SW Illinois; 21 miles E. of East Saint Louis.

•**ALBION**, City, Edwards County Seat; Pop. 2,295; Zip Code 62806; SE Illinois; Founded in 1818 by Morris Birkbeck and George Flower, English settlers who came to establish a colony; given the ancient and poetic name for England. Incorporated in 1869.

•**ALEDO**, City; Mercer County Seat; Pop. 3,877; Zip Code 61234; NW Illinois; A composite name given the town by soldiers who settled here in 1832. Incorporated in 1885.

•**ALEXIS**, Village, Mercer & Warren Counties; Pop. 1,081; Zip Code 60102; NW Illinois.

•**ALHAMBRA**, Village, Madison County; Pop. 643; Zip Code 62001; SW Illinois; Named after the famous Moorish kingdom.

•**ALMA**, Village, Marion County; Pop. 416; Zip Code 62807; S Central Illinois; 18 miles NE of Centralia; Founded 1855; Named after an early settler's wife.

•**ALPHA**, Village, Henry County; Pop. 819; Zip Code 61413; NW Illinois; Alpha was founded in 1871 and incorporated as a village in 1894. Given the Greek alphabet name signifying "first."

•**ALSIP**, Suburban village, Cook County; Pop. 17,083; Zip Code 60658; NE Illinois, just S of Chicago; Named after a family who owned a local brick factory.

•**ALTAMONT**, City, Effingham County; Pop. 2,394; Zip Code 62411; 19; Lat. 39-03-43 N long. 088-44-53 W; Central Illinois; Incorporated as a village in 1872, city 1901; Named for a highland area a mile to the west.

•**ALTON**, City, Madison County; Pop. 33,961; Zip Code 62002; Lat. 38-53-26 N long. 090-11-03 W; SW Illinois; On the bluffs overlooking the Mississippi River, and named for its height above the river.

•**ALTONA**, Village, Knox County; Pop. 621; Zip Code 61414; Lat. 41-06-53 N long. 090-09-52 W; NW Central Illinois; Founded 1868, incorporated in 1857 and named for its relatively high location.

•**AMBOY**, City, Lee County; Pop. 2,387; Zip Code 61310; Elev. 743; OLat. 41-42-51 N long. 089-19-43 W; named for Amboy, New Jersey.

•**ANDALUSIA**, Village, Rock Island County; Pop. 1,236; Zip Code 61232; Lat. 41-26-21 N long. 090-43-03 W; NW Illinois; On the Mississippi River; and named for the region in Spain.

•**ANNA**, City, Union County; Pop. 5,337; Zip Code 62906; Elev. 631; Lat. 37-27-37 N long. 089-14-49 W; SW Illinois; 28 miles SW of Marion. Anna, which was incorporated in 1865, and named after the wife of a pioneer.

•**ANNAWAN**, Village, Henry County; Pop. 912; Zip Code 61234; Elev. 625; Lat. 41-23-35 N long. 089-54-16 W; NW Illinois; Named after the 17th century Massachusetts Indian chief of the Wampanoag tribe.

•**ANTIOCH**, Lake resort village, Lake County; Pop. 4,417; Zip Code 60002; Lat. 42-28-38 Nlong. 088-05-44 W; NE Illinois; Antioch was settled in 1836, incorporated in 1857, and given the name of a Biblical city.

•**APPLE RIVER**, Village, Jo Daviess County; Pop. 471; Zip Code 61001; Lat. 42-30-18 N long. 090-05-55 W; NW Illinois; Named after the local river.

•**ARCOLA**, City, Douglas County; Pop. 2,713; Zip Code 61910; Elev. 678; Lat. 39-41-05 N long. 088-18-23 W; E Central Illinois; Named for a town in Italy, Arcola was platted in 1855 and incorporated in 1865.

•**ARENZVILLE**, Village, Cass County; Pop. 492; Zip Code 62611; Lat. 39-52-37 Nlong. 090-22-24 W; W Central Illinois; Founded 1840; Named for Francis Arenz and incorporated in 1893.

•**ARGENTA Village**, Macon County; Pop. 992; Zip Code 62501; Elev. 610; Lat. 39-58-55 N long. 088-49-22 W; Central Illinois; Known originally as Friends Creek, the village was founded in 1874 and was incorporated as a village in 1891.

•**ARLINGTON HEIGHTS**, Residential village, Cook & Lake Counties; Pop. 66,116; Zip Code 6005; Lat. 42-05-18 N long. 087-58-50 W; NE Illinois; NW suburb of Chicago; Settled in the 1830's, incorporated in 1887 and named for Arlington, VA.

•**AROMA PARK**, Village, Kankakee County; Pop. 669; Zip Code 60910; NE Illinois.

•**ARTHUR**, Village, Douglas & Moultrie Counties; Pop. 2,122; Zip Code 61911; E central Illinois; Originally an Amish colony, the village was platted in 1873, incorporated in 1877, and named after a prominent early settler.

•**ASHLAND**, Village, Cass County; Pop. 1,334; Zip Code 62612; SE corner of W central Illinois; Platted in 1857 and incorporated in 1869; Named after the Kentucky birthplace of Henry Clay.

•**ASHLEY**, City, Washington County; Pop. 629; Zip Code 62808; SW Illinois; Named for John Ashley, one of the early settlers.

•**ASHTON**, Village, Lee County; Pop. 1,1841, Zip Code 61006; Named for a banker who contributed a community center to the town.

•**ASSUMPTION**, City, Christian County; Pop. 1,251; Zip Code 62510; Central Illinois.

•**ASTORIA**, Town, Fulton County; Pop. 1,361; Zip Code 61501; W Central Illinois; The villages were combined and incorporated in 1839 and named for John Jacob Astor.

•**ATHENS**, City, Menard County; Pop. 1,158; Zip Code 62613; Central Illinois; 10 miles N of Springfield; Founded in 1831 and incorporated in 1859, and named for the classical Greek city.

•**ATKINSON**, Village, Henry County; Pop. 1,133; Zip Code 61235; NW Illinois, Founded in 1856 and named for an early settler.

•**ATLANTA**, City, Logan County; Pop. 1,807; Zip Code 61723; Central Illinois; 18 miles SW of Bloomington; Founded in 1853 as Xenia and later renamed for the city in Georgia.

•**ATWOOD**, Village, Douglas & Piatt Counties; Pop. 1,464; Zip Code 61913; E Central Illinois; Established in 1874, and incorporated in 1884. The name recalls a dense woods once found on the site, at-wood.

•**AUBURN**, City, Sangamon County; Pop. 3,603; Zip Code 62615; Central Illinois; Incorporated in 1865; Named after a famous mythical village in the work of English poet Oliver Goldsmith.

•**AUGUSTA**, Village, Hancock County; Pop. 740; Zip Code 62311; W Illinois; Founded in 1834, incorporated in 1859 and given the popular personal name.

•**AURORA**, Industrial city, Kane & Du Page Counties; Pop. 81,293; Zip Code 60505; Elev. 638; NE Illinois; The name Aurora, for the Roman goddess of dawn, was adopted by the two communities, and the town was incorporated in 1857.

•**AVON**, Village, Fulton County; Pop. 1,018; Zip Code 61415; W Central Illinois; Founded in 1852 and named after the famous English river.

•**BANNOCKBURN**, Village, Lake County; Pop. 1,275; Extreme NE Illinois; Named for Bannockburn, Scotland and incorporated in 1929.

•**BARRINGTON**, Village, Cook & Lake Counties; Pop. 9,029; Zip Code 60010: Lat. 42-09-14 N long. 088-08-10 W; NE Illinois; founded in 1845, and named after Great Barrington, Massachusetts.

•**BARRINGTON HILLS**, Village; Cook, Kane, Lake & McHenry Counties; Pop. 3,361; Zip Code 60010; Elev. ; Lat. N, long. W. Incorporated in the 1959, the village takes its name from nearby Barrington.

•**BARRY**, City, Pike County; Pop. 1,491; Zip Code 62312; Lat. 39-41-39 N long. 091-02-20 W; W Illinois; Founded in 1836 by veterans of the War of 1812 and incorporated as a city in 1859; named for Barre, Vermont.

•**BARTLETT**, Village, Cook & Du Page Counties; Pop. 13,254; Zip Code 60103; Lat. 41-59-42 N long. 088-11-08 W; NE Illinois; Founded in 1873 by Luther Bartlett, the first postmaster, who also bought the site in 1844; Incorporated in 1891.

•**BARTONVILLE**, Village, Peoria County; Pop. 6,033; Zip Code 61607; Lat. 40-39-01 N long. 089-39-07W; NW Central Illinois; Founded in 1881, the suburb grew rapidly and was incorporated in 1903.

•**BATAVIA**, Industrial city, Du Page & Kane Counties; Pop. 12,574; Zip Code 60510; Lat. 41-51-00 N 088-18-45 W; NE Illinois; On the Fox River, Batavia was founded in 1834 and given a Dutch name.

•**BATH**, Village, Mason County; Pop. 477; Zip Code 62617; Elev. 462; Lat. 40-11-36 N long. 090-08-27 W; Central Illinois; Founded in 1834, and in 1837 it was mapped by Abraham Lincoln then a surveyor. Named after the English city.

•**BEARDSTOWN**, City, Cass County; Pop. 6,313; Zip Code 62618; Lat. 40-01-03 N long. 090-25-27 W; Central Illinois; On the Illinois River, Beardstown was settled in 1819 as a ferry crossing and was originally called Beard's Ferry.

•**BECKEMEYER**, Village, Clinton County; Pop. 1,113; Zip Code 62219; Lat. 38-36-20 N long. 089-26-09 W; S Illinois; Established in 1905, the village was named for the Beckemeyer family, which owned a large portion of coal-producing land.

•**BEDFORD PARK**, Village, Cook County; Pop. 2,060; Zip Code 60638; Lat. 41-45-46 N long. 087-48-00 W; NE Illinois; Incorporated as a village in 1940.

•**BELLEVILLE**, City, St. Clair County; Pop. 39,853; Zip Code 62221; SW Illinois; Incorporated in 1819 and given a French name meaning "beautiful city.".

•**BELLEVUE**, Village, Peoria County; Pop. 2,050; N Central Illinois; Bellevue was a subdivsion of Peoria up until 1941, and given a French name meaning "beautiful view."

•**BELLWOOD**, Industrial village, Cook County; Pop. 19,812; Zip Code 60104; NE Illinois; Incorporated in 1900.

•**BEMENT**, Village, Platt County; Pop. 1,786; Zip Code 61813; Central Illinois; Founded in 1855, it was named for an official of the Great Western Railroad.

•**BENLD**, City, Macoupin County; Pop. 1,640; Zip Code 62009; SW Illinois; Established and incorporated as a village in 1900, it was named for Ben L. Dorsey, an early settler.

•**BENSENVILLE**, Village, Cook & Du Page Counties; Pop. 16,124; Zip Code 60106; NE Illinois; Named for Bensen, Germany and incorporated in 1894.

•**BENTON**, City, Franklin County; Pop. 7,763; Zip Code 62812; S Illinois; Founded in 1840, the city was named for Thomas Hart Benton, U.S. Senator from Missouri.

•**BERKELEY**, Village, Cook County; Pop. 5,467; Zip Code 60163; NE Illinois; Incorporated in 1924, it was named for Berkeley, California.

•**BERWYN**, Residential city, Cook County; Pop. 46,793; Zip Code 60402; NE Illinois; Named for a town in Pennsylvania, Berwyn was, unlike most Illinois cities, pre-planned by two realtors.

•**BETHALTO**, Villiage, Madison County; Pop. 8,609; SW Illinois; Bethalto's name came from combining "Bethel" (a chruch name) and "alto" from the nearby town of Alton.

•**BETHANY**, Village, Moutrie County; Pop. 1,550; Zip Code 61914; Central Illinois; The original settlement was known by the unlikely name of Marrowbone, conjured up by two trappers who ate the leftovers of the previous night's venison steak at this exact spot; The missionaries from the Bethany Cumberland Presbyterians of Tennessee changed it to its present designation in 1831.

•**BIGGSVILLE**, Village, Henderson County; Pop. 409; Zip Code 61418; Elev. 650; Lat. 40-51-13 N long. 090-51-53 W; W Illinois; Formerly known as Grove Farm (1856), it was incorporated as a village in 1879.

•**BISHOP HILL**, Village, Henry County; Pop. 166; Zip Code 61419; Lat. 41-12-06 N long. 090-07-08 W; NW Illinois; Bishop Hill is a restored Swedish village and Illinois' first commune (1846); It was named for Biskopskulla, Sweden, the birhplace of Erik Jansson, the religious communal leader and founder of the village.

•**BLOOMINGTON**, City; McLean County Seat; Pop. 44,330; Zip Code 61701; Elev. 829; Lat. 40-29-03- N long. 088-59-37 W; Central Illinois. Bloomington was settled in 1822 at a crossroads of several Indian trails, and for many years it was known as Keg Grove, supposedly because of a keg of liquor found there by a local Indian tribe. The name was eventually changed to Blooming Grove because of the profusion of widflowers that bloomed in the forest glades.

•**BLUE ISLAND**, City, Cook County; Pop. 21,701; Zip Code 60406; Lat. 41-39-26 long. 087-40-48 W; NE Illinois. Blue Island was first settled in 1835 by German and Italian pioneers and was named for the blue irises which grew in the area.

•**BLUE MOUND**, Village, Macon County; Pop. 1,310; Zip Code 62513; Lat. 39-42-04 N long. 089-07-23 W; Central Illinois. Descriptively named for a large glacial deposit, or mound, in the area covered with blue flowers in the spring.

•**BOURBONNAIS**, Town, Kankakee County; Pop. 13,290; Zip Code 60901; NE Illinois. Bourbonnais was the earliest settlement on the Kankakee River, established as a trading post in 1832. The town is named for Francois Bourbonnais, one of the French fur traders who started the post and went on to become historian of the area.

•**BRADFORD**, Town, Stark County; Pop. 924; Zip Code 61421; Elev. ; NW Central Illinois. Named after an early settler.

•**BRADLEY**, Village, Kanakee County; Pop. 9,523; Zip Code 61021; Elev. 648; NE Illinois. Bradley was founded in 1892 as North Kankakee but the name was changed later in honor of David Bradley who started an agricultural implement factory there.

•**BRAIDWOOD**, City, Will County; Pop. 3,421; Zip Code 60408; Elev. 585; NE Illinois. Braidwood was settled in 1865 when coal was accidentally found by a local resident who was drilling a well.

•**BREESE**, City, Clinton County; Pop. 3,518; Zip Code 62230; Elev. 458; SW Illinois. Breese was settled around 1860 and was named after Judge Sidney Breese, an Illinois jurist who once lived there. Incorporated in 1905.

•**BRIDGEPORT**, City, Lawerence County; Pop. 2,255; Zip Code 62417; Elev. 449; SE Illinois. Incorporated as a city in 1865 and named after the cityin Connecticut.

•**BRIDGEVIEW**, Village, Cook County; Pop. 14,059; Zip Code 60455; Lat. 412-45-00 N long. 087-48-15 W; NE Illinois. Bridgeview was incorporated in 1947.

•**BRIMFIELD**, Village, Peoria County; Pop. 894; Zip Code 61517; Elev. 653; Lat. 39-02-203 N long. 090-08-26 W; Central Illinois.

•**BROADLANDS**, Village, Champaign County; Pop. 344; Zip Code 61816; Lat. 39-54-31 N long. 087-59-39 W; E Illinois. Descriptively named for the local topography.

•**BROADVIEW**, residential suburb, Cook County; Pop. 8,630; Zip Code 60153; Elev. 62 Lat. 41-51-50 N long. 087-51-12 W; 5; NE Illinois; W of Chicago. Incorporated as a village in 1910, and named for a station of the Illinois Central Railway.

•**BROOKFIELD**, Residential village, Cook County; Pop. 19,237; Zip Code 60513; Elev. 62 Lat. 41-49-26 N long. 087-521-06 W; 0; NE Illinois. Brookfield was founded in 1893 following extensive land purchases by members of the Ogden, Armour, McCormick, and Rockefeller families. Then known as Grossdale, the name was changed to its present form in 1905.

•**BROOKPORT**, City, Massac County; Pop. 1,104; Zip Code 62910; Elev. 340; Lat. 37-07-25 N long. 088-37-49 W; S Illinois; On the Ohio River and just opposite Paducah, Kentucky. Brookport was incorporated in 1888.

•**BROWNSTOWN**, Village, Fayette County; Pop. 695; Zip Code 62418; Elev. 586; Lat. 38-59-45 N long. 088-57-10 W; S Central Illinois. Named for an early settler.

•**BRYANT**, Village, Fulton County; Pop. 333; Zip Code 61519; Lat. 40-27-58 N long. 090-05-30 W; W Central Illinois.

•**BUCKLEY**, Village, Iroquois County; Pop. 606; Zip Code 60918; Elev. 699; Lat. 40-35-49 N long. 088-02-17 W; E Illinois. Named for a pioneer farmer.

•**BUDA**, Village, Bureau County; Pop. 680; Zip Code 61314; N Illinois.

•**BUFFALO**, Village, Sangamon County; Pop. 505; Zip Code 62515; Elev. 703; Lat. 41-05-56 N long. 088-37-23 W; Central Illinois. Named for the American bison once found in the area.

•**BUFFALO GROVE**, Residential suburb; Lake and Cook Counties; Pop. 22,230; Zip Code 60090; NE Illinois. Named for the bison once local to the region.

•**BUNKER HILL**, City, Macoupin County; Pop. 1,687; Zip Code 62014; SW Central Illinois. Incorporated as a city in 1857, and named for the famous Revolutionary War battle.

•**BURLINGTON**, Village, Kane County; Pop. 433; Zip Code 60109; NE Illinois; 13 miles W of Elgin in a dairying, livestock, and farming area.

•**BURNHAM**, Village, Cook County; Pop. 4,039; Zip Code 60633; NE Illinois. Named for a settler.

•**BUSHNELL**, City, McDonough County; Pop. 3,797; Zip Code 61422; W Illinois. Bushnell, incorporated in 1865, was named for I.N. Bushnell, president of the Northern Cross Railroad.

•**BYRON**, City Ogle County; Pop. 2,037; Zip Code 61010; Elev. 729; NW Illinois. Founded in 1835 by New Englanders and named after poet Lord Byron.

•**CAHOKIA**, Village, St. Clair County; Pop. 18,969; Zip Code 62206; Elev. 407; SW Illinois; On the Mississippi River; originally an Indian village which became a French missionary post in 1699; The town derived its name from the Indian village which at that time housed about 2,000 Tamaroa and Cahokia natives.

•**CAIRO**, City, Alexander County Seat; Pop. 5,941; Zip Code 62914; Elev. 315; SW Illinois; at the confluence of the Ohio and Mississippi rivers. Pere Marquette and other explorers noted this finger of land, and in 1702 a French colony was established here with a fort and a tannery; Disease eventually wiped out most of the population. A subsequent settlement in 1818 was named Cairo by a Saint Louis merchant who thought it resembled the city in Egypt.

•**CALUMET CITY**, Industrial city, Cook County; Pop. 39,079; Zip Code 60409; Elev. 585; Lat. 41-36-56 N long. 087-31-46 W; NE Illinois. It was called West Hammond until 1924 when it gained its present name, which is derived from the French meaning "peace-pipe of the Indians."

•**CALUMET PARK**, Village, Cook County; Pop. 8,712; Zip Code 60643; Elev. 604; Lat. 41-39-46 N long. 087-39-38 W; NE Illinois. Originally known as Burr Oak, the name was changed to Calumet Park in 1925.

•**CAMBRIA**, Village, Williamson County; Pop. 1,087; Zip Code 62915; Lat. 37-46-53 N long. 089-07-09 WS Illinois.

•**CAMBRIDGE**, Village, Henry County Seat; Pop. 2,217; Zip Code 61238; Lat. 41-18-13 N long. 090-11-34 W; NW Illinois. Cambridge was incorporated in 1861 and named after the English university town.

•**CAMP POINT**, Town, Adams County; Pop. 1,294; Zip Code 62320; Elev. 743; Lat. 40-02-21 N long. 091-04-09 W; W Central Illinois; 29 miles NE of Quincy. Settled in 1870 by German immigrants, and descriptively named.

•**CANTON**, City, Fulton County; Pop. 14,772; Zip Code 61520; Elev. 655; Lat. 40-33-29 N long. 090-02-06 W; W Central Illinois. Canton was settled in 1825 by Isaac Swan, a native New Yorker who came to this spot and surveyed out a number of lots. He named his settlement Canton in the belief that it was located exactly on the opposite side of the world from Canton, China.

•**CAPRON**, Village, Boone County; Pop. 678; Zip Code 61012; Lat. 42-23-59 N long. 088-44-25 W; NE Illinois.

•**CARBON CLIFF**, Town, Rock Island County; Pop. 1,505; Zip Code 61239; Elev. 570; Lat. 41-29-41 N long. 090-23-26 W; NW Illinois. Named for the coal deposits found in the area.

•**CARBONDALE**, City, Jackson County; Pop. 26,144; Zip Code 62901; Elev. 416; Lat. 37-43-38 N long. 089-13-00 W; SW Illinois. Carbondale was founded in 1852 after the arrival of the Illinois Central Railroad, and it was subsequently named for the huge coalfields upon which it is built.

•**CARLINVILLE**, City, Macoupin County Seat; Pop. 5,433; Zip Code 62626; Elev. 627; Lat. 39-16-47 N long. 089-52-54 W; SW Central Illinois. The city was incorporated in 1837.

•**CARLYLE**, Town; Clinton County Seat; Pop. 3,386; Zip Code 62231; Elev. 461; Lat.38-36-37 N long. 089-22-21 W; S Central Illinois; 35 miles E of St. Louis; Incorporated in 1836 and named by English settlers in honor of Thomas Carlyle.

•**CARMI**, City, White county Seat; Pop. 6,238; Zip Code 62821; Elev. 383; Lat. 38-05-27 N long. 088-09-31 W; SE Illinois. Carmi was settled in 1816 and named for a Biblical character.

•**CAROL STREAM**, Residential suburb, DuPage County; Pop. 15,341; Zip Code 60187; Lat. 41-54-45 N long. 088-08-05 W; NE Illinois. Named for the daughter of developer, Jay Stream.

•**CARPENTERSVILLE**, Village, Kane County; Pop. 23,253; Zip Code 60110; Elev. 805; Lat. 42-07-16 N long. 088-15-28 W; NE Illinois. Carpentersville was settled in 1834 by Angelo Carpenter (thus the name) of Massachusetts.

•**CARRIER MILLS**, Village, Saline County; Pop. 2,214; Zip Code 62917; Elev. 391; Lat. 37-41-03 N long. 088-37-58 W; SE Illinois. Carrier Mills was established in 1894 and named after lumber magnate, William Carrier.

•**CARROLLTON**, City; Greene County Seat; Pop. 2,826; Zip Coe 62016; Elev. 625; Lat. 39-18-08 N long. 090-24-25 W; W Illinois; 30 miles NNW of Alton. Settled in 1818 and named in honor of Declaration of Independence signer, Charles Carrollton.

•**CARTERVILLE**, City, Williamson County; Pop. 23,253; Zip Code 62918; Elev. 457; Lat. 37-45-36 Nlong. 089-04-38 W; S Illinois; 5 miles SW of Herrin. Carterville was incorporated in 1892 and named for early farmer, Laban Carter.

•**CARTHAGE**, City; Hancock County Seat; Pop. 2,970; Zip Code 62321; Elev. 676; Lat. 41-55-08 N long. 089-18-49 W; W Illinois. Carthage was laid out in 1833 and named for the ancient city.

•**CARY**, Village; McHenry County; Pop. 6,646; Zip Code 60013; Elev. 825; Lat. 42-12-43 N long. 088-14-17 W; NE Illinois. Named in honorof pioneer William Clark.

•**CASEY**, City; Clark & Cumberland Counties; Pop. 3,026; Zip Code 62420; Elev. 648; Lat. 39-17-57 N long. 087-59-33 W; E Illinois. Incorporated in 1871 and named in honor of Lieutenant-Governor Zadok Casey.

•**CATLIN**, Village, Vermilion County; Pop. 2,207; Zip Code 61817; E Illinois. Named for J.M. Catlin, once president of the Great Western Railway Company.

•**CAVE-IN-ROCK**, Village, Hardin County; Pop. 464; Zip Code 62919; Elev. 340; SE Illinois; On the Ohio River. Cave-in-Rock is located in the hill country of the Illinois Ozarks and is named for the nearby natural cavern located midway between the summit of the river bluff and the waterline.

•**CEDARVILLE**, Village, Stephenson County; Pop. 705; Zip Code 61013; Elev. 781; N Illinois. Cedarville is the birthplace of Jane Addams, founder of Chicago's famous social center, Hull House (1889).

•**CENTRAL CITY**, Village, Marion County; Pop. 1,485; Elev. 498; S Illinois. Central City was settled by German immigrants, incorporated as a village in 1857, and named after the Illinois Central Railroad.

•**CENTRALIA**, City, Marion & Clinton Counties; Pop. 15,126; Zip Code 62801; Elev. 495; S Illinois. Founded in 1853 by members of the Illinois Central Railroad System, after which it is also named.

•**CERRO GORDO**, Village, Piatt County; Pop. 1,543; Zip Code 61818; Elev. I ; Central Illinois. The village was incorporated in 1873 and named for the Battle of Cerro Gordo in the Mexican American War.

•**CHAMPAIGN**, City, Champaign County; Pop. 57,176; Zip Code 61820; Elev. 740; E Illinois; Adjoining its sister city Urbana. Champaign was settled in 1854 and named for Champaign County, Ohio.

•**CHANDLERVILLE**, Village, Cass County; Pop. 834; Zip Code 62627; Elev. 464; Central Illinois. Chandlerville was named after and settled by Dr. Charles Chandler who hired young Abraham Lincoln to survey his land.

•**CHANNAHON**, Village, Will County; Pop. 3,806; Zip Code 60410; Elev. 530; NE Illinois. The name Channahon is derived from the Indian words meaning "meeting of the waters," descriptive of the village location at the junction of the the the Du Page and the Des Plains Rivers.

•**CHARLESTON**, City; Coles County Seat; Pop. 19,473; Zip Code 61920; Elev. 686; E Central Illinois. Charleston was settled in 1826 by Benjamin Parker and was later named for Charles Morton, its first postmaster.

•**CHATHAM**, Village, Sangamon County; Pop. 5,601; Zip Code 62629; Central Illinois. Named for the Earl of Chatham, William Pitt.

•**CHEBANSE**, Village, Iroquois-Kankakee County line; Pop. 1,195; Zip Code 60922; Elev. 667; E Illinois. The name is derived from the Indian words meaning "little duck."

•**CHENOA**, City, McLean County; Pop. 1,848; Zip Code 61726; Elev. 722; Lat. 40-44-30 N long. 088-43-11 W; Central Illinois. Chenoa was platted in 1856 by Matthew T. Scott and given an Indian name meaning "white dove."

•**CHERRY**, Village, Bureau County; Pop. 539; Zip Code 61317; Elev. 682; Lat. 41-25-37 N long. 089-12-48 W; N Illinois.

•**CHESTER**, City; Randolph County Seat; Pop. 5,337; Zip Code 62233; Elev. 381; Lat. 37-54-49 N long. 089-49-19 W; SW Illinois. Located on the Mississippi River near the mouth of the Kaskaskia River, Chester was founded in 1819 by an Ohio land company and named after the English city.

•**CHICAGO**, City; Cook & Du Page Counties; Pop. 3,005,072; Zip Code 606++; Elev. 596; Lat. 41-51-00 N long. 087-39-00 W; Pottawatomie Indians called this area "Checagou," evidently referring to the garlic, wild onion smell which permeated the air here.

•**CHICAGO RIDGE**, Village Cook County; Pop. 13,463; Zip Code 60415; Lat. 41-42-05 N long. 087-46-54 W; NE Illinois,

•**CHILLICOTHE**, City, Peoria County; Pop. 6,138; Zip Code 61523; Elev. 490; Lat. 40-55-20 N long. 089-29-10 W; Central Illinois. Incorporated in 1861 and named after Chillicothe, Ohio.

•**CHRISMAN**, City, Edgar County; Pop. 1,406; Zip Code 61923; Elev. 645; Lat. 39-48-13 N long. 087-40-25 W; E Illinois. Platted in 1872 by Matthias Chrisman.

•**CHRISTOPHER**, City, Franklin County; Pop. 3,081; Zip Code 62822; Lat. 37-58-21 N long. 089-03-12 W; S Illinois. Christopher, which was incorporated in 1910, developed as an important coal mining center for the area.

•**CICERO**, TOWN, Cook County; Pop. 61,233; Zip Code 60650; Elev. 606; Lat. 41-50-44 N long. 087-45-14 W; NE Illinois; E of Chicago. Cicero was founded in 1857 on a swampy lowland, and named after the great Roman orator.

•**CISSNA PARK**, Village, Iroquois County; Pop. 825; Zip Code 60924; Elev. 666; Lat. 40-33-53 Nlong. 087-53-35 W; E Illinois. Named for pioneer, Stephen Cissna.

•**CLARENDON HILLS**, Village, DuPage County; Pop. 6,832; Zip Code 60514; Lat. 41-47-51 Nlong. 087-57-17 W; NE Illinois; W of Chicago. Incorporated in 1924 and named for a famous English village.

•**CLAY CITY**, Village, Clay County; Pop. 1,042; Zip Code 62824; Elev. 433; Lat. 38-41-19 N long. 088-21-15 W; S Central Illinois. Settled in the early 1830's, Clay City is named after the county.

•**CLIFTON**, Village, Iroquois County; Pop. 1,386; Zip Code 60927; E Illinois.

•**CLINTON**, City; DeWitt County Seat; Pop. 7,953; Zip Code 61727; Elev. l746; Central Illinois; 19 miles N of Decatur. Settled in 1836, and named for Erie Canal builder, DeWitt Clinton.

•**COAL CITY**, City, Grundy County; Pop. 3,033; Zip Code 60416; Elev. 562; NE Illinois; 21 miles SSW of Joliet. Coal City was founded in 1875 as a site for bituminous coal mining.

•**COBDEN**, Village, Union County; Pop. 1,201; Zip Code 62920; Elev. 594; S Illinois. Cobden was incorporated in 1875 and named in honor of English investor, Sir Richard Cobden.

•**COLCHESTER**, City, McDonough County; Pop. 1,714; Zip Code 62326; W Illinois; 6 miles WSW of Macomb. Colchester, which was incorporated in 1867, was named for a coal town in England.

•**COLUMBIA**, City, Monroe County; Pop. 4,268; Zip Code 62236; Elev. 490; SW Illinois. Columbia was founded in the early 1800's and named patriotically.

•**CORDOVA**, Village, Rock Island County; Pop. 692; Zip Code 61242; Lat. 41-40-49 N long. 090-19-08 W; NW Illinois.

•**CORNELL**, Village, Livingston County; Pop. 601; Zip Code 61319; Elev. 638; Lat. 40-59-24 N long. 088-43-45 W; Central Illinois. Named for the famous New York merchant.

•**CORTLAND**, Town, DeKalb County; Pop. 1,012; Zip Code 60112; Lat. 41-55-12 N long. 088-41-19 W; N Illinois.

•**COULTERVILLE**, Village, Randolph County; Pop. 1,112; Zip Code 62237; Lat. 38-11-11 Nlong. 089-36-20 W; SW Illinois. Named for the Coulter brothers, early settlers from Tennessee.

•**COUNTRY CLUB HILLS**, Village, Cook County; Pop. 14,626; Zip Code 60477; Lat. 41-34-05 N long. 087-43-13 W; NE Illinois; S of Chicago. Named by its developers in 1958.

•**COUNTRYSIDE**, Village, Cook County; Pop. 6,509; Zip Code 60525; Lat. 41-46-58 N long. 087-52-41 W; NE Illinois. Named for its early rural history.

•**CREAL SPRINGS**, City, Williamson County; Pop. 849; Zip Code 62922; Elev. 473 ; Lat. 37-45-07 N long. 089-04-04 W; S Illinois.

•**CREST HILL**, Village, Will County; Pop. 9,210; Zip Code 60435; Lat. 41-33=-17 N long. 088-05-55 W; NE Illinois.

•**CRESTWOOD**, Village, Cook County; Pop. 10,688; Zip Code 61445; Lat. 41-39-94 N long. 087-45-09 W; NE Illinois. Named byits developers in the 1950's.

•**CRETE**, Village, Will County; Pop. 5,400; Zip Code 60417; Elev. 720; NE Illinois. Platted in 1849 and named for the island nation in the Mediterranean.

•**CREVE COEUR**, Village, Tazewell County; Pop. 6,908; Zip Code 61611; Central Illinois. Located on the Illinois River, the village was named after the first French fort built in the West and in Illinois (1680-1682).

•**CRYSTAL LAKE**, City, McHenry County; Pop. 18,456 Code 815; Zip Code 60014; NE Illinois; 13 miles N of Elgin. The city is named for the small lake around which it developed.

•**CUBA**, City, Fulton County; Pop. 1,645 Code 309; Zip Code 61427; W Central Illinois. Named for the island country of Cuba.

•**DALLAS CITY**, City, Hancock & Henderson Counties; Pop. 1,408; Zip Code 61330; W Illinois. Dallas City was settled in 1836, platted in 1848, and incorporated in 1859. It was named for George Dallas, vice-president of the United States from 1845 to 1849.

•**DANFORTH**, Village, Iroquois County; Pop. 550; Zip Code 60930; Elev. 658; E Illinois. Named for A. H. Danforth who purchased land here in 1850, and induced 30 families from the Netherlands to emigrate here.

•**DANVILLE**, City, seat of Vermilion County; Pop. 38,842; Zip Code 61832; E Illinois. Founded in 1765 on the site of a Piankashaw Indian village which was located next to the Vermilion River. Danville became known as Salt Works. After the brine supplies were depleted in the 1800's, it was renamed Danville for its surveyor.

•**DAWSON**, Village, Sangamon County; Pop. 537; Zip Code 62520; Central Illinois.

•**DECATUR**, City, seat of Macon County; Pop. 93,513; Zip Code 62525; Central Illinois. Decatur was founded and designated the seat of Macon County in 1829. Named for Commodore Stephen Decatur.

•**DEER CREEK**, Village, Tazewell-Woodford County lines; Pop. 688; Zip Code 61733; Elev. 670; Lat. 39-50-25 Nlong. 088-57-17 W; Central Illinois.

•**DEERFIELD**, Village, Cook & Lake Counties; Pop. 17,430; Zip Code 60015; Lat. 42-10-16 N long. 087-50-40 W; NE Illinois. Deerfield was founded in 1836 on the site of a Potawatomi Indian village. Incorporated in 1903.

•**DE KALB**, City, DeKalb County; Pop. 32,992; Zip Code 60115; Elev. 886; N Illinois. The city was named for Baron Johann De Kalb of the American Revolutionary Army, but for a long time was known as "Barb City" after Joseph E. Glidden, who invented twisted barbed wire there.

•**DELAVAN**, City, Tazewell County; Pop. 1,968; Zip Code 61734; Central Illinois. Founded in 1863 by Edward Cornelius Delavan of Rhode Island, who auctioned off parcels of land on Illinois' wild prairie. Incorporated in 1888.

•DEPUE (alt. DE PUE), Town, Bureau County; Pop. 1,864; Zip Code 61322; Elev. 472; Lat. 41-19-27 N long. 089-18-24 W; N Illinois. Depue was founded in the early 1800's on a glacial moraine by the Illinois River.

•DE SOTO, Village, Jackson County; Pop. 1,548; Zip Code 62929; Elev. 386; SW Illinois. Names for the famous Spanish explorer.

•DES PLAINS, City, Cook County; Pop. 53,479; Zip Code 60016; Elev. 643; Lat. 42-02-00 N long. 087-53-00 W; NE Illinois. Des Plaines was founded in the 1830's as Rand in honor of its first settler, Socrates Rand. It is located on the Des Plaines River, after which it was renamed in 1869.

DIVERNON, Village, Sangamon County; Pop. 1,066; Zip Code 62530; Central Illinois.

•DIXMOOR (alt. DIXMORE), Village, Cook County; Pop. 4,118; Zip Code 60406; NE Illinois; S of Chicago. Dixmoor was incorporated in 1922.

•DIXON, City, Lee County Seat; Pop. 15,730; Zip Code 61021; Elev. 659; N Illinois. Founded in 1830 by John Dixon, a trader who opened a tavern on the site.

•DOLTON, Village, Cook County; Pop. 24,653; Zip Code 60419; NE Illinois. Named for the pioneer Dolton brothers.

•DOWNERS GROVE, Village, Du Page County; Pop. 38,828; Zip Code 60515; Elev. 717; NE Illinois. Downers Grove was established by settler Pierce Downer at the crossroads of two Indian trails.

•DUNDEE, Village, Kane County; Pop. 4,706; Zip Code 60118; NE Illinois. Named for the place in Scotland.

•DUPO, Village, St. Clair County; Pop. 3,055; Zip Code 62239; Elev. 422; Lat. 38-30-58 N long. 090-12-37 W; SW Illinois. Dupo is located on the Mississippi River but was named after a nearby small creek crossed by a bridge. The name is contracted from Prairie duPont, French for "meadow of the bridge."

•DU QUOIN, City, Perry County; Pop. 6,554; Zip Code 62832; Elev 468; SW Illinois; 35 miles S of Centralia. Du Quoin, although settled at an earlier time, was actually founded in 1853 when the first settlement was moved to the site of a new railroad. It was named after Jean Baptiste du Quoigne, a French-Indian chief of the Kaskaskia whose village was nearby.

•DWIGHT, Village, Grundy & Livingston Counties; Pop. 4,146; Zip Code 60420; Elev. 641; Lat. 42-26-61 N long. 089-19-55 W; NE Illinois. Dwight was founded in 1854 and named for a civil engineer who worked on the nearby railroad.

•EARLVILLE, City, La Salle County; Pop. 1,389; Zip Code 60518; N Illinois. Earlville was named after the first postmaster's nephew.

•EAST ALTON, Village, Madison County; Pop. 7,159; Zip Code 62240; Elev. Lat. 38-52-49 N long. 090-06-40 W; 438; SW Illinois. Settled in 1800, East Alton developed as a river port. It was incorporated in 1894.

•EAST DUBUQUE, City, Joe Daviess County; Pop. 2,186; Zip Code 61025; Elev.; Lat. 42-29-32 Nlong. 090-38-34 W; 615; NW Illinois; Opposite Dubuque, Iowa on the east bank of the Mississippi River. The city was named for early French settler, Julien Dubuque.

•EAST DUNDEE, Village, Kane County; Pop. 2,616; Zip Code 60118; Elev. 739; Lat. 42-05-56 Nlong. 088-16-17 W; NE Illinois.

•EAST MOLINE, City, Rock Island County; Pop. 20,714; Zip Code 61244; Elev. 576; Lat. 40-56-52 Nlong. 090-18-36 W; NW Illinois; Near Moline. East Moline was incorporated in 1907.

•EAST PEORIA, City, Tazewell County; Pop. 21,546; Zip Code 61611; Elev. 478; Lat. 40-39-58 N long. 089-34-48 W; Central Illinois, near Peoria. East Peoria was settled in 1884 and called Blue Town. The name stems from the fact that the residents, many of whom were French, wore blue smocks which were unique to their native Alsace-Lorraine. The name was changed to East Peoria in 1889, and in 1919 the village was incorporated as a city.

•EAST SAINT LOUIS, City, St. Clair County; Pop. 54,966; Zip Code 62201; Elev. 418; Lat. 38-37-28 N long. 090-09-03 W; SW Illinois; Across from Saint Louis, Missouri on the Mississippi River. A village, known as Cahokia, was established as early as 1699 by French missionaries who hoped to civilize local Indian tribes. A new village was platted in 1818, and named Illinoistown. In 1859 the state legislature presented Illinoistown with a new charter incorporating it as a city and renaming it East Saint Louis.

•EDINBURGH, Village, Christian County; Pop. 1,194; Zip Code 62531; Central Illinois. Edinburgh, incorporated in 1872, was named after the city in Scotland.

•EDWARDSVILLE, City, Madison County seat; Pop. 12,437; Zip Code 62025; Elev. 554; SW Illinois. Edwardsville, founded in 1813, was named for Ninian Edwards, governor of Illinois Territory from 1809 to 1818 and one of the local landowners.

•EFFINGHAM, City; Effingham County seat; Pop. 11,238; SE Central Illinois. Named in honor of the 18th century Earl of Effingham who befriended the American colonies.

•ELBURN, Village, Kane County; Pop. 1,204; Zip Code 60119; Elev. 848; NE Illinois.

•ELDORADO, City, Saline County; Pop. 5,225; Zip Code 62930; Elev. 388. Eldorado was given a Spanish name for a mythical Indian kingdom where gold was abundant.

•ELGIN, City, Cook & Kane Counties; Pop. 63,798; Zip Code 60120; Elev. 717; NE Illinois. Elgin was founded in 1835 by James and Hezekiah Gifford, two settlers from New York.

•ELIZABETH, Village, Joe Daviess County; Pop. 774; Zip Code 61028; Elev. 790; NW Illinois. Situated on the banks of the Apple River, Elizabeth was founded in 1832. The village was named in honor of Elizabeth Armstrong, the woman who rallied the residents of the fort to a successful defense against a hostile Indian attack.

•ELK GROVE VILLAGE, Village, Cook & Du Page Counties; Pop. 28,907; Zip Code 60007; NE Illinois. Elk Grove Village, until 1960, was little more than a cornfield with scattered houses. That year Centrex Construction Company, a community planning enterprise, laid out a new town.

•ELMHURST, City DuPage County; Pop. 43,986; Zip Code 60126; Elev. 681; NE Illinois; 8 miles E of Wheaton. Elmhurst was founded in 1843 and was named for the area's stately elms, many of which still line the city's boulevards.

•ELMWOOD, City, Peoria County; Pop. 2,109; Zip Code 61529; Elev. 643; Lat. 40-46-40 N long. 089-57-59 W; Central Illinois; 19 miles WNW of Peoria. Elmwood was founded in 1864 after the discovery of a rich coal deposit on the site of the present city.

•ELMWOOD PARK, Village, Cook County; Pop. 23,840; Zip Code 60635; NE Illinois; W of Chicago. Elmwood Park grew as a commuter suburb of Chicago after its incorporation in 1914.

•**EL PASO**, City, Woodford County; Pop. 2,665; Zip Code 61738; Elev. 749; Lat. 41-55-16 N long. 087-48-33 W; N Central Illinois. El Paso, a leading agricultural center, was founded in 1854 and named after the city in Texas.

•**ELSAH**, Town, Jersey County; Pop. 982; Zip Code 62028; Elev. 429; Lat. 38-57-22 N long. 090-21-35 W; SW Illinois. Founded in 1847 by a woodchopper who settled there in hopes of selling wood to the steamboats. The tiny settlement which attracted woodchoppers, was first known as Jersey Landing, but the name was changed in 1853 (when it was platted as a town) by the first postmaster and later U.S. senator, James Semple. Semple named the town Elsah, a derivation of Ailsea, after his ancestral home in Scotland.

•**ELWOOD**, Village, Will County; Pop. 816; Zip Code 60421; Elev. 646; Lat. 41-24-14 N long. 088-06-42 W; NE Illinois.

•**ENFIELD**, Village, White County; Pop. 887; Zip Code 62835; Elev. 422; Lat. 40-17-55 N long. 089-29-06 W; SE Illinois. Enfield was settled in 1813.

•**ERIE**, Village, Whiteside County; Pop. 1,731; Zip Code 61250; NW Illinois. Erie is located on the site of an old Indian crossroad. The village was incorporated in 1872 and named after the Great Lake.

•**EUREKA**, City, Woodford County seat; Pop. 4,257; Zip Code 61530; Elev. 738; Lat. 40-43-17 N long. 089-16-22 W; Central Illinois. Founded in 1830, and given a Greek name meaning have found it."

•**EVANSTON**, City, Cook County; Pop. 73,278; Zip Code 60201; Elev. 603; NE Illinois.

•**EVERGREEN PARK**, Village, Cook County; Pop. 22,127; Zip Code 60642; NE Illinois. Descriptively named for the many evergreen trees.

•**FAIRBURY**, City, Livingston County; Pop. 3,514; Zip Code 61739; Elev. 686; NE Illinois.

•**FAIRFIELD**, City, Wayne County seat; Pop. 5,961; Zip Code 62837; Elev. 451; SE Illinois. Fairfield was settled in 1819 when a group of pioneers arrived with their wagons and declared "there was no fairer field for farms." The name was derived from this epitaph.

•**FAIRMOUNT**, Village, Vermillion County; Pop. 2,313; Zip Code 61841; SW Illinois.

•**FAIRMONT CITY**, Village, St. Clair County; Pop. 2,313 ; Zip Code 62201; Elev. 420; SW Illinois.

•**FARMER CITY**, City, De Witt County; Pop. 2,225; Zip Code 61842; Central Illinois. Farmer City has been variously known as Mount Pleasant, Hurley's Grove, and Santa Ana, but acquired its present name in 1869 just before the railroad laid its tracks through the settlement. Since the entire population consisted of farmers, the present name was adopted.

•**FINDLAY**, Village, Shelby County; Pop. 862; Zip Code 62534; Central Illinois.

•**FISHER**, Village, Champaign County; Pop. 1,573; Zip Code 61843; E Illinois. Named after town founder, Robert Fisher.

•**FITHIAN**, Village, Vermilion County; Pop. 540; Zip Code 61844; E Illinois. Named for Dr. William Fithian, early Danville settler and friend of Abraham Lincoln.

•**FLANAGAN**, Village, Livingston County; Pop. 972; Zip Code 61740; N Central Illinois.

•**FLORA**, City, Clay County; Pop. 5,390; Zip Code 62839; Elev. 490; Lat. 38-54-06 Nlong. 087-40-18 w; S Central Illinois. Flora named for the daughter of one of the founders, grew with the coming of the railroad in 1854.

•**FLOSSMOOR**, (alt. FLOSSMORE), Village, Cook County; Pop. 8,398; Zip Code 60422; NE Illinois. The name of the village is of Scotch derivation. It means "gently rolling countryside," an apt description for this golfer's paradise.

•**FOREST PARK**, Village, Cook County; Pop. 15,133; Zip Code 60130; Elev. 620; Lat. 41-52-46 N long. 087-48-49 W; W of Chicago and on the Des Plaines River.

•**FORREST**, Village, Livingston County; Pop. 1,242; Zip Code 61741; Elev. 688; E Central Illinois. Named for a banker who was a friend of the first railroad company to come to the area.

•**FORRESTON**, Village, Ogle County; Pop. 1,389; Zip Code 61030; Elev. 931; N Illinois. Descriptively named for the area's once forested hills.

•**FOX LAKE**, Village, Lake & McHenry Counties; Pop. 6,831; Zip Code 60020; Elev. 745; NE Illinois. Fox Lake was founded in 1839, incorporated in 1906, and named for the nearby lake.

•**FOX RIVER GROVE**, Village, McHenry County; Pop. 2,513 ; Zip Code 60021; Elev. 771; NE Illinois.

•**FRANKFORT**, Village, Will County; Pop. 4,348; Zip Code 60423; NE Illinois. Frankfort was named for its counterpart, Franfort-am-Main in Germany.

•**FRANKLIN PARK**, Village, Cook County; Pop. 17,554; Zip Code 60131; NE Illinois. Named for a 19th Century Chicago real estate developer.

•**FREEBURG**, Village, St. Clair County; Pop. 2,958; Zip Code 62243; SW Illinois.

•**FREEPORT**, City, Stephenson County seat; Pop. 26,062; Zip Code 61032; Elev. 781; N Illinois. Named by the wife of an early founder, who complained of many visitors coming to "Freeport."

•**FULTON**, City, Whiteside County; Pop. 3,925; Zip Code 61252; Elev. 597; NW Illinois. Fulton, an old river town founded in 1839, was named for the inventor of the steamboat, Robert Fulton (1765-815).

•**GALATIA**, Village, Saline County; Pop. 1,023; Zip Code 62935; Elev. 397; Lat. 37-50-26 N long. 088-36-33 W; SE Illinois.

•**GALENA**, City, Jo Daviess County seat; Pop. 3,897; Zip Code 61030; Elev. 603; Lat. 42-25-00 N long. 090-25-44 W; NW corner of Illinois; In about 1700 a Frenchman, Le Sueur, discovered that the local Indians were mining lead on the site. In 1807 the mines were placed under U.S. government protection. In 1826, by which time it had become more than a lead-mining camp, the town was laid out and named Galena, which is also the name for the sulphide lead ore extracted from the bedrock of the district.

•**GIBSON CITY**, City, SE Ford County; Pop. 3,504; Zip Code 60936; NE Central Illinois; Named after the founder's wife.

•**GIFFORD**, Village, Champaign County; Pop. 848; Zip Code 61847; E Central Illinois.

•**GILLESPIE**, City, SE Macoupin County; Pop. 3,719; Zip Code 62033; W Illinois.

•**GILMAN**, City, Iroquois County; Pop. 1,913; Zip Code 60938; Elev. 654; E Illinois; Named for an early settler.

•GIRARD, City, Macoupin County; Pop. 2,224; Zip Code 62640; SW Central Illinois; the personal name of a pioneer.

•GLASFORD, Town, Peoria County; Pop. 1,216; Zip code 61539; NW Central Illinois; Named for 19th century farmer Samuel Glasford.

•GLENCOE, Village, Cook County; Pop. 9,162; Zip Code 60022; Elev. 673; NE Illinois; Founded in 1836 and incorporated as a village in 1869; Name is a composite of "glen" suggestive of the site, and "coe" the maiden name of the wife of one of the founders, Walter S. Gurnee.

•GLENDALE HEIGHTS, City, Du Page County; Pop. 23,089; Zip Code 60137; NE Illinois; Given the name by its incorporators in 1959.

•GLEN ELLYN, Village, Du Page County; Pop. 23,852; Zip Code 60137; Elev. 766; NE Illinois; Originally a stage coach stop, Glen Ellyn was named after the wife, Ellyn, of one of the founders and the glen at the bottom of Cooper Hill; The new town was platted in 1851.

•GLENVIEW, Village, Cook County; Pop. 30,322; Zip Code 60025; NE Illinois; the village is named an early road.

•GLENWOOD, Village, Cook County; Pop. 10,425; Zip Code 60425; NE Ilinois; Settled in 1846 and named for the wooded glens then in existence.

•GODFREY, Village, Madison County; Pop.4000 ; Zip Code 62035; Elev. 438; SW Illinois; Named after Benjamin Godfrey, a retired Cape Cod sea captain, the community was founded in 1835.

•GOOD HOPE, Town, McDonough County; Pop. 448 ; Zip code 61438; Elev. 714; W Illinois; 6 miles N of Macomb. Naming Good Hope was a project in itself; It was platted as Sheridan in 1866 by J. E. Morris. The following year W. F. Blandin built a rival town bordering it to the west and called it Milan. The local post office, however, was already called Good Hope. Confusion set in as railway tickets went by the name Sheridan, conductors called out Milan, and all mail was addressed to Good Hope. To top it all off, some local residents went by the original name which was Clarkesville. The name Good Hope was finally agreed upon by all.

•GRAFTON, Town, Jersey County; Pop. 1020 ; Zip Code 62037; Elev. 446; Lat. 38-58-12 N long. 090-25-53 W; SW Illinois; On the confluence of the Mississippi and Illinois rivers.

•GRAND RIDGE, Village, La Salle County; Pop.681; Zip Code 61325; N Illinois; 8 miles S of Ottawa.

•GRAND TOWER, Town, Jackson County; Pop.727; Zip Code 62942; Elev. 367; Lat. 41-53-48 N long. 089-24-42 W; SW Illinois; The town was named for Tower Rock (q.v.), a natural stone sentinel 60 feet in height, in the Mississippi River.

•GRANITE CITY, City, Madison County; Pop. 36,257 ; Zip Code 62040; Elev. 431; Lat. 38-42-05 N long. 090-08-55 W; SW Illinois; Became an important city at the turn of the century, and was named for granite ware, its first product.

•GRANT PARK, Village, NE Kankakee County; Zip Code 60940; NE Illinois.

•GRANVILLE, City, Putnam County; Pop. 5209 ; Zip Code 61326; N Central Illinois.

•GRAYSLAKE, City, Lake County; Pop. 5241 ; Zip Code 60030; Elev. 799; NE corner of Illinois; Named for the lake at its western edge.

•GRAYVILLE, City, Edwards & White Counties; Pop. 2,313; Zip Code 62844; SE Illinois; On the Wabash River. Named for settler Thomas Gray.

•GREENFIELD, City, Greene County; Pop.1094; Zip Code 62044; W Illinois.

•GREEN OAKS, Village, Lake County Pop. 1408; Zip Code 60048; NE Illinois; E of Libertyville.

•GREEN ROCK, City, Henry County; Pop. 3298; Zip Code 61241; NW Illinois; On the Rock River just E of Moline.

•GREENUP, City, Cumberland County; Pop. ; Zip Code 62428; Elev. 554; E Illinois; Named for William C. Greenup, first clerk of the Illinois Territorial Legislature; Incorporated 1836.

•GREENVIEW, Village, Menard County; Pop. 819; Zip Code 62642; Central Illinois; 20 miles NW of Springfield.

•GREENVILLE, City, Bond County seat; Pop. 5209; Zip Code 62246; Elev. 563; Lat. 38-53-32 N long. 089-24-47 W; 47 miles ENE of East Saint Louis.

•GRIDLEY, Town, McLean County; Pop. 1241; Zip Code 61744; Elev. 752; Lat. 40-44-36 Nlong. 088-52-53 W; Central Illinois; Named for Asahel Gridley (1810-1881), a Civil War brigadier general from New York.

•GRIGGSVILLE, Town, Pike County; Pop. 1,185; Zip Code 62340; W Illinois; 5 miles W of the Illinois River; Named in honor of 1833 settler Richard Griggs.

•GURNEE, City, Lake County; Pop. 7003; Zip Code 60031; Lat. 39-53-57 N long. 090-03-00 W; E Illinois; On the shore of Lake Michigan and just N of Waukegan. Named for Walter S. Gurnee, one of city's founders.

•HAMBURG, Town, Hancock County; Pop. 163; Zip Code 62341; Elev. 510; Lat. 38-51-58 N long. 089-16-29 W; W Illinois; Founded 1852 by Artois Hamilton; Named for the German city.

•HAMMOND, Town, Piatt County; Pop. 557; Zip Code 61929; Elev. 678; Lat. 39-47-49 N long. 088-35-30 W; Central Illinois; Settled 1855.

•HAMPSHIRE, Town, Kane County; Pop. 1,732; Zip Code 60140; Elev. 900; Lat. 42-05-52 N long. 088-31-49 W; NE Illinois; Founded 1875 when Chicago, Milwaukee, St. Paul, and Pacific Railroad reached here; Once called Henpeck.

•HANOVER, town, Jo Daviess County; Pop. 1,083; Zip Code 61041; Elev. 630; Lat. 42-15-23 N long. 090-16-46 W; NW Illinois; Founded 1828 by Daniel Fowler and Charles Ames, named for Hanover, New Hampshire.

•HANOVER PARK, City, Cook and DuPage counties; Pop. 28,790; Zip Code 60103; Elev. 800; Lat. 41-59-58 N long. 088-08-42 W; NE Illinois.

•HARDIN, Town, Calhoun County Seat; Pop. 1,111; Zip Code 62047; Elev. 436; Lat. 39-09-24 N long. 090-37-04 W; W Illinois; Named to honor Col. John J. Hardin, killed leading a charge of the First Illinois Volunteers to Buena Vista during the Mexican War.

•HARRISBURG, City, Saline County Seat; Pop. 10,344; Zip Code 62946; Elev. 403; Lat. 37-44-18 N long. 088-32-26 W; SE Illinois; First settled by a sawmill proprietor, James Harris.

•HARTFORD, Town, Madison County; Pop. 1,877; Zip Code 62048; Elev. 420; Lat. 38-50-00 N long. 090-05-45 W; SW Illinois.

126

•**HARVARD**, City, McHenry County; Pop. 5,151; Zip Code 60033; Elev. 966; Lat. 42-25-20 N long. 088-36-49 W; NE Illinois; Incorporated 1869 and named for the American university.

•**HARVEY**, City, Cook County; Pop. 35,359; Zip Code 60426; Elev. 600; Lat. 41-36-36 N long. 087-38-48 W; Founded 1890 by Turlington W. Harvey, a Chicago land developer; Incorporated 1894.

•**HARWOOD HEIGHTS**, City, Cook County; Pop. 8,229; Zip Code 60656; Elev. 650; Lat. 41-58-02 N long. 087-48-27 W; NE Illinois; incorporated 1947. Name contrived from the "Har" of Harlem and the "wood" of Norwood Park Township.

•**HAVANA**, City, Mason County Seat; Pop. 2,681; Zip Code 62644; Elev. 470; Lat. 40-18-00 N long. 090-03-39 W; Central Illinois. Founded 1822 by Maj. Ossian M. Ross, a veteran of the War of 1812 and named for the capital of Cuba.

•**HAZEL CREST**, City, Cook County; Pop. 13,960; Zip Code 60429; Elev. 648; Lat. 41-34-18 N long. 087-41-40 W; NE Illinois Named for the hazel bushes found on the local area.

•**HAZEL DELL**, Town, Cumberland County; Pop. 13,960; Zip Code 62430; Elev. 600; Lat. 39-12-08 N long. 088-02-28 W; SE Central Illinois.

•**HAZEL GREEN**, Town, Cook County; Pop. 13,960; Zip Code 60482; Elev. 593; Lat. 41-41-00 N long. 087-44-24 W; NE Illinois.

•**HEBRON**, Town, McHenry County; Pop. 786; Zip Code 60034; Elev. 930; Lat. 42-28-18 N long. 088-25-56 EW; NE Illinois; named for the Biblical city.

•**HENNEPIN**, Town, Putnam County Seat; Pop. 713; Zip Code 61327; Elev. 500; Lat. 41-15-15 N long. 089-20-32 W; N Central Illiois; Named for Father Louis Hennepin (1660-1701), a Flemish missionary who was among the first Europeans to explore the region.

•**HENRY**, Town, Marshall County; Pop. 2,719; Zip Code 61537; Elev. 495; Lat. 41-06-41 N long. 089-21-23 W; N Central Illinois; Settled 1833; Named for Gen. James D. Henry of Black Hawk War fame.

•**HERRIN**, City, Williamson County; Pop. 10,151; Zip Code 62948; Elev. 420; Lat. 37-48-11 N long. 089-01-39 W; S Central Illinois.

•**HEYWORTH**, Town, McLean County; Pop. 1,592; Zip Code 61745; Elev. 749; Lat. 40-18-48 N long. 088-58-25 W; Central Illinois. Named for Laurence Heyworth, former member of Parliament and one of a group of English stockholders in the railroad.

•**HICKORY HILLS**, City, Cook County; Pop. 13,764; Zip Code 60457; Elev. 675; Lat. 41-43-32 N long. 087-49-30 W; NE Illinois; 15 miles SW of Chicago; Named by its incorporators in 1951.

•**HIGHLAND**, City, Madison County; Pop. 7,069; Zip Code 62249; Elev. 545; Lat. 38-44-22 N long. 089-40-16 W; SW Illinois; Named for its slightly higher elevation over the surrounding area.

•**HIGHLAND PARK**, City, Lake County; Pop. 30,260; Zip Code 60035; Elev. 690; Lat. 42-10-54 N long. 087-48-01 W; NE Illinois; first settled in 1847 as Port Clinton and Saint Johns; Named by Walter Gurnee, mayor of Chicago (1852-53) who bought the site in 1854.

•**HIGHWOOD**, City, Lake County; Pop. 5,344; Zip Code 60040; Elev. 685; Lat. 42-11-59 N long. 087-48-33 W; NE Illinois.

•**HILLSIDE**, City, Cook County; Pop. 8,263; Zip Code 60162; Elev. 659; Lat. 41-52-40 N long. 087-54-10 W; NE Illinois. Named by railroad 1905.

•**HINCKLEY**, Town, DeKalb County; Pop. 1,450; Zip Code 60520; Elev. 750; Lat. 41-46-08 N long. 088-38-27 W; N Central Illinois; Named for F.G. Hinckley, a 19th century railroad official.

•**HINSDALE**, City, DuPage and Cook counties; Pop. 16,715; Zip Code 60521; Elev. 725; Lat. 41-48-03 N long. 087-56-13 W; NE Illinois. Named for H. W. Hinsdale, a director of the Burlington Railroad; Incorporated 1873.

•**HODGKINS**, Town, Cook County; Pop. 1,972; Zip Code 60525; Elev. 600; Lat. 41-46-08 N long. 087-51-28 W; NE Illinois.

•**HOMETOWN**, City, Cook County; Pop. 5,297; Zip Code 60456; Elev. 620; Lat. 41-44-04 N long. 087-43-53 W; NE Illinois; SW suburb of Chicago; Named by its developers in 1950.

•**HOMEWOOD**, City, Cook County; Pop. 19,639; Zip Code 60430; Elev. 650; Lat. 41-33-26 N long. 087-39-56; NE Illinois; 22 miles SE of Chicago.

•**HOOPESTON**, City, Vermilion County; Pop. 6,391; Zip Cod 60942; Elev. 718; Lat. 40-28-02 N long. 087-40-06 W; E Illinois, Platted by three land companies in 1871 on the farm of Thomas Hoopes.

•**HOOPPOLE**, Town, Henry County; Pop. 237; Zip Code 61258; Elev. 620; Lat. 41-31-12 N long. 089-54-35 W; On the Green River; Received its name from the practice of coopers who cut hickory bands for their barrels in a nearby grove.

•**HOPEDALE**, Town, Tazewell County; Pop. 914; Zip Code 61747; Elev. 630; Lat. 40-25-15 N long. 089-24-52 W; Central Illinois.

•**HUNTLEY**, Town, McHenry County; Pop. 1,629; Zip Code 60142; Elev. 900; Lat. 42-10-05 N long. 088-25-41 W; NE Illinois; Founded 1851 by Thomas Stilwell Huntley as a station for the New Chicago and Northwestern Railway.

•**ILLIOPOLIS**, Town, Sangamon County; Pop. 1,123; Zip Code 62539; Elev. 602; Lat. 39-51-13 N long. 089-14-31 W; W Central Illinois.

•**INDIAN CREEK**, Town, Lake County; Pop. 235; Zip Code 60060; Elev. 741; Lat. 42-13-37 N long. 087-58-47 W; NE Illinois; Located on creek of same name, which is tributary of the Des Plaines River near Half Day.

•**INDUSTRY**, Town, McDonough County; Pop. 600; Zip Code 61440; Elev. 660; Lat. 40-19-40 N long. 090-36-25 W; W Illinois.

•**INVERNES**, Town, Cook County; Pop. 3,678; Zip Code 60067; Elev. 853; Lat. 42-07-05 N long. 088-05-46 W. Named after the place in Scotland.

•**IROQUOIS**, Town, Iroquois County; Pop. 227; Zip Code 60945; Elev. 660; Lat. 40-49-39 N long. 087-34-55 W; E Illinois; Name derived from Iroquois River, which was named because of an ancient battle that took place on its banks between the Iroquois and Illinois Indians.

•**IRVING**, Town, Montgomery County; Pop. 618; Zip Code 62051; Elev. 656; Lat. 39-12-21 N long. 089-24-16 W; SW Central Illinois.

•**IRVINGTON**, Town, Washington County; Pop. 772; Zip Code 62848; Elev. 530; Lat. 38-26-21 N long. 089-09-46 W.

•**ISLAND LAKE**, Town, Lake and McHenry Counties; Pop. 2,285; Zip Code 60042; Elev. 780; Lat. 42-16-34 N long. 088-11-31 W; NE Illinois; On a small lake created by damming Cotton Creek in 1936; Incorporated 1954.

•**ITASCA**, City, DuPage and Cook Counties; Pop. 7,720; Zip Code 60143; Elev. 686; Lat. 41-58-30 long. 088-00-26 W; NE Illinois, 20 miles WNW of Chicago.

•IUKA, Town, Marion County; Pop. 340; Zip Code 62849; Elev. 518; Lat. 38-36-58 N long. 088-47-25 W; S Central Illinois; Once named Middleton, name was changed by legislature in 1867 at request of the soldiers who had been in a battle of Iuka in the Civil War; Name is from Choctaw Indian word *i yuk hana*, meaning "where two roads cross."

•JACKSONVILLE, City, Morgan County Seat; Pop. 20,174; Zip Code 62650; Elev. 613; Lat. 39-44-02 N long. 090-13-44 W; W Illinois; Settled 1819 by brothers Seymour and Elisha Kellogg, veterans of the War of 1812; Incorporated 1867; Named for Gen. Andrew Jackson (1767-1845), seventh president of the U.S.

•JAMAICA, Town, Vermilion County; Pop. 281; Zip Code 61841; Elev. 677; Lat. 39-59-28 N long. 087-48-24 W; E Illinois; Near Fairmont; Named for island in the West Indies; Name may also be derived from that of an Arawakan tribe, Yamaye, which inhabited the island.

•JOHNSTON CITY, Town, Williamson County; Pop. 3,859; Zip Code 62951; Elev. 432; Lat. 37-49-14 N long. 088-55-39 W; S Central Illinois; Named for an early settler.

•JOLIET, City, Will County Seat; Pop. 78,165; Zip Code 60431; Elev. 564; Lat. 41-31-13 N long. 088-04-54 W; NE Illinois; Discovered by Father Mrquette and Louis Joliet 1673; Post office established 1833 and named Juliet; Name changed 1845 by legislature.

•JONESBORO, Town, Union County Seat; Pop. 1,845; Zip Code 62952; Elev. 568; Lat. 37-27-06 N long. 089-16-05 W; SE Illinois; 30 miles SW of Marion; First settled 1803.

•KANKAKEE, City; Kankakee County Seat; Pop. 29,812; Zip Code 60901; Elev. 663; Lat. 41-07-12 N long. 087-51-40 W; NE Illinois; Named for the river, word may be a corruption of a Potawatomi Indian word, *teh-yak-ki-ki*, meaning "swampy country."

•KANSAS, Town Edgar County; Pop. 793; Zip Code 61933; Elev. 710; Lat. 39-33-10 N long. 087-56-22 W; E Illinois; Named for Kansas Indians, a tribe of Siouan stock.

•KEITHSBURG, Town, Mercer County; Pop. 939; Zip Code 61442; Elev. 549; Lat. 41-05-58 N long. 090-56-33 W; NW Illinois; Named for a pioneer.

•KENILWORTH, Town, Cook County; Pop. 2,702; Zip Code 60043; Elev. 615; Lat. 42-05-09 N long. 087-43-03 W; NE Illinois; 17 miles NW of Chicago.

•KEWANEE, City, Henry County; Pop. 14,484; Zip Code 61443; Elev. 820; Lat. 41-14-44 N long. 089-55-29 W; NW Illinois; 38 miles ESE of Rock Island. Name derived from Ottawa Indian word, *ke-won-nee*, meaning "pairie hen."

•KILBOURNE, Town, Mason County; Pop. 378; Zip Code 62655; Elev. 493. Lat. 40-09-07 N long. 090-00-36 W.

•KILDEER, Town, Lake County; Pop. 1,597; Zip Code 60047; Elev. 780; Lat. 42-10-14 N long. 088-02-52 W; NE Illinois.

•KINCAID, Town, Christian County; Pop. 1,596; Zip Code 62540; Elev. 601; Lat. 39-35-19 N long. 089-24-52 W; Central Illinois; Named for James R. Kincaid of Springfield, a planner of the town.

•KIRKLAND, Town, DeKalb County; Pop. 1,151; Zip Code 60146; Elev. 7648; Lat. 42-05-33 N long. 088-51-04 W; NW Illinois.

•KIRKWOOD, Town, Warren County; Pop. 1,006; Zip Code 62447; Elev. 758; Lat. 40-51-57 N long. 090-44-54 W; NW Illinois.

•KNOXVILLE, Town, Knox County; Pop. 3,430; Zip Code 61484; Elev. 755; Lat. 40-45-29 N long. 089-46-55 W; W Illinois; Named in honor of Revolutionary War general Henry Knox.

•LADD, Town, Bureau County; Pop. 1,339; Zip Code 61329; Elev. 651; N Central Illinois; Founded 1890, and named after railroad builder George Ladd.

•LA GRANGE, City, Cook County; Pop. 15,349; Zip Code 60525; Elev. 650; NE Illinois; Named for LaGrange, Tennessee, former home of city's first president, Franklin D. Cossitt.

•LA GRANGE PARK, City, Cook County; Pop. 13,418; Zip Code 60525; Elev. 625; NE Illinois, named after nearby LaGrange.

•LA HARPE, Town, Hancock County; Pop. 1,459; Zip Code 61450; Elev. 691; W Illinois; Founded by and named for Benard de la Harpe, who headed a band of French explorers who tried to cross the 100 miles of trail from Fort Creve Coeur, at Peoria to the Mississippi River and were stopped here by storms in the mid-1700s.

•LAKE BLUFF, City, Lake County; Pop. 4,378; Zip Code 60044; Elev. 671; NE Illinois, descriptively named for its location on a bluff overlooking Lake Michigan.

•LAKE VILLA, Town, Lake County; Pop. 1,412; Zip Code 60046; Elev. 800; NE Illinois, named for the many nearby lakes.

•LAKEWOOD, Town, McHenry County; Pop. 1,242; Zip Code 60014; Elev. 894; NE Illinois; Near Crystal Lake.

•LAKE ZURICH, City, Lake County; Pop. 8,222; Zip Code 60047; Elev. 860; NE Illinois. Settled 1836 by *Daniel Wright*, a veteran of War of 1812; Incorporated 1896, and named for the Swiss city.

•LANSING, City, Cook County; Pop. 28,966; Zip Code 60438; Elev. 630; NE Illinois; Founded 1864 by brothers *John* and *Henry Lansing*.

•LEMONT, City, Cook and DuPage counties; Pop. 5,638; Zip Code 60439; Elev. 606; Lat. 41-40-25 N long. 088-00-06 W; NE Illinois; Name is French word meaning "mountain;" Incorporated June 9, 1873.

•LENA, Town, Stephenson County; Pop. 2,302; Zip Code 61048; Elev. 950; Lat. 42-22-46 N long. 089-49-20 W; N Central Illinois, 10 miles south of the Wisconsin line.

•LEXINGTON, Town, McLean County; Pop. 1,799; Zip Code 61753; Elev. 754; Lat. 40-38-29 N long. 088-47-00 W; Central Illinois,; named after the Revolutionary War battle.

•LIBERTYVILLE, City, Lake County; Pop. 16,487; Zip Code 60048; Elev. 700; Lat. 42-16-59 N long. 087-57-11 W; NE Illinois; Post office established April 16, 1838, and patriotically named.

•LINCOLN, City, Logan County Seat; Pop. 16,306; Zip Code 62656; Elev. 591; Lat. 40-08-54 N long. 089-21-53 W; W Illinois; 30 miles NNE of Springfield; Founded 1853; Named for Abraham Lincoln.

•LINCOLNSHIRE, Town, Lake County; Pop. 3,771; Zip Code 60015; Elev. 675; NE Illinois; 25 miles NW of Chicago on the Des Plaines River; Incorporated 1957, and named for Abe Lincoln.

•LINCOLNWOOD, City, Cook County; Pop. 11,850; Zip Code 60645; Elev. 600; Lat. 42-00-16 N long. 087-43-48 W; North of Chicago; Incorporated September 29, 1911, and named for President Abe Lincoln.

•LINDENHURST, City, Lake County; Pop. 6,202; Zip Code 60046; Elev. 800; Lat. 42-24-38 N long. 088-01-34 W; NE Illinois; named after the farm purchased for subdivision.

•LISLE, City, DuPage County; Pop. 13,622; Zip Code 60532; Elev. 682; Lat. 41-48-04 N long. 088-04-29 W; NE Illinois.

•LITCHFIELD, City, Montgomery County; Pop. 7,188; Zip Code 62056; Elev. 680; Lat. 41-09-48 N long. 087-35-12 W;S Central Illinois; Founded by and named for *Electus Bachus Litchfield*, born in Delphi, New York, in 1813.

•LOAMI, Town, Sangamon County; Pop. 770; Zip Code 62661; Elev. 630; Lat. 39-40-32 N long. 0898-50-48 W; W Central Illinois; Incorporated July 29, 1875.

•LOCKPORT, City, Will County; Pop. 8,883; Zip Code 60441; Elev. 604; Lat. 41-35-22 N long. 088-03-28 W; NE Illinois; site of locks that reverse the flow of the Chicago River, and of the device that raises the water level so that shipping can clear the divide between the Mississippi and St. Laurence valleys.

•LOMAX, Town, Henderson County; Pop. 605; Zip Code 61454; Elev. 550; Lat. 40-40-44 N long. 091-04-22 W; W Illinois; Incorporated November 4, 1913, and named for a prominent citizen.

•LOMBARD, City, DuPage County; Pop. 37,389; Zip Code 60148; Elev. 700; Lat. 41-52-48 N long. 088-00-28 W; NE Illinois; Incorporated March 29, 1869. First white settler was *Winslow Churchill* (1834). City was named for *Josiah Lombard,* who platted the town in the early 1860s.

•LONDON MILLS, Town, Fulton and Knox counties; Pop. 584; Zip Code 61544; Elev. 534; Lat. 40-42-38 N long. 090-15-58 W; W Central Illinois; Incorporated November 27, 1883.

•LOSTANT, Town, LaSalle County; Pop. 535; Zip Code 61334; Elev. 700; Incorporated February 16, 1865.

•LOUISVILLE, Town, Clay County Seat; Pop. 1,169; Zip Code 62858; Elev. 480; SE Central Illinois; Incorporated March 1, 1867; Named for a man called Lewis who owned a gristmill on the Little Wabash River.

•LOVES PARK, City, Winnebago County; Pop. 13,151; Zip Code 61111; Elev. 740; N Central Illinois; Incorporated April 30, 1947; Named for *Malcolm Love,* who bought 9,236-acre farm on the Rock River just north of Rockford.

•LYNDON, Town, Whiteside County; Pop. 782; Zip Code 61261; Elev. 614; NW Illinois; Incorporated March 3, 1874, named for a pioneer.

•LYNWOOD, Town, Cook County; Pop. 4,161; Zip Code 60411; NE Illinois; Incorporated December 23, 1959, and named by its developers.

•LYONS, City, Cook county; Pop. 9,888; Zip Code 60534; Elev. 625; NE Illinois; Post office established February 29, 1848; named after Lyons, France.

•MACKINAW, Town, Tazewell County; Pop. 1,338; Zip Code 61755; Elev. 680; Central Illinois; Incorporated January 21, 1840; Name is an Ojibway Indian word meaning "turtle."

•MACOMB, City McDonough County Seat; Pop. 19,847; Zip Code 61455; Elev. 700; W Illinois; First settled 1830 as Washington, later named for *Alexander Macomb,* Comander-in-Chief of the U.S. Army, 1828-41; Incorporated January 27, 1841.

•MACON, Town, Macon County; Pop. 1,295; Zip Code 62544; Elev. 721; Central Illinois; Reached by US 51; Founded 1835; Incorporated April 15, 1869, and named for the county.

•MADISON, City, Madison County; Pop. 5,900; Zip Code 62060; Elev. 410; SW Illinois; Named in honor of President James Madison.

•MAKANDA, Town, Jackson County; Pop. 407; Zip Code 62958; Elev. 437; Incorporated February 7, 1888.

•MANCHESTER, Town, Scott County; Pop. 387; Zip Code 62663; Elev. 696; Lat. 39-32-32 N long. 090-19-56 W; Incorporated February 21, 1861, and named for the English city.

•MANHATTAN, Town, Will County; Pop. 1,936; Zip Code 60442; Elev. 690; Lat. 541-25-21 N long. 087-59-09 w; NE Illinois; Incorporated December 20, 1886; Named for New York Island.

•MANITO, Town, Mason County; Pop. 1,803; Zip Code 61546; Elev. 500; Lat. 40-25-33 Nlong. 089-46-45 W; Central Illinois; Name is Algonquin Indian word meaning "the Great Spirit."

•MANSFIELD, Town, Piatt County; Pop. 918; Zip Code 61854; Elev. 727; E Central Illinois; Incorporated March 3, 1876, Named for a prominent citizen.

•MANTENO, Town, Kankakee County; Pop. 3,150; Zip Code 60950; Elev. 680; Lat. 41-15-02 N long. 087-49-53 W; E Illinois; Incorporated April 20, 1878; Named for half-Indian daughter of *Francois Bourbonnais, Jr.,* a nineteenth-century French scout for whom a Kankakee River village is named.

•MARINE, Town, Madison County; Pop. 956; Zip Code 62061; Elev. 528; Lat. 38-47-11 N long. 089-46-39 W; SW Illinois; Incorporated March 8, 1867.

•MARISSA, Town, St. Clair County; Pop. 2,577; Zip Code 62257; Elev. 448; Lat. 38-15-00 N long. 089-45-00 W; SW Illinois; Incorporated May 26, 1882; Named by an early settler from South Carolina, *James Wilson,* who picked it from his copy of Josephus' *History of the Jews.*

•MARKHAM, City, Cook County; Pop. 14,852; Zip Code 60426; Elev. 615; Lat. 41-35-37 N long. 087-41-41 W; NE Illinois; Incorporated October 23, 1925; Named for a former president of the Illinois Central Railroad.

•MAROA, Town, Macon County; Pop. 1,725; Zip Code 61756; Elev. 710; Lat. 40-02-11 N long. 088-57-25 W; Central Illinois; Incorporated March 7, 1867; Named when members of town council pulled letters from a hat.

•MARSEILLES, Town, LaSalle County; Pop. 4,716; Zip Code 61341; Elev. 504; Lat. 41-19-51 N long. 088-42-29 W; N Central Illinois; Incorporated February 21, 1861; Name, pronounced "Marsales," is taken from the old Mediterranean port.

•MARSHALL, Town, Clark County Seat; Pop. 3,461; Zip Code 62441; Elev. 641; Lat. 39-23-29 N long. 087-41-37 W; E Illinois; Incorporated February 10, 1853; Named for *John Marshall,* Chief Justice of U.S. Supreme Court.

•MARTINSVILLE, Town, Clark County; Pop. 1,304; Zip Code 62442; Elev. 574; Lat. 39-20-08 N long. 087-52-55 W; E Illinois; Platted 1833 by *Joseph Martin* on the north fork of the Embarras River.

•MARYVILLE, Town, Madison County; Pop. 1,928; Zip Code 62062; Elev. 582; SW Illinois; Named for the wife of a prominent citizen.

•MASCOUTAH, City, St. Clair County; Pop. 4,987; Zip Code 62258; Elev. 424; SW Illinois; Incorporated February 16, 1839; Name is Algonquin Indian word meaning "prairie."

•MASON, Town, Effingham County; Pop. 476; Zip Code 62443; Elev. 594; Lat. 38-57-11 N long. 088-37-25 W; Incorporated February 15, 1865.

•**MASON CITY**, Town, Mason County; Pop. 2,713; Zip Code 62664; Elev. 570; Lat. 40-12-08 N long. 089-41-53 W; Central Illinois; 28 miles north of Springfield; Platted 1857.

•**MATTESON**, City, Cook County; Pop. 10,177; Zip Code 60443; Elev. 701; Lat. 41-30-14 N long. 087-42-47 W; NE Illinois; Founded by German settlers in the 1850s; Named for *Gov. Joel A. Matteson.*

•**MATTOON**, City, Coles County; Pop. 19,075; Zip Code 61938; Elev. 726; Lat. 39-28-59 N long. 088-22-22 W; E Central Illinois; Named the engineer in charge of construction, *William Mattoon.*

•**MAYWOOD**, City, Cook County; Pop. 27,978; Zip Code 60153; Elev. 626; Lat. 41-52-45 N long. 087-50-35 W; NE Illinois; Founded 1860s by a group of New Englanders headed by *Col. W. T. Nichols,* who named settlement for his daughter May.

•**MAZON**, Town, Grundy County; Pop. 832; Zip Code 60444; Elev. 586; Lat. 41-14-29 N long. 088-25-10 W; NE Illinois; Incorporated April 30, 1895.

•**McHENRY**, City, McHenry County; Pop. 1,041; Zip Code 60050; Elev. 761; NE Illinois; On the Fox River, City was named for an army officer in the War of 1812 and the Black Hawk War of 1832.

•**McLEAN**, Town, McLean County; Pop. 830; Zip Code 61754; Elev. 700; Central Illinois; Incorporated January 23, 1873.

•**MECHANICSBURG**, Town, Sangamon County; Pop. 518; Zip Code 62545; Elev. 595; Lat. 39-48-34 N long. 089-23-50 W; Incorporated March 26, 1869; Once called Clear Creek.

•**MELROSE PARK**, City, Cook County; Pop. 20,460; Zip Code 60160; Elev. 640; Lat. 41-54-02 N long. 087-51-24 W; NE Illinois; named by its incorporators in the 1880s.

•**MENDOTA**, City, LaSalle County; Pop. 7,145; Zip Code 61342; Elev. 740; Lat. 41-32-50 N long. 089-07-03 W; N Central Illinois; Name comes from Dakota Indian word, *mdote,* meaning "mouth" or "junction of one river with another."

•**MEREDOSIA**, Town, Morgan County; Pop. 1,291; Zip Code 62665; Elev. 446; Lat. 39-49-52 N long. 090-33-34 W; W Central Illinois; At mouth of Meredosia Lake, Name said to be a corruption of the French *marais d'osier,* meaning "swamp of basket reeds."

•**MERRIONETTE PARK**, Town, Cook County; Pop. 2,047; Zip Code 60655; Elev. 620; Lat. 41-41-03 N long. 087-42-01 W; NE Illinois; Named for its sub-divider, J.E. Merrion.

•**METAMORA**, Town, Woodford County; Pop. 2,486; Zip Code 61548; Elev. 821; Lat. 40-47-26 N long. 089-21-38 W; N Central Illinois; Once called Black Partridge and Hanover, the final name was coined by playwright *John Stone,* as the name for *King Philip,* son of *Chief Massasoit,* killed 1676, in a popular play called "Metamora, or the Last of the Wampanoags."

•**METROPOLIS**, City; Massac County Seat; Pop. 7,124; Zip Code 62960; Elev. 345; Lat. 37-09-04 N long. 088-43-55 W; On Ohio River NW of Paducah, Kentucky, SE Illinois tip; named by developer William McBane when he founded the town in the 1830s.

•**METTAWA**, Town, Lake County; Pop. 325; Zip Code 60048; Elev. 675; Lat. 42-14-00 N long. 087-55-33 W; Incorporated January 25, 1960; Name is that of a Potawatomi chief.

•**MIDLOTHIAN**, City, Cook County; Pop. 14,174; Zip Code 60445; Elev. 615; Lat. 41-37-31 N long. 087-43-03 W; NE Illinois; Named

for a golf club built here in 1898 by *George R. Thorne,* then head of Montgomery Ward, and named for a shire in Scotland.

•**MILAN**, Town, Rock Island County; Pop. 6,248; Zip Code 61264; Elev. 570; Lat. 41-27-11 N long. 090-34-19 W; 4NW Illinois; Named for the Italian city.

•**MILFORD**, Town, Iroquois County; Pop. 1,711; Zip Code 60953; Elev. 670; Lat. 40-37-42 N long. 087-41-46 W; E Illinois; Named for a mill near a ford at the Hubbard Trail crossing of Sugar Creek.

•**MILLBURN**, Town, Lake County; Zip Code 60046: Lat. 42-25-33 N long. 088-00-14 W; Post office established January 24, 1848; Once called Strong's Neighborhood.

•**MILLEDGEVILLE**, Town, Carroll County; Pop. 1,222; Zip Code 61051; Elev. 749; Lat. 41-57-48 N long. 089-46-28 W; NW Illinois; Incorporated May 24, 1887; Name derived from the sawmill built in 1834 by *Jesse Kester,* an early settler, at the edge of the "ville".

•**MILLSTADT**, Town, St. Clair County; Pop. 2,738; Zip Code 62260; Elev. 620; Lat. 38-27-41 N long. 090-05-30 W; SW Illinois; Platted 1836 as Centerville; Name translated into German by residents because Illinois already had a post office of that name; Incorporated January 16, 1878.

•**MINIER**, Town, Tazewell County; Pop. 1,262; Zip Code 61759; Elev. 630; Lat. 40-26-01 N long. 089-18-47 W; Central Illinois; Incorporated July 17, 1872.

•**MINONK**, Town, Woodford County; Pop. 2,024; Zip Code 61760; Elev. 750; Lat. 40-54-16 N long. 089-02-04 W; N Central Illinois; Name derived from Algonquin words, *mino,* meaning "good" and *onk* meaning "place".

•**MINOOKA**, Town, Grundy and Will counties; Pop. 1,566; Zip Code 60447; Elev. 590; Lat. 41-27-19 N long. 088-15-42 W; NE Illinois; Incorporated March 27, 1869; Name is a corruption of Delaware Indian words *mino* ("good") and *oki* ("land").

•**MOKENA**, Town, Will County; Pop. 4,598; Zip Code 60448; Elev. 700; Lat. 41-31-34 N long. 087-53-21 W; NE Illinois; Incorporated May 24, 1880; Name is a variation of the Algonquin word for "turtle."

•**MOLINE** City, Rock Island County; Pop. 45,577; Zip Code 61265; Elev. 580; Lat. 41-30-24 N long. 090-30-54 W; NW Illinois; Settled 1847; Incorporated February 14, 1855; A corruption of the French word for mill.

•**MONEE**, Town, Will County; Pop. 1,007; Zip Code 60449; Elev. 800; Lat. 41-25-12 N long. 087-44-30 W; NE Illinois; Incorporated November 9, 1874; Name is Indian pronunciation of name of *Marie Lefevre* (1793-1866), Indian wife of *Joseph Baily,* a French trader.

•**MONTGOMERY**, Town, Kane and Kendall counties; Pop. 3,369; Zip Code 60538; Elev. 642; Lat. 41-43-50 N long. 088-20-45 W; NE Illinois; Montgomery was settled in 1840 by immigrants from Montgomery County in New York.

•**MONTICELLO**, City; Piatt County Seat; Pop. 4,760; Zip Code 61856; Elev. 675; Lat. 40-01-40 N long. 088-34-24 W; E Central Illinois; 25 miles NE of Decatur; Named by land promoters for the home of *Thomas Jefferson.*

•**MORRIS**, City; Grundy County Seat; Pop. 8,840; Zip Code 60450; Elev. 519; Lat. 41-21-26 N long 088-25-16 W; NE Illinois; Named for *Isaac N. Morris,* a canal commissioner for the Illinois and Michigan Canal (1848).

•MORRISON, Town, Whiteside County Seat; Pop. 4,624; Zip Code 61270; Elev. 716;Lat. 41-48-35 N long. 089-57-54 W; NW Illinois; named for an early settler.

•MORRISONVILLE, Town, Christian County; Pop. 1,212; Zip Code 62546; Elev. 625; Lat. 39-25-12 N long. 089-27-20 W; Central Illinois; Founded by and named by Col. J.L.D. Morrison, a veteran of the Civil War and son-in-law of Thomas Carlin, sixth governor of Illinois (1838-42).

•MORTON, City, Tazewell County; Pop. 13,640; Zip Code 61550; Elev. 710; Lat. 40-36-46 N long. 089-27-33 W; N Central Illinois; 10 miles SE of Peoria; Named for Marcus Morton, governor of Massachusetts (1840-44).

•MORTON GROVE, City, Cook County; Pop. 23,749; Zip Code 60053; Elev. 625; Lat. 42-02-26 N long. 087-46-57 W; NE Illinois; Named for Levi Parsons Morton (1824-1920), an official of the Chicago, Milwaukee, and St. Paul Railroad when it was built in 1872, and later Vice-President of the U.S. under President Benjamin Harrison.

•MOUND CITY, City; Pulaski County Seat; Pop. 1,113; Zip Code 62961; Elev. 327; Lat. 37-05-07 N long. 089-09-45 W; S Illinois; Named for the ancient Indian mounds in the area.

•MOUNDS, Town, Pulaski County; Pop. 1,699; Zip Code 62964; Elev. 423; Lat. 37-06-51 N long. 089-11-52 W; S Illinois; Named for Indian burial mounds nearby; Once called Beechwood, Junction, and Mound City Junction.

•MOUNT MORRIS, Town, Ogle County; Pop. 2,973; Zip Code 61054: Elev. 916; Lat. 42-03-01 N long. 089-25-52 W; Central Illinois.

•MOUNT OLIVE, Town, Macoupin County; Pop. 2,294; Zip Code 62069; Elev. 684; Lat. 39-04-20 N long. 089-43-38 W; SW Central Illinois; Named for the Biblical site. Incorporated October 1874.

•MOUNT PROSPECT, City, Cook County; Pop. 51,317; Zip Code 60056; Elev. 675; Lat. 42-03-59 N long. 087-56-14 W; NE Illinois; Named for a local geographic feature.

•MOUNT PULASKI, Town, Logan County; Pop. 1,792; Zip Code 62548; Elev. 650; Lat. 40-00-39 N long. 089-16-56 W; Central Illinois; The town is named for the famous Polish-American Revolutionary War hero.

•MOUNT STERLING, Town, Brown County Seat; Pop. 2178; Zip Code 62353; Elev. 706; Lat. 39-59-14 N long.090- 45-48 W; Illinois; Settled 1830 by Robert Curry, who named the town for the sterling quality of the soil.

•MOUNT VERNON, City; Jefferson County Seat; Pop. 16,445; Zip Code 62864; Elev. 500; Lat. 38-19-02 N long. 088-54-11 W; S Central Illinois; Named after George Washington's estate.

•MOUNT ZION, City, Macon County; Pop. 4,562; Zip Code 62549; Elev. 681; Lat. 39-46-17 N long. 088-52-27 W; given a Biblical name by its founders.

•MOWEAQUA, Town, Shelby and Christian Counties; Pop. 1,927; Zip Code 62250; Elev. 620; Lat. 39-37-29 N long. 089-0-108 W; Central Illinois; Name is Potawatmi Indian word meaning "weeping woman or "wolf woman."

•MULBERRY GROVE, Town, Bond County; Pop. 701; Zip Code 62262; Elev. 559; Lat. 38-55-30 N long. 089-16-08 W; S Central Illinois; descriptively named.

•MUNDELEIN, City, Lake County; Pop. 16,996; Zip Code 60060; Elev. 750; Lat. 38-55-30 N long. 089-16-08 W; NE Illinois; Named for George William Cardinal Mundelein; Once called Area.

•MURPHYSBORO, City; Jackson County Seat; Pop. 9,808; Zip Code 62966; Elev. 396; Lat. 37-45-52 N long. 089-20-06 W; SW Illinois.

•NAPERVILLE, City, DuPage and Will Counties; Pop. 42,330; Zip Code 60540; Elev. 700; Lat. 41-47-09 N long. 088-08-50 W; NE Illinois; Named for Joseph Naper, who built a sawmill and platted the townsite in 1832.

•NASHVILLE, Town; Washington County Seat; Pop. 3,136; Zip Code 62263; Elev. 532; Lat. 38-20-37 N long. 089-22-50 w; S Central Illinois; 20 miles SW of Centralia; Named by Tennesseans who platted town in 1830.

•NAUVOO, Town, Hancock County; Pop. 1,131; Zip Code 62354; Elev. 659; Lat. 40-33-00 N long. 091-23-05 w; W Illinois; On Mississippi River 45 miles north of Quincy.

•NEBO, Town, Pike County; Pop. 489; Zip Code 62447; Elev. 483; Lat. 39-26-33 N long. 090-47-27 W; E Central Illinois; Name derived from Iroquois Indian words, new ("supreme being"), and oga ("place").

•NEW ATHENS, Town, St. Clair County; Pop. 1,938; Zip Code 62264; Elev. 429; Lat. 38-19-35 N long. 089-52-37 W; SW Illinois; On the Kaskaskia River; Settled 1836 by French settlers who named town for city in Greece.

•NEW BADEN, Town, Clinton and St. Clair counties; Pop. 2,445; Zip Code 62265; Elev. 462; Lat. 38-32-06 N long. 089-42-02 W; SW Illinois; Named in 1855 by immigrants from Germany who named town for the spa in their homeland.

•NEW BOSTON, Town, Mercer County; Pop. 724; Zip Code 61272; Elev. 577; Lat. 41-10-13 N long. 090-59-48 W; NW Illinois; Incorporated February 21, 1859; Once called Dennison's Landing and Upper Yellow Banks.

•NEW LENOX, City, Will County; Pop. 5,771; Zip Code 60451; Elev. 675; Lat. 41-30-43 N long. 087-57-56 W; NE Illinois.

•NEWMAN, Town, Douglas County; Pop. 1,090; Zip Code 61942; Elev. 646; Lat. 39-47-55 N long. 087-59-09 w; E Central Illinois; Founded 1857 and named for B. Newman, son-in-law of the Methodist circuit rider, Peter Cartwright.

•NEWTON, Town; Jasper County Seat; Pop. 3,161; Zip Code 62448; Elev. 536; Lat. 38-59-27 N long. 088-09-45 W; SE Illinois; Named for Sgt. John Newton hero of the Revolutionary War.

•NILES, City, Cook County; Pop. 30,269; Zip Code 60648; Elev. 650; Lat. 42-01-08 N long. 087-48-10 W; NE Illinois; Once called Dutchman's Point and Lyttleton's Point, it derived its present name from pioneer newspaper owner William Ogden Niles.

•NOBLE, Town, Richland County; Pop. 830; Zip Code 62868; Elev. 478; Lat. 38-41-51 N long. 088-13-25 W; SE Illinois; Incorporated March 27, 1869.

•NOKOMIS, Town, Montgomery County; Pop. 2,666; Zip Code 62075; Elev. 670; Lat. 39-18-04 N long. 089-17-06 W; S Central Illinois; Named for the grandmother of Hiawatha in Longfellow's poem.

•NORMAL, City, McLean County; Pop. 35,601; Zip Code 61761; Elev. 790; Lat. 40-30-51 N long. 088-59-26 W; Central Illinois; Named for the first state Normal School, opened here, 1857.

•NORRIS CITY, Town, White County; Pop. 1,521; Zip Code 62869; Elev. 443; Lat.37-58-52 N long. 088-19-45 W; SE Illinois.

•NORTH BARRINGTON, Town, Lake County; Pop. 1,469; Zip Code 60010; Elev. 780; Lat. 42-12-28 N long. 088-08-26 W; NE Illinois; Incorporated November 2, 1959.

131

•**NORTHBROOK**, City, Cook County; Pop. 29,990; Zip Code 60062; Elev. 650; NE Illinois; NW suburb of Chicago.

•**NORTH CHICAGO**, City, Lake County; Pop. 38,272; Zip Code 60064; Elev. 650; Lat. 42-19-32 N long. 087-50-28 W; NE Illinois.

•**NORTHLAKE**, City, Cook County; Pop. 12,173; Zip Code 60164; Elev. 650-; Lat. 41-55-02 N long. 087-53-44 W; NE Illinois; NE suburb of Chicago.

•**OAKBROOK**, Town, DuPage and Cook counties; Pop. 6,646; Zip Code 60521; Elev. 660; Lat. 41-49-58 N long. 087-55-44 W; NE Illinois, named for the Oakbrook polo club.

•**OAK FOREST**, City, Cook County; Pop. 25,985; Zip Code 60452; Elev. 660; NE Illinois, descriptively named for the early forest cover.

•**OAKLAND**, Town, Coles County; Pop. 1,037; Zip Code 61943; Elev. 656; Lat. 39-39-14 N long. 088-01-34 W; SE Central Illinois.

•**OAK LAWN**, City, Cook County; Pop. 60,358; Zip Code 60453; Elev. 615; NE Illinois, 12 miles SW of Chicago, one of the largest suburbs of Chicago in Cook County.

•**OAK PARK**, City, Cook County; Pop. 54,895; Zip Code 60302; Elev. 620; NE Illinois, 10 miles west of Chicago; Founded 1833; Incorporated November 13, 1901; Initially called Oak Ridge because of a slight, tree-covered rise which has since disappeared due to grading and building.

•**OBLONG**, Town, Crawford County; Pop. 1,838; Zip Code 62449; Elev. 524; Lat. 39-00-07 N long. 087-54-32 W; In the Wabash River valley of SE Illinois; named for the town's shape in relation to the Embarras River.

•**ODIN**, Town, Marion County; Pop. 1,272; Zip Code 62870; Elev. 527; Lat. 38-37-02 N long. 089-03-08 W; S Central Illinois; Named for the Norse mythological figure.

•**OFALLON**, Town, St. Clari County; Pop. 10,184; Zip Code 62269; Elev. 550; SW Illinois; Near St. Louis and Mississippi River; Named for town site owner; settled, 1854.

•**OGLESBY**, Town, La Salle County; Pop. 3,976; Zip Code 61358; Elev. 465; Lat. 41-17-43 N long. 089-03-34 W; N Central Illinois; Named for *Gov. Richard J. Oglesby.*

•**OLNEY**, Town, Richland County Seat; Pop. 9,041; Zip Code 62450; Elev. 484; Lat. 38-43-51 N long. 088-05-07 W; SE Illinois; Named for *John Olney,* lawyer and Civil War lieutenant.

•**OLYMPIC FIELDS**, Town, Cook County; Pop. 4,126; Zip Code 60461; Lat. 41-30-48 N long. 087-40-27 W; NE Illinois; Developed 1926.

•**ONARGA**, Town, Iroquois County; Pop. 1,270; Zip Code 60955; Elev. 657; Lat. 40-42-54 N long. 088-00-22 W; NE Illinois; an Iroquois Indian word meaning "a place of rocky hills."

•**OQUAWKA**, Town, Henderson County Seat; Pop. 1,534; Zip Code 61469; Elev. 548;Lat. 40-55-55 N long. 00-56-49 W; NW Illinois; On Mississippi River; Name derived from the Indian, *Ozaukee,* meaning "yellow banks."

•**OREGON**, Town, Ogle County Seat; Pop. 3,558; Zip Code 61061; Elev. 702; Lat. 42-00-53 N long. 089-19-56 W; NW Illinois; 26 miles southwest of Rockford; On Rock River; An Indian name of uncertain meaning.

•**ORION**, Town, Henry County; Pop. 2,039; Zip Code 61273; Lat. 41-21-17 N long. 090-22-53 W; NW Illinois; Named for the heavenly constellation.

•**OTTAWA**, City; La Salle County Seat; Pop. 18,167; Zip Code 61350; Lat. 41-20-44 N long. 088-50-33 W; Northern Illinois; Named for the Ottawa Indian tribe.

•**PALATINE**, Town, Cook County; Pop. 31,945; Zip Code 60067; Lat. 42-06-37 N long. 088-02-03 W; Suburb of Chicago; Named for a division in Germany by that name.

•**PALESTINE**, Town, Crawford County; Pop. 1,730; Zip Code 62451; Elev. 450; Lat. 39-00-13 N long. 087-36-46 W; SE Illinois; Named after the Biblical country.

•**PALOS HEIGHTS**, Town, Cook County; Pop. 10,963; Zip Code 60463; Lat. 41-40-05 N long. 087-47-47 W.

•**PATOKA**, Town, Marion County; Pop. 667; Zip Code 62875; S Central Illinois; 17 miles north of Centralia; Named for an Indian chief.

•**PAWNEE**, Town, Sangamon County; Pop. 2,510; Zip Code 62875; W Central Illinois; Near Springfield. Named for the Pawnee Indians.

•**PAXTON**, Town; Ford County Seat; Pop. 4,269; Zip Code 60957; E Central Illinois; Near Champaign; settled, 1853, by Swedish immigrants.

•**PAYSON**, Town, Adams County; Pop. 1,071; Zip Code 62360; W Central Illinois; Near Quincy.

•**PEARL CITY**, Town, Stephenson County; Pop. 664; Zip Code 61062; Northern Illinois.

•**PECATONICA**, Town, Winnebago County; Pop. 1,727; Zip Code 61063; Northern Illinois; Near Rockford. A Sauk Indian word meaning "muddy."

•**PEKIN**, City; Peoria & Tazewell Counties; Tazewell County Seat; Pop. 33,967; Zip Code 61554; Elev. 479; N Central Illinois; Near Peoria. Named after Peking, China.

•**PEORIA**, city; Peoria County Seat; Pop. 135,000; Zip Code 616++; Elev. 608; /Central Illinois; Called Fort le Pe until about 1790 when it was first referred to as Piorias (the "s" was not pronounced), named after the Indians of the same name who populated the region when the first French explorers arrived.

•**PEOTONE**, Town, Will County; Pop. 2,833; Zip Code 60468; NE Illinois; 20 miles southeast of Joliet. A Potawatomi Indian word meaning "bring to this place."

•**PERU**, City, La Salle County; Pop. 10,862; Zip Code 61354; Elev. 459; Lat. 41-19-39 N long. 089-07-44 W; N Central Illinois; Founded, 1835; Named after Indian word meaning, "plenty of everything".

•**PESOTUM**, Town, Champaign County; Pop. 654; Zip Code 61863; Elev. 720; Lat. 39-54-53 N long. 088-16-24 W; E Central Illinois.

•**PETERSBURG**, Town, Menard County Seat; Pop. 2,390; Elev. 524; Lat. 38-35-30 N long. 087-49-52 W; W Central Illinois.

•**PHILO**, Town, Champaign County; Pop. 955; Zip Code 61864; Lat. 40-00-25 N long. 088-09-29 W; suburb of Champaign-Urbana.

•**PINCKNEYVILLE**, Town, Perry County Seat; Pop. 3,245; Zip Code 62274; Lat. 38-04-49 N long. 089-22-55 W; Southern Illinois. Named in honor of American Revolutionary War veteran Charles Pinckney.

•**PITTSBURG**, Town, Williamson County; Pop. 601; Zip Code 62974; Elev. 419; Lat. 38-52-17 N long. 089-12-42 W; Southern Illinois. Named after Pittsburg, Penn.

•**PITTSFIELD**, Town, Pike County Seat; Pop. 4,161; Zip Code 62363; Elev. 725; Lat. 39-36-28 N long. 090-48-18 W; Western Illinois; In between Mississippi and Illinois Rivers. Named after Pittsfield, Mass.

•**PLAINFIELD**, Town, Will County; Pop. 4,431; Zip Code 60544; Elev. 601; Lat. 41-37-37 N long. 088-12-14 W; NE Illinois; Near Joliet; Named for prairie topography; On Des Plaines River.

•**PLANO**, Town, Kendall County; Pop. 4,874; Zip Code 60545; Elev. 649; Lat. 41-39-46N long. 088-32-13 W; NE Illinois; 50 miles south west of Chicago; Settled, 1835.

•**PLEASANT HILL**, Town, Pike County; Pop. 1,110; Zip Code 62366; Lat. 40-36-47 N long. 088-44-49 W; Western Illinois.

•**PLYMOUTH**, Town, Hancock county; Pop. 640; Zip Code 62367; Elev. 4; Lat. 40-17-30 N long. 090-55-08 w; Western Illinois.

•**POCAHONTAS**, Town, Bond County; Pop. 862; Zip Code 62275; Elev. 515; LAt. 38-49-40 N long. 089-32-24 W; SW Illinois; 30 miles west of Vandalia; Named for the famous daughter of chief Powhatan of Virginia, who married John Wolf in 1614.

•**POLO**, Town, Ogle county; Pop. 2,629; Zip Code 61064; Elev. 836; Lat. 41-59-10 N long. 089-34-45 W; the town is named for 14th century explorer Marco Polo.

•**PONTIAC**, City; Livingston County Seat; Pop. 11,227; Zip Code 61764; Elev. 647; Lat. 40-52-51 N long. 088-37-47 W; NE Illinois; 57 miles southwest of Joliet; Named for Ottawa Indian chief; Founded, 1837.

•**POPLAR GROVE**, Town, Boone County; Pop. 820; Zip Code 61065; Elev. 908; Lat. 42-22-06 N long. 088-49-19 W; Northern Illinois; Descriptively named.

•**POSEN**, Town, Cook County; Pop. 4,321; Zip Code 60469; Elev. 605; Lat. 41-37-54 N long. 087-40-53 W; Named after the city in Poland.

•**POTOMAC**, Town, Vermillion County; Pop. 872; Zip Code 61865; Lat. 40-18-18 N long. 087-48-02 W; Eastern Illinois; Near Indiana border. Named after the Potomac River.

•**PRAIRIE CITY**, Town, McDonough County; Pop. 574; Zip Code 61470; Lat. 40-37-16 N long. 090-27-43 W; NW Illinois; Near Macomb. Named after its geography.

•**PRAIRIE DU ROCHER**, Town, Randolph County; Pop. 704; Zip Code 62277; Elev. 396; Lat. 38-04-59 N long. 090-005-45 W; Southern Illinois; On bluffs overlooking Mississippi River; Founded 1722 as a French settlement.

•**PRINCETON**, Town, Bureau County Seat; Pop. 7,324; Zip Code 61356; Lat. 41-22-05 N long. 089-27-53 W; N Central Illinois; Settled, 1833; Strong abolitionist community before Civil War; Named after Princeton, N.J.

•**PRINCEVILLE**, Town, Peoria County; Pop. 1,726; Zip Code 61559; Lat. 40-55-47 N long. 089-45-27 W; E Central Illinois. Settled by pioneer Daniel Prince and named for him.

•**PROPHETSTOWN**, Town, Whiteside County; Pop. 2,130; Zip Code 61277; Elev. 627; Lat. 41-40-17 N long. 089-56-10 W; NE Illinois; Near Rock Falls, on Rock River; Site of White Cloud's Village, who was known as the Indian prophet.

•**QUINCY**, City; Adams County Seat; Pop. 42,048; Zip Code 62301; Elev. 602; Lat. 39-56-08 N long. 091-24-35 W; Western Illinois; 132 miles southwest of Peoria; On Mississippi River bluffs; Named for *John Quincy Adams*, President at time of founding, 1825.

•**RAMSEY**, Town, Fayette County; Pop. 1,045; Zip Code 62080; Lat. 39-08-40 N long. 089-06-31 W; 087-53-47 W; S Central Illinois; Near Vandalia. Named for an early settler.

•**RANKIN**, Town, Vermillion County; Pop. 718; Zip Code 60960; Lat. 40-27-54 N long. 087-53-47 W; Eastern Illinois.

•**RANTOUL**, City, Champaign County, Pop. 20,083; Zip Code 61866; Elev. 758; Lat. 40-18-30 N long. 088-09-21 W; W Central Illinois; Near Champaign-Urbana; Named after Robert Rantoul, early railroad executive.

•**RAPID CITY**, Town, Rock Island County; Pop. 1,060; Zip Code 61278; Elev. 444; Lat. 41-34-54 N long. 090-2-0-36 W; NW Illinois.

•**RAYMOND**, Town, Montgomery County; Pop. 953; Zip Code 62560; Lat. 39-19-10 N long. 089-34-19 W; S Central Illinois.

•**RED BUD**, Town, Randolph County; Pop. 2,829; Zip Code 62278; Lat. 38-12-42 N long. 089-59-39 W; Southern Illinois; Named for red-bud trees which once grew near village site.

•**RICHMOND**, Town, McHenry County; Pop. 1,051; Zip Code 60071; Elev. 819; Northern Illinois; 80 miles northwest of Chicago. Named after Richmond, Virginia.

•**RIDGE FARM**, Town, Vermillion County; Pop. 1,084; Zip Code 61870; E Central Illinois.

•**RIDGWAY**, Town, Gallatin County; Pop. 1,228; Zip Code 62979; Southern Illinois; Named for *Dr. Robert Ridgway*, naturalist.

•**RIVERGROVE**, City, Cook County; Pop. 10,341; Zip Code 60171; Lat. 41-55-33 N long. 087-50-09 W; Named for its location on the Des Plaines River.

•**RIVERSIDE**, City, Cook County; Pop. 9,233; Zip Code 60546; Elev. 430; Lat. 41-50-06 N long. 087-49-22 W; Named for its riverside location.

•**RIVERTON**, Town, Sangamon County; Pop. 2,784; Zip Code 62561; Lat. 39-50-39 N long. 089-32-22 W; Suburb of Springfield. Located on the Sangamon River and so named.

•**ROANOKE**, Town, Woodford County; Pop. 2,010; Zip Code 61561; Lat. 40-47-46 N long. 089-11-50 W; 25 miles north of Bloomington. Named after Roanoke, Virginia.

•**ROBBINS**, City, Cook County; Pop. 7,905; Zip Code 60472; Elev. 602; Lat. 41-38-38 N long. 087-42-13 W; Chicago suburb; Near Blue Island.

•**ROBINSON**, Town; Crawford County Seat; Pop. 7,269; Zip Code 62454; Lat. 39-00-19 N long. 087-44-21 W. Named in honor of U.S. Senator John McCracken Robinson.

•**ROCHELLE**, Town, Ogle County; Pop. 8,945; Zip Code 61068; Elev. 793; Lat. 41-55-26 N long. 089-04-07 W; Northern Illinois; 27 miles south of Rockford; named after the area in France.

•**ROCHESTER**, Town, Sangamon County; Pop. 2,482; Zip Code 62563; Lat. 39-44-58 N long 089-31-54 W; Suburb of Springfield. Named after Rochester, New York.

•**ROCK FALLS**, Town, Whiteside County; Pop. 10,585; Zip Code 61071; Elev. 646; Lat. 41-46-47 N long. 089-41-20 W; Settled 1837; Descriptively named for its location on Rock River.

•**ROCKFORD**, city, Winnebago County; Pop. 139,211; Zip Code 611++; Elev. 715-742; It was named for the shallow rock-bottomed ford across the Rock River, which travelers on the Chicago-Galena line used before any settlement existed here.

•**ROCK ISLAND**, City, Rock Island County Seat; Pop. 46,928; Zip Code 61201; Elev. 563; Lat. 42-16-16 N long. 089-05-38 W; NW Illinois.

•**ROCKTON**, Town, Winnebago County; Pop. 2,304; Zip Code 61072; Lat. 42-27-46 N long. 089-05-42 W; Northern Illinois; On Rock River.

•**ROODHOUS**, Town, Greene County; Pop. 2,359; Zip Code 62082; Elev. 650; SW Illinois; 20 miles south of Jacksonville; Named for founder, *John Roodhouse*.

•**ROSCOE**, Town, Winnebago County; Pop. 1,387; Zip Code 61073; Lat. 42-24-48 N long. 089-00-33 W; Northern Illinois.

•**ROSELLE**, Village; Cook & Du Page Counties; Pop. 16,948; Zip Code 60101; Lat. 41-59-05 N long. 088-04-47 W; NW Suburb of Chicago. Named after pioneer Roselle Hough.

•**ROSEVILLE**, Town, Warren County; Pop. 1,246; Zip Code 61473; Elev. 736; Lat. 40-43-56 N long. 090-39-52 W; NW Illinois; Named for its famous flowers.

•**ROSICLARE**, Town, Hardin County; Pop. 1,409; Zip Code 62982; Lat. 37-25-25 N long. 088-20-46 W; On Ohio River. The town was named for Rose and Clair, the daughters of an early settler.

•**ROSSVILLE**, Town, Vermillion County; Pop. 1,355; Zip Code 60963; Elev. 700; Lat. 40-22-45 N long. 087-40-07 W; Named for *Jacob Ross*, early settler; Founded, 1857.

•**ROUND LAKE**, Town, Lake County; Pop. 2,578; Zip Code 60073; Lat. 42-21-12 N long. 088-05-36 W. Named for its location near Round Lake.

•**ROXANA**, Town, Madison County; Pop. 1,586; Zip Code 62084; Lat. 38-50-54 N long. 090-04-34 W; Near Alton.

•**ROYALTON**, Town, Franklin County; Pop. 1,300; Zip Code 62983; Lat. 37-52-37 N long. 089-06-52 W; Southern Illinois.

•**RUSHVILLE**, Town, Schuyler County Seat; Pop. 3,366; Zip Code 62671; Elev. 683; Named for Philadelphia physician, *Dr. William Rush.*

•**ST. ANNE**, Town, Kankakee County; Pop. 1,421; Zip Code 60964; Elev. 678; NE Illinois; Near Kankakee; Founded in 1852 by *Fr. Charles Chinquay*, of France.

•**ST. CHARLES**, Town, Du Page & Kane Counties; Pop. 17,492; Zip Code 60174; Elev. 802; NE Illinois; 33 miles northwest of Chicago; On Fox River.

•**ST. FRANCISVILLE**, Town, Lawrence County; Pop. 1,040; Zip Code 62460; SE Illinois. Named for St. Francis Xavier.

•**SALEM**, Town; Marion County Seat; Pop. 7,734; Zip Code 62881; Elev. 544; S Central Illinois; Founded, 1813; Incorporated, 1837 and given a Biblical name.

•**SANDOVAL**, Town, Marion County; Pop. 1,722; Zip Code 62882; Elev. 519; S Central Illinois.

•**SANDWICH**, Town, De Kalb & Kendall Counties; Pop. 5,244; Zip Code 60548; Elev. 657; NE Illinois; Named for Sandwich, Massachusetts by early settlers; 55 miles west of Chicago.

•**SAVANNAH**, Town, Carroll County; Pop. 4,529; Zip Code 61074; NW Illinois; Elev. 592; On Mississippi River; Named for grassy plains upon which it sits; Founded, 1828.

•**SAVOY**, Town, Champaign County; Pop. 2,253; Zip Code 61874; Lat. 40-03-17 N long. 088-15-06 W.

•**SENECA**, Town, Grundy & LaSalle Counties, Pop. 2,098; Zip Code 61360; Elev. 521; Lat. 41-18-40 N long. 088-36-35 W; N Central Illinois; Named for the Seneca Indians.

•**SESSER**, Town, Franklin County, Pop. 2,237; Zip Code 62884; Lat. 38-05-30 N long. 089-03-01 W; Southern Illinois. Named for railroad surveyor John Sesser.

•**SHABBONA**, Town, DeKalb County; Pop. 848; Zip Code 60550; Lat. 41-46-05 N long. 088-52-37 W; NE Illinois; Named for Potawatomi Indian Chief who befriended early settlers in region.

•**SHAWNEETOWN**, City; Gallatin County Seat; Pop. 1,829; Zip Code 62565; Lat. 37-42-47 N long. 088-11-12 W; Central Illinois; named after the Shawnee Indians.

•**SHELDON**, Town, Iroquois County Seat; Pop. 1,206; Zip Code 60966; Elev. 685; Lat. 40-46-09 N long. 087-33-50 W. The town is named in honor of an early railroad man.

•**SHERIDAN**, Town, LaSalle County; Pop. 714; Zip Code 60551; Lat. 41-31-48 N long. 088-40-47 W. Named in honor of Union general Phil Sheridan.

•**SIDELL**, Town, Champaign County; Pop. 914; Zip Code 61877; Lat. 39-54-35 N long. 087-49-16 W; E Central Illinois.

•**SIDNEY**, Town, Champaign County; Pop. 896; Zip Code 61877; Lat. 40-01-30 N long. 088-04-24 W; E Central Illinois.

•**SILVIS**, Town, Rock Island County; Pop. 7,199; Zip Code 61282; Elev. 576; Lat. 41-30-44 N long. 090-24-54 W; NE Illinois; near Rock Island and Moline. Named for 19th century settler R.S. Silvis.

•**SKOKIE**, City, Cook County; Pop. 60,327; Zip Code 60001; NE Illinois; 15 miles north of Chicago.

•**SOMONAUK**, Town, De Kalb & La Salle Counties; Pop. 1,344; Zip Code 60552; Lat. 41-38-01 N long. 088-40-52 W; NE Illinois. A Potawatomi Indian word meaning "paw-paw."

•**SORENTO**, Town, Bond County; Pop. 670; Zip Code 62086; Lat. 38-59-56 N long. 089-34-25 W; SW Illinois. Named after the Italian city.

•**SOUTH BELOIT**, Town, Winnebago County; Pop. 4,086; Zip Code 61080; Elev. 742; Lat. 42-29-35 N long. 089-02-12 W; Northern Illinois; Suburb of Beloit, Wisconsin.

•**SOUTH ELGIN**, Town, Kane County; Pop. 6,211; Zip Code 60177; Lat. 41-59-39 N long. 088-17-32 W; NE Illinois; Suburb of Elgin.

•**SOUTH HOLLAND**, City, Cook County; Pop. 24,679; Zip Code 60473; Elev. 600; Lat. 41-36-03 N long. 087-36-25 W; NE Illinois; 10 miles south of Chicago; Settled, 1840 by Dutch farmers.

•**SOUTH PEKIN**, Town, Tazewell County; Pop. 1,241; Zip Code 61564; Lat. 40-29-40 N long. 089-39-06 W; W Central Illinois; Suburb of Pekin.

•**SOUTH ROXANA**, Town, Madison County; Pop. 2,273; Zip Code 62087; Lat. 38-49-46 N long. 090-03-46 W.

•**SPARTA**, Town, Randolph County; Pop. 4,913; Zip Code 62286; Lat. 38-07-23 N long. 089-42-06 W; Southern Illinois. Named for the ancient Greek city.

•**SPRING VALLEY**, Town, Bureau County; Pop. 5,848; Zip Code 61362; Elev. 465; Lat. 41-19-39 N long. 089-11-59 W; N Central Illinois. Across Illinois River from LaSalle.

•**SPRINGFIELD**, City; Sangamon County Seat; Pop. 100,054; Zip Code 627+; Elev. 600. The capital of Illinois. Springfield was first settled in 1818 and in 1821 was named seat of the newly formed county. Transfer of the capital from Vandalia was led by the young county representative Abraham Lincoln who lived here until he became president of the U.S. in 1861.

•**STAUNTON**, Town, Macoupi County; Pop. 4,716; Zip Code 62088; Elev. 622; Lat. 39-00-44 N long. 089-47-28 W; SW Central Illinois; Founded, 1817 Named for an early settler.

•**STEELEVILLE**, Town, Randolph County; Pop. 2,249; Zip Code 62288; Lat. 38-00-26 N long. 089-39-30 W; SW Illinois. Named after early settler John Steele.

•**STEGER**, Village; Cook & Will Counties; Pop. 9,269; Zip Code 60465; Elev. 712; Lat. 41-28-12 N long. 087-38-11 W; Named after piano maker John Steger.

•**STERLING**, City, Whiteside County; Pop. 16,284; Zip Code 61081; Elev. 645; Lat. 41-47-19 N long. 089-41-46 W; NW Illinois.

•**TEUTOPOLIS**, Town, Effingham County; Pop. 1,406; Zip Code 62467; Elev. 601; Established, 1839 by a group of Germans from Cincinnati, Ohio.

•**THOMASBORO**, Town, Champaign County; Pop. 1,241; Zip Code 61878; Lat. 40-14-30 N long. 088-11-03 W. Named for an early settler.

•**THORNTON**, Town, Cook County; Pop. 3,023; Zip Code 60476; Lat. 41-34-05 N long. 087-36-29 W; NE Illinois.

•**TINLEY PARK**, Village, Cook and Will Counties; Pop. 25,959; Zip Code 60477; Lat. 41-34-24 N long. 087-47-04 W; Suburb of Chicago.

•**TOLEDO**, Town; Cumberland County Seat; Pop. 1,204; Zip Code 62468; Lat. 39-16-25 N long. 088-14-37 W; SE Central Illinois. Named after the city in Ohio.

•**TOLONO**, Town, Champaign County; Pop. 2,449; Zip Code 61880; Elev. 736; Lat. 39-59-10 N long. 088-15-32 W; Name coined by J. B. Calhoun of the Illinois Central Railroad.

•**TOLUCA**, Town, Marshall County; Pop. 1,478; Zip Code 61369; Lat. 41-00-08 N long. 089-08-00 W; N Central Illinois; Named after Toluca, Mexico.

•**TOULON**; City; Stark County Seat; Pop. 1,395; Zip Code 61483; Lat. 41-05-37 N long. 089-51-53 W; NW Central Illinois. Named after the French city.

•**TREMONT**, Town, Tazewell County; Pop. 2,098; Zip Code 61568; Lat. 40-31-39 N long. 089-29-33 W; N Central Illinois; Descriptively named for three local hills.

•**TRENTON**, Town, Clinton County; Pop. 2,507; Zip Code 62293; Elev. 498; Lat. 38-36-20 N long. 089-40-55 W; SW Illinois; Incorporated 1865. Named for Trenton, New Jersey.

•**TROY**, City, Madison County; Pop. 3,694; Zip Code 62294; Elev. 549; Lat. 38-43-45 N long. 089-52-59 W; SW Illinois; Established 1819; Named for New York town by land speculators; Incorporated, city, 1892.

•**TUSCOLA**, City, Douglas County Seat; Pop. 3,808; Zip Code 61953; Elev. 653; Lat. 39-47-57 N long. 088-16-59 W; E Illinois. A Choctaw Indian word meaning "warriors."

•**ULLIN**, Town Pulaski County; Pop. 537; Zip Code 62992: Lat. 37-16-37 N long. 089-11-00 W; Southern Illinois.

•**UNION**, Town, McHenry County; Pop. 625; Zip Code 60180; Lat. 40-17-15 N long. 089-22-01 W; NE Illinois.

•**VALIER**, Town, Franklin County; Pop. 722; Zip Code 62891; Lat. 38-00-55 N long. 089-02-33 W.

•**VALMEYER**, Town, Monroe County; Pop. 902; Zip Code 62295; Lat. 38-17-40 N long. 090-18-57 W.

•**VANDALIA**, City, Fayette County Seat; Pop. 5,343; Zip Code 62471; Elev. 503; Lat. 38-57-38 N long. 089-05-37 W; S Central Illinois; 30 miles N of Centralia; Second capital of Illinois (1819-39); On Kaskaskia River.

•**VENICE**, City, Madison County; Pop. 3,418; Zip Code 62090; Elev. 410; Lat. 38-40-20 N long. 090-10-11 W; SW Illinois; Settled, 1804; Incorporated, 1873; named because streets were often flooded by the river before levees were constructed.

•**VERMONT**, Town, Fulton County; Pop. 889; Zip Code 61484; Lat. 40-17-39 N long. 090-25-40 W; W Central Illinois. Named after the state.

•**VIENNA**, Town; Johnson County Seat; Pop. 1,431; Zip Code 62995; Elev. 405; Lat. 37-24-55 N long. 088-53-52 W; Southern Illinois. Named for the Austrian city.

•**VILLA PARK**, City, DuPage County; Pop. 23,096; Zip Code 60181; Lat. 41-53-23 N long. 087-59-20 W.

•**VIOLA**, Town, Mercer County; Pop. 1,140; Zip Code 61486; Elev. 797; Lat. 41-12-21 N long. 090-35-13 W; NW Illinois; Near Iowa River.

•**VIRDEN**, City, Macoupin & Sangamon Counties; Pop. 3,899 Zip Code 62690; Elev. 674; Lat. 39-30-03 N long. 089-46-04 W; SW Central Illinois; 30 miles south of Springfield. Named after the Virden Mine Company.

•**VIRGINIA**, City; Cass County Seat; Pop. 1,824; Zip Code 62691; Lat. 39-57-04 N long. 090-12-44 W; W Central Illinois; Elev. 619. Named after the state.

•**WADSWORTH**, Town, Lake County; Pop. 1,098; Zip Code 60083; Lat. 42-25-43 N long. 087-55-26 W; NE Illinois, Suburb of Chicago; On Des Plaines River.

•**WAMAC**, Town, Washington and Marion Counties; Pop. 1,672; Elev. 497; Lat. 38-30-32 N long. 089-08-26 W; Southern Illinois; Near Centralia. An acronym for Washington, Marion, and Clinton counties.

•**WARREN**, Town, Joe Daviess County; Pop. 1,602; Zip Code 61087; Elev. 1,005; Lat. 42-29-47 N long. 089-59-22 W; NE Illinois corner; Organized as town of Courtland, 1850; Renamed in 1853 in honor of town's founder's son, Warren.

•**WARRENSBURG**, Town, Macon County; Pop. 1,376; Zip Code 62573; Lat. 39-55-58 N long. 089-03-43 W; Central Illinois; Near Decatur.

•**WARRENVILLE**, Town, DuPage County; Pop. 7,185; Zip Code 60555; Elev. 693; Lat. 41-49-04 N long. 088-10-24 W; NE Illinois; 30 miles southwest of Chicago; On DuPage River. Named for 19th century settler Colonel Julius Warren.

•**WARSAW**, Town, Hancock County; Pop. 1,840; Zip Code 62397; Lat. 40-21-33 N long. 091-26-04 W. Named for the Polish city.

•**WASHINGTON**, City, Tazewell County; Pop. 10,292; Zip Code 61571; Elev. 766; Lat. 40-42-13 N long. 089-24-26 W; Central Illinois; 12 miles east of Peoria. Named in honor of George Washington.

•**WATAGA**, Town, Knox County; Pop. 996; Zip Code 61488; Lat. 41-01-31 N long. 090-16-47 W. A Cherokee Indian word meaning "River of Islands."

•**WATERLOO**, City; Monroe County Seat; Pop. 4,574; Zip Code 62298; Elev. 717; Lat. 38-20-09 N long. 090-08-59 W; SW Illinois; Named for the famous battle.

•**WATSEKA**, City; Iroquois County Seat; Pop. 5,457; Zip Code 60970; Elev. 634; Lat. 40-46-34 N long. 087-44-11 W; E Illinois; Renamed, 1865, in honor of *Watch-e-kee* (pretty woman), Potowatomi Indian and wife of *Gurdon Hubbard*, an early settler.

•**WAUCONDA**, City, Lake County; Pop. 5,662; Zip Code 60084; Elev. 800; Lat. 42-21-49 N long. 087-50-41 W; NE Illinois; Settled, 1836 on Bangs Lake by *Justus Bangs* ; Named by *Bangs* for a fictional Indian character.

•**WAUKEGAN**, City; Lake County Seat; Pop. 67,095; Zip Code 60085; Elev. 669; Lat. 42-21-49 N long. 087-50-41 W; NE Illinois. Site of Indian village known to seventeenth century explorers; Named for Indian word meaning "fort or trading post."

•**WAVERLY**, Town, Morgan County; Pop. 1,546; Zip Code 62692; Lat. 39-35-30 N long. 089-57-01 W; W Central Illinois. Named for the Waverly novels of Sir Walter Scott.

•**WAYNE**, Town, Du Page & Kane Counties; Pop. 940; Zip Code 60184; Lat. 41-57-03 N long. 088-14-32 W; NE Illinois. The town is named in honor of Revolutionary War general Antony Wayne.

•**WAYNE CITY**, Town, Wayne County; Pop. 1,132; Zip Code 62895; Lat. 38-20-43 N long. 088-35-16 W; SE Illinois. Named for General Antony Wayne.

•**WENONA**, Town, Marshall County; Pop. 1,014; Zip Code 61377; Elev. 696; N Central Illinois; Near Streator. A fictional Indian name used by Longfellow in his poem "Hiawatha."

•**WEST CHICAGO**, City, Du Page County; Pop. 12,444; Zip Code 60185; Lat. 41-53-05 N long. 088-12-14 W; NE Illinois; Near Wheaton.

•**WESTERN SPRINGS**, City, Cook County; Pop. 12,830; Zip Code 60558; Elev. 668; Lat. 41-48-35 Nlong. 087-54-02 W; NE Illinois; Named for local mineral springs believed to be medicinal, which have since dried up.

•**WEST FRANKFORT**, City, Franklin County; Pop. 9,414; Zip Code 62896; Southern Illinois.

•**WESTMONT**, City, Du Page County; Pop. 16,627; Zip Code 60559; Lat. 41-47-45 N long. 087-58-32 W; NE Illinois; Elev. 740; Near Hinsdale.

•**WESTVILLE**, City Vermillion County; Pop. 3,506; Zip Code 61883; Elev. 671; Lat. 40-02-32 N long. 087-38-19 W; E Illinois; Settled, 1873, by *W. P.* and *E. A. West*.

•**WHEATON**, City, Du Page County Seat; Pop. 42,772; Zip Code 60187; Elev. 753; Lat. 41-51-58 N long. 088-06-25 W; NE Illinois; 25 miles west of Chicago; Settled, 1838 by *Warren* and *Jesse Wheaton* ; Incorporated, 1853.

•**WHEELING**, City, Cook & Lake Counties; Pop. 23,266; Zip Code 60090; Elev. 650; Lat. 42-08-21 N long. 087-55-44 W; NE Illinois; 20 miles NW of Chicago; Settled, 1830 as a country store.

•**WHITEHALL**, Town, Greene county; Pop. 2,929; Zip Code 62092; Elev. 585; Lat. 39-26-13 N long. 090-24-11 W; SE Illinois; Founded, 1820; Named for the home of an early postmaster.

•**WILLIAMSVILLE**, Town, Sangamon County; Pop. 970; Zip Code 62693; Lat. 39-57-15 N long. 089-32-55 W; Central Illinois.

•**WILLOWSPRINGS**, Town, Cook County; Pop. 4,054; Zip Code 60480; Lat. 41-44-27 N long. 087-51-37 W. Descriptively named for an early springs.

•**WILMETTE**, Residential village, Cook County; Pop. 28,188; Zip Code 60091; Elev. 614; Lat. 42-04-20 N long. 087-43-22 W; NE Illinois; Suburb of Chicago; On Lake Michigan; Settled, 1829; Named for first white settler, *Antoine Quilmette*, a French Canadian whose Indian wife gained the land under a government treaty.

•**WILMINGTON**, City, Will County; Pop. 4,419; Zip Code 60481; Elev. 549; Lat. 41-18-28 N long. 088-08-48 W; NE Illinois.

•**WINCHESTER**, City, Scott County Seat; Pop. 1,705; Zip Code 62694; Elev. 546; Lat. 39-37-47 N long. 090-27-22 W; Founded, 1830; Named by a Kentucky settler who gained the honor from surveyors in exchange for a jug of whiskey.

•**WINFIELD**, Town, Du Page County; Pop. 4,393; Zip Code 60190; Lat. 41-51-42 N long. 088-09-39 W. Named in honor of Blackhawk War victor, General Winfield Scott.

•**WINNEBAGO**, Town, Winnebago County; Pop. 1,642; Zip Code 61088; Lat. 42-15-58 N long. 089-14-28 W; N Central Illinois. Named for the Winnebago Indians.

•**WINNETKA**, Village, Cook County; Pop. 12,697; Zip Code 60093; Elev. 651; Lat. 42-06-29 N long. 087-44-09 W; NE Illinois; 20 miles north of Chicago; Incorporated 1869; A Potawatomi Indian word meaning "beautiful land."

•**WINTHROP HARBOR**, Town, Lake County; Pop. 5,410; Zip Code 60096; Elev. 598; Lat. 42-28-44 N long. 087-49-25 W; NE Illinois corner. Named after the company which platted the town.

•**WITT**, Town, Montgomery County; Pop. 1,206; Zip Code 62094; Lat. 39-15-23 N long. 089-20-53 W.

•**WOOD DALE**, Town, Du Page County, Pop. 11,262; Zip Code 60191; Lat. 41-57-48 N long. 087-58-44 W.

•**WOOD RIVER**, City, Madison County; Pop. 12,292; Zip Code 62095; Elev. 430; SW Illinois; Named after the nearby Wood River.

•**WOODSTOCK**, City McHenry County Seat; Pop. 11,669; Zip Code 60098; Elev. 943; Lat. 42-18-53 N long. 088-26-55 W; NE Illinois; Named for Vermont town of early settlers in 1830s and 40s.

•**WORDEN**, Town, Madison County; Pop. 956; Zip Code 62097; Lat. 38-55-53 N long. 089-50-20 W.

•**WORTH**, Residential Village, Cook County; Pop. 11,573; Zip Code 60482; Lat. 41-41-23 N long. 087-47-50 W; NE Illinois; Chicago suburb.

•**WYANET**, Town, Bureau County; Pop. 1,055; Zip Code 61379; Elev. 656; Lat. 41-21-55 N long. 089-35-02 W; N Central Illinois; On Illinois and Mississippi Canal.

•**WYOMING**, Town, Stark County; Pop. 1,615; Zip Code 61491; Lat. 41-03-42 N long. 089-46-23 W; NW Central Illinois.

•**YATES CITY**, Town, Knox County; Pop. 856; Zip Code 61572; Lat. 40-46-43 N long. 090-00-53 W; W. Illinois; Named for *Gov. Richard Yates* (1861-65).

•**YORKVILLE**, Town, Kendall County Seat; Pop. 3,399; Zip Code 60560; Elev. 584; Lat. 41-38-28 N long. 088-26-50 W; NE Illinois; On Fox River.

•**ZEIGLER**, Town, Franklin County; Pop. 1,898; Zip Code 62999; Lat. 37-53-58 N Long. 089-03-07 W; Southern Illinois; Named for the Zeigler Coal Company.

•**ZION**, City, Lake County; Pop. 17,783; Zip Code 60099; Elev. 633; Lat. 42-26-46 N Long. 087-49-58 W; NE Illinois; Founded by a man who believed world to be flat and given a Biblical name.

INDIANA

•ADVANCE, Town; Boone County; Pop. 552; Zip Code 46102; Lat. 39-59-45 N long. 086-37-12 W; Settled in the 1820's and named for the progress the Midland Railway would bring to the community.

•AKRON, Town; Fulton County; Pop. 1,041; Zip Code 46910; Lat. 41-02-18 N long. 086-01-41 W; First laid out in 1838 and named after Akron, Ohio.

•ALAMO, Town; Montgomery County; Pop. 175; Zip Code 47916; Lat. 39-58-55 N long. 087-03-26 W; Founded in 1837 and named in honor of the historic fort in San Antonio, Texas.

•ALBANY, Town; Delaware & Randolph Counties; Pop. 2,625; Zip Code 47320; lat. 40-18-03 N long. 085-14-31 W; The town was founded in 1833 and named for Albany, New York.

•ALBION, Town; Noble County Seat; Pop. 1,632; Zip Code 46701; Lat. 41-23-44 N long. 085-25-28 W; Platted in 1846 and given the ancient name of Britian, Albion.

•ALEXANDRIA, City; Madison County; Pop. 6,030; Zip Code 46001; Lat. 40-15-46 N long. 085-40-33 W; Established in 1836 and named for the famous Egyptian city.

•ALFORDSVILLE, Town; Daviess County; Pop. 132; Lat. 38-33-38 N long. 086-56-54 W; The town's name honors James Alford, an early settler.

•ALTON, Town; Crawford County; Pop. 63; Lat. 38-07-21 N long. 086-25-04 W; Settled in 1838 and named after the town in England.

•ALTONA, Town; De Kalb County; Pop. 262; Lat. 41-21-05 N long. 085-09-18 W; The town is named after the city in Germany.

•AMBIA, Town; Benton County; Pop. 273; Zip Code 47917; Lat. 40-29-24 N long. 087-31-01 W.

•AMBOY, Town; Miami County; Pop. 450; Zip Code 46911; Lat. 40-36-05 N long. 085-55-44 W; Founded in 1873 and named for Ambialet, France.

•AMO, Town; Hendricks County; Pop. 436; Settled in 1850 and given the Latin name amo, a verb meaning "I love."

•ANDERSON, City; Madison County Seat; Pop. 64,421; Zip Code 46011; Lat. 40-48-05 N long. 095-36-14 W; Platted in 1823 and named after a local Delaware Indian chief, whose English name was William Anderson.

•ANDREWS, Town; Huntington County; Pop. 1,237; Lat. 41-45-12 N long. 093-45-25 W; Originally Antioch, the name was changed to Andrews to honor a local railroad official.

•ANGOLA, City; Steuben County Seat; Pop. 5,417; Settled in 1837 and named after Angola, New York.

•ARCADIA, Town; Hamilton County; Pop. 1,679; Zip Code 46030; Lat. 40-10-33 N long. 086-01-18 W; First settled in 1849 and named for the ancient Greek province noted for its pastoral beauty.

•ARGOS, Town; Marshall County; Pop. 1,548; Zip Code 46501; Lat. 41-41-50 N long. 086-14-42 W; Named in 1859 for the ancient Greek city.

•ASHLEY, Town; De Kalb & Steuben Counties; Pop. 841; Zip Code 46705; Lat. 41-31-38 N long. 085-03-56 W; The town was named in 1892 for a city in Pennsylvania.

•ATLANTA, Town; Hamilton County; Pop. 663; Zip Code 46031; Lat. 40-12-55 N long. 086-01-35 W; Settled in 1839 and later named after Atlanta, Georgia.

•ATTICA, City; Fountain County; Pop. 3,832; Zip Code 47918; Lat. 40-17-39 N long. 087-14-56 W; Established in 1825 and named for the ancient Greek province.

•AUBURN, City; De Kalb County; Pop. 8,085; Zip Code 46706; Lat. 41-22-01 N long. 085-03-32 W; Founded in 1836 and named for the English town.

•AURORA, City; Dearborn County Seat; Pop. 3,804; Zip Code 47001; lat. 39-03-25 N long. 084-54-05 W; Aurora was founded in 1819 and given the name for the Roman goddess of dawn.

•AUSTIN, Town; Scott County; Pop. 4,848; Zip Code 47102; Lat. 38-45-30 N long. 085-48-29 W; Mexican-American War veterans named the town after the city in Texas in the 1850's.

•AVILLA, Town; Noble County; Pop. 1,280; Zip Code 46710; Lat. 41-21-57 N long. 085-14-20 W; Settled in 1819 and named for the Spanish city of Avilla.

•BAINBRIDGE, Town; Putnam County; Pop. 644; Zip Code 46105; Lat. 39-45-40 N long. 086-48-43 W; Founded in 1824 and named in honor of navel hero William Bainbridge.

•BARGERSVILLE, Town; Johnson County; Pop. 1,639; Zip Code 46106; Lat. 39-31-15 N long. 086-10-04 W; The town was settled in 1850 and named in honor of Jefferson Barger.

•BATESVILLE, City; Franklin & Ripley Counties; Pop. 4,152; Zip Code 47006; Lat. 39-18-00 N long. 085-13-20 W; The city's name honors the pioneer Bates family.

•BATTLE GROUND, Town; Tippecanoe County; Pop. 812; Zip Code 47920; Lat. 40-30-30 N long. 086-50-30 W; The site of the Battle of Tippecanoe, the town is named after this fight.

•BEDFORD, City; Lawrence County Seat; Pop. 14,390; Zip Code 47421; Lat. 38-51-40 N long. 086-29-14 W; Platted in 1825 and named after Bedford County, Tennessee.

•BEECH GROVE, City; Marion County; Pop. 13,192; Zip Code 46107; Lat. 39-43-19 N long. 086-05-24 W; The town took its name from a nearby farm called Beech Grove Farm.

•BERNE, City; Adams County; Pop. 3,292; Zip Code 46711; Lat. 40-39-28 N long. 084-57-07 W; Swiss settlers platted the town in 1871 and named it after Berne, Switzerland.

•BETHANY, Town; Morgan County; Pop. 127; Lat. 39-10-26 N long. 086-03-55 W; The town's settlers named the town after the Biblical village.

•BEVERLY SHORES, Town; Porter County; Pop. 828; Zip Code 46301; Lat. 41-41-33 N long. 086-58-39 W; A fashionable residential village euphoniously named by its developer.

•BICKNELL, City; Knox County; Pop. 4,712; Zip Code 47512; Lat. 38-46-27 N long. 087-18-28 W; Named in 1869 in honor of pioneer John Bicknell.

•BIRDSEYE, Town; Dubois County; Pop. 534; Zip Code 47513; Lat. 38-19-00 N long. 086-41-45 W; The town was named by a local postmaster Rev. "Bird" Johnson who helped select the site.

•**BLOOMFIELD,** Town; Greene County Seat; Pop. 2,695; Zip Code 47424; Lat. 39-01-37 N long. 086-56-15 W; Founded in 1824 and named by town founder Hallet Dean for his birthplace in Bloomfield, New Jersey.

•**BLOOMINGDALE,** Town; Parke County; Pop. 405; Zip Code 47832; LAT. 39-50-00 N long. 087-14-59 W; Originally called Elevatis.

•**BLOOMINGTON,** City; Monroe County; Pop. 51,867; Zip Code 47401; Lat. 39-09-55 N long. 086-31-35 W; Settled in the early 1800's and named after a local settler, William Bloom.

•**BLOUNTSVILLE,** Town; Henry County; Pop. 208; Lat. 40-03-36 N long. 085-14-25 W; The town's name honors original landowner, Andrew Blount.

•**BLUFFTON,** City; Wells County; Pop. 8,623; Zip Code 46714; Lat. 40-44-19 N long. 085-10-18 W; Descriptively named for its location on the bluffs of the southern bank of the Wabash River.

•**BOONVILLE,** City; Warrick County Seat; Pop. 6,294; Zip Code 47601; Lat. 38-02-57 N long. 087-16-27 W.

•**BOSTON,** Town; Wayne County; Pop. 189; Zip Code 47324; Lat. 39-44-28 N long. 084-51-07 W; Settled in 1832 and named after Boston, Massachusetts.

•**BOSWELL,** Town; Benton County; Pop. 814; Zip Code 47921; Lat. 40-31-16 N long. 087-22-42 W; Charles Boswell settled here in 1872. The town is named after him.

•**BOURBON,** Town; Marshall County; Pop. 1,500; Zip Code 46504; Lat. 41-17-44 N long. 086-06-59 W; Settlers from Kentucky named their new home after Bourbon County, Kentucky.

•**BRAZIL,** City; Clay County Seat; Pop. 7,873; Zip Code 47834; Lat. 39-31-25 N long. 087-07-30 W; The city is named for the great country in South America.

•**BREMEN,** Town; Marshall County; Pop. 3,560; Zip Code 46506; Lat. 41-26-47 N long. 086-08-53 W; German settlers named their new home after Bremen, Germany.

•**BRISTOL,** Town; Elkhart County; Pop. 1,208; Zip Code 46507; Lat. 41-43-17 N long. 085-49-03 W; Settled in 1830 and named after Bristol, England.

•**BROOK,** Town; Newton County; Pop. 923; Zip Code 47922; Lat. 40-51-59 N long. 087-21-49 W; Descriptively named for a small stream that runs through the area.

•**BROOKLYN,** Town; Morgan County; Pop. 890; Zip Code 46111; Lat. 39-32-21 N long. 086-22-09 W; Brooklyn is named for its famous namesake in New York City.

•**BROOKSBURG,** Town; Jefferson County; Pop. 133; Lat. 38-44-11 N long. 085-14-37 W; Noah Brooks laid out the town in the 1840's. It is named after him.

•**BROOKSTON,** Town; White County; Pop. 1,696; Zip Code 47923; Lat. 40-36-10 N long. 086-52-02 W; The town's name honors railroad President James Brooks.

•**BROOKVILLE,** Town; Franklin County Seat; Pop. 2,873; Zip Code 47012; Lat. 39-25-23 N long. 085-00-46 W; Settled in 1808 and given one of its founder's mother's maiden name.

•**BROWNSBURG,** Town; Hendricks County; Pop. 6,206; Zip Code 46112; Lat. 39-50-36 N long. 086-23-52 W; Founded in 1835 and named after a local settler.

•**BROWNSTOWN,** Town; Jackson County; Pop. 2,693; Zip Code 47220; Lat. 38-52-44 N long. 086-02-31 W; The town's name remembers War of 1812 hero, General Jacob Brown.

•**BRUCEVILLE,** Town; Knox County; Pop. 646; Zip Code 47516; Lat. 38-45-34 N long. 087-24-56 W; Bruceville is named in honor of its first settler, Major William Bruce.

•**BRYANT,** Town; Jay County; Pop. 277; Zip Code 47326; Lat. 40-32-00 N long. 084-57-50 W; Established in 1872 and named for a railroad construction boss named Bryan.

•**BUNKER HILL,** Town; Miami County; Pop. 985; Zip Code 46914; Lat. 39-38-00 N long. 085-54-51 W; The town's name honors the famous Revolutionary War battle.

•**BURKET,** Town; Kosciusko County; Pop. 250; Zip Code 46508; Lat. 41-09-19 N long. 085-58-07 W; The town's name remembers its founder.

•**BURLINGTON,** Town; Carroll County; Pop. 678; Zip Code 46915; Lat. 40-28-49 N long. 086-23-41 W; Named after a Wyandotte Indian chief called Burlington.

•**BURNETTSVILLE,** Town; White County; Pop. 489; Zip Code 47926; Lat. 40-45-40 N long. 086-35-37 W; Burnetts Stream runs near the town. It is named after the stream.

•**BURNS HARBOR,** Town; Porter County; Pop. 925; Lat. 41-37-32 N long. 087-06-57 W; Named after an early settler.

•**BUTLER,** City; De Kalb County; Pop. 2,505; Zip Code 46721; Lat. 41-25-47 N long. 084-52-17 W; Originally called Norristown, the name was later changed to honor pioneer David Butler.

•**CADIZ,** Town; Henry County; Pop. 180; Lat. 39-57-05 N long. 085-29-12 W.

•**CAMBRIDGE CITY,** Town; Wayne County; Pop. 2,383; Zip Code 47327; Lat. 39-48-45 N long. 085-10-18 W; Originally a depot on the Whitewater Canal, it was named for the city in England.

•**CAMDEN,** Town; Carroll County; Pop. 620; Zip Code 46917; Lat. 40-36-31 N long. 086-32-24 W; Settled in 1833 and named for the city in New Jersey.

•**CAMPBELLSBURG,** Town; Washington County; Pop. 696; Zip Code 47108; Lat. 38-39-05 N long. 086-15-40 W; Founder Robert Campbell established the town in 1851. It is named for him.

•**CANNELBURG,** Town; Daviess County; Pop. 152; Zip Code 47519; Lat. 38-40-11 N long. 086-59-54 W; Settled in 1844 and named for the cannel coal mined near the site.

•**CANNELTON,** City; Perry County Seat; Pop. 2,238; Zip Code 47520; Lat. 37-54-41 N long. 086-44-40 W; Cannel coal is mined nearby and gives the town its name.

•**CARBON,** Town; Clay County; Pop. 303; Zip Code 47837; Lat. 39-35-52 N long. 087-07-07 W; Descriptively named for the coal, or carbon, deposits nearby.

•**CAREFREE,** Town; Crawford County; Pop. 41; Given this happy name by its founders.

•**CARLISLE,** Town; Sullivan County; Pop. 716; Zip Code 47838; Lat. 38-58-06 N long. 087-24-20 W; Settled in 1803 and named for Carlisle, Pennsylvania.

•**CARMEL,** City; Hamilton County; Pop. 18,072; Zip Code 46032; lat. 39-58-42 N long. 086-07-05 W; Early settlers named the city for the Biblical mountain.

•**CARTHAGE,** Town; Rush County; Pop. 883; Zip Code 46115; Lat. 39-44-18 N long. 085-34-19 W; First settled in 1834 and named for Carthage, North Carolina.

•**CASTLETON,** Town; Marion County; Pop. 80; Lat. 39-54-25 N long. 086-03-08 W; Founder Thomas Gentry named the town after his former home in Castleton, North Carolina.

•**CAYUGA,** Town; Vermillion County; Pop. 1,264; Zip Code 47928; Elev. 511; Lat. 39-56-55 N long. 087-27-35 W; Originally Eugene Station, it was later renamed after the Iroquois Indian word "Gwa-u-geh," or "the place of beginning a portage."

•**CEDAR GROVE,** Town; Franklin County; Pop. 213; Zip Code 47016; Lat. 39-21-23 N long. 084-42-48 W; Founded in 1837 and given a descriptive name.

•**CEDAR LAKE,** Town; Lake County; Pop. 8,630; Zip Code 46303; Lat. 41-21-53 N long. 087-26-28 W; Named for the red cedars along the shore of the nearby lake.

•**CLARKS HILL,** Town; Tippecanoe County; Pop. 664; Zip Code 47930; Lat. 40-14-49 N long. 086-43-30 W; Daniel Clark settled the town in the 1850's. It is named in his honor.

•**CLARKSVILLE,** Town; Clark County; Pop. 15,102; Lat. 40-01-56 N long. 085-54-45 W; Revolutionary War hero George Rogers Clark is remembered in the town's name.

•**CLAY CITY,** Town; Clay County; Pop. 885; Zip Code 47841; Lat. 39-16-36 N long. 087-06-46 W; Established in 1873 and named after the county.

•**CLAYPOOL,** Town; Kosciusko County; Pop. 464; Zip Code 46510; Lat. 41-07-45 N long. 085-52-50 W; Settled in 1841 and named after a local settler.

•**CLAYTON,** Town; Hendricks County; Pop. 696; Zip Code 46118; Lat. 39-41-21 N long. 086-31-21 W; The town's name honors Kentucky statesman, Henry Clay.

•**CLEAR LAKE,** Town; Steuben County; Pop. 308; Lat. 41-45-05 N long. 084-50-21 W; Incorporated in 1933 and named for nearby Clear Lake.

•**CLERMONT,** Town; Marion County; Pop. 1,469; Lat. 39-48-35 N long. 086-19-21 W; Originally Mechanicsburg, it was renamed in 1855 after a city in the eastern U. S.

•**CLIFFORD,** Town; Bartholomew County; Pop. 307; Zip Code 47226; Lat. 39-16-56 N long. 085-52-09 W; Given a local settler's name upon its founding in 1853.

•**CLINTON,** City; Vermillion County; Pop. 5,257; Zip Code 47842; Lat. 39-12-38 N long. 085-07-55 W; The name honors New York Governor De Witt Clinton, founder of the Erie Canal.

•**CLOVERDALE,** Town; Putnam County; Pop. 1,364; Zip Code 46120; Lat. 39-30-53 N long. 086-47-38 W; Descriptively named for the clover fields in the area.

•**COATESVILLE,** Town; Hendricks County; Pop. 479; Zip Code 46121; Lat. 39-41-16 N long. 086-40-13 W; Settled in the 1830's and probably named for a local settler.

•**COLFAX,** Town; Clinton County; Pop. 817; Zip Code 46035; Lat. 40-11-42 N long. 086-40-02 W; Named in honor of Hoosier Schuyler Colfax, who was a Vice President of the U. S. in the 1850's.

•**COLUMBIA CITY,** City; Whitley County; Pop. 5,071; Zip Code 46725; Lat. 41-09-26 N long. 085-29-18 W; Established in 1839 and given the popular name for America, Columbia.

•**COLUMBUS,** City; Bartholomew County Seat; Pop. 30,331; Zip Code 47201; Lat. 39-12-05 N long. 085-55-17 W; Originally called Tiptonia, but later changed to Columbus.

•**CONNERSVILLE,** City; Fayette County Seat; Pop. 16,755; Zip Code 47331; Lat. 39-38-25 N long. 085-15-44 W; Fur trader founded a town here in 1813. It is named after him.

•**CONVERSE,** Town; Grant & Miami Counties; Pop. 1,190; Zip Code 46919; Lat. 40-23-22 N long. 085-14-21 W; Platted in 1849 and named after a prominent landowner in the area.

•**CORUNNA,** Town; De Kalb County; Pop. 302; Zip Code 46730; Lat. 41-26-14 N long. 085-08-50 W; First settled in 1855 and named after Corunna, Michigan.

•**CORYDON,** Town; Harrison County Seat; Pop. 2,720; Zip Code 47846; Lat. 38-12-43 N long. 086-07-19 W; Named by General Henry Harrison after the shepard in the song "Pastoral Elegy."

•**COUNTRY CLUB HEIGHTS,** Town; Madison County; Pop. 95; Lat. 40-07-22 N long. 085-41-14 W; Descriptively named by its developers.

•**COVINGTON,** City; Fountain County; Pop. 2,889; Zip Code 47932; Lat. 40-08-30 N long. 087-23-41 W; Settled by Virginians and named after Covington, Virginia.

•**CRANDALL,** Town; Harrison County; Pop. 175; Zip Code 47114; Lat. 38-17-15 N long. 086-03-59 W; Founded by Cornelius Crawford and named for him.

•**CRANE,** Town; Martin County; Pop. 297; Zip Code 47522; Elev. 614; Lat. 38-53-28 N long. 086-54-14 W; Named for an early settler.

•**CRAWFORDSVILLE,** City; Montgomery County Seat; Pop. 13,310; Zip Code 47933; Elev. 769; Lat. 40-02-28 N long. 086-52-28 W; Settled in 1823 and named for U. S. Secretary of War, Colonel William Crawford.

•**CROMWELL,** Town; Noble County; Pop. 445; Zip Code 46732; Lat. 41-24-02 N long. 085-36-57 W; Founded in 1853 and named after Oliver Cromwell.

•**CROTHERSVILLE,** Town; Jackson County; Pop. 1,741; Zip Code 47229; Lat. 38-48-02 N long. 085-50-30 W; First established in 1835 and named after railroad superintendant Crothers.

•**CROWN POINT,** City; Lake County Seat; Pop. 16,364; Zip Code 46307; Lat. 41-25-01 N long. 087-21-55 W; Established in 1834 and named for a high point of land upon which stood the courthouse.

•**CROWS NEST,** Town; Marion County; Pop. 106; Lat. 39-51-29 N long. 086-10-07 W; Descriptively named by its settlers.

•**CULVER,** Town; Marshall County; Pop. 1,601; Zip Code 46511; Lat. 41-13-08 N long. 086-25-23 W; Originally Union Town, the name was changed to honor military academy founder, Henry H. Culver.

•**CUMBERLAND,** Town; Hancock & Miriam Counties; Pop. 3,375; Lat. 39-46-34 N long. 085-57-26 W; Named for the famous Cumberland Road which ran through Indiana.

•CYNTHIANA, Town; Posey County; Pop. 873; Zip Code 47612; Lat. 38-11-15 N long. 087-42-37 W; Settlers from Kentucky named the town after Cynthiana, Kentucky.

•DALE, Town; Spencer County; Pop. 1,696; Zip Code 47523; Lat. 38-10-08 N long. 086-59-24 W; Founded in 1843 and named after U. S. Congressman Robert Owen.

•DANA, Town; Vermillion County; Pop. 801; Zip Code 47847; Lat. 39-48-28 N long. 087-29-42 W; Railroad stockholder Charles Dana had the town named in his honor.

•DANVILLE, Town; Hendricks County Seat; Pop. 4,226; Zip Code 46122; Lat. 39-45-38 N long. 086-31-35 W; Settled in 1824 and named by the local circut judge for his brother Dan.

•DARLINGTON, Town; Montgomery County; Pop. 815; Zip Code 47940; Lat. 40-06-36 N long. 086-46-19 W; Quaker settlers named the town for the city in England.

•DARMSTADT, Town; Vanderburgh County; Pop. 1,261; Elev. 483; Lat. 38-05-57 N long. 087-34-44 W; German settlers named the town in 1860 after Darmstadt, Germany.

•DAYTON, Town; Tippecanoe County; Pop. 780; Zip Code 47941; Lat. 40-22-27 N long. 086-46-08 W; Established in 1827 and named after Dayton, Ohio.

•DE MOTTE, Town; Jasper County; Pop. 2,528; Zip Code 46310; Elev. 668; Lat. 41-11-42 N long. 087-11-55 W; Named for an early settler.

•DECATUR, City; Adams County Seat; Pop. 8,647; The city's name honors naval hero, Stephen Decatur.

•DECKER, Town; Knox County; Pop. 256; Zip Code 47524; Lat. 38-31-08 N long. 087-31-23 W; Founded by Issac Decker and named for him.

•DELPHI, City; Carroll County Seat; Pop. 3,036; Zip Code 46923; Elev. 580; Lat. 40-35-15 N long. 086-40-30   Named after the famous Greek shrine at Delphi.

•DENVER, Town; Miiiami County; Pop. 585; Zip Code 46926; Lat. 40-51-58 N long. 086-04-39 W; Probably named for the city in Colorado.

•DILLSBORO, Town; Dearborn County; Pop. 1,036; Zip Code 47018; Lat. 39-01-04 N long. 085-03-32 W; Settled in 1830 and named in honor of General James Dill.

•DUBLIN, Town; Wayne County; Pop. 980; Zip Code 47335; Lat. 39-48-44 N long. 085-12-32 W; Founded in the 1820's and named for the great Irish city.

•DUGGER, Town; Sullivan County; Pop. 1,110; Zip Code 47848; Lat. 39-04-10 N long. 087-15-36 W; F. M. Dugger founded the town in 1879. It is named after him.

•DUNE ACRES, Town; Porter County; Pop. 284; Lat. 41-38-58 N long. 087-05-09 W; Descriptively named after the famous Indiana Dunes.

•DUNKIRK, City; Blackford & Jay Counties; Pop. 3,180; Zip Code 47336; Lat. 40-45-23 N long. 40-45-23 N long. 086-23-37 W; Originally Quincy, the name was changed to recall Dunkirk, New York.

•DUNREITH, Town; Henry County; Pop. 187; Zip Code 47337; Lat. 39-48-12 N long. 085-26-19 W; The name is derived from early settler Emery Dunreith Coffin.

•DUPONT, Town; Jefferson County; Pop. 393; Zip Code 47231; Lat. 38-53-24 N long. 085-30-51 W; The town is named after the famous Dupont family.

•DYER, Town; Lake County; Pop. 9,538; Zip Code 46311; Lat. 41-29-39 N long. 087-31-18 W; Settled in the 1850's and named for a local settler.

•EARL PARK, Town; Benton County; Pop. 474; Zip Code 47942; Lat. 40-40-58 N long. 087-24-42 W; Named after prominent landowner Adam Earl who helped lay out the plan in 1872.

•EAST CHICAGO, City; Lake County; Pop. 39,798; Zip Code 46312; Lat. 41-38-21 N long. 087-27-17 W; Descriptively named for its location east of Chicago.

•EAST GERMANTOWN, Town; Wayne County; Pop. 441; Lat. 39-48-45 N long. 085-08-15 W; Also called Pershing, the town was named after German settlers from Pennsylvania who came here in the 1830's.

•EATON, Town; Delaware County; Pop. 1,805; Zip Code 47338; Lat. 40-20-25 N long. 40-20-25 N long. 085-21-03 W; Named for an early settler when the town was founded in 1854.

•ECONOMY, Town; Wayne County; Pop. 237; Zip Code 47339; Lat. 39-58-41 N long. 085-05-17 W; The original landowner subdivided his land to raise money and hence suggested this name in 1825.

•EDGEWOOD, Town; Madison County; Pop. 2,216; Lat. 40-06-12 N long. 085-44-03 W; Descriptively named for its location at the edge of a large forest.

•EDINBURGH, Town; Bartholomew & Johnson Counties; Pop. 4,856; Zip Code 46124; Lat. 39-21-15 N long. 085-58-00 W; The town is named after Edinburgh, Scotland.

•EDWARDSPORT, Town; Knox County; Pop. 452; Zip Code 47528; Lat. 38-48-43 N long. 087-15-08 W; The town is named after its founder, Henry Edwards.

•ELBERFELD, Town; Warrick County; Pop. 640; Zip Code 47613; Elev. 445; Lat. 38-09-35 N long. 087-26-54 W; Founded in 1885 and named by its German settlers after Elberfeld, Germany.

•ELIZABETH, Town; Harrison County; Pop. 175; Zip Code 47117; Lat. 38-07-16 N long. 085-58-27 W; Named for Elizabeth Veach whose husband donated the land for the town in 1812.

•ELIZABETHTOWN, Town; Bartholomew County; Pop. 611; Zip Code 47232; Lat. 39-08-06 N long. 085-48-48 W; The town's name honors the wife of the original landowner.

•ELKHART, City; Elkhart County; Pop. 41,049; Zip Code 46514; Lat. 41-40-55 N long. 085-58-36 W; Elkhart is named after the Elkhart River.

•ELLETTSVILLE, Town; Monroe County; Pop. 3,308; Zip Code 47429; Lat. 39-14-02 N long. 086-37-30 W; Named for early 19th century tavern owner Edward Elletts.

•ELNORA, Town; Daviess County; Pop. 755; Zip Code 47529; Lat. 38-52-42 N long. 087-05-09 W; Founded in 1885 and named for Elnora Griffith, the wife of a local merchant.

•ELWOOD, City; Madison & Tipton Counties; Pop. 10,867; Zip Code 46036; Lat. 40-16-37 N long. 085-50-31 W; Originally Quincy, the town was later named after Elwood Frazier, a resident of the town.

•ENGLISH, Town; Crawford County Seat; Pop. 623; Zip Code 47118; Lat. 38-20-04 N long. 086-27-51 W; Founded in 1839 and named for Indiana statesman, William English.

•**EVANSVILLE,** City; Vanderburgh County Seat; Pop. 129,667; Zip Code 47700; Lat. 37-58-29 N long. 087-33-21 W; The town's name honors General Robert Evans who settled here in 1817.

•**FAIRMOUNT,** Town; Grant County; Pop. 3,283; Zip Code 46928; Lat. 40-24-55 N long. 085-39-02 W; Named after the Fairmont Waterworks in Philadelphia when founded in 1850.

•**FAIRVIEW PARK,** Town; Vermillion County; Pop. 1,532; Lat. 39-40-49 N long. 087-25-03 W; A descriptive name for the area's attractive surroundings.

•**FARMERSBURG,** Town; Sullivan County; Pop. 1,242; Zip Code 47850; Lat. 39-14-55 N long. 087-22-55 W; Named Farmersburg in 1875 after the many farmers in the area.

•**FARMLAND,** Town; Randolph County; Pop. 1,543; Zip Code 47340; Lat. 40-11-16 N long. 085-07-39 W; Descriptively named for the rich farmland in the area.

•**FERDINAND,** Town; Dubois County; Pop. 2,199; Zip Code 47532; Elev. 541; Lat. 38-13-26 N long. 086-51-44 W; The town's name honors nineteenth century Austrian Emperor, Ferdinand.

•**FISHERS,** Town; Hamilton County; Pop. 2,010; Zip Code 46038; Lat. 39-57-20 N long. 086-00-50 W; Salathel Fisher founded the town 1872. It is named after him.

•**FLORA,** Town; Carroll County; Pop. 2,302; Zip Code 46929; Lat. 40-32-50 N long. 086-31-28 W; John Flora established the town in 1872. It is named after him.

•**FORT BRANCH,** Town; Gibson County; Pop. 2,490; Zip Code 47648; Lat. 38-15-04 N long. 087-34-52 W; The town is named after an early military outpost, Fort Branch.

•**FORT WAYNE,** City; Allen County Seat; Pop. 177,671; Zip Code 468+; Elev. 767. Until the close of the American Revolution this site was known as Miami Town for the Miami Indians led by Chief Little Turtle. He was defeated in 1794 by Gen. "Mad Anthony" Wayne, following which a fort was erected in his name.

•**FRANKLIN,** City; Johnson County; Pop. 11,573; Zip Code 46131; Lat. 39-28-50 N long. 086-03-18 W; Founded in 1811 and named in hnor of statesman, Benjamin Franklin.

•**FRANKTON,** Town; Madison County; Pop. 2,066; Zip Code 46044; Lat. 40-13-22 N long. 085-46-44 W; Francis "Frank" Sigler laid out the town in 1853. It is named for him.

•**FREDERICKSBURG,** Town; Washington County; Pop. 233; Zip Code 47120; Lat. 38-25-59 N long. 086-11-23 W; Frederick Royse founded the town in 1815. It is named in his honor.

•**FREMONT,** Town; Steuben County; Pop. 1,184; Zip Code 46737; Lat. 41-43-51 N long. 084-55-58 W; Founded in 1837 and named in honor of explorer J. C. Fremont.

•**FRENCH LICK,** Town; Orange County; Pop. 2,275; Zip Code 47432; Lat. 38-32-56 N long. 086-37-12 W; Descriptively named for its location near a famous salt spring and animal lick nearby.

•**FULTON,** Town; Fulton County; Pop. 396; Zip Code 46931; Lat. 40-56-50 N long. 086-15-46 W; The town is named after the county.

•**GALVESTON,** Town; Cass County; Pop. 1,821; Zip Code 46932; Lat. 40-34-44 N long. 086-11-25 W; Named after Galveston, Texas.

•**GARRETT,** City; De Kalb County; Pop. 4,880; Zip Code 46738; Lat. 41-20-58 N long. 085-08-08 W; The city's name honors B & O Railroad President John W. Garrett.

•**GARY,** City; Lake County; Pop. 151,855; Zip Code 464+; Lat. 41-35-36 N long. 087-20-47 W; Established in 1906 and named after Elbert Gary, Board Chairman of U. S. Steel.

•**GAS CITY,** City; Grant County; Pop. 6,325; Zip Code 46933; Elev. 853; Lat. 40-29-14 N long. 085-36-47 W; Descriptively named for natural gas deposits found here in 1887.

•**GASTON,** Town; Delaware County; Pop. 1,156; Zip Code 47342; Lat. 40-18-50 N long. 085-30-02 W; Originally New Corner, the name was changed when natural gas was discovered in the 1880's.

•**GENEVA,** Town; Adams County; Pop. 1,423; Zip Code 46740; Lat. 40-35-31 N long. 084-57-26 W; Founded in 1853 and named after the Swiss city.

•**GENTRYVILLE,** Town; Spencer County; Pop. 305; Zip Code 47537; Elev. 405; Lat. 38-06-15 N long. 087-01-59 W; Merchant James Gentry lived here in the 1850's. It is named after him.

•**GEORGETOWN,** Town; Floyd County; Pop. 1,492; Zip Code 47122; Lat. 41-13-55 N long. 084-51-56 W; Founded in 1833 and named for town father, George Waltz.

•**GLENWOOD,** Town; Fayette & Rush Counties; Pop. 370; Zip Code 46133; Elev. 1082; Lat. 39-37-33 N long. 085-18-01 W; A common descriptive name in the midwest's wooded areas.

•**GOODLAND,** Town; Newton County; Pop. 1,193; Zip Code 47948; Lat. 40-45-48 N long. 087-17-37 W; Descriptively named in 1861 for the surrounding fertile farmland.

•**GOSHEN,** City; Elkhart County Seat; Pop. 19,649; Zip Code 46526; Lat. 38-40-17 N long. 085-42-35 W; Named for a Biblical land of plenty to reflect the rich farmland in the area.

•**GOSPORT,** Town; Owen County; Pop. 1,337; Zip Code 47433; Lat. 39-21-03 N long. 086-40-01 W; The Goss brothers founded the town in 1829. It is named after them.

•**GRABILL,** Town; Allen County; Pop. 658; Zip Code 46741; Lat. 41-12-39 N long. 084-58-01 W; Settled in 1902 and named after local resident Joseph Grabill.

•**GRANDVIEW,** Town; Spencer County; Pop. 669; Zip Code 47615; Lat. 40-07-06 N long. 085-42-30 W; Established in 1851 and named after its bluff-top location which allows a view of the Ohio River in both directions.

•**GREENCASTLE,** City; Putnam County Seat; Pop. 8,414; Named after Greencastle, Pennsylvania.

•**GREENDALE,** Town; Dearborn County; Pop. 3,789; Zip Code 46135; Lat. 39-38-40 N long. 086-51-53 W; A descriptive name of the area's verdant surroundings.

•**GREENFIELD,** City; Hancock County Seat; Pop. 11,308; Zip Code 46140; Elev. 888; Lat. 39-47-06 N long. 085-46-10 W; Founded in 1828 and named after pioneer settler John Green.

•**GREENS FORK,** Town; Wayne County; Pop. 423; Zip Code 47345; Lat. 39-53-33 N long. 085-02-30 W; Named after nearby Green's Fork Stream when it was founded in 1818.

•**GREENSBORO,** Town; Henry County; Pop. 174; Zip Code 47344; Lat. 39-52-30 N long. 085-27-58 W; Settlers from Greensboro, North Carolina came here in 1830 and named the settlement for their own former home.

•**GREENSBURG,** City; Decatur County Seat; Pop. 9,255; Zip Code 47240; Lat. 39-20-14 N long. 085-29-01 W; Named after Greensburg, Pennsylvania.

•**GREENTOWN**, Town; Howard County; Pop. 2,253; Zip Code 46936; Elev. 844; Lat. 40-28-41 N long. 085-58-00 W; The town's name remembers Miami Indian, Chief Green.

•**GREENVILLE**, Town; Floyd County; Pop. 538; Zip Code 46936; Lat. 39-08-27 N long. 087-18-07 W; Settled in 1807 and named after Greenville Township.

•**GREENWOOD**, City; Johnson County; Pop. 19,300; Zip Code 46142; Lat. 36-36-49 N long. 086-06-24 W; Founded in 1864 and named after a local church.

•**GRIFFIN**, Town; Posey County; Pop. 192; Zip Code 47616; Lat. 38-12-15 N long. 087-54-53 W; Samuel Griffin was the town's first post. It is named in his honor.

•**GRIFFITH**, Town; Lake County; Pop. 17,227; Zip Code 46319; Lat. 41-31-42 N long. 087-25-25 W; Named in honor of railroad civil engineer, Benjamin Griffith.

•**HAGERSTOWN**, Town; Wayne County; Pop. 1,953; Zip Code 47346; Elev. 1008; Lat. 39-54-40 N long. 085-09-42 W; Settled in 1830 and named after Hagerstown, Maryland.

•**HAMILTON**, Town; De Kalb & Steuben Counties; Pop. 587; Zip Code 46742; Elev. 811; Lat. 40-20-41 N long. 086-37-05 W; Founded in 1823 and named in honor of Alexander Hamilton.

•**HAMLET**, Town; Starke County; Pop. 724; Zip Code 46532; Lat. 41-32-51 N long. 086-34-56 W; John Hamlet founded the town in 1863. It is named in his honor.

•**HAMMOND**, City; Lake County; Pop. 93,440; Zip Code 46320; Lat. 41-35-00 N long. 087-30-00 W; Named in honor of prominent meat packer George Hammond.

•**HANOVER**, Town; Jefferson County; Pop. 4,037; Zip Code 47243; Lat. 38-42-51 N long. 085-28-25 W; Founded in 1832 and named after Hanover, New Hampshire.

•**HARDINSBURG**, Town; Washington County; Pop. 298; Zip Code 47125; Lat. 39-07-19 N long. 084-50-51 W; The town was laid out in 1838 and Aaron Hardin and named for him.

•**HARMONY**, Town; Clay County; Pop. 608; Zip Code 47853; Lat. 39-32-12 N long. 087-06-21 W; Settled in 1839 and given this euphonious name.

•**HARTFORD CITY**, City; Blackford County Seat; Pop. 7,586; Zip Code 47348; Lat. 40-27-04 N long. 085-22-12 W; Originally Blackford, the name was changed in 1854 after Hartford, Connecticut.

•**HARTSVILLE**, Town; Bartholomew County; Pop. 379; Zip Code 47244; Lat. 39-16-03 N long. 085-41-53 W; The town is named for pioneer Gideon B. Hart.

•**HAUBSTADT**, Town; Gibson County; Pop. 1,389; Zip Code 47639; Lat. 38-12-18 N long. 087-34-27 W; Haubstadt, or Haub's City, remembers pioneer merchant Henry Haub.

•**HAZLETON**, Town; Gibson County; Pop. 371; Zip Code 47640; Lat. 38-29-20 N long. 087-32-30 W; Gervas Hazelton founded the town in 1856. It is named after him.

•**HEBRON**, Town; Porter County; Pop. 2,666; Zip Code 46341; Lat. 41-19-07 N long. 087-12-01 W; Given a Biblical name by the Rev. Hannan when it was laid out in 1844.

•**HIGHLAND**, Town; Lake County; Pop. 25,878; Lat. 41-33-13 N long. 087-27-07 W; Descriptively named for its location on higher ground than the surrounding area.

•**HILLSBORO**, Town; Fountain County; Pop. 558; Zip Code 47949; Lat. 40-06-32 N long. 087-11-08 W; Settled in 1826 and descriptively named for its location.

•**HOBART**, City; Lake County; Pop. 22,804; Zip Code 46342; Lat. 41-31-56 N long. 087-15-18 W; Founded in 1849 and named after Hobart Earle, brother of the town's founder.

•**HOLLAND**, Town; Dubois County; Pop. 688; Zip Code 47541; Lat. 38-14-44 N long. 087-02-10 W; Dutch settler Henry Kunz laid out the town in 1859 and named it for his native country.

•**HOLTON**, Town; Ripley County; Pop. 500; Zip Code 47023; Elev. 911; Lat. 39-04-30 N long. 085-23-14 W; Founded in 1854 by Jesse Holman and named Holton by its settlers to honor him.

•**HOMECROFT**, Town; Marion County; Pop. 833; Lat. 39-40-12 N long. 086-07-53 W; Named for a local settler.

•**HOPE**, Town; Bartholomew County; Pop. 1,852; Zip Code 47246; Lat. 39-18-14 N long. 085-46-17 W; Settled in 1836 and named after a Moravian settlement in North Carolina.

•**HUDSON**, Town; Steuben County; Pop. 445; Zip Code 46744; Lat. 41-31-58 N long. 085-04-52 W; Originally Benton, the name was changed to honor a local resident in 1875.

•**HUNTERTOWN**, Town; Allen County Seat; Pop. 1,267; Zip Code 46748; Lat. 41-13-42 N long. 085-10-21 W; Settled in 1836 and named after town founder William T. Hunter.

•**HUNTINGBURG**, City; Dubois County; Pop. 5,402; Zip Code 47542; Lat. 38-17-56 N long. 086-57-18 W; The town's founder, Joseph Geiger, hunted in the area before settling down and gave it this descriptive name.

•**HUNTINGTON**, City; Huntington County; Pop. 16,161; Zip Code 46750; Lat. 40-52-59 N long. 085-29-51 W; The city's name honors Samuel Huntington, a signer of the Declaration of Independence.

•**HYMERA**, Town; Sullivan County; Pop. 1,068; Zip Code 47855; Lat. 39-11-11 N long. 087-18-06 W; Founded in 1870 and named after the ancient Sicilian city of Himera.

•**INDIAN VILLAGE**, Town; St. Joseph County; Pop. 151; Lat. 41-02-54 N long. 085-10-21 W; Named for an Indain village that once occupied the site.

•**INDIANAPOLIS**, City; Marion County Seat; Pop. 698,753; Zip Code 46200; Lat. 39-46-06 N long. 086-09-29 W; Settled in 1820 and named after the Indiana (or Indian) territory.

•**INGALLS**, Town; Madison County; Pop. 911; Zip Code 46048; Elev. 869; Lat. 39-57-25 N long. 085-48-19 W; The town's name honors M. E. Ingalls, a railroad president.

•**JAMESTOWN**, Town; Boone & Hendricks Counties; Pop. 924; Zip Code 46147; Lat. 39-55-36 N long. 086-37-44 W; Founded in 1832 and named for James Matlock, a town founder.

•**JASONVILLE**, City; Greene County; Pop. 2,484; Zip Code 47438; Lat. 39-09-47 N long. 087-11-57 W; Jason Rogers purchased the land in 1853. The town is named after him.

•**JASPER**, City; Dubois County Seat; Pop. 9,136; Zip Code 47546; Lat. 38-23-29 N long. 086-55-52 W; Jasper's name honors Sgt. William Jasper, a Revolutionary War hero.

•JEFFERSONVILLE, City; Clark County Seat; Pop. 21,242; Zip Code 47130; Lat. 38-17-24 N long. 085-45-06 W; Named in honor of Thomas Jefferson.

•JONESBORO, Town; Grant County; Pop. 2,276; Zip Code 46938; Lat. 40-28-47 N long. 085-37-40 W; Named in honor of early settler Obediah Jones.

•JONESVILLE, Town; Bartholomew County; Pop. 221; Zip Code 47247; Lat. 39-03-38 N long. 085-53-23 W; Benjamin Jones founded the town in 1851. Named for him.

•JUDSON, Town; Parke County; Pop. 80; Zip Code 47856; Lat. 40-30-14 N long. 086-16-17 W; Settled in 1872 and named for Kentucky missionary Adoniram Judson who had died in 1850.

•KEMPTON, Town; Tipton County; Pop. 412; Zip Code 46049; Elev. 928; Lat. 40-17-18 N long. 086-13-47 W; Founded on land owned by David Kemp and named in his honor.

•KENDALLVILLE, City; Noble County; Pop. 6,881; Zip Code 46755; Lat. 41-26-29 N long. 085-15-54 W; The city's name honors postmaster General Amos Kendall, who served in the Jackson administration.

•KENNARD, Town; Henry County; Pop. 616; Zip Code 47351; Lat. 39-54-14 N long. 085-31-10 W; Jenkins Kennard, a prominent citizen, had the town named for him in 1882.

•KENTLAND, Town; Newton County Seat; Pop. 1,934; Zip Code 47951; Lat. 40-46-13 N long. 087-26-43 W; Founded by A. J. Kent and named in his honor.

•KIRKLIN, Town; Clinton County; Pop. 664; Zip Code 46050; Lat. 40-11-36 N long. 086-21-38 W; Nathan Kirk ran a tavern here in the 1830's. The town is named after him.

•KNIGHTSTOWN, Town; Henry County; Pop. 2,324; Zip Code 46148; Lat. 39-47-44 N long. 085-31-35 W; Named for John Knight, a construction engineer on the National Railroad.

•KNIGHTSVILLE, Town; Clay County; Pop. 765; Zip Code 47857; LAT. 39-31-33 N long. 087-06-45 W; Founded by A. W. Knight in 1867 and named for him.

•KNOX, City; Starke County Seat; Pop. 3,672; Zip Code 46534; Lat. 39-49-23 N long. 085-32-31 W; Settled in 1851 and named in honor of General Henry Knox, a member of Washington's cabinet.

•KOKOMO, City; Howard County Seat; Pop. 47,118; Zip Code 46901; Lat. 40-29-11 N long. 086-08-01 W; Named after a Miami Indian, Ko-ka-ma, or "the diver."

•KOUTS, Town; Porter County; Pop. 1,612; Zip Code 46347; Lat. 41-19-00 N long. 087-01-33 W; Railroad surveyors boarded with settler Barnardt Kouts in 1865. They named the town in his honor.

•LA CROSSE, Town; La Porte County; Pop. 678; Zip Code 46348; Lat. 41-19-03 N long. 086-53-29 W; The origin of the name is uncertain, it means either "the crossing," and referring to the junction of four railroads, or the game LaCrosse played by the Indians of the region.

•LA FONTAINE, Town; Wabash County; Pop. 945; Zip Code 46940; Lat. 40-40-26 N long. 085-43-17 W; Incorporated in 1862 and named for Chief La Fontaine, a Miami Indian chief.

•LACONIA, Town; Harrison County; Pop. 58; Zip Code 47135; Lat. 38-01-54 N long. 086-05-08 W; Founded in 1816 and named for the ancient city in Greece.

•LADOGA, Town; Mongtgomery County; Pop. 1,154; Zip Code 47954; Lat. 39-54-49 N long. 086-48-04 W; The town is named after the largest lake in Europe: Lake Ladoga.

•LAFAYETTE, City; Tippecanoe County Seat; Pop. 42,887; Zip Code 47901; Lat. 40-25-00 N long. 086-52-30 W; Settled in 1824 and named in honor of the Marquis De La Fayette.

•LAGRANGE, Town; Lagrange County; Pop. 2,156; Zip Code 46761; Lat. 41-38-30 N long. 085-25-00 W; Named after the Marquis De La Fayette country home near Paris.

•LAGRO, Town; Wabash County; Pop. 546; Zip Code 46941; Lat. 40-50-17 N long. 085-43-49 W; The town's name honors Chief LeGros, a Miami Indian chief in the 1820's.

•LAKE HART, Town; Morgan County; Pop. 216; Named for an early settler.

•LAKE STATION, City; Lake County; Pop. 14,085; Lat. 41-34-30 N long. 087-14-20 W; A descriptive name given by the town's founders.

•LA PAZ, Town; Marshall County; Pop. 652; Zip Code 46537; Lat. 41-27-35 N long. 086-18-30 W; Founded in 1873 and named for the city in South America.

•LA PORTE, City; La Porte County Seat; Pop. 21,781; Lat. 41-36-30 N long. 086-43-30 W; Settled in the 1830's and given a French name meaning "the door," to describe a natural opening in the forest.

•LAPEL, Town; Madison County; Pop. 1,875; Zip Code 46051; Lat. 40-04-06 N long. 085-50-54 W; Descriptive of a railroad right-of-way near the town which resembled a lapel, and provided a name for the town.

•LARWILL, Town; Whitley County; Pop. 284; Zip Code 46764; Lat. 41-10-50 N long. 085-37-32 W; Engineers William & Joseph Lariwill supervised the construction of the railroad through the town. It is named in their honor.

•LAUREL, Town; Franklin County; Pop. 800; Zip Code 47024; Lat. 39-30-03 N long. 085-11-11 W; Founded in 1836 and named for Laurel, Delaware.

•LAWRENCE, City; Marion County; Pop. 25,508; Lat. 39-50-19 N long. 086-01-31 W; Named in honor of U. S. Navy hero, Captain James Lawrence.

•LAWRENCEBURG, City; Dearborn County Seat; Pop. 4,390; Zip Code 47025; Lat. 39-05-27 N long. 084-51-00 W; Town founder Samuel C. Vance named the town for his wife's maiden name: Lawrence.

•LEAVENWORTH, Town; Crawford County; Pop. 348; Zip Code 47137; Lat. 38-11-59 N long. 086-20-39 W; Settled in 1818 and named for early landowners, the Leavenworths.

•LEBANON, City; Boone County Seat; Pop. 11,411; Zip Code 46052; Lat. 40-02-54 N long. 086-28-09 W; Tall hickory trees suggested the Biblical mountain known for its tall cedar trees to the town's founder.

•LEESBURG, Town; Kosciusko County; Pop. 623; Zip Code 46538; Lat. 41-19-55 N long. 085-51-00 W; Levi Lee founded the town in 1835. It is named for him.

•LEWISVILLE, Town; Henry County; Pop. 566; Zip Code 47352; Lat. 39-48-24 N long. 085-21-10 W; Named for town founder Lewis Freeman.

•**LIBERTY,** Town; Union County Seat; Pop. 1,844; Zip Code 47353; Lat. 39-38-08 N long. 084-55-52 W; Settlers from Virginia named it after Liberty, Virginia.

•**LIGONIER,** City; Noble County; Pop. 3,123; Zip Code 46767; Lat. 41-27-57 N long. 085-35-15 W; Settled in 1835 and named for Ligonier, Pennsylvania.

•**LINDEN,** Town; Montgomery County; Pop. 700; Zip Code 47955; Lat. 40-11-17 N long. 086-54-14 W; Named for the Linden tree when founded in 1852.

•**LINTON,** City; Greene County; Pop. 6,276; Zip Code 47441; Lat. 39-02-05 N long. 087-09-57 W; Settled as New Jerusalem in 1816, but later named after congressional candidate, Colonel William Linton.

•**LITTLE YORK,** Town; Washington County; Pop. 136; Zip Code 47139; Lat. 38-42-10 N long. 085-54-18 W; Settlers from New York named their new town after their old state.

•**LIVONIA,** Town; Washington County; Pop. 120; Lat. 38-33-25 N long. 086-16-39 W; Named by its early pioneers after the Baltic province in Russia.

•**LIZTON,** Town; Hendricks County; Pop. 456; Zip Code 46149; Lat. 39-53-12 N long. 086-32-36 W; Founded in 1851 ad New Elizabeth, the railroad shortened this to Lizton.

•**LOGANSPORT,** City; Cass County Seat; Pop. 17,866; Zip Code 46947; Lat. 40-45-16 N long. 086-21-24 W; Named after a Shawnee Indian, Captain Logain, who was killed in the U.S. Army during the War of 1812.

LONG BEACH, Town; La Porte County; Pop. 2,249; Lat. 41-44-44 N long. 086-51-03 W; A descriptive name given by the town's settlers.

•**LOOGOOTEE,** City; Martin County; Pop. 3,110; Zip Code 47553; Lat. 38-40-37 N long. 086-54-51 W; A coined name combining a railroad engineer's name: Lowe, and the original landowner: Gootee.

•**LOSANTVILLE,** Town; Randolph County; Pop. 306; Zip Code 47354; Lat. 40-01-27 N long. 085-10-58 W; A coined word meaning "the town opposite Licking Creek."

•**LOWELL,** Town; Lake County; Pop. 5,794; Zip Code 46356; Lat. 39-15-11 N long. 085-56-47 W; Settled in the 1830's and named for Lowell, Massachusetts.

•**LYNHURST,** Town; Marion County; Pop. 167; Lat. 39-45-32 N long. 086-14-53 W; Named for an early settler.

•**LYNN,** Town; Randolph County; Pop. 1,258; Zip Code 47355; Lat. 40-02-59 N long. 084-56-23 W; Founded in 1847 and named after an early settler.

•**LYNNVILLE,** Town; Warrick County; Pop. 563; Zip Code 47619; Lat. 38-11-46 N long. 087-17-48 W; John Lynn founded the town in 1839. It is named for him.

•**LYONS,** Town; Greene County; Pop. 785; Zip Code 47443; Lat. 38-59-21 N long. 087-04-56 W; Auditor Joe Lyon had the town named in his honor.

•**MACKEY,** Town; Gibson County; Pop. 165; Zip Code 47654; Lat. 38-15-08 N long. 087-23-30 W; Railroad entrepreneur O. J. Mackey founded the town in 1882. It is named in his honor.

•**MACY,** Town; Miami County; Pop. 288; Zip Code 46951; Lat. 40-57-33 N long. 086-07-38 W; Originally Lincoln, the name was later changed after a local resident.

•**MADISON,** City; Jefferson County Seat; Pop. 12,467; Zip Code 47250; Lat. 38-44-09 N long. 085-22-48 W; Settled in 1805 and named for President James Madison.

•**MARENGO,** Town; Crawford County; Pop. 885; Zip Code 47140; Lat. 38-22-32 N long. 086-20-41 W; The town's name remembers Napoleon's victory over the Austrians in 1800 at Morengo, Italy.

•**MARION,** City; Grant County Seat; Pop. 35,833; Zip Code 46952; Lat. 40-33-30 N long. 085-39-33 W; The town's name honors Revolutinary War hero, General Francis Marion.

•**MARKLE,** Town; Huntington & Wells Counties; Pop. 975; Zip Code 46770; Lat. 40-49-45 N long. 085-20-08 W; Settled in 1836 and named after a local resident.

•**MARKLEVILLE,** Town; Madison County; Pop. 428; Zip Code 46056; Lat. 39-58-40 N long. 085-36-53 W; John Markle founded the town in 1852. It is named after him.

•**MARSHALL,** Town; Parke County; Pop. 417; Zip Code 47859; Lat. 39-50-53 N long. 087-11-16 W; Landowner Mahlon Marshall donated the land for the town. It is named after him.

•**MARTINSVILLE,** City; Morgan County Seat; Pop. 11,214; Zip Code 46116; Elev. 607; Lat. 39-25-40 N long. 086-25-42 W; Founded in 1822 and named after county Commissioner John Martin.

•**MATTHEWS,** Town; Grant County; Pop. 737; Zip Code 46957; Lat. 40-23-19 N long. 085-29-58 W; Settled in 1833 and given a personal name of a local resident.

•**MAUCKPORT,** Town; Harrison County; Pop. 108; Zip Code 47142; Lat. 38-01-29 N long. 086-12-07 W; Founded in 1827 by Frederick Mauck and named for him.

•**MECCA,** Town; Parke County; Pop. 482; Zip Code 47860; Lat. 39-43-38 N long. 087-19-50 W; Settled in the 1840's and named for the Moslem city in Arabia.

•**MEDARYVILLLE,** Town; Pulaski County; Pop. 730; Zip Code 47957; Lat. 41-04-50 N long. 086-53-31 W; The town is named for Ohio statesman Joseph Medary.

•**MEDORA,** Town; Jackson County; Pop. 850; Zip Code 47260; Lat. 38-49-30 N long. 086-10-12 W; Founded in 1853 and named from Loro Byron's poem, "The Corsair."

•**MELLOTT,** Town; Fountain County; Pop. 298; Zip Code 47958; Lat. 40-09-55 N long. 087-08-52 W; John and Syrena Mellott founded the town in 1882. It is named after them.

•**MENTONE,** Town; Kosciusko County; Pop. 951; Zip Code 46539; Lat. 41-10-24 N long. 086-02-05 W; Named for the French city when founded in 1882.

•**MERIDIAN HILLS,** Town; Marion County; Pop. 1,798; Lat. 39-53-24 N long. 086-09-26 W; Descriptively named by its developers.

•**MEROM,** Town; Sullivan County; Pop. 360; Lat. 39-03-23 N long. 087-34-03 W; Founded in 1817 and named after the Biblical lake.

•**MERRILLVILLE,** Town; Lake County; Pop. 27,537; Lat. 41-28-58 N long. 087-19-58 W; Storekeeper Dudley Merrill left his name on the town.

•**MICHIANA SHORES,** Town; La Porte County; Pop. 464; Located on Lake Michigan, the name is a combination of Michigan and Indiana.

•**MICHIGAN CITY,** City; La Porte County; Pop. 36,248; Zip Code 46360; Lat. 41-42-27 N long. 086-53-42 W; Named for its location on Lake Michigan.

•MICHIGANTOWN, Town; Clinton County; Pop. 450; Zip Code 46057; Lat. 40-19-35 N long. 086-23-34 W; Descriptively named for the north-south Michigan Road which passes through the town.

•MIDDLEBURY, Town; Elkhart County; Pop. 1,673; Zip Code 46540; Lat. 39-15-51 N long. 087-07-08 W; Founded in 1835 and named after Middlebury, Vermont.

•MIDDLETOWN, Town; Henry County; Pop. 2,963; Zip Code 47356; Lat. 40-03-26 N long. 085-32-14 W; A locational and descriptive name given the town in 1829.

•MILAN, Town; Ripley County; Pop. 1,575; Zip Code 47031; Lat. 39-07-16 N long. 085-07-53 W; Named for the Italian city in 1831.

•MILFORD, Town; Kosciusko County; Pop. 1,154; Lat. 41-24-35 N long. 085-50-44 W; Named for a mill built here on the Turkey Creek ford.

•MILLERSBURG, Town; Elkhart County; Pop. 804; Lat. 41-31-40 N long. 085-41-40 W; Solomon Miller owned the land the town was built on. It is named in his honor.

•MILLHOUSEN, Town; Decatur County; Pop. 214; Zip Code 47261; Lat. 39-12-38 N long. 085-25-57 W; Settled in 1838 and named after the town in Germany.

•MILLTOWN, Town; Crawford & Harrison Counties; Pop. 1,006; Zip Code 47145; Lat. 38-20-32 N long. 086-16-34 W; Settled in 1827 and named as the site of a mill.

•MILTON, Town; Wayne County; Pop. 727; Zip Code 47357; Lat. 38-58-42 N long. 085-00-52 W; The location of several watermills, this fact suggested the name to the town's founders.

•MISHAWAKA, City; St. Joseph County; Pop. 38,279; Zip Code 46544; Lat. 41-39-43 N long. 086-09-31 W; A Potawatomi Indian word "M'seh-wah-keeoki" meaning "country of dead trees," referring to a tract of dead timber near here.

•MITCHELL, City; Lawrence County; Pop. 4,620; Zip Code 47446; Lat. 38-43-58 N long. 076-23-38 W; The town's name honors railroad engineer O. M. Mitchell.

•MODOC, Town; Randolph County; Pop. 248; Zip Code 47358; Lat. 40-02-43 N long. 085-07-35 W; Settled in 1882 and named after the Indian tribe.

•MONON, Town; White County; Pop. 1,537; Zip Code 47959; Lat. 40-52-04 N long. 086-52-44 W; A Potawatomi Indian word meaning "to carry."

•MONROE, Town; Adams County; Pop. 739; Zip Code 46772; Lat. 40-44-42 N long. 084-56-13 W; Named for President James Monroe when it was founded in 1832.

•MONROE CITY, Town; Knox County; Pop. 569; Zip Code 47557; Lat. 38-36-55 N long. 087-21-16 W; Named for early landowner Monroe Alton.

•MONROEVILLE, Town; Allen County; Pop. 1,361; Zip Code 46773; Lat. 40-58-29 N long. 084-52-06 W; The town is named after Monroe Township.

•MONTEREY, Town; Pulaski County; Pop. 236; Zip Code 46960; Lat. 41-09-25 N long. 086-28-58 W; Settled in 1849 and named after a battle in the Mexican-American War.

•MONTEZUMA, Town; Parke County; Pop. 1,344; Zip Code 47862; Lat. 39-47-34 N long. 087-22-15 W; The town's name remembrs the last Aztec emperor of Mexico.

•MONTGOMERY, Town; Daviess County; Pop. 388; Zip Code 47558; Lat. 38-39-45 N long. 087-02-46 W; Montgomery's name honors Revolutionary War hero, General Richard Montgomery.

•MONTICELLO, City; White County; Pop. 5,167; Zip Code 47960; Lat. 40-44-43 N long. 086-45-53 W; Named after Thomas Jefferson's famous Virginia home.

•MONTPELIER, City; Blackford County; Pop. 1,998; Zip Code 47359; Lat. 40-33-14 N long. 085-16-39 W; Early Vermont settlers named it after the city in Vermont.

•MOORELAND, Town; Henry County; Pop. 479; Zip Code 47360; Lat. 39-59-51 N long. 085-15-04 W; Named in 1882 after original landowner Miles Moore.

•MOORES HILL, Town; Dearborn County; Pop. 566; Zip Code 47032; Lat. 39-06-48 N long. 085-05-17 W; Founded in 1828 and named after mill owner Adam Moore.

•MOORESVILLE, Town; Morgan County; Pop. 5,391; Zip Code 46158; Lat. 39-36-46 N long. 086-22-27 W; Samuel Moore founded the town in 1824. It is named after him.

•MORGANTOWN, Town; Morgan County; Pop. 880; Zip Code 46160; Lat. 39-22-17 N long. 086-15-40 W; Settled in 1831 and named for the county, itself honoring Revolutionary War hero, General Daniel Morgan.

•MOROCCO, Town; Newton County; Pop. 1,335; Zip Code 47963; Lat. 40-56-46 N long. 087-27-12 W; Named after the country in North Africa when founded in 1851.

•MORRISTOWN, Town; Shelby County; Pop. 981; Zip Code 46161; Lat. 39-40-24 N long. 085-41-55 W; Samuel Morris co-founded the town in 1828. It is named for him.

•MOUNT AUBURN, Town; Wayne County; Pop. 194; Elev. 819; Lat. 39-23-33 N long. 085-53-37 W; Originally Black Hawk, the name was later changed to the commendatory Mount Auburn.

•MUNCIE, City; Delaware County Seat; Pop. 69,080; Zip Code 473+; Elev. 950. The name was called Munseytown from the Munsee tribe of the Delaware Indians which had at one time occupied the site. It was changed to Muncie in 1845.

•NASHVILLE, Town; Brown County Seat; Pop. 696; Zip Code 47448; Elev. 629; Lat. 39-12-26 N long. 086-15-04 W; Founded in 1834 and named for Nashville, Tennessee.

•NEW ALBANY, City; Floyd County Seat; Pop. 37,087; Zip Code 47150; Lat. 38-17-08 N long. 085-49-27 W; Named after Albany, New York when founded in 1813.

•NEW AMSTERDAM, Town; Harrison County; Pop. 31; Lat. 38-06-08 N long. 086-16-30 W; Settled in 1815 and named after the former Dutch name for New York.

•NEW CARLISLE, Town; St. Joseph County; Pop. 1,348; Zip Code 46552; Lat. 41-42-01 N long. 086-30-34 W; Richard Carlisle founded the town in 1835. It is named for him.

•NEW CASTLE, City; Henry County Seat; Pop. 20,025; Zip Code 47362; Lat. 39-55-44 N long. 085-22-13 W; Ezekial Leavell settled here in 1823 and named it for his former home in Kentucky.

•NEW CHICAGO, Town; Lake County; Pop. 3,273; Lat. 41-33-30 N long. 087-16-28 W; Founded in 1907 and named for nearby Chicago.

•NEW HARMONY, Town; Posey County; Pop. 945; Zip Code 47631; Lat. 38-07-47 N long. 087-56-06 W; First settled in 1814 and named for Harmonie, Pennsylvania.

•**NEW HAVEN,** City; Allen County; Pop. 6,706; Zip Code 46774; Lat. 41-04-14 N long. 085-00-52 W; Named after Neew Haven, Connecticut.

•**NEW MARKET,** Town; Montgomery County; Pop. 606; Zip Code 47965; Lat. 38-32-08 N long. 085-37-01 W; Founded after a fire, new businesses sprung up and suggested the name.

•**NEW MIDDLETOWN,** Town; Harrison County; Pop. 108; Zip Code 47160; Lat. 38-09-50 N long. 086-03-03 W; Originally Middletown, the "new" appelation was added in 1860.

•**NEW PALESTINE,** Town; Hancock County; Pop. 746; Zip Code 46163; Lat. 39-43-19 N long. 085-53-21 W; Given a Biblical name when founded in 1838.

•**NEW PEKIN,** Town; Washington County; Pop. 1,126; Zip Code 46553; Elev. 703; Lat. 38-32-11 N long. 085-55-43 W; Settled in 1852 near Pekin, and so named "New Pekin."

•**NEW PROVIDENCE,** Town; Clark County; Pop. 374; Founded in 1817 and given a Biblical name.

•**NEW RICHMOND,** Town; Montgomery County; Pop. 402; Zip Code 47967; Lat. 40-11-44 N long. 086-58-44 W; Pioneer Samuel Kincaid named the town after his former home in New Richmond, Ohio.

•**NEW ROSS,** Town; Montgomery County; Pop. 306; Zip Code 47968; Lat. 39-57-53 N long. 086-42-52 W; Innkeeper George Dorsey named the town after the English city of Ross.

•**NEW WHITELAND,** Town; Johnson County; Pop. 4,504; Lat. 39-33-29 N long. 086-05-43 W; Joel White founded the town in the mid-eighteenth century. It is named for him.

•**NEWBERRY,** Town; Greene County; Pop. 246; Zip Code 47449; Lat. 38-55-30 N long. 087-01-10 W; Named after Newberry, South Carolina when founded in 1830.

•**NEWBURGH,** Town; Warrick County; Pop. 2,886; Zip Code 47630; Lat. 37-56-40 N long. 087-24-19 W; Originally Sprinklesburg, it combined with a nearby village named Newburgh and took its name.

•**NEWPOINT,** Town; Decatur County; Pop. 298; Once called Crackway, it was later given the descriptive name "new point."

•**NEWPORT,** Town; Vermillion County Seat; Pop. 700; Zip Code 47966; Lat. 39-53-03 N long. 087-24-31 W; Named after Newport, Delaware.

•**NEWTOWN,** Town; Fountain County; Pop. 277; Zip Code 47969; Elev. 711; Lat. 40-12-15 N long. 087-08-52 W; The town's name honors Sgt. John Newton, a hero in the Revolutionary War.

•**NOBLESVILLE,** City; Hamilton County Seat; Pop. 12,030; Zip Code 46060; Lat. 40-02-44 N long. 086-00-31 W; Named in honor of James Noble, first U. S. Senator from Indiana.

•**NORTH CROWS NEST,** Town; Marion County; Pop. 78; Lat. 39-51-57 N long. 086-09-48 W; Descriptively named by its founders.

•**NORTH LIBERTY,** Town; St. Joseph County; Pop. 1,205; Zip Code 46554; Lat. 41-32-03 N long. 086-25-38 W; Named for its location in North Liberty Township.

•**NORTH MANCHESTER,** Town; Wabash County; Pop. 6,000; Zip Code 46962; Lat. 41-00-02 N long. 085-46-07 W; Settled in 1837 and named after Manchester, England.

•**NORTH SALEM,** Town; Hendricks County; Pop. 585; Zip Code 46165; Lat. 39-51-35 N long. 086-38-33 W; Founded in 1839 and named after a town in Kentucky.

•**NORTH VERNON,** City; Jennings County; Pop. 5,726; Zip Code 47265; Lat. 39-00-22 N long. 085-37-25 W; Named for its location north of Vernon. Vernon is named after George Washington's famous home.

•**NORTH WEBSTER,** Town; Kosciusko County; Pop. 699; Zip Code 46555; Lat. 41-19-32 N long. 085-41-52 W; Pioneer Malcolm Webster settled here in 1841. It is named for him.

•**OAKLAND CITY,** City; Gibson County; Pop. 3,172; Zip Code 47660; Lat. 38-20-19 N long. 087-20-42 W; Descriptively named in 1856 for its many oak groves.

•**OAKTOWN,** Town; Knox County; Pop. 776; Zip Code 47561; Lat. 38-52-16 N long. 087-26-29 W; Settled in 1867 and named for its many oak trees.

•**OOLITIC,** Town; Lawrence County; Pop. 1,491; Zip Code 47451; Lat. 38-54-03 N long. 086-31-31 W; Established in 1888 and given a descriptive name for the oolitic texture of the area's limestone.

•**ORESTES,** Town; Madison County; Pop. 543; Zip Code 46063; Lat. 40-16-10 N long. 085-43-41 W; The town is named after Orestes McMahan who was the son of the first postmaster.

•**ORLAND,** Town; Steuben County; Pop. 424; Zip Code 46776; Lat. 41-43-50 N long. 085-10-18 W; Founded in 1834 as the Vermont Settlement but later changed after the name of a popular hymn.

•**ORLEANS,** Town; Orange County; Pop. 2,145; Zip Code 47452; Lat. 38-39-42 N long. 068-25-35 W; Named to commemorate Andrew Jackson's victory at the Battle of New Orleans.

•**OSCEOLA,** Town; St. Joseph County; Pop. 1,855; Zip Code 46561; Lat. 41-39-54 N long. 086-04-33 W; Founded in 1837 and named after the famous Seminole Indian Chief, Osceola.

•**OSGOOD,** Town; Ripley County; Pop. 1,549; Zip Code 47037; Lat. 39-07-29 N long. 085-17-21 W; The town's name remembers the railroad surveyor who came through in 1857.

•**OSSIAN,** Town; Wells County; Pop. 1,928; Zip Code 46777; Lat. 40-52-50 N long. 085-09-59 W; Named for Ossian Hall, County Old, by Scottish settlers who arrived in 1846.

•**OTTERBEIN,** Town; Benton & Tippecanoe Counties; Pop. 1,118; Zip Code 47970; Lat. 40-29-26 N long. 087-05-47 W; Named in honor of pioneer settler Otterbein Brown.

•**OWENSVILLE,** Town; Gibson County; Pop. 1,255; Zip Code 47665; Lat. 38-16-19 N long. 087-41-16 W; Founded in 1817 and named after Kentuckian Thomas Owen.

•**OXFORD,** Town; Benton County; Pop. 1,313; Zip Code 47971; Lat. 40-31-11 N long. 087-14-52 W; Oxford's name recalls the famous English University town.

•**PALMYRA,** Town; Harrison County; Pop. 687; Zip Code 47164; Lat. 38-24-28 N long. 086-06-36 W; Settled in 1810 and named for the Biblical city of Palmyra.

•**PAOLI,** Town; Orange County Seat; Pop. 3,598; Zip Code 47454; Elev. 615; Lat. 38-33-22 N long. 086-28-06 W; The town is named in honor of Corsican patriot Pasquale Paoli.

•**PARAGON,** Town; Morgan County; Pop. 544; Zip Code 46166; Lat. 39-23-42 N long. 086-33-45 W; Settled in 1852 and given a commendatory name meaning "unsurpassed."

•**PARKER CITY,** Town; Randolph County; Pop. 1,414; Zip Code 47368; Lat. 40-11-20 N long. 085-12-15 W; Originally Morristown, the name was later changed to honor early settler Thomas Parker.

•**PATOKA,** Town; Gibson County; Pop. 819; Zip Code 47666; Lat. 38-24-25 N long. 087-35-08 W; Settled at the beginning of the nineteenth century and named after the Patoka River.

•**PATRIOT,** Town; Switzerland County; Pop. 264; Zip Code 47038; Lat. 38-50-19 N long. 084-49-37 W; Called Troy at first, the name was later changed to honor "patriots" of the Revolutionary War.

•**PENDLETON,** Town; Madison County; Pop. 2,132; Zip Code 46064; Lat. 39-59-51 N long. 085-44-48 W; The town is named after it's founder, Thomas Pendleton.

•**PENNVILLE,** Town; Jay County; Pop. 804; Zip Code 47369; Lat. 40-29-38 N long. 085-08-54 W; Settled in 1836 and named after William Penn.

•**PERRYSVILLE,** Town; Vermillion County; Pop. 528; Zip Code 47974; Lat. 40-03-05 N long. 087-26-00 W; Founded in 1826 and named in honor of War of 1812 naval hero, Oliver Perry.

•**PERU,** City; Miami County; Pop. 13,759; Zip Code 46970; Lat. 40-45-13 N long. 086-04-08 W; Estblished in 1838 and named after the South American country.

•**PETERSBURG,** City; Pike County Seat; Pop. 2,963; Zip Code 47567; Lat. 38-29-31 N long. 087-16-43 W.

•**PIERCETON,** Town; Kosciusko County; Pop. 1,046; Zip Code 46562; Lat. 41-12-01 N long. 085-42-20 W.

•**PINE VILLAGE,** Town; Warren County; Pop. 257; Lat. 40-27-01 N long. 087-15-16 W.

•**PITTSBORO,** Town; Hendricks County; Pop. 879; Zip Code 46167; Lat. 39-51-50 N long. 086-28-01 W.

•**PLAINFIELD,** Town; Hendricks County; Pop. 9,079; Zip Code 46168; Lat. 39-42-15 N long. 086-23-58 W.

•**PLAINVILLE,** Town; Daviess County; Pop. 551; Zip Code 47568; Lat. 38-48-22 N long. 087-09-08 W.

•**PLYMOUTH,** City; Marshall County Seat; Pop. 7,667; Zip Code 46563; Lat. 41-20-37 N long. 086-18-35 W.

•**PONETO,** Town; Wells County; Pop. 254; Zip Code 46781; Lat. 40-39-25 N long. 085-13-18 W.

•**PORTAGE,** City; Porter County; Pop. 27,186; Zip Code 46368; Lat. 41-34-33 N long. 087-10-34 W.

•**PORTER,** Town; Porter County; Pop. 2,955; Lt. 41-36-56 N long. 087-04-27 W; Named for navel hero David Porter, a commander in the War of 1812.

•**PORTLAND,** City; Jay County; Pop. 7,074; Zip Code 47371; Lat. 40-26-04 N long. 084-58-40 W; Portland is named after Portland, Maine, the home of many earlier settlers.

•**POSEYVILLE,** Town; Posey County; Pop. 1,249; Zip Code 47633; Lat. 38-10-12 N long. 087-46-59 W; Both the county and the town named after General Thomas Posey, an officer in the American Revolution.

•**POTTAWATTOMIE PARK,** Town; La Porte County; Pop. 266; Lat. 41-19-24 N long. 085-45-31 W; The town is named after one of the original Indian tribes in the area.

•**PRINCES LAKES,** Town; Johnson County; Pop. 935; A descriptive name given by the town founders.

•**PRINCETON,** City; Gibson County Seat; Pop. 8,980; Zip Code 47670; Lat. 38-21-19 N long. 087-34-03 W; Named in honor of Captain William Prince who arrived in the area in the early 1800's.

•**RAVENSWOOD,** Town; Marion County; Pop. 427; Lat. 39-53-17 N long. 086-07-52 W; A euphonious name given by the town's founders.

•**REDKEY,** Town; Jay County; Pop. 1,527; Zip Code 47373; Lat. 40-20-56 N long. 085-09-00 W; The town's name honors mid-nineteenth century settler James Redkey.

•**REMINGTON,** Town; Jasper County; Pop. 1,268; Zip Code 47977; Lat. 40-45-39 N long. 087-09-03 W; Originally called Carpenter's Creek, it was later named after a pioneer merchant.

•**RENSSELAER,** City; Jasper County Seat; Pop. 4,979; Zip Code 47978; Lat. 40-56-12 N long. 087-09-03 W; New York merchant James Van Rensselaer founded the town in 1837. It is named for him.

•**REYNOLDS,** Town; White County; Pop. 632; Zip Code 47980; Lat. 40-44-58 N long. 086-52-18 W; Named in honor of town founder Benjamin Reynolds.

•**RICHMOND,** City; Wayne County; Pop. 41,261; Zip Code 47374; Lat. 39-49-44 N long. 084-53-25 W; Settled in 1816 and named for the rich soil in the area.

•**RIDGEVILLE,** Town; Randolph County; Pop. 928; Zip Code 47380; Lat. 40-17-21 N long. 085-01-44 W; Founded in 1837 and descriptively named for its location on a ridge.

•**RILEY,** Town; Vigo County; Pop. 264; Zip Code 47871; Lat. 39-47-13 N long. 085-43-50 W; Named after the local township by the U. S. Post Office.

•**RISING SUN,** City; Ohio County Seat; Pop. 2,429; Zip Code 47040; Lat. 38-56-58 N long. 084-51-14 W; Descriptively named for the magnificent sunrises seen from the town.

•**RIVER FOREST,** Town; Madison County; Pop. 29; Lat. 40-06-35 N long. 085-43-38 W; Descriptively named by its founders.

•**ROACHDALE,** Town; Putnam County; Pop. 953; Zip Code 46172; Lat. 39-50-56 N long. 086-48-08 W; The town's name honors Judge Roach, a director of the local railroad.

•**ROANN,** Town; Wabash County; Pop. 548; Zip Code 46974; Lat. 40-54-42 N long. 085-55-28 W; The town is named for Roanne, France.

•**ROANOKE,** Town; Huntington County; Pop. 887; Zip Code 46783; Lat. 40-57-45 N long. 085-22-24 W; The town's name comes from the Roanoke Indians of Virginia.

•**ROCHESTER,** City; Fulton County Seat; Pop. 5,016; Zip Code 46975; Lat. 41-03-53 N long. 086-12-57 W; Founded in 1835 and named for Rochester, New York.

•**ROCKPORT,** City; Spencer County Seat; Pop. 2,598; Zip Code 47635; Lat. 37-52-59 N long. 087-02-58 W; Originally Hanging Rock, the town's name was later changed to the more euphonius Rockport.

•**ROCKVILLE,** Town; Parke County Seat; Pop. 2,776; Zip Code 47872; Lat. 39-45-45 N long. 087-13-45 W; Descriptively named for a large rock, now on the courthouse lawn.

•**ROME CITY,** Town; Noble County; Pop. 1,327; Zip Code 46784; Lat. 41-29-46 N long. 085-22-36 W; Settled in 1837 and named by Irish settlers after the city of Rome.

•**ROSEDALE,** Town; Parke County; Pop. 745; Zip Code 47874; Lat. 39-37-22 N long. 087-17-00 W; The town's name honors Chauncey Rose, prominent early settler.

•**ROSELAND,** Town; St. Joseph County; Pop. 824; Lat. 41-42-58 N long. 086-15-09 W; A descriptive name for the many wild roses in the area.

•**RUSSELLVILLE,** Town; Putnam County; Pop. 378; Zip Code 46175; Lat. 39-51-30 N long. 086-59-02 W; The town is named after its local township.

•**RUSSIAVILLE,** Town; Howard County; Pop. 974; Zip Code 46979; Lat. 40-25-03 N long. 086-16-17 W; Actually named Richardville, the town's name gradually migrated to Russiaville.

•**ST. JOE,** Town; De Kalb County; Pop. 549; Elev. 565; Lat. 38-24-00 N long. 085-48-30 W; Named for the nearby St. Joe River.

•**ST. JOHN,** Town; Lake County; Pop. 3,916; Zip Code 46373; Lat. 41-27-00 N long. 087-28-12 W; Founded in the 1830's and named for an early settler John Hack. The "Saint" title is euphonious.

•**ST. LEON,** Town; Dearborn County; Pop. 514; Lat. 39-17-31 N long. 084-48-26 W; Named by early settlers for a Catholic patron saint.

•**ST. PAUL,** Town; Decatur & Shelby Counties; Pop. 976; Zip Code 47272; Lat. 39-25-41 N long. 085-37-42 W; Settled in 1853 and named after an early settler, Jonathan Paul.

•**SALAMONIA,** Town; Jay County; Pop. 147; Zip Code 47381; Lat. 40-22-55 N long. 084-51-55 W; Founded in 1839 and named for the Salamonia River.

•**SALEM,** City; Washington County; Pop. 5,319; Zip Code 47167; Lat. 40-43-01 N long. 084-51-12 W; Settled in 1866 and named for Salem, Massachusetts.

•**SALTILLO,** Town; Washington County; Pop. 134; Lat. 38-39-54 N long. 086-17-21 W; Founded in 1849 and named after the Mexican city of Saltillo.

•**SANDBORN,** Town; Knox County; Pop. 575; Zip Code 47578; Lat. 38-53-47 N long. 087-11-12 W; Named in memory of a civil engineer on the Indianapolis and Vincennes Railroad.

•**SANTA CLAUS,** Town; Spencer County; Pop. 538; Zip Code 47579; Lat. 38-07-12 N long. 086-54-51 W; Obviously named for St. Nick of Chritsmas fame.

•**SARATOGA,** Town; Randolph County; Pop. 342; Zip Code 47382; Lat. 40-14-13 N long. 084-55-06 W; Established in 1875 and named after Saratoga, New York.

•**SCHERERVILLE,** Town; Lake County; Pop. 12,414; Lat. 41-30-02 N long. 087-27-41 W; Nicholas Schererville platted the town in 1866. It is named in his honor.

•**SCHNEIDER,** Town; Lake County; Pop. 364; Zip Code 46376; Lat. 41-11-13 N long. 087-26-54 W; The town is named after a 1900's era landowner.

•**SCOTTSBURG,** City; Scott County Seat; Pop. 5,078; Zip Code 47170; Elev. 443; Lat. 38-17-19 N long. 087-13-09 W; Named for railroad president Thomas Scott upon its founding in 1871.

•**SEELYVILLE,** Town; Vigo County; Pop. 1,367; Zip Code 47878; Lat. 39-29-31 N long. 087-16-02 W; Jonas Seely was the first postmaster. It is named after him.

•**SELLERSBURG,** Town; Clark County; Pop. 3,030; Zip Code 47172; Lat. 38-23-53 N long. 085-45-18 W; Moses Sellers co-founded the town in 1846. It is named after him.

•**SELMA,** Town; Delaware County; Pop. 1,052; Zip Code 47383; Lat. 40-11-30 N long. 085-16-08 W; Settled in 1852 and named after a local resident.

•**SEYMOUR,** City; Jackson County; Pop. 14,596; Zip Code 47274; Lat. 38-57-33 N long. 085-53-25 W; The town's name honors railroad superintendant Henry Seymour.

•**SHARPSVILLE,** Town; Tipton County; Pop. 620; Zip Code 46068; Elev. 881; Lat. 40-22-46 N long. 086-05-19 W; The town is named after early settler E. M. Sharp.

•**SHELBURN,** Town; Sullivan County; Pop. 1,260; Zip Code 47879; Lat. 39-10-42 N long. 087-23-37 W; Paschal Shelburne founded the town in 1855. It is named after him.

•**SHELBYVILLE,** City; Shelby County Seat; Pop. 14,878; Zip Code 46176; Lat. 39-31-17 N long. 085-46-37 W; The city takes its name from Shelby County.

•**SHERIDAN,** Town; Hamilton County; Pop. 2,214; Zip Code 46069; Elev. 949; Lat. 40-08-06 N long. 086-13-14 W; The town's name honors Civil War officer P. H. Sheridan.

•**SHIPSHEWANA,** Town; Lagrange County; Pop. 463; Zip Code 46565; Lat. 41-40-22 N long. 085-34-49 W; Named for a nearby lake, the lake's name is an Indian word meaning "vision of a lion."

•**SHIRLEY,** Town; Hancock & Henry Counties; Pop. 919; Zip Code 47384; Lat. 39-53-31 N long. 085-34-37 W; Settled in 1890 and named for railroad superintendant Joseph Shirley.

•**SHOALS,** Town; Martin County Seat; Pop. 960; Zip Code 47581; Lat. 38-39-59 N long. 086-47-28 W; Descriptively named for its location on a shallow place, or shoals, on the White River.

•**SIDNEY,** Town; Kosciusko County; Pop. 185; Zip Code 46566; Lat. 41-06-20 N long. 085-44-37 W; Founded in 1834 and named after the Sidney family, who were local landowners.

•**SILVER LAKE,** Town; Kosciusko County; Pop. 578; Zip Code 46982; Lat. 41-04-20 N long. 085-53-30 W; First settled in 1860 and named for nearby Silver Lake.

•**SOMERVILLE,** Town; Gibson County; Pop. 335; Zip Code 47683; Lat. 38-16-35 N long. 087-22-40 W; Originally Summitville, the post office changed the name because another town had prior claim to Summitville.

•**SOUTH BEND,** City; St. Joseph County Seat; Pop. 108,168; Zip Code 46600; Lat. 41-41-00 N long. 086-15-00 W; Descriptively named for its location on a bend in the St. Joseph's River.

•**SOUTH WHITLEY,** Town; Whitley County; Pop. 1,565; Zip Code 46787; Lat. 41-05-05 N long. 085-37-41 W; Founded in 1838 and named aftr the county.

•**SOUTHPORT,** City; Marion County; Pop. 2,254; Lat. 39-39-54 N long. 086-07-40 W; A locational name given the town when it was founded in 1852.

•**SPEEDWAY,** Town; Marion County; Pop. 12,634; Lat. 39-48-08 N long. 086-16-02 W; Named by the location of the Indianapolis Motor Speedway here.

•**SPENCER,** Town; Owen County Seat; Pop. 2,749; Zip Code 47460; Lat. 39-17-12 N long. 086-45-45 W; The town's name honors Captain Spier Spencer killed in the Battle of Tippecanoe.

•**SPICELAND,** Town; Henry County; Pop. 938; Zip Code 47385; Lat. 39-50-18 N long. 085-26-20 W; Descriptively named for the abundant spicebush in the area.

•**SPRING GROVE,** Town; Wayne County; Pop. 469; Lat. 39-50-54 N long. 084-53-39 W; A descriptive name given by the town's founders.

•**SPRING HILL,** Town; Marion County; Pop. 26; Lat. 39-37-12 N long. 086-07-06 W; Named for a large spring on a nearby hill.

•**SPRING LAKE,** Town; Hancock County; Pop. 236; Lat. 39-46-36 N long. 085-51-11 W; William Dye created an artificial lake here in 1884. The town is named for this lake.

•**SPRINGPORT,** Town; Henry County; Pop. 220; Zip Code 47386; Lat. 40-02-51 N long. 085-23-39 W; Founded in 1868 and named for a local spring.

•**SPURGEON,** Town; Pike County; Pop. 257; The origin of the name is unknown.

•**STATE LINE CITY,** Town; Warren County; Pop. 233; Zip Code 47982; Lat. 39-26-13 N long. 087-31-46 W; Descriptively named fot its location on the Indiana-Illinois state line.

•**STAUNTON,** Town; Clay County; Pop. 612; Zip Code 47881; Lat. 39-29-15 N long. 087-11-20 W; Founded in 1851 and named after Staunton, Virginia.

•**STILESVILLE,** Town; Hendricks County; Pop. 349; Zip Code 46180; Lat. 39-38-18 N long. 086-38-01 W; Established in 1828 and named for landowner, Jeremiah Stiles.

•**STINESVILLE,** Town; Monroe County; Pop. 227; Zip Code 47464; Lat. 39-17-55 N long. 086-39-08 W; Prominent landowner Eusebius Stine helped lay out the town in 1855. It is named after him.

•**STRAUGHN,** Town; Henry County; Pop. 329; Zip Code 47387; Lat. 39-48-32 N long. 085-17-29 W; Straughn's name honors pioneer settler Merriman Straughn.

•**SULLIVAN,** City; Sullivan County Seat; Pop. 4,738; Zip Code 47864; Lat. 39-05-43 N long. 087-24-21 W; Named in honor of Revolutionary War hero General Daniel Sullivan.

•**SULPHUR SPRINGS,** Town; Henry County; Pop. 345; Zip Code 47388; Lat. 38-12-43 N long. 086-28-30 W; A descriptive name given by the town's founders.

•**SUMMITVILLE,** Town; Madison County; Pop. 1,085; Zip Code 46070; Lat. 40-20-19 N long. 085-38-40 W; The town is descriptively named for its location on high ground.

•**SUNMAN,** Town; Ripley County; Pop. 920; Zip Code 47041; Lat. 39-14-13 N long. 085-05-41 W; Settled in 1856 and named in honor of prominent citizen Thomas Sunman.

•**SWAYZEE,** Town; Grant County; Pop. 1,120; Zip Code 46986; Lat. 40-30-30 N long. 085-49-32 W; Founded in 1881 and named for landowner James Swayzee.

•**SWEETSER,** Town; Grant County; Pop. 947; Zip Code 46987; Lat. 40-34-19 N long. 085-46-09 W; James Sweetser owned land in the area in the 1870's. It is named for him.

•**SWITZ CITY,** Town; Greene County; Pop. 300; Zip Code 47465; Lat. 39-16-30 N long. 087-03-12 W; Named after John Switz, a local landowner in the 1860's.

•**SYRACUSE,** Town; Kosciusko County; Pop. 2,572; Zip Code 46567; Lat. 41-25-40 N long. 085-45-09 W; The town is named after Syracuse, New York.

•**TELL CITY,** City; Perry County; Pop. 8,707; Zip Code 47586; Lat. 37-57-05 N long. 086-46-04 W; Named for the legendary Swiss hero, William Tell.

•**TENNYSON,** Town; Warrick County; Pop. 326; Zip Code 47637; Lat. 38-04-56 N long. 087-07-06 W; Settled in 1882 and named for poet Laureate Alfred, Lord Tennyson.

•**TERRE HAUTE,** City; Vigo County Seat; Pop. 61,020; Zip Code 47801; Lat. 39-28-00 N long. 087-24-50 W; Settled by the French in the 1700's and given a name meaning "high ground."

•**THORNTOWN,** Town; Boone County; Pop. 1,468; Zip Code 46071; Lat. 40-07-27 N long. 086-36-24 W; An English tran of an Indian name meaning "place of thorns."

•**TIPTON,** City; Tipton County Seat; Pop. 5,019; Zip Code 46072; Lat. 40-16-56 N long. 086-02-28 W; Named in honor of U. S. Senator from Indiana John Tipton who served from 1832 to 1839.

•**TOPEKA,** Town; Lagrange County; Pop. 869; Zip Code 46571; Lat. 41-32-21 N long. 085-32-23 W; A Shawnee Indian word for Jerusalem artichoke.

•**TOWN OF PINES,** Town; Porter County; Pop. 950; Lat. 41-40-55 N long. 086-57-37 W; A descriptive name given by the town's founders.

•**TRAFALGAR,** Town; Johnson County; Pop. 467; Zip Code 46181; Lat. 39-24-58 N long. 086-09-03 W; Founded in 1851 and named after the great English naval victory.

•**TRAIL CREEK,** Town; La Porte County; Pop. 2,581; Lat. 41-41-54 N long. 086-51-33 W; An English translation of a Indian name menaing "river road."

•**TROY,** Town; Perry County; Pop. 550; Zip Code 47588; Lat. 37-59-43 N long. 086-47-52 W; Settled in 1809 and named for the ancient city.

•**ULEN,** Town; Boone County; Pop. 192; Lat. 40-03-47 N long. 086-27-52 W; Named for an early settler.

•**UNION CITY,** City; Randolph County; Pop. 3,909; A patriotic name given the town upon its founding in 1849.

•**UNIONDALE,** Town; Wells County; Pop. 303; Zip Code 46791; Elev. 817; Lat. 40-49-50 N long. 085-14-30 W; The town is named after the local township.

•**UNIVERSAL,** Town; Vermillion County; Pop. 474; Zip Code 47884; Lat. 39-37-18 N long. 087-27-05 W; Settled in 1911 and named after the local Universal Mines.

•**UPLAND,** Town; Grant County; Pop. 3,331; Zip Code 46989; Lat. 40-28-32 N long. 085-29-40 W; Descriptively named in 1867 for its elevation between Union City and Logansport.

•**UTICA,** Town; Clark County; Pop. 473; Lat. 38-20-01 N long. 085-39-13 W; Named in 1816 for Utica, New York.

•**VALPARAISO,** City; Porter County Seat; Pop. 22,119; Zip Code 46383; Lat. 41-28-23 N long. 087-03-40 W; Settled in 1836 and named after the city in Chile, South America.

•**VAN BUREN,** Town; Grant County; Pop. 934; Zip Code 46991; Lat. 40-37-02 N long. 085-30-17 W; Originally Rood's Corner, the name was changed after the local township.

•**VEEDERSBURG,** Town; Fountain County; Pop. 2,245; Zip Code 47987; Lat. 40-06-47 N long. 087-15-45 W; Peter S. Veeder founded the town in 1872. It is named for him.

•**VERA CRUZ,** Town; Wells County; Pop. 117; Lat. 40-42-04 N long. 085-04-45 W; Founded in 1848 and named the Mexican city captured by American soldiers in 1847 during the Mexican-American War.

•**VERNON,** Town; Jennings County Seat; Pop. 329; Zip Code 47282; Lat. 38-59-05 N long. 085-36-34 W; Named for the home of George Washington upon its founding in 1815.

•**VERSAILLES,** Town; Ripley County Seat; Pop. 1,553; Zip Code 47042; Lat. 39-04-19 N long. 085-15-07 W; Named after the French town of Versailles.

•**VEVAY,** Town; Switzerland County Seat; Pop. 1,364; Zip Code 47043; Lat. 38-44-52 N long. 085-04-02 W; Swiss settlers named the town after the commune in Switzerland when they settled here in 1813.

•**VINCENNES,** City; Knox County Seat; Pop. 20,589; Zip Code 47591; Lat. 38-40-38 N long. 087-31-43 W; The town's name remembers an early French commander Francois-Marie Bissot, Sieur De Vincennes who was killed by Indians near here in 1736.

•**WABASH,** City; Wabash County Seat; Pop. 12,961; Zip Code 46992; Lat. 40-47-52 N long. 085-49-14 W; The town is named after the river. The word wabash is a Miami Indian name meaning "pure white," and referring to a limestone bed in the river.

•**WAKARUSA,** Town; Elkhart County; Pop. 1,270; Zip Code 46573; Elev. 847; Lat. 41-57-14 N long. 086-03-53 W; Named after the Wakarusa River in Kansas.

•**WALKERTON,** Town; St. Joseph County; Pop. 2,044; Zip Code 46574; Lat. 41-28-00 N long. 086-28-59 W; The town's name honors 1850's railroad promoter John Walker.

•**WALLACE,** Town; Fountain County; Pop. 90; Zip Code 47988; Lat. 39-59-11 N long. 087-08-54 W; Settled in 1832 and named in honor of Governor David Wallace.

•**WALTON,** Town; Cass County; Pop. 1,205; Zip Code 46994; Lat. 40-39-39 N long. 086-14-31 W; Settler Gilber Wall founded the town. It is named after him.

•**WANATAH,** Town; La Porte County; Pop. 843; Zip Code 46390; Lat. 41-25-50 N long. 086-53-54 W; An Indian name meaning "he who attacks his enemies."

•**WARREN,** Town; Huntington County; Pop. 1,250; Zip Code 46792; Lat. 40-40-58 N long. 085-25-38 W; Named in honor of Revolutionary War statesman Joseph Warren.

•**WARREN PARK,** Town; Marion County; Pop. 1,796; Lat. 39-46-55 N long. 086-03-01 W; Probably honoring Revolutionary War patriot Joseph Warren.

•**WARSAW,** City; Kosciusko County Seat; Pop. 10,586; Zip Code 46580; Lat. 41-14-17 N long. 085-51-11 W; Founded in 1836 and named after the capital of Poland.

•**WASHINGTON,** City; Daviess County Seat; Pop. 11,300; Zip Code 47501; Lat. 38-39-33 N long. 087-10-22 W; The city is named after George Washington.

•**WATERLOO,** Town; De Kalb County; Pop. 1,937; Zip Code 46793; Lat. 41-25-55 N long. 085-01-12 W; Settled in 1841 and named after the Battle of Waterloo.

•**WAVELAND,** Town; Montgomery County; Pop. 553; Zip Code 47989; Lat. 39-52-37 N long. 087-02-40 W; Pioneer John Milligan named the town for a Kentucky estate he liked.

•**WAYNETOWN,** Town; Montgomery County; Pop. 914; Zip Code 47990; Lat. 40-05-15 N long. 087-03-35 W; The town's name honors Revolutinary War General Anthony Wayne.

•**WEST BADEN SPRINGS,** Town; Orange County; Pop. 793; Zip Code 47469; Lat. 38-34-02 N long. 086-37-42 W; Named by an 1850's era medicine peddlar after the famous West Baden spa in Germany.

•**WEST COLLEGE CORNER,** Town; Union County; Pop. 605; Lat. 39-34-03 N long. 084-48-58 W; Descriptively named for its location west of College Corner, Ohio.

•**WEST HARRISON,** Town; Dearborn County; Pop. 328; Zip Code 47060; Lat. 39-15-39 N long. 084-49-15 W; Settled in 1813 and named after Harrison Township.

•**WEST LAFAYETTE,** City; Tippecanoe County; Pop. 21,197; Lat. 40-25-33 N long. 086-54-29 W; Originally Kingston, it was later changed to reflect its location west of Lafayette.

•**WEST LEBANON,** Town; Warren County; Pop. 934; Zip Code 47991; Lat. 40-16-12 N long. 087-23-12 W; Called Lebanon upon its founding in 1830, the West part was added to distinguish it from another Lebanon, Indiana.

•**WEST TERRE HAUTE,** Town; Vigo County; Pop. 2,814; Zip Code 47885; Lat. 39-27-54 N long. 087-27-00 W; Founded in 1836 and later given a locational name for its relation to Terro Haute.

•**WESTFIELD,** Town; Hamilton County; Pop. 2,788; Zip Code 46074; Lat. 40-02-34 N long. 086-07-39 W; Named by Quaker settlers in 1834 for a former home.

•**WESTPORT,** Town; Decatur County; Pop. 1,439; Zip Code 47283; Lat. 39-10-33 N long. 085-34-23 W; Settled in 1836 and given this descriptive name.

•**WESTVILLE,** Town; La Porte County; Pop. 2,858; Zip Code 46391; Lat. 41-32-29 N long. 086-54-02 W; A descriptive name for the area when the town was founded in 1852.

•**WHEATFIELD,** Town; Jasper County; Pop. 756; Zip Code 46392; Lat. 40-33-52 N long. 087-06-25 W; Founded in the 1870's and named for the chief agricultural crop.

•**WHEATLAND,** Town; Knox County; Pop. 532; Zip Code 47597; Lat. 38-39-49 N long. 087-18-34 W; Named for the good wheat production in the area.

•**WHITELAND,** Town; Johnson County; Pop. 1,961; Zip Code 46184; Lat. 39-33-00 N long. 086-04-47 W; First founded in 1863 and named for pioneer Joel White.

•**WHITESTOWN,** Town; Boone County; Pop. 497; Zip Code 46075; Lat. 39-59-50 N long. 086-20-45 W; The town's name honors Albert White, railroad president and local congressman.

•**WHITEWATER,** Town; Wayne County; Pop. 107; Lat. 39-56-41 N long. 084-49-52 W; Settled in 1828 and named after the Whitewater River.

•**WHITING,** City; Lake County; Pop. 5,713; Zip Code 46394; Lat. 41-40-47 N long. 087-29-40 W; The town's name remembers a railroad conductor involved in a trainwreck near here.

•**WILKINSON,** Town; Hancock County; Pop. 483; Zip Code 46186; Lat. 39-53-09 N long. 085-36-32 W; Named for the surveyors who measured the area in 1883.

•**WILLIAMS CREEK,** Town; Marion County; Pop. 427; Lat. 39-53-59 N long. 086-09-01 W; Named for a local pioneer family.

•**WILLIAMSPORT,** Town; Warren County Seat; Pop. 1,742; Zip Code 47993; Lat. 40-17-18 N long. 087-17-38 W; The town is named after the original landowner, William Harrison.

•**WINAMAC,** Town; Pulaski County Seat; Pop. 2,376; Zip Code 46996; Elev. 710; Lat. 41-03-05 N long. 086-36-11 W; A Potawatomi Indian name meaning "catfish."

•**WINCHESTER,** City; Randolph County Seat; Pop. 5,652; Zip Code 47394; Lat. 40-10-19 N long. 084-58-53 W; Settled in 1818 and named after the English city.

•**WINDFALL CITY,** Town; Tipton County; Pop. 899; Zip Code 46076; Lat. 40-21-47 N long. 085-57-23 W; Founded in 1853, the windfall is uncertain.

•**WINGATE,** Town; Montgomery County; Pop. 372; Zip Code 47994; Lat. 40-10-20 N long. 087-04-22 W; Pioneer John Wingate helped bring the railroad toi the area. It is named in his honor.

•**WINONA LAKE,** Town; Kosciusko County; Pop. 3,529; Zip Code 46590; Lat. 41-13-38 N long. 085-49-19 W; The town is named after the lake. Winona is a Sioux Indian name given to the first born female children.

•**WINSLOW,** Town; Pike County; Pop. 1,009; Zip Code 47598; Lat. 38-22-56 N long. 087-12-46 W; Named for an early settler.

•**WOLCOTT,** Town; White County; Pop. 916; Zip Code 47995; Lat. 40-45-29 N long. 087-02-30 W; The Wolcott family founded the town in 1861 and named it after themselves.

•**WOLCOTTVILLE,** Town; Lagrange & Noble Counties; Pop. 890; Zip Code 46795; Lat. 41-31-33 N long. 085-22-00 W; Named in honor of prominent businessman George Wolcott.

•**WOODBURN,** City; Allen County; Pop. 1,001; Zip Code 46797; Lat. 41-07-31 N long. 084-51-12 W; Founded in 1865 and named for settler John Woodburn.

•**WOODLAWN HEIGHTS,** Town; Madison County; Pop. 109; Lat. 40-07-08 N long. 085-41-37 W; A euphonious name given by the town's incorporators.

•**WORTHINGTON,** Town; Greene County; Pop. 1593; Zip Code 47471; Lat. 39-07-30 N long. 086-58-46 W; The town is named after Worthington, Ohio.

•**YEOMAN,** Town; Carroll County; Pop. 149; Lat. 40-40-04 N long. 086-43-27 W; Named in honor of a railroad official, one Colonel Yeoman.

•**YORKTOWN,** Town; Delaware County; Pop. 3,903; Zip Code 47396; Lat. 40-10-25 N long. 085-29-39 W; Established in 1836 and named for the York Tribe of the Delaware Indians.

•**ZIONSVILLE,** Town; Boone County; Pop. 3,937; Zip Code 46077; Elev. 849; Lat. 39-57-03 N long. 086-15-43 W; Settled in 1830 and named after pioneer William Zion.

IOWA

•**ACKLEY**, City; Franklin & Hardin Counties; Pop. 1,900; Zip Code 50601; Elev. 1092; Laid out in 1857 and named for J. W. Ackley.

•**ADAIR**, City; Adair & Guthrie Counties; Pop. 883; Zip Code 50002; Lat. 41-30-31 N long. 094-38-48 W; Named for Gen. John Adair, Governor of Kentucky.

•**ADEL**, City; Dallas County Seat; Pop. 2,846; Zip Code 50003; Lat. 41-37-02 N long. 094-01-49 W; An early spelling was Adell. Named for the location on a dell of North Racoon River.

•**AFTON**, City; Union County; Pop. 985; Zip Code 50830; Lat. 41-01-35 N long. 094-11-48 W; Laid out in 1854. The city was named after the Afton River in Scotland by Mrs. Baker, wife of one of the proprietors.

•**AGENCY**, City; Wapello County; Pop. 657; Zip Code 52530; Lat. 40-59-54 N long. 092-18-31 W; Named in 1838 for the Sac and Fox Indian Agency established here. After the Indians were removed to Kansas, the agency was abandoned, but the Fox Agency post office remained and the place became known as Agency.

•**AINSWORTH**, City; Washington County; Pop. 547; Zip Code 52201; Lat. 41-17-38 N long. 091-33-30 W; Named for D. H. Ainsworth, a Civil Engineer.

•**AKRON**, City; Plymouth County; Pop. 1,517; Zip Code 51001; Lat. 42-49-44 N long. 096-33-14 W; Possibly named after the city in Ohio. The name Akron means "summit" or "peak" in Greek.

•**ALBERT CITY**, City; Buena Vista County; Pop. 818; Zip Code 50510; Lat. 42-46-45 N long. 094-55-23 W.

•**ALBIA**, City; Monroe County Seat; Pop. 4,184; Zip Code 52531; Elev. 959; Lat. 41-01-30 N long. 092-47-56 W.

•**ALBION**, City; Marshall County; Pop. 739; Zip Code 50005; Lat. 42-06-44 N long. 092-59-54 W; Probably titled after the ancient name for England.

•**ALDEN**, City; Hardin County; Pop. 953; Zip Code 50006; Lat. 42-31-31 N long. 093-23-28 W; Named for Henry Alden, who settled there in 1854.

•**ALGONA**, City; Kossuth County Seat; Pop. 6,289; Zip Code 50511; Lat. 43-04-22 N long. 094-13-53 W; First known as Call's Grove for early residents, The name was changed to Algona, after Henry Schoolcraft's book "Algonquin", at the suggestion of Mrs. Call.

•**ALLISON**, City; Butler County Seat; Pop. 1,132; Zip Code 50602; Lat. 42-45-28 N long. 092-47-46 W. Named after an early settler.

•**ALMA** City; Buena Vista County; Pop. 1,720; Zip Code 51002; Lat. 42-40-27 N long. 095-18-35 W.

•**ALTON**, City; Sioux County; Pop. 986; Zip Code 51003; Lat. 42-58-49 N long. 096-01-09 W.

•**ALTOONA**, City; Polk County; Pop. 5,764; Zip Code 50009; Lat. 41-38-46 N long. 093-27-50 W; Named for its location at the highest elevation between the Des Moines and Mississippi Rivers. The name Altoona is derived from the latin word altus, meaning "high".

•**AMES**, City; Story County; Pop. 45,775; Zip Code 50010; Lat. 42-02-33 N long. 093-34-43 W; Named for Oakes Ames.

•**ANAMOSA**, City; Jones County Seat; Pop. 4,958; Zip Code 52205; Lat. 42-06-44 N long. 091-17-05 W; Laid out in 1845 and named Lexington. Renamed Anamosa to avoid duplication with another place called Lexington. Anamosa is derived from an Algonquin word meaning "little dog."

•**ANITA**, City; Cass County; Pop. 1,153; Zip Code 50020; Lat. 41-26-45 N long. 094-47-04 W. The city is named for Anita Cowles, niece of the surveyor who laid out the town.

•**ANKENY**, City; Polk County; Pop. 15,429; Zip Code 50021; Lat. 41-39-26 N long. 093-36-57 W. Named for founder J.F. Ankeny.

•**APLINGTON**, City; Butler County; Pop. 1,027; Zip Code 50604; Lat. 42-35-04 N long. 092-53-01 W.

•**ARCADIA**, City; Carroll County; Pop. 454; Zip Code 51430; Lat. 42-04-54 N long. 095-02-45 W. Given a pleasant name meaning "ideal countryside."

•**ARION**, City; Crawford County; Pop. 207; Zip Code 51520; Lat. 41-56-59 N long. 095-27-35 W.

•**ARLINGTON**, City; Fayette County; Pop. 498; Zip Code 50606; Lat. 42-44-18 N long. 091-40-25 W. Named for the area in Virginia.

•**ARMSTRONG**, City; Emmet County; Pop. 1,153; Zip Code 50514; Lat. 43-23-38 N long. 094-29-06 W. Named after an early settler.

•**ARNOLDS PARK**, City; Dickinson County; Pop. 1,051; Zip Code 51331; Lat. 43-21-17 N long. 095-07-47 W.

•**ASHTON**, City; Osceola County; Pop. 441; Zip Code 51232; Lat. 43-18-57 N long. 095-47-00 W.

•**ATALISSA**, City; Muscatine County; Pop. 360; Zip Code 52720; Lat. 41-34-11 N long. 091-09-51 W; Established in 1848. Probably named from Thomas Campbell's famous poem "Gertrude of Wyoming" in which a fictional Oneida chief, Outalissi, is mentioned.

•**ATKINS**, City; Benton County; Pop. 678; Zip Code 52206; Lat. 41-59-54 N long. 091-51-12 W.

•**ATLANTIC**, City; Cass County Seat; Pop. 7,789; Zip Code 50022; Elev. 1,215; Lat. 41-24-08 N long. 095-00-43 W. Named after the Atlantic Ocean.

•**AUBURN**, City; Sac County; Pop. 320; Zip Code 51433; Elev. 1,220; Lat. 42-17-09 N long. 094-52-44 W. Given the name of the village in Oliver Goldsmith's famous poem.

•**AUDUBON**, City; Audubon County Seat; Pop. 2,841; Zip Code 50025; Elev. 1,373; Lat. 41-43-28 N long. 094-55-47 W; Named for John James Audubon, a famous orinthologist.

•**AURELIA**, City; Cherokee County; Pop. 1,143; Zip Code 51005; Lat. 42-42-55 N long. 095-26-22 W. Named after Aurelia Blair.

•**AURORA**, City; Buchanan County; Pop. 248; Zip Code 50607; Lat. 42-37-08 N long. 091-43-32 W; The name is latin for "morning" or "dawn."

•**AVOCA**, City; Pottawattamie County; Pop. 1,650; Zip Code 51521; Lat. 41-16-46 N long. 095-50-10 W. Named for the Avoca River in Ireland.

•**AYRSHIRE**, City; Palo Alto County; Pop. 243; Zip Code 50515; Lat. 43-01-35 N long. 094-49-27 W; Named for the town in Scotland.

•**BADGER**, City; Webster County; Pop. 653; Zip Code 50516; Lat. 42-36-56 N long. 094-09-24 W.

•**BAGLEY,** City; Guthrie County; Pop. 370; Zip Code 50026; Elev. 1,106; Lat. 41-51-24 N long. 094-26-00 W. The city is named for an early farmer.

•**BANCROFT,** City; Kossuth County; Pop. 1,082; Zip Code 50517; Lat. 43-17-42 N long. 094-13-19 W. Named in honor of historian George Bancroft.

•**BARNUM,** City; Webster County; Pop. 198; Zip Code 50518; Lat. 42-30-30 N long. 094-221-04 W. Named after the famous 19th century showman.

•**BATAVIA,** City; Jefferson County; Pop. 525; Zip Code 52533; Lat. 40-59-41 N long. 092-09-46 W. Named after the Dutch city.

•**BATTLE CREEK,** City; Ida County; Pop. 919; Zip Code 51006; Elev. 1,194; Lat. 42-19-05 N long. 095-36-01 W; Named for a skirmish that took place here in 1849 between a government survey party and Sioux Indians.

•**BAXTER,** City; Jasper County; Pop. 951; Zip Code 50028; Lat. 41-49-52 N long. 093-09-40 W. Baxter was an early settler.

•**BAYARD,** City; Guthrie County; Pop. 637; Zip Code 50029; Elev. 1,135; Lat. 41-51-26 N long. 094-33-40 W.

•**BEACON,** City; Mahaska County; Pop. 530; Zip Code 52534; Lat. 41-16-14 N long. 092-40-33 W; Named in honor of Lord Beaconsfield.

•**BEACONSFIELD,** City; Ringgold County; Pop. 39; Zip Code 50030; Lat. 40-48-31 N long. 094-03-22 W; Most likely named for Lord Beaconsfield.

•**BEAVER,** City; Boone County; Pop. 85; Zip Code 50031; Lat. 42-02-09 N long. 094-08-25 W; The Fox Indians called this place Amaqua meaning "beaver," for the animals in the area. The English translation of the name was kept.

•**BEDFORD,** City; Taylor County Seat; Pop. 1,692; Zip Code 50833; Lat. 40-40-22 N long. 094-43-26 W. Named after the city in Massachusetts.

•**BELLE PLAINE,** City; Benton County; Pop. 2,903; Zip Code 52208; Lat. 41-53-52 N long. 092-16-21 W; A French name meaning "beautiful plain."

•**BELLEVUE,** City; Jackson County; Pop. 2,450; Zip Code 52031; Lat. 42-15-40 N long. 090-25-50 W; The name is French for "beautiful view."

•**BELMOND,** City; Wright County; Pop. 2,505; Zip Code 50421; Lat. 42-50-58 N long. 093-36-58 W. The city is named after early settler Belle Dumond.

•**BENNETT,** City; Cedar County; Pop. 458; Zip Code 52721; Lat. 41-43-48 N long. 090-58-33 W; Named for Chet Bennett, a railroad man.

•**BLANCHARD,** City; Page County; Pop. 101; Zip Code 51630; Lat. 40-35-13 N long. 095-13-28 W; An old French place name. Settlers from France and Canada gave the name Blanchard to many towns in the U. S.

•**BLOCKTON,** City; Taylor County; Pop. 280; Zip Code 50836; Lat. 40-37-13 N long. 094-28-50 W. Block was a pioneer.

•**BLOOMFIELD,** City; Davis County Seat; Pop. 2,849; Zip Code 52537; Lat. 40-45-07 N long. 092-25-15 W. The city's name was chosen at random by the county commissioners.

•**BLUE GRASS,** City; Scott County; Pop. 1,377; Zip Code 52726; Lat. 41-30-25 N long. 090-46-12 W; The city takes its name from a variety of grass that grows in Kentucky.

•**BONAPARTE,** City; Van Buren County; Pop. 489; Zip Code 52620; Lat. 40-42-51 N long. 091-48-18 W; Named in honor of Napoleon Bonaparte, first emperor of France, who sold the Louisiana Territory to the United States.

•**BONDURANT,** City; Polk County; Pop. 1,283; Zip Code 50035; Lat. 41-36-05 N long.. 093-28-41 W; The city was named for A. C. Bondurant.

•**BOONE,** City; Boone County Seat; Pop. 12,602; Zip Code 50036; Lat. 42-05-22 N long. 093-56-00 W; Named for Captain Boone, of the U.S. Dragoons, who captured the Des Moine Valley above Coon Forks.

•**BOYDEN,** City; Sioux County; Pop. 708; Zip Code 51234; Lat. 43-11-19 N long 096-00-55 W. Named in honor of a local railroad man.

•**BRANDON,** City; Buchanan County; Pop. 337; Zip Code 52210; Lat. 42-18-50 N long. 092-00-03 W.

•**BRAYTON,** City; Audubon County; Pop. 170; Zip Code 50042; Lat. 41-33-14 N long. 094-55-34 W. The city is named for a civil engineer who surveyed for the railroad here.

•**BREDA,** City; Carroll County; Pop. 502; Zip Code 51436; Lat. 42-10-38 N long. 094-58-40 W.

•**BRIDGEWATER,** City; Adair County; Pop. 233; Zip Code 50837; Lat. 41-14-30 N long. 094-40-26 W. Descriptively named.

•**BRIGHTON,** City; Washington County; Pop. 804; Zip Code 52540; Lat. 41-10-30 N long. 091-49-13 W; Probably named for Brighton, England.

•**BRITT,** City; Hancock County; Pop. 2,185; Zip Code 50423; Lat. 43-05-48 N long. 093-48-21 W. The town is named after a local newspaper editor.

•**BROOKLYN,** City; Poweshiek County; Pop. 1,509; Zip Code 52211; Lat. 41-44-14 N long. 092-26-53 W. Named for the city in New York.

•**BUFFALO,** City; Scott County; Pop. 1,441; Zip Code 52728; Lat. 41-27-23 N long. 090-43-24. Named for the Bison once found here.

•**BUFFALO CENTER,** City; Winnebago County; Pop. 1,233; Zip Code 50424; Lat. 43-23-05 N long. 093-56-14 W. Buffalo lived in the area when the settlers first arrived and this led to the city's name.

•**BURLINGTON,** City; Des Moines County Seat; Pop. 29,529; Zip Code 52601; Lat. 40-48-58 N long. 091-06-22 W; Named after the city of Burlington, Vermont.

•**BURT,** City; Kossuth County; Pop. 689; Zip Code 50522; Lat. 43-12-05 N long. 094-13-22 W; Called Burt after the President of the Union Pacific Railroad.

•**CALAMUS,** City; Clinton County; Pop. 452; Zip Code 52729; Lat. 41-49-33 N long. 090-45-29 W. Named for the wild marsh plant found in the area.

•**CALMAR,** City; Winneshiek County; Pop. 1,053; Zip Code 52132; Lat. 43-11-34 N long. 091-52-49 W.

•**CALUMET,** City; O'Brien County; Pop. 212; Zip Code 51009; Lat. 42-56-49 N long. 095-33-04 W; Calumet was a word used by the French for the Indian peace pipe. A possible reason for the name for the place might be that the Indians obtained pipestone in the area.

•**CAMANCHE,** City; Clinton County; Pop. 4,725; Zip Code 52730; A derivative of Comanche, the name of a Shoshone Indian tribe.

•**CAMBRIDGE,** City; Story County; Pop. 732; Zip Code 50046; Elev. 2,651; Lat. 41-55-00 N long. 093-30-23 W. Named for the English University city.

•**CARBON,** City; Adams County; Pop. 110; Zip Code 50839; Lat. 41-02-51 N long. 094-49-28 W; The name may have been given to the place to indicate the presence of coal deposits.

•**CARROLL,** City; Carroll County Seat; Pop. 9,705; Zip Code 51401; Lat. 42-01-19 N long. 094-50-53 W; Named for Charles Carroll, of Carrollton, Maryland.

•**CARSON,** City; Pottawattamie County; Pop. 3,438; Zip Code 51525; Lat. 41-14-06 N long. 095-25-15 W. Possibly named for explorer Kit Carson.

•**CARTER LAKE,** City; Pottawattamie County; Pop. 3,438; Lat. 41-17-26 N long. 095-55-04 W.

•**CASCADE,** City; Dubuque & Jones Counties; Pop. 1,912; Zip Code 52033; Lat. 42-17-49 N long. 091-01-01 W.

•**CEDAR FALLS,** City; Black Hawk County; Pop. 36,322; Zip Code 50613; Lat. 42-31-35 N long. 092-25-33 W; Named for its proximity to the Cedar River.

•**CEDAR RAPIDS,** City; Linn County Seat; Pop. 110,243; Zip Code 52400; Lat. 41-59-02 N long. 091-40-02 W; Located on and named for the Cedar River. The river was originally called Mosk-wah-wak-wah or "red cedar" by the Sauk-Fox Indians.

•**CENTER POINT,** City; Linn County; Pop. 1,591; Zip Code 52213; Lat. 42-11-38 N long. 091-47-03 W; Named for its geographical location.

•**CENTERVILLE,** City; Appanoose County Seat; Pop. 6,558; Zip Code 52544; Lat. 40-44-08 N long. 092-52-11 W; Most likely named for its central location.

•**CENTRAL CITY,** City; Linn County; Pop. 1,067; Zip Code 52214; Lat. 42-12-37 N long. 091-31-20 W. Descriptively named.

•**CENTRALIA,** City; Dubuque County; Pop. 106; Platted in 1850 and first called Dakotah. The name was later changed to Centralia.

•**CHARITON,** City; Lucas County Seat; Pop. 4,987; Zip Code 50049; Lat. 41-01-10 N long. 093-18-18 W; Named for an early French settler in this area, whose surname was similar to Chariton.

•**CHARLES CITY,** City; Floyd County Seat; Pop. 8,778; Zip Code 50616; Lat. 43-04-15 N long. 092-40-44 W. The city is named for Charles Kelly, son of the town's founder.

•**CHARLOTTE,** City; Clinton County; Pop. 442; Zip Code 52731; Lat. 41-57-37 N long. 090-27-54 W. Named for the city in Virginia.

•**CHARTER OAK,** City; Crawford County; Pop. 615; Zip Code 51439; Lat. 42-03-50 N long. 095-34-56 W. The town is named after a prominent oak tree.

•**CHELSEA,** City; Tama County; Pop. 376; Zip Code 52215; Elev. 792; Lat. 41-54-28 N long. 092-25-48 W. Named after the city in England.

•**CHEROKEE,** City; Cherokee County Seat; Pop. 7,004; Zip Code 51012; Lat. 42-44-28 N long. 095-33-16 W; Named for the Cherokee Indian tribe, which had no historical connection to the region. The first town named Cherokee was in Massachusetts. The name most likely came west with the settlers.

•**CHILLICOTHE,** City; Wapello County; Pop. 131; Zip Code 52548; Lat. 41-05-50 N long. 092-32-12 W; Derived from Chi-la-ka-tha, the name of one of the four divisions of the Shawnee Indian tribe.

•**CHURDAN,** City; Greene County; Pop. 540; Zip Code 50050; Elev. 1,110; Lat. 42-08-38 N long. 094-28-37 W.

•**CINCINNATI,** City; Appanoose County; Pop. 598; Zip Code 52549; Lat. 40-37-43 N long. 092-55-24 W. Named after the city in Ohio.

•**CLARENCE,** City; Cedar County; Pop. 1,001; Zip Code 52216; Lat. 41-52-40 N long. 091-02-57 W. Named for a prominent early settler.

•**CLARINDA,** City; Page County Seat; Pop. 5,458; Zip Code 51632; Lat. 40-47-08 N long. 095-01-34 W; Named for Clarinda Buck, the niece of the city founder.

•**CLARION,** City; Wright County Seat; Pop. 3,060; Zip Code 50525; Lat. 42-43-50 N long. 093-44-03 W; The name is derived from a French word, meaning "clear.

•**CLARKSVILLE,** City; Butler County; Pop. 1,424; Zip Code 50619; Lat. 42-47-13 N long. 092-40-43 W. Named for the city's founder.

•**CLAYTON,** City; Clayton County; Pop. 68; Lat. 42-54-14 N long. 091-08-50 W; Named in honor of John M. Clayton, Senator from Delaware.

•**CLEAR LAKE CITY,** City; Cerro Gordo County; Pop. 7,458; Lat. 43-08-17 N long. 093-22-45 W. Descriptively named for its location near the lake.

•**CLEGHORN,** City; Cherokee County; Pop. 275; Zip Code 51014; Lat. 42-48-44 N long. 095-42-52 W. Named in honor of a Dr. Cleghorn who donated land to the town in 1901.

•**COLFAX,** City; Jasper County; Pop. 2,211; Zip Code 50054; Lat. 41-40-49 N long. 093-15-30 W. Named in honor of U.S. Vice President, Schuyler Colfax.

•**COLLINS,** City; Story County; Pop. 451; Zip Code 50055; Lat. 41-55-06 N long. 093-17-54 W.

•**COLO,** City; Story County; Pop. 808; Zip Code 50056; Lat. 42-01-25 N long. 093-18-54 W. Railroad official John Blair remembered his favorite dog by naming the town after it.

•**COLUMBUS JUNCTION,** City; Louisa County; Pop. 1,429; Zip Code 52738; Lat. 41-16-48 N long. 091-21-38 W. Named for the discoverer of America.

•**CONRAD,** City; Grundy County; Pop. 1,133; Zip Code 50621; Lat. 42-13-04 N long. 092-52-23 W. Named for a pioneer.

•**COON RAPIDS,** City; Carroll County; Pop. 1,448; Zip Code 50058; Lat. 41-52-24 N long. 094-41-00 W; Named for nearby Coon Branch. The word coon is a colloquial abbreviation of racoon.

•**CORALVILLE,** City; Johnson County; Pop. 7,687; Lat. 41-40-35 N long. 091-34-49 W; Named for the coral formation underlying the town.

•**CORNING,** City; Adams County Seat; Pop. 1,939; Zip Code 50841; Lat. 40-59-15 N long. 094-44-26 W; The city took its name from famous merchant Erastus Corning.

•**CORRECTIONVILLE,** City; Woodbury County; Pop. 935; Zip Code 51016; Lat. 42-28-34 N long. 095-47-41 W; So named because it was situated on a surveying correction line.

•**CORWITH,** City; Hancock County; Pop. 480; Zip Code 50430; Lat. 42-59-52 N long. 093-57-41 W.

•**CORYDON,** City; Wayne County Seat; Pop. 1,818; Zip Code 50060; Lat. 40-45-34 N long. 093-19-24 W. Named after the English city.

•**COUNCIL BLUFFS,** City; Pottawattamie County Seat; Pop. 56,449; Zip Code 51501; Elev. 986; Lat. 41-09-10 N long. 095-35-59 W; The name originally came from bluffs on the Missouri River, 15 miles upstream from the present location of the city. Lewis and Clark held a conference with Oto and Missouri Indians at that site in 1804.

•**CRESCENT,** City; Pottawattamie County; Pop. 547; Zip Code 51526; Lat. 41-22-04 N long. 095-51-25 W. Descriptively named for the bluffs rising above the town.

•**CRESCA,** City; Howard County Seat; Pop. 3,860; Zip Code 52136; Lat. 43-22-23 N long. 092-07-30 W; The name was derived from latin and means "it grows."

•**CRESTON,** City; Union County Seat; Pop. 8,429; Zip Code 50801; Lat. 41-03-24 N long. 094-22-01 W; So named because it was located on a crest, the highest point on the Chicago, Burlington and Quincy Railroad line.

•**CRYSTAL LAKE,** City; Hancock County; Pop. 314; Zip Code 50432; Lat. 43-13-25 N long. 093-47-43 W. Named after the nearby lake.

•**CUMBERLAND,** City; Cass County; Pop. 351; Zip Code 50843; Lat. 41-16-11 N long. 094-53-05 W.

•**CUSHING,** City; Woodbury County; Pop. 270; Zip Code 51018; Elev. 1,327; Lat. 42-27-53 N long. 095-41-34 W.

•**CYLINDER,** City; Palo Alto County; Pop. 119; Zip Code 50528; Lat. 43-04-39 N long. 094-34-05 W. The city is named for nearby Cylinder Creek.

•**DAKOTA CITY,** City; Humboldt County Seat; Pop. 1,072; Zip Code 50529; Lat. 42-43-34 N long. 094-12-12 W; Named in 1855 by Edward McKnight. The word "Dakota" came from the name of the alliance of the Plains Indians.

•**DALLAS,** City; Marion County; Pop. 451; Zip Code 50062; Lat. 41-13-56 N long. 093-14-33 W; The city was named for George M. Dallas, Vice-President of the United States.

•**DALLAS CENTER,** City; Dallas County; Pop. 1,360; Zip Code 50063; Elev. 1,072; Lat. 41-41-21 N long. 093-58-00 W.

•**DANBURY,** City; Woodbury County; Pop. 492; Zip Code 51019; Lat. 42-14-01 N long. 095-44-14 W; Probably named for the town of Danbury in Essex, England.

•**DANVILLE,** City; Des Moines County; Pop. 994; Zip Code 52623; Lat. 40-51-40 N long. 091-18-19 W. Named for a local settler.

•**DAVENPORT,** City; Scott County Seat; Pop. 103,264; Zip Code 52800; Lat. 41-34-20 N long. 090-35-26 W; Named for Colonel Davenport, an early settler.

•**DAWSON,** City; Dallas County; Pop. 229; Zip Code 50066; Elev. 948; Lat. 41-50-12 N long. 094-13-05 W.

•**DAYTON,** City; Webster County; Pop. 941; Zip Code 50530; Lat. 42-15-48 N long. 094-05-24 W. Named after the city in Ohio.

•**DECATUR CITY,** City; Decatur County; Pop. 199; Zip Code 50067; Lat. 40-45-21 N long. 093-49-12 W; Named in honor of Commodore Stephen Decatur.

•**DECORAH,** City; Winneshiek County Seat; Pop. 7,991; Zip Code 52101; Lat. 43-18-57 N long. 091-48-15 W; The name came from a noted Winnebago Indian. Born in 1729, the son of Hopoekaw, a Winnebago woman and a French officer, Sabrevoir de Carrie, his last name was corrupted to Decorah.

•**DEDHAM,** City; Carroll County; Pop. 321; Zip Code 51440; Lat. 41-54-30 N long. 094-49-33 W.

•**DEEP RIVER,** City; Poweshiek County; Pop. 323; Zip Code 52222; Lat. 41-35-41 N long. 092-22-51 W; Named after a nearby creek.

•**DEFIANCE,** City; Shelby County; Pop. 383; Zip Code 51527; Elev. 1,283; Lat. 41-49-32 N long. 095-20-50 W.

•**DELAWARE,** City; Delaware County; Pop. 170; Zip Code 52036; Lat. 42-28-43 N long. 091-21-05 W; Named for Lord de la Narr, Governor and first Captain-General of Virginia.

•**DELHI,** City; Delaware County; Pop. 511; Zip Code 52223; Lat. 42-25-44 N long. 091-20-16 W; Probably named for the city in India.

•**DELTA,** City; Keokuk County; Pop. 482; Zip Code 52550; Lat. 41-19-18 N long. 092-19-47 W. Descriptively named.

•**DENISON,** City; Crawford County Seat; Pop. 6,675; Zip Code 51442; Lat. 42-00-51 N long. 095-20-04 W. The town is named after Baptist minister J.W. Denison.

•**DENVER,** City; Bremer County; Pop. 1,647; Zip Code 50622; Lat. 42-40-30 N long. 092-20-07 W. Named for the city in Colorado.

•**DES MOINES,** City; Polk County Seat; Pop. 191,003; Zip Code 50053; Lat. 41-36-25 N long. 093-43-15 W; Named after the Des Moines River. French explorers called the stream "Riviere des Moingouenas" after the Moingouena Indians. The name was shortened to Riviere des Morngs, and finally Riviere des Moines.

•**DEXTER,** City; Dallas County; Pop. 678; Zip Code 50070; Elev. 115; Lat. 41-31-08 N long. 094-13-49 W. Founded in 1865 and named for a racehorse.

•**DICKENS,** City; Clay County; Pop. 289; Zip Code 51333; Lat. 43-08-05 N long. 095-01-06 W. Named after the English novelist.

•**DIKE,** City; Grundy County; Pop. 987; Zip Code 50624; Lat. 42-27-53 N long. 092-38-09 W.

•**DONNELLSON,** City; Lee County; Pop. 972; Zip Code 52625; Lat. 40-38-20 N long. 091-34-16 W. Donnellson was a pioneer.

•**DOON,** City; Lyon County; Pop. 537; Zip Code 51235; Lat. 43-17-21 N long. 096-13-26 W; Named after the Doon River in Scotland.

•**DOUGHERTY,** City; Cerro Gordo County; Pop. 128; Zip Code 50433; Lat. 42-55-31 N long. 093-01-03 W; The city was named after one of its prominent residents, Daniel Dougherty.

•**DOW CITY,** City; Crawford County; Pop. 616; Zip Code 51528; Elev. 1,131; Lat. 41-55-11 N long. 095-26-30 W. Named for S.E. Dow, an early settler.

•**DRAKESVILLE,** City; Davis County; Pop. 212; Zip Code 52552; Lat. 40-48-01 N long 092-29-11 W; Laid out by John A. Drake, and named in his honor.

•**DUBUQUE,** City; Dubuque County Seat; Pop. 62,321; Zip Code 52001; Lat. 42-29-58 N long. 090-42-02 W; Named for Julien Dubuque, the first permanent white settler, who came to the area in 1797. An early name for the place was Dubuque's Lead Mines.

•DUMONT, City; Butler County; Pop. 815; Zip Code 50625; Lat. 42-45-13 N long. 092-58-35 W; Probably named for an early French settler.

•DUNCOMBE, City; Webster County; Pop. 504; Zip Code 50532; Lat. 42-28-18 N long. 094-01-11 W; The city was named for Hon. J. F. Duncombe.

•DUNDEE, City; Delaware County; Pop. 164; Zip Code 52018; Elev. 998; Lat. 42-34-45 N long. 091-33-04 W. Named for the city in Scotland.

•EAGLE GROVE, City; Wright County; Pop. 4,324; Zip Code 50533; Lat. 42-39-24 N long. 093-54-20 W; Named for the many eagles that built nests in a groove here.

•EARLHAM, City; Madison County; Pop. 1,140; Zip Code 50072; Lat. 41-29-41 N long. 094-07-07 W.

•EARLVILLE, City; Delaware County; Pop. 844; Zip Code 52041; Lat. 42-28-52 N long. 091-16-35 W; The city was named for its first settler, G. M. Earl.

•EARLY, City; Sac County; Pop. 670; Zip Code 50535; Lat. 42-27-43 N long. 095-09-04 W. Named for D.C. Early, a pioneer who settled here in the 1870s.

•EDGEWOOD, City; Clayton & Delaware Counties; Pop. 900; Zip Code 52042; Lat. 42-38-49 N long. 091-24-17 W.

•ELBERON, City; Tama County; Pop. 194; Zip Code 52225; Lat. 41-59-40 N long. 092-21-00 W.

•ELDON, City; Wapello County; Pop. 1,255; Zip Code 52554; Lat. 40-54-29 N long. 092-12-45 W. Eldon is named in honor of an early settler.

•ELDORA, City; Hardin County Seat; Pop. 3,063; Zip Code 50627; Elev. 1,088; Lat. 42-221-11 N long. 093-05-13 W; Derived from the Spanish words "el dorado", meaning "the gilded one."

•ELDRIDGE, City; Scott County; Pop. 3,279; Zip Code 52748; Lat. 41-39-29 N long. 090-35-04 W. Given the name of a prominent citizen.

•ELGIN, City; Fayette County; Pop. 702; Zip Code 52141; Lat. 42-57-52 N long. 091-37-55 W. Named after Elgin, Illinois.

•ELKADER, City; Clayton County Seat; Pop. 1,688; Zip Code 52043; Lat. 42-51-14 N long. 091-24-19 W. Named in 1845 for Algerian nationalist Abd-el-Kader.

•ELK HORN, City; Shelby County; Pop. 746; Elev. 1363; Lat. 41-35-30 N long. 095-03-35 W. Named after an elk horn once found in the area.

•ELK RUN HEIGHTS, City; Blkack Hawk County; Pop. 1,186; Lat. 42-28-01 N long. 092-15-23 W. Descriptively named.

•ELLIOTT, City; Montgomery County; Pop. 493; Zip Code 51532; Lat. 41-08-57 N long. 095-09-50 W.

•ELLSWORTH, City; Hamilton County; Pop. 480; Zip Code 50075; Lat. 42-18-25 N long. 093-34-28 W; Named for a banker who lived in Iowa Falls.

•ELMA, City; Howard County; Pop. 714; Zip Code 50628; Lat. 43-14-42 N long. 092-26-08 W.

•EMERSON, City; Mills County; Pop. 502; Zip Code 51533; Lat. 41-01-21 N long 095-27-08 W. Named in honor of the American philosopher R.W. Emerson.

•EMMETSBURG, City; Palo Alto County Seat; Pop. 4,621; Zip Code 50536; Lat. 43-06-18 N long. 094-41-01 W; Named in honor of Robert W. Emmet, an Irish patriot.

•EPWORTH, City; Dubuque County; Pop. 1,380; Zip Code 52045; Lat. 42-28-38 N long. 090-56-55 W; The city takes its name from the town in Lincolnshire, England.

•ESSEX, City; Page County; Pop. 1,001; Zip Code 51638; Lat. 40-49-43 N long. 095-17-50 W. Named for the county in England.

•ESTHERVILLE, City; Emmet County Seat; Pop. 7,518; Zip Code 51334; Lat. 43-24-18 N long. 094-48-17 W; Called Estherville, after the Esther A. Ridley, wife of one of the original proprietors.

•EVANSDALE, City; Black Hawk County; Pop. 4,798; Zip Code 50707; Lat. 42-28-09 N long. 092-16-51 W.

•EXIRA, City; Audubon County; Pop. 978; Zip Code 50076; Lat. 41-36-01 N long. 094-53-06 W. The city is named after Exira Eckman, the daughter of a local judge.

•FAIRBANK, City; Buchanon & Fayette Counties; Pop. 980; Zip Code 50629; Lat. 42-37-38 N long. 092-02-51 W.

•FAIRFAX, City; Linn County; Pop. 683; Zip Code 52228; Lat. 41-55-18 N long. 091-46-31 W. Named for the county in Virginia.

•FAIRFIELD, City; Jefferson County Seat; Pop. 9,428; Zip Code 52556; Elev. 778; Lat. 41-00-21 N long. 091-57-21 W. Descriptively named for the area's beauty.

•FARLEY, City; Dubuque County; Pop. 1,287; Zip Code 52046; Lat. 42-26-35 N long. 091-00-49 W. The town's name remembers railroad man J.P. Farley.

•FARMINGTON, City; Van Buren County; Pop. 869; Zip Code 52626; Elev. 569; Lat. 40-38-26 N long. 091-44-53 W. Named after the area's main economic activity: farming.

•FARRAGUT, City; Fremont County; Pop. 603; Zip Code 51639; Lat. 40-43-05 N long. 095-29-12 W; The city was named for Admiral Farragut.

•FAYETTE, City; Fayette County; Pop. 1,515; Zip Code 52142; Lat. 42-50-10 N long. 091-48-06 W; Named in honor of the Marquis de Lafayette, who served as French General in the American Army during the Revolutionary War.

•FENTON, City; Kassuth County; Pop. 394; Zip Code 50539; Lat. 43-13-20 N long. 094-24-24 W.

•FERTILE, City; Worth County; Pop. 372; Zip Code 50434; Lat. 43-16-07 N long. 093-25-21 W. Descritively named for the area's rich land.

•FLOYD, City; Floyd County; Pop. 408; Zip Code 50435; Lat. 43-07-54 N long. 092-44-18 W; Named for Sergeant Charles Floyd, a member of the Lewis and Clark expedition.

•FONDA, City; Pocahontas County; Pop. 863; Zip Code 50540; Lat. 42-34-58 N long. 094-50-44 W. Named by the town's first residents from the U.S. Post Office Directory.

•FONTANELLE, City; Adair County; Pop. 805; Zip Code 50846; Lat. 41-17-52 N long. 094-33-36 W; The city was either named after Louis Fontanelle, a trapper who worked for the American Fur Company, or for his son, Omaha Indian Chief Logan Fontanelle.

•FORT ATKINSON, City; Winneshiek County; Pop. 374; Zip Code 52144; Lat. 43-09-41 N long. 091-57-22 W. Named after an early military post.

•FORT DODGE, City; Webster County Seat; Pop. 29,423; Zip Code 50501; Lat. 42-30-23 N long. 094-11-16 W; Named after Senator Dodge of Wisconsin.

•FORT MADISON, City; Lee County Seat; Pop. 13,520; Zip Code 52627; Lat. 40-37-17 N long. 091-21-41 W; The city took its name from James Madison, President of the United States.

•FRANKLIN, City; Lee County; Pop. 261; Lat. 40-40-05 N long. 091-30-40 W; Like many places throughout the country, this city was named for Benjamin Franklin.

•FREDERICKSBURG, City; Bremer County; Pop. 223; Zip Code 50630; Lat. 42-58-11 N long. 092-13-07 W. Founded in 1856 and named after founder Frederick Padden.

•FREDERIKA, City; Bremer County; Pop. 223; Zip Code 50631; Lat. 42-52-58 N long. 092-18-36 W. The town's name remembers 19th century novelist Fredericka Bremer.

•FREMONT, City; Mahaska County; Pop. 730; Zip Code 52561; Lat. 41-12-49 N long. 092-26-19 W; The city was named for Gen. John C. Fremont.

•FRUITLAND, City; Muscatine County; Pop. 461; Zip Code 52749; Lat. 41-21-22 N long. 091-07-45 W. Descriptivley named for the local horticulture.

•GALVA, City; Ida County; Pop. 420; Zip Code 51020; Lat. 42-30-29 N long. 095-25-01 W.

•GARDEN GROVE, City; Decatur County; Pop. 297; Zip Code 50103; Lat. 40-50-35 N long. 093-35-16 W. Descriptively named.

•GARNAVIELLO, City; Clayton County; Pop. 723; Zip Code 52049; Lat. 42-53-17 N long. 091-11-50 W. Named after a town in Ireland.

•GARNER, City; Hancock County Seat; Pop. 2,908; Zip Code 50438; Lat. 43-06-01 N long. 093-36-33 W. The city's name remembers a prominent settler.

•GARRISON, City; Benton County; Pop. 411; Zip Code 52229; Lat. 42-08-44 N long. 092-08-25 W. Named after abolitionist William L. Garrison.

•GARWIN, City; Tama County; Pop. 626; Zip Code 50632; Lat. 42-05-32 N long. 092-40-30 W.

•GENEVA, City; Franklin County; Pop. 218; Zip Code 50633; Lat. 42-40-26 N long. 093-07-32 W. Named for the Swiss city.

•GEORGE, City; Lyon County; Pop. 1,241; Zip Code 51237; Lat. 43-21-03 N long. 095-58-35 W. Named after the founder.

•GILBERT, City; Story County; Pop. 805; Zip Code 50105; Lat. 42-06-52 N long. 093-36-59 W. Gilbert was a pioneer.

•GILBERTVILLE, City; Black Hawk County; Pop. 740; Zip Code 50634; Lat. 42-25-05 N long. 092-12-55 W.

•GOOSE LAKE, City; Clinton County; Pop. 274; Zip Code 52750; Lat. 41-58-03 N long. 090-22-58 W. Named after the nearby lake.

•GOWRIE, City; Webster County; Pop. 1,089; Zip Code 50543; Elev. 113; Lat. 42-19-02 N long. 094-18-06 W.

•GRAND JUNCTION, City; Greene County; Pop. 970; Zip Code 50107; Lat. 42-00-59 N long. 094-14-18 W; Named for its location

at the junction of the Keokuk and Des Moines and the Chicago and Northwestern Railroads.

•GRAND MOUND, City; Clinton County; Pop. 674; Zip Code 52751; Lat. 41-49-27 N long. 0909-38-52 W. Named for a nearby eroded glacial terminal moraine.

•GRANDVIEW, City; Louisa County; Pop. 473; Zip Code 52752; Lat. 41-16-33 N long. 091-11-18 W. Descriptively named.

•GRANGER, City; Dallas County; Pop. 619; Zip Code 50109; Lat. 41-45-44 N long. 094-49-57 W. The city's name honors railroad official Ben Granger.

•GRANT, City; Montgomery County; Pop. 143; Zip Code 50847; Lat. 41-08-37 N long. 094-59-41 W; Named in honor of Ulysses S. Grant.

•GRANVILLE, City; Sioux County; Pop. 336; Zip Code 51022; Lat. 42-58-53 N long. 095-53-30 W; The name is French for "large town."

•GRAVITY, City; Taylor County; Pop. 245; Zip Code 50848; Lat. 40-45-40 N long. 094-44-41 W; Settled in 1881 and named by early resident Sara Cox. She named the settlement Gravity because it was the main attraction in the area.

•GREELEY, City; Delaware County; Pop. 313; Zip Code 52050; Lat. 42-35-07 N long. 091-20-54 W. Named for the famous newspaper publisher Horace Greeley.

•GREENE, City; Butler County; Pop. 1,332; Zip Code 50636; Lat. 42-06-07 N long. 092-49-16 W; Named for Judge George Green of Linn County.

•GREENFIELD, City; Adair County Seat; Pop. 2,243; Zip Code 50849; Lat. 41-18-34 N long. 094-27-36 W; Greenfield took its name from the town in Massachusetts.

•GRIMES, City; Polk County; Pop. 1,973; Zip Code 50111; Lat. 41-39-41 N long. 093-47-29 W; Named for Senator Grimes.

•GRINNELL, City; Poweshiek County; Pop. 8,868; Zip Code 50112; Lat. 41-44-41 N long. 092-38-56 W; The city was named after one of its residents, Hon. W. H. Grinnell.

•GRISWOLD, City; Cass County; Pop. 1,176; Zip Code 51535; Lat. 41-13-58 N long. 095-07-58 W; Named for J. N. A. Griswold, a railroad official.

•GROETTINGER, City; Palo Alto County; Pop. 923; Zip Code 51342; Lat. 43-14-12 N long. 094-44-56 W.

•GRUNDY CENTER, City; Grundy County Seat; Pop. 2,880; Zip Code 50638; Elev. 1,026; Lat. 42-21-23 N long. 092-46-38 W; Grundy Center took its name from Felix Grundy, Senator from Tennessee.

•GUTHRIE CENTER, City; Guthrie County Seat; Pop. 1,713; Zip Code 50115; Elev. 1,150; Lat. 41-41-04 N long. 094-30-12 W; Named for Captain Edwin B. Guthrie.

•GUTTENBERG, City; Clayton County; Pop. 2,428; Zip Code 52052; Elev. 625; Lat. 42-44-32 N long. 091-05-30 W; Like the town of Guttenburg, New Jersey this city was named for the inventor of printing from moveable type.

•HAMBURG, City; Fremont County; Pop. 1,597; Zip Code 51640; Elev. 914; Lat. 40-36-16 N long. 095-39-27 W; Probably named for the city in Germany.

•HAMILTON, City; Marion County; Pop. 163; Zip Code 51016; Lat. 41-10-09 N long. 092-54-11 W; Named in honor of William W. Hamilton, President of the Senate in 1857.

•**HAMPTON,** City; Franklin County Seat; Pop. 4,630; Zip Code 50441; Lat. 42-44-31 N long. 093-12-08 W. Named for the eastern city.

•**HANCOCK,** City; Pottawattamie County; Pop. 254; Zip Code 51536; Lat. 41-23-24 N long. 095-21-44 W; Like many places throughout the United States, this city was named for John Hancock, signer of the Declaration of Independence.

•**HARLAN,** City; Shelby County Seat; Pop. 5,357; Zip Code 51537; Elev. 1250; Lat. 41-39-11 N long. 095-19-31 W; Named in honor of Senator Harlan.

•**HAWARDEN,** City; Sioux County; Pop. 2,722; Zip Code 51023; Lat. 42-59-45 N long. 096-29-06 W.

•**HAWKEYE,** City; Fayette County; Pop. 512; Lat. 42-56-19 N long. 091-57-00 W; Named either for Sauk Chief Black Hawk or from the character "Hawkeye" in James Fenimore Cooper's novel The Last of the Mohicans.

•**HAZLETON,** City; Buchanan County; Pop. 877; Zip Code 50641; Lat. 42-37-15 N long. 091-54-00 W.

•**HEDRICK,** City; Keokuk County; Pop. 847; Zip Code 52563; Lat. 41-10-21 N long. 092-18-31 W; Named for General Hedrick.

•**HEPBURN,** City; Page County; Pop. 42; Lat. 40-50-57 N long. 095-01-01 W; The city was named for Congressman Hepburn.

•**HIAWATHA,** City; Linn County; Pop. 4,825; Zip Code 52233; Lat. 42-02-09 N long. 091-40-55 W; Named for the Indian hero in Longfellow's poem, Song of Hiawatha.

•**HILLS,** City; Johnson County; Pop. 547; Zip Code 52235; Lat. 41-33-15 N long. 091-32-05 W. Descriptively named.

•**HINTON,** City; Plymouth County; Pop. 659; Zip Code 51024; Lat. 42-37-40 N long. 096-17-29 W.

•**HOLLAND,** City; Grundy County; Pop. 278; Zip Code 50642; Lat. 42-23-56 N long. 092-48-01 W. Named after the European country.

•**HOLSTEIN,** City; Ida County; Pop. 1,477; Zip Code 51025; Elev. 1437; Lat. 42-29-21 N long. 095-32-41 W.

•**HOPKINTON,** City; Delaware County; Pop. 774; Zip Code 52237; Lat. 42-20-38 N long. 091-14-54 W.

•**HOSPERS,** City; Sioux County; Pop. 655; Zip Code 51238; Lat. 43-04-19 N long. 095-54-15 W.

•**HUBBARD,** City; Hardin County; Pop. 852; Zip Code 50122; Lat. 42-18-20 N long. 093-18-00 W.

•**HUDSON,** City; Black Hawk County; Pop. 2,267; Zip Code 56643; Lat. 42-24-24 N long. 092-27-19 W. Named after the Hudson River.

•**HULL,** City; Sioux County; Pop. 1,714; Zip Code 51239: Lat. 43-11-19 N long. 096-08-00 W; Named for John Hull.

•**HUMBOLDT,** City; Humdoldt County; Pop. 4,794; Zip Code 50548; Lat. 42-43-15 N long. 094-12-54 W; The city was named for geographer, Baron Alexander von Humboldt.

•**HUMESTON,** City; Wayne County; Pop. 671; Zip Code 50123; Lat. 40-51-32 N long. 093-29-50 W.

•**IDA GROVE,** City; Ida County Seat; Pop. 2,285; Zip Code 51445; Elev. 1236; Lat. 42-20-42 N long. 095-28-17 W; Called Ida Grove by settlers from Ida Mountain in Greece.

•**INDEPENDENCE,** City; Buchanan County Seat; Pop. 6,392; Zip Code 50644; Lat. 42-28-07 N long. 091-53-21 W.

•**INDIANOLA,** City; Warren County Seat; Pop. 10,843; Zip Code 50125; Lat. 41-21-29 N long. 093-33-26 W.

•**INWOOD,** City; Lyon County; Pop. 755; Zip Code 51240; Lat. 43-18-26 N long. 096-25-54 W.

•**IOWA CITY,** City; Johnson County Seat; Pop. 50,508; Zip Code 52240; Lat. 41-39-40 N long. 091-31-48 W; Derived from the name of the Ioway Indian tribe. The word means "drowsy ones."

•**IOWA FALLS,** City; Hardin County; Pop. 6,174; Zip Code 50126; Lat. 42-31-21 N long. 093-15-04 W; Named for falls in the nearby Iowa River.

•**IRWIN,** City; Shelby County; Pop. 427; Zip Code 51446; Elev. 1264; Lat. 41-47-30 N long. 095-12-20 W.

•**JAMAICA,** City; Guthrie County; Pop. 275; Zip Code 50128; Elev. 1048; Lat. 41-50-46 N long. 094-18-34 W; Originally called Van Ness, the name was changed to avoid confusion with another town. The present name, Jamaica, is said to have been chosen randomly by pointing to a map blindfolded and landing on the island of Jamaica in the West Indies.

•**JANESVILLE,** City; Black Hawk & Bremer Counties; Pop. 840; Zip Code 56647. Called Janesville in honor of the wife of founder, John T. Barrick.

•**JEFFERSON,** City; Greene County Seat; Pop. 4,854; Zip Code 50129; Elev. 1078; Lat. 42-00-55 N long. 094-22-38 W; Like many towns throughout the country, this city was named for Thomas Jefferson.

•**JESUP,** City; Buchanan County; Pop. 2,343; Zip Code 50648; Lat. 42-28-32 N long. 092-03-49 W; Named for Morris K. Jesup of New York.

•**JEWELL JUNCTION,** City; Hamilton County; Pop. 1,145; Zip Code 50130; Lat. 42-18-25 N long. 093-38-24 W. Named for founder, David T. Jewell.

•**KALONA,** City; Washington County; Pop. 1,862; Zip Code 52247; Lat. 41-28-59 N long. 091-42-21 W.

•**KAMRAR,** City; Hamilton County; Pop. 225; Zip Code 50132; Lat. 42-23-32 N long. 093-43-45 W.

•**KANAWHA,** City; Hancock County; Pop. 756; Zip Code 50447; Lat. 42-56-16 N long. 093-47-35 W; Named after the Kanawha River in West Virginia.

•**KELLERTON,** City; Ringgold County; Pop. 278; Zip Code 50133; Lat. 40-42-39 N long. 094-02-59 W. Named for Judge Isaac Keller.

•**KELLEY,** City; Story County; Pop. 237; Zip Code 50134; Lat. 41-57-02 N long. 093-39-54 W.

•**KELLOGG,** City; Jasper County; Pop. 654; Zip Code 50135; Lat. 41-43-05 N long. 092-54-26 W; Named for an early settler.

•**KEOKUK,** City; Lee County Seat; Pop. 13,536; Zip Code 52632; Lat. 40-23-50 N long. 091-23-05 W; Named for Keokuk, U. S. Government appointed Chief of the Sauk Indians.

•**KEOSAUQUA,** City; Van Buren County Seat; Pop. 1,003; Zip Code 52565; Lat. 40-43-49 N long. 091-57-44 W; The name is an Indian word meaning "great bend" and refers to a bend in the Des Moines River.

•**KEOTA,** City; Keokuk County; Pop. 1,034; Zip Code 52248; Lat. 41-21-53 N long. 091-57-12 W; First called Keoton, a combination of the first three letters of Keokuk County and the last three of nearby Washington County. The name was later altered for easier pronunciation.

•**KESWICK,** City; Keokuk County; Pop. 300; Zip Code 50136; Lat. 41-27-20 N long. 092-14-19 W. Keswick was a pioneer's personal name.

•**KEYSTONE,** City; Benton County; Pop. 618; Zip Code 52249; Lat. 42-00-07 N long. 092-11-40 W.

•**KINGSLEY,** City; Plymouth County; Pop. 1,209; Zip Code 51028; Lat. 42-35-06 N long. 095-57-57 W; Named for Hon. J. T. Kingsley, a railroad official.

•**KIRKVILLE,** City; Wapello County; Pop. 220; Zip Code 52566; Lat. 41-09-31 N long. 092-30-18 W.

•**KLEMME,** City; Hancock County; Pop. 620; Zip Code 50449; Lat. 43-00-37 N long. 093-36-21 W.

•**KNOXVILLE,** City; Marion County Seat; Pop. 8,143; Zip Code 50138; Lat. 41-19-08 N long. 093-06-08 W. Named for General Henry Knox, the Secretary of War under Washington.

•**LACONA,** City; Warren County; Pop. 376; Zip Code 50139; Lat. 41-11-11 N long. 093-22-47 W.

•**LAKE CITY,** City; Calhoun County; Pop. 2,006; Zip Code 51449; Lat. 42-16-18 N long. 094-44-14 W. Named for its geography.

•**LAKE MILLS,** City; Winnebago County; Pop. 2,281; Zip Code 50450; Lat. 43-24-39 N long. 093-32-02 W.

•**LAKE PARK,** City; Dickinson County; Pop. 1,123; Zip Code 51347; Lat. 43-27-19 N long. 095-19-16 W.

•**LAKESIDE,** City; Buena Vista County; Pop. 589; Lat. 42-37-17 N long. 095-10-23 W. Descriptively named.

•**LAKE VIEW,** City; Sac County; Pop. 1,291; Zip Code 51450; Elev. 1,245; Lat. 42-17-57 N long. 095-04-07 W. Named for its view of the adjacent lake.

•**LAKOTA,** City; Kossuth County; Pop. 330; Zip Code 50451; Lat. 43-22-20 N long. 094-06-42 W; Derived from Dakota, the name for the Sioux Indian nation. Originally called Germania, for its many German residents, the town name was changed during World War I, due to anti-German sentiment.

•**LAMONI,** City; Decatur County; Pop. 2,705; Zip Code 50140; Lat. 40-37-34 N long. 093-55-32 W. A Mormon name meaning "righteous king."

•**LAMONT,** City; Buchanan County; Pop. 554; Zip Code 50650; Lat. 42-35-58 N long. 091-38-23 W; The name is probably of French origin and comes from "le mont" which means "the mountain."

•**LA MOTTE,** City; Jackson County; Pop. 322; Elev. 915; Lat. 42-17-45 N long. 090-37-15 W; Most likely named for Pierre Sieur de la Motte, a French captian.

•**LANSING,** City; Allamakee County; Pop. 1,181; Zip Code 51451; Lat. 43-22-14 N long. 091-13-12 W. The city was named after Lansing, Michigan.

•**LA PORTE CITY,** City; Black Hawk County; Pop. 2,324; Lat. 42-18-54 N long. 092-11-31 W; The name may either be from the French word meaning "door" or "opening", or from the La Porte family.

•**LARCHWOOD,** City; Lyon County; Pop. 701; Zip Code 51241; Lat. 43-27-23 N long. 096-27-03 W. Named for the many larch trees planted in the area by town founder J.W. Foll.

•**LARRABEE,** City; Cherokee County; Pop. 169; Zip Code 51029; Lat. 42-51-42 N long. 095-33-10 W. Larrabee was named for William Larrabee who was Governor of Iowa in 1886.

•**LATIMER,** City; Franklin County; Pop. 441; Zip Code 50452; Lat. 42-46-01 N log. 093-21-57 W.

•**LAURENS,** City; Pocahontas County; Pop. 1,606; Zip Code 50554; Lat. 42-50-48 N long. 094-50-43 W. The city was named for a nineteenth century resident.

•**LAWLER,** City; Chickasaw County; Pop. 534; Zip Code 52154; Lat. 43-04-16 N long. 092-10-36 W. Named for a prominent resident.

•**LAWTON,** City; Woodbury County; Pop. 447; Zip Code 51030; Elev. 1,179; Lat. 42-28-52 N long. 096-10-49 W.

•**LE CLAIRE,** City; Scott County; Pop. 2,899; Zip Code 52753; Lat. 41-35-52 N long. 0909-20-47 W; Named in honor of Antoine Le Clair, the founder of Davenport.

•**LE GRAND,** City; Marshall County; Pop. 921; Zip Code 50142; Lat. 42-00-20 N long. 092-46-26 W; The name is French for "the big one."

•**LEHIGH,** City; Webster County; Pop. 654; Zip Code 50557; Lat. 42-21-15 N long. 094-04-04 W; Named for the Lehigh River, a tributary of the Delaware in Pennsylvania. The name Lehigh is derived from a Delaware Indian word meaning "forked stream."

•**LEIGHTON,** City; Winnebago County; Pop. 274; Zip Code 50143; Lat. 41-20-20 N long. 092-47-02 W.

•**LE MARS,** City; Plymouth County Seat; Pop. 8,276; Elev. 1231; Lat. 42-47-39 N long. 096-09-55 W; The name is composed of the initials of the ladies who accompanied the city's founder on his first visit to the site.

•**LEON,** City; Decatur County Seat; Pop. 2,094; Zip Code 50144; Lat. 40-45-11 N long. 093-44-08 W. The name was chosen by the town's citizens in an 1854 petition to the legislature.

•**LESTER,** City; Lyon County; Pop. 274; Zip Code 51242; Lat. 43-26-32 N long. 096-20-06 W.

•**LETTS,** City; Louisa County; Pop. 473; Zip Code 52754; Lat. 41-19-42 N long. 091-14-13 W.

•**LEWIS,** City; Cass County; Pop. 497; Zip Code 51544; Lat. 41-18-18 N long. 095-04-41 W. Named for U.S. senator, Lewis Cass.

•**LIBERTYVILLE,** City; Jefferson County; Pop. 281; Zip Code 52567; Lat. 40-57-26 N long. 092-02-37 W.

•**LIME SPRINGS,** City; Howard County; Pop. 476; Zip Code 52155; Lat. 43-26-55 N long. 092-17-05 W; So named for springs in the rocks at this place.

•**LINCOLN,** City; Tama County; Pop. 202; Zip Code 50652; Lat. 42-15-51 N long. 092-41-15 W. Named in honor of Abraham Lincoln.

•**LINDEN,** City; Dallas County; Pop. 264; Zip Code 50146; Elev. 1,120; Lat. 41-38-34 N long. 094-16-16 W. The city was named after the beloved linden tree.

•**LINEVILLE,** City; Wayne County; Pop. 319; Zip Code 50147; Lat. 40-34-49 N long. 093-31-29 W; Situated on the Iowa-Missouri state line, the town was named in 1871 for its location. First known as Grand River.

•**LINN GROVE,** City; Buena Vista County; Pop. 205; Zip Code 51033; Lat. 42-53-32 N long. 095-14-37 W; Named for Hon. Lewis F. Linn, U. S. Senator from Missouri.

•**LISBON,** City; Linn County; Pop. 1,458; Zip Code 52253; Lat. 41-55-22 N long. 091-22-59 W. Lisbon takes its name from the great city in Portugal.

•**LITTLE ROCK,** City; Lyon County; Pop. 490; Lat. 43-26-39 N long. 095-52-59 W; Named after the Little Sioux River which was originally called "Petite riviere des Sioux" by the French.

•**LITTLE SIOUX,** City; Harrison County; Pop. 251; Elev. 103; Lat. 41-48-34 N long. 096-01-15 W.

•**LIVERMORE,** City; Humboldt County; Pop. 490; Zip Code 50558; Lat. 42-52-12 N long. 094-11-16 W.

•**LOGAN,** City; Harrison County Seat; Pop. 1,540; Zip Code 51546; Elev. 1,104; Lat. 41-38-41 N long. 095-47-44 W. Named in honor of Civil War general, John A. Logan.

•**LOHRVILLE,** City; Calhoun County; Pop. 521; Zip Code 51453; Lat. 42-16-27 N long. 094-33-15 W.

•**LONE ROCK,** City; Kossuth County; Pop. 169; Zip Code 50559; Lat. 43-13-23 N long. 094-18-59 W; Named for a single tree which stood on the prairie.

•**LONE TREE,** City; Johnson County; Pop. 1,014; Zip Code 52755; Lat. 41-29-17 N long. 091-25-33 W.

•**LONG GROVE,** City; Scott County; Pop. 596; Zip Code 52756; Lat. 41-41-51 N long. 090-34-57 W.

•**LORIMOR,** City; Union County; Pop. 405; Zip Code 50149; Lat. 41-07-42 N long. 094-03-37 W. Founded by Josiah Lorimar and named in his honor.

•**LOST NATION,** City; Clinton County; Pop. 524; Zip Code 52254; Lat. 41-58-06 N long. 090-50-36 W. A reference to the Indians.

•**LOVILIA,** City; Monroe County; Pop. 637; Zip Code 50150; Lat. 41-08-09 N long. 092-54-17 W.

•**MACEDONIA,** City; Pottawattamie County; Pop. 279; Zip Code 51549; Lat. 41-11-19 N long. 095-25-51 W. The city was named for the area in ancient Greece.

•**MADRID,** City; Boone County; Pop. 2,281; Zip Code 50156; Lat. 41-52-27 N long. 093-48-51 W. Named for the city in Spain.

•**MAGNOLIA,** City; Harrison County; Pop. 207; Lat. 41-41-45 N long. 095-52-35 W; Named for the magnolia trees at this place.

•**MALCOM,** City; Poweshiek County; Pop. 418; Zip Code 50157; Lat. 41-42-45 N long. 092-33-40 W; Named for an early Scotch settler.

•**MALLARD,** City; Palo Alto County; Pop. 407; Zip Code 50562; Lat. 42-55-06 N long. 094-41-23 W.

•**MALVERN,** City; Mills County; Pop. 1,244; Zip Code 51551; Lat. 41-00-04 N long. 095-32-28 W.

•**MANCHESTER,** City; Delaware County Seat; Pop. 4,942; Zip Code 52057; Lat. 42-31-03 N long. 091-24-31 W; The name was taken from "Chesterman" the city's original proprietor.

•**MANILLA,** City; Crawford County; Pop. 1,020; Zip Code 51454; Elev. 1317; Lat. 41-53-13 N long. 0-95-14-11 W.

•**MANLY,** City; Worth County; Pop. 1,496; Zip Code 50456; Elev. 1198; Lat. 43-17-21 N long. 093-12-16 W.

•**MANNING,** City; Carroll County; Pop. 1,609; Zip Code 51432; Elev. 1355; Lat. 41-54-28 N long. 095-08-21 W; Named for a merchant who lived here.

•**MANSON,** City; Calhoun County; Pop. 1,924; Zip Code 50563; Lat. 42-32-06 N long. 094-32-26 W; The name "Manson" came from one of the town's residents.

•**MAPLETON,** City; Monona County; Pop. 1,495; Zip Code 51034; Elev. 1157; Lat. 42-10-25 N long. 095-47-43 W.

•**MAQUOKETA,** City; Jackson County Seat; Pop. 6,313; Zip Code 52060; Lat. 42-03-51 N long. 090-40-14 W; Probably named for the Maquoketa River, which got its name from the Indian words meaning "there are bears" or "abundance of bears."

•**MARATHON,** City; Buena Vista County; Pop. 442; Zip Code 50565; Lat. 42-51-32 N long. 094-57-38 W. Probably named after the site in Greece.

•**MARBLE ROCK,** City; Floyd County; Pop. 419; Zip Code 50653; Lat. 42-58-05 N long. 092-52-08 W. Descriptively named for a local feature.

•**MARCUS,** City; Cherokee County; Pop. 1,206; Zip Code 51035; Lat. 42-49-23 N long. 095-48-34 W.

•**MARENGO,** City; Iowa County Seat; Pop. 2,308; Zip Code 52301; Lat. 41-47-25 N long. 092-04-07 W; Named for the battlefield in Italy.

•**MARION,** City; Linn County; Pop. 19,474; Zip Code 52302; Lat. 42-01-25 N long. 091-36-01 W; Named in honor of Gen. Francis Marioin.

•**MARNE,** City; Cass County; Pop. 162; Zip Code 51552; Lat. 41-27-03 N long. 095-06-12 W. Named after the area in France.

•**MARQUETTE,** City; Clayton County; Pop. 528; Zip Code 52158; Lat. 43-02-44 N long. 091-11-28 W; This city was named in honor of Jacques Marquette, the Jesuit priest who explored the Illinois and Mississipi valleys with Joliet. Named for Chief Justice John Marshall.

•**MARSHALLTOWN,** City; Marshall County Seat; Pop. 26,938; Zip Code 50158; Lat. 42-02-07 N long. 092-53-40 W.

•**MARTENSDALE,** City; Warren County; Pop. 438; Zip Code 50160; Lat. 41-22-19 N long. 093-44-24 W. Named for an early settler.

•**MASON CITY,** City; Cerro Gordo County Seat; Pop. 30,144; Zip Code 50401; Lat. 43-09-11 N long. 093-12-49 W.

•**MASSENA,** City; Cass County; Pop. 518; Zip Code 50853; Lat. 41-14-52 N long. 094-47-20 W; Named for French Marshall, Andre Massena.

•**MAXWELL,** City; Story County; Pop. 783; Zip Code 50161; Lat. 41-54-27 N long. 093-23-06 W.

•**MAYNARD,** City; Fayette County; Pop. 561; Zip Code 50655; Lat. 42-45-32 N long. 091-53-03 W.

•**MCGREGOR,** City; Clayton County; Pop. 945; Lat. 43-01-06 N long. 091-10-57 W; Named for Alexander McGregor, an early proprietor.

•**MECHANICSVILLE,** City; Cedar County; Pop. 1,166; Zip Code 52306; Lat. 41-53-56 N long. 091-13-57 W. The first settlers here were mechanics, and thus named the town.

•**MEDIAPOLIS,** City; Des Moines County; Pop. 1,685; Zip Code 52637; Lat. 41-00-38 N long. 091-09-28 W; Named for its location, halfway between Burlington and Washington.

•**MELBOURNE,** City; Marshall County; Pop. 732; Zip Code 50162; Lat. 41-56-20 N long. 093-06-27 W. Probably named after the Australian city.

•**MELCHER,** City; Marion County; Pop. 953; Zip Code 50163; Lat. 41-13-21 N long. 093-14-33 W.

•**MELROSE,** City; Monroe County; Pop. 953; Zip Code 52569; Lat. 40-58-37 N long. 093-03-13 W.

•**MENLO,** City; Guthrie County; Pop. 410; Zip Code 50164; Elev. 1,265; Lat. 41-32-37 N long. 094-24-09 W.

•**MERIDEN,** City; Cherokee County; Pop. 233; Zip Code 51037; Lat. 42-47-37 N long. 095-38-01 W. Originally called Hazzard, but later renamed by the Post Office.

•**MERRILL,** City; Plymouth County; Pop. 737; Zip Code 51038; Lat. 42-43-14 N long. 096-14-51 W. Named for a railroad man.

•**MIDDLETOWN,** City; Des Moines County; Pop. 487; Zip Code 52638; Lat. 40-49-46 N long. 091-15-02 W. Descriptively named for its location.

•**MILES,** City; Jackson County; Pop. 398; Zip Code 52064; Lat. 42-03-05 N long. 090-19-01 W; Found out by a man called Miles, and named for him.

•**MILFORD,** City; Dickinson County; Pop. 2,076; Zip Code 51351; Lat. 43-20-24 N long. 095-09-30 W. Named after an early mill site.

•**MILO,** City; Warren County; Pop. 778; Zip Code 50166; Lat. 41-17-18 N long. 093-26-31 W. Named for an early pioneer.

•**MILTON,** City; Van Buren County; Pop. 567; Zip Code 52570; Lat. 40-40-18 N long. 092-10-14 W. Named after the great English poet.

•**MINBURN,** City; Dallas County; Pop. 390; Zip Code 50167; Elev. 1,042; Lat. 41-45-25 N long. 094-02-18 W.

•**MINGO,** City; Jasper County; Pop. 303; Zip Code 50127; Lat. 41-46-43 N long. 093-12-21 W; The name may either have come from the eastren states where "mingo" was a term for certain Iroquois-speaking Indians, or from James Fenimore Cooper's books in which he called the enemies of the Delaware Indians, "mingos."

•**MISSOURI VALLEY,** City; Harrison County; Pop. 3,107; Zip Code 51555; Elev. 1,019; Lat. 41-33-29 N long. 095-54-38 W; The name "Missouri" came from the Indian word Miss-sou-li-au, which referred to "canoe men" or the Indians living east of the Mississippi River.

•**MITCHELL,** City; Mitchell County; Pop. 193; Lat. 43-19-19 N long. 092-52-03 W; Named for Irish patriot, John Mitchell.

•**MITCHELLVILLE,** City; Polk County; Pop. 1,530; Zip Code 50169; Lat. 41-39-55 N long. 093-21-39 W; Named for Thomas Mitchell.

•**MODALE,** City; Harrison County; Pop. 373; Zip Code 51556; Elev. 1,013; Lat. 41-36-58 N long. 096-02-47 W; The name is a combination of "Mo," the abbreviation for Missouri, plus dale, and is descriptive of the city's location near the Missouri River.

•**MONDAMIN,** City; Harrison County; Pop. 423; Zip Code 51557; Lat. 41-42-37 N long. 096-03-33 W; "Mondamin" is an Ojibwa Indian word meaning "corn."

•**MONMOUTH,** City; Jackson County; Pop. 210; Zip Code 52309; Lat. 42-04-31 N long. 090-52-37 W.

•**MONONA,** City; Clayton County; Pop. 1,530; Zip Code 52159; Lat. 43-03-18 N long. 091-23-38 W; Possibly named for the character "Monona" in Lewis Deffenbach's play, Oolaita, or the Indian Heroine.

•**MONROE,** City; Jasper County; Pop. 1,875; Zip Code 50170; Lat. 41-31-36 N long. 093-06-24 W; Like many American towns, this city was named for President James Monroe.

•**MONTEZUMA,** City; Poweshiek County Seat; Pop. 1,485; Zip Code 50171; Lat. 41-33-36 N long. 092-31-58 W; Named for Montezuma II, the Aztec ruler who was captured by the spanish, under Hernando Cortes, in 1520.

•**MONTICELLO,** City; Jones County; Pop. 3,641; Zip Code 52219; Lat. 42-14-14 N long. 091-25-22 W; Probably named for the famous Virginia estate of Thomas Jefferson.

•**MONTOUR,** City; Tama County; Pop. 387; Zip Code 50173; Lat. 41-58-27 N long. 092-42-45 W; Thought to be named for an early settler from Quebec, Canada.

•**MONTROSE,** City; Lee County; Pop. 1,038; Zip Code 52639; Elev. 530; Lat. 40-31-28 N long. 091-25-07 W. Originally called Mount of Roses, but later shortened to Montrose.

•**MOORHEAD,** City; Monona County; Pop. 264; Zip Code 51558; Elev. 1,200; Lat. 41-56-37 N long. 095-51-09 W.

•**MOORLAND,** City; Webster County; Pop. 257; Zip Code 50566; Lat. 42-26-24 N long. 094-17-13 W. Originally swampy land before being drained, the named recalls its former character.

•**MORAVIA,** City; Appanoose County; Pop. 706; Zip Code 52571; Lat. 40-54-16 N long. 092-49-03 W. Named after the province in central Europe.

•**MORNING SUN,** City; Louisa County; Pop. 959; Zip Code 52640; Lat. 41-05-43 N long. 091-14-41 W. Descriptively named.

•**MOULTON,** City; Appanoose County; Pop. 762; Zip Code 52572; Lat. 40-41-18 N long. 092-41-17 W; Named for an engineer of the Chicago, Burlington and Quincy Railroad.

•**MOUNT AUBURN,** City; Benton County; Pop. 188; Zip Code 52313; Lat. 42-15-35 N long. 092-05-40 W.

•**MOUNT AYR,** City; Ringgold County Seat; Pop. 1,938; Zip Code 50854; Lat. 40-43-01 N long. 094-14-16 W. Located on a high rolling prairie and descriptively named.

•**MOUNT PLEASANT,** City; Henry County Seat; Pop. 7,322; Zip Code 52641; Lat. 40-58-48 N long. 091-33-00 W.

•**MOUNT VERNON,** City; Linn County; Pop. 3,325; Zip Code 52314; Lat. 41-55-33 N long. 091-25-12 W; Probably named for George Washington's estate at Mount Vernon.

•**MOVILLE,** City; Woodbury County; Pop. 1,273; Zip Code 51039; Lat. 42-30-40 N long. 096-02-24 W; The name is a combination of "Mo," the abbreviation for Missouri, and "ville" which is French for "town."

•**NASHUA,** City; Chickasaw County; Pop. 1,846; Zip Code 50658; Lat. 42-57-04 N long. 092-31-58 W; The city got its name from Nashua, New York, the former home of resident, E. P. Greeley.

•**NEMAHA,** City; Sac County; Pop. 120; Zip Code 50567; Lat. 42-31-01 N long. 095-07-45 W; Either named for the Little Nemaha or the Nemaha River. The Indian word has been interpreted to mean "water of cultivation" or "muddy water."

•**NEOLA,** City; Pottawattamie County; Pop. 839; Zip Code 51559; Lat. 41-28-09 N long. 095-35-31 W.

•**NEVADA,** City; Story County Seat; Pop. 5,912; Zip Code 50201; Elev. 1,003; Lat. 42-01-02 N long. 093-27-51 W; Named by settlers from the state of Nevada. In Spanish "Nevada" means "snow-covered" and was applied to snow-capped peaks.

•**NEW ALBIN,** City; Allamakee County; Pop. 609; Zip Code 52160; Lat. 43-29-59 N long. 091-17-14 W.

•**NEWELL,** City; Buena Vista County; Pop. 913; Lat. 42-36-20 N long. 095-00-09 W.

•**NEW HAMPTON,** City; Chickasaw County Seat; Pop. 3,940; Zip Code 50659; Lat. 43-03-32 N long. 092-19-43 W. Named after the town in New Hampshire.

•**NEW HARTFORD,** City; Butler County; Pop. 764; Zip Code 50660; Lat. 42-34-09 N long. 092-37-27 W. The city was named after Hartford, Connecticut.

•**NEW LIBERTY,** City; Scott County; Pop. 136; Zip Code 52765; Lat. 41-43-04 N long. 090-52-44 W.

•**NEW LONDON,** City; Henry County; Pop. 2,043; Zip Code 52645; Lat. 40-56-30 N long. 091-24-22 W. Named after New London, Connecticut.

•**NEW MARKET,** City; Taylor County; Pop. 554; Zip Code 51646; Lat. 40-43-57 N long. 094-53-59 W.

•**NEW PROVIDENCE,** City; Hardin County; Pop. 249; Zip Code 50206; Elev. 1,130; Lat. 41-16-05 N long. 093-10-00 W.

•**NEW SHARON,** City; Mahaska County; Pop. 1,225; Zip Code 50207; Lat. 41-28-11 N long. 092-38-57 W.

•**NEWTON,** City; Jasper County Seat; Pop. 15,292; Lat. 41-41-59 N long. 093-02-52 W. Named in honor of a Revolutionary War soldier.

•**NEW VIENNA,** City; Dubuque County; Pop. 430; Zip Code 52065; Lat. 42-32-58 N long. 091-06-52 W.

•**NEW VIRGINIA,** City; Warren County; Pop. 512; Zip Code 50210; Lat. 41-11-01 N long. 093-43-53 W.

•**NODAWAY,** City; Adams County; Pop. 185; Zip Code 50857; Lat. 40-56-03 N long. 094-53-51 W; Named after the Nodaway River. "Nodaway" is an Algonquin Indian word meaning "Shake," often applied to their enemies.

•**NORA SPRINGS,** City; Floyd County; Pop. 1,572; Zip Code 50458; Lat. 43-08-49 N long. 093-00-38 W. Named after the local springs.

•**NORTHBORO,** City; Page County; Pop. 115; Zip Code 51647; Lat. 40-36-41 N long. 095-17-16 W.

•**NORTH LIBERTY,** City; Johnson County; Pop. 2,046; Lat. 41-44-57 N long. 091-35-52 W.

•**NORTHWOOD,** City; Worth County Seat; Pop. 2,193; Zip Code 50459; Lat. 43-26-47 N long. 093-13-09 W.

•**NORWALK,** City; Warren County; Pop. 2,676; Zip Code 50211; Lat. 41-30-27 N long. 093-36-47 W; Named from Norwalk, Connecticut.

•**NORWAY,** City; Benton County; Pop. 633; Zip Code 52318; Elev. 796; Lat. 41-54-18 N long. 091-54-56 W. Settled by Norwegians and who named the city for their former home.

•**OAKLAND,** City; Pottawattomie County; Pop. 1,552; Zip Code 51560; Elev. 1,103; Lat. 41-17-46 N long. 095-20-54 W. Named for the many oak trees once found here.

•**OCHEYEDON,** City; Osceola County; Pop. 599; Zip Code 51330; Lat. 43-24-55 N long. 095-38-36 W; Named for the Ocheyedan River and Mound. The name is derived from a Dakota Indian word meaning "little hill."

•**ODEBOLT,** City; Sac County; Pop. 1,299; Zip Code 51458; Elev. 1,377; Lat. 42-18-43 N long. 095-14-46 W; Taken from Odebeau, the name of a French trapper who lived alone by the creek at this place.

•**OELWEIN,** City; Fayette County; Pop. 7,564; Zip Code 50662; Lat. 42-39-17 N long. 091-55-04 W. The city was named after a German settler who donated land to the railroad.

•**OKOBOJI,** City; Dickinson County; Pop. 559; Zip Code 51355; Lat. 43-24-02 N long. 095-09-14 W; A Sioux name which has been interpreted as meaning "place of rest," "rushes," "a field of swamp grass" or "blue waters."

•**ONAWA,** City; Monona County Seat; Pop. 3,283; Zip Code 51040; Elev. 1,052; Lat. 42-02-28 N long. 096-05-39 W; Platted in 1857 by the Monona County Land Company and probably named for a song "Onaway" in Longfellow's poem, Hiawatha.

•**ONEIDA,** City; Delaware County; Pop. 61; Lat. 42-32-34 N long. 091-21-12 W; Named for the Oneida Indians who lived in the area around New York. The word "Oneida" means "standing stone."

•**ORANGE CITY,** City; Sioux County Seat; Pop. 4,588; Zip Code 51041; Lat. 42-59-56 N long. 096-04-15 W. Named for Prince William of Orange.

•**OSAGE,** City; Mitchell County Seat; Pop. 3,718; Zip Code 50454; Lat 43-22-53 N long. 092-43-33 W; Named for Orrin Sage, a banker from Wareham, Massachusetts. He signed his name O. Sage and was known for his generous donation to the town library.

•**OSCEOLA,** City; Clarke County Seat; Pop. 3,718; Zip Code 50213; Lat. 41-01-56 N long. 093-45-59 W; Names for Osceola, the famous Chief of the Florida Seminole Indians.

•**OSKALOOSA,** City; Mahaska County Seat; Pop. 10,629; Zip Code 52577; Lat. 41-17-21 N long. 092-38-16 W; Known for a short time as Mahaska, the name was changed to Oskaloosa in 1844. Possibly named for Ouskaloosa, a fictional character in the book, Osceola, or Fact and Fiction.

•**OSSIAN,** City; Winneshiek County; Pop. 829; Zip Code 52161; Lat. 43-09-51 N long. 091-46-17 W. Named after the Iowa poet John Ossian Porter.

•**OTTUMWA,** City; Wapello County Seat; Pop. 27,381; Zip Code 50570; Lat. 42-54-00 N long. 094-22-54 W; Named for the Fox Indian village of Ottumwah - noc, or Ottumwano, at this place, Possible meanings are "place of the lone chief" or "tumbling water."

•**OWASA,** City; Hardin County; Pop. 65; Elev. 1085; Lat. 42-26-01 N long. 093-12-25 W; Possibly named for a character in Henry Schoolcraft's book of "Owaissa," the bluebird in Longfellow's Hiawatha.

•**OXFORD,** City; Johnson County; Pop. 676; Zip Code 52322; Lat. 41-43-45 N long. 091-47-37 W. Named after the English city.

•**PACIFIC JUNCTION,** City; Mills County; Pop. 511; Zip Code 51561; Lat. 41-01-11 N long. 095-45-00 W. Named as a favorite stopping place for emigrants bound for the west coast.

•PALMER, City; Pocahontas County; Pop. 288; Zip Code 50571; Lat. 42-37-50 N long. 094-35-57 W.

•PALO, City; Linn County; Pop. 529; Zip Code 52324; Lat. 41-58-47 N long. 091-44-21 W; The name is a spanish word which means "stick."

•PANAMA, City; Shelby County; Pop. 229; Zip Code 51562; Elev. 1,325; Lat. 41-43-43 N long. 095-28-34 W; Probably named for "Pan-America." In Panama native languages the word may mean either "place where many fish are taken", or refer to a river lacking fish which was throught to be "unlucky" or "panema."

•PANORA, City; Guthrie County; Pop. 1,211; Zip Code 50216; Elev. 1,071; Lat. 41-42-23 N long. 094-21-54 W. The city's name is a contraction of "panorama."

•PARKERSBURG, City; Butler County; Pop. 1,968; Zip Code 50665; Lat. 42-34-52 N long. 092-47-32 W. The city was named after a prominent settler.

•PARNELL, City; Iowa County; Pop. 234; Zip Code 52325; Lat. 41-35-27 N long. 091-59-42 W. Named in honor of the famous Irish patriot.

•PATON, City; Greene County; Pop. 291; Zip Code 50217; Lat. 42-09-37 N long. 094-15-28 W.

•PAULINA, City; O'Brien County; Pop. 1,224; Zip Code 51046; Lat. 42-58-55 N long. 095-41-14 W.

•PELLA, City; Marion County; Pop. 8,329; Zip Code 50219; Lat. 41-24-25 N long. 092-54-56 W; Settled by Dutch immigrants and named "Pella" a word that to them meant "city of refuge."

•PEOSTA, City; Dubuque County; Pop. 120; Zip Code 52068; Lat. 42-27-37 N long. 090-50-44 W; Named for Peosta, an Indian warrior whose wife discovered lead in this area around 1780.

•PERRY, City; Dallas County; Pop. 7,053; Zip Code 50220; Elev. 998; Lat. 41-53-30 N long. 094-06-35 W. The city was named after a Colonel Perry, one of the owners of the Des Moines Valley Railroad.

•PERSIA, City; Harrison County; Pop. 355; Zip Code 51563; Elev. 1,273; Lat. 41-35-11 N long. 095-32-53 W. The city was named after the near eastern country.

•PETERSON, City; Clay County; Pop. 470; Zip Code 51047; Lat. 42-55-05 N long. 095-20-32 W.

•PIERSON, City; Woodbury County; Pop. 408; Zip Code 51048; Lat. 42-32-44 N long. 095-51-37 W.

•PISGAH, City; Harrison County; Pop. 307; Zip Code 51564; Elev. 1,060; Lat. 41-49-42 N long. 095-57-06 W.

•PLAINFIELD, City; Bremer County; Pop. 469; Zip Code 50666; Lat. 42-50-41 N long. 092-32-05 W. Named after the town in Illinois.

•PLANO, City; Appanoose County; Pop. 111; Zip Code 52581; Lat. 40-45-26 N long. 093-02-34 W. Settled by Seventh Day Adventists from Plano, Illinois.

•PLEASANT HILL, City; Polk County; Pop. 3,493; Zip Code 52767; Lat. 41-35-02 N long. 093-31-11 W. Descriptively named.

•PLEASANTVILLE, City; Marion County; Pop. 1,531; Zip Code 50225; Lat. 41-23-14 N long. 093-16-16 W.

•POMEROY, City; Calhoun County; Pop. 895; Zip Code 50575; Lat. 42-33-17 N long. 094-41-09 W.

•PORTSMOUTH, City; Shelby County; Pop. 240; Zip Code 51565; Elev. 1,237; Lat. 41-39-08 N long. 095-31-13 W. Named after the Connecticut town.

•POSTVILLE, City; Allamakee & Clayton Counties; Pop. 1,475; Zip Code 52162; Lat. 43-06-10 N long. 091-34-32 W. The city was named after settler, Joel Post, who arrived here in 1841.

•PRAIRIE CITY, City; Jasper County; Pop. 1,278; Zip Code 50228; Lat. 41-37-30 N long. 093-14-46 W. Settled in 1856 and descriptively named for the surrounding prairie.

•PRESCOTT, City; Adams County; Pop. 349; Zip Code 50859; Lat. 41-01-18 N long. 094-36-49 W.

•PRIMGHAR, City; O'Brien County Seat; Pop. 1,050; Zip Code 51245; Lat. 43-05-24 N long. 095-37-31 W; The name is a combination of the initials of the people present when the corner stone was laid.

•PRINCETON, City; Scott County; Pop. 965; Zip Code 52768; Lat. 41-40-29 N long. 090-20-25 W. Named after the city in New Jersey.

•PROMISE CITY, City; Wayne County; Pop. 149; Zip Code 52583; Lat. 40-44-28 N long. 093-08-52 W; Platted in 1855 and named for the hope of early settlers, that this would become an important center. It never did.

•PULASKI, City; Davis County; Pop. 267; Zip Code 52584; Lat. 40-41-51 N long. 092-16-58 W. The city's name honors the Polish-American Revolutionary War hero.

•QUASQUETON, City; Buchanan County; Pop. 599; Zip Code 52326; Lat. 42-23-37 N long. 091-45-07 W; Settled in 1842. The name was taken from the fox Indian language and is thought to mean "swiftly running water."

•QUIMBY, City; Cherokee County; Pop. 424; Zip Code 51049; Lat. 42-37-48 N long. 095-38-30 W.

•RADCLIFFE, City; Hardin County; Pop. 593; Zip Code 50230; Lat. 42-18-51 N long. 093-27-27 W.

•RALSTON, City; Carroll & Greene Counties; Pop. 108; Zip Code 51459; Lat. 42-02-19 N long. 094-37-52 W. Named after a circa 1890's officer of the American Express Company.

•RANDALL, City; Hamilton County; Pop. 171; Zip Code 50231; Lat. 42-13-39 N long. 093-35-40 W.

•RANDOLPH, City; Fremont County; Pop. 223; Zip Code 51649; Elev. 977; Lat. 40-52-33 N long. 095-34-15 W.

•RAYMOND, City; Black Hawk County; Pop. 655; Zip Code 50667; Lat. 42-31-51 N long. 092-15-08 W. Named after an early settler.

•READLYN, City; Bremer County; Pop. 858; Zip Code 50668; Lat. 42-42-26 N long. 092-13-37 W.

•REASNOR, City; Jasper County; Pop. 277; Zip Code 50232; Lat. 41-34-56 N long. 093-01-31 W.

•REDFIELD, City; Dallas County; Pop. 959; Zip Code 50233; Lat. 41-35-27 N long. 094-12-12 W; Named in honor of Colonel James Redfield, a Civil War soldier.

•RED OAK, City; Montgomery County Seat; Pop. 6,810; Zip Code 51566; Lat. 40-57-27 N long. 095-14-10 W; So named for a nearby grove of red oak trees.

•REINBECK, City; Grundy County; Pop. 1,808; Zip Code 50669; Lat. 42-19-02 N long. 092-36-05 W.

•**REMBRANDT,** City; Buena Vista County; Pop. 291; Zip Code 50576; Lat. 42-49-25 N long. 095-09-36 W. The town's name honors the Dutch painter.

•**REMSEN,** City; Plymouth County; Pop. 1,592; Zip Code 51050; Lat. 42-48-23 N long. 095-58-43 W. Named for landowner, Remsen Smith.

•**RENWICK,** City; Humboldt County; Pop. 410; Zip Code 50577; Lat. 42-49-53 N long. 093-58-39 W.

•**RICEVILLE,** City; Howard & Mitchell Counties; Pop. 919; Zip Code 50466; Lat. 43-21-37 N long. 092-33-01 W; Named for the three Rice brothers.

•**RICHLAND,** City; Keokuk County; Pop. 600; Zip Code 52585; Lat. 41-11-10 N long. 091-59-40 W. Descriptively named for the area's rich farm land.

•**RIDGEWAY,** City; Winneshiek County; Pop. 308; Zip Code 52165; Lat. 43-18-23 N long. 092-00-44 W.

•**RINGSTED,** City; Winneshiek County; Pop. 308; Zip Code 50578; Lat. 43-17-54 N long. 094-30-32 W.

•**RIPPEY,** City; Greene County; Pop. 304; Zip Code 50235; Elev. 1,077; Lat. 41-54-53 N long. 094-12-03 W; Named after Captain C. M. rippey, an early settler.

•**RIVERSIDE,** City; Washington County; Pop. 826; Zip Code 52327; Lat. 41-28-55 N long. 091-34-53; This city was named for its location.

•**ROCKFORD,** City; Floyd County; Pop. 1,012; Zip Code 50468; Lat. 43-03-21 N long. 092-57-01 W.

•**ROCK RAPIDS,** City; Lyon County Seat; Pop. 2,693; Zip Code 51246; Lat. 43-26-00 N long. 096-09-38 W; The city takes its name from its location near the falls of the Rock River.

•**ROCK VALLEY,** City; Sioux County; Pop. 2,706; Zip Code 51247; Lat. 43-12-11 N long. 096-17-42 W; Named for the Rock River.

•**ROCKWELL,** City; Cerro Gordo County; Pop. 1,039; Zip Code 50469; Lat. 42-59-16 N long. 093-10-18 W. Named after original landowner B.G. Rockwell.

•**ROCKWELL CITY,** City; Calhoun County Seat; Pop. 2,276; Zip Code 50579; Lat. 42-43-52 N long. 093-34-22 W. Named for settler J.M. Rockwell.

•**ROLAND,** City; Story County; Pop. 1,005; Zip Code 50236; Lat. 42-09-54 N long. 093-28-54 W.

•**ROLFE,** City; Pocohontas County; Pop. 796; Zip Code 50581; Lat. 42-48-41 N long. 094-32-01 W; Either named for the Englishman who married Pocahontas, or for the man who previously owned the townsite.

•**ROME,** City; Henry County; Pop. 113; Lat. 40-58-53 N long. 091-40-56 W; Probably named for Rome, Italy.

•**ROSE HILL,** City; Mahaska County; Pop. 214; Zip Code 52586; Lat. 41-19-15 N long. 092-27-32 W. Named after the many wild roses in the area.

•**ROWAN,** City; Wright County; Pop. 259; Zip Code 50470; Lat. 42-44-30 N long. 093-33-00 W.

•**ROYAL,** City; Clay County; Pop. 522; Zip Code 51357; Lat. 43-03-50 N long. 095-17-00 W.

•**RUDD,** City; Floyd County; Pop. 460; Zip Code 50471; Lat. 43-07-53 N long. 092-54-10 W.

•**RUSSELL,** City; Lucas County; Pop. 593; Zip Code 50238; Lat. 40-59-29 N long. 093-12-18 W. Russell is named for an early settler.

•**RUTHVEN,** City; Palo Alto County; Pop. 769; Zip Code 51358; Lat. 43-07-25 N long. 094-52-57 W. Named for the three Ruthven brothers who were among the first settlers.

•**RYAN,** City; Delaware County; Pop. 390; Zip Code 52330; Lat. 42-21-14 N long. 091-28-59 W. Named for an Irish settler.

•**SABULA,** City; Jackson County; Pop. 824; Zip Code 52070; Lat. 42-04-37 N long. 090-10-33 W. Named Sabula in 1846 to honor Mrs. Sabula Wood.

•**SAC CITY,** City; Sac County Seat; Pop. 3,000; Zip Code 50583; Lat. 42-25-19 N long. 095-00-03 W; Named for the Sac, or Sauk Indian tribe.

•**ST. ANSGAR,** City; Mitchell County; Pop. 1,100; Zip Code 50472; Elev. 1,171; Lat. 43-22-40 N long. 092-55-07 W. Given a religious name by Czech settlers.

•**ST. CHARLES,** City; Madison County; Pop. 507; Zip Code 50240; Lat. 41-18-03 N long. 093-12-28 W.

•**ST. MARYS,** City; Warren County; Pop. 111; Zip Code 50241; Elev. 1,033; Lat. 41-18-29 N long. 093-43-53 W.

•**SEARSBORO,** City; Poweshiek County; Pop. 134; Zip Code 50242; Lat. 41-35-23 N long. 092-38-51 W.

•**SERGEANT BLUFF,** City; Woodbury County; Pop. 2,416; Zip Code 51054; Elev. 1,092; Lat. 42-25-14 N long. 096-20-17 W; Established in 1854. The town was named for Sergeant Charles Floyd, the only man to die on the Lewis and Clark expedition. He was buried on a bluff on the Iowa side of the Missouri River.

•**SEYMOUR,** City; Wayne County; Pop. 1,036; Zip Code 52590; Lat. 40-40-49 N long. 093-07-22 W.

•**SHARPSBURG,** City; Taylor County; Pop. 114; Zip Code 50862; Lat. 40-48-18 N long. 094-38-30 W.

•**SHEFFIELD,** City; Franklin County; Pop. 1,224; Zip Code 50475; Lat. 42-54-22 N long. 093-12-15 W; Named for James Sheffield, a railroad contractor.

•**SHELBY,** City; Pottawamie & Shelby Counties; Pop. 665; Zip Code 51570; Like many places throughout the country, this city was named in honor of Gen. Isaac Shelby, Governor of Kentucky.

•**SHELDON,** City; O'Brien & Sioux Counties; Pop. 5,003; Zip Code 51201; Lat. 43-10-21 N long. 095-50-12 W; Named for Israel Sheldon, a stockholder in the first railroad to pass through town.

•**SHELL ROCK,** City; Butler County; Pop. 1,478; Zip Code 50670; Lat. 42-42-59 N long. 092-34-48 W.

•**SHELLSBURG,** City; Benton County; Pop. 771; Zip Code 52332; Lat. 42-05-36 N long. 091-51-50 W.

•**SHENANDOAH,** City; Fremont & Page Counties; Pop. 6,274; Zip Code 51602; Lat. 40-45-35 N long. 095-22-53 W; Said to be named for the Shenandoah Valley in Virginia which is similar to the Nishnabotna River Valley, in which the town is located.

•**SIBLEY,** City; Osceola County Seat; Pop. 3,051; Zip Code 51249; Lat. 43-24-10 N long. 095-44-41 W. Named in 1872 to honor General G.H. Sibley.

•**SIDNEY,** City; Fremont County Seat; Pop. 1,308; Zip Code 51652; Lat. 40-44-44 N long. 095-38-47 W. Named after Sidney, Ohio.

•**SIGOURNEY,** City; Keokiuk County Seat; Pop. 2,330; Zip Code 52591; Lat. 41-19-58 N long. 092-12-13 W; Called Sigourney aftr the poetess, Mrs. Lydia H. Sigourney.

•**SIOUX CENTER,** City; Sioux County; Pop. 4,588; Zip Code 51250; Lat. 43-04-39 N long. 096-10-41 W; Named for the Sioux Indinas. "Sioux" is the last part of "Nadouessioux," the derogatory Ojibwa-French name for the Dakotas.

•**SIOUX CITY,** City; Woodbury County Seat; Pop. 82,003; Zip Code 51100; Elev. 1,117; Lat. 42-30-05 N long. 096-23-43 W; Named for the Indians who lived in this part of the state.

•**SIOUX RAPIDS,** City; Buena Vista County; Pop. 897; Zip Code 50585; Lat. 42-53-26 N long. 095-08-33 W; A descriptive name for the falls on nearby Little Sioux River.

•**SLATER,** City; Story County; Pop. 1,312; Zip Code 50244; Lat. 41-54-10 N long. 093-39-06 W. Slater was an early settler.

•**SLOAN,** City; Woodbury County; Pop. 978; Zip Code 51055; Lat. 42-14-17 N long. 096-13-34 W.

•**SMITHLAND,** City; Woodbury County; Pop. 282; Zip Code 51056; Elev. 1,090; Lat. 42-13-53 N long. 095-55-34 W.

•**SOLDIER,** City; Monona County; Pop. 257; Zip Code 51572; Lat. 42-00-13 N long. 095-47-07 W; Named for the Soldier River which runs through this region.

•**SOLON,** City; Johnson County; Pop. 969; Zip Code 52333; Lat. 41-48-51 N long. 091-30-38 W. A Greek word meaning "wise man."

•**SOUTH ENGLISH,** City; Keokuk County; Pop. 211; Zip Code 52335; Lat. 41-27-10 N long. 092-05-09 W.

•**SPENCER,** City; Clay County Seat; Pop. 11,726; Zip Code 51301; Elev. 1,321; Lat. 43-08-32 N long. 095-08-28 W; This city was named in honor of George E. Spencer, U. S. Senator from Alabama.

•**SPILLVILLE,** City; Winneshiek County; Pop. 415; Zip Code 52168; Lat. 43-13-04 N long. 091-58-30 W.

•**SPIRIT LAKE,** City; Dickinson County Seat; Pop. 3,976; Zip Code 51360; Lat. 43-26-13 N long. 095-05-57 W; Named for nearby Spirit Lake. The Indians called the lake Minnewauken because they believed its waters were haunted by spirits.

•**SPRINGBROOK,** City; Jackson County; Pop. 149; Zip Code 52075; Lat. 42-10-03 N long. 090-28-44 W. Named for a local spring.

•**SPRINGVILLE,** City; Linn County; Pop. 1,165; Zip Code 52336; Lat. 42-03-30 N long. 091-26-19 W. Named for a nearby group of springs.

•**STACYVILLE,** City; Mitchell County; Pop. 538; Zip Code 50476; Lat. 43-26-01 N long. 092-46-56 W.

•**STANHOPE,** City; Hamilton County; Pop. 492; Zip Code 50246; Lat. 42-16-48 N long. 093-47-00 W.

•**STANLEY,** City; Buchanan County; Pop. 154; Zip Code 50671; Lat. 42-38-33 N long. 091-48-38. Stanley was an early settler.

•**STANTON,** City; Montgomnery County; Pop. 747; Zip Code 51573; Lat. 40-59-22 N long. 095-06-09 W. Named for Civil War cabinet officer Edwin Stanton.

•**STANWOOD,** City; Cedar County; Pop. 705; Zip Code 52337; Lat. 41-53-09 N long. 091-08-10 W. The city is named after a railroad official.

•**STATE CENTER,** City; Marshall County; Pop. 1,292; Zip Code 50247; Lat. 42-00-57 N long. 093-10-27 W; Descriptively named for its location at the center of the state.

•**STEAMBOAT ROCK,** City; Hardin County; Pop. 387; Zip Code 50672; Lat. 42-24-12 N long. 093-02-45 W; The city got its name from a large rock that resembles a steamboat found in a river nearby.

•**STOCKPORT,** City; Van Buren County; Pop. 272; Zip Code 52651; Lat. 40-52-26 N long. 091-50-26 W.

•**STORM LAKE,** City; Buena Vista County Seat; Pop. 8,814; Zip Code 50588; Lat. 42-38-00 N long. 095-10-54 W. Named after nearby Storm Lake.

•**STORY CITY,** City; Story County; Pop. 2,762; Zip Code 50248; Lat. 42-11-15 N long. 093-33-34 W; Platted in 1855 and named Fairview. With the establishment of the post office the following year, the town name was changed to Story City after Supreme Court Justice Joseph Story.

•**STRATFORD,** City; Hamilton & Webster Counties; Pop. 806; Zip Code 50249; Lat. 42-15-52 N long. 093-56-21 W. Named after Stratford, Connecticut.

•**STRAWBERRY POINT,** City; Clayton County; Pop. 1,463; Zip Code 52076; Lat. 42-41-22 N long. 091-32-35 W; Named by soldiers who camped here, for the abundance of wild strawberries in the area. The name became well-known and was kept after the town was platted in 1853.

•**STUART,** City; Adair & Guthrie Counties; Pop. 1,650; Elev. 1210; Lat. 41-30-31 N long. 094-25-16 W. Founded in 1869 by Charles Stuart.

•**SULLY,** City; Jasper County; Pop. 828; Zip Code 50251; Lat. 41-34-52 N long. 092-50-33 W.

•**SUMNER,** City; Bremer County; Pop. 2,335; Zip Code 50674; Lat. 42-51-04 N long. 092-06-30 W. The city's name honors abolitionist U.S. Senator Charles Sumner.

•**SUPERIOR,** City; Dickinson County; Pop. 188; Zip Code 51363; Lat. 43-25-53 N long. 094-56-42 W. Named after Lake Superior.

•**SUTHERLAND,** City; O'Brien County; Pop. 897; Zip Code 51058; Lat. 42-58-34 N long. 095-30-02 W. Sutherland was a prominent pioneer.

•**SWEA CITY,** City; Kossuth County; Pop. 813; Zip Code 50590; Lat. 43-22-52 N long. 094-18-22 W. The area was settled by Swedish emigrants who gave the town an affectionate nickname for Sweden.

•**SWISHER,** City; Johnson County; Pop. 654; Zip Code 52338; Lat. 41-50-56 N long. 091-42-21 W.

•**TABOR,** City; Fremont & Mills Counties; Pop. 1,088; Zip Code 51653; Lat. 40-53-59 N long. 095-39-02 W. A Biblical name given by the first settlers.

•**TAMA,** City; Tama County; Pop. 2,968; Zip Code 52339; Lat. 41-57-37 N long. 092-34-47 W; Named for Tama, a famous chief of the Fox Indians.

•**TEMPLETON,** City; Carroll County; Pop. 319; Zip Code 51463; Lat. 41-55-11 N long. 094-56-47 W.

•**TERRIL,** City; Dickinson County; Pop. 420; Zip Code 51364; Lat. 43-18-20 N long. 094-58-16 W.

•**THOMPSON,** City; Winnebago County; Pop. 668; Zip Code 50478; Lat. 43-21-55 N long. 093-46-21 W. Named after the original landowner.

•**THOR,** City; Humboldt County; Pop. 200; Zip Code 50591; Lat. 42-41-28 N long. 094-03-00 W. A settler's personal name.

•**THORNTON,** City; Cerro Gordo County; Pop. 442; Zip Code 50479; Lat. 42-56-45 N long. 093-22-42 W.

•**THURMAN,** City; Fremont County; Pop. 221; Zip Code 51654; Lat. 40-49-19 N long. 095-44-43 W.

•**TITONKA,** City; Kossuth County; Pop. 607; Zip Code 50480; Lat. 43-12-44 N long. 094-09-19 W; Titonka is a variation of the Sioux Indian words, meanig "big house."

•**TOLEDO,** City; Tama County Seat; Pop. 2,445; Zip Code 52342; Lat. 41-59-11 N long. 092-34-48 W. Named after Toledo, Ohio.

•**TORONTO,** City; Clinton County; Pop. 172; Zip Code 52343; Lat. 41-54-25 N long. 090-53-05 W; Named by George W. Thorn in 1844, for his former home of Toronto, Ontario.

•**TRAER,** City; Tama County; Pop. 1,703; Zip Code 50675; Lat. 42-11-22 N long. 092-27-12 W.

•**TREYNOR,** City; Pottawattamie County; Pop. 920; Zip Code 51575; Lat. 41-13-52 N long. 095-36-50 W.

•**TRIPOLI,** City; Bremer County; Pop. 1,280; Zip Code 50676; Lat. 42-48-24 N long. 092-15-50 W. Named after the North African city.

•**TRUESDALE,** City; Buena Vista County; Pop. 128; Zip Code 50592; Lat. 42-43-43 N long. 095-10-40 W. The city is named after railroad official W.H. Truesdale.

•**TURIN,** City; Monona County; Pop. 103; Zip Code 51059; Lat. 42-03-53 N long. 095-57-40 W. The city is named for Turin, Italy.

•**UNDERWOOD,** City; Pottawattamie County; Pop. 448; Zip Code 51519; Lat. 41-23-13 N long. 095-40-35 W.

•**UNION,** City; Hardin County; Pop. 515; Zip Code 50258; Lat. 42-13-45 N long. 093-02-38 W; Like many places in the United States, this city was named out of patriotic sentiment.

•**UNIVERSITY HEIGHTS,** City; Johnson County; Pop. 1,069; Lat. 41-39-18 N long. 091-33-24 W.

•**URBANA,** City; Benton County; Pop. 574; Zip Code 52345; Lat. 42-13-35 N long. 091-52-23 W.

•**URBANDALE,** City; Polk County; Pop. 17,869; Lat. 41-37-36 N long. 093-42-43 W. Descriptively named.

•**UTE,** City; Monona County; Pop. 479; Zip Code 51060; Lat. 42-03-53 N long. 095-42-42 W; The city was most likely named by the Northwestern Railroad, for the Ute Indians.

•**VAIL,** City; Crawford County; Pop. 490; Zip Code 51465; Lat. 42-03-27 N long. 095-12-18 W. Named for a railroad official.

•**VAN HORNE,** City; Benton County; Pop. 682; Zip Code 52346; Lat. 42-00-36 N long. 092-05-06 W.

•**VAN METER,** City; Dallas County; Pop. 747; Zip Code 50261; Lat. 41-32-10 N long. 093-57-41 W.

•**VENTURA,** City; Cerro Gordo County; Pop. 614; Zip Code 50482; Lat. 43-08-00 N long. 093-27-28 W.

•**VICTOR,** City; Iowa & Poweshiek Counties; Pop. 1,046; Zip Code 52347; Lat. 41-44-37 N long. 092-15-27 W.

•**VILLISCA,** City; Montgomery County; Pop. 1,434; Zip Code 50864; Lat. 40-55-38 N long. 094-59-13 W; Earlier spellings of the city name include Valiska and Vallisca. The name probably came from the Sauk and Fox Indian word "Waliska" or "evil spirit."

•**VINCENT,** City; Webster County; Pop. 207; Zip Code 50594; Lat. 42-35-24 N long. 094-02-25 W.

•**VINING,** City; Tama County; Pop. 96; Zip Code 52348; Lat. 41-58-50 N long. 092-24-54 W; Named for Hon. Plynn Vinton.

•**VINTON,** City; Benton County Seat; Pop. 5,040; Zip Code 52349; Lat. 42-10-12 N long. 092-01-09 W. Named after Congressman Plym Vinton.

•**VOLGA,** City; Clayton County; Pop. 310; Zip Code 52350; Lat. 42-05-30 N long. 091-23-09 W. Named for the great river in Russia.

•**WADENA,** City; Fayette County; Pop. 230; Zip Code 52169; Lat. 42-50-16 N long. 091-39-28 W; Named for Ojibwa Indian Chief, Wadena, who was wounded in the last battle between the Ojibwa and the Sioux in 1858.

•**WAHPETON,** City; Dickinson County; Pop. 372; Lat. 43-21-58 N long. 095-10-18 W; The name is taken from Wakhpetonwan or "dwellers among the leaves," one of the seven divisions of the Sioux nation.

•**WALFORD,** City; Benton & Linn Counties; Pop. 285; Zip Code 52351; Lat. 41-53-41 N long. 091-48-10 W.

•**WALKER,** City; Linn County; Pop. 733; Zip Code 52352; Lat. 42-17-20 N long. 091-46-43 W. Probably an early settler.

•**WALLINGFORD,** City; Emmet County; Pop. 256; Zip Code 51365; Lat. 43-19-25 N long. 094-46-17 W.

•**WALNUT,** City; Pottawattamie County; Pop. 897; Zip Code 51577; Lat. 41-16-46 N long. 095-50-10 W. Named after the walnut tree.

•**WAPELLO,** City; Louisa County Seat; Pop. 2,011; Zip Code 52653; Lat. 41-10-56 N long. 091-11-11 W; Named for Wapello, Chief of the Fox Indians.

•**WASHINGTON,** City; Washington County Seat; Pop. 6,584; Zip Code 52353; Lat. 41-17-51 N long. 091-41-13 W; Named in honor of George Washington.

•**WASHTA,** City; Cherokee County; Pop. 320; Zip Code 51061; Lat. 42-34-31 N long. 095-42-56 W; The name is a variation of the Dakota word "waste," which means "good."

•**WATERLOO,** City; Black Hawk County Seat; Pop. 75,985; Zip Code 50700; Lat. 42-29-47 N long. 092-20-37 W. The city is named after the great European battle.

•**WAUCOMA,** City; Fayette County; Pop. 308; Zip Code 52130; Lat. 42-59-56 N long. 092-02-44 W; Probably named for Waucoma Creek (now known as Badfish Creek) in Wisconsin.

•**WAUKEE,** City; Dallas County; Pop. 2,227; Zip Code 50263; Lat. 41-36-32 N long. 093-52-48 W; The name was most likely derived from "Milwaukee" came from Ojibwa INdian words meaning "good land." The name "Waukee" alone however, is meaningless.

•**WAUKON,** City; Allamakee County Seat; Pop. 3,983; Zip Code 52172; Lat. 43-16-59 N long. 091-29-15 W; Named for the Winnebago Chief, Waukon Decorah.

•**WAVERLY,** City; Bremer County Seat; Pop. 8,444; Zip Code 50677; Lat. 42-43-53 N long. 092-28-39 W. The city is named after Walter Scott's "Waverly" novels.

•**WAYLAND,** City; Henry County; Pop. 720; Zip Code 52654; Lat. 41-09-20 N long. 091-41-00 W.

•**WEBB,** City; Clay County; Pop. 222; Zip Code 51366; Lat. 43-00-43 N long. 095-10-59 W.

•**WEBSTER,** City; Keokuk County; Pop. 124; Zip Code 52355; Lat. 41-26-16 N long. 092-10-09 W; Named for Daniel Webster, a famous statesman.

•**WEBSTER CITY,** City; Hamilton County Seat; Pop. 8,572; Zip Code 50595; Lat. 42-27-42 N long. 093-48-35 W; Probably named in honor of Daniel Webster.

•**WELLMAN,** City; Washington County; Pop. 1,125; Zip Code 52356; Lat. 41-28-08 N long. 091-50-15 W.

•**WELLSBURG,** City; Grundy County; Pop. 761; Zip Code 50680; Lat. 42-26-00 N long. 092-55-34 W.

•**WELTON,** City; Clinton County; Pop. 119; Zip Code 52774; Lat. 41-54-29 N long. 090-35-430 W. Named for a town in England.

•**WESLEY,** City; Kossuth County; Pop. 598; Zip Code 50483; Lat. 43-05-30 N long. 094-01-10 W. Named for a local railroad man.

•**WEST BRANCH,** City; Cedar County; Pop. 1,867; Zip Code 52358; Lat. 41-37-27 N long. 091-09-53 W. Descriptively named for its location on a creek.

•**WEST BURLINGTON,** City; Des Moines County; Pop. 3,371; Zip Code 52655; Lat. 40-49-00 N long. 091-09-34 W.

•**WEST DES MOINES,** City; Polk County; Pop. 21,894; Lat. 41-34-38 N long. 093-42-40 W.

•**WESTFIELD,** City; Plymouth County; Pop. 199; Zip Code 51062; Lat. 42-45-32 N long. 096-36-24 W.

•**WESTGATE,** City; Fayette County; Pop. 263; Zip Code 50681; Lat. 42-45-20 N long. 091-59-54 W.

•**WEST LIBERTY,** City; Muscatine County; Pop. 2,723; Lat. 41-34-12 N long. 091-15-49 W.

•**WEST POINT,** City; Lee County; Pop. 1,133; Lat. 40-43-00 N long. 091-27-00 W.

•**WESTSIDE,** City; Crawford County; Pop. 387; Zip Code 51467; Lat. 42-04-32 N long. 095-06-39 W. Named by railroad officials for its western location to the roadbed.

•**WEST UNION,** City; Fayette County Seat; Pop. 2,783; Lat. 42-57-46 N long. 091-48-29 W.

•**WHAT CHEER,** City; Keokuk County; Pop. 803; Zip Code 50268; Lat. 41-23-55 N long. 092-21-18 W; The place was named What Cheer by a Scotch miner when he discovered coal in the area.

•**WHEATLAND,** City; Clinton County; Pop. 840; Zip Code 52777; Lat. 41-49-54 N long. 090-50-17 W. Named after the Pennsylvania estate of President James Buchanan.

•**WHITING,** City; Monona County; Pop. 734; Zip Code 51063; Lat. 42-08-23 N long. 096-09-24 W; Named for Senator Whiting.

•**WHITTEMORE,** City; Kossuth County; Pop. 647; Zip Code 50598; Lat. 43-04-00 N long. 094-24-22 W.

•**WILLIAMS,** City; Hamilton County; Pop. 410; Zip Code 50271; Lat. 42-29-10 N long. 093-32-35 W. Named in honor of U.S. Army major W. Williams.

•**WILLIAMSBURG,** City; Iowa County; Pop. 2,033; Zip Code 52361; Lat. 41-39-40 N long. 092-00-05 W; Named for an early settler.

•**WILLIAMSON,** City; Lucas County; Pop. 210; Zip Code 50272; Lat. 41-05-47 N long. 093-14-42 W.

•**WINFIELD,** City; Henry County; Pop. 1,042; Zip Code 52659; Lat. 41-07-47 N long. 091-26-51 W. Named in honor of General Winfield Scott.

•**WINTERSET,** City; Madison County Seat; Pop. 4,021; Zip Code 50273; Lat. 41-20-43 N long. 094-00-21 W.

•**WINTHROP,** City; Buchanan County; Pop. 767; Zip Code 50682; Lat. 42-28-27 N long. 091-44-00 W.

•**WIOTA,** City; Cass County; Pop. 181; Zip Code 50274; Lat. 41-23-59 N long. 094-53-50 W; An Indian word with several possible explanations. In the Sioux language it means "many moons," in Winnebago "much water." It has also been translated as "many snows."

•**WOODBINE,** City; Harrison County; Pop. 1,463; Zip Code 51579; Elev. 1,078; Lat. 41-44-18 N long. 095-41-51 W. Named for the popular flower.

•**WOODBURN,** City; Clarke County; Pop. 207; Zip Code 50275; Lat. 41-00-53 N long. 093-39-54 W.

•**WOODWARD,** City; Dallas County; Pop. 1,212; Zip Code 50276; Lat. 41-51-16 N long. 093-55-38 W. Named by the railroad for an early pioneer.

•**WORTHINGTON,** City; Dubuque County; Pop. 432; Zip Code 52078; Lat. 42-23-34 N long. 091-07-23 W.

•**WYOMING,** City; Jones County; Pop. 702; Zip Code 52230; Lat. 42-00-46 N long. 091-03-38 W; Named for the Wyoming Valley in Pennsylvania, the site of a famous massacre by British soldiers, Torries, and Iroquois Indinas in 1778.

•**YALE,** City; Guthrie County; Pop. 299; Zip Code 50277; Lat. 41-47-17 N long. 094-21-36 W. Named for the famous university.

•**YORKTOWN,** City; Page County; Pop. 123; Zip Code 51656; Lat. 40-44-10 N long. 095-09-23 W. The city is named after the final battle of the Revolutionary War.

•**ZEARING,** City; Story County; Pop. 630; Zip Code 50278; Lat. 42-09-33 N long. 093-17-25 W. Named for a Doctor Zearing who promised the town a church if it was named after him.

•**ZWINGLE,** City; Dubuque & Jackson Counties; Pop. 119; Zip Code 52079; Lat. 42-17-44 N long. 090-41-17 W; Named in honor of Ulrich Zwingle, a Swiss reformer.

KANSAS

•ABBYVILLE, City; Reno County; Pop. 123; Zip Code 67510; Elev. 1,650; Lat. 37-58-06 N long. 098-12-12 W; central Kansas; The town is named for the first child born there, Abbey McLean.

•ABILENE, City; Dickinson County Seat; Pop. 6,572; Zip Code 67410; Elev. 1,153; Lat. 38-55-08 N long. 097-13-09 W; E central Kansas; The town is named for the Roman city in ancient Syria, Abilene.

•ADMIRE, City; Lyon County; Pop. 158; Zip Code 66830; Elev. 1,230; Lat. 38-38-33 N long. 096-06-09 W; E Kansas; Admire is named after its founder Captain Jacob V. Admire.

•AGENDA, City; Republic County; Pop. 106; Zip Code 66930; Elev. 1,410; Lat. 39-42-25 N long. 097-25-47 W; N Kansas.

•AGRA, City; Phillips County; Pop. 321; Zip Code 67621; Elev. 1,851; Lat. 39-45-37 N long. 099-07-07 W; N Kansas; The city is named after Agra, India.

•ALBERT, City; Barton County; Pop. 236; Zip Code 67511; Elev. 2,615; Lat. 38-27-15 N long. 099-00-41 W; central Kansas; Albert's name recalls its first storekeeper, Albert Kreisinger.

•ALEXANDER, City; Rush County; Pop. 116; Zip Code 67513; Elev. 2,067; Lat. 38-28-12 N long. 099-33-02 W; central Kansas; Named in honor of Czar Alexander of Russia.

•ALLEN, City; Lyon County; Pop. 205; Zip Code 66833; Elev. 1,320; Lat. 38-39-20 N long. 096-10-20 W; E Kansas; Named after William Allen, a Democratic senator from Ohio.

•ALMA, City; Wabaunsee County Seat; Pop. 925; Zip Code 66401; Elev. 1,095; Lat. 39-00-55 N long. 096-17-15 W; E Kansas; Named after a stream in the Crimea in Russia.

•ALMENA, City; Norton County; Pop. 517; Zip Code 67622; Elev. 2,155; Lat. 39-53-26 N long. 099-42-37 W; N Kansas; Named for a local pioneer settler.

•ALTA VISTA, City; Wabaunsee County; Pop. 430; Zip Code 66834; Elev. 1,437; Lat. 37-32-52 N long. 099-38-03 W; E Kansas; Alta Vista, or High View, comes from its geographic location between Kaw and Neosho.

•ALTAMONT, City; Labette County; Pop. 1,054; Zip Code 67330;Elev. 910; Lat. 37-11-22 N long. 095-17-43 W; SE Kansas; The town is named after Altamont, Illinois.

•ALTON, City; Osborne County; Pop. 135; Zip Code 67623; Elev. 1,652; Lat. 39-27-59 N long. 098-56-43 W; N central Kansas; The city is named after Alton, Illinois.

•ALTOONA, City; Wilson County; Pop. 564; Zip Code 66710; Elev. 828; Lat. 37-31-27 N long. 095-39-41 W; SE Kansas; Altoona is named after Altoona, Pennsylvania.

•AMERICUS, City; Lyon County; Pop. 915; Zip Code 66835; Elev. 1,160; Lat. 38-30-24 N long. 096-15-45 W; central Kansas; The city is named after Americus, Georgia.

•ANDALE, City; Sedgwick County; Pop. 538; Zip Code 67001; Elev. 1,437; L;at. 37-47-29 N long. 097-37-47 W; S central Kansas; Andale's name was created by combining the names of Anderson and Dale.

•ANDOVER, City; Butler County; Pop. 2,801; Zip Code 67002; Elev. 1,350; Lat. 37-41-33 N long. 097-08-00 W; S Kansas; Andover is named after Andover, Massachusetts.

•ANTHONY, City; Harper County Seat; Pop. 2,661; Zip Code 67003; Elev. 1,350; Lat. 37-09-12 N long. 098-01-18 W; S Kansas; Named after Governor George Tobey Anthony.

•ARCADIA, City; Crawford County; Pop. 460; Zip Code 66711; Elev. 830; Lat. 37-38-30 N long. 094-37-36 W; SE Kansas; Named for the fertile region in ancient Greece.

•ARGONIA, City; Sumner County; Pop. 587; Zip Code 67004; Elev. 1,257; Lat. 37-15-56 N long. 097-46-02 W; S Kansas; A name from ancient Greek geography.

•ARKANSAS CITY, City; Cowley County; Pop. 13,201; Zip Code 67005; Elev. 1,100; Lat. 37-04-02 N long. 097-02-21 W; 50 mi. S of Wichita in S Kansas; The city is named after the Arkansas Indians.

•ARLINGTON, City; reno County; Pop. 631; Zip Code 67514; Elev. 1,610; Lat. 37-53-42 N long. 098-10-33 W; central Kansas; The city takes its name from Arlington, Virginia.

•ARMA, City; Crawford County; Pop. 1,676; Zip Code 66712; Elev. 1,003; Lat. 37-32-40 N long. 094-42-03 W; SE Kansas; Arma is named after coal businessman Arma Post.

•ASHLAND, City; Clark County Seat; Pop. 1,096; Zip Code 67831; Elev. 1,979; Lat. 37-11-19 N long. 099-46-01 W; S Kansas; The city is named after the ash tree.

•ASSARIA, City; Saline County; Pop. 414; Zip Code 67416; Elev. 1,282; Lat. 38-26-41 N long. 099-41-27 W; central Kansas; Assaria is a Hebrew word meaning "God helps."

•ATCHISON, City; Atchison County Seat; Pop. 11,407; Zip Code 66002; Elev. 950; Lat. 39-33-51 N long. 095-07-37 W; 20 mi. N of Leavenworth in NE Kansas; The town is named after Senator Atchison of Missouri.

•ATHOL, City; Smith County; Pop. 90; Zip Code 66932; Elev. 1,789; Lat. 39-45-52 N long. 098-55-01 W; N Kansas; Named after the wife of a railway official.

•ATLANTA, City; Cowley County; Pop. 256; Zip Code 67008; Elev. 1,433; Lat. 37-26-11 N long. 096-46-02 W; S Kansas; A name from Greek mythology.

•ATTICA, City; Harper County; Pop. 730; Zip Code 67009; Elev. 1,453; Lat. 37-14-34 N long. 098-13-36 W; S Kansas; The name for an ancient Greek province.

•ATWOOD, City; Rawlins County Seat; Pop. 1,665; Zip Code 67730; Elev. 2,850; Lat. 39-48-23 N long. 101-02-26 W; NW Kansas; Named for an early settler.

•AUBURN, City; Shawnee County; Pop. 890; Zip Code 66402; Elev. 1,080; Lat. 38-54-26 N long. 095-48-59 W; NE Kansas; The name of an imaginary village in Oliver Goldsmith's famous poem "Deserted Village."

•AUGUSTA, City; Butler County; Pop. 6,968; Zip Code 67010; Elev. 1,260; Lat. 37-40-54 N long. 096-58-32 W; 20 mi. E of Wichita in S Kansas; Town founder C. N. James named the town after his wife Augusta Boynton.

•AURORA, City; Cloud County; Pop. 130; Zip Code 67417; Elev. 1,476; Lat. 39-27-03 N long. 097-31-37 W; N Kansas; A Roman god of dawn.

•AXTELL, City; Marshall County; Pop. 470; Zip Code 66403; Elev. 1,368; Lat. 39-52-13 N long. 096-15-06 W; NE Kansas; The town is named after railroad official Jesse Axtell.

KANSAS

•**BALDWIN CITY,** City; Douglas County; Pop. 2,829; Zip Code 66006; Elev. 1,050; Lat. 38-46-36 N long. 095-11-02 W; E Kansas; The town is named after an Ohio educator.

•**BARNARD,** City; Lincoln County; Pop. 163; Zip Code 67418; Elev. 1,310; Lat. 39-11-246 N long. 098-02-40 W; central Kansas; Named after railroad man J. F. Barnard.

•**BARNES,** City; Washington County; Pop. 257; Zip Code 66933; Elev. 1,331; Lat. 39-42-37 N long. 096-52-19 W; N Kansas; Named in honor of railroad stockholder, A. S. Barnes.

•**BARTLETT,** City; Labette County; Pop. 163; Zip Code 67332; Elev. 890; Lat. 37-03-28 N long. 095-12-41 W; SE Kansas; Named by the railroad for A. G. Bartlett, a farmer who donated land to the station.

•**BASEHOR,** City; Leavenworth County; Pop. 1,483; Zip Code 66007; Elev. 984; Lat. 39-08-33 N long. 094-56-19 W; NE KS; The city is named after an early pioneer.

•**BAXTER SPRINGS,** City; Cherokee County; Pop. 4,773; Zip Code 66713; Lat. 37-23-34 N long. 097-16-49 W; SE corner of Kansas; Baxter Springs remembers squatter John L. Baxter who was killed in a land dispute.

•**BAZINE,** City; Ness County; Pop. 385; Zip Code 67516; Elev. 2,125; W central Kansas; The town is named after a French general of the Franco-Prussian War.

•**BEATTIE,** City; Marshall County; Pop. Zip Code 66406; Elev. 1,330; Lat. 39-51-45 N long. 096-24-58 W; NE Kansas; Beattie is named after Mayor A. Beattie who served as chief city official of St. Joseph.

•**BELLE PLAINE,** City; Sumner County; Pop. 1,706; Zip Code 67013; Elev. 1,230; S Kansas; Descriptively named for the beautiful prairie surrounding the town.

•**BELLEVILLE,** City; Republic County Seat; Pop. 2,805; Zip Code 66935; Elev. 1,550; Lat. 39-49-16 N long. 097-37-42 W; N Kansas; Named after the local postmaster's wife.

•**BELOIT,** City; Mitchell County Seat; Pop. 4,367; Zip Code 67420; Elev. 1,386; Lat. 39-27-48 N long. 098-06-26 W; 51 mi. NE of Salina in N central Kansas; Beloit takes its name from Beloit, Wisconsin.

•**BELPRE,** City; Edwards County; Pop. 154; Zip Code 67519; Elev. 2,090; Lat. 37-57-04 N long. 099-06-01 W; SW central Kansas; A French word meaning "pretty prairie."

•**BELVUE,** City; Pottawatomie County; Pop. 212; Zip Code 66407; Elev. 960; Lat. 39-12-51 N long. 096-10-38 W; NE Kansas; Descriptively named for the attractive environment.

•**BENEDICT,** City; Wilson County; Pop. 111; Zip Code 66714; Elev. 900; Lat. 37-37-30 N long. 095-44-35 W; SE Kansas; Named in honor of the Catholic order of Saint Benedict of Nursia.

•**BENNINGTON,** City; Ottawa County; Pop. 579; Zip Code 67422; Elev. 1,221; Lat. 39-01-55 N long. 097-35-30 W; NE central Kansas; Bennington is named after the city in Vermont.

•**BENTLEY,** City; Sedgwick County; Pop. 311; Zip Code 67016; Elev. 1,387; Lat. 37-53-07 N long. 097-30-55 W; S central Kansas; The city is named after lawyer O. H. Bentley who helped develop the railroad in the area.

•**BENTON,** City; Butler County; Pop. 609; Zip Code 67017; Elev. 1,375; Lat. 37-46-56 N long. 097-06-18 W; S Kansas; Benton is named after Thomas Benton Murdock, a Kansas legislator.

•**BERN,** City; Nemaha County; Pop. 220; Zip Code 66408; Elev. 1,281; Lat. 39-56-40 N long. 095-58-20 W; NE Kansas; Named by Swiss settlers for the city in Switzerland.

•**BEVERLY,** City; Lincoln County; Pop. 171; Zip Code 67423; Elev. 1,322; Lat. 39-00-49 N long. 097-58-23 W; central Kansas; Named after a city in Massachusetts.

•**BISON,** City; Rush County; Pop. 279; Zip Code 67520; Elev. 2,011; Lat. 38-31-13 N long. 099-11-45 W; central Kansas; Descriptively named after the once abundant bison in the area.

•**BLUE MOUND,** City; Linn County; Pop. 319; Zip Code 66010; Elev. 1,040; Lat. 38-05-25 N long. 095-00-34 W; E Kansas; Named after a local Indian feature.

•**BLUE RAPIDS,** City; Marshall County; Pop. 1,280; Zip Code 66411; Elev. 1,158; Lat. 39-40-39 N long. 096-39-42 W; NE Kansas; Descriptively named for a local water feature.

•**BLUFF CITY,** City; Harper County; Pop. 95; Zip Code 67018; Elev. 1,240; Lat. 37-04-28 N long. 097-51-50 W; S Kansas; Descriptively named for its location on a bluff.

•**BOGUE,** City; Graham County; Pop. 197; Zip Code 67625; Elev. 2,050; Lat. 39-21-26 N long. 099-41-14 W; NW central Kansas; A railroad engineer named Bogue had the town named after him for driving the first locomotive through the area.

•**BONNER SPRINGS,** City; Wyandotte County; Pop. 6,266; Zip Code 66012; Elev. 850; Lat. 39-03-41 N long. 094-53-03 W; 15 mi. W of Kansas City in NE Kansas; The city is named after its natural springs and an early pioneer.

•**BREWSTER,** City; Thomas County; Pop. 327; Zip Code 67732; Elev. 3,428; Lat. 39-21-42 N long. 101-22-26 W; NW Kansas; Named in honor of Rock Island Railway Director, L. D. Brewster.

•**BRONSON,** City; Bourbon County; Pop. 414; Zip Code 66716; Elev. 1,065; Lat. 37-53-42 N long. 095-04-20 W; NE Kansas; Fort Scott attorney Ira Bronson left his name on the town.

•**BROOKVILLE,** City; Saline County; Pop. 259; Zip Code 67425; Elev. 1,369; Lat. 38-46-25 N long. 097-51-58 W; central Kansas; The city is descriptively named for a local brook.

•**BROWNELL,** City; Ness County; Pop. 92; Zip Code 67521; Elev. 2,410; Lat. 38-38-26 N long. 099-44-35 W; W central Kansas; The town is named after a railroad attorney.

•**BUCKLIN,** City; Ford County; Pop. 786; Zip Code 67834; Elev. 2,412; S Kansas; Descriptively named.

•**BUFFALO,** City; Wilson County; Pop. 386; Zip Code 66717; Elev. 945; Lat. 37-42-32 N long. 095-41-56 W; SE Kansas; The town is named after the once plentiful buffalo.

•**BUHLER,** City; Reno County; Pop. 1,188; Zip Code 67522; Elev. 1,485; Lat. 38-08-12 N long. 097-46-22 W; central Kansas; Named in honor of Mennonite elder Bernard Buhler.

•**BUNKER HIL,** City; Russell County; Pop. 124; Zip Code 67626; Elev. 1,860; Lat. 38-52-28 N long. 098-42-08 W; central Kansas; The city is named after the famous Revolutionary War battle.

•**BURDEN,** City; Cowley County; Pop. 518; Zip Code 67019; Elev. 1,383; Lat. 37-18-52 N long. 096-45-12 W; S Kansas; Burden is named after an early settler.

•**BURDETT,** City; Pawnee County; Pop. 279; Zip Code 67523; Elev. 2,133; Lat. 38-11-31 N long. 099-31-32 W; central Kansas; Named for a local settler.

•**BURLINGAME,** City; Osage County; Pop. 1,239; Zip Code 66413; Elev. 1,055; Lat. 38-45-05 N long. 095-50-06 W; E Kansas; The city's name honors Massachusetts Senator, Anson Burlingame.

•**BURLINGTON,** City; Coffey County Seat; Pop. 2,901; Zip Code 66839; Elev. 1,037; Lat. 38-11-44 N long. 095-44-39 W; E Kansas; Named for the city in Iowa.

•**BURNS,** City; Marion County; Pop. 224; Zip Code 66840; Elev. 1,504; Lat. 38-05-32 N long. 096-53-11 W; E central Kansas; Named after a Santa Fe Railroad official.

•**BURR OAK,** City; Jewell County; Pop. 366; Zip Code 66936; Elev. 1,662; Lat. 39-52-11 N long. 098-18-16 W; N Kansas; Descriptively named for a local burr oak.

•**BURRTON,** City; Harvey County; Pop. 976; Zip Code Elev. 1,453; Lat. 38-01-29 N long. 097-40-23 W; SE central Kansas; The town is named after the commonplace burr oak stands in the area.

•**BUSHTON,** City; Rice County; Pop. 388; Zip Code 67427; Elev. 1,765; Lat 38-30-50 N long. 098-23-36 W; central Kansas; Bushton was descriptively named for the many attractive shrub-like bushes in the area.

•**CALDWELL,** City; Sumner County; Pop. 1,401; Zip Code 67022; Elev. 1,149; Lat. 37-02-01 N long. 097-36-25 W; S Kansas; Caldwell was named in honor of U. S. Senator Alexander Caldwell.

•**CAMBRIDGE,** City; Cowley County; Pop. 113; Zip Code 67023; Elev. 1,252; Lat. 37-19-03 N long. 096-39-59 W; S Kansas; The town is named after Cambridge, England.

•**CANEY,** City; Montgomery County; Pop. 2,284; Zip Code 67333; Elev. 770; Lat. 37-00-47 N long. 095-55-48 W; SE Kansas; The city is named for the nearby Caney River.

•**CANTON,** City; McPherson County; Pop. 926; Zip Code 67428; Elev. 590; Lat. 38-23-08 N long. 097-25-45 W; central Kansas; Canton Kansas is named after Canton, Ohio.

•**CARBONDALE,** City; Osage County; Pop. 1,518; Zip Code 66414; Elev. 1,087; Lat. 38-49-03 N long. 095-41-38 W; E Kansas; The city is descriptively named for the abundant coal resources in its area.

•**CASSODAY,** City; Butler County; Pop. 122; Zip Code 66842; Elev. 1,470; Lat. 38-02-21 N long. 096-38-05 W; S Kansas; Cassoday is named for a pioneer settler.

•**CAWKER CITY,** City; Mitchell County; Pop. 640; Zip Code 67430; Elev. 1,500; Lat. 39-30-37 N long. 098-26-01 W; N central Kansas; E. H. Cawker won the right to name the town in a poker game. He named it for himself.

•**CEDAR POINT,** City; Chase County; Pop. 66; Zip Code 66843; Elev. 1,240; Lat. 37-04-28 N long. 097-51-50 W; E central Kansas; The city is named for the cedar groves in the area.

•**CHASE,** City; Rice County; Pop. 753; Zip Code 67524; Elev. 1,718; Lat. 38-21-21 N long. 098-20-53 W; central Kansas; Chase is named for an official of the Santa Fe Railroad.

•**CHAUTAUQUA,** City; Chautauqua County; Pop. 156; ; Zip Code 67334; Elev. 903; Lat. 37-01-28 N long. 096-10-34 W; SE Kansas; Chautauqua is an Iroquois Indian name brought west by the vicinity's settlers.

•**CHENEY,** City; Sedgwick County; Pop. 1,404; Zip Code 67025; Elev. 1,385; Lat. 37-37-51 N long. 097-46-56 W; S central Kansas; Cheney is named for Santa Fe Railroad Director B. P. Cheney.

•**CHEROKEE,** City; Crawford County; Pop. 775; Zip Code 66724; Elev. 949; Lat. 37-20-45 N long. 094-49-31 W; SE KS; The name of a famous Indian people who lived in the southern U. S. before the coming of the whites.

•**CHERRYVALE,** City; Montgomery County; Pop. 2,769; Zip Code 67335; Elev. 850; Lat. 37-16-05 N long. 095-32-59 W; SE Kansas; The town's name refers to the wild black cherry and chokecherry which grew in the area.

•**CHETOPA,** City; Labette County; Pop. 1,751; Zip Code 67336; Elev. 824; Lat. 37-02-12 N long. 095-05-38 W; SE Kansas; The town is named for an Osage chief whose name meant "four houses."

•**CIMARRON,** City; Gray County Seat; Pop. 1,491; Zip Code 67835; Elev. 2,627; Lat. 37-48-20 N long. 100-20-45 W; SW Kansas; Cimarron is a Spanish word meaning "wild."

•**CIRCLEVILLE,** City; Jackson County; Pop. 164; Zip Code 66416; Elev. 1,103; Lat. 39-31-17 N long. 095-51-32 W; NE Kansas; The city is named after Circleville, Ohio.

•**CLAFLIN,** City; Barton County; Pop. 764; Zip Code 67525; Elev. 1,810; Lat. 38-31-25 N long. 098-32-04 W; central Kansas; The town was given the maiden surname of the town founder's wife, Miss O. P. Hamilton.

•**CLAY CENTER,** City; Clay County Seat; Pop. 4,948; Zip Code 67432; Elev. 1,333; Lat. 39-22-55 N long. 097-07-33 W; NW of Manhattan in NE central Kansas; Clay Center is named in honor of Kentucky statesman, Henry Clay.

•**CLAYTON,** City; Decatur & Norton Counties; Pop. 102; Zip Code 67629; Elev. 2,450; Lat. 39-44-14 N long. 100-10-40 W; N Kansas; Descriptively named for the clay on the roads in the area.

•**CLEARWATER,** City; Sedgwick County; Pop. 1,684; Zip Code 67026; Elev. 1,275; Lat. 37-30-14 N long. 097-30-03 W; S central Kansas; The town's name is a translation of an Indian word meaning "clearwater."

•**CLIFTON,** City; Clay & Washington Counties; Pop. 695; Zip Code 66937; Elev. 1,302; Lat. 39-34-02 N long. 097-17-12 W; N Kansas; The town was named after a well-liked government surveyor.

•**CLIMAX,** City; Greenwood County; Pop. 81; Zip Code 67027; Elev. 1,040; Lat. 37-43-17 N long. 096-13-31 W; SE Kansas; The origin of the town's name is uncertain.

•**CLYDE,** City; Cloud County; Pop. 909; Zip Code 66938; Elev. 1,300; Lat. 39-35-26 N long. 097-24-02 W; N Kansas; The town is named for the Clyde River in Scotland.

•**COATS,** City; Pratt County; Pop. 153; Zip Code 67028; Elev. 1,970; Lat. 37-30-39 N long. 098-49-26 W; S central Kansas; The city's name remembers railroad and town developer W. A. Coats.

•**COFFEYVILLE,** City; Montgomery County; Pop. 15,185; Zip Code 67337; Elev. 736; Lat. 37-06-17 N long. 095-27-03 W; 15 mi. S of Independence in SE Kansas; Colonel James Coffeyville founded a trading post here and left his name on the town.

•**COLDWATER,** City; Comanche County Seat; Pop. 989; Zip Code 67029; Elev. 2,112; Lat. 37-16-07 N long. 099-19-34 W; S Kansas; The city is named for the cool, sparkling water of a local spring.

•**COLLYER,** City; Trego County; Pop. 151; Zip Code 67631; Elev. 151; Lat. 39-02-21 N long. 100-07-07 W; W central Kansas; Collyer is named after pioneer settler, the Rev. Robert Collyer.

•**COLONY,** City; Anderson County; Pop. 474; Zip Code 66015; Elev. 1,130; Lat. 38-08-16 N long. 094-08-31 W; E Kansas; The town's name refers to its settlement as a colony by pioneers from Ohio.

•COLUMBUS, City; Cherikee County Seat; Pop. 3,426; Zip Code 66725; Elev. 910; Lat. 37-07-55 N long. 094-50-44 W; SE corner of Kansas; The town is named after the great Spanish-Italian explorer.

•COLWICH, City; Sedgwick County; Pop. 935; Zip Code 67030; Elev. 1,380; Lat. 37-46-52 N long. 097-32-15 W; S central Kansas; The town's name was created by combining two other place names.

•CONCORDIA, City; Cloud County Seat; Pop. 6,847; Zip Code 66901; Elev. 1,369; Lat. 39-34-03 N long. 097-39-26 W; 50 mi. N of Salina in N Kansas; The name reflects the agreement between the town's founders.

•CONWAY SPRINGS, City; Sumner County; Pop. 1,313; Zip Code 67434; Elev. 1,366; Lat. 37-23-26 N long. 097-38-43 W; S Kansas; The town is named after a Welsh settler called Conway.

•COOLIDGE, City; Hamilton County; Pop. 82; Zip Code 67836; Elev. 3,355; Lat. 38-02-30 N long. 102-00-25 W; W Kansas; The city's name honors Santa Fe Railroad president T. J. Coolidge.

•COPELAND, City; Gray County; Pop. 323; Zip Code 67837; Elev. 2,821; Lat. 37-32-27 N long. 100-37-40 W; SW Kansas; Copeland is named in honor of E. L. Copeland, one-time secretary-treasurer of the Santa Fe Railroad.

•CORNING, City; Nemaha County; Pop. 158; Zip Code 66417; Elev. 1,350; Lat. 39-39-27 N long. 096-01-40 W; NE Kansas; The city is named after Corning, New York.

•COTTONWOOD FALLS, City; Chase County Seat; Pop. 954; Zip Code 66845; Elev. 1,175; Lat. 38-22-09 N long. 096-32-29 W; E central Kansas; The town is named for the distinctive cottonwood trees found in the area.

•COUNCIL GROVE, City; Morris County Seat; Pop. 2,381; Zip Code 66846; Elev. 1,233; Lat. 38-42-46 N long. 096-34-26 W; E central Kansas; The town grew around a grove of trees used by the Indians and then the settlers as a meeting place.

•COURTLAND, City; Republic County; Pop. 377; Zip Code 66939; Elev. 1,499; Lat. 39-46-53 N long. 097-53-47 W; N Kansas; Courtland is named after Courtland, New York.

•COYVILLE, City; Wilson County; Pop. 98; Zip Code 66727; Elev. 885; Lat. 37-41-15 N long. 095-53-49 W; SE Kansas; The town is named after an early settler.

•CUBA, City; Republic County; Pop. 286; Zip Code 66940; Elev. 1,590; Lat. 39-48-01 N long. 097-27-19 W; N Kansas; The city of Cuba is named after the Caribbean country.

•CULVER, City; Ottawa County; Pop. 167; Zip Code 67435; NE central Kansas; Named after a pioneer settler.

•CUNNINGHAM, City; Kingman County; Pop. 540; Zip Code 67035; Elev. 1,705; Lat. 37-38-44 N long. 098-25-54 W; S central Kansas; First called Ninnescah, it was renamed for J. D. Cunningham during its rebuilding following a tornado.

•DAMAR, City; Rooks County; Pop. 204; Zip Code 67632; Elev. 2,106; Lat. 39-19-13 N long. 099-35-04 W; N Kansas; D. M. Marr owned the original townsite, it is named after him.

•DANVILLE, City; Harper County; Pop. 71; Zip Code 67036; Elev. 1,346; Lat. 37-17-07 N long. 097-53-02 W; S Kansas; The city is named after Danville, Ohio.

•DE SOTO, City; Johnson County; Pop. 2,061; Zip Code 66018; Elev. 842; Lat. 38-58-36 N long. 094-58-03 W; E Kansas; De Soto is named in honor of the great 16th century Spanish explorer.

•DEARING, City; Montgomery County; Pop. 475; Zip Code 67340; Elev. 770; Lat. 37-03-28 N long. 095-42-24 W; SE Kansas; Named for an early settler.

•DEERFIELD, City; Kearny County; Pop. 538; Zip Code 67838; Elev. 2,947; Lat. 37-59-00 N long. 101-08-10 W; W Kansas; Descriptively named for the many deer in the area when the settlers arrived.

•DELIA, City; Jackson County; Pop. 181; Zip Code 66418; Lat. 39-14-21 N long. 095-57-51 W; NE Kansas; The town's name honors pioneer Delia Cunningham.

•DELPHOS, City; Ottawa County; Pop. 570; Zip Code 67436; Elev. 1,300; Lat. 39-16-25 N long. 097-45-53 W; NE central Kansas; The city is named after the region in ancient Greece.

•DENISON, City; Jackson County; Pop. 231; Zip Code 66419; Elev. 1,050; Lat. 39-23-35 N long. 095-37-36 W; NE Kansas; Denison is named after Denison, Ohio.

•DENTON, City; Doniphan County; Pop. 156; Zip Code 66017; Elev. 1,078; Lat. 39-43-56 N long. 095-16-18 W; NE corner of Kansas; First settled by the four Denton brothers from England, it is named in their honor.

•DERBY, City; Sedgwick County; Pop. 9,786; Zip Code 67037; Elev. 1,275; Lat. 37-33-29 N long. 097-15-56 W; 15 mi. SE of Wichita in S central Kansas; The popular sport of horseracing led to the town being named for the famous track in England.

•DEXTER, City; Cowley County; Pop. 366; Zip Code 67038; Elev. 1,208; Lat. 37-10-38 N long. 096-42-39 W; S Kansas; The city is named after a famous racehorse.

•DIGHTON, City; Lane County Seat; Pop. 1,390; Zip Code 67839; Elev. 2,765; Lat. 38-28-53 N long. 100-27-50 W; W Kansas; Dighton is named after surveyor Richard Dighton.

•DODGE CITY, City; Ford County Seat; Pop. 18,001; Zip Code 67801; Elev. 2,550; Lat. 37-45-27 N long. 100-01-04 W; 120 mi. E of CO border in S Kansas; Dodge is named in honor of U. S. Army Colonel Richard Dodge.

•DORRANCE, City; Russell County; Pop. 220; Zip Code 67634; Elev. 1,730; Lat. 38-50-48 N long. 098-35-29 W; central Kansas; The city is named after Dorrance, Illinois.

•DOUGLASS, City; Butler County; Pop. 1,450; Zip Code 67039; Elev. 1,205; Lat. 37-30-26 N long. 097-00-47 W; S Kansas; The town is named after New York settler Captain Joseph Douglass.

•DOWNS, City; Osborne County; Pop. 1,324; Zip Code 67437; Elev. 1,484; Lat. 39-30-14 N long. 098-32-34 W; N central Kansas; The town is named in honor of railroad official Major William F. Downs.

•DRESDEN, City; Decatur County; Pop. 84; Zip Code 67635; Elev. 2,729; Lat. 39-37-18 N long. 100-25-00 W; NW Kansas; Dresden is named for the city in Germany.

•DUNLAP, City; Morris County; Pop. 82; Zip Code 66848; Elev. 1,186; Lat. 38-34-39 N long. 096-21-50 W; E central Kansas; Joseph Dunlap founded the town. It is named after him.

•DURHAM, City; Marion County; Pop. 130; Zip Code 67438; Elev. 1,396; Lat. 38-28-56 N long. 097-13-35 W; E central Kansas; The city is named for the county in England.

•DWIGHT, City; Morris County; Pop. 320; Zip Code 66849; Elev. 490; Lat. 38-50-42 N long. 096-35-30 W; E central Kansas; Dwight is named after an early pioneer.

•**EASTON,** City; Leavenworth County; Pop. 460; Zip Code 66020; Elev. 903; Lat. 39-20-40 N long. 095-06-56 W; NE Kansas; Named in honor of Easton, Pennsylvania.

•**EDGERTON,** City; Johnson County; Pop. 1,214; Zip Code 66021; Elev. 1,000; Lat. 38-45-53 N long. 095-00-37 W; E Kansas; The town's name honors a Santa Fe Railroad engineer, a Mr. Edgerton.

•**EDMOND,** City; Norton County; Pop. 56; Zip Code 67636; Elev. 2,119; Lat. 39-37-33 N: long. 099-49-23 W; N Kansas; Edmond is named for an early settler.

•**EDNA,** City; Labette County; Pop. 537; Zip Code 67342; Elev. 979; Lat. 37-03-31 N long. 095-213-23 W; SE Kansas; Named for the daughter of a local settler.

•**EDWARDSVILLE,** City; Wyandotte County; Pop. 3,364; Zip Code 66113; NE Kansas; The city's name remembers Union Pacific Railroad official John Edwards.

•**EFFINGHAM,** City; Atchison County; Pop. 634; Zip Code 66023; Elev. 1,138; Lat. 39-31-11 N long. 095-23-49 W; NE Kansas; Railroad promoter Effingham Nichols left his name on the town.

•**EL DORADO,** City; Butler County Seat; Pop. 10,510; Zip Code 67042; Elev. 1,344; Lat. 37-48-58 N long. 096-51-29 W; 28 mi. ENE of Wichita in S Kansas; The city is named for the mythical city of gold that brought Spanish explorers to the region in the 16th century.

•**ELBING,** City; Butler County; Pop. 175; Zip Code 67041; Elev. 1,440; Lat. 38-03-15 N long. 097-07-30 W; S Kansas; Mennonite settlers named the town after Elbing, Germany.

•**ELK CITY,** City; Montgomery County; Pop. 404; Zip Code 67344; Elev. 835; Lat. 37-17-24 N long. 095-54-32 W; SE Kansas; Descriptively named for the elk herds once common to the area.

•**ELK FALLS,** City; Elk County; Pop. 151; Zip Code 67345; Elev. 938; Lat. 37-22-33 N long. 096-11-57 W; SE Kansas; The Fall River creates a natural falls here in Elk County and hence the name.

•**ELKHART,** City; Morton County; Pop. 2,243; Zip Code 67950; Elev. 3,624; SW corner of Kansas; Elkhart is named after Elkhart, Indiana.

•**ELLINWOOD,** City; Barton County; Pop. 2,508; Zip Code 67526; Elev. 1,800; Lat. 38-21-22 N long. 098-34-43 W; central Kansas; The town's name remembers Santa Fe Railroad contractor, a Mr. Ellinwood.

•**ELLIS,** City; Ellis County; Pop. 2,062; Zip Code 67637; Elev. 2,117; Lat. 38-56-25 N long. 099-33-41 W; central Kansas; The city and the county are named for a Civil War hero.

•**ELLSWORTH,** City; Ellsworth County Seat; Pop. 2,465; Zip Code 67439; Elev. 1,550; Lat. 38-43-55 N long. 098-13-40 W; central Kansas; The town is named after Civil War Lieutenant Allen Ellsworth.

•**ELMDALE,** City; Chase County; Pop. 109; Zip Code 66850; Elev. 1,200; Lat. 38-22-17 N long. 096-38-42 W; E central Kansas; Elmdale's name recalls the elm trees once abundant in the area.

•**ELSMORE,** City; Allen County; Pop. 104; Zip Code 66732; Elev. 1,050; Lat. 37-47-42 N long. 095-08-54 W; SE Kansas; Originally named after the castle in Shakespeare's Hamlet, a mis-spelling left Elsinore changed to Elsmore

•**ELWOOD,** City; Doniphan County; Pop. 1,275; Zip Code 66024; Elev. 813; Lat. 39-45-42 N long. 094-52-42 W; NE corner of Kansas; first named Rose, the town was later reorganized by J. B. Elwood, and named after him.

•**EMPORIA,** City; Lyon County Seat; Pop. 25,287; Zip Code 66801; Elev. 1,150; Lat. 38-24-35 N long. 096-11-00 W; 52 mi. SW of Topeka, in E Kansas; Descriptively named for its market town origins.

•**ENGLEWOOD,** City; Clark County; Pop. 111; Zip Code 67840; Elev. 1,970; Lat. 37-02-18 N long. 099-58-47 W; S Kansas; Named after Englewood, Illinois.

•**ENSIGN,** City; Gray County; Pop. 209; Zip Code 67841; Elev. 2,719; Lat. 37-38-55 N long. 100-14-07 W; SW Kansas; G. L. Ensign founded the town, it is named for him.

•**ENTERPRISE,** City; Dickinson County; Pop. 839; Zip Code 67441; Lat. 38-54-13 N long. 097-07-08 W; E central Kansas; Originally Hoffman's Mills, the town fathers changed it to Enterprise to further its commercial ambitions.

•**ERIE,** City; Neosho County Seat; Pop. 1,415; Zip Code 66733; Lat. 37-34-04 N long. 095-14-31 W; SE Kansas; This Kansas city is named after New York's Lake Erie.

•**ESKRIDGE,** City; Wabaunsee County; Pop. 603; Zip Code 66423; Elev. 1,400; Lat. 38-51-28 N long. 096-06-20 W; E Kansas; Journalist Charles Eskridge left his name on the town.

•**EUDORA,** City; Douglas County; Pop. 2,934; Zip Code 66025; Elev. 880; Lat. 38-56-24 N long. 095-06-08 W; E Kansas; Eudora is an anglicized name of a Shawnee Indian woman.

•**EUREKA,** City; Greenwood County Seat; Pop. 3,425; Zip Code 67045; Elev. 1,084; Lat. 37-49-07 N long. 096-17-15 W; SE Kansas; Eureka is Greek for "I have found it." The name reflects the enthusiasm of its settlers.

•**EVEREST,** City; Brown County; Pop. 331; Zip Code 66424; Elev. 1,150; Lat. 39-40-38 N long. 095-25-32 W; NE Kansas; Colonel Aaron Everest was an attorney for the Union Pacific Railroad. The town is named for him.

•**FAIRVIEW,** City; Brown County; Pop. 258; Zip Code 66425; Elev. 1,230; Lat. 39-50-35 N long. 095-43-49 W; NE Kansas; Descriptively named for the pleasant view available from the townsite.

•**FAIRWAY,** City; Johnson County; Pop. 4,619; Zip Code ; E Kansas; An euphonious and descriptive name given by the town's early settlers.

•**FALL RIVER,** City; Greenwood County; Pop. 173; Zip Code 67047; Elev. 930; Lat. 37-36-24 N long. 096-01-43 W; SE Kansas; The city is named after the Fall River which runs from the Flint Hills.

•**FLORENCE,** City; Marion County; Pop. 729; Zip Code 66851; Elev. 1,280; Lat. 38-14-38 N long. 096-55-27 W; E central Kansas; Florence is named after the great Italian city.

•**FONTANA,** City; Miami County; Pop. 173; Zip Code 66026; Elev. 930; Lat. 38-25-34 N long. 094-50-12 W; E Kansas; Originally Old Fountain, the town was renamed Fontana for a nearby spring.

•**FORD,** City; Ford County; Pop. 272; Zip Code 67842; Elev. 2,406; Lat. 37-38-20 N long. 099-45-19 W; S Kansas; The city is named in honor of Civil-War-era Colonel James Ford.

•**FORMOSA,** City; Jewell County; Pop. 166; Zip Code 66942; Elev. 1,527; Lat. 39-46-34 N long. 097-59-24 W; N Kansas; The town is named after Formosa, the Portuguese name for Taiwan, meaning "beautiful isle."

•**FORT SCOTT,** City; Bourbon County Seat; Pop. 8,893; Zip Code 66701; Elev. 846; Lat. 37-49-55 N long. 094-42-11 W; 85 mi. S of Kansas City in SE Kansas; Fort Scott honors American General Winfield Scott.

173

•**FOWLER,** City; Meade County; Pop. 592; Zip Code 67844; Elev. 2,481; Lat. 37-22-45 N long. 100-11-41 W; SW Kansas; Named for an early settler.

•**FRANKFORT,** City; Marshall County; Pop. 1,038; Zip Code 66427; Elev. 1,150; Lat. 39-42-15 N long. 096-24-53 W; NE Kansas; The city is named after Frankfort, Germany.

•**FREDONIA,** City; Wilson County Seat; Pop. 3,047; Zip Code 66736; Elev. 893; Lat. 37-32-04 N long. 095-49-23 W; SE Kansas; The city is named after a popular name for America in the 19th century.

•**FRONTENAC,** City; Crawford County; Pop. 2,586; Zip Code 66762; SE Kansas; Frontenac is named after the famous French explorer.

•**FULTON,** City; Bourbon County; Pop. 194; Zip Code 66738; Elev. 850; Lat. 38-00-28 N long. 094-43-17 W; SE Kansas; Captain J. R. Fulton donated the land for the railroad station to the Santa Fe. The town is named after him.

•**GALENA,** City; Cherokee County; Pop. 3,587; Zip Code 66739; Elev. 941; Lat. 37-04-30 N long. 094-38-09 W; SE corner of Kansas; The city is named after Galena, Illinois.

•**GALESBURG,** City; Neosho County; Pop. 181; Zip Code 66740; Elev. 1,000; Latt. 37-28-22 N long. 095-21-23 W; SE Kansas; Scandinavian settlers from Illinois named the new town after Galesburg, Illinois.

•**GALVA,** City; McPherson County; Pop. 651; Zip Code 67443; Elev. 1,546; Lat. 38-22-52 N long. 097-32-20 W; central Kansas; Pioneers from Sweden named the town after Galva, Sweden.

•**GARDEN PLAIN,** City; Sedgwick County; Pop. 775; Zip Code 67050; Elev. 1,450; Lat. 37-39-49 N long. 097-41-17 W; S central Kansas; Descriptively named by its settlers for the area's garden-like fertility.

•**GARDNER,** City; Johnson County; Pop. 2,392; Zip Code 66030; Elev. 1,160; Lat. 38-48-35 N long. 094-55-03 W; E Kansas; Gardner's name honors Henry Gardner, Governor of Massachusetts in 1854.

•**GARFIELD,** City; Pawnee County; Pop. 277; Zip Code 67529; Elev. 2,075; Lat. 38-04-44 long. 099-14-35 W; central Kansas; The city is named in honor of U. S. President James Garfield.

•**GARNETT,** City; Anderson County Seat; Pop. 3,310; Zip Code 66032; Elev. 1,049; Lat. 38-16-54 N long. 095-14-44 W; E Kansas; Garnett's name honors an early settler.

•**GAS,** City; Allen County; Pop. 543; Zip Code 66742; Elev. 1,020; Lat. 37-55-26 N long. 095-20-48 W; SE Kansas; The city is named for the natural gas deposits in the vicinity.

•**GAYLORD,** City; Smith County; Pop. 203; Zip Code 67638; Elev. 1,592; Lat. 39-38-48 N long. 098-50-42 W; N Kansas; Gaylord was an early pioneer. The town is named after him.

•**GEM,** City; Thomas County; Pop. 101; Zip Code 67734; Elev. 3,090; Lat. 39-25-44 N long. 100-53-43 W; NW Kansas; The town's place name refers to the "precious" nature of the area.

•**GENESCO,** City; Rice County; Pop. 496; Zip Code 67444; Elev. 1,750; Lat. 38-30-51 N long. 098-12-39 W; central Kansas; The Kansas city is named after Genesco, New York.

•**GEUDA SPRINGS,** City; Cowley & Sumner Counties; Pop. 217; Zip Code 67051; S Kansas; The town is named for the "healing springs" nearby.

•**GIRARD,** City; Crawford County Seat; Pop. 2,888; Zip Code 66743; Elev. 986; Lat. 37-30-40 N long. 094-50-39 W; SE Kansas; Girard is named for an early French trader, Michael Girard.

•**GLADE,** City; Phillips County; Pop. 131; Zip Code 67639; Elev. 1,811; Lat. 39-41-00 N long. 099-18-41 W; N Kansas; The town is named after a Missouri Pacific Railroad engineer.

•**GLASGOW,** City; Cloud County; Pop. 710; Zip Code 67445; Elev. 1,320; Lat. 39-21-44 N long. 097-50-14 W; N Kansas; Scottish settlers named the town after Glasgow, Scotland.

•**GLEN ELDER,** City; Mitchell County; Pop. 491; Zip Code 67446; Elev. 1,424; Lat. 39-30-05 N long. 098-18-35 W; N central Kansas; Pioneers from Scotland gave this place its Scottish name.

•**GODDARD,** City; Sedgwick County; Pop. 1,427; Zip Code 67052; Elev. 1,465; Lat. 37-39-34 N long. 097-34-33 W; S central Kansas; In 1877 J. E. Goddard was the general manager of the Santa Fe Railroad. The town is named after him.

•**GOESSEL,** City; Marion County; Pop. 421; Zip Code 67053; Elev. 1,533; Lat. 38-14-47 N long. 097-20-51 W; E central Kansas; The town's name honors a heroic sea captain named Goessel who brought many of the area's Mennonite settlers across the Atlantic.

•**GOFF,** City; Nemaha County; Pop. 196; Zip Code 66428; Elev. 1,250; Lat. 39-39-51 N long. 095-55-51 W; NE Kansas; Named in honor of Central Union Pacific Railway official Edward Goff.

•**GOODLAND,** City; Sherman County Seat; Pop. 5,708; Zip Code 67735; Elev. 3,683; Lat. 39-20-53 N long. 101-42-33 W; 20 mi. E of the Colorado border in NW Kansas; Named after Goodland, Indiana.

•**GORHAM,** City; Russell County; Pop. 355; Zip Code 67640; Elev. 1,914; Lat. 38-52-53 N long. 099-01-31 W; central Kansas; Gorham is named for an early settler.

•**GOVE CITY,** City; Gove County Seat; 148; Zip Code 67736; Elev. 2,634; Lat. 38-57-31 N long. 100-29-06 W; The city's name honors Grenville Cove, a Civil War soldier.

•**GRAINFIELD,** City; Gove County; Pop. 417; Zip Code 67737; Elev. 2,813; Lat. 39-06-49 N long. 100-27-58 W; W Kansas; Descriptively named for the area's rich grain production.

•**GREAT BEND,** City; Barton County Seat; Pop. 16,608; Zip Code 67530; Elev. 1,849; Lat. 38-22-08 N long. 098-46-28 W; 53 mi. WNW of Hutchinson in central Kansas; Descriptively named for a great bend in the Arkansas River.

•**GREELEY,** City; Anderson County; Pop. 405; Zip Code 66033; Elev. 880; Lat. 38-22-04 N long. 095-07-45 W; E Kansas; Greeley is named for famous 19th century newspaper publisher Horace Greeley.

•**GREENLEAF,** City; Washington County; Pop. 462; Zip Code 66943; Elev. 1,417; Lat. 39-43-38 N long. 096-58-41 W; N Kansas; Named after a railroad man.

•**GREENSBURG,** City; Kiowa County Seat; Pop. 1,885; Zip Code 67054; Elev. 2,235; Lat. 37-36-11 N long. 099-17-34 W; S Kansas; Greensburg is named after a pioneer stage line owner.

•**GRENOLA,** City; Elk County; Pop. 335; Zip Code 67346; Elev. 1,117; Lat. 37-21-06 N long. 096-27-19 W; SE Kansas; Named after an early settler.

•**GRIDLEY,** City; Coffey County; Pop. 404; Zip Code 66852; Elev. 1,130; Lat. 38-05-50 N long. 095-52-53 W; E Kansas; Gridley is named for land promoter Walter Gridley.

•GRINNELL, City; Gove County; Pop. 410; Zip Code 67738; Elev. 2,910; Lat. 39-07-08 N long. 100-370-45 W; W Kansas; The town is named after Josiah Grinnell who also founded Grinnell, Iowa.

•GYPSUM, City; Saline County; Pop. 423; Zip Code 67448; Elev. 1,229; Lat. 38-42-28 N long. 097-25-18 W; central Kansas; The town is descriptively named for nearby gypsum mineral deposits.

•HADDAM, City; Washington County; Pop. 239; Zip Code 66944; Elev. 1,400; Lat. 39-51-16 N long. 097-18-08 W; N Kansas; According to legend an early settler referring to a rat infestation said "we've had em." The town was named by this phrase, or possibly after Haddam, Connecticut.

•HALSTEAD, City; Harvey County; Pop. 1,994; Zip Code 67056; Elev. 1,400; Lat. 38-00-10 N long. 097-30-24 W; SE central Kansas; Halstead is named in honor of Civil War newspaper correspondent Murat Halstead.

•HAMILTON, City; Greenwood County; Pop. 363; Zip Code 66853; Elev. 1,098; Lat. 37-58-43 N long. 096-09-41 W; SE Kansas; Hamilton is named after Revolutionary War patriot Alexander Hamilton.

•HANOVER, City; Washington County; Pop. 802; Zip Code 66945; Elev. 1,231; Lat. 39-53-32 N long. 096-52-26 W; N Kansas; Many German settlers came to Kansas from Hanover, Germany. The town's name remembers this origin.

•HANSTON, City; Hodgeman County; Pop. 257; Zip Code 67849; Elev. 2,160; Lat. 38-07-26 N long. 099-42-42 W; SW central Kansas; Benjamin Hann owned the townsite. It is named after him.

•HARDTNER, City; Barber County; Pop. 336; Zip Code 67057; Elev. 1,420; Lat. 37-00-48 N long. 098-38-58 W; S Kansas; Named for an early settler.

•HARPER, City; Harper County; Pop. 1,823; Zip Code 67058; Elev. 1,421; Lat. 37-16-56 N long. 098-01-26 W; S Kansas; Harper is named after a 19th century sergeant in the U. S. Army.

•HARTFORD, City; Lyon County; Pop. 551; Zip Code 66854; Elev. 1,085; Lat. 38-18-26 N long. 095-57-05 W; E Kansas; The city is named for the town in England.

•HARVEYVILLE, City; Wabaunsee County; Pop. 280; Zip Code 66431; Elev. 1,121; Lat. 38-47-18 N long. 095-57-36 W; E Kansas; The town is named in honor of Quaker missionary Henry Harvey.

•HAVANA, City; Montgomery County; Pop. 169; Zip Code 67347; Elev. 760; Lat. 37-05-41 N long. 095-56-17 W; SE Kansas; The city is named after Havana, Illinois.

•HAVEN, City; Reno County; Pop. 1,125; Zip Code 67543; Elev. 1,480; Lat. 37-56-06 N long. 097-46-49 W; central Kansas; Named after New Haven, Connecticut.

•HAVENSVILLE, City; Pottawatomie County; Pop. 183; Zip Code 66432; Elev. 1,200; Lat. 39-30-31 N long. 096-04-21 W; NE Kansas; The city's name is derived from New England's New Haven, Connecticut.

•HAVILAND, City; Kiowa County; Pop. 770; Zip Code 67059; Elev. 2,150; Lat. 37-36-58 N long. 099-03-55 W; S Kansas; The city is named in honor of distinguished Quaker Laura Haviland.

•HAYS, City; Ellis County Seat; Pop. 16,301; Zip Code 67601; Elev. 2,010; Lat. 38-52-35 N long. 099-19-26 W; 48 mi. NE of Great Bend in central Kansas; Named after the common agricultural grass, hay.

•HAYSVILLE, City; Sedgwick County; Pop. 8,006; Zip Code 67060; Elev. 1,275; Lat. 37-33-50 N long. 097-22-41 W; S of Wichita in S central Kansas; Named after the commonly grown hay.

•HAZELTON, City; Barber County; Pop. 143; Zip Code 67061; Elev. 1,360; Lat. 37-05-20 N long. 098-23-59 W; S Kansas; Named after a pioneer preacher.

•HEPLER, City; Crawford County; Pop. 165; Zip Code 66746; Elev. 1,000; Lat. 37-39-50 N long. 094-58-09 W; SE Kansas; Named after a pioneer settler.

•HERINGTON, City; Dickinson County; Pop. 2,930; Zip Code 67449; Elev. 1,350; Lat. 38-42-19 N long. 096-53-47 W; E central Kansas; Herington's name remembers pioneer rancher Monroe Herington.

•HERNDON, City; Rawlins County; Pop. 220; Zip Code 67739; Elev. 2,666; Lat. 39-54-27 N long. 100-46-57 W; NW Kansas; The city is named after Abraham Lincoln's early law partner, William Herndon.

•HESSTON, City; Harvey County; Pop. 3,013; Zip Code 67062; Elev. 1,476; Lat. 38-08-19 N long. 097-25-56 W; SE central Kansas; Hesston is named for its founder Abraham Hess.

•HIAWATHA, City; Brown County Seat; Pop. 3,702; Zip Code 66434; Elev. 1,136; Lat. 39-51-09 N long. 095-32-11 W; NE Kansas; The town is named after the famous Indian of Longfellow's poem.

•HIGHLAND, City; Doniphan County; Pop. 954; Zip Code 66035; Elev. 1,051; Lat. 39-51-33 N long. 095-16-00 W; NE corner of Kansas; Descriptively named for location in a "highland."

•HILL CITY, City; Graham County Seat__; 2,028; Zip Code 67642; Elev. 2,190; Lat. 39-21-57 N long. 099-50-44 W; NW central Kansas; The city is named after the original landowner, W. R. Hill.

•HILLSBORO, City; Marion County; Pop. 2,717; Zip Code 67063; Elev. 1,454; Lat. 38-21-10 N long. 097-12-05 W; E central Kansas; Hillsboro is named for pioneer landowner, John Hill.

•HOISINGTON, City; Barton County; Pop. 3,678; Zip Code 67544; Elev. 1,845; Lat. 38-31-06 N long. 098-46-37 W; central Kansas; The city is named for early prominent settler, Andrew J. Hoisington.

•HOLCOMB, City; Finney County; Pop. 816; Zip Code 67851; Elev. 2,885; Lat. 37-59-12 N long. 100-59-06 W; W Kansas; Named for a successful farmer, a Mr. Holcomb.

•HOLLENBURG, City; Washington County; Pop. 57; Zip Code 66946; Elev. 1,271; Lat. 39-58-51 N long. 096-59-33 W; N Kansas; Hollenburg is named after German adventurer Henry Hollenburg who settled here in 1858.

•HOLTON, City; Jackson County Seat; Pop. 3,132; Zip Code 66436; Elev. 1,095; Lat. 39-27-58 N long. 095-44-21 W; NE Kansas; Named in honor of wealthy banker Edward Holton.

•HOLYROOD, City; Ellsworth County; Pop. 567; Zip Code 67450; Elev. 1,805; Lat. 38-35-24 N long. 098-24-28 W; central Kansas; The city is named after the famous holyrood Abbey in Scotland.

•HOPE, City; Dickinson County; Pop. 468; Zip Code 67451; Elev. 1,400; Lat. 38-41-30 N long. 097-04-43 W; E central Kansas; Named after the Dutch community in Michigan.

•HORTON, City; Brown County; Pop. 2,130; Zip Code 66439; Elev. 1,082; Lat. 39-39-57 N long. 095-31-48 W; NE Kansas; Horton's name honors Kansas Supreme Court Judge Albert Horton.

•**HOWARD,** City; Elk County Seat; Pop. 965; Zip Code 67349; Elev. 1,040; Lat. 37-28-15 N long. 096-16-01 W; SE Kansas; The city's name honors General O. O. Howard, head of the Civil War era Freedman's Bureau.

•**HOXIE,** City; Sheridan County Seat; Pop. 1,462; Zip Code 67740; Elev. 2,700; Lat. 39-21-15 N long. 100-26-18 W; NW Kansas; Hoxie is named after railroad builder H. M. Hoxie.

•**HOYT,** City; Jackson County; Pop. 536; Zip Code 66440; Elev. 1,150; Lat. 39-14-57 N long. 095-42-10 W; NE Kansas; The city is named after lawyer George Hoyt who defended John Brown during his treason trial.

•**HUDSON,** City; Stafford County; Pop. 157; Zip Code 67545; Elev. 1,865; Lat. 38-06-29 N long. 098-39-42 W; central Kansas; The city is named after Hudson, Wisconsin.

•**HUGOTON,** City; Stevens County Seat; Pop. 3,165; Zip Code 67951; Elev. 3,111; SW Kansas; Hugoton is named in honor of 19th century French author Victor Hugo.

•**HUMBOLDT,** City; Allen County; Pop. 2,230; Zip Code 66748; Elev. 970; Lat. 37-48-48 N long. 095-26-10 W; SE Kansas; The famous German naturalist, Alexander Von Humboldt, left his name on this Kansas town.

•**HUNTER,** City; Mitchell County; Pop. 135; Zip Code 67452; Elev. 1,600; Lat. 39-13-57 N long. 098-23-50 W; N central Kansas; The town is named after a U. S. Senator from Virginia.

•**HURON,** City; Atchison County; Pop. 107; Zip Code 66038; Elev. 1,160; Lat. 39-38-16 N long. 095-21-03 W; NE Kansas; Huron is named after the Indian tribe of the old northwest.

•**HUTCHINSON,** City; Reno County Seat; Pop. 40,284; Zip Code 67501; Elev. 1,538; Lat. 38-03-44 N long. 097-57-11 W; 42 mi. WNW of Wichita in central Kansas; C. C. Hutchinson was an early pioneer preacher and Indian agent. The town is named for him.

•**INDEPENDENCE,** City; Montgomery County Seat; Pop. 10,598; Zip Code 67301; Elev. 826; Lat. 37-13-38 N long. 095-42-30 W; 58 mi. WSW of Pittsburg in SE Kansas; The city is named after Independence, Iowa.

•**INGALLS,** City; Gray County Seat; Pop. 274; Zip Code 67853; Elev. 2680; Lat. 37-49-42 N long. 100-27-07 W; SW Kansas; Ingalls is named after Kansas Senator John J. Ingalls.

•**INMAN,** City; McPherson County; Pop. 947; Zip Code 67546; Elev. 1527; Lat. 38-13-51 N long. 097-46-25 W; central Kansas; The city is named for Colonel Henry Inman.

•**IOLA,** City; Allen County; Pop. 6,938; Zip Code 66749; Elev. 965; Lat. 37-54-57 N long. 095-24-03 W; 15 mi. N of Chanute in SE Kansas; Iola is named after early settler Iola Colburn.

•**ISABEL,** City; Barber County; Pop. 137; Zip Code 67065; Elev. 1850; Lat. 37-28-08 N long. 098-33-08 W; S Kansas; cKS; Area Code The surveyor who laid out the town named it for his new born baby daughter, Isabel.

•**JAMESTOWN,** City; Cloud County; Pop. 440; Zip Code 66948; Elev. 1411; Lat. 39-35-56 N long. 097-51-32 W; N Kansas; The city is named after railroad vice-president James Pomeroy.

•**JENNINGS,** City; Decatur County; Pop. 194; Zip Code 67643; Elev. 2500; Lat. 39-40-53 N long. 100-17-25 W; NW Kansas; Jennings is named after a pioneer settler.

•**JETMORE,** City; Hodgeman County Seat; Pop. 862; Zip Code 67854; Elev. 2307; Lat. 38-04-52 N long. 099-53-45 W; SW Kansas;

Colonel Abraham Jetmore was a director of the Kansas Freedman's Relief Association. The town is named after him.

•**JEWELL,** City; Jewell County; Pop. 589; Zip Code 66949; Elev. 1550; Lat. 39-40-19 N long. 098-08-59 W; N Kansas; Jewell is named in honor of Colonel Lewis Jewell who was killed in the Civil War.

•**JOHNSON CITY,** City; Stanton County Seat; Pop. 1,244; Zip Code 67855; Elev. 3330; Lat. 37-34-06 N long. 101-45-04 W; SW Kansas; Named after an early settler.

•**JUNCTION CITY,** City; Geary County Seat; Pop. 19,305; Zip Code 66441; Elev. 1107; Lat. 39-05-35 N long. 096-49-24 W; 18 mi. SW of Manhattan in NE central Kansas; Descriptively named as a railroad junction.

•**KANOPOLIS,** City; Ellsworth County; Pop. 729; Zip Code 67454; Elev. 1574; Lat. 38-42-33 N long. 098-09-23 W; central Kansas; The town's name is a combination of "Kansas" and "polis."

•**KANORADO,** City; Sherman County; Pop. 217; Zip Code 67741; Elev. 3908; Lat. 39-20-12 N long. 102-02-17 W; NW Kansas; The city's name is a combination of Kansas and Colorado.

•**KANSAS CITY,** City; Wyandotte County Seat; Pop. 161,087; Zip Code 661++; Elev. 740; Lat. 39-06-27 N long. 094-40-11 W; at the confluence of the KS & MO Rivers in NE; Named after the state, itself named for the Kansas Indians.

•**KECHI,** City; Sedgwick County; Pop. 288; Zip Code 67067; Elev. 1380; Lat. 37-47-44 N long. 097-16-51 W; S central Kansas; Kechi is named after the Kechi Indians.

•**KENSINGTON,** City; Smith County; Pop. 681; Zip Code 66951; Elev. 1784; Lat. 39-45-58 N long. 099-01-57 W; N Kansas; The city is named after Kensington, England.

•**KINCAID,** City; Anderson County; Pop. 192; Zip Code 66039; Elev. 1045; Lat. 38-04-39 N long. 095-12-01 W; E Kansas; A railroad promoter named Kincaid left his name on the city.

•**KINGMAN,** City; Kingman County Seat; Pop. 3,563; Zip Code 67068 Elev. 1550; Lat. 37-31-37 N long. 097-59-30 W; S central Kansas; Kingman is named in honor of Samuel Kingman, who served as Chief Justice of the State Supreme Court.

•**KINSLEY,** City; Edwards County Seat; Pop. 2,074; Zip Code 67547; Elev. 2170; Lat. 37-55-15 N long. 099-24-40 W; SW central Kansas; The town is named after New England settler E. W. Kinsley.

•**KIOWA,** City; Barber County; Pop. 1,409; Zip Code 67070; Elev. 1330; Lat. 37-00-57 N long. 098-28-56 W; S Kansas; The city is named for the Kiowa Indians.

•**KIRWIN,** City; Phillips County; Pop. 249; Zip Code 67644; Elev. 1696; Lat. 39-40-18 N long. 099-07-22 W; N Kansas; Named for an early settler.

•**KISMET,** City; Seward County; Pop. 368; Zip Code 67859; Elev. 2775; Lat. 37-12-05 N long. 100-41-54 W; SW Kansas; Kismet is named after the Turkish word for "destiny."

•**LA CROSSE,** City; Rush County Seat; Pop. 1,618; Zip Code 67548; Elev. 2060; Lat. 38-31-50 N long. 099-18-18 W; central Kansas; The city is named after the famous Indian game.

•**LA CYGNE,** City; Linn County; Pop. 1,025; Zip Code 66040; Elev. 828; Lat. 38-20-44 N long. 094-45-40 W; E Kansas; Once the home of a flock of swans, La Cygne is French for swan.

•**LA HARPE,** City; Allen County; Pop. 687; Zip Code 66751; Elev. 1040; Lat. 37-54-57 N long. 095-17-57 W; SE Kansas; The city is named for 18th century explorer Bernard De La Harpe.

•**LAKE QUIVIRA,** City; Johnson & Wyandotte Counties; Pop. 1,087; E Kansas; Quivira was the name of a mystical land of treasure of the 16th century Spanish believed lay in central North America.

•**LAKIN,** City; Kearny County Seat; Pop. 1,823; Zip Code 67860; Elev. 3001; Lat. 37-56-34 N long. 101-15-35 W; W Kansas; David Lakin was a Santa Fe Railroad board member in the 1860's. The town is named after him.

•**LANCASTER,** City; Atchison County; Pop. 274; Zip Code 66041; Elev. 1150; Lat. 39-34-13 N long. 095-18-13 W; NE Kansas; Lancaster is named for the city in England.

•**LANE,** City; Franklin County; Pop. 249; Zip Code 66042; Elev. 910; Lat. 38-26-20 N long. 095-04-41 W; E Kansas; Lane is named in honor of James Lane, who served Kansas as its first U. S. Senator.

•**LANGDON,** City; Reno County; Pop. 84; Zip Code 67549; Elev. 908; Lat. 37-51-14 N long. 098-19-25 W; central Kansas; The city is named after an early settler.

•**LANSING,** City; Leavenworth County; Pop. 5,307; Zip Code 66043; Elev. 40 mi. NW of Topeka in NE Kansas; The town's name honors founder James W. Lansing.

•**LARNED,** City; Pawnee County Seat; Pop. 4,811; Zip Code 67550; Elev. 2004; Lat. 38-10-56 N long. 099-06-00 W; central Kansas; Larned is named after Colonel Benjamin Larned, Army Pay-Master-General in 1860.

•**LATHAM,** City; Butler County; Pop. 148; Zip Code 67072; Elev. 1470; Lat. 37-31-41 N long. 096-38-21 W; S Kansas; The town is named after railroad commissioner Latham Young.

•**LAWRENCE,** City; Douglas County Seat; Pop. 52,738; Zip Code 66044; Elev. 850; Lat. 38-57-32 N long. 095-14-51 W; 25 mi. E of Topeka in NE Kansas; The city of Lawrence, Kansas is named for town promoter Amos Lawrence.

•**LE ROY,** City; Coffey County; Pop. 701; Zip Code 66857; Elev. 1007; Lat. 38-15-19 N long. 095-38-03 W; E Kansas; Le Roy, Kansas is named after Le Roy, Illinois.

•**LEAVENWORTH,** City; Leavenworth County Seat; Pop. 5,307; Zip Code 66048; Elev. 900; Lat. 39-21-36 N long. 094-55-08 W; 22 mi. NW of Kansas City in NE Kansas; Leavenworth is named in honor of General Henry Leavenworth.

•**LEAWOOD,** City; Johnson County; Pop. 13,360; Zip Code 662++; Elev. S of Kansas City in E Kansas; The city's name honors retired policeman, Oscar G. Lea.

•**LEBANON,** City; Smith County; Pop. 440; Zip Code 66952; Elev. 1821; Lat. 39-48-34 N long. 098-33-20 W; N Kansas; Lebanon is named for the Biblical country to the north of Palestine.

•**LEBO,** City; Coffey County; Pop. 966; Zip Code 66858; Elev. 1157; Lat. 38-24-51 N long. 095-51-18 W; E Kansas; Lebo's name remembers Civil War merchant Joe Lebo.

•**LECOMPTON,** City; Douglas County; Pop. 576; Zip Code 66050; Elev. 950; Lat. 39-02-33 N long. 095-23-33 W; E Kansas; The town is named after pioneer Judge Samuel Lecompte.

•**LENEXA,** City; Johnson County; Pop. 18,639; Zip Code 662++; Elev. 10 mi. SW of Kansas City in E Kansas; Lenexa is an Indian name - probably an Indian woman's name.

•**LENORA,** City; Norton County; Pop. 444; Zip Code 67645; Elev. 2270; Lat. 39-36-36 N long. 100-00-12 W; N Kansas; Named after early pioneer Lenora Hanson.

•**LEON,** City; Butler County; Pop. 667; Zip Code 67074; Elev. 1350; Lat. 37-40-59 N long. 096-46-49 W; S Kansas; Leon, Kansas is named after Leon, Iowa.

•**LEONA,** City; Doniphan County; Pop. 73; Zip Code 66448; Elev. 950; Lat. 39-47-11 N long. 095-19-18 W; NE corner of Kansas; Leona is named for the first child born in the community.

•**LEONARDVILLE,** City; Riley County; Pop. 437; Zip Code 66449; Elev. 1385; Lat. 39-21-53 N long. 096-51-27 W; NE central Kansas; Originally called Alembic, the town's occupants changed the name to Leonardville, or "village of the lion heart."

•**LEOTI,** City; Wichita County Seat; Pop. 1,869; Zip Code 67861; Elev. 3305; Lat. 38-28-52 N long. 101-21-22 W; W Kansas; Named for an early female settler.

•**LEWIS,** City; Edwards County; Pop. 551; Zip Code 67552; Elev. 2140; Lat. 37-56-06 N long. 099-15-12 W; SW central Kansas; Lewis is named after M. M. Lewis, a journalist who dabbled in law and real estate.

•**LIBERAL,** City; Seward County Seat; Pop. 14,911; Zip Code 67901; Elev. 2836; on the Oklahoma border in SW Kansas; "Liberal refers to a generous pioneer who "liberally" supplied well water to local travellers.

•**LIEBENTHAL,** City; Rush County; Pop. 163; Zip Code 67553; Elev. 1976; Lat. 38-39-08 N long. 099-19-00 W; central Kansas; German settlers named the town, it means "valley of love."

•**LINCOLN CENTER,** City; Lincoln County Seat; Pop. 1,599; Zip Code 67455; Elev. central Kansas; The city's name honors President Abraham Lincoln.

•**LINCOLNVILLE,** City; Marion County; Pop. 235; Zip Code 66858; Elev. 1420; Lat. 38-29-32 N long. 096-57-34 W; E central Kansas; Lincolnville's name honors Abraham Lincoln.

•**LINDSBORG,** City; McPherson County; Pop. 3,155; Zip Code 67456; Elev. 1333; Lat. 38-34-39 N long. 097-40-31 W; central Kansas; Lind was a common Swedish surname of the area's settlers.

•**LINN,** City; Washington County; Pop. 483; Zip Code 66953; Elev. 1460; Lat. 39-40-54 N long. 097-05-07 W; N K S.; The city is named after a Missouri politician.

•**LINWOOD,** City; Leavenworth County; Pop. 343; Zip Code 66052; Elev. 800; Lat. 39-00-03 N long. 095-01-56 W; NE Kansas; Linwood was named for the local linwood trees.

•**LITTLE RIVER,** City; Rice County; Pop. 529; Zip Code 67457; Elev. 1590; Lat. 38-23-53 N long. 098-00-35 W; central Kansas; Descriptively named for a local geographic feature.

•**LOGAN,** City; Phillips County; Pop. 187; Zip Code 67646; Elev. 1970; Lat. 39-39-43 N long. 099-34-06 W; N Kansas; The town is named for General John Logan.

•**LONG ISLAND,** City; Phillips County; Pop. 187; Zip Code 67647; Elev. 2071; Lat. 39-56-53 N long. 099-31-59 W; N Kansas; The city is named after the great island of New York.

•**LONGFORD,** City; Clay County; Pop. 109; Zip Code 67458; Elev. 1350; Lat. 39-10-21 N long. 097-19-45 W; NE central Kansas; The city is named for Longford, Ireland.

•**LONGTON,** City; Elk County; Pop. 396; Zip Code 67352; Elev. 918; Lat. 37-22-56 N long. 096-05-15 W; SE Kansas; Longton is named for Longton, England.

•**LORRAINE,** City; Ellsworth County; Pop. 157; Zip Code 67459; Elev. 1781; Lat. 38-34-13 N long. 098-18-58 W; central Kansas; Named after the province in France.

•**LOST SPRINGS**, City; Marion County; Pop. 94; Zip Code 66859; Elev. 1490; Lat. 38-33-55 N long. 096-57-54 W; E central Kansas; Descriptively named for the springs tendency to go dry part of the year.

•**LOUISBURG**; city; Miami County; Pop. 1,744; Zip Code 66053; Elev. 1075; Lat. 38-37-10 N long. 094-40-51 W; E Kansas; Named in honor of the Bourbon Kings of France.

•**LOUISVILLE**, City; Pottawatomie County; Pop. 207; Zip Code 66450; Elev. 1000; Lat. 39-14-52 N long. 096-18-48 W; NE Kansas; Named after Louisville, Kentucky.

•**LUCAS**, City; Russell County; Pop. 524; Zip Code 67648; Elev. 1500; Lat. 39-03-31 N long. 098-32-15 W; central Kansas; The city takes its name from Lucas Place in Saint Louis.

•**LURAY**, City; Russell County; Pop. 295; Zip Code 67649; Elev. 1570; Lat. 39-06-51 N long. 098-41-28 W; central Kansas; The town is named after a city in Virginia.

•**LYNDON**, City; Osage County Seat; Pop. 1,132; Zip Code 66451; Elev. 1030; Lat. 38-36-35 N long. 095-41-11 W; E Kansas

•**LYONS**, City; Rice County Seat; Pop. 4,152; Zip Code 67554; Elev. 1700; Lat. 38-20-46 N long. 098-12-01 W; central Kansas; Lyons is named for Civil War hero General Nathaniel Lyon.

•**MACKSVILLE**, City; Stafford County; Pop. 546; Zip Code 67460; Elev. 2035; Lat. 37-57-31 N long. 098-58-08 W; central Kansas; The city is named after a prominent settler.

•**MADISON**, City; Greenwood County; Pop. 1,099; Zip Code 66860; Elev. 1100; Lat. 38-06-52 N long. 096-01-43 W; SE Kansas; Madison's name honors James Madison, the fourth President of the United States.

•**MAHASKA**, City; Washington County; Pop. 119; Zip Code 66955; Elev. 1600; Lat. 39-59-16 N long. 097-21-11 W; N Kansas; The name of a famous Sioux Indian chief, the name means "white cloud."

•**MAIZE**, City; Sedgwick County; Pop. 1,294; Zip Code 67101; Elev. 1350; Lat. 37-46-24 N long. 097-27-59 W; S central Kansas; Named by its settlers for the abundant corn crop grown here.

•**MANCHESTER**, City; Dickinson County; Pop. 98; Zip Code 67463; Elev. 1295; Lat. 39-05-36 N long. 097-19-16 W; E central Kansas; The city is named after Manchester, England.

•**MANHATTAN**, City; Pottawatomie & Riley Counties; Riley County Seat; Pop. 32,644; ; Zip Code 66502; Elev. 1020; Lat. 39-12-19 N long. 096-32-59 W; 50 mi. W of Topeka in NE central Kansas; This Kansas city is named after Manhattan Island in New York.

•**MANKATO**, City; Jewell County Seat; Pop. 1,205; Zip Code 66956; Elev. 1776; Lat. 39-47-04 N long. 098-12-21 W; N Kansas; Mankato is a Sioux Indian word meaning "blue earth."

•**MANTER**, City; Stanton County; Pop. 205; Zip Code 67862; Elev. 3490; Lat. 37-31-20 N long. 101-53-06 W; SW Kansas; Manter, Kansas is named after a local Santa Fe Railroad official.

•**MAPLE HILL**, City; Wabaunsee County; Pop. 381; Zip Code Elev. 960; Lat. 39-05-07 N long. 096-01-36 W; E Kansas; Descriptively named for its site: a hill with maple trees on it.

•**MAPLETON**, City; Bourbon County; Pop. 121; Zip Code 66754; Elev. 878; Lat. 38-00-52 N long. 094-53-01 W; SE Kansas; The city is named for the beloved maple tree found in the vicinity.

•**MARION**, City; Marion County Seat; Pop. 1,951; Zip Code 66861; Elev. 1307; Lat. 38-20-53 N long. 097-00-37 W; E central Kansas; Named in honor of Revolutionary War hero, General Francis Marion.

•**MARQUETTE**, City; McPherson County; Pop. 639; Zip Code 67464; Elev. 1385; Lat. 38-33-15 N long. 097-50-03 W; central Kansas; The city is named for the famous French explorer who travelled down the Mississippi in the late 1600's.

•**MARYSVILLE**, City; Marshall County Seat; Pop. 3,670; Zip Code 66508; Elev. 1202; Lat. 39-53-32 N long. 096-42-48 W; NE Kansas; The town is named after the wife of its founder, Mary Williams.

•**MATFIELD GREEN**, City; Chase County; Pop. 71; Zip Code 66862; Elev. 1430; Lat. 38-09-35 N long. 096-33-33 W; E central Kansas; The town is named after a suburb of London.

•**MAYETTA**, City; Jackson County; Pop. 287; Zip Code 66509; Elev. 1200; Lat. 39-20-20 N long. 095-43-13 W; NE Kansas; The city is named after an early woman settler.

•**MAYFIELD**, City; Sumner County; Pop. 128; Zip Code 67103; Elev. 1281; Lat. 37-15-46 N long. 097-32-45 W; S Kansas; Descriptively named by its settlers to reflect a young female settler's love of the nearby prairie, or May's field.

•**MCCRACKEN**, City; Rush County; Pop. 292; Zip Code 67556; Elev. 2141; Lat. 38-34-53 N long. 099-33-48 W; central Kansas; The town is named after a settler of Scotch descent.

•**MCCUNE**, City; Crawford County; Pop. 528; Zip Code 66753; Lat. 37-21-09 N long. 095-01-07 W; SE Kansas; A Scotch settler named McCune left his name on the town.

•**MCDONALD**, City; Rawlins County; Pop. 239; Zip Code 67745; Elev. 3360; Lat. 39-47-09 N long. 101-22-11 W; NW Kansas; McDonald is named for a Scottish settler.

•**MCLOUTH**, City; Jefferson County; Pop. 700; Zip Code 66054; Elev. 1180; Lat. 39-11-37 N long. 095-12-29 W; NE Kansas; McClouth is a Scottish name and recalls an early pioneer in the area.

•**MCPHERSON**, City; McPherson County Seat; Pop. 11,753; Zip Code 67460; Elev. 1504; Lat. 38-22-16 N long. 097-39-41 N; 27 mi. NE of Hutchinson in central Kansas; McPherson was an early pioneer of Scottish background who gave his name to the town.

•**MEADE**, City; Meade County Seat; Pop. 1,777; Zip Code 67864; Elev. 2497; Lat. 37-17-10 N long. 100-20-15 W; NW Kansas; The city is named after Civil War General, George Meade.

•**MEDICINE LODGE**, City; Barber County Seat; Pop. 2,384; Zip Code 67104; Elev. 1510; Lat. 37-17-03 N long. 098-34-53 W; S Kansas; Kiowa Indians took medicine baths in the nearby river, and thus gave it the name Medicine Lodge.

•**MELVERN**, City; Osage County; Pop. 481; Zip Code 66510; Elev. 1,012; Lat. 38-30-30 N long. 095-38-13 W; E Kansas; Melvern is named for a series of hills in Worcestershire, England.

•**MENLO**, City; Thomas County; Pop. 42; Zip Code 67746; Elev. 2,945; Lat. 39-21-15 N long. 100-43-31 W; NW Kansas; The origin of the town's name is uncertain.

•**MERIDEN**, City; Jefferson County; Pop. 707; Zip Code 66512; Elev. 970; Lat. 39-11-20 N long. 095-34-08 W; NE Kansas; Pioneer Newell Colby named the town after his former home in Meriden, New Hampshire.

•**MERRIAM**, City; Johnson County; Pop. 10,794; suburb of Kansas City in E Kansas; The city is named after the man who secured the railroad route for the town.

•**MILAN,** City; Sumner County; Pop. 135; Zip Code 67105; Elev. 1,221; Lat. 37-15-27 N long. 097-40-34 W; S Kansas; Milan Kansas is named after Milan, Italy.

•**MILDRED,** City; Allen County; Pop. 64; Zip Code 66055; Elev. SE Kansas; Businessman J. W. Wagner named the town for his daughter Mildred.

•**MILFORD,** City; Geary County; Pop. 465; Zip Code 66514; Elev. 1,194; Lat. 39-10-21 N long. 096-55-00 W; NE central Kansas; The town was the site of an early lumber mill.

•**MILTONVALE,** City; Cloud County; Pop. 588; Zip Code 67466; Elev. 1,373; Lat. 39-20-52 N long. 097-27-01 W; N Kansas; Milton-vale is named after a local settler.

•**MINNEAPOLIS,** City; Ottawa County Seat; Pop. 2,075; Zip Code 67467; Elev. 1,253; Lat. 39-07-32 N long. 097-42-07 W NE central Kansas; This Kansas town is named after the great city in Minnesota.

•**MINNEOLA,** City; Clark County; Pop. 712; Zip Code 67865; Elev. 2,548; Lat. 37-26-16 N long. 100-00-41 W; S Kansas; Named after the wife of an early settler.

•**MISSION,** City; Johnson County; Pop. 8,643; Zip Code 662++; E Kansas; The Rev. Thomas Johnson established a mission for the Indians here in 1829. The town is named after his church.

•**MISSION HILLS,** City; Johnson County; Pop. 3,904; Zip Code 662++; E Kansas; Named after the 1830's Indian mission founded here by Rev. Thomas Johnson.

•**MOLINE,** City; Elk County; Pop. 553; Zip Code 67353; Elev. 1,055; Lat. 37-21-53 N long. 096-18-31 W; SE Kansas; Settlers from Moline, Illinis named the town.

•**MONTEZUMA,** City; Gray County; Pop. 730; Zip Code 67867; Elev. 2,785; Lat. 37-35-46 N long. 100-26-28 W; SW Kansas; The city is named after the famous Aztec Indian ruler.

•**MORAN,** City; Allen County; Pop. 643; Zip Code 66755; Elev. 1,110; Lat. 37-55-01 N long. 095-10-11 W; SE Kansas; The town is named for an Irish settler who came here in the 19th century.

•**MORGANVILLE,** City; Clay County; Pop. 261; Zip Code 67468; Elev. 1,233; Lat. 39-28-05 N long. 097-12-17 W; NE central Kansas; The town is named for a prominent early settler.

•**MORLAND,** City; Graham County; Pop. 223; Zip Code 67650; Elev. 2,310; Lat. 39-21-02 N long. 100-04-22 W; NW central Kansas; Morland recalls the name of a pioneer settler.

•**MORRILL,** City; Brown County; Pop. 336; Zip Code 66515; Elev. 1,091; Lat. 39-55-45 N long. 095-41-32 W; NE Kansas; The town is named for E. N. Morrill who served as Governor of Kansas in 1894.

•**MORROWVILLE,** City; Washington County; Pop. 180; Zip Code 66958; Elev. 1,350; Lat. 39-50-41 N long. 097-10-19 W; N Kansas; Named in honor of legislator James C. Morrow.

•**MOSCOW,** City; Stevens County; Pop. 228; Zip Code 67952; Elev. 3,045; SW Kansas; The city is named after the great Russian city.

•**MOUND CITY,** City; Linn County Seat; Pop. 755; Zip Code 66056; Elev. 875; Lat. 38-08-35 N long. 094-48-44 W; E Kansas; Descriptively named for the Indian mounds nearby.

•**MOUND VALLEY,** City; Labette County; Pop. 381; Zip Code 67354; Elev. 850; Lat. 37-12-29 N LONG. 095-24-18 W; SE Kansas; The name of a row of hills in La Bette County.

•**MOUNDRIDGE,** City; McPherson County; Pop. 1,453; Zip Code 67107; Lat. 38-12-02 N long. 097-31-07 W; central Kansas; The name refers to a small hill above Black Kettle Creek.

•**MOUNT HOPE,** City; Sedgwick County; Pop. 791; Zip Code 67108; Elev. 1,440; Lat. 37-52-05 N long. 097-39-55 W; S central Kansas; The city is named after Mount Hope, Michigan.

•**MULBERRY,** City; Crawford County; Pop. 647; Zip Code 66756; Elev. 950; Lat. 37-33-27 N long. 094-37-12 W; SE Kansas; Descriptively named for the mulberry trees planted here.

•**MULLINVILLE,** City; Kiowa County; Pop. 339; Zip Code 67109; Elev. 2,330; Lat. 37-35-23 N long. 099-28-33 W; S Kansas; Mullin-ville is named after Judge Mullin, its founder.

•**MULVANE,** City; Sedgwick & Sumner Counties; Pop. 4,254; Zip Code 67110; Elev. 1,250; Lat. 37-28-38 N long. 097-14-26 W; S central Kansas; The city is named in honor of the Mulvane brothers who were Topeka bankers and land developers.

•**MUNDEN,** City; Republic County; Pop. 152; Zip Code 66959; Elev. 1,630; Lat. 39-54-44 N long. 097-32-14 W; N Kansas; Named after the city of Munden, Germany.

•**MUSCOTAH,** City; Atchison County; Pop. 248; Zip Code 66058; Elev. 964; Lat. 39-33-13 N long. 095-31-13 W; NE Kansas; Muscotah is an Indian name meaning "beautiful prairie."

•**NARKA,** City; Republic County; Pop. 120; Zip Code 66960; Elev. 1,585; Lat. 39-57-36 N long. 097-25-29 W; N Kansas; The town is named after the daughter of a Rock Island Railroad official.

•**NASHVILLE,** City; Kingman County; Pop. 127; Zip Code 67112; Elev. 1,740; Lat. 37-26-18 N long. 098-25-23 W; S central Kansas; The city is named for the southern city of Nashville, Tennessee.

•**NATOMA,** City; Osborne County; Pop. 515; Zip Code 67651; Elev. 1,834; Lat. 39-11-19 N long. 099-01-22 W; N central Kansas; Natoma is an Indian name of uncertain origin.

•**NEODESHA,** City; Wilson County; Pop. 3,414; Zip Code 66757; Elev. 819; Lat. 37-25-24 N long. 095-40-49 W; SE Kansas; An Osage Indian word meaning "muddy water."

•**NEOSHA FALLS,** City; Woodson County; Pop. 157; Zip Code 66758; Elev. 975; Lat. 38-00-12 N long. 095-33-16 W; SE Kansas; Neosha is an Indian word meaning "muddy water."

•**NEOSHA RAPIDS,** City; Lyon County; Pop. 289; Zip Code 66864; Elev. 1,090; Lat. 38-22-03 N long. 095-59-20 W; E Kansas; Descriptively named for the rapids on the Neosha River.

•**NESS CITY,** City; Ness County; Pop. 1,769; Zip Code 67560; Elev. 2,251; Lat. 38-27-21 N long. 099-54-16 W; W central Kansas; Ness City's name honors Corporal Noah Ness who was killed in the Civil War.

•**NETAWAKA,** City; Jackson County; Pop. 218; Zip Code 66516; Elev. 1,150; Lat. 39-36-14 N long. 095-43-10 W; NE Kansas; Netawaka is a Potawatomi Indian word meaning "grand view."

•**NEW CAMBRIA,** City; saline County; Pop. 175; Zip Code 67470; Elev. 1,196; Lat. 38-52-39 N long. 097-30-16 W; central Kansas.

•**NEWTON,** City; Harvey County Seat; Pop. 16,332; Zip Code 67114; Elev. 1,448; Lat. 38-02-48 N long. 097-20-39 W; 35 mi. E of Hutchinson in SE central Kansas; Newton is named after Newton, Mass.

•**NICKERSON,** City; Reno County; Pop. 1,292; Zip Code 67561; Elev. 1,593; Lat. 38-08-49 N long. 098-05-12 W; central Kansas; The city is named for a Santa Fe Railroad president.

•NIOTAZE, City; Chautauqua County; Pop. 104; Zip Code 67355; Elev. 765; Lat. 37-04-06 N long.096-00-43 W; SE Kansas; Named after Niota, Illinois.

•NORCATUR, City; Decatur County; Pop. 226; Zip Code 67653; Elev. 2,700; Lat. 39-50-07 N long. 100-11-15 W; NW Kansas; Norcatur is a combination of Norton and Decatur.

•NORTH NEWTON, City; Harvey County; Pop. 1,222; Zip Code 67117; Elev. 1,440; Lat. 38-04-21 N long. 097-20-39 W; SE central Kansas; Named for Newton, Kansas.

•NORTON, City; Norton County Seat; Pop. 3,400; Zip Code 67654; Elev. 2,300; Lat. 39-50-00 N long. 099-53-30 W; N Kansas; The town's name honors Civil War-era soldier Orloff Norton.

•NORTONVILLE, City; Jefferson County; Pop. 692; Zip Code 66060; Elev. 1,163; Lat. 39-25-02 N long.095-19-57 W; NE Kansas; Named for Civil War hero Orloff Norton.

•NORWICH, City; Kingman County; Pop. 476; Zip Code 67118; Elev. 1,490; Lat. 37-27-28 N long. 097-50-56 W; S central Kansas; Norwich is named for the village in England.

•OAK HILL, City; Clay County; Pop. 35; Zip Code 67472; Elev. 1,280; Lat. 39-14-48 N long.097-20-38 W; NE central Kansas; Descriptively named for its oak trees.

•OAKLEY, City; Logan & Thomas Counties; Pop. 2,343; Zip Code 67748; Elev. 350; W Kansas; Originally Carlyle, the name was changed to honor Miss Eliza Oakley.

•OBERLIN, City; Decatur County; Pop. 2,387; Zip Code 67749; Elev. 2,562; Lat. 39-49-35 N long. 100-31-20 W; NW Kansas; Oberlin, Kansas is named after Oberlin, Ohio.

•OFFERLE, City; Edwards County; Pop. 244; Zip Code 67563; Elev. 2,270; Lat. 37-53-23 N long. 099-33-39 W; SW central Kansas; Laurence Offerle surveyed the townsite. It is named after him.

•OGDEN, City; Riley County; Pop. 1,804; Zip Code 66517; Elev. 1,048; Lat. 39-06-40 N long. 096-42-25 W; NE central Kansas; Named in honor of Major Edmund Ogden.

•OKETO, City; Marshall County; Pop. 130; Zip Code 66518; Elev. 1,178; Lat. 39-57-45 N long. 096-35-50 W; NE Kansas; An abbreviated English name for Arkaketah, an Oto Indian chief in the 19th century.

•OLATHE, City; Johnson County Seat; Pop. 37,258; Zip Code 660++; Elev. 1,040; Lat. 38-52-50 N long. 094-48-39 W; 20 mi. SW of Kansas City in E Kansas; Olathe is a Shawnee Indian word meaning "beautiful."

•OLMITZ, City; Barton County; Pop. 140; Zip Code 67564; Elev. 2,010; Lat. 38-31-03 N long. 098-56-08 W; central Kansas; The city is named for a city in eastern Bohemia.

•OLPE, City; Lyon County; Pop. 477; Zip Code 66865; Elev. 1,200; Lat. 38-15-39 N long.096-10-03 W; E Kansas; Olpe is named after a German town.

•OLSBURG, City; Pottawatomie County; Pop. 166; Zip Code 66520; Lat. 39-25-50 N long. 096-36-47 W; NE Kansas; Named for an early Swedish settler.

•ONAGA, City; Pottawatomie County; Pop. 752; Zip Code 66521; Elev. 1,150; Lat. 39-29-26 N long.096-10-02 W; NE Kansas; Onaga is a Pottawatomie Indian personal name.

•ONEIDA, City; Nemaha County; Pop. 120; Zip Code 66522; Elev. 1,213; Lat. 39-51-55 N long. 095-56-28 W; NE Kansas; The city is named for a tribe of Iroquois Indians from the New York State area.

•OSAGE CITY, City; Osage County; Pop. 2,667; Zip Code 66523; Elev. 1,085; Lat. 38-38-03 N long. 095-49-29 W; E Kansas; Named after the Osage Indians.

•OSAWATOMIE, City; Miami County; Pop. 4,459; Zip Code 66064; Elev. 865; Lat. 38-29-51 N long. 094-57-09 W; E Kansas; Osawatomie is a combination of Osage and Pottawatomie.

•OSBORNE, City; Osborne County Seat; Pop. 2,120; Zip Code 67473; Elev. 1,554; Lat. 39-26-23 N long. 098-41-51 W; N central Kansas; Osborne's name honors Civil War veteran Vincent B. Osborne.

•OSKALOOSA, City; Jefferson County; Pop. 1,092; Zip Code 66066; Elev. 1,123; Lat. 39-12-56 N long. 095-18-54 W; NE Kansas; A Creek or Seminole Indian name meaning "black water."

•OSWEGO, City; Labette County Seat; Pop. 2,218; Zip Code 67356; Elev. 900; Lat. 37-09-56 N long. 095-06-32 W; SE Kansas; Named for a New York State Iroquois Indian tribe.

•OTIS, City; Rush County; Pop. 410; Zip Code 67565; Elev. 2,035; Lat. 38-31-55 N long. 099-02-58 W; central Kansas; Named in honor of Otis Modderwell.

•OTTAWA, City; Franklin County Seat; Pop. 11,016; Zip Code 66067; Elev. 901; Lat. 38-36-41 N long. 095-15-48 W; E Kansas; A Huron Indian name referring to a particular tribe, the name means "men of the bulrushes."

•OVERBROOK, City; Osage County; Pop. 930; Zip Code 66524; Elev. 1,220; Lat. 38-46-43 N long. 095-33-22 W; E Kansas; Early settlers named the town for a suburb of Philadelphia.

•OVERLAND PARK, City; Johnson County; Pop. 81,784; Zip Code 662++; S of Kansas City in E Kansas; Descriptively named for its location on a ridge which gave a panoramic view of the overland trail.

•OXFORD, City; Sumner County; Pop. 1,125; Zip Code 67119; Elev. 1,185; Lat. 37-16-18 N long. 097-10-10 W; S Kansas; Named after the great English univeristy town.

•OZAWKIE, City; Jefferson County; Pop. 472; Zip Code 66070; Elev. 1,000; Lat. 39-13-34 N long. 095-26-37 W; NE Kansas; Named after a well-known Sac Indian Chief, Ozawkie, or "yellow earth."

•PALCO, City; Rooks County; Pop. 329; Zip Code 67657; Elev. 2,280; Lat. 39-15-13 N long. 099-33-43 W; N Kansas; Palco is a combined name made by adding the names of two railroad workers: Palmer and Coe.

•PALMER, City; Washington County; Pop. 149; Zip Code 66962; Elev. 1,325; Lat. 39-38-01 N long. 097-08-16 W; N Kansas; Named for an early settler.

•PAOLA, City; Miami County Seat; Pop. 4,557; Zip Code 66071; Elev. 900; Lat. 38-34-20 N long. 094-53-33 W; E Kansas; With slight aleration the town is named after French linguist, Baptiste Peoria.

•PARADISE, City; Russell County; Pop. 89; Zip Code 67658; Elev. 1,695; Lat. 39-06-49 N long. 098-55-00 W; central Kansas; Religious early settlers named their new home after the Biblical "paradise."

•PARK, City; Gove County; Pop. 183; Zip Code 67751; Elev. 2,750; Lat. 39-06-42 N long. 100-21-32 W; W Kansas; Descriptively named for its park-like setting.

•PARKER, City; Linn County; Pop. 270; Zip Code 66072; Elev. 1,005; Lat. 38-19-42 N long. 094-59-11 W; E Kansas; Parker is named in honor of an early settler.

•**PARSONS,** City; Labette County; Pop. 12,898; Zip Code 67357; Elev. 907; Lat. 37-20-16 N long. 095-16-08 W; SE Kansas; Judge Levi Parsons, a New York Railroad promoter, brought the railroad to the area. It is named for him.

•**PARTRIDGE,** City; Reno County; Pop. 268; Zip Code 67566; Elev. 1,610; Lat. 37-57-54 N long. 098-05-33 W; central Kansas; The town is named after the common game bird.

•**PAWNEE ROCK,** City; Barton County; Pop. 409; Zip Code 67567; Lat. 38-15-53 N long. 098-58-51 W; central Kansas; Named after the Pawnee Indians as the site of an Indian battle between the Pawnees and the Comanches.

•**PAXICO,** City; Wabaunsee County; Pop. 168; Zip Code 66526; Elev. 990; Lat. 39-04-09 N long. 096-09-54 W; E Kansas; An anglicized version of the name of a Potawatomi Indian chief, Chief Pashqua.

•**PEABODY,** City; Marion County; Pop. 1,474; Zip Code 66866; Elev. 1,361; Lat. 38-10-26 N long. 097-06-31 W; E central Kansas; The town's name honors Boston philanthropist F. H. Peabody who was a Santa Fe Railroad director.

•**PENALOSA,** City; Kingman County; Pop. 31; Zip Code 67121; Elev. 1,725; Lat. 37-43-00 N long. 098-19-09 W; S central Kansas; The city is named after an early governor of Spanish New Mexico Don Diego Penalosa Berdugo.

•**PERRY,** City; Jefferson County; Pop. 907; Zip Code 66073; Elev. 850; Lat. 39-04-28 N long. 095-23-38 W; NE Kansas; Named for a prominent early settler.

•**PERU,** City; Chautauqua County; Pop. 286; Zip Code 67360; Elev. 784; Lat. 37-04-51 N long. 096-05-44 W; SE Kansas; Named for Peru, Illinois.

•**PHILLIPSBURG,** City; Phillips County Seat; Pop. 3,229; Zip Code 67661; Elev. 1,951; Lat. 39-42-59 N long. 099-22-18 W; NE Kansas; Phillipsburg is named after New York Tribune reporter, William A. Phillips.

•**PITTSBURG,** City; Crawford County; Pop. 18,770; Zip Code 66762; Elev. 944; Lat. 37-25-50 N long. 094-41-54 W; 30 mi. S of Fort Scott in SE Kansas

•**PLAINVILLE,** City; Rooks County; Pop. 2,458; Zip Code 67663; Elev. 2,143; Lat. 39-13-51 N long. 099-18-05 W; N Kansas; Descriptively named for the city's great plains location.

•**PLEASANTON,** City; Linn County; Pop. 1,303; Zip Code 66075; Elev. 861; Lat. 38-10-31 N long. 094-42-41 W; E Kansas; Named for General Alfred Pleasanton who served in Kansas in the 1850's.

•**PLEVNA,** City; Reno County; Pop. 115; Zip Code 67568; Elev. 1,684; Lat. 37-58-15 N long. 098-18-32 W; central Kansas; Plevna is a province in Bulgaria. This Kansas town is named for that place.

•**POMONA,** City; Franklin County; Pop. 868; Zip Code 66076; Elev. 965; Lat. 38-36-41 N long. 095-27-11 W; E Kansas; The town's name honors the queen of fruit, the apple.

•**PORTIS,** City; Osborne County; Pop. 172; Zip Code 67474; Elev. 1,542; Lat. 39-33-43 N long. 098-41-27 W; N central Kansas; Portis was a Missouri-Pacific Railroad vice-president. The town is named for that person.

•**POTWIN,** City; Butler County; Pop. 563; Zip Code 67123; Elev. 1,340; Lat. 37-56-14 N long. 097-01-08 W; S Kansas; Named for an early settler.

•**POWHATTAN,** City; Brown County; Pop. 95; Zip Code 66527; Elev. 1,203; Lat. 39-45-42 N long. 095-37-58 W; NE Kansas; Named for Indian Chief Powhattan, the father of Pochahontas.

•**PRAIRIE VIEW,** City; Phillips County; Pop. 145; Zip Code 67664; Elev. 2,200; Lat. 39-49-54 N long. 099-34-23 W; N Kansas; Descriptively named for the view of the prairie from the town.

•**PRAIRIE VILLAGE,** City; Johnson County; Pop. 24,657; Zip Code 66208; S of Kansas City in NE Kansas; Named for the location on the prairie.

•**PRATT,** City; Pratt County; Pop. 6,885; Zip Code 67124; Elev. 1,890; Lat. 37-38-18 N long. 098-49-10 W; 54 mi. WSW of Hutchinson in S cen Kansas; Pratt's name honors Civil War hero Caleb Pratt.

•**PRESCOTT,** City; Linn County; Pop. 319; Zip Code 66767; Elev. 880; Lat. 38-03-48 N long. 094-41-42 W; E Kansas; C. H. Prescott was auditor of the Fort Scott and Gulf Railroad. The town is named after him.

•**PRESTON,** City; Pratt County; Pop. 227; Zip Code 67569; Elev. 1,840; Lat. 37-45-27 N long. 098-33-21 W; S central Kansas; Named for a prominent settler.

•**PRETTY PRAIRIE,** City; Reno County; Pop. 655; Zip Code 67570; Elev. 1,576; Lat. 37-46-47 N long. 098-01-00 W; central Kansas; Descriptively named for its location on the prairie.

•**PRINCETON,** City; Franklin County; Pop. 244; Zip Code 66078; Elev. 966; Lat. 38-29-18 N long. 095-16-02 W; E Kansas; The city is named for Princeton, Illinois.

•**PROTECTION,** City; Comanche County; Pop. 684; Zip Code 67127; Elev. 1,850; Lat. 37-12-06 N long. 099-29-02 W; S Kansas

•**QUENEMO,** City; Osage County; Pop. 413; Zip Code 66528; Elev. 941; Lat. 38-34-47 N long. 095-31-33 W; E Kansas; The town is named after a famous Sac Chief, Quenemo.

•**QUINTER,** City; Gove County; Pop. 951; Zip Code 67752; Elev. 2,677; Lat. 39-04-12 N long. 100-14-04 W; W Kansas; Named after a popular preacher.

•**RADIUM,** City; Stafford County; Pop. 47; Zip Code 67571; Elev. 1,951; Lat. 38-10-25 N long. 098-53-31 W; central Kansas; Descriptively named for the element radium found in the area.

•**RAMONA,** City; Marion County; Pop. 116; Zip Code 67475; Elev. 1,433; Lat. 38-35-47 N long. 097-03-45 W; E central Kansas; The town is named after a popular novel.

•**RANDALL,** City; Jewell County; Pop. 154; Zip Code 66963; Elev. 1,457; Lat. 39-38-34 N long. 098-02-28 W; N Kansas; Named after Edward Randall, the original landowner.

•**RANDOLPH,** City; Riley County; Pop. 131; Zip Code 66554; Elev. 1,250; Lat. 39-25-42 N long. 096-45-25 W; NE central Kansas; Randolph's name honors its first postmaster, Gardner Randolph.

•**RANSOM,** City; Ness County; Pop. 448; Zip Code 67572; Elev. 2,511; Lat. 38-38-20 N long. 099-55-51 W; W central Kansas; Ransom's name honors General Thomas E. G. Ransom.

•**RANTOUL,** City; Franklin County; Pop. 212; Zip Code 66079; Elev. 892; Lat. 38-32-52 N long. 095-06-00 W; E Kansas; Named after U. S. Senator Rantoul from Massachusetts.

•**RAYMOND,** City; Rice County; Pop. 132; Zip Code 67573; Elev. 1,726; Lat. 38-16-49 N long. 098-24-45 W; central Kansas; Raymond's name honors a director of the Santa Fe Railroad.

•**READING**, City; Lyon County; Pop. 244; Zip Code 66868; Elev. 1,080; Lat. 38-31-06 N long. 095-57-26 W; E Kansas; Named for the English city.

•**REDFIELD**, City; Bourbon County; Pop. 185; Zip Code 66769; Elev. 853; Lat. 37-50-10 N long. 094-52-53 W; SE Kansas; Redfield is named for an early settler.

•**REPUBLIC**, City; Republic County; Pop. 223; Zip Code 66964; Elev. 1,500; Lat. 39-55-23 N long. 097-49-15 W; N Kansas; Republic is named after the Republican River.

•**REXFORD**, City; Thomas County; Pop. 204; Zip Code 67753; Elev. 2,955; Lat. 39-28-07 N long. 100-44-42 W; NW Kansas; Rexford is named for an early settler.

•**RICHFIELD**, City; Morton County Seat; Pop. 81; Zip Code 67953; Elev. 3,400; SW corner of Kansas; Descriptively named for the rich agricultural in the area.

•**RICHMOND**, City; Franklin County; Pop. 510; Zip Code 66080; Elev. 1,010; Lat. 38-24-00 N long. 095-15-03 W; E Kansas; Pioneer landowner John Richmond donated 40 acres to the railroad right-of-way. The town is named for him.

•**RILEY**, City; Riley County; Pop. 779; Zip Code 66531; Elev. 1,300; Lat. 39-17-54 N long. 096-49-32 W; NE central Kansas; Riley is named after an Irish railwayman.

•**ROBINSON**, City; Brown County; Pop. 324; Zip Code 66532; Elev. 955; Lat. 39-48-56 N long. 095-24-45 W; NE Kansas; Charles Robinson was the first state governor of Kansas.

•**ROELAND PARK**, City; Johnson County; Pop. 7,962; S suburb of Kansas City in NE Kansas; An euphonious name given by the town's developers.

•**ROLLA**, City; Morton County; Pop. 417; Zip Code 67954; SW corner of Kansas; Originally called Reit, a post office error resulted in it being spelled Rolla.

•**ROSE HILL**, City; Butler County; Pop. 1,557; Zip Code 67133; Elev. 1,240; Lat. 37-33-04 N long. 097-07-53 W; S Kansas; Probably named for the many wild roses growing near the town site.

•**ROSSVILLE**, City; Shawnee County; Pop. 1,045; Zip Code 66533; Elev. 930; Lat. 39-08-10 N long. 095-57-14 W; NE Kansas; Rossville is named in honor of prominent journalist William W. Ross who came to Kansas in 1855.

•**ROZEL**, City; Pawnee County; Pop. 219; Zip Code 67574; Elev. 2,073; Lat. 38-11-40 N long. 099-24-18 W; central Kansas; Named for the daughter of a land agent in Pawnee County.

•**RUSH CENTER**, City; Rush County; Pop. 207; Zip Code 67575; Elev. 1,995; Lat. 38-27-52 N long. 099-18-22 W; central Kansas; Rush Center is named after Captain Alexander Rush, a Civil War hero.

•**RUSSELL**, City; Russell County Seat; Pop. 5,427; Zip Code 67665; Elev. 1,826; Lat. 38-53-25 N long. 098-51-20 W; 37 mi. N of Great Bend in central Kansas; Russell's name honors Major Aura Russell who was killed during fighting in 1862.

•**SABETHA**, City; Brown & Nemaha Counties; Pop. 2,286; Zip Code 66534; Elev. 1,318; Lat. 39-54-12 N long. 095-48-10 W; NE Kansas; Sabetha is named after the well-known religious observance.

•**ST FRANCIS**, City; Cheyenne County; Pop. 1,610; Zip Code 67756; NW corner of Kansas; The city is named for Francis of Assisi, the Italian saint of the 13th century.

•**ST GEORGE**, City; Pottawatomie County; Pop. 309; Zip Code 66535; NE Kansas; The town is named for the popular English St. George, the dragon killer.

•**ST JOHN**, City; Stafford County Seat; Pop. 1,346; Zip Code 67576; central Kansas; St. John is named after the New Testament saint.

•**ST MARYS**, City; Pottawatomie County; Pop. 1,598; Zip Code 68536; NE Kansas; Named after the Virgin Mary.

•**ST PAUL**, City; Neosho County; Pop. 746; Zip Code 66771; SE Kansas; The city is named for the New Testament saint.

•**SALINA**, City; Saline County Seat; Pop. 41,843; Zip Code 67401; Lat. 38-49-37 N long. 097-36-20 W; 58 mi. NNE of Hutchinson in central Kansas; Salina is descriptively named for nearby salt deposits.

•**SATANTA**, City; Haskell County; Pop. 1,117; Zip Code 67870; Elev. 2,956; Lat. 37-26-14 N long. 100-59-19 W; SW Kansas; Santana was a Kiowa Indian chief. The town is named after him.

•**SAVONBURG**, City; Allen County; Pop. 113; Zip Code 66772; Elev. 950; Lat. 37-44-55 N long. 095-08-23 W; SE Kansas; Swedish settlers named this town, but the reason for their choice is uncertain.

•**SAWYER**, City; Pratt County; Pop. 213; Zip Code 67134; Elev. 1,910; Lat. 37-29-54 N long.098-40-50 W; S central Kansas; Sawyer was a director of the Santa Fe Railroad. The town is named for him.

•**SCAMMON**, City; Cherokee County; Pop. 501; Zip Code 66773; Elev. 900; Lat. 37-16-46 N long. 094-50-12 W; SE corner of Kansas; Scammon's name honors the four pioneer Scammon brothers.

•**SCANDIA**, City; Republic County; Pop. 480; Zip Code 66966; Elev. 1,450; Lat. 39-47-41 N long. 097-47-02 W; N Kansas; An anglicized name referring to settlers from Scandinavia.

•**SCHOENCHEN**, City; Ellis County; Pop. 209; Zip Code 67667; central Kansas; A German place name given by its early settlers, meaning "little beautiful one."

•**SCOTT CITY**, City; Scott County Seat; Pop. 4,154; Zip Code 67871; Elev. 2,978; Lat. 38-28-45 N long. 100-57-13 W; W Kansas; Named in honor of Sir Walter Scott, the 19th century English novelist."

•**SCRANTON** City; Osage County; Pop. 664; Code 66537; Elev. 1,123; Lat. 38-46-50 N long.095-44-25 W; E Kansas; The town is named after Scranton, Pennsylvania.

•**SEDAN**, City; Chautauqua County Seat; Pop. 1,579; Zip Code 67361; Elev. 862; Lat. 37-03-55 N long. 096-13-47 W; SE Kansas; Named for the city of Sedan, site of the final battle in the Franco-Prussion War.

•**SEDGWICK**, City; Harvey & Sedgwick Counties; Pop. 1,471; Zip Code 67135; Elev. 1,379; Lat. 37-55-03 N long. 097-25-35 W; S central Kansas; The town's name honors U. S. General Sedgwick who was a hero in the Civil War.

•**SELDEN**, City; Sheridan County; Pop. 266; Zip Code 67757; Elev. 2,837; Lat. 39-32-29 N long. 100-33-57 W; NW Kansas; Selden is named for an early settler.

•**SENECA**, City; Nemaha County Seat; Pop. 2,389; Zip Code 66538; Elev. 1,131; Lat. 39-50-12 N long. 096-03-54 W; NE Kansas; Seneca, Kansas is named after the Seneca Indians in New York.

•**SEVERANCE,** City; Doniphan County; Pop. 134; Zip Code 66081; Elev. 912; Lat. 39-46-06 N long. 095-15-04 W; NE corner of Kansas; Severance is named for one of its original landowners.

•**SEVERY,** City; Greenwood County; Pop. 447; Zip Code 67137; Elev. 1,120; Lat. 37-37-13 N long. 096-13-42 W; SE Kansas; Severy is named for a director of the Santa Fe Railroad.

•**SEWARD,** City; Stafford County; Pop. 88; Zip Code 67577; Elev. 1,913; Lat. 38-10-41 N long. 098-47-32 W; central Kansas; Named for William Seward, U. S. Secretary of State during the Civil War.

•**SHARON,** City; Barber County; Pop. 283; Zip Code 67138; Elev. 1,464; Lat. 37-14-49 N long.098-25-06 W; S Kansas; The city is named after the Biblical plain of Sharon.

•**SHARON SPRINGS,** City; Wallace County Seat; Pop. 982; Zip Code 67758; Elev. 3,471; Lat. 38-53-40 N long. 101-45-02 W; W Kansas; Named after Sharon Springs, New York.

•**SHAWNEE,** City; Johnson County; Pop. 29,653; Zip Code 662++; Elev. 3,471; Lat. 38-53-40 N long. 101-45-02 W; S suburb of Kansas City in E Kansas; Named for the Algonquin Indians, the Shawnees, who came to Kansas in the 1820's.

•**SILVER LAKE,** City; Shawnee County; Pop. 1,350; Zip Code 66539; Elev. 911; Lat. 39-06-13 N long. 095-51-33 W; NE Kansas; Descriptively named for the lake's silvery appearance.

•**SIMPSON,** City; Cloud & Mitchell Counties; Pop. 123; Zip Code 67478; Elev. 1,337; Lat. 39-23-03 N long. 097-55-53 W; N central Kansas; Named after U. S. Grant's middle name.

•**SMITH CENTER,** City; Smith County; Pop. 2,240; Zip Code 66967; Elev. 1,800; Lat. 39-46-47 N long. 098-47-00 W; N Kansas; The town and the county's name honors Civil War hero James Nelson Smith.

•**SMOLAN,** City; Saline County; Pop. 169; Zip Code 67479; Elev. 1,315; Lat. 38-44-19 N long. 097-40-53 W; central Kansas; Named after the province in Sweden.

•**SOLDIER,** City; Jackson County; Pop. 165; Zip Code 66540; Elev. 1,225; Lat. 39-32-08 N long. 095-57-54 W; NE Kansas; The bloody fighting in and around Kansas during the Civil War led to the town's being named soldier.

•**SOLOMON,** City; Dickinson County; Pop. 1,018; Zip Code 67480; Elev. 1,180; Lat. 38-55-09 N long. 097-22-03 W; E central Kansas; Solomon is named for an early French official.

•**SOUTH HAVEN,** City; Sumner County; Pop. 439; Zip Code 67140; Elev. 1,121; Lat. 37-02-59 N long. 097-24-00 W; S Kansas; Named after New Haven, Connecticut.

•**SOUTH HUTCHINSON,** City; Reno County; Pop. 2,226; central Kansas; Named after C. C. Hutchinson, preacher and Indian agent.

•**SPEARVILLE,** City; Ford County; Pop. 693; Zip Code 67876; Elev. 2,460; Lat. 37-50-58 N long. 099-45-21 W; S Kansas; Boston financier Alden Spear had interests in the Santa Fe Railroad. The town is named after him.

•**SPEED,** City; Phillips County; Pop. 41; Zip Code N Kansas; James Speed was U.S. Attorney-General in Lincoln's cabinet. The town is named for him.

•**SPIVEY,** City; Kingman County; Pop. 83; Zip Code 67142; Elev. 1,510; Lat. 37-26-55 N long. 098-09-55 W; S central Kansas; The town is named for a director of the Santa Fe Railroad.

•**SPRING HILL,** City; Johnson & Miami Counties; Pop. 2,005; Zip Code 66083; Elev. 1,050; Lat. 38-44-46 N long. 094-49-48 W; E Kansas; Named after Spring Hill, Alabama.

•**STAFFORD,** City; Stafford County; Pop. 1,425; Zip Code 67578; Elev. 1,858; Lat. 37-57-53 N long. 098-35-55 W; central Kansas; Named in honor of Civil War hero Captain Lewis Stafford.

•**STARK,** City; Neosho County; Pop. 143; Zip Code 66775; Elev. 1,050; Lat. 37-41-20 N long. 095-08-36 W; SE Kansas; Stark's name honors Revolutionary War hero John Stark.

•**STERLING,** City; Rice County; Pop. 2,312; Zip Code 67579; Elev. 1,640; Lat. 38-12-52 N long. 098-12-16 W; central Kansas; Named for the father of two early settlers, Sterling Rosan.

•**STOCKTON,** City; Rooks County Seat; Pop. 1,825; Zip Code 67669; Elev. 1,792; Lat. 39-26-15 N long. 099-16-04 W; N Kansas; Descriptively named as a cattle-raising town.

•**STRONG CITY,** City; Chase County; Pop. 675; Zip Code 66869; Elev. 1,182; Lat. 38-23-44 N long. 096-32-12 W; E central Kansas; Named in honor of William B. Strong, president of the Santa Fe Railroad.

•**SUBLETTE,** City; Haskell County Seat; Pop. 1,293; Zip Code 67877; Elev. 2,918; Lat. 37-28-47 N long. 100-50-33 W; SW Kansas; Sublette is named for pioneer William L. Sublette.

•**SUMMERFIELD,** City; Marshall County; Pop. 158; Zip Code 66541; Elev. 1,511; Lat. 39-59-46 N long. 096-20-57 W; NE Kansas; Elias Summerfield was a local railroad official. The town is named for him.

•**SYLVAN GROVE,** City; Lincoln County; Pop. 376; Zip Code 67481; Elev. 1,445; Lat. 39-00-45 N long. 098-23-33 W; central Kansas; Descriptively named for the attractive trees found near the town.

•**SYLVIA,** City; Reno County; Pop. 353; Zip Code 67581; Elev. 1,738; Lat. 37-57-33 N long. 098-24-32 W; central KS ; Named after the general manager of the Santa Fe Railroad's wife, Sylvia Peters.

•**SYRACUSE,** City; Hamilton County Seat; Pop. 1,654; Zip Code 67878; Elev. 3,233; Lat. 37-58-54 N long. 101-44-56 W; W Kansas; Named for the ancient Greek city of the same name.

•**TAMPA,** City; Marion County; Pop. 113; Zip Code 67483; Elev. 1,424; Lat. 38-32-52 N long. 097-09-08 W; E central Kansas; Tampa, Kansas is named after Tampa, Florida.

•**TESCOTT,** City; Ottawa County; Pop. 331; Zip Code 67484; Elev. 1,294; Lat. 39-00-41 N long. 097-52-29 W; NE central Kansas; Tescott is named for pioneer T. E. Scott.

•**THAYER,** City; Neosho County; Pop. 517; Zip Code 66776; Elev. 1,033; Lat. 37-29-17 N long. 095-28-15 W; SE Kansas; Boston railway promoter Nathaniel Thayer left his name on the town.

•**TIMKEN,** City; Rush County; Pop. 99; Zip Code 67582; Elev. 1,963; Lat. 38-28-24 N long. 099-10-37 w; central Kansas; The Timken family came to Kansas from Germany. The town is named after them.

•**TIPTON,** City; Mitchell County; Pop. 321; Zip Code 67485; Elev. 1,604; Lat. 39-20-14 N long. 098-28-24 W; N central Kansas; Named for an early settler.

•**TONGANOXIE,** City; Leavenworth County; Pop. 1,864; Zip Code 66086; Elev. 853; Lat. 39-06-26 N long. 095-04-40 W; NE Kansas; Tonganoxie is named for a Delaware Indian chief.

•**TOPEKA,** City; Shawnee County Seat; Pop. 115,266; Zip Code 666++; Elev. 1,000; Lat. 39-02-19 N long. 095-41-25 W; 55 mi. W of Kansas City in NE Kansas; A Kaw Indian word meaning a place "to find small potatoes."

•**TORONTO,** City; Woodson County; Pop. 466; Zip Code 66777; Elev. 950; Lat. 37-47-55 N long. 095-56-51 W; SE Kansas; Toronto is a Huron Indian name menaing "gateway." It is also the name of a great Canadian city.

•**TOWANDA,** City; Butler County; Pop. 1,332; Zip Code 67144; Elev. 1,300; Lat. 37-47-40 N long. 096-59-46 W; S Kansas; An Iroquois Indian name imported by early settlers from New York.

•**TREECE,** City; Cherokee County; Pop. 194; Zip Code 66778; Elev. 840; Lat. 37-00-10 N long. 094-50-36 W; SE corner of Kansas; Treece may be named for an early settler.

•**TRIBUNE,** City; Greeley County Seat; Pop. 955; Zip Code 67879; Elev. 3,616; Lat. 38-28-22 N long. 101-46-16 W; W Kansas; Tribune is named after the New York Tribune newspaper.

•**TROY,** City; Doniphan County Seat; Pop. 1,240; Zip Code 66087; Elev. 1,099; Lat. 39-47-06 N long. 095-05-19 W; NE corner of Kansas; Troy is named for the great city of Greek mythology.

•**TURON,** City; Reno County; Pop. 481; Zip Code 67583; Elev. 1,760; Lat. 37-48-23 N long. 098-25-37 W; central Kansas; Turon is an anglicized version of Turin, the Italian city.

•**TYRO,** City; Montgomery County; Pop. 289; Zip Code 67364; Elev. 891; Lat. 37-02-20 N long. 095-49-09 W; SE Kansas; Named by its settlers to reflect their inexperience. The word means "novice."

•**UDALL,** City; Cowley County; Pop. 891; Zip Code 67146; Elev. 1,267; Lat. 37-23-24 N long. 097-07-17 W; S Kansas; Udall is named for an early settler.

•**ULYSSES,** City; Grant County Seat; Pop. 4,653; Zip Code 67880; Elev. 3,057; Lat. 37-35-02 N long. 101-21-46 W; SW Kansas; Named for the famous Greek hero, known for "his many devices."

•**UNIONTOWN,** City; Bourbon County; Pop. 371; Zip Code 66779; Elev. 895; Lat. 37-50-46 N long. 094-58-34 W; SE Kansas; Uniontown was named for its being a bastion of anti-slavery "free state" sentiment.

•**UTICA,** City; Ness County; Pop. 275; Zip Code 67584; Elev. 2,618; Lat. 38-38-37 N long. 100-10-04 W; W central Kansas; Utica is named for the ancient Roman city.

•**VALLEY CENTER,** City; Sedgwick County; Pop. 3,300; Zip Code 67147; Elev. 1,345; Lat. 37-50-06 N long. 097-22-18 W; S central Kansas; Descriptively named for the major geographical feature of the area.

•**VALLEY FALLS,** City; Jefferson County; Pop. 1,189; Zip Code 66088; Elev. 950; Lat. 39-20-36 N long. 095-27-34 W; NE Kansas; Originally called Grasshopper Falls, unhappy settlers renamed it.

•**VERMILLION,** City; Marshall County; Pop. 191; Zip Code 66544; Elev. 1,240; Lat. 39-43-10 N long. 096-15-52 W; NE Kansas; Named after the Vermillion River, itself named for its red sandstone bottom.

•**VICTORIA,** City; Ellis County; Pop. 1,328; Zip Code 67671; Elev. 1,940; Lat. 38-51-13 N long. 099-08-59 W; central Kansas; The city's name honors Britians' Queen Victoria.

•**VIOLA,** City; Sedgwick County; Pop. 199; Zip Code 67149; Elev. 1,335; Lat. 37-28-57 N long. 097-38-37 W; S central Kansas; Named after Viola, Illinois.

•**VIRGIL,** City; Greenwood County; Pop. 169; Zip Code 66870; Elev. 1,000; Lat. 37-58-52 N long. 096-00-30 W; SE Kansas; The town is named after the great Roman poet.

•**WAKEENEY,** City; Trego County Seat; Pop. 2,388; Zip Code 67672; W central Kansas; The town's name is a composite honoring its developers, a Mr. Warren and a Mr. Keeney.

•**WAKEFIELD,** City; Clay County; Pop. 803; Zip Code 67487; Elev. 1,148; Lat. 39-13-07 N long. 097-01-01 W; NE central Kansas; Named for the city in England.

•**WALDO,** City; Russell County; Pop. 75; Zip Code 67673; Elev. 1,711; Lat. 39-07-12 N long. 098-47-52 W; central Kansas; Waldo is named after a Union Pacific Railroad official.

•**WALDRON,** City; Harper County; Pop. 29; Zip Code 67150; Elev. 1,246; Lat. 37-00-08 N long. 098-10-45 W; S Kansas; Named for a local settler.

•**WALLACE,** City; Wallace County; Pop. 86; Zip Code 67761; Elev. 3,311; Lat. 38-54-45 N long. 101-35-32 W; W Kansas; The town of Wallace is named for Civil War hero General William Wallace.

•**WALNUT,** City; Crawford County; Pop. 308; Zip Code 66780; Elev. 930; Lat. 37-36-09 N long. 095-04-31 W; SE Kansas; Descriptively named for the many walnut trees once found in the area.

•**WALTON,** City; Harvey County; Pop. 269; Zip Code 67151; Elev. 1,537; Lat. 38-07-05 N long. 097-15-19 W; SE central Kansas; Walton's name remembers a prominent Santa Fe Railroad stockholder.

•**WAMEGO,** City; Pottawatomie County; Pop. 3,159; Zip Code 66547; Elev. 990; Lat. 39-12-11 N long. 096-18-28 W; NE Kansas; Named for an early Pottawatomie Indian chief.

•**WASHINGTON,** City; Washington County Seat; Pop. 1,488; Zip Code 66968; Elev. 1,335; Lat. 39-48-57 N long. 097-03-05 W; N Kansas; The city's name honors General George Washington.

•**WATERVILLE,** City; Marshall County; Pop. 694; Zip Code 66548; Elev. 1,176; Lat. 39-41-34 N long. 096-44-56 W; NE Kansas; Named after Waterville, New York.

•**WATHENA,** City; Doniphan County; Pop. 1,418; Zip Code 66090; Elev. 823; Lat. 39-45-37 N long. 094-56-55 W; NE corner of Kansas; The town is named for a Kickapoo Indian chief.

•**WAVERLY,** City; Coffey County; Pop. 671; Zip Code 66871; Elev. 1,131; Lat. 38-23-39 N long. 095-36-22 W; E Kansas; The town is named for the chief character in Sir Waltr Scott's novel Waverly.

•**WEBBER,** City; Jewell County; Pop. 53; Zip Code 66970; Elev. 1,670; Lat. 39-56-09 N long. 098-02-01 W; N Kansas; Named for an early settler.

•**WEIR,** City; Cherokee County; Pop. 705; Zip Code 66781; Elev. 920; Lat. 37-18-45 N long. 094-46-30 W; SE corner of Kansas; Descriptively named for a local water project.

•**WELLINGTON,** City; Sumner County Seat; Pop. 8,212; Zip Code 67152; Elev. 1,230; Lat. 37-16-00 N long. 097-23-52 W; 30 mi. S of Wichita in S Kansas; Wellington's name remembers the famous English general, the Duke of Wellington.

•**WELLSVILLE,** City; Franklin County; Pop. 1,363; Zip Code 66092; Elev. 2,116; Lat. 38-43-14 N long. 095-04-36 W; E Kansas; Wellsville is named for an early settler.

•**WEST MINERAL**; City; Cherokee County; Pop. ,229; Zip Code 66782; Elev. 900; Lat. 37-17-02 N long. 094-55-40 W; SE corner of Kansas; Descriptively named for the numerous minerals including coal in the area.

•**WEST PLAINS,** City; Meade County; Pop. 1,044; Area Code 319; Zip Code SW Kansas; Named for its location on the plains of Kansas.

•**WESTMORELAND,** City; Pottawatomie County Seat; Pop. 598; Zip Code 66549; Elev. 1,168; Lat. 39-26-25 N long. 096-30-19 W; NE Kansas; The city is named for the English county.

•**WESTPHALIA,** City; Anderson County; Pop. 204; Zip Code 66093; Elev. 1,100; Lat. 38-10-48 N long. 095-29-22 W; E Kansas; German settlers gave the town the name of a state in Germany.

•**WESTWOOD,** City; Johnson County; Pop. 1,783; E Kansas.; A descriptive geographical term given by the early settlers.

•**WETMORE,** City; Nemaha; 376; Zip Code 66550; Elev.1,150; Lat. 39-38-12 N long. 095-48-44 W; NE Kansas; The town's name honors W. T. Wetmore, vice-president of the Central Branch Railroad.

•**WHITE CITY,** City; Morris County; Pop. 534; Zip Code 66872; Elev. 1,470; Lat. 38-47-41 N long. 096-44-12 W; E central Kansas; The town's name honors railroad superintendant F. C. White.

•**WHITE CLOUD,** City; Doniphan County; Pop. 234; Zip Code 66094; Elev. 888; Lat. 39-58-26 N long. 095-18-05 W; NE corner of Kansas; The town is named after an Iowa Indian Chief, White Cloud.

•**WHITEWATER,** City; Butler County; Pop. 751; Zip Code 67154; Elev. 1,370; Lat. 37-57-41 N long. 097-08-47 W; S Kansas; The city is named for the color of the Whitewater River, itself named for its color -caused by the white limestone of its bed.

•**WHITING,** City; Jackson County; Pop. 270; Zip Code 66552; Elev. 1,113; Lat. 39-35-15 N long. 095-36-35 W; NE Kansas; Given the maiden name of Senator Promeroy's wife.

•**WICHITA,** City; Sedgwick County Seat; Pop.279,272; Zip Code 672++; Elev. 1,305; Lat. 37-46-54 N long. 097-12-25 W; 177 mi. SW of Kansas City in S central Kansas; Named for a tribe of the Pawnee Indians: The Wichitas.

•**WILLIAMSBURG,** City; Franklin County; Pop. 362; Zip Code 66095; Elev. 1,138; Lat. 38-28-55 N long. 095-27-53 W; E Kansas; The town's name honors local farmer William Scofield.

•**WILLIS,** City; Brown County; Pop. 85; Zip Code 66435; NE Kansas; State legislator Martin Willis had the town named for him.

•**WILMORE,** City; Comanche County; Pop. 97; Zip Code 67155; Elev. 2,022; Lat. 37-19-56 N long. 099-12-27 W; S Kansas; Wilmore is named for a pioneer family.

•**WILSEY,** City; Morris County; Pop. 179; Zip Code 66873; Elev. 1,510; Lat. 38-38-03 N long. 096-40-27 W; E central Kansas; Named after a 19th century pioneer.

•**WILSON,** City; Ellsworth County; Pop. 978; Zip Code 67490; Elev. 1,689; Lat. 38-49-39 N long. 098-28-34 W; central Kansas; The town is named after Colonel Hierd Wilson.

•**WINCHESTER,** City; Jefferson County; Pop. 570; Zip Code 66097; Elev. 1,190; Lat. 39-19-18 N long. 095-16-01 W; NE Kansas; Named for the English city.

•**WINDOM,** City; McPherson County; Pop. 160; Zip Code 67491; Elev. 1,950; Lat. 38-23-02 N long. 097-54-47 W; central Kansas; Windom's name honors William Windom, U. S. Senator from Minnesota.

•**WINONA,** City; Logan County; Pop. 258; Zip Code 67764; Elev. 3,329; W Kansas; Named after Wenonah in Longfellow's poem "Hiawatha."

•**WOODBINE,** City; Dickinson County; Pop. 172; Zip Code 67492; Elev. 1,250; Lat. 38-47-50 N long. 096-57-42 W; E central Kansas; The town is named after the ornamental shrub, the woodbine.

•**WOODSTON,** City; Rooks County; Pop. 157; Zip Code 67675; Elev. 1,712; Lat. 39-27-13 N long. 099-05-44 W; N Kansas; Named after pioneer Charles C. Woods.

•**YATES CENTER,** City; Woodson County Seat; Pop. 1,998; Zip Code 66783; Elev. 1,136; Lat. 37-52-49 N long. 095-43-46 W; SE Kansas; Named for an early settler.

•**ZENDA,** City; Kingman County; Pop. 146; Zip Code 67159; Elev. 1,663; Lat. 37-26-38 N long. 098-16-52 W; S central Kansas; Zenda is named after Anthony Hope's novel The Prisoner of Zenda.

•**ZURICH,** City; Rooks County; Pop. 185; Zip Code 67676; Elev. 2,214; Lat. 39-13-57 N long. 099-25-52 W; N Kansas; Named after Zurich, Switzerland.

KENTUCKY

•**ALBANY,** City; Clinton County Seat; Pop. 2,083; Zip Code 42602; Elev. 964; Lat. 36-41-27 N long. 085-08-05 W; S Kentucky. Named for the capital of New York.

•**ALEXANDRIA,** City; Campbell County Seat; Pop. 4,735; Zip Code 41001; Elev. 823; Lat. 38-49-23 N long. 084-25-41 W; N Kentucky. Settled in the 1790s by pioneer *Frank Spilman* who came from Virginia, and probably named the new town after Alexandria, Virginia.

•**ALLEN,** City; Floyd County; Pop. 338; Zip Code 41601; Elev. 638; Lat. 37-36-34 N long. 082-43-40 W; E Kentucky. On the west bank of the Levisa Fork at the gateway to Beaver Valley.

•**ALLENSVILLE,** City; Todd County; Pop. 170; Zip Code 42204; Elev. 581; Lat. 36-43-00 N long. 087-03-58 W; SW Kentucky. The city was settled in the early 1800's and named for a pioneer family.

•**ANCHORAGE,** City; Jefferson County; Pop. 1,726; Zip Code 40223; Lat. 38-16-00 N long. 085-31-59 W; N central Kentucky. A residential suburb of Louisville. When the town was incorporated , in 1876, it was renamed for the estate of Capt. J.W. Goslee, A steamboat pilot, who, when he retired and built his home at Hobb's Station, said he wished "to anchor there for life."

•**ARLINGTON,** City; Carlisle County; Pop. 511; Zip Code 42021; Elev. 347; Lat. 36-47-25 N long. 089-00-46 W; SW Kentucky. Originally called Neville when it was founded in the 1870's, railroad officials changed it to Arlington after a resemblence of the local topography to that site in Virginia.

•**ASHLAND,** City; Boyd County; Pop. 27,064; Zip Code 41101; Elev. 558; Lat. 38-28-42 N long. 082-38-17 W. In Eastern Kentucky.

•**AUBURN,** City; Logan County; Pop. 1,467; Zip Code 42206; Elev. 642; Lat. 36-51-51 N long. 086-42-37 W; S Kentucky. Settled in the early 1800's as Federal Grove, the name was changed in the 1860's after Auburn, New York.

•**AUDUBON PARK,** City; Jefferson County; Pop. 1,571; Lat. 38-12-14 N long. 085-43-31 W; N central Kentucky. The town's name honors famous American naturalist *James Audubon.*

•**AUGUSTA,** City; Bracken County; Pop. 1,455; Zip Code 41002; Elev. 444; Lat. 38-46-18 N long. 084-00-21 W; NE Kentucky. Situated on the high bank of the Ohio River.

•**BANCROFT,** City; Jefferson County; Pop. 725; Lat. 37-09-57 N long. 087-14-51W; N central Kentucky. The city is named for a pioneer settler.

•**BARBOURMEADE,** City; Jefferson County; Pop. 1,038; Zip Code 40906; Lat. 38-17-50 N long. 085-36-12 W; N central Kentucky. *Thomas* and *Richard Barbour* were pioneer settlers in the region. The town was named for them when it was incorporated in 1962.

•**BARBOURVILLE,** City; Knox County Seat; Pop. 3,333; Zip Code 40906; Elev. 975; Lat. 36-51-59 N long. 083-53-20 W; SE Kentucky. When Knox County was created in 1799, it included 5,000 acres belonging to *Richard Barbour,* a Virginian. The town was named in his honor.

•**BARDSTOWN,** City; Nelson County Seat; Pop. 6,155; Zip Code 40004; Elev. 647; Lat. 37-48-33 N long. 085-28-01 W; central Kentucky. First known as Salem, Bardstown was renamed for *William Baird* (or *Bard*) of Pennsylvania, one of the owners of the 100-acre tract on which the town was laid out.

•**BARDWELL,** City; Carlisle County Seat; Pop. 988; Zip Code 42023; Elev. 390; Lat. 36-52-14 N long. 089-00-35 W; SW Kentucky. The last established county of the Jackson Purchase, derived its name from a bored well here, which supplied trains with water.

•**BEATTYVILLE,** City; Lee County Seat; Pop. 1,068; Zip Code 41311; Elev. 666; Lat. 37-34-18 N long. 083-42-25 W; E Kentucky. Founded as Taylor's Landing, the name was changed in 1850 to honor pioneer *Samuel Beatty* who donated the land for the town.

•**BEAVER DAM,** City; Ohio County; Pop. 3,185; Zip Code 42320; Elev. 414; Lat. 37-24-07 N long. 086-52-33 W; W central Kentucky.

•**BEDFORD,** City; Trimble County Seat; Pop. 835; Zip Code 40006; Elev. 982; Lat. 38-35-33 N long. 085-19-04 W; N Kentucky. Settled in 1808 by pioneer *Richard Bell,* and named after his former home of Bedford, Virginia.

•**BEECHWOOD VILLAGE,** City; Jefferson County; Pop. 1,462; Elev. 540; Lat. 38-15-17 N long. 085-37-53 W; N central Kentucky. Originally the name comes from the abundance of beech trees in the area.

•**BELLEFONTE,** City; Greenup County; Pop. 908; Lat. 38-29-33 N long. 082-41-25 W; NE Kentucky. Founded in 1918 and named for the historic Bellefonte Iron Furnace which had been established in the area the previous century.

•**BELLEVUE,** City; Campbell County; Pop. 7,678; Zip Code 41073; Elev. 549; Lat. 39-06-23 N long. 084-28-44 W; N Kentucky. Founded in 1866 and named after the adjacent hillside estate of *General James Taylor.*

•**BENTON,** City; Marshall County Seat; Pop. 3,700; 42025; Zip Code 42025; Lat. 36-51-26 N long. 088-21-01 W; W Kentucky. The town was named for *Thomas Hart Benton* (1782-1858), the United States Senator from Missouri.

•**BEREA,** City; Madison County; Pop. 8,226; Zip Code 40403; Elev. 943; Lat. 37-34-07 N long. 084-17-47 W; E central Kentucky. Settled in the 1850's and given the Biblical name of Berea, where *St. Paul* had once preached.

•**BLOOMFIELD,** City; Nelson County; Pop. 954; Zip Code 40008; Elev. 657; Lat. 37-54-37 N long. 085-19-00 W; central Kentucky. Founded in 1799 by *Dr. John Bemiss* of Rochester, N.Y.

•**BOWLING GREEN,** City; Warren County Seat; Pop. 40,450; Zip Code 42101; Elev. 469; Lat. 36-59-25 N long. 086-26-37 W; S KY 65 mi. SE of Owensboro. The county court had held its sessions in the home of *Robert Moore.* The visiting lawyers and court officials long used the yard about Moore's house as a green for playing bowls, as did many people in the town. From this custom Bowling Green derived its name.

•**BRADFORDSVILLE,** City; Marion County; Pop. 331; Zip Code 40009; Elev. 682; Lat. 37-29-39 N long. 085-08-56 W; central Kentucky. Founded in the early 1800's and named after hunter *Peter Bradford.*

•**BRANDENBURG,** City; Meade County Seat; Pop. 1,831; Zip Code 40108; Elev. 356; Lat. 37-59-56 N long. 086-10-10 W; NW central Kentucky. Incorporated in 1825, it bears the name of *Col. Solomon Brandenburg,* an early settler who had seen service in the War of 1812.

•**BRODHEAD,** City; Rockcastle County; Pop. 686; Zip Code 40409; Elev. 940; Lat. 37-24-15 N long. 084-24-50 W; SE central

Kentucky. Originally a stage coach stop called Stigall's Station, the site was renamed by the railroad in 1868 after U.S. *Senator Richard Brodhead.*

•**BROMLEY,** City; Kenton County; Pop. 844; Elev. 606; Lat. 39-04-55 N long. 084-33-37 W; N Kentucky.

•**BROOKSVILLE,** City; Bracken County Seat; Pop. 680; Zip Code 41004; Elev. 925; Lat. 38-40-57 N long. 084-03-57 W; NE Kentucky.

•**BROWNSBORO VILLAGE,** City; Jefferson County; Pop. 410; Lat. 38-15-47 N long. 085-39-57 W; N central Kentucky. The city is named after Kentucky's first senator, *John Brown.*

•**BURGIN,** City; Mercer County; Pop. 1,008; Zip Code 40310 ; Elev. 893; Lat. 37-45-12 N long. 084-46-00 W; central Kentucky. Settler *Temple Burgin* donated the land to the railroad in 1874 and the grateful railroad named the town after him.

•**BURKESVILLE,** City; Cumberland County Seat; Pop. 2,051; Zip Code 42717; Elev. 581; Lat. 36-47-25 N long. 085-22-14 W; S Kentucky. Founded in 1798 by *Samuel Burks* and named in his honor.

•**CADIZ,** City; Trigg County Seat; Pop. 1,661; Zip Code 42211; Elev. 468; Lat. 36-51-54 N long. 087-50-07 W; SW Kentucky. Trigg County was named for *Col. Stephen Trigg,* a Virginian who was a well-known Indian fighter.

•**CALHOUN,** City; McLean County Seat; Pop. 1,080; Zip Code 42327; Elev. 392; Lat. 37-32-20 N long. 087-15-30 W; W Kentucky. *John Calhoun,* for whom the town was named, was the first circuit judge of old Fort Vienna, and United States Congressman for one term (1835-39).

•**CALVERT CITY,** City; Marshall County; Pop. 2,338; Zip Code 42029; Lat. 37-02-00 N long. 088-21-00 W; W Kentucky. *P. W. Calver* gave the right-of-way for the railroad in exchange for his name on the new town.

•**CAMARGO,** City; Montgomery County; Pop. 1,301; Lat. 37-59-39 N long. 083-53-16 W; E Kentucky. Veterans of the 1846 Mexican War named the town after the city in Mexico.

•**CAMPBELLSVILLE,** City; Taylor County Seat; Pop. 8,715; Zip Code 42718; Lat. 37-20-36 N long. 085-20-31 W; central Kentucky. Founded in 1817 and named for pioneer *Andrew Campbell.* The town incorporated in 1838.

•**CARLISLE,** City; Nicholas County Seat; Pop. 1,757; Zip Code 40311; Elev. 879; Lat. 38-18-43 N long. 084-01-39 W; NE Kentucky. Established in 1816 and named after Carlisle, Pennsylvania.

•**CARROLLTON,** City; Carroll County Seat; Pop. 3,967; Zip Code 41008; Elev. 484; Lat. 38-40-51 N long. 085-10-46 W; N Kentucky. Incorporated in 1794 under the name of *Port William.* In 1838 it was renamed in honor of *Charles Carroll* of Carrollton, Maryland, signer of the Declaration of Independence.

•**CATLETTSBURG,** City; Boyd County Seat; Pop. 3,005; Zip Code 41129; Elev. 552; Lat. 38-24-17 N long. 082-36-02 W; NE Kentucky. The town and near-by Catletts Creek were named for *Sawney Catlett,* who came from Virginia in 1808 and established a trading post that, for more than 50 years, served trappers and hunters of the Ohio and Big Sandy River regions.

•**CAVE CITY,** City; Barren County; Pop. 2,098; Zip Code 42127; Elev. 613; Lat. 37-08-1 N long. 085-57-25 W; S Kentucky. This is cave country.

•**CENTRAL CITY,** City; Muhlenberg County; Pop. 5,214; Zip Code 42330; Elev. 462; Lat. 37-17-38 N long. 087-07-24 W; W Kentucky.

•**CLARKSON,** City; Grayson County; Pop. 666; Zip Code 42726; Lat. 37-29-43 N long. 086-13-17 W; W central Kentucky. Founded as Grayson Springs after the nearby resort, the name was changed in 1882 for *Manoah Clarkson,* the proprietor of the resort.

•**CLAY,** City; Webster County; Pop. 1,356; Zip Code 42404; Elev. 628; Lat. 37-28-36 N long. 087-49-12 W; W Kentucky. Settled in 1837 and named in honor of Kentucky Statesman *Henry Clay.*

•**CLAY CITY,** City; Powell County; Pop. 1,276; Zip Code 40312; Elev. 628; Lat. 37-51-33 N long. 083-55-07 W; E Kentucky.

•**CLINTON,** City; Hickman County Seat; Pop. 1,720; Zip Code 42031; Elev. 389; Lat. 36-40-02 N long. 088-59-36 W; SW Kentucky.

•**CLOVERPORT,** City; Breckinridge County; Pop. 1,585; Zip Code 40111; Elev. 386; Lat. 37-50-00 N long. 086-37-58 W; NW Kentucky. A river town established in 1808.

•**COLD SPRING,** City; Campbell County; Pop. 2,117; Zip Code 41076; Elev. 859; Lat. 39-01-18 N long. 084-26-24 W; N Kentucky. Descriptively named for a cold, clear spring which was the town's water supply in the early days.

•**COLUMBIA,** City; Adair County Seat; Pop. 3,710; Zip Code 42728; Elev. 750; Lat. 37-06-10 N long. 085-18-23 W; S central Kentucky.

•**CORBIN,** City; Knox & Whitley Counties; Pop. 8,075; Zip Code 40701; Elev. 1,046; Lat. 36-56-55 N long. 084-05-49 W; SE Kentucky. First called Cummins, the name was changed in 1885 to honor the *Rev. James Corbin,* a local minister.

•**COVINGTON,** City; Kenton County Seat; Pop. 49,013; Zip Code 41000; Lat. 39-05-01 N long. 084-30-31 W; N Kentucky.

•**CRESCENT SPRINGS,** City; Kenton County; Pop. 1,951; Lat. 39-03-05 N long. 084-34-54 W; N Kentucky. Settled in 1785 and given a nickname of the Cincinnati Southern Railroad--The "Crescent Road."

•**CUMBERLAND,** City; Harlan County; Pop. 3,712; Zip Code 40823; Elev. 1,430; Lat. 36-58-41 N long. 082-59-19 W; SE Kentucky. Known as Poor Fork until 1926, when it was renamed after the Cumberland River.

•**CYNTHIANA,** City; Harrison County Seat; Pop. 5,881; Zip Code 41031; Elev. 718; Lat. 38-23-25 N long. 084-17-39 W; N Kentucky. Established in 1793 and incorporated in 1806, Cynthiana was named for *Cynthia* and *Anna,* two daughters of the first settler, *Robert Harrison.*

•**DANVILLE,** City; Boyle County Seat; Pop. 12,942; Zip Code 40422; Elev. 955; Lat. 37-38-09 N long. 085-27-21 W; central KY 30 mi. SSW of Lexington. It was founded in 1775.

•**DAYTON,** City; Campbell County; Pop. 6,979; Zip Code 41074; Elev. 520; Lat. 39-06-46 N long. 084-28-22 W; N Kentucky. Founded in 1849 as Brooklyn, the town may have been named after Dayton, Ohio.

•**DRAKESBORO,** City; Muhlenbert County; Pop. 798; Zip Code 42337; Lat. 37-13-03 N long. 087-02-56 W; W Kentucky. *William Drake* was a pioneer settler who came to the area in the 1860's. The town was named for him when it incorporated in 1888.

•**DRY RIDGE,** City; Grant County; Pop. 1,250; Zip Code 41035; Elev. 929; Lat. 38-40-55 N long. 084-35-24 W; N Kentucky. Originally called Campbell's Station, it was settled before 1792 near a mineral spring later valued for its medicinal properties.

•**EARLINGTON,** City; Hopkins County; Pop. 2,011; Zip Code 42410; Elev. 422; Lat. 37-16-27 N long. 087-30-43 W; W Kentucky.

•**EDDYVILLE,** City; Lyon County Seat; Pop. 1,949; Zip Code 42038; Elev. 436; Lat. 37-05-40 N long. 088-04-49 W; W Kentucky. On the bank of the Cumberland River, was so named because of eddies in the river above and below the city.

•**EDMONTON,** City; Metcalfe County Seat; Pop. 1,401; Zip Code 42129; Elev. 800; Lat. 36-58-48 N long. 085-36-44 W; S Kentucky. Named for *Edmond Rogers*, a soldier of Virginia, who came to Kentucky after the Revolutionary War. He acquired 20,000 acres of land and a large number of slaves, and laid out a town here.

•**ELIZABETHTOWN,** City; Hardin County Seat; Pop. 15,380; Zip Code 42701; Elev. 708; Lat. 37-41-38 N long. 085-51-33 W; central KY 40 mi. S of Louisville.

•**ELKHORN CITY,** City; Pike County; Pop. 1,446; Zip Code 41522; Elev. 790; Lat. 37-18-14 N long. 082-21-04 W; E Kentucky. Pioneer *William Ramey* settled here in 1810, and named the site for an elk's horn he found in the vicinity.

•**ELKTON,** City; Todd County Seat; Pop. 1,815; Zip Code 42220; Elev. 602; Lat. 36-48-36 N long. 087-09-15 W; SW Kentucky. Descriptively named as the watering hole of a large elk herd prior to pioneer times.

•**ELSMERE,** City; Kenton County; Pop. 7,203; Lat. 39-00-45 N long. 084-36-17 W; N Kentucky. Settled in the 1880's and named after a street in Norwood, Ohio by a town founder.

•**EMINENCE,** City; Henry County; Pop. 2,260; Zip Code 40019; Elev. 939; Lat. 38-22-12 N long. 085-10-50 W; N Kentucky.

•**EVARTS,** City; Harlan County; Pop. 1,234; Zip Code 40828; Lat. 36-51-57 N long. 083-11-26 W; SE Kentucky. Founded in the 1850's and named for a pioneer family.

•**FAIRVIEW,** City; Kenton County; Pop. 198; Zip Code 42221; Lat. 37-54-05 N long. 085-06-25 W; N Kentucky.

•**FALMOUTH,** City; Pendleton County Seat; Pop. 2,482; Zip Code 41010; Elev. 525; Lat. 38-40-36 N long. 084-19-49 W; N Kentucky. First settled in 1776, the town was established in 1799 by Virginians who named it for Falmouth, Virginia.

•**FERGUSON,** City; Pulaski County; Pop. 1,009; Zip Code 42533; Lat. 36-46-46 N long. 086-58-38 W; SE central Kentucky. The Cincinnati Southern Railroad founded the town in 1906 for its workers in the area. It is named in honor of *Attorney Edward Ferguson* who helped found the railroad.

•**FLATWOODS,** City; Greenup County; Pop. 8,354; Zip Code 41139; Elev. 689; Lat. 38-31-21 N long. 082-43-02 W; NE Kentucky. Originally called Advance, the name was changed to Flatwoods when the town incorporated in 1938. The town's name is descriptive of the local topography.

•**FLEMING-NEON,** City; Letcher County; Pop. 1,195; Zip Code 41816; SE Kentucky. Established in 1913 as Fleming after coal company president *George Fleming*, it later merged with nearby Neon.

•**FLEMINGSBURG,** City; Fleming County Seat; Pop. 2,835; Zip Code 41041; Elev. 850; Lat. 38-25-20 N long. 083-44-02 W; NE Kentucky. Named for *John Fleming*, a Virginian, who, with his half-brother, *George Stockton*, came down the Ohio in a canoe to Marysville in 1787.

•**FLORENCE,** City; Boone County; Pop. 15,586; Zip Code 41042; Elev. 935; Lat. 38-59-56 N long. 084-37-36 W; N KY SW of Cincinnati, Ohio.

•**FORT MITCHELL,** City; Kenton County; Pop. 7,297; Zip Code 41017; Lat. 39-03-34 N long. 084-32-51 W; N Kentucky. One of a series of forts built in the 1860's to defend Cincinnati. It is named in honor of *General Ormsby Mitchel* who designed the forts.

•**FORT THOMAS,** City; Campbell County; Pop. 16,012; Zip Code 41075; Elev. 852; Lat. 39-04-30 N long. 084-26-59 W; N KY 5 mi. SE of Covington. Named after *General George Henry Thomas*.

•**FRANKFORT,** City; Franklin County Seat; Pop. 25,973; Zip Code 40601; Elev. 00510; Lat. 38-12-03 N long. 084-52-24 W.

•**FRANKLIN,** City; Simpson County Seat; Pop. 7,738; Zip Code 42143; Elev. 717; Lat. 36-43-20 N long. 086-34-38 W; S KY 20 mi. S of Bowling Green. It was founded in 1820, named for *Benjamin Franklin*.

•**GEORGETOWN,** City; Scott County Seat; Pop. 10,972; Zip Code 40324; Elev. 866; Lat. 36-53-21 N long. 083-03-19 W; N central KY approx 10 mi. N of Lexington. Incorporated by the Virginia Legislature in 1790, and named for *George Washington*.

•**GERMANTOWN,** City; Bracken & Mason Counties; Pop. 347; Zip Code 41044; Elev. 490; Lat. 38-39-17 N long. 083-57-53 W; NE Kentucky. Pennsylvania Germans settled here in 1788 and named the town after their ethnic heritage.

•**GHENT,** City; Carroll County; Pop. 439; Zip Code 41045; Lat. 38-44-15 N long. 085-03-30 W; N Kentucky. Founded in 1809 by 13 families from the Rappahannock River region of Virginia, and named in 1814 by *Henry Clay* for the Belgian city where the peace treaty between the United States and Great Britain was signed.

•**GLASGOW,** City; Barren County Seat; Pop. 12,958; Zip Code 42141; Elev. 780; Lat. 36-59-45 N long. 085-54-43 W; S KY 30 mi. E of Bowling Green. It was named for Glasgow, Virginia, in 1799.

•**GLENCOE,** City; Gallatin County; Pop. 354; Zip Code 41046; Elev. 544; Lat. 38-42-52 N long. 084-49-22 W; Founded in the 1860's and named for the Glencoe Valley in Scotland.

•**GLENVIEW MANOR,** City; Jefferson County; Pop. 212; Zip Code 40025; Lat. 38-17-15 N long. 085-38-13 W; N central Kentucky.

•**GRAND RIVERS,** City; Livingston County; Pop. 428; Zip Code 42045; Lat. 37-00-11 N long. 088-14-04 W; W Kentucky.

•**GRAYMOOR,** City; Jefferson County; Pop. 1,194; Lat. 38-16-23 N long. 085-37-23 W; N central Kentucky. Incorporated in 1959, the community is named after a Catholic monastery in Garrison, New York.

•**GRAYSON,** City; Carter County Seat; Pop. 3,423; Zip Code 41143; Elev. 752; Lat. 38-19-57 N long. 082-56-55 W; NE Kentucky. Named for *Col. Robert Grayson*, an aide of *George Washington*. After the revolution he received a large land grant in the area.

•**GREENSBURG,** City; Green County Seat; Pop. 2,377; Zip Code 42743; Elev. 583; Lat. 37-15-39 N long. 085-29-56 W; central Kentucky. Named for *Gen. Nathanael Greene*, a general of the Revolutionary Army.

•**GREENUP,** City; Greenup County; Pop. 1,386; Zip Code 41144; Elev. 478; Lat. 38-34-23 N long. 082-49-49 W; NE Kentucky. Named for *Christopher Greenup*, Governor of Kentucky (1804-1808). The town was known as Greenupsburg until 1872 when the name was changed to avoid confusion with Greensburg in Green County.

•**GREENVILLE,** City; Muhlenberg County Seat; Pop. 4,631; Zip Code 42345; Elev. 538; Lat. 37-12-04 N long. 087-10-44 W; W Kentucky. Named for *General John Peter Gabriel Muhlenberg* (1746-1807), a Lutheran minister of Virginia, who left his pulpit at the beginning of the Revolutionary War to become a military officer.

•**GUTHRIE,** City; Todd County; Pop. 1,361; Zip Code 42234; Elev. 548; SW Kentucky. Once a railroad center named for *James Guthrie*, president of the Louisville & Nashville R.R. in 1867, when the town was incorporated.

•**HARDINSBURG,** City; Breckinridge County Seat; Pop. 2,211; Zip Code 40143; Elev. 715; Lat. 37-46-48 N long. 086-27-38 W; NW central Kentucky. Established in 1780 as a fort built by *Capt. William Hardin*, soldier and frontiersman, who was known to the Indians as "Big Bill."

•**HARLAN,** City; Harlan County Seat; Pop. 3,024; Zip Code 40831; Elev. 1,197; Lat. 36-50-35 N long. 083-19-19 W; SE Kentucky. First called Mount Pleasant, the town was later renamed to honor *Maj. Silas Harlan*, who came to Kentucky from Virginia in 1774, and was killed while leading his command at the Battle of Blue Licks (August 19, 1782).

•**HARTFORD,** City; Ohio County Seat; Pop. 2,512; Zip Code 42347; Elev. 425; Lat. 37-27-04 N long. 086-54-33 W; W central KY; It is by hills that rise 650 to 700 feet. At the time of its founding in 1790, Hartford was called Deer Crossing, from which "hart-ford" was evolved.

•**HAWESVILLE,** City; Hancock County Seat; Pop. 1,036; Zip Code 42348; Elev. 423; Lat. 37-54-00 N long. 086-45-18 W; NW central Kentucky. Incorporated in 1836, it was named for *Richard Hawes*, who owned the land on which the town site was platted.

•**HAZARD,** City; Perry County Seat; Pop. 5,429; Zip Code 41701; Elev. 833; Lat. 37-14-58 N long. 083-11-36 W; SE Kentucky. Named by men who served under *Oliver Hazard Perry* in the Battle of Lake Erie, September 10, 1813.

•**HENDERSON,** City; Henderson County Seat; Pop. 24,834; Zip Code 42420; Elev. 382; Lat. 37-50-10 N long. 087-35-24 W; NW KY 10 mi. S of Evansville, Indiana. Founded by the Transylvania Company (later known as the Richard Henderson Company) in 1797, on 200,000 acres granted to the company by the State. The first settlement, made in and around the old stockaded village of Red Banks, was named for *Col. Richard Henderson*, leader of the company.

•**HICKMAN,** City; Fulton County Seat; Pop. 2,894; Zip Code 42050; Elev. 306; Lat. 37-27-32 N long. 085-33-36 W; SW Kentucky. In 1834 a large part of the area was purchased by a Tennessee settler who named it Hickman in honor of his wife's family.

•**HIGHLAND HEIGHTS,** City; Campbell County; Pop. 4,435; Lat. 39-01-59 N long. 084-27-07 W; N Kentucky. Founded in 1927 as a suburb of Cincinnati, it is descriptively named for its elevation.

•**HILLVIEW,** City; Bullitt County; Pop. 5,196; Lat. 37-17-57 N long. 086-13-43 W; central Kentucky. Given a euphonious name by the town founders.

•**HODGENVILLE,** City; Larue County Seat; Pop. 2,459; Zip Code 42748; Elev. 720; Lat. 37-34-26 N long. 085-44-24 W; central Kentucky. In 1789 *Robert Hodgen* erected a mill on his land. The town was named after him.

•**HOPKINSVILLE,** City; Christian County Seat; Pop. 27,318; Zip Code 42240; Lat. 36-51-56 N long. 087-29-19 W. In 1797 *Bartholomew Wood* The settlement was named to honor *Gen. Samuel Hopkins*, a hero of the War of 1812.

•**INDEPENDENCE,** City; Kenton County Seat; Pop. 7,998; Zip Code 41051; Elev. 903; Lat. 38-56-35 N long. 084-32-39 W; Settled in the 1830's and, as the seat of the now county of Kenton, given the name Independence to mark its separation from Campbell County.

•**IRVINE,** City; Estill County Seat; Pop. 2,889; Zip Code 40336; Lat. 37-42-02 N long. 083-58-26 W; Established in 1812 and named in honor of *Colonel William Irvine*, a Revolutionary War hero.

•**IRVINGTON,** City; Breckinridge County; Pop. 1,409; Zip Code 40146; Elev. 620; Lat. 37-52-49 N long. 086-17-02 W; Founded in 1888 and named by railroad engineer *Eugene Cornwall* for his former home in Irvington, New York.

•**JACKSON,** City; Breathitt County Seat; Pop. 2,651; Zip Code 41339; Lat. 37-21-57 N long. 082-43-59 W; Named for President Andrew Jackson.

•**JAMESTOWN,** City; Russell County Seat; Pop. 1,441; Zip Code 42629. Elev. 1024; Lat. 37-29-54 N long. 082-08-13 W; First called Jacksonville in honor of *Andrew Jackson*. By 1826 the Whigs came into power and, resenting the tribute to their opponent, changed the names to *Jamestown*, honoring *James Wooldridge* who had donated 110 acres for a town site.

•**JEFFERSONTOWN,** City; Jefferson County; Pop. 15,795; Elev. 711; Lat. 38-11-39 N long. 085-33-52 W; *Abraham Bruner* settled here in 1797 and named the town after *Thomas Jefferson*.

•**JEFFERSONVILLE,** City; Montgomery County; Pop. 1,528; Zip Code 40337; Elev. 817; Lat. 37-58-25 N long. 083-50-31 W; Founded in the early 1800's the town was named for *Thomas Jefferson*. The post office opened in 1866 and the incorporated in 1876.

•**JUNCTION CITY,** City; Boyle & Lincoln Counties; Pop. 2,045; Zip Code 40440; Elev. 986; Lat. 37-35-12 N long. 084-47-38 W; Founded by the railroad in 1866 as Goresburg, the name was changed in 1882 when another railroad reached the main line at this point.

•**KUTTAWA,** City; Lyon County; Pop. 560; Zip Code 42055; Elev. 466; Lat. 37-03-32 N long. 088-07-57 W; Settled in the 1860's and given an Indian word meaning "Great Wilderness."

•**LA CENTER,** City; Ballard County; Pop. 1,044; Zip Code 42056; Lat. 37-04-36 N long. 088-58-25 W. Laid out in 1903 and descriptively named for its location in the center of the county.

•**LA GRANGE,** City; Oldham County Seat; Pop. 2,971; Zip Code 40032. Elev. 867; Lat. 38-24-27 N long. 085-22-44 W; Named for the French estate of *General Lafayette*.

•**LANCASTER,** City; Garrard County Seat; Pop. 3,365; Zip Code 40446. Elev. 1032; Lat. 37-37-10 N long. 084-34-41 W; Settled in 1798 by pioneers from Lancaster, Pennsylvania, who designed and named it for their native city.

•**LAWRENCEBURG,** City; Anderson County Seat; Pop. 5,167; Zip Code 40342. Elev. 791; Lat. 38-02-14 N long. 084-53-48 W; Named in honor of *Capt. James Lawrence*, commander of the *Chesapeake*, whose last words were "Don't give up the ship."

•**LEBANON,** City; Marion County Seat; Pop. 6,590; Zip Code 40033; Elev. 797; Lat. 37-34-11 N long. 085-15-10 W; Founded in 1815 and named for the abundance of cedars which reminded the pioneers of the Cedars of Biblical Lebanon.

•**LEBANON JUNCTION,** City; Bullitt County; Pop. 1,581; Zip Code 40150; 37-50-04 N long. 085-43-55 W. Founded in the 1850's and named for its railroad connection to Lebanon.

•**LEITCHFIELD,** City; Grayson County Seat; Pop. 4,533; Zip Code 42754; Lat. 37-28-48 N long. 086-17-38 W. Named for *Maj. David Leitch,* who owned the land on which this county seat was settled.

•**LEWISPORT,** City; Hancock County Seat; Pop. 1,832; Zip Code 42351; Elev. 394; Lat. 37-56-13 N long. 086-54-08 W. Founded in 1839 as a flatboat landing, and named after *Dr. John Lewis,* an early settler.

•**LEXINGTON,** City; Fayette County Seat; Pop. 204,165; Zip Code 405++; Lat. 38-02-57 N long. 084-30-01 W; The city was named after the Battle of Lexington by Robert Patterson, Simon Kenton, and others who in June 1775 were camped nearby while on their way to build a fort near the Kentucky River.

•**LIBERTY,** City; Casey County Seat; Pop. 2,206; Zip Code 42539; Elev. 797; Lat. 37-19-06 N long. 084-56-22 W; Named by veterans of the Revolutionary War who came to this section from Virginia in 1791.

•**LIVERMORE,** City; McLean County; Pop. 1,672; Elev. 408; Lat. 37-29-35 N long. 087-07-55 W; Settled in the 1830's and named after pioneer *James Livermore.*

•**LIVINGSTON,** City; Rockcastle County; Pop. 334; Zip Code 40445; Elev. 889; Lat. 37-17-52 N long. 084-12-54 W; Founded in the 1840's and named in honor of *James Livingston,* an early pioneer.

•**LOCKPORT,** City; Henry County; Pop. 84; Zip Code 40036; Lat. 38-26-09 N long. 084-58-02 W; The city is named for an adjacent river construction, Lock No. 2.

•**LONDON,** City; Laurel County Seat; Pop. 4,002; Zip Code 4074++; Elev. 1255; Lat. 37-07-44 N long. 084-05-00 W; Founded in 1826 and named after the great English city.

•**LONE OAK,** City; McCracken County; Pop. 443; Elev. 745'; Lat. 37-25-32 N long. 086-04-18 W; Estabished as Pepper's Mill in the 1870's, it was renamed in 1892 after a large oak tree that stood near the post office.

•**LORETTO,** City; Marion County; Pop. 954; Zip Code 40037; Elev. 744; Lat. 37-38-07 N long. 085-24-03 W; The Sisters of Loretto founded an academy here in 1812. When the post office opened in 1833, it took their name.

•**LOUISA,** City; Lawrence County Seat; Pop. 1,832; Zip Code 41230; Lat. 38-06-51 N long. 082-36-12 W; Named for *Louisa, Duchess of Cumberland.* During the Napoleonic wars thousands of bearskins were collected along the Big Sandy and Kanawha Rivers and sent from Louisa down river to New Orleans, and thence to Europe, where they were made into headpieces for Napoleon's grenadiers.

•**LOUISVILLE,** City; Jefferson County Seat; Pop. 298,451; Zip Code 402++; Elev. 462; Lat. 38-15-15 N long. 085-45-34 W; As a gesture of gratitude for the aid given by Louis XVI and the French Nation to the American Revolution, the city was named Louisville.

•**LUDLOW,** City; Kenton County; Pop. 4,959; Zip Code 41016; Lat. 39-05-33 N long. 084-32-51 W; *Israel Ludlow* laid out the town in 1836. It is named after him.

•**LYNCH,** City; Harlan County; Pop. 1,614; Zip Code 40855; Lat. 36-57-58 N long. 082-55-21 W; Developed by the United States Coal & Coke Company.

•**LYNDON,** City; Jefferson County; Pop. 1,553; Zip Code 40222; Lat. 38-15-24 N long. 085-36-06 W; Established after the Civil War and named by local landowner *Alvin Wood* after *William Linn,* one of *George Roger Clark's* officers.

•**MADISONVILLE,** City; Hopkins County Seat; Pop. 16,979; Zip Code 42431; Elev. 470; Lat. 37-19-41 N long. 087-29-56 W; Named for James Madison.

•**MANCHESTER,** City; Clay County Seat; Pop. 1,838; Zip Code 40962; Elev. 870; Lat. 37-09-13 N long. 083-45-43 W; Founded in 1807 as Greenville, but renamed a few years later to promote local industry after the model of the great English industrial city.

•**MARION,** City; Crittenden County Seat; Pop. 3,392; Zip Code 40264; Elev. 594; Lat. 37-19-58 N long. 088-04-52 W; Established in 1842 and named in honor of Revolutionary War hero *General Francis Marion.*

•**MAYFIELD,** City; Graves County Seat; Pop. 10,705; Zip Code 42066; Lat. 36-44-30 N long. 088-38-12 W; Founded in 1819 and named after a notorious local kidnapping of a wealthy planter called *Mayfield.*

•**MAYSVILLE,** City; Mason County Seat; Pop. 7,983; Zip Code 41056; Lat. 38-38-28 N long. 083-44-40 W; Established in 1787 and named for *John May,* a local government official.

•**MCHENRY,** City; Ohio County; Pop. 582; Zip Code 42354; Elev. 426; Lat. 37-22-55 N long. 086-55-21 W; Settled in the 1850's as Hamelton, but renamed in 1874 to honor *Col. Henry McHenry,* U.S. Congressman in Kentucky's 4th District.

•**MCKEE,** City; Jackson County Seat; Pop. 759; Zip Code 40447; Elev. 1030; Lat. 37-25-49 N long. 083-59-53 W; *George McKee* was a state legislator here in the 1850's. It is named for him.

•**MIDDLESBOROUGH,** City; Bell County; Pop. 12,251; Zip Code 40965; Elev. 1138; Lat. 36-36-30 N long. 083-43-00 W; First settled in 1810 as Yellow Creek, but renamed in the 1890's by English land investors for Middlesborough, England.

•**MIDWAY,** City; Woodford County; Pop. 1,445; Zip Code 40347; Elev. 523; Lat. 37-08-16 N long. 087-46-52 W; The Lexington and Ohio Railroad founded the town in 1835 and named it for its location halfway between Lexington and Frankfort.

•**MILLERSBURG,** City; Bourbon County; Pop. 987; Zip Code 40348; Lat. 38-18-07 N long. 084-08-51 W; *Major John Miller* founded the town in 1798. The post office opened in 1804.

•**MONTEREY,** City; Owen County; Pop. 186; Elev. 487; Lat. 38-10-21 N long. 084-18-32 W; Founded in 1805 as Williamsburg, then called Cedar Creek, and finally Monterey to commemorate the battle fought in 1847 during the Mexican-American war.

•**MONTICELLO,** City; Wayne County Seat; Pop. 5,677; Zip Code 42633; Lat. 37-59-32 N long. 084-33-01 W; Established in 1801 and named for Jefferson's famous home.

•**MOREHEAD,** City; Rowan County Seat; Pop. 7,789; Zip Code 40351; Elev. 505; Lat. 37-16-16 N long. 087-10-35 W; Founded as Tripplet in 1817, but changed to Morehead in 1856. The town's name honors Kentucky governor *James Morehead.*

•**MORGANFIELD,** City; Union County Seat; Pop. 3,781; Zip Code 42437; Elev. 437; Lat. 37-41-00 N long. 087-55-00 W; Settled in the early 1800's and named in honor of *General Daniel Morgan,* who received the land for his Revolutionary War service.

•**MORGANTOWN,** City; Butler County Seat; Pop. 2,000; Zip Code 42261; Elev. 573; Lat. 37-13-32 N long. 086-41-01 W.

•**MORTONS GAP,** City; Hopkins County; Pop. 1,201; Lat. 37-14-12 N long. 087-28-31 W; *Thomas Morton* settled near the natural gap in the mountains in 1804. The subsequent town on the site was named for him.

•**MOUNT OLIVET,** City; Robertson County Seat; Pop. 346; Zip Code 41064; Elev. 958; Lat. 38-31-53 N long. 084-02-13 W; The city was founded in 1820 and given a Biblical name. It incorporated in 1851.

•**MOUNT STERLING,** City; Montgomery County Seat; Pop. 5,820; Zip Code 40353; Elev. 1027; Lat. 38-03-23 N long. 083-56-36 W; Settled in the late 1700's as "Little Mountain Town," the name was changed in 1792 after the city in Scotland.

•**MOUNT VERNON,** City; Rockcastle County Seat; Pop. 2,334; Zip Code 40456; Lat. 38-01-32 N long. 084-29-43 W; Founded in 1811 and named for *Washington's* famous home in Virginia.

•**MOUNT WASHINGTON,** City; Bullitt County; Pop. 3,997; Zip Code 40047; Elev. 688; Lat. 38-03-00 N long. 085-32-45 W; Known as Crossroads in the early 1800's, it's name was changed in 1830 to honor *George Washington.*

•**MUNFORDVILLE,** City; Hart County Seat; Pop. 1,783; Zip Code 42765; Elev. 612; Lat. 37-16-20 N long. 085-53-28 W; Central Kentucky. Pioneer *Richard Munford* settled here in 1816. The town is named in his honor.

•**MURRAY,** City; Calloway County Seat; Pop. 14,248; Zip Code 42071; Elev. 515; Lat. 36-36-37 N long. 088-18-53 W; 20 m ESE of Mayfield in SW Kentucky. Murray was founded in 1842 and named for U.S. Congressman *John Murray.*

•**NEBO,** City; Hopkins County; Pop. 269; Zip Code 42441; Lat. 37-23-01 N long. 087-38-34 W; W. Ky. Nebo was named for Biblical Mt. Nebo when it was founded in 1840.

•**NEW CASTLE,** City; Henry County Seat; Pop. 832; Zip Code 40050; Elev. 844; Lat. 38-26-00 N long. 085-10-11 W; N. Kentucky. Established in 1798 and named for the city in Pennsylvania.

•**NEW HAVEN,** City; Nelson County; Pop. 926; Zip Code 40051; Lat. 37-39-28 N long. 085-35-28 W; central Kentucky. Founded in 1820 and named for New Haven, Connecticut by a pioneer fond of that place.

•**NEWPORT,** City; Campbell County Seat; Pop. 21,587; Zip Code 41071; Lat. 39-05-29 N long. 084-29-45 W; E of Covington in N KY. Established in 1792 and named for *Captain Christopher Newport* who brought the first colonists to Jamestown in 1607.

•**NICHOLASVILLE,** City; Jessamine County Seat; Pop. 10,400; Zip Code 40356; Lat. 37-52-50 N long. 084-34-23 W; 10 m. SSW of Lexington in E central Kentucky. The city was founded in 1806 and named for *General George Nicholas,* Kentucky's first Attorney General.

•**OAK GROVE,** City; Christian County; Pop. 2,088; Zip Code 42262; Lat. 37-20-39 N long. 086-45-17 W; SW Kentucky. The city is descriptively named after a grove of oak trees.

•**OAKLAND,** City; Warren County; Pop. 264; Zip Code 42159; Elev. 579; Lat. 37-02-31 N long. 086-14-54 W; S Kentucky. Pioneer storekeeper *William Radford* named the town in 1859 for the many oak trees in the area.

•**OLIVE HILL,** City; Carter County; Pop. 2,539; Zip Code 41164; Elev. 760; Lat. 38-18-00 N long. 083-10-27 W; NE Kentucky. Founded in the early 1800's and incorporated in 1838. The origin of the name is unknown.

•**OWENSBORO,** City; Daviess County Seat; Pop. 54,450; Zip Code 42302; Lat. 37-46-27 N long. 087-06-48 W; 85 m. WSW of Louisville in NW Kentucky. First called Yellow Banks, the name was changed in 1816 to honor *Colonel Abraham Owen* who had been killed fighting Indians at the Battle of Tippencanoe.

•**OWENTON,** City; Owen County Seat; Pop. 1,341; Zip Code 40359; Elev. 960; Lat. 38-32-11 N long. 084-50-31 W; N Kentucky. Founded in 1822 and named after Kentucky Indian fighter *Colonel Abraham Owen.*

•**OWINGSVILLE,** City; Bath County Seat; Pop. 1,419; Zip Code 40360; Lat. 38-08-41 N long. 083-45-51 W; NE Kentucky. *Thomas Owings* donated land to the town in 1811. It is named for him.

•**PADUCAH,** City; McCracken County Seat; Pop. 29,315; Zip Code 42002. Lat. 37-05-00 N long. 088-36-00 W; William Clark, who was made Superintendent of Indian Affairs for Missouri (1822-1836), laid out the town site in 1827 , and named it for his Chickasaw friend, Chief Paduke.

•**PAINTSVILLE,** City; Johnson County Seat; Pop. 3,815; Zip Code 41240; Lat. 37-48-52 N long. 082-48-26 W; E Kentucky. *Rev. Henry Dixon* established the town in 1826, and named it for the many painted figures of animals found on tree trunks in the area.

•**PARIS,** City; Bourbon County Seat; Pop. 7,935; Zip Code 40361; Lat. 38-12-35 N long. 084-15-11 W; 20 m. NE of Lexington in NE Kentucky. Started in 1789 as Hopewell, but renamed in 1790 to honor France's help in the Revolutionary War.

•**PARK HILLS,** City; Kenton County; Pop. 3,500; Lat. 39-04-17 N long. 084-31-56 W; N Kentucky. Settled in the middle 1800's, but not given its present name until 1926 for its location near Devon Park.

•**PEWEE VALLEY,** City; Oldham County; Pop. 982; Zip Code 40056; Lat. 38-18-38 N long. 085-29-15 W; N Kentucky.

•**PIKEVILLE,** City; Pike County Seat; Pop. 4,756; Zip Code 4150++; Lat. 37-28-45 N long. 082-31-08 W; E Kentucky. Founded in 1825 and named in honor of *Zebulon Pike,* a U.S. Army officer who explored the early west.

•**PINEVILLE,** City; Bell County Seat; Pop. 2,599; Zip Code 40977; Elev. 1015; Lat. 36-45-43 N long. 083-41-42 W; SE Kentucky. Known as Cumberland Ford when it was founded in 1818, the name was eventually changed to reflect the many pine trees in the area.

•**PLEASUREVILLE,** City; Henry & Shelby Counties; Pop. 837; Zip Code 40057; Elev. 838; Lat. 38-28-41 N long. 083-36-13 W; N central Kentucky. The first settlers arrived in 1784 and named the place Bantatown.A chance remark by a pleased visitor led to its being given the current name in the 1820's.

•**POWDERLY,** City; Muhlenberg County; Pop. 848; Zip Code 42367; Lat. 37-14-13 N long. 087-09-33 W; W Kentucky. *Terence Powderly* opened a coal mine here in 1887. The town is named for him.

•**PRESTONBURG,** City; Floyd County Seat; Pop. 4,011; Zip Code 41653; Lat. 37-39-56 N long. 082-46-18 W; E Kentucky. The city was founded in 1797 on *John Preston's* 100,000 acre land grant. It is named for him.

•**PRINCETON,** City; Caldwell County Seat; Pop. 7,073; Zip Code 42445; Lat. 37-06-33 N long. 087-52-55 W; 40 m. E of Paducah in W Kentucky. Founded as Eddy's Grove, it was renamed in 1817 to honor pioneer *William Prince.*

•**PROSPECT,** City; Jefferson County; Pop. 1,981; Zip Code 40059; Lat. 38-20-42 N long. 085-36-56 W; N central Kentucky. Established as a railroad station, the view from a nearby hill led people to admire the "prospect," hence, the town's name.

•**PROVIDENCE,** City; Webster County; Pop. 4,434; Zip Code 42450; Elev. 736; Lat. 36-52-01 N long. 083-54-42 W; W Kentucky. Settled in the 1820's and named after Providence, Rhode Island.

•RACELAND, City; Greenup County; Pop. 1,970; Zip Code 41169; Lat. 38-32-24 N long. 082-43-43 W; NE Kentucky. Called Chinnville for many years, it was renamed in 1925 when a racetrack opened nearby.

•RADCLIFF, City; Hardin County; Pop. 14,519; Zip Code 40160; Lat. 37-50-25 N long. 085-56-57 W; Central Kentucky. Founded in 1919 and named for a popular army officer, one Major Radcliff.

•ROCHESTER, City; Butler County; Pop. 289; Zip Code 42273; Lat. 37-12-45 N long. 086-53-35 W; W central Kentucky. Established in the 1830's and named for Rochester, New York.

•RUSSELL, City; Greenup County; Pop. 3,824; Zip Code 41169; Lat. 38-31-02 N long. 082-41-52 W; NE Kentucky. Established in 1869 by John Russell, a mining executive, and named for him.

•RUSSELL SPRINGS, City; Russell County; Pop. 1,831; Zip Code 42642; Lat. 37-03-22 N long. 085-05-19 W; S Kentucky. Founded as a health resort, the Russell Springs post office opened in 1855.

•RUSSELLVILLE, City; Logan County Seat; Pop. 7,520; Zip Code 42276; Elev. 595; Lat. 36-50-43 N long. 086-53-14 W; 35 m. E ofHopkinsville in S Kentucky. Russelville began in 1795 and named for Revolutionary war hero General William Russell.

•SACRAMENTO, City; McLean County; Pop. 538; Zip Code 42372; Elev. 497; Lat. 37-24-57 N long. 087-15-56 W; W Kentucky. Founded in the 1850's during the California gold rush and named after Sacramento, California.

•ST CHARLES, City; Hopkins County; Pop. 405; Zip Code 42453; Lat. 37-11-10 N long. 087-33-21 W; W Kentucky. Incorporated as St. Charles in 1874. The origin of the name is unknown.

•ST MATTHEWS, City; Jefferson County; Pop. 13,354; Zip Code 402++; Lat. 38-15-10 N long. 085-39-21 W; E suburb of Louisville in N central Kentucky. Settled in the late 1840's and named for a local church.

•ST REGIS PARK, City; Jefferson County; Pop. 1,735; Lat. 38-13-36 N long. 085-37-00 W; N central Kentucky. Incorporated in 1853 and named for a local Catholic church.

•SALEM, City; Livingston County; Pop. 833; Zip Code 42078; Elev. 448; Lat. 37-15-52 N long. 088-14-39 W; W Kentucky. The old log houses of the early settlers who came here with their slaves from Virginia and Carolina, once dotted this region.

•SALYERSVILLE, City; Magoffin County Seat; Pop. 1,352; Zip Code 41465; Elev. 854; Lat. 37-45-09 N long. 083-04-08 W; E Kentucky. When Magoffin County was formed in 1860, the town's name was changed to honor Sam Salyers, the district's legislative representative.

•SANDERS, City; Carroll County; Pop. 332; Zip Code 41083; Lat. 38-39-19 N long. 084-56-50 W; N Kentucky. Nathaniel Sanders founded the town in 1816. It is named for him.

•SCIENCE HILL, City; Pulaski County; Pop. 655; Zip Code 42553; Elev. 1117; Lat. 37-10-37 N long. 084-38-09 W; SE central Kentucky. Scientist William Bobbitt collected many rock samples on the site, and his investigations gave the town its name.

•SCOTTSVILLE, City; Allen County Seat; Pop. 4,278; Zip Code 42164; Elev. 760; Lat. 36-45-12 N long. 086-11-26 W; S central Kentucky. Named for Gen. Charles Scott, fourth Governor of Kentucky.

•SEBREE, City; Webster County; Pop. 1,516; Zip Code 42455; Elev. 404; Lat. 37-26-09 N long. 083-28-24 W; W Kentucky. Colonel E. G. Sebree founded the town in 1868. It is named for him.

•SHELBYVILLE, City; Shelby County Seat; Pop. 5,308; Zip Code 40065; Elev. 791; Lat. 38-12-43 N long. 085-13-25 W; 20 m. W of Frankfort in n central Kentucky. Founded in 1792 and named, as was the county, for Isaac Shelby, Kentucky's first Governor.

•SHEPHERDSVILLE, City; Bullitt County Seat; Pop. 4,454; Zip Code 40165; Elev. 449; Lat. 37-59-18 N long. 085-42-57 W; central Kentucky. Pioneer Adam Shepard built a mill here in 1793. The town is named for him.

•SHIVELY, City; Jefferson County; Pop. 16,819; Zip Code 40216; Lat. 38-12-00 N long. 085-49-22 W; S suburb of Louisville in N central Kentucky. The Shiverly family settled here in 1780 and left their name on the subsequent town.

•SILVER GROVE, City; Campbell County; Pop. 1,260; Zip Code 41085; Elev. 494; Lat. 39-02-04 N long. 084-23-25 W; N Kentucky. The railroad created the town in 1912 and named it for a nearby grove of silver popular trees.

•SMITHFIELD, City; Henry County; Pop. 137; Zip Code 40068; Elev. 891; Lat. 38-23-12 N long. 085-15-25 W; N Kentucky. Incorporated in 1870 and named for railroad president Thomas Smith.

•SOMERSET, City; Pulaski County Seat; Pop. 10,649; Zip Code 42564; Lat. 37-05-31 N long. 084-36-15 W; 40 m. S of Danville in SE central Kentucky. Named for the Duke of Somerset, and made the seat of Pulaski County by court order in 1801.

•SONORA, City; Hardin County; Pop. 416; Zip Code 42776; Lat. 37-31-27 N long. 085-53-35 W; Central Kentucky. The railroad established the town in 1859. The name Sonora remembers the name of a Mexican-born railroad contractor.

•SOUTHGATE, City; Campbell County; Pop. 2,833; Zip Code 41071; Lat. 39-04-19 N long. 084-28-22 W; Founded in 1907 and named in honor of pioneer Richard Southgate who had lived in the area one hundred years earlier.

•SPARTA, City; Gallatin/Owen County; Pop. 192; Zip Code 41086; Elev. 503; Lat. 38-40-37 N long. 084-54-25 W; Settled in 1800 and named for a local grist mill.

•SPRINGFIELD, City; Washington County Seat; Pop. 3,179; Zip Code 40069; Elev. 773; Lat. 37-41-07 N long. 085-13-20 W; Established in 1793 and named for the area's many springs.

•STANFORD, City; Lincoln County Seat; Pop. 2,764; Zip Code 40484; Elev. 946; Lat. 37-31-52 N long. 084-39-43 W; three original counties of the Kentucky District of Virginia formed in 1780.

•STURGIS, City; Union County; Pop. 2,293; Zip Code 42459; Lat. 37-32-48 N long. 087-59-02 W; Sturgis was found in 1886 as a coal mining town. It is named after the original landowner Samuel Sturgis.

•TAYLOR MILL, City; Kenton County; Pop. 4,509; Lat. 38-59-51 N long. 084-29-47 W; Although not incorporated until 1956, it was named for a mill founded in 1790 by pioneer James Taylor.

•TOLLESBORO, City; Lewis County; Pop. 808; Zip Code 41189; Elev. 816; Lat. 38-33-34 N long. 083-34-34 W; Founded in the 1840's and named after the pioneer Tolle family who had arrived in the area in 1809.

•TOMKINSVILLE, City; Monroe County Seat; Pop. 4,366; Zip Code 42167; Elev. 923; Lat. 36-42-08 N long. 085-41-30 W; The town grew around a store built in 1809. It was named in honor of U.S. Vice President Daniel Tompkins.

•TRENTON, City; Todd County; Pop. 465; Zip Code 42286; Lat. 36-43-26 N long. 087-15-46 W; Settled in 1796 as Lewisburg, and renamed in 1819 after Trenton, New Jersey.

•**UNIONTOWN**, City; Union County; Pop. 1,169; Zip Code 42461; Lat. 37-46-31 N long. 087-55-50 W; The towns of Francisburg and Locust Port merged in 1840. The new name resulted.

•**UPTON**, City; Hardin & Larue Counties; Pop. 731; Zip Code 42784; Elev. 744; Lat. 37-27-54 N long. 085-53-36 W; Founded as Leesville in 1841, but renamed to Upton by pioneer *George Upton* in 1856.

•**VANCEBURG**, City; Lewis County Seat; Pop. 1,939; Zip Code 41179; Elev. 525; Lat. 38-35-57 N long. 083-19-08 W.

•**VERSAILLES**, City; Woodford County Seat; Pop. 6,427; Zip Code 40383; Lat. 38-03-09 N long. 084-43-48 W; Named by *General Calmes* for Versailles, France, as a tribute to *Louis XVI* for his timely aid in the Revolutionary War.

•**VICCO**, City; Perry County; Pop. 456; Zip Code 41773; Lat. 37-12-56 N long. 083-03-42 W; The town's initial stand for the Virginia Iron Coal and Coke Company.

•**VILLA HILLS**, City; Kenton County; Pop. 4,402; N Kentucky. The town's name reflects the nearby Catholic monastery Villa Madonna founded in 1903.

•**VINE GROVE**, City; Hardin County; Pop. 3,583; Zip Code 40175; Elev. 682; Lat. 37-48-36 N long. 085-58-53 W; Settled in the 1850's and named for the many wild grape vines on the town site.

•**WALLINS CREEK**, City; Harlan County; Pop. 459; Zip Code 40873; Lat. 36-49-52 N long. 083-25-01 W; SE Kentucky. A pioneer surveyor named *Wallis* was killed near here. It is named for him.

•**WALTON**, City; Boone County; Pop. 1,651; Zip Code 41094; Elev. 930; Lat. 38-52-12 N long. 084-36-48 W; N Kentucky. Founded in 1786 and named for an early settler.

•**WARSAW**, City; Gallatin County Seat; Pop. 1,328; Zip Code 41095; Elev. 495; Lat. 38-47-00 N long. 084-54-06 W; N central Kentucky. The town was founded in 1815 and named after the popular novel "Thaddeus of Warsaw."

•**WASHINGTON**, City; Mason County; Pop. 624; Zip Code 41096; Elev. 547; Lat. 38-36-57 N long. 083-48-31 W; NE Kentucky. Chartered in 1787 and named in honor of *George Washington.*

•**WATER VALLEY**, City; Graves County; Pop. 395; Zip Code 42085; SW Kentucky. Descriptively named for its water resources, and tendency to flood during heavy rains.

•**WAVERLY**, City; Union County; Pop. 434; Zip Code 42462; Lat. 37-42-35 N long. 087-48-46 W; W Kentucky. The town was established in 1870 and named for the nephew of founder *Hugh McElroy.*

•**WAYLAND**, City; Floyd County; Pop. 601; Zip Code 41666; Lat. 37-26-42 N long. 082-48-19 W; E Kentucky. Founded in 1913 and named for U.S. Senator *Clarence Wayland Watson.*

•**WELLINGTON**, City; Jefferson County; Pop. 653; Zip Code 40387; Elev. 1202; Lat. 38-12-59 N long. 085-40-09 W; N central Kentucky. Wellington began in 1880 and is named for town founder *Wellington Davis.*

•**WEST POINT**, City; Hardin County; Pop. 1,339; Zip Code 40177; Elev. 438; Lat. 37-59-58 N long. 085-56-37 W; Central Kentucky. Founded in 1796 and descriptively named for its location on the Ohio River.

•**WHEATCROFT**, City; Webster County; Pop. 325; Zip Code 42463; Elev. 372; Lat. 37-29-24 N long. 087-51-46 W; W Kentucky. Named in honor of Englishman *Irving Wheatcroft* who laid out the town in 1899.

•**WHEELWRIGHT**, City; Floyd County; Pop. 865; Zip Code 41669; Elev. 1102; Lat. 37-19-57 N long. 082-43-16 W; E Kentucky. Established in 1916 as a coal mining town and named in honor of coal company president *Jere Wheelwright.*

•**WHITE PLAINS**, City; Hopkins County; Pop. 859; Zip Code 42464; Elev. 412; Lat. 37-11-01 N long. 087-23-01 W; W Kentucky. First settled in 1853 and named for the open, prairie-like plain it is found on.

•**WHITESBURG**, City; Letcher County Seat; Pop. 1,525; Zip Code 41858; Elev. 1164; Lat. 37-07-06 N long. 082-49-37 W; SE Kentucky. Named for *C. White,* a member of the legislature when the county was formed.

•**WHITESVILLE**, City; Daviess County; Pop. 788; Zip Code 42378; Lat. 37-40-59 N long. 086-52-17 W; NW Kentucky. *Dr. William White* founded the town in 1844. It is named for him.

•**WICKLIFFE**, City; Ballard County Seat; Pop. 1,044; Zip Code 42087; Lat. 36-57-53 N long. 089-05-21 W; W Kentucky.

•**WILDER**, City; Campbell County; Pop. 633; N Kentucky. Established in 1935 and named for prominent eye doctor *William Wilder.*

•**WILDWOOD**, City; Jefferson County; Pop. 309; Lat. 38-14-58 N long. 085-34-23 W; N central Kentucky. Descriptively named by its early settlers.

•**WILLIAMSBURG**, City; Whitley County Seat; Pop. 5,560; Zip Code 40769; Elev. 951; Lat. 36-44-36 N long. 084-09-35 W; SE Kentucky. Named for *Col. William Whitley,* a pioneer renowned as an Indian fighter.

•**WILLIAMSTOWN**, City; Grant County Seat; Pop. 2,502; Zip Code 41097; Elev. 974; Lat. 38-38-17 N long. 084-33-38 W; N Kentucky. It was named for *William Arnold,* who in 1820 gave the land for the public buildings, and free timber to all who purchased lots from him.

•**WILMORE**, City; Jessamine County; Pop. 3,787; Zip Code 40390; Lat. 37-51-43 N long. 084-39-42 W; E central Kentucky. Founded in 1877 and named for local landowner *John Wilmore.*

•**WINCHESTER**, City; Clark County Seat; Pop. 15,216; Zip Code 40391; Lat. 37-59-24 N long. 084-10-47 W; 20 mi. E of Lexington in E central Kentucky. The settlement incorporated in 1793, was named for Winchester, Virginia, the former home of *John Baker,* its founder.

•**WOODLAND HILLS**, City; Jefferson County; Pop. 839; Lat. 38-14-25 N long. 085-31-27 W; N central Kentucky. Founded in 1955 and given a descriptive name.

•**WOODLAWN PARK**, City; Jefferson County; Pop. 1,052; Lat. 38-15-41 N long. 085-37-45 W; N central Kentucky. Founded in 1854 and named for the Woodlawn Race Track.

LOUISIANA

•**ABBEVILLE,** City; Vermilion County Seat; Pop. 12,391; Zip Code 70510; Elev. 18; Lat. 29-58-28 N long. 092-07-27 W; 20 mi. SSW of Lafayette in S Louisiana. Established as a town in 1845. Named for the city in France.

•**ABITA SPRINGS,** City; St. Tammany County; Pop. 1,072; Zip Code 70420; Lat.30-28-31 N long. 090-02-02 W; SE Louisiana. The town takes its name from the Choctaw Indian word for spring.

•**ADDIS,** Town; West Baton Rouge County; Pop. 1,320; Zip Code 70710; Elev. 19; Lat. 30-21-32 N long. 091-15-39 W; SE central Louisiana.

•**ALBANY,** Village; Livingston County; Pop. 857; Zip Code 70711; Elev. 41; Lat. 30-29-57 N long. 090-35-00 W; SE Louisiana. The village is named after the city in New York State.

•**ALEXANDRIA,** City; Rapides County Seat; Pop. 51,565; Zip Code 71301; Elev. 82; Lat. 31-16-51 N long. 092-28-35 W; 100 mi. NW of Baton Rouge in central Louisiana. Town named after the daughter of the original surveyor.

•**AMITE CITY,** Town; Tangipahoa County Seat; Pop. 4,301; Zip Code 70422; Lat. 30-42-08 N long. 090-34-39 W; SE Louisiana. A Tangipahoa Indian word meaning friendly, the French translated the word to amite.

•**ANACOCO,** Village; Vernon County; Pop. 90; Zip Code 71403; Lat. 31-14-57 N long. 093-20-25 W; W Louisiana.

•**ANGIE,** Village; Washington County; Pop. 311; Zip Code 70426; Elev. 142; Lat. 30-57-53 N long. 089-48-41 W; E Louisiana. The Village takes it's name from the wife of an early settler.

•**ARCADIA,** Town; Bienville County Seat; Pop. 3,403; Zip Code 71001; Elev. 360; Lat. 32-33-01 N long. 092-55-15 W; NW Louisiana. Town named for the 18th century French colony in Nova Scotia.

•**ARNAUDVILLE,** Town; St. Landry & St. Martin Counties; Pop. 1,679; Zip Code 70512; Elev. 29; Lat. 30-23-55 N long. 091-55-57 W; S central Louisiana. The town is named for French settler M. Arnaud.

•**ASHLAND,** Village; Natchitoches County; Pop. 307; Zip Code 71002; Elev. 238; Lat. 32-07-33 N long. 093-06-04 W; NW central Louisiana.

•**ATHENS,** Village; Claiborne County; Pop. 419; Zip Code 71003; Elev. 299; Lat. 32-39-05 N long. 093-01-19 W; N Louisiana. Settled in the 1830's and named after the ancient Greek city.

•**ATLANTA,** Village; Winn County; Pop. 127; Zip Code 71404; Lat. 31-48-19 N long. 092-44-43 W; N central Louisiana. The village is named for the city in Georgia.

•**BAKER,** City; East Baton Rouge County; Pop. 12,865; Zip Code 70714; Lat. 30-35-08 N long. 091-10-17 W; 10 mi. N of Baton Rouge in SE central Louisiana. The town's name comes from an early pioneer in Baton Rouge.

•**BALDWIN,** Town; St. Mary County; Pop. 2,644; Zip Code 70514; Lat. 29-50-01 N long. 091-32-58 W; S Louisiana.

•**BALL,** Town; Rapides County; Pop. 3,405; Zip Code 71405; Lat. 31-25-02 N long. 092-24-39 W; central Louisiana.

•**BASILE,** Town; Evangeline County; Pop. 2,635; Zip Code 70515; Elev. 46; Lat. 30-29-03 N long. 092-36-06 W; S central Louisiana. Settled in 1905 the town is named after its first inhabitant, Basile Fontenot.

•**BASKIN,** Village; Franklin County; Pop. 286; Zip Code 71219; Lat. 32-15-04 N long. 091-44-36W; NE Louisiana.

•**BASTROP,** City; Morehouse County Seat; Pop. 15,527; Zip Code 71220; Elev. 126; Lat. 32-46-42 N long. 091-55-00 W; 24 mi. NNE of Monroe in N Louisiana. Named after one of the large French land grants in the from which a number of parishes were set up.

•**BATON ROUGE,** City; East Baton Rouge County Seat; Pop. 219,486; Zip Code 70800; Lat. 30-27-05 N long. 091-08-35 W; 78 mi. WNW of New Orleans in SE central Louisiana. Possibly the name of an indian chief, or a site of an indian massacre, the name means red staff.

•**BELCHER,** Village; Caddo County; Pop. 436; Zip Code 71004; Lat. 32-45-13 N long. 093-49-57 W; NW corner of Louisiana.

•**BENTON,** Town; Bossier County Seat; Pop. 1,864; Zip Code 71006; Elev. 215; Lat. 32-41-19 N long. 093-44-23 W; NW Louisiana.

•**BERNICE,** Town; Union County; Pop. 1,956; Zip Code 71222; Lat. 32-49-40 N long. 092-39-28 W; N Louisiana.

•**BERWICK,** Town; St.Mary County; Pop. 4,466; Zip Code 70342; Lat. 29-41-25 N long. 091-13-11 W; S Louisiana.

•**BIENVILLE,** Village; Bienville County; Pop. 249; Zip Code 71008; Elev. 238; Lat. 32-21-23 N long. 092-58-48 W; NW Louisiana. The village is named after French explorer Jean Baptiste Le Moyne De Bienville.

•**BLANCHARD,** Village; Caddo County; Pop. 1,128; Zip Code 71009; Lat. 32-31-35 N long. 093-44-24 W; NW corner of Louisiana. Named for a French settler, Blanchard.

•**BOGULSA,** City; Washington County; Pop. 16,976; Zip Code 70427; Lat. 30-46-52 N long. 089-51-25 W; 60 mi. NNE of New Orleans in E Louisiana. A Choctaw Indian name that means black creek.

•**BONITA,** Village; Morehouse County; Pop. 503; Zip Code 71223; Lat. 32-55-13 N long. 091-40-22 W; N Louisiana.

•**BOSSIER CITY,** City; Bossier County; Pop. 49,969; Zip Code 711+; E suburb of Shreveport in NW Louisiana. The city is named for General Pierre Bossier, an early French commander.

•**BOYCE,** Town; Rapides County; Pop. 1,198; Zip Code 71409; Elev. 84; Lat. 31-23-32 N long. 092-40-16 W; central Louisiana.

•**BREAUX BRIDGE,** City; St. Martin County; Pop. 5,922; Zip Code 70517; Lat. 30-16-18 N long. 091-54-19 W; 8 mi. ENE of Lafayette in E Louisiana. Named for an early French settler, Breaux.

•**BROUSSARD,** Town; Lafayette County; Pop. 2,923; Zip Code 70518; Lat. 30-08-49 N long. 091-57-48 W; S Louisiana. Named for settler Joseph Broussard who was a captain in the French militia.

•**BRUSLY,** Town; West Baton Rouge County; Pop. 1,762; Zip Code 70719; Lat. 30-23-14 N long. 091-14-15 W; SE central Louisiana. The town gets its name from the French verb to burn, and refers to the settlement's original clearing.

•**BRYCELAND,** Village; Bienville County; Pop. 94; Zip Code 71014; Elev. 264; Lat. 32-27-00 N long. 092-59-00; NW Louisiana. The village is named after the Bryce family whose plantation stood on the townsite.

•**BUNKIE,** Town; Avoyelles County; Pop. 5,364; Zip Code 71322; Lat. 30-57-12 N long. 092-11-06 N; 28 mi. SSE of Alexandria in central Louisiana. Originally called Irion, the town later took the nickname of the founder's daughter.

•**CALVIN,** Village; Winn County; Pop. 263; Zip Code 71410; Lat. 31-57-56 N long. 092-46-43 W; N central Louisiana.

•**CAMPTI,** Town; Natchitoches County; Pop. 1,069; Zip Code 71411; Lat. 31-53-50 N long. 093-07-03 W; NW central Louisiana. Named by the early settlers in honor of a local Indian chief.

•**CANKTON,** Village; St. Landry County; Pop. 303; S central Louisiana.

•**CARENCO,** Town; Lafayette County; Pop. 3,712; Zip Code 70520; Lat. 30-19-16 N long. 092-02-48 W; S Louisiana.

•**CASTOR,** Village; Bienville County; Pop. 195; Zip Code 71060; Elev. 165; Lat. 32-15-04 N long. 093-09-59 W; NW Louisiana. Named by the French for the abundance of beavers.

•**CHATAIGNIER,** Village; Evangeline County; Pop. 431; Zip Code 70524; Lat. 30-34-10 N long. 092-19-09 W; S central Louisiana. Chataignier is the French word for Chestnut Tree, which were formerly found in profusion in the area.

•**CHATHAM,** Town; Jackson County; Pop. 714; Zip Code 71226; Lat. 32-18-30 N long. 092-26-58 W; N Louisiana.

•**CHENEYVILLE,** Town; Rapides County; Pop. 865; Zip Code 71325; Elev. 63; Lat. 31-00-41 N long. 092-17-09 W; central Louisiana. The town is named after William Cheney, who led a group of settlers here in 1811.

•**CHOUDRANT,** Village; Lincoln County; Pop. 809; Zip Code 71227; Elev. 188; Lat. 32-31-44 N long. 092-30-46 W; N Louisiana. Either named for an pioneer settler, or the French word for cauldron.

•**CHURCH POINT,** Town; Acadia; Pop. 4,599; Zip Code 70525; Elev. 46; Lat. 30-24-12 N long. 092-12-52 W; S Louisiana.

•**CLARENCE,** Village; Natchitoches County; Pop. 612; Zip Code 71414; Elev. 118; Lat. 31-49-25 N long. 093-01-35 W; NW central Louisiana. Originally called Tiger Island, the village changed its name after the war between the states to honor a prominent citizen.

•**CLARKS,** Village; Caldwell County; Pop. 931; Zip Code 71415; Elev. 133; Lat. 32-01-36 N long. 092-08-15 W; N central Louisiana.

•**CLAYTON,** Village; Concordia County; Pop. 1,204; Zip Code 71326; Elev. 61; Lat. 31-45-29 N long. 091-32-14 W; E central Louisiana. Named for American statesman Henry Clay.

•**CLINTON,** Town; East Feliciana County Seat; Pop. 1,919; Zip Code 70722; Elev. 209; Lat. 30-51-47 N long. 091-00-59 W; E Louisiana. Named for De Witt Clinton, governor of New York and builder of the Erie Canal.

•**COLFAX,** Town; Grant County Seat; Pop. 1,680; Zip Code 71417; Elev. 100; Lat. 31-31-15 N long. 092-42-23 W; central Louisiana. The town was maned during reconstruction for Grant's vice-president, Schuyler Colfax.

•**COLLINSTON,** Village; Morehouse County; Pop. 439; Zip Code 71229; Elev. 82; Lat. 32-41-18 N long. 091-52-13 W; N Louisiana.

•**COLUMBIA,** Town; Caldwell County Seat; Pop. 687; Zip Code 71418; Elev. 66; Lat. 32-06-07 N long. 092-04-36 W; N central Louisiana. Settled in 1827 by Daniel Humphries who gave the town the popular name for America.

•**CONVERSE,** Village; Sabine County; Pop. 449; Zip Code 71419; Lat. 31-46-50 N long. 093-41-47 W; W Louisiana. The town is named for Colonel James Converse.

•**COTTON VALLEY,** Town; Webster County; Pop. 1,445; Zip Code 71018; Lat. 32-48-53 N long. 093-25-02 W; NW Louisiana. Named after the region's major agricultural activity.

•**COTTONPORT,** Town; Avoyelles County; Pop. 1,911; Zip Code 71327; Elev. 56; Lat. 30-59-16 N long. 092-03-09 W; central Louisiana. The town takes its name from being a center of cotton transport.

•**COUSHATTA,** Town; Red River County Seat; Pop. 2,084; Zip Code 71019; Elev. 145; Lat. 32-01-56 N long. 093-20-22 W; NW Louisiana. Named for the Choctaw Indian word for white reed-break.

•**COVINGTON,** City; St. Tammany; Pop. 7,892; Zip Code 70433; Lat. 30-28-45 N long. 090-06-06 W; 37 mi. N of New Orleans in SE Louisiana. First called Wharton, the name was changed in 1816 to honor General Leonard Covington who fought in the War of 1812.

•**CROWLEY,** City; Acadia County Seat; Pop. 16,036; Zip Code 70526; Lat. 30-12-56 N long. 092-22-16 W; 24 mi. W of Lafayette in S Louisiana. Originally called Houstch, the town is named after a section hand on the Southern Pacific railroad of the 1880's.

•**CULLEN,** Town; Webster County; Pop. 1,869; Zip Code 71021; Lat. 32-58-06 N long. 093-26-48 W; NW Louisiana.

•**DE QUINCY,** Town; Calcasieu County; Pop. 3,966; Zip Code 70633; Elev. 65; Lat. 30-27-05 N long. 093-25-58 W; SW Louisiana.

•**DE RIDDER,** City; Beauregard & Vernon Counties; Beauregard County Seat; Pop. 11,057; Zip Code 70634; 42 mi. N of Lake Charles in SW Louisiana.

•**DELCAMBRE,** Town; Iberia & Vermilion Counties; Pop. 2,216; Zip Code 70528; Lat. 29-56-58 N long. 091-59-15 W; S Louisiana. Named in honor of Frenchman Desire Delcambre.

•**DELHI,** Town; Richland County; Pop. 3,290; Zip Code 71232; Lat. 32-27-40 N long. 091-29-19 W; NE Louisiana. Named by settler John Bishop for the great city in India.

•**DELTA,** Village; Madison County; Pop. 295; Zip Code 71233; Lat. 32-18-56 N long. 090-55-28 W; NE Louisiana. Named for its physical geography near the Mississippi River.

•**DENHAM SPRINGS,** City; Livingston County; Pop. 8,412; Zip Code 70726; Lat. 30-24-31 N long. 090-53-58 W; E of Baton Rouge in SE Louisiana. Named after the mineral springs discovered by William Denham in 1827.

•**DODSON,** Village; Winn County; Pop. 469; Zip Code 71422; Elev. 232; Lat. 32-04-55 N long. 092-39-31 W; N central Louisiana. Originally called Pyburn, it was renamed after a prominent settler.

•**DONALDSONVILLE,** City; Ascension County Seat; Pop. 7,901; Zip Code 70346; Lat. 30-05-59 N long. 090-59-45 W; 28 mi. SSE of Baton Rouge in SE Louisiana. In 1806 a New Orleans Englishman, William Donaldson, bought a large tract of land and offered it to the state for a capitol. In 1822 the town incorporated and took his name.

•**DOWNSVILLE,** Village; Lincoln & Union Counties; Pop. 213; Zip Code 71234; Elev. 253; Lat. 31-54-01 N long. 092-14-37 W; N Louisiana.

•**DOYLINE,** Village; Webster County; Pop. 801; Zip Code 71023; Elev. 223; Lat. 32-31-45 N long. 093-24-34 W; NW Louisiana.

•**DRY PRONG,** Village; Grant County; Pop. 526; Zip Code 71423; Elev. 196; Lat. 31-34-38 N long. 092-31-48 W; central Louisiana.

•**DUBACH,** Town; Lincoln County; Pop. 1,161; Zip Code 71235; Elev. 142; Lat. 32-41-55 N long. 092-39-26 W; N Louisiana.

•**DUBBERLY,** Village; Webster County; Pop. 421; Zip Code 71024; Elev. 256; Lat. 32-32-32 N long. 093-14-06 W; NW Louisiana.

•**DUSON,** Town; Lafayette County; Pop. 1,253; Zip Code 70529; Lat. 30-14-03 N long. 092-11-10 W; S Louisiana.

•**ELIZABETH,** Town; Allen County; Pop. 454; Zip Code 70638; Lat. 30-52-04 N LONG. 092-47-28 W; SW Louisiana.

•**ELTON,** Town; Jefferson Davis County; Pop. 1,450; Zip Code 70532; Elev. 50 Lat. 30-28-50 N long. 092-41-38 W; SW Louisiana.

•**EPPS,** Village; West Carroll County; Pop. 672; Zip Code 71237; Lat. 32-36-12 N long. 091-28-29 W; NE Louisiana.

•**ERATH,** Town; Vermiliom County; Pop. 2,133; Zip Code 70533; Elev. 9; Lat. 29-57-23 N long. 092-01-55 W; S Louisiana.

•**EROS,** Village; Jackson County; Pop. 158; Zip Code 71238; Elev. 192; Lat. 32-23-37 N long. 092-25-16 W; N Louisiana.

•**ESTHERWOOD,** Village; Acadia County; Pop. 691; Zip Code 70534; Elev. 15; Lat. 30-10-49 N long. 092-27-42 W; S Louisiana.

•**EUNICE,** City; Acadia & St. Landry Counties; Pop. 12,479; Zip Code 70535; Elev. 49; Lat. 30-28-49 N long. 092-25-17 W; 32 mi. NW of Lafayette in S central Louisiana. Founded in 1894 by C.C. Duson and named after his wife.

•**EVERGREEN,** Town; Avoyelles County; Pop. 272; Zip Code 71333; Lat. 30-57-24 N long. 092-06-31 W; central Louisiana.

•**FARMERVILLE,** Town; Union County Seat; Pop. 3,768; Zip Code 71241; Elev. 113; Lat. 32-46-25 N long. 092-24-08 W; N Louisiana.

•**FENTON,** Village; Jefferson Davis County; Pop. 491; Zip Code 70640; Elev. 34; Lat. 30-15-00 N long. 092-49-03 W; SW Louisiana..

•**FERRIDAY,** Town; Concordia County; Pop. 4,472; Zip Code 71334; Elev. 63; Lat. 31-37-36 N long. 091-32-24 W; E central Louisiana. Named for John Ferriday who owned the land upon which the town was built in 1903.

•**FISHER,** Village; Sabine County; Pop. 325; Zip Code 71426; Elev. 336; Lat. 31-29-33 N long. 093-27-59 W; W Louisiana.

•**FLORIEN,** Village; Sabine County; Pop. 964; Zip Code 71429; Elev. 253; Lat. 31-26-41 N long. 093-27-28 W; W Louisiana. Established in the late nineteenth century and named for Florien Giauque, a rich landowner.

•**FOLSOM,** Village; St. Tammany County; Pop. 319; Zip Code 70437; Lat. 30-37-44 N long. 090-11-19 W; SE Louisiana.

•**FOREST,** Village; West Carroll County; Pop. 299; Zip Code 71242; Lat. 32-47-36 N long. 091-24-38 W; NE Louisiana.

•**FOREST HILL,** Village; Rapides County; Pop. 494; Zip Code 71430; Elev. 167; Lat. 31-02-42 N long. 092-31-45 W; central Louisiana. Originally called Bismark, the town's later name recalls the Choctaw Indian village upon the site.

•**FRANKLIN,** City; St. Mary County Seat; Pop. 9,584; Zip Code 70538; Lat. 29-47-38 N long. 091-30-08 W; S Louisiana. Founded in 1800 by a former Pennsylvanian to honor Benjamin Franklin.

•**FRANKLINTON,** Town; Washington County Seat; Pop. 4,119; Zip Code 70438; Elev. 155; Lat. 30-50-53 N long. 090-08-56 W; E Louisiana.

•**FRENCH SETTLEMEMT,** Village; Livingston County; Pop. 761; Zip Code 70733; Elev. 14 Lat. 30-03-51 N long. 090-50-14 W; SE Louisiana.

•**GEORGETOWN,** Village; Grant County; Pop. 381; Zip Code 71432; Elev. 96; Lat. 31-45-52 long. 092-23-07 W; central Louisiana.

•**GIBSLAND,** Town; Bienville County; Pop. 1,354; Zip Code 71028; Elev. 294; Lat. 32-31-23 N long. 093-02-55 W; NW Louisiana. The town began as railroad junction on the former plantation of Dr.Gibs and hence the name.

•**GILBERT,** Village; Franklin County; Pop. 800; Zip Code 71336; Lat. 32-02-51 N long. 091-39-16 W; NE Louisiana.

•**GILLIAM,** Village; Caddo County; Pop. 244; Zip Code 71029; Lat. 32-49-34 N long. 093-50-44 W; NW corner of Louisiana.

•**GLENMORA,** Town; Rapides County; Pop. 1,479; Zip Code 71433; Elev. 136; Lat. 30-59-19 N long. 092-34-13 W; central Louisiana.

•**GOLDEN MEADOW,** Town; Lafourche County; Pop. 2,282; Zip Code 70357; Elev. 2; Lat. 29-23-06 N long. 090-16-22 W; SE Louisiana. Named for the level, grassy marshes of nearby Bayou LaFourche.

•**GOLDONNA,** Village; Natchitoches County; Pop. 526; Zip Code 71030; Elev. 144; Lat. 32-01-04 N long. 092-54-14 W; NW central Louisiana.

•**GONZALES,** City; Ascension County; Pop. 7,287; Zip Code 70737; Lat. 30-13-52 N long. 090-55-11 W; SE Louisiana. Named in 1887 for a local settler.

•**GRAMBLING,** Town; Lincoln County; Pop. 4,226; Zip Code 71245; Elev. 305; Lat. 32-31-13 N long. 092-42-31 W; N Louisiana.

•**GRAMERCY,** Town; St. James County; Pop. 3,211; Zip Code 70052; Lat. 30-03-02 N long. 090-41-26 W; SE Louisiana.

•**GRAND CANE,** Village; De Soto County; Pop. 252; Zip Code 71032; Elev. 302; Lat. 32-05-01 N long. 093-48-35 W; NW Louisiana. Founded in 1848 and named for a large canebreak on the town's site.

•**GRAND COTEAU,** Town; St. Landry County; Pop. 1,165; Zip Code 70541; Elev. 53; Lat. 30-25-06 N long. 092-02-47 W; SE central Louisiana. In French the town's name means "great hill", and refers to a large hill in the community.

•**GRAND ISLE,** Town; Jefferson County; Pop. 1,982; Zip Code 70358; Lat. 290-13-56 N long. 090-00-19 W; SE Louisiana. One of the several islands lying along the north shore of the Gulf of Mexico. It is seven miles long and hence the name.

•**GRAYSON,** Village; Caldwell County; Pop. 564; Zip Code 71435; Elev. 163; Lat. 32-03-07 N long. 092-06-03 W; N central Louisiana.

•**GREENSBURG,** Town; St. Helena County Seat; Pop. 662; Zip Code 70441; Elev. 223; Lat. 30-49-32 N long. 090-39-50 W; E Louisiana.

•**GREENWOOD,** Village; Caddo County; Pop. 1,043; Zip Code 71033; Elev. 244; Lat. 32-26-37 N long. 093-58-31 W; NW corner Louisiana.

•**GRETNA,** City; Jefferson County Seat; Pop. 20,615; Zip Code 70053; On Mississippi River in SE Louisiana.

•**GROSSE TETE,** Village; Iberville County; Pop. 749; Zip Code 70740; S Louisiana. In French the name means "large head".

•**GUEYDAN,** Town; Vermilion County; Pop. 1,695; Zip Code 70542; S Louisiana.

•**HALL SUMMIT,** Village; Red River County; Pop. 276; Zip Code 71034; Elev. 233; Lat. 31-01-34 N long. 091-55-57 W; NW Louisiana.

•**HAMMOND,** City; Tangipahoa County; Pop. 15,043; Zip Code 70401; Lat. 30-30-37 N long. 090-26-34 W; 45 mi. E of Baton Rouge in SE Louisiana. Named for Peter Hammond, a Swede, who came to Louisana in the early nineteenth century.

•**HARAHAN,** City; Jefferson County; Pop. 11,384; Zip Code 701+; W of New Orleans in SE Louisiana.

•**HARRISONBURG,** Village; Catahoula County Seat; Pop. 610; Zip Code 71340; Lat. 31-46-02 N long. 091-49-24 W; central Louisiana. Founded several decades before the civil war the town takes its name from an early settler.

•**HAUGHTON,** Town; Bossier County; Pop. 1,510; Zip Code 71037; Elev. 237; Lat. 32-31-57 N long. 093-30-14 W; NW Louisiana.

•**HAYNESVILLE,** Town; Claiborne County; Pop. 3,454; Zip Code 71038; Elev. 360; Lat. 32-57-41 N long. 093-08-24 W; N Louisiana. The town is named for Samuel Haynes, a local farmer.

•**HEFLIN,** Village; Webster County; Pop. 279; Zip Code 71039; Elev. 272; Lat. 32-27-30 N long. 093-15-59 W; NW Louisiana.

•**HENDERSON,** Town; St. Martin County; Pop. 1,560; Zip Code 70517; S Louisiana. The town's name honors James Henderson, an 1812 war hero.

•**HESSMER,** Town; Avoyelles County; Pop. 743; Zip Code 71341; Elev. 78; Lat. 31-03-21 N long. 092-07-18 W; central Louisiana.

•**HODGE,** Village; Jackson County; Pop. 708; Zip Code 71247; Elev. 191; Lat. 32-16-35 N long. 092-43-22 W; N Louisiana. The village is named for A.J. Hodge, a prominent Louisana conservationalist.

•**HOMER,** Town; Claiborne County Seat; Pop. 4,307; Zip Code 71040; Elev. 281; Lat. 32-47-19 N long. 093-03-27 W; N Louisiana. The town is named for the famous ancient Greek writer.

•**HORNBECK,** Town; Vernon County; Pop. 470; Zip Code 71439; Lat. 31-19-47 N long. 093-23-48 W; W Louisiana.

•**HOSSTON,** Village; Caddo County; Pop. 480; Zip Code 71043; Lat. 32-53-03 N long. 093-52-45 W; NW corner of Louisiana.

•**HOUMA,** City; Terrebonne County Seat; Pop. 32,602; Zip Code 70360; Lat. 29-36-05 N long. 090-43-14 W; 50 mi. WSW of New Orleans in SE Louisiana. The "city is named for the Houma Indians who lived in the in the eighteenth century.

•**IDA,** Village; Caddo County; Pop. 306; Zip Code 71044; Elev. 286; Lat. 33-00-10 N long. 093-53-34 W; NW corner of Louisiana. Named for an early settler's wife.

•**INDEPENDENCE,** Town; Tangipahoa County; Pop. 1,684; Zip Code 70443; Elev. 93; Lat. 30-38-03 N long. 090-30-08 W; SE Louisiana. Commemorative name of the signing of the Declaration of Independence.

•**IOTA,** Town; Acadia County; Pop. 1,326; Zip Code 70543; Lat. 30-19-28 N long. 092-29-37 W; S Louisiana.

•**IOWA,** Town; Calcasieu County; Pop. 2,437; Zip Code 70647; Elev. 25; Lat. 30-14-30 N long. 093-01-19 W; SW Louisiana. The town is named in honor of the state of Iowa.

•**JACKSON,** Town; East Feliciana County; Pop. 3,133; Zip Code 70748; Lat. 30-49-47 N long. 091-12-16 W; E Louisiana. Following the American victory at the battle of New Orleans the town of Buncombe became Jackson to honor Andrew Jackson.

•**JAMESTOWN,** Village; Bienville County; Pop. 131; Zip Code 71045; Elev. 227; Lat. 32-20-27 N long. 093-12-36 W; NW Louisiana. The village is named for the first English settlement in Virginia.

•**JEAN LAFITTE,** Town; Jefferson County; Pop. 541; SE Louisiana. Named after Nicholas Lafitte, a French privateer who helped the Americans fight the British in the War of 1812.

•**JEANERETTE,** City; Iberia County; Pop. 6,511; Zip Code 70544; Lat. 29-54-55 N long. 091-40-17 W; 32 mi. SE of Lafayette in S Louisiana. Believed to be named for the French pirate and American war hero Jean Lafitte.

•**JENA,** Town; LaSalle County Seat; Pop. 4,332; Zip Code 71342; Elev. 157; Lat. 31-41-12 N long. 092-07-29 W; central Louisiana. The town's name honors Napolean's great victory at Jena.

•**JENNINGS,** City; Jefferson Davis County Seat; Pop. 12,401; Zip Code 70546; Elev. 22; Lat. 30-13-15 N long. 092-39-18 W; 35 mi. E of Lake Charles in SW Louisiana. Named after Jennings Mc-Comb, the engineer in charge of building the Southern Pacific Railroad in the area.

•**JONESBORO,** Town; Jackson County Seat; Pop. 5,061; Zip Code 71251; Elev. 215; Lat. 32-14-28 N long. 092-42-33 W; 40 mi. WSW of Monroe in N Louisiana. Founded during the Civil War the town is named for an early settler.

•**JUNCTION CITY,** Village; Claiborne & Union Counties; Pop. 727; Zip Code 71749; N Louisiana. So called because the town lies on the border between Louisana and Arkansas.

•**KAPLAN,** City; Vermiliom County; Pop. 5,016; Zip Code 70548; Lat. 30-00-12 N long. 092-17-13 W; 23 mi. SW of Lafayette in S Louisiana.

•**KEATCHIE,** Town; De Soto County; Pop. 342; Zip Code 71046; Elev. 336; Lat. 32-10-34 N long. 093-54-48 W; NW Louisiana. The town takes its name from the Caddo Indian word for panther.

•**KENNER,** City; Jefferson County; Pop. 66,382; Zip Code 70062; Lat. 29-59-17 N long. 090-14-34 W; 12 mi. W of New Orleans in SE Louisiana. The town grew up on the plantation of Minor Kenner and took his name.

•**KENTWOOD,** Town; Tangipahoa County; Pop. 2,667; Zip Code 70444; Lat. 30-55-52 N long. 090-31-11 W; SE Louisiana. Named after Amos Kent, the first settler, who came here in 1854 and built a sawmill and brickyard.

•**KILBOURNE,** Village; West Carroll County; Pop. 286; Zip Code 71253; Lat. 32-59-53 N long. 091-18-50 W; NE Louisiana. The village is named after the place in Ireland.

•**KILLIAN,** Village; Livingston County; Pop. 611; SE Louisiana. Named by early Irish settlers to recall their homeland.

•**KINDER,** Town; Allen County; Pop. 2,603; Zip Code 70648; Elev. 49; Lat. 30-29-12 N long. 092-50-44 W; SW Louisiana.

•**KROTZ SPRINGS,** Town; St. Landry County; Pop. 1,374; Zip Code 70750; Elev. 26; Lat. 30-32-14 N long. 091-45-14 W; S central Louisiana. Named for the original owner of the land upon which the springs were discovered.

•**LAFAYETTE,** City; Lafayette County Seat; Pop. 81,961; Zip Code 70501; Elev. 41; Lat. 30-12-57 N long. 092-01-48 W; 55 mi. WSW of Baton Rouge in S Louisiana. Named in honor of the French general and Revolutionary War hero Lafayette.

•**LAKE ARTHUR,** Town; Jefferson Davis County; Pop. 3,615; Zip Code 70549; Lat. 30-04-54 N long. 092-40-28 W; SW Louisiana. Named after an early settler.

•**LAKE CHARLES,** City; Calcasieu County Seat; Pop. 75,051; Zip Code 706--; Elev. 20; Lat. 30-12-35 N long. 093-12-21 W; 13 mi. NNE of Calcasieu Lake in SW Louisiana. One of the original settlers, Carlos Salia, changed his name to Charles Sallier and gave his new name to the lake.

•**LAKE PROVIDENCE,** Town; East Carroll County Seat; Pop. 6,361; Zip Code 71254; Elev. 106; Lat. 32-48-07 N long. 091-10-31 W; 60 mi. ENE of Monroe in the NE corner of Louisiana. Named by grateful boatmen who had negotiated treacherous currents and avoided nearby pirates.

•**LECOMPTE,** Town; Rapides County; Pop. 1,661; Zip Code 71346; Elev. 74; Lat. 31-05-23 N long. 092-24-01 W; central Louisiana. The town takes its name from an early settler.

•**LEESVILLE,** City; Vernon County Seat; Pop. 9,054; Zip Code 71446; 53 mi. W of Alexandria in W Louisiana. Founded in 1871 the city honors General Robert E. Lee.

•**LEONVILLE,** Village; St. Landry County; Pop. 1,143; Zip Code 70551; Lat. 30-28-06 N long. 091-58-47 W; S central Louisiana. Named after one of its mulatto founders following the Civil War.

•**LILLIE,** Village; Union County; Pop. 172; Zip Code 71256; Elev. 114; Lat. 32-55-04 N long. 092-39-36 W; N Louisiana. Named for the sweetheart of an early pioneer.

•**LISBON,** Village; Claiborne County; Pop. 138; Zip Code 71048; Elev. 344; Lat. 32-47-44 N long. 092-51-40 W; N Louisiana. The village is named after the great city in Portugal.

•**LIVINGSTON,** Town; Livingston County Seat; Pop. 1,260; Zip Code 70754; Lat. 30-30-08 N long. 090-44-49 W; SE Louisiana. The town honors the Livingston brothers. Robert Livingston advised Jefferson to make the Louisana Purchase.

•**LIVONIA,** Village; Pointe Coupee County; Pop. 980; Zip Code 70755; Lat. 30-33-22 N long. 091-33-14 W; SE central La. Named for a former province in Russia.

•**LOCKPORT,** Town; Lafourche County; Pop. 2,424; Zip Code 70374; Lat. 29-38-39 N long. 090-32-11 W; SE Louisiana. Situated on a bayou the town is named for locks on a nearby canal.

•**LOGANSPORT,** Town; De Soto County; Pop. 1,565; Zip Code 71049; Elev. 204; Lat. 31-58-08 N long. 093-56-58 W; NW Louisiana. Founded in the 1830's the town was named for the Logan brothers who ran the local ferry.

•**LONGSTREET,** Village; De Soto County; Pop. 281; Zip Code 71050; Elev. 330; Lat. 32-05-48 N long. 093-57-04 W; NW Louisiana. The village is named for the Confederate General James Longstreet.

•**LOREAUVILLE,** Village; Iberia County; Pop. 860; Zip Code 70552; S Louisiana. Named for a French settler Loreau.

•**LUCKY,** Village; Bienville County; Pop. 370; NW Louisiana. Named for good fortune by its early pioneers.

•**LUTCHER,** Town; St. James County; Pop. 4,730; Zip Code 70071; Lat. 30-02-46 N long. 090-41-54 W; SE Louisiana. Lutcher is named after an original settler.

•**MADISONVILLE,** Town; St. Tammany County; Pop. 799; Zip Code 70447; Lat. 30-24-11 N long. 090-09-44 W; SE Louisiana. The town honors President James Madison.

•**MAMOU,** Town; Evangeline County; Pop. 3,194; Zip Code 70554; Lat. 30-37-59 N long. 092-24-59 W; S central Louisiana. Believed to be a corruption of the French word for mammoth, whose fossil remains have been found in the area.

•**MANDEVILLE,** Town; St. Tammany County; Pop. 6,076; Zip Code 70448; Lat. 30-21-37 N long. 090-04-07 W; SE Louisiana. The name honors Frenchman, Bernard De Mandeville, one of the wealthiest persons in Louisana.

•**MANGHAM,** Town; Richland County; Pop. 867; Zip Code 71259; Elev. 74; Lat. 32-18-29 N long. 091-46-42 W; NE Louisiana.

•**MANSFIELD,** City; De Soto County Seat; Pop. 6,485; Zip Code 71052; Elev. 330; Lat. 32-01-26 N long. 093-42-43 W; 33 mi. S of Shreveport in NW Louisiana. A prominent planter in ante bellum days.

•**MANSURA,** Town; Avoyelles County; Pop. 2,074; Zip Code 71350; Elev. 77; Lat. 31-03-31 N long. 092-02-52 W; central Louisiana.

•**MANY,** Town; Sabine County Seat; Pop. 3,988; Zip Code 71449; Elev. 321; Lat. 31-33-58 N long. 093-28-26 W; W Louisiana. Established in 1843 the town recalls Colonel Many who commanded nearby Fort Jesup.

•**MARINGOUIN,** Town; Iberville County; Pop. 1,291; Zip Code 70757; Elev. 23; Lat. 30-29-22 N long. 091-32-21 W; S Louisiana. The early French called the place Maringouin, a large tropical mosquito.

•**MARION,** Village; Union County; Pop. 989; Zip Code 71260; Elev. 202; Lat. 32-54-09 N long. 092-14-37 W; N Louisiana. Marion honors revolutionary war hero Francis Marion, also known as the Swamp Fox.

•**MARKSVILLE,** Town; Avoyelles County Seat; Pop. 5,113; Zip Code 71351; Elev. 82; Lat. 31-07-47 N long. 092-03-44 W; central Louisiana. Named for Mark Elishe, whose wagon broke down on this spot, and who started a trading post here.

•**MAURICE,** Village; Vermilion County; Pop. 478; Zip Code 70555; Elev. 23; Lat. 30-06-23 N long. 092-07-27 W; S Louisiana.

•**MELVILLE,** Town; St. Landry County; Pop. 1,764; Zip Code 71353; Elev. 33; Lat. 30-41-32 N long. 091-44-36 W; S central Louisiana. The town's name honors American author Herman Melville.

•**MER ROUGE,** Village; Morehouse County; Pop. 802; Zip Code 71261; Lat. 32-46 N long. 091-47-29 W; N Louisiana. A flood deposited so much red mud in the it resembled the Red Sea, hence the name.

•MERMENTAU, Village; Acadia County; Pop. 771; Zip Code 70556; Lat. 30-11-14 N long. 092-34-52 W; S Louisiana. An early French family who lived in the and gave the village their name.

•MERRYVILLE, Town; Beauregard County; Pop. 1,286; Zip Code 70653; Lat. 30-45-29 N long. 093-31-49 W; SW Louisiana.

•MINDEN, City; Webster County Seat__; Pop. 15,074; Zip Code 71055; Elev. 259; Lat. 32-36-17 N long. 093-18-35 W; 28 mi. E of Shreveport in NW Louisiana. Founded in 1836 and named after a town on the Weser River in Germany.

•MONROE, City; Ouachita County Seat; Pop. 57,597; Zip Code 712+; Elev. 74; Lat. 32-29-39 N long. 092-05-27 W; 100 mi. E of Shreveport in N Louisiana. Formerly called Fort Miro, the name was changed in 1819 to honor the first steamboat, the "James Monroe", to ascend to Ouachita River.

•MONTGOMERY, Town; Grant County; Pop. 843; Zip Code 71454; Elev. 165; central Louisiana. So named by a local minister's wife who persuaded the town's people to call the place Montgomery after her birthplace in Alabama.

•MONTPELIER, Village; St. Helena County; Pop. 219; E Louisiana. Named for the French city.

•MOORINGSPORT, Town; Caddo County; Pop. 911; Zip Code 71060; Lat. 32-41-09 N long. 093-56-37 W; NW corner of Louisiana. Named to reflect the town's position on Lake Caddo.

•MOREAUVILLE, Village; Avoyelles County; Pop. 853; Zip Code 71355; Lat. 31-01-57 N long. 091-58-30 W; central Louisiana. The village recalls a French general whom Napolean exiled to America.

•MORGAN CITY, City; St. Mary County; Pop. 16,114; Zip Code 70380; Lat. 29-41-52 N long. 091-14-00 W; 53 mi. S of Baton Rouge in S Louisiana. Morgan City came into being around 1850, and got its name from the President of the local railroad.

•MORSE, Village; Acadia County; Pop. 835; Zip Code 70559; Lat. 30-07-19 N long. 092-29-50 W; S Louisiana. Probably named in honor of Samuel Morse, inventor of the telegraph.

•MOUND, Village; Madison County; Pop. 40; Zip Code 71262; NE Louisiana. So called because of the numerous Indian mounds in the region.

•MOUNT LEBANON, Town; Bienville County; Pop. 105; NW Louisiana. The large stands of timber and fetile soil reminded the original settlers of biblical Lebanon.

•NAPOLEONVILLE, Town; Assumption County Seat; Pop. 829; Zip Code 70390; Lat. 29-56-15 N long. 091-01-39 W; SE Louisiana. A French settler who fought under Napoleon named the town for his former commander.

•NATCHEZ, Village; Natchitoches County; Pop. 527; Zip Code 71456; NW central Louisiana. In remembrance of the Natchez Indians who formerly lived in the area.

•NATCHITOCHES, City; Natchitoches County Seat; Pop. 16,664; Zip Code 71457; 52 mi. NW of Alexandria in NW central Louisiana. Named for a tribe of Caddo Inidans. It translates as "chestnut eaters".

•NEW IBERIA, City; Iberia County Seat; Pop. 32,766; Zip Code 70560; Lat. 30-00-16 N long. 091-49-17 W; 20 mi. SSE of Lafayette in S Louisiana. Called Iberia by the Canary Islanders who settled here after old Spain. Changed in 1868 to distinguish it from the County Seat.

•NEW ORLEANS, City; Orleans County Seat; Pop. 557,482; Zip Code 701+; Lat. 29-58-06 N long. 090-04-36 W; between Miss. River & L. Pontchartrain in SE L Founded in 1718, the city's name honored Duc d'Orleans, then Regent of France.

•NEW ROADS, Town; Pointe Coupee County Seat; Pop. 3,924; Zip Code 70760; Elev. 32; Lat. 30-41-52 N long. 091-26-13 W; SE central Louisiana. So named after the Bayou Sara Road was constructed in the in 1847.

•NEWELLTON, Town; Tensas County; Pop. 1,726; Zip Code 71357; Elev. 79; Lat. 32-04-20 N long. 091-14-19 W; NE Louisiana. The town is named after its founder, Edward Newell, who settled here in 1832.

•NEWLLANO, Village; Vernon County; Pop. 2,213; Zip Code 71461; W Louisiana. The village is near the famous LLano cooperative colony. The name remained after the colony's demise.

•NOBLE, Village; Sabine County; Pop. 194; Zip Code 71462; Elev. 281; W Louisiana. Given the name by Anglicans who settled here in the 1830s.

•NORTH HODGE, Village; Jackson County; Pop. 573; N Louisiana. In memory of A.J. Hodge, a noted Louisana Conservationalist.

•OAK GROVE, Town; West Carroll County Seat; Pop. 2,214; Zip Code 71263; Lat. 32-51-45 N long. 091-23-09 W; NE Louisiana. Called this by its founders for the many oak groves in the .

•OAK RIDGE, Village; Morehouse County; Pop. 257; Zip Code 71264; Elev. 92; Lat. 32-37-31 N long. 091-46-17 W; N Louisiana.

•OAKDALE, City; Allen County; Pop. 7,155; Zip Code 70053; Elev. 117; 37 mi. SSW of Alexandria in SW Louisiana.

•OBERLIN, Town; Allen County Seat; Pop. 7,155; Zip Code 70655; Elev. 75; Lat. 30-37-14 N long. 092-45-47 W; SW Louisiana. The town recalls Jean Frederic Oberlin, a French clergyman and teacher.

•OIL CITY, Town; Caddo County; Pop. 1,323; Zip Code 71061; Lat. 32-44-41 N long. 093-58-33 W; NW corner of Louisiana. The town is almost the exact center of the great Caddo oil strike of 1906.

•OLLA, Town; LaSalle County; Pop. 1,603; Zip Code 71465; Elev. 155; central Louisiana. Named for Olla Mills, the daughter of one of the town's founders.

•OPELOUSAS, City; St. Landry County Seat; Pop. 18,903; Zip Code 70570; Elev. 70; Lat. 30-31-46 N long. 092-05-02 W; 22 mi. N of Lafayette in S central Louisiana. In honor of the Opelousas Indians who lived in the before the Europeans arrived.

•PALMETTO, Village; St. Landry County; Pop. 327; Zip Code 71358; Lat. 30-42-57 N long. 091-54-24 W; S central Louisiana. So named because of thick growth of palmettoes in the vicinity.

•PATTERSON, Town; St. Mary County; Pop. 4,584; Zip Code 70392; Elev. 12; Lat. 29-41-45 N long. 091-18-13 W; S Louisiana. After its first settler, Captain Patterson, who owned several plantations in the .

•PEARL RIVER, Town; St. Tammany County; Pop. 1,693; Zip Code 70452; Lat. 30-22-16 N long. 089-45-00 W; SE Louisiana. Pearl River is named for its river which flows south into the Mississippi Sound.

•PINE PRAIRIE, Village; Evangeline County; Pop. 734; Zip Code 70576; Elev. 123; Lat. 30-46-51 N long. 092-25-15 W; S central

LOUISIANA

Louisiana. So called by the Acadian settlers because of the extensive prairie mixed with stands of pine .

•**PINEVILLE,** City; Rapides County; Pop.12,034; Zip Code 71360; Lat. 31-19-16 N long. 092-25-06 W; 5 mi. NE of Alexandria in central Louisiana. After the extensive pine forest that once occupied the area.

•**PIONEER,** Village; West Carroll County; Pop. 221; Zip Code 71266; Lat. 32-44-11 N long. 091-26-02 W; NE Louisiana. A commemoration of the early settlers.

•**PLAIN DEALING,** Town; Bossier County; Pop. 1,213; Zip Code 71064; Elev. 265; Lat. 32-54-25 N long. 093-41-56 W; NW Louisiana. Founded in 1887 and named for its civic ideal.

•**PLAQUEMINE,** City; Iberville County Seat; Pop. 7,521; Zip Code 70764; 13 mi. SSW of Baton Rouge in S Louisiana. The city is probably named from the French word for plate, but may have signified persimmons after the numerous persimmon trees.

•**PLEASANT HILL,** Village; Sabine County; Pop. 776; Zip Code 71065; W Louisiana. So called because of the distinctive geographic feature.

•**POLLOCK,** Town; Grant County; Pop. 399; Zip Code 71467; Elev. 129; central Louisiana. Originally called Oaction, the name was later changed to honor Captain J.W. Pollock who built a lumber mill.

•**PONCHATOULA,** City; Tangipahoa County; Pop. 5,469; Zip Code 70454; Lat. 30-26-06 N long. 090-26-25 W; 41 mi. NNW of New Orleans in SE Louisiana. The Chowtaw Indian word for hanging hair, believed to refer to nearby Spanish Moss trees.

•**PORT ALLEN,** City; West Baton Rouge County Seat; Pop. 6,114; Zip Code 70767; Lat. 30-27-53 N long. 091-12-46 W; on Miss. R. in SE central Louisiana. The city is named after General Henry Allen who served as the Confederate governor of Louisana in 1864.

•**PORT BARRE,** Town; St. Landry County; Pop. 2,625; Zip Code 70577; Lat. 30-33-21 N long. 091-57-31 W; S central Louisiana.

•**PORT VINCENT,** Village; Livingston County; Pop. 450; SE Louisiana. Named for a local ferryman who was the first man to sail a schooner from Lake Mallrepas up the Amite River.

•**POWHATAN,** Village; Natchitoches County; Pop. 279; Zip Code 71066; Elev. 127; Lat. 31-52-22 N long. 093-11-57 W; NW central Louisiana. The village commemorates the Indian village found by the first English settlers of Virginia in 1607.

•**PROVENCAL,** Village; Natchitoches County; Pop. 695; Zip Code 71468; Elev. 210; NW central Louisiana. Named after a region in France.

•**QUITMAN,** Village; Jackson County; Pop. 231; Zip Code 71268; Latf. 32-20-52 N long. 092-42-16 W; N Louisiana.

•**RAYNE,** City; Acadia County; Pop. 9,066; Zip Code 70578; Elev. 32; Lat. 30-14-08 N long. 092-16-05 W; 16 mi. W of Lafayette in S Louisiana.

•**RAYVILLE,** Town; Richland County Seat; Pop. 4,610; Zip Code 71269; Lat. 32-28-26 N long. 091-45-20 W; NE Louisiana. Named in honor of John Ray, who had large land holdings in the area.

•**REEVES,** Village; Allen County; Pop. 199; Zip Code 70658; Elev. 45; Lat. 30-31-11 N long. 093-02-29 W; SW Louisiana.

•**RICHMOND,** Village; Madison County; Pop. 505; NE Louisiana. The village is named after the city in Virginia.

•**RIDGECREST,** Town; Concordia County; Pop. 895; E central Louisiana. Named for the descriptive geographic feature of the town.

•**RINGGOLD,** Town; Bienville County; Pop. 1,655; Zip Code 71068; Lat. 32-19-39 N long. 093-17-02 W; NW Louisiana. In honor of Samuel Ringgold, a professional soldier killed in the Mexican war.

•**ROBELINE,** Village; Natchitoches County; Pop. 238; Zip Code 71469; NW central Louisiana. Said to be named for an early settler who journeyed here via the San Antonia Trace.

•**RODESSA,** Village; Caddo County; Pop. 337; Zip Code 71069; Elev. 261; Lat. 32-58-18 N long. 093-59-42 W; NW corner of Louisiana.

•**ROSEDALE,** Village; Iberville County; Pop. 658; Zip Code 70772; Lat. 30-26-27 N long. 091-27-12 W; S Louisiana. Named for the flower.

•**ROSELAND,** Town; Tangipahoa County; Pop. 1,346; Zip Code 70456; Elev. 132; Lat. 30-45-45 N long. 090-30-59 W; SE Louisiana. The town is named for the famous flower.

•**ROSEPINE,** Village; Vernon County; Pop. 953; Zip Code 70659; Elev. 221; Lat. 30-55-12 N long. 093-16-55 W; W Louisiana.

•**RUSTON,** City; Lincoln County Seat; Pop. 20,585; Zip Code 71270; Elev. 319; Lat. 32-31-36 N long. 092-38-14 W; 33 mi. W of Monroe in N Louisiana.

•**ST. FRANCISVILLE,** Town; West Feliciana County Seat; Pop. 1,471; Zip Code 70775; E central Louisiana. Probably named after a monastery honoring St. Francis of Assisi.

•**ST. JOSEPH,** Town; Tensas County Seat; Pop. 1,687; Zip Code 71366; NE Louisiana. Named in honor of St. Joseph.

•**ST. MARTINVILLE,** City; St. Martin County Seat; Pop. 7,965; Zip Code 70582; 13 mi. ESE of Lafayette in S Louisiana. The city takes its name from the fourth century Christian bishop Martin of Tours.

•**SALINE,** Village; Bienville County; Pop. 293; Zip Code 71070; Elev. 183; Lat. 32-09-43 N long. 092-58-38 W; NW Louisiana. Located on a bayou near a salt dome, the town was named in 1839.

•**SAREPTA,** Village; Webster County; Pop. 831; Zip Code 71071; Elev. 254; Lat. 32-53-39 N long. 093-27-01 W; NW Louisiana.

•**SCOTT,** Town; Lafayette County; Pop. 2,239; Zip Code 70583; Lat. 30-14-03 N long. 092-05-43 W; S Louisiana.

•**SHONGALOO,** Village; Webster County; Pop. 163; Zip Code 71072; Lat. 32-56-29 N long. 093-17-54 W; NW Louisiana. The village takes its name from the Chowtaw Indian word for cypress tree.

•**SHREVEPORT,** City; Bossier & Caddo Couties; Caddo County Seat; Pop. 205,820; Zip Code 711+; Lat. 32-28-32 N long. 093-45-59 W; 18 mi. E of the Texas border in NW corner of LA; Named in honor of Captain Henry Miller Shreve, an American engineer and steamboat builder, who opened the Red River to navigation in the 1830s.

•**SIBLEY,** Village; Webster County; Pop. 1,211; Zip Code 71073; Elev. 244; Lat. 32-32-31 N long. 093-17-38 W; NW Louisiana.

•**SICILY ISLAND,** Village; Catahoula County; Pop. 691; Zip Code 71368; Lat. 31-50-50 N long. 091-39-32 W; central Louisiana. Named by an early explorer for its resemblance to his native Sicily.

•**SIKES,** Village; Winn County; Pop. 226; Zip Code 71473; Elev. 154; N central Louisiana. The town is named for an early settler.

•**SIMMESPORT,** Town; Avoyelles County; Pop. 2,293; Zip Code 71369; Elev. 43; Lat. 30-59-01 N long. 091-48-33 W; central Louisiana.

•**SIMPSON,** Village; Vernon County; Pop. 534; Zip Code 71474; W Louisiana. Named for one of the early settlers.

•**SIMSBORO,** Village; Lincoln County; Pop. 553; Zip Code 71275; Elev. 348; Lat. 32-31-58 N long. 092-47-10 W; N Louisiana.

•**SLAUGHTER,** Town; East Feliciana County; Pop. 729; Zip Code 70777; Elev. 133; Lat. 30-43-00 N long. 091-08-37 W; E Louisiana.

•**SLIDELL,** City; St. Tammany County; Pop. 26,718; Zip Code 70458; Elev. 9; Lat. 30-16-46 N long. 089-46-22 W; 30 mi. NE of New Orleans in SE Louisiana. Named for the Confederate commissioner to France whose capture by the U.S. Navy in 1862 almost precipitated a war with Britain.

•**SORRENTO,** Town; Ascension County; Pop. 1,197; Zip Code 70778; Elev. 7; SE Louisiana. The town takes its name from the region in Italy.

•**SOUTH MANSFIELD,** Village; De Soto County; Pop. 419; NW Louisiana.. A prominent planter in ante bellum Louisana gave his name to the town.

•**SPEARSVILLE,** Village; Union County; Pop. 181; Zip Code 71277; Lat. 32-56-13 N long. 092-36-14 W; N Louisiana..

•**SPRINGFIELD,** Town; Livingston County; Pop. 424; Zip Code 70462; Elev. 16; Lat. 30-25-31 N long. 090-32-36 W; SE Louisiana. Named for the city in Massachusetts, itself named after the town in Essex, England.

•**SPRINGHILL,** City; Webster County; Pop. 6,516; Zip Code 71075; Lat. 33-00-02 N long. 093-27-47 W; 38 mi. NNW of Shreveport in NW Louisiana.

•**STERLINGTON,** Town; Ouachita County; Pop. 1,400; Zip Code 71280; Lat. 32-41-51 N long. 092-03-39 W; N Louisiana.

•**STONEWALL,** Town; De Soto County; Pop. 1,175; Zip Code 71078; Lat. 32-16-58 N LONG. 083-49-23 W; NW Louisiana. Founded after the Civil War, the town is named for the famous Confederate general Stonewall Jackson.

•**SULPHUR,** City; Calcasieu County; Pop. 19,709; Zip Code 70663; Lat. 30-13-22 N long. 093-21-28 W; 10 mi. W of Lake Charles in SW Louisiana. The town takes its name from a nearby large sulphur dome discovered in 1905.

•**SUN,** Village; St. Tammany County; Pop. 338; Zip Code 70463; Lat. 30-39-06 N long. 089-54-37 W; SE Louisiana. Named for the sun by its founders.

•**SUNSET,** Town; St. Landry County; Pop. 2,300; Zip Code 70584; Lat. 30-22-25 N long. 092-05-13 W; S central Louisiana. Given a descriptive name by its founders.

•**TALLULAH,** City; Madison County Seat; Pop. 10,392; Zip Code 71282; Elev. 87; Lat. 32-24-33 N long. 091-11-29 W; 57 mi. E of Monroe in NE Louisiana. An old Cherokee Indian word whose meaning has been lost. Another tradition has a love-smitten railroad engineer name the city for a sweetheart.

•**TANGIPAHOA,** Village; Tangipahoa County; Pop. 493; Zip Code 70465; Elev. 179; Lat. 30-52-36 N long. 090-30-38 W; SE Louisiana. The name for a local Indian tribe. It is believed to mean "cornstalk gatherers".

•**THIBODAUX,** City; Lafourche County Seat; Pop. 15,810; Zip Code 70301; Lat. 29-47-20 N long. 090-49-46 W; 49 mi. WSW of New Orleans in SE Louisiana. Originally a trading post the town is named in honor of Henry Thibodaux, a prominent official who donated land to the community in 1820.

•**TICKFAW,** Village; Tangipahoa County; Pop. 571; Zip Code 70466; Elev. 64; Lat. 30-34-36 N long. 090-29-08 W; SE Louisiana. A Choctaw Indian name meaning pine rest.

•**TULLOS,** Town; La Salle & Winn Counties; Pop. 772; Zip Code 71479; central Louisiana.

•**TURKEY CREEK,** Village; Evangeline County; Pop. 366; Zip Code 70585; Elev. 130; Lat. 30-52-26 N long. 092-24-48 W; S central Louisiana. Named for the once abundant wild turkey.

•**URANIA,** Town; La Salle County; Pop. 849; Zip Code 71480; Elev. 92; central Louisiana.

•**VARNADO,** Village; Washington County; Pop. 249; Zip Code 70467; E Louisiana.

•**VIDALIA,** Town; Concordia County Seat; Pop. 5,936; Zip Code 71373; Elev. 65; Lat. 31-34-33 N long. 091-25-41 W; E central Louisiana. Established in 1801 by Spanish landowner Don Jose Vidal who donated public land and had the town named in his honor.

•**VIENNA,** Town; Lincoln County; Pop. 519; N Louisiana. Named by the early settlers after a town in Georgia, probably named for the famous Austrian city.

•**VILLE PLATTE,** Town; Evangeline County Seat; Pop. 9,201; Zip Code 70586; Lat. 30-41-21 N long. 092-16-47 W; 35 mi. NNW of Lafayette in S central Louisiana. The town was settled by French people who called it "flat town" because it lies on a prairie.

•**VINTON,** Town; Calcasieu County; Pop. 3,631; Zip Code 70668; Elev. 19; Lat. 30-11-30 N long. 093-34-49 W; SW Louisiana. Founded in 1888 and named after a town in Iowa.

•**VIVIAN,** Town; Caddo County; Pop. 4,146; Zip Code 71082; Lat. 32-52-20 N long. 093-59-08 W; NW corner of Louisiana. Named for the wife of an early pioneer.

•**WALKER,** Town; Livingston County; Pop. 2,957; Zip Code 70785; Lat. 30-29-35 N long. 090-51-11 W; SE Louisiana. Originally called Milton Oldfield, the town's name was changed to Walker in 1870 to honor the local Congressman.

•**WASHINGTON,** Town; St. Landry County; Pop. 1,266; Zip Code 70589; Elev. 63; Lat. 30-36-50 N long. 092-03-31 W; S central Louisiana. Settled in 1800 the town is named after George Washington.

•**WATERPROOF,** Town; Tensas County; Pop. 1,339; Zip Code 71375; Elev. 83; Lat. 31-48-21 N long. 091-23-14 W; NE Louisiana. The town has been moved several times due to Mississippi River flooding. During the third flood the whole region except one waterproof knoll was under water. The town subsequntly moved to the knoll and acquired the name.

•**WELSH,** Town; Jefferson Davis County; Pop. 3,515; Zip Code 70591; Lat. 30-14-12 N long. 092-48-57 W; SW Louisiana. Named for its original settler Miles Welsh who journeyed here in an ox-drawn wagon.

•**WEST MONROE,** City; Ouachita County; Pop. 14,993; Zip Code 71291; Elev. 88; Lat. 32-30-53 N long. 092-09-27 W; N Louisiana. Named after the steamboat "James Monroe", the first steamboat to ascend the Ouachita River.

•**WESTLAKE,** Town; Calcasieu County; Pop. 5,246; Zip Code 70669; Elev. 16; Lat. 30-14-59 N long. 093-15-29 W; SW Louisiana.

•**WESTWEGO,** City; Jefferson County; Pop. 12,663; Zip Code 70094; Elev. 5; Lat. 29-37-43 N long. 089-19-11 W; 8 mi. WSW of New Orleans in SE Louisiana. During the gold rush it was a point of departure for westbound traveler and gradually acquired the name.

•**WHITE CASTLE,** Town; Iberville County; Pop. 2,160; Zip Code 70788; Lat. 30-10-06 N long. 091-08-50 W; S Louisiana. The town is named for the plantation house built in the early nineteenth century by Thomas Vaughn.

•**WILSON,** Village; East Feliciana County; Pop. 656; Zip Code 70789; Elev. 256; Lat. 30-55-36 N long. 091-06-51 W; E Louisiana.

•**WINNFIELD,** City; Winn County Seat; Pop. 7,311; Zip Code 71483; Elev. 143; 45 mi. N of Alexandria in N central Louisiana. Both the town and the parish named for Walter O. Winn, a prominent Louisana lawyer.

•**WINNSBORO,** Town; Franklin County Seat; Pop. 5,921; Zip Code 71295; Lat. 32-09-42 N long. 091-43-05 W; 33 mi. SE of Monroe in NE Louisiana. Named in honor of Walter Winn, a prominent lawyer from Alexandria.

•**YOUNGSVILLE,** Village; Lafayette County; Pop. 1,053; Zip Code 70592; Lat. 30-05-52 N long. 091-59-35 W; S Louisiana.

•**ZACHARY,** City; East Baton Rouge County; Pop. 7,297; Zip Code 70791; Lat. 30-35-04 N long. 091-10-48 W; SE central Louisiana. The town is named in honor of President Zachary Taylor.

•**ZWOLLE,** Town; Sabine County; Pop. 2,602; Zip Code 71486; Elev. 148; W Louisiana. Founded in 1896 and named for the Zwolle family.

MAINE

•ABBOT; Town; Piscataquis County; Pop. 576; Zip Code 04406; Elev. 458; Lat. 45-11-07 N long. 069-27-11 W; N central Maine. The town is named for Professor John Abbot, Treasurer of Bowdoin College.

•ACTON, Town; York County; Pop. 1,228; Zip Code 04001; SW; Lat. 43-32-03 N long. 070-45-35 W; coastal Maine. The town takes its name from the town in England.

•ADDISON, Town; Washington County; Pop. 1,061; Zip Code 04606; Elev. 17; SE corner; Lat. 44-37-13 N long. 067-44-45 W; coastal Maine. Addison is named in honor of 18th century English author Joseph Addison.

•ALBION, Town; Kennebec County; Pop. 1,551; Zip Code 04910; SW Maine. Lat. 44-31-28 N long. 069-26-30 W; The town is named aftr England's ancient name.

•ALEXANDER, Town; Washington County; Pop. 385; Zip Code; SE corner; coastal Maine. Named in honor of Alexander Baring, Lord Ashburton, who with Daniel Webster settled the Northeastern boundary dispute.

•ALFRED, Town; York County; Pop. 1,890; Zip Code 04002; SW; Lat. 43-28-31 N long. 070-42-58 W; coastal Me. The town's name remembers Alfred the Great, 9th century King of England.

•ALLAGASH, Town; Aroostook County; Pop. 448; Zip Code; N Maine. An Abnaki Indian word meaning "bark cabin."

•ALNA, Town; Lincoln County; Pop. 425; Zip Code 04535; S; Lat. 44-06-25 N long. 069-36-22 W; coastal Maine. The town takes its name from the latin alnus, alder tree.

•ALTON, Town; Penobscot County; Pop. 468; Zip Code; E central Maine. Named after Alton, South Hampton, England.

•AMHERST, Town; Hancock County; Pop. 203; Zip Code; SE; coastal Maine. Named for Amherst, Maine, which in turn honored Lord Amherst in colonial times.

•AMITY, Town; Aroostook County; Pop. 168; Zip Code; N Maine. The name recalls the friendship of the early settlers.

•ANDOVER, Town; Oxford County; Pop. 850; Zip Code 04216; Elev. 723; W Maine. Lat. 44-38-07 N long. 070-45-00 W; Named after Andover, Massachusetts.

•APPLETON, Town; Knox County; Pop. 818; Zip Code; S; coastal Maine. Samuel Appleton, an early settler, gave his name to the town.

•ARGYLE, Unorganized; Penobscot County; Pop. 225; Zip Code; E central Maine. Named aftre the city of Argyle in Scotland.

•ARROWSIC, Town; Sagadahoc County; Pop. 305; Zip Code; S; coastal Maine. An Abnaki Indian word translated as "place of obstruction."

•ASHLAND, Town; Aroostook County; Pop. 1,865; Zip Code 04732; Elev. 572; Lat. 46-37-54 N long. 068-24-06 W; N Maine. The town is named for Ashland, Henry Clay's former name.

•ATHENS, Town; Somerset County; Pop. 802; Zip Code 04912; Elev. 344; Lat. 44-55-36 N long. 069-40-22 W; W Maine. Named for the famous city in Greece.

•ATKINSON, Town; Piscataquis County; Pop. 306; Zip Code; N central Maine. Named for Judge Atkinson, who owned a great deal of land in this area.

•AUGUSTA, City,; Kennebec County; Pop. 21,819; Zip Code 04330; Lat. 44-19-04 N long. 069-46-08 W; 25 mi. NE of Lewiston in SW Maine. The city is named in honor of Pamela Augusta Dearborn, the daughter of Revolutionary War General Harry Dearborn.

•AURORA, Town; Hancock County; Pop. 110; Zip Code 04408; Lat. 44-50-57 N long. 068-19-55 W; SE; coastal Maine. Named after the goddess of dawn by Reverend Srluster Williams.

•AVON, Town; Franklin County; Pop. 475; W Maine. The town's name commemorated the Avon River in England.

•BAILEYVILLE, Town; Washington County; Pop. 2,188; Zip Code ; SE corner; coastal Maine. Named for either an early settler Thomas Bailey, or the two Bailey brothers who were local landowners.

•BALDWIN, Town; Cumberland County; Pop. 1,140; SW; coastal Maine. The town's name comes from Loammi Baldwin, an early settler.

•BANCROFT, Town; Aroostook County; Pop. 61; N Maine. Named in honor of historian George Bancroft, whose brother was town historian.

•BANGOR, City; Penobscot County; Pop. 31,643; Zip Code 04401; Elev. 158; Lat. 44-49-27 N long. 068-44-48 W; 60 mi. NE of Augusta in E central Maine. Probably named for the hymn "Bangor" by Reverend Seth Noble.

•BAR HARBOR, Town; Hancock County; Pop. 4,124; Zip Code 04609; Lat. 44-23-16 N long. 068-12-29 W; SE. coastal Maine. Named for Bar Island located in the harbor.

•BARING, Plantation; Washington County; Pop. 308; SE corner; coastal Maine. Named in honor of Alexander Baring, Lord Ashburton.

•BATH, City; Sagadahoc County; Pop. 10,246; Zip Code 04530; Elev. 79; Lat. 43-54-53 N long. 069-49-30 W; 28 mi. NE of Portland in S; coastal Maine. Named by Colonel Dummer Sewall for Bath, England.

•BEALS, Town; Washington County; Pop. 695; Zip Code 04611; Lat. 44-31-11 N long. 067-36-57 W; SE corner; coastal Maine. The first settler, Manwaring Beal, gave his name to this town.

•BEAVER COVE, Town; Piscataquis County; Pop. 56; N central Maine. A descriptive name for the large beaver population once in area.

•BEDDINGTON, Town; Washington County; Pop. 36; SE corner; coastal Maine. The town is anmed after Beddington, England.

•BELFAST, City; Waldo County; Pop. 6,243; Zip Code 04915; Elev. 103; Lat. 44-25-35 N long. 069-00-56 W; 30 mi. SSW of Bangor in S; coastal Maine. So called after the home city of many Irish settlers.

•BELGRADE, Town; Kennebec County; Pop. 2,043; Zip Code 04917; Lat. 44-27-01 N long. 069-50-00 W; SW Maine. Named aftre Belgrade, Yugoslavia.

•BELMONT, Town; Waldo County; Pop. 520; S coastal Maine. George Watson, one of the town's founding fathers, gave it the name Belmont, or beautiful mountain.

•**BENEDICTA,** Town; Aroostook County; Pop. 225; Zip Code 04733; Elev. 619; Lat. 45-47-51 N long. 068-24-48 W; N Maine. The town gets its name from Bishop Benedict Fenwick, and original landowner.

•**BENTON,** Town; Kennebec County; Pop. 2,188; SW Maine. The name honors Thomas Hart Benton, a prominent Democrat and congressman.

•**BERWICK,** Town; York County; Pop. 4,149; Zip Code 03901; Elev.182; SW; coastal Maine. Named for Berwick, Dorsetshire, England.

•**BETHEL,** Town; Oxford County; Pop. 2,340; Zip Code 04217; Lat. 44-24-37 N long. 070-47-36 W; W MRE. The town takes its name from the biblical town Bethel.

•**BIDDEFORD,** City; York County; Pop. 19,638; Zip Code 04005; Lat. 43-28-50 N long. 070-27-06 W; on the Saco R. oppo of Saco in SW Maine. Early settlers named the city for Bideford, England.

•**BINGHAM,** Town; Somerset County; Pop. 1,184; Zip Code 04920; Elev. 371; Lat. 45-03-31 N long. 069-52-45 W; W Maine. Named for William Bingham, who owned great traces of Maine at one time.

•**BLAINE,** Town; Aroostook County; Pop. 922; Zip Code 04734; Lat. 46-30-16 N long. 067-52-12 W; N Maine. One time presidential candidate James G. Blaine had the town named in his honor.

•**BLANCHARD,** Plantation; Piscataquis County; Pop. 64; Zip Code ; N central Maine. Named for Charles Blanchard who was co-owner of the township.

•**BLUE HILL,** Town; Hancock County; Pop. 1,644; Zip Code 04614; Lat. 44-24-53 N long. 068-35-30 W; SE; coastal Maine. The town gets its descriptive name from a blue bug imported by the spruce and pine trees nearby.

•**BOOTHBAY,** Town; Lincoln County; Pop. 2,308; Zip Code 04537; Elev. 127; Lat. 43-52-31 N long. 069-38-05 W; S; coastal Maine. Supposedly named in 1764 by a local agent testifying before a legislative committee in charge of names. He is reported to have described the bay as "snug as a booth," and the committee accepted that name.

•**BOOTHBAY HARBOR,** Town; Lincoln County; Pop. 2,207; Zip Code 04536; Lat. 43-51-01 N long. 069-36-53 W; S; coastal Maine. Named in 1764 after a local agent described the harbor as "snug as a booth."

•**BOWDOIN,** Town; Sagadahoc County; Pop. 1,629; S; coastal Maine. The town is named for James Bowdoin, Governor of Massachusetts in 1785-86.

•**BOWDOINHAM,** Town; Sagadahoc County; Pop. 1,828; Zip Code 04008; Lat. 44-00-31 N long. 069-53-58 W; S; coastal Maine. Named for a early landholder, Dr. Peter Bowdoin.

•**BOWERBANK,** Town; Piscataquis County; Pop. 27; N central Maine. The second owner of the townshop's land, London merchant named Bowerbank, had it called in his honor.

•**BRADFORD,** Town; Penobscot County; Pop. 888; Zip Code 04410; Elev. 235; Lat. 45-03-59 N long. 069-03-53 W; E central Maine. The town is named aftre Bradford, Massachusetts.

•**BRADLEY,** Town; Penobscot County; Pop. 1,149; Zip Code 04411; Lat. 44-55-18 N long. 068-37-53 W; E central Maine. Named for Bradley Blackman, an early settler and prominent citizen.

•**BREMEN,** Town; Lincoln County; Pop. 598; S; coastal Maine. Named for Bremen, Germany.

•**BREWER,** City; Penobscot County; Pop. 9,017; Zip Code 04412; Lat. 44-47-06 N long. 068-45-39 W; on Penobscot R. opp. of Bangor in E cen Maine. The city's name honors Colonel John Brewer, an early settler from Massachusetts.

•**BRIDGEWATER,** Town; Aroostook County; Pop. 742; Zip Code 04735; Elev. 428; Lat. 46-25-27 N long. 067-50-40 W; N Maine. As is the case for other Maine towns, Bridgewater takes its name from the town in Massachusetts.

•**BRIDGTON,** Town; Cumberland County; Pop. 3,528; Zip Code 04009; Elev. 294; Lat. 44-03-13 N long. 070-42-48 W; SW; coastal Maine. Named in honor of Moody Bridges, an early landowner.

•**BRISTOL,** Town; Lincoln County; Pop. 2,095; Zip Code 04539; Elev. 73; Lat. 43-57-25 N long. 069-30-44 W; S; coastal Maine. Reflecting the origin of many Maine settlers, the town takes its name from the city in England.

•**BROOKLIN,** Town; Hancock County; Pop. 619; Zip Code 04616; Elev. 125; Lat. 44-15-58 N long. 068-34-17 W; SE; coastal Maine. A descriptive name pointing out the brook boundary to the adjacent township.

•**BROOKS,** Town; Waldo County; Pop. 804; Zip Code 04921; Elev. 387; Lat. 44-32-58 N long. 069-07-20 W; S; coastal Maine. The town's name honors Governor John Brooks of Massachusetts.

•**BROOKSVILLE,** Town; Hancock County; Pop. 753; Zip Code 04617; SE; coastal Maine. Named after Governor John Brooks of Massachusetts, who held office between 1816 - 20.

•**BROWNFIELD,** Town; Oxford County; Pop. 767; Zip Code 04010; Elev. 424; Lat. 43-56-12 N long. 070-54-36 W; W Maine. Named in honor of Captain Henry Brown for U. S. service in the French and Indian War.

•**BROWNVILLE,** Town; Piscataquis County; Pop. 1,545; Zip Code 04414; Lat. 45-18-24 N long. 069-02-18 W; N central Maine. Named after an early settler, Francis Brown, who built a mill here in 1812.

•**BRUNSWICK,** Town; Cumberland County; Pop. 17,366; Zip Code 04011; Elev. 67; Lat. 43-54-42 N long. 069-57-55 W; 23 mi. NE of Portland in Sw; coastal Maine. Early settlers named the town for the Brunswick area of Germany.

•**BUCKFIELD,** Town; Oxford County; Pop. 1,333; Zip Code 04220; Lat. 44-17-25 N long. 070-21-54 W; W Maine. Abijah Buck, an early settler, had the town named after him.

•**BUCKSPORT,** Town; Hancock County; Pop. 4,345; Zip Code 04416; Elev. 43; Lat. 44-34-57 N long. 068-47-28 W; SE; coastal Maine. Named after its founder, Colonel Jonathan Buck, who built a mill nearby in 1764.

•**BURLINGTON,** Town; Penobscot County; Pop. 322; Zip Code 04417; Lat. 45-12-29 N long. 068-25-33 W; E central Maine. Named for the town in Massachusetts.

•**BURNHAM,** Town; Waldo County; Pop. 951; Zip Code 04922; Elev. 161; Lat. 44-41-31 N long. 069-25-54 W; S; coastal Maine. The town's name honors an early 1800's doctor and settler.

•**BUXTON,** Town; York County; Pop. 5,775; 15 mi. W of Portland in SW Maine. A pioneer settler from England named the town for his former city in England.

•**BYRON,** Town; Oxford County; Pop. 114; W Maine. The town's name honors the famous English poet George Gordon, or Lord Byron.

•**CALAIS,** City; Washington County; Pop. 4,262; Zip Code 04619; Elev. 19; Lat. 54-10-25 N long. 067-16-24 W; SE corner; coastal

Maine. the city is named for Calais, France, and may commemorate French assisting in the Revolutionary War.

•**CAMBRIDGE,** Town; Somerset County; Pop. 445; Zip Code 04923; Elev. 356; Lat. 45-01-23 N long. 069-28-10 W; W Maine. Named in 1834 for the University town in England.

•**CAMDEN,** Town; Knox County; Pop. 4,584; Zip Code 04843; Elev. 33; Lat. 44-15-57 N long. 069-09-42 W; S; coastal Maine. Camden's name honors Charles Pratt, Earl of Camden.

•**CANAAN,** Town; Somerset County; Pop. 1,189; Zip Code 04924; Elev. 236; Lat. 44-45-45 N long. 069-33-40 W; W Maine. Toe town's people considered their area as boutiful as the promised land and gave it the biblical name.

•**CANTON,** Town; Oxford County; Pop. 831; Zip Code 04221; Lat. 44-28-06 N long. 070-18-59 W; W Maine. Canton is named for Canton, Massachusetts.

•**CAPE ELIZABETH,** Town; Cumberland County; Pop. 7,838; Zip Code 04107; 7 mi. S of Portland in SW; coastal Maine. Named for Princess Elizabeth, eldest daughter of King James I.

•**CARATUNK,** Plantation; Somerset County; Pop. 84; Zip Code 04925; Elev. 549; Lat. 45-13-59 N long. 069-59-33 W; W Maine. An Abnaki Indian word meaning "crooked stream."

•**CARIBOU,** City; Aroostook County; Pop. 9,919; Zip Code 04736; Elev. 442; Lat. 46-52-00 N long. 068-00-33 W; 13 mi. N of Presque Island in N Maine. Named in 1829 for the area's once abundant Caribou population.

•**CARMEL,** Town; Penobscot County; Pop. 1,695; Zip Code 04419; Lat. 44-47-53 N long. 069-03-07 W; E central Maine. The first settler, Reverend Paul Ruggles, named this town to commemorate Elijah's experience on Mount Carmel.

•**CARRABASSETT VALLEY,** Town; Franklin County; Pop. 107; W Maine. An Abnaki Indian name meaning either "place of small moose" or "place of sturgeon."

•**CARROLL,** Plantation; Penobscot County; Pop. 175; E central Maine. Named in honor of Daniel Carroll, a signer of the U. S. Constitution.

•**CARTHAGE,** Town; Franklin County; Pop. 438; W Maine. The town is named after the classical city of Carthage in North Africa.

•**CARY,** Plantation; Aroostook County; Pop. 229; N Maine. Cary is named after Shepard Cary, once a loading lumberman of the county.

•**CASCO,** Town; Cumberland County; Pop. 2,243; Zip Code 04013; Lat. 44-00-17 N long. 070-31-32 W; SW; coastal Maine. An Abnaki Indian name meaning "great blue heron."

•**CASTINE,** Town; Hancock County; Pop. 1,304; Zip Code 04421; Lat. 45-24-42 N long. 068-02-25 W; SE; coastal Maine. the town's name remembers Baron Vincent De St. Castine, a resident from 1667-97.

•**CASTLE,** HILL; Town; Pop. Aroostook County; Elev. 0,"509; 207; N Maine. the descriptive name commerates a large log building which resembled a castle.

•**CASWELL,** Plantation; Aroostook County; Pop. 586; N Maine. Named for the Caswell family, who owned the first farm in the township.

•**CENTERVILLE,** Town; Washington County; Pop. 28; SE corner; coastal Maine. So called because the town is in the center of the county.

•**CENTRAL AROOSTOOK,** Unorganized; Aroostook County; Pop. 16; N Maine. A descriptive name for the site's location.

•**CHAPMAN,** Town; Aroostook County; Pop. 406; N Maine. The original survivor, Chris Chapman, carved his name on the town's corner posts and gave it his name.

•**CHARLESTOWN,** Town; Penobscot County; Pop. 1,037; Zip Code 04422; Elev. 471; Lat. 45-05-07 N long. 069-02-31 W; E central Maine. Named for Charlestown, Massachusetts.

•**CHARLOTTE,** Town; Washington County; Pop. 300; SE corner; coastal Maine. A settler, David Blanchard, named the town for his wife in 1821.

•**CHELSEA,** Town; Kennebec County; Pop. 2,522; SW Maine. the town is named after Chelsea, Massachusetts.

•**CHERRYFIELD,** Town; Washington County; Pop. 983; Zip Code 04622; Elev. 54; Lat. 44-35-55 N long. 067-55-35 W; SE corner; coastal Maine. The town is named for an early cherry orchard.

•**CHESTER,** Town; Penobscot County; Pop. 434; E central Maine. An early settler, Samuel Chesley, named the town for his former name in Chester, New Hampshire.

•**CHESTERVILLE,** Town; Franklin County; Pop. 869; W Maine. Named for either Chester, New Hampshire or the hymn "Chester."

•**CHINA,** Town; Kennebec County; Pop. 2,918; Zip Code 04926; SW Maine. The name of an hymn the early settler's liked.

•**CLIFTON,** Town; Penobscot County; Pop. 462; E central Maine. A descriptive name reflecting the town's cliffs.

•**CLINTON,** Town; Kennebec County; Pop. 2,696; Zip Code 04927; Elev. 124; Lat. 44-39-00 N long. 069-29-40 W; SW Maine. Clinton's name honors De Witt Clinton, builder of the Erie Canal.

•**CODYVILLE,** Plantation; Washington County; Pop. 43; SE corner; coastal Maine. Named for an early settler.

•**COLUMBIA,** Town; Washington County; Pop. 275; SE corner; coastal Maine. The town's patriotic citizen's called it "Columbia," for America.

•**COLUMBIA FALLS,** Town; Washington County; Pop. 517; Zip Code 04623; Lat. 44-39-18 N long. 067-43-43 W; SE corner; coastal Maine. Given the name for "America."

•**CONNOR,** Unorganized; Aroostook County; Pop. 574; N Maine. Named for Selden Connor, one-time Governor of Maine.

•**COOPER,** Town; Washington County; Pop. 105; SE corner; coastal Maine. Cooper is named in honor of General John Cooper, a landowner and one-time Sheriff of the county.

•**CORINNA,** Town; Penobscot County; Pop. 1,887; Zip Code 04928; Lat. 44-55-16 N long. 069-15-44 W; E central Maine. Named after the daughter of the first landowner, Dr. John Warren.

•**CORINTH,** Town; Penobscot County; Pop. 1,711; E central Maine. Corinth's remembers the ancient Greek city.

•**CORNISH,** Town; York County; Pop. 1,047; Zip Code 04020; Elev. 353; Lat. 43-48-12 N long. 070-48-18 W; SW; coastal Maine. Named for the county of Cornwall in England.

•**CORNVILLE,** Town; Somerset County; Pop. 838; W Maine. A descriptive name for the abundant local Indian corn.

MAINE

•CRANBERRY ISLES, Town; Hancock County; Pop. 198; Zip Code 04625; Lat. 44-15-10 N long. 068-16-20 W; SE; coastal Maine. The town is descriptively named for the numerous cranberry patches.

•CRAWFORD, Town; Washington County; Pop. 86; SE corner; coastal Maine. Crawford's name honors William Harris Crawford, former Secretary of the Treasury.

•CRIEHAVEN, Unorganized; Knox County; Pop. 5; S; coastal Maine. Named about 1848 and honoring Robert Crie, the owner of the area, who opened his home to shipwrecked sailors.

•CUMBERLAND, Town; Cumberland County; Pop. 5,284; Zip Code 04021; 14 mi. NNW of Portland in SW; coastal Maine. William, Duke of Cumberland, and King George II gave his name to the town.

•CUSHING, Town; Knox County; Pop. 795; Zip Code 04563; Elev. 41; Lat. 43-58-55 N long. 069-17-21 W; S; coastal Maine. Named in honor of Thomas Cushing, one-time Lieutenant-Governor of Massachusetts.

•CUTLER, Town; Washington County; Pop. 726; Zip Code 04626; Elev. 20; Lat. 44-39-35 N long. 067-12-23 W; SE corner; coastal Maine. The town is named after Joseph Culter of Massachusetts, an early settler.

•DALLAS, Plantation; Franklin County; Pop. 146; W Maine. Probably named for George M. Dallas, a Vice-President of the United States.

•DAMARISCOTTA, Town; Lincoln County; Pop. 1,493; Zip Code 04543; Elev. 69; Lat. 44-01-48 N long. 069-31-59 W; S; coastal Maine. An Abnaki Indian word translated as "plenty of fish."

•DANFORTH, Town; Washington County; Pop. 826; Zip Code 04424; Lat. 45-39-37 N long. 067-52-00 W; SE corner; coastal Maine. The town's name comes from an early large landowner.

•DAYTON, Town; York County; Pop. 882; SW; coastal Maine. The town is named for Jonathan Dayton, youngest member of the Constitutional Convention and speaker of the House of Representatives.

•DEBLOIS, Town; Washington County; Pop. 44; SE corner; coastal Maine. T. A. Deblois, President of the Bank of Portland, owned much of the town and gave it his name.

•DEDHAM, Town; Hancock County; Pop. 841; SE; coastal Maine. Reubon Gregg, an early settler, named the town for his former home of Dedham, Massachusetts.

•DEER ISLE, Town; Hancock County; Pop. 1,492; Zip Code 04627; Lat. 44-13-24 N long. 068-40-51 W; SE; coastal Maine. A descriptive name referring to the area's once large deer population.

•DENMARK, Town; Oxford County; Pop. 672; Zip Code 04022; Lat. 43-52-55 N long. 070-47-46 W; W Maine. Believed to be named for the European Country.

•DENNISTOWN, Plantation; Somerset County; Pop. 30; W Maine. Probably named for an early settler.

•DENNYSVILLE, Town; Washington County; Pop. 296; Zip Code 04628; Elev. 57; Lat. 44-53-55 N long. 067-13-41 W; SE corner; coastal Maine. Named either for an Indian, John Denny, or Nicholas Denys, pioneer historian and Lieutenant Governor of Acadia.

•DETROIT, Town; Somerset County; Pop. 744; Zip Code 04929; Elev. 207; Lat. 44-47-36 N long. 069-17-50 W; W Maine. A French word referring to "the straits" of the Sebasticook River.

•DEXTER, Town; Penobscot County; Pop. 4,286; Zip Code 04930; Lat. 45-01-12 N long. 069-17-31 W; E central Maine. The town honors Samuel Dexter, unsuccessful Democratic candidate for Governor of Massachusetts in 1816.

•DIXFIELD, Town; Oxford County; Pop. 2,389; Zip Code 04224; Elev. 417; Lat. 44-32-12 N long. 070-27-29 W; W Maine. Dr. Elijah Dix agreed to build the town a library if they would name the community for him. The town got its library.

•DIXMONT, Town; Penobscot County; Pop. 812; Zip Code 04932; Elev. 543; Lat. 44-40-48 N long. 069-09-55 W; E central Maine. Th tpwn is named for Dr. Elijah Dix, a large landowner.

•DOVER-FOXCROFT, Town; Piscataquis County; Pop. 4,323; Zip Code 04426; Elev. 356; Lat. 45-11-12 N long. 069-13-08 W; N central Maine. So called as the result of this.

•DRESDEN, Town; Lincoln County; Pop. 998; Zip Code 04342; Lat. 44-06-25 N long. 069-43-38 W; S; coastal Maine. Named after the city in Germany.

•DREW, Plantation; Penobscot County; Pop. 57; E central Maine. Probably named for an early settler.

•DURHAM, Town; Androscoggin County; Pop. 2,074; SW Maine. Named by prominent landowner Colonel Royal for his former home in England.

•DYER BROOK, Town; Aroostook County; Pop. 275; N Maine. The origin of the town's name is unknown.

•EAGLE LAKE, Town; Aroostook County; Pop. 1,019; Zip Code 04739; Elev. 603; Lat. 47-02-25 N long. 068-35-50 W; N Maine. Major Hastings Strickland named the town in 1839 for bald eagles sighted nearby.

•EAST CENTRAL WASHINGTON, Unorganized; Washington County; Pop. 625; SE corner; coastal Maine. Named for George Washington.

•EAST FRANKLIN, Unorganized; Franklin County; Pop. 2; W Maine. Named for Benjamin Franklin.

•EAST HANCOCK, Unorganized; Hancock County; Pop. 44; SE; coastal Maine. The name honors John Hancock, Governor of Massachusetts and signer of the Declaration of Independence.

•EAST MACHIAS, Town; Washington County; Pop. 1,233; Zip Code 04630; Elev. 43; Lat. 44-44-27 N long. 067-23-32 W; SE corner; coastal Maine. An Abnaki Indian word meaning "bad little falls.

•EAST MILLINOCKET, Town; Penobscot County; Pop. 2,372; Zip Code 04430; Lat. 45-37-28 N long. 068-34-41 W; E central Maine. Great northern engineers built a paper mill and marked their blueprints "east of Millinocket". The "of" was later dropped and the town took its present name.

•EASTBROOK, Town; Hancock County; Pop. 262; SE; coastal Maine. So called because drainage of the southern half of the town flows into the East Branch Union River.

•EASTON, Town; Aroostook County; Pop. 1,305; Zip Code 04740; Lat. 46-38-30 N long. 067-54-42 W; N Maine. So called because the town lies on the east line of Aroostock County and of Maine.

•EASTPORT, Town; Washington County; Pop. 1,982; Zip Code 04631; Lat. 44-54-22 N long. 066-59-40 W; SE corner; coastal Maine. The town's name refers to its easterly location and was assigned by Captain Wopley Yeaton.

206

•**EDDINGTON,** Town; Penobscot County; Pop. 1,769; E central Maine. Colonel Jonathan Eddt, a soldier from Massachusetts, gave the town its name.

•**EDGECOMB,** Town; Lincoln County; Pop. 841; S; coastal Maine. The colonists gave the town the name after Lord Edgecomb, a friend of the American colonies before the Revoluationary War.

•**EDINBURG,** Town; Penobscot County; Pop. 126; E central Maine. the local roadbuilder, John Bennoch, named the town for Edinburg, Scotland.

•**ELIOT,** Town; York County; Pop. 4,948; Zip Code 03903; SW; coastal Maine. The town's name honors Robert Eliot, a member of the provincial council of New Hampshire in colonial days.

•**ELLIOTSVILLE,** Plantation; Piscataquis County; Pop. 26; N central Maine. Named for Elliot G. Vaughn, who owned the land in the area.

•**ELLSWORTH,** City; Hancock County; Pop. 5,179; Zip Code 04605; Lat. 44-33-26 N long. 068-27-00 W; 27 mi. SE of Bangor in SE Maine. The city is named for Oliver Ellsworth, a delegate to the Constitutional Convention from Massachusetts.

•**EMBDEN,** Town; Somerset County; Pop. 536; W Maine. Named for the city in Germany.

•**ENFIELD,** Town; Penobscot County; Pop. 1,397; Zip Code 04433; Elev. 211; Lat. 44-48-58 N long. 069-06-50 W; E central Maine. Believed to be named for Enfield, England.

•**ETNA,** Town; Penobscot County; Pop. 758; Zip Code 04434; Elev. 234; Lat. 44-48-58 N long. 069-06-50 W; E central Maine. Named by Benjamin Friend for Mount Etna in Sicily.

•**EUSTIS,** Town; Franklin County; Pop. 582; Zip Code 04936; Elev. 1172; Lat. 45-12-55 N long. 070-28-38 W; W Maine. Charles L. Eustis owned part of the township and gave it his name.

•**EXETER,** Town; Penobsoct County; Pop. 823; Zip Code 04435; Elev. 310; Lat. 44-58-15 N long. 069-08-40 W; E central Maine. Early settlers named the town for their former city of Exeter, New Hampshire.

•**FAIRFIELD,** Town; Somerset County; Pop. 6,113; Zip Code 04937; Elev. 142; Lat. 44-35-12 N long. 069-35-54 W; 4 mi. N of Waterville in W Maine. A descriptive name for the town's beautiful surroundings.

•**FALMOUTH,** Town; Cumberland County; Pop. 6,853; 6 mi. N of Portland in SW; coastal Maine. The town is named for Falmouth, England.

•**FARMINGDALE,** Town; Kennebec County; Pop. 2,535; SW Maine. The town's name suggests the many farms in the vicinity.

•**FARMINGTON,** Town; Franklin County; Pop. 6,730; Zip Code 04938; Elev. 425; Lat. 44-40-05 N long. 070-09-02 W; 26 mi. WNW of Waterville in W Maine. A descriptive name for the good farming in the region.

•**FAYETTE,** Town; Kennebec County; Pop. 812; SW Maine. Name in honor of Marquis de la Fayette, French soldier and Revolutionary War hero.

•**FORT FAIRFIELD,** Town; Aroostook County; Pop. 4,376; Zip Code 04742; Lat. 46-45-54 N long. 067-50-19 W; N Maine. One time site of a fort named in honor of John Fairfield, an early governor of Maine.

•**FORT KENT,** Town; Aroostook County; Pop. 4,826; Zip Code 04743; Elev. 350; Lat. 45-15-00 N long. 068-35-54 W; N Maine. The town was a site of a fort named in honor of an early governor of Maine, Edward Kent.

•**FRANKFORT,** Town; Waldo County; Pop. 783; Zip Code 04438; Lat. 44-36-26 N long. 068-52-35 W; S; coastal Maine. Either referring to the original home of many early German settlers, or as a compliment to Cont Henri Luther from Frankfort, who held large land tracts in the area.

•**FRANKLIN,** Town; Hancock County; Pop. 979; Zip Code 04634; Lat. 44-31-52 N long. 068-09-24 W; SE; coastal Maine. One of many town's name d in honor of Benjamin Franklin.

•**FREEDOM,** Town; Waldo County; Pop. 458; Zip Code 04941; Lat. 44-31-52 N long. 069-17-49 W; S; coastal Maine. Named furing the War of 1812 by citizens determined to retain their freedom.

•**FREEPORT,** Town; Cumberland County; Pop. 5,863; Zip Code 04032; Elev. 130; Lat. 43-51-36 N long. 070-05-51 W; 16 mi. NNE of Portland in SW; coastal Maine. Probably a descriptive name for the port's asseccibility, but possibly named for Sir Anthony Freeport, a character in one of Joseph Addison's plays.

•**FRENCHBORO,** Town; Hancock County; Pop. 43; Zip Code 04635; Lat. 44-07-06 N long. 068-19-45 W; SE; coastal Maine. Probably referring to early French settlers.

•**FRENCHVILLE,** Town; Aroostook County; Pop. 1,450; Zip Code 04745; Lat. 46-40-54 N long. 069-20-12 W; N Maine. A descriptive name referring to the large French-Canadian population.

•**FRIENDSHIP,** Town; Knox County; Pop. 1,000; Zip Code 04547; Lat. 43-59-05 N long. 069-20-12 W; S; coastal Maine. A descriptive compliment of the town's citizens.

•**FRYEBURG,** Town; Oxford County; Pop. 2,715; Zip Code 04037; Elev. 430; W Maine. The town's name remembers the original area landowner, Captain Joseph Frye.

•**GARDINER,** City; Kennebec County; Pop. 6,485; Zip Code 04345; Elev. 122; Lat. 44-14-06 N long. 069-46-31 W; 8 mi. S of Augusta in SW Maine. Named for an early large landowner, Dr. Sylvester Gardiner.

•**GARFIELD,** Plantation; Aroostook County; Pop. 107; N Maine. Named in honor of U. S. President James Garfield.

•**GARLAND,** Town; Penobscot County; Pop. 718; Zip Code 04939; E central Maine. The town takes its name from Joseph Garland, the first settler who arrived in 1802.

•**GEORGETOWN,** Town; Sagadahoc County; Pop. 735; Zip Code 04548; Lat. 43-48-12 N long. 069-45-25 W; S; coastal Maine. Named for either King George I, or nearby Fort St. George.

•**GILEAD,** Town; Oxford County; Pop. 191; W Maine. Named for the Balm of Gilead.

•**GLENBURN,** Town; Penobscot County; Pop. 2,319; E central Maine. A descriptive Scottish term meaning "a small stream in a narrow valley."

•**GORHAM,** Town; Cumberland County; Pop. 10,101; Zip Code 04038; Elev. 212; Lat. 43-40-44 N long. 070-26-38 W; 10 mi. W of Portland in SW; coastal Maine. The town is named after Captain John Gorham who served in King Phillip's War.

•**GOULDSBORO,** Town; Hancock County; Pop. 1,574; Lat. 44-29-13 N long. 068-07-34 W; SE; coastal Maine.

•**GRAND ISLE,** Town; Aroostook County; Pop. 719; Zip Code 04746; Lat. 47-18-22 N long. 068-09-17 W; N Maine. The town takes its name from the large island in the St. John River.

•**GRAND LAKE STREAM,** Plantation; Washington County; Pop. 198; Zip Code 04637; Elev. 303; Lat. 45-10-43 N long. 067-46-29 W; SE corner; coastal Maine. A descriptive geographical name.

•**GRAY,** Town; Cumberland County; Pop. 4,344; Zip Code 04039; Elev. 301; Lat. 43-53-08 N long. 070-19-46 W; SW; coastal Maine. Named in honor of Thomas Gray, an early large landowner in Massachusetts.

•**GREAT POND,** Plantation; Hancock County; Pop. 45; SE; coastal Maine. A descriptive name for the large pond in the area.

•**GREENBUSH,** Town; Penobscot County; Pop. 1,064; E central Maine. A descriptive name for the nearby green woods.

•**GREENE,** Town; Androscoggin County; Pop. 3,037; Zip Code 04236; Elev. 316; Lat. 44-10-45 N long. 070-08-27 W; SW Maine. the town's name honors Revolutionary War General Greene.

•**GREENFIELD,** Town; Penobscot County; Pop. 194; E central Maine. Probably named by early settlers for their former home in Greenfield, Massachusetts.

•**GREENVILLE,** Town; Piscataquis County; Pop. 1,839; Zip Code 04441; Elev. 1038; Lat. 45-27-40 N long. 069-36-04 W; N central Maine.

•**GREENWOOD,** Town; Oxford County; Pop. 653; W Maine. Probably named after Alexander Greenwood, the area's early surveyor.

•**GUILFORD,** Town; Piscataquis County; Pop. 1,793; Zip Code 04443; Lat. 45-18-12 N long. 069-20-54 W; N central Maine. Named for the first name child born in the town, Moses Guilford Law.

•**HALLOWELL,** City; Kennebec County; Pop. 2,502; Zip Code 04347; Lat. 44-16-25 N long. 069-47-26 W; SW Maine. the city gets its name from a prominent landowner, Benjamin Hallowell, who received large tracts in the Kennebec patent.

•**HAMLIN,** Plantation; Aroostook County; Pop. 340; N Maine. Named in honor of Hannibal Hamlin, a Vice-President of the United States.

•**HAMMOND,** Plantation; Aroostook County; Pop. 73; N Maine. Probably named for an early settler.

•**HAMPDEN,** Town; Penobscot County; Pop. 5,250; Zip Code 04444; Elev. 132; Lat. 44-44-38 N long. 068-50-22 W; 7 mi. S of Bangor in E central Maine. the town is named in honor of 17th century English patriot, John Hampden.

•**HANCOCK,** Town; Hancock County; Pop. 1,409; Zip Code 04640; Lat. 44-31-39 N long. 068-15-18 W; SE; coastal Maine. The town's name honors John Hancock, a Governor of Massachusetts, and famous signer of the Declaration of Independence.

•**HANOVER,** Town; Oxford County; Pop. 256; Zip Code 04237; Elev. 635; Lat. 44-29-44 N long. 070-41-48 W; W Maine. The town's pioneers named it after the province in Germany from which they had come.

•**HARMONY,** Town; Somerset County; Pop. 755; 207; Zip Code 04942; Elev. 316; Lat. 44-58-27 N long. 069-32-48 W; W Maine. The wife of Deacon John Moses gave the town it's name to describe the good feeling among the early settlers.

•**HARPSWELL,** Town; Cumberland County; Pop. 3,796; SW; coastal Maine. The pioneer Denning family named the town after Harpswell, England.

•**HARRINGTON,** Town; Washington County; Pop. 859; Zip Code 04643; Lat. 44-37-15 N long. 067-48-55 W; SE corner; coastal Maine. Named by the original English survivor for a British noble, and kept by the first settlers when the town was incorporated.

•**HARRISON,** Town; Cumberland County; Pop. 1,667; Zip Code 04040; Lat. 44-06-34 N long. 070-41-04 W; SW; coastal Maine. fthe town is named for Harrison Gray Otis, one of the early large landowners.

•**HARTFORD,** Town; Oxford County; Pop. 480; W Maine. Named after Hartford, Connecticut.

•**HARTLAND,** Town; Somerset County; Pop. 1,669; Zip Code 04943; Elev. 258; Lat. 44-53-01 N long. 069-26-58 W; W Maine. Either referring to the large deer herds or its position in the hills.

•**HAYNESVILLE,** Town; Aroostook County; Pop. 169; Zip Code 04446; Lat. 45-49-34 N long. 067-59-22 W; N Maine. Named in 1835 for a local storekeeper, Alvin Haynes.

•**HEBRON,** Town; Oxford County; Pop. 665; Zip Code 04238; Elev. 576; Lat. 44-11-53 N long. 070-24-28 W; W Maine. A bilical name possibly chosen by the Hebron Baptist society in 1791.

•**HERMON,** Town; Penobscot County; Pop. 3,170; E central Maine. Named by the original settlers for the biblical Mount Hermon.

•**HERSEY,** Town; Aroostook County; Pop. 67; N Maine. 1894 prohibition candidate for governor of Maine, General Samuel Hersey, had the town named in his honor.

•**HIGHLAND,** Plantation; Somerset County; Pop. 60; W Maine. A descriptive name for the area.

•**HIRAM,** Town; Oxford County; Pop. 1,067; Zip Code 04041; Elev. 369; Lat. 43-52-44 N long. 070-48-35 W; W Maine. The first settlers chose to name the town after the biblical King Hiram of Tyre.

•**HODGDON,** Town; Aroostook County; Pop. 1,084; N Maine. The town's name remembers prominent landowner John Hodgdon.

•**HOLDEN,** Town; Penobscot County; Pop. 2,554; E central Maine. Named for either Holden, Massachusetts or a Dr. Holden.

•**HOLLIS,** Town; York County; Pop. 2,892; Zip Code 04042; SW; coastal Maine. The name honors the Duke of Newcastle, whose family name was Hollis.

•**HOPE,** Town; Knox County; Pop. 730; Zip Code 04847; S; coastal Maine. Either named by the early settlers as a "land of hope," or so called by the town's surveyor James Malcolm.

•**HOULTON,** Town; Aroostook County; Pop. 6,766; Zip Code 07430; Elev. 366; Lat. 46-07-34 N long. 067-50-30 W; 22 mi. N of Grand Lake in N Maine. Named for Joseph Houlton, a local landowner, who settled in the area around 1810.

•**HOWLAND,** Town; Penobscot County; Pop. 1,602; Zip Code 04448; Lat. 45-14-27 N long. 068-39-25 W; E central Maine. The town is named for Matflower pioneer, John Howland.

•**HUDSON,** Town; Penobscot County; Pop. 797; Zip Code 04449; Lat. 44-59-52 N long. 068-53-09 W; E central Maine. The town is named after Hudson, Massachusetts.

•**INDUSTRY,** Town; Franklin County; Pop. 563; W Maine. Named by the Reverend J. Thompson's wife for the character of the town's people.

•**ISLAND FALLS,** Town; Aroostook County; Pop. 981; 207; Zip Code 04747; Lat. 46-00-20 N long. 068-16-18 W; N Maine. A descriptive name.

•**ISLE AU HAUT,** Town; Knox County; Pop. 57; Zip Code 04645; S; coastal Maine. Named by French explorer Samuel De Champlain and meaning "high island."

•**ISLEBORO,** Town; Waldo County; Pop. 521; Zip Code 04848; Lat. 44-18-23 N long. 068-54-17 W; S; coastal Maine. A descriptive name for the town's island location.

•**JACKMAN,** Town; Somerset County; Pop. 1,003; Zip Code 04945; Elev. 1172; Lat. 45-37-58 N long. 070-15-35 W; W Maine. Named for an early settler family, the Jackmans.

•**JACKSON,** Town; Waldo County; Pop. 346; Zip Code 04945; S; coastal Maine. Named in honor of Revolutionary War hero, General Henry Jackson.

•**JAY,** Town; Franklin County; Pop. 5,080; Zip Code 04239; Lat. 44-30-19 N long. 070-13-04 W; 28 mi. N of Lewiston in W Maine. The town's name honors John Jay, first Chief Justice of the United States.

•**JONESBORO,** Town; Washington County; Pop. 553; Zip Code 04648; Elev. 19; Lat. 44-39-41 N long. 067-34-33 W; SE corner; coastal Maine. John Coffin Jones received a large grant in the area in 1789 and gave his name to the town.

•**JONESPORT,** Town; Washington County; Pop. 1,512; Zip Code 04649; Lat. 44-31-48 N long. 067-36-36 W; SE corner; coastal Maine. Originally a part of Jonespbro, the town's name recalls the first landowner John C. Jones.

•**KENDUSKEAG,** Town; Penobscot County; Pop. 1,210; Zip Code 04450; Elev. 127; Lat. 44-55-14 N long. 068-55-58 W; E central Maine. An Agnoki Indian word meaning "ell weir plogg."

•**KENNEBUNK,** Town; York County; Pop. 6,621; Zip Code 04043; Lat. 43-23-09 N long. 070-32-36 W; 8 mi. S of Biddeford in SW Maine. An Ignaki Indian term meaning "long sandbar."

•**KENNEBUNKPORT,** Town; York County; Pop. 2,952; Zip Code 04046; Lat. 43-22-22 N long. 070-26-26 W; SW; coastal Maine. An Indian word meaning "long sandbar."

•**KINGFIELD,** Town; Franklin County; Pop. 1,083; Zip Code 04947; Elev. 560; Lat. 44-57-28 N long. 070-53-19 W; W Maine. Named in honor of William King, first governor of Maine.

•**KINGMAN,** Unorganized; Penobscot County; Pop. 281; Zip Code 04451; Elev. 341; Lat. 45-32-55 N long. 068-12-07 W; E central Maine. Named in honor of R. S. Kingman, owners of a large tannery.

•**KINGSBURY,** Plantation; Piscataquis County; Pop. 4; N central Maine. A pprominent landowner, Judge Sanford Kingsbury, had the area named for him.

•**KITTERY,** Town; York County; Pop. 9,314; Zip Code 03904; Elev. 22; across the bay from Portsmouth, NH in SW Maine. The town's name remembers the kitten-point manor in Kingsweare, Devon, England.

•**LAGRANGE,** Town; Penobscot County; Pop. 509; Zip Code 04453; Elev. 314; Lat. 45-09-58 N long. 068-50-46 W; E central Maine. The town's name recalls the Marquis De Lafayette's estate "LaGrange."

•**LAMOINE,** Town; Hancock County; Pop. 953; SE; coastal Maine. The town is named for an early French settler De Lamoine.

•**LEBANON,** Town; York County; Pop. 3,239; SW; coastal Maine. The first settlers gave the biblical name to the town.

•**LEE,** Town; Penobscot County; Pop. 688; Zip Code 04455; E central Maine. Early settler Stephen Lee gave his name to the town.

•**LEEDS,** Town; Androscoggin County; Pop. 1,463; SW Maine. The first pioneers named it for their former name in England.

•**LEVANT,** Town; Penobscot County; Pop. 1,117; Zip Code 04456; Lat. 44-52-12 N long. 068-55-58 W; E central Maine. Frenh settlers from the Levant plateau in Nova Scotia named the town for their former home.

•**LEWISTON,** City; Androscoggin County; Pop. 40,481; Zip Code 04240; Elev. 121; Lat. 44-05-53 N long. 070-11-50 W; 30 mi. N of Portland in SW Maine. Folklore says a drunken Indian named Lewis drown in the city's falls and had them named after him. The city takes its name from the falls.

•**LIBERTY,** Town; Waldo County; Pop. 694; Zip Code 04949; Lat. 44-25-35 N long. 069-0056 W; S; coastal Maine. The town desired to show its love of freedom in its name.

•**LIMERICK,** Town; York County; Pop. 1,356; Zip Code 04048; Lat. 43-41-18 N long. 070-47-34 W; SW; coastal Maine. Named in 1787 by pioneer James Sullivan for his former name of Limerick, Ireland.

•**LIMESTONE,** Town; Aroostook County; Pop. 8,719; Zip Code 04750; Elev. 521; Lat. 46-55-05 N long. 067-50-21 W; 18 mi. NNE of Presque Isle in N Maine. A descriptive name for the town's limestone deposits.

•**LIMINGTON,** Town; York County; Pop. 2,203; Zip Code 04049; Elev. 474; Lat. 43-43-48 N long. 070-42-44 W; SW; coastal Maine. Named for either Limington in Somersetshire, or Hampshire, England.

•**LINCOLN,** Town; Penobscot County; Pop. 5,066; Zip Code 04457; Lat. 45-21-51 N long. 068-30-16 W; 42 mi. N of Bangor in E central Maine. Named for Enoch Lincoln, sixth governor of Maine.

•**MACHIAS,** Town; Washington County; Pop. 2,458; Zip Code 04654; Elev. 70; Lat. 44-42-53 N long. 067-27-47 W; SE corner; coastal Maine. An Abnaki Indian word meaning "bad little falls."

•**MACHIASPORT,** Town; Washington County; Pop. 1,108; Zip Code 04655; Lat. 44-41-49 N long. 067-23-50 W; SE corner; coastal Maine.",The town takes its name from an Indian word meaning "bad little falls."

•**MACWAHOC,** Plantation; Aroostook County; Pop. 126; N Maine. An Abnoki Indian work meaning "wet ground" or "fog".

•**MADAWASKA,** Town; Aroostook County; Pop. 5,282; Zip Code 04756; Elev. 595; Lat. 47-21-21 N long. 068-19-53 W; 17 mi. ENE of Fort Kent in N Maine. A Micmac Indian word meaning "where one river ends into another," or "having its outlet reeds.

•**MADISON,** Town; Somerset County; Pop. 4,367; Zip Code 04950; Elev. 297; Lat. 44-48-04 N long. 069-52-43 W; W Maine. Named for the Madison Bridge over the Kennebec River, itself named for James Madison, fourth President of the United States.

•**MADRID,** Town; Franklin County; Pop. 178; W Maine. The town is named for the city of Madrid in Spain.

•**MAGALLOWAY,** Plantation; Oxford County; Pop. 79; W Maine. An Malecite Indian word meaning "many caribou."

•**MANCHESTER,** Town; Kennebec County; Pop. 1,949; Zip Code 04351; Lat. 44-19-33 N long. 069-51-46 W; SW Maine. The first settlers named their now name in Maine after their old one in Masachusetts.

•**MAPLETON,** Town; Aroostook County; Pop. 1,895; Zip Code 04757; Elev. 548; Lat. 46-40-50 N long. 068-09-43 W; N Maine. The town is named for its maple trees.

•**MARIAVILLE,** Town; Hancock County; Pop. 168; SE; coastal Maine. The town's name remembers Maria Matilda, the daughter of Maine land baron, William Bingham.

•**MARS HILL,** Town; Aroostook County; Pop. 1,892; Zip Code 04758; Elev. 435; Lat. 46-30-46 N long. 067-51-56 W; N Maine. The town takes its name from a verse in the Bible which mentions a Mars Hill where Paul preached. Read by a chaplain to a survey crew working the area.

•**MARSHFIELD,** Town; Washington County; Pop. 416; SE corner; coastal Maine. A descriptive name pointing out the town's marshlands.

•**MASARDIS,** Town; Aroostook County; Pop. 328; Zip Code 04759; N Maine. An Abnaki Indian term meaning "place of white clay."

•**MATINICUS ISLE,** Plantation; Knox County; Pop. 66; Zip Code 04851; Lat. 43-51-49 N long. 068-53-26 W; S; coastal Maine.

•**MATTAWAMKEAG,** Town; Penobscot County; Pop. 1,000; Zip Code 04459; Elev. 217; Lat. 45-30-56 N long. 068-21-22 W; E central Maine. An Abnaki Indian term meaning "fishing place beyond the gravel bar." The same word used by an Micmac Indian would mean "on a sand bar".

•**MAXFIELD,** Town; Penobscot County; Pop. 64; E central Maine. The town's name comes from the second settler Joseph McIntosh. His farm became known as "Mac's field," and the present spelling evolved.

•**MECHANIC FALLS,** Town; Androscoggin County; Pop. 2,616; Zip Code 04256; Elev. 304; Lat. 44-06-02 N long. 070-22-58 W; SW Maine. Descriptively named for early local industries and the "mechanics" who worked there.

•**MEDDYBEMPS,** Town; Washington County; Pop. 119; Zip Code 04657; Elev. 174; Lat. 45-02-08 N long. 067-21-26 W; SE corner; coastal Maine. A Passamaquody-Abnaki term meaning "plenty of fish."

•**MEDFORD,** Town; Piscataquis County; Pop. 163; N central Maine. A descriptive name for the middle ford of the Piscataquis River where the town lies.

•**MEDWAY,** Town; Penobscot County; Pop. 1,871; Zip Code 04460; Elev. 296; Lat. 45-37-25 N long. 068-34-41 W; E central Maine. A descriptive name for the towns location midway between Banger and the county's north boundary.

•**MERCER,** Town; Somerset County; Pop. 448; W Maine. Honoring Revolutionary War hero Brigadier General Hugh Mercer.

•**MERRILL,** Town; Aroostook County; Pop. 285; N Maine. Named for Captain William Merrill, a landowner the region about 1840.

•**MEXICO,** Town; Oxford County; Pop. 3,698; Zip Code 04257; Lat. 44-33-39 N long. 070-32-37 W; W Maine. Named for Mexico, which was rebelling against Spain in 1818 when the town was incorporated.

•**MILBRIDGE;** Town; Washington; Zip Code 04658; Elev. 21; Lat. 44-32-23 N long. 067-53-05 W; SE corner; coastal Maine. Named after a mill and bridge built in the town in the 1830's by Mr. Gordiner.

•**MILFORD,** Town; Penobscot County; Pop. 2,160; Zip Code 04461; Lat. 44-56-41 N long. 068-38-29 W; E central Maine. Named after their previous name of Milford, Massachusetts by early settlers.

•**MILLINOCKET,** Town; Penobscot County; Pop. 7,567; Zip Code 04462; Elev. 358; Lat. 45-39-27 N long. 068-42-40 W; 54 mi. SW of Houlton in E central Maine. An Abnaki Indian word meaning "this place is admirable."

•**MILO,** Town; Piscataquis County; Pop. 2,624; Zip Code 04463; Lat. 45-15-04 N long. 068-58-57 W; N central Maine. Theopuilus Sargent, an early settler, nemed the town for the classical Greek athlete, Mild of Crotond.

•**MINOT,** Town; Androscoggin County; Pop. 1,631; Zip Code 04258; Elev. 2631; Lat. 44-05-11 N long. 070-19-22 W; SW Maine. The town's name honors Judge Minot, an early member of the General Court of Massachusetts.

•**MONMOUTH,** Town; Kennebec County; Pop. 2,888; Zip Code 04259; Elev. 270; Lat. 44-14-13 N long. 070-02-08 W; SW Maine. General Henry Dearborn named the town to commemorate the Battle of Monmouth in the American Revolution.

•**MONROE,** Town; Waldo County; Pop. 657; Zip Code 04951; Lat. 44-36-55 N long. 069-01-08 W; coastal Maine. In honor of James Monroe, fifth President of the United States.

•**MONSON,** Town; Piscataquis County; Pop. 804; Zip Code 04464; Lat. 45-17-15 N long. 069-30-13 W; N central Maine. The area was land granted to the Hebron Academy, which was in Monson, Massachusetts.

•**MONTICELLO,** Town; Aroostook County; Pop. 950; Zip Code 04760; Elev. 392; Lat. 46-18-35 N long. 067-50-34 W; N Maine. The town's name honors Jefferson name and estate of Monticello.

•**MONTVILLE,** Town; Waldo County; Pop. 631; S; coastal Maine. A descriptive name meaning "mountain town."

•**MOOSE RIVER,** Town; Somerset County; Pop. 252; W Maine. A descriptive name for the large moose population.

•**MORRILL,** Town; Waldo County; Pop. 506; Zip Code 04952; Elev. 238; Lat. 44-26-42 N long. 069-09-07 W; S. coastal Maine. The town's name honors Anson P. Morrill, Governor of Maine from 1855 - 58.

•**MOSCOW,** Town; Somerset County; Pop. 570; W Maine. The town was surveyed in 1812 the year the Russians repulsed Napoleon and hence the name.

•**MOUNT CHASE,** Town; Penobscot County; Pop. 233; E central Maine. Named for a Maine forest agent who searched for timber thieves in the area.

•**MOUNT DESERT,** Town; Hancock County; Pop. 2,063; Zip Code 04660; Lat. 44-21-57 N long. 068-19-56 W; SE; coastal Maine. Named by the French for the many bare peaks in the area.

•**MOUNT VERNON,** Town; Kennebec County; Pop. 1,021; Zip Code 04352; Elev. 339; Lat. 44-30-04 N long. 069-59-10 W; SW Maine. The town's name honors George Washington's estate Mount Vernon.

•**NAPLES,** Town; Cumberland County; Pop. 1,833; Zip Code 04055; Lat. 43-58-19 N long. 070-36-34 W; SW; coastal Maine. The town is named after Naples, Italy.

•**NEW CANADA,** Town; Aroostook County; Pop. 269; N Maine. So called as a result of the many French-Canadians living here.

•NEW GLOUCESTER, Town; Cumberland County; Pop. 3,180; Zip Code 04260; Lat. 43-57-23 N long. 070-16-08 W; SW; coastal Maine. Settlers from Glouster, Massachusetts named their now town for their previous home.

•NEW LIMERICK, Town; Aroostook County; Pop. 513; Zip Code 04761; Lat. 46-06-04 N long. 067-57-35 W; N Maine. Many of the early settlers were from Limerick, Maine, and so gave that name to their new town.

•NEW PORTLAND, Town; Somerset County; Pop. 651; Zip Code 04954; Lat. 44-53-01 N long. 070-06-10 W; W Maine. Early settlers who had been burned out by Indian raids on Falmouth named their now town for Portland, Maine.

•NEW SHARON, Town; Franklin County; Pop. 969; Zip Code 04955; Elev. 369; Lat. 44-38-22 N long. 070-01-53 W; W Maine. the first pioneers were from Sharon, Massachusetts and so named their now town.

•NEW SWEDEN, Town; Aroostook County; Pop. 737; Zip Code 04762; Elev. 866; Lat. 46-56-29 N long. 068-07-20 W; N Maine. Swedish settlers decided to call their now town after the mother country.

•NEW VINEYARD, Town; Franklin County; Pop. 607; Zip Code 04956; Lat. 44-48-15 N long. 070-07-18 W; W Maine. New settlers from Martha's Vineyard in Massachusetts named the town in 1791.

•NEWBURGH, Town; Penobscot County; Pop. 1,228; E central Maine. Given by early settlers and meaning "new Town."

•NEWFIELD, Town; York County; Pop. 644; Zip Code 04056; Elev. 406; Lat. 43-38-52 N long. 070-50-46 W; SW; coastal Maine. A descriptive name meaning "newfields".

•NEWPORT, Town; Penobscot County; Pop. 2,755; Zip Code 04953; Elev. 202; Lat. 44-50-17 N long. 069-16-02 W; E central Maine. A descriptive name for an Indian portage between the Penobscot and Sebasticook Rivers known as "new portage."

•NEWRY, Town; Oxford County; Pop. 235; Zip Code 04261; Elev. 642; Lat. 44-29-10 N long. 070-47-18 W; W Maine. Named by its first settlers for their former home in Newry, County Down, Ireland.

•NORRIDGEWOCK, Town; Somerset County; Pop. 2,552; Zip Code 04957; Elev. 204; Lat. 44-42-26 N long. 069-47-10 W; W Maine. An Abnaki Indian term meaning "little falls with smooth water above and below." Probably the name of an Indian chief Norridwog.

•NORTH BERWICK, Town; York County; Pop. 2,878; Zip Code 03906; Elev. 147; SW; coastal Maine. Named for Berwick, Dorsetshire in England.

•NORTH FRANKLIN, Unorganized; Franklin County; Pop. 28; W Maine. Named in honor of Benjamin Franklin.

•NORTH HAVEN, Town; Knox County; Pop. 373; Zip Code 04853; Elev. 20; Lat. 44-07-38 N long. 068-52-39 W; S; coastal Maine. A descriptive name given by the early settlers.

•NORTH OXFORD, Unorganized; Oxford County; Pop. 37; W Maine. Named by David Leonard, an early settler for Oxford Massachusetts.

•NORTH PENOBSCOT, Unorganized; Penobscot County; Pop. 246; E central Maine. An Abnoki or Malecite Indian term meaning "at the descending rocks."

•NORTH WASHINGTON, Unorganized; Washington County; Pop. 393; SE corner; coastal Maine. The name honors President George Washington.

•NORTH YARMOUTH, Town; Cumberland County; Pop. 1,919; SW; coastal Maine. Called by early settlers North Yarmouth to distinguish it from Yarmouth, Massachusetts.

•NORTHEAST PISCATAQUIS, Unorganized; Piscataquis County; Pop. 132; N central Maine. An Abnaki Indian term meaning "at the river branch."

•NORTHEAST SOMERSET, Unorganized; Somerset County; Pop. 301; W Maine. Named after Somerset, England.

•NORTHFIELD, Town; Washington County; Pop. 88; SE corner; coastal Maine. Named for the large fields north of the town of Machias.

•NORTHPORT, Town; Waldo County; Pop. 958; S; coastal Maine. Named by early settlers for its location in the north part of the old ducktrap plantation.

•NORTHWEST AROOSTOOK, Unorganized; Aroostook County; Pop. 101; N Maine. A Micmac Indian term meaning "shining river."

•NORTHWEST HANCOCK, Unorganized; Hancock County; SE; Coastal Me. Named in honor of John Hancock, signer of the Declaration of Independence and Governor of Massachusetts.

•NORTHWEST PISCATAQUIS, Unorganized; Piscataquis County; Pop. 99; N central Maine. An Abnaki Indian term meaning "at the river barnch.

•NORWAY, Town; Oxford County; Pop. 4,042; Zip Code 04268; Elev. 383; Lat. 44-12-39 N long. 070-32-16 W; W Maine. The town's people Petitioned for their township to be called "Norage" or Indian for "falls." When the petition came back a clerk at the legislature had "corrected" the spelling to Norway.

•OAKFIELD, Town; Aroostook County; Pop. 847; Zip Code 04763; Elev. 565; Lat. 46-05-57 N long. 068-09-37 W; N Maine. Named in 1866 by the oldest resident, James Timonsy, for the nearby oaks and fields.

•OAKLAND, Town; Kennebec County; Pop. 5,162; Zip Code 04963; Elev. 238; Lat. 44-32-54 N long. 069-43-01 W; 5 mi. W of Waterville in SW Maine. A descriptive name for the area's oak trees.

•OLD ORCHARD BEACH, Town; York County; Pop. 6,291; Zip Code 04064; Lat. 43-29-55 N long. 070-23-07 W; SW; coastal Maine. Named for an orchard planted by Thomas Rogers in 1638.

•OLD TOWN, City; Penobscot County; Pop. 8,422; Zip Code 04468; Elev. 108; Lat. 44-55-54 N long. 068-39-48 W; 11 mi. NNE of Bangor in E central Maine. The city's name reflects continuous occupation since 1669.

•ORIENT, Town; Aroostook County; Pop. 97; Zip Code 04471; Lat. 45-48-50 N long. 067-50-25 W; N Maine. Located on the east boundary of Maine, and hence given the name for "east."

•ORLAND, Town; Hancock County; Pop. 1,645; Zip Code 04472; Lat. 44-34-15 N long. 068-44-26 W; SE; coastal Maine. Supposedly named by settler Joseph Gross in 1764 when he found an oar on the shore of the river.

•ORONO, Town; Penobscot County; Pop. 10,578; Zip Code 04473; Elev. 132; Lat. 44-53-22 N long. 068-40-15 W; 8 mi. NNE of Bangor in E central Maine. Named for Chief Joseph Orono of the Penobscot Indians.

•ORRINGTON, Town; Penobscot County; Pop. 3,244; Zip Code 04474; Lat. 44-43-53 N long. 068-49-46 W; E central Maine. Named by Parson Noble as a misspelling on the town's incorporation application, or possibly given by an agent of the Massachusetts General Courts that they liked the name.

211

•OTISFIELD, Town; Oxford County; Pop. 897; W Maine. Probably named for the landholdings of an early settler.

•OWLS HEAD, Town; Knox County; Pop. 1,633; Zip Code 04854; Lat. 44-04-56 N long. 069-03-36 W; S; coastal Maine. A descriptive name for the areas shape. So called by Governor Thomas Pownal in 1759.

•OXBOW, Plantation; Aroostook County; Pop. 84; Lat. 46-25-11 N long. 068-28-04 W; N Maine. A descriptive name for a bend in the Birch River.

•OXFORD, Town; Oxford County; Pop. 3,143; Zip Code 04270; Lat. 44-07-58 N long. 070-29-38 W; W Maine.

•PALERMO, Town; Waldo County; Pop. 760; Zip Code 04354; Elev. 366; Lat. 44-24-30 N long. 069-28-24 W; S; coastal Maine. Following a popular 18th century practice, the town is named after the European city of Palermo, Italy.

•PALMYRA, Town; Somerset County; Pop. 1,485; Zip Code 04965; Elev. 310; Lat. 44-50-46 N long. 069-21-38 W; W Maine. Named by pioneer Warren family after their daughter Palmyra.

•PARIS, Town; Oxford County; Pop. 4,168; Zip Code 04271; Lat. 44-15-32 N long. 070-29-49 W; W Maine. Named in honor of the great French city, or possibly after for Alfon Paris, a leading Democrat who helped in Maine's separation from Massachusetts.

•PARKMAN, Town; Piscataquis County; Pop. 621; N central Maine. Named for Samuel Parkman, an early settler.

•PARSONSFIELD, Town; York County; Pop. 1,089; SW; coastal Maine. the town takes its name from an early landowner, Thomas Parsons.

•PASSADUMKEAG, Town; Penobscot County; Pop. 430; Zip Code 04475; Elev. 143; Lat. 45-11-04 N long. 068-36-52 W; E central Maine. An Abnaki Indian word meaning "rapids over gravelbeds."

•PASSAMAQUODDY INDIAN TOWNSHIP, Indian Reservation; Washington County; Pop. 423; SE corner; coastal Maine. A Malecite Indian term meaning "plenty of polluck fish."

•PASSAMAQUODDY PLEASANT POINT, Indian Reservation; Washington County; Pop. 549; SE corner; coastal Maine. Named by the Indians for the abundant cod fishing in the area.

•PATTEN, Town; Penobscot County; Pop. 1,368; Zip Code 04765; Elev. 546; Lat. 45-56-43 N long. 068-29-37 W; E central Maine. The town's name comes from an early settler, Amos Patten, who purchased the township in 1830.

•PEMBROKE, Town; Washington County; Pop. 920; Zip Code 04666; Elev. 19; Lat. 44-57-13 N long. 067-09-52 W; SE corner; coastal Maine. An early settler, Jerry Burgin, for Pembroke, Wales.

•PENOBSCOT, Town; Hancock County; Pop. 1,104; Zip Code 04476; Elev. 54; Lat. 44-27-40 N long. 068-42-30 W; SE; coastal Maine. An Abnaki Indian term meaning "at the descending river rocks."

•PENOBSCOT INDIAN ISLAND, Indian Reservation; Penobscot County; Pop. 458; E central Maine. An Abnaki on Malette Indian term meaning "at the descending river rocks".

•PERHAM, Town; Aroostook County; Pop. 437; Zip Code 04766; Elev. 630; Lat. 46-50-35 N long. 068-12-09 W; N Maine. Named in honor of Sidngy Perham, an early governor of Maine.

•PERKINS, Unorganized; Sagadahoc County; Pop. 2; S; coastal Maine. Named for a local settler family.

•PERRY, Town; Washington County; Pop. 737; Zip Code 04667; Lat. 44-58-22 N long. 067-04-44 W; SE corner; coastal Maine. In honor of Oliver H. Perry, the War of 1812 naval hero.

•PERU, Town; Oxford County; Pop. 1,564; Zip Code 04272; Lat. 44-30-18 N long. 070-24-32 W; W Maine. The town's name honors Peru which attained its independence in 1821 the same year the town was incorporated.

•PHILLIPS, Town; Franklin County; Pop. 1,092; Zip Code 04966; Elev. 571; Lat. 44-49-21 N long. 070-20-36 W; W Maine. Jonathan Phillips of Boston, an early pioneer, had the town named in his honor.

•PHIPPSBURG, Town; Sagadahoc County; Pop. 1,527; Zip Code 04562; Elev. 49; Lat. 43-49-12 N long. 069-49-01 W; S; coastal Maine. In honor of Sir William Phipps, Governor of Massachusetts in 1692.

•PITTSFIELD, Town; Somerset County; Pop. 4,125; Zip Code 04967; Elev. 223; Lat. 44-46-52 N long. 069-23-08 W; W Maine. Landowner William Pitts of Boston, gave this town its name.

•PITTSTON, Town; Kennebec County; Pop. 2,267; SW Maine. In honor of the John Pitt family who was instrumental in settling the area.

•PLYMOUTH, Town; Penobscot County; Pop. 811; Zip Code 04969; Lat. 44-45-59 N long. 069-12-40 W; E central Maine. The town is named for Plymouth, Massachusetts.

•POLAND, Town; Androscoggin County; Pop. 3,578; Zip Code 04273; Lat. 44-03-40 N long. 070-23-41 W; SW Maine. Either for an old hymn Poland" or after the European country.

•PORTAGE LAKE, Town; Aroostook County; Pop. 562; Zip Code 04768; Elev. 641; Lat. 46-45-26 N long. 068-28-30 W; N Maine. A descriptive term referring to the portage between the lake and nearby Machias Lake.

•PORTER, Town; Oxford County; Pop. 1,222; Zip Code 04068; Elev. 411; Lat. 43-47-45 N long. 070-55-58 W; W Maine. Dr. Aaron Porter owned much of the town, and as its leading citizen had it named in his honor.

•PORTLAND, City; Cumberland County; Pop. 61,572; Zip Code 041+; Lat. 43-40-12 N long. 070-16-38 W; Seaport city on Casco Bay in SW Maine. Named in honor of the English city in Dorsetshire.

•POWNAL, Town; Cumberland County; Pop. 1,189; Zip Code 04069; Lat. 43-54-00 N long. 070-14-11 W; SW; coastal Maine. The town is named for one time Governor of Massachusetts, Thomas Pownal.

•PRENTISS, Plantation; Penobscot County; Pop. 205; E central Maine. The area takes its name from prominent landowner Henry E. Prentiss.

•PRESQUE ISLE, City; Aroostook County; Pop. 11,172; Zip Code 04769; Elev. 446; Lat. 46-41-43 N long. 068-00-13 W; 40 mi. N of Houlton in N Maine. An early French name meaning "almost an island," or in other words a peninsula.

•PRINCETON, Town; Washington County; Pop. 994; Zip Code 04668; Elev. 211; Lat. 45-13-13 N long. 067-34-25 W; SE corner; coastal Maine. An original settler, Ebenezer Rolfe, named the now town after his old home in Massachusetts.

•PROSPECT, Town; Waldo County; Pop. 511; lat. 44-24-21 N long. 068-01-50 W; S; coastal Maine. A descriptive name for the beautiiiful higher elevation view from the center of the township.

•**RANDOLPH,** Town; Kennebec County; Pop. 1,834; SW Maine. Named by early settlers for Randolph, Massachusetts.

•**RANGELEY,** Town; Franklin County; Pop. 1,023; Zip Code 04970; Elev. 1545; Lat. 44-58-05 N long. 070-38-41 W; W Maine. The town is named for Squire Rangeley of Yorkshire, England who bought the area in 1825.

•**RAYMOND,** Town; Cumberland County; Pop. 2,251; Zip Code 04071; Lat. 44-54-45 N long. 069-24-42 W; SW; coastal Maine. Named in honor of Captain Williamn Raymond, who served in the early Indian Wars.

•**READFIELD,** Town; Kennebec County; Pop. 1,943; Zip Code 04355; Elev. 300; Lat. 44-23-20 N long. 069-57-56 W; SW Maine. Supposedly named for Peter Norson who was an avid reader.

•**RICHMOND,** Town; Sagadahoc County; Pop. 2,627; Zip Code 04357; Elev. 31; Lat. 44-05-39 N long. 069-48-35 W; S; coastal Maine. The town's name recalls fort Richmond, named for the Duke of Richmond and built in 1719.

•**RIPLEY,** Town; Somerset County; Pop. 439; W Maine. In honor of General Eleazer Ripley, an officer in the War of 1812.

•**ROBBINSTON,** Town; Washington County; Pop. 492; Zip Code 04671; Lat. 45-04-30 N long. 067-06-30 W; SE corner; coastal Maine. The town is named for the Robbins brothers who were the original land grantees.

•**ROCKLAND,** City; Knox County; Pop. 7,919; Zip Code 04841; Elev. 35; Lat. 44-08-26 N long. 069-09-07 W; 37 mi. ESE of Augusta in S Maine. The cities' name refers to its limestone querries.

•**ROCKPORT,** Town; Knox County; Pop. 2,749; Zip Code 04856; Elev. 66; Lat. 44-11-16 N long. 069-05-38 W; S; coastal Maine. A descriptive name for the port's rocky terrain.

•**ROME,** Town; Kennebec County; Pop. 627; SW Maine. The town is named for the external city, rome, in Italy.

•**ROQUE BLUFFS,** Town; Washington County; Pop. 244; SE corner; coastal Maine. Named by H. P. Garner for nearby Roque Island.

•**ROXBURY,** Town; Oxford County; Pop. 373; Zip Code 04275; Lat. 44-40-12 N long. 070-35-36 W; W Maine. The town is called after its namesake in Massachusetts.

•**RUMFORD,** Town; Oxford County; Pop. 8,240; Zip Code 04276; Lat. 44-33-03 N long. 070-32-55 W; W Maine. Named in honor of Sir Benjamin Thompson, Count of Rumford.

•**SABATTUS,** Town; Androscoggin County; Pop. 3,081; Zip Code 04280; Lat. 44-07-20 N long. 070-04-25 W; SW Maine. The town's name remembers Sabattus, a chief of the Anasagunticooks Indians, who was killed in the area.

•**SACO,** City; York County; Pop. 12,921; Zip Code 04072; Lat. 43-30-42 N long. 070-26-37 W; N of Biddeford on the Saco R. in SW Maine. An Abnaki Indian term meaning "flowing out."

•**ST. AGATHA,** Town; Aroostook County; Pop. 1,035; Zip Code 04772; Lat. 47-14-36 N long. 068-18-32 W; N Maine. the town takes its name from the local St. Agatha Church.

•**ST. ALBANS,** Town; Somerset County; Pop. 1,400; Zip Code 04971; W Maine. Named for St. Albons, England.

•**ST. FRANCIS,** Plantation; Aroostook County; Pop. 839; Zip Code 04774; Elev. 597; Lat. 47-10-14 N long. 068-53-26 W; N Maine. Probably named for the famous Catholic saint of Assisi.

•**ST. GEORGE,** Town; Knox County; Pop. 1,948; Zip Code 04857; Elev. 113; Lat. 44-01-09 N long. 069-12-12 W; S; coastal Maine. For St. George the patron saint of England. Named by Captain George Wetmouth in 1600 when he claimed the area for England.

•**SANFORD,** Town; York County; Pop. 18,020; Zip Code 04073; Lat. 43-26-24 N long. 070-46-23 W; 15 mi. W of Biddefordin SW Maine. Named in honor of early settlers John Sanford's children.

•**SANGERVILLE,** Town; Piscataquis County; Pop. 1,219; Zip Code 04479; Elev. 518; Lat. 45-10-22 N long. 069-21-27 W; N central Maine. The town is named for Colonel Calvin Sanger of Sherborn, Massachusetts who owned land in this area.

•**SCARBOROUGH,** Town; Cumberland County; Pop. 11,347; Zip Code 04074; Elev. 17; Lat. 43-34-45 N long. 070-21-13 W; 7 mi. S of Portland in SW; coastal Maine. The town is named for Scarborough, Yorkshire, England.

•**SEARSMONT,** Town; Waldo County; Pop. 782; Zip Code 04973; Elev. 227; Lat. 44-21-44 N long. 069-11-58 W; S; coastal Maine. Named after large landowner, David Sears.

•**SEARSPORT,** Town; Waldo County; Pop. 2,309; Zip Code 04974; Elev. 60; Lat. 44-27-35 N long. 068-55-00 W; S; coastal Maine. David Sears, who held much of the original grant, had the town named in his honor.

•**SEBAGO,** Town; Cumberland County; Pop. 974; Zip Code 04075; Elev. 284; Lat. 43-45-32 N long. 070-31-32 W; SW; coastal Maine. An Abnaki Indian word meaning "big lake".

•**SEBEC,** Town; Piscataquis County; Pop. 469; Zip Code 04481; Elev. 358; Lat. 45-16-18 N long. 069-06-58 W; N central Maine. An Abnaki Indian term meaning "much water."

•**SEBOEIS,** Plantation; Penobscot County; Pop. 53; Zip Code 04484; Lat. 45-53-51 N long. 068-25-58 W; E central Maine. An Abnaki Indian word meaning "little stream."

•**SEBOOMOOK LAKE,** Unorganized; Somerset County; Pop. 37; W Maine. An Abnaki Indian term meaning "at or near the large stream".

•**SEDGWICK,** Town; Hancock County; Pop. 795; Zip Code 04676; Lat. 44-18-08 N long. 068-37-08 W; SE; coastal Maine. The town's name honors Major Robert Sedgwick of Charleston, Massachusetts, a soldier in the French and Indian wars.

•**SHAPLEIGH,** Town; York County; Pop. 1,370; Zip Code 04076; Lat. 43-32-23 N long. 070-50-48 W; SW; coastal Maine. Shapleigh's name remembers Englishman Nicholas Shapleigh, who was a major landowner at Kittery-Point.

•**SHERMAN,** Town; Aroostook County; Pop. 1,021; Zip Code 04776; N Maine. The town is named in honor ofSenator John Sherman of Ohio, noted statesman, financier, and aboliitionist.

•**SHIRLEY,** Town; Piscataquis County; Pop. 242; Zip Code 04485; N central Maine. Named by local citizens to honor Joesph Kelsot, a representative to the legislature from Shirley, Massachusetts.

•**SIDNEY,** Town; Kennebec County; Pop. 2,052; SW Maine. The town's name honors Englishman Phillip Sidney.

•**SKOWHEGAN,** Town; Somerset County; Pop. 8,098; Zip Code 04976; Lat. 44-46-24 N long. 069-43-13 W; 15 mi. NNW of Waterville in W Maine. An Abnaki word meaning "place of waiting - a fish spearing place."

•**SMITHFIELD,** Town; Somerset County; Pop. 748; Zip Code 04978; Lat. 44-37-52 N long. 069-49-42 W; W Maine. Named for Reverend Herny Smith, an early settler.

•**SMYRNA,** Town; Aroostook County; Pop. 354; Zip Code 04780; N Maine. The town's name after the ancient city of Smyrna, Turkey.

•**SOLON,** Town; Somerset County; Pop. 827; Zip Code 04979; Elev. 405; Lat. 44-56-59 N long. 069-51-39 W; W Maine. The town is named for Solon, Lowgiver and Sage, in ancient Greece.

•**SORRENTO,** Town; Hancock County; Pop. 276; Zip Code 04677; Lat. 44-28-23 N long. 068-11-30 W; SE; coastal Maine. Either named for Sorrento, Italy, or a Mr. Soren who founded a summer resort.

•**SOUTH AROOSTOOK,** Unorganized; Aroostook County; Pop. 261; N Maine. A Micmac word meaning "beautiful" or "sshining river".

•**SOUTH FRANKLIN,** Unorganized; Franklin County; Pop. 48; W Maine. The area is named in honor of Benjamin Franklin.

•**SOUTH OXFORD,** Unorganized; Oxford County; Pop. 348; W Maine. The area is named after Oxford, Massachusetts.

•**SOUTH PORTLAND,** City; Cumberland County; Pop. 22,712; Zip Code 04106; SE suburb of Portland in SW Maine. The city is named for Portland in Dorsethire, England.

•**SOUTH THOMASTON,** Town; Knox County; Pop. 1,064; Zip Code 04858; Lat. 43-59-45 N long. 069-07-07 W; S; coastal Maine. The town's name honors Major General John Thomas, who fought in the Revolutionary War.

•**SOUTHEAST PISCATAQUIS,** Unorganized; Piscataquis County; Pop. 183; N central Maine. An Abnaki Indian word meaning "at the river branch."

•**SOUTHWEST HARBOR,** Town; Hancock County; Pop. 1,855; Zip Code 04679; Elev. 468; Lat. 44-16-00 N long. 068-18-44 W; SE; coastal Maine. A descriptive name.

•**SQUARE LAKE,** Unorganized; Aroostook County; Pop. 604; N Maine. Ironically a mistranslation of an Indian word meaning "round."

•**STANDISH,** Town; Cumberland County; Pop. 5,946; Zip Code 04084; Elev. 433; Lat. 43-44-10 N long. 070-33-08 W: 15 mi. NW of Portland in SW Maine. Named in honor of Migs Standish, Militant leader of the Patriots colony.

•**STARKS,** Town; Somerset County; Pop. 440; W Maine. The town's name honors General John Stark, hero of the Revolutionary War.

•**STEUBEN,** Town; Washington County; Pop. 970; Zip Code 04680; Lat. 44-30-35 N long. 067-58-02 W; SE corner; coastal Maine. For Barow Steuben, the German officer who helped the cause during the Revolutionary War.

•**STOCKHOLM,** Town; Aroostook County; Pop. 319; Zip Code 04783; Elev. 554; Lat. 47-02-32 N long. 068-08-26 W; N Maine. Swedish immigrants named their new town for the Great City in Sweden.

•**STOCKTON SPRINGS,** Town; Waldo County; Pop. 1,230; Zip Code 04981; Lat. 44-29-21 N long. 068-51-33 W; S; coastal Maine. Named by N. G. Hichborn for Stockton, a seaport town in England. The "springs" were a local descriptive addition.

•**STONINGTON,** Town; Hancock County; Pop. 1,273; Zip Code 04681; Lat. 44-09-21 N long. 068-40-16 W; SE; coastal Maine. A descriptive name for the area's good granite quarries.

•**STOW,** Town; Oxford County; Pop. 186; W Maine. The town is named after Stow, Massachusetts.

•**STRONG,** Town; Franklin County; Pop. 1,506; Zip Code 04983; Elev. 501; Lat. 44-48-28 N long. 070-13-13 W; W Maine. In honor of Caleb Strong, the governor of Massachusetts who signed the incorporation papers.

•**SULLIVAN,** Town; Hancock County; Pop. 967; SE; coastal Maine. Named for Daniel Sullivan, an early settler.

•**SUMNER,** Town; Oxford County; Pop. 613; W Maine. In honor of Increase Sumner, an early governor of Massachusetts.

•**SURRY,** Town; Hancock County; Pop. 894; Zip Code 04684; Lat. 44-29-47 N long. 068-30-34 W; SE; coastal Maine. The town is named for Surry, England.

•**SWANS ISLAND,** Town; Hancock County; Pop. 337; Zip Code 04685; Lat. 44-08-42 N long. 068-27-13 W; SE; coastal Maine. Named for Englishman James Swan, an 18th century land speculator in Maine.

•**SWANVILLE,** Town; Waldo County; Pop. 873; S; coastal Maine. the town's name reflects a number of "Swan" families in the vicinity.

•**SWEDEN,** Town; Oxford County; Pop. 163; W Maine. The first settlers named the town after the country in Europe.

•**TALMADGE,** Town; Washington County; Pop. 40; SE corner; coastal Maine. For Benjamin Talmadge, who purchased the town's land in 1804.

•**TEMPLE,** Town; Franklin County; Pop. 518; Zip Code 04984; Lat. 44-41-00 N long. 070-13-44 W; W Maine. Named by the first settlers for their former home in Temple, New Hampshire.

•**THE FORKS,** Plantation; Somerset County; Pop. 72; W Maine. A descriptive name for where the dead river empties into the Kennebec River.

•**THOMASTON,** Town; Knox County; Pop. 2,900; Zip Code 04861; Lat. 44-04-45 N long. 069-10-23 W; S; coastal Maine. In honor of Major General Jon Thomas, a general in the revolution.

•**THORNDIKE,** Town; Waldo County; Pop. 603; Zip Code 04986; Elev. 275; Lat. 44-34-41 N long. 069-16-47 W; S; coastal Maine. Named for Israel Thorndike, one of the early landowners.

•**TOPSFIELD,** Town; Washington County; Pop. 240; Zip Code 04490; Lat. 45-25-07 N long. 067-44-10 W; SE corner; coastal Maine. The first settler, Nehsmiah Kindsland, named the town for his former home in Topsfield, Massachusetts.

•**TOPSHAM,** Town; Sagadahoc County; Pop. 6,431; Zip Code 04086; Lat. 43-55-37 N long. 069-57-56 W; on the mouth of the Androscoggin R. in S Maine. Settlers from Topsham, England gave their former home's name to the now town.

•**TREMONT,** Town; Hancock County; Pop. 1,222; SE; coastal Maine. A descriptive name for the tree-covered mountains.

•**TRENTON,** Town; Hancock County; Pop. 718; SE; coastal Maine. In honor of the Battle of Trenton during the Revolutionary War.

•**TROY,** Town; Waldo County; Pop. 701; Zip Code 04987; Elev. 472; Lat. 44-39-49 N long. 069-14-27 W; S; coastal Maine. The first citizens named their town for the classical city of Homer.

•**TURNER,** Town; Androscoggin County; Pop. 3,539; Zip Code 04282; Elev. 303; Lat. 44-15-09 N long. 070-22-04 W; SW Maine. In honor of Reverend Charles Turne,r resident in the area before 1786 and a state senator to Massachusetts.

•**UNION,** Town; Knox County; Pop. 1,569; Zip Code 04862; Elev. 97; Lat. 44-12-45 N long. 069-16-40 W; S; coastal Maine. Referring to the political union formed to incorporate the town.

•**UNITY,** Town; Waldo County; Pop. 495; Zip Code 04988; Lat. 44-39-49 N long. 069-14-27 W; S; coastal Maine. A descriptive name for the democratic political unity at the townships founding.

•**UNITY,** Unorganized; Kennebec County; Pop. 37; SW Maine. Named after Unity township in Waldo County.

•**UPTON,** Town; Oxford County; Pop. 65; W Maine. Named for Upton, Massachusetts.

•**VAN BUREN,** Town; Aroostook County; Pop. 3,557; Zip Code 04785; Lat. 47-09-21 N long. 067-56-17 W; N Maine. In honor of Martin Van Buren, the President of the United States during the Aroostock War.

•**VANCEBORO,** Town; Washington County; Pop. 256; Zip Code 04491; Elev. 392; Lat. 45-33-31 N long. 067-25-45 W; SE corner; coastal Maine. The town is named for William Vance, a prominent landowner in Baring Township.

•**VASSALBOROUGH,** Town; Kennebec County; Pop. 3,410; Zip Code 04989; Lat. 44-27-37 N long. 069-40-44 W; SW Maine. Named either for Florentine Vassal of London, an original proprietor of the Plymouth colony, or William Vassal, a prominent Massachusetts citizen.

•**VERONA,** Town; Hancock County; Pop. 559; SE; coastal Maine. The town is named for Verona, Italy.

•**VIENNA,** Town; Kennebec County; Pop. 454; Zip Code 04360; Elev. 396; Lat. 44-31-55 N long. 069-58-59 W; SW Maine. The town is named for Vienna, Austria.

•**VINALHAVEN,** Town; Knox County; Pop. 1,211; Zip Code 04863; Lat. 44-02-53 N long. 068-50-16 W; S; coastal Maine. The town's name honors John Vinal, a Boston merchant who assisted the first settlers in getting clear title to the land.

•**WAITE,** Town; Washington County; Pop. 130; Zip Code 04492; SE corner; coastal Maine. Named in honor of Benjamin Waite, Calais Lumberman.

•**WALDO,** Town; Waldo County; Pop. 495; S; coastal Maine. The town is named for Englishman Samuel Waldo who held the vast Waldo land potent from English crown.

•**WALDOBORO,** Town; Lincoln County; Pop. 3,985; Zip Code 04572; Lat. 44-05-43 N long. 069-22-38 W; S; coastal Maine. Named for General Waldo who fought the French in 1754 and later helped the early settlers of Maine.

•**WALLAGRASS,** Town; Aroostook County; Pop. 653; N Maine. Either an Abnaki Indian word meaning "shallow, full of weeds," or a Micmac word meaning "good river."

•**WALTHAM,** Town; Hancock County; Pop. 186; SE; coastal Maine. Named for Waltham, Massachusetts.

•**WARREN,** Town; Knox County; Pop. 2,566; Zip Code 04864; Lat. 44-07-18 N long. 069-14-33 W; S; coastal Maine. The town's name honors General Joseph Warren, who fell in the Battle of Bunker Hill.

•**WASHBURN,** Town; Aroostook County; Pop. 2,028; Zip Code 04786; Elev. 483; Lat. 46-46-57 N long. 068-09-00 W; N Maine. In honor of Israel Washburn, one time governor of Maine.

•**WASHINGTON,** Town; Knox County; Pop. 954; Zip Code 04574; Lat. 44-16-21 N long. 069-22-20 W; S; coastal Maine. Named in honor og General George Washington.

•**WATERFORD,** Town; Oxford County; Pop. 951; Zip Code 04088; Lat. 44-10-52 N long. 070-42-55 W; W Maine. A descriptive name for the area's many ponds and brooks.

•**WATERVILLE,** City; Kennebec County; Pop. 17,779; Zip Code 04901; Lat. 44-33-06 N long. 069-38-33 W; 18 mi. N of Augusta in SW Maine. A descriptive name referring to the city's location on the Kennebec River.

•**WAYNE,** Town; Kennebec County; Pop. 680; Zip Code 04284; Lat. 44-20-57 N long. 070-04-04 W; SW Maine. Named in honor of General "Mad" Anthony Wayne, Revolutionary War soldier and hero.

•**WELD,** Toen; Franklin County; Pop. 435; Zip Code 04285; Elev. 767; Lat. 44-41-54 N long. 070-25-12 W; W Maine. Named for Benjamin Weld, an early settler and landowner.

•**WELLINGTON,** Town; Piscataquis County; Pop. 287; Zip Code 04990; Elev. 571; Lat. 45-02-16 N long. 069-35-48 W; N central Maine. The town's name honors the famous Duke of Wellington.

•**WEST BATH,** Town; Sagadahoc County; Pop. 1,309; S; coastal Maine. The origin of the name is unknown.

•**WEST CENTRAL FRANKLIN,** Unorganized; Franklin County; Elev. 207; W Maine. In honor of Benjamin Franklin.

•**WEST FORKS,** Plantation; Somerset County; Pop. 72; Zip Code 04985; Lat. 45-20-09 N long. 069-58-07 W; W Maine. A descriptive name for the areas locatoinbetween the Kennebec And the Dead Rivers.

•**WEST GARDINER,** Town; Kennebec County; Pop. 2,113; SW Maine. the town takes its name from Dr. Sylvester Gardiner, an early landowner.

•**WEST PARIS,** Town; Oxford County; Pop. 1,390; Zip Code 04289; Elev. 486; Lat. 44-19-35 N long. 070-34-40 W; W Maine. Named for the capital of France.

•**WESTBROOK,** City; Cumberland County; Pop. 14,976; Zip Code 04092; Lat. 43-41-13 N long. 070-21-17 W; 7 mi. W of Portland in SW Maine. The city is named after Colonel Thomas Westbrook.

•**WESTFIELD,** Town; Aroostook County; Pop. 647; Zip Code 04787; Lat. 46-34-11 N long. 067-55-25 W; N Maine. The first settlers named the town after Westfield, Massachusetts.

•**WESTMANLAND,** Plantation; Aroostook County; Pop. 53; N Maine. Swedish settlers name the area after the Westmanland district in Sweden.

•**WESTON,** Town; Aroostook County; Pop. 155; Zip Code 04494; N Maine. The town is named for the surveyor who laid it out in 1835, a Mr. Weston.

•**WHITEFIELD,** Town; Lincoln County; Pop. 1,606; Zip Code 04362; Lat. 44-10-14 N long. 069-37-50 W; S; coastal Maine. The town takes it name from George Whitefield, Minister from England.

•**WHITING,** Town; Washington County; Pop. 335; Zip Code 04691; Elev. 37; Lat. 44-47-27 N long. 067-10-38 W; SE corner; coastal Maine. the town is named for Timothy Whiting, an early settler.

MAINE

•**WHITNEY,** Unorganized; Penobscot County; E central Maine. Named for the Whitney family who were early settlers.

•**WHITNEYVILLE,** Town; Washington County; Pop. 264; Zip Code 04692; Lat. 44-43-12 N long. 067-31-26 W; SE corner; coastal ME ; The area is named for colonel Joseph Whitney, who built a dam on the river and established a mill.

•**WILLIMANTIC,** Town; Piscataquis County; Pop. 164; N central Maine. The town takes its name from the Willimantic Thread Company, which had a factory in the town inthe 1880's.

•**WILTON,** Town; Franklin County;; Pop. 4,382; Zip Code 04294; Elev. 642; Lat. 44-35-29 N long. 070-13-33 W; W Maine. Abraham Butterfield of Wilton, New Hampshire, offered to pay for the town's incorporation if the citizens would name it for him. They did.

•**WINDHAM,** Town; Cumberland County; Pop. 11,282; 15 mi. NW of Portland in SW Maine. Named for Windham, England.

•**WINDSOR,** Town; Kennebec County; Pop. 1,702; Zip Code 04363; Elev. 297; Lat. 44-18-41 N long. 069-34-54 W; SW Maine. The town is named for the English royal house.

•**WINN,** Town; Penobscot County; Pop. 503; Zip Code 04495; Lat. 45-29-12 N long. 068-22-23 W; E central Maine. the town takes it name from John M. Winn, who owned much of the land.

•**WINSLOW,** Town; Kennebec County; Pop. 8,057; Zip Code 04901; SE suburb of Waterville in SW Maine. the town's name hoors General John Winslow, who helped construct Fort Holifax.

•**WINTER HARBOR,** Town; Hancock County; Pop. 1,120; Zip Code 04693; Elev. 11; Lat. 44-23-44 N long. 068-05-05 W; SE; coastal Maine. A descriptive name for the harbor which does not freeze in the winter.

•**WINTERPORT,** Town; Waldo County; Pop. 2,675; Zip Code 04496; Lat. 44-38-00 N long. 068-50-55 W; S; coastal Maine. A descriptive name for the town's fine harbor on the Penabscot River.

•**WINTERVILLE,** Plantation; Aroostook County; Pop. 235; Zip Code 04788; Elev. 1012; Lat. 46-58-12 N long. 068-34-12 W; N Maine. PPossibly name for the severe winters.

•**WINTHROP,** Town; Kennebec County; Pop. 5,889; Zip Code 04364; Elev. 225; Lat. 44-18-25 N long. 069-58-31 W; 10 mi. W of Augusta in SW Maine. The town is named for Governor John Winthrop, first colonial governor of Massachusetts.

•**WISCASSET,** Town; Lincoln County; Pop. 2,832; Zip Code 04578; Lat. 44-00-20 N long. 069-40-02 W; S; coastal Maine. An Abnaki Indian term meaning "at the hidden outlet."

•**WOODLAND,** Town; Aroostook County; Pop. 1,369; Zip Code 04694; Lat. 45-09-14 N long. 067-24-33 W; N Maine. A descriptive name for the nearby woods.

•**WOODSTOCK,** Town; Oxford County; Pop. 1,087; W Maine. A descriptive name for the areas woods.

•**WOODVILLE,** Town; Penobscot County; Pop. 226; E central Maine. The Benjamin Stanwood family named the town for the local woods.

•**WOOLWICH,** Town; Sagadahoc County; Pop. 2,156; Zip Code 04579; Lat. 43-55-00 N long. 069-48-17 W; S; coastal Maine. The town is named for Woollllwich, England.

•**WYMAN,** Unorganized; Franklin County; Pop. 7; W Maine. Named for Miles Wyman, an early Maine guide.

•**YARMOUTH,** Town; Cumberland County; Pop. 6,585; Zip Code 04096; Lat. 43-48-03 N long. 070-11-35 W; 10 mi. N of Portland in SW Maine. The town is named for Yarmouth, England.

MARYLAND

•**ABERDEEN,** Town; Harford County; Pop. 11,533; Zip Code 21001; Elev. 16; Lat. 38-15-15 N long. 076-44-38 W; Incorporated in 1892 and named Aberdeen by the first postmaster, a Mr. Winston of Aberdeen, Scotland.

•**ACCIDENT,** Town; Garrett County; Pop. 246; Zip Code 21520; Lat. 39-27-44 N long. 076-16-46 W; So named because the first two surveyors in the 1770's surveyed and claimed the same piece of land.

•**ANNAPOLIS,** City; Anne Arundel County Seat; Pop. 31,740; Zip Code 214+; Elev. 270; Lat. 38-48-50 N long. 076-53-54 W; Annapolis, or city of Anna, comes from Queen Anne of England.

•**BALTIMORE,** City; Pop. 786,775; Zip Code 212+; Lat. 39-17-25 N long. 076-36-45 W; The city is named in honor of George Calvert, Lord Baltimore of the Barony of Baltimore in Ireland.

•**BARCLAY,** Town; Queen Anne's County; Pop. 132; Zip Code 21607; Elev. 69; Lat. 39-08-39 N long. 075-51-52 W; Barclay is named for an early settler.

•**BARNESVILLE,** Town; Montgomery County; Pop. 141; Zip Code 20838; Lat. 39-13-14 N long. 077-22-40 W; Named after an early early settler family, the Barnes, who came to Maryland in 1678.

•**BARTON,** Town; Allegany County; Pop. 617; Zip Code 21521; Elev. 1251; Lat. 39-31-50 N long. 079-01-04 W; Coal developer Andrew Shaw founded the town and named it in honor of his father's birthplace in Barton, England.

•**BEL AIR,** Town; Harford County Seat; Pop. 7,814; Zip Code 21014; Lat. 39-32-09 N long. 076-20-55 W; A French word meaning "fine air."

•**BERLIN,** Town; Worcester County; Pop. 2,162; Zip Code 21811; Elev. 45; Lat. 38-19-21 N long. 075-13-05 W; The town's name is a combination of the English name Burleigh and Inn.

•**BERWYN HEIGHTS,** Town; Prince George's County; Pop. 3,135; Lat. 38-59-38 N long. 076-54-39 W; Founded in 1883 and named after the Berwyn Mountains in Wales.

•**BETTERTON,** Town; Kent County; Pop. 356; Zip Code 21610; Lat. 39-21-57 N long. 076-03-45 W; Descriptive name by its first settlers.

•**BLADENSBURG,** Town; Prince George's County; Pop. 7,691; Zip Code 20710; Elev. 45; Lat. 38-56-21 N long. 076-56-03 W; Founded in 1742 and named for Thomas Bladen, the governor of Maryland in 1742.

•**BOONSBORO,** Town; Washington County; Pop. 1,908; Zip Code 21713; Lat. 38-57-00 N long. 075-51-37 W; Pioneers George and William Boone settled here in 1774. The town is named in their honor.

•**BOWIE,** City; Prince George's County; Pop. 33,695; Zip Code 207+; Lat. 39-00-24 N long. 076-46-46 W; The name honors Oden Bowie, the thirty-seventh governor of Maryland.

•**BRENTWOOD,** Town; Prince George's County; Pop. 2,988; Zip Code 20722; Lat. 38-56-35 N long. 076-57-25 W; A post World War I development, the town is named for the old pineer family, the Brents.

•**BROOKEVILLE,** Town; Montgomery County; Pop. 120; Zip Code 20833; Named after early surveyor James Brooke.

•**BROOKVIEW,** Town; Dorchester County; Pop. 78; Lat. 38-34-31 N long. 075-47-47 W; Descriptively named for the view by its settlers.

•**BRUNSWICK,** Town; Frederick County; Pop. 202; Zip Code 21716; Elev. 247; Lat. 39-18-51 N long. 077-37-41 W; Early Germans settlers named the town after the area in Germany.

•**BURKITTSVILLE,** Town; Frederick County; Pop. 202; Zip Code 21718; Lat. 39-23-37 N long. 077-37-45 W; Founded in 1829 and named for settler Henry Burkitt.

•**CAMBRIDGE,** City; Dorchester County Seat; Pop. 11,703; Zip Code 21613; Lat. 38-33-47 N long. 076-04-45 W; Established in 1684 and named for England's famous university town.

•**CAPITOL HEIGHTS,** Town; Prince George's County; Pop. 3,271; Zip Code 20743; Elev. 109; Lat. 38-53-06 N long. 076-54-58 W; A descriptive name as the town is slightly elevated and near Washington, D. C.

•**CECILTON,** Town; Cecil County; Pop. 508; Zip Code 21913; Elev. 79; Lat. 39-24-14 N long. 075-52-04 W; The town is named in honor of Cecil Calvert, second Lord Baltimore.

•**CENTREVILLE,** Town; Queen Anne's County Seat; Pop. 2,018; Zip Code 21617; Lat. 39-20-11 N long. 077-19-48 W; Founded in 1792 and named for its location in the county.

•**CHARLESTOWN,** Town; Cecil County; Pop. 720; Zip Code 21914; Lat. 39-33-22 N long. 078-58-30 W; Incorporated in 1742 and named in honor of the fifth Lord Baltimore.

•**CHESAPEAKE BEACH,** Town; Calvert County; Pop. 1,408; Zip Code 20732; Lat. 38-41-10 N long. 076-32-06 W; Incorporated in 1894 and descriptively named for its location on Chesapeake Bay.

•**CHESAPEAKE CITY,** Town; Cecil County; Pop. 899; Zip Code 21915; Lat. 39-31-51 N long. 075-48-28 W; Founded in 1804 and named after the Chesapeake Bay.

•**CHESTERTOWN,** Town; Kent County Seat; Pop. 3,300; Zip Code 21620; Lat. 39-12-32 N long. 076-04-01 W; Established in 1708 and named for its location on the Chester River.

•**CHEVERLY,** Town; Prince George's County; Pop. 5,751; Lat. 38-55-41 N long. 076-54-58 W; The town is named for the village of Cheverly in Warwickshire, England.

•**CHEVY CHASE SECTION FOUR,** Town; Montgomery County; Pop. 2,903; Lat. 38-58-49 N long. 077-04-55 W; The town is named after the Chevy Chase Land Company who developed the area in the 1890's.

•**CHEVY CHASE VILLAGE,** Town; Montgomery County; Pop. 2,118; Named for the Chevy Chase Land Development Company.

•**CHURCH CREEK,** Town; Dorchester County; Pop. 124; Zip Code 21622; Lat. 38-30-07 N long. 076-09-09 W; Descriptively named for a small creek, once the site of a Catholic Church.

•**CHURCH HILL,** Town; Queen Anne's County; Pop. 319; Zip Code 216+; Lat. 39-20-38 N long. 077-28-31 W; Founded in 1802 and descriptively named as the site of several churches.

•**CLEAR SPRING,** Town; Washington County; Pop. 477; Zip Code 21722; Lat. 39-39-22 N long. 077-55-55 W; Established in 1821 and named for an adjacent spring.

•**COLLEGE PARK,** City; Prince George's County; Pop. 23,614; Zip Code 207+; Lat. 38-58-50 N long. 076-56-14 W; Founded at the turn of the century and named after the nearby Maryland Agricultural College.

•COTTAGE CITY, Town; Prince George's County; Pop. 1,122; Lat. 38-56-17 N long. 076-56-55 W; Established in the 1920's and named descriptively when a builder constructed a group of cottages.

•CRISFIELD, City; Somerset County; Pop. 2,924; Zip Code 21817; Elev. 4; Lat. 37-59-00 N long. 075-51-15 W; The town is named for nineteenth century railroad developer, John Crisfield.

•CUMBERLAND, City; Allegany County Seat; Pop. 25,933; Zip Code 215+; Lat. 39-39-10 N long. 078-45-46 W; Founded in 1754 as a military fort and named for Georoge II's son, William Augustus, Duke of Cumberland.

•DEER PARK, Town; Garrett County; Pop. 486; Lat. 39-23-56 N long. 076-49-49 W; Descriptively named for the great abundance of deer during colonial days.

•DELMAR, Town; Wicomico County; Pop. 1,232; Elev. 55; Lat. 38-27-21 N long. 075-34-40 W; Established in 1859 and coined by adding the opening syllables of Delaware and Maryland.

•DENTON, Town; Caroline County Seat; Pop. 1,927; Zip Code 21629; Lat. 38-53-04 N long. 075-49-39 W; Originally called Edenton in honor of Sir Robert Eden, the last royal governor of Maryland, the letter "E" was dropped during the Revolutionary War.

•DISTRICT HEIGHTS, City; Prince George's County; Pop. 6,799; Lat. 38-51-27 N long. 076-53-23 W; A District of Columbia suburb descriptively named for its 280 feet height.

•EAGLE HARBOR, Town; Prince George's County; Pop. 45; Lat. 38-34-04 N long. 076-41-11 W; Incorporated in 1929 and named from pioneer days for the eagles in the vicinity.

•EAST NEW MARKET, Town; Dorchester County; Pop. 230; Zip Code 21631; Lat. 38-35-56 N long. 075-55-35 W; Founded in 1803 and given this descriptive name.

•EASTON, Town; Talbot County Seat; Pop. 7,536; Zip Code 21601; Elev. 38; Lat. 38-46-27 N long. 076-04-36 W; Established in the eighteenth century and named for Easton, Somersetshire, England.

•EDMONSTON, Town; Prince George's County; Pop. 1,109; Lat. 38-56-48 N long. 076-55-53 W; The town is named for a prominent early settler family named Edmonston.

•ELDORADO, Town; Dorchester County; Pop. 93; Elev. 9; Lat. 38-35-03 N long. 075-47-22 W; The town takes its name from the nearby Becky Taylor farm.

•ELKTON, Town; Cecil County Seat; Pop. 6,468; Zip Code 21921; Lat. 36-36-2 N long. 075-50-01 W; 4At the head of the Elk River, both the town and river takes their name from the abundant colonial elk herds.

•EMMITSBURG, Town; Frederick County; Pop. 1,552; Zip Code 21727; Elev. 449; Lat. 39-42-16 N long. 077-19-38 W; Laid out in 1785 by Irish emigrant Samuel Emmit.

•FAIRMOUNT HEIGHTS, Town; Prince George's County; Pop. 1,616; Lat. 38-54-03 N long. 076-54-57 W; An ironical name given by early settlers as the elevation isn't large.

•FEDERALSBURG, Town; Caroline County; Pop. 1,952; Zip Code 21632; Lat. 38-41-39 N long. 075-46-26 W; Established in 1789 and named after a federalist party convention held here in 1812.

•FOREST HEIGHTS, Town; Prince George's County; Pop. 2,999; Lat. 38-48-34 N long. 076-59-54 W; Descriptively named by a real estate company in 1941 for its location on a hill side above the Potomac River.

•FREDERICK, City; Frederick County Seat; Pop. 27,557; Zip Code 217+; Elev. 290; Lat. 39-24-51 N long. 077-24-39 W; Laid out in 1745 and named for the sixth Lord Baltimore, Frederick Calvert.

•FRIENDSVILLE, Town; Garrett County; Pop. 511; Zip Code 21531; Elev. 1497; Lat. 39-39-49 N long. 079-24-20 W; The town is named in honor of the area's first settler, John Friend.

•FROSTBURG, City; Allegany County; Pop. 7,715; Zip Code 21532; Elev. 2075; Lat. 39-39-29 N long. 078-55-43 W; The city is named after the Frosts, who ran a tavern in the area in 1812.

•FRUITLAND, City; Wicomico County; Pop. 2,694; Zip Code 21826; Elev. 39; Lat. 38-19-19 N long. 075-37-14 W; The railroad reached the area in 1867. The production of strawberries gave the town its descriptive name.

•FUNKSTOWN, Town; Washington County; Pop. 1,103; Zip Code 21734; Lat. 39-36-32 N long. 077-42-17 W; Named after Henry Funk, who was granted land in the area in 1754.

•GAITHERSBURG, City; Montgomery County; Pop. 26,424; Zip Code 208+; Elev. 508; Lat. 39-08-36 N long. 077-12-06 W; The town's name honors the Gaither family, who were among the earliest colonial settlers in the area.

•GALENA, Town; Kent County; Pop. 374; Zip Code 21635; Lat. 39-20-26 N long. 075-52-45 W; Galena takes its name from a small deposit of galena, or lead, mined in the area in the early 1800's.

•GALESTOWN, Town; Dorchester County; Pop. 142; Lat. 38-33-58 N long. 075-42-55 W; Named for 18th century pioneer George Gale.

•GARRETT PARK, Town; Montgomery County; Pop. 1,178; Zip Code 20896; Elev. 314; Lat. 39-02-17 N long. 077-05-36 W; Incorporated in 1891 and named after John Garrett, then president of the Baltimore and Ohio Railroads.

•GLEN ECHO, Town; Montgomery County; Pop. 229; Zip Code 20812; Lat. 38-58-08 N long. 077-08-340 W; A scenic, hilly area given this euphonious name by nineteenth century settlers.

•GLENARDEN, Town; Prince George's County; Pop. 4,993; Elev. 110; Lat. 38-55-45 N long. 076-51-43 W; A euphonious name meaning "forest glen."

•GOLDSBORO, Town; Caroline County; Pop. 188; Zip Code 21636; Lat. 39-02-02 N long. 075-47-13 W; Originally called Oldtown, the name was later changed in honor of 1870's landowner, Dr. G. W. Goldsborough.

•GRANTSVILLE, Town; Garrett County; Pop. 498; Zip Code 21536; Elev. 2300; Lat. 39-41-42 N long. 079-09-05 W; The town's name remembers settler Daniel Grant, who came to the area in 1785.

•GREENBELT, City; Prince George's County; Pop. 16,000; Zip Code 207+; Lat. 39-00-16 N long. 076-52-33 W; A New Deal model community built in 1935 and descriptively named for its surrounding ring of parkland.

•GREENSBORO, Town; Caroline County; Pop. 1,253; Zip Code 21639; Lat. 38-58-25 N long. 075-48-19 W; Founded in 1732 as Choptank Bridge and later changed to Greensboro after a local farmer.

•HAGERSTOWN, City; Washington County Seat; Pop. 34,132; Zip Code 217+; Lat. 39-38-30 N long. 077-43-13 W; Settled by Captain Johnathan Hager and named Hagerstown in his honor.

•HAMPSTEAD, Town; Carroll County; Pop. 1,293; Zip Code 21074; Lat. 39-36-17 N long. 076-51-01 W; Established in 1786 and named for Hampstead, England.

•HANCOCK, Town; Washington County; Pop. 1,887; Zip Code 21750; Elev. 448; Lat. 39-41-56 N long. 078-10-48 W; Pioneer Joseph Hancock settled in the area in 1749, the town is named after him.

•HAVRE DE GRACE, City; Harford County; Pop. 8,763; Zip Code 21078; Lat. 39-32-57 N long. 076-05-31 W; The town was settled in 1659 as Lower Ferry. Lafayette remarked on the area's resemblance to Le Havre, France during a visit in 1782. The town's name was changed in his honor in 1795.

•HEBRON, Town; Wicomico County; Pop. 714; Zip Code 21830; Elev. 43; Lat. 38-25-12 N long. 075-41-17 W; Pioneer settlers named the town for the Biblical city of Herbon in Israel.

•HENDERSON, Town; Caroline County; Pop. 156; Zip Code 21640; Lat. 39-04-27 N long. 075-45-59 W; Settled in the 1850's as Mellville's Crossroads, but later changed to Henderson for a local family.

•HIGHLAND BEACH, Town; Anne Arundel County; Pop. 8; Lat. 38-55-49 N long. 076-27-58 W; A summer resort on Chesapeake Bay, the town is descriptively named for land overlooking the shore.

•HILLSBORO, Town; Caroline County; Pop. 180; Zip Code 21641; Elev. 47; Lat. 38-55-00 N long. 075-56-21 W; Descriptively named by early settlers.

•HURLOCK, Town; Dorchester County; Pop. 1,690; Zip Code 21643; Lat. 38-37-27 N long. 075-51-17 W; The town is named for early merchant John M. Hurlock, who built the first store in the area in 1869.

•HYATTSVILLE, City; Prince George's County; Pop. 12,709; Zip Code 207+; Lat. 38-57-21 N long. 076-56-45 W; The city is named for pioneer Christopher Hyatt who settled in the area in 1845.

•INDIAN HEAD, Town; Charles County; Pop. 1,381; Zip Code 20640; Lat. 38-36-00 N long. 077-09-45 W; Named by early pioneers for a high wooded point on the Potomac River.

•KEEDYSVILLE, Town; Washington County; Pop. 476; Zip Code 21756; Elev. 404; Lat. 39-29-10 N long. 077-42-00 W; Originally called Centerville, the name was changed in the 1860's to Keedysville for the many Keedy family members in the area.

•KENSINGTON, Town; Montgomery County; Pop. 1,822; Zip Code 20895; Lat. 39-01-32 N long. 077-04-36 W; Named after the district in London by its settlers.

•KITZMILLERVILLE, Town; Garrett County; Pop. 387; Settled in the early 1800's and named for Ebenezer Kitzmiller who ran a saw mill nearby.

•LA PLATA, Town; Charles County Seat; Pop. 2,484; Zip Code 20646; Elev. 193; Lat. 38-31-45 N long. 076-58-32 W; The railroad and the first post office arrived in 1873 and took the name of the Chapman farm, "Le Plateau." This name was later shortened to La Plata.

•LANDOVER HILLS, Town; Prince George's County; Pop. 1,428; Lat. 38-56-35 N long. 076-53-33 W; Named after the Welch city of Landovery.

•LAUREL, City; Prince George's County; Pop. 12,103; Zip Code 207+; Lat. 39-05-57 N long. 076-50-55 W; The city is named for the abundant laurel trees of the colonial era.

•LAYTONSVILLE, Town; Montgomery County; Pop. 195; Elev. 609; Lat. 39-12-43 N long. 077-08-35 W; Originally called Goshen Mills, the name was later changed to Laytonsville, after early settler John Layton.

•LEONARDTOWN, Town; St. Mary's County Seat; Pop. 1,448; Zip Code 20650; Elev. 87; Lat. 38-17-28 N long. 076-38-10 W; Established in the 1690's and named in 1733 for the fourth Lord Baltimore, Benedict Leonard Calvert.

•LOCH LYNN HEIGHTS, Town; Garrett County; Pop. 503; Elev. 2438; Lat. 39-23-35 N long. 079-22-24 W; Named in 1894 after settler David Lynn and given the additional Scottish name for lake.

•LONACONING, Town; Allegany County; Pop. 1,420; Zip Code 21539; Lat. 39-33-57 N long. 078-58-50 W; An Algonquian Indian name meaning "where there is a beautiful summit."

•LUKE, Town; Allegany County; Pop. 329; Lat. 39-28-30 N long. 079-03-26 W; The town is named for the Luke family who emigrated to the area from Scotland in the 1850's.

•MANCHESTER, Town; Carroll County; Pop. 1,830; Zip Code 21088; Lat. 39-39-40 N long. 076-53-07 W; Founded in the 1790's by Captain Richard Richards who named it after Manchester, England.

•MIDLAND, Town; Allegany County; Pop. 601; Zip Code 21542; Elev. 1694; Lat. 39-35-24 N long. 078-57-00 W; Established in 1902 and named for the Midlands area of England.

•MILLINGTON, Town; Kent & Queen Anne's Counties; Pop. 546; Zip Code 216+; Elev. 27; Lat. 39-15-29 N long. 075-50-15 W; Named in 1827 after early settler Richard Millington.

•MORNINGSIDE, Town; Prince George's County; Pop. 1,395; Lat. 38-49-48 N long. 076-53-30 W; Developed in the 1940's and given a romantic name by the developers.

•MOUNT AIRY, Town; Carroll & Frederick Counties; Pop. 2,450; Zip Code 217+; Incorporated in 1854 and descriptively named for its location on an 800 ft. ridge.

•MOUNT RAINIER, City; Prince George's County; Pop. 7,361; Zip Code 20712; Lat. 38-56-29 N long. 076-57-55 W; Named by several army officers from the Seattle area for Mt. Rainier in Washington state.

•MOUNTAIN LAKE PARK, Town; Garrett County; Pop. 1,597; Lat. 39-23-54 N long. 079-22-55 W; Descriptively named by the town's developers.

•MYERSVILLE, Town; Frederick County; Pop. 432; Zip Code 21773; Elev. 669; Lat. 39-30-18 N long. 077-34-00 W; Pioneer James Stottlemyer settled in the area in 1742. The last part of his name later became the town's name.

•NEW CARROLLTON, City; Prince George's County; Pop. 12,632; Lat. 38-58-11 N long. 076-52-49 W; Named for pioneer Charles Carroll who owned large tracts of land in colonial Maryland.

•NEW MARKET, Town; Frederick County; Pop. 306; Zip Code 21774; Elev. 551; Lat. 39-22-57 N long. 077-16-11 W; Named by early settlers after New Market, England.

•NEW WINDSOR, Town; Carroll County; Pop. 799; Zip Code 21776; Lat. 39-32-31 N long. 077-06-30 W; Originally called Sulphur Springs, the name was changed in 1816 after Windsor, England.

•NORTH BEACH, Town; Calvert County; Pop. 1,504; Zip Code 20714; Lat. 38-42-26 N long. 076-31-53 W; Descriptively named by its developers.

•**NORTH BRENTWOOD,** Town; Prince George's County; Pop. 580; Lat. 38-56-43 N long. 076-57-07 W; Settled after World War I by commuters from Washington D. C., and named after the pioneer Brent family.

•**NORTH EAST,** Town; Cecil County; Pop. 1,469; Zip Code 21901; Elev. 10; Lat. 39-36-00 N long. 075-56-30 W; Established as a settlement in 1716 and descriptively named for being at the head of the Northeast River.

•**OAKLAND,** Town; Garrett County Seat; Pop. 1,994; Zip Code 21550; Lat. 39-30-11 N long. 076-06-53 W; Descriptively named in the nineteenth century for the abundance of oak trees.

•**OCEAN CITY,** Town; Worcester County; Pop. 4,946; Zip Code 21842; Elev. 8; Lat. 38-20-11 N long. 075-05-07 W; Founded in 1875 and descriptively named for its location on Sinepuxent Bay.

•**OXFORD,** Town; Talbot County; Pop. 754; Zip Code 21654; Lat. 38-41-11 N long. 076-10-19 W; Settled in 1635 as Thread Haven, but changed in 1702 to honor England's great university town.

•**PERRYVILLE,** Town; Cecil County; Pop. 2,018; Zip Code 219+; Lat. 39-33-36 N long. 076-04-18 W; Purchased by Captain Richard Perry in 1710, it passed into the hands of his descendants and retained his name.

•**PITTSVILLE,** Town; Wicomico County; Pop. 519; Zip Code 21850; Lat. 38-23-43 N long. 075-24-48 W; Named after a Dr. H. R. Pitts, who was president of a small railroad in the area in the 1860's.

•**POCOMOKE CITY,** City; Worcester County; Pop. 3,558; Zip Code 21851; Lat. 38-04-32 N long. 075-34-06 W; The town is named for its location on the Pocomoke River. Pocomoke is an Algonquian Indian word meaning "broken ground."

•**POOLESVILLE,** Town; Montgomery County; Pop. 3,428; Zip Code 20837; Lat. 39-08-45 N long. 077-25-02 W; The town was named in 1793 after Joseph Poole, the son of the original settler.

•**PORT DEPOSIT,** Town; Cecil County; Pop. 664; Zip Code 21904; Lat. 39-36-17 N long. 076-06-56 W; Renamed in 1812 for its function as a port of deposit for the lumber trade.

•**PORT TOBACCO VILLAGE,** Town; Charles County; Pop. 40; Zip Code 20677; Named for its location on Port Tobacco Creek. Port Tobacco is a corruption of the Algonquian Indian word, Potapaco, meaning "a jutting inlet."

•**PRESTON,** Town; Caroline County; Pop. 498; Zip Code 21655; Lat. 38-42-42 N long. 075-54-31 W; The town was named Preston in 1856 in honor of prominent Baltimore lawyer Alexander Preston.

•**PRINCESS ANNE,** Town; Somerset County Seat; Pop. 1,499; Zip Code 21853; Lat. 38-12-10 N long. 075-41-34 W; The town was laid out in 1733 and named foir Princess Anne, the daughter of King George II.

•**QUEEN ANNE,** Town; Queen Anne's & Talbot Counties; Pop. 181; Zip Code 216+; Elev. 39; Lat. 38-55-15 N long. 075-57-20 W; The town is named Anne, Queen of England in the early 18th century.

•**QUEENSTOWN,** Town; Queen Anne's County; Pop. 491; Zip Code 21658; Lat. 38-57-02 N long. 076-57-54 W; Named after the county which was named in 1707 for Queen Anne of England.

•**RIDGELY,** Town; Caroline County; Pop. 933; Zip Code 216+; Elev. 70; Lat. 38-56-52 N long. 075-53-05 W; Named in honor of the Rev. Greenbury W. Ridgely, who was a law partner of Henry Clay.

•**RISING SUN,** Town; Cecil County; Pop. 1,160; Zip Code 21911; Elev. 388; Lat. 39-41-52 N long. 076-03-47 W; Rising Sun is named after an early tavern with a rising sun on its shingle.

•**RIVERDALE,** Town; Prince George's County; Pop. 4,748; Zip Code 20737; Lat. 39-05-57 N long. 076-32-10 W; H=Descriptively named around 1800 for its location on the upper reaches of the Anacostia River.

•**ROCK HALL,** Town; Kent County; Pop. 1,511; Zip Code 21661; Lat. 39-16-07 N long. 077-31-35; The town is named after a colonial mansion made of local white sandstone, built nearby in 1812.

•**ROCKVILLE,** City; Montgomery County Seat; Pop. 43,811; Zip Code 208+; Elev. 451; Lat. 39-05-02 N long. 077-09-11 W; The city's name honors the lovely rock creek nearby.

•**ROSEMONT,** Town; Frederick County; Pop. 305; Lat. 39-14-14 N long. 076-38-06 W; Named descriptively by its developers.

•**ST. MICHAELS,** Town; Talbot County; Pop. 1,301; Zip Code 21663; Lat. 38-47-06 N long. 076-13-29 W; The town was named for St. Michaels Church, which was built here in 1690.

•**SALISBURY,** City; Wicomico County Seat; Pop. 16,429; Zip Code 218+; Lat. 38-21-38 N long. 075-35-59 W; Founded in 1732 and named Salisbury for the city in England.

•**SEAT PLEASANT,** City; Prince George's County; Pop. 5,217; Lat. 38-53-46 N long. 076-54-25 W; Called originally Chesapeake Junction, the name was changed in 1906 to the pleasant sounding current name.

•**SECRETARY,** Town; Dorchester County; Pop. 487; Zip Code 21664; Lat. 38-36-33 N long. 075-56-52 W; Incorporated in 1900 and named for its local stream, Secretary Creek.

•**SHARPSBURG,** Town; Washington County; Pop. 721; Zip Code 21782; Elev. 413; Lat. 39-27-27 N long. 077-44-57 W; Laid out in 1763 and named after Gov. Horatio Sharp.

•**SHARPTOWN,** Town; Wicomico County; Pop. 654; Zip Code 21861; Lat. 39-08-11 N long. 076-13-08 W; The town is named in honor of colonial era governor, Horatio Sharp.

•**SMITHSBURG,** Town; Washington County; Pop. 833; Zip Code 21783; Lat. 39-39-17 N long. 077-34-23 W; The town was founded by Christopher Smith in the early 1800's. It is named in his honor.

•**SNOW HILL,** Town; Worcester County Seat; Pop. 2,192; Zip Code 21863; Elev. 21; Lat. 38-10-37 N long. 075-23-35 W; Snow Hill was founded in 1686 and named for the Snow Hill district of London.

•**SOMERSET,** Town; Montgomery County; Pop. 1,101; Lat. 38-57-57 N long. 077-05-47 W; Founded in colonial days and named for the county in England.

•**SUDLERSVILLE,** Town; Queen Anne's County; Pop. 443; Zip Code 21668; Elev. 67; Lat. 39-11-13 N long. 075-51-33 W; The town is sited on the pioneer Sudler estate. The Sudler's were here as early as 1694.

•**SYKESVILLE,** Town; Carroll County; Pop. 1,712; Zip Code 21784; Lat. 39-22-25 N long. 076-58-05 W; The town is named after English businessman James Sykes who established several mills in the area.

•**TAKOMA PARK,** City; Montgomery & Prince George's Counties; Pop. 16,231; Named after Mt. Takoma in Washington by 1880's real estate developer Benjamin Gilbert.

•**TANEYTOWN,** City; Carroll County; Pop. 2,618; Zip Code 21787; Elev. 524; Lat. 39-39-28 N long. 077-10-29 W; Named for the prominent local Taney family who reached the area in the 1660's.

•**TEMPLEVILLE,** Town; Caroline & Queen Anne's Counties; Pop. 96; Zip Code 216+; Lat. 39-08-10 N long. 075-45-59 W; The town is named for the prominent local Temple family. One of its members was a governor of Delaware.

•**THURMONT,** Town; Frederick County; Pop. 2,934; Zip Code 21788; Elev. 523; Lat. 39-37-25 N long. 077-24-40 W; Founded in 1751 and given the name of a prominent local family.

•**TRAPPE,** Town; Talbot County; Pop. 739; Zip Code 21673; Lat. 38-39-30 N long. 076-03-30 W; The town's name remembers its location in colonial days as a wolf trap.

•**UNION BRIDGE,** Town; Carroll County; Pop. 927; Zip Code 21791; Lat. 39-34-08 N long. 077-10-38 W; Named in 1810 for a bridge uniting two small nearby villages.

•**UNIVERSITY PARK,** Town; Prince George's County; Pop. 2,536; Lat. 38-58-13 N lon. 076-56-32 W; Descriptively named by its developers.

•**UPPER MARLBORO,** Town; Prince George's County Seat; Pop. 828; Zip Code 20772; Lat. 38-48-57 N long. 076-45-00 W; Settled in 1704, the year of John Churchill Marlborough's great victory at Blenheim, and named in his honor.

•**VIENNA,** Town; Dorchester County; Pop. 300; Zip Code 21869; Lat. 38-29-05 N long. 075-49-30 W; A phonetic translation of an Indian name Unnakokossimmon, a chief of the Nanticoke Indians about 1677.

•**WALKERSVILLE,** Town; Frederick County; Pop. 2,212; Zip Code 21793; Elev. 320; Lat. 39-29-10 N long. 077-21-08 W; Named in honor of the Walkers, early Scotch settlers in the area.

•**WASHINGTON GROVE,** Town; Montgomery County; Pop. 527; Zip Code 20880; Lat. 39-08-23 N long. 077-10-32 W; Named by its settlers after the U. S. Capitol.

MASSACHUSETTS

•**ABINGTON**, Town; Plymouth County; Pop. 13,517; Zip Code 02351; Elev. 104; Lat. 42-06.4'N, Long. 70-56.8'W; 5 miles NE of Brockton in SE Massachusetts.

•**ACTON**, Town; Middlesex County; Pop. 17,544; Zip Code 01720; Elev. 150; Lat. 42-29.2'N, Long. 71-26.0'W.

•**ACUSHNET**, Town; Bristol County; Pop. 8,704; Zip Code 02743; Elev. 138; (Indian, "A Bathing Place") was completely devastated during King Philip's War.

•**ADAMS**, Town; Berkshire County; Pop. 10,381; Zip Code 01220; Lat. 42-37.5'N, Long. 73-07.0'W; Settled 1762; in NW Massachusetts; The town of Adams was named in honor of *Samuel Adams*, Revolutionary War propagandist.

•**AGAWAM**, Town; Hampden County; Pop. 26,281; Zip Code 01001; Elev. 85; Settled 1635; Inc. 1855; 5 miles SW of Springfield in SE central Massachusetts; The Agawam (Indian *Agaam*, or "Crooked River") River meanders along the northern boundary of the town.

•**ALFORD**, Town; Berkshire County; Pop. 394; Zip Code 01230; Elev. 960; Settled about 1740; Located SW Massachusetts; Named in honor of *John Alford*, founder of the Alford professorship of Moral Philosophy at Harvard University.

•**AMESBURY**, Town; Essex County; Pop. 13,971; Zip Code 01913; Elev. 90; Lat. 42-51.4'N, Long. 70-55.9'W; Settled 1645; Inc. 1668; Northern most town in Massachusetts; 25 miles NE of Lowell in NE Massachusetts, on the Merrimack River.

•**AMHERST**, Town; Hampshire County; Pop. 33,229; Zip Code 01002; Elev. 30; Lat. 42-22.6'N, Long. 72-31.3'W; 20 miles N of Springfield in W Massachusetts.Named for *Lord Jeffrey Amherst*, a British general in the French and Indian War.

•**ANDOVER**, Town; Essex County; Pop. 26,370; Zip Code 01810; Elev. 92; Lat. 42-39.5'N, Long. 71-08.4'W; Settled 1642; 9 miles E of Lowell in NE Massachusetts; it was named Andover for the English home of early settlers.

•**ASHBURNHAM**, Town; Worcester County; Pop. 4,075; Zip Code 01420; Elev. 1,037; Settled 1736; Located North Central Massachusetts at the junction of State 101 and Hwy. 12.

•**ASHBY**, Town; Middlesex County; Pop. 2,311; Zip Code 01431; Is on elevated land, bordering on Rindge, New Hampshire.

•**ASHFIELD**, Town; Franklin County; Pop. 1,458; Zip Code 01330; Elev. 1,360; Settled 1743; NW Massachusetts.

•**ASHLAND**, Town; Middlesex County; Pop. 9,165; Zip Code 01721; Lat. 42-15.7'N, Long 71-27.8'W; E Massachusetts.

•**ATHOL**, Town; Worcester County; Pop. 10,635; Zip Code 01331; Elev. 550; Lat. 42-35.6'N, Long. 72-13.7'W; Settled 1735; Named by *John Murray*, one of the leading proprietors, who thought that the scenery resembled that about Blair Castle, the home of the Scottish *Duke of Atholl.*

•**ATTELBORO**, City; Bristol County; Pop. 34,196; Zip Code 02701; Lat. 41-56.7"N, Long 71-17.1'W; Located in SE Massachusetts.

•**AUBURN**, Town; Worcester County; Pop. 14,845; Zip Code 01501; Lat. 42-11.7'N, Long. 71-50.1'W;

•**AVON**, Town; Norfolk County; Pop. 5,026; Zip Code 02322; Elev. 180; Lat. 42-07.7'N, Long 71.02.5'W; Settled before 1700; in

E Massachussets.Its present name was suggested by the town schoolmaster to honor the Bard of Avon.

•**AYER**; Town Middlesex County; Pop. 6,993; Zip Code 014+; Lat. 42-33.7'N, Long 71-35.4'W.

•**BARNSTABLE**, Town; Seat of Barnstable County; Pop. 30,898; Zip Code 02630; Lat. 41-42.0'N, 70-18.0'W; Settled 1637; on S shore of Cape Cod, 65m. SE of Boston in SE Mass.

•**BARRE**, Town; Worcester County; Pop. 4,102; Zip Code 01005; Elev. 650; Lat. 42-24.3'N, Long 72-06.4'W; Settled 1720; 60 miles SW of Boston in central Massachusetts.

•**BECKETT**, Town; Berkshire County; Pop. 1,339; Zip Code 01223; Elev. 1,207; W Massachusetts.

•**BEDFORD**, Town; Middlesex County; Pop. 13,067; Zip Code 01730; Elev. 118; Lat. 42-24.4'N, Long 71-17.6'W; Settled 1640; 10 miles S of Lowell in NE Massachusetts.

•**BELCHERTOWN**, Town; Hampshire County; Pop. 8,339; Zip Code 01007; Lat. 42-16.6'N, Long. 72-24.1'W; Settled 1731; 15m. N of Springfield in Mass.; was named for Jonathan Belcher, late Governor of the Province.

•**BELLINGHAM**, Town; Norfolk County; Pop. 14,300; Zip Code 02019; Elev. 240; Settled 1713; 20m. SE of Worcester in E Massachussets.

•**BELMONT**, Middlesex County; Pop. 26,100; Zip Code 02178; Lat. 42-24.9'N, Long 71-10.5'W.

•**BERLIN** Town; Worcester County; Pop. 2,215; Zip Code 01503; Central Massachusetts. Bounded N by Bolton, E by Marlborough and W by Boyleston and Sterling.

•**BERNARDSTON**, Town; Franklin County; Pop. 1,750; Zip Code 01337; Elev. 353; Settled 1738; Located N central Mass.; The name was shortened to Fall Town and later changed to Bernardstown, in honor of Sir Francis Barnard, Provincial Governor of Massachusetts under George III.

•**BEVERLY**, City; Essex County; Pop. 37,655; Zip Code 01915; Elev. 21; Lat. 42-33.0'N, Long. 70-52.9'W; NE Massachusetts.

•**BILLERICA**, Town; Middlesex County; Pop. 36,727; Zip Code 01821; Elev. 126; Lat. 42 -33.6'N, Long. 71 -16.1'W; Settled 1637; NE Mass; home of the Wamesit tribe, and one of the Praying Indian towns, was originally called Shawsheen, the Indian name. It was later named Billericay, for the town in Essex, England.

•**BLACKSTONE**, Town; Worcester County; Pop. 6,570; Zip Code 01504; Elev. 190; Settled 1662; 20m SE of Worcester in S. Mass; was named for the Rev. William Blackstone, an Episcopalian clergyman who was the first white settler on the banks of the local river, also named for him.

•**BLANDFORD** Town; Hampden County; Pop. 1,038; Zip Code 01008; Elev. 1,440; Settled 1735; SW Mass.; Provincial Governor Shirley, who arrived from England on the ship Blandford, denied the petition of the inhabitants for another name and instead named it for his crossing vessel.

•**BOSTON**, City; State Capitol and Seat of Suffolk County; Pop. 562,994; Zip Code 021++; Elev. 8; Lat. 42-21.7'N, Long. 71-03.5'W; Settled in 1625; on Atlantic Coast and Massachusetts Bay in SE Massachusetts. Originally called Shawmet or Trimountain, in 1630 it officially received its present name after the Boston in Lincolnshire from where most of the Puritan leaders had come.

•**BOURNE**, Town; Barnstable County; Pop. 13,874; Zip Code 02532; Elev. 19; Settled about 1640; On Cape Cod Canal, 14m. W of Barnstable in SE Mass.; originally the village of Monument it was renamed for its most prominent citizen, *Jonathan Bourne*.

•**BROCKTON**, City; Plymouth County; Pop. 95,172; Zip Code 024+; Elev. 120. Originally part of Bridgewater, the land was deeded by the Indians in 1649. The name Brockton was adopted in 1874. In 1649 these lands were deeded by the Indians to Miles Standish and John Alden for about thirty dollars.

•**BROOKFIELD**, CDP; Worcester County; Pop. 1,037; Zip Code 01506; Elev. 714; Lat. 42-12-50 N, long. 072-06-10 W. Settled in 1664 and incorporated in 1718, Brookfield was originally known as Quabaug.

•**BROOKLINE**, CDP; Norfolk County; Pop. 55,062; Zip Code 021+; Elev. 120; Lat. 42-19-50 N, long. 071-08-00 W. Named by Judge Sewall for the brook that ran at the back of his property along the border of his estate.

•**BUCKLAND**, Town; Franklin County; Pop.1,864; Zip Code 01338; Elev. 690; Lat. 42-35-32 N, long. 072-47-32 W. Buckland was named in colonial times for buck-shooting incidents.

•**BURLINGTON**, Town; Middlesex County; Pop. 23,486; Zip Code 01803; Elev. 218; Lat. 42-30-17 N, long. 071-11-46. The origin of the name is uncertain, but speculation has it that the first settlers named the town with a corrupted version of an English place name.

•**CAMBRIDGE** City; Seat of Middlesex County; Pop. 95,322; Zip Code 021+ Zone; Elev. 9; Lat. 42-21.9'N; Long. 71-06.3'W; Settled 1630; town dates back over three centuries. Following a bequest by John Harvard for a college, the common court ruled "New towne shall henceforth be called Cambridge," the name of the Old English University town.

•**CANTON** Town; Norfolk County; Pop. 18,182; Zip Code 02021; Elev. 113; Lat. 42-09.1'N, Long. 71-08.9'W; Settled 1630; 15m. SW of Boston in E Massachusetts; received its present name by geographical whim of a prominent citizen who estimated that the town was exactly antipodal to Canton, China.

•**CARVER** Town; Plymouth County; Pop. 6,988; Zip Code 02330; 8 m SSW of Plymouth and 38 m. SE of Boston. Carver derived it name from the first governor of Plymouth colony.

•**CHARLEMONT**, Town; Franklin County; Pop. 1,149; Zip Code 01339; Elev. 555; Settled about 1742; NW Massachusetts; 15m. W of Greenfield and 105m. WNW of Boston.

•**CHARLESTOWN**, Part of Boston; Suffolk County; Zip Code 021++ ;The town and the river were named in honor of Charles I, the reigning king in England at the time of settlement.

•**CHATHAM**, Town; Barnstable County; Pop. 6,071; Zip Code 02633; Lat. 41-41.0'N, Long. 69-57.7'W; Elev. 59; SE Massachusetts on the Atlantic coast being extreme eastern point of the state, Incorporated 1712.

•**CHELMSFORD**, Town; Middlesex County; Pop. 31,174; Zip Code 01824; Elev. 149; Lat. 42-35.8'N, Long, 71-21.0'W; Settled 1633; 5m. SE of Lowell in NE Massachusetts; was settled by people from Concord and Woburn, and named for Chelmsford in Essex, England.

•**CHELSEA**, City; Suffolk County; Pop. 25,431; Zip Code 02150; Elev. 20; Lat. 42-23.4'N, Long. 71-02.3'W; 5m. NE of Boston in E Massachusetts.

•**CHESHIRE**, Town; Berkshire County; Pop. 3,124; Zip Code 01225; Elev. 945; Settled 1766; NE of Pittsfield in NW Massachusetts on the Hoosic River.

•**CHESTER**, Town; Hampden County; Pop. 2,318; Zip Code 01011; Elev. 601; Settled 1760; Inc. 1765; SW Massachusetts.

•**CHESTERFIELD**, Town; Hampshire County; Pop. 1,000; Zip Code 01012; Elev. 1440; Settled 1760; W. Massachusetts, originally called New Hingham, was eventually named for the polished Earl of Chesterfield.

•**CHICOPEE**, City; Hampden County; Pop. 55,112; Zip Code 010+; Elev. 92; Lat. 42-08-55 N, long. 072-36-30 W. The town is named for the Chicopee River. Chicopee is an Indian menaing "birch bark place."

•**CLINTON**, Town; Worcester County; Pop. 12,771; Zip Code 01510; Elev. 328; Lat. 42-25.2'N, Long 71-41.0'W; Settled 1654; Inc. 1850; 10 miles NE of Worcester in N Central Massachusetts.

•**COHASSET**, Town; Norfolk County; Pop. 7,174; Zip Code 02025; Elev. 50; Lat. 42-14-30 N, Long. 070-48-15 W. Settled 1647; formerly part of Hingham. Cohasset is an Indian term meaning "rocky place."

•**COLRAIN**, Town; Franklin County; Pop. 1,552; Zip Code 01320; Elev. 620; Settled 1735; NW Massachusetts on Highway 112; was settled originally by Scotch-Irish from northern Ireland, was presumably named for Lord Coleraine, an Irish peer.

•**CONCORD**, Town; Middlesex County; Pop. 16,293; Zip Code 01742; Elev. 135; Lat. 42-27.7'N, Long. 42-21.0'W; Settled 1635; S of Lowell in NE Massachusetts, is situated where the Sudbury and Assabet join to form the Concord River. In 1635 the settlers purchased from the Massachusetts tribe a plantation described as "Concord" commemorates this friendship, a friendship that was never broken.

•**CONWAY**, Town; Franklin County; Pop. 1,213; Zip Code 01341; Elev. 300; Settled in 1762 it was named for General Henry Conway, a member of the British ministry popular in the colonies after he secured repeal of the Stamp Act in 1766.

•**DALTON**, Town; Berkshire County; Pop. 6,797; Zip Code 01226; 5m NE of Pittsfield in W Massachusetts.

•**DANVERS**, Town; Essex County; Pop. 24,100; Zip Code 01923; Lat. 42-34.2'N, Long. 70-56.2'W; 15m. NE of Boston in NE Massachusetts.

•**DARTMOUTH**, Town; Bristol County; Pop. 23,966; Zip Code 02714; Elev. 240; Settled 1650; Inc. 1664; Located in SE Massachusetts., 6 miles SW of the city of New Bedford, the town was named for the port city in England.

•**DEDHAM**, Town; Seat of Norfolk County; Pop. 25,298; Zip Code 02026; Elev. 111; Lat. 42-14.9'N, Long. 71-10.3'W; 10m. SW of Boston in E. Massachusetts. on the Charles River.

•**DENNIS** Town; Barnstable County; Pop. 12,360; Zip Code 02638; Elev. 160; Settled 1639; 5m. NE of Barnstable on Cape Cod in SE Massachusetts; was named for the Rev. Josiah Dennis, pastor of the first meeting house.

•**DIGHTON** Town; Bristol County; Pop. 5,352; Zip Code 02715; Elev. 29; Settled 1678; 10m. N. of Fall River in SE Massachusetts.

•**DOVER** Town; Norfolk County; Pop. 4,703; Zip Code 02030; Lat. 42-14.8'N, Long. 71-17.0'W SE Massachusetts. Suburban.

•**DRACUT** Town; Middlesex County; Pop. 21,249; Zip Code 01826; Lat. 42-40.1'N, Long. 71-18.2'W; it lies twenty-seven miles N of Boston.

•**DUDLEY** Town; Worcester County; Pop. 8,717; Zip Code 01570. The town was named in honor of Paul and William Dudley, who were among the first proprietors.

•DUXBURY, Town; Plymouth County; Pop. 11,807; Zip Code 02332; Elev. 31; Lat. 42-02.6'N, Long. 71-40.2'W; Settled 1624; Inc. 1637; on Plymouth Bay, 20m. SE of Brockton in SE. Massachusetts. The origin of the name is uncertain, but it may have been taken from the Lancastershire seat of the Standish family.

•EAST BRIDGEWATER, Town; Plymouth County; Pop. 9,945; Zip Code 02333; Elev. 68; Settled 1649; Inc. 1823; 5m. SE of Brockton in SE Massachusetts.

•EAST BROOKFIELD, Town; Worcester County; Pop. 1,955; Zip Code 01515; Elev. 621; Settled 1664; Located central Massachusetts; is one of the youngest towns in the State.

•EASTHAM, Town; Bristol County; Pop. 3,466; Zip Code 02642; Elev. 36; Settled 1644 Inc. 1651; in SE Massachusetts just S of Cape Cod.

•EASTHAMPTON, Town; Hampshire County; Pop. 15,580; Zip Code 01027; Lat. 42-16.0'N, 72-40.3'W; Elev. 169; Settled 1664; Inc. 1809; W central Massachusetts.

•EAST LONGMEADOW, Town; Hampden County; Pop. 12,905; Zip Code 01028; Lat. 42-03.9'N, Long. 72-30.7'W; SE of Springfield in S central Massachusetts.

•EASTON, Town; Bristol County; Pop. 16,623; Zip Code 02334; Elev. 124; Settled 1694; Inc. 1725; 5m. SW of Brockton in Massachusetts.

•EGARTOWN, Town; Seat of Dukes County; Pop. 2,204; Zip Code 02539; Lat. 41-23.3'N, Long. 70-31.0'W; Elev. 10; Settled 1642; was first called Nunnepog (Indian, Fresh Pond), and, when incorporated in 1671, was named for Edgar, son of James II.

•ERVING, Town; Franklin County; Pop. 1,326; Zip Code 01344; Elev. 474; Settled 1801; 10m. NE of Greenfield and 85m. NW of Boston in N Massachusetts. The town land was sold to John Erving of Boston in 1752.

•ESSEX, Town; Essex County; Pop. 2,978; Zip Code 01929; Elev. 27; Lat. 42-38.0'N, 70-46.8'W; Settled 1634; 20m. NE of Boston in NE Massachusetts. Named for Essex, England.

•EVERETT, City; Middlesex County; Pop. 37,195; Zip Code 02149; Elev. 31; Lat. 42-24.3'N, 71-03.7'W; Settled 1649; 5m. N of Boston in NE Massachusetts. The town was incorporated under the name of Everett, in honor of the illustrious orator, statesman, and scholar Edward Everett.

•FAIRHAVEN, Town; Bristol County; Pop. 15,759; Zip Code 02719; Elev. 45; Lat. 41-38.6'N. 70-54.6'W; Settled 1660; Inc. 1812; on Buzzards Bay across the harbor from New Bedford in SE Massachusetts.

•FALL RIVER, City; Seat of Bristol County; Pop. 92,574; Zip Code 027++; Elev. 39; Lat. 41-25.5'N, Long. 71-09.6'W; Settled 1656; Inc. Town 1803; 10m. NW of New Bedford, at the mouth of the Taunton River in SE Massachusetts. The present name of the city dates from 1834, and originated from the Indian name of the Quequechan River ("Falling Water"), which runs through the city and gives power to its mills.

•FALMOUTH, Town; Barnstable County; Pop. 23,640; Zip Code 025+; Lat. 41-33.2'N, Long. 70-37.1'W; Elev. 44; Settled about 1660; 1686; 15m. SE of New Bedford near Buzzards Bay in SE Massachusetts.

•FITCHBURG, City; Seat of Worcester County; Pop. 39,580; Zip Code 01420; Elev. 458; Lat. 42-35.0'N, Long. 71-47.8'W was settled in 1740 and chartered as a city in 1872.

•FLORIDA, Town; Berkshire County; Pop. 730; Zip Code 01343; Elev. 2,180; Settled 1783; 125m. NW of Boston.

•FOXBOROUGH, Town; Norfolk County; Pop. 14,148; Zip Code 02035; Elev. 296; Settled 1704; W of Brockton in E Massachusetts; was named for Charles James Fox, British champion of the American Colonies.

•FRAMINGHAM, Town; Middlesex County; Pop. 65,113; Zip Code 01701; Elev. 189; Lat. 42-16.6'N, Long. 71-24.9'W; Settled 1650; Inc. 1700; 20m. SW of Boston in E Massachusetts.

•FRANKLIN, Town; Norfolk County; Pop. 18,217; Zip Code 02038; Elev. 294; Lat. 42-05.1'N, Long 71-24.0'W; Settled 1660; 20m. W of Brockton in S Massachusetts. Named in honor of the great statesman, scholar, and humanist, Benjamin Franklin. He was not insensible to the honor, and, after wavering for some time between presenting a church bell or a collection of books to his municipal namesake, he decided in favor of the books because it is said he "considered sense more essential than sound."

•GARDNER, City; Worcester County; Pop. 17,900; Zip Code 01440; Elev. 1030; Lat. 42-34.0'N, Long. 71-58.9'W; Settled 1764; Inc. Town 1785; City 1923; 10m. W of Fitchburg in N Massachusetts.

•GEORGETOWN, Town; Essex County; Pop. 5,687; Zip Code 01833; Elev. 74; Lat. 42-43.5'N, Long. 70-59.4'W; Settled 1639; Inc. 1838; NE Massachusetts.

•GLOUCESTER, City; Essex County; Pop. 27,768; Zip Code 01930; Elev. 57; Lat. 42-36.8'N, Long. 70-39.9'W; Settled 1623; Inc. Town 1642; City 1873; 30m. NE of Boston in NE Massachusetts comprises the whole of the granite peninsula of Cape Ann.

•HANSON, Town; Plymouth County; Pop. 8,617; Zip Code 02341; Elev. 66; Settled 1632; Inc. 1820; 8m. SE of Brockton in SE Massachusetts; named for Alexander Conte Hanson, a patriot, assaulted by a Baltimore mob in 1812 for criticizing the Federal administration.

•HARDWICK, Town; Worcester County; Pop. 2,272; Zip Code 01037; Elev. 986; Settled 1737; in central Mass.; Hardwick was purchased in 1686 from the Nipmuck Indians by eight Roxbury residents. At first called Lambstown, the district was incorporated as Hardwick, probably for Philip York, first Lord Hardwick.

•HARVARD, Town; Worcester County; Pop. 12,170; Zip Code 01451 Elev. 390; Lat 42-30.1'N, Long. 72-35.0'W; Settled 1704; 10m. SE of Fitchburg in central Massachusetts; Harvard was named in honor of John Harvard, first patron of Harvard University.

•HARWICH, Town; Barnstable County; Pop. 8,971; Zip Code 02645; Elev. 80; Settled 1670; 10m. E of Barnstable in SE Massachusetts. Queen Elizabeth called the English village for which it was named "Happy-go-lucky Harwich," a term that can be applied to this charming namesake.

•HATFIELD, Town Hampshire County; Pop. 3,045; Zip Code 01038; Located on the Connecticut River in W. Massachusetts.

•HAVERHILL, City; Essex County; Pop. 46,865; Zip Code 01830; Elev. 59; Lat. 42-46.6'N, Long. 71-04.6'NW; Settled 1640; 15m. NE of Lowell in NE corner of Massachusetts. The Reverend John Ward named the plantation for the quiet market town of Haverhill, England, in 1640.

•HINGHAM,, Town; Plymouth County; Pop. 20,339; Zip Code 02043; Elev. 21; Lat. 42-14.5'N. Long. 70-53.3'W; Settled 1633; 10m. SE of Boston, on Massachusetts Bay in SE Massachusetts; is named for the former English home of most of its settlers.

•HINSDALE, Town; Berkshire County; Pop. 1,707; Zip Code 01235; Elev. 1,431; Settled 1763; 10m. SE of Pittsfield in W central Massachusetts. It was named for Rev. Theodore Hinsdale, who came here and founded a church in 1795.

•HOLBROOK, Town; Norfolk County; Pop. 11,140; Zip Code 02343; Elev. 200; Lat. 42-09.2'N, Long. 71-00.5'W; Settled 1710; 5 m. N of Brockton in E. Massachusetts.

•HOLDEN, Town; Worcester County; Pop. 13,336; Zip Code 01520; Elev. 855; Lat. 42-21.1'N, Long. 71-51.6'W; Settled 1723; 10m. NW of Worcester in central Massachusetts; Holden is in a town once known as the "North Half" of Worcester; at its incorporation, it was named for Samuel Holden, a London merchant whose philanthropies aided the Colonies.

•HOLLISTON, Town; Middlesex County; Pop. 12,622; Zip Code 01746; Elev. 198; Lat. 42-12.0'N, Long. 71-25.7'W; Settled about 1659; 20m. SE of Worcester in E Massachusetts; Holliston was named for Thomas Hollis, an early benefactor of Harvard College.

•HOLYOKE, City; Hampden County; Pop. 44,678; Zip Code 01040; Elev. 152; Lat. 42-12.2'N, Long. 72-36.5'W; Settled 1745; City 1873; 10m. N of Springfield in SW Massachusetts, on the Connecticut River.

•HOPKINTON, Town; Misslesex County; Pop. 7,114; Zip Code 01748; Elev. 439; Lat. 42-13.8'N, Long. 71-31.3'W; 30 miles SW of Boston.

•HUDSON, Town Middlesex County; Pop. 16,408; Zip Code 01749; Lat. 42-23.4'N, Long. 71-34.4'W.

•HULL, Town; Plymouth County; Pop. 9,714; Zip Code 02045; Lat. 42-18.2'N, Long. 70-54.5'W.

•HUMAROCK, Included in Scituate; Plymouth County; Zip Code 02047.

•HUNTINGTON, Town; Hamnpshire County; Pop. l,804; Zip Code 01050 Elev. 381; W. Massachusetts; settled in 1769, at first called Norwich, was later renamed for Charles F. Huntington.

•HYANNIS, Barnstable County; Pop. 9,000; Zip Code 02601; on Cape Cod in SE Massachusetts. Resort community.

•IPSWICH, Part of Cambridge; Middlesex County; Pop. 5,600; Elev. 30; Settled in 1633; NE corner of Massachusetts; settled by a group of 12 pioneers, and named for the town of Ipswich, in England. Its Indian name was Deperion, a name applied to several other places in the country, signifying a fishing station.

•KINGSTON, Town; Plymouth County; Pop. 7,362; Zip Code 02364; Lat. 41-59.9'N, Long. 70-44.0'W; SE Massachusetts. The territory of this town was formerly a part of Plymouth, and set off, and called Jones' River parish, in 1717.

•LANCASTER, Town; Worcester County; Pop. 6,334; Zip Code 01523; 34 mi. NW of Boston; Central Massachusetts.

•LANESBOROUGH, Town; Berkshire County; Pop. 3,131; Zip Code 01237; Elev. 1210; Settled 1753; 5m. N of Pittsfield in NW Massachusetts; was originally known as New Framingham, but was incorporated as Lanesborough in honor of the beautiful Irish Countess of Lanesborough, a court favorite and a friend of the then Governor of Massachusetts.

•LAWRENCE, City, Seat of Essex County; Pop. 63,175; Zip Code 018++ Elev. 43; Lat. 42-42.5'N, Long. 73-15.1'W; Settled 1655; Inc. Town 1847; 10m. NE of Lowell in NE Massachusetts on the Merrimack River.

•LEE, Town; Berkshire County; Pop. 6,274; Zip Code 01238; Elev. 888; Lat. 42-18.6'N, Long 73-15.1'W; Settled 1760; Inc. 1777; 10m. S of Pittsfield in W. Massachusetts; named for General Charles Lee, later notorious for his treason to Washington.

•LEICESTER, Town; Worcester County; Pop. 9,446; Zip Code 01524; Elev. 1009; Settled 1713; Inc. 1722; Located central Massachusetts.

•LENOX, Town, Berkshire County; Pop. 6,513; Zip Code 01240; Elev. 1,210; Lat. 42-21.5'N, Long. 73-17.0'W; Settled 1750; 5m. S of Pittsfield in W Massachusetts; was named for Charles Lenox, Duke of Richmond, a defender of Colonial rights.

•LEOMINSTER, City; Worcester County; Pop. 34,508; Zip Code 01453; Elev. 409; Lat. 42-31.6'N, Long. 71-45.5'W; Settled 1653; 5m SE of Fitchburg in Central Massachusetts.

•LEVERETT, Town; Franklin County; Pop. 1,471; Zip Code 01054; Elev. 430; Settled 1713; 10m SE of Greenfield in NW Massachusetts.

•LEXINGTON, Town; Middlesex County; Pop. 29,479; Zip Code 02173; Elev. 201; Lat. 42-26.9'N, Long. 71-13.5'W; Settled 1642; 10 m. NW of Boston in NE Massachusetts.

•LINCOLN, Town; Middlesex County; Pop. 7,098; Zip Code 01773; Lat. 42-4.6'N, Long. 71-18.2'W; this town was once a part of Concord, Lexington, and Weston.

•LITTLETON, Town; Middlesex County; Pop. 6,970; Zip Code 01460; Elev. 230; Lat. 42-32.3'N, Long. 71-30-7'W; Settled about 168; 10m. SW of Lowell in NE Massachusetts. This township was granted in 1714, and named for George Littleton, a member of the British parliament. Its Indian name was Nashobah.

•LONGMEADOW, Town; Hampden County; Pop. 16,301; Elev. 55, Settled 1644; Located S central Massachusetts on Connecticut River just S of Springfield. (The "long meddowe") purchased from the Indians in 1636, rapidly became a substantial settlement.

•LOWELL, City; Seat of Middlesex County; Pop. 92,418; Zip Code 018+; Elev. 110; Lat. 42-38.2'N, Long 71-18.8'W; Settled 1653; 25m. NW of Boston on Merrimack River at Pawtucket Falls in NE Massachusett. Named for Francis Cabot Lowell.

•LUDLOW, Town; Hampden County; Pop. 18,150; Zip Code 01056; Elev. 239; Settled 1751; 5m. NE of Springfield in SW Massachusetts; originally known as Stony Hill.

•LUNENBURG, Town; Worcester County; Pop. 8,405; Zip Code 01462; Elev. 377; Settled 1721; 5m. E of Fitchburg in N Massachusetts. This was originally a part of "Turkey Hills", or Fitchburg, and was so called in compliment to George II, or to the Duke of Lunenburg.

•LYNN, City; Essex County; Pop. 78,471; Zip Code 019++; Elev. 34; Lat. 42-27.8'N, Long. 70-56.9'W; Settled 1629; 10m. NE of Boston on Lynn Harbor; the city was named in honor of King Lynn in Norfolk County, England.

•LYNNFIELD, Town; Essex County, Pop. 11,267; Zip Code 01940; Elev. 90; Lat. 42-32.3'N., Long. 71-03.0'W; Settled 1638-39; 10m. NE of Boston in NE Massachusetts.

•MALDEN, City; Middlesex County; Pop. 53,386; Zip Code 02148; Elev. 9; Lat. 42-25.6'N, Long. 71-04.4'W; Settled 1640; 5m. N of Boston in NE Massachusetts.

•MANCHESTER, Town; Essex County; Pop. 5,404; Zip Code 01944; Elev. 14; Lat. 42-34.5'N, Long. 70-46.4'W; Settled 1626-27; Inc. 1645; 20 m. NE of Boston on the Atlantic Ocean in NE Massachusetts.

•**MANSFIELD**, Town; Bristol County; Pop. 13,453; Zip Code 02048; Elev. 178; Lat. 42-01.5'N, Long. 71-13.0'W; Settled 1659; was named for Lord Mansfield and occupies the site of an Indian winter camping ground.

•**MARBLEHEAD**, Town; Essex County; Pop. 20,126; Zip Code 01945; Elev. 15; Lat. 42-30.2'N, Long 70-51.1'W; Settled 1629; Reckless, hardbitten fishermen from Cornwall and the Channel Islands settled Marblehead (Marble Harbor) in 1629 as a plantation of Salem.

•**MARION** Town; Plymouth County; Pop. 3,932; Zip Code 02738; Elev. 29; Settled 1679; NE of New Bedford in SE Massachusetts on Buzzards Bay; was set off from Rochester and named for General Francis Marion, southern Revolutionary hero.

•**MARLBOROUGH** City; Middlesex County; Pop. 30,617; Zip Code 01752; Elev. 386; Settled 1657; NE of Worcester in Massachusetts; was the site of an Indian plantation called Okammakamefit.

•**MARSHFIELD**, Town; Plymouth County; Pop. 20,016, Zip Code 02050; Elev. 24; Settled 1632; 15m. E of Brockton in SE Massachusetts.

•**MASHPEE**, Town; Barnstable County; Pop. 3,700; Zip Code 02649; Elev. 51; Settled 1660; SE Massachusetts; in an area with picturesque ponds, groves, streams, and stretches of woodland. Mashpee-Indian term for "standing Water" or "Great Pond".

•**MATTAPOISETT**, Town; Plymouth County; Pop. 5,597; Zip Code 02730; Elev. 9; Lat. 41-39.6'N; Long. 70-49.0'W; Settled 1750; 5m. NE of New Bedford on Buzzards Bay in SE Massachusetts; (Indian "Place of Rest").

•**MAYNARD**, Town; Middlesex County; Pop. 9,590; Zip Code 01754, Elev. 176; Lat. 42-26.0'N; Long. 71-27.0'W; Settled 1638; NE Massachusetts on the Assabet River; Amory Maynard, from whom the town took its name, founded the original textile mill, out of which grew American Woolen Company.

•**MEDFIELD**, Town; Norfolk County; Pop. 10,220; Zip Code 02052; Elev. 179; Lat. 42-11.2'N, Long. 71-18.2'W; Settled and Incorporated in 1651; 15m. SW of Boston in E Massachusetts.

•**MEDFORD**, City; Middlesex; Pop. 58,076; Zip Code 02155; Elev. 12.

•**MEDWAY**, Town; Norfolk County; Pop. 8,447; Zip Code 02053; Elev. 184; Lat. 42-08.4'N, Long. 71-23.8'W; Settled 1657; 20m. SW of Boston in E Massachusetts.

•**MELROSE**, City; Suffolk County; Pop. 30,050; Zip Code 021+; Elev. 55; Lat. 42-27.4'N, Long. 71-03.8'W; Settled 1629; 5m. N of Boston in NE Massachusetts. Formerly a part of Malden, this district was known locally as the North End of North Malden.

•**MENDON**, Town; Worcester County; Pop. 3,108; Zip Code 01756; Elev. 420; Settled 1660; 15m. SE of Worcester in S Massachusetts; originally Quinshepauge, renamed for Mendon, England.

•**MERRIMAC**, Town; Essex County; Pop. 4,451; Zip Code 01860; Elev. 105; Settled 1638; Located NE of Lowell in NE Massachusetts; named by the Indians "Swift Waters"

•**METHUEN**, Town; Essex County; Pop. 36,701; Zip Code 01841; Elev. 105; Lat. 42-43.6'N, Long 71-11.3'W; Settled 1642; NE Massachusetts; formerly in Haverhill until 1725, was named for Lord Paul Methuen.

•**MIDDLEBOROUGH**, Town; Plymouth County; Pop. 16,404, Code 02360; Elev. 110; Settled 1660; Inc. 1660; 15m. S of Brockton in SE Massachusetts; was known to the Indians as Nemasket.

•**MIDDLETON**, Town; Essex County; Pop. 4,135; Zip Code 01949; Elev. 95; Lat. 42-35.6'N, Long. 71-00.9'W; Settled 1659; 15m. SE of Lowell in NE Massachusetts.

•**MILFORD**, Town; Worcester County; Pop. 23,390; Zip Code 01757; Elev. 257; Lat. 42-08.3'N, Long. 71-31.3'W; Elev. 257; Lat. 42-08.3'N, Long. 71-31.3'W; Elev. 257; Settled 1662; 15m. SE of Worcester in E Massachusetts.

•**MILLBURY**, Town; Worcester County; Pop. 11,828; Zip Code 01527; Elev. 407; Lat. 42-11.6'N, Long. 71-45.5'W; Settled 1716; 5m. S of Worcester in central Massachusetts S of Worcester City.

•**MILLIS**, Town; Norfolk County; Pop. 6,908; Zip Code 02054; Lat. 42-10.3'N, Long. 71-21.5'W.

•**MILLVILLE**, Town; Worcester County; Pop. 1,693; Zip Code 01529; Elev. 225; Settled 1662; Incorporated 1916; SE of Worcester in S Massachusetts.

•**MILTON**, Town; Norfolk County; Pop. 25,860; Zip Code 021++ Elev. 24; Lat. 42-15.2'N, Long. 71-04.6'W; Settled 1636; Located 5m. S of Boston in E Massachusetts; originally Uncataquisset (Indian "Head of Tidewater").

•**MONSON**, Town; Hampden County; Pop. 7,315; Zip Code 01057; S Massachusetts; 20 miles E of Springfield.

•**MONTAGUE**, Town; Franklin County; Pop. 8,011; Zip Code 01351; W Massachusetts.

•**MONTEREY**, Town; Berkshire County; Pop. 818; Zip Code 01245; Elev. 1,200; Settled 1739; Inc. 1847; W Massachusetts; formerly a district of Tyringham, was named for the American victory in the Mexican War.

•**NAHANT**, Town; Essex County; Pop. 3,947; Zip Code 01908; Lat. 42-25.5'N, Long. 71-55.0'W; NE Massachusetts.

•**NANTUCKET**, Town; Seat of Nantucket County; Pop. 5,087; Zip Code 02554; Lat. 41-16.9'N, Long. 70-06.1'W; Elev. 12; Settled 1641; Incorporated, 1687; Located on Nantucket Island, near the harbor, takes its name from the Indian *Nanticut*; population includes all communities on island.

•**NATICK**, Town; Middlesex County; Pop. 29,461; Zip Code 01760; NE Massachusetts.

•**NEW BEDFORD**, City; Seat of Bristol County; Pop. 98,478; Zip Code 027++ Elev. 9; Lat. 41-38.2'N, Long. 70-55.8'W; Settled 1640; Until its incorporation as New Bedford, "Bedford Village" was a part of the town of Dartmouth. Joseph Russell, known as the "Father of New Bedford" gave the town its name in honor of the Duke of Bedford.

•**NEW SALEM**, Town; Franklin County; Pop. 688; Zip Code 01355; Elev. 1030; Settled 1737; Incorporated 1753; New Salem was named for Salem because the original proprietors were residents of that town.

•**NEWBURY**, Town; Essex County; Pop. 4,529; Elev. 40; Settled and Incorporated 1635; NE corner of Massachusetts.

•**NEWBURYPORT**, Town; Seat of Essex County; Pop. 15,900; Zip Code 01950; Elev. 26; Lat. 42-48.7'N, Long. 70-52.5'W; Settled 1635; 25 miles NE of Lowell in NE Massachusetts, at the mouth of Merrimack River.

•**NEWTON**, City; Middlesex County; Pop. 83,622; Zip Code 021++; Elev. 142; Lat. 42-20.9'N; Long. 71-11.6'W; Settled 1639; Incorporated Town 1691; 5 miles W of Boston in NE Massachusetts.

•**NORFOLK**, Town; Norfolk County; Pop. 6,363; Zip Code 02056; Lat. 42-07.0'N, Long. 71-19.5'W; Located in eastern Massachusetts; 21 miles SW of Boston.

•**NORTH ADAMS**, City; Berkshire County; Pop. 18,063; Zip Code 01247; Lat. 42-41.9'N, Long. 73-06.6'W; Settled about 1767; Located NW Massachusetts.

•**NORTHAMPTON**, City; Seat of Hampshire County; Pop. 29,286; Zip Code 01060; Elev. 138; Lat. 42-19.2'N, Long. 72-37.8'W; Settled 1654; 15 miles N of Springfield in W Massachusetts on the Connecticut River.

•**NORTH ANDOVER**, Town; Essex County; Pop. 20,129; Zip Code 01845; Lat. 42-42.0'N, Long. 71-07.8'W; NE Massachusetts.

•**NORTH ATTLEBOROUGH**, Town; Bristol County; Pop. 21,075; Zip Code 027++; Elev. 183; Lat. 41-59.0'N, Long. 71-19.8'W; Settled 1669; SE Massachusetts.

•**NORTH BROCKFIELD**, Town; Worcester County; Pop. 4,150; Zip Code 01535; Lat. 42-16-13 N, long. 072-05-02. This town, formerly the second parish of Brookfield, was incorporated as North Brookfield in 1812.

•**NORTH CARVER**, Town; Plymouth County; Pop. included in Carver; Zip Code 02355; Elev. 114; Lat. 41-55-07 N, long. 070-47-57 W. Incorporated in 1790 and named for John Carver, the first governor of Plymouth Colony.

•**NORTH READING**, Town; Middlesex County; Pop. 11,455; Zip Code 01864; Elev. 80; Lat. 42-34-27 N, long. 071-04-39. Settled in 1651 and incorporated in 1853.

•**NORTHBOROUGH**, Town; Worcester County; Pop. 5,670; Zip Code 01532; Elev. 303; Lat. 42-19-07 N, long. 071-38-30 W. Incorporated 1775, the town was once part of Marlborough.

•**NORTHBRIDGE**, Town; Worcester County; Pop. 12,246; Zip Code 01588; Elev. 302; Lat. 42-06-45 N, long. 071-40-14 W. Until 1772, the town was the northern part of Uxbridge. The town was then known as *Whitinsville* after Paul Whitin opened a cotton textile factory.

•**NORTHFIELD**, Town; Franklin County; Pop. 2,386; Zip Code 01360; Elev. 262; Lat. 42-41-15 N, long. 072-26-47 W. First settled in 1673, the town is named for its northern situation in the county.

•**NORTON**, Town; Bristol County; Pop. 2, 035; Zip Code 02766; Elev. 104; Lat. 41-58-21 N, long. 071-11-06 W. Settled in 1669 and named for the town in England.

•**NORWELL**, Town; Plymouth County; Pop. 9,162; Zip Code 02061; Lat. 42-09-40 N, long. 070-47-38 W. Located in SE Massachusetts in an agricultural region.

•**NORWOOD**, Town; Norfolk County; Pop. 29,711; Zip Code 02062; Elev. 149; Lat. 41-57-08 N, long. 070-48-31 W. Settled in 1678 and named for Norwood, England.

•**OAK BLUFFS**, Town; Dukes County; Pop. 1,984; Area Code 617; Zip Code 02557; Lat. 41-27.2'N, Long. 70D34.0'W; Settled 1642; Incorporated 1880; Located on Martha's Vineyard Isle in the NE section of the isle; is an attractive town which greatly increases its population in the summer. The Algonquin name for this tract of land was Ogkeshkuppe ("Damp Thicket"), but the earliest English name, given in 1646 by Thomas Mayhew, the first proprietor, was Easternmost Chop of Holmes' Hole. Mayhew granted it to John Dagget.

•**OAKHAM**, Town; Worcester County; Pop. 994; Area Code 617; Zip Code 01068; Central Massachusetts. This was once a part of Rutland, and called "Rutland West Wing." The first minister in this town was the Rev. John Strickland, a Presbyterian, in 1768. His successor was the Rev. Daniel Tomlinson, a Congregationalist, in 1786.

•**ORANGE**, Town; Franklin County; Pop. 6,844; Area Code 413; Zip Code 01364; Elev. 505; Settled about 1746; Incorporated 1810; 15 miles E of Greenfield in N Massachusetts; was named in honor of William, Prince of Orange. On the banks of a rapid river, the town was destined to become a manufacturing center.

•**ORLEANS**, Town; Barnstable County; Pop. 5,306; Area Code 617; Zip Code 02653; Lat. 41-47.4'N, Long. 69-59.5'w;; Elev. 35; Settled 1693; Incorporated 1797; 20 miles NE of Barnstable in SE Massachusetts, on an inlet of the Atlantic Ocean; was presumable named for Louis Phillippe, Duke of Orleans, who visited New England in 1797. The settlers were engaged in shipping, shell fisheries, and salt works. Windmills and surf mills were used to pump the sea water for the latter into vats on the shore.

•**OTIS**, Town; Berkshire County; Pop. 963; Area Code 413; Zip Code 02153; Elev. 1,240; Settled 1735; Incorporated 1778; NW Massachusetts; was named for Harison Gray Otis, then Speaker of the House of Representatives.

•**OXFORD**, Town; Worcester County; Pop. 11,680; Area Code 617; Elev. 516; Settled 1687; Incorporated 1693; 10 miles SW of Worcester in S central Massachusetts just W of Hwy. 52; named for Oxford, England, is on land purchased from the Nipmucks in 1681. The first attempted settlements made by French Huguenots were abandoned owing to Indian depredations. Permanent settlement was made by the English in 1713.

•**PEABODY**, City; Essex County; Pop. 45,976; Area Code 617; Zip Code 01960; Lat. 42-31.3'N, Long. 70-55.5'W; 15 miles SE of Lowell in NE corner of Massachusetts. Named Peabody in 1868 and incorporated in 1916.

•**PELHAM**, Town, Hampshire County; Pop. 1,112; Area Code 413; Elev. 800; Settled 1738; Incorporated 1743; Located central Massachusetts. At its incorporation it was named for Lord Pelham, then traveling in the Colony.

•**PEMBROKE**, Town; Plymouth County; Pop. 13,487; Area Code 617; Zip Code 02359; Elev. 160; Settled 1650; Incorporated 1712; 10 miles E of Brockton in SE Massachusetts.

•**PEPPERELL**, Town; Middlesex County; Pop. 8,061; Area Code 617; Zip Code 01463; Elev. 193; Lat. 42-40.0'N, Long. 71-34.6'W; Settled 1720; Incorporated 1753; 10m. NE of Fitchburg in NE Massachusetts; was named for Sir William Pepperell, a hero of the Battle of Louisburg.

•**PERU**, Town, Berkshire County; Pop. 633; Area Code 413; Elev. 2295; Settled 1767; Incorporated 1771; Located NE Massachusetts on State 143; the highest village in the state, is perched on the summit of the Green Mt. Range. First called Patridgefield, it was incorporated 1806 under its present name on the suggestion of the Rev. John Leland "because," he said, "it is like the Peru of South America, a mountain town, and if no gold or silver mines are under her rocks, she favors hard money and begins with a "P."

•**PETERSHAM**, Town; Worcester County; Pop. 1,024; Area Code 617; Zip Code 01366; Elev. 1,100; Settled 1733; Incorporated 1754; Located in central Massachusetts; was first called Nichewaug and Volunteers Town, and later named for Petersham in Surrey, England.

•**PHILLIPSTON**, Town, Worcester County; Pop. 953; Area Code 617; Elev. 914; Settled 1751; Incorporated 1814; located in central Massachusetts; named for William Phillips, for 12 successive terms Lieutenant-Governor of the State.

•**PITTSFIELD**, City; Seat of Berkshire County; Pop. 51,974; Area Code 617; Zip Code 01201; Elev. 1,038; Lat. 42-26.8'N, Long. 73-15.2'W; Settled 1752; Incorporated Town 1761; City 1889; 40m. WNW of Springfield in W Massachusetts on the Housatonic River.

•**PLAINVILLE**, Town; Norfolk County; Pop. 5,857; Area Code 617; Zip Code 027+; Elev. 207; Settled 1661; Inc. 1905; 30m. SE of Boston in SE Massachusetts.

•**PLYMOUTH**, Town; Seat of Plymouth County; Pop. 35,913; Area Code 617; Zip Code 02367; Elev. 29; Lat. 41-57.3'N, Long. 70-40.3'W; Settled 1620; Incorporated Town 1620; 20 miles SE of Brockton in E Massachusetts on Plymouth Bay.

•**PLYMPTON**, Town; Plymouth County; Pop. 1,974; Area Code 617; Zip Code 02367; Elev. 79; Settled 1662; Inc. 1707; Located SE Massachusetts on State 58; because of its geographic propinquity to Plymouth, it was named for Plympton, a borough near Plymouth, England.

•**PRINCETON**, Town; Worcester County; Pop. 2,425; Area Code 617; Zip Code 01541; Elev. 949; Settled 1743; Incorporated 1771; 15m. NW of Worcester in central Massachusetts on State 62; was named for the Rev. Thomas Prince, associate pastor of Old South Church in Boston, 1718.

•**PROVINCETOWN**, Town and Harbor, Barnstable County; Pop. 3,536; Area Code 617; Zip Code 02657; Elev. 11; Lat. 42-03.0'N, Long. 70-11.4'W; Settled 1700; Incorporated 1727; on N tip of Cape Cod in SE Massachusetts.

•**QUINCY**, City; Norfolk County; Pop. 84,743; Zip Code 021+; Elev. 42; Lat 42-15.1'N; Long. 71-00.1'W; Settled in 1625 by Thomas Morton. First known as Merrymount later renamed Quincy in honor of Colonel John Quincy, an eminent citizen who had occupied nearby Mount Wollaston.

•**RAYNHAM**, Town; Bristol County; Pop. 9,076; Zip Code 02767; Elev. 51; Settled 1652; Incorporated 1731; 10 miles SW of Brockton in SE Massachusetts named in honor of Lord Townshend of Rainham, England.

•**RANDOLPH**, Town; Norfolk County; Pop. 28,218; Zip Code 02368; Elev. 225; Lat. 42-09.7'N, Long. 71-02.3'W; Settled about 1710; 5 miles N of Brockton in E Massachusetts; It was named Randolph in honor of Peyton Randolph, first President of the Continental Congress.

•**READING**, Town; Middlesex County; Pop. 22,678; Zip Code 01867; Elev. 107; Lat.42-31.5'N, Long. 71-06.2'W; Settled 1639; Incorporated 1644; 10 miles N of Boston in NW Massachusetts.

•**REHOBOTH**, Town; Bristol County; Pop. 7,570; Zip Code 02769; Elev. 256; Settled 1636; 10 miles NW of Fall River in SE Massachusetts.

•**REVERE**, City; Suffolk County; Pop. 42,423; Zip Code 02151; Elev. 15; Lat. 42-24.5'N, Long. 71-00.9'W; Settled 1630; 5 miles NE of Boston in NE Massachusetts. Named in honor of Paul Revere.

•**RICHMOND**, Town; Berkshire County; Pop. 1,659; Zip Code 01254; Elev. 1107; Settled 1760; NW Massachusetts; Was originally called Yokumtown, incorporated as Richmont, but in 1785 became Richmond in honor of Charles Lennox, Duke of Richmond, and defender of Colonial rights.

•**ROCHESTER**,Town; Plymouth County; Pop. 3,190; Zip Code 02770; Elev. 140; Settled 1638; Incorporated 1686; E Massachusetts; First known as Sippician, the town was named Rochester for the English home of some of its settlers.

•**ROCKLAND**, Town; Plymouth County; Pop. 15,695; Zip Code 02370; Elev. 124; Lat. 42-08.0'N, Long. 70-54.8'W; Elev. 124; Settled 1673; Incorporated 1874; 6 miles ENE of Brockton in SE Massachusetts.

•**ROCKPORT**, Town; Essex County; Pop. 6,345; Zip Code 01966; Elev. 61; Lat. 42-39.4'N, Long. 70-37.1'W; Settled 1690; Incorporated 1840; is on the Granite peninsula off Cape Ann in E Massachusetts.

•**ROWLEY**, Town; Essex County; Pop. 3,867; Zip Code 01969; Elev. 59; Lat. 42-43.0'N, Long. 70-52.6'W; Settled 1638; Incorporated 1639; 5 miles N of Ipswich in NE Massachusetts.

•**ROYALSTON**, Town; Worcester County; Pop. 955; Zip Code 01368; Elev. 817; Settled 1762; N Massachusetts.

•**RUSSELL**, Town; Hampden County; Pop. 1,570; Zip Code 01071; Elev. 266; Settled 1782; SE Massachusetts.

•**RUTLAND**, Town; Worcester County; Pop. 4,334; Zip Code 01543; Elev. 1,001; Settled 1716; Incorporated 1722; 10 miles NW of Worcester in central Massachusetts.

•**SALEM**, City; Seat of Essex County; Pop. 38,220; Zip Code 01970; Elev. 13; Lat. 42-31.3'N, Long. 70-53.3'W; Settled 1626; 15 miles NE of Boston in NE Massachusetts on the Atlantic Ocean. Named by early settlers, who chose the Hebrew term meaning "city of peace."

•**SALISBURY**, Town; Essex County; Pop. 5,973; Zip Code 01950; Elev. 15; Settled in 1638; Incorporated 1640; Located in the most NE part of Massachusetts.

•**SANDWICH**, Town, Barnstable County; Pop. 8,727; Zip Code 02563; Elev. 15; Lat. 41-45.6'N, Long. 70-29.6'W; Settled 1637; Incorporated 1639; S of Cape Cod in SE Massachusetts; named for the town in England.

•**SAUGUS**, Town; Essex County; Pop. 24,746; Zip Code 01906; Elev. 20; Lat. 42-27.9'N, Long. 71-00.7'W; Settled 1630; Incorporated 1815; 10 miles NNE of Boston not far from Massachusetts Bay. Named for the river that runs through town.

•**SAVOY**, Town; Berkshire County; Pop. 644; Zip Code 01256; W Massachusetts.

•**SCITUATE**, Town; Plymouth County; Pop. 17,317; Zip Code 02066; Elev. 46; Lat. 42-11.8'N, Long. 70-43.5'W; Settled 1630, 15 miles ENE of Brockton in SE Massachusetts.

•**SEEKONK**, Town; Bristol County; Pop. 12,269; Zip Code 02771; Elev. 140; Settled 1636; Incorporated 1812; 10 miles NW of Fall River in SE Massachusetts. The name (Indian, "Black Goose") indicates an abundance of these birds prior to the coming of the white men.

•**SHARON**, Town, Norfolk County; Pop. 13,601; Zip Code 02067; Elev. 234; Lat. 42-07.4'N, Long. 71-10.6'W; Settled 1650; 10 miles WNW of Brockton in SE Massachusetts; lies in the territory once known as Massapoag ("Great Waters"). incorporated in 1765, by the name of Stoughtonham, but the name became unpopular, and was soon changed to the more euphonic and scriptural name of Sharon.

•**SHEFFIELD**, Town; Berkshire County; Pop. 2,743; Zip Code 01257; Elev. 607; Settled 1726; Inc. 1733; 25 miles SW of Pittsfield in SW corner of Massachusetts.

•**SHELBURNE** (alt. SHELBURNE FALLS), Town; Franklin County; Pop. 2,002; Zip Code 01370; Elev. 700; Settled 1756-6; NW Massachusetts; was once known as Deerfield Pasture or Deerfield Northwest. In 1760 the town was named for the second Earl of Shelburne.

•**SHIRLEY**, Town; Middlesex County; Pop. 5,124; Zip Code 01464; Elev. 283; Settled 1720; Incorporated 1753; 5 miles SE of Fitchburg in NE Massachusetts.

•**SHUTESBURY**, Town; Franklin County; Pop. 1,049; Zip Code 01072; Elev. 1,000; Settled 1735; Incorporated 1761; Central Massachusetts just west of the Quabbin Reservoir. Originally part of a grant called Roadtown, the town was named for Samuel Shute, one-time Governor of the Bay Colony.

•**SHREWSBURY**, Town, Worcester County; Pop. 22,674; Zip Code 01545; Elev. 671; Lat. 42-17.8'N; Long. 71-42.7'W; Settled 1722; 5 miles ENE of Worcester in Central Massachusetts. It is named for Charles Talbot, Duke of Shrewsbury.

•**SOMERSET**, Town; Briston County; Pop. 18,813; Zip Code 027++; Elev. 17; Lat. 41-46.5'N, Long. 71-07.6'W; Settled 1677; Incorporated 1790; 5 miles N of Fall River in SE Massachusetts. Named for Somerset, England.

•**SOMERVILLE**, City; Middlesex County; Pop. 77,372; Zip Code 021++;Z Elev. 41; Lat. 42-22.8'N, Long. 71-05.5'W; Settled 1630; 5 miles NW of Boston in NE Massachusetts.

•**SOUTHAMPTON**, Town; Hampshire County; Pop. 4,137; Zip Code 01073; Elev. 229; Lat. 42-36.8'N, Long. 70-52.5'W; Settled 1732; Incorporated 1775; 10 miles NW of Springfield in W central Massachusetts; was named for Southampton, England.

•**SOUTHBOROUGH**, Town; Worcester County; Pop. 6,193; Zip Code 01772 Lat. 42-18.4'N, Long. 71-31.5'W; 15 mile E of Westboro in central Massachusetts.

•**SOUTHBRIDGE**, Town; Worcester County; Pop. 16,665; Zip Code 01550; Lat. 42-04.6'N, Long. 72-02.1'W; 15 miles SW of Worcester in central Massachusetts.

•**SOUTH EGREMONT**, Berkshire County; Pop. included in Egremont Zip Code 01258; Elev. 740; Settled 1730; was named in honor of Charles Windham, Earl of Egremont, a liberal and a friend of the American cause in the Revolution.

•**SOUTH HADLEY**, Town; Hampshire County; Pop. 16,399; Zip Code 01075; Elev. 246; Settled 1659; N of Springfield in W Massachusetts.

•**SOUTHWICK**, Town; Hampden County; Pop. 7,382; Zip Code 01077; Elev. 260; Lat. 42-03.3'N, Long. 72-46.2'W; Settled 1770; in S Massachusetts; was named for an English village.

•**SPENCER**, Town; Worcester County; Pop. 10,774; Zip Code 01562; Elev. 860; Lat. 42-14.7'N, Long. 71-59.5'W; Settled 1721; 11 miles W of Worcester city in central Massachusetts; was named for Lieutenant-Governor Spencer Phipps, instrumental in securing the town's district status.

•**SPRINGFIELD**, City; Seat of Hampden County; Pop. 152,319; Zip Code 011++; Elev. 69; Lat. 42-06.0'N, Long. 72-35.3'W; Settled in 1636; 5 miles N of Connecticut border in SW Massachusetts; pair.

•**SQUANTUM**, Uninc. Village, Suffolk County; Zip Code 031++; Elev. 31; E. Massachusetts; Suburb of Boston.

•**STERLING**, Town; Worcester County; Pop. 5,440; Zip Code 01564; Elev. 500; Settled 1720; 10 miles S of Fitchburg in central Massachusetts; was named for Lord Stirling.

•**STOCKBRIDGE**, Town; Berkshire County; Pop. 2,328; Zip Code 01262; Elev. 839; Settled 1734; located western Massachusetts on State 41 just miles from the N.Y. State line; was named for an English municipality.

•**STONEHAM**, Town; Suffolk County; Pop. 21,419; Zip Code 02180; Elev. 147; Lat. 42-29.0'N, Long. 71-06.0'W; Settled 1645; Inc. 1725; 10 miles N of Boston in NE Massachusetts.

•**STOUGHTON**, Town; Norfolk County; Pop. 26,710; Zip Code 02072; Elev. 239; Lat. 42-07.5'N, Long. 71-06.0'W; Settled 1713; Inc. 1743; 20 miles S of Boston in SE Massachusetts; was named for William Stoughton, (1694-1791), Lieutenant-Governor of Massachusetts.

•**STOW**, Town; Middlesex County; Pop. 5,144; Zip Code 01775; Elev. 330; Lat. 42-26.2'N, Long. 71-30.4'W; Settled 1650; 20 miles NW of Boston in NE Massachusetts.

•**STURBRIDGE**, Town; Worcestr County; Pop. 5,976; Zip Code 01566; Elev. 622; Settled 1729; Incorporated 1738; 20 miles SW of Worcester in central Massachusetts.

•**SUDBURY**, Town; Middlesex County; Pop. 14,027; Zip Code 01776; Elev. 165; Lat. 42-23.0'N, Long. 71-24.7'W; Settled 1638; 20 miles W of Boston in E Massachusetts on the Sudbury River.

•**SUNDERLAND**, Town; Franklin County; Pop. 2,929; Zip Code 01375; Elev. 142; Settled 1713; 10 miles SE of Greenfield in central Massachusetts on the Connecticut River.

•**SUTTON**, Town, Worcester County; Pop. 5,855; Zip Code 01527; Elev. 346; Settled 1716; 10 miles SE of Worcester in S Massachusetts.

•**SWAMPSCOTT**, Town; Essex County; Pop. 13,837; Zip Code 01907; Elev. 127; Lat. 42-28.0'N, Long. 70-55.4'W; Settled 1629; 10 miles NE of Boston in NE Massachusetts, on the Massachusetts Bay.

•**SWANSEA**, Town, Essex County; Pop. 15,424; Zip Code 02777; Elev. 120; Settled 1632; Incorporated 1668; 5 miles NW of Fall River in SE Massachusetts.

•**TAUNTON**, City; Briston County; Pop. 45,001; Zip Code 02780; Elev. 37; Lat. 41-53.9'N, Long. 71-05.9'W; Settled 1638; 15 miles N of Fall River in SE Massachusetts.

•**TEMPLETON**, Town; Worcester County; Pop. 6,070; Zip Code 01468; Elev. 964; Settled 1751; 15 miles W of Fitchburg in central Massachusetts.

•**TEWKSBURY**, Town; Middlesex County; Pop. 24,635; Zip Code 01876; Elev. 105; Lat. 42-35.7'N, Long. 71-14.0'W; Settled 1637; Incorporated 1734; 5 miles SE of Lowell in NE Massachusetts; is named after a town in England; formerly the site of an Indian village called Wamesitt.

•**TOPSFIELD**, Town; Essex County; Pop. 5,709; Zip Code 01983; Elev. 85; Lat. 42-38.2'N, Long. 70-57.1'W; Settled about 1635, 20 miles E of Boston in NE Massachusetts.

•**TRURO**, Town; Barnstable County; Pop. 1,486; Zip Code 02666; Elev. 12; Settled 1700; Incorporated on Cape Cod known as "the wrist of the bended arm of Massachusetts," was settled by the Pamet Proprietors, organized about 1689.

•**TYNGSBOROUGH**, Town; Middlesex County; Pop. 5,683; Zip Code 01879; Elev. 112; Lat. 42-40.6'N, Long. 71-25.5'W; Settled

1661; 10 miles NW of Lowell in NE Massachusetts; is a town on the banks of the Merrimack River, named for the Tyng family, whose coat of arms became its official seal.

•**UPTON**, Town; Worcester County; Pop. 3,886; Zip Code 01568; Elev. 240; Lat. 42-10.5'N, Long. 71-37.2'W; Settled 1728; Incorporated 1735; 15 miles SE of Worcester in central Massachusetts; was named for a village in Worcestershire, England.

•**UXBRIDGE**, Town; Worcester County; Pop. 8,374; Zip Code 01569; Elev. 259; Settled 1662; Incorporated 1727; 15 miles SE of Worcester in S Massachusetts; called "Wacantuck" by the Indians.

•**VINEYARD HAVEN**, Included with town of Tisbury, Dukes County; Zip Code 02568; Elev. 20; Lat. 41-27.2'N, Long. 70-36.4'W; Settled 1660; On Martha's Vineyard (N) in SE Massachusetts; is a summer resort.

•**WALES**, Town; Hampden County; Pop. 1,177; Elev. 890; Settled 1726; 20 miles SE of Springfield in SW Massachusetts; Originally incorporated as South Brimfield, the town was renamed for James Lawrence Wales in 1828, in acknowledgement of a $2,000 legacy.

•**WALPOLE**, Town; Norfolk County; Pop. 18,859; Zip Code 02081; Elev. 155; Lat. 42-08.7'N, Long. 71-15.0'W; Settled 1659; 20 miles SW of Boston in E Massachusetts; was named for Sir Robert Walpole, English statesman.

•**WALTHAM**, City; Middlesex County; Pop. 58,200; Zip Code 02154; Elev. 48; Lat. 42-22.6'N, Long. 71-14.2'W; Settled 1634; 10 miles W of Boston in E Massachusetts on the Charles River. In 1738, after much agitation and considerable disagreement, the West Precinct of Watertown was incorporated as the township of Waltham, a name which means Forest Home, *walt* signifying a forest or wood, and *ham* a dwelling or home.

•**WARE**, Town; Hampshire County; Pop. 8,953; Zip Code 01082; Elev. 488; Lat. 42-15.6'N, Long. 72-14.3'W; Settled 1717; 20 miles ENE of Springfield in W Massachusetts; was called Nenameseck "Fishing Weir" by the Indians, a name applied also to the river, where salmon were caught.

•**WAREHAM**, Town; Plymouth County; Pop. 18,457; Zip Code 02571; Elev. 8; Lat. 41-45.7'N, Long. 70-43.4'W; Settled 1678; Incorporated 1739; 15 miles ENE of New Bedford in SE Massachusetts.

•**WATERTOWN**, Town; Middlesex County; Pop. 34,384; Zip Code 02172; Lat. 42-21.9'N, Long 71-11.1'W; Settled 1630; 5 miles W of Boston in NE Massachusetts; the colonists named it Watertown because it was so well watered.

•**WAYLAND**, Town; Middlesex County; Pop. 12,170; Zip Code 01778; Elev. 140; Lat. 42-21.8'N, Long. 71-21.5'W; Settled 1638; Incorporated 1835; 15 miles W of Boston in NE Massachusetts; was named for Francis Wayland, clergyman and president of Brown University (1827-55).

•**WEBSTER**, Town; Worcester County; Pop. 14,480; Zip Code 01570; Elev. 458; Lat. 42-03.0'N, Long. 71-52.7'W; settled 1713; located in S central Massachusetts just minutes from the Conn.-Massachusetts state line; was named for Daniel Webster.

•**WELLEFLEET**, Town; Barnstable County; Pop. 2,2204; Zip Code 02667; Elev. 5; Lat. 41-56.4'N, Long. 70-02.1'W; Settled 1724; Incorporated 1763; Located SE Massachusetts.

•**WELLESLEY**, Town; Norfolk County; Pop. 27,209; Zip Code 021+; Elev. 140; Lat. 42-17.8'N, Long. 71-17.5'W; E Massachusetts. The name Wellesley is an adaptatioin of the family name of Samuel Welles.

•**WENDELL**, Town; Franklin County; Pop. 694; Zip Code 01379; Elev. 500; Settled 1754; 10 miles SE of Greenfield in NW Massachusetts; named in honor of Judge Oliver Wendell of Boston.

•**WENHAM**, Town; Essex County; Pop. 3,897; Zip Code 01984; Lat. 42-36.4'N, Long. 71-21.5'W; this town was formerly a part of Salem.

•**WEST BOYLSTON**, Town; Worcester County; Pop. 6,204; Zip Code 01583; Elev. 495; Settled 1642; 5 miles N of Worcester in central Massachusetts.

•**WEST BRIDGEWATER**, Town; Plymouth County; Pop. 6,359; Zip Code 02379; Elev. 92; Settled 1651; 5 miles S of Brockton in E Massachusetts.

•**WEST NEWBURY**, Town; Essex County; Pop. 2,861; ZipCode 01985; Elev. 180; Settled 1635; Incorporated 1819; 20 miles NE of Lowell in NE Massachusetts.

•**WEST SPRINGFIELD**, Town; Hampden County; Pop. 26,960; Zip Code 01089; Elev. 103; Settled 1660; on Connecticut River across from Springfield in SE Massachusetts.

•**WEST STOCKBRIDGE**, Town; Berkshire County; Pop. 1,280; Zip Code 01266; Elev. 744; Settled 1766; Incorporated 1775; NW Massachusetts.

•**WEST TISBURY**, Town; Dukes County; Pop. 1,010; Zip Code 02568; Elev. 10; Settled 1669; located on Martha's Vineyard Isle in SE Massachusetts; named for the English birthplace of Governor Thomas Mayhew, was first known as *Tackhum-Min-Eyi* or *Takemmy* (Indian, "The Place Where One Goes to Grind Corn".

•**WESTBOROUGH**, Town; Worcester County; Pop. 13,619; Zip Code 01581; Lat. 42-16.l'N, Long. 71-36.7'W; 10 miles N of Worcester in Central Massachusetts.

•**WESTFIELD**, City; Hampden County; Pop. 36,465; Zip Code 01085; Lat. 42-07-2'N, Long. 72-45.1'W; S Massachusetts. At the time of its incorporation, in 1669, it was the most western settlement in the colony of Massachusetts, and from that circumstance it derived its name.

•**WESTFORD**, Town; Middlesex County; Pop. 13,434; Zip Code 01886; 10 miles SW of Lowell in NE Massachusetts.

•**WESTMINSTER**, Town; Worcester County; Pop. 5,139; Zip Code 01473; Elev. 724; Settled 1737; Incorporated 1759; 5 miles SW of Fitchburg in N central Massachusetts.

•**WESTON**, Town; Middlesex County; Pop. 11,169; Zip Code 02193; Lat. 42-22.0'N, Long 71-18.2'W; 10 miles W of Boston in NE section of Massachusetts.

•**WESTPORT**, Town; Bristol County; Pop. 13,763; Zip Code 02790; 10 miles W of New Bedford in SE Massachusetts.

•**WESTWOOD**, Town; Norfolk County; Pop. 13,212; Zip Code 02090; Elev. 102; Lat. 42-12.9'N, Long. 71-13.6'W; Settled 1640; Incorporated 1897.

•**WEYMOUTH**, Town; Norfolk County; Pop. 55,601; Zip Code 021+; Elev. 42; Lat. 42-13.3'N, Long. 70-57.2'W; Settled 1630; Incorporated 1635; 10 miles SE of Boston in E Massachusetts.

•**WHATELY**, Town; Franklin County; Pop. 1,341; Zip Code 01093; Elev. 183; Settled 1672; 10 miles S of Greenfield in NW Massachusetts; is named by Governor Hutchinson for Thomas Whately of England.

•**WHITINSVILLE**, Included in Northbridge; Worcester County; Pop. Est. 5,300; Zip Code 01588; E Central Massachusetts.

•**WHITMAN**, Town; Plymouth County; Pop. 13,557; Zip Code 02382; Elev. 76; Lat. 42-02.8'N, Long. 70-56.1'W; Settled 1670; 5 miles E of Brockton in SE Massachusetts; known as "Little Comfort", or South Abington, Whitman was named for Augustus Whitman when it became a separate town.

•**WILBRAHAM**, Town; Hampden County; Pop. 12,053; Zip Code 01095; 10 miles E of Springfield in SW area of Massachusetts.

•**WILLIAMSBURG**, Town; Hampshire County; Pop. 2,237; Zip Code 01096; Elev. 500; settled 1735; located W central Massachusetts.

•**WILLIAMSTOWN**, Town, Berkshire County; Pop. 8,741; Zip Code 01267; Elev. 603; Lat. 42-42.7'N, Long. 73-12.0'W; Settled 1749; Incorporated 1765; 20 miles N of Pittsfield in W Massachusetts. Named for Colonel Ephraim Williams who was killed in the French and Indian War.

•**WILMINGTON**, Town; Middlesex County; Pop. 17,471; Zip Code 01887; Elev. 100; Lat. 42-32.9'N, Long. 71-10.4'W; Settled 1639; Incorporated 1730; 10 miles SE of Lowell in NE Massachusetts; was named in honor of Lord Wilmington, a member of the British Privy Council.

•**WINCHEDON**, Town; Worcester County; Pop. 7,019, Zip Code 01475; Elev. 992; Lat. 42-40.9'N, Long. 72-03.1'W; Settled 1753; 15 miles from Fitchburg; is known at the "Toy Town". First known as Ipswich Canada, it received its present name of an old English town at its incorporation.

•**WINCHESTER**, Town; Middlesex County; Pop. 20,701; Zip Code 01890; Lat. 42-27.0'N, Long. 71-08.0'W; 10 miles NW of Boston in NE section of the state.

•**WINDSOR**, Town; Berkshire County; Pop. 598; Zip Code 01270; Elev. 2030; Settled 1767; 10 miles NE of Pittsield in NW Massachusetts.

•**WINTHROP**, Town, Suffolk County; Pop. 19,294; Zip Code 02152; Lat. 42-22.5'N, Long. 70-59.0'W; 5 miles ENE of Boston in eastern part of the state.

•**WOBURN**, City; Middlesex County; Pop. 36,626; Zip Code 01801; Elev. 83; Lat. 42-28.9'N, Long. 71-09.0'W; Settled 1640; 10 miles NNW of Boston in NE Massachusetts.

•**WORCESTER**, City; Seat of Worcester County; Pop. 161,799; Zip Code 016++; Elev. 492; Lat. 42-16.3'N, Long. 71-47.7'W; Settled 1673; Inc. Town 1722; 35 miles W of Boston in central Massachusetts.

•**YARMOUTH**, Town, Barnstable County; Pop. 18,449; Zip Code 02675; Elev. 24; Settled 1639; 5 miles E of Barnstable in SE Massachusetts.

MICHIGAN

•ADDISON, Village; Lenawee County; Pop. 655 Zip Code 49220; Elev. 658; Lat. 41-59-11 N long. 084-20-50 W; Orignally called Nanetall, the name was changed to Addison after Banker Addison J. Comstock.

•ADRIAN, City; Lenawee County; Pop. 21,186; Zip Code 49221; Lat. 41-53-51 N long. 084-02-14 W; The wife of an early settler named it after the Roman Emperor Hadrian, but it was incorporated as Adrian.

•AHMEEK, Village; Keweenaw County; Pop. 210; Zip Code 49901; Lat. 47-17-56 N long. 088-23-47 W; Ahmeek is a Chippewa Indian word for beaver, so named for the once abundant animals.

•AKRON, Village; Tuscola County; Pop. 538; Zip Code 48701; Lat. 43-34--5 N long. 083-30-51 W; Incorporated in 1910 and named after Akron, Ohio.

•ALANSON, Village; Emmet County; Pop. 508; Zip Code 49706; Elev. 615; Lat. 45-26-39 N long. 084-47-12 W; The town was named for a railroad official, Alanson Cook, when the railroad came through the area in 1882.

•ALBION, City; Calhoun County; Pop. 11,059; Zip Code 49224; Lat. 42-14-35 N long. 084-45-11 W; Settled in 1835 and named after Albion, New York.

•ALGONAC, City; St. Clair County; Pop. 4,412; Zip Code 48001; Lat. 42-37-06 N long. 082-31-52 W; Established in the early 1800's and named after the Algonquin Indians.

•ALLEGAN, City; Allegan County Seat; Pop. 4,576; Zip Code 49010; Elev. 658; Lat. 42-31-45 N long. 085-51-19 W; Incorporated in 1838 and named after the Allegan Indians.

•ALLEN, Village; Hillsdale County; Pop. 266; Zip Code 49227; Lat. 41-57-25 N long. 084-46-04 W; Captain Moses Allen arrived in 1827. The town is named after him.

•ALLEN PARK, City; Wayne County; Pop. 34,196; Zip Code 48101; Lat. 42-15-27 N long. 083-12-40 W; Incorporated in 1927 and named after pioneer businessman Lewis Allen.

•ALMA, City; Gratiot County; Pop. 9,652; Zip Code 488+; Elev. 736; Lat. 43-22-44 N long. 084-39-35 W; Settled in 1853 and named after pioneer daughter, Alma Gargett.

•ALMONT, Village; Lapeer County; Pop. 1,857; Zip Code 48003; Lat. 42-55-14 N long. 083-02-42 W; Incorporated in 1855 and named in honor of Mexican General John N. Almonte.

•ALPENA, City; Alpena County Seat; Pop. 12,214; Zip Code 49707; Lat. 45-03-42 N long. 083-25-58 W; Settled in the 1830's and later given the Chippewa Indian word for partridge.

•ALPHA, Village; Iron County; Pop. 229; Zip Code 49902; Lat. 46-02-38 N long. 088-22-37 W; Alpha began as an iron mining settlement in the 1880's. It was given the first name of the Greek alphabet.

•ANN ARBOR, City; Washtenaw County Seat; Pop. 107,316; Zip Code 481+; Lat. 42-17-00 N long. 083-44-45 W. The first settler's wife was named Ann, and the area had abundant groves of trees, hence the name Ann Arbor.

•APPLEGATE, Village; Sanilac County; Pop. 257; Zip Code 48401; Lat. 43-21-19 N long. 082-38-14 W; Settled in 1856 and named in honor of Oregon Trail pioneer Jesse Applegate.

•ARMADA, Village; Macomb County; Pop. 1,392; Zip Code 48005; Lat. 42-50-39 N long. 082-53-04 W; Incorporated in 1867 and given this name by its early settlers.

•ASHLEY, Village; Gratiot County; Pop. 570; Zip Code 48806; Elev. 671; Lat. 43-11-12 N long. 084-28-28 W; Founded in 1884 and named in honor of railroad builder, John M. Ashley.

•ATHENS, Village; Calhoun County; Pop. 960; Zip Code 49011; Elev. 896; Lat. 42-05-19 N long. 085-14-05 W; The first settlers arrived in 1831 and named the town for their former home in Athens, New York.

•AU GRES, City; Arenac County; Pop. 768; Zip Code 48703; Elev. 589; Lat. 44-02-55 N long. 083-41-45 W; Named by early French explorers for the "gritty stone" in the area.

•AUBURN, City; Bay County; Pop. 1,921; Zip Code 48611; Lat. 43-36-12 N long. 084-04-11 W; Named Auburn in 1877 after the deserted village in English poet Oliver Goldsmith's work.

•AUGUSTA, Village; Kalamazoo County; Pop. 913; Zip Code 49012; Lat. 42-20-11 N long. 085-21-08 W; Settled in 1832 and named after Augusta, Maine.

•BAD AXE, City; Huron County Seat; Pop. 3,184; Zip Code 48413; Elev. 765; Lat. 43-48-07 N long. 083-00-03 W; An early surveyor found a used ax at his campsite here and named it Bad Ax on his map, the name stuck.

•BALDWIN, Village; Lake County Seat; Pop. 674; Zip Code 49304; Elev. 838; Lat. 43-54-04 N long. 085-51-06 W; The town's name honors Henry Baldwin, Governor of Michigan in 1872.

•BANCROFT, Village; Shiawassee County; Pop. 618; Zip Code 48414; Elev. 854; Lat. 42-52-43 N long. 084-03-50 W; Settled in 1877 and named after the Bancroft Mining Company.

•BANGOR, City; Van Buren County; Pop. 2,001; Zip Code 49013; Elev. 658; Lat. 42-18-45 N long. 086-06-47 W; Founded in 1837 and named after Bangor, Maine.

•BARAGA, Village; Baraga County; Pop. 1,055; Zip Code 499+; Elev. 614; Lat. 46-46-43 N long. 088-29-20 W; In 1843 the Rev. Frederic Baraga opened a mission for the Indians. The town is named in his honor.

•BARODA, Village; Berrien County; Pop. 627; Zip Code 49101; Lat. 41-57-27 N long 086-29-08 W; Incorporated in 1907 and named for a city in India.

•BARRYTON, Village; Mecosta County; Pop. 422; Zip Code 49305; Elev. 976; Lat. 43-45-09 N long. 085-08-49 W; Founded by Frank Barry in 1894 and named after him.

•BARTON HILLS, Village; Washtenaw County; Pop. 357; Lat. 42-19-19 N long. 083-46-08 W; Named after an early settler.

•BATTLE CREEK, City; Calhoun County; Pop. 35,724; Zip Code 4901+; Lat. 42-19-16 N long. 085-10-47 W; An early surveying party fought with Indians on this stream's banks, and gave it this descriptive name.

•BAY CITY, City; Bay County Seat; Pop. 41,593; Zip Code 4870+; Lat. 43-35-40 N long. 083-53-20 W; Settled in the 1830's and named for its position on the Saginaw Bay.

•BEAR LAKE, Village; Manistee County; Pop. 388; Zip Code 49614; Lat. 44-25-15 N long. 086-08-53 W; Founded in 1863 and named for the nearby Bear Lake.

•BEAVERTON, City; Gladwin County; Pop. 1,025; Zip Code 48612; Lat. 43-52-56 N long. 084-29-05 W; A town since 1875, it is named after Beaverton, Ontario.

•BELDING, City; Ionia County; Pop. 5,634; Zip Code 4880+; Lat. 43-05-52- N long. 085-13-44 W; Hiram Belding founded a silk goods business here in 1855. The town is named after him.

•BELLAIRE, Village; Antrim County Seat; Pop. 1,063; Zip Code 49615; Elev. 616; Lat. 44-58-49 N long. 085-12-40 W; Founded on the property of Ambrose Palmer known for its pure air, and so descriptively named.

•BELLEVILLE, City; Wayne County; Pop. 3,366; Zip Code 48111; Lat. 42-12-17 N long. 083-29-07 W; A French name meaning "beautiful town" given by early settlers.

•BELLEVUE, Village; Eaton County; Pop. 1,289; Zip Code 49021; Lat. 42-26-36 N long. 085-01-05 W; Descriptively named for its pleasant surroundings.

•BENTON HARBOR, City; Berrien County; Pop. 14,707; Zip Code 49022; Lat. 42-07-00 N long. 086-27-15 W; Founded in 1863 and named in honor of U. S. Senator Thomas Hart Benton.

•BENZONIA, Village; Benzie County; Pop. 466; Zip Code 49616; Lat. 44-37-17 N long. 086-05-57 W; An English corruption of the French "Bec Sae", or "sawbill duck."

•BERKLEY, City; Oakland County; Pop. 18,637; Lat. 42-30-11 N long. 083-11-01W; Incorporated in 1923 and named for a local school.

•BERRIEN SPRINGS, Village; Berrien County; Pop. 2,042; Zip Code 4910+; Lat. 41-56-47 N long. 086-20-20 W; Settled in the 1830's and named in honor of John Berrien, U. S. Attorney General during the Jackson administration.

•BESSEMER, City; Gogebic County Seat; Pop. 2,553; Zip Code 49911; Elev. 1432; Lat. 45-28-53 N long. 090-03-10 W; Established in 1884 as a mining town and named for Sir Henry Bessemer who invented the Bessemer smelting process.

•BEULAH, Village; Benzie County Seat; Pop. 454; Zip Code 49617; Lat. 44-37-55 N long. 086-05-27 W; Settled in the 1880's and named after Biblical Beulah.

•BEVERLY HILLS, Village; Oakland County; Pop. 11,598; Elev. 1395; Lat. 46-30-49 N long. 087-36-24 W; Incorporated in 1958 and named after the Beverly Hills housing subdivision.

•BIG RAPIDS, City; Mecosta County Seat; Pop. 14,361; Zip Code 49307; Lat. 43-41-53 N long. 085-29-01 W; Located on the biggest rapids of the Muskego River, and so descriptively named.

•BINGHAM FARMS, Village; Oakland County; Pop. 529; Elev. 716; Lat. 42-30-57 N long. 083-16-24 W; Incorporated in 1955 and named after Bingham farm.

•BIRCH RUN, Village; Saginaw County; Pop. 1,196; Zip Code 48415; Elev. 635; Lat. 43-15-03 N long. 083-47-39 W; Settled in 1852 and named after Birch Creek.

•BIRMINGHAM, City; Oakland County; Pop. 21,689; Zip Code 4800+; Lat. 42-32-48 N long. 083-12-41 W; Founded in 1819 and named after Birmingham, England.

•BLISSFIELD, Village; Lenawee County; Pop. 3,107; Zip Code 49228; Elev. 694; Lat. 41-49-57 N long. 083-51-45 W; The village is named after the first settler, Hervey Bliss, who came here in 1824.

•BLOOMFIELD HILLS, City; Oakland County; Pop. 3,985; Zip Code 48013; Lat. 42-35-01 N long. 083-14-44 W; Settled first in 1820 and named for its township.

•BLOOMINGDALE, Village; Van Buren County; Pop. 537; Zip Code 49026; Lat. 42-22-58 N long. 085-57-25 W; Incorporated in 1881 and named for its location in a "blooming" valley.

•BOYNE CITY, City; Charlevoix County; Pop. 3,348; Zip Code 49712; Lat. 45-13-00 N long. 085-00-50 W; The first settlers arrived in 1856 and built near the Boyne River. This river remembers another in Ireland.

•BOYNE FALLS, Village; Charlevoix County; Pop. 378; Zip Code 49713; Lat. 45-10-05 N long. 084-54-58 W; Established in 1874 and named for the nearby Boyne River.

•BRECKENRIDGE, Village; Gratiot County; Pop. 1,495; Zip Code 48615; Lat. 43-24-29 N long. 084-28-30 W; The town was settled in 1872 and named for an early mill owner.

•BREEDSVILLE, Village; Van Buren County; Pop. 244; Zip Code 49027; Lat. 42-20-47 N long. 08604-23 W; An early pioneer, Silas Breed, built the first sawmill. The village is named for him.

•BRIDGMAN, City; Berrien County; Pop. 2,235; Zip Code 49106; Lat. 41-56-35 N long. 086-33-25 W; Once called Charlotteville, it was later changed to Bridgman after a local lumber company owner.

•BRIGHTON, City; Livingston County; Pop. 4,268; Zip Code 48116; Lat. 42-31-46 N long. 083-46-49 W; Founded in 1832 by settlers from Brighton, New York.

•BRITTON, Village; Lenawee County; Pop. 693; Zip Code 49229; Lat. 41-59-12 N long. 083-49-52 W; Storekeeper John Britton paid the Wabash Railroad $500 to have them name the station (and town) after him.

•BRONSON, City; Branch County; Pop. 2,271; Zip Code 49028; Lat. 41-52-20 N long. 085-11-41 W; The first white settler, Jebez Bronson, came to the area in 1828. The town is named after him.

•BROOKLYN, Village; Jackson County; Pop. 1,110; Zip Code 49230; Elev. 992; Lat. 42-06-21 N long. 084-14-54 W; First settled in 1833 and named after Brooklyn, New York.

•BROWN CITY, City; Sanilac & Lapeer Counties; Pop. 1,163; Zip Code 4841+; Founded in 1879 by the Brown brothers and named for them.

•BUCHANAN, City; Berrien County; Pop. 5,142; Zip Code 49107; Lat. 41-49-38 N long. 086-21-40 W; White settlers came here in 1833. The town is named for President Franklin Buchanan.

•BUCKLEY, Village; Wexford County; Pop. 357; Zip Code 49620; Lat. 44-30-16 N long. 085-40-37 W; Founded in 1905 and named for the local Buckley and Douglas Lumber Company.

•BURLINGTON, Village; Calhoun County; Pop. 367; Zip Code 49029; Elev. 923; Lat. 42-06-24 N long. 085-04-47 W; A number of veterans of the War of 1812 who served on the gunboat Burlington settled here and named the town after the vessel.

•BURR OAK, Village; St. Joseph County; Pop. 853; Zip Code 49030; Elev. 883; Lat. 41-50-50 N long. 085-19-07 W; Settled in 1835 and descriptively named for the many Burr Oaks in the area.

•BURTON, City; Genesee County; Pop. 29,976; Lat. 43-00-28 N long. 084-17-05 W; The town is named after an early settler.

•BYRON, Village; Shiawasee County; Pop. 689; Zip Code 48418; Lat. 42-49-22 N long. 083-56-40 W; The village is named after the township.

•CADILLAC, City; Wexford County Seat; Pop. 10,199; Zip Code 49601; Elev. 1328; Lat. 44-15-07 N long 085-24-04 W; The city is named after French explorer Antoine De La Mothe Cadillac, the founder of Detroit.

•**CALDEONIA**, Village; Kent County; Pop. 722; Zip Code 49316; Lat. 42-47-21 N long. 085 31-00 W; Settled in 1838 and named after Caldeonia, N. Y.

•**CALUMET**, Village; Houghton County; Pop. 1,013; Zip Code 4991+; Elev. 1208; Lat. 47-14-48 N long. 088-27-14 W; Founded in the 1860's and given the name Calumet, the strong bowl of an Indian peace pipe.

•**CAMDEN**, Village; Hillsdale County; Pop. 420; Zip Code 49232; Lat. 41-45-08 N long. 084-45-28 W; The second postmaster, Easton Chester, named the town for Camden, New York.

•**CAPAC**, Village; St. Clair County; Pop. 1,377; Zip Code 48014; Lat. 43-00-45 N long. 082-55-41 W; Founded in 1857 and named for the 16th century Inca emperor, Huayna Capac.

•**CARLETON**, Village; Monroe County; Pop. 2,786; Zip Code 48117; Lat. 42-03-33 N long. 083-23-27 W; Laid out in 1872 and named in honor of Will Carleton, a popular Michigan poet.

•**CARO**, Village; Tuscola County Seat; Pop. 4,317; Zip Code 48723; Lat. 43-29-28 N long. 083-23-49 W; Settled in the 1850's and given a shortened version of the name Cairo.

•**CARSON CITY**, City; Montcalm County; Pop. 1,229; Zip Code 48811; Lat. 43-10-37 N long. 084-50-47 W; The city's name honors explorer Kit Carson.

•**CARSONVILLE**, Village; Sanilac County; Pop. 622; Zip Code 48419; Elev. 823; Lat. 43-25-37 N long. 082-40-17 W; Pioneer Arthur Carson built a store here in 1864. The village is named in his honor.

•**CASEVILLE**, Village; Huron County; Pop. 851; Zip Code 48725; Lat. 43-56-28 N long. 083-16-17 W; The first white settlers came in 1836. The village is named after prominent landowner Leonard Case.

•**CASNOVIA**, Village; Kent & Muskegon Counties; Pop. 348; Zip Code 49318; Elev. 881; Lat. 43-14-05 N long. 085-47-26 W; Founded in 1850, the name is Latin for our "new home."

•**CASPIAN**, City; Iron County; Pop. 1,038; Zip Code 49915; Elev. 1492; Lat. 46-03-51 N, long. 088-37-53 W. First platted in 1908 to provide more housing for the nearby Caspian, Baltic and Fogarty Mines. It moved to its present site in 1909.

•**CASS CITY**, Village; Tuscola County; Pop. 2,258; Zip Code 48726; Elev. 743; Lat. 43-36-03 N, long. 083-10-29 W. Located near the forks of the Cass River, the village was incorporated in 1863 and named for the river.

•**CASSOPOLIS**, Village; Cass County Seat; Pop. 1,933; Zip Code 49031; Elev. 902; Lat. 41-54-42 N, long. 086-00-36 W. Incorporated in 1863 and named Cassapolis for territorial governor Lewis Cass. The spelling was changed to Cassopolis in 1865 by the town's first newspaper.

•**CEDAR SPRINGS**, City; Kent County; Pop. 2,615; Zip Code 49319; Lat. 43-13-24 N, long. 085-33-05 W. First platted in 1859 and named for the numerous springs and dense growth of cedar in the area at that time.

•**CEMENT CITY**, Village; Jackson & Lenawee Counties; Pop. 539; Zip Code 49233; Lat. 42-04-12 N, long. 084-19-50 W. Originally named Woodstock in 1838, the village was renamed Cement City upon the arrival of a cement company in 1901.

•**CENTER LINE**, City; Macomb County; Pop. 9,293; Zip Code 48015; Lat. 42-29-06 N, long. 083-01-40 W. Three Indian trails ran north through the area. The town was named by the French for its location on the middle trail.

•**CENTRAL LAKE**, Village; Antrim county; Pop. 895; Zip Code 49622; Elev. 635; Lat. 45-04-12, long. 085-15-52. Named for its location on the shore of Central Lake.

•**CENTREVILLE**, Village; St. Joseph County Seat; Pop. 1,202; Zip Code 49032; Elev. 826; Lat. 41-55-24 N, long. 085-31-42. Incorporated in 1837 and named for its location in the center of the county.

•**CHARLEVOIX**, City; Charlevoix County Seat; Pop. 3,296; Zip Code 4971+; Lat. 45-19-05 N long. 085-15-30 W; The city began as a fisherman's colony. It is named after Jesuit missinary, Pierre F. X. Charlevoix.

•**CHARLOTTE**, City; Eaton County Seat; Pop. 8,251; Zip Code 48813; Elev. 917; Lat. 42-33-49 N long. 084-50-09 W; The city is named after the wife of early landowner, Edmond Bostwick.

•**CHATHAM**, Village; Alger County; Pop. 315; Zip Code 49816; Lat. 46-20-52 N long. 086-55-44 W; Founded in 1897 and named after Chatham, Ontario.

•**CHEBOYGAN**, City; Cheboygan County Seat; Pop. 5,106; Zip Code 49721; Lat. 45-38-49 N long. 084-28-28 W; Settled in 1846 and given an Indian name meaning "chippewa water."

•**CHELSEA**, Village; Washtenaw County; Pop. 3,816; Zip Code 48118; Lat. 42-19-05 N long. 084-01-14 W; The first white settler came in 1834. It is named after Chelsea, Massachusetts.

•**CHESANING**, Village; Saginaw County; Pop. 2,656; Zip Code 48616; Lat. 43-11-05 N long. 084-06-54 W; Settled in 1839 and given an Indian name meaning "big rock."

•**CLARE**, City; Clare & Isabella Counties; Pop. 3,300; Zip Code 48617; Elev. 841; Lat. 43-49-10 N long. 084-46-07 W; Established in 1940 and named after County Clare in Ireland.

•**CLARKSTON**, Village; Oakland County; Pop. 968; Zip Code 48016; Lat. 42-44-09- N long. 083-25-08 W; The Clark brothers platted the town in 1840, it is named in their honor.

•**CLARKSVILLE**, Village; Ionia County; Pop. 348; Zip Code 48815; Elev. 826; Lat. 42-50-32 N long. 085-14-33 W. Originally Skipperville, the first postmaster had it renamed Clarksville.

•**CLAWSON**, City; Oakland County; Pop. 15,103; Zip Code 48398; Elev. 667; Lat. 42-32-00 N long. 083-08-47 W; Grocer John Lawson applied for a post office in his name, but the authorities named it "Clawson" by mistake.

•**CLAYTON**, Village; Lenawee County; Pop. 396; Zip Code 49235; Elev. 891; Lat. 41-51-48 N long. 084-14-11 W; Settled in 1836 and named in honor of the Rev. Clayton, a Presbyterian minister.

•**CLIFFORD**, Village; Lapeer County; Pop. 406; Zip Code 48727; Lat. 43-18-53 N long. 083-10-45 W; Founded in 1862 and named after Clifford Lyman, the son of the town's founder.

•**CLIMAX**, Village; Kalamazoo County; Pop. 619; Zip Code 49034; Lat. 42-14-18 N long. 085-20-06 W; Settled in 1835 and originally called Climax Prairie, the name was shortened to Climax in 1874.

•**CLINTON**, Village; Lenawee County; Pop. 2,342; Zip Code 49236; Lat. 42-04-19 N long. 083-58-18 W; Established in 1831 and named in honor of De Witt Clinton.

•**CLIO**, City; Genesee County; Pop. 2,669; Zip Code 48420; Lat. 43-10-39 N long. 083-44-03 W; Originally Varna, the name was changed to Clio in 1866.

•**COLDWATER,** City; Branch County Seat; Pop. 9,461; Zip Code 49036; Elev. 969; Lat. 41-56-25 N long. 085-00-02 W; Founded in 1832 and named after the Coldwater River.

•**COLEMAN,** City; Midland County; Pop. 1,429; Zip Code 48618; Elev. 757; Lat. 43-45-24 N long. 084-35-09 W; Incorporated in 1887 and named after early landowner, Seymour Coleman.

•**COLOMA,** City; Berrien County; Pop. 1,833; Zip Code 4903+; Elev. 649; Lat. 42-11-10 N long. 086-18-30 W; Settled in 1834 as Dickerville, and named after Coloma, California.

•**COLON,** Village; St. Joseph County; Pop. 1,190; Zip Code 49040; Lat. 41-57-30 N long. 085-19-30 W; A nearby lake had the shape of a colon, so early settlers descriptively named the town after that feature.

•**COLUMBIAVILLE,** Village; Lapeer County; Pop. 953; Zip Code 48421; Elev. 780; Lat. 43-09-24 N, long. 083-24-38 W. A prominent early settler came from Columbia County, New York, and so named the new town.

•**CONCORD,** Village; Jackson County; Pop. 900; Zip Code 49237; Lat. 42-10-40 N long. 084-38-35 W; The first settlers came in 1832, and soon established a harmonious community. They gave the town the name of Concord to reflect this fact.

•**CONSTANTINE,** Village; St. Joseph County; Pop. 1,680; Zip Code 49042; Lat. 41-50-28 N long. 085-40-07 W; Originally Meek's Mill, the name was changed in 1835 to honor the first christian Roman Emperor, Constantine the Great.

•**COOPERSVILLE,** City; Ottawa County; Pop. 2,889; Zip Code 49404; Lat. 43-03-50 N long. 985-56-05 W; Early settler Benjamin Cooper donated land to the railroad and had the railroad depot, and the town named after him.

•**COPEMISH,** Village; Manistee County; Pop. 287; Zip Code 49625; Elev. 808; Lat. 44-28-54 N, long. 085-55-21 W. Founded in 1889 and given a descriptive Indian name meaning "big beech tree."

•**COPPER CITY,** Village; Houghton County; Pop. 244; Zip Code 49917; Elev. 877; Lat. 47-17-01 N, long. 088-23-13 W. Incorporated in 1917 and named after the copper mining region.

•**CORUNNA,** City; Shiawassee County Seat; Pop. 3,206; Zip Code 48817; Lat. 42-58-55 N, long. 084-07-04 W. Settled in 1836 and named after Corunna, Spain.

•**CROSWELL,** City; Sanilac County; Pop. 2,073; Zip Code 48422; Elev. 736; Lat. 43-16-32 N long. 082-37-16 W; Originally Davisville, the town was renamed in 1877 in honor of Charles Croswell, Governor of Michigan.

•**CRYSTAL FALLS,** City; Iron County Seat; Pop. 1,965; Zip Code 49920; Elev. 1517; Lat. 46-05-53 N long. 088-20-02 W; Descriptively named for the beautiful falls on the nearby Paint River.

•**CUSTER,** Village; Mason County; Pop. 341; Zip Code 49405; Elev. 698; Lat. 43-57-07 N long. 086-13-10 W; Founded in 1876 and named in honor of General George Custer.

•**DAGGETT,** Village; Menominee County; Pop. 274; Zip Code 49821; Lat. 45-27-49 N long. 087-36-23 W; Started in 1876 by Thomas Faulkner who gave the town his wife's maiden surname, Daggett.

•**DANSVILLE,** Village; Ingham County; Pop. 479; Zip Code 48819; Lat. 42-33-21 N, long. 084-18-12 W. Pioneer Daniel Crossman platted the village in 1857, it is named after him.

•**DAVISON,** City; Genesee County; Pop. 6,087; Zip Code 48423; Elev. 799; Lat. 43-02-05 N long. 083-31-05 W; The town is named in honor of early pioneer Norman Davidson.

•**DEARBORN,** City; Wayne County; Pop. 90,660; Zip Code 4812+; Lat. 42-19-20 N long. 083-10-35 W; First settled in 1795 and later named in honor of General Henry Dearborn, American Commander in the War of 1812.

•**DEARBORN HEIGHTS,** City; Wayne County; Pop. 67,706; Zip Code 48127; Lat. 42-20-13 N long. 083-16-24 W; Once part of Dearborn, it's name recalls General Henry Dearborn.

•**DECATUR,** Village; Van Buren County; Pop. 1,915; Zip Code 49045; Lat. 42-06-29 N long. 085-58-28 W; Settled in 1847 and named for American war hero Stephen Decatur.

•**DECKERVILLE,** Village; Sanilac County; Pop. 887; Zip Code 48427; Lat. 43-31-36 N long. 082-44-07 W; The village's name remembers prominent lumberman, Charles Decker.

•**DEERFIELD,** Village; Lenawee County; Pop. 957; Zip Code 49238; Elev. 673; Lat. 41-53-20 N long. 083-46-44 W; Settled in 1826 and descriptively named for the many deer in the area.

•**DE TOUR VILLAGE,** Village; Chippewa County; Pop. 466; Zip Code 49725; Elev. 613; Lat. 45-59-40 N, long. 083-54-10 W. Descriptively named as the point where the navigator turns for Mackinac Island and the Straits.

•**DETROIT,** City; Wayne County Seat; Pop. 1,203,339; Zip Code 482+; Lat. 42-19-53 N long. 083-02-45 W; Founded in 1701 by French explorer Antoine De La Mothe, and given the descriptive French name for "strait."

•**DE WITT,** City; Clinton County; Pop. 3,165; Zip Code 48820; Lat. 42-50-32, long. 084-34-09. Settled in the 1830's and named in honor of Dewitt Clinton.

•**DEXTER,** Village; Washtenaw County; Pop. 1,524; Zip Code 48130; Elev. 862; Lat. 42-20-18 N long. 083-53-19 W; Judge Samuel Dexter settled here in 1824. The town is named for him.

•**DIMONDALE,** Village; Eaton County; Pop. 1,008; Zip Code 48821; Isaac Dimond built a sawmill here in 1856. The town is named after him.

•**DOUGLAS,** Village; Allegan County; Pop. 948; Zip Code 49406; Lat. 42-38-36 N long. 086-12-02 W; Settled in 1851 and named either for the town of Douglas on the Isle of Man, or after American statesman Stephen Douglas.

•**DOWAGIAC,** City; Cass County; Pop. 6,307; Zip Code 49047; Elev. 772; Lat. 41-59-03 N long. 086-06-31 W; Platted in 1848 and given an English version of an Indian word meaning "foraging ground."

•**DRYDEN,** Village; Lapeer County; Pop. 650; Zip Code 48428; Elev. 919; Lat. 42-56-46 N, long. 083-07-26 W. Settled in 1840 and named in honor of English poet John Dryden.

•**DUNDEE,** Village; Monroe County; Pop. 2,575; Zip Code 48131; Lat. 41-57-26 N long. 083-39-35 W; The first white settler arrived in 1823 and named after Dundee, Scotland.

•**DURAND,** City; Shiawassee County; Pop. 4,238; Zip Code 48429; Elev. 796; Lat. 42-54-43 N long. 083-59-05 W; The city's name honors George Durand, U. S. Representative for the 6th district in 1875.

•**EAGLE,** Village; Clinton County; Pop. 155; Zip Code 48822; Lat. 42-48-28 N long. 084-47-19 W; Established in 1834 and named after the township.

•**EAST DETROIT,** City; Macomb County; Pop. 38,280; Zip Code 48021; Lat. 42-28-06 N long. 082-57-20 W; Detroit means "strait" in French.

•**EAST GRAND RAPIDS,** City; Kent County; Pop. 10,914; Elev. 756; Lat. 42-56-28 N long. 085-36-36 W; Incorporated in 1891 and named for its location in relation to Grand Rapids.

•**EAST JORDAN,** City; Charlevoix County; Pop. 2,185; Zip Code 49727; Lat. 45-09-29 N long. 085-07-27 W; Descriptively named for its location on the east side of the Jordan river.

•**EAST LAKE,** Village; Manistee County; Pop. 514; Elev. 660; Lat. 44-14-40 N, long. 086-17-46 W. The village is on the east shore of Manistee Lake and is descriptively named.

•**EAST LANSING,** City; Ingham County; Pop. 48,309; Zip Code 4882+; Lat. 42-44-13 N long. 084-29-02 W; Settled in 1849 and named for its location near Lansing.

•**EAST TOWAS,** City; Iosco County; Pop. 2,584; Zip Code 48730; Elev. 689; Lat. 44-16-46 N long. 083-29-25 W; Incorporated in 1895 and descriptively named for its location east of Tawas City.

•**EATON RAPIDS,** City; Eaton County; Pop. 4,510; Zip Code 48827; Elev. 871; Lat. 42-30-33 N long. 084-39-21 W; John Eaton was Secretary of War in the cabinet of Andrew Jackson. The town took his name and the descriptive reference to the nearby rapids on the Grand River.

•**EAU CLAIRE,** Village; Berrien County; Pop. 573; Zip Code 49111; Lat. 41-59-06 N, long. 086-17-59 W. A sparkling creek inspired early settlers to name the town Eau Claire, or "clear water."

•**ECORSE,** City; Wayne County; Pop. 14,447; Lat. 42-14-44 N long. 083-08-45 W; Early French settlers named the river: Riviere Aux Ecorse, or "Bark Creek."

•**EDMORE,** Village; Montcalm County; Pop. 1,176; Zip Code 48829; Elev. 965; Lat. 43-24-29 N long. 085-02-19 W; Founded by Edwin Moore in 1878 and given a contraction of his name.

•**EDWARDSBURG,** Village; Cass County; Pop. 1,135; Zip Code 4911+; Elev. 829; Lat. 41-47-44 N long. 086-04-51 W; Settled in 1828 and named by the town's first merchant, Thomas Edwards, for himself.

•**ELBERTA,** Village; Benzie County; Pop. 556; Zip Code 49628; Lat. 44-37-10 N, long. 086-13-35 W. Originally called Frankfort, the town's name was changed in 1911 to honor the locally grown Elberta peach.

•**ELK RAPIDS,** Village; Antrim County; Pop. 1,504; Zip Code 49629; Elev. 587; Lat. 44-53-44 N long. 085-24-59 W; Platted in 1852 and named by an early settler for a pair of Elk Horns found in a nearby stream.

•**ELKTON,** Village; Huron County; Pop. 953; Zip Code 48731; Elev. 647; Lat. 43-49-10 N long. 083-10-51 W; An early blacksmith killed a large elk nearby and named the town after this event.

•**ELLSWORTH,** Village; Antrim County; Pop. 436; Zip Code 49729; Elev. 621; Lat. 45-09-56 N, long. 085-14-46 W. The town's name honors Civil War hero Ephraim Ellsworth.

•**ELSIE,** Village; Clinton County; Pop. 1,022; Zip Code 4881+; Lat. 43-05-19 N long. 084-23-13 W; Founded in 1857 and given the name of the postmaster's baby daughter.

•**EMMETT,** Village; St. Clair County; Pop. 285; Zip Code 48022; Elev. 775; Lat. 42-59-26 N, long. 082-45-54 W. The town's name honors Irish patriot Robert Emmett.

•**EMPIRE,** Village; Leelanau County; Pop. 340; Zip Code 49630; Elev. 619; Lat. 44-48-40 N long. 086-03-36 W; The Schooner Empire became icebound here in 1863. The town was named after the vessel.

•**ESCANABA,** City; Delta County Seat; Pop. 14,359; Zip Code 49829; Elev. 598; Lat. 45-44-43 N long. 087-03-52 W; First called Sandy Point, it was later given a Choppewa Indian name meaning "flat rock."

•**ESSEXVILLE,** City; Bay County; Pop. 4,370; Zip Code 48732; Lat. 43-36-55 N long. 083-50-31 W; Settled in 1850 by Ransom Essex and named after him.

•**ESTRAL BEACH,** Village; Monroe County; Pop. 463; Lat. 41-59-03 N, long. 083-14-09. Incorporated in 1925. Estral is Spanish for "star."

•**EVART,** City; Osceola County; Pop. 1,931; Zip Code 49631; Lat. 43-54-02 N long. 085-15-29 W; Civil War veteran Perry Everts settled in the area. The town is named after him.

•**FAIRGROVE,** Village; Tuscola County; Pop. 691; Zip Code 48733; Lat. 43-31-25 N long. 083-32-36 W; Settled in 1852 and descriptively named for a beautiful grove of trees near the village.

•**FARMINGTON,** City; Oakland County; Pop. 11,035; Zip Code 48018; Lat. 42-27-52 N long. 083-22-35 W; The first settlers came from Farmington, New York. They named their new town after the old.

•**FARMINGTON HILLS,** City; Oakland County; Pop. 57,922; Named after Farmington, New York.

•**FARWELL,** Village; Clare County; Pop. 804 Zip Code 48622; Lat. 43-50-06 N, 084-52-01 W. Founded in 1870 and named in honor of railroad investor Samuel Farwell.

•**FENNVILLE,** City; Allegan County; Pop. 962; Zip Code 49408; Lat. 42-35-38 N long. 086-06-06 W; Pioneer Elam Fenn built a sawmill here in 1862. The town is named after him.

•**FENTON,** City; Genesee County; Pop. 8,098; Zip Code 48430; Lat. 42-47-52 N long. 083-42-18 W; Lawyer William Fenton platted the town in 1837. It is named after him.

•**FERNDALE,** City; Oakland County; Pop. 26,202; Elev. 649; Lat. 42-27-38 N long. 083-08-05 W; Founded in 1917 and descriptively named for the many ferns in the area.

•**FERRYSBURG,** City; Ottawa County; Pop. 2,441; Zip Code 49409; Lat. 43-05-04 N long. 086-13-13 W; Established in 1857 by the Ferry brothers and named in honor of their father.

•**FIFE LAKE,** Village; Grand Traverse County; Pop. 402; Zip Code 49633; Elev. 1038; Lat. 44-34-37 N, long. 085-21-02 W. Fife Lake is named after state highway commissioner William Fife.

•**FLAT ROCK,** City; Wayne County; Pop. 6,872; Zip Code 48134; Elev. 772; Lat. 45-49-33 N long. 087-11-00 W; Settled in 1821 and descriptively named for the smooth rock bed of the nearby Huron River.

•**FLINT,** City; Genesee County Seat; Pop. 159,576; Zip Code 4850+; Lat. 43-00-45 N long. 083-41-15 W; First settled in 1819 and descriptively named for the Flint River which runs through the town.

•**FLUSHING,** City; Genesee County; Pop. 8,643; Zip Code 48433; Lat. 43-03-47 N long. 083-51-04 W; Settled in the 1830's and named after its township.

•**FORESTVILLE,** Village; Sanilac County; Pop. 159; Zip Code 48434; Elev. 635; Lat. 43-39-43 N, long. 082-36-34 W. Heavily timbered when the pioneers arrived, it is descriptively named.

•**FOUNTAIN,** Village; Mason County; Pop. 195; Zip Code 49410; Lat. 44-02-48 N, long. 086-10-43 W. Established in 1882 and named after a local spring.

•**FOWLER,** Village; Clinton County; Pop. 1,029; Zip Code 48835; Elev. 743; Lat. 43-00-06 N long. 084-44-23 W; Originally called Dalles, the name was changed in 1867 after local landowner J. N. Fowler.

•**FOWLERVILLE,** Village; Livingston County; Pop. 2,292; Zip Code 48836; Lat. 42-39-38 N long. 084-04-23 W; Pioneer Ralph Fowler settled here in 1836. The town is named in his honor.

•**FRANKENMUTH,** City; Saginaw County; Pop. 3,746; Zip Code 48734; Lat. 43-19-54 N long. 083-44-17 W; German settles arrived in 1845. It's name combines Franconia, a district in Germany, and the German word "muth," or courage.

•**FRANKFORT,** City; Benzie County; Pop. 1,597; Zip Code 49635; Elev. 600; Lat. 44-38-01 N long. 086-14-04 W; Settled in 1850 and named after Frankfort, Germany.

•**FRANKLIN,** Village; Oakland County; Pop. 2,874; Elev. 833; Lat. 42-31-20 N long. 083-18-22 W; Pennsylvania settlers arrived in the 1820's and named the town after Benjamin Franklin.

•**FRASER,** City; Macomb County; Pop. 14,560; Zip Code 48026; Lat. 42-32-21 N, long. 082-56-58 W. Named for Alex Fraser, who founded the village in 1957.

•**FREEPORT,** Village; Barry County; Pop. 479; Zip Code 49325; Lat. 42-45-58 N, long. 085-18-48 W. Founded by the Roush brothers who named it after Freeport, Ohio, their former home.

•**FREE SOIL,** Village; Mason County; Pop. 212; Zip Code 49411; Elev. 677; Lat. 44-06-25 N, long. 086-13-00 W. Named for the Free Soil anti-slavery party.

•**FREMONT,** City; Newaygo County; Pop. 3,672; Zip Code 49412; Elev. 823; Lat. 43-28-03 N, long. 085-56-31 W. The town was originally named Weaversville. It was renamed Fremont in 1882 in honor of Civil War general John C. Fremont.

•**FRUITPORT,** Village; Muskegon County; Pop. 1,137; Zip Code 49415; Lat. 43-07-55 N, long. 086-09-17 W; Settled in 1868 and descriptively named as a lake port in a fruit growing region.

•**GAASTRA,** City; Iron County; Pop. 404; Zip Code 49927; Lat. 46-03-30 N, long. 088-36-21 W. Originally owned by Alfred Kidder, building contractor Douwe Gaastra platted the village in 1908. It is named after him.

•**GAGETOWN,** Village; Tuscola County; Pop. 428; Zip Code 48735; Lat. 43-39-26 N long. 083-14-42 W; The town is named after its first postmaster, James Gage.

•**GAINES,** Village; Genesee County; Pop. 440; Zip Code 48436; Lat. 42-52-21 N, long. 083-54-51 W. Settled in the 1830's and named in honor of General E. P. Gaines.

•**GALESBURG,** City; Kalamazoo County; Pop. 1,811; Zip Code 49053; Lat. 42-17-19 N long. 085-25-05 W; Pioneer George Gale founded the town in 1835. It is named after him.

•**GALIEN,** Village; Berrien County; Pop. 692; Zip Code 49113; Elev. 679; Lat. 41-47-53 N, long. 086-29-57 W. The town was settled in 1853 and named in honor of French explorer Reno De Galien.

•**GARDEN,** Village; Delta County; Pop. 296; Zip Code 49835; Elev. 618; Lat. 45-46-29 N, long. 086-33-02 W. Descriptively named by its early settlers for the fertile soil.

•**GARDEN CITY,** City; Wayne County; Pop. 35,667; Zip Code 48135; Elev. 636; Lat. 42-19-32 N long. 083-19-52 W; Founded in the depression and platted into lots large enough for vegetable gardens.

•**GAYLORD,** City; Otsego County Seat; Pop. 3,012; Zip Code 49735; Elev. 1349; Lat. 45-01-39 N long. 084-40-29 W; Originally called Barnes, it was renamed in 1874 for railroad lawyer A. S. Gaylord.

•**GIBRALTAR,** City; Wayne County; Pop. 4,446; Elev. 584; Lat. 42-05-42 N long. 083-11-23 W; Settled in 1811 and named after the Gibraltar and Flat Rock Company.

•**GLADSTONE,** City; Delta County; Pop. 4,536; Zip Code 49837; Elev. 601; Lat. 45-51-10 N long. 087-01-18 W; Founded in 1887 and named for famous British prime minister William E. Gladstone.

•**GLADWIN,** City; Gladwin County Seat; Pop. 2,476; Zip Code 48624; Elev. 786; Lat. 43-58-51 N long. 084-29-11 W; First called Cedar, but later named for British soldier, Major Henry Gladwin.

•**GOBLES,** City; Van Buren County; Pop. 811; Zip Code 49055; Elev. 815; Lat. 42-21-39 N long. 085-52-46 W; The Goble family were the first settlers in 1864. The town is named after them.

•**GOODRICH,** Village; Genesee County; Pop. 797; Zip Code 48438; Elev. 894; Lat. 42-55-01 N long. 083-30-23 W; Settled in 1835 by the Goodrich brothers and named in their honor.

•**GRAND BEACH,** Village; Berrien County; Pop. 227; Lat. 41-46-24 N, long. 086-47-51 W. Descriptively named for its location on the shores of Lake Michigan.

•**GRAND BLANC,** City; Genesee County; Pop. 6,862; Zip Code 4843+; Lat. 42-55-39 N long. 083-37-48 W; Originally Grumlaw in 1823, it was later named after a husky white trader the Indians called "grand blanc", or big white.

•**GRAND HAVEN,** City; Ottawa County Seat; Pop. 11,860; Zip Code 49417; Lat. 43-03-47 N long. 086-13-46 W; Settled in 1833 and named for its location on the Grand River.

•**GRAND LEDGE,** City; Eaton County; Pop. 6,929; Zip Code 48837; Lat. 42-45-12 N long. 084-44-47 W; On the Grand River, the name was suggested to early settlers by a great ledge of rocks nearby.

•**GRAND RAPIDS,** City; Kent County Seat; Pop. 181,602; Zip Code 4950+; Lat. 46-45-57 N long. 089-16-32 W; Descriptively named for its location near a rapids of the Grand River when settled in the 1820's.

•**GRANDVILLE,** City; Kent County; Pop. 12,417; Zip Code 49418; Elev. 604; Lat. 42-54-35 N long. 085-45-47 W; Grandville is named for its location on the Grand River.

•**GRANT,** City; Newaygo County; Pop. 683; Zip Code 49327; Elev. 835; Lat. 43-20-10 N, long. 085-48-39 W. The city is named in honor of General U. S. Grant.

•**GRASS LAKE,** Village; Jackson County; Pop. 970; Zip Code 49240; Elev. 996; Lat. 42-15-03 N long. 084-12-47 W; Settled in 1829 and named for a nearby grassy lake.

•**GRAYLING,** City; Crawford County Seat; Pop. 1,794; Zip Code 49739; Elev. 1137; Lat. 44-39-41 N long. 084-42-53 W; The city is named after the graying trout which were plentiful in the area in pioneer days.

•**GREENVILLE**, City; Montcalm County; Pop. 8,007; Zip Code 48838; Lat. 43-10-39 N long. 085-15-10 W; Founded by John Green in 1844 and named in his honor.

•**GROSSE POINTE**, City; Wayne County; Pop. 5,910; Lat. 42-23-10 N long. 082-54-43 W; The city is named for the point which projects into Lake St. Clair and forms the eastern boundary of the township.

•**GROSSE POINTE FARMS**, City; Wayne County; Pop. 10,556; Lat. 42-24-33 N long. 082-53-31 W; Once part of Grosse Pointe, the town became an independent city in 1893.

•**GROSSE POINTE PARK**, City; Wayne County; Pop. 13,657; Lat. 42-22-23 N long. 082-56-15 W; Incorporated in 1907, the town is named after nearby Grosse Pointe.

•**GROSSE POINTE SHORES**, Village; Macomb & Wayne Counties; Pop. 3,122; Elev. 586; Lat. 42-26-12 N, long. 082-52-37 W. Originally Claireview, it was incorporated as Grosse Point Shores in 1911.

•**GROSSE POINTE WOODS**, City; Wayne County; Pop. 18,895; Elev. 587; Lat. 42-26-37 N long. 082-54-25 W; Incorporated as Lochmoor in 1926, but renamed Grosse Pointe Woods in 1939.

•**HAMTRAMCK**, City; Wayne County; Pop. 21,223; Lat. 42-23-34 N long. 083-02-59W; The city is named after American Revolutionary War soldier, Colonel John F. Hamtramck.

•**HANCOCK**, City; Houghton County; Pop. 5,114; Zip Code 49930; Elev. 686; Lat. 47-07-37 N long 088-34-51 W; Incorporated in 1875 and named after Revolutionary War patriot, John Hancock.

•**HARBOR BEACH**, City; Huron County; Pop. 2,005; Zip Code 48441; Elev. 610; Lat. 43-50-41 N long. 082-39-05 W; Founded in 1837 as Sand Beach, the name was changed in 1889, to better describe the area.

•**HARBOR SPRINGS**, City; Emmet County; Pop. 1,561; Zip Code 4973+; Lat. 45-25- 54 N long. 084-59-31 W; Incorporated in 1881 and named for its natural harbor and abundant local springs.

•**HARPER WOODS**, City; Wayne County; Pop. 16,570; Lat. 42-25-59 N long. 082-55-27 W; Settled in the 1850's and renamed in 1949 in honor of prominent Detroit citizen Walter Harper and the heavily wooded area around the community.

•**HARRIETTA**, Village; Wexford County; Pop. 139; Zip Code 49638; Elev. 1112; Lat. 44-18-36 N, long. 085-41-52 W. Pioneer railroad builder named the town in 1889 by combining the names of his father, Harry, and his fiancee, Henriette.

•**HARRISON**, City; Clare County Seat; Pop. 1,701; Zip Code 48625; Elev. 1186; Lat. 44-01-09 N long. 084-47-58 W; Incorporated in 1885 and named in honor of President William Henry Harrison.

•**HARRISVILLE**, City; Alcona County; Pop. 556; Zip Code 48740; Lat. 44-39-23 N long. 083-17-41 W; The town is named in honor of early settlers Benjamin Harris, and his sons Levi and Henry.

•**HART**, City; Oceana County Seat; Pop. 1,890; Zip Code 49420; Lat. 43-41-54 N long. 086-21-50 W; Settled in 1856 and named for early pioneer Wellington Hart.

•**HARTFORD**, City; Van Buren County; Pop. 2,492; Zip Code 49057; Lat. 42-12-24 N long. 086-10-00 W; Originally Hartland, it was renamed to Hartford in 1837 due to a postal conflict with another town.

•**HASTINGS**, City; Barry County Seat; Pop. 6,403; Zip Code 49058; Elev. 797; Lat. 42-38-45 N long. 085-17-27 W; Settled in 1836 and named in honor of bank president, E. P. Hastings, who owned the townsite.

•**HAZEL PARK**, City; Oakland County; Pop. 20,919; Zip Code 48030; Lat. 42-27-45 N long. 083-06-15 W; Incorporated in 1942 and named after the many hazlenut bushes in the area.

•**HERSEY**, Village; Osceola County; Pop. 364; Zip Code 49639; Lat. 43-50-55 N long. 085-26-40 W; Trapper Nathan Hershey arrived here in 1843. The town is named after him.

•**HESPERIA**, Village; Newaygo & Oceana Counties; Pop. 876; Zip Code 49421; Lat. 43-343-08 N, long. 086-02-22 W. Incorporated in 1883 and named after the classical goddess of gardens.

•**HIGHLAND PARK**, City; Wayne County; Pop. 27,755; Lat. 42-23-45 N long. 085-25-11 W; Descriptively named for its location on a ridge.

•**HILLMAN**, Village; Montmorency County; Pop. 372; Zip Code 49746; Elev. 813; Lat. 45-03-33 N long. 083-54-04 W; Established in 1880 by John Hillman Stevens and named after him.

•**HILLSDALE**, City; Hillsdale County Seat; Pop. 7,434; Zip Code 49242; Lat. 41-55-12 N long. 084-37-50 W; Incorporated in 1847 and descriptively named for the local geography of hills and dales.

•**HOLLAND**, City; Allegan & Ottawa Counties; Pop. 26,281; Zip Code 49422; Lat. 42-27-15 N, long. 086-06-32 W. Dutch settlers arrived in 1847 and named the new town for their former home.

•**HOLLY**, Village; Oakland County; Pop. 4,885; Zip Code 48442; Elev. 937; Lat. 42-47-31 N long. 083-37-40 W; Settled in the 1840's and named after the holly bushes in the area.

•**HOMER**, Village; Calhoun County; Pop. 1,786; Zip Code 49245; Elev. 994; Lat. 42-08-45 N long. 084-48-32 W; Early settlers came from the Homer, New York area, and named their new home after their old one.

•**HONOR**, Village; Benzie County; Pop. 281; Zip Code 49640; Lat. 44-39-50 N, long. 086-01-05 W. Founded in 1895 and named for the baby daughter of a local business executive.

•**HOPKINS**, Village; Allegan County; Pop. 536; Zip Code 49328; Elev. 704; Lat. 42-37-25 N, long. 085-45-37 W. Named after Stephen Hopkins, a signer of the Declaration of Independence.

•**HOUGHTON**, City; Houghton County Seat; Pop. 7,504; Zip Code 4992+; Elev. 607; Lat. 47-07-19 N long. 088-34-08 W; Settled in 1852 and named after pioneer state geologist Douglass Houghton.

•**HOWARD CITY**, Village; Montcalm County; Pop. 1,099; Zip Code 49329; Lat. 43-23-44 N long. 085-28-04 W; Incorporated in 1873 and named after Detroit railroad attorney, William A. Howard.

•**HOWELL**, City; Livingston County Seat; Pop. 6,979; Zip Code 4884+; Elev. 922; Lat. 42-36-26 N long. 083-55-46 W; Settled in 1834 and named for a friend of one of the early pioneers, Thomas Howell.

•**HUBBARDSTON**, Village; Clinton & Ionia Counties; Pop. 421; Zip Code 48845; Lat. 43-05-32 N, long. 084-50-32 W. Although the area was settled in the 1850's, the village was incorporated in 1867 and named in honor of town founder, Thomas Hubbard.

•**HUDSON,** City; Lenawee County; Pop. 2,545; Zip Code 49247; Elev. 918; Lat. 41-51-18 N long. 084-21-14 W; The first settler arrived in 1833 and named the town in honor of Dr. Daniel Hudson of Geneva, New York.

•**HUDSONVILLE,** City; Ottawa County; Pop. 4,841; Zip Code 49426; Lat. 42-52-15 N long. 085-51-54 W; The city is named after its first postmaster, Homer Hudson.

•**HUNTINGTON WOODS,** City; Oakland County; Pop. 6,935; Lat. 42-28-50 N long. 083-10-01 W; Descriptively named for the small game hunting in the surrounding timber areas.

•**IMLAY CITY,** City; Lapeer County; Pop. 2,496; Zip Code 48444; Elev. 830; Lat. 43-01-29 N long. 083-04-40 W; Connecticut speculator William Imlay bought acreage in the area in 1836. The town was organized in 1850 and named after him.

•**INKSTER,** City; Wayne County; Pop. 35,205; Zip Code 48141; Elev. 628; Lat. 42-17-39 N long. 083-18-36 W; Settled in 1825 and named after early settler, Robert Inkster.

•**IONIA,** City; Ionia County Seat; Pop. 5,908; Zip Code 48846; Elev. 660; Lat. 42-59-14 N long. 085-04-16 W; Ionia was settled in the 1830's and named for the ancient Greek province.

•**IRON MOUNTAIN,** City; Dickinson County Seat; Pop. 8,355; Zip Code 49801; Elev. 1138; Lat. 45-49-13 N long. 088-03-57 W; The town is named for the nearby iron ore mine.

•**IRON RIVER,** City; Iron County; Pop. 2,425; Zip Code 49801; Elev. 1510; Lat. 46-05-34 N long. 088-38-32 W; Descriptively named for its location near the Nanaimo iron mine.

•**IRONWOOD,** City; Gogebic County; Pop. 7,696; Zip Code 49938; Elev. 1503; Lat. 46-27-17 N long. 090-10-15 W; Settled in 1885 and named after prominent mining organizer, James Wood.

•**ISHPEMING,** City; Marquette County; Pop. 7,538; Elev. 1411; Zip Code 49849; Settled in 1856 and given a Chippewa Indian name meaning "high place."

•**ITHACA,** City; Gratiot County Seat; Pop. 2,948; Zip Code 48847; Lat. 43-17-30 N long. 084-36-27 W; The city's early settlers came from New York state and named the town after Ithaca, New York.

•**JACKSON,** City; Jackson County Seat; Pop. 39,735; Zip Code 4920+; Lat. 42-14-45 N long. 084-24-05 W; Settled in 1827 and named after President Andrew Jackson.

•**JONESVILLE,** Village; Hillsdale County; Pop. 2,170; Zip Code 49250; Lat. 41-59-03 N long. 084-39-43 W; Pioneer Benaiah Jones came here in 1829. The town is named after him.

•**KALAMAZOO,** City; Kalamazoo County Seat; Pop. 79,802; Zip Code 4900+; Lat. 42-17-30 N long. 085-35-14 W; An English variation of the Indian word Kilalamazoo, or "reflecting river."

•**KALEVA,** Village; Manistee County; Pop. 445; Zip Code 49645; Lat. 44-22-24 N, long. 086-00-37 W. Settled by Finnish pioneers and named after Finland's national epic, the Kalevala.

•**KALKASKA,** Village; Kalkaska County Seat; Pop. 1,639; Zip Code 49646; Elev. 1035; Lat. 44-44-03 N long. 085-10-33 W; Established in 1873 and given a Chippewa Indian word whose meaning is unknown.

•**KEEGO HARBOR,** City; Oakland County; Pop. 3,099; Lat. 42-36-29 N long. 083-20-38 W; Developed in 1902 and named after the Keego fish.

•**KENT CITY,** Village; Kent County; Pop. 863; Zip Code 49330; Elev. 800; Lat. 43-13-12 N long. 085-45-04 W; Both the village and the county names honor noted New York jurist, James Kent.

•**KENTWOOD,** City; Kent County; Pop. 30,449; Elev. 689; Lat. 42-52-10 N long. 085-38-41 W; Named after New York jurist Jamews Kent.

•**KINDE,** Village; Huron County; Pop. 598; Zip Code 48445; Lat. 43-56-22 N long. 082-59-49 W; Incorporated in 1903 and named after storekeeper John Kinde.

•**KINGSFORD,** City; Dickinson County; Pop. 5,290; Lat. 45-47-42 N, long. 088-04-19 W. The city was planned by the Ford Motor Company and named for Ford executive Edward G. Kingsford.

•**KINGSLEY,** Village; Grand Traverse County; Pop. 664; Zip Code 49649; Elev. 878; Lat. 45-55-33 N, long. 087-15-47 W. First platted by Judson W. Kingsley on part of his homestead, the village was incorporated in 1890 and named for him.

•**KINGSTON,** Village; Tuscola County; Pop. 417; Zip Code 48741; Lat. 43-24-52 N, long. 083-11-09 W. The name honors the village's first settler, Alanson K. King.

•**LAINGSBURG,** City; Shiawassee County; Pop. 1,145; Zip Code 48848; Lat. 42-53-25 N, long. 084-21-05 W. Founded in 1836 by Dr. Peter Laing and named for him.

•**LAKE ANN,** Village; Benzie County; Pop. 235; Zip Code 49650; Lat. 44-43-26 N, long. 085-50-35 W. The first settler beside the lake named it Lake Ann, after his wife. The village took its name from the lake.

•**LAKE CITY,** City; Missaukee County Seat; Pop. 843; Zip Code 49651; Elev. 1260; Lat. 44-20-07 N, long. 085-12-54 W. Named for its location beside Missaukee Lake.

•**LAKE LINDEN,** Village; Houghton County; Pop. 1,181; Zip Code 49945; Lat. 47-11-39 N, long. 088-24-26 W. Descriptively named for its location near Torch Lake and for the linden trees that grow there.

•**LAKE ODESSA,** Village; Ionia County; Pop. 2,171; Zip Code 48849; Lat. 42-47-05 N, long. 085-08-18 W. Named after Odessa Township and its nearby lakes.

•**LAKE ORION,** Village; Oakland County; Pop. 2,913; Zip Code 48035; Lat. 42-47-04 N long. 083-14-23 W; Originally Canandiagua City, the name was changed in 1859 after the well-known constellation.

•**LAKEVIEW,** Village; Montcalm County; Pop. 1,153; Zip Code 48850; Lat. 41-50-00 N long. 086-41-34 W; Settled in 1858 and named descriptively for its location on the banks of Tamarack Lake.

•**L'ANSE,** Village; Baraga County Seat; Pop. 2,496; Zip Code 49946; Elev. 682; Lat. 46-45-24 N long. 088-27-10 W; A French Indian mission here in 1660 was named L'Anse. More than two centuries later the incorporating village kept the name.

•**LANSING,** City; Clinton, Eaton & Ingham Counties; Capital of Michigan; Pop. 130,414; Zip Code 489+; Lat. 42-43-57 N, long. 084-33-20 W. Settlers arrived in the 1830's and named the town after Revolutionary War hero, John Lansing.

•**LAPEER,** City; Lapeer County Seat; Pop. 6,224; Zip Code 48446; Lat. 43-03-05 N long. 083-19-08 W; Once a French trading village, its name is an anglicized version of the French La Pierre.

•**LATHRUP VILLAGE,** City; Oakland County; Pop. 4,641; Elev. 703; Lat. 42-29-47 N long. 083-13-22 W; Founded by real estate developer Louise Lathrup in 1926, the village is named in her honor.

MICHIGAN

•LAURIUM, Village; Houghton County; Pop. 2,676; Elev. 1246; Lat. 47-14-15 N long. 088-26-35 W; Laurium was the name of a silver mining district in ancient Greece, this Michigan village had a prominent copper mine and took the name of its ancient mining namesake.

•LAWRENCE, Village; Van Buren County; Pop. 903; Zip Code 49064; Lat. 42-13-09 N, long. 086-03-05 W. Founded in 1835 and named after the township.

•LAWTON, Village; Van Buren County; Pop. 1,556; Zip Code 49065; Lat. 42-10-02 N long. 085-50-49 W; Pioneer Nathan Lawton donated ten acres to the Michigan Central Railroad in 1849. The town is named in his honor.

•LENNON, Village; Shiawassee County; Pop. 483; Zip Code 48449; Named in honor of railroad builder Peter Lennon.

•LEONARD, Village; Oakland County; Pop. 423; Zip Code 48038; Elev. 1003; Lat. 42-51-55 N, long. 083-08-34 W. The village was founded by Leonard Rowland in 1882 and named after him.

•LE ROY, Village; Osceola County; Pop. 293; Zip Code 49655; Lat. 44-02-17 N, long. 085-27-14 W. Settled in 1872 and named after federal land agent Le Roy Carr.

•LESLIE, City; Ingham County; Pop. 2,116; Zip Code 49251; Elev. 935; Lat. 42-27-05 N long. 084-25-57 W; Originally called Meekersville, a later settler renamed the town for the Leslie family of New York.

•LEXINGTON, Village; Sanilac County; Pop. 766; Zip Code 48450; Elev. 623; Lat. 43-16-05 N long. 082-31-51 W; Founded in the 1840's and named after the Revolutionary War battle.

•LINCOLN, Village; Alcona County; Pop. 361; Zip Code 48742; Lat. 44-41-05 N, long. 083-24-44 W. Settled in 1885 and named in honor of President Abraham Lincoln.

•LINCOLN PARK, City; Wayne County; Pop. 45,087; Zip Code 48146; Elev. 587; Lat. 42-15-02 N long. 083-10-43 W; Laid out in 1906 and named for Abraham Lincoln.

•LINDEN, Village; Genesee County; Pop. 2,173; Zip Code 48451; Lat. 42-48-52 N long. 083-46-57 W; First settled in 1835 and named for the Linden trees in the area.

•LITCHFIELD, City; Hillsdale County; Pop. 1,364; Zip Code 49252; Lat. 42-02-38 N long. 084-45-27 W; The town was founded in 1834 and named after Litchfield, Connecticut.

•LIVONIA, City; Wayne County; Pop. 104,728; Zip Code 4815+; Elev. 638; Lat. 42-22-06 N long. 083-21-10 W; The first settlers in the region came from Livonia, New York and gave that name to the town.

•LOWELL, City; Kent County; Pop. 3,673; Zip Code 49331; Lat. 42-56-01 N long. 085-20-31 W; Incorporated in 1863 and named after Lowell, Massachusetts.

•LUDINGTON, City; Mason County; Pop. 8,917; Zip Code 49431; Elev. 584; Lat. 43-57-19 N long. 086-27-09 W; Settled in 1847 and named for timber investor James Ludington.

•LUNA PIER, City; Monroe County; Pop. 1,443; Lat. 41-48-25 N long. 083-26-33W; Established in 1929 and given the Latin name for moon with the descriptive pier.

•LUTHER, Village; Lake County; Pop. 414; Zip Code 49656; Lat. 44-02-25 N, long. 085-40-57 W. Originally called Wilson, it was later renamed for the lumber firm of Luther and Wilson.

•LYONS, Village; Ionia County; Pop. 708; Zip Code 48851; Lat. 42-58-55 N, long. 084-56-49 W. Settled in 1836 and named Lyons by Lucius Lyon.

•MACKINAC ISLAND, City; Mackinac County; Pop. 479; Zip Code 49757; Lat. 45-50-57 N long. 084-37-08 W; The French settled the island in 1780. The name is a shortened version of the Indian place name Michilimackinac.

•MACKINAW CITY, Village; Cheboygan & Emmet Counties; Pop. 820; Zip Code 49701; Lat. 45-47-02 N, long. 084-43-40 W. A fur trading post in 1673, the name is a shortened version of Fort Michilimackinac.

•MADISON HEIGHTS, City; Oakland County; Pop. 35,211; Lat. 42-29-09 N long. 083-06-19 W; Incorporated in 1955 and named after President James Madison.

•MANCELONA, Village; Antrim County; Pop. 1,433; Zip Code 49659; Lat. 44-54-08 N long. 085-03-39 W; Established in 1889 and named for the daughter of its first settlers.

•MANCHESTER, Village; Washtenaw County; Pop. 1,685; Zip Code 48158; Lat. 42-09-01 N long. 084-02-16 W; Settled in 1833 and named after Manchester Township in Ontario County, New York.

•MANISTEE, City; Manistee County Seat; Pop. 7,559; Zip Code 49660; Lat. 44-14-40 N long. 086-19-27 W; Founded in the 1840's and given an Indian name meaning "spirit of the woods."

•MANISTIQUE, City; Schoolcraft County Seat; Pop. 3,948; Zip Code 49854; Lat. 45-57-28 N long. 086-14-46 W; The city was founded in 1871 and given an Ojibawa Indian name meaning "vermillion river."

•MANTON, City; Wexford County; Pop. 1,190; Zip Code 49663; Lat. 44-24-39 N long. 085-23-56 W; Settled in 1874 by George Manton, who became the first postmaster and had the town named after him.

•MAPLE RAPIDS, Village; Clinton County; Pop. 683; Zip Code 48853; Lat. 43-06-17 N, long. 084-41-31 W. Descriptively named for its location near a rapids on the Maple River.

•MARCELLUS, Village; Cass County; Pop. 1,137; Zip Code 49067; Lat. 42-01-33 N long. 085-48-56 W; Platted in 1870 and named after the famous Roman general.

•MARINE CITY, City; St. Clair County; Pop. 4,423; Zip Code 48039; Elev. 588; Lat. 42-43-10 N long. 082-29-32 W; Originally Yankee Point, but later descriptively renamed for its location at the mouth of the Belle River.

•MARION, Village; Osceola County; Pop. 816; Zip Code 49665; Lat. 44-06-09 N, long. 085-08-49 W. Settled in the 1880's and named after the first postmaster's wife.

•MARLETTE, Village; Sanilac County; Pop. 1,762; Zip Code 48453; Lat. 43-19-37 N long. 083-04-49 W; Incorporated in 1881 and named for two early Irish settlers.

•MARQUETTE, City; Marquette County Seat; Pop. 23,338; Zip Code 49855; Elev. 628; Lat. 46-32-37 N long. 087-23-43 W; Established in 1850 and named in honor of French Jesuit missionary, Jacques Marquette.

•MARSHALL, City; Calhoun County Seat; Pop. 7,123; Zip Code 4906+; Elev. 916; Lat. 42-16-20 N long. 084-58-48 W; Settled in 1830 and named for U. S. Chief Justice John Marshall.

•**MARTIN,** Village; Allegan County; Pop. 447; Zip Code 49070; Elev. 832; Lat. 42-32-13 N, long. 085-38-30 W. The village was settled in 1836 and named after President Martin Van Buren.

•**MARYSVILLE,** City; St. Clair County; Pop. 7,335; Zip Code 48040; Lat. 42-54-45 N long. 082-29-13 W; Begun as a sawmill town in 1843, the name honors Mary Mills, the wife of a local lumber businessman.

•**MASON,** City; Ingham County Seat; Pop. 6,012; Zip Code 48854; Lat. 47-08-28 N long. 088-27-56 W; Founded in 1836 and named for Governor Steven T. Mason.

•**MATTAWAN,** Village; Van Buren County; Pop. 2,125; Zip Code 49071; Lat. 42-12-34 N long. 085-47-04 W; Railroad attorney Nathaniel Chesbrough platted the village in 1845 and named it after a town on the Hudson River in New York.

•**MAYBEE,** Village; Monroe County; Pop. 490; Lat. 42-00-14N, long. 083-30-56 W. Developed as a charcoal manufacturing site, it was named for sawmill owner Abram Maybee.

•**MCBAIN,** City; Missaukee County; Pop. 519; Zip Code 49657; Lat. 44-11-37 N, long. 085-12-48 W. Founded in 1887 by Gillis Mc-Bain and named for him.

•**MCBRIDE,** Village; Montcalm County; Pop. 252; Zip Code 4852; Elev. 964; Lat. 43-21-15 N, long. 085-02-34 W. Pioneer Alexander McBride built a sawmill here in 1874. The town is named after him.

•**MECOSTA,** Village; Mecosta County; Pop. 421; Zip Code 49332; Lat. 43-37-13 N long. 085-13-35 W; The first white settler arrived in 1851. The village is named after Mecosta County.

•**MELVIN,** Village; Sanilac County; Pop. 171; Zip Code 48454; Lat. 43-11-11 N, 082-51-42 W. The town began around a saloon and was named for an early citizen.

•**MELVINDALE,** City; Wayne County; Pop. 12,313; Lat. 42-16-57 N long. 083-10-31 W; Settled in 1870 and Oakwood Heights but later renamed to honor local philantropist Melvin Wilkinson.

•**MEMPHIS,** City; Macomb & St. Clair Counties; Pop. 1,171 Zip Code 48041; Lat. 42-53-47 N, long. 082-46-08 W. The city was founded in 1834 and named after the ancient Egyptian city of Memphis.

•**MENDON,** Village; St. Joseph County; Pop. 949; Zip Code 49072; Elev. 852; Lat. 42-00-23 N long. 085-27-00 W; The town's first settlers came from Mendon, Massachusetts, and named the new town for the old.

•**MENOMINEE,** City; Menominee County Seat; Pop. 10,088; Zip Code 49858; Lat. 45-06-28 N long. 087-36-51 W; Settled in 1836 and named after the Menominee Indians.

•**MERRILL,** Village; Saginaw County; Pop. 850; Zip Code 48637; Elev. 671; Lat. 43-24-35 N long. 084-19-44 W; The town was settl-ed in the 1870's and named in honor of railroadman N. W. Merrill.

•**MESICK,** Village; Wexford County; Pop. 374; Zip Code 49668; Lat. 44-24-19 N, long. 085-42-48 W. The village was platted in 1890 by Howard Mesick and named after him.

•**METAMORA,** Village; Lapeer County; Pop. 552; Zip Code 48455; Lat. 42-56-29 N long. 083-17-21 W; Settled in 1850 and given an Indian name meaning "hills."

•**MICHIANA,** Village; Berrien County; Pop. 329; Lat. 41-45-51 N long. 086-48-48 W; Descriptively named for its location which is partly in Indiana and partly in Michigan.

•**MIDDLEVILLE,** Village; Barry County; Pop. 1,800; Zip Code 49333; Elev. 726; Originally Thornapple, the name was later changed to Middleville because the town was near Middle Village.

•**MIDLAND,** City; Bay & Midland Counties; Midland County Seat; Pop. 37,250; Zip Code 48640; Elev. 629; Lat. 43-36-56 N, long. 084-14-50 W. Settled in 1836 and named for its locatin in the mid-dle of the state.

•**MILAN,** City; Washtenaw County; Pop. 3,263; Zip Code 48160; Once called Tolanville, it was renamed Milan in 1836 after the ci-ty in Italy.

•**MILFORD,** Village; Oakland County; Pop. 5,044; Zip Code 48042; Elev. 945; Platted in 1836 and descriptively named for the excellent water-mill resources of the nearby Huron River.

•**MILLERSBURG,** Village; Presque Isle County; Pop. 231; Zip Code 49759; Lat. 45-20-04 N, long. 084-03-39 W. Founded in 1897 and named in honor of town founder, C. R. Miller.

•**MILLINGTON,** Village; Tuscola County; Pop. 1,236; Zip Code 48746; Lat. 43-16-53 N long. 083-31-47 W; Incorporated in 1877 and descriptively named for the many mills along its creek.

•**MINERAL HILLS,** Village; Iron County; Pop. 257; Lat. 46-06-48 N, long. 088-38-52 W. Incorporated in 1918 and descriptively named for the rich iron bearing hills in the area.

•**MONROE,** City; Monroe County Seat; Pop. 23,527; Zip Code 4813+; Lat. 41-54-59 N long. 083-23-52 W; Originally a French settlement, it was later named in honor of President James Monroe.

•**MONTAGUE,** City; Muskegon County; Pop. 2,337; Zip Code 49437; Lat. 43-25-00 N long. 086-21-25 W; Founded in 1874 and named for pioneer William Montague Ferry.

•**MONTROSE,** Village; Genesee County; Pop. 1,715; Zip Code 48457; Lat. 43-10-36 N long. 083-53-34 W; Scottish pioneer John Farquharson named the town Montrose to impress his Scottish friends.

•**MORENCI,** City; Lenawee County; Pop. 2,127; Zip Code 49256; Lat. 41-43-10 N long. 084-13-05 W; Settled in 1835 and named for a local pioneer.

•**MORLEY,** Village; Mecosta County; Pop. 507; Zip Code 49336; Lat. 43-29-27 N, long. 085-26-38 W. Incorporated in 1870 and named for a local pioneer.

•**MORRICE,** Village; Shiawassee County; Pop. 733; Zip Code 48857; Lat. 42-50-19 N, long. 084-10-42 W. Incorporated in 1884 and named in honor of the Morrice brothers who settled here in the 1830's.

•**MOUNT CLEMENS,** City; Macomb County Seat; Pop. 18,810; Zip Code 48043; Elev. 614; Lat. 42-35-50 N, long. 082-52-41 W; Christian Clemens settled the site in 1818. The town is named after him.

•**MOUNT MORRIS,** City; Genessee County; Pop. 3,246; Zip Code 48458; Elev. 794; Lat. 43-07-07 N, long. 083-41-42 W. Nam-ed by early settlers for their former home, Mount Morris, New York.

•**MOUNT PLEASANT,** City; Isabella County Seat; Pop. 23,746; Zip Code 48858; Elev. 649; Lat. 42-27-26 N, long. 086-14-50 W. Chosen as the county seat in 1860, Mount Pleasant was first incorporated as a village in 1875, then as a city in 1889.

•**MUIR,** Village; Ionia County; Pop. 698; Zip Code 48860; Elev. 655; Lat. 42-59-45 N, long. 084-56-33 W. Named for railroad superintendent H.K. Muir, whose efforts helped bring the Muskegon and Western Railroad through the village.

•**MULLIKEN,** Village; Eaton County; Pop. 550; Zip Code 48861; Lat. 42-45-44 N, long. 084-53-47 W. Named for the contractor who built the railroad that runs through the village.

•**MUNISING,** City; Alger County Seat; Pop. 3,083; Zip Code 49862; Lat. 46-24-40 N, long. 086-38-52 W. The name comes from "minissing," an Indian word meaning "island in a lake," or "near the island."

•**MUSKEGON,** City; Muskegon County Seat; Pop. 40,823; Zip Code 494+; Elev. 625; Lat. 43-14-03 N, long. 086-14-54 W. The name is Indian for "river with marshes." It was originally occupied by Potawatomi Indians. Established as a trading post by Frenchman Baptiste Recollet in 1810. Incorporated in 1869.

•**MUSKEGON HEIGHTS,** City; Muskekgon County; Pop. 14,611; Zip Code 49444; Lat. 43-12-04 N, long. 086-14-20 W. After the lumbering era ended, the Muskegon Improvement Company subsidized new industries here. First incorporated as a village in 1891, then as a city in 1903.

•**NASHVILLE,** Village; Barry County; Pop. 1,620; Zip Code 49073; Lat. 42-36-10 N long. 085-05-35 W; Founded in 1865 and named after railroad engineer George Nash.

•**NEGAUNEE,** City; Marquette County; Pop. 5,187; Elev. 1375; Lat. 46-29-57 N long. 087-36-42 W; Settled in 1846 and given a Chippewa Indian name meaning "pioneer."

•**NEW BALTIMORE,** City; Macomb County; Pop. 5,445; Zip Code 48047; Lat. 42-40-52 N long. 082-44-13 W; The first settlers arrived in 1796. It was named New Baltimore in 1855 and incorporated in 1867.

•**NEW BUFFALO,** City; Berrien County; Pop. 2,832; Zip Code 49117; Lat. 41-47-38 N long. 086-44-38 W; Early settlers from New York named the new city after Buffalo, New York.

•**NEW ERA,** Village; Oceana County; Pop. 534; Zip Code 49446; Elev. 754; Lat. 43-33-33 N, long. 086-20-44 W. Founded in 1870 and descriptively named by its early settlers for their new beginnings.

•**NEW HAVEN,** Village; Macomb County; Pop. 1,878; Zip Code 48048; Lat. 42-43-46 N long. 082-48-05 W; Incorporated in 1869 and named after New Haven, Connecticut.

•**NEW LOTHROP,** Village; Shiawassee County; Pop. 646; Zip Code 48460; Lat. 43-07-00 N, long. 083-58-12 W. Settled in the 1830's and named after William Lothrop who gave bells to the Methodist Church.

•**NEWAYGO,** City; Newaygo County; Pop. 1,257; Zip Code 49337; Elev. 633; Lat. 43-25-11 N long. 085-48-00 W; Incorporated in 1867 and named for Chippewa Indian chief Naw-wa-goo.

•**NEWBERRY,** Village; Luce County Seat; Pop. 2,124; Zip Code 49868; Elev. 788; Lat. 46-21-18 N, long. 085-30-34 W; Originally Grant Corner, it was later renamed in honor of Detroit industrialist Truman Newberry.

•**NILES,** City; Berrien County; Pop. 13,087; Zip Code 4912+; Elev. 658; Lat. 41-49-47 N long. 086-15-15 W; Settled in 1829 and named in honor of Baltimore newspaper publisher, Hezekiah Niles.

•**NORTH ADAMS,** Village; Hillsdale County; Pop. 565; Zip Code 49262; Elev. 1196; Lat. 41-58-15 N, long. 084-31-33 W. The town began around a tavern in 1835. It is named for its location in Adams Township.

•**NORTH BRANCH,** Village; Lapeer County; Pop. 893; Zip Code 48461; Lat. 43-13-46 N long. 083-11-48 W; Founded in 1856 and descriptively named for its location on the north branch of the Flint River.

•**NORTH MUSKEGON,** City; Muskegon County; Pop. 4,020; Elev. 621; Lat. 43-15-22 N long. 086-16-03 W; An old lumber boom town, the city is named for its location north of Muskegon.

•**NORTHVILLE,** City; Oakland & Wayne Counties; Pop. 5,698; Zip Code 48167; Elev. 829; Lat. 42-25-52 N, long. 083-29-00 W. Settlers arrived here in 1825 and named the town for its location north of Plymouth Township.

•**NORTON SHORES,** City; Muskegon County; Pop. 22,018; Elev. 612; Lat. 43-10-08 N long. 086-15-50 W; Named after an early settler.

•**NORWAY,** City; Dickinson County; Pop. 2,915; Zip Code 49870; Norwegian miner Anton Odell settled here in 1877 and named it for his home country.

•**NOVI,** City; Oakland County; Pop. 22,528; Zip Code 48050; Elev. 909; Lat. 42-28-50 N long. 083-28-32 W; First settled in 1825 and given the Latin word for "now" by its pioneers.

•**OAK PARK,** City; Oakland County; Pop. 31,561; Lat. 42-21-30 N long. 085-15-25 W; Incorporated in 1927 and named after the Oak Park subdivision.

•**OAKLEY,** Village; Saginaw County; Pop. 412; Zip Code 48649; Lat. 43-08-23 N, long. 084-10-05 W. Settled in the 1840's and named for Judge Oakley of Dutchess County, New York, a relative of one of the founders.

•**OLIVET,** City; Eaton County; Pop. 1,589; Zip Code 49076; Lat. 42-26-29 N long. 084-55-27 W; The Rev. John Shipherd founded a colony here in 1844 and named it after Mount Olivet in the Bible.

•**OMER,** City; Arenac County; Pop. 408; Zip Code 48749; Lat. 44-02-51 N long. 083-51-16 W; Settled in the 1860's and called Homer until a postal conflict led to its shortening to Omer.

•**ONAWAY,** City; Presque Isle County; Pop. 1,080; Zip Code 49765; Lat. 45-21-27 N long. 084-13-26 W; Platted in 1886 and named after an Indian maiden.

•**ONEKAMA,** Village; Manistee County; Pop. 597; Zip Code 49675; Lat. 44-21-49 N long. 086-12-18 W; First settled in 1845 and given an Indian name which meant "portage."

•**ONSTED,** Village; Lenawee County; Pop. 667; Zip Code 49265; Elev. 989; Lat. 42-00-22 N long. 084-11-24 W; Founded by William Onsted in 1884 and named in honor of his father.

•**ONTONAGON,** Village; Ontonagon County Seat; Pop. 2,182; Zip Code 49953; Elev. 642; Lat. 46-52-16 N long. 089-18-50 W; Platted in 1854 and given a Chippewa Indian name meaning "bowl", and referring to the mouth of a nearby river.

•**ORCHARD LAKE VILLAGE,** City; Oakland County; Pop. 1,795; Elev. 961; Lat. 42-34-59 N long. 083-21-34 W; The Indians called the area "apple place" for its many wild apple trees. The community's founders followed this tack by namein it Orchard Lake Village.

•**ORTONVILLE,** Village; Oakland County; Pop. 1,190; Zip Code 48462; Elev. 941; Lat. 42-51-08 N long. 083-26-35 W; Pioneer Amos Orton built a sawmill here in 1848. The town is named after him.

•**OTSEGO,** City; Allegan County; Pop. 3,798; Zip Code 49078; Lat. 42-27-38 N long. 085-41-47 W; Pioneer Samuel Foster settled here in 1831. The town is named after Otsego County, New York.

•OTTER LAKE, Village; Genesee & Lapeer Counties; Pop. 456; Zip Code 48464; Lat. 43-12-48 N, long. 083-27-16 W. Named for the nearby lake which once held an abundant otter population.

•OVID, Village; Clinton County; Pop. 1,712; Zip Code 48866; Lat. 43-00-21 N long. 084-22-18 W; Settled in 1834 and named after Ovid, New York.

•OWENDALE, Village; Huron County; Pop. 308; Zip Code 48754; Elev. 643; Lat. 43-43-45 N long. 083-16-05 W; Pioneer John Owen ran a large sawmill in the settlement's early days. The town is named after him.

•OWOSSO, City; Shiawassee County; Pop. 16,457; Zip Code 48867; Lat. 42-59-52 N long. 084-10-36 W; The town's name remembers Chief Owasso who held the land prior to their displacement by white settlers.

•OXFORD, Village; Oakland County; Pop. 2,753; Zip Code 48051; Elev. 1057; Lat. 42-49-29 N long. 083-15-53 W; Founded in 1836 and named for the many oxen teams owned by the settlers.

•PARCHMENT, City; Kalamazoo County; Pop. 1,809; Lat. 42-19-41 Nlong. 085-34-11 W; The town was founded in 1909 when a paper mill was established.

•PARMA, Village; Jackson County; Pop. 875; Zip Code 49269; Elev. 992; Lat. 42-15-30 N long. 084-35-59 W; Settled in 1833 and named for Parma, New York.

•PAW PAW, Village; Van Buren County Seat; Pop. 3,218; Zip Code 49079; Lat. 42-13-04 N long. 085-53-28 W; The first settler arrived here in 1832. The town is named for the Paw Paw River and the Paw Paw fruit growing on its banks.

•PECK, Village; Sanilac County; Pop. 608; Zip Code 48466; Lat. 43-15-31 N long. 082-49-03 W; Incorporated in 1903 and named after an early settler.

•PELLSTON, Village; Emmet County; Pop. 565; Zip Code 49769; Elev. 702; Lat. 45-33-10 N, long. 084-47-02 W. Pioneer William Pells founded the village in 1876. It is named after him.

•PENTWATER, Village; Oceana County; Pop. 1,169; Zip Code 49449; Elev. 689; Lat. 43-46-54 N long. 086-25-59 W; Settled in the 1850's and named for nearby Pentwater Lake.

•PERRINTON, Village; Gratiot County; Pop. 448; Zip Code 48871; Lat. 43-10-58 N, long. 084-40-45 W. Founded in 1886 and named in honor of a St. John's lawyer with large land interests.

•PERRY, City; Shiawassee County; Pop. 2,048; Zip Code 48872; Elev. 889; Lat. 42-49-35 N long. 084-13-10 W; The town was established in 1850 and named for its location in Perry Township.

•PETERSBURG, City; Monroe County; Pop. 1,218; Zip Code 49270; Lat. 41-54-04 N long. 083-42-54 W; Incorporated in 1869 and named for pioneer Richard Peters.

•PETOSKEY, City; Emmet County Seat; Pop. 6,090; Zip Code 49770; Elev. 786; Lat. 45-22-24 N long. 084-58-19 W; Founded as an Indian mission in 1852 and given a corrupt version of the Chippewa Indian name meaning "rising sun."

•PEWAMO, Village; Ionia County; Pop.488; Zip Code 48873; Lat. 43-00-04 N, long. 084-50-49 W. Begun in 1859 and named for an early Indian chief.

•PIERSON, Village; Montcalm County; Pop. 216; Zip Code 49339; Elev. 900; Lat. 43-19-11 N long. 085-29-52 W; The village was founded by pioneer David Pierson in 1856 and named after him.

•PIGEON, Village; Huron County; Pop. 1,250; Zip Code 48755; Lat. 43-49-48 N long. 083-16-12 W; Incorporated in 1902 and named for the nearby Pigeon River.

•PINCKNEY, Village; Livingston County; Pop. 1,389; Zip Code 48169; Lat. 42-27-24 N long. 083-56-47 W; Town founder William Kirkland began the village in 1836 and named it after his brother Charles Pinckney Kirkland.

•PINCONNING, City; Bay County; Pop. 1,428; Zip Code 48650; Lat. 43-51-13 N long. 083-57-54 W; The town is named after the nearby Pinconning River.

•PLAINWELL, City; Allegan County; Pop. 3,763; Zip Code 49080; Lat. 42-26-24 N long. 085-38-56 W; Settled in 1833 and named after the township.

•PLEASANT RIDGE, City; Oakland County; Pop. 3,224; Lat. 42-28-16 N long. 083-08-32 W; Founded in 1913 and named after a local road.

•PLYMOUTH, City; Wayne County; Pop. 9,984; Zip Code 48170; Lat. 46-27-53 N long. 089-58-46 W; The first settler built his log cabin here in 1825. The name remembers the Pilgrim colony of Plymouth, Massachusetts.

•PONTIAC, City; Oakland County Seat; Pop. 76,270; Zip Code 48033; Elev. 943; Lat. 42-38-20 N long. 083-17-28 W; Incorporated in 1861 and named for an Ottawa Indian chief.

•PORT AUSTIN, Village; Huron County; Pop. 839; Zip Code 48467; Lat. 44-02-46 N, long. 082-59-39 W. Originally Byrd's Creek, it was later renamed for lumber mill owner, P. C. Austin.

•PORT HOPE, Village; Huron County; Pop. 369; Zip Code 48468; Lat. 43-56-27 N, long. 082-42-46 W. Two early residents managed to land here while adrift in a small skiff and they named the place Point Hope.

•PORT HURON, City; St. Clair County Seat; Pop. 33,901; Zip Code 4806+; Lat. 42-58-15 N long. 082-25-30 W; Founded in 1828 and named after the Huron Indians.

•PORT SANILAC, Village; Sanilac County; Pop. 598; Zip Code 48469; Lat. 43-25-51 N long. 082-32-33 W; Settled in the 1840's and named after the county.

•PORTAGE, City; Kalamazoo County; Pop. 38,215; Zip Code 49081; Lat. 42-12-04 N long. 085-34-48 W; The first white settler arrived in 1830. The town is named after its chief stream, Portage Creek.

•PORTLAND, City; Ionia County; Pop. 3,947; Zip Code 48875; Lat. 42-52-09 N long. 084-54-11 W; Incorporated in 1869 and named for its excellent boat loading facilities.

•POSEN, Village; Presque Isle County; Pop. 270; Zip Code 49776; Lat. 42-52-09 N, long. 084-54-11 W. Polish settles who arrived in 1870 named the town after the province of Poznan in Poland.

•POTTERVILLE, City; Eaton County; Pop. 1,504; Zip Code 48876; Lat. 42-37-45 N long. 084-44-20 W; Settled in 1844 by Linus Potter and named for him.

•POWERS, Village; Menominee County; Pop. 498; Zip Code 49874; Elev. 869; Lat. 45-41-24 N long. 087-31-33 W; The town is named after pioneer settler L. K. Powers.

•PRESCOTT, Village; Ogemaw County; Pop. 332; Zip Code 48756; Lat. 44-11-31 N long. 083-55-51 W; Pioner railroadman C.H. Prescott established a railroad here in 1880. The town is named after him.

•QUINCY, Village; Branch County; Pop. 1,567; Zip Code 49082; Elev. 1017; Lat. 41-56-39 N long. 084-53-02 W; Established in 1833 and named after Quincy, Massachusetts.

•RAVENNA, Village; Muskegon County; Pop. 951; Zip Code 49451; Founded in 1844 and named after Ravenna, Ohio.

•READING, City; Hillsdale County; Pop. 1,200; Zip Code 49274; Lat. 41-50-22 N long. 084-44-53 W; White settlement began in the 1840's. The town is named after Reading, Pennsylvania.

•REED CITY, City; Osceola County Seat; Pop. 2,214; Zip Code 49677; Elev. 1039; Lat. 43-52-30 N long. 085-30-36 W; The town is named after founder James M. Reed.

•REESE, Village; Tuscola County; Pop. 1,652; Zip Code 48757; Elev. 628; Lat. 43-27-02 N long. 083-41-47 W; The town's name honors railroad superintendant G. W. Reese.

•RICHLAND, Village; Kalamazoo County; Pop. 487; Zip Code 49083; Lat. 42-22-23 N long. 085-27-18 W; Organized in 1832 and named for its township.

•RICHMOND, City; Macomb County; Pop. 3,513; Zip Code 48062; Lat. 42-48-33 N long. 082-45-21 W; Founded in the 1830's and named for Richmond, New York.

•RIVER ROUGE, City; Wayne County; Pop. 12,839; Elev. 584; Lat. 42-16-24 N long. 083-08-04 W; Originally a French settlement, it was named for the River Rouge, or Red River.

•RIVERVIEW, City; Wayne County; Pop. 14,534; Lat. 43-26-53 N long. 085-39-09W; Founded in 1906 and named for its locaton on the Detroit River.

•ROCHESTER, City; Oakland County; Pop. 7,202; Zip Code 4806+; Elev. 749; Lat. 42-40-50 N long. 083-08-02 W; Settled in 1817 and named for Rochester, New York.

•ROCKFORD, City; Kent County; Pop. 3,037; Zip Code 4934+; Elev. 693; Lat. 43-07-12 N long. 085-33-36 W; Originally Laphamville, the town was renamed Rockford in 1865.

•ROCKWOOD, City; Wayne County; Pop. 3,377; Zip Code 48173; Lat. 42-04-15 N long. 083-14-48 W; The first settlers arrived in 1834. The town was named Rockwood in 1872.

•ROGERS CITY, City; Presque Isle County Seat; Pop. 3,922; Zip Code 49779; Lat. 45-25-17 N ong. 083-49-06 W; The town's name remembers pioneer lumberman William E. Rogers.

•ROMEO, Village; Macomb County; Pop. 3,536; Zip Code 48065; Lat. 42-48-10 N long. 083-00-47 W; Pioneer Ashael Bailey settled here in 1822. The town was named after Shakespeare's great character in 1827.

•ROMULUS, City; Wayne County; Pop. 24,853; Zip Code 48174; Lat. 42-13-20 N long. 083-23-48 W; The first pioneers arrived in 1827, and named the town after Romulus, New York.

•ROOSEVELT PARK, City; Muskegon County; Pop. 4,019; Incorporated in 1946 and named in honor of President Franklin Roosevelt.

•ROSCOMMON, Village; Roscommon County Seat; Pop. 834; Zip Code 48653; Elev. 1130; Lat. 44-29-54 N, long. 084-35-31 W. Settled in 1845 and named after a county in Ireland.

•ROSEBUSH, Village; Isabella County; Pop. 336; Zip Code 48878; Lat. 43-41-57 N, 084-46-04 W. Pioneer James Bush platted the town and named it after his wife Rose.

•ROSE CITY, City; Ogemaw County; Pop. 661; Zip Code 48654; Lat. 44-25-17 N long. 084-07-00 W; Incorporated in 1892 and named for pioneer storekeeper Allan S. Rose.

•ROSEVILLE, City; Macomb County; Pop. 54,376; Zip Code 4806+; Lat. 42-29-50 N long. 082-56-14 W; The city is named in honor of its first postmaster William C. Rose.

•ROYAL OAK, City; Oakland County; Pop. 70,795; Zip Code 4806+; Lat. 42-29-22 N long. 083-08-41 W; The place was named by Governor Lewis Cass for a large oak tree in the area which reminded him of the famous Royal Oak of Scotland.

•SAGINAW, City; Saginaw County Seat; Pop. 77,384; Zip Code 4860+; Lat. 43-25-10 N long. 083-57-03 W; First settled in 1816 and named Saginaw, or place of the Sauk Indians.

•ST. CHARLES, Village; Saginaw County; Pop. 2,257; Zip Code 48655; Elev. 593; Lat. 43-17-49 N long. 084-08-26 W; Rough and ready lumberjacks dubbed the town's first storekeeper, Charles Kimberly, St. Charles for his fastidious ways.

•ST. CLAIR, City; St. Clair County; Pop. 4,780; Zip Code 48079; Lat. 42-49-15 N, 082-29-10 W. The city takes its name from nearby St. Clair Lake.

•ST. CLAIR SHORES, City; Macomb County; Pop. 76,210; Zip Code 4808+; Elev. 585; Lat. 42-29-49 N, long. 082-53-20 W. Descriptively named for its location on the shore of St. Clair Lake.

•ST. IGNACE, City; Mackinac County Seat; Pop. 2,632; Zip Code 49781; Lat. 45-52-07 N, long. 084-43-40 W. French Jesuits founded the St. Ignace mission here in 1671.

•ST. JOHNS, City; Clinton County Seat; Pop. 7,299; Zip Code 48879; Elev. 794; The town was laid out by state official John Swegles. A Baptist minister added the word Saint to his name to christen the town.

•ST. JOSEPH, City; Berrien County Seat; Pop. 9,614; Zip Code 49085. The city is descriptively named for its location on the St. Joseph River.

•ST. LOUIS, City; Gratiot County; Pop. 4,094; Zip Code 48880. Platted in 1855 and named for St. Louis, Missouri.

•SALINE, City; Washtenaw County; Pop. 6,482; Zip Code 48176; Lat. 42-10-00 N long. 083-46-54 W; Platted in 1832 and named for the Saline River.

•SAND LAKE, Village; Kent County; Pop. 388; Zip Code 49343; Lat. 44-19-09 N, long. 083-41-05 W. Pioneer Fred Whitmore named the village for its location by a Shoal lake.

•SANDUSKY, City; Sanilac County Seat; Pop. 2,213; Zip Code 48471; Elev. 774; Lat. 43-25-13 N long. 082-49-47 W; Founded in 1870 by Wildman Mills and named after Sandusky, Ohio.

•SANFORD, Village; Midland County; Pop. 875; Zip Code 48657; Lat. 43-40-22 N long. 084-22-50 W; Pioneer Charles Sanford settled here in 1864. The town is named after him.

•SARANAC, Village; Ionia County; Pop. 1,420; Zip Code 48881; Elev. 644; Lat. 42-55-46 N long. 085-12-47 W; Incorporated in 1869 and named after a New York resort town.

•SAUGATUCK, Village; Allegan County; Pop. 1,047; Zip Code 49453; Lat. 42-39-18 N long. 086-12-07 W; Settled in 1830 and named the Pottawattomi Indian word for river's mouth.

•SAULT STE. MARIE, City; Chippewa County; Pop. 14,423; Zip Code 4978+; Elev. 613; Lat. 46-29-43 N long. 084-20-43 W; The first European settlement in Michigan, it was named for its location on the height's overlooking the rapids (Sault), and after the Virgin Mary.

•**SCHOOLCRAFT,** Village; Kalamazoo County; Pop. 1,353; Zip Code 49087; Lat. 42-06-51 N long. 085-38-16 W; Platted in 1831 and named in honor of Michigan's Indian agent, Henry Rowe Schoolcraft.

•**SCOTTVILLE,** City; Mason County; Pop. 1,241; Zip Code 49454; Elev. 678; Lat. 43-57-17 N long. 086-16-48 W; The town was founded in the 1870's and named after one of its founders, a Mr. Scott.

•**SEBEWAING,** Village; Huron County; Pop. 2,052; Zip Code 48759; Elev. 585; Lat. 43-43-56 N long. 083-27-04 W; Settled in 1845 and given an Indian name meaning "crooked creek."

•**SHELBY,** Village; Oceana County; Pop. 1,624; Zip Code 49455; Lat. 43-36-31 N long. 086-21-50 W; The town's name honors General Isaac Shelby who led the attack that captured Detroit from the British in the War of 1812.

•**SHEPHERD,** Village; Isabella County; Pop. 1,489; Zip Code 48883; Lat. 43-31-28 N long. 084-41-41 W; The town was founded by lumberman Issac Shepherd in the 1850's.

•**SHERIDAN,** Village; Montcalm County; Pop. 664; Zip Code 48884; Lat. 43-12-44 N, long. 085-04-25 W. First settled in 1851 and later named in honor of General Phillip Sheridan.

•**SHERWOOD,** Village; Branch County; Pop. 353; Zip Code 49089; Elev. 883; Lat. 42-00-05 N, long. 085-14-19 W. The town's first settler came from Sherwood Forest, England.

•**SHOREHAM,** Village; Berrien County; Pop. 740; Elev. 605; Lat. 42-03-54 N long. 086-29-42 W; Incorporated in 1930 and descriptively named for its location along Lake Michigan.

•**SOUTH HAVEN,** City; Van Buren County; Pop. 5,939; Elev. 618; Lat. 42-24-11 N long. 086-16-25 W; The first settlers arrived in 1831. The town is descriptively named for its location south of Grand Haven.

•**SOUTH LYON,** City; Oakland County; Pop. 5,238; Zip Code 48178; Elev. 919; Lat. 42-27-38 N long. 083-39-06 W; Descriptively named for its location in the township of Lyons.

•**SOUTH RANGE,** Village; Houghton County; Pop. 861; Zip Code 49963; Elev. 1140; Lat. 47-04-12 N, long. 088-38-35 W. Founded by a mining company in 1902 and named for its location at the south end of the county.

•**SOUTH ROCKWOOD,** Village; Monroe County; Pop. 1,354; Zip Code 48179; Lat. 42-03-50 N Long. 083-15-40 W; The town was founded in 1863 and named after Rockwood, Ontario.

•**SOUTHFIELD,** City; Oakland County; Pop. 75,500; Zip Code 4807+; Elev. 684; Lat. 42-28-24 N long. 083-13-19 W; Settled in 1823 and named for its location in Southfield Township.

•**SOUTHGATE,** City; Wayne County; Pop. 32,014; Elev. 591; Lat. 42-12-25 N long. 083-11-38 W; Incorporated in 1955 and descriptively named for its location on the southern boundary of Detroit.

•**SPARTA,** Village; Kent County; Pop. 3,368; Zip Code 49345; Elev. 753; Lat. 43-09-39 N long. 085-42-36 W; Founded in 1848 and named after the famous ancient Greek city.

•**SPRING LAKE,** Village; Ottawa County; Pop. 2,726; Zip Code 49456; Elev. 594; Lat. 43-04-37 N l ong. 086-11-49 W; Originally Hopkins Mill, it was renamed Spring Lake for its location on Spring Lake.

•**SPRINGFIELD,** City; Calhoun County; Pop. 5,907; Lat. 42-19-35 N long. 085-14-21 W; Established in 1904 and named for Springfield, Illinois.

•**SPRINGPORT,** Village; Jackson County; Pop. 675; Zip Code 49284; Lat. 42-22-42 N, 084-41-55 W. John Oyer founded the town in 1836. It was renamed for the many springs in the area in 1838.

•**STAMBAUGH,** City; Iron County; Pop. 1,426; Zip Code 49964; Elev. 1539; Lat. 46-04-52 N long. 088-37-37 W; Founded in 1882 and named for prominent businessman, John Stambaugh.

•**STANDISH,** City; Arenac County Seat; Pop. 1,271; Zip Code 48658; Elev. 631; Lat. 43-58-59 N long. 083-57-32 W; Pineer John Standish built a mill here in 1871. The town is named for him.

•**STANTON,** City; Montcalm County Seat; Pop. 1,315; Zip Code 48888; Elev. 919; Lat. 43-17-33 N long. 085-04-53 W; Founded in 1860 and named in honor of Secretary of War Edwin Stanton in 1863.

•**STANWOOD,** Village; Mecosta County; Pop. 209; Zip Code 49346; Lat. 43-34-43 N, long. 085-26-57 W. Settled in 1870 and descriptively named for a large stand of timber in the area.

•**STEPHENSON,** City; Menominee County; Pop. 976; Zip Code 4981+; Lat. 45-24-55 N long. 087-36-27 W; Begun in the 1870's and named for U. S. Congressman Samuel Stephenson.

•**STERLING,** Village; Arenac County; Pop. 457; Zip Code 48659; Elev. 759; Lat. 44-02-00 N, long. 084-01-22 W. Incorporated in 1917 and named for lumberman William C. Sterling.

•**STERLING HEIGHTS,** City; Macomb County; Pop. 108,998; Lat. 42-34-49 N long. 083-01-49 W; Settled in 1835 and named in honor of pioneer Azariah Sterling.

•**STEVENSVILLE,** Village; Berrien County; Pop. 1,273; Zip Code 49127; Elev. 635; Lat. 42-00-52 N long. 086-31-10 W; Landowner Thomas Stevens platted the village in the 1870's. It is named in his honor.

•**STOCKBRIDGE,** Village; Ingham County; Pop. 1,222; Zip Code 49285; Lat. 42-27-04 N long. 084-10-50 W; Platted by settler Silas Beebe who named the village after the township.

•**STURGIS,** City; St. Joseph County; Pop. 9,525; Zip Code 49091; Lat. 41-47-57 N long. 085-25-09 W; Judge John Sturgis arrived in 1827. The town finally took his name in 1857.

•**SUNFIELD,** Village; Eaton County; Pop. 589; Zip Code 48890; Elev. 866; Lat. 42-45-44 N long. 084-59-33 W; Settled in the 1830's and named for its township.

•**SUTTONS BAY,** Village; Leelanau County; Pop. 505; Zip Code 49682; Lat. 44-58-36 N long. 085-39-02 W; Descriptively named for its location on Grand Traverse Bay on land owned by Harry Sutton.

•**SWARTZ CREEK,** City; Genesee County; Pop. 5,017; Zip Code 48473; Lat. 42-57-26 N long. 083-49-50 W; Settled in 1836 and named after Swartz (German for black) Creek.

•**SYLVAN LAKE,** City; Oakland County; Pop. 1,954; Lat. 42-36-41 N long. 083-19-43 W; Organized in 1921 and named for its location on Sylvan Creek.

•**TAWAS CITY,** City; Iosco County Seat; Pop. 1,965; Zip Code 4876+; Elev. 587; Lat. 44-16-10 N long. 083-30-53 W; Platted in 1855 and named for the Ottawas Indians.

•**TAYLOR,** City; Wayne County; Pop. 77,497; Zip Code 48180; Elev. 615; Lat. 42-14-27 N long. 083-16-11 W; Established in 1847 and named in honor of General Zachary Taylor.

•**TECUMSEH,** City; Lenawee County; Pop. 7,305; Zip Code 49286; Lat. 42-00-14 N long. 083-56-42 W; Founded in 1824 and named after the famous Shawnee Indian chief.

•**TEKONSHA,** Village; Calhoun County; Pop. 755; Zip Code 49092; Lat. 42-05-36 N, long. 084-59-09 W. Settled in the 1830's and named for Pottawattomi Chief Tekon-qua-sha.

•**THOMPSONVILLE,** Village; Benzie County; Pop. 329; Zip Code 49683; Elev. 793; Lat. 44-31-13 N long. 085-56-38 W; Incorporated in 1892 and named for lumberman Sumner Thompson.

•**THREE OAKS,** Village; Berrien County; Pop. 1,761; Zip Code 49128; Elev. 679; Lat. 41-47-55 N long. 086-36-38 W; First settled in 1850 and descriptively named for three white-oak trees growing on the town site.

•**THREE RIVERS,** City; St. Joseph County; Pop. 6,979; Zip Code 49093; Lat. 41-56-38 N long. 085-37-57 W; Platted in the 1830's and descriptively named for the confluence of the St. Joseph, Rocky, and portage Rivers.

•**TRAVERSE CITY,** City; Grand Traverse County Seat; Pop. 15,393; Zip Code 4968+; Elev. 599; Lat. 44-45-47 N long. 085-37-14 W; French explorers named the larger of two indentations on Michigan's west coast, La Grande Traverse. The town began in 1851 and took that name.

•**TRENTON,** City; Wayne County; Pop. 22,734; Zip Code 48183; Lat. 42-08-22 N long. 083-10-42 W; First established in 1827 as Truaxton, but later renamed Trenton for a limestone strata under the town.

•**TROY,** City; Oakland County; Pop. 67,003; Zip Code 4800+; Elev. 833; Lat. 43-44-35 N long. 086-01-09 W; First settled in 1822 and named for Troy, New York.

•**TURNER,** Village; Arenac County; Pop. 187; Zip Code 48765; Lat. 44-08-33 N, long. 083-47-16 W. The town was founded and named by pioneer Joseph Turner.

•**TUSTIN,** Village; Osceola County; Pop. 264; Zip Code 49688; Lat. 44-06-09 N long. 085-27-32 W; Settled in 1872 and named for Dr. J. P. Tustin.

•**TWINING,** Village; Arenac County; Pop. 195; Zip Code 48766; Lat. 44-06-47 N long. 083-48-27 W; The village is named after early lumberman Frederick Twining.

•**UBLY,** Village; Huron County; Pop. 858; Zip Code 48475; Elev. 789; Lat. 43-42-36 N long. 082-55-54 W; Originally Pagett's Corners, the name was changed to that of a city in England.

•**UNION CITY,** Village; Branch & Clahoun Counties; Pop. 1,667; Zip Code 49094; Lat. 42-04-00 N, long. 085-08-10 W. Incorporated in 1866 and named for the union of the St. Joseph and Coldwater Rivers in the county.

•**UNIONVILLE,** Village; Tuscola County; Pop. 578; Zip Code 48767; Lat. 43-39-13 N long. 083-27-58 W; Settled in the 1850's and named after Union, Ohio.

•**UTICA,** City; Macomb County; Pop. 5,239; Zip Code 4807+; Lat. 42-37-34 N long. 083-02-01 W; Platted in 1829 and named for Utica, New York.

•**VANDALIA,** Village; Cass County; Pop. 443; Zip Code 49095; Elev. 877; Lat. 41-55-01 N long. 085-54-53 W; Laid out in 1851 and named for Vandalia, New York.

•**VANDERBILT,** Village; Otsego County; Pop. 526; Zip Code 49795; Lat. 45-08-34 N long. 084-39-37 W; Settled in 1875 and named in honor of the Vanderbilt family of New York.

•**VASSAR,** City; Tuscola County; Pop. 2,673; Zip Code 4876+; Lat. 43-22-19 N long. 083-35-00 W; Founded in 1849 and named for Matthew Vassar, founder of Vassar College.

•**VERMONTVILLE,** Village; Eaton County; Pop. 832; Zip Code 49096; Elev. 928; Lat. 42-37-44 N long. 085-01-27 W; The Rev. Sylvester Cochrane organized a colony of Vermontiers and settled here in 1836. They named the town for their former home.

•**VERNON,** Village; Shiawassee County; Pop. 2,676; Zip Code 48476; Lat. 42-56-21 N long. 084-01-46 W; Settled in 1833 and named for George Washington's estate, Mount Vernon.

•**VICKSBURG,** Village; Kalamazoo County; Pop. 2,214; Zip Code 49097; Elev. 860; Lat. 42-07-12 N long. 085-31-58 W; Originally Brady, the name was amended in 1871 to Vicksburg, possibly after the great Civil War battle.

•**WAKEFIELD,** City; Gogebic County; Pop. 2,592; Zip Code 49968; Elev. 1550; Lat. 46-28-31 N long. 089-56-23 W; First settled in 1884, pioneer George Wakefield platted the town in 1885.

•**WALDRON,** Village; Hillsdale County; Pop. 572; Zip Code 49288; Elev. 900; Lat. 41-43-40 N long. 084-25-08 W; Settlers from New York arrived in 1835. The town was named for U. S. Congressman Henry Waldron.

•**WALKER,** City; Kent County; Pop. 15,097; Elev. 742; Lat. 43-00-05 N long. 085-46-05 W; Settled by Canadians and named for its township.

•**WALKERVILLE,** Village; Oceana County; Pop. 296; Zip Code 49459; Elev. 870; Lat. 43-42-52 N, long. 086-07-28 W. Plattted in 1883 and named for a local settler.

•**WALLED LAKE,** City; Oakland County; Pop. 4,750; Zip Code 48088; Elev. 939; Lat. 42-32-16 N long. 083-28-52 W; The city was settled in the 1830's along Square Mile Lake. The lake's appearance led to the name "Walled Lake."

•**WARREN,** City; Macomb County; Pop. 161,173; Zip Code 4808+; Lat. 42-28-39 N long. 083-01-40 W; Originally Alba in 1838, the town was named General Joseph Warren who was killed at the Battle of Bunker Hill.

•**WATERVLIET,** City; Berrien County; Pop. 1,873; Zip Code 49098; Lat. 42-11-12 N long. 086-15-38 W; Founded in 1833 and named after Watervliet, New York.

•**WAYLAND,** City; Allegan County; Pop. 2,025; Zip Code 49348; Lat. 42-40-26 N long. 085-38-41 W; Colonel Isaac Barnes settled here in 1837, and named for Wayland, New York.

•**WAYNE,** City; Wayne County; Pop. 21,143; Zip Code 4818+; Elev. 658; Lat. 42-16-53 N long. 083-23-11 W; Organized in 1835 and named for General Anthony Wayne.

•**WEBBERVILLE,** Village; Ingham County; Pop. 1,531; Zip Code 48892; Lat. 42-40-01 N long. 084-10-27 W; First settled in 1837 and named for postmaster Hubert Webber.

•**WEST BRANCH,** City; Ogemaw County Seat; Pop. 1,786; Zip Code 48661; Elev. 959; Lat. 44-16-35 N long. 084-14-19 W; The railroad arrivedin 1871. The town is located on the west branch of the Rifle River.

•**WESTLAND,** City; Wayne County; Pop. 84,684; Zip Code 48185; Lat. 42-19-27 N long. 083-24-01 W; Incorporated in 1966 and named for its location west of Detroit.

•**WESTPHALIA,** Village; Clinton County; Pop. 889; Zip Code 48894; Elev. 761; Lat. 42-55-46 N long. 084-47-55 W; Farmers from Westphalia, Germany came to the area in 1836 and named the new town for their old province.

•**WHITE CLOUD,** City; Newaygo County Seat; Pop. 1,103; Zip Code 49349; Elev. 871; Lat. 43-33-01 N long. 085-46-19 W; Settled in the 1870's as Morganville, it was renamed White Cloud in 1877.

•**WHITE PIGEON,** Village; St. Joseph County; Pop. 1,481; Zip Code 49099; Lat. 41-47-53 N long. 085-38-36 W; First settled in 1827 and named for Indian Chief White Pigeon.

•**WHITEHALL,** City; Muskegon County; Pop. 2,837; Zip Code 4946+; Elev. 593; Lat. 43-24-36 N long. 086-20-55 W; Platted in 1859 and named for its location on White Lake.

•**WHITTEMORE,** City; Iosco County; Pop. 438; Zip Code 48770; Lat. 44-14-01 N, long. 083-48-11 W. Founded in 1879 and named for settler Frank Whittemore.

•**WILLIAMSTON,** City; Ingham County; Pop. 2,996; Zip Code 48895; Lat. 42-41-20 N long. 084-16-59 W; Settled in 1834 and named for lumberman O. B. Williams.

•**WIXOM,** City; Oakland County; Pop. 6,713; Zip Code 48096; Elev. 930; Lat. 42-31-29 N long. 083-32-11 W; Lewis Norton settled here in 1830. The town is named after early settler Willard Wixom.

•**WOLVERINE,** Village; Cheboygan County; Pop. 364; Zip Code 49799; Lat. 45-16-24 N, long. 084-36-16 W. The town is named after the once abundant state animal: the wolverine.

•**WOLVERINE LAKE,** Village; Oakland County; Pop. 4,947; Lat. 42-33-24 N long. 083-28-26 W; Platted in 1881 and named for Michigan's state animal, the wolverine.

•**WOODHAVEN,** City; Wayne County; Pop. 10,902; Zip Code 48183; Lat. 42-08-20 N, long. 083-14-30 W. Incorporated in 1961 and named by its developers.

•**WOODLAND,** Village; Barry County; Pop. 431; Zip Code 48897; Elev. 875; Lat. 42-43-36 N, long. 085-08-01 W. Settled in 1837 and descriptively named for its location in thick woods.

•**WYANDOTTE,** City; Wayne County; Pop. 34,006; Zip Code 48192; Lat. 46-53-24 N, long. 088-52-31 W. The city is named for the Indian tribe which had a village here at one time.

•**WYOMING,** City; Kent County; Pop. 59,616; Zip Code 49509; Elev. 646; Lat. 42-54-48 N, long. 085-42-19 W. The village of Wyoming had been formed by 1859. It was incorporated as a city in 1958.

•**YALE,** City; St. Clair County; Pop.1,814; Zip Code 48097; Lat. 43-07-48 N, long. 082-47-54 W. The name honors Yale University.

•**YPSILANTI,** City; Washtenaw County; Pop. 24,031; Zip Code 48197; Lat. 42-14-28 N, long. 083-36-47 W. Named for General Demetrius Ypsilanti, a Greek war of independence hero.

•**ZEELAND,** City; Ottawa County; Pop. 4,764; Zip Code 49464; Elev. 646; Lat. 42-48-45 N, long. 086-01-07 W. Named by Dutch colonists for the province which had been their home in the Netherlands.

•**ZILWAUKEE,** City; Saginaw County; Pop. 2,201; Lat. 43-28-35 N, long. 083-55-14 W. Named by sawmill owners Daniel and Solomon Johnson who hoped German immigrant workers would confuse the name with Milwaukee and so be lured to the town.

MINNESOTA

•**ADA,** City; Norman County Seat; Pop. 1,971; Zip Code 56510; Elev. 907; Lat. 47-18-02 N long. 096-30-43 W; The town's name remembers Ada Fisher, the daughter of railroad superintendant William H. Fisher.

•**ADAMS,** City; Mower County; Pop. 797; Zip Code 55909; Lat. 43-33-58 N long. 092-43-00 W; The city is named in honor of John Adams, the second President of the United States.

•**ADRIAN,** City; Nobles County; Pop. 1,336; Zip Code 56110; Elev. 1541; Lat. 43-37-59 N long. 095-55-59 W; The city's name recalls Adrian Islein, the mother of prominent railroad director, Adrian Iselin.

•**AFTON,** City; Washington County; Pop. 2,550; Zip Code 55001; Lat. 44-53-59 N long. 092-46-53 W; Robert Burn's poem "Afton Water provided the city's name when it was organized in 1855.

•**AITKIN,** City; Aitkin County Seat; Pop. 1,770; Zip Code 56431; Elev. 1217; Lat. 46-32-02 N long. 093-42-16 W; Fur trader William Aitkin gave his name to the city and county.

•**AKELEY,** City; Hubbard County; Pop. 486; Zip Code 56433; Lat. 47-00-07 N long. 094-43-35 W; The city is named for locally prominent 19th century businessman, Healy Akeley.

•**ALBANY,** City; Stearns County; Pop. 1,569; Zip Code 56307; Lat. 45-39-40 N long. 094-35-27 W; Settled in 1863 and named for the capitol of New York state.

•**ALBERT LEA,** City; Freeborn County Seat; Pop. 19,190; Zip Code 56007; Lat. 43-39-01 N long. 093-21-58 W; The city takes its name from early explorer Albert Miller who mapped the region in 1835.

•**ALBERTA,** City; Stevens County; Pop. 145; Zip Code 56207; Lat. 45-34-40 N long. 096-03-18 W; Named in honor of Alberta Lindsey, wife of a local farmer.

•**ALBERTVILLE,** City; Wright County; Pop. 564; Zip Code 55301; Lat. 45-14-03 N long. 093-39-35 W; Named by the Great Northern railway after one of its employees.

•**ALDEN,** City; Freeborn County; Pop. 687; Zip Code 56009; Lat. 43-40-07 N long. 093-34-42 W; The city was incorporated in 1879 and is believed to be named for an early settler.

•**ALEXANDRIA,** City; Douglas County Seat; Pop. 7,608; Zip Code 56308; Lat. 45-50-16 N long. 095-21-46 W; Named in honor of Alexander Kinkaid, the first settler in the area.

•**ALPHA,** City; Jackson County; Pop. 180; Zip Code 56111; Elev. 1387; Lat. 43-38-07 N long. 094-51-57 W; Founded in 1895 and given the name of the first letter of the Greek alphabet.

•**ALTURA,** City; Winona County; Pop. 354; Zip Code 55910; Lat. 44-04-34 N long. 091-58-43 W; The city is named for the famous city in Valencia, Spain.

•**ALVARADO,** City; Marshall County; Pop. 385; Zip Code 56710; Lat. 48-11-37 N long. 096-59-41 W; The town is named for a seaport in Mexico.

•**AMBOY,** City; Blue Earth County; Pop. 606; Zip Code 56010; Lat. 43-53-20 N long. 094-09-35 W; The city's first postmaster, Robert Richardson, named the new town after his former home in Illinois.

•**ANDOVER,** City; Anoka County; Pop. 9,387; The city is named for the town in Massachusetts.

•**ANNANDALE,** City; Wright County; Pop. 1,568; Zip Code 55302; Lat. 45-15-51 N long. 094-07-43 W; The town's name remembers the Scottish seaport of Annan.

•**ANOKA,** City; Anoka County Seat; Pop. 15,634; Zip Code 55304; Lat. 45-10-15 N long. 093-19-15 W; The city's name is a Sioux word meaning "on both sides and is thought to refer to the Rum River which runs through the town.

•**APPLE VALLEY,** City; Dakota County; Pop. 21,818; Zip Code 55124; The city is named descriptively because of local fruit production.

•**APPLETON,** City; Swift County; Pop. 1,842; Zip Code 56208; Lat. 45-12-04 N long. 096-01-14 W; Originally called Phelps, it was renaned Appleton in 1872 after the town in Wisconsin.

•**ARCO,** City; Lincoln County; Pop. 96; Zip Code 56113; Lat. 44-22-50 N long. 096-10-52 W; Named in 1900 by local railroad officials after an ancient city in Italy.

•**ARDEN HILLS,** City; Ramsey County; Pop. 8,012; The city's name remembers the Ardennes forest of northern France.

•**ARGYLE,** City; Marshall County; Pop. 741; Zip Code 56713; Elev. 847; Lat. 48-19-45 N long. 096-49-06 W; The city's name remembers a county in Scotland.

•**ARLINGTON,** City; Sibley County; Pop. 1,779; Zip Code 55307; Lat. 44-36-35 N long. 094-04-38 W; Named for the famous estate in Washington D.C.

•**ASKOV,** City; Pine County; Pop. 350; Zip Code 55704; Lat. 46-11-28 N long. 092-46-43 W; Named for an early settler.

•**ATWATER,** City; Kandiyohi County; Pop. 1,128; Zip Code 56209; Lat. 45-08-03 N long. 094-46-44 W; The town was founded in 1869 and named for E.D. Atwater, an official of the St. Paul and Pacific Railway Co.

•**AUDUBON,** City; Becker County; Pop. 383; Zip Code 56511; Lat. 46-51-49 N long. 095-58-48 W; The city is named in honor of the great American ornithologist, John Audubon.

•**AURORA,** City; St. Louis County; Pop. 2,670; Zip Code 55705; Lat. 47-31-38 N long. 092-14-01 W; A latin name meaning "morning."

•**AUSTIN,** City; Mower County Seat; Pop. 23,020; Zip Code 55912; Lat. 43-40-48 N long. 092-58-24 W; Founded in the late 1850s and named for the first settler, Austin Nichols.

•**AVOCA,** City; Murray County; Pop. 201; Zip Code 56114; Lat. 43-56-51 N long. 095-38-45 W; The city is named for a river in Ireland made famous by poet Thomas Moore.

•**AVON,** City; Stearns County; Pop. 804; Zip Code 56310; Elev. 1129; Lat. 45-36-41 N long. 094-26-55 W; Named for the famous river Avon in England.

•**BABBITT,** City; St. Louis County; Pop. 2,435; Zip Code 55706; Lat. 47-42-24 N long. 091-56-42 W; The town is named for an early settler.

•**BACKUS,** City; Cass County; Pop. 255; Zip Code 56435; Lat. 46-49-13 N long. 094-30-49 W; Backus is named in honor of Edward Backus, a well known Minneapolis lumberman.

•**BADGER,** City; Roseau County; Pop. 320; Zip Code 56714; Elev. 1082; Lat. 48-46-51 N long. 096-01-14 W; The city takes its name from nearby Badger Creek.

•BAGLEY, City; Clearwater County Seat; Pop. 1,321; Zip Code 56621; Elev. 1441; Lat. 47-31-26 N long. 095-23-58 W; The town's settlers named it for Sumner Bagley, a pioneer lumberman.

•BALATON, City; Lyon County; Pop. 752; Zip Code 56115; Elev. 1523; 44-14-02 N long. 095-54-23 W; The city's name recalls Lake Balaton in western Hungary.

•BARNESVILLE, City; Clay County; Pop. 2,207; Zip Code 56514; Lat. 46-38-39 N long. 096-24-29 W; Early farmer George Barnes founded this railway town and gave it his name.

•BARNUM, City; Carlton County; Pop. 464; Zip Code 55707; Elev. 1103; Lat. 46-30-14 N long. 092-41-08 W; The town is named for George Barnum, an official of the St. Paul and Duluth railway.

•BARRETT, City; Grant County; Pop. 388; Zip Code 56311; Elev. 1166; Lat. 45-54-42 N long. 095-53-12 W; The city's name honor Civil War hero and local farmer General Theodore H. Barrett.

•BARRY, City; Big Stone County; Pop. 43; Zip Code 56210; Lat. 45-33-30 N long. 096-33-40 W; The Barry brothers, early settlers from Massachusetts, gave the city their name.

•BATTLE LAKE, City; Otter Tail County; Pop. 708; Zip Code 56515; Elev. 1372; Lat. 46-17-00 N long. 095-42-51 W; Named after a Ojibway-Sioux battle which took place around 1795.

•BAUDETTE, City; Lake of the Woods Seat; Pop. 1,170; Zip Code 56623; Lat. 48-42-53 N long. 094-35-59 W; The city is named for an early French trapper.

•BAXTER, City; Crow Wing County; Pop. 2,625; Zip Code 56401; The city's name honors Luther Baxter, soldier, attorney, and state representative in the 1870s.

•BAYPORT, City; Washington County; Pop. 2,932; Zip Code 55003; Lat. 45-01-04 N long. 092-47-00 W; The town is descriptively named for a local bay.

•BEARDSLEY, City; Big Stone County; Pop. 344; Zip Code 56211; Lat. 45-33-18 N long. 096-43-53 W; The town is situated on the former farm of early settler W.W. Beardsley and so named.

•BEAVER BAY, City; Lake County; Pop. 283; Zip Code 55601; Lat. 47-15-38 N long. 091-17-57 W; Descriptively named for the once-plentiful beaver of the area.

•BEAVER CREEK, City; Rock County; Pop. 260; Zip Code 56116; Lat. 43-36-48 N long. 096-21-55 W; The city was founded in 1872 and named for the excellent fur trapping of that day.

•BECKER, City; Sherburne County; Pop. 601; Zip Code 55308; Lat. 45-23-36 N long. 093-52-18 W; The town is named for attorney and mayor of St. Paul, George Becker, who lived in years 1829-1904.

•BEJOU, City; Mahnomen County; Pop. 109; Zip Code 56516; Elev. 1222; Lat. 47-26-33 N long. 095-58-25 W; A shortened version of the French greeting "Bonjour."

•BELGRADE, City; Stearns County; Pop. 805; Zip Code 56312; Elev. 1266; Lat. 45-27-15 N long. 095-00-07 W; The town is named after the city in Serbia.

•BELLE PLAINE, City; Scott County; Pop. 2,754; Zip Code 56011; Lat. 44-37-20 N long. 093-45-54 W; Named by its first settlers and meaning in French "beautiful plain."

•BELLINGHAM, City; Lac qui Parle; Pop. 290; Zip Code 56212; Lat. 45-08-09 N long. 096-16-55 W; The city is named after early settler Robert Bellingham.

•BELTRAMI, City; Polk County; Pop. 134; Zip Code 56517; Elev. 903; Lat. 47-32-38 N long. 096-31-48 W; The city is named for Italian exile Giacomo Beltrami who explored the area in 1823.

•BELVIEW, City; Redwood County; Pop. 438; Zip Code 56214; Lat. 44-36-10 N long. 095-19-55 W; The city's name means "beautiful view" in French.

•BEMIDJI, City; Beltrami County Seat; Pop. 10,949; Zip Code 56601; Lat. 47-32-08 N long. 094-49-01 W; The town is named for an Ojibway Indian chief.

•BENA, City; Cass County; Pop. 153; Zip Code 56626; Lat. 47-20-27 N long. 094-12-21 W; The city acquired its name from the Ojibway Indian word for "partridge."

•BENSON, City; Swift County Seat; Pop. 3,656; Zip Code 56215; Lat. 45-18-54 N long. 095-36-08 W; Ben Benson settled in the area in 1869 and began a mercantile business. The town was subsequently named for him.

•BERTHA, City; Todd County; Pop. 510; Zip Code 56437; Lat. 46-16-00 N long. 095-03-28 W; Incorporated in 1897 and named for Mrs. Bertha Riston, the first woman settler.

•BETHEL, City; Anoka County; Pop. 272; Zip Code 55005; Lat. 45-22-15 N long. 093-13-43 W; An early settler, Moses Twitchell, named the city after his former home: Bethel, Maine.

•BIG FALLS, City; Koochiching County; Pop. 490; Zip Code 56627; Lat. 48-37-13 N long. 093-12-19 W; Descriptively named for the large waterfall on the edge of the town.

•BIG LAKE, City; Sherburne County; Pop. 2,210; Zip Code 55309; Elev. 942; The town took its name from the adjacent lake.

•BIGELOW, City; Nobles County; Pop. 249; Zip Code 56117; Lat. 43-30-19 N long. 095-41-10 W; The town is named in honor of Charles Bigelow, a prominent lumber and insurance businessman.

•BIGFORK, City; Itasca County; Pop. 457; Zip Code 56628; Elev. 1318; Lat. 47-44-57 N long. 093-39-53 W; Descriptively named for the town's location on the Big Fork of the Rainy River.

•BINGHAM LAKE, City; Cottonwood County; Pop. 222; Zip Code 56118; Lat. 43-54-36 N long. 095-002-48 W; Incorporated in 1900, the name recalls K.S. Bingham, U.S. Senator and Michigan governor in the pre-Civil War era.

•BIRD ISLAND, City; Renville County; Pop. 1,372; Zip Code 55310; Lat. 44-45-43 N long. 094-53-28 W; The city is descriptively named for a nearby marshy island which sheltered a large wild bird population in pioneer days.

•BIWABIK, City; St. Louis County; Pop. 1,428; Zip Code 55708; Elev. 1448; Lat. 47-30-47 N long. 092-24-02 W; An Ojibway Indian word meaning "iron."

•BLACKDUCK, City; Beltrami County; Pop. 653; Zip Code 56630; Elev. 1383; Lat. 47-45-36 N long. 094-29-10 W; Named after nearby Black Duck Lake. So called because of the common ring-necked duck.

•BLAINE, City; Anoka County; Pop. 28,558; Zip Code 55434; Founded in 1862 and named for prominent Republican Senator (Maine) and Presidential canidate, James Blaine.

•BLOMKEST, City; Kandiyohi County; Pop. 200; Zip Code 56216; Lat. 44-56-32 N long. 095-01-11 W; The derivation of the town's name is not known.

•**BLOOMING PRAIRIE,** City; Steele County; Pop. 1,969; Zip Code 55917; Lat. 43-52-03 N long. 093-03-16 W; First settled in 1856 and descriptively named for the abundant Spring prairie flowers.

•**BLOOMINGTON,** City; Hennepin County; Pop. 81,831; Zip Code 55420; Early settlers named the city after their home town in Illinois.

•**BLUE EARTH,** City; Faribault County Seat; Pop. 4,132; Zip Code 56013; Lat. 43-38-17 N long. 094-06-04 W; The city takes its name from the river where a blue-green clay is found.

•**BLUFFTON,** City; Otter Tail County; Pop. 206; Zip Code 56518; Lat. 46-27-57 N long. 095-13-47 W; Founed in 1878 and named for the high banks of the Leaf River along the southern boundary of the city.

•**BOVEY,** City; Itasca County; Pop. 813; Zip Code 55709; Lat. 47-17-39 N long. 093-25-41 W; The town is named after an early settler.

•**BOYD,** City; Lac qui Parle; Pop. 329; Zip Code 56218; Lat. 44-51-00 N long. 095-54-00 W; Boyd is named after an officer of the Minneapolis and St. Louis Railweay Company.

•**BRAHAM,** City; Isanti Couny; Pop. 1,051; Zip Code 55006; Lat. 45-43-25 N long. 093-10-20 W; Originally a railway village named by the Great Northern Railway for one of its officers.

•**BRAINERD,** City; Crow Wing County Seat; Pop. 11,489; Zip Code 56401; Lat. 46-24-07 N long. 094-17-37 W; The city was founded in 1870 and named in honor of the wife of the President of the Northern Pacific Railway Company.

•**BRANCH,** City; Chisago County; Pop. 1,866; Settled in 1872 and named for the North Branch of the Sunrise River, which flows through the town.

•**BRECKENRIDGE,** City; Wilkin County Seat; Pop. 3,909; Zip Code 56520; Lat. 46-15-54 N long. 096-35-05 W; Founded in 1858 and named in honor of John C. Breckenridge,vice-president of the United States and later a general in the Confederate States.

•**BREWSTER,** City; Nobles County; Pop. 559; Zip Code 56119; Lat. 43-41-41 N long. 095-27-45 W; Named after Brewster, Massachusetts: that name honoring William Brewster, one of the original Mayflower pilgrims.

•**BRICELYN,** City; Faribault County; Pop. 487; Zip Code 56014; Lat. 43-33-50 N long. 093-51-49 W; John Brice, the original landowner, gave his name to the city.

•**BROOKLYN PARK,** City; Hennepin County; Pop. 43,332; Zip Code 55429; The town gets its name from the city and borough of New York.

•**BROOKS,** City; Red Lake County; Pop. 173; Zip Code 56715; Lat. 47-48-58 N long. 096-00-26 W; The town is named for an early settler.

•**BROOTEN,** City; Stearns County; Pop. 647; Zip Code 56316; Lat. 45-30-13 N long. 095-07-23 W; Founded in 1886 and named for one of its early Scandinivian settlers.

•**BROWERVILLE,** City; Todd County; Pop. 693; Zip Code 56438; Lat. 46-05-15 N long. 094-52-06 W; Early pioneer, Abraham Bower, gave his name to the town.

•**BROWNS VALLEY,** City; Traverse County; Pop. 887; Zip Code 56219; Elev. 1283; Lat. 45-35-29 N long. 096-50-13 W; Founded in 1866 by Joseph Brown and named in his honor after his death in 1870.

•**BROWNSDALE,** City; Mower County; Pop. 691; Zip Code 55918; Lat. 45-44-33 N long. 092-51-58 W; The city was founded by the Brown Brothers in the 1850s. It received their name when incorporated in 1876.

•**BROWNSVILLE,** City; Houston County; Pop. 418; Zip Code 55919; Lat. 43-41-10 N long. 091-16-40 W; Originally a steamboat landing set up by Job and Charles Brown who settled in Minnesota in 1848. The town grew up around the landing.

•**BROWNTON,** City; McLeod County; Pop. 697; Zip Code 55312; Elev. 1021; Lat. 44-43-59 N long. 094-21-04 W; Named in honor of local farmer and Civil War captain, Alonzo Brown.

•**BUCKMAN,** City; Morrison County; Pop. 171; Zip Code 56317; Lat. 45-53-51 N long. 094-05-52 W; Clarence Buckman, one of the area's first settlers, had the city named in his honor.

•**BUFFALO,** City; Wright County Seat; Pop. 4,560; Zip Code 55313; Elev. 967; Lat. 45-11-12 N long. 093-52-19 W; The town is named after Buffalo Lake, itself so designated by Indian traders because of the many Buffalo fish in the lake.

•**BUFFALO LAKE,** City; Renville County; Pop. 782; Zip Code 55314; Elev. 1074; Lat. 44-44-12 N long. 094-37-05 W; The city is named for nearby Buffalo Lake.

•**BUHL,** City; St. Louis County; Pop. 1,284; Zip Code 55713; Elev. 1533; Lat. 47-29-36 N long. 092-46-37 W; Located near the famous Mesabi iron mining range and named in honor of Frank Buhl, president of the Sharon Iron Ore Co.

•**BURNSVILLE,** City; Dakota County; Pop. 35,674; Zip Code 55337; Canadian emigrant William Burns, who arrived in 1853, left his name on the city.

•**BUTTERFIELD,** City; Watonwan County; Pop. 634; Zip Code 56120; Lat. 43-57-19 N long. 094-47-03 W; Named in honor of its first settler, William Butterfield.

•**BYRON,** City; Olmsted County; Pop. 1,715; Zip Code 55920; Elev. 1262; Lat. 44-02-02 N long. 092-38-51 W; Incorporated in 1873 and named after Port Byron, New York at the suggestion of a prominent businessman who had formerly lived there.

•**CALEDONIA,** City; Houston County Seat; Pop. 2,691; Zip Code 55921; Elev. 1174; Lat. 43-37-50 N long. 091-28-49 W; Settled in 1851 and given the ancient Roman name for Scotland.

•**CALLAWAY,** City; Becker County; Pop. 238; Zip Code 56521; Elev. 1370; Lat. 46-58-54 N long. 095-54-24 W; William Callaway, general agent for the Soo Railway in 1906, had the town named after him.

•**CALUMET,** City; Itasca County; Pop. 469; Zip Code 55716; Elev. 1392; Lat. 47-19-33 N long. 093-19-08 W; The town is named after the calumet, the ceremonial smoking pipe used by the Sioux Indians to solemnize special occasions.

•**CAMBRIDGE,** City; Isanti County Seat; Pop. 3,170; Zip Code 55008; Elev. 962; Lat. 45-34-12 N long. 093-13-26 W; Settlers from Maine named the town after their former home: Cambridge, Massachusetts.

•**CAMPBELL,** City; Wilkin County; Pop. 286; Zip Code 56522; Lat. 46-05- N long. 096-24-19 W; The Great Northern Railway Company gave the town this popular Scottish name, possibly after one of their officers.

•**CANBY,** City; Yellow Medicine; Pop. 2,143; Zip Code 56220; Lat. 44-42-42 N long. 096-16-06 W; The city is named in honor of Brigadier General Edward Canby, Civil War hero and Indian fighter.

•**CANNON FALLS,** City; Goodhue County; Pop. 2,653; Zip Code 55009; Elev. 838; Lat. 44-30-39 N long. 092-54-17 W; Settled in 1854 and named by early American explorers after the Cannon River.

•**CANTON,** City; Fillmore County; Pop. 386; Zip Code 55922; Elev. 1345; Lat. 43-31-37 N long. 091-54-58 W; Settled in 1851 and named for Canton, Ohio; itself named for Canton, China.

•**CARLOS,** City; Douglas County; Pop. 364; Zip Code 56319; Lat. 45-58-21 N long. 095-18-14 W; The city is named for Lake Carlos.

•**CARLTON,** City; Carlton County Seat; Pop. 862; Zip Code 55718; Elev. 1091; Lat. 46-3907 N long. 092-25-04 W; The city, as well as the county, is named in honor of Reuban B. Carlton, who settled in the area in 1847.

•**CARVER,** City; Carver County; Pop. 642; Zip Code 55315; Lat. 44-45-54 N long. 093-37-47 W; The city and the county are named for Captain Johnathan Carver, who explored the area in 1847.

•**CASS LAKE,** City; Cass County; Pop. 1,001; Zip Code 56633; Lat. 47-22-48 N long. 094-36-00 W; The city and county are named in honor of Lewis Cass, explorer, U.S. Senator, and Secretry of State in 1857-60.

•**CENTER CITY,** City; Chisago County Seat; Pop. 458; Zip Code 55012; Lat. 45-23-38 N long. 092-49-00 W; So called because of the town's central location between Chisago City and Taylor's Fall.

•**CEYLON,** City; Martin County; Pop. 543; Zip Code 56121; Lat. 43-31-54 N long. 094-37-51 W; Originally a railway town, it was named for the island of Ceylon in the Indian Ocean.

•**CHAMPLIN,** City; Hennepin County; Pop. 9,006; Zip Code 55316; Lat. 45-10-35 N long. 093-23-21 W; Settled in 1852 and named for Erza Champlin, Civil War soldier and state legislator.

•**CHANDLER,** City; Murray County; Pop. 344; Zip Code 56122; Elev. 1651; Lat. 43-55-45 N long. 095-56-57 W; The town's name honors John A., Chandler, who worked for the Chicago, Milwaukee, and St. Paul Railway in the area for over forty years.

•**CHANHASSEN,** City; Carver County; Pop. 6,359; Zip Code 55317; Elev. 976; Lat. 44-52-08 N long. 093-31-30 W; Settled in 1852 and given the Sioux Indian word meaning sugar maple, or "the tree of sweet juice."

•**CHASKA,** City; Carver County Seat; Pop. 8,346; Zip Code 55318; Lat. 44-48-03 N long. 093-37-26 W; A Sioux Indian word meaning "first born child."

•**CHATFIELD,** City; Fillmore County; Pop. 2,055; Zip Code 55923; Lat. 43-50-46 N long. 092-11-02 W; Judge Andrew Chatfield presided over the first court held in the county and give his name to the city in 1858.

•**CHISAGO CITY,** City; Chisago County; Pop. 1,634; Zip Code 55013; Lat. 45-22-09 N long. 092-53-20 W; The city and county takes its name from a Chippewa Indian word meaning "large and beautiful lake."

•**CHISHOLM,** City; St. Louis County; Pop. 5,930; Zip Code 55719; Elev. 1578; Lat. 47-29-09 N long. 092-51-42 W; The city is named in honor of Archibald Chisholm, one of the chief explorers of the Mesabi iron ore range.

•**CHOKIO,** City; Stevens County; Pop. 559; Zip Code 56221; Lat. 45-34-23 N long. 096-10-21 W; Chokio is a Sioux Indian word meaning "middle."

•**CIRCLE PINES,** City; Anoka County; Pop. 3,321; Zip Code 55014; Lat. 45-09-26 N long. 093-08-00 W; A euphonious name given to the town by its incorporators.

•**CLARA CITY,** City; Chippewa County; Pop. 1,574; Zip Code 56222; Elev. 1062; Lat. 44-57-23 N long. 095-21-48 W; Named in honor of the wife of Theodor Koch, who helped settle the area.

•**CLAREMONT,** City; Dodge County; Pop. 591; Zip Code 55924; Lat. 44-02-43 N long.092-59-45 W; Settled by New Hampshire pioneers in 1858, who gave it the name of their former town.

•**CLARISSA,** City; Todd County; Pop. 663; Zip Code 56440; Lat. 46-07-56 N long. 094-56-52 W; Lewis Bishoffsheim settled in the area in 1877, and named the town in honor of his wife.

•**CLARKFIELD,** City; Yellow Medicine; Pop. 1,171; Zip Code 56223; Lat. 44-47-33 N long. 095-48-134 W; Founded in 1884 and named after a local railroad official.

•**CLARKS GROVE,** City; Freeborn County; Pop. 620; Zip Code 56016; Lat. 43-45-50 N long. 093-20-16 W; The town was settled in 1890 and named after early pioneer J. Mead Clark.

•**CLEARBROOK,** City; Clearwater County; Pop. 579; Zip Code 56634; Lat. 47-41-45 N long. 095-25-39 W; Descriptively named for the nearby brook.

•**CLEARWATER,** City; Wright County; Pop. 379; Zip Code 55320; Lat. 45-25-11 N long. 094-03-10 W; Named after the Clearwater River which flows into the Mississippi.

•**CLEMENTS,** City; Redwood County; Pop. 227; Zip Code 56224; Lat. 44-22-49 N long. 095-03-23 W; Founded in 1902 and named in honor of Peter O. Clements, an early settler-farmer.

•**CLEVELAND,** City; Le Sueur County; Pop. 699; Zip Code 56017; Elev. 1051; Lat. 44-19-32 N long. 093-49-38 W; Ohio settlers in 1858 named the city after their former home.

•**CLIMAX,** City; Polk County; Pop. 273; Zip Code 56523; Lat. 47-36-34 N long. 096-49-13 W; The town's founder named the town from an advertisement for "Climax Tobacco.

•**CLINTON,** City; Big Stone County; Pop. 622; Zip Code 56225; Lat. 45-27-39 N long. 096-26-36 W; Named by early settlers in honor of DeWitt Clinton, builder of the Erie Canal.

•**CLITHERALL,** City; Otter Tail County; Pop. 121; Zip Code 56524; Elev. 1348; Lat. 46-16-24 N long. 095-37-37 W; The city's name honors Major George Clitherall, who ran the U.S. Land Office in Otter Tail City in the late 1850s.

•**CLONTARF,** City; Swift County; Pop. 196; Zip Code 56226; Elev. 1050; Lat. 45-22-38 N long. 095-40-43 W; Settled in 1877 by Irish settlers who named the town for a suburb of Dublin.

•**CLOQUET,** City; Carlton County; Pop. 11,142; Zip Code 55720; Elev. 1204; Lat. 46-42-50 N long. 092-26-23 W; Named after the nearby Cloquet River.

•**COKATO,** City; Wright County; Pop. 2,056; Zip Code 55321; Elev. 1052; Lat. 45-04-33 N long. 094-11-24 W; Settled in 1856 and given the Sioux name Cokato, which means "at the middle.

•**COLD SPRING,** City; Stearns County; Pop. 2,294; Zip Code 56320; Elev. 1091; Lat. 45-27-22 N long. 094-25-16 W; Natural mineral springs gave the town its name.

•**COLERAINE,** City; Itasca County; Pop. 1,116; Zip Code 55722; Lat. 47-17-59 N, long. 093-25-48 W. Named in honor of Thomas Cole who had an influential role in this Mesabi Range town.

•**COLOGNE,** City; Carver County; Pop. 545; Zip Code 55322; Elev. 948; Lat. 44-46-06 N, long. 093-46-37 W. German settlers named the town for the city in their homeland.

251

•**COLUMBIA HEIGHTS,** City; Anoka County; Pop. 20,029; Zip Code 55421. A euphonious name given to a suburb of Minneapolis by Thomas Lowry, who was an early settler.

•**COMFREY,** City; Brown County; Pop. 548; Zip Code 56019; Elev. 1301; Lat. 44-06-49 N, long. 094-54-09 W. The city takes its name from a nearby post office called after the famous medicinal plant.

•**COMSTOCK,** City; Clay County; Pop. 110; Zip Code 56525; Lat. 46-39-23 N, long. 096-44-28 W. The town's name honors Solomon Comstock, both a state and Congressional representative for the area.

•**CONGER,** City; Freeborn County; Pop. 183; Zip Code 56020; Elev. 1289; Lat. 43-36-57 N, long. 093-32-10 W. Railway officials of the Chicago, Rock Island, and Pacicic Railroad named the town after a company employee.

•**COOK,** City; St. Louis County; Pop. 800; Zip Code 55723; Elev. 1306; Lat. 47-51-15 N, long. 092-41-18 W. Founded in 1903 and honoring Wirth Cook, a lumber businessman from Duluth who was instrumental in its founding.

•**COON RAPIDS,** City; Anoka County; Pop. 35,826; Zip Code 55433; A descriptively named suburb of Minneapolis.

•**CORCORAN,** City; Hennepin County; Pop. 4,252. Patrick Corcoran, the first school teacher and postmaster, gave his name to the town in 1858.

•**CORRELL,** City; Big Stone County; Pop. 83; Zip Code 56227; Lat. 45-13-50 N, long. 096-09-43 W. Railway officers of the Chicago, Milwaukee, and St. Paul railroad named the city after an employee.

•**COSMOS,** City; Meeker County; Pop. 571; Zip Code 56228; Lat. 44-55-56 N, long. 094-40-26 W. Early settler, Daniel Hoyt, gave the town the Greek name meaning "orderly universe."

•**COTTAGE GROVE,** City; Washington County; Pop. 18,994; Zip Code 55016; Lat. 25-45-39 N, long. 053-25-05 W. Settled in the 1840s and given a descriptive name for the intermingled farms and groves of trees.

•**COTTONWOOD,** City; Lyon County; Pop. 924; Zip Code 56229; Lat. 44-36-23 N, long. 095-40-39 W. Named for the nearby lake with its cottonwood trees along the shore.

•**COURTLAND,** City; Nicollet County; Pop. 399; Zip Code 56021; Lat. 44-16-17 N, long. 094-20-26 W. Founded in 1858 and named for Cortland county in New York.

•**CROMWELL,** City; Carlton County; Pop. 229; Zip Code 55726; Elev. 1311; Lat. 46-40-52 N, long. 092-52-25 W. Named by Northern Pacific Railway officials after the famous English puritan Oliver Cromwell.

•**CROOKSTON,** City; Polk County Seat; Pop. 8,628; Zip Code 56716; Lat. 47-46-35 N, long. 096-36-30 W. The town is named in honor of Colonel William Crooks who was the chief engineer of the first railroad through the area.

•**CROSBY,** City; Crow Wing County; Pop. 2,218; Zip Code 56441; Elev. 1261; Lat. 46-29-40 N, long. 094-00-17 W. The town's name honors George Crosby, a former manager of the local iron mines.

•**CROSSLAKE,** City; Crow Wing County; Pop. 1,064; Zip Code 56442; Lat. 46-39-25 N, long. 094-08-37 W. A descriptive name given the city.

•**CRYSTAL,** City; Hennepin County; Pop. 25,543; Zip Code 55428; Given its current name in 1887 after nearby Crystal Lake.

•**CURRIE,** City; Murray County; Pop. 359; Zip Code 56123; Lat. 44-04-13 N, long. 095-39-53 W. The city was founded in 1872 by the Currie family who engaged in flour milling and merchandising.

•**CUYUNA,** City; Crow Wing County; Pop. 157. The town's name honors Cuyler Adams and his dog Una. Adams discovered and owned the iron mine in the area.

•**CYRUS,** City; Pope County; Pop. 334; Zip Code 56323; Elev. 1138; Lat. 45-37-45 N, long. 095-41-50 W. Founded in 1882 and given a common Christian name.

•**DAKOTA,** City; Winona County; Pop. 350; Zip Code 55925; Elev. 691; Lat. 43-54-50 N, long. 091-21-24 W. The town's name is a Sioux word meaning "alliance or confederation."

•**DALTON,** City; Otter Tail County; Pop. 248; Zip Code 56324; Lat. 46-10-17 N, long. 095-54-48 W. Founded in the 1880s and named in honor of Ole C. Dahl who was the original landowner.

•**DANUBE,** City; Renville County; Pop. 590; Zip Code 56230; Lat. 44-47-36 N, long. 095-06-04 W. The city's name recalls the large and famous river in Europe.

•**DANVERS,** City; Swift County; Pop. 152; Zip Code 56231; Elev. 1027; Lat. 45-17-02 N, long. 095-45-16 W. Early settlers named the city for their former home in Massachusetts.

•**DARFUR,** City; Watonwan County; Pop. 139; Zip Code 56022; Elev. 1148; Lat. 44-03-18 N, long. 094-50-02 W. Incorporated at the turn of the century and named after an area in the Sudan.

•**DARWIN,** City; Meeker County; Pop. 282; Zip Code 55324; Elev. 1132; Lat. 45-05-45 N, long. 094-23-32 W. The city's name honors Darwin Litchfield, chief stockholder of the Great Northern Railway Co.

•**DASSEL,** City; Meeker County; Pop. 1,066; Zip Code 55325; Elev. 1091; Lat. 45-04-41 N, long. 094-17-33 W. Renamed in 1871 to honor Bernard Dassel, who at that time was the secretary of the Great Northern Railroad.

•**DAWSON,** City; Lac qui Parle County; Pop. 139; Zip Code 56232; Elev. 1058; Lat. 44-55-48 N, long. 096-03-15 W. The town was founded in 1885 and named in honor of William Dawson, a banker who owned land in the area.

•**DAYTON,** City; Hennepin County; Pop. 4,070; Zip Code 55327; Lat. 45-14-27 N, long. 093-31-27 W. Lyman Dayton, railroad president and local real estate investor, gave his name to the town in the 1850s.

•**DE GRAFF,** City; Swift County; Pop. 179; Zip Code 56233; Lat. 45-15-46 N, long. 095-28-02 W. Andrew De Graff built the Great Northern Railroad line in this area in the post Civil War era. The town is named in honor.

•**DEEPHAVEN,** City; Hennepin County; Pop. 3,716; Zip Code 55391; The town is descriptively named for its excellent harbor.

•**DEER CREEK,** City; Otter Tail County; Pop. 392; Zip Code 56527; Elev. 1393; Lat. 46-23-19 N, long. 095-18-54 W. Deer Creek flows through the town and gave its name to the community.

•**DEER RIVER,** City; Itasca County; Pop. 907; Zip Code 56636; Elev. 1291; Lat. 47-21-17 N long. W. The Ojibway Indians called the place Wawashkeshini; the white settlers translated this to "Deer River."

•**DEERWOOD,** City; Crow Wing County; Pop. 580; Zip Code 56444; Elev. 1277; Lat. 46-29-42 N, long. 093-55-23 W. A descriptive name given by early settlers for the plentiful deer in the nearby woods.

•**DELANO,** City; Wright County; Pop. 2,480; Zip Code 55328; Elev. 944; Lat. 45-02-33 N; long. 093-46-50 W. Francis R. Delano served as superintendent of the St. Paul and Pacific Railrod and as a state representative in the 1860s and the 1870s. The city is named in his honor.

•**DELAVAN,** City; Faribault County; Pop. 262; Zip Code 56023; Elev. 1063; Lat. 43-46-00 N long. 094-01-06 W. The town was incorporated in 1877 and named for Oren Delavan Brown, a railroad official with the Southern Minnesota Railroad.

•**DELHI,** City; Redwood County; Pop. 96; Zip Code 56283; Alfred Cook, a local flour miller, named the new community for his former home of Delhi, Ohio.

•**DELLWOOD,** City; Washington County; Pop. 751; Founded in 1882 and given the euphonious name of Dellwood.

•**DENHAM,** City; Pine County; Pop. 48; Zip Code 55728; The city is named for an early pioneer family.

•**DENNISON,** City; Goodhue County; Pop. 176; Zip Code 55018; Lat. 44-24-30 N, long. 093-02-04 W. Morris Dennison owned the land upon which the city was founded in 1856. It is named in his honor.

•**DENT,** City; Otter Tail County; Pop. 167; Zip Code 56528; Lat. 46-35-07 N, long. 095-43-14 W. Founded in 1904 and named for a local railroad official.

•**DETROIT LAKES,** City; Becker County Seat; Pop. 7,106; Zip Code 56578; Lat. 46-51-01 N, long. 095-41-06 W. An early French explorer noticed a long, sand bar bifurcated part of the lake and created a strait (or detroit in French).

•**DEXTER,** City; Mower County; Pop. 279; Zip Code 55926; Lat. 43-43-10 N, long. 092-41-52 W. The city is named for Dexter Parrity, the first settler, who came to the area in 1857.

•**DILWORTH,** City; Clay County; Pop. 2,585; Zip Code 56529; Lat. 46-53-20 N, long. 096-39-39 W. Northern Pacific Railwy officials named the city for one of their employees.

•**DODGE CENTER,** City; Dodge County; Pop. 1,816; Zip Code 55927; Elev. 1293; Lat. 44-01-44 N, long. 092-51-27 W. Incorporated in 1872 in Dodge County and so named because of its central position in the county.

•**DONALDSON,** City; Kittson County; Pop. 84; Zip Code 56720; Lat. 48-34-31 N, long. 096-53-38 W. Captain Hugh Donaldson, who managed a large farm in the area had the town named in his honor.

•**DONNELLY,** City; Stevens County; Pop. 317; Zip Code 56235; Lat. 45-41-14 N, long. 096-00-40 W. Politician and author Ignatius Donnelly owned a farm near the town. It is named in his honor.

•**DORAN,** City; Wilkin County; Pop. 77; Zip Code 56530; Lat. 46-11-01 N, long. 096-29-08 W. Michael Doran, a prominent local farmer and businessman, had the town named in his honor.

•**DOVER,** City; Olmsted County; Pop. 312; Zip Code 55929; Lat. 43-58-26 N, long. 092-07-58 W. Early settlers gave the city the name of Dover after their former home in New Hampshire.

•**DOVRAY,** City; Murray County; Pop. 87; Zip Code 56125; Lat. 44-03-18 N, long. 095-32-48 W. Founded in 1879 and named for a Norwegian village.

•**DULUTH,** City; St. Louis County Seat; Pop. 92,811; Zip Code 558+; Elev. 620; Lat. 46-47-21 N, long. 092-06-55 W. Originally occupied by the Sioux and then the Chippewa Indians the area was visited in 1679 by Daniel Greysolon Sieur du Luth for whom Duluth was named.

•**EAGAN,** City; Dakota County; Pop. 20,532; Zip Code 55121; Founded in 1861 and named for one of the first settlers, Patrick Eagan.

•**EAGLE LAKE,** City; Blue Earth County; Pop. 1,470; Zip Code 56024; Elev. 1014; Lat. 44-09-34 N long. 093-53-01 W; Nearby Eagle Lake gave the town its name. The lake was so named due to the many bald eagles nesting around it.

•**EAST BETHEL,** City; Anoka County; Pop. 6,626; Zip Code 55005; Moses Twitchell, an early settler, named the town for his former home in Bethel, Maine.

•**EAST GRAND FORKS,** City; Polk County; Pop. 8,537; Zip Code 56721; Lat. 47-55-47 N long. 097-01-17 W; The city is descriptively named as it is on the east side of the Red River across from Grand Forks, North Dakota.

•**EASTON,** City; Faribault County; Pop. 283; Zip Code 56025; Lat. 43-45-58 N long. 093-54-07 W; The town was founded in 1874 and named for one of the original landowners, Jason Easton.

•**ECHO,** City; Yellow Medicine; Pop. 334; Zip Code 56237; Lat. 44-37-15 N long. 095-24-51 W; Founded in 1874 and called Echo since no other town had this name.

•**EDEN PRAIRIE,** City; Hennepin County; Pop. 16,263; Zip Code 55344; Descriptively named in 1852 by Governor Ramsey for the beautiful natural prairie on the town's southern boundary.

•**EDEN VALLEY,** City; Meeker County; Pop. 763; Zip Code 55329; Lat. 45-19-28 N long. 094-32-43 W; St. Paul, Minneapolis, and Sault Ste. Marie Railway officers gave the town this euphonious name.

•**EDGERTON,** City; Pipestone County; Pop. 1,123; Zip Code 56128; Elev. 1573; Lat. 43-52-21 N long. 096-07-45 W; The town's name honors General Alonzo Edgerton who was a state senator and later a U.S. Senator in the 1880s.

•**EDINA,** City; Hennepin County; Pop. 46,073; Zip Code 55424; Incorporated in 1888 and named after a local flour mill, itself named for a place near Edinburgh, Scotland.

•**EFFIE,** City; Itasca County; Pop. 141; Zip Code 56639; Elev. 1381; Lat. 47-50-30 N long. 093-38-30 W; The town was named for the daughter of its postmaster.

•**EITZEN,** City; Houston County; Pop. 226; Zip Code 55931; Lat. 43-30-21 N long. 091-27-31 W; Early settlers from Germany named the town for their former home.

•**ELBOW LAKE,** City; Grant County Seat; Pop. 1,358; Zip Code 56531; Elev. 1222; Lat. 45-59-30 N long. 095-58-10 W; Descriptively named for the nearby lake which resembles an arm bent at the elbow.

•**ELGIN,** City; Wabasha County; Pop. 667; Zip Code 55932; Lat. 44-07-46 N long. 092-15-00 W; Settled in 1855 and named for the town and county in Scotland.

•**ELIZABETH,** City; Otter Tail County; Pop. 195; Zip Code 56533; Lat. 46-22-51 N long. 096-07-38 W; Founded in 1870 and named for the wife of merchant Rudolph Niggler.

•**ELK RIVER,** City; Sherburne County Seat; Pop. 6,785; Zip Code 55330; Elev. 900; Lat. 45-18-21 N long. 093-34-13 W; The town takes its name from the river which in turn was named by early settlers for the large elk herds in the vicinity.

•**ELKO,** City; Scott County; Pop. 274; Zip Code 55020; Lat. 44-33-51 N long. 093-19-22 W; Believed to be named by early pioneers for a former home.

•ELKTON, City; Mower County; Pop. 139; Zip Code 55933; Lat. 43-39-47 N long. 092-42-13 W; Founded in 1887 and given this name by the Chicago Great Western Railway.

•ELLENDALE, City; Steele County; Pop. 555; Zip Code 56026; Lat. 43-52-21 N long. 093-18-08 W; The town was named in honor of Mrs C.J. Ives (Ellen Dale), the wife of the President of the Chicago, Rock Island, and Pacific Railway.

•ELLSWORTH, City; Nobles County; Pop. 629; Zip Code 56129; Lat. 43-31-02 N long. 096-01-16 W; Founded in 1885 and named in honor of early pioneer Eugene Ellsworth.

•ELMORE, City; Faribault County; Pop. 882; Zip Code 56027; Lat. 43-30-25 N long. 094-03-59 W; After its founding in 1855 as Dobson, the name was changed to honor well known Wisconsin civic leader Andrew Elmore.

•ELROSA, City; Stearns County; Pop. 214; Zip Code 56325; Lat. 45-33-47 N long. 094-56-50 W; Founded by the Soo Railway, the town's name origin is uncertain.

•ELY, City; St. Louis County; Pop. 4,820; Zip Code 55731; Lat. 47-54-15 N long. 091-51-18 W; Financier Arthur Ely who helped open up the Vermillion Range had the town named in his honor.

•ELYSIAN, City; Le Sueur County; Pop. 454; Zip Code 56028; Lat. 44-12-04 N long. 093-40-07 W; Setted in 1858 and named for the Greek heaven, the Elysian Fields.

•EMILY, City; Crow Wing County; Pop. 588; Zip Code 56447; Lat. 46-44-22 N long. 093-58-17 W; The name comes from Emily Lake, itself believed to be named for the wife of an early lumberman.

•EMMONS, City; Freeborn County; Pop. 465; Zip Code 56029; Lat. 43-30-12 N long. 093-29-59 W; The city is named in honor of Henry Emmons, a local merchant and later state legislator.

•ERHARD, City; Otter Tail County; Pop. 194; Zip Code 56534; Lat. 46-30-01 N long. 096-05-34 W; Alexander Erhard's house served as the site of the town's organizational meeting and first election. The town was named in his honor.

•ERSKINE, City; Polk County; Pop. 585; Zip Code 56535; Lat. 47-39-51 N long. 096-00-30 W; John Quincy Erskine, a prominent local banker, left his name on the town.

•EVAN, City; Brown County; Pop. 90; Zip Code 56238; Lat. 44-21-44 N long. 094-50-30 W; Martin Norseth, the town's first postmaster, named his post office Evan in honor of his wife Eva. The town took the name.

•EVANSVILLE, City; Douglas County; Pop. 571; Zip Code 56326; Elev. 1359; Lat. 46-00-24 N long. 095-41-06 W; The town's name honors the first mail carrier in the area, who was killed in the Sioux outbreat of 1862.

•EVELETH, City; St. Louis County; Pop. 5,042; Zip Code 55734; Elev.; Lat. 47-27-40 N long. 092-32-58 W; The city is named for a woodsman named Eleveth who scouted the area for lumber interests in the 1890s.

•EXCELSIOR, City; Hennepin County; Pop. 2,523; Zip Code 55331; Lat. 44-54-28 N long. 093-34-12 W; The city was established by the Excelsior Pioneer Association in 1852. "Excelsior refers to the famous Longfellow poem.

•EYOTA, City; Olmsted County; Pop. 1,244; Zip Code 55934; Elev. 1241; Lat. 43-58-43 N long. 092-15-26 W; A Sioux word meaning the "the greatest.

•FAIRFAX, City; Renville County; Pop. 1,405; Zip Code 55332; Lat. 44-31-36 N long. 094-43-00 W; Named by the President of the Minneapolis and St. Louis Railway for his native county in Virginia.

•FAIRMONT, City; Martin County Seat; Pop. 11,506; Zip Code 56031; Lat. 43-38-48 N long. 094-27-36 W; A descriptive name referring to the city's positon overlooking Central Chain of Lakes.

•FARIBAULT, City; Rice County Seat; Pop. 16,241; Zip Code 55021; Lat. 44-17-20 N long. 093-16-24 W; The city is named for early settler and merchant Alexander Faribault who arrived in the area in 1826.

•FARMINGTON, City; Dakota County; Pop. 4,370; Zip Code 55024; Elev. 904; Lat. 44-38-12 N long. 093-08-35 W; A descriptive name for the many farms originally in the area.

•FARWELL, City; Pope County; Pop. 77; Zip Code 56329; Lat. 45-45-003 N long. 095-37-16 W; Founded as a railway town in 1887 and euphonious in origin.

•FEDERAL DAM, City; Cass County; Pop. 192; Zip Code 56641; Lat. 47-14-15 N long. 094-12-23 W; A descriptive name referring to the reservoir dam on nearby Leech Lake River.

•FELTON, City; Clay County; Pop. 264; Zip Code 56536; Elev. 910; Lat. 47-04-09 N long. 096-30-18 W; The town takes its name from the railway statoin S. M. Felton, a Great Northern railroad officer.

•FERGUS FALLS, City; Otter Tail County Seat; Pop. 12,519; Zip Code 56537; Lat. 46-18-03 N long. 096-05-46 W; The name honors James Fergus who organized and financed the original settlement of the town.

•FERTILE, City; Polk County; Pop. 869; Zip Code 56540; Lat. 47-32-04 N long. 096-16-54 W; Early settlers from Fertile, Iowa gave their new home their old home's name.

•FIFTY LAKES, City; Crow Wing County; Pop. 263; Zip Code 56448; Lat. 46-44-45 N long. 094-03-49 W; A descriptive name for the many lakes in the area.

•FINLAYSON, City; Pine County; Pop. 202; Zip Code 55735; Lat. 46-12-14 N long. 092-59-08 W; Sawmill owner David Finlayson had the town named in his honor.

•FISHER, City; Polk County; Pop. 453; Zip Code 56723; Lat. 47-47-59 N long. 096-48-05 W; Originally a steamboat port and later a railway terminal, the name honors St. Paul and Duluth Railroad President William H. Fisher.

•FLENSBURG, City; Morrison County; Pop. 256; Zip Code 56328; Lat. 45-51-04 N long. 094-33-57 W; Early settles named the town for their former home, a seaport in Prussia.

•FLOODWOOD, City; St. Louis County; Pop. 648; Zip Code 55736; Lat. 46-56-02 N long. 092-54-55 W; A descriptive name taken from floodewater river which was formerly blocked by large rafts of driftwood.

•FOLEY, City; Benton County Seat; Pop. 1,606; Zip Code 56329; Lat. 45-39-52 N long. 093-54-57 W; The town is named in honor of one of its founders, John Foley.

•FOREST LAKE, City; Washington County; Pop. 4,596; Zip Code 55025; Elev. 909; Lat. 45-16-22 N long. 092-58-55 W; Descriptively named as the town was situated on the west end of a lake with great timber growth along its shores. .

•FORESTON, City; Mille Lacs County; Pop. 283; Zip Code 56330; Lat. 45-44-01 N long. 093-42-35 W; Descriptively named as the town was partially encompossed by a forest.

•FOSSTON, City; Polk County; Pop. 1,599; Zip Code 56542; Elev. 1298; Lat. 47-34-40 N long. 095-44-50 W; The city takes its name from pioneer merchant Louis Foss.

•FOUNTAIN, City; Fillmore County; Pop. 327; Zip Code 55935; Elev. 1305; Lat. 43-44-32 N long. 092-07-30 W; A large spring named "fountain spring" gave the town its name.

•FOXHOME, City; Wilkin County; Pop. 161; Zip Code 56543; Elev. 1029; Lat. 46-16-39 N long. 096-18-46 W; Robert A. Fox, a real estate developer, owned the land upon which the town was founded and had it named after him.

•FRANKLIN, City; Renville County; Pop. 512; Zip Code 55333; The town's name is one of many in 29 states honoring Benjamin Franklin.

•FRAZEE, City; Becker County; Pop. 1,284; Zip Code 56544; Lat. 46-43-43 N long. 095-41-54 W; Randoph Frazee served in the Minesota state legislature in 1875 and ran a lumber mill business. The town is named in his honor.

•FREEBORN, City; Freeborn County; Pop. 323; Zip Code 56032; Lat. 43-45-57 N long. 093-33-18 W; A member of the Minnesota Territorial Legislature in the 1850's, both the county and town are named in his honor.

•FREEPORT, City; Stearns County; Pop. 563; Zip Code 56331; Lat. 45-41-49 N long. 094-42-134 W; Early settlers from Freeport, Illinois gave the same name to their new home.

•FRIDLEY, City; Anoka County; Pop. 30,228; Zip Code 55432; Abram Fridley was a prosperous farmer and member of the state legislature. The town is named in his honor.

•GEORGETOWN, City; Clay County; Pop. 124; Zip Code 56546; Elev. 1247; Lat. 47-04-37 N long. 096-47-34 W; Founded as Hudson Bat Trading Post in 1859 and named for one of their employees.

•GHENT, City; Lyon County; Pop. 356; Zip Code 56239; Elev. 1164; Lat. 44-30-045 N long. 095-53-41 W; The arrival of a group of Belgian colonists in 1880 caused Grandview to be renamed Ghent, a city in Belgium.

•GIBBON, City; Sibley County; Pop. 787; Zip Code 55335; Lat. 45-35-58 N long. 094-51-32 W; The city's name honors Gengam John Gibbon who was stationed in Minesota in the 1800's.

•GILBERT, City; St. Louis County; Pop. 2,721; Zip Code 55741; Lat. 47-28-56 N long. 092-27-31 W; Founded in 1908 the city's name honors E. A. Gilbert, a well-known Duluth businessman.

•GILMAN, City; Benton County; Pop. 156; Zip Code 56333; Lat. 45-44-04 N long. 093-57-13 W; Charles Gilman served Minnesota in the state legislature and as the register of the U. S. Land Office in St. Cloud. He was both Lieutenant Governor and state librarian in the 1880's and 1890's. The town's name remembers his many contributions.

•GLENCOE, City; McLeod County Seat; Pop. 4,396; Zip Code 55336; Lat. 45-49-34 N long 094-45-03 W; The town was founded in 1855 and named for Glencoe, Scotland.

•GLENVILLE, City; Freeborn County; Pop. 851; Zip Code 56036; Lat. 43-34-14 N long. 093-14-57 W; Formerly Shell rock the community was renamed Glenville by local railway officials in 1898.

•GLENWOOD, City; Pope County Seat_; Pop. 2,523; Zip Code 56334; Lat. 45-39-23 N long. 095-25-03 W; Descriptively named for the great valley along the southside of Lake Minnewaska.

•GLYNDON, City; Clay County; Pop. 882; Zip Code 56547; Elev. 922; Lat. 46-46-56 N long. 096-34-15 W; Founded in 1872 and named by officials of the Northern Pacific Railroad Co., the name remembers Burton and poet Mrs. Edward W. Searing whose pen name was Howard Glyndon.

•GOLDEN VALLEY, City; Hennepin County; Pop. 22,775; Zip Code 55427; Near Minneapolis the city is descriptively named for its small valley and lake.

•GONVICK, City; Clearwater County; Pop. 362; Zip Code 56664; Lat. 47-44-24 N long. 095-30-43 W; Martin Gonvick, an early Norwegian pioneer, gave the town his name.

•GOOD THUNDER, City; Blue Earth County; Pop. 560; Zip Code 56037; Lat. 44-00-23 N long. 094-04-10 W; The town's name remembers Winnebagoe Indian chief Good Thunder whose village was nearby.

•GOODHUE, City; Goodhue County; Pop. 657; Zip Code 55027; Lat. 44-23-04 N long. 092-34-12 W; James M. Goodhue was the first printer and newspaperman in Minnesota. The town honors his memory.

•GRACEVILLE, City; Big Stone County; Pop. 780; Zip Code 56240; Elev. 1116; Lat. 45-34-07 N long. 096-26-16 W; The town was settled by Catholics in the late 1870's. They named their new home after Thomas Grace, Bishop of St. Paul.

•GRANADA, City; Martin County; Pop. 377; Zip Code 56039; Lat. 47-45-13 N long. 090-20-26 W; The city is named for the famous Kinsoam and town in Spain.

•GRAND MARAIS, City; Cook County Seat; Pop. 1,289; Zip Code 55604; Elev. 688; Lat. 47-45-13 N long. 090-20-26 W; Early French trappers descriptively named the town "Great Marsh" for its original feature.

•GRAND MEADOW, City; Mower County; Pop. 965; Zip Code 55936; Elev. 1341; Lat. 43-42-28 N long. 092-34-15 W; The city was founded on an extensive prairie and hence so named.

•GRAND RAPIDS, City; Itasca County Seat; Pop. 7,934; Zip Code 55774; Elev. 1290; Lat. 47-13-44 N long. 093-30-08 W; Descriptively named after the adjacent rapids on the Mississippi River.

•GRANITE FALLS, City; Yellow Medicine Seat; Pop. 3,451; Zip Code 56241; The Minnesota River forms a falls over large granite outcrops and thus the city took the name.

•GREEN ISLE, City; Sibley County; Pop. 357; Zip Code 55338; Elev. 1000; Lat. 44-40-43 N long. 094-00-44 W; Irish immigrant Christopher Dolan suggested the name as on allusion to Ireland. The townspeople took the name.

•GREENBUSH, City; Roseau County; Pop. 817; Zip Code 56726; Lat. 48-41-57 N long. 096-11-19 W; The city took its name from evergreen spruce trees visible from an early pioneer wagon road.

•GREENWALD, City; Stearns County; Pop. 259; Zip Code 56335; Elev. 1263; Settled by Germans, the town was given the name which means green grass.

•GREY EAGLE, City; Todd County; Pop. 338; Zip Code 56336; Elev. 1222; The town takes its name from a gray eagle shot in the area in 1868.

•GROVE CITY, City; Meeker County; Pop. 596; Zip Code 56243; Lat. 45-09-03 N long. 094-40-22 W; The city's name points out the many original forest groves in the vicinity.

•GRYGLA, City; Marshall County; Pop. 216; Zip Code 56727; Lat. 48-18-00 N long. 095-37-18 W; The town is named in honor of Frank Grygla, a well-known Polish patriot and descendant of a noble Polish family.

•GULLY, City; Polk County; Pop. 116; Zip Code 56646; Lat. 47-46-05 N long. 095-37-21 W; A descriptive name for a glacier-created gully that is near the town.

•HACKENSACK, City; Cass County; Pop. 285; Zip Code 56452; Lat. 46-55-53 N long. 094-31-17 W; The town is named for Hackensack, New Jersey.

•HADLEY, City; Murray County; Pop. 137; Zip Code 56133; Lat. 43-59-59 N long. 095-51-21 W; An old English name found in several New England states, and given to this city in Murray county.

•HALLOCK, City; Kittson County Seat; Pop. 1,405; Zip Code 56728; Elev. 817; Lat. 48-46-20 N long. 096-56-20 W; The town is named for Charles Hallock who was a well-known sportsman and journalist and who built a hotel in the city in 1890.

•HALMA, City; Kittson County; Pop. 97; Zip Code 56729; Elev. 1001; Lat. 48-39-37 N long. 096-35-32 W; Early Norwegian settlers named the town for a place in Norway.

•HALSTAD, City; Norman County; Pop. 690; Zip Code 56548; Elev. 872; Lat. 47-21-09 N long. 096-49-47 W; The town's name remembers Ole Halstad, an early pioneer farmer who emigrated from Norway.

•HAMBURG, City; Carver County; Pop. 475; Zip Code 55339; Lat. 44-43-48 N long. 093-57-43 W; The great German city on the river Elbe provided the name for the town.

•HAMMOND, City; Wabasha County; Pop. 178; Zip Code 55938; Pioneer farmer, Joseph Hammond, owned the land upon which the village was founded and hence its name. .

•HAMPTON, City; Dakota County; Pop. 299; Zip Code 55031; Elev. 980; Lat. 44-36-28 N long. 092-57-56 W; Founded in 1858 and named for a town in Connecticut.

•HANCOCK, City; Stevens County; Pop. 877; Zip Code 56244; Elev. 1151; Lat. 45-29-44 N long. 095-47-10 W; Early missionary, teacher, and local historian Joseph Hancock had the town named in his honor.

•HANLEY FALLS, City; Yellow Medicine; Pop. 265; Zip Code 56245; Elev. 1046; Lat. 44-41-43 N long. 095-37-07 W; The town's name honors an officer of the Minneapolis and St. Louis Railroad Co. which reached the town in 1884.

•HANOVER, City; Wright County; Pop. 647; Zip Code 55341; Lat. 45-09-32 N long. 093-39-17 W; German immigrants, the Vellbrecht brothers, named the town after their birthplace in Germany.

•HANSKA, City; Brown County; Pop. 429; Zip Code 56041; Lat. 44-09-32 N long. 094-29-45 W; Hanska is a Siux word meaning "lone" which the Indians named the adjacent lake, and in turn named the town. .

•HARDWICK, City; Rock County; Pop. 279; Zip Code 56134; Elev. 607; Lat. 43-46-40 N long. 096-11-55 W; The city's name honors J. L. Hardwick, one time master builder of the Burlington Railway Co. .

•HARMONY, City; Fillmore County; Pop. 1,133; Zip Code 55939; Lat. 43-33-05 N long. 091-59-51 W; Early pioneers gave their new town the euphonious name Harmony.

•HARRIS, City; Chisago County; Pop. 678; Zip Code 55032; Elev. 902; Lat. 45-34-45 N long. 092-58-30 W; Incorporated in 1884 and named in honor of Phillip Harris, an officer of St. Paul and Duluth Railway Co.

•HARTLAND, City; Freeborn County; Pop. 322; Zip Code 56042; Elev. 1252; Lat. 43-48-13 N long. 093-29-20 W; Settlers from Hartland, Vermont named their new town after the old one in 1857.

•HASTINGS, City; Dakota County Seat; Pop. 12,827; Zip Code 55033; Elev. 730; Lat. 44-40-25 N long. 092-49-59 W; The town's name recalls Gasson L. Henry Hastings Sibley who defended the state during the 1862 Sioux uprisig.

•HATFIELD, City; Pipestone County; Pop. 87; Zip Code 56135; Lat. 44-00-10 N long. 096-19-38 W; Named by early settlers for another town in Massachusetts.

•HAWLEY, City; Clay County; Pop. 1,634; Zip Code 56549; Lat. 46-47-16 N long. 096-18-30 W; Originally called Bethel but renamed to honor Gov. Joseph Hawley, Civil War hero and U.S. Senator.

•HAYWARD, City; Freeborn County; Pop. 294; Zip Code 56043; Lat. 43-39-06 N long. 093-13-09 W; Hayward is named in honor of David Hayward, one of the earliest settlers.

•HECTOR, City; Renville County; Pop. 1,252; Zip Code 55342; Elev. 1078; Lat. 44-44-36 N long. 094-42-39 W; Settlers from Hector, New York gave the town its name.

•HENDERSON, City; Sibley County; Pop. 739; Zip Code 56044; Lat. 44-31-53 N long. 093-54-18 W; Early settler and newspaperman Joseph Brown named the town in honor of his grandfather, Andrew Henderson.

•HENDRICKS, City; Lincoln County; Pop. 737; Zip Code 56136; Lat. 44-30-28 N long. 096-25-38 W; The town takes its name from nearby Lake Hendricks. The lake's name honors Thomas A. Hendricks, Vice-President of the U.S. in 1885.

•HENDRUM, City; Norman County; Pop. 336; Zip Code 56550; Lat. 47-15-54 N long. 096-48-35 W; Norwegian emigrant farmers named the town for a district in Norway.

•HENNING, City; Otter Tail County; Pop. 832; Zip Code 56551; Lat. 46-19-16 N long. 095-26-22 W; Founded in 1878 the town was renamed Henning in 1884 to honor John O. Henning, the town druggist.

•HERMAN, City; Grant County; Pop. 600; Zip Code 56248; Elev. 1073; Lat. 45-48-33 N long. 096-08-10 W; Herman Trett, land agent of the St. Paul and Pacific Railway, had the town named in his honor.

•HERON LAKE, City; Jackson County; Pop. 783; Zip Code 56137; Lat. 43-47-54 N long. 095-19-36 W; The town is named from Heron Lake. The lake is named Heron from a Sioux Indian name which translates "nesting place of herons.".

•HEWITT, City; Todd County; Pop. 299; Zip Code 56453; Lat. 46-18-30 N long. 095-04-40 W; The city's name honors nearby farmer, Jenry Hewitt.

•HIBBING, City; St. Louis County; Pop. 21,193; Zip Code 55746; Lat. 47-25-22 N long. 092-55-13 W; German immigrant Frank Hibbing was a large invester in the Mesabi Iron Mines. The town is named in his honor. .

•HILL CITY, City; Aitkin County; Pop. 533; Zip Code 55748; Lat. 46-59-21 N long. 093-36-00 W; A descriptive name for the glacial moraine (hill) which dominates the immediate vicinity.

•HILLS, City; Rock County; Pop. 598; Zip Code 56138; Lat. 43-31-49 N long. 096-21-38 W; Railway President Frederick Hills left his name on town.

•HINCKLEY, City; Pine County; Pop. 963; Zip Code 55037; Elev. 1031; Lat. 46-01-02 N long. 092-56-16 W; Named in honor of Isaac Hinckley, president of the Philadelphia and Baltimore Railway Co.

•**HOFFMAN,** City; Grant County; Pop. 631; Zip Code 56339; Elev. 1254; Lat. 45-50-00 N long. 095-47-05 W; The town's name honors Robert C. Hoffman, who was the chief engineer of the Minneapolis, St. Paul and South Ste. Maine Railway.

•**HOKAH,** City; Houston County; Pop. 686; Zip Code 55941; Lat. 43-45-26 N long. 091-20-51 W; A Sioux Indian chief named Hokah once lived with his village nearby and gave the town its name.

•**HOLDINGFORD,** City; Stearns County; Pop. 635; Zip Code 56340; Lat. 45-43-52 N long. 094-28-18 W; Pioneer Randolph Holding named this site as a fording point of the south stream of the two rivers.

•**HOLLANDALE,** City; Freeborn County; Pop. 290; Zip Code 56045; Lat. 43-45-36 N long. 093-10-40 W; Named by Dutch settlers for the old country.

•**HOPKINS,** City; Hennepin County; Pop. 15,336; Zip Code 55334; The city is named for its one time postmaster, Harley Hopkins.

•**HOUSTON,** City; Houston County; Pop. 1,057; Zip Code 55943; Elev. 684; Lat. 43-45-41 N long. 091-33-18 W; Found in the 1850's and named for General Sam Houston of Texas.

•**HOWARD LAKE,** City; Wright County; Pop. 1,240; Zip Code 55349; Elev. 1018; Lat. 45-03-33 N long. 094-03-50 W; Early surveyors named the nearby lake for English humanitarian, John Howard. The town is named from the lake.

•**HOYT LAKES,** City; St. Louis County; Pop. 3,186; Zip Code 55750; Elev. 1469; Lat. 47-30-36 N long. 092-08-35 W; The city is named in honor of businessman Elton Hoyt II.

•**HUGO,** City; Washington County; Pop. 3,771; Zip Code 55038; Elev. 935; Lat. 45-10-15 N long. 093-04-30 W; The town's name honors Trevanion Hugo, an English engineer who settled in Minnesota and later became mayor of Duluth (1900-1904).

•**HUMBOLDT,** City; Kittson County; Pop. 111; Zip Code 56731; Lat. 48-55-18 N long. 097-05-41 W; The city is named in honor of Baron Alexander von Humboldt, the famous German scientist and naturalist.

•**HUTCHINSON,** City; McLeod County; Pop. 9,244; Zip Code 55350; Elev. 1056; Lat. 44-53-27 N long. 094-22-11 W; The city is named after two of its founders, the Hutchinson brothers.

•**IHLEN,** City; Pipestone County; Pop. 129; Zip Code 56140; Lat. 43-54-36 N long. 096-21-54 W; The original owner of the town's land, Casper Ihlen, had the town named in his honor.

•**INDEPENDENCE,** City; Hennepin County; Pop. 2,640; The city was named by its townfolk in honor of the 4th of July.

•**INTERNATIONAL FALLS,** City; Koochiching County Seat; Pop. 5,611; Zip Code 56649; Elev. 1128; Lat. 48-36-18 N long. 093-17-52 W; A descriptive name for the town's location on the international Canadian-American boundary.

•**INVER GROVE HEIGHTS,** City; Dakota County; Pop. 17,171; Irish settler John McGroartt named the town for a town in Ireland.

•**IONA,** City; Murray County; Pop. 248; Zip Code 56141; Lat. 43-54-53 N long. 095-47-06 W; Founded in 1880 and named for a small island off the west coast of Scotland, known for its ancient abbey.

•**IRON JUNCTION,** City; St. Louis County; Pop. 134; The town is a railway junction for the shipment of iron ore from the Mesobi Range, hence the name.

•**IRONTON,** City; Crow Wing County; Pop. 537; Zip Code 56455; Lat. 46-28-08 N long. 094-01-28 W; Descriptively named after the large U. S. Steel camp mill in the town.

•**ISANTI,** City; Isanti County; Pop. 858; Zip Code 55040; Lat. 45-29-30 N long. 093-14-55 W; The name of the eastern Sioux who lived here before the coming of the white man.

•**ISLAND VIEW,** City; Koochiching County; Pop. 101; The city is descriptively named.

•**ISLE,** City; Mille Lacs County; Pop. 573; Zip Code 56342; Lat. 46-08-46 N long. 093-27-32 W; A port on Mille Lacs protected from storms by great island.

•**IVANHOE,** City; Lincoln County Seat; Pop. 761; Zip Code 56142; Lat. 44-27-37 N long. 096-14-54 W; Founded in 1900 and named for the home of Sir Walter Scott's novel.

•**JACKSON,** City; Jackson County Seat; Pop. 3,797; Zip Code 56143; Elev. 1479; Lat. 43-37-12 N long. 095-01-55 W; The town is named for Henry Jackson, who was the first merchant in the city of St. Paul.

•**JANESVILLE,** City; Waseca County; Pop. 1,897; Zip Code 56048; Lat. 44-07-04 N long. 093-42-21 W; Founded in 1856 and named for a popular local settler, Mrs. Jane Sprague.

•**JASPER,** City; Pipestone County; Pop. 731; Zip Code 56144; Lat. 43-51-00 N long. 096-24-00 W; The town was incorporated in 1889 and named for the deposits of red quartzite, or jasper, found nearby.

•**JEFFERS,** City; Cottonwood County; Pop. 437; Zip Code 56145; Lat. 44-03-40 N long. 095-11-40 W; The town was founded on land owned by George Jeffers, and named in his honor.

•**JENKINS,** City; Crow Wing County; Pop. 219; Lumberman George Jenkins founded the town and had it named in his honor.

•**JOHNSON,** City; Big Stone County; Pop. 57; Zip Code 56250; Lat. 45-34-11 N long. 096-17-36 W; The city is named for an early settler.

•**JORDAN,** City; Scott County; Pop. 2,663; Zip Code 55352; Lat. 44-40-08 N long. 093-37-47 W; Founded in 1872 and named after much argument for the Biblical Jordan River.

•**KANDIYOHI,** City; Kandiyohi County; Pop. 447; Zip Code 56251; Elev. 1223; Lat. 45-07-51 N long. 094-55-36 W; The name is a Sioux Indian word meaning "where the buffalo fish come.".

•**KARLSTAD,** City; Kittson County; Pop. 934; Zip Code 56732; Elev. 1048; Lat. 48-34-43 N long. 096-30-33 W; Named by early Swedish settlers for Karlstad, Sweden.

•**KASOTA,** City; Le Sueur County; Pop. 739; Zip Code 56050; Lat. 44-17-21 N long. 093-57-18 W; A Sioux Indian word meaning "cleared off" and referring to the nearby prairie.

•**KASSON,** City; Dodge County; Pop. 2,827; Zip Code 55944; Elev. 1242; Lat. 44-01-53 N long. 092-45-06 W; The town is named in honor of original landowner, J. H. Kasson.

•**KEEWATIN,** City; Itasca County; Pop. 1,443; Zip Code 55753; Elev. 1469; Lat. 47-24-15 N long. 093-09-13 W; An Ojibway Indian word meaning "the northwest-wind."

•**KELLIHER,** City; Beltrami County; Pop. 324; Zip Code 56650; Elev. 1361; Lat. 47-56-37 N long. 094-27-00 W; A one time lumbering town, it was named in honor of lumber agent A. O. Kelliher.

•**KELLOGG,** City; Wabasha County; Pop. 440; Zip Code 55945; Lat. 44-18-31 N long. 091-59-41 W; Railroad officials named the town for a company vendor.

•**KENNEDY,** City; Kittson County; Pop. 405; Zip Code 56733; Lat. 48-38-36 N long. 096-54-28 W; The city is named in honor of railway director and banker John Stewart Kennedy, who was well-known for his humantarian work.

•**KENNETH,** City; Rock County; Pop. 95; Zip Code 56147; Lat. 43-45-23 N long. 096-04-16 W; Founded in 1900 and named for the son of a nearby farmer.

•**KENSINGTON,** City; Douglas County; Pop. 331; Zip Code 56343; Lat. 45-46-44 N long. 095-41-40 W; The town was incorporated in 1891 and named for the western section of London, England.

•**KENT,** City; Wilkin County; Pop. 121; Zip Code 56553; Lat. 46-26-11 N long. 096-40-52 W; The city was named by Great Northern Railway officers for the county in England.

•**KENYON,** City; Goodhue County; Pop. 1,529; Zip Code 55946; Lat. 44-15-48 N long. 092-59-09 W; The town waws settled in 1858 and named for a merchant who founded a general store.

•**KERKHOVEN,** City; Swift County; Pop. 761; Zip Code 56252; Elev. 1109; Lat. 45-11-27 N long. 095-18-44.

•**KERRICK,** City; Pine County; Pop. 79; Zip Code 55729; Lat. 46-22-11 N long. 092-33-10 W; Named in honor of Cassius Kerrick who worked for the Great Northern Railway Co.

•**KETTLE RIVER,** City; Carlton County; Pop. 174; Zip Code 55757; Elev. 1182; Lat. 46-29-07 N long. 092-52-40 W; The town is named after the river. Kettle is a translation of an Ojibway Indian name.

•**KIESTER,** City; Faribault County; Pop. 670; Zip Code 56051; Lat. 43-32-43 N long. 093-42-30 W; The city's name honors Jacob Kiester who became historian of Faribault County.

•**KIKENNY,** City; Le Sueur County; Pop. 177; Zip Code 56052; Lat. 44-18-46 N long. 093-33-53 W; Named by Irish settlers for the county in Ireland.

•**KIMBALL PRAIRIE,** City; Stearns County; Pop. 651; Frye Kimball was an early settler in the county. The town is named in his honor.

•**KINBRAE,** City; Nobles County; Pop. 40; Founded in 1879 and given its Scottish name by officers of the Dundee Land Company.

•**KINGSTON,** City; Meeker County; Pop. 141; The site was settled in 1856 and named by lawyer Geroge Nourse. Kingston is a common English place name.

•**KINNEY,** City; St. Louis County; Pop. 447; Zip Code 55758; Lat. 47-30-44 N long. 092-43-44 W; Named in honor of O. D.Kinney who discovered the iron deposits of Virginia, Minnesota.

•**LA CRESCENT,** City; Houston County; Pop. 3,674; Zip Code 55947; Lat. 43-49-35 N long. 091-18-24 W; Settled in 1851 and named in contrast to La Crosse, Wisconsin across the Mississipi River.

•**LA SALLE,** City; Watonwan County; Pop. 115; Zip Code 56056; Founded in 1899 and named for the famous French explorer Robert Cavelier (De La Salle.).

•**LAFAYETTE,** City; Nicollett County; Pop. 507; Zip Code 56054; Elev. 1014; Lat. 44-27-01 N long. 094-23-37 W; Founded in 1858 and named in honor of Revolutionary War hero Marquis de Lafayette.

•**LAKE BENTON,** City; Lincoln County; Pop. 869; Zip Code 56149; Lat. 44-15-28 N long. 096-17-22 W; Explorers Nicolett and Fremont named the nearby lake for Fremont's father-in-law, U. S. Senator Thomas Hart Benton.

•**LAKE BRONSON,** City; Kittson County; Pop. 298; Zip Code 56734; Lat. 48-44-05 N long. 096-39-24 W; The town takes its name from early farmer Giles Bronson, a well-known sportsman.

•**LAKE CITY,** City; Wabasha County; Pop. 4,505; Zip Code 55041; Elev. 701; Lat. 44-26-42 N long. 092-16-13 W; A descriptive name for the town next to Lake Popin.

•**LAKE CRYSTAL,** City; Blue Earth County; Pop. 2,078; Zip Code 56055; Elev. 1000; Lat. 44-06-20 N long. 094-13-20 W; Explorers Nicollett and Fremont named the nearby lake for its crystal waters. The town took the lake's name.

•**LAKE ELMO,** City; Washington County; Pop. 5,296; Zip Code 55042; Lat. 44-59-38 N long. 092-54-58 W; Originally called Bass Lake, but renamed to "St. Elmo" after a popular novel.

•**LAKE LILLIAN,** City; Kandiyohi County; Pop. 329; Zip Code 56243; Lat. 44-56-43 N long. 094-52-33 W; Artist and writer, Edwin Whitefield, was part of the exploring party in 1856. The lake and later the town are named in honor of his wife Lillian.

•**LAKE PARK,** City; Becker County; Pop. 716; Zip Code 56554; Lat. 46-53-12 N long. 096-05-58 W; Founded in 1841 and named after an Indian word which loosely translates as "the lakes with the beautiful parks."

•**LAKE WILSON,** City; Murray County; Pop. 380; Zip Code 56151; Lat. 43-59-42 N long. 095-57-13 W; Prominent landowner, Johnathan Wilson, named the nearby lake for himself. The town is named after the lake.

•**LAKEFIELD,** City; Jackson County; Pop. 1,845; Zip Code 56150; Elev. 1476; Lat. 43-40-49 N long. 095-10-22 W; The town is named for the adjacent Heron Lake.

•**LAKELAND,** City; Washington County; Pop. 1,812; Zip Code 55043; Lat. 44-57-27 N long. 092-45-52 W; The town's name comes from being on Lake St. Croix.

•**LAKEVILLE,** City; Dakota County; Pop. 14,790; Zip Code 55044; Elev. 974; Lat. 44-40-33 N long. 093-15-01 W; The town's received its name from the adjacent Lake Marion.

•**LAMBERTON,** City; Redwood County; Pop. 1,032; Zip Code 56142; Elev. 1151; Lat. 44-13-54 N long. 095-15-48 W; The town's name remembers Henry W. Lamberton who was a prominent civic leader.

•**LANCASTER,** City; Kittson County; Pop. 368; Zip Code 56735; Lat. 48-51-15 N long. 0-96-48-09 W; Early settlers gave the town the name of the county in England.

•**LANESBORO,** City; Fillmore County; Pop. 923; Zip Code 55949; Elev. 846; Lat. 43-43-15 N long. 091-57-42 W; Settlers from Lanesboro, Massachusetts named the town after their old home.

•**LAPORTE,** City; Hubbard County; Pop. 160; Zip Code 56461; Lat. 47-13-04 N long. 094-46-17 W; A French name meaning "the door," and probably referring to early trade routes through the area's lakes.

•LE CENTER, City; Le Sueur County Seat; Pop. 1,967; Zip Code 56057; Elev. 1052; Lat. 44-23-28 N long. 093-43-18 W; Organized in 1890 at the exact geographic centr of the county and hence the name.

•LE ROY, City; Mower County; Pop. 930; Zip Code 55951; Lat. 43-30-38 N long. 092-30-00 W; Orignally a railway village, railroad officers gave it this common French place name.

•LE SUEUR, City; Le Sueur County; Pop. 3,763; Zip Code 56058; Lat. 44-28-07 N long. 093-53-30 W; The city and county are named for early French explorer Pierre Charles La Sueur who explored the region in 1689.

•LESTER PRAIRIE, City; McLeod County; Pop. 1,229; Zip Code 55354; Elev. 1004; Lat. 44-53-08 N long. 094-02-21 W; The city was founded in 1888 and named in honor of Mr. and Mrs. John Lester, the original townsite landowners.

•LEWISTON, City; Winona County; Pop. 1,226; Zip Code 55952; Lat. 43-59-02 N long. 091-51-54 W; S. J. Lewis, an early settler, had the town named in his honor.

•LEWISVILLE, City; Watonwan County; Pop. 273; Zip Code 56060; Lat. 43-55-25 N long. 094-26-01 W; The town honored one of its early pioner families, the Lewis family, by its choice of their name.

•LINDSTROM, City; Chisago County; Pop. 1,972; Zip Code 55045; Lat. 45-23-28 N long. 092-51-00 W; Swedish farmer and pioneer Daniel Lindstrom came to the region in the mid 1800's. The town is named after him.

•LISMORE, City; Nobles County; Pop. 276; Zip Code 56155; Lat. 43-44-59 N long. 095-56-47 W; A baronial village in Ireland provided the name for this new world town.

•LITCHFIELD, City; Meeker County Seat; Pop. 5,904; Zip Code 55355; Lat. 45-07-35 N long. 094-30-48 W; Originally called Ness, the town later changed its name to honor the local Litchfield brothers who were railroad contractors.

•LITTLE FALLS, City; Morrison County Seat; Pop. 7,250; Zip Code 56345; Lat. 45-57-00 N long. 094-25-09 W; Incorporated in 1879, the town's name describes the rapids of the adjacent Mississipi River.

•LITTLEFORK, City; Koochiching County; Pop. 918; Zip Code 56653; Lat. 48-23-44 N long. 093-33-31 W; Located on the little fork of the Rainy River and so descriptively named.

•LONG LAKE, City; Hennepin County; Pop. 1,747; Zip Code 55356; Elev. 981; Lat. 44-58-59 N long. 093-34-20 W; The city gets its name from nearby descriptively named Long Lake.

•LONG PRAIRIE, City; Todd County Seat; Pop. 2,859; Zip Code 56347; Lat. 45-58-33 N long. 094-51-29 W; The Long Prairie River flows through the county and names the town.

•LONSDALE, City; Rice County; Pop. 1,160; Zip Code 55046; Lat. 44-31-57 N long. 093-25-39 W; Named by settlers from Rhode Island for a town in their former state.

•LORETTO, City; Hennepin County; Pop. 297; Zip Code 55357; Lat. 45-03-15 N long. 093-38-07 W; Founded in 1886 and named via a Catholic man's society for a pilgrimage shrine in Italy.

•LOWRY, City; Pope County; Pop. 283; Zip Code 56349; Lat. 45-42-14 N long. 095-31-20 W; Thomas Lawry was a prominent Minneapolis civil leader in the late 1800's. The town is named in his honor.

•LUCAN, City; Redwood County; Pop. 262; Zip Code 56255; Lat. 44-24-38 N long. 095-24-51 W; Irish settlers named their new home after a village near Dublin, Ireland.

•LUVERNE, City; Rock County Seat; Pop. 4,568; Zip Code 56156; Lat. 43-39-35 N long. 096-12-38 W; Named for an early pioneer settler.

•LYLE, City; Mower County; Pop. 576; Zip Code 55953; Lat. 43-30-12 N long. 092-56-31 W; Judge Robert Lyle lived in the area in the 1850's and 1860's. The town's name honors him.

•LYND, City; Lyon County; Pop. 304; Zip Code 56157; Elev. 1320; Lat. 44-23-24 N long. 095-53-39 W; Fur trader James Lynd was killed in the 1862 Sioux uprising. The town was given his name in 1873.

•MABEL, City; Fillmore County; Pop. 861; Zip Code 55954; Elev. 1134; Lat. 43-31-11 N long. 091-45-55 W; Railroad engineer Frank Adams memorialized his deceased young daughter by giving the town her name.

•MADELIA, City; Watonwan County; Pop. 2,130; Zip Code 56062; Elev. 1029; Lat. 44-02-47 N long. 094-25-31 W; Founded in 1857 the name is an elision of Madeline, the daughter of an original landowner.

•MADISON, City; Lac qui Parle Seat; Pop. 2,212; Zip Code 56256; Lat. 45-00-50 N long. 096-11-23 W; Settled in 1877 and named by a pioneer for his former home in Madison, Wisconsin.

•MADISON LAKE, City; Blue Earth County; Pop. 592; Zip Code 56063; Lat. 44-12-12 N long. 093-48-50 W; Named for adjoining Madison Lake, itself named for fourth President of the United States, James Madison.

•MAGNOLIA, City; Rock County; Pop. 234; Zip Code 56158; Lat. 43-38-45 N long. 096-04-38 W; Founded in 1872 and named for Magnolia, Wisconsin from whence an early settler had come.

•MAHNOMEN, City; Mahnomen County Seat; Pop. 1,283; Zip Code 56557; Lat. 47-18-56 N long. 095-58-04 W; The Ojibway Indian word for "wild rice.".

•MANKATO, City; Blue Earth County Seat; Pop. 28,651; Zip Code 56001; A Sioux Indian word meaning "blue-green earth." Home of the well-known American artist Jeanne Regis.

•MANTORVILLE, City; Dodge County Seat; Pop. 705; Zip Code 55955; Lat. 44-03-58 N long. 092-45-23 W; Lumber businessman C. Peter Mantor was a leading force in establishment of the town. It was named in his family's honor.

•MAPLE GROVE, City; Hennepin County; Pop. 20,525; A descriptive name for the many sugar maple trees in the area.

•MAPLE LAKE, City; Wright County; Pop. 1,132; Zip Code 55358; Lat. 45-14-03 N long. 094-00-36 W; The city takes its name from nearby Maple Lake. Woodlands of sugar maple are abundant in the area.

•MAPLE PLAIN, City; Hennepin County; Pop. 1,421; Zip Code 55359; Found in 1868 and named for the many sugar maple groves in the area.

•MAPLETON, City; Blue Earth County; Pop. 1,516; Zip Code 56065; Lat. 43-55-29 N long. 093-57-44 W; Named after the Maple River, itself named for the many maple trees near the river.

•MARBLE, City; Itasca County; Pop. 757; Zip Code 55764; Lat. 47-19-47 N long. 093-18-36 W; The town is named for an early pioneer family.

•**MARIETTA,** City; Lac qui Parle; Pop. 279; Zip Code 56257; Lat. 45-00-38 N long. 096-25-11 W; The Minneapolis and St. Louis Raiway Co. founded the town in the 1880's and named it in honor of settlers from Marietta, Ohio.

•**MARINE ON ST. CROIX,** City; Washington County; Pop. 543; Zip Code 55047; Lat. 45-11-52 N long. 092-46-13 W; The name Marine comes from an Illinois lumber company who set up a lumber mill in 1839. The St. Croix refers to the large St. Croix lake.

•**MARSHALL,** City; Lyon County Seat; Pop. 11,161; Zip Code 56258; Lat. 44-26-46 N long. 095-47-35 W; Incorporated in 1876 and named for former Governor Marshall.

•**MAYER,** City; Carver County; Pop. 388; Zip Code 55360; Elev. 979; Lat. 44-53-11 N long. 093-52-59 W; Named by Great Northern Railway officials for a company officer.

•**MAYNARD,** City; Chippewa County; Pop. 428; Zip Code 56260; Elev. 1029; Lat. 44-54-10 N long. 095-27-50 W; Great Northern Railwy superintendant John Spicer named the town in honor of his brother-in-law.

•**MAZEPPA,** City; Wabasha County; Pop. 680; Zip Code 55956; Elev. 931; Lat. 44-16-27 N long. 092-32-34 W; The Cossack Chief Ivan Mazeppa lent his name to the town via a famous poem by Byron.

•**MCGRATH,** City; Aitkin County; Pop. 81; Zip Code 56350; Lat. 46-14-38 N long. 093-16-20 W; Named for an early settler.

•**MCGREGOR,** City; Aitkin County; Pop. 447; Zip Code 55760; Elev. 1233; Lat. 46-36-11 N long 093-18-35 W; A Great Northern Railway village whose name recalls pioneer Scotch settlers.

•**MCINTOSH,** City; Polk County; Pop. 681; Zip Code 56556; Elev. 1223; Lat. 47-38-02 N long. 095-53-12 W; A hotel proprietor who was part Scotch and part Ojibway Indian owned the land on which the town was founded.

•**MCKINLEY,** City; St. Louis County; Pop. 230; Zip Code 55761; Elev. 1438; Lat. 47-30-45 N long. 092-24-41 W; Organized as a iron mining village and named for the McKinley brothers who owned the local mine.

•**MEDFORD,** City; Steele County; Pop. 775; Zip Code 55049; Lat. 44-10-18 N long. 093-14-47 W; Townspeople named the city for the ship Medford upn which the son of town organizer William Collins had been born.

•**MEDINA,** City; Hennepin County; Pop. 2,623; Formerlly called Hamburg the town's citizens changed it to the name of the famous Arabic city of Medina in 1858.

•**MELROSE,** City; Stearns County; Pop. 2,409; Zip Code 56352; Elev. 1213; Lat. 45-36-32 N long. 094-50-18 W; A compound name formed by pioneer Warren Aalgy from his two daughter's names: Melissa and Rose.

•**MENAHGA,** City; Wadena County; Pop. 980; Zip Code 56464; Lat. 46-45-16 N long. 095-05-51 W; The Ojibway Indian word for blueberry.

•**MENDOTA HEIGHTS,** City; Dakota County; Pop. 7,288; Zip Code 55150; A descriptive name for an elevated part of the Mendota area.

•**MENTOR,** City; Polk County; Pop. 219; Zip Code 56736; Lat. 47-41-54 N long. 096-08-28 W; Originally a railway town and named for Menton, Ohio.

•**MIDDLE RIVER,** City; Marshall County; Pop. 349; Zip Code 56737; Named for the tributary of the Snake River which flows through the central part of the county.

•**MILACA,** City; Mille Lacs County Seat; Pop. 2,104; Zip Code 56353; Elev. 1079; Lat. 45-45-07 N long. 093-39-06 W; Originally called Oak City, the name was latre changed to a shortened version of Mille Locs, the county name.

•**MILAN,** City; Chippewa County; Pop. 417; Zip Code 56262; Elev. 1005; Lat. 45-06-35 N long. 095-54-54 W; Founded in 1880's and named for the famous city in northern Italy.

•**MINNEAPOLIS,** City; Hennepin County Seat; Pop. 370,951; Zip Code 554++; The city's name is a compound of the Sioux word Minnehaha, or "laughing waters," and polis, the Greek word for city.

•**MINNESOTA CITY,** City; Winona County; Pop. 265; Zip Code 55959; Lat. 44-05-41 N long. 091-44-56 W; A Sioux Indian word meaning "clouded water," and referring to the river at flood stage when it becomes turbid and clouded with sediment.

•**MINNESTRISTA,** City; Hennepin County; Pop. 3,236; A Sioux Indian name adopted by early settlers meaning "crooked waters" and refering to the shape of the many lakes in the area.

•**MIZPAH,** City; Koochiching County; Pop. 129; Zip Code 56660; Elev. 1385; Lat. 48-21-45 N long. 093-36-59 W; Early settlers ggave the town the name Mizpah, which is an Old Testament Hebrew word for watchtower. It is also a salutation meaning "the Lord be with you.".

•**MONTEVIDEO,** City; Chippewa County Seat; Pop. 5,845; Zip Code 56265; Lat. 44-56-49 N long. 095-43-02 W; The name Montevideo is Latin for "mount of vision." Early settlers named the town after seeing the adjacent Minnesota and Choppowa River valleys.

•**MONTGOMERY,** City; Le Sueur County; Pop. 2,349; Zip Code 56069; Elev. 1065; Lat. 44-26-22 N long. 093-34-24 W; The town was settled in the 1850's and named in honor of Revolutionary War hero General Richard Montgomery.

•**MONTICELLO,** City; Wright County; Pop. 3,111; Zip Code 55362; Settled in the 1850's and given the name Monticello, or "little mountain" for a hill two miles from the town.

•**MOORHEAD,** City; Clay County Seat; Pop. 29,998; Zip Code 56560; Lat. 46-52-08 N long. 096-44-08 W; The town was settled in the 1870's as the Northern Pacific Railway comes through the area. The town took the name of William G. Moorhead who was a Great Northern Director of that time.

•**MOOSE LAKE,** City; Carlton County; Pop. 1,408; Zip Code 55767; Elev. 1062; Lat. 46-27-09 N long. 092-45-35 W; The city is named for the nearby lake. The Ojibway Indians gave it that name in their own language for the abundant moose in the area.

•**MORA,** City; Kanabec County Seat; Pop. 2,890; Zip Code 55051; Elev. 1010; Lat. 45-52-28 N long. 093-17-19 W; Landowner Myron Kent named the site in the 1880's from a city in Sweden.

•**MORGAN,** City; Redwood County; Pop. 975; Zip Code 56266; Lat. 44-24-59 N long. 094-55-28 W; The town was named in honor of soldier, explorer, and writer Lewis Henry Morgan who passed through the area in the early 1860's.

•**MORRIS,** City; Stevens County Seat; Pop. 5,367; Zip Code 56267; Elev. 1133; Lat. 45-35-11 N long. 095-54-41 W; Founded in the early 1870's and named in honor of railroad engineer, Charles Morris.

•**MORRISTOWN,** City; Rice County; Pop. 639; Zip Code 55052; Lat. 44-13-26 N long. 093-26-46 W; Morristown was settled in the 1850's and named in honor of Minister Jonathon Nunes who died here in 1856.

•**MORTON,** City; Renville County; Pop. 549; Zip Code 56270; Lat. 44-33-12 N long. 094-59-01 W; Morton was founded in the 1880's and named by officers of the Minneapolis and St. Louis Railway.

•**MOTLEY,** City; Morrison County; Pop. 444; Zip Code 56466; Lat. 46-31-43 N long. 094-39-07 W; The town was settled in the 1870's and named by officers of the Northern Pacific Railway Co. It's exact derivation is unknown.

•**MOUND,** City; Hennepin County; Pop. 9,280; Zip Code 55364; Elev. 942; Lat. 44-15-14 N long. 092-14-25 W; The town is descriptively named for the numerous abnormal mounds in the area.

•**MOUNDS VIEW,** City; Ramsey County; Pop. 12,593; The city has a small group of glacier-deposit hills extending through it to a height of 200 ft. above the countryside.

•**MOUNTAIN IRON,** City; St. Louis County; Pop. 4,134; Zip Code 55768; Elev. 1474; Lat. 47-31-36 N long. 092-37-24 W; Named for the first iron ore mine to ship iron from the Mesabi range in 1892.

•**MOUNTAIN LAKE,** City; Cottonwood County; Pop. 2,277; Zip Code 56159; Elev. 1305; Lat. 43-56-30 N long. 094-55-49 W; The town is named after mountain lake which had a large flat island in it.

•**NASHWAUK,** City; Itasca County; Pop. 1,419; Zip Code 55769; Lat. 47-22-25 N long. 093-14-01 W; The town's name comes from the Nashauk River in New Brunswick.

•**NASSAU,** City; Lac qui Parle; Pop. 115; Zip Code 56272; Lat. 45-04-04 N long. 096-26-26 W; German settlers named the town after an area in Germany.

•**NELSON,** City; Douglas County; Pop. 209; Zip Code 56355; Lat. 45-53-15 N long. 095-16-34 W; Founded in 1875 and named after U.S. Senator Knute Nelson from Minnesota.

•**NEVIS,** City; Hubbard County; Pop. 332; Zip Code 56467; Elev. 1470; Lat. 46-57-54 N long. 094-51-08 W; Scottish settlers named the town for Bev Nevis Mountain in Scotland.

•**NEW AUBURN,** City; Sibley County; Pop. 331; Zip Code 55366; Elev. 1002; Lat. 44-40-28 N long. 094-13-44 W; Settlers from Auburn, New York arrived in the late 1850's and gave the town its name.

•**NEW BRIGHTON,** City; Ramsey County; Pop. 23,269; Zip Code 55112; The town takes its name from Brighton, Massachusetts which like New Brighton was a meat-packing center.

•**NEW GERMANY,** City; Carver County; Pop. 347; Zip Code 55367; Lat. 44-53-02 N long. 093-58-07 W; The city was named in honor of the many German settlers in the area.

•**NEW HOPE,** City; Hennepin County; Pop. 23,087; A descriptive name given by early settles and embodying their wishes for the new city.

•**NEW LONDON,** City; Kandiyohi County; Pop. 812; Zip Code 56273; Lat. 45-18-08 N long. 094-56-25 W; Pioneer Louis Larson named the city for his former home of New London, Wisconsin.

•**NEW PRAGUE,** City; Scott County; Pop. 2,952; Zip Code 56071; Lat. 44-31-15 N long. 093-35-32 W; New Prague was settled in the 1850's and named for the ancient European city of Prague.

•**NEW RICHLAND,** City; Waseca County; Pop. 1,263; Zip Code 56072; Elev. 1184; Lat. 43-53-44 N long. 093-28-21 W; Settlers from Wisconsin named the new city after Richland County in Wisconsin.

•**NEW ULM,** City; Brown County Seat; Pop. 13,755; Zip Code 56073; Lat. 44-18-45 N long. 094-27-59 W; German colonists named the city for Ulm, Germany.

•**NEWPORT,** City; Washington County; Pop. 3,323; Zip Code 55055; Elev. 743; Lat. 43-19-33 N long. 089-47-33 W; Mrs. James Hugunin, the wife of an early settler, named the town for a similarily called city on the east coast.

•**NICOLLET,** City; Nicollet County; Pop. 709; Zip Code 56074; Lat. 44-16-42 N long. 094-11-16 W; Named in honor of explorer Nicolas Nicollet who mapped the area in the 1830's.

•**NISSWA,** City; Crow Wing County; Pop. 1,407; Zip Code 56468; Elev. 1231; Lat. 46-30-54 N long. 094-14-00 W; An Objibway Indian name "in the middle."

•**NORTH BRANCH,** City; Chisago County; Pop. 1,597; Zip Code 55056; Lat. 45-30-36 N long. 092-58-22 W; Founded in the 1870's and descriptively named for the north branch of the Sunrise River.

•**NORTH MANKATO,** City; Nicollet County; Pop. 9,145; Zip Code 56001; The city is on the Minnesota River opposite Mankato, and hence its descriptive name.

•**NORTH OAKS,** City; Ramsey County; Pop. 2,846; A euphonious name given the city by its founders.

•**NORTH ST. PAUL,** City; Ramsey County; Pop. 11,921; Zip Code 55109; Originaly called Castle, it was later renamed to reflect its proximity to St. Paul.

•**NORTHFIELD,** City; Rice County; Pop. 12,562; Zip Code 55057; Lat. 44-27-26 N, long. 093-09-45 W. The city is named in honor of John North who laid out the town and later became a U. S. Judge in California.

•**NORWOOD,** City; Carver County; Pop. 1,219; Zip Code 55368; Lat. 44-46-06 N, long. 093-55-52 W. The village was founded in the 1870's and named by an early pineer for a personal friend.

•**OAK PARK HEIGHTS,** City; Washington County; Pop. 2,591. The area was originally covered with oak timber and subsequent city names reflect this history.

•**OAKDALE,** City; Washington County; Pop. 12,123. The town was covered with white and burr oak trees, and the forest gave the city its name.

•**ODESSA,** City; Big Stone County; Pop. 177; Zip Code 56276; Lat. 45-15-24 N, long. 096-19-22 W. The town is named for the Russion Black Sea port.

•**ODIN,** City; Watonwan County; Pop. 134; Zip Code 56160; Lat. 43-51-55 N, long. 094-44-32 W. The city was settled in the 1860's and named for a god in Norse mythogoy.

•**OGEMA,** City; Becker County; Pop. 215; Zip Code 56569; Lat. 47-06-03 N, long. 095-55-49 W. An Ojibway Indian term meaning "chief.".

•**OGILVIE,** City; Kanabec County; Pop. 423; Zip Code 56358; Elev. 1047; Lat. 45-49-48 N, long. 093-29-10 W. The town is named for Oric Ogilvie Whited, a prominent lawyer and landowner in the area.

•**OKABENA,** City; Jackson County; Pop. 263; Zip Code 56161; Elev. 1424; Lat. 43-44-25 N, long. 095-19-02 W. A Sioux Indian term meaning "the nesting place of the herons.".

•**OKLEE,** City; Red Lake County; Pop. 536; Zip Code 56742; Lat. 47-50-32 N, long. 095-51-03 W. The town is named for early Scandanvian settler, Ole K. Lee.

•**OLIVIA,** City; Renville County Seat; Pop. 2,802; Zip Code 56277; Lat. 44-46-35 N, long. 094-59-14 W. The city is named after the first railroad agent, a woman named Olive.

•**ONAMIA,** City; Mille Lacs County; Pop. 691; Zip Code 56359; Lat. 46-04-15 N, long. 093-39-53 W. An Ojibuay Indian name whose meaning is uncertain.

•**ORMSBY,** City; Watonwan County; Pop. 181; Zip Code 56162; Lat. 43-50-50 N, long. 094-41-58 W. Founded at the turn of the century and named in honor of a Colonel Ormsby of Iowa.

•**ORONO,** City; Hennepin County; Pop. 6,845. Settlers from Maine gave the town the name of a city in Maine, itself called after a Penobscot Indain chief.

•**ORONOCO,** City; Olmsted County; Pop. 574; Zip Code 55960; Lat. 44-09-54 N, long. 092-32-16 W. Settled in the 1850's and named by Dr. Hector Galloway for the Orinoco River in South America.

•**ORR,** City; St. Louis County; Pop. 294; Zip Code 55771; Elev. 1304; Lat. 48-03-28 N, long. 092-49-32 W. The town takes its name from former postmaster and general store owner, William Orr.

•**ORTONVILLE,** City; Big Stone County Seat; Pop. 2,550; Zip Code 56278; Lat. 45-16-30 N, long. 096-25-39 W. The town began in the 1870's and was named for founder Cornelius Orton, who was a prominent local businessman.

•**OSAKIS,** City; Douglas County; Pop. 1,355; Zip Code 56360; Lat. 45-52-01 N, long. 095-08-36 W. The city is named after the lake, which in turn gets its name from the Souk Indians who once lived in the area.

•**OSLO,** City; Marshall County; Pop. 379; Zip Code 56744; Elev. 1295; Lat. 48-11-39 N, long. 097-07-47 W. Named by Norwegian settlers for the capital of Norway.

•**OSSEO,** City; Hennepin County; Pop. 2,974; Zip Code 55369; Lat. 45-04-36 N, long. 093-23-19 W. The city takes its name from the "The Song of Hiawatha" by Longfellow.

•**OSTRANDER,** City; Fillmore County; Pop. 293; Zip Code 55961; Lat. 43-36-41 N, long. 092-25-06 W. Founded in the 1890's and given the name of two brothers, the Ostranders, who originally owned the land.

•**OTTERTAIL,** City; Otter Tail County; Pop. 239; Zip Code 56571; Lat. 46-29-02 N, long. 095-36-13 W. The city is named after Otter-tail Lake which had a long narrow sand bar in it resembling an otter's tail.

•**OWATONNA,** City; Steele County Seat; Pop. 18,632; Zip Code 55060; Lat. 44-05-01 N, long. 093-12-58 W. A Sioux Indian word meaning "straight river.".

•**PALISADE,** City; Aitkin County; Pop. 155; Zip Code 56469; Lat. 46-43-20 N, long. 093-29-20 W. The town is named for a descriptive geological feature.

•**PARK RAPIDS,** City; Hubbard County Seat; Pop. 2,976; Zip Code 56470; Lat. 46-55-14 N, long. 095-03-48 W. Original landowner, Frank Rice, named the town for the park like groves and the rapids on the nearby Fish Hook river.

•**PARKERS PRAIRIE,** City; Otter Tail County; Pop. 917; Zip Code 56361; Elev. 1464; Lat. 46-08-12 N, long. 095-24-54 W. An early settler owned a large piece of land on the nearby prairie and left his name on the city.

•**PAYNESVILLE,** City; Stearns County; Pop. 2,140; Zip Code 56362; Lat. 45-25-07 N, long. 094-45-18 W. Settler Edwin Paynes arrived in the area in 1857. The town was named in his honor.

•**PEASE,** City; Mille Lacs County; Pop. 174; Zip Code 56363; Lat. 45-41-49 N, long. 093-38-51 W. Great Northern Railway officers named the town.

•**PELICAN RAPIDS,** City; Otter Tail County; Pop. 867; Zip Code 56572; Lat. 46-34-17 N, long. 096-05-07 W. Incorporated in 1882 the city's site had the adjacent Pelican River flowing over buildings and creating rapids.

•**PEMBERTON,** City; Blue Earth County; Pop. 208; Zip Code 56078; Lat. 44-00-30 N, long. 093-46-58 W. The origin of the city's name is uncertain.

•**PENNOCK,** City; Kandiyohi County; Pop. 410; Zip Code 56279; Elev. 1131; Lat. 45-08-39 N, long. 095-10-20 W. Geroge Pennock, one time superintendant of the Great Northern Railway, had the town named in his honor.

•**PEQUOT LAKES,** City; Crow Wing County; Pop. 681; Zip Code 56472; Elev. 1280; Lat. 46-36-08 N, long. 094-11-15 W. The city is named for an Algonquian Indian tribe that once lived in eastern Connecticut.

•**PERHAM,** City; Otter Tail County; Pop. 2,086; Zip Code 56573; Lat. 46-35-31 N, long. 095-34-25 W. The town's name honors Josiah Perham.

•**PERLEY,** City; Norman County; Pop. 124; Zip Code 56574; Lat. 47-10-35 N, long. 096-48-04 W. Perley is named in honor of George Perley - Minnesota lawyer and state representataive.

•**PETERSON,** City; Fillmore County; Pop. 291; Zip Code 55962; Lat. 43-47-17 N, long. 091-51-30 W. The town is named after Pewter Petrson Haslerud, a Norwegian pioneer and member of the state legislature.

•**PIERZ,** City; Morrison County; Pop. 1,018; Zip Code 56364; Lat. 46-02-58 N, long. 094-04-34 W. The city is named in honor of Francis Xavier Pierz, a Catholic missionary to the Ojibway Indians in the mid 1850's.

•**PILLAGER,** City; Cass County; Pop. 341; Zip Code 56473; Elev. 1209; Lat. 46-19-37 N, long. 094-28-43 W. An early trader in the mid 1760's was robbed of his goods here by the Ojibways. He labled them "pillagers" and the name stuck to the place.

•**PINE CITY,** City; Pine County Seat; Pop. 2,489; Zip Code 55063; Elev. 950; Lat. 45-49-34 N, long. 092-58-17 W. A descriptive name for the extensive stands of white and red pine originally in the district.

•**PINE ISLAND,** City; Goodhue County; Pop. 1,986; Zip Code 55963; Lat. 44-12-10 N, long. 092-39-20 W. Settled in 1854, the name is a translation of an Indian word and refers to a secure winter camp ground sheltered by the island's pines.

•**PINE RIVER,** City; Cass County; Pop. 881; Zip Code 56474; Lat. 46-43-47 N, long. 094-23-35 W. The town takes its name from the river - itself named for the abundant pine stands once in the area.

•**PIPESTONE,** City; Pipestone County Seat; Pop. 4,887; Zip Code 56164; Elev. 1738; Lat. 43-59-44 N long. 096-19-04 W; Both the city and the county are named for a celebrated Indian quarry of red pipestone.

•PLAINVIEW, City; Wabasha County; Pop. 2,416; Zip Code 55964; Elev. 1155; Lat. 44-09-50 N long. 092-09-56 W; A descriptive name referring to the plain view available of the surrounding countryside.

•PLATO, City; McLeod County; Pop. 390; Zip Code 55370; Lat. 44-46-27 N long. 094-01-17 W; The city is named for the famous Greek idealistic philosopher.

•PLYMOUTH, City; Hennepin County; Pop. 31,615; Zip Code 55441; The city's name remembers Plymouth, England and Plymouth, Massachusetts where the Pilgrams landed in 1620-21.

•PRESTON, City; Fillmore County Seat; Pop. 1,478; Zip Code 55965; Lat. 43-40-17 N long. 092-04-20 W; Settled in 1853 and named by a local millowner for his millwright, Luther Preston.

•PRINCETON, City; Mille Lacs County; Pop. 3,146; Zip Code 55371; Elev. 983; Lat. 45-34-18 N long. 093-35-13 W; Named in honor of John Prince who helped lay out the town in 1855.

•PRINSBURG, City; Kandiyohi County; Pop. 557; Zip Code 56281; Elev. 1104; Lat. 44-55-58 N long. 095-11-00 W; Martin Prins, a landowner from Holland, came to the area in 1884. The town honors his memory.

•PRIOR LAKE, City; Scott County; Pop. 7,284; Zip Code 55372; Lat. 44-43-00 N long. 093-25-20 W; Named in honor of Charles Prior, who was superintendant of the Minnesota section of the Chicago, Milwaukee, and St. Paul Railway during the years 1871-86.

•PROCTOR, City; St. Louis County; Pop. 3,180; Zip Code 55810; The city's name remembers James Proctor Knott, a U.S. Congressman from Kentucky, who made a humorous speech to congress in 1871 ridiculing Duluth. The speech helped the city by its advertisement.

•QUAMBA, City; Kanabec County; Pop. 122; Zip Code 55064; The town was named by officials of the Great Northern Railway Company - its exact meaning is unknown.

•RAMSEY, City; Anoka County; Pop. 10,093; The city's name honors Alexander Ramsey, the first governor of the Minnesota territory, 1849-53.

•RANDALL, City; Morrison County; Pop. 527; Zip Code 56475; Lat. 46-05-16 N long. 094-30-09 W; Incorporated in 1900 and named for John H. Randall, an official of Northern Pacific Railway Company.

•RANDOLPH, City; Dakota County; Pop. 351; Zip Code 55065; Lat. 44-31-40 N long. 093-01-00 W; The town is named after a local railway official.

•RAYMOND, City; Kandiyohi County; Pop. 723; Zip Code 56282; Lat. 45-00-53 N long. 095-14-16 W; Founded in 1887 and named for Raymond Spicer, the son of a prominent pioneer.

•RED LAKE FALLS, City; Red Lake County Seat; Pop. 1,732; Zip Code 56750; Elev. 1037; Lat. 47-53-06 N long. 096-16-40 W; Descriptively named for the falls on the Red Lake River at the site of the town.

•RED WING, City; Goodhue County; Pop. 13,736; Zip Code 55066; Lat. 44-33-27 N long. 092-32-25 W; The town is the site of an early missionary outpost named for a great Dakota chief of that era.

•REDWOOD FALLS, City; Redwood County Seat; Pop. 5,210; Zip Code 56283; Elev. 1044; Lat. 44-32-21 N long. 095-06-59 W; The city's name comes from the nearby falls of the Redwood River.

•REMER, City; Cass County; Pop. 396; Zip Code 56672; Elev. 1340; Lat. 47-03-35 N long. 093-58-25 W; Remer is named after the Remer brothers who were prominent in the founding of the town.

•RENVILLE, City; Renville County; Pop. 1,493; Zip Code 56284; Elev. 1069; Lat. 44-47-24 N long. 095-12-30 W; The town and county are named for Joseph Renville, a French-Indian soldier, trapper, and historical informant on the Sioux in the early 1800's.

•RICHFIELD, City; Hennepin County; Pop. 37,851; Zip Code 55423; The town was settled in 1849 and given the common English town name: Richfield.

•RICHMOND, City; Stearns County; Pop. 867; Zip Code 56368; Elev. 1119; Lat. 45-27-19 N long. 094-31-08 W; The town is named after an early settler.

•ROBBINSDALE, City; Hennepin County; Pop. 14,442; Zip Code 55442; The city is named for Andrew Robbins, one of the town's original landowners.

•ROCHESTER, City; Olmsted County Seat; Pop. 57,855; Zip Code 559++; The city was incorporated in 1858 and named after Rochester, N. Y.

•ROCK CREEK, City; Pine County; Pop. 890; Zip Code 55067; Elev. 938; Lat. 45-45-18 N long. 092-57-09 W; Named for a creek that flows into the St. Croix River.

•ROCKFORD, City; Wright County; Pop. 2,408; Zip Code 55373; Elev. 916; Lat. 45-05-40 N long. 093-42-24 W; Founded in 1855 and named for a rocky ford of the Crow River where a sawmill was built.

•ROLLINGSTONE, City; Winona County; Pop. 528; Zip Code 55869; Elev. 759; Lat. 44-06-03 N long. 091-48-58 W; The town is named after its river. Its Dakota Indian name was "the stream where the stone rolls.".

•ROOSEVELT, City; Roseau County; Pop. 124; Zip Code 56673; Elev. 1163; Lat. 48-48-15 N long. 095-05-46 W; The town is named in honor of Theodore Rossevelt, President of the United States, 1901-09.

•ROSE CREEK, City; Mower County; Pop. 371; Zip Code 55970; Lat. 43-32-39 N long. 092-52-06 W; The town is named after Rose Creek which is a tributary of the Cedar River.

•ROSEAU, City; Roseau County Seat; Pop. 2,272; Zip Code 56751; Elev. 1048; Lat. 48-51-00 N long. 095-45-37 W; The city and the county are named for the Roseau River.

•ROSEMOUNT, City; Dakota County; Pop. 5,083; Zip Code 55068; Lat. 44-44-00 N long. 093-07-31 W; The city is named for the village of Rosemount in Ireland.

•ROSEVILLE, City; Ramsey County; Pop. 35,820; Zip Code 55113; The city's name honors early pioneer Isaac Rose, who settled here in 1843.

•ROTHSAY, City; Wilkin County; Pop. 476; Zip Code 56579; Elev. 1209; Lat. 46-29-12 N long. 096-15-13 W; Rothsay takes its name from the seaport thirty miles west of Glasgow, Scotland.

•ROUND LAKE, City; Nobles County; Pop. 480; Zip Code 56167; Lat. 43-32-21 N long. 095-28-07 W; The city was named for nearby Round Lake at the request of an early large landowner in the area.

•ROYALTON, City; Morrison County; Pop. 660; Zip Code 56373; Lat. 45-49-56 N long. 094-17-20 W; Named by early settlers for their former home in Vermont.

•**RUSH CITY,** City; Chisago County; Pop. 1,198; Zip Code 55069; Elev. 917; Lat. 45-40-59- N long. 092-58-00 W; Founded in 1868 as a railway depot, the town is named for the Rush River.

•**RUSHFORD,** City; Fillmore County; Pop. 1,478; Zip Code 55971; Elev. 726; Lat. 43-48-22 N long. 091-49-23 W; Settled in 1853 and taking its name from Rush Creek - a tributary to the Root River.

•**RUSHMORE,** City; Nobles County; Pop. 387; Zip Code 56168; Lat. 43-37-06 N long. 095-47-46 W; The town is named for pioneer merchant, S. M. Rushmore.

•**RUSSELL,** City; Lyon County; Pop. 412; Zip Code 56159; Elev. 1527; Lat. 44-19-06 N long. 095-57-10 W; The town is named in honor of Russell Spicer, who was the son of the builder of the area's branch railway.

•**SABIN,** City; Clay County; Pop. 446; Zip Code 56580; Lat. 46-46-29 N long. 096-39-05 W; The town is named in honor of Dwight Sabin, a prominent Minnesota businessman and U. S. Senator (1883-89).

•**SACRED HEART,** City; Renville County; Pop. 666; Zip Code 56285; Lat. 44-47-11 N long. 095-20-52 W; An early trapper wore a bearskin hat -sacred to the Sioux- he became known as "sacred hat" man - gradually this became sacred heart.

•**ST. ANTHONY,** City; Stearns County; Pop. 78. The town is named after an early church.

•**ST. CHARLES,** City; Winona County; Pop. 2,184; Zip Code 55972; Founded in 1870 and named for St. Charles of Italy.

•**ST. CLAIR,** City; Blue Earth County; Pop. 655; Zip Code 56080; Originally called Hilton, the town's name was changed to St. Clair by officers of the Chicago, Milwaukee and St. Paul Railway.

•**ST. CLOUD,** City; Stearns County Seat; Pop. 42,566; Zip Code 56301; Town founder John Wilson named the town after Napoleons palace of St. Cloud outside Paris.

•**ST. FRANCIS,** City; Anoka County; Pop. 1,184; Zip Code 55070; The city is named for St. Francis of Assisi who founded the Franciscan order.

•**ST. JAMES,** City; Watonwan County Seat; Pop. 4,346; Zip Code 56081; The president and director of the St.Paul and Sioux city railway named the town "St. James" after forgetting a proposed Sioux Indian name.

•**ST. JOSEPH,** City; Stearns County; Pop. 2,994; Zip Code 54082; The town is named after its original church.

•**ST. LOUIS PARK,** City; Hennepin County; Pop. 42,931; Zip Code 55426; The town is named after the Minneapolis and St. Louis Railway.

•**ST. MICHAEL,** City; Wright County; Pop. 1,519; Zip Code 55376; The city takes its name from the church built in 1856.

•**ST. PAUL,** City; Ramsey County Seat; Pop. 270,230; Zip Code 551++; Father Lucian Galtier convinced the first settlers to rename their community after St. Paul.

•**ST. PAUL PARK,** City; Washington County; Pop. 4,864; Zip Code 55071; Named for the Christian saint.

•**ST. PETER,** City; Nicollet County Seat; Pop. 9,056; Zip Code 56082; Named in honor of Pierre (Peter) Charles Le Seuer, the famous French explorer.

•**SANBORN,** City; Redwood County; Pop. 518; Zip Code 56083; Lat. 44-12-37 N long. 095-07-35 W; The city's name honors Sherburn Sanborn - an official of the Chicago and Northwestern Railway Co.

•**SANDSTONE,** City; Pine County; Pop. 1,594; Zip Code 55072; Lat. 46-07-36 N long. 092-51-30 W; The town was named for its extensive sandstone quarries in the nearby bluffs on the Kettle River.

•**SARTELL,** City; Stearns County; Pop. 3,427; Zip Code 56377; Lat. 45-37-10 N long. 094-12-12 W; Joseph Sartell settled here in 1854. He established a sawmill and raised his family. The town is named in his honor.

•**SAUK CENTRE,** City; Stearns County; Pop. 3,709; Zip Code 56378; Elev. 1246; Lat. 45-44-42 N long. 094-57-27 W; The town takes its name from its position on the Sauk River.

•**SAUK RAPIDS,** City; Benton County; Pop. 5,793; Zip Code 56379; Organized in 1854 and so named for the nearby rapids.

•**SAVAGE,** City; Scott County; Pop. 3,954; Zip Code 55378; Formerly called Hamilton and named in honor of famous horsebreeder Marion W. Savage.

•**SEBEKA,** City; Wadena County; Pop. 774; Zip Code 56477; Named by Great Northern Railway Engineer, Colonel William Crooks after an Ojibuay Indian word meaning "the village beside the river."

•**SHAKOPEE,** City; Scott County Seat; Pop. 9,941; Zip Code 55379; Lat. 44-47-36 N long. 093-31-41 W; Shakopee was a Sioux chief who lived near the townsite. The city kept his name.

•**SHERBURN,** City; Martin County; Pop. 1,275; Zip Code 56171; Lat. 43-39-06 N long. 094-43-29 W; The city's name honors the wife of a railroad company official.

•**SHOREVIEW,** City; Ramsey County; Pop. 17,300; Descriptively named for its view of the Mississipi River.

•**SHOREWOOD,** City; Hennepin County; Pop. 4,646; A euphonious name decided upon by the town's incorporators.

•**SILVER BAY,** City; Lake County; Pop. 2,917; Zip Code 55614; Lat. 47-32-24 N long. 090-53-52 W; So named because of the play of the light on Lake Superior.

•**SILVER LAKE,** City; McLeod County; Pop. 698; Zip Code 55381; Lat. 44-54-10 N long. 094-11-44 W; The town is named for its location next to Silver Lake.

•**SLAYTON,** City; Murray County Seat; Pop. 2,420; Zip Code 56172; Elev. 1608; Lat. 43-59-08 N long. 095-45-10 W; The town is named aftr Charles Slayton, the town's founder and original landowner.

•**SLEEPY EYE,** City; Brown County; Pop. 3,581; Zip Code 56085; Elev. 1030; Lat. 44-18-15 N long. 094-43-33 W; The city is named for a chief of the Lower Sisseton Sioux.

•**SOUTH HAVEN,** City; Wright County; Pop. 205; Zip Code 55382; Elev. 1115; Lat. 45-17-36 N long. 094-13-13 W; So named because of its location between Southside and Fair Haven Townships.

•**SOUTH INTERNATIONAL FALLS,** City; Koochiching County; Pop. 2,806; Zip Code 56679; Lat. 48-34-52 N long. 093-24-04 W; The city's name notes its location on the internatinal boundary at Koochiching Falls.

•**SOUTH ST. PAUL,** City; Dakota County; Pop. 21,235; Zip Code 55075; Lat. 43-02-44 N long. 089-14-40 W; A descriptive geographic name for the city's relation to St. Paul.

•**SPICER,** City; Kandiyohi County; Pop. 909; Zip Code 56288; Elev. 1171; Lat. 45-13-52 N long. 094-56-12 W; Founded in 1886 and named in honor of John Spicer who owned the site.

•**SPRING GROVE,** City; Houston County; Pop. 1,275; Zip Code 55974; Lat. 43-33-37 N long. 091-38-16 W; The town is named for its founding geographic points of reference - a spring and a grove.

•**SPRING PARK,** City; Hennepin County; Pop. 1,465; Zip Code 55384; Lat. 44-56-08 N long. 093-37-39 W; A pleasant sounding name created by the town's incorporators.

•**SPRING VALLEY,** City; Fillmore County; Pop. 2,616; Zip Code 55975; Lat. 43-41-05 N long. 092-22-40 W; The city is named for several large springs within several miles of the city limits.

•**SPRINGFIELD,** City; Brown County; Pop. 2,303; Zip Code 56087; Elev. 1026; Lat. 44-11-15 N long. 094-58-53 W; The town may either be named after Springfield, Massaachusetts, or a large spring nearby.

•**STACY,** City; Chisago County; Pop. 996; Zip Code 55079; Lat. 45-23-52 N long. 092-59-01 W; Established in 1875 and named in honor of pioneer Dr. Stacy Collins.

•**STAPLES,** City; Todd County; Pop. 2,887; Zip Code 56479; Lat. 46-21-24 N long. 094-47-35 W; The town's name honors an early lumberman named Staples who established a mill in the town.

•**STARBUCK,** City; Pope County; Pop. 1,224; Zip Code 56381; Elev. 1162; Lat. 45-36-49 N long. 095-31-53 W; Founded in 1882 and named by Norther Pacific Railroad officials for a company empoyee.

•**STEPHEN,** City; Marshall County; Pop. 898; Zip Code 56757; Lat. 48-26-54 N long. 096-52-22 W; Stephen is named in honor of George Stephen, a prominent stockholder in the Great Northern Railway.

•**STEWART,** City; McLeod County; Pop. 616; Zip Code 55385; Elev. 1062; Lat. 44-43-25 N long. 094-29-31 W; Incorporated in 1888 and named in honor of the town's founder Dr. D. A. Stewart.

•**STEWARTVILLE,** City; Olmsted County; Pop. 3,925; Zip Code 55976; Elev. 1240; Lat. 43-51-14 N long. 092-29-37 W; Charles Stewart built a mill here in 1858. The town is named in his honor.

•**STILLWATER,** City; Washington County Seat; Pop. 12,290; Zip Code 55082; Lat. 44-58-54 N long. 092-47-12 W; Named for the calm lake nearby and in honor of Stillwater, Maine.

•**STURGEON LAKE,** City; Pine County; Pop. 222; Zip Code 55783; Elev. 1074; Lat. 46-23-16 N long. 092-49-29 W; The town is named for the adjacent Sturgeon Lake.

•**SUNBURG,** City; Kandiyohi County; Pop. 130; Zip Code 56289; Lat. 45-20-49 N long. 095-14-17 W; A euphonious and descriptive name given by the town's founders.

•**TACONTIE,** City; Itasca County; Pop. 331; Zip Code 55786; Lat. 47-19-16 N long. 093-24-08 W; The town is named for adjacent mineral deposits.

•**TAUNTON,** City; Lyon County; Pop. 177; Zip Code 56291; Elev. 1175; Lat. 44-35-43 N long. 096-04-02 W; Chicago and Northwestern Railway official C. C. Wheeler, named the town after Taunton, Mass.

•**TAYLORS FALLS,** City; Chisago County; Pop. 623; Zip Code 55084; Elev. 744; Lat. 45-24-41 N long. 092-39-15 W; Founded in 1850 and named in honor of pioneer Jesse Taylor.

•**THIEF RIVER FALLS,** City; Pennington County Seat; Pop. 9,105; Zip Code 56701; Elev. 1133; Lat. 46-02-19 N long. 096-18-20 W; The city is named after the adjacent Thief River.

•**TONKA BAY,** City; Hennepin County; Pop. 1,354; A Sioux Indian word meaning "water."

•**TOWER,** City; St. Louis County; Pop. 640; Zip Code 55790; Lat. 47-48-27 N long. 092-16-57 W; Named in honor of Charlemagne Tower of Philadelphia, a prominent businessman in the development of Minnesota's iron industry.

•**TRACY,** City; Lyon County; Pop. 2,478; Zip Code 56175; Elev. 1398; Lat. 44-14-07 N long. 095-37-15 W; Tracy's name honors John F. Tracy, a former president of the Chicago and Northwestern Railway.

•**TRIMONT,** City; Martin County; Pop. 805; Zip Code 56176; Lat. 43-45-29 N long. 094-42-44 W; Descriptively named for local geographic features.

•**TROSKY,** City; Pipestone County; Pop. 113; Zip Code 56177; Lat. 43-53-25 N long. 096-15-12 W; Probably named for an early settler.

•**TRUMAN,** City; Martin County; Pop. 1,392; Zip Code 56088; Lat. 43-49-43 N long. 094-26-02 W; The town's name honors Truman Clark, son of a railway vice-president.

•**TWIN LAKES,** City; Freeborn County; Pop. 210; Zip Code 56089; Lat. 43-33-42 N long. 093-25-52 W; A descriptive geographic name for the nearby twin lakes.

•**TWIN VALLEY,** City; Norman County; Pop. 907; Zip Code 56584; Lat. 47-15-38 N long. 096-15-27 W; Descriptively named for the town's location between the Wild Rice River and its tributary.

•**TWO HARBORS,** City; Lake County Seat; Pop. 4,039; Zip Code 55616; Lat. 47-01-36 N long. 091-40-30 W; The city is situated on two bays and is so named Two Harbors.

•**TYLER,** City; Lincoln County; Pop. 1,353; Zip Code 56178; Elev. 1733; Lat. 44-16-31 N long. 096-07-46 W; The town's name honors C. B. Tyler, local newspaperman and banker.

•**ULEN,** City; Clay County; Pop. 514; Zip Code 56585; Lat. 46-59-20 N long. 096-15-30 W; The town's first settler was Ole Ulen. It is named in his honor.

•**UNDERWOOD,** City; Otter Tail County; Pop. 332; Zip Code 56586; Lat. 46-17-02 N long. 095-52-01 W; The town's name honors Adoniram Underwood, newspaperman and state representative.

•**UPSALA,** City; Morrison County; Pop. 400; Zip Code 56384; Lat. 45-48-48 N long. 094-34-06 W; The city is named for the famous university town in Sweden.

•**UTICA,** City; Winona County; Pop. 249; Zip Code 55979; Lat. 43-58-43 N long. 091-56-52 W; The city is named after Utica, New York.

•**VADNAIS HEIGHTS,** City; Ramsey County; Pop. 5,111; Named in honor of John Vadnais, early pioneer settler.

•**VERGAS,** City; Otter Tail County; Pop. 287; Zip Code 56587; Lat. 46-39-14 N long. 095-48-16 W; Probably named for an early settler.

•**VERMILLION,** City; Dakota County; Pop. 438; Zip Code 55085; Lat. 44-40-25 N long. 092-57-53 W; Descriptively named for the bright red sandstone found on the banks of the Vermillion River.

•**VERNDALE,** City; Wadena County; Pop. 504; Zip Code 56481; Elev. 1349; Lat. 46-23-430 N long. 095-00-37 W; Lucas Smith built the first house in the area. The town is named in honor of his granddaughter, Verne Smith.

•**VERNON CENTER,** City; Blue Earth County; Pop. 365; Zip Code 56090; Lat. 43-57-53 N long. 094-10-17 W; Settled in 1855 and named for Mount Vernon, Ohio.

•**VESTA,** City; Redwood County; Pop. 360; Zip Code 56292; Lat. 44-30-33 N long. 095-24-59 W; Settled in 1868 and named for the ancient Roman goddess Vesta.

•**VICTORIA,** City; Carver County; Pop. 1,425; Zip Code 55386; Lat. 44-51-51 N long. 093-38-31 W; A railway town, its name honors Britian's Queen, Victoria.

•**VIKING,** City; Marshall County; Pop. 129; Zip Code 56760; Lat. 48-13-04 N long. 096-24-08 W; Named for the famous Scandanavian raiders of medevil Europe.

•**VILLARD,** City; Pope County; Pop. 275; Zip Code 56385; Lat. 45-42-51 N long. 095-16-10 W; The town's name honors Henry Villard, president of the Northern Pacific Railway Company.

•**VINING,** City; Otter Tail County; Pop. 87; Zip Code 56588; Elev. 1387; Lat. 46-15-57 N long. 095-31-44 W; Named by officials of the Northern Pacific Railway after a town in Iowa.

•**VIRGINIA,** City; St. Louis County; Pop. 11,056; Zip Code 55792; Elev. 1437; Lat. 47-31-27 N long. 092-31-34 W; Named for the state of Virginia by an early lumberman from that state.

•**WABASHA,** City; Wabasha County Seat; Pop. 2,372; Zip Code 55981; Lat. 44-22-45 N long. 092-02-02 W; The hereditary name of three generations of Mississippi Sioux Indians.

•**WABASSO,** City; Redwood County; Pop. 745; Zip Code 56293; Lat. 44-24-06 N long. 095-15-33 W; Founded in 1899 and given an Ojibway Indian name from Longfellow's "Song of Hiawatha," meaning "rabbit."

•**WACONIA,** City; Carver County; Pop. 2,638; Zip Code 55387; Elev. 991; Lat. 44-50-56 N long. 093-46-57 W; A Sioux Indian word meaning "spring" or "fountain."

•**WADENA,** City; Wadena County Seat; Pop. 4,699; Zip Code 56482; Lat. 46-26-07 N long. 095-08-18 W; The site of an early trading post it is an Ojibway Indian word meaning "little round hill."

•**WAHKON,** City; Mille Lacs County; Pop. 271; Zip Code 56386; Lat. 46-07-03 N long. 093-31-14 W; ;;A Sioux Indain word meaning "sacred" or "holy."

•**WAITE PARK,** City; Stearns County; Pop. 3,496; The town's name honors Henry C. Waite, businessman and state representataive.

•**WALDORF,** City; Waseca County; Pop. 249; Zip Code 56091; Lat. 43-56-01 N long. 093-40-56 W; The town is named after a city in Maryland.

•**WALKER,** City; Cass County Seat; Pop. 970; Zip Code 56484; Lat. 47-05-56 N long. 094-34-57 W; The town's name honors Thomas B. Walker who held extensive lumber and land interests in Cass County.

•**WALNUT GROVE,** City; Redwood County; Pop. 753; Zip Code 56180; Elev. 1212; Lat. 44-13-28 N long. 095-28-17 W; The town is named for a grove of black walnut trees a mile west of the village.

•**WALTERS,** City; Faribault County; Pop. 118; Zip Code 56092; Lat. 43-36-14 N long. 093-40-24 W; Named by officials of the Chicago, Rock Island, and Pacific Railway Company for one of their employees.

•**WALTHAM,** City; Mower County; Pop. 176; Zip Code 55982; Lat. 43-49-39 N long. 092-52-39 W; Founded in 1885 and named for the city of Waltham, Massachusetts.

•**WANAMINGO,** City; Goodhue County; Pop. 717; Zip Code 55983; Lat. 44-18-10 N long. 092-47-30 W; An Indian name of uncertain origin.

•**WANDA,** City; Redwood County; Pop. 118; Zip Code 56294; Lat. 44-19-05 N long. 095-12-46 W; An Ojibway Indian word meaning "forgetfulness."

•**WARBA,** City; Itasca Couunty; Pop. 150; Zip Code 55793; Lat. 47-07-51 N long. 093-17-06 W; An Ojibway Indian word meaning "soon."

•**WARREN,** City; Marshall County Seat; Pop. 2,105; Zip Code 56762; Elev. 854; Lat. 48-11-43 N long. 096-46-13 W; Founded in 1879 and named in honor of Charles Warren, the general passanger agent of the St.Paul, Minneapolis, and Manitoba Railway Company.

•**WARROAD,** City; Roseau County; Pop. 1,216; Near the Warroad River, the are originally belonged to no one tribe but was a transit zone for war parties.

•**WASECA,** City; Waseca County Seat; Pop. 8,219; Zip Code 56093; Elev. 1151; Lat. 44-04-38 N long. 093-29-56 W; A Siux Indian word meaning "rich or fertile."

•**WATERTOWN,** City; Carver County; Pop. 1,818; Zip Code 55388; Lat. 44-57-55 N long. 093-50-48 W; Settled in 1856 and served by six lakes and a river the town has a good water supply.

•**WATERVILLE,** City; Le Sueur County; Pop. 1,717; Zip Code 56096; Lat. 44-13-14 N long. 093-33-19 W; Descriptively named for the nearby lakes and rivers.

•**WATKINS,** City; Meeker County; Pop. 757; Zip Code 55389; Lat. 45-18-58 N long. 094-24-36 W; Named by officers of the Soo railway Company for a company employee.

•**WATSON,** City; Chippewa County; Pop. 238; Zip Code 56295; Elev. 1031; Lat. 45-00-27 N long. 095-48-01 W; Chicago, Milwaukee, and St. Paul Railway officers named the town in honor of one of their employees.

•**WAUBUN,** City; Mohnomen County; Pop. 390; Zip Code 56589; Lat. 47-11-05 N long. 095-56-37 W; An Ojibway Indian word meaning "east" or "dawn."

•**WAVERLY,** City; Wright County; Pop. 470; Zip Code 55390; Elev. 998; Lat. 45-03-52 N long. 093-57-55 W; Settled in 1869 and named by early pioneers for their former home in Waverly, New York.

•**WAYZATA,** City; Hennepin County; Pop. 3,621; Zip Code 55391; Lat. 44-57-31 N long. 093-29-32 W; A Dakota Soiux word meaning "at the pines, the north."

•**WELCOME,** City; Martin County; Pop. 855; Zip Code 56181; Elev. 1235; Lat. 43-40-09 N long. 094-37-08 W; A railway village named in honor of Alfred Welcome, a nearby farmer.

•**WELLS,** City; Faribault County; Pop. 2,777; Zip Code 56097; Lat. 43-44-39 N long. 093-47-03 W; Named after the maiden surname of early settler Mrs. Clark Wells Thompson.

•**WENDELL,** City; Grant County; Pop. 216; Zip Code 56590; Lat. 46-02-00 N long. 096-06-13 W; Founded in the 1880's and named for a town in Massachusetts.

•**WEST CONCORD,** City; Dodge County; Pop. 762; Zip Code 55985; Lat. 44-09-10 N long. 092-54-04 W; Founded in 1885 and given this euphonious name by officials of the Chicago Great Western Railway.

•**WEST ST. PAUL,** City; Dakota County; Pop. 18,527; Adjacent to St.Paul, the city was named by early Catholic missionaries after the New Testament's St.Paul.

•**WEST UNION,** City; Todd County; Pop. 74; Zip Code 56389; Lat. 45-48-02 N long. 095-04-59 W; Founded in 1867 and named for the American union.

•**WESTBROOK,** City; Cottonwood County; Pop. 978; Zip Code 56183; Elev. 1422; Lat. 44-02-41 N long. 095-26-07 W; Founded in 1870 and named for the west branch of Highwater Creek.

•**WESTPORT,** City; Pope County; Pop. 50; Founded in 1882 and given a common eastern town name.

•**WHALAN,** City; Fillmore County; Pop. 119; Zip Code 55986; Elev. 793; Lat. 43-44-03 N long. 091-54-42 W; The town was founded in 1868 and named for the original landowner, John Whaalahan

•**WHEATON,** City; Traverse County Seat; Pop. 1,969; Zip Code 56296; Elev. 1019; Lat. 45-48-09 N long. 096-29-48 W; The town's name honors early surveyor, Daniel T.Wheaton.

•**WHITE BEAR LAKE,** City; Remsey County; Pop. 22,538; The town is named from nearby White Bear Lake. The lake was sacred to the Siuux Indians.

•**WILDER,** City; Jackson County; Pop. 120; Zip Code 56184; Lat. 43-49-50 N long. 095-14-56 W; The city's name honors 19th century businessman and industrialist Amherst H. Wilder.

•**WILLERNIE,** City; Washington County; Pop. 654; Zip Code 55090; Lat. 45-03-17 N long. 092-57-38 W; Named after a prominent citizen.

•**WILLIAMS,** City; Lake of the Woods; Pop. 217; Zip Code 56686; Lat. 48-46-12 N long. 094-57-12 W; Named for an early settler.

•**WILLOW RIVER,** City; Pine County; Pop. 303; Zip Code 55795; Elev. 1038; Lat. 46-19-12 N long. 092-49-58 W; The town is named for the river. The river is named for the many willows along its banks.

•**WILMAR,** City; Kandiyohi County Seat; Pop. 15,895; A European stockholder of the St. Paul and Pacific Railroad Company had the town named in his honor.

•**WILMONT,** City; Nobles County; Pop. 380; Zip Code 56185; Lat. 43-45-45 N long. 095-49-30 W; The town's name is derived from the township name: Wilmont.

•**WILTON,** City; Beltrami County; Pop. 176; Zip Code 56687; Lat. 47-30-17 N long. 095-00-04 W; The town was given this common English name, already used in the east and Canada.

•**WINDOM,** City; Cottonwood County Seat; Pop. 4,666; Zip Code 56101; Elev. 1364; Lat. 43-52-17 N long. 095-06-52 W; The town is named in honor of William Windom, U. S. Senator and cabinet officer in the late 1800's.

•**WINGER,** City; Polk County; Pop. 200; Zip Code 56592; Lat. 47-32-07 N long. 095-59-14 W; Norwegian farmers name the town for an area in central Norway.

•**WINNEBAGO,** City; Faribault County; Pop. 1,869; Zip Code 56098; Lat. 43-45-55 N long. 094-10-08 W; The city is named after the Winnebago Indian tribe.

•**WINONA,** City; Winona County Seat; Pop. 25,075; Zip Code 55942; Lat. 44-01-03 N long. 091-33-32 W; The city's name remembers a prominent Dakota Indian woman Winona.

•**WINSTED,** City; McLeod County; Pop. 1,522; Zip Code 55395; Lat. 44-57-51 N long. 094-02-42 W; Early settler Eli Lewis named the town after his former home in Connecticut.

•**WINTHROP,** City; Sibley County; Pop. 1,376; Zip Code 55396; Elev. 1018; Lat. 44-32-33 N long. 094-21-56 W; Incorporated in 1891 and named by officers of the Minneapolis and St. Louis Railway.

•**WINTON,** City; St. Louis County; Pop. 276; Zip Code 55796; Lat. 47-55-42 N long. 091-47-52 W; The town's name honors early lumberman Wiliam Winton.

•**WOLF LAKE,** City; Becker County; Pop. 67; Zip Code 56593; Lat. 46-48-23 N long. 095-21-07 W; Descriptively named by early settlers for the nearby large lake with a wolf's shape.

•**WOLVERTON,** City; Wilkin County; Pop. 126; Zip Code 56594; Lat. 46-33-48 N long. 096-44-01 W; The town's name remembers physician W. D. Wolverton, the township's original landowner.

•**WOOD LAKE,** City; Yellow Medicine; Pop. 420; Zip Code 56297; Lat. 44-39-16 N long. 095-32-01 W; Named for the nearby large lake fringed with timber.

•**WOODBURY,** City; Washington County; Pop. 10,297; The town's name honors Judge Levi Woodbury, U. S. Senator and Supreme Court Justice.

•**WOODLAND,** City; Hennepin County; Pop. 526; Descriptively named for the area's forests.

•**WOODSTOCK,** City; Pipestone County; Pop. 180; Zip Code 56186; Lat. 44-00-36 N long. 096-05-53 W; Named after Woodstock, Illinois and Woodstock, Vermont.

•**WORTHINGTON,** City; Nobles County Seat; Pop. 10,243; Zip Code 56187; Elev. 998; Lat. 43-37-17 N long. 095-35-56 W; Founded in 1872 and named in honor of the prominent Worthington family of Ohio.

•**WRENSHALL,** City; Carlton County; Pop. 333; Zip Code 55797; Elev. 1041; Lat. 46-37-31 N long. 092-26-17 W; The town is named in honor of Northern Pacific Railway Co. supervisor, C. C. Wrenshall.

•**WRIGHT,** City; Carlton County; Pop. 162; Zip Code 55798; Elev. 1303; Lat. 46-40-26 N long. 093-00-29 W; The town's name honors pioneer developer and land surveyor George B. Wright.

•**WYKOFF,** City; Fillmore County; Pop. 482; Zip Code 55990; Elev. 1322; Lat. 43-42-08 N long. 092-15-25 W; Incorporated in 1876 the town's name honors railroad surveyor, C.G. Wykoff.

•**WYOMING,** City; Chisago County; Pop. 1,559; Zip Code 55092; Lat. 45-20-07 N long. 092-59-30 W; Named after the Wyoming Valley in Luzerne County, Pennsylvania.

•**YOUNG AMERICA,** City; Carver County; Pop. 1,237; Zip Code 55397; Lat. 44-46-49 N long. 093-54-49 W; Incorporated in 1879 and given this progressive name by its early settlers.

•**ZIMMERMAN,** City; Sherburne County; Pop. 1,074; Zip Code 55398; Lat. 45-26-34 N long. 093-35-21 W; The town is named for an early farmer-settler.

•**ZUMBRO FALLS,** City; Wabasha County; Pop. 208; Zip Code 55991; Lat. 44-17-22 N long. 092-25-35 W; The town is descriptively named for the adjacent falls on the Zumbro River.

•**ZUMBROTA,** City; Goodhue County; Pop. 2,129; Zip Code 55992; Elev. 1005; Lat. 44-17-34 N long. 092-40-17 W; A compound French and Dakota word referring to the nearby Zumbro River.

MISSISSIPPI

•**ABBEVILLE,** Town; Lafayette County; Pop. 448; Zip Code 38601; Elev 361; Lat. 34-24-39 N long. 089-36-32 W; Named after the city in France.

•**ABERDEEN,** City; Monroe County Seat; Pop. 7,184; Zip Code 39730; Lat. 33-49-30 N long. 088-33-25 W; The town is named for the city in Scotland.

•**ACKERMAN,** Town; Choctaw County Seat; Pop. 1,567; Zip Code 39735 ; Elev 520; Lat. 33-18-39 N long. 089-10-12 W; Named for a local settler.

•**ALLIGATOR,** Town; Bolivar County; Pop. 256; Zip Code 38720; Lat. 34-05-21 N long. 090-43-09 W; The town is named after the famous local reptile.

•**AMORY,** City; Monroe County; Pop. 7,307; Zip Code 38821; Lat. 33-59-17 N long. 088-28-43 W; Amory is the family name of an early settler.

•**ANGUILLA,** Town; Sharkey County; Pop. 950; Zip Code 38721; Lat. 32-58-28 N long. 090-49-56 W; The town is named after the West Indian island.

•**ARCOLA,** Town; Washington County; Pop. 588; Zip Code 38722; Lat. 33-21-23 N long. 090-56-20 W; Derived from the Spanish word for "arch."

•**ARTESIA,** Town; Lowndes County; Pop. 526; Zip Code 39736; Elev 244; Lat. 33-24-49 N long. 088-38-33 W; Named for the presence of Artesian wells.

•**ASHLAND,** Town; Benton County Seat; Pop. 532; Zip Code 38603; Elev 645; Lat. 34-50-00 N long. 089-1034 W; The town is named after the famous Kentucky estate of Henry Clay.

•**BALDWYN,** City; Lee & Prentiss Counties; Pop. 3,427; Zip Code 38824; Elev 365; Lat. 34-30-25 N long. 088-38-27 W; The town's name honors a prominent Mississippi pioneer.

•**BASSFIELD,** Town; Jefferson Davis County; Pop. 325; Zip Code 39421; Lat. 31-29-43 N long. 089-44-25 W; A family name, the town is named after a local settler.

•**BATESVILLE,** City; Panola County Seat; Pop. 4,692; Zip Code 38606 ; Elev 150; Lat. 34-19-06 N long. 089-57-07 W; The town's name honors a settler named Bates.

•**BAY SPRINGS,** Town; Jasper County Seat; Pop. 1,884;Zip Code 39422; Lat. 31-58-25 N long. 089-17-20 W; A descriptive name for a local spring.

•**BAY ST. LOUIS,** City; Hancock County Seat; Pop. 7,891; Zip Code 39520; Lat. 30-19-07 N long. 089-20-05 W; Originally Shieldsborough, the name later reversed to an even earlier name: Bay St. Louis. The French explorer named it this in 1699 after King Louis IX.

•**BEAUMONT,** Town; Perry County; Pop. 1,112; Zip Code 39423; Elev 95 ; Lat. 31-10-15 N long. 088-55-27 W; A personal family name of an early settler.

•**BELMONT,** Town; Tishomingo County; Pop. 1,420; Zip Code 38827; Lat. 34-30-46 N long. 088-12-52 W; Either a family name or a commendatory descriptive.

•**BELZONI,** City; Humphreys County Seat; Pop. 2,982; Zip Code 39038; Lat. 33-10-47 N long. 090-29-20 W; The city is named for an early Italian immigrant named Belzoni.

•**BENOIT,** Town; Bolivar County; Pop. 499; Zip Code 38725; Lat. 33-39-04 N long. 091-00-42 W; Named for a settler of French descent.

•**BENTONIA,** Town; Yazoo County; Pop. 518; Zip Code 39040; Elev 188 ; Lat. 32-38-45 N long. 090-21-57 W; The town's name honors a settler named Benton.

•**BEULAH,** Town; Bolivar County; Pop. 431; Code 38726; Zip Code 38726; Lat. 33-47-23 N long. 090-58-53 W; A Biblical name for a blessed land.

•**BILOXI,** City; Harrison County Seat; Pop. 49,311; Zip Code 395+; Elev. 25. Ft. Maurepas, across the bay from the present city, was the first capital of the French Territory. Biloxi was named for the Biloxi tribe of the Sioux Indians who originally occupied the area. The name means "the first people."

•**BLUE MOUTAIN,** Town; Tippah County; Pop. 867; Zip Code 38610; Lat. 34-40-13 N long. 089-01-29 W; A descriptive geographic name.

•**BLUE SPRINGS,** Village; Union County; Pop. 131; Zip Code 38828; Lat. 34-23-59 N long. 088-52-16 W; So named for the water color in the local springs.

•**BOLTON,** Town; Hinds County; Pop. 664; Zip Code 39401; Elev 217; Lat. 32-20-45 N long. 090-27-33 W; The name of an early settler.

•**BOONEVILLE,** City; Prentiss County Seat; Pop. 6,199; Zip Code 38829; Lat. 34-39-37 N long. 088-33-40 W; The city is named in honor of pioneer Daniel Boone.

•**BOYLE,** Town; Bolivar County; Pop. 888; Zip Code 38730; Elev 139; Lat. 33-42-21 N long. 0900-43-25 W; A personal name of an early settler.

•**BRANDON,** City; Rankin County Seat; Pop. 9,626; Zip Code 39042; Elev 486; Lat. 32-16-18 N long. 089-59-11 W; Named in honor of Governor Gerard Brandon who served from 1825 to 1831.

•**BROOKHAVEN,** City; Lincoln County Seat; Pop. 10,800; Zip Code 39601; Elev 487; Lat. 31-34-53 N long. 090-26-58 W; Settled in 1818 and given an euphonious name by its founders.

•**BROOKSVILLE,** Town; Naxubee County; Pop. 1,038; Zip Code 39739; Elev 277; Lat. 33-14-00 N long. 088-34-48 W; Descriptively named for several local brooks.

•**BRUCE,** Town; Calhoun County; Pop. 2,208; Zip Code 38915; Lat. 33-59-42 N long. 089-20-44 W; The personal name of an early settler.

•**BUDE,** Town; Franklin County; Pop. 1,092; Zip Code 39630; Elev 232; Lat. 31-27-44 N long. 090-51-17 W; Probably named for a local pioneer settler.

•**BURNSVILLE,** Town; Tishomingo County; Pop. 889; Zip Code 38833; Elev 465; Lat. 34-50-19 N long. 088-18-51 W; The town's name honors a pioneer named Burns.

•**BYHALIA,** Town; Marshall County; Pop. 757; Zip Code 38611; Elev 369; Lat. 34-52-17 N long. 089-41-24 W; An Indian word meaning "great oaks."

•**CALDEONIA,** Village; Lowndes County; Pop. 497; Zip Code 39740; Elev 339; Lat. 33-41-03 N long. 088-19-14 W; The ancient name for Scotland transplanted to this new location.

•**CALHOUN CITY,** Town; Calhoun County; Pop. 2,033; Zip Code 38916; Lat. 33-51-22 N long. 089-18-41 W; Named in honor of statesman John C. Calhoun.

•**CANTON,** City; Madison County Seat; Pop. 11,116; Zip Code 39046; Lat. 32-36-55 N long. 090-02-27 W; Either referring to Canton, China, or the French word for administrative sub-division.

•**CARTHAGE,** City; Leake County Seat; Pop. 3,453; Zip Code 39051; Lat. 32-44-18 N long. 089-32-02 W; The city is named after the ancient North African city.

•**CARY,** Town; Sharkey County; Pop. 470; Zip Code 39054; Lat. 32-48-24 N long. 090-55-40 W; The name of an early settler.

•**CENTREVILLE,** Town; Amite & Wilkinson Counties; Pop. 1,844; Zip Code 39631; Elev 380; Lat. 31-05-16 N long. 091-03-31 W; Descriptively named for its location.

•**CHARLESTON,** City; Tallahatchie County Seat; Pop. 2,878; Zip Code 38921; Lat. 34-00-23 N long. 090-03-07 W; Named after the city in South Carolina.

•**CLARKSDALE,** City; Coahoma County Seat; Pop. 21,137; Zip Code 38614; Lat. 34-12-00 N long. 090-34-23 W; The town is named after English immigrant John Clark.

•**CLEVELAND,** City; Bolivar County Seat; Pop. 14,524; Zip Code 38732; Lat. 33-44-21 N long. 090-43-25 W; The city takes its name from the city in Ohio.

•**CLINTON,** City; Hinds County; Pop. 14,660; Zip Code 39056; Elev 381; Lat. 32-20-28 N long. 090-19-06 W; The city's name honors 1820's New York Governor DeWitt Clinton.

•**COFFEEVILLE,** Town; Yalabusha County Seat; Pop. 1,129; Zip Code 38922; Lat. 33-58-48 N long. 089-40-39 W; So named because coffee was traded here extensively.

•**COLDWATER,** Town; Tate County; Pop. 1,505; Zip Code 38618; Lat. 34-41-24 N long. 089-58-31 W; A descriptive name given by the town's founders.

•**COLLINS,** City; Covington County Seat; Pop. 2,131; Zip Code 39428; Lat. 31-38-28 N long. 089-33-25 W; A personal name for an early settler.

•**COLUMBIA,** City; Marion County Seat; Pop. 7,733; Zip Code 39429; Lat. 31-17-39 N long. 089-49-50 W; The popular name for America.

•**COLUMBUS,** City; Lowndes County Seat; Pop. 27,383; Zip Code 39701; Lat. 33-34-15 N long. 088-25-11 W; Named after the discoverer of America: Columbus.

•**COMO,** Town; Panola County; Pop. 1,378; Zip Code 38619; Lat. 34-31-00 N long. 089-56-14 W; Founded in 1856 and named for Lake Como in Italy.

•**CORINTH,** City; Alcorn County Seat; Pop. 13,839; Zip Code 38834; Elev 455; Lat. 34-54-13 N long. 088-34-00 W; Originally Cross City, the name was changed in 1857 to Corinth, after the ancient Greek city.

•**CRAWFORD,** Town; Lowndes County; Pop. 495; Zip Code 39743; Elev 321; Lat. 33-18-13 N long. 088-37-16 W; The personal name of an early settler.

•**CRENSHAW,** Town; Panola & Quitman Counties; Pop. 1,019; Zip Code 38621; Lat. 34-30-15 N long. 090-11-56 W; The family name of a prominent early settler.

•**CROWDER,** Town; Panola & Quitman Counties; Pop. 789; Zip Code 38622; Lat. 34-10-25 N long. 090-08-10 W; A prominent family name in the settlement of this region.

•**CRUGER,** Town; Holmes County; Pop. 540; Zip Code 38924; Lat. 33-19-15 N long. 090-14-04 W; Probably named for an early 19th century pioneer.

•**CRYSTAL SPRINGS,** City; Copiah County; Pop. 4,902; Zip Code 39059; Elev 464; Lat. 31-59-05 N long. 090-21-31 W; A descriptive name for the quality of the water at the local springs.

•**DE KALB,** Town; Kemper County Seat; Pop. 1,159; Zip Code 39328; Elev 464 ; Lat. 32-45-50 N long. 088-38-53 W; Named in honor of the German Baron De Kalb, who came to America in 1776 to fight for American independence.

•**DECATUR,** Town; Newton County Seat; Pop. 1,148; Zip Code 39327; Lat. 32-26-14 N long. 089-06-45 W; The town's name honors early naval hero Stephen Decatur.

•**DERMA,** Town; Calhoun County; Pop. 793; Zip Code 38839; Lat. 33-51-21 N long. 089-17-06 W; The origin of the town's name is uncertain.

•**DREW,** City; Sunflower County; Pop. 2,528; Zip Code 38737; Elev 139; Lat. 33-48-40 N long. 090-31-40 W; A family name for an early pioneer.

•**DUCK HILL,** Town; Montgomery County; Pop. 706; Zip Code 38925; Lat. 33-37-52 N long. 089-42-55 W; Descriptively named for a large hill east of town associated with a Choctaw Indian chief called "duck."

•**DUMAS,** Town; Tippah County; Pop. 312; Zip Code 38625; Elev 623; Lat. 34-38-25 N long. 088-50-18 W; The town is named after the popular French novelist of the 19th century.

•**DUNCAN,** Town; Bolivar County; Pop. 501; Zip Code 38740; Lat. 34-02-30 N long. 090-44-36 W; A Scottish name, probably a local settler.

•**DURANT,** City; Holmes County; Pop. 2,889; Zip Code 39063; Elev 269; Lat. 33-04-32 N long. 089-51-23 W; The personal name of an early settler.

•**ECRU,** Town; Pontotoc County; Pop. 687; Zip Code 38841; Lat. 34-21-18 N long. 089-01-13 W; W. C. Falkner named the town after the color of the paint on the local railroad station.

•**EDWARDS,** Town; Hinds County; Pop. 1,515; Zip Code 39066; Lat. 32-19-52 N long. 090-36-24 W; The name of one of the town's founders.

•**FLORA,** Town; Madison County; Pop. 1,507; Zip Code 39071; Elev 256; Lat. 32-32-37 N long. 090-18-29 W; From a personal name of an early female settler.

•**FLORENCE,** Town; Rankin County; Pop. 1,111; Zip Code 39073; Elev 316; Lat. 32-09-154 N long. 090-07-47 W; Named for the wife of a local settler.

•**FOREST,** City; Scott County Seat; Pop. 5,229; Zip Code 39074; Elev 485; Lat. 32-21-40 N long. 089-27-45 W; Descriptively named for the area's main vegetation.

•**FRENCH CAMP,** Village; Choctaw County; Pop. 306; Zip Code 39745; Lat. 33-17-37 N long. 089-24-01 W; Named after a group of French speaking people who occupied the site as a camp.

•**FRIARS POINT**, Town; Coahoma County; Pop. 1,400; Zip Code 38631; Lat. 34-22-03 N long. 090-38-27 W; Descriptively named for a early settler in the county's history.

•**FULTON**, City; Itawamba County Seat; Pop. 3,238; Zip Code 38843; Elev 341; Lat. 34-16-06 N long. 088-24-47 W; Named in honor of the steamboat's inventor Robert Fulton.

•**GEORGETOWN**, Town; Copiah County; Pop. 343; Zip Code 39078; Elev 236; Lat. 31-52-18 N long. 090-10-02 W; Named after the town's founder.

•**GLOSTER**, Town; Amite County; Pop. 1,726; Zip Code 39638; Elev 434; Lat. 31-11-43 N long. 091-01-11 W; Named after the engineer who built the railroad through here in the 1880's.

•**GOLDEN**, Town; Tishomingo County; Pop. 292; Zip Code 38847; Lat. 34-29-21 N long. 088-11-20 W; A commendatory name given the place by its settlers.

•**GOODMAN**, Town; Holmes County; Pop. 1,285; Zip Code 39079; Lat. 32-58-08 N long. 089-54-42 W; A personal name of an early settler.

•**GREENVILLE**, City; Washington County Seat; Pop. 40,613; Zip Code 38701; Lat. 33-24-41 N long. 091-00-29 W; Incorporated in 1870 and descriptively named for the lush vegetation of this Mississippi River town.

•**GREENWOOD**, City; Leflore County Seat; Pop. 20,115; Zip Code 38912; Lat. 33-39-27 N long. 090-05-15 W; Descriptively named for the area's thick forests.

•**GRENADA**, City; Grenada County Seat; Pop. 12,641; Zip Code 38901; Lat. 33-46-35 N long. 089-48-24 W; Named for the West Indian island.

•**GULFPORT**, City; Harrison County Seat; Pop. 39,676; Zip Code 39501; Lat. 30-23-52 N long. 089-04-49 W; Descriptively named for its location on the Gulf of Mexico.

•**GUNNISON**, Town; Bolivar County; Pop. 708; Zip Code 38746; Elev 155 ; Lat. 33-56-40 N long. 090-56-29 W; Named for an early settler in the county.

•**GUNTOWN**, Town; Lee County; Pop. 359; Zip Code 38849; Elev 384; Lat. 34-26-24 N long. 088-3942 W; Virginia tory, James Gunn, fled here during the American Revolution. The town is named after him.

•**HATTIESBURG**, City; Forrest & Lamar Counties; Forest County Seat; Pop. 40,829; Zip Code 39401; Elev 161 ; Lat. 31-18-07 N long. 089-17-57 W; Founded by Captain Hardy in the 1880's and named for his wife Hattie.

•**HAZLEHURST**, City; Copiah County Seat; Pop. 4,437; Zip Code 39083; Elev 479 ; Lat. 31-51-48 N long. 090-23-41 W; Named in honor of railroad civil engineer Goerge Hazelhurst in 1857.

•**HEIDELBERG**, Town; Jasper County; Pop. 1,098; Zip Code 39439; Elev 324 ; Lat. 31-53-03 N long. 088-59-18 W; The town is named after the famous German city.

•**HERMANDO**, City; De Soto County Seat; Pop. 2,969; Zip Code 38632; Lat. 34-49-33 N long. 089-59-24 W; The town is named for the Spanish explorer Hernando De Soto.

•**HICKORY**, Town; Newton County; Pop. 670; Zip Code 39332; Lat. 32-19-04 N long. 089-01-23 W; Named in honor of "ol Hickory" Andrew Jackson.

•**HICKORY FLAT**, Town; Benton County; Pop. 458; Zip Code 38633; Lat. 34-36-50 N long. 089-11-13 W; Descriptively named for the topography and the nearby hickory trees.

•**HOLLANDALE**, City; Washington County; Pop. 4,336; Zip Code 38748; Lat. 33-10-30 N long. 090-51-15 W; Named for Dutch immigrants who settled here.

•**HOLLY SPRINGS**, City; Marshall County Seat; Pop. 7,285; Zip Code 38635; Lat. 34-46-19 N long. 089-26-50 W; A descriptive name for a spring surrounded by holly trees.

•**HORN LAKE**, City; De Soto County; Pop. 4,326; Zip Code 38637; Lat. 34-57-54 N long. 090-01-51 W; A descriptive name for the lake's shape.

•**HOUSTON**, City; Chickasaw County Seat; Pop. 3,747; Zip Code 38851; Lat. 33-56-13 N long. 088-59-59 W; Named in honor of Texas patriot Sam Houston.

•**INDIANOLA**, City; Sunflower County Seat; Pop. 8,221; Zip Code 38749; Lat. 33-26-49 N long. 090-45-10 W; A place name coined from Indian and a Latin-like ending.

•**INVERNESS**, Town; Sunflower County; Pop. 1,034; Zip Code 38753; Elev 119 ; Lat. 33-21-10 N long. 090-35-23 W; The town is named after the city in Scotland.

•**ISOLA**, Town; Humphreys County; Pop. 834; Zip Code 38754; Lat. 33-15-48 N long. 090-35-28 W; The Italian word "island," probably implies isolation.

•**ITTA BENA**, City; Leflore County; Pop. 2,904; Zip Code 38941; Lat. 33-29-39 N long. 090-19-37 W; The origin of this unusual name is uncertain.

•**IUKA**, City; Tishomingo County Seat; Pop. 2,846; Zip Code 38852; Elev 569 ; Lat. 34-48-46 N long. 088-11-22 W; Iuka is the name of a Chickasaw Indian chief of the early 1800's.

•**JACKSON**, City; Hinds County Seat; Pop. 202,893; Zip Code 39200; Elev 294; Lat. 32-18-39 N long. 090-10-43 W; Jackson's name honors President Andrew Jackson.

•**JONESTOWN**, Town; Coahoma County; Pop. 1,231; Zip Code 38639; Lat. 34-19-15 N long. 090-27-08 W; A personal name for one of the early settlers.

•**KILMICHAEL**, Town; Montgomery County; Pop. 906; Zip Code 39747; Elev 357; Lat. 33-26-25 N long. 089-34-17 W; An Irish name given by settlers from Eire.

•**KOSCIUSKO**, City; Attala County Seat; Pop. 7,415; Zip Code 39090; Elev 488; Lat. 33-03-13 N long. 089-35-19 W; Incorporated in 1836 and named in honor of the Polish noble who fought with the Americans in the Revolutionary War.

•**LAKE**, Town; Scott County; Pop. 504; Zip Code 39092; So named for its location near a lake.

•**LAMBERT**, Town; Quitman County; Pop. 1,624; Zip Code 38643 ; Lat. 34-12-08 N long. 090-17-07 W; The name of an early settler.

•**LAUREL**, City; Jones County Seat; Pop. 21,897; Zip Code 39440; Lat. 31-42-14 N long. 089-07-34 W; The city is named after the the laurel tree.

•**LEAKESVILLE**, Town; Greene County Seat; Pop. 1,120; Zip Code 39451; Lat. 31-09-24 N long. 088-33-31 W; A settler neamed Leakes left his name on the town.

•**LELAND**, City; Washington County; Pop. 6,667; Zip Code 38756; Elev 126 ; Lat. 33-24-25 N long. 090-53-34 W; The family name of 19th century pioneers.

•LENA, Town; Leake County; Pop. 231; Zip Code 39094; Lat. 32-35-34 N long. 089-35-29 W; An Indian name, possibly meaning "man."

•LEXINGTON, City; Holmes County Seat; Pop. 2,628; Zip Code 39095; Lat. 33-06-54 N long. 090-03-06 W; Named after the famous Revolutionary War battle.

•LIBERTY, Town; Amite County Seat; Pop. 669; Zip Code 39645; Elev 361 ; Lat. 31-09-30 N long. 090-48-18 W; Patriotically named for the popular virtue.

•LONG BEACH, City; Harrison County; Pop. 7,967; Zip Code 39560; Lat. 30-21-02 N long. 089-09-08 W; Descriptively named for a geographic feature.

•LOUIN, Town; Jasper County; Pop. 338; Zip Code 39338; Lat. 32-04-31 N long. 089-15-11 W; The family name of a pioneer.

•LOUISE, Town; Humphreys County; Pop. 400; Zip Code 39097; Lat. 32-59-05 N long. 090-35-55 W; Named for the wife or daughter of an early settler.

•LOUISVILLE, City; Winston County Seat; Pop. 7,323; Zip Code 39339; Lat. 33-07-10 N long. 089-03-21 W; Named after the city in Kentucky.

•LUCEDALE, City; George County Seat; Pop. 2,429; Zip Code 39452; Elev 282; Lat. 30-55-07 N long. 088-35-29 W; The city takes the name of the Luce family.

•LULA, Town; Coahoma County; Pop. 394; Zip Code 38644; Lat. 34-27-11 N long. 090-28-34 W; The name of the wife of a local settler.

•LUMBERTON, City; Lamar County; Pop. 2,210; Zip Code 39455; The local lumber industry named the town.

•LYON, Town; Coahoma County; Pop. 531; Zip Code 38645; Lat. 34-13-03 N long. 090-32-28 W; The personal name of one of the town's founders.

•MABEN, Town; Oktibbeha & Webster Counties; Pop. 855; Zip Code 39750; Lat. 33-33-15 N long. 089-05-13 W; Named for a prominent local family.

•MACON, City; Noxubee County Seat; Pop. 2,396; Zip Code 39341; Lat. 33-06-48 N long. 088-33-33 W; Named after the city in Georgia.

•MADISON, Town; Madison County; Pop. 2,241; Zip Code 39110; Elev 335 ; Lat. 32-27-31 N long. 090-06-47 W; The town is named after President James Madison.

•MAGEE, City; Simpson County; Pop. 3,497; Zip Code 39111; Elev 430 ; Lat. 31-52-06 N long. 089-43-33 W; An anglo-saxon name brought by a pioneer in the county.

•MAGNOLIA, City; Pike County Seat; Pop. 2,461; Zip Code 39652; Elev 319; Lat. 31-09-05 N long. 090-27-26 W; The city is named after the many beautiful magnolia trees in the area.

•MANTACHIE, Town; Itawamba County; Pop. 732; Zip Code 38855; Elev 356 ; Lat. 34-19-20 N long. 088-29-32 W; The town is named after the Chickasaw Indian chief Man-at-chee.

•MARIETTA, Town; Prentiss County; Pop. 298; Zip Code 38856; Elev 382 ; Lat. 34-30-04 N long. 088-28-06 W; Named after the city in Ohio.

•MARION, Town; Lauderdale County; Pop. 771; Zip Code 39342; Lat. 32-25-08 N long. 088-39-06 W; The town's name honors Revolutionary War hero Francis Marion.

•MARKS, City; Quitman County Seat; Pop. 2,260; Zip Code 38646; Elev 166; Lat. 34-15-10 N long. 090-16-36 W; The city is named for an early inhabitant.

•MATHISTON, Town; Choctaw & Webster Counties; Pop. 632; Zip Code 39752; Lat. 33-32-04 N long. 089-07-43 W; Named after the prominent Mathis family.

•MAYERSVILLE, Town; Issaquena County Seat; Pop. 378; Zip Code 39113; Lat. 32-54-13 N long. 091-03-11 W; The personal name of an early settler.

•MCCOMB, City; Pike County; Pop. 12,331; Zip Code 39648; Lat. 31-13-50 N long. 090-27-31 W; The city is named in honor of 1850's railroad president Colonel H. S. McComb.

•MCLAIN, Town; Greene County; Pop. 688; Zip Code 39456; Lat. 31-06-13 N long. 088-49-32 W; Named after an early settler.

•MEADVILLE, Town; Franklin County Seat; Pop. 575; Zip Code 39653; Lat. 31-28-16 N long. 090-53-39 W; The old English word for "meadow."

•MOORHEAD, City; Sunflower County; Pop. 2,358; Zip Code 38761; Lat. 33-26-59 N long. 090-30-04 W; Moorhead's name remembers a pioneer in the area.

•MORGAN CITY, Town; Leflore County; Pop. 319; Zip Code 38946; Lat. 33-22-48 N long. 090-21-04 W; Named for an early settler.

•MORTON, City; Scott County; Pop. 3,303; Zip Code 39117; Lat. 32-20-54 N long. 089-39-13 W; A personal name recalling a pioneer in the county.

•MOSS POINT, City; Jackson County; Pop. 18,998; Zip Code 39563; A descriptive name for the vegetation in the vicinity.

•MOUND BAYOU, City; Bolivar County; Pop. 2,917; Zip Code 38762; Elev 143; Lat. 33-52-48 N long. 090-43-34 W; The city is named after Indian mounds to the northeast and southeast of the city.

•MOUNT OLIVE, Town; Covington County; Pop. 993; Zip Code 39119; Elev 461; Lat. 31-45-26 N long. 089-39-12 W; The town is named after the Biblical hill in Jerusalem.

•MYRTLE, Town; Union County; Pop. 402; Zip Code 38650; Elev 398; Lat. 34-33-29 N long. 089-07-02 W; named after the myrtle tree.

•NATCHEZ, City; Adams County Seat; Pop. 22,015; Zip Code 39120; Lat. 31-34-06 N long. 091-21-56 W; An Indian tribal name.

•NETTLETON, Town; Lee & Monroe Counties; Pop. 1,911; Zip Code 38858; Elev 266; Lat. 34-05-23 N long. 088-37-19 W; Nettleton is named after a prominent early resident.

•NEW ALBANY, City; Union County Seat; Pop. 7,072; Zip Code 38652; Elev 364; Lat. 34-29-27 N long. 089-00-40 W; Named after Albany, Georgia.

•NEWHEBRON, Village; Lawrence County; Pop. 470; Zip Code 39140; Elev 364; Lat. 31-43-37 N long. 089-58-43 W; Named after the Biblical city.

•NEWTON, City; Newton County; Pop. 3,708; Zip Code 39345; Elev 415; Lat. 32-19-12 N long. 089-09-41 W; Both a common place name and a common personal name.

•NORTH CARROLLTON, Town; Carroll County; Pop. 859; Zip Code 38947; Lat. 33-30-59 N long. 089-55-05 W.

•NOXAPATER, Town; Winston County; Pop. 516; Zip Code 39346; Elev 491; Lat. 32-59-15 N long. 089-03-43 W; A Choctaw Indian word of uncertain origin.

•OAKLAND, Town; Yalobusha County; Pop. 540; Zip Code 38948; Elev 410; Lat. 34-03-09 N long. 089-54-58 W; Named for the many oak trees in the county.

•OCEAN SPRINGS, City; Jackson County; Pop. 14,504; Zip Code 39564; Lat. 30-25-33 N long. 088-49-01 W; Descriptively named for its geographic location.

•OKOLONA, City; Chickasaw County Seat; Pop. 3,409; Zip Code 38860; Elev 231; Lat. 34-03-56 N long. 088-44-52 W; The origin of the name is uncertain.

•OLIVE BRANCH, City; De Soto County; Pop. 2,067; Zip Code 38654; Elev; Lat. 34-57-07 N long. 089-49-12 W; The town's name refers to a peaceful ending to a conflict between the Indians and the settlers in 1832.

•OSYKA, Town; Pike County; Pop. 581; Zip Code 39657; Lat. 31-00-26 N long. 090-28-00 W; An Choctaw Indian word meaning "eagle."

•OXFORD, City; Lafayette County Seat; Pop. 9,882; Zip Code 38655; Elev 416; Lat. 34-22-10 N long. 089-31-18 W; Oxford takes its name from the famous University town in England.

•PACE, Town; Bolivar County; Pop. 519; Zip Code 38764; Elev 140; Lat. 33-47-33 N long. 090-51-39 W; Pace is named for an early settler.

•PACHUTA, Town; Clarke County; Pop. 256; Zip Code 39347; Lat. 32-02-56 N long. 088-52-30 W; A Creek Indian word meaning town.

•PASCAGOULA, City; Jackson County Seat; Pop. 29,318; Zip Code 39563; Elev 16; Lat. 30-23-52 N long. 088-31-22 W; An Indian tribal name.

•PASS CHRISTIAN, City; Harrison County; Pop. 5,014; Zip Code 39571; Elev 10; Lat. 30-19-23 N long. 089-14-16 W; Descriptively named for its location on a channel called Christian's Pass.

•PEARL, City; Rankin County; Pop. 20,778; Zip Code 39208; Descriptively named for the local pearl fishery.

•PELAHATCHIE, Town; Rankin County; Pop. 1,445; Zip Code 39145; Elev 359; Lat. 32-18-57 N long. 089-47-29 W; A Choctaw Indian word meaning "hurricane-stream."

•PETAL, City; Forrest County; Pop. 8,476; Zip Code 39465; Lat. 31-20-36 N long. 089-15-07 W; Named for the many beautiful flowers in the vicinity.

•PHILADELPHIA, City; Neshoba County Seat; Pop. 6,434; Zip Code 39350; Elev 424; Lat. 32-46-23 N long. 089-06-52 W; The city is named after the metropolis in Pennsylvania.

•PICAYUNE, City; Pearl River County; Pop. 10,361; Zip Code 39466; Elev 61; Lat. 30-31-54 N long. 089-40-01 W; The city is named after a newspaper, the New Orleans Picayune.

•PICKENS, Town; Holmes County; Pop. 1,386; Zip Code 39146; Elev 232; Lat. 32-53-07 N long. 089-58-03 W; The town is named for an early settler.

•PLANTERSVILLE, Town; Lee County; Pop. 920; Zip Code 38862; Elev 300; Lat. 34-12-26 N long. 088-39-46 W; The town was named for the many planters in the before the Civil War.

•PONTOTOC, City; Pontotoc County Seat; Pop. 4,723; Zip Code 38863; Elev 501; Lat. 34-14-43 N long. 089-01-28 W; A Chickasaw Indian word meaning "battle at the cat-tails."

•POPE, Village; Panola County; Pop. 208; Zip Code 38658; Lat. 34-13-02 N long. 089-56-43 W; Pope is named after a pioneer settler.

•POPLARVILLE, City; Pearl River County Seat; Pop. 2,562; Zip Code 39470; Elev 317; Lat. 30-50-26 N long. 089-32-10 W; Named for the many poplar trees in the vicinity.

•PORT GIBSON, City; Claiborne County Seat; Pop. 2,371; Zip Code 39150; Lat. 31-57-33 N long. 090-58-54 W; Town founder Samuel Gibson arrived here in 1788. The town is named for him.

•PRENTISS, Town; Jefferson Davis County Seat; Pop. 1,465; Zip Code 39474; Elev 336; Lat. 31-35-48 N long. 089-52-14 W; An early settler named Prentiss left his name on the town.

•PURVIS, City; Lamar County Seat; Pop. 2,256; Zip Code 39475; Elev 381; Lat. 31-08-35 N long. 089-24-28 W; The name of an early settler in the area.

•QUITMAN, City; Clarke County Seat; Pop. 2,632; Zip Code 39355; Elev 434; Lat. 32-02-37 N long. 088-43-16 W; Quitman is named after an early settler in the region.

•RALEIGH, Town; Smith County Seat; Pop. 998; Zip Code 39153; Elev 544; Lat. 32-01-22 N long. 089-27-09 W; The town is named for the city in North Carolina.

•RAYMOND, Town; Hinds County Seat; Pop. 1,967; Zip Code 39154; Elev 321; Lat. 32-15-27 N long. 090-25-14 W; Raymond is named after a prominent pioneer.

•RICHLAND, City; Rankin County; Pop. 3,955; Zip Code 39218; An allusion to the region's many resources.

•RICHTON, Town; Perry County; Pop. 1,205; Zip Code 39476; Lat. 31-20-50 N long. 088-56-23 W; Named after an early settler.

•RIDGELAND, City; Madison County; Pop. 5,461; Zip Code 39157; Elev 353; Lat. 32-25-15 N long. 090-08-04 W; Descriptively named for the town's location.

•RIENZI, Town; Alcorn County; Pop. 423; Zip Code 38865; Elev 437; Lat. 34-45-49 N long. 088-31-51 W; An Italian settler named Rienzi left his name on the town.

•RIPLEY, City; Tippah County Seat; Pop. 4,271; Zip Code 38663; Lat. 34-43-57 N long. 088-56-51 W; Ripley is named after an early pioneer.

•ROLLING FORK, City; Sharkey County Seat; Pop. 2,590; Zip Code 39070; Lat. 32-36-49 N long. 091-01-11 W; The city is named for the Rolling Fork Plantation.

•ROSEDALE, City; Bolivar County Seat; Pop. 2,793; Zip Code 38769; Elev 145; Lat. 33-51-20 N long. 091-01-38; Named for the many beautiful rose plantings in the .

•ROXIE, Town; Franklin County; Pop. 591; Zip Code 39661; Elev 232; Lat. 31-30-06 N long. 091-03-57 W; Roxie is named after an early settler.

•RULEVILLE, City; Sunflower County; Pop. 3,332; Zip Code 38771; Elev 135; Lat. 33-43-38 N long. 090-32-50 W; The town's name refers to either an early inhabitant, or to some local bit of history.

•SALIS, Town; Attala County; Pop. 211; Zip Code 39160; Lat. 33-01-23 N long. 089-45-55 W; Named for a local settler.

•**SALTILLO,** Town; Lee County; Pop. 1,271; Zip Code 38866; Lat. 34-22-34 N long. 088-41-06 W; A city in Mexico occupied by American troops in the 1846 war.

•**SANDERSVILLE,** Town; Jones County; Pop. 800; Zip Code 39477; Elev 286; Lat. 31-46-39 N long. 089-02-06 W; Named after a prominent early settler.

•**SARDIS,** Town; Panola County Seat; Pop. 2,278; Zip Code 38666; Elev 379; LR. 34-26-08 N long 089-55-10 W; A city mentioned in the Book of Revelation.

•**SCHLATER,** Town; Leflore County; Pop. 429; Zip Code 38952; Lat. 33-38-27 N long. 090-20-58 W; Schlater is named after an early settler.

•**SCOOBA,** Town; Kemper County; Pop. 511; Zip Code 39358; Lat. 32-49-45 N long. 088-28-43 W; A Choctaw Indian word meaning "reed thicket."

•**SEBASTOPOL,** Town; Scott County; Pop. 314; Code; Zip Code 39359; Lat. 32-33-59 N long. 089-20-06 W; The town is named after the city in southern Russia.

•**SEMINARY,** Town; Covington County; Pop. 327; Zip Code 39479; Elev 268; Lat. 31-33-35 N long. 089-29-39 W; Named for a local seminary.

•**SENATOBIA,** City; Tate County Seat; Pop. 5,013; Zip Code 38668; Lat. 34-37-09 N long. 089-58-02 W; A corruption of a Chowtaw Indian word meaning "sycamore."

•**SHANNON,** Town; Lee County; Pop. 680; Zip Code 38868; Lat. 34-06-57 N long. 088-42-44 W; Either a personal name or after a river in Ireland.

•**SHAW,** City; Bolivar & Sunflower Counties; Pop. 2,461; Zip Code 38773; Elev 134; Lat. 33-37-31 N long. 090-45-48 W; Shaw's name remembers a founder of the community.

•**SHELBY,** City; Bolivar County; Pop. 2,540; Zip Code 38774; Elev 157; Lat. 33-56-54 N long. 090-45-47 W; A personal name, probably for an early settler.

•**SHUBUTA,** Town; Clarke County; Pop. 626; Zip Code 39360; Elev 197; Lat. 31-53-12 Nlong. 088-41-02 W; A Chowtaw Indian word meaning "smooky."

•**SHUQUALAK,** Town; Noxubee County; Pop. 554; Zip Code 39361; Elev 217; Lat. 32-58-44 N long. 088-34-12 W; A Choctaw Indian word of uncertain meaning.

•**SILVER CITY,** Town; Humphreys County; Pop. 378; Zip Code 39166; Lat. 33-05-41 N long. 090-29-34 W; Descriptiveluy named for a local historical event.

•**STONEWALL,** Town; Clarke County; Pop. 1,345; Zip Code 39363; Elev 235; Lat. 32-08-03 N long. 088-47-16 W; Named in honor of Confederate General Stonewall Jackson.

•**STURGIS,** Town; Oktibbeha County; Pop. 269; Zip Code 39769; Elev 336; Lat. 33-20-44 N long. 089-03-04 W; Sturgis is named for a local settler.

•**SUMMIT,** Town; Pike County; Pop. 1,753; Zip Code 39666; Elev 431; Lat. 31-17-06 N long. 090-27-54 W; A descriptive geographic name for the town's location.

•**SUMNER,** Town; Tallahatchie County Seat; Pop. 452; Zip Code 38957; Lat. 33-58-16 N nlong. 090-22-08 W; Named after the county in South Carolina.

•**SUMRALL,** Town; Lamar County; Pop. 1,197; Zip Code 39482; Elev 290; Lat. 31-25-10 N long. 089-32-54 W; Named after a local resident.

•**SUNFLOWER,** Town; Sunflower County; Pop. 1,027; Zip Code 38778; Lat. 33-32-54 N long. 090-32-11 W; Named for the many sunflowers growing in the region.

•**TAYLOR,** Village; Lafayette County; Pop. 301; Zip Code 38673; Elev 325; Lat. 34-16-17 N long. 089-35-22 W; Named after Zachary Taylor.

•**TAYLORSVILLE,** Town; Smith County; Pop. 1,387; Zip Code 39168; Lat. 31-49-50 N long. 089-25-35 W; Named in honor of President Zachary Taylor.

•**TCHULA,** Town; Holmes County; Pop. 1,931; Zip Code 39169; Lat. 33-11-06 N long. 090-13-29 W; A Chowtaw word meaning "boundary."

•**TERRY,** Town; Hinds County; Pop. 655; Zip Code 39170; Elev 295; Lat. 32-14-46 N long. 090-13-57 W; Terry is named for a local resident.

•**THAXTON,** Town; Pontotoc County; Pop. 404; Zip Code 38871; Elev 436; Lat. 34-18-34 N long. 089-10-47 W; The town is named after a settler called Thaxton.

•**TISHOMINGO,** Town; Tishomingo County; Pop. 387; Zip Code 38873; Lat. 34-38-11 N long. 088-13-42 W; The town's name remembers a well-known Chickasaw Indian chief.

•**TOCCOPOLA,** Town; Pontotoc County; Pop. 184; Zip Code 38874; Elev 412; Lat. 34-15-23 N long. 089-13-58 W; A Choctaw Indian word of uncertain meaning.

•**TREMONT,** Town; Itawamba County; Pop. 379; Code; Zip Code 38876; Lat. 34-14-08 N long. 088-15-30 W; Named in honor of a prominent early settler.

•**TUNICA,** Town; Tunica County Seat; Pop. 1,361; Zip Code 38676; Lat. 34-541-48 N long. 090-22-46 W; The name of an Indian tribe.

•**TUPELO,** City; Lee County Seat; Pop. 23,905; Zip Code 38801; Elev 290; Lat. 34-14-57 N long. 088-43-09 W; The city is named after the black gum, or tupelo tree.

•**TUTWILER,** Town; Tallahatchie County; Pop. 1,174; Zip Code 38963; Lat. 34-00-56 N long. 090-26-12 W; Tutwiler is named after a local resident.

•**TYLERTOWN,** Town; Walthall County; Pop. 1,976; Zip Code 39667; Elev 293; Lat. 31-07-04 N long. 090-08-40 W; Probably named after President John Tyler.

•**UNION,** Town; Neshoba & Newton Counties; Pop. 1,931; Zip Code 39365; Elev 291; Lat. 32-34-18 N long. 089-07-11 W; A political and patriotic reference to the United States.

•**UTICA,** Town; Hinds County; Pop. 865; Zip Code 39175; Lat. 32-06-10 N long. 090-37-00 W; The town is named after the city in New York.

•**VAIDEN,** Town; Carroll County Seat; Pop. 924; Zip Code 39176; Lat. 33-19-53 N long. 089-44-33 W; The town's name recalls an early settler.

•**VARDAMON,** Town; Calhoun County; Pop. 1,009; Zip Code 38878; Lat. 33-52-54 N long. 089-10-46 W; Named after a pioneer in the region.

•VERONA, Town; Lee County; Pop. 2,497; Zip Code 38879; Lat. 34-11-30 N long. 088-43-21 W; The town is named after the Italian city.

•VICKSBURG, City; Warren County; Pop. 25,434; Zip Code 39180; Lat. 32-20-26 N long. 090-52-10 W; The city is named after Newitt Vick, a Methodist minister and an early settler.

•WALNUT, Town; Tipah County; Pop. 513; Zip Code 38683; Elev 162; Lat. 34-56-54 N long. 088-54-10 W; : The town is named after the many walnut trees in the county.

•WALNUT GROVE, Town; Leake County; Pop. 439; Zip Code 39189; Lat. 32-35-43 N long. 089-27-33 W; Descriptively named for a nearby grove of walnut trees.

•WATER VALLEY, City; Yalobusha County Seat; Pop. 4,417; Zip Code 38965; Lat. 34-09-28 N long. 089-37-48 W; A descriptive name given the by its settlers.

•WAVELAND, City; Hancock County; Pop. 4,186; Zip Code 39576; Lat. 30-17-08 N long. 089-22-44 W; Named for a local geographic description.

•WAYNESBORO, City; Wayne County Seat; Pop. 5,349; Zip Code 39367; Elev 190; Lat. 31-40-39 N long. 088-38-54 W; The city is named in honor of general Anthony Wayne, Revolutionary War hero.

•WEBB, Town; Tallahatchie County; Pop. 782; Zip Code 38966; Lat. 33-56-51 N long. 090-20-44 W; Named for a prominent early settler.

•WEIR, Town; Choctaw County; Pop. 553; Zip Code 39772; Elev 467; Lat. 33-15-52 N long. 089-17-19 W; Either a personal name or referring to a weir in a local dam.

•WESSON, Town; Copiah County; Pop. 1,313; Zip Code 39191; Elev 461; Lat. 31-45-53 N long. 090-21-48 W; Wesson is named for a pioneer inhabitant.

•WEST, Town; Holmes County; Pop. 253; Zip Code 39192; Lat. 33-11-54 N long. 089-46-58 W; Named after one of its founders.

•WEST POINT, City; Clay County Seat; Pop. 8,811; Zip Code 39773; Lat. 33-36-06 N long. 088-38-46 W; A descriptive name for the town's location.

•WIGGINS, City; Stone County Seat; Pop. 3,205; Zip Code 39550; Lat. 30-53-36 N long. 089-09-52 W; The name of an early settler.

•WINONA, City; Montgomery County Seat; Pop. 6,177; Zip Code 38967; Lat. 33-29-03 N, long. 089-44-13 W. Winona is a Sioux Indian word, meaning "first born daughter."

•WOODVILLE, Town; Wilkinson County Seat; Pop. 1,512; Zip Code 39669; Elev. 560; Lat. 31-06-06 N, long. 091-17-52 W. Located in the SW corner of Mississippi, in an area of truck and livestock farming.

•YAZOO CITY, City; Yazoo County Seat; Pop. 12,426; Zip Code 39194; Elev. 120; Lat. 32-51-14 N, long. 090-24-22 W. Named for Yazoo County, which was named for the Yazoo River. Yazoo was the name of an early Indian tribe of the area; to the Indians, the river was known as "the river of death." Yazoo literally means "to blown on a horn."

MISSOURI

•**ADRIAN**, City; Bates County; Pop. 1,484; Zip Code 64720; Elev. 868; Lat. 38-23-51 N long. 094-21-05 W; N. Missouri. According to some sources, this city is named for one of the four sons of the influential Mr. Talmage who was a General Passenger Agent for the Missouri Pacific Railroad. Other sources cite the name as coming from the Roman Emperor Hadrian, or Adrian.

•**ADVANCE**, City; Stoddard County; Pop. 1,054; Zip Code 63730; Elev. 361; Lat. 37-06-16 N long. 089-54-38 W; SE Missouri. The city was named after an ideal, from which many Missouri place names are derived. For example: *Liberty, Independence, Fairplay* and *Liberal*. Founded in 1910.

•**AGENCY**, Town; Buchanan County; Pop. 419; Zip Code 64401; Elev. 838; Lat. 39-38-41 N long. 094-44-23 W; NW Missouri. Once known as Agency Ford because the agency of the Sac and Fox Indians was located at this point, where the road from Clay County to the Blacksnake Hills crossed the ford.

•**AIRPORT DRIVE**, Village; Jasper County; Pop. 702; Elev. 964; Lat. 37-08-33 N long. 094-30-38 W; SW Missouri.

•**ALBA**, City; Jasper County; Pop. 474; Zip Code 64830; Elev. 989; Lat. 37-14-18 N long. 094-25-02 W; SW Missouri. Is named after its first postmaster. Founded in 1882.

•**ALBANY**, City; Seat of Gentry County; Pop. 2,152; Zip Code 64402; Elev. 915; Lat. 40-14-55 N long. 094-19-51 W; NW Missouri. First called Ashton, the name was changed in 1857 by an act of the legislature to Albany, after the capital of New York.

•**ALEXANDRIA**, City; Clark County; Pop. 417; Zip Code 63430; Elev. 498; Lat. 40-21-34 N long. 091-27-19 W; NE Missouri. Named for the Greek classical word or Alexdria, Egypt.

•**ALMA**, City; Lafayette County; Pop. 445; Zip Code 64001; Lat. 39-05-43 N long. 093-32-42 W; W Missouri. Named in 1879 by the founder, John M. Woodson's daughter.

•**ALTAMONT**, Town; Daviess County; Pop. 192; Zip Code 64620; Elev. 1004; Lat. 39-53-19 N long. 094-05-20 W; NW Missouri. Means "high mountain." Named in 1890 because of its elevation of 1002 feet at the railroad depot.

•**ALTENBURG**, City; Perry County; Pop. 280; Zip Code 63732; Elev. 577; Lat. 37-37-51 N long. 089-35-07 W; E Missouri. Named in 1839 its earliest settlers for the capital of the Dutchy of Saxe-Altenburg, Germany.

•**AMITY**, Town; DeKalb County; Pop. 74; Zip Code 64422; Lat. 39-52-15 N long. 094-26-08 W; NW Missouri. Named in 1870 in the idealistic sense meaning peaceful relationship.

•**AMSTERDAM**, City; Bates County; Pop. 231; Zip Code 64723; Lat. 38-20-59 N long. 094-35-20 W; W Missouri. Was named in 1891 for Amsterdam, Holland for its earliest settler homeland.

•**ANDERSON**, City; McDonald County; Pop. 1,237; Zip Code 64831; Elev. 904; Lat. 36-39-02 N long. 094-26-36 W; SW Missouri. Named for a nearby resident.

•**ANNAPOLIS**, City; Iron County; Pop. 370; Zip Code 63620; Lat. 37-21-37 N long. 090-41-51 W; SE Missouri. Named after Annapolis, Maryland in 1876.

•**ANNISTON**, Town; Mississippi County; Pop. 320; Zip Code 63820; Lat. 36-49-33 N long. 089-19-40 W; SE Missouri. Named in 1895 for the same place name in Alabama.

•**APPLETON CITY**, City; St. Clair County; Pop. 1,257; Zip Code 64724; Elev. 836; Lat. 38-11-26 N long. 094-01-45 W; W Missouri. Called Appleton City because the publishing house of D. Appleton, through William H. Appleton of New York made a large donation for a public library.

•**ARBYRD**, City; Dunklin County; Pop. 704; Zip Code 63821; Elev. 268; Lat. 36-03-03 N long. 090-14-19 W; SE Missouri. Named by its early land owner in 1915 by combining his initials with his last name, A.R. Byrd.

•**ARCADIA**, City; Iron County; Pop. 683; Zip Code 63621; Elev. 926; Lat. 37-35-17 N long. 090-37-44 W; SE Missouri. Named for the classical place name.

•**ARCHIE**, City; Cass County; Pop. 753; Zip Code 64725; Elev. 832; Lat. 38-28-54 N long. 094-21-15 W; W Missouri. Named for Mr. Talmage's son. Mr. Talmage was a General Passenger Agent for the Missouri Pacific Railroad.

•**ARGYLE**, Town; Maries and Osage Counties; Pop. 216; Zip Code 65001; Elev. 719; Lat. 38-17-40 N long. 092-01-25 W; S central Missouri. Named by early settlers for their homeland in Scotland.

•**ARNOLD**, City; Jefferson County; Pop. 19,141; Zip Code 63010; Lat. 38-35-58 N long. 090-22-39 W; E Missouri. Named for early landowner J. L. Arnold in 1915.

•**ASH GROVE**, City; Greene County; Pop. 1,157; Zip Code 65604; Elev. 1,048; Lat. 37-18-55 N long. 093-35-06 W; SW Missouri. Named in 1853 for a nearby grove of ash trees.

•**ASHLAND**, City; Boone County; Pop. 1,021; Zip Code 65010; Elev. 900; Lat. 38-46-28 N long. 092-15-25 W; Central Missouri. Named for the home of *Henry Clay* in Kentucky.

•**AURORA**, City; Lawrence County; Pop. 6,437; Zip Code 65605; Elev. 1,351; Lat. 36-58-15 N long. 093-43-04 W; 30 miles SW of Springfield in SW Missouri. Named for the mythological goddess of the morning.

•**AUXVASSE**, City; Callaway County; Pop. 858; Zip Code 65231; Elev. 875; Lat. 39-01-05 N long. 091-53-49 W; Central Missouri. Named for the French word "vasse" meaning muddy or miry, because the stream at Auxvasse was hard to cross at some points.

•**AVA**, City; Seat of Douglas County; Pop. 2,761; Zip Code 65608; Elev. 1283; Lat. 36-57-07 N long. 092-39-37 W; S Missouri. Named in the allegorial sense for a place in Assyria.

•**AVONDALE**, City; Clay County; Pop. 612; Zip Code 64010; Lat. 39-09-15 N long. 094-32-48 W; NW Missouri. Is named in the literary sense from Shakespeare.

•**BAGNELL**, Town; Miller County; Pop. 71; Elev. 587; Lat. 38-13-36 N long. 092-36-05 W; Central Missouri. Founded in 1882. The town was named for William Bagnell, the railroad contractor.

•**BALLWIN**, City; St. Louis County; Pop. 12,750; Zip Code 63011; Elev. 659; Lat. 38-35-42 N long. 090-32-46 W; E Missouri. Named after *John Ball*, who settled the area in 1804 and owned the land on which the town was laid out.

•**BARING**, City; Knox County; Pop. 206; Zip Code 63531; Lat. 40-14-39 N long. 092-12-20 W; NW Missouri. Named for Baring Brothers of England in 1889. The brothers made a large loan to establish this town.

•**BATES CITY**, Village; Lafayette County; Pop. 199; Zip Code 64011; Elev. 880; Lat. 39-00-22 N long. 094-04-20 W; W Missouri.

•**BATTLEFIELD**, Town; Greene County; Pop. 1,227; Zip Code 65619; Lat. 37-06-56 N long. 093-22-12 W; SW Missouri.

•**BELLA VILLA**, City; St. Louis County; Pop. 758; Lat. 38-32-28 N long. 090-16-48 W; E Missouri.

•**BELL CITY**, City; Stoddard County; Pop. 539; Zip Code 63735; Elev. 326; Lat. 37-01-25 N long. 089-49-11 W; SE Missouri.

•**BELLEFONTAINE NEIGHBORS**, City; St. Louis County; Pop. 12,082; Lat. 38-44-25 N long. 090-13-35 W; E Missouri. Bellfontaine Neighbors is named for the French word meaning "beautiful spring" or fountain.

•**BELTON**, City; Cass County; Pop. 12,708; Zip Code 64012; Elev. 1,106; Lat. 38-48-43 N long. 094-31-54 W; 10 miles S of Kansas City in W Missouri. (1,106 altitude), was platted in 1871.

•**BENTON**, City; Seat of Scott County; Pop. 674; Zip Code 63736; Elev. 440; Lat. 37-05-52 N long. 089-33-45 W; SE Missouri. Named for Thomas Hart Benton who was a Senator, 1821-1851. He was also known as "Old Bullion."

•**BERKELEY**, City; St. Louis County; Pop. 16,146; Zip Code 63134; Lat. 38-45-16 N long. 090-19-52 W; E. Missouri.

•**BERNIE**, City; Stoddard County; Pop. 1,975; Zip Code 63822; Elev. 303; Lat. 36-40-08 N long. 089-58-07 W; SE Missouri.

•**BETHANY**, City; Seat of Harrison County; Pop. 3,095; Zip Code 64424; Elev. 916; Lat. 36-36-42 N long. 090-04-09 W; 45 miles NW of Chillicothe in N. Missouri.

•**BEVERLY HILLS**, City; St. Louis County; Pop. 712; Area Code 317; fLat. 38-42-00 N long. 090-17-32 W; E Missouri.

•**BEVIER**, City; Macon County; Pop. 733; Zip Code 63532; Elev. 791; Lat. 39-44-49 N long. 092-33-50 W; N. Missouri. Named after well-known Confederate leader *Col. Robert Bevier* of Kentucky.

•**BILLINGS**, City; Christian County; Pop. 911; Zip Code 65610; Elev. 1,366; Lat. 37-04-03 N long. 093-33-07 W; SW Missouri. Founded in 1872 and named after a Mr. Billings who paid $1000 to local churches for the honor.

•**BIRCH TREE**, City; Shannon County; Pop. 622; Zip Code 65438; Elev. 990; Lat. 36-59-28 N long. 091-29-33 W; S Missouri. Was named for a large birch that stood on the bank of a creek near the site of an early post office.

•**BISMARCK**, City; St. Francois County; Pop. 1,625; Zip Code 63624; Lat. 37-46-09 N long. 090-37-29 W; E Missouri. Named by the German-Americans in the making of Missouri after the town of Bismarck, Germany.

•**BLACK JACK**, City; St. Louis County; Pop. 5,293; Elev. 596; Lat. 38-47-36 N long. 090-16-02 W; E Missouri.

•**BLAND**, City; Grasconade and Osage Counties; Pop. 662; Zip Code 65014; Elev. 1023; Lat. 38-18-06 N long. 091-37-58 W; E central Missouri. Named for *Richard P. Bland*, a member of Congress.

•**BLOOMFIELD**, City; Seat of Stoddard County; Pop. 1,795; Zip Code 63825; Elev. 497; Lat. 36-53-09 N long. 089-55-45 W; SE Missouri. Named in 1835 after the large field of flowers the founders noticed.

•**BLOOMSDALE**, City; Ste. Greneviève County; Pop. 397; Zip Code 63627; Elev. 500; Lat. 38-00-34 N long. 090-13-04 W; E Missouri.

•**BLUE SPRINGS**, City; Jackson County; Pop. 25,927; Zip Code 64015; Lat. 39-01-01 N long. 094-16-53 W; 10 miles SE of Independence in W. Missouri. Named after a spring of water falling from the hillside into a tributary of Little Blue River.

•**BOLCKOW**, Town; Andrew County; Pop. 245; Zip Code 64427; Lat. 40-06-47 N long. 094-49-19 W; NW Missouri. Platted by *John Anderson* and *Benjamin A. Conrad*. Named in 1868 after a famous employee of the railroads.

•**BOLIVAR**, City; Seat of Polk County; Pop. 5,919; Zip Code 65613; Elev. 1056; Lat. 37-36-52 N long. 093-24-37 W; SW Missouri. Named in 1840 after the city, Bolivar, Tennessee.

•**BONNE TERRE**, City; St. Francois County; Pop. 3,797; Zip Code 63628; Elev. 828; Lat. 37-55-23 N long. 090-33-19 W; 50 miles SSW of St. Louis in E Missouri. The names means "good earth" in French.

•**BOONVILLE**, City; Seat of Cooper County; Pop. 6,959; Zip Code 65233; Elev. 675; Lat. 38-58-25 N long. 092-44-35 W; 25 miles W of Columbia in central Missouri. Named for *Daniel Boone*.

•**BOURBON**, City; Crawford County; Pop. 1,259; Zip Code 65441; Elev. 932; Lat. 38-09-17 N long. 091-14-38 W; SE central Missouri. According to some sources, the town was named after Bourbon, Kentucky in 1825. Other sources say the twon was named for an old post office in the area which had been named Bourbon after the brand of whiskey.

•**BOWLING GREEN**, City; Seat of Pike County; Pop. 3,022; Zip Code 63334; Elev. 876; Lat. 39-20-31 N long. 091-11-42 W; E. Missouri. Platted in 1826 and named for the Kentucky home of many of the town's early residents.

•**BRANSON**, City; Taney County; Pop. 2,550; Zip Code 65616; Elev. 723; Lat. 36-38-37 N long. 093-13-06 W; S Missouri. Named in 1881 after R. S. Branson, the first postmaster.

•**BRAYMER**, City; Caldwell County; Pop. 986; Zip Code 64624; Lat. 39-35-13 N long. 093-47-45 W; NW Missouri. Founded in 1887. Named for *Judge Daniel Braymer*, a banker.

•**BRECKENRIDGE**, City; Caldwell County; Pop. 523; Zip Code 64625; Elev. 927; Lat. 39-45-44 N long. 093-48-15 W; NW Missouri. Platted in 1858 and named for John C. Breckenridge, Kentuckian, Vice President under Buchanan, 1857-61, and candidate for President against Lincoln, 1860.

•**BRECKENRIDGE HILLS**, Village; St. Louis County; Pop. 5,666; Lat. 38-42-52 N long. 090-22-02 W; E. Missouri.

•**BRENTWOOD**, City; St. Louis County; Pop. 8,209; Zip Code 63144; Elev. 490; Lat. 38-37-03 N long. 090-20-57 W; 10 miles W of St. Louis in E Missouri. Named after Brent who laid out the town.

•**BRIDGETON**, City; St. Louis County; Pop. 18,445; Zip Code 63044; Lat. 38-44-38 N long. 090-24-49 W; E. Missouri.

•**BRONAUGH**, Town; Vernon County; Pop. 209; Zip Code 64728; Lat. 37-41-39 N long. 094-28-07 W; W. Missouri. Named in 1886 after W. C. Bronough who was a landowner.

•**BROOKFIELD**, City; Linn County; Pop. 5,555; Zip Code 64628; Elev. 910; Lat. 39-47-04 N long. 093-04-24 W; 25 miles E of Chillicothe in N Missouri.

•**BROOKLINE**, Village; Greene County; Pop. 211; Zip Code 65619; Elev. 1286; Lat. 37-09-48 N long. 093-25-12 W; SW Missouri.

•BROWNING, City; Linn and Sullivan Counties; Pop. 368; Lat. 40-02-07 N long. 093-09-44 W; N Missouri. Founded in 1872. The name first suggested for the town was Linnivan, since it was located near the Linn and Sullivan County lines. But it was finally named to honor Mrs. Browning, the wife of an official of the C., B & Q. Railroad.

•BRUMLEY, Town; Miller County; Pop. 109; Zip Code 65017; Elev. 751; Lat. 38-05-11 N long. 092-29-12 W; Central Missouri. Founded in 1869 and named for an early settler, *John Brumley.*

•BRUNSWICK, City; Chariton County; Pop. 1,272; Zip Code 65236; Elev. 652; Lat. 39-25-24 N long. 093-07-49 W; N central Missouri. The town was laid out in 1836, one mile below the mouth of Grand River, by the Reverend James Keyte, and named for his former English home, Brunswick Terrace.

•BUCKLIN, City; Linn County; Pop. 713; Zip Code 64631; Elev. 910; Lat. 39-46-54 N long. 092-53-24 W; N. Missouri. Founded in 1854 and named for *Major James H. Bucklin,* Chief Engineer of the J. & St. J. Railway Company.

•BUCKNER, City; Jackson County; Pop. 2,848; Zip Code 64016; Elev. 749; Lat. 39-07-57 N long. 094-11-54 W; W. Missouri. Began as a station on the Missouri Pacific railroad in 1875. Named for Mr. Buckner who lived on a hill nearby.

•BUFFALO, City; Seat of Dallas County; Pop. 2,217; Zip Code 65622; Elev. 1200; Lat. 37-38-38 N long. 093-05-32 W; SW central Missouri. Named for the large herds of buffalo that once lived in the territory.

•BURLINGTON JUNCTION, City; Nodaway County; Pop. 657; Zip Code 64428; Elev. 944; Lat. 4-26-44 N long. 095-03-57 W; NW Missouri.

•BUTLER, City; Seat of Bates County; Pop. 4,107; Zip Code 64730; Elev. 866; Lat. 38-15-31 N long. 094-19-49 W; 30 miles N of Nevada in W Missouri. (866 alt), was platted in 1854 and named for William O. Butler, officer in the Mexican War.

•CABOOL, City; Texas County; Pop. 2,090; Zip Code 65689; Elev. 1253; Lat. 37-07-26 N long. 092-06-04 W; S Missouri.

•CAINSVILLE, City; Harrison County; Pop. 496; Zip Code 64632; Lat. 40-26-18 N long. 093-46-34 W; N Missouri. Founded in 1837 by James Nash. Named for *John C. Calhoun,* a statesman from South Carolina.

•CALEDONIA, Village; Washington County; Pop. 162; Zip Code 63631; Elev. 924; Lat. 37-45-48 N long. 090-46-22 W; E Missouri. Named after the town of Caledonia, Scotland.

•CALIFORNIA, City; Seat of Moniteay County; Pop. 3,381; Zip Code 65018; Elev. 889; Lat. 38-37-39 N long. 092-33-59 W; 20 miles W of Jefferson City in central Missouri. Named in 1856 by returning prospectors from California after the gold rush. It is a Spanish word.

•CAMDEN, City; Ray County; Pop. 219; Zip Code 64017; Elev. 713; Lat. 39-11-50 N long. 094-01-22 W; NW Missouri. Laid out by *Edward M. and Elizabeth R. Samuel* and *Amos and Judith C. Rees.* Named in 1845 after Earl Camden of England, a leader of the Whig Party.

•CAMDENTON, City; Seat of Camden County; Pop. 2,303; Zip Code 65020; Elev. 1043; Lat. 38-00-29 N long. 092-44-40 W; S central Missouri. Named in 1930 after Earl Camden of England.

•CAMERON, City; Clinton and DeKalb Counties; Pop. 4,519; Area Code 816; Zip Code 64429; Elev. 1,036; Lat. 39-44-25 N long. 094-14-27 W; 45 miles NNE of Kansas City in NW Missouri. Cameron was platted in 1855 and named for Colonel Elisha

Cameron of Clay County, father-in-law of Samuel McCorkle, one of the town's founders.

•CAMPBELL, City; Dunklin County; Pop. 2,134; Zip Code 63933; Lat. 36-29-36 N long. 090-04-30 W; SE Missouri. Named in 1886 for Judge Alexander Campbell.

•CANALOU, City; New Madrid County; Pop. 369; Zip Code 63828; Elev. 289; Lat. 36-45-18 N long. 089-41-13 W; SE Missouri.

•CANTON, City; Lewis County; Pop. 2,435; Zip Code 63435; Elev. 494; Lat. 40-07-30 N long. 091-37-30 W; NE Missouri. Canton, oldest town (1830) in Lewis County, is named for Canton, Ohio, and extends from the high bottomland along the Mississippi River to the bluffs on the west.

•CAPE GIRARDEAU, City; Cape Girardeau County; Pop. 34,361; Zip Code 63701; Elev. 347; Lat. 37-18-21 N long. 089-31-05 W; 30 miles NNW of confluence with Ohio River in SE Missouri. Named in 1812 for Ensign Sierer Girardah or De Girardot, a prosperous fur trader.

•CARL JUNCTION, City; Jasper County; Pop. 3,937; Zip Code 64834; Lat. 37-10-36 N long. 094-33-55 W; SW Missouri.

•CARROLLTON, City; Seat of Carroll County; Pop. 4,700; Zip Code 64633; Elev. 665; Lat. 39-21-30 N long. 093-29-44 W; 30 miles South of Chillicothe in NW central Missouri. When Carroll County, named for Charles Carroll, a signer of the Declaration of Independence, was organized January 2, 1833, John Standley donated land for the county seat, which was platted and had its first sale of lots March 31, 1834.

•CARTERVILLE, City; Jasper County; Pop 1,973; Zip Code 64835; Elev. 1,003; Lat. 37-08-57 N long. 094-26-34 W; SW Missouri.

•CARTHAGE, City; Seat of Jasper County; Pop. 11,104; Zip Code 64836; Elev. 941; Lat. 37-10-35 N long. 094-18-36 W; 15 miles NE of Joplin in SW Missouri. The town, which was selected as the seat of Jasper County, was platted in 1842 and named for the ancient commerical center of northern Africa.

•CASSVILLE, City; Seat of Barry County; Pop. 2,091; Zip Code 65625; Elev. 1324; Lat. 36-40-37 N long. 093-52-07 W; SW Missouri. The town was named in honor of *Lewis Cass,* the Secretary of the Navy under President Tyler.

•CEDAR CITY, City; Callaway County; Pop. 665; Zip Code 65022; Lat. 38-35-50 N long. 092-10-46 W; Central Missouri. Laid out by *David Kenney.* Named in 1870 for the many cedar trees in the region.

•CENTERVILLE, City; Seat of Reynolds County; Pop. 241; Zip Code 63633; Elev. 742; Lat. 37-26-06 N long. 090-57-30 W; SE Missouri. Named in 1847 for its central location in the county. Selected as county seat by *Ayers Hudspeth, John Miller* and *Moses Carty.*

•CHAFFEE, City; Scott County; Pop. 3,241; Zip Code 63740; Lat. 37-10-48 N long. 089-39-18 W; 10 miles SW of Cape Girardeau in SE Missouri. Named for General A. R. Chaffee, who fought in the Spanish-American War.

•CHARLESTON, City; Seat of Mississippi County; Pop. 5,230; Zip Code 63834; Elev. 327; Lat. 36-55-15 N long. 089-21-02 W; 30 miles SSE of Cape Girardeau in SE Missouri. Named in 1837 after the city of Charleston, South Carolina.

•CHILLICOTHE, City; Seat of Livingston County; Pop. 9,089; Zip Code 64601; Elev. 798; Lat. 39-47-43 N long. 093-33-08 W; 75 miles NE of Kansas City in N Missouri. The seat of Livingston County, the town was platted in 1837 and named for Chillicothe, Ohio. The name is Shawnee Indian for "the big town where we live."

•**CLARENCE**, City; Shelby County; Pop. 1,147; Zip Code 63437; Elev. 825; Lat. 39-44-31 N long. 092-15-30 W; NE Missouri. Platted in 1857 by John Duff, a railroad contractor, the town is said to have been named for one of his children.

•**CLARK**, City; Randolph County; Pop. 304; Zip Code 65243; Elev. 867; Lat. 39-16-52 N long. 092-20-33 W; N central Missouri.

•**CLARKSBURG**, City; Moniteau County; Pop. 352; Zip Code 65025; Elev. 897; Lat. 38-39-33 N long. 092-39-48 W; Central Missouri. Named in honore of *Hiram Clark*, pioneer and first postmaster.

•**CLARKTON**, City; Dunklin County Pop. 1,228; Zip Code 63837; Elev. 273; Lat. 36-27-06 N long. 089-58-01 W; SE Missouri. (273 alt), Platted in 1860. The town was first named Bach but later changed to Clarkton in honor of *Henry E. Clark*, one of the contractors of the old Weaverville-Clarkton plank road, sometimes called the "Devil's Washboard."

•**CLAYTON**, City; Seat of St. Louis County; Pop. 14,219; Zip Code 631+; Lat. 38-38-33 N long. 090-19-25 W; 10 miles W of St. Louis in E Missouri. Named in 1877 for *Ralph Clayton*, an early landowner who donated one hundred acres of his farm to the new county.

•**CLEVELAND**, Town; Cass County; Pop. 485; Zip Code 64734; Lat. 38-40-45 N long. 094-35-36 W; W Missouri. Named in 1900 after Grover Cleveland.

•**CLINTON**, City; Seat of Henry County; Pop. 8,366; Zip Code 64735; Elev. 750; Lat. 38-22-07 N long. 093-46-41 W; 40 miles SW of Sedalia in W Missouri. Named in 1833 after the popular DeWitt Clinton, the Governor of New York.

•**COLE CAMP**, City; Benton County; Pop. 1,022; Zip Code 65325; Elev. 1018; Lat. 38-27-36 N long. 093-12-09 W; W central Missouri.

•**COLUMBIA**, City; Seat of Boone County; Pop. 62,061; Zip Code 65201; Elev. 748; Lat. 38-57-06 N long. 092-20-02 W; 25 miles N of Jefferson City in central Missouri. Named in 1819 for Columbia, Kentucky.

•**CONCORDIA**, City; Lafayette County; Pop. 2,129; Zip Code 64020; Elev. 782; Lat. 38-59-00 N long. 093-34-06 W; W Missouri.

•**CONWAY**, City; Laclede County; Pop. 601; Zip Code 65632; Lat. 37-30-07 N long. 092-49-15 W; S central Missouri.

•**COOTER**, Town; Pemiscot County; Pop. 479; Zip Code 63839; La 36-02-48 N long. 089-48-36 W; SE Missouri. Named in 1854 for the Coutre family, one of whom was a merchant in New Madrid in 1795.

•**COSBY**, Town; Andrew County; Pop. 148; Zip Code 64436; Lat. 39-51-51 N long. 094-40-41 W; NW Missouri.

•**COTTLEVILLE**, Town; St. Charles County; Pop. 184; Zip Code 63338; Lat. 38-44-46 N long. 090-39-14 W; E Missouri. Established in 1839 by *Captain Lorenzo Cottle* who served in the Black Hawk and Florida Wars.

•**COUNTRY CLUB**, Village; Andrew County; Pop. 1,234; Zip Code 641+; Lat. 39-49-56 N long. 094-49-17 W; NW Missouri.

•**COWGILL**, City; Caldwell County; Pop. 267; Zip Code 64637; Lat. 39-33-33 N Long. NW Missouri. Established in 1887. Named for *Judge James Cowgill*, a prominent citizen of the county.

•**CRAIG**, City; Holt County; Pop. 379; Zip Code 64437; Elev. 868; Lat. 40-11-41 N long. 095-22-15 W; NW Missouri. Established in 1868 and named in honor of *General James Craig*, a member of Congress.

•**CRANE**, City; Stone County; Pop. 1,185; Zip Code 65633; Elev. 1122; Lat. 36-54-19 N long. 093-34-17 W; SW Missouri.

•**CREIGHTON**, City; Cass County; Pop. 301; Zip Code 64739; Lat. 38-29-41 N long. 094-04-23 W; W Missouri. Named in 1855 for an early settler, John Creighton.

•**CRESTWOOD**, City; St. Louis County; Pop. 12,815; Elev. 621; Lat. 38-33-25 N long. 090-22-54 W.

•**CREVE COEUR**, City; St. Louis County; Pop. 12,694; Zip Code 63141; Elev. 644; Lat. 38-39-39 N long. 090-25-21 W; E Missouri. Named the Dutch fortress Crevecoeur.

•**CRYSTAL CITY**, City; Jefferson County; Pop. 3,573; Zip Code 63019; Elev. 420; Lat. 38-13-16 N long. 090-22-44 W; 30 miles S of St. Louis in E Missouri. Named in 1868 for the inexhaustible riches in the soil and the mineral wealth.

•**CUBA**, City; Crawford County; Pop. 2,120; Zip Code 65453; Elev. 1015; Lat. 38-03-46 N long. 091-24-12 W; SE central Missouri. The town was given its name by two former gold miners from California, who wished to perpetuate the memory of a holiday they had spend on the "Isle of Cuba."

•**CURRYVILLE**, City; Pike County; Pop. 323; Zip Code 63339; Elev. 816; Lat. 39-20-44 N long. 091-20-41 W; E Missouri. Named for *Perry A. Curry* who laid out the town in 1867.

•**DADEVILLE**, Village; Dade County; Pop. 216; Zip Code 65635; Lat. 37-28-49 N long. 093-40-25 W; SW Missouri. Named for Captain Francis L. Dade who was killed in the Seminole War in 1835.

•**DARLINGTON**, Town; Gentry County; Pop. 131; Zip Code 64438; Elev. 836; Lat. 40-11-54 N long. 094-2345 W; NW Missouri.

•**DEARBORN**, City; Buchanan and Platte Counties; Pop. 547; Zip Code 64439; Elev. 881; Lat. 39-31-19 N long. 094-46-11 W; NW Missouri. Named for *General Henry Dearborn*, Secretary of War under Thomas Jefferson.

•**DE KALB**, Town; Buchanan County; Pop. 245; Zip Code 64440; Lat. 39-35-13 N long. 094-55-30 W; NW Missouri. Founded in 1839 by *James G. Finch*. The town was first called Bloomington but changed to DeKalb in 1851 in honore or *Baron John De Kalb* of Bavaria, who fell at Camden.

•**DELLWOOD**, City; St. Louis County; Pop. 6,200; Elev. 537; Lat. 38-44-58 N long. 090-17-08 W; E Missouri.

•**DELTA**, City; Cape Girardeau County; Pop. 524; Zip Code 63744; Elev. 337; Lat. 37-11-48 N long. 089-44-10 W; SE Missouri.

•**DES ARC**, Village; Iron County; Pop. 237; Zip Code 63636; Lat. 37-16-57 N long. 090-38-14 W; SE Missouri. Means "the bow" or "bend". Named for a big bend in the railroad near the town.

•**DESLOGE**, City; St. Francois County; Pop. 3,481; Zip Code 63601; Lat. 37-52-22 N long. 090-31-40 W; E Missouri. Named in honor of *Firmin Desloge*, president of a mining company.

•**DE SOTO**, City; Jefferson County; Pop. 5,993; Zi Code 63020; Elev. 509; Lat. 38-08-22 N long. 090-33-18 W; 40 miles SSW of St. Louis in E Missouri. Named in 1857 for *Fernando De Soto* who discovered the Mississippi River in 1541.

•**DES PERES**, City; St. Louis County; Pop. 8,254; Zip Code 63131; Lat. 38-36-03 N long. 090-25-58 W; 10 miles W of St. Louis in E Missouri.

•**DEXTER**, City; Stoddard County; Pop. 7,043; Zip Code 63841; Elev. 323; Lat. 36-47-45 N long. 089-57-28 W; 25 miles E of Poplar Bluff in SE Missouri. Named in 1873 for a race horse.

•**DIAMOND**, Town; Newton County; Pop. 766; Zip Code 64840; Elev. 1,169; Lat. 36-59-43 N long. 094-18-57 W; SW Missouri. Named by Joseph Smith. The original name was Adam-Ondi-Ahman, but the Mormon settlement shortened the spelling to Di-amon, Diamong or Diamond.

•**DIGGINS**, Village; Webster County; Pop. 245; Zip Code 65636; Elev. 1651; Lat. 37-10-21 N long. 092-51-15 W; S Missouri.

•**DIXON**, City; Pulaski County; Pop. 1,402; Zip Code 65459; Elev. 1167; Lat. 37-59-30 N long. 092-05-37 W; S central Missouri.

•**DONIPHAN**, City; Seat of Ripley County; Pop. 1,921; Zip Code 63935; Elev. 344; Lat. 36-37-15 N long. 090-49-24 W; S Missouri. On the north bank of the Current. Settled about 1847, Doniphan was named for *Colonel Alexander Doniphan* of Mexican War fame.

•**DOWNING**, City; Schuyler County; Pop. 462; Zip Code 63536; Elev. 873; Lat. 40-29-15 N long. 092-22-09 W; N Missouri. Founded by Henry Downing and named in his honor.

•**DREXEL**, City; Bates and Cass Counties; Pop. 908; Zip Code 64742; Elev. 992; Lat. 38-28-46 N long. 094-36-30 W; W Missouri. Named for the owner of a local pioneer store.

•**DUQUESNE**, Village; Jasper County; Pop. 1,252; Elev. 1072; Lat. 37-04-36 N long. 094-27-33 W; SW Missouri.

•**EASTON**, City; Buchanan County; Pop. 313; Zip Code 64443; Lat. 39-43-20 N long. 094-38-29 W; NW Missouri.

•**EAST PRAIRIE**, City; Mississippi County; Pop. 3,713; Zip Code 63845; Elev. 307; Lat. 36-46-47 N long. 089-23-08 W; 40 miles S of Cape Girardeau in SE Missouri. Named to give direction with relation to other places.

•**EDGAR SPRINGS**, City; Phelps County; Pop. 271; Zip Code 65462; Lat. 37-42-16 N long. 091-51-59 W; S central Missouri.

•**EDGERTON**, City; Platte County; Pop. 584; Zip Code 64444; Lat. 39-30-18 N long. 094-37-59 W; NW Missouri.

•**EDINA**, City; Seat of Knox County; Pop. 1,520; Zip Code 63537; Elev. 816; Lat. 40-10-03 N long. 092-10-212 W; NE Missouri. Named in 1839 for the town of Edina, Scotland. Selected by a commission as the seat of Knox County in 1845.

•**ELDON**, City; Miller County; Pop. 4,342; Zip Code 65026; Elev. 934; Lat. 38-20-54 N long. 092-34-53 W; 25 miles SW of Jefferson City in cental Missouri. Named in 1881 for one of the railroad officials.

•**EL DORADO SPRINGS**, City; Cedar County; Pop. 3,868; Zip Code 64744; Elev. 913; Lat. 37-52-37 N long. 094-01-16 W; 20 miles E of Nevada in W Missouri.

•**ELLINGTON**, City; Reynolds County; Pop. 1,215; Zip Code 63638; Elev. 670; Lat. 37-14-30 N long. 090-58-07 W; SE Missouri.

•**ELLISVILLE**, City; St. Louis County; Pop. 6,233; Lat. 38-35-33 N long. 090-35-13 W; E Missouri. Named for Vespuccio Ellis, onetime United States Consul to Venezuela, was settled by Captain Harvey Ferris, who came from Kentucky about 1836.

•**ELSBERRY**, City; Lincoln County; Pop. 1,272; Zip Code 63343; Lat. 39-10-00 N long. 090-46-51 W; E Missouri. Named in 1879 for *Robert T. Elsberry,* one of the early homesteaders.

•**ELVINS**, City; St. Francois County; Pop. 1,548; Elev. 765; Lat. 37-50-12 N long. 090-31-58 W; E Missouri. Named for *Polite Elvins,* a member of Congress.

•**EMMA**, City; Lafayette and Saline Counties; Pop. 267; Zip Code 65327; Elev. 759; Lat. 38-58-18 N long. 093-29-40 W; W central Missouri. Named in 1895 for the daughter of a Lutheran minister at Concordia.

•**ESSEX**, City; Stoddard County; Pop. 545; Zip Code 63846; Elev. 300; Lat. 36-48-45 N long. 089-51-41 W; SE Missouri.

•**ESTHER**, City; St. Francois County; Pop. 1,038; Lat. 37-51-01 N long. 090-29-55 W; E Missouri. Named in 1901 for the daughter of Harry Cantwell, a business man.

•**EUREKA**, City; St. Louis County; Pop. 3,862; Zip Code 63025; Elev. 461; Lat. 38-30-09 N long. 090-37-40 W; E Missouri. Said to have been named by the surveying engineer of the Missouri Pacific Railroad, who found that a route through this valley would eliminate many cuts and grades.

•**EXCELSIOR SPRINGS**, City; Clay and Ray Counties; Pop. 10,424; Zip Code 64024; Elev. 801; Lat. 39-20-21 N long. 094-13-33 W; 25 miles NE of Kansas City in NW Missouri.

•**EXETER**, City; Barry County; Pop. 588; Zip Code 65647; Elev. 1559; Lat. 36-40-20 N long. 093-56-27 W; SW Missouri. Named after the town of Exeter in England. Exeter was laid out for *George A. Purdy* in September 1880.

•**FAIRFAX**, City; Atchison County; Pop. 835; Zip Code 64446; Lat. 40-20-19 N long. 095-23-35 W; NW Missouri. Laid out in 1881 by *Charles E. Perkins.*

•**FAIRVIEW**, Town; Newton County; Pop. 282; Zip Code 64842; Lat. 36-49-03 N long. 094-05-17 W; SW Missouri.

•**FARBER**, City; Audrain County; Pop. 503; Zip Code 63345; Elev. 767; Lat. 39-16-21 N long. 091-34-28 W; NE central Missouri. Laid out by *Thomas W. Carter* in 1872. Named for *Silas W. Farber.*

•**FARMINGTON**, City; Seat of St. Francois County; Pop. 8,270; Zip Code 63640; Elev. 973; Lat. 37-46-51 N long. 090-25-18 W; 60 miles S of St. Louis in E Missouri.

•**FAYETTE**, City; Seat of Howard County; Pop. 2,983; Zip Code 65248; Elev. 661; Lat. 39-08-45 N long. 092-41-01 W; 25 miles NW of Columbia in N central Missouri. Named for Marquis Jean Paul de Lafayette of France.

•**FENTON**, City; St. Louis County; Pop. 2,417; Zip Code 63026; Lat. 38-30-47 N long. 090-26-09 W; E Missouri.

•**FERGUSON**, City; St. Louis County; Pop. 24,740; Zip Code 63135; Elev. 554; Lat. 38-44-39 N long. 090-18-22 W; 10 miles NNW of St. Louis in E Missouri. Named in 1876 for one of the early settlers, William B. Ferguson.

•**FESTUS**, City; Jefferson County; Pop. 7,574; Zip Code 63028; Elev. 395; Lat. 38-13-14 N long. 090-232-45 W; 30 miles S of St. Louis in E Missouri. The story goes that when Festus was platted in 1878, it was called Tanglefoot - either for the gait of homeward-bound roisterers, or for the town's principal product, which caused it - but that as the village grew in size and dignity, a more respectable name was demanded. The village fathers consequently opened a Bible at random, intending to adopt the first proper name they saw. "Then Agrippa said unto Festus, I would also hear the man myself," is the passage upon which searching finger came to rest.

•**FISK**, Town; Butler County; Pop. 450; Zip Code 63940; Elev. 334; Lat. 36-46-55 N long. 090-12-31 W; SE Missouri.

•**FLAT RIVER**, City; St. Francois County; Pop. 4,443; Zip Code 63601; Elev. 796; Lat. 37-51-04 N long. 090-31-14 W; 55 miles SSW of St. Louis in E Missouri.

•**FLORISSANT**, City; St. Louis County; Pop. 55,372; Zip Code 630+; Elev. 575; Lat. 38-47-21 N long. 090-19-21 W; E. Missouri. Named Florissant (flowering) by its first French settlers, and called St. Ferdinand by Spanish authorities, the village was known as St. Ferdinand de Floorissant until 1939, when it officially became Florissant. Most of the streets were named for either French or Spanish saints.

•**FORDLAND**, City; Webster County; Pop. 569; Zip Code 65652; Elev. 1,592; Lat. 37-09-27 N long. 092-56-26 W; S Missouri. Founded in 1881. Named for *J.S. Ford* of the K.C., Ft. Scott and Mem. Railroad.

•**FORSYTH**, City; Seat of Taney County; Pop. 1,010; Zip Code 65653; Elev. 696; Lat. 36-41-06 N long. 093-07-11 W; S Missouri.

•**FREDERICKTOWN**, City; Seat of Madison County; Pop. 4,036; Zip Code 63645; Elev. 722; Lat. 37-33-35 N long. 090-17-38 W; 45 miles WNW of Cape Girardeau in SE Missouri.

•**FREEBURG**, Village; Osage County; Pop. 554; Zip Code 65035; Elev. 899; Lat. 38-18-54 N long. 091-55-21 W; central Missouri.

•**FREEMAN**, City; Cass County; Pop. 485; Zip Code 64746; Elev. 349; Lat. 38-37-06 N long. 094-30-18 W; W Missouri.

•**FRONTENAC**, City; St. Louis County; Pop. 3,654; Lat. 38-38-08 N long. 090-24-54 W; 10 miles W of St. Louis in E Missouri.

•**FULTON**, City; Seat of Callaway County; Pop. 11,046; Zip Code 65251; Elev. 818; Lat. 38-50-48 N long. 091-56-52 W; 25 miles NNE of Jefferson City in central Missouri. Was founded as the county seat in June 1825, and named Volney for Count Constantin Volney, French scientist and atheist. Two months later, its name was changed to honor Robert Fulton, American scientist, artist, and marine engineer.

•**GALENA**, City; Seat of Stone County; Pop. 423; Zip Code 65656; Elev. 985; Lat. 36-48-19 N long. 093-27-59 W; SW Missouri. Named in 1853 for the large amounts of riches of the soil and mineral wealth; such as iron ore.

•**GALLATIN**, City; Seat of Daviess County; Pop. 2,063; Zip Code 64640; Elev. 931; Lat. 39-54-52 N long. 093-57-43 W; NW Missouri. County, on the south bank of Grand River. Platted in 1837 and named for Albert Gallatin, Secretary of the Treasury (1801-13).

•**GARDEN CITY**, City; Cass County; Pop. 1,021; Zip Code 64747; Elev. 916; Lat. 38-33-40 N long. 094-11-28 W; W Missouri.

•**GENTRY**, Village; Gentry County; Pop. 126; Zip Code 64453; Elev. 888; Lat. 40-19-54 N long. 094-25-12 W; NW Missouri. Named for Col. Richard Gentry, who fell in the Florida War.

•**GIDEON**, City; New Madrid County; Pop. 1,240; Zip Code 63848; Elev. 269; Lat. 36-27-07 N long. 089-55-09 W; SW Missouri. Named in 1900 for Frank Gideon, a merchant.

•**GILMAN CITY**, City; Daviess and Harrison Counties; Pop. 414; Zip Code 64642; Elev. 979; Lat. 40-08-37 N long. 093-52-18; NW Missouri.

•**GLADSTONE**, City; Clay County; Pop. 24,990; Zip Code 641+; Lat. 39-12-14 N long. 094-33-16 W; NW Missouri. Named after the famous prime minister in England.

•**GLASGOW**, City; Chariton and Howard Counties; Pop. 1,284; Zip Code 65254; Elev. 622; Lat. 39-13-38 N long. 092-50-47 W; N central Missouri. Named for James Glasgow, a St. Louis merchant, the town was laid out in 1836 after three earlier attempts to establish a river port in the vicinity had failed.

•**GLENDALE**, City; St. Louis County; Pop. 6,035; Elev. 825; Lat. 40-29-12 N long. 092-45-48 W; 10 miles SW of St. Louis in E Missouri.

•**GOLDEN CITY**, City; Barton County; Pop. 900; Zip Code 64748; Lat. 37-23-35 N long. 094-05-37 W; SW Missouri. Named because some gold was found there. Golden City was originally laid out in 1867 but replatted in 1870 by *F. C. Brock.*

•**GOODMAN**, Town; McDonald County; Pop. 1,030; Zip Code 64843; Elev. 1254; Lat. 36-44-30 N long. 094-23-56 W; SW Missouri.

•**GORDONVILLE**, Town; Cape Girardeau County; Pop. 267; Zip Code 63752; Lat. 37-18-40 N long. 089-40-45 W; SE Missouri.

•**GOWER**, City; Buchanan and Clinton Counties; Pop. 1,276; Elev. 941; Lat. 39-36-39 N long. 094-35-57 W; Zip Code 64454; NW Missouri. Named in 1870 for *A. G. Gower*, Division Superintendent of the railroad.

•**GRAIN VALLEY**, City; Jackson County; Pop. 1,327; Lat. 39-00-54 N long. 094-11-54 W; W Missouri. Surveyed in 1878 for *Joseph Peters.* Named for the grain production in the area.

•**GRANBY**, City; Newton County; Pop. 1,908; Zip Code 64844; Elev. 1,142; Lat. 36-55-09 N long. 094-15-18 W; SW Missouri. Named for the town of Granby, Massachusetts.

•**GRANDVIEW**, City; Jackson County; Pop. 24,502; Lat. 38-53-09 N long. 094-31-58 W; 5 miles S of Kansas City in W Missouri.

•**GRANT CITY**, City; Seat of Worth County; Pop. 1,068; Zip Code 64456; Elev. 1136; Lat. 40-29-15 N long. 094-24-39 W; NW Missouri. Named in 1863 for Ulysses S. Grant.

•**GRANTWOOD**, Town; St. Louis County; Pop. 1,002; Elev. 605; Lat. 38-33-15 N long. 090-20-42 W; E Missouri.

•**GREEN CITY**, City; Sullivan County; Pop. 719; Zip Code 63545; Elev. 1059; Lat. 40-16-07 N long. 092-57-11 W; N Missouri.

•**GREENFIELD**, City; Seat of Dade County; Pop. 1,394; Zip Code 65661; Elev. 1087; Lat. 37-24-55 N long. 093-50-27 W; SW Missouri. Named for the local features.

•**GREENTOP**, Village; Adair and Schuyler Counties; Pop. 538; Zip Code 63546; Elev. 911; Lat. 40-20-49 N long. 092-34-08 W; N Missouri.

•**GREENWOOD**, City; Jackson County; Pop. 1,315; Zip Code 64034; Elev. 953; Lat. 38-51-06 N long. 094-20-37 W; W Missouri.

•**HALE**, City; Carroll County; Pop. 529; Zip Code 64643; Lat. 39-36-13 N long. 093-20-32 W; NW central Missouri. Founded in 1833. Named for *John P. Hale* of Carrollton.

•**HAMILTON**, City; Caldwell County; Pop. 1,582; Zip Code 64644; Elev. 996; Lat. 39-44-37 N long. 093-59-53 W; NW Missouri, named by *Albert G. Davis* "partly in honor of *Alexander Hamilton,* and partly for *Joseph Hamilton,* a brilliant lawyer of olden times, and a gallant soldier who was killed under *Gen. Harrision* at the battle of the Thames, in Canada, Oct. 5, 1813, during the war with Great Britain."

•**HANLEY HILLS**, Village; St. Louis County; Pop. 2,439; Lat. 38-41-09 N long. 090-19-26 W; E Missouri.

•**HANNIBAL**, City; Marion and Ralls Counties; Pop. 18,811; Zip Code 63401; Elev. 488; Lat. 39-42-30 N long. 091-212-30 W; NE Missouri. In 1819, the Hannibal Company was formed and the village near Bear Creek was named Hannibal, taking the name Hannibal, from the historic Carthagenian General.

•**HARDIN**, City; Ray County; Pop. 688; Zip Code 64035; Lat. 39-16-15 N long. 093-50-03 W; NW Missouri. Named in honor of *Charles H. Hardin* who later became governor of Missouri.

•**HARRISONVILLE**, City; Seat of Cass County; Pop. 6,372; Zip Code 64701; Elev. 904; Lat. 38-39-12 N long. 094-20-55 W; 30 miles S of Independence in W Missouri.

•**HARTVILLE**, City; Seat of Wright County; Pop. 576; Zip Code 65667; Lat. 37-15-03 N long. 092-30-37 W; S Missouri. Named for Isaac Hart, an early settler.

•**HAYTI**, City; Pemiscot County; Pop. 3,964; Zip Code 63851; Elev. 256; Lat. 36-14-01 N long. 089-44-58 W; 5 miles NW of Caruthersville in SE Missouri. Named for the town of Hayti, West Indies.

•**HAZELWOOD**, City; St. Louis County; Pop 12,935; Zip Code 630+; Lat. 38-46-17 N long. 090-22-15 W; E Missouri.

•**HENRIETTA**, City; Ray County; Pop. 4214; Zip Code 64036; Elev. 694; Lat. 39-14-03 N long. 093-56-07 W; NW Missouri.

•**HERCULANEUM**, City; Jefferson County; Pop. 2,293; Zip Code 63048; Elev. 407; Lat. 38-16-06 N long. 090-22-48 W; E Missouri.

•**HERMANN**, City; Seat of Gasconade County; Pop. 2,695; Zip Code 65041; Elev. 520; Lat. 38-42-15 N long. 091-26-14 W; E central Missouri. Founded by the German Settlement Association of Philadelphia in 1837. Named for Hermann, Germany.

•**HERMITAGE**, City; Seat of Hickory County; Pop. 384; Zip Code 65668; Elev. 1,210; Lat. 37-56-29 N long. 093-18-58 W; SW central Missouri.

•**HIGBEE**, City; Randolph County; Pop. 817; Zip Code 65257; Lat. 39-18-17 N long. 092-30-45 W; N central Missouri.

•**HIGGINSVILLE**, City; Lafayette County; Pop. 4,595; Zip Code 64037; Elev. 800; Lat. 39-04-21 N long. 093-43-01 W; 40 miles NW of Sedalia in W Missouri.

•**HILLSBORO**, City; Seat of Jefferson County; Pop. 1,508; Zip Code 63050; Elev. 802; Lat. 38-13-56 N long. 090-33-46 W; E Missouri. Selected as the county seat by an act of the legislature in 1839. First named Monticello for the hill just to the south, the name soon changed to Hillsboro.

•**HOLCOMB**, City; Dunklin County; Pop. 632; Zip Code 63852; Lat. 36-23-57 N long. 090-01-25 W; SW Missouri.

•**HOLDEN**, City; Johnson County; Pop. 2,195; Zip Code 64040; Elev. 844; Lat. 38-42-51 N long. 093-59-28 W; W Missouri. Named for Major N.B. Holden, member of the State Legislature.

•**HOLLIDAY**, Village; Monroe County; Pop. 168; Zip Code 65258; Elev. 788; Lat. 39-29-40 N long. 092-07-43 W; NE Missouri.

•**HOLLISTER**, City; Taney County; Pop. 1,439; Zip Code 65672; Elev. 735; Lat. 36-37-16 N long. 093-12-55 W; S Missouri.

•**HOLT**, City; Clay and Clinton Counties; Pop. 276; Zip Code 64048; Lat. 39-27-10 N long. 094-20-31 W; NW Missouri. According to some sources this city was named for *Dr. David Rice Holt,* a member of the State Legislature. Other sources say it was named in honor of *Jerre A. Holt,* an early settler.

•**HOMESTOWN**, City; Pemiscot County; Pop. 306; Lat. 36-19-55 N long. 089-49-33 W; SE Missouri.

•**HOPKINS**, City; Nodaway County; Pop. 634; Zip Code 64461; Elev. 1046; Lat. 40-33-03 N long. 094-49-09 W; NW Missouri. Founded in 1871. named for *A.L. Hopkins,* a railroad agent.

•**HOUSTON**, City; Seat of Texas County; Pop. 2,157; Zip Code 65483; Lat. 37-19-34 N long. 091-57-21 W; S Missouri. Established in 1845, the county seat was platted and named for General Samuel Houston, first president of the Texas Republic.

•**HOWARDVILLE**, City; New Madrid County; Pop. 536; Lat. 36-34-05 N long. 089-36-02 W; SE Missouri.

•**HUMANSVILLE**, City; Polk County; Pop. 907; Zip Code 65674; Lat. 37-47-40 N long. 093-34-40 W; SW Missouri.

•**HUNTLEIGH**, City; St. Louis County; Pop. 428; Lat. 38-36-57 N long. 090-24-38 W; E Missouri.

•**HUNTSVILLE**, City; Seat of Randolph County; Pop. 1,657; Zip Code 65259; Elev. 800; Lat. 39-26-26 N long. 092-32-42 W; N central Missouri. Platted in 1831 and named for *Daniel Hunt,* one of the first settlers in the vicinity, and one of the donors of the town site.

•**IBERIA**, City; Miller County; Pop. 852; Zip Code 65486; Elev. 932; Lat. 38-05-25 N long. 092-17-33 W; central Missouri. Named for the town of Iberia, Louisiana.

•**ILLMO** City; Scott County; Pop. 1,368; Zip Code 63754; Lat. 37-13-11 .l long. 089-30-32 W; SE Missouri. Named by blending Illinois plus Missouri.

•**INDEPENDENCE**, City; Clay and Seat of Jackson Counties; Pop. 111,806; Zip Code 640+; Elev. 949; Lat. 39-05-28 N long. 094-24-55 W; 10 miles E of Kansas City in NW Missouri.

•**IONIA**, Town; Benton and Pettis Counties; Pop. 131; Zip Code 65335; Lat. 38-30-15 N long. 093-19-26 W; W central Missouri. Laid out in 1866 by *Henry Pollard.* Named for the Greek and Roman classics.

•**IRONTON**, City; Seat of Iron County; Pop. 1,743; Zip Code 63650; Elev. 919; Lat. 37-35-50 N long. 090-37-38 W; SE Missouri. Named for the inexhaustible riches of the soil and the mineral wealth.

•**JACKSON**, City; Seat of Cape Girardeau County; Pop. 7,827; Zip Code 63755; Elev. 497; Lat. 37-22-56 N long. 089-39-58 W; 10 miles NW of Cape Girardeau in SE Missouri. Platted as a town and named for General Andrew Jackson.

•**JACKSONVILLE**, Village; Randolph County; Pop. 130; Zip Code 65260; Elev. 851; Lat. 37-33-30 N long. 092-25-21 W; N central Missouri. Named for Hancock Jackson, pre-Civil Governor of Missouri and Randolph County resident, was established as a railroad stop in 1858.

•**JASPER**, City; Jasper County; Pop. 1,012; Zip Code 64755; Elev. 946; Lat. 37-20-10 N long. 094-18-04 W; SW Missouri.

•**JEFFERSON CITY**, City; Callaway and Seat of Cole Counties; Capital of Missouri; Pop. 33,619; Zip Code 665101; Elev. 702; Lat. 38-34-36 N long. 092-10-24 W; Central Missouri. Named for Thomas Jefferson.

•**JENNINGS**, City; St. Louis County; Pop. 17,026; Zip Code 63136; Elev. 515; Lat. 38-43-09 N long. 090-15-37 W; 5 miles N of St. Louis in E Missouri.

•**JONESBURG**, City; Montgomery County; Pop. 614; Zip Code 63551; Elev. 900; Lat. 38-51-12 N long. 091-18-21 W; E central Missouri.

•**KAHOKA**, City; Seat of Clark County; Pop. 2,101; Zip Code 63445; Elev. 703; Lat. 40-25-13 N long. 091-43-10 W; NE Missouri. Platted 1856, which derives its name from that of the Gawakie Indians -"the lean ones."

•**KEARNEY**, City; Clay County; Pop. 1,433; Zip Code 64060; Elev. 849; Lat. 39-22-04 N long. 094-21-43 W; NW Missouri. Founded in 1867 and named after Fort Kearney.

•**KENNETT**, City; Seat of Dunklin County; Pop. 10,145; Zip Code 63857; Elev. 258; Lat. 36-14-10 N long. 090-03-20 W; 20 miles W of Caruthersville in SE Missouri. In 1849 the name was changed to Buytler and, a few years later, to Kennett, in honor of Dr. Luther M. Kennett, Mayor of St. Louis (1849-52).

•**KEYTESVILLE**, City; Seat of Chariton County; Pop. 689; Zip Code 65261; Elev. 643; Lat. 39-26-04 N long. 092-56-17 W; N central Missouri. Platted in 1830 by the Reverend James Keyte, is the seat of Chariton County.

•**KIMBERLING**, City; Stone County; Pop. 1,285; Zip Code 65686; Lat. 39-25-54 N long. 092-29-20 W; SW Missouri.

•**KIMMSWICK**, City; Jefferson County; Pop. 207; Zip Code 63053; Elev. 409; Lat. 38-21-55 N long. 090-21-46 W; E Missouri. Founded in October, 1859 by *Theodoro Kimm* and named in his honor.

•**KINGDOM CITY**, Village; Callaway County; Pop. 146; Zip Code 65262; Elev. 800; Lat. 38-57-35 N long. 091-55-55 W; Central Missouri.

•**KINGSTON**, City; Seat of Caldwell County; Pop. 280; Zip Code 64650; Elev. 1,005; Lat. 39-38-39 N long. 094-02-18 W; NW Missouri. Named for Judge Austin A. King, governor of Missouri 1848-52.

•**KINLOCH**, City; St. Louis County; Pop. 4,455; Zip Code 63040; Lat. 38-44-24 N long. 090-19-35 W; E Missouri.

•**KIRKSVILLE**, City; Seat of Adair County; Pop. 17,167; Zip Code 63501; Elev. 969; Lat. 40-11-41 N long. 092-34-59 W; 55 miles N of Moberly in N Missouri. Kirksville was founded in 1841 as the seat of Adair County, which was organized in that year. According to tradition, Mr. and Mrs. Jesse Kirk gave the commissioners a turkey dinner on condition that the town be named for them.

•**KIRKWOOD**, City; St. Louis County; Pop. 27,987; Zip Code 631+; Elev. 640; Lat. 38-35-00 N long. 090-24-24 W; 15 miles W of St. Louis in E Missouri. The town was incorporated in 1865 and named in honor of James P. Kirkwood, then chief engineer of the railroad.

•**KNOB NOSTER**, City; Johnson County; Pop. 2,040; Zip Code 65336; Elev. 793; Lat. 38-45-54 N long. 093-33-23 W; W Missouri. Founded in 1856, the town takes its name from two prominent mounds or knobs called "Our Knobs" on the prairie nearby.

•**LA BELLE**, City; Lewis County; Pop. 845; Zip Code 63447; Elev. 738; Lat. 40-07-01 N long. 091-54-45 W; NE Missouri. Laid out in November, 1871. The name LaBelle means "the beautiful", probably suggested by the town's pretty location.

•**LADUE**, City; St. Louis County; Pop. 9,376; Lat. 38-38-59 N long. 090-22-50 W; 40 miles W of St. Louis in E Missouri.

•**LA GRANGE**, City; Lewis County; Pop. 1,217; Zip Code 63448; Elev. 484; Lat. 40-02-34 N long. 091-29-51 W; NE Missouri.

•**LAKE LOTAWANA**, City; Jackson County; Pop. 1,875; Zip Code 64063; Lat. 38-55-23 N long. 094-14-38 W; W Missouri.

•**LAKE OZARK**, City; Camden and Miller Counties; Pop. 427; Zip Code 65049; Elev. 703; Lat. 38-11-55 N long. 092-38-19 W; S central Missouri. Formed by the impounding of the waters of the Osage River, is one of the largest wholly artificial lakes in the United States. Broken by innumerable coves that give it the shape of an octopus, it is 129 miles long, has a 1,300-mile, irregular shoreline, wooded in oak, hickory, elm, wild crab, and other trees, and covers an area of 95 square miles.

•**LAMAR**, City; Seat of Barton County; Pop. 4,053; Zip Code 64759; Elev. 980; Lat. 37-29-42 N long. 094-16-35 W; 30 miles NNE of Joplin in SW Missouri. Founded in 1856, and named for Mirabeau B. Lamar, President of the Texas Republic, (1838-41).

•**LA MONTE**, City; Pettis County; Pop. 1,054; Zip Code 65337; Elev. 860; Lat. 38-46-27 N long. 093-25-28 W; W central Missouri.

•**LANAGAN**, Town; McDonald County; Pop. 440; Zip Code 64847; Elev. 854; Lat. 36-36-29 N long. 094-26-51 W; SW Missouri.

•**LANCASTER**, City; Seat of Schuyler County; Pop. 855; Zip Code 63548; Elev. 979; Lat. 40-31-15 N long. 092-31-40 W; N Missouri. Publicized as the birthplace of Rupert Hughes, has been seat of Schuyler County since its organization in 1845. He was editor on *Godey's Magazine, Current Literature, The Criterion,* and *Encyclopedia Britannica.* His published works include novels, juvenile books, and plays.

•**LA PLATA**, City; Macon County; Pop. 1,423; Zip Code 63549; Elev. 930; Lat. 40-01-24 N long. 092-29-29 W; N Missouri. Laid out in 1855. The name translates from Spanish as "silver."

•**LATHROP**, City; Clinton County; Pop. 1,732; Zip Code 64465; Elev. 1,071; Lat. 39-32-54 N long. 094-19-47 W; NW Missouri. Founded in 1857 by *J.S. Harris,* land commissioner of the Hannibal and St. Joseph Railroad. Lathrop was named for the township in which it was located.

•**LAWSON**, City; Clay and Ray Counties; Pop. 1,688; Zip Code 64062; Lat. 39-26-18 N long. 094-12-14 W; NW Missouri. Founded in June, 1870 by the St. Joseph Land Company. Named in honor of *L.M. Lawson* of Donnell, Lawson & Company, a New York Banking House.

•**LEAWOOD**, Village; Newton County; Pop. 631; Lat. 37-02-13 N long. 094-29-48 W; NW Missouri.

•**LEBANON**, City; Seat of Laclede County; Pop. 9,507; Zip Code 65536; Elev. 1,265; Lat. 37-40-50 N long. 092-39-49 W; 25 miles South of East end of Lake of the Ozarks in South central Missouri.

•**LEE'S SUMMIT**, City; Cass and Jackson Counties; Pop. 28,741; Zip Code 64063; Elev. 1,050; Lat. 38-54-39 N long. 094-22-55 W; 20 miles SE of Kansas City in W Missouri.

•**LESLIE**, Village; Franklin County; Pop. 108; Zip Code 63056; Lat. 38-25-04 N long. 091-13E-55 W; Missouri.

•**LEWIS AND CLARK VILLAGE**, Town; Buchanan County; Pop. 131; Lat. 39-32-35 N long. 095-03-09 W; NW Missouri.

•**LEWISTOWN**, Town; Lewis County; Pop. 502; Zip Code 63452; Elev. 725; Lat. 40-05-10 N long. 091-48-47 W; NE Missouri. Surveyed July 1, 1871 by *Charles Peter.* The town was named after Lewis County.

•**LEXINGTON**, City; Seat of Lafayette County; Pop. 5,063; Zip Code 64067; Elev. 688; Lat. 39-11-05 N long. 093-52-47 W; 35 miles E of Independence in W Missouri. The town was platted, and named for Lexington, Kentucky, former home of many of its settlers.

•**LIBERAL**, City; Barton County; Pop. 701; Zip Code 64762; Elev. 885; Lat. 37-33-29 N long. 094-31-11 W; SW Missouri. Founded in 1880 by G. H. Walser (1834-1910), a disciple of Robert C. Ingersoll. Walser, born in Indiana, served in the Civil War, and lived for a time in Rockport before moving to Lamar, where he conceived the idea of establishing a refuge for free-thinkers. Walser purchased land and platted Liberal.

•**LIBERTY**, City; Seat of Clay County; Pop. 16,251; Zip Code 64068; Elev. 850; Lat. 38-41-21 N long. 091-57-33 W; 15 miles NNE of Kansas City in NW Missouri.

•**LICKING**, City; Texas County; Pop. 1,272; Zip Code 65542; Elev. 1259; Lat. 37-29-58 N long. 091-51-25 W; S Missouri. Surveyed in 1878 and named for a buffalo lick.

•**LILBOURN**, City; New Madrid County; Pop. 1,463; Zip Code 63862; Lat. 36-35-32 N long. 089-36-55 W; SE Missouri.

•**LINCOLN**, City; Benton County; Pop. 819; Zip Code 65338; Lat. 38-23-27 N long. 093-20-04 W; W central Missouri. Named for *Abraham Lincoln*.

•**LINN**, City; Seat of Osage County; Pop. 1,211; Zip Code 65051; Elev. 897; Lat. 38-29-09 N long. 091-51-01 W; Central Missouri. Named in honor of United States Senator Lewis F. Linn.

•**LINN CREEK**, Town; Camden County; Pop. 242; Zip Code 65052; Elev. 722; Lat. 38-02-17 N long. 092-42-41 W; S central Missouri.

•**LINNEUS**, City; Seat of Linn County; Pop. 421; Zip Code 64653; Elev. 837; Lat. 39-52-43 N long. 093-11-19 W; N Missouri.

•**LITHIUM**, Village; Perry County; Pop. 81; Lat. 37-50-00 N long. 089-53-09 W; E Missouri. Founded in 1882 and named for the metal lithium.

•**LONE JACK**, Village; Jackson County; Pop. 420; Zip Code 64070; Elev. 1,012; Lat. 38-52-20 N long. 094-10-22 W; W Missouri. Founded in 1841. Lone Jack received its name from a blackjack tree near a spring which served as a prairie landmark.

•**LOUISBURG**, Village; Dallas County; Pop. 140; Zip Code 65685; Lat. 37-45-28 N long. 093-08-21 W; SW central Missouri.

•**LOUISIANA**, City; Pike County; Pop. 4,261; Zip Code 63353; Elev. 469; Lat. 39-26-56 N long. 091-03-05 W; 25 miles SE of Hannibal in E Missouri. Laid out by *Samuel K. Caldwell* and *Joel Shaw* in 1818, and named for the State of Louisiana.

•**LUDLOW**, Town Livingston County; Pop. 178; Lat. 39-39-18 N long. 093-42-07 W; Zip Code 64656; N Missouri.

•**LUPUS**, Town; Moniteau County; Pop. 50; Elev. 574; Lat. 38-50-46 N long. 092-27-11 W; Central Missouri. Originally called "Wolf's Point", the name was later changed to Lupus, the Latin word for wolf.

•**LUTESVILLE**, City; Bollinger County; Pop. 865; Zip Code 63762; Elev. 417; Lat. 37-18-01 N long. 089-58-52 W; SE Missouri. Named after *Eli Lutz*. Founded in 1869.

•**MACON**, City; Seat of Macon County; Pop. 5,680; Zip Code 63552; Elev. 874; Lat. 39-44-32 N long. 092-28-21 W; 25 miles N of Moberly in N Missouri. Macon was named, as was the county, for *Nathaniel Macon* (1757-1837), Revolutionary War soldier and United States Senator from North Carolina.

•**MADISON**, City; Monroe County; Pop. 656; Zip Code 65263; Elev. 801; Lat. 39-28-25 N long. 092-12-35 W; NE Missouri.

•**MALDEN**, City, Dunklin County; Pop. 6,096; Zip Code 63863; Elev. 294; Lat. 36-33-25 N long. 089-57-59 W; 30 miles ESE of Poplar Bluff in SE Missouri. Named for Malden, Massachusetts.

•**MANCHESTER**, City; St. Louis County; Pop. 6,191; Zip Code 63011; Elev. 512; Lat. 38-35-49 N long. 090-30-33 W; 15 miles W of St. Louis in E Missouri. Probably named for "old Mr. Manchester" who lived in the vicinity as early as 1795.

•**MANSFIELD**, City, Wright County; Pop. 1,423; Zip Code 65704; Elev. 1,476; Lat. 37-06-24 N long. 092-34-50 W; S Missouri.

•**MAPLEWOOD**, City; St. Louis County; Pop. 10,960; Zip Code 63143; Elev. 520; Lat. 38-36-45 N long. 090-19-28 W; 5 miles W of St. Louis in E Missouri.

•**MARCELINE**, City; Linn County; Pop. 2,938; Zip Code 64658; Elev. 858; Lat. 39-42-43 N long. 092-56-53 W; 35 miles NW of Moberly in N Missouri. Founded in 1887 and named for the wife of a railroad official.

•**MARIONVILLE**, City; Lawrence County; Pop. 1,920; Zip Code 65705; Elev. 1,351; Lat. 37-00-11 N long. 093-38-14 W; SW Missosuri.

•**MARLBOROUGH**, Village; St. Louis County; Pop. 2,012; Lat. 38-58-36 N long. 094-33-43 W; E Missouri.

•**MARQUAND**, City; Madison County; Pop. 397; Zip Code 63655; Elev. 571; Lat. 37-25-45 N long. 090-10-05 W; SW Missouri. Named after *W. G. Marquand* who donated to the local church.

•**MARSHALL**, City; Seat of Saline County; Pop. 12,781; Zip Code 65340; Elev. 779; Lat. 39-07-23 N long. 093-11-48 W; 30 miles N of Sedalia in W central Missouri. Settled in 1839 by immigrants from Virginia, Tennessee, and Kentucky, on a site known as Elk's Hill, was named for *John Marshall*, Chief Justice of the United States Supreme Court.

•**MARSHFIELD**, City; Seat of Webster County; Pop. 3,871; Zip Code 65706; Elev. 1,487; Lat. 37-20-19 N long. 092-54-25 W; 25 miles ENE of Springfield in S Missouri. Named in honor of the Massachusetts home of *Daniel Webster*.

•**MARSTON**, City; New Madrid County; Pop. 742; Zip Code 63866; Lat. 36-31-08 N long. 089-36-45 W; SE Missouri.

•**MARTINSBURG**, Town; Audrain County; Pop. 309; Zip Code 65264; Elev. 807; Lat. 39-06-08 N long. 091-38-51 W; NE central Missouri. Founded in 1857 by *William R. Martin* and named in his honor.

•**MARTINSVILLE**, Town; Harrison County; Pop. 44; Zip Code 64467; Elev. 1076; Lat. 40-20-19 N long. 094-09-41 W; N Missouri. Laid out in 1856 by *Willis Log* and named for *Zadoc Martin*, a miller.

•**MARYVILLE**, City; Seat of Nodaway County; Pop. 9,558; Zip Code 64468; Elev. 1,036; Lat. 40-20-46 N long. 094-52-20 W; 40 miles N of St. Joseph in NW Missouri. Was selected for the seat of newly organized Nodaway County in September of 1845, it was named in honor of *Mrs. Mary Graham*, the first white woman to live within the limits of the town.

•**MATTHEWS**, City, New Madrid County; Pop. 547; Zip Code 63867; Elev. 310; Lat. 36-45-33 N long. 089-35-12 W; SE Missouri.

•**MAYSVILLE**, City; Seat of DeKalb County; Pop. 1,187; Zip Code 64469; Elev. 974; Lat. 39-53-21 N long. 094-21-42 W; NW Missouri. Established in 1845 as the seat of DeKalb County. Marysville was located and surveyed by *G. W. McPherson*.

•**MEMPHIS**, City; Seat of Scotland County; Pop. 2,105; Zip Code 63555; Elev. 801; Lat. 40-27-28 N long. 092-10-16 W; NE Missouri. Built on land donated by *Samuel Cecil* for the seat of Scotland County. First settled in 1838.

•**MENDON**, Town; Chariton County; Pop. 252; Lat. 39-35-23 N long. 093-08-04 W; Zip Code 64660; N central Missouri. Founded in 1871.

•**META**, City; Osage County; Pop. 336; Zip Code 65058; Elev. 610; Lat. 38-18-45 N long. 092-09-57 W; Central Missouri.

•**MEXICO**, City; Seat of Audrain County; Pop. 12,276; Zip Code 65265; Elev. 800; Lat. 39-10-11 N long. 091-52-58 W; 30 miles ENE of Columbia in NE central Missouri.

•**MIAMI**, City; Saline County; Pop. 177; Zip Code 65344; Lat. 39-19-17 N long. 093-13-40 W; W central Missouri. At the foot of the nearby bluffs, a group of Miami Indians established a village before 1810.

•**MIDWAY**, Village; Newton County; Pop. 223; Zip Code 65201; Lat. 38-59-06 N long. 092-26-57 W; SW Missouri. Named for its location midway between Columbia and Rocheport.

•**MILAN**, City; Seat of Sullivan County; Pop. 1,947; Zip Code 63556; Elev. 969; Lat. 40-12-08 N long. 093-07-30 W; N Missouri. Surveyed in 1845 by *Wilson Baldridge* as the seat of Sullivan County.

•**MILLER**, City; Lawrence County; Pop. 795; Zip Code 65707; Lat. 37-12-53 N long. 093-50-23 W; SW Missouri.

•**MILL SPRINGS**, Village; Wayne County; Pop. 257; Zip Code 63952; Lat. 37-03-43 N long. 090-41-02 W; Established in November, 1871. Named for the mill which was run by a large spring there.

•**MINDENMINES**, City; Barton County; Pop. 318; Zip Code 64769; Elev. 968; Lat. 37-28-17 N long. 094-35-23 W; SW Missouri. Platted April 19, 1883 by *R. J. Tucker.*

•**MOBERLY**, City; Randolph County; Pop. 13, 418; Zip Code 65270; Elev. 872; Lat. 39-25-06 N long. 092-26-17 W; 35 miles N of Columbia in N central Missouri. Named for *Col. William E. Moberly,* President of the road which is now part of the Wabash Railroad.

•**MOKANE**, Town; Callaway County; Pop. 293; Zip Code 65059; Elev. 534; Lat. 38-40-30 N long. 091-52-27 W; Central Missouri. Named for the Missouri, Kansas and Topeka Railroad in 1849.

•**MOLINE ACRES**, City; St. Louis County; Pop. 2,774; Lat. 38-44-49 N long. 090-14-24 W; E Missouri.

•**MONETT**, City; Barry and Lawrence Counties; Pop. 6,148; Zip Code 65708; Elev. 1,302; Lat. 36-55-44 N long. 093-55-39 W; 35 miles SE of Joplin in SW Missouri. Named in 1887 for the general passenger agent of the New York Central Railroad.

•**MONROE CITY**, City; Marion and Monroe Counties; Pop. 2,557; Zip Code 63456; Elev. 748; Lat. 39-39-13 N long. 091-44-04 W; NE Missouri. Named for *James Monroe* in 1856.

•**MONTGOMERY CITY**, City; Seat of Montgomery County; Pop. 2,101; Zip Code 63361; Elev. 816; Lat. 38-58-39 N long. 091-30-17 W; E central Missouri.

•**MONTICELLO**, Town; Seat of Lewis County; Pop. 134; Zip Code 63457; Lat. 40-07-06 N long. 091-42-43 W; NE Missouri. Selected in September, 1833 as the seat of Lewis County. Named for *Thomas Jefferson's* home at Monticello, Virginia.

•**MOREHOUSE**, City; New Madrid County; Pop. 1,220; Elev. 302; Lat. 36-50-50 N long. 089-41-07 W; SE Missouri.

•**MORLEY**, Town; Scott County; Pop. 745; Zip Code 63767; Lat. 37-02-37 N long. 089-36-37 W; SE Missouri.

•**MORRISVILLE**, Town; Polk County; Zip Code 65710; Lat. 37-28-52 N long. 093-25-38 W; SW Missouri. Named for *Morris Mitchell,* who founded the town in 1870.

•**MOSBY**, City; Clay County; Pop. 284; Zip Code 64073; Lat. 39-18-56 N long. 094-17-37 W; NW Missouri. Named for the Mosby family.

•**MOUND CITY**, City; Holt County; Pop. 1,447; Zip Code 64470; Elev. 877; Lat. 40-07-52 N long. 095-13-53 W; NW Missouri. The name is derived from a low mound of hill upon which a portion of the town is built.

•**MOUNTAIN GROVE**, City; Wright County; Pop. 3,974; Zip Code 65711; Elev. 1,463; Lat. 37-07-50 N long. 092-15-48 W; 40 miles NW of West Plains in S Missouri. Named for the distinctive local beautiful landscapes.

•**MOUNTAIN VIEW**, City; Howell County; Pop. 1,664; Zip Code 65548; Elev. 1,123; Lat. 36-59-430 N long. 091-42-13 W; S Missouri.

•**MOUNT VERNON**, City; Seat of Lawrence County; Pop. 3,341; Zip Code 65712; Lat. 37-06-13 N long. 093-49-06 W; 30 miles WSW of Springfield in SW Missouri. Named in 1845 for the home of *George Washington.*

•**NAPOLEAN**, City; Lafayette County; Pop. 271; Zip Code 64074; Elev. 750; Lat. 39-07-53 N long. 094-04-14 W; W Missouri.

•**NAYLOR**, City; Ripley County; Pop. 602; Zip Code 63953; Elev. 304; Lat. 36-34-31 N long. 090-36-14 W; S Missouri.

•**NEELYVILLE**, City; Butler County; Pop. 474; Zip Code 63954; Elev. 307; Lat. 36-33-42 N long. 090-30-22 W; SE Missouri. Named for the Neely family.

•**NEOSHO**, City; Seat of Newton County; Pop. 9,493; Zip Code 64850; Elev. 1,039; Lat. 36-52-08 N long. 094-22-04 W; 15 miles SSE of Joplin in SW Missouri. (1,039 alt.), called by the Osage Indian word for clear water because of the large spring near the center of the town.

•**NEVADA**, City; Seat of Vernon County; Pop. 9,044; Zip Code 64772; Elev. 874; Lat. 37-50-21 N long. 094-21-16 W; 55 miles N of Joplin in W Missouri.

•**NEWARK**, Town; Knox County; Pop. 105; Zip Code 63458; Lat. 39-59-35 N long. 091-58-22 W; NE Missouri. Named for Newark, New Jersey in 1837.

•**NEW BLOOMFIELD**, City; Callaway County; Pop. 519; Zip Code 65063; Elev. 841; Lat. 38-43-13 N long. 092-05-28 W; Central Missouri.

•**NEW FLORENCE**, City; Montgomery County; Pop. 731; Zip Code 63363; Lat. 38-54-37 N long. 091-26-53 W; E central Missouri. Founded in 1857 by *Judge Lewis* and named after his only daughter Florence.

•**NEW HAVEN**, City; Franklin County; Pop. 1,581; Zip Code 63068; Lat. 38-36-30 N long. 091-13-08 W; E Missouri. First known as Miller's Landing but renamed for New Haven, Connecticut in 1858.

•**NEW LONDON**, City; Seat of Ralls County; Pop. 1,161; Zip Code 63459; Elev. 600; Lat. 39-35-07 N long. 091-24-03 W; NE Missouri. Named for New London, England in 1819.

•**NEW MADRID**, City; Seat of New Madrid County; Pop. 3,204; Elev. 305; Lat. 36-35-11 N long. 089-31-40 W; SE Missouri.

•**NEWTONIA**, Town; Newton County; Pop. 224; Zip Code 64853; Elev. 1203; Lat. 36-52-36 N long. 094-11-07 W; SW Missouri.

•**NIANGUA**, City; Webster County; Pop. 376; Zip Code 65713; Elev. 1435; Lat. 37-23-14 N long. 092-49-57 W; S Missouri. Named by the Indians for natural features, streams, or mountains.

•**NIXA**, City; Christian County; Pop. 2,662; Zip Code 65714; Lat. 37-02-36 N long. 093-17-39 W; SW Missouri.

•**NOEL**, City; McDonald County; Pop. 1,161; Zip Code 64854; Elev. 828; Lat. 36-32-44 N long. 094-29-06 W; SW Missouri. Named for *C.W. and W.J. Noel,* livestock raisers and saw mill owners.

•**NORBORNE**, City; Carroll County; Pop. 931; Zip Code 64668; Lat. 39-18-09 N long. 093-40-38 W; NW Missouri. Founded in 1868. Named for Norborne B. Coats, promoter of the town.

•**NORMANDY**, City; St. Louis County; Pop. 5,174; Zip Code 63121; Lat. 38-43-31 N long. 090-17-48 W; 5 miles NW of St. Louis in E Missouri. Named for Normandy, France.

•**NOVINGER**, City; Adair County; Pop. 626; Zip Code 63559; Lat. 40-13-55 N long. 092-42-30 W; N Missouri. Named for *John C. Novinger* who laid out the town on his land in 1879.

•**OAK GROVE**, City; Jackson and Lafayette Counties; Pop. 4,067; Zip Code 64075; Lat. 38-13-32 N long. 091-09-04 W; W Missouri.

•**ODESSA**, City; Lafayette County; Pop. 3,088; Zip Code 64076; Elev. 932; Lat. 38-59-57 N long. 093-57-12 W; 30 miles E of Independence in W Missouri.

•**O'FALLON**, City; St. Charles County; Pop. 8,654; Zip Code 63366; Elev. 535; Lat. 38-13-32 N long. 091-09-04 W; 30 miles NW of St. Louis in E Missouri. It was founded in 1857 and named for *Col. John O'Fallon,* St. Louis capitalist and director of the old North Missouri Railway.

•**OLD APPLETON**, Town; Cape Girardeau County; Pop. 80; Zip Code 63770; Elev. 401; SE Missouri.

•**OLIVETTE**, City; St. Louis County; Pop. 8,039; Zip Code 63132; Elev. 660; Lat. 38-39-55 N long. 090-22-33 W.

•**ORAN**, City; Scott County; Pop. 1,266; Zip Code 63771; Elev. 347; Lat. 37-05-06 N long. 089-39-19 W; SE Missouri. Founded in 1869. Named by a retired sea-captain, who once visited the city in Algeria.

•**OREGON**, City; Seat of Holt County; Pop. 901; Zip Code 64473; Elev. 1,094; Lat. 39-59-13 N long. 095-08-41 W; NW Missouri. Oregon was laid out as the seat of justice in June of 1841 and named in honor of the Oregon country, which was then attracting the first of a long procession of immigrants.

•**ORONOGO**, City; Jasper County; Pop. 525; Zip Code 64855; Elev. 975; Lat. 37-11-18 N long. 094-28-12 W; SW Missouri. Name may have been a distorted Spanish name, after the many Spanish speaking immigrants that were flooding into the state at that time.

•**ORRICK**, City; Ray County; Pop. 922; Zip Code 64077; Lat. 39-12-46 N long. 094-07-21 W; NW Missouri. Laid out by the North Missouri Railroad Company in March, 1869. Named for W. W. Orrick, who worked for the railroad.

•**OSBORN**, City; Clinton and DeKalb Counties; Pop. 381; Zip Code 64474; Lat. 36-34-50 N long. 090-12-41 W; NW Missouri. Founded by the Hannibal and St. Joseph Railroad and named for *Col. William Osborn* of Waterville, New York.

•**OSCEOLA**, City; Seat of St. Clair County; Pop. 841; Zip Code 64778; Elev. 750; Lat. 38-02-48 N long. 093-42-15 W; W Missouri.

The settlers laid out a town, which they named for Osceola, a Seminole Indian chief who was captured in 1837 after a two-year war with the United States.

•**OVERLAND**, City; St. Louis County; Pop. 19,620; Zip Code 63114; Elev. 641; Lat. 38-42-04 N long. 090-21-44 W; 10 miles WNW of St. Louis in E Missouri.

•**OWENSVILLE**, City; Gasconade County; Pop. 2,241; Zip Code 65066; Elev. 935; Lat. 38-20-44 N long. 091-30-05 W; E central Missouri. Named for a storekeeper, named Owen.

•**OZARK**, City; Seat of Christian County; Pop. 2,980; Zip Code 65721; Elev. 1,177; Lat. 37-01-15 N long. 093-12-21 W; SW Missouri.

•**PACIFIC**, City; Franklin and St. Louis Counties; Pop. 4,410; Zip Code 63069; Elev. 467; Lat. 38-28-55 N long. 090-44-29 W; 35 miles W of St. Louis in E Missouri.

•**PAGEDALE**, City; St. Louis County; Pop. 4,542; Lat. 38-41-00 N long. 090-18-28 W; E Missouri.

•**PALMYRA**, City; Seat of Marion County; Pop. 3,469; Zip Code 63461; Elev. 652; Lat. 39-47-39 N long. 091-31-23 W; 10 miles NW of Hannibal in NE Missouri. The town was platted in 1819 and named for the Syrian city built by King Solomon, probably because it, too, was founded in the wilderness.

•**PARIS**, City; Seat of Monroe County; Pop. 1,598; Zip Code 65275; Elev. 673; Lat. 39-28-51 N long. 092-00-04 W; NE Missouri. Named for the city of Paris, France.

•**PARKVILLE**, City; Platte County; Pop. 1,997; Zip Code 641+; Elev. 754; Lat. 39-11-42 N long. 094-40-55 W; NW Missouri.

•**PARKWAY**, Village; Franklin County; Pop. 254; Zip Code 641+; Elev. 748; Lat. 38-20-17 N long. 090-58-11 W; E Missouri.

•**PARMA**, City; New Madrid County; Pop. 1,081; Zip Code 63870; Elev. 281; Lat. 36-36-49 N long. 089-48-59 W; SE Missouri. Named for the town of Parma, Italy.

•**PASADENA HILLS**, Village; St. Louis County; Pop. 1,221; Lat. 38-42-30 N long. 090-17-34 W; E Missouri.

•**PASADENA PARK**, Village; St. Louis County; Pop. 531; Lat. 38-42-38 N long. 090-17-53 W; E Missouri.

•**PASSAIC**, Town; Bates County; Zip Code 64777; Elev. 865; Lat. 38-19-19 N long. 094-20-53 W; W Missouri. Named for the town of Passaic, New Jersey.

•**PAYNESVILLE**, Town; Pike County; Pop. 85; Zip Code 63371; Lat. 39-15-45 N long. 090-54-01 W; E Missouri.

•**PECULIAR**, City; Cass County; Pop. 1,571; Zip Code 64078; Elev. 1,006; Lat. 38-43-09 N long. 094-27-30 W; W Missouri. Received its name when a group of spiritualists under the leadership of Mrs. Jane Hawkins came to Cass Countyj in search of a home. George Moore, Carry Nation's father, took Mrs. Hawkins and some of her followers to look at a farm for which he had the agency. As they came over a hilltop and saw the valley below, Mrs. Hawkins exclaimed: "That's peculiar! It is the vary place I saw in a vision in Connecticut." Thus, when the spiritualists bought the farm and laid out a town in 1868, they named it Peculiar.

•**PERRY**, City; Ralls County; Pop. 836; Zip Code 63462; Elev. 683; Lat. 39-25-52 N long. 091-40-30 W; NE Missouri.

•**PERRYVILLE**, City; Seat of Perry County; Pop. 7,343; Zip Code 63775; Elev. 570; Lat. 37-43-27 N long. 089-51-40 W; 35 miles

NNW of Cape Girardeau in E Missouri. Named for Captain James Perry, who won the Battle of Lake Erie.

•**PEVELY**, city; Jefferson County; Pop. 2,732; Zip Code 63070; Elev. 440; Lat. 38-17-00 N long. 090-23-42 W; E Missouri.

•**PICKERING**, Town; Nodaway County; Pop. 215; Zip Code 64476; Elev. 1022; Lat. 40-27-03 N long. 094-50-31 W; NW Missouri. Named after *Pickering Clark,* a railroad official.

•**PIEDMONT**, City; Wayne County; Pop. 2,359; Zip Code 63957; Elev. 502; Lat. 37-09-16 N long. 090-41-44 W; SE Missouri. From the French "pied" meaning "foot" and "mont" meaning "mountain." Piedmont was laid out by a railroad company.

•**PIERCE CITY**, City; Lawrence County; Pop. 1,391; Zip Code 65723; Elev. 1199; Lat. 36-56-40 N long. 094-00-15 W; SW Missouri. Founded in 1870. Named for *Andrew Pierce* of Boston, President of the St. Louis and San Francisco Railroad.

•**PINE LAWN**, City; St. Louis County; Pop. 6,662; Lat. 38-41-41 N long. 090-16-42 W; E Missouri. Named for the woodland paradise that Missouri once was.

•**PINEVILLE**, Town; Seat of McDonald County; Pop. 504; Zip Code 64856; Elev. 899; Lat. 36-35-40 N long. 094-23-02 W; SW Missouri. Named for nearby pine lands.

•**PLATTE CITY**, City; Seat of Platte County; Pop. 2,114; Zip Code 64079; Elev. 805; Lat. 39-22-13 N long. 094-46-56 W; NW Missouri.

•**PLATTSBURG**, City; Seat of Clinton County; Pop. 2,095; Zip Code 64477; Elev. 953; Lat. 39-33-56 N long. 094-26-52 W; NW Missouri.

•**PLEASANT HILL**, City; Cass County; Pop. 3,301; Zip Code 64080; Elev. 909; Lat. 38-47-15 N long. 094-16-09 W; W Missouri. Named for the natural beauty of the local surroundings.

•**PLEASANT VALLEY**, City; Clay County; Pop. 1,545; Lat. 39-12-59 N long. 094-29-02 W; NW Missouri.

•**POCAHONTAS**, Town; Cape Girardeau County; Pop. 130; Zip Code 63779; Lat. 37-30-04 N long. 089-38-20 W; SE Missouri. Named for famous Indian princess.

•**POLO**, City; Caldwell County; Pop. 583; Zip Code 64671; Lat. 39-33-08 N long. 094-02-26 W; NW Missouri. Settled in 1867 by *Isaac Webb* and *Groge Wilkinson.* Named after the town of Polo, Illinois.

•**POPLAR BLUFF**, City; Seat of Butler County; Pop. 17,139; Zip Code 63901; Elev. 436; Lat. 36-45-25 N long. 090-23-34 W; 65 miles WSW of Cape Girardeau in SE Missouri.

•**PORTAGE DES SIOUX**, City; St. Charles County; Pop. 488; Zip Code 63373; Lat. 38-55-30 N long. 090-20-39 W; E Missouri. So named because the Indians carried their canoes across the peninsula here between the Mississippi and Missouri Rivers.

•**PORTAGEVILLE**, City; New Madrid County; Pop. 3,470; Zip Code 63873; Elev. 271; Lat. 36-25-31 N long. 089-41-58 W; SE Missouri.

•**POTOSI**, City; Seat of Washington County; Pop. 2,528; Zip Code 63664; Elev. 905; Lat. 37-56-11 N long. 090-47-16 W; 60 miles SW of St. Louis in E Missouri. Named for the town of Potosi, South America.

•**PRATHERSVILLE**, Village; Clay County; Pop. 141; Lat. 39-01-05 N long. 092-19-18 W; NW Missouri.

•**PRINCETON**, City; Seat of Mercer County; Pop. 1,264; Zip Code 64673; Elev. 839; Lat. 40-24-03 N long. 093-34-49 W; N Missouri.

Platted in 1846 and incorporated in 1853, Princeton is the seat of Mercer County, named for General Hugh Mercer, who fought with Washington in the Battle of Princeton (New Jersey). the name of the city commemorates the battle, which took place January 3, 1777.

•**PURDIN**, City; Linn County; Pop. 243; Zip Code 64674; Lat. 39-57-07 N long. 093-09-56 W; N Missouri. Named after *Allen W. Purdin,* owner of the land on which the town was laid out.

•**PURDY**, City; Barry County; Pop. 928; Zip Code 65734; Lat. 36-49-02 N long. 093-55-14 W; SW Missouri. Named for *George A. Purdy,* an enterprising citizen. Founded in 1880.

•**PUXICO**, City; Stoddard County; Pop. 833; Zip Code 63960; Elev. 370; Lat. 36-56-59 N long. 090-09-30 W; SE Missouri. Named for a well-known Indian chief, Puxico.

•**QUEEN CITY**, City; Schuyler County; Pop. 783; Zip Code 63561; Elev. 1,003; Lat. 40-24-33 N long. 092-34-03 W; N Missouri. Founded in 1867 by *Dr. George W. Wilson,* as the "Queen of the prairies."

•**QUILIN**, Town; Butler County; Pop. 545; Zip Code 63961; Lat. 36-35-45 N long. 090-14-50 W; SE Missouri.

•**RAVENWOOD**, Town; Nodaway County; Pop. 436; Zip Code 64479; Lat. 40-21-08 N long. 094-40-25 W; NW Missouri.

•**RAYMORE**, City; Cass County; Pop. 3,154; Zip Code 64083; Elev. 1104; Lat. 38-48-07 N long. 094-27-09 W; W Missouri. Named for Messrs. Ray and Moore, two St. Louis railroad men.

•**RAYTOWN**, City; Jackson County; Pop. 31,759; Zip Code 641+; Lat. 39-00-31 N long. 094-27-48 W; W Missouri. Once a postal station and assembly place for wagon trains on the Santa Fe Trail and in 1840 a cross-roads trading village.

•**RAYVILLE**, Town; Ray County; Pop. 197; Zip Code 64084; Lat. 39-20-54 N long. 094-03-46 W; NW Missouri. Founded in 1871. First called Hallard or Haller Station. Later named after the county in which it is located.

•**REA**, Town; Andrew County; Pop. 78; Zip Code 64480; Elev. 1059; Lat. 40-03-43 N long. 094-45-52 W; NW Missouri. Named for Judge Joseph Rea.

•**READINGS**, Village; Newton County; Pop. 222; Lat. 39-29-29 N long. 091-07-56 W; SW Missouri.

•**REPUBLIC**, City; Greene County; Pop. 4,485; Zip Code 65738; Elev. 1,311; Lat. 37-07-12 N long. 093-28-48 W; SW Missouri.

•**RHINELAND**, Town; Montgomery County; Pop. 172; Zip Code 65069; Elev. 517; Lat. 38-43-03 N long. 091-31-02 W; E central Missouri. Founded in 1853 by Germans and named in honor of the Rhine River.

•**RICHARDS**, Town; Vernon County; Pop. 117; Zip Code 64778; Lat. 37-54-26 N long. 094-33-25 W; W Missouri.

•**RICH HILL**, City; Bates County; Pop. 1,471; Zip Code 64779; Elev. 805; Lat. 38-05-47 N long. 094-21-39 W; W Missouri. Named by the first postmaster, *E. W. Ratekin,* for the town's location on a hill underlaid with coal.

•**RICHLAND**, City; Camden, Laclede, and Pulaski Counties; Pop. 1,922; Zip Code 65556; Lat. 37-51-24 N long. 092-24-18 W; S central Missouri.

•**RICHMOND**, City; Seat of Ray County; Pop. 5,499; Zip Code 64085; Elev. 890; Lat. 39-16-430 N long. 093-58-36 W; 40 miles ENE of Kansas City in NW Missouri. Named for the city of Richmond, Virginia, founded by Colonel William Byrd in 1733.

MISSOURI

•**RICHMOND HEIGHTS**, City; St. Louis County; Pop. 11,516; Zip Code 63117; Elev. 469; Lat. 38-37-43 N long. 090-19-10 W; 5 miles W of St. Louis in E Missouri. Named for Richmond, Virginia

•**RISCO**, City; New Madrid County; Pop. 446; Zip Code 63874; Lat. 36-33-12 N long. 089-49-04 W; SE Missouri.

•**RIVERMINES**, Village; St. francois County; Pop. 414; Lat. 37-50-54 N long. 090-31E-52 W; Missouri.

•**RIVERSIDE**, City; Platte County; Pop. 3,206; Zip Code 64168; Lat. 36-02-33 N long. 090-20-14 W; NW Missouri.

•**RIVERVIEW**, Village; St. Louis County; Pop. 3,367; Elev. 860; Lat. 38-16-33 N long. 093-04-10 W; E Missouri.

•**ROCKAWAY BEACH**, Town; Taney County; Pop. 110; Zip Code 65740; Lat. 36-41-57 N long. 093-09-35 W; S Missouri.

•**ROCK HILL**, City; St. Louis County; Pop. 5,702; Lat. 38-36-27 N long. 090-22-42 W; 10 miles W of St. Louis in E Missouri.

•**ROCK PORT**, City; Seat of Atchinson County; Pop. 1,511; Zip Code 64482; Elev. 935; Lat. 40-24-36 N long. 095-30-52 W; NW Missouri.

•**ROCKVILLE**, City; Bates County; Pop. 281; Zip Code 64780; Elev. 784; Lat. 38-04-17 N long. 094-04-46 W; W Missouri. Laid out in 1868 by *William L. Hardesty*. Rockville was named for the excellent white sandstone quarries in the area.

•**ROGERSVILLE**, Town; Greene and Webster Counties; Pop. 741; Zip Code 65742; Lat. 37-07-01 N long. 093-03-20 W; SW Missouri. Named for *Dr. Rogers*, a pioneer.

•**ROLLA**, City; Seat of Phelps County; Pop. 13,303; Zip Code 65401; Elev. 1,120; Lat. 37-57-05 N long. 091-46-16 W; S central Missouri. George Coppedge, nostalgic for his North Carolina home, asked that it be named Raleigh. This last proposal was accepted and the name was spelled as Coppedge pronounced it, Rolla.

•**RUSH HILL**, Town; Audrain County; Pop. 140; Zip Code 65280; Lat. 39-12-36 N long. 091-43-17 W; NE central Missouri. Laid out by Reusch and Hill and named for its two original owners.

•**SAGINAW**, Village; Newton County; Pop. 293; Zip Code 64864; Lat. 37-01-26 N long. 094-28-05 W; SW Missouri. Named for the city of Saginaw, Michigan.

•**ST. ANN**, City; St. Louis County; Pop. 15,523; Zip Code 63074; Lat. 38-43-38 N long. 090-22-59 W; E Missouri.

•**ST. CHARLES**, City; Seat of St. Charles County; Pop. 37,379; Zip Code 63301; Elev. 536; Lat. 38-47-02 N long. 090-28-52 W; 20 miles NW of St. Louis in E Missouri. Named for St. Charles Borromeo because it was the purpose of the vicar of Pontoise to establish a seminary here where Indians could be educated.

•**ST. CLAIR**, City; Franklin County; Pop. 3,485; Zip Code 63077; Elev. 770; Lat. 38-20-43 N long. 090-58-51 W; 50 miles SW of St. Louis in E Missouri. Named for General Arthur St. Clair, who was governor of the Northwest territory.

•**ST. JAMES**, City; Phelps County; Pop. 3,328; Zip Code 65559; Elev. 1,069; Lat. 37-59-50 N long. 091-36-51 W; 10 miles E of Rolla in S central Missouri. Named directly for St. James the Apostle, but indirectly also Thomas James, its founder.

•**ST. JOHN**, City; St. Louis County; Pop. 7,854; Zip Code 63114; Elev. 1075; Lat. 37-53-21 N long. 092-22-46 W; E Missouri. Named for old Fort San Juan del Misuri built by the Spaniards.

•**ST. JOSEPH**, City; Seat of Buchanan County; Pop. 76,691; Zip Code 645+; Lat. 39-46-07 N long. 094-50-47 W; 45 miles NNW of Kansas City in NW Missouri. Named for founder *Joseph Robidoux*, an early French trader and settler.

•**ST. LOUIS**, City; St. Louis County; Pop. 453,085; Zip Code 631+; Elev. 657. Settlement was finalized in 1764 on a site first selected in 1763 by Pierre Laclede Liguest, partner in Maxent, Laclede and Company. Named for Louis IX, Crusader King of France and patron saint of Louis XV.

•**ST. PETERS**, City; St. Charles County; Pop. 15,700; Zip Code 63376; Elev. 445; Lat. 38-48-01 N long. 090-37-35 W; E Missouri. Dates from 1820, was platted as a village in 1868. Named after the Jesuit mission established here in the early days.

•**ST. ROBERT**, City; Pulaski County; Pop. 1,735; Zip Code 65583; Lat. 37-49-41 N long. 092-10-39 W; S central Missouri.

•**ST. THOMAS**, Town; Cole County; Pop. 337; Zip Code 65076; Lat. 38-22-06 N long. 092-13-00 W; Central Missouri.

•**SALEM**, City; Seat of Dent County; Pop. 4,454; Zip Code 65560; Elev. 1,182; Lat. 37-38-44 N long. 091-32-09 W; 25 miles SSE of Rolla in Se central Missouri.

•**SALISBURY**, City; Chariton County; Pop. 1,975; Zip Code 65281; Lat. 39-25-26 N long. 092-48-05 W; N central Missouri. Named for Judge Lucien Salsbury, a founder.

•**SARCOXIE**, City; Jasper County; Pop. 1,381; Zip Code 64862; Lat. 37-04-09 N long. 094-06-59 W; SW Missouri. Founded in 1834 and first called Centerville from its location on Center Creek. In 1839, at the suggestion of *Hon. James S. Rains,* the name was changed to Sarcoxie, in honor of an old and freidnly Shawnee chief who lived near a spring in the present town limits. Sarcoxie means "Rising Sun."

•**SAVANNAH**, City; Seat of Andrew County; Pop. 4,184; Zip Code 64485; Elev. 1,115; Lat. 39-56-30 N long. 094-49-48 W; 15 miles North of St. Joseph in NW Missouri. Savannah, near the geographical center of the county, was platted in 1841, the year Andrew County was created. It was named for Savannah, Georgia.

•**SCOTT CITY**, City; Scott County; Pop. 3,262; Lat. 37-13-00 N long. 089-31-28 W; Zip Code 63780.

•**SEDALIA**, City; Seat of Pettis County; Pop. 20,927; Zip Code 65301; Elev. 907; Lat. 38-42-16 N long. 093-13-41 W; 60 miles W of Jefferson City in W central Missouri. Pioneer George Smith plated the town, which he named Sedville in honor of his daughter Sarah, whom he called "Sed." On October 16, 1860, General Smith filed a second plat, including the original Sedville, and called it Sedalia.

•**SEDGEWICKVILLE**, Village; Bollinger County; Pop. 115; Zip Code 63781; Elev. 642; Lat. 37-30-58 N long. 089-54-25 W; SE Missouri.

•**SELIGMAN**, City; Barry County; Pop. 508; Zip Code 65745; Elev. 1540; Lat. 36-31-21 N long. 093-56-22 W; SW Missouri. Founded in 1880. Some sources say Seligman was named for a railroad official. Others say it was named in honor of *Mrs. Seligman,* a banker's wife, who made a generous gift for the building of a church.

•**SENATH**, City; Dunklin County; Pop. 1,728; Area Code 417; Zip Code 63876; Elev. 250; SE Missouri. A cotton town, was established by its first postmaster, A. W. Douglass, in 1882, and named for his wife, Mrs. Senath Hale Douglass.

•**SENECA**, City; Newton County; Pop. 1,853; Area Code 417; Zip Code 64865; Elev. 865; SW Missouri. Named for an Indian tribe

288

that was moved to Indian Territory a few miles west of the town. The word is a corruption of the Dutch word "Sinnekaas", a term applied to them.

•SEYMOUR, City; Webster County; Pop. 1,535; Area Code 417; Zip Code 65746; Elev. 1,642; S Missouri.

•SHELBINA, City; Shelby County; Pop. 2,169; Area Code 317; Zip Code 63468; Elev. 779; NE Missouri. Named for Isaac Shelby of Kentucky, Governor.

•SHELBYVILLE, City; Seat of Shelby County; Pop. 645; Zip Code 63469; Elev. 768; Lat. 39-48-21 N long. 092-02-29 W; NE Missouri.

•SHERIDAN, Town; Worth County; Pop. 220; Zip Code 64486; Lat. 40-31-05 N long. 094-36-53 W; NW Missouri.

•SHREWSBURY, City; St. Louis County; Pop. 5,077; Lat. 38-35-25 N long. 090-20-12 W; E Missouri.

•SIBLEY, Village; Jackson County; Pop. 382; Zip Code 64088; Elev. 746; Lat. 39-10-43 N long. 094-11-35 W; W Missouri. An early Jackson County settlement named for General George C. Sibley, early factor of Fort Osage and a surveyor of the Santa Fe Trail.

•SIKESTON, City; New Madrid and Scott Counties; Pop. 17,431; Zip Code 63801; Elev. 325; Lat. 36-52-36 N long. 089-35-16 W; 30 miles S of Cape Girardeau in SE Missouri. Named for John Sikes, who laid out the town.

•SILVER CREEK, Village; Newton County; Pop. 519; Lat. 37-02-26 N long. 094-28-21 W; SW Missouri.

•SLATER, City; Saline County; Pop. 2,492; Zip Code 65349; Elev. 853; Lat. 39-13-05 N long. 093-04-08 W; W central Missouri. Founded in 1880. Named for Col. John F. Slater of Chicago, director of the C & A Railroad.

•SMITHVILLE, City; Clay County; Pop. 1,873; Zip Code 64089; Lat. 39-23-13 N long. 094-34-51 W; NW Missouri. Named after pioneer Humphrey Smith who settled in 1822.

•SOUTH GREENFIELD, Village; Dade County; Pop. 110; Zip Code 65752; Elev. 943'; Lat. 37-22-34 N long. 093-50-27 W; SW Missouri.

•SOUTH WEST CITY, City; McDonald County; Pop. 516; Zip Code 64863; Elev. 949; Lat. 36-30-53 N long. 094-36-40 W; SW Missouri. Founded in 1870. Named for the location of the town in the southwest corner of the county and state.

•SPICKARD, City; Grundy County; Pop. 389; Lat. 40-14-38 N long. 093-35-39 W; N Missouri. Named for W. W. Spickard, a pioneer.

•SPRINGFIELD, City; Greene Country Seat; Pop. 13,116; Zip Code 658+; Elev. 1345. Traditions vary as to the origin of the city's name. One account relates that it was named for the former home of one of the early settlers. Another states that John Polk Campbell, who staked an early claim here, chose Springfield because there was a field on a hill and a spring under it.

•STANBERRY, City; Gentry County; Pop. 1,387; Zip Code 64489; Elev. 886; Lat. 40-13-04 N long. 094-32-17 W; NW Missouri. Named for John J. Stanberry, original owner of the townsite.

•STEELE, City; Pemiscot County; Pop. 2,419; Zip Code 63877; Elev. 244; Lat. 36-05-02 N long. 089-49-45 W; SW Missouri. Named for L. L. Steele, a merchant.

•STEELVILLE, City; Seat of Crawford County; Pop. 1,470; Zip Code 65565; Elev. 755; Lat. 37-58-05 N long. 091-21-17 W; SE

Missouri. The first settler here was William Britton, who built a log house and a small gristmill on Yadkin Creek in 1833. The village was named for James Steel, who arrived two years later.

•STEWARTSVILLE, City; De Kalb County; Pop. 832; Zip Code 64490; Lat. 39-45-03 N long. 094-29-47 W; NW Missouri. Laid out in 1854. Named for Robert M. Stewart, Governor of the state in 1857.

•STOCKTON, City; Seat of Cedar County; Pop. 1,432; Zip Code 65785; Elev. 965; Lat. 37-41-56 N long. 093-47-45 W; W Missouri. Named for Commodore Robert Field Stockton, who helped Fremont to conquer California.

•STOTTS CITY, City; Lawrence County; Pop. 232; Zip Code 65756; Lat. 37-06-13 N long. 093-56-58 W; SW Missouri.

•STOUTLAND, Village; Camden and Laclede Counties; Pop. 232; Zip Code 65567; Elev. 1171; Lat. 37-48-51 N long. 092-30-50 W; S central Missouri.

•STOVER, City; Morgan County; Pop. 1,041; Zip Code 65078; Elev. 1052; Lat. 38-26-27 N long. 092-59-30 W; Central Missouri. Named after Col. John Stover, one time Congressman.

•STRAFFORD, City; Greene County; Pop. 1,121; Zip Code 65757; Elev. 1,478; Lat. 37-16-06 N long. 093-07-01 W; SW Missouri.

•STURGEON, City; Boone County; Pop. 901; Zip Code 65284; Elev. 851; Lat. 39-14-03 N long. 092-16-50 W; Central Missouri. Laid out in 1856 by the Sturgeon Town Company. Named for Isaac H. Sturgeon, a Superintendent of the North Misouri Railroad.

•SUGAR CREEK, City; Clay and Jackson Counties; Pop. 4,305; Zip Code 640+; Lat. 39-06-35 N long. 094-26-40 W; 10 miles E of Kansas City in NW Missouri. Named for the sugar maple trees found in the area.

•SULLIVAN, City; Crawford and Franklin County; Pop. 5,461; Zip Code 63080; Elev. 971; Lat. 38-12-29 N long. 091-09-37 W; The town was established as Mt. Helicon in 1856, but the officials of the St. Louis-San Francisco Railway changed the name in 1860 to honor Stephen Sullivan, who had donated the right of way through the village.

•SUMMERSVILLE, City; Shannon and Texas Counties; Pop. 551; Zip Code 65571; Lat. 37-10-45 N long. 091-39-24 W; S Missouri. Named by the Missourians for the town of Summerville, Kentucky.

•SUNRISE BEACH, Village; Camden and Morgan Counties; Pop. 148; Zip Code 65079; Lat. 38-10-33 N long. 092-47-03 W; S central Missouri.

•SUNSET HILLS, City; St. Louis County; Pop. 4,363; Lat. 38-32-20 N long. 090-24-26 W; E Missouri.

•SWEET SPRINGS, City; Saline County; Pop. 1,694; Zip Code 65351; Elev. 683; Lat. 38-57-49 N long. 093-24-53 W; W central Missouri.

•SYCAMORE HILLS, Village; St. Lois County; Pop. 741; Elev. 655; Lat. 38-42-03 N long. 090-20-59 W; E Missouri.

•TALLAPOOSA, City; New Madrid County; Pop. 197; Zip Code 63878; Lat. 36-30-29 N long. 089-49-09 W; SE Missouri.

•TANEYVILLE, Village; Taney County; Pop. 300; Zip Code 65759; Elev. 1075; Lat. 36-44-29 N long. 093-02-03 W; S Missouri. Named for the county in which it is located.

•TAOS, City; Cole County; Pop. 759; Elev. 710; Lat. 39-34-39 N long. 094-50-05 W; Central Missouri.

•**TARKIO**, City; Atchinson County; Pop. 2,375; Zip Code 64491; Elev. 916; Lat. 40-26-25 N long. 095-22-39 W; NW Missouri. Tarkio was laid out in August of 1880 by *Charles E. Perkins.*. The name is Indian for "walnut", or "a place where walnuts grow."

•**THAYER**, City; Oregon County; Pop. 2,211; Zip Code 65791; Elev. 518; Lat. 36-31-28 N long. 091-32-17 W; S Missouri. Named Nathaniel Thayer of Boston, an important stockholder.

•**TINA**, Town; Carroll County; Pop. 202; Zip Code 64682; NW central Missouri. Named for the daughter of E. M. Gilchrist, a railroad man.

•**TINDALL**, Town; Grundy County; Pop. 104; Elev. 787; Lat. 40-09-40 N long. 093-36-29 W; N Missouri.

•**TIPTON**, City; Moniteau County; Pop. 2,155; Zip Code 65081; Elev. 922; Lat. 38-39-20 N long. 092-46-47 W; Central Missouri. Is named for Tipton Sealey, who donated land for the townsite.

•**TRACY**, City; Platte County; Pop. 310l; Zip Code 64079; Elev. 778; Lat. 39-22-37 N long. 094-47-34 W; NW Missouri. Founded in 1872 and named for *J.W. Tracey,* a Rock Island Railroad Superintendent.

•**TRENTON**, City; Seat of Grundy County; Pop. 6,811; Zip Code 64683; Elev. 822; Lat. 40-04-44 N long. 093-36-59 W; 20 miles N of Chillicothe in N Missouri. It was probably named for Trenton, New Jersey.

•**TRIMBLE**, Town; Clinton County; Pop. 262; Zip Code 64492; Elev. 931; Lat. 39-28-16 N long. 094-33-52 W; NW Missouri.

•**TROY**, City; Seat of Lincoln County; Pop. 2,624; Zip Code 63379; Elev. 573; Lat. 38-58-46 N long. 090-58-50 W; E Missouri. Platted in 1819 and named for Troy, New York by *Joshua N. Robbins.*

•**TURNEY**, Town; Clinton County; Pop. 379; Zip Code 64493; Lat. 39-38-09 N long. 094-19-16 W; NW Missouri.

•**TUSCUMBIA**, Town; Seat of Miller County; Pop. 241; Elev. 742; Lat. 38-13-59 N long. 092-27-30 W; Central Missouri. Named for the town of Tuscumbia, Alabama. Located in the Osage River Valley.

•**TWIN OAKS**, Village; St. Louis County; Pop. 426; Lat. 38-33-53 N long. 090-29-47 W; E Missouri.

•**UNION**, City; Seat of Franklin County; Pop. 5,506; Zip Code 63084; Elev. 568; Lat. 38-26-44 N long. 091-00-20 W; 50 miles WSW of St. Louis in E Missouri. Named by the Missourians for the high ideals they always had and were fond of naming places for them.

•**UNION STAR**, Town; De Kalb County; Pop. 423; Zip Code 64494; Lat. 39-58-50 N long. 094-35-39 W; NW Missouri.

•**UNIONVILLE**, City; Seat of Putnam County; Pop. 2,178; Zip Code 63565; Elev. 1067; Lat. 40-28-37 N long. 093-00-11 W; N Missouri.

•**UNITY VILLAGE**, Town; Jackson County; Pop. 202; Zip Code 64063; Lat. 38-57-05 N long. 094-24-05 W; W Missouri.

•**UNIVERSAL CITY**, City; St. Louis County; Pop. 42,738; Zip Code 63130; E Missouri.

•**UPLANDS PARK**, Village; St. Louis County; Pop. 544; Lat. 38-41-35 N long. 090-16-56 W; E Missouri.

•**URBANA**, City; Dallas County; Pop. 329; Zip Code 65767; Lat. 37-50-32 N long. 093-10-00 W; SW central Missouri. Named for the town of Urbana, Illinois.

•**URICH**, City; Henry County; Pop. 509; Zip Code 64788; Lat. 38-27-35 N long. 094-00-02 W; W Missouri. Founded in 1871. Named for the French *General Uhrich,* who defended Strasburg against the Prussians.

•**VALLEY PARK**, City; St. Louis County; Pop. 3,232; Zip Code 63088; Elev. 421; Lat. 38-32-57 N long. 090-29-33 W; 15 miles W of St. Louis in E Missouri. Named for the distinctive local features and the beauty of their landscapes.

•**VAN BUREN**, Town; Seat of Carter County; Pop. 850; Zip Code 63965; Elev. 1,345; Lat. 36-59-44 N long. 091-00-52 W; SE Missouri. Named after *President Van Buren.*

•**VANDALIA**, City; Audrain County; Pop. 3,170; Zip Code 63382; Elev. 768; Lat. 39-18-39 N long. 091-29-18 W; NE central Missouri. Named for the town of Vandalia, Illinois.

•**VANDUSER**, Village; Scott County; Pop. 320; Zip Code 63784; Elev. 313; Lat. 36-59-26 N long. 089-41-08 W; SE Missouri.

•**VERONA**, Town; Lawrence County; Pop. 592; Zip Code 65769; Elev. 1,273; Lat. 36-57-50 N long. 093-47-44 W; SW Missouri. Named for Verona, Italy.

•**VERSAILLES**, City; Seat of Morgan County; Pop. 2,406; Zip Code 65084; Elev. 1,037; Lat. 38-25-53 N long. 092-50-27 W; Central Missouri. Founded in 1834. Named after the palace in France.

•**VIENNA**, City; Seat of Maries County; Zip Code 65582; Elev. 873; Lat. 38-11-12 N long. 091-56-49 W; S central Missouri. Named after the city in Austria. Vienna became the seat of Maries County in 1855.

•**VINITA PARK**, City; St. Louis County; Pop. 2,283; Lat. 38-41-24 N long. 090-20-33 W; E Missouri.

•**WACO**, Town; Jasper County; Pop. 129; Zip Code 64869; Lat. 37-14-49 N long. 094-35-57 W; SW Missouri. Named for the town of Waco, Texas.

•**WAKENDA**, Town; Carroll County; Pop. 98; Zip Code 64687; Lat. 39-18-51 N long. 093-22-37 W; NW Central Missouri.

•**WALKER**, Town; Vernon County; Pop. 325; Zip Code 64790; Elev. 852; Lat. 37-53-55 N long. 094-13-55 W; W Missouri. Platted in 1870 and named for *Hiram F. Walker,* an early resident.

•**WALNUT GROVE**, City; Greene County; Pop. 504; Zip Code 65770; Lat. 37-24-40 N long. 093-32-58 W; SW Missouri. Named for the many walnut trees found in the area.

•**WARDELL**, Town; Pemiscot County; Pop. 299; Zip Code 63879; Lat. 36-21-05 N long. 089-49-04 W; SE Missouri. Named for the founder of the town, Warren.

•**WARRENSBURG**, City; Seat of Johnson County; Pop. 13,807; Zip Code 64093; Elev. 803; Lat. 38-45-46 N long. 093-44-09 W; 30 miles W of Sedalia in W Missouri.

•**WARRENTON**, City; Seat of Warren County; Pop 3,219; Zip Code 63383; Elev. 943; Lat. 38-48-41 N long. 091-08-29 W; E Missouri.

•**WARSAW**, City; Seat of Benton County; Pop. 1,494; Zip Code 65355; Elev. 687; Lat. 38-14-35 N long. 093-22-54 W; W central Missouri.

•**WASHBURN**, City; Barry County; Pop. 289; Zip Code 65772; Lat. 36-35-13 N long. 093-57-57 W; SW Missouri. Named after *Samuel Washburn,* a pioneer who settled Washburn's prairie in 1828. The town was settled in 1840.

•**WASHINGTON**, City; Franklin County; Pop. 9,251; Zip Code 63090; Elev. 546; Lat. 38-33-29 N long. 091-00-43 W; 50 miles E of St. Louis in E Missouri.

•**WAVERLY**, Town; Lafayette County; Pop. 941; Zip Code 64096; Elev. 684; Lat. 39-12-34 N long. 093-31-03 W; W Missouri. Named for the book by Sir Walter Scott.

•**WAYLAND**, City; Clark County; Pop. 498; Zip Code 63472; Elev. 535; Lat. 40-23-40 N long. 091-34-59 W; NE Missouri. Founded in 1880 and named for *Jerre Wayland,* a pioneer.

•**WAYNESVILLE**, City; Seat of Pulaski County; Pop. 2,879; Zip Code 65583; Elev. 806; Lat. 37-49-43 N long. 092-12-02 W; S central Missouri. In 1839 when the town was platted, Harvey Wood secured the post office and named it for "Mad Anthony" Wayne.

•**WEATHERBY LAKE**, City; Platte County; Pop. 1,446; Lat. 39-14-16 N long. 094-41-45 W; NW Missouri.

•**WEBB CITY**, City; Jasper County; Pop. 7,309; Zip Code 64870; Elev. 1,003; Lat. 37-08-47 N long. 094-27-46 W; SW Missouri. Until 1873 the site of Webb City was part of the fertile acres belonging to John C. Webb, whose corn and wheat farm consisted of a quarter-section bounded on the east by the Carter farm.

•**WEBSTER GROVES**, City; St. Louis County; Pop. 23,097; Zip Code 63119; Elev. 507; Lat. 38-35-33 N long. 090-21-26 W; 10 miles W of St. Louis in E Missouri. Named for Daniel Webster of Marshfield, Massachusetts (1782-1852) who was an unsuccessful candidate for the Whig nomination.

•**WELDON SPRING HEIGHTS**, Town; St. Charles County; Pop. 144; Lat. 38-42-18 N long. 090-41-14 W; E Missouri. Named for settlers *Joseph and John Weldon* and the nearby springs.

•**WELLINGTON**, City; Lafayette County; Pop. 780; Zip Code 64097; Elev. 716; Lat. 39-08-03 N long. 093-58-57 W; W Missouri. Platted in 1837.

•**WELLSTON**, City; St. Louis County; Pop. 4,495; Zip Code 631+; Lat. 38-40-22 N long. 090-17-57 W; E Missouri. Named for Erastus Wells, who developed the streetcar system of St. Louis.

•**WELLSVILLE**, City; Montgomery County; Pop. 1,546; Zip Code 63384; Lat. 39-04-19 N long. 091-34-12 W; E central Missouri. Founded in 1856 by *Judge Wells* and named in his honor.

•**WENTZVILLE**, City; St. Charles County; Pop. 3,193; Zip Code 63385; Elev. 675; Lat. 38-48-41 N long. 090-51-10 W; E Missouri. Was founded in 1855 and named for the chief of the St. Louis, Kansas City & Northern Railway.

•**WESTBORO**, Village; Atchinson County; Pop. 188; Zip Code 64498; Lat. 40-32-05 N long. 095-19-08 W; NW Missouri. Laid out in 1881 by *Charles E. Perkins.*

•**WESTON**, City; Platte County; Pop. 1,440; Zip Code 64098; Elev. 773; Lat. 39-24-40 N long. 094-54-05 W; NW Missouri. An important tobacco market, is half-hidden in a pinched little valley between Missouri River bluffs.

•**WESTPHALIA**, City; Osage County; Pop. 285; Zip Code 65085; Elev. 622; Lat. 38-26-31 N long. 091-59-57 W; Central Missouri. Named for the town of Westphalia, Germany.

•**WEST PLAINS**, City; Seat of Howell County; Pop. 7,741; Zip Code 65775; Elev. 991; Lat. 36-43-41 N long. 091-51-08 W; 90 miles ESE of Springfield in S Missouri. The county seat, laid out a year later, was named for its level site.

•**WHEATLAND**, City; Hickory County; Pop. 364; Zip Code 65779; Lat. 37-56-46 N long. 093-24-03 W; SW central Missouri. Founded in 1869. Named for the inexhaustible riches of the soil.

•**WHEATON**, City; Barry County; Pop. 548; Zip Code 64874; Lat. 36-45-46 N long. 094-03-21 W; SW Missouri.

•**WHITEWATER**, Town; Cape Girardeau County; Pop. 161; Zip Code 63785; Elev. 370; Lat. 37-14-13 N long. 089-47-47 W; SE Missouri.

•**WILLARD**, City; Greene County; Pop. 1,799; Zip Code 65781; Lat. 37-18-18 N long. 093-25-42 W; SW Missouuri.

•**WILLIAMSVILLE**, City; Wayne County; Pop. 418; Zip Code 63967; Elev. 392; Lat. 36-58-16 N long. 090-32-58 W; SE Missouri. Named for *Asa E. Williams* who founded the town in 1822.

•**WILLOW SPRINGS**, City; Howell County; Pop. 2,215; Zip Code 65793; Elev. 1,238; Lat. 36-59-32 N long. 091-58-11 W; S Missouri. Named for the many willow trees found in the area.

•**WINCHESTER**, City; St. Louis County; Pop. 2,237; Elev. 673; Lat. 40-19-04 N long. 091-36-40 W; E Missouri.

•**WINDSOR**, City; Henry and Pettis Counties; Pop. 3,058; Zip Code 65360; Lat. 38-31-56 N long. 093-31-19 W; W central Missouri. Founded in 1855 and known for a time as Belmont. the name wa changed to Windsor, after Windsor Castle in England, by an act of the legislature on December 9, 1859.

•**WINFIELD**, City; Lincoln County; Pop. 592; Zip Code 63389; Elev. 446; Lat. 38-59-50 N long. 090-44-18 W; E Missouri.

•**WINONA**, City; Shannon Conty; Zip Code 65588; Lat. 37-00-35 N long. 091-19-24 W; S Missouri. Originally located in a pine forest. Named for Longfellow's "Winona" in "Hiawatha."

•**WINSTON**, Town; Daviess County; Pop. 246; Zip Code 64689; Elev. 1,044; Lat. 39-52-12 N long. 094-08-23 W; NW Missouri.

•**WORTH**, Town; Worth County; Pop. 137; Zip Code 64499; Elev. 923; Lat. 40-24-18 N long. 094-26-38 W; NW Missouri.

•**WRIGHT CITY**, City; Warren County; Pop. 1,179; Zip Code 63390; Elev. 727; Lat. 38-49-39 N long. 091-01-12 W; E Missouri. Founded in 1857 and named for *H.C. Wright,* an early settler.

•**WYACONDA**, City; Clark County; Pop. 359; Zip Code 63474; Elev. 756; Lat. 40-23-23 N long. 091-55-37 W; NE Missouri. Founded in 1888. The Sioux Indians bellieved thier diety "Wyaconda" lived at the mouth of the local stream.

•**WYATT**, City; Mississippi County; Pop. 441; Zip Code 63882; Elev. 320; Lat. 36-54-33 N long. 089-13-21 W; SE Missouri.

•**ZALMA**, Village; Bollinger County; Pop. 121; Zip Code 63787; Lat. 37-08-41 N long. 090-04-34 W; SE Missouri. Named for Zalma Block, a friend of Louis Houck, a railroad builder.

MONTANA

•**ALBERTON,** Town; Mineral County; Pop. 368; Zip Code 59846; Elev. 2880; Lat. 47-01-53 N long. 114-19-32 W; Named for the Alberts, a pioneer family who came to the area from Canada in 1870.

•**ANACONDA-DEER LODGE,** City; Deer Lodge County Seat; Pop. 12,518; Zip Code 59711; Elev. 5265; Lat. 46-07-41 N long. 112-57-10 W; Michael Hickey established a copper mine here and named it from a newspaper editorial which stated that Grant's army was "encircling Lee's forces like a giant anaconda." The word anaconda struck Hickey as a good name.

•**BAINVILLE,** Town; Roosevelt County; Pop. 245; Zip Code 59212; Lat. 48-08-23 N long. 104-13-05 W; First called Kilva, later renamed in honor of C. M. Bain, an early resident.

•**BAKER,** City; Fallon County Seat; Pop. 2,354; Zip Code 59313; Lat. 46-22-00 N long. 104-16-22 W; Originally known as Lorraine. In 1908 the name was changed to Baker after A. G. Baker, a railroad man.

•**BEARCREEK,** Town; Carbon County; Pop. 61; Zip Code 59007; Elev. 4578; Lat. 45-09-35 N long. 109-09-19 W; Founded in 1906 and named for the bears that came for berries along a nearby creek.

•**BELGRADE,** Town; Gallatin County; Pop. 2,336; Zip Code 59714; Elev. 4454; Lat. 45-46-32 N long. 111-10-51 W; Named in 1889 by a Serbian capitalist for his former home of Belgrade.

•**BELT,** City; Cascade County; Pop. 825; Zip Code 59412; Elev. 3571; Lat. 47-23-05 N long. 110-55-22 W; First known as Castner, after founder, John Castner. Later renamed for nearby Belt Butte, a nearby mountain which has a belt or girdle of rocks around it.

•**BIG SANDY,** Town; Chouteau County; Pop. 835; Zip Code 59520; Elev. 2712; Lat. 48-10-30 N long. 110-06-27 W; The Indians called a creek near here un-es-putcha-eka or "big sandy creek." The town was named for the stream.

•**BIG TIMBER,** City; Sweet Grass County Seat; Pop. 1,690; Zip Code 59011; Lat. 45-50-00 N long. 109-56-57 W; Large cottonwood trees along a nearby creek suggested the name for this city.

•**BILLINGS,** City; Yellowstone County Seat; Pop. 66,798; Zip Code 59002; Lat. 45-55-37 N long. 108-41-06 W; Named in honor of Frederick Billings, a lawyer, railroad promoter and philanthropist.

•**BOULDER,** Town; Jefferson County Seat; Pop. 1,441; Zip Code 59632; Elev. 4904; Lat. 46-14-10 N long. 112-07-09 W; Established about 1860 and named for the massive rocks found in the valley.

•**BOZEMAN,** City; Gallatin County Seat; Pop. 21,645; Zip Code 59715; Elev. 4810; Lat. 45-40-32 N long. 111-02-41 W; The city takes its name from John Bozeman, an explorer who guided the first train of immigrants into the Gallatin Valley. An early name for the city was "Missouri."

•**BRIDGER,** Town; Carbon County; Pop. 724; Zip Code 59014; Lat. 45-17-28 N long. 108-54-50 W; Named in honor of Jim Bridger, an early white explorer. Earlier known as Georgetown and Stringtown.

•**BROADUS,** Town; Powder River County Seat; Pop. 712; Zip Code 59317; Elev. 3029; Lat. 45-26-47 N long. 105-24-08 W; The town was named for the Broaddus family, pioneers who settled along the Powder River.

•**BROADVIEW,** Town; Yellowstone County; Pop. 120; Zip Code 59015; Lat. 46-05-57 N long. 108-52-36 W; Dr. Sudduth, a local rancher, suggested the name because of the view from his house.

•**BROCKTON,** Town; Roosevelt County; Pop. 374; Zip Code 59213; Elev. 1959; Lat. 48-09-03 N long. 104-54-53 W; The town is located on the prairie a few miles from Twin Buttes, a famous landmark where Sioux and Crow Indians fought.

•**BROWNING,** Town; Glacier County; Pop. 1,226; Zip Code 59417; Lat. 48-33-21 N long. 113-01-04 W; The United States commissioner of Indian affairs named this town, which is the agency headquarters for the Blackfoot Indian Reservation.

•**BUTTE-SILVER BOW,** City; Silver Bow County Seat; Pop. 37,205; First called Butte City for Big Butte peak which stands northwest of the town. Silver Bow, the name of the adjoining town, came from Silver Bow Creek.

•**CASCADE,** Town; Cascade County; Pop. 773; Zip Code 59421; Elev. 3378; Lat. 47-16-18 N long. 111-42-06 W; So named for falls of "cascades" on the Missouri River.

•**CHESTER,** Town; Liberty County Seat; Pop. 963; Zip Code 59522; Elev. 3132; Lat. 48-30-42 N long. 110-57-59 W; The first telegraph operator here selected the name Chester, after his hometown in Pennsylvania.

•**CHINOOK,** City; Blaine County Seat; Pop. 1,660; Zip Code 59523; Elev. 2438; Lat. 48-35-13 N long. 109-13-49 W; Originally called Belknap, then Dawes, renamed Chinook, an Indian word meaning "warm wind."

•**CHOTEAU,** City; Teton County Seat; Pop. 1,798; Zip Code 59422; Elev. 3820; Lat. 47-48-36 N long. 112-11-03 W; First known as Old Agency, later renamed in honor of Pierre Chouteau, Jr., president of the American Fur Company.

•**CIRCLE,** Town; McCone County Seat; Pop. 931; Zip Code 59215; Lat. 47-25-05 N long. 105-35-07 W; Named for the circle brand of an early Montana cow outfit owned by Cross and Twiggly.

•**CLYDE PARK,** Town; Park County; Pop. 283; Zip Code 59018; Elev. 4868; Lat. 45-53-01 N long. 110-36-29 W; Earlier known as Sunnyside. The name was changed to Clyde Park after local ranchers imported Clydesdale horses from England.

•**COLUMBIA FALLS,** City; Flathead County; Pop. 3,112; Zip Code 59912; Lat. 48-22-22 N long. 114-11-05 W; So named because the townsite was originally intended for a location near falls on the Flathead River which is part of the headwaters of the Columbia River.

•**COLUMBUS,** Town; Stillwater County Seat; Pop. 1,439; Zip Code 59019; Elev. 3600; Lat. 45-38-26 N long. 109-15-17 W; Early names included Stillwater, Eagle's Nest and Sheep Dip. It was named Columbus in 1894.

•**CONRAD,** City; Pondera County Seat; Pop. 3,074; Zip Code 59425; Lat. 48-10-17 N long. 111-57-00 W; Originally called Rondera. Renamed about 1884 for W. G.Conrad of the Conrad Investment Company.

•**CULBERTSON,** Town; Roosevelt County; Pop. 887; Zip Code 59218; Elev. 1933; Lat. 48-08-47 N long. 104-30-58 W; The town takes its name from Alexander Culbertson, an early fur trapper.

•**CUT BANK,** City; Glacier County Seat; Pop. 3,688; Zip Code 59427; Lat. 48-38-01 N long. 112-20-02 W; The deep gorge made by nearby Cut Bank Creek suggested the name for this city.

•**DARBY,** Town; Ravali County; Pop. 581; Zip Code 59829; Elev. 3888; Lat. 46-01-15 N long. 114-10-45 W; The town was named in honor of its first postmaster, James R. Darby.

•**DEER LODGE,** City; Powell County Seat; Pop. 4,023; Zip Code 59722; Elev. 4521; Lat. 46-23-48 N long. 112-43-42 W; The Indians called this valley "Lodge of the White Tailed Deer." Settlers named this city Cottonwood, then LaBarge City and finally Deer Lodge.

•**DENTON,** Town; Fergus County; Pop. 356; Zip Code 59430; Elev. 3603; Lat. 47-19-07 N long. 109-56-41 W; Named for the Dent brothers who owned the land on which the town was built.

•**DILLON,** City; Beaverhead County Seat; Pop. 3,976; Zip Code 59724; Elev. 5096; Lat. 44-43-34 N long. 112-42-03 W; The city was named in honor of Sidney Dillon, president of the Union Pacific Railroad.

•**DODSON,** Town; Phillips County; Pop. 158; Zip Code 59524; Lat. 48-23-42 N long. 108-14-31 W; Dodson was named for the man who owned the trading post and saloon here before the coming of the Great Northern Railroad.

•**DRUMMOND,** Town; Granite County; Pop. 414; Zip Code 59832; Elev. 3948; Lat. 46-39-58 N long. 113-08-42 W; First called Drummond Camp after an early trapper named Drummond.

•**DUTTON,** Town; Teton County; Pop. 359; Zip Code 59433; Elev. 3716; Lat. 47-50-53 N long. 111-42-49 W; Founded in the early 1900's and named for Mr. Dutton, a freight and passenger agent for the railroad.

•**EAST HELENA,** Town; Lewis and Clark County; Pop. 1,647; Zip Code 59635; Elev. 3874; Lat. 46-35-31 N long. 111-54-57 W; Settled about 1900 and named for its location east of the city of Helena.

•**EKALAKA,** Town; Carter County Seat; Pop. 620; Zip Code 59324; Lat. 45-53-24 N long. 104-32-58 W; The name is derived from the Indian word Ijkalaka meaning "swift one". Ijkalaka was the name of Sitting Bull's niece.

•**ENNIS,** Town; Madison County; Pop. 660; Zip Code 59729; Elev. 4939; Lat. 45-20-19 N long. 111-43-57 W; William Ennis settled here in 1879 and built a store. The town was later named in his honor.

•**EUREKA,** Town; Lincoln County; Pop. 1,119; Zip Code 59917; Elev. 2566; Lat. 48-52-44 N long. 115-03-02 W; Built on the banks of the Tobacco River, the town was first supported by a sawmill trade. It now has a flouishing Christmas tree industry.

•**FAIRFIELD,** Town; Teton County; Pop. 650; Zip Code 59436; Elev. 3977; Lat. 47-37-02 N long. 111-58-46 W; Nearby hay and grain fields suggested the name for this town.

•**FAIRVIEW,** City; Richland County; Pop. 1,366; Zip Code 59221; Lat. 47-51-13 N long. 104-02-58 W; So named for the city's beautiful view of the lower Yellowstone Valley.

•**FLAXVILLE,** Town; Daniels County; Pop. 142; Zip Code 59222; Lat. 48-48-17 N long. 105-10-20 W; Originally located two and a half miles southwest of the present site and called Boyer. The townsite relocated when the railroad was built, and was renamed for the flax that grew in the area.

•**FORSYTH,** City; Rosebud County Seat; Pop. 2,553; Zip Code 59327; Elev. 2526; Lat. 46-15-51 N long. 106-40-46 W; Named in honor of General James W. Forsyth who came up the Yellowstone River by steamer and landed here.

•**FORT BENTON,** City; Chouteau County Seat; Pop. 1,693; Zip Code 59442; Elev. 2632; Lat. 47-49-10 N long. 110-39-49 W; The city was originally a trading post, named in honor of Senator Thomas Hart Benton.

•**FROID,** Town; Roosevelt County; Pop. 323; Zip Code 59226; Lat. 48-20-10 N long. 104-29-20 W: The name is French meaning "cold" and was probably descriptive of the winters in this northern town.

•**FROMBERG,** Town; Carbon County; Pop. 469; Zip Code 59029; Elev. 3527; Lat. 45-23-31 N long. 108-54-22 W; First called Gebo, then Poverty Flats, and finally Fromberg. The post office was established here in 1903.

•**GERALDINE,** Town; Chouteau County; Pop. 305; Zip Code 59446; Elev. 3135; Lat. 47-36-09 N long. 110-15-56 W; The town was named for Geraldine, wife of Wiliam Rockefeller, director of the Milwaukee Railroad.

•**GLASGOW,** City; Valley County Seat; Pop. 4,455; Zip Code 59230; Lat. 48-11-51 N long. 106-37-44 W; Founded in 1887 and named for Glasgow, Scotland.

•**GLENDIVE,** City; Dawson County Seat; Pop. 5,978; Zip Code 59330; Elev. 2078; Lat. 47-06-26 N long. 104-42-28 W; Named for nearby Glendive Creek, which was originally called Glendale Creek by Sir St. George Gore, a wealthy Irishman.

•**GRASS RANGE,** Town; Fergus County; Pop. 139; Zip Code 59032; Lat. 47-01-43 N long. 108-48-08 W; Established about 1883 and named for the surrounding grassy prairie.

•**GREAT FALLS,** City; Cascade County Seat; Pop. 56,725; Zip Code 59401; Elev. 3334; Lat. 47-30-15 N long. 111-17-09 W; In 1805 Lewis and Clark discovered "great falls" on the river here. Nearly eighty years later, the city was founded and given that name.

•**HAMILTON,** City; Ravalli County Seat; Pop. 2,661; Zip Code 59840; Elev. 3572; Lat. 46-14-52 N long. 114-09-39 W; The Northern Pacific Railroad purchased right-of-way here from J. W. Hamilton and named the city in his honor.

•**HARDIN,** City; Big Horn County Seat; Pop. 3,300; Zip Code 59034; Elev. 2902; Lat. 45-43-46 N long. 107-36-44 W; The president of the Lincoln Land Company named this town after his friend, Samuel Hardin.

•**HARLEM,** City; Blaine County; Pop. 1,023; Zip Code 59526; Elev. 2371; Lat. 48-31-51 N long. 108-46-46 W; Founded in 1889. For many years, this was a trading post for the Fort Belknap Indian Reservation.

•**HARLOWTON,** City; Wheatland County Seat; Pop. 1,181; Zip Code 59036; Lat. 46-26-12 N long. 109-50-04 W; Originally known as Merino. Renamed Harlowton in 1900, after railroad builder, Richard Harlow.

•**HAVRE,** City; Hill County Seat; Pop. 10,891; Zip Code 59501; Elev. 2494; Lat. 48-33-16 N long. 109-40-40 W; First called Bull Hook Bottoms, then Bull Hook siding. Homesteaders Simon Pepin and Gus DesCelles changed the name to Havre in honor of their birthplace in France.

•**HELENA,** City; Lewis and Clark County Seat; Capital of Montana; Pop. 23,938; Zip Code 59601; Elev. 4090; Lat. 46-35-28 N long. 112-02-01 W; First known as Last Chance Gulch, the city was renamed in 1864 at the suggestion of John Somerville who came from Helena, Minnesota.

•**HINGHAM,** Town; Hill County; Pop. 186; Zip Code 59528; Elev. 3032; Lat. 48-33-22 N long. 110-25-09 W; Established about 1910 as a shipping station for livestock and grain.

•**HOBSON,** Town; Judith Basin County; Pop. 261; Zip Code 59452; Elev. 4078; Lat. 46-59-45 N long. 109-52-22 W; Named in honor of S. S. Hobson, a local cowboy and rancher.

•**HOT SPRINGS,** Town; Sanders County; Pop. 601; Zip Code 59845; Elev. 2829; Lat. 47-36-34 N long. 114-40-20 W; So named for the natural hot springs located here.

•**HYSHAM,** Town; Treasure County Seat; Pop. 449; Zip Code 59038; Elev. 2661; Lat. 46-17-21 N long. 107-13-45 W; Founded about 1907 and named for Charles J. Hysham, a trail herder who worked at a local ranch.

•**ISMAY,** Town; Custer County; Pop. 31; Zip Code 59336; Lat. 46-29-57 N long. 104-47-37 W; Established as a station on the Milwaukee Road and named for Isabelle and Mary Peck, daughters of George W. Peck, General Consul for the railroad.

•**JOLIET,** Town; Carbon County; Pop. 580; Zip Code 59041; Lat. 45-29-01 N long. 108-58-35 W; A railroad official named this town for his former home in Joliet, Illinois.

•**JORDAN,** Town; Garfield County Seat; Pop. 485; Zip Code 59337; Elev. 2598; Lat. 47-19-11 N long. 106-54-32 W; Founded by Arthur Jordan, who requested the town be named in honor of a friend in Miles City who was also called Jordan.

•**JUDITH GAP,** City; Wheatland County; Pop. 213; Zip Code 59453; Lat. 46-40-43 N long. 109-45-12 W; So named because of its location in a "gap" in the Little Belt Mountains which offered the easiest way to reach Judith Basin.

•**KALISPELL,** City; Flathead County Seat; Pop. 10,648; Zip Code 59901; Lat. 48-11-50 N long. 114-18-47 W; The city takes its name from the Kalispel Indians who were part of the Flathead tribe.

•**KEVIN,** Town; Toole County; Pop. 208; Zip Code 59454; Elev. 3329; Lat. 48-44-46 N long. 111-57-50 W; Established about 1910 and named for Thomas Kevin, an official of the Alberta Railway and Irrigation Company Railway.

•**LAUREL,** City; Yellowstone County; Pop. 5,481; Zip Code 59044; Elev. 3297; Lat. 45-40-20 N long. 108-46-08 W; Founded about 1899. Laurel was the site of shipping yards for the Northern Pacific, Great Northern and Chicago, Burlingotn and Quincy Railroads.

•**LAVINA,** Town; Golden Valley County; Pop. 164; Zip Code 59046; Lat. 46-17-39 N long. 108-56-13 W; Begun as a trading post and stagestation. Lavina was named for the daughter of the housekeeper of Mr. Vance, an early settler.

•**LEWISTOWN,** City; Fergus County Seat; Pop. 7,104; Zip Code 59445; Elev. 3963; Lat. 46-45-03 N long. 109-45-04 W; Earlier known as Reed's Fort for Major A. S. Reed. Later renamed in honor of Major William H. Lewis.

•**LIBBY,** City; Lincoln County Seat; Pop. 2,748; Zip Code 59923; Lat. 48-23-16 N long. 115-33-12 W; George Davis, an early settler, suggested the name Libby, in honor of his daughter.

•**LIMA,** Town; Beaverhead County; Pop. 272; Zip Code 59739; Elev. 6256; Lat. 44-38-18 N long. 112-35-28 W; Henry Thompson named this town after his home of Lima, Wisconsin.

•**LIVINGSTON,** City; Park County Seat; Pop. 6,994; Zip Code 59047; Elev. 4503; Lat. 45-39-40 N long. 110-33-34 W; First called Clark's City. Renamed in 1882 for Crawford Livingston, director of the Northern Pacific Railroad.

•**LODGE GRASS,** Town; Big Horn County; Pop. 771; Zip Code 59050; Elev. 3363; Lat. 4-18-48 N long. 107-21-49 W; Named for a nearby creek which the Crow Indians called "Greasy Grass." The words for grease and lodge are similar in the Crow language, and the name was mistranslated as Lodge Grass.

•**MALTA,** City; Phillips County Seat; Pop. 2,367; Zip Code 59538; Elev. 2255; Lat. 48-21-15 N long. 107-52-12 W; A railroad official named this city after the island of Malta in the Mediterranean.

•**MANHATTAN,** Town; Gallatin County; Pop. 988; Zip Code 59741; Elev. 4243; Lat. 45-51-27 N long. 111-20-05 W; Originally called Hamilton, then Moreland. The name was changed to Manhattan in 1891, for the Manhattan Company of New York which had land holdings in the area.

•**MEDICINE LAKE,** Town; Sheridan County; Pop. 408; Zip Code 59247; Elev. 1951; Lat. 48-30-06 N long. 104-30-19 W; Indians named a nearby lake, Medicine Lake, because they found medicinal herbs and roots along its shores.

•**MELSTONE,** Town; Musselshell County; Pop. 238; Zip Code 59054; Lat. 46-35-46 N long. 107-52-03 W; Named for Melvin Stone, a newspaper man, who was on the train with railroad officials who selected the names for towns along the line.

•**MILES CITY,** City; Custer County Seat; Pop. 9,602; Zip Code 59301; Elev. 2358; Lat. 46-24-26 N long. 105-50-23 W; Known as Milestown, then Miles City, in honor of General Nelson Miles.

•**MISSOULA,** City; Missoula County Seat; Pop. 33,388; Zip Code 59801; Elev. 3200; Lat. 46-51-26 N long. 114-00-57 W; First called Missoula Mills. The name Missoula is probably of Indian origin, meaning either "The River of Awe," "sparkling waters" or "by the chilling waters."

•**MOORE,** Town; Fergus County; Pop. 229; Zip Code 59464; Elev. 4171; Lat. 46-58-27 N long. 109-41-36 W; Named in honor of a Mr. Moore of Philadelphia who contributed financially to the building of the "Jaw Bone" railroad.

•**NASHUA,** Town; Valley County; Pop. 495; Zip Code 59248; Elev. 2063; Lat. 48-08-01 N long. 106-21-30 W; Located at the joining of Porcupine Creek and the Milk River. These two streams run into the Missouri River a few miles from the town. The name Nashua is believed to be Indian for the "meeting of two streams."

•**NEIHART,** Town; Cascade County; Pop. 91; Zip Code 59465; Elev. 5635; Lat. 46-56-10 N long. 110-44-08 W; The town was named for James I. Neihart, a prospector who discovered minerals near here.

•**OPHEIM,** Town; Valley County; Pop. 210; Zip Code 59250; Elev. 3265; Lat. 48-51-21 N long. 106-24-27 W; Named for Alfred S. Opheim, the town's second postmaster.

•**OUTLOOK,** Town; Sheridan County; Pop. 122; Zip Code 59252; Lat. 48-53-21 N long. 104-46-36 W; Said to be so named when a stranger entering the saloon here was told "lookout!" and avoided being hit by a hurled glass. The word was turned around and the name for the town became Outlook.

•**PHILIPSBURG,** Town; Granite County Seat; Pop. 1,138; Zip Code 59858; Elev. 5270; Lat. 46-20-10 N long. 113-17-45 W; Settled about 1864 and named for Phillip Deidesheimer, first superintendent of the St. Louis Montana Gold and Silver Mining Company.

•**PLAINS,** Town; Sanders County; Pop. 1,116; Zip Code 59859; Elev. 2468; Lat. 47-27-41 N long. 114-53-03 W; Originally called Horse Plains because the Indians spent the winters here with their horses. Later shortened to Plains.

•**PLENTYWOOD,** City; Sheridan County Seat; Pop. 2,476; Zip Code 59254; Lat. 48-46-31 N long. 104-33-14 W; So named because a cattle outfit driving across the treeless prairie found firewood here.

•**PLEVNA,** Town; Fallon County; Pop. 191; Zip Code 59344; Lat. 46-25-07 N long. 104-31-07 W; Bulgarian settlers named this town after Plevna, the city in their homeland.

•**RICHEY,** Town; Dawson County; Pop. 417; Zip Code 59259; Lat. 47-38-39 N long. 105-04-00 W: Named in honor of Clyde C. Richey, the town's first postmaster.

•**RONAN,** City; Lake County; Pop. 1,530; Zip Code 59864; Lat. 47-31-40 N long. 114-05-59 W; This city takes its name from Major Peter Ronan, who wrote a history of the Flathead Indians.

•**ROUNDUP,** City; Musselshell County Seat; Pop. 2,119; Zip Code 59072; Elev. 3226; Lat. 46-26-53 N long. 108-32-20 W; Once a "roundup" place for cattle which grazed in the valley, the city was founded about 1883.

•**RYEGATE,** Town; Golden Valley County Seat; Pop. 273; Zip Code 59074; Lat. 46-18-04 N long. 109-15-26 W; Rye fields in the area suggested the name for this town.

•**SACO,** Town; Phillips County; Pop. 252; Zip Code 59261; Elev. 2175; Lat. 48-27-30 N long. 107-20-21 W; "Either named for the Sack-on Indian tribe of Maine, or from Sacajawea, a guide on the Lewis and Clark Expedition.

•**ST. IGNATIUS,** Town; Lake County; Pop. 877; Zip Code 59865; Lat. 47-19-10 N long. 114-05-36 W; Founded as a Catholic mission in 1854 and named for St. Ignatius Loyola, the founder of the Society of Jesus.

•**SCOBEY,** City; Daniels County Seat; Pop. 1,382; Zip Code 59263; Elev. 2507; Lat. 48-47-27 N long. 105-25-12 W; Named for Major C.R.A. Scobey, an agent of the Fort Peck Indian Reservation.

•**SHELBY,** City; Toole County Seat; Pop. 3,142; Zip Code 59474; Elev. 3286; Lat. 48-30-14 N long. 111-51-22 W; Founded in 1891 and named for Peter P. Shelby, general manager of the Montana-Central Railroad.

•**SHERIDAN,** Town; Madison County; Pop. 646; Zip Code 59749; Lat. 45-27-37 N long. 112-11-40 W; Established about 1866 and named in honor of General Philip H. Sheridan of Civil War fame.

•**SIDNEY,** City; Richland County Seat; Pop. 5,726; Zip Code 59270; Elev. 1931; Lat. 47-42-45 N long. 104-09-19 W; Named for Sidney Walters, a settler.

•**STANFORD,** Town; Judith Basin County Seat; Pop. 595; Zip Code 59479; Elev. 4284; Lat. 47-08-53 N long. 110-13-02 W; Settlers Calvin and Edward Bowers named this town after their former home of Stanfordville, New York.

•**STEVENSVILLE,** Town; Ravalli County; Pop. 1,207; Zip Code 59870; Elev. 3370; Lat. 46-30-28 N long. 114-05-18 W; Established about 1868 and named for Isaac Ingle Stevens.

•**SUNBURST,** Town; Toole County; Pop. 476; Zip Code 59482; Elev. 3348; Lat. 48-52-50 N long. 111-54-17 W; William George Davis suggested the name Sunburst, descriptive of the way the sun rose over the valley.

•**SUPERIOR,** Town; Mineral County Seat; Pop. 1,054; Zip Code 59872; Elev. 2744; Lat. 47-11-36 N long. 114-53-28 W; An early settler named this town after his former home of Superior, Wisconsin.

•**TERRY,** City; Prairie County Seat; Pop. 929; Zip Code 59349; Elev. 2253; Lat. 46-47-20 N long. 105-18-38 W; Founded about 1882 and named for General Alfred H. Terry.

•**THOMPSON FALLS,** Town; Sanders County Seat; Pop. 1,478; Zip Code 59873; Elev. 2419; Lat. 47-35-49 N long. 115-20-33 W; Named for David Thompson, a fur trader who worked this area around 1809.

•**THREE FORKS,** Town; Gallatin County; Pop. 1,247; Zip Code 59752; Elev. 3968; Lat. 45-53-36 N long. 111-32-56 W; Located near the joining of the Madiosn, Gallatin and Jefferson River forks with the Missouri River.

•**TOWNSEND,** City; Broadwater County Seat; Pop. 1,587; Zip Code 59644; Elev. 3848; Lat. 46-19-09 N long. 111-30-53 W; Townsend was named for an official of the Northern Pacific Railroad.

•**TROY,** Town; Lincoln County; Pop. 1,088; Zip Code 59935; Elev. 1888; Lat. 48-27-38 N long. 115-53-27 W; First called Lake City, then Troy after Troy Morrow, a local resident.

•**TWIN BRIDGES,** Town; Madison County; Pop. 437; Zip Code 59754; Elev. 4627; Lat. 45-32-22 N long. 112-20-02 W; Named for two bridges which span the Jefferson river near town.

•**VALIER,** Town; Pondera County; Pop. 640; Zip Code 59486; Elev. 3805; Lat. 48-18-15 N long. 112-15-15 W; The town was named for Peter Valier, who supervised the building of the Montana Western Railroad.

•**VIRGINIA CITY,** Town; Madison County Seat; Pop. 192; Zip Code 59755; Elev. 5822; Lat. 45-17-42 N long. 111-56-28 W; In 1864 this became the first incorporated town in Montana. First named Varina for the wife of Jefferson Davis, it was later corrupted to Virginia.

•**WALKERVILLE,** City; Silver Bow County; Pop. 887; Named for the Walker brothers who operated the Alice Mine near here.

•**WEST YELLOWSTONE,** Town; Gallatin County; Pop. 735; Zip Code 59758; Elev. 6667; Lat. 44-39-39 N long. 111-06-14 W; Located at the western entrance to Yellowstone Park. The town was originally called Yellowstone. Renamed West Yellowstone in 1920.

•**WESTBY,** Town; Sheridan County; Pop. 291; Zip Code 59275; Lat. 48-52-16 N long. 104-03-21 W; Once the most westerly town in North Dakota. The town moved across the border to Montana when the railroad came. Danish settlers named it "west" for its location and "by" meaning town.

•**WHITE SULPHUR SPRINGS,** City; Meagher County Seat; Pop. 1,302; Zip Code 59645; Lat. 46-32-46 N long. 110-53-55 W; So named because white deposits were found around the sulphur hot springs here.

•**WHITEFISH,** City; Flathead County; Pop. 3,703; Named for a nearby lake which in turn was named for the numerous whitefish that lived there.

•**WHITEHALL,** Town; Jefferson County; Pop. 1,030; Zip Code 59759; Lat. 45-52-15 N long. 112-05-46 W; E. G. Brooke built a large white ranch house here and named it for its resemblence to a similar building in Whitehall, Illinois. That later became the name for the town.

•**WIBAUX,** Town; Wibaux County Seat; Pop. 782; Zip Code 59353; Lat. 46-59-06 N long. 104-11-17 W; Named for Pierre Wibaux, a French Hugenot who settled here.

•**WINIFRED,** Town; Fergus County; Pop. 155; Zip Code 59489; Lat. 47-33-06 N long. 109-22-42 W; Either named for Winifred Sewall, daughter of Ed. D. Dewall, or for Winifred Rockefeller.

295

NEBRASKA

•**ABIE,** Village; Butler County; Pop. 107; Lat. 41-20-03 N long. 096-56-55 W; Named Abie in 1877, for Abagail Stevens, the wife of the man who filed the application.

•**ADAMS,** Village; Gage County; Pop. 395; Zip Code 68301; Lat. 40-27-30 N long. 096-30-35 W; The village was named for settler John O. Adams, who founded Adams Township in 1873.

•**AINSWORTH,** City; Brown County Seat; Pop. 2,256; Zip Code 69210; Lat. 42-32-54 N long. 099-51-26 W; Incorporated in 1883 and named for Captain James E. Ainsworth, a chief engineer for the railroad company.

•**ALBION,** City; Boone County Seat; Pop. 1,997; Zip Code 68620; Elev. 1916; Lat. 41-41-16 N long. 098-00-05 W; Named after Albion, Michigan. "Albion" is the poetical name for England.

•**ALDA,** Village; Hall County; Pop. 601; Zip Code 68810; Elev. 3751; Lat. 40-52-14 N long. 098-28-07 W; First called Pawnee. Later named for the first white child born in the town.

•**ALEXANDRIA,** Village; Thayer County; Pop. 255; Zip Code 68303; Lat. 40-14-49 N long. 097-23-15 W; Established in 1871 and named in honor of S.J. Alexander, the Nebraska Secretary of State.

•**ALLEN,** Village; Dixon County; Pop. 390; Zip Code 68710; Lat. 42-24-54 N long. 096-50-38 W; Named for pioneer, Henry Allen, who homesteaded this land in 1870.

•**ALLIANCE,** City; Box Butte County Seat; Pop. 9,869; Zip Code 69301; Lat. 42-06-13 N long. 102-52-03 W; First called Grand Lake. Later named by G.W. Holdrege, who is said to have selected Alliance because it was a single word, different from and name in the state and was near the beginning of the alphabet.

•**ALMA,** City; Harlan County Seat; Pop. 1,369; Zip Code 68920; Lat. 40-06-06 N long. 099-21-37 W; The townsite was selected in part by N.P. Cook of the Cheyenne Colony, and named for his daughter.

•**ALVO,** Village; Cass County; Pop. 144; Zip Code 68304; Lat. 40-52-17 N long. 096-23-03 W; The postoffice in Washington, D.C. named this village without any apparent reference to a specific person or place.

•**AMHERST,** Village; Buffalo County; Pop. 269; Zip Code 68812; Lat. 40-50-14 N long. 099-16-06 W; John N. Hamilton, railroad president, named the village after Amherst College in Massachusetts.

•**ANOKA,** Village; Boyd County; Pop. 24; Probably named after Anoka, Minnesota, which was taken from the Dakota Indian word meaning "on both sides."

•**ANSELMO,** Village; Custer County; Pop. 187; Zip Code 68813; Lat. 41-37-03 N long. 099-51-53 W; Platted in 1886 and named for Anselmo B. Smith, a civil engineer for the Lincoln Town-Site Company.

•**ANSLEY,** Village; Custer County; Pop. 644; Zip Code 68814; Lat. 41-17-17 N long. 099-22-51 W; Settled in 1886 and named for a lady who investedin real estate when the town was founded.

•**ARAPAHOE,** City; Furnas County; Pop. 1,107; Zip Code 68922; Lat. 40-18-17 N long. 099-53-46 W; Taken from the name of the Indian tribe. The word *Arapahoe* means "traders."

•**ARCADIA,** Village; Valley County; Pop. 412","; Zip Code 68815; Lat. 41-25-28 N long. 099-07-27 W; First called Brownville, for settler, Porter Brown. Laid out in 1885 and named Arcadia by Mrs. Samuel A. Hawthorne, who understood the meaning of the name to be "the feast of flowers."

•**ARLINGTON,** Village; Washington County; Pop. 1,117; Zip Code 68002; Lat. 41-27-13 N long. 096-21-18 W; Originally called Bell Creek, for the Bell family who settled at a nearby creek. In 1882, the name was changed to Arlington, after the city in Virginina.

•**ARNOLD,** Village; Custer County; Pop. 813; Zip Code 69120; Lat. 41-25-25 N long. 100-11-41 W; Laid out in 1883 and named in honor of George Arnold who settled in the area about 1875.

•**ARTHUR,** Village; Arthur County Seat; Pop. 124; Zip Code 69121; Lat. 41-34-15 N long. 101-41-19 W; Named after the county, which in turn was named oin honor of President Chester A. Arthur.

•**ASHLAND,** City; Saunders County; Pop. 2,274; Zip Code 68003; Lat. 41-02-34 N long. 096-22-16 W; Organized in 1870 and named for the home in Kentucky of statesman, Henry Clay.

•**ASHTON,** Village; Sherman County; Pop. 273; Zip Code 68817; Lat. 41-14-50 N long. 098-47-39 W; Settler Joh P. Taylor, named this village after his former home in Ashton, Illinois.

•**ATKINSON,** City; Holt County; Pop. 1,521; Zip Code 68713; Lat. 42-31-48 N long. 098-58-38 W; Settled in 1876 and named in honor of Colonel John Atkinson of Detroit, who had large land holdings in the area.

•**ATLANTA,** Village; Phelps County; Pop. 102; Zip Code 68923; Elev. 2339; Lat. 40-22-08 N long. 099-28-24 W; 4Either named for Atlanta, Georgia or for Atlanta, Illinois, which got its name from the city in Georgia.

•**AUBURN,** City; Nemaha County Seat; Pop. 3,482; Zip Code 68305; Lat. 40-23-18 N long. 095-50-33 W; Comprisedof two towns orginally named Sheridan and Calvert. They were incorporated under the name Auburn, after Auburn, New York.

•**AURORA,** City; Hamilton County Seat; Pop. 3,717; Zip Code 68818; Lat. 40-47-30 N long. 097-58-19 W; David Stone, a settler, named this cityfor his wife's former home of Aurora, Illinois.

•**AVOCA,** Village; Cass County; Pop. 242; Zip Code 68307; Lat. 40-47-40 N long. 096-07-03 W; Platted in 1857 and named for Avoca Precinct. The name may have come from Thomas Moore's poem "Sweet Vale of Avoca."

•**AXTELL,** Village; Kearney County; Pop. 602; Zip Code 68924; Lat. 40-28-41 N long. 099-07-34 W; Named for the engineer of a Burlington passenger train.

•**AYR,** Village; Adams County; Pop. 112; Zip Code 68925; Lat. 40-26-10 N long. 098-26-28 W; Established in 1878 and named for Dr. Ayr, a director of the Burlington and Missouri River Railroad.

•**BANCROFT,** Village; Cuming County; Pop. 552; Zip Code 68004; Lat. 42-00-36 N long. 096-34-19 W; Named in honor of George Bancroft, American historian.

•**BARADA,** Village; Richardson County; Pop. 36; Located in Barada Precinct which was named for an early settler, Antoine Barada.

•**BARNESTON,** Village; Gage County; Pop. 155; Zip Code 68309; Lat. 40-02-48 N long. 096-34-20 W; Named for Francis M. Barnes, a member of the townsite company that established the village.

•BARTLETT, Village; Wheeler County Seat; Pop. 144; Zip Code 68622; Lat. 41-52-59 N long. 098-33-04 W; Founded about 1885 by Ezra Bartlett Hitchell and named in his honor.

•BARTLEY, Village; Red Willow County; Pop. 342; Zip Code 69020; Lat. 40-15-03 N long. 100-18-25 W; Platted in 1886 and named for Rev. Allen Bartley, a homesteader and Methodist Episcopal minister.

•BASSETT, City; Rock County Seat; Pop. 1,009; Zip Code 68714; Lat. 42-35-02 N long. 099-32-16 W; This city was named for J.W. Bassett, a rancher, who brought the first herd of cattle into the state in 1871.

•BATTLE CREEK, Village; Madison County; Pop. 948; Zip Code 68715; Lat. 42-00-38 N long. 097-35-02 W; The village took its name from a nearby creek, which was said to be the site of a battle between Nebraska volunteer militiamen and Pawnee Indians.

•BAYARD, City; Morrill County; Pop. 1,435; Zip Code 69334; Lat. 41-45-22 N long. 103-19-24 W; In 1887 Millard and Jap Senteny named this town for their former home of Bayard, Iowa.

•BAZILE MILLS, Village; Knox County; Pop. 54; So called after an early mill, built here on Bazile Creek. The name Bazile probably came from Bazeilles, France.

•BEATRICE, City; Gage County Seat; Pop. 12,891; Zip Code 68310; Lat. 40-16-04 N long. 096-44-29 W; Incorporated in 1858 and named for Julia Beatrice Kinney, daughter of Judge J.F. Kinney of the Utah Supreme Court.

•BEAVER CITY, City; Furnas County Seat; Pop. 775; Zip Code 68926; Lat. 099-49-39 W; Named for its location in the Beaver River valley.

•BEAVER CROSSING, Village; Seward County; Pop. 458; Zip Code 68313; Lat. 40-46-39 N long. 097-16-47 W; Platted in 1887 and named for a place nearby where the overland trail from Leavenworth crossed Beaver Creek.

•BEE, Village; Seward County; Pop. 192; Zip Code 68314; Lat. 41-00-22 N long. 097-03-28 W; Located in one of sixteen precincts in Seward County labelled A through P. This village is in Precinct B and was therefore named Bee.

•BEEMER, Village; Cuming County; Pop. 853; Zip Code 68716; Lat. 41-55-44 N long. 096-48-32 W; First called Rockcreek. The townsite was later changed and the village renamed for A.D. Beemer.

•BELDEN, Village; Cedar County; Pop. 151; Zip Code 68717; Lat. 097-12-19 W; Named for Scott Belden, a paymaster on the railroad from Sioux City to O'Neill.

•BELGRADE, Village; Nance County; Pop. 195; Zip Code 68623; Lat. 41-28-04 N long. 098-04-06 W; James Main named this village after Belgrade, Serbia because he thought the landscape resembled that of the city on the Danube.

•BELLEVUE, City; Sarpy County; Pop. 21,813; Zip Code 68005; Lat. 41-09-14 N long. 095-54-31 W; The oldest city in Nebraska. Fur trader, Manuel Lisa came herein 1805 and named it Bellevue because it was a *belle vue* or "beautiful view."

•BELLWOOD, Village; Butler County; Pop. 407; Zip Code 68624; Lat. 41-20-36 N long. 097-14-26 W; Named in honor of Jesse D. Bell, who founded the town and planted rows of trees here.

•BELVIDERE, Village; Thayer County; Pop. 158; Zip Code 68315; Lat. 40-15-15 N long. 097-33-28 W; Possibly named after Belvidere, Illinois or New Jersey. Belvidere is derived from an Italian word *belvedere* meaning "beautiful to see."

•BENEDICT, Village; York County; Pop. 228; Zip Code 68316; Lat. 41-00-20 N long. 097-36-24 W; Incorporated in 1890 and named in honor of E.C. Benedict, president of the Kansas City and Omaha Railroad.

•BENKELMAN, City; Dundy County Seat; Pop. 1,235; Zip Code 69021; Lat. 40-02-58 N long. 101-31-52 W; First called Collinsville, after early settler, Moses Collins. Later renamed for J.G. Benkelman, another settler.

•BENNET, Village; Lancaster County; Pop. 523; Zip Code 68317; Lat. 40-40-52 N long. 096-30-04 W; Platted in 1871 and name for John Bennett, a railroad official and local resident.

•BENNINGTON, Village; Douglas County; Pop. 631; Zip Code 68007; Lat. 41-21-49 N long. 096-09-23 W; The village was named after Bennington, Vermont, which took its name from Governor Bennington Wentworth of New Hampshire.

•BERTRAND, Village; Phelps County; Pop. 775; Zip Code 68927; Lat. 40-31-39 N long. 099-37-54 W; Organized in 1885 and named for an official of the Chicago, Burlington and Quincy Railroad.

•BERWYN, Village; Custer County; Pop. 104; Zip Code 68819; Lat. 41-21-03 N long. 099-30-00 W; First called Janesville. The name Berwyn is said to be after a railroad surveyor.

•BIG SPRINGS, Village; Deuel County; Pop. 505; Zip Code 69122; Elev. 3367; Lat. 41-03-42 N long. 102-04-28 W; Named for a big spring located here.

•BLADEN, Village; Webster County; Pop. 298; Zip Code 68928; Lat. 40-19-25 N long. 098-35-44 W; This village was platted in 1886 by the Lincoln Land Company.

•BLAIR, City; Washington County Seat; Pop. 6,418; Zip Code 680+; Lat. 41-32-41 N long. 096-08-32 W; Platted in 1869 and named in honor of John I. Blair, a railroad financeer, who owned land here.

•BLOOMFIELD, City; Knox County; Pop. 1,393; Zip Code 68718; Lat. 42-35-53 N long. 097-38-42 W; Named for Bloomfield Dyer, an early landowner.

•BLOOMINGTON, Village; Franklin County; Pop. 138; Zip Code 68929; Lat. 40-05-23 N long. 099-02-15 W; This village was probably named after Bloomington, Illinois.

•BLUE HILL, City; Webster County; Pop. 883; Zip Code 68930; Lat. 40-15-00 N long. 098-26-57 W; First called Belmont. Later named Blue Hill for the city's location in the hills near the Blue River.

•BLUE SPRINGS, City; Gage County; Pop. 521; Zip Code 68318; Lat. 40-08-05 N long. 096-39-40 W; Established in 1857 and named for several springs near the Blue River, known as "Blue Springs."

•BOYS TOWN, Village; Douglas County; Pop. 622; Zip Code 68010; Lat. 41-15-40 N long. 096-07-54.

•BRADSHAW, Village; York County; Pop. 383; Zip Code 68319; Lat. 40-52-57 N long. 097-44-52 W; J.M. Richards helped establish this village in 1890 and named it for his wife, whose maiden name was Mary Bradshaw.

•BRADY, Village; Lincoln County; Pop. 377; Zip Code 69123; Lat. 40-55-22 N long. 100-40-49 W; Named for Mr. Brady, one of the earliest settlers here, who was killed by Indians, or according to some accounts, by a French companion.

•BRAINARD, Village; Butler County; Pop. 275; Zip Code 68626; Lat. 41-10-56 N long. 097-00-00 W; The village was named in honor of David Brainard, a missionary to the Indians.

•**BREWSTER,** Village; Blaine County Seat; Pop. 46; Zip Code 68821; Lat. 41-56-14 N long. 099-51-53 W; Founded by George W. Brewster, a newspaper man, and named in his honor.

•**BRIDGEPORT,** City; Morrill County Seat; Pop. 1,668; Zip Code 69336; Lat. 41-39-57 N long. 103-05-48 W; The city was named for a local bridge over the North Platte River.

•**BRISTOW,** Village; Boyd County; Pop. 123; Zip Code 68719; Lat. 42-53-40 N long. 098-34-32 W; Named for Benjamin H. Bristow, U.S. Secretary of the Treasury under President Grant.

•**BROADWATER,** Village; Morrill County; Pop. 161; Zip Code 69125; Lat. 41-35-51 N long. 102-50-57 W; Mr. Moeller, president of the Union Pacific Railroad, named this village in honor of his personal friend, General Broadwater.

•**BROCK,** Village; Nemaha County; Pop. 189; Zip Code 68320; Lat. 40-28-49 N long. 095-57-35 W; Named for Mr. Brock, a railroad superintendent, also said to be a local resident.

•**BROKEN BOW,** City; Custer County Seat; Pop. 3,979; Zip Code 68822; Elev. 2475; Lat. 41-24-16 N long. 099-38-17 W; Platted in 1882 and named for a broken bow and arrow found at an Indian campsite near here.

•**BROWNVILLE,** Village; Nemaha County; Pop. 203; Zip Code 68321; Lat. 40-23-57 N long. 095-39-34 W; Founded in 1856 and named for Richard Brown who owned the site.

•**BRULE,** Village; Keith County; Pop. 438; Zip Code 69127; Lat. 41-05-45 N long. 101-53-18 W; The village takes its name from the Brule tribe of the Teton Sioux Indians.

•**BRUNING,** Village; Thayer County; Pop. 330; Zip Code 68322; Lat. 40-20-10 N long. 097-33-50 W; Named for early settlers, Frank Bruning and his brother.

•**BRUNO,** Village; Butler County; Pop. 154; Zip Code 68001; Lat. 41-20-01 N long. 096-56-56 W; Moravian settlers named this village after the city of Brno or Brunn in Moravia. It was later corrupted to Bruno.

•**BRUNSWICK,** Village; Antelope County; Pop. 190; Zip Code 68720; Lat. 42-20-11 N long. 097-58-12 W; Named after Brunswick, Germany, a center for the beet industry. Settler, Henry Nagle, suggested the name after he raised an immense sugar beet on his farm.

•**BURCHARD,** Village; Pawnee County; Pop. 122; Zip Code 68323; Lat. 40-08-59 N long. 096-20-56 W; Named for Mr. Burchard, a local minister.

•**BURR,** Village; Otoe County; Pop. 101; Zip Code 68324; Lat. 40-32-04 N long. 096-18-05 W; First called Burr Oak after a grove of the trees near here. The name was shortened to avoid confusion with the town of Burr Oak, Kansas.

•**BURWELL,** City; Garfield County Seat; Pop. 1,383; Zip Code 68823; Lat. 41-46-53 N long. 099-08-05 W; Platted in 1883 by Frank Webster and first called Webster's Town. Later named for Miss Burwell, the fiance of Frank Webster's brother.

•**BUSHNELL,** Village; Kimball County; Pop. 187; Zip Code 69128; Lat. 41-13-41 N, long. 103-53-33 W. Named for Mr. Bushnell, a civil engineer on the Union Pacific Railroad.

•**BUTTE,** Village; Boyd County Seat; Pop. 529; Zip Code 68722; Elev. 1811; Lat. 42-55-47 N, long. 098-50-22 W. Named for a rocky elevation at the south end of the village.

•**BYRON,** Village; Thayer County; Pop. 154; Zip Code 68325; Lat. 40-00-19 N, long. 097-46-06 W. The village takes its name from Lord Byron, the English poet.

•**CAIRO,** Village; Hall County; Pop. 737; Zip Code 68824; Lat. 41-00-08 N, long. 098-36-28 W. The Lincoln Land Company named this village, probably after Cairo, Egypt.

•**CALLAWAY,** Village; Custer County; Pop. 579; Zip Code 68825; Lat. 41-17-30 N, long. 099-55-06 W. Platted in 1885 and named for S.R. Callaway, general manager of the Union Pacific Railroad.

•**CAMBRIDGE,** City; Furnas County; Pop. 1,206; Zip Code 69022; Lat. 40-16-56 N, long. 100-10-14 W. First called Medicine Creek. Later renamed after Cambridge, Massachusetts.

•**CAMPBELL,** Village; Franklin County; Pop. 441; Zip Code 68932; Lat. 40-17-41 N, long. 098-43-53 W. Named for Mr. Campbell, a member of the townsite company that founded this village.

•**CARLETON,** Village; Thayer County; Pop. 160; Zip Code 68326; Lat. 40-18-07 N, long. 097-40-29 W. Originally named Coldrain, or Coleraine on some old maps. The owner of the townsite later renamed the village in honor of his son, Carleton.

•**CARROLL,** Village; Wayne County; Pop. 246; Zip Code 68723; Lat. 42-16-30 N, long. 097-11-23 W. Named in honor of Charles Carroll, one of the signers of the Declaration of Independence.

•**CEDAR BLUFFS,** Village; Saunders County; Pop. 632; Zip Code 68015; Lat. 41-23-48N, long. 096-36-35 W. The village takes its name from a nearby bluff with cedar trees overlooking the Platte River.

•**CEDAR CREEK,** Village; Cass County; Pop. 311; Zip Code 68016; Lat. 41-02-00 N, long. 096-06-04 W. Laid out in 1865 and named for a nearby creek that had cedar trees along its banks.

•**CEDAR RAPIDS,** Village; Boone County; Pop. 447; Zip Code 68627; Lat. 41-33-24 N, long. 098-08-49 W. Named for its location on the Cedar River.

•**CENTER,** Village; Knox County Seat; Pop. 123; Zip Code 68724; Lat. 42-36-27 N, long. 097-52-26 W. So named because of its situation at the center of Knox County.

•**CENTRAL CITY,** City; Merrick County Seat; Pop. 3,083; Zip Code 68826; Lat. 41-06-48 N, long. 097-59-52 W. Named for its central location in Nebraska's agricultural region.

•**CERESCO,** Village; Saunders County; Pop. 836; Zip Code 68017; Lat. 41-03-30 N, long. 096-38-37 W. Settlers, Richard Nelson and Hod Andrus, named this after their former home of Ceresco, Michigan.

•**CHADRON,** City; Dawes County Seat; Pop. 5,933; Zip Code 69337; Lat. 42-49-30 N, long. 102-59-46 W. Platted in 1885 and named for Pierre Chadron, a French-Indian trapper who lived in this area.

•**CHAMBERS,** Village; Holt County; Pop. 390; Zip Code 68725; Lat. 42-12-18 N, long. 098-44-51 W. W.D. Matthews of the *Frontier* named this town after his friend B.F. Chambers, register of the land office in Niobrara.

•**CHAPMAN,** Village; Merrick County; Pop. 349; Zip Code 68827; Lat. 41-01-15 N, long. 098-09-35 W. Named after the roadmaster for the Union Pacific Railroad.

•**CHAPPELL,** City; Deuel County Seat; Pop. 1,095; Zip Code 69129; Lat. 41-05-42 N, long. 102-27-52 W. Laid out and named for John Chappell, president of the Union Pacific Railroad.

•**CHESTER,** Village; Thayer County; Pop. 435; Zip Code 68327; Lat. 40-00-36 N, long. 097-37-09 W. Laid out in 1880 by the Lincoln Land Company.

•CLARKS, Village; Merrick County; Pop. 445; Zip Code 68628; Lat. 41-13-02 N, long. 097-50-18 W. This village was named for Silas Henry H. Clark, acting head of the Union Pacific Railroad.

•CLARKSON, City; Colfax County; Pop. 817; Zip Code 68629; Lat. 41-43-29 N, long. 097-07-18 W. Platted in 1886 and named for T.S. Clarkson, first postmaster of Schuyler, Nebraska, who helped establish an office here.

•CLATONIA, Village; Gage County; Pop. 273; Zip Code 68328; Lat. 40-27-49 N, long. 096-51-03 W. Originally a part of Clay County. The village was named after Clatonia Creek, which took its name from the county.

•CLAY CENTER, City; Clay County Seat; Pop. 962; Zip Code 68933; Lat. 40-31-15 N, long. 098-03-10 W. Surveyed in 1879 and named for its location at the center of Clay County.

•CLEARWATER, Village; Antelope County; Pop. 409; Zip Code 68726; Lat. 42-10-18 N, long. 098-11-22 W. Originally called Antelope. Later named Clearwater after a nearby creek.

•CODY, Village; Cherry County; Pop. 177; Zip Code 69211; Lat. 42-56-15 N, long. 101-14-51 W. Named for Thomas Cody, a foreman of the water supply construction gang when the railroad was built here.

•COLERIDGE, Village; Cedar County; Pop. 673; Zip Code 68727; Lat. 42-30-19 N, long. 097-12-09 W. Called Coleridge after Lord Coleridge, who was visiting the United States at the time the village was established.

•COLON, Village; Saunders County; Pop. 148; Zip Code 68018; Lat. 41-17-51 N, long. 096-36-27 W. The first postmaster here named the office after his former home of Colon, Michigan. It later was adopted as the name for the village.

•COLUMBUS, City; Platte County Seat; Pop. 17,328; Zip Code 68601; Lat. 41-25-56 N, long. 097-21-21 W. Laid out in 1856 by the Columbus Company, a group of men who formerly lived in Columbus, Ohio.

•COMSTOCK, Village; Custer County; Pop. 168; Zip Code 68828; Lat. 41-33-22 N, long. 099-14-29 W. Named for W.H. Comstock, who moved a store building from Wescott to this townsite.

•CONCORD, Village; Dixon County; Pop. 145; Zip Code 68728; Lat. 42-23-00 N, long. 096-59-19 W. Marvin Hughitt, a railroad president named this village after the Concord bridge battlesite in Massachusetts.

•COOK, Village; Johnson County; Pop. 341; Zip Code 68329; Lat. 40-30-36 N, long. 096-09-39 W. Mr. Cook, who owned land in the area, named this town in honor of his children.

•CORDOVA, Village; Seward County; Pop. 129; Zip Code 68330; Lat. 40-42-58 N, long. 097-21-00 W. Established in 1887 and named Hunkins, after C.W. Hunkins, the first postmaster. Changed to Cordova after Cordova, Spain.

•CORNLEA, Village; Platte County; Pop. 40; Zip Code 68630; Lat. 41-40-43 N, long. 097-33-55 W. Laid out in 1886. The name is a combination of the words "corn" and "lea" meaning cornland.

•CORTLAND, Village; Gage County; Pop. 403; Zip Code 68331; Lat. 40-30-19 N, long. 096-42-23 W. The name was suggested by railroad officials, probably after Cortland, New York.

•COTESFIELD, Village; Howard County; Pop. 82; Zip Code 68829; Lat. 41-21-30 N, long. 098-37-59 W. Named in honor of Miss Coates who with General Augiur and his daughter made a visit to the area.

•COWLES, Village; Webster County; Pop. 48; Platted in 1878 and named in honor of W.D. Cowles, who was a frieght agent for the Burlington and Missouri River Railroad.

•COZAD, City; Dawson County; Pop. 4,453; Zip Code 69130; Lat. 40-51-42 N, long. 099-59-03 W. Settled about 1873 by pioneers from Ohio. They named the city for John J. Cozad, the head of their company.

•CRAB ORCHARD, Village; Johnson County; Pop. 82; Zip Code 68332; Lat. 40-19-59 N, long. 096-25-14 W. Named for a crab-apple orchard originallyfound at the townsite.

•CRAIG, Village; Burt County; Pop. 237; Zip Code 68019; Lat. 41-47-06 N, long. 096-21-41 W. Named for William Stewart Craig, who owned the land on which the town was built.

•CRAWFORD, City; Dawes County; Pop. 1,315; Zip Code 69339; Lat. 42-40-54 N, long. 103-24-35 W. This city was named for Captain Jack Crawford, a poet, scout and soldier, who was stationed at Fort Robinson in the 1880's.

•CREIGHTON, City; Knox County; Pop. 1,341; Zip Code 68729; Lat. 42-29-12 N, long 097-54-12 W. Named in honor of John A. Creighton of Omaha, founder of the John A. Creighton Medical College of Creighton University.

•CRESTON, Village; Platte County; Pop. 210; Zip Code 68631; Lat. 41-42-30 N, long. 097-21-38 W. Named for its location on the crest of a hill overlooking the Elkhorn and Platte Rivers.

•CRETE, City; Saline County; Pop. 4,872; Zip Code 68333; Lat. 40-37-24 N, long. 096-57-15 W. Platted in 1870 and named Blue River City. A post office to the north of the town was named Crete, after Crete, Illinois. The two places were eventually consolidated as a single city called Crete.

•CROFTON, Village; Knox County; Pop. 948; Zip Code 68730; Lat. 42-43-47 N, long. 097-29-40 W. Named by J.T.M. Pierce, wither for his former home of Crofton Court England, or after an Englishman named Crofton.

•CROOKSTON, Village; Cherry County; Pop. 86; Zip Code 69212; Lat. 42-55-34 N, long. 100-45-05 W. Platted in 1894 and named after W.T. Crook, a yard master for the railroad.

•CULBERTSON, Village; Hitchcock County; Pop. 767; Zip Code 69024; Lat. 40-13-46 N, long. 10050-05 W. Named for Mr. Culbertson, a well-known Indian agent.

•CURTIS, City; Frontier County; Pop. 1,014; Zip Code 69025; Lat. 40-37-54 N, long. 100-30-51 W. Named after nearby Curtis Creek. The creek was named for a trapper who settled in the area.

•CUSHING, Village; Howard County; Pop. 48; The village was named for James Cushing, an early settler.

•DAKOTA CITY, City; Dakota County Seat; Pop. 1,440; Zip Code 68731; Lat. 42-24-59 N, long. 096-25-02 W. Surveyed and platted bythe Dakota CityLand Companyin 1855-56. Named for the Dakota Indians.

•DALTON, Village; Cheyenne County; Pop. 345; Zip Code 69131; Lat. 41-24-32 N, long. 102-58-19 W. The village began as a station for the railroad and was probably named for Dalton, Massachusetts.

•DANBURY, Village; Red Willow County; Pop. 143; Zip Code 60926; Lat. 40-02-16 N, long. 100-24-03 W. The first postmaster, George Gilbert, named this town for his former home of Danbury, Connecticut.

•DANNEBROG, Village; Howard County; Pop. 356; Zip Code 68831; Lat. 41-07-09 N, long. 098-32-39 W. Danish settlers named this village in honor of the flag of Denmark.

•**DAVENPORT,** Village; Thayer County; Pop. 445; Zip Code 68335; Lat. 40-18-46 N, long. 097-48-38 W. Laid out in 1872 and named for Davenport, Iowa.

•**DAVEY,** Village; Lancaster County; Pop. 190; Zip Code 68336; Lat. 40-58-58 N, long. 096-40-06 W. Platted in 1886 and named for Michael Davey, who owned the land on which the townsite was located.

•**DAVID CITY,** City; Butler County Seat; Pop. 2,514; Zip Code 68632; Lat. 41-15-22 N, long. 097-07-30 W. The city was named after Mrs. Miles, whose maiden name was David, because she deed a large tract of land for the townsite.

•**DAWSON,** Village; Richardson County; Pop. 215; Zip Code 68337; Lat. 40-07-36 N, long. 095-49-49 W. Sometimes called Noraville. The town was laid out in 1871 and named Dawson, for settler Joshua Dawson, who built a flour and feed mill here.

•**DAYKIN,** Village; Jefferson County; Pop. 207; Zip Code 68338; Lat. 40-19-09 N, long. 097-18-00 W. Named for John Daykin, who owned land here.

•**DECATUR,** Village; Burt County; Pop. 723; Zip Code 68020; Lat. 42-00-27 N, long. 096-15-05 W. Located in 1855 by the Decatur Town and Ferry Company and named for Stephen Decatur, a member of the company.

•**DENTON,** Village; Lancaster County; Pop. 164; Zip Code 68339; Lat. 40-44-21 N, long. 096-50-35 W. Laid out in 1871 and Daniel M. Denton, a homesteader.

•**DESHLER,** City; Thayer County; Pop. 997; Zip Code 68340; Lat. 40-08-24 N, long. 097-43-19 W. Named for John Deshler, the original owner of the townsite.

•**DE WITT,** Village; Saline County; Pop. 642; Incorporated in 1857 and named for Mr. DeWitt, said to be a railroad man.

•**DEWEESE,** Village; Clay County; Pop. 69; Zip Code 68934; Lat. 40-21-15 N, long. 098-08-09 W. The village was named for James W. Deweese, an attorney for the Burlington Railroad.

•**DICKENS,** Village; Lincoln County; Pop. 24; Named in honor of the English author, Charles Dickens.

•**DILLER,** Village; Jefferson County; Pop. 311; Zip Code 68342; Lat. 40-06-31 N, long. 096-56-06 W. Laid out in 1881 and named for H.H. Diller, an early settler.

•**DIX,** Village; Kimball County; Pop. 275; Zip Code 69133; Lat. 41-13-52 N, long. 103-29-14 W. Dix was named after Dixon, Illinois, the former home of Margaret Robertson, a landowner.

•**DIXON,** Village; Dixon County; Pop. 127; Zip Code 68732; Lat. 42-24-56 N, long. 096-59-45 W. Located in Dixon County which was named for an early pioneer.

•**DODGE,** Village; Dodge County; Pop. 815; Zip Code 68633; Lat. 41-43-12 N, long. 096-52-48 W. Platted by the Pioneer Town-Site Company in 1886 and named for George A. Dodge, a settler.

•**DONIPHAN,** Village; Hall County; Pop. 696; Zip Code 68832; Elev. 1940; Lat. 40-46-35 N long. 098-22-00 W: Either named for Colonel John Doniphan, an attorney for the railroad, or for Colonel Alexander William Doniphan.

•**DORCHESTER,** Village; Saline County; Pop. 611; Zip Code 68343; Lat. 40-38-49 N long. 097-06-50 W; Originally called DeWitt. Later changed to Dorchester, either after a suburb of Boston, Massachusetts, or after Dorchester, England.

•**DOUGLAS,** Village; Otoe County; Pop. 207; Zip Code 68344; Lat. 40-35-304 N long. 096-23-19 W; First called Hendricks after an early settler. Later changed to Douglas, for a girl from the Douglas family, which owned land here.

•**DUNCAN,** Village; Platte County; Pop. 410; Zip Code 68634; Lat. 41-23-20 N long. 097-29-26 W; Laid out in 1871 as Jackson. Later renamed, either for a resident, or after the town of Duncan, Illinois.

•**DU BOIS,** Village; Pawnee County; Pop. 178; Zip Code 68345; Lat. 40-02-10 N long. 096-02-50 W; Named in honor of Mr. Du Bois, chief engineer of the first railroad built here.

•**DUNBAR,** Village; Otoe County; Pop. 216; Zip Code 68346; Lat. 40-40-00 N long. 096-01-38 W; First called Wilson, then Dennison, and finally Dunbar, after either Thomas Dunbar, an early resient, or John Dunbar, a landowner.

•**DUNNING,** Village; Blaine County; Pop. 182; Zip Code 68833; Lat. 41-49-39 N long. 100-06-10 W; Established in Dunning Precinct as a station on the Chicago, Burlington and Quincy Railroad. The precinct was named for an early resident.

•**DWIGHT,** Village; Butler County; Pop. 221; Zip Code 68635; Lat. 41-04-53 N long. 097-01-00 W; First called Lone Star. Later changed to Dwight, because many of the town settlers were from Dwight, Illinois.

•**EAGLE,** Village; Cass County; Pop. 832; Zip Code 68347; Lat. 40-48-57 N long. 096-25-44 W; Probably named for the eagles that once lived in the area. The village has also been called Sunlight.

•**EDDYVILLE,** Village; Dawson County; Pop. 121; Zip Code 68834; Lat. 41-00-39 N long. 099-37-25 W; Railroad promoters named this town after Eddyville, Iowa, which was named for J.P. Eddy, a trader.

•**EDGAR,** City; Clay County; Pop. 705; Zip Code 68935; Lat. 40-22-09 N long. 097-57-55 W; First called Eden. Later changed to Edgar, in honor of the son of pioneer, Ed Graham.

•**EDISON,** Village; Furnas County; Pop. 210; Zip Code 68936; Lat. 40-16-4 N long. 099-46-27 W; The post office and the village were named for Edaward Rohr, who was nicknamed Eddie.

•**ELBA,** Village; Howard County; Pop. 218; Zip Code 68835; Lat. 41-17-06 N long. 098-34-06 W; Founded in 1882 and named for the "elbow curve" in the railroad to the south of town.

•**ELGIN,** City; Antelope County; Pop. 807; Zip Code 68636; Lat. 41-58-56 N long. 098-04-54 W; E. Gailey, a post office official, selected the name Elgin, after Elgin, Illinois.

•**ELK CREEK,** Village; Johnson County; Pop. 144; Zip Code 68348; Lat. 40-17-11 N long. 096-07-31 W; The village was called Elk Creek after the nearby stream, which was named for the elk that lived in the area.

•**ELKHORN,** City; Douglas County; Pop. 1,344; Zip Code 68022; Lat. 41-17-08 N long. 096-14-03 W; Incorporated in 1856 and called Elkhorn or Elkhorn Station for its location on the Elkhorn River.

•**ELM CREEK,** Village; Buffalo County; Pop. 862; Zip Code 68836; Elev. 2262; Lat. 40-43-04 N long. 099-22-28 W; The village took its name from a nearby creek which had elm trees growing along its banks.

•ELMWOOD, Village; Cass County; Pop. 598; Zip Code 68349; Lat. 40-50-31 N long. 096-17-36 W; Named for a grove of elm trees that grew nearby.

•ELSIE, Village; Perkins County; Pop. 133; Zip Code 69134; Lat. 40-50-52 N long. 101-23-07 W; Either named for Elsie Perkins, daughter of Charles E. Perkins, after whom the county was named, of for a daughter of merchant, Joseph Perkins.

•ELWOOD, Village; Gosper County Seat; Pop. 716; Zip Code 68937; Lat. 40-35-21 N long. 099-51-41 W; Named for Elwood Thomas, who owned a farm near here.

•ELYRIA, Village; Valley County; Pop. 62; Zip Code 68837; Lat. 41-40-48 N long. 099-00-18 W; First called Eldon. The name was changed to Elyria to avoid confusion with another Eldon inthe state.

•EMERSON, Village; Dixon County; Pop. 874; Zip Code 68733; Lat. 42-16-41 N long. 096-43-30 W; Platted in 1883 and named in honor of author, Ralph Waldo Emerson.

•EMMET, Village; Holt County; Pop. 73; Zip Code 68734; Lat. 42-28-26 N long. 098-48-15 W; Settlers named this town for the Irish patriot, Robert Emmet.

•ENDICOTT, Village; Jefferson County; Pop. 198; Zip Code 68350; Lat. 40-04-48 N long. 097-05-43 W; Named in honor of William C. Endicott, U.S. Secretary of War under President Cleveland.

•ERICSON, Village; Wheeler County; Pop. 132; Zip Code 68637; Lat. 41-46-44 N long. 098-40-40 W; The village was named for Christensen Erickson and his two sons, Eric and Peter. Peter homesteaded land here and sold it for the development of the townsite.

•EUSTIS, Village; Frontier County; Pop. 460; Zip Code 69028; Lat. 40-39-41 N long. 100-01-44 W; Named for P.S. Eustis, a passenger agent for the Burlington Railroad.

•EWING, Village; Holt County; Pop. 520; Zip Code 68735; Lat. 42-15-42 N long. 098-20-36 W; Established in 1874 and named for James Ewing, the first postmaster.

•EXETER, Village; Fillmore County; Pop. 807; Zip Code 68351; Elev. 2552; Lat. 40-38-35 N long. 097-26-55 W; Settlers from Exeter, New Hampshire named this village after their former home.

•FAIRBURY, City; Jefferson County Seat; Pop. 4,885; Zip Code 68352; Lat. 40-08-23 N long. 097-10-33 W; Woodford G. McDowell platted the cityin 1869 and named it for his former home of Fairbury, Illinois.

•FAIRFIELD, City; Clay County; Pop. 543; Zip Code 68938; Lat. 40-25-59 N long. 098-05-59 W; First called White Elm, later Frankfort. The name was changed to Fairfield, probably after Fairfield, Illinois or Iowa, to avoid confusion with another town named Frankfort in the state.

•FAIRMONT, Village; Fillmore County; Pop. 767; Zip Code 68354; Lat. 40-38-05 N long. 097-35-03 W; Pioneers called this place Hesperia. It was later named Fairmont, because of its elevated location and fine view.

•FALLS CITY, City; Richardson County Seat; Pop. 5,374; Zip Code 68355; Lat. 40-08-23 N long. 095-35-19 W; Named for its location on the Great Nemaha River. The city was incorporated in 1860.

•FARNAM, Village; Dawson County; Pop. 268; Zip Code 69029; Lat. 40-42-23 N long. 100-12-57 W; Started in 1887 and named for Henry W. Farnam, a railroad builder.

•FARWELL, Village; Howard County; Pop. 165; Zip Code 68838; Lat. 41-12-55 N long. 098-37-38 W; First settled by Polish immigrants and called Posen. The name was later changed to Farwell, the Danish word for "goodbye."

•FILLEY, Village; Gage County; Pop. 172; Zip Code 68357; Lat. 40-17-07 N long. 096-31-56 W; Founded in 1882 by Elijah Filley and named in his honor.

•FIRTH, Village; Lancaster County; Pop. 384; Zip Code 68358; Lat. 40-32-03 N long. 096-36-10 W; Laid out in 1873 and named for Superintendent Firth of the Atchison and Nebraska Railroad.

•FORDYCE, Village; Cedar County; Pop. 148; W; Zip Code 68736; Lat. 42-41-55 N long. 097-21-41 W; Named for William B. Fordyce, a train dispatcher for the railroad.

•FORT CALHOUN, City; Washington County; Pop. 641; Zip Code 68023; Lat. 41-27-18 N Long. 096-01-25 W; Earlier known as Fort Atkinson, after Brevet Brigadier General Henry Atkinson. Later renamed for J.C. Calhoun, U.S. Secretary of War.

•FOSTER, Village; Pierce County; Pop. 81; Zip Code 68737; Lat. 42-16-25 N long. 097-39-48 W; The village was named for George Foster, a station agent for the railroad, who owned land near here.

•FRANKLIN, City; Franklin County Seat; Pop. 1,167; Zip Code 68939; Lat. 40-05-47 N Long. 098-57-13 W; Settled in 1879 and named in honor of Benjamin Franklin.

•FREMONT, City; Dodge County Seat; Pop. 23,979; Zip Code 68025; Lat. 41-25-42 N long. 096-29-33 W; Platted in 1856 and named for John C. Fremont, the western explorer.

•FRIEND, City; Saline County; Pop. 1,079; Zip Code 68359; Lat. 40-38-59 N long. 097-17-06 W; Surveyed in 1873 and named for Charles E. Friend, who owned a farm here, and became the town's first postmaster and storekeeper.

•FULLERTON, City; Nance County Seat; Pop. 1,506; Zip Code 68638; Lat. 41-21-44 N long. 097-58-32 W; The city was surveyed and platted in 1878, and named for early settler Randall Fuller.

•FUNK, Village; Phelps County; Pop. 189; Zip Code 68940; Lat. 40-27-30 N long. 099-15-01 W; Settled about 1887 and named for P.C. Funk, and early resident.

•GANDY, Village; Logan County; Pop. 53; Named for James Gandy,an early settler, who built the first court house in Logan County.

•GARLAND, Village; Seward County; Pop. 257; Zip Code 68360; Lat. 40-56-42 N long. 096-59-00 W; German settlers named this village Germantown. It was later changed to Garland in honor of a local soldier, Ray Garland, who died in France during the World War.

•GARRISON, Village; Butler County; Pop. 68; Surveyed by a Mr. Sargent, who named the village for William Lloyd Garrison, the famous anti-slavery leader.

•GENEVA, City; Fillmore County Seat; Pop. 2,400; Zip Code 68361; Lat. 40-31-32 N long. 097-35-43 W; The city was established on land owned by Colonel J.A. McCaully, and his daughter Emma, named it after Geneva, New York.

•GENOA, City; Nance County; Pop. 1,090; Zip Code 68640; Lat. 41-26-47 N long. 097-44-03 W; Mormons settled here in 1857 and named the city after Genoa, Italy.

•GERING, City; Scotts Bluff Seat; Pop. 7,760; Zip Code 69341; Lat. 41-50-16 N long. 103-39-46 W; The city was named for Martin Gering, a member of the original town-site company and a Civil War veteran.

301

•**GIBBON**, City; Buffalo County; Pop. 1,531; Zip Code 68840; Lat. 40-44-51 N long. 098-50-31 W; Named for Major-General John Gibon who served in the Mexican and the Civil War.

•**GILEAD**, Village; Thayer County; Pop. 69; Zip Code 68362; Lat. 40-08-45 N long. 097-24-49 W; Located in Gilead Precinct, which was named for Mount Gilead in Palestine.

•**GILTNER**, Village; Hamilton County; Pop. 400; Zip Code 68841; Lat. 41-43-25 N long. 097-00-13 W; Platted in 1886 and first called Bromfield. The name was changed to Giltner in honor of Rev. Henry M. Giltner, a Presbyterian minister and missionary.

•**GLENVILLE**, Village; Clay County; Pop. 363; Zip Code 68941; Lat. 40-30-02 N long. 098-15-03 W; First known Georgetown, or Dogtown because at one time the town had more dogs than people. Later changed to Glenville, which was shortened to Glenvil to avoid confusion with other Glenvilles.

•**GOEHNER**, Village; Seward County; Pop. 165; Zip Code 68364; Lat. 40-49-58 N long. 097-13-043 W; Platted in 1887 and named for John F. Goehner, a merchant and member of the Nebraska State Legislature.

•**GORDON**, City; Sheridan County; Pop. 2,167; Zip Code 69343; Lat. 42-48-31 N long. 102-12-00 W: Named for John Gordon who traveled in this area with a pioneer wagon train.

•**GOTHENBURG**, City; Dawson County; Pop. 3,479; Zip Code 69138; Elev. 2997; Lat. 40-55-57 N long. 100-09-38 W; E.G. West named this city after Gothenburg, Sweden.

•**GRAFTON**, Village; Fillmore County; Pop. 185; Zip Code 68365; Lat. 40-37-50 N long. 097-42-50 W; Started as a railroad station, the village was probably named for Grafton, Massachusetts.

•**GRAND ISLAND**, City; Hall County Seat; Pop. 33,180; Zip Code 688+; Lat. 40-55-43 N long. 098-21-03 W; Laid out in 1866 and named after a large island in the Platte River.

•**GRANT**, City; Perkins County Seat; Pop. 1,270; Zip Code 69140; Elev. 3148; Lat. 40-50-35 N long. 101-43-26 W; Named in honor of President Ulysses S. Grant.

•**GREELEY CENTER**, Village; Greeley County Seat; Pop. 597; Named for its location at the center of Greeley County. The county was named for Horace Greeley.

•**GREENWOOD**, Village; Cass County; Pop. 587; Zip Code 68366; Lat. 40-57-42 N long. 096-26-29 W; The village was named after nearby Greenwood Creek, which took its name from an early settler.

•**GRESHAM**, Village; York County; Pop. 320; Zip Code 68367; Lat. 41-01-40 N long. 097-23-56 W; Platted in 1887 by the Pioneer Town-Site Company and named for Walter Quinton Gresham, U.S. Secretary of State under President Cleveland.

•**GRETNA**, City; Sarpy County; Pop. 1,609; Zip Code 68028; Lat. 38-34-10 N long. 090-13-41 W; Probably named for Gretna Green, in Dumfriesshire, Scotland.

•**GROSS**, Village; Boyd County; Pop. 2; The village was named for B.B. Gross, a homesteader who also became the town's first postmaster.

•**GUIDE ROCK**, Village; Webster County; Pop. 344; Zip Code 68942; Lat. 40-04-25 N long. 098-19-48 W; Named after a nearby rocky bluff that rises above the old bed of the Republican River and was a prominent landmark for early pioneers.

•**GURLEY**, Village; Cheyenne County; Pop. 212; Zip Code 69141; Lat. 41-19-16 N long. 102-58-27 W.

•**HADAR**, Village; Pierce County; Pop. 286; The name was taken from the German word *hader* meaning "argument" after two early settlers had a dispute here.

•**HAIGLER**, Village; Dundy County; Pop. 225; Zip Code 69030; Lat. 40-00-37 N long. 101-56-13 W; Named for Jacob Haigler, a prominent landowner who had a cattle business here.

•**HALLAM**, Village; Lancaster County; Pop. 290; Zip Code 68368; Lat. 40-32-13 N long. 096-47-06 W; Laid out by the Kansas Town and Land Company in 1892.

•**HALSEY**, Village; Thomas County; Pop. 144; Zip Code 69142; Lat. 41-54-12 N long. 100-16-16 W; Named for Halsey Yates, a surveyor for the railroad.

•**HAMLET**, Village; Hayes County; Pop. 74; Zip Code 69031; Lat. 40-23-02 N long. 101-14-05 W; First called Hudson after its founder. The name Hamlet meaning "a small town" was chosen later because there was already another Hudson in the state.

•**HAMPTON**, Village; Hamilton County; Pop. 419; Zip Code 68843; Lat. 40-52-49 N long. 097-53-05 W; Platted in 1879 and called Murray. Later changed to Hampton to avoid confusion with another town named Murray along the railroad.

•**HARBINE**, Village; Jefferson County; Pop. 50; Laid out in 1881 and named for Colonel Thomas Harbine.

•**HARDY**, Village; Nuckolls County; Pop. 232; Zip Code 68943; Lat. 40-00-33 N long. 097-56-23 W; The village was named after an official of the Burlington Railroad.

•**HARRISON**, Village; Sioux County Seat; Pop. 361; Zip Code 69346; Lat. 42-41-18 N long. 103-52-56 W; First called Bowen, after John S. Bowen of Blair Nebraska. The post office in Washington later changed the name to Harrison, after President Benjamin Harrison.

•**HARTINGTON**, City; Cedar County Seat; Pop. 1,730; Zip Code 68739; Lat. 42-37-14 N long. 097-15-48 W; Named for Lord Hartington, who had visited the United States a few years earlier.

•**HARVARD**, City; Clay County; Pop. 1,217; Zip Code 68944; Lat. 40-37-07 N long. 098-05-40 W; Officials of the chicago, Burlington and Quincy Railroad named this city after Harvard University in Massachusetts.

•**HASTINGS**, City; Adams County Seat; Pop. 23,045; Zip Code 68901; Lat. 40-35-19 N long. 098-23-38 W; Named in honor of Colonel D. T. (or T.D.) Hastings, of the St. Joseph and Grand Island Railroad.

•**HAYES CENTER**, Village; Hayes County Seat; Pop. 231; Zip Code 69032; Lat. 40-30-31 N long. 101-01-09 W; Established in 1885 and named for its location at the center of Hayes County.

•**HAY SPRINGS**, Village; Sheridan County; Pop. 794; Zip Code 69347; Lat. 42-41-01 N long. 102-41-22 W; The town name is descriptive of its location in meadow lands fed by numerous springs.

•**HAZARD**, Village; Sherman County; Pop. 75; Zip Code 68844; Lat. 41-05-29 N long. 099-04-36 W; It is said that when a conference was held to decide the village name, one man said he would "hazard some name," and that remark suggested the town name of Hazard.

•**HEARTWELL**, Village; Kearney County; Pop. 87; Zip Code 68945; Lat. 40-34-19 N long. 098-47-23 W; Established along the railroad and named for J.B. Heartwell, president of the Nebraska Loan and Trust Company, and a former state senator.

•**HEBRON,** City; Thayer County Seat; Pop. 1,906; Zip Code 68370; Lat. 40-10-11 N long. 097-35-01 W; Pioneer settlers who were associated with the Disciples of Christ named this city after Hebron, Palestine, which is mentioned in the Bible.

•**HEMINGFORD,** Village; Box Butte County; Pop. 1,023; Zip Code 69348; Lat. 42-19-07 N long. 103-04-20 W; Joseph Hare named this village after his former home of Hemmingford in Canada, changing the spelling to just one *m*.

•**HENDERSON,** City; York County; Pop. 1,072; Zip Code 68371; Lat. 40-46-47 N long. 097-48-39 W; Settled about 1866 and named for pioneers David Henderson and his son John.

•**HENDLEY,** Village; Furnas County; Pop. 39; Zip Code 68946; Lat. 40-07-50 N long. 099-58-18 W; Named for Mr. Hendley, and early resident.

•**HENRY,** Village; Scotts Bluff County; Pop. 155; The village was named for Henry Nichols, a boy who drowned in the Platte River a year before the town was established.

•**HERMAN,** Village; Washington County; Pop. 340; Zip Code 68029; Lat. 41-40-29 N long. 096-12-55 W; Platted in 1871 and named for Samuel Herman, a conductor on the Omaha and Northwestern Railroad.

•**HERSHEY,** Village; Lincoln County; Pop. 633; Zip Code 69143; Lat. 41-09-22 N long. 101-00-03 W; Named about 1890 for J.H. Hershey, a rancher and prominent landowner.

•**HICKMAN,** Village; Lancaster County; Pop. 687; Zip Code 68372; Lat. 40-37-18 N long. 096-37-51 W; Laid out in 1872 by C.H. Hickman and named in his honor.

•**HILDRETH,** Village; Franklin County; Pop. 394; Zip Code 68947; Lat. 40-20-11 N long. 099-02-36 W; Named for Carson Hildreth who owned the land on which the village was built.

•**HOLBROOK,** Village; Furnas County; Pop. 297; Zip Code 68948; Lat. 40-18-14 N long. 100-00-35 W; First called Burton's Bend after Ben Burton's Indian Trading Post at a bend in the Republican River. Later named Holbrook for a railroad official.

•**HOLDREGE,** City; Phelps County Seat; Pop. 5,624; Zip Code 68949; Lat. 40-26-20 N long. 099-22-20 W; Established in 1883 and named for George W. Holdredge, Superintendent of the Chicago, Burlington and Quincy Railroad.

•**HOLSTEIN,** Village; Adams County; Pop. 241; Zip Code 68950; Lat. 40-27-46 N long. 098-39-09 W; Platted in 1887 and named after the Schleswig-Holstein peninsula in Germany.

•**HOMER,** Village; Dakota County; Pop. 564; Zip Code 68030; Lat. 42-19-11 N long. 096-29-43 W; Surveyed in 1874 and named for Homer, the Greek poet.

•**HOOPER,** City; Dodge County; Pop. 932; Zip Code 68031; Lat. 41-36-46 N long. 096-32-47 W; Named for Hon. Samuel Hooper, a member of Congress during the Civil War.

•**HORDVILLE,** Village; Hamilton County; Pop. 155; Zip Code 68846; Lat. 41-04-48 N long. 097-52-58 W; Settled in 1907 and named for T.B. Hord, who once owned land in this area.

•**HOSKINS,** Village; Wayne County; Pop. 306; Zip Code 68740; Lat. 42-06-39 N long. 097-18-21; Named for a member of the land company that established this town.

•**HOWARD CITY,** Village; Howard County; Pop. 228; Probably named after the county, which was named for General Oliver Otis Howard of Civil War fame.

•**HOWELLS,** Village; Colfax County; Pop. 677; Zip Code 68641; Platted in 1886 and named for J.S. Howell, a prominent resident. The railroad company called this town Howells, and the post office called it Howell.

•**HUBBARD,** Village; Dakota County; Pop. 234; Zip Code 68741; Elev. 1172; Lat. 42-23-08 N long. 096-35-25 W; Laid out in 1880 and anmed in honor of Judge Asahel W. Hubbard, president of the Covington, Columbus and Black Hills Railroad.

•**HUBBELL,** Village; Thayer County; Pop. 71; Zip Code 68375; Lat. 40-00-36 N long. 097-29-43 W; The Lincoln Land and Loan Company laid out his town in 1880 and named it for Hubbell H. Johnson, who owned the land on which the site was located.

•**HUMBOLDT,** City; Richardson County; Pop. 1,176; Zip Code 68376; Lat. 40-09-57 N long. 095-56-43 W; Founded by O.J. Tinker who probably named the city for Baron Friedrich Heinrich Alexander von Humboldt, the famous German scientist.

•**HUMPHREY,** City; Platte County; Pop. 799; Zip Code 68642; Lat. 41-39-03 N long. 097-29-40 W; Plated in 1880 and named for Humphrey, New York, the former home of Mrs. Leach, the town's postmistriss.

•**HUNTLEY,** Village; Harlan County; Pop. 64; Zip Code 68951; Lat. 40-12-34 N long. 099-17-25 W; Named for Mr. Huntley, a railroad official who was instrumental in securing right-of-way for the tracks.

•**HYANNIS,** Village; Grant County Seat; Pop. 336; Zip Code 69350; Lat. 41-59-54 N long. 101-45-38 W; A railroad official named this town after Hyannis, Massachusetts.

•**IMPERIAL,** City; Chase County Seat; Pop. 1,941; Zip Code 69033; Elev. 3284; Lat. 40-31-05 N long. 101-38-31 W; Laid out by homesteader Thomas Mercier who came from Canada and named this city either for a town in his former country, or for the British Imperial Government.

•**INDIANOLA,** City; Red Willow County; Pop. 856; Zip Code 69034; Lat. 40-14-06 N long. 100-25-07 W; I. Starbuck named this city after his former home of Indianola, Iowa.

•**INMAN,** Village; Holt County; Pop. 181; Zip Code 68742; Lat. 42-22-57 N long. 098-31-47 W; Established about 1881 and named for W.H. Inman, an early settler and storekeeper.

•**ITHACA,** Village; Saunders County; Pop. 156; Zip Code 68033; Lat. 41-09-44 N long. 096-32-18 W; The county surveyor suggested the name Ithaca, after Ithaca, New York.

•**JACKSON,** Village; Dakota County; Pop. 287; Zip Code 68743; Elev. 1120; Lat. 42-26-51 N long. 096-33-50 W; First called Franklin. The name was changed to Jackson because there was already another Franklin in the state.

•**JANSEN,** Village; Jefferson County; Pop. 204; Zip Code 68377; Lat. 40-11-05 N long. 097-04-56 W; Named for Peter Jansen, a Mennonite immigrant who acted as proprietor of this town.

•**JOHNSON,** Village; Nemaha County; Pop. 87; Zip Code 68378; Lat. 40-24-22 N long. 096-00-59 W; Laid out in 1869 and named for Julius A. Johnson who owned the land on which the village was built.

•**JOHNSTOWN,** Village; Brown County; Pop. 78; Zip Code 69214; Lat. 42-34-20 N long. 100-03-15 W; Homesteaded by John Berry, a mail stagecoach driver. The village was named in his honor.

•**JULIAN,** Village; Nemaha County; Pop. 87; Zip Code 68379; Lat. 40-31-12 N long. 095-52-04 W; Named for Julian Bahaud, a Frenchman who owned several farms in the area.

•**JUNIATA,** Village; Adams County; Pop. 703; Zip Code 68955; Lat. 40-35-20 N long. 098-30-20 W; Named after the Juniata River in Pennsylvania.

•**KEARNEY,** City; Buffalo County Seat; Pop. 21,158; Zip Code 68847; Elev. 2153; Lat. 40-42-03 N long. 099-04-43 W; First called Fort Childs, then Kearney Junction, and finally Kearney. The present name comes from General Stephen Watts Kearny, who served in the War of 1812 and the Mexican War.

•**KENESAW,** Village; Adams County; Pop. 854; Zip Code 68956; Lat. 40-37-16 N long. 098-39-25 W; Surveyed in 1872. The village was named for the battle of Kenesaw Mountain in Georgia in 1864.

•**KENNARD,** Village; Washington County; Pop. 372; Zip Code 68034; Lat. 41-28-23 N long. 096-12-09 W; Incorporated in 1895 and named for Hon. Thomas P. Kennard, Nebraska's first Secretary of State.

•**KILGORE,** Village; Cherry County; Pop. 76; Zip Code 69216; Elev. 2919; Lat. 42-56-22 N long. 100-57-27 W; Named for an early settler.

•**KIMBALL,** City; Kimball County Seat; Pop. 3,120; Zip Code 69145; Lat. 41-13-59 N long. 103-39-28 W; Originally called Antelopeville, for the antelope that lived in the area. Renamed Kimball in 1885, for Thomas L. Kimball, vice-president and general manager of the Union Pacific Railroad.

•**LAMAR,** Village; Chase County; Pop. 60; Zip Code 69035; Lat. 40-34-20 N long. 101-58-42 W; Named in honor of Lucius Q.C. Lamar, U.S. Secretary of the Interior under President Cleveland.

•**LAUREL,** City; Cedar County; Pop. 508; Zip Code 68745; Lat. 42-25-38 N long. 097-05-24 W; W.M. Martin organized the Original Town-Site Company of Laurel, and named this city for his daughter Laura.

•**LAWRENCE,** Village; Nuckolls County; Pop. 350; Zip Code 68957; Lat. 40-17-28 N long. 098-15-32 W; Named for an official of the Burlington Railroad.

•**LEBANON,** Village; Red Willow County; Pop. 102; Zip Code 69036; Lat. 40-02-56 N long. 100-16-19 W; Mr. Bradbury, the first postmaster, suggested the name Lebanon, after the Cedars of Lebanon in the Bible.

•**LEIGH,** Village; Colfax County; Pop. 509; Zip Code 68643; Lat. 41-42-18 N long. 097-14-16 W; Built on land originally owned by A.M. Walling, and named in honor of his wife, whose maiden name was Leigh.

•**LESHARA,** Village; Saunders County; Pop. 133; The village was named for Pita Lesharu, a Pawnee Indian chief.

•**LEWELLEN,** Village; Garden County; Pop. 368; Zip Code 69147; Lat. 41-19-51 N long. 102-08-23 W; Named for Frank Lewellen who ran the first store and post office here about 1887.

•**LEWISTON,** Village; Pawnee County; Pop. 102; Zip Code 68380; Lat. 40-14-34 N long. 096-24-19 W; Either named for a local resident, or for the town of Lewiston, Maine.

•**LEXINGTON,** City; Dawson County Seat; Pop. 6,898; Zip Code 68850; Lat. 40-46-50 N long. 099-44-25 W; First called Plum Creek. Later changed to Lexington, after the Battle of Lexington of the Revolutionary War.

•**LIBERTY,** Village; Gage County; Pop. 105; Zip Code 68381; Lat. 40-05-17 N long. 096-28-43 W; Situated in Liberty Township. The village took its name from the post office established in this vicinity.

•**LINCOLN,** City; Lancaster County Seat; Pop. 171,932; Zip Code 685+; Lat. 40-48-40 N long. 096-40-02 W; First called Lancaster, after the county. Located as the state capital in 1867 and renamed in honor of Abraham Lincoln.

•**LINDSAY,** Village; Platte County; Pop. 383; Zip Code 68644; Lat. 41-42-03 N long. 097-41-21 W; John Walker, an early settler named this town after Lindsay in Ontario, Canada.

•**LINWOOD,** Village; Butler County; Pop. 119; Zip Code 68036; Lat. 41-24-44 N long. 096-55-54 W; Sara Johnson, a settler, suggested the name Linwood for the linn or basswood trees that grew in the area.

•**LITCHFIELD,** Village; Sherman County; Pop. 256; Zip Code 68852; Lat. 41-09-26 N long. 099-09-09 W; Laid out in 1886 and probably named after Litchfield, Connecticut.

•**LODGEPOLE,** Village; Cheyenne County; Pop. 413; Zip Code 69149; Elev. 3830; Lat. 41-08-52 N long. 102-38-10 W; Named after nearby Lodgepole Creek, which got its name because Indians used to cut lodgepoles for their teepees from trees that grew near the stream.

•**LONG PINE,** City; Brown County; Pop. 521; Zip Code 69217; Lat. 42-32-02 N long. 099-41-54 W; Settled in 1878 and named after Long Pine Creek. The stream was named for the pine trees that grew along its bluffs.

•**LOOMIS,** Village; Phelps County; Pop. 447; Zip Code 68958; Lat. 40-28-38 N long. 099-30-29 W; Organized about 1885 and named for N.H. Loomis, a railroad man.

•**LORTON VILLAGE,** Village; Otoe County; Pop. 47; Platted in 1881 and named Delta. Later called Cio, and finally, Lorton, after Robert Lorton, who owned a wholesale grocery business.

•**LOUISVILLE,** Village; Cass County; Pop. 1,022; Zip Code 68037; Elev. 1044; Lat. 40-59-49 N long. 096-09-32 W; Laid out in 1857. The village was probably named after Louisville, Kentucky.

•**LOUP CITY,** City; Sherman County Seat; Pop. 1,368; Zip Code 68853; Lat. 41-16-40 N long. 098-58-03 W; Named for its location in the Loup Valley. The word *loup* is the French translation of the Pawnee Indian named *skidi* meaning "wolf."

•**LUSHTON,** Village; York County; Pop. 33; Surveyed in 1887 and named for Mr. Lush, a railroad official.

•**LYNCH,** Village; Boyd County; Pop. 357; Zip Code 68746; Lat. 42-50-00 N long. 098-27-50 W; The town was probably named after an early settler.

•**LYONS,** City; Burt County; Pop. 1,214; Zip Code 68038; Lat. 41-56-14 N long. 096-28-27 W; Named for Waldo Lyon, a settler who came here from Arizona about 1869.

•**MADISON,** City; Madison County Seat; Pop. 1,950; Zip Code 68748; Lat. 41-49-40 N long. 097-27-26 W; Settled in 1868 and probably named for the county, which took its name from President James Madison.

•**MADRID,** Village; Perkins County; Pop. 284; Zip Code 69150; Elev. 3300; Lat. 40-51-00 N long. 101-32-21 W; First known as Trail City. Later platted and named Madrid, after Madrid, Spain.

•**MAGNET,** Village; Cedar County; Pop. 59; Zip Code 68749; Lat. 42-27-17 N long. 097-28-19 W; Established in 1893. B.E. Smith named this town after the magnet stone found here, saying that the place would "attract people as the magnet attracts iron."

•**MALCOLM,** Village; Lancaster County; Pop. 355; Zip Code 68402; Lat. 40-54-26 N long. 096-51-54 W; Laid out in 1877 and named for Malcolm A. Showers, who owned land here.

•MALMO, Village; Saunders County; Pop. 100; Zip Code 68040; Lat. 41-15-57 N long. 096-43-13 W; Settled by Swedes who named this village after Malmo, Sweeden.

•MANLEY, Village; Cass County; Pop. 124; Zip Code 68403; Lat. 40-55-04 N long. 096-09-56 W; Originally called Summit. Later named Manley, possibly for a rancher who lived in the area.

•MARQUETTE, Village; Hamilton County; Pop. 303; Zip Code 68854; Lat. 41-00-22 N long. 098-00-36 W; Platted in 1882 and named for Thomas M. Marquette, a member of the Lincoln Land Company.

•MARSLAND, Village; Dawes County; Pop. 27; Zip Code 69354; Lat. 42-26-43 N long. 103-18-08 W; Named for Thomas Marsland, general frieght agent of the Chicago, Burlington and Quincy Railroad.

•MARTINSBURG, Village; Dixon County; Pop. 100; Elev. 1252; Settled in 1872 and named for Jonathan Martin, an early resident.

•MASKELL, Village; Dixon County; Pop. 76; Zip Code 68751; Lat. 42-41-25 N long. 096-58-59 W; The Saint Paul Town-Site Company named this village for A.H. Maskell, who owned land in the area.

•MASON CITY, Village; Custer County; Pop. 196; Zip Code 68855; Lat. 41-13-15 N long. 099-17-57 W; Possibly named by settlers from Mason County, Virginia, or in honor of Judge O.P. Mason of Lincoln.

•MAXWELL, Village; Lincoln County; Pop. 410; Zip Code 69151; Elev. 2711; Lat. 41-04-26 N long. 100-31-22 W; Earlier known as McPherson after the nearby fort which was named for Major-General James B. McPherson. Later changed to Maxwell, after a railroad official.

•MAYWOOD, Village; Frontier County; Pop. 332; Zip Code 69038; Lat. 40-39-32 N long. 100-37-19 W; Originally called Laird, after James Laird. Renamed Maywood for May Wood, daughter of Israel Wood, who owned the land on which the town was built.

•MCCOOK, City; Red Willow County Seat; Pop. 8,404; Zip Code 69001; Lat. 40-12-18 N long. 100-37-42 W; Laid out in 1882 and called Fairview. Later changed to McCook, after Major-General Alexander McDowell McCook of Civil War fame.

•MCCOOL JUNCTION, Village; York County; Pop. 404; Zip Code 68401; Lat. 40-44-37 N long. 097-35-44 W; Located at a junction of the Chicago, Burlington and Quincy Railroad, and probably named for a local resident.

•MCGREW, Village; Scotts Bluff County; Pop. 110; Zip Code 69353; Lat. 41-44-55 N long. 103-24-52 W; Named for an Omaha resident who promoted the townsite here.

•MCLEAN, Village; Pierce County; Pop. 46; Zip Code 68747; Lat. 42-23-06 N long. 097-28-01 W; Probably named for McLean, Ohio.

•MEAD, Village; Saunders County; Pop. 506; Zip Code 68041; Lat. 41-13-37 N long. 096-29-17 W; First called Alvin, then Saunders, after the county. It was later changed to Mead, for Mr. Mead, a railroad official.

•MEADOW GROVE, Village; Madison County; Pop. 400; Zip Code 68752; Lat. 42-01-48 N long. 097-44-04 W; Named for a grove of trees that grew near the meadow here.

•MELBETA, Village; Scotts Bluff County; Pop. 151; Zip Code 69355; Lat. 41-46-53 N long. 103-30-54 W; The town was a railroad shipping place for beets, and was named from the German word *melbeta* said to mean "sugar beets."

•MEMPHIS, Village; Saunders County; Pop. 89; Zip Code 68042; Lat. 41-05-39 N long. 096-25-53 W; Settlers from Tennessee named this for their former home of Memphis in that state.

•MERNA, Village; Custer County; Pop. 389; Zip Code 68856; Lat. 41-29-03 N long. 099-45-32 W; Samuel Dunning, the first postmaster, suggested the name in honor of his daughter, Merna.

•MERRIMAN, Village; Cherry County; Pop. 159; Zip Code 69218; Lat. 42-55-06 N long. 101-47-57 W; First spelled Merryman. The town was named for John Merriman, a train master for the railroad.

•MILFORD, City; Seward County; Pop. 2,108; Zip Code 68405; Lat. 40-46-21 N long. 097-02-56 W; Settled in 1864 by J.L. Davison who built a mill at Weeping Water Falls just above a ford on the Blue River, thus suggesting the name for the town, Milford.

•MILLER, Village; Buffalo County; Pop. 147; Zip Code 68858; Lat. 40-55-40 N long. 099-23-30 W; The village was named for Dr. George L. Miller, who once owned land in the area.

•MILLIGAN, Village; Fillmore County; Pop. 332; Zip Code 68406; Lat. 40-29-56 N long. 097-23-11 W; Named for an official of the Kansas City and Omaha Railroad.

•MINATARE, City; Scotts Bluff County; Pop. 969; Zip Code 69356; Lat. 41-48-41 N long. 103-29-57 W; The city was named for the Minnetaree tribe of the Sioux Indians.

•MINDEN, City; Kearney County Seat; Pop. 2,939; Zip Code 68959; Elev. 2172; Lat. 40-29-53 N long. 098-57-02 W; Fred Bredemier, the city's first postmaster, named this for his former home of Minden, Germany.

•MITCHELL, City; Scotts Bluff County; Pop. 1,956; Zip Code 69357; Lat. 41-56-34 N long. 103-48-37 W; Named after nearby Fort Mitchell, which was named in honor of David D. Mitchell.

•MONOWI, Village; Boyd County; Pop. 18; The name is an Indian word meaning "flowers." At the time the town was founded there were many wildflowers growing in the area.

•MONROE, Village; Platte County; Pop. 294; Zip Code 68647; Lat. 41-28-26 N long. 097-35-48 W; Leander Gerrard and his brother founded this town in 1889 and named it in honor of President James Monroe.

•MOOREFIELD, Village; Frontier County; Pop. 36; Zip Code 69039; Elev. 2824; Lat. 40-41-12 N long. 100-24-04 W; Named for Mr. Moore, who originally owned the land on which the town was established.

•MORRILL, Village; Scotts Bluff County; Pop. 1,097; Zip Code 69358; Lat. 41-57-56 N long. 103-55-35 W; The village was named after Charles H. Morrill, who owned property here and was president of the Lincoln Land Company.

•MORSE BLUFF, Village; Saunders County; Pop. 132; Zip Code 68648; Lat. 41-25-56 N long. 096-45-52 W; Named in honor of Charles W. Morse, who once owned the land on which the town was located. "Bluff" was added to the name to avoid confusion with another place along the railroad line called Morse.

•MULLEN, Village; Hooker County Seat; Pop. 720; Zip Code 69152; Lat. 42-02-35 N long. 101-02-42 W; Railroad officials named this town after a contractor who worked in the area.

•MURDOCK, Village; Cass County; Pop. 242; Zip Code 68407; Lat. 40-55-29 N long. 096-16-44 W; Named after a member of the town-site company that established this village.

305

•**MURRAY,** Village; Cass County; Pop. 465; Zip Code 68409; Lat. 40-54-53 N long. 095-55-38 W; Originally called Fairview. The name was changed to Murray for Rev. George L. Murray, a United Presbyterian minister, and influential man in the town.

•**NAPER,** Village; Boyd County; Pop. 136; Zip Code 68755; Lat. 42-57-49 N long. 099-05-46 W; Homesteaded by Ralph Naper, who donated eighty acres for the townsite and named the village after himself.

•**NAPONEE,** Village; Franlkn County; Pop. 160; Zip Code 68960; Lat. 40-04-30 N long. 099-08-13 W; Settled in 1870 and named after a town in Canada.

•**NEBRASKA CITY,** City; Otoe County Seat; Pop. 7,127; Zip Code 68410; Lat. 40-40-43 N long. 095-51-37 W; First incorporated in 1855 and named after the state. The state got its name from the Indian word for the Platte River.

•**NEHAWKA,** Village; Cass County; Pop. 270; Zip Code 68413; Elev. 992; Lat. 40-49-43 N long. 095-59-21 W; The name Nehawka is a white man's approximation of the Indian name *Nigahoe* for a nearby creed. The name means "rustling water."

•**NELIGH,** City; Antelope County Seat; Pop. 1,893; Zip Code 68756; Lat. 42-07-51 N long. 098-01-40 W; Platted in 1873 and named for John D. Neligh, an early settler and landowner.

•**NELSON,** City; Nuckolls County Seat; Pop. 733; Zip Code 68961; Lat. 40-12-01 N long. 098-03-57 W; Surveyed in 1873 and named for C. Nelson, who owned the land on which the city was established.

•**NEMAHA,** Village; Nemaha County; Pop. 209; Zip Code 68414; Lat. 40-20-22 N long. 095-40-31 W; Incorporated in 1856 and named for the Nemaha River. The Otoe Indinas called the river *Nimaha* meaning "miry water."

•**NENZEL,** Village; Cherry County; Pop. 28; Zip Code 69219; Lat. 42-55-42 N long. 101-06-04 W; Named for George Nenzel, who owned the land on which the town was built.

•**NEWCASTLE,** Village; Dixon County; Pop. 348; Zip Code 68757; Lat. 42-39-10 N long. 096-52-33 W; Gustavus Smith built the first house here and called it his "new castle." That later became the name for the town.

•**NEWMAN GROVE,** City; Madison County; Pop. 930; Zip Code 68758; Lat. 41-44-42 N long. 097-46-30 W; Named for a grove of cottonwood trees that grew nearby on land belonging to Newman Warren.

•**NEWPORT,** Village; Rock County; Pop. 141; Zip Code 68759; Lat. 42-36-01 N long. 099-19-23 W; The village was named after the Newport Bridge which spans the Niobrara River about ten miles north of town.

•**NICKERSON,** Village; Dodge County; Pop. 254; Zip Code 6804; Lat. 41-32-13 N long. 096-28-11 W; Founded by Reynolds K. Nickerson, a contractor for the railroad, and named in his honor.

•**NIOBRARA,** Village; Knox County; Pop. 419; Zip Code 68760; Lat. 42-45-16 N long. 098-01-42 W; Named for the Niobrara River. Omaha and Ponca Indians called the river *Nibthatha* or "spreading water."

•**NORA,** Village; Nuckolls County; Pop. 24; Mr. Whiting, who owned a farm near here, selected the name Nora, after Nora, Illinois.

•**NORFOLK,** City; Madison County; Pop. 19,449; Zip Code 68738; Lat. 42-06-09 N long. 097-26-39 W; Residents wanted to name this city Nor'fork, a contraction of North Fork, because of the town's location of the north fork of the river. The post office changed the spelling to Norfolk.

•**NORMAN,** Village; Kearney County; Pop. 58; Zip Code 68963; Lat. 40-28-51 N long. 098-47-20 W; The village was named for John and Carl Norman who owned eighty acres on which the town was built.

•**NORTH BEND,** City; Dodge County; Pop. 1,368; Zip Code 68649; Lat. 41-27-46 N long. 096-46-51 W; Named for its location on the bend farthest to the north in the Platte River.

•**NORTH LOUP,** Village; Valley County; Pop. 405; Zip Code 68859; Lat. 41-29-43 N long. 098-46-18 W; The village was named for its location in the vally of the North Loup River.

•**NORTH PLATTE,** City; Lincoln County Seat; Pop. 24,479; Zip Code 69101; Lat. 41-08-00 N long. 100-46-15 W; Laid out in 1866 and named for the nearby North Platte River.

•**OAK,** Village; Nuckolls County; Pop. 79; Zip Code 68964; Lat. 40-14-09 N long. 097-54-12 W; Named for a grove of oak trees that grew along the Little Blue River.

•**OAKDALE,** Village; Antelope County; Pop. 410; Zip Code 68761; Lat. 42-04-09 N long. 097-58-00 W; Platted in 1872 and named for the many oak trees in the region.

•**OAKLAND,** City; Burt County; Pop. 1,393; Zip Code 68045; Elev. 1287; Lat. 41-50-05 N long. 096-27-55 W; Platted in 1872 and named for the many oak trees in the region.

•**OBERT,** Village; Cedar County; Pop. 44; Zip Code 68762; Lat. 42-41-23 N long. 097-01-37 W; First called Oberton, after a railroad officer. The name was shortened to Obert to avoid confusion with another town called Overton.

•**OCONTO,** Village; Custer County; Pop. 176; Zip Code 68860; Lat. 41-08-30 N long. 099-45-41 W; Either named for a man called Oconto, or from Oconto County, Wisconsin, which took its name from the Menominee Indian word for "place of the pickeral."

•**OCTAVIA,** Village; Butler County; Pop. 127; Zip Code 68650; Lat. 41-20-52 N long. 097-03-31 W; Laid out in 1857 and named for Octavia Speltz, wife of a prominent farmer in the area.

•**ODELL,** Village; Gage County; Pop. 322; Zip Code 68415; Lat. 40-02-55 N long. 096-48-11 W; Founded in 1880 and named for Le Grand Odell, an early settler.

•**OGALLALA,** City; Keith County Seat; Pop. 5,638; Zip Code 69153; Lat. 41-07-33 N long. 101-43-01 W; The city was named for the Oglala (or Ogalalla) tribe of the Teton Sioux Indians.

•**OHIOWA,** Village; Fillmore County; Pop. 135; Zip Code 68416; Lat. 40-24-41 N long. 097-27-00 W; The name is a combination of Ohio and Iowa, the former home states of early settlers here.

•**OMAHA,** City; Douglas County Seat; Pop. 311,681; Zip Code 68046; Lat. 38-22-55 N long. 089-37-37 W; Founded in 1854 and named for the Omaha Indians. The word *Omaha* means "upstream people."

•**O'NEILL,** City; Holt County Seat; Pop. 4,049; Named for General O'Neill, who settled here in 1874.

•**ONG,** Village; Clay County; Pop. 104; Platted in 1886 and first called Greenberry, for Greenberry L. Fort, a landowner. Later named for Judge J.E. Ong, who owned the land on which the town was built.

•**ORCHARD,** Village; Antelope County; Pop. 482; Zip Code 68764; Elev. 1946; Lat. 42-20-16 N long. 098-14-15 W; Settled in 1880. The village was named for a large apple orchard planted here.

•**ORD,** City; Valley County Seat; Pop. 2,658; Zip Code 68862; Lat. 41-36-06 N long. 098-55-45 W; Surveyed in 1874 and named for General E.O.C. Ord who commanded the military department of the Platte.

•**ORLEANS,** Village; Harlan County; Pop. 527; Zip Code 68966; Lat. 40-07-54 N long. 099-27-17 W; First called Melrose. Later named for either Orleans, Massachusetts, or for Orleans, France.

•**OSCEOLA,** City; Polk County Seat; Pop. 975; Zip Code 68651; Lat. 41-10-49 N long. 097-32-48 W; Platted in 1872 and named in honor of Osceola, the Seminole Indian chief.

•**OSHKOSH,** City; Garden County Seat; Pop. 1,057; Zip Code 69154; Lat. 41-24-28 N long. 102-20-430 W; Alfred W. Grumaer suggested the named after his former home of Oshkosh, Wisconsin.

•**OSMOND,** City; Pierce County; Pop. 871; Zip Code 68765; Lat. 42-21-33 N long. 097-35-42 W; Probably named for an official of the Chicago, Burlington and Quincy Railroad.

•**OTOE,** Village; Otoe County; Pop. 197; Zip Code 68417; Lat. 40-43-30 N long. 096-07-31 W; German settlers first called this town Berlin. the name was changed to Otoe, after Otoe County, during the World War.

•**OVERTON,** Village; Dawson County; Pop. 633; Zip Code 68863; Lat. 40-44-21 N long. 099-32-00 W; Named in 1871 for a government official in charge of guarding workmen when they built the railroad here.

•**OXFORD,** Village; Furnas County; Pop. 1,109; Zip Code 68967; Lat. 40-15-15 N long. 099-37-51 W; First called Grand View. Later named for a nearby ford in the Republican River where ox teams used to cross. Some sources say the name came from Oxford, Ohio, or from Oxford Univeristy in England.

•**PAGE,** Village; Holt County; Pop. 172; Zip Code 68766; Lat. 42-24-02 N long. 098-25-04 W; Homesteaded by the Page family and named in their honor. Mrs. Selinda Page was the town's first postmistress.

•**PALISADE,** Village; Hitchcock County; Pop. 401; Zip Code 69040; Lat. 40-20-50 N long. 101-06-17 W; Samuel True named the village Palisade because he thought the breaks around the town resembled palisades.

•**PALMER,** Village; Merrick County; Pop. 487; Zip Code 68864; Lat. 41-13-14 N long. 098-15-24 W; The village was probably named for a Burlington Railroad official.

•**PALMYRA,** Village; Otoe County; Pop. 512; Zip Code 68418; Lat. 40-42-12 N long. 096-23-36 W; Founded in 1870 and named for the ancient city of Palmyra in Asia Minor.

•**PANAMA,** Village; Lancaster County; Pop. 160; Zip Code 68419; Lat. 40-36-00 N long. 096-30-25 W; Probably named for the Isthmus of Panama and the Panama canal which was in the news around the time this village was established.

•**PAPILLION,** City; Sarpy County Seat; Pop. 6,399; Elev. 1029; Named for nearby Papillion Creek. In French *papillon* means "butterfly."

•**PAWNEE CITY,** City; Pawnee County Seat; Pop. 1,156; Zip Code 68420; Lat. 40-06-34 N long. 096-09-21 W; Incorporated in 1858 and named for the Pawnee Indians.

•**PAXTON,** Village; Keith County; Pop. 568; Zip Code 69155; Lat. 41-07-33 N long. 101-21-11 W; Named for W.A. Paxton, a resident of Omaha, Nebraska.

•**PENDER,** Village; Thurston County Seat; Pop. 1,318; Zip Code 68047; Lat. 42-06-42 N long. 096-42-34 W; First known as Athens. Later moved two miles north and named for John Pender, director of the Chicago, St. Paul, Minneapolis and Omaha Railroad.

•**PERU,** City; Nemaha County; Pop. 998; Zip Code 68421; Lat. 40-28-52 N long. 095-43-49 W; Settlers from Peru, Illinois named this city for their former hometown.

•**PETERSBURG,** Village; Boone County; Pop. 381; Zip Code 68652; Lat. 41-51-10 N long. 098-04-46 W; Settled in 1887 and named for John Peters, who owned the land on which the village was established.

•**PHILLIPS,** Village; Hamilton County; Pop. 405; Zip Code 68865; Lat. 40-53-54 N long. 098-12-51 W; Named for Captain R.O. Phillips, who established townsites for the Lincoln Land Company.

•**PICKRELL,** Village; Gage County; Pop. 184; Zip Code 68422; Lat. 40-22-34 N long. 096-43-40 W; Laid out in 1884 and named for William Pickrell, who owned part of the original townsite.

•**PIERCE,** City; Pierce County Seat; Pop. 1,535; Zip Code 68767; Elev. 1579; Lat. 42-11-51 N long. 097-31-20 W; Settled in 1870 and, like the county, was named in honor of President Franklin Pierce.

•**PILGER,** Village; Stanton County; Pop. 400; Zip Code 68768; Lat. 42-00-32 N long. 097-03-12 W; Named for Peter Pilger, who owned the land on which the village was located.

•**PLAINVIEW,** City; Pierce County; Pop. 1,483; Zip Code 68769; Lat. 42-21-00 N long. 097-47-11 W; First called Roseville, after postmaster, Charles Rose. Later named for its location on high ground, and also for the town of Plainview, Minnesota.

•**PLYMOUTH,** Village; Jefferson County; Pop. 506; Zip Code 68424; Lat. 40-18-09 N long. 096-59-13 W; Settlers from New England named this for thier former home at Plymouth, Massachusetts.

•**POLK,** Village; Polk County; Pop. 440; Zip Code 68654; Lat. 41-04-31 N long. 097-46-53 W; Named after the county, which was named in honor of President James K.Polk.

•**PONCA,** City; Dixon County Seat; Pop. 1,057; Zip Code 68770; Lat. 42-32-13 N long. 096-46-15 W; Surveyed in 1856 and named for the Ponca Indians, who once lived in the area.

•**POTTER,** Village; Cheyenne County; Pop. 369; Zip Code 69156; Lat. 41-13-07 N long. 103-18-50 W; Named for General Potter, who commanded troops in western Nebraska and owned shares in the Union Pacific Railway.

•**PRAGUE,** Village; Saunders County; Pop. 285; Zip Code 68050; Lat. 41-19-18 N long. 096-48-25 W; Settled by Bohemians who suggested the name, after the city of Prague in their home country.

•**PRESTON,** Village; Richardson County; Pop. 45; First called Bluffton, then Sac. James S. Eatough, a storekeeper suggested the name be changed to Preston, after his hometown in England.

•**PRIMROSE,** Village; Boone County; Pop. 102; Zip Code 68655; Lat. 41-37-22 N long. 098-14-15 W; Laid out on land owned by David Primrose, and named in his honor.

•PROSSER, Village; Adams County; Pop. 98; Zip Code 68868; Lat. 40-41-15 N long. 098-34-35 W; Named for T.J. Prosser, who was superintendent of the construction crew that built the railroad through town.

•RALSTON, City; Douglas County; Pop. 5,143; The city was named for Mr. Ralston, a prominent businessman and early resident.

•RANDOLPH, City; Cedar County; Pop. 1,106; Zip Code 68771; Lat. 42-21-23 N long. 097-19-27 W; F.H. Peavey named this city in honor of Lord Randolph Churchill of England.

•RAVENNA, City; Buffalo County; Pop. 1,296; Zip Code 68869; Elev. 2018; Lat. 41-01-39 N long. 098-54-49 W; First called Beaver Creek. Later renamed for the ancient Italian city of Ravenna.

•RAYMOND, Village; Lancaster County; Pop. 179; Zip Code 68428; Lat. 40-57-17 N long. 096-46-48 W; Platted in 1860 and named for I.M. Raymond, a wholesale grocer.

•RED CLOUD, City; Webster County Seat; Pop. 1,300; Zip Code 68970; Lat. 40-05-07 N long. 098-31-21 W; Named in honor of Red Cloud, chief of the Teton-Sioux Indians.

•REPUBLICAN CITY, Village; Harlan County; Pop. 231; Zip Code 68971; Lat. 40-05-55 N long. 099-13-14 W; Settled in 1871 nad named for its location on the Republican River.

•REYNOLDS, Village; Jefferson County; Pop. 125; Zip Code 68429; Lat. 40-03-36 N long. 097-20-08 W; The town was named for Mr. Reynolds, the father of a contractor for the railroad.

•RICHLAND, Village; Colfax County; Pop. 114; Zip Code 68657; Lat. 41-26-09 N long. 097-12-40 W; Platted in 1884 and first called Spitley. The name was later changed to Richland, probably descriptive of the surrounding country.

•RISING CITY, Village; Butler County; Pop. 392; Zip Code 68658; Lat. 41-11-51 N long. 097-17-45 W; The village was named for A.W. and S.W. Rising, who owned the townsite.

•RIVERDALE, Village; Buffalo County; Pop. 204; Zip Code 68870; Lat. 40-47-05 N long. 099-09-38 W; Named for its location in the Wood River valley of the Platte River.

•RIVERTON, Village; Franklin County; Pop. 212; Zip Code 68972; Lat. 40-05-17 N long. 098-45-30 W; Settled in 1871. Possibly named for its location on the Republican River, or after Riverton, Iowa.

•ROCA, Village; Lancaster County; Pop. 130; Zip Code 68430; Lat. 40-39-29 N long. 096-39-31 W; A stone quarrying town, laid out in 1876. The name Roca was chosen because it is Spanish for "rock" or "stone."

•ROCKVILLE, Village; Sherman County; Pop. 116; Zip Code 68871; Lat. 41-07-05 N long. 098-49-48 W; Named for nearby Rock Creek, which got its name from the lime rocks in its bed.

•ROGERS, Village; Colfax County; Pop. 89; Zip Code 68659; Lat. 41-27-49 N long. 096-54-40 W; Plattd in 1866 and named for a railroad official.

•ROSALIE, Village; Thurston County; Pop. 224; Zip Code 68055; Lat. 42-03-20 N long. 096-30-32 W; The village was named for Rosalie LaFlesche, daughter of Joseph LaFlesche, an Omaha Indian chief.

•ROSELAND, Village; Adams County; Pop. 254; Zip Code 68973; Elev. 1972; Lat. 40-28-10 N long. 098-33-38 W; B.F. Evans, the town's first postmaster, selectedthe name Roseland, for the many wild roses in the area.

•ROYAL, Village; Antelope County; Pop. 86; Zip Code 68773; Lat. 42-19-57 N long. 098-07-27 W; First called Savage. Later changed to Royal, after Mr. Royal Thayer.

•RULO, City; Richardson County; Pop. 261; Zip Code 68431; Lat. 40-03-03 N long. 095-25-40 W; Laid out in 1857 and named for Mrs. Rouleau, who owned the townsite. The spelling was later corrupted to Rulo.

•RUSHVILLE, City; Sheridan County Seat; Pop. 1,217; Zip Code 69360; Lat. 42-42-59 N long. 102-27-23 W; Named after nearby Rush Creek, which got its name from the rushes growing in the area.

•RUSKIN, Village; Nuckolls County; Pop. 224; Zip Code 68974; Lat. 40-08-37 N long. 097-52-14 W; The village was named in honor of John Ruskin, English author and art critic.

•ST. EDWARD, City; Boone County; Pop. 891; Zip Code 68660; Lat. 41-34-15 N long. 097-52-00 W; This city was named for Father Edward Serrels, a prominent Catholic priest at Notre Dame University in South Bend, Indiana.

•ST. HELENA, Village; Cedar County; Pop. 111; Zip Code 68774; Lat. 42-48-44 N long. 097-14-51 W; Carl C.P. Myer, the first settler, selected the name St. Helena about 1858.

•ST. PAUL, City; Howard County Seat; Pop. 2,094; Zip Code 68873; Lat. 41-15-19 N long. 098-24-52 W; Phineas W. Hitchcock, a U.S. Senator from Nebraska, suggested the name St. Paul in honor of the first settlers, J.N. and N.J. Paul.

•SALEM, Village; Richardson County; Pop. 221; Zip Code 68433; Lat. 40-04-31 N long. 095-43-25 W; Laid out in 1855 and named Salem, the biblical name for "city of peace."

•SANTEE, Village; Knox County; Pop. 388; Named for the Santee Sioux Indians.

•SARGENT, City; Custer County; Pop. 828; Zip Code 68874; Lat. 41-38-25 N long. 099-22-06 W; Laid out in 1883. Mrs. George Sherman, the postmistress anmed the city after friends of hers in Illinois.

•SARONVILLE, Village; Clay County; Pop. 63; Rev. Haterius, a Swedish Lutheran minister, established a church here he called Saron, after the village in Sweden. The town later became Saronville, from the church name.

•SCHUYLER, City; Colfax County Seat; Pop. 1,940; Zip Code 68661; Lat. 41-26-52 N long. 097-03-31 W; Named for Schuyler Colfax, Vice-President of the United States.

•SCOTIA, Village; Greeley County; Pop. 349; Zip Code 6875; Elev. 1906; Lat. 41-28-02 N long. 098-41-57 W; An early settler named this village for Scotland, his former homeland.

•SCOTTSBLUFF, City; Scotts Bluff County; Pop. 14,156; Zip Code 69361; Lat. 41-51-47 N long. 103-39-35 W; The city took its name from Scottsbluff, a high ridge in the Platte Valley where the body of mountaineer, Hiram Scott was found.

•SCRIBNER, City; Dodge County; Pop. 1,011; Zip Code 68057; Lat. 41-39-54 N long. 096-39-42 W; Named for Charles Scribner, the famous publisher in New York.

•SENECA, Village; Thomas County; Pop. 90; Zip Code 69161; Lat. 42-02-37 N long. 100-49-43 W; Started as a railroad station and named for the Seneca Indians.

•SEWARD, City; Seward County Seat; Pop. 5,713; Zip Code 68434; Lat. 40-54-47 N long. 097-05-34 W; The city was named after the county, which took its named from William H. Seward, U.S. Secretary of State under President Lincoln.

•**SHELBY,** Village; Polk County; Pop. 724; Zip Code 68662; Lat. 41-11-50 N long. 097-25-33 W; Laid out in 1879 and first called Arcade. Later named Shelby, for a Union Pacific Railroad official.

•**SHELTON,** Village; Buffalo County; Pop. 1,046; Zip Code 68876; Lat. 40-46-44 N long. 098-43-40 W; First called Wood River Center. Later named Shelton, after N. Shelton, an auditor for the railroad.

•**SHICKLEY,** Village; Fillmore County; Pop. 413; Zip Code 68436; Lat. 40-24-52 N long. 097-43-25 W; Named for Fillmore Schickley, owner of the townsite and an attorney for the railroad.

•**SHOLES,** Village; Wayne County; Pop. 27; Established in 1902 and named for Lyman Sholes, a railroad official.

•**SHUBERT,** Village; Richardson County; Pop. 267; Zip Code 68437; Elev. 1123; Lat. 40-14-07 N long. 095-41-01 W; Named for Henry W. Shubert, an early settler.

•**SIDNEY,** City; Cheyenne County Seat; Pop. 6,010; Zip Code 691+; Lat. 41-08-21 N long. 102-58-49 W; The city was named for Sidney Dillon, an attorney for the Union Pacific Railroad Company.

•**SILVER CREEK,** Village; Merrick County; Pop. 496; Zip Code 68663; Lat. 41-19-15 N long. 097-39-39 W; Named for Silver Creek, a nearby stream.

•**SMITHFIELD,** Village; Gosper County; Pop. 68; Elev. 2545; E.B. Smith owned the field on which the town was located, and the village was therefore named in his honor.

•**SNYDER,** Village; Dodge County; Pop. 387; Zip Code 68664; Lat. 41-42-10 N long. 096-47-12 W; Platted in 1886 and named for Conrad Schneider who owned the townsite and became the first postmaster.

•**SOUTH BEND,** Village; Cass County; Pop. 107; Zip Code 68058; Lat. 41-00-11 N long. 096-14-58 W; Laid out in 1857 and named for its location on the south bend of the Platte River.

•**SOUTH SIOUX CITY,** City; Dakota County; Pop. 9,339; Zip Code 68776; Lat. 42-28-14 N long. 096-24-19 W; Named for the Sioux Indians who had a reservation near here.

•**SPALDING,** Village; Greeley County; Pop. 645; Zip Code 68665; Lat. 41-41-18 N long. 098-21-43 W; Established by an Irish Catholic association and named in honor of its president, Bishop Spalding.

•**SPENCER,** Village; Boyd County; Pop. 596; Zip Code 68777; Lat. 42-52-25 N long. 098-41-59 W; Mr. Sterns, the first postmaster named this town after his former home of Spencer, Iowa.

•**SPRAGUE,** Village; Lancaster County; Pop. 168; Zip Code 68438; Lat. 40-37-38 N long. 096-44-35 W; Surveyed in 1888 by a man called Sprague, and named in his honor.

•**SPRINGFIELD,** City; Sarpy County; Pop. 782; Zip Code 68059; Lat. 41-05-00 N long. 096-07-53 W; Platted in 1881 and named for the many springs in the area.

•**SPRINGVIEW,** Village; Keya Paha County Seat; Pop. 326; Zip Code 68778; Lat. 42-49-10 N long. 099-44-53 W; Named for a spring that once flowed near the center of town.

•**STAMFORD,** Village; Harlan County; Pop. 214; Zip Code 68977; Lat. 40-08-02 N long. 099-35-38 W; First called Carisbrook. When the railroad came through, the town was moved and renamed for Stamford, Connecticut.

•**STANTON,** City; Stanton County Seat; Pop. 1,603; Zip Code 68779; Lat. 41-56-59 N long. 097-13-20 W; Platted in 1871 by S.L.

Halman, who named the city for his wife, whose maiden name was Stanton.

•**STAPLEHURST,** Village; Seward County; Pop. 306; Zip Code 68439; Lat. 40-58-26 N long. 097-10-22 W; Ebenezar Jull settled here about 1873 and named the town after his former home of Staplehurst, England.

•**STAPLETON,** Village; Logan County Seat; Pop. 340; Zip Code 69163; Lat. 41-28-40 N long. 100-30-41 W; Harry O'Neill suggested the name Stapleton, after a friend of his who helped promote the townsite.

•**STEELE CITY,** Village; Jefferson County; Pop. 306; Zip Code 68440; Named for Dudley M. Steele, president of the St. Joseph and Denver City Railroad.

•**STEINAUER,** Village; Pawnee County; Pop. 108; Zip Code 68441; Lat. 40-12-26 N long. 096-13-59 W; Settled about 1856 and named for Joseph A. Steinauer, who became the town's first postmaster.

•**STELLA,** Village; Richardson County; Pop. 289; Zip Code 68442; Lat. 40-13-51 N long. 095-46-25; Laid out in 1881 and named for Stella Clark, daughter of J.W. Clark, owner of the townsite.

•**STERLING,** Village; Johnson County; Pop. 526; Zip Code 68443; Lat. 40-27-34 N long. 096-22-42 W; John Mann, an early settler, named this village for his former home of Sterling, Illinois.

•**STOCKHAM,** Village; Hamilton County; Pop. 68; Platted in 1887 and named for Joseph Stockham, a member of the town board of trustees.

•**STOCKVILLE,** Village; Frontier County Seat; Pop. 45; Zip Code 69042; Lat. 40-31-49 N long. 100-22-53 W; Established in 1872 and so named because the settlers were mostly cattlemen and it was a stocktown.

•**STRANG,** Village; Fillmore County; Pop. 59; Zip Code 68444; Lat. 40-24-48 N long. 097-35-07 W; Named for A.L. Strang, a local resident who donated a windmill for a town pump.

•**STRATTON,** Village; Hitchcock County; Pop. 499; Zip Code 69043; Lat. 40-14-56 N long. 101-09-58 W; Founded in 1883 and named for Mrs. Stratton, an early settler.

•**STROMSBURG,** City; Polk County; Pop. 1,290; Zip Code 68666; Lat. 41-06-59 N long. 097-35-32 W; Surveyed in 1872. Swedish settlers named it Stromsburg, after a suburb of Stockholm, Sweden.

•**STUART,** Village; Holt County; Pop. 641; Zip Code 68780; Lat. 42-35-57 N long. 099-08-28 W; Settled about 1879 and named for Peter Stuart, who owned the townsite.

•**SUMNER,** Village; Dawson County; Pop. 254; Zip Code 68878; Elev. 4990; Lat. 40-57-00 N long. 099-30-24 W; Laid out in 1890. The village was named for Senator Charles Sumner of Massachusetts.

•**SUPERIOR,** City; Nuckolls County; Pop. 2,502; Zip Code 68978; Lat. 40-01-13 N long. 098-03-58 W; So named for the superior land along the railroad here, as compared to other places.

•**SURPRISE,** Village; Butler County; Pop. 60; Zip Code 68667; Lat. 41-06-17 N long. 097-18-29 W; Settlers here were surprised to find much better land than they expected, so they named the town Surprise.

•**SUTHERLAND,** Village; Lincoln County; Pop. 1,238; Zip Code 69165; Lat. 41-09-30 N long. 101-07-37 W; Laid out in 1869 and named for Mr. Sutherland, an official of the Union Pacific Railroad.

•**SUTTON,** City; Clay County; Pop. 1,416; Zip Code 689+; Elev. 1680; Lat. 40-36-04 N long. 097-56-13 W; Settled about 1870 and named after Sutton, Massachusetts.

•**SWANTON,** Village; Saline County; Pop. 131; Zip Code 68445; Lat. 40-22-47 N long. 097-04-39 W; First called Morris, after an early settler. Later named Swanton after nearby Swan Creek.

•**SYRACUSE,** City; Otoe County; Pop. 1,638; Zip Code 68446; Lat. 40-39-19 N long. 096-10-45 W; George Warner named the precinct for his former hometown of Syracuse, New York.

•**TABLE ROCK,** Village; Pawnee County; Pop. 393; Zip Code 68447; Lat. 40-10-48 N long. 096-05-38 W; Incorporated in 1860 and named for a large, flat-topped rock east of town.

•**TALMAGE,** Village; Otoe County; Pop. 246; Zip Code 68448; Lat. 40-31-53 N long. 096-01-29 W; Platted in 1881 and named for Thomas DeWitt Talmage, superintendent of a division of the Missouri Railroad.

•**TAMORA,** Village; Seward County; Pop. 50; Surveyed in 1879. The name Tamora is said to come from the word "tomorrow," or possibly from the Tamoria tribe of Indians.

•**TARNOV,** Village; Platte County; Pop. 63; First called Burrows. Later changed to Tarnov, probably after Tarnow, Galicia.

•**TAYLOR,** Village; Loup County Seat; Pop. 278; Zip Code 68879; Lat. 41-46-12 N long. 099-22-51 W; Established about 1881 and named for Ed Taylor, a pioneer.

•**TECUMSEH,** City; Johnson County Seat; Pop. 1,926; Zip Code 68450; Lat. 40-22-21 N long. 096-11-28 W; Laid out in 1856 and first called Frances after the wife of General Johnson. Later named for Tecumseh, the Indian chief.

•**TEKAMAH,** City; Burt County; Pop. 1,886; Zip Code 68061; Lat. 41-46-37 N long. 096-13-10 W; Founded in 1854 on an old Indian camping ground. The name is of Indian origin, possibly meaning "big cottonwood" or "field of battle."

•**THEDFORD,** Village; Thomas County Seat; Pop. 313; Zip Code 69166; Lat. 41-58-40 N long. 10-34-30 W; Probably named after the town of Thedford in Ontario, Canada.

•**THURSTON,** Village; Thurston County; Pop. 139; Zip Code 68062; Lat. 42-10-51 N long. 096-41-53 W; First known as Flournoy. Later named for U.S. Senator John M. Thurston from Nebraska.

•**TILDEN,** City; Madison County; Pop. 1,012; Zip Code 68781; Lat. 42-02-36 N long. 097-49-51 W; Originally called Burnett after a railroad official. Renamed for Samuel J. Tilden, statesman from New York.

•**TOBIAS,** Village; Saline County; Pop. 138; Zip Code 68453; Lat. 40-25-03 N long. 097-20-15 W; Named for Tobias Castor, a prominent citizen. First called Castor, but later changed to Tobias, to avoid confusion with the town of Custer.

•**TRENTON,** Village; Hitchcock County Seat; Pop. 796; Zip Code 69044; Lat. 40-10-27 N long. 101-00-47 W; Probably named for Trenton, New Jersey.

•**TRUMBULL,** Village; Clay County; Pop. 216; Zip Code 68980; Lat. 40-40-38 N long. 098-16-34 W; The village was named for a railroad official.

•**UEHLING,** Village; Dodge County; Pop. 273; Zip Code 68063; Lat. 41-44-02 N long. 096-30-17 W; Platted in 1906 and named for Theodore Uehling, a settler who came to Nebraska in 1860.

•**ULYSSES,** Village; Butler County; Pop. 270; Zip Code 68669; Lat. 41-04-17 N long. 097-12-05 W; Named in honor of Ulysses S. Grant.

•**UNADILLA,** Village; Otoe County; Pop. 291; Zip Code 68454; Lat. 40-40-51 N long. 096-16-07 W; I.N. White named this village after his former hometown of Unadilla, New York. The word *unadilla* is Iroquois for "meeting place."

•**UNION,** Village; Cass County; Pop. 307; Zip Code 68455; Lat. 40-48-44 N long. 095-55-17 W; Townspeople selected the name Union for their sympathies with the north during the Civil War.

•**UPLAND,** Village; Franklin County; Pop. 192; Zip Code 68981; Lat. 40-19-08 N long. 098-53-57 W; So named for its location on high ground.

•**UTICA,** Village; Seward County; Pop. 689; Zip Code 68456; Lat. 40-53-45 N long. 097-20-35 W; Named after the city of Utica in New York.

•**VALENTINE,** City; Cherry County Seat; Pop. 2,829; Zip Code 69201; Lat. 42-52-25 N long. 100-32-56 W; The city was named for Edward Kimball Valentine, a congressman for this district.

•**VALLEY,** City; Douglas County; Pop. 1,716; Zip Code 680+; Lat. 41-19-46 N long. 096-25-42 W; Earlier named Platte Sanders, after John Sanders. When the town was incorporated the name Platte was omitted and replaced with Valley.

•**VALPARAISO,** Village; Saunders County; Pop. 484; Zip Code 68065; Lat. 41-04-48 N long. 096-49-54 W; First called Raccoon Forks for three creeks that joined here. Later named Valparaiso because it was considered the "valley of paradise."

•**VENANGO,** Village; Perkins County; Pop. 230; Zip Code 69168; Elev. 359; Lat. 40-45-47 N long. 102-02-21 W; Probably named for Venango, Pennsylvania.

•**VERDIGRE,** Village; Knox County; Pop. 617; Zip Code 68783; Lat. 42-35-51 N long. 098-02-03; First called Verdigris after a nearby creek, which took its name from the green copper ore in the area. The spelling was later corrupted to Verdigre.

•**VERDON,** Village; Richardson County; Pop. 278; Zip Code 68457; Lat. 40-08-51 N long. 095-42-37 W; Laid out in 1882 and named Verdon, possibly from the word *verdure.*

•**VIRGINIA,** Village; Gage County; Pop. 90; The town was named in honor of Miss Virginia Lewis.

•**WACO,** Village; York County; Pop. 225; Zip Code 68460; Lat. 40-53-43 N long. 097-27-45 W; Miss Chapin, who donated land for the townsite named this for her former home of Waco, Texas.

•**WAHOO,** City; Saunders County Seat; Pop. 3,555; Zip Code 68066; Lat. 41-12-47 N long. 096-37-10; The name may have come either from the "wahoo" or "burning bush" that grows in the area, or from an Indian word for a species of elm.

•**WAKEFIELD,** City; Dixon County; Pop. 1,125; Zip Code 68784; Lat. 42-15-58 N long. 096-52-00 W; Founded in 1881 and named for L.W. Wakefield, an engineer for the railroad surveying party.

•**WALLACE,** Village; Lincoln County; Pop. 349; Zip Code 69169; Lat. 40-50-19 N long. 101-10-01 W; The head of the Lincoln Town-Site Company named this town for his son-in-law, Wallace.

•**WALTHILL,** Village; Thurston County; Pop. 847; Zip Code 68067; Lat. 42-08-58 N long. 096-29-19 W; Settled about 1906 and named for Walter Hill who helped organize the town.

•**WASHINGTON,** Village; Washington County; Pop. 113; Zip Code 68068; Lat. 41-23-47 N long. 096-12-37 W; Platted in 1887 and named for the county, which took its name from George Washington.

•**WATERBURY,** Village; Dixon County; Pop. 92; Zip Code 68785; Lat. 42-27-30 N long. 096-44-01 W; Named for a nearby spring that provided water for the railroad.

•**WATERLOO,** Village; Douglas County; Pop. 450; Zip Code 68069; Lat. 41-17-14 N long. 096-17-12 W; Laid out in 1871 and named for Waterloo, the battlefield in Belgium.

•**WAUNETA,** Village; Chase County; Pop. 746; Zip Code 69045; Lat. 40-24-57 N long. 101-22-04 W; Early settlers named this town after the popular song *Juanita.* The spelling was changed to Wauneta to avoid confusion with the town of Juniata.

•**WAUSA,** Village; Knox County; Pop. 647; Zip Code 68786; Lat. 42-29-50 N long. 097-32-01 W; Named in honor of Gustavus Vasa, the first Protestant King of Sweden. The spelling was changed to Wausa to correspond to the pronunciation.

•**WAVERLY,** City; Lancaster County; Pop. 1,726; Zip Code 68462; Lat. 40-54-43 N long. 096-31-39 W; Established in 1868 and named for *Waverley,* the historical novel by Sir Walter Scott.

•**WAYNE,** City; Wayne County Seat; Pop. 5,240; Zip Code 68787; Lat. 42-14-08 N long. 097-01-03 W; Named after the county, which was named for General Anthony Wayne.

•**WEEPING WATER,** City; Cass County; Pop. 1,109; Zip Code 68463; Lat. 40-52-05 N long. 096-08-21 W; The city was named after a nearby creek which the French called *L'Eau qui Pleure* or "water that weeps."

•**WELLFLEET,** Village; Lincoln County; Pop. 83; Zip Code 69170; Lat. 40-45-14 N long. 100-43-39 W; The village was named after Wellfleet, Massachusetts, which is said to be derived from the words "whale fleet."

•**WESTERN,** Village; Saline County; Pop. 336; Zip Code 68464; Lat. 40-23-35 N long. 097-11-42 W; Established in 1872 and named for Mr. West, a homesteader.

•**WESTON,** Village; Saunders County; Pop. 286; Zip Code 68070; Lat. 41-11-37 N long. 096-44-27 W; Officials of the Union Pacific Railroad selected the name for this town.

•**WEST POINT,** City; Cuming County Seat; Pop. 3,609; Zip Code 68788; Lat. 41-50-15 N long. 096-42-33 W; So named because when it was first settled it was the most westerly populated point in the Elkhorn River valley.

•**WHITNEY,** Village; Dawes County; Pop. 72; First called Dawes City, later Earth Lodge. It was finally named Whitney, in honor of Peter Whitney, a townsite agent for the railroad.

•**WILBER,** City; Saline County Seat; Pop. 1,624; Zip Code 68465; Lat. 40-28-51 N long. 096-57-35 W; Laid out about 1872 by Professor C.D. Wilber and named in his honor.

•**WILCOX,** Village; Kearney County; Pop. 379; Zip Code 68982; Lat. 40-21-50 N long. 099-10-12 W; Founded by Henry Wilcox and named for him.

•**WILSONVILLE,** Village; Furnas County; Pop. 189; Zip Code 69046; Elev. 2304; Lat. 40-06-43 N long. 100-06-17 W; The town was named for the Wilson brothers, early settlers to this area.

•**WINNEBAGO,** Village; Thurston County; Pop. 902; Zip Code 68071; Lat. 42-14-09 N long. 096-28-20 W; Named for the Winnebago tribe of Indians.

•**WINNETOON,** Village; Knox County; Pop. 82; Zip Code 68789; Lat. 42-30-40 N long. 097-57-36 W; W.F. Fitch, a railroad official, named this village after a farm in Wisconsin.

•**WINSIDE,** Village; Wayne County; Pop. 439; Zip Code 68790; Lat. 42-10-37 N long. 097-10-30 W; So named for what was considered to be a "winning" location at the side of the railroad tracks.

•**WINSLOW,** Village; Dodge County; Pop. 143; Zip Code 68072; Lat. 41-36-37 N long. 096-30-15 W; Officials of the Great Northern Railroad selected the name for this town.

•**WISNER,** City; Cuming County; Pop. 1,335; Zip Code 68791; Lat. 41-59-22 N long. 096-54-51 W; Established about 1865 and named for Samuel P. Wisner, vice-president of the railroad company.

•**WOLBACH,** Village; Greeley County; Pop. 301; Zip Code 68882; Lat. 41-23-36 N long. 098-23-27 W; The town was named for S.N. Wolbach, who once owned a great deal of land here.

•**WOOD LAKE,** Village; Cherry County; Pop. 89; Zip Code 69221; Lat. 42-38-15 N long. 100-13-47 W; Named for a nearby lake with trees on its shore.

•**WOOD RIVER,** City; Hall County; Pop. 1,334; Zip Code 68883; Lat. 40-49-18 N long. 098-35-58 W; Established about 1871 and named for its location on the banks of the Wood River.

•**WYMORE,** City; Gage County; Pop. 1,841; Zip Code 68466; Lat. 40-07-13 N long. 096-40-01 W; The city was named for Samuel Wymore, who donated land to the railroad.

•**WYNOT,** Village; Cedar County; Pop. 222; Zip Code 68792; Lat. 42-44-22 N long. 097-10-08 W; The name comes from the words "why not." It is said that a German settler here was in the habit of answering questions with the word "why not" and this caught on and became the name for the town.

•**YORK,** City; York County Seat; Pop. 7,723; Zip Code 68467; Lat. 40-55-11 N long. 097-32-31 W; Platted in 1896 and probably named for an early settler.

•**YUTAN,** Village; Saunders County; Pop. 631; Zip Code 68073; Lat. 41-14-38 N long. 096-23-55 W; Named in honor of Ietan, an Otoe Indian chief.

NEVADA

•ALAMO, Township; Lincoln County; Pop. 1,126; Zip Code 89001; Lat. 37-21-52 N long. 115-09-46 W; Founded about 1900 and named for poplar trees that grew in the area. The Spanish word for poplar is alamo.

•ARGENTA, Township; Lander County; Pop. 3,646; Elev. 4596; Lat. 40-40-28 N long. 116-42-17 W; A railroad shiping point for barium, the township was named "Argenta" the traditional name for the native ore.

•AUSTIN, Township; Lander County; Pop. 436; Zip Code 89310; Elev. 6527; Lat. 39-29-35 N long. 117-04-11 W; In 1883 David Buel laid out the townsite and named it for Alvah C. Austin, is friend and partner. Other sources claim the township was named for John Austin, a pioneer.

•BEATTY, Township; Nye County; Pop. 3,524; Zip Code 89003; Lat. 36-54-22 N long. 116-45-39 W; Named in honor of M. M. Beatty, a ranch owner who was locally known as "old man" or "Jim" Beatty.

•BOULDER CITY, City; Clark County; Pop. 9,590; Zip Code 89005; Lat. 35-58-00 N long. 114-49-36 W; Originally the construction camp for Hoover Dam (earlier known as Boulder Dam). The city was named from Boulder Canyon.

•BUNKERVILLE, Township; Clark County; Pop. 492; Zip Code 89007; Lat. 36-46-21 N long. 114-07-30 W; Formerly called Mesquite. Renamed for Edweard Bunker, a missionary who came here about 1877.

•CALIENTE, City; Lincoln County; Pop. 982; Zip Code 89008; Elev. 4395; Lat. 37-36-53 N long. 114-30-43 W; First called Dutch Flat, later Culverwell Ranch, and Clover or Cloverdale Staion. In 1901 the town was laid out and named "Calientes" or "hot" after nearby hot springs.

•CARLIN, City; Elko County; Pop. 1,232; Zip Code 89821; Lat. 40-35-25 N long. 116-28-44 W; Settled in the 1860's and named in honor of William Passmore Carlin, a Union Army officer.

•CARSON CITY, City; Capital of Nevada; Pop. 32,022; Zip Code 89701; Elev. 4665; Lat. 39-08-57 N long. 119-46-55 W; First known as Eagle Station. In 1858 Major William M. Omsby purchased the land and laid out a town he called Carson City.

•DAYTON, Township; Lyon County; Pop. 4,376; Zip Code 89403; Lat. 39-14-11 N long. 119-35-30 W; Pioneers called their campsite here Ponderers Rest. Later named were Halls Station, Gold Creek Station, McNarlins Station, Chinatown, Mineral Rapids, Nevada City, Clinto, and finally Dayton after John Day, a surveyor.

•EAST FORK, Township; Douglas County; Pop. 14,053; So named for the east fork of the Carson River.

•ELKO, City; Elko County Seat; Pop. 8,758; Zip Code 89801; Elev. 5067; Lat. 40-49-56 N long. 115-45-43 W; Laid out about 1869. Railroad officials probably selected the name Elko, a typical railroad town name.

•ELY, City; White Pine County Seat; Pop. 4,882; Zip Code 89301; Elev. 6427; Lat. 39-14-48 N long. 114-53-08 W; Located in 1869 or 1870 by George Lamb and called Murry Creek Station. Later renamed for Smith Ely who built a copper furnace in the town.

•ESMERALDO, Township; Esmeraldo County; Pop. 777; So named for the county, which took its name either from the Spanish word for emerald, or from the gypsy girl in Victor Hugo's The Hunchback of Notre-Dame.

•EUREKA, Township; Eureka County; Pop. 798; Zip Code 89316; Elev. 6481; Lat. 39-30-46 N long. 115-57-40 W; The township was named for the Eureka mining district. Prospectors were said to have showed "eureka" (I have found it) when they made a discovery here in 1864.

•FALLON, City; Churchill County Seat; Pop. 4,262; Zip Code 89406; Elev. 3963; Lat. 39-27-12 N long. 118-44-36 W; Established in 1896 and named for Michael Fallon, a settler.

•GABBS, City; Nye County; Pop. 811; Zip Code 89409; Lat. 38-51-56 N long. 117-55-11 W; First called Toiyabe in 1942. Renamed the following year for pallontologist, William M. Gabbs.

•GERLACH, Township; Wahoe County; Pop. 583; Zip Code 89412; Lat. 40-39-14 N long. 119-21-18 W; Settled about 1906 and named for the Gerlach Land and Cattle Company.

•GOLD RUN, Township; Humboldt County; Pop. 780; Earlier known as Gold Run Mining District and Adelaide. The district was named after Gold Run Creek.

•GOODSPRINGS, Township; Clark County; Pop. 1,003; Elev. 3718; Lat. 35-49-57 N long. 115-26-00 W; Joseph Good, a prospector, settled at the springs in 1868 and they wre called Good Sprngs. The town took its name from his original settlement.

•HAWTHORNE, Township; Mineral County; Pop. 5,166; Zip Code 89415; Lat. 38-31-24 N long. 118-37-10 W; The town was named in honor of William Hawthorn, a cattleman and justice of the peace.

•HENDERSON, City; Clark County; Pop. 24,363; Zip Code 89015; Lat. 36-02-46 N long. 114-58-45 W; Established about 1944 and named in honor of Senator Charles Henderson.

•JACKPOT, Township; Elko County; Pop. 809; Zip Code 89825; Lat. 41-59-15 N long. 114-40-13 W; A gambling center, Jackpot was named in 1959 for the winnings at the slot machines.

•JARBRIDGE, Township; Elko County; Pop. 33; Zip Code 89826; Lat. 41-52-28 N long. 115-25-52 W; Established in 1910 and named for Jourbridge Canyon which the Shoshones called Jahabich or "devil."

•LAKE, Township; Pershing County; Pop. 3,408; So named for numerous lakes in the area.

•LAS VEGAS, City; Clark County Seat; Pop. 164,674; Zip Code 891+; Lat. 36-10-15 N long. 115-10-15 W; Traders on the Old Spanish Trail camped here and named this place Las Vegas, spanish for fertile or marshy plains.

•LOGAN, Township; Clark County; Pop. 1,087; Settled about 1864 and called St. Joseph. Renamed in 1895 when the post office was established in honor of a prominent settler, Robert Logan.

•LOVELOCK, City; Pershing County Seat; Pop. 1,680; Zip Code 89419; Lat. 40-10-49 N long. 118-28-15 W; First known as Big Meadows. Later renamed for settler, George Lovelock.

•MASON VALLEY, Township; Lyon County; Pop. 5,050; Named in honor of Henry "Hock" A. Mason, who settled in the area about 1859.

•MCDERMITT, Township; Humboldt County; Pop. 1,159; Zip Code 89421; Lat. 41-59-21 N long. 117-46-26 W; Named in honor of Colonel McDermit, who was killed in an Indian ambush in 1865.

•**MESQUITE,** Township; Clark County; Pop. 922; Zip Code 89024; Elev. 1608; Lat. 36-48-22 N long. 114-03-48 W; The name is descriptive of the mesquite which grows in the area.

•**MINA,** Township; Mineral County; Pop. 484; Zip Code 89422; Elev. 4546; Lat. 38-23-31 N long. 118-06-30 W; The name is Spanish for "mine" or "ore."

•**MOAPA,** Township; Clark County; Pop. 702; Zip Code 89025; Elev. 1709; Lat. 36-40-21 N long. 114-37-12 W; The name "Moapa" comes from the Moapariats or "mosquite creek people," a band of southern Painte Indians.

•**MOUNTAIN CITY,** Township; Elko County; Pop. 1,216; Zip Code 89831; Lat. 41-50-20 N long. 115-57-51 W; Settled about 1860 and named for the natural surroundings.

•**NELSON,** Township; Clark County; Pop. 10,059; Elev. 2954; Lat. 35-42-29 N long. 114-49-26 W; Platted in 1905 and named for prospector, Charles Nelson, who was murdered at his mine near here.

•**NEW RIVER,** Township; Churchill County; Pop. 13,917; So named when the Carson River flooded in 1862 creating a new channel which became known as New River.

•**NORTH LAS VEGAS,** City; Clark County; Pop. 42,739; Zip Code 89030; Lat. 36-12-24 N long. 115-07-34 W; So named for its location, north of the city of Las Vegas.

•**OVERTON,** Township; Clark County; Pop. 1,752; Zip Code 89040; Lat. 36-32-34 N long. 114-26-35 W; The town is said to have been named "Overtown" after the settlement was moved from the river bank to a hill overlooking the old site.

•**PAHRUMP,** Township; Nye County; Pop. 1,358; Zip Code 89041; Lat. 36-12-22 N long. 115-59-12 W; First established about 1891. The name is probably derived from Indian words meaning "water stone,", "people of the meadows," "great spring," or "cave from which water flows."

•**PANACA,** Township; Lincoln County; Pop. 758; Zip Code 89042; Elev. 4738; Lat. 37-47-26 N long. 114-23-01 W; Named for the Panacker Ledge. Pa-na-ka is a southern Painte word meaning "metal."

•**PARADISE VALLEY,** Township; Humboldt County; Pop. 286; Zip Code 89426; Lat. 41-29-38 N long. 117-32-03 W; Established in 1866 and named for the valley in which it was located. When prospectors first explored here in 1863, the valley was like an oasis or a "paradise."

•**PIOCHE,** Township; Lincoln County; Pop. 794; Zip Code 89043; Elev. 6064; Lat. 37-55-51 N long. 114-27-01 W; First called Ely after John H. ely. Later renamed in honor of F.L.A. Pioche, a San Francisco banker who owned property here.

•**RENO,** City; Washoe County Seat; Pop. 100,756; Zip Code 89500; Elev. 4498; Lat. 39-31-39 N long. 119-49-04 W; Originally called Fuller's Crossing, latre Lakes Crossing. With the coming of the railroad the city was renamed for Jesse Lee Reno, an army officer.

•**ROUND MOUNTAIN,** Township; Nye County; Pop. 574; Zip Code 89045; Lat. 38-42-46 N long. 117-04-04 W; Named for a nearby low, round-top mountain at the base of the Toquima Range.

•**SCHURZ,** Township; Mineral County; Pop. 567; Zip Code 89427; Elev. 4126; Lat. 38-57-04 N long. 118-48-30 W; Established about 1891 and named for Carl Schurz, statesman and author.

•**SEARCHLIGHT,** Township; Clark County; Pop. 620; Zip Code 89046; Lat. 35-27-51 N long. 114-55-14 W; Named for the sear-chlight mining area, which in turn was named for Lloyd Searchlight, the owner of claims in the district.

•**SMITH VALLEY,** Township; Lyon County; Pop. 853; Named for the Smith party of herdsmen who settled here in 1859. The group included Timothy B. Smith, R. B. Smith and Cyrus "Adobe" Smith.

•**SPARKS,** City; Washoe County; Pop. 40,780; Zip Code 89431; Lat. 39-35-51 N long. 119-44-57 W; Founded about 1903 as Harriman. Renamed in honor of John Sparks, Governor of Nevada.

•**TAHOE,** Township; Douglas County; Pop. 5,368; Named for Lake Tahoe. The name Tahoe came from the Indian word "Tah-hoe-ee" meaning big lake or water.

•**TECOMA,** Township; Elko County; Pop. 231; Lat. 41-19-13 N long. 114-04-50 W; Named for the famous Tecoma mines.

•**TONOPAH,** Township; Nye County; Pop. 2,680; Zip Code 89049; Elev. 6030; Lat. 38-04-03 N long. 117-13-47 W; Formerly known as Butler. The name Tonopah is Indian for "hidden spring," brush water springs," or "water brush."

•**UNION,** Township; Humboldt County; Pop. 7,209; Elev. 6669; Lat. 40-10-03 N long. 116-01-25 W; Founded about 1863 as the Union Mining District. "Union" was a popular in place-naming during the Civil War.

•**VERDI,** Township; Washoe County; Pop. 1,256; Zip Code 89439; Elev. 4905; Lat. 39-31-10 N long. 119-59-23 W; Formerly called O'Neils Crossing. Railroad officials changed the name to Verdi, in honor of the Italian operatic composer.

•**VIRGINIA,** Township; Storey County; Pop. 1,459; The town was named in honor of a prospector who came to the region in 1851.

•**WADSWORTH,** Township; Washoe County; Pop. 1,012; Zip Code 89442; Elev. 4076; Lat. 39-37-48 N long. 119-17-10 W; Established in 1854 as a trading post. It became known as Drytown and Lower Emigrant Crossing. In 1868 railroad officials named the town in honor of James Samuel Wadsworth, an army officer.

•**WELLS,** City; Elko County; Pop. 1,218; Zip Code 89833; Lat. 40-30-21 N long. 115-20-52 W; Established as a railroad station and called Humboldt Wells after nearby springs known as "wells." The name of the city was later shortened to wells.

•**WINNEMUCCA,** City; Humboldt County Seat; Pop. 4,140; Zip Code 89445; Elev. 4299; Lat. 40-58-47 N long. 117-43-39 W; First called French Ford or French Bridge, later Centerville. In 1868, C.B.O. Bannon named this city Winnemucca in honor of the famous Indian chief.

•**YERINGTON,** City; Lyon County Seat; Pop. 2,021; Zip Code 89447; Elev. 4384; Lat. 38-59-11 N long. 119-09-44 W; Earlier known as Poison, Pizen, Switch and Greenfield. Renamed for Henry Marvin Yerington, Superintendent of the Virginia and Truckee Railroad.

NEW HAMPSHIRE

•ACWORTH, Town; Sullivan County; Pop. 590; Zip Code 03601; Lat. 43-13-00 N long. 072-17-34 W; Acworth was named in 1766 for Sir Jacob Acworth, a British admiral accociated with the West Indies trade.

•ALEXANDRIA, Town; Grafton County; Pop. 706; The town is named after Alexandria, Virginia, which is famous as the starting point of the French and Indian war.

•ALLENSTOWN, Town; Merrimack County; Pop. 4,398; The town was named in 1721 in honor of Governor Samuel Allen of Massachusetts.

•AMHERST, Town; Hillsborough County; Pop. 8,243; Zip Code 03031; The town's name commemorates the popular English commander during the French-Indian War, Lord Jeffrey Amherst.

•ANDOVER, Town; Merrimack County; Pop. 1,587; Zip Code 03216; Lat. 43-26-13 N long. 071-49-20 W; Named by Dr. Anthony Emery in 1779 for Andover, Massachusetts.

•ANTRIM, Town; Hillsborough County; Pop. 2,208; Zip Code 03440; Lat. 43-01-47 N long. 071-56-23 W; Early settler Phillip Riley named his new home after his former home in Country Antrim, Ireland.

•ASHLAND, Town; Grafton County; Pop. 1,807; Zip Code 03217; Lat. 43-41-53 N long. 071-38-03 W; The town's name comes from Henry Clay's Kentucky estate, Ashland.

•ATKINSON, Town; Rockingham County; Pop. 4,397; Zip Code 03811; Lat. 42-50-31 N long. 071-09-35 W; Founded in 1767 and named in honor of Colonel Theodore Atkinson whose farm covered the townsite.

•AUBURN, Town; Rockingham County; Pop. 2,883; Zip Code 03032; First called Chester Woods, later Auburn after the English poet Goldsmith's verse.

•BARRINGTON, Town; Strafford County; Pop. 4,404; Zip Code 03825; Lat. 43-12-47 N long. 070-59-48 W; Barrington's name honors English governor of Massachusetts, Samuel Snute of Barrington Hall.

•BATH, Town; Grafton County; Pop. 761; Zip Code 03740; Lat. 44-10-05 N long. 071-57-56 W; The town's name honors English statesman William Pultengy, the first Earl of Bath.

•BEDFORD, Town; Hillsborough County; Pop. 9,481; Zip Code 03142; The city's name honors Lord John Russell, fourth Duke of Bedford in 1732.

•BENNINGTON, Town; Hillsborough County; Pop. 890; Zip Code 03442; Lat. 43-00-02 N long. 071-55-33 W; The city was named in 1842 to commemorate the Revolutionary War Battle of Bennington, Vermont, which occurred on August 14, 1777.

•BENTON, Town; Grafton County; Pop. 333; Originally Coventry, the town's name became Benton in 1840 in honor of U. S. Senator Thomas Hart Benton.

•BERLIN, City; Coos County; Pop. 13,084; Zip Code 03570; Lat. 44-26-58 N long. 071-11-13 W; The city is named after Berlin, Massachusetts.

•BETHLEHAM, Town; Grafton County; Pop. 1,784; Zip Code 03574; Elev. 1,426; Lat. 44-16-46 N long. 071-41-17 W; Incorporated on December 27, 1799 and named to commemorate the Christmas season.

•BOSCAWEN, Town; Merrimack County; Pop. 3,435; Named in 1761 in honor of English Admiral Edward Boscawen, who led the squadron which captured the French fortress of Louisburg in 1758.

•BRENTWOOD, Town; Rockingham County; Pop. 2,004; Brentwood is named after Brentwood, England. Brentwood was once the descriptive "burnt wood."

•BRIDGEWATER, Town; Grafton County; Pop. 606; The town's founding families were from Bridgewater, Massachusetts, and so named their new home.

•BRISTOL, Town; Grafton County; Pop. 2,198; Zip Code 03222; Lat. 43-35-34 N long. 071-44-18 W; The town had a fine sand, useful in making ceramics, similar to the variety made in Bristol, England. The name followed from this connection.

•BROOKLINE, Town; Hillsborough County; Pop. 1,766; Zip Code 03033; Founded in 1769 as West Holis, it was renamed in 1798 at the suggestion of prominent landowner Benjamin Shattuck, who was from Brookline, Massachusetts.

•CAMPTON, Town; Grafton County; Pop. 1,694; Zip Code 03285; Lat. 43-49-42 N long. 071-39-05; Governor Benning Wentworth named the site in honor of his business friend, Spencer Compton, Earl of Wilmington. Compton became spelled Campton.

•CANAAN, Town; Grafton County; Pop. 2,456; Zip Code 03741; Elev. 945; Lat. 43-35-42 N long. 072-00-52 W; Named after Canaan, Connecticut. Canaan is a Biblical name from the Old Testament.

•CANDIA, Town; Rockingham County; Pop. 2,989; Zip Code 03034; Governor Benning Wentworth named it in 1873 for the largest city on the Greek island of Crete.

•CANTERBURY, Town; Merrimack County; Pop. 1,410; Zip Code 03224; Elev. 595; Lat. 43-20-06 N long. 071-33-48 W; Founded in 1727 and named in honor of William Wake, Archbishop of Canterbury.

•CHARLESTOWN, Town; Sullivan County; Pop. 4,417; Zip Code 03603; Lat. 43-14-21 N long. 072-25-23 W; Named in 1753 in honor of British Admiral Sir Charles Knowles.

•CHESTER, Town; Rockingham County; Pop. 2,006; Zip Code 03036; Elev. 464. Named for the city in England.

•CHICHESTER, Town; Merrimack County; Pop. 1,492; Founded in 1724 and named in honor of Thomas Holles, Earl of Chichester.

•CLAREMONT, City; Sullivan County; Pop. 14,557; Zip Code 03743; Elev. 561; Lat. 43-18-47 N long. 072-20-35 W; The city's name remembers the great English palace, Claremont, home of the Earl of Clare.

•CONCORD, City; Merrimack County; Pop. 30,400; Zip Code 033++; Elev. 288; Lat. 43-13-02 N long. 071-32-42 W; The capital of New Hampshire, Concord is the Latin word for "peace" and signifies a resolved boundary dispute in colonial times.

•CORNISH, Town; Sullivan County; Pop. 1,390; Zip Code 03745; Elev. 843; Founded in 1763 as a supply depot for the Royal Navy, and named for Admiral Sir Samuel Cornish.

•CROYDON, Town; Sullivan County; Pop. 457; The town is named after the well-known London suburb of Croydon.

•DANBURY, Town; Merrimack County; Pop. 680; Zip Code 03230; Elev. 825; Lat. 43-31-27 N long. 071-51-43 W; The city is named after Danbury, England.

•**DANVILLE,** Town; Rockingham County; Pop. 1,318; Zip Code 03819; Lat. 42-54-43 N long. 071-07-27 W; Settled in 1694 by several pioneers whose christian names were Daniel. The town's name remembers that coincidence.

•**DEERFIELD,** Town; Rockingham County; Pop. 1,979; Zip Code 03037; Elev. 552; Incorporated in 1766 and named after Deerfield, Massachusetts by early settlers.

•**DEERING,** Town; Hillsborough County; Pop. 1,041; The town is named in honor of the family name of New Hampshire Governor John Wentworth's wife, the Deerings.

•**DERRY,** Town; Rockingham County; Pop. 18,875; Zip Code 03038; Elev. 290; Incorporated in 1827 and named for the Isle of Derry in Ireland.

•**DORCHESTER,** Town; Grafton County; Pop. 244; Established in 1761 and named for the city in England.

•**DOVER,** City; Strafford County; Pop. 22,377; Zip Code 03820; Lat. 43-11-31 N long. 070-52-40 W; Dover was settled in 1623 and had many early names. In 1641 it was named in honor of English soldier and lawyer, Robert Dover.

•**DUNBARTON,** Town; Merrimack County; Pop. 1,174; Dunbarton is named after Dunbartonshire in Scotland on the River Clyde.

•**DURHAM,** Town; Strafford County; Pop. 10,652; Zip Code 03824; Lat. 43-08-00 N long. 070-55-31 W; Incorporated in 1732 and named for seventeenth century English Bishop of Durham, Richard Barnes.

•**EAST KINGSTON,** Town; Rockingham County; Pop. 1,135; Zip Code 03827; Elev. 124; Lat. 42-55-29 N long. 071-00-25 W; Originally part of Kingston, it became a separate city in 1738. Kingston, itself, was established in 1694 and named in honor of the fifth Earl of Kingston-on-Hull.

•**EASTON,** Town; Grafton County; Pop. 124; Originally called Eastern Landaff, the name was gradually corrupted to Eastern, then Easton.

•**ENFIELD,** Town; Grafton County; Pop. 3,175; Zip Code 03748; Elev. 776; Lat. 43-38-44 N long. 072-08-55 W; Originally named Relhan, early settlers named the town after their former home in Enfield, Connecticut.

•**EPPING,** Town; Rockingham County; Pop. 3,460; Zip Code 03042; Chartered in 1741 and named by Massachusetts Governor Jonathan Belcher after Epping Forest, a park-suburb of London.

•**EPSOM,** Town; Merrimack County; Pop. 2,743; Zip Code 03234; Lat. 43-13-23 N long. 071-20-04 W; Established in 1727 and named for Epsom, England, a famous horse-racing town.

•**EXETER,** Town; Rockingham County; Pop. 11,024; Zip Code 03833; Lat. 42-59-07 N long. 070-57-01 W; Settled in 1638 and named after Exeter, England.

•**FARMINGTON,** Town; Strafford County; Pop. 4,630; Zip Code 03835; Lat. 43-23-35 N long. 071-03-52 W; Set up 1798 and descriptively named for the area's many fertile farms.

•**FRANCESTOWN,** Town; Hillsborough County; Pop. 830; Zip Code 03043; Named in 1772 for Royal Governor John Wentworth's beautiful wife, Frances Deering Wentworth.

•**FRANCONIA,** Town; Grafton County; Pop. 743; Zip Code 03580; Lat. 44-13-43 N long. 071-44-49 W; A mountainous area it was named Franconia in 1782 after the Franconian Alps in Germany.

•**FRANKLIN,** City; Merrimack County; Pop. 7,901; Zip Code 03235; Elev. 335; Lat. 43-26-42 N long. 071-39-18 W. Named in honor of patriot Benjamin Franklin.

•**FREMONT,** Town; Rockingham County; Pop. 1,333; Zip Code 03044; Elev. 158; Settled as Poplin in 1764, the town was renamed in 1854 to honor Republican Presidential hopeful, John C. Fremont.

•**GOFFSTOWN,** Town; Hillsborough County; Pop. 11,315; Zip Code 03045; Elev. 306; Chartered in 1748 by the New Hampshire provincial government and named for Colonel John Goffe who was among the first settlers.

•**GOSHEN,** Town; Sullivan County; Pop. 549; Zip Code 03752; Lat. 43-16-42 N long. 072-08-01 W; Incorporated in 1791 and named by settlers who had relatives in Goshen, Connecticut.

•**GRAFTON,** Town; Grafton County; Pop. 739; Zip Code 03240; Lat. 43-33-29 N long. 071-56-57 W; Chartered in 1761 and named for Augustus Henry Fitzroy, Duke of Grafton.

•**GRANTHAM,** Town; Sullivan County; Pop. 704; Zip Code 03753; Elev. 962; Lat. 43-29-24 N long. 072-08-14 W; Incorporated in 1761 and named in honor of English diplomat, Thomas Robinson, Baron of Grantham.

•**GREENFIELD,** Town; Hillsborough County; Pop. 972; Zip Code 03047; Elev. 843; Settled in 1753 and descriptively named for the town's location between hills on fertile, level ground.

•**GREENLAND,** Town; Rockingham County; Pop. 2,129; Zip Code 03840; Lat. 43-02-09 N long. 070-49-58 W; One of the earliest towns to be settled (1638), it's name honors pioneer Henry Greenland.

•**GREENVILLE,** Town; Hillsborough County; Pop. 1,988; Zip Code 03048; Incorporated in 1872 and descriptively named for the area's fertile agriculture.

•**GROTON,** Town; Grafton County; Pop. 255; Settled after the Revolutionary War and named after Groton, Massachusetts.

•**HAMPSTEAD,** Town; Rockingham County; Pop. 3,785; Zip Code 03841; Elev. 329; Lat. 42-52-33 N long. 071-10-50 W; Named Hampstead in 1749 in honor of the English home of colonial friend, William Pitt, Earl of Chatham.

•**HAMPTON,** Town; Rockingham County; Pop. 10,493; Zip Code 03842; Lat. 42-56-22 N long. 070-50-09 W; Founded in 1638 and named after Hampton, England.

•**HAMPTON FALLS,** Town; Rockingham County; Pop. 1,372; Zip Code 03844; Lat. 42-54-59 N long. 070-52-06 W; Originally part of Hampton, it became independent in 1726 and changed its name to reflect its location on the Taylor River.

•**HANCOCK,** Town; Hillsborough County; Pop. 1,193; Zip Code 03449; Lat. 42-58-22 N long. 071-58-56 W; Settled in 1764 and named in honor of Revolutionary patriot John Hancock.

•**HANOVER,** Town; Grafton County; Pop. 9,119; Zip Code 03755; Elev. 531; Lat. 43-42-07 N long. 072-17-32 W; Established in 1761 and named for Hanover parish in eastern Connecticut.

•**HAVERHILL,** Town; Grafton County; Pop. 3,445; Zip Code 03765; Lat. 44-01-59 N long. 072-03-54 W.

•**HEBRON,** Town; Grafton County; Pop. 349; Zip Code 03241; Lat. 43-41-29 N long. 071-48-24 W; Originally part of Groton, early saettlers renamed it after Hebron, Connecticut.

•HENNIKER, Town; Merrimack County; Pop. 3,246; Zip Code 03242; Lat. 43-10-50 N long. 071-49-17 W; Governor Wentworth named the town in 1768 in honor of London merchant, Sir John Henniker.

•HILL, Town; Merrimack County; Pop. 736; Zip Code 03242; Lat. 43-31-19 N long. 071-41-17 W; Incorporated in 1753 as Chester, and renamed in 1837 for popular New Hampshire governor Isaac Hill.

•HILLSBOROUGH, Town; Hillsborough County; Pop. 3,437; Zip Code 03244; Elev. 580; Lat. 43-06-58 N long. 071-53-37 W; Founded as a defensive outpost against Indian attacks, and named in 1748 for Will Hills, Earl of Hillsborough.

•HOLDERNESS, Town; Grafton County; Pop. 1,586; Zip Code 03245; Lat. 43-43-54 N long. 071-35-20 W; Granted in 1751 to Robert Darcy, fourth Earl of Holderness.

•HOLLIS, Town; Hillsborough County; Pop. 4,679; Zip Code 03049; The town was established in 1746 by Governor Benning Wentworth and named in honor of the powerful Hollis family.

•HOOKSETT, Town; Merrimack County; Pop. 7,303; Zip Code 03106; Descriptively named for the hook shaped bend in the adjacent Merrimack River.

•HOPKINTON, Town; Merrimack County; Pop. 3,861; Settlers from Hopkinton, Massachusetts named the town after their former home. Hopkinton, Massachusetts was named in honor of Edward Hopkins, a prosperous London merchant in 1715.

•HUDSON, Town; Hillsborough County; Pop. 14,022; Zip Code 03051; Founded in 1741 and later named after the Hudson river.

•KEENE, City; Cheshire County Seat; Pop. 21,449; Zip Code 03431; Elev. 486; Lat. 42-56-23 N long. 072-17-17 W; Granted in the 1750's and named in honor of Sir Benjamin Keene of England, a businessman and diplomat.

•KENSINGTON, Town; Rockingham County; Pop. 1,322; Granted in the 1730's and named in honor of Edward Rich, Earl of Holland and Baron Kensington.

•KINGSTON, Town; Rockingham County; Pop. 4,111; Zip Code 03848; Elev. 139; Lat. 42-56-25 N long. 071-03-02 W; Established in 1694 and named by its settlers after Kingston, Massachusetts.

•LACONIA, City; Belknap County Seat; Pop. 15,575; Zip Code 03246; Lat. 43-32-31 N long. 071-28-49 W; Founded in 1855 and given the name of a region of ancient classical Greece.

•LANDAFF, Town; Grafton County; Pop. 266; Incorporated in 1774 and named in honor of the Bishop of Leandaff, a Welsh bishopric in Cardiff, Wales.

•LANGDON, Town; Sullivan County; Pop. 437; Founded in 1787 and named in honor of New Hampshire's second Governor, John Landgon.

•LEBANON, City; Grafton County; Pop. 11,134; Zip Code 03766; Elev. 595; Lat. 43-38-35 N long. 072-15-27 W; Early settlers from Lebanon, Connecticut founded the town. Lebanon is a Biblical semetic word meaning "white" (as in snow covered.).

•LEE, Town; Strafford County; Pop. 2,111; Established in 1766 and named in honor of English General Charles Lee, an officer during the French-Indian Wars.

•LEMPSTER, Town; Sullivan County; Pop. 637; Zip Code 03606; Elev. 1,416; Lat. 43-14-23 N long. 072-12-46 W; Originally a defensive town, it was named after Sir Thomas Farmer of Lempster in 1761.

•LINCOLN, Town; Grafton County; Pop. 1,313; Zip Code 03251; Elev. 811; Lat. 44-01-35 N long. 071-40-07 W; Named in 1764 in honor of Henry Clinton, ninth Earl of Lincoln.

•LISBON, Town; Grafton County; Pop. 1,517; Zip Code 03585; Elev. 599; Lat. 44-13-30 N long. 071-54-25 W; Granted in 1763 and later named (1824) after Lisbon, Portugal.

•LITCHFIELD, Town; Hillsborough County; Pop. 4,150; First Naticook, then Brenton, and finally, in 1749, Litchfield. It was named in honor of George Henry Lee, Earl of Litchfield.

•LITTLETON, Town; Grafton County; Pop. 5,558; Zip Code 03561; Elev. 822; Lat. 44-18-19 N long. 071-46-14 W; Named Littleton in 1784 in honor of Colonel Moses Little, a Revolutionary War soldier.

•LONDONDERRY, Town; Rockingham County; Pop. 13,598; Zip Code 03053; Named in 1722 by emigrants from Londonberry in northern Ireland.

•LOUDON, Town; Merrimack County; Pop. 2,454; Zip Code 03301; Chartered in 1773 and named in honor of John Campbell, fourth Earl of Loudoun.

•LYMAN, Town; Grafton County; Pop. 281; Granted in 1761 and named in honor of English General Phineas Lyman.

•LYME, Town; Grafton County; Pop. 1,289; Zip Code 03768; Lat. 43-48-34 N long. 072-09-42 W; Chartered in 1761 and named after Lyme Regis in England.

•LYNDEBOROUGH, Town; Hillsborough County; Pop. 1,070; Zip Code 03082; Settled in 1735 and later named in honor of prominent lawyer Benjamin Lynde.

•MADBURY, Town; Strafford County; Pop. 987; The area was named Madbury by Sir Francis Champernowne who came to America in the 1640's. He named his estate in honor of his farm, Madbury, in England.

•MANCHESTER, City; Hillsborough County Seat; Pop. 90,936; Zip Code 03100; Lat. 42-59-09 N long. 071-27-23 W; Originally Derryfield in 1751, the town was later renamed for the famous English industrial city, Manchester.

•MASON, Town; Hillsborough County; Pop. 792; Mason's name honors Captain John Mason, New Hampshire's founder, who in 1631 sent over a group of colonists and founded the first settlements.

•MERRIMACK, Town; Hillsborough County; Pop. 15,406; Zip Code 03054; Founded in 1722 as part of Naticook, and renamed in 1746 for its location on the Merrimack River.

•MIDDLETON, Town; Strafford County; Pop. 734; Chartered in 1749 and named in honor of Sir Charles Middleton, a British naval officer.

•MILFORD, Town; Hillsborough County; Pop. 8,685; Zip Code 03055; Elev. 263; Incorporated in 1794 and desriptively named for the location of an early mill site.

•MILTON, Town; Strafford County; Pop. 2,438; Zip Code 03851; Lat. 43-24-48 N long. 070-59-05 W; The site of early water mills on the Salmon Falls River, the town took this descriptive name in 1802 upon incorporation.

•MONROE, Town; Grafton County; Pop. 619; Zip Code 03771; Elev. 534; Lat. 44-15-38 N long. 072-03-22 W; Incorporated in 1854 and named in honor of James Monroe, fifth President of the United States.

•**MOUNT VERNON,** Town; Hillsborough County; Pop. 1,444; Zip Code 03057; Mount Vernon was named in 1803 after George Washington's Virginia estate.

•**NASHUA,** City; Hillsborough County Seat; Pop. 67,865; Zip Code 03060; Elev. 169; Originally Dunstable, the name was changed in 1836 to Nashua after the Nashua River. The river is named after the Nashaway Indians. Nashaway translates "beautiful river with pebbly bottom."

•**NEW BOSTON,** Town; Hillsborough County; Pop. 1,928; Zip Code 03070; Settled in 1736 and named after Boston, Massachusetts.

•**NEW CASTLE,** Town; Rockingham County; Pop. 936; Zip Code 03854; Lat. 43-03-53 N long. 070-42-48 W; Incorporated in 1693 and named after Fort William and Mary, known as "the Castle," built on the town site to defend against Indian attacks.

•**NEW IPSWICH,** Town; Hillsborough County; Pop. 2,433; Zip Code 03071; Granted in 1735 and named after Ipswich, Massachusetts. Ipswich refers to the Saxon Queen Ebba and "wich" which means village, or "ebba village."

•**NEW LONDON,** Town; Merrimack County; Pop. 2,935; Zip Code 03256; Lat. 43-24-59 N long. 071-58-21 W; Founded in 1753 as Heidlebourg, it became New London after the Revolution, and then New London.

•**NEWBURY,** Town; Merrimack County; Pop. 961; Zip Code 03255; Lat. 43-19-22 N long. 066-02-20 W; Settled in 1753 as Dantzic and eventually (1837) becoming Newbury after Newbury, Massachusetts.

•**NEWFIELDS,** Town; Rockingham County; Pop. 817; Zip Code 03856; Lat. 43-02-09 N long. 070-56-27 W; Originally part of Exeter, the name was changed to Newfields in 1895. On the Squamscott River, it was named Newfields for the beautiful meadows adjacent the river.

•**NEWMARKET,** Town; Rockingham County; Pop. 4,290; Zip Code 03857; Elev. 626; Lat. 43-04-32 N long. 070-56-27 W; Granted town status in 1737 and named after Newmarket in County Suffolk, England.

•**NEWPORT,** Town; Sullivan County; Pop. 6,229; Zip Code 03773; Elev. 797; Lat. 43-21-44 N long. 072-10-17 W; Incorporated in 1761 and named in honor of English soldier and statesman Henry Newport, Earl of Bradford.

•**NEWTON,** Town; Rockingham County; Pop. 3,068; Zip Code 03858; Lat. 42-52-00 N long. 071-02-18 W; Chartered as "Newtown" in 1749, it was renamed Newton in 1846.

•**NORTH HAMPTON,** Town; Rockingham County; Pop. 3,425; Zip Code 03862; Lat. 42-54-00 N long. 070-49-30 W; At first a part of Hampton, it became a separate city in 1742. Hampton comes from Hampton, England.

•**NORTHFIELD,** Town; Merrimack County; Pop. 3,051; Established in 1780 and named Northfield from an original name of North Hill.

•**NORTHWOOD,** Town; Rockingham County; Pop. 2,175; Zip Code 03261; Elev. 559; Lat. 43-11-45 N long. 071-06-07 W; Settled in 1763 and descriptively named for its forests.

•**NOTTINGHAM,** Town; Rockingham County; Pop. 1,952; Zip Code 03290; Elev. 260; Established in 1722 and named in honor of Daniel Finch, second Earl of Nottingham.

•**ORANGE,** Town; Grafton County; Pop. 197; Granted in 1769 as Cardigan, the name was changed to Orange after the Revolution for the nearby deposits of orange-yellow ochre.

•**ORFORD,** Town; Grafton County; Pop. 928; Zip Code 03777; Elev. 419; Lat. 43-54-22 N long. 072-08-18 W; Chartered in 1761 and named in honor of Robert Walpole, Earl of Orford.

•**PELHAM,** Town; Hillsborough County; Pop. 8,090; Zip Code 03076; Elev. 152; Incorporated in 1746 and named in honor of Henry Pelham, then Prime Minister of England.

•**PEMBROKE,** Town; Merrimack County; Pop. 4,861; Granted in 1728 and named Pembroke in 1759 in honor of Henry Herbert, ninth Earl of Pembroke.

•**PETERBOROUGH,** Town; Hillsborough County; Pop. 4,895; Zip Code 03458; Elev. 723; Lat. 42-51-41 N long. 071-57-52 W; Named in 1738 for Charles Mordaunt, a famous English admiral, and third Earl of Petersborough.

•**PIERMONT,** Town; Grafton County; Pop. 507; Zip Code 03779; Elev. 568; Lat. 43-58-13 N long. 072-04-54 W; Named in 1764 after the Piedmont in the Italian Alps. The spelling was changed to Piermont, but the idea was to compare the two area's natural beauties.

•**PITTSFIELD,** Town; Merrimack County; Pop. 2,889; Zip Code 03263; Elev. 501; Lat. 43-17-40 N long. 071-19-58 W; Pittsfield's name honors Wiliam Pitt, Prime Minister of England, and friend to the colonies in the years before the Revolution.

•**PLAINFIELD,** Town; Sullivan County; Pop. 1,749; Zip Code 03781; Elev. 528; Lat. 43-32-06 N long. 072-21-23 W; Founded in 1761 at the beginning of the reign of King George III, and named after Plainfield, Connecticut.

•**PLAISTOW,** Town; Rockingham County; Pop. 5,609; Zip Code 03865; Elev. 104; Lat. 42-50-25 N long. 071-05-46 W; Plaistow is an open space near a village's center where sports or games are played on holidays.

•**PLYMOUTH,** Town; Grafton County; Pop. 5,094; Zip Code 03264; Elev. 514; Lat. 43-45-19 N long. 071-41-21 W; Granted in 1763 and named after Plymouth, Massachusetts.

•**PORTSMOUTH,** City; Rockingham County; Pop. 26,254; Zip Code 03801; Elev. 21; Lat. 43-04-25 N long. 070-47-14 W; One of New Hampshire's original settlements, the town was named after Portsmouth, England by New Hampshire founder Captain John Mason.

•**RANDOLPH,** Town; Coos County; Pop. 274; Originally Durand, the town was renamed Randloph in honor of Virginia Senator John Randolph in 1824.

•**RAYMOND,** Town; Rockingham County; Pop. 5,453; Zip Code 03077; Elev. 205; Named in 1764 in honor of Captain William Raymond of Beverly, Massachusetts who received land in the area for military services against the French in Canada.

•**ROCHESTER,** City; Strafford County; Pop. 21,560; Zip Code 03867; Lat. 43-18-18 N long. 070-58-32 W; Founded in the seventeenth century and named in honor of Lawrence Hyoe, Earl of Rochester.

•**RUMNEY,** Town; Grafton County; Pop. 1,212; Zip Code 03266; Lat. 43-48-17 N long. 071-48-43 W; Granted in 1761 and named in honor of Robert Marsham, second Baron of Rumney.

•**RYE,** Town; Rockingham County; Pop. 4,508; Zip Code 03870; Lat. 43-00-35 N long. 070-46-27 W; The first settlement in New Hampshire in 1623. The town was later named for the English port town of Rye.

•**SALEM,** Town; Rockingham County; Pop. 24,124; Zip Code 03079; Elev. 131; Founded as part of Meuthllen, Massachusetts and renamed Salem in 1741 after Salem, Massachusetts.

•**SALISBURY,** Town; Merrimack County; Pop. 781; Zip Code 03268; Lat. 43-22-42 N long. 071-42-56 W; Granted in 1736 and named Baker's Town after a well-known explorer. The town was renamed in 1768 after Salisbury, Massachusetts.

•**SANDOWN,** Town; Rockingham County; Pop. 2,057; Zip Code 03873; Lat. 42-55-37 N long. 071-11-14 W; Incorporated in 1756 and named for the English resort on the Isle of Wight.

•**SEABROOK,** Town; Rockingham County; Pop. 5,917; Zip Code 03871; Elev. 56; Lat. 42-53-28 N long. 070-52-25 W; Incorporated in 1768 and named after the Seabrook River which flows into the Atlantic Ocean.

•**SHELBURNE,** Town; Coos County; Pop. 318; Chartered in 1769 and named in honor of William Fitzmaurice, Earl of Shelbuyrne, who was a staunch ally of the colonies in the days before the Revolution.

•**SOMERSWORTH,** City; Strafford County; Pop. 10,350; Zip Code 03878; Elev. 204; Lat. 43-15-07 N long. 070-52-09 W; Incorporated in 1754 the origin of the town's name is uncertain.

•**SOUTH HAMPTON,** Town; Rockingham County; Pop. 660; Chartered in 1742 and originally one of the Hampton border towns, it is named for Hampton, England.

•**SPRINGFIELD,** Town; Sullivan County; Pop. 532; Governor John Wentworth granted the town in 1769. After the Revolution (1794) it changed its name from "Protectworth" to Springfield.

•**STARK,** Town; Coos County; Pop. 470; Originally named Percy in 1774, but later (1832) renamed to honor New Hampshire's Revolutionary War hero General John Stark.

•**STEWARTSTOWN,** Town; Coos County; Pop. 943; Granted in 1770 and named in honor of Sir John Stuart, Lord Bute, who was influential at the Court of George III.

•**STRATFORD,** Town; Coos County; Pop. 989; Zip Code 03884; Early settlers (1773) named the town for nearby Stratford, Connecticut.

•**STRATHAM,** Town; Rockingham County; Pop. 2,507; Zip Code 03885; Incorporated in 1716 and named after Streatham, a district near London, England.

•**SUGAR HILL,** Town; Grafton County; Pop. 397; Zip Code 03585; One of the youngest towns in New Hampshire, it is named for a large grove of sugar maples.

•**SUNAPEE,** Town; Sullivan County; Pop. 2,312; Zip Code 03782; Elev. 1,008; Lat. 43-23-10 N long. 072-05-11 W; Founded as Sunapee in 1768, it was renamed after nearby Sunappe Lake. Sunapee is an Algonquin Indian word meaning "goose lake."

•**SUTTON,** Town; Merrimack County; Pop. 1,091; Settled in 1748 and named after Sutton, Massachusetts.

•**TEMPLE,** Town; Hillsborough County; Pop. 692; Zip Code 03084; Elev. 1,005; Incorporated in 1768 and named for New Hampshire's last royal lieutenant governor.

•**THORNTON,** Town; Grafton County; Pop. 952; Established in 1763 and named for New Hampshire surgeon and patriot Dr. Matthew.

•**UNITY,** Town; Sullivan County; Pop. 1,092; Founded in 1753 and later named to commemorate settlement of a legal dispute over ownership of the grant.

•**WARNER,** Town; Merrimack County; Pop. 1,963; Zip Code 03278; Elev. 445; Lat. 43-16-50 N long. 071-48-58 W; Incorporated as Warner after a prominent Portsmouth citizen, it was named in 1774, one of the last towns established under English rule.

•**WARREN,** Town; Grafton County; Pop. 650; Zip Code 03279; Lat. 43-55-27 N long. 071-53-41 W; Granted in 1764 and named in honor of Admiral Sir Peter Warren, who was best known for his role in the capture of the French fortress of Louisburg in 1745.

•**WASHINGTON,** Town; Sullivan County; Pop. 411; Zip Code 03280; Lat. 43-10-36 N long. 072-06-00 W; Established in 1776 and named in honor of General George Washington.

•**WEARE,** Town; Hillsborough County; Pop. 3,232; Zip Code 03281; Incorporated in 1764 and named after pioneer settler and the town's first clerk, Colonel Meshech Weare.

•**WEBSTER,** Town; Merrimack County; Pop. 1,095; Established in 1860 and named for the great American lawyer and statesman, Daniel Webster.

•**WENTWORTH,** Town; Grafton County; Pop. 527; Zip Code 03282; Lat. 43-52-05 N long. 071-54-21 W; The town's name honors colonial governors John and Benning Wentworth.

•**WHITEFIELD,** Town; Coos County; Pop. 1,681; Zip Code 03598; Elev. 956; Lat. 44-22-33 N long. 071-36-33 W; Granted on July 4, 1774, the last town chartered under the Englsih provincial government, and named in honor of the famous English evangelist, George Whitefield.

•**WILMOT,** Town; Merrimack County; Pop. 725; Zip Code 03287; Elev. 683; Lat. 43-25-02 N long. 071-53-25 W; Settled in 1807 and named in honor of Dr. James Wilmot, a prominent English clergyman and friend to the colonies in the days before the Revolution.

•**WILTON,** Town; Hillsborough County; Pop. 2,669; Zip Code 03086; Elev. 357; Laid out in the 1730's as a defensive town against Indian raids, and named by Governor Benning Wentworth for a friend, famous English sculptor, Sir Joseph Wilton.

•**WINDHAM,** Town; Rockingham County; Pop. 5,664; Zip Code 03087; Elev. 200; Founded in the mid-1700's and named in honor of Sir Charles Windham, Earl of Egremont, and a friend to the colonies before the Revolution.

•**WOODSTOCK,** Town; Grafton County; Pop. 1,008; Zip Code 03293; Called Pegline when established in 1763, and renamed Woodstock in 1840 after the famous palace in England.

NEW JERSEY

•ABSECON, City; Atlantic County; Pop. 6,787; Zip Code 08021; Elev. 24; Lat. 39-25-42 N long. 074-29-46 W; 5 miles NW of Atlantic City in SE New Jersey on the Atlantic Ocean; is named from Absegami (an Indian tribe) meaning place of the swans.

•ALLAMUCHY, Township; Warren County; Pop. 2,541; Zip Code 07820; Elev. 620; Lat. 40-55-18 N long. 074-48-38 W; NW New Jersey; named from the Indian meaning "place within the hills."

•ALLENDALE, Borough; Bergen County; Pop. 5,900; Zip Code 07401; Elev. 375; Lat. 41-02-29 N long. 074-07-46 W; 10 miles N of Paterson in NE New Jersey; named after *Col. Wm. C. Allen*, who was a surveyor for the Erie Railroad.

•ALLENHURST, Borough; Monmouth County; Pop. 875; Zip Code 07711; Elev. 24; Lat. 40-14-10 N long. 074-00-04 W; E Central New Jersey; on the Atlantic; named for an early resident, *Abner Allen.*

•ALLENTOWN, Borough; Monmouth County; Pop. 1,967; Zip Code 08501; Elev. 82; Lat. 40-10-40 N long. 074-35-02 W; E Central New Jersey on the coast; named for *Nathan Allen*, who was the son-in-law of *Robert Burnet* an early settler of this area.

•ALLOWAY, Township; Salem County; Pop. 2,669; Zip Code 08001; Elev. 41; Lat. 39-33-39 N long. 075-21-46 W; SW New Jersey; named for an Indian chief *Aloes Alloway.*

•ALPHA, Borough; Warren County; Pop. 2,653; Zip Code 08865; Elev. 273; Lat. 40-40-01 N long. 075-09-28 W; 5 miles SE of Phillipsburg in NW New Jersey; named after the Alpha Cement Works Company.

•ALPINE, Borough; Bergen County; Pop. 1,557; Zip Code 07620; Elev. 410; Lat. 40-57-21 N long. 073-55-54 W; NE New Jersey; named after the Alps Mountains in Europe.

•ANDOVER, Borough; Sussex County; Pop. 865; Zip Code 07821; Elev. 634; Lat. 40-59-09 N long. 074-44-33 W; is the site of Andover Mine were parts of a tract of 11,000 acres obtained from *William Penn's* heirs.

•ASBURY PARK, City; Monmouth County; Pop. 16,675; Zip Code 07712; Elev. 21; Lat. 40-13-13 N long. 074-00-45 W; 25 miles SE of Perth Amboy in NE Central New Jersey, on the Atlantic Coast; named after the first Methodist bishop in America who was *Francis Asbury.*

•ATLANTIC CITY, City; Atlantic County; Pop. 40,199; Elev. 8; Lat. 39-21-51 N long. 074-25-24 W; 60 miles SE of Philadelphia in SE New Jersey on the Atlantic Ocean, from where it derives its name.

•ATLANTIC HIGHLANDS, Borough; Monmouth County; Pop. 4,895; Zip Code 07716; Elev. 26; Lat. 40-24-28 N long. 074-02-05 W; E Central New Jersey; named after the Ocean.

•AUDUBON, Borough; Camden County; Pop. 9,546; ; Zip Code 08105; Elev. 58; Lat. 39-53-27 N long. 075-04-24 W; 5 miles SE of Camden in SW New Jersey; named after *John James Audubon*, the naturalist and founder of the Audubon Society.

•AVALON, Borough; Cape May County; Pop. 2,192; Elev. 6; Lat. 39-06-04 N long. 074-43-05 W; S New Jersey; named after the island of Welsh mythology.

•AVON BY THE SEA, Borough; Monmouth County; Pop. 2,286; Zip Code 07717; Elev. 22; Lat. 40-11-32 N long. 074-00-59 W; E Central New Jersey of the Atlantic Coast; named after Avon, England.

•BARNEGAT, Township; Ocean County; Pop. 8.568; Zip Code 08005; Elev. 35; Lat. 39-45-11 N long. 074-13-24 W; located on the eastern coast of New Jersey. The town's name was originally, but never officially Barendegat (Dutch, breaker's inlet).

•BARRINGTON, Borough; Camden County; Pop. 7,426; Zip Code 08007; Elev. 81; Lat. 39-51-53 N long. 075-03-20 W; 5 miles SE of Camden in SW New Jersey.

•BAY HEAD, Borough; Ocean County; Pop. 1,336; Zip Code 08742; Elev. 5; Lat. 40-04-18 N long. 074-03-17 W; E Coastal; derives its name from the location at the head of Barnegat Bay.

•BAYONNE, City; Hudson County; Pop. 65,047; Zip Code 07002; Elev. 27; Lat. 40-40-07 N long. 074-06-53 W; 5 miles SW of Jersey City in NE New Jersey; named after Bayonne, France.

•BEACH HAVEN, Borough; Ocean County; Pop. 1,714; Zip Code 08008; Elev. 10; Lat. 39-33-33 N long. 074-14-37 W; E New Jersey.

•BEACHWOOD, Borough; Ocean County; Pop. 7,687; Zip Code 08722; Elev. 25; Lat. 39-56-20 N long. 074-11-36 W; located in Eastern New Jersey.

•BEDMINSTER, Township; Somerset County; Pop. 2,469; Zip Code 07921; Elev. 198; Lat. 40-40-50 N long. 074-38-45 W; named for Bedminster, England.

•BELLEVILLE, Town; Essex County; Pop. 35367; Zip Code 07109; Elev. 69; Lat. 40-47-37 N long. 074-09-02 W; located in NE New Jersey; is an old Dutch settlement on the steep bank of Passaic River. The name is French, meaning "beautiful city."

•BELLMAWR, Borough; Camden County; Pop. 13,752; Zip Code 08031; Elev. 44; Lat. 39-52-03 N long. 075-05-42 W; located in SW New Jersey, 5 miles South of Camden; Named for *Ernest C. Bell*, horse breeder.

•BELMAR, Borough; Monmouth County; Pop. 6,771; Zip Code 07719; Elev. 19; Lat. 40-10-42 N long. 074-01-20 W; located in E New Jersey; is named for the Italian word meaning "beautiful sea."

•BELVIDERE, Town; Warren County; Pop. 2,475; Zip Code 07823; Elev. 257; Lat. 40-49-47 N long. 075-04-41 W; name is Italian word meaning "beautiful to see."

•BERGENFIELD, Borough; Bergen County; Pop. 25,568; Zip Code 07621; Elev. 92; Lat. 40-55-39 N long. 073-59-52 W; located in NE New Jersey.

•BERKELEY HEIGHTS, Township; Union County; Pop. 12,549; Zip Code 07922; Elev. 220; Lat. 40-41-00 N long. 074-26-35 W; located in NE New Jersey; named after *Lord John Berkeley*, Proprietor.

•BERLIN, Borough; Camden County; Pop. 5,786; Zip Code 08009; Elev. 155; Lat. 39-47-28 N long. 074-55-46 W; 15 miles SE of Camden in SW New Jersey; named for Berlin, Germany.

•BERNARDSVILLE, Borough; Somerset County; Pop. 6,715; Zip Code 07924; Elev. 400; Lat. 40-43-07 N long. 074-34-11 W; located in N New Jersey; named after *Francis Bernard*, Governor 1758-60.

•BEVERLY,, City; Burlington County; Pop. 2,919; Zip Code 08010; Elev. 28; Lat. 40-03-55 N long. 074-55-10 W; located in S New Jersey; named for Beverly, England.

•BLACKWOOD TERRACE, Township (also included in Deptford Township); Gloucester County; Pop. 900; Zip Code 08096; Elev. 30; Lat. 39-48-18 N long. 075-05-10 W; located in SW New Jersey.

•BLAIRSTOWN, Township; Warren County; Pop. 4,360; Zip Code 07825; Elev. 350; Lat. 40-58-58 N long. 074-57-39 W; located in NW New Jersey.

•**BLOOMFIELD**, Town; Essex County; Pop. 47,792; Zip Code 07003 ; Elev. 131; Lat. 40-48-24 N long. 074-11-09 W; located in NE New Jersey; Originally known as Wardsesson (Ind. crooked place), it got its present name when a town meeting decided in 1796 to honor *Joseph Bloomfield*, Revolutionary general and later Governor (1810-1812).

•**BLOOMINGDALE**, Borough; Passaic County; Pop. 7,867; Zip Code 07403; Elev. 257; Lat. 41-00-07 N long. 074-19-37 W; located in N New Jersey; name is descriptive of location.

•**BLOOMSBURY**, Borough; Hunterdon County; Pop. 864; Zip Code 08804; Elev. 279; Lat. 40-39-14 N long. 075-05-13 W; located in NW New Jersey.

•**BOGOTA**, Borough; Bergen County; Pop. 8344; Zip Code 07603; Elev. 100; Lat. 40-52-34 N long. 074-01-49 W; located in NE New Jersey; named for Bogert family, early settlers.

•**BOONTOWN**, Town; Morris County; Pop. 8,620; Zip Code 07005; Elev. 431; Lat. 40-54-09 N long. 074-24-27 W; located N of New Jersey; Named after Governor Thomas Boone, 1760-61. Settled in 1762.

•**BORDENTOWN**, City; Burlington County; Pop. 4,441; Zip Code 08505; Elev. 72; Lat. 40-08-46 N long. 074-42-44 W; located in S New Jersey; Established by *Joseph Borden*, for whom the town was named.

•**BOUND BROOK**, Borough; Somerset County; Pop. 9,710; Zip Code 08805; Elev. 48; Lat. 40-34-06 N long. 074-32-20 W; located in North Central New Jersey.

•**BRADLEY BEACH**, Borough; Monmouth County; Pop. 4,772; Zip Code 07720; Elev. 26; Lat. 40-12-08 N long. 074-00-45 W; named after *James A. Bradley*, founder.

•**BRANCHVILLE**, Borough; Sussex County; Pop. 870; Zip Code 07826; Elev. 529; Lat. 41-08-47 N long. 074-45-10 W; located in N New Jersey; named Branchville as it's the main branch of Paulins Kill.

•**BRICK**, Township; Ocean County; Pop. 53,629; Zip Code 08723; located in E New Jersey; named after *Joseph W. Brick*, resident.

•**BRIDGETON**, City; Seat of Cumberland County; Pop. 18,795; Zip Code 08302; Elev. 40; Lat. 39-25-38 N long. 075-14-04 W; located in SW New Jersey; A bridge built across Cohansey Creek about 1716 gave the hamlet the name of Conhansy Bridge. Later it was changed to Bridge Town and then to Bridgeton.

•**BRIDGEWATER**, Township; Somerset County; Pop. 29,175; Zip Code 08807; located in N New Jersey; named after Bridgewater, England.

•**BRIELLE**, Borough; Monmouth County; Pop. 4,086; Zip Code 08730; Elev. 12; Lat. 40-06-28 N long. 074-03-25 W; located in E New Jersey; Named after commune in Holland.

•**BRIGANTINE**, City; Atlantic County; Pop. 8,318; Zip Code 08203; Elev. 8; Lat. 39-24-36 N long. 074-21-54 W; located in SE New Jersey; named after Brigantine, a ship wrecked about 1710 in this area.

•**BUDD LAKE**, Unincorporated; Morris County; Pop. 3,168; Zip Code 07828; Elev. 940; Lat. 40-52-16 N long. 074-44-04 W; named for *John Budd* an early landowner.

•**BUENA**, Borough; Atlantic County; Pop. 3,642; Zip Code 08310; Elev. 108; Lat. 39-30-49 N long. 074-55-30 W; located in SE New Jersey; named for battle of Buena Vista, Mexican War.

•**BURLINGTON**, City; Burlington County; Pop. 10,246; Zip Code 08016; Elev. 12; Lat. 40-04-16 N long. 074-51-55 W; located in S New Jersey; named for Burlington, England.

•**BUTLER**, Borough; Morris County; Pop. 7,616; Zip Code 07405; Elev. 315; Lat. 41-00-13 N long. 074-20-31 W; located in N New Jersey; named for an early landowner.

•**CALDWELL**, Borough; Essex County; Pop. 7,624; Zip Code 07006; Elev. 411; Lat. 40-50-23 N long. 074-16-37 W; located in NE New Jersey; named after a "fighting parson" during the Revolution, *Rev. James Caldwell*.

•**CALIFON**, Borough; Hunterdon County; Pop. 1,023; Zip Code 07830; Elev. 411; Lat. 40-43-10 N long. 074-50-10 W; located in NW New Jersey; named for California.

•**CAMDEN**, City; Camden County; Pop. 84,910; Zip Code 081++; Elev. 23; Lat. 39-55-33 N long. 075-07-12 W; located in SW New Jersey; Named Camden for the first Earl of Camden, the nobleman who befriended the Colonies during their disputes with the mother country.

•**CAPE MAY**, City; Cape May County; Pop. 4,853; Zip Code 08204; Elev. 14; Lat. 38-56-06 N long. 074-54-23 W; named for explorer *Cornelius Jacobsen Mey* who sailed past in 1623 - 14 years after *Henry Hudson*.

•**CARLSTADT**, Borough; Bergen County; Pop. 6.166; Zip Code 07072; Elev. 94; Lat. 40-50-25 N long. 074-05-28 W; located in NE New Jersey; The town, first called Tailor Town because many of the inhabitants worked for New York tailors, was later renamed Carlstadt (Carl's town) for *Dr. Carl Klein*.

•**CARNEY'S POINT**, Township; Salem County; Pop. 2,680; Zip Code 08069; Elev. 19; Lat. 39-42-40 N long. 07528-14 W; located in SW New Jersey; 6 miles NE of Perth Amboy in Central New Jersey by Staten Island.

•**CARTERET**, Borough; Middlesex County; Pop. 20,598; Zip Code 07008; Elev. 12; Lat. 40-34-38 N long. 074-13-43 W; located in Central New Jersey; named after the first English Governor, *Philip Carteret*.

•**CEDAR GROVE**, Township; Essex County; Pop. 12,600; Zip Code 07009; Elev. 24; Lat. 39-09-45 N long. 074-46-01 W; located in NE New Jersey; descriptive name for stands of cedars.

•**CHATHAM**, Borough; Morris County; Pop. 8,537; Zip Code 07928; Elev. 244; Lat. 40-44-27 N long. 074-23-03 W; 5 miles SE of Morristown in N New Jersey; located 10 miles West of Newark; named for the Earl of Chatham who was friendly to the colonists.

•**CHERRY HILL**, Township; Camden County; Pop. 68,785; Zip Code 080; Elev. 90; Lat. 40-55-15 N long. 074-02-20 W; E of Camden in W central New Jersey.

•**CHESTER**, Borough; Morris County; Pop. 1,433; Zip Code 07930; Elev. 846; Lat. 40-47-03 N long. 074-41-50 W; located in North Central New Jersey Named for Chestershire, England.

•**CINNAMINSON**, Township; Burlington County; Pop. 16,072; Zip Code 08077; Elev. 70; Lat. 39-59-48 N long. 074-59-35 W; located in S central New Jersey; descriptive name meaning "stone" and minna meaning "island."

•**CLARK**, Township; Union County; Pop. 16,699; Zip Code 07066; Elev. 80; Lat. 40-38-27 N long. 074-18-40 W; located in NE New Jersey; named after a signer of the Declaration of Independence, *Abraham Clark*.

•**CLAYTON**, Borough; Gloucester County; Pop. 6,013; Zip Code 08312; Elev. 130; Lat. 39-39-36 N long. 075-05-33 W; located in SW New Jersey.

•**CLEMENTON**, Borough; Camden County; Pop. 5,764; Zip Code 08021; Elev. 96; 39-48-41 N long. 074-59-00 W; SE of Camden in SW NewJersey; named for *Samuel Clements*, industrialist.

•**CLIFFSIDE PARK**, Borough; Bergen County; Pop. 21,464; Zip Code 07010; Elev. 57; Lat. 40-49-17 N long. 073-59-17 W; on the Hudson River, across from New York City, 10 miles NE of Jersey City; named for its location "Park by the cliffs."

•**CLIFTON**, City; Passaic County; Pop. 74,388; Zip Code 070; Elev. 233; Lat. 40-51-30 N long. 074-09-51 W; located in N New Jersey; named for location under Weasel Mountain.

•**CLINTON**, Town; Hunterdon County; Pop. 1,910; Zip Code 08809; Elev. 195; Lat. 40-52-45 N long. 074-18-55 W; located in NW New Jersey; named for Governor of New York *De Witt Clinton*.

•**CLOSTER**, Borough; Bergen County; Pop. 8,164; Zip Code 07624; Elev. 51; Lat. 40-58-23 N long. 073-57-43 W.

•**COLLINGSWOOD**, Borough; Camden County; Pop. 15,838; Zip Code 08108; Elev. 20; Lat. 39-55-05 N long. 075-04-18 W; located in SW New Jersey, NE of Camden; named after the Mother of *Edward Collings Knight*.

•**COLONIA**, Unincorporate village; Somerset County; Pop. 23,200; Elev. 60; Lat. 40-34-28 N long. 074-18-09 W; NE New Jersey; In a suburban-residential area SW of Rahway.

•**COLTS NECK**, Township; Monmouth County; Pop. 7,888; Zip Code 07722; Elev. 125; Lat. 40-17-15 N long. 074-10-22 W; located in E New Jersey; was originally named Caul's Neck for an early settler. It became a famous breeding place for race horses, and a story persists that a colt of the renowned race horse, *Old Fashioned*, fell and broke its neck here.

•**CONVENT STATION**, included in Morristown; Morris County; Pop. est. 1,300; Zip Code 07961; located in N New Jersey.

•**COOKSTOWN**, included in New Hanover and North Hanover townships; Burlington County; Pop. est. 300; Zip Code 08511; Elev. 90; Lat. 40-02-56 N long. 074-33-46 W; located in S New Jersey.

•**CRANBURY**, Township; Middlesex County; Pop. 1,927; Zip Code 08512; Elev. 110; Lat. 40-18-58 N long. 074-30-51 W; located in Central New Jersey; named for wild cranberries.

•**CRANFORD**, Township; Union County; Pop. 24,573; Zip Code 07016; Elev. 70; Lat. 40-39-30 N long. 074-18-00 W; located in NE New Jersey; named for the *Crane* family.

•**CRESSKILL**, Borough; Bergen County; Pop. 7,609; Zip Code 07626; Elev. 43; Lat. 40-56-29 N long. 073-57-35 W; located in NE New Jersey; descriptive name, meaning steam full of cresses.

•**DEAL**, Borough; Monmouth County; Pop. 1,952; Zip Code 07723; Elev. 33; Lat. 40-14-35 N long. 074-00-04 W; located in E New Jersey; named for Deal, England.

•**DEERFIELD**, Township; Cumberland County; Pop. 2,523; Zip Code 08313; Elev. 120; Lat. 39-31-25 N long. 075-14-11 W; located in SW New Jersey. Named for Deerfield, Massachusetts.

•**DELANCO**, Township; Burlington County; Pop. 3,730; Zip Code 08075; Elev. 20; Lat. 40-03-02 N long. 074-57-14 W; located in S central New Jersey; named for the location on the Delaware River and Rancocas Creek.

•**DELRAN**, Township; Burlington County; Pop. 14,811; Zip Code 08075; located in S New Jersey.

•**DEMAREST**, Borough; Bergen County; Pop. 4,963; Zip Code 07627; Elev. 38; Lat. 40-57-26 N long. 073-57-50 W; located in NE New Jersey 15 miles NE of Paterson; named by *Demarest* family, early settlers.

•**DENNIS**, Township; Cape May County; Pop. 3,989; Zip Code 08214; located in S New Jersey.

•**DENVILLE**, Township; Morris County; Pop. 15,380; Zip Code 07834; Elev. 540; Lat. 40-53-32 N long. 074-28-40 W; named for *Daniel Denton*, a landowner; at its southwestern tip is Indian Lake.

•**DEPTFORD**, Township; Gloucester County; Pop. 23,473; Zip Code 08096; located in SW New Jersey; named for Deptford, England.

•**DOVER**, Town; Morris County; Pop. 14,681; Zip Code 07801; Elev. 585; Lat. 40-53-02 N long. 074-33-45 W; located in N New Jersey; named for Dover, New Hampshire.

•**DUMONT**, Borough; Bergen County; Pop. 18,334; Zip Code 07628; Elev. 104; Lat. 40-56-26 N long. 073-59-50 W; located in NE New Jersey; named for the first mayor.

•**DUNELLEN**, Borough; Middlesex County; Pop. 6,593; Zip Code 08812; Elev. 58; Lat. 40-35-21 N long. 074-28-20 W; located in Central New Jersey 9 miles NE of New Brunswick; was conceived, planned and established (1868) by the Central R.R. of New Jersey. Railroad president De Forest took the first name of a friend, *Ellen Betts*, and prefixed the "dun" because he liked the sound of the combination.

•**EAST BRUNSWICK**, Township; Middlesex County; Pop. 37,711; Zip Code 08816; located in Central New Jersey.

•**EAST HAVOVER**, Township; Morris County; Pop. 9,319; Zip Code 07936; located in N New Jersey.

•**EAST ORANGE**, City; Essex County; Pop. 77,025; Zip Code 070; Elev. 166; Lat. 40-46-02 N long. 074-12-19 W; located in NE New Jersey; is the largest of "The Oranges" and closest to the center of Newark.

•**EAST RUTHERFORD**, Borough; Bergen County; Pop. 7,849; Zip Code 07073; Elev. 48; Lat. 40-50-02 N long. 074-05-51 W; located in NE New Jersey; North of Newark; is separated from Rutherford only by the tracks of the Erie R.R.

•**EATONTOWN**, Borough; Monmouth County; Pop. 12,703; Zip Code 07724; Elev. 46; Lat. 40-17-46 N long. 074-03-05 W; 5 miles NW of Asbury Park in E New Jersey; was named for *Thomas Eaton*, who came here from Rhode Island before 1685.

•**EDGEWATER**, Borough; Bergen County; Pop. 4,628; Zip Code 07020; Elev. 55; Lat. 40-49-37 N long. 073-58-34 W; located in NE New Jersey; named for location along the Hudson River.

•**EDISON**, Township; Middlesex County; Pop. 70,193; Zip Code 088; Elev. 100; Lat. 39-31-07 N long. 074-24-45 W; located in Central New Jersey; named after *Thomas Alva Edison*.

•**EGG HARBOR CITY**, City; Atlantic County; Pop. 4,618; Zip Code 08215; Elev. 58; Lat. 39-31-43 N long. 074-38-54 W; located in S Central New Jersey. Named for its Gull's eggs.

•**ELIZABETH**, City; Union County; Pop. 106,201; Zip Code 072; Elev. 36; Lat. 40-39-50 N long. 074-12-40 W; located in NE New Jersey; *Philip Carteret*, the first English governor of New Jersey, named it Elizabethtown in honor of the wife of his cousin, *Sir George Carteret*.

•**ELMER**, Borough; Salem County; Pop. 1,569; Zip Code 08318; Elev. 118; Lat. 39-35-42 N long. 075-10-14 W; located in SW New Jersey; is named for *L.Q.C. Elmer*, New Jersey Supreme Court Justice.

321

•ELMWOOD PARK, Borough; Bergen County; Pop. 18,377; Zip Code 07407; Elev. 50; Lat. 40-54-14 N long. 074-07-08 W; located in NE New Jersey; originally Eat Paterson; SE of Paterson in N New Jersey.

•EMERSON, Borough; Bergen County; Pop. 7,793; Zip Code 07630; Elev. 46; Lat. 40-58-34 N long. 074-01-36 W; located in NE New Jersey; is named for author, *Ralph Waldo Emerson*.

•ENGLEWOOD, City; Bergen County; Pop. 23,701; Zip Code 076; Elev. 44; Lat. 40-53-34 N long. 073-58-23 W; located in NE New Jersey.

•ENGLEWOOD CLIFFS, Borough; Bergen County; Pop. 5,698; Zip Code 07632; Elev. 371; Lat. 40-53-07 N long. 073-57-10 W; located in NE New Jersey; is named for position atop Palisades.

•ENGLISHTOWN, Borough; Monmouth County; Pop. 976; Zip Code 07726; Elev. 70; Lat. 40-17-50 N long. 074-21-31 W; located in E New Jersey; is where *Washington* made his headquarters, June 27, 1778, the night before the Battle of Monmouth. *Washington* slept in the house of *Dr. James English*, the night before the battle.

•ESSEX FELLS, Borough; Essex County; Pop. 2,363; Zip Code 201; Elev. 387; Lat. 40-49-28 N long. 074-17-06 W; located in NE New Jersey; named for *John Fells*.

•ESTELL MANOR, City; Atlantic County; Pop. 848; Zip Code 08319; Elev. 78; Lat. 39-24-43 N long. 074-44-34 W; located in S central New Jersey; The name is derived from the D'Estail family, French Huguenots who settled here in 1671.

•FAIR HAVEN, Borough; Monmouth County; Pop. 5,679; Zip Code 07701; Elev. 30; Lat. 40-21-38 N long. 074-02-19 W; located in E New Jersey; name is the remark of a ship's Captain.

•FAIR LAWN, Borough; Bergen County; Pop. 32,229; Zip Code 07410; Elev. 100; Lat. 40-56-25 N long. 074-07-56 W; located in NE New Jersey; name of the *Ackerson* estate.

•FAIRVIEW, Borough; Bergen County; Pop. 10,519; Zip Code 07022; Elev. 308; Lat. 40-48-45 N long. 073-59-58 W; located in NE New Jersey; named for the view of the Hackensack Valley.

•FANWOOD, Borough; Union County; Pop. 7,767; Zip Code 07023; Elev. 184; Lat. 40-38-27 N long. 074-2302 W; located in NE New Jersey; was named for *Miss Fannie Wood*, a writer, daughter of Jersey Central R.R. official.

•FARMINGDALE, Borough; Monmouth County; Pop. 1,348; Zip Code 07727; Elev. 79; Lat. 39-22-34 N long. 075-06-36 W; located in E New Jersey; named for center of farming area.

•FLEMINGTON, Borough; Hunterdon County; Pop. 4,132; Zip Code 08822; Elev. 160; Lat. 40-30-44 N long. 074-51-35 W; located in NW New Jersey; *Philip Kase* is generally credited as being the town's first settler, although the community takes its name from *Samuel Fleming*.

•FLORENCE, Township; Burlington County; Pop. 9,084; Zip Code 08518; Elev. 20; Lat. 40-07-10 N long. 074-48-21 W; located in S New Jersey; named for Florence, Italy.

•FLORHAM PARK, Borough; Morris County; Pop. 9,359; Zip Code 07932; Elev. 200; Lat. 40-47-16 N long. 074-23-19 W; located in N New Jersey.

•FORT LEE, Borough; Bergen County; Pop. 32,449; Zip Code 07024; Elev. 313; Lat. 40-51-03 N long. 073-58-14 W; located in NE New Jersey; named after Revolutionary fort, for *Major General Charles Lee*.

•FRANKLIN, Borough; Sussex County; Pop. 4,486; Zip Code 07416; Elev. 621; Lat. 41-07-19 N long. 074-34-51 W; located in N New Jersey; named after *Benjamin Franklin*.

•FRANKLIN LAKES, Borough; Bergen County; Pop. 8,769; Zip Code 07417; Elev. 399; Lat. 41-01-00 N long. 074-12-22 W; located in NE New Jersey; named for *William Franklin*, last Royal Governor of New Jersey.

•FRANKLIN PARK, Township; Somerset County; Pop. 31,116; Zip Code 08823; Elev. 130; Lat. 40-26-20 N long. 074-32-08 W; located in N New Jersey; named for *Benjamin Franklin* ; was an early Dutch community.

•FRANKLINVILLE, Township; Gloucester County; Pop. 12,396; Zip Code 08322; Elev. 98; Lat. 39-37-05 N long. 075-04-34 W; located in SW New Jersey.

•FREEHOLD, Borough; Monmouth County; Pop. 10,020; Zip Code 07728; Elev. 178; Lat. 40-15-36 N long. 074-16-27 W; located in E New Jersey; Scotch settlers chose the name of Monmouth Court House from Monmouthshire in England. By 1795 a post office was opened, under the shorter name of Monmouth. Six years later the name was changed to Freehold by postal authorities to avoid confusion with other Monmouths in the county.

•FRENCHTOWN, Borough; Hunterdon County; Pop. 1,573; Zip Code 08825; Elev. 141; Lat. 40-31-34 N long. 075-03-43 W; located in NW New Jersey; is on the bank of the Delaware River. Named for fugitives from French Revolution.

•GARFIELD, Bergen County; Pop. 26,803; Zip Code 07026; Elev. 80; Lat. 40-52-53 N long. 074-06-49 W; located in NE New Jersey; named after *President James A. Garfield*.

•GARWOOD, Borough; Union County; Pop. 4,752; Zip Code 07027; Elev. 86; Lat. 40-39-34 N long. 074-19-24 W; located in NE New Jersey; is named for the *Unami* clan of Indians.

•GIBBSBORO, Borough; Camden County; Pop. 2,510; Elev. 89; Lat. 39-50-17 N long. 074-57-55 W; located in SW New Jersey.

•GLASSBORO, Borough; Gloucester County; Pop. 14,574; Zip Code 08028; Elev. 144; Lat. 39-42-10 N long. 075-06-44 W; located in SW New Jersey; named for it's early glass industry.

•GLEN RIDGE, Borough; Essex County; Pop. 7,855; Zip Code 07028; Elev. 187; Lat. 40-48-19 N long. 074-12-15 W; located in NE NewJersey; descriptive name for a ridge in glen formed by Toney's Brook.

•GLEN ROCK, Borough; Bergen County; Pop. 11,497; Zip Code 07452; Elev. 114; Lat. 40-57-46 N long. 074-08-00 W; located in NE New Jersey; named by ridge in glen formed by Toney's Brook.

•GREENWICH, Township; Cumberland County; Pop. 973; Zip Code 08323; Elev. 14; Lat. 39-23-23 N long. 075-20-20 W; located in SW New Jersey; named after Greenwich, England.

•GUTTENBERG, Town; Hudson County; Pop. 7,340; Zip Code 07093; Elev. 240; Lat. 40-47-31 N long. 074-00-15 W; located in NE NewJersey; name is a German word meaning, "good village."

•HACKENSACK, City; Bergen County; Pop. 36,039; Zip Code 076; Elev. 20; Lat. 40-53-09 N long. 074-02-38 W; located in NE New Jersey; the name Hackensack is supposed to be of Indian origin, but the exact derivation is vague.

•HACKETTSTOWN, Town; Warren County; Pop. 8,850; Zip Code 07840; Elev. 560; Lat. 40-51-14 N long. 074-49-46 W; located in NW New Jersey; Mts. Originally called Helm's Mills or Musconetcong, it became known as Hackettstown about the middle of the eighteenth century after *Samuel Hackett*, largest landowner in the district.

•**HADDONFIELD**, Borough; Camden County; Pop. 12,345; Zip Code 08033; Elev. 571; Lat. 39-53-29 N long. 075-02-17 W; located in SW New Jersey, 10 miles W of Camden; was founded by a Quaker girl of 20, *Elizabeth Haddon*. In 1710 *Elizabeth* was sent over from England by her father, who had no sons, to develop 400 acres of land. Within a year the young woman had started her colony, erected a home, and married *John Estaugh*, Quaker missionary, because she had the courage to propose to him. Longfellow tells the tory of the romance with the "Theologian's Tale" in Tales of a Wayside Inn.

•**HADDON HEIGHTS**, Borough; Camden County; Pop. 8,361; Zip Code 08035; Elev. 60; Lat. 39-52-38 N long. 075-03-54 W; located in SW New Jersey; is named after *Elizabeth Haddon*, settler.

•**HAINESPORT**, Township; Burlington County; Pop. 3,236; Zip Code 08036; Elev. 41; Lat. 39-59-01 N long. 074-49-39 W; located in S New Jersey; is named for *Barclay Haines* an early resident.

•**HALEDON-NORTH HALEDON**, Borough; Passaic County; Pop. 8,177; Zip Code 075; Elev. 259; Lat. 40-56-08 N long. 074-11-12 W; located in N New Jersey; is named after Haledon, England.

•**HAMBURG**, Borough; Sussex County; Pop. 1,832; Zip Code 07419; Elev. 453; Lat. 41-09-12 N long. 074-34-36 W; located in N New Jersey; Named after Hamburg, Germany.

•**HAMILTON**, Township; Mercer County; Pop. 82,801; Zip Code 08690; Elev. 100; Lat. 40-12-25 N long. 074-04-54 W; was originally known as the Crossroads in Nottingham Township, and later was called Nottingham Square. The name was changed in 1842 to honor *Alexander Hamilton*.

•**HAMMONTON**, Town; Atlantic County; Pop. 12,298; Zip Code 08037; Elev. 100; Lat. 39-38-11 N long. 074-48-10 W; located in SE New Jersey.

•**HAMPTON**, Borough; Hunterdon County; Pop. 1,614; Zip Code 08827; Elev. 496; Lat. 40-42-25 N long. 074-57-23 W; located in NW New Jersey; is named for *Jonathan Hampton*, donor of church land.

•**HARRINGTON PARK**, Borough; Bergen County; Pop. 4,532; Zip Code 07640; Elev. 50; Lat. 40-59-01 N long. 073-58-49 W; located in NE New Jersey; is named after *Harring* family, settlers.

•**HARRISON**, Town; Hudson County; Pop. 12,242; Zip Code 07020; Elev. 30; Lat. 40-44-47 N long. 074-09-24 W; located in NE New Jersey; is named after *President William Henry Harrison*.

•**HARRISON**, Township; Gloucester County; Pop. 3,585; Zip Code 08039; Elev. 10; located in SW New Jersey; settled by Quakers at some time after 1673, Named after *President William Henry Harrison*.

•**HARVEY CEDARS**, Borough; Ocean County; Pop. 363; Zip Code 08008; Elev. 9; Lat. 39-42-22 N, long. 074-08-04 W. Located in E. New Jersey, the island's oldest settlement drew whalers from Long Island and New England soon after the war of 1812.

•**HASBROUCK HEIGHTS**, Borough; Bergen County; Pop. 12,166; Zip Code 07604; Elev. 130; Lat. 40-51-29 N, long. 074-04-52 W. The town was founded by the Kip family in 1685, but the name was taken from another Dutch colonist.

•**HAWORTH**, Borough; Bergen County; Pop. 3,509; Zip Code 07641; Elev. 90; Lat. 40-57-39 N, long. 073-59-26 W. The borough is named for Haworth, England.

•**HAWTHORNE**, Borough; Passaic County; Pop. 18,200; Zip Code 075+; Elev. 100; Lat. 40-56-57 N, long. 074-09-15 W. The borough is named after novelist Nathaniel Hawthorne.

•**HAZLET**, Township; Monmouth County; Pop. 23,013; Zip Code 07730; Elev. 60; Lat. 40-24-56 N, long. 074-11-29 W. Located in E. New Jersey. Hazlet is named after an early settler.

•**HELMETTA**, Borough; Middlesex County; Pop. 955; Zip Code 08828; Elev. 44; Lat. 40-22-36 N, long. 074-25-30 W. Named after Etta Helme, the daughter of a snuff factory owner.

•**HEWITT**, included West Milford; Passaic County; Pop. 22,750; Zip Code 07421; Elev. 420; Lat. 41-08-30 N, long. 074-18-40 W. Named for Abram S. Hewitt, ironmaster, mayor of New York.

•**HIGH BRIDGE**, Borough; Hunterdon County; Pop. 3,435; Zip Code 08829; Elev. 332; Lat. 40-40-01 N, long. 074-53-46 W. Located in NW New Jersey. Descriptively named as a route through the Musconetcong Mountains.

•**HIGHLAND PARK**, Borough; Middlesex County; Pop. 13,396; Zip Code 08904; Elev. 99; Lat. 40-29-45 N, long. 074-25-29 W. A suburb of New Brunswick, it is divided from that city by the Raritan River. An Indian village was on the townsite in 1675, when the place was known as Raritan Falls, from a small cascade.

•**HIGHLANDS**, Borough; Monmouth County; Pop. 5,187; Zip Code 07732; Lat. 40-24-13 N, long. 073-59-31 W. Formerly Parkertown, Highlands is a fishing village and summer resort close by the ocean.

•**HIGHTSTOWN**, Borough; Mercer County; Pop. 4,581; Zip Code 08520; Elev. 84; Lat. 40-16-10, N, long. 074-31-25 W. Founded in 1721, the town was named for John Hight, an early landowner and miller. In 1834 it became a station on the Camden and Amboy R.R., the first railroad built in New Jersey.

•**HILLSDALE**, Borough; Bergen County; Pop. 10,495; Zip Code 07642; Elev. 83; Lat. 41-00-09 N, long. 074-02-27 W. Located in NE New Jersey and descriptively named for its "dale among the hills."

•**HILLSIDE**, Township; Union County; Pop. 21,440; Zip Code 07205; Elev. 100; 40-42-04 N, long. 074-13-50 W. Located in NE New Jersey. Descriptively named for a local geographic feature, part of the nearby Watchung Mountains.

•**HOBOKEN**, City; Hudson County; Pop. 42,460; Zip Code 07030; Elev. 5; Lat. 40-44-38 N, long. 074-01-58 W. *Hobocan Hacking*, meaning "land of the tobacco pipe," was the Lenni Lenape Indian name for this territory. It was settled by the Dutch of New Amsterdam as early as 1640. In 1804 Col. John Stevens bought the whole area and called it the "New City of Hoboken." It separated from North Bergen and was incorporated as a city in 1855.

•**HO HO KUS**, Borough; Bergen County; Pop. 4,129; Zip Code 07423; Elev. 113; Lat. 40-59-47 N, long. 074-06-06 W. In colonial times Hohokus was known as Hoppertown because of an early settler. The present name comes from the Chihohokies Indian word *Mehohokus*, meaning "red cedar."

•**HOLMDEL**, Township; Monmouth County; Pop.8,447; Zip Code 07733; Elev. 100; Lat. 40-20-42 N, long. 074-11-04 W. The township is named for the Holmes family, leading landowners and descendants of the Rev. Obadiah Holmes, who came from England in 1638 and became pastor of the Baptist Church at Newport, R.I. in 1676.

•**HOPATCONG**, Borough; Sussex County; Pop.15,531; Zip Code 07843; Elev. 1,000; Lat. 40-55-58 N; long. 074-39-35 W. The borough is named for Hokunk, "above," peek, "body of water," and "hill," and Saconk, "outlet."

•HOPE, Township; Warren County; Pop. 1,468; Zip Code 07844; Elev. 433; Lat. 40-54-40 N, long. 074-58-04 W. Moravian colonists from Bethlehem, Pa. settled here in 1774. It was named "Hope of Immortality" by Moravian missionaries.

•HOPEWELL, Borough; Mercer County; Pop. 2,001; Zip Code 08525; Elev. 200; Lat. 40-23-21 N, long. 074-45-44 W. Named after "The Hopewell," which brought settlers.

•HOWELL, Township; Monmouth County; Pop. 25,065; Zip Code 07731; located in E New Jersey. Named for Richard Howell, Governor 1792-1801.

•INDIAN MILLS, Burlington County; Zip Code 08080; Elev. 77; Lat. 39-47-38 N, long. 074-44-41 W. The site of the first Indian reservation on the continent, it was established in 1758. The 3,000-acre tract was called Edge Pillock or Edge-Pe-lick. Friends of the Indians renamed it Brotherton. The last of the tribesmen sold the land in 1801 and left to join kinsmen in the Lake Oneida Reservation, New York. Indian Mills today is a settlement of cranberry pickers and a few farmers.

•IRVINGTON, Town; Essex County; Pop. 61,493; Zip Code 07111; Elev. 185; located in NE New Jersey. The town is named for Washington Irving, author.

•ISELIN, included in Woodbridge; Middlesex County; Pop. 18,400; Zip Code 08830; Elev. 64; Lat. 40-34-31 N, long. 074-19-22 W. Named for the Iselin family, prominent in New York financial and international yacht-racing circles.

•ISLAND HEIGHTS, Borough; Ocean County; Pop. 1,575; Zip Code 08732; Elev. 30; Lat. 39-56-31 N, long. 074-09-01 W. The borough is descriptively named for its location.

•JACKSON, Township; Ocean County; Pop. 25,644; Zip Code 08527; Elev. 120; Lat. 39-46-35 N, long. 074-51-46 W. The town is named for President Andrew Jackson.

•JAMESBURG, Borough; Middlesex County; Pop. 4,114; Zip Code 08831; Elev. 65; Lat. 40-21-09 N, long. 074-26-26 W. The borough is named for miller and stage owner James Buckelew.

•JERSEY CITY, City; Hudson County Seat; Pop. 223,532; Zip Code 073+; Elev. 11. This city was first important as a gateway to the Dutch traders who settled Manhattan. The first permanent settlement was probably around 1629. Important to the city's growth was construction of a railroad tunnel to New York--first attempted in 1874--not completed until 1910.

•JERSEYVILLE, Monmouth County; Pop. 70; Zip Code 07728; Elev. 157; Lat. 40-14-21 N long. 074-13-47 W; located in Central Eastern New Jersey on Hwy. 33.

•JOHNSONBURG, included in Frelinghuysen; Warren County; Pop. est. 200; Area Code 201; Zip Code 07846; Elev. 573; Lat. 40-57-52 N long. 074-52-44 W; located in NW New Jersey.

•KEANSBURG, Borough; Monmouth County; Pop. 10,613; Zip Code 07734; Elev. 13; Lat. 40-26-30 N long. 074-07-49 W; located in E New Jersey; is named after John Kean, U.S. Senator 1899-1911.

•KEARNY, Town; Hudson County; Pop. 35,735; Zip Code 07032; Elev. 104; Lat. 40-46-06 N long. 074-08-45 W; located in NE New Jersey just NE of Newark; Kearny was named for Maj. Gen. Philip Kearny, brilliant cavalry officer who lived in the town when he was not fighting.

•KENILWORTH, Borough; Union County; Pop. 8,221; Zip Code 07033; Elev. 91; Lat. 40-40-35 N long. 074-17-28 W; located in NE New Jersey; is named for Kenilworth Castle, England.

•KENVIL, included Roxbury; Morris County; Pop. 1,700; Zip Code 07847; Elev. 720; Lat. 40-52-47 N long. 074-37-08 W; located in N New Jersey.

•KEYPORT, Borough; Monmouth County; Pop. 7,413; Zip Code 07735; Elev. 25; Lat. 40-25-59 N long. 074-12-00 W; located in E New Jersey.

•KINGSTON, included Franklin; Somerset County; Pop. est. 900; Zip Code 08528; Elev. 110; Lat. 40-22-31 N long. 074-36-50 W; located in N New Jersey. Named for King William II.

•KINNELON, Borough; Morris County; Pop. 7,770; Zip Code 07405; Elev. 760; Lat. 41-00-06 N long. 074-22-03 W; located in N New Jersey; is named after Francis S. Kinney, founder.

•LAFAYETTE, Township; Sussex County; Pop. 1,614; Zip Code 07848; Elev. 533; Lat. 41-05-54 N long. 074-41-20 W; located in N New Jersey; is named for Marquis de la Fayette.

•LAKEHURST, Borough; Ocean County; Pop. 2,908; Zip Code 08733; Elev. 72; Lat. 40-00-52 N long. 074-18-42 W; located in E New Jersey on Hwy. 40.

•LAKEWOOD, Township; Ocean County; Pop. 38,464; Zip Code 08701; Elev. 91; Lat. 40-05-52 N long. 074-13-05 W; located in eastern New Jersey.

•LAMBERTVILLE, City; Hunterdon County; Pop. 4,044; Zip Code 08530; Elev. 76; Lat. 40-21-57 N long. 074-56-36 W; located in NW New Jersey; Known first as Coryel's Ferry and then as Georgetown, Lambertville received its present name when John Lambert opened the first post office shortly after the War of 1812.

•LANDING, (Shore Hills); included Roxbury; Morris County; Pop. 3,064; Zip Code 07850; Elev. 940; Lat. 40-54-18 N long. 074-39-56 W; located in N New Jersey.

•LAUREL SPRINGS, Borough; Camden County; Pop. 2,249; Zip Code 08021; Elev. 82; Lat. 39-49-12 N long. 075-00-24 W; located in SW New Jersey; descriptive name meaning "Medical Springs in laurel grove."

•LAVALLETTE, Borough; Ocean County; Pop. 2,072; Zip Code 08735; Elev. 5; Lat. 39-58-13 N long. 074-04-09 W; located in E New Jersey; is named for Admiral Lavallette of the U.S. Navy.

•LAWNSIDE, Borough; Camden County; Pop. 3,042; Zip Code 08045; Elev. 112; Lat. 39-51-59 N long. 075-01-43 W; located in SW New Jersey; was one of the first Black-owned and Black-governed boroughs in New Jersey, and one of the few such towns in the United States. It was founded during the antislavery agitation of a century ago.

•LAWRENCEVILLE, Township; Mercer County; Pop. 19,724; Zip Code 08648; Elev. 130; Lat. 40-17-50 N long. 074-43-48 W; located in Central New Jersey; was a post village incorporated in 1798 as Maidenhead, the name being changed in 1816 to honor Capt. James Lawrence ("Don't give up the ship!").

•LEBANON, Borough; Hunterdon County; Pop. 820; Zip Code 08833; Elev. 296; Lat. 40-38-30 N, long. 074-50-11 W. Founded in 1731 by German immigrants and named for Mt. Lebanon, Palestine.

•LEONIA, Borough; Bergen County; Pop. 8,027; Zip Code 07605; Elev. 100; Lat. 40-51-41 N long. 073-59-19 W; located in NE New Jersey; named was taken from Fort Lee.

•LINCOLN PARK, Borough; Morris County; Pop. 8,806; Zip Code 07035; Elev. 200; Lat. 40-31-12 N long. 074-23-09 W; located in N New Jersey; is named after President Abraham Lincoln.

•**LINCROFT**, included in Middletown Township; Monmouth County; Pop. est. 4,100; Zip Code 07738; Elev. 66; Lat. 40-19-50 N long. 074-07-17 W; Named for Anglo-Saxon description, "Small Field of Flax."

•**LINDEN**, City; Union County; Pop. 37,836; Zip Code 07036; Elev. 37; Lat. 40-37-19 N long. 074-14-42 W; located in NE New Jersey; named for trees brought from Germany.

•**LINDENWOLD**, Borough; Camden County; Pop. 18,196; Zip Code 08021; Elev. 50; Lat. 39-49-27 N long. 074-59-53 W; located in SW New Jersey.

•**LINWOOD**, City; Atlantic County; Pop. 6,144; Zip Code 08221; Elev. 28; Lat. 39-20-23 N long. 074-34-32 W; located in SE New Jersey.

•**LITTLE FALLS**, Township; Passaic County; Pop. 11,496; Zip Code 07424; Elev. 360; Lat. 40-52-08 N long. 074-12-31 W; located in N New Jersey; named for lesser falls of Passaic River.

•**LITTLE FERRY**, Borough; Bergen County; Pop. 9,399; Zip Code 07643; Elev. 10; Lat. 40-51-10 N long. 074-02-33 W; located in NE New Jersey; named for a colonial ferry.

•**LITTLE SILVER**, Borough; Monmouth County; Pop. 5,548; Zip Code 07739; Elev. 38; Lat. 40-20-12 N long. 074-02-51 W; located in E New Jersey; named for payment to Indians.

•**LITTLE YORK**, included in Alexandria and York; Hunterdon County; Pop. est. 125; Zip Code 08834; Elev. 380; Lat. 40-36-40 N long. 075-04-35 W; located in NW New Jersey.

•**LIVINGSTON**, Township; Essex County; Pop. 28,040; Zip Code 07039; Elev. 410; Lat. 40-47-45 N long. 074-18-55 W; located in NE New Jersey, 5 miles West of Newark; is named for *William Livingston*, New Jersey's Revolutionary Governor and one of the signers of the Constitution.

•**LODI**, Borough; Bergen County; Pop. 23,956; Zip Code 07644; Elev. 43; Lat. 40-52-56 N long. 074-05-01 W; located in NE New Jersey; named after Lodi, Italy.

•**LONG BEACH**, Township; Ocean County; Pop. 3,488; Zip Code 08008; Elev. 10; Lat. 39-41-08 N long. 074-08-43 W; located in E New Jersey; named for strip of beach bounding Barnegat Bay.

•**LONG BRANCH**, City; Monmouth County; Pop. 29,819; Zip Code 07740; Elev. 19; Lat. 40-18-15 N long. 073-59-34 W; is on the New Jersey coast.

•**LONGPORT**, Borough; Atlantic County; Pop. 1,275; Zip Code 08403; Elev. 6; Lat. 39-18-51 N long. 074-31-31 W; located in SE New Jersey; named after *John Long*, landowner.

•**LONG VALLEY**, included in Washington; Morris County; Pop. 1,645; Area Code 201; Zip Code 07853; Elev. 532; Lat. 40-47-09 N long. 074-46-50 W.

•**LYNDHURST**, Township; Bergen County; Pop. 20,326; Zip Code 07071; Elev. 60; Lat. 40-48-43 N long. 074-07-29 W; located in NE New Jersey; First called New Barbados Neck by an early settler from Barbados, its name was changed in honor of *Lord Lyndhurst*, a frequent visitor.

•**MADISON**, Borough; Morris County; Pop. 15,357; Zip Code 07940; Elev. 261; Lat. 40-45-35 N long. 074-25-03 W; located in N New Jersey; West of Newark. Named after *President James Madison*.

•**MAGNOLIA**, Borough; Camden County; Pop. 4,881; Zip Code 08049; Elev. 79; Lat. 39-35-20 N long. 074-43-27 W; located in SW New Jersey; was known in Civil War days as Greenland, not from the climate but because of the greenish tinge of the soil The town was renamed for the blossoms of magnolia trees in this area.

•**MAHWAH**, Township; Bergen County; Pop. 12,127; Zip Code 07430; Elev. 300; Lat. 41-05-19 N long. 074-08-39 W; located in NE New Jersey; descriptive name meaning "meeting place.".

•**MANASQUAN,** Borough; Monmouth County; Pop. 5,354; Zip Code 08736; Elev. 28; Lat. 40-07-34 N, long. 074-02-59 W. Located on the Manasquan River in E New Jersey. The Indian name of this place means "an enclosure with a house," the braves parking their wives here for safety while they went hunting and fishing. Descriptive name from *Menach'hen* meaning "island" and *esquand* meaning "door."

•**MANTOLOKING**, Borough; Ocean County; Pop.433; Zip Code 07838; Elev. 7; Lat. 40-02-21 N, long. 074-03-01 W. Named for the sub-tribe, Mantua, Iekau, "sand" and ink, "place."

•**MANTUA**, Township; Gloucester County; Pop. 9,193; Zip Code 08051; Elev. 66; Lat. 39-49-03 N long. 075-11-39 W; located in SW New Jersey; named for sub-tribe, Mantua.

•**MANVILLE**, Borough; Somerset County; Pop. 11,278; Zip Code 08835; Elev. 44; Lat. 40-32-27 N long. 074-35-17 W; located in N New Jersey.

•**MAPLE SHADE**, Township; Burlington County; Pop. 20,525; Zip Code 08052; Elev. 50; Lat. 39-57-09 N long. 074-59-34 W; located in S New Jersey.

•**MAPLEWOOD**, Township; Essex County; Pop. 22,950; Zip Code 07040; Elev. 140; Lat. 40-46-26 N long. 074-16-26 W; located in NE New Jersey.

•**MARGATE CITY**, City; Atlantic County; Pop. 9,179; Zip Code 08402; Elev. 8; Lat. 39-19-40 N long. 074-30-14 W; located in SE New Jersey; Named after Margate, England.

•**MARLBORO**, Township; Monmouth County; Pop. 17,560; Zip Code 07746; Elev. 190; Lat. 40-18-55 N long. 074-14-48 W; located in central eastern New Jersey on Hwy. 79; Named for marl beds.

•**MARLTON**, Burlington County; Zip Code 08053; Elev. 100; Lat. 39-53-28 N long. 074-55-20 W; located in SW New Jersey, its named for the mining of marl from pits in this area.

•**MATAWAN**, Borough; Monmouth County; Pop. 8,837; Zip Code 07747; Elev. 55; Lat. 40-24-53 N long. 074-13-48 W; located in E New Jersey; descriptive name meaning "where two rivers come together" or mechawanienk, "ancient path."

•**MAYWOOD**, Borough; Bergen County; Pop. 9,895; Zip Code 07607; Elev. 94; Lat. 40-54-09 N long. 074-03-44 W; located in NE New Jersey.

•**MEDFORD**, Township; Burlington County; Pop. 17,471; Zip Code 08055; Elev. 80; Lat. 39-54-03 N long. 074-49-26 W; located in S central New Jersey on Hwy. 541, S of 70; founded by Quakers before 1759. *Mark Reeve* visited Medford, Mass., and was so much impressed with the place that he induced his neighbors in 1828 to name their town for it.

•**MEDFORD LAKES**, Borough; Burlington County; Pop. 4,958; Zip Code 08055; Elev. 80; Lat. 39-51-30 N, long. 074-48-12 W. Named for the local lake, itself named after Medford, Massachusetts.

•**MENDHAM**, Borough; Morris County; Pop. 4,883; Zip Code 07945; Elev. 648; Lat. 40-46-33 N long. 074-36-04 W; located in North central New Jersey on Hwy. 24; Named after Myndham, England.

•MERCERVILLE, included in Hamilton; Mercer County; Pop. 15,000; Zip Code 08619; Elev. 90; Lat. 40-14-13 N long. 074-41-13 W; located in central W New Jersey, The present name honors *Gen. Hugh Mercer*, fatally wounded in the Battle of Princeton.

•MERCHANTVILLE, Borough; Camden County; Pop. 3,972; Zip Code 08109; Elev. 82; Lat. 39-56-50 N long. 075-04-01 W; located in SW New Jersey.

•METUCHEN, Borough; Middlesex County; Pop. 13,762; Zip Code 08840; Elev. 117; Lat. 40-32-35 N long. 074-21-49 W; located in central New Jersey. Named after *Chief Matochshegan*.

•MICKLETON, included in East Greenwich; Gloucester County; Zip Code 08056; Elev. 68; Lat. 39-47-24 N long. 075-14-17 W; located in SW New Jersey.

•MIDDLESEX, Borough; Middlesex County; Pop. 13,480; Zip Code 08846; Elev. 63; Lat. 40-34-21 N long. 074-29-35 W; located in N central New Jersey. Named after Middlesex, England.

•MIDLAND PARK, Borough; Bergen County; Pop. 7,381; Zip Code 07432; Elev. 350; Lat. 40-59-21 N, long. 074-08-28 W. Named for its location "amid Bergen hills."

•MILLBURN, Township; Essex County; Pop. 19,543; Zip Code 07041; Elev. 140; Lat. 40-44-22 N long. 074-18-16 W; located in NE New Jersey; named for Burn which supplied power for paper and other mills.

•MILLTOWN, Borough; Middlesex County; Pop. 7,136; Zip Code 08850; Elev. 65; Lat. 40-27-22 N long. 074-26-37 W; located in central New Jersey; named for early gristmills.

•MILLVILLE, City; Cumberland County; Pop. 25,281; Zip Code 08332; Elev. 37; Lat. 39-24-07 N long. 075-02-23 W; located in SW New Jersey; was originally Shingle Landing, later Maurice River Bridge and The Bridge. Settled as a establishment of a mill town and so named.

•MONMOUTH BEACH, Borough; Monmouth County; Pop. 3,318; Zip Code 07750; Elev. 12; Lat. 40-19-49 N long. 073-58-55 W; located in E New Jersey.

•MONTCLAIR, Town; Essex County; Pop. 38,321; Zip Code 070; Elev. 337; Lat. 40-49-33 N long. 074-12-34 W; located in NE New Jersey; given a French name meaning "bright mountain."

•MONTVALE, Borough; Bergen County; Pop. 7,318; Zip Code 07645; Elev. 310; Lat. 41-02-48 N, long. 074-01-24 W. Montvale is named for the topograpy of the area.

•MONTVILLE, Township; Morris County; Pop. 14,290; Zip Code 07045; Elev. 300; Lat. 40-54-53 N, long. 074-23-03 W. Descriptively named for the mountainous terrain of its location.

•MOORESTOWN, Township; Burlington County; Pop. 15,596; Zip Code 08057; Elev. 76; Lat. 39-58-01 N, long. 074-56-35 W. Named after Thomas Moore, poet.

•MORGANVILLE, included in Marlboro; Monmouth County; Pop. 900; Zip Code 07751; Elev. 115; Lat. 40-22-35 N, long. 074-14-41 W. The town is named for an early settler.

•MORRIS PLAINS, Borough; Morris County; Pop. 5,305; Zip Code 07950; Elev. 399; Lat. 40-49-18 N, long. 074-28-53 W. Named for Lewis Morris, the first governor of New Jersey.

•MORRISTOWN, Town; Morris County Seat; Pop. 16,614; Zip Code 07960; Elev. 327; Lat. 40-47-48 N, long. 074-28-55 W. First settled in 1710, the new village was originally named West Hanover. In 1739 a new county was laid out and named in honor of Lewis Morris, the state's first governer. The township of Morris was legally defined during the first session of the Morris County court that same year.

•MOUNTAIN LAKES, Borough; Morris County; Pop. 4,153; Zip Code 07046; Elev. 513; Lat. 40-53-41 N, long. 074-26-00 W. Name given for twin lakes.

•MOUNTAINSIDE, Borough; Union County; Pop. 7,118; Zip Code; 07092; Elev. 142; Lat. 40-40-20, long. 074-21-28 W. Descriptively named for its location in wooded hills.

•MOUNT ARLINGTON, Borough; Morris County; Pop. 4,251; Zip Code 07856; Elev. 1000; Lat. 40-55-33 N, long. 074-38-07 W. Named after Henry Bennet, Earl of Arlington.

•MOUNT EPHRAIM, Borough; Camden County; Pop. 4,251; Zip code 08059; Elev. 70; Lat. 39-52-42 N, long 075-05-35 W. The town was a Colonial settlement. Stagecoach companies operating between Camden, Philadelphia and the coast chose Ephraim Albertson's tavern here as a station.

•MOUNT HOLLY, Township; Burlington County Seat; Pop. 10,818; Zip Code 08060; Elev. 52; Lat. 39-59-34 N, long. 074-47-17 W. The area was first settled in 1676. In 1796 the County Seat was transferred from Burlington to Mount Holly. The town's name is descriptive of a hill covered with holly trees.

•MOUNT LAUREL, Township; Burlington County; Pop. 17,714; Zip Code 08054; Elev. 80; Lat. 39-56-02, long. 074-53-29 W. Descriptive name for hill covered with laurel.

•NATIONAL PARK, Borough; Gloucester County; Pop. 3,552; Zip Code 08063; Elev. 20; Lat. 39-51-57 N, long. 075-10-45 W. The name is derived from Red Bank Battlefield National Park.

•NEPTUNE CITY, Borough; Monmouth County; Pop. 5,276; Elev. 15; Lat. 40-12-00 N, long. 074-01-42 W. Named for the Roman god of the ocean.

•NEW BRUNSWICK, City; Middlesex County; Pop. 41,442; Zip Code 089; Elev. 42; Lat. 40-29-10 N long. 074-27-08 W; The name Brunswick, in honor of *King George I*, also Duke of Brunswick, first appears in court records of 1724.

•NEW EGYPT, Village, included in Plumsted township; Ocean County; Pop. 1,769; Zip Code 08533; Elev. 78; Lat. 40-04-03 N long. 074-31-52 W; located in Central New Jersey; At the time of the Revolution the village was known as Timmons Mills. After the victory at Trenton in December, 1776, *Washington* needed grain for his army. *Benjamin Jones*, one of the General's New Jersey advisors, had a large quantity of buckwheat flour and cornmeal stored at the mills; he sent his secretary, *Joseph Curtis*, to bring the milled grain to Trenton. Hailing the welcome arrival, *Washington* said: "Joseph has been in Egypt and gotten the corn."

•NEWARK, City; Essex County Seat; Pop. 330,104; Zip Code 071+; Elev. 146. The source of the name is unknown. It was long thought the inspiration came from Newark-on-Trent, the supposed English home of Rev. Abraham Pierson, pastor of the first church. More likely is the possibility that it came from the Biblical "New Ark" meaning a new project.

•NEWFIELD, Borough; Gloucester County; Pop. 1,563; Zip Code 08344; Elev. 110; Lat. 39-32-47 N long. 075-01-31 W; located in SW New Jersey; descriptive name for a new town.

•NEWFOUNDLAND, included in West Milford; Passaic County; Pop. est. 550; Zip Code 07435; Elev. 760; Lat. 41-02-47 N long. 074-26-08 W; located in N New Jersey; Name derived from Pioneer's report, "The only land we found."

•NEW MILFORD, Borough; Bergen County; Pop. 16,876; Zip Code 07646; Elev. 33; Lat. 40-56-06 N long. 074-01-10 W; located in NE New Jersey; named after Milford, Pa.

•NEW PROVIDENCE, Borough; Union County; Pop. 12,426; Zip Code 07974; Elev. 220; Lat. 40-41-54 N long. 074-24-07 W; located in NE New Jersey.

•**NEWTON**, Town; Sussex County; Pop. 7,748; Zip Code 07860; Elev. 636; Lat. 41-03-29 N long. 074-45-11 W; located in N New Jersey; called by the Indians Chinchewunska (side hill town).Descriptive name meaning a "new town."

•**NORTH ARLINGTON**, Borough; Bergen County; Pop. 16,587; Zip Code 07032; Elev. 122; Lat. 40-47-18 N long. 074-08-01 W; located in NE New Jersey.

•**NORTH BRUNSWICK**, Township; Middlesex County; Pop. 22,220; Zip Code 08902; located in Central New Jersey.

•**NORTHFIELD**, City; Atlantic County; Pop. 7,795; Zip Code 08225; Elev. 33; Lat. 39-22-13 N long. 074-33-02 W; located in SE New Jersey.

•**NORTH PLAINFIELD**, Borough; Somerset County; Pop. 19,108; Zip Code 07060; Elev. 100; Lat. 40-37-48 N long. 074-25-40 W; located in N New Jersey.

•**NORTHVALE**, Borough; Bergen County; Pop. 5,046; Zip Code 07647; Elev. 82; Lat. 41-00-23 N long. 073-56-58 W; located in NE New Jersey; named for location and topography.

•**NORTH WILDWOOD**, City; Cape May County; Pop. 4,714; Zip Code 08260; Elev. 6; Lat. 39-00-02 N long. 074-47-59 W; located in S New Jersey.

•**NORWOOD**, Borough; Bergen County; Pop. 4,413; Zip Code 07648; Elev. 90; Lat. 40-59-53 N long. 073-57-44 W; located in NE New Jersey; named for location; north woods of county.

•**NUTLEY**, Town; Essex County; Pop. 28,998; Zip Code 07110; Elev. 91; Lat. 40-49-20 N long. 074-09-37 W; located in NE New Jersey; Named for a resident's estate.

•**OAKHURST**, included in Ocean Township; Monmouth County; Pop. est. 4,600; Zip Code 07755; Elev. 40; Lat. 40-16-15 N long. 074-01-00 W; located in NE New Jersey.

•**OAKLAND**, Borough; Bergen County; Pop. 13,443; Zip Code 07436; Elev. 282; Lat. 41-00-47 N long. 074-15-53 W; located in NE New Jersey; Named for white oak trees.

•**OAKLYN**, Borough; Camden County; Pop. 4,223; Zip Code 08107; Elev. 28; Lat. 39-54-03 N long. 075-05-06 W; located in SW New Jersey.

•**OCEAN**, Township, Monmouth County; Pop. 23,570; Zip Code 07712; located in E New Jersey; named for location on the Atlantic Ocean.

•**OCEAN CITY**, City; Cape May County; Pop. 13,949; Zip Code 08226; Elev. 4; Lat. 39-16-39 N long. 074-34-30 W; located in S New Jersey; named for location on the Atlantic Ocean.

•**OCEAN GATE**, Borough; Ocean County; Pop. 1,385; Zip Code 08740; Elev. 7; Lat. 39-55-36 N long. 074-08-03 W; located in E New Jersey; named for location on the Atlantic Ocean Coast.

•**OCEAN GROVE**, included in Neptune; Monmouth County; Pop. est. 4,200; Zip Code 07756; Elev. 20; Lat. 40-12-43 N long. 074-00-25 W; located in NE New Jersey, S of Asbury Park.

•**OCEANPORT**, Borough; Monmouth County; Pop. 5,888; Zip Code 07757; Elev. 24; Lat. 40-19-05 N long. 074-00-56 W; located in E New Jersey.

•**OGDENSBURG**, Borough; Sussex County; Pop. 2,737; Zip Code 07439; Elev. 677; Lat. 41-04-54 N long. 074-35-34 W; located in N New Jersey; named for *Robert Ogden*, distiller and mine owner.

•**OLD BRIDGE**, Township; Middlesex County; Pop. 51,515; Zip Code 08857; Elev. 30; Lat. 40-24-53 N long. 074-21-57 W; located in Central New Jersey.

•**OLD TAPPAN**, Borough; Bergen County; Pop. 4,168; Zip Code 07675; Elev. 50; Lat. 41-00-38 N long. 073-59-30 W; located in NE New Jersey; named for sub-tribe, Tappans.

•**OLDWICK**, Village, included in Tewksburg township; Hunterdon County; Pop. est. 450; Zip Code 08858; Elev. 240; Lat. 40-40-21 N long. 074-44-52 W; located in NW New Jersey; is an old settlement known as Smithfield in Colonial days and later as New Germantown. Anglo-Saxon name meaning "old town."

•**ORADELL**, Borough; Bergen County; Pop. 8,658; Zip Code 07649; Elev. 110; Lat. 40-57-31 N long. 074-02-14 W; located in NE New Jersey; named derived from Latin ora, meaning "edge" and dell.

•**ORANGE**, City; Essex County; Pop. 31,136; Zip Code 070; Elev. 204; Lat. 40-46-14 N long. 074-13-59 W; located in NE New Jersey; Orange was settled in 1678 with the aristocratic name of the Mountain Plantations. It is believed to have been afterward renamed in honor of *William*, Prince of Orange, who became *William III* of England.

•**OXFORD**, Township; Warren County; Pop. 1,659; Zip Code 07863; Elev. 500; Lat. 40-48-11 N long. 074-59-24 W; located in NW New Jersey; Named after *John Axford*, settler.

•**PALISADES PARK**, Borough; Bergen County; Pop. 13,372; Zip Code 07650; Elev. 150; Lat. 40-50-53 N long. 073-59-53 W; located in NE New Jersey; named for palisades of Hudson River.

•**PALMYRA**, Borough; Burlington County; Pop. 7,085; Zip Code 08065; Elev. 20; Lat. 40-00-25 N long. 075-01-43 W; located in S New Jersey; named after Palmyra, Syria, meaning "palm trees."

•**PARAMUS**, Borough; Bergen County; Pop. 26,474; Zip Code 07652; Elev. 58; Lat. 40-56-40 N long. 074-04-33 W; located in NE New Jersey; is an old Dutch farm community. Name derived from peram-sepus, meaning "pleasant stream."

•**PARK RIDGE**, Borough; Bergen County; Pop. 8,515; Zip Code 07656; Elev. 226; Lat. 41-02-15 N long. 074-02-28 W; located in NE New Jersey; named for location, on a ridge.

•**PARSIPPANY** (Troy Hills), Township; Morris County; Pop. 49,868; Zip Code 07054; Elev. 300; Lat. 40-51-28 N long. 074-25-35 W; located in N New Jersey; Named for *Parlin* family.

•**PASSAIC**, City; Passaic County; Pop. 52,463; Zip Code 07055; Elev. 102; Lat. 40-51-24 N long. 074-07-44 W; located in N New Jersey; Dutch traders were the first settlers of Passaic (Ind., *peaceful valley*).

•**PATERSON**, City; Seat of Passaic County; Pop. 137,970; Zip Code 075; Elev. 100; Lat. 40-55-00 N long. 074-10-20 W; located in N New Jersey.

•**PAULSBORO**, Borough; Gloucester County; Pop. 6,944; Zip Code 08066; Elev. 9; Lat. 39-49-49 N long. 075-14-27 W; located in SW New Jersey; the town dates back to 1681, when 250 colonists settled in the section. *Phillip Paul*, for whom the settlement was named, arrived in 1685.

•**PEAPACK**, Borough; Somerset County; Pop. 2,038; Zip Code 07977; Elev. 300; Lat. 40-43-00 N long. 074-39-25 W; located in N New Jersey; descriptive name meaning Pe "water" and pack "roots."

•**PEMBERTON**, Borough; Burlington County; Pop. 1,198; Zip Code 08068; Elev. 60; Lat. 39-58-19 N, long. 074-41-00 W. Named after James Pemberton, landowner.

•PENNINGTON, Borough; Mercer County; Pop. 19,724; Zip Code 08534; Elev. 211; Lat. 40-19-42 N, 074-47-28 W. The village was first known as Queenstown, in honor of Queen Anne, but because of its insignificant size people began to refer to it derisively as Penny Town. About 1747 it became permanently known as Pennington, a corruption of Pennytown.

•PENNS GROVE, Borough; Salem County; Pop. 5.760; Zip Code 08069; Elev. 12; Lat. 39-43-46 N long. 075-28-06 W; located in SW New Jersey; named after *William Penn.*

•PENNSAUKEN, Township; Camden County; Pop. 33,775; Zip Code 081+. Located in SW New Jersey, named after William Penn and sauk meaning "water inlet or outlet."

•PENNSVILLE, Township; Salem County; Pop. 13,848; Zip Code 08070; Elev. 19; Lat. 39-39-12 N long. 075-31-01 W; located in SW New Jersey; named for *William Penn.*

•PEQUANNOCK, Township; Morris County; Pop. 13,776; Zip Code 07440; Elev. 180; Lat. 40-57-08 N long. 074-17-57 W; located in N New Jersey; named after sub-tribe, Pequannuc.

•PERTH AMBOY, City; Middlesex County; Pop. 38,951; Zip Code 088++; Elev. 155; Lat. 40-30-24 N long. 074-15-57 W; located in Central New Jersey; was part of a large tract purchased from the Indians in 1651 by *Augustine Herman,* a Staten Island Dutchman. The Indians had called this point of land Ompoge (large level piece of ground). Through a series of corruptions it became Amboy and then Amboy Point.

•PHILLIPSBURG, Town; Warren County; Pop. 16,647; Zip Code 08865; Elev. 314; Lat. 40-41-37 N long. 075-11-26 W; located in North central New Jersey on the Delaware River; was long ago the site of an Indian Village called Chintewink. Named for *William Phillips,* settler.

•PINE HILL, Borough; Camden County; Pop. 8,684; Zip Code 08021; Elev. 170; Lat. 39-47-03 N long. 074-59-33 W; located in SW New Jersey. Descriptively named for the terrain and wood cover.

•PISCATAWAY, Township; Middlesex County; Pop. 42,223; Zip Code 08854; Elev. 120; Lat. 40-29-57 N long. 074-23-58 W; located in Central New Jersey; named for Piscataqua, Me.

•PITMAN, Borough; Gloucester County; Pop. 9,744; Zip Code 08071; Elev. 132; Lat. 39-43-58 N long. 075-07-55 W; located in SW New Jersey; named for *Rev. Charles Pitman.*

•PLAINFIELD, City; Union County; Pop. 45,555; Zip Code 070++; Elev. 110; Lat. 40-38-01 N long. 074-24-28 W; located in NE New Jersey. Descriptively named by its colonial settlers.

•PLAINSBORO, Township; Middlesex County; Pop. 5,605; Zip Code 08536; Elev. 80; Lat. 40-20-00 N long. 074-36-03 W; located in Central New Jersey.

•PLEASANTVILLE, City; Atlantic County; Pop. 13,435; Zip Code 08232; Elev. 22; Lat. 39-23-23 N long. 074-31-28 W; located in SE New Jersey; named for its surroundings, by *Dr. Daniel Ingersoll.*

•POINT PLEASANT, Borough; Ocean County; Pop. 17,747; Zip Code 08742; Elev. 18; Lat. 40-04-59 N long. 074-04-07 W; located in E New Jersey; named for location, on Atlantic Ocean and Manasquan Inlet.

•POINT PLEASANT BEACH, Borough; Ocean County; Pop. 5,415; Zip Code 08742; Elev. 14; Lat. 40-05-28 N long. 074-02-54 W; located in E New Jersey; named for location on Atlantic.

•POMPTON PLAINS, included in Pequanock; Morris County; Pop. 8,000; Zip Code 07444; Elev. 181; Lat. 40-58-05 N, long. 074-17-46 W. Named for a subtribe.

•PORT ELIZABETH, included in Maurice River; Cumberland County; Pop. 500; Zip Code 08348; Elev. 15; Lat. 39-18-48 N, long. 074-58-53 W. Named for Elizabeth Bodely, who purchased the property in 1790.

•PORT REPUBLIC, City; Atlantic County; Pop. 837; Zip Code 08540; Elev. 17; Lat. 39-31-14 N, long. 074-29-10 W. Named for the U.S. Republic.

•PRINCETON, Borough; Mercer County; Pop. 12,035; Zip Code 08540; Elev. 215; Lat. 40-20-55 N long. 074-39-34 W; located in W New Jersey; in 1724 the residents chose the name of Prince's Town (later shortened to Princeton) supposedly because of the proximity to King's Town (Kingston).

•QUINTON, Township; Salem County; Pop. 2,887; Zip Code 08072; Elev. 20; Lat. 39-32-45 N long. 075-24-4 W; located in SW New Jersey.

•RAHWAY, City; Union County; Pop. 26,723; Zip Code 070++; Elev. 25; Lat. 40-36-29 N long. 074-16-41 W; located in NE New Jersey; descriptive name derived from Rechouwakie meaning "place of sands."

•RAMSEY, Borough; Bergen County; Pop. 12,899; Zip Code 07446; Elev. 373; Lat. 41-03-26 N long. 074-08-29 W; located in NE New Jersey. The town's name honors a colonial settler.

•RANDOLPH, Township; Morris County; Pop. 17,828; Zip Code 07869; located in N New Jersey. The town is named after Revolutionary War-era settler and businessman, Benjamin Randolph.

•RARITAN, Borough; Somerset County; Pop. 6,128; Zip Code 08869; Elev. 76; Lat. 40-34-10 N long. 074-38-00 W; located in N New Jersey; named after sub-tribe, Naraticong.

•READINGTON, Township; Hunterdon County; Pop. 10,855; Zip Code 08870; Elev. 200; Lat. 40-34-07 N long. 074-44-17 W; located in NW New Jersey; named for *John Reading,* Governor, 1757-1758.

•RED BANK, Borough; Monmouth County; Pop. 12,031; Zip Code 07701; Elev. 53; Lat. 40-20-49 N long. 074-03-53 W; located in E New Jersey; owes its name to the Navesink river's clay banks.

•RIDGEFIELD, Borough; Bergen County; Pop. 10,294; Zip Code 07657; Elev. 150; Lat. 40-50-03 N long. 074-00-33 W; located in NE New Jersey. Named for the gently undulating ridges found in the region.

•RIDGEFIELD PARK, Village; Bergen County; Pop. 12,738; Zip Code 07660; Elev. 96; Lat. 40-51-25 N long. 074-01-19 W; located in NE New Jersey. The town is named after Ridgefield.

•RIDGEWOOD, Village; Bergen County; Pop. 25,208; Zip Code 074+; Elev. 144; Lat. 40-58-45 N long. 074-07-01 W; located in NE New Jersey; named for location. The town's name is descriptive of its terrain.

•RINGWOOD, Borough; Passaic County; Pop. 12,625; Zip Code 07456; Elev. 508; Lat. 41-06-48 N long. 074-14-45 W; located in NE New Jersey. Founded in the 1760's and descriptively named for the mountainous terrain "ringed with woods."

•RIVERDALE, Borough; Morris County; Pop. 2,530; Zip Code 07457; Elev. 232; located in N New Jersey. Riverdale is named for its location near the Pequannock River.

•RIVERSIDE, Township; Burlington County; Pop. 7,941; Zip Code 08075; Elev. 20; Lat. 40-01-56 N long. 074-57-28 W; located in S New Jersey; named for location on the Delaware.

•**RIVERTON**, Borough; Burlington County; Pop. 3,068; Zip Code 08077; Elev. 60; Lat. 40-00-41 N long. 075-00-55 W; located in S New Jersey. Named for its proximity to a river.

•**RIVER EDGE**, Borough; Bergen County; Pop. 11,111; Zip Code 07661; Elev. 35; Lat. 40-55-43 N long. 074-02-25 W; located in NE New Jersey; named for location on the Hackensack River.

•**RIVER VALE**, Township; Bergen County; Pop. 9,489; Zip Code 07675; Elev. 56; Lat. 40-59-43 N long. 074-00-45 W; located in NE New Jersey; named for location on the Hackensack River.

•**ROCHELLE PARK**, Township; Bergen County; Pop. 5,603; Elev. 63; Lat. 40-54-26 N, long. 074-04-32 W. The town is named after La Rochelle, France.

•**ROCKAWAY**, Borough/Township; Morris County; Pop. 19,850; Zip Code 07866; Elev. 534; Lat. 40-54-04 N long. 074-30-53 W; located in N New Jersey; Descriptive name derived from Rechouwakie meaning "place of sands."

•**ROEBLING**, included in Florence; Burlington County; Pop. est. 3,600; Zip Code 08554; Elev. 40; Lat. 40-06-57 N long. 074-47-12 W; located on the Delaware River; is a company town established by *John A. Roebling*, founder of the large steel-cable factory known to engineers all over the world for its part in building the Brooklyn Bridge and in supplying cables for the George Washington Bridge, the Golden Gate Bridge and other big suspension bridges.

•**ROOSEVELT**, Borough; Monmouth County; Pop. 835; Zip Code 08555; Elev. 152; Lat. 40-13-12 N, long. 074-28-25 W. Named for President Theodore Roosevelt.

•**ROSELAND**, Borough; Essex County; Pop. 5,330; Zip Code 07068; Elev. 356; Lat. 40-49-14 N long. 074-17-39 W; located in NE New Jersey.

•**ROSELLE**, Borough; Union County; Pop. 20,641; Zip Code 072+; Elev. 51; Lat. 40-39-51 N long. 074-15-49 W; located in NE New Jersey.

•**ROSELLE PARK**, Borough; Union County; Pop. 13,377; Zip Code 072++; Elev. 85; Lat. 40-39-52 N long. 074-15-53 W; located in NE New Jersey.

•**RUMSON**, Borough; Monmouth County; Pop. 7,623; Zip Code 07760; Elev. 15; Lat. 40-22-19 N long. 073-59-58 W; located in E New Jersey; named after *Chief Alumson.*

•**RUNNEMEDE**, Borough; Camden County; Pop. 9,461; Zip Code 08078; Elev. 64; Lat. 39-51-08 N long. 075-04-06 W; located in SW New Jersey, S of Camden City; In 1844 the name Runnemede was adapted from the meadow near London where *King John* signed the Magna Carta.

•**RUTHERFORD**, Borough; Bergen County; Pop. 19,068; Zip Code 070++; Elev. 98; Lat. 40-49-35 N long. 074-06-26 W; located in NE New Jersey; the name was taken from *John Rutherford*, son of a retired British officer but an active patriot and personal friend of *Washington.*

•**SADDLE BROOK**, Township; Bergen County; Pop. 14,084; Zip Code 07662; Elev. 50; Lat. 40-53-56 N long. 074-05-35 W; located in NE New Jersey.

•**SADDLE RIVER**, Borough; Bergen County; Pop. 2,763; Zip Code 07458; Elev. 175; Lat. 41-01-54 N long. 074-06-09 W; located in NE New Jersey; named for stream and valley in Argyleshire, Scotland.

•**SALEM**, City; Salem County; Pop. 6,959; Zip Code 08079; Elev. 19; Lat. 39-34-18 N long. 075-28-03 W; located in SW New Jersey. The city is named for a Hebrew name meaning "peace."

•**SAYREVILLE**, Borough; Middlesex County; Pop. 29,969; Zip Code 08872; Elev. 41; Lat. 40-27-33 N long. 074-21-41 W; located in Central New Jersey.

•**SCOTCH PLAINS**, Township; Union County; Pop. 20,744; Zip Code 07076; Elev. 150; Lat. 40-39-19 N long. 074-23-25 W; located in NE New Jersey; is where a group of Scottish Presbyterian and Quaker immigrants came here in 1684 after refusing to swear allegiance to the British Crown. Named after *George Scott*, leader of the Scottish settlers.

•**SEA BRIGHT**, Borough; Monmouth County; Pop. 1,812; Zip Code 07760; Elev. 4; Lat. 40-21-41 N long. 073-58-28 W; located in E New Jersey; named for Sea Bright, England.

•**SEA GIRT**, Borough; Monmouth County; Pop. 2,650; Zip Code 08750; Elev. 19; Lat. 40-07-55 N long. 074-02-06 W; located in E New Jersey; named for Estate of Commander *Robert F. Stockton.*

•**SEA ISLE CITY**, City; Cape May County; Pop. 2,644; Zip Code 08243; Elev. 6; Lat. 39-09-12 N long. 074-41-36 W; located in S New Jersey.

•**SEASIDE HEIGHTS**, Borough; Ocean County; Pop. 1,802; Zip Code 08751; Elev. 7; Lat. 39-56-39 N long. 074-04-24 W; located in E New Jersey; named for location on strip of beach.

•**SEASIDE PARK**, Borough; Ocean County; Pop. 1,795; Zip Code 08752; Elev. 6; Lat. 39-55-36 N long. 074-04-39 W; located in E New Jersey; named for location on strip of beach.

•**SECAUCUS**, Town; Hudson County; Pop. 13,719; Zip Code 07094; Elev. 12; Lat. 40-47-22 N long. 074-03-25 W; located in NE New Jersey; descriptive name from Sukit meaning "black snake."

•**SHILOH**, Borough; Cumberland County; Pop. 604; Elev. 118; Lat. 39-27-32 N, long. 075-17-58 W. Founded in 1705 by Seventh-Day Baptists fleeing from persecution in England, the settlement, located along Cohansey Creek, was first known as Cohansey, named for an Indian Chief. In 1771, when the Baptists were moving an old frame church 2 miles to Cohansey, the reached Six Corners here at sundown on a Friday. Work ceased and religious services were begun. Their pastor used as his text, "The Ark of the Lord resteth at Shiloh," and by common consent the named of the community was changed to Shiloh.

•**SHIP BOTTOM**, Borough; Ocean County; Pop. 1,427; Zip Code 08008; Elev. 10; Lat. 39-38-34 N long. 074-10-51 W; located in E New Jersey; it's odd name is the center of controversy of date and detail rather than event. One tradition is that in 1817 *Capt. Stephen Willits* during a storm came upon a ship aground, bottom up. His men heard tapping inside and chopped a hole with an axe. Out stepped a beautiful young girl, whom they carried to shore, where she thanked them in a strange tongue, sank to her knees, and drew the sign of the cross on the sand. She was sent to New York and never heard from again.

•**SHREWSBURY**, Borough; Monmouth County; Pop. 2,962; Zip Code 07701; Elev. 25; Lat. 40-19-46 N long. 074-03-43 W; located in E New Jersey; named after Shrewsbury, England.

•**SOMERDALE**, Borough; Camden County; Pop. 5,900; Zip Code 08083; Elev. 83; Lat. 39-50-38 N long. 075-01-23 W; located in SW New Jersey.

•**SOMERSET**, Village, included in Franklin township; Somerset County; Zip Code 08873; Elev. 60; Lat. 40-16-34 N long. 074-50-58 W; located in N New Jersey. Named after Somersetshire, England.

•**SOMERS POINT**, City; Atlantic County; Pop. 10,330; Zip Code 08244; Elev. 31; Lat. 39-19-03 N long. 074-35-42 W; located SE New Jersey; named for *John Somers*, landowner.

•**SOMERVILLE**, Borough; Somerset County; Pop. 11,973; Zip Code 08876; Elev. 54; Lat. 40-34-27 N long. 074-36-37 W; located in N Central New Jersey; Named after Somersetshire, England.

•**SOUTH AMBOY**, City; Middlesex County; Pop. 8,322; Zip Code 08879; Elev. 54; Lat. 40-28-40 N long. 074-17-28 W; Named after the Earl of Perth.

•**SOUTH BOUND BROOK**, Borough; Somerset County; Pop. 4,331; Zip Code 08880; Elev. 45; Lat. 40-33-12 N long. 074-31-55 W; located in N Central New Jersey.

•**SOUTH HACKENSACK**, Township; Bergen County; Pop. 2,229; Zip Code 076++; Elev. 11; Lat. 40-51-45 N long. 074-02-54 W; located in NE New Jersey.

•**SOUTH ORANGE**, Township; Essex County; Pop. 15,864; Zip Code 07079; Elev. 141; located in NE New Jersey.

•**SOUTH PLAINFIELD**, Borough; Middlesex County; Pop. 20,521; Zip Code 07080; Elev. 67; Lat. 40-34-45 N long. 074-24-43 W; located in Central New Jersey.

•**SOUTH RIVER**, Borough; Middlesex County; Pop. 14,361; Zip Code 08882; Elev. 50; Lat. 40-26-47 N long. 074-23-11 W; Named for tributary of the Raritan River.

•**SOUTH TOMS RIVER**, Borough; Ocean County; Pop. 3,954; Zip Code 08757; Elev. 31; Lat. 39-56-31 N long. 074-12-17 W; located in E New Jersey.

•**SPARTA**, Township; Sussex County; Pop. 13,333; Zip Code 07871; Elev. 712; Lat. 41-02-00 N long. 074-38-20 W; located in N New Jersey; historic Greek name.

•**SPOTSWOOD**, Borough; Middlesex County; Pop. 7,840; Zip Code 08884; Elev. 30; Lat. 40-23-30 N long. 074-23-56 W; located in Central New Jersey; named for Spottswoode, Scotland.

•**SPRINGFIELD**, Township; Union County; Pop. 13,955; Zip Code 07081; Elev. 100; Lat. 40-02-35 N long. 074-38-45 W; located in NE New Jersey. Named because of abundant springs and brooks.

•**SPRING LAKE**, Borough; Monmouth County; Pop. 4,215; Zip Code 07762; Elev. 25; Lat. 40-09-12 N long. 074-01-43 W; located in E New Jersey; descriptive name meaning "fresh water stream."

•**STANHOPE**, Borough; Sussex County; Pop. 3,638; Zip Code 07874; Elev. 882; Lat. 40-54-10 N long. 074-42-34 W; located in N New Jersey.

•**STILLWATER**, Township; Sussex County; Pop. 3,887; Zip Code 07875; Elev. 460; Lat. 41-02-09 N long. 074-52-43 W; located in N New Jersey.

•**STIRLING**, included in Passaic; Morris County; Zip Code 07980; Elev. 240; Lat. 40-40-19 N long. 074-29-43 W; named after *Gen. William. Alexander*, Lord Stirling, Revolution.

•**STOCKTON**, Borough; Hunterdon County; Pop. 643; Zip Code 08559; Elev. 85; Lat. 40-24-28 N long. 074-58-43 W; located in NW New Jersey; named after *Stockton* family.

•**STONE HARBOR**, Borough; Cape May County; Pop. 1,187; Zip Code 08247; Elev. 5; Lat. 39-03-03 N long. 074-45-30 W; located in S New Jersey.

•**STRATFORD**, Borough; Camden County; Pop. 8,005; Zip Code 08084; Elev. 70; Lat. 39-49-36 N, long. 075-00-57 W. Named for Stratford-on-Avon, England.

•**SUCCASUNNA**, Village, Morris County; Pop. 7,400; Zip Code 07876; Elev. 710; Lat. 40-52-06 N long. 074-38-27 W; located in N Central New Jersey . Name derived from sukit meaning "black" and assan meaning "stone."

•**SUMMIT**, City; Union County; Pop. 21,071; Zip Code 07901; Elev. 388; Lat. 40-44-29 N long. 074-21-36 W; located in NE New Jersey; named for location on the Watchung Mountains.

•**SURF CITY**, Borough; Ocean County; Pop. 1,571; Zip Code 08008; Elev. 6; Lat. 39-39-43 N long. 074-09-56 W; located in E New Jersey on Long Beach Island which is on the Atlantic Coast.

•**SUSSEX**, Borough; Sussex County; Pop. 2,418; Zip Code 07461; Elev. 464; Lat. 41-12-35 N long. 074-36-29 W; located in N New Jersey. Named after Sussex, England.

•**SWEDESBORO**, Borough; Gloucester County; Pop. 2,031; Zip Code 08085; Elev. 68; Lat. 39-44-51 N long. 075-18-39 W; located in SW New Jersey; named after Swedish settlers.

•**TEANECK**, Township; Bergen County; Pop. 39,007; Zip Code 07666; Elev. 92; Lat. 40-53-51 N long. 074-00-59 W; located in NE New Jersey; Dutch name meaning "on a neck" of land.

•**TENAFLY**, Borough; Bergen County; Pop. 13,552; Zip Code 07670; Elev. 52; Lat. 40-55-31 N long. 073-57-48 W; located in NE New Jersey; Dutch word meaning "on a meadow" or "garden meadow."

•**TINTON FALLS**, Borough; Monmouth County; Pop. 7,740; Zip Code 07724; Elev. 88; Lat. 40-18-15 N long. 074-06-03 W; located in E New Jersey; named for Tintern Manor of *Col. Lewis Morris*.

•**TOMS RIVER**, Township; Ocean County; Pop. 7,303; Zip Code 087++; Elev. 20; Lat. 39-57-13 N long. 074-11-54 W; located in E New Jersey; is on the northern banks of Tom River, a waterway discovered in 1673 by the surveyor, *Capt. William Tom.*

•**TOTOWA**, Borough; Passaic County; Pop. 11,448; Zip Code 075++; Elev. 260; Lat. 40-54-18 N long. 074-12-37 W; located in N New Jersey.

•**TOWACO**, included in Montrille; Morris County; Zip Code 07082; Elev. 200; Lat. 40-55-19 N long. 074-20-45 W; located in N New Jersey; was formerly known as Whitehall. Named for Sub-tribe, Towakan.

•**TRENTON**, City; Mercer County seat and capital of New Jersey; Pop. 92,124; Zip Code 086++; Elev. 50; Lat. 40-13-01 N long. 074-44-36 W; located in W New Jersey. Named after a prominent setler.

•**TUCKERTON**, Borough; Ocean County; Pop. 2,472; Zip Code 08087; Elev. 23; Lat. 39-36-11 N long. 074-20-26 W; located on the Eastern New Jersey coast. Named after *Ebenezer Tucker*, resident.

•**UNION**, Township; Union County; Pop. 50,184; Zip Code 07083; Elev. 300; Lat. 40-40-10 N long. 074-55-28 W; located in NE New Jersey; descriptive name for union of several communities.

•**UNION BEACH**, Borough; Monmouth County; Pop. 6,354; Zip Code 07735; Elev. 9; Lat. 40-26-47 N long. 074-10-43 W; located in E New Jersey.

•**UNION CITY**, City; Hudson County; Pop. 55,593; Zip Code 07087; Elev. 189; Lat. 40-46-46 N long. 074-01-27 W; located in NE NewJersey.

•**VENTNOR CITY**, City; Atlantic County; Pop. 11,704; Zip Code 08406; Elev. 11; Lat. 39-20-25 N long. 074-28-40 W; located in SE New Jersey; named for Ventnor, England.

•**VERNON**, Township; Sussex County; Pop. 16,302; Zip Code 07462; Elev. 60; Lat. 39-53-50 N long. 075-01-56 W; located in N New Jersey; named after *Edward Vernon*, English admiral.

•**VERONA**, Borough; Essex County; Pop. 14,166; Zip Code 07044; Elev. 348; Lat. 40-49-47 N long. 074-14-26 W; located in NE New Jersey; Named for Verona, Italy.

•**VIENNA**, Village; Warren County; Zip Code 07880; Elev. 580; Lat. 40-52-07 N long. 074-53-22 W; located in NW New Jersey; Named after Vienna Foundry.

•**VINCENTOWN**, included in Southampton; Burlington County; Pop. est. 800; Zip Code 08088; Elev. 40; Lat. 39-56-02 N long. 074-44-56 W; located in S New Jersey; on the banks of Stop-the-Jade Run.

•**VINELAND**, City; Cumberland County; Pop. 53,750; Zip Code 08360; Elev. 106; Lat. 39-29-10 N long. 075-01-34 W; located in S Central New Jersey; Named Vineland for its 19th century vineyard development.

•**VOORHEES**, Township; Camden County; Pop. 12,919; Zip Code 08043; Elev. 105; Lat. 40-28-52 N long. 074-29-01 W; located in SW New Jersey; named after *Van Voor Hees* family, Dutch settlers.

•**WALDWICK**, Borough; Bergen County; Pop. 10,802; Zip Code 07463; Elev. 181; Lat. 41-00-38 N long. 074-07-06 W; located in NE NewJersey; Anglo-Saxon word meaning "village in a grove."

•**WALL**, Borough; Monmouth County; Pop. 18,952; Zip Code 07719; located in E New Jersey; named after *Ganet D. Wall*, U.S. Senator 1835-1841.

•**WALLINGTON**, Borough; Bergen County; Pop. 10,741; Zip Code 07057; Elev. 14; Lat. 40-51-11 N long. 074-06-51 W; located in NE New Jersey; named after *Walling Jackobs*.

•**WALPACK**, Township, Sussex County; Pop. 150; Zip Code 07881. The name is derived from Walpekat, meaning "very deep water."

•**WANAQUE**, Borough; Passaic County; Pop. 10,025; Zip Code 07465; Elev. 240; Lat. 41-02-17 N long. 074-17-40 W; located in N New Jersey; descriptive name meaning "place where the sassafras tree grows."

•**WARETOWN**, included in Ocean; Ocean County; Pop. est. 900; Zip Code 08758; Elev. 14; Lat. 39-47-29 N long. 074-11-44 W; located on Eastern coast of New Jersey; was named for *Abraham Waeir*, an early settler, who died in 1768.

•**WASHINGTON**, Borough; Warren County; Pop. 6,429; Zip Code 07882; Elev. 463; Lat. 40-45-30 N long. 074-58-47 W; located in NW New Jersey; Named after *President George Washington*.

•**WATCHUNG**, Borough; Somerset County; Pop. 5,290; Zip Code 07060; Elev. 181; Lat. 40-38-16 N long. 074-27-05 W; located in N New Jersey; derived from Watschee meaning "hill."

•**WATERFORD**, Township; Camden County; Pop. 8,126; Zip Code 08089; Elev. 125; Lat. 39-43-23 N long. 074-50-58 W; located in S Central New Jersey was first named for a glassworks founded in 1824. Renamed for Waterford, England.

•**WAYNE**, Township; Passaic County; Pop. 46,474; Zip Code 07470; Elev. 180; Lat. 40-55-31 N long. 074-16-37 W; located in N New Jersey; named after General "Mad Anthony" Wayne, of the Revolution.

•**WEEHAWKEN**, Township; Hudson County; Pop. 13,168; Zip Code 07087; Elev. 189; Lat. 40-46-10 N long. 074-01-15 W; located in NE New Jersey; descriptive name meaning "place of gulls."

•**WENONAH**, Borough; Gloucester County; Pop. 2,303; Zip Code 08090; Elev. 27; Lat. 39-47-40 N long. 075-08-57 W; located in SW New Jersey; named after the mother of Hiawatha.

•**WEST CALDWELL**, Borough; Essex County; Pop. 11,407; Zip Code 07006; Elev. 240; Lat. 40-50-27 N long. 074-18-08 W; located in NE New Jersey.

•**WEST DEPTFORD**, Township; Gloucester County; Pop. 18,002; Zip Code 08066; located in SW New Jersey.

•**WESTFIELD**, Town; Union County; Pop. 30,447; Zip Code 070++; Elev. 126; Lat. 40-39-32 N long. 074-20-52 W; located in NE New Jersey; named after undeveloped section, "the west fields".

•**WEST LONG BRANCH**, Borough; Monmouth County; Pop. 7,380; Zip Code 07764; Elev. 27; Lat. 40-17-25 N long. 074-01-05 W; located in E New Jersey.

•**WEST MILFORD**, Township; Passaic County; Pop. 22,750; Zip Code 07480; Elev. 710; Lat. 41-07-52 N long. 074-22-04 W; located in N New Jersey; named after Milford, Connecticut.

•**WEST NEW YORK**, Town; Hudson County; Pop. 39,194; Zip Code 07093; Elev. 185; Lat. 40-47-16 N long. 074-00-53 W; located in NE New Jersey.

•**WEST ORANGE**, Town; Essex County; Pop. 39,510; Zip Code 07052; Elev. 368; Lat. 40-47-55 N long. 074-14-22 W; located in NE New Jersey.

•**WEST PATERSON**, Borough; Passaic County; Pop. 11,293; Zip Code 07424; Elev. 400; Lat. 40-53-23 N long. 074-11-43 W; located in N New Jersey.

•**WESTVILLE**, Borough; Gloucester County; Pop. 4,786; Zip Code 08093; Elev. 16; Lat. 39-52-04 N long. 075-07-55 W; located in SW New Jersey; named after *Thomas West*.

•**WESTWOOD**, Borough; Bergen County; Pop. 10,714; Zip Code 07675; Elev. 75; Lat 40-59-28 N long. 074-01-59 W; located in NE New Jersey.

•**WHARTON**, Borough; Morris County; Pop. 5,485; Zip Code 07885; Elev. 700; Lat. 40-53-35 N long. 074-34-56 W; located in N New Jersey; named for Wharton Steel Company.

•**WHIPPANY**, Morris County; Zip Code 07981; Elev. 201; Lat. 40-49-28 N long. 074-25-03 W; located in N New Jersey; descriptive name derived from Winit meaning "tooth" and onk meaning "place."

•**WILDWOOD**, City; Cape May County; Pop. 4,913; Zip Code 08260; Elev. 8; Lat. 38-59-30 N long. 074-48-55 W; located in S New Jersey; descriptive name meaning "abundance of wild flowers".

•**WILDWOOD CREST**, Borough; Cape May County; Pop. 4,149; Elev. 9; Lat. 38-58-29 N, long. 074-50-02 W. Descriptive name meaning "abundance of wild flowers."

•**WILLIAMSTOWN**, included in Monroe; Gloucester County; Pop. est. 4,075; Elev. 160; Lat. 39-41-10 N long. 074-59-44 W; located in S Central New Jersey; vegetables. Williamstown has gradually lived down its early name of Squankum (Ind., place of the evil god). The name was brought here in 1772 from Squankum, Monmouth County, by *Deacon Israel Williams* ; 70 years later the town was named for the deacon himself.

•**WILLINGBORO**, Township; Burlington County; Pop. 39,912; Zip Code 08046; Elev. 60; Lat. 40-01-40 N long. 074-52-10 W; located in S New Jersey; named for Willingboro, England.

•**WINDSOR**, included in Washington; Mercer County; Pop. est. 400; Zip Code 08561; Elev. 100; Lat. 40-14-32 N long. 074-34-54 W; located in Central New Jersey; Windsor was named by the English who settled here about 1714.

•**WINSLOW**, Township; Camden County; Pop. 20,034; Zip Code 08095; Elev. 114; Lat. 39-39-26 N long. 074-51-46 W; located in SW New Jersey; named for glassworks.

•**WOODBINE**, Borough; Cape May County; Pop. 2,809; Zip Code 08270; Elev. 40; Lat. 39-14-30 N long. 074-48-6 W; located in S New Jersey.

•**WOODBRIDGE**, Township; Middlesex County; Pop. 90,074; Zip Code 07095; Elev. 30; Lat. 40-33-27 N long. 074-17-06 W; located in Central New Jersey; The community was settled by 1665 by Puritans from Massachusetts Bay and New Hampshire. Named after *Rev. John Woodbridge*, leader of settlers from Massachusetts.

•**WOODBURY**, City; Gloucester County; Pop. 10,353; Zip Code 08096; Elev. 57; Lat. 39-50-17 N long. 075-09-11 W; located in SW New Jersey, is the seat of Gloucester County; named after *John Wood*, settler.

•**WOODBURY**, Borough; Gloucester County; Pop. 3,460; Zip Code 08097; Elev. 74; Lat. 39-49-01 N long. 075-09-20 W; located in SW New Jersey; named after *John Wood*, settler.

•**WOODCLIFF LAKE**, Borough; Bergen County; Pop. 5,644; Zip Code 07675; Elev. 249; Lat. 41-01-24 N long. 074-04-01 W; located in NE New Jersey; named for location on lake in the woods under a cliff.

•**WOODLYNNE**, Borough; Camden County; Pop. 2,578; Zip Code 08017; Elev. 20; located in SW New Jersey; is where Borough Hall stands on the Site Of Mark Newbie's Bank, said to have been the first bank of issue in America. Named for Linden trees.

•**WOOD-RIDGE**, Borough; Bergen County; Pop. 7,929; Zip Code 070++; Elev. 188; Lat. 40-50-44 N long. 074-05-18 W; located in NE New Jersey.

•**WOODSTOWN**, Borough; Salem County; Pop. 3,250; Zip Code 08098; Elev. 47; Lat. 39-39-05 N long. 075-19-43 W; located in SW New Jersey on Hwy. 40; Named after settler, *Jackanias Wood*.

•**WRIGHTSTOWN**, Borough; Burlington County; Pop. 3,031; Zip Code 08562; Elev. 133; located in S New Jersey; named for donor of street site, *John Wright*.

•**WYCKOFF**, Township; Bergen County; Pop. 15,500; Zip Code 07481; located in NE New Jersey; named for Wicaugh, England.

NEW MEXICO

•**ALAMOGORDO,** City; Otero County Seat; Pop. 24,024; Zip Code 87510; Lat. 36-12-28 N long. 106-19-06 W; Settled in 1898 and given the Spanish name meaning "large cottonwood".

•**ALBUQUERQUE,** City; Bernalillo County Seat; Pop. 331,767; Zip Code 87100; Lat. 35-05-46 N long. 106-35-37. W; Established in 1706 and named in honor of Don Francisco Enriquez, the 34th viceroy of New Spain.

•**ARTESIA,** City; Eddy County; Pop. 10,385; Zip Code 88210; Elev. 3379'; Lat. 32-50-17 N long. 104-24-39 W; Founded in 1903 and named after the artesian water wells nearby.

•**AZTEC,** City; San Juan County Seat; Pop. 5,512; Zip Code 87410; Lat. 36-49-37 N long. 107-59-47 W; Aztec was named for the Aztec Indians of Mexico and founded in 1890.

•**BAYARD,** Village; Grant County; Pop. 3,036; Zip Code 88023; Lat. 32-45-28 N long. 108-07-53 W; Named for an early military post, Fort Bayard.

•**BELEN,** City; Valencia County; Pop. 5,617; Zip Code 87002; Lat. 34-40-12 N long. 106-46-18 W; Founded in 1740 and given the name meaning "Bethlehem."

•**BERNALILLO,** Town; Sandoval County Seat; Pop. 2,763; Zip Code 87001; Elev. 5052'; Lat. 35-25-39 long. 106-26-22 W; Possibly named for a Catholic missionary, Fray Jaun Bernal, who was martyred in 1680.

•**BLOOMFIELD,** City; San Juan County; Pop. 4,881; Zip Code 87413; Lat. 36-42-37 N long. 107-58-41 W; First settled in 1878 and named for an early pioneer.

•**BOSQUE FARMS,** Village; Valencia County; Pop. 3,353; Zip Code 87006; Lat. 34-33-36 N long. 106-47-19 W; The town's name is Spanish for "woods."

•**CAPITAN,** Village; Lincoln County; Pop. 762; Zip Code 88316; Elev. 6351'; Lat. 33-32-35 N long. 105-34-16 W; The town is named after the nearby Capitan Mountains.

•**CARLSBAD,** City; Eddy County Seat; Pop. 25,496; Zip Code 88220; Elev. 3111'; Lat. 32-24-58 N long. 104-14-10 W; Established in 1888 and named for the famous Carlsbad Springs in Bohemia after discovery of a local mineral spring.

•**CARRIZOZO,** Town; Lincoln County Seat; Pop. 1,222; Zip Code 88301; Lat. 33-38-26 N long. 105-52-28 W; Founded in 1900 and named after the Carrizo Springs.

•**CAUSEY,** Village; Roosevelt County; Pop. 81; Zip Code 88113; Lat. 33-52-07 N long. 103-07-17 W; Causey is named for a pioneer buffalo hunter.

•**CENTRAL,** Village; Grant County; Pop. 1,968; Zip Code 88026; Lat. 32-46-16 N long. 108-08-56 W; Descriptively named in 1887 for its central location in the county.

•**CHAMA,** Village; Rio Arriba County; Pop. 1,090; Zip Code 87520; Lat. 36-54-15 N long. 106-35-08 W; The village is named for the Chama River.

•**CIMARRON,** Village; Colfax County; Pop. 888; Zip Code 87714; Elev. 6428'; Lat. 36-30-31 N long. 104-55-00 W; A generalized Spanish word meaning "wild or unruly."

•**CLAYTON,** Town; Union County Seat; Pop. 2,968; Zip Code 88415; Elev. 5053'; Lat. 36-27-47 N long. 103-10-55 W; Founded in 1887 and named for Clayton Dorsey, son of an Arkansas senator.

•**CLOUDCROFT,** Village; Otero County; Pop. 521; Zip Code 88317; Elev. 8663'; Lat. 32-57-29 N long. 105-44-48 W; Located at 8,640 feet and descriptively named for its position "in the clouds."

•**CLOVIS,** City; Curry County Seat; Pop. 31,194; Zip Code 88101; Lat. 34-24-15 N long. 103-15-58 W; Settled in 1906 and named for an early Frankish king.

•**COLUMBUS,** Village; Luna County; Pop. 414; Zip Code 88029; Elev. 4064'; Lat. 31-49-36 N long. 107-38-00 W; Founded in 1891 and named for the famous explorer.

•**CORONA,** Village; Lincoln County; Pop. 236; Zip Code 88318; Lat. 34-14-43 N long. 105-35-49 W; Settled in 1902 and named by the railroad for a local hill in the shape of a crown.

•**CORRALES,** Village; Bernalillo & Sandoval Counties; Pop. 2,791; Zip Code 870+; Lat. 35-13-37 N long. 106-36-51 W; A Spanish name meaning "enclosure."

•**CUBA,** Village; Sandoval County; Pop. 609; Zip Code 87013; Elev. 6908'; Lat. 36-01-13 N long. 107-04-11 W; Settled in 1879 and named for a nearby place called Cubeta meaning "little trough."

•**DEMING,** City; Luna County Seat; Pop. 9,964; Zip Code 88030; Lat. 32-15-29 N long. 107-45-16 W; The town is named after Mary Ann Deming, an early pioneer.

•**DES MOINES,** Village; Union County; Pop. 178; Zip Code 88418; Lat. 36-46-12 N long. 103-49-55 W; The village is named after Des Moines, Iowa.

•**DEXTER,** Town; Chaves County; Pop. 882; Zip Code 88230; Lat. 33-11-29 N long. 104-22-15 W; Founded in 1903 and named after Dexter, Iowa.

•**DORA,** Village; Roosevelt County; Pop. 168; Zip Code 88115; Elev. 4288'; Lat. 33-56-15 N long. 103-19-53 W; Named for the first postmaster's daughter Dora Humphrey.

•**EAGLE NEST,** Village; Colfax County; Pop. 202; Zip Code 87710; Elev. 8203'; Lat. 36-33-13 N long. 105-16-01 W; The village is named for the golden eagles living in nearby mountains.

•**ELIDA,** Town; Roosevelt County; Pop. 202; Zip Code 88116; Lat. 33-56-42 N long. 103-39-12 W; First settled in 1902 and named after a city in Ohio.

•**ENCINO,** Village; Torrance County; Pop. 155; Zip Code 88321; Lat. 34-38-49 N long. 105-27-09 W; A Spanish word meaning "oak grove."

•**ESPANOLA,** City; Rio Arriba & Santa Fe Counties; Pop. 6,803; Zip Code 875+; A Spanish word meaning "new spain."

•**ESTANCIA,** Town; Torrance County Seat; Pop. 830; Zip Code 87016; Elev. 6107'; Lat. 34-45-19 N long. 106-03-26 W; Estancia is Spanish for "large estate."

•**EUNICE,** City; Lea County; Pop. 2,970; Zip Code 88231; Lat. 32-26-23 N long. 103-08-45 W; The city is named after Eunice Carlson, the daughter of the original homesteader.

•**FARMINGTON,** City; San Juan County; Pop. 30,729; Zip Code 87401; Lat. 36-45-47 N long. 108-10-18 W; Descriptively named by early ranchers for the area's function as a "farming town."

•FLOYD, Village; Roosevelt County; Pop. 146; Zip Code 88118; Elev. 4153'; Lat. 33-53-50 N long. 103-31-31 W; The first postmaster Simon Lane named the town for a freind.

•FOLSOM, Village; Union County; Pop. 73; Zip Code 88419; Lat. 36-50-52 N long. 103-54-43 W; The village is named after President Grover Cleveland's wife Francis Folsom.

•FORT SUMNER, Village; De Baca County Seat; Pop. 1,421; Zip Code 88119; Elev. 4049'; Lat. 34-28-18 N long. 104-14-23 W; Named in honor of General Edmond Sumner, an early Civil War era commander.

•GALLUP, City; McKinley County Seat; Pop. 18,161; Zip Code 873++; Lat. 35-31-20 N long. 108-44-29 W; Established in 1881 and named for the AT & SF Railroad official David Gallup.

•GRADY, Village; Curry County; Pop. 122; Zip Code 88120; Lat. 34-49-18 N long. 103-18-54 W; The village is named after early postmaster Pearl Grady.

•GRANTS, City; Valencia County; Pop. 11,451; Zip Code 870++; Lat. 35-10-00 N long. 107-52-08 W; Grants is named for the Grant brothers who were local railroad contractors.

•GRENVILLE, Village; Union County; Pop. 39; Zip Code 88424; Lat. 36-35-16 N long. 103-36-39 W; Founded in the 1880's and named after a prominent early pioneer.

•HAGERMAN, Town; Chaves County; Pop. 936; Zip Code 88232; Elev. 3425'; Lat. 33-06-37 N long. 104-19-35 W; Hagerman is named for railroad president J. J. Hagerman, president of a local railroad.

•HATCH, Village; Dona Ana County; Pop. 1,028; Zip Code 87937; Elev. 4057'; Lat. 32-39-50 N long. 107-09-23 W; General Edward Hatch commanded the local military district here in the 1880's. The town is named for him.

•HOBBS, City; Lea County; Pop. 28,794; Zip Code 882++; Lat. 32-41-59 N long. 103-08-30 W; The Hobbs family were the first homesteaders. The town is named after them.

•HOPE, Village; Eddy County; Pop. 111; Zip Code 88250; Elev. 4086'; Lat. 32-48-43 N long. 104-44-19 W; Settled in 1884 and named for a bet between two homesteaders, one of whom "hoped" the other would lose the toss to name the town.

•HOUSE, Village; Quay County; Pop. 117; Zip Code 88121; Lat. 34-38-28 N long. 103-54-42 W; Lucie House settled here in 1902. The town is named for her.

•HURLEY, Town; Grant County; Pop. 1,616; Zip Code 88043; Lat. 32-41-52 N long. 108-07-32 W; Hurley is named after the Chino mine's manager, J. E. Hurley.

•JAL, City; Lea County; Pop. 2,675; Zip Code 88252; Lat. 32-07-04 N long. 103-11-07 W; Pioneer rancher John A. Lynch founded the JAL Ranch nearby. The town is named for that ranch.

•JEMEZ SPRINGS, Village; Sandoval County; Pop. 316; Zip Code 87025; Lat. 35-46-20 N long. 106-40-51 W; A Spanish translation of an Indian word "hay mish," or "people."

•LAKE ARTHUR, Town; Chaves County; Pop. 327; Zip Code 88253; Elev. 3378'; Lat. 32-59-49 N long. 104-21-33 W; Pioneer Arthur Russell settled here in 1893. The town is named after him.

•LAS CRUCES, City; Dona Ana County Seat; Pop. 45,086; Zip Code 880++; Lat. 32-19-53 N long. 106-42-41 W; An old burial ground with its crosses gave the town its Spanish name meaning "the crosses."

•LAS VEGAS, City; San Miguel County Seat; Pop. 14,322; Zip Code 877++; Elev. 6436'; Lat. 35-35-59 N long. 105-13-02 W; Las Vegas is Spanish for "meadows."

•LOGAN, Village; Quay County; Pop. 735; Zip Code 88426; Elev. 3819'; Lat. 35-22-19 N long. 103-25-05 W; The village is named in honor of a Texas ranger commander.

•LORDSBURG, City; Hidalgo County Seat; Pop. 3,195; Zip Code 880++; Elev. 4258'; Lat. 32-20-34 N long. 108-42-20 W; Settled in 1880 and named for a local railroad construction engineer.

•LOS LUNAS, Village; Valencia County Seat; Pop. 3,525; Zip Code 87031; Elev. 4852'; Lat. 34-48-53 N long. 106-43-37 W; Named after an early settler family, the Lunas.

•LOS RANCHOS DE ALBUQUERQUE, Village; Bernalillo County; Pop. 2,702; Zip Code 87107; Lat. 35-09-43 N, long. 106-38-32 W. The village's named comes from the Los Ranchos de Albuquerque Grant, a large land grant N of Albuquerque made by the crown of Spain to Diego Montoya in 1694.

•LOVING, Village; Eddy County; Pop. 1,355; Zip Code 88256; Lat. 32-17-24 N long. 104-05-45 W; Swiss pioneers settled here in 1893 and named for it for early rancher John Loving.

•LOVINGTON, City; Lea County Seat; Pop. 9,727; Zip Code 88260; Lat. 32-56-42 N long. 103-20-55 W; Founded around 1900 and named for settler R. F. Love.

•MAGDALENA, Village; Socorro County; Pop. 1,022; Zip Code 87825; Elev. 6573'; Lat. 34-06-31 N long. 107-13-53 W; Settled in 1884 and named after Biblical Mary Magdalene.

•MAXWELL, Village; Colfax County; Pop. 316; Zip Code 87728; Elev. 5931'; Lat. 36-32-25 N long. 104-32-21 W; The village is named after pioneer Lucien Maxwell who received a land grant here.

•MELROSE, Village; Curry County; Pop. 649; Zip Code 88124; Lat. 34-24-53 N long. 103-38-21 W; Railway officials named the town after Melrose, Ohio in 1906.

•MESILLA, Town; Dona Ana County; Pop. 2,029; Zip Code 88046; Lat. 32-17-36 N long. 106-46-49 W; Mesilla is Spanish for "little table."

•MILAN, Village; Valencia County; Pop. 3,747; Zip Code 87021; Lat. 35-10-11 N, long. 107-53-25 W. The town is named for Salvador Milan, the original landowner.

•MORIARTY, City; Torrance County; Pop. 1,276; Zip Code 87035; Elev. 6217'; Lat. 34-59-59 N long. 106-02-45 W; Michael Moriarty came to the area in the 1880's for a health cure, and settled permanently.

•MOSQUERO, Village; Harding & San Miguel Counties; Harding County Seat; Pop. 197; Zip Code 877+; Elev. 5688; Lat. 35-46-28 N long. 103-57-09 W; The town's name is Spanish for "swarm of flies."

•MOUNTAINAIR, Town; Torrance County; Pop. 1,170; Zip Code 87036; Elev. 6499'; Lat. 34-31-04 N long. 106-14-18 W; Descriptively named for its location at the top of the Abo Pass.

•PECOS, Village; San Miguel County; Pop. 885; Zip Code 87552; Elev. 6923'; Lat. 35-34-21 N long. 105-40-25 W; A Spanish translation of an Indian word meaning "place of water."

•PORTALES, City; Roosevelt County Seat; Pop. 9,940; Zip Code 88130; Elev. 4009'; Lat. 34-10-59 N long. 103-20-09 W; Founded in 1898 and named for the nearby caves, or "portales."

•**QUESTA,** Village; Taos County; Pop. 608; Zip Code 87556; Elev. 7392'; Lat. 36-42-16 N long. 105-35-30 W; Questa is Spanish for "slope."

•**RATON,** City; Colfax County Seat; Pop. 8,225; Zip Code 87740; Lat. 36-53-41 N long. 104-26-08 W; Raton is Spanish for "mouse or rat."

•**RED RIVER,** Town; Taos County; Pop. 332; Zip Code 87558; Elev. 8650'; Lat. 36-42-24 N long. 105-24-15 W; Descriptively named for its red color.

•**RESERVE,** Village; Catron County Seat; Pop. 439; Zip Code 87830; Lat. 33-43-00 N long. 108-45-27 W; There is a U. S. forest ranger headquarters here; the town is named for the adjacent U. S. forest reserves.

•**ROSWELL,** City; Chaves County Seat; Pop. 39,676; Zip Code 882++; Elev. 3573'; Lat. 33-23-12 N long. 104-31-32 W; Settled in 1869 and named for Roswell Smith, a gambler who helped found the town.

•**ROY,** Village; Harding County; Pop. 381; Zip Code 87743; Elev. 5888'; Lat. 35-57-03 N long. 104-11-14 W; The Roy brothers settled here in 1901. The town is named for them.

•**RUIDOSO,** Village; Lincoln County; Pop. 4,260; Zip Code 88345; Lat. 33-19-54 N long. 105-39-39 W; Ruidoso is Spanish for "noisy" and refers to a fast flowing creek that runs through the town.

•**RUIDOSO DOWNS,** Village; Lincoln County; Pop. 949; Zip Code 88346; Lat. 33-19-45 N long. 105-35-15 W; The town is named after a local stream.

•**SAN JON,** Village; Quay County; Pop. 341; Zip Code 88434; Elev. 4022'; Lat. 35-06-23 N long. 103-19-29 W; San Jon is probably a corruption of "zanjon," or "deep gulley."

•**SAN YSIDRO,** Village; Sandoval County; Pop. 199; Zip Code 87053; Lat. 35-33-49 N long. 106-46-15 W; The village is named after eleventh century Spanish saint, St. Isidore.

•**SANTA FE,** City; Santa Fe County Seat; Pop. 48,899; State Capital; Zip Code 875+; Elev. 6989; Lat. 35-40-27 N long. 105-57-14 W; Santa Fe is Spanish for "holy faith."

•**SANTA ROSA,** City; Guadalupe County Seat; Pop. 2,469; Zip Code 884++; Elev. 4599'; Lat. 34-49-56 N long. 104-37-22 W; The city was settled in 1865 and named for St. Rose of Lima.

•**SILVER CITY,** Town; Grant County Seat; Pop. 9,887; Zip Code 880++; Elev. 5938'; Lat. 32-47-43 N long. 108-09-08 W; First settled in 1870 and named for the local silver deposits.

•**SOCORRO,** City; Socorro County Seat; Pop. 7,576; Zip Code 87801; Lat. 34-03-00 N long. 106-53-36 W; Socorro is Spanish for "help, or aid."

•**SPRINGER,** Town; Colfax County; Pop. 1,696; Zip Code 877++; Elev. 5832'; Lat. 36-20-54 N long. 104-47-34 W; Springer was settled in 1879 and named for the Springer brothers.

•**TAOS,** Town; Taos County Seat; Pop. 3,369; Zip Code 87571; Elev. 6952'; Lat. 36-25-06 N long. 105-33-41 W; Taos is a Spanish translation of an Indian word "to-o-ta," or "red willow place."

•**TATUM,** Town; Lea County; Pop. 896; Zip Code 88267; Lat. 33-15-05 N long. 103-18-40 W; James Tatum founded the first store here in 1909. It is named for him.

•**TEXICO,** City; Curry County; Pop. 958; Zip Code 88135; Lat. 34-23-28 N long. 103-03-08 W; Texico is a combined word formed by joining the names Texas and New Mexico.

•**TIJERAS,** Village; Bernalillo County; Pop. 311; Zip Code 87059; Lat. 35-04-51 N long. 106-23-15 W; A pioneer surname whose name translates as "scissors."

•**TRUTH OR CONSEQUENCES,** City; Sierra County Seat; Pop. 5,219; Zip Code 87901; Elev. 4242'; Lat. 33-08-11 N long. 107-15-15 W; Originally known as Hot Springs, the name was changed in 1950 after the then popular T. V. show.

•**TUCUMCARI,** City; Quay County Seat; Pop. 6,765; Zip Code 884++; Elev. 4086'; Lat. 35-10-32 N long. 103-43-21 W; The city is named for the Tucumcari Mountains nearby.

•**TULAROSA,** Village; Otero County; Pop. 2,536; Zip Code 88352; Lat. 33-04-59 N long. 106-01-40 W; Tularosa is Spanish for "reddish reeds or willows."

•**VAUGHN,** Town; Guadalupe County; Pop. 737; Zip Code 88353; Lat. 34-36-04 N long. 105-12-59 W; Founded around 1900 and named for Major G. W. Vaughn, a Civil Engineer for the AT & SF Railroad.

•**WAGON MOUND,** Village; Mora County; Pop. 416; Zip Code 877++; Elev. 6195'; Lat. 36-03-32 N long. 105-07-12 W; The village is named after a local rocky formation that resembles a covered wagon.

•**WILLARD,** Village; Torrance County; Pop. 166; Zip Code 87063; Elev. 6107'; Lat. 34-35-43 N long. 106-01-42 W; Named for Willard Hopewell, son of railroad promoter W. S. Hopewell.

•**WILLIAMSBURG,** Village; Sierra County; Pop. 433; Zip Code 87942; Lat. 33-06-31 N long. 107-17-47 W; Named for an early pioneer settler.

NEW YORK

•ACRA, Village; Greene County; Pop. 400; Zip Code 12405; Elev. 668; Lat. 42-18-39 N long. 074-03-21 W; E. N.Y.; named for the Syrian city.

•ADAMS, Village and Town; Jefferson County; Pop. 1,699 and 4,368; Zip Code 13605; Elev. 600; Lat. 43-48-33 N long. 076-01-28 W; N N.Y. 15 m. S of Watertown just E of Interstate 81. Named for President John Adams.

•AKRON, Village; Erie County; Pop. 2,970; Zip Code 14001; Lat. 43-01-15 N long. 078-29-44 W; NW N.Y. on State 93, 15 m. E of Buffalo in W N.Y. Akron is a Greek word meaning summit.

•ALABAMA, Town; Genessee County; Pop. 1,923; Zip Code 14003; Lat. 43-05-47 N long. 078-23-28 W; 35 m. W of Buffalo on State 63 in NW N.Y. Named for the state.

•ALBANY, City; Albany County seat and Capital of New York; Pop. 101,767; Zip Code 12201; Elev. 18 to 300; Lat. 42-39-09 N long. 073-45-24 W; E New York; 150 m. N of New York City; On Hudson River. Named after the Duke of Albany.

•ALBION, Village and Town; Seat of Orleans County; Pop. 4,898 and 6,425; Zip Code 14411; Lat. 43-14-47 N long. 078-11-38 W; NW N.Y. Given the ancient name for England.

•ALDEN, Village and Town; Erie County; Pop. 2,490 and 10,101; Zip Code 14004; Elev. 866; Lat. 42-54-00 N long. 078-29-32 W; 20 m. NE of Buffalo in NW N.Y.; Named for the English town.

•ALEXANDER, Village and Town; Genesee County; Pop. 483 and 2,639; Zip Code 14005; Elev. 940; Lat. 42-54-04 N long. 078-15-25 W; NW N.Y. 30 m. E of Buffalo; Named for Alexander Rea, first settler and State Senator.

•ALFRED, Village and Town; Allegany County; Pop. 4,957 and 6,193; Zip Code 14802; Elev. 1,760; Lat. 42-15-15 N long. 077-47-27 W; 10 m. SW of Hornell in SW N.Y. Named for an early settler.

•ALLEGANY, Village and Town; Cattaraugus County; Pop. 2,078 and 8,560; Zip Code 14706; Elev. 1,425; Lat. 42-05-24 N long. 078-29-40 W; on the Allegany River in SE N.Y. An Indian word meaning "beautiful.

•ALMA, Town; Allegany County; Pop. 925; Zip Code 14708; Elev. 1552; Lat. 42-00-45 N long. 078-03-29 W; SW N.Y. just north of the Pennsylvania border. A Latin word meaning "nourishing."

•ALTAMONT, Village; Albany County; Pop. 1,277; Zip Code 12009; Elev. 451; Lat. 42-42-02 N long. 074-02-03 W; 8 m. W of Albany in E N.Y. The name means "high mountain."

•ALTONA, Town; Clinton County; Pop. 2,082; Zip Code 12910; Lat. 44-53-18 N long. 073-39-22 W; in the northern corner of the state.

•AMAGANSETT, Included in East Hampton; Suffolk County; Pop. 1,800; Zip Code 11930; Elev. 32; Lat. 40-58-25 N long. 072-08-39 W; SE N.Y.; an Indian name meaning "well."

•AMENIA, Town; Dutchess County; Pop. 6,266; Zip Code 12510; Elev. 573; Lat. 41-50-57 N long. 073-33-26 W; E New York.

•AMITYVILLE, Village; Suffolk County; Pop. 9,085; Zip Code 11701; Elev. 25; Lat. 40-40-44 N long. 073-25-03 W; on Great South Bay on the south shore of Long Island in SE N.Y.; name means "friendship town."

•AMSTERDAM, City; Montgomery County; Pop. 21,838; Zip Code 12010; Elev. 289; Lat. 42-56-19 N long. 0874-11-19 W; 28 miles NW of Albany in N N.Y.; the name recalls the early Dutch settlement.

•ANDOVER, Village and Town; Allegany County; Pop. 1,119 and 1,949; Zip Code 14806; Elev. 1665; Lat. 42-09-23 N long. 077-47-45 W; S N.Y. Named for the city in England.

•ANGOLA, Village; Erie County; Pop. 2,295; Zip Code 14006; Elev. 689; Lat. 42-38-18 N long. 079-01-41 W; Western coast of N.Y., named for the country in Africa.

•ARCADE, Village and Town; Wyoming County; Pop. 2,060 and 3,719; Zip Code 14009; Lat. 42-32-02 N long. 078-25-24 W; named for the district in ancient Greece.

•ATHENS, Village and Town; Greene County; Pop. 1,728 and 3,411; Zip Code 12015; Lat. 42-15-37 N long. 073-48-36 W; named after the Greek city.

•ATLANTIC BEACH, Village; Nassau County; Pop. 1,773; Zip Code 11509; Lat. 40-35-20 N long. 073-43-46 W; at the western point of Long Beach on western Long Island in SE N.Y. Descriptively named for its location.

•ATTICA, Village and Town; Wyoming County; Pop. 2,658 and 5,690; Zip Code 14011; Lat. 42-51-51 N long. 078-16-50 W; NW N.Y. Named after the district in ancient Greece.

•AUBURN, City; Seat of Cayuga County; Pop. 32,442; Zip Code 13021; Lat. 42-55-54 N long. 076-33-59 W; on the end of Lake Owasco. Named after the village in Goldsmith's poem.

•AUSTERLITZ, Town; Columbia County; Pop. 12,017; Zip Code 12017; Elev. 1,210; Lat. 42-18-42 N long. 073-28-25 W; on the eastern border of N.Y. *Martin Van Buren*, an ardent admirer of *Napoleon*, named this town Austerlitz.

•AVON, Village and Town; Livingston County; Pop. 3,009 and 6,185; Zip Code 14414; Elev. 651; Lat. 42-54-43 N long. 077-44-45 W; on the Genesee River, in western N.Y. Named after the famous English river.

•BABYLON, Village; Suffolk County; Pop. 12,380; Zip Code 117+; Lat. 40-41-44 N long. 073-19-34 W; on the S shore of Long Island. Named for the Biblical city.

•BAINBRIDGE, Village and Town; Chenango County; Pop. 1,597 and 3,343; Zip Code 13733; Elev. 1,000; Lat. 42-17-36 N long. 075-28-47 W; on the Susquehanna River in S N.Y. Named in honor of naval hero William Bainbridge.

•BALDWINSVILLE, Village; Onondaga County; Pop. 6,434; Zip Code 13027; Elev. 423; Lat. 43-09-31 N long. 076-19-59 W; on the Seneca River.

•BALLSTON, Town; Saratoga County; Pop. 7,707; Zip Code 12019; located in E N.Y. Named for a prominent settler.

•BANGOR, Town; Franklin County; Pop. 1,966; Zip Code 12966; Lat. 44-48-44 N long. 074-23-52 W; in NE N.Y. Named for the town in Wales.

•BARTON, Town; Tioga County; Pop. 8,696; Zip Code 13734; Lat. 42-02-34 N long. 076-26-56 W; from a personal name.

•BATAVIA, City; Seat of Genesee County; Pop. 16,667; Zip Code 14020; Elev. 890; Lat. 42-59-53 N long. 078-11-16 W; in NW N.Y. named for the Dutch republic to which the proprietors belonged.

•BATH, Village and Town; Seat of Steuben County; Pop. 6,038 and 12,278; Zip Code 14810; Elev. 1,104; Lat. 42-20-13 N long. 077-19-05 W; in S N.Y. Named for the English city.

•**BAYVILLE**, Village; Nassau County; Pop. 7,019; Zip Code 11709; Elev. 40; Lat. 40-54-38 N long. 073-33-45 W; on the NW tip of Long Island in SE N.Y. Descriptively named for its location.

•**BEACON**, City; Dutchess County; Pop. 12,908; Zip Code 12508; Elev. 150; Lat. 41-30-17 N long. 073-58-12 W; on the Hudson River across from Neaburgh in SE N.Y. Named after nearby Mt. Beacon.

•**BEDFORD**, Town; Westchester County; Pop. 15,085; Zip Code 10506; Lat. 40-41-19 N long. 073-57-20 W; in SE N.Y. just W of the Connecticut border; named after the town in England.

•**BELFAST**, Town; Allegany County; Pop. 1,488; Zip Code 14711; Lat. 42-20-34 N long. 078-06-42 W; in S N.Y. Named after the Irish city.

•**BELMONT**, Village; Seat of Allegany County; Pop. 1,024; Zip Code 14813; Elev. 1418; Lat. 42-13-23 N long. 078-02-05 W; in SW N.Y. The village is named after *August P. Belmont*, financier and sportsman.

•**BERNE**, Town; Albany County; Pop. 2,515; Zip Code 12023; Lat. 42-37-31 N long. 074-08-02 W; in E N.Y. settled in 1750; and named for the native Swiss city of *Jacob Weidman*.

•**BINGHAMTON**, City; Broome County seat; Pop. 55,745; Zip Code 13901; Elev. 845; Lat. 42-05-55 N long. 075-55-06 W; S central New York; Named in honor of *William Bingham*, a Philadelphia merchant.

•**BOLIVAR**, Village and Town; Allegany County; Pop. 1,348 and 2,499; Zip Code 14715; Elev. 1,609; Lat. 42-04-00 N long. 078-10-05 W; in S N.Y. Named for the famous Latin American liberator.

•**BOMBAY**, Town; Franklin County; Pop. 1,249; Zip Code 12914; Elev. 189; Lat. 44-56-20 N long. 074-34-05 W; in N N.Y. Named after the Indian city.

•**BOSTON**, Town; Erie County; Pop. 7,691; Zip Code 14025; Elev. 727; Lat. 42-37-44 N long. 078-44-16 W; in W N.Y. Named after Boston, Massachusetts.

•**BRIGHTWATERS**, Village; Suffolk County; Pop. 3,290, Zip Code 11718; Lat. 40-43-15 N long. 073-61-04 W; on Great South Bay on Long Island. Descriptively named.

•**BROADALBIN**, Village and Town; Fulton County; Pop. 1,426 and 4,095; Zip Code 12025; Elev. 820; Lat. 43-03-31 N long. 074-11-49 W; settled in 1770; was named by its Scottish population when the post office was established in 1804.

•**BROCKPORT**, Village; Monroe County; Pop. 9,767; Zip Code 14420; Elev. 539; Lat. 43-12-49 N long. 077-56-22 W; from a personal name.

•**BRONX**, Borough, Seat of Bronx County; Pop. 1,162,632; Zip Code 104+; in N part of N.Y. City. Named after the early Dutch settler Jonas Bronck.

•**BROOKHAVEN**, Town; Suffolk County; Pop. 364,764; Zip Code 11719; Lat. 40-46-45 N long. 072-54-57 W; E of Patchogue, on Long Island in SE N.Y. Named for an early stream.

•**BROOKLYN**, Borough; Seat of Kings County; Pop. 2,218,441; Zip Code 112+; Elev. 1381; Lat. 42-25-59 N long. 078-44-55 W; a residential borough located in SW Long Island. An English version of a Dutch word refering to a local brook.

•**BUFFALO**, City; Erie County Seat; Pop. 357,384; Zip Code 14201; Elev. 600; Lat. 42-53-11 N long. 078-52-43 W; NW New York; The name, according to local historian *Roy W. Nagle*, is enigmatic, because no buffalo ever existed in the area.

•**BYRON**, Town; Genesee County; Pop. 2,246; Zip Code 14422; Elev. 616; Lat. 43-04-47 N long. 078-03-51 W; Named for the English poet.

•**CAIRO**, Town; Greene County; Pop. 4,619; Zip Code 12413; Elev. 340; Lat. 42-17-56 N long. 073-59-56 W; Named after the great Egyptian city.

•**CALEDONIA**, Village and Town; Livingston County; Pop. 2,189 and 4,042; Zip Code 14423; Elev. 666; Lat. 42-58-23 N long. 077-51-11 W; Given the ancient name for Scotland.

•**CAMBRIDGE**, Village and Town; Washington County; Pop. 1,822 and 1,850; Zip Code 12816; Elev. 500; Lat. 43-01-41 N long. 073-22-54 W; E N.Y. Named for the English University town.

•**CAMDEN**, Village and Town; Oneida County; Pop. 2,643 and 4,908; Zip Code 13316; Lat. 43-20-04 N long. 075-44-54 W; Named in honor of Lord Camden, who supported the American cause before the Revolution.

•**CAMPBELL**, Town; Steuben County; Pop. 3,794; Zip Code 14821; Lat. 42-48-20 N long. 075-37-03 W; Named for the famous Scottish clan.

•**CANAAN**, Town; Columbia County; Pop. 1,663; Zip Code 12029; Elev. 847; Lat. 42-24-43 N long. 073-26-51 W; Given the Biblical name.

•**CANAJOHARIE**, Village and Town; Montgomery County; Pop. 2,401 and 4,133; Zip Code 13317; Elev. 311; Lat. 42-54-20 N long. 074-34-20 W; on Mohawk River, the name, from the Indian meaning, "the pot that washes itself", refers to a large pothole at the entrance to Canajoharie Gorge.

•**CANANDAIGUA**, City; Seat of Ontario County; Pop. 10,361; Zip Code 14424; Elev. 766; Lat. 42-52-07 N long. 077-20-09 W; an Iroquoian Indian word meaning "town site."

•**CANASTOTA**, Village; Madison County; Pop. 4,765; Zip Code 13032; Lat. 43-04-46 N long. 075-45-04 W; an Iroquoian Indian word meaning "lone pine grove."

•**CANEADEA**, Town; Allegany County; Pop. 2,426; Zip Code 14717; Lat. 42-23-11 N long. 078-09-14 W; SW N.Y.; name is Indian for "where heaven meets earth."

•**CANISTEO**, Village and Town; Steuben County; Pop. 2,679 and 3,967; Zip Code 14823; Elev. 1132; Lat. 42-16-13 N long. 077-36-22 W; on Canisteo River. An Indian word refering to the pickerel fish.

•**CANTON**, Village and Town; Seat of St. Lawrence County; Pop. 7,064 and 11,576; Zip Code 13617; Elev. 409; Lat. 44-35-44 N long. 075-10-10 W; Named for the Chinese city.

•**CARMEL**, Town; Seat of Putnam County; Pop. 27,867; Zip Code 10512; Elev. 520; Lat. 41-25-48 N long. 073-40-50 W. Named after the Biblical mountain.

•**CARTHAGE**, Village; Jefferson County; Pop. 3,659; Zip Code 13619; Elev. 742; Lat. 43-58-41 N long. 075-36-35. Named after the ancient North African country.

•**CASTILE**, Village and Town; Wyoming County; Pop. 1,131 and 2,861; Zip Code 14427; Lat. 42-37-44 N long. 078-03-17 W. For the Spanish kingdom.

•**CATSKILL**, Village and Town; Seat of Greene County; Pop. 4,699 and 11,337; Zip Code 12414; Elev. 75; Lat. 42-13-02 N long. 073-51-54 W; on W side of Hudson River, named by the Dutch for the wildcats that occasionally came down from the hills, where they roamed in large numbers.

•**CEDARHURST**, Village; Nassau County; Pop. 6,190; Zip Code 11516; Lat. 40-37-22 N long. 073-43-29 W; on Long Island. Descriptively named for the numerous cedar trees.

•**CHAMPLAIN**, Village and Town; Clinton County; Pop. 1,400 and 5,845; Zip Code 12919; Elev. 152; Lat. 44-59-11 N long. 073-26-49 W; NE N.Y. Named in honor of the early French explorer.

•**CHATEAUGAY**, Village and Town; Franklin County; Pop. 866 and 1,859; Zip Code 12920; Elev. 972; Lat. 44-55-35 N long. 074-04-48 W; named for the adjoining Canadian land grant owned by *Charles Lemoyne*, founder of an eminent Canadian family.

•**CHATHAM**, Village and Town; Columbia County; Pop. 2,001 and 4,286; Zip Code 12037; Elev. 473; Lat. 42-21-51 N long. 073-35-43 W. Named in honor of Lord Chatham, William Pitt.

•**CHAUTAUQUA**, Town; Chautauqua County; Pop. 4,734; Zip Code 14722; Lat. 42-12-35 N long. 079-28-01 W; on Chautauqua Lake in SW corner of N.Y. An Indian word refering to a lost legend.

•**CHAZY**, Town; Clinton County; Pop. 3,777; Zip Code 12921; Lat. 44-53-23 N long. 073-26-11 W; near Lake Champlain. Named in honor of Lieutenant de Chezy, who was killed here in 1666.

•**CHEEKTOWAGA**, Town; Erie County; Pop. 109,385; Zip Code 142+; E of Buffalo in W N.Y. An Iroquoian Indian word meaning "crab apple place."

•**CHEMUNG**, Town; Chemung County; Pop. 2,424; Zip Code 14825; Elev. 847; Lat. 42-00-30 N long. 076-37-27 W. An Iroquoian Indian word meaning "big horn."

•**CHESTER**, Village and Town; Orange County; Pop. 1,910 and 6,845; Zip Code 10918; Lat. 41-21-45 N long. 074-16-18 W; SE N.Y. Named after the city in England.

•**CHITTENANGO**, Village; Madison County; Pop. 4,281; Zip Code 13037; Lat. 43-02-42 N long. 075-52-01 W; 16 m. E of Syracuse in central N.Y. An Iroquoian Indian word whose meaning is uncertain.

•**CICERO**, Town; Onondaga County; Pop. 24,431; Zip Code 13039; Lat. 43-10-32 N long. 076-07-11 W. Named after the famous Roman writer.

•**CINCINNATUS**, Town; Cortland County; Pop. 1,155; Zip Code 13040; Elev. 1046; Lat. 42-32-32 N long. 075-53-46 W. The town is named after the ancient Roman hero.

•**CLAREDON**, Town; Orleans County; Pop. 2,149; 716; Zip Code 14429; Lat. 43-11-36 N long. 078-03-54 W. Named for the Earl of Claredon.

•**CLARENCE**, Town; Erie County; Pop. 18,126; Zip Code 14031; Lat. 42-58-36 N long. 078-35-32 W; W N.Y. For a personal name.

•**CLAVERACK**, Town; Columbia County; Pop. 6,095; Zip Code 12513; Lat. 42-13-30 N long. 073-44-06 W. A Dutch word meaning "clover stretch."

•**CLAY**, Town; Onondaga County; Pop. 52,046; Zip Code 13041; Lat. 43-11-09 N long. 076-10-22 W; Central N.Y. Refering to the local soil type.

•**CLINTON**, Village; Oneida County; Pop. 2,106; Zip Code 13323; Lat. 43-02-54 N long. 075-22-44 W. Named in honor of Governor DeWitt Clinton.

•**CLYDE**, Village; Wayne County; Pop. 2,498; Zip Code 14433; Elev. 400; Lat. 43-05-03 N long. 076-52-11 W; on N.Y. Named after the river in Scotland.

•**COBLESKILL**, Village and Town; Schoharie County; Pop. 5,257 and 7,030; Zip Code 12043; Elev. 932; Lat. 42-40-40 N long. 074-29-09 W; SW of Amsterdam in E N.Y. Named after Jacob Kobell, an early Dutch settler.

•**COEYMANS**, Town; Albany County; Pop. 7,878; Zip Code 12045; Lat. 42-28-26 N long. 073-47-34 W; E N.Y. Named after Dutch settler Barent Coeymans.

•**COHOCTON**, Village and Town; Steuben County; Pop. 887 and 2,454; Zip Code 14826; Lat. 42-30-08 N long. 077-30-27 W. An Iroquoian Indian word meaning "log-in-the-water."

•**COHOES**, City; Albany County; Pop. 18,158; Zip Code 12047; Lat. 42-46-27 N long. 073-42-02 W. An Indian word meaning "pine tree."

•**COLDEN**, Town; Erie County; Pop. 3,127; Zip Code 14033; Lat. 42-38-39 N long. 078-41-06 W; named for *Cadwallader Colden*, historian.

•**COLD SPRING**, Village; Putnam County; Pop. 2,161; Zip Code 10516; Elev. 1349; Lat. 42-05-49 N long. 078-51-54 W; on *Hudson River*.

•**COLONIE**, Village and Town; Albany County; Pop. 8,835 and 74,534; Zip Code 12212; Lat. 42-43-04 N long. 073-50-02 W; NW of Albany. Named after an early settlement.

•**CONESUS**, Town; Livingston County; Pop. 1,972; Zip Code 14435; Elev. 1199; Lat. 42-43-08 N long. 077-40-36 W; An Indian word meaning "berry place."

•**COOPERSTOWN**, Village; Otsego County Seat; Pop. 2,336; Zip Code 13326; Elev. 1,240; Lat. 42-42-02 N long. 074-55-29 W; E central New York; *William Cooper* bought land here in 1785, and soon founded the settlement which bears his name.

•**COPAKE**, Town; Columbia County; Pop. 2,336; Zip Code 12516; Elev. 620; Lat. 42-06-12 N long. 073-33-02 W; E N.Y.; An Indian word meaning "snake pond."

•**CORINTH**, Village and Town; Saratoga County; Pop. 2,698 and 5,199; Zip Code 12822; Lat. 43-14-40 N long. 073-49-58 W; Named after the ancient Greek city.

•**CORNING**, City; Steuben County; Pop. 12,894; Zip Code 14830; Elev. 937; Lat. 42-08-34 N long. 077-03-18 W; on Chemung River. Named after founder Erastus Corning."

•**CORNWALL**, Town; Orange County; Pop. 10,756; Zip Code 12518; Lat. 41-26-41 N long. 074-00-58 W; on Hudson River S of Newburgh in SE N.Y. Named for the county in England.

•**CORTLAND**, City; Seat of Cortland County; Pop. 20,094; Zip Code 13045; Lat. 42-36-04 N long. 076-10-51 W; 30 m. S of Syracuse; was first settled in 1792 and named for the prominent Van Cortlandt family.

•**COXSACKIE**, Village and Town; Greene County; Pop. 2,761 and 5,976; Zip Code 12051; Lat. 42-21-03 N long. 073-48-12 W; on Hudson River. An Indian word meaning "stream outlet."

•**CUBA**, Village and Town; Allegany County; Pop. 1,701 and 3,394; Zip Code 14727; Elev. 1500; Lat. 42-13-03 N long. 078-16-32 W. Named for the Caribbean island.

•**CUDDEBACKVILLE**, Orange County; Zip Code 12729; Lat. 41-28-02 N long. 074-35-39 W; was named for *Abraham A. Cuddeback*, believed to be the first white settler, who arrived here about 1792.

•**DANNEMORA**, Village and Town; Clinton County; Pop. 3,767 and 4,709; Zip Code 12929; Elev. 1,400; Lat. 44-43-17 N long. 073-43-27 W; named for the city in Sweden because of the high quality of its iron deposits.

•**DAYTON**, Town; Cattaraugus County; Pop. 1,976; Zip Code 14041; Elev. 1,322; Lat. 42-25-01 N long. 078-58-38 W. From a personal name.

•**DEFERIET**, Village; Jefferson County; Pop. 326; Zip Code 13628; Elev. 641; Lat. 44-02-08 N long. 075-41-03 W; N central N.Y.; The place was named for *Baroness Jenika de Derriet*, who about 1830 built a beautiful mansion, called the Hermitage on the bank of the Black River.

•**DELHI**, Village and Town; Seat of Delaware County; Pop. 3,377 and 5,302; Zip Code 13753; Elev. 1370; Lat. 42-16-41 N long. 074-54-59 W; on the Delaware River in S N.Y. At the suggestions of citizens the community was named for Delhi, India.

•**DENMARK**, Town; Lewis County; Pop. 2,448; Zip Code 13631; Lat. 43-53-59 N long. 075-34-58 W; N central N.Y.; named after the Kingdom in Northwestern Europe.

•**DEPAUVILLE**, Jefferson County; Zip Code 13632; Elev. 297; Lat. 44-08-18 N long. 076-03-57 W; was named for *Francis Depau*, early settler, who in 1834-5 built the stone Depauville Union Church.

•**DEPEW**, Village; Erie County; Pop. 19,819; Zip Code 14043; Elev. 680; Lat. 42-54-14 N long. 078-41-33 W; W New York.

•**DEPEYSTER**, Town; St. Lawrence County; Pop. 896; Zip Code 13633; was named after a wealthy New York merchant.

•**DOLGEVILLE**, Village; Herkimer County; Pop. 2,607; Zip Code 13329; Elev. 800; Lat. 43-06-03 N long. 074-46-24 W; was named in 1881 for *Alfred Dolge*, a businessman who transformed the village of Brockett's Bridge into a factory town of several thousand workers.

•**DRYDEN**, Village and Town; Tompkins County; Pop. 1,758 and 12,138; Zip Code 13053; Lat. 42-29-27 N long. 076-17-51 W. Named for the English poet.

•**DUANESBURG**, Town; Schenectady County; Pop. 4,710; Zip Code 12056; Elev. 720; Lat. 42-45-43 N long. 074-08-03 W; was named for *James Duane* (1733-97), jurist, land speculator, and mayor of Manhattan (1748-9).

•**DUNDEE**, Village; Yates County; Pop. 1,551; Zip Code 14837; Elev. 994; Lat. 42-31-24 N long. 076-58-37 W. Named for the city in Scotland.

•**DUNKIRK**, City; Chautauqua County; Pop. 15,255; Zip Code 14048; Elev. 600; Lat. 42-28-46 N long. 079-20-03 W; in SW N.Y. on Lake Erie. Named after the French channel port.

•**EAST AURORA**, Village; Erie County; Pop. 6,824; Zip Code 14052; Elev. 926; Lat. 42-46-04 N long. 078-36-49 W; 15 m. E SE of Buffalo in W N.Y.; in violation of its name, lies 90 m. W of Aurora.

•**EAST HAMPTON**, Town and Village; Suffolk County; Pop. 14,044 and 1,845; Zip Code 11937; Elev. 36; Lat. 40-57-48 N long. 071-11-00 W; on Long Island, on Atlantic Ocean 20 m. W of Montauk Point in SE N.Y.; was settled in 1648, and named for the English county.

•**EAST ROCKAWAY**, Village; Nassau County; Pop. 10,886; Zip Code 11518; Lat. 40-38-31 N long. 073-40-12 W; on Long Island 20 m. E of New York City.

•**EATON**, Town; Madison County; Pop. 5,169; Zip Code 13334; Elev. 1200; Lat. 42-50-59 N long. 075-36-44. From a personal name.

•**EDEN**, Town; Erie County; Pop. 7,337; Zip Code 14057; Lat. 42-39-08 N long. 078-53-50 W. Given a Biblical name.

•**ELBA**, Village and Town; Genesee County; Pop. 751 and 2,501; Zip Code 14058; Elev. 761; Lat. 43-04-38 N long. 078-11-14 W. Named for the island of Napolean's exile.

•**ELBRIDGE**, Village and Town; Onondaga County; Pop. 1,098 and 5,876; Zip Code 13060; Lat. 43-02-04 N long. 076-26-54 W; Central N.Y. From a personal name.

•**ELLENVILLE**, Village; Ulster County; Pop. 4,407; Zip Code 12428; Elev. 360; Lat. 41-43-01 N long. 074-23-46 W; named for the wife of an early settler.

•**ELLICOTTVILLE**, Village and Town; Cattaraugus County; Pop. 716 and 1,671; Zip Code 14731; Elev. 1,549; Lat. 42-16-30 N long. 078-40-23 W; was named for *Joseph Ellicott*, Holland Land Company surveyor.

•**ELMA**, Town; Erie County; Pop. 10,579; Lat. 42-51-03 N long. 078-38-26 W; W N.Y. Named for the many Elm trees once in the area.

•**ELMIRA**, City; Chemung County seat; Pop. 35,363; Zip Code 14901; Elev. 860; Lat. 42-05-23 N long. 076-48-29 W; S central New York; Named for *Elmira Teall*, daughter of an early settler.

•**ELMSFORD**, Village; Westchester County; Pop. 3,327; Zip Code 10523; Lat. 41-03-18 N long. 073-49-14 W; 26 m. N of New York in SE N.Y. So named for the many elm trees in the area.

•**ENDICOTT**, Broome County; Pop. 14,457; Zip Code 13760; Elev. 840; Lat. 42-05-54 N long. 076-02-59 W; 8 m. W of Binghamton in S N.Y. Named for a prominent citizen.

•**ESOPUS**, Town; Ulster County; 47,584; Zip Code 12429; at the mouth of Roundout in the Catskill Mts. in SE N.Y.; Lat. 41-49-40 N long. 073-57-56 W. In 1615 Dutch traders established a trading post at the mouth of Roundout Creek and named it Esopus.

•**ESSEX**, Town; Essex County; Pop. 884; Zip Code 12936; NE N.Y.; Lat. 44-18-36 N long. 073-21-11 W; Named after the English county.

•**EVANS MILLS**, Village; Jefferson County; Pop. 653; Zip Code 13637; Elev. 431; N. N.Y.; Lat. 44-05-17 N long. 075-48-27 W; *Ethni Evans*, New Hampshire millwright, who settled here in 1803, gave his name to the hamlet.

•**FAIRPORT**, Village; Monroe County; Pop. 5,958; Zip Code 14450; Lat. 43-05-55 N long. 077-26-32 W; 10 m. E of Rochester in W N.Y. Descriptively named.

•**FALCONER**, Village; Chautauqua County; Pop. 2,786; Zip Code 14733; SW N.Y.; Elev. 1262; Lat. 42-07-07 N long. 079-11-55.

•**FALLSBURG**, Town; Sullivan County; Pop. 9,801; Zip Code 12733; SE N.Y.; Elev. 1162; Lat. 41-43-55 N long. 074-36-06 W; Named for a local geographical feature.

•**FARMINGDALE**, Village; Nassau County; Pop. 7,940; Zip Code 11735; Lat. 40-43-57 N long. 073-26-45 W; 30 M. E of New York City on Long Island in SE N.Y.

•**FINE**, Town; St. Lawrence County; Pop. 2,243; Zip Code 13639; Elev. 960; Lat. 44-14-52 N long. 075-08-17 W.

•**FISHKILL**, Village and Town; Dutchess County; Pop. 1,733 and 15,668; Zip Code 12524; Elev. 200; Lat. 41-32-08 N long. 073-5-58 W; on the Hudson River. An anglicized version of a Dutch word meaning "fish stream."

•**FLEISCHMANNS**, Village; Delaware County; Pop. 350; Zip Code 12430; Elev. 1,515; Lat. 42-09-19 N long. 074-31-58 W; named after a prominent citizen.

•**FLORAL PARK**, Village; Nassau County; Pop. 16,778; Zip Code 110+; Lat. 40-43-25 N long. 073-42-19 W; in S N.Y. on Long Island. Descriptively named.

•**FLORIDA**, Village; Orange County; Pop. 1,932; Zip Code 10921; Lat. 41-19-54 N long. 074-21-26 W; . Named for the state.

•**FONDA**, Village; Seat of Montgomery County; Pop. 1,006; Zip Code 12068; Elev. 294; Lat. 42-57-16 N long. 074-22-37 W; on Mohawk River 12 m. W of Amsterdam in E N.Y. Settled early in the eighteenth century by the Dutch, the place was known as Caughnawaa (Indian, "On the rapids"). In 1851 the town took its present name.

•**FORESTPORT**, Town; Oneida County; Pop. 1,371; Zip Code 13338; Lat. 43-26-31 N long. 075-12-27 W. Named for the once abundant forest.

•**FORT COVINGTON**, Town; Franklin County; Pop. 1,812; Zip Code 12937; Elev. 181; Lat. 44-59-21 N long. 074-29-42 W; on the N tip of N.Y. In the autumn of 1812 *General Wade Hampton*, guarding the border, built a blockhouse here.

•**FORT EDWARD**, Village and Town; Washington County; Pop. 3,563 and 6,476; Zip Code 12828; Elev. 144; Lat. 43-16-01 N long. 073-35-06 W; on Hudson River 38 m. N of Troy in E New York.

•**FORT JOHNSON**, Village; Montgomery County; Pop. 647; Zip Code 12070; Elev. 300; N N.Y.; Lat. 42-57-30 N long. 074-14-00 W; During the French and Indian War a palisade was built around the settlement named for *Sir William Johnson.*

•**FORT PLAIN**, Village; Montgomery County; Pop. 2,538; Zip Code 12229; Elev. 317; Lat. 42-55-53 N long. 074-37-23 W; on the Mohawk River, 23 m. W of Amsterdam in E N.Y.; at the confluence of Otsquago Creek and the Mohawk River. Named for its level geography.

•**FRANKFORT**, Village and Town; Herkimer County; Pop. 2,989 and 7,652; Zip Code 13340; Elev. 400; Lat. 43-02-20 N long. 075-04-15 W; named after the German city.

•**FRANKLIN**, Village and Town; Delaware County; Pop. 442 and 2,431; Zip Code 13775; Lat. 42-20-26 N long. 075-09-56 W. Named in honor of Benjamin Franklin.

•**FRANKLINVILLE**, Village and Town; Cattaraugus County; Pop. 1,874 and 3,085; Zip Code 14737; Elev. 1,549; Lat. 42-20-13 N long. 078-27-30 W; the name honors Benjamin Franklin.

•**FREDONIA**, Village; Chautauqua County; Pop. 11,071; Zip Code 14063; Elev. 728; Lat. 42-26-24 N long. 079-19-55 W; SW corner of N.Y., given an early name for America.

•**FREEDOM**, Town; Cattaraugus County; Pop. 1,842; Zip Code 14065; Lat. 42-29-05 N long. 078-19-53 W.

•**FREEPORT**, Village; Nassau County; Pop. 38,168; Zip Code 11520; Lat. 40-39-27 N long. 073-35-01 W; on S shore of Long Island.

•**FRIENDSHIP**, Town; Allegany County; Pop. 2,151; Zip Code 14739; Elev. 1514; Lat. 42-12-23 N long. 078-08-16 W.

•**FULTON**, City; Oswego County; Pop. 13,274; Zip Code 13069; Elev. 364; Lat. 43-19-22 N long. 076-25-03 W; 24 m. NW of Syracuse in central N.Y. Named in honor of inventor Robert Fulton.

•**GAINESVILLE**, Village and Town; Wyoming County; Pop. 334 and 2,140; Zip Code 14066; Lat. 42-38-27 N long. 078-08-03 W.

•**GALWAY**, Village and Town; Saratoga County; Pop. 246 and 3,020; Zip Code 12074; Lat. 43-01-07 N long. 074-01-55 W. Named after the Irish city.

•**GARDEN CITY**, Village; Nassau County; Pop. 23,019; Zip Code 11530; Lat. 40-43-36 N long. 073-38-05 W; 18 m. E. N.Y. City on Long Island in SE N.Y.; a planned town named by its developers.

•**GARDINER**, Town; Ulster County; Pop. 3,550; Zip Code 12525; Elev. 308; Lat. 41-40-47 N long. 074-09-03 W.

•**GENESEO**, Village and Town; Seat of Livingston County; Pop. 6,744 and 8,670; Zip Code 14454; Elev. 800; Lat. 42-47-45 N long. 077-49-02 W; in Genesee Valley in W central N.Y. The name is from the Indian word meaning beautiful valley.

•**GENEVA**, City; Seneca and Ontario Counties; Pop. 15,068; Zip Code 14456; Elev. 494; Lat. 42-52-08 N long. 076-58-41 W; at N end of Seneca Lake in W N.Y. Named for the Swiss city.

•**GENOA**, Town; Cayuga County; Pop. 1,921; Zip Code 13071; Lat. 42-40-04 N long. 076-32-10 W. Named for the Italian city.

•**GERMANTOWN**, Town; Columbia County; Pop. 1,920; Zip Code 12526; Elev. 1703; Lat. 42-09-31 N long. 078-16-50 W; about 1,200 of the German Palatines brought over in 1710 by *Governor Hunter* to make tar and other naval stores were settled on Livingston land in this area.

•**GERRY**, Town; Chautauqua County; Pop. 2,022; Zip Code 14740; Elev. 1302; Lat. 42-11-36 N long. 079-14-56 W. Named for a prominent citizen.

•**GHENT**, Town; Columbia County; Pop. 4,627; Zip Code 12075; Lat. 42-19-45 N long. 073-36-58 W; SE N.Y. Named after the Belgium city.

•**GILBOA**, Town; Schoharie County; Pop. 1,083; Zip Code 12076; Lat. 42-23-50 N long. 074-26-47 W. Named after the Biblical battle.

•**GLEN COVE**, City; Nassau County; Pop. 24,516; Zip Code 11542; Lat. 40-51-44 N long. 073-38-03 W; NE of N.Y. City on Long Island's N shore in SE New York.

•**GLENS FALLS**, City, Warren County; Pop. 15,884; Zip Code 12801; Elev. 348; Lat. 43-18-34 N long. 073-38-40 W; in E N.Y. Descriptively named.

•**GLOVERSVILLE**, City; Fulton County; Pop. 17,751; Zip Code 12078; Elev. 800; Lat. 43-03-10 N long. 074-20-39 W; 12 m. NW of Amsterdam in E N.Y.; Named for its outstanding industry.

•**GORHAM**, Town; Ontario County; Pop. 3,722; Zip Code 14461; Lat. 42-47-56 N long. 077-07-55 W. From a personal name.

•**GOSHEN**, Village and Town; Seat of Orange County; Pop. 4,869 and 10,475; Zip Code 10924; Elev. 439; Lat. 41-24-07 N long. 074-19-29 W; S N.Y.; The settlers who came to this place in the early decades of the eighteenth century believed that the fertility of the rich soil would rival that of the Biblical land of Goshen.

•GOUVERNEUR, Village and Town; St.Lawrence County; Pop. 4,287 and 6,655; Zip Code 13642; Elev. 447; Lat. 44-20-12 N long. 075-27-48 W; N N.Y.; is on both banks of the Oswegatchie (Indian, "black water flowing out") River. *Gouverneur Morris* purchased land here in 1798, and seven years later the village was settled.

•GOWANDA, Village; Erie and Cattaraugus County; Pop. 2,718; Zip Code 14070; Elev. 760; Lat. 42-27-47 N long. 078-56-10 W; in SW N.Y. An Indian word meaning "surrounded by a hill."

•GRAFTON, Town; Rensselaer County; Pop. 1,622; Zip Code 12082; Elev. 1472; Lat. 42-46-08 N long. 073-27-05 W; located in W N.Y. Named for the English town.

•GRAND ISLAND, Town; Erie County; Pop. 16,766; Zip Code 14072; W N.Y. Descriptively named.

•GRANVILLE, Village and Town; Washington County; Pop. 2,689 and 5,527; Zip Code 12832; Elev. 407; Lat. 43-24-28 N long. 073-15-36 W; in E N.Y.; was originally called Bishop's Corners when its first settlers, many of them Quakers, arrived from Vermont in 1781.

•GREAT NECK, Village; Nassau County; Pop. 9,045; Zip Code 110+; Lat. 40-48-02 N long. 073-43-44 W; in S N.Y. Named for the dominant geographical feature.

•GREECE, Town; Monroe County; Pop. 81,316; Zip Code 14616; Lat. 43-12-35 N long. 077-41-36 W; W N.Y. Named for the country.

•GREENE, Village and Town; Chenango County; Pop. 1,762 and 5,736; Zip Code 13778; Elev. 924; Lat. 42-19-45 N long. 075-46-13 W. The name honors General Nathanael Greene.

•GREENPORT, Village; Suffolk County; Pop. 2,288; Zip Code 11944; Lat. 41-06-12 N long. 072-21-35 W; between Gardiner Bay and Long Island Sound on the N tip of Long Island in SE New York.

•GREENVILLE, Town; Green County; Pop. 2,820; Zip Code 12083; Elev. 708; Lat. 42-24-55 N long. 074-01-21 W. Descriptively named.

•GREENWICH, Village and Town; Washington County; Pop. 1,955 and 4,278; Zip Code 12834; Lat. 43-05-26 N long. 073-29-57 W. Named for the English town near London.

•GREIG, Lewis County; Pop. 1,135; Zip Code 13345; Lat. 43-40-53 N long. 075-21-18 W. From a personal name.

•GROTON, Village and Town; Tompkins County; Pop. 2,294 and 5,195; Zip Code 13073; Elev. 1,026; Lat. 42-35-16 N long. 076-22-02 W; named after the English town.

•GROVELAND, Town; Livingston County; Pop. 2,123; Zip Code 14462; Lat. 42-39-53 N long. 077-46-12 W. Descriptively named after its once numerous tree groves.

•GUILDERLAND, Town; Albany County; Pop. 26,462; Zip Code 12084; Elev. 210; Lat. 42-42-16 N long. 073-54-43 W; E N.Y. Named for the province in the Netherlands.

•HADLEY, Town; Saratoga County; Pop. 1,348; Zip Code 12835; Lat. 43-19-02 N long. 073-50-55 W. Named after the town in England.

•HAGUE, Town; Warren County; Pop. 767; Zip Code 12836; Elev. 328; Lat. 43-44-43 N long. 073-29-56 W; on Lake George in E N.Y. Named for the Dutch city.

•HALESITE, Suffolk County; Zip Code 11743; Lat. 40-53-18 N long. 073-24-57 W; SE N.Y. on Long Island; was named for the American martyr, *Nathan Hale.*

•HAMBURG, Village and Town; Erie County; Pop. 10,591 and 53,292; Zip Code 14075; Elev. 825; Lat. 42-42-57 N long. 078-49-47 W; 10 m. S of Buffalo in W N.Y. Hamburg was settled by German immigrants about 1808.

•HAMILTON, Village and Town; Madison County; Pop. 3,719 and 6,031; Zip Code 13346; Elev. 1126; Lat. 42-49-37 N long. 075-32-42 W; SW of Utica in central N.Y.; Settled 1792 and named for Alexander Hamilton.

•HAMLIN, Town; Monroe County; Pop. 7,676; Zip Code 14464; Lat. 43-18-11 N long. 077-55-17 W. Named after the German town.

•HANCOCK, Village and Town; Delaware County; Pop. 1,523; Zip Code 13783; Elev. 920; Lat. 41-57-14 N long. 075-16-51 W; S N.Y. Named for the prominent Hancock family.

•HANNAWA FALLS, Hamlet; St. Lawrence County; Zip Code 13647; Elev. 560; Lat. 44-36-44 N long. 074-58-17 W; 2 m. S of Potsdam on the Racquette River in N N.Y.; spreading from the falls of the same name.

•HANNIBAL, Village and Town; Oswego County; Pop. 667; Zip Code 13074; Elev. 327; Lat. 43-19-16 N long. 076-34-45 W; central N.Y.; named after the famous Carthagian general.

•HARPERSFIELD, Town; Delaware County; Pop. 1,491; Zip Code 13786; Elev. 1,752; Lat. 42-26-18 N long. 074-41-16 W; central N.Y. on Hwy. 23. Settled in 1771 by *Colonel John Harper* from Cherry Valley.

•HARRISON, Village and Town; Westchester County; Pop. 22,999; Zip Code 10528; Lat. 40-58-08 N long. 073-42-47 W. From a personal name.

•HARTFORD, Town; Washington County; Pop. 1,754; Zip Code 12838; Elev. 390; Lat. 43-21-49 N long. 073-23-39 W. Named after the town in England.

•HASTINGS-ON-HUDSON, Village; Westchester County; Pop. 8,550; Zip Code 10706; Elev. 199; Lat. 41-00-10 N long. 073-52-45 W; on Hudson River 18 m. N of New York in SE N.Y.; named for the English birthplace of *William Saunders*, a local manufacturer.

•HAVERSTRAW, Village and Town; Rockland County; Pop. 8,826 and 31,923; Zip Code 10927; Elev. 20; Lat. 41-11-51 N long. 073-57-54 W; on W shore of Hudson River 32 m. N of New York in SE N.Y. Named after an early Dutch settler.

•HECTOR, Town; Schuyler County; Pop. 3,769; Zip Code 14841; Lat. 42-30-02 N long. 076-52-22 W. Named for the mythological hero.

•HEMPSTEAD, Village and Town; Nassau County; Pop. 40,377 and 737,903; Zip Code 115+; Lat. 40-42-22 N long. 073-37-09 W; 20 m. E of N.Y. City on Long Island in SE N.Y.; named for the town in the Netherlands.

•HENRIETTA, Town; Monroe County; Pop. 36,084; Zip Code 14467; Elev. 596; Lat. 43-03-33 N long. 077-36-45 W; W N.Y. From a personal name.

•HERKIMER, Village and Town; Seat of Herkimer County; Pop. 8,339; and 10,975; Zip Code 13350; Elev. 407; Lat. 43-01-32 N long. 074-59-11 W; NE central N.Y. In 1777, *General Nicholas Herkimer* marched to the Battle of Oriskany. The town is named for him.

•HIGHLAND FALLS, Village; Orange County; Pop. 4,215; Zip Code 10928; Elev. 200; Lat. 41-22-09 N long. 073-58-00 W; on Hudson River 5 m. S SW of Newburgh in SE N.Y. Named for the local falls.

•HILLSDALE, Town; Columbia County; Pop. 1,607; Zip Code 12529; Elev. 686; Lat. 42-10-44 N long. 073-31-35 W. Descriptively named.

•HILTON, Village; Monroe County; Pop. 4,152; Zip Code 14468; Lat. 43-17-17 N long. 077-47-37 W. From a personal name.

•HOLLAND, Town; Erie County; Pop. 3,435; Zip Code 14080; Elev. 1111; Lat. 42-38-28 N long. 078-32-31 W. Named after the Netherlands.

•HOLLEY, Village; Orleans County; Pop. 1,886; Zip Code 14470; Lat. 43-13-35 N long. 078-01-37 W. Named for an early settler.

•HOMER, Village; Cortland County; Pop. 3,636; Zip Code 13077; Elev. 1133; Lat. 42-38-13 N long. 076-10-45 W; 28 m. S of Syracuse in central N.Y.; was first settled in 1791 and named for the ancient Greek poet.

•HONEOYE FALLS, Village; Monroe County; Pop. 2,403; Zip Code 14472; Elev. 668; Lat. 42-57-08 N long. 077-35-26 W. Named for the local falls.

•HOOSICK, Town; Rensselaer County; Pop. 6,749; Zip Code 12089; Elev. 480; Lat. 42-51-45 N long. 073-19-43 W; on the Hoosic River, named from the Indian meaning "stony place".

•HORNELL, City; Steuben County; Pop. 10, 225; Zip Code 14843; Elev. 1164; Lat. 42-19-40 N long. 077-39-41 W; 56 m. S of Rochester in S N.Y. The city was named for George Hornell, an Indian trader who purxhased the site in 1793, built the first gristmill and the first tavern, and became the leading citizen of the upper Canisteo Valley.

•HORSEHEADS, Village and Town; Chemung County; Pop. 7,338 and 20,216; Zip Code 14845; Elev. 898; Lat. 42-10-01 N long. 076-49-15 W; 5 m. N of Elmira in S New York.

•HUDSON, City; Seat of Columbia County; Pop. 7,925; Zip Code 12534; Elev. 100; Lat. 42-15-10 N long. 073-47-29 W; on E bank of Hudson River 28 m. S of Albany in SE N.Y.; is built on a slope that rises from the Hudson River.

•HUME, Town; Allegany County; Pop. 2,034; Zip Code 14745; Elev. 1,281; Lat. 42-28-22 N long. 078-08-12 W. Named after an early settler.

•HUNTINGTON, Town; Suffolk County; Pop. 201,559; Zip Code 11743; Lat. 40-52-05 N long. 073-25-34 W; on N shore of Long Island in SE N.Y. The name recalls the towns first vocation.

•HURLEY, Town; Ulster County; Pop. 7,049; Zip Code 12443; Lat. 41-55-28 N long. 074-03-42 W; first called Nieuw Dorp (Dutch, "new village"), was renamed in 1669 for Francis Loveace Baron Hurley of Ireland.

•HYDE PARK, Town; Dutchess County; Pop. 20,719; Zip Code 12538; Elev. 184; Lat. 41-47-05 N long. 073-56-01 W; on E bank of Hudson River 6 m. N of Poughkeepsie in SE N.Y.; was once called Stoutenburgh, for Jacobus Stoutenburgh, the first settler.

•ILION, Village; Herkimer County; Pop. 9,156; Zip Code 13357; Elev. 410; Lat. 43-00-54 N long. 075-02-09 W; on Mohawk River 11 m. E SE of Utica in NE central N.Y. A Greek word for the name Troy.

•INDIAN LAKE, Town; Hamilton County; Pop. 1,410; Zip Code 12842; Elev. 1752; Lat. 43-46-57 N long. 074-16-20 W. Named after the area's original settlers.

•INLET, Town; Hamilton County; Pop. 327; Zip Code 13360; Lat. 43-45-16 N long. 074-47-36 W. Descriptively named.

•IRONDEQUOIT, Town; Monroe County; Pop. 57,585; Zip Code 14617. An Iroquoian word meaning "bay."

•IRVINGTON, Village; Westchester County; Pop. 5,783; Zip Code 10533; Elev. 175; Lat. 41-02-20 N long. 073-51-56 W; on Hudson River 22 m. N of N.Y. and 3 m. S of Tarrytown in SE N.Y. Named for Washington Irving.

•ISCHUA, Town; Cattaraugus County; Pop. 774; Zip Code 14746; Lat. 42-14-51 N long. 078-24-00 W. In a pocket along Ischua Creek among quarried hills.

•ISLAND PARK, Village; Nassau County; Pop. 4,847; Zip Code 11558; Lat. 40-36-15 N long. 073-33-92 W; on Atlantic Ocean 29 m E SE of N.Y. in SE N.Y. Named for its location.

•ISLIP, Town; Suffolk County; Pop. 298,895; Zip Code 11751; Elev. 16; Lat. 40-43-47 N long. 073-12-39 W; on Long Island on Great South Bay, about 10 m. W of Patchogue in SE N.Y. Named after the English town.

•ITHACA, City; Tompkins County Seat; Pop. 28,846; Zip Code 14850; Elev. 900; Lat. 42-26-26 N long. 076-29-49 W; S central New York; Named for legendary ancient Greek home of Ulysses by U.S. Surveyor General Simeon DeWitt.

•JAMAICA, part of Queens Borough; Seat of Queens County; Zip Code 114+; Lat. 40-41-29 N long. 073-48-22 W; on Long Island in SE N.Y. Named after the Caribbean island.

•JAMESTOWN, City; Chautauqua County; Lat. 42-05-49 N long. 079-14-08 W; Named for the first English settlement in North America.

•JAY, Town; Essex County; Pop. 2,206; Zip Code 12941; Lat. 44-22-30 N long. 073-43-43 W; Named after John Jay.

•JEFFERSON, Town; Schoharie County; Pop. 1,105; Zip Code 12093; Elev. 1873; Lat. 42-28-52 N long. 074-36-39 W. The town's name honors Thomas Jefferson.

•JERICHO, Nassau County; Pop. 14,200; Zip Code 11753; Elev. 1393; Lat. 44-47-39 N long. 073-39-47 W; on Long Island in SE N.Y. Named after the Biblical city.

•JOHNSBURG, Town; Warren County; Pop. 2,171; Zip Code 12843; Elev. 1287; Lat. 43-37-06 N long. 073-57-42 W. Named after an early settler.

•JOHNSON CITY, Village; Broome County; Pop. 17,115; Zip Code 13790; Elev. 847; Lat. 42-06-56 N long. 075-57-33 W. From a personal name.

•JOHNSTOWN, City; Seat of Fulton County; Pop. 9,345; Zip Code 12095; Elev. 660; Lat. 43-00-24 N long. 074-22-05 W; 11 m. W NW of Amsterdam in E N.Y.; is on the Cayadutta Plateau. It was named for Sir William Johnson, who settled here in 1762 at the height of his picturesque life as a frontier statesman and empire builder.

•JORDAN, Village; Onondaga County; Pop. 1,362; Zip Code 13080; Lat. 43-03-55 N long. 076-28-24 W. Given a Biblical name.

•KEESEVILLE, Village; Clinton and Essex Counties; Pop. 2,025; Zip Code 12944; Elev. 503; Lat. 44-30-18 N long. 073-28-50 W; 12 m. S of Plattsburgh in NE N.Y.; was settled by Quaker John Keese, who arrived in 1806.

•KENDALL, Town; Orleans County; Pop. 2,378; Zip Code 14476; Elev. 338; Lat. 43-19-38 N long. 078-02-10 W. Named for an early settler.

•**KENMORE**, Village; Erie County; Pop. 18,475; Zip Code 14217; Lat. 42-57-57 N long. 078-52-13 W; on Niagara River 5 m. N of Buffalo in W N.Y. From the name of a prominent citizen.

•**KINDERHOOK**, Village and Town; Columbia County; Pop. 1,365 and 7,632; Zip Code 12106; Elev. 256; Lat. 42-23-43 N long. 073-41-54 W; E of Hudson River in SE N.Y.; Kinderhook (Dutch "children's corner") is a village whose Dutch settlers brought the village name with them.

•**KINGS POINT**, Village; Nassau County; Pop. 5,208; Zip Code 11024; Elev. 26; Lat. 40-49-11 N long. 073-44-08 W: near Great Neck, Long Island, New York.

•**KINGSTON**, City; Seat of Ulster County; Pop. 24,427; Zip Code 12401; Elev. 150; Lat. 41-55-37 N long. 073-59-52 W; on Hudson River 15 m.

•**KIRKWOOD**, Town; Broome County; Pop. 5,839; Zip Code 13795; Lat. 42-02-23 N long. 075-47-51 W. Named for an early settler.

•**KNOX**, Town; Albany County; Pop. 2,476; Zip Code 12107; Lat. 42-40-16 N long. 074-06-58 W. Named in honor of patriot Henry Knox.

•**LACKAWANNA**, City; Erie County; Pop. 22,730; Zip Code 14218; Elev. 600; Lat. 42-49-32 N long. 078-49-25 W; S of Buffalo; was named for the steel company that moved from Scranton, Pennsylvania, and erected its plant here in 1899.

•**LA FARGEVILLE**, Jefferson County; Zip Code 13656; Elev. 381; Lat. 44-11-41 N long. 075-57-59 W; N N.Y.; settled in 1816 by *Reuben Andrus* and named for *John LaFarge*, large landholder.

•**LA FAYETTE**, Town; Onondaga County; Pop. 4,473; Zip Code 13085; Elev. 1,160; Lat. 42-53-32 N long. 076-06-20 W. Named for Revolutionary War hero, the Marquis de La Fayette.

•**LAKE GEORGE**, Village and Town; Seat of Warren County; Pop. 1,042 and 3,402; Zip Code 12845; Elev. 353; Lat. 43-25-34 N long. 073-42-46 W.

•**LAKE GROVE**, Village; Suffolk County; Pop. 9,683; Zip Code 11755; Elev. 119; Lat. 40-51-10 N long. 073-06-56 W; 7 m. NE of Islip in SE N.Y. Named for tree groves once in the area.

•**LAKE LUZERNE**, Town; Warren County; Pop. 2,674; Zip Code 12846; Lat. 43-18-46 N long. 073-50-07 W. Named after the famous Swiss Lake.

•**LAKE PLACID**, Village; Essex County; Pop. 2,474; Zip Code 12946; Elev. 1,880; Lat. 44-16-46 N long. 073-58-49 W; in Adirondack Mts. Named for nearby Lake Placid.

•**LAKEWOOD**, Village; Chautauqua County; Pop. 3,931; Zip Code 14750; Elev. 1329; Lat. 42-06-15 N long. 079-20-00 W; on Chautaqua Lake 5 m. W of Jamestown in SW corner of New York.

•**LANCASTER**, Village and Town; Erie County; Pop. 13,049 and 30,130; Zip Code 14086; Lat. 42-54-02 N long. 078-40-14 W; in W N.Y. 11 m. E of Buffalo; Named after the English county.

•**LANSING**, Village and Town; Tompkins County; Pop. 3,031 and 8,301; Zip Code 14882; Elev. 415; Lat. 43-26-35 N long. 076-27-01 W. Named in honor of jurist John Lansing.

•**LARCHMONT**, Village; Westchester County; Pop. 6,268; Zip Code 10538; Elev. 100; Lat. 40-55-40 N long. 073-45-08 W; on Long Island Sound in S N.Y. Descriptive of the Larch trees once found in the area.

•**LAWRENCE**, Village; Nassau County; Pop. 6,183; Zip Code 11559; Lat. 40-36-56 N long. 073-43-48 W; on Long Island 16 m. E SE of New York in SE N.Y. Named after naval hero James Lawrence.

•**LEBANON**, Town; Madison County; Pop. 1,126; Zip Code 13085; Lat. 42-46-53 N long. 075-38-53 W. Named for the Biblical country.

•**LEROY** Village and Town; Genesee County; Pop. 4,890 and 8,013; Zip Code 14482; Elev. 869; 24 m. SW of Rochester in W N.Y. Named for a prominent citizen.

•**LEWISTON**, Village and Town; Niagara County; Pop. 3,321 and 16,185; Zip Code 14092; Elev. 363; Lat. 43-10-21 N long. 079-02-10 W; W New York; along the Niagara River.

•**LEXINGTON**, Town; Greene County; Pop. 807; Zip Code 12452; Elev. 1331; Lat. 42-14-25 N long. 074-21-57 W. Named for the city in Massachusetts.

•**LIBERTY**, Village and Town; Sullivan County; Pop. 4,293 and 9,931; Zip Code 12754; Elev. 1,509; Lat. 41-48-04 N long. 074-44-49 W. Descriptively of its citizens wishes.

•**LIMA**, Village; Livingston County; Pop. 2,033; Zip Code 14485; Lat. 42-54-17 N long. 077-36-42 W. Named for the city in Peru.

•**LIMESTONE**, Village; Cattaraugus County; Pop. 464; Zip Code 14753; Elev. 1407; Lat. 42-01-38 N long. 078-37-47 W. Descriptively named after the local mineral.

•**LINDENHURST**, Village; Suffolk County; Pop. 26,896; Zip Code 11757; Elev. 27; Lat. 40-41-12 N long. 073-22-26 W; 35 m. E of N.Y. A popular personal name.

•**LISBON**, Town; St.Lawrence County; Pop. 3,555; Zip Code 13658; Elev. 358; Lat. 44-43-38 N long. 075-19-17 W. Named after the city in Portugal.

•**LITTLE FALLS**, City; Herkimer County; Pop. 6,153; Zip Code 13365; Elev. 440; Lat. 43-02-36 N long. 074-51-36 W; 20 m. E of Utica in NE central N.Y. Named for the local feature.

•**LIVERPOOL**, Village; Onondaga County; Pop. 2,844; Zip Code 13088; Elev. 380; Lat. 43-06-23 N long. 076-13-05 W; 5 m. N of Syracuse in central N.Y. Named for the English city.

•**LIVINGSTON**, Town; Columbia County; Pop. 3,052; Zip Code 12541; Lat. 42-08-31 N long. 073-46-42 W. Named for a signer of the Declaration of Independence.

•**LIVONIA**, Village and Town; Livingston County; Pop. 1,238 and 5,753; Zip Code 14487; Elev. 1047; Lat. 42-49-17 N long. 077-40-08 W. Named after the Baltic province.

•**LOCKE**, Town; Cayuga County; Pop. 1,747; Zip Code 13092; Elev. 800; Lat. 42-39-38 N long. 076-25-52 W. Named after the English philosopher.

•**LOCKPORT**, City; Seat of Niagara County; Pop. 24,857; Zip Code 14094; Elev. 660; Lat. 43-10-14 N long. 078-41-26 W; grew around the series of locks built to carry the Erie Canal through the Lockport gorge.

•**LONG BEACH**, City; Nassau County; Pop. 34,022; Zip Code 11561; Lat. 40-35-18 N long. 073-39-30 W; It sits on the shifting sands of the W end of the Outer Barrier.

•**LOWVILLE**, Village and Town; Seat of Lewis County; Pop. 3,382 and 4,595; Zip Code 13367; Elev. 865; Lat. 43-47-12 N long. 075-29-32 W; 26 m. SE of Watertown in N central N.Y..

•**LYNBROOK**, Village Nassau County; Pop. 20,500; Zip Code 11563; Elev. 21; Lat. 40-39-17 N long. 073-40-20 W; on S shore of Long Island 18 m. E of New York City in SE N.Y. Named for an early settler.

•**LYONS**, Village and Town; Seat of Wayne County; Pop. 4,160 and 6,078; Zip Code 14489; Elev. 438; Lat. 43-03-51 N long. 076-59-26 W. Named after the city in France.

•**LYSANDER**, Town; Onondaga County; Pop. 13,889; Zip Code 13094; Elev. 418; Lat. 43-12-23 N long. 076-27-34 W. Named for the ancient Spartan general.

•**MACEDON**, Village and Town; Wayne County; Pop. 1,388 and 6,490; Zip Code 14502; Elev. 478; Lat. 43-04-09 N long. 077-17-57 W. Named for the ancient Greek province.

•**MADISON**, Village and Town; Madison County; Pop. 395 and 2,315; Zip Code 13402; Lat. 42-53-56 N long. 075-30-45 W. Named for James Madison.

•**MADRID**, Town; St. Lawrence County; Pop. 1,856; Zip Code 13660; Lat. 44-45-01 N long. 075-07-53 W. Named after the Spanish city.

•**MAINE**, Town; Broome County; Pop. 5,256; Zip Code 13802; Elev. 919; Lat. 42-11-33 N long. 076-03-41 W. The town is named for the state.

•**MALONE**, Village and Town; Seat of Franklin County; Pop. 7,645 and 11,215; Zip Code 12953; Elev. 722; Lat. 44-50-55 N long. 074-17-430 W; 45 m. W NW of Plattsburg in NE N.Y.; The place was settled by Vermonters in 1802; the name bestowed in honor of *Edmund Malone*, Shakespearian scholar.

•**MALVERNE**, Village; Nassau County; Pop. 9,257; Zip Code 11565; Lat. 40-40-44 N long. 073-40-28 W; on Long Island 17 m. E of New York in SE N.Y. Named after the hills in England.

•**MAMARONECK**, Village and Town; Westchester County; Pop. 17,501 and 28,817; Zip Code 10543; Elev. 47; Lat. 40-56-55 N long. 073-43-59 W; on Long Island Sound 22 m. NE of New York in SE New York; (Indian, "he assembles the people"); first settled by English farmers about 1650.

•**MANCHESTER**, Village and Town; Ontario County; Pop. 1,681 and 9,039; Zip Code 14504; Elev. 590; Lat. 42-58-11 N long. 077-13-50 W; 24 m. SE of Rochester in W N.Y., in the Finger Lakes resort area. The early residents named the place after Manchester, England.

•**MANHATTAN**, Borough; New York Conty; Pop. 1,148,124; Zip Code 100+; in SE N.Y. part of New York City. Named after the local Indian tribe.

•**MARCELLUS**, Village and Town; Onondaga County; Pop. 1,880 and 6,188; Zip Code 13108; Lat. 42-58-58 N long. 076-20-27 W. Named after the Roman hero.

•**MARCY**, Town; Oneida County; Pop. 6,425; Zip Code 13403; Lat. 43-10-14 N long. 075-17-31 W. From a settler's name.

•**MARION**, Town; Wayne County; Pop. 4,471; Zip Code 14505; Elev. 463; Lat. 43-08-36 N long. 077-11-22 W. Named in honor of Revolutionary War general Francis Marion.

•**MARYLAND**, Town; Otsego County; Pop. 1,680; Zip Code 12116; Lat. 42-32-11 N long. 074-53-13 W. Named after the state.

•**MASSAPEQUA PARK**, Village; Nassau County; Pop. 19,791; Zip Code 11762; Elev. 24; Lat. 40-40-49 N long. 073-27-20 W; on Long Island in SE New York.

•**MASSENA**, Village and Town; St. Lawrence County; Pop. 12,838 and 14,842; Zip Code 13662; Elev. 1,340; Lat. 44-55-41 N long. 074-53-32 W. Named in honor of French general Andre Massena.

•**MECHANICVILLE**, City; Saratoga County; Pop. 5,481; Zip Code 12118; Elev. 104; Lat. 42-54-10 N long. 073-41-16 W; On Hudson River 17 m. N of Albany in E N.Y. Named for early local industry.

•**MEDINA**, Village; Orleans County; Pop. 6,391; Zip Code 14103; Elev. 542; Lat. 43-13-12 N long. 078-23-14 W; Named after the city in Arabia.

•**MENDON**, Town; Monroe County; Pop. 5,434; Zip Code 14506; Lat. 42-59-52 N long. 077-30-17 W. Named after the town in England.

•**MEXICO**, Village and Town; Oswego County; Pop. 1,619 and 4,770; Zip Code 13114; Elev. 384; Lat. 43-27-34 N long. 076-13-45 W. Named for the country.

•**MIDDLEBURGH**, Village and Town; Schoharie County; Pop. 1,356 and 2,970; Zip Code 12122; Elev. 650; Lat. 42-35-53 N long. 074-20-03 W; founded in 1712 by *John Conrad Weiser* and the first group of Palatine pioneers.

•**MIDDLEPORT**, Village; Niagara County; Pop. 1,999; Zip Code 14105; Elev. 540; Lat. 42-47-26 N long. 075-33-37 W; 30 m. E NE of Niagara Falls in W N.Y.; it sprang up as a settlement upon completion of the Erie Canal in 1825, and took its name from its location midway between Lockport and Albion.

•**MIDDLESEX**, Town; Yates County; Pop. 1,124; Lat. 42-42-17 N long. 077-16-19 W. Named for the English county.

•**MIDDLETOWN**, City; Orange County; Pop. 21,455; Zip Code 10940; Elev. 559; Lat. 41-26-45 N long. 074-25-24 W; 23 m. W of Newburgh in SE N.Y. Named for its location.

•**MILLERTON**, Village; Dutchess County; Pop. 1,020; Zip Code 12546; Elev. 701; Lat. 41-57-13 N long. 073-30-40 W. Named for early water mills.

•**MINEOLA**, Village; Seat of Nassau County; Pop. 20,673; Zip Code 11501; Lat. 40-44-57 N long. 073-38-28 W; on Long Island 20 m. E of New York in SE N.Y. An Indian word meaning "much water."

•**MINETTO**, Town; Oswego County; Pop. 1,903; Zip Code 13115; Lat. 43-23-53 N long. 076-28-40 W.

•**MINOA**, Village; Onondaga County; Pop. 3,552; Zip Code 13116; Lat. 43-04-34 N long. 076-00-04 W. Named after the ancient Greek city.

•**MOHAWK**, Village; Herkimer County; Pop. 2,954; Zip Code 13407; Elev. 407; Lat. 43-00-41 N long. 075-00-16 W; on Mohawk River, named after the Indian tribe.

•**MOIRA**, Town; Franklin County; Pop. 2,629; Zip Code 12957; Lat. 44-49-05 N long. 074-33-22 W. From a personal name.

•**MONROE**, Village and Town; Orange County; Pop. 5,987 and 14,942; Zip Code 10950; Elev. 679; Lat. 41-19-50 N long. 074-11-14 W; 15 m. SW of Newburgh in SE N.Y. Named after James Monroe.

•**MONTEZUMA**, Town; Cayuga County; Pop. 1,125; Zip Code 13117; Elev. 400; Lat. 43-00-36 N long. 076-42-13 W. The name recalls the Aztec Indian King.

•**MONTGOMERY**, Village and Town; Orange County; Pop. 2,318 and 16,554; Zip Code 12549; Elev. 354; Lat. 41-31-39 N long.

074-14-14 W; SE N.Y. Named in honor of general Richard Montgomrery, Revolutionary War hero.

•**MONTICELLO**, Village; Seat of Sullivan County; Pop. 6,297; Zip Code 12701; Lat. 41-39-20 N long. 074-41-23 W; 42 m. W of Poughkeepsie in SE N.Y. Named for Jefferson's Virginia estate.

•**MONTOUR FALLS**, Village; Schuyler County; Pop. 1,791; Zip Code 14865; Elev. 480; Lat. 42-20-50 N long. 076-50-44 W; 16 m. N of Elmira in SW central N.Y. near the N point of Seneca Lake. Nearby are seven glens, each with a distinctive claim to beauty in cascades, caverns, waterfalls, amphitheaters, and high and angular cliffs.

•**MORAVIA**, Village and Town; Cayuga County; Pop. 1,565 and 2,614; Zip Code 13118; Lat. 42-42-45 N long. 076-25-19 W. Named for the province in Europe.

•**MORIAH**, Town; Essex County; Pop. 5,124; Zip Code 12960; Elev. 950; Lat. 44-02-46 N long. 073-30-20 W. Named after the Biblical mountain.

•**MORRISVILLE**, Village; Madison County; Pop. 2,711; Zip Code 13408; Lat. 44-41-35 N long. 073-33-45 W. Named for the prominent Morris family.

•**MOUNT VERNON**, City; Westchester County; Pop. 66,023; Zip Code 14075; Elev. 100; Lat. 42-45-14 N long. 078-53-27 W; SE New York; N New York City suburb; Named for *George Washington's* Virginia estate.

•**NAPLES**, Village and Town; Ontario County; Pop. 1,226 and 2,339; Zip Code 14512; Elev. 800; Lat. 42-36-55 N long. 077-24-10 W; Named for the Italian city.

•**NASSAU**, Village and Town; Rensselaer County; Pop. 1,286 and 4,489; Zip Code 12123; Elev. 403; Lat. 42-30-57 N long. 073-36-38 W. Named by Dutch settlers after the title of the Prince of Orange.

•**NEVERSINK**, Town; Sullivan County; Pop. 2,850; Zip Code 12765; Elev. 1633; Lat. 41-50-50 N long. 074-37-10 W. An English version of an Indian word meaning "point-at."

•**NEWARK**, Village; Wayne County; Pop. 10,022; Zip Code 14513; Elev. 457; Lat. 43-02-48 N long. 077-05-44 W. Named for the town in England.

•**NEW BALTIMORE**, Town; Greene County; Pop. 3,046; Zip Code 12124; Lat. 42-26-46 N long. 073-47-20 W. Named after Lord Baltimore.

•**NEW BERLIN**, Village and Town; Chenango County; Pop. 1,371 and 2,993; Zip Code 13411; Lat. 42-37-27 N long. 075-19-55 W. Named after the German city.

•**NEW BREMEN**, Town; Lewis County; Pop. 2,339; Zip Code 13412; Lat. 43-50-16 N long. 075-26-26 W. Named by German settlers.

•**NEWBURGH**, City; Orange County; Pop. 23,116; Zip Code 12550; Elev. 139; Lat. 41-30-12 N long. 074-00-39 W; on Hudson River; lies above the broad expanse of Newburgh Bay. The present name was given to the settlement in 1762 in honor of the town in Scotland on the River Tay.

•**NEW CITY**, Unincorporated; Seat of Rockland County; Pop. 27,344; Zip Code 10956; Elev. 163; Lat. 41-08-51 N long. 073-59-23 W; SE New York.

•**NEWFANE**, Town; Niagara County; Pop. 9,274; Zip Code 14108; Elev. 345; Lat. 43-17-12 N long. 078-42-38 W; W N.Y. Named for settler John Fane.

•**NEWFIELD**, Town; Tompkins County; Pop. 4,394; Zip Code 14867; Lat. 42-21-43 N long. 076-35-28 W. Descriptively named.

•**NEW HARTFORD**, Village and Town; Oneida County; Pop. 2,323 and 21,105; Zip Code 13413; Lat. 43-04-24 N long. 075-17-17 W; central N.Y. Named after the city in England.

•**NEW HAVEN**, Town; Oswego County; Pop. 2,414; Zip Code 13121; Elev. 418; Lat. 43-28-47 N long. 076-18-56 W.

•**NEW HYDE PARK**, Village; Nassau County; Pop. 9,875; Zip Code 11040; Lat. 40-44-06 N long. 073-41-18 W; on Long Island in SE New York.

•**NEW LEBANON**, Town; Columbia County; Pop. 2,313; Zip Code 12125; Elev. 720; Lat. 42-27-50 N long. 073-23-49 W.

•**NEW PALTZ**, Village and Town; Ulster County; Pop. 4,906 and 10,135; Zip Code 12561; Elev. 236; Lat. 41-44-51 N long. 074-05-14 W; Early in 1678, 12 families loaded their possessions in three oxcarts and established their new home, which they called New Paltz after their first refuge, the Rheinish Pfalz.

•**NEW ROCHELLE**, City; Westchester County; Pop. 70,519; Zip Code 10801; Elev. 94; Lat. 40-54-41 N long. 073-46-58 W; SE New York; 16 m. NE of New York City boundary; on Long Island Sound; In 1688 a small group of Huguenot refugees landed at what is now Bonnefoi Point. and named the settlement for their old home in France, La Rochelle.

•**NEW SCOTLAND**, Town; Albany County; Pop. 8,960; Zip Code 12127; Lat. 42-37-43 N long. 073-54-50 W.

•**NEW WINDSOR**, Town; Orange County; Pop. 19,512; Zip Code 12550; Elev. 160; Lat. 41-28-36 N long. 074-01-27 W; a Newburgh suburb.

•**NEW YORK**, City; Pop. 7,035,348; Zip Code 100+; Elev. 0-410. Named New Amsterdam when William Verhulst was governor in 1625; renamed New York in 1664 when Col. Richard Nicolls siezed the town for King Charles II of England. Since 1898 Greater New York has been composed of five boroughs; Bronx, Brooklyn, Manhattan, Queens, and Richmond.

•**NIAGARA FALLS**, City; Niagara County; Pop. 71,344; Zip Code 14301; Elev. 575; Lat. 43-05-40 N long. 079-03-25 W; NW New York; On Niagara River at the Falls; 20 m. N of Buffalo. what is undisputably the most famous natural feature in New York state, Niagara Falls.

•**NORFOLK**, Town; St. Lawrence County; Pop. 4,975; Zip Code 13667; Elev. 257; Lat. 44-48-03 N long. 074-59-29 W. Named for the English county.

•**NORTH COLLINS**, Village and Town; Erie County; Pop. 1,509 and 3,801; Zip Code 14111; Elev. 830; Lat. 42-35-43 N long. 078-56-29 W; was settled about 1809 by Quakers, who in 1813 built the first meetinghouse.

•**NORTHPORT**, Village; Suffolk County; Pop. 7,640; Zip Code 11768; Lat. 40-54-03 N long. 073-20-37 W; N coast of Long Island in SE N.Y. Named for its location.

•**NORTH SALEM**, Town; Westchester County; Pop. 4,562; Zip Code 10560; Lat. 41-20-05 N long. 073-34-18 W.

•**NORTH SYRACUSE**¡, Village; Onondaga County; Pop. 7,965; Zip Code 13212; Lat. 43-08-05 N long. 076-07-49 W; 8 m. N NE of Syracuse in central New York.

•**NORTH TONAWANDA**, City; Niagara County; Pop. 35,717; Zip Code 14120; Elev. 575; Lat. 43-02-19 N long. 078-51-52 W; 10 m. E of Niagara Falls in W N.Y..

•**NORWICH**, City; Seat of Chenango County; Pop. 8,070; Zip Code 13815; Elev. 1,015; Lat. 42-31-52 N long. 075-31-26 W; 36 m. N NE of Binghamton in S central N.Y. Named after the city in England.

•**NUNDA**, Village and Town; Livingston County; Pop. 1,168 and 2,695; Zip Code 14517; Elev. 944; Lat. 42-34-46 N long. 077-56-34 W; An Indian word meaning "hilly."

•**NYACK**, Village; Rockland County; Pop. 6,455; Zip Code 10960; Lat. 41-05-26 N long. 073-55-06 W; on W shore of Hudson River 25 m. N of N.Y. in SE N.Y. An Indian word meaning "point-land."

•**OAKFIELD**, Village and Town; Genesee County; Pop. 1,795 and 3,210; Zip Code 14125; Elev. 753; Lat. 43-03-57 N long. 078-16-12 W. Named for the local Oak trees.

•**OCEANSIDE**, Nassau County; Zip Code 11572; Lat. 40-38-19 N long. 073-38-26 W; W end of Long Island in SE N.Y. The first white settlers, a group of fishermen who arrived here nearly 200 years ago, called the settlement Christian Hook but the name was changed to Oceanville in 1864 and Oceanside in 1889.

•**OGDENSBURG**, City; St.Lawrence County; Pop. 12,372; Zip Code 13669; Elev. 275; Lat. 44-41-39 N long. 075-29-12 W; on St.Lawrence River. The town was named for *Colonel Samuel Ogden*, who purchased the site in 1792 and promoted its resettlement after the British evacuation.

•**OLD WESTBURY**, Village; Nassau County; Pop. 3,245; Zip Code 11568; Lat. 40-47-19 N long. 073-36-00 W; on W central Long Island SE of Roslyn; SE N. Y.

•**OLEAN**, City; Cattaraugus County; Pop. 18,188; Zip Code 14760; Elev. 1,440; Lat. 42-04-39 N long. 078-25-48 W; on Allegheny River in SW N.Y. Named for the first white child born here.

•**ONEIDA**, City; Madison County; Pop. 10,779; Zip Code 13421; Elev. 437; Lat. 43-05-33 N long. 075-39-06 W; 5 m. SE of Oneida Lake ; is the geographic center of the state. Named for the Indian tribe.

•**ONEONTA**, City; Otsego County; Pop. 14,810; Zip Code 13820; Elev. 1,120; Lat. 42-27-10 N long. 075-03-51 W; on Susquehanna River 45 m. S of Utica in central N.Y.; (Indian for "stony place") is called the City of Hills.

•**ONONDAGA**, Town; Onondaga County; Pop. 17,825; Zip Code 13215; central N.Y.; means "People of the Mountains."

•**ONTARIO**, Town; Wayne County; Pop. 7,452; Zip Code 14519; Lat. 43-13-15 N long. 077-17-00 W; abt. 17 m. NE of Rochester in W N.Y. Named for the Indian tribe.

•**ORCHARD PARK**, Village and Town; Erie County; Pop. 3,666 and 24,353; Zip Code 14127; Lat. 42-46-03 N long. 078-44-39 W; Descriptively named.

•**ORISKANY**, Village; Oneida County; Pop. 1,676; Zip Code 13424; Lat. 43-09-26 N long. 075-19-59 W; on Mohawk River 7 m. W NW of Utica in central N.Y.; occupies the site of the Indian village of Oriska, name means "nettles."

•**ORWELL**, Town; Oswego County; Pop. 1,024; Zip Code 13426; Elev. 808; Lat. 43-34-29 N long. 075-59-48 W. Named for an early settler.

•**OSSINING**, Village and Town; Westchester County; Pop. 20,228 and 30,722; Zip Code 10562; Lat. 41-09-46 N long. 073-51-43 W; on E bank of Hudson River overlooking Tappan Zee, name means "little-stones."

•**OSWEGATCHIE**, Town; St.Lawrence County; Pop. 3,184; Zip Code 13670; Elev. 1372; Lat. 44-10-58 N long. 075-04-14 W. An Iroquoian word meaning "black-water."

•**OSWEGO**, Seat of Oswego County; Pop. 19,737; Zip Code 13126; Elev. 295; Lat. 43-27-19 N long. 076-30-39 W; on Lake Ontario at mouth of Oswego River; The name, from the Indian, means "pouring out of waters".

•**OTEGO**, Village and Town; Otsego County; Pop. 1,091 and 2,800; Zip Code 13825; Lat. 42-23-50 N long. 075-10-26 W. An Iroquoian word meaning "to have fire there."

•**OVID**, Village and Town; Seat of Seneca County; Pop. 669 and 2,582; Zip Code 14521; Lat. 42-40-35 N long. 076-49-24 W; W central N.Y. Named for the Roman poet.

•**OWASCO**, Town; Cayuga County; Pop. 3,617; Zip Code 13130; Lat. 42-51-18 N long. 076-27-56 W. Indian for "Lake at floating bridge."

•**OWEGO**, Village and Town; Seat of Tioga County; Pop. 4,389 and 20, 488; Zip Code 13827; Elev. 818; Lat. 42-06-12 N long. 076-15-45 W; came into existence on the site of Ah-wah-ga (where the valley widens), one of the Indian towns destroyed by the *Sullivan-Clinton* troops in 1779.

•**OXFORD**, Village and Town; Chenango County; Pop. 1,766 and 3,967; Zip Code 13830; Elev. 982; Lat. 42-26-31 N long. 075-35-53 W. Named after the English town.

•**OYSTER BAY**, Town; Nassau County; Pop. 305,407; Zip Code 11771; Lat. 40-51-56 N long. 073-31-57 W; on Long Island on inlet of Long Island Sound in SE N.Y. Descriptively named.

•**PAINTED POST**, Village; Steuben County; Pop. 2,189; Zip Code 14870; Elev. 950; Lat. 42-09-43 N long. 077-05-40 W; Painted Post was so named because of a red-painted oaken post that was once here, probably erected as a memorial either to an Indian victory or to an Indian chief.

•**PALMYRA**, Village and Town; Wayne County; Pop. 3,730 and 7,651; Zip Code 14522; Elev. 470; Lat. 43-03-50 N long. 077-14-01 W; Named after the ancient city.

•**PARIS**, Town; Oneida County; Pop. 4,458; Zip Code 13429; Elev. 1,481; Lat. 43-00-02 N long. 07518-51 W; central N.Y.; named for early settler *Issac Paris Jr.*.

•**PARISHVILLE**, Town; St. Lawrence County; Pop. 1,951; Zip Code 13672; Elev. 903; Lat. 44-37-43 N long. 074-48-51 W.

•**PATCHOGUE**, Village; Suffolk County; Pop. 11,300; Zip Code 11772; Lat. 40-45-56 N long. 073-00-56 W; on S shore of Long Island, named for an Indian tribe.

•**PATTERSON**, Town; Putnam County; Pop. 7,255; Zip Code 12563; Elev. 400; Lat. 41-30-49 N long. 073-36-24 W; SE N.Y.; The present name - after *Matthew Patterson*, an early settler - was adopted in 1808.

•**PAVILION**, Town; Genesee County; Pop. 2,385; Zip Code 14525; Lat. 42-52-34 N long. 078-01-23 W.

•**PAWLING**, Village and Town; Dutchess County; Pop. 1,961 and 5,674; Zip Code 12564; Elev. 420; Lat. 41-33-43 N long. 073-36-11 W; 20 m. SE of Poughkeepsie in SE N.Y.; was settled about 1740 by English Quakers.

•**PEEKSKILL**, City; Westchester County; Pop. 18,247; Zip Code 10566; Elev. 120; Lat. 43-32-48 N long. 075-57-54 W; on Hudson River 39 m. N of New York in SE N.Y.; takes its name from Peeks's Kill, the creek along its northern boundary named for *Jan Peek*, a Dutch trader who settled on its bank in 1665.

•**PELHAM**, Village and Town; Westchester County; Pop. 6,825 and 12,913; Zip Code 10803; Elev. 100; Lat. 40-54-35 N long. 073-48-30 W; is on land purchased by *Thomas Pell* in 1664 from the Siwanoy Indians.

•**PENFIELD**, Town; Monroe County; Pop. 27,154; Zip Code 14526; Lat. 43-07-49 N long. 077-28-33 W; 7 m. SE of Rochester in W New York.

•**PENN YAN**, Village; Seat of Yates County; Pop. 5,241; Zip Code 14527; Elev. 767; Lat. 42-39-39 N long. 077-03-15 W; at outlet of Lake Keuka 30 m. SW of Auburn in W N.Y.; Controversy between the settlers from Pennsylvania and New England over a name for the place was compromised by combining the first syllables of Pennsylvania and Yankee.

•**PERRY**, Village and Town; Wyoming County; Pop. 4,193 and 5,436; Zip Code 14530; Elev. 1,320; Lat. 42-42-56 N long. 078-00-21 W; 37 m. SE of Rochester in W N.Y. Named after naval hero Oliver Perry.

•**PERU**, Town; Clinton County; Pop. 5,341; Zip Code 12972; Elev. 300; Lat. 44-34-42 N long. 073-31-38 W; NE corner of N.Y.; was named by some stretch of the imagination for the South American country because of its proximity to the mountains.

•**PETERSBURG**, Town; Rensselaer County; Pop. 1,370; Zip Code 12138; Lat. 42-44-58 N long. 073-20-26 W; E N.Y.; 20 miles E of Troy.

•**PHELPS**, Village and Town; Ontario County; Pop. 2,006 and 6,515; Zip Code 14532; Elev. 522; Lat. 42-57-27 N long. 077-03-28 W. Named for an early settler.

•**PHILADELPHIA**, Village and Town; Jefferson County; Pop. 864 and 1,428; Zip Code 13673; Elev. 490; Lat. 44-09-16 N long. 075-42-33 W. Named after the Pennsylvania city.

•**PHOENIX**, Village; Oswego County; Pop. 2,350; Zip Code 13135; Lat. 43-13-52 N long. 076-18-04 W; 14 m. N NW of Syracuse in central N.Y. Named for the Greek mythological bird.

•**PIERMONT**, Village; Rockland County; Pop. 2,313; Zip Code 10968; Lat. 41-02-31 N long. 073-55-07 W; on Hudson River 22 m. N of New York in SE N.Y. The town took its name from the mile-long pier of the Erie Railroad.

•**PITTSFORD**, Village and Town; Monroe County; Pop. 1,569 and 26,701; Zip Code 14534; Elev. 500; Lat. 43-05-26 N long. 077-30-55 W.

•**PLATTEKILL**, Town; Ulster County; Pop. 7,411; Zip Code 12568; Elev. 140; Lat. 41-37-03 N long. 074-04-35 W. A Dutch word meaning "flat-water."

•**PLATTSBURGH**, City; Seat of Clinton County; Pop. 12,074; Zip Code 12901; Elev. 135; Lat. 44-41-58 N long. 073-27-12 W; on W shore of Lake Champlain, 20 m. S of Canadian border in NE corner of New York.

•**PLEASANTVILLE**, Village; Westchester County; Pop. 6,757; Zip Code 10570; Lat. 42-15-39 N long. 079-25-43 W; 30 m. N NE of N.Y. in SE N.Y. Descriptively named by its settlers.

•**PLYMOUTH**, Town; Chenango County; Pop. 1,514; Zip Code 13832; Lat. 42-37-01 N long. 075-36-10 W; Central N.Y. Named for the town in Massachusetts.

•**POESTENKILL**, Town; Rensselaer County; Pop. 3,647; Zip Code 12140; Elev. 484; Lat. 42-41-25 N long. 073-33-54 W; near Troy in E N.Y. Named for an early Dutch settler.

•**POMONA**, Village; Rockland County; Pop. 2,424; Zip Code 10970; Lat. 41-10-01 N long. 074-02-37 W; SE N.Y. Named after the Roman goddess of fruit.

•**POMPEY**, Town; Onondaga County; Pop. 4,512; Zip Code 13138; Elev. 1,700; Lat. 42-53-56 N long. 076-00-59 W. Named for the Roman general.

•**PORT BYRON**, Village; Cayuga County; Pop. 1,400; Zip Code 13140; Elev. 400; Lat. 43-02-04 N long. 076-37-27 W; NW N.Y. Named for the English poet.

•**PORT CHESTER**, Village; Westchester County; Pop. 23,472; Zip Code 10573; Lat. 41-00-06 N long. 073-39-58 W; on Long Island Sound 25 m. NE of New York in SE N.Y.; first known as Saw Log Swamp and later as Saw Pit, was settled about 1650.

•**PORT HENRY**, Village; Essex County; Pop. 1,438; Zip Code 12974; Elev. 600; Lat. 44-02-54 N long. 073-27-37 W; NE New York.

•**PORT JEFFERSON**, Village; Suffolk County; Pop. 6,673; Zip Code 11777; Elev. 12; Lat. 40-56-47 N long. 073-04-11 W; on Long Island, on Long Island Sound.

•**PORT JERVIS**, City; Orange County; Pop. 8,680; Zip Code 12771; Elev. 442; Lat. 41-22-30 N long. 074-41-35 W; on Delaware River 38 m. W of Newburgh in SE N.Y.; calls itself the Tri-State City.

•**PORT WASHINGTON**, Village; Nassau County; Pop. 15,923; Zip Code 11050; Lat. 40-49-32 N long. 073-41-55 W; SE N.Y. on N shore of Long Island.

•**PORTLAND**, Town; Chautauqua County; Pop. 4,394; Zip Code 14769; Elev. 760; Lat. 42-22-47 N long. 079-28-04 W; SW New York.

•**POTSDAM**, Village and Town; St.Lawrence County; Pop. 10,676 and 17,466; Zip Code 13676; Lat. 44-40-11 N long. 074-58-54 W; 27 m. E of Ogdensburg in N N.Y. Named for the city in Germany.

•**POUGHKEEPSIE**, City; Dutchess County Seat; Pop. 29,677; Zip Code 12601; Elev. 175; Lat. 41-42-01 N long. 073-55-17 W; SE New York; on Hudson River; midway between New York City and Albany; Name is modified from Indian word meaning "tree-covered lodge by the little water place".

•**POUND RIDGE**, Town; Westchester County; Pop. 4,016; Zip Code 10576; Lat. 41-12-31 N long. 073-34-31 W; SE New York.

•**PRATTSBURG**, Town; Steuben County; Pop. 1,641; Zip Code 14873; Lat. 42-31-26 N long. 077-17-21 W; S New York.

•**PREBLE**, Town; Cortland County; Pop. 1,635; Zip Code 13141; Lat. 42-44-07 N long. 076-08-55 W; N central New York.

•**PULASKI**, Village; Oswego County; Pop. 2,417; Zip Code 13142; Lat. 43-34-01 N long. 076-07-41 W; near Lake Ontario 30 m. S SW of Watertown in central N.Y. Named in honor of the Polish-American Revolutionary War hero.

•**PULTENEY**, Town; Steuben County; Pop. 1,267; Zip Code 14874; Elev. 1049; Lat. 42-31-30 N long. 077-10-03 W; is named after *Sir William Pulteney*, head of the London Associates.

•**PUTNAM VALLEY**, Town; Putnam County; Pop. 8,959; Zip Code 10579; Lat. 41-20-09 N long. 073-52-28 W; SE New York.

•**QUEENS BOROUGH**, Queens County; Pop. 1,886,550; located in SE N.Y. on Long Island.

•**QUEENSBURY**, Town; Warren County; Pop. 18,970; Zip Code 12801; Elev. 293; Lat. 43-22-38 N long. 073-36-49 W; NE New York.

•**QUOGUE**, Village; Suffolk County; Pop. 970; Zip Code 11959; Lat. 40-49-23 N long. 072-36-36 W; SE N.Y. on Long Island. Resort. An Indian word meaning "trembling river."

•**RANDOLPH**, Village and Town; Cattaraugus County; Pop. 1,393 and 2,588; Zip Code 14772; Elev. 1278; Lat. 42-09-43 N long. 078-58-32 W; SW corner of N.Y. Named for a prominent colonial citizen.

•**RAVENA**, Village; Albany County; Pop. 3,092; Zip Code 12143; Elev. 182; Lat. 42-28-06 N long. 073-49-00 W; on the Hudson River 11 m. S of Albany in E N.Y. Named after the Italian city.

•**RED HOOK**, Village and Town; Dutchess County; Pop. 1,686 and 8,353; Zip Code 12571; Elev. 218; Lat. 41-59-42 N long. 073-52-33 W; SE N.Y.; Elev. 200; was called Roode Hoeck by early Dutch navigators because of the profusion of red berries they saw growing on the hillsides.

•**RENSSELAER**, City; Rensselaer County; Pop. 9,006; Zip Code 12144; Lat. 42-38-33 N long. 073-44-36 W; across Hudson River from Albany in E N.Y. The city, formed in 1897 by the union of the villages of East Albany, Greenbush and Bath-on-the-Hudson, stands on ground that was part of Rensselaerswyck, most successful of the patroonships.

•**RHINEBECK**, Village and Town; Dutchess County; Pop. 2,519 and 6,926; Zip Code 12572; Elev. 200; Lat. 41-55-36 N long. 073-54-47 W; near East bank of the Hudson River 16 m. N of Poughkeepsie.

•**RICHFIELD SPRINGS**, Village; Otsego County; Pop. 1,561; Zip Code 13439; Elev. 1,300; Lat. 42-51-12 N long. 074-59-09 W; 20 m. SE of Utica in central N.Y.; came to prominence in 1820 when the Great White Sulphur Springs became popular.

•**RICHLAND**, Town; Oswego County; Pop. 5,553; Zip Code 13144; Elev. 529; Lat. 43-34-10 N long. 076-02-53 W; central N.Y. Descriptively named.

•**RICHMOND BOROUGH**, Borough; Richmond County; Pop. 349,601; SW part of New York city in SE N.Y. As of 1975 officially known as Staten Island. The borough, a roughly triangular island is 37 square miles in area.

•**RIPLEY**, Town; Chautauqua County; Pop. 3,238; Zip Code 14775; Elev. 730; Lat. 42-16-01 N long. 079-42-39 W; SW corner of N.Y.; Elev. 370'. Named for an early settler.

•**RIVERHEAD**, Town; Seat of Suffolk County; Pop. 20,204; Zip Code 11901; Lat. 40-55-01 N long. 072-39-45 W; on the Peconic River, E end of Long Island in SE N.Y.; settled in 1690.

•**ROCHESTER**, City; Monroe County Seat; Pop. 241,539; Zip Code 14601; Elev. 500; Lat. 43-09-17 N long. 077-36-57 W; N New York; 80 miles NW of Syracuse; Purchased in 1803 by *Colonel William Fitzhugh*, *Major Charles Carroll*, and *Colonel Nathaniel Rochester*, all from Maryland. In 1811 Colonel Rochester offered lots for sale; on May 5, 1812, IIn 1817 the village was incorporated as Rochesterville.

•**ROCKVILLE CENTRE**, Village; Nassau County; Pop. 25,384; Zip Code 11570; Elev. 31; Lat. 40-39-31 N long. 073-38-30 W; on Long Island, ; owes its name to the Long Island Smiths, of whom there were so many that qualifying names were needed to distinguish the various clans. Hence an odd list; "Bull", "Tangier", "Wait", and "Rock" Smiths. To the last-named family belonged the *Reverend Mordecai "Rock" Smith*, for whom the village was named.

•**ROME**, City; Oneida County Seat; Pop. 43,732; Zip Code 13440; Elev. 440. Earlier known as Lynchville, in 1819 incorporated as the village of Rome, the name being in tribute to the "heroic defense of the republic made here."

•**ROMULUS**, Town; Seneca County; Pop. 2,459; Zip Code 14541; Elev. 330; Lat. 42-45-08 N long. 076-50-02 W; W central N.Y. Named for the mythological founder of Rome.

•**RONKONKOMA**, Village; Suffolk County; Pop. 16,000; Zip Code 11779; Elev. 111; Lat. 40-48-55 N long. 073-06-46 W; SE N.Y. in central Long Island; the name means "fishing place."

•**ROOSEVELT**, Village; Nassau County; Pop. 15,008; Zip Code 11575; Lat. 40-40-43 N long. 073-35-22 W; SE N.Y. on Long Island; named for the Roosevelt family.

•**ROSE**, Town; Wayne County; Pop. 2,676; Zip Code 14542; Elev. 418; Lat. 43-09-13 N long. 076-52-44 W; W central New York.

•**ROSENDALE**, Town; Ulster County; Pop. 5,890; Zip Code 12472; Lat. 41-50-38 N long. 074-04-57 W; SE New York.

•**ROSLYN**, Village; Nassau County; Pop. 2,120; Zip Code 11576; Lat. 40-47-59 N long. 073-39-05 W; on Long Island abt. 4 m. N of Mineola in SE N.Y. Named for the wife of an early settler.

•**ROTTERDAM**, Town; Schenectady County; Pop. 29,445; Zip Code 12303; E N.Y. Named after the Dutch city.

•**ROUSES POINT**, Village; Clinton County; Pop. 2,257; Zip Code 12979; Elev. 116; Lat. 44-59-38 N long. 073-21-55 W; at the upper end of Lake Champlain at Canadian border. Named for an early settler.

•**ROXBURY**, Town; Delaware County; Pop. 2,286; Zip Code 12474; Elev. 1,470; Lat. 42-17-02 N long. 074-33-55 W; 18 m. E of Delhi in S N.Y. An English word meaning "rocky."

•**RUSH**, Town; Monroe County; Pop. 3,001; Zip Code 14543; Lat. 42-59-45 N long. 077-38-45 W; W N.Y. Named for the rush reeds in the vicinity.

•**RUSHFORD**, Town; Allegany County; Pop. 1,121; Zip Code 14777; Lat. 42-23-32 N long. 078-15-14 W; S N.Y. Named after an early settler.

•**RUSSELL**, Town; St. Lawrence County; Pop. 1,634; Zip Code 13684; Elev. 582; Lat. 44-25-46 N long. 075-09-01 W; N N.Y. Named for a prominent citizen.

•**RYE**, City; Westchester County; Pop. 15,055; Zip Code 10580; Elev. 47; Lat. 40-58-50 N long. 073-41-03 W; on Long Island Sound; settled in 1660.

•**SACKETS HARBOR**, Village; Jefferson County; Pop. 1,017; Zip Code 13685; Elev. 278; Lat. 43-56-46 N long. 076-07-10 W; on Lake Ontario 11 m. W SW of Watertown in N New York.

•**SAG HARBOR**, Village; Suffolk County; Pop. 2,483; Zip Code 11963; Lat. 40-59-52 N long. 072-17-35 W; 25 m. W of Montauk Point at the W end of Long Island in SE N.Y. Sag is an Indian word meaning "outlet of the stream."

•**SAINT JAMES**, Village; Suffolk County; Pop. 11,000; Zip Code 11780; Lat. 40-52-44 N long. 073-09-26 W; SE New York.

•**SALAMANCA**, City; Cattaraugus County; Pop. 6,849; Zip Code 14779; Elev. 1,380; Lat. 42-09-28 N long. 078-42-55 W; in SW N.Y. When the Atlantic and Great Western railroad company built shops and yards here, the grateful citizens named their village in honor of one of the important stockholders.

•**SALINA**, Town; Onondaga County; Pop. 37,380; Zip Code 132+; central N.Y. Sallina is Spanish for salt.

•**SAN REMO**, Village; Suffolk County; Pop. 8,700; Elev. 163; Lat. 40-52-55 N long. 073-13-16 W; SE N.Y.; named after an Italian town.

•**SAND LAKE**, Town; Rensselaer County; Pop. 6,957; Zip Code 12153; Lat. 42-38-14 N long. 073-32-28 W; E N.Y. Descriptively named.

•**SANDY CREEK**, Village and Town; Oswego County; Pop. 762 and 3,258; Zip Code 13145; Elev. 498; Lat. 43-38-39 N long. 076-05-11 W; W New York.

•**SANGERFIELD**, Town; Oneida County; Pop. 2,409; Zip Code 13455; Lat. 42-54-50 N long. 075-22-46 W; W central N.Y. Named after a local citizen.

•**SARANAC**, Town; Clinton County; Pop. 3,379; Zip Code 12981; Lat. 44-39-05 N long. 073-44-38 W; NE N.Y. An Indian word of uncertain meaning.

•**SARANAC LAKE**, Village; Essex and Franklin Counties; Pop. 5,580; Zip Code 12983; Elev. 1,540; Lat. 44-19-46 N long 074-07-54 W; near Lower Saranac Lake 36 m. S of Malone in NE New York.

•**SARATOGA SPRINGS**, City; Saratoga County; Pop. 23,901; Zip Code 12866; Elev. 330; Lat. 43-04-59 N long. 073-47-06 W; in E N.Y. Famed for its mineral springs. Large numbers of wild animals, attracted by the saline properties of the water, made this section a favorite hunting ground for the Indians, who called it Saraghoga (place of swift water).

•**SARDINIA**, Town; Erie County; Pop. 2,801; Zip Code 14134; Elev. 1398; Lat. 42-32-28 N long. 078-30-30 W; W N.Y. Named after the famous island in the Mediterranean.

•**SAUGERTIES**, Village and Town; Ulster County; Pop. 3,879 and 17,880; Zip Code 12477; Elev. 100; Lat. 42-04-39 N long. 073-57-12 W; on W side of Hudson River 11 m. N of Kingston in SE N.Y. Named after the first Dutch settler.

•**SAVANNAH**, Town; Wayne County; Pop. 1,879; Zip Code 13146; Elev. 426; Lat. 43-04-02 N long. 076-45-36 W; W central N.Y. A Carib Indian word meaning "meadow."

•**SAVONA**, Village; Steuben County; Pop. 939; Zip Code 14879; Lat. 42-17-19 N long. 077-13-07 W; S N.Y. Named after the Italian city.

•**SAYVILLE**, Village; Suffolk County; Pop. 15,300; Zip Code 11782; Lat. 40-44-09 N long. 073-04-57 W; SE N.Y.; on S shore of Long Island at the Great South Bay.

•**SCARBOROUGH**, Village; Westchester County; Zip Code 10510; Lat. 41-08-09 N long. 073-51-32 W; SE N.Y.; Named after the town in England.

•**SCARSDALE**, Village and Town; Westchester County; Pop. 17,625 and 17,625; Zip Code 10583; Elev. 200; Lat. 41-00-18 N long. 073-47-06 W; It takes its name from the Manor of Scarsdale, of which its site was a part, established by *Caleb Heathcote*, who came from Scarsdale, Derbyshire, England, in 1701.

•**SCHAGHTICOKE**, Village and Town; Rensselaer County; Pop. 681 and 7,134; Zip Code 12154; Lat. 42-54-00 N long. 073-35-09 W; E N.Y. An Indian word meaning "branching stream."

•**SCHENECTADY**, City; Seat of Schenectady County; Pop. 67,877; Zip Code 123; Elev. 220; Lat. 42-48-51 N long. 073-56-24 W; E N.Y. Mohawk Indians called the present city site Schonowe (big flats). The Indian original of the name Schenectady (at the end of the pine plains) referred to the sites of both Albany and Schenectady as the termini of the aboriginal portage between the Hudson and Mohawk Rivers.

•**SCHROON LAKE**, Village; Essex County; Zip Code 12870; Elev. 840; Lat. 43-50-19 N long. 073-45-41 W; lies at the head of Schroon Lake. The name is believed to have been given by French scouts in the early eighteenth century, who compared the beauty of the long slim body of water with that of the young widow of *Paul Scarron*, the consort of Louis XIV.

•**SCHUYLER FALLS**, Town; Clinton County; Pop. 4,174; Zip Code 12985; Elev. 429; Lat. 44-37-43 N long. 073-33-30 W; named in honor of General Phillip Schuyler.

•**SCHUYLERVILLE**, Village; Saratoga County; Pop. 1,265; Zip Code 12871; Lat. 43-06-00 N long. 073-34-56 W; on W bank of Hudson River 32 m. N of Albany in E N.Y.; Elev. 140'

•**SCIO**, Town; Allegany County; Pop. 1,969; Zip Code 14880; Lat. 42-10-17 N long. 077-58-44 W; S N.Y. Named after the Greek island.

•**SCOTIA**, Village; Schenectady County; Pop. 7,241; Zip Code 12303; Elev. 240; Lat. 42-49-35 N long. 073-57-53 W; 25 m. NW of Albany in E N.Y.; the village takes its name from the Latin name of Scotland, the native land of *Alexander Lindsey Glen*.

•**SEA CLIFF**, Village; Nassau County; Pop. 5,351; Zip Code 11579; Lat. 40-50-56 N long. 073-38-43 W; on W Long Island in SE N.Y. Descriptively named.

•**SELDEN**, Village; Suffolk County; Pop. 21,800; Zip Code 22784; Lat. 40-51-59 N long. 073-02-10 W; SE N.Y. on central Long Island. Named for a local settler.

•**SENECA FALLS**, Village and Town; Seneca County; Pop. 7,481 and 9,894; Zip Code 13148; Elev. 465; Lat. 42-54-38 N long. 076-47-49 W; on Seneca River. Named after the Seneca Indians.

•**SENNETT**, Town; Cayuga County; Pop. 2,547; Zip Code 13150; Elev. 598; Lat. 42-59-41 N long. 076-31-59 W; W central N.Y. From a personal name.

•**SHANDAKEN**, Town; Ulster County; Pop. 2,912; Zip Code 12480; Lat. 42-07-12 N long. 074-23-45 W; SE N.Y. An Indian word meaning "hemslock."

•**SHELTER ISLAND**, Town and Island; Suffolk County; Pop. 2,060; Zip Code 11964; Lat. 41-04-05 N long. 072-20-21 W; an island in Gardiners Bay off the NE coast of Long Island in SE N.Y. As early as 1652 Quakers sought refuge on the island.

•**SHERIDAN**, Town; Chautauqua County; Pop. 2,656; Zip Code 14135; Lat. 42-29-18 N long. 079-14-15 W; on State 20 in SW corner of the state; was named after *General Philip Sheridan*.

•**SHIRLEY**, Village; Suffolk County; Pop. 8,200; Zip Code 11967; Lat. 42-34-36 N long. 078-54-50 W; SE N.Y.; On Long Island; a family name.

•**SHORTSVILLE**, Village; Ontario County; Pop. 1,717; Zip Code 14548; Lat. 42-57-21 N long. 077-13-16 W; 7 m. N of Canandaigua in W central New York.

•**SIDNEY**, Village and Town; Delaware County; Pop. 4,851 and 6,852; Zip Code 13838; Elev. 900; Lat. 42-18-53 N long. 075-23-31 W; named for a prominent citizen.

•**SILVER CREEK**, Village; Chautauqua County; Pop. 3,113; Zip Code 14136; Elev. 640; Lat. 42-32-39 N long. 079-10-01 W; on Lake Erie 28 m. S of Buffalo in SW Corner of N.Y.; The village that grew up around it took its name from another Silver Creek flowing into Lake Erie.

•**SKANEATELES**, Village and Town; Onondaga County; Pop. 2,777 and 7,774; Zip Code 13152; Lat. 42-56-49 N long. 076-25-46 W; at N end of Skaneateles Lake 8 m. E of Auburn in central N.Y. An Indian word meaning "long lake."

•**SLOAN**, Village; Niagara County; Pop. 5,216; Lat. 42-53-36 N long. 078-47-39 W; W N.Y.; 6 m. E of downtown Buffalo in a residential area.

•**SLOATSBURG**, Village; Rockland County; Pop. 3,157; Zip Code 10974; Elev. 320; Lat. 41-09-16 N long. 074-11-36 W; near New Jersey state line ; the Sloat House is a brick Greek Revival structure built by *Isaac Sloat* in the early 1800's on the front of a much older one-story house erected by his father Isaac, for whom the village was named.

•**SMITHTOWN**, Town; Suffolk County; Pop. 116,460; Zip Code 11787; Elev. 73; Lat. 40-51-21 N long. 073-12-04 W; SE N.Y.; named after a prominent resident.

•**SODUS**, Village and Town; Wayne County; Pop. 1,788 and 9,484; Zip Code 14551; Elev. 475; Lat. 43-14-16 N long. 077-03-42 W; an Indian word of uncertain meaning.

•**SOLVAY**, Village; Onondaga County; Pop. 7,107; Zip Code 132+; Elev. 503; Lat. 43-03-29 N long. 076-12-28 W; 5 m. W of Syracuse in central N.Y. Named after the Solvay chemical process.

•**SOMERS**, Town; Westchester County; Pop. 13,152; Zip Code 10589; Elev. 300; Lat. 41-19-41 N long. 073-41-10 W; in SE N.Y. Named for a local resident.

•**SOUND BEACH**, Village; Suffolk County; Pop. 5,400; Zip Code 11789; Elev. 60; Lat. 40-57-22 N long. 072-58-06 W; SE N.Y.; On N shore of Long Island. Descriptively named.

•**SOUTH GLENS FALLS**, Village; Saratoga County; Pop. 3,727; Zip Code 12801; Elev. 345; Lat. 43-17-57 N long. 073-38-08 W; 17 m. NE of Sarasota Springs in E N.Y. Across the Hudson River to the N is Glens Falls which named this village.

•**SOUTH HUNTINGTON**, Village; Suffolk County; Pop. 8,946; Lat. 40-49-25 N long. 073-23-57 W; SE N.Y. in central Long Island, 3 m. S of Huntington.

•**SOUTHAMPTON**, Village and Town; Suffolk County; Pop. 4,021 and 42,796; Zip Code 11968; Lat. 40-53-03 N long. 072-23-24 W; on Long Islands S shore in SE N.Y.; named for the English city.

•**SOUTHOLD**, Town; Suffolk County; Pop. 19,140; Zip Code 11971; Lat. 41-03-53 N long. 072-25-36 W; 18 m. NE of Riverhead on the N end of Long Island in SE New York.

•**SOUTHPORT**, Village; Chemung County; Pop. 8,865; Elev. 889; Lat. 42-03-17 N long. 076-49-10 W; S N.Y.; near Pennsylvania state line and 2 m. S of Elmira near the Chemung River.

•**SPENCERPORT**, Village; Monroe County; Pop. 3,428; Zip Code 14559; Elev. 528; Lat. 43-11-11 N long. 077-48-15 W; 10 m. NW of Rochester in W part of the state. From a personal name.

•**SPRING VALLEY**, Village; Rockland County; Pop. 20,580; Zip Code 10977; Lat. 41-06-47 N long. 074-02-39 W; in SE N.Y.; is known for its fruit farms and as a resort.

•**SPRINGVILLE**, Village; Erie County; Pop. 4,271; Zip Code 14141; Elev. 1,341; Lat. 42-30-30 N long. 078-40-03 W; 27 m. SE of Buffalo in W New York.

•**SPRINGWATER**, Town; Livingston County; Pop. 2,134; Zip Code 14560; Elev. 970; Lat. 42-38-14 N long. 077-35-46 W; 40 m. S of Rochester in W central New York.

•**STAFFORD**, Town; Genesee County; Pop. 2,507; Zip Code 14143; Elev. 996; Lat. 42-58-54 N long. 078-04-27 W; W N.Y. Named after the town in England.

•**STAMFORD**, Village and Town; Delaware County; Pop. 1,237 and 2,150; Zip Code 12167; Elev. 1,827; Lat. 42-24-26 N long. 074-36-53 W; in S N.Y. Named after a town in England.

•**STATEN ISLAND**, Island; Richmond County; Pop. 349,601; Zip Code 103+; in SE N.Y. W of Long Island in New York Bay. A Dutch word refering to the governing legislature of Holland in the 17th century.

•**STEPHENTOWN**, Town; Rensselaer County; Pop. 2,049; Zip Code 12168; Elev. 878; Lat. 42-32-55 N long. 073-22-28 W; in E New York.

•**STERLING**, Town; Cayuga County; Pop. 3,264; Zip Code 13156; Lat. 43-19-33 N long. 976-38-43 W; in central N.Y. Named after a prominent citizen.

•**STILLWATER**, Village and Town; Saratoga County; Pop. 1,586; Zip Code 12170; Lat. 42-03-32 N long. 079-13-08 W; on the Hudson River in N N.Y. about 20 m. N of Albany. Descriptively named.

•**STOCKTON**, Town; Chautauqua County; Pop. 2,316; Zip Code 14784; Elev. 1328; Lat. 42-19-03 N long. 079-21-22 W; in the SW corner of New York.

•**STONY BROOK**, Village; Suffolk County; Pop. 6,391; Zip Code 11790; Elev. 88; Lat. 40-55-32 N long. 073-08-29 W; SE N.Y.; on Smithtown Bay N of Long Island.

•**STONY POINT**, Town; Rockland County; Pop. 12,841; Zip Code 10980; Elev. 120; Lat. 42-33-04 N long. 073-44-50 W; in SE N.Y; derives its name from the rocky bluff that projects into the Hudson.

•**STUYVESANT**, Town; Columbia County; Pop. 2,207; Zip Code 12173; Elev. 100; Lat. 42-23-25 N long. 073-46-55 W; in SE N.Y. Named after the famous Dutch governor of New York.

•**SUFFERN**, Village; Rockland County; Pop. 10,785; Zip Code 10901; Elev. 500; Lat. 41-06-53 N long. 074-09-00 W; 30 m. NW of N.Y.City in SE N.Y. Named for an early pioneer family.

•**SYOSSET**, Village; Nassau County; Pop. 10,200; Zip Code 11791; Lat. 40-49-34 N long. 073-30-09 W; SE N.Y. on Long Island.

•**SYRACUSE**, City; Onondaga County Seat; Pop. 170,292; Zip Code 400; Lat. 43-02-53 N long. 076-08-52 W; Central New York; *Abraham Walton* purchased 250 acres of the reservation from the state for $6,650, and after extensive draining of the swamps and clearing of the marshes, he named the area Syracuse, after the ancient Greek city in Sicily.

•**TAPPAN**, Village; Rockland County; Pop. 6,100; Zip Code 10983; Elev. 80; Lat. 42-11-44 N long. 074-08-03 W; SE N.Y.; 5 m. S of Nyack near the Hudson River. Named after the Indian tribe.

•**TARRYTOWN**, Village; Westchester County; Pop. 10,608; Zip Code 10591; Elev. 70; Lat. 42-33-32 N long. 073-57-05 W; on the Hudson River in SE N.Y. According to *Washington Irving*, was named by irate Dutch farm women who complained that their husbands lingered too long at the village tavern after depositing produce at the Philipse wharf; but more serious historians say that "tarry" is a corruption of the Dutch word "tarwe" (wheat).

•**TERRYVILLE**, Village; Suffolk County; Pop. 6,000; Elev. 154; Lat. 40-54-32 N long. 073-03-56 W; SE N.Y. on Long Island.

•**TICONDEROGA**, Village and Town; Essex County; Pop. 2,2921 and 5,419; Zip Code 12883; Elev. 154; Lat. 43-50-55 N long. 073-25-26 W; NE N.Y. on the neck of land connecting Lake George and Lake Champlain. The name is a variation of the Indian Cheonderoga (between two waters, or where the waters meet).

•**TIVOLI**, Village; Dutchess County; Pop. 701; Zip Code 12583; Elev. 152; Lat. 42-03-30 N long. 073-54-35 W; SE N.Y. Here in 1798-1802 *Peter de Labigarre*, who came to America after the French Revolution, built the Chateau de Tivoli, the first unit of a projected model community.

•**TONAWANDA**, City; Erie County; Pop. 18,701; Zip Code 14150; Elev. 575; Lat. 43-01-13 N long. 078-52-50 W; 9 m. N of Buffalo in W N.Y. An Iroquoian word meaning "swift water."

•**TROY**, City; Rensselaer County seat; Pop. 56,614; Zip Code 12180; Elev. 34; Lat. 42-43-42 N long. 073-41-32 W; E New York, on E bank of Hudson River at mouth of Mohawk River. The name Troy was adopted at a public meeting in Ashley's Tavern on January 5, 1789.

•**TRUMANSBURG**, Village; Tompkins County; Pop. 1,724; Zip Code 14886; Elev. 1,000; Lat. 42-32-32 N long. 076-39-59 W; in S central N.Y. The name was misspelled for that of its first settler *Abner Treman*, who was a Revolutionary veteran who came here in 1792.

•**TUCKAHOE**, Village; Westchester Conty; Pop. 6,274; Zip Code 10707; Elev. 120; Lat. 40-53-56 N long. 072-24-41 W; 18 m. N NE of New York in SE N.Y. The name means "wild tuber."

•**TULLY**, Village and town; Onondaga county; Pop. 1,065 and 2,414; Zip Code 13159; Elev. 1252; Lat. 42-47-53 N long. 076-06-35 W; Central N.Y. Named for the famous Roman orator.

•**TUPPER LAKE**, Village and Lakes; Franklin County; Pop. 4,470; Zip Code 12986; Elev. 1,569; named for a prominent citizen.

•**TYRONE**, Town; Schuyler conty; Pop. 1,475; Zip Code 14887; Lat. 42-24-29 N long. 077-03-31 W; in SW central N.Y. Named after the county in Ireland.

•**UNADILLA**, Village and town; Otsego County; Pop. 1,366 and 4,023; Zip Code 13849; Elev. 1,023; Lat. 42-19-31 N long. 075-18-46 W; in central N.Y. An Iroquoian word meaning "place of meeting."

•**UNION**, town; Broome County; Pop. 61,160; Zip Code 13760; Lat. 42-52-04 N long. 075-53-15 W; in S N.Y.; named because two British armies met here during the Revolutionary War.

•**UNION SPRINGS**, Village; Cayuga County; Pop. 1,201; Zip Code 13160; Elev. 419; Lat. 42-50-23 N long. 076-41-37 W; in central N.Y.; takes its name from the numerous sulphur and salt springs in the vicinity.

•**UTICA**, city; Oneida County seat; pop. 75,435; Zip Code 13501; Elev. 500; Lat. 43-06-03 N long. 075-13-59 W; Central New York; 90 m. W of Albany. The original name for Utica was the Indian Yahnundasis, or "around the hill", in reference to this area where trails passed through the foothills. "Utica" was chosen as the name by a chance selection from a hatful of paper slips, and is derived from the name of the ancient city on the Mediterranean coast of Tunisia.

•**VALATIE**, Village; Columbia County; Pop. 1,605; Zip Code 12184; Lat. 42-24-48 N long. 073-40-25 W; in SE N.Y. A Dutch word meaning "little valley."

•**VALHALLA**, Village; Westchester County; Pop. 6,600; Zip Code 10595; Lat. 41-04-29 N long. 073-46-32 W; SE N.Y. In German mythology, the home of the Gods.

•**VALLEY STREAM**, Village; Nassau County; Pop. 35,597; Zip Code 115+; Lat. 40-39-51 N long. 073-42-32 W; 18 m. from the Manhattan Bridge; SE New York.

•**VERNON**, Village and Town; Oneida County; Pop. 1,381 and 5,364; Zip Code 13476; Elev. 580; Lat. 43-04-46 N long. 075-32-23 W; Central N.Y. Named after the famous British admiral.

•**VERONA**, Town; Oneida County; Pop. 6,652; Zip Code 13478; Elev. 501; Lat. 43-08-17 N long. 075-34-16 W; in central N.Y. Named after the Italian city.

•**VESTAL**, Town; Broome County; Pop. 27,234; Zip Code 13850; Lat. 42-05-06 N long. 076-03-15 W; in S N.Y. Named after a local resident.

•**VICTOR**, Village and Town; Ontario County; Pop. 2,362 and 5,768; Zip Code 14564; Elev. 580; Lat. 42-58-57 N long. 077-24-33 W; in W New York.

•**VOORHEESVILLE**, Village; Albany County; Pop. 3,310; Zip Code 12186; Elev. 332; Lat. 42-39-14 N long. 073-55-45 W; in E central N.Y.; was named after *Walker and Gmelin Voorhees*.

•**WALDEN**, Village; Orange County; Pop. 5,648; Zip Code 12586; Elev. 647; Lat. 42-54-42 N long. 078-47-05 W; NW of Newburgh in SE New York.

•**WALTON**, Village and Town; Delaware County; Pop. 3,331 and 5,836; Zip Code 13856; Elev. 1226; Lat. 42-10-10 N long. 075-07-47 W; in S N.Y. Named after an early settler.

•**WALWORTH**, Town; Wayne County; Pop. 5,280; Zip Code 14568; Elev. 541; Lat. 43-08-21 N long. 077-16-21 W; in W N.Y. Named for a prominent citizen.

•**WANTAGH**, Village; Nassau County; Pop. 22,300; Zip Code 11793; Lat. 40-41-01 N long. 073-30-38 W; SE N.Y. Named after an early Indian chief.

•**WAPPINGERS FALLS**, Village; Dutchess County; Pop. 5,071; Zip Code 12590; Elev. 116; Lat. 41-35-47 N long. 073-54-41 W; 8 m. S of Poughkeepsie near the Hudson River in SE N.Y.; named for the 75-foot cascade in Wappinger Creek that has provided water power since the place was settled.

•**WARRENSBURG**, Town; Warren County; Pop. 3,796; Zip Code 12885; Elev. 720; is on the shore of the Schroon River; was named for *James Warren*, who settled here in 1804.

•**WARSAW**, Village and Town; Seat of Wyoming County; Pop. 3,617 and 5,050; Zip Code 14569; Elev. 1,000; Named for the Polish capital.

•**WARWICK**, Village and Town; Orange County; Pop. 4,319 and 21,001; Zip Code 10900; Elev. 558; 40 m. NW of New York City in S N.Y.; settled in 1746 by English immigrants from Warwickshire.

•**WASHINGTONVILLE**, Village; Orange County; Pop. 2,384; Zip Code 10992; in S N.Y. Named in honor of George Washington.

•**WATERFORD**, Village and Town; Saratoga County; Pop. 2,412 and 7,191; Zip Code 12188; Elev. 38; 10 m. N of Albany on the Hudson River in E New York.

•**WATERLOO**, Village and Town; Seat of Seneca County; Pop. 5,297 and 7,778; Zip Code 13165; Elev. 450; named after the great European battle.

•**WATERTOWN**, City; Seat of Jefferson County; Pop. 27,900; Zip Code 13601; Elev. 478; 10 m. E of Lake Ontario in N N.Y.; In 1800 five New Englanders hacked their way up from the Mohawk Valley, stopped at the rocky Black River Falls, and named the site Watertown.

•**WATERVLIET**, City; Albany County; Pop. 11,322; Zip Code 12189. A Dutch word for "water stream."

•**WATKINS GLEN**, Village; Seat of Schuyler County; Pop. 2,425; Zip Code 14891; Elev. 477; 18 m. N of Elmira in SW central New York.

•**WAVERLY**, Village; Tioga County; Pop. 4,755; Zip Code 14892; Elev. 839; 15 m. SE of Elmira in SE New York.

•**WARWARSING**, Town; Ulster County; Pop. 12,868; Zip Code 12489; in SE New York.

•**WEBSTER**, Village and Town; Monroe County; Pop. 5,486 and 28,895; Zip Code 14580; Lat. 43-12-44 N long. 077-25-49 W; 10 m. NE of Rochester in W N.Y. Named for an early settler.

•**WELLSVILLE**, Village and Town; Allegany County; Pop. 5,764 and 8,646; Zip Code 14895; Elev. 1,517; Lat. 42-07-19 N long. 077-56-54 W; in SW N.Y.; settled in 1795; It was settled in 1795 and named for *Gardiner Wells*, early settler and chief landowner.

•**WEST BABYLON**, Village; Suffolk County; Pop. 32,100; Zip Code 11704; Lat. 40-43-05 N long. 073-21-17 W; SE N.Y.; 1 m. W of Babylon near the Great South Bay of Long Island.

•**WESTBURY**, Village; Nassau County; Pop. 13,802; Zip Code 11590; Lat. 43-12-53 N long. 076-42-40 W; 2-1/2 m. E of Mineola and 23 m. E of N.Y. City on Long Island in SE N.Y..

•**WESTFIELD**, Village and Town; Chautauqua County; Pop. 3,451 and 5,065; Zip Code 14787; Elev. 754; Lat. 42-19-20 N long. 079-34-42.

•**WESTHAMPTON BEACH**, Village; Suffolk County; Pop. 1,626; Zip Code 11978; Lat. 40-48-11 N long. 072-36-54 W; on W half of Long Island in SE N.Y.; at the point where the Outer Barrier all but joins the mainland.

•**WEST HAVERSTRAW**, Village; Rockland County; Pop. 9,152; Lat. 41-12-34 N long. 073-59-09 W; in SE part of New York.

•**WESTMORELAND**, Town; Oneida County; Pop. 5,454; Zip Code 13490; Lat. 43-06-58 N long. 075-24-15 W; in central N.Y. Named after the county in England.

•**WEST POINT**, SE N.Y.; United States Military Academy and Village; Orange County; Zip Code 10996; Elev. 161; Lat. 41-23-29 N long. 073-57-23 W; On the Hudson River; 50 m. N of New York City; Established March 16, 1802; Named for its position on the river.

•**WEST SENECA**, Town; Erie County; Pop. 51,204; Zip Code 14224; in W New York.

•**WHITEHALL**, Village and Town; Washington County; Pop. 3,232 and 4,414; Zip Code 12887; Elev. 123; Lat. 43-33-20 N long. 073-24-15 W; is midway between New York and Montreal on the Hudson-Champlain trail.

•**WHITE PLAINS**, City; Seat of Westchester County; Pop. 46,799; Zip Code 106+; Elev. 467; on W bank of Hudson River. Descriptive of the area in the winter.

•**WHITESBORO**, Village; Oneida County; Pop. 4,462; Zip Code 13492; Elev. 140; Lat. 43-07-19 N long. 075-17-31 W; 5 m. NW of Utica in central N.Y. on the Mohawk River. *Judge Hugh White* (1733-1812) left his Middletown, Connecticut, home in 1784, shipped by water to Albany, overland to Schenectady, and up the Mohawk by boat to his western frontier.

•**WILLIAMSON**, Town; Wayne County; Pop. 6,275; Zip Code 14589; Elev. 452; Lat. 43-13-26 N long. 077-11-11 W; 25 m. NE of Rochester in W N.Y. Named for an early settler.

•**WILLISTON PARK**, Village; Nassau County; Pop. 8,201; Zip Code 11596; Elev. 127; Lat. 40-45-23 N long. 073-38-43 W; 18 m. E of New York City on Long Island in SE New York.

•**WILLSBORO**, Town; Essex County; Pop. 1,759; Zip Code 12996; Elev. 150; Lat. 44-21-26 N long. 073-23-33 W; 25 m. S of Plattsburg in NE New York.

•**WILTON**, Town; Saratoga County; Pop. 7,232; Zip Code 12866; Elev. 348; Lat. 43-10-48 N long. 073-44-41 W; in E N.Y. Named for a prominent citizen.

•**WINDHAM**, Town; Greene County; Pop. 1,641; Zip Code 12496; Lat. 42-18-26 N long. 074-15-09 W; in E central N.Y. Named for the English town.

•**WINDSOR**, Village and Town; Broome County; Pop. 1,134 and 5,877; Zip Code 13865; Lat. 42-04-33 N long. 075-38-27 W; in central S N.Y. Named for the castle in England.

•**WOLCOTT**, Village and Town; Wayne County; Pop. 1,491 and 4,019; Zip Code 14590; Elev. 378; Lat. 43-13-14 N long. 076-48-55 W; in N central N.Y. 47 m. E of Rochester.

•**WOODSTOCK**, Town; Ulster County; Pop. 6,733; Zip Code 12498; Elev. 560; Lat. 42-19-18 N long. 074-00-49 W; in E central New York.

•**WURTSBORO**, Village; Sullivan County; Pop. 1,135; Zip Code 12790; Elev. 560; Lat. 41-34-36 N long. 074-29-15 W; in SE New York.

•**WYOMING**, Village; Wyoming County; Zip Code 716; Zip Code 14591; Elev. 987; Lat. 42-49-35 N long. 078-05-24 W; 30 m. SW of Batavia in NW N.Y. An Indian word meaning "big flats."

•**YONKERS**, City; Westchester County; Pop. 194,601; Zip Code 10701; Elev. 30; Lat. 40-55-52 N long. 073-53-57 W; SE New York; NE New York City Suburb. An Indian village - Nappeckamack - stood on the site of Yonkers, which was part of the Kekeskick Purchase (1639) made by the Dutch West India Company from the Indians. The city site was included in a grant of land made in 1646 by the company to *Adriaen Cornelissen Van der Donck*, the first lawyer and the first historian of New Netherland. By reason of his wealth and social position Van der Donck enjoyed the courtesy title of "jonker," the Dutch equivalent of "his young lordship," from which was derived the name of the city.

•**YORK**, Town; Livingston County; Pop. 3,208; Zip Code 14592; Elev. 787; Lat. 42-52-16 N long. 077-53-08 W; in W N.Y. Named for the county in England.

•**YORKSHIRE**, Town; Cattaraugus County; Pop. 3,629; Zip Code 14173; Elev. 1,438; Lat. 42-31-48 N long. 078-28-23 W; 37 m. SW of Buffalo in SW New York.

•**YOUNGSTOWN**, Village; Niagara County; Pop. 2,196; Zip Code 14174; Elev. 290; Lat. 43-14-50 N long. 079-03-01 W; in W N.Y.; 35 m. N of Buffalo.

NORTH CAROLINA

•**ABERDEEN,** Town; Moore County; Pop. 1,945; Zip Code 28315; Lat. 35-07-56 N long. 079-25-39 W; Originally Blue's Crossing, the name was later changed to Aberdeen after the Scotish seaport.

•**AHOSKIE,** Town; Hertford County; Pop. 4,887; Zip Code 27910; Elev. 53; Lat. 36-17-24 N long. 076-59-15 W; An Indian name of uncertain origin used by the settlement as early as 1719.

•**ALAMANCE,** Village; Alamance County; Pop. 320; Zip Code 27201; Lat. 36-07-40 N long. 079-29-03 W; The town is named after the Great Alamance Creek.

•**ALBEMARLE,** City; Stanly County Seat; Pop. 15,110; Zip Code 28001; Elev. 505; Lat. 35-21-16 N long. 080-11-46 W; Named after George Monck, Duke of Albemarle, one of the original Lord proprietors.

•**ALIANCE,** Town; Pamlico County; Pop. 616; Zip Code 28509; Lat. 35-08-51 N long. 076-48-50 W; Named after the Rarmer's Alliance Movement of the 1890's.

•**ANDREWS,** Town; Cherokee County; Pop. 1,621; Zip Code 28901; The town's name honors railroad promoter A. B. Andrews.

•**ANGIER,** Town; Harnett County; Pop. 1,709; Zip Code 27501; Elev. 301; Lat. 35-30-29 N long. 078-44-27 W; Colonel John C. Angier helped found the town. It is named in his honor.

•**ANSONVILLE,** Town; Anson County; Pop. 794; Zip Code 28007; Elev. 326; Lat. 35-06-06 N long. 080-06-32 W; The town is named after the county. Anson county's name honors Lord Anson, a British admiral of pre-revolution days.

•**APEX,** Town; Wake County; Pop. 2,847; Zip Code 27502; Lat. 35-44-01 N long. 078-51-07 W; Descriptively named as the highest point (it was thought) between Richmond, Va. and Jacksonville, Fla. on the railroad line.

•**ARAPAHOE,** Town; Pamlico County; Pop. 467; Zip Code 28510; Lat. 35-01-31 N long. 076-49-36 W; Founded in 1886 and named after a local race horse.

•**ARCHDALE,** City; Guilford & Randolph Counties; Zip Code 27263; Pop. 5,745; Elev. 869; Lat. 35-54-52 N, long. 079-58-20 W. The town's name honors John Archdale, a colonial governor of Carolina.

•**ARLINGTON,** Town; Yadkin County; Pop. 872; Originally an English village name transferred to Virginia and the Carolinas.

•**ASHEBORO,** City; Randolph County; Pop. 15,252; Zip Code 272+; Lat. 35-42-18 N long. 079-49-12 W; Named in honor of Governor Samuel Ashe who held office in 1795.

•**ASHEBORO SOUTH,** (CDP); Randolph County Seat; Pop. 2,445; Zip Code 272+; Descriptively named for its location to the south of Asheboro.

•**ASHEBORO WEST,** (CDP); Randolph County; Pop. 1,491; Zip Code 272+; Descriptively named for its location to the west of Asheboro.

•**ASHEVILLE,** City; Buncombe County Seat; Pop. 53,583; Zip Code 288+; Elev. 2134; Asheville's name remembers Samuel Ashe who was governor of North Carolina from 1795-98.

•**ASKEWVILLE,** Town; Bertie County; Pop. 227; Elev. 19; Founded in the 1890's and named for a local family.

•**ATKINSON,** Town; Pender County; Pop. 298; Zip Code 28421; Elev. 63; Lat. 34-31-31 N long. 078-10-22 W; An engineer named Aktinson helped finish the railroad through the town. It was named for him in 1909.

•**ATLANTIC BEACH,** Town; Carteret County; Pop. 941; Zip Code 28512; Elev. 8; Lat. 34-42-08 N long. 076-44-06; Descriptively named for its location on the Atlantic Ocean.

•**AULANDER,** Town; Bertie County; Pop. 1,214; Zip Code 27805; Lat. 077-07-10; The town's incorporators intended to name it Orlando, but kept the different spelling to distinguish it from the city in Florida.

•**AURORA,** Town; Beaufort County; Pop. 698; Zip Code 27806; Elev. 8; Lat. 35-18-13 N long. 076-47-13 W; The town is named after an old county newspaper called the Aurora Borealis.

•**AUTRYVILLE,** Town; Sampson County; Pop. 228; Zip Code 28318; Elev. 113; Lat. 34-59-54 N long. 078-38-26 W; Settled in the 1880's and named in honor of merchant J. L. Autry.

•**AYDEN,** Town; Pitt County; Pop. 4,361; Zip Code 28513; Lat. 35-28-02 N long. 077-25-22 W; Named after an early settler.

•**BADIN,** (CDP); Stanly County; Pop. 1,514; Zip Code 28009; Elev. 515; Lat. 35-24-44 N long. 080-07-47 W; Probably named after a pioneer settler.

•**BAILEY,** Town; Nash County; Pop. 685; Zip Code 27807; Elev. 774; Lat. 35-46-48 N long. 078-06-52; Incorporated in 1908 in honor of pioneer settler, Joe Bailey.

•**BAKERSVILLE,** Town; Mitchell County Seat; Pop. 373; Zip Code 28705; Elev. 2460; Lat. 36-00-48 N long. 082-09-29 W; "','"','"" ,"Incorporated in 1868 and named in honor of 18th century settler, David Baker.

•**BALFOUR,** (CDP); Henderson County; Pop. 1,772; Zip Code 28706; Lat. 35-20-48 N long. 082-29-03 W; The town's name honors 1880's businessman and railroad agent Captain William Balfour Troy.

•**BANNER ELK,** Town; Avery County; Pop. 1,087; Zip Code 286+; Elev. 3739; Lat. 36-09-42 N long. 081-52-20; The Banner family settled near here on the Elk River in the early 1800's. The town is named after them.

•**BARKER HEIGHTS,** (CDP); Henderson County; Pop. 1,267; This community in Henderson County is named after an early settler.

•**BATH,** Town; Beaufort County; Pop. 207; Zip Code 27808; Lat. 35-28-16 N long. 076-48-43 W; Settled in 1690 and named in honor of John Granville, Earl of Bath in pre-revolution days.

•**BATTLEBORO,** Town; Edgecomb & Nash Counties; Pop. 632; Zip Code 27809; Elev. 136; Lat. 36-02-40 N long. 077-45-05 W; Founded in 1840 as a railroad depot and named after the Battle brothers who were stockholders in the railroad.

•**BAYBORO,** Town; Pamlico County Seat; Pop. 759; Zip Code 28515; Elev. 12; Lat. 35-08-33 N long. 076-46-12 W; Named after the Bay River, itself named for the many bay trees along its banks.

•**BEARGRASS,** Town; Martin County; Pop. 82; Descriptively named for its location on a tributary of Beargrass Swamp.

•BEAUFORT, Town; Carteret County Seat; Pop. 3,826; Zip Code 28516; Lat. 34-43-16 N long. 076-39-08 W; The town's name honors Henry Somerset, Duke of Beaufort around the town's founding in 1715.

•BELHAVEN, Town; Beaufort County; Pop. 2,430; Zip Code 27810; Elev. 4; Lat. 35-32-27 N long. 076-37-21 W; Incorporated in 1899, the town's name means "beautiful harbor."

•BELMONT, City; Gaston County; Pop. 4,607; Zip Code 28012; Elev. 685; Lat. 35-14-56 N long. 081-02-26 W; Named in honor of August Belmont, a New York banker and financier at the turn of the century.

•BENSON, Town; Johnston County; Pop. 2,792; Zip Code 27504; Lat. 35-22-54 N long. 078-32-56 W; The town's name honors pioneer landowner, M. C. Benson.

•BESSEMER CITY, City; Gaston County; Pop. 4,787; Zip Code 28016; Elev. 904; Lat. 35-17-01 N long. 061-16-49 W; Incorporated in 1893 and named in honor of Sir Henry Bessemer who discovered the process for converting cast iron to steel.

•BETHEL, Town; Pitt County; Pop. 1,825; Zip Code 27812; Elev. 594; Lat. 35-48-25 N long. 077-22-38 W; Settled prior to the Civil War and named after the Bethel Methodist Church.

•BEULAVILLE, Town; Duplin County; Pop. 1,060; Zip Code 28518; Lat. 34-55-14 N long. 077-46-21 W; A Biblical name given by the town's pioneer settlers.

•BILTMORE FOREST, Town; Buncombe County; Pop. 1,499; The town is named after an experimental forest established on the Vanderbilt estate in the 1890's.

•BISCOE, Town; Montgomery County; Pop. 1,334; Zip Code 27209; Elev. 610; Lat. 35-21-36 N long. 079-46-45 W; Originally Filo, the town's name was changed to honor Major Henry Biscoe, a lumber merchant.

•BLACK CREEK, Town; Wilson County; Pop. 523; Zip Code 27813; Elev. 126; Lat. 35-38-09 N long. 077-56-01 W; The town is named for nearby Black Creek.

•BLACK MOUNTAIN, Town; Buncombe County; Pop. 4,083; Zip Code 28711; Elev. 2400; Lat. 35-37-10 N long. 082-19-29 W; The town is named after the local Black Mountain Range. The range is named for the dark foliage of the balsam fir.

•BLANDENBORO, Town; Bladen County; Pop. 1,428; Zip Code 28320; Elev. 111; Lat. 34-32-29 N long. 078-47-38 W; Named in honor of English soldier and politician Martin Bladen, who lived from 1680-1746.

•BLOWING ROCK, Town; Caldwell & Watauga Counties; Pop. 1,337; Zip Code 28605; Elev. 3579; Lat. 36-07-16 N long. 081-39-59 W; Incorporated in 1889 and named for a rock formation whose shape creates an updraft and returns light articles thrown from it.

•BOGER CITY, (CDP); Lincoln County; Pop. 2,252; The town's name honors Robert Boger who founded a textile mill here.

•BOILING SPRING LAKES, City; Brunswick County; Pop. 998; Zip Code 280+; Elev. 878; Lat. 35-14-55 N long. 081-40-02 W; Incorporated in 1961 and named after the nearby Boiling Springs.

•BOILING SPRINGS, Town; Cleveland County; Pop. 2,381; Zip Code 280+; The community is descriptively named for its location near Boiling Spring.

•BOLIVIA, Town; Brunswick County; Pop. 252; Zip Code 28422; Elev. 40; Lat. 34-03-36 N long. 078-08-38 W; Incorporated in 1911 and named for the country in South America.

•BOLTON, Town; Columbus County; Pop. 563; Zip Code 28423; Elev. 66; Lat. 34-19-03 N long. 078-24-29 W; Founded in 1889 and named after the Bolton Lumber Company.

•BOONE, Town; Watauga County Seat; Pop. 10,191; Zip Code 286+; Elev. 3266; Lat. 36-12-53 N long. 081-40-13 W; The city is named in honor of pioneer Daniel Boone.

•BOONVILLE, Town; Yadkin County; Pop. 1,028; Zip Code 27011; Elev. 1066; Incorporated in 1895 and named after pioneer Daniel Boone.

•BOSTIC, Town; Rutherford County; Pop. 476; Zip Code 28018; Elev. 920; Lat. 35-21-37 N long. 081-50-09 W; The town's name honors George Bostic, the first mayor in 1893.

•BREVARD, City; Transylvania County Seat; Pop. 5,323; Zip Code 28712; Elev. 2230; Lat. 35-13-57 N long. 082-44-07 W; The city is named after Revolutionary War era teacher and surgeon Ephriam Brevard.

•BRIDGETON, Town; Craven County; Pop. 461; Zip Code 28519; Lat. 35-07-52 N long. 077-01-57 W; Incorporated in 1907 and named for the bridge which crosses the Neuse River here.

•BROADWAY, Town; Lee County; Pop. 908; Zip Code 27505; Elev. 472; Lat. 35-27-20 N long. 079-03-09 W; Named for a broad meadow in the pine forest which covered the area in the 1870's.

•BROGDEN, (CDP); Wayne County; Pop. 2,988; Elev. 157; Named in honor of Cutis Brogden, a governor of North Carolina in the 19th century.

•BROOKFORD, Town; Catawba County; Pop. 467; Holbrook and Shuford founded a mill here and had their names combined to name the town.

•BRUNSWICK, Town; Columbus County; Pop. 223; Zip Code 28424; Elev. 68; Lat. 34-17-12 N long. 078-42-10 W; The town's name remembers King George I, Duke of Brunswick and Lunenberg.

•BRYSON CITY, Town; Swain County Seat; Pop. 1,556; Zip Code 28713; Elev. 1736; Lat. 35-25-42 N long. 083-26-51 W; Captain Thaddeus Bryson was a founder of Charleston. Bryson City remembers his contribution.

•BUIES CREEK, (CDP); Harnett County; Pop. 1,939; Zip Code 27506; Lat. 35-24-30 N long. 078-44-20 W; Named after an early settler.

•BUNN, Town; Franklin County; Pop. 505; Zip Code 27508; Elev. 275; Lat. 35-57-35 N long. 078-15-06 W; Incorporated in 1913 and named after local resident Green Bunn.

•BURGAW, Town; Pender County; Pop. 1,586; Zip Code 28425; Elev. 49; Lat. 34-33-08 N long. 077-55-24 W; Probably named after a local settler.

•BURLINGTON, City; Alamance County; Pop. 37,266; Zip Code 272+; Elev. 663; Lat. 36-06-04 N long. 079-27-23 W; ","","","Originally called "Company Shops" for the railroad repair yards located here, the name was changed in 1887.

•BURNSVILLE, Town; Yancey County Seat; Pop. 1,452; Zip Code 28714; Elev. 497; Lat. 35-54-57 N long. 082-18-03 W; Founded in 1833 and named after War of 1812 privateer Otway Burns.

•BUTNER, (CDP); Granville County; Pop. 4,240; Zip Code 27509; Lat. 36-08-26 N long. 078-45-07 W; Butner's name honors General Henry Wolfe Butner for whom a nearby World War II camp was named.

•**CALABASH,** Town; Brunswick County; Pop. 128; Called Pea Landing until 1880 when it was named for the gourds found in the area.

•**CALPYSO,** Town; Duplin County; Pop. 689; Zip Code 28325; Elev. 167; Lat. 35-09-23 N long. 078-06-19 W; Incorporated in 1913 and named for a sea nymph in Homer's Odyssey.

•**CAMERON,** Town; Moore County; Pop. 225; Zip Code 28326; Lat. 35-19-32 N long. 079-15-04 W; Named in honor of a railroad civil engineer who surveyed the road bed in the area.

•**CAMP LEJEUNE,** (CDP); Onslow County; Pop. 30,764; General John Lejeune was the World War I Marine Commandant. The town is named in his honor.

•**CANDOR,** Town; Montgomery County; Pop. 868; Zip Code 27229; Elev. 730; Lat. 35-17-39 N long. 079-44-42 W; Incorporated in 1891 and named after the virtue of "Franicness."

•**CANTON,** Town; Haywood County; Pop. 4,631; Zip Code 28716; Elev. 2609; Lat. 35-34-50 N long. 082-50-46 W; Named Canton in 1893 after Canton, Ohio.

•**CAPE CARTERET,** Town; Carteret County; Pop. 944; Both the cape and the town are named after Sir John Carteret, who was an original Lord Proprietor of the Carolinas.

•**CAROLINA BEACH,** Town; New Hanover County; Pop. 2,000; Zip Code 28428; Elev. 5; Lat. 34-02-37 N long. 077-53-54 W; Descriptively named for its Atlantic Ocean location in New Hanover County.

•**CARRBORO,** Town; Orange County; Pop. 7,336; Zip Code 27510; Lat. 35-54-55 N long. 079-04-37 W; Named Carrboro in 1913 after textile mill owner Julian Carr who founded a mill here.

•**CARTHAGE,** Town; Moore County Seat; Pop. 925; Zip Code 28327; Lat. 35-17-47 N long. 079-23-56 W; Founded in the late 1700's and named for the ancient Mediterrean city.

•**CARY,** Town; Wake County; Pop. 21,763; Zip Code 27511; Lat. 35-46-11 N long. 078-47-44 W; Settled in the 1860's and later named after Ohio Senator Samuel Carey.

•**CASAR,** Town; Cleveland County; Pop. 346; Zip Code 28020; Elev. 1125; Lat. 35-30-46 N long. 081-37-03 W; The spelling is supposed to refer to Julius Caeser, but was incorrrectly given.

•**CASHIERS,** Town; Jackson County; Pop. 553; Zip Code 28717; Lat. 35-06-24 N long. 083-05-40 W; Founded in the 1830's and named after a local settler.

•**CASTALIA,** Town; Nash County; Pop. 358; Zip Code 27816; Elev. 310; Lat. 36-04-57 N long. 078-03-27; Schoolmaster David Richardson named the town after the Castalian Springs from Greek mythology in 1853.

•**CASTLE HAYNE,** (CDP); New Hanover County; Pop. 1,087; Zip Code 28429; Elev. 19; Lat. 34-21-13 N long. 077-54-02 W; Captain Roger Hauyne built a large home, or "castle" here prior to the Revolutionary War. By 1882 the town had taken its current name.

•**CENTERVILLE,** Town; Franklin County; Pop. 135; Elev. 340; Descriptively named for its location between Warrenton and Louisburg.

•**CERRO GORDO,** Town; Columbus County; Pop. 295; Zip Code 28430; Elev. 97; Lat. 34-19-24 N long. 078-55-46 W; The town's name commemorates the American victory at Cerro Gordo in 1847 during the Mexican-American War.

•**CHADBOURN,** Town; Columbus County; Pop. 1,975; Zip Code 28431; Elev. 107; Lat. 34-19-22 N long. 078-49-33 W; Incorporated in 1883 and named for a lumber merchant family.

•**CHADWICK ACRES,** Town; Onslow County; Pop. 15; Incorporated in 1961 and named by its developers, possibly for an early settler.

•**CHAPEL HILL,** Town; Durham & Orange Counties; Pop. 32,421; Zip Code 275+; Lat. 35-55-27 N long. 079-01-26 W; Settled in the 1790's and named after the New Hope Chapel which once stood at the hill's crossroads.

•**CHARLOTTE,** City; Mecklenburg County Seat; Pop. 314,447; Zip Code 282+; Lat. 35-12-59 N long. 080-49-57 W; The city is named after Charlotte Sophia, Queen of George III.

•**CHERRYVILLE,** City; Gaston County; Pop. 4,844; Zip Code 28021; Lat. 35-22-52 N long. 081-23-36 W; Descriptively named for a row of cherry trees planted parallel to the post road.

•**CHINA GROVE,** Town; Rowan County; Pop. 2,081; Zip Code 280+; Lat. 35-33-15 N long. 080-35-35 W; Settled in 1823 and named for the many chinaberry trees growing in the area.

•**CHOCOWINITY,** Town; Beaufort County; Pop. 644; Zip Code 27817; Lat. 35-31-02 N long. 077-05-52 W; An Indian name meaning "fish from many waters."

•**CLAREMONT,** City; Catawba County; Pop. 880; Zip Code 28610; Elev. 981; Lat. 35-42-54 N long. 081-08-37 W; Incorporated in 1893 and named for Clare Sigmon, an early settler.

•**CLARKTON,** Town; Bladen County; Pop. 664; Zip Code 28433; Lat. 34-29-18 N long. 078-39-22; Originally Brown Marsh Station, it was renamed in 1863 for John Clark.

•**CLAYTON,** Town; Johnston County; Pop. 4,091; Zip Code 27520; Lat. 35-38-52 N long. 078-27-26 W; Named in honor of Delaware Senator John Clayton who served in the 1850's.

•**CLEMMONS,** (CDP); Forsyth County; Pop. 7,401; Zip Code 27012; Elev. 832; The town's name honors Revolutionary War era settler Peter Clemmons.

•**CLEVELAND,** Town; Rowan County; Pop. 595; Zip Code 27013; Elev. 819; Named in 1887 in honor of President Grover Cleveland.

•**CLINTON,** City; Sampson County Seat; Pop. 7,552; Zip Code 28328; Elev. 152; Lat. 34-59-48 N long. 078-19-33 W; Founded on land owned by Richard Clinton (1721-96), the town was named after him.

•**CLYDE,** Town; Haywood County; Pop. 1,008; Zip Code 28721; Elev. 2539; Lat. 35-34-38 N long. 082-54-35 W; Clyde's name remembers a railroad engineer who helped build the line here in the 1880's.

•**COATS,** Town; Harnett County; Pop. 1,385; Zip Code 27521; Elev. 314; Lat. 35-24-24 N long. 078-40-18 W; Incorporated in 1905 and named in honor of town elder Tom Coats.

•**COFIELD,** Village; Herford County; Pop. 465; Zip Code 27922; Elev. 43; Lat. 36-21-24 N long. 076-54-25 W; The origin of the town's name is uncertain.

•**COLERAIN,** Town; Bertie County; Pop. 284; Zip Code 27924; Lat. 36-11-57 N long. 076-45-54 W; Settled in the early 1700's and named for Coleraine County, Ireland.

•**COLUMBIA,** Town; Tyrrell County Seat; Pop. 758; Zip Code 27925; Elev. 5; Lat. 35-55-07 N long. 076-14-58 W; Originally Elizabeth Town, the name was changed in 1801 to the poetic name for the United States.

•**COLUMBUS,** Town; Polk County Seat; Pop. 727; Zip Code 28722; Elev. 1109; Lat. 35-15-04 N long. 082-11-51 W; The town's name honors Dr. Columbus Mills, a state legislator who helped found the county.

•**COMO,** Town; Hertford County; Pop. 89; Zip Code 27818; Elev. 74; Lat. 36-30-18 N long. 077-00-17 W; Named after Lake Como in Italy upon its founding in 1883.

•**CONCORD,** City; Cabarrus County; Pop. 16,942; Zip Code 280+; Elev. 704; The town's founders argued over the site for the settlement. When they came to agreement they named the town "Concord."

•**CONETOE,** Town; Edgecombe County; Pop. 215; Zip Code 27819; Elev. 48; Lat. 35-48-46 N long. 077-26-59 W; The town is named for nearby Conetoe Creek.

•**CONOVER,** City; Catawba County; Pop. 4,245; Zip Code 28613; Elev. 1062; Lat. 35-42-48 N long. 081-13-04 W; Named in honor of Italian sculptor Canova.

•**CONWAY,** Town; Northampton County; Pop. 678; Zip Code 27820; Lat. 36-26-08 N long. 077-13-42 W; Founded in the 1830's and later named after the wife of a railroad official.

•**COOLEEMEE,** (CDP); Davie County; Pop. 1,448; Zip Code 27014; Elev. 663; An Indian word meaning "place where the white oak grows."

•**CORNELIUS,** Town; Mecklenburg County; Pop. 1,460; Zip Code 28031; Elev. 831; Lat. 35-29-20 N long. 080-51-29 W; Founded in 1893 and named after textile mill stockholder Joe Cornelius.

•**COVE CITY,** Town; Craven County; Pop. 500; Zip Code 28523; Elev. 47; Lat. 35-11-18 N long. 077-19-29 W; Founded in 1859 and descriptively named for a local feature.

•**CRAMERTON,** Town; Gaston County; Pop. 1,869; Zip Code 28032; Elev. 633; Lat. 35-14-09 N long. 081-04-35 W; Established in 1906 as Mayesworth, and changed to honor textile mill owner Stuart Cramer, who set up a business here.

•**CREEDMOOR,** City; Granville County; Pop. 1,641; Zip Code 275+; Lat. 36-07-15 N long. 078-41-05 W; Started as "Need More," but later changed to the more respectable "Creedmoor."

•**CRESWELL,** Town; Washington County; Pop. 426; Zip Code 27928; Lat. 35-52-12 N long. 076-23-32 W; Settled in the 1820's and later named after U. S. Postmaster General, A. J. Creswell in 1885.

•**CRICKET,** (CDP); Wilkes County; Pop. 2,307; Established in 1888 and given its name by the post office.

•**CROSSNORE,** Town; Avery County; Pop. 297; Zip Code 28616; Lat. 36-01-21 N long. 081-55-46 W; The town's name remembers merchant store owner, George Crossnore.

•**DALLAS,** Town; Gaston County; Pop. 3,340; Zip Code 28034; Elev. 784; Lat. 35-18-57 N long. 081-10-32 W; Named in honor of U. S. Vice President George Dalles (1792-1864).

•**DANBURY,** Town; Stokes County Seat; Pop. 140; Zip Code 27016; Elev. 825; Lat. 36-24-32 N long. 080-12-42 W; Descriptively and historically named for the "Danbury" plantation of Governor Alexander Martin.

•**DAVIDSON,** Town; Iredell & Mecklenburg Counties; Pop. 3,241; Zip Code 28036; Lat. 35-29-59 N long. 080-51-07 W; The town is named in honor of Revolutionary War hero General William Lee Davidson.

•**DELLVIEW,** Town; Gaston County; Pop. 7; Incorporated in 1925 by the Dell brothers and named after themselves.

•**DENTON,** Town; Davidson County; Pop. 949; Zip Code 27239; Elev. 698; Lat. 35-37-36 N long. 080-06-44 W; Incorporated in 1907 and named after Denton, Texas.

•**DILLSBORO,** Town; Jackson County; Pop. 179; Zip Code 28725; Elev. 1983; Lat. 35-22-10 N long. 083-14-57 W; William Dills founded the town in 1889. It is named in his honor.

•**DOBSON,** Town; Surry County Seat; Pop. 1,222; Zip Code 27017; Elev. 1259; Lat. 36-23-43 N long. 080-43-15 W; Established in the 1850's and named after a prominent citizen.

•**DORTCHES,** Town; Nash County; Pop. 885; Elev. 194; First settled in 1890 and named for a local family.

•**DOVER,** Town; Craven County; Pop. 600; Zip Code 28526; Elev. 63; Lat. 35-13-09 N long. 077-26-11 W; Named after a local plantation, itself named after Dover, England.

•**DREXEL,** Town; Burke County; Pop. 1,392; Zip Code 28619; Lat. 35-45-38 N long. 081-36-09 W; The town incorporated in 1913 and was named after the well-known Drexel family of Philadelphia.

•**DUBLIN,** Town; Bladen County; Pop. 477; Zip Code 28332; Elev. 123; Lat. 34-39-16 N long. 078-43-26 W; Incorporated in 1913 and named after Dublin, Ireland.

•**DUNN,** City; Harnett County; Pop. 8,962; Zip Code 28334; Lat. 35-18-34 N long. 078-36-30 W; The town's name honors railroad construction engineer Bennett Dunn.

•**DURHAM,** City; Durham County Seat; Pop. 100,831; Zip Code 277+; Elev. 394; Lat. 35-59-47 N long. 078-54-27 W; Established in 1851 and named in honor of Dr. Bartlett Durham.

•**EARL,** Town; Cleveland County; Pop. 206; Zip Code 28038; Lat. 35-11-39 N long. 081-31-58 W; Incorporated in 1889 and named for landowner Abel Earl.

•**EAST ARCADIA,** Town; Bladen County; Pop. 461; Originally Marville, it was later renamed East Arcadia.

•**EAST BEND,** Town; Yadkin County; Pop. 602; Zip Code 27018; Elev. 1069; Lat. 36-14-19 N long. 080-30-19 W; Descriptively named for a bend in the nearby Yadkin River.

•**EAST FLAT ROCK,** (CDP); Henderson County; Pop. 3,365; Zip Code 28726; Elev. 2207; Lat. 35-17-13 N long. 082-24-58 W; The town is named for a nearby open-faced granite quarry.

•**EAST LAURINBURG,** Town; Scotland County; Pop. 536; Named in honor of the McLaurin family who emigrated to the area from Scotland.

•**EAST MARION,** (CDP); McDowell County; Pop. 1,851; Named after Revolutionary War hero General Francis Marion.

•**EAST ROCKINGHAM,** (CDP); Richmond County; Pop. 5,190; The town's name honors Charles Watson-Wentworth, second Marquis of Rockingham, and pro-colonial British statesman.

•**EAST SPENCER,** Town; Rowan County; Pop. 2,150; Zip Code 28039; Elev. 747; Lat. 35-40-40 N long. 080-25-56 W; The town is named after railroad president Samuel Spencer.

•**EASTOVER,** (CDP); Cumberland County; Pop. 1,075; Descriptively named by its early settlers.

•**EDEN,** City; Rockingham County; Pop. 15,672; Zip Code 27288; Elev. 589; Lat. 36-30-07 N long. 079-44-57 W; Founded in 1967 and named for William Byrd's nearby estate, Land of Eden.

•**EDENTON,** Town; Chowan County Seat; Pop. 5,357; Zip Code 27932; Lat. 36-03-42 N long. 076-36-22 W; Edenton's name remembers Governor Charles Eden who ruled in colonial days.

•**ELIZABETH CITY,** City; Pasquotank County; Pop. 14,004; Zip Code 279+; Lat. 36-17-16 N long. 076-13-49 W; The town is named after the wife of landowner Adam Tooley who was the original proprietor.

•**ELIZABETHTOWN,** Town; Bladen County; Pop. 3,551; Zip Code 28337; Elev. 85; Lat. 34-38-00 N long. 078-32-57 W; Settled in the 1770's and named after Queen Elizabeth I.

•**ELK PARK,** Town; Avery County; Pop. 535; Zip Code 28622; Elev. 3182; Lat. 36-09-27 N long. 081-58-55 W; The town's name remembers the elk herds once found in the area.

•**ELKIN,** Town; Surry & Wilkes Counties; Pop. 2,858; Zip Code 28621; Lat. 36-15-15 N long. 080-51-43 W; Incorporated in 1889 and named after the nearby river.

•**ELLENBORO,** Town; Rutherford County; Pop. 560; Zip Code 28040; Elev. 1046; Lat. 35-19-31 N long. 081-45-28 W; Incorporated in 1889 and named for the daughter of a local railroad president.

•**ELLERBE,** Town; Richmond County; Pop. 1,415; Zip Code 28338; Lat. 35-04-07 N long. 079-45-48 W; Incorporated in 1911 and named after local developer W. T. Ellerbee.

•**ELM CITY,** Town; Wilson County; Pop. 1,561; Zip Code 278+; Elev. 143; Lat. 35-48-16 N long. 077-51-48 W; Descriptively named for the many elm trees in the area.

•**ELON COLLEGE,** Town; Alamance County; Pop. 2,873; Zip Code 27244; Elev. 710; Lat. 36-06-06 N long. 079-30-07 W; Elon is Hebrew for oak and descriptively refers to the many oak trees in the area.

•**EMERALD ISLE,** Town; Carteret County; Pop. 865; Descriptively named for its location on the Atlantic Ocean.

•**ENFIELD,** Town; Halifax County; Pop. 2,995; Zip Code 27823; Elev. 113; Lat. 36-10-44 N long. 077-40-08 W; Enfield is named after Enfield, England.

•**ENKA,** (CDP); Buncombe County; Pop. 5,567; Zip Code 28728; Elev. 2059; Lat. 35-32-25 N long. 082-38-21 W; The town is named after the American Enka Corporation which has a textile mill here.

•**ENOCHVILLE,** (CDP); Rowan County; Pop. 2,646; Elev. 847; The town's name comes from the St. Enoch's Evanglical Church.

•**ERWIN,** Town; Harnett County; Pop. 2,828; Zip Code 28339; Lat. 35-19-32 N long. 078-40-28 W; Textile mill operator William Erwin ran a mill here in the 1920's. It is named after him.

•**EUREKA,** Town; Wayne County; Pop. 303; A Greek word meaning "I have found it."

•**EVERETTS,** Town; Martin County; Pop. 213; Zip Code 27825; Elev. 66; Lat. 35-50-00 N long. 077-10-15 W; Incorporated in 1891 and named for the local Everetts family.

•**FAIR BLUFF,** Town; Columbus County; Pop. 1,095; Zip Code 28439; Lat. 34-18-34 N long. 079-01-41 W; Descriptively named for its attractive location.

•**FARMVILLE,** Town; Pitt County; Pop. 4,707; Zip Code 27828; Lat. 35-35-47 N long. 077-35-24 W; Descriptively named for its location in rich farming country.

•**FAYETTEVILLE,** City; Cumberland County Seat; Pop. 59,507; Zip Code 283+; Lat. 35-03-35 N long. 078-52-51 W; The town's name honors the Marquis De Lafayette, French Revolutionary war hero.

•**FLAT ROCK,** (CDP); Surry County; Pop. 1,922; Zip Code 28731; Elev. 2217; Lat. 36-30-21 N long. 080-34-43 W; Descriptively named for the nearby open-faced granite quarry.

•**FOREST CITY,** Town; Rutherford County; Pop. 7,688; Zip Code 28043; Elev. 999; Lat. 35-19-14 N long. 081-51-44 W; Incorporated in 1877 and named in honor of lumber merchant Forest Davis.

•**FOUNTAIN,** Town; Pitt County; Pop. 424; Zip Code 27829; Lat. 35-40-21 N long. 077-38-27 W; Local merchant Robert Fountain had the town named after him.

•**FOUR OAKS,** Town; Johnston County; Pop. 1,049; Zip Code 27524; Elev. 211; Lat. 35-26-42 N long. 078-25-46 W; Descriptively named in 1889 for four oak sprouts growing out of a nearby cut oak stump.

•**FOXFIRE,** Village; Moore County; Pop. 153; Named descriptively by its early settlers.

•**FRANKLIN,** Town; Macon County Seat; Pop. 2,640; Zip Code 28734; Elev. 2113; Lat. 35-10-53 N long. 083-22-39 W; The town is named in honor of Jesse Franklin who was Governor of North Carolina in 1820.

•**FRANKLINTON,** Town; Franklin County; Pop. 1,394; Zip Code 27525; Lat. 36-06-17 N long. 078-27-21 W; The town is named after Revolutionary War statesman Ben Franklin.

•**FRANKLINVILLE,** Town; Randolph County; Pop. 607; Zip Code 27248; Lat. 35-44-39 N long. 079-41-19 W; Franklinville's name honors 1820's governor of North Carolina Jesse Franklin.

•**FREMONT,** Town; Wayne County; Pop. 1,736; Zip Code 27830; Elev. 153; Lat. 35-32-24 N long. 077-55-32 W; Incorporated in 1867 and named in honor of railroad engineer Col. S. L. Fremont.

•**FUQUAY-VARINA,** Town; Wake County; Pop. 3,110; Zip Code 27526; Lat. 35-35-29 N long. 078-48-13 W; The town of Fuquay was named for early settlers. It merged with Varina in 1963 and took its present name.

•**GARDEN CREEK,** (CDP); McDowell County; Pop. 1,161; Elev. 1223; Descriptively named by its early settlers for the garden-like creek running near the town.

•**GARLAND,** Town; Sampson County; Pop. 885; Zip Code 28441; Elev. 137; Lat. 34-47-14 N long. 078-23-39 W; Augustus Garland was Attorney General of the U. S. in 1885. It is named in his honor.

•**GARNER,** Town; Wake County; Pop. 10,073; Zip Code 27529; Elev. 370; Lat. 35-42-13 N long. 078-36-58 W; Incorporated in 1883 and named in honor of H. C. Garner, the town's founder.

•**GARYSBURG,** Town; Northampton County; Pop. 1,434; Zip Code 27831; Lat. 36-26-29 N long. 077-33-47 W; Settled in the early 1800's and named for an early settler.

•**GASTON,** Town; Northampton County; Pop. 883; Zip Code 27832; Elev. 180; Lat. 36-29-51 N long. 077-38-42 W; The town's name remembers Judge William Gaston.

•**GASTONIA,** City; Gaston County Seat; Pop. 47,333; Zip Code 280+; Elev. 816; Lat. 35-16-03 N long. 081-09-41 W; Named in honor of Judge William Gaston who was a member of Congress and a judge of the Supreme Court of North Carolina.

•**GATESVILLE,** Town; Gates County Seat; Pop. 363; Zip Code 27938; Elev. 4.7; Lat. 36-24-24 N long. 076-45-12 W; Gatesville's name honors General Horatio Gates, American victor at the Battle of Saratoga.

•**GIBSON,** Town; Scotland County; Pop. 533; Zip Code 28343; Lat. 34-45-30 N long. 079-36-19 W; Noah Gibson was the town's first postmaster. It is named in his honor.

•**GIBSONVILLE,** Town; Alamance & Guilford Counties; Pop. 2,865; Zip Code 27249; Elev. 720; Lat. 36-06-22 N long. 079-32-20 W; The town is named for pre-Civil War landowner Joseph Gibson.

•**GLEN ALPINE,** Town; Burke County; Pop. 645; Zip Code 28628; Elev. 1206; Lat. 35-43-35 N long. 081-46-40 W; Incorporated in 1883 and named by the railroad.

•**GLEN RAVEN,** (CDP); Alamance County; Pop. 2,755; A descriptive term glen added to that of raven, which recalls an early businessman's fondness for hunting crows.

•**GODWIN,** Town; Cumberland County; Pop. 233; Zip Code 28344; Elev. 155; Lat. 35-13-06 N long. 078-40-44 W; Settler Issac Godwin granted the railroad its right-of-way. It is named in his honor.

•**GOLDSBORO,** City; Wayne County; Pop. 31,871; Zip Code 27530; Lat. 35-21-52 N long. 077-58-02 W; Named in honor of railroad engineer Major Matthew Goldsborough.

•**GOLDSBORO NORTHWEST,** (CDP); Wayne County; Pop. 1,397; The name honors railroad engineer Matthew Goldsborough.

•**GOLDSTON,** Town; Chatham County; Pop. 353; Zip Code 27252; Elev. 424; Lat. 35-35-29 N long. 079-19-38 W; The town was built on land owned by Joseph Goldston. It is named after him.

•**GORMON,** (CDP); Durham County; Pop. 2,662; Named after an early settler.

•**GRAHAM,** City; Alamance County Seat; Pop. 8,674; Zip Code 27253; Lat. 36-04-38 N long. 079-23-50 W; Settled in 1849 and named after Governor William Graham.

•**GRANITE FALLS,** Town; Caldwell County; Pop. 2,580; Zip Code 28630; Lat. 35-47-56 N long. 081-25-39 W; The town is named after adjacent Granaite Falls, a 35-foot waterfall on Gunpowder Creek.

•**GRANITE QUARRY,** Town; Rowan County; Pop. 1,294; Zip Code 28072; Elev. 802; Lat. 35-36-43 N long. 080-26-58 W; Incorporated in 1901 and named for nearby local quarries.

•**GREENSBORO,** City; Guilford County Seat; Pop. 155,642; Zip Code 274+; Lat. 36-03-14 N long. 079-45-07 W; The city's name remembers Revolutionary War hero General Nathaniel Green.

•**GREENVILLE,** City; Pitt County; Pop. 35,740; Zip Code 278+; Lat. 35-36-14 N long. 077-22-31 W; In honor of Revolutionary War General Nathaniel Green.

•**GRIFTON,** Town; Lenoir & Pitt Counties; Pop. 2,179; Zip Code 28530; Lat. 35-22-12 N long. 077-26-22 W; Renamed Grifton in 1889 to honor a local merchant.

•**GRIMESLAND,** Town; Pitt County; Pop. 453; Zip Code 27837; Lat. 35-33-48 N long. 077-11-34 W; Originally Boyd's Ferry, the name was changed in 1887 to honor Confederate General J. B. Grimes.

•**GROVER,** Town; Cleveland County; Pop. 597; Zip Code 28073; Elev. 840; Lat. 35-10-21 N long. 081-27-23 W; The town is named in honor of President Grover Cleveland.

•**HALF MOON,** (CDP); Onslaw County; Pop. 3,592; Elev. 30; The community is named after nearby Half Moon Creek.

•**HALIFAX,** Town; Halifax County Seat; Pop. 253; Zip Code 27839; Elev. 133; Lat. 36-19-33 N long. 077-35-27 W; Incorporated in 1760 and named after George Montagu, second Earl of Halifax.

•**HAMILTON,** Town; Martin County; Pop. 638; Zip Code 27840; Lat. 35-56-41 N long. 077-12-25 W; Incorporated in 1804 and named after Alexander Hamilton.

•**HAMLET,** City; Richmond County; Pop. 4,720; Zip Code 28345; Lat. 34-53-58 N long. 079-41-37 W; Settled in 1875 and given the descriptive name for its size at that time.

•**HARKERS ISLAND,** (CDP); Carteret County; Pop. 1,901; Zip Code 28531; Lat. 34-41-52 N long. 076-33-43 W; Incorporated in 1957 and named after the second owner Ebenezer Harker.

•**HARRELLS,** Town; Duplin & Sampson Counties; Pop. 255; Zip Code 28444; Elev. 88; Lat. 34-44-03 N long. 078-12-00 W; Named in honor of 19th century merchant Abner Harrell.

•**HARRELLSVILLE,** Town; Hertford County; Pop. 151; Zip Code 27942; Elev. 65; Lat. 36-18-10 N long. 076-47-30 W; Originally Bethel the name was changed in 1847 to honor Abner Harrell.

•**HARRISBURG,** Town; Cabarrus County; Pop. 1,433; Zip Code 28075; Lat. 35-19-25 N long. 080-39-01 W; The town is named after a local family.

•**HASSELL,** Town; Martin County; Pop. 109; Zip Code 27841; Elev. 79; Lat. 35-54-27 N long. 077-16-33 W; First settled in the 1870's and named after Baptist Church elder Sylvester Hassell.

•**HAVELOCK,** City; Craven County; Pop. 17,718; Zip Code 285+; Lat. 34-52-41 N long. 076-54-14 W; Named in 1857 in honor of British war hero Sir Henry Havelock.

•**HAW RIVER,** Town; Alamance County; Pop. 1,858; Zip Code 27258; Lat. 36-05-42 N long. 079-21-29 W; The town is named after the river. The river is named for the black haw bushes growing along its banks.

•**HAYESVILLE,** Town; Clay County Seat; Pop. 376; Zip Code 28904; Elev. 1890; Incorporated in 1891 and named after state assemblyman George Hayes.

•**HAYWOOD,** Town; Chatham County; Pop. 190; Founded in 1796 as Lyons, but renamed in 1800 after John Haywood, state treasurer at the time.

•**HAZELWOOD,** Town; Haywood County; Pop. 1,811; Zip Code 28738; Elev. 2724; Lat. 35-32-30 N long. 083-00-10 W; Descriptively named for the many hazelnuts growing in the vicinity.

•**HENDERSON,** City; Vance County Seat; Pop. 13,522; Zip Code 27536; Elev. 509; Lat. 36-19-11 N long. 078-24-03 W; The town's name honors N. C. Supreme Court Chief Justice Leonard Henderson who sat from 1829-1833.

•**HENDERSONVILLE,** City; Henderson County Seat; Pop. 6,862; Zip Code 287+; Elev. 2146; Lat. 35-18-50 N long. 082-28-21 W; Named in honor of Justice Leonard Henderson of the N. C. Supreme Court.

•**HENRIETTA,** (CDP); Rutherford County; Pop. 1,412; Zip Code 28076; Elev. 104; Lat. 35-15-45 N long. 081-47-44 W; Founded in 1887 and named in honor of the mother-in-law of textile mill founder Simpson B. Tanner.

•**HERTFORD,** Town; Perquimans County Seat; Pop. 1,941; Zip Code 279+; Lat. 36-07-35 N. long 076-15-09 W; Incorporated in 1758 and named after Hertford, England.

•**HICKORY,** City; Burke & Catawba Counties; Pop. 20,757; Zip Code 286+; Elev. 1163; Lat. 35-44-20 N long. 081-21-09 W; The town's name remembers a hickory log tavern built at the site in the 1850's.

•**HICKORY NORTH,** (CDP); Catawba County; Pop. 4,322; Named after an 1850's era hickory tavern.

•**HIGH POINT,** City; Davidson, Guilford & Randolph Counties; Pop. 63,380; Zip Code 272+; Elev.939; Lat. 35-50-09 N, long. 079-42-43. The highest point on the North Carolina railroad, this fact named the town.

•**HIGH SHOALS,** City; Gaston & Lincoln Counties; Pop. 586; Zip Code 28077; Elev. 724; Lat. 35-24-09 N long. 081-12-06 W; Settled in 1750 and named for a series of rocky shoals in the river.

•**HIGHLANDS,** Town; Macon County; Pop. 653; Zip Code 28741; Elev. 3835; Lat. 35-02-57 N long. 083-11-50 W; Incorporated in 1879 and named for its elevation.

•**HILDEBRAN,** Town; Burke County; Pop. 628; Zip Code 28637; Elev. 1264; Lat. 35-43-08 N long. 081-25-48 W; Named for J. A. Hildebran, a local lumber merchant, when the town was incorporated in 1899.

•**HILLSBOROUGH,** Town; Orange County; Pop. 3,019; Zip Code 27278; Elev. 624; Lat. 36-04-40 N long. 079-06-36 W; Settled in 1754 and named in honor of Wills Hill, Earl of Hillsborough.

•**HOBGOOD,** Town; Halifax County; Pop. 483; Zip Code 27843; Lat. 36-01-32 N long. 077-23-40 W; Named in honor of educator Franklin Hobgood.

•**HOFFMAN,** Town; Richmond County; Pop. 389; Zip Code 28347; Lat. 35-01-39 N long. 079-33-05 W; Founded in the 1870's and named for railroad president Richard C. Hoffman.

•**HOLDEN BEACH,** Town; Brunswick County; Pop. 232; Named after an early settler and its beach location.

•**HOLLY RIDGE,** Town; Onslow County; Pop. 465; Zip Code 28445; Elev. 50; Lat. 34-25-55 N long. 077-33-59 W; The town is located on a slight ridge, which was once covered with holly trees.

•**HOLLY SPRINGS,** Town; Wake County; Pop. 688; Zip Code 27540; Lat. 35-38-59 N long. 078-50-05 W; Descriptively named for holly trees growing near a local spring.

•**HOLLY VIEW FOREST-HIGHLAND PARK,** (CDP); Surry County; Pop. 1,647; Descriptively named by its developers.

•**HOLLYVILLE,** Village; Pamlico County; Pop. 100; Incorporated in 1907 and named for local trees.

•**HOOKERTON,** Town; Greene County; Pop. 460; Zip Code 28538; Lat. 35-25-19 N long. 077-35-20 W; Incorporated in 1817 on land owned by William Hooker and named after him.

•**HOPE MILLS,** Town; Cumberland County; Pop. 5,412; Zip Code 28348; Elev. 109; Lat. 34-58-26 N long. 078-56-52 W; Originally known as Rockfish, the name was changed in 1891 when the mills were built.

•**HOT SPRINGS,** Town; Madison County; Pop. 678; Zip Code 28743; Elev. 1334; Lat. 35-53-43 N long. 082-49-48 W; The town is named for local thermal springs.

•**JACKSON,** Town; Northampton County Seat; Pop. 720; Zip Code 27845; Lat. 36-23-14 N, long. 077-25-09 W. Named for President Andrew Jackson.

•**JACKSONVILLE,** City; Onslow County Seat; Pop. 17,056; Zip Code 285+. The city is named in honor of President Andrew Jackson.

•**JACKSONVILLE EAST,** (CDP); Onslow County; Pop. 3,700; Zip Code 28540; Elev. 15; ;Named in honor of President Andrew Jackson.

•**JAMES CITY,** (CDP); Craven County; Pop. 2,953; A freeman's camp was here in 1865. The town is named for Horace James, a union chaplain who supervised the camp.

•**JAMESTOWN,** Town; Guilford County; Pop. 2,148; Zip Code 27282; Elev. 775; Lat. 35-52-32 N long. 079-37-26 W; Founded in 1770 and named in honor of Quaker settler James Mendenhall.

•**JAMESVILLE,** Town; Martin County; Pop. 604; Zip Code 27846; Lat. 35-48-37 N long. 076-53-54 W; Originally Jamestown, after the Virginia city, the name was later changed to Jamesville.

•**JEFFERSON,** Town; Ashe County Seat; Pop. 1,086; Zip Code 28640; Lat. 36-25-11 N long. 081-28-25 W; Established in 1803 and named after President Thomas Jefferson.

•**JENKINS HEIGHTS,** (CDP); Gaston County; Pop. 1,156; Named for its location and after an early settler.

•**JONESVILLE,** Town; Yadkin County; Pop. 1,752; Zip Code 28642; Elev. 913; Lat. 36-13-50 N long. 080-50-12 W; Founded in 1811 and named after local settler Hardy Jones.

•**KANNAPOLIS,** (CDP); Cabarrus & Rowan Counties; Pop. 34,564; Zip Code 280+; Lat. 35-30-30 N long. 080-37-53 W; Established in 1905 and named after the Cannon Mills textile family.

•**KELFORD,** Town; Bertie County; Pop. 254; Zip Code 27847; Elev. 92; Lat. 36-10-53 N long. 077-13-25 W; Incorporated in 1893 and named after a ford in Scotland.

•**KENANSVILLE,** Town; Duplin County Seat; Pop. 931; Zip Code 28349; Lat. 34-57-47 N long. 077-57-50 W; Incorporated in 1852 and named in honor of Revolutionary War officer General James Kenan.

•**KENLY,** Town; Johnston & Wilson Counties; Pop. 1,433; Zip Code 27542; Lat. 35-35-34 N long. 078-07-26 W; Settled in the 1870's and named for railroad official J. I. Kenly.

•**KERNERSVILLE,** Town; Forsyth County; Pop. 6,802; Zip Code 272+; Elev. 1023; Lat. 36-07-23 N long. 080-09-33 W; Settled in 1756 and named after landowner Joseph Kerner.

•**KILL DEVIL HILLS,** Town; Dare County; Pop. 1,796; Zip Code 27948; Lat. 36-01-14 N long. 075-40-06 W; Incorporated in 1953 and given a legendary name that refers to Carolina Rum, strong enough to "kill the devil."

359

•**KING**, (CDP); Stokes County; Pop. 8,757; Zip Code 27021; Lat. 36-16-54 N long. 080-21-22 W; Named for an early settler, Oscar King.

•**KINGS GRANT**, (CDP); New Hanover County; Pop. 6,562; A descriptively historical name.

•**KINGS MOUNTAIN**, City; Cleveland & Gaston Counties; Pop. 9,080; Zip Code 28086; Elev. 1003; Lat. 35-14-45 N long. 081-19-56 W; Descriptively named after a nearby small mountain range.

•**KINSTON**, City; Lenoir County Seat; Pop. 25,234; Zip Code 285+; Elev. 44; Lat. 35-16-05 N long. 077-34-42 W; Originally Kingston, the name was changed after the Revolution to Kinston.

•**KITTRELL**, Town; Vance County; Pop. 225; Zip Code 27544; Lat. 36-13-06 N long. 078-26-27 W; Incorporated in 1885 and named in honor of landowner George Kittrell.

•**KNIGHTDALE**, Town; Wake County; Pop. 985; Zip Code 27545; Lat. 35-47-20 N long. 078-28-47 W; Founded in 1927 and named for H. H. Knight who chartered the town.

•**KURE BEACH**, Town; New Hanover County; Pop. 611; Zip Code 28449; Lat. 34-00-05 N long. 077-55-07 W; The Kure family came here in 1867. The town is named after them.

•**LA GRANGE**, Town; Lenoir County; Pop. 3,147; Zip Code 28551; Elev. 113; Lat. 35-18-16 N long. 077-47-27 W; Named after Lafayette's estate near Paris.

•**LAKE LURE**, Town; Rutherford County; Pop. 488; Zip Code 28746; Lat. 35-26-07 N long. 082-12-52 W; Descriptively named for the "lure fishing."

•**LAKE WACCAMAW**, Town; Columbus County; Pop. 1,133; Zip Code 28450; Elev. 63; Lat. 34-18-46 N long. 078-31-47 W; Both the town and lake are named for an 18th century tribe of Indians.

•**LANDIS**, Town; Rowan County; Pop. 2,092; Zip Code 28088; Lat. 35-33-16 N long. 080-36-11 W; Incorporated in 1901 and named after Judge Kenesaw Mountain Landis.

•**LANSING**, Town; Ashe County; Pop. 194; Zip Code 28643; Elev. 2699; Lat. 36-29-43 N long. 081-30-27 W; Named for an early settler.

•**LASKER**, Town; Northampton County; Pop. 96; Zip Code 27848; Lat. 36-20-53 N long. 077-18-21 W; Incorporated in 1895 and named after Hezekiah Lasker, a railroad conductor.

•**LATTIMORE**, Town; Cleveland County; Pop. 237; Zip Code 28089; Elev. 925; Lat. 35-19-00 N long. 081-39-38 W; Settled in 1880 and named after first postmaster Audley Lattimore.

•**LAUREL HILL**, (CDP); Scotland County; Pop. 2,314; Zip Code 28351; Lat. 34-48-31 N long. 079-32-22 W; Founded in the late 1700's and named for the laurel growing on the hill.

•**LAUREL PARK**, Town; Henderson County; Pop. 764; Incorporated in 1925 and named for the laurel growing in the park like-setting.

•**LAURINBURG**, City; Scotland County Seat; Pop. 11,480; Zip Code 28352; Elev. 227; Lat. 34-46-15 N long. 079-27-35 W; Named for the McLaurin family who were early Scotch settlers.

•**LAWNDALE**, Town; Cleveland County; Pop. 469; Zip Code 28090; Elev. 817; Lat. 35-24-47 N long. 081-33-44 W; Incorporated in 1903 and named after the green lawns of a prominent citizen.

•**LEGGETT**, Town; Edgecombe County; Pop. 99; Elev. 63; Founded in 1895 and named for a local settler.

•**LENOIR**, City; Caldwell County Seat; Pop. 13,748; Zip Code 286+; Elev. 1182; Established in 1841 and named in honor of Revolutionary War hero, General William Lenoir.

•**LEWISTON**, Town; Bertie County; Pop. 459; Elev. 77; Incorporated in 1881 and named after the Lewis family.

•**LEWISVILLE**, (CDP); Forsyth County; Pop. 4,547; Zip Code 27023; Elev. 973; Lat. 36-05-57 N long. 080-25-08 W; The city is named in honor of early settler Lewis Lagenauer.

•**LEXINGTON**, City; Davidson County; Pop. 15,711; Zip Code 272+; Elev. 809; Lat. 35-48-57 N long. 080-15-26 W; Incorporated in 1827 and named after the Revolutionary War Battle of Lexington.

•**LIBERTY**, Town; Randolph County; Pop. 1,997; Zip Code 27298; Elev. 1651; Lat. 35-51-14 N long. 079-34-11 W; The town is named after an erly 1800's plantation.

•**LILESVILLE**, Town; Anson County; Pop. 588; Zip Code 28091; Lat. 34-58-03 N long. 079-59-15 W; Settled in the 1820's and named for Nelson Liles, a local merchant.

•**LILLINGTON**, Town; Harnett County Seat; Pop. 1,948; Zip Code 27546; Lat. 35-24-00 N long. 078-48-54 W; Named in honor of Revolutionary War patriot Alexander Lillington.

•**LINCOLNTON**, Town; Lincoln County Seat; Pop. 4,879; Zip Code 280+; Lat. 35-28-06 N long. 081-14-42 W; Incorporated in 1786 and named after Revolutionary War General, Benjamin Lincoln.

•**LINDEN**, Town; Cumberland County; Pop. 365; Zip Code 28356; Lat. 35-15-08 N long. 078-44-51 W; Settled in the early 1800's and named for nearby linden trees.

•**LINVILLE**, Town; Avery", "244; Zip Code 28646; Lat. 36-04-16 N long. 081-52-10 W; The town is named for its location on the Linville River.

•**LITTLETON**, Town; Halifax County; Pop. 820; Zip Code 27850; Elev. 376; Lat. 36-25-54 N long. 077-54-41 W; Named after state Senator William Little who served from 1804 to 1806.

•**LOCUST**, City; Stanly County; Pop. 1,590; Zip Code 28097; Elev. 742; Lat. 35-15-41 N long. 080-25-34 W; Incorporated in 1905 and named for a large nearby locust tree.

•**LONG BEACH**, Town; Brunswick County; Pop. 1,844; Descriptively named for its location along the Atlantic Ocean.

•**LONGVIEW**, Town; Burke & Catawba Counties; Pop. 3,587; Zip Code 28601; Elev. 23; Originally Penelope, the name was changed in 1907 to the descriptive Longview.

•**LOUISBURG**, Town; Franklin County Seat; Pop. 3,238; Zip Code 27549; Elev. 224; Lat. 36-08-28 N long. 078-12-12 W; Founded in 1779 and named after French King Louis 16th.

•**LOVE VALLEY**, Town; Iredell County; Pop. 55; Probably named after an early settler.

•**LOWELL**, Town; Gaston County; Pop. 2,917; Zip Code 28098; Elev. 770; Lat. 35-15-59 N long. 081-06-41 W; Incorporated in 1879 and named after Lowell, Massachusetts.

•**LUCAMA**, Town; Wilson County; Pop. 1,070; Zip Code 27851; Elev. 134; Lat. 35-38-41 N long. 078-00-38 W; Incorporated in 1889 and named by combining the first two letters of the three Borden sisters: Lucy, Carrie, and Mary.

•**LUMBER BRIDGE,** Town; Robeson County; Pop. 171; Zip Code 28357; Elev. 193; Lat. 34-53-17 N long. 079-04-25 W; Incorporated in 1891 and named after a local lumber bridge.

•**LUMBERTON,** City; Robeson County Seat; Pop. 18,241; Zip Code 283+; Elev. 137; Lat. 34-35-51 N long. 079-00-35 W; The town is named after its position on the Lumber River.

•**MACCLESFIELD,** Town; Edgecombe County; Pop. 504; Zip Code 27852; Lat. 35-45-11 N long. 077-40-13 W; Incorporated in 1901 and named after Macclesfield, England.

•**MACON,** Town; Warren County; Pop. 153; Zip Code 27551; Elev. 385; Lat. 36-26-20 N long. 078-05-02 W; Named after Nathaniel Macon, member of Congress from 1815 to 1828.

•**MADISON,** Town; Rockingham County; Pop. 2,806; Zip Code 27025; Elev. 574; Lat. 36-23-12 N long. 079-58-06 W; Settled in 1818 and named after President James Madison.

•**MAGGIE VALLEY,** Town; Haywood County; Pop. 202; Zip Code 28751; Lat. 35-31-01 N long. 083-05-59 W; Established in 1909 and named after the daughter of the postmaster.

•**MAGNOLIA,** Town; Duplin County; Pop. 592; Zip Code 28453; Lat. 34-53-46 N long. 078-03-20 W; Descriptively named in 1857 for the many magnolia trees nearby.

•**MAIDEN,** Town; Catawba & Lincoln Counties; Pop. 2,574; Zip Code 28650; Elev. 900; Lat. 35-35-08 N long. 081-11-10 W; The town is named for the profusion of maidencane growing nearby when it was settled.

•**MANTEO,** Town; Dare County Seat; Pop. 902; Zip Code 27954; Elev. 5; Lat. 35-54-22 N long. 075-40-13 W; Incorporated in 1899 and named for the Indian Chief Manteo, who was taken by Sir Walter Raleigh to England in 1584.

•**MAR-MAC,** (CDP); Wayne County; Pop. 3,366; The origin of the town's name is uncertain.

•**MARION,** City; McDowell County Seat; Pop. 3,684; Zip Code 28752; Elev. 1395; Lat. 35-40-48 N long. 082-00-16 W; Named in honor of Revolutionary War leader, General Francis Marion.

•**MARS HILL,** Town; Madison County; Pop. 2,126; Zip Code 28754; Elev. 2325; Lat. 35-49-38 N long. 082-33-00 W; The town is named after a hill in Athens, Greece.

•**MARSHALL,** Town; Madison County Seat; Pop. 809; Zip Code 28753; Lat. 35-47-50 N long. 082-41-02 W; Named in honor of Chief Justice of the U. S. Supreme Court John Marshall.

•**MARSHVILLE,** Town; Union County; Pop. 2,011; Zip Code 28103; Elev. 555; Lat. 34-59-22 N long. 080-21-55 W; Incorporated in 1877 and named for the Marsh family who donated land for a school to the community.

•**MARVEN,** Town; Anson County; Pop. 765; Named after a local family.

•**MASONBORO,** (CDP); New Hanover County; Pop. 3,881; Settlea in the late 1700's and named after a number of masons who settled here.

•**MATTHEWS,** Town; Mecklenburg County; Pop. 1,648; Zip Code 281+; Lat. 35-07-06 N long. 080-43-26 W; Incorporated in 1879 and named after an official of the Central Carolina Railroad.

•**MAXTON,** Town; Robeson & Scotland Counties; Pop. 2,711; Zip Code 28364; Lat. 34-44-12 N long. 079-20-52 W; Originally "Shoe Heel," the name was later changed to note the many

families of Scottish descent living in the area whose names began with Mc or Mac.

•**MAYODAN,** Town; Rockingham County; Pop. 2,627; Zip Code 27027; Lat. 36-24-42 N long. 079-58-15 W; The town was incorporated in 1899 and named by combining the first letters of the nearby Mayo and Dan Rivers.

•**MAYSVILLE,** Town; Jones County; Pop. 877; Zip Code 28555; Elev. 40; Lat. 34-54-21 N long. 077-13-41 W; Known as "Young's Cross Roads," the name was later changed after a local resident.

•**MCADENVILLE,** Town; Gaston County; Pop. 947; Zip Code 28101; Lat. 35-15-24 N long. 081-04-51 W; Named after Rufus McAden, speaker of the N. C. House of Representatives in 1866.

•**MCDONALD,** Town; Robeson County; Pop. 117; Turpentine distiller Peter McDonald ran a business here which attracted a railroad station. It is named after him.

•**MCFARLAN,** Town; Anson County; Pop. 133; Zip Code 28102; Lat. 34-48-50 N long. 079-58-19 W; The town is named after Cheraw and Salisbury Railroad President Alan McFarland.

•**MCLEANSVILLE,** (CDP); Guilford County; Pop. 1,176; Zip Code 27301; Elev. 763; Lat. 36-06-38 N long. 079-52-48 W; A Scotch family from Ulster settled in this area and left their name on the town.

•**MEBANE,** Town; Alamance & Orange Counties; Pop. 2,782; Zip Code 27302; Lat. 36-05-38 N long. 079-15-48 W; Incorporated in 1880 and named for a local tavern then over a century old.

•**MONROE,** City; Union County Seat; Pop. 12,639; Zip Code 28110; Elev. 595; Lat. 34-59-08 N long. 080-32-45 W; Incorporated in 1844 and named for President James Monroe.

•**MONTREAT,** Town; Buncombe County; Pop. 741; Zip Code 28757; Incorporated in 1967 and named by condensing "mountain retreat."

•**MOORESBORO,** City; Cleveland County; Pop. 405; Zip Code 28114; Elev. 902; Lat. 35-17-49 N long. 081-41-42 W; First settled in the 1780's and named after Lem Moore, an early settler.

•**MOORESVILLE,** Town; Iredell County; Pop. 8,575; Zip Code 28115; Elev. 911; Lat. 35-35-04 N long. 080-48-34 W; The town is named after 1857 Mayor John F. Moore.

•**MORAVIAN FALLS,** (CDP); Wilkes County; Pop. 1,552; Zip Code 28654; Elev. 1192; Lat. 36-05-45 N long. 081-10-56 W; A natural waterfall occurs here, so named because of its discovery in 1752 by Moravian surveyors.

•**MOREHEAD CITY,** Town; Carteret County; Pop. 4,359; Zip Code 28557; Elev. 16; Lat. 34-42-04 N long. 076-49-45 W; Incorporated in 1861 and named for John Morehead, onetime governor of South Carolina.

•**MORGANTON,** City; Burke County; Pop. 13,763; Zip Code 28655; Lat. 35-44-18 N long. 081-41-32 W; Established in the 1770's and named in honor of Revolutionary War leader General Daniel Morgan.

•**MORGANTOWN,** (CDP); Almance County; Pop. 1,988; Named in honor of Revolutionary War General, Daniel Morgan.

•**MORRISVILLE,** Town; Wake County; Pop. 251; Zip Code 27560; Lat. 35-49-26 N long. 078-49-37 W; First settled in 1840 and named after local landowner Jerry Morris.

•MOUNT AIRY, City; Surry County; Pop. 6,862; Zip Code 270+; Elev. 1104; Lat. 36-30-00 N long. 080-35-26 W; Incorporated in 1869 and named after a local mountain.

•MOUNT GILEAD, Town; Montgomery County; Pop. 1,423; Zip Code 27306; Lat. 35-12-52 N long. 079-59-56 W; Settled in 1830 and named for the Biblical mountain.

•MOUNT HOLLY, City; Gaston County; Pop. 4,530; Zip Code 28120; Elev. 632; Lat. 35-17-45 N long. 081-01-24 W; Settled around 1800 and named for the town in New Jersey.

•MOUNT OLIVE, Town; Duplin & Wayne Counties; Pop. 4,876; Zip Code 28365; Elev. 112; Lat. 35-11-27 N long. 078-03-46 W; Incorporated in 1870 and named after the Biblical Mount of Olives.

•MOUNT PLEASANT, Town; Cabarrus County; Pop. 1,210; Zip Code 28124; Elev. 629; Lat. 35-24-08 N long. 080-25-53 W; Settled in 1750 and named for its pleasant elevated location.

•MOUNTAIN HOME, (CDP); Henderson County; Pop. 1,387; Zip Code 28758; A descriptive name given by its first settlers.

•MULBERRY, (CDP); Wilkes County; Pop. 2,270; Descriptively named for the local vegetation.

•MURFREESBORO, Town; Hertford County; Pop. 3,007; Zip Code 27855; Lat. 36-26-26 N long. 077-06-08 W; Named after William Murfree, a colonial and Revolutionary War leader.

•MURPHY, Town; Cherokee County Seat; Pop. 2,070; Zip Code 28906; Elev. 1583; Incorporated in 1851 and named for political leader Archibald Murphey.

•MYRTLE GROVE, (CDP); New Hanover County; Pop. 2,552; Elev. 27; Descriptively named for the myrtle groves in the area.

•NAGS HEAD, Town; Dare County; Pop. 1,020; Zip Code 27959; Lat. 35-58-13 N long. 075-38-21 W; Named according to a popular legend where norses (or "nags") carrying laterns were used to lure ships to wreck on the beach and subsquent pillage.

•NASHVILLE, Town; Nash County Seat; Pop. 2,678; Zip Code 27856; Lat. 35-58-09 N long. 077-58-00 W; The town's name honors General Francis Nash, a brilliant American officer who was killed during the Revolutionary War.

•NAVASSA, Town; Brunswick County; Pop. 439; The origin of the town's name is uncertain.

•NEW BERN, City; Craven County; Pop. 14,557; Zip Code 285+; Elev. 15; Lat. 35-05-39 N long. 077-04-36 W; Settled in 1710 and named after Bern, Switzerland.

•NEW HOPE, (CDP); Wayne County; Pop. 6,685; Named by the town's settlers for their hopes for the community.

•NEW LONDON, Town; Stanly County; Pop. 454; Zip Code 28127; Elev. 697; Lat. 35-26-35 N long. 080-13-13 W; Incorporated in 1891 and named after the city in Connecticut.

•NEW RIVER STATION, (CDP); Onslow County; Pop. 5,401; The town is named for its proximity to the New River.

•NEWLAND, Town; Avery County; Pop. 722; Zip Code 28657; Elev. 3621; Lat. 36-05-14 N long. 081-55-34 W; The town is named for William C. Newland, North Carolina's Lieutenant Governor in 1909.

•NEWPORT, Town; Carteret County; Pop. 1,883; Zip Code 28570; Elev. 21; Lat. 34-48-03 N long. 076-52-21 W; Incorporated in 1866 and named for Newport, Rhode Island.

•NEWTON, City; Catawba County Seat; Pop. 7,624; Zip Code 28658; Elev. 969; Lat. 081-13-09 W; Named in honor of Issac Newton Wilson, son of the assembly member who introduced the bill to found the county.

•NEWTON GROVE, Town; Sampson County; Pop. 564; Zip Code 28366; Elev. 185; Lat. 35-15-01 N long. 078-21-24 W; Incorporated in 1879 and named for Sir Issac Newton.

•NORLINA, Town; Warren County; Pop. 901; Zip Code 27563; Elev. 437; Lat. 36-26-41 N long. 078-11-40 W; The name is a composite created by adding North and Carolina together.

•NORMAN, Town; Richmond County; Pop. 252; Zip Code 28367; Lat. 35-10-14 N long. 079-43-19 W; Founded in 1910 and named after local lumber merchant Flim Norman.

•NORTH BELMONT, (CDP); Gaston County; Pop. 10,762; Elev. 728; The town is named after New York City financier August Belmont.

•NORTH CONCORD, (CDP); Cabarrus County; Pop. 2,095; The area was settled around 1800 and named for the peaceful resolution of a dispute about the town's location.

•NORTH HENDERSON, (CDP); Vance County; Pop. 1,832; Named in honor of North Carolina Supreme Court Justice Leonard Henderson (1773-1833).

•NORTH WILKESBORO, Town; Wilkes County; Pop. 3,260; Zip Code 286+; Elev. 1016; ;Lat. 36-10-02 N long. 081-07-57 W; Named in honor of English political leader John Wilkes who supported the colonies during the pre-revolution era.

•NORWOOD, Town; Stanly County; Pop. 1,818; Zip Code 28128; Elev. 813; Lat. 35-13-30 N long. 080-07-00 W; Incorporated in 1881 and named for the first postmaster William Norwood.

•OAK CITY, Town; Martin County; Pop. 475; Zip Code 27857; Elev. 84; Lat. 35-57-36 N long. 077-18-22 W; Founded as Conoho in 1895, but changed to Oak City in 1905.

•OAKBORO, Town; Stanly County; Pop. 587; Zip Code 28129; Lat. 35-13-22 N long. 080-19-28 W; Incorporated in 1915 and descriptiveluy named by its settlers.

•OCEAN ISLE BEACH, Town; Brunswick County; Pop. 143; Descriptively named for its location on the Atlantic Ocean.

•OLD FORT, Town; McDowell County; Pop. 752; Zip Code 28762; Elev. 1438; Once the site of a fort to protect the settlers from the Cherokee Indians, the name is derived from this 1770's outpost.

•ORIENTAL, Town; Pamlico County; Pop. 536; Zip Code 28571; Elev. 10; Founded in 1870 and named after the federal ship Oriental which had sunk nearby in 1862.

•ORRUM, Town; Robeson County; Pop. 167; Zip Code 28369; Lat. 34-27-47 N long. 079-00-25 W; Incorporated in 1903, the first name choice was Orton, but this was in use, so the sound-alike Orrum became the name.

•OXFORD, City; Granville County Seat; Pop. 7,603; Zip Code 27565; Lat. 36-18-20 N long. 078-35-12 W; First incorporated in 1816 and named after a local large plantation called "Oxford."

•**PANTEGO**, Town; Beaufort County; Pop. 185; Zip Code 27860; Elev. 7; Lat. 35-35-25 N long. 076-39-40 W; The town is named for its location on Pantego Creek.

•**PARKTON**, Town; Robeson County; Pop. 564; Zip Code 28371; Elev. 186; Lat. 34-54-10 N long. 079-00-41 W; Settled in the 1880's and descriptively named the area's use by farmers to "park" their teams while waiting to take the train.

•**PARKWOOD**, (CDP); Durham County; Pop. 3,420; In 1953 the community of Hallison changed its name for that of nearby deserted Parkwood.

•**PARMELE**, Town; Martin County; Pop. 484; Zip Code 27861; Elev. 74; Lat. 35-49-02 N long. 077-18-40 W; Incorporated in 1893 and named for the Parmele-Eccleston Lumber Co.

•**PATTERSON SPRINGS**, Town; Cleveland County; Pop. 731; Zip Code 28661; Lat. 36-00-00 N long. 081-33-49 W; Settled in the 1880's and named for an early settler Arthur Patterson.

•**PEACHLAND**, Town; Anson County; Pop. 506; Zip Code 28133; Elev. 446; Lat. 34-59-44 N long. 080-15-48 W; Incorporated in 1895 and named for a large peach orchard nearby.

•**PEMBROKE**, Town; Robeson County; Pop. 2,698; Zip Code 28372; Elev. 172; Lat. 34-40-50 N long. 079-11-29 W; The town's name honors railroad official Pembroke Jones.

•**PENELOPE**, (CDP); Burke County; Pop. 1,348; Named after the wife of an early settler.

•**PHILLIPSVILLE**, (CDP); Haywood County; Pop. 1,642; The town is named for an early settler.

•**PIKEVILLE**, Town; Wayne County; Pop. 662; Zip Code 27863; Elev. 142; Lat. 35-29-46 N long. 077-59-02 W; Named for Nathan Pike, the second owner of the townsite land.

•**PILOT MOUNTAIN**, Town; Surry County; Pop. 1,090; Zip Code 27041; Elev. 1152; Lat. 36-23-03 N long. 080-28-04 W; Standing 1500 feet above the surrounding countryside, it has served as a landmark, or pilot, for the Indians and settlers who followed.

•**PINE KNOLL SHORES**, Town; Carteret County; Pop. 646; A descriptive name given by the town's founders.

•**PINE LEVEL**, Town; Johnston County; Pop. 953; Zip Code 27568; Elev. 52; Lat. 35-30-41 N long. 078-14-43 W; Incorporated in 1874 and descriptively named for the level pine forests in the area.

•**PINE VALLEY**, (CDP); New Hanover County; Pop. 3,438; The town is named for its geographic site and the forest cover originally blanketing it.

•**PINEBLUFF**, Town; Moore County; Pop. 935; Zip Code 28373; Lat. 35-06-25 N long. 079-28-13 W; Incorporated in 1899 and named for the longleaf pine in the area.

•**PINEHURST**, (CDP); Moore County; Pop. 3,421; Zip Code 28374; Lat. 35-11-57 N long. 079-28-08 W; The town is named for its location in a pine forest.

•**PINETOPS**, Town; Edgecombe County; Pop. 1,465; Zip Code 27864; Lat. 35-47-20 N long. 077-38-16 W; Settled around 1900 and named for the pine forests in the area.

•**PINEVILLE**, Town; Mecklenburg County; Pop. 1,525; Zip Code 28134; Lat. 35-05-00 N long. 080-53-25 W; Named for its location among pine forests.

•**PINEY GREEN-WHITE OAK,** (CDP); Onslow County; Pop. 6,058; Elev. 41; The town is named after an 18th century plantation.

•**PINK HILL**, Town; Lenoir County; Pop. 644; Zip Code 28572; Lat. 35-03-17 N long. 077-44-42 W; The town is named after a colonial-era plantation.

•**PISGAH FOREST**, (CDP); Transylvania County; Pop. 1,899; Zip Code 28768; The name Pisgah is probably of Indian origin, bu its meaning is uncertain.

•**PITTSBORO**, Town; Chatham County; Pop. 1,332; Zip Code 27228; Lat. 35-46-59 N long. 079-08-28 W; The town's name remembers William Pitt, British statesman, who defended American rights in the years before the Revolution.

•**PLEASANT GARDEN**, (CDP); Guilford County; Pop. 1,991; Zip Code 27313; Lat. 35-57-32 N long. 079-45-49 W; Descriptively named for the area's pleasant surroundings.

•**PLEASANT HILL**, (CDP); Wilkes County; Pop. 1,278; Zip Code 27866; Lat. 36-32-00 N long. 077-32-12 W; Descriptively named for the area's ideal environment.

•**PLYMOUTH**, Town; Washington County Seat; Pop. 4,571; Zip Code 27962; Elev. 6; Lat. 35-51-43 N long. 076-44-49 W; Incorporated in 1807 and named for Plymouth, Massachusetts.

•**POLKTON**, Town; Anson County; Pop. 762; Zip Code 28135; Elev. 305; Lat. 35-00-14 N long. 080-12-09 W; Named in honor of Leonidas Polk, a nineteenth century agricultural leader.

•**POLKVILLE**, City; Cleveland County; Pop. 528; Zip Code 28136; Elev. 1079; Lat. 35-25-18 N long. 081-38-36 W; Named after an early settler.

•**POLLOCKSVILLE**, Town; Jones County; Pop. 318; Zip Code 28573; Elev. 23; Lat. 35-00-18 N long. 077-13-13 W; Founded in the 1770's and named after a local settler.

•**POPLAR TENT**, (CDP); Cabarrus County; Pop. 2,764; The community is named for its association with large groves of poplar trees.

•**POWELLSVILLE**, Town; Bertie County; Pop. 320; Zip Code 27967; Lat. 36-13-32 N long. 076-55-56 W; Incorporated in 1887 and named for a local family.

•**PRINCETON**, Town; Johnston County; Pop. 1,034; Zip Code 27569; Elev. 152; Lat. 35-27-59 N long. 078-09-32 W; Originally Boon Hill, the name was changed to Princeton in 1873.

•**PRINCEVILLE**, Town; Edgecombe County; Pop. 1,508; The town was incorporated in 1885 and named after Turner Prince, a local resident.

•**PROCTORVILLE**, Town; Robeson County; Pop. 205; Zip Code 28375; Elev. 120; Lat. 34-28-21 N long. 079-01-58 W; The town's name honors Edward Proctor, Jr. who helped promote the Raleigh and Charleston Railroad.

•**RAEFORD**, City; Hoke County Seat; Pop. 3,630; Zip Code 283+; Lat. 35-03-18 N long. 079-20-47 W; Incorporated in 1901 and named by combining the last two syllables of the town's founders: MacRae and Williford.

•**RALEIGH**, City; State Capital; Wake County Seat; Pop. 150,255; Zip Code 276+; Lat. 35-47-28 N long. 078-39-54 W; Settled in the late 1700's and named for Sir Walter Raleigh.

•**RAMSEUR,** Town; Randolph County; Pop. 1,162; Zip Code 27316; Lat. 35-43-47 N long. 079-39-15 W; Incorporated in 1895 and named in honor of Confederate Major General Stephen D. Ramseur.

•**RANDLEMAN,** City; Randolph County; Pop. 2,156; Zip Code 27317; Lat. 35-49-05 N long. 079-48-04 W; First settled in the early 1800's as Dicks, the name was later changed to Randleman in honor of a local mill owner.

•**RAYNHAM,** Town; Robeson County; Pop. 83; Settled in 1884 and named after a parish in Norfolk, England.

•**RED OAK,** Town; Nash County; Pop. 314; Zip Code 27868; Lat. 36-02-12 N long. 077-54-17 W; The town was settled in the 1880's and named for a grove of red oaks on the site.

•**RED SPRINGS,** Town; Robeson County; Pop. 3,607; Zip Code 28377; Lat. 34-48-46 N long. 079-11-03 W; Local spring water has a reddish tint due to iron oxides in the water. This condition named the town.

•**RICH SQUARE,** Town; Northampton County; Pop. 1,057; Zip Code 27869; Lat. 36-16-24 N long. 077-17-18 W; Settled in 1750 and named for an old map description which referred to the soil's fertility as the "rich square."

•**RICHFIELD,** Town; Stanly County; Pop. 373; Zip Code 28137; Elev. 661; Lat. 35-28-14 N long. 080-15-46 W; Named for the local Ritchie family.

•**RICHLANDS,** Town; Onslow County; Pop. 825; Zip Code 28574; Lat. 34-53-55 N long. 077-32-43 W; Descriptively named for the area's fertility.

•**ROANOKE RAPIDS,** City; Halifax County; Pop. 14,702; Descriptively named for its location at a rapids on the Roanoke River.

•**ROBBINS,** City; Moore County; Pop. 1,256; Zip Code 27325; Elev. 415; Lat. 35-26-00 N long. 079-34-41 W; Originally Mechanicsville, the name was changed in 1943 to honor local textile mill owner Karl Robbins.

•**ROBBINSVILLE,** Town; Graham County Seat; Pop. 1,370; Zip Code 28771; Elev. 2064; The town was established in 1872 and named after the local Robbins family.

•**ROBERSONVILLE,** Town; Martin County; Pop. 1,981; Zip Code 27871; Lat. 35-49-20 N long. 077-15-14 W; Incorporated in 1870 and named in honor of Confederate Civil War veteran Henry Roberson.

•**ROCKINGHAM,** City; Richmond%+_","8,300","0",""","",", Zip Code 28379; Elev. 211; Lat. 34-55-38 N long. 079-46-01 W; Named in honor of Charles Watson-Wentworth, 2nd marquis of Rockingham, British statesman who backed American Independence.

•**ROCKWELL,** Town; Rowan County; Pop. 1,339; Zip Code 28138; Elev. 786; Lat. 35-33-00 N long. 080-24-29 W; Descriptively named for the good water available from a nearby rockwell.

•**ROCKY MOUNT,** City; Edgecombe & Nash Counties; Pop. 41,283; Zip Code 2780+; Lat. 35-57-30 N long. 077-47-55 W; The city is named after rocky ledges near the adjacent Tar River.

•**ROLESVILLE,** Town; Wake County; Pop. 381; Zip Code 27571; Elev. 442; Lat. 35-55-25 N long. 078-27-27 W; Incorporated in 1837 and named after an early settler, William Roles.

•**RONDA,** Town; Wilkes County; Pop. 457; Zip Code 28670; Elev. 935; Lat. 36-13-19 N long. 080-56-32 W; The town was incorporated in 1907 and given a shortened name version of a local estate "roundabout."

•**ROPER,** Town; Washington County; Pop. 795; Zip Code 27970; Lat. 35-52-30 N long. 076-36-24 W; First settled in 1706 as Lees Mills, the name was changed in 1884 for lumber businessman John L. Roper.

•**ROSE HILL,** Town; Duplin County; Pop. 1,508; Zip Code 28458; Elev. 94; Lat. 34-49-33 N long. 078-01-46 W; the town is named for the many wild roses growing in the area.

•**ROSEBORO,** Town; Sampson County Seat; Pop. 1,227; Zip Code 28382; Elev. 137; Lat. 34-57-06 N long. 078-30-39 W; Incorporated in 1891 and named in honor of railroad official George Rose.

•**ROSEWOOD,** (CDP); Wayne County; Pop. 4,003; Elev. 128; Descriptively named for the many wild roses in the area.

•**ROSMAN,** Town; Transylvania County; Pop. 512; Zip Code 28772; The town was named by combining the names of businessmen Rosenthal and Ormansky.

•**ROWLAND,** Town; Robeson County; Pop. 1,841; Zip Code 28383; Elev. 151; Lat. 34-32-07 N long. 079-17-28 W; Incorporated in 1889 and named after Confederate Officer Colonel Alfred Rowland.

•**ROXBORO,** City; Person County; Pop. 7,532; Zip Code 27573; Lat. 36-23-40 N long. 078-59-01 W; Settled in the 1790's and named for Roxburgh, Scotland.

•**ROXOBEL,** Town; Bertie County; Pop. 278; Zip Code 27872; Lat. 36-12-07 N long. 077-14-28 W; Founded in 1800 and later named after a popular novel Roxobel.

•**RURAL HALL,** Town; Forsyth County; Pop. 1,336; Zip Code 27045; Elev. 998; Lat. 36-12-43 N long. 080-16-58 W; First settled after the Revolutionary War and named for its rural setting.

•**RUTH,** Town; Rutherford County; Pop. 381; Elev. 1034; Incorporated in 1893 as Hampton, but later changed to Ruth.

•**RUTHERFORD COLLEGE,** Town; Burke County; Pop. 1,108; Zip Code 28671; Lat. 35-45-01 N long. 081-31-31 W; Incorporated in 1872 and named for John Rutherford who donated the land for nearby Rutherford College.

•**RUTHERFORDTON,** Town; Rutherford County Seat; Pop. 3,434; Zip Code 28139; Elev. 929; Lat. 35-22-06 N long. 081-57-28 W; Founded in 1787 and named for General Griffith Rutherford, American Revolutionary War leader.

•**ST. PAULS,** Town; Robeson County; Pop. 1,639; Zip Code 28384; Elev. 170; Lat. 34-48-06 N long. 078-58-10 W; Incorporated in 1909 and named for a local Presbyterian Church.

•**ST. STEPHENS,** (CDP); Catawba County; Pop. 10,797; The town is named after a former Church of England parish.

•**SALEM,** (CDP); Burke County; Pop. 2,823; Elev. 1234; Settled in the 1800's and given a name which means "peace."

•**SALEMBURG,** Town; Sampson County; Pop. 742; Zip Code 28385; First settled in the 1870's and named after a local school: The Salem Academy.

•**SALISBURY,** City; Rowan County Seat; Pop. 22,677; Zip Code 28144; Elev. 746; Lat. 35-39-25 N long. 080-29-07 W; Established in 1755 and named for the city in England.

•**SALUDA,** City; Polk County; Pop. 607; Zip Code 28773; Elev. 209; Founded in 1878 and given an Indian name which means "corn river."

•**SANFORD,** City; Lee County Seat; Pop. 14,773; Zip Code 27237; Lat. 35-33-11 N long. 079-14-17 W; Incorporated in 1874 and named after Colonel C. O. Sanford, an engineer for the Chatham Railroad.

•**SARATOGA,** Town; Wilson County; Pop. 381; Zip Code 27873; Lat. 35-39-12 N long. 077-46-33 W; An Indian name from the New York area whose meaning is uncertain.

•**SCOTLAND NECK,** Town; Halifax County; Pop. 2,834; Zip Code 27874; Elev. 103; Lat. 36-07-38 N long. 077-25-23 W; Settled in 1722 and named by Scottish settlers for their former home.

•**SEABOARD,** Town; Northampton County; Pop. 687; Zip Code 27876; Elev. 130; Lat. 36-29-09 N long. 077-26-36 W; Incorporated in 1877 and named for the Seaboard Railroad.

•**SEAGATE,** (CDP); New Hanover County; Pop. 3,422; First settled in 1890 and named for its location on a sound bordering the Atlantic Ocean.

•**SEAGROVE,** Town; Randolph County; Pop. 294; Zip Code 27341; Lat. 35-32-18 N long. 079-46-28 W; Incorporated in 1913 and named after a local railroad official.

•**SELMA,** Town; Johnston County; Pop. 4,762; Zip Code 27576; Lat. 35-32-09 N long. 078-17-01 W; Originally Mitchenor's Station, the name was changed in 1873 after Selma, Alabama.

•**SEVEN SPRINGS,** Town; Wayne County; Pop. 166; Zip Code 28578; Lat. 35-13-34 N long. 077-50-39 W; Descriptively named as the site of seven local springs.

•**SEVERN,** Town; Northampton County; Pop. 309; Zip Code 27877; Lat. 36-30-55 N long. 077-11-19 W; Incorporated in 1919 and named after railroad stockholder Severn Ayers.

•**SHADY FOREST,** Town; Brunswick County; Pop. 43; Descriptively named for the town's location.

•**SHALLOTE,** Town; Brunswick County; Pop. 680; Zip Code 28459; Elev. 10; Lat. 33-54-23 N long. 078-26-39 W; Named from the Shallote River, itself named for a small onion-like plant growing in the vicinity.

•**SHARPSBURG,** Town; Edgecombe, Nash & Wilson Counties; Pop. 997; Zip Code 27878; Elev. 145; Lat. 35-51-55 N long. 077-49-44 W; First settled in 1851 and named for local settler John Jay Sharp.

•**SHELBY,** City; Cleveland County Seat; Pop. 15,310; Zip Code 281+; Elev. 853; Lat. 35-17-22 N long. 081-32-19 W; Named in honor of Colonel Issac Shelby, an American Revolutionary War commander.

•**SILER CITY,** Town; Chatham County; Pop. 4,446; Zip Code 27344; Elev. 598; Lat. 35-43-23 N long. 079-27-46 W; Incorporated in 1887 and named for an early settler-merchant.

•**SILVER LAKE,** (CDP); New Hanover County; Pop. 3,678; Originally Dew's Mill until 1922 when the present name was adopted.

•**SIMPSON,** Village; Pitt County; Pop. 407; Zip Code 27879; Lat. 35-34-30 N long. 077-16-32 W; Incorporated in 1923 and named for a local settler.

•**SIMS,** Town; Wilson County; Pop. 192; Zip Code 27880; Elev. 202; Lat. 35-45-40 N long. 078-03-34 W; The town is named for W.W. Simms. It was incorporated in 1923.

•**SMITHFIELD,** Town; Johnston County Seat; Pop. 7,288; Zip Code 27577; Lat. 35-30-21 N long. 078-20-38 W; Founded in the 1770's and named for local landowner John Smith.

•**SNOW HILL,** Town; Greene County Seat; Pop. 1,374; Zip Code 28580; Lat. 35-27-14 N long. 077-40-28 W; The town is named after a local plantation.

•**SOUTH BELMONT,** (CDP); Gaston County; Pop. 2,068; Elev. 710; Named for New York banker and financier August Belmont.

•**SOUTH GASTONIA,** (CDP); Gaston County; Pop. 4,767; The town is named in honor of Judge William Gaston (1778-1844).

•**SOUTH GOLDSBORO,** (CDP); Wayne County; Pop. 2,531; Named in honor of railroad engineer Major Matthew Goldsborough.

•**SOUTH HENDERSON,** (CDP); Vance County; Pop. 2,384; The city's name honors Leonard Henderson, Chief Justice of the North Carolina Supreme Court from 1829 to 1833.

•**SOUTH WELDON,** (CDP); Halifax County; Pop. 1,801; Settled in the 1820's and named for landowner Daniel Weldon.

•**SOUTHERN PINES,** Town; Moore County; Pop. 8,620; Zip Code 28387; Elev. 512; Lat. 35-10-19 N long. 079-23-44 W; Originally Vineland, it was later renamed for its location on the edge of a pine forest.

•**SOUTHERN SHORES,** Town; Dare County; Pop. 395; Descriptively named for its location on the south coast of the North Banks area.

•**SOUTHPORT,** City; Brunswick County Seat; Pop. 2,824; Zip Code 28461; Lat. 33-56-12 N long. 078-04-00 W; Named Southport in 1889 for its location as the most southern seaport of North Carolina.

•**SPARTA,** Town; Alleghany County Seat; Pop. 1,687; Zip Code 28675; Elev. 2939; Lat. 36-30-22 N long. 081-07-04 W; The town is named after the famous ancient Greek city.

•**SPEED,** Town; Edgecombe County; Pop. 95; Zip Code 27881; Lat. 35-57-58 N long. 077-26-28 W; Founded in 1901 and named for E.T. Speed, a local resident.

•**SPENCER,** Town; Rowan County; Pop. 2,938; Zip Code 28159; Elev. 751; Lat. 35-41-29 N long. 080-26-11 W; The town's name honors railway president Samuel Spencer.

•**SPENCER MOUNTAIN,** Town; Gaston County; Pop. 169; Named in memory of Revolutionary loyalist-turned-patriot, Zachariah Spencer.

•**SPINDALE,** Town; Rutherford County; Pop. 4,246; Zip Code 28160; Elev. 1094; Lat. 35-21-24 N long. 081-55-32 W; Founded in 1916 and descriptively named for its location in a valley with a number of cotton mills.

•**SPRING HOPE,** Town; Nash County; Pop. 1,254; Zip Code 27882; Elev. 130; Lat. 35-56-31 N long. 078-06-43 W; Incorporated in 1889 and named for a settler's hope that a nearby spring would always be a source of good water.

•**SPRING LAKE,** Town; Cumberland County; Pop. 6,273; Zip Code 28390; Lat. 35-10-15 N long. 078-58-25 W; Incorporated in 1951 and named by its founders.

•**SPRUCE PINE,** Town; Mitchell County; Pop. 2,282; Zip Code 28777; Elev. 2517; The town is named after a large spruce pine which grew near a local tavern.

•**STALEY,** Town; Randolph County; Pop. 204; Zip Code 27355; Lat. 35-47-55 N long. 079-32-54 W; The town incorporated in 1901 and took the name of Confederate veteran Colonel John Staley.

•**STALLINGS,** Town; Union County; Pop. 1,826; Named for cotton industrialist J. M. Stallings.

•**STANFIELD,** Town; Stanly County; Pop. 463; Zip Code 28163; Elev. 628; Lat. 35-14-01 N long. 080-25-43 W; The town is named after an early settler.

•**STANLEY,** Town; Gaston County; Pop. 2,341; Zip Code 28164; Elev. 856; Lat. 35-21-44 N long. 081-06-09 W; Incorporated in 1897 as Brevard Station, but renamed in 1893 for nearby Stanley Creek.

•**STANLEYVILLE,** (CDP); Forsyth County; Pop. 5,039; Elev. 941; The city is named after an early settler.

•**STANTONSBURG,** Town; Wilson County; Pop. 920; Zip Code 27883; Lat. 35-36-15 N long. 077-49-22 W; Incorporated in 1817 and named after the first mayor, Willie Stanton.

•**STAR,** Town; Montgomery County; Pop. 816; Zip Code 27356; Elev. 649; Lat. 35-24-09 N long. 079-46-58 W; Local merchant Angus Leach named the town for its high elevation and good visibility in all directions.

•**STATESVILLE,** City; Iredell County Seat; Pop. 18,622; Zip Code 28677; Elev. 923; Lat. 35-51-03 N long. 080-56-10 W; Established just after North Carolina became a state in 1789 and named for that occasion.

•**STATESVILLE WEST,** (CDP); Iredell County; Pop. 1,905; The town's name commemorates North Carolina's joining of the Union in 1789.

•**STEDMAN,** Town; Cumberland County; Pop. 723; Zip Code 28391; Elev. 129; Lat. 35-00-49 N long. 078-41-32 W; Incorporated in 1913 and named for Major Charles Stedman, president of the North Carolina Railroad.

•**STEM,** Town; Granville County; Pop. 222; Zip Code 27581; Elev. 476; Lat. 36-12-04 N long. 078-43-26 W; The town is named for a local family. It incorporated in 1911.

•**STOKESDALE,** (CDP); Guilford County; Pop. 1,070; Zip Code 27357; Lat. 36-14-48 N long. 079-59-14 W; Originally called Pine, the name was later changed in honor of Governor Montford Stokes.

•**STONEVILLE,** Town; Rockingham County; Pop. 1,054; Zip Code 27048; Elev. 824; Lat. 36-27-50 N long. 079-54-30 W; Settled in 1857 and named for the Rev. Frank Stone.

•**STONEWALL,** Town; Pamlico County; Pop. 360; Zip Code 28583; Lat. 35-08-06 N long. 076-44-51 W; First called Jackson, and renamed in 1871 in honor of Confederate War hero, "Stonewall" Jackson.

•**STONY POINT,** (CDP); Alexander County; Pop. 1,150; Zip Code 28678; Elev. 1060; Lat. 35-52-07 N long. 081-03-03 W; Settled in 1789 and descriptively named for the rocky formations in the area.

•**SWANSBORO,** Town; Onslow County; Pop. 976; Zip Code 28584; Lat. 34-41-38 N long. 077-05-36 W; The town's name remembers early colonial legislator Samuel Swann, who served in the mid-1700's.

•**SYLVA,** Town; Jackson County Seat; Pop. 1,699; Zip Code 28779; Elev. 2036; First settled in 1861 and named after carpenter William D. Sylva.

•**TABOR CITY,** Town; Columbus County; Pop. 2,710; Zip Code 28463; Elev. 106; Lat. 34-08-58 N long. 078-52-33 W; Settled in the 1880's and named for the Mount Tabor Presbyterian Church.

•**TAR HEEL,** Town; Bladen County; Pop. 118; Zip Code 28392; Elev. 134; Lat. 34-44-02 N long. 078-47-23 W; Named for an appelation given Revolutionary North Carolina troop by the British, i.e. "tar heels."

•**TARBORO,** Town; Edgecombe County; Pop. 8,634; Zip Code 27886; Lat. 35-53-35 N long. 077-31-56 W; Named for the nearby Tar River when settled in 1732.

•**TAYLORSVILLE,** Town; Alexander County; Pop. 1,103; Zip Code 28681; Elev. 1247; Lat. 35-55-22 N long. 081-10-29 W; Founded in 1847 and named in honor of General Zachary Taylor.

•**TEACHEY,** Town; Duplin County; Pop. 373; Zip Code 28464; Elev. 69; Lat. 34-45-59 N long. 078-00-35 W; Possibly named for Edward Teach, or "Blackbeard," who haunted North Carolina waters in the early 1700's.

•**THOMASVILLE,** City; Davidson County; Pop. 14,144; Zip Code 273+; Lat. 35-53-06 N long. 080-04-52 W; The city was established in 1852 and named for its founder, John W. Thomas.

•**TOAST,** (CDP); Surry County; Pop. 2,339; Zip Code 27049; Elev. 1066; Lat. 36-29-43 N long. 080-37-45 W; Probably named for baked or roasted bread.

•**TOPSAIL BEACH,** Town; Pender County; Pop. 264; Elev. 12; Descriptively named for local residents practice of watching the topsoils of sailing ships approaching.

•**TRENT WOODS,** Town; Craven County; Pop. 1,177; Incorporated in 1959 and named for its location on the Trent River.

•**TRENTON,** Town; Jones County Seat; Pop. 407; Zip Code 28585; Elev. 28; Lat. 35-03-48 N long. 077-21-06 W; Named for the Trent River upon its incorporation in 1874.

•**TRINITY,** (CDP); Randolph County; Pop. 6,887; Zip Code 27370; Elev. 794; Lat. 35-32-43 N long. 079-15-28 W; Named after Trinity College when the town incorporated in 1869.

•**TROUTMAN,** Town; Iredell County; Pop. 1,360; Zip Code 28166; Elev. 946; Lat. 35-41-56 N long. 080-53-23 W; Settled just prior to the Civil War and named after Mrs. Annie Troutman and her sons.

•**TROY,** Town; Montgomery County Seat; Pop. 2,702; Zip Code 27371; Elev. 664; Lat. 35-21-41 N long. 079-53-42 W; Either named for the ancient city of Troy or a N. C. state legislator of the early 1800's.

•**TRYON,** Town; Polk County; Pop. 1,796; Zip Code 28782; Elev. 1085; Named after nearby Tryon Mountain, itself named for William Tryon, who served as colonial governor from 1765-71.

•**TURKEY,** Town; Sampson County; Pop. 417; Zip Code 28393; Lat. 34-59-28 N long. 078-11-07 W; The town takes its name from nearby Turkey Creek.

•**VALDESE,** Town; Burke County; Pop. 3,364; Zip Code 28690; Elev. 1203; Lat. 35-44-39 N long. 081-33-59 W; First settled in 1893 by Italian immigrants, the name is Italian for "valley of our Lord."

•**VALLEY HILL,** (CDP); Henderson County; Pop. 2,396; Descriptively named by its settlers.

•**VANCEBORO,** Town; Craven County; Pop. 833; Zip Code 28586; Elev. 22; Lat. 35-18-00 N long. 077-09-14 W; Originally Durgantown, the name was changed in 1877 in honor of Governor Z. B. Vance.

•**VANDEMERE,** Town; Pamlico County; Pop. 335; Zip Code 28587; Lat. 35-11-05 N long. 076-40-13 W; Former Union army surgeon Dr. Abbot settled here in the 1870's. He and his wife named the town; a Dutch word meaning "from the sea."

•**VASS,** Town; Moore County; Pop. 828; Zip Code 28394; Lat. 35-15-19 N long. 079-16-52 W; Incorporated in 1907 and named for William Vass, the treasurer of the Raleigh and Gaston Railroad.

•**VIRGILINA,** Town; Granville County; Pop. 48; On the Virginia-North Carolina border, the name is a composite of the two state's names.

•**WACO,** Town; Cleveland County; Pop. 322; Zip Code 28169; Elev. 934; Lat. 35-21-41 N long. 081-25-47 W; First settled in the 1850's and named for Waco, Texas.

•**WADE,** Town; Cumberland County; Pop. 474; Zip Code 28395; Elev. 142; Lat. 35-09-55 N long. 078-44-05 W; Landowner N. G. Wade donated the railroad right-of-way, the town is named after him.

•**WADESBORO,** Town; Anson County Seat; Pop. 4,206; Zip Code 28170; Elev. 522; Lat. 34-57-43 N long. 080-04-41 W; Named Wadesboro in 1787 to honor Revolutionary War patriot, Colonel Thomas Wade.

•**WAGRAM,** Town; Scotland County; Pop. 617; Zip Code 28396; Lat. 34-53-16 N long. 079-22-02 W; The town is named for the Napoleonic Battle of Wagram.

•**WAKE FOREST,** Town; Wake County; Pop. 3,780; Zip Code 27587; Elev. 395; Lat. 35-58-53 N long. 078-30-29 W; Wake County was largely forest when it was settled, and hence got this name.

•**WALLACE,** Town; Duplin & Pender Counties; Pop. 2,903; Zip Code 28466; Elev. 59; Lat. 34-44-09 N long. 077-59-47 W; The town's name honors Stephen Wallace, vice-president of the Atlantic Coast Railroad.

•**WALNUT COVE,** Town; Stokes County; Pop. 1,147; Zip Code 27052; Elev. 689; Lat. 36-17-42 N long. 080-08-20 W; Settled in the 1880's and descriptively named for a grove of walnut trees.

•**WALSTONBURG,** Town; Greene County; Pop. 181; Zip Code 27888; Lat. 35-35-40 N long. 077-42-04 W; The town's name remembers plantation owner Seth Walston who owned tracts of land here after the Civil War.

•**WANCHESE,** (CDP); Dare County; Pop. 1,105; Zip Code 27981; Elev. 9; Lat. 35-50-44 N long. 075-38-16 W; The town is named for an Indian taken back to England by Sir Walter Raleigh's 1584 expedition.

•**WARRENTON,** Town; Warren County Seat; Pop. 908; Zip Code 27589; Elev. 395; Lat. 36-23-47 N long. 078-09-23 W; Incorporated in 1779 and named in honor of Revolutionary War patriot Joseph Warren who was killed at the Battle of Bunker Hill.

•**WARSAW,** Town; Duplin County; Pop. 2,910; Zip Code 28398; Elev. 160; Lat. 35-00-03 N long. 078-05-37 W; Incorporated in 1855 and named after a popular novel Thaddeus of Warsaw.

•**WASHINGTON,** City; Beaufort County; Pop. 8,418; Zip Code 27889; Elev. 8; Lat. 35-32-26 N long. 077-02-16 W; Settled before the Revolutionary War and later named in George Washington's honor.

•**WATHA,** Town; Pender County; Pop. 196; Zip Code 28471; Elev. 60; Lat. 34-38-51 N long. 077-57-30 W; Incorporated in 1909, the town's name is a corruption of Hiawatha.

•**WAXHAW,** Town; Union County; Pop. 1,208; Zip Code 28173; Elev. 664; Lat. 34-55-31 N long. 080-44-36 W; The town takes its name from the long vanished Waxhaw Indians.

•**WAYNESVILLE,** Town; Haywood County Seat; Pop. 6,765; Zip Code 28786; Settled in 1800 and named in honor of Revolutionary War hero, General Anthony Wayne.

•**WEAVERVILLE,** Town; Buncombe County; Pop. 1,495; Zip Code 28787; Elev. 2176; Settled as Pine Cabin, the name was changed in 1873 to honor local educator the Rev. M. Weaver.

•**WEBSTER,** Town; Jackson County; Pop. 200; Zip Code 28788; Incorporated in 1859 and named for American statesman, Daniel Webster.

•**WELCOME,** (CDP); Davidson County; Pop. 3,243; Zip Code 27374; Elev. 859; Lat. 35-54-35 N long. 080-15-27 W; A compromise name arrived at during argumentative discussions over the town's title.

•**WELDON,** Town; Halifax County; Pop. 1,844; Zip Code 27890; Lat. 36-24-56 N long. 077-36-10 W; First settled in the 1820's and named after Daniel Weldon, a local landowner.

•**WENDELL,** Town; Wake County; Pop. 2,222; Zip Code 27591; Lat. 35-46-55 N long. 078-22-08 W; Named for Oliver Wendell Holmes upon its incorporation in 1903.

•**WEST CONCORD,** (CDP); Cabarrus County; Pop. 5,859; A compromise name reached and commented on by naming the town after the decision, or concord.

•**WEST JEFFERSON,** Town; Ashe County; Pop. 822; Zip Code 28694; Lat. 36-24-03 N long. 081-29-20 W; Named in honor of President Thomas Jefferson.

•**WEST MARION,** (CDP); McDowell County; Pop. 1,596; The city's name honors Revolutionary patriot, General Francis Marion.

•**WEST ROCKINGHAM,** (CDP); Richmond County; Pop. 2,093; Named in honor of the 2nd Maquis of Rockingham, a British advocate of American independence before the Revolution.

•**WHISPERING PINES,** Village; Moore County; Pop. 1,160; A residential community developed in 1962.

•**WHITAKERS,** Town; Edgecombe & Nash Counties; Pop. 924; Zip Code 27891; Elev. 134; Lat. 36-06-21 N long. 077-42-50 W; Incorporated in 1872 and named after the local Whitaker Brothers.

•**WHITE LAKE,** Town; Bladen County; Pop. 968; The town is named after the adjacent lake, itself named for its clear water and sandy bottom.

•**WHITEVILLE,** City; Columbus County; Pop. 5,565; Zip Code 28472; Elev. 66; Lat. 34-19-41 N long. 078-42-14 W; Incorporated in 1832 on land owned by James White, and so named after him.

•**WILKESBORO**, Town; Wilkes County Seat; Pop. 2,335; Zip Code 28697; Elev. 1042; Lat. 36-08-37 N long. 081-09-52 W; Named in honor of John Wilkes, an English leader who stood up for the colonists prior to the Revolution.

•**WILLIAMSBORO**, Town; Vance County; Pop. 59; Elev. 428; Incorporated in 1808 and named for Judge John Williams.

•**WILLIAMSTON**, Town; Martin County; Pop. 6,159; Zip Code 27892; Lat. 35-48-36 N long. 077-05-38 W; Incorporated in 1779 and named for Revolutionary War hero Colonel William Williams.

•**WILMINGTON**, City; New Hanover County; Pop. 44,000; Zip Code 284+; Chartered in 1740 and named for the Earl of Wilmington.

•**WILSON**, City; Wilson County Seat; Pop. 34,424; Zip Code 278+; Lat. 35-43-38 N long. 077-54-52 W; Settled around 1800 and named in honor of war hero Captain Louis D. Wilson.

•**WINDEMERE**, (CDP); New Hanover County; Pop. 4,115; Named after a town in England.

•**WINDSOR**, Town; Bertie County; Pop. 2,126; Zip Code 27983; Lat. 36-03-22 N long. 076-56-44 W; Incorporated in 1766 and named after the royal castle in England.

•**WINFALL**, Town; Perquimans County; Pop. 634; Zip Code 27985; Lat. 36-12-54 N long. 076-27-51 W; A descriptive name given by the town's founders concerning its origins.

•**WINGATE**, Town; Union County; Pop. 2,615; Zip Code 28174; Elev. 576; Lat. 34-59-00 N long. 080-26-55 W; Originally "Ames Turnout," it was later renamed for a local settler.

•**WINSTON-SALEM**, City; Forsyth County Seat; Pop. 131,885; Zip Code 271; Elev. 912; Lat. 36-06-06 N long. 080-15-20 W; Formed in 1913 by the union of the town's of Winston and Salem.

•**WINTER PARK**, (CDP); New Hanover County; Pop. 4,504; Elev. 45; A community descriptively named for its winter time look.

•**WINTERVILLE**, Town; Pitt County; Pop. 2,052; Zip Code 28590; Elev. 72; Lat. 35-31-46 N long. 077-24-13 W; Named for an early settler.

•**WINTON**, Town; Hertford County; Pop. 825; Zip Code 27986; Elev. 45; Lat. 36-23-34 N long. 076-55-56 W; Incorporated in 1766 on land owned by Benjamin Winton.

•**WOODFIN**, Town; Buncombe County; Pop. 3,260; Named after the Wood family, local settlers.

•**YADKINVILLE**, Town; Yadkin County Seat; Pop. 2,216; Zip Code 27055; Lat. 36-07-57 N, long. 080-39-32 W. The town's name comes from the Indian word "reatkin."

•**YANCEYVILLE**, CDP; Caswell County Seat; Pop. 1,511; Zip Code 27379; Lat. 36-24-09 N, long. 079-20-06 W. Yanceyville is named after Bartlett Yancey, a prominent politician of the state.

NORTH DAKOTA

•**ABERCROMBIE,** City; Richland County; Pop. 260; Zip Code 58001; Elev. 936; Lat. 46-26-33 N long. 096-43-30 W; The town is named after Fort Abercrombie, a military post in intermittent use in the 1860's.

•**ADAMS,** City; Walsh County; Pop. 303; Zip Code 58210; Lat. 48-25-41 N long. 098-04-32 W; Named by early settlers for Adams County, Wisconsin.

•**ALAMO,** City; Williams County; Pop. 122; Zip Code 58830; Elev. 2115; Lat. 48-34-44 N long. 103-27-46 W; Alamo is Spanish for cottonwood. The town is named for both the nearby cottonwood stands and the famous mision in Texas.

•**ALEXANDER,** City; McKenzie County; Pop. 358; Zip Code 58831; Lat. 47-50-22 N long. 103-38-36 W; Founded in 1905 and named for prominent political leader Alexander McKenzie.

•**ALMONT,** City; Morton County; Pop. 146; Zip Code 58520; Lat. 46-43-18 N long. 101-30-32 W; Founded in 1906 and named for nearby Altamount Buttes, a glacial moraine.

•**ANAMOOSE,** City; McHenry County; Pop. 355; Zip Code 58710; Lat. 47-52-58 N long. 100-14-17 W; The town's name honors U. S.District Court Judge Chales Anamoose.

•**ANETA,** City; Nelson County; Pop. 341; Zip Code 58212; Elev. 1503; Lat. 47-40-46 N long. 097-59-32 W; Aneta is named for Mrs. Annetta Mitchell who was the first woman resident of the townsite.

•**ANTLER,** City; Bottineau County; Pop. 101; Zip Code 58711; Elev. 2430; Lat. 48-58-17 N long. 101-17-02 W; Descriptively named for a set of streams flowing through the area which resembles a deer's horns.

•**ARGUSVILLE,** City; Cass County; Pop. 147; Zip Code 58005; Lat. 47-03-21 N long. 096-56-05 W; The town is named after the Farge Argus newspaper, which was the first daily newspaper in North Dakota.

•**ARTHUR,** City; Cass County; Pop. 445; Zip Code 58006; Lat. 47-06-18 N long. 097-13-03 W; The town's name honors U. S. President Chester A. Arthur.

•**ASHLEY,** City; McIntosh County Seat; Pop. 1,192; Zip Code 58413; Lat. 46-02-08 N long. 099-22-17 W; The railroad came through in 1887. Railroad officials named it for Ashley Morrow who was part of the construction company.

•**BALTA,** City; Pierce County; Pop. 139; Zip Code 58313; Elev. 1542; Lat. 48-10-03 N long. 100-02-11 W; Early Russian immigrants named the town for Balta in the Russian Ukraine.

•**BEACH,** City; Stark County; Pop. 1,274; Zip Code 58621; Lat. 46-54-54 N long. 104-00-14 W; Named for a local settler.

•**BELFIELD,** City; Stark County; Pop. 1,274; Zip Code 58622; Elev. 2592; Lat. 46-53-05 N long. 103-11-53 W; The town is named for the beautiful prairie bluebell flowers on the nearby hills.

•**BERTHOLD,** City; Ward County; Pop. 485; Zip Code 58710; Lat. 48-19-49 N long. 101-49-45 W; Bartholmew Berthold established a trading post at the townsite in 1845. Later a fort, the town was named in his honor.

•**BEULAH,** City; Mercer County; Pop. 2,878; Zip Code 58523; Elev. 1750; Lat. 47-15-53 N long. 101-46-46 W; Originally called Troy, New York, the name was later changed to Beulah after a niece of the land company agent.

•**BINFORD,** City; Griggs County; Pop. 293; Zip Code 58416; Lat. 47-33-38 N long. 098-20-40 W; Originally called Blooming Prairie, the town was renamed Binford for the attorney representing the original landowners.

•**BISBEE,** City; Towner County; Pop. 257; Zip Code 583+; Lat. 48-37-25 N long. 099-30-03 W; The town's name remembers Civil War veteran Colonel Bisbee who lived nearby.

•**BISMARCK,** City; Burleigh County Seat and Capital of North Dakota; Pop. 44,485; Zip Code 585+; Lat. 46-48-51 N long. 100-47-06 W; Northern Pacific Railroad officials named the town for Germany's famous Chancelor, Otto Von Bismark.

•**BOTTINEAU,** City; Bottineau County Seat; Pop. 2,829; Zip Code 58318; Elev. 1635; Lat. 48-49-38 N long. 100-26-30 W; The city's name honors early explorer Pierre Bottineau.

•**BOWBELLS,** City; Burke County Seat; Pop. 587; Zip Code 58721; Lat. 48-48-14 N long. 102-14-51 W; Named by English stockholders of the Soo railroad for the famous Bow Bells in London, England.

•**BOWMAN,** City; Bowman County Seat; Pop. 2,071; Zip Code 58623; Elev. 2960; Lat. 46-10-52 N long. 103-23-53 W; Originally called Lowden, the name was changed to honor William Bowman, a well-known territorial legislator.

•**BUFFALO,** City; Cass County; Pop. 226; Zip Code 58011; Elev. 1197; Lat. 46-55-16 N long. 097-32-58 W; The town is named for Buffalo, New York.

•**BURLINGTON,** City; Ward County; Pop. 762; Zip Code 587+; Lat. 48-16-44 N long. 101-25-36 W; Originally called Colton, the name was changed in 1884 to Burlington, for Burlington, Iowa.

•**CANDO,** City; Towner County Seat; Pop. 1,496; Zip Code 58324; Elev. 1486; Lat. 48-26-25 N long. 099-11-52 W; Established in 1884 and given the name "can do" by county commissioners overruling a challenge to their authority.

•**CARRINGTON,** City; Foster County Seat; Pop. 2,641; Zip Code 58421; Elev. 1587; Lat. 47-26-59 N long. 099-07-11 W; The town was named in honor of M.D.Carrington, General Manager of a land company with large holdings in the area.

•**CARSON,** City; Grant County Seat; Pop. 469; Zip Code 58529; Lat. 46-25-12 N long. 101-34-00 W; Early settlers coined the name to honor pioneer businessmen Frank Carter and the Pederson brothers.

•**CASSELTON,** City; Cass County; Pop. 1,661; Zip Code 58012; Elev. 936; Lat. 46-54-07 N long. 097-12-43 W; Named in honor of Northern Pacific Railway president George Cass.

•**CAVALIER,** City; Pembina County Seat; Pop. 1,505; Zip Code 58220; Lat. 48-47-33 N long. 097-37-22 W; The town is named in honor of Charles Cavalier, the earliest settler.

•**CENTER,** City; Oliver County Seat; Pop. 900; Zip Code 58530; Lat. 47-07-03 N long. 101-17-56 W; The town's early residents named it for its central location in the county.

•**COGSWELL,** City; Sargent County; Pop. 227; Zip Code 58017; Lat. 46-06-22 N long. 097-46-59 W; Founded in 1889 and named after a Soo Railroad official.

•**COLEHARBOR,** City; McLean County; Pop. 150; Zip Code 58531; Lat. 47-32-37 N long. 101-13-06 W; Named by Soo Railroad officials for one of their employees, W. A.Cole.

•**COLUMBUS,** City; Burke County; Pop. 325; Zip Code 58727; Lat. 48-54-19 N long. 102-46-48 W; The town takes its name from the second postmaster, Columbus Larson.

•**COOPERSTOWN,** City; Griggs County Seat; Pop. 1,308; Zip Code 58425; Elev. 1437; Lat. 47-26-38 N long. 098-07-12 W; The town is named in honor of Rollin C. Cooper, well-to-do farmers who settled the area in 1880.

•**CROSBY,** City; Divide County Seat; Pop. 1,469; Zip Code 58730; Elev. 1964; Lat. 48-54-47 N long. 103-17-29 W; In 1903 local lawyer S. A. Crosby platted the area and founded the town. It is named in his honor.

•**DAVENPORT,** City; Cass County; Pop. 195; Zip Code 58021; Lat. 46-42-50 N long. 097-04-01 W; Founded in 1872 and named by one of the town's founders for Alice Davenport, wife of the Governor of Massachusetts.

•**DAWSON,** City; Kidder County; Pop. 144; Zip Code 58428; Lat. 46-52-04 N long. 099-45-06 W; Founded in 1873 and named in honor of farmer and banker J. Dawson Thompson.

•**DES LACS,** City; Ward County; Pop. 212; Zip Code 58733; Elev. 1931; Lat. 48-15-22 N long. 101-33-32 W; The town is named after the river and lakes of the same name.

•**DEVILS LAKE,** City; Ramsey County Seat; Pop. 7,442; Zip Code 58301; Elev. 1475; Lat. 48-06-46 N long. 098-51-44 W; Originally called Creelsburg, the town's name was later changed to Devil's Lake after the nearby lake.

•**DICKINSON,** City; Stark County Seat; Pop. 15,924; Zip Code 586+; Elev. 2417; Lat. 46-52-57 N long. 102-47-24 W; The town is named after the original landowner Wells S. Dicinson.

•**DRAKE,** City; McHenry County; Pop. 479; Zip Code 58736; Elev. 1682; Lat. 47-55-17 N long. 100-22-21 W; Herman Drake homesteaded the town in 1899. Soo Railroad Comapny officials named it in his honor.

•**DRAYTON,** City; Pembina County; Pop. 1,082; Zip Code 58225; Elev. 801; Lat. 48-33-45 N long. 097-10-29 W; Canadian settlers named the town after their former home in Drayton, Ontario.

•**DUNN CENTER,** City; Rolette County; Pop. 625; Zip Code 58626; Elev. 2182; Lat. 47-21-13 N long. 102-37-21 W; Named for an early settler.

•**ELGIN,** City; Grant County; Pop. 930; Zip Code 58533; Elev. 1545; Lat. 46-23-53 N long. 101-50-48 W; Originally called Staley, the name was changed to Elgin when a local citizen suggested the name after his Elgin watch.

•**ELLENDALE,** City; Dickey County Seat; Pop. 1,967; Zip Code 58436; Elev. 1456; Lat. 46-00-06 N long. 098-31-27 W; A railroad townsite, it is named in honor of Mary Ellen Dale Merrill, the wife of the local railroad superintendant.

•**EMERADO,** City; Grand Forks County; Pop. 596; Zip Code 58228; Lat. 47-55-00 N long. 097-21-59 W; The town's name derives from Emery Farm, part of the original townsite.

•**ENDERLIN,** City; Cass & Ransom Counties; Pop. 1,151; Zip Code 58027; Lat. 46-37-09 N long. 097-36-02 W; A humorous corruption of "end of the line," and referring to a temporary terminus of the railroad.

•**ESMOND,** City; Benson County; Pop. 337; Zip Code 58332; Elev. 1623; Lat. 48-02-01 N long. 099-45-59 W; Founded in 1901 and named by railroad construction engineer E. Smith after Thackeray's novel "Henry Esmond."

•**FAIRMOUNT,** City; Richland County; Pop. 480; Zip Code 58030; Elev. 984; Lat. 46-03-22 N long. 096-35-57 W; Founded in 1881 and named by original settlers after Fairmount Park in Philadelphia, Pa.

•**FARGO,** City; Cass County Seat; Pop. 61,308; Zip Code 58102; Lat. 46-52-45 N Long. 096-47-44 W; Founded in 1871 and named by Northern Pacific Railroad officials in honor of William Fargo, the founder of Wells-Fargo.

•**FESSENDEN,** City; Wells County Seat; Pop. 761; Zip Code 58438; Elev. 1608; Lat. 47-39-01 N long. 099-37-26 W; Named in honor of surveyor, General Cortez Fessenden who surveyed the area in the early 1880's.

•**FINLEY,** City; Steele County Seat; Pop. 718; Zip Code 58230; Elev. 1457; Lat. 47-30-54 N long. 097-50-06 W; Originally called Gilbert it was renamed in 1896 to honor Great Northern Railway Vice-President, W. W. Finley.

•**FLASHER,** City; Morton County; Pop. 410; Zip Code 585+; Lat. 46-27-14 N long. 101-13-42 W; The town was founded in 1902 and named in honor of homesteader Mabel Flasher.

•**FORDVILLE,** City; Walsh County; Pop. 326; Zip Code 58231; Elev. 1144; Lat. 48-15-08 N long. 097-47-53 W; Originally called Medford, the name was combined with Belleville to give Fordville.

•**FORMAN,** City; Sargent County Seat; Pop. 629; Zip Code 58032; Lat. 46-06-26 N long. 097-38-06 W; Founded in 1883 and named after Colonel Colnglius Forman who settled in the area.

•**FORT YATES,** City; Sioux County Seat; Pop. 771; Zip Code 58528; Lat. 46-24-46 N long. 100-38-13 W; The town is named in honor of Captain George Yates who was killed at Custer's last stand in 1876.

•**FULLERTON,** City; Dickey County; Pop. 107; Zip Code 58441; Elev. 1455; Lat. 46-09-47 N long. 098-25-39 W; Original landowner E. F. Sweet settled in the area in 1882. He named the town for his father-in-law, P. C. Fuller.

•**GACKLE,** City; Logan County; Pop. 456; Zip Code 58442; Lat. 46-37-35 N long. 099-08-21 W; Founded in 1903 and named for merchant George Gackle.

•**GALESBURG,** City; Traill County; Pop. 165; Zip Code 58035; Lat. 47-16-11 N long. 097-24-35 W; Named after the original landowner J. H. Gale who settled in the area in 1883.

•**GARRISON,** City; McLean County; Pop. 1,830; Zip Code 58540; Elev. 1920; Lat. 47-39-18 N long. 101-24-45 W; The town is named from Garrison Stream. The stream was named in 1864 by troops garrisoned at nearby Fort Stevenson.

•**GILBY,** City; Grand Forks County; Pop. 283; Zip Code 58235; Lat. 48-05-09 N long. 097-28-12 W; The town is named for the Gibley brothers who were early settlers.

•**GLADSTONE,** City; Stark County; Pop. 317; Zip Code 58630; Elev. 2354; Lat. 46-51-35 N long. 102-34-09 W; Early settlers named the town for English statesman William Gladstone.

•**GLEN ULLIN,** City; Morton County; Pop. 1,125; Zip Code 58631; Elev. 2072; Lat. 46-48-48 N long. 101-49-51 W; Founded in 1883 and given a gaelic name. Glen means valley and ullin is froman English ballad, Lord's Ullin Daughter.

•**GRAFTON,** City; Walsh County Seat; Pop. 5,293; Zip Code 58237; Elev. 826; Lat. 48-25-04 N long. 097-24-37 W; The first settler, Thomas Cooper, named the town for his wife's former home in Grafton County New Hampshire.

•**GRAND FORKS,** City; Grand Forks County Seat; Pop. 43,765; Zip Code 58201; Elev. 834; Lat. 47-56-12 N long. 097-12-00 W; French for traders named the site Grand Forks for the union of the Red River and Red Lake River.

•GWINNER, City; Sargent County; Pop. 725; Zip Code 58020; Elev. 1263; Lat. 46-11-58 N long. 097-57-38 W; Northern Pacific Railway officials named the town in honor of Major Stockholder and European banker Arthur Gwinner.

•HALLIDAY, City; Dunn County; Pop. 355; Zip Code 58636; Elev. 2044; Lat. 47-21-05 N long. 102-20-15 W; The town's name honors Nathan Haliday, the first postmaster.

•HANKINSON, City; Richland County; Pop. 1,158; Zip Code 58041; Elev. 1067; Lat. 46-04-26 N long. 096-53-37 W; Civil War soldier Richard Hankinson homesteaded the site. The town is named in his honor.

•HARVEY, City; Wells County; Pop. 2,527; Zip Code 58341; Elev. 1600; Lat. 47-46-10 N long. 099-55-49 W; The town's name honors Colonel James Harvey, a director and stockholder of the Soo Railroad.

•HARWOOD, City; Cass County; Pop. 326; Zip Code 58042; Elev. 889; Lat. 46-58-41 N long. 096-52-41 W; The town is named after Fargo real-estate agent A. J. Harwood who invested heavily in the region.

•HATTON, City; Traill County; Pop. 787; Zip Code 58240; Elev. 1081; Lat. 47-38-16 N long. 097-27-33 W; The town's name honors assistant U. S. Postmaster Frank Hatton.

•HAZEN, City; Mercer County; Pop. 2,365; Zip Code 58545; Elev. 1743; Lat. 47-24-09 N long. 101-32-27 W; The city was founded in 1885 and named for assistant U.S.Postmaster, A. D. Hazen.

•HEBRON, City; Morton County; Pop. 1,078; Zip Code 58638; Elev. 2167; Lat. 46-54-23 N long. 102-02-39 W; Originally called Knife River, the name was changed to Hebron, a Biblical valley in 1904.

•HETTINGER, City; Adams County Seat; Pop. 1,739; Zip Code 58639; Lat. 46-00-00 N long. 102-37-57 W; U. S. surveyor E. A. Williams named the town after his father-in-law, Mathias Hettinger.

•HILLSBORO, City; Traill County Seat; Pop. 1,600; Zip Code 580+; Elev. 908; Lat. 47-20-45 N long. 097-13-10 W; Founded in 1880 as Comstock, but later renamed Hillsboro to honor railroad magnate James J. Hill.

•HOPE, City; Steele County; Pop. 406; Zip Code 58046; Elev. 1240; Lat. 47-19-31 N long. 097-43-01 W; Founded in 1882 and named for Hope Steele, wife of the land company treasurer who bought 50,000 acres of wheat land from the railroad for one dollar per acre.

•HUNTER, City; Cass County; Pop. 369; Zip Code 58048; Elev. 978; Lat. 47-11-36 N long. 097-13-22 W; The town's name remembers John C. Hunter who owned extensive landholdings in the area.

•INKSTER, City; Grand Forks County; Pop. 135; Zip Code 58244; Elev. 1029; Lat. 48-09-14 N long. 097-38-44 W; The town is named for the first settler George Inkster.

•JAMESTOWN, City; Stutsman County Seat; Pop. 16,280; Zip Code 584+; Elev. 1413; Lat. 46-54-12 N long. 098-42-30 W; The town is located on the James River. Construction Engineer T. L. Rosser, a Virginian, named it after Jamestown in Virginia.

•KENMARE, City; Ward County; Pop. 1,456; Zip Code 58746; Lat. 48-40-36 N long. 102-04-40 W; Settled in the 1890's and named for a community in Ireland.

•KILLDEER, City; Dunn County; Pop. 790; Zip Code 58640; Elev. 1433; Lat. 47-22-11 N long. 102-45-10 W; The town is named for the nearby ten-mile long Killdeer hills.

•KULM, City; La Moure County; Pop. 570; Zip Code 58456; Lat. 46-18-09 N long. 098-56-56 W; The city's name honors settlers from Kulm, Russian and Kulm, Germany.

•LA MOURE, City; La Moure County Seat; Pop. 1,077; Zip Code 58458; Lat. 46-21-25 N long. 098-17-34 W; Founded in 1882 and named in honor of pioneer and territorial politician Judson La Moure.

•LARIMORE, City; Grand Forks County; Pop. 1,524; Zip Code 58251; Elev. 1136; Lat. 47-54-21 N long. 097-37-42 W; The town is named in honor of Bonanza farmer N. G. Larimore who held 15,000 acres in the area.

•LEEDS, City; Benson County; Pop. 678; Zip Code 583+; Elev. 1514; Lat. 48-11-14 N long. 099-19-13 W; Officials of the Great Northern and Northern Pacific Railroads named the town after Leeds, England.

•LEONARD, City; Cass County; Pop. 289; Zip Code 58052; Lat. 46-39-00 N long. 097-14-46 W; The town is named in honor of pioneer settler Leonard Stroble.

•LINTON, City; Emmons County Seat; Pop. 1,561; Zip Code 58552; Elev. 1708; Lat. 46-16-01 N long. 100-14-01 W; Established in 1899 and named in honor of George Lynn, a prominent pioneer attorney.

•LISBON, City; Ransom County Seat; Pop. 2,283; Zip Code 58054; Elev. 1091; Lat. 46-26-17 N long. 097-41-15 W; Early settlers named the new town for their former homes in Illinois and New York.

•MADDOCK, City; Benson County; Pop. 677; Zip Code 58348; Elev. 588; Lat. 47-57-41 N long. 099-31-41 W; Originally called Ellwood, but later renamed Maddock to honor early settlers.

•MANDAN, City; Morton County Seat; Pop. 15,513; Zip Code 58554; Elev. 1657; The town is named in honor of the Mandan Indians.

•MAPLETON, City; Cass County; Pop. 306; Zip Code 58059; Elev. 808; Lat. 46-53-27 N long. 097-02-23 W; Founded in 1876 and named for its location on the Maple River.

•MAYVILLE, City; Traill County; Pop. 2,255; Zip Code 58219; Elev. 976; Lat. 47-27-28 N long. 096-53-02 W; An early settler, Alvin Arnold, named the town for his second daughter, May.

•MCCLUSKY, City; Sheridan County Seat; Pop. 658; Zip Code 58463; Elev. 1925; Lat. 47-28-58 N long. 100-26-32 W; The city is named for William McClusky, who settled in the area in 1902.

•MEDINA, City; Stutsman County; Pop. 521; Zip Code 58467; Lat. 46-53-29 N long. 099-14-15 W; Founded in 1873 and originally called Midway. The name was later changed to Medina.

•MICHIGAN CITY, City; Nelson County; Pop. 502; Zip Code 58224; Elev. 1516; Lat. 48-09-26 N long. 097-55-47 W; In the 1880's settlers from Michigan named the town after their former home.

•MILNOR, City; Sargent County; Pop. 716; Zip Code 58060; Lat. 46-15-36 N long. 097-27-19 W; Northern Pacific Railroad officials named the town for two of their employees.

•MINOT, City; Ward County Seat; Pop. 32,843; Zip Code 58701; Lat. 48-19-38 N long. 101-18-54 W; Founded in 1886 and named for Eastern Railroad investor Henry Davis Minot.

•MINTO, City; Walsh County; Pop. 592; Zip Code 58261; Elev. 820; Lat. 48-17-35 N long. 097-22-30 W; Settled by Canadians who named it for their former home in Canada.

•**MOHALL,** City; Renville County Seat; Pop. 1,049; Zip Code 58761; Elev. 1639; Lat. 48-45-58 N long. 101-30-28 W; The town is named for Martin O. Hall who settled in the area in 1901.

•**MOTT,** City; Hettinger County Seat; Pop. 1,315; Zip Code 58646; Elev. 2377; Lat. 46-22-24 N long. 102-19-24 W; The town's name honors C. W. Mott, a general agent for the Northern Pacific Railroad.

•**MUNICH,** City; Cavalier County; Pop. 300; Zip Code 58352; Lat. 48-40-09 N long. 098-49-49 W; Town founder William Budge named the city for the famous town in Germany.

•**NAPOLEON,** City; Logan County Seat; Pop. 1,103; Zip Code 58561; Lat. 46-30-22 N long. 099-46-16 W; Founded in 1886 and named for Napoleon Goodsill, the president of the local land company.

•**NEW ENGLAND,** City; Hettinger County; Pop. 825; Zip Code 58647; Elev. 2592; Lat. 46-32-25 N long. 102-52-00 W; Founded in 1887 by New Englanders and named for their former regional home.

•**NEW ROCKFORD,** City; Eddy County Seat; Pop. 1,791; Zip Code 58356; Lat. 47-40-47 N long. 099-08-10 W; Pioneer Charles Gregory named the town for his former home in Rockford, Illinois.

•**NEW TOWN,** City; Mountrail County; Pop. 1,335; Zip Code 58763; Lat. 47-58-52 N long. 102-28-44 W; Founded in 1950 to replace several towns flooded by the Garrison Dam Reservoir.

•**NORTHWOOD,** City; Grand Forks County; Pop. 1,240; Zip Code 58267; Elev. 1113; Lat. 47-44-04 N long. 097-34-25 W; Early settlers from Northwood, Iowa gave the town its name.

•**OAKES,** City; Dickey County; Pop. 2,112; Zip Code 58474; Elev. 1313; Lat. 46-08-19 N long. 098-05-12 W; The town is named in honor of Northern Pacific Railway manager Thomas Oakes.

•**PAGE,** City; Cass County; Pop. 329; Zip Code 58064; Lat. 47-09-46 N long. 097-34-24 W; A large landowner named Colonel Morton named the town in honor of his brother-in-law, E. E. Page.

•**PARK RIVER,** City; Walsh County; Pop. 1,844; Zip Code 58270; Elev. 1006; Lat. 48-23-44 N long. 097-44-36 W; Named for the Park River which flows through the town.

•**PARSHALL,** City; Mountrail County; Pop. 1,059; Zip Code 58770; Lat. 47-57-11 N long. 102-07-58 W; Founded in 1913 and named in honor of George Parshall, a pioneer stage coach driver.

•**PEMBINA,** City; Pembina County; Pop. 673; Zip Code 58271; Lat. 48-58-02 N long. 097-14-41 W; Derived from the Chippewa Indian word for "summer berry."

•**PLAZA,** City; Mountrail County; Pop. 222; Zip Code 58771; Lat. 48-01-30 N long. 101-57-32 W; Founded in 1906 and descriptively named for a plaza in the town's business district.

•**PORTAL,** City; Burke County; Pop. 238; Zip Code 58772; Lat. 48-59-42 N long. 102-32-38 W; Founded in the 1890's as a railroad division point and named for its closeness to the international border.

•**RAY,** City; Williams County; Pop. 766; Zip Code 58849; Lat. 48-18-15 N long. 103-10-00 W; Founded in 1901 and named in honor of early pioneer Ray Payton.

•**REEDER,** City; Adams County; Pop. 355; Zip Code 58649; Lat. 46-06-19 N long. 102-56-30 W; The town is named in honor of Milwaukee Railroad Engineer, E. A. Reeder.

•**RHAME,** City; Bowman County; Pop. 222; Zip Code 58651; Lat. 46-13-57 N long. 103-39-21 W; Settled in 1907 and named for railroad district engineer, Mitchell Rhame.

•**ROLETTE,** City; Rolette County; Pop. 667; Zip Code 58366; Elev. 1623; Lat. 48-39-46 N long. 099-50-11 W; The town's name honors pioneer fur trader and legislator Joseph Rolette.

•**ROLLA,** City; Rolette County Seat; Pop. 1,538; Zip Code 8367; Lat. 48-51-40 N long. 099-36-51 W; The city's name is either a contraction of the county name or is named after Rolla, Missouri.

•**RUGBY,** City; Pierce County Seat; Pop. 3,335; Zip Code 58315; Elev. 1550; Lat. 48-30-21 N long. 100-10-29 W; Founded in 1885 and named by English railroad stockholders for Rugby, England.

•**ST. JOHN,** City; Rolette County; Pop. 401; Zip Code 58369; Lat. 48-56-43 N long. 099-42-31 W; An old trading centr, St. John was named by an early settler for his former home of St. John, Canada.

•**SAWYER,** City; Ward County; Pop. 417; Zip Code 58781; Elev. 1542; Lat. 48-05-21 N long. 101-03-03 W; Founded in 1882 and named by Soo railroad officials for a company employee named Sawyer.

•**SCRANTON,** City; Bowman County; Pop. 415; Zip Code 58653; Lat. 46-08-55 N long. 103-08-16 W; Established in 1907 and named for another coal mining town, Scranton, Pa.

•**SELFRIDGE,** City; Sioux County; Pop. 273; Zip Code 58568; Elev. 2184; Lat. 46-02-29 N long. 100-55-26 W; Named either for a Soo railroad official or an early army aviator hero.

•**SHERWOOD,** City; Renville County; Pop. 294; Zip Code 58782; Lat. 48-57-41 N long. 101-37-49 W; The town is named for original landowner Sherwood Sleeper.

•**SHEYENNE,** City; Eddy County; Pop. 307; Zip Code 58374; Lat. 47-49-37 N long. 099-06-57 W; The town is named after the river. The river, in turn, is named for the Chetening Indians.

•**STANLEY,** City; Mountrail County Seat; Pop. 1,631; Zip Code 58784; Lat. 48-18-45 N long. 102-23-01 W; Settled in 1895 and named for an early homesteader, King Stanley.

•**STANTON,** City; Mercer County Seat; Pop. 623; Zip Code 58571; Elev. 1701; Lat. 47-19-14 N long. 101-22-57 W; The McGrath brothers settled here in 1882 and gave it their mother's maiden name.

•**STEELE,** City; Kidder County Seat; Pop. 796; Zip Code 58482; Elev. 1865; Lat. 46-51-11 N long. 099-55-05 W; In 1881 Colonel Wilbur Steele platted a townsite on his homestead. The town is named in his honor.

•**STRASBURG,** City; Emmons County; Pop. 623; Zip Code 5573; Elev. 1804; Lat. 46-08-04 N long. 100-09-50 W: Founded in 1902 and named for the city in Europe's Rhineland.

•**SURREY,** City; Ward County; Pop. 999; Zip Code 58785; Elev. 1625; Lat. 48-14-03 N long. 101-07-54 W; Founded in 1900 and named by railroad officials for Surrey, England.

•**TAPPEN,** City; Kidder County; Pop. 271; Zip Code 58487; Lat. 46-52-15 N long. 099-37-47 W; Tappen is named after Bonanza farmer S. Tappen who ran a 10,000 acre farm here in the 1880's.

•**THOMPSON,** City; Grand Forks County; Pop. 785; Zip Code 58278; Lat. 47-46-36 N long. 097-06-20 W; Originally called Norton, but renamed for the first postmaster, Albert Thompson.

•TIOGA, City; Williams County; Pop. 1,597; Zip Code 58852; Elev. 2238; Lat. 48-23-56 N long. 102-56-15 W; Settlers from Tioga, New York settled here in 1902. The name is an Iroquois Indian word meaning "peaceful valley."

•TOWNER, City; McHenry County Seat; Pop. 867; Zip Code 58788; Elev. 1186; Lat. 48-20-53 N long. 100-24-18 W; Settled in 1886 and named for Colonel O. M. Towner, a Civil War veteran, and an early rancher.

•TURTLE LAKE, City; McLean County; Pop. 707; Zip Code 58575; Elev. 1875; Lat. 47-31-19 N long. 100-53-12 W; The town is named for the nearby turtle-shaped lake.

•UNDERWOOD, City; McLean County; Pop. 1,329; Zip Code 58576; Elev. 2026; Lat. 47-27-14 N long. 101-08-13 W; Founded in 1903 and named in honor of local railroad vice-president Fred Underwood.

•UPHAM, City; McHenry County; Pop. 227; Zip Code 58789; Elev. 1445; Lat. 48-34-53 N long. 100-43-48 W; Founded in 1905 and named in honor of explorer and geologist Dr. Warren Upham.

•VALLEY CITY, City; Barnes County Seat; Pop. 7,774; Zip Code 58072; Elev. 1222; Lat. 46-55-34 N long. 097-59-55 W; Founded in 1881 and given a descriptive name.

•VELVA, City; McHenry County; Pop. 1,101; Zip Code 58790; Lat. 48-03-34 N long. 100-55-53 W; Soo railroad officials descriptively named the town for the velvet-like appearance of the Mouse River Valley.

•WAHPETON, City; Richland County Seat; Pop. 9,064; Zip Code 58024; Elev. 963; Lat. 46-18-06 N long. 096-44-19 W; The town is named after the local Indian tribe, the Wahpetons.

•WALHALLA, City; Pembina County; Pop. 1,429; Zip Code 58282; Lat. 48-55-13 N long. 097-55-11 W; An English translation of a German word meaning "home of the gods."

•WASHBURN, City; McLean County Seat; Pop. 1,767; Zip Code 58577; Elev. 1731; Lat. 47-17-16 N long. 101-01-31 W; The town was founded in 1882 and named by its founders for C. C. Washburn, the Governor of Wisconsin in 1872.

•WATFORD CITY, City; McKenzie County Seat; Pop. 2,119; Zip Code 58854; Lat. 47-48-07 N long. 103-16-56 W; Originally named Banks, the local physician, V. G. Morris, renamed it for his former home in Ontario, Canada.

•WEST FARGO, City; Cass County; Pop. 10,099; Zip Code 58078; Lat. 46-54-48 N long. 096-49-23 W; Originally called Haggart, the town's name was changged to West Fargo to reflect its proximity to Fargo, N. D.

•WILLISTON, City; Williams County Seat; Pop. 13,336; Zip Code 58801; Elev. 1882; Lat. 48-09-17 N long. 103-37-28 W; Great Northern Railroad Director James Hill named the town after his friend D. Willis James of New York.

•WILTON, City; McLean County; Pop. 688; Zip Code 58579; Elev. 2183; Lat. 47-09-36 N long. 100-47-06 W; Minneapolis flour magnate W. D.Washburn founded the town in 1898 and named it for his former hone in Maine.

•WISHEK, City; McIntosh County; Pop. 1,345; Zip Code 58495; Lat. 46-15-36 N long. 099-33-44 W; Surveyed in 1898 and named in honor of original landowner John Wishek.

•WYNDMERE, City; Richland County; Pop. 550; Zip Code 58008; Elev. 1059; Lat. 46-15-58 N long. 096-59-51 W; Settled in the 1880's and given an English peace name meaning "narrow marshy lane."

OHIO

•ABERDEEN, Village; Brown County; Pop. 1,532; Zip Code 45101; Elev. 500; Lat. 38-39-20 N long. 083-45-40 W; SW Ohio; Named for the Scottish city.

•ADA, Village; Hardin County; Pop. 5,646; Zip Code 45810; Lat. 40-46-10 N long. 083-49-22 W; 6 m. E of Lima in NW Ohio; Established in 1853 as Johnstown.

•ADDYSTON, Village; Hamilton County; Pop. 1,200; Zip Code 45001; Elev. 510; Lat. 39-08-12 N long. 084-42-33 W; SW Ohio; Had a few settlers as early as 1789, but did not become a town until 1871 when *Matthew Addy* of Cincinnati established a large pipe foundry here.

•AKRON, City; Seat of Summit County; Pop. 237,005; Zip Code 443+; Elev. 950; Lat. 41-04-53 N long. 081-31-09 W; on the little Cuyahoga River, Akron is derived from the Greek akros, meaning "high".

•ALLIANCE, City; Mahoning and Stark Counties; Pop. 24,322; Zip Code 44601; Elev. 1174; Lat. 40-54-55 N long. 081-06-22 W; 14 m. NE of Canton in NE central Ohio; In 1805, three rival towns sprang up near by and prospered--Greedom, Williamsport, and Mount Union. In 1854 the four communities were united under the name Alliance, and the town was incorporated in 1889.

•AMANDA, Village; Fairfield County; Pop. 721; Zip Code 43102; Lat. 39-38-58 N long. 082-44-40 W; 30 m. SE of Columbus in central Ohio; the village was named by *William Hamilton*, surveyor.

•AMBERLEY, Village; Hamilton County; Pop. 3,428; Elev. 803; Lat. 39-12-17 N long. 084-25-41 W; m. NE of Cincinnati in SW Ohio; is mainly a suburban community.

•AMELIA, Village, Clermont County; Pop. 1,104; Zip Code 45102; Lat. 39-01-42 N long. 084-13-04 W; SW Ohio; 21 m. SE of Cincinnati.

•AMESVILLE, Village; Athens County; Pop. 247; Zip Code 45711; Lat. 39-24-02 N long. 081-57-21 W; SE Ohio; in a recreational region near several rivers.

•AMHERST, City; Lorain County; Pop. 10,620; Zip Code 44001; Lat. 41-23-52 N long. 082-13-21 W; 25 m. SW of Cleveland in N Ohio. Named after the city in New Jersey.

•AMSTERDAM, Village; Jefferson County; Pop. 783; Zip Code 43903; Lat. 40-28-25 N long. 080-55-23 W; approximately 21 m. NW of Steubenville in E Ohio. Named for the Dutch city.

•ANDOVER, Village; Ashtabula County; Pop. 1,205; Zip Code 44004; Elev. 1,095; Lat. 41-36-24 N long. 080-34-21 W; NE Ohio. Named after the city in Maine.

•ANSONIA, Village, Darke County; Pop. 1,271; Zip Code 45303; Elev. 1009; Lat. 40-12-52 N long. 084-38-13 W; W Ohio.

•ANTIOCH, Village; Monroe County; Pop. 112; Zip Code 43710; Lat. 39-45-58 N long. 083-16-18 W; SE Ohio; Near the Ohio River. Named after the Biblical city.

•ANTWERP, Village; Paulding County; Pop. 1,768; Zip Code 45813; Elev. 732; Lat. 41-10-53 N long. 084-44-26 W; NW Ohio; named by Hollanders and Germans who settled here.

•APPLE CREEK, Village; Wayne County; Pop. 742; Zip Code 44606; Lat. 40-45-06 N long. 081-50-22 W; SE of Wooster in NE Ohio. Descriptively named.

•ARCANUM, Village; Darke County; Pop. 2,017; Zip Code 45304; Lat. 39-59-28 N long. 084-33-08 W; W Ohio; 14 m. SE of Greenville along Twin Creek.

•ARCHBOLD, Village; Fulton County; Pop. 3,322; Zip Code 43502; Elev. 734; Lat. 41-31-17 N long. 084-18-26 W; NW Ohio.

•ARLINGTON, Village; Fulton County; Pop. 3,322; Zip Code 45814; Elev. 869; Lat. 40-53-47 N long. 083-39-01 W; Ohio. The village was named after the district in Virginia.

•ASHLAND, City; Seat of Ashland County; Pop. 20,252; Zip Code 44805; Elev. 1,077; Lat. 40-52-07 N long. 082-19-06 W; N central Ohio, NE of Mansfield. In 1822 the growing town was renamed Ashland, after *Henry Clay's* estate at Lexington, Kentucky.

•ASHLEY, Village; Delaware County; Pop. 1,056; Zip Code 43003; Elev. 989; Lat. 40-24-32 N long. 082-57-20 W; 40 m. N of Columbus on the E shore of the Delaware Reservoir in central Ohio.

•ASHTABULA, City; Ashtabula County; Pop. 23,354; Zip Code 44004; Elev. 688; Lat. 41-51-54 N long. 080-47-24 W; 50 m. NE of Cleveland in NE Ohio; lies on the shore of Lake Erie. The name is an Indian word thought to mean "River of Many Fish."

•ASHVILLE, Village; Pickaway County; Pop. 2,046; Zip Code 43103; Elev. 709; Lat. 39-42-56 N long. 082-57-11 W; S central Ohio; 30 m. S of Columbus.

•ATHENS, City; Seat of Athens County; Pop. 19,801; Zip Code 45701; Elev. 723; Lat. 39-19-45 N long. 082-06-05 W; 30 m. W of Marietta; named after the famous Greek city.

•ATTICA, Village; Seneca County; Pop. 867; Zip Code 44807; Lat. 41-03-53 N long. 082-53-16 W; on a branch of the Sandusky River in N Ohio; was named for the town in New York.

•AURORA, City; Portage County; Pop. 8,174; Zip Code 44202; Elev. 1130; Lat. 41-19-03 N long. 081-20-44 W; 21 m. SE of Cleveland and 21 m. NE of Akron in NE Ohio. Given the Roman name for the goddess of Dawn.

•AVON, City; Lorain County; Pop. 7,265; Zip Code 44011; Elev. 670; Lat. 41-27-06 N long. 082-02-08 W; S of Lake Erie shoreline in N Ohio. Named for the English river.

•AVON LAKE, City; Lorain County; Pop. 13,184; Zip Code 44012; Elev. 628; Lat. 41-30-19 N long. 082-01-42 W; 19 m. W of Cleveland in NE Ohio.

•BAINBRIDGE, Village; Ross County; Pop. 1,030; Zip Code 45612; Elev. 716; Lat. 39-13-39 N long. 083-16-14 W; S central Ohio The village was named for *Commander William Bainbridge*, War of 1812 fame.

•BALTIMORE, Village; Fairfield County; Pop. 2,694; Zip Code 43105; Lat. 39-50-43 N long. 082-36-03 W; S central Ohio; 30 m. SE of Columbus.

•BARBERTON, City; Summit County; Pop. 29,732; Zip Code 44203; Elev. 969; Lat. 41-00-46 N long. 081-36-19 W; 7m. SW of Akron NE Ohio; Barberton was laid out in 1891 by *Ohio Columbus Barber*.

•BARNESVILLE, Village; Belmont County; Pop. 4,640; Zip Code 43713; Lat. 39-59-17 N long. 081-10-36 W; 40 m. SW of Steubenville in SE Ohio; in a hilly region. The town was named after *James Barnes* who was the founder in 1808.

•BATAVIA, Village; Seat of Clermont County; Pop. 1,890; Zip Code 45103; Elev. 594; Lat. 39-04-37 N long. 084-10-37 W; on the E fork of the Miami River, 20 m. E of Cincinnati in SW Ohio.

•**BAY VILLAGE**, City; Cuyahoga County; Pop. 17,839; Zip Code 44140; Elev. 630; Lat. 41-29-05 N long. 081-55-20 W; NE Ohio; is a suburb of Cleveland overlooking Lake Erie.

•**BEACHWOOD**, City; Cuyahoga County; Pop. 9,618; Zip Code 44122; Lat. 41-27-52 N long. 081-30-32 W;   NE Ohio; Near Cleveland on Lake Erie; Suburban.

•**BEDFORD**, City; Cuyahoga County; Pop. 15,003; Zip Code 44146; Elev. 946; Lat. 41-23-35 N long. 081-32-12 W; 10 m. SE of Cleveland in NE Ohio; was the site of a temporary settlement by Moravian missionaries in 1786; The name was chosen after the same town in Connecticut.

•**BEDFORD HEIGHTS**, City; Cuyahoga County; Pop. 13,187; Lat. 41-25-01 N long. 081-31-39 W.

•**BELLAIRE**, City; Belmont County; Pop. 8,231; Zip Code 43906; Elev. 653; Lat. 40-00-45 N long. 080-45-39 W; 35 m. S of Steubenville on the Ohio River in E Ohio.

•**BELLBROOK**, City; Greene County; Pop. 5,182; Zip Code 45305; Elev. 796; Lat. 39-38-08 N long. 084-04-15 W; 14 m. SE of Dayton in SW Ohio; suburban; is named after *Stephen Bell* in 1816.

•**BELLEFONTAINE**, City; Seat of Logan County; Pop. 11,798; Zip Code 43311; Elev. 1,251; Lat. 40-21-40 N long. 083-45-35 W; is 30 m. N of Springfield in W Ohio;was named for the springs of limestone according to an early writer.

•**BELLEVUE**, City; Huron and Sandusky Counties; Pop. 8,193; Zip Code 44811; Elev. 753; Lat. 41-16-25 N long. 082-50-30 W; 15 m. SW of Sandusky in N Ohio; first settled in 1815; Named in 1839 by *James Bell*, who was then building the Mad River and Lake Erie Railroad from Sandusky.

•**BELMORE**, Village; Putnam County; Pop. 45815; Zip Code 45815; Elev. 736; Lat. 41-09-12 N long. 083-56-16 W; NW Ohio; 20 m. NE of Ottawa.

•**BELOIT**, Village; Mahoning County; Pop. 1,100; Zip Code 44609; Elev. 1132; Lat. 40-55-23 N long. 080-59-38 W; E Ohio; 30 m. SWof Youngstown. Named for the French explorer.

•**BELPRE**, City; Washington County; Pop. 7,155; Zip Code 45714; Elev. 622; Lat. 39-16-26 N long. 081-34-23 W; S Ohio; It's name means beautiful meadows in French.

•**BEREA**, City; Cuyahoga County; Pop. 19,636; Zip Code 44017; Elev. 788; Lat. 41-21-58 N long. 081-51-16 W; 10 m. SW of Cleveland in N Ohio.

•**BETHEL**, Village; Clermont County; Pop. 2,230; Zip Code 45106; Elev. 892; Lat. 38-57-49 N long. 084-04-51 W; SW Ohio; 30 m. SE of Cincinnati. A Biblical name meaning hope.

•**BETHESDA**, Village; Belmont County; Pop. 1,453; Zip Code 43719; Lat. 40-00-58 N long. 081-04-22 W; E Ohio; Hilly region.

•**BEVERLY**, Village; Washington County; Pop. 1,468; Zip Code 45715; Elev. 631; Lat. 39-32-52 N long. 081-38-23 W; SE Ohio; was settled in 1789.

•**BEXLEY**, City; Franklin County; Pop. 13,396; Zip Code 43209; Elev. 775; Lat. 39-58-08 N long. 082-56-16 W; E side of Columbus in central Ohio.

•**BLANCHESTER**, Village; Clinton County; Pop. 3,302; Zip Code 45107; Elev. 953; Lat. 40-43-55 N long. 083-38-37 W; approx. 30 m. NE of Cincinnati in SW Ohio; The town was first settled in 1832.

•**BLOOMVILLE**, Village, Seneca County; Pop. 1,020; Zip Code 44818; Lat. 41-03-07 N long. 083-00-54 W; N Central Ohio.

•**BLUE ASH**, City; Hamilton County; Pop. 9,482; Lat. 39-13-55 N long. 084-22-42 W; NE of Cincinnati; Residential.

•**BLUFFTON**, Village; Allen County; Pop. 3,308; Zip Code 45817; Elev. 824; Lat. 40-53-43 N long. 083-53-20 W; 14 m. NE of Lima in NW Ohio; founded in 1833, took its present name from a Mennonite community in Indiana.

•**BOLIVAR**, Village; Tuscarawas County; Pop. 989; Zip Code 44612; Lat. 40-39-00 N long. 081-27-08 W; E Ohio. Named in honor of the great South American librator.

•**BOTKINS**, Village; Shelby County; Pop. 1,376; Zip Code 45306; Elev. 1011; Lat. 40-28-04 N long. 084-10-50 W; W Ohio; Rural.

•**BOWLING GREEN**, City; Seat of Wood County; Pop. 25,745; Zip Code 43402; Elev. 700; Lat. 41-22-29 N long. 083-39-05 W; 20 m. SW of Toledo in NW central Ohio; Laid out in 1835 and named by *Joseph Gordon* for his home town in Kentucky.

•**BRADFORD**, Village; Miami County; Pop. 2,171; Zip Code 45308; Elev. 989; Lat. 40-07-56 N long. 084-25-51 W; 15 m. W of Greenville.

•**BRADNER**, Village; Wood County; Pop. 1,172; Zip Code 43406; Lat. 41-19-27 N long. 083-26-19 W; NW Ohio.

•**BRATENAHL**, Village; Cuyahoga County; Pop. 1,483; Zip Code (with Cleveland); Lat. 41-32-33 N long. 081-37-35 W; NE Ohio; On Lake Erie.

•**BRECKSVILLE**, City; Cuyahoga County; Pop. 10,133; Zip Code 44141; Elev. 955; Lat. 41-19-11 N long. 081-37-37 W; was settled about 1811 and named for *John* and *Robert Breck*, early land owners in the region.

•**BREMEN**, Village; Fairfield County; Pop. 1,435; Zip Code 43107; Lat. 39-42-06 N long. 082-25-37 W; 10 m. E of Lancaster in N central Ohio; is named for the German City.

•**BREWSTER**, Village; Stark County; Pop. 2,312; Zip Code 44613; Lat. 40-42-25 N long. 081-35-54 W; NE Ohio; 18 m. SW of Canton; Along the Sugar Creek.

•**BRIDGEPORT**, Village; Belmont County; Pop. 2,642; Zip Code 43912; Elev. 660; Lat. 40-04-11 N long. 080-44-25 W; on the Ohio River in E Ohio; across the river is Wheeling, West Virginia.

•**BRILLIANT**, Village; Jefferson County; Pop. 1,756; Zip Code 43913; Lat. 40-15-53 N long. 080-37-35 W; E Ohio; On the Ohio River, 7 m. S of Steubenville.

•**BROADVIEW HEIGHTS**, City; Cuyahoga County; Pop. 10,909; Zip Code (with Cleveland); Lat. 41-18-50 N long. 081-41-07 W; NE Ohio; Suburban development, 20 m. S of Cleveland.

•**BROOKLYN**, City; Cuyahoga County; Pop. 12,324; Zip Code 44144; Elev. 765; Lat. 41-26-23 N long. 081-44-08 W; NE Ohio; S suburb of Cleveland; Named after the city in New York.

•**BROOK PARK**, City; Cuyahoga Coutny; Pop. 26,195; Zip Code 44142; Lat. 41-23-54 N long. 081-48-17 W; NE Ohio; SW suburb of Cleveland.

•**BROOKVILLE**, Village; Montgomery County; Pop. 4,317; Zip Code 45309; Elev. 1033; Lat. 39-50-12 N long. 084-24-41 W; SW central Ohio; 20 m. NW of Dayton.

•**BRUNSWICK**, City; Medina County; Pop. 27,645; Zip Code 44212; Lat. 41-14-17 N long. 081-50-31 W; 25 m. SW of Cleveland in N Ohio; is named for Brunswick township.

•**BRYAN**, City; Seat of Williams County; Pop. 7,880; Zip Code 43506; Elev. 764; Lat. 41-28-29 N long. 084-33-09 W; 50 m. W of Toledo in NW Ohio; is named for *Hon. John A. Bryon* who held offices in the state and also developed this part of the state.

•**BUCYRUS**, City; Seat of Crawford County; Pop. 13,413; Zip Code 44820; Elev. 1,006; Lat. 40-48-30 N long. 082-58-32 W; 20 m. NE of Marion in N central Ohio, along the Sandusky River; Because *Cyrus*, a leader of the ancient Persians, was one of the founder's favorite heroes, and because the country was attractive, he is said to have named the community by prefixing Cyrus with "bu", signifying "beautiful".

•**BURTON**, Village; Geauga County; Pop. 1,401; Zip Code 44021; Elev. 1,310; Lat. 41-28-14 N long. 081-08-43 W; NE Ohio; near the Cuyahoga River; is named for the son of the founder.

•**BYESVILLE**, Village; Guernsey County; Pop. 4,050; Zip Code 45820; Elev. 804; Lat. 39-58-11 N long. 081-32-12 W; E Ohio; named for *Jonathan Bye*, who built the first flour mill in the vicinity early in the nineteenth century.

•**CADIZ**, Village; Seat of Harrison County; Pop. 4,050; Zip Code 43907; Elev. 1,280; Lat. 40-16-22 N long. 080-59-49 W; 20 m. SW of Steubenville in E Ohio. Named after the Spanish city.

•**CALDWELL**, Village; Seat of Noble County; Pop. 1,942; Zip Code 43724; Elev. 744; Lat. 39-44-52 N long. 081-31-00 W; 27 m. N of Marietta in a rich coal mining region in SE Ohio. Founded in 1857, it is named for the owners of the town site.

•**CAMBRIDGE**, City; Seat of Guernsey County; Pop. 13,450; ; Zip Code 43725; Elev. 799; 20 m. NE of Zanesville in E Ohio. 1806 *Jacob Gomber* and *Zacheus Beatty* laid out the town and named it for Cambridge, Maryland, from which came many of the first settlers.

•**CAMDEN**, Village; Preble County; Pop. 1,965; Zip Code 45311; Lat. 39-46-01 N long. 080-56-42 W; SW Ohio; On Seven mile Creek, 19 m. N of Hamilton. Named for the city in New Jersey.

•**CAMPBELL**, City; Mahoning County; Pop. 11,591; Zip Code 44405; Lat. 41-04-42 N long. 080-35-58 W; on the Mahoning River, 5 m. SE of Youngstown in NE Ohio; Suburb.

•**CANAL FULTON**, Village; Stark County; Pop. 3,481; Zip Code 44614; Elev. 947; Lat. 40-53-23 N long. 081-35-52 W; NE Ohio; Formerly Milan, it changed its name name to Canal Fulton in honor of *Robert Fulton*, inventor of the steamboat.

•**CANFIELD**, City; Mahoning County; Pop. 5,530; Zip Code 44406; Elev. 1,161; Lat. 41-01-30 N long. 080-45-40 W; 10 m. SW of Youngstown in NE Ohio; named for *Johnathan Canfield* an early landowner.

•**CANTON**, City; Seat of Stark County; Pop. 94,635; Zip Code 444 + zone; Elev. 1,050; Lat. 40-47-56 N long. 081-22-43 W; 20 m. SE of Akron in NE Ohio. The city takes its name from the famous Chinese port.

•**CARDINGTON**, Village; Morrow County; Pop. 1,665; Zip Cdoe 43315; Elev. 1014; Lat. 40-30-02 N long. 082-53-37 W; N central Ohio; 14 m. SE of Marion.

•**CAREY**, Village; Wyandot County; Pop. 3,681; Zip Code 43316; Elev. 823; Lat. 40-57-09 N long. 083-22-57 W; 15 m. SE of Findlay NW central Ohio; the place was named for *Judge John Carey.*

•**CARLISLE**, Village; Warren and Montgomery Counties; Pop. 4,271; Zip Code 45005; Lat. 39-44-44 N long. 081-21-50 W; 15 m. SW of Dayton in SW Ohio; Between the Twin and Miami Rivers; Near Middletown.

•**CARROLLTON**, Village; Seat of Carroll County; Pop. 3,054; Zip Code 44615; Elev. 1130; Lat. 40-34-22 N long. 081-05-09 W; 20 m. SE of Canton in E Ohio; was named for *Charles Carroll* who signed the Declaration of Independence.

•**CEDARVILLE**, Village; Greene County; Pop. 2,804; Zip Code 45314; Elev. 1,055; Lat. 39-44-39 N long. 083-48-31 W; NE of Xenia in SW central Ohio; was named for cedar trees in the area. The place was formerly known as Milford but was changed for postal reasons.

•**CELINA**, City; Seat of Mercer County; Pop. 9,127; Zip Code 45822; Elev. 768; Lat. 40-32-56 N long. 084-34-13 W; on the W end of Lake St. Marys in W Ohio; was named for a New York town, Salina. Settled in 1834.

•**CENTERVILLE**, City; Montgomery County; Pop. 18,953; Zip Code 454--; Lat. 39-58-33 N long. 080-57-56 W; 10 m. S of Dayton in SW central Ohio. Named for its geographical position.

•**CHAGRIN FALLS**, City; Cuyahoga County; Pop. 4,306; Zip Code 44022; Elev. 985; Lat. 41-25-47 N long. 081-23-27 W; NE Ohio; Lies in a wide loop of the Chagrin River, which is said to have been named by *Moses Cleaveland* and his party of surveyors. The Indian word meaning clear water sounds like Shagreen.

•**CHARDON**, Village; Seat of Geauga County; Pop. 4,417; Zip Code 44024; Elev. 1,230; Lat. 41-36-51 N long. 081-08-57 W; 25 m. NE of Cleveland in NE Ohio; The town is named for *Peter Chardon Brooks*, first owner of the site.

•**CHAUNCEY**, Village; Athens County; Pop. 1,048; Zip Code 45719; Elev. 659; Lat. 39-23-52 N long. 082-07-46 W; SE Ohio.

•**CHESAPEAKE**, Village; Lawrence County; Pop. 1,382; Zip Code 45619; Lat. 38-25-40 N long. 082-27-26 W; S Ohio; On the Ohio River across from Huntington, West Virginia. Named after the Chesapeake Bay.

•**CHEVIOT**, City; Hamilton County; Pop. 9,842; Lat. 39-09-25 N long. 084-36-48 W; 10 m. NW of Cincinnati in SW Ohio.

•**CHILLICOTHE**, City; Seat of Ross County; Pop. 23,384; Zip Code 45601; Elev. 643; Lat. 39-19-59 N long. 082-58-57 W; A Shawnee Indian word meaning "a place where people dwell."

•**CINCINNATI**, City; Pop. 383,114; Elev. 683; Lat. 39-09-43 N long. 084-27-25 W; Cincinnati was named by *Gen. Arthur St. Clair* in 1709 in honor of the "Order of Cincinnati" - an association of American Revolution Veterans.

•**CIRCLEVILLE**, City; Seat of Pickaway County; Pop. 11,682; Zip Code 43114; Elev. 702; Lat. 39-36-02 N long. 082-56-46 W; on Scioto River 25 m. S of Columbus in S central Ohio. Circleville was laid out inside the round enclosure from which it took its name.

•**CLEVELAND**, City; Cuyahoga County Seat; Pop. 572,657; Zip Code 441 +; Elev. 665. The city was named for General Moses Cleaveland who platted a town site here for the Connecticut Land Company in 1796. Legend has it that the simplified spelling resulted when a newly launched newspaper called itself the Cleveland Gazette and Commercial Register, dropping the first "A" so that the name would more neatly fit its masthead.

•**CLEVELAND HEIGHTS**, City; Cuyahoga County; Pop. 56,308; Zip Code 44118; Elev. 915; Lat. 41-31-12 N long. 081-33-23 W; 10 m. E of Cleveland on an Appalachian Plateau above Lake Erie in NE Ohio.

•**CLEVES**, Village; Hamilton County; Pop. 2,109; Zip Code 45002; Elev. 496; Lat. 39-09-42 N long. 084-44-57 W; SW Ohio; the village was named for early proprietor *John Cleves Symmes.*

•**COLUMBUS**, City; Franklin County Seat; Pop. 562,462; Zip Code 430+,432+; Elev. 760. This city, the state capital, was named in honor of Christopher Columbus by the Honorable Joseph Foos, a senator from Franklin County, in 1816.

•**CORTLAND**, Village; Trumbull County; Pop. 5,001; Zip Code 44410; Lat. 41-19-49 N long. 080-43-32 W; Named by the Company Railroad that came through here in the 1800's. The place was originally known as Baconsburgh for *Enos Bacon* who owned a store here in 1829.

•**COSHOCTON**, City; Seat of Coshocton County; Pop. 13,418; Zip Code 43812; Elev. 770; Lat. 40-16-19 N long. 081-51-35 W; SE central Ohio; The town's name was probably taken from one of two Delaware Indian names: Cush-og-wenk, meaning "black bear town", or Coshoc-gung, meaning "union of waters".

•**COVINGTON**, Village; Miami County; Pop. 2,614; Zip Code 45318; Elev. 930; Lat. 40-07-02 N long. 084-21-14 W; 5 m. W of Piqua in SW Ohio; on Stillwater Creek.

•**CRAIG BEACH**, Village; Mahoning County; Pop. 1,666; Lat. 41-07-01 N long. 080-59-01 W; On a widened area of the Mahoning River, W of Youngstown.

•**CRESTLINE**, City; Crawford County; Pop. 5,404; Zip Code 44827; Lat. 40-47-15 N long. 082-44-12 W; 10 m. W of Mansfield on the Sandusky River in N central Ohio; The name comes from the watershed located here.

•**CRESTON**, Village; Wayne County; Pop. 1,821; Zip Code 44217; Elev. 985; Lat. 40-59-13 N long. 081-53-38 W; NE Central Ohio.

•**CRIDERSVILLE**, Village; Auglaize County; Pop. 1,841; Zip Code 45806; Elev. 890; Lat. 40-39-15 N long. 084-09-03 W; 10 m. S of Lima in W central Ohio.

•**CROOKSVILLE**, Village; Perry County; Pop. 2,773; Zip Code 43731; Lat. 39-46-08 N long. 082-05-32 W; 10 m. S of Zanesville in SE central Ohio.

•**CUSTAR**, Village; Wood County; Pop. 254; Zip Code 43511; Lat. 41-17-05 N long. 083-50-40 W; 17 m. SW of Bowling Green in NW Ohio; rural.

•**CUYAHOGA FALLS**, City; Summit County; Pop. 43,708; Zip Code 442+; Lat. 41-08-02 N long. 081-29-05 W; 5 m. N of Akron in NE Ohio; Named because it lies along a rapids area of the Cuyahoga River.

•**CYGNET**, Village; Wood County; Pop. 646; Zip Code 43413; Lat. 41-14-24 N long. 083-38-36 W; 10 m. S of Bowling Green in central Ohio.

•**DALTON**, Village; Wayne County; Pop. 1,351; Zip Code 44618; Lat. 40-47-56 N long. 081-41-44 W; 7 m. W of Massillon in NE central Ohio.

•**DANVILLE**, Village; Knox County; Pop. 1,123; Zip Code 43014; Lat. 39-08-41 N long. 083-44-17 W; N central Ohio.

•**DAYTON**, City; Seat of Montgomery County; Pop. 1ᴗ0,323; Zip Code 454+; Lat. 39-45-32 N long. 084-11-30 W; in SW Ohio. Named for the early landowner *Johnathan Dayton*, who plotted the town in 1795.

•**DEER PARK**, City; Hamilton County; Pop. 6,501; Zip Code 45236; Lat. 39-12-19 N long. 084-23-41 W; 10 m. NE of Cincinnati in SW corner of Ohio.

•**DEFIANCE**, City; Seat of Defiance County; Pop. 16,783; Zip Code 43512; Elev. 712; Lat. 41-17-04 N long. 084-21-21 W; 40 m. NW of Lima in NW Ohio; Named for Fort Defiance.

•**DE GRAFF**, Village; Logan County; Pop. 1,361; Zip Code 43318; Elev. 1007; Lat. 40-18-43 N long. 083-54-57 W; 12 m. SW of Bellefontaine in W central Ohio.

•**DELAWARE**, City; Seat of Delaware County; Pop. 17,629; Zip Code 43015; Elev. 900; Lat. 40-17-55 N long. 083-04-05 W; central Ohio. The Delaware Indians, for whom the city and the county are named, had a village here.

•**DELPHOS**, City; Allen and Van Wert Counties; Pop. 7,317; Zip Code 45833; Elev. 750; 10 m. NW of Lima in NW Ohio.

•**DELTA**, Village; Fulton County; Pop. 2,750; Zip Code 43515; Lat. 41-34-25 N long. 084-00-19 W; Approx. 25 m. W of Toledo.

•**DENNISON**, Village; Tuscarawas County; Pop. 3,391; Zip Code 44621; Elev. 862; Lat. 40-23-36 N long. 081-20-02 W; 30 m. S of Canton in E Ohio; Named for *William Dennison*, a Civil War governor of Ohio.

•**DOVER**, City; Tuscarawas County; Pop. 11,500; Zip Code 44622; Elev. 900; Lat. 40-31-14 N long. 081-28-27 W; E Ohio. Named after the English city.

•**DOYLESTOWN**, Village; Wayne County; Pop. 2,487; Zip Code 44230; Lat. 40-58-12 N long. 081-41-48 W; NE central Ohio.

•**DUBLIN**, Village; Delaware and Franklin Counties; Pop. 3,851; Zip Code 43017; Elev. 805; Lat. 41-00-11 N long. 080-47-09 W; Central Ohio; on the W bank of the Scioto River; named after the city of the same name in Ireland.

•**EAST CANTON**, Village; Stark County; Pop. 1,719; Zip Code 44730; Elev. 1,050; Lat. 40-47-14 N long. 081-16-58 W; 5 m. E of Canton in NE Ohio; originally named as Osnaburg, the name was changed to East Canton in 1918.

•**EAST CLEVELAND**, City; Cuyahoga County; Pop. 36,694; Zip Code 44112; Elev. 730; Lat. 41-31-59 N 081-34-45 W; NE Ohio; Suburb of Cleveland.

•**EASTLAKE**, City; Lake County; Pop. 21,954; Zip Code 44094; NE Ohio; 20 m. NE of Cleveland on Lake Erie shoreline.

•**EAST LIVERPOOL**, City; Columbiana County; Pop. 16,517; Zip Code 43920; Elev. 686; Lat. 40-37-07 N long. 080-20 m. N of Steubenville in E Ohio; Named because many of the inhabitants had come from the English city of Liverpool. Later the name was changed to East Liverpool.

•**EAST PALESTINE**, City; Columbiana County; Pop. 5,303; Zip Code 44413; Elev. 1,015; Lat. 40-50-02 N long. 080-32-26 W; 20 m. S of Youngstown in E Ohio; Established in 1828 by *Thomas McCalla* and *William Grate*.

•**EATON**, City; Seat of Preble County; Pop. 6,830; Zip Code 45320; Elev. 1,040; Lat. 39-44-38 N long. 084-38-12 W; 20 m. W of Dayton in SW Ohio; was founded in 1806 and named after *General William Eaton*, hero of the Tripolitan War of 1805.

•**EDGERTON**, Village; Williams County; Pop. 1,815; Zip Code 43517; Lat. 41-26-55 N long. 084-44-53 W; 40 m. NE of Fort Wayne, Indiana in NW Ohio; is named for a land developer of this area of the state, *Alfred P. Edgerton*.

•**ELIDA**, Village; Allen County; Pop. 1,335; Zip Code 45807; Lat. 40-47-19 N long. 084-12-14 W; NW Ohio; 7 m. NW of Lima.

•**ELMORE**, Village; Ottawa County; Pop. 1,270; Zip Code 43416; Lat. 41-28-34 N long. 083-17-45 W; N Ohio; On the Portage River, just off the Ohio Turnpike (U.S. 80).

•**ELMWOOD PLACE**, Village; Hamilton County; Pop. 2,822; Zip Code 45216; Lat. 39-11-14 N long. 084-29-17 W; SW Ohio; On Mill Creek just N of Cincinnati city center.

•**ELYRIA**, City; Seat of Lorain County; Pop. 57,039; Zip Code 440+; Elev. 730; Lat. 41-22-06 N long. 082-06-28 W; N Ohio; Settlement began in 1817 when *Heman Ely*, a New Englander, acquired 12,500 acres around the falls of the Black River. The name was derived by combining Ely with ria, because his wife's name was Maria.

•**ENGLEWOOD**, City; Montgomery County; Pop. 11,320; Zip Code 45322; Elev. 922; Lat. 39-52-39 N long. 084-18-08 W; 10 m. NW of Dayton in SW Ohio.

•**ENON**, Village; Clark County; Pop. 2,595; Zip Code 45323; Lat. 39-52-41 N long. 083-56-13 W; W Ohio; 10 m. SW of Springfield.

•**EUCLID**, City; Cuyahoga County; Pop. 59,951; Zip Code 44117; Elev. 648; Lat. 41-35-35 N long. 081-31-37 W; on Lake Erie in N Ohio; suburb of Cleveland, first settled in 1798, was named for the Greek mathematician by surveyors in the party of *Moses Cleaveland*.

•**FAIRBORN**, City; Greene County; Pop. 29,747; Zip Code 45324; Lat. 39-49-15 N long. 084-01-10 W; 10 m. NE of Dayton in SW Ohio; the name came from combining the names of two towns, in 1950.

•**FAIRFAX**, Village; Hamilton County; Pop. 2,233; Lat. 39-08-43 N long. 084-23-36 W; SW Ohio; N of Cincinnati; a residential area.

•**FAIRFIELD**, City; Butler County; Pop. 30,816; Zip Code 45014; Lat. 39-20-45 N long. 084-33-38 W; 20 m. N of Cincinnati in SW Ohio.

•**FAIRLAWN**, City; Summit County; Pop. 6,105; Zip Code 44313; Elev. 1005; Lat. 41-07-40 N long. 081-36-36 W; NE central Ohio; Residential area on the Cuyahoga River, just N of Akron.

•**FAIRVIEW PARK**, City; Cuyahoga County; Pop. 19,283; Zip Code 44126; Lat. 41-26-29 N 081-51-52 W; NE Ohio; 10 m. SW of Cleveland city center.

•**FINDLAY**, City; Seat of Hancock County; Pop. 35,533; Zip Code 45840; Elev. 777; Lat. 41-02-39 N long. 083-39-00 W; 4l m. S of Toledo in NW Ohio; named for Fort Findlay, one of the outposts built here under the direction of *General Hull* during his march to Detroit in the War of 1812.

•**FLUSHING**, Village; Belmont County; Pop. 1,272; Zip Code 43977; Elev. 1132; Lat. 40-08-58 N long. 081-03-59 W; Approx. 40 m. SW of Steubenville in E Ohio in a former coal mining area. The village was named for a place in Holland.

•**FOREST PARK**, City; Hamilton County; Pop. 18,770; Elev. 836; Lat. 39-17-25 N long. 084-30-15 W; Zip Code 454+; Approx. 20 m. N of downtown Cincinnati.

•**FORT RECOVERY**, Village; Mercer County; Pop. 1,366; Zip Code 45846; Elev. 948; Lat. 40-24-46 N long. 084-46-35 W; W Ohio; Fort Recovery is the site of *Gen. Arthur St.Clair's* defeat in 1791, and of *General Anthony Wayne's* "recovery" of the area in 1793, after the erection of a fort here.

•**FORT SHAWNEE**, Village; Allen County; Pop. 4,533; Elev. 866; Lat. 40-41-12 N long. 084-08-16 W; NW Ohio; nearby is the Shawnee State Forest, the largest forested area in Ohio, covering 33,410 acres.

•**FOSTORIA**, City; Seneca County; Pop. 15,717; Zip Code 44830; Elev. 780; Lat. 41-09-25 N long. 083-25-01 W; N Ohio. Because

C.W.Foster had much to do with local development in the real-estate, merchandising, and banking fields, the community was named for him.

•**FRANKFORT**, Village; Ross County; Pop. 1,016; Zip Code 45628; Elev. 740; Lat. 41-38-38 N long. 083-51-23 W; S. Ohio.

•**FRAZEYBURG**, Village; Muskingum County; Pop. 1,022; Zip Code 43822; Lat. 40-07-02 N long. 082-07-10 W; 15 m. N of Zanesville in a hilly region in SE central Ohio; was named for *Samuel Frazey*.

•**FREMONT**, City; Seat of Sandusky County; Pop. 17,887; Zip Code 43420; Elev. 636; Lat. 41-21-01 N long. 083-07-19 W; 45 m. W of Cleveland on the Sandusky River in N Ohio; named for the explorer *John C. Fremont*.

•**GALENA**, Village; Delaware County; Pop. 358; Zip Code 43021; Lat. 40-12-54 N long. 082-52-48 W; Central Ohio on the Hoover Reservoir N of Columbus; Recreational facilities.

•**GALION**, City; Crawford County; Pop. 12,391; Zip Code 44833; Elev. 1,169; Lat. 40-44-01 N long. 082-47-24 W; 15 m. W of Mansfield in N central Ohio; Settled by German Lutherans from Pennsylvania in 1831.

•**GALLIPOLIS**, City; Seat of Gallia County; Pop. 5,576; Zip Code 45631; Elev. 576; Lat. 38-48-35 N long. 082-12-09 W; on the Ohio River, 30 m. NE of Ironton in S Ohio near the West Virginia border. Gallipolis was established in 1790. It was the third settlement in Ohio.

•**GAMBIER**, Village; Knox County; Pop. 2,056; Zip Code 43022; Lat. 40-22-32 N long. 082-23-50 W; 5 m. E of Mount Vernon on the Walhonding River in N central Ohio; named for *Lord James Gambler*, an English Admiral.

•**GARFIELD HEIGHTS**, City; Cuyahoga County; Pop. 33,380; Zip Code 441+; Lat. 41-25-01 N long. 081-36-22 W; NE Ohio, S suburb of Cleveland bordered to the W by the Cuyahoga River-Ohio Canal; Residential, with some industry.

•**GARRETTSVILLE**, Village; Portage County; Pop. 1,769; Zip Code 44231; Lat. 41-17-03 N long. 081-05-48 W; 20 m. W of Warren in NE Ohio; named for *Col. John Garrett* who was the first settler here.

•**GATES MILLS**, Village; Cuyahoga County; Pop. 2,236; Zip Code 44040; Lat. 41-31-03 N long. 081-24-13 W; 15 m. E of Cleveland, outside of the busy metropolitan area in NE Ohio; named for *Halsey Gates* who settled here in 1812.

•**GENEVA**, City; Ashtabula County; Pop. 6,655; Zip Code 44041; Elev. 685; Lat. 39-39-43 N long. 082-26-01 W; 10 m. SW of Astabula in NE Ohio; named for Switzerland town.

•**GENEVA-ON-THE-LAKE**, Village; Ashtabula County; Pop. 1,634; Zip Code 44043; Elev. 605; Lat. 41-51-34 N long. 080-57-15 W; N of the city of Geneva in NE Ohio, on Lake Erie shoreline.

•**GENOA**, Village; Ottawa County; Pop. 2,213; Zip Code 43430; Lat. 41-31-05 N long. 083-21-33 W; N Ohio; 15 m. S of Lake Erie shoreline and 20 m. SE of Toledo.

•**GEORGETOWN**, Village; Seat of Brown County; Pop. 3,467; Zip Code 45121; Elev. 930; Lat. 38-51-52 N long. 083-54-15 W; SW Ohio near the Ohio River. It was surveyed in 1819 and named for Georgetown, Kentucky.

•**GERMANTOWN**, Village; Montgomery County; Pop. 5,015; Zip Code 45327; Elev. 756; Lat. 39-35-02 N long. 081-19-04 W; 15 m. SW of Dayton in SW central Ohio; Early settlers of German descent gave this town its name after the same town name in Pennsylvania.

•**GETTYSBURG**, Village; Darke County; Pop. 545; Zip Code 45328; Lat. 40-06-41 N long. 084-29-43 W; Central Ohio; Rural community named after the city in Pennsylvania.

•**GIBSONBURG**, Village; Sandusky County; Pop. 2,479; Zip Code 43431; Lat. 41-23-04 N long. 083-19-14 W; N Ohio; 24 m. SE of Toledo.

•**GIRARD**, City; Trumbull County; Pop. 12,517; Zip Code 44420; Elev. 866; Lat. 41-09-14 N long. 080-42-06 W; NE Ohio; named for *Stephen Girard*, philanthropist and founder of Girard College at Philadelphia, Pennsylvania.

•**GLANDORF**, Village; Putnam County; Pop. 746; Zip Code 45848; Lat. 41-01-44 N long. 084-04-45 W; NW central Ohio, along the Ottawa River; named by the early settlers of German descent for the town in Germany.

•**GLENDALE**, Village; Hamilton County; Pop. 2,368; Zip Code 45246; Elev. 630; Lat. 39-16-14 N long. 084-27-34 W; 15 m. N of Cincinnati in SW Ohio.

•**GLENMONT**, Village; Holmes County; Pop. 270; Zip Code 44628; Elev. 881; Lat. 40-31-12 N long. 082-05-51 W; NE central Ohio; 22 m. S of Wooster.

•**GNADENHUTTEN**, Village; Tuscarawas County; Pop. 1,320; Zip Code 44629; Elev. 835; Lat. 40-21-30 N long. 081-26-04 W; 10 m. S of New Philadelphia on the Tuscarawas River in E central Ohio. A group of Christian Indians led by *Joshua*, a Mohican elder, came here in 1772 and founded this town, calling it after the German word for "tents of grace," which they had learned from Moravian missionaries.

•**GOLF MANOR**, City; Hamilton County; Pop. 4,317; Lat. 39-11-14 N long. 084-26-47 W; SW Ohio; Residential development just N of downtown Cincinnati; In a hilly area; named for the golf facilities in the city.

•**GORDON**, Village; Darke County; Pop. 230; Zip Code 45329; Lat. 39-55-50 N long. 084-30-31 W; W Ohio; 15 m. SE of Greenville in a corn farming region; Near Indiana state line.

•**GRAFTON**, Village; Lorain County; Pop. 2,231; Zip Code 44044; Lat. 41-16-21 N long. 082-03-17 W; N Ohio, along the Black River just S of Elyria.

•**GRAND RAPIDS**, Village; Wood County; Pop. 962; Zip Code 43522; Elev. 654; Lat. 41-24-43 N long. 083-51-52 W; NW Ohio; Along the Maumee River, 7 m. W of Bowling Green; Residential area, with a large state park nearby.

•**GRAND RIVER**, Village; Lake County; Pop. 412; Zip Code 44045; Lat. 41-44-10 N long. 081-16-53 W; NE Ohio; 2 m. S of Lake Erie shoreline and just W of the Grand River's mouth; mostly residential.

•**GRANDVIEW HEIGHTS**, City; Franklin County; Pop. 7,420; Zip Code (with Columbus); Lat. 40-11-08 N long. 083-58-13 W; Central Ohio; On the Olentangy River, just W of downtown Columbus

•**GRANVILLE**, Village; Licking County; Pop. 3,851; Zip Code 43023; Elev. 960; Lat. 40-04-05 N long. 082-31-11 W; 10 m. W of Newark in a rich farming area in central Ohio; named for the town in Massachusetts.

•**GRATIOT**, Village; Licking and Muskingum Counties; Pop. 227; Zip Code 43740; Elev. 988; Lat. 39-57-04 N long. 082-12-58 W; off U.S. Highway 70, 10 m. W of Zanesville in SE Central Ohio. The place is named for *General Charles Gratiot* who was a chief of Army engineer that built a National Road between Columbus in Zanesville.

•**GRAYSVILLE**, Village; Monroe County; Pop. 112; Zip Code 45734; Lat. 39-39-56 N long. 081-10-26 W; SE Ohio in the E Wayne National Forest.

•**GREEN CAMP**, Village; Marion County; Pop. 475; Zip Code 43322; Lat. 40-31-55 N long. 083-12-38 W; Central Ohio; On the Scioto River where it branches off the Little Scioto River; Former Indian camp.

•**GREENFIELD**, City; Seat of Highland County; Pop. 5,034; Zip Code 45123; Lat. 39-21-07 N long. 083-22-58 W; 20 m. W of Chillicothe along Paint Creek in S Ohio. The name describes the locality.

•**GREENHILLS**, City; Hamilton County; Pop. 4,927; Zip Code 45218; Elev. 968; Lat. 39-16-05 N long. 084-31-23 W; SW Ohio, N suburb of Cincinnati, first developed in 1937 by the Federal Works Project Administration.

•**GREEN SPRINGS**, Village; Sandusky and Seneca Counties; Pop. 1,568; Zip Code 44836; N Ohio; 10 m. SE of Fremont.

•**GREENVILLE**, City; Darke County; Pop. 13,002; Zip Code 45331; Elev. 1,020; Lat. 40-06-10 N long. 084-37-59 W; 30 m. NW of Dayton in W Ohio. Site of Fort Greenville, built in 1793. Once the home of *Tecumseh*, Shawnee Indian chief. The place is named for *Gen. Nathaniel Greene*.

•**GREENWICH**, Village; Huron County; Pop. 1,458; Zip Code 44837; Elev. 1,031; Lat. 41-01-48 N long. 082-30-57 W; N Ohio; in a large farming area. Named for Greenwich, CT.

•**GROVE CITY**, City; Franklin County; Pop. 16,793; Zip Code 43123; Elev. 835; Lat. 39-52-53 N long. 083-05-35 W; Central Ohio; Just S of Columbus; Named by *William F. Bruck* for the description of the area.

•**GROVEPORT**, Village; Franklin County; Pop. 3,286; Zip Code 43125; Lat. 39-52-42 N long. 082-53-02 W; Central Ohio; Between the Hocking River and Big Walnut Creek, SE of Columbus city center; First named Wert's Grove by *Jacob Wert* in 1843 for the walnut groves here. A year later, nearby, *John Rareysport*, a great horse trainer, started a settlement. In 1846 the names were combined.

•**GROVER HILL**, Village; Paulding County; Pop. 486; Zip Code 45849; Lat. 41-01-09 N long. 084-28-36 W; NW Ohio; 20 m. SW of Defiance; Rural center.

•**HAMILTON**, City; Seat of Butler County; Pop. 63,189; Zip Code 450 + zone; Lat. 39-23-58 N long. 084-33-41 W; 20 m. N of Cincinnati in SW Ohio. It lies on the Great Miami River; named after *Alexander Hamilton*.

•**HAMLER**, Village; Henry County; Pop. 625; Elev. 714; Lat. 41-13-45 N long. 084-02-03 W; NW Ohio; 20 m. E of Defiance; Rural trading community.

•**HANGING ROCK**, Village; Lawrence County; Pop. 353; Zip Code 45635; Elev. 550; Lat. 38-33-36 N long. 082-43-16 W; S Ohio; At the end of the crescent formed by the Ohio River; It takes its name from the cliff of sandstone 400 feet high, the top of which juts out over the wall like the cornice of a house. The village was founded in 1820.

•**HARRISON**, Village; Hamilton County; Pop. 5,855; Zip Code 45030; Elev. 820; Lat. 39-15-43 N long. 084-49-12 W; SW Ohio; Named for *Gen. William Henry Harrison*.

•**HARTFORD**, Village; Licking County; Pop. 444; Zip Code 44424; Lat. 41-18-41 N long. 080-34-07 W; E central Ohio; Rural. Named for the city in Connecticut. In 1798 this land was deeded to *Ephriam Root* and *Urial Holmes*.

•HARVEYSBURG, Village; Warren County; Pop. 425; Zip Code 45032; Lat. 39-30-13 N long. 084-00-38 W; 29 m. SE of Dayton along Caesar's Creek in SW Ohio. Named for *George Harvey* and was platted in 1815.

•HAYESVILLE, Village; Ashland County; Pop. 514; Zip Code 44838; Elev. 1,244; Lat. 40-46-23 N long. 082-15-45 W; N central Ohio. In 1830 *Linus Hayes*, tavern owner, and the *Reverend John Cox* laid out the village.

•HEATH, City; Licking County; Pop. 6,961; Zip Code 43055; Lat. 40-01-22 N long. 082-26-41 W; S central Ohio; Just W of Newark.

•HEBRON, Village; Licking County; Pop. 2,036; Zip Code 43025; Elev. 889; Lat. 39-57-42 N long. 082-29-29 W; S central Ohio; 9 m. SW of Newark on a branch of the Licking river. Named after the Biblical region.

•HICKSVILLE, Village; Defiance County; Pop. 3,743; Zip Code 43526; Elev. 766; Lat. 41-17-35 N long. 084-45-43 W; 20 m. W of Defiance, just W of the Indiana state line in NW Ohio. Named for *Henry W. Wicks* who laid out this town in 1836 with a New York state group named "American Land Co."

•HIGGINSPORT, (alt. GINSPORT), Village; Brown County; Pop. 343; Zip Code 45131; Lat. 38-47-23 N long. 083-58-03 W; SW Ohio; Named for *Robert Higgins* who in 1894 settled here.

•HILLIARD, City; Franklin County; Pop. 7,996; Zip Code 43026; Lat. 40-02-00 N long. 083-09-30 W; S central Ohio; W of Columbus; Named for the man who laid out this place in 1853.

•HILLSBORO, City; Seat of Highland County; Pop. 6,344; Zip Code 45133; Elev. 1,129; Lat. 39-12-08 N long. 083-36-42 W; S Ohio. Descriptively named.

•HOLGATE, Village; Henry County; Pop. 1,320; Zip Code 43527; Elev. 714; Lat. 41-14-56 N long. 084-07-59 W; NW Ohio; 11 m. S of Napoleon.

•HOLLOWAY, Village; Belmont County; Pop. 455; Zip Code 43985; Lat. 40-09-44 N long. 081-07-58 W; E Ohio; 40 m. SW of Steubenville; Named for the Holloway family from Virginia in 1827. *Issac Holloway* platted the town in 1883.

•HUBBARD, City; Trumbull County; Pop. 9,262; Zip Code 44425; Elev. 935; Lat. 41-09-23 N long. 080-34-10 W; NE Ohio; 10 m. N of Youngstown, just W of the Pennsylvania state line; This town was named for *Nehemiah Hubbard*, who purchased the surrounding township in 1801.

•HUDSON, Village; Summit County; Pop. 4,612; Zip Code 44236; Elev. 1,409; Lat. 41-14-24 N long. 081-26-27 W; 10 m. NE of Akron in NE Ohio. In 1799, *David Hudson* and a group from Connecticut settled this site.

•HURON, City; Erie County; Pop. 7,075; Zip Code 44839; Elev. 599; Lat. 41-22-25 N long. 082-33-17 W; 10 m. ESE of Sandusky in N Ohio; at the mouth of the Huron River. Named for the Indian tribe.

•INDEPENDENCE, City; Cuyahoga County; Pop. 6,612; Zip Code 44131; Elev. 728; Lat. 41-23-40 N long. 081-38-27 W; NE Ohio; Just S of Cleveland along the old Ohio Canal; Industrial suburb.

•IRONTON, City; Seat of Lawrence County; Pop. 14,178; Zip Code 45638; Elev. 547; Lat. 38-32-12 N long. 082-40-59 W; S Ohio; On the Ohio River across from the Kentucky state line; Named after iron ore was discovered here in 1826.

•ITHACA, Village; Darke County; Pop. 133; Zip Code (Rural); Lat. 39-56-14 N long. 084-33-12 W; W Ohio; Farming community 15 m. S of Greenville.

•JACKSON, City; Seat of Jackson County; Pop. 6,670; Zip Code 45640; Elev. 670; Lat. 39-03-07 N long. 082-38-12 W; S Ohio; Platted in 1817. Named after *Gen. Andrew Jackson.*

•JACKSONVILLE, Village; Athens County; Pop. 654; Zip Code 45740; Lat. 38-54-29 N long. 083-26-24 W; 15 m. N of Athens in central Wayne National Forest in SE central Ohio; Named for *Andrew Jackson.*

•JAMESTOWN, Village; Greene County; Pop. 1,703; Zip Code 45335; Elev. 1,053; Lat. 39-39-29 N long. 083-44-06 W; SW Ohio; Named for Jamestown, VA.

•JEFFERSON, Village; Seat of Ashtabula County; Pop. 2,964; Zip Code 44047; Elev. 700; Lat. 41-44-19 N long. 080-46-12 W; NE corner of Ohio; 10 m. S of Ashtabula. Named for *Thomas Jefferson.*

•JEFFERSON, Village; Madison County; Pop. 4,433; Zip Code 43162; Lat. 39-48-50 N long. 082-45-39 W; SW central Ohio; 15 m. W of Columbus. Named for *Thomas Jefferson.*

•JEFFERSONVILLE, Village; Fayette County; Pop. 1,247; Zip Code 43128; Elev. 1049; Lat. 39-39-13 N long. 083-33-50 W; SW central Ohio near Paint Creek; Named for *Thomas Jefferson.*

•JERUSALEM, Village; Monroe County; Pop. 237; Zip Code 43747; Lat. 39-51-06 N long. 081-05-33 W; SE Ohio; Named, as were many towns in the area, for a Biblical city.

•JEWETT, Village; Harrison County; Pop. 976; Zip Code 43986; Lat. 40-22-04 N long. 081-00-20 W; E Ohio; 25 m. W of Steubenville in a coal mining area.

•JOHNSTOWN, Village; Licking County; Pop. 3,158; Zip Code 43031; Elev. 1,166; Lat. 40-09-13 N long. 082-41-07 W; 20 m. NE of Columbus in N central Ohio. Named for *Capt. James Johnston* who was an early landowner.

•JUNCTION CITY, Village; Perry County; Pop. 754; Zip Code 43748; Lat. 39-43-16 N long. 082-17-56 W; SE central Ohio; 18 m. E of Lancaster; On a railroad line; Named for a railroad junction.

•KALIDA, Village; Putnam County; Pop. 1,019; Zip Code 45853; Elev. 727; Lat. 40-58-58 N long. 084-11-58 W; 20 m. N of Lima in NW Ohio along the Ottawa River. Named for the Greek word meaning beautiful.

•KENT, City; Portage County; Pop. 26,142; Zip Code 44240; Elev. 1097; Lat. 41-09-13 N long. 081-21-29 W; 10 m. E of Akron on the Cuyahoga River in NE central Ohio.

•KETTERING, City; Montgomery County; Pop. 61,223; Zip Code 454+; Lat. 39-41-22 N long. 084-10-08 W; SW Ohio; On thesouthern outskirts of Dayton; Named after *Charles F. Kettering.*

•KILLBUCK, Village; Holmes County; Pop. 938; Zip Code 44637; Elev. 808; Lat. 40-29-42 N long. 081-59-05 W; NE central Ohio; First settled in 1811, was named for the Indian, *Killbuck*, who figured in the region's history.

•KINGSTON, Village; Ross County; Pop. 1,299; Zip Code 45644; Elev. 797; Lat. 39-28-26 N long. 082-54-39W; S central Ohio; 11 m. NE of Chillicothe in a rolling farmlands region.

•KIRKERSVILLE, Village; Licking County; Pop. 622; Zip Code 43033; Lat. 39-57-34 N long. 082-35-45 W; 22 m. E of Columbus along a branch of the Licking River in central Ohio.

•KIRTLAND, City; Lake County; Pop. 5,915; Zip Code (with Euclid); Elev. 660; Lat. 41-37-44 N long. 081-21-42 W; a suburban village on the brow of a hill overlooking the Chargrin River.

•**KIRTLAND HILLS**, Village; Lake County; Pop. 498; Lat. 41-37-26 N long. 081-18-26 W; NE Ohio.

•**LAFAYETTE**, Village; Allen County; Pop. 487; Zip Code 45854; Elev. 1,013; Lat. 40-45-37 N long. 083-56-55 W; NW Ohio; Near Lima; Named for the French marquis who aided Washington in the Revolutionary War.

•**LAGRANGE**, Village; Lorain County; Pop. 1,253; Zip Code 44050; N Ohio; Elev. 825; Lat. 41-14-14 N long. 082-07-12 W; 10 m. S of Elyria near the Black River.

•**LAKEMORE**, Village; Summit County; Pop. 2,746; Zip Code 44250; Lat. 41-01-15 N long. 081-26-10 W; NE Ohio; Just SE of Akron onthe N tip of Springfield Lake.

•**LAKEVIEW**, Village; Logan County; Pop. 1,089; Zip Code 43331; Lat. 39-55-19 N long. 081-26-00 W; W Ohio, on Indian Lake, 15 m. NW of Bellefontaine; Descriptively named for its lakeside location.

•**LAKEWOOD**, City; Cuyahoga County; Pop. 61,921; Zip Code 44107; Elev. 685; Lat. 41-28-55 N long. 081-47-54 W; NE Ohio; On Lake Erie; named for its setting along the wooded shore of Lake Erie.

•**LANCASTER**, City; Seat of Fairfield County; Pop. 34,925; Zip Code 43130; Elev. 898; Lat. 39-42-49 N long. 082-35-58 W; S central Ohio; Named for Lancaster, PA.

•**LA RUE**, Village; Marion County; Pop. 862; Zip Code 43332; 13 m. W of Marion on the Scioto River in central Ohio. Named for land owner *William LaRue.*

•**LEBANON**, City; Seat of Warren County; Pop. 9,602; Zip Code 45036; Elev. 969; Lat. 39-36-28 N long. 081-16-24 W; 20 m. E of Hamilton in SW Ohio; was founded in 1803 and named after the Biblical country.

•**LEESBURG**, Village; Highland County; Pop. 1,021; Zip Code 45135; Elev. 1,025; Lat. 39-20-42 N long. 083-33-11 W; SW central Ohio; 10 m. N of Hillsboro.

•**LEIPSIC**, Village; Putnam County; Pop. 2,170; Zip Code 45856; Elev. 766; Lat. 41-05-54 N long. 083-59-05 W; 30 m. N of Lima in NW Ohio. Named by the settlers for their hometown in Germany.

•**LEWISBURG**, Village; Preble County; Pop. 1,452; Zip Code 45338; Elev. 1,019; Lat. 39-50-46 N long. 084-32-23 W; 22 m. NW of Dayton in SW Ohio; Industrial center of a large agricultural region.

•**LEXINGTON**, Village; Richland County; Pop. 3,826; Zip Code 44904; Elev. 1,180; Lat. 40-40-43 N long. 082-34-57 W; 10 m. SW of Mansfield in N central Ohio; Laid out in 1812, and named in honor of Lexington, Massachusetts.

•**LIMA**, City; Seat of Allen County; Pop. 47,354; Zip Code 458+; Elev 878; Lat. 40-44-33 N long. 084-06-19 W; NW Ohio, named after the city in South America.

•**LINCOLN HEIGHTS**, City; Hamilton County; Pop. 5,214; Zip Code (with Cincinnati); Lat. 39-14-20 N long. 084-27-20 W; SW Ohio; N suburb of Cincinnati, set amidst the hills encircling the city.

•**LINDSEY**, Village; Sandusky County; Pop. 572; Zip Code 43442; Lat. 41-25-08 N long. 083-13-17 W; N Ohio; 30 m. SE of Toledo and approx. 10 m. W of Sandusky Bay.

•**LISBON**, Seat of Columbia County; Pop. 3,157; Zip Code 44432; Elev. 955; Lat. 39-51-39 N long. 083-38-07 W; 15 m. NW of East Liverpool in E Ohio; Founded in 1802 and named for the great city in Portugal.

•**LOCKLAND**, City; Hamilton County; Pop. 4,256; Zip Code 45215; SW Ohio; Just N of Cincinnati on Mill Creek.

•**LODI**, Village; Median County; Pop. 2,924; Zip Code 44254; Elev. 927; Lat. 41-02-00 N long. 082-00-44 W; N Ohio. Named after Bonaparte's Italian Campaign victory, the Battle of Lodi.

•**LOGAN**, City; Seat of Hocking County; Pop. 6,557; Zip Code 43138; Elev. 728; Lat. 39-32-24 N long. 082-24-26 W; S Ohio; Named for the Mingo Chief.

•**LONDON**, City; Seat of Madison County; Pop. 6,916; Zip Code 43140; Elev. 1,046; Lat. 39-53-11 N long. 083-26-54 W; SW central Ohio. Named after the English city.

•**LORAIN**, City; Lorain County; Pop. 74,580; Zip Code 440+; Elev. 610; Lat. 41-27-10 N long. 082-10-57 W; 25 m. W of Cleveland in N Ohio where Black River flows into Lake Erie; Named for the French, Lorraine by *Judge Herman Ely* from his European travels.

•**LOUDONVILLE**, Village; Ashland County; Pop. 2,933; Zip Code 44842; Elev. 974; Lat. 40-38-07 N long. 082-14-00 W; N central Ohio; Named after *James Loudon,* Priest who laid out the town with *Stephen Butler* in 1814.

•**LOUISVILLE**, City; Stark County; Pop. 7,839; Zip Code 44641; Elev. 900; Lat. 38-59-34 N long. 083-27-52 W; 5 m NE of Canton in NE central Ohio; A land owner named *Henry Loutzenheiser* named the place after his son *Lewis Heald.*

•**LOVELAND**, City; Hamilton and Clermont Counties; Pop. 9,096; Zip Code 45140; Elev. 728; Lat. 39-17-59 N long. 084-15-48 W; SW Ohio; 16 m. NE of Cincinnati on the Little Miami River; Named for *Colonel Loveland.*

•**LOWELLVILLE**, Village; Mahoning County; Pop. 1,559; Zip Code 44436; Lat. 41-02-07 N long. 080-32-12 W; 5 m. SE of Youngstown in NE Ohio.

•**LYNCHBURG**, Village; Highland County; Pop. 1,207; Zip Code 45142; Lat. 40-44-28 N long. 080-59-58 W; 15 m. NW of Hillsboro in S Ohio. Named by early settlers from Virginia for their original hometown.

•**LYNDHURST**, City; Cuyahoga County; Pop. 18,093; Zip Code 44124; Lat. 41-31-12 N long. 081-29-20 W; NE Ohio; Approx. 10 m. E of downtown Cleveland in a residential area.

•**LYONS**, Village; Fulton County; Pop. 593; Zip Code 43533; Elev. 771; Lat. 41-41-58 N long. 084-04-13 W; NW Ohio; 50 m. W of Toledo, just S of the Michigan state line.

•**MACEDONIA**, City; Summit County; Pop. 6,562; Zip Code 44056; Elev. 989; Lat. 41-18-49 N long. 081-30-31 W; NE Ohio; At a midpoint between Cleveland and Akron; Named for the ancient kingdom in Europe.

•**MADEIRA**, City; Hamilton County; Pop. 9,342; Zip Code 45243; Elev. 772; Lat. 39-11-27 N long. 084-21-49 W; SW Ohio; Approx. 15 m. NE of Cincinnati in a residential area.

•**MADISON**, Village; Lake County; Pop. 2,278; Zip Code 44057; Elev. 744; Lat. 41-46-16 N long. 081-03-00 W; 15 m. SW of Ashtabula in NE Ohio; Named for *President James Madison.*

•**MAGNOLIA**, Village; Carroll and Stark Counties; Pop. 984; Zip Code 44643; Lat. 40-39-04 N long. 081-17-57 W; 15 m. S of Canton along Sandy Creek in NE Ohio; *Richard Elson* founded the place in 1834. and built a mill, which he named after the magnolia flower.

•**MALTA**, Village; Morgan County; Pop. 960; Zip Code 43758; Elev. 671; Lat. 39-38-57 N long. 081-51-44 W; SE Ohio; Across the Muskingum River from McConnelsville; Named after the famous island.

•**MALVERN**, Village; Carroll County; Pop. 1,023; Zip Code 44644; Elev. 997; Lat. 40-41-30 N long. 081-10-53 W; 16 m. SE of Canton on Sandy Creek in E Ohio; Named after the town in Pennsylvania by the two landowners, *Joseph Tidbald* and *Lewis Vail*.

•**MANCHESTER**, Village; Adams County; Pop. 2,333; Zip Code 45144; Elev. 511; Lat. 38-41-17 N long. 083-36-34 W; S Ohio; Named after Manchester, England.

•**MANSFIELD**, City; Seat of Richland County; Pop. 53,907; Zip Code 449 + zone; Elev. 1,240; Lat. 40-45-30 N long. 082-30-56 W; Ncentral Ohio; Named in 1808 under the direction of *Jared Mansfield*, Surveyor General of the United States.

•**MANTUA**, Village; Portage County; Pop. 1,041; Zip Code 44255; Lat. 41-17-02 N long. 081-13-27 W; 30 m. SE of Cleveland in NE Ohio on the Cuyahoga River. Named for a town in Italy, by *John Leavitt*.

•**MAPLE HEIGHTS**, City; Cuyahoga County; Pop. 29,465; Zip Code 44137; Lat. 41-24-55 N long. 081-33-58 W; NE Ohio; SE suburb of Cleveland; Residential area named for the trees which line many of the streets.

•**MARIEMONT**, Village; Hamilton County; Pop. 3,274; Zip Code 45227; Elev. 650; Lat. 39-08-42 N long. 084-22-28 W; SW Ohio; Overlooking the Little Miami River; Laid out in 1922 on land owned by *Marie Emery* of Cincinnati.

•**MARIETTA**, City; Seat of Washington County; Pop. 16,462; Zip Code 45750; Elev. 620; Lat. 39-24-55 N long. 081-27-18 W; SE Ohio; 45 m. SE of Zanesville where the Ohio and Muskingum Rivers merge; Named after *Queen Marie Antoinette* of France for her assistance in the American Revolution.

•**MARION**, City; Seat of Marion County; Pop. 37,071; Zip Code 43302; Elev. 986; Lat. 40-35-19 N long. 083-07-43 W; Central Ohio; Named for General Francis Marion, a Revolutionary War hero.

•**MARSHALLVILLE**, Village; Wayne County; Pop. 794; Zip Code 44645; Lat. 40-54-08 N long. 081-44-03 W; NE Ohio; 25 m. SW of Akron.

•**MARTINS FERRY**, City; Belmont County; Pop. 9,304; Zip Code 43935; Elev. 660; Lat. 40-05-45 N long. 080-43-29 W; E Ohio; In 1835, the place was known as Martinsville after *Ebenezer Martin*. The name was later changed by the post office to Martins Ferry.

•**MARYSVILLE**, City; Seat of Union County; Pop. 7,403; Zip Code 43040; Elev. 999; Lat. 39-56-50 N long. 081-36-13 W; W central Ohio; Settled in 1816 by *Jonathan Summers*, and platted in 1820 by *Samuel Culbertson*, who named the village for his daughter Mary.

•**MASON**, City; Warren County; Pop. 8,696; Zip Code 45040; Lat. 39-21-36 N long. 084-18-36 W; SW Ohio; 20 m. E of Cincinnati in a hilly residential area.

•**MASSILLON**, City; Stark County; Pop. 30,422; Zip Code 44646; Elev. 1,030; Lat. 40-47-48 N long. 081-31-18 W; 10 m. W of Canton in NE central Ohio. Named after the famous French divine Jean Batiste Massillon.

•**MAUMEE**, City; Lucas County; Pop. 15,752; Zip Code 43537; Lat.41-33-46 N long. 083-39-14 W; NW Ohio; adjacent to and S of Toledo on the Maumee River; Early a trading post and fort (1680) later the British Ft. Miami (1764). The present name is a variation of Miami.

•**MAYFIELD**, Village; Cuyahog County; Pop. 3,552; Lat. 39-29-41 N long. 084-22-22 W; 15 m. E of Cleveland in NE Ohio; Residential.

•**MAYFIELD HEIGHTS**, City; Cuyahoga County; Pop. 21,383; Lat. 41-31-09 N long. 081-27-29 W; 15 m. E of Cleveland, just S of Village of Mayfield; Residential development.

•**MCARTHUR**, Village; Seat of Vinton County; Pop. 1,919; Zip Code 45651; Elev. 767; Lat. 39-14-47 N long. 082-28-43 W; S Ohio; named McArthurstown for *General Duncan McArthur*, later governor of Ohio.

•**MCCOMB**, Village; Hancock County; Pop. 1,606; Zip Code 45858; Elev. 778; Lat. 41-06-27 N long. 083-47-34 W; NW Ohio; 10 m. NW of Findlay.

•**MCDONALD**, Village; Trumbull County; Pop. 3,738; Zip Code 44437; Lat. 39-51-45 N long. 081-50-50 W; NE Ohio; just S of Niles and Warren.

•**MECHANICSBURG**, Village; Champaign County; Pop. 1,782; Zip Code 43044; Lat. 40-04-19 N long. 083-33-23 W; W Ohio; 30 m. W of Columbus in a farming region.

•**MEDINA**, City; Seat of Medina County; Pop. 15,307; Zip Code 44256; Elev. 1,086; Lat. 41-08-18 N long. 081-51-50 W; 20 m. NW of Akron in N Ohio. The name was changed to Medina in 1825 for the ancient capital of Arabia.

•**MENDON**, Village; Mercer County; Pop. 747; Zip Code 45862; Lat. 40-40-24 N long. 084-31-08 W; W Ohio; Just S of the Saint Marys river.

•**MENTOR**, City; Lake County; Pop. 41,903; Area Zip Code 44060; Elev. 65; Lat. 41-39-58 N long. 081-20-23 W; NE Ohio, just S of the Lake Erie shoreline; Named for the great teacher from Greek history.

•**MENTOR-ON-THE-LAKE**, City; Lake County; Pop. 7,894; Zip Code 44060; Lat. 41-42-18 N long. 081-21-38 W; Just S of Lake Erie shoreline.

•**MIAMISBURG**, City; Montomery County; Pop. 15,327; Zip Code 45342; Elev. 711; Lat. 39-38-34 N long. 084-17-12 W; SW Ohio; Named for its location on the Great Miami River, S of Dayton.

•**MIDDLEBURG HEIGHTS**, City; Cuyahoga County; Pop. 16,228; Zip Code (With Parma); Lat. 41-21-41 N long. 081-48-47 W; 15 m. SW of Cleveland in a suburban-resdiential area.

•**MIDDLEFIELD**, Village; Geauga County; Pop. 2,001; Zip Code 44062; Elev. 1126; Lat. 41-27-43 N long. 081-04-26 W; NE Ohio; Named this for its geographic location between Warren and Painesville.

•**MIDDLE POINT**, Village; Van Wert County; Pop. 709; Zip Code 45863; NW Ohio; At the midpoint of a large bend in the Auglaize River, 8 m. E of Van Wert city.

•**MIDDLEPORT**, Village; Meigs County; Pop. 2,967; Zip Code 45760; Elev. 564; Lat. 39-00-06 N long. 082-02-56 W; SE Ohio; 40 m. SW of Marietta.

•**MIDDLETOWN**, City; Butler County; Pop. 43,693; Zip Code 45042; Lat. 39-30-54 N long. 084-23-54 W; SW Ohio; On the Miami River, 35 m. N of Cincinnati; Named for its location between Dayton and Cincinnati.

•**MILAN**, Village; Erie and Huron Counties; Pop. 1,564; Zip Code 44846; Elev. 602; Lat. 41-17-51 N long. 082-36-20 W; N Ohio; Named after the famous Italian city.

•**MILFORD**, Village; Clermont County; Pop. 5,227; Zip Code 45150; Lat. 39-10-31 N long. 084-17-40 W; SW Ohio; 12 m. NE of Cincinnati in an industrial area.

•**MILLERSBURG**, Village; Seat of Holmes County; Pop. 3,225; Zip Code 44654; Elev. 818; Lat. 40-33-16 N long. 081-55-05 W; NE central Ohio; Named after *Charles Miller* who settled here in 1824 along with *Adam Johnson.*

•**MINERVA**, Village; Stark & Carroll Counties; Pop. 4,547; Zip Code 44657; Elev. 1,050; Lat. 40-43-47 N long. 081-06-20 W; NE central Ohio on the Sandy River. It was named for the niece of *John Whitacre,* the founder.

•**MINERVA PARK**, Village; Franklin County; Pop. 1,617; Lat. 40-04-35 N long. 082-56-38 W; central Ohio.

•**MINGO JUNCTION**, City, Jefferson County; Pop. 4,844; Zip Code 43938; Elev. 675; Lat. 40-19-18 N long. 080-36-36 W; E Ohio; On the Ohio River.

•**MINSTER**, Village; Auglaize County; Pop. 2,556; Zip Code 45864; Elev. 967; Lat. 40-23-35 N long. 084-22-34 W; W Ohio; On E shore of Loramie Lake.

•**MOGADORE**, Village; Portage & Summit Counties; Pop. 4,192; Zip Code 44260; Lat. 41-02-47 N long. 081-23-53 W; NE Ohio; Named after the city of the same name in Morocco, North Africa.

•**MONROE**, Village; Warren County; Pop. 4,259; Zip Code 45050; Elev. 823; Lat. 39-26-25 N long. 084-21-44 W; SW Ohio; Approx. 30 m. N of Cincinnati. Named after *President James Monroe.*

•**MONTGOMERY**, City; Hamilton County; Pop. 15,090; Zip Code 45242; Lat. 39-13-41 N long. 084-21-15 W; SW Ohio; 15 m. NE of Cincinnati in a residential area.

•**MONTPELIER**, Village; Williams County; Pop. 4,426; Zip Code 43543; Elev. 860; 50 m. W of Toledo in NW Ohio on the St. Joseph River; Named after the French city.

•**MORAINE**, City; Montgomery County; Pop. 5,250; Lat. 39-42-22 N long. 084-13-10 W; 5 m. S of Dayton in SW Ohio. Named after the local geological feature.

•**MORROW**, Village; Warren County; Pop. 1,247; Zip Code 45152; Elev. 640; Lat. 39-21-16 N long. 084-07-38 W; SW Ohio; Settled in 1844 and named for *Jeremiah Morrow,* Governor of Ohio from 1822 to 1826.

•**MOUNT GILEAD**, Village; Seat of Morrow County; Pop. 2,894; Zip Code 43338; Elev. 1,083; Lat. 40-32-57 N long. 082-49-39 W; Named to honor Mount Gilead, Virginia.

•**MOUNT HEALTHY**, City; Hamilton County; Pop. 7,553; Zip Code 45231; Elev. 855; Lat. 39-14-01 N long. 084-32-45 W; SW Ohio; 14 m. N of Cincinnati surrounding a large hill by the same name.

•**MOUNT ORAB**, Village; Brown County; Pop. 1,869; Zip Code 45154; Elev. 922; Lat. 39-01-39 N long. 083-55-11 W; SW Ohio; In a hilly region near Lake Grant.

•**MOUNT STERLING**, Village; Madison County; Pop. 1,616; Zip Code 43149; Elev. 906; Lat. 39-43-10 N long. 083-15-55 W; SW central Ohio; On Deer Creek; 23 m. SW of Columbus.

•**MOUNT VERNON**, City; Seat of Knox County; Pop. 14,362; Zip Code 43050; Lat. 40-23-36 N long. 082-29-09 W; 35 m. NE of Columbusin central Ohio on the Kokosing River. Named after George Washington's estate.

•**MUNROE FALLS**, Village; Summit County; Pop. 4,729; Zip Code 44262; Lat. 41-08-40 N long. 081-26-24 W; NE central Ohio; Named for founder Edmund Munroe.

•**NAPOLEON**, City; Seat of Henry County; Pop. 8,615; Zip Code 43545; Elev. 689; Lat. 41-23-32 N long. 084-07-31 W; NW Ohio. Named in honor of the great French soldier.

•**NAVARRE**, Village; Stark County; Pop. 1,344; Zip Code 44662; Elev. 940; Lat. 40-43-28 N long. 081-31-20 W; NE Ohio; Named in honor of *King Henry IV* of France and Navarre by the French speaking wife of *James Duncan.*

•**NELSONVILLE**, City; Athens County; Pop. 4,571; Zip Code 45764; Elev. 1,044; Lat. 39-27-31 N long. 082-13-55 W; S Ohio; Originally known as Englishtown, the town changed its name in 1824 to honor *Daniel Nelson,* the settlement's most enterprising citizen.

•**NEVADA**, Village; Wyandot County; Pop. 946; Zip Code 44849; Lat. 40-49-09 N long. 083-07-50 W; NW central Ohio; 10 m. W of Bucyrus in a rich farming area. Named in 1852 for the boundary of the Sierra Nevada Mountains.

•**NEW ALBANY**, Village; Franklin County; Pop. 398; Zip Code 43054; Lat. 40-56-32 N long. 080-50-10 W; Central Ohio; 13 m. NE of Columbus. Named for Albany, New York.

•**NEWARK**, City; Seat of Licking County; Pop. 41,162; Zip Code 43055; Elev. 836; Lat. 40-03-29 N long. 082-24-05 W; 35 m. E of Columbus. Founded in 1802 by *General William Schenck,* the settlement was named after a New Jersey community.

•**NEW BOSTON**, Village; Scioto County; Pop. 3,177; Zip Code 45662; Lat. 38-45-08 N long. 082-56-13 W; S Ohio; On the Ohio River, 5 m. E of Portsmouth; Named after Boston, Massachusetts.

•**NEW BREMEN**, Village; Auglaize County; Pop. 2,401; Zip Code 45869; Elev. 941; Lat. 40-26-13 N long. 084-22-47 W; W central Ohio; On the St. Marys River. Named for the city in Germany.

•**NEWBURGH HEIGHTS**, Village; Cuyahoga County; Pop. 2,671; Zip Code 441+; Lat. 41-27-00 N long. 081-39-49 W; NE Ohio; Just S of downtown Cleveland off the Willow Freeway (U.S.77).

•**NEW CARLISLE**, City; Clark County; Pop. 6,435; Zip Code 45344; Elev. 906; Lat. 39-56-10 N long. 084-01-32 W; W central Ohio; 12 m. W of Springfield. Named after Carlisle, New Jersey.

•**NEWCOMERSTOWN**, Village; Tuscarawas County; Pop. 3,955; Zip Code 43832; Elev. 849; Lat. 40-16-20 N long. 081-36-22 W; E Ohio; It was to this place that the second wife of *Chief Eagle Feather* called "the newcomer" by his first wife, *Mary Harris,* fled after circumstantial evidence pointed to her guilt in his murder. it is said to have taken its final name from "the newcomer."

•**NEW CONCORD**, Village; Muskingum County; Pop. 1,858; Zip Code 43762; Lat. 39-59-37 N long. 081-44-03 W; 8 m. W of Cambridge in SE central Ohio. Named after Concord, Massachusetts.

•**NEW LEBANON**, Village; Montgomery County; Pop. 4,498; Zip Code 45345; Elev. 913; Lat. 39-44-43 N long. 084-23-06 W; 10 m. W of Dayton in SW Ohio. Named after the Biblical country.

•**NEW LEXINGTON**, Village; Perry County Seat; Pop. 5,174; Zip Code 43764; Elev. 958; Lat. 39-42-50 N long. 082-12-31 W; SE central Ohio; 19 m. SW of Zanesville. Named for the famous town in Massachusetts.

•**NEW LONDON**, Village; Huron County; Pop. 2,439; Zip Code 44851; 45 m. SW of Cleveland near the Vermillion River in N central Ohio. The village is named for the city in Connecticut.

•**NEW MADISON**, Village; Darke County; Pop. 1,016; Zip Code 45346; Lat. 39-58-04 N long. 084-42-33 w; W Ohio; 11 m. S of Greenville.

•**NEW MIAMI**, Village; Butler County; Pop. 2,991; Lat. 39-26-05 N long. 084-32-13 W; E Ohio. Named after the local Miami Indians.

•**NEW MIDDLETOWN**, Village; Mahoning County; Pop. 2,189; Zip Code 4442; Lat. 40-51-52 N long. 080-54-55 W; 12 m. SE of Youngstown.

•**NEW PHILADELPHIA**, City; Seat of Tuscarawas County; Pop. 16,921; Zip Code 44663; Elev. 901; Lat. 40-29-23 N long. 081-26-45W; E Ohio; Founded by *John Kinisely* in 1804.

•**NEW RICHMOND**, Village; Clermont County; Pop. 2,773; Zip Code 45157; Elev. 510; Lat. 38-56-55 N long. 084-16-48 W; SW Ohio; is a union of two villages.

•**NEWTON FALLS**, City; Trumbull County; Pop. 4,954; Zip Code 44444; Elev. 924; Lat. 41-11-18 N long. 080-58-42 W; NE Ohio; On the Mahoning River, 10 m. W of Warren.

•**NEWTOWN**, Village; Hamilton County; Pop. 1,816; Zip Code 45244; Lat. 39-07-28 N long. 084-21-42 W; SW Ohio; Just E of Cincinnati. Descriptively named upon its founding.

•**NEW VIENNA**, Village; Clinton County; Pop. 1,133; Zip Code 45159; Lat. 39-19-25 N long. 083-41-28 W; SW central Ohio; 13 m. SE of Wilmington. Named for the Austrian capital.

•**NEW WASHINGTON**, Village; Crawford County; Pop. 1,211; Zip Code 44854; Lat. 40-57-44 N long. 082-51-16 W; N central Ohio; 20 m. NW of Mansfield. The village is named after George Washington.

•**NILES**, City; Trumball County; Pop. 23,072; Zip Code 44446; Elev. 912; Lat. 41-10-58 N long. 080-45-56 W; Just S of Warren in NE central Ohio. Named after a Baltimore newspaper editor.

•**NORTH BALTIMORE**, Village; Wood County; Pop. 3,124; Zip Code 45872; Lat. 41-10-58 N long. 083-40-42 W; NW Ohio; 20 m. S of Bowling Green.

•**NORTH BEND**, Village; Hamilton County; Pop. 545; Zip Code 45052; Elev. 510; Lat. 39-09-09 N long. 084-44-53 W; SW Ohio; On a bend in the Ohio River, 10 m. W of Cincinnati. Named after the northern most bend in the Ohio River.

•**NORTH CANTON**, City; Stark County; Pop. 14,189; Zip Code 447+; Elev. 1160; Lat. 40-52-33 N long. 081-24-09 W; NE central Ohio; Just N of city of Canton; Site of Walsh College.

•**NORTH COLLEGE HILL**, City; Hamilton County; Pop. 11,066; Zip Code 45239; Elev. 712; Lat. 39-13-06 N long. 084-33-03 W; 10 m. N of Cincinnati in SW Ohio; Suburban.

•**NORTHFIELD**, Village; Summit County; Pop. 2,918; Zip Code 44067; Elev. 1044; Lat. 41-20-42 N long. 081-31-43 W; 20 m. S of Cleveland in NE Ohio; The first earlier settlers were from Massachusetts and named it after their hometown.

•**NORTH KINGSVILLE**, Village; Ashtabula County; Pop. 2,922; Zip Code 44068; Elev. 715; Lat. 41-54-21 N long. 080-41-26 W; NE Ohio; Just S of the Lake Erie shoreline; Suburban.

•**NORTH OLMSTED**, City; Cuyahoga County; Pop. 36,480; Zip Code 44070; Lat. 41-24-56 N long. 081-55-25 W; NE Ohio; 15 m. W of Cleveland, just S of the Lake Erie shoreline; Suburban.

•**NORTH RIDGEVILLE**, City; Lorain County; Pop. 21,237; Zip Code 44039; Lat. 41-22-13 N long. 082-02-43 W; N Ohio; N suburb of Elyria; Residential.

•**NORTH ROYALTON**, City; Cuyahoga County; Pop. 17,705; Zip Code 44133; Elev. 1197; Lat. 41-18-49 N long. 081-43-29 W; NE Ohio; 20 m. S of Cleveland in a residential area.

•**NORTHWOOD**, Village; Wood County; Pop. 5,482; Zip Code (with Toledo); Lat. 40-28-22 N long. 083-43-57 W; NW Ohio; Across the Maumee River from Toledo in a residential area.

•**NORTON**, City; Summit County; Pop. 12,241; Zip Code 44203; Elev. 946; Lat. 40-26-02 N long. 083-04-26 W; NE central Ohio; Residential suburb, just S of Akron and Barberton.

•**NORWALK**, City; Seat of Huron County; Pop. 14,348; Zip Code 44857; Elev. 719; Lat. 41-14-33 N long. 082-36-57 W; N central Ohio; It was named for the Connecticut town because many of its settlers left that State to make homes here on their "Firelands" grants.

•**NORWOOD**, City; Hamilton County; Pop. 26,126; Zip Code 452+; Lat. 39-09-20 N long. 084-27-35 W; SW Ohio; surrounded by the city of Cincinnati.

•**OAK HARBOR**, Village; Ottawa County; Pop. 2,683; Zip Code 43449; N Ohio; On the Portage River, 11 m. W of Port Clinton. Named for the many oaks once in the area.

•**OAK HILL**, Village; Jackson County; Pop. 1,715; Zip Code 45656; Elev. 967; Lat. 40-24-51 N long. 082-14-28 W; 12 m. S of the city of Jackson.

•**OAKWOOD**, City; Montgomery County; Pop. 9,404; Zip Code (with Dayton); Elev. 64; Lat. 41-23-09 N long. 081-29-20 W; SW central Ohio; A suburb of Dayton.

•**OAKWOOD**, Village; Cuyahoga County; Pop. 3,783; Zip Code (with Cleveland); Lat. 39-43-31 N long. 084-10-27 W; 15 m. SE of Cleveland in NE Ohio. Residential suburb.

•**OBERLIN**, City; Lorain County; Pop. 8,600; Zip Code 44074; Lat. 41-17-38 N long. 082-13-03W; N Ohio; 20 m. SW of Cleveland. Named after *Rev. Johann Friedrich Oberlin* it was one of the first colleges to admit Black students.

•**OBETZ**, Village; Franklin County; Pop. 3,098; Lat. 39-52-44 N long. 082-57-03 W; central Ohio.

•**OLMSTED FALLS**, City; Cuyahoga County; Pop. 5,868; Zip Code 44138; Elev. 774; Lat. 41-22-30 N long. 081-54-30 W; NE Ohio; 15 m. SW of Cleveland along Rocky Creek.

•**ONTARIO**, Village; Richland County; Pop. 4,122; Zip Code 44862; Lat. 40-45-34 N long. 082-35-25 W; N central Ohio; Just W of Mansfield. Named after the Canadian province.

•**ORANGE**, Village; Cuyahoga County; Pop. 2,368; Zip Code (with Cleveland); Lat. 40-17-17 N long. 081-40-59 W; Suburban-residential.

•**OREGON**, City; Lucas County; Pop. 18,682; Zip Code 436+; Lat. 41-38-37 N long. 083-29-13 W; 10 m. E of Toledo in NW Ohio, just S of Maumee Bay. Named after the state.

•**ORRVILLE**, City; Wayne County; Pop. 7,507; Zip Code 44667; Elev. 1064; Lat. 40-50-37 N long. 081-45-51 W; 44 m. S of Cleveland in NE central Ohio.

•**OTTAWA**, Village; Seat of Putnam County; Pop. 3,870; Zip Code 45875; Elev. 729; Lat. 41-01-09 N long. 084-02-50 W; NW Ohio; 20 m. N of Lime. The village was Est. in 1833, shortly after the last of the Ottawa Indians had been removed to their western reservations.

•**OTTAWA HILLS**, Village; Lucas County; Pop. 4,053; Lat. 41-39-51 N long. 083-38-36 W; NW Ohio.

•OXFORD, City; Butler County; Pop. 17,669; Zip Code 45056; Elev. 972; Lat. 39-30-25 N long. 084-44-43 W; SW Ohio; 25 m. SW of Dayton, named for the great English university town.

•PAINESVILLE, City; Seat of Lake County; Pop. 16,351; Zip Code 44077; Elev. 702; Lat. 41-43-28 N long. 081-14-45 W; 30 m. NEof Cleveland in NE Ohio; It was named for *General Edward Paine,* an officer in the Revolutionary War, who arrived here in the early 1800's.

•PANDORA, Village; Putnam County; Pop. 977; Zip Code 45877; Elev. 773; Lat. 40-56-53 N long. 083-57-40 W; NW Ohio; 18 m. NE ofLima. Named for the Greek mythological character.

•PARMA, City; Cuyahoga County; Pop. 92,578; Zip Code 441+; Lat. 41-24-17 N long. 081-43-23 W; 10 m. S of Cleveland in N Ohio; named after the Italian city.

•PATASKALA, Village; Licking County; Pop. 2,285; Zip Code 43062; Lat. 39-59-44 N long. 082-40-28 W; 20 m. E of Columbus in central Ohio; farming area. Named for the Indian word meaning "Salt Lick."

•PAULDING, Village; Seat of Paulding County; Pop. 2,760; Zip Code 45879; Elev. 723; Lat. 41-08-17 N long. 084-34-50 W; 40 m. NW of Lima in NW Ohio; Named for, one of the three men that captured *Major Andre* during the Revolution, *John Paulding* of Peekskill, NY.

•PAYNE, Village; Paulding County; Pop. 1,397; Zip Code 45880; Elev. 753; Lat. 41-04-39 N long. 084-43-38 W; NW Ohio; 35 m. E of Fort Wayne, Indiana.

•PEEBLES, Village; Adams County; Pop. 1,791; Zip Code 45660; Elev. 813; Lat. 38-56-56 N long. 083-24-21 W; Approx. 30 m. NW of Portsmouth in S Ohio.

•PEPPER PIKE, City; Cuyahoga County; Pop. 6,175; Elev. 1050; Lat. 41-28-42 N long. 081-27-50 W; 10 m. E of Cleveland in N Ohio.

•PERRYSBURG, City; Wood County; Pop. 10,196; Zip Code 43551; Elev. 628; Lat. 41-33-25 N long. 083-37-38 W; NW Ohio; Overlooks the Maumee River and the city of Maumee; Named for the War of 1812 hero *Com. Oliver Hazard Perry.*

•PICKERINGTON, Village; Fairfield & Franklin Counties; Pop. 3,887; Zip Code 43147; Elev. 842; Lat. 39-53-03 N long. 082-45-13 W; 10 m. NW of Lancaster; Named for the *Abraham Pickerington* who bought land here in 1811.

•PIKETON, Village; Pike County; Pop. 1,726; Zip Code 45661; Elev. 578; Lat. 39-04-05 N long. 083-00-52 W; S Ohio; 10 m. S of Waverley; Named for *General Zebulon Montgomery Pike.*

•PIONEER, Village; Williams County; Pop. 1,127; Zip Code 43554; Elev. 874; Lat. 41-40-48 N long. 084-33-11 W; NW corner, Ohio;Just S of Michigan state line.

•PIQUA, City; Miami County; Pop. 20,466; Zip Code 45358; Elev. 899; Lat. 40-08-41 N long. 084-14-33 W; W Ohio; Situated on the Great Miami River. Named for a tribe of the Shawnee who established themselves in this region after 1763. The name, Piqua, means "a man risen out of the ashes."

•PLAIN CITY, Village; Madison & Union Counties; Pop. 2,114; Zip Code 43064; Elev. 935; Lat. 40-06-27 N long. 083-16-03 W; SW central Ohio. Laid out in 1818 by *Issac Bigelow,* named Plain City in 1851 because it is situated on Big Darby Plain.

•PLEASANT HILL, Village; Miami County; Pop. 1,056; Zip Code 45359; Lat. 39-40-17 N long. 082-30-29 W; W central Ohio.

•PLYMOUTH, Village; Huron and Richland Counties; Pop. 1,941; Zip Code 44865; Lat. 41-49-33 N long. 080-44-46 W; N central Ohio; On the W branch of the Huron River, named after the city in Massachusetts.

•POMEROY, Village; Seat of Meigs County; Pop. 2,781; Zip Code 45769; Elev. 590; Elev. 39-01-39 N long. 082-02-02 W; SE Ohio, 40 m. SE of Marietta. Named for *Samuel Pomeroy,* a Boston merchant who in 1804 purchased 262 acres of land on the site of the city.

•PORT CLINTON, City; Seat of Ottawa County; Pop. 7,229; Elev. 580; Lat. 41-30-43 N long. 082-56-16 W; N Ohio; 30 m. SE of Toledo. The town was named in honor of *DeWitt Clinton,* New York governor.

•PORTSMOUTH, City; Seat of Scioto County; Pop. 25,993; Zip Code 45662; Elev. 527; Lat. 38-43-54 N long. 082-59-52 W; S Ohio; Was founded in 1803 by a Virginia land speculator, *Major Henry Massie.*

•POWELL, Village; Delaware County; Pop. 381; Zip Code 43065; Elev. 922; Lat. 40-18-21 N long. 081-42-07 W; Central Ohio; approx. 15 m. N of downtown Columbus.

•POWHATAN POINT, Village; Belmont County; Pop. 2,183; Zip Code 43942; Elev. 638; Lat. 39-51-36 N long. 080-48-56 W; E Ohio.

•PROSPECT, Village; Marion County; Pop. 1,164; Zip Code 43342; Lat. 40-27-01 N long. 083-11-19 W; Central Ohio; Along the Scioto River, 12 m. S of Marion.

•QUAKER CITY, Village; Guernsey County; Pop. 694; Zip Code 43773; Lat. 39-58-12 N long. 081-17-58 W; E Ohio; 16 m. E of Cambidge.

•RACINE, Village; Meigs County; Pop. 913; Zip Code 45771; Elev. 601; Lat. 38-58-16 N long. 081-54-52 W; SE Ohio; On the Ohio River, 25 m. NE of Gallipolis.

•RAVENNA, City; Seat of Portage County; Pop. 11,956; Zip Code 44266; Elev. 1,138; Lat. 41-09-27 N long. 081-14-32 W; NE Ohio; It was named for the Italian city after its settlement in 1799 from Ohio.

•READING, City; Hamilton County; Pop. 12,819; Elev. 660; Lat. 40-50-06 N long. 081-01-53 W; SW Ohio; 10 m. NE of the city in a residential area. Reading was given its present name in honor of *Redingbo, William Penn's* son-in-law.

•REYNOLDSBURG, City; Franklin County; Pop. 20,513; Zip Code 43068; Lat. 39-57-17 N long. 082-48-44 W; Central Ohio; 10 m. E of Columbus.
The current name is in honor of *John C. Reynolds.*

•RICHFIELD, Village; Summit County; Pop. 3,424; Zip Code 44286; Elev. 1,148; Lat. 41-14-23 N long. 081-38-18 W; NE Ohio.

•RICHMOND HEIGHTS, City; Cuyahoga County; Pop. 10,090; Zip Code 44143; Lat. 41-33-10 N long. 081-30-37 W; NE Ohio; 15 m. NE of Cleveland in a residential area just S of Lake Erie.

•RICHWOOD, Village; Union County; Pop. 2,176; Zip Code 43344; Lat. 40-25-35 N long. 083-17-49 W; 15 m. S of Marion in W central Ohio.

•RIPLEY, Village; Brown County; Pop. 2,193; Zip Code 45167; Elev. 447; Lat. 38-44-44 N long. 083-50-42 W; SW Ohio. The current name is in honor of *Gen. Eleazer Wheelock Ripley.*

•RITTMAN, City; Wayne & Medina Counties; Pop. 6,066; Zip Code 44270; Elev. 979; Lat. 40-58-41 N long. 081-46-56 W; 40 m. S of Cleveland.

•ROCKY RIVER, City; Cuyahoga County; Pop. 21,070; Zip Code 44116; Lat. 41-28-32 N long. 081-50-22 W; NE Ohio; At the mouth of the Rocky River on Lake Erie, 10 m. W of Cleveland city center.

•ROSSFORD, City; Wood County; Pop. 5,983; Zip Code 43460; Elev. 630; Lat. 41-36-35 N long. 083-33-52 W; NW Ohio.

•RUSSELLS POINT, Village; Logan County; Pop. 1,158; Zip Code 43348; Lat. 40-28-16 N long. 083-53-34 W; W Ohio; On S Indian Lake, 13 m. NW of Bellefontaine.

•SABINA, Village; Clinton County; Pop. 2,807; Zip Code 45169; Elev. 1,051; Lat. 39-29-19 N long. 083-38-13 W;; SW Ohio; 11 m. NE of Wilmington.

•ST. CLAIRSVILLE, City; Seat of Belmont County; Pop. 5,425; Zip Code 43950; Elev. 1,260; Lat. 40-04-50 N long. 080-54-01 W; E Ohio; Named for *Arthur St.Clair*, first governor of the Northwest Territory.

•ST. MARYS, City; Auglaize County; Pop. 8,368; Zip Code 45885; Elev. 926; Lat. 40-32-32 N long. 084-23-22 W; 80 m. NW of Columbus in W Ohio; Named for an early church.

•SALEM, City; Columbia County; Pop. 12,865; Zip Code 44460; Elev. 1,230; Lat. 40-54-03 N long. 080-51-25 W; 20 m. , New Jersey; SW of Youngstown in E Ohio; named after Salem, Massachusetts.

•SALINEVILLE, Village; Columbia County; Pop. 1,637; Zip Code 43945; Elev. 950; Lat. 40-37-21 N long. 080-50-17 W; 18 m. W of East Liverpool in E Ohio; Named for the salt springs in the area.

•SPRINGFIELD, City; Clark County Seat; Pop. 72,263; Zip Code 455+; Elev. 980. Incorporated a town in 1801; city in 1850. Christened Springfield because of the spring water flowing down the hills that bordered the valley of Buck Creek.

•STEUBENVILLE, City; Jefferson County Seat; Pop. 26,287; Zip Code 43952; Elev. 830. This town became a city in 1851 and named after Fort Steuben which was named after Baron von Steuben, a Prussian drill master and Revolutionary War supporter.

•SUGARCREEK, Village; Tuscarawas County; Pop. 1,969; Zip Code 44681; Lat. 39-22-56 N long. 082-04-45 W; 8 m. W of Dover in E Ohio; Along a branch of the Sugar Creek; Named in 1818 after the township.

•SUNBURY, Village; Delaware County; Pop. 1,895; Zip Code 43074; Elev. 965; Lat. 40-14-33 N long. 082-51-33 W; Central Ohio; 12 m. SE of Delaware city.

•SWANTON, Village; Fulton County; Pop. 3,423; Zip Code 43558; Lat. 41-35-19 N long. 083-53-28 W; NW Ohio.

•SYCAMORE, Village; Wyandot County; Pop. 1,057; Zip Code 44882; Elev. 826; Lat. 39-17-00 N long. 084-19-01 W; 14 m. S of Tiffin in NW central Ohio. Named for the creek that runs through the place.

•SYLVANIA, City; Lucas County; Pop. 15,556; Zip Code 43560; Lat. 41-43-08 N long. 083-42-47 W; W Ohio; 11 m. NW of Toledo, just S of the Michigan state line.

•TALLMADGE, City; Summit County; Pop. 15,238; Zip Code 44278; Elev. 1114; Lat. 41-06-05 N long. 081-26-31 W; NE central Ohio; Just E of Akron; Named in honor of founder Colonel Benjamin Tallmadge.

•TIFFIN, City; Seat of Seneca County; Pop. 19,567; Zip Code 44883; Elev. 761; Lat. 41-06-52 N long. 083-10-41 W; N Ohio; On the Sandusky River, Named Tiffin, after *Edward Tiffin*, first governor of Ohio.

•TILTONSVILLE, Village; Jefferson County; Pop. 1,755; Zip Code 43963; Lat. 40-10-00 N long. 080-42-00 W; E Ohio; On the Ohio River, about 20 m. S of Steubenville. Named after *John Tilton* who platted out the town in 1806.

•TIPP CITY, City; Miami County; Pop. 5,601; Zip Code 45371; Lat. 39-57-30 N long. 084-10-20 W; W central Ohio; Along the Miami River about 7 m. S of Troy.

•TOLEDO, City; Lucas County Seat; Pop. 354,558; Zip Code 436+; Elev. 587. The first permanent settlement here was named Port Lawrence which, a year later, merged with Vistula, a river settlement to the north. The residents chose the name Toledo. Legend has it that it was suggested by Willard J. Daniels, a merchant, because it "is easy to pronounce, pleasant in sound, and there is no other city by that name on the American Continent."

•TORONTO, City; Jefferson County; Pop. 6,869; Zip Code 43964; Elev. 695; Lat. 40-27-51 N long. 080-36-04 W; E Ohio; Toronto was named after the Canadian city.

•TRENTON, City; Butler County; Pop. 6,375; Zip Code 45067; Elev. 653; Lat. 39-28-51 N long. 084-27-28 W; 35 m. N of Cincinnati in SW Ohio; named after Trenton, New Jersey.

•TROY, City; Seat of Miami County; Pop. 19,008; Zip Code 45373; Elev. 840; Lat. 40-02-22 N long. 084-12-12 W; W central Ohio. The city is named after Troy, New York.

•TUSCARAWAS, Village; Tuscarawas County; Pop. 920; Zip Code 44682; Lat. 40-23-41 N long. 081-24-26 W; E central Ohio; 10 m. S of New Philadelphia; Named for the river which flows nearby.

•TWINSBURG, City; Summit County; Pop. 7,627; Zip Code 44087; Elev. 985; Lat. 41-18-45 N long. 081-26-25 W; NE Ohio; Clusters about its six-acre village square, a gift of the Wilcox twins, *Moses and Aaron*, for whom the town was named.

•UHRICHSVILLE, City; Tuscarawas County; Pop. 6,139; Zip Code 44683; Elev. 856; Lat. 40-23-35 N long. 081-20-48 W; E Ohio; Settled in 1804 by *Michael Uhrich* of Pennsylvania.

•UNION, Village; Montgomery County; Pop. 5,109; Zip Code 45322; Lat. 39-53-52 N long. 084-18-23 W; SW central Ohio.

•UNIVERSITY HEIGHTS, City; Cuyahoga County; Pop. 15,380; Zip Code 44118; Elev. 600; Lat. 41-29-52 N long. 081-32-15 W; 10 m. W of Cleveland in NE Ohio.

•UPPER ARLINGTON, City; Franklin County; Pop. 35,624; Zip Code 43221; Lat. 39-30-58 N long. 084-22-35 W; Central Ohio; Just NW of Columbus.

•URBANA, City; Seat of Champaign County; Pop. 10,774; Zip Code 43078; Elev. 1,031; Lat. 40-06-30 N long. 083-45-09 W; W central Ohio.

•UTICA, Village; Knox and Licking Counties; Pop. 2,235; Zip Code 43080; Elev. 961; Lat. 40-14-03 N long. 082-27-05 W; Central Ohio; On the Licking River, 14 m. N of Newark. In 1815 first known as Wilmington the name was changed to Utica for the city in New York.

•VANDALIA, City; Montgomery County; Pop. 13,164; Zip Code 45377; Elev. 994; Lat. 39-53-26 N long. 084-11-56 W; SW Ohio; Settled in 1838, and when it apeared that the National Road would end here instead of at Vandalia, Illinois, the community took the name of the Illinois town.

•VAN WERT, City; Seat of Van Wert County; Pop. 11,022; Zip Code 45891; Elev. 788; Lat. 40-52-10 N long. 084-35-03 W; NW Ohio; 70 m. SW of Toledo. Named for *Issac Van Wart*, Revolutionary war hero. Spelling of name was modified later.

•**VERMILLION**, City; Erie and Lorain Counties; Pop. 11,011; Zip Code 44089; Elev. 664; Lat. 41-25-19 N long. 082-21-53 W; on Lake Erie in N Ohio just E of Sandusky; settled in 1808, lies along the winding Vermilion River.

•**VERSAILLES**, Village; Darke County; Pop. 2,300; Zip Code 45380; Elev. 978; Lat. 40-13-21 N long. 084-29-04 W; W Ohio; 40 m. NW of Dayton. Named after the French estate.

•**WADSWORTH**, City; Medina County; Pop. 15,187; Zip Code 44281; Elev. 1,173; Lat. 41-01-32 N long. 081-43-48 W; NE central Ohio; 35 m. S of Cleveland. Named after the township which was named for *Gen. Elijah Wadsworth* who was the largest landowner in the Western Reserve.

•**WAPAKONETA**, City; Seat of Auglaize County; Pop. 8,379; Zip Code 45895; Elev. 898; Lat. 40-34-04 N long. 084-11-37 W; According to local history, Wapaghkonetta (the town's original name) was derived from the names of an Indian chief and his squaw, Wapaugh and Konetta.

•**WARREN**, City; Seat of Trumball County; Pop. 55,471; Zip Code 444+; Elev. 904; Lat. 41-14-15 N long. 080-49-07 W; 15 m. NW of Youngstown in NE Ohio; Named for *Moses Warren*, a county surveyor, in 1798.

•**WASHINGTON COURT HOUSE**, City; Seat of Fayette County; Pop. 12,648; Zip Code 43160; Elev. 973; Lat. 39-32-11 N long. 083-26-21 W; 30 m. NW of Chillicothe in SW Ohio; Originally named Washington, the city adopted the larger name in 1810 after the first court of common pleas was held in the cabin of one of the town's resident's, *John Devault.*

•**WATERVILLE**, Village; Lucas County; Pop. 3,885; Zip Code 43567; Elev. 654; Lat. 41-30-03 N long. 083-43-06 W; NW Ohio; Platted in 1818 by *John Pray.*

•**WAUSEON**, Village; Seat of Fulton County; Pop. 6,170; Zip Code 4356; Elev. 757; Lat. 41-32-57 N long. 084-08-30 W; W of Toledo in NW Ohio.

•**WAVERLY CITY**, City; Seat of Pike County; Pop. 4,573; Zip Code 45690; Elev. 604; 15 m. S of Chillicothe in S Ohio; founded in 1829 and named after the novelist, *Scott Waverly.*

•**WESTON**, Village; Wood County; Pop. 1,700; Zip Code 43569; Lat. 41-20-41 N long. 083-47-50 W; NW Ohio; 8 m. W of Bowling Green; Residential area.

•**WEST SALEM**, Village; Wayne County; Pop. 1,356; Zip Code 44287; Elev. 1,092; Lat. 40-58-17 N long. 082-06-36 W; NE central Ohio; Laid out in 1834 by the *Rickel brothers.*

•**WEST UNION**, Village; Seat of Adams County; Pop. 2,790; Zip Code 45693; Elev. 967; Lat. 38-47-40 N long. 083-32-43 W; 55 m. SE of Cincinnati, 10 m. N of Kentucky state line in S Ohio.

•**WHITEHALL**, City; Franklin County; Pop. 21,295; Zip Code 43213; Central Ohio; 6 m. E of Columbus, over-looking the city on Big Walnut Creek; Named after the famous English estate.

•**WHITEHOUSE**, Village; Lucas County; Pop. 2,132; Zip Code 43571; NW Ohio; 20 m. SW of Toledo in a section outside of the city area.

•**WICKLIFFE**, City; Lake County; Pop. 16,800; Zip Code 44092; 15 m. NE of Cleveland, just S of the Lake Erie shoreline.

•**WILLARD**, Cit; Huron County; Pop. 5,666; Zip Code 44890; N central Ohio; 20 m. N of Mansfield.

•**WILLIAMSBURG**, Village; Clermont County; Pop. 1,948; Zip Code 45176; SW Ohio; On the E Fork of the Miami River, 25 m. E of Cincinnati. Named for the town in Virginia.

•**WILLOUGHBY**, City; Lake County; Pop. 19,290; Zip Code 44094; Elev. 649; 20 m. NE of Cleveland in NE Ohio. Originally called Chagrin, this city was named for an instructor in the Willoughby Medical College.

•**WILLOWICK**, City; Lake County; Pop. 17,758; Zip Code 44094; 10 m. NE of Cleveland, in a suburban area near Willoughby on Lake Erie in NE Ohio; Residential.

•**WILMINGTON**, City; Seat of Clinton County; Pop. 10,442; Zip Code 45177; Elev. 1,033; Lat. 39-26-43 N long. 083-49-43 W; 30 m. SE of Dayton; Founded in 1810. Named after Wilmington, N.C. and originally known as Clinton.

•**WINCHESTER**, Village; Adams County; Pop. 1,086; Zip Code 45697; Lat. 38-56-30 N long. 083-39-03 W; S Ohio; 45 m. E of Cincinnati.

•**WOODSFIELD**, Village; Seat of Monroe County; Pop. 3,127; Zip Code 43793; Elev. 1213; Lat. 39-45-45 N long. 081-06-56 W; 30 m. NE of Marietta in SE Ohio; Archibald Woods founded the town in 1815.

•**WOODVILLE**, Village; Sandusky County; Pop. 2,053; Zip Code 43469; Lat. 39-15-18 N long. 084-00-40 W; N Ohio; 25 m. SE of Toledo. Named for the man who laid the town out in 1838, *Amos Wood.*

•**WOOSTER**, City; Seat of Wayne County; Pop. 19,273; Zip Code 44691; Elev. 910; Lat. 40-48-18 N long. 081-56-07 W; NE central Ohio. Named for the Revolutionary War general, *David Wooster.*

•**WORTHINGTON**, City; Franklin County; Pop. 14,956; Zip Code 43085; Elev. 908; Lat. 40-05-35 N long. 083-01-05 W; Central Ohio; 10 m. N of Columbus; Named Worthington after a parish in Connecticut, in 1803.

•**WYOMING**, City; Hamilton County; Pop. 8,247; Zip Code (with Cincinnati); Lat. 39-13-52 N long. 084-27-57 W; SW Ohio; 10 m. N of Cincinnati in a residential area; Named for the county in Pennsylvania.

•**XENIA**, Seat of Greene County; Pop. 24,712; Zip Code 45385; Elev. 925; Lat. 39-41-05 N long. 083-55-47 W; 15 m. SE of Dayton and 3 m. E of the Little Miami River in SW Ohio.

•**YELLOW SPRINGS**, Village; Greene County; Pop. 4,074; Zip Code 45387; Elev. 974; Lat. 39-48-23 N long. 083-53-13 W; SW Ohio; 9 m. S of Springfield in a great metal It was founded in 1804, and took its name from the yellow discharges of the neighboring iron springs whose health-giving waters attracted visitors here for several decades.

•**YORKVILLE**, Village; Belmont and Jefferson Counties; Pop. 1,443; Zip Code 43971; Elev. 669; Lat. 40-09-16 N long. 080-42-38 W; E Ohio; Named for its early settlers, who came from York, Pennsylvania.

•**YOUNGSTOWN**, City; Seat of Mahoning County; Pop. 115,429; Zip Code 445+; Elev. 861; Lat. 41-05-59 N long. 080-38-59 W; On Mahoning river 45 m. E of Akron in NE Ohio. Named after pioneer *John Young* of Whitestown, New York, and his party of settlers, who arrived in 1797.

•**ZANESVILLE**, City; Seat of Muskingum County; Pop. 28,600; Zip Code 43701; Lat. 39-56-25 N long. 082-00-48 W;. On Muskingum river 50 m. E of Columbus in SE central Ohio; The land once belonged to *Issac Zane*, about whom center many of the lusty events in early Ohio History.

•**ZOAR**, Village; Tuscarawas County; Pop. 262; Zip Code 44697; Lat. 40-36-51 N long. 081-25-21 W; 15 m. S of Canton along the Tuscarawas River in E central Ohio. The town was named for the biblical city to which Lot fled after leaving Sodom.

OKLAHOMA

•ACHILLE, Town; Bryan County; Pop. 480; Zip Code 74720; Elev 685; Lat. 33-50-08 N long. 096-23-11 W; The town's name is loosely based on a Cherokee word "astila" which means "fire."

•ADA, City; Pontotoc County Seat; Pop. 15,902; Zip Code 74820; Elev 1010; Lat. 34-46-32 N long. 096-40-05 W; The town is named for the daughter of the first postmaster, William Reed.

•ADAIR, Town; Mayes County; Pop. 508; Zip Code 74330; Elev 680; Lat. 36-26-18 N long. 095-16-11 W; Adair is named after William Penn Adair, a well-known Cherokee leader.

•ADDINGTON, Town; Jefferson County; Pop. 141; Zip Code 73520; Elev 946; Lat. 34-14-42 N long. 097-57-43 W; The town is named in honor of first postmaster, James P. Addington.

•AFTON, Town; Ottawa County; Pop. 1,174; Zip Code 74331; Elev 792; Lat. 36-39-29 N long. 094-56-20 W; Railroad surveyor Anton Aires named his daughter for the Afton River in Scotland. The town was named in her honor.

•AGRA, Town; Lincoln County; Pop. 354; Zip Code 74824; Lat. 35-53-34 N long. 096-51-52 W; The town's developer named it from the word agriculture.

•ALBION, Town; Pushmataha County; Pop. 165; Zip Code 74521; Lat. 34-39-49 N long. 095-05-49 W; Named by Englishman John Bailey for the old Roman name of Britian.

•ALDERSON, Town; Pittsburg County; Pop. 366; Zip Code 74522; Lat. 34-54-07 N long. 095-41-27 W; Alderson's name remembers an employee of the Chowtac, Oklahoma, and Gulf Railroad.

•ALEX, Town; Grady County; Pop. 769; Zip Code 73002; Elev 1048; Lat. 34-54-41 N long. 097-46-59 W; The town's name honors the first postmaster, William Alexander.

•ALINE, Town; Alfalfa County; Pop. 313; Zip Code 73716; Elev 1281; Lat. 36-30-40 N long. 098-26-51 W; Named after Marie Aline, daughter of well-known settler Erza Hartshorn.

•ALLEN, Town; Hughes & Pontotoc Counties; Pop. 998; Zip Code 74825; Lat. 34-52-45 N long. 096-24-18 W; The town is named for the son of a deputy U. S. Marshall, Allen McCall.

•ALTUS, City; Jackson County Seat; Pop. 23,101; Zip Code 73521; Elev 1395; Lat. 34-38-39 N long. 099-19-13 W; After the original townsite was destroyed in a flood, the settlers moved to higher ground and named the new town "altus" or latin for "high."

•ALVA, City; Woods County Seat; Pop. 6,416; Zip Code 73717; Lat. 36-48-00 N long. 098-39-59 W; Alva was named for Alva Adams, one time governor of the state of Colorado.

•AMBER, Town; Grady County; Pop. 416; Zip Code 73004; Lat. 34-25-25 N long. 097-36-33 W; A descriptive name for the amber colored countryside.

•AMES, Town; Major County; Pop. 314; Zip Code 73718; Elev 1226; Lat. 36-14-36 N long. 098-11-05 W; The town is named in honor of Henry Ames, an official of the Denver, Enid, and Gulf Railroad.

•AMETT, Town; Ellis County Seat; Pop. 714; The town is named after an early settler.

•AMORITA, Town; Alfalfa County; Pop. 66; Zip Code 73719; Elev 1212; Lat. 36-56-07 N long. 098-17-44 W; Amorita is named in honor of Amorita Ingersoll, the wife of a local railroad company.

•ANODARKO, City; Caddo County Seat; Pop. 6,378; Zip Code 73005; Lat. 35-04-21 N long. 098-14-30 W; A Cadoo Indian name for one of the Cadoo tribes.

•ANTLERS, Town; Pushmataha County Seat; Pop. 2,989; Zip Code 74523; Elev 508; Lat. 34-14-06 N long. 095-36-57 W; An early camping place was marked by a pair of antlers. The town took its name from this trail mark.

•APACHE, Town; Caddo County; Pop. 1,560; Zip Code 73006; Elev 1300; Lat. 34-53-36 N long. 098-21-42 W; A Zuni Indian word meaning "enemy."

•ARAPAHO, Town; Custer County Seat; Pop. 851; Zip Code 73620; Elev 1669; Lat. 35-34-32 N long. 098-57-32 W; An Indian word meaning "cloud men."

•ARDMORE, City; Carter County Seat; Pop. 23,689; Zip Code 73401; Lat. 34-11-02 N long. 097-03-14 W; Named by early settlers for Ardmore, Pennsylvania.

•ARKOMA, Town; Le Flore County; Pop. 2,175; Zip Code 74901; Lat. 35-20-58 N long. 094-26-28 W; Near the state line the word is a joining of Arkansas and Oklahoma.

•ASHER, Town; Pottawatomie County; Pop. 659; Zip Code 74826; Lat. 34-59-27 N long. 096-55-39 W; The town is named in honor of its founder, G. M. Asher.

•ASHLAND, Town; Pittsburg County; Pop. 72; Zip Code 74524; Lat. 34-45-56 N long. 096-04-16 W; Named by the U. S. Post Office.

•ATOKA, City; Atoka County Seat; Pop. 3,409; Zip Code 74525; Elev 583; Lat. 34-23-02 N long. 096-07-46 W; The town is named for Captain Atoka, a Choctaw ball-player.

•AVANT, Town; Osage County; Pop. 461; Zip Code 74001; Elev 681; Lat. 36-29-16 N long. 096-03-30 W; Avant's name remembers Ben Avant, a prominent Osage Indian.

•AVARD, Town; Woods County; Pop. 51; Named for the wife of the first postmaster, Frank Todd.

•BARNSDALL, City; Osage County; Pop. 1,501; Zip Code 74002; Elev 773; Lat. 36-33-39 N long. 096-09-32 W; The town is named after the Barnsdall Oil Company.

•BARTLESVILLE, City; Osage & Washington Counties; Washington County Seat; Pop. 34,568; Zip Code 74003; Lat. 36-44-58 N long. 095-58-34 W; Jacob Bartles established a trading post here in 1879. The town is named in his honor.

•BEAVER, City; Beaver County Seat; Pop. 1,939; Zip Code 73932; Elev 2393; Lat. 36-48-49 N long. 100-31-28 W; The town is named after the adjacent Beaver River.

•BEGGS, City; Okmulgee County; Pop. 1,428; Zip Code 74421; Elev 732; Lat. 35-44-27 N long. 096-04-20 W; Begg's name honors C. H. Beggs, Vice-President of a local railroad.

•BENNINGTON, Town; Bryan County; Pop. 302; Zip Code 74723; Lat. 34-00-16 N long. 096-02-13 W; The town was named after Bennington, Vermont - site of a Revolutionary War battle.

•BERNICE, Town; Delaware County; Pop. 318; The town's name honors Benice Lundy, daughter of a well-known local family.

•BESSIE, Town; Washita County; Pop. 245; Zip Code 73622; Lat. 35-23-01 N long. 098-59-12 W; The Blackwell, Enid, and Southwestern Railroad was popularly known as the "Bessie."

•BETHANY, City; Oklahoma County; Pop. 22,130; Zip Code 73008; Lat. 35-30-47 N long. 097-35-04 W; Named after the Biblical community near Jerusalem.

•BETHEL ACRES, Town; Pottawatomie County; Pop. 2,314; Zip Code 74724; Elev 874; Lat. 34-21-29 N long. 094-50-51 W; Bethel is a Hebrew word meaning "house of god."

•BIG CABIN, Town; Craig County; Pop. 252; Zip Code 74332; Lat. 36-25-20 N long. 095-13-22 W; The town is named after Big Cabin Creek. The creek, in turn, was named for a large plank cabin on the Texas road.

•BILLINGS, Town; Noble County; Pop. 632; Zip Code 74630; Elev 1020; Lat. 36-32-02 N long. 097-26-28 W; Rock Island Railroad agent named the town after his wife's maiden surname.

•BINGER, Town; Caddo County; Pop. 791; Zip Code 73009; Lat. 35-18-31 N long. 098-20-31 W; The town's name honors Binger Hermann, commissioner of the General Land Office from 1897 to 1903.

•BIXBY, City; Tulsa & Wagoner Counties; Pop. 6,969; Zip Code 74008; Lat. 35-57-29 N long. 095-52-54 W; The town's name honors Tam Bixby, chairman of the Dawes Commission.

•BLACKBURN, Town; Pawnee County; Pop. 114; The town is named for U. S. Senator Joseph Blackburn of Kentucky.

•BLACKWELL, City; Kay County; Pop. 8,400; Zip Code 74631; Elev 1014; Lat. 36-47-51 N long. 097-17-21 W; Named for its founder Andrew Blackwell.

•BLAIR, Town; Jackson County; Pop. 1,092; Zip Code 73526; Lat. 34-46-42 N long. 099-20-03 W; The name honors John Blair, a local railroad official.

•BLANCHARD, Town; Grady & McClain Counties; Pop. 1,616; Zip Code 73010; Elev 1276; Lat. 35-08-21 N long. 097-39-25 W; Founded in 1906 and named after town founder, W. G. Blanchard.

•BLUEJACKET, Town; Craig County; Pop. 247; Zip Code 74333; Lat. 36-50-02 N long. 095-04-22 W; The first postmaster, Charles Bluejacket, gave his name to the town.

•BOISE CITY, City; Cimarron County Seat; Pop. 1,761; Zip Code 73933; Elev. 4165; Lat. 36-43-47 N long. 102-30-21 W; Named in 1908 for Boise, Idaho.

•BOKCHITO, Town; Bryan County; Pop. 628; Zip Code 74726; Elev 637; Lat. 34-01-14 N long. 096-08-20 W; A Choctaw Indian word meaning "big creek."

•BOKOSHE, Town; Le Flore County; Pop. 556; Zip Code 74930; Lat. 35-11-23 N long. 094-47-20 W; A Choctaw Indian word meaning "little creek."

•BOLEY, Town; Okfuskee County; Pop. 423; Zip Code 74829; Lat. 35-29-38 N long. 096-28-56 W; Founded in 1903 and named for the local railroad roadmaster, W. H. Boley.

•BOSWELL, Town; Choctaw County; Pop. 702; Zip Code 74727; Elev 597; Lat. 34-01-39 N long. 095-52-00 W; Formerly called Mayhew, Boswell honors civic leader and engineer, A. V. Boswell.

•BOWLEGS, Town; Seminole County; Pop. 522; Zip Code 74830; Lat. 35-08-35 N long. 096-40-15 W; In Seminole County; the town is named for Billy Bowlegs, a Seminole chief.

•BOYNTON, Town; Muskogee County; Pop. 518; Zip Code 74422; Lat. 35-38-54 N long. 095-39-17 W; The town is named for E. W.Boynton - a chief engineer for a local railway company.

•BRADLEY, Town; Grady County; Pop. 284; Zip Code 73011; Lat. 34-52-29 N long. 097-42-41 W; Bradley's name honors local rancher Winters P. Bradley.

•BRAGGS, Town; Muskogee County; Pop. 351; Zip Code 74423; Elev 559; Lat. 35-39-57 N long. 095-11-27 W; The town is named after local landowner Soloman Braggs.

•BRAMAN, Town; Kay County; Pop. 355; Zip Code 74632; Lat. 36-55-21 N long. 097-19-57 W; Railroad developer Dwight Braman left his name on the town.

•BRAY, Town; Stephens County; Pop. 591; Zip Code 73012; Lat. 34-38-28 N long. 097-48-31 W; Bray takes its name from the first postmaster, Thomas Bray.

•BRECKENRIDGE, Town; Garfield County; Pop. 261; The town is named in honor of Breckenridge Jones, president of the Denver, Enid, and Gulf Railway.

•BRIDGEPORT, City; Caddo County; Pop. 115; The site of a stage crossing of the Canadian River, travellers waited for low water to cross - hence the name.

•BRISTOW, City; Creek County; Pop. 4,702; Zip Code 74010; Lat. 35-49-45 N long. 096-23-10 W; Founded in 1898 and named for Kansas Senator Joseph Bristow.

•BROKEN ARROW, City; Tulsa & Wagoner Counties; Pop. 35,761; Zip Code 740+; Elev. 753; Lat. 36-02-00 N long. 095-48-20 W; Near Tulsa the name comes from a Creek Indian ceremony after the Civil War to symbolize the war's end.

•BROKEN BOW, City; McCurtain County; Pop. 3,965; Zip Code 74728; Lat. 34-01-28 N long. 094-44-00 W; Founded in 1911 and named by pioneer Dirks family for their former home in Nebraska.

•BROMIDE, Town; Coal & Johnston Counties; Pop. 180; Zip Code 74530; Elev. 707; Lat. 34-25-19 N long. 096-29-49 W; Once called Zenobia, the town was renamed after a local mineral springs.

•BROOKSVILLE, Town; Pottawatomie County; Pop. 46; Named in honor of the first postmaster, Alfred H. Brooks.

•BUFFALO, Town; Harper County Seat; Pop. 1,381; Zip Code 73834; Lat. 36-50-02 N long. 099-37-19 W; The town is named for nearby Buffalo Creek.

•BURBANK, Town; Osage County; Pop. 161; Zip Code 74633; Elev 1026; Lat. 36-41-47 N long. 096-43-33 W; Founded in 1907 and named descriptively for a bluff along Salt Creek covered with cockleburs.

•BURLINGTON, Town; Alfalfa County; Pop. 206; Zip Code 73722; Elev 1218; Lat. 36-54-00 N long. 098-25-22 W; Named by early settlers for Burlington, Iowa.

•BURNS FLAT, Town; Washita County; Pop. 2,431; Zip Code 73624; Lat. 35-21-24 N long. 099-10-53 W; Named for the town of Burns immediately to the south.

•BUTLER, Town; Custer County; Pop. 388; Zip Code 73625; Lat. 35-38-11 N long. 099-11-10 W; Founded in 1898 and named for Major General Matthew Butler, a Civil War officer.

•BYARS, Town; McClain County; Pop. 353; Zip Code 74831; Lat. 34-53-47 N long. 097-06-44 W; Byars is named in honor of local rancher Nathan Byars.

•BYNG, Town; Pontotoc County; Pop. 833; Byng's name honors British Army officer Sir Julian Byng.

•BYRON, Town; Alfalfa County; Pop. 67; Zip Code 73723; Elev 1190; Lat. 36-54-06 N long. 098-17-33 W; Founded in 1894 and named for a relative of the first postmaster.

•CAMERON, Town; Le Flore County; Pop. 365; Zip Code 74902; Elev 489; Lat. 35-14-27 N long. 094-29-19 W; Established in 1888 and named for mining superintendent William Cameron.

•CANADIAN, Town; Pittsburg County; Pop. 279; Zip Code 74425; Lat. 35-10-26 N long. 095-39-08 W; A supply point during the Civil War, the town took its name from the nearby Canadian River.

•CANEY, Town; Atoka County; Pop. 147; Zip Code 74533; Lat. 34-13-57 N long. 096-12-40 W; Founded in 1888 and named for the Caney switch on a nearby railway.

•CANTON, Town; Blaine County; Pop. 854; Zip Code 73724; Elev 1591; Lat. 36-03-21 N long. 098-35-22 W; Established in 1905 and named for nearby Cantonment, a onetime military reservation.

•CANUTE, Town; Washita County; Pop. 676; Zip Code 73626; Lat. 35-25-13 N long. 099-16-45 W; Originally called Oak the town was renamed for the famous King Canute of Denmark.

•CAPRON, Town; Woods County; Pop. 54; Zip Code 73725; Elev. 1293; Lat. 36-53-34 N long. 098-34-38 W; The town was named for Captain Allyn Capron, a commander in the Spanish-American War.

•CARMEN, Town; Alfalfa County; Pop. 516; Zip Code 73726; Elev. 1354; Lat. 36-34-46 N long. 098-27-23 W; Founded in 1901 and named for Carmen Diaz, the wife of the president of Mexico.

•CARNEGIE, Town; Caddo County; Pop. 2,016; Zip Code 73015; Elev. 1309; Lat. 35-06-21 N long. 098-35-58 W; The town is named for industrialist Andrew Carnegie.

•CARNEY, Town; Lincoln County; Pop. 622; Zip Code 74832; Lat. 35-48-15 N long. 097-00-44 W; Called Cold Springs originally, the town's name was changed to Carney in honor of its founder.

•CARRIER, Town; Garfield County; Pop. 259; Zip Code 73727; Elev 1339; Lat. 36-28-34 N long. 098-01-32 W; Founded in 1897 and named in honor of merchant Solomon Carrier.

•CARTER, Town; Beckham County; Pop. 367; Zip Code 73627;

•CASHION, Town; Kingfisher & Logan Counties; Pop. 547; Zip Code 73016; Lat. 35-47-47 N long. 097-41-00 W; The town's name honors Spanish-American War hero Roy Cashion.

•CASTLE, Town; Okfuskee County; Pop. 130; Zip Code 74833; Lat. 35-28-17 N long. 096-22-57 W; Local landowner Mannford Castle gave the town his name.

•CATOOSA, City; Rogers County; Pop. 1,772; Zip Code 74015; Lat. 36-11-19 N long. 095-44-48 W; A Cherokee Indian word meaning "new settlement place."

•CEDAR RIDGE, Town; Pawnee County; A descriptive name give the town after a grove of cedar trees.

•CEMENT, Town; Caddo County; Pop. 884; Zip Code 73017; Lat. 34-55-55 N long. 098-08-20 W; Founded in 1902 and named after nearby cement operations.

•CENTRAHOMA, City; Coal County; Pop. 166; Zip Code 74534; Elev. 711; Lat. 34-36-28 N long. 096-20-42 W; A coined name from "central Oklahoma."

•CHANDLER, City; Lincoln County Seat; Pop. 2,926; Zip Code 74834; Lat. 35-42-23 N long. 096-52-44 W; The name honors George Chandler, assistant secretary of the interior under President Harrison.

•CHATTANOOGA, Town; Comanche & Tillman Counties; Pop. 403; Zip Code 73528; Lat. 34-25-27 N long. 098-39-14 W; Established in 1903 and named after Chattanooga, Tennessee.

•CHECOTAH, City; McIntosh County; Pop. 3,454; Zip Code 74426; Elev. 652; Lat. 35-28-12 N long. 095-31-16 W; Founded in 1886 and named for a Creek Chief, Samuel Checote.

•CHELSEA, City; Rogers County; Pop. 1,754; Zip Code 74016; Lat. 36-32-06 N long. 095-25-44 W; Charles Peach, a local railroad official, named the town for his former home in England in 1882.

•CHEROKEE, City; Alfalfa County Seat; Pop. 2,105; Zip Code 73728; Elev 1181; Lat. 36-46-14 N long. 098-22-38 W; Established in 1894 and named after the Cherokee Indian nation.

•CHEYENNE, Town; Roger Mills County Seat; Pop. 1,207; Zip Code 73628; Lat. 35-36-46 N long. 099-40-18 W; Named after the Cheyenne Indian tribe.

•CHICKASHA, City; Grady County Seat; Pop. 15,828; Zip Code 73018; Elev 1096; Lat. 35-02-04 N long. 097-56-56 W. The site of the town was included in the "Swinging Ring" cattle ranch owned by an intermarried citizen of the Chickasaw Indian Nation, the western border of which was nearby.

•CHOCTAW, City; Oklahoma County; Pop. 7,520; Zip Code 73020; Lat. 35-28-48 N long. 097-16-10 W; The city derives its name from the Choctaw Coal and Railway Company.

•CHOUTEAU, Town; Mayes County; Pop. 1,559; Zip Code 74337; Lat. 36-11-15 N long. 095-20-30 W; Founded in 1871 and named in honor of the Chouteau family.

•CLAREMORE, City; Rogers County Seat; Pop. 12,085; Zip Code 74017; Lat. 36-18-46 N long. 095-36-30 W; Established in 1874 and named for an Osage Indain chief, Clermont.

•CLAYTON, Town; Pushmataha County; Pop. 833; Zip Code 74536; Lat. 34-35-13 N long. 095-21-19 W; The town is named for Clayton, Missouri.

•CLEO SPRINGS, Town; Major County; Pop. 514; Zip Code 73729; Elev. 283; Lat. 36-24-31 N long. 098-26-08 W; Named for nearby Cleo Springs.

•CLEVELAND, City; Pawnee County; Pop. 2,972; Zip Code 74020; Elev 777; Lat. 36-18-23 N long. 096-27-54 W; The town is named in honor of Grover Cleveland.

•CLINTON, City; Custer County; Pop. 8,796; Zip Code 73601; Elev 1592; Lat. 35-30-36 N long. 098-58-29 W; Founded in 1903 and named for a territorial jurist, Clinton F. Irwin.

•COALGATE, City; Coal County Seat; Pop. 2,001; Zip Code 74538; Elev 623; Lat. 34-31-17 N long. 096-13-18 W; The town got its name from nearby coal mines.

•COLBERT, Town; Bryan County; Pop. 1,122; Zip Code 74733; Lat. 33-51-22 N long. 096-29-59 W; Colbert's name honors early settler, Benjamin Colbert.

•COLCORD, Town; Delaware County; Pop. 530; Zip Code 74338; Lat. 36-15-35 N long. 094-41-14 W; The town's name remembers Charles Colcord, an early resident of Oklahoma City.

•COLE, Town; McClain County; Pop. 309; The original landowner, Preslie Cole, had the town named in his honor.

•COLLINSVILLE, City; Rogers & Tulsa Counties; Pop. 3,556; Zip Code 74021; Lat. 36-21-57 N long. 095-50-06 W; Founded in 1897 and named for Dr. H. H. Collins, an early settler.

•COLONY, Town; Washita County; Pop. 185; Zip Code 73021; Lat. 35-20-53 N long. 098-40-39 W; Colony took its name from the Seger Colony, founded by pioneer John Seger.

•COMANCHE, City; Stephens County; Pop. 1,937; Zip Code 73529; Elev 984; Lat. 34-21-59 N long. 097-58-15 W; Named after the famous Indian tribe.

•COMMERCE, City; Ottawa County; Pop. 2,556; Zip Code 74339; Lat. 36-56-28 N long. 094-52-33 W; Named by local settlers after their ambitions.

•COOPERTON, Town; Kiowa County; Pop. 31; Established in 1902 and named in honor of Captain George Cooper, an early pioneer.

•COPAN, Town; Washington County; Pop. 960; Zip Code 74022; Lat. 36-54-01 N long. 095-55-20 W; The city takes its name from the Honduran city.

•CORN, Town; Washita County; Pop. 542; Zip Code 73024; Lat. 35-22-38 N long. 098-46-56 W; The original post office was in a cornfield, hence the name.

•CORNISH, Town; Jefferson County; Pop. 115; Established in the 1890's and named for rancher John Cornish.

•COUNCIL HILL, Town; Muskogee County; Pop. 141; Zip Code 74428; Lat. 35-33-23 N long. 095-39-11 W; A well-known landmark used by the Creek Indians for various ceremonies.

•COVINGTON, Town; Garfield County; Pop. 715; Zip Code 73730; Lat. 36-18-28 N long. 097-35-20 W; John Covington, a well-known pioneer, left his name on the town.

•COWETA, City; Wagoner County; Pop. 4,554; Zip Code 74429; Elev 654; Lat. 36-03-06 N long. 095-41-51 W; Presbyterian missionaries named the town after a Creek Indian town in Alabama.

•COWLINGTON, Town; Le Flore County; Pop. 546; Founded in the 1880's and named for early pioneer, A. F. Cowling.

•COYLE, Town; Logan County; Pop. 345; Zip Code 73027; Lat. 35-57-27 N long. 097-14-10 W; Founded in 1899 and named in honor of a prominent citizen of Guthrie, a Mr. William Coyle.

•CRESCENT, City; Logan County; Pop. 1,651; Zip Code 73028; Lat. 36-00-15 N long. 097-36-40 W; Settled in the 1890's and descriptively named for a nearby crescent-shaped oak grove.

•CROMWELL, Town; Seminole County; Pop. 337; Zip Code 74837; Lat. 35-20-37 N long. 096-27-04 W; Oil producer Joe Cromwell gave his name to the town in the 1920's.

•CROWDER, Town; Pittsburg County; Pop. 431; Zip Code 74430; Lat. 35-07-33 N long. 095-39-56 W; Originally called Juanita, the town's name was changed to honor early pioneer Dr. W. E. Crowder.

•CURCHECE, Town; Pawnee County; Pop. 7; Named for an early settler.

•CUSHING, City; Payne County; Pop.7,720; Zip Code 74023. Marshall Cushing, assistant to the Postmaster General, had the town named in his honor.

•CUSTER CITY, Town; Custer County; Pop. 530; Zip Code 73639; Elev. 1769; Lat. 35-39-43 N long. 098-53-06 W; Named in honor of General George Custer who was killed in 1876 while fighting the Sioux Indians.

•CYRIL, Town; Caddo County; Pop. 1,220; Zip Code 73029; Lat. 34-53-02 N long. 098-12-06 W; The original landowner, Cyril Lookingglass, had the town named in his honor.

•DACOMA, Town; Woods County; Pop. 226; Zip Code 73731; Elev. 1366; Lat. 36-39-32 N long. 098-33-40 W; A coined word combining Dakota and Oklahoma.

•DAVENPORT, Town; Lincoln County; Pop. 974; Zip Code 74026; Lat. 35-42-15 N long. 096-45-44 W; The first postmaster, Nettie Davenport, gave the town her family name.

•DAVIDSON, Town; Tillman County; Pop. 501; Zip Code 73530; Lat. 34-14-37 N long. 099-04-53 W; Davidson is named in hnor of A. J. Davidson, a Director of a local railroad.

•DAVIS, City; Murray County; Pop. 2,782; Zip Code 73030; Elev 846; Lat. 34-30-07 N long. 097-06-58 W; Merchant Samuel Davis left his name on the town.

•DEER CREEK, Town; Grant County; Pop. 174; Zip Code 74636; Elev 1085; Lat. 36-48-19 N long. 097-31-17 W; The town is named for adjacent Deer Creek, a tributary of the Arkansas River.

•DEL CITY, City; Oklahoma County; Pop. 28,424; A part of the Oklahoma City area, the town is named for Delaphens Campbell, the daughter of the original landowner.

•DELAWARE, Town; Nowata County; Pop. 544; Zip Code 74027; Lat. 36-46-45 N long. 095-38-21 W; The town's name remembers the Delaware Indians.

•DEPEW, Town; Creek County; Pop. 682; Zip Code 74028; Lat. 35-47-57 N long. 096-30-13 W; Found in 1901 and named for Chauncey Depew, U. S. Senator from New York.

•DEVAL, City; Cotton County; Pop. 186; Zip Code 73531; Lat. 34-11-42 N long. 098-35-18 W; The town is named in honor of its first postmaster.

•DEWAR, City; Okmulgee County; Pop. 1,048; Zip Code 74431; Lat. 35-27-21 N long. 095-56-21 W; Established in 1909 and named for a local railraod official, William Dewar.

•DEWEY, City; Washington County; Pop. 3,545; Zip Code 74029; Lat. 36-47-48 N long. 095-56-05 W; Founded in 1899 and named for Spanish-American War hero, Admiral George Dewey.

•DIBBLE, Town; McClain County; Pop. 348; Zip Code 73031; Lat. 35-02-04 N long. 097-37-49 W; Local ranchers John and James Dibble left their name on the town.

•DICKSON, Town; Carter County; Pop. 996. Named for an early pioneer.

•DILL CITY, Town; Washita County; Pop. 649; Zip Code 73641; Lat. 35-16-57 N long. 099-07-49 W; Named for prominent Washita Conty resident D. S. Dill.

•DISNEY, Town; Mayes County; Pop. 464; Zip Code 74340; Lat. 36-28-33 N long. 095-01-18 W; The town's name honors U. S. Congressman, Wesley Disney.

•DOUGHERTY, Town; Murray County; Pop. 210; Zip Code 73032; Elev. 773; Lat. 34-23-54 N long. 097-02-56 W; Founded in 1887 and honoring William Dougherty, a Texas banker.

•DOUGLAS, Town; Garfield County; Pop. 89; Zip Code 73733; Lat. 36-15-38 N long. 097-40-00 W; Formerly called Onyx but later renamed in honor of Douglas Frantz, a prominent citizen.

•DOVER, Town; Kingfisher County; Pop. 570; Zip Code 73734; Lat. 35-58-58 N long. 097-54-39 W; The town is named after Dover, England.

OKLAHOMA

•**DRUMMOND,** Town; Garfield County; Pop. 482; Zip Code 73735; Elev 1241; Lat. 36-18-02 N long. 098-02-01 W; Drummond is named after local railway official Harry Drummond.

•**DRUMRIGHT,** City; Creek County Pop. 3,162; Zip Code 74030; Lat. 35-59-11 N long. 096-36-55 W; The original landowner, Aaron Drumright, had the town named in his honor.

•**DUNCAN,** City; Stephens County Seat; Pop. 22,517; Zip Code 73533; Elev 1126; Lat. 34-28-09 N long. 097-59-42 W; Founded in 1884 and named for William Chickawaw, an original settler.

•**DURANT,** City; Bryan County Seat; Pop. 11,972; Zip Code 74701; Lat. 33-59-51 N long. 096-23-08 W; Established in the 1870's and named in honor of the well-known Durant family.

•**EAST NINNEKAH,** Town; Grady County; Pop. 1,085; The city takes its name from the Choctaw Indian word Ninek, meaning "night" or "darkness."

•**EDMOND,** City; Oklahoma County; Pop. 34,637; Zip Code 730+; Elev. 1,200; Lat. 35-32-46 N, long. 098-22-50 W. Named for a railroad official.

•**ELGIN,** Town; Comanche County; Pop. 1,003; Zip Code 73538; Lat. 34-46-27 N, long. 098-17-28 W. The town is named after Elgin, Illinois.

•**ELK CITY,** City; Beckham County; Pop. 9,579; Zip Code 73644; Elev. 1,928; Lat. 35-24-51 N, long. 099-24-44 W. Named for Elk Creek, which skirts the town's limits.

•**EL RENO,** City; Canadian County Seat; Pop. 15,486; Zip Code 73036; Lat. 35-31-56 N long. 097-57-14 W; Founded in 1889 and named for nearby Fort Reno.

•**ELMORE CITY,** Town; Garvin County; Pop. 582; Zip Code 73035; Lat. 34-37-23 N long. 097-23-44 W; The town is named for pioneer J. O. Elmore.

•**ENID,** City; Garfield County Seat; Pop. 50,363; Zip Code 73701; Elev. 1246; Lat. 36-25-08 N long. 097-51-55 W; Established in 1893 and taken from the Idylls of the King by Tennyson.

•**ERICK,** City; Beckham County; Pop. 1,375; Zip Code 73645; Lat. 35-12-47 N long. 099-52-12 W; The town's developer, Beeks Erick, had the town named in his honor.

•**EUFAULA,** City; McIntosh County Seat; Pop. 3,092; Zip Code 74432; Elev. 617; Lat. 35-17-09 N long. 095-34-57 W; Eufaula was the name of a Creek Indian village in Alabama. It means "they left here and went to other places."

•**FAIRFAX,** Town; Osage County; Pop. 1,073; Zip Code 74637; Elev 342; Lat. 36-34-26 N long. 096-42-15 W; The town is named in honor of Fairfax County; in Virginia.

•**FAIRLAND,** Town; Ottawa County; Pop. 1,073; Zip Code 74343; Elev 838; Lat. 36-45-21 N long. 094-50-37 W; A descriptive name for the many prairie flowers in the area.

•**FAIRMONT,** Town; Garfield County; Pop. 419; Zip Code 73736; Elev 1202; Lat. 36-21-33 N long. 097-42-06 W; John Murphy of Enid named the town after Fairmount School in Wichita, Kansas.

•**FAIRVIEW,** City; Major County Seat; Pop. 3,370; Zip Code 73737; Lat. 36-16-40 N long. 098-28-38 W; The town has a scenic location in a wooded valley east of the Glass Mountains.

•**FANSHOWE,** Town; Le Flore County; Pop. 416; Zip Code 74935; Elev 545; Lat. 34-56-59 N long. 094-54-31 W; Founded in 1891 and named for a local settler.

•**FARGO,** Town; Ellis County; Pop. 409; Zip Code 73840; Elev. 2101; Lat. 36-22-17 N long. 099-37-26 W; The town took its name from the Wells, Fargo, and Company.

•**FAXON,** Town; Comanche County; Pop. 140; Zip Code 73540; Lat. 34-27-37 N long. 098-34-39 W; Established in 1902 and named for Ralph Faxon, Secretary to U. S. Senator Chester Long from Kansas.

•**FLETCHER,** Town; Comanche County; Pop. 1,074; Zip Code 73541; Lat. 34-48-59 N long. 098-14-25 W; In Comanche County; the town was named for pioneer Fletcher Dodge.

•**FORAKER,** Town; Osage County; Pop. 34; In Osage County; the town took its name from U. S. Senator from Ohio, Joseph Foraker.

•**FOREST PARK,** Town; Oklahoma County; Pop. 1,148; A part of Oklahoma City and descriptivgely named for the oak groves in the town.

•**FORGAN,** Town; Beaver County; Pop. 611; Zip Code 73938; Lat. 36-54-25 N long. 100-32-17 W; The town is named for Chicago banker James B. Forgan.

•**FORT COBB,** Town; Caddo County; Pop. 760; Zip Code 73038; Elev 1255; Lat. 35-06-00 N long. 098-26-14 W; Established in 1859 and named for Howell Cobb, Secretary of the Treasury under President Buchanan.

•**FORT GIBSON,** Town; Muskagee County; Pop. 2,483; Zip Code 74434; Lat. 35-48-18 N long. 095-15-04 W; Founded in 1824, the fort was named for Colonel George Gibson, U. S. Army Commissary Dept.

•**FORT SUPPLY,** Town; Woodward County; Pop. 559; Zip Code 73841; Elev. 1994; Lat. 36-30-23 N long. 099-23-10 W; Established in 1868 as a supply base for General Custer's Indian campaigns.

•**FORT TOWSON,** Town; Choctaw County; Pop. 789; Zip Code 74735; Lat. 34-01-06 N long. 095-15-56 W; Set up as an army base in 1824 and named for Nathan Towson, U. S. Army paymaster general.

•**FOSS,** City; Washita County; Pop. 188; Zip Code 73647; Elev 1629; Lat. 35-27-21 N long. 099-10-11 W; The city is named for early resident J. M. Foss.

•**FOYIL,** Town; Rogers County; Pop. 191; Zip Code 74031; Lat. 36-26-08 N long. 095-31-04 W; In Rogers County; the town was named for its first postmaster, Alfred Foyil.

•**FRANCIS,** Town; Pontotoc County; Pop. 365; Zip Code 74844; Lat. 34-52-44 N long. 096-35-10 W; In Pontotoc County; the town is named for early day rancher David Francis.

•**FREDERICK,** City; Tillman County Seat; Pop. 6,153; Zip Code 73542; Lat. 34-23-31 N long. 099-00-50 W; Formerly Gosnell, the town's name was changed to honor Frederick Van Blarcom, the son of a prominent railraod developer.

•**FREEDOM,** Town; Woods County; Pop. 339; Zip Code 73842; Lat. 36-46-09 N long. 099-06-43 W; Founded in 1901 and given this cheerful name.

•**GAGE,** Town; Ellis County; Pop. 667; Zip Code 73843; Elev 2136; Lat. 36-19-03 N long. 099-45-31 W; In Ellis County;, Gage is named in honor of Lyman Gage, William McKinley's Secretary of the Treasury.

•**GANS,** Town; Sequoyah County; Pop. 346; Zip Code 74936; Lat. 35-23-22 N long. 094-41-35 W; The town is named after the Gann brothers, two local Cherokees.

•**GARBER,** City; Garfield County; Pop. 1,215; Zip Code 73738; Elev 1177; Lat. 36-26-16 N long. 097-34-50 W; Once called McCardie, the name was changed in 1894 to honor early resident Martin Garber.

•**GARVIN,** Town; McCurtain County; Pop. 162; Zip Code 74736; Elev. 494; Lat. 33-57-12 N long. 094-56-04 W; In McCurtain County; the town is named for Choctaw Indian chief Isaac Garvin.

•**GATE,** Town; Beaver County; Pop. 146; Zip Code 73844; Elev 2230; Lat. 36-50-59 N long. 100-03-14 W; The town was located at the entrance to the old neutral strip and hence took this name.

•**GEARY,** City; Blaine & Canadian Counties; Pop. 1,700; Zip Code 73040; Elev 1541; Lat. 35-37-38 N long. 098-18-50 W; Established in 1892 and named for Indian scout Ed Geary.

•**GENE AUTRY,** Town; Carter County; Pop. 178; Zip Code 73436; Lat. 34-16-55 N long. 097-01-55 W; Formerly the town of Berwyn, the name was changed in 1942 to honor the movie star.

•**GERONIMO,** Town; Comanche County; Pop. 726; Zip Code 73543; Lat. 34-29-10 N long. 098-22-49 W; The town is named for the famous Apache Indian chief.

•**GLENCOE,** Town; Payne County; Pop. 490; Zip Code 74032; Elev 1064; Lat. 36-13-29 N long. 096-55-40 W; Named after Glencoe, Scotland.

•**GLENPOOL,** City; Tulsa County; Pop. 2,706; Zip Code 74033; Lat. 35-57-23 N long. 096-00-34 W; The town is named after Ida Glenn, the original landowner of the townsite.

•**GOLDSBY,** Town; McClain County; Pop. 603; In McClain County; the town is named for early resident Frank Goldsby.

•**GOLTRY,** Town; Alfalfa County; Pop. 305; Zip Code 73739; Elev. 1380; Lat. 36-32-00 N long. 098-08-51 W; Formerly called Karoma the town was renamed in honor of local businessman Charles Goltry.

•**GOODWELL,** Town; Texas County; Pop. 1,186; Zip Code 73939; Elev 3293; Lat. 36-35-38 N long. 101-37-40 W; The Rock Island Railroad drilled a water well on the site which proved to be good water, hence the name.

•**GORE,** Town; Sequoyah County; Pop. 445; Zip Code 74435; Lat. 35-31-49 N long. 095-07-04 W; The town's name honors U. S. Senator Thomas P. Gore.

•**GOTEBO,** Town; Kiowa County; Pop. 457; Zip Code 73041; Elev. 1430; Lat. 35-04-16 N long. 098-52-10 W; In Kiowa County; the town is named a chief of the Kiowa Indians.

•**GOULD,** Town; Harmon County; Pop. 318; Zip Code 73544; Lat. 34-39-54 N long. 099-46-25 W; The town is named for its first postmaster John Gould.

•**GRACEMONT,** Town; Caddo County; Pop. 503; Zip Code 73042; Lat. 35-11-14 N long. 098-15-14 W; The first postmaster Alice Bailey coined the name after two of her friends: Grace and Montgomery.

•**GRANDFIELD,** City; Tillman County; Pop. 1,445; Zip Code 73546; Elev 1456; Lat. 34-13-46 N long. 098-41-20 W; The town's name honors U. S. Postmaster General Charles Grandfield.

•**GRANITE,** Town; Greer County; Pop. 1,617; Zip Code 73547; Lat. 34-57-42 N long. 099-23-01 W; Founded in 1889 and named for the large granite formations in the nearby Wichita Mountains.

•**GREENFIELD,** Town; Blaine County; Pop. 233; Zip Code 73043; Lat. 35-43-38 N long. 098-22-37 W; The town is named for its first postmaster, Henry Greenfield.

•**GROVE,** Town; Delaware County; Pop. 3,378; Zip Code 74344; Lat. 36-35-27 N long. 094-47-31 W; The nearby Round Grove Civil War landmark gave the town its name.

•**GUTHRIE,** City; Logan County Seat; Pop. 10,312; Zip Code 73044; Lat. 35-52-43 N long. 097-25-31 W; Capital of the Oklahoma Territory, the city was named for Kansas jurist, John Guthrie.

•**GUYMAN,** City; Texas County Seat; Pop. 8,492; Zip Code 73942; Elev. 3121; Lat. 36-41-10 N long. 101-28-56 W; The town's name honors E.T. Guyman, the original developer.

•**HALL PARK,** Town; Cleveland County; Pop. 577; Near the city of Norman, Hall is named after original developer Ike Hall.

•**HALLETT,** Town; Pawnee County; Pop. 186; Zip Code 74034; Lat. 36-13-45 N long. 096-34-06 W; The town's name remembers Lieutenant Charles Hallett of the nineteenth Kansas Cavalry.

•**HAMMON,** Town; Custer & Roger Mills Counties; Pop. 866; Zip Code 73650; Elev 1736; Lat. 35-37-30 N long. 099-22-40 W; Founded in 1894 and named for Indian agent J. H. Hammon.

•**HANNA,** Town; McIntosh County; Pop. 157; Zip Code 74845; Elev 678; Lat. 35-12-24 N long. 095-53-15 W; Originally called Hasson, the town's name remembers long time resident Hanna Bullett.

•**HARDESTY,** Town; Texas County; Pop. 243; Zip Code 73944; Elev 2911; Lat. 36-36-51 N long. 101-11-36 W; Founded in 1887 and named after rancher A. J. Hardesty.

•**HARRAH,** Town; Oklahoma County; Pop. 2,897; Zip Code 73045; Lat. 35-29-10 N long. 097-09-56 W; Businessman and civic leader Frank Harrah had the town take his name.

•**HARRIS,** Town; McCurtain County; Pop. 192; Harris is named after Choctaw jurist Henry C. Harris.

•**HARTSHORNE,** City; Pittsburg County; Pop. 2,380; Zip Code 74547; Elev 705; Lat. 34-50-36 N long. 095-33-33 W; Founded in 1890 and named for railroad official Dr. Charles Hartshorne.

•**HASKELL,** Town; Muskogee County; Pop. 1,953; Zip Code 74436; Lat. 35-49-12 N long. 095-40-33 W; Formerly Sanokla, the town is named after Charles Haskell, longtime resident.

•**HASTINGS,** Town; Jefferson County; Pop. 246; Zip Code 73548; Lat. 34-12-58 N long. 098-06-15 W; The town's name remembers W. w. Hastings, a lonetime town resident.

•**HAWORTH,** Town; McCurtain County; Pop. 341; Zip Code 74740; Lat. 33-50-38 N long. 094-38-43 W; The town is named after railroad surveyor John Haworth.

•**HEADRICK,** Town; Jackson County; Pop. 223; Zip Code 73549; Lat. 34-37-31 N long. 099-08-10 W; In Jackson County; the town is named for its original landowner T. B. Headrick.

•**HEALDTON,** City; Carter County; Pop. 3,769; Zip Code 73438; Lat. 34-13-58 N long. 097-29-12 W; Founded in the 1880's and named after prominent resident Charles Heald.

•**HEAVENER,** City; Le Flore County; Pop. 2,776; Zip Code 74937; Elev 562; Lat. 34-53-16 N long. 094-36-14 W; Established in the 1890's and named for Joseph Heavener, a well-known merchant.

•**HELENA,** Town; Alfalfa County; Pop. 710; Zip Code 73741; Elev 1397; Lat. 36-32-50 N long. 098-16-08 W; The town is named after its first postmaster, Helen S. Monroe.

•**HENDRIX,** Town; Bryan County; Pop. 106; Zip Code 74741; Lat. 33-46-30 N long. 096-24-15 W; In Bryan County;, the town is named after its first postmaster, James Hendrix.

•**HENNESSEY,** Town; Kingfisher County; Pop. 2,287; Zip Code 73742; Lat. 36-06-27 N long. 097-53-55 W; The town's name commemorates freight hauler Pat Hennessey who was killed in an Indian massacre in 1874.

•**HENRYETTA,** City; Okmulgee County; Pop. 6,432; Zip Code 74437; Lat. 35-28-23 N long. 095-55-47 W; In Okmulgee County; the town is named after Henry and Etta Ray Beard.

•**HOBART,** City; Kiowa County Seat; Pop. 4,735; Zip Code 73651; Elev. 1,550; Lat. 35-01-41 N, long. 099-05-39 W. Named for Garrett A. Hobart, vice president 1897-1899.

•**HOLDENVILLE,** City; Hughes County Seat; Pop. 5,469; Zip Code 74848; Elev. 866; Lat. 35-05-02 N, long. 096-23-41 W. Named for nearby Lake Holdenville.

•**HOLLIS,** City; Harmon County Seat; Pop. 2,958; Zip Code 73550; Elev. 1,615; Lat. 34-41-08 N, long. 099-55-02 W. Part of the Red River Territory, which Texas claimed prior to a Supreme Court decision in 1896.

•**HOMINY,** City; Osage County; Pop. 3,130; Zip Code 74035; Elev 792; Lat. 36-24-49 N long. 096-23-32 W; A corruption of the word harmony - possibly referring to a religious mission in Kansas.

•**HOOKER,** City; Texas County; Pop. 1,788; Zip Code 73945; Lat. 36-51-39 N long. 101-12-43 W; The town is named for local rancher Joseph Hooker.

•**HOWE,** Town; Le Flore County; Pop. 562; Zip Code 74940; Lat. 34-56-59 N long. 094-38-09 W; The town is named for Kansas Railroad Director, Dr. Herbert Howe.

•**HUGO,** City; Choctaw County Seat; Pop. 7,172; Zip Code 74743; Lat. 34-00-32 N long. 095-30-41 W; Hugo is named in honor of the great French novelist, Victor Hugo.

•**HULBERT,** Town; Cherokee County; Pop. 633; Zip Code 74441; Lat. 34-56-04 N long. 095-53-30 W; Hulbert is in Cherokee County; and is named for Ben Hulbert, a well-known Cherokee.

•**HUNTER,** Town; Garfield County; Pop. 276; Zip Code 74640; Elev 1094; Lat. 36-34-04 N long. 097-39-39 W; The town is named after original landowner Charles Hunter.

•**HYDRO,** Town; Blaine & Caddo Counties; Pop. 938; Zip Code 73048; Elev 1557; Lat. 35-32-53 N long. 098-34-42 W; The town is named for the good well water locally available.

•**IDABEL,** City; McCurtain County Seat; Pop. 7,622; Zip Code 74745; Elev. 489; Lat. 33-53-30 N long. 094-48-56 W; Founded around 1904 and named for Ida and Belle Purnell, the daughters of a local railroad official.

•**INDIAHOMA,** Town; Comanche County; Pop. 364; Zip Code 73552; Elev 1335; Lat. 34-36-44 N long. 098-45-05 W; A coined word combining Indian and Oklahoma.

•**INDIANOLA,** Town; Pittsburg County; Pop. 254; Zip Code 74442; Lat. 35-09-57 N long. 095-46-31 W; A combined word: Indian and the Choctaw word olah, or "this side of."

•**INOLA,** Town; Rogers County; Pop. 1,550; Zip Code 74036; Elev 600; Lat. 36-09-06 N long. 095-35-19 W; A Cherokee word meaning "black fox."

•**JAY,** Town; Delaware County Seat; Pop. 2,100; Zip Code 74346; Elev 1035; Lat. 36-25-11 N long. 094-47-50 W; The county seat of Delaware County;, Jay is named for Jay Washbourne, the grandson of a Cherokee missinary.

•**JENKS,** City; Tulsa County; Pop. 5,876; Zip Code 74037; Lat. 36-01-22 N long. 095-58-04 W; In Tulsa County; the town is named after early resident Elmer Jenks.

•**JENNINGS,** Town; Pawnee County; Pop. 395; Zip Code 74038; Elev 932; Lat. 36-10-44 N long. 096-34-06 W; Founded in 1893 and named for original landowner George Jennings.

•**JET,** Town; Alfalfa County; Pop. 352; Zip Code 73749; Lat. 36-40-03 N long. 098-10-44 W; Established in 1894 and named for its first postmaster, W. M. Jett.

•**JONES,** Town; Oklahoma County; Pop. 2,270; Zip Code 73049; Lat. 35-33-50 N long. 097-17-25 W; The town is named in honor of C. G. Jones, an Oklahoma City industriailist and railroad promoter.

•**KANSAS,** Town; Dalaware County; Pop. 491; Zip Code 74347; Lat. 36-12-15 N long. 094-47-49 W; Early settlers named the town after the state of Kansas.

•**KAW CITY,** City; Kay County; Pop. 283; Zip Code 74641; Lat. 36-50-20 N long. 096-50-12 W; The town is named after the Kaw Indian tribe.

•**KELLYVILLE,** Town; Creek County; Pop. 960; Zip Code 74039; Lat. 35-56-25 N long. 096-12-45 W; Merchant James Kelly gave his name to the town.

•**KEMP,** Town; Bryan County; Pop. 178; Zip Code 74747; Lat. 33-46-11 N long. 096-21-07 W; Kemp was founded in 1890 and named after Jackson Kemp, a prominent Chickasaw Indian.

•**KENDRICK,** Town; Lincoln County; Pop. 132; Zip Code 74040; Lat. 35-47-05 N long. 096-46-15 W; Kendrick's name honors Santa Fe Railway Vice President, J. W. Kendrick.

•**KENEFIC,** Town; Bryan County; Pop. 140; Zip Code 74748; Lat. 34-08-51 N long. 096-21-42 W; The town's name honors William Kenefic, President of the Kansas, Oklahoma and Gulf Railroad.

•**KEOTA,** Town; Haskell County; Pop. 661; Zip Code 74941; Elev 4353; Lat. 35-15-34 N long. 094-55-10 W; A Choctaw Indian word meaning "the fire gone out," and referring to an entire tribe destroyed by disease.

•**KETCHUM,** Town; Craig County; Pop. 326; Zip Code 74349; Elev 772; Lat. 36-27-19 N long. 095-02-09 W; In Craig County; the town is named for longtime resident James Ketchum.

•**KEYES,** Town; Cimarron County; Pop. 557; Zip Code 73947; Elev 954; Lat. 36-48-31 N long. 102-15-03 W; The town's name honors Santa Fe Railway President, Henry Keyes.

•**KIEFER,** Town; Creek County; Pop. 912; Zip Code 74041; Lat. 35-56-39 N long. 096-03-41 W; Formerly called Praper, the town is named for Smith Kiefer, an early resient.

•**KINGFISHER,** City; Kingfisher County Seat; Pop. 4,245; Zip Code 73750; Lat. 35-51-15 N long. 097-55-55 W; The town gets is name from Kingfisher Creek.

•**KINGSTON,** Town; Marshall County; Pop. 1,171; Zip Code 73439; Lat. 33-59-430 N long. 096-43-17 W; Kingston gets its name from early resident Jeh King.

•KINTA, Town; Haskell County; Pop. 303; Zip Code 74552; Lat. 35-07-11 N long. 095-14-11 W; Kinta is an Indain word for "beaver".

•KIOWA, Town; Pittsburg County; Pop. 866; Zip Code 74553; Elev 744; Lat. 34-43-22 N long.095-54-04 W; Named for the Kiowa Indian tribe.

•KNOWLES, Town; Beaver County; Pop. 44; Zip Code 74553; Elev 744; Lat. 34-43-22 N long. 095-54-04 W; The town is named for a local school teacher, F.E. Knowles.

•KONAWA, City; Seminole County; Pop. 1,711; Zip Code 74849; Elev 967; Lat. 34-57-34 N long. 096-45-44 W; A Seminole Indian word meaning "a string of beads."

•KREBS, City; Pittsburg County; Pop. 1,754; Zip Code 74554; Lat. 34-55-39 N long. 095-43-07 W; The town is named for Judge Edmund Krebs, a Choctaw jurist.

•KREMLIN, Town; Garfield County; Pop. 301; Zip Code 73753; Elev 1116; Lat. 36-32-54 N long. 097-49-45 W; Named for the Kremlin in Moscow, Russia.

•LAHOMA, Town; Garfield County; Pop. 537; Zip Code 73754; Elev 1236; Lat. 36-23-11 N long. 098-05-07 W; A diminutive name for Oklahoma.

•LAMAR, Town; Hughes County; Pop. 121; Zip Code 74850; Elev 763; Lat. 35-05-50 N long. 096-07-38 W; Named after an early pioneer.

•LAMONT, Town; Grant County; Pop. 571; Zip Code 74643; Elev 1011; Lat. 36-41-27 N long. 097-33-33 W; The town is named in honor of Daniel Lamont, President Cleveland's Secretary of War.

•LANGLEY, Town; Mayes County; Pop. 582; Zip Code 74350; Lat. 36-27-51 N long. 095-03-04 W; Langley's name honors J. Howard Langley, who was chairman of the Grand River Dam Authority.

•LANGSTON, Town; Logan County; Pop. 443; Zip Code 73050; Lat. 35-56-28 N long. 097-15-10 W; Black educator and U. S. Congressman, John M. Langston had the town named in his honor.

•LAVERNE, Town; Harper County; Pop. 1,563; Zip Code 73848; Lat. 36-42-25 N long. 099-53-44 W; Founded in the 1890's and named for early settler Laverne Smith.

•LAWTON, City; Comanche County Seat; Pop. 80,054; Zip Code 73501; Lat. 34-36-47 N long. 098-24-57 W; The town's name honors General Henry Lawton who was killed during the Philippine insurrection.

•LE FLORE, Town; Le Flore County; Pop. 322; Zip Code 74942; Lat. 34-53-36 N long. 094-58-47 W; Founded in the 1880's and named after the settler Le Flore family.

•LEEDEY, Town; Dewey County; Pop. 499; Zip Code 73654; Lat. 35-52-07 N long. 099-20-47 W; Leedey is named after its first postmaster, Amos Leedey.

•LEHIGH, City; Coal County; Pop. 284; Zip Code 74556; Elev 611; Lat. 34-28-21 N long. 096-13-28 W; The town is named after Lehigh, Pennsylvania.

•LENAPAH, Town; Nowata County; Pop. 350; Zip Code 74042; Lat. 36-51-06 N long. 095-38-01 W; A variant name on the original name of the Delaware Indians.

•LEON, Town; Love County; Pop. 120; Zip Code 73441; Lat. 33-52-39 N long. 097-25-54 W; Founded in 1883 and given the Spanish name for "lion."

•LEROY, Town; Pawnee County; Pop. 9; A joint name honoring local residents Lee Jordan and Roy De Master.

•LEXINGTON, Town; Cleveland County; Pop. 1,731; Zip Code 73051; Elev. 1034; Lat. 35-00-57 N long. 097-19-53 W; The town is named after Lexington, Kentucky.

•LINDSAY, City; Garvin County; Pop. 3,454; Zip Code 73052; Lat. 34-50-20 N long. 097-36-39 W; Named for the town's original landowner, Lewis Lindsay.

•LOCO, City; Stephens County; Pop. 215; Zip Code 73442; Lat. 34-19-51 N long. 097-40-40 W; Named after Locoweed, a herb in the pea family, famous for being poisonous to livestock.

•LOCUST GROVE, Town; Mayes County; Pop. 1,179; Zip Code 74352; Lat. 36-12-04 N long. 095-09-59 W; Site of a Civil War battle, the town is named after a prominent grove of locust trees.

•LONE GROVE, Town; Carter County; Pop. 3,369; Zip Code 73443; Lat. 34-10-31 N long. 097-15-59 W; Descriptively named for a single grove of trees.

•LONE WOLF, Town; Kiowa County; Pop. 613; Zip Code 73655; Elev. 1577; Lat. 34-59-20 N long. 099-14-39 W; The town's name honors Kiowa Indian Chief, Lone Wolf.

•LONGDALE, Town; Blaine County; Pop. 405; Zip Code 73755; Elev 1655; Lat. 36-08-01 N long. 098-32-57 W; Named after the original landowner in the town, W. H. Long.

•LOOKEBA, Town; Caddo County; Pop. 221; Zip Code 73053; Elev 142; Lat. 35-21-41 N long. 098-22-00 W; The three developers of the town, Lowe, Kelly, and Baker, gave the town their name.

•LOVELAND, Town; Tillman County; Pop. 21; Zip Code 73553; Lat. 34-18-11 N long. 098-46-22 W; Founded in the early 1900's and given a euphonious name by merchant E. T. Duncan.

•LOYAL, Town; Kingfisher County; Pop. 112; Zip Code 73756; Elev 1115; Lat. 35-58-15 N long. 098-06-57 W; Formerly called Keil the name was changed in 1918 to show loyalty to the United States.

•LUTHER, Town; Oklahoma County; Pop. 1,159; Zip Code 73054; Lat. 35-38-14 N long. 097-13-06 W; Founded in the 1890's and named in honor of Oklahoma City businessman Luther Jones.

•MACOMB, Town; Pottawatomie County; Pop. 58; Zip Code 74852; Lat. 35-08-57 N long. 097-0042 W; The town is named after J. Macomb, an engineer for the Santa Fe Railway Company.

•MADILL, City; Marshall County Seat; Pop. 3,173; Zip Code 73446; Elev 789; Lat. 34-05-17 N long. 096-46-17 W; Railroad attorney George Madill had the town named in his honor.

•MANCHESTER, Town; Grant County; Pop. 146; Zip Code 73758; Elev 1277; Lat. 36-59-27 N long. 098-01-40 W; The town was named after Manchester, England.

•MANGUM, City; Greer County Seat; Pop. 3,833; Zip Code 73554; Elev 1606; Lat. 34-52-38 N long. 099-30-14 W; Named after the town's original landowner, A. S. Magnum.

•MANITOU, Town; Tillman County; Pop. 322; Zip Code 73555; Elev 1255; Lat. 34-30-29 N long. 098-58-44 W; An Algonquian Indian word for God.

•MANNFORD, Town; Tulsa County; Zip Code 74044; Lat. 36-07-08 N long. 096-20-44 W; Named for an early settler.

•MANNSVILLE, Town; Johnston County; Pop. 568; Zip Code 73447; Lat. 34-11-15 N long. 096-51-29 W; The town is named after its first postmaster, Wallace Mann.

•MARAMEC, Town; Pawnee County; Pop. 101; Zip Code 74045; Lat. 36-14-19 N long. 096-40-52 W; The name is an Algonquina Indian word meaning "fish."

•MARBLE CITY, Town; Sequoyah County; Pop. 294; Zip Code 74945; Lat. 35-34-56 N long. 094-48-53 W; The city is descriptively named for surrounding rock formations.

•MARIETTA, City; Love County Seat; Pop. 2,494; Zip Code 73448; Lat. 33-56-09 N long. 097-07-08 W; The city is named after Marietta, Pennsylvania.

•MARLAND, Town; Noble County; Pop. 340; Zip Code 74644; Elev 1013; Lat. 36-33-41 N long. 097-09-03 W; The town's name honors E.W. Marland, a governor of Oklahoma.

•MARLOW, City; Stephens County; Pop. 5,017; Zip Code 73055; Elev 1312; Lat. 34-39-01 N long. 097-57-05 W; The city was named after the nearby Marlow Ranch.

•MARSHALL, Town; Logan County; Pop. 372; Zip Code 73056; Lat. 36-09-33 N long. 097-37-25 W; Town founder S. T.Rice named the new town after his former home, Marshaltown, Iowa.

•MARTHA, Town; Jackson County; Pop. 219; Zip Code 73556; Lat. 34-43-37 N long. 099-23-09 W; Founded in 1889 and named for a Baptist minister's daughter, Martha Medlin.

•MAUD, City; Pottawatomie & Seminole Counties; Pop. 1,444; Zip Code 74854; Elev 966; Lat. 35-07-54 N long. 096-46-46 W; Established in 1896 and named for local resident Maud Tinkle.

•MAYSVILLE, Town; Garvin County; Pop. 1,396; Zip Code 73057; Elev 943; Lat. 34-49-07 N long. 097-24-35 W; Founded in 1878 and named for the Mayes brothers ranchers.

•MCALESTER, City; Pittsburg County Seat; Pop. 17,255; Zip Code 74501; Lat. 34-56-03 N long. 095-46-08 W; Founded in 1873 and named in honor of businessman and second Lieutenant Governor of Oklahoma, John McAlester.

•MCCURTAIN, Town; Haskell County; Pop. 549; Zip Code 74944; Lat. 35-09-12 N long. 094-57-46 W; The town's name honors Choctaw Chief, Green McCurtain.

•MCLOUD, Town; Pottawatomie County; Pop. 4,061; Zip Code 74851; Lat. 35-25-46 N long. 097-05-12 W; Railroad attorney John McCloud had the town named in his honor.

•MEAD, Town; Bryan County; Pop. 143; Zip Code 73449; Lat. 34-00-04 N long. 096-30-35 W; The town is named for Chickasaw Indian Minor Mead.

•MEDFORD, City; Grant County Seat; Pop. 1,419; Zip Code 73759; Lat. 36-48-25 N long. 097-44-09 W; The town is named for Medford, Massachusetts.

•MEDICINE PARK, Town; Comanche County; Pop. 437; Zip Code 73557; Lat. 34-43-44 N long. 098-29-55 W; Medicine Creek is named for the local creek.

•MEEKER, Town; Lincoln County; Pop. 1,032; Zip Code 74855; Lat. 35-30-06 N long. 096-54-06 W; The town's name remembers Julian Meeker, the original landowner.

•MERIDIAN, Town; Logan County; Pop. 78; Zip Code 73058; Elev. 2260; Lat. 35-50-32 N long. 097-14-54 W; A descriptive name for the town located on the Indian meridian.

•MIAMI, City; Ottawa County Seat; Pop. 14,237; Zip Code 743+; Elev 798; Lat. 36-53-12 N long. 094-52-47 W; The town's name honors the nearby Miami Indians.

•MIDWEST CITY, City; Oklahoma County; Pop. 49,559; Near Oklahoma City the town was named after the adjoining Midwest air bse.

•MILBURN, Town; Johnston County; Pop. 376; Zip Code 73450; Elev 721; Lat. 34-14-36 N long. 096-33-06 W; Named in honor of W. J. Milburn, a pioneer resident.

•MILL CREEK, Town; Johnston County; Pop. 431; Zip Code 74856; Elev 1011; Lat. 34-22-56 N long. 096-49-30 W; In Johnston County; the town is named for adjacent Mill Creek.

•MILLERTON, Town; McCurtain County; Pop. 262; Zip Code 74750; Lat. 33-59-02 N long. 095-00-49 W; Original landowner, Benedict Miller, left his name on the town.

•MINCO, City; Grady County; Pop. 1,489; Zip Code 73059; Lat. 35-19-12 N long. 097-55-48 W; The town's name is an Indian word meanig "chief."

•MOFFETT, Town; Sequoyah County; Pop. 269; Zip Code 74946; Lat. 35-24-58 N long. 095-26-44 W; The wife of a local farmer, Martha Moffett Payne, gave her name to the town.

•MOORE, City; Cleveland County; Pop. 35,063; Santa Fe Railroad conductor Al Moore had the town named in his honor.

•MOORELAND, Town; Woodward County; Pop. 1,383; Zip Code 73852; Lat. 36-26-45 N long. 099-07-21 W; A descriptive name for the "moor" like landscape near the town.

•MORRIS, City; Okmulgee County; Pop. 1,288; Zip Code 74455; Elev. 710; Lat. 35-36-21 N long. 095-51-24 W; Railroad official H. E. Morris had the town named in his honor.

•MORRISON, Town; Noble County; Pop. 671; Zip Code 73061; Lat. 36-17-43 N long. 097-00-35 W; Original landowner, James Morrison, gave his name to the town.

•MOUNDS, Town; Creek County; Pop. 1,086; Zip Code 74047; Elev. 722; Lat. 35-52-30 N long. 096-03-31 W; A descriptive name for the large twin mounds near the townsite.

•MOUNTAIN PARK, Town; Kiowa County; Pop. 557; Zip Code 73559; Elev 1365; Lat. 34-41-52 N long. 098-57-06 W; Formerly called Buford the town took its name from the nearby Wichita Mountains.

•MOUNTAIN VIEW, Town; Kiowa County; Pop. 1,189; Zip Code 73062; Elev. 1336; Lat. 35-06-06 N long. 098-44-36 W; Descriptively named for the view of the adjacent Wichita Mountains.

•MULDROW, Town; Sequoyah County; Pop. 2,538; Zip Code 74948; Lat. 35-24-25 N long. 094-35-52 W; Founded in 1887 and named for Henry Muldrow, Congressman and assistant Secretary of State.

•MULHALL, Town; Logan County; Pop. 301; Zip Code 73063; Elev. 945; Lat. 36-04-00 N long. 097-24-19 W; Founded in 1890 and named for rancher Zack Mulhall.

•MUSKOGEE, City; Muskogee County Seat; Pop. 40,011; Zip Code 74401; Lat. 35-45-01 N long. 095-21-52 W; Established in 1872 and given the alternate name for the Creek Indians.

•MUSTANG, City; Canadian County; Pop. 7,496; Zip Code 73064; Lat. 35-23-14 N long. 097-43-16 W; Named for adjacent Mustang Creek.

•**MUTUAL,** Town; Woodward County; Pop. 135; Zip Code 73853; Elev 1873; Lat. 36-13-49 N long. 099-10-00 W; The post office assigned the name to the town.

•**NARDIN,** Town; Kay County; Pop. 98; Zip Code 74646; Lat. 36-48-22 N long. 097-26-36 W; The name honors George Nardin, an early settler.

•**NASH,** Town; Grant County; Pop. 301; Zip Code 73761; Lat. 36-40-02 N long. 098-02-42 W; The first postmaster, Clark Nash, had the town named for him.

•**NEW ALLUWE,** Town; Nowata County; Pop. 129; Alluwe is a Delaware Indian word menaing "superioir."

•**NEWCASTLE,** Town; McClain County; Pop. 3,076; Zip Code 73065; Named after Newcastle, Texas.

•**NEWKIRK,** City; Kay County Seat; Pop. 2,413; Zip Code 74647; Elev 1154; Lat. 36-52-53 N long. 097-03-25 W; A descriptive name applied when the site was chosen two miles from a Santa Fe railway stop known as Kirk.

•**NICHOLS HILLS,** City; Oklahoma County; Pop. 4,171; The city's name honors Oklahoma civic leader G. A.Nichols.

•**NICOMA PARK,** City; Oklahoma County; Pop. 2,588; Zip Code 73066; Lat. 35-29-36 N long. 097-19-43 W; A coined word combining the original landowner's name, G. A. Nichols and Oklahoma.

•**NOBLE,** Town; Cleveland County; Pop. 3,497; Zip Code 73068; Lat. 35-08-34 N long. 097-22-58 W; The town's name recalls John Noble, President Benjamin Harrison's Secretary of the Interior.

•**NORMAN,** City; Cleveland County Seat; Pop. 68,020; Zip Code 730+; Lat. 35-13-37 N long. 097-25-08 W; Named for Sante Fe Railroad surveyor Aubrey Norman.

•**NORTH MIAMI,** Town; Ottawa County; Pop. 544; Zip Code 74358; Lat. 36-55-24 N long. 094-53-05 W; Miami was the name of a nearby Indian tribe.

•**NOWATA,** City; Nowata County Seat; Pop. 4,270; Zip Code 74048; Lat. 36-41-53 N long. 095-38-03 W; A Delawre Indian word meaning "welcome."

•**OAKLAND,** Town; Marshall County; Pop. 485; Zip Code 73452; Lat. 34-05-58 N long. 096-47-33 W; The town is named for the oak groves in the vicinity.

•**OAKS,** Town; Delaware County; Pop. 591; Zip Code 74359; Lat. 36-10-52 N long. 094-50-53 W; Founded in 1842 as a mission and descriptively named for the oak trees nearby.

•**OAKWOOD,** Town; Dewey County; Pop. 140; Zip Code 73658; Lat. 35-55-52 N long. 098-41-51 W; Descriptively named for the adjacent oak forest.

•**OCHELATA,** Town; Washington County; Pop. 480; Zip Code 74051; Lat. 36-36-16 N long. 095-58-44 W; The town is named after Cherokee Indian Chief, Ochelata.

•**OILTON,** City; Creek County; Pop. 1,244; Zip Code 74052; Lat. 36-04-59 N long. 096-35-06 W; Descriptively named during the great oil boom of 1915.

•**OKARCHE,** Town; Canadian & Kingfisher Counties; Pop. 1,064; Zip Code 73762; Lat. 35-43-31 N long. 097-58-37 W; Early settler Charles Hunter coined the name from Oklahoma, Arapaho, and Cheyenne.

•**OKAY,** Town; Wagoner County; Pop. 554; Zip Code 74446; Lat. 35-50-46 N long. 095-18-41 W; The town got its name from the local OK Truck Manufacturing Company.

•**OKEENE,** Town; Blaine County; Pop. 1,601; Zip Code 73763; Elev. 1218; Lat. 36-07-00 N long. 098-19-03 W; Settler Elmer Brodrick combined the words Oklahoma, Cherokee, and Cheyenne.

•**OKEMAH,** City; Okfuskee County Seat; Pop. 3,381; Zip Code 74859; Lat. 35-25-51 N long. 096-18-22 W; Town developer H. B.Dexter gave the town a creek Indian name menaing "big chief."

•**OKLAHOMA CITY,** City; Canadian, Cleveland, McClain, Oklahoma & Pottawatomie Counties; Oklahoma County Seat; Capital of Oklahoma; Pop. 403,213; Zip Code 731+; Lat. 35-29-21 N long. 097-31-02 W; In Choctaw Indian language the name means "red people."

•**OKMULGEE,** City; Okmulgee County Seat; Pop. 16,263; Zip Code 74447; Lat. 35-37-20 N long. 095-57-45 W; The name of a Creek town in Alabama.

•**OKTAHA,** Town; Muskogee County; Pop. 376; Zip Code 74450; Lat. 35-34-37 N long. 095-28-27 W; The name of a well-known Creek chief of the civil War period.

•**OOLOGAH,** Town; Rogers County; Pop. 798; Zip Code 74053; Elev. 657; Lat. 36-26-50 N long. 095-42-24 W; A Cherokee Indian chief, the name means "dark cloud."

•**OPTIMA,** Town; Texas County; Pop. 133; Zip Code 73948; Lat. 36-45-26 N long. 101-21-10 W; A Latin word meaning "the best possible result."

•**ORLANDO,** Town; Logan County; Pop. 218; Zip Code 73073; Lat. 36-08-59 N long. 097-22-38 W; The town's founder named it for a relative, Orlando Hysell.

•**OSAGE,** Town; Osage County; Pop. 243; Zip Code 74054; Lat. 36-17-29 N long. 096-24-42 W; Named for the Osage Indians.

•**OWASSO,** City; Tulsa County; Pop. 6,149; Zip Code 74055; Lat. 36-16-12 N long. 095-50-59 W; An Osage word meaning "end" and descriptively applied to a branch of the Santa Fe Railroad.

•**PADEN,** Town; Okfuskee County; Pop. 448; Zip Code 74860; Lat. 35-30-25 N long. 096-34-10 W; The town's name honors the first postmaster, Benjamin F. Paden.

•**PANAMA,** Town; Le Flore County; Pop. 1,164; Zip Code 74951; Lat. 35-10-17 N long. 094-40-10 W; Named after the country in Central America.

•**PAOLI,** Town; Garvin County; Pop. 573; Zip Code 73074; Elev 962; Lat. 34-49-37 N long. 097-15-37 W; The town is named after Paoli, Pennsylvania.

•**PARADISE HILL,** Town; Sequoyah County; Pop. 154; A descriptive name for the town's pleasant surroundings.

•**PAULS VALLEY,** City; Garvin County Seat; Pop. 5,664; Zip Code 73075; Elev 876; Lat. 34-44-14 N long. 097-13-09 W; The city is named in honor of early settler Smith Paul.

•**PAWHUSKA,** City; Osage County Seat; Pop. 4,771; Zip Code 74009; Elev 818; Lat. 35-57-29 N long. 095-52-54 W; The name of an Osage Indian chief, it means "white hair."

•**PAWNEE,** City; Pawnee County Seat; Pop. 1,688; Zip Code 74058; Elev. 866; Lat. 36-21-09 N long. 096-41-46 W; Named after the Pawnee Indians.

•PENSACOLA, Town; Mayes County; Pop. 82; The town is named after "Pensacola," the ranch of prominent Cherokee Indian Joseph Martin.

•PERKINS, Town; Payne County; Pop. 1,762; Zip Code 74059; Lat. 35-58-29 N long. 097-02-00 W; Founded in 1890 and named for U. S. Senator from Kansas, B. W. Perkins.

•PERRY, City; Noble County Seat; Pop. 5,796; Zip Code 73077; Lat. 36-17-31 N long. 097-17-25 W; The Perry's were a prominent Choctaw Indian family. The town is named after them.

•PICHER, City; Ottawa County; Pop. 2,180; Zip Code 74360; Lat. 36-59-28 N long. 094-49-58 W; The town is named after W.S. Picher of the Eagle-Picher Lead Company.

•PIEDMONT, Town; Canadian & Kingfisher Counties; Pop. 2,016; Zip Code 73078; Lat. 35-38-27 N long. 097-44-36 W; Named for the Piedmont region of the eastern United States.

•PITTSBURG, Town; Pittsburg County; Pop. 305; Zip Code 74560; Lat. 34-42-37 N long. 095-50-57 W; The town is named after Pittsburgh, Pennsylvania.

•POCOLA, Town; Le Flore County; Pop. 3,268; A Choctaw Indian word meaning "ten" and referring to the distance to nearby Fort Smith.

•PONCA CITY, City; Kay County; Pop. 26,238; Zip Code 74601; Elev. 1022; Lat. 36-44-59 N long. 097-00-24 W; An Indian word meaning "sacred leader."

•POND CREEK, City; Grant County; Pop. 949; Zip Code 73766; Elev. 1048; Lat. 36-40-13 N long. 097-47-57 W; Descriptively named for an embayed pond in a local creek.

•PORTER, Town; Wagoner County; Pop. 642; Zip Code 74454; Lat. 35-52-03 N long. 095-31-07 W; The town is named for Pleasant Porter, a Creek Indian Chief.

•POTEAU, City; Le Flore County Seat; Pop. 7,089; Zip Code 74953; Lat. 35-03-05 N long. 094-37-06 W; The name is derived from the adjacent Porteau, or "post," River.

•PRAGUE, City; Lincoln County; Pop. 2,208; Zip Code 74864; Lat. 35-29-02 N long. 096-41-11 W; The town is named after the famous city in Europe.

•PRUE, Town; Osage County; Pop. 554; Zip Code 74060; Lat. 36-15-22 N long. 096-16-06 W; Henry Prue, the original landowner, gave his name to the town.

•PRYOR CREEK, City; Mayes County Seat; Pop. 8,483; Pryor Creek is located a few miles from the city. The town is named for this stream.

•PURCELL, City; McClain County Seat; Pop. 4,638; Zip Code 73080; Elev 1106; Lat. 35-00-37 N long. 097-21-46 W; Santa Fe Railway Director E.B. Purcell had the town named in his honor.

•PUTNAM, Town; Dewey County; Pop. 74; Zip Code 73659; Elev. 1971; Lat. 35-51-26 N long. 098-57-51 W; The town's name honors Revolutinary War hero Israel Putnam.

•QUAPAW, Town; Ottawa County; Pop. 1,097; Zip Code 74363; Lat. 36-56-32 N long. 094-43-52 W; The town is named for the Quapaw Indians. The name means "downstream people."

•QUAY, Town; Pawnee & Payne Counties; Pop. 50; Quay's name honors a U. S. Senator from Pennsylvania, M. S. Quay.

•QUINLAN, Town; Woodward County; Pop. 64; Well-known local ranchers, the Quinlans, had the town named in their honor.

•QUINTON, Town; Pittsburg County; Pop. 1,228; Zip Code 74561; Elev. 619; Lat. 35-07-15 N long. 095-21-59 W; The town is named after Martha Quinton, a prominent Choctaw Indian.

•RALSTON, Town; Pawnee County; Pop. 495; Zip Code 74650; Elev 815; Lat. 36-30-14 N long. 096-43-48 W; The town is named after J. H. Ralston, the original landowner-developer.

•RAMONA, Town; Washington County; Pop. 567; Zip Code 74061; Lat. 36-31-49 N long. 095-55-14 W; Formerly Banton, the name was changed in 1899 for the novel Ramona by Helen Hunt Jackson.

•RANCHWOOD MANOR, Town; Cleveland County; Pop. 296; A pleasant sounding name given by the town's developers.

•RANDLETT, Town; Cotton County; Pop. 461; Zip Code 73562; Lat. 34-10-36 N long. 098-27-41 W; Randlett is named in honor of Kiowa-Comanche Indian agent, James Randlett.

•RATLIFF CITY, Town; Carter County; Pop. 350; Zip Code 73081; Lat. 34-26-33 N long. 097-31-04 W; Founded in the 1950's and named for a local merchant, Ollie Ratliff.

•RATTAN, Town; Pushmataha County; Pop. 332; Zip Code 74562; Lat. 34-11-58 N long. 095-24-45 W; The town is named after Rattan, Texas.

•RAVIA, Town; Johnston County; Pop. 487; Zip Code 73455; Elev 760; Lat. 34-14-39 N long. 096-45-32 W; Ravia's name remembers early pioneer settler Joseph Ravia.

•RED OAK, Town; Latimer County; Pop. 676; Zip Code 74563; Lat. 34-56-54 N long. 095-04-45 W; Descriptively named for a well-known red oak tree in the town's center.

•RED ROCK, Town; Noble County; Pop. 376; Zip Code 74651; Lat. 36-27-40 N long. 097-10-46 W; The town is named after a tributary to the Arkansas River, Red Rock Creek.

•REDBIRD, Town; Wagoner County; Pop. 199; Zip Code 74458; Elev. 610; Lat. 35-53-08 N long. 095-34-58 W; Established in 1902 and named for an Indian chief.

•RENTIESVILLE, Town; McIntosh County; Pop. 78; Zip Code 74459; Elev 589; Lat. 35-31-15 N long. 095-29-36 W; The site of a Civil War battle, the town is named after its original developer, William Rentie.

•REYDON, Town; Roger Mills County; Pop. 252; Zip Code 73660; Lat. 35-39-12 N long. 099-55-17 W; Formerly called Rankin, the town was renamed for a town in England.

•RINGLING, Town; Jefferson County; Pop. 1,561; Zip Code 73456; Lat. 34-10-09 N long. 097-35-45 W; The town's name honors famous circus owner, John Ringling.

•RINGWOOD, City; Major County; Pop. 389; Zip Code 73768; Lat. 36-23-03 N long. 098-14-30 W; Descriptively named as the original site was ringed by a circle of trees.

•RIPLEY, Town; Payne County; Pop. 451; Zip Code 74062; Lat. 36-00-59 N long. 096-54-19 W; The town is named for William P. Ripley, who was the president of the Santa Fe Railroad Company.

•ROCKY, Town; Washita County; Pop. 242; Zip Code 73661; Lat. 35-09-31 N long. 099-03-15 W; Early merchant W. F.Schultz built his store with rock. The town was named after the store.

•ROFF, Town; Pontotoc County; Pop. 729; Zip Code 74865; Elev. 1254; Lat. 34-37-31 N long. 096-50-21 W; Rancher J. T.Roff gave his name to the town.

•ROLAND, Town; sequoyah County; Pop. 1,472; Zip Code 74954; Lat. 35-25-07 N long. 094-30-19 W; Formerly called Garrison, the town's name was changed to Roland in 1904.

•ROOSEVELT, Town; Kiowa County; Pop. 396; Zip Code 73564; Lat. 34-50-56 N long. 099-01-06 W; Named for President Theordore Roosevelt.

•ROSSTON, Town; Harper County; Pop. 66; Zip Code 73855; Lat. 36-48-36 N long. 099-55-52 W; Founded in 1912 and given a coined name of two early settlers, R.H. Ross and A. R. Rallston.

•RUSH SPRINGS, Town; Grady County; Pop. 1,451; Zip Code 73082; Lat. 34-46-42 N long. 097-57-37 W; Named for the well-known Chisholm Trail watering site, Rush Springs.

•RYAN, Town; Jefferson County; Pop. 1,083; Zip Code 73565; Lat. 34-03-02 N long. 097-57-59 W; The town is named for early pioneer Stephen Ryan.

•ST. LOUIS, Town; Pottawatomie County; Pop. 109; Zip Code 74866; Elev 1017; Lat. 35-04-18 N long. 096-51-44 W; The town is named after the famous city in Missouri.

•SALINA, Town; Mayes County; Pop. 1,115; Zip Code 74365; Lat. 36-17-48 N long. 095-09-12 W; The name is a variant of Saline, so called because of a nearby salt works.

•SALLISAW, City; Sequoyah County Seat; Pop. 6,403; Zip Code 74955; Lat. 35-27-47 N long. 094-47-10 W; The town is named after Sallisaw Creek. Sallisaw means "salt provisions."

•SAND SPRINGS, City; Osage & Tulsa Counties; Pop. 13,246; Zip Code 74063; Lat. 36-07-41 N, long. 096-02-46 W. Named for the adjacent springs on the north bank of the Arkansas River.

•SAPULPA, City; Creek County Seat; Pop. 15,853; Zip Code 74066; Lat. 35-59-41 N long. 096-06-20 W; The town's name is derived from a Creek Indian leader who lived nearby, Sus-pul-ber.

•SASAKWA, Town; Seminole County; Pop. 335; Zip Code 74867; Elev 839; Lat. 34-56-52 N long. 096-32-00 W; Sasakwa is a Creek Indian word meaning "goose".

•SAVANNA, Town; Pittsburg County; Pop. 828; Zip Code 74565; Elev 729; Lat. 34-49-43 N long. 095-50-23 W; A railroad manager, Robert Stevens, had a private railroad car called Savanna. The town takes its name from that car.

•SAYRE, City; Beckham County Seat; Pop. 3,177; Zip Code 73662; Lat. 35-18-07 N long. 099-38-16 W; The town's name honors railroad developer, Robert Sayre.

•SEILING, City; Dewey County; Pop. 1,103; Zip Code 73663; Elev 1744; Lat. 36-08-52 N long. 098-55-28 W; Seiling is named for its original landowner, Louis Seiling.

•SEMINOLE, City; Seminole County; Pop. 8,590; Zip Code 748+; Lat. 35-14-08 N long. 096-40-46 W; The city is named after the Seminole Indians.

•SENTINEL, City; Washita County; Pop. 1,016; Zip Code 73664; Lat. 35-09-37 N long. 099-09-58 W; Established in 1899, the town is named after a local newspaper, the Herald Sentinel.

•SHADY GROVE, Town; Pawnee County; Pop. 2; A descriptive name given by early settlers.

•SHADY POINT, Town; Le Flore County; Pop. 235; Zip Code 74956; Elev. 447; Lat. 35-07-50 N long. 094-39-30 W; Formerly called Harrison, the name was changed to Shady Point in 1894.

•SHAMROCK, Town; Creek County; Pop. 218; Zip Code 74068; J. M. Thomas, the first postmaster, named the town for his former home in Illinois.

•SHARON, Town; Woodward County; Pop. 171; Zip Code 73857; Lat. 36-16-29 N long. 099-20-11 W; The town is named for the original landowner, Alexander Sharon.

•SHATTUCK, Town; Ellis County; Pop. 1,759; Zip Code 73858; Elev 2268; Lat. 36-16-12 N long. 099-52-30 W; The town's name honors George Shattuck, a one-time director of the Santa Fe Railway Company.

•SHAWNEE, City; Pottawatomie County Seat; Pop. 26,506; Zip Code 74801; Lat. 35-19-54 N long. 096-58-33 W; The city takes its name from the Shawnee Indians. Shawnee is an Algonquian Indian word meaning "southerner."

•SHIDLER, Town; Osage County; Pop. 708; Zip Code 74652; Elev 1167; Lat. 36-46-52 N long. 096-39-24 W; E. S. Shidler, the original landowner, had the town named in his honor.

•SKEDEE, Town; Pawnee County; Pop. 117; Named for the "skidi," or "wolf," tribe of the Pawnee Confederacy.

•SKIATOOK, Town; Osage & Tulsa Counties; Pop. 3,596; Zip Code 74070; Elev 834; Lat. 36-21-57 N long. 096-W; Founded in 1880 and named for a prominent Osage Indian, Skiatooka.

•SLICK, Town; Creek County; Pop. 187; Zip Code 74071; Elev. 719; Lat. 35-46-40 N long. 096-16-01 W; The town's name honors prominent oil producer, Thomas Slick.

•SMITH VILLAGE, Town; Oklahoma County; Pop. 82; Part of the Oklahoma City area, the town was named after the original landowner, Rose Smith.

•SMITHVILLE, Town; McCurtain County; Pop. 133; Zip Code 74957; Lat. 34-28-07 N long. 094-38-26 W; The town is named after long-time local Choctaw resident, Joshua Smith.

•SNYDER, City; Kiowa County; Pop. 1,848; Zip Code 73566; Elev 1364; Lat. 34-39-43 N long. 098-56-55 W; First postmaster Margaret Snyder had the town named in her honor.

•SOPER, Town; Choctaw County; Pop. 465; Zip Code 74759; Lat. 34-01-59 N long. 095-41-36 W; The town's name honors P. L. Soper, a U. S. attorney.

•SOUTH COFFEYVILLE, Town; Nowata County; Pop. 873; Zip Code 74072; Lat. 36-59-38 N long. 095-37-04 W; The town is just across the state line south of Coffeyville, Kansas - hence the name.

•SPARKS, Town; Lincoln County; Pop. 772; Zip Code 74869; Elev 846; Lat. 35-36-40 N long. 096-49-09 W; Sparks is named for George Sparks who was a director of the Fort Smith and Western Railway.

•SPAVINAW, Town; Mayes County; Pop. 623; Zip Code 74366; Lat. 36-23-34 N long. 095-03-06 W; Founded in 1892 and given phonetic equivalent to two French words cepee and vineux meaning "young growths" of trees.

•SPENCER, City; Oklahoma County; Pop. 4,064; Zip Code 73084; Lat. 35-29-09 N long. 097-22-08 W; Spencer is named after railroad developer A. M. Spencer.

•**SPERRY,** Town; Tulsa County; Pop. 1,276; Zip Code 74073; Lat. 36-17-45 N long. 095-59-33 W; The town is named for an English adaptation, Sperry, of settler Henry Spybucks's last name.

•**SPIRO,** Town; Le Flore County; Pop. 2,221; Zip Code 74959; Lat. 35-14-32 N long. 094-37-27 W; Named for Abram Spiro of Ft. Smith, Arkansas.

•**SPRINGER,** Town; Carter County; Pop. 679; Zip Code 73458; Elev 917; Lat. 34-18-48 N long. 097-07-54 W; The town is named in honor of pioneer cattleman, W.A. Springer.

•**STERLING,** Town; Comanche County; Pop. 702; Zip Code 73567; Lat. 34-44-47 N long. 098-10-00 W; Texas ranger Captain Charles Sterling had the town named in his honor.

•**STIDHAM,** Town; McIntosh County; Pop. 60; Zip Code 74461; Elev 633; Lat. 35-21-59 N long. 095-42-08 W; Creek Indian leader George Stidham left his name on the town.

•**STIGLER,** City; Haskell County Seat; Pop. 2,630; Zip Code 74462; Elev 583; Lat. 35-19-43 N long. 095-03-14 W; Town developer Joseph Stigler had the town named in his honor.

•**STILLWATER,** City; Payne County Seat; Pop. 38,268; Zip Code 740+; Lat. 36-07-22 N long. 097-04-07 W; The city takes its name from the nearby tributary of the Cimarron, Stillwater Creek.

•**STILWELL,** City; Adair County; Pop. 2,369; Zip Code 74960; Elev 1112; Lat. 35-48-52 N long. 094-37-24 W; Arthur Stilwell, developer of the Kansas City Southern Railway, had the town named in his honor.

•**STONEWALL,** Town; Pontotoc County; Pop. 672; Zip Code 74871; Lat. 34-39-06 N long. 096-31-24 W; The town's name commemorates General "Stonewall" Jackson, military hero of the confederacy.

•**STRANG,** Town; Mayes County; Pop. 126; Zip Code 74367; Lat. 36-24-45 N long. 095-08-14 W; The town is named for Clarita Strang Kenefic, wife of a local railroad developer.

•**STRATFORD,** Town; Garvin County; Pop. 1,459; Zip Code 74872; Elev 1110; Lat. 34-47-42 N long. 096-57-32 W; Named for the town of Stratford-on Avon in England.

•**STRINGTOWN,** Town; Atoka County; Pop. 1,047; Zip Code 74569; Lat. 34-28-06 N long. 096-03-13 W; Originally called Springtown, the name was changed on the 1870's to Stringtown.

•**STROUD,** City; Lincoln County; Pop. 3,139; Zip Code 74079; Lat. 35-44-46 N long. 096-39-08 W; Established in 1892 and named for early day merchant James Stroud.

•**STUART,** Town; Hughes County; Pop. 235; Zip Code 74570; Lat. 34-53-57 N long. 096-05-50 W; Stuart is named in honor of territorial jurist, Charles Stuart.

•**SULPHUR,** City; Murray County Seat; Pop. 5,516; Zip Code 73086; Lat. 34-31-54 N long. 096-54-54 W; Descriptively named for the nearby sulphur springs.

•**TAFT,** Town; Muskogee County; Pop. 489; Zip Code 74463; Lat. 35-45-37 N long. 095-32-59 W; Named for President William Taft.

•**TAHLEQUAH,** City; Cherokee County Seat; Pop. 9,708; Zip Code 74464; Lat. 35-54-25 N long. 094-58-31 W; The word is an old Cherokee place name which the settlers borrowed for their use.

•**TALALLA,** Town; Rogers County; Pop. 191; Zip Code 74080; Elev. 685; Lat. 36-31-35 N long. 095-42-07 W; Named in honor of Cherokee Civil War soldier, Captain Talala.

•**TALIHINA,** Town; Le Flore County; Pop. 1,387; Zip Code 74571; Lat. 34-45-14 N long. 095-03-28 W; Talihina is the Choctaw Indian word for "railroad."

•**TALOGA,** Town; Dewey County Seat; Pop. 446; Zip Code 73667; Elev. 1708; Lat. 36-02-24 N long. 098-57-46 W; A creek Indian word meaning "rock."

•**TATUMS,** Town; Carter County; Pop. 281; Zip Code 73087; Lat. 34-29-02 N long. 097-27-33 W; The first postmaster, Lee Tatums, left his name on the town.

•**TECUMSEH,** City; Pottawatomie County; Pop. 5,123; Zip Code 74873; Lat. 35-15-31 N long. 096-55-55 W; The town is named for the famous Shawnee Indian chief.

•**TEMPLE,** Town; Cotton County; Pop. 1,339; Zip Code 73568; Elev. 1007; Lat. 34-16-11 N long. 098-14-04 W; The town's name honors Temple Hiliston, the son of Sam Houston.

•**TERLTON,** Town; Pawnee County; Pop. 155; Zip Code 74081; Lat. 36-11-05 N long. 096-29-23 W; Ira Terrell, a member of the first territorial legislature, had the town named in his honor.

•**TERRAL,** Town; Jefferson County; Pop. 604; Zip Code 73561; Lat. 33-59-06 N long. 097-45-14 W; The first postmaster, John Terral, had the town named in his honor.

•**TEXHOMA,** Town; Texas County; Pop. 785; Zip Code 73949; Elev. 3487; Lat. 36-29-57 N long. 101-47-00 W; A coined name combining Texas and Oklahoma.

•**TEXOLA,** Town; Beckham County; Pop. 106; Zip Code 73668; Lat. 35-13-03 N long. 099-59-27 W; A coined name created by combining Texas and Oklahoma.

•**THACKERVILLE,** Town; Love County; Pop. 431; Zip Code 73459; Lat. 33-47-40 N long. 097-08-20 W; The town is named for early settler Zachariah Thacker.

•**THOMAS,** Town; Custer County; Pop. 1,515; Zip Code 73669; Lat. 35-44-56 N long. 098-45-00 W; Pioneer attorney William Thomas left his name on the city.

•**TIPTON,** Town; Tillman County; Pop. 1,475; Zip Code 73570; Elev 1303; Lat. 34-30-06 N long. 099-08-12 W; Conductor John Tipton who worked for a local railroad had the town named in his honor.

•**TISHOMINGO,** City; Johnston County Seat; Pop. 3,212; Zip Code 73460; Elev. 693; Lat. 34-14-19 N long. 096-40-56 W; The town's name remembers the great Chickasaw Indian chief.

•**TONKOWA,** City; Kay County; Pop. 3,524; Zip Code 74653; Lat. 36-40-43 N long. 097-18-22 W; Named for the Tonkowa Indian tribe.

•**TRYON,** Town; Lincoln County; Pop. 435; Zip Code 74875; Lat. 35-52-04 N long. 096-57-40 W; Tryon is named in honor of original landowner Fred Tryon.

•**TULLAHASEE,** Town; Wagoner County; Pop. 145; Zip Code 74466; Lat. 35-50-15 N long. 095-25-56 W; A Creek Indian word meaning "old town."

•**TULSA,** City; Osage & Tulsa Counties; Tulsa County Seat; Pop. 360,919; Zip Code 741+; Lat. 36-09-21 N long. 095-58-31 W; A borrowed Creek Indian place name for an Indain town in Alabama.

•**TUPELO,** City; Coal County; Pop. 542; Zip Code 74572; Elev 689; Lat. 34-36-05 N long. 096-25-10 W; Named for Tupelo, Mississippi.

•**TUTTLE,** Town; Grady County; Pop. 3,051; Zip Code 73089; Lat. 35-18-18 N long. 097-46-48 W; Named in honor of local rancher James Tuttle.

•**TYRONE,** Town; Texas County; Pop. 928; Zip Code 73951; Elev 2921; Lat. 36-57-18 N long. 101-03-57 W; Tyrone is named after county Tyrone in Ireland.

•**UNION CITY,** Town; Canadian County; Pop. 558; Zip Code 73090; Lat. 35-23-25 N long. 097-56-13 W; Founded in 1889 and named for the American "union."

•**VALLEY BROOK,** Town; Oklahoma County; Pop. 921; Part of Oklahoma City's area - given a euphonious name by its incorporators.

•**VALLIANT,** Town; McCurtain County; Pop. 927; Zip Code 74764; Elev 512; Lat. 34-00-00 N long. 095-05-37 W; The town is named after F. W. Valliant, who was chief engineer on the Arkansas and Choctaw Railroad.

•**VELMA,** City; Stephens County; Pop. 831; Zip Code 73091; Elev 1044; Lat. 34-27-23 N long. 097-40-18 W; The town is named after the daughter of a local merchant, Velma Dobbins.

•**VERA,** Town; Washington County; Pop. 182; Zip Code 74082; Lat. 36-27-05 N long. 095-53-03 W; Founded in 1899 and named for Vera Duncan, the daughter of settler James Duncan.

•**VERDEN,** Town; Grady County; Pop. 625; Zip Code 73092; Lat. 35-05-01 N long. 098-05-14 W; Named for original landowner, A. N. Verden.

•**VIAN,** Town; Sequoyah County; Pop. 1,521; Zip Code 74962; Lat. 35-29-58 N long. 094-58-13 W; Derived from the French word "viande," or "meat."

•**VICI,** Town; Dewey County; Pop. 845; Zip Code 73859; Elev. 2265; Lat. 36-08-55 N long. 099-17- 55 W; "Founded in 1900 and named for the last word in the Latin phrase veni, vidi, vici.

•**VINITA,** City; Craig County Seat; Pop. 6,740; Zip Code 74301; Lat. 36-31-18 N long. 095-08-31 W; The town is named in honor of Vinnie Ream, a well-known sculptress.

•**WAGONER,** City; Wagoner County Seat; Pop. 6,191; Zip Code 74467; Lat. 35-57-29 N long. 095-22-12 W; Train dispatcher "Big Foot" Wagoner of Parsons, Kansas had the town named after him.

•**WAINWRIGHT,** Town; Muskogee County; Pop. 182; Zip Code 74468; Lat. 35-36-49 N long. 095-33-49 W; The town's name honors W. H. Wainwright, a local banker.

•**WAKITA,** Town; Grant County; Pop. 526; Zip Code 73771; Elev. 1175; Lat. 36-52-56 N long. 097-54-50 W; A Cherokee word meaning "water collected in a depression."

•**WALTERS,** City; Cotton County Seat; Pop. 2,778; Zip Code 73572; Lat. 34-21-15 N long. 098-17-58 W; The town's name honors a prominent citizen, William R. Walter.

•**WANETTE,** Town; Pottawatomie County; Pop. 473; Zip Code 74878; Lat. 34-57-50 N long. 097-02-11 W; Established in 1894 and given a variant name of a popular song, "Jaunita."

•**WANN,** Town; Nowata County; Pop. 156; Zip Code 74083; Lat. 36-54-56 N long. 095-47-57 W; Wann is named after a well-known local Cherokee Indian, Robert Wann.

•**WAPANUCKA,** Town; Johnston County; Pop. 472; Zip Code 73461; Elev 617; Lat. 34-22-31 N long. 096-25-30 W; A Delaware Indian word meaning "eastern people."

•**WARNER,** Town; Muskogee County; Pop. 1,310; Zip Code 74469; Lat. 35-29-42 N long. 095-18-18 W; The town is named for William Warner, U.S. Senator from Missouri.

•**WARR ACRES,** City; Oklahoma County; Pop. 9,940; Founded in 1948 and named in honor of Oklahoma City civic leader C.B. Warr.

•**WARWICK,** Town; Lincoln County; Pop. 167; Founded in 1892 and named for the county in England.

•**WASHINGTON,** Town; McClain County; Pop. 477; Zip Code 73093; Elev. 1149; Lat. 35-06-08 N long. 097-28-42 W; Caddo Indian Chief, George Washington, gave his name to the town.

•**WATONGA,** City; Blaine County Seat; Pop. 4,139; Zip Code 73772; Lat. 35-50-52 N long. 098-24-51 W; Established in 1892 and named for an Arapaho chief. Translated his name means "black coyote.

•**WATTS,** Town; Adair County; Pop. 316; Zip Code 74964; Lat. 36-06-33 N long. 094-34-06 W; The town is named for a chief of the Chickamauga Cherokees, John Watts.

•**WAUKOMIS,** Town; Garfield County; Pop. 1,551; Zip Code 73773; Elev. 1238; Lat. 36-16-48 N long. 097-54-05 W; According to legend certain railroad officials were stranded and had to "walk home." The name is a phonetic variation of this phrase.

•**WAURIKA,** City; Jefferson County Seat; Pop. 2,258; Zip Code 73573; Elev. 881; Lat. 34-10-08 N long. 098-00-02 W; An Indian word meaning "pure water."

•**WAYNE,** Town; McClain County; Pop. 621; Zip Code 73095; Lat. 34-55-07 N long. 097-18-47 W; The town is named after Wayne, Pennsylvania.

•**WAYNOKA,** City; Woods County; Pop. 1,377; Zip Code 73860; Elev 1476; Lat. 36-35-10 N long. 098-52-31 W; A Cheyenne Indian word meaning "sweet watrr."

•**WEATHERFORD,** City; Custer County; Pop. 9,640; Zip Code 73096; Elev. 1647; Lat. 35-31-50 N long. 098-42-12 W; Deputy Marshal William Weatherford gave his name to the town.

•**WEBB CITY,** Town; Osage County; Pop. 157; Named for the original landowner Horace Webb.

•**WEBBERS FALLS,** Town; Muskogee County; Pop. 461; Zip Code 74470; Lat. 35-30-54 N long. 095-07-40 W; The town's name remembers local Cherokee Chief, Walter Webber.

•**WELCH,** Town; Craig County; Pop. 697; Zip Code 74369; Lat. 36-56-28 N long. 095-05-36 W; The town is named after railroad official A. L. Welch.

•**WELEETKA,** Town; Okfuskee County; Pop. 1,195; Zip Code 74880; Lat. 35-21-42 N long. 096-05-51 W; A Creek Indian word meaning "running water."

•**WELLSTON,** Town; Lincoln County; Pop. 802; Zip Code 74881; Lat. 35-41-31 N long. 097-04-04 W; Indian trader Christian Wells left his name on the town.

•**WESTVILLE,** Town; Adair County; Pop. 1,049; Zip Code 74965; Elev 1139; Lat. 35-59-28 N long. 094-33-51 W; Local resident Samuel West had the town named in his honor.

•**WETUMKA,** City; Hughes County; Pop. 1,725; Zip Code 74883; Lat. 35-14-07 N long. 096-14-12 W; A Creek Indian word meaning "tumbling water."

•**WEWOKA,** City; Seminole County Seat; Pop. 5,480; Zip Code 74884; Lat. 35-09-03 N long. 096-29-51 W; A Creek Indian word meaning "roaring water."

•**WHITEFIELD,** Town; Haskell County; Pop. 240; Zip Code 74472; Lat. 35-15-04 N long. 095-14-24 W; Methodist leader and pioneer Bishop George Whitefield had the town named in his honor.

•**WILBURTON,** City; Latimer County Seat; Pop. 2,996; Zip Code 74578; Lat. 34-55-01 N long. 095-18-37 W; The city's name honors Elisha Wilbur, president of the Lehigh Valley Railroad.

•**WILLOW,** Town; Greer County; Pop. 11; Zip Code 73673; Lat. 35-01-49 N long. 099-30-50 W; The town is named after the first postmaster, William O'Connell.

•**WILSON,** City; Carter County; Pop. 1,585; Zip Code 73463; Elev 699; Lat. 34-09-46 N long. 097-25-22 W; The town is named in honor of local merchant J. H. Wilson.

•**WOODLAWN PARK,** Town; Oklahoma County; Pop. 167; Adjacent to Oklahoma City and given this pleasant sounding name by its developers.

•**WOODVILLE,** Town; Marshall County; Pop. 94; Zip Code 73466; Lat. 33-58-06 N long. 096-39-13 W; The town's name remembers L. L. Wood, a well-known Chickasaw Indian resident.

•**WOODWARD,** City; Woodward County Seat; Pop. 13,610; Zip Code 738+; Lat. 36-25-59 N long. 099-24-11 W; The town's name honors Brinton Woodward, a Santa Fe Railroad Company Director.

•**WRIGHT CITY,** Town; McCurtain County; Pop. 1,168; Zip Code 74766; Elev 399; Lat. 34-03-31 N long. 095-00-01 W; The town's name honors World War I soldier William Wright, the first local boy killed in action.

•**WYANDOTTE,** Town; Ottawa County; Pop. 336; Zip Code 74370; Elev 761; Lat. 36-47-55 N long. 094-43-27 W; An Iroquoian Indian word meaning "islanders."

•**WYNNEWOOD,** City; Garvin County; Pop. 2,615; Zip Code 73098; Elev. 896; Lat. 34-38-39 N, long. 097-09-48 W. The center of a farming region, especially noted for its production of pecans.

•**YUKON,** City; Canadian County; Pop. 17,112; Zip Code 73099; Elev. 1,298; Lat. 35-30-03 N, long. 097-44-50 W. Laid out in 1891 by the Spencer Brothers, who owned the site.

OREGON

•**ADAIR VILLAGE,** City; Benton County; Pop. 589; The town is named after the former U. S. Army base camp Adair. Lieutenant Henry Adair was a World War I era military hero.

•**ADAMS,** City; Umatilla County; Pop. 240; Zip Code 97810; Elev. 1513; Lat. 45-46-03 N long. 118-33-41 W; The town's name remembers original settler John F. Adams.

•**ADRIAN,** City; Malheur County; Pop. 162; Zip Code 97901; Lat. 43-44-27 N long. 117-04-15 W; The town was founded in the early 1900's and named after sheepman, James Adrian.

•**ALBANY,** City; Benton & Linn Counties; Linn County Seat; Pop. 26,546; Zip Code 97321; Elev. 212; Lat. 44-38-12 N long. 123-06-17 W; Founded in 1848 and named after Albany, New York.

•**AMITY,** City; Yamhill County; Pop. 1,092; Zip Code 97101; Lat. 45-06-57 N long. 123-12-22 W; Settled in the mid-1800's and named for an amicable settlement of a local school dispute.

•**ANTELOPE,** City; Wasco County; Pop. 39; Zip Code 97001; Elev. 2632, Lat. 44-54-39 N long. 120-43-18 W; Descriptively named for the abundant antelope of pioneer days.

•**ARLINGTON,** City; Gilliam County; Pop. 521; Zip Code 97812; Elev. 2851; Lat. 45-43-01 N long. 120-11-59 W; Established in 1881 and named for the famous Virginia home of Robert E. Lee.

•**ASHLAND,** City; Jackson County; Pop. 14,943; Zip Code 97520; Elev. 1951; Lat. 42-11-41 N long. 122-42-30 W; Named in 1852 for Henry Clay's birthplace near Ashland, Kentucky.

•**ASTORIA,** City; Clatsop County Seat; Pop. 9,998; Zip Code 97103; Elev. 18; Lat. 46-11-17 N long. 123-49-48 W; The city was founded in 1813 and named in honor of fur trade magnate John Jacob Astor.

•**ATHENA,** City; Umatilla County; Pop. 965; Zip Code 97813; Elev. 1710; Lat. 45-48-43 N long. 118-29-22 W; Originally Centerville, the name was changed in 1889 to the more romantic Athena. Athena was the Greek goddess of war and industry.

•**AUMSVILLE,** City; Marion County; Pop. 1,432; Zip Code 97325; Elev. 363; Lat. 44-50-28 N long. 122-52-11 W; Aumus was the nickname of early settler Amos M. Davis. The town was named in his honor.

•**AURORA,** City; Marion County; Pop. 523; Zip Code 97002; Elev. 133; Lat. 45-13-52 N long. 122-45-17 W; Settled in 1857 and later named Aurora, the Roman goddess of dawn.

•**BAKER,** City; Baker County Seat; Pop. 9,471; Zip Code 97814; Elev. 3443; Lat. 44-46-42 N long. 117-49-42 W; The town's name honors Edward D. Baker, U. S. Senator from Oregon and Civil War hero.

•**BANDON,** City; Coos County; Pop. 2,311; Zip Code 97411; Elev. 67; Lat. 43-07-09 N long. 124-24-26 W; Settled in the 1870's and named by an Irish settler for Bandon, Ireland.

•**BANKS,** City; Washington County; Pop. 489; Zip Code 971+; Lat. 45-37-08 N long. 123-06-47 W; Banks is named in honor of pioneer resident Robert.

•**BARLOW,** City; Clackamas County; Pop. 105; Elev. 101; Lat. 45-15-07 N long. 122-43-10 W; The town is named after pioneer settler William Barlow.

•**BAY CITY,** City; Tillamook County; Pop. 986; Zip Code 97107; Elev. 18; Lat. 45-31-22 N long. 123-53-17 W; Established in 1888 and named after Bay City, Michigan.

•**BEAVERTON,** City; Washington County; Pop. 30,582; Zip Code 970+; Elev. 189; Lat. 45-29-14 N long. 122-48-09 W; Settled in 1869 and named for the many beaver once in the area.

•**BEND,** City; Deschutes County Seat; Pop. 17,263; Zip Code 977+; Elev. 3629; Lat. 44-03-30 N long. 121-18-51 W; Descriptively named for its location on a bend of the Deschutes River.

•**BOARDMAN,** City; Moorow County; Pop. 1,261; Zip Code 97818; Lat. 45-50-24 N long. 119-41-58 W; Settled in 1916 and named for town founder Sam Boardman.

•**BONANZA,** Town; Klamath County; Pop. 270; Zip Code 97623; Elev. 4116; Lat. 42-11-56 N long. 121-24-18 W; Bonanza is Spanish for "prosperity." Well-developed irrigation water supplies suggested this name to its early settlers.

•**BROOKINGS,** City; Curry County; Pop. 3,384; Zip Code 97415; Lat. 42-03-10 N long. 124-16-58 W; Settled at the beginning of the 20th century and named in honor of lumberman Robert S. Brookings.

•**BROWNSVILLE,** City; Linn County; Pop. 1,261; Zip Code 97327; Elev. 356; Lat. 44-23-37 N long. 122-59-01 W; The city was established in 1853 and named for Hugh Brown who started a store in the area.

•**BURNS,** City; Harney County Seat; Pop. 3,579; Zip Code 977+; Elev. 4148; Lat. 43-35-11 N long. 119-03-11 W; Pioneer George McGowan named the town after poet Robert Burns.

•**BUTTE FALLS,** Town; Jackson County; Pop. 428; Zip Code 97522; Elev. 2536; Lat. 42-32-36 N long. 122-33-52 W; Descriptively named for the town's location on the falls of Big Butte Creek.

•**CANBY,** City; Clackamas County; Pop. 7,659; Zip Code 97013; Elev. 153; Lat. 45-15-47 N long. 122-41-29 W; The town's name honors General Edward Canby who was killed by Modoc Indians on April 11, 1873.

•**CANNON BEACH,** City; Clatsop County; Pop. 1,187; Zip Code 971+; Lat. 45-53-31 N long. 123-57-37 W; In 1846 the U. S. Navy Schooner Shark was wrecked near the Columbia River shore. An iron cannon from the wreck named the beach, and later the town.

•**CANYON CITY,** Town; Grant County Seat; Pop. 639; Zip Code 97820; Elev. 3198; Lat. 44-23-23 N long. 118-56-57 W; Descriptively named for its location in a canyon.

•**CANYONVILLE,** City; Douglas County; Pop. 1,288; Zip Code 97417; Elev. 785; Lat. 42-55-39 N long. 123-16-48 W; Situated at the end of Canyon Creek Canyon, and thus descriptively named.

•**CARLTON,** City; Yamhill County; Pop. 1,302; Zip Code 97111; Elev. 199; Lat. 45-17-40 N long. 123-10-31 W; Established in 1874 and named for early settler John Carl.

•**CASCADE LOCKS,** City; Hood River County; Pop. 838; Zip Code 97014; Lat. 45-40-12 N long. 121-53-22 W; Named for the cascade locks constructed in 1888.

•**CAVE JUNCTION,** City; Josephine County; Pop. 1,023; Zip Code 97523; Elev. 1295; Lat. 42-09-47 N long. 123-38-49 W; Named for its location on the highway which branches to the Oregon caves.

•**CENTRAL POINT,** City; Jackson County; Pop. 6,357; Zip Code 97502; Elev. 1278; Lat. 42-22-34 N long. 122-54-55 W; Descriptively named for the cross of two pioneer wagon trails of the Rogue River valley.

•**CHILOQUIN,** City; Klamath County; Pop. 778; Zip Code 97604; Elev. 4179; Lat. 42-34-40 N long. 121-51-54 W; The name of a Klamath Indian chief Chaloquin.

•**CITY OF THE DALLES,** City; Wasco County; Pop. 10,820; Zip Code 97058. Dalles is a French word meaning "flag stone" which was applied to the narrows of the Columbia River. The town's name reflects its location on the river.

•**CLATSKANIE,** City; Columbia County; Pop. 1,648; Zip Code 97016; Elev. 33; Lat. 46-06-05 N long. 123-12-20 W; An old Indian place name for a spot in the Nehalem Valley, white settlers named the river for it, and the town also.

•**COBURG,** City; Lane County; Pop. 699; Zip Code 97401; Elev. 400; Lat. 44-08-14 N long. 123-03-55 W; Blacksmith Thomas Kane named the town for a well-known local stallion.

•**COLUMBIA,** City; Columbia County; Pop. 678; Zip Code 97018; Elev. 24; Lat. 45-53-25 N long. 122-48-21 W; Founded in 1867 and named after the Columbia River.

•**CONDON,** City; Gilliam County Seat; Pop. 783; Zip Code 97823; Elev. 2844; Lat. 45-14-04 N long. 120-11-02 W; Condon was established in 1884 and named for lawyer Harvey C. Condon.

•**COOS BAY,** City; Goos County; Pop. 14,424; Zip Code 97420; Elev. 11; Lat. 43-22-05 N long. 124-12-57 W; The city is named after its bay on the Pacific. The Coos Indians named the bay.

•**COQUILLE,** City; Coos County Seat; Pop. 4,481; Zip Code 97423; Elev. 50; Lat. 43-10-38 N long. 124-11-11 W; Once the home of the Ku-kwil-tunne Indians, french trappers translated this name as Coquille.

•**CORNELIUS,** City; Washington County; Pop. 4,055; Zip Code 97113; Elev. 179; Lat. 45-31-12 N long. 123-03-31 W; Named for pioneer Colonel T. R. Cornelius who came to Oregon in 1845.

•**CORVALLIS,** City; Benton County Seat; Pop. 40,960; Zip Code 9733+; Elev. 225; Lat. 44-33-53 N long. 123-15-39 W; Named by pioneer Joseph Avery in 1853, the name is a latin compound word meaning "heart of the valley."

•**COTTAGE GROVE,** City; Lane County; Pop. 7,148; Zip Code 97424; Elev. 641; Lat. 43-47-52 N long. 123-03-30 W; The first postmaster, G. C. Pearce, had his home in a nearby oak grove and so named the settlement Cottage Grove.

•**COVE,** City; Union County; Pop. 451; Zip Code 97824; Lat. 45-17-48 N long. 117-48-25 W; Descriptively named for its location where Mill Creek flows from the Wallowa Mountains.

•**CRESWELL,** City; Lane County; Pop. 1,770; Zip Code 97426; Elev. 547; Lat. 43-55-05 N long. 123-01-24 W; The town's name honors U. S. Postmaster General from 1869-74, John A. Creswell.

•**CULVER,** City; Jefferson County; Pop. 514; Zip Code 97734; Elev. 2636; Lat. 44-31-33 N long. 121-12-43 W; The town took the ancestoral name of its first postmaster O. G. Collver as its name.

•**DALLAS,** City; Polk County Seat; Pop. 8,530; Zip Code 97338; Elev. 326; Lat. 44-55-10 N long. 123-18-57 W; The city is named after U. S. Vice-President George Dalles who served from 1845-49.

•**DAYTON,** City; Yamhill County; Pop. 1,409; Zip Code 97114; Lat. 45-13-15 N long. 123-04-30 W; Settled in 1848 and named after Dayton, Ohio.

•**DAYVILLE,** Town; Grant County; Pop. 199; Zip Code 97825; Lat. 44-28-06 N long. 119-32-05 W; The town is named after the John Day River. John Day was an explorer with the Astor expedition.

•**DEPOE BAY,** City; Lincoln County; Pop. 723; Zip Code 97341; Elev. 58; Lat. 44-48-31 N long. 124-03-43 W; An Indian associated with an early army supply depot acquired the nick name "Depot," and this later became Depoe.

•**DETROIT,** City; Marion County; Pop. 367; Zip Code 97342; Lat. 44-44-03 N long. 122-08-55 W; Established in 1891 and named after Detroit, Michigan.

•**DONALD,** City; Marion County; Pop. 267; Zip Code 97020; Elev. 195; Lat. 45-13-21 N long. 122-50-17 W; Donald's name remembers R. L. Donald, a railroad construction official.

•**DRAIN,** City; Douglas County; Pop. 1,148; Zip Code 97435; Elev. 292; Lat. 43-39-32 N long. 123-19-03 W; The city was named after pioneer-settler, Charles Drain.

•**DUFUR,** Town; Wasco County; Pop. 560; Zip Code 97021; Elev. 1320; Lat. 45-27-12 N long. 121-07-46 W; Founded in 1878 and named in honor of Andrew and Burnham Dufur, local farmers.

•**DUNDEE,** City; Yamhill County; Pop. 1,223; Zip Code 97115; Elev. 190; Lat. 45-16-42 N long. 123-00-35 W; Named after Dundee, Scotland by pioneer William Reid.

•**DURHAM,** City; Washington County; Pop. 707; Elev. 142; Lat. 45-24-08 N long. 122-45-06 W; Durham's name remembers pioneer lumberman Albert A. Durham.

•**EAGLE POINT,** City; Jackson County; Pop. 2,764; Zip Code 97524; Elev. 1305; Lat. 42-28-22 N long. 122-48-06 W; Settled in 1872 and named for nearby rocky cliffs, the nesting place of many eagles.

•**EASTSIDE,** City; Coos County; Pop. 1,601; Zip Code 97420; Elev. 61; Lat. 43-21-49 N long. 124-11-30 W; On the eastside of Coos Bay, and so descriptively named.

•**ECHO,** City; Umatilla County; Pop. 624; Zip Code 97826; Elev. 638; Lat. 45-44-33 N long. 119-11-40 W; The town is named in honor of Echo Koontz, the daughter of a pioneer family.

•**ELGIN,** City; Union County; Pop. 1,701; Zip Code 97827; Elev. 2716; Lat. 45-33-54 N long. 117-54-59 W; Once called Fishtrap, the first postmaster named the town for a song about the "wreck of the Lady Elgin."

•**ELKTON,** City; Douglas County; Pop. 155; Zip Code 97436; Elev. 149; Lat. 43-38-16 N long. 123-34-01 W; Settled in 1850 and descriptively named for its location on Elk Creek.

•**ENTERPRISE,** City; Wallowa County Seat; Pop. 2,003; Zip Code 97828; Elev. 3756; Lat. 45-25-35 N long. 117-16-40 W; Named in 1887 after the pioneer virtue.

•**ESTACADA,** City; Clackamas County; Pop. 1,419; Zip Code 97023; Lat. 45-17-23 N long. 122-19-57 W; A spanish word meaning "staked out, or marked off."

•**EUGENE,** City; Lane County Seat; Pop. 105,624; Zip Code 974+; Elev. 419; Lat. 44-03-08 N long. 123-05-08 W; Eugene Skinner claimed this land in 1847. The city is named after him.

•**FAIRVIEW,** City; Multnomah County; Pop. 1,749; Zip Code 97024; Elev. 125; Lat. 43-13-01 N long. 124-04-21 W; Settled in the 1850's and given the name of a Methodist Church.

•**FALLS CITY,** City; Polk County; Pop. 804; Zip Code 97344; Elev. 370; Lat. 44-51-59 N long. 123-26-05 W; Descriptively named for the nearby falls on the Little Luckiamute River.

•**FLORENCE,** City; Lane County; Pop. 4,411; Zip Code 97439; Elev. 23; Lat. 43-58-58 N long. 124-05-55 W; Florence is named in honor of early Oregon State Senator, A. B. Florence.

•FOREST GROVE, City; Washington County; Pop. 11,499; Zip Code 9711+; Lat. 45-31-12 N long. 123-06-34 W; Named in 1851 for the homestead of pioneer settler J. Q. Thornton.

•FOSSIL, Town; Wheeler County Seat; Pop. 535; Zip Code 97830; Elev. 2654; Lat. 44-59-54 N long. 120-12-54 W; Founded in the 1870's and named after the numerous fossils in the area.

•GARIBALDI, City; Tillamook County; Pop. 999; Zip Code 97118; Elev. 10; Lat. 45-33-36 N long. 123-54-35 W; Pioneer Daniel Bayley settled here in the 1860's and named the town for the great Italian patriot, Giuseppe Garibaldi.

•GASTON, City; Washington County; Pop. 471; Zip Code 97119; Lat. 45-26-11 N long. 123-08-18 W; The town's name remembers Joseph Gaston, pioneer railroad promoter.

•GATES, City; Linn & Marion Counties; Pop. 455; Zip Code 97346; Elev. 942; Lat. 44-45-23 N long. 122-24-56 W; Settled in 1882 and named after Mrs. Gates, one of the oldest pioneer settlers.

•GEARHART, City; Clatsop County; Pop. 967; Zip Code 97138; Elev. 16; Lat. 46-01-28 N long. 123-54-36 W; The town is named after pioneer Philip Gearhart.

•GERVAIS, City; Marion County; Pop. 1,144; Zip Code 97026; Elev. 184; Lat. 45-06-30 N long. 122-53-47 W; French trapper Joseph Gervais came to Oregon in 1811, the town is named for him.

•GLADSTONE, City; Clackamas County; Pop. 9,500; Zip Code 97027; Lat. 45-22-51 N long. 122-35-37 W; Established in 1890 and named for British statesman William E. Gladstone.

•GLENDALE, City; Douglas County; Pop. 712; Zip Code 97442; Elev. 1423; Lat. 42-44-11 N long. 123-25-20 W; Settled in the 1880's and named for either Glendale, Massachusetts, or Glendale, Scotland.

•GOLD BEACH, City; Curry County Seat; Pop. 1,515; Zip Code 97444; Elev. 51; Lat. 42-24-27 N long. 124-25-14 W; The city is named after the placer gold operations conducted here in the 1850's.

•GOLD HILL, City; Jackson County; Pop. 904; Zip Code 97525; Gold Hill was the site of a gold discovery in Southern Oregon and was so named.

•GRANITE, City; Grant County; Pop. 17; Elev. 4689; Lat. 44-48-34 N long. 182-25-00 W; Descriptively named for the abundant granite rocks in the region.

•GRANTS PASS, City; Josephine County Seat; Pop. 14,997; Zip Code 975+; Elev. 948; Lat. 42-26-21 N long. 123-19-38 W; Founded in the 1860's and named in honor of U. S. Grant.

•GRASS VALLEY, City; Sherman County; Pop. 164; Zip Code 97029; Elev. 2252; Lat. 45-21-37 N long. 120-47-04 W; Incorporated in 1900.

•GREENHORN, City; Baker & Grant Counties; Lat. 44-42-29 N long. 118-29-25 W; The town is named for the many amateur miners who came to the area in the 1860's gold rush.

•GRESHAM, City; Multnomah County; Pop. 33,005; Zip Code 97030; Elev. 323; Lat. 45-29-54 N long. 122-25-49 W; Gresham's name honors Civil War General Walter Q. Gresham.

•HAINES, City; Multnomah County; Pop. 33,005; Zip Code 97833; Elev. 3333; Lat. 44-54-42 N long. 117-56-16 W; Founded in 1884 and named for "Judge" I. D. Haines, who was the original landowner.

•HALFWAY, Town; Baker County; Pop. 380; Zip Code 97834; Elev. 2663; Lat. 44-52-51 N long. 117-06-49 W; Founded in 1887 and descriptively named for its location between Pine and Cornucopia.

•HAMMOND, Town; Clatsop County; Pop. 516; Zip Code 97121; Elev. 9; Lat. 46-12-01 N long. 123-57-01 W; Hammond is named for Pacific Coast businessman Andrew H. Hammond.

•HAPPY VALLEY, City; Clackamas County; Pop. 1,499; Lat. 45-26-49 N long. 122-31-45 W; An early settler named the town for its hospitable and happy residents.

•HARRISBURG, City; Linn County; Pop. 1,881; Zip Code 97446; Elev. 309; Lat. 44-16-27 N long. 123-10-10 W; Incorporated in 1866 and named for Harrisburg, Pennsylvania.

•HELIX, City; Umatilla County; Pop. 155; Zip Code 97835; Elev. 1754; Lat. 45-50-59 N long. 118-39-21 W; An early resident suffered an infection of the helix of the ear about the time the town was being named - somehow the name was chosen.

•HEPPNER, City; Morrow County Seat; Pop. 1,498; Zip Code 97836; Elev. 1955; Lat. 45-21-12 N long. 119-33-24 W; The town is named after Henry Heppner, who opened the first store here in 1873.

•HERMISTON, City; Umatilla County; Pop. 9,408; Zip Code 97838; Elev. 457; Lat. 45-50-26 N long. 119-17-18 W; Pioneer Colonel F. McNaught named the town after an unfinished novel by Robert Louis Stevenson, Wier of Hermiston.

•HILLSBORO, City; Washington County Seat; Pop. 27,664; Zip Code 9712+; Lat. 45-31-23 N long. 122-59-19 W; The city is named after David Hill who settled in Oregon in 1842.

•HINES, City; Harney County; Pop. 1,632; Zip Code 97738; Elev. 4157; Lat. 43-33-51 N long. 119-04-48 W; Hines is named after the Edward Hines Lumber Company.

•HOOD RIVER, City; Hood River County Seat; Pop. 4,329; Zip Code 97031; Lat. 45-42-20 N long. 121-31-13 W; The city is named for the nearby Hood River.

•HUBBARD, City; Marion County; Pop. 1,640; Zip Code 97032; Elev. 182; Lat. 45-10-57 N long. 122-48-24 W; Named in honor of pioneer settler Charles Hubbard who came to Oregon in 1847.

•HUNTINGTON, City; Baker County; Pop. 539; Zip Code 97907; Elev. 2108; Lat. 44-21-05 N long. 117-15-56 W; The town's name remembers the Huntington brothers who settled here in 1882.

•IDANHA, City; Linn & Marion Counties; Pop. 319; Zip Code 97350; Elev. 1718; Lat. 44-42-10 N long. 122-04-39 W; Incorporated in 1895 and located on the North Santiam River. Named by an early settler.

•IMBLER, City; Union County; Pop. 292; Zip Code 97841; Elev. 2731; Lat. 45-27-35 N long. 117-57-40 W; Settled in the 19th century and named for the Imblers, a pioneer family.

•INDEPENDENCE, City; Polk County; Pop. 4,024; Zip Code 97351; Elev. 168; Lat. 44-51-05 N long. 123-11-08 W; Settler E. A. Thorp came to Oregon in 1845. He named Independence after Independence, Missouri.

•IONE, City; Morrow County; Pop. 345; Zip Code 97843; Elev. 1085; Lat. 45-30-05 N long. 119-49-25 W; Pioneer E. G. Sperry named the town for Ione Arthur.

•IRRIGON, City; Morrow County; Pop. 700; Zip Code 97844; Elev. 297; Lat. 45-53-45 N long. 119-29-25 W; Settled around 1900 and named by combining the words "irrigation," and "Oregon."

•ISLAND CITY, Town; Union County; Pop. 477; Lat. 45-20-28 N long. 118-02-37 W; Descriptively named for its location on an island formed by a slough of the Grande Ronde River.

•JACKSONVILLE, City; Jackson County; Pop. 2,030; Zip Code 97530; Elev. 1569; Lat. 42-18-49 N long. 122-57-57 W; The city is named for its location on Jackson Creek.

•JEFFERSON, City; Marion County; Pop. 1,702; Zip Code 9735+; Elev. 230; Lat. 44-43-11 N long. 123-00-33 W; The town is named for President Thomas Jefferson.

•JOHN DAY, City; Grant County; Pop. 2,012; Zip Code 97845; Elev. 3084; Lat. 44-24-58 N long. 118-57-07 W; The town is named after the John Day River. John Day was an explorer and trapper with the Astor expedition in 1811.

•JOHNSON CITY, City; Clackamas County; Pop. 378; Lat. 43-08-23 N long. 124-10-42 W; The town is named after its developer, Delbert Johnson.

•JORDAN VALLEY, Town; Malheur County; Pop. 473; Zip Code 97910; Elev. 4389; Lat. 42-58-27 N long. 117-03-12 W; Established in the 1870's and named for the Biblical Jordan Valley.

•JOSEPH, City; Wallowa County; Pop. 999; Zip Code 97846; Elev. 4190; Lat. 45-21-16 N long. 117-13-43 W; The town's name remembers Chief Joseph who fought a war here with the White's in the nineteenth century.

•JUNCTION CITY, City; Lane County; Pop. 3,320; Zip Code 97448; Elev. 327; Lat. 44-13-10 N long. 123-12-16 W; Descriptively named as the site of joining of two main railroad lines.

•KING CITY, City; Washington County; Pop. 1,853; Zip Code 97224. A recent community, its developers gave it a "royalty" theme, and hence the name.

•KLAMATH FALLS, City; Klamath County Seat; Pop. 16,661; Zip Code 976+; Lat. 42-13-30 N long. 121-46-50 W; On the falls of the Link River in Klamath County, the town is thus named. Klamath was the name of the local Indian tribe when the whites came.

•LAFAYETTE, City; Yamhill County; Pop. 1,215; Zip Code 97127; Lat. 45-14-40 N long. 123-06-49 W; Founded in 1846 and named after Lafayette, Indiana.

•LA GRANDE, City; Union County Seat; Pop. 11,354; Zip Code 978+; Elev. 2771; Lat. 45-19-29 N long. 118-05-12 W; Settled in the 1860's and given the name "the grand" to reflect the surrounding Grande Ronde Valley and its impressive views.

•LAKE OSWEGO, City; Clackamas, Multnomah & Washington Counties; Pop. 22,868; Zip Code 97034; Elev. 100; Lat. 45-25-15 N long. 122-40-10 W; Descriptively named for its position on Lake Oswego. The lake is named after Oswego, New York.

•LAKESIDE, City; Coos County; Pop. 1,453; Zip Code 97449; Elev. 29; Lat. 43-34-33 N long. 124-10-26 W; Located on Tenmile Lake and so descriptively named.

•LAKEVIEW, Town; Lake County Seat; Pop. 2,770; Zip Code 97630; Elev. 4798; Lat. 42-11-20 N long. 120-20-41 W; The town's name was chosen for its view of Goose Lake.

•LEBANON, City; Linn County; Pop. 10,413; Zip Code 97355; Lat. 44-32-12 N long. 122-54-21 W; Named by early settlers for Lebanon, Tennessee.

•LEXINGTON, Town; Morrow County; Pop. 307; Zip Code 97839; Lat. 45-26-43 N long. 119-41-00 W; Prominent pioneer William Penland named the town for his former home in Lexington, Kentucky.

•LINCOLN CITY, City; Lincoln County; Pop. 5,469; Zip Code 973+; Lat. 44-57-30 N long. 124-01-00 W; In 1964 three local communities combined under the name of Lincoln. Lincoln is the county name and honors Abraham Lincoln.

•LONEROCK, City; Gilliam County; Pop. 26; Descriptively named for a 100 ft. high rock landmark near the center of the community.

•LONG CREEK, Town; Grant County; Pop. 252; Zip Code 97856; Elev. 3772; Lat. 44-42-51 N long. 119-06-11 W; Descriptively named for a long creek in Grant County.

•LOSTINE, City; Wallowa County; Pop. 250; Zip Code 97857; Lat. 45-30-14 N long. 117-25-23 W; Named by a pioneer for Lostine, Kansas, probably his former home.

•LOWELL, City; Lane County; Pop. 661; Zip Code 97438; Elev. 741; Lat. 43-55-07 N long. 122-46-57 W; Settled in the 1850's and named for Lowell, Maine.

•LYONS, City; Linn County; Pop. 877; Zip Code 97358; Elev. 659; Lat. 44-46-29 N long. 122-36-50 W; The town is named after the pioneer family that established the town.

•MADRAS, City; Jefferson County Seat; Pop. 2,235; Zip Code 97741; Lat. 44-38-01 N long. 121-07-42 W; Named by an early merchant for cotton cloth from Madras, India.

•MALIN, City; Klamath County; Pop. 539; Zip Code 97632; Lat. 42-00-46 N long. 121-24-27 W; Named by Czechoslovakian settlers who founded the community in 1909, after their former home town in Czechoslovakia.

•MANZANITA, City; Tillamook County; Pop. 443; Zip Code 97130; Elev. 111; Lat. 45-43-07 N long. 123-56-02 W.

•MAUPIN, City; Wasco County; Pop. 495; Zip Code 97037; Elev. 1041; Lat. 45-10-31 N long. 121-04-49 W; The town's name remembers central Oregon pioneer Howard Maupin.

•MAYWOOD PARK, City; Multnomah County; Pop. 1,083; Incorporated in 1967 and named by the developer's family for the beautiful woods in the during May.

•MCMINNVILLE, City; Yamhill County Seat; Pop. 14,080; Zip Code 97128; Elev. 160; Lat. 45-12-37 N long. 123-11-51 W; Pioneer William Newby named the town for his birthplace in McMinnville, Tennessee.

•MEDFORD, City; Jackson County Seat; Pop. 39,603; Zip Code 975+; Elev. 383; Lat. 42-19-36 N long. 122-52-28 W; Named by railroad engineer David Loring for the town's location on the middle ford of Bear Creek.

•MERRILL, City; Klamath County; Pop. 809; Zip Code 97633; Elev. 4067; Lat. 42-01-31 N long. 121-35-58 W; The town is named for early pioneer Nathan S. Merrill.

•METOLIUS, City; Jefferson County; Pop. 451; Zip Code 97741; Elev. 2530; Lat. 44-35-12 N long. 121-10-38 W; Named after a tributary of the Deschutes River, it is an Indian word meaning "salmon-water."

•MILL CITY, City; Linn & Marion Counties; Pop. 1,565; Zip Code 97360; Elev. 827; Lat. 44-45-15 N long. 122-28-37 W; Located on the North Santiam River, and named for an early sawmill.

•MILLERSBURG, City; Linn County; Pop. 562; Elev. 242; Lat. 44-40-52 N long. 123-03-37 W; Named for the pioneer Miller family who have lived there for more than a hundred years.

•MILTON-FREEWATER, City; Umatilla County; Pop. 5,086; Zip Code 97862; Elev. 1033; Lat. 45-55-58 N long. 118-23-12 W; Milton and Freewater merged in 1951 and thereafter had a joint name.

•**MILWAUKIE**, City; Clackamas & Multnomah Counties; Pop. 17,931; Zip Code 97222; Lat. 45-26-47 N long. 122-38-17 W; Settled in 1847 and named for Milwaukee, Wisconsin.

•**MITCHELL**, Town; Wheeler County; Pop. 183; Zip Code 97750; Elev. 748; Lat. 44-18-20 N long. 122-41-20 W; Mitchell's name honors U. S. Senator J. H. Mitchell who served Oregon in the years 1873-79.

•**MOLALLA**, City; Clackamas County; Pop. 2,992; Zip Code 97038; Elev. 373; Lat. 45-08-51 N long. 122-34-33 W.

•**MONMOUTH**, City; Polk County; Pop. 5,594; Zip Code 97361; Elev. 201; Lat. 44-50-55 N long. 123-13-58 W; Settled in 1853 and named for Monmouth, Illinois.

•**MONROE**, City; Benton County; Pop. 412; Zip Code 97456; Elev. 288; Lat. 44-18-51 N long. 123-17-44 W; Founded in 1853 and named in honor of James Monroe, fifth President of the United States.

•**MONUMENT**, City; Grant County; Pop. 192; Zip Code 97864; Elev. 2008; Lat. 44-49-10 N long. 119-25-12 W; Settled in the 1870's and named for a nearby mountain which resembles a monument.

•**MORO**, City; Sherman County Seat; Pop. 336; Zip Code 97039; Elev. 1808; Lat. 45-29-03 N long. 120-43-48 W; The town was founded in the late 1860's and named after Moro, Illinois.

•**MOSIER**, City; Wasco County; Pop. 340; Zip Code 97040; Elev. 121; Lat. 45-41-01 N long. 121-23-46 W; The town's name remembers pioneer-founder J. H. Mosier, who began the community in 1853.

•**MOUNT ANGEL**, City; Marion County; Pop. 2,876; Zip Code 97362; Elev. 168; Lat. 45-04-05 N long. 122-47-56 W; Named in 1883 after Engelberg, Switzerland. Angel is anglized Engle.

•**MOUNT VERNON**, City; Grant County; Pop. 569; Zip Code 97865; Elev. 2871; Lat. 44-25-04 N long. 119-06-45 W; The town is named for a well-known black stallion of the 1870's.

•**MYRTLE CREEK**, City; Douglas County; Pop. 3,365; Zip Code 97457; Elev. 640; Lat. 43-01-13 N long. 123-17-31 W; Myrtle Creek was descriptively named for the groves of Oregon Myrtle in the area.

•**MYRTLE POINT**, City; Coos County; Pop. 2,859; Zip Code 97458; Elev. 90; Lat. 43-03-54 N long. 124-08-16 W; The town is named for the abundance of Oregon Myrtle.

•**NEHALEM**, Town; Tillamook County; Pop. 258; Zip Code 97131; Lat. 45-43-13 N long. 123-53-34 W; Nehalem's name remembers the Nehalem Indians who lived there before the white man came.

•**NEWBERG**, City; Yamhill County; Pop. 10,394; Zip Code 97132; Elev. 176; Lat. 45-18-01 N long. 122-58-19 W; The first postmaster, Sebastian Brutscher, named the town after Neuberg, Germany.

•**NEWPORT**, City; Lincoln County; Pop. 7,519; Zip Code 9736+; Elev. 177; Lat. 44-38-13 N long. 124-03-08 W; Named in 1868 after Newport, Rhode Island.

•**NORTH BEND**, City; Coos County; Pop. 9,779; Zip Code 97459; Elev. 23; Lat. 43-24-24 N long. 124-13-23 W; Captain A. M. Simpson named the town descriptively for its location near Coos Bay in 1856.

•**NORTH PLAINS**, City; Union County; Pop. 430; Zip Code 97133; Lat. 45-35-50 N long. 122-59-32 W; The name in use since pioneer days whose original designation is uncertain.

•**NORTH POWDER**, City; Union County; Pop. 430; Zip Code 97867; Elev. 3256; Lat. 45-01-43 N long. 117-55-08 W; The city was named descriptively for its location on the North Powder River.

•**NYSSA**, Town; Malheur County; Pop. 2,862; Zip Code 97913; Elev. 2177; Lat. 43-52-37 N long. 116-59-38 W; Named by a Greek section hand for a mythological nymph who reared the infant Bacchus.

•**OAKLAND**, City; Douglas County; Pop. 886; Zip Code 97462; Elev. 430; Lat. 43-25-20 N long. 123-17-50 W; Descriptively named for the oak trees around the original townsite.

•**OAKRIDGE**, City; Lane County; Pop. 3,729; Zip Code 97463; Elev. 1209; Lat. 43-44-48 N long. 122-27-38 W; Established in 1912 and named for the oak-covered ridge forming part of the town.

•**ONTARIO**, City; Malheur County; Pop. 8,814; Zip Code 979+; Elev. 2154; Lat. 44-01-36 N long. 116-57-43 W; Pioneer James Virtue named it after his birthplace, Ontario, Canada.

•**OREGON CITY**, City; Clackamas County Seat; Pop. 14,673; Zip Code 97045; Lat. 45-21-27 N long. 122-36-20 W; Founded in 1842 and named for the state.

•**PAISLEY**, City; Lake County; Pop. 343; Zip Code 97636; Elev. 4369; Lat. 42-41-38 N long. 120-32-42 W; Named by early Scotish settlers for Paisley, Scotland.

•**PORTLAND**, City; Clackamas, Multnomah & Washington Counties; Multnomah County Seat; Pop. 366,383; Zip Code 972+; Elev. 77. The largest city and principle port of Oregon, Portland was founded in 1845 and incorporated in 1851. It was named for the city in Maine. During the 1860's and 1870's it was a supply center for the gold rushes of the Northwest.

•**POWERS**, City; Coos County; Pop. 819; Zip Code 97466; Lat. 45-54-43 N long. 119-18-10 W; The town was named for lumber businessman A. H. Powers in 1914.

•**PRAIRIE CITY**, City; Grant County; Pop. 1,106; Zip Code 978+; Lat. 44-27-48 N long. 118-42-32 W; Descriptively named by early miners for the surrounding locale.

•**PRESCOTT**, City; Columbia County; Pop. 73; Elev. 25; Lat. 46-02-57 N long. 122-53-10 W; The city was named for the owners of the local sawmill.

•**PRINEVILLE**, City; Crook County Seat; Pop. 5,276; Zip Code 97754; Elev. 2952; Lat. 44-18-45 N long. 121-09-47 W; Barney Prine, the town's first merchant, had the town named after him.

•**RAINIER**, City; Columbia County; Pop. 1,655; Zip Code 97048; Elev. 24; Lat. 46-05-21 N long. 122-56-05 W; Settled in 1851 and named after Mount Rainier. Peter Rainier was a Rear-Admiral in the Royal Navy.

•**REDMOND**, City; Deschutes County; Pop. 6,452; Zip Code 97756; Elev. 2997; Lat. 44-16-22 N long. 121-10-22 W; The town's name remembers pioneer Frank Redmond who settled in the area in 1905.

•**REEDSPORT**, City; Douglas County; Pop. 4,984; Zip Code 97467; Elev. 10; Lat. 43-42-09 N long. 124-05-44 W; Reedsport honors Alfred Reed, an early pioneer in the area.

•**RICHLAND**, Town; Baker County; Pop. 181; Zip Code 97870; Lat. 44-46-09 N long. 117-10-03 W; The land's fertile soil led to this descriptive name.

•**RIDDLE**, City; Douglas County; Pop. 1,265; Zip Code 97469; Elev. 705; Lat. 42-57-04 N long. 123-21-47 W; Riddle is named after pioneer William Riddle who settled here in 1851.

•**RIVERGROVE,** City; Clackamas & Washington Counties; Pop. 314; Lat. 45-23-29 N long. 122-43-56 W; Incorporated in 1971 and combining the names Tualatin River and Lake Grove.

•**ROCKAWAY,** City; Tillamook County; Pop. 906; Zip Code 97136; Elev. 16; Lat. 45-36-49 N long. 123-56-31 W; The city is named after the rockaway summer resorts in Rockaway, Long Island.

•**ROGUE RIVER,** City; Jackson County; Pop. 1,308; Zip Code 97537; Elev. 1001; Lat. 42-26-10 N long. 123-10-15 W; Named after the Rogue River Indians.

•**ROSEBURG,** City; Douglas County Seat; Pop. 16,644; Zip Code 97470; Elev. 459; Lat. 43-13-00 N long. 123-20-26 W; Aaron rose settled here in 1851. The town is named in his honor.

•**RUFUS,** City; Sherman County; Pop. 352; Zip Code 97050; Elev. 206; Lat. 45-41-42 N long. 120-44-05 W; Rufus is named after the original settler Rufus C. Wallis.

•**ST. HELENS,** City; Columbia County Seat; Pop. 7,064; Zip Code 9705+; Elev. 73; Lat. 45-51-51 N long. 122-48-19 W; Descriptively named for its location near Mount St. Helens.

•**ST. PAUL,** City; Marion County; Pop. 312; Zip Code 97137; Elev. 170; Lat. 45-12-41 N long. 122-58-32 W; The town is named after the Saint Paul Mission established here in 1839.

•**SALEM,** City; Marion & Polk Counties; Marion County Seat; Capital of Oregon; Pop. 89,233; Zip Code 973+; Elev. 154. The capital of Oregon was settled in 1840 by a group of Methodist ministers on a site known as Chemetka, Indian for "place of peace." This was translated to the Biblical name of Salem.

•**SANDY,** City; Clackamas County; Pop. 2,905; Zip Code 97055; Lat. 45-23-51 N long. 122-15-37 W; The city is near the Sandy River and so descriptively named.

•**SCAPPOOSE,** City; Columbia County; Pop. 3,213; Zip Code 97056; Elev. 61; Lat. 45-45-16 N long. 122-52-35 W; Scappoose is an Indian word meaning "gravel plain."

•**SCIO,** City; Linn County; Pop. 579; Zip Code 97374; Elev. 317; Lat. 44-42-18 N long. 122-50-53 W; The city is named after Scio, Ohio. Scio, or Chios, is an island off Turkey.

•**SCOTTS MILLS,** City; Marion County; Pop. 249; Zip Code 97375; Lat. 45-02-35 N long. 122-40-02 W; Pioneers Robert and Thomas Scott ran a sawmill here in the 1860's. The town is named after this operation.

•**SEASIDE,** City; Clatsop County; Pop. 5,193; Zip Code 97138; Lat. 45-59-36 N long. 123-55-17 W; The city is named after a well-known hotel and resort, the Seaside House.

•**SENECA,** City; Grant County; Pop. 285; Zip Code 97873; Elev. 4666; Lat. 44-08-05 N long. 118-58-14 W; The town is named after Judge Seneca Smith of Portland.

•**SHADY COVE,** City; Jackson County; Pop. 1,097; Zip Code 97539. The town is on the Rogue River and is descriptive of a little nook on the river bank.

•**SHANIKO,** City; Wasco County; Pop. 30; Zip Code 97057; Elev. 3341; Lat. 45-00-14 N long. 120-45-04 W; Pioneer rancher August Scherneckau settled in Oregon after the Civil War. The Indians mispronounced the name Shaniko.

•**SHERIDAN,** City; Yamhill County; Pop. 2,249; Zip Code 97378; Lat. 45-05-58 N long. 123-23-37 W; The town is named after Philip Henry Sheridan, soldier and Civil War hero.

•**SHERWOOD,** City; Washington County; Pop. 2,386; Zip Code 97140; Elev. 205; Lat. 45-21-24 N long. 122-50-20 W; Originally Smockville, the name was changed in 1891 to Sherwood, after Sherwood, Michigan, or possibly England's Sherwood Forest.

•**SILETZ,** City; Lincoln County; Pop. 1,001; Zip Code 97357; Elev. 131; Lat. 44-43-19 N long. 123-55-08 W: The city is named after the Siletz River, itself named for the Siletz Indians.

•**SILVERTON,** City; Marion County; Pop. 5,168; Zip Code 97381; Elev. 249; Lat. 45-00-19 N long. 122-46-55 W; Settled in the 1840's and named for its location on Silver Creek.

•**SISTERS,** City; Deschutes County; Pop. 696; Zip Code 97759; Elev. 3186; Lat. 44-17-28 N long. 121-32-53 W; The city is east of the Cascades, and descriptively named for the nearby three sister peaks.

•**SODAVILLE,** Town; Linn County; Pop. 171; Lat. 44-29-05 N long. 122-52-14 W; The town is descriptively named for a nearby mineral springs.

•**SPRAY,** Town; Wheeler County; Pop. 155; Zip Code 97874; Elev. 1798; Lat. 44-50-04 N long. 119-47-36 W; John Spray came to Oregon in 1864. He founded Spray in 1900. The town is named in his honor.

•**SPRINGFIELD,** City; Lane County; Pop. 41,621; Zip Code 974+; Elev. 456; Lat. 44-02-47 N long. 123-01-15 W; Settled in 1849 and named for a natural spring on the site.

•**STANFIELD,** City; Umatilla County; Pop. 1,568; Zip Code 97875; Lat. 45-46-50 N long. 119-12-58 W; Founded in the 1880's and named after U. S. Senator Robert N. Stanfield.

•**STAYTON,** City; Marion County; Pop. 4,396; Zip Code 9738+; Elev. 457; Lat. 44-48-03 N long. 122-47-36 W; Established in 1872 and named after Drury S. Stayton, who founded the town.

•**SUBLIMITY,** City; Marion County; Pop. 1,077; Zip Code 97385; Elev. 548; Lat. 44-49-47 N long. 122-47-36 W; Sublimity was founded in 1852 and descriptively named for the "sublime scenery" in the adjacent vicinity.

•**SUMMERVILLE,** Town; Union County; Pop. 132; Zip Code 97876; Lat. 45-29-19 N long. 118-00-07 W; Settled in 1865 and named for pioneer Alexander Sommerville.

•**SUTHERLIN** City; Douglas County; Pop. 4,560; Zip Code 97479; Elev. 540; Lat. 43-23-25 N long. 123-18-41 W; The city's name honors pioneer horticulturalist Fendel Sutherlin.

•**SWEET HOME,** City; Linn County; Pop. 6,921; Zip Code 97386; Elev. 525; Lat. 44-23-52 N long. 122-44-06 W; An early pioneer named the "sweet home valley," the name was taken for the town.

•**TALENT,** City; Jackson County; Pop. 2,577; Zip Code 97540; Elev. 1635; Lat. 42-14-45 N long. 122-47-15 W; A. P. Talent founded the town in the 1880's. It is named after him.

•**TANGENT,** City; Linn County; Pop. 478; Zip Code 97389; Elev. 246; Lat. 44-32-29 N long. 123-06-25 W; The town is on a straight 20 mile segment of the Southern Pacific Railroad Line, and so suggested "a tangent."

•**TIGARD,** City; Washington County; Pop. 14,286; Zip Code 97223; Elev. 166; Lat. 45-25-53 N long. 122-46-13 W; Wilson M. Tigard came to Oregon in 1852. The town is named after him.

•**TILLAMOOK,** City; Tillamook County Seat; Pop. 3,981; Zip Code 971+; Elev. 16; Lat. 45-27-23 N long. 123-50-34 W; Tillamook was the name of a tribe of Salish Indians who lived in the area.

•TOLEDO, City; Lincoln County Seat; Pop. 3,151; Zip Code 97391; Elev. 59; Lat. 44-37-18 N long. 123-56-14 W; Settled in 1868 and named by a homesick pioneer after Toledo, Ohio.

•TROUTDALE, City; Multnomah County; Pop. 5,908; Zip Code 97060; Elev. 73; Lat. 45-32-22 N long. 122-23-10 W; Originally Sandy, the name was changed to describe a nearby pond stocked with trout.

•TUALATIN, City; Clackamas & Washington Counties; Pop. 7,348; Zip Code 97062; Elev. 123; Lat. 45-23-03 N long. 122-45-46 W; An Indian word meaning "sluggish" and referring to the Tualatin River.

•TURNER, City; Marion County; Pop. 1,116; Zip Code 97392; Lat. 44-50-36 N long. 122-57-06 W; The city's name honors pioneer Henry L. Turner.

•UKIAH, City; Umatilla County; Pop. 249; Zip Code 97880; Elev. 3353; Lat. 45-08-03 N long. 118-55-53 W; Settled in 1890 and named for Ukiah, California.

•UMATILLA, City; Umatilla County; Pop. 3,199; Zip Code 97882; Elev. 296; Lat. 45-55-03 N long. 119-20-29 W; The Umatilla were among the original Indians in the area.

•UNION, City; Union County; Pop. 2,062; Zip Code 97883; Elev. 2788; Lat. 45-12-31 N long. 117-51-51 W; Founded in 1862 and named by patriotic citizens for the embattled "union."

•UNITY, City; Baker County; Pop. 115; Zip Code 97884; Lat. 44-26-15 N long. 118-11-30 W; The original town post office was moved after a "unity" meeting concerning its location. The name stuck on the new site.

•VALE, City; Malheur County Seat; Pop. 1,558; Zip Code 97918; Lat. 43-58-56 N long. 117-14-14 W; Named by early settlers for a vale, or valley.

•VENETA, City; Lane County; Pop. 2,449; Zip Code 97487; Lat. 44-02-56 N long. 123-20-59 W; Founded in 1913 by E. E. Hunter, and named for his daughter, Veneta Hunter.

•VERNONIA, City; Columbia County; Pop. 1,785; Zip Code 97064; Elev. 621; Lat. 45-51-32 N long. 123-11-30 W; Ozias Cherrington was one of the town's founders. The town is named after his daughter Vernonia.

•WALDPORT, City; Lincoln County; Pop. 1,274; Zip Code 97376; Elev. 11; Lat. 44-25-37 N long. 124-04-03 W; Named in the 1880 by combining the German word wald, or forest, with the English word "port."

•WALLOWA, City; Wallowa County; Pop. 847; Zip Code 97885; Elev. 2948; Lat. 45-34-13 N long. 117-31-38 W; Wallowa is a Nez Perce Indian word describing a structure of stakes for catching fish.

•WARRENTON, City; Clatsop County; Pop. 2,493; Zip Code 97146; Lat. 46-09-55 N long. 123-55-21 W; The city is named in honor of D. K. Warrenton, an early settler.

•WASCO, City; Sherman County; Pop. 415; Zip Code 97065; Elev. 1270; Lat. 45-35-31 N long. 120-41-49 W; Named after the Wasco Indians who once lived on the Columbia River.

•WATERLOO, Town; Linn County; Pop. 221; Lat. 44-29-39 N long. 122-49-27 W; Named after the famous battle which led to Napoleon's downfall.

•WESTFIR, City; Lane County; Pop. 312; Zip Code 97492; Lat. 43-45-27 N long. 122-29-43 W; Named for the great quantity of douglas fir in the area.

•WEST LINN, City; Clackamas County; Pop. 12,956; Zip Code 97068; Elev. 128; Lat. 45-21-57 N long. 122-36-40 W; Settled in the 1840's and named for U. S. Senator Lewis Linn of Missouri, who urged the American settlement of Oregon.

•WESTON, City; Umatilla County; Pop. 719; Zip Code 97886; Elev. 1838; Lat. 45-48-50 N long. 118-25-25 W; Established in the 1860's and named for Weston, Missouri.

•WHEELER, City; Tillamook County; Pop. 319; Zip Code 97147; Elev. 18; Lat. 45-41-21 N long. 123-52-46 W; Prominent Portland lumberman C. H. Wheeler had the town named in his honor.

•WILLAMINA, City; Polk & Yamhill Counties; Pop. 1,749; Zip Code 97396 Elev. 225; Lat. 45-04-44 N long. 123-29-05 W; The city is named after Willamina Creek. The creek is named after the first white woman in the area, Mrs. Willamina Williams.

•WILSONVILLE, City; Clackamas & Washington Counties; Pop. 2,920; Zip Code 97070; Lat. 45-18-00 N long. 122-46-21 W; Settled in the 1870's and named after pioneer Charles Wilson.

•WINSTON, City; Douglas County; Pop. 3,359; Zip Code 97496; Elev. 534; Lat. 43-07-21 N, long. 123-24-41 W. Founded in 1893 and named for its first postmaster, Elijah Winston.

•WOODBURN, City; Marion County; Pop. 11,196; Zip Code 97071; Elev. 183; Lat. 45-08-38 N, long. 122-51-15 W. Descriptively named for the main energy source of its settlers.

•WOOD VILLAGE, City; Multnomah County; Pop. 2,253; Lat. 45-32-04 N, long. 122-25-03 W. Founded in World War II and named in honor of Portland Real Estate Agent, Lester J. Wood.

•YAMHILL, City; Yamhill County; Pop. 690; Zip Code 97148; Lat. 45-20-30 N, long. 123-11-10 W. The town is named for the nearby river, itself named for the Yamel Indians.

•YONCALLA, City; Douglas County; Pop. 805; Zip Code 97499; Lat. 43-35-55 N, long. 123-16-56 W. The town is named for a nearby mountain. Yoncalla is an Indian word meaning "eagle."

PENNSYLVANIA

•**AARONSBURG**, Village; Centre County; Pop. 500; Zip Code 16820; Elev. 1200; Lat. 40-53-59 N long. 077-27-13 W; 0 m. NW of Lewisburg in central Pennsylvania; settled in 1775; named for *Aaron Levy*, who founded the town in 1786.

•**ABBOTTSTOWN**, Borough; Adams County; Pop. 689; Zip Code 17301; Elev. 544; Lat. 39-53-11 N long. 076-59-06 W; S Pennsylvania; on Beaver Creek.

•**ABERDEEN**, Unincorporated Village; Lackawanna County; Pop. 40; Zip Code 18444; part of Madison township in NE Pennsylvania.

•**ABINGTON**, Township; Montgomery County; Pop. 59,084; Zip Code 19001; Elev. 350; Lat. 40-07-14 N long. 075-07-06 W; SE Pennsylvania; Founded in 1714, when the Abington Presbyterian Church was built.

•**ACADEMY CORNERS**, Village; Tioga County; Pop. 50; Zip Code 16929; 5 m. S of New York State Line in N central Pennsylvania; named for old Union Academy, which was established in this region.

•**ACKERMANVILLE**, Village; Northampton County; Pop. 350; Zip Code 18010; Elev. 500; Lat. 40-50-21 N long. 075-13-11 W; 10 m. N of Easton in E central Pennsylvania.

•**ACME**, Village; Westmoreland County; Pop. 300; Zip Code 15610; Elev. 1,920; Lat. 40-07-36 N long. 079-25-44 W; near Mount Pleasant in SE central Pennsylvania.

•**ACMETONIA**, Village; Allegheny County; Pop. 1,200; Zip Code 15024; located near Pittsburgh in W Pennsylvania.

•**ACOSTA**, Village; Somerset County; Pop. 500; Zip Code 15520; Elev. 1,880; Lat. 40-06-37 N long. 079-04-09 W; S Pennsylvania.

•**ADAH** (alt. ANTRAM), Village; Fayette County; Pop. 600; Zip Code 15410; Elev. 920; Lat. 39-53-47 N long. 079-55-20 W; SW Pennsylvania.

•**ADAMS DALE**, Village; Schuylkill County; Pop. 160; Zip Code 17972; Elev. 510; Lat. 40-38-10 N long. 076-07-42 W; near Schuylkill Haven in E central Pennsylvania.

•**ADAMS HILL**, Village; Westmoreland County; Pop. 120; Zip Code 15642; near E Pittsburgh in SW Pennsylvania.

•**ADAMSBURG**, Borough; Westmoreland County; Pop. 236; Zip Code 15611; Elev. 1,200; Lat. 40-18-42 N long. 079-39-23 W; near Jeannette in SW Pennsylvania; named for *President John Adams.*

•**ADAMSTOWN**, Borough; Berks and Lancaster Counties; Pop. 1,119; Zip Code 19501; Elev. 500; Lat. 40-14-28 N long. 076-03-24 W; SE Pennsylvania. *William Bird,* an ironmaster, obtained a patent for 356 acres here in 1739;

•**ADAMSVILLE**, Village; Crawford County; Pop. 150; Zip Code 16110; Elev. 1,040; Lat. 41-30-40N long. 080-22-12; 15 m. SW of Meadville in NW Pennsylvania.

•**ADDISON**, Borough; Somerset County; Pop. 259; Zip Code 15411; Elev. 2,026; Lat. 39-44-50 N long. 079-20-22 W; near Maryland state line and Youghiogheny Reservoir in S Pennsylvania.

•**ADELAIDE**, Village; Fayette County; Pop. 150; Zip Code 15425; Lat. 40-02-36 N long. 079-37-27 W; near Connellsville in SW Pennsylvania.

•**ADMIRE**, Village; York County; Pop. 50; Zip Code 17364; Lat. 39-57-43 N long. 076-52-15 W; 10 m. W of York in SSE Pennsylvania.

•**ADRIAN**, Village; Armstrong County; Pop. 150; Zip Code 16210; Elev. 1,080; Lat. 40-53-05 N long. 079-32-17 W; 10 m. N of Kittanning in W central Pennsylvania.

•**AIKEN**, Village; McKean County; Pop. 125; Zip Code 16744; Elev. 2210; Lat. 41-52-41 N long. 078-34-41 W; near Bradford in N central Pennsylvania.

•**AIRVILLE**, Village; York County; Pop. 85; Zip Code 17302; Elev. 780; Lat. 39-49-56 N long. 076-24-24 W; 20 m. SW of Lancaster in SE Pennsylvania; is located near the Susquehanna River.

•**AKELEY**, Village; Warren County; Pop. 70; Zip Code 16345; Elev. 1242; Lat. 41-57-53 N long. 079-07-52 W; on Conewango Creek near New York state line in NW Pennsylvania.

•**AKRON**, Borough; Lancaster County; Pop. 3,471; Zip Code 17501; Elev. 400; Lat. 40-09-24 N long. 076-12-09 W; SE Pennsylvania; was settled by Germans in the 1800s and was incorporated as a borough in 1884.

•**ALBA**, Borough; Bradford County; Pop. 222; Zip Code 16910; Elev. 1,340; Lat. 41-42-18 N long. 076-49-43 W; N Pennsylvania.

•**ALBANY**, Village; Berks County; Pop. 1,109; Zip Code 19529; Lat. 40-02-16 N long. 079-52-18 W; SE Pennsylvania; named for *James II* whose Scottish title was Duke of Albany.

•**ALBION**, Borough; Erie County; Pop. 1,818; Zip Code 16401; Elev. 904; Lat. 41-53-26 N long. 080-22-00 W; NW Pennsylvania; was settled in 1815. First known as Jackson Cross Roads.

•**ALBION**, Village; Jefferson County; Pop. 100; Zip Code 15767; near Punxsutawney in W central Pennsylvania.

•**ALBRIGHTSVILLE**, Village; Carbon County; Pop. 150; Zip Code 18210; Elev. 1,600; Lat. 41-00-52 N long. 075-36-05 W; on Muddy Run; approx. 15 m. N of Jim Thorpe in central Pennsylvania.

•**ALBURTIS**, Borough; Lehigh County; Pop. 1,428; Zip Code 18011; Elev. 440; Lat. 40-30-39 N long. 075-36-12 W; near Allentown in E Pennsylvania.

•**ALDAN**, Borough; Delaware County; Pop. 4,671; Elev. 120; Lat. 39-55-17 N long. 075-17-18 W; suburb of Chester in SE Pennsylvania.

•**ALDEN**, Village; Suzerne County; Pop. 800; Zip Code 18634; Lat. 41-10-55 N long. 076-00-46 W; E central Pennsylvania; suburb of Nanticoke and Wilkes-Barre.

•**ALDENVILLE**, Village; Wayne County; Pop. 50; Zip Code 18401; Elev. 1,220; Lat. 41-38-48 N long. 075-21-51 W; on White Oak Pond near Honesdale in NE Pennsylvania.

•**ALDOVIN**, Village; Wyoming County; Pop. 100; Zip Code 18657; Lat. 41-37-02 N long. 075-56-19 W; 10 m. N of Tunkhannock in NE PA near Lake Carey.

•**ALEXANDRIA**, Borough; Huntingdon County; Pop. 435; Zip Code 16611; Elev. 700; Lat. 40-33-23 N long. 078-05-53 W; on Juniata River's Frankstown branch; in Appalachian Mountains and near Huntington in S central Pennsylvania.

•**ALFARATA**, Village; Mifflin County; Pop. 150; Zip Code 16611; Elev. 700; Lat. 40-33-59 N long. 078-07-07 W; suburb of Lewiston on Juniata River in S central Pennsylvania; named for "Alfrata, the Maid of Juniata," heroine of a local folk song.

•**ALFORD**, Village; Susquehanna County; Pop. 50; Zip Code 18826; Lat. 41-48-24 N long. 075-46-30W; NE Pennsylvania.

•**ALICIA**, Village; Fayette County; Pop. 50; Zip Code 15417; on Manongahela River near Brownsville in SW Pennsylvania.

•**ALINDA**, Village; Perry County; Pop. 50; Zip Code 17040; Lat. 40-20-47 N long. 077-17-05W; near New Bloomfield and Harrisburg area.

•**ALIQUIPPA**, Borough; Beaver County; Pop. 17,094; Zip Code 15001; Elev. 725; Lat. 40-38-12 N long. 080-14-25 W; W Pennsylvania. It was named for an Iroquois Indian Queen, *Aliquippa*, who is said to have lived on the site of McKeesport in the 1750s. The name may mean "hat" in Iroquoian. *Aliquippa* was called "Queen of the Delaware", although she was probably Mohawk.

•**ALLEGHENY**, Village; Allegheny County; Pop. 650; Zip Code 15076; W central Pennsylvania; unincorporated suburb of Pittsburgh.

•**ALLEGHENYVILLE**, Village; Berks County; Pop. 50; Zip Code 19540; Lat. 40-14-03 N long. 075-59-20 W; E Pennsylvania; suburb of Reading.

•**ALLEMANS**, Village; Clearfield County; Pop. 70; Zip Code 16639; Elev. 1,778; Lat. 40-43-36 N long. 078-24-15 W; Central Pennsylvania.

•**ALLEN**, Village; Cumberland County; Pop. 400; Zip Code 17001; Elev. 510; near Harrisburg in S central Pennsylvania.

•**ALLEN**, Township; Northampton County; Pop. 1,856; Zip Code 18067; named for *William Allen*, who was Chief Justice of PA (1750-74) and received 3,000 acres here in 1748.

•**ALLENPORT**, Borough; Washington County; Pop. 735; Zip Code 15412; Lat. 40-05-53 N long. 079-50-57 W; SW Pennsylvania.

•**ALLENSVILLE**, Village; Mifflin County; Pop. 350; Zip Code 17002; Elev. 98; Lat. 40-32-09 N long. 077-49-02 W; 10 m. NE of Huntington in S central Pennsylvania.

•**ALLENTOWN**, City; Seat of Lehigh County; Pop. 103,758; Zip Code 181 + zone; Elev. 364; near Bethlehem and Easton in E Pennsylvania; incorporated as a borough in 1811 and as a city in 1867. Originally known as Northampton Town, the city was first settled by German immigrants in the 1720s.

•**ALLISON**, Village; Fayette County; Pop. 1,040; Zip Code 15413; Elev. 1,060; Lat. 39-59-20 N long. 079-51-54 W; SW Pennsylvania.

•**ALLISON HEIGHTS**, Village; Fayette County; Pop. 100; Zip Code 15413; Elev. 1,060; Lat. 39-59-10 N long. 079-52-44 W; SW Pennsylvania; suburb of Allison.

•**ALLISON PARK**, Borough; Allegheny County; Pop. 5,600; Zip Code 15101; Elev. 861; W Pennsylvania; suburb of Pittsburgh.

•**ALSACE MANOR**, Village; Berks County; Pop. 300; Zip Code 19560; Elev. 912; Lat. 40-23-59 N long. 075-51-39 W; near Reading in SE Pennsylvania.

•**ALTAMONT**, Village; Schuylkill County; Pop. 450; Zip Code 17931; Lat. 40-47-10 N long. 076-13-31 W; near Mahoney City in E central Pennsylvania.

•**ALTOONA**, City; Blair County; Pop. 57,078; Zip Code 166 plus zone; Elev. 1,171; Lat. 40-31-07 N long. 078-23-42 W; S central Pennsylvania.

•**ALUM BANK (alt. PLEASANTVILLE)**, Village; Bedford County; Pop. 280; Elev. 1,240; Lat. 40-10-50 N long. 078-36-50 W; on Juniata River in S Pennsylvania; named for pure alum deposits found here.

•**ALUTA**, Village; Northampton County; Pop. 700; Zip Code 18064; Lat. 40-46-15 N long. 075-19-02 W; E Pennsylvania.

•**ALVERDA**, Village; Indiana County; Pop. 700; Zip Code 15710; Elev. 1,917; Lat. 40-37-49 Nlong. 078-51-26 W; 25 m. N of Johnstown in W central Pennsylvania; name means "all green."

•**ALVERTON**, Village; Westmoreland County; Pop. 400; Zip Code 15612; Elev. 1,100; Lat. 40-08-24 N long. 079-35-15 W; W central Pennsylvania.

•**AMBLER**, Borough; Montgomery County; Pop. 6,628; Zip Code 19002; Lat. 40-09-16 N long. 075-13-19 W; SE Pennsylvania. Named for a prominent family of early settlers one of which *Joseph Amber* settled here in 1723.

•**AMBRIDGE**, Borough; Beaver County; Pop. 9,575; Zip Code 15003; Elev. 775; Lat. 40-35-21 N long. 080-13-31 W; W Pennsylvania. It was named for the American Bridge Company, which bought the community called Harmony Society here in 1901.

•**AMBRIDGE HEIGHTS**, Village; Beaver County; Pop. 2,000; Zip Code 15003; Elev. 751; Lat. 40-35-30 N long. 080-12-43 W; suburb of Ambridge in Pittsburgh area, in W Pennsylvania.

•**AMEND**, Village; Fayette County; Pop. 300; Zip Code 15401; Lat. 39-52-22 N long. 079-47-22 W; near Uniontown in SW Pennsylvania.

•**AMITY**, Village; Washington County; Pop. 170; Zip Code 15311; Elev. 1,204; Lat. 40-49-51 N long. 078-24-02 W; 10 m. S of Washington in SW Pennsylvania. It was laid out in 1797, the village grew up around Amity Presbyterian Church; named for "the religious and social amity which the people decided to foster."

•**AMSBRY**, Village; Cambria County; Pop. 100; Zip Code 16641; Lat. 40-32-11 N long. 078-33-23 W; W central Pennsylvania.

•**ANALOMINK**, Village; Monroe County; Pop. 150; Zip Code 18320; Elev. 530; Lat. 41-03-04 N long. 075-13-15 W; E Pennsylvania.

•**ANCIENT OAKS**, Village; Lehigh County; Pop. 1,800; Zip Code 18062; Lat. 40-32-50 N long. 075-35-23 W; E central Pennsylvania; suburb of Allentown.

•**ANDALUSIA**, City; Bucks County; Pop. 4,500; Zip Code 19020; Elev. 37; Lat. 40-04-10 N long. 074-58-18 W;near Philadelphia in SE Pennsylvania; on Delaware River; named for 95 acre estate of *Charles T. Biddle* which he named for Southern region of Spain.

•**ANDREAS**, Village; Schuylkill County; Pop. 110; Zip Code 18211; Elev. 591; Lat. 40-45-06 N long. 075-47-34 W; E central Pennsylvania.

•**ANGELS**, Village; Wayne County; Pop. 100; Zip Code 18445; Lat. 41-16-41 N long. 075-22-04 W; NE Pennsylvania.

•**ANITA**, Village; Jefferson County; Pop. 600; Zip Code 15711; Elev. 1,500; Lat. 41-00-05 N long. 078-57-48 W; near Punsatavney in mountainous region in W central Pennsylvania.

•**ANNVILLE**, Elev. 420; Lat. 40-19-46 N long. 076-30-56 W; on Quitapahilla Creek, was formerly called Millerstown for *Abraham Miller*, who laid it out in 1762; but the name was changed, at Miller's suggestion, to honor his wife *Ann*.

PENNSYLVANIA

•**APOLLO**, Borough; Armstrong County; Pop. 2,212; Zip Code 15613; Elev. 809; LAt. 40-34-53 N long. 079-34-00 W; W Pennsylvania; once known as Warren for an Indian trader who often stopped here, it was renamed in 1848 by *Dr. Robert McKisson*, physician, poet, and student of the classics.

•**ARCHBALD**, Borough; Lackawanna County; Pop. 6,295; Zip Code 18403; Elev. 919; Lat. 40-48-31 Nlong. 079-31-19W; NE Pennsylvania. It was called White Oak Run until 1846 when the Delaware and Hudson Canal Company began exploiting its coal deposits and named it for *James Archbald*, a company engineer.

•**ARNOT**, Village; Tioga County; Pop. 300; Zip Code 16911; Elev. 1,687; Lat. 41-39-45 N long. 077-07-24 W; near Tioga River in N Pennsylvania.

•**ARONA**, Borough; Westmoreland County; Pop. 446; Zip Code 15617; Elev. 1,000; Lat. 40-16-09 N long. 079-39-42 W; SW Pennsylvania.

•**ASHFIELD**, Village; Carbon County; Pop. 200; Zip Code 18212; Elev. 550; Lat. 40-47-04 N long. 075-42-50 W; E central Pennsylvania.

•**ASHLAND**, Borough; Schuylkill County; Pop. 4,737; Zip Code 17921; Elev. 885; Lat. 40-46-54 N long. 076-20-46 W; E central Pennsylvania. Named for *Henry Clay's* estate in Lexington, Kentucky by *Samuel Lewis* in 1847.

•**ASHLEY**, Borough; Luzerne County; Pop. 3,512; Zip Code 18706; Elev. 643; Lat. 41-12-37 N long. 075-53-49 W; E Pennsylvania. Town was known as Scrabbletown, Coalville, Skunktown, Peestone, Hightown, Newton, Hendricksburg, Nanticoke Junction and Alberts since it was settled in 1810. Current name was adopted in 1871 for a prominent family of coal operators including *Herfert Henry Ashley* of Wilkes-Barre.

•**ASHVILLE**, Borough; Cambria County; Pop. 383; Zip Code 16613; Elev. 1,680; Lat. 40-33-36 N long. 078-32-56 W; SW central Pennsylvania.

•**ASPERS**, Village; Adams County; Pop. 275; Zip Code 17304; Elev. 651; Lat. 39-58-46 Nlong. 077-13-23 W; Pennsylvania.

•**ASPINWALL**, Borough; Allegheny County; Pop. 3,284; Zip Code 15215; Elev. 800; Lat. 40-29-29 N long. 079-54-18 W; SW Pennsylvania; founded in 1796 and named for the *Aspinwall* family, early landowners; on Allegheny River.

•**ASTON**, Borough & Township; Delaware County; Pop. 6,900 (Township 13,704); Zip Code 19014; Elev. 200; suburb of Philadelphia near Delaware state line and Delaware River.

•**ASYLUM**, Township; Bradford County; Pop. 843; Lat. 41-42-47 N long. 076-20-02 W;Towanda area. Colony was originally established in 1794 for refugees of the French Revolution, promoted by *Robert Morris* and *John Nicholson*.

•**ATGLEN**, Borough; Chester County; Pop. 669; Zip Code 19310; Elev. 504; Lat. 39-56-57 N long. 075-58-26 W; SE Pennsylvania.

•**ATHENS**, Borough; Bradford County; Pop. 3,662; Zip Code 18810; Elev. 772; Lat. 41-57-26 N long. 076-31-06 W; N Pennsylvania. Athens took the name of the township, founded in 1786, and named for the capital of Greece; probably because the ring of hills surrounding the city resembles the Greek metropolis.

•**ATHOL**, Village; Berks County; Zip Code 200; Zip Code 19502; Elev. 280; 45 m. N of Philadelphia in SE Pennsylvania.

•**ATLANTIC**, Village; Clearfield County; Pop. 100; Zip Code 16651; Lat. 40-50-41 N long. 078-23-43 W; Central Pennsylvania.

•**ATLANTIC**, Village; Crawford County; Pop. 175; Zip Code 16111; Elev. 1,150; NW Pennsylvania.

•**ATLAS**, Village; Northumberland County; Pop. 1,527; Zip Code 17851; Elev. 1,160; Lat. 40-47-59 N long. 076-25-41 W; near Mt. Carmel and Kulpmont in E central Pennsylvania.

•**ATLASBURG**, Village; Washington County; Pop. 550; Zip Code 15004; Elev. 1,120; Lat. 40-20-28 N long. 080-22-59 W; SW Pennsylvania.

•**AUBURN**, Borough; Schuylkill County; Pop. 999; Zip Code 17922; Elev. 500; Lat. 40-35-54 N long. 076-05-37 W; E central Pennsylvania.

•**AUDENREID**, Village; Carbon County; Pop. 180; Zip Code 18201; Lat. 40-54-38 N long. 075-59-31 W; near Hazleton in E central Pennsylvania.

•**AUDUBON**, Montgomery County; Pop. 4,400; Zip Code 19407; Elev. 200; Lat. 40-54-38 N long. 075-59-31 W; SE Pennsylvania; unincorporated suburb of Norristown and Philadelphia. Located on the Perkiomen Creek, this borough is nearby the former estate of *John James Audubon*, the ornithologist for whom it was named.

•**AULTMAN**, Village; Indiana County; Pop. 300; Zip Code 15713; Elev. 1,120; Lat. 40-33-50 N long. 079-15-40 W; N central Pennsylvania.

•**AUSTINBURG**, Village; Tioga County; Pop. 100; Zip Code 16928; Lat. 41-59-35 N long. 077-29-42 W; N Pennsylvania.

•**AVALON**, Borough; Allegheny County; Pop. 6,240; Elev. 727; Lat. 41-50-20 N long. 076-52-27 W; SW Pennsylvania. First settled in late 1700s by Irish trader *James Taylor*. Originally known as Birmingham for *Captain John Birmingham* who purchased land from *Taylor*. In 1874, it was incorporated as West Bellevue, and in 1894 the name was changed to Avalon, a Celtic word meaning "orchard," or "land of apples."

•**AVELLA**, Village; Washington County; Pop. 1,109; Zip Code 15312; Elev. 960; Lat. 40-16-30 N long. 080-27-39W; approx. 25 m. SW of Pittsburgh in W Pennsylvania.

•**AVIS**, Borough; Clinton County; Pop. 1,718; Zip Code 17721; Elev. 600; Lat. 41-11-05 N long. 077-18-51 W; Central Pennsylvania; named for *Avis Cochran*, daughter of one of the chief promoters of the town in the early 20th century.

•**AVOCA**, Borough; Luzerne County; Pop. 3,536; Zip Code 18641; Elev. 660; Lat. 41-20-23 N long. 075-44-12 W; E Pennsylvania; at the junction of the Lackawanna and Wyoming Valleys, was originally named Pleasant Valley.

•**AVON**, Village; Lebanon County; Pop. 1,271; Zip Code 17042; Lat. 40-20-44 N long. 076-23-25 W; SE central Pennsylvania; suburb of Lebanon.

•**AVONDALE**, Borough; Chester County; Pop. 891; Zip Code 19311; Elev. 227; Lat. 39-49-24 N long. 075-47-01 W; on White Clay Creek in SE Pennsylvania; in agricultural area; mainly producing mushrooms.

•**AVONMORE**, Borough; Westmoreland County; Pop. 1,234; Zip Code 15618; Elev. 880; Lat. 40-31-44 N long. 079-27-42 W; SW Pennsylvania.

•**AXEMANN**, Village; Center County; Pop. 150; Zip Code 16823; Elev. 900; Lat. 40-53-24 N long. 077-45-38W; near Bellefonte in central Pennsylvania; named for *William and Harvey Mann*.

412

•**BACHMANVILLE**, Village; Dauphin County; Pop. 100; Zip Code 17033; Lat. 40-14-33 N long. 076-35-42 W; near Hershey in SE central Pennsylvania.

•**BADEN**, Borough; Beaver County; Pop. 5,318; Zip Code 15005; Elev. 673; Lat. 40-38-06 N long. 080-13-42 W;on Ohio River, just N of Ambridge in W Pennsylvania; residential; incorporated as a borough 1868.

•**BAEDERWOOD**, Borough; Montgomery County; Pop. 1,300; Zip Code 19046; Lat. 40-06-24 N long. 075-08-33 W; residential suburb of Philadelphia.

•**BAGGALEY**, Village; Westmoreland County; Pop. 450; Zip Code 15063; Lat. 40-16-06 N long. 079-22-22 W; near Latrobe in W Pennsylvania.

•**BAIDLAND**, Village; Washington County; Pop. 800; Zip Code 15063; Lat. 40-11-41 N long. 079-58-16 W; W Pennsylvania.

•**BAINBRIDGE**, Village; Lancaster County; Pop. 650; Zip Code 17502; Elev. 320; Lat. 40-05-27 N long. 076-40-04 W; on Susquehanna River in SE Pennsylvania; named for *Cmdr. William Bainbridge* in 1817.

•**BAIR**, Village; York County; Pop. 200; Zip Code 17405; Elev. 462; Lat. 39-54-19 N long. 076-49-41 W; 10 m. W of York in S Pennsylvania.

•**BAIRDFORD**, Village; Allegheny County; Pop. 950; Zip Code 15006; Elev. 900; Lat. 40-25-57 N long. 079-16-45 W; 15 m. NE of Pittsburgh in SE Pennsylvania.

•**BAKERS SUMMIT**, Village; Bedford County; Pop. 125; Zip Code 16614; Elev. 1,440; Lat. 40-15-45 N long. 078-25-18 W; 20 m. S of Altoona in S Pennsylvania.

•**BAKERSTOWN**, Village; Allegheny County; Pop. 1,000; Zip Code 15007; Elev. 1,107; Lat. 40-39-03 N long. 079-56-12 W; 20 m. NE of Pittsburgh in W Pennsylvania.

•**BAKERSVILLE**, Village; Somerset County; Pop. 200; Zip Code 15501; Elev. 2093; Lat. 40-02-32 N long. 079-13-00 W; 10 m. NW of Somerset in S Pennsylvania; Laurel Hill; near ski and camping areas.

•**BALA-CYNWYD**, Borough; Montgomery County; Pop. 8,600; Zip Code 19004; Elev. 304; Lat. 40-00-27 N long. 075-14-04 W; SE Pennsylvania; NW suburb of Philadelphia.

•**BALD EAGLE**, Township; Clinton County; Pop. 1,282; Lat. 40-43-19 N long. 078-11-08 W; named for Indian Chief who once lived here.

•**BALDWIN**, Borough; Allegheny County; Pop. 24,598; Lat. 10-20-17 N long. 079-58-45 W; SW Pennsylvania; S suburb of Pittsburgh; named for locomotive originator *Mathias Bladwin*.

•**BALLIETTSVILLE**, Town; Lehigh County; Pop. 320; Zip Code 18037; Lat. 40-40-42 N long. 075-34-27 W; near Allentown in E Pennsylvania.

•**BALLY**, Borough; Berks County; Pop. 1,051; Zip Code 19503; Elev. 480; Lat. 40-24-08 N long. 075-35-15 W; SE Pennsylvania. It was laid out in 1742 on ground owned by the Society of Jesus, was later named for the *Reverend Augustin Bally, S.J.*.

•**BALSINGER**, Village; Fayette County; Pop. 100; Zip Code 15484; Lat. 39-53-46 N long. 079-47-57 W; near Uniontown in S Pennsylvania.

•**BANGOR**, Borough; Northampton County; Pop. 5,006; Zip Code 18013; Elev. 514; Lat. 40-51-56 N long. 075-12-25 W; E Pennsylvania. It was founded in 1773 and named for a slate producing city in Wales, is the center of PA's slate quarrying area.

•**BANNING**, Village; Fayette County; Pop. 200; Zip Code 15428; Lat. 40-07-10 N long. 079-45-06 W; 35 m. SE of Pittsburgh in SW Pennsylvania.

•**BARBOURS**, Village; Lycoming County; Pop. 100; Zip Code 17701; Elev. 740; Lat. 41-23-35 N long. 076-47-59 W; N central suburb of Williamsport.

•**BARESVILLE**, Village; York County; Pop. 1,700; Zip Code 17331; near Hanover in S Pennsylvania.

•**BAREVILLE**, Village; Lancaster County; Pop. 800; Zip Code 17540; Lat. 40-05-32 N long. 076-09-22 W; NE of Lancaster in SE Pennsylvania.

•**BARNES**, Village; Warren County; Pop. 200; Zip Code 16347; Elev. 1479; Lat. 41-11-31 N long. 079-58-33 W; near Sheffield in N Pennsylvania.

•**BARNESBORO**, Borough; Cambria County; Pop. 2,741; Zip Code 15714; Elev. 1,446; Lat. 40-39-45 N long. 078-46-49 W; SW central Pennsylvania. *Thomas Barnes*, a coal mine operator, laid out the town in 1891 after first coal was discovered.

•**BARNESVILLE**, Village; Schuylkill County; Pop. 200; Zip Code 18214; Elev. 1,064; Lat. 40-48-52 N long. 076-01-52 W; E central Pennsylvania.

•**BARNSLEY**, Village; Chester County; Pop. 125; Zip Code 19363; Elev. 554; Lat. 39-45-56 N long. 075-59-21 W; near Oxford in SE Pennsylvania.

•**BARREE**, Village; Huntingdon County; Pop. 150; Zip Code 16615; Elev. 720; Lat. 40-35-07 N long. 078-06-03 W; S central Pennsylvania.

•**BARRVILLE**, Village; Mifflin County; Pop. 100; Zip Code 17084; Elev. 883; Lat. 40-39-47 N long. 077-40-37 W; in Stone Mountain range in central Pennsylvania.

•**BART**, Village and Township; Lancaster County; Pop. 250 (township, 1,838); Zip Code 17503; Elev. 678; 15 m. SE of Lancaster in SE Pennsylvania; named for the abbreviation of the title Baronet, for *Sir William Keith, Bart.*, provincial governor of PA (1717-26).

•**BARTO**, Village; Berks County; Pop. 70; Zip Code 19504; Elev. 460; Lat. 40-23-28 N long. 075-36-38 W; SE Pennsylvania.

•**BATH**, Borough; Northampton County; Pop. 1,952; Zip Code 18014; Lat. 40-43-32 N long. 075-23-40 W; E Pennsylvania.

•**BATH ADDITION**, Village; Bucks County; Pop. 800; Zip Code 19007; Lat. 40-06-27 N long. 074-51-56 W; SE Pennsylvania; suburb of Philadelphia included with Bristol.

•**BAUERSTOWN**, Village; Allegheny County; Pop. 2,700; Zip Code 15209; Lat. 40-29-45 Nlong. 079-58-36 W; W Pennsylvania; suburb of Pittsburgh.

•**BAUMSTOWN**, Village; Berks County; Pop. 400; Zip Code 19508; Elev. 206; Lat. 40-16-49 N long. 075-48-19 W; 48 m. NW of Philadelphia in SE central Pennsylvania.

•**BAUSMAN**, Village; Lancaster County; Pop. 450; Zip Code 17504; Lat. 40-01-27 Nlong. 076-19-52 W; SE Pennsylvania.

•**BAXTER**, Village; Jefferson County; Pop. 75; Zip Code 15829; Lat. 41-08-04 N long. 079-09--00W; W central Pennsylvania.

•**BEACH HAVEN**, Village; Luzerne County; Pop. 450; Zip Code 18601; Lat. 41-04-06 N long. 076-10-34 W; NE Pennsylvania.

•BEACH LAKE, Village; Wayne County; Pop. 240; Zip Code 18405; Elev. 1,300; Lat. 41-36-06 N long. 075-09-01 W; near Honesdale in NE Pennsylvania; resort town on Beach Lake.

•BEALSVILLE, Borough; Washington County; Pop. 588; Zip Code 15313; Elev. 1,136; Lat. 40-03-55 N long. 080-01-26 W; SW Pennsylvania.

•BEAR CREEK, Village and Township; Luzerne County; Pop. 200 (township, 2,450); Zip Code 18602; Elev. 1,670; Lat. 41-10-43 N long. 075-45-24 W; near Wilkes-Barre in NE Pennsylvania; on W bank of Bear Creek. Named for numerous bears in region when it was first settled.

•BEAR LAKE, Borough; Warren County; Pop. 249; Zip Code 16402; Elev. 1,550; Lat. 41-59-36 N long. 079-30-11 W; NW Pennsylvania.

•BEAR ROCKS, Village; Fayette County; Pop. 500; Zip Code 15610; Lat. 40-07-22 N long. 079-27-43 W; in Chestnut Ridge region in SW Pennsylvania.

•BEAR VALLEY, Village; Northumberland County; Pop. 100; Zip Code 17872; Lat. 40-46-21 N long. 076-34-40 W; near Shamokin in central Pennsylvania.

•BEARTOWN, Village; Franklin County; Pop. 165; Zip Code 17268; Lat. 39-44-42 N long. 077-30-04 W; S Pennsylvania.

•BEATTY, Village; Westmoreland County; Pop. 100; Zip Code 15650; Lat. 40-18-06 N long. 079-25-07 W; SW Pennsylvania.

•BEAVER, Borough; Seat of Beaver County; Pop. 5,441; Zip Code 15009; Elev. 723; Lat. 40-41-43 N long. 080-18-18 W; 25 m. NW of Pittsburgh in W Pennsylvania.

•BEAVER BROOK, Village; Luzerne County; Pop. 375; Zip Code 18201; Lat. 40-55-05 N long. 075-59-23 W; NE Pennsylvania; incorporated with Hazleton.

•BEAVERDALE, Village; Cambria County; Pop. 1,579; Zip Code 15921; Elev. 1,929; 80 m. W of Pittsburgh in W central Pennsylvania.

•BEAVER FALLS, City; Beaver County; Pop. 12,525; Zip Code 15010; Elev. 758; Lat. 40-45-07 N long. 080-19-10 W; 30 m. NW of Pittsburgh in W Pennsylvania; on W bank of Beaver River where it forms falls. Laid out in 1806, the town was called Brighton by the Constable brothers of Brighton, England. However, after New Brighton was founded, the name was changed to Beaver Falls in 1866 by members of the Harmony Society.

•BEAVER MEADOWS, Borough; Carbon County; Pop. 1,078; Zip Code 18216; Elev. 1,355; Lat. 40-55-41 N long. 075-54-45 W; near Hazleton in E Pennsylvania; named for nearby Beaver Creek.

•BEAVERSPRINGS, Village; Snyder County; Pop. 725; Zip Code 17812; Elev. 591; Lat. 40-44-46 N long. 077-12-35 W; near Beavertown in central Pennsylvania.

•BEAVERTOWN, Borough; Snyder County; Pop. 853; Zip Code 17813; Elev. 651; 8 m. W of Middleburg in central Pennsylvania; clothing is important industry; named for beaver colonies once numerous here.

•BECCARIA, Village and Township; Clearfield County; Pop. 200, (township, 1,877); Zip Code 16616; Lat. 40-46-12 N long. 078-26-54 W; Central Pennsylvania; named for Italian publicist and philosopher Cesare the Marquis of Beccaria (1735-94).

•BECHTELSVILLE, Borough; Berks County; Pop. 832; Zip Code 19505; Elev. 420; Lat. 40-22-24 N long. 075-37-46 W; SE Pennsylvania.

•BEDFORD, Borough; Seat of Bedford County; Pop. 3,326; Zip Code 15522; Elev. 1,060; Lat. 40-01-07 N long. 078-30-15 W; S Pennsylvania; was settled about 1750 and first named Raystown for a Scottish trader named John Wray who had a post here.

•BEDMINSTER, Village and Township; Bucks County; Pop. 350 (township, 3,252); Zip Code 18910; Elev. 440; Lat. 40-25-33 N long. 075-10-46 W; approx. 35 m. N of Philadelphia in SE Pennsylvania.

•BEECH CREEK, Borough; Clinton County; Pop. 760; Zip Code 16822; Elev. 617; Lat. 41-04-33 N long. 077-35-20 W; on E bank of Beech Creek in central Pennsylvania; near Lock Haven.

•BEERSVILLE, Village; Northampton County; Pop. 175; Zip Code 18067; Lat. 40-44-47 N long. 075-28-16 W; near Northampton in E Pennsylvania.

•BELFAST, Village; Northampton County; Pop. 275; Zip Code 18064; Elev. 520; Lat. 40-46-50 N long. 075-16-42 W; 10 m. NW of Easton in E Pennsylvania.

•BELFAST JUNCTION, Village; Northampton County; Pop. 100; Zip Code 18042; Lat. 40-46-04 N long. 075-16-22 W; near Belfast and incorporated with Easton.

•BELLA VISTA, Village; Lycoming County; Pop. 150; Zip Code 17754; Lat. 41-14-52 N long. 076-52-49 W; NE central Pennsylvania.

•BELLEFONTE, Borough; Seat of Centre County; Pop. 6,300; Zip Code 16823; Elev. 749; Lat. 40-54-48 N long. 077-46-43 W; Central Pennsylvania. Bellefonte (French, beautiful fountain), was surveyed in 1769 and settled shortly afterward, occupies seven hills at the southeastern base of Bald Eagle Mountain. The name is attributed, in story, to Talleyrand's exclamation of pleasure upon seeing the Big Spring here during his exile from France in 1794-5.

•BELLEGROVE, Village; Lebanon County; Pop. 300; Zip Code 17003; Lat. 40-22-01 N long. 076-32-57 W; SE central Pennsylvania.

•BELLEVUE, Borough; Allegheny County; Pop. 10,128; Zip Code 15202; Elev. 727; Lat. 40-29-38 N long. 080-03-07 W; SW Pennsylvania; suburb of Pittsburgh; on Ohio River. Name means "beautiful view" in French, given for the sight obtained from a nearby hill. In colonial times Bellevue was a Delaware Indian hunting ground under Chief Killbuck. White settlement began in 1802. Incorporated, 1867.

•BELMONT, Borough; Cambria County; Pop. 1,800; Zip Code 15904; Lat. 40-17-14 N long. 078-53-23 W; W central Pennsylvania; suburb of Johnstown.

•BELMONT HILLS, Borough; Bucks County; Pop. 1,300; Zip Code 19020; Lat. 40-02-03 N long. 075-15-29 W; unincorporated suburb of Philadelphia near Trevoze in SE Pennsylvania.

•BELMONT HOMES, Village; Cambria County; Pop. 350; Zip Code 15904; unincorporated suburb of Johnstown in W central Pennsylvania; residential.

•BELSANO, Village; Cambria County; Pop. 350; Zip Code 15922; Elev. 1,187; Lat. 40-31-10 N long. 078-52-17 W; 10 m. W of Ebensburg in S central Pennsylvania; founded in 1830 and named for a town in Italy.

•BEN AVON, Borough; Allegheny County; Pop. 2,134; Elev. 727; Lat. 40-30-29 N long. 080-05-00 W; suburb to NW of Pittsburgh in SW Pennsylvania; incorporated borough in 1891; name is Scottish for "hill by the waters."

•BEN AVON HEIGHTS, Borough; Allegheny County; Pop. 398; Lat. 40-30-49 N long. 080-04-24 W; SW Pennsylvania.

•BENDERSVILLE, Borough; Adams County; Pop. 533; Zip Code 17306; Elev. 740; Lat. 39-58-57 N long. 077-14-59 W; S Pennsylvania.

•BENEZETT, Village and Township; Elk County; Pop. 175 (township 353); Zip Code 15821; Elev. 1,020; Lat. 41-19-00 N long. 078-23-12 W; N central Pennsylvania; on the Trout Run and Bennett branch of the Sinnemahoning River.

•BENFER, Village; Snyder County; Pop. 75; Zip Code 17812; Elev. 607; Lat. 40-46-22 N long. 077-12-32 W; Central Pennsylvania.

•BENS CREEK, Village; Cambria and Somerset Counties; Pop. 500; Zip Code 15905;Lat. 40-16-57 N long. 078-56-12 W; S central Pennsylvania.

•BENTLEYCREEK, Village; Bradford County; Pop. 130; Zip Code 14894; Lat. 40-12-30 N long. 078-55-41 W; just S of New York state line in N Pennsylvania.

•BENTLEYVILLE, Borough; Washington County; Pop. 2,525; Zip Code 15314; Elev. 960; Lat. 40-07-00 N long. 080-00-31 W; approx. 25 m. S of Pittsburgh in SW Pennsylvania; named for *Sheshbazzar Bentley, Jr.*, who laid out the town in 1816.

•BENTON, Borough; Columbia County; Pop. 981; Zip Code 17814; Elev. 760; Lat. 41-11-42 N long. 076-23-02 W; 15 m. N of Bloomsburg in E central Pennsylvania; named in honor of *Col. Thomas H. Benton*, popular U.S. Senator from Missouri; incorporated in 1850.

•BERKELEY HILLS, Borough; Allegheny County; Pop. 3,700; Zip Code 15237; Lat. 40-31-54 N long. 080-00-14 W; unincorporated suburb of Pittsburgh in W Pennsylvania.

•BERKLEY, Village; Berks County; Pop. 200; Zip Code 19605; Lat. 40-25-45 N long. 075-56-05 W; suburb of Reading in SE Pennsylvania.

•BERLIN, Borough; Somerset County; Pop. 1,999; Zip Code 15530; Elev. 1,163; Lat. 39-55-14 N long. 078-57-29 W; 40 m. S of Johnstown in S Pennsylvania; on a ridge in Brothers Valley; named by Germans who settled here in 1769; coal mining and farming region.

•BERLINSVILLE, Village; Northampton County; Pop. 300; Zip Code 18088; Lat. 40-46-07 N long. 075-34-27 W; 15 m. NE of Bethlehem in E Pennsylvania.

•BERNE, Village; Berks County; Pop. 65; Zip Code 19506; Elev. 334; Lat. 40-31-26 N long. 076-00-07 W; SE Pennsylvania; settled in early 1700s by emigrants from the Berne region in Switzerland.

•BERRYSBURG, Borough; Dauphin County; Pop. 447; Zip Code 17005; Elev. 700; Lat. 40-36-07 N long. 076-48-44 W; SE central Pennsylvania.

•BERWICK, Borough; Columbia County; Pop. 12,189; Zip Code 18603; Elev. 505; Lat. 41-03-16 N long. 076-14-01 W; E central Pennsylvania. It is named for Berwick upon Tweed, an English town on the Scottish border.

•BERWINSDALE, Village; Clearfield County; Pop. 60; Zip Code 16656; Lat. 40-49-09 N long. 078-35-51 W; Central Pennsylvania.

•BERWYN, Borough; Chester County; Pop. 9,300; Zip Code 19312; Elev. 500; Lat. 40-02-41 N long. 075-26-21 W; residential suburb W of Philadelphia in SE Pennsylvania.

•BESCO, Village; Washington County; Pop. 100; Zip Code 15322; Lat. 39-59-06 N long. 080-01-26 W; SW Pennsylvania.

•BESSEMER, Borough; Lawrence County; Pop. 1,293; Zip Code 16112; Elev. 1,100; Lat. 40-23-40 N long. 079-51-16 W; 10 m. W of New Castle in W Pennsylvania; named for *Sir Henry Bessermer*, inventor of an economical process to make steel that revolutionized the industry.

•BETHANY, Borough; Wayne County; Pop. 282; Elev. 1,070; Lat. 41-36-47 N long. 075-17-05 W; near Honesdale in NE Pennsylvania.

•BETHEL, Village and Township; Berks County; Pop. 600 (township, 2,600); Zip Code 19501; Elev. 525; 40 m. E of Harrisburg in SE Pennsylvania.

•BETHEL PARK, Borough; Allegheny County; Pop. 34,755; Zip Code 15102; Elev. 1,200; SW Pennsylvania; suburb of Pittsburgh.

•BETHLEHEM, City; Lehigh and Northampton Counties; Pop. 70,419; Zip Code 180 + zone; Elev. 237; Lat. 40-51-42 N long. 078-43-50 W; borders on Allentown in E Pennsylvania; on the Lehigh River. Founded in 1741 by the Moravian Brethren, Bethlehem was named on Christmas Eve that year when the congregation and their leader, *Count Nicholas Ludwig*, sang an old German hym meaning "Bethlehem gave us that which makes life rich."

•BEVERLY ESTATES, Borough; Lancaster County; Pop. 500; Zip Code 17601; Lat. 40-04-27 N long. 076-18-08 W; suburb of Lancaster in SE central Pennsylvania.

•BEVERLY HEIGHTS, Village; Lebanon County; Pop. 100; Zip Code 17042; Lat. 40-24-21 N long. 076-28-30 W; SE central Pennsylvania.

•BEYER, Village; Indiana County; Pop. 180; Zip Code 16211; Elev. 1,200; Lat. 40-47-11 N long. 079-12-05 W; W central Pennsylvania.

•BIESECKER GAP, Village; Franklin County; Pop. 150; Zip Code 17268; Lat. 39-47-15 N long. 077-32-03 W; S Pennsylvania.

•BIGLERVILLE, Borough; Adams County; Pop. 991; Zip Code 17307; Elev. 649; Lat. 39-55-49 N long. 077-14-54 W; 7 m. N of Gettysburg in S Pennsylvania; surveyed in 1817, the town is the center of a fruit growing region.

•BIG RUN, Borough; Jefferson County; Pop. 822; Zip Code 15715; Elev. 1,286; Lat. 41-04-53 N long. 077-40-05 W; 7 m. N of Punxsutawney in W central Pennsylvania; founded in 1822 and named for a stream that flows into Stump Creek here; coal mining and farming area.

•BINGEN, Village; Northampton County; Pop. 250; Zip Code 18015; near Bethlehem in E Pennsylvania; named for Bingen region in Germany.

•BIRCHRUNVILLE, Village; Chester County; Pop. 300; Zip Code 19321; Elev. 390; Lat. 40-07-46 N long. 075-38-17 W; SE Pennsylvania.

•BIRD IN HAND, Village; Lancaster County; Pop. 700; Zip Code 17505; Elev. 355; Lat. 40-02-19 N long. 076-10-57 W; 0 m. SW of Reading in SE Pennsylvania; named for an early inn that displayed a sign reading "a bird in the hand is worth two in the bush;" Tavern was rebuilt three times over original 18th century site.

•BIRDSBORO, Borough; Berks County; Pop. 3,481; Zip Code 19508; Elev. 190; Lat. 40-15-52 N long. 075-48-16 W; 11 m. W of Pottstown in SE Pennsylvania; on Schuylkill River; founded in 1740; named for ironmaster *William Bird*.

•BISHOP, Village; Washington County; Pop. 400; Zip Code 15057; Elev. 970; Lat. 40-19-14 N long. 080-11-14 W; 20 m. SW of Pittsburgh in SW Pennsylvania.

•BLACK HORSE, Village; Montgomery County; Pop. 370; Zip Code 19401; Elev. 704; Lat. 89-59-08 N long. 075-57-19 W; -suburb of Norristown in SE Pennsylvania.

•BLACK LICK, Village; Indiana County; Pop. 1,074; Zip Code 15716; Elev. 967;Lat. 40-28-45 N long. 079-12-00 W; near Blainsville on Conemaugh River Reservoir in W central Pennsylvania. Settled in 1807 and laid out in 1860, this town was named for a nearby coal-black creek, which once contained a salt lick.

•BLAIN, Borough; Perry County; Pop. 274; Zip Code 17006; Elev. 720; Lat. 40-20-18 N long. 077-30-46 W; 40 m. W of Harrisburg in S central Pennsylvania; on Sherman Creek.

•BLAINE HILL, Village; Allegheny County; Pop. 1,300; Zip Code 15037; Lat. 40-16-25 N long. 079-52-31 W; SE suburb of Pittsburgh in W Pennsylvania.

•BLAIRSVILLE, Borough; Indiana County; Pop. 4,166; Zip Code 15717; Elev. 1,012; Lat. 40-25-52 N long. 079-15-40W; W central Pennsylvania. Located on the Conemaugh River, Blairsville was settled in 1792 and named for Captain John Blair, of Blair's Gap, who was among the first promoters of the turnpike and canal-portage system.

•BLAKELY, Borough; Lackawana County; Pop. 7,438; Zip Code 18447; Elev. 872; Lat. 41-28-51 N long. 075-35-42 W; NE Pennsylvania; suburb of Scranton; on Lackawana River; named for Captain Johnston Blakely, naval commander during the War of 1812.

•BLANCHARD, Village; Centre County; Pop. 750; Zip Code 16826; Elev. 650; Lat. 40-39-26 N long. 079-49-43 W; Central Pennsylvania.

•BLANDBURG, Village; Cambria County; Pop. 775; Zip Code 16619; Elev. 2,047; Lat. 40-41-13 N long. 078-24-40 W; in Allegheny Mountain Range in W central Pennsylvania.

•BLANDON, Village; Berks County; Pop. 1,113; Zip Code 19510; Elev. 400; Lat. 40-26-28 N long. 075-53-14 W; suburb of Reading in SE central Pennsylvania.

•BLOOMFIELD, Borough; Seat of Perry County; Pop. 1,109; Zip Code 152 + zone; Lat. 40-27-39 N long. 079-57-04 W; S central Pennsylvania.

•BLOOMINGDALE, Village; Lancaster County; Pop. 1,200; Zip Code 17601; Lat. 40-49-29 Nlong. 075-51-02 W; suburb of Lancaster of SE Pennsylvania.

•BLOOMSBURG, Town; Seat of Columbia County; Pop. 11,717; Zip Code 17815; Elev. 482; Lat. 40-25-46 N long. 076-00-49 W; E central Pennsylvania. It lies at the foot of Spectator Bluff, and on Fishing Creek. Ludwig Eyer laid it out in 1802, and the name was chosen in honor of Samuel Bloom, who had been a county commissioner when the old Bloom Township was organized in 1797.

•BLOSSBURG, Borough; Tioga County; Pop. 1,757; Zip Code 16912; Elev. 1,348; Lat. 41-40-46 N long. 077-03-51 W; N Pennsylvania. First known as Peters Camp; Renamed for Aaron Bloss, who opened a tavern here in 1802.

•BLOSSOM HILL, Village; Lancaster County; Pop. 1,300; Zip Code 17601; Lat. 39-44-45 Nlong. 079-53-50 W; suburb of Lancaster in SE Pennsylvania.

•BLUE BALL, Village; Lancaster County; Pop. 700; Zip Code 17506; Elev. 469; Lat. 40-07-07 N long. 076-02-51 W; 45 m. W of Chester in SE Pennsylvania; founded in 1766 by Robert Wallace who opened an inn and tavern here called the "Blue Ball," which was a favorite stopping place for marketing farmers.

•BLUE BELL, Village; Montgomery County; Pop. 1,600; Zip Code 19422; Elev. 360; Lat. 40-09-08 N long. 075-16-00 W; northern suburb of Philadelphia in SE Pennsylvania.

•BOALSBURG, Village; Centre County; Pop. 950; Zip Code 16827; Elev. 1,100; Lat. 40-46-32 N long. 077-47-34 W; near State College in central Pennsylvania. Laid out in 1810, this village was named for Capt. David Boal, a native Irishman who settled here in 1798.

•BOBTOWN, Village; Greene County; Pop. 1,055; Zip Code 15315; Lat. 39-45-40 N long. 079-58-54 W; near Dunkard Creek in SW Pennsylvania.

•BOILING SPRINGS, Village; Cumberland County; Pop. 1,521; Zip Code 17007; Lat. 40-08-59 N long. 077-07-43 W; 15 m. SW of Harrisburg; rural.

•BOOTHWYN, Borough; Delaware County; Pop. 7,100; Zip Code 19061; Elev. 100;Lat. 39-49-48 N long. 075-26-31 W; suburb of Philadelphia in SE Pennsylvania; residential.

•BOSTON, Borough; Allegheny County; Pop. 1,200; Zip Code 15135; Elev. 760; Lat. 40-18-43 N long. 079-49-24 W suburb of Pittsburgh to SE.

•BOSWELL, Borough; Somerset County; Pop. 1,480; Zip Code 15531; Lat. 40-09-41 N long. 079-01-45 W; S Pennsylvania.

•BOWMANSTOWN, Borough; Carbon County; Pop. 1,078; Zip Code 18030; Elev. 437; E Pennsylvania. Founded in 1796. It occupies the flat center of a large mountain-rimmed bowl.

•BOYERS, Village; Butler County; Pop. 300; Zip Code 16020; Elev. 1,200; Lat. 41-06-30 N long. 079-53-57 W; W Pennsylvania.

•BOYERTOWN, Borough; Berks County; Pop. 4,428; Zip Code 19512; Elev. 386; Lat. 40-20-01 N long. 075-38-16 W; 25 m. S of Allentown in SE central Pennsylvania. First settled in 1720 and founded in 1834, this town was named for Henry Boyer, early settler.

•BRACKENRIDGE, Borough; Allegheny County; Pop. 4,297; Zip Code 15014; Elev. 757; Lat. 40-36-29 N long. 079-44-29 W; N suburb of Pittsburgh in SW Pennsylvania; named for Brackenridge family, prominent in the area during the nineteenth century; incorporated as a borough, 1901.

•BRADDOCK, Borough; Allegheny County; Pop. 5,634; Zip Code 15104; Elev. 700; Lat. 40-24-12 N long. 079-52-07 W; 10 m. E of Pittsburgh in SW Pennsylvania; incorporated as a borough, 1867 and named for Gen. Edward Braddock who was fatally wounded nearby in a battle with the French and Indians in 1755; an important steel and coal manufacturing center around the turn of the century.

•BRADENVILLE, Village; Westmoreland County; Pop. 1,200; Zip Code 15620; Elev. 1,100; Lat. 40-19-17 N long. 079-20-25 W; near Latrobe in W central Pennsylvania.

•BRADFORD, City; McKean County; Pop. 11,211; Zip Code 16701; Elev. 1,443; Lat. 41-57-21 N long. 078-38-39 W; 4 m. S of New York state line in N Pennsylvania. First known as Littleton, for the county's first landowner *Col. L.C. Little* of Boston, the name was changed to honor *William Bradford* when *Daniel Kingsbury* purchased the land in 1850.

•**BRADFORD HILLS**, Village; Chester County; Pop. 300; Zip Code 19335; Lat. 40-00-11 N long. 075-38-54 W; suburb of Philadelphia in SE Pennsylvania.

•**BRENTWOOD**, Borough; Allegheny County; Pop. 11,907; Zip Code 15227; Elev. 884; Lat. 40-22-14 N long. 079-58-30 W; SW Pennsylvania. It was incorporated in 1915 with the merger of the villages of Brentwood, Whitehall, and Point View.

•**BRIAR CREEK**, Borough; Columbia County; Pop. 637; Lat. 41-02-45 N long. 076-16-57 W; E central Pennsylvania.

•**BRIDGEPORT**, Borough; Montgomery County; Pop. 4,843; Zip Code 19405; Lat. 39-55-56 N long. 077-18-43 W; SE Pennsylvania.

•**BRIDGEVILLE**, Borough; Allegheny County; Pop. 6,154; Zip Code 15017; Lat. 40-21-22 N long. 080-06-37 W; SW Pennsylvania.

•**BRIDGEWATER**, Borough; Beaver County; Pop. 879; Elev. 710; W Pennsylvania.

Bridgewater, across the Beaver River from Rochester, was consolidated with Sharon in 1868, 70 years after *Major Robert Darragh* erected the first building and opened the first store.

•**BRISTOL**, Borough; Bucks County; Pop. 10,867; Zip Code 19007; Elev. 21; Lat. 40-06-02 N long. 074-51-08 W; 20 m. NE of Philadelphia in SE PA, on the Delaware River. First settled in 1697 and designated as Bucks County Seat in 1705. Named for the western seaport in England, where some of *William Penn's* ancestors lived.

•**BROCKTON**, Village; Schuylkill County; Pop. 550; Zip Code 17925; Elev. 700; Lat. 40-44-54 N long. 076-04-08 W; 10 m. N of Pottsville in E central Pennsylvania.

•**BROCKWAY**, Borough; Jefferson County; Pop. 2,376; Zip Code 15824; Elev. 1,445; Lat. 41-14-57 N long. 078-47-59 W; W central Pennsylvania. First settled in 1822 by *Alonzo and Chauncey Brockway*, they named the town for themselves 14 years later.

•**BRODHEADSVILLE**, Village; Monroe County; Pop. 500; Zip Code 18322; Elev. 675; Lat. 40-55-28 N long. 075-23-39 W; 20 m. NW of Easton in E Pennsylvania; near Weir Mountain range, near ski resorts; named for *David Brodhead*, who established a Moravian mission nearby in 11739.

•**BROOKHAVEN**, Borough; Delaware County; Pop. 7,912; Zip Code 19015; Elev. 119; Lat. 39-52-09 N long. 075-22-58 W; SE Pennsylvania.

•**BROOKSIDE**, Borough; Erie County; Pop. 1,800; Zip Code 16510; Lat. 40-19-55 N long. 080-03-20 W; 2 m. W of Lake Erie shore and the city of Erie in NW Pennsylvania; residential.

•**BROOKVILLE**, Borough; Seat of Jefferson County; Pop. 4,568; Zip Code 15825; Elev. 1,269; Lat. 41-09-40 N long. 079-05-00 W; approx. 80 m. NW of Pittsburgh in W central Pennsylvania; on Red Bank Creek and three of its tributaries. First settled in 1801, but not laid out and named until 1830, when it became the county seat and was christened for the various brooks flowing in and around town.

•**BROOMALL**, Borough; Delaware County; Pop. 25,040; Zip Code 19008; Elev. 350; Lat. 39-58-53 N long. 075-21-25 W; 15 m. NW of Philadelphia in SE Pennsylvania; residential; incorporated as the township of Marple.

•**BROWNSTOWN**, Village; Lancaster County; Pop. 800; Zip Code 17508; Elev. 320; Lat. 40-32-54 N long. 079-30-48 W; NE suburb of Lancaster in S Pennsylvania; near airport.

•**BROWNSVILLE**, Borough; Fayette County; Pop. 4,043; Zip Code 15417; Elev. 900; Lat. 40-22-01 N long. 076-04-35 W; SW Pennsylvania. Combined with South Brownsville borough since 1933.

•**BRUNNERVILLE**, Village; Lancaster County; Pop. 300; Zip Code 17543; Elev. 520; Lat. 40-11-05 N long. 076-17-06 W; near Lititz in S Pennsylvania; site of a Ephrata Cloister.

•**BRYN GWELED**, Village; Bucks County; Pop. 500; Zip Code 18966; N of Philadelphia and near Southampton in SE Pennsylvania; residential suburb.

•**BRYN MAWR**, Unincorporated town; Montgomery and Delaware Counties; Pop. 9,500 (including college); Zip Code 19010; Elev. 413; Lat. 40-18-14 N long. 080-05-13 W; NW suburb of Philadelphia in SE Pennsylvania. Name means "great hill" in Welsh.

•**BUCK HILL FALLS**, Village; Monroe County; Pop. 400; Zip Code 18323; Elev. 1,360; Lat. 41-11-16 N long. 075-15-58 W; 32 m. SE of Scranton in E Pennsylvania; in Pocono Mountains and named for the natural falls nearby; resort and skiing area.

•**BUCKINGHAM**, Village and Township; Bucks County; Pop. 500; Zip Code 18912; Elev. 217; Lat. 40-19-25 N long. 075-03-37 W; N suburb of Philadelphia in SE Pennsylvania; founded in 1702.

•**BULLY HILL**, Village; Venango County; Pop. 60; Zip Code 16323; Lat. 41-22-08 N long. 079-49-35 W; Just S of Franklin in NW Pennsylvania; site of Venango County Museum.

•**BURGETTSTOWN**, Borough; Washington County; Pop. 1,867; Zip Code 15021; Elev. 989; Lat. 40-22-55 N long. 080-23-35 W; 20 m. W of Pittsburgh in SW Pennsylvania; named for Fort Burgett, which was erected here during the Revolutionary War by Sebastian Burgett, a native of Germany. His son, *George Burgett*, laid out the town in 1795.

•**BURNHAM**, Borough; Mifflin County; Pop. 2,457; Zip Code 17009; Elev. 520; Lat. 40-38-19 N long. 077-34-08 W; Central Pennsylvania. First known as Freedom Forge, and later as Logan, the town was renamed in 1911 for *William Burnham*, official of a local steel plant.

•**BURNT CABINS**, Village; Fulton County; Pop. 125; Zip Code 17215; Elev. 900'.Lat. 40-04-41 N long. 077-53-45 W; Burnt Cabins is at the foot of Cove Mountain, was so named because the cabins of early squatters here were burned down by order of the provincial government after the Indians had complained against white encroachment on their lands.

•**BUSHKILL**, Pop. 500 (summer 1,000); Elev. 641; Lat. 41-05-36 N long. 075-00-08 W; name means "little river" in Dutch; was settled in 1812.

•**BUSHKILL CENTER**, Village; Northampton County; Pop. 135; Zip Code 18064; Elev. 695; Lat. 40-47-37 N long. 075-19-30 W; E central Pennsylvania; named for the creek that flows nearby.

•**BUTLER**, City; Seat of Butler County; Pop. 17,026; Zip Code 16001; Elev. 1,011; Lat. 40-51-40 N long. 079-53-44 W; 33 m. N of Pittsburgh in W Pennsylvania. Built on rolling hills originally owned by *Robert Morris* of Philadelphia, financier of the American Revolution, was laid out in 1803, and named for *Richard Butler* of York County, a lieutenant colonel with Morgan's Rifles in 1777, an Indian agent in Ohio in 1787, and a major general in the St. Clair expedition of 1791, in which he was killed. The city is bisected by Conoquenessing Creek.

•**CABOT**, Village; Butler County; Pop. 400; Zip Code 16023; Elev. 1,200; Lat. 40-45-53 N long. 079-46-00 W; on Penn Central rail line SE of Butler.

•**CAIRNBROOK**, Village; Somerset County; Pop. 800; Zip Code 15924; Elev. 2,200; Lat. 40-07-08 N long. 078-49-06 W; on Shade Creek and Penn Central rail line from Johnstown, approx. 20 m. N.

•**CALIFORNIA**, Borough; Washington County; Pop. 5,703; Zip Code 15419; Elev. 800; Lat. 40-28-32 N long. 075-20-51 W; 40 m. S of Pittsburgh in SW Pennsylvania; annexed to E Pike Run Township in 1954; site of California State College. It was laid out in 1849, shortly after the discovery of gold in California, when this alluring name was in everyone's mouth.

•**CALUMET**, Village; Westmoreland County; Pop. 800; Zip Code 15621; Elev. 1,080; Lat. 40-12-39 N long. 079-29-08 W; E suburb of Pittsburgh in W central Pennsylvania.

•**CAMBELLTOWN**, Village; Lebanon County; Pop. 1,355; Zip Code 17010; Elev. 440; Lat. 40-16-39 N long. 076-35-08 W; 20 m. E of Harrisburg and near Hershey in SE central Pennsylvania.

•**CAMBRIA HEIGHTS**, Village; Cambria County; Pop. 500; Zip Code 15906; in the hills near Johnstown in S Pennsylvania; name is derived from the old poetic word for Wales, "Cymry."

•**CAMERON**, Village; Cameron County; Pop. 75; Zip Code 15834; Elev. 960; once a thriving lumbering and mining town. The village and the county were named for *Simon Cameron* (1799-1889) of Lancaster County, who controlled the Republican Party in Pennsylvania for more than three decades. He was the first Secretary of War under *Lincoln* and several times a member of the United States Senate.

•**CAMBRIDGE SPRINGS**, Borough; Crawford County; Pop. 2,102; Zip Code 16403; Elev. 1,181; Lat. 41-48-13 N long. 080-03-24 w; NW Pennsylvania. It is on French Creek. *Dr. John H. Gray* found a mineral spring here in 1884 while prospecting for oil.

•**CANONSBURG**, Borough; Washington County; Pop. 10,459; Zip Code 15317; Elev. 931; Lat. 40-15-45 N long. 080-11-15 W; 17 m. SW of Pittsburgh in SW Pennsylvania. It was settled about 1773 and laid out in 1787 by *Colonel John Canon*, militia officer and member of the State assembly.

•**CANTON**, Borough; Bradford County; Pop. 1,959; Zip Code 17724; Elev. 1,255; Lat. 41-39-23 N long. 076-51-13 W; 30 m. NE of Williamsport in N Pennsylvania. It was founded in 1800 and named for the Connecticut town by early settlers.

•**CARBONDALE**, City; Lackawanna County; Pop. 11,255; Zip Code 18407; Elev. 1,078; Lat. 41-34-25 N long. 075-30-08 W; on Lackawanna River, 16 m. NE of Scranton in NE Pennsylvania. It had been an anthracite town since 1814, when *William Wurts*, a Philadelphia merchant, owner of large tracts in the vicinity, and *David Nobles*, a hunter who knew the region, opened veins and obtained coal for exhibition and appraisal in New York and Philadelphia.

•**CARLISLE**, Borough; Seat of Cumberland County; Pop. 18,314; Zip Code 17013; Elev. 478; Lat. 40-12-05 N long. 077-11-21 W; 15 m. W of Harrisburg in S Pennsylvania. *Molly Pritcher*, the famous Revolutionary War fighter and nurse, died and was buried here. The Carlisle Barracks (Civil War), have been preserved nearby.

•**CARNEGIE**, Borough; Allegheny County; Pop. 10,099; Zip Code 15106; Elev. 769; Lat. 40-24-31 N long. 080-05-01 W; 6 m. W of Pittsburgh in SW Pennsylvania. The community was named for *Andrew Carnegie*.

•**CARNOT**, Village; Allegheny County; Pop. 4,000; Zip Code 15108; Lat. 40-31-10 N long. 080-13-18 W; NW suburb of Pittsburgh in SW Pennsylvania; near Coraopolis in a hilly area.

•**CARROLLTOWN**, Borough; Cambria County; Pop. 1,395; Zip Code 15722; Elev. 2,140; Lat. 40-36-10 N long. 078-42-32 W; SW central Pennsylvania. It was laid out in 1840, was named by *Prince Demetrius Gallitzin* for *John Carroll* who, in 1788, became the first Roman Catholic Bishop in the United States and 20 years later was Archbishop of Baltimore. His cousin, *Charles Caroll*, signed the Declaration of Independence, and later resided here.

•**CASHTOWN**, Village; Adams County; Pop. 250; Zip Code 17310; Elev. 745; Lat. 39-53-04 N long. 077-21-35 W; 8 m. W of Gettysburg in S Pennsylvania. It is said to have been named for an early tavernkeeper's insistence that all patrons pay cash. An old tavern, possibly the legendary one, stands here, built in 1797. Nearby is the Conewago Mission, one of the first Jesuit outposts when it was built in 1817.

•**CASSVILLE**, Borough; Huntingdon County; Pop. 183; Zip Code 16623; Elev. 1,241; Lat. 40-17-35 N long. 078-01-38 W; S central Pennsylvania. Named for Cass Township, which was named in 1843 for the statesman, *Lewis Cass* shortly after the public welcome he had received in Philadelphia upon his return from France, where he had served as United States ambassador.

•**CASTLE SHANNON**, Borough; Allegheny County; Pop. 10,164; Zip Code 15234; Elev. 1,040; Lat. 40-21-53 N long. 080-01-21 W; 8 m. S of Pittsburgh in SW Pennsylvania; on Saw Mill Run; suburban area.

•**CATASAUQUA**, Borough; Lehigh County; Pop. 7,944; Zip Code 18032; Elev. 320; Lat. 40-39-17 N long. 075-28-30 W; on Lehigh River, N of Allentown in E Pennsylvania. Site of Allentown-Bethlehem-Easton Airport. In 1853 the growing town was incorporated as Catasauqua, for the creek flowing nearby, a name corrupted from the Delaware Indian phrase *gotto-shacki*, "burnt ground", "parched land," or "the earth thirsts".

•**CATAWISSA**, Borough; Columbia County; Pop. 1,568; Zip Code 17820; Lat. 40-57-07 N long. 076-27-36 W; E central Pennsylvania; on Susquehanna River near a group of "growing fat." The Indian hunters may have killed a deer along the stream in the season when deer fatten. Catawissa was laid out in 1787 by *William Hughes*, a Berks County Quaker.

•**CENTERPORT,** Borough; Berks County; Pop. 246; Zip Code 19516; Elev. 340; Lat. 40-29-14 N, long. 076-00-17 W. NW of Reading, on Irish Creek.

•**CENTERVILLE**, Borough; Crawford County; Pop. 245; Zip Code 16404; Lat. 41-44-28 N, long. 079-45-42 W. Near Oil Creek in a farming area.

•**CENTERVILLE**, Borough; Washington County; Pop. 4,207; Zip Code 15301; Elev. 1,160; Lat. 40-10-53 N, long. 080-15-52 W. First settled in 1766, Centerville was laid out in 1821 as a pike town and was named for its position between Uniontown and Washington.

•**CENTRAL CITY,** Borough; Somerset County; Pop. 1,496; Zip Code 15926; Lat. 40-05-11 N, long. 078-50-15 W. Terminal of the Penn Central rail line is here.

•**CENTRALIA**, Borough; Columbia County; Pop. 1,017; Zip Code 17927; Elev. 1,484; Lat. 40-48-17 N, long. 076-20-32 W. Founded in 1826 and named for its then strategic commercial situation.

•**CENTRE HALL**, Borough; Centre County; Pop. 1,233; Pop. 814; Zip Code 16828; Elev. 1,320; Lat. 40-50-51 Nlong. 077-41-11 w; Central Pennsylvania. Named for its central position in Penn's Valley, one of the state's finest hunting and fishing sections.

•CHADDS FORD, Village; Delaware County; Pop. 250; Zip Code 19317; Elev. 168; Lat. 39-52-18 Nlong. 075-35-30 W; SE Pennsylvania. Named for *John Chadds*, son of *Francis Chadds*, or *Chadsey*, who emigrated from Wiltshire in 1689, and settled on a tract that included all the present village of Chadds Ford.

•CHALFANT, Borough; Allegheny County; Pop. 1,119. Eastern suburb of Pittsburg in a low density residential area.

•CHALFONT, Borough; Bucks County; Pop. 2,802; Zip Code 18914; Elev. 225; Lat. 40-24-31 N long. 079-50-21 W; SE Pennsylvania. Chalfont, originally Butlers Mill, was renamed for *Chalfont St. Giles*, an English parish where *William Penn* is buried.

•CHAMBERSBURG, Borough; Seat of Franklin County; Pop. 16,174; Zip Code 17201; Elev. 620; Lat. 39-56-15 N long. 077-39-41 W; 50 m. SW of Harrisburg in S Pennsylvania. *Benjamin Chambers* settled on this tract as miller, sawyer, trader, physician, militia colonel, judge, and arbitrator and the town was formally laid out in 1764.

•CHARLEROI, Borough; Washington County; Pop. 5,717; Zip Code 15022; Elev. 761; Lat. 40-08-16 N long. 079-53-54 W; m. S of Pittsburgh in SW Pennsylvania. It is the trading center of this glass manufacturing region. It was laid out in 1890 as the site of a large glass plant, and named Charleroi for an industrial town of that name in Belgium.

•CHATHAM, Village; Chester County; Pop. 300; Zip Code 19318; Elev. 400; Lat. 39-51-12 N long. 075-49-19 W; suburb of Philadelphia in SE Pennsylvania; named for the English statesman *William Pitt*, the Earl of Chatham.

•CHELTENHAM, Village; Montgomery County; Pop. 6,500; Zip Code 19012; Elev. 130; Lat. 40-03-39 N long. 075-05-40 W; N suburb of Philadelphia in SE Pennsylvania; seat of a large township by the same name.

•CHERRY CITY, Village (uninc.); Allegheny County; Pop. 4,000; Zip Code 15223; Lat. 40-29-41 N long. 079-57-47 W; NE suburb of Pittsburgh that grew substantially after World War II; on the Allegheny River.

•CHERRY TREE, Borough; Indiana County; Pop. 520; Zip Code 15724; Elev. 1,365; Lat. 40-43-35 N long. 078-48-25 W; W central Pennsylvania. Known to the Indians as Canoe Place, it was renamed for the cherry tree that was used to determine one of the boundaries of the territory conveyed to the Pennsylvania Proprietaries by the Fort Stanwix Treaty of 1768.

•CHESTER, City; Delaware County seat; Pop. 45,705; Zip Code 19013; Elev. 23: Lat. 39-50-58 N long. 075-21-22 W; 15 m. SW of Philadelphia on the Delaware River. It is the second oldest settlement in Pennsylvania. The city, center of an industrial area and the second port of PA, was named by *William Penn* allegedly in honor of *Lord Chester*.

•CHESTER HEIGHTS, Borough; Delaware County; Pop. 1,302; Zip Code 19017; Elev. 340: Lat. 39-53-24 N long. 075-28-33 W; SE Pennsylvania.

•CHESTER HILL, Borough; Clearfield County; Pop. 1,054; Zip Code 16866; Elev. 1,440: Lat. 40-53-23 N long. 078-13-43 W; on the Moshannon Creek near Phillipsburg in W Pennsylvania.

•CHESWICK, Borough; Allegheny County; Pop. 2,336; Zip Code 15024; Lat. 40-32-30 N long. 079-47-58 W; 12 m. NE of Pittsburgh in an industrial-mining area in SW Pennsylvania; on Allegheny River.

•CHICORA, Borough; Butler County; Pop. 1,192; Zip Code 16025; Elev. 1,247; Lat. 40-56-53 N long. 079-44-35 W; 10 m. NE of Butler

in W Pennsylvania; on B&O Railroad line; name was changed from Millerstown in 1956.

•CHRISTIANA, Borough; Lancaster County; Pop. 1,183; Zip Code 17509; Elev. 494: Lat. 39-57-17 N long. 075-59-50 W; SE Pennsylvania. Christiana was not named, as has often been asserted, for *King Christian* and *Queen Christiana* of Sweden, but for *Christiana*, the first wife of *William Noble*, who built the first house and started a machine-shop here in 1833.

•CHURCHILL, Borough; Allegheny County; Pop. 4,285; Zip Code 15221; Elev. 1,100: Lat. 40-26-18 N long. 079-50-36 W; E suburb of Pittsburgh in SW Pennsylvania.

•CHURCHVILLE, Village; Bucks County; Pop. 2,600; Zip Code 18966; Lat. 40-09-53 N long. 078-30-45 W; near Southampton in SE Pennsylvania; N suburb of Philadelphia.

•CLAIRTON, City; Allegheny County; Pop. 12,188; Zip Code 15025; Elev. 960: Lat. 40-17-32 N long. 079-52-55 W; SW Pennsylvania. The origin of the city's name is not certain. One can be fairly sure the the name Clairton has been made by adding the locative suffix ton ("town") to *Clair* ("clear, bright, or illustrious"), the second syllable of the surname St. Clair or its variant form, Sinclair. The current traditional explanation is that the name Clairton is derived from the name of *Samuel Sinclair*, who once owned a tract of 215 acres of land on which part of the present city is built.

•CLARION, Borough; Seat of Clarion County; Pop. 6,664; Zip Code 16214; Elev. 1,491: Lat. 41-12-53 N long. 079-23-08 W; 28 m. SE of Oil City in W Pennsylvania.

•CLARKS SUMMIT, Borough; Lackawanna County; Pop. 5,272; Zip Code 18411; Elev. 1,240: Lat. 41-29-19 N long. 075-42-32 W; 5 m. NW of Scranton in NE Pennsylvania; residential. Clark's Summit has strong ties with Clarks Green, the adjacent borough. Both were named for *Deacon William Clark* who in 1799 cleared the triangular "Green"; the "Summit" was the peak of a grade on the Legett's Gap Railroad, northern division of the Lackawanna and Western.

•CLAYSBURG, Village (uninc.); Blair County; Pop. 1,516; Zip Code 16625; Elev. 1,148'.Lat. 40-17-48 N long. 078-27-00 W; Claysburg is a narrow town set on a mountainside, and threaded by the Frankstown branch of the Juniata River; the town was founded in 1804 by *John Ulrich Zeth*.

•CLAYSVILLE, Borough; Washington County; Pop. 1,029; Zip Code 15323; Elev. 1,001: 38 m. SW of Pittsburgh in SW Pennsylvania. It was named by its founder for *Henry Clay*, probably because he championed both the National Highway and a protective tariff on coal, once the comunity's chief support.

•CLEARFIELD, Borough; Seat of Clearfield County; Pop. 7,580; Zip Code 16830; Elev. 1,112: Lat. 41-01-38 N long. 078-26-22 W; 50 m. N of Altoona in W central Pennsylvania. It is named for nearby Clearfield Creek, so called because buffalo are supposed to have cleared the undergrowth from large tracts along the creek "so as to give them the appearance of cleared fields."

•CLEARVIEW, Village; Lancaster County; Pop. 1,200; Zip Code 17601; 2 m. N of Lancaster in SE central Pennsylvania; residential.

•CLEONA, Borough; Lebanon County; Pop. 2,003; Zip Code 17042; Elev. 460: Lat. 40-20-14 N long. 076-28-33 W; just W of Lebanon in SE central Pennsylvania; residential.

•CLIFFORD, Village; Susquehanna County; Pop. 350; Zip Code 18413; Elev. 1,080: Lat. 41-38-56 N long. 075-35-57 W; NE Pennsylvania; a crossroads town on the East Branch of Tunkhannock Creek, settled in 1800 by *Adam Miller.*

•CLIFTON HEIGHTS, Borough; Delaware County; Pop. 7,320; Zip Code 19018; Elev. 109: Lat. 39-55-45 N long. 075-17-48 W; SE Pennsylvania; settled in the last decade of the eighteenth century and incorporated as a borough in 1885.

•CLYMER, Borough; Indiana County; Pop. 1,761; Zip Code 15728; Elev. 1,218: Lat. 40-40-05 N long. 079-00-43 W; 10 m. NE of Indiana in W central Pennsylvania; on Two Lick Creek. Clymer was laid out in 1905 by the Dixon Run Land Company, which chose this name in honor of *George Clymer,* a PA signer of the Declaration of Independence and one of the framers of the Constitution of the United States.

•COALDALE, Borough; Schuylkill County; Pop. 2,762; Zip Code 18218; Elev. 1,040: 15 m. SE of Hazleton in E central Pennsylvania; on Highway 209. Incorporated in 1906, it owes its existence and its name to a dale containing rich deposits of anthracite coal.

•COATESVILLE, City; Chester County; Pop. 10,698; Zip Code 19320; Elev. 381: 38 m. W of Philadelphia in SE Pennsylvania. It became a post-office in 1812; and its first postmaster was *Moses Coates,* who owned a large tract of land now occupied by the town.

•COCHRANTON, Borough; Crawford; County; Pop. 1,240; Zip Code 16314; Elev. 582:Lat. 41-31-12 N long. 080-02-55 W; approx. 10 m. SE of Meadville in NW Pennsylvania; on French Creek; residential.

•COLLEGEVILLE, Borough; Montgomery County; Pop. 3,406; Zip Code 19426; Elev. 200: Lat. 40-11-08 N long. 075-27-07 W; 20 m. NW of Philadelphia in SE Pennsylvania. Originally known as Perkiomen Bridge and then as Freeland.

•COLONIAL PARK, Village; Dauphin County; Pop. 9000; Zip Code 17109; Lat. 40-18-02 N long. 076-48-36 W; NE suburb of Harrisburg in SE central Pennsylvania; home of many city workers.

•COLUMBIA, Borough; Lancaster County; Pop. 10,466; Zip Code 17512; Elev. 255: Lat. 40-02-01 N long. 076-30-17 W; 12 m. W of Lancaster in SE PA -received its name at the time it was being considered as one of many possible sites for the national capital.

•COLUMBUS, Village; Warren County; Pop. 500; Zip Code 16405; Elev. 1,425: Lat. 41-56-27 N long. 079-34-55 W; NW Pennsylvania; named for the legendary discoverer of North America.

•COLWYN, Borough; Delaware County; Pop. 2,851; Zip Code 19023; Elev. 50: Lat. 39-54-44 N long. 075-15-15 W; 10 m. SW of downtown Philadelphia on Cobbs Creek (the city boundary) in SE Pennsylvania.

•CONNELLSVILLE, City; Fayette County; Pop. 10,319; Zip Code 15425; Elev. 890: Lat. 40-01-04 N long. 079-35-23 W; 47 m. SE of Pittsburgh in SW PA -ccupies the site of an early Shawnee village. *Zachariah Connell* and several other pioneers came to this vicinity in 1770 about the time coal was discovered here, and 23 years later *Connell* laid out a village.

•CONSHOHOCKEN, Borough; Montgomery County; Pop. 8,475; Zip Code 19428; Elev. 220: Lat. 40-04-45 N long. 075-18-07 W; 11 m. NW of Philadelphia on the Schuylkill River in SE Pennsylvania; suburban. "Conshohocken" is an Indian name meaning "pleasant valley."

•CONWAY, Borough; Beaver County; Pop. 2,747; Zip Code 15027; Elev. 760: Lat. 40-39-35 N long. 080-14-22 W; 19 m. NW of Pittsburgh on E bank of the Ohio River in W Pennsylvania; suburban-industrial community.

•CONYNGHAM, Borough; Luzerne County; Pop. 2,242; Zip Code 18219; Elev. 940: Lat. 40-59-31 N long. 076-03-25 W; 5 m. W of Hazleton in an old mining area in E Pennsylvania.

•COOPERSBURG, Borough; Lehigh County; Pop. 2,595; Zip Code 18036; Elev. 539: Lat. 40-30-41 N long. 075-23-27 W; 10 m. S of Allentown in E Pennsylvania; founded in 1780.

•COPLAY, Borough; Lehigh County; Pop. 3,130; Zip Code 18037; Elev. 380: Lat. 40-40-12 N long. 075-29-45 W; on Lehigh River, N of Allentown in E Pennsylvania; suburban; name is Indian for "smooth running stream."

•CORAOPOLIS, Borough; Allegheny County; Pop. 7,308; Zip Code 15108; Elev. 730: Lat. 40-31-06 N long. 080-10-01 W; 10 m. NW of Pittsburgh in SW Pennsylvania. -was settled about 1760. According to some, the name comes from the Greek *Koreopolis,* "maiden city," but others hold that it was named for *Cora Watson,* daughter of an influential citizen..

•CORNWALL, Borough; Lebanon County; Pop. 2,653; Zip Code 17016; Elev. 680: Lat. 40-16-25 N long. 076-24-23 W; SE central Pennsylvania; served by major rail lines heading to and from Lebanon, 3 m. north. Site of the old Cornwall Blast Furnace. Named for a region in England.

•CORNWELLS HEIGHTS, Village; Bucks County; Pop. 8,200; Zip Code 19020; Elev. 60:Lat. 40-04-36 N long. 074-56-57 W; 12 m. NE of downtown Philadelphia in SE Pennsylvania; on the Delaware River.

•CORRY, City; Erie County; Pop. 7,149; Zip Code 16407; Elev. 1,429: Lat. 41-55-13 N long. 079-38-26 W; 28 m. SE of Erie in NW Pennsylvania; on S branch of the French Creek. -born in 1861 when the rights of way of two railroads intersected on *Hiram Corry's* farm, was nursed on the oil discovered by *Drake* at Titusville, some 25 miles to the south.

•COUDERSPORT, Borough; Seat of Potter County; Pop. 2,791; Zip Code 16915; Elev. 1,650: Lat. 41-46-29 N long. 078-01-15 W; N PA, near the New York state line. Coudersport was named for *Jean Samuel Couderc,* of the Amsterdam banking firm that had managed the interests of those exiled Frenchmen of Asylum who had invested in the Ceres Land Company. The final letter in *M. Couderc's* name was dropped for the sake of euphony.

•CRAFTON, Borough; Allegheny County; Pop. 7,623; Zip Code 15205; Elev. 880: Lat. 40-26-06 N long. 080-03-59 W; SE suburb of Pittsburgh in SW Pennsylvania; on Chartiers Creek; It was laid out about 1870 by *Charles C. Craft,* and named in honor of his father, *James S. Craft,* a prominent Pittsburgh lawyer, from whom he inherited the land on which the town is built.

•CREIGHTON, Village; Allegheny County; Pop. 2,081; Zip Code 15030; Elev. 800: Lat. 40-35-14 N long. 079-46-43 W; suburb of Pittsburgh. It grew up about a tavern erected here in 1792.

•CRESSONA, Borough; Schuylkill County; Pop. 1,810; Zip Code 17929; Elev. 600: Lat. 40-37-36 N long. 076-11-35 W; E central Pennsylvania. It was named for *John Chapman Cresson,* who laid out the town. He was a civil engineer in Philadelphia, manager of the Schuylkill Navigation Company, president of the Mine Hill and Schuylkill Haven Railroad Company, and chief engineer of Fairmount Park in Philadelphia.

•CROYDON, Village; Bucks County; Pop. 9,800; Zip Code 19020; Lat. 40-05-14 N long. 074-54-14 W; 10 m. NE of downtown Philadelphia in SE Pennsylvania; on Neshaminy Creek; named for a suburb of London, England.

•**CRUM LYNNE**, Village; Delaware County; Pop. 3,700; Zip Code 19022; Elev. 20: Lat. 39-52-20 N long. 075-19-42 W; SW suburb of Philadelphia near Chester, in SE Pennsylvania.

•**CURWENSVILLE**, Borough; Clearfield County; Pop. 3,116; Zip Code 16833; Elev. 1,167: Lat. 40-58-32 N long. 078-31-31 W; W central Pennsylvania. The first settlement occurred in 1812, 14 years after *John Curwen* obtained title to the tract. *Curwen* never resided here, however. Curwensville State Park is nearby.

•**DALE**, Borough; Cambria County; Pop. 1,906; Zip Code 15902; Elev. 1,250: Lat. 40-24-58 N long. 075-36-58 W; suburb of Johnstown in SW central Pennsylvania; in a hilly area.

•**DALLAS**, Borough; Luzerne County; Pop. 2,679; Zip Code 18612; Elev. 1,128: Lat. 41-20-10 Nlong. 075-57-49 W; 10 m. NW of Wilkes-Barre in E Pennsylvania. It took its name from the Philadelphia author, lawyer, statesman, and financier, *Alexander James Dallas*, who won fame by his efficient administration as Secretary of the Treasury in 1814-17.

•**DALLASTOWN**, Borough; York County; Pop. 3,949; Zip Code 17313; Elev. 880; Lat. 39-53-58 Nlong. 076-38-26 W; 10 m. SE Named in honor of *George Mifflin Dallas* of Philadelphia, who served as United States Senator from PA in 1831, as Vice-President of the United States during *Polk's* administration, and as minister to Great Britain from 1856 to 1861. *George M. Dallas* was the son of *Alexander J. Dallas.*

•**DARBY**, Borough; Delaware County; Pop. 11,513; Zip Code 19023; Elev. 50; Lat. 39-55-06 N long. 075-15-34 W; m. SW of downtown Philadelphia in SE Pennsylvania; in a residential area along Darby Creek. It was so called for old pearing as "Derbytown" in 1698. Three centuries ago the form Darby was used quite as frequently as Derby.

•**DAVIDSON HEIGHTS**, Village; Beaver County; Pop. 2,000; Zip Code 15001; Suburb of Aliquippa in W Pennsylvania.

•**DENVER**, Borough; Lancaster County; Pop. 2,018; Zip Code 17517; Elev. 380; Lat. 40-13-59 Nlong. 076-08-15 W; 15 m. NE of Lancaster in SE Pennsylvania.

•**DERRY**, Borough; Westmoreland County; Pop. 3,072; Zip Code 15627; Elev. 1050; Lat. 41-11-18 N long. 076-27-42 W; 35 m. E of Pittsburgh in SW Pennsylvania. It was named for the Northern Irish town that was known as Derry before the British took control and renamed it Londonderry.

•**DEVON**, Village; Chester County; Pop. 4,500; Zip Code 19333; Elev. 495; Lat. 40-02-57 N long. 075=-25-46 W; 10 m. NW of Philadelphia in SE Pennsylvania; Devereux Foundation is located here.

•**DICKSON CITY**, Borough; Lackawanna County; Pop. 6,699; Zip Code 18519; Elev. 752; Lat. 41-28-17 Nlong. 075-36-29 W; NE Pennsylvania. It was named for *Thomas Dickson*, president of the Delaware and Hudson Canal Company (1869-84), merges with Blakely on one side and Scranton on the other. *William H. Richmond*, of Scranton, opened coal drifts here in 1859; the following year the first breaker was erected.

•**DILLSBURG**, Borough; York County; Pop. 1,733; Zip Code 17019; Elev. 580; Lat. 40-06-39 Nlong. 077-02-07 W; 15 m. S of Harrisburg in S Pennsylvania; reached by U.S. Highway 15, where a roadside picnic area marks the outskirts of town.

•**DONORA**, Borough; Washington County; Pop. 7,524; Zip Code 15033; Elev. 780; Lat. 40-10-24 N long. 079-51-28 W; SW Pennsylvania. It was an important industrial town founded in 1900 on the west bank of the Monongahela River. It is named for *William H. Donner*, president of the town's developing company, and *Nora Mellon*, wife of *Andrew W. Mellon.*

•**DORMONT**, Borough; Allegheny County; Pop. 11,275; Zip Code 15216; Elev. 1,220; Lat. 40-23-45 N long. 080-02-00 W; S suburb of Pittsburgh in SW Pennsylvania; population declined in the 1970s. The ornate and somewhat pretentious name Dormont, from the French *d'or mont*, "mount of gold," was suggested by *Gilbert M. Brown*, who became the first burgess of Dormont. The name refers to the beautiful hills on which the town is built and to the wonderful opportunities that they offered.

•**DOVER**, Borough; York County; Pop. 1,910; Zip Code 17315; Elev. 431; Lat. 40-00-06 N long. 076-51-02 W; S Pennsylvania; on Fox Run Creek at the foot of the Conewago Mountains; residential town named for the English port city.

•**DOWNINGTOWN**, Borough; Chester County; Pop. 7,650; Zip Code 19335; Elev. 264; Lat. 40-00-23 N long. 075-42-13 W; SE Pennsylvania. It is on the East Branch of Brandywine Creek, was settled by emigrants from Birmingham, England. First known as Milltown, it was renamed for *Thomas Downing*, who purchased a mill here in 1739, and was incorporated as a borough in 1859.

•**DOYLESTOWN**, Borough; Seat of Bucks County; Pop. 8,717; Zip Code 18901; Elev. 355; Lat. 40-18-36 N long. 075-07-49 W; 25 m. N of Philadelphia in SE Pennsylvania. It was settled in 1735 by *William Doyle*, was once an overnight stop of stage travelers between Easton and Philadelphia.

•**DRAVOSBURG**, Borough; Allegheny County; Pop. 2,511; Zip Code 15034; Elev. 800; Lat. 40-21-02 Nlong. 079-53-11 W; SE suburb of Pittsburgh, on the Mongahela River in SW Pennsylvania; bordered by the Allegheny County Airport. The town was named for *John F. Drava*, pioneer coal operator.

•**DREXEL HILL**, Village; Delaware County; Pop. 30,000; Zip Code 19026; Elev. 210; Lat. 39-56-49 N long. 075-17-33 W; 6 m. W of Philadelphia, along the Darby Creek in SE Pennsylvania; in a residential area.

•**DUBLIN**, Borough; Bucks County; Pop. 1,565; Zip Code 18917; Lat. 40-22-18 N long. 075-12-07 W; SE Pennsylvania.

•**DUBOIS**, City; Clearfield County; Pop. 9,290; Zip Code 15801; Elev. 1,339; Lat. 41-07-09 N long. 078-45-37 W; 100 m. N of Pittsburgh in W central Pennsylvania. It is bisected by Sandy Lick Creek, lies in a narrow basin at the lowest pass in the Alleghenies. In 1880 the town was incorporated under the name of DuBois, given in honor of *John DuBois*, its most important citizen.

•**DUNBAR**, Borough; Fayette County; Pop. 1,369; Zip Code 15431; Elev. 1,000; Lat. 39-58-40 N long. 079-36-53 W; 7 m. NE of Uniontown in a farming area in SW Pennsylvania. *Col. Thomas Dunbar* was defeated by a French and Indian army here in 1755. His name was given to the new town shortly afterwards.

•**DUNCANNON**, Borough; Perry County; Pop. 1,645; Zip Code 17020; Elev. 260; Lat. 40-23-53 N long. 077-02-01-24 W; m. N of Harrisburg on the Susquehanna River, in S central Pennsylvania.

•**DUNCANSVILLE**, Borough; Blair County; Pop. 1,355; Zip Code 16635; Elev. 1,020; Lat. 40-25-24 N long. 078-26-03 W; 4 m. SW of Lakemont in S central Pennsylvania. It was founded by *Samuel Duncan* ; at the same time *Jacob Walter* owned a site to the east called Walterstown; the two met on a bridge spanning Blair Creek and tossed a penny to decide what the common name should be.

•**DUNMORE**, Borough; Lackawanna County; Pop. 16,781; Zip Code 18512; Elev. 939; Lat. 41-25-11 N long. 075-37-58 W; NE Pennsylvania. It was settled in 1783 by *William Allsworth*, a convivial shoemaker. Called Buckstown until 1840, it was renamed for the second son of the fifth Earl of Dunmore.

421

•**DUPONT**, Borough; Luzerne County; Pop. 3,460; Zip Code 18641; Elev. 701; Lat. 41-19-30 N long. 075-44-45 W; E Pennsylvania. It was founded in 1917 and named for the *duPonts*, operators of a nearby powder plant, is set in a hollow.

•**DUQUESNE**, City; Allegheny County; Pop. 10,094; Zip Code 15110; Elev. 841; Lat. 40-22-53 N long. 079-51-36 W; SW Pennsylvania. It was incorporated in 1891. The name came from old Fort Duquesne, which was built at the forks of the Ohio in 1754, and named in honor of the *Marquis Duquesne de Menneville*, then governor of New France.

•**DURYEA**, Borough; Luzerne County; Pop. 5,415; Zip Code 18642; Elev. 589; Lat. 41-20-38 N long. 075-44-20 W; E Pennsylvania. It was named for *Abram Duryea*, who opened coal mines here in 1845. For a time the settlement was known as Babyton because of the mixture of tongues occasioned by the influx of immigrant miners. *Duryea* was a colonel in the Civil War of the fifth New York Infantry.

•**EAST BERLIN**, Borough; Adams County; Pop. 1,054; Zip Code 17316; Elev. 430; Lat. 39-56-15 N long. 076-58-44 W; along the Conewago Creek in S Pennsylvania; named by German settlers.

•**EAST BRADY**, Borough; Clarion County; Pop. 1,153; Zip Code 16028; Elev. 1,080; Lat. 40-59-09 N long. 079-36-48 W; on Brady's Bend of the Allegheny River in W Pennsylvania. It was laid out in 1866 and named for *Captain Brady*. During the Revolutionary War, *Captain Brady's* father and brother were killed by Indians. The captain swore vengeance and for many years led expeditions against his enemies.

•**EAST CONEMAUGH**, Borough; Cambria County; Pop. 2,128; Zip Code 15909; Elev. 1,240; Lat. 40-20-55 N long. 078-53-02 W; 1 m. N of Johnstown in SW central Pennsylvania. It dates back to a time when it was necessary to use the prefix East to distinguish this town from the older borough of Conemaugh, which was consolidated with Johnstown about 130 years ago. The Conemaugh River, which became famous at the time of the Johnstown flood in 1889, has given its name to East Conemaugh. The name is derived from the Indian *Connemach*, which signifies "otter creek."

•**EAST FAXON**, Village; Lycoming County; Pop. 4,000; Zip Code 17706; 1 m. E of Williamsport along the Susquehanna River in E central Pennsylvania; residential suburb.

•**EAST GREENVILLE**, Borough; Montgomery County; Pop. 2,456; Zip Code 18041; Elev. 415; Lat. 40-24-23 Nlong. 075-30-08 W; 20 m. S of Allentown on the main rail lines between that city and Philadelphia; SE Pennsylvania; also near Perkiomen Creek.

•**EAST LANSDOWNE**, Borough; Delaware County; Pop. 2,806; Zip Code 19050; Elev. 130; Lat. 39-56-44 Nlong. 075-15-42 W; 5 m. W of downtown Philadelphia along Cobbs Creek in SE Pennsylvania.

•**EAST LAWN**, Village; Northampton County; Pop. 18064; Zip Code 18064; Lat. 40-45-01 N long. 075-17-41 W; suburb of Easton and Allentown-Bethlehem in E Pennsylvania.

•**EAST MCKEESPORT**, Borough; Allegheny County; Pop. 2,940; Zip Code 15035; Elev. 1,200; Lat. 40-22-59 N long. 079-48-24 W; near McKeesport in SW Pennsylvania; incorporated about 1895. Site of the Bliss Speedway, near State Highway 48.

•**EAST NORRITON**, Village; Montgomery County; Pop. 11,837; Zip Code 19401; near Norristown in SE Pennsylvania; residential.

•**EAST PETERSBURG**, Borough; Lancaster County; Pop. 3,600; Zip Code 17520; Elev. 380; Lat. 40-06-00 N long. 076-21-16 W; 5 m. N of Lancaster in SE Pennsylvania.

•**EAST PITTSBURGH**, Borough; Allegheny County; Pop. 2,493; Zip Code 15112; Elev. 1,000; Lat. 40-23-44 N long. 079-50-20 W;

adjacent to Pittsburgh in SW Pennsylvania; near Monongahela River in a residential area.

•**EAST STROUDSBURG**, Borough; Monroe County; Pop. 8,039; Zip Code 18301; Elev. 430; Lat. 40-59-58 N long. 075-10-54 W; E Pennsylvania. Originally just an extension of Stroudsburg, it is almost as large and important today as the older town.

•**EAST WASHINGTON**, Borough; Washington County; Pop. 2,241; Zip Code 15301; Elev. 1,220; Lat. 40-10-25 N long. 080-14-16 W; adjacent to Washington in SW Pennsylvania. The historic Lemoyne House is located here.

•**EASTON**, City; Northampton County seat; Pop. 26,069; Zip Code 18042; Elev. 271; Lat. 41-07-38 N long. 079-32-28 W; on Delaware River, E of Allentown in E Pennsylvania; near Phillipsburg, New Jersey. The town was named Easton, at the proprietor's wish, for the Northamptonshire estate (Easton-Weston) of *Lord Pomfret*, Penn's father-in-law.

•**EBENSBURG**, Borough; Seat of Cambria County; Pop. 4,096; Zip Code 15931; Elev. 2,022; Lat. 40-29-06 N long. 078-43-30 W; 18 m. NE of Johnstown in SW central Pennsylvania; on N branch of Conemaugh Creek. It was founded in the early 1800's by the *Reverend Rees Lloyd*, a religious dissenter and leader of Welsh immigrants. *Rev. Lloyd* named the town for his son, *Eber*, who died in childhood.

•**ECHO**, Village; Armstrong County; Pop. 50; Zip Code 16222; Lat. 40-51-00 N long. 079-19-39 W; W Pennsylvania. It took its name from the three ravines that meet here and cause sounds to echo.

•**ECONOMY**, Borough; Beaver County; Pop. 9,538; Zip Code 15005; Elev. 1,180; W Pennsylvania; incorporated in 1958. In 1825 the Harmony Society moved into PA, bought about three thousand acres of land, and founded the town and the township of Economy.

•**EDDYSTONE**, Borough; Delaware County; Pop. 2,555; Zip Code 19013; Elev. 20; Lat. 39-51-36 N long. 075-20-41 W; 15 m. SW of Philadelphia in SW PA, on the Delaware River; port facilities along the riverfront.

•**EDGEWOOD**, Borough; Allegheny County; Pop. 4,382; Zip Code 15218; Elev. 920; Lat. 40-25-55 N long. 079-52-54 W; E suburb of Pittsburgh in SW Pennsylvania; in a residential area.

•**EDGEWORTH**, Borough; Allegheny County; Pop. 1,738; Zip Code 15143; Elev. 723; Lat. 40-33-04 N long. 080-11-35 W; NW of Pittsburgh in SW PA, on Ohio River.

•**EDINBORO**, Borough; Erie County; Pop. 6,324; Zip Code 16412; Elev. 1,210; Lat. 41-52-27 N long. 080-07-55 W; 20 m. S of Lake Erie Shore in NW Pennsylvania; named for city in Scotland.

•**EDWARDSVILLE**, Borough; Luzerne County; Pop. 5,729; Zip Code 18704; Elev. 760; Lat. 41-16-10 N long. 075-55-00 W; 3 m. NW of Wilkes-Barre in E Pennsylvania. It was incorporated in 1884, was named for *Daniel Edwards*, superintendent of the Kingston Coal Company, whose mining operations opened here soon after the borough was incorporated..

•**ELIZABETH**, Borough; Allegheny County; Pop. 1,892; Zip Code 15037; Elev. 731; Lat. 40-16-09 N long. 079-53-24 W; SE suburb of Pittsburgh in SW Pennsylvania. It was laid out in 1787 by *Stephen Bayard* and named in honor of his bride, *Elizabeth Mackay Bayard*, daughter of *Colonel Aeneas Mackay*, once commandant at Fort Pitt.

•**ELIZABETHTOWN**, Borough; Lancaster County; Pop. 8,233; Zip Code 17022; Elev. 462; Lat. 40-09-10 N long. 076-36-11 W; 15 m. SE of Harrisburg in SE Pennsylvania. It was named for the wife of *Captain Barnabas Hughes* who purchased the tavern and the original Harris tract in 1750.

•ELKLAND, Borough; Tioga County; Pop. 1,974; Zip Code 16920; Elev. 1,130; Lat. 41-59-10 N long. 077-18-40 W; just S of New York state line in N Pennsylvania.

•ELLSWORTH, Borough; Washington County; Pop. 1,228; Zip Code 15331; Elev. 1,060; Lat. 40-06-43 N long. 080-01-03 W; 30 m. S of Pittsburgh in SW PA, in an old coal mining region.

•ELLWOOD CITY, Borough; Beaver and Lawrence Counties; Pop. 9,998; Zip Code 16117; Elev. 900; 10 m. N of Beaver Falls in W PA, on the Shenango River. It was laid out in 1890 by the Pittsburgh Company, and was named in honor of *Colonel I.L. Ellwood* of Indiana, who pioneered the manufacturing of wire fencing.

•EMMAUS, Borough; Lehigh County; Pop. 11,001; Zip Code 18049; Elev. 433; Lat. 40-32-22 Nlong. 075-29-50 W; 5 m. S of Allentown in E Pennsylvania. It was founded shortly after 1740 by the Moravians, was called successively Maguntchi (Ind. "place of the bears") and Salzburg. Not until 1761, when *Bishop August Spangenberg*, founder of the Moravian Church in America, conducted a feast here, was it named for the biblical town of Emmaus. In the succeeding years one "m" was dropped from the name, but in 1939 the earlier spelling was officially restored.

•EMPORIUM, Borough; Seat of Cameron County; Pop. 2,837; Zip Code 15834; Elev. 1,031; Lat. 41-30-44 N long. 078-14-07 W; on Bucktail Trail, near New York state line in N central Pennsylvania. Emporium is the Latinized form of the Greek word for "market, or centre of trade." The name Emporium, which was assumed by the county-seat at the time of its incorporation in 1864.

•ENOLA, Village; Cumberland County; Pop. 7,000; Zip Code 17025; Elev. 400; Lat. 40-17-24 N long. 076-56-03 W; across the Susquehanna River from Harrisburg in S Pennsylvania; The erroneous popular explanation of this peculiar name is that the call for the lonely telegraph tower which once stood across the river from Harrisburg was the word *alone*, and that the name Enola was suggested by spelling this word backward. In point of fact, the name Enola has been traced to *Amanda Gingrich Underwood* who once lived in Mechanicsburg, Pennsylvania.

•EPHRATA, Borough; Lancaster County; Pop. 11,095; Zip Code 17522; Elev. 380; Lat. 40-10-47 N long. 076-10-45 W; 12 m. NE of Lancaster in SE Pennsylvania; site of the historic Ephrata Clioster along a scenic route. The German Seventh-Day Adventists established a monastic community here in 1735.

•ERIE, City; Erie County seat; Pop. 118,964; Zip Code 165+; Elev. 709; Lat. 42-07-45 N long. 080-05-07 W; on Lake Erie, 90 m. W of Buffalo, New York in NW Pennsylvania. Erie's first known inhabitants were Indians of the Eriez nation, from which the lake and later the city received their names. They were exterminated by the Seneca about 1654, and for decades thereafter the region remained under control of the Iroquois Confederacy.

•ETNA, Borough; Allegheny County; Pop. 4,534; Zip Code 15223; Elev. 750; Lat. 40-30-15 N long. 079-56-57 W; SW Pennsylvania. Etna, appropriately named for Sicily's famed volcano, is a town of flaming furnaces, iron works, and steel mills. Etna's history as an industrial town dates form 1832 when an ironmaking establishment was set up here. It became a borough in 1868.

•EVANS CITY, Borough; Butler County; Pop. 2,299; Zip Code 16033; Elev. 940; Lat. 40-46-09 N long. 080-03-47 W; W Pennsylvania. Evans City was settled in 1796 by *Robert Boggs*, who exchanged a mare for a 400-acre tract on which he built a cabin and a mill. In 1836, *Thomas B. Evans* laid out the village, after buying half of *Boggs'* land.

•EVERETT, Borough; Bedford County; Pop. 1,828; Zip Code 15537; Elev. 1,106; Lat. 40-00-41 N long. 078-22-25 W; 42 m. S of Altoona in S Pennsylvania; in the Tussey Mountains.

•EXETER, Borough; Luzerne County; Pop. 5,493; Zip Code 18643; Elev. 591; Lat. 41-19-14 N long. 075-49-10 W; E Pennsylvania. Exeter was named for Exeter Township, organized in 1790 by settlers from Exeter, Rhode Island.

•EXTON, Village; Chester County; Pop. 2,000; Zip Code 19341; Elev. 370; Lat. 40-01-44 Nlong. 075-37-16 W; 25 m. NW of Philadelphia in SE Pennsylvania; in a suburban area.

•FAIRCHANCE, Borough; Fayette County; Pop. 2,106; Zip Code 15436; Lat. 39-49-29 N long. 079-45-17 W; 6 m. S of Uniontown in a rural area of SW Pennsylvania.

•FAIRFIELD, Borough; Adams County; Pop. 591; Zip Code 17320; Elev. 608; Lat. 39-47-14 N long. 077-22-08 W; 8 m. SW of Gettysburg in S Pennsylvania; in a hilly, densely forested area.

•FAIRHOPE, Village; Fayette County; Pop. 2,500; Zip Code 15012; Lat. 39-50-24 N long. 078-47-32 W; 2 m. E of Belle Vernon along the Monongahela River in SW Pennsylvania.

•FAIRLESS HILLS, Village; Bucks County; Pop. 12,500; Zip Code 19030; Elev. 100; Lat. 40-10-46 Nlong. 074-51-20 W; NE suburb of Philadelphia in SE Pennsylvania; a residential area extending from Levittown.

•FARRELL, City; Mercer County; Pop. 8,645; Zip Code 16121; Elev. 853; Lat. 41-12-44 N long. 080-29-49 W; W Pennsylvania. Farrell was incorporated as South Sharon in 1901, it was renamed in 1911 to honor *James A. Farrell*, president of the United States Steel Corporation.

•FAYETTEVILLE, Village; Franklin County; Pop. 2,400; Zip Code f17222; Elev. 800; Lat. 40-26-20 N long. 080-12-50 W; 7 m. SE of Chambersburg in S Pennsylvania; named for *General la Fayette*.

•FERNDALE, Borough; Cambria County; Pop. 2,204; Zip Code 18921; Lat. 40-32-01 N long. 075-10-45 W; S suburb of Johnstown in SW central Pennsylvania; residential.

•FLEETWOOD, Borough; Berks County; Pop. 3,422; Zip Code 19522; Elev. 440; Lat. 40-27-14 N long. 075-49-06 W; 15 m. NE of Reading in SE Pennsylvania. In 1859, the growing settlement took the name of Fleetwood after a prominent English capitalist, who encouraged the construction of the railroad.

•FLEMINGTON, Borough; Clinton County; Pop. 1,416; Zip Code 19522; Elev. 440; Lat. 41-07-35 N long. 077-28-19 W; Central Pennsylvania; named for *John Fleming*, an associate justice in Lycoming County (1798), who once owned this site.

•FLOURTOWN, Village; Montgomery County; Pop. 5,000; Zip Code 19031; Elev. 169; Lat. 40-06-12 N long. 075-12-46 W; SE Pennsylvania. Flourtown, founded in 1743, was once noted for its flour trade; farmers came to buy supplies and have their wheat ground by the millers along the Wissahickon River.

•FOLCROFT, Borough; Delaware County; Pop. 8,231; Zip Code 19032; Elev. 70; Lat. 39-53-27 N long. 075-17-03 W; SW suburb of Philadelphia in SE Pennsylvania.

•FORD CITY, Borough; Armstrong County; Pop. 3,923; Zip Code 16226; Elev. 785; Lat. 40-46-20 N long. 079-31-48 W; W Pennsylvania. Ford City, off U.S. Highway 422 on the Allegheny River, was named for *Captain John B. Ford*, "father of the plate glass industry in America," who erected a factory here in 1887.

•**FOREST CITY**, Borough; Susquehanna County; Pop. 1,924; Zip Code 18421; Elev. 1,480; Lat. 41-39-05 N long. 075-28-01 W; 20 m. NE of Scranton in NE Pennsylvania.

•**FOREST HILLS**, Borough; Allegheny County; Pop. 8,198; Zip Code 15221; Elev. 1,080; Lat. 40-58-28 N long. 077-02-59 W; E suburb of Pittsburgh, off U.S. Highway 30 in SW Pennsylvania.

•**FORT LITTLETON**, Village; Fulton County; Pop. 130; Zip Code 17223; Elev. 785; Lat. 40-03-46 Nlong. 077-57-50 W; S Pennsylvania; a collection of frame houses at the foot of a slope, was founded in 1756, the year the fort was built.

•**FORT LOUDON**, Village; Franklin County; Pop. 900; Zip Code 17224; Elev. 641'Lat. 39-54-53 N long. 077-54-18 W; .

•**FORT WASHINGTON**, Village; Montgomery County; pop. 4,000; Zip Code 19034; Elev. 174; Lat. 40-08-30 N long. 075-12-34 W; 18 m. N of Philadelphia. Fort Washington was named for General Washington's encampment.

•**FORTY FORT**, Borough; Luzerne County; Pop. 5,590; Zip Code 18704; Elev. 554; Lat. 41-16-44 N long. 075-52-43 W; E Pennsylvania; named for the first 40 settlers who came to the valley.

•**FOUNTAIN HILL** , Borough; Lehigh County; Pop. 4,805; Zip Code 18015; Elev. 360; Lat. 40-36-05 N long. 075-23-44 W; 1 m. W of Bethlehem in E Pennsylvania; in a residential area.

•**FOX CHAPEL**, Borough; Allegheny County; Pop. 5,049; Zip Code 15238; Elev. 980; NE suburb of Pittsburgh in SW Pennsylvania.

•**FRACKVILLE**, Borough; Schuylkill County; Pop. 5,308; Zip Code 17931; Elev. 1,476; Lat. 40-47-02 N long. 076-13-50 W; 20 m. SW of Hazleton in E central Pennsylvania.

•**FRANKLIN**, City; Seat of Venango County; Pop. 8,146; Zip Code 16323; Elev. 1,017; Lat. 40-20-32 N long. 078-53-06 W; 70 m. N of Pittsburgh in NW Pennsylvania. The town was laid out for the county seat in 1795 on a tract of 1,000 acres belonging to the state and took its name from Fort Franklin.

•**FREDERICKTOWN**, Village; Washington County; Pop. 1,000; Zip Code 15333; Elev. 790; Lat. 40-00-09 N long. 079-59-54 W; SW Pennsylvania. The town was named for its founder, *Frederick Wise*, in 1790.

•**FREEDOM**, Borough; Beaver County; Pop. 2,272; Zip Code 15042; Elev. 703; Lat. 40-45-47 N long. 076-56-23 W; on bend of Ohio River in W Pennsylvania.

•**FREELAND**, Borough; Luzerne County; Pop. 4,285; Zip Code 18224; Elev. 1,880; Lat. 41-01-00 N long. 075-53-51 W; 10 m. NE of Hazelton in E Pennsylvania. The Donop plot became generally known as "free land"; that is, land that could be purchased, as distinguished from the coal companies' land, which was not for sale. *Mr. Donop* preferred to name his new town Freehold, a name that it retained until the establishment of a post-office in 1874. The postal authorities objected to this name because of the nearness and importance of Freehold in New Jersey; and the townspeople then adopted the nickname, Freeland.

•**FREEPORT**, Borough; Armstrong County; Pop. 2,381; Zip Code 16229; Elev. 775; Lat. 40-40-26 N long. 079-41-06 W; W Pennsylvania. Freeport, at the confluence of the Allegheny and Kiskiminetas Rivers and Buffalo Creek, in a fertile farming country with valuable orchard and dairy interests, was laid out in 1796 by *William and David Todd* as a free port for river craft.

•**GALETON**, Borough; Potter County; Pop. 1,462; Zip Code 16922; Elev. 1,315; Lat. 41-43-59 N long. 077-38-32 W; at the forks of Pine Creek, near Lyman Run State Park in N Pennsylvania.

•**GALLITZIN**, Borough; Cambria County; Pop. 2,315; Zip Code 16641; Elev. 2,167; Lat. 40-28-56 N long. 078-33-07W; 10 m. W of Altoona in SW central Pennsylvania; on a scenic route. Gallitzin bears the name of the priest, *Prince Demetrius Augustine Gallitzin*, one of the pioneers of Cambria County. *Prince Gallitzin*, the son of a Russian diplomat and the scion of an ancient and noble family, moved to Baltimore on his *wanderjahr* in 1792 at the age of 22.

•**GEISTOWN**, Borough; Cambria County; Pop. 3,304; Zip Code 15904; Elev. 1,900; 6 m. SE of Johnstown in SW central Pennsylvania.

•**GETTYSBURG**, Borough; Seat of Adams County; Pop. 7,194; Zip Code 17325; Elev. Lat. 3-49-51 N long. 077-13-53 W; S Pennsylvania. About ten years before Adams County was organized, *James Gettys*, who has been described as "a man of brains, force of character, and resources," scenting the certainty of a new county and the possibility of securing an eligible site for the county-seat, bought a tract of land and laid out a village, which he called Gettys-town. The name of the little town which he planned and plotted was destined to become famous throughout the world and memorable in history as the name of a bloody battlefield, on which the great Rebellion was to be checked and the fate of the Union decided.

•**GIRARD**, Borough; Erie County; Pop. 2,615; Zip Code 16417; Elev. 831; Lat. 42-00-01 N long. 080-19-06 W; 10 m. SW of Erie on Elk Creek in NW Pennsylvania. Settlement occurred prior to 1800; named for *Stephen Girard*, a Philadelphia merchant who owned land in the vicinity, it was incorporated as a borough in 1846.

•**GLASSPORT**, Borough; Allegheny County; Pop. 6,242; Zip Code 15045; Elev. 755; Lat. 40-19-29 N long. 079-53-33 W; SW Pennsylvania; on the east bank of the Monongahela, named in 1888 when the United States Glass Company established a plant here. The borough was incorporated in 1902.

•**GLEN ROCK**, Borough; York County; Pop. 1,662; Zip Code 17327; Elev. 560; Lat. 39-47-35 N long. 076-43-50 W; 15 m. S of York in a farming region in S Pennsylvania.

•**GLENOLDEN**, Borough; Delaware County; Pop. 7,633; Zip Code 19036; Elev. 90; 5 m. SW of central Philadelphia in SE Pennsylvania; residential.

•**GLENSHAW**, Village; Allegheny County; Pop. 18,000; Zip Code 15116; Elev. 1,060; Lat. 40-31-58 N long. 079-58-04 W; NW suburb of Pittsburgh in SW Pennsylvania; Pine Creek flows through this hilly residential community.

•**GLENSIDE**, Village; Montgomery County; Pop. 17,000; Zip Code 19038; Elev. 260; Lat. 40-06-08 N long. 075-09-09 W; one of the largest suburbs N of Philadelphia in SE Pennsylvania.

•**GRATERFORD**, Village; Montgomery County; Pop. 800; Zip Code 19426; Elev. 140; Lat. 40-13-32 N long. 075-27-18 ; 10 m. E of Pottstown; founded in 1756 and named for *Jacob Kreater*.

•**GREELEY**, Village; Pike County; Pop. 400 (summer 1,000); Zip Code 18425; Elev. 1,100'. Lat. 41-25-16 N long. 074-59-44 W; Greeley, where in 1842 *Horace Greeley*, publisher of the New York *Tribune* (1841-72), founded a colony based on the Utopian Socialist ideas of *Francois Marie Charles Fourier* (1772-1837). *Fourier's* plan proposed the organization of society into self-sufficient groups of 1,600, called phalanxes, each inhabiting a phalanstery.

•**GREEN TREE**, Borough; Allegheny County; Pop. 5,722; Zip Code 15242; Elev. 1,100; Lat. 40-24-42 N long. 080-02-45 W; S suburb of Pittsburgh which includes Mann Oak and Parkway Center; SW Pennsylvania.

•**GREENCASTLE**, Borough; Franklin County; Pop. 3,679; Zip Code 17225; Elev. 580; S of Chambersburg in S Pennsylvania; on a scenic route (181); laid out in 1782 by *Colonel John Allison* and named for his native town, a tiny seaport in County Donegal, Ireland.

•**GREENSBURG**, City; Seat of Westmoreland County; Pop. 17,558; Zip Code 15601; Elev. 1,110; Lat. 340-18-05 N long. 079-32-21 W; 30 m. E of Pittsburgh in SE Pennsylvania. About this time a town was laid out on the land of *Christopher Truby*, and named Greensburg in honor of *General Nathaniel Greene* (1742-86), under whom had fought many a Scotch-Irish soldier from Westmoreland.

•**GREENVILLE**, Borough; Mercer County; Pop. 7,730; Zip Code 16125; Elev. 963; Lat. 41-00-38 N long. 078-36-16 W; 70 m. N of Pittsburgh in W Pennsylvania. The town, which was long called West Greenville, is generally believed to have been named for *General Nathaniel Greene*. No other plausible or authoritative explanation has ever been given.

•**GROVE CITY**, Borough; Mercer County; Pop. 8,162; Zip Code 16127; Elev. 1,246; Lat. 41-09-28 Nlong. 080-05-20 W; 55 m. N of Pittsburgh in W Pennsylvania; site of Grove City College.

•**HALLAM**, Borough; York County; Pop. 1,428; Zip Code 17406; Elev. 380; Lat. 40-00-17 N long. 076-36-16 W; 5 m. NE of York along a scenic route; named by early settler *Samuel Blunston* for his native town of Upper Hallam in Yorkshire, England.

•**HALLSTEAD**, Borough; Susquehanna County; Pop. 1,280; Zip Code 18822; Elev. 884; Lat. 41-57-40 N long. 075-44-37 W; on N branch of Susquehanna River in NE Pennsylvania; was named for *William F. Hallstead*, an official of the Lackawanna Railroad.

•**HAMBURG**, Borough; Berks County; Pop. 4,011; Zip Code 19526; Elev. 387; Lat. 40-33-20 N long. 075-58-56 W; 17 m. N of Reading in SE Pennsylvania; founded in 1779, is on the east bank of the Schuylkill.

•**HANOVER**, Borough; York County; Pop. 14,890; Zip Code 17331; Elev. 599; Lat. 41-11-08 N long. 075-58-57 W; 8 m. N of Massachusetts state line in S Pennsylvania. To please the German settlers, the town was, at the suggestion of Michael Danner, who owned a large tract of land southeast of the site, formally christened Hanover for his native Hanover in Germany.

•**HARMONY**, Borough; Butler County; Pop. 1,334; Zip Code 16037; Elev. 913; Lat. 40-48-05 N long. 080-07-39 W; W Pennsylvania. Harmony is the site of the first settlement of the Harmony Society, organized in 1805 by *George Rapp*, for more than 40 years the religious and industrial leader of the Harmony Society.

•**HARRISBURG**, City, Dauphin County seat and capital of Pennsylvania; Pop. 53,113; Zip Code 171 + zone; Elev. 374; Lat. 40-16-25 N long. 076-53-05 W; 100 m. W of Philadelphia on the Susquehanna River in S central Pennsylvania. Lying on the east bank of the *John Harris*, a Yorkshireman, licensed in 1705 as an Indian trader, settled at Paxtang about 1712 and established a trading post and ferry. The town is named for him.

•**HARVEYS LAKE**, Borough; Luzerne County; Pop. 2,318; Zip Code 18618; Elev. 1,287; Lat. 41-23-00 N long. 076-01-30 W; N of Wilkes-Barre in E Pennsylvania.

•**HATFIELD**, Borough; Montgomery County; Pop. 2,533; Zip Code 19440; Elev. 340; Lat. 39-52-40 N long. 079-44-22 W; N suburb of Philadelphia, 10 m. W of Dylestown in SE Pennsylvania.

•**HAVERTOWN**, Village; Delaware County; Pop. 35,000; Zip Code 19083; Lat. 39-58-51 N long. 075-18-32 W; NW suburb of Philadelphia in SE Pennsylvania; a large bedroom community for city commuters.

•**HAWLEY**, Borough; Wayne County; Pop. 1,181; Zip Code 18428; Elev. 896; Lat. 41-28-33 N long. 075-10-57 W; 25 m. E of Scranton in NE Pennsylvania.

•**HAWTHORN**, Borough; Clarion County; Pop. 547; Zip Code 16230; Elev. 1,000; Lat. 41-01-12 N long. 079-16-29 W; on Red Bank Creek in W Pennsylvania; in a rural area.

•**HAZLETON**, City; Luzerne County; Pop. 27,318; Zip Code 18201; Elev. 1,624; Lat. 40-57-30 N long. 075-58-30 W; E Pennsylvania. Hazleton, named for Hazel Creek.

•**HEIDELBERG**, Borough; Allegheny County; Pop. 1,606; Zip Code 15106; Elev. 820; Lat. 40-23-32 Nlong. 080-05-28 W; 4 m. S of Central Pittsburgh in SW Pennsylvania; named by German founders for the medieval city in their native land. A large race track is located here.

•**HERSHEY**, Village (Unincorporated); Zip Code 17033; Elev. 400; Lat. 40-17-09 N long. 076-39-02 W; 15 m. E of Harrisburg. Hershey is the privately owned and planned community of *M.S. Hershey*, (see Biographies) a former Lancaster caramel manufacturer, who bought a cornfield here in 1903 and created a chocolate manufacturing center.

•**HIGHSPIRE**, Borough; Dauphin County; Pop. 2,959; Zip Code 17034; Elev. 299; Lat. 40-12-39 N long. 076-47-29 W; 5 m. SE of Harrisburg in SE central Pennsylvania. It is said to have been named for the old church spire here that served as a landmark for Susquehanna River boatmen.

•**HOLLIDAYSBURG**, Borough; Seat of Blair County; Pop. 5,897; Zip Code 16648; Elev. 953; Lat. 40-25-38 N long. 078-23-21 W; 5 m. S of Altoona in W central Pennsylvania. The settlement was founded in 1768 by *Adam and William Holliday*, Irish immigrants, at a time when Indians were still fighting white encroachment.

•**HOKENDAUQUA**, Village; Lehigh County; Pop. 2,000; Zip Code 18052; Lat. 40-39-43 N long. 075-29-29 W; N suburb of Allentown along the Lehigh River in E Pennsylvania; name is Indian for "searching for land," which probably came about as tribesmen observed the first white land surveyors here.

•**HOMER CITY**, Borough; Indiana County; Pop. 2,248; Zip Code 15748; Elev. 1,023; Lat. 40-32-36 N long. 079-09-45 W; 7 m. S of town Indiana in W central Pennsylvania; founded in 1854.

•**HOMESTEAD**, Borough; Allegheny County; Pop. 5,092; Zip Code 15120; Elev. 852; Lat. 40-24-21 N long. 079-54-44 W; adjoining Pittsburgh in SW Pennsylvania. Homestead, originally Amity Homestead, and renamed when incorporated as a borough in 1880. The settlement was laid out in 1871 by a Pittsburgh corporation called the Homestead Bank and Life Insurance Company. The town took its name from this company. It happened, however, that one of the farms which the company bought belonged to *Abdiel McClure*, who lived in a fine old farmhouse locally known as "the McClure homestead," embowered in a clump of trees. Many believe that this stately old homestead suggested the name of the town.

•**HONESDALE**, Borough; Seat of Wayne County; Pop. 5,128; Zip Code 18431; Elev. 982; Lat. 41-34-36 N long. 075-15-33 W; 24 m. NE of Scranton in NE Pennsylvania. In 1826, *Philip Hone*, mayor of New York City, later president of the Delaware & Hudson Canal Company, came to the settlement to push construction of a canal that would divert the flow of coal to his city.

•**HOUSTON**, Borough; Washington County; Pop. 1,568; Zip Code 15342; Elev. 960; Lat. 40-14-47 N long. 080-12-42 W; 18 m. SW of Pittsburgh in SW Pennsylvania.

•HOUTZDALE, Borough; Clearfield County; Pop. 1,222; Zip Code 16651; Elev. 1,518; Lat. 40-49-30 N long. 078-21-05 W; 30 m. NE of Altoona in W central Pennsylvania. Town was named for *Dr. Daniel Houtz*, who owned the land upon which it was built in 1870.

•HUGHESTOWN, Borough; Luzerne County; Pop. 1,783; Elev. 760; Lat. 41-19-37 N long. 075-46-25 W; residential suburb of Wilkes-Barre in E Pennsylvania, just NE of Pittston.

•HUGHESVILLE, Borough; Lycoming County; Pop. 2,174; Zip Code 17737; Elev. 483; Lat. 41-14-28 N long. 076-43-27 W; 15 m. E of Williamsport in N central Pennsylvania. Hughesville was laid out in 1816 by *Jeptha Hughes*, who called it Hughesburg. In 1827, when the post office was established, the name was changed to Hughesville.

•HULMEVILLE, Borough; Bucks County; Pop. 1,014; Zip Code 19047; Elev. 40; Lat. 40-08-35 N long. 074-54-41 W; NE suburb of Philadelphia in SE Pennsylvania.

•HUMMELSTOWN, Borough; Dauphin County; Pop. 4,267; Zip Code 17036; Elev. 370; Lat. 40-15-55 N long. 076-42-31 W; SE central Pennsylvania. Hummelstown, founded about 1740 by *Frederick Hummel* and known as Frederickstown until his death in 1780. During the Revolution Hummelstown was an important depot of arms and munitions for garrisons and forts situated to the west and the north.

•HUNTINGDON, Borough; Seat of Huntingdon County; Pop. 7,042; Zip Code 16652; Elev. 630; Lat. 40-29-05 N long. 078-00-38 W; 35 m. E of Altoona in S central Pennsylvania. Huntingdon was originally called standing stone. The settlement was laid out in 1767 by *Dr. William Smith*, first Provost of the University of Pennsylvania, and named for *Selina Hastings*, Countess of Huntingdon, who had responded liberally to *Smith's* appeal for funds to aid the university.

•HYNDMAN, Borough; Bedford County; Pop. 1,106; Zip Code 15545; Elev. 934; Lat. 39-49-23 N long. 078-43-06 W; On Wills Creek, 50 m. SW of Altoona in S Pennsylvania. Hyndman was first called Bridgeport, for which, at the time of its incorporation in 1877, the name Hyndman was substituted, in honor of *E.K. Hyndman*, president of the Pittsurgh and Western Railroad.

•IMPERIAL, Village; Allegheny County; Pop. 2,000; Zip Code 15126; Elev. 940; Lat. 40-26-58 N long. 080-14-41 W; NW suburb of Pittsburgh in SW Pennsylvania. The town was laid out by the Imperial Coal Company in 1879, and was named for their Imperial Mine.

•INDIANA, Borough; Seat of Indiana County; Pop. 16,051; Zip Code 15701; Elev. 1,310; Lat. 40-37-17 N long. 079-09-10 W; 46 m. NE of Pittsburgh in W central Pennsylvania. Indiana, founded in 1805, when *George Clymer* of Philadelphia, one of the signers of the Declaration of Independence, donated 250 acres for county buildings, it was probably named for the Territory of Indiana, which Congress formed from the Northwest Territory in 1800.

•INDUSTRY, Borough; Beaver County; Pop. 2,417; Zip Code 15052; Elev. 695; Lat. 40-38-40 N long. 080-24-59 W; W Pennsylvania.

•INGRAM, Borough; Allegheny County; Pop. 4,346; Zip Code 15205; Elev. 880; Lat. 40-26-46 N long. 080-04-04 W; S suburb of Pittsburgh in SW Pennsylvania.

•IRWIN, Borough; Westmoreland County; Pop. 4,995; Zip Code 15642; Elev. 879; Lat. 40-19-28 N long. 079-42-05 W; 20 m. SE of Pittsburgh in SW Pennsylvania.

•JACOBUS, Borough; York County; Pop. 1,396; Zip Code 17407; 10 m. S of York in S Pennsylvania.

•JEANNETTE, City; Westmoreland County; Pop. 13,106; Zip Code 15644; Elev. 1,040; Lat. 40-19-41 N long. 079-36-56 W; 23 m. SE of Pittsburgh in SW Pennsylvania; named for the wife of *H. Sellers McKee*, who in 1889 helped to establish a glass works that led to the transformation of a farm site into an industrial city.

•JEFFERSON, Borough; Allegheny County; Pop. 8,643; Zip Code 15025; Elev. 780; Lat. 41-12-21 N long. 079-33-19 W; SE suburb of Pittsburgh in SW Pennsylvania; incorporated in 1950 as a residential subdivision; named for *Thomas Jefferson*.

•JENKINTOWN, Borough; Montgomery County; Pop. 4,942; Zip Code 19046; Elev. 250; Lat. 40-05-45 N long. 075-07-32 W; in suburb of Philadelphia in SE Pennsylvania; low density houses and country clubs are in vicinity. Jenkintown was named for the Welsh pioneer, *William Jenkins*, who settled here before 1697. The place was called Jenkins'-town as early as 1759.

•JERMYN, Borough; Lackawanna County; Pop. 2,411; Zip Code 18433; Elev. 952; Lat. 41-31-51 N long. 075-32-45 W; NE Pennsylvania. Jermyn, which with Mayfield forms the so-called "twin boroughs," was named by the Delaware and Hudson Canal Company for *John Jermyn*, a wealthy English merchant, and much of the subsequent immigration was from Great Britain.

•JERSEY SHORE, Borough; Lycoming County; Pop. 4,631; Zip Code 17740; Elev. 603; 16 m. W of Williamsport on Susquehanna River in N central Pennsylvania. Jersey Shore, settled in 1785 by several families from New Jersey, was named by settlers on the opposite shore of the river.

•JESSUP (alt. Winton), Borough; Lackawanna County; Pop. 4,974; Zip Code 18434; Elev. 872; Lat. 41-28-07 Nlong. 075-33-45 W; NE Pennsylvania. This community, settled in 1849, was successively calley Saymour, and Mount Vernon; when *William W. Winton* established a coal breaker and laid out some semblance of a town in 1874, the townsmen named it for him.

•JOHNSONBURG, Borough; Elk County; Pop. 3,938; Zip Code 15845; Elev. 1,453; Lat. 41-29-26 Nlong. 078-40-31 W; 100 m. NE of Pittsburgh in NW central Pennsylvania. Johnsonburg, at the forks of the Clarion River, was laid out in 1888. It is said to have received its name from *John Johnson*, the traditional pioneer settler in that region, who about 50 years before the towns was laid out, occupied a small cabin at the junction of the east and west branches of the Clarion River, near the center of the present town.

•JOHNSTOWN, City; Cambria County; Pop. 35,496; Zip Code 159+; Elev. 1,184; Lat. 40-19-36 N long. 078-55-20 W; 75 m. E of Pittsburgh in SW central Pennsylvania. Johnstown is squeezed firmly between narrow valley walls. The city was named for *Joseph Johns, Jahns, or Yahns* (as the name was variously spelled), a native Switzerland, who came to America in 1769, at the age of 19. He first Conemaugh in 1831, and three years later the legislature formally changed its name to Johnstown.

•JOLLYTOWN, Village; Greene County; Pop. 30; Zip Code 16229; SE Pennsylvania; named for *Titus Jolly*, who once owned land on this spot.

•JOSEPHINE, Village; Indiana County; Pop. 500; Zip Code 15750; Elev. 1,020; Lat. 39-43-42 N long. 080-19-19 W; founded in 1905 and named for the wife of a partner in a local steel company. An exodus occured after this plant suspended operations about 1926.

•KANE, Borough; McKean County; Pop. 4,916; Zip Code 16735; Elev. 2,000; Lat. 41-39-46 N long. 078-48-41 W; on E border of the Allegheny National Forest in N Pennsylvania.

•**KENHORST**, Borough; Berks County; Pop. 3,187; Zip Code 19607; Elev. 310; Lat. 40-18-38 N long. 075-56-23 W; residential suburb of Reading in SE Pennsylvania.

•**KENNETT SQUARE**, Borough; Chester County; Pop. 4,715; Zip Code 19348; Elev. 268; Lat. 39-50-48 N long. 075-42-43 W; 12 m. NW of Wilmington, Delaware in SE Pennsylvania. Kennett Square, settled in 1686 by *Francis Smith*, who had come from Kennett, a village in Wiltshire, England, the major shipping center for fresh mushrooms, it also has a large mushroom cannery.

•**KENSINGTON**, Residential village; Philadelphia County; Pop. (incl. with Philadelphia); Zip Code 19125; SE Pennsylvania. which was incorporated as Kensington, after the English village which is now a part of London.

•**KING OF PRUSSIA (BRANDYWINE VILLAGE)**, Village; Montgomery County; Pop. 11,000; Zip Code 19406; Elev. 190'. Lat. 40-05-21 N long. 075-23-47 W; King of Prussia had its nucleus in the King of Prussia Inn, which the first proprietor, a native of Prussia, named for the Brandenburg prince, who in 1701 transformed Prussia from a duchy into a kingdom, taking the title of *King Frederick I.*

•**KINGSTON**, Borough; Luzerne County; Pop. 15,681; Zip Code 18704; E Pennsylvania. The name of Kingston was borrowed from Kingston in Rhode Island, from which some of the "first 40" of the early settlers had migrated.

•**KITTANNING**, Borough; Set of Armstrong County; Pop. 5,432; Zip Code 16201; Elev. 807; Lat. 40-48-59- N long. 079-31-20 W; 43 m. NE of Pittsburgh in W Pennsylvania; on Allegheny River. Kittanning stretches along the eastern bank of the Allegheny. Kittanning was laid out in 1803 by *Judge George Rose*. From this place a famous Indian trail known as "the Kittanning Path" led across the mountains to Standing Stone, now Huntingdon.

•**KNOX**, Borough; Clarion County; Pop. 1,364; Zip Code 16232; Elev. 1,400; Lat. 41-14-04 N long. 079-32-15 W; 20 m. SE of Oil City in W Pennsylvania.

•**KNOXVILLE**, Borough; Tioga County; Pop. 650; Zip Code 16928; Elev. 1,241; Lat. 40-25-11 N long. 079-59-42 W; at the foot of 2,200' Fork Hill in N Pennsylvania.

•**KOPPEL**, Borough; Beaver County; Pop. 1,146; Zip Code f16136; Elev. 890; Lat. 40-50-03 N long. 080-19-21 W; W Pennsylvania. Koppel was named for *Arthur Koppel* of Germany, who established a freight car factory here a few years before World War I.

•**KOSSUTH**, Village; Clarino County; Pop. 50; Zip Code 16331; Elev. 1,540; Lat. 41-17-05 N long. 079-34-27 W; 12 m. NW of Clarion in W Pennsylvania. Kossuth received its name from the Hungarian patriot and revolutionary leader, *Louis Kossuth*, who wcs a political exile in the United States in 1852. He was very popular in the United States during his prime.

•**KULPMONT**, Borough; Northumberland County; Pop. 3,675; Zip Code 17834; Elev. 900; Lat. 40-47-36 N long. 076-28-22 W; E central Pennsylvania; founded in 1875 and incorporated as a borough in 1914.

•**KUTZTOWN**, Borough; Berks County; Pop. 4,040; Zip Code 19530; Elev. 450; Lat. 40-23-55 N long. 076-19-20 W; 18 m. N of Reading in SE Pennsylvania. Kutztown was founded in 1771 and named for *George Kutz*, who laid it out.

•**LACEYVILLE**, Borough; Wyoming County; Pop. 498; Zip Code 18623; Elev. 656; Lat. 41-38-45 N long. 076-09-42 W; NE Pennsylvania.

•**LACKAWAXEN**, Village; Pike County; Pop. 500; Elev. 647'. Lat. 41-28-55 N long. 074-59-11 W; Lackawaxen (Ind. "swift waters" or "where the way forks"), founded in 1770.

•**LAFAYETTE HILL**, Village; Montgomery County; Pop. 5,500; suburb of Philadelphia; also known as Barren Hill.

•**LAFLIN**, Borough; Luzerne County; Pop. 1,650; Elev. 727; Lat. 41-17-20 N long. 075-48-21 W; 4 m. N of Wilkes-Barre in E Pennsylvania, on Gardner's Creek.

•**LAKE CITY**, Borough; Erie County; Pop. 2,384; Zip Code 16423; Elev. 721; Lat. 41-21-53 N long. 078-53-09 W; NW Pennsylvania. Name changed from North Girard in 1954. Located on Lake Erie shore, 15 m. SE of Erie.

•**LANCASTER**, City; Lancaster County Seat; Pop. 54,632; Zip Code 176+; Lat. 40-02-16 N long. 076-18-21 W; 64 m. W of Philadelphia in SE Pennsylvania; near the Susquehanna River. Both county and town were named by *John Wright*, chief magistrate, for his home shire of Lancaster, England.

•**LANDISVILLE**, Village; Lancaster County; Pop. 2,000; Zip Code 17538; Elev. 403; Lat. 40-20-57 N long. 075-06-49 W; German residential town, was laid out in 1808.

•**LANGHORNE**, Borough; Bucks County; Pop. 1,697; Zip Code 19047; Elev. 220; Lat. 40-10-28 N long. 074-55-23 W; SE Pennsylvania. Named for early settler *Jeremiah Langhorne*, chief justice of the province in 1739-43. Today it is a suburb of Philadelphia, mainly residential.

•**LANGHORNE MANOR**, Borough; Bucks County; Pop. 1,103; Zip Code 19047; Elev. 200; Lat. 40-10-01 N long. 074-55-05 W; 1 m. N of Langhorne in SE Pennsylvania; also a suburb of Philadelphia.

•**LANDSDALE**, Borough; Montgomery County; Pop. 16,526; Zip Code 19446 Lat. 40-14-29 N long. 075-17-03 W; 24 m. NW of Philadelphia in a suburban area in SE Pennsylvania.

•**LANSDOWNE**, Borough; Delaware County; Pop. 11,891; Zip Code 19050; Elev. 205; Lat. 39-56-17 N long. 075-16-20 W; SE Pennsylvania; was probably named for *Lord Lansdowne.*

•**LANDSFORD**, Borough; Carbon County; Pop. 4,466; Zip Code 18232; Elev. 1,100; Lat. 40-49-54 N long. 075-52-58 W; E Pennsylvania; founded in 1846 and named for *Asa Lansford Foster*, mining engineer, coal operator, and early champion of the public school system.

•**LAPORTE**, Borough; Seat of Sullivan County; Pop. 230; Zip Code 18626; Elev. 1,966; Lat. 41-25-26 N long. 076-29-40 W; NE central Pennsylvania. Laporte, the smallest county seat in Pennsylvania, was laid out in 1850 by *Michael Meylert*, who named both the township and the village for his friend, *John Laporte*, who was speaker of the General Assembly in 1832, a member of Congress from 1832 to 1836 and the last surveyor-general of Pennsylvania, serving from 1845-1851.

•**LARKSVILLE**, Borough; Luzerne County; Pop. 4,410; Elev. 940; Lat. 41-14-42 N long. 075-55-52 W; E suburb of Wilkes-Barre in E Pennsylvania; a mining borough originally called Blidtown, was renamed in 1895 in honor of *Peggy Lark*, who had owned the village site and died here at the reputed age of 106.

•**LATROBE**, Borough; Westmoreland County; Pop. 10,799; Zip Code 15650; Elev. 1,006; Lat. 40-19-16 N long. 079-22-47 W; 41 m. SE of Pittsburgh in SW Pennsylvania. Latrobe, on Loyalhanna Creek, was named for *Benjamin Henry Latrobe, Jr.*, son of the father of architecture in the United States.

•**LAUGHLINTOWN**, Village; Westmoreland County; Pop. 750; Zip Code 15655; Elev. 1,274; Lat. 40-12-43 N long. 079-11-53 W; at the base of Laurel Hill, was founded in 1797 by *Robert Laughlin*.

427

•**LAUREL RUN**, Borough; Luzerne County; Pop. 715; Elev. 900; Lat. 41-13-20 N long. 075-51-48 W; Suburb of Wilkes-Barre in E Pennsylvania.

•**LAURELDALE**, Borough; Berks County; Pop. 4,047; Zip Code 19605; Elev. 380; N suburb of Reading in SE Pennsylvania.

•**LEBANON**, City; Seat of Lebanon County; Pop. 25,711; Zip Code 17042; Elev. 468; Lat. 40-20-27 N long. 076-24-42 W; 80 m. NW of Philadelphia in SE central Pennsylvania. Lebanon lies on a branch of Quitapahilla (Ind. "spring which flows from among pines") Creek between the South and Blue Mountains. Laid out in 1756 by *George Steitz*, the settlement was first known as Steitztown. Cedar trees growing in the vicinity may have reminded the Moravian settlers of the Biblical "cedars of Lebanon," and thus inspired its name.

•**LEECHBURG**, Borough; Armstrong County; Pop. 2,682; Zip Code 15656; Elev. 789' W Pennsylvania.Lat. 40-30-16 N long. 079-45-49 W; Leechburg, on the Kiskiminetas, was laid out in 1828 by *David Leech*, a native of Meicer County.

•**LEESPORT**, Borough; Berks County; Pop. 1,258; Zip Code 19533; Elev. 340; Lat. 40-26-49 N long. 075-58-00 W; SE Pennsylvania; name changed from West Leesport in 1950.

•**LEETSDALE**, Borough; Allegheny County; Pop. 1,604; Zip Code 15056; Elev. 714; Lat. 40-33-47 N long. 080-12-31 W; suburb of Pittsburgh in SE Pennsylvania; settled by *William Leet* in 1796.

•**LEHIGHTON**, Borough; Carbon County; Pop. 5,826; Zip Code 18235; Elev. 478; Lat. 40-50-01 N long. 075-42-51 W; 26 m. NW of Allentown in E Pennsylvania. Lehighton is on a plateau overlooking river and valley. The town was laid out in 1794 by *Colonel Jacob Weiss* and *William Henry*, and took its name from the Lehigh River, on which it is situated.

•**LEVITT**, Unincorporated village; Bucks County; Pop. 7,200; Zip Code 19053; Elev. 60; 25 m. NE of Philadelphia in SE Pennsylvania. Levitt is a large residential area. Community was planned by the *Levitt brothers* in the 1950s, who also developed a Levittown on Long Island, N.Y.

•**LEWISBURG**, Borough; Seat of Union County; Pop. 5,407; Zip Code 17837; Elev. 461; Lat. 40-57-52 N long. 076-53-05 W; 10 m. NW of Sunbury in central Pennsylvania, on Susquehanna River. Laid out in 1785, the settlement was named for *Ludwig (Lewis) Doerr*, storekeeper and early settler.

•**LEWIS RUN**, Borough; McKean County; Pop. 677; Zip Code 16738; Elev. 1,551; Lat. 41-52-15 N long. 078-39-42 W; N Pennsylvania. Lewis Run is on a plain at the southern edge of the Bradford oil field, and bisected by the stream for which it is named.

•**LEWISTOWN**, Borough; Seat of Mifflin County; Pop. 9,830; Zip Code 17044; Elev. 495; Lat. 40-35-57 N long. 077-34-18 W; Pennsylvania. Lewistown, near the western end of Lewistown Narrows, was laid out in 1790, and named Lewistown in honor of *William Lewis*, an ironmaster, who then owned and operated Hope Furnace, which was situated in old Derry Township, a few miles west of the new town.

•**LIBERTY**, Borough; Allegheny County; Pop. 3,112; Elev. 1,648; Lat. 40-19-31 N long. 079-51-23 W; Pennsylvania. Liberty began its history as a blockhouse. In the village center is the site of the Liberty Blockhouse erected as a provision station and refuge in 1792 during construction of Blockhouse or Williamson Road, between Northumberland and Canoe Camp.

•**LIGONIER**, Borough; Westmoreland County; Pop. 1,917; Zip Code 15658; Elev. 1,200; Lat. 40-14-35 N long. 079-14-16 W; out in 1816 and named for Fort Ligonier, erected in 1758 by *Colonel*

Henry Bouquet and named for a noted English soldier of French extraction, Field Marshal *Sir John Louis Ligonier*, who was raised to an earldom in 1766.

•**LILY**, Borough; Cambria County; Pop. 1,462; Zip Code 15938; Elev. 1,904; Lat. 40-25-33 N long. 078-37-13 W; hilly area, 20 m. SW of Altoona in SW central Pennsylvania.

•**LINCOLN**, Borough; Allegheny County; Pop. 1,428; Elev. 1,100; Lat. 40-11-47 N long. 076-12-05 W; in 1958 from Lincoln Township; suburb of Pittsburgh in SW Pennsylvania.

•**LINESVILLE**, Borough; Zip Code 16424; Elev. 1,050; Lat. 41-39-22 N long. 080-25-27 W; received its name from *Amos Line*, who was employed as a surveyor by the Pennsylvania Population Company, and who laid out the town about 1825.

•**LITITZ**, Borough; Lancaster County; Pop. 7,590; Zip Code 17543; Elev. 360; Lat. 40-09-26 N long. 076-18-26 W; of Lancaster in SE Pennsylvania. Lititz was laid out in 1757 by Moravian missionaries from Bethlehem, and named for a barony in Moravia.

•**LITTLESTOWN**, Borough; Adams County; Pop. 2,870; Zip Code 17340; Elev. 640; Lat. 40-31-13 N long. 079-01-34 W; S Pennsylvania. *Adam Klein*, a German immigrant, began this settlement in 1765. Early on, the village was known both as Petersburg and Kleine-staedtel. Finally the latter name stuck, and was translated into "Littlestown."

•**LOCK HAVEN**, City; Seat of Clinton County; Pop. 9,617; Zip Code 17745; Elev. 579; Lat. 41-08-13 N long. 077-26-50 W; on the Susquehanna River in the Bald Eagle Mountains in central Pennsylvania. Lock Haven was christened because the canal had a *lock* here, and the river furnished an excellent harbor, or *haven*, for rafts.

•**LOGANVILLE**, Borough; Zip Code 17342; Elev. 782; Lat. 39-51-20 N long. 076-42-28 W; Pennsylvania. Loganville was laid out about 1820 and named for *Colonel Henry Logan*, York County representative in Congress.

•**LORETTO**, Borough; Cambria County; Pop. 1,395; Zip Code 15940; Elev. 2,102; Lat. 40-30-11 N long. 078-37-50 W; SW of Altoona in SW central Pennsylvania. Loretto was named for the celebrated religious shrine in Italy near the Adriatic Sea by the priest *Demetrius Gallatzin*.

•**LOWER BURRELL**, City; Westmoreland County; Pop. 13,200; Zip Code 15068; Elev. 760; Lat. 40-33-11 N long. 079-45-27 W; N suburb of Pittsburgh in SE Pennsylvania.

•**LUZERNE**, Borough; Luzerne County; Pop. 3,703; Zip Code 18709; Elev. 570; Lat. 39-59-57 N long. 079-57-47 W; suburb of Wilkes-Barre in E Pennsylvania.

•**LYKENS**, Borough; Dauphin County; Pop. 2,181; Zip Code 17048; Elev. 677; Lat. 40-34-00 N long. 076-42-03 W; central Pennsylvania; founded in 1826, one year after the discovery of anthracite at the lower end of Short Mountain. It is named for *Andrew Lycan*, or *Lykens*, who had settled here in 1732.

•**MACUNGIE**, Borough; Lehigh County; Pop. 1,899; Zip Code 18062; Elev. 380; Lat. 40-30-57 N long. 075-33-20 w; of Allentown on Swope Creek, in E Pennsylvania; Indian name means "feeding place of the bears."

•**MAHAFFEY**, Borough; Clearfield County; Pop. 513; Zip Code 15757; Elev. 1,323; Lat. 40-52-22 N long. 078-42-38 W; on west branch of the Susquehanna River in W central Pennsylvania.

•**MAHANOY CITY**, Borough; Schuylkill County; Pop. 6,167; Zip Code 17948; Elev. 1,256; Lat. 40-48-45 N long. 076-08-31 W;hanoy was derived from the language of the Delawares, the word mahoni meaning a "lick", a term used in pioneer days to denote saline deposits where deer congregate.

•**MALVERN**, Borough; Chester County; Pop. 2,999; Zip Code 19355; Elev. 550; Lat. 40-02-10 N long. 075-30-51 W; suburb of Philadelphia near Paoli, in SE Pennsylvania; residential area.

•**MANCHESTER**, Borough; York County; Pop. 2,027; Zip Code 17345; Elev. 500; Lat. 40-27-18 N long.080-01-12 W; Pennsylvania. Named for the large industrial city in England, Manchester in Pennsylvania has a few industries of its own.

•**MANHEIM**, Borough; Lancaster County; Pop. 5,015; Zip Code 17545; Elev. 339; Lat. 40-09-48 N long. 076-23-43 W SE Pennsylvania.

•**MANOR**, Borough; Westmoreland County; Pop. 2,235; Zip Code 15665; Elev. 1,000; Lat. 40-37-57 N long. 078-59-02 W; lvania; named for one of the manors owned by the *Penn* family, which once stood here.

•**MANSFIELD**, Borough; Tioga County; Pop. 3,322; Zip Code 16933; Elev. 1,174; Lat. 41-48-26 N long. 077-04-40 W;SW of Elmira, N.Y. in N Pennsylvania; named in 1824 for *Asa Mann*, an early settler.

•**MARIETTA**, Borough; Lancaster County; Pop. 2,740; Zip Code 17547; Elev. 261; Lat. 40-03-25 N long. 076-33-09 W; 22 m. SE of Harrisburg on Susquehanna River in SE Pennsylvania. The town was originally two distinct settlements, - New Haven, laid out by *David Cook* in 1803, and Waterford, laid out at "Anderson's Ferry," by *James Anderson* in 1804. In 1812 the two villages were incorporated under one charter as Marietta, a name said to have been compounded of *Mary* and *Etta*, the first names of *Mrs. Cook* and *Mrs. Anderson*, the wives of the two founders.

•**MARS**, Borough; Butler County; Pop. 1,803; Zip Code 16046; Elev. 1,031; Lat. 40-41-45 Nlong. 080-00-43 W; of Pittsburg in W Pennsylvania.

•**MARTINSBURG**, Borough; Blair County; Pop. 2,231; Zip Code 16662; Elev. 1,407; Lat. 40-18-40 N long. 078-19-28 W; Pennsylvania.

•**MARYSVILLE**, Borough; Perry County; Pop. 2,452; Zip Code 17053; Elev.460; N of Harrisburg, on Susquehanna River in S central Pennsylvania.

•**MASONTOWN**, Borough; Fayette County; Pop. 4,909; Zip Code 15461; Elev. 1,050; Lat. 40-11-28 N long. 078-15-38 W; ut this town in 1798. Settlers subsequently named it for him.

•**MASTHOPE**, Village; Pike County; Pop. 500; name is an anglicization of an Indian word meaning "glass beads." Today it is a ski resort.

•**MATAMORAS**, Borough; Pike County; Pop. 2,111; Zip Code 18336; Elev. 868; Lat. 40-26-24 N long. 076-56-01 W; Delaware River, near New York and New Jersey state lines in NE Pennsylvania.

•**MAYFIELD**, Borough; Lackawanna County; Pop. 1,812; Zip Code 18433; Elev. 952; Lat. 41-32-27 N long. 075-32-11 W; NE Pennsylvania; was developed prior to 1840 by *John Gibson*, who sold out in 1874 to the Delaware and Hudson Canal Company.

•**MCADOO**, Borough; Schuylkill County; Pop. 2,940; Zip Code 18237; Elev. 1,836; Lat. 40-54-36 N long. 075-59-30 W; in 1880 and later named by postal authorities for *William Gibbs McAdoo*.

•**MCCLURE**, Borough; Snyder County; Pop. 1,024; Zip Code 17841; Elev. 700; Lat. 40-06-14 N long. 079-33-15 W; Pennsylvania; was founded in 1867 and named for *Alexander Kelley McClure* (1828-1909), journalist, politician, and author. McClure was one of the founders of the Republican Party. The town was formerly called Stricktown for a noted Indian fighter.

•**MCCONNELLSBURG**, Borough; Seat of Fulton County; Pop. 1,178; Zip Code 17233; Elev. 955; Lat. 39-55-57 N long. 077-59-57 W;lvania.

•**MCDONALD**, Borough; Allegheny and Washington Counties; Pop. 2,772; Zip Code 15057; Elev. 1,020; Lat. 40-22-15 N long. 080-14-06 W; Pennsylvania. McDonald was laid out in 1781, and took its name from old Fort McDonald, which was built during the Revolutionary War on the land of *John McDonald*, who settled here in 1775.

•**MCKEESPORT**, City; Allegheny County; Pop. 31,012; Zip Code 151+; Elev. 750; Lat. 40-20-52 N long. 079-51-52 W; lvania. McKeesport is at the junction of the Youghiogheny and Monongahea Rivers. *David McKee*, a north country Irishman who settled here in 1755, acquired title to 844 acres and in 1755 obtained ferry privileges from Colonial authorities. The town is named after his family.

•**MCSHERRYSTOWN**, Borough; Adams County; Pop. 2,764; Zip Code 17344; Elev. 571; Lat. 39-48-26 N long. 077-00-42 W; settler, *Patrick McSherry*, who came here in 1765.

•**MEADVILLE**, City; Seat of Crawford County; Pop. 15,544; Zip Code 16335; Elev. 1,078; Lat. 41-38-29 N long. 080-09-06 W; vania, on French Creek. Meadville is in the western foothills of the Alleghenies, was settled in 1788 by *David Mead*, his brothers, and other pioneers from Sunburgh, who made the first white settlement in Northwestern Pennsylvania.

•**MECHANICSBURG**, Borough; Cumberland County; Pop. 9,487; Zip Code 17055; Elev. 460; Lat. 40-33-42 N long. 080-24-11 W; vania. Named for the large number of mechanics who worked in the foundries and machine shops here.

•**MEYERSDALE**, Borough; Somerset County; Pop. 2,581; Zip Code 15552; Elev. 2,054; 18. Lat. 39-48-49 N long. 079-01-30 W; NW of Cumberland, Maryland in S Pennsylvania; was laid out in a valley in 1844 and named for *Peter Meyers*, an early settler who converted his farm into building lots.

•**MIDDLETOWN**, Borough; Dauphin County; Pop. 10,122; Zip Code 17057; Elev. 355; Lat. 41-55-38 N long. 076-41-57 W; 8 m. SE of Harrisburg in SE central Pennsylvania, on Susquehanna River. Middletown, halfway between Lancaster and Carlisle, was founded in 1755.

•**MIDLAND**, Borough; Beaver County; Pop. 4,310; Zip Code 15059; Elev. 750; Lat. 40-37-57 N long. 080-26-48 W; 7 m. E of east Liverpool, Ohio in W Pennsylvania. Midland, on the north bank of the Ohio River, is a smoky steel-producing center named for the Midland Steel Company.

•**MIDWAY**, Borough; Washington County; Pop. 1,187; Zip Code 15060; Elev. 1,120; Lat. 39-48-30 N long. 077-00-11 W; SW Pennsylvania; so named because it is located between Pittsburgh and Steubenville, Ohio.

•**MILESBURG**, Borough; Centre County; Pop. 1,309; Zip Code 16853; Elev. 700; Lat. 40-56-390 N long. 077-47-07 W; Central Pennsylvania; was founded in 1793 by *General Samuel Miles*, Indian fighter, patriot, landowner, iron manufacturer, and onetime mayor of Philadelphia (1790).

•**MILLERSBURG**, Borough; Dauphin County; Pop. 2,770; Zip Code 17061; Elev. 397; 28 m. N of Harrisburg in SE central Pennsylvania, on Susquehanna River. Settlement was made in 1790 by *Daniel* and *John Miller*, brothers, who owned 400 acres here.

•**MILLERSVILLE**, Borough; Lancaster County; Pop. 7,668; Zip Code 17551; Elev. 360; suburb of Lancaster in SE Pennsylvania; site of Millersville State College, with 4,700 students.

•**MILLVALE**, Borough; Allegheny County; Pop. 4,754; Zip Code 15209; Elev. 900; SW Pennsylvania.

•**MILTON**, Borough; Northumberland County; Pop. 6,730; Zip Code 17847; Elev. 473; Lat. 40-54-35 N long. 079-13-01 W; 23 m. SE of Williamsport in E central Pennsylvania, on the Susquehanna River.

•**MINERSVILLE**, Borough; Schuylkill County; Pop. 5,635; Zip Code 17954; Elev. 820; Lat. 40-20-32 N long. 078-55-33 W; E central Pennsylvania. Named for the fact that a large number of its people have from the beginning been coal miners.

•**MONACA**, Borough; Beaver County; Pop. 7,661; Zip Code 15061; Elev. 720; Lat. 40-41-14 N long. 080-16-18 W; 2 m. S of Beaver in W Pennsylvania.

•**MONESSEN**, City; Westmoreland County; Pop. 11,928; Zip Code 15062; Elev. 756; Lat. 40-08-54 N long. 079-53-17 W; 22 m. S of Pittsburgh in SW Pennsylvania, on Monongahela River. The name Monessen is a curious hybrid compound, formed by combining the first syllable of Monongahela with Essen, the name of the greatest iron town in Germany, the home of the famous Krupp works. The original meaning of the name Essen has been lost; it has no connection with *Eisen*, the German word fo *iron*.

•**MONONGAHELA**, City; Washington County; Pop. 5,950; Zip Code 15063 Elev. 754; Lat. 40-12-11 N long. 079-55-35 W; 18 m. S of Pittsburgh in SW Pennsylvania, on Monongahela River. The name "Monongahela" is a form of the Indian *Menaun-gehilla*, meaning "river with the sliding banks."

•**MONROEVILLE**, Borough; Allegheny County; Pop. 30,977; Zip Code 15146; Elev. 1,980; 13 m. E of Pittsburgh in SW Pennsylvania; residential suburb.

•**MONTOURSVILLE**, Borough; Lycoming County; Pop. 5,403; Zip Code 17754; Elev. 525; Lat. 41-15-15 Nlong. 076-55-15 W; near Williamsport in N central Pennsylvania, on Susquehanna River. The site, once occupied by the Indian village of Otzinachson, was given in 1768 to *Andrew Montour*, a half-breed Indian interpreter, for his loyalty to the provincial government.

•**MOOSIC**, Borough; Lackawanna County; Pop. 6,068; Zip Code 18507; Elev. 650; Lat. 41-21-12 N long. 075-44-19 W; NE Pennsylvania; named for the great herds of moose that once roamed the Lackawanna River Valley. Suburb of Scranton.

•**MORTON**, Borough; Delaware County; Pop. 2,412; Zip Code 19070; Elev. 130; Lat. 39-54-35 N long. 075-19-26 W; SW suburb of Philadelphia in SE of Pennsylvania. Named for *John Morton*, who may have cast the deciding vote from Pennsylvania in favor of the Declaration of Independence, and who signed the historic document.

•**MOSCOW**, Borough; Lackawanna County; Pop. 1,536; Zip Code 18444; Elev. 1,600; Lat. 41-20-12 N long. 075-31-08 W; 12 m. SE of Scranton in NE Pennsylvania.

•**MOUNT OLIVER**, Borough; Allegheny County; Pop. 4,576; Zip Code 15210; Elev. 1,100; Lat. 40-24-51 N long. 079-59-17 W; SW Pennsylvania. The origin of the name "Oliver" is not definitely known, although some think the name is derived from *Oliver Ormsby* who owned several hundred acres of land here in 1840, and the next year it was apportioned among his eight children.

•**MOUNTVILLE**, Borough; Lancaster County; Pop. 1,505; Zip Code 17554; Elev. 440; Lat. 40-02-21 N long. 076-25-52 W; SE Pennsylvania.

•**MUNCY**, Borough; Zip Code 17756; Pop. 497; Lat. 41-12-20 N long. 076-47-09 W; 12 m. E of Williamsport on the Susquehanna River in N central Pennsylvania. Muncy was laid out in 1797, and named for the Munsee Indians.

•**MYERSTOWN**, Borough; Zip Code 17067; Elev. 472; Lat. 40-02-37 N long. 077-11-23 W; 8 m. E of Lebanon in SE central Pennsylvania.

•**NANTICOKE**, City; Luzerne County; Pop. 13,044; Zip Code 18634; Elev. 640; Lat. 41-12-19 N long. 076-00-19 W; Suburb of Wilkes-Barre, on Susquehanna River. Nanticoke received its name from a tribe of Indians.

•**NARBETH**, Borough; Montgomery County; Pop. 4,496; Zip Code 19072; Elev. 285; Lat. 40-00-30 N long. 075-15-39 W; NW suburb of Philadelphia in SE Pennsylvania.

•**NAZARETH**, Borough; Northampton County; Pop. 5,443; Zip Code 18064; Elev. 485; Lat. 40-44-25 N long. 075-18-36 W; 13 m. NE of Allentown in E Pennsylvania; Nazareth was the second Moravian settlement in Pennsylvania.

•**NESQUEHONING**, Borough; Carbon County; Pop. 3,346; Zip Code 18240; Elev. 801; Lat. 40-51-52 N long. 075-48-41 W; 28 m. S of Wilkes-Barre in E Pennsylvania. Nesquehoning is an Indian term meaning "at the black lick," or "narrow valley".

•**NEW BEAVER**, Borough; Lawrence County; Pop. 1,885; suburb of Beaver Falls in W Pennsylvania; incorporated in 1960 from Big Beaver Township.

•**NEW BETHLEHEM**, Borough; Clarion County; Pop. 1,441; Zip Code 16242; Elev. 1,075; LAT. 41-00-06 N LONG. 079-19-54 W; 36 m. SE of Oil City in W Pennsylvania.

•**NEW BRIGHTON**, Borough; Beaver County; Pop. 7,364; Zip Code 15066; Elev. 750; LAT. 40-43-49 N LONG. 080-18-37 W; just S of Beaver Falls in W Pennsylvania. Named for the great English sea resort.

•**NEW BRITAIN**, Borough; Bucks County; Pop. 2,519; Zip Code 18901; Elev. 300; LAT. 40-17-56 N LONG. 075-10-53 W; N suburb of Philadelphia in SE Pennsylvania; named for the industrial city in Connecticut by west-moving pioneers.

•**NEW CASTLE**, City; Seat of Lawrence County; Pop. 33,621; Zip Code 161+; Elev. 806; LAT. 41-00-13 N LONG. 080-20-50 W; 44 m. NW of Pittsburgh in W Pennsylvania, on the Shenango River. Named the spot for Newcastle upon Tyne, the English industrial city.

•**NEW CUMBERLAND**, Borough; Cumberland County; Pop. 8,051; Zip Code 17070; Elev. 308; Lat. 40-13-56 N long. 076-53-06 W; .s Suburb of Harrisburg in S Pennsylvania, on the Susquehanna River. It was named for the county it sits in, which is Welsh for "land of compatriots."

•**NEW EAGLE**, Borough; Washington County; Pop. 2,617; Zip Code 15067; Elev. 840; Lat. 40-12-28 N long. 079-56-50 W; 16 m. S of Pittsburgh in SW Pennsylvania, on Monogahela River.

•**NEW GALILEE**, Borough; Beaver County; Pop. 596; Zip Code 16141; Elev. 960; Lat. 40-50-08 N long. 080-23-59 W; suburb of Pittsburgh and Beaver Falls in W Pennsylvania; named by religious settlers for Jesus homeland.

•**NEW HOLLAND**, Borough; Lancaster County; Pop. 4,147; Zip Code 17557; Elev. 495; Lat. 40-06-06 N long. 076-05-08 W; 13 m. NE of Lancaster in a tobacco and corn farming region.

•**NEW KENSINGTON**, City; Westmoreland County; Pop. 17,660; Zip Code 15068; Elev. 614; Lat. 40-34-11 N long. 079-45-54 W; 16 m. NE of Pittsburgh in SW Pennsylvania, on Allegheny River. New Kensington probably took its name from the London district of Kensington.

•**NEW OXFORD**, Borough; Adams County; Pop. 1,921; Zip Code 17350; Elev. 560; Lat. 39-51-49 N long. 077-03-22 W; S Pennsylvania; was laid out in 1792. The name was inspired by the English medieval university town.

•**NEW STANTON**, Borough; Westmoreland County; Pop. 2,600; Zip Code 15672; Elev. 980; Lat. 40-13-09 N long. 079-36-35 W; SW Pennsylvania.

•**NEWTOWN**, Borough; Bucks County; Pop. 2,419; Zip Code 18940; Elev. 150; Lat. 40-50-57 N long. 078-15-42 W; 22 m. NE of Philadelphia.

•**NEW WILMINGTON**, Borough; Lawrence County; Pop. 2,774; Zip Code 16142; Elev. 950; Lat. 41-07-20 N long. 080-19-59 W; 9 m. N of New Castle in W Pennsylvania; on Little Neshannock Creek, was incorporated from Wilmington Township in 1863.

•**NEWELL**, Borough; Fayette County; Pop. 629; Zip Code 15466; Elev. 800; SE Pennsylvania; incorporated in 1952 from Jefferson Township.

•**NORRISTOWN**, Borough; Seat of Montgomery County; Pop. 34,648; Zip Code 194+; Elev. 83; Lat. 40-07-17 N long. 075-20-25 W; located on the Schuylkill River 15 miles NW of Philadelphia in SE Pennsylvania; is in a fertile rolling section of the Schuylkill Valley. On October 7, 1704, Isaac Norris and William Trent purchased the land now occupied by the borough for 50 cents an acre. The town is named for him.

•**NORTHAMPTON**, Borough; Northampton County; Pop. 8,240; Zip Code 18067; Elev. 320; 5 miles N of Allentown in E Pennsylvania. This borough is named for the county of the same name.

•**NORTH APOLLO**, Borough; Armstrong County; Pop. 1,487; Zip Code 15673; Elev. 900; Lat. 40-35-46 N long. 079-33-21 W; W Pennsylvania.

•**NORTH BELLE VERNON**, Borough; Westmoreland County; Pop. 2,425; Zip Code rural; Elev. 900; Lat. 40-07-45 N long. 079-52-06 W; SW Pennsylvania.

•**NORTH BRADDOCK**, Borough; Allegheny County; Pop. 8,711; Zip Code ; Elev. 1,220; Lat. 40-23-56 N long. 079-50-28 W; 10 miles E of Pittsbuqua in SW Pennsylvania; Incorporated in 1897 and named for its southern neighbor, Braddock. Metal products are manufactured.

•**NORTH EAST**, Borough; Erie County; Pop. 4,568; Zip Code 16428; Elev. 800; Lat. 42-12-56 N long. 079-50-04 W; 15 miles NE of Erie in NW Pennsylvania on Lake Erie; The town is named for North East Township, which occupies the northeast corner of the Erie Triangle, a wedge-shaped slice of land once claimed by New York, Massachusetts, and Connecticut.

•**NORTH IRWIN**, Borough; Westmoreland County; Pop. 1,016 ; Elev. 1,104; Lat. 40-20-15 N long. 079-42-49 W; E suburb of Pittsburgh in SW Pennsylvania.

•**NORTH WALES**, Borough; Montgomery County; Pop. 3,391; Zip Code 19454; Elev. 380; Lat. 40-12-39 N long. 075-16-43 W; 20 miles N of Philadelphia in SE Pennsylvania.

•**NORTH YORK**, Borough; York County; Pop. 1,755; Zip Code 17371; Elev. 380; Lat. 39-58-41 N long. 076-44-00 W; Just N of the city of York in S Pennsylvania.

•**NORTHUMBERLAND**, Borough; Northumberland County; Pop. 3,636; Zip Code 17857; Elev. 452; Lat. 40-53-30 N long. 076-47-52 W; 28 miles SE of Williamsport in E central Pennsylvania; On the Susquehanna River; was laid out in 1772 on a wedge of land formed by the junction of the two branches of the Susquehanna River; and was named for the newly-formed county it sits in.

•**NORVELT**, Village; Westmoreland County; Pop. 1,800; Zip Code 15674; Elev. 1,040; Lat. 40-12-29 N long. 079-29-52 W; SW

Pennsylvania. Norvelt was named by combining the final syllables of *Mrs. Eleanor Roosevelt's* first and last names.

•**NORWOOD**, Borough; Delaware County; Pop. 6,647; ; Zip Code 19074; Elev. 50; Lat. 39-53-30 N long. 075-18-00 W; 9 miles SW of Philadelphia in SE Pennsylvania.

•**OAKDALE**, Borough; Allegheny County; Pop. 1,955; Zip Code 15071; Elev. 900; Lat. 40-59-31 N long. 075-55-14 W; S suburb of Susquehanna in SW Pennsylvania.

•**OAKMONT**, Borough; Allegheny County; Pop. 7,0939; Zip Code 15139; Elev. 840; Lat. 40-31-18 N long. 079-50-33 W; 11 miles NE of Pittsburgh.

•**OBERLIN**, Village; Dauphin County; Pop. 3,500; Zip Code 17113; Lat. 40-14-29 N long. 076-48-54 W; Suburb of Harrisburg near Steelton. Named for the preacher, *Jean F. Oberlin*, who was a preacher in the Alsace-Lorraine region of France.

•**OGONTZ**, Village; Montgomery County; Pop. (incl. with Elkins Park); Named for an Indian chief who converted to Christianity and became a missionary to his people. A campus of Pennsylvania State University is here.

•**OHIOVILLE**, Borough; Beaver County; Pop. 4,217; Elev. 1,100; Lat. 40-40-45 Nl ong. 080-29-42 W; 25 miles SW of New Castle in W Pennsylvania; Incorporated in the early 1960s.

•**OIL CITY**, City; Venango County; Pop. 13,881; Zip Code 16301; Elev. 1,029; Lat. 40-24-08 N long. 078-38-25 W; 90 miles N of Pittsburgh in NW Pennsylvania; on the Allegheny River at the mouth of Oil Creek, and once the site of a Seneca village, emerged in 1860 as an important oil center. It owes its name to the rise and growth of the petroleum business.

•**OLD FORGE**, Borough; Lackawanna County; Pop. 9,304; Zip Code 185+zone; 6 miles SW of Scranton in NE Pennsylvania; founded in 1789 when a forge was built by *Dr. William Hooker Smith*, the pioneer physician of this region.

•**OLEONA**, Village; Elev. 1,250; Lat. 41-33-22 N long. 077-42-07 W; was the principal site of the colony established in 1852 by the Norwegian violin virtuoso, *Ole Borneman Bull*, who wished "to found a New Norway, consecrated to liberty, baptized with independence, and protected by the Union's mighty flag."

•**OLYPHANT**, Borough; Lackawanna County; Pop. 5,204; Zip Code 18447; Elev. 790; Lat. 41-28-06 N long. 075-36-12 W; 5 miles NE of Scranton in NE Pennsylvania; *James Ferris* erected the first house here in 1789. Olyphant was named in honor of *George Talbot Olyphant* of New York, who became president of the Delaware and Hudson Canal Company in 1858.

•**ORANGEVILLE**, Borough; Columbia County; Pop. 507; Zip Code 17859; Elev. 580; Lat. 41-04-41 N long. 076-24-53 W; E central Pennsylvania; Named by early settlers for Orange County, New York.

•**ORBISONIA**, Borough; Huntingdon County; Pop. 506; Zip Code 17243; Elev. 628; Lat. 40-14-34 N long. 077-53-36 W; S cen. Pennsylvania; was founded in 1760 and named for *Thomas E. Orbison*, early landowner.

•**OREGON**, Village; Lancaster County; Pop. 100; Zip Code 17543; Elev. 343; Lat. 40-00-00 N long. 076-14-43 W; near Lititz; was formerly called Catfish after the tasty denizens of nearby Lititz Creek.

•**ORRSTOWN**, Borough; Franklin County; Pop. 247; Zip Code 17244; Elev. 620; Lat. 40-03-31 N long. 077-36-37 W; S Pennsylvania.

431

•**ORWIGSBURG**, Borough; Schuylkill County; Pop. 2,700; Zip Code 17961; Elev. 640; Lat. 40-39-17 N long. 076-06-04 W; 5 miles SE of Pottsville in E central Pennsylvania; Laid out and named by *Peter Orwig* in 1796. It was Schuylkill County seat in 1811 to 1851, when the seat moved to Pottsville.

•**OXFORD**, Borough; Chester County; Pop. 3,633; Zip Code 19363; Elev. 507; Lat. 39-47-07 N long. 075-58-45 W; in SE Pennsylvania; founded in 1801 and was named for the English university town.

•**PAINT**, Borough; Somerset County; Pop. 1,177; Lat. 40-14-37 N long. 078-50-57 W; in S Pennsylvania.

•**PALMERTON**, Borough; Carbon County; Pop. 5,455; Zip Code 18071; Elev. 420; Lat. 40-48-05 N long. 075-36-38 W; 15 miles NW of Allenton in E Pennsylvania; laid out in 1898 by the New Jersey Zinc Company and named for *Stephen J. Palmer*, company president, was incorporated as a borough in 1913.

•**PALMYRA**, Borough; Lebanon County; Pop. 7,228; Zip Code 17078; Elev. 450; Lat. 40-18-32 N long. 076-35-37 W; 15 miles E of Harrisburg in SE cen. Pennsylvania; was settled by *John Palm*, who came to America from Germany in 1749. *Palm* called his settlement Palmstown, but several years later the place was renamed for the ancient Syrian city.

•**PAOLI**, Village; Chester County; Pop. 5,835; Zip Code 19301; Elev. 452; Lat. 40-02-31 N long. 075-28-36 W; 15 miles NW of Philadelphia; took its name from the General Paoli Tavern, destroyed by fire in 1906, which had been named for *General Pasquale Paoli*, the Corsican patriot.

•**PARKESBURG**, Borough; Chester County; Pop. 2,578; Zip Code 19365; Elev. 539; Lat. 39-57-31 Nl ong. 075-55-11 W; in SE Pennsylvania; named for the old and influential Parkes family. Wooden and metal skids are made in Parkesburg.

•**PARKSIDE**, Borough; Delaware County; Pop. 2,464; Elev. 100; Lat. 39-51-51 N long. 075-22-44 W; SW suburb of Philadelphia in SE Pennsylvania.

•**PATTON**, Borough; Cambria County; Pop. 2,441; Zip Code 16668; Elev. 1,750; Lat. 40-38-02 N long. 078-39-02 W; 20 miles NW of Altoon in SW central Pennsylvania; Named for *Col. John Patton* of Curwensville; The seldom seen Valley Mine is near town; where mining history is preserved and displayed.

•**PAUPACK**, Village; Pike County; Pop. 400; Zip Code 18451; Elev. 1,540; Lat. 41-23-46 N long. 075-11-48 W; E Pennsylvania.

•**PAXTANG**, Borough; Dauphin County; Pop. 1,646; Zip Code 17111; Elev. 400; Lat. 40-15-32 N long. 076-49-56 W; SE central Pennsylvania.

•**PEN ARGYL**, Borough; Northampton County; Pop. 3,388; Zip Code 18072; Elev. 831; Lat. 40-52-07 N long. 075-15-19 W; 20 miles NE of Allentown in E Pennsylvania.

•**PENBROOK**, Borough; Dauphin County; Pop. 1,006; Zip Code 17103; Elev. 490; Lat. 40-16-31 N long. 076-50-54 W; 5 miles Ne of Harrisburg in SE central Pennsylvania.

•**PENN**, Borough; Westmoreland County; Pop. 619; Zip Code 15675; Elev. 980; Lat. 40-19-44 N long. 079-38-29 W; E suburb of Pittsburgh in SW Pennsylvania; Named for William Penn.

•**PENNDEL**, Borough; Bucks County; Pop. 2,703; Zip Code 19047; Elev. 100; suburb of Philadelphia in Pennsylvania; Named for William Penn.

•**PENNSBURG**, Borough; Montgomery County; Pop. 2,339; Zip Code 18073; Lat. 40-23-27 N long. 075-29-33 W; 40 miles N of Philadelphia in SE Pennsylvania.

•**PERKASIE**, Borough; Bucks County; Pop. 5,241; Zip Code 18944; Elev. 400; Lat. 40-22-19 N long. 075-17-35 W; 20 miles SE of Allentown in SE Pennsylvania.

•**PERRYOPOLIS**, Borough; Fayette County; Pop. 2,139; Zip Code 15473; Elev. 741; Lat. 40-05-13 N long. 079-45-03 W; in SW Pennsylvania; was laid out in 1814 and named for the naval hero, *Oliver Hazard Perry*.

PHILADELPHIA, City: Philadelphia County Seat; Pop. 1,681,185; Zip Code ; Elev. 110; Lat. 39-57-08 N long. 075-09-51 W; Fourth largest of American cities, it is long-recognized as the birthplace of the nation. It was also the first citadel of high finance in the New World and for a time its largest settlement. William Penn and his early settlers would not recognize the sprawling commercial and industrial giant Philadelphia has become today. Penn's former "greene country towne" now covers over 130 square miles and while Penn wasn't able to see his city grow, he was able to plan it. He had soured on England's rigidity and crooked streets, and today the central part of Philadelphia is a neat network of straight north-south and east-west thoroughfares. Only after the Quaker colonizer had acquired the Pennsylvania grant from Charles II in 1681 did the "City of brotherly love " come into existence.

•**PHILIPSBURG**, Borough; Centre County; Pop. 3,464; Zip Code 16866; Elev. 1,433; Lat. 40-53-47 N long. 078-13-15 W; 28 miles NE of Altoona in central Pennsylvania; was founded in 1797 by two Englishmen, *Henry* and *James Phillips*.

•**PHOENIXVILLE**, Borough; Chester County; Pop. 14,165; Zip Code 19460; Elev. 127; Lat. 40-07-49 N long. 075-30-55 W; 10 miles W of Norristown on the Schuylkill River in SE Pennsylvania.

•**PINE GROVE**, Borough; Schuylkill County; Pop. 2,244; ; Zip Code 17963; Elev. 540; Lat. 40-29-07 N long. 078-37-15 W; in E cen. Pennsylvania.

•**PITCAIRN**, Borough; Allegheny County; Pop. 4,175; Zip Code 15140; Elev. 880; Lat. 40-24-11 N long. 079-46-42 W; 13 miles E of Pittsburgh in SW Pennsylvania; The town was incorporated under the name of Pitcairn in honor of *Robert Pitcairn*, then superintendent of the Pittsburgh division of the Pennsylvania Railroad. Pitcairn means "cairn-croft."

•**PITTSBURGH**, City; Allegheny County Seat; Pop. 424,205; Zip Code 152+; Elev. 744; Lat. 40-26-26 N long. 079-59-46 W; Pennsylvania's second city of importance and one of the greatest steel centers of the world embraces the forks where the Monongahela and Allegheny Rivers unite to form the Ohio. Named for the great British statesman, the elder *William Pitt*, this city in western Pennsylvania had its origin in a cluster of log cabins built near Fort Pitt after 1758.

•**PITTSTON**, City; Luzerne County; Pop. 9,930; Zip Code 186+; Elev. 570; Lat. 41-19-33 N long. 075-47-23 W; 10 miles NE of Wilkes-Barre on the Susquehanna River in E Pennsylvania; was named for the elder *William Pitt*, British statesman and friend of the Colonies.

•**PLEASANTVILLE**, Borough; Bedford County; Pop. 275; Zip Code 16341; Elev. 1,240; Lat. 40-37-19 N long. 079-44-13 W; in S Pennsylvania; The natural deposits of alum in this area caused this borough's original name of Alum Bank.

•**PLYMOUTH**, Borough; Luzerne County; Pop. 7,605; Zip Code 18651; Elev. 540; Lat. 41-14-25 N long. 075-56-42 W; W suburb of Wilkes-Barre on the Susquehanna River in E Pennsylvania; named and incorporated from Plymouth Township, one of the five townships formed by the Susquehanna Company on December 28, 1768. Its name was derived from Plymouth in Litchfield County, Connecticut. The Connecticut town was doubtless named for Plymouth in Massachusetts, the oldest settlement in New

England. The Pilgrim Fathers called their town Plymouth because the *Mayflower* had sailed from Plymouth in Devonshire, which lies at the mouth of the River Plym.

•**POINT MARION**, Borough; Fayette County; Pop. 1,642; Zip Code 15474; Elev. 815; Lat. 39-44-20 N long. 079-53-56 W; 20 miles SW of Uniontown in SW Pennsylvania; at the confluence of the Cheat and Monongahela Rivers, was laid out in 1842, and named for *General Francis Marion*, the "Swamp Fox" of the Revolution.

•**POLK**, Borough; Venango County; Pop. 1,884; Zip Code 16342; Elev. 1,116; Lat. 41-22-01 N long. 079-55-46 W; 15 miles SW of Oil City in NW Pennsylvania; settled about 1798, took form in 1839 when *Aaron McKissick* purchased the site and laid out a village. When incorporated in 1886, it was named for *President James K. Polk*.

•**PORT ALLEGANY**, Borough; McKean County; Pop. 2,593; Zip Code 16743; Elev. 1,484; Lat. 41-48-39 N long. 078-16-48 W; 20 miles SE of Olean, New York on the Allegheny River in N Pennsylvania; was the center of the tremendous lumbering operations along the Allegheny River that reached their peak between 1830 and 1840.

•**PORTAGE**, Borough; Cambria County; Pop. 3,510; Zip Code 15946; Elev. 1,700; 20 miles NE of Johnstown in a coal mining region in SW cen. Pennsylvania; named for the old Portage Railroad, which once extended from Hollidaysburg to Johnstown.

•**PORTLAND**, Borough; Northampton County; Pop. 540; Zip Code 18351; Elev. 293; Lat. 40-55-23 N long. 075-05-49 W; in E Pennsylvania; was founded in 1845 by *Captain James Ginn*, of Portland, Maine.

•**POTTSTOWN**, Borough; Montgomery County; Pop. 22,729; Zip Code 19464; Elev. 138; Lat. 40-14-43 N long. 075-39-00 W; 15 miles SE of Reading in SE Pennsylvania; is at the junction of Manatawny (Ind. "place where we drink") Creek and the Schuylkill River. About 1754, *John Potts*, a prominent ironmaster whose father had been asociated with *Rutter*, laid out a town, and in 1815 the place was incorported as the borough of Pottstown.

•**PRINGLE**, Borough; Luzerne County; Pop. 1,221; Zip Code 18704; Elev. 660; Lat. 41-16-41 N long. 075-53-51 W; near Wilkes-Barre in E Pennsylvania.

•**PROSPECT**, Borough; Butler County; Pop. 1,016; Zip Code 16052; Elev. 1.369; Lat. 40-54-16 N long. 080-02-48 W; in W Pennsylvania; in an early agricultural section, first settled in 1796. Today it is a residential suburb of Butler.

•**PUNXSUTAWNEY**, Borough; Jefferson County; Pop. 7,479; Zip Code 15767; Elev. 1,236; Lat. 40-56-37 N long. 078-58-16 W; 80 miles NE of Pittsburgh on Mahoning Creek in W cen. Pennsylvania. Shawnee wigwam villages once occupied the site. Swarms of gnats, plagued early settlers and their livestock. Indians called the insects *ponkies* (living dust and ashes), and the village was called *Ponkis Utenink* (land of the ponkies), from which the present name evolved.

•**QUAKERTOWN**, Borough; Bucks County; Pop. 8,867; Zip Code 18951; Elev. 499; Lat. 40-26-30 N long. 075-20-31 W; 15 miles SE of Allentown in SE Pennsylvania; was founded by Quakers from Gwynedd, Wales in 1715.

•**RADNOR**, Urban Township; Delaware County; Elev. 250; Lat. 40-02-46 N long. 075-21-37 W; in W Pennsylvania; residential suburb. Settled and named in 1683 by Quakers from Radnorshire, Wales.

•**RAMEY**, Borough; Clearfield County; Pop. 568; Zip Code 16671; Elev. 1,610; Lat. 40-47-53 N long. 078-23-51 W; in W cen.Pennsylvania.

•**RANKIN**, Borough; Allegheny County; Pop. 2,892; Zip Code 15201; Elev. 747; Lat. 40-24-45 N long. 079-52-46 W; 5 miles E of Pittsburgh, on the Monongahela River in SW Pennsylvania. About 1870 a man named *Thomas Rankin* bought a farm, built a house, and lived where the town now stands. At that time Rankin's house was the only one in sight, and the Baltimore and Ohio Railroad made it a stopping place, callin the station Rankin.

•**READING**, City; Seat of Berks County; Pop. 78,582; Zip Code 196+; Elev. 264; Lat. 40-20-08 N long. 075-55-38 W; 70 miles NW of Philadelphia on the Schuylkill River in SE Pennsylvania; on the Schuylkill River's bank in southeastern *Penn* named it for the seat of Berkshire, England, the name of which was derived from the Saxon words *rhedin*, a fern, and *ing*, a meadow.

•**RED LION**, Borough; York County; Pop. 5,824; Zip Code 17356; Elev. 910; Lat. 40-28-50 N long. 075-36-59 W; 10 miles SE of York in S Pennsylvania; named for a tavern bult here in colonial times, which had a lion painted red as its emblem.

•**RENOVO**, Borough; Clinton County; Pop. 1,812; Zip Code 17764; Elev. 668; Lat. 41-19-35 N long. 077-45-04 W; 60 miles NW of Williamsport in central Pennsylvania; located on the Susquehanna River in a soft coal mining region; takes its name from the Latin verb *renovo*, "I renew."

•**RICHLAND**, Borough; Lebanon County; Pop. 1,470; Zip Code 17087; Elev. 490; Lat. 40-35-48 N long. 078-29-09 W; in SE cen. Pennsylvania.

•**RICHLANDTOWN**, Borough; Bucks County; Pop. 1,180; Zip Code 18955; Elev. 520; Lat. 40-28-12 N long. 075-19-15 W; in SE Pennsylvania.

•**RIDGWAY**, Borough; Seat of Elk County; Pop. 5,604; Zip Code 15853; Elev. 1,381; Lat. 41-25-13 N long. 078-43-44 W; 20 miles N of DuBois in NW cen. Pennsylvania; in a crook of the Clarion River at the mouth of Elk Creek, occupies part of an 80,000-acre tract purchased in 1817 by *Jacob Ridgway*, a prominent Philadelphia Quaker merchant.

•**RIMERSBURG**, Borough; Clarion County; Pop. 1,096; Zip Code 16248; Elev. 1,450; Lat. 41-02-29 N long. 079-30-12 W; in W Pennsylvania; *John Rimer* settled here in 1829 and later opened a tavern.

•**RIVERSIDE**, Borough; Northumberland County; Pop. 2.266; Zip Code 17868; Elev. 500; Lat. 40-17-00 N long. 078-55-21 W; in E central Pennsylvania; annexed to Gearheart township in 1950.

•**ROBESONIA**, Borough; Berks County; Pop. 1,748; Zip Code 19551; Elev. 453; Lat. 40-21-06 N long. 076-08-05 W; in SE Pennsylvania; was founded in 1855 and named for an early settler, *Andrew Robeson*. *Robeson* was an immigrant from Sweden who eventually became wealthy and powerful in his community.

•**ROCHESTER**, Borough; Beaver County; Pop. 4,759; Zip Code 15074; Elev. 707; Lat. 40-42-08 N long. 080-17-12 W; in W Pennsylvania; at the confluence of the Beaver and Ohio Rivers, where the latter turns southwestward. The name Rochester was not used until 1838, when *Ovid Pinney* named it for his native Rochester, New York.

•**ROCKLEDGE**, Borough; Montgomery County; Pop. 2,538; Zip Code 19111; Elev. 200; Lat. 40-04-52 N long. 075-05-24 W; 10 miles NE of Philadelphia in SE Pennsylvania; a large shopping mall graces this residential suburb.

•ROME, Borough; Bradford County; Pop. 426; Zip Code 18837; Elev. 830: Lat. 41-51-30 N long. 076-20-28 W; in N Pennsylvania; named for the city in New York by the first settlers.

•ROSETO, Borough; Northampton County; Pop. 1,484; Zip Code 18013; Elev. 720:Lat. 40-52-50 N long. 075-12-54 W; near Bangor in E Pennsylvania.

•ROSE VALLEY, Borough; Delaware County; Pop. 1,038; Elev. 150: SW suburb of Philadelphia in SE Pennsylvania.

•ROYALTON, Borough; Dauphin County; Pop. 981; Zip Code 17101; Elev. 300: Lat. 40-11-14 N long. 076-43-39 W; suburb of Harrisburg in SE cen. Pennsylvania.

•ROYERSFORD, Borough; Montgomery County; Pop. 4,243; Zip Code 19468; Elev. 180: Lat. 40-11-03 N long. 075-32-18 W; 5 miles N of Phoenixville in a residential area in SE Pennsylvania.

•RURAL VALLEY, Borough; Armstrong County; Pop. 1,033; Zip Code 16249; Elev. 1,111: Lat. 40-11-13 N long. 080-20-56 W; in W Pennsylvania.

•RUSSELL, Village; Warren County; Pop. 800; Elev. 1,233: Lat. 41-56-29 N long. 079-08-07 W; 5 miles S of New York state line in NW Pennsylvania; was laid out in 1843 on part of an extensive tract owned by *Robert Russell.*

•RUTLEDGE, Borough; Delaware County; Pop. 934; Zip Code 19070; Elev. 130: Lat. 39-54-06 N long. 075-19-44 W; SW suburb of Philadelphia in SE Pennsylvania.

•SAEGERTOWN, Borough; Crawford County; Pop. 942; Zip Code 16433; Elev. 1,120:Lat. 41-43-08 N long. 080-08-52 W; in NW Pennsylvania.

•ST. CLAIR, Borough; Schuylkill County; Pop. 4,037; Zip Code 17970; Elev. 749:Lat. 40-24-59 N long. 079-58-18 W; 5 miles NW of Pottsville in E cen. Pennsylvania; was founded in 1831, Saint Clair took the name of *St. Clair Nichols,* who owned the farm on which the town was built.

•ST. LAWRENCE, Borough; Berks County; Pop. 1,376; Elev. 360: Lat. 40-19-37 N long. 075-52-20 W; in SE Pennsylvania.

•ST. MARYS, Borough; Elk County; Pop. 6,417; Zip Code 15857; Elev. 1,702: Lat. 41-25-40 N long. 078-33-40 W; near New York state line in NW central Pennsylvania; in 1842 Philadelphia and Baltimore German Catholics, who had fled the "Know Nothing" persecution, settled on land owned by the German Catholic Brotherhood. As the date of settlement was the feast of the Immaculate Conception of the Virgin Mary, and as the name of the first white woman who set foot on the new town was also Mary, the settlers called the place Saint Mary's.

•ST. PETERSBURG, Borough; Clarion County; Pop. 452; Zip Code 16054; Elev. 1,400:Lat. 41-09-42 N long. 079-39-11 W; in W Pennsylvania; the "borough" was first called Petersburg in honor of *Judge Richard Peters* of Philadelphia, who once owned the town site.

•SALLADASBURG, Borough; Lycoming County; Pop. 273; Elev. 650: Lat. 41-16-38 N long. 077-13-34 W; in N cen. Pennsylvania; named for founder, *Jacob P. Sallada.*

•SALTILLO, Borough; Huntingdon County; Pop. 373; Zip Code 17253; Elev. 780: Lat. 40-12-38 N long. 078-00-25 W; in S cen. Pennsylvania; named for the large city in NE Mexico.

•SALTSBURG, Borough; Indiana County; Pop. 964; Zip Code 15681; Elev. 852: Lat. 40-29-11 N long. 079-27-06 W; 30 miles NE of Pittsburgh in W cen. Pennsylvania. Tradition credits a *Mrs.*

Deemer with the discovery of salt deposits here when she found the food she cooked in water that trickled from rocks along the Conemaugh had a salty taste.

•SAXONBURG, Borough; Butler County; Pop. 1,336; Zip Code 16056; Elev. 1,300: Lat. 40-45-14 N long. 079-48-37 W; NE suburb of Pittsburgh in W Pennsylvania; is all that now remains of an ambitious German colony, named for their former home in Old Saxony. The founder of this colony, *John A. Roebling,* afterward became a civil engineer and a builder of suspension bridges.

•SAYRE, Borough; Bradford County; Pop. 6,951; Zip Code 18840; Elev. 772: Lat. 41-58-44 N long. 076-30-57 W; 20 miles SE of Elmire, New York in N Pennsylvania; was a small railway settlement until the Lehigh Valley Railroad constructed a roundhouse and shops here in 1871 and named the place for *Robert H. Sayre,* superintendent of the road.

•SCALP LEVEL, Borough; Cambria County; Pop. 1,186; Elev. 1,840: Lat. 40-14-59 N long. 078-50-57 W; in SW cen. Pennsylvania.

•SCHUYLKILL HAVEN, Borough; Schuylkill County; Pop. 5,977; Zip Code 17972; Elev. 526: Lat. 40-37-50 N long. 076-10-17 W; 5 miles S of Pottsville in E cen. Pennsylvania; The completion in 1825 of the Schuylkill Canal between Philadelphia and a point just north of Schuylkill Haven gave the town its name and its principal support for six decades.

•SCOTTDALE, Borough; Westmoreland County; Pop. 5,833; Zip Code 15683; Elev. 1,061: Lat. 40-06-01 N long. 079-35-14 W; 15 miles NE of Uniontown in a coal mining and agricultural area in SW Pennsylvania; on Jacobs Creek, originally named Fountain Mills, was renamed for *Thomas A. Scott,* president of the Pennsylvania Railroad, after a spur was extended to the town in 1873.

•SCRANTON, City; Lackawanna County seat; Pop. 87,378; Zip Code 185+; Elev. 741:Lat. 41-24-32 N long. 075-39-46 W; In 1840 two brothers, *George W.* and *Selden T. Scranton,* came to the settlement from New Jersey. At that time it was a community of five weather-beaten old houses. Attracted by the abundance of iron ore and anthracite nearby, the *Scrantons* and their partners-*William Henry, Sanford Grant,* and *Philip Mattes* -organized the firm of Scranton, Grant, and Company, and built a forge here. This firm was the nucleus of the Lackawanna Iron and Steel Company. Despite many discouragements, they finally succeeded in manufacturing iron with anthracite as a fuel. In 1845 the Scrantons named the place Harrison in honor of *President William Henry Harrison.* The post office at Scrantonia was established in 1850. Less than a year later the name of the town and post office was simplified as Scranton.

•SELINSGROVE, Borough; Snyder County; Pop. 5,227; Zip Code 17870; Elev. 445: Lat. 40-47-56 N long. 076-51-45 W; 5 miles S of Sunbury on the W banks of the Susquehanna River in central Pennsylvania; was laid out in 1790 by *Anthony Selin,* a Swiss soldier of fortune who accompanied *Lafayette* to America.

•SELLERSVILLE, Borough; Bucks County; Pop. 3,143; Zip Code 18960; Elev. 336:Lat. 40-21-14 N long. 075-18-19 W; 20 miles SE of Allentown in SE Pennsylvania; a narrow town founded in 1738, *Samuel Sellers* operated Old Sellers Tavern, a three-story stuccoed stone building that served as an early stage stop along the road to Allentown.

•SEVEN SPRINGS, Borough; Fayette and Somerset Counties; Pop. 30; Elev. 1,480: Lat. 40-01-23 N long. 079-17-51 W; in S Pennsylvania; incorporated in 1964.

•SEWARD, Borough; Westmoreland County; Pop. 675; Zip Code 15954; Elev. 1,140:Lat. 40-24-51 N long. 079-01-13 W; in SW Pennsylvania.

•SEWICKLEY, Borough; Allegheny County; Pop. 4,778; Zip Code 15143; Elev. 720: Lat. 40-32-11 N long. 080-11-05 W; 10 miles NW of Pittsburgh on the Ohio River in SW Pennsylvania; named for an Indian tribe.

•SHAMOKIN, City; Northumberland County; Pop. 10,357; Zip Code 17872; Elev. 730: in E central Pennsylvania; was laid out in 1835, named from the old Indian village that once stood at its mouth, on the present site of Sunbury, 18 miles west of the borough of Shamokin. The Delawares called this village *Schachamekhan*, which signifies "eel stream." Another form of the name was *Schahamokink*, or "the place of eels."

•SHARON, City; Mercer County; Pop. 19,057; Zip Code 16416; Elev. 853: Lat. 41-13-59 Nlong. 080-29-37 W; 15 miles NE of Youngstown, Ohio on the Ohio River in W Pennsylvania; named, probably, by some Bible-reading pioneer who likened its flat topography to the plain of Sharon in Palestine.

•SHARON HILL, Borough; Delaware County; Pop. 6,221; Zip Code 19079; in SE Pennsylvania.

•SHARPSBURG, Borough; Allegheny County; Pop. 4,351; Zip Code 15215; Elev. 741:Lat. 39-54-23 N long. 075-16-19 W; 5 miles NE of Pittsburgh on the Allegheny River in SW Pennsylvania; In this community, founded in 1826 by *James Sharp* and incorporated as a borough in 1841, the eight-year-old *Howard J. Heinz* began his billion dollar business by selling the produce of his mother's garden patch. *James Sharp* kept a temperance hotel here until his death in 1861.

•SHARPSVILLE, Borough; Mercer County; Pop. 5,375; Zip Code 16150; Elev. 950:Lat. 41-15-33 N long. 080-28-20 W; 20 miles NW of New Castle in an industrial area in W Pennsylvania; named for *James Sharp*, one of the original owners of the town site.

•SHEAKLEYVILLE, Borough; Mercer County; Pop. 155; Zip Code 16151; Elev. 1.282:Lat. 41-26-34 N long. 080-12-29 W; in W Pennsylvania.

•SHEFFIELD, Village; Warren County; Pop. 1,500; Zip Code ; Elev. 1,336: Lat. 41-42-14 N long. 079-02-09 W; 10 miles SE of Warren in NW Pennsylvania.

•SHELOCTA, Borough; Indiana County; Pop. 139; Zip Code 15774; Elev. 990: Lat. 40-39-21 N long. 079-18-08 W; in W cen. Pennsylvania.

•SHENANDOAH, Borough; Schuylkill County; Pop. 7,589; Zip Code 17976; Elev. 1,300; Lat. 40-49-13 N long. 076-12-04 W; 10 miles N of Pottsville in E central Pennsylvania; was first settled in 1835; mining on a large scale began in 1862 when a land company laid out the town.

•SHICKSHINNY, Borough; Luzerne County; Pop. 1,192; Zip Code 18655; Elev. 520; Lat. 41-09-11 N long. 076-09-02 W; E Pennsylvania; is named for the indian meaning "five mountains."

•SHILLINGTON, Borough; Berks County; Pop. 5,601; Zip Code 19607; Elev. 350; Lat. 40-18-28 N long. 075-57-57 W; 5 miles SW of Reading in SE Pennsylvania. Samuel Shilling laid out this town in 1860 when he decided to locate his 130 acre farm. The town was also named after this earlier farmer a very short time after he settled here.

•SHIMERVILLE, Village; Lehigh County; Pop. 85; Zip Code rural; Elev. 248; Lat. 40-29-42 N long. 075-31-36 W; near Emmaus in E Pennsylvania; was laid out on land bought by *John Shimer* in 1792.

•SHINGLEHOUSE, Borough; Potter County; Pop. 1,310;; Zip Code 16748; Elev. 1,490; Lat. 41-57-49 N long. 078-11-28 W; located in N Pennsylvania; is named for an old English pioneer clapboard house with shingles, belonging to a French immigrant named *Jaudrie* about 1806.

•SHIPPENSBURG, Borough; Cumberland and Franklin Counties; Pop. 5,261; Zip Code 17257;; Elev. 649; Lat. 40-03-02 N long. 077-31-14 W; is located 10 miles N of Chambersburg in S Pennsylvania. Shippensburg is the oldest town in Pennsylvania, with the exception of York that is W of the Susquehanna River. It was founded in 1730 by *Edward Shippen*, who in 1737 was said to have had been the biggest person, the biggest house, and the biggest coach in Philadelphia.

•SHIPPENVILLE, Borough; Clarion County; Pop. 558; ; Zip Code 16254; Elev. 1,208;Lat. 41-15-01 N long. 079-27-35 W; W Pennsylvania; was laid out by *Judge Henry Shippen*, in its early years was known as an iron center.

•SHIPPINGPORT, Borough; Beaver County; Pop. 255; Zip Code 15077; Elev. 780; Lat. 40-37-55 N long. 080-24-51 W; is located on the Ohio River in W Pennsylvania; So named because is is a coal shipment point.

•SHIRLEYSBURG, Borough; Huntingdon County; Pop. 147; Zip Code 17260; Elev. 606; Lat. 40-17-52 N long. 077-52-28 W; is located in S central Pennsylvania on the Aughwick Creek, was the site of the Indian town of Aughwick, or Old Town, where the noted Indian trader, *George Croghan*, had an early trading post. The white man's town was founded in 1757 and named for Fort Shirley. Here in 1754 *Conrad Weiser*, Indian interpreter and provincial agent, conferred with the Iroquoian representative, *Tanacharison*, and chiefs of the Shawnee and Delaware.

•SHREWSBURY, Borough; York County; Pop. 2,688; Zip Code 17361; Elev. 735; Lat. 39-46-07 N long. 076-40-48 W; Founded in 1739 by immigrants from Shrewsbury, England.

•SHRINESTOWN, Village; York County; Pop. 200; Zip Code ; Elev. 257; near Manchester in S Pennsylvania; founded in 1800, was for more than 50 years a flourishing cigar-manufacturing center. Once the site of an Indian village, it was named for *John Shrine*, an early settler. Well-kept houses are scattered on a hillside.

•SINKING SPRING, Borough; Berks County; Pop. 2,617; Zip Code 19608; Elev. 345; Lat. 40-19-38 N long. 076-00-41 W; 5 miles W of Reading in a red brick residential area in SE Pennsylvania; was founded in 1793 and named for the Sinking Spring, 402 Penn Ave., which fills in each February when water begins to ooze from the frost-packed ground but dries up before summer.

•SKINNERS EDDY, Village; Wyoming County; Pop. 60; Zip Code 18623; Elev. 649;Lat. 41-38-29 N long. 076-08-49 W; near Laceyville in NE Pennsylvania; a tavern was erected by *Ebenezer Skinner* in 1792, for an eddy in the Susquehanna made this a convenient stopping place for boatmen.

•SLATINGTON, Borough; Lehigh County; Pop. 4,277; Zip Code 18080; Elev. 367;Lat. 40-44-54 N long. 075-36-44 W; 15 miles NW of Allentown in E Pennsylvania; is a slate center where quarrying began in 1845.

•SLIGO, Borough; Clarion County; Pop. 798; Zip Code 16255; Elev. 769; Lat. 40-38-36 N long. 079-41-31 W; in W Pennsylvania; is bisected by Big Licking and Little Licking Creeks. Sligo Furnace, built in 1845 by four men from Sligo, Ireland, was shut down after the panic of 1873.

•SLIPPERY ROCK, Borough; Butler County; Pop. 3,047; Zip Code 16057; Elev. 1,302; Lat. 41-03-50 N long. 080-03-24 W; 10 miles

NW of Butler in W Pennsylvania; was called Ginger Hill by early settlers from the local tavern keeper's practice of giving away plenty of ginger with the whiskey he sold.

•**SMETHPORT**, Borough; Seat of McKean County; Pop. 1,797; Zip Code 16749; Elev. 1,486; Lat. 41-48-40 N long. 078-26-42 W; 20 miles S of Bradford in N Pennsylvania; was named for *Raymond* and *Theodore de Smeth*, Dutch bankers and business agents of the exiled French nobility in their dealings with the Ceres Land Company.

•**SMITHFIELD**, Borough; Fayette County; Pop. 1,084; Zip Code 25478; Elev. 986; Lat. 39-48-11 N long. 079-48-29 W; in SW Pennsylvania; was laid out in 1799 and incorporated as a borough in 1916.

•**SNOW SHOE**, Borough; Centre County; Pop. 852; Zip Code 16874; Elev. 1,572; Lat. 41-01-51 N long. 077-56-59 W; S of Clarence in central Pennsylvania; was named for "Snow Shoe Camp Survey," so called, it is supposed, because the surveyor found snowshoes at a deserted Indian camp here in 1773.

•**SOMERSET**, Borough; Seat of Somerset County; Pop. 6,474; Zip Code 15501; Elev. 2,250; Lat. 40-00-30 N long. 079-04-42 W; 30 miles S of Johnstown in S Pennsylvania; was originally called Brunerstown, after *Ulrich Bruner*, who arrived in 1787.

•**SOUDERTON**, Borough; Montgomery County; Pop. 6,657; Zip Code 18964; Elev. 428; Lat. 40-18-42 N long. 075-19-32 W; 5 miles N of Lansdale in SE Pennsylvania; was founded in 1876 but much older in settlement.

•**SPANGLER**, Borough; Cambria County; Pop. 2,399; Zip Code 15775; Elev. 1,470; Lat. 40-38-34 N long. 078-46-23 W; 20 miles NW of Altoona in a coal mining region in SW Pennsylvania; when it was incorporated in 1893, Spangler was named for *Colonel J.L. Spangler* of Bellefonte.

•**SPARTANSBURG**, Borough; Crawford County; Pop. 403; Zip Code 16434; Elev. 1,450;Lat. 41-49-26 N long. 079-41-02 W; in NW Pennsylvania; named because of the spartan character of the town's early settlers.

•**SPEERS**, Borough; Washington County; Pop. 1,425; Zip Code 15012; Elev. 767; Lat. 40-07-28 N long. 079-52-48 W; W of Belle Vernon in SW Pennsylvania; is on the west bank of the Monongahela River, named for *Apollos Speers*, and closely identified with the early development of the Monongahela Valley.

•**SPRING CITY**, Borough; Chester County; Pop. 3,389; Zip Code 19475; Elev. 150;Lat. 40-10-36 N long. 075-32-53 W; 30 miles NW of Philadelphia on the Schuylkill River in SE Pennsylvania; it was at first called Springville from a large spring situated at the corner of Yost and Main Streets. About 1872, when the post office was established and the town incorporated, the name was changed to Spring City because there was already one Springville in Pennsylvania.

•**SPRINGDALE**, Borough; Allegheny County; Pop. 4,418; Zip Code 15144; Elev. 801; Lat. 40-32-27 N long. 079-47-043 W; 15 miles NE of Pittsburgh on the Allegheny River in SW Pennsylvania; is along a sweeping curve of the Allegheny River. Settled in 1795, it was later named for springs in a nearby hollow.

•**SPRINGFIELD**, Urban Village and Township; Delaware County; Pop. 29,000; Zip Code 19064; Elev. 220; Lat. 41-50-57 N long. 076-44-46 W; 15 miles W of Philadelphia in a residential area in SE Pennsylvania; probably named for Springfield, Massachusetts.

•**SPRING MILLS**, Village; Centre County; Pop. 600; Zip Code 16875; Elev. 52; Lat. 40-51-12 Nl ong. 077-34-04 W; in cen. Pennsylvania; on Penn's Creek, was part of the "Manor of Succoth," held by the Penns until 1791.

•**SPRUCE CREEK**, Village; Huntingdon County; Pop. 140; Elev. 777; Lat. 40-36-34 N long. 078-08-09 W; in S cen. Pennsylvania; at the confluence of Spruce Creek and the Little Juniata River, was settled prior to 1763.

•**STATE COLLEGE**, Borough; Seat of Centre County; Pop. 36,082; Zip Code 16801; Elev. 1,191; Lat. 40-47-36 N long. 077-51-37 W; 50 miles NE of Altoona in central Pennsylvania; located in the Nittany Valley between the Bald Eagle Ridge (NW) and the Seven Mountains (SE).

•**STEELTON**, Borough; Dauphin County; Pop. 6,484; Zip Code 17113; Elev. 306; Lat. 40-14-07 N long. 076-50-30 W; in SE cen. Pennsylvania; *Rudolph* and *Henry Kelker*, who owned land adjoining the steel works, first called the town Baldwin in honor of *Matthew Baldwin*, a large stockholder in the steel company. The post office renamed it Steel Works in 1871, and nine years later steel works superintendant *Luther Bent* suggested its present name.

•**STOCKDALE**, Borough; Washington County; Pop. 641; Zip Code 15483; Elev. 765; Lat. 40-05-00 N long. 079-50-54 W; in SW Pennsylvania; named for the dairy cows that have grazed on the land here.

•**STOCKERTON**, Borough; Northampton County; Pop. 661; Zip Code 18083; Elev. 374; in E Pennsylvania; bisected by Bushkill Creek, was named for *Andrew Stocker*, who laid out the village in 1774.

•**STODDARTSVILLE**, Village; Luzerne and Monroe Counties; Pop. 30; Elev. 1,589; Lat. 41-07-47 N long. 075-37-43 W; a center for hunters, on the west bank of the Lehigh River, was laid out in 1815 by *John Stoddart*.

•**STRASBURG**, Borough; Lancaster County; Pop. 1,999; Zip Code 17579; Elev. 480;Lat. 39-58-59 N long. 076-11-04 W; 10 miles SE of Lancaster in SE Pennsylvania; The LeFevres or Ferrees, and other French immigrants settled this town in 1733,

•**STROUDSBURG**, Borough; Seat of Monroe County; Pop. 5.148; Zip Code 18360; Elev. 420; Lat. 40-59-12 N long. 075-11-42 W; 30 miles N of Easton in E Pennsylvania; lies among the Pocono foothills at the confluence of McMichaels, Pocono, and Brodhead Creeks. In 1776 *Colonel Jacob Stroud*, a veteran of the French and Indian War, erected a stockaded house here and called it Fort Penn.

•**SUGAR NOTCH**, Borough; Luzerne County; Pop. 1,191; Zip Code 18706; Elev. 740; Lat. 41-11-49 Nlong. 075-55-43 W; in E Pennsylvania; named for the mountain gap nearby, covered in sugar maples.

•**SUGARCREEK**, Borough; Venango County; Pop. 5,954; Zip Code 16301; Lat. 41-25-17 N long. 079-52-53 W; 10 miles W of Oil Creek in NW Pennsylvania; incorporated in 1968.

•**SUMMERHILL**, Borough; Cambria County; Pop. 725; Zip Code 15958; Elev. 1,540; Lat. 40-22-41 N long. 078-45-39 W; in SW central Pennsylvania; originally named Somerhill for *Joseph* and *David Somer*, two landowners in the area.

•**SUMMIT HILL**, Borough; Carbon County; Pop. 3,418; Zip Code 18250; Elev. 1,410; Lat. 40-50-27 N long. 075-52-31 W; in E Pennsylvania; so named because it is at the summit of Sharp Mountain; an excellent view of the countryside is seen from here.

•**SUNBURY**, City; Seat of Northumberland County; Pop. 12,292; Zip Code 17801; Elev. 450; Lat. 40-51-45 N long. 076-47-41 W; 50 miles N of Harrisburg on the Susquehanna River in E central Pennsylvania; is bounded roughly by the Shamokin Creek and the Susquehanna River. Etymologically Sunbury signifies "the city of the sun."

•**SUSQUEHANNA DEPOT**, Borough; Susquehanna County; Pop. 1,994; Elev. 920; Lat. 41-56-36 N long. 075-36-00 W; in NE Pennsylvania; named for the county and river flowing through it. Near New York state line in a farming region.

•**SUTERVILLE**, Borough; Westmoreland County; Pop. 863; Zip Code 15083; Elev. 800; Lat. 40-14-10 N long. 079-47-58 W; in SW Pennsylvania.

•**SWARTHMORE**, Borough; Delaware County; Pop. 5,950; Zip Code 19081; Elev. 190; Lat. 39-54-07 N long. 075-21-01 W; 10 miles SW of Philadelphia in SE Pennsylvania; named for Swarthmore Hall, home of *George Fox* (1624-91), founder of the Society of Friends.

•**SWISSVALE**, Borough; Allegheny County; Pop. 11,345; Zip Code 15218; Elev. 920; Lat. 40-25-25 N long. 079-52-59 W; 5 miles E of Pittsburgh in SW Pennsylvania; was built up on the farm of *James Swisshelm*, who inherited it from his father, *John*. The name Swissvale is said to have been invented by *Jane Gray Swisshelm*, the wife of the proprietor.

•**SWOYERSVILLE**, Borough; Luzerne County; Pop. 5,795; Zip Code 18704; Elev. 840; Lat. 41- 17-30 N long. 075-52-30 W; 5 miles N of Wilkes-Barre in E Pennsylvania; named for *Henry Swoyer*, early coal operator.

•**SYKESVILLE**, Borough; Jefferson County; Pop. 1,537; Zip Code 15865; Elev. 1,352; Lat. 41-03-01 Nlong. 078-49-21 W; 5 miles SW of DuBois in a farming area in W central Pennsylvania; settled in 1861 and named for *Jacob Sykes*, sawmill owner of the 1880's.

•**TAMAQUA**, Borough; Schuylkill County; Pop. 8,843; Zip Code 18252; Elev. 805; Lat. 40-47-50 N long. 075-58-11 W; 15 miles NE of Pottsville in E central Pennsylvania; laid out in 1829 by the Lehigh Coal and Navigation Company, Tamaqua was named for the creek flowing by. *Tamaque* was a Delaware Indian word meaning "beaver."

•**TARENTUM**, Borough; Allegheny County; Pop. 6,419; Zip Code 15084; Elev. 737; Lat. 40-36-05 N long. 079-45-36 W; in SW Pennsylvania; settled in the last decade of the eighteenth century when a gristmill wa erected on Bull Creek, was laid out in 1829 by *Judge Henry Marie Brackenridge*, and given this classical name for the town. He was a scholar and a student of ancient history and the classical languages, and he may have been attracted by the name of the ancient city in southern Italy which the Romans called Tarentum, and which the Greeks had previously named Taras from the small stream on which the old Greek colony was planted.

•**TAYLOR**, Borough; Lackawanna County; Pop. 7,246; Zip Code ; Elev. 680; Lat. 41-23-41 N long. 075-42-25 W; 5 miles SW of Scranton in NE Pennsylvania; was named for the late *Moses Taylor*, a prominent New York merchant and capitalist, who had extensive business interests in the place that now bears his name.

•**TELFORD**, Borough; Bucks and Montgomery Counties; Pop. 3,507; Zip Code 18969; Elev. 420; Lat. 40-19-19 N long. 075-19-42 W; 25 miles E of Reading in SE Pennsylvania.

•**TEMPLE**, Borough; Berks County; Pop. 1,486; Zip Code 19560; Elev. 380; Lat. 40-24-31 N long. 075-55-19 W; in SE Pennsylvania; near Reading; named for an old hotel sign that bore the words, "Stop at Solomon's Temple." Solomon was the innkeeper's name.

•**THOMAS MILLS**, Village; Somerset County; Pop. 100; Zip Code 15935; Elev. 1,410; Lat. 40-39-42 N long. 078-39-48 W; rural town near Hollsopple in S Pennsylvania; was named for the flour mill erected in 1836 by *John Thomas*.

•**THOMPSON**, Borough; Susquehanna County; Pop. 303; Zip Code 18465; Elev. 1,640; Lat. 41-51-49 N long. 075-30-53 W; in NE Pennsylvania; named for an early settler.

•**THROOP**, Borough; Lackawanna County; Pop. 4,166; Zip Code 18512; Elev. 860; Lat. 41-27--05 N long. 075-36-44 W; 5 miles NE of Scranton in NE Pennsylvania; was named in honor of *Dr. Benjamin Henry Throop*, the pioneer physician of Scranton. *Doctor Throop*.

•**TITUSVILLE**, Borough; Crawford County; Pop. 6,884; Zip Code 16354; 15 miles N of Oil City in an agricultural region in NW Pennsylvania on Oil Creek;

•**TOPTON**, Borough; Berks County; Pop. 1,818; Zip Code 19562; Elev. 480; Lat. 40-30-12 N long. 075-42-06 W; in SE Pennsylvania.

•**TOBYHANNA**, Village; Monroe County; Pop. 900; Zip Code 18466; Elev. 1,940; Lat. 41-10-38 N long. 075-25-02 W; in E Pennsylvania; name means "older stream," from an Indian word.

•**TOWANDA**, Borough; Seat of Bradford County; Pop. 3,526; Zip Code 18848; Elev. 837; Lat. 41-46-03 N long. 076-26-35 W; 50 miles NW of Wilkes-Barre in a mountainous resort area in N Pennsylvania; (Ind. "where we bury the dead"), occupies a slope on the west shore of the Susquehanna, at the convergence of three valleys.

•**TOWER CITY**, Borough; Schuylkill County; Pop. 1,667; Zip Code 17980; Elev. 800; Lat. 40-35-21 N long. 076-33-10 W; 25 miles W of Pottsville in E central Pennsylvania; was built on reclaimed marsh lands in 1868 by *Charlemagne Tower*.

•**TRAFFORD**, Borough; Allegheny and Westmoreland Counties; Pop. 3,662; Zip Code 15085; Elev. 820; Lat. 40-23-08 N long. 079-45-33 W; E suburb of Pittsburgh in SW Pennsylvania.

•**TRAINER**, Borough; Delaware County; Pop. 2,056; Elev. 29; Lat. 39-49-39 N long. 075-24-53 W; SW suburb of Philadelphia in SE Pennsylvania; grew up around grist and saw mills established by *David Trainer*.

•**TRAPPE**, Borough; Montgomery County; Pop. 1,800; Elev. 300; Lat. 40-11-56 N long. 075-28-36 W; in SE Pennsylvania; The origin of the name is uncertain, though many historians declare than an early tavern's high stoop caused it to be called *treppe* (steps) by the German settlers, and that a corrupted form of the word came into popular use as the village name. Another explanation is that the tavern's high steps often became a "trap" for the unsteady feet of steady patrons.

•**TREMONT**, Borough; Schuylkill County; Pop. 1,796; Zip Code 17981; Elev. 760; Lat. 40-37-42 N long. 076-23-15 W; in E central Pennsylvania.

•**TULLYTOWN**, Borough; Bucks County; Pop. 2,277; Zip Code 19007; Elev. 20; Lat. 40-08-21 N long. 074-48-54 W; E suburb of Philadelphia in SE Pennsylvania.

•**TUNKHANNOCK**, Borough; Seat of Wyoming County; Pop. 2,144; Zip Code 18657; Elev. 613; Lat. 41-32-19 N long. 075-56-49 W; 20 miles NW of Scranton in NE Pennsylvania; is at the confluence of Tunkhannock Creek and the Susquehanna's North Branch The township and the village of Tunkhannock were named for the Tunkhannock Creek. This name is a corruption of *Tank-hanne*, "a small stream." The earliest form of the name was *Tenkghanacke*, which may be identified with Tagh-ka-nick, an Indian name in New York, and with Taconic in Massachusetts and Connecticut. Tenkghanacke, Taghkanick, and Taconic are all apparently the same Algonquin word in different forms. The common interpretation of this name is "forest, or wilderness."

•**TURTLE CREEK**, Borough; Allegheny County; Pop. 6,959; Zip Code 15145; Elev. 900; Lat. 40-24-21 N long. 079-49-31 W; in SW Pennsylvania; was settled about 1765. The settlement grew into a pleasant suburban community, stimulated by the laying of the Greensburg turnpike, and was incorporated in 1892. The name is a translation of the Indian words for the peace, *Tulpewi-sysu*.

•**TYRONE**, Borough; Blair County; Pop. 6,346; Zip Code 16686; Elev. 909; Lat. 40-40-14 N long. 078-14-20 W; 15 miles NE of Altoona in S central Pennsylvania; (Irish, the land of Owen), was settled in 1850, but emigrants from North Ireland had penetrated the region earlier. They named the place for their native county of Tyrone.

•**ULSTER**, Village; Bradford County; Pop. 400; Elev. 742; Lat. 41-50-45 N long. 076-30-08 W; in N Pennsylvania; was the site of a trading post in 1765. Named by Irish immigrants for their homeland.

•**UNION CITY**, Borough; Erie County; Pop. 3,263; Zip Code 16438; Elev. 1,300; Lat. 41-53-58 N long. 079-50-44 W; 20 miles SE of Erie in NW Pennsylvania.

•**UNION DALE**, Borough; Susquehanna County; Pop. 321; Zip Code 18470; Elev. 1,660; Lat. 41-43-00 N long. 075-29-33 W; in NE Pennsylvania.

•**UNIONTOWN**, City; Seat of Fayette County; Pop. 14,023; Zip Code 15401; Elev. 1,023; Last. 40-42-17 N long. 078-49-51 W; 45 miles SE of Pittsburgh in SW Pennsylvania.

•**UPLAND**, Borough; Delaware County; Pop. 3,458; Elev. 60; Lat. 39-51-09 N long. 075-22-5 W; SW suburb of Philadelphia, near Chester in SE Pennsylvania.

•**VALLEY FORGE**, Urban Village; Chester County; Pop. 450; Zip Code 19481; Elev. 150; Lat. 40-05-49 N long. 075-28-12 W; 20 miles NW of Philadelphia in a rural-residential area in SE Pennsylvania; located on the Schuylkill River; was *George Washington's* winter headquarters in 1777-78, a state park commemorates his army's bravery.

•**VANDERBILT**, Borough; Fayette County; Pop. 689; Zip Code 15486; Elev. 900; Lat. 40-01-59 N long. 079-39-42 W; in SW Pennsylvania.

•**VANDERGRIFT**, Borough; Westmoreland County; Pop. 6,823; Zip Code 15690; Elev. 860; Lat. 40-36-10 N long. 079-33-54 W; 30 miles NE of Pittsburgh in SW Pennsylvania; steel milling and coal mining are the major industries.

•**VANDLING**, Borough; Lackawanna County; Pop. 557; Zip Code 18421; Elev. 1,600; Lat. 41-37-59 N long. 075-28-15 W; near Forest City in NE Pennsylvania.

•**VANPORT**, Village; Beaver County; suburb of Beaver Falls in W Pennsylvania; named for *Martin Van Buren* during his 1836 presidential campaign.

•**VENANGO**, Borough; Crawford County; Pop. 298; Zip Code 16440; Elev. 1,130; Lat. 40-41-04 N long. 080-19-45 W; in NW Pennsylvania; originally an Indian village; Name means "a tract of level, fertile ground," or "a mink," or "bull thistles."

•**VERONA**, Borough; Allegheny County; Pop. 3,179; Zip Code 15147; Elev. 860; Lat. 40-30-23 N long. 079-50-36 W; in SW Pennsylvania; named for the Northern Italian city.

•**VERSAILLES**, Borough; Allegheny County; Pop. 2,150; Elev. 850; Lat. 40-18-56 N long. 079-49-53 W; 15 miles SE of Pittsburgh on the Youghiogheny River in SW Pennsylvania; named for the palace of French kings to commemorate the earliest settlers of western Pennsylvania.

•**VILLANOVA**, Urban Village; Delaware County; Pop. 5,000; Zip Code 19085; Elev. 430; Lat. 40-02-14 Nl ong. 075-20-58 W; 10 miles NW of Philadelphia in a residential area in SE Pennsylvania; Villanova University, with about 8,000 students, is located here. The village's name means "new town."

•**WALLINGFORD**, Urban Village; Delaware County; Pop. 4,000; Elev. 160; Lat. 39-53-27 N long. 075-21-48 W; SW suburb of Philadelphia in SE Pennsylvania; residential; named for town in Connecticut.

•**WALNUTPORT**, Borough; Northampton County; Pop. 2,007; Zip Code 18088; Elev. 380; Lat. 40-45-15 N long. 075-35-57 W; in E Pennsylvania.

•**WAMPUM**, Borough; Lawrence County; Pop. 851; Zip Code 16157; Elev. 783; Lat. 40-53-17 N long. 080-20-18 W; in W Pennsylvania; settled in 1796 on the Beaver River, was incorporated as a borough in 1876. The name is a contraction of Wampumpeak (Ind. "a string of shell beads").

•**WARMINSTER**, Urban Village; Bucks County; Pop. 37,200; Zip Code 18974; Elev. 310; Lat. 40-12-24 N long. 075-06-00 W; 20 miles NE of Philadelphia in a residential area in SE Pennsylvania; Burpee Seed Company has its national headquarters here, as does the Society for Individual Liberty.

•**WARREN**, Borough; Seat of Warren County; Pop. 12,146; Zip Code 16365; Elev. 1,185; Lat. 41-50-38 N long. 079-08-43 W; 20 miles S of Jamestown, New York in NW Pennsylvania; near the mouth of the Conewago Creek, on the Allegheny River.

•**WASHINGTON**, City; Seat of Washington County; Pop. 18,363; Zip Code 15301; Elev. 1,039; Lat. 40-12-08 N long. 077-28-42 W; 30 miles SW of Pittsburgh in SW Pennsylvania; The site, once known as Catfish's Camp, was a Delaware Indian village, the headquarters of *Chief Tingoocqua*. A town laid out in 1781 shortly became the county seat of newly created Washington County. Incorporated as a borough in 1810, Washington was chartered as a city in 1924.

•**WATSONTOWN**, Borough; Northumberland County; Pop. 2,311; Zip Code 17777; Elev. 500; Lat. 41-05-04 N long. 076-51-51 W; in E central Pennsylvania; named for *John Watson*, who bought 610 acres here in 1792, and two years later laid out the town.

•**WAYMART**, Borough; Wayne County; Pop. 1,248; Zip Code 18472; Elev. 1,400; Lat. 41-34-49 N long. 075-24-31 W; in NE Pennsylvania; a state hospital is located outside of town.

•**WAYNESBORO**, Borough; Franklin County; Pop. 9,726; Zip Code 17268; Elev. 713; Lat. 39-45-21 Nlong. 077-34-41 W; 10 miles NE of Hagerstown, Maryland in S Pennsylvania; set in a natural hollow and was laid out in 1797 by *John Wallace*, who had served under *General Anthony Wayne*.

•**WAYNESBURG**, Borough; Seat of Greene County; Pop. 4,482; Zip Code 15370; Elev. 1,035; Lat. 39-53-47 N long. 080-10-46 W; 50 miles S of Pittsburgh in SW Pennsylvania; was laid out in 1796 and named for *General Anthony Wayne*, whose Indian battles allowed for extensive settlement of western Pennsylvania in the early 1800s.

•**WEATHERLY**, Borough; Carbon County; Pop. 2,891; Zip Code 18255; Elev. 1,095; 10 miles E of Hazleton in E Pennsylvania; The town was settled in 1840 and named for the clockmaker, *David Weatherly*.

•**WELLSBORO**, Borough; Seat of Tioga County; Pop. 3,085; Zip Code 16901; Elev. 1,308; Lat. 41-44-55 N long. 077-18-03 W; 4 40 miles SW of Elmira, New York in N Pennsylvania; The town was laid out in 1806 by *Benjamin W. Morris*, a land agent who arrived in 1799 and gave the settlement his wife's maiden name. *Mary Wells Morris* and her brothers promoted their town to be the seat of the new county of Tioga in 1806.

•**WESLEYVILLE**, Borough; Erie County; Pop. 3,998; Zip Code 165+; Elev. 730; Lat. 42-08-25 N long. 080-00-55 W; in NW Pennsylvania; was laid out by *John Shadduck* in 1828 and named for *John Wesley*, founder of Methodism.

•**WEST CHESTER**, Borough; Seat of Chester County; Pop. 17,435; Zip Code 19380; Elev. 455; Lat. 39-57-38 N long. 075-36-21 W; 25 miles W of Philadelphia in SE Pennsylvania; is within cannon sound of Brandywine, Paoli, Valley Forge, and other hallowed places of the Revolution.

•**WESTFIELD**, Borough; Tioga County; Pop. 1,268; Zip Code 16950; Elev. 1,370; 50 miles SW of Elmira, New York in N Pennsylvania; named for Westfield, Massachusetts by *Henry Trowbridge*, who established a woolen mill here in the early 1800s.

•**WEST GROVE**, Borough; Chester County; Pop. 1,820; Zip Code 19390; Elev. 400; Lat. 39-49-19 N long. 075-49-40 W; residential suburb of Philadelphia in SE Pennsylvania.

•**WEST HAZLETON**, Borough; Luzerne County; Pop. 4,871; Zip Code 18201; Elev. 1,700; Lat. 40-57-31 N long. 075-59-47 W; adjacent to Hazleton in E Pennsylvania; residential.

•**WEST HOMESTEAD**, Borough; Allegheny County; Pop. 3,128; Zip Code 15120; Elev. 1,000; Lat. 40-23-38 N long. 079-54-44 W; SE suburb of Pittsburgh, adjacent to Homestead in SW Pennsylvania; on the Monongahela River.

•**WEST KITTANNING**, Borough; Armstrong County; Pop. 1,591; Zip Code 16201; Elev. 980; Lat. 40-48-37 Nlong. 079-31-47 W; W of Kittanning in W Pennsylvania.

•**WEST MIFFLIN**, Borough; Allegheny County; Pop. 26,279; Zip Code 15122; Elev. 1,000; Lat. 40-46-48 N long. 080-20-19 W; SE suburb of Pittsburgh in SW Pennsylvania.

•**WEST READING**, Borough; Berks County; Pop. 4,507; Zip Code 19611; Elev. 320; Lat. 40-20-01 N long. 075-56-52 W; on Schuylkill River, across from Reading in SE Pennsylvania; laid out in 1873 and incorporated in 1907.

•**WEST YORK**, Borough; York County; Pop. 4,526; Zip Code 174+; Elev. 400; Lat. 39-57-09 N long. 076-45-06 W; 5 miles W of York in S Pennsylvania; includes in its 320 acres the 160-acre farm of *Henry Ebert*, for whose ancestors the town was originally named Eberton.

•**WESTMONT**, Borough; Cambria County; Pop. 6,113; Zip Code 16603; Elev. 1,795; near Altoona in a highlands area in SW cen. Pennsylvania.

•**WHEATLAND**, Borough; Mercer County; Pop. 1,132; Zip Code 16161; Elev. 900; Lat. 40-02-22 N long. 076-21-05 W; in W Pennsylvania; laid out about 1865 by *James Wood*, a Philadelphia Democrat who named the town for *President James Buchanan's* Lancaster County estate.

•**WHITEHALL**, Borough; Allegheny County; Pop. 15,206; Zip Code 18052; Elev. 1,200; Lat. 41-06-59 Nlong. 076-37-55 W; S suburb of Pittsburgh in SW Pennsylvania.

•**WHITE OAK**, Borough; Allegheny County; Pop. 9,480; Zip Code 15131; Elev. 1,100; Lat. 40-20-15 Nlong. 079-48-34 W; S suburb of Pittsburgh in SW Pennsylvania.

•**WHITEMARSH**, Township and Village; Montgomery County; Pop. 15,886; Elev. 203; 15 miles N of Philadelphia on the Wissahocken Creek in SE Pennsylvania.

•**WILKES-BARRE**, City; Seat of Luzerne County; Pop. 51,117; Zip Code 187+; Elev. 575; Lat. 41-14-45 N long. 075-52-54 W; 20 miles SW of Scranton in NE Pennsylvania.

•**WILKINSBURG**, Borough; Allegheny County; Pop. 23,669; Zip Code 15221; Elev. 922; Lat. 40-26-30 N long. 079-52-56 W; 10 miles E of Pittsburgh in SW Pennsylvania; settled in 1780 and known successively as McNairsville and Rippeysville, was incorporated in 1887. Its name was changed to honor *Judge William Wilkins*, Minister to Russia and *President Tyler's* Secretary of War.

•**WILLIAMSBURG**, Borough; Blair County; Pop. 1,400; Zip Code 16693; Elev. 885; Lat. 40-27-43 N long. 078-12-00 W; in S central. Pennsylvania.

•**WILLIAMSPORT**, City; Seat of Lycoming County; Pop. 33,401; Zip Code 17701; in N central Pennsylvania.

•**WILLOW GROVE**, Urban Village; Montgomery County; Pop. 21,000; Zip Code 19090; Elev. 284; Lat. 40-57-12 N long. 080-22-59 W; 15 miles N of Philadelphia in SE Pennsylvania.

•**WILMERDING**, Borough; Allegheny County; Pop. 2,421; Zip Code 15148; Elev. 900; Lat. 40-23-27 N long. 079-48-37 W; 10 miles E of Pittsburgh in SW Pennsylvania; was at first a railroad station, built about 1885, on land originally owned by *Major William B. Negley*. The name Wilmerding was suggested by *Robert Pitcairn*, then superintendent of the Pittsburgh division of the Pennsylvania Railroad, Negley's wife, *Joanna Wilmerding Negley*. Wilmerding was the family name of her mother.

•**WILSON**, Borough; Northampton County; Pop. 7,564; Zip Code 15025; near Easton in an industrial area in E Pennsylvania.

•**WINDBER**, Borough; Somerset County; Pop. 5,585; Zip Code 15963; Elev. 1,600; Lat. 40-14-23 N long. 078-50-07 W; in S Pennsylvania; was selected by the Pennsylvania Railroad Company in 1897 for its new station at this point. This name, which was suggested by E.J. Berwind, the chief stockholder in the Berwind-White Coal company, was formed by transposing the two syllables of the family name Berwind.

•**WIND GAP**, Borough; Northampton County; Pop. 2,651; Zip Code 18091; Elev. 841; in E Pennsylvania; incorporated as a borough in 1893 and named for the Wind Gap to the north.

•**WINDSOR**, Borough; York County; Pop. 1,205; Zip Code 17366; Elev. 660; Lat. 39-54-58 N long. 076-35-05 W; bin S Pennsylvania; named for Windsor, England by *Thomas Armor*, who was justice of the township in the 1750s.

•**WOMELSDORF**, Borough; Berks County; Pop. 1,827; Zip Code 19567; Elev. 434; Lat. 40-21-42 N long. 076-11-04 W; in SE Pennsylvania; founded by Germans in 1723, was called Middletown until 1762, when it was renamed for *John Womelsdorf*, leader of emigrants from the German Palatinate.

•**WORMLEYSBURG**, Borough; Cumberland County; Pop. 2,772; Zip Code 17043; Elev. 320; Lat. 40-15-46 N long. 076-54-51 W; suburb of Harrisburg in S Pennsylvania.

•**WYOMING**, Borough; Luzerne County; Pop. 3,655; Zip Code 18644; Elev. 557; Lat. 41-18-42 N long. 075-50-16 W; 5 miles NE of Wilkes-Barre on the Susquehanna River in E Pennsylvania; Is the Site of the Battle of Wyoming, where valley settlers fought an invading party of Tories, known as Butler's Rangers, and a band of Iroquois on July 3, 1778.

•**WYOMISSING**, Borough; Berks County; Pop. 6,551; Zip Code 19610; Elev. 320; Lat. 40-19-46 N long. 075-57-56 W; 45 miles W of Reading in SE Pennsylvania; residential suburb; name is derived from an Indian phrase meaning "place of flats."

•**YEADON**, Borough; Delaware County; Pop. 11,727; Zip Code 19050; Elev. 100; Lat. 39-56-20 N long. 075-15-21 W; 5 miles SW of Philadelphia in SE Pennsylvania; residential.

•**YORK**, City; Seat of York County; Pop. 44,619; Zip Code 174+; 10 miles WSW of the Susquehanna River in SE Pennsylvania. Named by Richard, Thomas and John Penn, probably to honor their royal patron and benefactor of their family, the Duke of York, but possibly in memory of the ancient English city of York.

•**YOUNGSVILLE**, Borough; Warren Borough; 2,006; Zip Code 16371; Elev. 1,211; 10 miles W of Warren in NW Pennsylvania; settled in 1795 by *John McKinney*, and named for *Matthew Young*, who taught school from his tent here beginning in 1796.

•**YOUNGWOOD**, Borough; Westmoreland County; Pop. 3,749; Zip Code 15697; Elev. 976; 30 miles E of Pittsburgh in an industrial area in SW Pennsylvania.

•**ZELIENOPLE**, Borough; Butler County; Pop. 3,502; Zip Code 16063; Elev. 906; 30 miles NW of Pittsburgh, W Pennsylvania; was laid out on Connoquenessing Creek in 1802 by *Baron Dettmar Basse*, who later sold half of his 10,000-acre tract to *Father Rapp* for the latter's Harmony colony. The Baron named the settlement for his daughter, nicknamed *Zelie*.

RHODE ISLAND

•BARRINGTON, Town; Bristol County; Pop. 16,174; Zip Code 02806; Lat. 41-43-44 N, long. 071-18-38 W. Settled in 1677, incorporated by Massachusetts in 1717, then by Rhode Island in 1770, the town was named in honor of English theologian Lord Barrington, an advocate of religious toleration.

•BRISTOL, Town; Bristol County Seat; Pop. 20,128; Zip Code 02809; Lat. 41-40-52 N, long. 071-16-00 W. Named for Bristol, England.

•BURRILLVILLE, Town; Providence County; Pop. 13,164. Named for James Burrill, Jr., Attorney-General of the state who later became a chief justice and U.S. Senator.

•CENTRAL FALLS, City; Providence County; Pop, 16,995; Lat. 41-53-26 N long. 071-23-34 W; Descriptively named for its location.

•CHARLESTOWN, Town; Washington County; Pop. 4,800; Zip Code 02813; Lat. 41-22-46 N, long. 071-44-44 W. Incorporated in 1738 and named for King Charles II, who had granted Rhode Island its charter in 1663.

•COVENTRY, Town; Kent County; Pop. 27,065; Zip Code 02816; Lat. 41-41-26 N, long. 071-34-00 W. Named for Coventry, England.

•CRANSTON, City; Providence County; Pop, 71,992; Lat. 41-46-47 N long. 071-26-16 W; Named after an early settler.

•CUMBERLAND, Town; Providence County; Pop. 27,069; Zip Code 02864; Lat. 41-54-32 N, long. 071-23-32 W. Previously known as Attleboro Gore, the name was changed to honor Prince William, Duke of Cumberland.

•EAST GREENWICH, Town; Kent County Seat; Pop. 10,211; Zip Code 02818; Lat. 41-39-48 N, long. 071-27-33 W. The name is derived from a district of London in Kent County, England.

•EAST PROVIDENCE, City; Providence County; Pop, 50,980; Elev. 59; Lat. 41-48-49 N long. 071-22-14 W; Named by Roger Williams in 1636 for "God's merciful providence."

•EXETER, Town; Washington County; Pop. 4,453; Zip Code 02822; Lat. 41-34-37 N, long. 071-32-21 W. The town is named for Exeter, England.

•FOSTER, Town; Providence County; Pop. 3,370; Zip Code 02825; Lat. 41-51-10 N, long. 071-45-39 W. Incorporated in 1781 and named for Theodore Foster, a U.S. Senator who owned property in the town.

•GLOCESTER, Town; Providence County; Pop. 7,550. Named for Gloucester, England.

•HOPKINTON, Town; Washington County; Pop. 6,406; Zip Code 02833; Lat. 41-27-41 N, long. 071-46-40 W. Named in 1757 for Governor Stephen Hopkins.

•JAMESTOWN, Town; Newport County; Pop. 4,040; Zip Code 02835; Lat. 41-29-22 N, long. 071-21-51 W. Named in honor of James II, Duke of York and Albany.

•JOHNSTON, Town; Providence County; Pop. 24,907; Zip Code 02919; Lat. 41-49-18 N, long. 071-29-44 W. Incorporated in 1759 and named for Augustus Johnston, Attorney-General of the colony from 1757-1765.

•LINCOLN, Town; Providence County; Pop. 16,949; Zip Code 02865; Lat. 41-53-47 N, long. 071-24-55 W. Named for President Abraham Lincoln in 1871.

•LITTLE COMPTON, Town; Newport County; Pop.3,085; Zip Code 02837; Lat. 41-30-28 N, long. 071-10-25 W. Named for the town in England.

•MIDDLETOWN, Town; Newport County; Pop. 17,216; Zip Code 02840; Lat. 41-32-44 N, long. 071-17-31 W. Named for its central location on the island of Rhode Island.

•NARRAGANSETT, Town; Washington County; Pop. 12,088; Zip Code 02882; Lat. 41-23-24 N, long. 071-28-24 W. The town takes its name from the Indian tribe which at one time lived in this territory.

•NEWPORT, City; Newport County Seat; Pop. 29,259; Zip Code 02840; Lat. 41-29-32 N long. 071-18-45 W; Settled and named in 1639 after several English towns.

•NEW SHOREHAM, Town; Washington County; Pop. 620. Incorporated in 1672 and named for a place in England.

•NORTH KINGSTOWN, Town; Washington County; Pop. 21,938; Zip Code 02852; Lat. 41-37-35 N, long. 071-27-17. Incorporated as King's Towne in 1674, the name was changed to Rochester in 1686, then changed back to its original name in 1689. In 1723 the town was divided into North and South Kingstown.

•NORTH PROVIDENCE, Town; Providence County; Pop. 29,188. Named for its location, north of Providence.

•NORTH SMITHFIELD, Town; Providence County; Pop. 9,972. The name indicates the town's geographical location north of Smithfield.

•PAWTUCKET, City; Providence County; Pop. 71,204; Zip Code 02860; Lat. 41-52-32 N long. 071-22-53 W; An Algonquian Indian word meaning "falls-in-the-river."

•PORTSMOUTH, Town; Newport County; Pop. 14,257; Zip Code 02871; Lat. 41-36-03 N, long. 071-15-00 W. Founded in 1638 by colonists from Massachusetts Bay Colony and named for Portsmouth, England.

•PROVIDENCE, City; Providence County Seat; Pop. 156,804; Zip Code 029+; Lat. 41-49-24 N long. 071-25-32 W; A thankful reference by the state's early settlers to "divine providence."

•RICHMOND, Town; Washington County; Pop. 4,018. Probably named for Edward Richmond, attorney-general of the colony from 1677-1680.

•SCITUATE, Town; Providence County; Pop. 8,405. Settlers from Scituate, Massachusetts came here in 1710 and named the town for their former home.

•SMITHFIELD, Town; Providence County; Pop. 16,886. The origin of the town's name is uncertain; however, the land on which the Quaker Meeting House was built was deeded by a party named Smith, and the town may have been named in his honor.

•SOUTH KINGSTOWN, Town; Washington County; Pop. 20,414. Formerly part of Kingstown, which was divided in 1723 into North and South Kingstown.

•TIVERTON, Town; Newport County; Pop. 13,526; Zip Code 02878; Lat. 41-37-31 N, long. 071-12-27 W. Named for Tiverton, England, the town was previously known as Pocasset, for the Pocasset Indians from whom the land was purchased.

•WARREN, Town; Bristol County; Pop. 10,640; Zip Code 02885; Lat. 41-43-30 N, long. 071-16-10 W. Incorporated in 1747 and named for Sir Peter Warren, a British Navy admiral.

•WARWICK, City; Kent County; Pop. 87,123; Zip Code 028+; Elev. 64; Lat. 41-43-00 N long. 071-26-22 W; Named for the town and county in England.

•**WEST KINGSTON,** Washington County Seat; Zip Code 02892; Lat. 41-28-55 N, long. 071-49-40 W. The name refers to the town's location.

•**WEST WARWICK,** Town; Kent County; Pop. 27,026; Zip Code 02893; Lat. 41-42-08 N, long. 071-30-14 W. Named in honor of the Earl of Warwick, who had been appointed Governor-in-Chief and Lord High Admiral in the Colonies.

•**WESTERLY,** Town; Washington County; Pop. 18,580; Zip Code 02891; Lat. 41-22-29 N, long. 071-49-40 W. Named for its location in the most westerly part of the state.

•**WOONSOCKET,** City; Providence County; Pop, 45,914; Zip Code 02895; Elev. 162; Lat. 42-00-07 N long. 071-30-25 W; An Algonquian Indian word meaning "steep descent."

SOUTH CAROLINA

•**ABBEVILLE**, City; Abbeville County Seat; Pop. 5,863; Zip Code 29620; Elev. 597; Lat. 34-10-42 N long. 082-22-39.

•**AIKEN**, City; Aiken County Seat; Pop. 14,978; Zip Code 298+; Lat. 33-33-56 N long. 081-44-01 W.

•**ALLENDALE**, Town; Allendale County Seat; Pop. 4,400; Zip Code 29810; Elev. 191; Lat. 33-00-22 N long. 081-18-12 W.

•**ANDERSON**, City; Anderson County Seat; Pop. 27,313; Zip Code 29621; Elev. 771; Lat. 34-30-42 N long. 082-38-58 W.

•**ANDREWS**, Town; Georgetown & Williamsburg Counties; Pop. 3,129; Zip Code 29510; Elev. 37; Lat. 33-27-12 N long. 079-34-42 W.

•**ARCADIA LAKES**, Town; Richland County; Pop. 611; Zip Code 29320; Lat. 34-57-48 N long. 081-59-15 W; Arcadia is an old English name for the ideal garden-like environment. The town's beautiful surroundings suggested the name.

•**AYNOR**, Town; Horry County; Pop. 643; Zip Code 29511; Elev. 104; Lat. 33-59-55 N long. 079-11-57 W; Named after an early settler.

•**BAMBERG**, Town; Bamberg County Seat; Pop. 3,672; Zip Code 29003; Elev. 168; The town as well as the county are named in honor of the prominent Bamberg family.

•**BARNWELL**, City; Barnwell County Seat; Pop. 5,572; Zip Code 29812; Lat. 33-14-41 N long. 081-21-42 W; The town's name honors Revolutionary War hero General John Barnwell.

•**BATESBURG**, Town; Lexington & Saluda Counties; Pop. 4,023 Zip Code 29006; Elev. 649; Named after Captain Tom Bates, a Civil War captain and prominent citizen.

•**BEAUFORT**, City; Beaufort County Seat; Pop. 8,634; Zip Code 29902; Elev. 11; Founded in 1710 and named in honor of the Duke of Beaufort.

•**BELTON**, City; Anderson County; Pop. 5,312; Zip Code 29627; Elev. 885; Lat. 34-31-24 N long. 082-29-36 W; Judge John Belton was a lwayer, railroad president, and historian. The town is named in his honor.

•**BENNETTSVILLE**, City; Marlboro County Seat; Pop. 8,774; Zip Code 29512; Lat. 34-36-51 N long. 079-41-28 W; The city's name honors Thomas Bennet, governor of South Carolina in 1820.

•**BETHUNE**, Town; Kershaw County; Pop. 481; Zip Code 29009; Elev. 283; Named in 1899 for a prominent citizen.

•**BISHOPVILLE**, Town; Lee County Seat; Pop. 3,429; Zip Code 29010; Elev. 226; The town is named after Dr. Jacob Bishop who owned land and ran a store in the area.

•**BLACKSBURG**, Town; Cherokee County; Pop. 1,873; Zip Code 29702; Elev. 768; Originally Stark's Folly, the town was later renamed to honor the Black family who were well-to-do landowners.

•**BLACKVILLE**, Town; Barnwell County; Pop. 2,840; Zip Code 29817; Lat. 33-21-03 N long. 081-16-04 W; Railroad developer Alexander Black helpted establish the South Carolina railroad. The town is named in his honor.

•**BLENHEIM**, Town; Marlboro County; Pop. 202; Zip Code 29516; Elev. 120; Lat. 34-30-36 N long. 079-39-08 W; The town is named for the famus Blenheim Castle in England.

•**BLUFFTON**, Town; Beaufort County; Pop. 541; Zip Code 29910; Elev. 25; Lat. 32-14-19 N long. 080-51-50 W; Descriptively named for its location on the May River.

•**BLYTHEWOOD**, Town; Richland County; Pop. 92; Zip Code 29016; Elev. 504; Named for the nearby Blythewood Academy following the Civil War.

•**BONNEAU**, Town; Berkeley County; Pop. 401; Zip Code 29431; Elev. 62; Lat. 33-18-26 N long. 079-58-20 W; The town is named for the Bonneau family, who were Huguenot pioneers.

•**BOWMAN**, Town; Orangeburg County; Pop. 1,137; Zip Code 29018; Elev. 39; The town's name honors the Bowman family, who were large landowners.

•**BRANCHVILLE**, Town; Orangeburg County; Pop. 1,769; Zip Code 29432; Elev. 125; Lat. 33-15-10 N long. 080-48-56 W; Descriptively named for a branch of the South Carolina railway.

•**BRUNSON**, Town; Hampton County; Pop. 590; Zip Code 29911; Elev. 138; Lat. 32-55-30 N long. 081-11-21 W; Named for an early settler.

•**BURNETTOWN**, Town; Aiken County; Pop. 359; Burnettown's name remembers an early settler.

•**CALHOUN FALLS**, Town; Abbeville County; Pop. 2,491; Zip Code 29828; Lat. 34-05-27 N long. 082-35-52 W; Originally Terryville, the town was renamed to honor Colonel J. E. Calhoun.

•**CAMDEN**, City; Kershaw County Seat; Pop. 7,462; Zip Code 29020; Settled in 1733 and named in honor of Lord Camden, who defended the colonies in Parliment.

•**CAMERON**, Town; Calhoun County; Pop. 536; Zip Code 29030; Lat. 33-33-33 N long. 080-42-41 W; Cameron is a Scotch clan name bestowed by early settlers.

•**CAMPOBELLO**, Town; Spartanburg County; Pop. 472; Zip Code 29322; Elev. 848; Lat. 35-06-57 N long. 082-08-44 W; Incorporated in 1881 and named Campa Bella, or "beautiful fields."

•**CARLISLE**, Town; Union County; Pop. 503; Zip Code 29031; Lat. 34-35-31 N long. 081-27-58 W; Originally fish dam, the name was later changed to honor Methodist minister, Coleman Carlisle.

•**CAYCE**, City; Lexington County; Pop. 11,701; Zip Code 29033; Lat. 33-58-02 N long. 081-04-31 W; The town's name remembers John Cayce whose house figured in local Revolutionary War history.

•**CENTRAL**, Town; Pickens County; Pop. 1,914; Zip Code 29630; Elev. 910; Lat. 34-43-23 N long. 082-46-45 W; Descriptively named for its location between Atlanta and Charlotte.

•**CHAPIN**, Town; Lexington County; Pop. 311; Zip Code 29036; Lat. 34-09-55 N long. 081-21-08 W; Named in honor of early settler Tom Chapin.

•**CHAPPELLS**, Town; Newberry County; Pop. 109; Zip Code 29037; Lat. 34-10-49 N long. 081-52-04 W; An early settler family, the Chappells, left their name on the town.

•**CHARLESTON**, City; Charleston County Seat; Pop. 69,510; Zip Code 29401; Elev. 118; Lat. 32-46-30 N long. 079-56-23 W; Settled in 1670 and named in honor of King Charles II.

•**CHERAW**, Town; Chesterfield County; Pop. 5,654; Zip Code 29520; Elev. 157; Lat. 34-41-51 N long. 079-53-18 W; The town was settled in 1752 and named after the local Cheraw Indians.

•**CHESNEE,** Town; Spartanburg County; Pop. 1,069; Zip Code 29323; Elev. 913; Lat. 35-08-52 N long. 081-51-45 W; The Chesnee family settled in the area in the 1750's and held large land grants. The town is named after them.

•**CHESTER,** City; Chester County Seat; Pop. 6,820; Zip Code 29706; Elev. 549; Lat. 34-42-32 N long. 081-12-52 W; Settlers from Chester, Pennsylvania came to the area in 1785. They named their new home after the old.

•**CHESTERFIELD,** Town; Chesterfield County Seat; Pop. 1,432; Zip Code 29709; Lat. 34-44-11 N long. 080-05-08 W; Settled in the late 1700's and named in honor of the Earl of Chesterfield.

•**CLEMSON,** City; Anderson & Pickens Counties; Pop. 8,118; Zip Code 29631; Lat. 34-40-58 N long. 082-48-06 W; The town is named after Clemson College, that name honoring its founder Thomas Clemson.

•**CLINTON,** City; Laurens County; Pop. 8,596; Zip Code 29325; Elev. 676; Lat. 34-28-15 N long. 081-52-43 W; Founded in 1850 and named for lawyer Colonel Henry Clinton Young.

•**CLIO,** Town; Marlboro County; Pop. 1,031; Zip Code 29525; Lat. 34-35-08 N long. 079-3229 W; Originally Ivy's Cross Roads, the name was changed to a coined word created by placing together initials of circulars signed by English writer Addison in the Spectator: Chelsea, London, Islington, and Office.

•**CLOVER,** Town; York County; Pop. 3,451; Zip Code 29710; Elev. 814; Lat. 35-06-39 N long. 081-13-40 W; Early settlers found white clover growing abundantly in the area. They named the town after this clover.

•**COLUMBIA,** City; Richland County Seat; Pop. 99,296; Zip Code 292+; Lat. 34-00-36 N long. 081-00-08 W; Founded in 1786 and given the patriotic name for America.

•**CONWAY,** City; Horry County Seat; Pop. 10,240; Zip Code 29526; Lat. 33-50-42 N long. 079-03-26 W; Settled as Kingston, but renamed in 1801 in honor of Revolutionary War hero, general Robert Conway.

•**COPE,** Town; Orangeburg County; Pop. 167; Zip Code 29038; Lat. 33-22-48 N long. 081-00-24 W; Named for an early settler.

•**CORDOVA,** Town; Orangeburg County; Pop. 202; Zip Code 29039; Elev. 252; Lat. 33-26-14 N long. 080-55-01 W; Originally Smoaks, the name was later changed to the better sounding Cordova by Atlantic Coast Railroad Company.

•**COTTAGEVILLE,** Town; Colleton County; Pop. 371; Zip Code 29435; Lat. 32-58-26 N long. 080-29-30 W; The widow of Methodist minister, Mrs. H. H. Durant, needed a home, which the communnity built. It was subsequently named for that "cottage."

•**COWARD,** Town; Florence County; Pop. 428; Zip Code 29530; Lat. 33-58-20 N long. 079-44-55 W; Named for an early settler.

•**COWPENS,** Town; Spartanburg County; Pop. 2,023; Zip Code 29330; Lat. 35-01-20 N long. 081-48-14 W; Cattle were raised in the area prior to the Revolutionary War, the name was later adopted.

•**CROSS HILL,** Town; Laurens County; Pop. 604; Zip Code 29332; Elev. 587; Lat. 34-18-16 N long. 081-59-00 W; Descriptively named by its settlers.

•**DARLINGTON,** City; Darlington County Seat; Pop. 7,989; Zip Code 295+; Lat. 34-18-24 N long. 079-52-32 W; Founded in 1798 and either named after Darlington, England, or Colonel Darlington of the Revolutionary War.

•**DENMARK,** City; Bamberg County; Pop. 4,434; Zip Code 29042; Elev. 244; Lat. 33-19-19 N long. 081-08-30 W; Originally Graham's Turnout, it was renamed to honor the Denmark family, who promoted the railroad.

•**DILLON,** City; Dillon County Seat; Pop. 7,042; Zip Code 29536; Elev. 113; Lat. 34-25-05 N long. 079-22-14 W; Named in honor of prominent Irish settler, J. W. Dillion, who helped build the railroad in the county.

•**DONALDS,** Town; Abbeville County; Pop. 1,366; Zip Code 29638; Elev. 762; Lat. 34-22-41 N long. 082-20-42 W; Named for an early settler.

•**DUE WEST,** Town; Abbeville County; Pop. 1,366; Zip Code 29639; Lat. 34-19-57 N long. 082-23-16 W; Originally called Duett's Corner, the present name is a corruption.

•**DUNCAN,** Town; Spartanburg County; Pop. 1,259; Zip Code 29334; Lat. 34-56-11 N long. 082-08-11 W; Founded as Vernon, but renamed in 1876 as Duncan, after a local settler.

•**EASLEY,** City; Pickens County; Pop. 14,264; Zip Code 29640; Elev. 1091; Lat. 34-50-12 N long. 082-37-12 W; Easley is named after prominent railroad attorney, William K. Easley.

•**EASTOVER,** Town; Richland County; Pop. 899; Zip Code 29044; Elev. 190; Lat. 33-52-44 N long. 080-41-22 W; Descriptively named by its early settlers.

•**EDGEFIELD,** Town; Edgefield County Seat; Pop. 2,713; Zip Code 29824; Lat. 33-47-15 N long. 081-55-49 W; Founded in 1798 and descriptively named as the "edge" of South Carolina at that time.

•**EDISTO BEACH,** Town; Colleton County; Pop. 193; The town's name recalls early Indians, the Adusta, also the name of their chief.

•**EHRHARDT,** Town; Bamberg County; Pop. 353; Zip Code 29081; Elev. 146; Lat. 33-05-49 N long. 081-00-44 W; Named for an early settler.

•**ELGIN,** Town; Kershaw County; Pop. 595; Zip Code 29045; Elev. 420; Lat. 34-10-22 N long. 080-47-43 W; Once called St. Luke's, the railroad changed the name in 1895.

•**FAIRFAX,** Town; Allendale & Hampton Counties; Pop. 2,154; Zip Code 29827; Elev. 136; Lat. 32-57-09 N long. 081-13-58 W; Settled in 1872 and named after historic Lord Fairfax of Virginia.

•**FLORENCE,** City; Florence County Seat; Pop. 30,062; Zip Code 29501; Elev. 149; Lat. 34-12-18 N long. 079-45-05 W; Settled in 1888 and named in honor of a railroad president's daughter, Miss Florence Harllee.

•**FOLLY BEACH,** City; Charleston County; Pop. 1,478; Zip Code 29439; Lat. 32-39-23 N long. 079-56-09 W; Named for a particular incidents in the town's history.

•**FOREST ACRES,** City; Richland County; Pop. 6,033; Descriptively named for the once abundant forests.

•**FORT LAWN,** Town; Chester County; Pop. 471; Zip Code 29714; Elev. 556; Lat. 34-41-48 N long. 080-53-53 W; The town is named after an early fort.

•**FORT MILL,** Town; York County; Pop. 4,162; Zip Code 29715; Elev. 668; Lat. 35-00-32 N long. 080-56-35 W; A fort for the Catawba Indians was founded in 1796 near a mill. The name followed from this fact.

•**FOUNTAIN INN**, Town; Greenville & Laurens Counties; Pop. 4,226; Zip Code 29644; Elev. 872; Lat. 34-41-18 N long. 082-11-23 W; An overnight stop during stagecoach days, the spot was named for a fountain near the station.

•**FURMAN**, Town; Hampton County; Pop. 13,453; Zip Code 29921; Elev. 112; Lat. 32-41-01 N long. 081-11-27 W; The town was established in 1901 and is named for black woman, Mum Lizzie Furman.

•**GAFFNEY**, City; Cherokee County Seat; Pop. 13,453; Zip Code 29340; Elev. 769; Lat. 35-04-25 N long. 081-38-17 W; Captain Michael Gaffney settled in the area in 1804 and started the town. It is named after him.

•**GASTON**, Town; Lexington County; Pop. 960; Zip Code 29053; Lat. 33-49-08 N long. 081-05-19 W; Named for an early settler.

•**GEORGETOWN**, City; Georgetown County Seat; Pop. 10,144; Zip Code 294+; Elev. 18; Lat. 33-22-06 N long. 079-17-24 W; Founded in the 1760's and named in honor of King George II.

•**GIFFORD**, Town; Hampton County; Pop. 385; Zip Code 29923; Elev. 139; Lat. 32-51-33 N long. 081-14-10 W; Gifford is named after an early settler.

•**GILBERT**, Town; Lexington County; Pop. 211; Zip Code 29054; Elev. 529; Lat. 33-55-25 N long. 081-23-28 W; Named after a prominent early settler.

•**GOOSE CREEK**, City; Berkeley County; Pop. 17,811; Zip Code 29445; Lat. 32-59-430 N long. 080-02-32 W; Descriptively named by wealthy planters for the winding creek which reminded them of a goose's neck.

•**GRAY COURT**, Town; Laurens County; Pop. 988; Zip Code 29645; Lat. 34-36-39 N long. 082-06-54 W; Originally Dorran's, the name was later changed to honor the Grey family, prominent plantation owners.

•**GREAT FALLS**, Town; Chester County; Pop. 2,601; Zip Code 29055; Elev. 467; Lat. 34-34-25 N long. 080-54-04 W; Descriptively named for its location on the falls of the Catawba River.

•**GREELEYVILLE**, Town; Williamsburg County; Pop. 593; Zip Code 29056; Elev. 79; Lat. 33-34-55 N long. 079-59-25 W; Legend has it that the town is named for famous newspaperman, Horace Greeley.

•**GREENVILLE**, City; Greenville County Seat; Pop. 58,242; Zip Code 29601; Lat. 34-50-56 N long. 082-24-08 W; Settled in the 1780's and named in honor of Revolutionary War hero, General Nathaniel Greene.

•**GREENWOOD**, City; Greenwood County Seat; Pop. 21,613; Zip Code 29646; Elev. 665; Lat. 34-11-34 N long. 082-09-02 W; Originally Woodville, the name was changed in 1850 to "Greenwood," after the nearby home of Judge John McGehee.

•**GREER**, City; Greenville & Spartanburg Counties; Pop. 10,525; Zip Code 29651; Elev. 1016; Lat. 34-56-21 N long. 082-13-01 W; Incorporated in 1875 and named after a local family.

•**HAMPTON**, Town; Hampton County Seat; Pop. 3,143; Zip Code 29913; Elev. 95; Lat. 32-55-04 N long. 081-04-45 W; The town is named in honor of Governor Wade Hampton, who was in office from 1876 to 1879.

•**HARDEEVILLE**, Town; Jasper County; Pop. 1,250; Zip Code 29927; Elev. 20; Lat. 32-16-43 N long. 081-04-22 W; Hardeeville is named for an early settler.

•**HARLEYVILLE**, Town; Dorchester County; Pop. 606; Zip Code 29448; Elev. 92; Lat. 33-12-52 N long. 080-26-56 W; Named for an early settler.

•**HARTSVILLE**, City; Darlington County; Pop. 7,631; Zip Code 29550; Lat. 34-22-57 N long. 080-04-31 W; Incorporated in 1891 and named after the Hart family.

•**HEATH SPRINGS**, Town; Lancaster County; Pop. 979; Zip Code 29058; Elev. 687; Lat. 34-35-49 N long. 080-40-10 W; Descriptively named after nearby Heath's Spring, a mineral spring.

•**HEMINGWAY**, Town; Williamsburg County; Pop. 853; Zip Code 29554; Elev. 53; Lat. 33-44-28 N long. 079-28-42 W; Once called Lamberts, it was renamed in 1908 for the Hemingway family, who were prominent English planters.

•**HICKORY GROVE**, Town; York County; Pop. 344; Zip Code 29717; Elev. 485; Lat. 34-58-45 N long. 081-24-53 W; Descriptively named for the many hickory groves in the area.

•**HODGES**, Town; Greenwood County; Pop. 154; Zip Code 296+; Lat. 34-17-24 N long. 082-14-48 W; Named after an early pioneer family.

•**HOLLY HILL**, Town; Orangeburg County; Pop. 1,785; Zip Code 29059; Elev. 108; Lat. 33-19-33 N long. 080-24-37 W; Descriptively named for a nearby hill covered with holly.

•**HOLLYWOOD**, Town; Charleston County; Pop. 729; Zip Code 29449; Lat. 32-44-02 N long. 080-14-24 W; Originally Cross Roads, it was renamed to reflect the many holly trees in the area.

•**HONEA PATH**, Town; Abbeville & Anderson Counties; Pop. 4,114; Zip Code 296+; Lat. 34-29-48 N long. 082-17-07 W; An Indian name meaning "great path."

•**INMAN**, City; Spartanburg County; Pop. 1,554; Zip Code 29349; Elev. 986; Lat. 35-02-43 N long. 082-05-28 W; The town's name honors Southern Railway official, Samuel M. Inman.

•**IRMO**, Town; Lexington & Richland Counties; Pop. 3,957; Zip Code 29063; Lat. 34-05-21 N long. 081-11-12 W; Named for an early settler.

•**ISLE OF PALMS**, City; Charleston County; Pop. 3,421; Zip Code 29451; Lat. 32-47-33 N long. 079-46-34 W; Descriptively named for the many palms in the area.

•**IVA**, Town; Anderson County; Pop. 1,369; Zip Code 29655; Lat. 34-18-12 N long. 082-39-51 W; The town's name honors Iva Cook, daughter of a pioneer family.

•**JACKSON**, Town; Aiken County; Pop. 1,771; Zip Code 29831; Elev. 204; Lat. 33-19-53 N long. 081-47-32 W; Named after President Andrew Jackson.

•**JAMESTOWN**, Town; Berkeley County; Pop. 193; Zip Code 29453; Elev. 40; Lat. 33-17-04 N long. 079-41-45 W; The town's name remembers an early Huguenot settlement on the Santee River, named for King James of England.

•**JOHNSONVILLE**, City; Florence County; Pop. 1,421; Zip Code 29555; Elev. 94; Lat. 33-48-58 N long. 079-27-03 W; Named for an early settler.

•**JOHNSTON**, Town; Edgefield County; Pop. 2,624; Zip Code 29832; Elev. 661; Lat. 33-49-46 N long. 081-48-03 W; Johnston's name honors W. P. Johnston, president of the Southern Railway Company.

•**JONESVILLE**, Town; Union County; Pop. 1,188; Zip Code 29353; Elev. 682; Lat. 34-50-07 N long. 081-40-54 W; The town remembers Charlie Jones, an early settler.

•**KERSHAW,** Town; Lancaster County; Pop. 1,993; Zip Code 29067; Elev. 522; Lat. 34-32-48 N long. 080-34-51 W; The towns name honors Colonel Joseph Kershaw, a Revolutionary War hero.

•**KINGSTREE,** Town; Williamsburg County Seat; Pop. 4,147; Zip Code 29556; Lat. 33-40-12 N long. 079-49-50 W; In colonial days, trees marked with an arrow sign were reserved for the royal Navy's sailing ships. The town was named for a large white pine on the Black River so marked.

•**KLINE,** Town; Barnwell County; Pop. 315; Named for an early settler.

•**LAKE CITY,** City; Florence County; Pop. 5,636; Zip Code 29560; Elev. 77; Lat. 33-52-01 N long. 079-45-27 W; Named either for its location near Lake Swamp or after the Lake family, who were pioneer settlers.

•**LAKE VIEW,** Town; Dillon County; Pop. 939; Zip Code 29563; Lat. 34-20-34 N long. 079-10-06 W; An early mill created an artificial lake and cause the site to be named "Lake View."

•**LAMAR,** Town; Darlington County; Pop. 1,333; Zip Code 29069; Lat. 34-10-08 N long. 080-03-55 W; Once known as Devil's Woodyard, its name was changed in 1880 to hnor J. Q. Lamar, a member of President Cleveland's cabinet.

•**LANCASTER,** City; Lancaster County Seat; Pop. 9,603; Zip Code 29720; Lat. 34-42-17 N long. 080-47-15 W; Settled in the 1790's and named for Lancaster, Pennsylvania, the former name of many early settlers.

•**LANDRUM,** City; Spartanburg County; Pop. 2,141; Zip Code 29356; Lat. 35-10-43 N long. 082-10-56 W; The first house in the village was built by Reverend John Landrum. The city is named in his honor.

•**LANE,** Town; Williamsburg County; Pop. 554; Zip Code 29564; Elev. 70; Lat. 33-31-18 N long. 079-52-52 W; Named for an early settler.

•**LATTA,** Town; Dillon County; Pop. 1,804; Zip Code 29565; Lat. 34-20-13 N long. 079-25-54 W; Founed in 1888 and named for an official of the Atlantic Coast Line Railroad.

•**LAURENS,** City; Laurens County Seat; Pop. 10,587; Zip Code 29360; Lat. 34-30-31 N long. 082-00-18 W; Established in 1798 and named in honor of statesman and member of the Continental Congress, Henry Laurens.

•**LEESVILLE,** Town; Lexington County; Pop. 2,296; Zip Code 29070; Elev. 656; Lat. 33-55-16 N long. 081-28-02 W; The town is named in honor of Colonel John Lee, a prominent citizen.

•**LEXINGTON,** Town; Lexington County Seat; Pop. 2,131; Zip Code 29072; Elev. 392; Lat. 33-59-01 N long. 081-14-16 W; The town's names the Battle of Lexington in the early part of the Revolutionary War.

•**LIBERTY,** Town; Pickens County; Pop. 3,167; Zip Code 29657; Elev. 1005; Lat. 34-47-04 N long. 082-41-56; Once called Salubrity, the name was changed during the Revolution to Liberty.

•**LINCOLNVILLE,** Town; Charleston County; Pop. 808; Settled by blacks after the Civil War and named in honor of President Abraham Lincoln.

•**LITTLE MOUNTAIN,** Town; Newberry County; Pop. 282; Zip Code 29075; Lat. 34-11-40 N long. 081-24-33 W; Named for a nearby hill called Little Mountain.

•**LIVINGSTON,** Town; Orangeburg County; Pop. 166; Mrs. Lavinia Livingston donated land to the town and had it named in her honor.

•**LOCKHART,** Town; Union County; Pop. 85; Zip Code 29364; Elev. 422; Lat. 34-47-32 N long. 081-27-36 W; The town is named for a pioneer miller named Lockhart.

•**LODGE,** Town; Colleton County; Pop. 145; Zip Code 29082; Elev. 111; Lat. 33-04-22 N long. 080-56-25 W; The town is named after Hope Masonic Lodge No. 122.

•**LORIS,** City; Horry County; Pop. 2,193; Zip Code 29569; Elev. 99; Lat. 34-03-20 N long. 078-53-07 W; Loris is probably named after an early settler.

•**LOWNDESVILLE,** Town; Abbeville County; Pop. 197; Zip Code 29659; Lat. 34-12-37 N long. 082-38-54 W; Lowings is named after an early settler.

•**LOWRYS,** Town; Chester County; Pop. 225; The Lowry family settled in the4 area in the 1750's. The town is named after them.

•**LURAY,** Town; Hampton County; Pop. 149; Zip Code 29932; Elev. 140; Lat. 32-48-53 N long. 081-14-21 W; Founded in 1893 and named after Luray Caverns in Virginia.

•**LYMAN,** Town; Spartanburg County; Pop. 1,067; Zip Code 29365; Lat. 34-56-47 N long. 082-07-27 W; Originally called Lyman, the town's name was changed to honor Arthur Lyman, who directed a large textile mill in the area.

•**LYNCHBURG,** Town; Lee County; Pop. 534; Zip Code 29080; Lat. 34-03-44 N long. 080-04-38 W; Descriptively named for its location on the Lynch River.

•**MANNING,** City; Clarendon County Seat; Pop. 4,746; Zip Code 29102; Lat. 33-42-56 N long. 080-17-18 W; Manning's name honors Richard Manning, who was governor from 1824 - 26.

•**MARION,** City; Marion County Seat; Pop. 7,700; Zip Code 29571; Elev. 77; Lat. 34-10-39 N long. 079-23-55 W; Founded in 1800 and named in honor of Revolutionary War hero, General Francis Marion.

•**MAULDIN,** City; Greenville County; Pop. 8,245; Zip Code 29662; Elev. 942; Lat. 34-46-51 N long. 082-18-20 W; Named for an early settler.

•**MAYESVILLE,** Town; Sumter County; Pop. 663; Zip Code 29104; Elev. 326; Lat. 33-59-12 N long. 080-12-33 W; Mayesville is named after a pioneer settler.

•**MCBEE,** Town; Chesterfield County; Pop. 774; Zip Code 29101; Lat. 34-28-14 N long. 080-15-27 W; Named by railroad officials in 1900 in honor of Bunch McBee.

•**MCCLELLANVILLE,** Town; Charleston County; Pop. 436; Zip Code 29458; Elev. 9; Lat. 33-05-11 N long. 079-27-44 W; The town's name remembers a prominent colonial family, the Mc-Clellans.

•**MCCOLL,** Town; Marlboro County; Pop. 2,677; Zip Code 29570; Elev. 185; Lat. 34-40-09 N long. 079-32-35 W; Settled in 1759 and later named for D. D. McColl, president of a local railroad.

•**MCCONNELLS,** Town; York County; Pop. 171; Zip Code 29726; Elev. 698; Lat. 34-52-19 N long. 081-13-39 W; The town is named for an early settler.

•**MCCORMICK,** Town; McCormick County Seat; Pop. 1,725; Zip Code 29835; Lat. 33-54-44 N long. 082-17-39 W; The town's name honors Cyrus McCormick, the inventor of the McCormick reaper.

•**MEGGETT**, Town; Charleston County; Pop. 249; Zip Code 29460; Lat. 32-43-03 N long. 080-14-18 W; Meggett's name remembers original landowner William Meggett, who was also a prosperous cotton planter.

•**MONCKS CORNER**, Town; Berkeley County Seat; Pop. 3,699; Zip Code 29461; Elev. 56; Lat. 33-11-39 N long. 080-00-53 W; Thomas Monck purchased the townsite as part of a plantation in 1735. The town is named after him.

•**MONETTA**, Town; Aiken & Saluda Counties; Pop. 108; Zip Code 29105; Elev. 634; Lat. 33-51-16 N long. 081-36-39 W; Founded in 1888 and according to legend named for an Indian princess buried nearby.

•**MOUNT CARMEL**, Town; McCormick County; Pop. 182; Zip Code 29840; Elev. 546; Lat. 34-00-14 N long. 082-36-01 W; Given this biblical name by early settlers.

•**MOUNT CROGHAN**, Town; Chesterfield County; Pop. 146; Zip Code 29727; Elev. 449; Lat. 34-46-14 N long. 080-13-37 W; The town's name remembers French Revolutionary War soldier Major Croghan.

•**MOUNT PLEASANT**, Town; Charleston County; Pop. 13,838; Zip Code 29464; Elev. 24; Lat. 32-48-17 N long. 079-51-46 W; Originally Haddrell's Point, the name was later changed to reflect the site's "pleasant" location.

•**MULLINS**, City; Marion County; Pop. 6,068; Zip Code 29574; Elev. 101; Lat. 34-12-22 N long. 079-15-21 W; Incorporated in 1872 and named in honor of railroad president William Mullins.

•**MYRTLE BEACH**, City; Horry County; Pop. 18,758; Zip Code 29577; Elev. 30; Lat. 33-39-22 N long. 078-55-59 W; Descriptively named for the Myrtle business found in the area.

•**NEESES**, Town; Orangeburg County; Pop. 557; Zip Code 29107; Lat. 33-31-58 N long. 081-07-30 W; Founded in 1890 by J. W. Neece and named in his honor.

•**NEWBERRY**, Town; Newberry County Seat; Pop. 9,866; Zip Code 29108; Elev. 503; Lat. 34-16-31 N long. 081-36-54 W; Established in 1789 and named in honor of Revolutionary War hero, Captain John Newberry.

•**NEW ELLENTON**, Town; Aiken County; Pop. 2,628; Zip Code 29809; Lat. 33-25-13 N long. 081-41-13 W; Named for the wife of an early pioneer.

•**NICHOLS**, Town; Marion County; Pop. 606; Zip Code 29581; Elev. 61; Lat. 34-13-56 N long. 079-08-52 W; Named in honor of prominent businessman A. B. Nichols, who helped develop the community in the 1850's.

•**NINETY SIX**, Town; Greenwood County; Pop. 2,249; Zip Code 29666; Lat. 34-10-22 N long. 082-01-13 W; Founded in 1730 and named after the distance from Charleston to Keowee.

•**NORRIS**, Town; Pickens County; Pop. 903; Zip Code 29667; Elev. 999; Lat. 34-45-51 N long. 082-45-46 W; The town grew around the Norris Cotton Mill and took its name.

•**NORTH**, Town; Orangeburg County; Pop. 1,304; Zip Code 29076; Lat. 33-33-10 N long. 081-07-12 W; Captain John North was an early settler and prominent landowner. He contributed land to the town and its settlers named it in his honor.

•**NORTH AUGUSTA**, City; Aiken County; Pop. 13,593; Zip Code 29841; Lat. 33-30-41 N long. 081-56-29 W.

•**OLANTA**, Town; Florence County; Pop. 699; Zip Code 29114; Elev. 118; Lat. 33-56-04 N long. 079-55-50 W; Originally called Bealah, the name was changed in 1909 by the U. S. Post Office.

•**OLAR**, Town; Bamberg County; Pop. 381; Zip Code 29843; Elev. 381; Lat. 33-12-00 N long. 081-10-51 W; Named for an early settler.

•**ORANGEBURG**, City; Orangeburg County Seat; Pop. 14,933; Zip Code 29115; Elev. 245; Lat. 33-29-56 N long. 080-51-44 W; Founded in 1768 and named for William of Orange, son-in-law of King George II.

•**PACOLET**, Town; Spartanburg County; Pop. 1,556; Zip Code 29372; Lat. 34-54-06 N long. 081-45-32 W; The town is named after the Pacolet River.

•**PACOLET MILLS**, Town; Spartanburg County; Pop. 686; Zip Code 29373; Lat. 34-54-58 N long. 081-44-45 W; Named for the Pacolet River.

•**PAGELAND**, Town; Chesterfield County; Pop. 2,720; Zip Code 29728; Elev. 654; Lat. 34-46-29 N long. 080-23-23 W; Established in 1904 and named for an early resident.

•**PAMPLICO**, Town; Florence County; Pop. 1,213; Zip Code 29583; Lat. 33-59-42 N long. 079-34-14 W; The origin of the town's name is uncertain.

•**PARKSVILLE**, Town; McCormick County; Pop. 157; Zip Code 29844; Elev. 348; Lat. 33-46-58 N long. 082-12-55 W; Settled in 1758 and named for Indian trader Antony Park.

•**PATRICK**, Town; Chesterfield County; Pop. 375; Zip Code 29584; Elev. 223; Lat. 34-34-25 N long. 080-02-41 W; Founded in 1902 and named for railroad agent John T. Patrick.

•**PEAK**, Town; Newberry County; Pop. 82; Zip Code 29122; Lat. 34-14-13 N long. 081-19-22 W; The town is named for H. T. Peak, the first superintendant of the Columbia and Greenville Railway Company.

•**PELION**, Town; Lexington County; Pop. 213; Zip Code 29123; Elev. 390; Lat. 33-45-54 N long. 081-14-29 W; Named after an early settler.

•**PELZER**, Town; Anderson County; Pop. 130; Zip Code 29669; Lat. 34-38-41 N long. 082-27-42 W; The town was founded by Francis J. Pelzer and named in his honor.

•**PENDLETON**, Town; Anderson County; Pop. 3,154; Zip Code 29670; Elev. 859; Lat. 34-39-12 N long. 082-46-53 W; The town was settled in 1790 and named for Virginia Jurist Henry Pendleton.

•**PERRY**, Town; Aiken County; Pop. 273; Zip Code 29124; Lat. 33-37-30 N long. 081-18-27 W; Perry is named after an early settler.

•**PICKENS**, Town; Pickens County Seat; Pop. 3,199; Zip Code 29671; Elev. 1110; Lat. 34-53-02 N long. 082-42-18 W; Pickens is named in honor of Revolutionary War hero, General Andrew Pickens.

•**PINERIDGE**, Town; Lexington County; Pop. 1,287; Descriptively named for the white pine forests in the area.

•**PINEWOOD**, Town; Sumter County; Pop. 689; Zip Code 29125; Lat. 33-44-20 N long. 080-27-48 W; Descriptively named for the many pine trees in the region.

•**PLUM BRANCH**, Town; McCormick County; Pop. 73; Zip Code 29845; Elev. 471; Lat. 33-51-00 N long. 082-15-30 W; Plums grow in the region and gave the town its descriptive name.

•**POMARIA**, Town; Newberry County; Pop. 271; Zip Code 29126; Elev. 404; Lat. 34-15-54 N long. 081-24-58 W; Pomaria is latin for fruit and describes the region's horticultural production.

447

•PORT ROYAL, Town; Beaufort County; Pop. 2,977; Zip Code 29935; Lat. 32-22-40 N long. 080-41-16 W; The town was named by French explorer Jean Ribaut in 1562 for its good harbor.

•PROSPERITY, Town; Newberry County; Pop. 672; Zip Code 29127; Elev. 541; Lat. 34-00-33 N long. 080-17-07 W; Originally called Frog Level, the name was changed by majority petition to the more positive "prosperity."

•RAVENEL, Town; Charleston County; Pop. 1,655; Zip Code 29470; Elev. 38; Lat. 32-46-43 N long. 080-14-21 W; The town is named for an early settler.

•REEVESVILLE, Town; Dorchester County; Pop. 241; Zip Code 29471; Elev. 12; Lat. 33-12-15 N long. 080-38-41 W; Reevesville's name honors an early settler.

•RICHBURG, Town; Chester County; Pop. 269; Zip Code 29729; Elev. 584; Lat. 34-43-05 N long. 081-01-02 W; The soil is very fertile in the area and to this descriptive name.

•RIDGELAND, Town; Jasper County Seat; Pop. 1,143; Zip Code 29912; Elev. 62; Lat. 32-35-19 N long. 080-55-31 W; Situated on a high ridge and so descriptively named.

•RIDGE SPRING, Town; Saluda County; Pop. 969; Zip Code 29129; Lat. 33-50-43 N long. 081-39-46 W; The town is founded on a ridge with a nearby spring and so named.

•RIDGEVILLE, Town; Dorchester County; Pop. 603; Zip Code 29472; Elev. 75; Lat. 33-05-55 N long. 080-19-02 W; Originally called Timothy Creek, but later renamed to reflect its location on a ridge.

•RIDGEWAY, Town; Fairfield County; Pop. 343; Zip Code 29130; Elev. 34-18-16 N long. 080-57-34 W; Located on the watershed of Fairfield County and so descriptively named for its topography.

•ROCK HILL, City; York County; Pop. 35,344; Zip Code 29730; Elev. 667; Lat. 34-55-52 N long. 081-01-23 W; Railroad construction crews here to blast a roadbed through the hill and so gave it a descriptive name.

•ROWESVILLE, Town; Orangeburg County; Pop. 388; Zip Code 29133; Elev. 166; Lat. 33-22-22 N long. 080-50-02 W; The Rowe family settled in the area in 1740. The town is named after them.

•RUBY, Town; Chesterfield County; Pop. 256; Zip Code 29741; Elev. 381; Lat. 34-44-33 N long. 080-11-06 W; Called Flint Hill when settled in 1875. In 1890 the name Ruby was chosen by contest to replace the old title.

•ST. GEORGE, Town; Dorchester County Seat; Pop. 2,134; Zip Code 29477; Elev. 102; Lat. 33-11-11 N long. 080-34-33 W; During colonial times the area was part of St. George Parish and ultimately so named when settled.

•ST. MATTHEWS, Town; Calhoun County Seat; Pop. 2,496; Zip Code 29135; Lat. 33-39-55 N long. 080-46-46 W; Once called Lewisburg, the name was later changed in honor of St. Matthews Parish.

•SALEM, Town; Oconee County; Pop. 194; Zip Code 29676; Elev. 1061; Lat. 34-53-33 N long. 082-58-30 W; Salem is named after Salem, Massachusetts.

•SALLEY, Town; Aiken County; Pop. 584; Zip Code 29137; Lat. 33-33-44 N long. 081-18-18 W; The town is named in honor of prominent early settler, D. H. Salley.

•SALUDA, Town; Saluda County Seat; Pop. 2,752; Zip Code 29138; Lat. 34-00-12 N long. 081-46-03 W; The city and the river are named after the Indian tribe that once occupied the area.

•SANTEE, Town; Orangeburg County; Pop. 612; Zip Code 29142; Lat. 33-29-05 N long. 080-28-38 W; The town is named after the Santee River. Santee is an Indian word meaning "haven."

•SCRANTON, Town; Florence County; Pop. 861; Zip Code 29591; Elev. 95; Lat. 33-55-05 N long. 079-44-48 W; Scranton is named after the city in Pennsylvania.

•SELLERS, Town; Marion County; Pop. 388; Zip Code 29592; Lat. 34-16-53 N long. 079-28-43 W; John Seller was a prominent farmer in the community. The town is named in his honor.

•SENECA, Town; Oconee County; Pop. 7,436; Zip Code 29678; Elev. 950; Lat. 34-40-52 N long. 082-56-22 W; The town is named after a pre-colonial Cherokee Indian town of Sinica.

•SHARON, Town; York County; Pop. 323; Zip Code 29742; Elev. 652; Lat. 34-57-04 N long. 081-20-22 W; The town is named after the Sharon Church.

•SILVERSTREET, Town; Newberry County; Pop. 200; Zip Code 29145; Lat. 34-13-08 N long. 081-42-40 W; Silvery-looking plants once lined the major street and gave the town its name.

•SIMPSONVILLE, Town; Greenville County; Pop. 9,037; Zip Code 29681; Elev. 865; Lat. 34-43-26 N long. 082-18-17 W; Named for an early settler named Simpson.

•SIX MILE, Town; Pickens County; Pop. 470; Zip Code 29682; Elev. 1027; Lat. 34-48-23 N long. 082-49-15 W; The town is six miles from Charlestown and so named.

•SMOOKS, Town; Colleton County; Pop. 165; Zip Code 29481; Lat. 33-05-24 N long. 080-48-31 W Named for an early settler.

•SMYRNA, Town; York County; Pop. 47; Zip Code 29743; Elev. 520; Lat. 35-02-25 N long. 081-24-24 W; The name of the Presbyterian Church formed in 1843, the name was adopted for the town.

•SOCIETY HILL, Town; Darlington County; Pop. 848; Zip Code 29593; Elev. 166; Lat. 34-30-38 N long. 079-51-00 W; Originally Long Bluff, the name was later changed to note the academy founded on the site by the St. David's Society.

•SOUTH CONGAREE, Town; Lexington; Pop. 2,113; Named by Irish settlers for a place in the old country.

•SPARTANBURG, City; Spartanburg County Seat; Pop. 43,968; Zip Code 293+; Elev. 816; Lat. 34-56-37 N long. 081-57-44 W; The Spartan militia was formed in the area in 1776 and fought honorably throughout the American Revolution. The town is named in their honor.

•SPRINGDALE, Town; Lexington County; Pop. 2,985; Descriptively named for the verdant countryside.

•SPRINGFIELD, Town; Orangeburg County; Pop. 604; Zip Code 29146; Elev. 300; Lat. 33-29-50 N long. 081-16-52 W; Settled in 1756 and finally named for an early settler, a Mr. Spring.

•STARR, Town; Anderson County; Pop. 241; Zip Code 29684; Elev. 771; Lat. 34-22-40 N long. 082-41-41 W; The town is named in honor of a C & W C Railroad official.

•STUCKEY, Town; Williamsburg County; Pop. 222; The town is named after an erly settler.

•SULLIVAN'S ISLAND, Town; Charleston County; Pop. 1,867; Zip Code 29482; Lat. 32-45-43 N long. 079-50-31 W; Sullivan was an early settler and the town is named after him.

•**SUMMERTON,** Town; Clarendon County; Pop. 1,173; Zip Code 29148; Lat. 33-36-32 N long. 080-21-08 W; A summer resort before the Civil War, it was noted for its warm, balmy weather, and descriptively named.

•**SUMMERVILLE,** Town; Charleston & Dorchester Counties; Pop. 6,368; Zip Code 29483; Elev. 75; Lat. 33-00-57 N long. 080-10-36 W; The town was used by rich planters and given a resort name.

•**SUMTER,** City; Sumter County Seat; Pop. 24,890; Zip Code 29150; Elev. 169; Lat. 33-54-40 N long. 080-20-52 W; Incorporated in 1798 and named in honor of Revolutionary War soldier, General Thomas Sumter.

•**SURFSIDE BEACH,** Town; Horry County; Pop. 2,522; The town is descriptively named for its location.

•**SWANSEA,** Town; Lexington County; Pop. 888; Zip Code 29160; Lat. 33-44-19 N long. 081-05-57 W; The town is named after Swansea, the city in England.

•**SYCAMORE,** Town; Allendale County; Pop. 261; Zip Code 29846; Elev. 153; Lat. 33-02-12 N long. 081-13-19 W; Sycamore trees grow abundantly in the area, so the townspeople gave their community this descriptive name.

•**TATUM,** Town; Marlboro County; Pop. 101; Zip Code 29594; Elev. 199; Lat. 34-38-39 N long. 079-35-10 W; Originally called Mount Washington, the name was changed to Tatum after an early settler.

•**TIMMONSVILLE,** Town; Florence County; Pop. 2,112; Zip Code 29161; Elev. 150; Lat. 34-08-03 N long. 079-56-32 W; The Timmons family were early settlers in the community, and the town is named after them.

•**TRAVELERS REST,** City; Greenville County; Pop. 3,107; Zip Code 29690; Lat. 34-58-17 N long. 082-26-15 W; An old stage coach stop, the town was named for its function as an overnight rest stop.

•**TRENTON,** Town; Edgefield County; Pop. 404; Zip Code 29847; Elev. 621; Lat. 33-44-30 N long. 081-50-26 W; Once called Pine House, the city was renamed for Trenton, New Jersey.

•**TROY,** Town; Greenwood County; Pop. 705; Zip Code 29848; Lat. 33-59-16 N long. 082-17-37 W; Troy is named after Troy, New York.

•**TURBEVILLE,** Town; Clarendon County; Pop. 549; Zip Code 29162; Elev. 131; Lat. 33-53-19 N long. 080-01-04 W; The town's name recalls an early settler.

•**ULMER,** Town; Alldndale County; Pop. 91; Zip Code 29849; Elev. 164; Lat. 33-03-27 N long. 081-16-14 W; Ulmer is named after one of its original settlers.

•**UNION,** City; Union County Seat; Pop. 10,523; Zip Code 29379; Elev. 639; Lat. 34-43-08 N long. 081-36-33 W; The city was founded in 1765 and named after a multi-denominational church.

•**VANCE,** Town; Orangeburg County; Pop. 89; Zip Code 29163; Lat. 33-26-16 N long. 080-25-09 W; Vance is named for an early settler.

•**VARNVILLE,** Town; Hampton County; Pop. 1,948; Zip Code 29944; Elev. 111; Lat. 32-51-16 N long. 081-04-59 W; Established in 1873 and named in honor of Methodist minister Berry Varn.

•**WAGENER,** Town; Aiken County; Pop. 903; Zip Code 29164; Lat. 33-38-55 N long. 081-21-42 W; The town's name honors C. G. Wagener, a well-known early pioneer.

•**WALHALLA,** Town; Oconee County Seat; Pop. 3,977; Zip Code 29691; Elev. 1027; Lat. 34-46-05 N long. 083-03-49 W; Named by the German colonization society in 1850, the word is the English "valhall," or garden of the gods.

•**WALTERBORO,** City; Colleton County; Pop. 6,036; Zip Code 29488; Elev. 69; Lat. 32-57-01 N long. 080-39-37 W; Once called Ireland Creek, the name was changed to honor an erly citizen named Walter.

•**WARD,** Town; Saluda County; Pop. 98; Zip Code 29166; Elev. 672; Lat. 33-51-33 N long. 081-43-57 W; The Ward family emigrated from England in 1819 and later operated a stagcoach in the South.

•**WARE SHOALS,** Town; Abbeville, Greenwood & Laurens Counties; Pop. 2,370; Zip Code 29692; Elev. 642; Lat. 34-24-11 N long. 082-15-06 W; A shortened version of the descriptive "beware shoals".

•**WATERLOO,** Town; Laurens County Seat; Pop. 200; Zip Code 29384; Lat. 34-21-44 N long. 082-03-18 W; Named after the great Battle of the Napoleonic Wars.

•**WELLFORD,** City; Spartanburg County; Pop. 2,143; Zip Code 29385; Lat. 34-57-19 N long. 082-06-09 W; Incorporated in 1882 and named in honor of Southern Railway Director, P. A.Wellford.

•**WEST COLUMBIA,** City; Lexington County; Pop. 10,409; Formerly Brookland, the name was changed to West Columbia in 1938.

•**WESTMINSTER,** Town; Oconee County; Pop. 3,114; Zip Code 29693; Elev. 935; Lat. 34-39-57 N long. 083-05-38 W; The town is named for the Westminister Union Church.

•**WEST UNION,** Town; Oconee County; Pop. 300; Zip Code 29696; Lat. 34-45-25 N long. 083-02-31 W; Temperance leader Joseph Greshman named the town "West of Temperance Union", which was shortened to West Union.

•**WHITMIRE,** Town; Newberry County; Pop. 2,038; Zip Code 29178; Lat. 34-30-14 N long. 081-36-51 W; The town's name honors settler and trader George Whitmire.

•**WILLIAMS,** Town; Colleton County; Pop. 205; Zip Code 29493; Lat. 33-02-52 N long. 080-50-05 W; Williams is named after an early settler.

•**WILLIAMSTON,** Town; Anderson County; Pop. 4,310; Zip Code 29697; Elev. 826; Lat. 34-37-02 N long. 082-28-44 W; Named in memory of its founder, W. A. Williams.

•**WILLISTON,** Town; Barnwell County; Pop. 3,173; Zip Code 29853; Elev. 353; Lat. 33-24-06 N long. 081-25-22 W; An early settler, Willis, gave his name to the town.

•**WINDSOR,** Town; Aiken County; Pop. 55; Zip Code 29856; Elev. 391; Lat. 33-29-04 N long. 081-29-08 W; Named before the American Revolution for Windsor, England.

•**WINNSBORO,** Town; Fairfield County Seat; Pop. 2,919; Zip Code 29180; Lat. 34-22-06 N long. 081-05-05 W; Incorporated in 1785 and named for Colonel Richard Winn, an officer in the Revolutionary War.

•**WOODRUFF,** Town; Spartanburg County; Pop. 5,171; Zip Code 29388; Elev. 189; Lat. 34-44-21 N long. 082-02-04 W; Thomas Woodruff was the town's first settler. It was named in his honor.

•**YEMASSEE,** Town; Beaufort & Hampton Counties; Pop. 1,048; Zip Code 29945; Elev. 25; Lat. 32-41-17 N long. 080-50-53 W; The town is named for the Yemassee Indians.

•**YORK,** City; York County Seat; Pop. 6,412; Zip Code 29745; Elev. 756; Lat. 34-59-37 N, long. 081-14-19 W. Named for the town in England.

SOUTH DAKOTA

•ABERDEEN, City; Brown County Seat; Pop. 25,956; Zip Code 57401; Elev. 1304; Lat. 45-27-46 N long. 098-28-47 W; Founded in 1881 and named by railroad officials for Aberdeen, Scotland.

•AGAR, Town; Sully County; Pop. 139; Zip Code 57520; Elev. 1851; Lat. 44-50-15 N long. 100-04-19 W; The town was founded in 1910 and named in honor of county commissioner Charles Agar.

•AKASKA, Town; Walworth County; Pop. 49; Zip Code 57420; Elev. 3505; Lat. 45-19-35 N long. 100-07-00 W; A siux Indian word meaning "a woman who lives with several men."

•ALBEE, Town; Grant County; Pop. 23; Zip Code 57210; Elev. 1768; Lat. 45-03-06 N long. 096-33-04 W; Albee's name remembers early train dispatcher W. C. Albee.

•ALCESTER, City; Union County; Pop. 885; Zip Code 57001; Lat. 43-01-24 N long. 096-37-36 W; The town was founded in 1879 and named for a colonel in the British Army.

•ALEXANDRIA, City; Hanson County Seat; Pop. 588; Zip Code 57311; Lat. 43-39-06 N long. 097-46-40 W; The town's name honors Alexander Mitchell, one time president of the Milwaukee Railroad.

•ALPENA, Town; Jerauld County; Pop. 288; Zip Code 57312; Lat. 44-10-54 N long. 098-21-58 W; The town was plotted in 1883 and named for Alpena, Michigan by local railroad officials.

•ALTAMONT, Town; Deuel County; Pop. 58; Founded in the 1880's and named for the highest point in the county.

•ANDOVER, Town; Day County; Pop. 139; Zip Code 57422; Elev. 1482; Lat. 45-24-27 N long. 097-54-04 W; Andover is named after Andover, Massachusetts.

•ARDMORE, Town; Fall River County; Pop. 16; Established in 1889 and named for the town's schoolteacher, Dora Moore. The name evolved to "Ardmore."

•ARLINGTON, City; Brookings & Kingsbury Counties; Pop. 991; The town is named after Arlington, Virginia.

•ARMOUR, City; Douglas County Seat; Pop. 819; Zip Code 57313; Elev. 1523; Lat. 43-19-03 N long. 098-21-04 W; Founded in 1886 and named in honor of Phillip D. Armour, industrialist and railroad director.

•ARTAS, Town; Campbell County; Pop. 43; Zip Code 57423; Elev. 1813; Lat. 45-53-09 N long. 099-48-28 W; Artas was established in 1901 and given a Greek name "artos" or "bread." A descriptive name refering to the region's wheat growing virtues.

•ARTESIAN, Town; Sanborn County; Pop. 227; Zip Code 57314; Elev. 1317; Lat. 44-00-30 N long. 097-55-09 W; Originally called Dianna, but later changed to Artesion for its location in a great artesian basin.

•ASHTON, City; Spink County; Pop. 154; Zip Code 57524; Elev. 1291; Lat. 44-59-24 N long. 098-29-53 W; Founded in 1879 and named by early settlers for the groves of ash trees.

•ASTORIA, Town; Deuel County; Pop. 154; Zip Code 57213; Lat. 44-33-21 N long. 096-32-24 W; Established in 1900 and named for Astoria, Oregon.

•AURORA, Town; Brookings County; Pop. 507; Zip Code 57002; Lat. 44-17-03 N long. 096-41-05 W; At its founding in 1880 its first settlers gave the town the name of the Roman gods of dawn.

•AVON, City; Bon Homme County; Pop. 576; Zip Code 57315; Elev. 1608; Lat. 43-00-09 N long. 098-03-28 W; The post office was founded in 1879 and named by the first postmaster for Shaakespeare's "Avon."

•BADGER, Town; Kingsbury County; Pop. 99; Zip Code 57214; Lat. 44-29-09 N long. 097-12-25 W; Badger was founded in 1906 and named for the nearby lake.

•BALTIC, Town; Minnehaha County; Pop. 679; Zip Code 57003; Elev. 1510; Lat. 43-45-33 N long. 096-44-05 W; Founded in 1881 and named for the Baltic Sea.

•BANCROFT, Town; Kingsbury County; Pop. 41; Zip Code 57316; Lat. 44-29-34 N long. 097-45-04 W; L. L. Bancroft started a newspaper in the town in 1884. The town later took his name.

•BATESLAND, Town; Shannon County; Pop. 163; Zip Code 57716; Lat. 43-07-44 N long. 102-06-04 W; The town is named for C. A. Bates, the government surveyor who plotted the area.

•BELLE FOURCHE, City; Butte County Seat; Pop. 4,692; Zip Code 57717; Elev. 3023; Lat. 44-39-49 N long. 103-50-50 W; Situated on the Belle Fourche River and thus descriptively named.

•BELVIDERE, Town; Jackson County; Pop. 80; Zip Code 57521; Lat. 43-49-57 N long. 101-17-29 W; Settlers from Belvidere, Illinois named the town for their former home.

•BERESFORD, City; Lincoln & Union Counties; Pop. 1,865; Zip Code 57004; Elev. 1498; Lat. 43-04-59 N long. 096-46-30 W; Originally called Paris, but later changed to Beresford after Admiral Lord Charles Beresford who had a financial interest in the local railroad.

•BIG STONE CITY, City; Grant County; Pop. 672; Zip Code 57216; Elev. 977; Lat. 45-17-34 N long. 096-28-07 W; Located on Big Stone Lake and descriptively named.

•BISON, Town; Perkins County Seat; Pop. 457; Zip Code 57620; Elev. 2460; Lat. 45-31-21 N long. 102-27-57 W; Founded in 1907 and named for the American Bison, commonly called the Buffalo.

•BLUNT, City; Hughes County; Pop. 424; Zip Code 57522; Elev. 1619; Lat. 44-30-15 N long. 099-59-20 W; Settled in 1882 and named in honor of John Blunt, Chief Engineer of the North Western Railroad.

•BONESTEEL, City; Gregory County; Pop. 358; Zip Code 57317; Elev. 1963; Lat. 43-04-28 N long. 098-56-43 W; Pioneer H. E. Bonesteel settled in the territory in 1872. He later started a well-known freight company.

•BOWDLE, City; Edmunds County; Pop. 644; Zip Code 57428; Elev. 2004; Lat. 45-27-07 N long. 099-39-20 W; Laid out in 1886 and named in honor of C. C. Bowdle, pioneer banker.

•BOX ELDER, City; Pennington County; Pop. 3,186; Zip Code 57719; Elev. 3030; Lat. 44-06-59 N long. 103-03-46 W; The town is named after Box Elder Creek.

•BRADLEY, Town; Clark County; Pop. 135; Zip Code 57217; Elev. 1795; Lat. 45-05-32 N long. 097-38-38 W; E. R. Bradley broke up a fight between a railroad official and a group of labaorers. Grateful railroad officials named the town for him.

•BRANDON CITY, City; Minnehaha County; Pop. 2,589; Zip Code 57005; Elev. 1357; Lat. 43-35-25 N long. 096-33-32 W; The town is named after Brandon, Vermont.

•**BRANDT,** Town; Deuel County; Pop. 129; Zip Code 57218; Elev. 1851; Lat. 44-39-52 N long. 096-37-27 W; Founded in 1884 and named after the Reverand P. O. Brandt.

•**BRENTFORD,** Town; Spink County; Pop. 91; Zip Code 57429; Lat. 45-09-32 N long. 098-19-06 W; Established in 1905 and named after Brentford, England.

•**BRIDGEWATER,** City; McCook County; Pop. 653; Zip Code 57319; Lat. 43-32-57 N long. 097-29-48 W; Originally called Nation, railroad workers carrying their drinking water across a bridge led to the now name.

•**BRISTOL,** City; Day County; Pop. 445; Zip Code 57219; Elev. 1790; Lat. 45-20-32 N long. 097-44-51 W; Founded in 1881 and named for Bristol, England.

•**BRITTON,** City; Marshall County Seat; Pop. 1,590; Zip Code 57430; Elev. 1358; Lat. 45-47-42 N long. 097-45-08 W; Platted in 1881 and named for Col. Issac Britton, the general manager of the Dakota and Great Southern Railroad.

•**BROOKINGS,** City; Brookings County Seat; Pop. 14,951; Zip Code 57006; Elev. 1623; Lat. 44-18-51 N long. 096-47-01 W; Platted in 1879 as Ada, the name was changed to honor Judge Wilmot Brookings, a prominent early pioneer.

•**BRUCE,** City; Brookings County; Pop. 254; Zip Code 57220; Elev. 1620; Lat. 44-26-14 N long. 096-53-28 W; Founded in 1881 and renamed for B. K. Bruce, a well-known negro statesman.

•**BRYANT,** City; Hamlin County; Pop. 388; Zip Code 57221; Lat. 44-25-20 N long. 097-28-06 W; Platted in 1887 and named for an official of the Milwaukee land company.

•**BUFFALO,** Town; Harding County Seat; Pop. 453; Zip Code 57720; Elev. 2877; Lat. 45-34-51 N long. 103-32-37 W; The town is named after the once numerous Buffalo herds.

•**BUFFALO GAP,** Town; Custer County; Pop. 186; Zip Code 57722; Elev. 3260; Lat. 43-29-32 N long. 103-18-41 W; Named for the large buffalo herds once found in the area.

•**BURKE,** City; Gregory County Seat; Pop. 859; Zip Code 57523; Elev. 1745; Lat. 43-10-48 N long. 099-17-32 W; Founded in 1904 and named in honor of state legislator Charles Burke.

•**BUSHNELL,** Town; Brookings County; Pop. 76; Frank Bushnell owned the land upon which the town was founded. It is named in his honor.

•**BUTLER,** Town; Day County; Pop. 22; Zip Code 57222; Elev. 1822; Lat. 45-15-11 N long. 097-42-41 W; Established in 1887 and named after Harrison butler who deeded the land to the town.

•**CAMP CROOK,** Town; Harding County; Pop. 100; Zip Code 57724; Lat. 45-33-08 N long. 103-58-31 W; Founded in 1884 and named for General George Crook, a well-known Indian fighter in the 1870's.

•**CANISTOTA,** City; McCook County; Pop. 626; Zip Code 57012; Elev. 1549; Lat. 43-35-39 N long. 097-17-30 W; Founded in 1883 and given an Indian name meanign "board on the water."

•**CANOVA** Town; Miner County; Pop. 194; Zip Code 57321; Lat. 43-52-46 N long. 097-30-10 W; Settled in 1883 and named for Antonia Canova, a famous Italian sculptor.

•**CANTON,** City; Lincoln County Seat; Pop. 2,886; Zip Code 57013; Lat. 43-18-05 N long. 096-35-33 W; Canton is named after Canton, China. Early settlers thought their town opposite that great Chinses city.

•**CARTER,** Town; Tripp County; Pop. 7; Zip Code 57526; Lat. 43-23-27 N long. 100-12-14 W; The town was platted in 1909 and named in honor of Jervis Carter, who was a local U. S. land office registrar.

•**CARTHAGE,** City; Miner County; Pop. 274; Zip Code 57323; Lat. 44-10-16 N long. 097-42-53 W; Established in the early 1880's and named after Carthage, New York.

•**CASTLEWOOD,** City; Hamlin County; Pop. 557; Zip Code 57223; Lat. 44-43-30 N long. 097-01-45 W; Named after "Castlewood," the home of hero Henry Esmond in Thackery's novel.

•**CAVOUR,** Town; Beadle County; Pop. 117; Zip Code 57324; Elev. 1310; Lat. 44-22-15 N long. 098-02-28 W; Named in 1880 to honor Carriello Benno, Count Cavour, Italian statesman and patriot.

•**CENTERVILLE,** City; Turner County; Pop. 892; Zip Code 57014; Elev. 1226; Lat. 43-07-10 N long. 096-57-45 W; Named in 1872 for its location between Swan Lake and Vermillion.

•**CENTRAL CITY,** City; Lawrence County; Pop. 232; Founded in 1877 and named for its location between lead and deadwood.

•**CHAMBERLAIN,** City; Brule County Seat; Pop. 2,258; Zip Code 57325; Elev. 1465; Lat. 43-48-26 N long. 099-19-33 W; Milwaukee Railroad director Selah Chamberlain gave his name to the town when it was founded in 1881.

•**CHANCELLOR,** Town; Turner County; Pop. 257; Zip Code 57015; Elev. 1367; Lat. 43-22-19 N long. 096-59-10 W; Early German farmers/settlers named the town after Otto Bismarck, Germany's "Iron Chancellor."

•**CHELSEA,** Town; Faulk County; Pop. 41; The local town development company named the town after Chelsea, England in 1907.

•**CLAIRE CITY,** Town; Roberts County; Pop. 87; Zip Code 57224; Lat. 45-51-23 N long. 097-06-13 W; Town founder A. Feeney named the town for his wife Claire. It was established in 1913.

•**CLAREMONT,** Town; Brown County; Pop. 180; Zip Code 57432; Lat. 45-40-21 N long. 098-00-50 W; The Great Northern Railway founded the town in 1886 and named it for Claremont, New Hampshire.

•**CLARK,** City; Clark County Seat; Pop. 1,351; Zip Code 57225; Elev. 1845; Lat. 44-52-44 N long. 097-44-02 W; Founded in 1882 and named in honor of territorial legislator Newton Clark.

•**CLEAR LAKE,** City; Deuel County Seat; Pop. 1,310; Zip Code 57226; Elev. 1800; Lat. 44-45-05 N long. 096-41-04 W; Settled in 1884 and descritpvely named for the nearby "clear lake."

•**COLMAN,** City; Moody County; Pop. 501; Zip Code 57017; Lat. 43-59-04 N long. 096-49-00 W; Originally called Sankey, the name was changed to honor the Colman Lumber Company.

•**COLOME,** City; Tripp County; Pop. 361; Zip Code 57528; Elev. 2268; Lat. 43-15-35 N long. 099-43-01 W; Founded in 1905 and named for the Colome brothers who established the town.

•**COLTON,** City; Minnehaha County; Pop. 757; Zip Code 57018; Elev. 1304; Lat. 43-47-16 N long. 096-56-03 W; Railroad builder J. E. Colton had the town named after him in 1898 after donating a park to the community.

•**COLUMBIA,** City; Brown County; Pop. 161; Zip Code 57433; Elev. 2479; Lat. 45-36-59 N long. 098-18-34 W; Originally Richmond, the name was changed due to a postal conflict to the patriotic "Columbia."

•CONDE, City; Spink County; Pop. 259; Zip Code 57434; Elev. 1314; Lat. 45-09-32 N long. 098-05-32 W; French settlers named the town after the famous french Conde family in 1886.

•CORONA, Town; Roberts County; Pop. 126; Zip Code 57227; Lat. 45-20-11 N long. 096-46-12 W; Named by its early settlers for Corona, New York.

•CORSICA, City; Douglas County; Pop. 644; Zip Code 57328; Lat. 43-25-18 N long. 098-24-34 W; Many Corsicans helped build the railroad in the area. The town was named in their honor in 1905.

•COTTONWOOD, Town; Jackson County; Pop. 4; Originally called Ingham after an early settler, the name was later changed to the descriptive Cottonwood for the nearby Cottonwood Creek.

•CRESBARD, Town; Faulk County; Pop. 221; Zip Code 57435; Lat. 45-10-05 N long. 098-56-47 W; Founded in 1906 and given a coined name made by combining the names of two early settlers, John Cressey and Fred Baird.

•CROOKS, Town; Minnehaha County; Pop. 594; Zip Code 57020; Lat. 43-39-45 N long. 096-48-40 W; The town's name honors W. A.Crooks, the town's first postmaster.

•CUSTER, City; Custer County Seat; Pop. 1,830; Zip Code 57730; Elev. 5318; Lat. 43-45-54 N long. 103-35-35 W; Established in 1875 and named in honor of George Armstrong Custer, who was killed fighting the Sioux Indians the following year.

•DALLAS, Town; Gregory County; Pop. 199; Named for Dallas, Texas in 1907. G. M. Dalles was Vice-President of the United States in 1844.

•DANTE, Town; Charles Mix County; Pop. 83; Zip Code 57329; Lat. 43-02-21 N long. 098-11-03 W; Dante was founded in 1908 and named after the great Italian author and poet.

•DAVIS, Town; Turner County; Pop. 100; Zip Code 57021; Elev. 1250; Lat. 43-15-28 N long. 096-59-39 W; The town began in 1893 and was named for Jackson Davis, the original landowner.

•DE SMET, City; Kingsbury County Seat; Pop. 1,237; Zip Code 57231; Elev. 1905; Lat. 44-23-13 N long. 097-32-59 W; Incorporated in 1883 and named in honor of Father Peter John De Smet, who spent his life ministering to the Indians in the nineteenth century.

•DEADWOOD, City; Lawrence County Seat; Pop. 2,035; Zip Code 57732; Elev. 4537; Lat. 44-22-41 N long. 103-43-36 W; Descriptively named in 1876 for its location in Deadwood Gulch.

•DELL RAPIDS, City; Minnehaha County; Pop. 2,389; Zip Code 57022; Elev. 1498; Lat. 43-49-31 N long. 096-42-28 W; Incorporated in 1871.

•DELMONT, City; Douglas County; Pop. 290; Zip Code 57330; Lat. 43-15-57 N long. 098-09-58 W; Delmont was founded in 1886 and named for an official of the Milwaukee Railroad Company.

•DIMOCK, Town; Hutchinson County; Pop. 140; Zip Code 57331; Lat. 43-28-33 N long. 097-59-42 W; A surveyor named Dimock charted the railroad link in 1885. Railroad officials named the town for him in 1910.

•DOLAND, City; Spink County; Pop. 381; Zip Code 57436; Elev. 1358; Lat. 44-53-56 N long. 098-05-47 W; Settled in 1882 and named in honor of F. H. Doland, who was a director of the North Western Railroad, and a local landowner.

•DOLTON, Town; Turner County; Pop. 47; Zip Code 57023; Lat. 43-29-32 N long. 097-23-06 W; Incorporated in 1907 and named after a director of the townsite development company.

•DRAPER, Town; Jones County; Pop. 138; Zip Code 57531; Elev. 2257; Lat. 43-55-36 N long. 100-31-53 W; Established in 1906 and named for Milwaukee Railroad conductor, C. A. Draper.

•DUPREE, City; Ziebach County Seat; Pop. 562; Zip Code 57622; Lat. 44-36-18 N long. 101-29-56 W; Settled in 1910 and named after early rancher and trader, Fred Dupris.

•EAGLE BUTTE, Town; Dewey County; Pop. 435; Zip Code 57625; Lat. 45-00-00 N long. 101-12-54 W; Founded in 1910 and descriptively named for nearby Eagle Butte.

•EGAN, City; Moody County; Pop. 248; Zip Code 57024; Lat. 44-00-00 N long. 096-39-00 W; Elev. @ Settled in 1880 and named for a Milwaukee railroad official.

•ELK POINT, City; Union County Seat; Pop. 1,661; Zip Code 57025; Elev. 1127; Lat. 42-41-05 N long. 096-40-51 W; The town is descriptively named after nearby Elk Point on the Missouri River.

•ELKTON, City; Brookings County; Pop. 632; Zip Code 57026; Elev. 1751; Lat. 44-14-34 N long. 096-28-58 W; Platted in the 1880's and named after Elkton, Maryland.

•EMERY, City; Hanson County; Pop. 399; Zip Code 57332; Elev. 1382; Lat. 43-36-02 N long. 097-37-13 W; First settled in 1881 and named in honor of original landowner S. M. Emery.

•ERWIN, Town; Kingsbury County; Pop. 66; Zip Code 57233; Lat. 44-29-23 N long. 097-26-28 W; The town's name honors its first postmaster, James Erwin Hollister.

•ESTELLINE, City; Hamlin County; Pop. 719; Zip Code 57234; Lat. 44-34-30 N long. 096-53-58 W; The town's name remembers the daughter of the original landowner, D. J. Spalding.

•ETHAN, Town; Davison County; Pop. 351; Zip Code 57334; Elev. 1344; Lat. 43-32-49 N long. 097-59-06 W; The town was platted in 1883, and named for Revolutionary War patriot Ethan Allen.

•EUREKA, City; McPherson County; Pop. 1,360; Zip Code 57434; Elev. 1891; Lat. 45-46-08 N long. 099-37-22 W; Settled in 1887 by enthusiastic Russo-Germen homesteaders who suggested the Greek word Eureka, or "I have found it," as the town's name.

•FAIRBURN, Town; Custer County; Pop. 41; Zip Code 57738; Elev. 3289; Lat. 43-41-03 N long. 103-11-51 W; Located on an attractive creek, the town's name means "fair," "burn," or Scotch for "fair stream."

•FAIRFAX, Town; Gregory County; Pop. 225; Zip Code 57335; Elev. 1932; Lat. 43-01-25 N long. 098-53-21 W; Established in 1890 and named after Fairfax County, Virginia.

•FAIRVIEW, Town; Lincoln County; Pop. 90; Zip Code 57027; Elev. 1213; Lat. 43-13-16 N long. 096-28-49 W; Located on the beautiful Sioux River Valley, and so descriptively named.

•FAITH, City; Meade County; Pop. 576; Zip Code 57626; Lat. 45-01-11 N long. 102-02-21 W; The town is believed to be named in honor of Faith Rockefeller, wife of an important Milwaukee Railroad stockholder.

•FARMER, Town; Hanson County; Pop. 27; Zip Code 57336; Elev. 1394; Lat. 43-43-16 N long. 097-41-16 W; A fertile landscape inspired early settler Joseph Altenhofer to describe the area as a "farmers paradise." The name stuck to the town.

•FAULKTON, City; Faulk County Seat; Pop. 981; Zip Code 57438; Elev. 1589; Lat. 45-02-01 N long. 099-07-23 W; The city was platted in 1886 and named in honor of Andrew Faulk, third governor of the Dakota territory.

•**FLANDREAU,** City; Moody County Seat; Pop. 2,114; Zip Code 57028; Elev. 1570; Lat. 44-02-50 N long. 096-35-21 W; Settled in 1857 and named in honor of Judge Charles Flandreau of St. Paul, Minnesota.

•**FLORENCE,** Town; Codington County; Pop. 190; Zip Code 57235; Lat. 45-03-18 N long. 097-20-00 W; Named by North Western Railroad officials for the wife of a personal friend.

•**FORT PIERRE,** City; Stanley County Seat; Pop. 1,789; Zip Code 57532; Lat. 44-21-17 N long. 100-22-17 W; One of the oldest white settlements in South Dakota, the town is named after the old fort.

•**FRANKFORT,** City; Spink County; Pop. 209; Zip Code 57440; Elev. 5336; Lat. 44-52-27 N long. 098-18-21 W; Settled in 1882 and named for the famous German city.

•**FREDERICK,** Town; Brown County; Pop. 307; Zip Code 57441; Lat. 45-50-06 N long. 098-30-25 W; Established in 1882 and named for the son of a Milwaukee railroad official.

•**FREEMAN,** City; Hutchinson County; Pop. 1,462; Zip Code 57029; Lat. 43-20-57 N long. 097-26-07 W; The site of a large settlement of Mennonites, the town is named for an early settler.

•**FRUITDALE,** Town; Butte County; Pop. 88; Founded in 1910 and named by original landowner Henry Stearns for the many fruit varieties growing in the area.

•**FULTON,** Town; Hanson County; Pop. 108; Zip Code 57340; Elev. 1328; Lat. 43-43-35 N long. 097-49-21 W; The town is named in honor of inventor Robert Fulton.

•**GARDEN CITY,** Town; Clark County; Pop. 104; Zip Code 57236; Lat. 44-57-37 N long. 097-34-49 W; Settled in 1889 and given this descriptive name for its picturesque surroundings.

•**GARRETSON,** City; Minnehaha County; Pop. 963; Zip Code 57030; Elev. 1481; Lat. 43-42-59 N long. 096-29-13 W; Incorporated in 1891 and named for Sioux City banker, A. S. Garretson.

•**GARY,** City; Deuel County; Pop. 354; Zip Code 57237; Elev. 1483; Lat. 44-47-38 N long. 096-26-39 W; Established in 1877 and named in honor of H. B. Gary, an early day mail agent.

•**GAYVILLE,** Town; Yankton County; Pop. 407; Zip Code 57031; Elev. 1165; Lat. 42-53-26 N long. 097-10-18 W; The post office was established in 1872 and named after the first postmaster, Elkanah Gay.

•**GEDDES,** City; Charles Mix County; Pop. 303; Zip Code 57342; Elev. 1620; Lat. 43-15-17 N long. 098-41-43 W; Founded in 1900 and named after Milwaukee railroad official, D. C. Geddes.

•**GETTYSBURG,** City; Potter County Seat; Pop. 1,623; Zip Code 57442; Elev. 2061; Lat. 45-00-48 N long. 099-56-56 W; Settled in the 1880's by Civil War veterans who named the town after the great Civil War battle.

•**GLENHAM,** Town; Walworth County; Pop. 169; Zip Code 57631; Elev. 1709; Lat. 45-32-05 N long. 100-16-18 W; Established in 1900 and descriptively named for its location in a glen.

•**GOODWIN,** Town; Deuel County; Pop. 139; Zip Code 57238; Lat. 44-52-40 N long. 096-51-23 W; Originally known as Prairie Siding, the name was later changed to Goodwin after local railroad official George Goodwin.

•**GREGORY,** City; Gregory County; Pop. 1,503; Zip Code 575+; Elev. 2166; Settled in 1904 and named after Gregory County.

•**GRENVILLE,** Town; Day County; Pop. 119; Zip Code 57239; Lat. 45-27-46 N long. 097-23-17 W; Incorporated in 1918 and descriptively named for the grass-covered hills nearby.

•**GROTON,** City; Brown County; Pop. 1,230; Zip Code 57439; Elev. 1308; Lat. 45-19-52 N long. 098-05-57 W; The city is named after Groton, Massachusetts.

•**HARRISBURG,** Town; Lincoln County; Pop. 558; Zip Code 57032; Elev. 1425; Lat. 43-25-47 N long. 096-41-47 W; The town was named for its first postmaster in 1873.

•**HARROLD,** Town; Hughes County; Pop. 196; Zip Code 57536; Elev. 1796; Lat. 44-31-30 N long. 099-44-20 W; Settled in 1881 and named for railroad official Harrold McCullough.

•**HARTFORD,** City; Minnehaha County; Pop. 1,207; Zip Code 57033; Elev. 1568; Lat. 43-37-15 N long. 096-57-08 W; Early settlers from connecticut named the town for their former name in 1881.

•**HAYTI,** Town; Hamlin County Seat; Pop. 371; Zip Code 57241; Lat. 44-39-38 N long. 097-12-18 W; Meeting to discuss the town's name, early settlers tied some hay together for fuel and decided on that name as an inspiration.

•**HAZEL,** Town; Hamlin County; Pop. 94; Zip Code 57242; Elev. 1766; Lat. 44-45-39 N long. 097-23-02 W; Founded in 1888 on land owned by pioneer C. A. Bowley, and named for his daughter Hazel.

•**HECLA,** City; Brown County; Pop. 435; Zip Code 57446; Elev. 1299; Lat. 45-53-02 N long. 098-09-04 W; The town was settled in 1886 and named for a volcano in Iceland.

•**HENRY,** Town; Codington County; Pop. 217; Zip Code 57243; Lat. 44-52-58 N long. 097-28-00 W; Henry is named in honor of its first settler, J. E. Henry.

•**HERMOSA,** Town; Custer County; Pop. 251; Zip Code 57744; Elev. 3303; Lat. 43-50-16 N long. 103-10-53 W; Founded in 1886 and given the Spanish name meaning "beautiful".

•**HERREID,** City; Campbell County; Pop. 570; Zip Code 57632; Elev. 1682; Lat. 45-49-42 N long. 100-04-16 W; The town's name honors Charles Herreid, Governor of South Dakota in 1907.

•**HERRICK,** Town; Gregory County; Pop. 115; Zip Code 57538; Elev. 2155; Lat. 43-06-39 N long. 099-11-15 W; Town founder Samuel Herrick left his name on the town.

•**HETLAND,** Town; Kingsbury County; Pop. 66; Zip Code 57244; Elev. 1733; Lat. 44-22-34 N long. 097-13-50 W; Established in 1880 and named for pioneer homesteader, John Hetland.

•**HIGHMORE,** City; Hyde County Seat; Pop. 1,055; Zip Code 57345; Elev. 1888; Lat. 44-31-14 N long. 099-26-16 W; Originally called Siding No. S., the name was changed to reflect its position on high ground in the area.

•**HILL CITY,** Town; Pennington County; Pop. 535; Zip Code 57745; Elev. 4979; Lat. 43-55-44 N long. 103-34-21 W; Settled during the gold rush of 1876 and named for its location in the Black Hills.

•**HITCHCOCK,** Town; Beadle County; Pop. 132; Zip Code 57348; Lat. 44-37-33 N long. 098-24-33 W; Called Clarkesville in the beginning, railroad officials later changed to honor an early settler named Hitchcock.

•**HOSMER,** City; Edmunds County; Pop. 385; Zip Code 57448; Elev. 1906; Lat. 45-34-48 N long. 099-29-08 W; Named in 1887 and the maiden name of the wife of a settler named Arnold.

•HOT SPRINGS, City; Fall River County Seat; Pop. 4,742; Zip Code 57747; Elev. 3464; Lat. 43-26-14 N long. 103-28-22 W; Located on a hot springs used by the Indians, the first settlers gave it a descriptive name.

•HOVEN, Town; Potter County; Pop. 615; Zip Code 57450; Elev. 1902; Lat. 45-14-39 N long. 099-46-28 W; Founded in 1883 and named after townsite landowners Peter and Matt Hoven.

•HOWARD, City; Miner County Seat; Pop. 1,169; Zip Code 57349; Elev. 1572; Lat. 44-00-46 N long. 097-31-28 W; Howard's name remembers the son of Judge J. D. Farmer, the original townsite owner, who died while a young man.

•HUDSON, Town; Lincoln County; Pop. 388; Zip Code 57034; Elev. 1221; Lat. 43-07-41 N long. 096-27-16 W; Settled in 1868 and named by early settlers for their former home in Hudson, Iowa.

•HUMBOLDT, Town; Minnehaha County; Pop. 487; Zip Code 57035; Elev. 1308; Lat. 43-38-33 N long. 097-05-07 W; Founded in the 1880's and named for Baron Alexander von Humboldt, the famous German naturalist.

•HURLEY, City; Turner County; Pop. 419; Zip Code 57036; Elev. 1293; Lat. 43-16-51 N long. 097-05-21 W; Platted in 1883 and named after R. E. Hurley, Chief Engineer of the North Western Railroad.

•HURON, City; Beadle County Seat; Pop. 13,000; Zip Code 57350; Lat. 44-21-23 N long. 098-13-00 W; Settled in 1880 and named after the Huron Indians.

•INTERIOR, Town; Jackson County; Pop. 62; Zip Code 57750; Elev. 2378; Lat. 43-43-38 N long. 101-59-02 W; Descriptively named for its position inside the Badland's Wall.

•IPSWICH, City; Edmunds County Seat; Pop. 1,153; Zip Code 57451; Lat. 45-26-55 N long. 099-01-42 W; Settled in 1883 and named after Ipswich, England.

•IRENE, Town; Clay, Turner & Yankton Counties; Pop. 523; Zip Code 57037; Elev. 1364; Lat. 43-04-58 N long. 097-09-31 W; The town's name honors Irene Fry, the daughter of the original landowner.

•IROQUOIS, City; Beadle & Kingsbury Counties; Pop. 348; Zip Code 57353; Elev. 1398; Lat. 44-22-00 N long. 097-51-04 W; Founded in the 1880's and named for the Iroquois Indians.

•ISABEL, City; Dewey County; Pop. 332; Zip Code 57633; Lat. 45-23-24 N long. 101-24-36 W; The city's name honors a daughter of a Milwaukee railroad official.

•JAVA, City; Walworth County; Pop. 261; Zip Code 57452; Elev. 2079; Lat. 45-30-16 N long. 099-52-54 W; Milwaukee Railroad officials named the town after "Java" coffee.

•JEFFERSON, Town; Union County; Pop. 592; Zip Code 57038; Elev. 1119; Lat. 42-36-12 N long. 096-33-36 W; The town is named in honor of thomas Jefferson.

•KADOKA, City; Jackson County Seat; Pop. 832; Zip Code 57543; Elev. 2458; Lat. 43-50-06 N long. 101-35-29 W; Founded in 1906 and named a Sioux word meaning "opening" and refering to the town's location along the Badland's wall.

•KENNEBEC, Town; Lyman County Seat; Pop. 334; Zip Code 57544; Elev. 1690; Lat. 43-54-13 N long. 099-51-42 W; Established in 1905 and named by Milwaukee railroad officials.

•KEYSTONE, Town; Pennington County; Pop. 295; Zip Code 57751; Elev. 4323; Lat. 43-53-48 N long. 103-25-07 W; The town was founded in 1891 and named after a nearby mine.

•KIMBALL, City; Brule County; Pop. 752; Zip Code 57355; Elev. 1788; Lat. 43-44-47 N long. 098-57-18 W; Incorporated in 1883 and named in honor of surveyor J. W. Kimball.

•KRANZBURG, Town; Codington County; Pop. 136; Zip Code 57245; Lat. 44-53-35 N long. 096-54-54 W; Platted in 1879 and named after the four Kranz brothers, who were pioneer settlers.

•LA BOLT, Town; Grant County; Pop. 94; Zip Code 57246; Elev. 1392; Lat. 45-02-55 N long. 096-40-30 W; The town's name remembers Alfred La Bolt, an early landowner.

•LAKE ANDES, City; Charles Mix County Seat; Pop. 1,029; Zip Code 573+; Lat. 43-09-28 N long. 098-32-10; Founded in 1904 and named for nearby Lake Andes.

•LAKE CITY, Town; Marshall County; Pop. 46; Zip Code 57247; Elev. 1466; Lat. 45-43-34 N long. 097-24-40 W; Established in 1914 and descriptively named for its location in South Dakota's lake region.

•LAKE NORDEN, City; Hamlin County; Pop. 417; Zip Code 57248; Elev. 1864; Lat. 44-34-50 N long. 097-12-24 W; Platted in 1908 and named for nearby Lake Norden.

•LAKE PRESTON, City; Kingsbury County; Pop. 789; Zip Code 57249; Lat. 44-21-48 N long. 097-22-29 W; Nearby Lake Preston gave its name to the town in 1881.

•LANE, Town; Jerauld County; Pop. 83; Zip Code 57358; Elev. 2882; Lat. 44-04-05 N long. 098-25-14 W; The town's name remembers T. W. Lane, who was the original landowner.

•LANGFORD, Town; Marshall County; Pop. 307; Zip Code 57454; Elev. 1376; Lat. 45-36-13 N long. 097-49-46 W; Landford is named after original landowner Sam Langford.

•LEAD, City; Lawrence County; Pop. 4,330; Zip Code 57754; Lat. 44-20-54 N long. 103-45-58 W; Founded as Washington in 1876 and renamed "lead", or gold-bearing vein, in 1877.

•LEBANON, Town; Potter County; Pop. 129; Zip Code 57455; Lat. 45-04-08 N long. 099-45-48 W; Platted in 1887 and named for the country in the Middle East.

•LEMMON, City; Perkins County; Pop. 1,871; Zip Code 57638; Elev. 1698; Lat. 45-56-08 N long. 102-09-30 W; The town's name honors G. E. Lemmon, a well-known early cowboy.

•LENNOX, City; Lincoln County; Pop. 1,827; Zip Code 57039; Elev. 2577; Lat. 43-21-21 N long. 096-53-32 W; Settled in 1879 and named for Milwaukee railroad official, Ben Lennox.

•LEOLA, City; McPherson County Seat; Pop. 645; Zip Code 57456; Elev. 1596; Lat. 45-43-13 N long. 098-56-11 W; The city is named in honor of Leola Hayes, the daughter of an early pioneer family.

•LESTERVILLE, Town; Yankton County; Pop. 156; Zip Code 57040; Elev. 1380; Lat. 43-02-09 N long. 097-35-23 W; Originally called Moscow, the town's first postmaster, A. S. Duning, had the town renamed Lester for his first grandson.

•LETCHER, Town; Sanborn County; Pop. 221; Zip Code 57359; Elev. 1308; Lat. 43-53-51 N long. 098-08-15 W; The town is named after original landowner O. T. Letcher.

•LILY, Town; Day County; Pop. 38; Zip Code 57250; Elev. 1845; Lat. 45-10-36 N long. 097-40-52 W; Settled in 1887 and named for the first postmaster's sister, Lily.

•LONG LAKE, Town; McPherson County; Pop. 117; Zip Code 57457; Lat. 45-51-20 N long. 099-12-21 W; The town is named for a nearby lake.

•LOYALTON, Town; Edmunds County; Pop. 6; Civil War veterans from New Hampshire settled the area in 1887,a and gave the town this complimentary name.

•MARION, City; Turner County; Pop. 830; Zip Code 57043; Lat. 43-25-25 N long. 097-15-34 W; Established in 1879 and named after the daughter of a Milwaukee railroad official.

•MARTIN, City; Bennett County Seat; Pop. 1,018; Zip Code 57551; Lat. 43-10-31 N long. 101-43-54 W; The town's name honors U. S. Congressman Eben Martin, who represented South Dakota in 1908-12.

•MARVIN, Town; Grant County; Pop. 52; Zip Code 57251; Lat. 45-15-39 N long. 096-54-50 W; Founded as Grant's Siding and named after a Marvin Safe Company vault in the town.

•MCINTOSH, City; Corson County Seat; Pop. 418; Zip Code 57641; Elev. 2301; Lat. 45-55-20 N long. 101-18-54 W; McIntosh takes its name from the McIntosh Construction company, who worked here on the Milwaukee Railroad in 1909.

•MELLETTE, City; Spink County; Pop. 192; Zip Code 57461; Elev. 1296; Lat. 45-09-12 N long. 098-30-02 W; Settled in 1878 and named in honor of the first governor of South Dakota, Arthur Melette.

•MENNO, City; Hutchinson County; Pop. 793; Zip Code 57045; Elev. 1326; Lat. 43-14-10 N long. 097-34-52 W; Founded in 1879 and named for a large colony of Mennonites in the area.

•MIDLAND, Town; Haakon County; Pop. 277; Zip Code 57552; Elev. 1879; Lat. 44-04-09 N long. 101-09-07 W; Established in 1890 and descriptively named for its location halfway between the Missouri and Cheyenne Rivers.

•MILBANK, City; Grant County Seat; Pop. 4,120; Zip Code 57252; Elev. 1150; Lat. 45-13-07 N long. 096-38-06 W; Railroad director Jeremiah Milbank donated a $15,000 church to the now town, and had it named in his honor.

•MILLER, City; Hand County Seat; Pop. 1,931; Zip Code 57362; Elev. 1578; Lat. 44-31-17 N long. 098-59-14 W.

•MISSION, City; Todd County; Pop. 748; Zip Code 57555; Elev. 2581; Lat. 43-18-21 N long. 100-39-24 W; S. J. Kimmel founded the town in 1915 and descriptively named it for the many churches in the area.

•MISSION HILL, Yankton County; Pop. 197; Zip Code 57046; Lat. 42-55-18 N long. 097-16-50 W; Rev. C. B. Nichols named the town for a nearby hill in 1894.

•MITCHELL, City; Davison County Seat; Pop. 13,916; Zip Code 57301; Lat. 43-42-34 N long. 098-01-35 W; The town's name honors Alexander Mitchell, President of the Milwaukee Railroad in 1879.

•MOBRIDGE, City; Walworth County; Pop. 4,174; Zip Code 57601; Elev. 1676; Lat. 45-32-20 N long. 100-26-03 W; Established in 1906 and named for a railroad bridge across the Missouri River.

•MONTROSE, City; McCook County; Pop. 396; Zip Code 57048; Elev. 1480; Lat. 43-41-53 N long. 097-10-56 W; Settled in 1880 and named after a Walter Scott novel Legend of Montrose.

•MORRISTOWN, Town; Corson County; Pop. 127; Zip Code 57645; Lat. 45-56-12 N long. 101-43-02 W; Named after prominent rancher Nels P. Morris, whose cattle drives led to the founding of the town.

•MOUND CITY, Town; Campbell County Seat; Pop. 111; Zip Code 57646; Elev. 1722; Lat. 45-43-24 N long. 100-04-10 W; Nearby Indian mounds gave the town its descriptive.

•MOUNT VERNON, City; Davison County; Pop. 402; Zip Code 57363; Elev. 1411; Lat. 43-42-39 N long. 098-15-28 W; Founded in the 1880's and named for George Washington's estate, Mount Vernon.

•MURDO, City; Jones County Seat; Pop. 723; Zip Code 57559; Elev. 2326; Lat. 43-53-10 N long. 100-42-20 W; Murdo's name honors early cattleman Murdo McKenzie.

•NEW EFFINGTON, Town; Roberts County; Pop. 261; Zip Code 57255; Elev. 1108; Lat. 45-51-19 N long. 096-55-21 W; Effington was moved in 1913 and became New Effington. It had been named for the first girl born in the town.

•NEWELL, City; Butte County; Pop. 638; Zip Code 57760; Elev. 2853; Lat. 44-42-56 N long. 103-24-46 W; Founded in 1910 and named in honor of reclamation engineer, F. H. Newell.

•NEW UNDERWOOD, Town; Pennington County; Pop. 517; Zip Code 57761; Elev. 2839; Lat. 44-05-32 N long. 102-50-10 W; Established in 1906 and named for Johnny Underwood, the partner of the original landowner.

•NEW WITTEN, Town; Tripp County; Pop. 134; Settled in 1910 and named for a local government land agent.

•NISLAND, Town; Butte County; Pop. 216; Zip Code 57762; Elev. 2857; Lat. 44-40-20 N long. 103-32-51 W; The town was founded in 1909 on the land of pioneer Nils Sorenson. It is named in his honor.

•NORTH SIOUX CITY, City; Union County; Pop. 1,992; Zip Code 57049; Elev. 1100; Lat. 42-31-37 N long. 096-28-56 W; Named after the Sioux Indians.

•NORTHVILLE, Town; Spink County; Pop. 138; Zip Code 57465; Elev. 1279; Lat. 45-09-12 N long. 098-35-08 W; Platted in 1881 and given a descriptive name as the northern point of North Western Railroad.

•NUNDA, Town; Lake County; Pop. 60; Zip Code 57050; Lat. 44-09-33 N long. 097-01-04 W; Pioneer settler John Fleming named the township for his former home in Nunda, Vermont.

•OACOMA, Town; Lyman County; Pop. 289; Zip Code 57365; Elev. 1390; Lat. 43-48-01 N long. 099-23-23 W; Founded in 1890 and given a Sioux Indian name meaning "a place between". The name refers to the town's location between the Missouri River and its bluffs.

•OELRICHS, Town; Fall River County; Pop. 124; Zip Code 57763; Lat. 43-10-43 N long. 103-13-47 W; Established in 1885 and named in honor of prominent rancher Harry Oelrichs.

•OLDHAM, City; Kingsbury County; Pop. 222; Zip Code 57051; Lat. 44-13-38 N long. 097-18-08 W; Originally Huffman the name was changed by Milwaukee railroad officials to honor Oldham Carrot, a farmer who granted the right-of-way tot he railroad.

•OLIVET, Town; Hutchinson County; Pop. 96; Zip Code 57052; Elev. 1220; Lat. 43-14-34 N long. 097-40-38 W; Two early settlers named the town after their former home in Olivet, Michigan.

•ONAKA, Town; Faulk County; Pop. 70; Zip Code 57466; Lat. 45-11-29 N long. 099-27-48 W; A Sioux Indian word meaning "places."

•ONIDA, City; Sully County Seat; Pop. 851; Zip Code 57564; Lat. 44-42-11 N long. 100-03-59 W; New York settlers founded the place in 1883 and named it after Oneida, New York.

•ORIENT, Town; Faulk County; Pop. 87; Zip Code 57467; Lat. 44-54-05 N long. 099-05-09 W; Started in 1887 and named by Milwaukee railroad officials for the far east.

•ORTLEY, Town; Roberts County; Pop. 80; Originally Anderson, but later renamed after an Indian who lived in the area.

•PARKER, City; Turner County Seat; Pop. 999; Zip Code 57053; Elev. 1372; Lat. 43-23-53 N long. 097-08-16 W; Settled in 1879 and named after railroad official Kimball Parker.

•PARKSTON, City; Hutchinson County; Pop. 1,545; Zip Code 57366; Elev. 1396; Lat. 43-23-36 N long. 097-59-12 W; Parkston's name recalls the original landowner, R. S. Parke.

•PEEVER, Town; Roberts County; Pop. 232; Zip Code 57257; Lat. 45-32-25 N long. 096-57-22 W; Landowner T. H. Peever named the town after himself.

•PHILIP, City; Haakon County Seat; Pop. 1,088; Zip Code 57567; Elev. 2162; Lat. 44-02-17 N long. 101-39-36 W; Cattleman James Philip had the town named in his honor in 1907.

•PIERPONT, Town; Day County; Pop. 184; Zip Code 57468; Lat. 45-29-39 N long. 097-49-49 W; Settled in 1883 and named after a Milwaukee railroad official.

•PIERRE, City; Hughes County Seat; Capital of South Dakota; Pop. 11,973; Zip Code 57501; Elev. 1484; Lat. 44-22-03 N long. 100-20-14 W; Settled in 1878 and named for Fort Pierre just across the Missouri River.

•PLANKINTON, City; Aurora County Seat; Pop. 644; Zip Code 57368; Elev. 1525; Lat. 43-42-59 N long. 098-29-09 W; Organized in 1881 and named after Milwaukee Railroad Director, John H. Plankinton.

•PLATTE, City; Charles Mix County; Pop. 1,334; Zip Code 57369; Elev. 1612; Lat. 43-23-16 N long. 098-50-30 W; Dutch settlers named the town for nearby Platte Creek in 1882.

•POLLOCK, Town; Campbell County; Pop. 355; Zip Code 57648; Elev. 1665; Lat. 45-53-54 N long. 100-17-51 W; Originally called Harba but renamed to honor pioneer settler James Pollock.

•PRESHO, City; Lyman County; Pop. 760; Zip Code 57568; Lat. 43-54-20 N long. 100-03-29 W; Settled in 1905 and named for J. S. Presho, an early trader.

•PRINGLE, Town; Custer County; Pop. 105; Zip Code 57773; Lat. 43-36-31 N long. 103-35-47 W; Rancher W. H. Pringle owned the local water rights, and wound up with the town named for him.

•PUKWANA, Town; Brule County; Pop. 234; Zip Code 57370; Elev. 1549; Lat. 43-46-41 N long. 099-11-06 W; Founded in 1881 and given an "Indian" name from Longfellow's poem Hiawatha.

•QUINN, Town; Pennington County; Pop. 80; Zip Code 57775; Elev. 2606; Lat. 43-59-11 N long. 102-07-24 W; Established in 1907 and named for pioneer rancher Michael Quinn.

•RAMONA, Town; Lake County; Pop. 241; Zip Code 57054; Elev. 1800; Lat. 44-07-08 N long. 097-12-51 W; Platted in 1886 and named after a Swiss settler family, the Ramons.

•RAPID CITY, City; Pennington County Seat; Pop. 46,492; Zip Code 57701; Elev. 3247; Lat. 44-06-00 N long. 103-09-07 W; Settled in 1876 and named for Rapid Creek which flows through the town.

•RAYMOND Town; Clark County; Pop. 106; Zip Code 57258; Elev. 1456; Lat. 44-54-41 N long. 097-56-12 W; North Western Railroad Engineer had the town named for him in 1909.

•REDFIELD, City; Spink County Seat; Pop. 3,027; Zip Code 57469; Elev. 1303; Lat. 44-52-12 N long. 098-30-59 W; Redfield was named in honor of North Western Railroad official J. B. Redfield.

•REE HEIGHTS, Town; Hand County; Pop. 88; Zip Code 57371; Elev. 1729; Lat. 44-31-01 N long. 099-12-00 W; Descriptively named for its location near the Ree hills.

•RELIANCE, Town; Lyman County; Pop. 190; Zip Code 57569; Elev. 1796; Lat. 43-52-54 N long. 099-36-00 W; Settled in 1905 and given this popular name by the local townsite officials.

•REVILLO, Town; Grant County; Pop. 158; Zip Code 57259; Elev. 3059; Lat. 4-00-52 N long. 096-34-12 W; His name was spelled backward, but the town is named for popular railroad man, J. S. Oliver.

•ROCKHAM, Town; Faulk County; Pop. 52; Zip Code 57470; Elev. 1396; Lat. 44-54-14 N long. 098-48-57 W; Named for Rockham, Australia in 1886.

•ROSCOE, City; Edmunds County; Pop. 370; Zip Code 57471; Elev. 1830; Lat. 45-27-03 N long. 099-20-01 W; Founded in 1877 and named for U. S. Senator Roscoe Conkling of New York.

•ROSHOLT, Town; Roberts County; Pop. 446; Zip Code 57260; Elev. 1047; Lat. 45-52-00 N long. 096-43-59 W; Established in 1913 and named for railroad construction man, Julius Rosholt.

•ROSLYN, Town; Day County; Pop. 261; Zip Code 57261; Elev. 1865; Lat. 45-29-23 N long. 097-29-16 W; The town's name is a coined word made by combining the names of nearby Lakes Rosholt and Linn.

•ROSWELL, Town; Miner County; Pop. 19; Milwaukee Railroad President Roswell Miller had the town named in his honor in 1883.

•ST. FRANCIS, Town; Todd County; Pop. 766; Zip Code 57572; Lat. 43-08-38 N long. 100-54-04 W; The town is named after the nearby St. Francis Indian School.

•ST. LAWRENCE, Town; Hand County; Pop. 223; Zip Code 57373; Lat. 44-30-54 N long. 098-56-07 W; Settled in 1881 and named for the St. Lawrence.

•SALEM, City; McCook County Seat; Pop. 1,486; Zip Code 57058; Elev. 1527; Lat. 43-43-34 N long. 097-23-14 W; The first postmaster, O. S. Pender, named the town for his former home in Salem, Massachusetts.

•SCOTLAND, City; Bon Homme County; Pop. 1,022; Zip Code 57059; Elev. 1348; Lat. 43-08-42 N long. 097-43-09 W; Platted in 1879 and named by Scottish settlers for their former home.

•SELBY, City; Walworth County Seat; Pop. 884; Zip Code 57472; Elev. 1912; Lat. 45-30-18 N long. 100-01-54 W; Founded in 1899 and named after a local railroad official.

•SENECA, Town; Faulk County; Pop. 103; Zip Code 57473; Elev. 1907; Lat. 45-03-41 N long. 099-30-42 W; Named by its founders after Seneca, New York.

•SHERMAN, Town; Minnehaha County; Pop. 100; Zip Code 57060; Lat. 43-45-24 N long. 096-27-42 W; Territorial banker E. A. Sherman had the town named in his honor in 1888.

•SINAI, Town; Brookings County; Pop. 129; Zip Code 57061; Lat. 44-14-46 N long. 097-02-38 W; Named for nearby Lake Sinai in 1907.

•SIOUX FALLS, City; Lincoln & Minnehaha Counties; Minnehah County Seat; Pop. 81,343; Zip Code 570+, 571+; Elev. 1442; Lat. 43-31-11 N long. 096-33-23 W. Settled in 1857 and descriptively named for its location on the falls of the Big Sioux River.

•**SISSETON,** City; Roberts County Seat; Pop. 2,789; Zip Code 57262; Elev. 1204; Lat. 45-39-49 N long. 097-02-58 W; Settled in the late 1860's and named after Fort Sisseton.

•**SOUTH SHORE,** Town; Codington County; Pop. 241; Zip Code 57263; Elev. 1862; Lat. 45-06-14 N long. 096-55-53 W; Named for its location in the South Shore of Punished Woman Lake.

•**SPEARFISH,** City; Lawrence County; Pop. 5,251; Zip Code 57783; Elev. 3643; The city was founded in 1876 and after nearby Spearfish Creek.

•**SPENCER,** City; McCook County; Pop. 380; Zip Code 57374; Elev. 1381; Lat. 43-43-43 N long. 097-35-36 W; Settled in the 1880's and named for Omaha Railford official Hugh Spencer.

•**SPRINGFIELD,** City; Bon Homme County; Pop. 1,377; Zip Code 57062; Elev. 1275; Lat. 42-51-07 N long. 097-53-43 W; Incorporated in 1879 and descriptively named for the many springs in the area.

•**STICKNEY,** Town; Aurora County; Pop. 409; Zip Code 57375; Lat. 43-35-28 N long. 098-27-21 W; Platted in 1905 and named after Milwaukee Railway official, J. B. Stickney.

•**STOCKHOLM,** Town; Grant County; Pop. 95; Zip Code 57264; Lat. 45-05-59 N long. 096-47-50 W; Founded in 1896 by Swedish settlers and named for the capital of Sweden.

•**STRANDBURG,** Town; Grant County; Pop. 79; Zip Code 57265; Lat. 45-02-39 N long. 096-45-31 W; John Strandburg, the first postmaster, left his name on the town.

•**STRATFORD,** Town; Brown County; Pop. 82; Zip Code 57474; Lat. 45-18-58 N long. 098-18-15 W; The name was chosen by officials of the Minneapolis and St. Louis Railway.

•**STURGIS,** City; Meade County Seat; Pop. 5,184; Zip Code 57784; Elev. 3440; The town's name honors Lieutenant J. G.Sturgis who was killed in 1876 in the Custer massacre.

•**SUMMIT,** Town; Roberts County; Pop. 290; Zip Code 57266; Lat. 45-18-15 N long. 097-02-14 W; Descriptively named for the town's 2000 feet altitude.

•**TABOR,** Town; Bon Homme County; Pop. 460; Zip Code 57063; Elev. 1364; Lat. 42-56-37 N long. 097-39-39 W; Settled in 1872 by Czech emigrants who named the town for a city in Bohemia.

•**TEA,** Town; Lincoln County; Pop. 729; Zip Code 57064; Elev. 1486; Lat. 43-26-49 N long. 096-50-05 W; Originally called Bryon, a postal conflict required a town meeting that went on to "tea time." The settlers promptly adopted the name.

•**TIMBER LAKE,** City; Dewey County Seat; Pop. 660; Zip Code 57656; Lat. 45-25-01 N long. 101-04-30 W; The town is named for the nearby lake.

•**TOLSTOY,** Town; Potter County; Pop. 97; Zip Code 57475; Elev. 1997; Lat. 45-12-32 N long. 099-36-23 W; Founded in 1907 and named for the great Russian writer.

•**TORONTO,** Town; Deuel County; Pop. 236; Zip Code 57268; Lat. 44-34-08 N long. 096-38-16 W; Established in 1884 by Daniel McCraney, a settler from Canada.

•**TRENT,** Town; Moody County; Pop. 197; Zip Code 57065; Elev. 1531; Lat. 43-54-25 N long. 096-39-27 W; Founded as Brookfield, but later renamed by railroad officials.

•**TRIPP,** City; Hutchinson County; Pop. 804; Zip Code 57376; Lat. 43-13-22 N long. 097-58-05 W; Barlett Tripp served as territorial chief justice in 1886 when the town was founded. It is named in his honor.

•**TULARE,** Town; Spink County; Pop. 238; Zip Code 57476; Elev. 1322; Lat. 44-44-05 N long. 098-30-37 W; Descriptively named as a marshy region with abundant reeds.

•**TYNDALL,** City; Bon Homme County Seat; Pop. 1,253; Zip Code 57066; Elev. 1422; Lat. 42-59-09 N long. 097-51-55 W; Incorporated in 1887 and named in honor of British scientist, John Tyndall.

•**UTICA,** Town; Yankton County; Pop. 100; Zip Code 57067; Lat. 42-58-48 N long. 097-29-45 W; Named after Utica, New York.

•**VALLEY SPRINGS,** City; Minnehaha County; Pop. 801; Zip Code 57068; Elev. 1392; Lat. 43-34-54 N long. 096-26-52 W; Settled in 1872 and named for the many springs in the area.

•**VEBLEN,** City; Marshall County; Pop. 368; Zip Code 57270; Lat. 45-51-40 N long. 097-17-07 W; Founded in 1900 and named for the first homesteader J. E. Veblen.

•**VERDON,** Town; Brown County; Pop. 7; A slight mis-spelling of the French town of Verdun, which it was named for in 1886.

•**VERMILLION,** City; Clay County Seat; Pop. 9,582; Zip Code 57069; Elev. 1931; Lat. 42-45-30 N long. 096-54-59 W; Founded in 1859 and named for the adjacent Vermillion River.

•**VIBORG,** City; Turner County; Pop. 812; Zip Code 57070; Elev. 1304; Lat. 43-10-13 N long. 097-04-48 W; Settled in 1886 and named by Danish settlers for a city in Denmark.

•**VIENNA,** Town; Clark County; Pop. 90; Originally named Stusted, the name was changed in 1888 in honor of the great European city.

•**VILAS,** Town; Miner County; Pop. 28; Established in 1883 and named in honor of Postmaster General of the United States, W. F. Vilas.

•**VIRGIL,** Town; Beadle County; Pop. 37; Zip Code 57379; Lat. 44-17-29 N long. 098-25-46 W; The town began in the 1880's and was named for the Latin poet Virgil.

•**VOLGA,** City; Brookings County; Pop. 1,221; Zip Code 57071; Elev. 1634; Lat. 44-19-29 N long. 096-55-29 W; Settled in the 1880's and named for the great river in Russia.

•**VOLIN,** Town; Yankton County; Pop. 156; Zip Code 57072; Elev. 1185; Lat. 42-57-29 N long. 097-10-51 W; The town is named for pioneer settler, Henry Volin.

•**WAGNER,** City; Charles Mix County; Pop. 1,453; Zip Code 57380; Elev. 1448; Lat. 43-04-29 N long. 098-17-52 W; Laid out in 1900 and named in honor of postmaster Walt Wagner.

•**WAKONDA,** Town; Clay County; Pop. 383; Zip Code 57073; Elev. 1377; Lat. 43-00-36 N long. 097-06-11 W; Platted in 1888 and given a Sioux name meaning "holy."

•**WALL,** Town; Pennington County; Pop. 542; Zip Code 57729; Elev. 2818; Lat. 44-15-19 N long. 102-12-29 W; Founded in 1907 near the Badlands National Monument wall and descriptively named for its location.

•**WALLACE,** Town; Codington County; Pop. 90; Zip Code 57272; Lat. 45-04-58 N long. 097-28-45 W; Named for the original town landowner.

•**WARD,** Town; Moody County; Pop. 43; Zip Code 57074; Lat. 44-09-16 N long. 096-27-54 W; Settled in the 1880's and named after Dakota railroad promoter, James A. Ward.

•**WARNER,** Town; Brown County; Pop. 322; Zip Code 57479; Elev. 1298; Lat. 45-19-28 N long. 098-29-59 W; Warner is named for early settler, Warren Tarbox.

•**WASTA,** Town; Pennington County; Pop. 99; Zip Code 57791; Elev. 2313; A Sioux Indian word meaning "good."

•**WATERTOWN,** City; Codington County Seat; Pop. 15,649; Zip Code 57201; Elev. 1739; Lat. 44-54-13 N long. 097-07-02 W; The city was founded in 1875 and named for Watertown, New York.

•**WAUBAY,** City; Day County; Pop. 675; Zip Code 57256; Elev. 1814; Lat. 45-20-10 N long. 097-12-24 W; The city was named in 1885 for nearby Waubay Lake.

•**WEBSTER,** City; Day County Seat; Pop. 2,417; Zip Code 57274; Elev. 1847; Lat. 45-19-56 N long. 097-31-07 W; Platted in 1881 and named for the first settler, J. B. Webster.

•**WENTWORTH,** Village; Lake County; Pop. 193; Zip Code 57075; Lat. 43-59-47 N long. 096-57-43 W; Founded in 1879 and named for the first settler, George Wentworth.

•**WESSINGTON,** City; Beadle County; Pop. 304; Zip Code 57381; Elev. 1415; Lat. 44-27-28 N long. 098-41-56 W; Settled in 1880 and named for the nearby Wessington Hills.

•**WESSINGTON SPRINGS,** City; Jerauld County Seat; Pop. 1,203; Zip Code 57382; Elev. 1687; Lat. 44-04-48 N long. 098-34-03 W; So named because the town's springs arise from the Wessington hills.

•**WESTPORT,** Town; Brown County; Pop. 122; Zip Code 57481; Lat. 45-38-58 N long. 098-29-58 W; The town was named for a Milwaukee railroad official.

•**WHITE,** City; Brookings County; Pop. 474; Zip Code 57276; Elev. 1777; Lat. 44-26-09 N long. 096-38-33 W; Platted in 1884 and named for the original settler, W. H. White.

•**WHITE LAKE,** City; Aurora County; Pop. 414; Zip Code 57383; Lat. 43-43-42 N long. 098-42-51 W; First known as Siding 36, it was later named for nearby White Lake.

•**WHITE RIVER,** City; Mellette County Seat; Pop. 561; Zip Code 57579; Lat. 43-34-04 N long. 100-44-34 W; Founded in 1911 and named after the adjacent White River.

•**WHITE ROCK,** Town; Roberts County; Pop. 10; Descriptively named for a large grey rock landmark near the town.

•**WHITEWOOD,** City; Lawrence County; Pop. 821; Zip Code 57793; Elev. 3748; Platted in 1888 and named for the numerous birch and aspen trees in the area.

•**WILLOW LAKE,** City; Clark County; Pop. 375; Zip Code 57271; Lat. 44-42-23 N long. 097-29-55 W; Settled in 1882 and named for a nearby lake.

•**WILMOT,** City; Roberts County; Pop. 507; Zip Code 57279; Lat. 45-24-32 N long. 096-51-34 W; The town is named in honor of distinguished Judge Wilmot Brookings, a well-known early pioneer.

•**WINFRED,** Town; Lake County; Pop. 81; Zip Code 57076; Elev. 1710; Lat. 43-59-49 N long. 097-21-40 W; Founded in 1882 and named for the daughter of an early settler.

•**WINNER,** City; Tripp County Seat; Pop. 3,472; Zip Code 57580; Lat. 43-22-26 N long. 099-51-39 W; Named as the winner of the railroad right-of-way contest in the area.

•**WOLSEY,** Town; Beadle County; Pop. 437; Zip Code 57384; Lat. 44-24-32 N long. 098-28-24 W; Settled in 1882 and named after Cardinal Thomas Wolsey, a 16th century British prelate.

•**WOOD,** Town; Mellette County; Pop. 134; Zip Code 57585; Lat. 43-29-39 N long. 100-28-45 W; A. K. Wood founded the town in 1910. It is named in his honor.

•**WOONSOCKET,** City; Sanborn County Seat; Pop. 799; Zip Code 57385; Elev. 1307; Lat. 44-03-18 N long. 098-16-16 W; Settled in 1883 and named after Woonsocket, Rhode Island.

•**YANKTON,** City; Yankton County Seat; Pop. 12,011; Zip Code 57079. The name comes from the Sioux Indian name "Ihanktonwan," meaning "end village."

TENNESSEE

ADAMS, Town; Robertson County; Pop. 600; Zip Code 37010; Elev. 560; Lat. 36-34-41 N long. 087-04-02; Adams is named after the sixth president of the United States, John Quincy Adams.

ADAMSVILLE, Town; McNairy County; Pop. 1,453; Zip Code 38310; Elev. 518; Lat. 35-14-24 N long. 088-23-28 W; Named after an early pioneer.

ALAMO, Town; Crockett County Seat; Pop. 2,615; Zip Code 38001; Elev. 367; Lat. 35-47-03 N long. 089-06-59 W; The town's name commemorates the Texas battle.

ALCOA, City; Blount County; Pop. 6,870; Zip Code 37701; Lat. 35-47-02 N long. 083-59-02 W; Named after the Alcoa Aluminum Company.

ALEXANDRIA, Town; De Kalb County; Pop. 689; Zip Code 37012; Elev. 709; 36-04-36 N long. 086-02-07 W; Named after the Egyptian city.

ALLARDT, City; Fentress County; Pop. 654; Zip Code 38504; Lat. 36-22-44 N long. 084-52-58 W; A personal name from an early land owner.

ALTAMONT, Town; Grundy County Seat; Pop. 679; Zip Code 37301; Elev. 1870; Lat. 35-26-00 N long. 085-43-24 W; A Spanish word meaning "High Mountain."

ARDMORE, City; Giles County; Pop. 835; Zip Code 384+; Lat. 34-59-23 N long. 086-50-39 W; Named after Ardmore, Ireland.

ARLINGTON, Town; Shelby County; Pop. 1,778; Zip Code 38002; Lat. 35-16-51 N long. 089-39-46 W; The town is named for Arlington, Virginia.

ASHLAND CITY, Town; Cheatham County Seat; Pop. 2,329; Zip Code 37015; Elev. 438; Lat. 36-16-16 N long. 087-03-34 W; Named after Henry Clay's Kentucky home.

ATHENS, City; McMinn County Seat; Pop. 12,080; Zip Code 37303; Elev. 867; Lat. 35-26-39 N long. 084-36-01 W; Named after the famous Greek city of classical times.

ATOKA, Town; Tipton County; Pop. 691; Zip Code 38004; Elev. 434; Lat. 35-26-10 N long. 089-46-430 W; An indian name of uncertain meaning.

ATWOOD, Town; Carroll County; Pop. 1,143; Zip Code 38220 Elev. 448; Lat. 35-58-19 N long. 088-40-43 W; Atwood's name honors an early settler.

AUBURNTOWN, Town; Cannon County; Pop. 204; Zip Code 37016; Elev. 679; Lat. 35-56-39 N long. 086-05-46 W; The town is named after Auburn, New York.

BAXTER, Town; Putnam County; Pop. 1,411; Zip Code 38544; Elev. 1031; Lat. 36-09-14 N long. 085-38-21 W; Baxter's name recalls an early landowner.

BEERSHEBA SPRINGS, Town; Grundy County; Pop. 643; Zip Code 37305; Elev. 1845; Lat. 35-27-43 N long. 085-39-51 W; Given a biblical name by its early settlers.

BELL BUCKLE, Town; Bedford County; Pop. 450; Zip Code 37020; Elev. 837; Lat. 35-35-26 N long. 086-21-04 W; Descriptively named for a historical incident in the town's beginnings.

BELLE MEADE, City; Davidson County; Pop. 3,182; The city's name means "Beautiful Meadow."

BELLS, Town; Crockett County; Pop. 1,571; Zip Code 38006; Lat. 35-42-53 N long. 089-05-11 W; Descriptively named after local church bells.

BENTON, Town; Polk County Seat; Pop. 1,115; Zip Code 37307; Elev. 748; Lat. 35-10-32 N long. 084-39-04 W; Benton's name recalls a pioneer.

BERRY HILL, City; Davidson County; Pop. 1,113; Descriptively named for the wild berries growing in the area.

BETHEL SPRINGS, Town; McNairy County; Pop. 873; Zip Code 38315; Elev. 462; Lat. 35-13-57 N long. 088-36-21 W; Bethel is a biblical term meaning "Hope."

BIG SANDY, Town; Benton County; Pop. 650; Zip Code 38221; Lat. 36-14-01 N long. 088-04-51 W; Named after local soil conditions.

BLAINE, City; Grainger County; Pop. 1,147; Zip Code 37709; Elev. 937; Lat. 36-09-20 N long. 083-42-08 W; Named after a prominent politician.

BLUFF CITY, Town; Sullivan County; Pop. 1,121; Zip Code 37618; Elev. 1429; Lat. 36-27-48 N long. 082-15-26 W; Descriptively named for its topography.

BOLIVAR, City; Hardeman County Seat; Pop. 6,597; Zip Code 38008; Elev. 453; Lat. 35-15-31 N long. 088-59-55 W; The city's name honors the great South American liberator.

BRADEN, City; Fayette County; Pop. 293; Zip Code 38010; Elev. 315; Lat. 35-22-47 N long. 089-33-58 W; The city is named after a prominent citizen.

BRADFORD, Town; Gibson County; Pop. 1,146; Zip Code 38316; Elev. 366; Lat. 36-04-29 N long. 088-48-39 W; Bradford was an early settler in the area.

BRENTWOOD, City; Williamson County; Pop. 9,431; Zip Code 37027; Elev. 725; Lat. 36-01-41 N long. 086-47-14 W; Named for a famous English estate.

BRIGHTON, Town; Tipton County; Pop. 976; Zip Code 38011; Lat. 35-29-00 N long. 089-43-22 W; The town is named after the English resort city.

BRISTOL, City; Sullivan County; Pop. 23,986; Zip Code 37620; Lat. 36-34-35 N long. 082-11-21 W; The city is named after Bristol, England.

BROWNSVILLE, Town; Haywood County Seat; Pop. 9,307; Zip Code 38012; Elev. 390; Lat. 35-35-36 N long. 089-15-37 W; Named for an early pioneer.

BRUCETON, Town; Carroll County; Pop. 1,579; Zip Code 38317; Elev. 412; Lat. 36-02-05 N long. 088-14-37 W; Bruce was a pioneer settler who left his name on the town.

BULLS GAP, Town; Hawkins County; Pop. 821; Zip Code 37711; Elev. 1153; Lat. 36-15-15 N long. 083-04-57 W; Descriptively named for a local topographic feature.

BURLISON, Town; Tipton County; Pop. 386; Zip Code 38015; Lat. 35-33-17 N long. 089-47-47 W; Named after a pioneer.

BURNS, Town; Dickson County; Pop. 777; Zip Code 37029; Elev. 794; Lat. 36-03-10 N long. 087-18-47 W; Burns is named after the Scottish poet Robert Burns.

BYRDSTOWN, Town; Pickett County Seat; Pop. 884; Zip Code 38549; Elev. 1037; Lat. 36-34-13 N long. 085-07-49 W; Possibly a descriptive name.

•**CALHOUN,** Town; McMinn County; Pop. 590; Zip Code 37309; Lat. 35-17-45 N long. 084-44-43 W; Calhoun's name honors the prominent 19th century southern politician.

•**CAMDEN,** Town; Benton County Seat; Pop. 3,279; Zip Code 38320; Elev. 460; Lat. 36-03-32 N long. 088-05-50 W; The town is named after the city in New Jersey, site of a revolutionary war battle.

•**CARTHAGE,** Town; Smith County Seat; Pop. 2,672; Zip Code 37030; Elev. 515; Lat. 36-14-37 N long. 085-56-53 W; Named after the ancient North African city.

•**CARYVILLE,** Town; Campbell County; Pop. 2,039; Zip Code 37714; Elev. 1095; Lat. 36-17-35 N long. 084-12-49 W; Cary was the family name of an early settler.

•**CEDAR HILL,** Town; Robertson County; Pop. 420; Zip Code 37032; Lat. 36-33-07 N long. 087-00-00 W; The town is named descriptively for the cedar trees originally found in the area.

•**CELINA,** Town; Clay County Seat; Pop. 1,580; Zip Code 38551; Elev. 562; Lat. 36-32-54 N long. 085-30-08 W; Celina is named after the wife of a pioneer.

•**CENTERVILLE,** Town; Hickman County Seat; Pop. 2,824; Zip Code 37033; Elev. 634; Lat. 35-47-35 N long. 087-26-58 W; Named for its location to other towns in the area.

•**CHAPEL HILL,** Town; Marshall County; Pop. 861; Zip Code 37034; Lat. 35-37-46 N long. 086-41-43 W; Originally the site of a chapel on a hill and so named.

•**CHARLESTON,** Town; Bradley County; Pop. 756; Zip Code 37310; Elev. 688; Lat. 35-17-14 N long. 084-45-30 W; The town is named after the city in South Carolina.

•**CHARLOTTE,** Town; Dickson County Seat; Pop. 788; Zip Code 37036; Elev. 631; Lat. 36-10-42 N long. 087-20-24 W; Named after Charlotte Robertson, the wife of Richard Napier.

•**CHATTANOOGA,** City; Hamilton County Seat; Pop. 169,565; Zip Code 37400; Elev. 685; Lat. 35-00-24 N long. 085-12-09 W; A creek indian word meaning "Rock Rising to a Point."

•**CHURCH HILL,** Town; Hawkins County; Pop. 4,110; Zip Code 37642; Elev. 1249; Lat. 36-32-19 N long. 082-40-47 W; Descriptively named for a local church on a hill.

•**CLARKSBURG,** Town; Carroll County; Pop. 400; Zip Code 38324; Lat. 35-52-39 N long. 088-24-06 W; Clark was an early landowner.

•**CLARKSVILLE,** City; Montgomery County Seat; Pop. 54,777; Zip Code 37040; Lat. 36-31-53 N long. 087-21-31 W; Named in honor of General George Rogers Clark.

•**CLEVELAND,** City; Bradley County Seat; Pop. 26,415; Zip Code 373+; Lat. 35-08-55 N long. 084-52-00 W; Named after Cleveland, Ohio.

•**CLIFTON,** Town; Wayne County; Pop. 773; Zip Code 38425; Elev. 403; Lat. 35-23-02 N long. 087-59-40 W; Descriptively named for the local topography.

•**CLINTON,** Town; Anderson County Seat; Pop. 5,245; Zip Code 37716; Lat. 36-05-22 N long. 084-08-15 W; Named in honor of Erie canal builder DeWitt Clinton.

•**COALMONT,** Town; Grundy County; Pop. 625; Zip Code 37313; Lat. 35-20-19 N long. 085-42-32 W; Descriptively named for the coal deposits in the area.

•**COLLEGEDALE,** City; Hamilton County; Pop. 4,607; Zip Code 37315; Lat. 35-02-42 N long. 085-02-54 W; The city is named after a local college.

•**COLLIERVILLE,** Town; Shelby County; Pop. 7,839; Zip Code 38017; Elev. 387; Lat. 35-02-37 N long. 089-39-47 W; Descriptively named for the coal operations in the area.

•**COLLINWOOD,** City; Wayne County; Pop. 1,064; Zip Code 38450; Elev. 1056; Lat. 35-10-18 N long. 087-44-21 W; The city is named for an early settler.

•**COLUMBIA,** City; Maury County Seat; Pop. 25,767; Zip Code 38401; Lat. 35-36-45 N long. 087-02-29 W; The city is named after Columbia, South America.

•**COOKEVILLE,** City; Putnam County Seat; Pop. 20,350; Zip Code 38501; Elev. 118; Lat. 36-10-52 N long. 085-28-28 W; Cookeville's name honors Major Richard Cooke who fought in the Mexican-American war.

•**COPPERHILL,** Town; Polk County; Pop. 418; Zip Code 37317; Elev. 1476; Lat. 34-59-20 N long. 084-22-13 W; Named for a local copper deposit.

•**CORNERSVILLE,** Town; Marshall County; Pop. 722; Zip Code 37047; Elev. 893; Lat. 35-21-34 N long. 086-50-19 W; The town is named as the site of an early crossroads.

•**COTTAGE GROVE,** Town; Henry County; Pop. 117; Zip Code 38224; Lat. 36-22-40 N long. 088-28-38 W; Named for an early cottage on the site in a grove of trees.

•**COVINGTON,** City; Tipton County Seat; Pop. 6,065; Zip Code 38019; Elev. 339; Lat. 35-34-28 N long. 089-41-57 W; Leonard W. Covington was a general in the War of 1812. The town is named for them.

•**COWAN,** City; Franklin County; Pop. 1,790; Zip Code 37318; Lat. 36-15-39 N long. 086-39-03 W; The city is named for a pioneer family.

•**CRAB ORCHARD,** Town; Cumberland County; Pop. 1,065; Zip Code 37723; Elev. 1671; Lat. 35-54-34 N long. 084-52-40 W; The site of a crab apple orchard and, hence, so named.

•**CROSS PLAINS,** City; Robertson County; Pop. 655; Zip Code 37049; Elev. 749; Lat. 36-33-00 N long. 086-41-50 W; Descriptively named for the area's role as a pioneer route.

•**CROSSVILLE,** City; Cumberland County Seat; Pop. 6,394; Zip Code 38555; Elev. 1863; Lat. 35-56-46 N long. 085-01-30 W; Named for its location at the junction of the Nashville-Knoxville Road and the Kentucky-Chattanooga Stock Road.

•**CUMBERLAND CITY,** Town; Stewart County; Pop. 276; Zip Code 37050; Elev. 390; Lat. 36-23-10 N long. 087-37-55 W; The town is named for Cumberland County, England.

•**CUMBERLAND GAP,** Town; Claiborne County; Pop. 263; Zip Code 37724; Elev. 1302; Lat. 36-35-45 N long. 083-39-53 W; The town is named for the local geographic feature.

•**DANDRIDGE,** Town; Jefferson County Seat; Pop. 1,383; Zip Code 37725; Elev. 1000; Lat. 36-01-00 N long. 083-24-55 W; Named for the city in Kentucky, itself named after Martha Dandridge Curtis, George Washington's wife.

•**DAYTON,** City; Rhea County Seat; Pop. 5,913; Zip Code 37321; Elev. 694; Lat. 35-01-10 N long. 085-10-54 W; The city is named for Dayton, Ohio.

•**DECATUR**, Town; Meigs County Seat; Pop. 1,069; Zip Code 37322; Elev. 788; Lat. 35-30-53 N long. 084-47-24 W; Named after War of 1812 naval hero Stephen Decatur.

•**DECATURVILLE**, Town; Decatur County Seat; Pop. 1,004; Zip Code 38329; Elev. 517; Lat. 35-34-51 N long. 088-07-09 W; The town's name honors War of 1812 naval hero Stephen Decatur.

•**DECHERD**, Town; Franklin County; Pop. 2,233; Zip Code 37324; Elev. 960; Lat. 35-12-36 N long. 086-04-55 W; Decherd was an early settler.

•**DENMARK**, Town; Madison County; Pop. 51; Zip Code 38391; Elev. 466; Lat. 35-31-30 N long. 089-00-15 W; The town is named for the country in Europe.

•**DICKSON**, City; Dickson County; Pop. 7,040; Zip Code 37055; Elev. 794; Lat. 36-04-33 N long. 087-22-38 W; Dickson's name honors an early pioneer.

•**DOVER**, Town; Stewart County Seat; Pop. 1,197; Zip Code 37058; Elev. 400; Lat. 36-29-12 N long. 087-50-27 W; Named after the English city.

•**DOWELLTOWN**, Town; De Kalb County; Pop. 341; Zip Code 37059; Lat. 36-00-53 N long. 085-56-39 W; Dowelltown is named after an early settler.

•**DOYLE**, Town; White County; Pop. 344; Zip Code 38559; Elev. 965; Lat. 35-51-06 N long. 085-30-43 W; The city is named after an Irish settler.

•**DRESDEN**, Town; Weakley County Seat; Pop. 2,256; Zip Code 38225; Elev. 425; Lat. 36-17-05 N long. 088-42-26 W; The town is named after the famous German city.

•**DUCKTOWN**, City; Polk County; Pop. 583; Zip Code 37326; Lat. 35-04-32 N long. 084-27-16 W; Named for the many wild ducks in the area.

•**DUNLAP**, City; Sequatchie County Seat; Pop. 3,681; Zip Code 37327; Elev. 722; Lat. 35-22-17 N long. 085-23-21 W; Dunlap was a pioneer.

•**DYER**, City; Gibson County; Pop. 2,419; Zip Code 38330; Elev. 360; Lat. 36-04-02 N long. 088-59-38 W; Robert Dyer was a famous Indian fighter. The town is named for him.

•**DYERSBURG**, City; Dyer County Seat; Pop. 15,856; Zip Code 38024; Lat. 36-02-12 N long. 089-22-59 W; Named in honor of Indian fighter Robert Dyer.

•**ELKTON**, Town; Giles County; Pop. 540; Zip Code 38455; Lat. 35-03-06 N long. 086-53-14 W; The town is named after the once plentiful elk herds in the area.

•**ENGLEWOOD**, Town; McMinn County; Pop. 1,840; Zip Code 37329; Elev. 869; Lat. 35-25-20 N long. 084-29-11 W; Named after the English village.

•**ENVILLE**, Town; Chester & McNairy Counties; Pop. 287; Zip Code 38332; Elev. 427; Lat. 35-23-11 N long. 088-25-47 W; The origin of the town's name are uncertain.

•**ERIN**, City; Houston County Seat; Pop. 1,614; Zip Code 37061; Lat. 36-19-05 N long. 087-41-48 W; Named by an Irish settler for his homeland.

•**ERWIN**, City; Unicoi County Seat; Pop. 4,739; Zip Code 37650; Elev. 1675; Lat. 36-08-09 N long. 082-24-48 W; Named in honor of Dr. J. N. Erwin who donated land to the community.

•**ESTILL SPRINGS**, Town; Franklin County; Pop. 1,324; Zip Code 37330; Elev. 945; Lat. 35-15-44 N long. 086-07-41 W; James Estill was a famous Indian fighter. The town is named for him.

•**ETHRIDGE**, City; Lawrence County; Pop. 548; Zip Code 38456; Lat. 35-19-26 N long. 087-18-17 W; Named by combining a personal name with a local geographical feature.

•**ETOWAH**, City; McMinn County; Pop. 3,758; Zip Code 37331; Elev. 807; Lat. 35-19-35 N long. 084-31-40 W; A Creek Indian word meaning "Village."

•**FAIRVIEW**, City; Williamson County; Pop. 3,648; Zip Code 37062; Elev. 1002; Lat. 35-59-14 N long. 087-06-56 W; Descriptively named for its view.

•**FAYETTEVILLE**, City; Lincoln County Seat; Pop. 7,559; Zip Code 37334; Elev. 71; Lat. 35-09-05 N long. 086-34-34 W; Named in honor of revolutionary war hero General Marquis Lafayette.

•**FINGER**, Town; McNairy County; Pop. 245; Zip Code 38334; Elev. 431; Lat. 35-21-35 N long. 088-35-49 W; Descriptively named for a long and thin geographical feature.

•**FRANKLIN**, City; Williamson County Seat; Pop. 12,407; Zip Code 37064; Elev. 648; Lat. 35-56-57 N long. 086-52-34 W; The city is named after Benjamin Franklin.

•**FRIENDSHIP**, Town; Crockett County; Pop. 763; Zip Code 38034; Elev. 403; Lat. 35-54-29 N long. 089-14-55 W; Named by its settlers after the virtue.

•**FRIENDSVILLE**, Town; Blount County; Pop. 694; Zip Code 37737; Lat. 35-45-40 N long. 084-08-25 W; NAmed by its settlers for friendship.

•**GADSDEN**, Town; Crockett County; Pop. 683; Zip Code 38337; Elev. 422; Lat. 35-46-35 N long. 088-59-31 W; Gadsen is named in honor of South Carolina soldier and diplomat James Gadsen.

•**GAINESBORO**, Town; Jackson County Seat; Pop. 1,119; Zip Code 38562; Elev. 565; Lat. 36-21-15 N long. 085-39-28 W; Named for Edmund P. Gaines.

•**GALLATIN**, City; Sumner County Seat; Pop. 17,191; Zip Code 37066; Elev. 526; Lat. 36-23-08 N long. 086-26-18 W; The city's name honors Albert Gallatin, Secretary of the Treasury, under Presidents John Adams and Thomas Jefferson.

•**GALLAWAY**, City; Fayette County; Pop. 804; Zip Code 38036; Elev. 285; Lat. 35-19-40 N long. 089-37-07 W; Gallaway owned land here in the early 1800's. The town is named for him.

•**GARLAND**, Town; Tipton County; Pop. 301; Named for U.S. Senator Augustus Hill.

•**GATLINBURG**, City; Sevier County; Pop. 3,210; Zip Code 37738; Elev. 1289; Lat. 35-42-52 N long. 083-30-34 W; Named for a pioneer.

•**GERMANTOWN**, City; Shelby County; Pop. 20,459; Named for the ethnic origin of the area's early settlers.

•**GIBSON**, Town; Gibson County; Pop. 458; Zip Code 38338; Lat. 35-52-32 N long. 088-50-38 W; John Gibson served under Andrew Jackson in the War of 1812. The town is named for him.

•**GLEASON**, Town; Weakley County; Pop. 1,335; Zip Code 38229; Lat. 36-13-12 N long. 088-36-41 W; Gleason was an early settler.

•**GOODLETTSVILLE,** City; Davidson & Sumner Counties; Pop. 8,327; Zip Code 37072; Elev. 509; Lat. 36-18-03 N long. 086-43-27 W; The city takes its name from early settlers, the Goodlett family.

•**GORDONSVILLE,** Town; Smith County; Pop. 893; Zip Code 38563; Lat. 36-10-44 N long. 085-55-50 W; Named for a pioneer family.

•**GRAND JUNCTION,** City; Hardman County; Pop. 360; Zip Code 38039; Elev. 575; Lat. 35-02-57 N long. 089-11-01 W; Descriptively named as a crossroads.

•**GRAYSVILLE,** Town; Rhea County; Pop. 1,380; Zip Code 37338; Elev. 725; Lat. 35-26-45 N long. 085-04-57 W; Gray was an early settler.

•**GREENBACK,** City; Loudon County; Pop. 546; Zip Code 37742; Elev. 902; Lat. 35-39-32 N long. 084-10-14 W; Probably descriptive of the local vegetation.

•**GREENBRIER,** Town; Robertson County; Pop. 3,180; Zip Code 37073; Elev. 664; Lat. 36-25-43 N long. 086-48-17 W; Named for the local thorny vine, Smilax Rotundifolia.

•**GREENEVILLE,** Town; Greene County Seat; Pop. 14,097; Zip Code 37743; Elev. 1531; Lat. 36-13-18 N long. 082-48-13 W; The town is named in honor of Revolutionary War General Nathaniel Greene.

•**GREENFIELD,** Town; Weakley County; Pop. 2,109; Zip Code 38230; Elev. 433; Lat. 36-09-28 N long. 088-48-03 W; The town is named for its lush agriculture.

•**HALLS,** Town; Lauderdale County; Pop. 2,444; Zip Code 38040; Lat. 35-52-36 N long. 089-23-46 W; Halls is named after a local settler.

•**HARRIMAN,** City; Roane County; Pop. 8,303; Zip Code 37748; Lat. 35-56-09 N long. 084-32-56 W; The city is named in honor of General Walter Harriman, a former Governor of New Hampshire.

•**HARTSVILLE,** Town; Trousdale County Seat; Pop. 2,674; Zip Code 37074; Elev. 474; Lat. 36-23-18 N long. 086-09-30 W; James Hart was an early settler. The town is named for him.

•**HENDERSON,** City; Chester County Seat; Pop. 4,449; Zip Code 38340; Elev. 462; Lat. 35-26-22 N long. 088-38-47 W; Named for James Henderson who fought in the War of 1812.

•**HENDERSONVILLE,** City; Sumner County; Pop. 26,561; Zip Code 37075; Elev. 459; Lat. 36-17-30 N long. 086-37-16 W; The city is named after War of 1812 Soldier James Henderson.

•**HENNING,** Town; Lauderdale County; Pop. 638; Zip Code 38041; Elev. 293; Lat. 35-40-27 N long. 089-34-21 W; The town is named after a pioneer.

•**HENRY,** Town; Henry County; Pop. 295; Zip Code 38231; Elev. 547; Lat. 36-12-17 N long. 088-25-00 W; Henry is named for an early land owner.

•**HICKORY VALLEY,** Town; Hardeman County; Pop. 252; Zip Code 38042; Elev. 564; Lat. 35-09-16 N long. 089-07-26 W; Descriptively named for the hickory trees in the surrounding valley.

•**HOHENWALD,** City; Lewis County Seat; Pop. 3,922; Zip Code 38462; Elev. 976; Lat. 35-32-52 N long. 087-33-34 W; Swiss settlers gave the town a German name meaning "High Forest."

•**HOLLOW ROCK,** Town; Carroll County; Pop. 955; Zip Code 38342; Elev. 424; Lat. 36-02-11 N long. 088-16-22 W; Named after a local geological oddity.

•**HORNBEAK,** Town; Obion County; Pop. 452; Zip Code 38232; Elev. 474; Lat. 36-19-53 N long. 089-17-35 W; The town is named after a local geographical feature.

•**HORNSBY,** Town; Hardeman County; Pop. 401; Zip Code 38044; Lat. 35-13-34 N long. 088-49-57 W; Hornsby was a prominent pioneer.

•**HUMBOLDT,** City; Gibson County Seat; Pop. 10,209; Zip Code 38343; Elev. 357; Lat. 35-49-32 N long. 088-54-40 W; The city's name honors the great German naturalist Alexander Humboldt.

•**HUNTINGDON,** Town; Carroll County Seat; Pop. 3,962; Zip Code 38344; Lat. 36-00-21 N long. 088-25-05 W; Named for the great hunting the first settlers found in the area.

•**HUNTLAND,** Town; Franklin County; Pop. 983; Zip Code 37345; Lat. 35-03-00 N long. 086-15-54 W; Descriptively named for the area's excellent hunting.

•**HUNTSVILLE,** Town; Scott County Seat; Pop. 519; Zip Code 37756; Lat. 36-24-33 N long. 084-29-07 W; Hunting formed an important part of pioneer life in the area. The name recalls that time.

•**IRON CITY,** City; Lawrence County; Pop. 482; Zip Code 38463; Elev. 559; Lat. 35-02-08 N long. 087-30-20 W; The city is named after a local iron foundry.

•**JACKSBORO,** Town; Campbell County Seat; Pop. 1,620; Zip Code 37757; Elev. 1070; Lat. 36-19-32 N long. 084-11-16 W; Jacksboro is named in honor of John F. Jack, early Tennessee legislator and judge.

•**JACKSON,** City; Madison County Seat; Pop. 49,131; Zip Code 38301; Elev. 401; Lat. 35-39-19 N long. 088-52-30 W; Jackson's name honors President Andrew Jackson.

•**JAMESTOWN,** City; Fentress County Seat; Pop. 2,364; Zip Code 38556; Elev. 1716; Lat. 36-26-19 N long. 084-55-51 W; Named after the city in Virginia.

•**JASPER,** Town; Marion County Seat; Pop. 2,633; Zip Code 37347; Elev. 622; Lat. 35-03-38 N long. 085-39-24 W; The town's name honors Sgt. William Jasper0 who fought in the Revolutionary War.

•**JEFFERSON CITY,** Town; Jefferson County; Pop. 5,612; Zip Code 37760; Lat. 36-07-15 N long. 083-29-31 W; Named in honor of President Thomas Jefferson.

•**JELLICO,** City; Campbell County; Pop. 2,798; Zip Code 37762; Elev. 982; Lat. 36-34-39 N long. 084-07-47 W; Originally Jerrico, but subsequently mis-spelled to Jellico.

•**JOHNSON CITY,** City; Carter & Washington Counties; Washington County Seat; Pop. 39,753; Zip Code 376+; Elev. 1635; Lat. 36-18-57 N long. 082-21-16 W; Named for President Andrew Johnson.

•**JONESBORO,** Town; Washington County Seat; Pop. 2,829; Zip Code 37659; Elev. 1692; Lat. 36-17-46 N long. 082-27-58 W; Jonesboro's name honors North Carolina politician Willie Jones.

•**KENTON,** Town; Gibson & Obion Counties; Pop. 1,551; Zip Code 38233; Lat. 36-12-03 N long. 089-00-39 W; Named for Simon Kenton, a famous Indian fighter of the early 1800's.

•**KINGSPORT,** City; Hawkins & Sullivan Counties; Pop. 32,027; Zip Code 376+; Lat. 36-33-30 N long. 082-32-47 W; Colonel James King built a mill here. The town is named for him.

•**KINGSTON,** City; Roane County Seat; Pop. 4,441; Zip Code 37763; Lat. 35-52-20 N long. 084-30-45 W; Kingston is named in honor of Major Roger King, Revolutionary War soldier.

TENNESSEE

•**KINGSTON SPRINGS,** Town; Cheatham County; Pop. 1,017; Zip Code 37082; Lat. 36-05-50 N long. 087-06-50 W; The town is named after the springs.

•**KNOXVILLE,** City; Knox County Seat; Pop. 183,139; Zip Code 37900; Lat. 35-58-39 N long. 083-56-05 W; The city is named in honor of Revolutionary War General Henry Knox.

•**LA FAYETTE,** City; Macon County Seat; Pop. 3,808; The city is named for the French-American Revolutionary War hero.

•**LA FOLLETTE,** City; Campbell County; Pop. 8,176; Zip Code 37766; Lat. 36-22-37 N long. 084-07-06 W; The city is named after Harvey La Follette, president of the La Follette iron and coal company.

•**LA GRANGE,** Town; Fayette County; Pop. 185; Zip Code 38046; Lat. 35-02-45 N long. 089-14-21 W; Named for the country estate of the Marquis de Lafayette.

•**LA VERGNE,** City; Rutherford County; Pop. 5,495; Zip Code 37086; Lat. 36-00-58 N long. 086-33-53 W; Given a French name by its settlers.

•**LAKE CITY,** Town; Anderson County; Pop. 2,335; Zip Code 37769; Elev. 855; Lat. 36-13-10 N long. 084-09-28 W; Descriptively named for a nearby lake.

•**LAWRENCEBURG,** City; Lawrence County Seat; Pop. 10,175; Zip Code 38464; Lat. 35-14-48 N long. 087-19-37 W; Lawrenceburg is named in honor of Captain James Lawrence, a naval hero in the War of 1812.

•**LEBANON,** City; Wilson County Seat; Pop. 11,872; Zip Code 37087; Elev. 507; Lat. 36-12-29 N long. 086-18-02 W; The community was named after biblical Lebanon.

•**LOBELVILLE,** City; Perry County; Pop. 993; Zip Code 37097; Elev. 501; Lat. 35-45-33 N long. 087-47-02 W; Lobel was an early settler. The town is named for him.

•**LOOKOUT MOUNTAIN,** Town; Hamilton County; Pop. 1,886; Zip Code 37350; Lat. 34-58-41 N long. 085-21-08 W; Descriptively named for a local mountain.

•**LORETTO,** City; Lawrence County; Pop. 1,612; Zip Code 38469; Elev. 833; Lat. 35-04-25 N long. 087-26-25 W; Founded in 1872 and named after the area in Italy.

•**LOUDON,** Town; Loudon County Seat; Pop. 3,940; Zip Code 37774; Lat. 35-44-01 N long. 084-20-36 W; The town is named for British soldier John Campbell, 4th Earl of Loudon, who commanded British armies during the early port of the French Indian War.

•**LUTTRELL,** Town; Union County; Pop. 962; Zip Code 37779; Elev. 1065; Lat. 36-12-15 N long. 083-44-40 W; Named for a prominent pioneer.

•**LYNCHBURG,** Town; Moore County Seat; Pop. 668; Zip Code 37352; Lat. 35-16-58 N long. 086-22-29 W; Descriptively named for a nearly famous beech tree that was used for hanging criminals.

•**LYNNVILLE,** Town; Giles County; Pop. 383; Zip Code 38472; Elev. 755; Lat. 35-22-45 N long. 087-00-10 W; Named after the town in Massachusetts.

•**MADISONVILLE,** Town; Monroe County Seat; Pop. 2,884; Zip Code 37354; Elev. 968; Lat. 35-31-16 N long. 084-21-34 W; The town is named after0 President James Madison.

•**MANCHESTER,** City; Coffee County Seat; Pop. 7,250; Zip Code 37355; Elev. 1063; Lat. 35-28-21 N long. 086-04-59 W; The town is named after Manchester, England.

•**MARTIN,** City; Weakley County; Pop. 8,898; Zip Code 38237; Elev. 413; Lat. 36-20-30 N long. 088-51-13 W; Named for a pioneer.

•**MARYVILLE,** City; Blount County Seat; Pop. 17,480; Zip Code 37801; Elev. 940; Lat. 35-46-17 N long. 083-57-59 W; Maryville's name honors Mary Grainger Blount, the wife of Governor William Blount.

•**MASON,** Town; Tipton County; Pop. 471; Zip Code 38049; Lat. 35-24-42 N long. 089-31-49 W; Named for a pioneer family.

•**MAURY CITY,** Town; Crockett County; Pop. 989; Zip Code 38050; Elev. 346; Lat. 35-48-56 N long. 089-13-36 W; The town is named for Abram Maury, a U.S. Congressman from Tennessee in the 1830's.

•**MAYNARDVILLE,** City; Union County Seat; Pop. 924; Zip Code 37807; Lat. 36-14-35 N long. 083-48-11 W; The city is named for Congressman Horace Maynard who served the area during the Civil War.

•**MCEWEN,** Town; Humphreys County; Pop. 1,352; Zip Code 37101; Elev. 836; Lat. 36-06-22 N long. 087-37-55 W; The town's name honors a prominent local family.

•**MCKENZIE,** City; Carrol, Henry & Weakley Counties; Pop. 5,405; Zip Code 38201; Elev. 495; Lat. 36-08-12 N long. 088-31-25 W; Named after a pioneer.

•**MCLEMORESVILLE,** Town; Carroll County; Pop. 311; Zip Code 38235; Lat. 35-59-08 N long. 088-34-45 W; The town's name recalls a prominent settler.

•**MCMINNVILLE,** City; Warren County Seat; Pop. 10,683; Zip Code 37110; Lat. 35-42-12 N long. 085-45-43 W; Named after an early settler.

•**MEDINA,** Town; Gibson County; Pop. 687; Zip Code 38355; Elev. 505; Lat. 35-48-20 N long. 088-46-13 W; Medina is named for the famous Arabian city.

•**MEDON,** Town; Madison County; Pop. 162; Zip Code 38356; Elev. 478; Lat. 35-27-22 N long. 088-51-45 W; Medon is named after an early land owner.

•**MEMPHIS,** City; Shelby County Seat; Pop. 646,356; Zip Code 37501; Named after the ancient capital of lower Egypt.

•**MICHIE,** Town; McNairy County; Pop. 530; Zip Code 38357; Lat. 35-03-44 N long. 088-24-38 W; Michie's name remembers an early land owner.

•**MIDDLETON,** Town; Hardeman County; Pop. 596; Zip Code 38052; Elev. 409; Lat. 35-03-49 N long. 088-53-22 W; Descriptively named for its location in the area.

•**MILAN,** City; Gibson County; Pop. 8,083; Zip Code 38358; Elev. 420; Lat. 35-55-10 N long. 088-45-35 W; The city takes its name from the famous Italian town.

•**MILLEDGEVILLE,** Town; Chester, Hardin & McNairy Counties; Pop. 392; Zip Code 38359; Elev. 118; Lat. 35-22-35 N long. 088-21-54 W; The town is named for Revolutionary War hero John Milledge.

•**MONTEAGLE,** Town; Grundy County; Pop. 680; Zip Code 37356; Lat. 35-14-24 N long. 085-49-53 W; Named after the nearby mountain.

•**MONTEREY,** Town; Putnam County; Pop. 2,610; Zip Code 38574; Elev. 1875; Lat. 36-08-41 N long. 085-15-56 W; Named after the battle in the Mexican-American War.

•**MORRISON,** Town; Warren County; Pop. 587; Zip Code 37357; Elev. 1076; Lat. 35-35-42 N long. 085-49-29 W; The town isnamed for one of its founders.

•**MORRISTOWN,** City; Hamblen County Seat; Pop. 19,683; Zip Code 37814; Lat. 36-13-02 N long. 083-17-29 W; Named for the three Morris brothers who settled here in 1783.

•**MOSCOW,** Town; Fayette County; Pop. 499; Zip Code 38057; Elev. 356; Lat. 35-03-34 N long. 089-24-00 W; Moscow is named after the famous city in Russia.

•**MOSHEIM,** Town; Greene County; Pop. 1,539; Zip Code 37818; Elev. 1298; Lat. 36-11-24 N long. 082-57-26 W; Mosheim is named for a local settler.

•**MOUNT PLEASANT,** Town; Maury County; Pop. 3,375; Zip Code 38474; Elev. 675; Lat. 35-32-08 N long. 087-12-23 W; Descriptively named foru the local geography and scenery.

•**MOUNTAIN CITY,** Town; Johnson County Seat; Pop. 2,125; Zip Code 37683; Elev. 2429; Lat. 36-28-42 N long. 081-48-11 W; Descriptively named for its location in a valley surrounded by mountains.

•**MURFREESBORO,** City; Rutherford County Seat; Pop. 32,845; Zip Code 37130; Elev. 619; Lat. 35-50-56 N long. 086-22-43 W; The city is named for Revolutionary War hero Col. Hardy Murfree.

•**NASHVILLE,** City; Davidson County Seat and Capital of Tennessee; Pop. 455,651; Zip Code 372+; Elev. 440. Founded in 1779 by James Robertson and John Donelson on land formerly serving as a French trading post. It originally was occupied by Shawnee Indians. Named Fort Nashborough for Gen. Francis Nash and renamed in 1784 to its present name.

•**NEW JOHNSONVILLE,** City; Humphreys County; Pop. 1,824; Zip Code 37134; Elev. 429; Lat. 36-00-55 N long. 087-57-49 W; Named after an early settler.

•**NEW MARKET,** City; Jefferson County; Pop. 1,216; Zip Code 37820; Lat. 36-06-08 N long. 083-32-38 W; Descriptively named for the town's commerce.

•**NEW TAZEWELL,** Town; Claiborne County; Pop. 1,677; Zip Code 37825; Lat. 36-26-06 N long. 083-36-03 W; New Tazewell's name honors Littelton W. Tazewell, a U.S. Senator from Virginia in 1824.

•**NEWBERN,** Town; Dyer County; Pop. 2,794; Zip Code 38059; Elev. 376; Lat. 36-06-50 N long. 089-15-47 W; The town is named after the city in Switzerland.

•**NEWPORT,** City; Cocke County Seat; Pop. 7,580; Zip Code 37821; Elev. 1055; Lat. 35-57-45 N long. 083-11-10 W; Descriptively named for its location on the bank of the French Broad River.

•**NORRIS,** City; Anderson County; Pop. 1,374; Zip Code 37828; Lat. 36-12-59 N long. 084-03-49 W; George Norris, a U.S. Senator from Nebraska, helped bring the Tennessee valley authority project. The town is named after him.

•**OAK HILL,** City; Davidson County; Pop. 4,609; Descriptively named for the oaks in the vicinity.

•**OAK RIDGE,** City; Anderson & Roane Counties; Pop. 27,662; Zip Code 37830; Lat. 35-58-34 N long. 084-18-03 W; Descriptively named after the area's oak covered ridge.

•**OAKLAND,** Town; Fayette County; Pop. 472; Zip Code 38060; Elev. 382; Lat. 35-13-34 N long. 089-30-52 W; The town is named for the oak trees in the area.

•**OBION,** Town; Obion County; Pop. 1,282; Zip Code 38240; Elev. 290; Lat. 36-15-40 N long. 089-11-08 W; An indian word meaning "Many Forks."

•**OLIVER SPRINGS,** Town; Anderson, Morgan & Roane Counties; Pop. 3,659; Zip Code 37840; Elev. 785; Lat. 36-02-29 N long. 084-20-27 W; The town is named after the nearby springs.

•**ONEIDA,** Town; Scott County; Pop. 3,029; Zip Code 37841; Lat. 36-30-08 N long. 084-30-33 W; The town is named after the Indian tribe.

•**ORLINDA,** Town; Robertson County; Pop. 382; Zip Code 37141; Elev. 720; Lat. 36-35-57 N long. 086-42-50 W; Named for the wife of an early settler.

•**PALMER,** Town; Grundy County; Pop. 1,027; Zip Code 37365; Elev. 1810; Lat. 35-21-21 N long. 085-33-38 W; Palmer was a 19th century land owner.

•**PARIS,** City; Henry County Seat; Pop. 10,728; Zip Code 38242; Elev. 519; Lat. 36-18-01 N long. 088-19-03 W; The city is named for the French capital.

•**PARROTTSVILLE,** Town; Cocke County; Pop. 118; Zip Code 37843; Lat. 36-00-23 N long. 083-05-30 W; Parrottsville's name honors the town's founders.

•**PARSONS,** Town; Decatur County; Pop. 2,422; Zip Code 38363; Elev. 497; Lat. 35-38-53 N long. 088-07-22 W; Named after a local farmer.

•**PEGRAM,** Town; Cheatham County; Pop. 1,081; Zip Code 37143; Elev. 549; Lat. 36-06-05 N long. 087-03-00 W; The town took the name of a pioneer.

•**PETERSBURG,** Town; Lincoln & Marshall Counties; Pop. 681; Zip Code 37144; Elev. 747; Lat. 35-18-57 N long. 086-38-17 W; Peters was a prominent local citizen.

•**PHILADELPHIA,** City; Loudon County; Pop. 507; Zip Code 37846; Elev. 863; Lat. 35-40-27 N long. 084-24-10 W; The city is named after the metropolis in Pennsylvania.

•**PIGEON FORGE,** City; Sevier County; Pop. 1,822; Named for an iron foundry on the Little Pigeon River.

•**PIKEVILLE,** Town; Bledsoe County Seat; Pop. 2,085; Zip Code 37367; Elev. 865; Lat. 35-36-19 N long. 085-11-23 W; The town is named after an early road.

•**PLEASANT HILL,** Town; Cumberland County; Pop. 371; Zip Code 38578; Elev. 1902; Lat. 35-58-27 N long. 085-11-43 W; Descriptively named by its settlers after the garden-like setting.

•**RIDGELY,** Town; Lake County; Pop. 1,932; Zip Code 38080; Elev. 280; Lat. 36-15-49 N long. 089-29-01 W; Located on a ridge and so named.

•**RIDGETOP,** Town; Davidson & Robertson Counties; Pop. 1,225; Zip Code 37152; Lat. 36-16-43 N long. 086-46-16 W. Descriptively named for its location.

•**RIPLEY,** Town; Lauderdale County Seat; Pop. 6,366; Zip Code 38063; Elev. 459; Lat. 35-44-32 N long. 089-31-50 W; Named in honor of War of 1812 General Eleazer W. Ripley.

•**RIVES,** Town; Obion County; Pop. 386; Zip Code 38253; Elev. 300; Lat. 36-21-18 N long. 089-02-52 W; Rives was an early settler.

•**ROCKFORD,** City; Blount County; Pop. 567; Zip Code 37853; Lat. 35-49-58 N long. 083-56-29 W; Descriptively named for a Rocky Ford.

•**ROCKWOOD,** City; Roane County; Pop. 5,767; Zip Code 37854; Lat. 35-52-08 N long. 084-40-56 W; Descriptive of the rugged, wooded area.

•**ROGERSVILLE,** Town; Hawkins County Seat; Pop. 4,368; Zip Code 37857; Elev. 1294; Lat. 36-24-06 N long. 083-00-16 W; Named after Joseph Rogers who settled in the area in 1785.

•**ROSSVILLE,** Town; Fayette County; Pop. 379; Zip Code 38066; Elev. 313; Lat. 35-02-39 N long. 089-32-40 W; Given an early settler's name.

•**RUTHERFORD,** Town; Gibson County; Pop. 1,378; Zip Code 38369; Lat. 36-07-38 N long. 088-59-21 W; Named after American Revolutionary War General Griffith Rutherford.

•**RUTLEDGE,** Town; Grainger County Seat; Pop. 1,058; Zip Code 37861; Elev. 1015; Lat. 36-16-39 N long. 083-31-08 W; Named in honor of General George Rutledge.

•**ST. JOSEPH,** City; Lawrence County; Pop. 897; Zip Code 38481; Lat. 35-02-08 N long. 087-30-20 W; The city is named after the biblical Joseph, husband of Virgin Mary.

•**SALTILLO,** Town; Hardin County; Pop. 434; Zip Code 38370; Lat. 35-22-55 N long. 088-12-40 W; Named for a nearby salt lick.

•**SAMBURG,** Town; Obion County; Pop. 465; Zip Code 38254; Lat. 36-22-52 N long. 089-21-04 W; Samburg is named after a local resident.

•**SARDIS,** Town; Henderson County; Pop. 301; Zip Code 38371; Lat. 35-26-38 N long. 088-17-33 W; Given a biblical name by its settlers.

•**SAULSBURY,** Town; Hardeman County; Pop. 156; Zip Code 38067; Lat. 35-02-52 N long. 089-05-12 W; The town is named after a pioneer.

•**SAVANNAH,** City; Hardin County Seat; Pop. 6,992; Zip Code 38372; Lat. 35-13-31 N long. 088-14-18 W; Savannah is named for the port city in Georgia.

•**SCOTTS HILL,** Town; Decatur & Henderson Counties; Pop. 668; Zip Code 38374; Elev. 519; Lat. 35-30-49 N long. 088-14-28 W; Descriptively named for a local hill.

•**SELMER,** Town; McNairy County Seat; Pop. 3,979; Zip Code 38375; Elev. 442; Lat. 35-10-07 N long. 088-35-16 W; Named after Selma, Alabama, but mis-spelled.

•**SEVIERVILLE,** City; Sevier County Seat; Pop. 4,566; Zip Code 37862; Elev. 903; Lat. 35-49-22 N long. 083-33-23 W; The town's name honors Tennessee's first Governor, John Sevier.

•**SHARON,** Town; Weakley County; Pop. 1,134; Zip Code 38255; Elev. 414; Lat. 36-14-11 N long. 088-49-38 W; The town is named for a pioneer's wife.

•**SHELBYVILLE,** City; Bedford County Seat; Pop. 13,530; Zip Code 37160; Elev. 765; Lat. 35-29-03 N long. 086-27-08 W; Shelbyville's name honors Revolutionary War hero Colonel Isaac Shelby.

•**SIGNAL MOUNTAIN,** Town; Hamilton County; Pop. 5,818; Zip Code 37377; Lat. 35-07-31 N long. 085-19-27 W; Descriptively named for its function during pioneer days.

•**SILERTON,** Town; Chester County; Pop. 2; Zip Code 38377; Lat. 35-20-28 N long. 088-47-47 W.

•**SLAYDEN,** Town; Dickson County; Pop. 69; Zip Code 37165; Lat. 36-17-38 N long. 087-28-14 W; Slayden is named after an early land owner.

•**SMITHVILLE,** Town; De Kalb County Seat; Pop. 3,839; Zip Code 37166; Elev. 1032; Lat. 35-57-13 N long. 085-49-02 W; The town is named after a prominent settler family.

•**SMYRNA,** Town; Rutherford County; Pop. 8,839; Zip Code 37167; Elev. 1030; Lat. 35-59-13 N long. 086-30-57 W; Named after an ancient Greek sea port.

•**SNEEDVILLE,** Town; Hancock County Seat; Pop. 1,110; Zip Code 37869; Elev. 1169; Lat. 36-32-03 N long. 083-12-45 W; William H. Sneed served as a congressman in 1855. The town is named for him.

•**SODDY-DAISY,** City; Hamilton County; Pop. 8,388; Zip Code 37379; Lat. 35-15-48 N long. 085-10-34 W; A combined name created by the union of two towns.

•**SOMERVILLE,** Town; Fayette County Seat; Pop. 2,264; Zip Code 38068; Lat. 35-14-25 N long. 089-20-59 W; The town's name honors a Lieutenant Somerville who was killed during the Creek Indian War.

•**SOUTH FULTON,** City; Obion County; Pop. 2,735; Named after the inventor of the steamboat.

•**SOUTH PITTSBURG,** City; Marion County; Pop. 3,636; Zip Code 37380; Elev. 624; Lat. 35-01-16 N long. 085-42-40 W; Named after the city in Pennsylvania.

•**SPARTA,** Town; White County Seat; Pop. 4,864; Zip Code 38583; Elev. 885; Lat. 35-55-58 N long. 085-28-06 W; Sparta is named after the ancient Greek city.

•**SPENCER,** Town; Van Buren County Seat; Pop. 1,126; Zip Code 38585; Elev. 1820; Lat. 35-44-45 N long. 085-27-23 W; Named after the Spencer family who were early settlers.

•**SPRING HILL,** Town; Maury & Williamson Counties; Pop. 989; Zip Code 37174; Elev. 438; Lat. 35-45-13 N long. 086-55-29 W; Descriptively named after a local spring.

•**SPRINGFIELD,** City; Robertson County Seat; Pop. 10,814; Zip Code 37172; Elev. 677; Lat. 36-30-02 N long. 086-52-58 W; Named after a spring in the area.

•**STANTON,** Town; Haywood County; Pop. 540; Zip Code 38069; Elev. 314; Lat. 35-27-44 N long. 089-24-00 W; Stanton is probably named after a pioneer settler.

•**STANTONVILLE,** Town; McNairy County; Pop. 271; Zip Code 38379; Lat. 35-09-30 N long. 088-25-36 W; Named after a pioneer settler.

•**SURGOINSVILLE,** Town; Hawkins County; Pop. 1,536; Zip Code 37873; Elev. 1136; Lat. 36-28-02 N long. 082-51-24 W.

•**SWEETWATER,** City; Monroe County; Pop. 4,725; Zip Code 37874; Elev. 917; Lat. 35-36-18 N long. 084-27-51 W; The city is named for its location in the Sweetwater Valley.

•**TAZEWELL,** Town; Claiborne County Seat; Pop. 2,090; Zip Code 37879; Lat. 36-27-07 N long. 083-34-14 W; The town's name honors 19th century U.S. Senator Henry Tazewell.

•**TELICO PLAINS,** Town; Monroe County; Pop. 698; Zip Code 37385; Lat. 35-21-39 N long. 084-17-44 W; The origin of the town's name is uncertain.

•**TENNESSEE RIDGE,** City; Houston & Stewart Counties; Pop. 1,325; Zip Code 37178; Elev. 742; Lat. 36-19-02 N long. 087-45-59 W; Given a combination of the state's name with a local geographical feature.

•**TIPTONVILLE,** Town; Lake County Seat; Pop. 2,438; Zip Code 38079; Elev. 301; Lat. 36-22-31 N long. 089-28-44 W; Named in honor of Indian fighter Jacob Tipton.

•**TOONE,** Town; Hardeman County; Pop. 355; Zip Code 38381; Elev. 395; Lat. 35-21-06 N long. 088-57-02 W; Toone is named after a 19th century settler.

•**TRACY CITY,** Town; Grundy County; Pop. 1,356; Zip Code 37387; Elev. 1829; Lat. 35-15-38 N long. 085-44-09 W; Named after a prominent settler.

•**TRENTON,** City; Gibson County Seat; Pop. 4,601; Zip Code 38382; Elev. 338; Lat. 35-58-23 N long. 088-56-30 W; The city's name honors the site of an important Revolutionary War battle.

•**TREZEVANT,** Town; Carroll County; Pop. 921; Zip Code 38258; Elev. 464; Lat. 36-00-42 N long. 088-37-14 W; A name made by combining Trezibond and Levant.

•**TRIMBLE,** Town; Dyer & Obion Counties; Pop. 722; Zip Code 38259; Elev. 293; Lat. 36-12-09 N long. 089-11-06 W; The town's name honors U.S. Supreme Court Justice Robert Trimble.

•**TROY,** Town; Obion County; Pop. 1,093; Zip Code 38260; Elev. 378; Lat. 36-20-09 N long. 089-09-31 W; Troy is named after the famous Homeric City.

•**TULLAHOMA,** City; Coffee & Franklin Counties; Pop. 15,800; Zip Code 37388; Elev. 1071; Lat. 35-21-12 N long. 086-12-17 W; A Muskogean Indian term meaning "Red Town."

•**UNION CITY,** City; Obion County Seat; Pop. 10,436; Zip Code 38261; Elev. 337; Lat. 36-25-21 N long. 089-02-41 W; Named after the union of the United States.

•**VANLEER,** Town; Dickson County; Pop. 401; Zip Code 37181; Elev. 849; Lat. 36-14-04 N long. 087-26-35 W; The town is named for a prominent settler.

•**VIOLA,** Town; Warren County; Pop. 149; Zip Code 37394; Elev. 995; Lat. 35-31-59 N long. 085-46-21 W; Viola is named for a pioneer's wife.

•**VONORE,** Town; Monroe County; Pop. 528; Zip Code 37885; Elev. 852; Lat. 35-35-21 N long. 084-14-33 W; Given the name of an early pioneer.

•**WARTBURG,** City; Morgan County Seat; Pop. 761; Zip Code 37887; Lat. 36-06-01 N long. 084-35-47 W; Named for Wartburg, Germany.

•**WARTRACE,** Town; Bedford County; Pop. 540; Zip Code 37183; Elev. 824; Lat. 35-31-33 N long. 086-20-03 W; Descriptively named for a path through the forest used by Indian War parties.

•**WATAUGA,** City; Carter County; Pop. 376; Zip Code 37694; Elev. 1451; Lat. 36-21-54 N long. 082-17-28 W; A Cherokee Indian word meaning "Beautiful River."

•**WATERTOWN,** City; Wilson County; Pop. 1,300; Zip Code 37184; Elev. 667; Lat. 36-06-00 N long. 086-08-08 W; Named after a nearby body of water.

•**WAVERLY,** City; Humphreys County Seat; Pop. 4,405; Zip Code 37185; Elev. 546; Lat. 36-05-04 N long. 087-47-21 W; The city is named after a very popular Sir Walter Scott novel.

•**WAYNESBORO,** City; Wayne County Seat; Pop. 2,109; Zip Code 38485; Lat. 35-18-50 N long. 087-45-38 W; The city is named in honor of Revolutionary War hero General Anthony Wayne.

•**WESTMORELAND,** Town; Sumner County; Pop. 1,754; Zip Code 37186; Lat. 36-33-58 N long. 086-14-54 W; Named after a county in England.

•**WHITE BLUFF,** Town; Dickson County; Pop. 2,055; Zip Code 37187; Elev. 819; Lat. 36-06-25 N long. 087-13-17 W; The town is named for its local geographic feature.

•**WHITE HOUSE,** City; Robertson & Sumner Counties; Pop. 2,225; Zip Code 37188; Elev. 862; Lat. 36-28-14 N long. 086-39-10 W; Named for a local landmark.

•**WHITE PINE,** Town; Jefferson County; Pop. 1,900; Zip Code 37890; Elev. 1140; Lat. 36-06-23 N long. 083-17-10 W; Descriptively named for the White Pine groves in the area.

•**WHITEVILLE,** Town; Hardeman County; Pop. 1,270; Zip Code 38075; Lat. 35-19-33 N long. 089-08-44 W; A pioneer named White gave his name to the town.

•**WHITWELL,** City; Marion County; Pop. 1,783; Zip Code 37397; Lat. 35-12-11 N long. 085-30-59 W; Whitwell was an early settler.

•**WINCHESTER,** City; Franklin County Seat; Pop. 5,821; Zip Code 37398; Elev. 965; Lat. 35-11-09 N, long. 086-06-33 W. The city is named in honor of General James Winchester, pioneer Indian fighter and legislator.

•**WOODBURY,** Town; Cannon County Seat; Pop. 2,160; Zip Code 37190; Elev. 735; Lat. 35-49-19 N, long. 086-04-06 W. Originally Danville, the name was changed to reflect the forested areas nearby.

•**WOODLAND MILLS,** City; Obion County; Pop. 526; Zip Code 38271; Elev. 368; Lat. 36-30-13 N, long. 089-03-56 W. Descriptively named for a local mill and the surrounding forests.

•**YORKVILLE,** Town; Gibson County; Pop. 272; Zip Code 38389; Lat. 36-06-00 N, long. 089-07-12 W. The city is named in honor of World War I infantry hero Alvin C. York.

TEXAS

•ABE, Village; Houston County; Pop. Rural; E Texas. *Abraham B. Thomas* was the first postmaster of this village in 1887, and the townspeople used his "nickname" when the post office was established.

•ABERDEEN, Village; Collingsworth County; Pop. Rural; NE Texas. The *Earl of Aberdeen* (Scotland) owned the Rocking Chair Ranch, which had one of its headquarters here.

•ABERNATHY, City; Hale & Lubbock Counties; Pop. 2,904; Zip Code 79311; NW Texas; 19 m. N of Lubbock.

•ABILENE, City; Jones & Taylor Couties; Taylor County Seat; Pop. 98,315; Elev. 1,179; Lat. 32-29.9 N, Long. 99-42.8 W; NW central Texas; 150 m. W of Fort Worth; was named for Abilene, Kansas.

•ACALA, Village; Hudspeth County; Pop. 25; W Texas, on Reo Grande, 55 m. SE of El Paso. Named for a type of cotton, originally grown in Acala, Mexico and brought here by *W.T. Young* in 1921.

•ACAMPO, Village; Shackelford County; N central Texas. Mexican immigrants worked on the Missouri, Kansas and Texas Railroad here, and lived in temporary housing known as Acampos. This stock loading station was then named for these shacks.

•ACKERLY, City; Dawson & Martin Counties; Pop. 317; Zip Code 79713; NW Texas; 25 m. NW of Big Spring in a rural area.

•ACTON, Village; Hood County; Pop. 130; N central Texas. This town was once known as Comanche Peak, but the name was changed to memorialize a townswoman named "Miss Acton". It may also signify "Oak Town", because of the large numbers of oaks in the area.

•ADDISON, City; Dallas County; Pop. 5,506; Zip Code 75001; Lat. 32-57.5 N, Long. 96-49.8 W; N suburb of Dallas. Town population has risen 10 times during the 1970s.

•ADDRAN, Village; Hopkins County; Pop. Rural; NE Texas. An Add-Ran College once operated near this place; today it has become Texas Christian University.

•ADRIAN, City; Oldham County; Pop. 228; Zip Code 79001; Lat. 35-16.3 N, Long. 102 -40.2 W; NW Texas; 23 m. E of New Mexico state line.

•AFTON, Village; Dickens County; Pop. 100; Zip Code 79220; NW Texas; 110 m. NE of Lubbock. A school teacher, *Myra Velley*, was elected to decide on a name for this town in 1900. She opted for a name suggesting the nature of Cottonwood Creek, which flows nearby. The song, "Flow Gently, Sweet Afton" inspired her.

•AGUA DULCE, City; Nueces County; Pop. 917; Zip Code 78330; Lat. 27-47.1 N, Long. 97-54.6 W; S coastal Texas; 25 m. W of Corpus Christi. Name means "sweet water", indicating that of nearby Agua Dulce Creek.

•ALAMO, City; Hidalgo County; Pop. 5,810; Zip Code 78516; S Texas; 10 m. E of McAllen. The town was first known as Ebenezer in 1909, when a town was settled here by the Alamo Land and Sugar Company. Later named Swallow but was changed to honor the shrine of Texas Liberty in San Antonio, Alamo is a Spanish word meaning "cottonweed tree".

•ALAMO HEIGHTS, City; Bexar County; Pop. 6,243; Zip Code 782 + zone; Lat. 29-28.4 N, Long. 98-27.8 W; S central Texas; N residential suburb of San Antonio.

•ALBA, Town; Rains & Wood Counties; Pop. 568; Zip Code 75410; Lat. 32-47.6 N, Long. 95-37.8 W; NE Texas; 65 m. E of Dallas. The town's name means "white" in Latin, which indicates the policy of the early, post-Civil War settlement here which did not admit blacks within its limits.

•ALBANY, City; Shackelford County Seat; Pop. 2,453; Zip Code 76430; Elev. 1,429; Lat. 32-43.6 N, Long. 99-17.7 W; N central Texas; 35 m. NE of Abilene. Named for Albany, New York, this city was an early supply point on the Western Trail to Dodge City.

•ALEDO, City; Parker County; Pop. 1,028; Zip Code 76008; Lat. 32-41.7 N, Long. 97-36.1 W; N Texas; 15 m. W of Fort Worth.

•ALGOA, Village; Galveston County; Pop. 135; E coastal Texas. Many sources show that a British ship Algoa crashed on the shore here during a storm in September 1900. However, the town was named in 1887, so the local legend does not stand up to the facts.

•ALICE, City; Jim Wells County Seat; Pop. 20,853; Zip Code 78332; Elev. 205; Lat. 27-45.0 N, Long. 98-04.7 W; S Texas, 43 m. W of Corpus Christi. The town was founded as a depot for the San Antonio and Aransas Pass Railroad in 1880. It was named for one of the founder's daughters of the King Ranch.

•ALLEN, City; Collin County; Pop. 8,303; Zip Code 75002; Lat. 33-06.2 N, Long. 96-40.3 W; NE Texas; 30 m. NE of Dallas; suburban population has increased 800 percent in the 1970's.

•ALLEYTON, Pop. Est. 375; Zip Code 78935; Lat. 29-42.4 N, Long. 96-29.3 W; SE Texas; was founded in 1824.

•ALLRED, Village; Yoakum County; NW Texas; 10 m. E of New Mexico state line. *James V. Allred* was governor of Texas when this town was founded (1938) by a (Mr. Young) and his associates.

•ALPINE, City; Brewster County Seat; Pop. 5,455; Zip Code 79830; Elev. 4,481; Lat. 30-21.6 N, Long. 103-39.6 W; SW Texas. Cradled in a valley between towering mountains, Alpine was founded in 1882 with the coming of the railroad. Originally named Murphyville. Named after a random selection of the zip code directory by early townspeople who picked Alpine, Alabama. "Alpine" seemed apt to *Walter Garnett*, because of the mountainous terrain here.

•ALTIAR, Village; Colorado County; Pop. 80; Zip Code 77412; SE central Texas, on Colorado River, 80 m. W of Houston. Altair was named for a bright star by amateur astronomer *"Curly" Jones* in 1890.

•ALTO, Town; Cherokee County; Pop. 1,200; Zip Code 75925; Elev. 433; Lat. 31-31.0 N, Long. 95-04.4 W; E Texas, 50 m. S of Tyler; on a divide between the Neches and Angelina Rivers. The town's name is a Spanish word meaning "high" by *Captain Henry Berryman* in 1849.

•ALTOGA, Village; Colin County; Pop. 348; NE Texas. The citizens of this community were known for their cooperative spirit, under their leader *Dock Owensby*. Owensby wanted to call the town "All Together Now", but the federal government of the 1890's would not accept such an unorthodox name. Altoga is a compromise of that original phrase.

•ALVARADO, City; Johnson County; Pop. 2,685; Zip Code 76009; Lat. 32-24.0 N, Long. 97-12.8 W; N Texas, 28 m. SW of Dallas.

•ALVIN, City; Brazoria County; Pop. 16,110; Zip Code 77611; Lat. 29-25.5 N, Long. 95-14.6 W; SE Texas, 25 m. SE of Houston.

•ALVORD, Town; Wise County; Pop. 862; Zip Code 76225; Lat. 33-21.6 N, Long. 97-41.8 W; N Texas; 45 m. NW of Fort Worth.

468

•**AMARILLO**, City; Potter & Randall Counties; Potter County Seat; Pop. 149,230; Elev. 3,676; Lat. 35-12.5 N, Long. 101-50.0 W; NW Texas, 320 m. NW of Fort Worth. The selection of the name Amarillo (yellow) is said by some to have been due to the nearness of Amarillo Creek, named because of its yellow banks, while others insist that the name resulted from the yellow flowers that blanketed the prairies in spring. At any rate the name so pleased Sanborn, who ran the hotel and several business houses, that he had them all painted a bright yellow.

•**ANAHUAC**, City; Chambers County Seat; Pop. 1,860; Zip Code 77514; Lat. 29-46.3 N, Long. 94-41.0 W; on Trinity Bay of Galveston Bay in SE Texas; the city is named for the Indian Aztec meaning "plain near the water". Past names Chambersia and Perry's Point (before 1870).

•**ANDERSON**, Village; Grimes County Seat; Pop. 300; Zip Code 77830; Elev. 215; Lat. 30-29.4 N, Long. 95-59.2 W; E Texas, 90 miles NW of Houston; Established in 1834 on the old La Bahia Road.

•**ANDREWS**, City; Andrews County Seat; Pop. 11,010; Zip Code 79714; Lat. 32-19.2 N, Long. 102-32.8 W; NW Texas; named after *Richard Andrews* who was the first soldier to die in the Texas Revolution during the battle of Concepcion.

•**ANGLETON**, City; Brazoria County Seat; Pop. 13,873; Zip Code 77515; SE Texas, 40 m. S of Houston in a flat coastal wetlands area. Named for *G.W. Angle*, an early developer.

•**ANNONA**, Town; Red River County; Pop. 471; Zip Code 75550; NE Texas, 55 m. W of Texarkana; Named in 1884 for an unidentified Indian girl.

•**ANTHONY**, Town; El Paso County; Pop. 2,644; Zip Code 88021; Elev. 3,800; W Texas, 25 m. NW of El Paso at New Mexico state line. Anthony was named for *Saint Anthony* of Padua by a Spanish-speaking woman named *Shrina* who owned a chapel in the area. Originally named in 1881 La Tuna meaning "prickly pear cactus" in Spanish.

•**ANTON**, City; Hockley County; Pop. 1,187; Zip Code 79313; Lat. 33-48.7 N, Long. 102-09.9 W; NW Texas, 25 m. NW of Lubbock.

•**APPLEBY**, City; Nacogdoches County; Pop. 453; Zip Code 75961; Lat. 31-42.9 N, Long. 94-36.3 W; E Texas, 10 m. NE of Nacogdoches.

•**APPLE SPRINGS**, Village; Trinity County; Pop. 130; Zip Code 75926; E Texas; In Davy Crockett National Forest. Named for the apple trees growing near the springs at this spot. Original name: May Apple Springs. Founded in 1884.

•**AQUILLA**, City; Hill County; Pop. 130; Zip Code 76622; Lat. 31-51.1 N, 97-13.0 W; NE Texas, 11 miles S of Hillsboro; name may be Indian, or derived from the Spanish word for "eagle".

•**ARANSAS PASS**, City; Aransas, Nueces & San Patricio Counties; Pop. 7,173; Zip Code 78336; Elev. 20; 27-59.1 N, Long. 97-09.0 W; S Texas.

•**ARCADIA**, Village; Galveston County; Zip Code 77517; Lat. 29-23.0 N, Long. 95-07.0 W; SE Texas, 20 m. NW of Galveston. Named for the ancient region of Greece, poetically referred to as a tranquil wonderland.

•**ARCHER CITY**, City; Archer County Seat; Pop. 1,859; Zip Code 76351; Elev. 1,041; Lat. 33-35.7 N, Long. 98-37.6 W; N Texas, 30 m. S of Wichita Falls.

•**ARLINGTON**, City; Tarrant County; Pop. 161,192; Elev. 616; Lat. 32-44.2 N, Long. 97-06.8 W; N Texas, 13 m. E of Fort Worth in a residential-industrial suburban area.

•**ARTHUR CITY**, Village; Lamar County; Zip Code 75411; Elev. 426; Lat. 33-52.1 N, Long. 95-30.5 W; NE Texas, on Red River, just S of Oklahoma.
Arthur City is at or near the site of one of the French trading posts known to have been established on the Red River.

•**ASHERTON**, City; Dimmit County; Pop. 1,637; Zip Code 78827; Lat. 28-26.6 N, Long. 99-45.5 W; S Texas, 43 miles SE of Eagle Pass.

•**ASPERMONT**, Town; Stonewall County Seat; Pop. 1,349; Zip Code 79502; Elev. 1,773; Lat. 33-08.3 N, Long. 100-13.6 W; NW Texas; originally called Sunflower Flat by ranchers in the late 1880's. The site was donated by *A.L. Rhomberg* in 1889 and named it for its descriptive location "rough mountain" from the Latin.

•**ATHENS**, City; Henderson County Seat; Pop. 10,085; Zip Code 75751; Elev. 490; Lat. 32-12.3 N, Long. 95-51.2 W; NE Texas, 70 miles SE of Dallas. Originally named Alvin but later named in 1850 by *Mrs. Dull Averitt* for Athens, Greece because she thought Athens would be the cultural center of eastern Texas. Interestingly, the town is built on seven hills, as is the ancient Greek city. Some locals would argue that Mrs. Averitt named the town for her native Athens, Georgia, however.

•**ATLANTA**, City; Cass County; Pop. 6,189; Zip Code 75551; Elev. 264; Lat. 33-06.9 N, Long. 95-10.1 W; NE Texas, 25 m. S of Texarkana. Established in 1872 with building of the Texas and Pacific Railroad, the town was named for Atlanta, Georgia by early settlers.

•**AUDREY**, Town; Denton County; Pop. 956; Zip Code 76227; Lat. 33-18.3 N, Long. 96-59.2 W; N Texas; originally known as Ornego, present name was selected randomly by townspeople when the post office opened here in 1881. The man whose choice won in the town lottery is said to have used the name of his girlfriend.

•**AUSTIN**, City; State Capital; Travis & Williamson Counties; Travis County Seat; Pop. 345,496; Zip Code 787; Elev. 650; Lat. 30-16.9 N, Long. 97-44.5 W; Central Texas; 85 m. N of San Antonio on the Colorado River, which is dammed in seven places here. The town is named for Stephen Austin who was killed at the Alamo.

•**AUSTWELL**, City; Refugio County; Pop. 280; Zip Code 77950; Lat. 28-23.4 N, Long. 96-50.5 W; S Texas, on San Antonio Bay, 55 m. N of Corpus Christi. It was named after two of the area's earliest settlers, *Preston R. Austin* and *Jesse C. McDowell*, who owned large ranches here.

•**AVERY**, Town; Red River County; Pop. 513; Zip Code 75554; Elev. 476; Lat. 33-33.0 N, Long. 94-46.9 W; NE Texas, 45 m. W of Texarkana.

•**AVINGER**, Town; Cass County; Pop. 677; Zip Code 75630; Lat. 32-53.9 N, Long. 94-33.3 W; NE Texas, 50 m. SW of Texarkana in a wooded area. Nearby is the Lake-O-The Pines.

•**AVOCA**, Village; Jones County; Pop. 121; Zip Code 79503; NE central Texas; 30 m. N of Abilene. The Texas Railroad came through here in 1893, and *J.L. Crostwaite* of Avo moved his general store to the station. Crostwaite added the ending "ca" to give the town is present name.

•**AZLE**, City; Parker & Tarrant Counties; Pop. 5,822; Zip Code 76020; Lat. 32-53.9 N, Long. 97-32.4 W; N Texas, 20 m. NW of Fort Worth

•**BAIRD**, City; Callahan County Seat; Pop. 1,696; Zip Code 79504; Elev. 1,708; Lat. 32-23.6 N, Long. 99-23.7 W; N central Texas, 20 m. E of Abilene. It was established in 1880 when the Texas and Pacific Railroad was built. This railroad switching point was named for director *Matthew Baird*, who drove the first Texas and Pacific stake in 1875.

•**BALCH SPRINGS**, City; Dallas County; Pop. 13,746; Zip Code 75180; Lat. 32-43.1 N, Long. 96-38.2 W; NE Texas, E suburb of Dallas.

•**BALLINGER**, City; Runnels County Seat; Pop. 4,207; Zip Code 76821; Elev. 1,637; W central Texas, 35 m. NE of San Angelo on the Colorado River.

•**BALMORHEA**, City; Reeves County; Pop. 568; Zip Code 79718; Elev. 3,205; Lat. 30-59.1 N, Long. 103-44.5 W; W Texas; on Toyah Creek and Balmorhea Lake, 35 m. S of Pecos. Land promoters established this town in 1906, on a 14,000 acre tract of hilly land fed by San Solomon Springs. Balmorhea was named for its three promoters, *Balcon, Morrow and Rhea*.

•**BANDERA**, City; Bandera County Seat; Pop. 947; Zip Code 78003; Elev. 1,258; Lat. 29-43.6 N, Long. 99-04.5 W; SW central Texas; 50 m. NW of San Antonio. The name probably comes from *General Bandera*, a Spanish Indian fighter in San Antonio. The name is also a Spanish word meaning "flag".

•**BANGS**, City; Brown County; Pop. 1,716; Zip Code 76823; Lat. 31-43.0 N, Long. 99-07.9 W; Central Texas, 10 m. W of Brownwood.

•**BANKERSMITH**, Village; Gillespie and Kendall Counties; Pop. Rural; S central Texas. *Temple D. Smith* was the first president of a bank in near by Fredericksburg. Townspeople knew him as "Banker Smith", and named this tiny village for him.

•**BARDWELL**, City; Ellis County; Pop. 335; Zip Code 75101; Lat. 32-15.9 N, Long. 96-41.8 W; NE central Texas.

•**BARKSDALE**, Village; Edwards County; Pop. 71; Zip Code 78828; Elev. 1,498; S central Texas; On N fork of the Nueces River along a scenic, hilly route (Texas Hwy. 55). The first settler called this place "Dixie" in 1876, but it was later named for *Louis Barksdale* who moved here about 1880.

•**BARTLETT**, City; Bell & Williamson Counties; Pop. 1,567; Zip Code 76511; central Texas; 20 m. S of Temple in a rural area.

•**BASTROP**, City; Bastro County Seat; Pop. 3,789; Zip Code 78602; Elev. 369; Lat. 30-06.7 N, Long. 97-18.8 W; S central Texas; on a navigable point in the Colorado River, 30 m. SE of Austin. Bastrop was founded in the 1830's. In 1837 the town was incorporated. Its name honors the *Baron de Bastrop*, a friend of *Moses Austin*, who claimed he was from Holland. However, he was actually born in Dutch Gukyana of ordinary Dutch parents. He had been an accused embezzler in his homeland.

•**BAY CITY**, City; Matagorda County Seat; Pop. 17,837; Zip Code 77414; Elev. 55; Lat. 28-58.9 N, Long. 95-58.2 W; on Colorado River, 65 m. SW of Houston.

•**BAYSIDE**, Town; Refugio County; Pop. 381; Zip Code 78340; Lat. 28-05.6 N, Long. 97-12.8 W; S Texas; On Copano Bay, 24 m. N of Corpus Christi.

•**BAYTOWN**, City; Chambers & Harris Counties; Pop. 56,923; Elev. 26; Lat. 29-43.1 N, Long. 94-58.6 W; E Texas, 15 m. E of Houston on W Galveston Bay.

•**BEAUMONT**, City; Jefferson County Seat; Pop. 118,102; Elev. 21; Lat. 30-04.9 N, Long. 94-05.7 W; SE Texas on Neches River, 85 m. NE of Houston. About 1835, *Henry Millard*, member of a land-purchasing group known as Thomas B. Huling and Company of Jasper County, purchased 50 acres of land from *Noah Trevis*, and in October a town was laid out. Of numerous stories regarding its name, one asserts that Millard named it Beaumont for his brother-in-law, *Jefferson Beaumont*, another, that Beaumont (Fr., "beautiful Hill"), was chosen because of a slight elevation southeast of town.

•**BECKVILLE**, City; Panola County; Pop. 945; Zip Code 75631; Lat. 32-14.15 N,, Long. 92-27.4 W; NE Texas; 18 m. S of Longview.

•**BEDFORD**, City; Tarrant County; Pop. 20,821; Zip Code 76021; Lat. 32-50.6 N, Long. 97-08.2 W; N Texas; NE suburb of Fort Worth, near the International Airport. Population doubled during 1970's.

•**BEEVILLE**, City; Bee County Seat; Pop. 14,574; Zip Code 78102; Elev. 214; Lat. 28-24.1 N, Long. 97-44.8 W; S Texas, 45 m. NW of Corpus Christi. Beeville was named for *General Barnard E. Bee*, who was founder of the Texas Republic Army, and later Secretary of War for the independent nation.

•**BELLAIRE**, City; Harris County; Pop. 14,950; Zip Code 77401; Elev. 41; SE Texas; W suburb of Houston, surrounded by that city's limits.

•**BELLEVUE**, City; Clay County; Pop. 352; Zip Code 76228; N Texas; 33 m. SE of Wichita Falls; Name means "pretty view" in French.

•**BELLS**, Town; Grayson County; Pop. 846; Zip Code 75414; NE Texas, 12 m. E of Sherman. The original name here was Gospel Ridge, for the many houses of worship along the hills. On Sundays, the chaotic chiming of all of the church bells caused Texas and Pacific Railroad planners to dub the place "Bells". That name stuck.

•**BELMONT**, Gonzales County; Zip Code 78604; Lat. 29-31.5 N, Long. 97-41.1 W; S central Texas; 45 m. NE of San Antonio. Name is from the French, meaning, "beautiful hill."

•**BELTON**, City; Bell County Seat; Pop. 10,666; Zip Code 76513; Lat. 31-02.9 N, Long. 97-27.9 W; Central Texas; 7 m. W of Temple, near Belton Lake and Stillhouse Hollow Reservoir; Recreational area.

•**BENAVIDES**, City; Duval County; Pop. 1,978; Zip Code 78341; Lat. 27-35.8 N, Long. 98-24.5 W; S Texas; 55 m. SW of Corpus Christi; Rural.

•**BEN BOLT**, Village; Jim Wells County; Pop. 110; Zip Code 78342; SE Texas. This tiny hamlet was founded in 1906 and named for an early settler. It was platted by *Tom Collins*, who thought of a local ballad called "Ben Bolt and Sweet Alice," when naming the place, since the town of Alice was only seven miles away.

•**BENJAMIN**, City; Knox County Seat; Pop. 257; Zip Code 79505; Elev. 1,456; Lat. 33-35.0 N, Long. 99-47.6 W; N Texas; 80 m. N of Abilene near the Salt Fork of the Brazos River; and the South Wichita River.

•**BERTRAM**, City; Burnet County; Pop. 824; Zip Code 78605; Lat. 30-44.5 N, Long. 98-03.2 W; Central Texas; 35 m. NW of Austin.

•**BESSMAY**, Village; Jasper County; Pop. 1,669; E Texas. *J.H.Kirby*, a lumber mill owner here, around the turn of the century, named the place for his daughter.

•**BEVERLY**, McLennan County; Zip Code 76711; Elev. 430; Lat. 31-31.5 N, Long. 97-08.5 W; Central Texas; suburb of Waco.

•**BIG FOOT**, Village; Frio County; Pop. 75; Zip Code 78005; S Texas; 30 m. S of San Antonio; Named for *William "Big Foot" Wallace*, a famous Indian fighter; settled in 1854 by *Bob Connally* and others, including Wallace.

•**BIG LAKE**, City; Reagan County Seat; Pop. 3,404; Zip Code 76932; Elev. 2,678; Lat. 31-11.5 N, Long. 101-28.1 W; W Texas; 60 m. SW of San Angelo on a lake by the same name.

•**BIG SANDY**, Town; Upshur County; Pop. 1,258; Zip Code 75755; Lat. 32-35.0 N, Long. 95-06.6 W; NE Texas; 100 m. E of Dallas on the Sabine River.

•**BIG SPRING**, City; Howard County Seat; Pop. 24,804; Zip Code 79720; Elev. 2,397; Lat. 32-15.0 N, Long. 101-28.4 W; NW Texas; 90 m. W of Abilene on Sulphur Springs Creek. It was named for a large spring, now dry, was formerly a frontier watering place where buffalo hunters and bone gatherers erected their hide and wood huts.

•**BIG WELLS**, City; Dimmit County; Pop. 939; Zip Code 78830; Lat. 28-34 3 N, Long. 99-34.0 W; S Texas; 90 m. SW of San Antonio.

•**BISHOP**, Town; Nueces County; Pop. 3,706; Zip Code 78343; Lat. 27-35.0 N, Long. 97-48.0 W; S Texas; 6 m. NE of Kingsville.

•**BIROME**, Village; Hill County; Pop. 30; Zip Code 76625; NE central Texas; Near Hillsboro; Named for *Bickam and Jerome Cartwright* by their grandfather, *R.L.Cartwright*

•**BLACKWELL**, Town; Coke & Nolan Counties; Pop. 286; Zip Code 79506; Lat. 32-05.1 N, Long. 100-19.2 W; NW Texas; 45 m. SW of Abilene near Oak Creek Reservoir.

•**BLANCO**, City; Blanco County; Pop. 1,179; Zip Code 78606; Elev. 1,350; Lat. 30-06.1 N, Long. 98-25.3 W; Central Texas; 50 m. N of San Antonio, on Blanco River.

•**BLANKET**, Town; Brown County; Pop. 388; Zip Code 76432; Lat. 31-49.4 N, Long. 98-47.2 W; Central Texas; 10 m. NE of Brownwood. In 1852, surveyors of the region saw Indian blankets here, which had been spread over sumac bushes near a creek as shelter from a downpour. The surveyors liked the obvious name for the creek, which was later given to the village that grew along its banks.

•**BLOOMBURG**, Town; Cass County; Pop. 419; Zip Code 75556; Lat.33-08.3 N, Long. 94-03.5 W; NE Texas; at Arkansas state line.

•**BLOOMING GROVE**, Town; Navarro County; Pop. 823; Zip Code 76626; Lat. 32-05.6 N, 96-43.2 W; NE central Texas; 50 m. S of Dallas, near Navarro Mills Lake.

•**BLOSSOM**, Town; Lamar County; Pop. 1,487; Zip Code 75416; Lat. 33-39.7 N, Long. 95-23.3 W; NE Texas; 10 m. E of Paris, Texas; Named for wildflowers growing here.

•**BLUE RIDGE**, Town; Collin County; Pop. 442; Zip Code 75004; Lat. 33-17.9 N, Long. 96-24.1 W; NE Texas; 35 m. NE of Dallas in a rural area.

•**BLUM**, Town; Hill County; Pop. 357; Zip Code 76627; NE central Texas; 40 m. S of Fort Worth.

•**BOERNE**, City; Kendall County Seat; Pop. 3,229; Zip Code 78006; Elev. 1,405; Lat. 29-47.2 N, Long. 98-43.6 W; S central Texas; 30 m. NW of San Antonio.
Members of the German colony of Bettina founded Boerne in 1849. After two years they moved to the site of the present town, which was named for *Ludwig Boerne*, a poet who was one of its founders.

•**BOGATA**, Town; Red River County; Pop. 1,508; Zip Code 75417; Lat. 33-28.1 N, Long. 95-12.9 W; NE Texas; 25 m. SE of Paris. Bogata was supposed to be named for the capital of Columbia - Bogata; but the postmaster's embellished handwriting was interpreted as Bogata.

•**BONHAM**, City; Fannin County Seat; Pop. 7,338; Zip Code 75418; Elev. 568; Lat. 33-34.8 N, Long. 96-10.8 W; NE Texas; 25 m. E of Sherman in a residential area, S of Red River. The town was named for Alamo defender *James Butler Bonham*.

•**BOOKER**, Town; Lipscomb & Ochiltree Counties; Pop. 1,219; Zip Code 79005; Lat. 36-27.2 N, Long. 100-32.3 W; NW Texas; 16 m. NE of Perrytown.

•**BORGER**, City; Hutchinson County; Pop. 15,837; Zip Code 79007; Lat. 35-39.4 N, Long. 101-23.6 W; NW Texas; 45 m. NE of Amarillo, near Lake Meredith.

•**BOSTON**, Village; Bowie County Seat; Pop. included in New Boston; Zip Code 78887; NE Texas; 25 m. W of Texarkana; Named for Boston, Massachusetts.

•**BOVINA**, City; Parmer County; Pop. 1,499; Zip Code 79009; Lat. 34-30.8 N, Long. 102-53.2 W; NW Texas; near New Mexico state line on Running Water Creek. The town was originally known as Bull Town. The newer name also suggests the amount of steers that inhabit the region.

•**BOWIE**, City; Montague County; Pop. 5,610; Zip Code 76230; Lat. 33-33.7 N, Long. 97-51.0 W; N Texas; 40 m. SE of Wichita Falls; Named for *James A. Bowie*, famous pioneer and maker of a knife that still bears his name.

•**BOYD**, Town; Wise County; Pop. 889; Zip Code 76023; Lat. 33-04.6 N, Long. 97-34.0 W; N Texas; 20 m. NW of Fort Worth along the West Fork of the Trinity River.

•**BRACKETTVILLE**, City; Kinney County Seat; Pop. 1,676; Zip Code 78832; Elev. 1,020; Lat. 29-19.0 N, Long. 100-24.7 W; SW Texas; 40 m. N of Eagle Pass near the Anachacho Mountains.

•**BRADY**, City; McCulloch County Seat; Pop. 5,969; Zip Code 76825; Elev. 1,670; Central Texas; 77 m. SE of San Angelo.

•**BRAZORIA**, City; Brazoria County; Pop. 3,025; Zip Code 77422; Elev. 32; Lat. 29-02.6 N, Long. 95-34.2 W; SE Texas; 50 m. S of Houston on the Brazos River.

•**BRECKENRIDGE**, City; Stephens County Seat; Pop. 6,921; Zip Code 76024; Elev. 1,200; Lat. 32-45.3 N, Long. 98-54.2 W; N central Texas; E of Hubbard Creek Lake, 48 m. NE of Abilene. The city was named for Buchanan's Vice President, *John C. Breckenridge* (1857-61).

•**BREMOND**, City; Robertson County; Pop. 1,025; Zip Code 76629; Lat. 31-09.9 N, Long. 96-40.5 W; E central Texas; 40 m. SE of Waco.

•**BRENHAM**, City; Washington County Seat; Pop. 10,966; Zip Code 77833; Elev. 350; Lat. 30-10.0 N, Long. 96-23.6 W; SE central Texas.

•**BRIAR**, City; Parker, Tarrant & Wise Counties; Pop. 1,810; N Texas; 20 m. NW of Fort Worth near Eagle Mountain Lake.

•**BRIDGE CITY**, City; Orange County; Pop. 7,667; Zip Code 77611; Lat. 30-01.2 N, Long. 93-50.9 W; E Texas; 5 m. N of Port Arthur, near Sabine Lake.

•**BRIDGEPORT**, City; Wise County; Pop. 3,737; Zip Code 76026; Elev. 754; Lat. 33-12.6 N, Long. 97-45.4 W; N Texas; 35 m. NW of Fort Worth along the West Fork of the Trinity River, near Lake Bridgeport.

•**BROADDUS**, Town; San Augustine County; Pop. 225; Zip Code 75929; Lat. 31-18.4 N, Long. 94-16.1 W; E Texas; On Angelina Bayou of Sam Rayburn Reservoir, within the Angelina National Forest.

•**BRONSON**, City; Sabine County; Pop. 254; Zip Code 75930; Lat. 31-20.6 N, Long. 94-00.7 W; E Texas; 85 m. N of Beaumont near the Sabine National Forest.

•**BRONTE**, Town; Coke County; Pop. 983; Zip Code 76933; Elev. 1,893; Lat. 31-53.3 N, Long. 100-17.6 W; W central Texas; 30 m. N of San Angelo. The town, originally called Oso, and then Bronco, was renamed for novelist *Charlotte Bronte* in 1890. Bronte's writings were very popular at the time.

•**BROOKSHIRE**, City; Waller County; Pop. 2,175; Zip Code 77423; Elev. 168; Lat. 29-47.2 N, Long. 95-57.2 W; SE Texas; 35 m. W of Houston.

•**BROWNDEL**, City; Jasper County; Pop. 228; E Texas; Named for *John Wilcox Brown*, whose wife's name was *Dell*, in 1903. Brown's Maryland Trust Company financed this lumbering village.

•**BROWNFIELD**, City; Terry County Seat; Pop. 10,387; Zip Code 79316; Elev. 3,312; Lat. 33-10.8 N, Long. 102-16.5 W; NW Texas; 40 m. SW of Lubbock.

•**BROWNSBORO**, City; Henderson County; Pop. 582; Zip Code 75756; NE Texas; 18 m. W of Tyler.

BROWNSVILLE, City; Cameron County Seat; Pop. 84,997; Elev. 35; Lat. 25-54.3 N, Long. 97-30.2 W; S Texas; on Rio Grande River, 145 m. S of Corpus Christi.

•**BROWNWOOD**, City; Brown County Seat; Pop. 19,203; Zip Code 76801; Elev. 1,342; Lat. 31-42.6 N, Long. 98-58.6 W; Central Texas; 100 m. E of San Angelo, S of Lake Brownwood.

•**BRUCEVILLE**, (alt. Eddy), City; Falls & McLennan Counties; Pop. 1,038; Zip Code 76630; Central Texas; 17 m. S of Waco.

•**BRYAN**, City; Brazos County Seat; Pop. 44,337; Zip Code 77801; Elev. 367; Lat. 30-40.4 N, Long. 96-22.2 W; E central Texas; 100 m. NE of Austin near the Brazos River.

•**BRYSON**, City; Jack County; Pop. 579; Zip Code 76027; Lat. 33-09.6 N, Long. 98-23.2 W; N Texas; 55 m. S of Wichita Falls, near site of old Fort Richardson.

•**BUCKHOLTS**, Town; Milam County; Pop. 388; Zip Code 76518; Lat. 30-02.4 N, Long. 97-07.4 W; Central Texas; 20 m. SE of Temple.

•**BUDA**, City; Hays County; Pop. 597; Zip Code 78610; Lat. 30-04.9 N, Long. 97-50.6 W; S central Texas; 11 m. SW of Austin. Name is from the Spanish word for widow, viuda, for a women who lived here in the early settlement days. The town may also have been known as "the City of Widows". It was organized in 1887.

•**BUFFALO**, City; Leon County; Pop. 1,507; Zip Code 75831; Elev. 4; Lat. 31-27.7 N, Long. 96-03.9 W; E central Texas; 110 m. SE of Dallas.

•**BUFFALO GAP**, Town; Taylor County; Pop. 387; Zip Code 79508; Elev. 1,179; Lat. 32-16.9 N, Long. 99-49.6 W; NW central Texas; 13 m. S of Abilene. Buffalo also passed through this gap in the Callahan divide, hence the name.

•**BULLA**, Village; Bailey County; Pop. 105; Zip Code 79320; NW Texas. *W.B. and To Newsome* founded a town here on their ranchlands in 1924. At first the town was called Newsome, but then was renamed for *Bula Oaks*, daughter of a local real estate agent.

•**BULLARD**, Town; Cherokee & Smith Counties; Pop. 681; Zip Code 75757; Elev. 500; Lat. 32-08.3 N, Long. 95-19.2 W; NE Texas; 15 m. S of Tyler.

•**BUNA**, Village; Jasper County; Pop. 1,500; Zip Code 77612; Elev. 76; E Texas; 120 m. NE of Houston.

•**BUNKER HILL**, Village; City; Harris County; Pop. 3,750; E Texas; W suburb of Houston; Named for the Revolutionary War battle site.

•**BURKBURNETT**, City; Wichita County; Pop. 10,668; Zip Code 76354; Elev. 1,040; Lat. 34-05.9 N, Long. 98-34.2 W; N Texas; 11 m. N of Wichita Falls near the Oklahoma State line. The 6666 Ranch originally encompassed this community, then known as Nesterville. *Theodore Roosevelt* hunted wolves here in 1905, and stayed with ranch owner *Burk Burnett*. According to the local story, *President Roosevelt* personally recommended the town's new name in 1907, remembering the rancher's hospitality.

•**BURKE**, City; Angelina County; Pop. 322; Zip Code 75941; Lat. 31-13.9 N, Long. 94-46.1 W; E Texas; 7 m. S of Lufkin.

•**BURLESON**, City; Johnson & Tarrant Counties; Pop. 11,734; Zip Code 76028; Lat. 32-32.5 N, Long. 97-19.3 W; N central Texas; 12 m. S of Fort Worth; Named for *Colonel Edward Burleson*.

•**BURNET**, Town; Burnet County Seat; Pop. 3,410; Zip Code 78611; Elev. 1,319; Lat. 30-45.4 N, Long. 98-13.7 W; Central Texas; 45 m. NW of Austin near Inks Lake.

•**BURTON**, Town; Washington County; Pop. 325; Zip Code 77835; Lat. 30-11.0 N, Long. 96-41.8 W; SE central Texas, 55 m. E of Austin in a rural area; Named for *Major Isaac Burton*, commander of the Horse Marines in southeast Texas.

•**BUSHLAND**, Village; Potter County; Pop. 130; Zip Code 79012; NW Texas. Although the prairies here are covered in bushes, this village was named for its original landowner, *W.H. Bush* of Chicago. His relatives, *Charles and William Bush* were also prominent here; hence the "Bushland" name.

•**BYERS**, City; Clay County; Pop. 556; Zip Code 76357; Lat. 34-04.2 N, Long. 98-11.4 W; N Texas; 23 m. NE of Wichita Falls, near the Oklahoma state line.

•**BYNUM**, Town; Hill County; Pop. 232; Zip Code 76631; Lat. 31-58.3 N, Long. 97-00.2 W; NE central Texas; 8 m. SE of Hillsboro.

•**CACTUS**, Town; Moore County; Pop. 898; Zip Code 79013; Lat. 36-02.3 N, Long. 101-59.7 W; NW Texas; near Dumas. The presence of the prickly desert plants led to the name of this town. Before the first houses could be built here in the late 1940's, large numbers of cactus had to be removed.

•**CADDO MILLS**, City; Hunt County; Pop. 1,060; Zip Code 75005; Lat. 33-03.9 N, Long. 96-14.4 W; NE Texas; 8 m. SW of Greenville; Named for the Indian tribe that once lived near this site.

•**CALDWELL**, City; Burleson County Seat; Pop. 2,953; Zip Code 77836; Elev. 402; Lat. 30-32.1 N, Long. 96-41.6 W; E central Texas; 65 m. NE of Austin in a resort area. Founded in 1840, Caldwell was once Milam County seat. It was named for *Mathew "Old Paint" Caldwell*, a noted Indian fighter and signer of the Texas Declaration of Independence.

•**CALVERT**, City; Robertson County; Pop. 1,732; Zip Code 77837; Elev. 335; Lat. 30-58.7 N, Long. 96-40.3 W; E central Texas; 20 m. NE of Bryan. Most of the town looks much as it did in Victorian times. Named for a descendant of *Lord Baltimore*, *Robert Calvert*, a plantation owner who donated the townsite.

•**CAMERON**, City; Milam County Seat; Pop. 5,721; Zip Code 76520; Elev. 402; Lat. 30-51.3 N, Long. 96-58.6 W; Central Texas; On Little River, 50 m. S of Waco. Cameron was settled before the Texas Revolution and named for *Captain Ewen Cameron*, one of the state's first cowboys, whose statue is on the courthouse lawn.

•**CAMP VERDE**, Village; Kerr County; Pop. 41; Zip Code 78010; Elev. 1,800; SW central Texas; 16 m. S of Kerrville in the Hill County region.

•**CAMP WOOD**, City; Real County; Pop. 728; Zip Code 78833; Elev. 1,449; Lat. 29-40.1 N, 100-00.7 W; SW central Texas; 40 m. N of Uvalde near the Neches River. The city received its name from the old United States military post.

•**CANADIAN**, Town; Hemphill County Seat; Pop. 3,491; Zip Code 79014; Elev. 2,340; Lat. 35-54.6 N, Long. 100-23.1 W; NW Texas; 100 m. NE of Amarillo. Lying in a curve of the Canadian River, Canadian was first known as Hogtown, then as Desperado City.

•**CANTON**, City; Van Zandt County Seat; Pop. 2,845; Zip Code 75103; Elev. 540; Lat. 32-33.1 N, Long. 95-51.9 W; NE Texas; 60 m. SE of Dallas in a farming and livestock raising region. Canton is a French word meaning a "district" or other geographic division, similar to a county.

•**CANYON**, City; Randall County Seat; Pop. 10,724; Zip Code 79015; Elev. 3,566; NW Texas; 15 m. S of Amarillo. Near by is the Palo Duro Canyon, for which the city was named.

•**CARBON**, Town; Eastland County; Pop. 281; Zip Code 76435; Lat. 32-16.1 N, Long. 98-49.8 W; N central Texas; 60 m. SE of Abilene; named for the petroleum and other carbon materials mined here.

•**CARMINE**, City; Fayette County; Pop. 239; Zip Code 78932; Lat. 30-09.0 N, Long. 96-41.2 W; SE central Texas; 70 m. E of Austin.

•**CARRIZO SPRINGS**, City; Dimmit County Seat; Pop. 6,886; Zip Code 78834; Elev. 602; Lat. 28-31.4 N, Long. 99-51.6 W; S Texas; 45 m. E of Eagle Pass.

•**CARROLLTON**, City; Collin, Dallas & Denton Counties; Pop. 40,591; Elev. 500; Lat. 32-57.1 N, Long. 96-54.6 W; NE Texas; suburb of Dallas (NW); Population has increased three times here during the 1970's.

•**CARTHAGE**, City; Panola County Seat; Pop. 6,447; Zip Code 75633; Elev. 302; Lat. 32-09.4 N, Long. 94-20.3 W; E Texas; 25 m. S of Marshall. It was named for Carthage, Mississippi by *Mr. Major Holland*, an early settler.

•**CASTROVILLE**, City; Medina County; Pop. 1,821; Zip Code 78009; Elev. 787; Lat. 29-21.3 N, Long. 98-52.6 W; S central Texas; 30 m. SW of San Antonio, on a bend in the Medina River.
  Castroville is a bit of old Alsace-Lorraine, uprooted and transplanted beside the Medina River. Castroville was founded in 1844 by a group of colonists under *Count Henri de Castro* (who, however, signed all papers Henry Castro), and was named in his honor.

•**CEDAR HILL**, City; Dallas & Ellis Counties; Pop. 6,849; Zip Code 75104; Lat. 32-35.3 N, Long. 96-57.5 W; NE Texas; 20 m. SW of Dallas; Residential suburb that is growing rapidly.

•**CEDAR PARK**, City; Williamson County; Pop. 3,474; Zip Code 78613; Lat. 30-30.4 N, Long. 97-49.2 W; Central Texas; N suburb of Austin; Incorporated during the 1970s.

•**CELESTE**, Town; Hunt County; Pop. 716; Zip Code 75423; Lat. 33-17.6 N, Long. 96-11.8 W; NE Texas; 12 m. NE of Greenville.

•**CELINA**, Town; Collin County; Pop. 1,520; Zip Code 75009; Lat. 33-19.4 N, Long. 96-47.1 W; NE Texas; 30 m. N of Dallas; Named for county; in Ohio.

•**CENTER**, City; Shelby County Seat; Pop. 5,827; Zip Code 75935; Elev. 345; Lat. 31-47.7 N, Long. 94-10.8 W; E Texas; 50 m. S of Longview. Quick to take advantage of this, *Jesse Amason* donated 50 acres for a town site that was named Center.

•**CENTER CITY**, Village; Mills County; Pop. 75; Central Texas. Town is situated near approximate center of the state. Center Oak, which the pioneers believed marked the exact center of Texas, still stands by a concrete wall.

•**CENTERVILLE**, City; Leon County Seat; Pop. 799; Zip Code 75833; Elev. 353; Lat. 31-15.6 N, Long. 95-58.7 W; E central Texas; 40 m. SW of Palestine.

•**CHANDLER**, Town; Henderson County; Pop. 1,308; Zip Code 75758; Lat. 32-18.4 N, Long. 95-28.9 W; NE Texas; 10 m. W of Tyler.

•**CHANNING**, Town; Hartley County Seat; Pop. 304; Zip Code 79018; Lat. 35-41.0 N, Long. 102-20.0 W; NW Texas; 64 m. NW of Amarillo.

•**CHARLOTTE**, City; Atascosa County; Pop. 1,443; Zip Code 78011; Lat. 2-51.8 N, Long. 98-42.5 W; S Texas; 45 m. S of San Antonio.

•**CHESTER**, Town; Tyler County; Pop. 305; Zip Code 75936; Lat. 30-55.5 N, Long. 94-35.9 W; E Texas; 75 m. NW of Beaumont. This town was named for *Chester A. Arthur*, U.S. President (1881-85), by *U.G. Feagin*, who bought land here from the Trinity and Sabine Timber Company.

•**CHICO**, City; Wise County; Pop. 890; Zip Code 76030; Lat. 33-17.6 N, Long. 97-48.0 W; N Texas; 12 m. NE of Decatur; named for Chico, California. Chico is Spanish for "little".

•**CHILDRESS**, City; Childress County Seat; Pop. 5,817; Zip Code 79201; Elev. 1,877; Lat. 34-25.2 N, Long. 100-12.7 W; NW Texas; 120 m. NW of Wichita Falls. It was named for *George Campbell Childress*, author of the Texas Declaration of Independence.

•**CHILLICOTHE**, City; Hardeman County; Pop. 1,052; Zip Code 79225; Elev. 1,400; Lat. 34-15.3 N, Long. 99-31.2 W; N Texas; 85 m. NW of Wichita Falls. The name means "big town where we live" in Indian.

•**CHINA**, City; Jefferson County; Pop. 1,351; Zip Code 77613; Lat. 30-02.9 N, Long. 94-20.2 W; SE Texas; 11 m. W of Beaumont; Named for Chinese immigrants that have lived here.

•**CHIRENO**, City; Nacogdoches County; Pop. 371; Zip Code 75937; Lat. 31-29.9 N, Long. 94-21.1 W; E Texas; 19 m. SE of Nacogdoches, near the Angelina Bayou.

•**CHRISTINE**, City; Atascosa County; Pop. 392; Zip Code 78012; S Texas; 40 m. S of San Antonio.

•**CHRISTOVAL**, Village; Tom Green County; Pop. 216; Zip Code 76935; Elev. 2,000; W central Texas; 20 m. S of San Angelo. One old settler, *Christopher Columbus Doty*, gave the town its name about 1889.

•**CIBOLO**, City; Guadalupe County; Pop. 549; Zip Code 78108; S central Texas; Near Seguin. Cibolo is a Spanish word meaning buffalo, itself taken from an Indian word.

•**CISCO**, City; Eastland county; Pop. 4,517; Zip Code 76437; Elev. 1,608; Lat. 32-23.1 N, Long. 98-58.8 W; N central Texas; 45 m. E of Abilene. Cisco was the first town west of Fort Worth to have two railroads. It was named for *J.J. Cisco*, leading railroad promoter of the 1860's.

•**CLAIRMONT**, Village; Kent County; Pop. 35; Lat. 33-09.9 N, Long. 100-45.1 W; NW Texas; 80 m SE of Lubbock. Formerly seat of Kent County.

•**CLARENDON**, City; Donley County Seat; Pop. 2,220; Zip Code 79226; Elev. 2,727; Lat. 34-56.3 N, Long. 100-53.4 W; NW Texas. It is the offspring of one of the first settlements in the Panhandle. Old Clarendon was founded in 1878 by a Methodist minister, *Lewis Carhard*, who named the place for his wife, *Clara*.

•**CLARKSVILLE**, City; Red River County Seat; Pop. 4,917; Zip Code 75426; Elev. 442; Lat. 33-36.6 N, Long. 95-03.1M W; NE Texas.

•**CLAUDE**, City; Armstrong County Seat; Pop. 1,112; Zip Code 79019; Elev. 3,405; Lat. 35-06.5 N, Long. 95-03.1 W; NW Texas; 28 m. E of Amarillo.

•**CLEBURNE**, City; Johnson County Seat; Pop. 19,218; Zip Code 76031; Elev. 764; Lat. 32-21.2 N, Long. 97-23.4 W; N central Texas; 55 m. SW of Dallas on the West Buffalo Creek in a wooded, hilly area. It was established in 1854 and first known as Camp Henderson. In 1867, the name was changed to honor Confederate *General Pat Cleburne*.

•**CLEVELAND**, City; Liberty County; Pop. 5,977; Zip Code 77327; Lat. 30-20.5 N, Long. 95-05.4 W; E Texas; 45 m. NE of Houston; Named for *Grover Cleveland*, twenty-fourth U.S.President.

•**CLIFTON**, City; Bosque County; Pop. 3,063; Zip Code 76634; Elev. 670; Lat. 31-47.0 N, Long. 97-34.6 W; Central Texas on Bosque River, 32 m. NW of Waco; named for cliffs by the river.

•**CLINT**, Town; El Paso County; Pop. 1,314; Zip Code 79836; Elev. 3,630; Lat. 31-35.4 N, Long. 106-13.5 W; W Texas; Suburb of El Paso. Many adobe houses grace this little town.

•**CLYDE**, Town; Callahan County; Pop. 2,562; Zip Code 79510; Lat. 32-24.4 N, Long. 99-29.8 W; N central Texas; 15 m. E of Abilene. *Robert Clyde* established a railroad worker's camp here in 1881.

•**COAHOMA**, Town; Howard County; Pop. 1,069; Zip Code 79511; Lat. 32-17.6 N, Long. 101-18.3 W; W Texas; 10 m. E of Big Spring; Name is Indian for "signal", because of a hill nearby known as Signal Mountain.

•**COCKRELL HILL**, City; Dallas County; Pop. 3,262; Zip Code 75211; Lat. 32-44.3 N, Long. 96-53.4 W; NE Texas; Suburb of Dallas; Residential.

•**COLDSPRING**, City; San Jacinto County Seat; Pop. 569; Zip Code 77331; Elev. 356; Lat. 30-35.6 N, Long. 95-07.8 W; E Texas; In Sam Houston National Forest, near Lake Livingston. Coldspring was founded in 1847 as Coonskin. Name successively changed to Fireman's Hill and Coldspring, for the cold mountain waters here.

•**COLEMAN**, City; Coleman County Seat; Pop. 5,960; Zip Code 76834; Elev. 1,710; Lat. 31-49.9 N, Long. 99-25.6 W; Central Texas; 30 m. W of Brownwood near the geographic center of the state; Named for *Robert M. Coleman*.

•**COLLEGE STATION**, City; Brazos County; Pop. 37,272; Zip Code 77840; Elev. 308; Lat. 30-36.9 N, Long. 96-20.7 W; E central Texas; 4 m. SE of Bryan. Home of the Texas Agricultural and Mechanical University (commonly called "Texas A&M"), the state's first public institution of higher learning. It was established in 1876 and granted university status in 1963, and has made important contributions to the development of Texas agriculture.

•**COLLEYVILLE**, City; Tarrant County; Pop. 6,700; Zip Code 76034; Lat. 32-52.8 N, Long. 97-09.3 W; N Texas; Suburb of Fort Worth.

•**COLMESNEIL**, City; Tyler County; Pop. 553; Zip Code 75938; Lat. 30-54.4 N, Long. 94-25.1 W; E Texas; 60 m. N of Beaumont.

•**COLORADO CITY**, City; Mitchell County Seat; Pop. 5,405; Zip Code 79512; Elev. 2,067; Zip Code 79512; Lat. 32-23.7 N, Long. 100-51.9 W; NW central Texas; on Colorado River, 30 m. E of Big Springs.

•**COLUMBUS**, City; Colorado County Seat; Pop. 3,923; Zip Code 78934; Elev. 207; Lat. 29-42.3 N, Long. 96-32.8 W; SE central Texas; 65 m. W of Houston.

•**COMANCHE**, City; Comanche County Seat; Pop. 4,075, Zip Code 76442; Elev. 1,358; Lat. 31-53.9 N, Long. 98-36.2 W; Central Texas; 33 m. NE of Brownwood. Established as a trade center for the surrounding ranches in 1858, Comanche was plagued by fighting between colonists and Indians.

•**COMBES**, Town; Cameron County; Pop. 1,441; Zip Code 78535; Lat. 26-15.0 N, Long. 97-44.7Z W; S Texas; Suburb of Brownsville.

•**COMBINE**, City; Dallas & Kaufman Counties; Pop. 688; NE Texas.

•**COMMERCE**, City; Hunt County; Pop. 8,136; Zip Code 75428; Elev. 546; Lat. 33-14.8 N, Long. 95-54.1 W; NE Texas; 60 m. NE of Dallas. Commerce is a shipping center for the agricultural "Blacklands Belt" of Texas.

•**COMFORT**, Village; Kendall County; Pop. 1,226; Zip Code 78013; Elev. 1,437; S central Texas; 45 m. NW of San Antonio on the edge of the Guadalupe River Valley. Comfort was established by German settlers in 1854. Wearied by their journey from New Braunfels, the small group was so happy to see the picturesque site and pure water they named it "Camp Comfort".

•**COMO**, Town; Hopkins County; Pop. 554; Zip Code 75431; Lat. 33-03.3 N, Long. 95-28.3 W; NE Texas; 10 m. SE of Sulphur Springs.

•**CONCAN**, Village; Uvalde County; Pop. 71; Zip Code 78838; Elev. 1,260; SW central Texas; in Frio River, 21 m N of Uvalde. Settled about 1840, Concan may have been named for the Mexican gambling game of "Coon Can", from the spanish work Conquian.

•**CONROE**, City; Montgomery County Seat; Pop. 18,034; Elev. 213; Lat. 30-18.8 N, Long. 95-21.4 W; E Texas; 35 m. N of Houston.

•**COOLIDGE**, Town; Limestone County; Pop. 810; Zip Code 76635; Lat. 31-45.3 N, Long. 96-38.9 W; E central Texas; 90 m. S of Dallas.

•**COOPER**, City; Delta County Seat; Pop. 2,338; Zip Code 75432; Elev. 495; Lat. 33-22.5 N, Long. 95-41.7 W; NE Texas; 70 m. NE of Dallas, between North and South Sulphur Rivers.

•**COPPELL**, City; Dallas & Denton Counties; Pop. 3,826; Zip Code 75019; Lat. 32-57.1 N, Long. 97-00.5 W; NE Texas; NW suburb of Dallas, near the International Airport.

•**COPPERAS COVE**, City; Coryell County; Pop. 19,469; Zip Code 76522; Lat. 31-07.5 N, Long. 97-54.1 W; Central Texas; on SW border of Fort Hood Military Reservation. Named for the creek flowing nearby, which seeped a mineral that resembled the sulfate copperas.

•**CORPUS CHRISTI**, City; Kleberg, Nueces & San Patricio Counties; Nueces County Seat; Pop. 231,999; Elev. 35; Lat. 27-46.8 N, Long. 97-23.9 W; S Texas; 130 m. SE of San Antonio at Nueces River mouth. Its name was taken from that given the bay by the Spaniard, *Alonso Alvarez de Pineda*, who, in 1519, claimed the outer island and the land beyond for his king.

•**COTULLA**, City; LaSalle County Seat; Pop. 3,912; Zip Code 78014; Elev. 442; Lat. 28-26.2 N, Long. 99-14.1 W; S Texas; On Nueces River, 60 m. N of Laredo.

•**COVINGTON**, City; Hill County; Pop. 259; Zip Code 76636; Lat. 32-10.6 N, Long. 97-15.6 W; NE central Texas; 45 m. S of Fort Worth in a rural area.

•**CRANDALL**, City; Kaufman County; Pop. 831; Zip Code 75114; Lat. 32-37.7 N, Long. 96-27.4 W; NE Texas; 25 m. SE of Dallas.

•**CRANE**, City; Crane County Seat; Pop. 3,622; Zip Code 79731; Lat. 31-23.9 N, Long. 102-21.0 W; W Texas; 32 m. S of Odessa in a ranching region.

•**CRANFILLS GAP**, City; Bosque County; Pop. 341; Zip Code 76637; Lat. 31-46.3 N, Long. 97-49.5 W; Central Texas; 50 m. NW of Waco.

•**CRAWFORD**, Town; McLennan County; Pop. 610; Zip Code 76638; Lat. 31-32.0 N, Long. 97-26.5 W; Cen tral Texas; 15 m. W of Waco.

•**CROCKETT**, City; Houston County Seat; Pop. 7,405; Zip Code 75835; Elev. 350; Lat. 31-19.1 N, Long. 95-27.4 W; E Texas; 33 m. S of Palestine. It was named for *Davy Crockett*, who is said to have camped, while on his way to the Alamo, under a large oak near a spring about 500 feet from Crockett Circle.

•**CROSBYTON**, City; Crosby County Seat; Pop. 2,289; Zip Code 79322; Elev. 3,000; Lat. 33-39.7 N, Long. 101-14.2 W; NW Texas; At "Crown of Cap Rock".

•**CROSS PLAINS**, Town; Callahan County; Pop. 1,240; Zip Code 76443; Lat. 32-07.7 N, Long. 99-11.3 W; N central Texas; 40 m. SE of Abilene.

•**CROWELL**, City; Foard County Seat; Pop. 1,509; Zip Code 79227; Elev. 1,463; Lat. 33-59.0 N, Long. 99-43.4 W; N Texas; 80 m. W of Wichita Falls.

•**CROWLEY**, City; Tarrant County; Pop. 5,852; Zip Code 76036; Lat. 32-34.6 N, Long. 97-21.6 W; N Texas; S suburb of Fort Worth in a growing residential area.

•**CRYSTAL CITY**, City; Zavala County Seat; Pop. 8,334; Zip Code 78839; Elev. 580; Lat. 28-40.8 N, Long. 99-49.6 W; S Texas. The town was named for the clear well water pumped in the vicinity by early settlers. It was founded in 1907 and became county seat 21 years later.

•**CUERO**, City; DeWitt County Seat; Pop. 7,124; Zip Code 77954; Elev. 177; Lat. 29-05.6 N, Long. 97-17.4 W; S Texas; On Guadalupe River, 28 m. NW of Victoria. Cuero received its name from the creek on which it is lo cated. This creek, called Arroyo del Cuero (Creek of the Rawhide) by the Spanish as early as 1745, was so named because of the exceedingly boggy banks in which wild cattle and buffa loes, seeking water, became mired and unable to extricate themselves. Mexicans and Indians killed the helpless beasts chiefly for their hides, which were a medium of exchange.

•**CUSHING**, City; Nacogdoches County; Pop. 518; Zip Code 75760; Elev. 420; Lat. 31-48.7 N, Long. 94-50.5 W; E Texas; 20 m. NW of Nacogdoches; a lumbering and agricultural center.

•**CUT AND SHOOT**, Town; Montgomery County; Pop. 568; Zip Code 77302; Lat. 30-20.1 N, Long. 95-21.2 W; E Texas; N of Houston in a rural area. The name may have arisen from the cry of revenge from townsmen who discovered the local preacher had been philandering with their wives. Most sources, however, claim it is derived from a dispute over the shape of a church steeple. The town was incorporated during the 1970s.

•**DAINGERFIELD**, Town; Morris County Seat; Pop. 3,030; Zip Code 75638; Elev. 402; Lat. 33-01.9 N, Long. 94-43.6 W; NE Texas.

The town was named by early settlers (1840s) for *Captain London Daingerfield*, who was killed in a battle with Indians on this site. It is one of the smallest county seats in Texas.

•**DAISETTA**, City; Liberty County; Pop. 1,177; Zip Code 77533; Lat. 30-06.8 N, Long. 94-38.8 W; E Texas; 35 m. W of Beaumont. Named for two early townswomen, *Daisy Barrett* and *Etta White*. It was settled in about 1850, but was not officially founded until 1921, after oil had been drilled nearby.

•**DALHART**, City; Dallam & Hartley Counties; Dallam County Seat; Pop. 6,854; Zip Code 79022; Elev. 3,985; Lat. 36-04.2 N, Long. 102-31.4 W; NW Texas; 75 m. NW of Amarillo. Since this city is located near the line between Dallam and Hartley Counties, early rancher *Ora Atkinson* suggested its present name. It had also been known as Twist and Denrock, because it grew at the junction of the Denver City and Rock Island railroad lines after 1901.

•**DALLAS**, City; Collin, Dallas, Denton, Kaufman & Rockall Counties; Dallas County Seat; Pop. 904,078; Zip Code 752+; Elev. 512; Lat. 32-46.6 N, Long. 96-48.7 W; NE Texas; On Trinity River, 35 m. E of Fort Worth. The origin of the town's name is uncertain, one group of historians believing it was named for *George Mifflin Dallas*, a Pennsylvanian who 3 years later became Vice President of the United States; another group say that the name honored *Commander Mifflin Dallas* ; a third that the town was named for *Joseph Dallas*, a friend of *John Neely Bryan*, who came to the region from Washington County, Arkansas, in 1843, and settled at Cedar Springs, now within the Dallas city limits. in 1852 to *Alexander Cockrell* for $7,000.

•**DANBURY**, City; Brazoria County; Pop. 1,357; Zip Code 77534; Lat. 29-13.7 N, Long. 95-20.3 W; SE Texas; 25 m. NW of the Brazosport area.

•**DANEVANG**, Village; Wharton County; Pop. 61; Zip Code 77432; SE Texas; 11 m. S of El Campo in an area of cotton farming. It was founded in 1894 by Danes, whose descendants comprise a large part of the population. The name is Danish for "Danish Meadow".

•**DARROUZETT**, Town; Lipscomb County; Pop. 444; Zip Code 79024; Lat. 36-26.7 N, Long. 100-19.8 W; NW Texas; on a creek just S of Oklahoma state line.

•**DAWSON**, Town; Navarro County; Pop. 747; Zip Code 76639; Lat. 31-53.8 N, Long. 96-42.8 W; NE central Texas; Named for *Captain Nicholas M. Dawson* of the Texas Revolution.

•**DAYTON**, City; Liberty County; Pop. 4,908; Zip Code 77535; Lat. 30-02.8 N, Long. 94-53.5 W; E Texas; 25 m. NE of Houston; Named for early settler by the name of *Day*.

•**DE KALB**, Town; Bowie County; Pop. 2,217; Zip Code 75559; Elev. 407; Lat. 33-30.5 N Long. 94-37.0 W; NE Texas; 27 m. N of Texarkana. DeKalb was founded about a half mile north of its present location, was named in honor of *Baron de Kalb* (1721-1780), a German general in the American Revolutionary Army.

•**DE LEON**, City; Comanche County; Pop. 2,478; Zip Code 76444; Elev. 1,268; Lat. 32-06.6 N, Long. 98-32.3 W; Central Texas; 83 m. SE of Abilene. Founded in 1881, De Leon was named for the nearby Leon River, which was named for *Alonso de Leon*, an early Mexican explorer.

•**DECATUR**, City; Wise County Seat; Pop. 4,104; Zip Code 76234; Elev. 1,097; Lat. 33-13.9 N, Long. 97-35.2 W; N Texas; 40 m. NW of Fort Worth. The town was first settled in the 1850s and known as Taylorville but renamed for Stephen Decatur, a War of 1812 naval hero.

•**DEER PARK**, City; Harris County; Pop. 22,648; Zip Code 77536; Elev. 50; Lat. 29-42.5 N, Long. 95-07.5 W; SE Texas; Suburb, 17 m. SE of Houston, near the Galveston Bay along the ship channel.

475

•**DEL RIO**, City; Val Verde County Seat; Pop. 30,034; Zip Code 78840; Elev. 948; Lat. 29-21.8 N, Long. 100-53.7 W; SE Texas; 145 m. W of San Antonio. The town was named for San Felipe del Rio (Saint Philip of the River).

•**DELL CITY**, City; Hudspeth County; Pop. 495; Zip Code 79837; Elev. 3,698; Lat. 31-56.2 N, Long. 105-12.0 W; W Texas; 90 m. NE of El Paso in a rural ranchland area near the New Mexico state line.

•**DENISON**, City; Grayson County; Pop. 23,884; Zip Code 75020; Elev. 767; Lat. 33-45.0 N, Long. 96-32.8 W; NE Texas; 10 m. N of Sherman near the Oklahoma state line.

•**DENTON**, City; Denton County Seat; Pop. 48,063; Zip Code 76201; Elev. 620; Lat. 33-13.2 N, Long. 97-08.2 W; N Texas; 35 m. NE of Fort Worth. Named for an early Texas preacher called Denison.

•**DEPORT**, City; Lamar & Red River Counties; Pop. 724; Zip Code 75435; Lat. 33-31.5 N; NE Texas; 15 m. SE of Paris in a farming region.

•**DESOTO**, City; Dallas County; Pop. 15,538; Zip Code 75115; Lat. 32-35.3 N, Long. 96-51.4 W; NE Texas; 17 m. SW of Dallas in a residential area that has grown enormously in recent years.

•**DETROIT**, Town; Red River County; Pop. 805; Zip Code 75436; Elev. 482; Lat. 33-39.5 N, Long. 95-15.9 W; NE Texas; 20 m. E of Paris. The town was named for the Michigan city by early settlers.

•**DEVINE**, City; Medina County; Pop. 3,756; Zip Code 78016; Elev. 670; Lat. 29-08.3 N, Long. 98-54.4 W; S central Texas; 27 m. SW of San Antonio.

•**DIBOLL**, City; Angelina County; Pop. 5,227; Zip Code 75941; Lat. 31-11.1 N, Long. 94-47.0 W; E Texas; 100 m. NE of Houston, near the Neches River.

•**DICKENS**, City; Dickens County Seat; Pop. 409; Zip Code 79229; Elev. 2,468; Lat. 33-37.3 N, Long. 100-50.1 W; NW Texas; 65 m. E of Lubbock. Named after *J.Dickens*, an early settler and fighter at the Alamo.

•**DICKINSON**, Village; Galveston County; Pop. 7,505; Zip Code 77539; Lat. 29-27.6 N, Long. 95-03.0 W; SE Texas; 15 m. N of Galveston in a residential suburban area.

•**DILLEY**, City; Frio County; Pop. 2,579; Zip Code 78017; Lat. 28-40.3 N, Long. 99-10.2 W; S Texas; 65 m. SW of San Antonio in a rural region; Named for *George M. Dilley* of the International and Great Northern Railroad, from Palestine, Texas.

•**DIME BOX**, (alt. OLD DIME BOX), Village; Lee County; Pop. 313; Zip Code 77853; Central Texas; 40 m. NE of Austin. Stagecoach drivers and railroaders carried mail to and from this settlement in early times for a fee of 10 cents. The mail was delivered to a special box erected by the citizens. In 1943, Dime Box received recognition when it "Contributed 100 percent" to the March of Dimes, the first U.S. town to do so.

•**DIMMITT**, City; Castro County Seat; Pop. 5,019; Zip Code 79027; Lat. 34-33.0 N, Long. 102-18.9 W; NW Texas; 60 m. SW of Amarillo in a ranching region; Named for *Philip Dimmit*.

•**DODGE**, Village; Walker County; Pop. 150; Zip Code 77334; E Texas; 10 m. E of Huntsville in the Sam Houston National Forest. *C.G. Dodge* of the Dodge-Phelps Construction Company which built rail lines through town, gave it its name.

•**DONIE**, Village; Freestone County; Pop. 206; Zip Code 75838; E central Texas; 50 m. E of Waco. The name may originate from *Dovie*, since *Edward Dovie* was an important rancher in the area. It may also come from *Dovie Prairie*, which locals say was an early name for the region. In any case, the post office misread the intended name when they recorded this railroad village in 1898.

•**DOUGLASSVILLE**, Town; Cass County; Pop. 228; Zip Code 75560; Lat. 33-11.5 N, Long. 94-21.3 W; NE Texas; 30 m. SW of Texarkana. Douglassville was founded in 1853. The log cabin erected in 1854 by *John Douglass* still stands, somewhat modernized. During the era of settlement, plantation owners had large numbers of slaves; their descendants still farm the cotton fields. The heavily timbered area is also important for sawmilling.

•**DRISCOLL**, City; Nueces County; Pop. 648; Zip Code 78351; Lat. 27-40.5 N, Long. 98-05.4 W; S Texas; 20 m. SW of Corpus Christi.

•**DUBLIN**, City; Erath County; Pop. 2,723; Zip Code 76446; Elev. 1,450; Lat. 32-05.1 N, Long. 98-20.6 W; N central Texas; 50 m. NE of Brownwood. The name, despite its Celtic sound, has a purely local origin. It was derived from a huge double log cabin erected by early-day citizens as a protection against Indians. "Dublin' in" was a term for a retreat to the cabin, and the town became known as Doublin, later contracted to Dublin. an Irish railroad man added to the impression that the town had an Irish origin by giving many of the streets Celtic names.

•**DUMAS**, City; Moore County Seat; Pop. 12,194; Zip Code 79029; Elev. 3,668; Lat. 35-51.5 N, Long. 101-58.3 W; NW Texas; 50 m. N of Amarillo. It was named for *Louis Dumas*, president of a company that founded this county seat in 1892. Oil was discovered in 1926.

•**DUNCANVILLE**, City; Dallas County; Pop. 27,781; Zip Code 751+; Lat. 32-39.0 N, Long. 96-54.5 W; NE Texas; Suburb of Dallas, in a residentail area that has doubled in population during the 1970s.

•**DUNDEE**, Village; Archer County; Pop. 60; Zip Code 76358; Elev. 1,143; N Texas; 27 m. SE of Wichita Falls. Farms and ranches surround this quiet town named for the port city of Scotland.

•**EAGLE PASS**, City; Maverick County Seat; Pop. 21,407; Zip Code 78852; Elev. 797; Lat. 28-42.6 N, Long. 100-30.0 W; SW Texas; on Rio Grande, 130 m. SW of San Antonio; Across river from Piedras Negras, Mexico. Eagle Pass is a tourist resort of narrow streets and Mexican border atmosphere, which during the days of the war with Mexico, was the site of a U.S. military encampment at the crossing of the Rio Grande. It was named Camp Eagle Pass from the daily flight of an eagle back and forth cross the river to its nest in a huge cottonwood tree on the Mexican bank.

•**EARLY**, City; Brown County; Pop. 2,313; Zip Code 76801; Lat. 31-44.6 N, Long. 98-56.5 W; Central Texas; 1 m. NE of Brownwood; Residential.

•**EARTH**, City; Lamb County; Pop. 1,512; Zip Code 79031; Lat. 34-14.0 N, Long. 102-24.4 W; NW Texas; 40 m. W of Plainview. Named during a sandstorm, Earth is strung out along U.S. Highway 70.

•**EASTLAND**, City; Eastland County Seat; Pop. 3,747; Zip Code 76448; Elev. 1,421; Lat. 32-23.9 N, Long. 98-49.1 W; N central Texas; 55 m. E of Abilene.

•**EASTON**, City; Gregg & Rusk Counties; Pop. 333; Zip Code 75641; Lat. 32-23.2 N, Long. 94-35.1 W; NE Texas; Suburb of Longview.

•**EDCOUCH**, City; Hidalgo County; Pop. 3,092; Zip Code 78538; Lat. 26-17.6 N, Long. 97-57.9 W; S Texas; 15 m. NW of Harlingen in a citrus farming area.

•**EDEN**, City; Concho County; Pop. 1,294; Zip Code 76837; Elev. 2,046; Lat. 31-13.1 N, Long. 99-50.6 W; W central Texas; 45 m. SE of San Angelo.

•**EDGEWOOD**, Town; Van Zandt County; Pop. 1,413; Zip Code 75117; Lat. 32-41.8 N, Long. 95-53.3 W; NE Texas; 35 m. E of Dallas in a rural area.

•**EDINBURG**, City; Hidalgo County Seat; Pop. 24,075; Zip Code 78539; Elev. 91; Lat. 26-18.1 N, Long. 98-09.7 W; S Texas; 55 m. NW of Brownsville. It was first named Chapin for an early promoter and renamed in 1911.

•**EDMONSON**, Town; Hale County; Pop. 291; Zip Code 79032; Lat. 34-16.9 N, Long. 101-54.0 W; NW Texas; 10 m. NW of Plainview in a ranching region.

•**EDNA**, City; Jackson County Seat; Pop. 5,650; Zip Code 77957; Elev. 72; Lat. 28-58.7 N, Long. 96-38.8 W; SE Texas; 95 m. SW of Houston.

•**EL CAMPO**, City; Wharton County; Pop. 10,462; Zip Code 77437; Elev. 110; Lat. 29-11.6 N, Long. 96-16.2 W; SE Texas; 70 m. SW of Houston. When incorporated in 1902, the city fathers used Spanish words for its name.

•**EL PASO**, City; El Paso County Seat; Pop. 425,259; Zip Code 799+; Elev. 3,762; Lat. 31-45.3 N, Long. 106-28.8 W; W Texas. El Paso is the lowest natural pass in that region of deserts and mountains where the westernmost tip of Texas touches the borders of Mexico and New Mexico. It was named for "the pass" of the early Spanish conquistodores.

•**ELDORADO**, Town; Schleicher County Seat; Pop. 2,061; Zip Code 76936; Elev. 2,410; Lat. 30-51.6 N, Long. 100-36.0 W; W central Texas; 45 m. S of San Angelo. First a stage station known as Verand, it was located in Vermont Pasture. The town was moved on top of the divide in 1895 and took its Spanish name, which means "the gilded one."

•**ELECTRA**, City; Wichita County; Pop. 3,755; Zip Code 76360; Elev. 1,229; Lat. 34-02.0 N, Long. 98-54.9 W; N Texas; 30 m. NW of Wichita Falls. Electra was named by *W.T. Waggone* for his daughter.

•**ELGIN**, City; Bastrop County; Pop. 4,535; Zip Code 78621; Lat. 30-20.7 N, Long. 97-22.1 W; S central Texas; 22 m. E of Austin. It was named for *Robert M. Elgin*, who was land commissioner for the Houston and Texas Central Railroad after the Civil War.

•**ELKHART**, Town; Anderson County; Pop. 1,317; Zip Code 75839; Lat. 31-37.5 N, Long. 95-34.8 W; E Texas; 15 m. S of Palestine. This town may have been named for a friendly Indian chief, or for an abandoned covered wagon that had an elk carved on it; hence "elk cart."

•**ELMATON**, Village; Matagorda County; Pop. 165; Zip Code 77440; SE coastal Texas; near Bay City; Name is Spanish for "The Killer", but origin is disputed.

•**ELMENDORF**, City; Bexar County; Pop. 492; Zip Code 78112; Lat. 29-15.2 N, Long. 98-20.0 W; S central Texas; 15 m. SE of San Antonio.

•**ELSA**, City; Hidalgo County; Pop. 5,061; Zip Code 78543; Lat. 26-17.6 N, Long. 97-59.6 W; S Texas; 20 m. W of Harlingen.

•**EMHOUSE**, Town; Navarro County; Pop. 197; Zip Code 75110; Lat. 32-09.7 N, Long. 96-34.7 W; NE central Texas; 10 m. NW of Corsicana; Rural.

•**EMORY**, City; Rains County Seat; Pop. 813; Zip Code 75440; Elev. 464; Lat. 32-52.4 N, Long. 95-45.9 W; NE Texas; 30 m. SE of Greenville. Emory was named for *Emory Rains*, first settler in the area in 1848.

•**ENCINAL**, City; La Salle County; Pop. 704; Zip Code 78019; Lat. 28-02.3 N, Long. 99-21.3 W; S Texas; 36 m. N of Laredo; Named for the live oaks found in the region, from the Spanish word "encina".

•**ENCINO**, Village; Brooks County; Pop. 110; Zip Code 78353; S Texas; 50 m. N of McAllen; Name comes from a 1831 Mexican land grant, which called the place La Encantada y Encina del Pozo or "The Enchanted Place and Live Oak in a Hole", because of a large tree surrounded by depressed earth that stood out on the landscape.

•**ENNIS**, City; Ellis County; Pop. 12,110; Zip Code 75119; Elev. 548; Lat. 32-20.0 N, Long. 96-37.8 W; NE central Texas; 30 m. SE of Dallas.

•**EOLA**, Village; Concho County; Pop. 218; Zip Code 76937; W central Texas; 20 m. E of San Angelo; Named for the Roman god of the winds, *Aeolus*. An Indian word, "eola", also refers to wind.

•**ESTELLINE**, Town; Hall County; Pop. 258; Zip Code 79233; Elev. 1,759; Lat. 34-32.8 N, Long. 100-26.4 W; NW Texas; On Red River, 15 m. NW of Childress.

•**EULESS**, City; Tarrant County; Pop. 24,002; Zip Code 76039; Lat. 32-50.2 N, Long. 97-05.0 W; N Texas; 15 m. NE of Fort Worth in a rapidly changing agricultural - residential area.

•**EUSTACE**, City; Henderson County; Pop. 541; Zip Code 75124; Lat. 32-18.3 N, Long. 96-00.5 W; NE Texas; 45 m. SE of Dallas near Cedar Creek Lake.

•**EVANT**, Town; Coryell & Hamilton Counties; Pop. 425; Zip Code 76525; Lat. 31-28.5 N, Long. 98-09.2 W; Central Texas; 63 m. W of Waco.

•**EVERMAN**, City; Tarrant County; Pop. 5,387; Zip Code 76140; Lat. 32-37.9 N, Long. 97-17.2 W; N Texas; 5 m. SE of Fort Worth in a residential area.

•**FAIRFIELD**, City; Freestone County Seat; Pop. 3,505; Zip Code 75840; Elev. 461; Lat. 31-43.5 N, Long. 96-09.8 W; E central Texas; 60 m. E of Waco.

•**FAIRVIEW**, City; Wise County; Pop. 180; Zip Code 770+; Lat. 32-21.4 N, Long. 101-31.2 W; N Texas; Rural.

•**FALFURRIAS**, City; Brooks County Seat; Pop. 6,103; Zip Code 78355; Elev. 119; Lat. 27-13.5 N, Long. 98-08.6 W; S Texas; 75 m. SW of Corpus Christi. Falfurrias is Spanish for "Heart's Delight', the name of a local wildflower.

•**FALLS CITY**, City; Karnes County; Pop. 580; Zip Code 78113; Lat. 28-59.1 N, Long. 98-01.1 W; S Texas; 35 m. SE of San Antonio at a small falls in the San Antonio River.

•**FARMERS BRANCH**, City; Dallas County; Pop. 24,863; Zip Code 75234; Lat. 32-56.3 N, Long. 96-54.2 W; NE Texas; N suburb of Dallas in a growing residential area; Named because it was once an agricultural village on a large branch of the Trinity River.

•**FARMERSVILLE**, City; Collin County; Pop. 2,360; Zip Code 75031; Lat. 33-09.7 N, Long. 96-21.6 W; NE Texas; 15 m. W of Greenville; so named because of its agricultural character.

•**FARWELL**, City; Parmer County Seat; Pop. 1,354; Zip Code 79325; Lat. 34-22.9 N, Long. 103-02.3 W; NW Texas; 90 m. SW of

Amarillo. This city was named for the *Farwell brothers*, who received a land grant reaching into ten counties, as payment for building the capital at Austin.

•**FATE**, City; Rockwall County; Pop. 263; Zip Code 75032; NE Texas. Fate was named for local citizen *LaFeyette Peyton*, who owned a cotton gin, or for early sheriff *LaFayette Brown*. In either case, Fate is a shortening of their name.

•**FAYETTEVILLE**, Town; Fayette County; Pop. 356; Zip Code 78940; Lat. 29-54.2 N, Long. 96-40.5 W; SE central Texas; 15 m. E of LaGrange; First settled by Czechoslovakian immigrants.

•**FERRIS**, City; Dallas & Ellis Counties; Pop. 2,228; Zip Code 75125; Lat. 32-32.2 N, Long. 96-40.0 W; NE central Texas; 35 m. N of Corsicana.

•**FISCHER**, Village; Comal County; Pop. 20; Zip Code 78623; Elev. 1,200; S central Texas. Established in 1853 by *Herman Fischer*, this village began as a small general store. The post office; established in 1875, has never failed to have a *Fischer* as Post Master.

•**FLATONIA**, Town; Fayette County; Pop. 1,070; Zip Code 78941; Lat. 29-41.3 N, Long. 97-06.6 W; SE central Texas; 50 m. SE of Austin. Named for *F.W. Flato*, an early settler among the early Czech immigrants who first came here.

•**FLORENCE**, Town; Williamson County; Pop. 744; Zip Code 76527; Lat. 30-50.6 N, Long. 97-47.6 W; Central Texas; 50 m. N of Austin in a rural area.

•**FLORESVILLE**, City; Wilson County Seat; Pop. 4,381; Zip Code 78114; Elev. 389; Lat. 29-08.2 N, Long. 98-09.9 W; S central Texas; 20 m. SE of San Antonio. It was named for early rancher, *Don Francisco Flores de Abrego*, who moved here from Mexico in 1832.

•**FLOYDADA**, City; Floyd County Seat; Pop. 4,193; Zip Code 79235; Elev. 3,137; Lat. 33-59.2 N, Long. 101-20.4 W; NW Texas; 40 m. NE of Lubbock. It is named for Alamo hero *Dolphin Floyd*.

•**FOLLETT**, City; Lipscomb County; Pop. 547; Zip Code 79034; Lat. 36-25.9 N, Long. 100-08.4 W; Nw Texas; At NE corner of the Panhandle, near the Oklahoma state line.

•**FORNEY**, Town; Kaufman County; Pop. 2,483; Zip Code 75126; Lat. 32-44.9 N, Long. 96-28.2 W; NE Texas; 20 m. E of Dallas near E Fork of the Trinity River.

•**FORSAN**, City; Howard County; Pop. 239; Zip Code 79733; W Texas; 15 m. S of Big Spring; Named for the four areas of sands that were believed to be oil-producing in the late 1920s.

•**FORT DAVIS**, Village; Jeff Davis County Seat; Pop. 787; Zip Code 79734; Elev. 5,050; W Texas; 180 m. SE of El Paso in the Davis Mountains. It was named after *Jefferson Davis*, then U.S. Secretary of War.

•**FORT GATES**, City; Coryell County; Pop. 777; Elev. 795; 39 m. W of Waco; Named fort built in 1849 as a unit in the earliest line of U.S. defense posts, behind which the western settlement of Texas began.

•**FORT GRIFFIN**, Village; Schackelford County; Pop. 96; Elev. 1,275; N central Texas; 47 m. NE of Abilene; is one of the most famous of Texas frontier towns.

•**FORT MCKAVETT**, Village; Menard County; Pop. 103; Elev. 2,155; Central Texas; 65 m. SE of San Angelo. It named for *Captain Henry McKavett*, killed in the Battle of Monterrey in Mexico.

•**FORT STOCKTON**, City; Pecos County Seat; Pop. 8,688; Zip Code 79735; Elev. 3,052; Lat. 30-53.3 N, Long. 102-53.0 W; W Texas; 150 m. W of San Angelo.

•**FORT WORTH**, City; Tarrant County Seat; Pop. 385,141; Zip Code 761+; Elev. 670; Lat. 32-45.0 N, Long. 97-17.7 W; N Texas; 30 m. W of Dallas. The camp was named Fort Worth in honor of *General William Jenkins Worth*, Mexican War hero.

•**FRANKLIN**, City; Robertson County Seat; Pop. 1,349; Zip Code 77856; Elev. 450; Lat. 31-01.6 N, Long. 96-29.0 W; E central Texas; 30 m. NW of Bryan in a farming area.

•**FRANKSTON**, Town; Anderson County; Pop. 1,255; Zip Code 75763; Elev. 389; Lat. 32-02.9 N, Long. 85-30.2 W; E Texas; 25 m. SW of Tyler.

•**FRANNIN**, Village; Goliad County; Pop. 94; Zip Code 77960; S Texas; 17 m. SW of Victoria; Named for Texas Revolutionary figure *James W. Fannin, Jr.*

•**FREDERICKSBURG**, Town; Gillespie County Seat; Pop. 6,412; Zip Code 78624; Elev. 1,743; Lat. 30-16.4 N, Long. 98-52.2 W; Central Texas; 70 m. NW of San Antonio. It was named *Frederick the Great* of Prussia.

•**FREEPORT**, City; Brazoria County; Pop. 13,444; Zip Code 77541; Elev. 5; Lat. 28-57.1 N, Long. 95-21.3 W; SE Texas; 60 m. S of Houston at point where Brazos River flows into the Gulf.

•**FREER**, City; Duval County; Pop. 3,213; Zip Code 78357; Lat. 27-52.9 N. Long. 95-21.3 W; S Texas; 60 m. NE of Laredo.

•**FRIENDSWOOD**, City; Galveston & Harris Counties; Pop. 10,719; Zip Code 77546; Lat. 29-32.0 N, Long. 95-12.0 W; SE Texas; Suburb of Galveston.

•**FRIJOLE**, Village; Culberson County; Pop. (Rural); Elev. 5,500; W Texas; S of New Mexico state line off U.S. Highway 62/180. In 1916, townspeople voted on a name for their new post office and agreed on the Spanish name for bean.

•**FRIONA**, City; Parmer County; Pop. 3,809; Zip Code 79035; Lat. 34-38.3 N, Long. 102-43.2 W; NW Texas; 65 m. SW of Amarillo. This city was called Frio, for the creek flowing nearby, but since another Texas town had taken the name before, the ending - na - was added for the post office records.

•**FRISCO**, City; Collin & Denton Counties; Pop. 3,420; Zip Code 75034; Lat. 33-09.1 N, Long. 96-49.4 W; NE Texas; 20 m. N of Dallas; Probably named for the California city of San Francisco during the great Gold Rush.

•**FRITCH**, City; Hutchinson & Moore Counties; Pop. 2,299; Zip Code 79036; Elev. 3,200; Lat. 35-38.3 N, Long. 101-35.9 W; NW Texas; on E shore of Lake Meredith, 33 m. N of Amarillo.

•**FROST**, Town; Navarro County; Pop. 564; Zip Code 76641; Lat. 32-04.8 N, Long. 96-48.5 W; NE central Texas; 45 m. NE of Waco in a cotton farming region; Named for railroad man *S. M. Frost*.

•**FRUITVALE**, City; Van Zandt County; Pop. 367; Zip Code 75127; NE Texas; 45 miles E of Dallas in a rural area; Name is descriptive.

•**FULSHEAR**, Town; Fort Bend County; Pop. 594; Zip Code 77441; Lat. 29-41.2 N, Long. 95-53.8 W; SE Texas; Near Rosenburg, SW of Houston.

•**FULTON**, Town; Aransas County; Pop. 725; Zip Code 78358; Elev. 6; Lat. 28-03.6 N, Long. 97-02.2 W; S Texas; S of Rockport; Named for the Coleman-Fulton Cattle Company.

•**GAIL**, Village; Borden County Seat; Pop. 189; Zip Code 79738; Elev. 2,510; W Texas; 36 m. W of Snyder. *Gail Borden*, Texas pioneer and inventor of a process for condensing milk, gave this town and county their names.

•**GAINESVILLE**, City; Cooke County Seat; Pop. 14,081; Zip Code 76240; Elev. 730; Lat. 33-37.6 N, Long. 97-08.3 W; N Texas; 35 m. W of Sherman.

•**GALENA PARK**, City; Harris County; Pop. 9,879; Zip Code 77547; Lat. 29-44.0 N, Long. 95-13.8 W; SE Texas; Named for the lead ore found here.

•**GALLATIN**, City; Cherokee County; Pop. 132; Zip Code 75764; Lat. 31-53.7 N, Long. 95-08.4 W; E Texas; 10 m. SE of Jacksonville; Named for *Albert Gallatin*, early nineteenth century politician.

•**GALVESTON**, City; Galveston County Seat; Pop. 61,902; Zip Code 775+; Elev. 6 to 17; Lat. 29-18.0 N, Long. 94-47.7 W; SE coastal Texas; 50 m. SE of Houston. It was named in honor of *Count Bernardo de Galvez*, Viceroy of Mexico.

•**GANADO**, Town; Jackson County; Pop. 1,770; Zip Code 77962; Elev. 71; Lat. 29-02.4 N, Long. 96-30.8 W; SE Texas; 90 m. SW of Houston. It is the Spanish word for "cattle".

•**GARDEN CITY**, Village; Glasscock County Seat; Pop. 293; Zip Code 79739; W Texas; 22 m. S of Big Spring in a ranching area. Originally, the town was called Gardner City, for postmaster *William Gardner*. However, Washington record keepers misspelled the name when the first post office was established in 1886.

•**GARLAND**, City; Collin, Dallas & Rockwall Counties; Pop. 138,857; Zip Code 750+; Elev. 540; Lat. 32-54.5 N, Long. 96-38.2 W; NE Texas; 15 m. NE of Dallas; Residential suburb.

•**GARRISON**, Town; Nacogdoches County; Pop. 1,059; Zip Code 75946; Lat. 31-49.4 N, Long. 94-29.6 W; E Texas; 28 m. NE of Nacogdoches.

•**GATESVILLE**, City; Coryell County Seat; Pop. 6,260; Zip Code 76528; Elev. 795; Lat. 31-26.1 N, Long. 97-44.6 W; Central Texas; 40 m. W of Waco. It was named for Fort Gates, a frontier post established in 1849 as a unit in the earliest line of U.S. Government defenses, behind which settlement of the western part of the country began.

•**GEORGETOWN**, City; Williamson County Seat; Pop. 9,468; Zip Code 78626; Elev. 750; Lat. 30-38.0 N, Long. 97-40.6 W; Central Texas; 30 m. N of Austin.

•**GEORGE WEST**, City; Live Oak County Seat; Pop. 2,627; Zip Code 78022; Elev. 162; Lat. 28-20.1 N, Long. 98-06.9 W; S Texas; 60 m. NW of Corpus Christi. Ranchman *George West* built this town.

•**GERONIMO**, Village; Guadalupe County; Pop. 150; Zip Code 78115; S central Texas; Near Seguin. The village is named for the Apache Indian Chief, *Geronimo*, who once led battles in this region.

•**GIDDINGS**, City; Lee County Seat; Pop. 3,950; Zip Code 78942; Elev. 520; Lat. 30-10.9 N, Long. 96-56.2 W; Central Texas; 50 m. E of Austin.

•**GILMER**, City; Upshur County Seat; Pop. 5,167; Zip Code 75644; Elev. 370; Lat. 32-43.8 N, Long. 94-56.9 W; NE Texas; 110 m. E of Dallas.

•**GLADEWATER**, City; Gregg & Upshur Counties; Pop. 6,548; Zip Code 75647; Elev. 333; Lat. 32-32.7 N, Long. 94-56.3 W; NE Texas.

Originally established at a different site and called St. Clair, the town was moved to location on Texas and Pacific Railroad in 1872 and renamed for Glade Creek.

•**GLAZIER**, Hemphill County; Pop. 20; Zip Code 79037; Elev. 2,601; Lat. 36-00.8 N, Long. 100-15.9 W; NW Texas.

•**GLEN ROSE**, City; Somervell County Seat; Pop. 2,075; Zip Code 76043; Elev. 680; Lat. 32-14.2 N, Long. 97-45.4 W; N central Texas; 50 m. SW of Fort Worth on the Paluxy River.

•**GODLEY**, Town; Johnson County; Pop. 614; Zip Code 76044; Lat. 32-26.9 N, Long. 97-40.4 W; N central Texas; 30 m. S of Fort Worth.

•**GOLDSMITH**, City; Ector County; Pop. 409; Zip Code 79741; Lat. 31-59.1 N, Long. 102-37.0 W; W Texas; 25 m. NW of Odessa.

•**GOLDTHWAITE**, City; Mills County Seat; Pop. 1,783; Zip Code 76844; Elev. 1,580; Lat. 31-27.2 N, Long. 98-34.2 W; Central Texas; 88 m. W of Waco.

•**GOLIAD**, City; Goliad County Seat; Pop. 1,990; Zip Code 77963; Elev. 167; Lat. 28-40.1 N, Long. 97-23.4 W; S Texas; 20 m. SW of Victoria. Goliad grew around a mission and presidio established here by the Spaniards in 1749.

•**GONZALES**, City; Gonzales County Seat; Pop. 7,152; Zip Code 78629; Elev. 301; Lat. 29-30.1 N, Long. 97-27.0 W; S central Texas; On both sides of Guadalupe River, 55 m. SE of Austin. It was named for *Don Rafael Gonzales*, then provisional governor of the Mexican province of Caohila and Texas.

•**GOODRICH**, City; Polk County; Pop. 350; Zip Code 77335; Lat. 30-36.3 N, Long. 94-56.8 W; E Texas; 60 m. N of Houston, near Lake Livingston.

•**GORDON**, City; Palo Pinta County; Pop. 516; Zip Code 76453; Lat. 32-32.8 N, Long. 98-22.4 W; N central Texas; 30 m. SW of Mineral Wells.

•**GOREE**, City; Knox County; Pop. 524; Zip Code 76363; Lat. 33-28.2 N, Long. 99-31.4 W; N Texas; 65 m. SW of Wichita Falls in a rural area.

•**GORMAN**, City; Eastland County; Pop. 1,258; Zip Code 76454; Lat. 32-12.4 N, Long. 98-40.8 W; N central Texas; 60 m. SE of Abilene in a farm region.

•**GRAFORD**, City; Palo Pinto County; Pop. 495; Zip Code 76045; Lat. 32-56.1 N, Long. 98-14.4 W; N central Texas; 12 m. NW of Mineral Wells; so named because it lies between Graham and Weatherford.

•**GRANBURY**, City; Hood County Seat; Pop. 3,332; Zip Code 76048; Elev. 725; Lat. 32-26.8 N, Long. 97-47.4 W; N central Texas; 40 m. SW of Fort Worth along the Brazos River. Picturesquely situated on Lake Granbury, Granbury was settled in 1854 by *Thomas Lambert* who united it with the settlement called Stockton to form nucleus of Granbury.

•**GRAND PRAIRIE**, City; Dallas, Ellis & Tarrant Counties; Pop. 71,462; Zip Code 750+; Elev. 528; Lat. 32-44.9 N, Long. 96-59.7 W; NE Texas; 12 m. W of Dallas, at E edge of Grand Prairie region of state.

•**GRAND SALINE**, City; Van Zandt County; Pop. 2,709; Zip Code 75140; Elev. 407; Lat. 32-40.5 N, Long. 95-42.7 W; NE Texas; 65 m. E of Dallas. The town is built on a hill surrounded by salt flats.

•**GRANDFALLS**, Town; Ward County; Pop. 635; Zip Code 79742; Lat. 31-20.4 N, Long. 102-51.1 W; W Texas; 40 m. SW of Odessa near falls of the Pecos River.

•GRANDVIEW, City; Johnson County; Pop. 1,205; Zip Code 76050; Lat. 32-16.2 N, Long. 97-10.9 W; N central Texas; 14 m. SE of Cleburne in a farming and ranching area; Named for the long vistas of flatlands here.

•GRANGER, City; Williamson County; Pop. 1,236; Zip Code 76530; Lat. 30-43.1 N, Long. 97-26.4 W; Central Texas; 25 m. S of Temple; Named for *General Gordon Granger.*

•GRANITE SHOALS, City; Burnet County; Pop. 634; Zip Code 78654; Central Texas; Named for the rock along the Colorado River banks here.

•GRAPELAND, City; Houston County; Pop. 1,634; Zip Code 75844; Lat. 31-29.5 N, Long. 95-28.8 W; E Texas; 20 m. S of Palestine.

•GRAPEVINE, City; Dallas & Tarrant Counties; Pop. 11,801; Zip Code 76051; Lat. 32-56.3 N, Long. 47-04.6 W; N Texas; 20 m. NE of Fort Worth; An industrial suburb in a rapidly growing area.

•GREENVILLE, City; Hunt County Seat; Pop. 22,161; Zip Code 75401; Elev. 554; Lat. 33-08.3 N, Long. 96-06.8 W; NE Texas; 50 m. NE of Dallas.

•GREGORY, City; San Patricio County; Pop. 2,739; Zip Code 78359; Elev. 32; Lat. 27-55.5 N, Long. 97-17.6 W; S Texas; 11 m. NE of Corpus Christi, across the bay.

•GROESBECK, City; Limestone County Seat; Pop. 3,373; Zip Code 76642; Elev. 477; Lat. 31-31.2 N, Long. 96-32.1 W; E central Texas; 35 m. E of Waco. Groesbeck was dedicated in 1870 as townsite by Houston and Texas Central Railroad and named for one of its directors.

•GROOM, Town; Carson County; Pop. 736; Zip Code 79039; Lat. 35-12.2 N, Long. 101-06.3 W; NW Texas; 40 m. E of Amarillo in the Panhandle ranching county.

•GROVES, City; Jefferson County; Pop. 17,090; Zip Code 77619; Lat. 29-57.2 N, Long. 93-54.0 W; SE Texas; S of Port Arthur.

•GROVETON, City; Trinity County Seat; Pop. 1,262; Zip Code 75845; Lat. 31-03.5 N, Long. 95-07.6 W; E Texas; 40 m. NE of Huntsville in a lumbering area; large stands of pine gave the place its name.

•GRUVER, City; Hansford County; Pop. 1,216; Zip Code 79040; Lat. 36-15.8 N, Long. 101-25.4 W; NW Texas; 45 m. N of Borger in a ranching area.

•GUNTER, Town; Grayson County; Pop. 849; Zip Code 75058; Lat. 33-26.9 N, Long. 96-44.7 W; N Texas; 20 m. SW of Sherman.

•GUSTINE, Town; Comanche County; Pop. 416; Zip Code 76455; Lat. 31-50.7 N, Long. 98-24.2 W; Central Texas; 35 m. NE of Grownwood.

•GUTHRIE, Village; King County Seat; Pop. 140; Zip Code 79235; NW Texas; On S Wichita River; 95 m. E of Lubbock; Ranch supply center named for an early settler.

•HALLETTSVILLE, City; Lavaca County Seat; Pop. 2,865; Zip Code 77964; Elev. 232; Lat. 29-26.5 N, Long. 96-56.5 W; SE central Texas; 80 m. SE of Austin on Lavaca River.

•HALLSVILLE, City; Harrison County; Pop. 1,556; Zip Code 75650; Lat. 32-30.3 N, Long. 94-34.5 W; NE Texas; 12 m. W of Marshall.

•HALTOM CITY, City; Tarrant County; Pop. 29,014; Zip Code 76117; N Texas; 5 m. NE of Fort Worth in a growing residential area.

•HAMILTON, City; Hamilton County Seat; Pop. 3,189; Zip Code 79520; Lat. 31-42.2 N, Long. 98-07.4 W; Central Texas; 60 m. NW of Waco.

•HAMILTON, City; Jones County; Pop. 3,189; Zip Code 79520; Elev. 1,750; Lat. 32-53.0 N, Long. 100-07.6 W; NW central Texas; 40 m. NW of Abilene.

•HAPPY, Town; Randall & Swisher Counties; Pop. 674; Zip Code 79042; Lat. 34-44.6 N, Long. 101-51.6 W; NW Texas; 35 m. S of Amarillo. Spring water discovered by cowboys was so delightful in this dry flatlands area that early white settlers adopted the old Indian name for the region, "happy hunting grounds".

•HARDIN, Town; Liberty County; Pop. 779; Zip Code 77561; Lat. 30-09.2 N, Long. 94-44.3 W; E Texas; Named for *John Wesley Hardin,* outlaw.

•HARKER HEIGHTS, City; Bell County; Pop. 7,345; Zip Code 76541; Central Texas; Suburb of Temple; Residential.

•HARLINGEN, City; Cameron County; Pop. 43,543; Zip Code 78550; Elev. 36; Lat. 26-11.5 n, Long. 97-41.8 W; S Texas; 26 m. N of Brownsville in Lower Rio Grande Valley. Named for a city in The Netherlands, Harlingen was incorporated in 1905.

•HART, City; Castro County; Pop. 1,008; Zip Code 79043; Lat. 34-23.2 N, Long. 102-06.9 W; NW Texas; 25 m. NW of Plainview; Named for *Simeon Hart,* early rancher and developer.

•HASKELL, City; Haskell County Seat; Pop. 3,782; Zip Code 79521; Elev. 2,553; Lat. 33-09.5 N, Long. 99-43.9 W; N Texas; 50 m. N of Abilene.

•HASLET, City; Tarrant County; Pop. 262; Zip Code 76052; Lat. 32-58.5 N, Long. 97-20.9 W; N Texas; Near Fort Worth.

•HAWKINS, City; Wood County; Pop. 1,302; Zip Code 75765; Lat. 32-35.3 N, Long. 95-12.3 W; NE Texas; 25 m. W of Longview.

•HAWLEY, City; Jones County; Pop. 679; Zip Code 79525; Lat. 32-36.7 N, Long. 99-48.7 W; NW central Texas; Rural.

•HEARNE, City; Robertson County; Pop. 5,418; Zip Code 77859; Elev. 305; Lat. 30-52.6 N, Long. 96-35.5 W; E central Texas; 55 m. SE of Waco.

•HEBBRONVILLE, Village; Jim Hogg County Seat; Pop. 4,050; Zip Code 78361; Elev. 550; S Texas; On Noriacitas Creek, 53 m. E of Laredo in a cattle ranching area.

•HEDLEY, Town; Donley County; Pop. 380; Zip Code 79237; Lat. 34-52.1 N, Long. 100-39.4 W; NW Texas; 75 m. SE of Amarillo.

•HEMPHILL, City; Sabine County Seat; Pop. 1,353; Zip Code 75948; Elev. 257; Lat. 31-20.4 N, Long. 93-50.9 W; E Texas; 80 m. N of Beaumont; Named for *John Hemphill,* a Republic of Texas justice.

•HEMPSTEAD, City; Waller County Seat; Pop. 3,456; Zip Code 77445; Elev. 251; Lat. 30-05.8 N, Long. 96-04.6 W; SE Texas; 50 m. W of Houston.

•HENDERSON, City; Rusk County Seat; Pop. 11,473; Zip Code 75652; Elev. 505; Lat. 32-09.1 N, Long. 94-48.0 W; E Texas; 22 m. S of Longview.

•HENRIETTA, City; Clay County Seat; Pop. 3,149; Zip Code 76365; Elev. 886; Lat. 33-48.8 N, Long. 98-11.8 W; N Texas.

•HEREFORD, City; Deaf Smith County Seat; Pop. 15,853; Zip Code 79045; Elev. 3,806; Lat. 34-49.3 N, Long. 102-23.9 W; NW Texas. It was named for early herds of Hereford cattle.

•**HERMLEIGH**, Scurry County; Pop. 725; Zip Code 79526; Elev. 2,392; NW central Texas; 10 m. SE of Snyder. Citizens voted in 1907 to name the town Hermlin for founders *Harry Harlin* and *R.C. Herm*, but documenters in Washington changed the suggestion to a more euphonious one.

•**HICO**, City; Hamilton County; Pop. 1,375; Zip Code 76457; Lat. 31-58.9 N, Long. 98-01.9 W; Central Texas; 70 m. NW of Waco. Founder *J.R.Alford* named this town for his native town in Kentucky. It may also come from the name of the local Indian tribe, also spelled Hueco.

•**HIDALGO**, City; Hidalgo County; Pop. 2,288; Zip Code 78557; Lat. 26-06.3 N, Long. 98-15.6 W; S Texas; Just N of Renyosa, Mexico on the Rio Grande. This town, named for Mexican Revolutionary leader *Miguel Hidalgo* (1753-1811), has survived floods, bandit raids and droughts.

•**HIGGINS**, City; Lipscomb County; Pop. 702; Zip Code 79046; Elev. 2,569; Lat. 32-07.2 N, Long. 100-01.5 W; NW Texas; 1 m. W of Oklahoma state line at NE corner of Panhandle.

•**HILLSBORO**, City; Hill County Seat; Pop. 7,397; Zip Code 76645; Elev. 634; Lat. 32-00.5 N, Long. 97-07.6 W; NE central Texas; 35 m. N of Waco.

•**HITCHCOCK**, City; Galveston County; Pop. 6,655; Zip Code 77563; Lat. 29-20.9 N, Long. 95-01.1 W; SE Texas; 6 m. NW of Galveston; Named for *Colonel E.A. Hitchcock*, Mexican War soldier.

•**HOLLAND**, Town; Bell County; Pop. 863; Zip Code 76534; Lat. 30-52.7 N, Long. 97-24.2 W; Central Texas; 15 m. S of Temple.

•**HOLLIDAY**, City; Archer County; Pop. 1,349; Zip Code 76366; Elev. 1,055; Lat. 33-48.8 N, Long. 98-41.5 W; N Texas; 14 m. SW of Wichita Falls.

•**HONDO**, City; Medina County Seat; Pop. 6,057; Zip Code 78861; Elev. 887; Lat. 29-20.9 N, Long. 99-08.6 W; S central Texas; 40 m. W of San Antonio. City was named for the Hondo River.

•**HONEY GROVE**, City; Fannin County; Pop. 1,973; Zip Code 75446; Elev. 668; Lat. 33-35.1 N, Long. 95-54.5 W; NE Texas; 22 m. W of Paris.

•**HOOKS**, City; Bowie County; Pop. 2,507; Zip Code 75561; Elev. 375; Lat. 33-28.0 N, Long. 94-15.5 W; NE Texas; 15 m. W of Texarkana. It was named for landowner *Warren Hooks*.

•**HOUSTON**, City; Fort Bend, Harris & Waller Counties; Harris County Seat; Pop. 1,594,086; Zip Code 770+; Elev. 53; Lat. 29-45.8 N, Long. 95-21.7 W; SE Texas; on Buffalo Bayou, 50 m. NW of Galveston Bay. The founders named the town for *Sam Houston*.

•**HOWE**, Town; Grayson County; Pop. 2,072; Zip Code 75059; Lat. 33-30.4 N, Long. 96-36.9 W; NE Texas; 10 m. S of Sherman, in a farming area.

•**HUGHES SPRINGS**, City; Cass County; Pop. 2,196; Zip Code 75656; Elev. 378; Lat. 33-00.0 N, Long. 94-38.0 W; NE Texas; 60 m. SW of Texarkana. Situated on site of old Choctaw Indian village, the city was named for *Reece Hughes* who visited area on buffalo hunt in 1829 and returned in 1839 to settle here.

•**HUMBLE**, City; Harris County; Pop. 6,729; Zip Code 773+; Elev. 92; Lat. 29-59.9 N, Long. 95-16.0 W; SE Texas; 20 m. NE of Houston. It was originally named for the Humble Oil Company, now Exxon Corporation, which in turn was named for town founder *P.S. Humble*.

•**HUNTINGTON**, City; Angelina County; Pop. 1,672; Zip Code 75949; Lat. 31-16.9 N, Long. 94-34.4 W; E Texas; 10 m. SE of Lufkin; Residential.

•**HUNTSVILLE**, City; Walker County Seat; Pop. 23,936; Zip Code 77340; Elev. 401; Lat. 30-43.4 N, Long. 95-33.0 W; E Texas; 70 m. N of Houston.

•**HURST**, City; Tarrant County; Pop. 31,420; Zip Code 76053; Lat. 32-48.7 N, Long. 97-09.4 W; N Texas; NE suburb of Fort Worth; Name is Anglo-Saxon for "wooded hill."

•**HUTCHINS**, City; Dallas County; Pop. 2,996; Zip Code 75141; Lat. 32-38.9 N, Long. 96-42.7 W; NE Texas; S suburb of Dallas.

•**HUTTO**, Town; Williamson County; Pop. 659; Zip Code 78634; Lat. 30-32.7 N, Long. 97-32.7 W; Central Texas; 26 m. NE of Austin.

•**IDALOU**, Town; Lubbock County; Pop. 2,348; Zip Code 79329; Lat. 33-39.8 N, Long. 101-40.7 W; NW Texas; 11 m. NE of Lubbock. *Ida Bassett* and *Lou Bacon*, founding mothers of this town, gave it its name.

•**IMPACT**, Town, Taylor County; Pop. 54; N central Texas; N suburb of Abilene; Incorporated in 1960 and named by an advertising man. The Impact Advertising Company offered the only liquor sales in the Abilene area until 1978.

•**INDEPENDENCE**, Village; Washington County; Pop. 140; Elev. 321; E central Texas; 30 m. S of Bryan. Original name Coles Settlement; name changed in 1836 to commemorate independence of Texas from Mexico.

•**INGLESIDE**, City; San Patricio County; Pop. 5,436; Zip Code 78362; Lat. 27-52.9 N, Long. 97-12.7 W; S Texas; across bay from Corpus Christi.

•**INGRAM**, Village; Kerr County; Pop. 1,949; Zip Code 78025; Elev. 1,600; Central Texas; 5 m. W of Kerrville. On north bank of Guadalupe River, city founded 1883 by *J.C.W. Ingram* who built a store and conducted church services.

•**IOWA PARK**, Town; Wichita County; Pop. 6,184; Zip Code 76367; Lat. 33-57.1 N, Long. 98-39.9 W; N Texas; 11 m. W of Wichita Falls; a small airport serves this community.

•**IRAAN**, City; Pecos County; Pop. 1,358; Zip Code 79744; Elev. 2,200;; Lat. 30-54.8 N, Long. 101-53.9 W; W Texas; 95 m. S of Odessa. Name, chosen in a contest, combines names of the townsite owners, *Ira and Ann Yates*.

•**IREDELL**, City; Bosque County; Pop. 407; Zip Code 76649; Lat. 31-59.1 N, Long. 97-52.2 W; Central Texas; 60 m. NW of Waco.

•**IRION COUNTY**, W central Texas; 1,073 sq. miles; Pop. 1,397; Seat - Mertzon; Est. March 7, 1889; Named after *Robert Anderson Irion*, a Texas Republic leader.

•**IRVING**, City; Dallas County; Pop. 109,943; Zip Code 750+; Elev. 460; Lat. 32-48.8 N, Long. 96-56.2 W; NE Texas; 9 m. W of Dallas.

•**ITALY**, Town; Ellis County; Pop. 1,306; Zip Code 76651; Elev. 576; Lat. 32-11.0 N, Long. 96-53.0 W; NE central Texas; 45 m. S of Dallas. *Gabriel J. Penn* named the town after returning from a visit to Italy and discovering similar weather and terrain in this area.

•**ITASCA**, City; Hill County; Pop. 1,600; Zip Code 76055; Elev. 704; Lat. 32-09.5 N, Long. 97-08.9 W; NE central Texas; 45 m. S of Fort Worth. It was named by a railroad worker for Lake Itasca, Minnesota, and was formally established in 1881.

•**JACKSBORO**, City; Jack County Seat; Pop. 4,000; Zip Code 76056; Elev. 1,074; Lat. 33-13.1 N, Long. 98-09.8 W; N Texas; 60 m. NW of Fort Worth.

•**JACKSONVILLE**, City; Cherokee County; Pop. 12,264; Zip Code 75766; Elev. 516; Lat. 31-57.9 N, Long. 95-16.5 W; E Texas; 30 m. S of Tyler.

•**JASPER**, City; Jasper County Seat; Pop. 6,959; Zip Code 75951; Elev. 221; E Texas; 80 m. N of Beaumont. The building of *John Bevil's* log cabin in 1824 marked the beginning of this settlement, which was named in honor of *Sergeant William Jasper*, South Carolina hero of the American Revolution.

•**JAYTON**, Town; Kent County; Pop. 638; Zip Code 79528; Elev. 2,016; Lat. 33-14.9 N, Long. 100-34.4 W; NW Texas; 80 m. SE of Lubbock.

•**JEFFERSON**, City; Marion County Seat; Pop. 2,643; Zip Code 75657; Elev. 191; Lat. 32-45.7 N, Long. 94-20.8 W; NE Texas; 15 m. N of Marshall on Caddo Lake. It is named in honor of President Thomas Jefferson.

•**JEWETT**, City; Leon County; Pop. 597; Zip Code 75846; Lat. 31-21.6 N, Long. 96-08.7 W; E central Texas; 60 m. E of Waco.

•**JOHNSON CITY**, City; Blanco County Seat; Pop. 872; Zip Code 78636; Elev. 1,197; Lat. 30-16.6 N, Long. 98-24.6 W; Central Texas; 50 m. W of Austin in ragged hills near the Edwards Plateau; Named for pioneer *Johnson* family, ancestors of *Lyndon B. Johnson*.

•**JOSHUA**, City; Johnson County; Pop. 1,470; Zip Code 76058; Lat. 32-27.7 N, Long. 96-23.3 W; N central Texas; 30 m. S of Fort Worth in a growing residential area.

•**JOURDANTON**, City; Atascosa County Seat; Pop. 2,743; Zip Code 78026; Elev. 491; Lat. 28-54.8 N, Long. 98-32.6 W; S Texas; 50 m. S of San Antonio.

•**JUNCTION**, City; Kimble County Seat; Pop. 2,593; Zip Code 76849; Elev. 2,180; Lat. 30-29.4 N, Long. 99-46.3 W; W central Texas; 100 m. SE of San Angelo.

•**JUSTIN**, City; Denton County; Pop. 920; Zip Code 76247; Lat. 33-05.2 N, Long. 97-17.9 W; N Texas; Suburb of Denton.

•**KARNACK**, Village; Harrison County; Pop. 775; Zip Code 75661; Elev. 237; NE Texas; 15 m. NE of Longview on Caddo Lake. The city is named for a point of ancient historical reference in Egypt.

•**KARNES CITY**, Town; Karnes County Seat; Pop. 3,296; Zip Code 78118; Elev. 404; Lat. 28-53.1 N, Long. 97-54.0 W; S Texas; 50 m. SE of San Antonio. Name honors *Henry W. Karnes*, Texas Revolutionary figure and Indian fighter.

•**KATY**, City; Fort Bend, Harris & Waller Counties; Pop. 5,660; Zip Code 774+; Lat. 29-47.1 N, Long. 95-49.3 W; SE Texas; Residential area near Houston; Named for "The Katy", a common name for the Missouri, Kansas and Texas Railroad.

•**KAUFMAN**, City; Kaufman County Seat; Pop. 4,658; Zip Code 75142; Elev. 440; Lat. 32-35.3 N, Long. 96-18.6 W; NE Texas; 30 m. SE of Dallas.

•**KEENE**, City; Johnson County; Pop. 3,013; Zip Code 76059; Elev. 890; Lat. 32-23.7 N, Long. 97-19.6 W; N central Texas; 25 m. S of Fort Worth. This growing town was named for a leader in the Seventh Day Adventist Church, whose members dominate the community.

•**KEMAH**, City; Galveston County; Pop. 1,304; Zip Code 77565; Lat. 29-32.7 N, Long. 95-01.3 W; SE Texas; 12 m. N of Galveston on the Bay; Name is Indian for "facing the winds," since the place received blusters from Galveston Bay.

•**KEMP**, Town; Kaufman County; Pop. 1,035; Zip Code 75143; Lat. 32-26.4 N, Long. 96-13.8 W; NE Texas; 45 m. SE of Dallas in a cattle raising area.

•**KENDLETON**, Town; Fort Bend County; Pop. 606; Zip Code 77451; Elev. 102; Lat. 29-27.0 N, Long. 95-59.6 W; SE Texas; 45 m. S of Houston.

•**KENEDY**, City; Karnes County; Pop. 4,356; Zip Code 78119; Elev. 271; Lat. 28-49.1 N, Long. 97-51.1 W; S Texas; 60 m. SE of San Antonio.

•**KENNARD**, City; Houston County; Pop. 424; Zip Code 75847; Lat. 31-21.7 N, Long. 95-11.1 W; E Texas; In Davy Crockett National Forest; Rural.

•**KENNEDALE**, City; Tarrant County; Pop. 2,594; Zip Code 76060; Lat. 32-38.8 N, Long. 97-13.2 W; N Texas; 8 m. SE of Fort Worth.

•**KERENS**, City; Navarro County; Pop. 1,582; Zip Code 75144; Lat. 32-07.8 N, Long. 96-13.7 W; NE central Texas; 14 m. E of Corsicana in a farming area; Fertilizers are manufactured.

•**KERMIT**, City; Wingler County Seat; Pop. 8,015; Zip Code 79745; Elev. 2,890; Lat. 31-51.5 N, Long. 103-05.6 W; W Texas; 45 m. W of Odessa. The town was named for *President Theodore Roosevelt's* 21 year old son in 1910.

•**KERRVILLE**, City; Kerr County Seat; Pop. 15,276; Zip Code 78028; Lat. 30-02.8 N, Long. 99-08.4 W; SW central Texas; 65 m. NW of San Antonio on the Guadalupe River.

•**KILGORE**, City; Gregg & Rusk Counties; Pop. 10,968; Zip Code 75662; Elev. 371; NE Texas; 120 m. E of Dallas.

•**KILLEEN**, City; Bell County; Pop. 46,296; Zip Code 765+; Elev. 833; Central Texas; 30 m. W of Temple. City is edged by 218,000-acre Fort Hood. Named for *Frank Kileen*, a civil engineer of the Santa Fe Railroad that built across county in 1822.

•**KINGSLAND**, Village; Llano County; Pop. 2,216; Zip Code 78639; Elev. 856; Central Texas; 60 m. NW of Austin in Highland Lakes area.

•**KINGSVILLE**, City; Kleberg County Seat; Pop. 28,808; Zip Code 78363; Lat. 27-31.0 N, Long. 97-52.0 W; S Texas; 30 m. SW of Corpus Christi. It is named for the local King Ranch.

•**KIRBYVILLE**, City; Jasper County; Pop. 1,972; Zip Code 75956; Elev. 101; Lat. 30-39.7 N, Long. 93-53.6 W; E Texas; 40 m. N of Beaumont. Town was named for sawmill operator *John Kirby*.

•**KIRVIN**, Town; Freestone County; Pop. 107; Zip Code 75848; Lat. 31-45.9 N, Long. 96-19.8 W; E central Texas.

•**KNOX CITY**, City; Knox County; Pop. 1,546; Zip Code 79529; Lat. 33-25.1 N, Long. 99-48.8 W; N Texas; 60 m. N of Abilene. The town is named for *General Henry Knox*.

•**KOSSE**, Town; Limestone County; Pop. 484; Zip Code 76653; Lat. 31-18.4 N, Long. 96-37.8 W; E central Texas; 40 m. SE of Waco.

•**KOUNTZE**, City; Hardin County Seat; Pop. 2,716; Zip Code 77625; Elev. 85; Lat. 30-22.4 N, Long. 94-18.9 W; E central Texas; 40 m. SE of Tyler.

•**KRESS**, City; Swisher County; Pop. 783; Zip Code 79052; Lat. 34-22.0 N, Long. 101-45.1 W; NW Texas; 10 m. N of Plainview in a ranching area.

•**KRUM**, City; Denton County; Pop. 917; Zip Code 76249; Lat. 33-15.7 N, Long. 97-14.4 W; N Texas; Suburb of Denton.

•**KYLE**, Town; Hays County; Pop. 2,093; Zip Code 78640; Lat. 29-59.3 N, Long. 97-52.7 W; S central Texas; 20 m. SW of Austin.

•**LA COSTE**, City; Medina County; Pop. 862; Zip Code 78039; Lat. 29-18.6 N, Long. 98-48.8 W; S central Texas; 24 m. W of San Antonio.

•**LA FERIA**, City; Cameron County; Pop. 3,395; Zip Code 78559; S Texas; 8 m. W of Harlingen near the Rio Grande in a lush tropical and citrus fruit-growing area.

•**LA GRANGE**, City; Fayette County Seat; Pop. 3,768; Zip Code 78945; Elev. 272; SE central Texas; 65 m. SE of Austin on the Colorado River.

•**LA JOYA**, City; Hidalgo County; Pop. 2.018; Zip Code 78560; Lat. 26-13.7 N, Long. 98-26.8 W; S Texas; Near the Rio Grande; Name is taken from Spanish word for "jewel".

•**LA WARD**, City; Jackson County; Pop. 218; Zip Code 77970; SE Texas; 40 m. E of Victoria; Named for early settler *Lafayette Ward*.

•**LADONIA**, Town; Fannin County; Pop. 761; Zip Code 75449; Lat. 33-25.4 N, Long. 95-56.9 W; NE Texas; 80 m. NE of Dallas; Name is from Spanish word "La Dona", meaning "the lady".

•**LAKE DALLAS**, City; Denton County; Pop. 3,177; Zip Code 75065; Elev. 581; N Texas; N suburb of Dallas.

•**LAKE JACKSON**, City; Brazoria County; Pop. 19,102; Zip Code 77566; Lat. 29-02.6 N, Long. 95-26.5 W; SE Texas; 30 m. SW of Galveston on the Gulf, considered part of the Brazosport area.

•**LAKE TANGLEWOOD**, Village; Randall County; Pop. 485; NW Texas.

•**LAKE WORTH**, City; Tarrant County; Pop. 4,394; Zip Code 76135; N Texas; 9 m. W of downtown Fort Worth. This village grew around the 5,000 acre reservoir by the same name.

•**LA MARQUE**, City; Galveston County; Pop. 15,372; Zip Code 77568; Elev. 17; SE Texas; 13 m. W of Galveston in a residential area. This city, once known as Buttermilk Station, became La Marque after the Civil War when post mistress *Madame St. Ambrose* renamed it. The name is French for "the mark."

•**LAMESA**, City; Dawson County Seat; Pop. 11,790; Zip Code 79331; Elev. 2,975; Lat. 32-44.1 N, Long. 101-57.5 W; NW Texas; 65 m. S of Lubbock. Cotton, cattle and black-eyed peas are the mainstays of this town. Its position on the plains at the edge of Cap Rock gave LaMesa its name, which makes one word of the Spanish "la mesa", "the table".

•**LAMPASAS**, City; Lampasas County Seat; Pop. 6,165; Zip Code 76550; Elev. 1,025; Lat. 31-04.0 N, Long. 98-11.1 W; Central Texas; 60 m. NW of Austin. Named for the Spanish word for *water lily*.

•**LANCASTER**, City; Dallas County; Pop. 14,807; Zip Code 751+; Lat. 32-35.4 N, Long. 96-45.2 W; NE Texas; S suburb of Dallas in a growing residential area.

•**LANEVILLE**, Village; Rusk County; Pop. 200; Zip Code 75667; Elev. 415; E Texas; 40 m. SE of Tyler. Developed in the 1880s near the Angelina River, Laneville was named because it grew around a junction of four lanes.

•**LANGTRY**, Val Verde County; Zip Code 78871; Elev. 1,315; Lat. 29-48.5 N, Long. 101-33.5 W; SW Texas; Just N of Mexico border on Rio Grande.

•**LA PORTE**, City; Harris County; Pop. 14,062; Zip Code 77571; Elev. 28; Lat. 29-39.9 N, Long. 95-01.0 W; SE Texas; On Galveston Bay, 15 m. E of Houston. It was given its name "The Door" by French settlers in 1889 when the city was founded on upper Galveston Bay.

•**LAREDO**, City; Webb County Seat; 91,449; Zip Code 780+; Elev. 438; S Texas 140 m. SW of San Antonio on the Rio Grande. On May 15, 1755, with three or four families, *Thomas Sanchez* formally founded the Villa de Laredo.

•**LA VERNIA**, City; Wilson County; Pop. 632; Zip Code 78121; Lat. 29-21.1 N, Long. 98-06.8 W; S central Texas; 20 m. E of San Antonio. Town was settled by *William Wiseman* and his family in 1850. Originally named "Live Oak Grove," it was changed in 1859 to the Spanish name for "the tree," or "the green."

•**LAVON**, Town; Collin County; Pop. 185; Zip Code 75066; NE Texas; 30 m. NE of Dallas on a lake by the same name; Residential - recreational.

•**LAWN**, Town; Taylor County; Pop. 390; Zip Code 79530; NW central Texas; 35 m. S of Abilene; Named for the residential yards in town.

•**LEAGUE CITY**, City; Galveston County; Pop. 16,578; Zip Code 77573; Lat. 29-30.5 N, Long. 95-05.6 W; SE Texas; 20 m. NW of Galveston; Residential.

•**LEAKEY**, City; Real County Seat; Pop. 468; Zip Code 78873; Elev. 1,609; Lat. 29-43.7 N, Long. 99-45.8 W; SW central Texas; 40 m. N of Uvalde.

•**LEANDER**, City; Williamson County; Pop. 2,179; Zip Code 78641; Lat. 30-34.8 N, Long. 97-51.2 W; Central Texas; 20 m. NW of Austin.

•**LEFORS**, Town; Gray County; Pop. 829; Zip Code 79054; Lat. 35-26.2 N, Long. 100-48.4 W; NW Texas; 11 m. SE of Pampa.

•**LEONA**, Town; Leon County; Pop. 165; Zip Code 75850; Lat. 31-09.3 N, Long. 95-58.1 W; E central Texas; 50 m. NE of Leona on Boggy Creek.

•**LEONARD**, City; Fannin County; Pop. 1,421; Zip Code 75452; Elev. 704; Lat. 33-23.0 N, Long. 96-14.9 W; NE Texas; 30 m. SE of Sherman.

•**LEROY**, City; McLennan County; Pop. 253; Zip Code 76654; Lat. 31-43.8 N, Long. 97-00.8 W; Central Texas; Near Waco.

•**LEVELLAND**, City; Hockley County Seat; Pop. 13,809; Zip Code 79336; Elev. 3,523; Lat. 33-35.2 N, Long. 102-22.7 W; NW Texas; 30 m. W of Lubbock. Appropriately named for the surrounding terrain.

•**LEWISVILLE**, City; Denton County; Pop. 24,273; Zip Code 24,145; Elev. 484; Lat. 33-02.8 N, Long. 96-59.8 W; N Texas; 15 m. SE of Denton.

•**LEXINGTON**, Town; Lee County; Pop. 1,065; Zip Code 78947; Lat. 30-24.8 N, Long. 97-00.5 W; Central Texas; 40 m. NE of Austin.

•**LIBERTY**, City; Liberty County Seat; Pop. 7,945; Zip Code 77575; Elev. 30; Lat. 30-03.3 N, Long. 94-47.7 W; E Texas; 40 m. NE of Houston. Liberty was first named Atascosita, from its position on a frontier highway, the Atascosita Road. Later called Liberty Town, it sent a delegation to the San Felipe de Austin Convention of 1832, and in 1836 a company from Liberty joined *Sam Houston's* army in time to fight the Battle of San Jacinto.

•**LINDALE**, Town; Smith County; Pop. 2,180; Zip Code 75771; Lat. 32-30.9 N, Long. 95-24.7 W; NE Texas; 80 m. SE of Dallas.

•**LINDEN**, City; Cass County Seat; Pop. 2,443; Zip Code 75563; Elev. 270; Lat. 33-00.7 N, Long. 94-22.0 W; NE Texas; 35 M. N of Marshall. Linden was named for a town in a popular poem by *Thomas Campbell.*

•**LIPSCOMB**, Village; Lipscomb County Seat; Pop. 160; Zip Code 79056; Elev. 2,450; NW Texas at NE Panhandle on Wolf Creek. Settled in 1880 on Wolf Creek, it was named for *Abner Smith Lipscomb,* Texas Secretary of State under *Mirabeau B. Lamar.*

•**LITTLE RIVER**, City; Bell County; Pop. 1,155; Zip Code 76554; Lat. 30-59.3 N, Long. 47-21.9 W; Central Texas; 5 m. S of Temple on a river by the same name.

•**LIVERPOOL**, Village; Brazoria County; Pop. 602; Zip Code 77577; Lat. 29-17.6 N, Long. 95-16.6 W; SE Texas; Named for English port city because it lies on the Gulf Coast.

•**LIVINGSTON**, Town; Polk County Seat; Pop. 4,928; Zip Code 77351; Elev. 194; Lat. 30-42.6 N, Long. 94-56.2 W; E Texas; 70 m. NE of Houston.

•**LLANO**, City; Llano County Seat; Pop. 3,071; Zip Code 78643; Elev. 1,029; Lat. 30-45.0 N, Long. 98-40.6 W; Central Texas; 65 m. NW of Austin. Name means "level land" in an Indian language.

•**LOCKHART**, City; Caldwell County Seat; Pop. 7,953; Zip Code 78644; Elev. 518; Lat. 29-53.2 N, Long. 97-40.2 W; S Central Texas; 30 m. S of Austin; Named for townsite owner and Texas soldier *Byrd Lockhart.*

•**LOCKNEY**, Town; Floyd County; Pop. 2,334; Zip Code 79241; Lat. 34-07.3 N, Long. 101-26.6 W; NW Texas; 20 m. SE of Plainview in a ranching area.

•**LOLITA**, Village; Jackson County; Pop. 1,200; Zip Code 77971; SE Texas; 30 m. E of Victoria. The town was named in 1910 for *Lolita Reese,* who claimed as her ancestors a soldier at the battle of San Jacinto and a member of the Mier Expedition. The name was nearly changed during the 1950s when the movie *Lolita* scandalized townspeople.

•**LOMETA**, City; Lampasas County; Pop. 666; Zip Code 76853; Elev. 1,484; Lat. 31-12.0 N, Long. 98-23.5 W; Central Texas; 90 m. NW of Austin; Name is from Spanish Lomita, or "little hill." entertainment.

•**LONE OAK**, Town; Hunt County; Pop. 467; Zip Code 75453; Lat. 32-59.7 N, Long. 95-56.7 W; NE Texas; 15 m. SE of Greenville.

•**LONE STAR**, Town; Morris County; Pop. 2,036; Zip Code 75668; Lat. 32-55.1 N, Long. 94-42.6 W; NE Texas; 40 m. NW of Marshall. Incorporated in 1948, Lone Star was named for the Lone Star Steel Company, which in turn was taken from the state's nickname.

•**LONGVIEW**, City; Gregg & Harrison Counties; Gregg County Seat; Pop. 62,762; Zip Code 756+; Elev. 339; Lat. 32-29.5 N, Long. 94-44.0 W; NE Texas; 65 m. W of Shreveport, Louisiana.

•**LORAINE**, Town; Mitchell County; Pop. 929; Zip Code 79532; Lat. 32-24.5 N, Long. 100-42.7 W; NW central Texas. A landowner named the place for his wife, *Loraine Crandall.*

•**LORENA**, Town; McLennan County; Pop. 619; Zip Code 76655; Lat. 31-23.1 N, Long. 97-12.9 W; Central Texas; 10 m. S of Waco.

•**LORENZO**, Town; Crosby County; Pop. 1,394; Zip Code 79343; Lat. 33-40.4 N, Long. 101-32.2 W; NW Texas; 25 m. E of Lubbock.

•**LOS ANGELES**, Village; La Salle County; Pop. 140; Zip Code 78014; S Texas; 75 m. N of Laredo. Town was developed in 1923 by San Antonio land company. One promoter believed the area was similar to that of Los Angeles, California.

•**LOS PRESNOS**, City; Cameron County; Pop. 2,173; Zip Code 78566; Lat. 26-04.3 N, Long. 97-28.6 W; S Texas; 12 m. N of Brownsville. Its name is Spanish for "the ash trees."

•**LOTT**, City; Falls County; Pop. 865; Zip Code 76656; Elev. 522; Lat. 31-12.3 N, Long. 97-02.0 W; Central Texas; 26 m. NE of Temple on a small lake.

•**LOVELADY**, City; Houston County; Pop. 509; Zip Code 75851; Lat. 31-07.7 N, Long. 95-26.6 W; E Texas; 33 m. N of Huntsville.

•**LUBBOCK**, City; Lubbock County Seat; Pop. 173,979; Zip Code 794+; Elev. 3,241; Lat. 33-35.0 N, Long. 101-50.6 W; NW Texas; 110 m. S of Amarillo. Nmaed after *Thomas Lubbock,* a Confederate leader.

•**LUCKENBACH**, Village; Gillespie County; Pop. 25; Central Texas. *Mrs. Albert Luckenbach* established the post office here in 1886. It was discontinued in 1975.

•**LUEDERS**, City; Jones County; Pop. 420; Zip Code 79533; Lat. 32-47.8 N, Long. 99-37.3 W; NW central Texas; On Clear Fork of the Brazos River, 30 m. N of Abilene.

•**LUFKIN**, City; Angelina County Seat; Pop. 28,562; Zip Code 75901; Elev. 326; Lat. 31-20.8 N, Long. 94-43.5 W; E Texas; 115 m. N of Houston.

•**LULING**, City; Caldwell County; Pop. 5,039; Zip Code 78648; Elev. 418; Lat. 29-40.8 N, Long. 97-38.8 W; S central Texas; 55 m. NE of San Antonio.

•**LUMBERTON**, City; Hardin County; Pop. 2,480; Zip Code 77711; E Texas; 20 m. N of Beaumont in a heavily timbered area.

•**LYFORD**, Town; Willacy County; Pop. 1,618; Zip Code 78569; Lat. 26-24.5 N, Long. 97-47.5 W; S Texas; 15 m. N of Harlingen.

•**LYONS**, Burleson County; Zip Code 77863; Lat. 30-23.2 N, Long. 96-33.8 W; E central Texas; 20 m. SE of Bryan; Named for early shopkeeper *W.A. Lyon.*

•**LYTLE**, City; Atascosa, Bexar & Medina Counties; Pop. 1,920; Zip Code 78052; Lat. 29-13.9 N, Long. 98-47.8 W; S Texas; 20 m. SW of San Antonio.

•**MABANK**, Town; Kaufman county; Pop. 1,437; Zip Code 75147; Lat. 32-21.9 N, Long. 96-06.1 W; NE Texas; 55 m. SE of Dallas on N shore of Cedar Creek Lake. *Dodge Mason* and *Tom Eubank* were early settlers here. Parts of each of their names were used for the name of this town.

•**MADISONVILLE**, City; Madison County Seat; Pop. 3,660; Zip Code 77864; Elev. 278; Lat. 30-57.0 N, Long. 95-54.8 W; E central Texas. Named for fourth President of the United States it is today the center for cotton, cattle and lumber in the region.

•**MAGNOLIA**, Town; Montgomery County; Pop. 867; Zip Code 77355; Lat. 30-12.6 N, Long. 95-45.1 W; E Texas; 40 m. NW of Houston.

•**MALAKOFF**, City; Henderson County; Pop. 2,082; Zip Code 75148; Lat. 32-10.2 N, Long. 96-00.8 W; NE Texas; 25 m. E of Corsicana at S tip of Cedar Creek Lake.

•**MALONE**, Town; Hill County; Pop. 315; Zip Code 76660; Lat. 31-54.9 N, Long. 96-53.7 W; NE central Texas; 15 m. SE of Hillsboro.

•**MANOR**, City; Travis County; Pop. 1,044; Zip Code 78653; Lat. 30-20.5 N, Long. 97-33.4 W; Central Texas; 10 m. NE of Austin; Residential.

•**MANSFIELD**, City; Johnson & Tarrant Counties; Pop. 8,092; Zip Code 76063; Lat. 32-33.9 N, Long. 97-08.5 W; N Texas; 15 m. SE of Fort Worth; Residential. City was named for early settlers *R.S. Mann* and *Julian Field*.

•**MANVEL**, City; Brazoria County; Pop. 3,549; Pop. 713; Zip Code 77578; Lat. 29-27.8 N, Long. 95-21.4 W; SE Texas; 20 m. S of Houston.

•**MARATHON**, Village; Brewster County; Pop. 718; Zip Code 79842; Elev. 4,043; W Texas. It was named by a sea captain who thought the area looked like Marathon, Greece.

•**MARBLE FALLS**, Town; Burnet County; Pop. 3,252; Zip Code 78654; Elev. 764; Lat. 30-34.5 N, Long. 98-16.4 W; Central Texas; On the Colorado River, 40 m. NW of Austin. This town in the Hill Country was named for nearby Colorado River waterfalls over marble out-croppings.

•**MARFA**, City; Presidio County Seat; Pop. 2,466; Zip Code 79843; Elev. 4,668; Lat. 30-18.5 N, Long. 104-01.1 W; W Texas; 175 m. SE of El Paso.

•**MARIETTA**, City; Cass County; Pop. 169; Zip Code 75566; Lat. 33-10.3 N, Long. 94-32.7 W; NE Texas; 70 m. N of Marshall.

•**MARION**, City; Guadalupe County; Pop. 674; Zip Code 78124; S central Texas; 25 m. NE of San Antonio; Named for *General Francis Marion.*

•**MARQUEZ**, City; Leon County; Pop. 231; Zip Code 77865; Lat. 31-14.4 N, Long. 96-15.2 W; E central Texas; 60 m. N of Bryan.

•**MARSHALL**, City; Harrison County Seat; Pop. 24,921; Zip Code 75670; Elev. 375; 32-33.0 N, Long. 94-23.0 W; NE Texas; 70 m. S of Texarkana. Marshall, named for U.S. *Chief Justice John Marshall,* was established in 1841.

•**MART**, City; McLennan County; Pop. 2,324; Zip Code 76664; Lat. 31-32.6 N, Long. 96-49.6 W; Central Texas; 17 m. E of Waco.

•**MASON**, City; Mason County Seat; Pop. 2,153; Zip Code 76856; Elev. 1,450; Lat. 30-45.0 N, Long. 99-14.0 W; Central Texas; 120 m. NW of San Antonio near the Llano River. Named after *Charles H. Mason,* who was killed during the Mexican War.

•**MATADOR**, Town; Motley County Seat; Pop. 1,052; Zip Code 79244; Elev. 2,347; Lat. 34-00.7 N, Long. 100-49.3 W; NW Texas; 60 m. SE of Plainview. Named for its promixity to the great Matador Ranch.

•**MATHIS**, City; San Patricio County; Pop. 5,667; Zip Code 78368; Elev. 161; Lat. 28-05.8 N, Long. 97-49.7 W; S Texas; 40 m. NW of Corpus Christi.

•**MAUD**, City; Bowie County; Pop. 1,059; Zip Code 75567; Elev. 284; Lat. 33-20.2 N, Long. 94-20.7 W; NE Texas; 20 m. SW of Texarkana.

•**MAYPEARL**, City; Ellis county; Pop. 626; Zip Code 76064; Lat. 32-18.6 N, Long. 97-00.8 W; NE central Texas; 35 m. S of Dallas. The town, incorporated in 1914, was named for *May Pearl Trammel,* wife of a railroad engineer.

•**MCALLEN**, City; Hidalgo County; Pop. 67,042; Zip Code 78501; Lat. 26-12.1 N, Long. 98-13.8 W; S Texas; 50 m. NW of Brownsville, near the Rio Grande.

•**MCCAMEY**, City; Upton County; Pop. 2,436; Zip Code 79752; Elev. 2,241; Lat. 31-08.2 N, Long. 102-13.5 W; W Texas; 100 m. W of San Angelo. Then an oil driller named *McCamey* hit a gusher. In less than a year, McCamey was brawling boom town of 10,000 housed in tents and hastily constructed buildings.

•**MCGREGOR**, City; McLennan County; Pop. 4,513; Zip Code 76657; Elev. 713; Lat. 31-26.6 N, Long. 97-24.4 W; Central Texas; 19 m. W of Waco.

•**MCKINNEY**, City; Collin County Seat; Pop. 16,249; Zip Code 75069; Elev. 612; Lat. 33-11.9 N, Long. 96-37.1 W; NE Texas; 30 m. S of Sherman. Settled in 1845, city and county were named for *Collin McKinney,* a signer of the Texas Declaration of Independence and leader in establishment of the Disciples of Christ (Christian Church) in Texas.

•**MCLEAN**, Town; Gray County; Pop. 1,160; Zip Code 79057; Lat. 35-14.0 N, Long. 100-36.1 W; NW Texas; 70 m. E of Amarillo.

•**MEADOW**, Town; Terry County; Pop. 571; Zip Code 79345; Lat. 33-20.2 N, Long. 102-12.3 W; NW Texas; 20 m. SW of Lubbock.

•**MELISSA**, Town; Collin County; Pop. 604; Zip Code 75071; Lat. 33-17.1 N, Long. 96-34.4 W; NE Texas; 40 m. N of Dallas.

•**MELVIN**, Town; McCulloch County; Pop. 202; Zip Code 76858; Lat. 31-11.8 N, Long. 99-34.7 W; Central Texas; 50 m. E of San Angelo.

•**MEMPHIS**, City; Hall County Seat; Pop. 3,352; Zip Code 79245; Elev. 2,067; Lat. 34-43.5 N, Long. 100-32.5 W; NW Texas.

•**MENARD**, City; Menard County Seat; Pop. 1,697; Zip Code 76859; Elev. 1,960; Lat. 30-55.1 N, Long. 99-47.2 W; W central Texas; on the San Saba River, 65 m. SE of San Angelo. Named after *Michael Branaman Menard,* founder of Galveston.

•**MENTONE**, Village; Loving County Seat; Pop. 91; Zip Code 79754; Elev. 2,683; W Texas.

•**MERCEDES**, City; Hidalgo County; Pop. 11,851; Zip Code 78570; Elev. 61; Lat. 26-09.0 N, Long. 97-54.9 W; S Texas; 18 m. W of Harlingen. had its establishment in 1906, in the early days of the citrus boom, and was named for *Mercedes Diaz,* wife of the then President of Mexico.

•**MERIDIAN**, City; Bosque County Seat; Pop. 1,330; Zip Code 76665; Elev. 791; Lat. 31-55.5 N, Long. 97-39.3 W; Central Texas; 40 m. NW of Waco; Named because it lies at the ninety-eighth meridian.

•**MERKEL**, Town; Taylor County; Pop. 2,493; Zip Code 79536; Lat. 32-28.2 N, Long. 100-00.8 W; NW central Texas; 15 mi. W of Abilene.

•**MERTZON**, Town; Irion County Seat; Pop. 687; Zip Code 76941; Elev. 2,184; Lat. 31-15.5 N, Long. 100-49.0 W; W central Texas; 28 m. SW of San Angelo. Established 1910 as stop on Kansas City, Mexico and Orient Railroad; named for a director of the line.

•**MESQUITE**, City; Dallas County; Pop. 67,053; Elev. 491; Zip Code 751+; Lat 32-45.9 N, Long. 96-35.8 W; NE Texas; 10 m. E of Dallas. Named for nearby Mesquite Creek.

•**MEXIA**, City; Limestone County; Pop. 7,094; Zip Code 76667; Elev. 534; Lat. 31-40.9 N, Long. 96-28.8 W; E central Texas; 30 m. S of Corsicana. Established 1871, named for Mexican *General Jose Antonio Mexia* whose family donated townsite.

•**MIAMI**, City; Roberts County Seat; Pop. 813; Zip Code 79059; Elev. 2,802; Lat. 35-41.5 N, Long. 100-38.3 W; NW Texas. The town was named for an Algonquian Indian tribe, native to Ohio; the word *Miami* meant "sweetheart".

•**MIDLAND**, City; Midland County Seat; Pop. 70,525; Zip Code 797+; Elev. 2,779; Lat. 31-59.7 N, Long. 102-04.7 W; W Texas; 20 m. NE of Odessa. Named for location halfway between Fort Worth and El Paso.

•**MIDLOTHIAN**, City; Ellis County; Pop. 3,219; Zip Code 76065; Lat. 32-28.9 N, Long. 96-59.1 W; NE central Texas; 20 m. SW of Dallas. It was named by a railroad workers for the county in Scotland.

•**MILANO**, Town; Milam County; Pop. 468; Zip Code 76556; Lat. 30-42.6 N, Long. 96-51.9 W; Central Texas; 40 m. SE of Temple. Name was originally Milam, as in the county name, but was changed by post office authorities to avoid duplication. Today it bears the name of a great Northern Italian city.

•**MILES**, City; Runnels County; Pop. 720; Zip Code 76861; Elev. 1,800; Lat. 31-35.7 N, Long. 100-10.9 W; W central Texas; 20 m. NE of San Angelo. Named for *Jonathan Miles,* pioneer cattleman and railroad contractor.

•**MILLSAP**, Town; Parker County; Pop. 439; Zip Code 76066; Lat. 32-44.8 N, Long. 88-00.6 W; N central Texas; 33 m. W of Fort Worth.

•**MINEOLA**, City; Wood County; Pop. 4,346; Zip Code 75773; Lat. 32-39.7 N, Long. 95-29.3 W; NE Texas; 20 m. N of Tyler.

•**MINERAL WELLS**, City; Palo Pinto & Parker Counties; Pop. 14,468; Zip Code 76067; Elev. 925; Lat. 32-48.4 N, Long. 98-06.8 W; N central Texas; 50 m. W of Fort Worth. Discovery of medicinal qualities in waters made city nationally famous in the nineteenth century.

•**MISSION**, City; Hidalgo County; Pop. 22,589; Zip Code 78572; Elev. 134; Lat. 26-12.9 N, Long. 98-19.5 W; S Texas; 6 m. W of McAllen. Town was laid out on the LaLomita Rancho; property of the Oblate Fathers, who, carrying on the work started by Franciscans 100 years before, founded a chapel in 1824 on the north bank of the Rio Grande, south of town.

•**MISSOURI CITY**, City; Fort Bend & Harris Counties; Pop. 24,533; Zip Code 774+; Lat. 29-37.0 N, Long. 95-32.1 W; SE Texas; 10 m. SW of Houston; Residential. Named because a number of settlers had read advertisements for the townsite in their local newspapers in Missouri.

•**MOBEETIE**, Town; Wheeler County; Pop. 291; Zip Code 79061; Lat. 35-30.8 N, Long. 100-26.2 W; NW Texas; 30 m. E of Pampa in NE Panhandle.

•**MONAHANS**, City; Ward & Winkler Counties; Ward County Seat; Pop. 8,397; Zip Code 79756; Elev. 2,613; Lat. 31-35.7 N, Long. 102-53.5 W; W Texas; 140 m. W of San Angelo.

•**MONT BELVIEU**, City; Chambers County; Pop. 1,730; Zip Code 77580; Lat. 29-51.0 N, Long. 94-53.4 W; SE Texas; 15 m. N of Baytown; Name means "Beautiful Old Hill."

•**MONTAGUE**, Village; Montague County Seat; Pop. 400; Zip Code 79754; N Texas; 20 m. S of Red River in a farming area. Named for *Daniel Montague,* a pioneer; Red River and Oklahoma state line form N boundary.

•**MONTGOMERY**, City; Montgomery County; Pop. 258; Zip Code 77356; Lat. 30-23.4 N, Long. 95-41.8 W; E Texas; Near W outskirts of Sam Houston National Forest; Named for *Richard Montgomery,* Revolutionary War general.

•**MOODY**, Town; McLennan County; Pop. 1,385; Zip Code 76557; Elev. 783; Lat. 30-50.6 N, Long. 97-24.8 W; Central Texas; 25 m. SW of Waco. Renamed in 1881 to honor *Col. W.L. Moody,* director of the Gulf, Colorado and Santa Fe Railroad, when that line was built through.

•**MORTON**, City; Cochran County Seat; Pop. 2,674; Zip Code 79346; Elev. 3,758; Lat. 33-43.5 N, Long. 102-45.6 W; NW Texas; 40 m. S of Bailey.

•**MOULTON**, Town; Lavaca County; Pop. 1,009; Zip Code 77975; Lat. 29-34.7 N, Long. 97-08.8 W; SE central Texas; 75 m. NE of San Antonio.

•**MOUNT CALM**, City; Hill County; Pop. 393; Zip Code 76673; Lat. 31-45.5 N, Long. 96-52.9 W; NE central Texas; 35 m. SE of Hillsboro on Navasota River.

•**MOUNT ENTERPRISE**, City; Rusk County; Pop. 485; Zip Code 75681; Elev. 480; Lat. 31-55.1 N, Long. 94-40.9 W; E Texas; 20 m. S of Henderson/

•**MOUNT PLEASANT**, City; Titus County Seat; Pop. 11,003; Zip Code 75455; Elev. 416; Lat. 33-09.3 N, Long. 94-58.1 W; NE Texas; 65 m. SW of Texarkana. The town was named for its pleasant wooded location.

•**MOUNT VERNON**, Town; Franklin County Seat; Pop. 2,025; Zip Code 75457; Elev. 476; Lat. 33-11.2 N, Long. 95-13.2 W; NE Texas. The area first settled in 1830 by *Joshua T. Johnson,* has been known as *Keith* and *Lone Star.* In 1875, the new name was chosen, honoring *George Washington's* plantation.

•**MOUNTAIN HOME**, Village; Kerr County; Pop. 96; Zip Code 78058; Elev. 2,135; S central Texas; 18 m. NW of Kerrville.

•**MUENSTER**, City; Cooke County; Pop. 1,408; Zip Code 76252; Elev. 970; Lat. 33-39.1 N, Long. 97-22.6 W; N Texas; 60 m. N of Fort Worth. Founded in 1889 by two brothers, Muenster was named for a city in their fatherland.

•**MULESHOE**, City; Bailey County Seat; Pop. 4,842; Zip Code 79347; Elev. 3,789; Lat. 34-13.4 N, Long. 102-43.4 W; NW Texas; 70 m. NW of Lubbock. Muleshoe is in the center of the Muleshoe Ranch from which it took its name.

•**MULLIN**, Town; Mills County; Pop. 213; Zip Code 76864; Lat. 31-33.4 N, Long. 98-39.9 W; Central Texas; 22 m. SE of Brownwood.

•**MUNDAY**, City; Knox County; Pop. 1,738; Zip Code 76371; Lat. 33-26.8 N, Long. 99-37.6 W; N Texas; 73 m. SW of Witchita Falls in a farming region.

•**MURCHISON**, Town; Henderson County; Pop. 513; Zip Code 75778; Lat. 32-16.6 N, Long. 95-44.9 W; NE Texas; 27 m. W of Tyler.

•**NACOGDOCHES**, City; Nacogdoches County Seat; Pop. 27,149; Zip Code 75961; Elev. 283; E Texas. The Nacogdoches tribe had a permanent village on the site, and beside an Indian trail the Spaniards built their mission.

•**NAPLES**, Town; Morris County; Pop. 1,908; Zip Code 75568; Lat. 33-12.1 N, Long. 94-41.0 W; NE Texas; 65 m. SW of Texarkana; Named for the Italian city.

•NATALIA, City; Medina County; Pop. 1,264; Zip Code 78059; Elev. 686; Lat. 29-11.3 N, Long. 98-51.7 W; S central Texas; 25 m. SW of downtown San Antonio.

•NAVASOTA, City; Grimes County; Pop. 5,971; Zip Code 77868; Elev. 215; Lat. 30-23.3 N, Long. 96-05.3 W; E central Texas; 60 m. NW of Houston.

•NAZARETH, City; Castro County; Pop. 299; Zip Code 79063; Lat. 34-32.6 N, Long. 102-06.3 W; NW Texas; 50 m. S of Amarillo. A Catholic priest named the town for *Jesus'* town.

•NEDERLAND, City; Jefferson County; Pop. 16,855; Zip Code 77627; Elev. 25; Lat. 29-58.5 N, Long. 93-59.5 W; SE Texas; 7 m. SE of Beaumont. It was founded in 1896 by colonists from The Netherlands. The name means "lowland" in Dutch.

•NEEDVILLE, City; Fort Bend County; Pop. 1,428; Zip Code 77461; Lat. 29-23.9 N, Long. 95-50.3 W; SE Texas; 38 m. SW of Houston. The post office was called Needville because the local settlers were needy.

•NEWARK, City; Wise County; Pop. 466; Zip Code 76071; Lat. 33-00.0 N, Long. 97-29.0 W; N Texas; 20 m. N of Fort Worth; Named for New Jersey town.

•NEW BADEN, Town; Robertson County; Zip Code 77870; Elev. 427; E central Texas. It was established in 1880 by *J.G. Meyer*, colonizer who worked with a land company that brought in cultured German colonists principally from Baden.

•NEW BOSTON, Town; Bowie County; Pop. 4,628; Zip Code 75570; Lat. 33-27.6 N, Long. 94-25.3 W; NE Texas; 25 m. E of Texarkana. Named because it is adjacent to and was founded after the town of Boston.

•NEW BRAUNFELS, City; Coman & Guadalupe Counties; Comal County Seat; Pop. 22,402; Zip Code 78130; Elev. 750; Lat. 29-42.0 N, Long. 98-07.7 W; S central Texas; 30 m. NE of San Antonio. Here the quixotic *Prince Carl Zum Solms-Braunfels,* for whom the city is named, established a German settlement in 1845, and, surrounding himself with a retinue of velvet-clad courtiers and soldiers who wore brilliant plumes.

•NEW DEAL, Town; Lubbock County; Pop. 637; Zip Code 79350; Lat 33-44.1 N, Long. 101-50.2 W; NW Texas; 7 m. N of Lubbock. During *President Roosevelt's* "New Deal" era, a school was established here, and townspeople gave their post office a pro-per thank-you.

•NEW LONDON, City; Rusk County; Pop. 942; Zip Code 75682; Elev. 510; Lat. 32-14.8 N, Long. 94-56.3 W; E Texas; 10 m. W of Henderson.

•NEW SUMMERFIELD, City; Cherokee County; Pop. 319; Zip Code 75780; Lat 31-59.9 N, Long. 95-05.7 W; E Texas; 30 m. SE of Tyler.

•NEW ULM, Village; Austin County; Pop. 650; Zip Code 78950; SE Texas; 75 m. W of Houston; Named for the city in Germany by early settlers.

•NEW WAVERLY, Town; Walker County; Pop. 824; Zip Code 77358; Elev. 362; Lat. 30-32.3 N, Long. 95-28.9 W; E Texas; 70 m. N of Houston in Sam Houston National Forest.

•NEWCASTLE, City; Young County; Pop. 688; Zip Code 76372; Elev. 1,126; Lat. 33-11.6 N, Long. 98-44.4 W; N Texas; 50 m. S of Wichita Falls. It was founded in 1908. Because of early coal-mining interest it was named after famous English coal-mining city.

•NEWTON, City; Newton County Seat; Pop. 1,620; Zip Code 75966; Lat. 30-50.9 N, Long. 93-45.6 W; E Texas. Named after *John Newton,* a soldier in the American Revolution.

•NIXON, City; Gonzales & Wilson Counties; Pop. 2,008; Zip Code 78140; Elev. 396; Lat. 29-16.2 N, Long. 97-45.9 W; S central Texas; 45 m. SE of San Antonio.

•NOCONA, City; Montague County; Pop. 2,992; Zip Code 76255; Elev. 988; Lat. 33-47.4 N, Long. 97-43.8 W; N Texas; 50 m. E of cWichita Falls. Nocona was named for *Peta Nocona,* an Indian chief.

•NOME, City; Jefferson County; Pop. 550; Zip Code 77629; Lat. 30-02.1 N, Long. 94-25.4 W; SE Texas; 15 m. W of Beaumont. The town was founded in 1894 as Buttfield, but wa changed nine years later when a mapmaker wrote "Name?" on a drawing of this site. The printers misprinted it as Nome. Another explana-tion may be that it was named for Nome, Alaska, because both Texas and Alaska were experiencing booms, from oil and gold, at that time.

•NORDHEIM, City; DeWitt County; Pop. 369; Zip Code 78141; Lat. 28-55.4 N, Long. 97-36.5 W; S Texas; 22 m. SW of Cuero; Name is German for "North Home."

•NORMANGEE, Town; Leon & Madison Counties; Pop. 636; Zip Code 77871; Lat. 31-01.8 N, Long. 96-07.0 W; E central Texas.

•NORSE, Village, Pop. 110; E Central Texas; 75 mi. SW of Dallas. King Olav V of Norway visited this tiny community in 1982, on Cleng Peerson's 200th birthday.

•NOVICE, City; Coleman County; Pop. 201; Zip Code 79538; Lat. 31-59.4 N, Long. 99-37.4 W; Central Texas; 40 m. SE of Abilene.

•OAKWOOD, Town; Leon County; Pop. 606; Zip Code 75855; Lat. 31-35.1 N, Long. 95-51.0 W; E central Texas; 20 m. SW of Palestine in a rural area; Name is descriptive.

•O'Brien, City; Pop. 212; Zip Code 79539; Lat. 33-22.8 N, Long. 99-50.6 W; N Texas; 70 m. N of Abilene.

•ODEM, City; San Patricio County; Pop. 2,363; Zip Code 78370; Lat. 27-57.0 N, Long. 97-35.0 W; S Texas; 18 m. NW of Corpus Christi in a farming area.

•ODESSA, City; Ector County Seat; Pop. 90,027; Zip Code 797+; Elev. 2,890; Lat. 31-51.5 N, Long. 102-22.5 W; W Texas. It is said that name originated from Russian railroad laborers who com-pared wide, flat prairies with their homeland on steppes of Russia.

•O'DONNELL, City; Dawson & Lynn Counties; Pop. 1,200; Zip Code 79351; Elev. 3,000; Lat. 32-58.0 N, Long. 101-49.8 W; NW Texas; 43 m. S of Lubbock.

•OGLESBY, City; Coryell County; Pop. 470; Zip Code 76561; Lat. 31-25.0 N, Long. 97-30.4 W; Central Texas; 20 m. SW of Waco.

•OLNEY, City; Young County; Pop. 4,060; Zip Code 76374; Elev. 1,184; Lat. 33-22.1 N, Long. 98-45.4 W; N Texas; 45 m. S of Wichita Falls. Named to honor *Richard Olney,* Secretary of State in *Grover Cleveland's* cabinet.

•OLTON, City; Lamb County Seat; Pop. 2,235; Zip Code 79064; Elev. 3,615; Lat. 34-10.8 N, Long. 102-08.1 W; NW Texas; 25 m. W of Plainview in a ranching region.

•OMAHA, City; Morris County; Pop. 960; Zip Code 75571; Lat. 33-10.9 N, Long. 94-44.1 W; NE Texas; 50 m. SW of Texarkana.

•**ONALASKA**, City; Polk County; Pop. 386; Zip Code 77360; Lat. 30-48.3 N, Long. 95-07.1 W; E Texas. *T.G. Rowe*, lumber company owner, named this town for *Oonalaska* in *Thomas Campbell's* poem, *Pleasures of Hope*, in the mid-1800s.

•**ORANGE**, City; Orange County Seat; Pop. 23,628; Zip Code 77630; Elev. 20; Lat. 30-05.5 N, Long. 93-44.2 W; E Texas; 20 m. E of Beaumont on the Sabine River. Named for the wild orange groves along the banks of the Sabine River.

•**ORANGE GROVE**, City; Jim Wells County; Pop. 1,212; Zip Code 78372; Lat. 27-57.5 N, Long. 97-56.2 W; S Texas; 30 m. W of Corpus Christi; Name is descriptive.

•**ORCHARD**, Town; Fort Bend County; Pop. 408; Zip Code 77464; Lat. 29-36.2 N, Long. 95-57.9 W; SE Texas; 10 m. W of Rosenberg.

•**ORE CITY**, City; Upshur County; Pop. 1,050; Zip Code 75683; Lat. 32-47.9 N, Long. 94-43.0 W; NE Texas; 30 m. NW of Marshall, near Lake O' The Pines.

•**OVERTON**, City; Rusk & Smith Counties; Pop. 2,430; Zip Code 75684; Elev. 507; Lat. 32-16.4 N, Long. 94-58.7 W; E Texas; 24 m. E of Tyler. Laid out 1873 when Missouri Pacific Railroad was built; named for a pioneer family.

•**OZONA**, Town; Crockett County Seat; Pop. 3,764; Zip Code 76943; W Texas; Elev. 2,348; 70 m. SE of San Angelo in a sage-covered area.

•**PADUCAH**, Town; Cottle County Seat; Pop. 2,216; Zip Code 79248; Elev. 1,886; Lat. 34-00.8 N, Long. 100-18.4 W; NW Texas; 100 m. NW of Wichita Falls. The town's first residents hailed from Paducah, Kentucky, and named their new home for it.

•**PAINT ROCK**, Town; Concho County Seat; Pop. 256; Zip Code 76866; Elev. 1,640; Lat. 31-30.5 N, Long. 99-55.3 W; W central Texas; 30 m. E of San Angelo. town is today a wool shipping center. Founded in 1879, Paint Rock was named for extensive group of Indian pictographs painted on limestone cliffs bordering Concho River.

•**PALACIOS**, Town; Matagorda County; Pop. 4,667; Zip Code 77465; Elev. 17; Lat. 28-42.0 N, Long. 96-12.8 W; SE Texas; 90 m. SW of Houston. Settled in 1903, in an area named by shipwrecked Spaniards who supposedly saw a vision of *tres palacios* (three palaces).

•**PALESTINE**, City; Anderson County Seat; Pop. 15,948; Zip Code 75801; Elev. 510; Lat. 31-45.8 N, Long. 95-37.9 W; E Texas; 45 m. SW of Tyler; Named for Palestine, Illinois.

•**PALMER**, Town; Ellis County; Pop. 1,187; Zip Code 75152; Elev. 468; Lat. 32-25.8 N, Long. 96-40.2 W; NE central Texas; 30 m. SE of Dallas. It was named for *Martin Palmer*, a participant in the Battle of San Jacinto.

•**PALO PINTO**, Village; Palo Pinto County Seat; Pop. 350; Zip Code 76072; N central Texas; 10 m. W of Mineral Wells. Name means "painted tree" or "stick" in Spanish. It is a farm trading center.

•**PAMPA**, City; Gray County Seat; Pop. 21,396; Zip Code 79065; Elev. 3,234; Lat. 35-32.3 N, Long. 100-57.7 W; NW Texas; 55 m. NE of Amarillo. Pampa is so named because of the resemblance of the encircling prairies to the Argentine pampas.

•**PANHANDLE**, Town; Carson County Seat; Pop. 2,226; Zip Code 79068; Elev. 3,451; Lat. 35-20.8 N, Long. 101-22.7 W; NW Texas; 28 m. NE of Amarillo. Named for its location in Texas Panhandle, it became the county seat upon organization of Carson County in 1888.

•**PANNA MARIA**, Village; Karnes County; Pop. 96; Zip Code 78144; Elev. 325; S Texas; On the San Antonio River; 50 m. SE of San Antonio. Established in 1854 by Polish Catholics; in fulfillment of vow, immigrants named their new town Panna Maria, meaning Virgin Mary in Polish.

•**PANTEGO**, Town; Tarrant County; Pop. 2,431; Zip Code 760+; Lat. 32-43.3 N, Long. 97-09.0 W; N Texas; Suburb of Fort Worth.

•**PARIS**, City; Lamar County Seat; Pop. 25,498; Zip Code 75460; Lat. 33-39.6 N, Long. 95-33.3 W; NE Texas; 95 m. NE of Dallas.

•**PASADENA**, City; Harris County; Pop. 112,560; Zip Code 775+; Elev. 34; Lat. 29-42.8 N, Long. 95-12.7 W; SE Texas; 3 m. E of Houston. Name is Spanish for "Land of Flowers", chosen for blooming meadows along Vince's Bayou.

•**PEARLAND**, City; Brazoria & Harris Counties; Pop. 13,248; Zip Code 775+; Lat. 29-33.8 N, Long. 95-17.1 W; SE Texas; 12 m. S of Houston; Residential.

•**PEARSALL**, City; Frio County Seat; Pop. 7,383; Zip Code 78061; Elev. 641; Lat. 28-53.5 N, Long. 99-05.8 W; S Texas. Established on International-Great Northern Railroad in 1880.

•**PECOS**, City; Reeves County Seat; Pop. 12,855; Zip Code 79772; Elev. 2,850; W Texas; 75 m. SW of Odessa on the Pecos River. One of the country's earliest versions of the popular western spectacle, the rodeo, as today practiced is credited to Pecos.

•**PENELOPE**, Town; Hill County; Pop. 235; Zip Code 76676; Lat. 31-51.5 N, Long. 96-55.6 W; NE central Texas.

•**PERRYTON**, City; Ochiltree County Seat; Pop. 7,991; Zip Code 79070; Elev. 2,942; Lat. 36-23.6 N, Long. 100-48.4 W; NW Texas; 120 m. NE of Amarillo, near Oklahoma state line. The town was formed in 1919, largely by citizens of Ochiltree, Texas and Gray, Oklahoma, who moved to the new town site hauling their homes intact, hitched to tractors.

•**PETERSBURG**, Town; Hale County; Pop. 1,633; Zip Code 79250; Lat. 33-52.1 N, Long. 101-35.8 W; NW Texas; 28 m. SE of Plainview.

•**PETROLIA**, City; Clay County; Pop. 755; Zip Code 76377; Lat. 34-00.7 N, Long. 98-14.0 W; N Texas; 15 m. NE of Wichita Falls. The town was founded as Oil City in 1901, but when it was moved to the new railroad tracks, townspeople renamed it. A large oil field is nearby.

•**PFLUGERVILLE**, City; Travis County; Pop. 745; Zip Code 78660; Lat. 30-26.4 N, Long. 97-37.3 W; Central Texas; 12 m. N of Austin.

•**PHARR**, City; Hidalgo County; Pop. 21,381; Zip Code 78577; Elev. 107; Lat. 26-11.6 N, Long. 98-11.0 W; S Texas. Established in 1909, named after Henry N. Pharr, sugar planter from Louisiana.

•**PILOT POINT**, Town; Denton County; Pop. 2,211; Zip Code 76258; N Texas; 20 m. NE of Denton; Named because it is on a high ridge overlooking a forested valley. George Newcomb platted the town in 1853.

•**PINELAND**, City; Sabine County; Pop. 1,111; Zip Code 75968; Elev. 267; Lat. 31-15.0 N, Long. 93-58.4 W; E Texas; 20 m. N of Jasper in the Sabine National Forest. This lumber mill town has its homes spread out amid the piney woods.

•**PINE SPRINGS**, Village; Culberson County; Pop. 20; Elev. 5,634; W Texas; On U.S. Hwy. 62/180 near Guadalupe Mountains National Park. The Butterfield Overland Mail Route passed through this tiny station, beginning in 1858. Tumbled stone ruins and a historical marker are all that remain today.

•**PITTSBURG**, City; Camp County Seat; Pop. 4,245; Zip Code 75686; Elev. 392; Lat. 32-59.6 N; Long. 94-58.0 W; NE Texas; 50 m. N of Tyler. A heavily timbered area, also a commercial center for farming, poultry and livestock.

•**PLAINS**, Town; Yoakum County Seat; Pop. 1,457; Zip Code 79355; Elev. 3,400; Lat. 33-11.2 N; Long. 102-49.7 W; NW Texas; 32 m. W of Brownfield. First land claim was filled here in 1890's by family who lived in a dugout, but whose possesions included a piano.

•**PLAINVIEW**, City; Hale County Seat; Pop. 22,187; Zip Code 79072; Elev. 3,366; Lat. 34-11.0 N; Long. 101-42.5 W; NW Texas; 40 m. N of Lubbock. Plainview was founded in the 1880's as a dugout town. Named for its magnificent view of plains.

•**PLANO**, City; Collin & Denton Counties; Pop. 72,331; Zip Code 750+; Elev. 655; Lat. 33-01.2 N; Long. 96-42.0 W; NE Texas. Town was established as Fillmore in 1848, but changed to the Spanish word for "plain" due to its location on the broad, level blacklands prairies in 1851.

•**PLEASANTO**, City; Atascosa County; Pop. 6,346; Zip Code 78064; Elev. 365; Lat. 28-57.5 N; Long. 98-29.3 W; S Texas; 32 m. S of San Antonio. Settled in the 1850's, Pleasanto was one of the cattle concentration points on the old Western Trail to Dodge City, Kansas.

•**POINT**, City; Rains County; Pop. 468; Zip Code 75472; Lat. 32-55.9 N; Long. 95-52.2 W; NE Texas; 17 m. SE of Greenville. Name was originally Rice's Point, for an early settler.

•**POINT COMFORT**, City; Calhoun County; Pop. 1,125; Zip Code 77978; Lat. 28-40.7 N; Long. 96-33.3 W; S Texas; 5 m. across Lavaca Bay from Port Lavaca.

•**POINTBLANK**, City; San Jacinto County; Pop. 325; Zip Code 77364; Lat. 30-44.7 N; Long. 95-12.8 W; E Texas; On Lake Livingston in the Sam Houston National Forest. Florence Dissiway, an early settler and governess to a prominent family, named it Blanc Point because the area "was without obstacles in the way," referring to the flat country. The name was later turned around and spelled differently.

•**PONDER**, Town; Denton County; Pop. 297; Zip Code 76259; N Texas; 10 m. W of Denton; Named for early settler W.A. Ponder.

•**PORT ARANSAS**, City; Aransas & Nueces Counties; Pop. 1,968; Zip Code 78373; S Texas; 30 m. NE of Corpus Christi at Aransas Pass to Gulf of Mexico. The city is on Mustang Island, reached by causeway and free, 24-hour ferry service.

•**PORT ARTHUR**, City; Jefferson County; Pop. 61,195; Zip Code 77640; Elev. 4; Lat. 29-54.0 N, Long. 93-55.8 W; SE Texas; 90 m. E of Houston on Sabine Lake. Having fixed upon the Lake Sabine shores as the site of his dream city, in 1895 Arthur Stilwell caused a town site to be surveyed which he named Port Arthur in his honor.

•**PORT ISABEL**, City; Cameron County; Pop. 3,769; Zip Code 78578; Elev. 8; Lat. 26-04.6 N, Long. 97-12.4 W; S Texas; 120 m. S of Corpus Christi on the Gulf. This resort and fishing town was settled by Mexican ranchers as early as 1770, but today hotels, motels and boat slips dominate the scene.

•**PORT LAVACA**, City; Calhoun County Seat; Pop. 10,911; Zip Code 77979; Elev. 22; Lat. 28-36.8 N, Long. 96-37.5 W; S Texas; 70 m. NE of Corpus Christi. Founded by the Spanish in 1815, the early town was called La Vaca (the cow), the Lavaca River having been thus named by La Salle.

•**PORT MANSFIELD**, Village; Willacy County; Pop. 731; Zip Code 78598; Elev. 11; S coastal Texas; 37 m. NE of Harlingen on the Gulf Coast. People of Willacy County, employing own financing, set about creating port; built wharves, docks and turning basin; laid out townsite, and called it Port Mansfield.

•**PORT NECHES**, City; Jefferson County; Pop. 13,944; Zip Code 77651; Lat. 29-59.5 N, Long. 93-57.7 W; SE Texas; 10 m. NW of Port Arthur on the Neches River.

•**PORTLAND**, City; Nueces & San Patricio Counties; Pop. 12,023; Zip Code 78374; Lat. 27-52.5 N, Long. 97-19.7 W; S Texas; 8 m. N of Corpus Christi across the bay. Oil and gas refining are important in this port town.

•**POST**, City; Garza County Seat; Pop. 3,961; Zip Code 79356; Elev. 2,590; Lat. 33-11.6 N; Long. 101-22.9 W; NW Texas; 40 m. SE of Lubbock. Founded in 1907 by C.W. Post, of Battle Creek, Michigan, a cereal manufacturer and philanthropist, who dreamed of having here a model town where agriculture and industry were to round out its civic existence.

•**POTEET**, City; Atascosa County; Pop. 3,086; Zip Code 78065; Elev. 525; S Texas. In center of truck-farming region; called the "Strawberry Capital of Texas."

•**POTH**, Town; Wilson County; Pop. 1,461; Zip Code 78147; Lat. 29-04.1 N, Long. 98-04.9 W; S central Texas; 30 m. SE of San Antonio.

•**POTTSBORO**, Town; Grayson County; Pop. 895; Zip Code 75076; Lat. 33-45.6 N, Long. 96-39.9 W; NE Texas; 10 m. NW of Sherman in a rural area.

•**POWELL**, Town; Navarro County; Pop. 111; Zip Code 75153; Lat. 32-06.9 N, Long. 96-19.7 W; NE central Texas; 8 m. E of Corsicana.

•**POYNOR**, Town; Henderson County; Pop. 272; Zip Code 75782; Elev. 402; Lat. 32-04.4 N, Long. 95-36.0 W; NE Texas; 30 m. SW of Tyler; Named for D.A. Paynor, a railroad surveyor who came here in 1900.

•**PRAIRIE VIEW**, City; Waller County; Pop. 3,993; Zip Code 77445; Elev. 250; Lat. 30-05.7 N, Long. 95-59.3 W; SE Texas. Named for plantation home of Col. Jack Kirby.

•**PREMONT**, City; Jim Wells County; Pop. 2,984; Zip Code 78375; Lat. 27-21.5 N, Long. 98-07.4 W; S Texas; 27 m. S of Alice.

•**PRESIDIO**, Village; Presidio County; Pop. 1,720; Zip Code 79845; Elev. 2,594; W Texas; 200 m. SE of El Paso on the Rio Grande. Spanish priests came here in the late sixteenth century. In 1684, a formal establishment of a group of missions was made under the name La Junta de los Rios ("junction of the rivers"). In 1830, the name was changed to Presidio del Norte, which was eventually shortened.

•**PROSPER**, Town; Collin County; Pop. 675; Zip Code 75078; Lat. 33-14.1 N, Long. 96-48.1 W; NE Texas; 6 m. NW of McKinney.

•**PUTNAM**, Town; Callahan County; Pop. 116; Zip Code 76469; Lat. 32-22.2 N, Long. 99-11.8 W; N central Texas; 26 m. E of Abilene.

•**PYOTE**, Town; Ward County; Pop. 382; Zip Code 79777; Lat. 31-32.0 N, Long. 103-07.5 W; W Texas; 20 m. NE of Pecos; Name is derived from peyote, a native cactus. First settled on a rail line in the 1880's.

•**QUANAH**, City; Hardeman County Seat; Pop. 3,890; Zip Code 79252; Elev. 1,568; Lat. 34-17.6 N, Long. 99-44.5 W; N Texas; 80 m. NW of Wichita Falls. The city was named for Quanah Parker, one-time war chief of the Comanches.

•**QUEEN CITY**, City; Cass County; Pop. 1,748; Zip Code 75572; Lat. 33-08.9 N, Long. 94-09.1 W; NE Texas; 15 m. S of Texarkana.

•**QUEMADO**, Village; Maverick County; Pop. 426; Zip Code 78877; SW Texas; Named for the Spanish word for "burned", since a dry valley nearby appears so.

•**QUINLAN**, City; Hunt County; Pop. 1,002; Zip Code 75474; Lat. 32-54.6 N, Long. 96-08.3 W; NE Texas; 40 m. E of Dallas near Lake Tawakoni.

•**QUITAQUE**, City; Briscoe County; Pop. 696; Zip Code 79255; Elev. 2,570; NW Texas; 70 m. NE of Lubbock; Named for the Quitaca Indians. It may also be from an Indian word for "horse manure," describing the two buttes nearby.

•**QUITMAN**, City; Wood County Seat; Pop. 1,893; Zip Code 75783; Elev. 414; Lat. 32-47.7 N, Long. 95-27.0 W; NE Texas; 65 m. NW of Marshall. Quitman is commercial center for farming, livestock, oil, headquarters for electric co-op.

•**RALLS**, City; Crosby County; Pop. 2,422; Zip Code 79357; Lat. 33-40.8 N, Long. 101-23.3 W; NW Texas.

•**RANGER**, City; Eastland County; Pop. 3,142; Zip Code 76470; Elev. 1,429; Lat. 32-28.1 N, Long. 98-40.2 W; N central Texas; 60 m. E of Abilene. Founded in 1881 and named for a camp of Texas Rangers, near which the tent village of the first citizens took shape.

•**RAKIN**, City; Upton County Seat; Pop. 1,216; Zip Code 79778; Lat. 31-13.4 N, Long. 101-56.3 W; W Texas; 55 m. SE of Odessa in oil and cattle country.

•**RAYMONDVILLE**, City; Willacy County Seat; Pop. 9,493; Zip Code 78580; Elev. 40; Lat. 26-28.8 N, Long. 97-46.9 W; S Texas; 20 m. N of Harlingen. Raymondville is a commercial center for an irrigated fruit and vegetable area.

•**RED OAK**, City; Ellis County; Pop. 1,882; Zip Code 75154; Lat. 32-31.0 N, Long. 96-48.3 W; NE central Texas; 20 m. S of Dallas.

•**REFUGIO**, Town; Refugio County Seat; Pop. 3,898; Zip Code 78377; Elev. 50; Lat. 28-18.3 N, Long. 97-16.5 W; S Texas. Refugio was founded in 1790 when Franciscan monks built Mission Nuestra Senora Del Refugio (Mission of Our Lady of Refuge), which was first destroyed in wars between Karankawas and Comanches, and later bombarded by the Mexican Army in 1836.

•**REKLAW**, Town; Cherokee & Rusk Counties; Pop. 305; Zip Code 75784; Lat. 31-51.7 N, Long. 94-59.3 W; E Texas. The town was named for Margaret Walker, landowner. Her name was spelled backwards because another Texas town had been registered as Walker already.

•**RHOME**, City; Wise County; Pop. 478; Zip Code 76078; Lat. 33-03.2 N, Long. 97-28.4 W; N Texas; 25 m. N of Fort Worth.

•**RICE**, City; Ellis & Navarro Counties; Pop. 439; Zip Code 75155; Lat. 32-14.6 N, Long. 96-30.1 W; NE central Texas; 10 m. SE of Ennis.

•**RICHARDSON**, City; Collin & Dallas Counties; Pop. 72,496; Zip Code 750+; Elev. 630; Lat. 32-57.2 N, Long. 96-43.5 W; NE Texas; N suburb of Dallas. The settlement was called Breckenridge before Civil War. The town grew around new station on T & NO Railroad when built through area in 1872; renamed for railroad official.

•**RICHLAND**, Town; Navarro County; Pop. 260; Zip Code 76681; Lat. 31-55.6 N, Long. 96-25.5 W; NE central Texas; 10 m. S of Corsicana; Named for good soil in vicinity.

•**RICHLAND SPRINGS**, Town; Pop. 420; Zip Code 76871; Lat. 31-16.4 N, Long. 98-56.7 W; Central Texas; 50 m. SE of Brownwood.

•**RICHMOND**, Town; Fort Bend County; Pop. 9,692; Zip Code 77469; Elev. 104; Lat. 29-34.7 N, Long. 95-45.9 W; SE Texas; 30 m. SW of Houston. Richmond was settled in 1822 by Austin's colonists, this is among the oldest Anglo-American towns in the State.

•**RIESEL**, City; McLennan County; Pop. 691; Zip Code 76682; Lat. 31-28.5 N, Long. 96-55.3 W; Central Texas; 12 m. SE of Waco.

•**RIO GRANDE CITY**, Village; Starr County Seat; Pop. 8,887; Zip Code 78582; Elev. 238; Lat. 26-22.7 N, Long. 98-48.8 W; S Texas. Occupied by Spanish settlers of Escandon in 1753, and founded as a town in 1847 by Henry Clay Davis, a soldier of fortune. Long known locally as Rancho Davis, it was for years an important stop for the river steamers plying the Rio Grande.

•**RIO HONDO**, Town; Cameron County; Pop. 1,673; Zip Code 78583; Lat. 26-14.2 N, Long. 97-35.0 W; S Texas; 10 m. NE of Harlingen; Name means "deep river."

•**RIO VISTA**, City; Johnson County; Pop. 509; Zip Code 76093; Lat. 32-14.1 N, Long. 97-22.6 W; N central Texas.

•**RISING STAR**, Town; Eastland County; Pop. 1,204; Zip Code 76471; Lat. 32-05.9 N, Long. 98-58.0 W; N central Texas; 28 m. N of Brownwood. This town was assigned its name by the post office in 1880, after *T.W. Anderson* made two other suggestions, "Rising Sun" and "Star."

•**RIVER OAKS**, City; Tarrant County; Pop. 6,890; Zip Code 770+; Lat. 32-46.3 N, Long. 97-23.7 W; N Texas; suburb of Fort Worth.

•**ROANOKE**, City; Denton County; Pop. 910; Zip Code 76262; Lat. 32-59.9 N, Long. 91-13.7 W; N Texas; 20 m. N of Fort Worth.

•**ROARING SPRINGS**, Town; Motley County; Pop. 315; Zip Code 79256; Elev. 2,520; Lat. 33-53.9 N, Long. 100-31.5 W; NW Texas; 80 m. NE of Lubbock; Named for springs three miles south in a canyon near the Tongue River. Once an Indian camp.

•**ROBERT LEE**, City; Coke County Seat; Pop. 1,202; Zip Code 76945; Elev. 1,850; Lat. 31-53.8 N, Long. 100-29.2 W; W central Texas. Promoted as townsite in 1889 by two Confederate soldiers; name honors *Robert E. Lee*.

•**ROBINSON**, City; McLennan County; Pop. 6,074; Zip Code 76706; Lat. 31-28.1 N, Long. 97-06.9 W; Central Texas; 5 m. S of Waco.

•**ROBSTOWN**, City; Nueces County; Pop. 12,100; Zip Code 78380; Lat. 27-47.4 N, Long. 97-40.1 W; S Texas; 25 m. W of Corpus Christi. Named for *"Rob" Driscoll, Jr.,* whose father began a large ranch here in 1905.

•**ROBY**, City; Fisher County Seat; Pop. 814; Zip Code 79543; Lat. 32-44.7 N, Long. 100-22.6 W; NW central Texas; 20 m. N of Sweetwater. An electric co-op has its headquarters for a vast ranching area here.

•**ROCKDALE**, City; Milam County; Pop. 5,611; Elev. 462; Zip Code 76567; Central Texas; 60 m. NE of Austin. Oil refining and cottonseed processing are important industries.

•**ROCKPORT**, City; Aransas County Seat; Pop. 3,686; Zip Code 78382; Elev. 20; S Texas. Established in 1867 as shipping point for wool, hides, bones and tallow.

•**ROCKSPRINGS**, Town; Edwards County Seat; Pop. 1,317; Zip Code 78880; Elev. 2,450; SW central Texas; 115 m. SE of San

Angelo. Established 1891, named for springs prized as water source by wagon trains and Indians.

•**ROCKWALL**, City; Rockwall County Seat; Pop. 5,939; Zip Code 75087; Elev. 552; NE Texas; 20 m. NE of Dallas. It was named because of a curious subterranean geologic formation, which resembles a rock wall of artificial construction.

•**ROMA**, City; Starr County; Pop. 3,384; Zip Code 78584; Elev. 243; S Texas; 88 m. SE of Laredo on the Rio Grande. Settled in 1765 by Indians occupying the vistas (civil village) of Escandon's colony at Mier. Ranchers took up holdings on the north bank of the river, where gradually a settlement developed.

•**ROMERO**, Village; Hartley County; Pop. 25; Elev. 4,101; NW Texas. This tiny settlement dates back to an era long before the coming of the non-Latin ranchers. New Mexicans from Taos and Santa Fe came into this section in the early 1800's on large, organized buffalo hunts.

•**ROPESVILLE**, City; Hockley County; Pop. 489; Zip Code 79358; NW Texas; 20 m. SW of Lubbock. First choice for the town name was Lariat, but since that had already been taken, local ranchers had to settle on "Ropes" ville in 1920.

•**ROSCOE**, City; Nolan County; Pop. 1,628; Zip Code 79545; Elev. 2,391; Lat. 32-26.6 N, Long. 100-32.2 W; NW Texas. Grain is the main product shipped from this railroad stop.

•**ROSEBUD**, City; Falls County; Pop. 2,076; Zip Code 76570; Elev. 392; Lat. 31-04.4 N, Long. 96-58.6 W; Central Texas; 32 m. S of Waco. Czechs and Germans settled this area and made its reputation for being filled with rose plants.

•**ROSENBERG**, City; Fort Bend County; Pop. 17,995; Zip Code 77471; Elev. 106; Lat. 29-33.5 N, Long. 95-48.5 W; SE Texas. The population is largely of German, Bohemian and Polish birth descent. Founded in 1883 with the construction of the railroad.

•**ROSHARON**, Village; Brazoria County; Pop. 435; Zip Code 77583; SE Texas; Named by early settler, *George Collins*, for the wildflowers here that reminded him of roses in his native England.

•**ROSS**, City; McLennan County; Pop. 200; Zip Code 76684; Lat. 31-43.1 N, Long. 97-07.1 W; Central Texas; 18 m. N of Waco.

•**ROTAN**, City; Fisher County; Pop. 2,284; Zip Code 79546; Lat. 32-51.4 N, Long. 100-27.8 W; NW central Texas; 30 m. N of Sweetwater.

•**ROUND ROCK**, City; Travis & Williamson Counties; Pop. 11,812; Zip Code 78664; Elev. 709; Lat. 30-30.6 N, Long. 97-40.7 W; Central Texas; 15 m. N of Austin. Established 1850, named for large round rock in bed of Brushy Creek.

•**ROUND TOP**, Town; Fayette County; Pop. 87; Zip Code 78954; Elev. 390; SE central Texas. Established in 1835 as Jones Post Office. In 1854, Round Top Academy was founded; advertised tuition for the five month session was $10. School closed in 1861.

•**ROWENA**, Village; Runnels County; Pop. 466; Zip Code 76875; Central Texas; 29 m. NE of San Angelo in a rural area producing cotton and grains. The son of a railroad official named the town for his girlfriend, Rowena, in 1901.

•**ROWLETT**, City; Dallas & Rockwall Counties; Pop. 7,522; Zip Code 75088; Lat. 32-54.2 N, Long. 96-34.0 W; NE Texas; Suburb of Dallas.

•**ROXTON**, City; Lamar County; Pop. 735; Zip Code 75477; Lat. 33-32.8 N, Long. 95-43.6 W; NE Texas; 15 m. SW of Paris.

•**ROYSE CITY**, City; Collin & Rockwall Counties; Pop. 1,566; Zip Code 75089; NE Texas; 30 m. NE of Dallas.

•**SAN DIEGO**, City; Duval & Jim Wells Counties; Duval County Seat; Pop. 5,225; Zip Code 78384; Elev. 312; Lat. 27-45.8 N, Long. 98-14.3 W; S Texas; 50 m. W of Corpus Christi. San Diego was once an important cattle shipping point which required Ranger detachments to cope with its gun-toting citizens and cowboys, and with the bands of rustlers that infested the back country.

•**SAN SABA**, Town; San Saba County Seat; Pop. 2,336; Zip Code 76877; Elev. 1,210; Lat. 31-11.7 N, Long. 98-43.1 W; Central Texas; 80 m. W of Temple. Settled in 1854 and named for scenic river on which it is located.

•**SANTA ANNA**, Town; Coleman County; Pop. 1,535; Zip Code 76878; Elev. 1,743; Lat. 31-44.5 N, Long. 99-19.6 W; Central Texas; 80 m. E of San Angelo. Named for its location at the foot of Santa Anna Mountain.

•**SANTA ROSA**, Town; Cameron County; Pop. 1,535; Zip Code 78593; Lat. 26-15.6 N, Long. 97-49.6 W; S Texas; 8 m. NW of Harlingen.

•**SARATOGA**, Village; Hardin County; Pop. 100; Zip Code 77585; Elev. 83; E Texas; 30 m. NW of Beaumont. Settled a decade before Civil War, it was named for Saratoga N.Y., because of medicinal springs.

•**SARITA**, Town; Kenedy County; Pop. 185; Zip Code 78385; Elev. 34; S Coastal Texas; 20 m. S of Kingsville in a rural area. Named for *Sarita Kenedy*, grand-daughter of *Mifflin Kenedy*.

•**SASPAMCO**, Village; Wilson County; Pop. 262; S central Texas; Named for San Antonio Sewer Pipe and Manufacturing Company, only industry in this community.

•**SAVOY**, City; Fannin County; Pop. 855; Zip Code 75479; Lat. 33-36.0 N, Long. 96-22.1 W; NE Texas; 13 m. E of Sherman; Named for landowner *William Savoy*.

•**SCHERTZ**, City; Bexar, Comal & Guadalupe Counties; Pop. 7,262; Zip Code 78154; S central Texas; 15 m. NE of San Antonio.

•**SCHULENBURG**, City; Fayette County; Pop. 2,469; Zip Code 78956; Elev. 344; Lat. 29-40.9 N, Long. 96-54.1 W; SE central Texas; 78 m. SE of Austin. Germans and Bohemians settled this town.

•**SCOTLAND**, City; Archer & Clay Counties; Pop. 367; Zip Code 76379; Lat. 33-39.5 N, Long. 98-28.3 W; N Texas; 20 m. S of Wichita Falls. Named for land promotor *Henry Scott* of Toronto, Canada, in 1907. It was incorporated in the 1970's.

•**SCOTTSVILLE**, City; Harrison County; Pop. 245; Zip Code 75688; Elev. 390; Lat. 32-32.4 N, Long. 94-14.2 W; NE Texas; 12 m. W of Louisiana state line. Founded in 1834, this town was one of the oldest camp meeting sites in the state.

•**SEABROOK**, City; Chambers, Galveston & Harris Counties; Pop. 4,670; Zip Code 77586; Lat. 29-33.8 N, Long. 95-01.5 W; SE Texas; Suburb of Houston.

•**SEADRIFT**, City; Calhoun County; Pop. 1,277; Zip Code 77983; Lat. 28-24.9 N, Long. 96-42.5 W; S Texas; 30 m. SE of Victoria on San Antonio Bay.

•**SEAGOVILLE**, City; Dallas & Kaufman Counties; Pop. 7,304; Zip Code 75159; Lat. 32-38.3 N, Long. 96-32.3 W; NE Texas; 20 m. SE of Dallas.

•**SEAGRAVES**, City; Gaines County; Pop. 2,596; Zip Code 79359; Lat. 32-36.3 N, Long. 102-34.1 W; NW Texas; 60 m. SW of Lubbock.

•SEGUiN, City; Guadalupe County Seat; Pop. 17,854; Zip Code 78155; Elev. 553; Lat. 29-34.2 N, Long. 97-58.2 W; S central Texas; 30 m. NE of San Antonio. Named in 1839 for *Colonel Juan N. Seguin,* who commanded the only detachment of Texas-born Mexicans in the Battle of San Jacinto.

•SELMA, City; Bexar, Comal & Guadalupe Counties; Pop. 528; Zip Code 75689; Elev. 750; S central Texas; 10 m. NE of San Antonio; settled by German immigrants.

•SEMINOLE, City; Gaines County Seat; Pop. 6,080; Zip Code 79360; Lat. 32-43.2 N, Long. 102-38.8 W; NW Texas; 80 m. SW of Lubbock in a ranchland area; Named for the Indian tribe native to the area in 1906.

•SERBIN, Village; Lee County; Pop. 90; Elev. 520; Central Texas; 50 m. E of Austin. In 1855, five hundred Wendish colonists began building the log settlement of Serbin. This community became the cultural center of the Wends in America.

•SEYMOUR, City; Baylor County Seat; Pop. 3,657; Zip Code 76380; Elev. 1,290; Lat. 33-35.4 N, Long. 99-15.6 W; N Texas; 50 m. SW of Wichita Falls. Settled in 1878 by a group from Oregon.

•SHAFTER, Village; Presidio County; Pop. 31; Zip Code 79850; Elev. 4,000; W Texas. Established as silver mining town in the early 1880's.

•SHALLOWATER, City; Lubbock County; Pop. 1,932; Zip Code 79363; Lat. 33-41.3 N, Long. 101-59.7 W; NW Texas; 11 m. NE of Lubbock; Named because well water was not very far underground.

•SHAMROCK, City; Wheeler County; Pop. 2,834; Zip Code 79079; Elev. 2,281; Lat. 35-13.0 N, Long. 100-14.9 W; NW Texas; 90 m. E of Amarillo. In 1883, British noblemen, headed by the *Baron of Tweedmouth* and the *Earl of Aberdeen,* purchased land here. The domain was called the Rocking Chair Ranch, from its brand; but Texas cowboys dubbed it the Nobility Ranch. When it failed, the noblemen returned to England, leaving the town names of Tweedy, Shamrock, Wellington, Clarendon, and Aberdeen.

•SHELBYVILLE, Shelby County; Zip Code 75973; Lat. 31-45.6 N, Long. 94-04.7 W; E Texas; 40 m. S of Longview near Sabine National Forest. Shelbyville was founded about 1817, and has been variously called Tenaha, Nashville, and Shelbyville, the last in honor of *General Isaac Shelby.*

•SHEPHERD, City; San Jacinto County; Pop. 1,674; Zip Code 77371; Lat. 30-29.9 N, Long. 94-59.9 W; E Texas; 53 m. N of Houston; Named for early settler, *B.A. Shepherd.*

•SHERMAN, City; Grayson County Seat; Pop. 30,413; Zip Code 75090; Elev. 720; Lat. 33-38.4 N, Long. 96-36.3 W; NE Texas; 60 m. N of Dallas. Organized in 1846. First laid out a short distance west of present location, but because of scarce firewood and water, moved to present site in 1848.

•SHINER, City; Lavaca County; Pop. 2,213; Zip Code 77984; Elev. 350; Lat. 29-25.8 N, Long. 97-10.2 W; SE central Texas; 70 m. E of San Antonio. Founded in 1887; a trade center for Czech and German farmers.

•SIERRA BLANCA, Village; Hudspeth County; Pop. 573; Zip Code 79851; Elev. 4,512; W Texas. Meeting site of nation's second transcontinental rail route in 1881, named for Sierra Blanca Mountain northwest of town.

•SILSBEE, City; Hardin County; Pop. 7,684; Zip Code 77656; Elev. 79; Lat. 30-20.8 N, Long. 94-11.1 W; E Texas. Established in 1892 around a logging camp of *John H. Kirby.*

•SKELLYTOWN, Town; Carson County; Pop. 899; Zip Code 79080; Lat. 35-34.2 N, Long. 101-10.6 E; NW Texas; 13 m. SE of Borger; Named for the Skelly Oil Company, which began drilling here in the 1930's.

•SLATON, City; Lubbock County; Pop. 6,804; Zip Code 79364; Elev. 3,040; Lat. 33-26.0 N, Long. 101-38.6 W; NW Texas; 16 m. SE of Lubbock at a railroad division point.

•SMILEY, City; Gonzales County; Pop. 439; Zip Code 78159; Lat. 29-16.2 N, Long. 97-38.2 W; S central Texas; 50 m. SE of San Antonio.

•SMITHVILLE, City; Bastrop County; Pop. 3,470; Zip Code 78957; Elev. 324; Lat. 30-00.6 N, Long. 97-09.8 W; S central Texas; 40 m. SE of Austin in a forested area, rich in varied agriculture.

•SNYDER, City; Scurry County Seat; Pop. 12,705; Zip Code 79549; Elev. 2,316; Lat. 32-43.6 N, Long. 100-54.7 W; NW central Texas; 90 m. NW of Abilene. The townsite was laid out in 1882, and county was organized two years later.

•SOMERSET, City; Bexar County; Pop. 1,096; Zip Code 78069; Lat. 29-13.5 N, Long. 98-39.5 W; S central Texas; 20 m. SW of San Antonio.

•SOMERVILLE, City; Burleson County; Pop. 1,824; Zip Code 77879; Elev. 250; Lat. 30-20.7 N, Long. 96-31.7 W; E central Texas; 30 m. SW of Bryan; named for early resident *Albert Somerville.*

•SONORA, City; Sutton County Seat; Pop. 3,856; Zip Code 76950; Elev. 2,120; Lat. 30-34.0 N, Long. 100-38.7 W; SE central Texas; 60 m. S of San Angelo. Settled in 1889 on the Dry Fork of the Devil's River. On the western slope of the Edwards Plateau, Sonora began as trading post on Old San Antonio-El Paso Road.

•SOUR LAKE, City; Hardin County; Pop. 1,807; Zip Code 77659; Lat. 30-08.5 N, Long. 94-24.8 W; E Texas; 14 m. W of Beaumont near the Big Thicket national preserve.

•SOUTH HOUSTON, City; Harris County; Pop. 13,293; Zip Code 77587; Elev. 44; Lat. 29-39.8 N, Long. 95-14.2 W; SE Texas; 11 m. SE of Houston. The town was nearly destroyed by a Gulf storm in 1915.

•SOUTHLAKE, City; Denton & Tarrant Counties; Pop. 2,808; Zip Code 76051; Lat. 32-56.5 N, Long. 97-06.9 W; N Texas; suburb of Fort Worth.

•SOUTH PADRE ISLAND, Town; Cameron County; Pop. 791; Zip Code 78597; Elev. 5; S Texas; incorporated in 1974, small city is on southern tip of storied Padre Island just across Laguna Madre, the body of water separating island from mainland.

•SPEARMAN, City; Hansford County Seat; Pop. 3,413; Zip Code 79081; Elev. 3,105; Lat. 36-11.8 N, Long. 101-11.6 W; NW Texas; 80 m. NE of Amarillo. Established in the 1920's when North Texas and Santa Fe Railroad built across Hansford County; named for railroad executive.

•SPLENDORA, City; Montgomery County; Pop. 721; Zip Code 77372; Lat. 30-14.0 N, Long. 95-09.7 W; E Texas; 40 m. N of Houston. The first postmaster named this town for its abundance of beautiful wildflowers.

•SPOFFORD, City; Kinney County; Pop. 77; Zip Code 78882; Lat. 29-10.4 N, Long. 100-24.8 W; SE Texas.

•SPRINGLAKE, Town; Lamb County; Pop. 222; Zip Code 79082; Lat. 34-13.9 N, Long. 102-18.4 W; NW Texas; 35 m. W of Plainview.

•**SPRINGTOWN**, City; Parker County; Pop. 1,658; Zip Code 76092; Lat. 32-58.1 N, Long. 97-41.0 W; N central Texas; 35 m. NW of Fort Worth; residential.

•**SPRING VALLEY**, City; Harris County; Pop. 3,353; Zip Code 752+; Lat. 29-47.2 N, Long. 95-30.9 W; SE Texas; Suburb of Houston.

•**SPUR**, City; Dickens County; Pop. 1,690; Zip Code 79370; Elev. 2,274; Lat. 33-28.4 N, Long. 100-51.5 W; NW Texas; 55 m. E of Lubbock. Founded in 1909 and named for the Old Spur Ranch (Espuela Land and Cattle Company).

•**STAFFORD**, Town; Fort Bend & Harris Counties; Pop. 4,755; Zip Code 77477; Lat. 29-36.8 N, Long. 95-33.7 W; SE Texas; 20 m. SW of Houston.

•**STAMFORD**, City; Haskell & Jones Counties; Pop. 4,542; Zip Code 79553; Elev. 1,603; Lat. 32-56.6 N, Long. 99-48.1 W; NW central Texas; 40 m. N of Abilene. Developed in 1899 as project of Texas Central Railroad, named after Connecticut home town of the railroad president.

•**STANTON**, City; Martin County Seat; Pop. 2,314; Zip Code 79782; Elev. 2,664; Lat. 32-07.8 N, Long. 101-47.6 W; NW Texas; 19 m. NE of Midland. Founded by monks who established a small Roman Catholic colony of German immigrants. It was called Mariensfeld in 1881. The name was changed in 1890 in honor of *Abraham Lincoln's* Secretary of War, *Edwin M. Stanton.*

•**STEPHENVILLE**, City; Erath County Seat; Pop. 11,881; Zip Code 86401; Elev. 1,283; Lat. 32-13.2 N, Long. 98-12.4 W; N central Texas; 60 m. SW of Fort Worth. Stephenville began in 1850 with settlement by *Stephens brothers* in area; one brother, *John,* donated original townsite.

•**STERLING CITY**, City; Sterling County Seat; Pop. 915; Zip Code 76951; Elev. 2,295; Lat. 31-50.2 N, Long. 100-59.5 W; W central Texas; 40 m. NW of San Angelo. The town grew from ranch headquarters of *W.S. Sterling,* Indian fighter and buffalo hunter in late 1880's.

•**STINNETT**, City; Hutchinson County Seat; Pop. 2,222; Zip Code 79083; Elev. 3,173; Lat. 35-49.7 N, Long. 101-26.5 W; NW Texas; 40 m. N of Amarillo at N Canadian River Valley. Established in 1901, it is a trade center and livestock shipping point in the High Plains.

•**STOCKDALE**, City; Wilson County; Pop. 1,265; Zip Code 78160; Lat. 29-14,2 N, Long. 97-57.5 W; S central Texas; named for a Civil War Lieutenant Governor of Texas, *Fletcher Stockdale.*

•**STONEWALL**, Village; Gillespie County; Pop. 245; Zip Code 78671; Elev. 1,512; Central Texas; 65 m. W of Austin on Pedernales Creek. Established in 1870, and named for Confederate *Gen. Stonewall Jackson.*

•**STRATFORD**, Town; Sherman County Seat; Pop. 1,917; Zip Code 79084; Elev. 3,690; Lat. 36-20.2 N, Long. 102-04.4 W; NW Texas; 80 m. NW of Amarillo on Coldwater Creek. Early settler *Colonel Walter Cotton* named the place for *Robert E. Lee's* birthplace in Virginia.

•**STRAWN**, City; Palo Pinto County; Pop. 694; Zip Code 76475; Elev. 992; Lat. 32-33.0 N, Long. 98-30.0 W; N central Texas; 70 m. E of Abilene. Oil development in the 1930's added to town's prosperity. Before petroleum was discovered, coal mining was important.

•**STREETMAN**, Town; Freestone & Navarro Counties; Pop. 415; Zip Code 75859; Lat. 31-52.7 N, Long. 96-19.3 W; E central Texas.

•**STUDY BUTTE**, Village; Brewster County; Pop. 120; Elev. 2,500; W Texas; 80 m. S of Alpine in a mountainous area. The wild, harsh area of the Big Bend region was for centuries only the retreat of bandits, smugglers and fierce Apache and Comanche warriors.

•**SUDAN**, City; Lamb County; Pop. 1,091; Zip Code 79371; Elev. 3,752; NW Texas; 50 m. NW of Lubbock. Named for the grass that is one of the principal crops in the region. It is the center of a large ranching region of yucca-covered prairies.

•**SUGAR LAND**, City; Fort Bend County; Pop. 8,826; Zip Code 774+; Elev. 82; Lat. 29-37.1 N, Long. 95-37.8 W; SE Texas; 20 m. SW of Houston. The Imperial Sugar company once owned one of the largest sugar plantations and refineries in the world here on 12,500 acres of land.

•**SULPHUR SPRINGS**, City; Hopkins County Seat; Pop. 12,804; Zip Code 75482; Elev. 530; Lat. 33-08.2 N, Long. 95-36.2 W; NE Texas; 25 m. E of Greenville. First known as Bright Star, the name was changed in 1871 when mineral springs were advertised.

•**SUNDOWN**, City; Hockley County; Pop. 1,511; Zip Code 79372; NW Texas; Named by early landowner *R.L. Slaughter* for a movie he had seen being filmed on his property in Mexico.

•**SUNRAY**, Town; Moore County; Pop. 1,952; Zip Code 79086; Lat. 36-01.2 N, Long. 101-49.4 W; NW Texas; 45 m. NW of Borger; Named for the Sunray Oil Company in 1931.

•**SWEENY**, Town; Brazoria County; Pop. 3,538; Zip Code 77480; Elev. 38; Lat. 29-02.5 N, Long. 95-41.8 W; SE Texas; 27 m. W of Freeport. It was built on the old *John Sweeny* plantation of the 1830's.

•**SWEETWATER**, City; Nolan County Seat; Pop. 12,242; Zip Code 79556; Elev. 2,164; Lat. 32-28.2 N, Long. 100-24.5 W; NW Texas; 40 m. W of Abilene. Begun in in 1877 when a trader, *Billy Knight,* following the buffalo hunters and Government surveyors, opened a store in a dugout on the banks of Sweetwater Creek.

•**TAFT**, City; San Patricio County; Pop. 3,686; Zip Code 78390; Elev. 54; Lat. 27-58.7 N, Long. 97-24.0 W; S Texas; 20 m. N of Corpus Christi. Named for *Charles P. Taft,* half-brother of *President William H. Taft.*

•**TAHOKA**, City; Lynn County Seat; Pop. 3,262; Zip Code 79373; Elev. 3,090; Lat. 33-10.0 N, Long. 101-47.8 W; NW Texas; 30 m. S of Lubbock near Tahoka Lake. Named for nearby Tahoka Lake, a natural spring-fed lake whose Indian name meant fresh or clear water.

•**TALCO**, City; Titus County; Pop. 751; Zip Code 75487; Elev. 358; Lat. 33-21.6 N, Long. 95-06.1 W; NE Texas; 35 m. SE of Paris. Named by a local merchant for the Texas, Arkansas and Louisiana Candy Company.

•**TALPA**, Town; Coleman County; Pop. 122; Zip Code 76882; Lat. 31-46.6 N, Long. 99-42.5 W; Central Texas; 40 m. W of Brownwood.

•**TATUM**, City; Panola & Rusk Counties; Pop. 1,339; Zip Code 75691; Elev. 385; Lat. 32-18.8 N, Long. 94-31.1 W; E Texas; 17 m. S of Longview. Established in 1885 when Santa Fe Railroad was built through, Townsite donated by *Tatum* family settlers in area.

•**TAYLOR**, City; Williamson County; Pop. 10,619; Zip Code 76574; Elev. 583; Lat. 30-34.2 N, Long. 97-24.5 W; Central Texas; 35 m. NE of Austin. Cotton, oil and dairy farming are important in the vicinity. The town was settled by Germans and Czechs.

•**TEAGUE**, City; Freestone County; Pop. 3,390; Zip Code 75860; Elev. 497; Lat. 31-37.6 N, Long. 96-16.9 W; E central Texas; 55 m. E of Waco. Named for niece of railroad magnate *B.F. Yoakum.*

•**TEE PEE CITY**, Village; Motley County; Pop. (Rural), Elev. 1,800; Settled 1879; NW Texas; Near the Pease River and Paducah. Settled by Anglo-Americans in 1879 on a site that had long been a favorite camping ground of the Comanches. It derived its name from the large number of teepee circles found by the first settlers.

•**TEHUACANA**, Town; Limestone County; Pop. 265; Zip Code 76686; Lat. 31-44.5 N, Long. 96-32.7 W; E central Texas; 40 m. NE of Waco. Founded about 1844 and named for an Indian tribe that had a village in the vicinity.

•**TELFERNER**, Village; Victoria County; Pop. 304; Zip Code 77988; Elev. 96; Lat. 28-51.0 N, Long. 96-53.4 W; S Texas; 8 m. NE of Victoria. Named for the Italian Count Telferner, who conceived the idea of building a railroad from New York to Mexico City.

•**TEMPLE**, City; Bell County; Pop. 42,483; Zip Code 765+; Elev. 630; Lat. 31-05.8 N, Long. 97-20.6 W; Central Texas; 32 m. S of Waco. Established in 1880. It first grew up as a railroad town on Gulf, Colorado and Santa Fe Railroad, and Missouri, Kansas and Texas lines.

•**TENAHA**, Town; Shelby County; Pop. 1,005; Zip Code 75974; Elev. 351; Lat. 31-56.7 N, Long. 94-14.7 W; E Texas; 45 m. S of Longview. The name is from the Indian word TENEHA, meaning "muddy water."

•**TERRELL**, City; Kaufman County; Pop. 13,225; Zip Code 75160; Elev. 530; Lat. 32-44.4 N, Long. 96-16.8 W; NE Texas. First settled in 1848. The town was organized about 1873 when the railroad was built.

•**TEXARKANA**, City; Bowie County; Pop. 31,271; Zip Code 755+; Elev. 295; Lat. 33-25.9 N, Long. 94-02.7 W; NE Texas; on the Texas-Arkansas Line, 20 miles southeast of the Oklahoma border. It is the twin city of Texarkana, Oklahoma. Founded in 1873 when the Texas and Pacific Railway came into the district. Established at the point where the tracks crossed the Texas-Arkansas Line. The place was called Texarkana, a name compounded of the first syllable of Texas, the first two of Arkansas, and the last syllable of Louisiana.

•**TEXAS CITY**, City; Galveston County; Pop. 41,403; Zip Code 775+; Elev. 12; Lat. 29-23.7 N, Long. 94-53.6 W; SE Texas; 15 m. N of Galveston on the bay. Original bay-front community was called Shoal Point.

•**TEXHOMA**, Town; Sherman County; Pop. 358; Zip Code 73949; NW Texas; Just S of Oklahoma state line. Many businesses are located on Oklahoma side.

•**THOMPSONS**, Town; Fort Bend County; Pop. 240; Zip Code 77481; Lat. 29-29.9 N, Long. 95-35.4 W; SE Texas.

•**THORNDALE**, City; Milam & Williamson Counties; Pop. 1,300; Zip Code 76577; Elev. 460; Lat. 30-36.9 N, Long. 97-12.3 W; Central Texas; 45 m. S of Temple. Three Spanish missions were built in the area near Thorndale: San Francisco Xavier de Horcasitas (St. Francis Xavier of Horcasitas), established in 1748; San Ildefonso (St. Alphonsus), established in 1749, and Nuestra Senora de la Candelaria (Our Lady of Candlemas), built in 1749. They were abandoned in 1755.

•**THORNTON**, Town; Limestone County; Pop. 498; Zip Code 76687; Lat. 31-24.5 N, Long. 96-34.4 W; E central Texas.

•**THRALL**, Town; Williamson County; Pop. 573; Zip Code 76578; Elev. 569; Lat. 30-35.4 N, Long. 97-17.9 W; Central Texas; 45 m. S of Temple. The town has, during two periods of its history, been the scene of oil booms.

•**THREE RIVERS**, City; Live Oak County; Pop. 2,133; Zip Code 78071; Elev. 155; Lat. 28-27.8 N, Long. 98-10.9 W; S Texas; At junction of Frio, Atascosa, and Nueces Rivers, for which it was named.

•**THROCKMORTON**, Town; Throckmorton County Seat; Pop. 1,174; Zip Code 76083; Elev. 1,700; Lat. 33-10.8 N, Long. 99-10.6 W; N Texas; 70 m. SW of Wichita Falls. Established in 1879.

•**THURBER**, Village; Erath County; Pop. 8; Elev. 1,100; N central Texas; 80 m. E of Abilene. Founded in 1888 by Texas & Pacific Coal Company.

•**TILDEN**, Village; McMullen County Seat; Pop. 500; Zip Code 78072; Elev. 245; S Texas; 65 m. S of San Antonio. In bend of Frio River, originally called Dog Town from local ranchers' habit of using packs of trained dogs to round up cattle in the brush country. Town was probably named for *Samuel J. Tilden*, Democratic candidate for president in 1876.

•**TIMPSON**, City; Shelby County; Pop. 1,164; Zip Code 75975; Lat. 31-54.4 N, Long. 94-24.1 W; E Texas; 50 m. S of Longview.

•**TIOGA**, Town; Grayson County; Zip Code 76271; Lat. 33-27.9 N, Long. 96-55.0 W; NE Texas; 28 m. NE of Denton; Name is Iroquoian for "at the forks."

•**TOLAR**, City; Hood County; Pop. 415; Zip Code 76476; Elev. 1,013; Lat. 32-23.3 N, Long. 97-55.2 W; N central Texas; 45 m. SW of Fort Worth. Petrified wood, found in vicinity, has been used here to build homes and stores.

•**TOM BEAN**, Town; Grayson County; Pop. 811; Zip Code 75489; Lat. 33-31.3 N, Long. 96-29.0 W; NE Texas. The town, named for railroad surveyor *Tom Bean*, grew up after the Cotton Belt Railroad came through in 1887.

•**TOMBALL**, City; Harris County; Pop. 3,996; Zip Code 77375; Lat. 30-05.8 N, Long. 95-36.9 W; SE Texas; Suburb of Houston; Named for *Thomas H. Ball*, a congressman from Houston.

•**TOYAH**, Town; Reeves County; Pop. 165; Zip Code 79785; W Texas; 19 m. SW of Pecos; The name is derived from an Indian word meaning "much water", which does not describe this region.

•**TRENT**, Town; Taylor County; Pop. 313; Zip Code 79561; Lat. 32-29.3 N, Long. 100-07.4 W; NW central Texas; 17 m. E of Sweetwater.

•**TRENTON**, Town; Fannin County; Pop. 691; Zip Code 75490; Lat. 33-25.8 N, Long. 96-20.4 W; NE Texas; Named by an early settler who liked the sound of the New Jersey city's name.

•**TRICKHAM**, Village; Coleman County; Pop. 40; Central Texas; 60 m. SE of Abilene. Named for a storekeeper here in the late 1800's who loved to play practical jokes on his customers. "Trick 'em" was the original nickname of merchant, *Tom Peters*.

•**TRINIDAD**, City; Henderson County; Pop. 1,130; Zip Code 75163; Lat. 32-08.6 N, Long. 96-05.6 W; NE Texas; 20 m. E of Corsicana; Name is Spanish for "trinity."

•**TRINITY**, City; Trinity County; Pop. 2,452; Zip Code 75862; Elev. 226; Lat. 30-56.8 N, Long. 95-22.4 W; E Texas. The town was settled in 1868 on land of New York and Texas Land Company.

•**TROUP**, City; Cherokee & Smith Counties; Pop. 1,911; Zip Code 75789; NE Texas; 15 m. SE of Tyler. Named in the 1850's for Georgia *Governor George M. Troup*.

•**TROY**, Town; Bell County; Pop. 1,353; Zip Code 76579; Lat. 32-08.6 N, Long. 95-07.2 W; Central Texas; 15 m. NE of Temple.

•**TULIA**, City; Swisher County Seat; Pop. 5,033; Zip Code 79088; Elev. 3,501; Lat. 34-32.3 N, Long. 101-46.0 W; NW Texas; 45 m. S of Amarillo. Tulia is a city that began in 1890 when *W.G. Connor* started a post office on the prairie.

•**TURKEY**, City; Hall County; Pop. 644; Zip Code 79261; Lat. 34-23.5 N, Long. 100-53.8 W; NW Texas; 95 m. SE of Amarillo in a ranching area where hoards of wild turkeys once roamed.

•**TUSCOLA**, Town; Taylor County; Pop. 660; Zip Code 79562; Lat. 32-12.4— N, Long. 99-47.9 W; NW central Texas; 15 m. S of Abilene; Named for the county in Michigan; Indian for "warrior prairie."

•**TYE**, Town; Taylor County; Pop. 1,378; Zip Code 79563; Lat. 32-27.3 N, Long. 99-52.2 W; NW central Texas; 7 m. NE of Abilene, near Dyess Airforce Base.

•**TYLER**, City; Smith County Seat; Pop. 69,995; Zip Code 757+; Elev. 558; Lat. 32-20.7 N, Long. 95-18.1 W; NE Texas. The city, founded in the 1840's, was named for *John Tyler*, tenth president of the United States, who signed the joint resolution under which Texas was admitted to the Union.

•**UNCERTAIN**, Village; Harrison County; Pop. 176; NE Texas; On Caddo Lake. Name may relate to the "uncertain landing" of early steamboats here, or to a fish buyer who didn't always show up for local fishermen.

•**UNION GROVE**, Village; Upshur County; Pop. 344; Elev. 300; NE Texas; 15 m. NW of Longview. *John O'Byrne* moved here from Ireland in the 1890's and planted shamrocks from seeds.

•**UNIVERSAL CITY**, City; Bexar County; Pop. 10,720; Zip Code 78148; Lat. 29-32.6 N, Long. 98-17.4 W; S central Texas; 12 m. NE of San Antonio in a residential area.

•**UTOPIA**, Village; Uvalde County; Pop. 360; Zip Code 78884; SW Texas; 45 m NE of Uvalde in a hilly area. Settled in 1852 by *Captain William Ware*, a veteran of the Battle of San Jacinto. The town was not known as Utopia until 1885. Schoolteacher *George Barker* named it for its pleasant surroundings.

•**UVALDE**, City; Uvalde County Seat; Pop. 14,178; Zip Code 78801; Elev. 913; Lat. 39-12.7 N, Long. 99-47.3— W; SE Texas; 80 m. SW of San Antonio. Uvalde was named in honor of *Juan de Ugalde* (the present spelling being a corruption of his name), a Spanish military leader, who in 1790 defeated the Apaches in what is now Uvalde Canyon.

•**VALENTINE**, Town; Jeff Davis County; Pop. 328; Zip Code 79854; Lat. 30-35.1 N, Long. 104-29.8 W; W Texas; 140 m. SE of El Paso near the Sierra Vieja Mountains. So named because the railroad reached the townsite on Valentine's Day, 1882.

•**VALLEY MILLS**, City; Bosque & McLennan Counties; Pop. 1,236; Zip Code 76689; Lat. 31-39.5 N, Long. 97-28.1 W; Central Texas; 21 m. NW of Waco.

•**VALLEY VIEW**, Town; Cooke County; Pop. 514; Zip Code 76272; Lat. 33-29.3 N, Long. 97-09.8 W; N Texas; 10 m. S of Gainesville.

•**VAN**, City; Van Zandt County; Pop. 1,881; Zip Code 75790; Lat. 32-31.4 N, Long. 95-38.3 W; NE Texas; 25 m. NE of Tyler; Named for early settlers *Vannie and Henry Vance Tunnell*.

•**VAN ALSTYNE**, Town; Grayson County; Pop. 1,860; Zip Code 75095; Lat. 33-25.4 N, Long. 96-34.7 W; NE Texas; 15 m. S of Sherman.

•**VAN HORN**, Town; Culberson County Seat; Pop. 2,772; Zip Code 79855; Elev. 4,010; Lat. 31-02.6 N, Long. 104-49.8 W; W Texas; 100 m. SE of El Paso. Named for Van Horn Wells, a frontier watering place a short distance to the south.

•**VAN ORMY**, Village; Bexar County; Pop. 264; Zip Code 78073; S Texas; S suburb of San Antonio on the Medina River; Named for *Count Adolph Von Ormy* of Austria, who owned 2,300 acres here in the 1880's.

•**VANDERBILT**, Village; Jackson County; Pop. 660; Zip Code 77991; SE Texas; 30 m. E of Victoria; Named for a captain in the Civil War whose barge sunk in the Navidad River. Town originated in 1904.

•**VANDERPOOL**, Village; Bandera County; Pop. 20; Zip Code 78885; SE central Texas; Elev. 1,610; 35 m. SW of Kerrville. The town received its name from early settler *L.B. Vanderpool*) when a post office was granted in 1885.

•**VEGA**, Town; Oldham County Seat; Pop. 900; Zip Code 79092; Elev. 4,030; Lat. 35-14.7 N, Long. 102-25.7 W; NW Texas; 30 m. W of Amarillo; Cattle and grains are chief export items.

•**VENUS**, Town; Johnson County; Pop. 518; Zip Code 76084; Lat. 32-25.8 N, Long. 97-06.2 W; N central Texas; 30 m. SW of Dallas; Named by a town founder for the natural beauty of the area.

•**VERNON**, City; Wilbarger County Seat; Pop. 12,695; Zip Code 76384; Elev. 1,205; Lat. 34-09.1 N, Long. 99-17.0 W; N Texas; 15 m. W of Oklahoma state line. Founded in 1880, Vernon was on the busy Western Trail, and so its stores carried large amounts of supplies for those crossing the western wilderness, especially cattlemen.

•**VICTORIA**, City; Victoria County Seat; Pop. 50,703; Zip Code 77901; Elev. 93; Lat. 28-48.3 N, Long. 97-00.3 W; S Texas; 90 m. NE of Corpus Christi. Named for *General Guadalupe Victoria*, later Mexico's first president.

•**VIDOR**, City; Orange County; Pop. 12, 117; Zip Code 77662; Elev. 2; Lat. 30-07.4 N, Long. 94-00.8 W; E Texas; 7 m. NE of Beaumont. Named for the Miller-Vidor Lumber Company, which operated here around the turn of the century.

•**VINEGARONE**, Village; Val Verde County; Pop. (Rural), Elev. 1,800; Settled in the early 1920s; SW Texas, on Dry Devils Creek. Vinegarone was named for the area it is in, known to cowboys as Vinegarone Hollow because of the great number of large whip scorpions - of the variety called *vinegarones* found there. The insects emit a vinegar-like odor when alarmed.

•**WACO**, City; McLennan County Seat; Pop. 101,261; Zip Code 767+; Lat. 31-32.8 N, Long. 97-08.5 W; Central Texas; 100 m. S of Dallas on the Brazos River. A Methodist missionary, *Joseph P. Sneed*, came to the region in 1849 and preached the first sermon in a log cabin.

•**WAELDER**, City; Gonzales County; Pop. 942; Zip Code 78959; Elev. 367; Lat. 29-41.7 N, Long. 97-17.9 W; S central Texas; 75 m. NE of San Antonio.

•**WAKE VILLAGE**, City; Bowie County; Pop. 3,865; Zip Code 75501; NE Texas; Named during World War II after Battle of Wake Island. It began as a housing project for defense factory workers.

•**WALLER**, City; Harris & Waller Counties; Pop. 1,241; Zip Code 77484; Elev. 250; Lat. 30-03.6 N, Long. 95-55.5 W; SE Texas; 40 m. NW of Houston.

•**WALLIS**, City; Austin County; Pop. 1,138; Zip Code 77485; Lat. 29-37.7 N, Long. 96-03.7 W; SE central Texas; 40 m. W of Houston.

•**WALNUT SPRINGS**, City; Bosque County; Pop. 613; Zip Code 76690; Lat. 32-03.4 N, Long. 97-45.0 W; Central Texas; 50 m. NW of Waco; Name is descriptive.

•**WASHINGTON**, Village; Washington County; Pop. 265; Zip Code 77880 Elev. 260; Lat. 30-19.5 N, Long. 96-09.4 W; SE central Texas; 35 m. SE of Bryan, on the muddy waters of the Brazos River. Founded in 1835, the town was first called Washington-on-the-Brazos.

•**WASKOM**, City; Harrison County; Pop. 1,793; Zip Code 75692; Elev. 371; Lat. 32-28.8 N, Long. 94-03.8 W; NE Texas; 16 m. E of Longview; Established in 1850. Originally known as Powellton. Name changed to Waskom Station in 1872 to honor man who was instrumental in bringing Southern Pacific Railroad through the community.

•**WATAUGA**, City; Tarrant County; Pop. 10,284; Zip Code 76148; Lat. 32-51.7 N, Long. 97-15.8 W; N Texas; Name is Cherokee, meaning unknown.

•**WAXAHACHIE**, City; Ellis County Seat; Pop. 14,624; Zip Code 75165; Elev. 530; Lat. 32-23.6 N, Long. 96-50.9 W; NE central Texas; 25 m. S of Dallas. The name derives from an Indian word meaning "cow (or buffalo) creek."

•**WEATHERFORD**, City; Parker County Seat; Pop. 12,049; Zip Code 76086; Elev. 864; Lat. 32-45.6 N, Long. 97-47.9 W; N central Texas; 30 m. W of Fort Worth. Established in the 1850's and named after *Jefferson Weatherford*, a member of the Texas Senate.

•**WEBSTER**, City; Harris County; Pop. 2,168; Zip Code 77598; Lat. 29-32.2 N, Long. 95-06.9 W; SE Texas; Suburb of Houston.

•**WECHES**, Village; Houston County; Pop. 26; Elev. 450; E central Texas; In Davy Crockett National Forest. A rural community first settled before 1847. Originally called Neches, the citizens chose Weches when a post office application revealed the first name was already in use.

•**WEIMAR**, City; Colorado County; Zip Code 78962; Lat. 29-42.2 N, Long. 96-46.8 W; SE central Texas; 90 m. W of Houston near the Colorado River. Named by German settlers for their native towns.

•**WELLINGTON**, City; Collingsworth County Seat; Pop. 3,043; Zip Code 79095; Elev. 1,980; Lat. 34-51.3 N, Long. 100-13.0 W; NW Texas; 95 m. SE of Amarillo. Named for the *Duke of Wellington*.

•**WELLMAN**, Town; Terry County; Pop. 239; Zip Code 79378; Lat. 33-02.8 N, Long. 102-25.6 W; NW Texas; 11 m. SW of Brownfield.

•**WELLS**, Town; Cherokee County; Pop. 926; Zip Code 75976; Lat. 31-29.2 N, 94-56.4 W; E Texas.

•**WESLACO**, City; Hidalgo County; Pop. 19,331; Zip Code 78596; Elev. 75; Lat. 26-09.5 N, Log. 97-59.5 W; S Texas; 45 m. NW of Brownsville. The name comes from the initials of W.E. Stewart Land Company that promoted the townsite in the irrigated Rio Grande Valley in 1919.

•**WEST**, City; McLennan County; Pop. 2,485; Zip Code 76691; Lat. 31-48.1 N, Long. 97-05.6 W; Central Texas; 17 m. N of Waco in a farming area.

•**WEST COLUMBIA**, City; Brazoria County; Pop. 4,109; Zip Code 77486; Elev. 34; Lat. 29-08.6 N, Long. 95-38.8 W; SE Texas; 40 m. SW of Galveston. In 1826, after he had laid out the town site on the Brazos River, *Joseph Bell* cleared a two mile long avenue through the prairie, and at its farthest end started this town, which he called Columbia.

•**WESTBROOK**, City; Mitchell County; Pop. 298; Zip Code 79565; Lat. 32-21.2 N, Long. 101-00.9 W; NW central Texas.

•**WHARTON**, City; Wharton County Seat; Pop. 9,033; Zip Code 77488; Elev. 111; Lat. 29-18.6 N, Long. 96-06.0 W; SE Texas; 55 m.

SW of Houston. Named for *William and John Wharton*, brothers, prominent during the Texas Revolution.

•**WHEELER**, Town; Wheeler County Seat; Pop. 1,584; Zip Code 79096; Elev. 2,520; Lat. 35-26.7 N, Long. 100-16.4 W; NW Texas; 107 m. E of Amarillo. The post office was established when area became "thickly settled" by five families living in dugouts within two-mile radius. The town became seat of Wheeler County in 1906.

•**WHITE DEER**, Town; Carson County; Pop. 1,210; Zip Code 79097; Lat. 35-25.8 N, Long. 101-10.36 W; NW Texas; Named for a nearby creek. Town moved in 1908 to be near Santa Fe rail lines.

•**WHITE SETTLEMENT**, City; Tarrant County; Pop. 13,508; Zip Code 76108; Lat. 32-45.6 N, Long. 97-27.0 W; N Texas; W suburb of Fort Worth.

•**WHITEFACE**, Town; Cochran County; Pop. 463; Zip Code 79379; Lat. 33-36.2 N, Long. 102-36.8 W; NW Texas; 40 m. W of Lubbock; Named by rancher *C.C. Slaughter* for his "white-faced" cattle, the Herefords.

•**WHITESBORO**, City; Grayson County; Pop. 3,197; Zip Code 76273; Elev. 783; Lat. 33-39.4 N, Long. 96-54.4 W; NE Texas; 60 m. N of Dallas.

•**WHITEWRIGHT**, Town; Fannin & Grayson Counties; Pop. 1,757; Zip Code 75491; Lat. 33-30.8 N, Long. 96-23.7 W; NE Texas; 50 m. NE of Dallas.

•**WHITNEY**, Town; Hill County; Pop. 1,631; Zip Code 76692; Elev. 585; 57.0 N, Long. 97-19.2 W; NE central Texas; 30 m. N of Waco. Established in 1879 when the Texas Central Railroad crossed Hill County; named for *Charles Whitney* of New York, a major railroad stockholder.

•**WICHITA FALLS**, City; Archer & Wichita Counties; Wichita County Seat; Pop. 94,201; Zip Code 763+; Elev. 946; Lat. 33-54.2 N, Long. 98-29.6 W; N Texas; 16 miles S of Texas-Oklahoma Line. There are several legends regarding the name "Wichita," but according to the Smithsonian Institution the name is "of uncertain meaning and origin." *John Gould*, columnist of the *Wichita Daily Times*, was convinced the name means "men from the north." "Falls" was used in the town's name because of a five-foot waterfall which in early years existed in the river.

•**WILLS POINT**, City; Van Zandt County; Pop. 2,631; Zip Code 75169; Elev. 532; NE Texas; 50 m. E of Dallas; Marketing and shipping center.

•**WILSON**, City; Lynn County; Pop. 578; Zip Code 79381; Lat. 33-19.0 N, Long. 101-43.6 W; NW Texas; 22 m. SE of Lubbock. Named after *James Charles Wilson*, a Mier expedition adventurer.

•**WINBERLY**, Unincorporated Town; Hays County; Pop. 3,065; Zip Code 78676; Elev. 967;; S central Texas; 35 m. SW of Austin. Established 1848, a center of resort and retirement development in central Texas Hill Country.

•**WINDOM**, Town; Fannin County; Pop. 276; Zip Code 75492; Lat. 33-34.0 N, Long. 95-59.9 W; NE Texas; 35 m. E of Sherman.

•**WINDTHORST**, Town; Archer & Clay Counties; Pop. 409; Zip Code 76389; Elev. 900; Lat. 33-34.4 N, Long. 98-26.3 W; N Texas; 24 m. S of Wichita Falls. German immigrants founded the town in 1891.

•**WINFIELD**, Town; Titus County; Pop. 349; Zip Code 75493; Lat. 33-10.1 N, Long. 95-06.7 W; NE Texas; 65 m. NE of Tyler.

•**WINK**, City; Winkler County; Pop. 1,182; Zip Code 79789; Lat. 31-45.3 N, Long. 103-09.4— W; W Texas; 50 m. W of Odessa; Named for first part of Winkler County.

•**WINNSBORO**, City; Frankling & Wood Counties; Pop. 3,458; Zip Code 75494; Elev. 533; Lat. 32-57.5 N, Long. 95-17.4 W; NE Texas; 105 m. E of Dallas. Founded in 1854 as a trade center at intersection of two main roads, and first known as Crossroads. Name changed to honor early settler, *John E. Wynn.* Spelling was supposedly changed by a newspaper editor in the 1870s because of a shortage of "ys" in his type.

•**WINONA**, Town; Smith County; Pop. 443; Zip Code 75792; Lat. 32-29.4 N, Long. 95-10.2 W; NE Texas; 11 m. NE of Tyler; Named for the daughter of a railroad executive, *Winona Douglass.*

•**WINTERS**, City; Runnels County; Pop. 3,061; Zip Code 79567; Lat. 31-57.6 N, Long. 99-57.9 W; W central Texas; 50 m. NE of San Angelo; Named for early settler, *J.N. Winters.*

•**WOLFE CITY**, City; Hunt County; Pop. 1,594; Zip Code 75496; Lat. 33-22.1 N, Long. 96-04.3 W; NE Texas; 15 m. N of Greenville.

•**WOLFFORTH**, Town; Lubbock County; Pop. 1,701; Zip Code 79382; Lat. 33-30.3 N, Long. 102-00.9 W; NW Texas; 8 m. SW of Lubbock; Named for early settler *George Wolforth*, whose name was misspelled on the records.

•**WOODSBORO**, Town; Refugio County; Pop. 1,974; Zip Code 78393; Elev. 48; Lat. 28-14.3 N, Long. 97-19.5 W; S Texas; 50 m. NW of Corpus Christi in a vast ranching area.

•**WOODSON**, Town; Throckmorton County; Pop. 291; Zip Code 76091; Lat. 33-01.0 N, Long. 99-03.3 W; N Texas.

•**WOODVILLE**, Town; Tyler County Seat; Pop. 2,821; Zip Code 75979; Elev. 232; Lat. 30-46.5 N, Long. 94-25.3 W; E Texas; 55 m. NW of Beaumont. Named for *George T. Wood*, second governor of Texas.

•**WORTHAM**, Town; Freestone County; Pop. 1,187; Zip Code 76693; Lat. 31-47.2 N, Long. 96-27.8 W; E central Texas; 25 m. S of Corsicana.

•**WYLIE**, City; Colling County; Pop. 3,152; Zip Code 75098; Lat. 33-00.8 N, Long. 96-32.5 W; NE Texas; 22 m. NE of Dallas.

•**YANTIS**, Town; Wood County; Pop. 210; Zip Code 75497; Lat. 32-55.7 N, Long. 95-34.6 W; NE Texas; 45 m. N of Tyler.

•**YARD**, Village; Anderson County; Pop. 18; NE central Texas; Near Palestine; Named by a storekeeper-postmaster in 1903 after a townsperson purchased a yard of cloth in his store.

•**YOAKUM**, City; De Witt & Lavaca Counties; Pop. 6,148; Zip Code 77995; Elev. 322; SE central Texas; 90 m. E of San Antonio. Yoakum was founded on a league of land granted to *John May* of Ireland in 1835. Named after *Henderson King Yoakum*, pioneer and historian.

•**YORKTOWN**, City; DeWitt County; Pop. 2,498; Zip Code 78164; Elev. 266; Lat. 28-59.0 N, Long. 97-30.0 W; S Texas; 65 m. SE of San Antonio. First settler in 1846 was *John York.* Road from Indianola to San Antonio, surveyed in 1848, went by way of the York home, and the surveyor, *Charles Eckhardt*, built a home at the site of Yorktown.

•**ZAPATA**, Zapata County Seat; Lat. 26-54.5 N, Long. 99-16.3 W; S Texas; On Falcon Lake near the Mexican border; is one of the oldest towns in the Lower Rio Grande Valley. Here an independent civil settlement of Spanish ranchmen - Revilla, now Guerrero, Mexico, was found on land granted by *Jose de Escandon* in 1750 and spread northward across the Rio Grande. Zapata appeared on the maps of 1858 as Carrizo and on the maps of 1868 as Bellville. It was named for pioneer *Antonio Zapata.*

•**ZAVALLA**, City; Angelina County; Pop. 762; Zip Code 75980; Elev. 228; Lat. 31-09.5 N, Long. 94-25.6 W; E Texas; 20 m. SE of Lufkin. Named for an old settlement near Jasper that was the seat of government for the De Zavala colony in 1829. For some reason the modern name is spelled with two l's.

UTAH

•**ALPINE,** City; Utah County; Pop. 2,649; Descriptively named for its elevated location in the Wasatch Mountains which provides "alpine" views.

•**ALTA,** Town; Salt Lake County; Pop. 381; Zip Code 84092; Alta is Spanish for "high." At 9500 feet elevation this ex-minig town evolved to famous ski resort is aptly named.

•**ALTAMONT,** Town; Duchesne County; Pop. 247; Zip Code 84002; Elev 6375; Lat. 40-24-01 N long 110-17-35 W; Descriptively named for its elevation, the name means "high mountain."

•**AMERICAN FORK,** City; Utah County; Pop. 12,417; Zip Code 84003; Lat. 40-21-59 N long. 111-47-35 W; Settled in 1850 near the Fork River, the name American Fork was chosen to contrast with nearby Spanish Fork.

•**ANNABELLA,** Town; Sevier County; Pop. 463; Zip Code 84711; Elev 5301; Lat. 38-42-28 N long. 112-03-37 W; Named for the wife of an early settler.

•**AURORA,** Town; Sevier County; Pop. 874; Zip Code 84620; Elev 5187; Lat. 38-55-19 N long. 111-56-11 W; A Latin word meaning "dawn."

•**BEAR RIVER CITY,** Town; Box Elder County; Pop. 540; Zip Code 84301; Lat. 41-37-08 N long. 112-07-47 W; The town is named after the Bear River which empties into the Great Salt Lake.

•**BEAVER,** City; Beaver County County; Pop. 1,792; Zip Code 84713; Elev 5898; Lat. 38-16-45 N long. 112-38-21 W; Named after the Beaver River, itself descriptively named for the once plentiful fur bearing animals.

•**BICKNELL,** Town; Wayne County; Pop. 296; Zip Code 84715; Lat. 38-20-28 N long. 111-32-32 W; Bicknell is named for businessman Thomas Bicknell.

•**BLANDING,** City; San Juan County; Pop. 3,118; Zip Code 84510; Elev 6105; Lat. 37-12-55 N long. 109-11-04 W; First called Red Mesa and later changed to Blanding, the maiden name of Mrs. Thomas Bicknell.

•**BOUNTIFUL,** City; Davis County; Pop. 32,877; Zip Code 84054; Lat. 40-51-29 N long. 111-53-52 W; Early settlers gave their town this grateful descriptive name for its fertility.

•**BRIAN HEAD,** Town; Iron County; Pop. 77; Zip Code 84719; A high point in south-west Utah, the town is named for a member of the U. S. geological survey.

•**BRIGHAM CITY,** City; Box Elder County Seat; Pop. 15,596; Zip Code 84304; Lat. 41-50-12 N long. 112-00-20 W; The city's name honors Mormon pioneer Brigham Young.

•**CANNONVILLE,** Town; Garfield County; Pop. 134; Zip Code 84718; Named after an early settler.

•**CASTLE,** City; Emery County Seat; Pop. 1,910; Located on the San Rafael River in Castle Valley an so named.

•**CEDAR,** City; Iron County; Pop. 10,972; Zip Code 84720; Founded in 1851 and named for the abundant scrub cedar in the area.

•**CEDAR CITY,** City; Iron County; Pop. 10,972; Zip Code 84720; Founded in 1851 and named for the abundant scrub cedar in the area.

•**CEDAR FORT,** Town; Utah County; Pop. 269; Named after the abundant scrub cedar in the area.

•**CENTERFIELD,** Town; Sanpete County; Pop. 653; Zip Code 84622; Lat. 39-07-37 N long. 111-49-08 W; Named for its location in the county.

•**CENTERVILLE,** City; Davis County; Pop. 8,069; Zip Code 84014; Lat. 40-54-14 N long. 111-53-10 W; Central to the local area and thus given this descriptive name.

•**CHARLESTON,** Town; Wasatch County; Pop. 320; The town is named after the city in South Carolina.

•**CIRCLEVILLE,** Town; Piute County; Pop. 445; Zip Code 84723; Elev 6063; Lat. 38-10-19 N long. 112-16-16 W; A geographic and descriptive name for the circular contour of the town's valley.

•**CLARKSTON,** Town; Cache County; Pop. 562; Zip Code 84305; Elev 4884; Lat. 41-55-11 N long. 112-03-15 W; Named for an early pioneer settler.

•**CLEARFIELD,** City; Davis County; Pop. 17,982; Zip Code 84015; Elev; Lat. 41-06-42 N long. 112-01-17 W; Descriptively named by the first settlers.

•**CLEVELAND,** Town; Emery County; Pop. 522; Zip Code 84518; Lat. 39-20-49 N long. 110-50-55 W; Named in honor of Grover Cleveland, the 24th President of the United States.

•**CLINTON,** City; Davis County; Pop. 5,777; Clinton is named after the famous governor of New York.

•**COALVILLE,** City; Summit County Seat; Pop. 1,031; Zip Code 84017; Elev 5586; Lat. 40-55-09 N long. 111-23-37 W; The first coal deposits in Utah were found in the area and gave the town its name.

•**CORINNE,** City; Box Elder County; Pop. 512; Zip Code 84307; A railroad boom town in the late 1800's, it was named after a town entrepreneur's daughter.

•**CORNISH,** Town; Cache County; Pop. 181; Zip Code 84308; Named for the local crop.

•**DELTA,** City; Millard County; Pop. 1,930; Zip Code 84624; Lat. 39-21-13 N long. 112-34-33 W; The town is located in the dry Sevier Lake in a region of river delta. This geography named the town.

•**DEWEYVILLE,** Town; Box Elder County; Pop. 311; Zip Code 84309; Named for a prominent early citizen.

•**DRAPER,** City; Salt Lake County; Pop. 5,530; Zip Code 84020; Lat. 40-31-41 N long. 111-52-04 W; Draper is named for an early settler.

•**DUCHESNE,** City; Duchesne County Seat; Pop. 1,677; Zip Code 84021; Lat. 40-09-59 N long. 110-23-53 W; A French trapper named Du Chesne worked the United Basin in the 1840's and gave his name to the river and the town.

•**EAST CARBON,** City; Carbon County; Pop. 1,942; Zip Code 84520; Lat. 39-32-37 N long. 110-24-46 W; Named for the large coal deposits nearby.

•**EAST LAYTON,** City; Davis County; Pop. 3,531; The city is named after an early settler.

•**ELK RIDGE,** Town; Utah County; Pop. 381; Once the home of numerous elk before the white man came, the town's name remembers this heritage.

•**ELMO,** Town; Emery County; Pop. 300; Zip Code 84521; Elev 5694; Lat. 39-23-22 N long 110-48-44 W; Named for an early settler.

•**ELSINORE,** Town; Sevier County; Pop. 612; Zip Code 84724; Lat. 38-40-58 N long. 112-08-59 W; Named by Mormom settlers from Elsinore, Denmark for their former home.

•**EMERY,** Town; Emery County; Pop. 372; Zip Code 84522; Elev 6262; Lat. 38-55-34 N long. 111-14-43 W; Named in honor of George Emery, Utah's territorial governor from 1875-1880.

•**ENOCH,** Town; Iron County; Pop. 678; Named by Mormom settlers after Biblical patriarch Enoch.

•**ENTERPRISE,** City; Washington County; Pop. 905; Zip Code 84725; Lat. 37-34-22 N long. 113-42-48 W; The site of a major irrigation project in the 1890's, this work led to the town's being labeled enterprise.

•**EPHRAIM,** City; Sanpete County; Pop. 2,810; Zip Code 84627; Elev; Lat. 39-21-41 N long. 111-35-15W; A Biblical name given by the Mormom settlers.

•**ESCALANTE,** Town; Garfield County; Pop. 652; Zip Code 84716; Elev 5812; Lat. 37-55-28N long. 111-25-37 W; The town is named in honor of Spanish explorer Fray Francisco Silvestre De Escalante who explored the region in 1776.

•**EUREKA,** City; Juab County; Pop. 670; Zip Code 84628; Elev 6442; Lat. 39-57-09 N long. 112-06-50 W; An historic mining district the town's name is Greek, meaning "Iave found it." The discovery refers to a vein of precious metal.

•**FAIRVIEW,** City; Sanpete County; Pop. 916; Zip Code 84629; Lat. 39-37-42 N long. 111-26-19 W; Descriptively named for the city's scenic resources.

•**FARMINGTON,** City; Davis County Seat; Pop. 4,691; Zip Code 84025; Elev 4302; Lat. 40-59-06 N long. 111-53-13 W; The city's name reflects the area's main economic activity.

•**FAYETTE,** Town; Sanpete County; Pop. 165; Zip Code 84630; Named by Mormom settlers after Fayette, New York where Joseph Smith founded the Mormom church in 1830.

•**FERRON,** City; Emery County; Pop. 1,718; Zip Code 84523; Lat. 39-05-23 N long. 111-07-40 W; Ferron is named for the original surveyor of Emery and Carbon counties, A. D. Ferron.

•**FIELDING,** Town; Box Elder County; Pop. 325; Zip Code 84311; Elev 4367; Lat. 41-48-42 N long. 112-06-50 W; Named for an early settler.

•**FILLMORE,** City; Millard County Seat; Pop. 2,083; Zip Code 84631; Elev 5135; Lat. 38-58-12 N long. 112-19-51 W; Named in honor of President Millard Fillmore who signed the Utah Territory Act in 1850.

•**FOUNTAIN GREEN,** City; Sanpete County; Pop. 578; Zip Code 84632; Elev 6025; Lat. 39-37-41 N long. 111-38-24 W; A descriptive name for the area's rich agriculture.

•**GARDEN CITY,** Town; Rich County; Pop. 259; Zip Code 84028; Lat. 41-55-32 N long. 111-23-12 W; The city's rich agriculture led to this name.

•**GARLAND,** City; Box Elder County; Pop. 1,405; Zip Code 84312; Elev 5273; Lat. 41-44-40 N long. 112-09-43 W; Garland is named after an early settler.

•**GLENDALE,** Town; Kane County; Pop. 237; Zip Code 84710; Elev 5824; Lat. 37-26-20 N long. 112-28-37 W; A common descriptive name often given to western communities.

•**GLENWOOD,** Town; Sevier County; Pop. 447; Zip Code 84730; A descriptive name referring to meadow - like openings, or glens, in the local forests.

•**GOSHEN,** Town; Utah County; Pop. 582; Zip Code 84633; Elev; Lat. 39-57-01 N long. 111-53-55 W; A Biblical name reflecting the area's desirability for farming and ranching.

•**GRANTSVILLE,** City; Tooele County; Pop. 4,419; Zip Code 84029; Lat. 40-35-54 N long. 112-27-55 W; Named in honor of General, and later, President U. S. Grant.

•**GREEN RIVER,** City; Emery & Grand Counties; Pop. 1,048; Zip Code 84525; Lat. 38-59-41 N long. 110-09-29 W; Named by early Spanish explorers Rio Verde, or Green River, for its characteristic water color.

•**GUNNISON,** City; Sanpete County; Pop. 1,255; Zip Code 84630; Lat. 39-13-30 N long. 111-51-23 W; The town's nameonors Captain J. W. Gunnisn, explorer and surveyor, who was killed by the Ute Indians in 1853.

•**HARRISVILLE,** City; Weber County; Pop. 1,371; The city is named after a local settler.

•**HATCH,** Town; Garfield County; Pop. 121; Zip Code 84735; Elev 6917; Lat. 37-38-52 N long 112-25-51 W; Hatch is named after a settler in the area.

•**HEBER,** City; Wasatch County Seat; Pop. 4,362; Zip Code 84032; Elev 5595; Lat. 40-29-12 N long. 111-26-14 W; Heber's name remembers Mormom counselor Heber C. Kimball.

•**HELPER,** City; Darbon County; Pop. 2,724; Zip Code 84526; Lat. 39-41-14 N long. 110-51-07 W; A railroad station on a steep grade, additional "helper" locomotives were added here to cross the mountains. The practice led to this name.

•**HENEFER,** Town; Summit County; Pop. 547; Zip Code 84033; Lat. 41-01-21 N long. 111-29-39 W; Named after a local inhabitant.

•**HENRIEVILLE,** Town; Garfield County; Pop. 167; Zip Code 84736; Lat. 37-33-44 N long. 111-59-42 W; A local settler named Henry gave the town its name.

•**HIAWATHA,** Town; Carbon County; Pop. 249; Zip Code; Named for the legendary Mowark Indian hero of Longfellow's famous poem.

•**HINCKLEY,** Town; Millard County; Pop. 464; Zip Code 84635; Lat. 39-20-00 N ong. 112-40-24 W; Named for a local settler.

•**HOLDEN,** Town; Millard County; Pop. 364; Zip Code 84636; Lat. 39-05-59 N long. 112-16-34 W; A common personal name recalling a pioneer family.

•**HONEYVILLE,** Town; Box Elder County; Pop. 915; Zip Code 84314; Lat. 41-38-05 N long. 112-04-44 W; Descriptively named for the beekeeping activities in the area.

•**HOWELL,** Town; Box Elder County; Pop. 176; Zip Code 84316; Elev 4556; Lat. 41-46-59 N long. 112-26-20 W; A common personal name recalling an early settler in the area.

•**HUNTINGTON,** City; Emery County; Pop. 2,316; Zip Code 84528; Elev 5791; Lat. 39-19-31 N long. 110-57-33 W; Named for a prominent local settler.

•**HUNTSVILLE,** Town; Weber County; Pop. 577; Zip Code 84317; Elev 4929; Lat. 41-15-36 N long. 111-45-57 W; The town's name honors Captain Jefferson Hunt of the Mormom battalion in the Mexican-American War.

•**HURRICANE,** City; Washington County; Pop. 2,361; Zip Code 84737; Elev 3266; Lat. 37-10-29 N long. 113-17-15 W; A spanish word meaning "cyclone," but here referring to a violent storm.

•**HYDE PARK**, City; Cache County; Pop. 1,495; Zip Code 84318; Lat. 41-47-58 N long. 111-49-13 W; Named after the famous residential area of London.

•**HYRUM**, City; Cache County; Pop. 3,952; Zip Code 84319; Lat. 41-37-57 N long. 111-51-18 W; The city is named after a Biblical character.

•**KAMAS**, City; Summit County; Pop. 1,064; Zip Code 84036; Lat. 40-37-21 N long. 111-16-13 W; The town is named after the edible camassia quamash plant which resembles a hyacinth.

•**KANAB**, City; Kane County Seat; Pop. 2,148; Zip Code 84741; Kanab is a Ute Indian word for "willow."

•**KANARRAVILLE**, Town; Iron County; Pop. 255; Zip Code 84742; The town is named after a Pah Ute Indian Chief, Kanarra.

•**KANOSH**, Town; Millard County; Pop. 435; Zip Code 84637; Elev 5015; Lat. 38-48-18 N long. 112-26-19 W; Kanosh is named after a famous Indian Chief, Kanosh.

•**KINGSTON**, Town; Piute County; Pop. 146; Zip Code 84743; Named after 19th century geologist Clarence King.

•**KOOSHAREM**, Town; Sevier County; Pop. 183; Zip Code 84744; Elev 6914; Lat. 38-30-43 N long. 111-52-56 W; A Ute Indian word referring to an edible tuber.

•**LA VERKIN**, Town; Washington County; Pop. 1,174; Zip Code 84745; Lat. 37-12-08 N long. 113-16-02 W; A shortened and corrupted version of a nearby stream's name: Rio De La Virgen.

•**LAKETOWN**, Town; Rich County; Pop. 271; Zip Code 84038; Elev 5988; Lat. 41-49-13 N long. 111-19-00 W; Descriptively named for its lakeside location.

•**LAYTON**, City; Davis County; Pop. 22,862; Zip Code 84041; Lat. 41-04-27 N long. 111-57-26 W; Named for an early settler.

•**LEAMINGTON**, Town; Millard County; Pop. 113; Zip Code 84638; Leamington's name recalls one of its early settlers.

•**LEEDS**, Town; Washington County; Pop. 216; Zip Code 84746; Named after Leeds, England.

•**LEHI**, City; Utah County; Pop. 6,848; Zip Code 84043; Elev 4562; Lat. 40-23-31 N long. 111-48-51 W; Named after the Book of Mormom colonizer of America.

•**LEVAN**, Town; Juab County; Pop. 453; Zip Code 84639; Elev 5314; Lat. 39-33-24 N long. 111-51-40 W; A shortened version of "levant", or "the lands of the surnrise."

•**LEWISTON**, City; Cache County; Pop. 1,438; Zip Code 84308; Elev 4506; Lat. 41-58-00 N long. 111-57-24 W; Named for an early settler.

•**LINDON**, City; Utah County; Pop. 2,796; Often mistaken by settlers for Linden trees, the name may spring from the cottonwood tree, which is common to the area.

•**LOA**, Town; Wayne County Seat; Pop. 364; Zip Code 84747; Lat. 38-24-03 N long. 111-38-29 W; Loa is a Hawaiian word meaning "long."

•**LOGAN**, City; Cache County Seat; Pop. 26,844; Zip Code 84321; Lat. 41-43-19 N long. 111-49-26 W; The town is named after Plains Indian Chief Logan Fontanglle.

•**LYNNDYL**, Town; Millard County; Pop. 90; Zip Code 84640; Elev 4784; Lat. 39-31-15 N long. 112-22-34 W; Named after Lynn, Massachusetts with the euphonious suffix "dyl" added.

•**MANILA**, Town; Daggett County Seat; Pop. 272; Zip Code 84046; Lat. 40-59-36 N long. 109-43-23 W; Named after the city of Manila in the Phillipines.

•**MANTI**, City; Sanpete County Seat; Pop. 2,080; Zip Code 84642; Lat. 39-15-49 N long. 111-38-13W; A city mentioned in the Book of Mormom, and the source of this town's name.

•**MANTUA**, Town; Box Elder County; Pop. 484; A corruption of the word manteau, or loose cloak.

•**MAPLETON**, City; Utah County; Pop. 2,726; Named after the beloved maple tree.

•**MARYSVALE**, Town; Piute County; Pop. 359; Zip Code 84750; Lat. 38-26-56 N long. 112-13-38 W; Originally named by the Spanish for the Virgin Mary.

•**MAYFIELD**, Town; Sanpete County; Pop. 397; Zip Code 84643; Lat. 39-07-07 N long. 111-42-30 W; A common name referring to an early settler.

•**MEADOW**, Town; Millard County; Pop. 265; Zip Code 84644; Lat. 38-53-17 N long. 112-24-32 W; Descriptively named for its most prominent feature.

•**MENDON**, City; Cache County; Pop. 663; Zip Code 84325; Lat. 41-42-29 N long. 111-58-51 W; Named after Mendon, Massachusetts, itself named after Mendon, England.

•**MIDVALE**, City; Salt Lake County; Pop. 10,144; Zip Code 84047; Lat. 40-36-59 N long. 111-52-47 W; The city is descriptively named for its location in the surroundig valley.

•**MIDWAY**, City; Wasatch County; Pop. 1,194; Zip Code 84049; Lat. 40-31-02 N long. 111-28-16 W; Located between two farming areas, the area's settlers called it Midway.

•**MILFORD**, City; Beaver County; Pop. 1,293; Zip Code 84751; Elev 4957; Lat. 38-23-34 N long.113-00-29 W; The city was named after an ore reduction mill, and a nearby river ford.

•**MILLVILLE**, Town; Cache County; Pop. 848; Zip Code 84326; Lat. 41-40-49 N long. 111-49-36 W; Descriptively named as the site of several mills.

•**MOAB**, City; Grand County Seat; Pop. 5,333; Zip Code 84532; The city is named after the Biblical kingdom of Moab.

•**MONA**, Town; Juab County; Pop. 536; Zip Code 84645; Elev 4916; Lat. 39-49-00 N long. 111-51-26 W; Possibly named by Welsh immigrants for a county in Wales.

•**MONROE**, City; Sevier County; Pop. 1,476; Zip Code 84739; Lat. 38-37-54 N long. 112-13-00 W; Named in honor of President James Monroe.

•**MONTICELLO**, City; San Juan County Seat; Pop. 1,929; Zip Code 84535; Elev 7066; Lat. 37-52-14 N long. 109-20-21 W; Monticello means "little mountain." There is a small mountain near the town, and so it is descriptively named.

•**MORGAN CITY**, City; Morgan County Seat; Pop. 1,896; Zip Code 84050; Elev 5064; Lat. 41-02-17 N long. 111-40-27 W; The city is named after Jedediah Morgan Grant, counselor to Brigham Young.

•**MORONI**, City; Sanpete County; Pop. 1,086; Zip Code 84623; Elev 5520; Lat. 39-28-33 N long. 111-28-15 W; The Mormoms believe the angel Moroni appeared to Joseph Smith and told him to start the Mormom Church.

•**MOUNT PLEASANT**, City; Sanpete County; Pop. 2,049; Zip Code 84647; Elev 5924; Lat. 39-32-33 N long. 111-27-19 W; Descriptively named for the pleasant environment.

•**MURRAY**, City; Salt Lake County; Pop. 25,750; Zip Code 84107; The name honors Utah territorial Governoir Eli Murray who goverened from 1880-86.

•**NEPHI**, City; Juab County Seat; Pop. 3,285; Zip Code 84648; Elev 5133; Lat. 39-42-36 N long. 111-49-50 W; The city is named after the prophet Nephi, an important figure in the Book of Mormom.

•**NEW HARMONY**, Town; Washington County; Pop. 117; Zip Code 84757; Elev 5306; Lat. 37-28-39 N long. 113-18-11 W; A euphonious name given the place by its settlers.

•**NEWTON**, Town; Cache County; Pop. 623; Zip Code 84327; Lat. 41-51-37 N long. 111-59-31 W; A common English name - the town is named after a local settler.

•**NORTH OGDEN**, City; Weber County; Pop. 9,309; Named after Hudson Bay Company Peter Skene Ogden.

•**NORTH SALT LAKE**, City; Davis County; Pop. 5,548; Zip Code 84054; The city is descriptively named for the Great Salt Lake.

•**OAK CITY**, Town; Millard County; Pop. 389; Zip Code 84649; Elev 5105; Lat. 39-22-37 N long. 112-20-24 W; The town is descriptively named for the many oaks in the area.

•**OAKLEY**, Town; Summit County; Pop. 470; Zip Code 84055; Lat. 40-43-34 N long. 111-16-50 W; Named after the many local oaks.

•**OGDEN**, City; Weber County Seat; Pop. 64,407; Zip Code 84400; Lat. 41-13-37 N long. 111-57-26 W; Peter Ogden was an early Hudson Bay factor in Utah. The city is named after him.

•**ORANGEVILLE**, City; Emery County; Pop. 1,309; Zip Code 84537; The town is named after Orange Seeley, an early pioneer.

•**ORDERVILLE**, Town; Kane County; Pop. 423; Zip Code 84537; Elev 5772; Lat. 39-13-32 N long. 111-02-54 W; The name recalls a Mormon economic order established in the pioneering days but later abandoned.

•**OREM**, City; Utah County; Pop. 52,399; Zip Code 84057; Lat. 40-17-08 N long. 111-41-25 W; The town is named after an early railway builder.

•**PANGUITCH**, City; Garfield County Seat; Pop. 1,343; Zip Code 84717; Lat. 37-37-44 N long. 112-10-06 W; A Pah Ute Indian word meaning "fish."

•**PARADISE**, Town; Cache County; Pop. 542; Zip Code 84328; Lat. 41-34-10 N long. 111-50-06 W; Descriptively and euphonious-ly named by the town's settlers.

•**PARK CITY**, City; Summit & Wasatch Counties; Pop. 2,823; Zip Code 84060; Lat. 40-38-52 N long. 111-29-26 W; Descriptively named after Parley's Park to the north.

•**PAROWAN**, City; Iron County Seat; Pop. 1,836; Zip Code 84761; A Pah Ute Indian word meaning "marsh people," and referring to the original local inhabitants.

•**PAYSON**, City; Utah County; Pop. 8,246; Zip Code 84651; Lat. 40-02-17 N long. 111-43-50 W; Probably named after a local settler.

•**PERRY**, City; Box Elder County; Pop. 1,084; The town's name honors a prominent early pioneer.

•**PLAIN CITY**, City; Weber County; Pop. 2,379; A descriptive name for the local geography.

•**PLEASANT GROVE**, City; Utah County; Pop. 10,669; Zip Code 84062; Lat. 40-20-55 N long. 111-45-15 W; Originally Battle Creek as a result of Indian-settler fights, later settlers changed it to the more euphonious "Pleasant Grove."

•**PLEASANT VIEW**, City; Weber County; Pop. 3,983; Named after the attractive local environment.

•**PLYMOUTH**, Town; Box Elder County; Pop. 238; Zip Code 84330; Lat. 41-52-26 N long. 112-08-33 W; The town is named after Plymouth, Massachusetts.

•**PRICE**, City; Carbon County Seat; Pop. 9,086; Zip Code 84501; Lat. 39-36-02 N long. 110-48-06 W; Both the town and the river are named for pioneer settler, William Price.

•**PROVIDENCE**, City; Cache County; Pop. 2,675; Zip Code 84332; Lat. 41-42-14 N long. 111-49-14 W; Named after the city in Rhode Island.

•**PROVO**, City; Utah County Seat; Pop. 73,907; Zip Code 84064; Elev 4549; Lat. 41-39-42 N long. 111-10-58 W; Provo's name remembers French-Canadian explorer and mountain man, Etienne Provot.

•**RANDOLPH**, Town; Rich County Seat; Pop. 659; The town is named after Randolph Stewart, who was its founder.

•**REDMOND**, Town; Sevier County; Pop. 619; Zip Code 84652; Lat. 39-00-07 N long. 111-51-47 W; Probably a descriptive name for the area's soil or rocks.

•**RICHFIELD**, City; Sevier County Seat; Pop. 5,482; Zip Code 84657; Lat. 38-51-00 N long. 111-58-02 W; A descriptive name given by the area's early settlers.

•**RICHMOND**, City; Cache County; Pop. 1,705; Zip Code 84333; Elev 4607; Lat. 41-55-16 N long. 111-48-24 W; The city is named after one of several similarly named cities on the east coast of the United States.

•**RIVER HEIGHTS**, City; Cache County; Pop. 1,211; A geographic descriptive name for the town's immediate locality.

•**RIVERDALE**, City; Weber County; Pop. 3,841; A dscriptive name for the area's geography.

•**RIVERTON**, City; Salt Lake County; Pop. 7,293; Zip Code 84065; Elev 4435; Lat. 40-34-28 N long. 111-56-54 W; Named for its location near a local river.

•**ROOSEVELT**, City; Duchesne County; Pop. 3,842; Zip Code 84066; Elev 5100; Lat. 40-27-19 N long. 110-04-21 W; The city is named after President Theodore Roosevelt.

•**ROY**, City; Weber County; Pop. 19,694; Zip Code 84067; Lat. 41-11-14 N long. 112-01-10 W; Named after a prominent local settler.

•**RUSH VALLEY**, Town; Tooele County; Pop. 356; Zip Code 84069; Lat. 40-14-15 N long. 112-26-22 W; A descriptive name for the area's local vegetation.

•**ST. GEORGE**, City; Washington County Seat; Pop. 11,350; Zip Code 84746; Elev 2761; Lat. 37-14-22 N long. 113-21-13 W.

•**SALEM**, City; Utah County; Pop. 2,233; Zip Code 84653; Lat. 40-03-03 N long. 111-40-08 W; The town has a Biblical name meaning "peace."

•**SALINA,** City; Sevier County; Pop. 1,992; Zip Code 84654; Lat. 38-57-25 N long. 111-51-12 W; A Spanish name meaning "salt marsh or pond."

•**SALT LAKE CITY,** City; Salt Lake County Seat and Capital of Utah; Pop. 163,033; Zip Code 84100; Lat. 40-45-26 N long. 111-52-29 W; The city is named for the Great Salt Lake near it.

•**SANDY CITY,** City; Salt Lake County; Pop. 51,022; Zip Code 84070; Lat. 40-34-52 N long. 111-52-24 W; Descriptively named for local soil types.

•**SANTA CLARA,** Town; Washington County; Pop. 1,091; Zip Code 84738; Lat. 37-10-13 N long. 113-40-25 W; A Spanish name menaing "Saint Clara."

•**SANTAQUIN,** City; Utah County; Pop. 2,175; Zip Code 84655; Lat. 40-06-16 N long. 111-54-30 W; A Pau Ute Indian chief who found several battles with the Mormoms.

•**SCIPIO,** Town; Millard County; Pop. 257; Zip Code 84656; Mormom settlers named the town after the great Roman general who destroyed Carthage.

•**SCOFIELD,** Town; Carbon County; Pop. 105; Named after a prominent early settler.

•**SMITHVILLE,** City; Cache County; Pop. 4,993; Zip Code 84335; Elev. 4595; Lat. 41-50-44 N, long. 111-52-00 W. Located in N. Utah, in an area of livestock and dairy farms.

•**SOUTH JORDAN,** City; Salt Lake County; Pop. 7,492; Named by the pioneers after the Jordan River.

•**SOUTH OGDEN,** City; Weber County; Pop. 11,366; Named in honor of 19th century Hudson Bay factor Peter Ogden.

•**SOUTH SALT LAKE,** City; Salt Lake County; Pop. 10,561; The city is named by its proximity to Salt Lake.

•**SOUTH WEBER,** City; Davis County; Pop. 1,575; Named in honor of early mountain man John Weber.

•**SPANISH FORK,** City; Utah County; Pop. 9,825; Zip Code 84660; Lat. 40-06-37 N long. 111-38-42 W; The Fork River comes down here from the Wasatch Mountains. It is called Spanish Fork because a Spanish exploration group followed it into the Utah Valley in 1776.

•**SPRING CITY,** City; Sanpete County; Pop. 671; Zip Code 84662; Elev 5826; Lat. 39-28-40 N long. 111-29-35 W; Named for the occurrence of local springs.

•**SPRINGDALE,** Town; Washington County; Pop. 258; Zip Code 84763; Lat. 37-09-40 N long. 113-02-26 W; Local springs and the surroundings named the town.

•**SPRINGVILLE,** City; Utah County; Pop. 12,101; Zip Code 84663; Lat. 40-11-04 N long. 111-37-02 W; A large spring occurs at the base of the Wasatch Mountains near here. The town is named for this spring.

•**STERLING,** Town; Sanpete County; Pop. 199; Zip Code 84665; Probably a commendatory name, as in a "sterling town."

•**STOCKTON,** Town; Tooele County; Pop. 437; Zip Code 84071; Lat. 40-27-18 N long. 112-21-42 W; The town is named after Stockton, California.

•**SUNNYSIDE,** City; Carbon County; Pop. 611; Zip Code 84539; Lat. 39-32-58 N long. 110-23-09 W; A descriptive name for the town sunny location.

•**TABIONA,** Town; Duchesne County; Pop. 152; Zip Code 84072; Elev 6517; Lat. 38-16-58 N long. 111-28-32 W; A Ute Indian Chief named Tabby organized his tribe into a confederacy. Tabiona is named after him.

•**TOOELE,** City; Tooele County Seat; Pop. 14,335; Zip Code 84074; Lat. 40-31-58 N long. 112-17-55 W; An English corruption of the Spanish word "tule," or the common bulrush.

•**TOQUERVILLE,** Town; Washington County; Pop. 277; Zip Code 84774; Lat. 37-14-28 N long. 113-16-54 W; A Pah Ute word for "black montain."

•**TORREY,** Town; Wayne County; Pop. 140; Zip Code 84775; The town is named after a local settler with the family name Torrey.

•**TREMONTON,** City; Box Elder County; Pop. 3,464; Zip Code 84337; Elev 4290; Lat. 41-41-59 N long. 112-09-11 W; The city was named by French-Canadian trappers who called the area "tres monton", or "three hills."

•**TRENTON,** Town; Cache County; Pop. 447; Zip Code 84338; Lat. 41-54-43 N long. 111-56-18 W; The town is named after Trenton, New Jersey.

•**TROPIC,** Town; Garfield County; Pop. 338; Zip Code 84718; Elev 6295; Lat. 37-33-50 N long. 112-03-15 W; The town's founders gave it this physiogeographic name.

•**UINTAH,** Town; Weber County; Pop. 439; Zip Code 84008; Lat. 39-59-00 N long. 109-10-36 W; A branch of the Pah Ute Indian tribe, the Unitah left their name on the area.

•**VERNAL,** City; Uintah County Seat; Pop. 6,600; Zip Code 84078; Lat. 40-27-22 N long. 109-31-39 W; Settled in 1879 and given a name meaning "spring."

•**VERNON,** Town; Tooele County; Pop. 181; Zip Code 84080; Lat. 40-14-15 N long. 112-26-22 W; The town's name honors founder Joseph Vernon.

•**VIRGIN,** Town; Washington County; Pop. 169; Zip Code 84779; A descriptive name given by its settlers for the area's unspoiled beauty.

•**WALES,** Town; Sanpete County; Pop. 153; Zip Code 84667; Mormom immigrants from Wales gave their new home the title of their former one.

•**WALLSBURG,** Town; Wasatch County; Pop. 239; Zip Code 84082; Lat. 40-23-13 N long. 111-25-08 W; Descriptively named for canyon-like features nearby.

•**WASHINGTON,** City; Washington County; Pop. 3,092; Zip Code 84780; The city is named after George Washington.

•**WELLINGTON,** City; Carbon County; Pop. 1,406; Zip Code 84542; Elev 5413; Lat. 39-32-30 N long. 110-43-48 W; The city is named in honor of the Great British commander of the Napoleionic Wars.

•**WELLSVILLE,** City; Cache County; Pop. 1,952; Zip Code 84339; Lat. 41-38-02 N long. 111-56-15 W; Settled in 1856 and named after Mormom military commander Daniel Wells.

•**WENDOVER,** Town; Tooele County; Pop. 1,099; Zip Code 84034; Lat. 40-02-17 N long. 114-59-56 W; A compound word: the verb wend and the adverb over.

•**WEST BOUNTIFUL,** City; Davis County; Pop. 3,556; Named for the assessment the pioneers gave the place.

•**WEST JORDAN,** City; Salt Lake County; Pop. 26,794; Zip Code 84084; Lat. 40-36-07 N, long. 111-58-22 W. Named for its geographical location and after the Biblical country.

•**WEST POINT,** City; Davis County; Pop. 2,170. The town is named for its geographical features.

•**WOODS CROSS,** City; Davis County; Pop. 4,263; Zip Code 84087; Lat. 40-52-20 N, long. 111-53-39 W. Descriptively named by its settlers for the local feature.

VERMONT

•ADDISON, Town; Addison County; Pop. 889; The town was named in honor of the great English statesman Joseph Addison who died in 1719.

•ALBANY, Town; Orleans County; Pop. 705; Zip Code 05820; Elev. 956'; Lat. 44-43-49 N long. 072-22-49 W; Originally called Lutterloh, the name was later changed to Albany after that city in New York.

•ALBURG, Town; Grand Isle County; Zip Code 05440; Elev. 124'; Lat. 44-58-31 N long. 073-18-05 W; Founded by Ira Allen, the town's name is a contraction of Allenburg.

•ANDOVER, Town; Windsor County; Pop. 350; Zip Code 05501; The town is named after Andover in Hampshire, England

•ARLINGTON, Town; Bennington County; Pop. 2,184; Zip Code 05250; Lat. 43-04-14 N long. 073-09-08; The town is named in Honor of Augustus Henry Fitzroy, the fourth Earl of Arlington, and a friend of the American colonies.

•ATHENS, Town; Windham County; Pop. 250; Settled in the late 1700's and named for the classical Greek city.

•BAKERSFIELD, Town; Franklin County; Pop. 852; Zip Code 05441; Elev. 736'; Lat. 44-46-53 N long. 072-48-16; Settler Joseph Baker bought the town in 1788, and named it after himself.

•BALTIMORE, Town; Windsor County; Pop. 181; Baltimore takes its name from Baltimore, Maryland.

•BARNARD, Town; Windsor County; Pop. 790; Zip Code 05031; Elev. 1335'; Barnard takes its name from colonial Governor Francis Bernard, who served as Governor of the Massachusetts Bay colony from 1760-69.

•BARRE, City; Washington County; Pop. 9,824; Zip Code 05641; Elev. 609'; Lat. 44-11-56 N long. 072-30-08 W; Chartered in 1781 and named after Barre, Massachusetts.

•BARRE, Town; Washington County; Pop. 7,090; Founded in the 1790's and named after Barre, Massachusetts.

•BARTON, Town; Orleans County; Pop. 2,990; Zip Code 05822; Elev. 952; Lat. 44-44-57 N long. 072-10-38 W; Settled after the Revolutionary War and named for Colonel William Barton.

•BELLOWS FALLS, Village; Windham County; Pop. 3,456; Zip Code 05101; Elev. 299'; Named after an early settler and its location.

•BELVIDERE, Town; Lamoille County; Pop. 218; Zip Code 05442; Elev. 924'; Lat. 44-45-08 N long. 072-41-17; Landowner John Kelly named the town after Lake Belvedere in Ireland.

•BENNINGTON, Town; Bennington County Seat; Pop. 15,815; Zip Code 05201; Elev. 681'; Lat. 42-52-46 N long. 073-11-47; Bennington honors Royal Governor Benning Wentworth who chartered many areas and towns in Vermont.

•BENSON, Town; Rutland County; Pop. 739; The town's name honors Revolutionary War patriot Egbert Benson.

•BERKSHIRE, Town; Franklin County; Pop. 1,116; Settled in 1780 and named after Berkshire County, Massachusetts.

•BERLIN, Town; Washington County; Pop. 2,454; Granted in 1763 and named after Berlin, Massachusetts.

•BETHEL, Town; Windsor County; Pop. 1,715; Zip Code 05032; Elev. 543'; Chartered in 1779 and given the biblical name of Bethel.

•BLOOMFIELD, Town; Essex County; Pop. 188; Named in 1830 for its descriptive connotations associated with flowers and blossoms.

•BOLTON, Town; Chittenden County; Pop. 715; Named by Governor Wentworth for the Duke of Bolton.

•BRADFORD, Town; Orange County; Pop. 2,191; Zip Code 05033; Originally Mooretown, the name was changed after the Revolution to honor early Massachusett Governor William Bradford.

•BRAINTREE, Town; Orange County; Pop. 1,065; Chartered in 1781 and named after Braintree, Massachusetts, itself named after Braintree in Essex, England.

•BRANDON, Town; Rutland County; Pop. 4,194; Zip Code 05733; Elev. 431'; Lat. 43-47-48 N long. 073-05-21 W; Originally named Neshobe and later renamed after Brandon Bay in Ireland.

•BRATTLEBORO, Town; Windham County; Pop. 11,886; Zip Code 05301; Elev. 240'; Lat. 42-51-06 N long. 072-33-52 W; Granted by Benning Wentworth and named for a Grantee, Colonel William Brattle.

•BRIDGEWATER, Town; Windsor County; Pop. 867; Zip Code 05034; Granted in 1761 and named in honor of Francis Egerton, third Duke of Bridgewater, who became famous for his construction of the first canals in Britain.

•BRIDPORT, Town; Addison County; Pop. 997; Zip Code 05734; Lat. 43-59-04 N long. 073-19-00; The town is named after English Channel port of Bridport.

•BRIGHTON, Town; Essex County; Pop. 1,557; Granted in 1780 and named after the English Resort town.

•BRISTOL, Town; Addison County; Pop. 3,293; Zip Code 05443; Elev. 571'; Lat. 44-08-18 N long. 073-04-54 W; Originally Pocock, the name was changed in 1789 after Bristol, Rhode Island.

•BROOKFIELD, Town; Orange County; Pop. 959; Zip Code 05036; Elev. 1276'; Brookfield is named after Brookfield, Massachusetts.

•BROOKLINE, Town; Windham County; Pop. 310; Grassy brook flows through the town in an almost perfect straight line, and gave the town its name.

•BROWNINGTON, Town; Orleans County; Pop. 708; Granted in 1782 and named for two Grantees, Daniel and Timothy Brown.

•BRUNSWICK, Town; Essex County; Pop. 82; Established in 1761 and named to honor the English Hanover King George III, who was also the Duke of Brunswick-Lungburg.

•BURKE, Town; Caledonia County; Pop. 1,385; The town was named to honor English Statesman Edmund Burke.

•BURLINGTON, City; Burlington & Chittenden County Seats; Pop. 37,712; Zip Code 05401; Elev. 113'; Lat. 44-29-02 N long. 073-13-12 W; Incorporated in 1864, the city was named after the Earl of Burlington in the 18th century.

•CABOT, Town; Washington County; Pop. 958; Zip Code 05647; Elev. 1064'; Lat. 44-24-14 N long. 072-18-26 W; Chartered in the 1780's and named for the Cabot family.

•CALAIS, Town; Washington County; Pop. 1,207; Zip Code 05648; Lat. 44-22-28 N long. 072-29-45 W; Granted in 1781 and named for the French Channel port.

•CAMBRIDGE, Town; Lamoille County; Pop. 2,019; Zip Code 05444; Elev. 455'; Lat. 44-38-39 N long. 072-52-37 W; Chartered in 1781 and named for Cambridge, Massachusetts.

•CANAAN, Town; Essex County; Pop. 1,196; Zip Code 05901; Lat. 44-59-44 N long. 071-42-40 W; Chartered in 1782 and given the biblical name for the promised land.

•CASTLETON, Town; Rutland County; Pop. 3,637; Zip Code 05735; Elev. 439'; Lat. 43-36-38 N long. 073-10-56 W; Settled in the late 1700's and named after Castleton, England.

•CAVENDISH, Town; Windsor County; Pop. 1,355; Zip Code 05142; Elev. 929'; The town was named to honor William Cavendish, the fourth Duke of Devonshire (1720-64), and an influential British peer.

•CHARLESTON, Town; Orleans County; Pop. 851; The town is named after Charlestown, South Carolina where Commodore Abraham Whipple put up a heroic defense in 1780.

•CHARLOTTE, Town; Chittenden County; Pop. 2,561; Zip Code 05445; Elev. 169'; Lat. 44-18-31 N long. 073-15-17 W; Granted in 1762 and named for Charlotte Sophia of Mecklenburg-Strelitz, the wife of George III.

•CHELSEA, Town; Orange County Seat; Pop. 1,091; Zip Code 05038; Originally Turnersburgh, the name was changed in 1794 after Chelsea, Connecticut.

•CHESTER, Town; Windsor County; Pop. 2,791; Zip Code 05143; Elev. 623'; Originally called New Flamstead, the name was changed in 1766 to honor Prince George Augustus Frederick, the eldest son of British Monarch George III.

•CHITTENDEN, Town; Rutland County; Pop. 927; Zip Code 05737; Lat. 43-42-27 N long. 072-56-59 W; Chittenden was named for Vermont's first Governor, Thomas Chittenden.

•CLARENDON, Town; Rutland County; Pop. 2,372; Named by Governor Benning Wentworth for Clarendon in Wiltshire, England.

•COLCHESTER, Town; Chittenden County; Pop. 12,629; Zip Code 05446; Lat. 44-32-31 N long. 073-08-59 W; Named in 1763 to honor prominent British Nobleman William Henry Nassau du Zurlostine, Baron of Colchester.

•CONCORD, Town; Essex County; Pop. 1,125; Zip Code 05824; Elev. 859'; Lat. 44-25-42 N long. 071-53-21 W; Founded in 1780 and named after Concord, Massachusetts.

•CORINTH, Town; Orange County; Pop. 904; Zip Code 05039; Granted in 1764 by Benning Wentworth and named for the ancient Greek city.

•CORNWALL, Town; Addison County; Pop. 993; The town is named for the Maritime County in England.

•COVENTRY, Town; Orleans County; Pop. 674; Zip Code 05825; Elev. 718'; Lat. 44-51-58 N long. 072-16-02 W; Chartered in 1780 and named after Coventry, Connecticut.

•CRAFTSBURY, Town; Orleans County; Pop. 844; Zip Code 05826; Lat. 44-38-11 N long. 071-37-34 W; Among the original charter members was Colonel Ebenezer Crafts. The town is named for him.

•DANBY, Town; Rutland County; Pop. 992; Zip Code 05739; Lat. 43-20-44 N long. 072-59-56 W; Named by Benning Wentworth in honor of Basil Fielding, sixth Earl of Denbigh.

•DANVILLE, Town; Caledonia County; Pop. 1,705; Zip Code 05828; Lat. 44-24-40 N long. 066-08-34 W; Chartered in 1786 and named to honor famous French cartographer Jean Baptiste Bourguignon d'Anville.

•DERBY, Town; Orleans County; Pop. 4,222; Zip Code 05829; Lat. 44-57-22 N. long. 072-08-13 W. Named for the town and county in England. Chartered just before the end of the Revolutionary War and named after Derby, Connecticut.

•DORSET, Town; Bennington County; Pop. 1,648; Zip Code 05251; Elev. 962'; Lat. 43-15-13 N long. 073-06-02 W; Named in honor of Lionel Sackville, the first Duke of Dorset.

•DOVER, Town; Windham County; Pop. 666; Incorporated in 1810 and named after Dover, New Hampshire.

•DUMMERSTON, Town; Windham County; Pop. 1,574; The town is named for an 18th century Lieutenant Governor of Massachusetts, William Dummer.

•DUXBURY, Town; Washington County; Pop. 877; Duxbury was granted in 1763 and named after Duxbury, Massachusetts.

•EAST HAVEN, Town; Essex County; Pop. 280; Zip Code 05837; Lat. 44-39-52 N long. 071-53-14 W; Established in 1790 and named for East Haven, Connecticut.

•EAST MONTPELIER, Town; Washington County; Pop. 2,205; Zip Code 05651; Elev. 728'; Lat. 44-16-12 N long. 072-29-30 W; Originally part of Montpelier, and so descriptively named.

•EDEN, Town; Lamoille County; Pop. 612; Zip Code 05652; Elev. 1112'; Lat. 44-42-28 N long. 072-32-50 W; Settled after the Revolutionary War and named for the biblical paradise.

•ELMORE, Town; Lamoille County; Pop. 421; Granted to a group of Revolutionary War veterans, among them Colonel Samuel Elmore, for whom the town was named.

•ENOSBURG, Town; Franklin County; Pop. 2,070; Zip Code 05450; Elev. 422'; Lat. 44-54-10 N long. 072-48-14 W; Charted in 1780 and named after the first grantee, General Roger Enos.

•ESSEX, Town; Chittenden County; Pop. 14,392; Zip Code 05451; Lat. 44-30-42 N, long. 073-03-36. Named for Essex, England.

•ESSEX JUNCTION, Village, Chittenden , Pop. 7,033; Zip Code 05452; Elev. 347'; Lat. 44-29-31 N long. 073-06-56 W; Granted in 1763 and named after Essex, England.

•FAIR HAVEN, Town; Rutland County; Pop. 2,819; Zip Code 05731; Lat. 43-42-22 N long. 073-18-43 W; Settled in the 1780's and given a commendatory name.

•FAIRFAX, Town; Franklin County; Pop. 1,805; Zip Code 05454; Lat. 44-39-59 N long. 073-00-43 W; Fairfax is named after Thomas Fairfax, the sixth Baron Fairfax who immigrated to Virginia in 1747.

•FAIRFIELD, Town; Franklin County; Pop. 1,493; Zip Code 05455; Lat. 44-48-04 N long. 072-56-43 W; The town is named after Fairfield, Connecticut.

•FAIRLEE, Town; Orange County; Pop. 770; Zip Code 05045; Settled in the late 1700's and named after a town on the Isle of Wight. The name means "a beautiful meadow."

•**FAYSTON,** Town; Washington County; Pop. 657; The town is named in honor of Vermont's prominent 18th century family.

•**FERDINAND,** Town; Essex County; Pop. 12; Named by Governor Benning Wentworth in 1761 to honor Prince Karl Wilhelm Ferdinand, a relative of King George III.

•**FERRISBURG,** Town; Addison County; Pop. 2,117; Zip Code 05456; Elev. 218'; Lat. 44-12-24 N long. 073-14-52 W; Ferrisburg is named after one of its founders, Benjamin Ferris.

•**FLETCHER,** Town; Franklin County; Pop. 626; Chartered in 1781 and named for Revolutionary War General Samuel Fletcher.

•**FRANKLIN,** Town; Franklin County; Pop. 1,006; Zip Code 05457; Elev. 453'; Lat. 44-58-57 N long. 072-55-07 W; Originally named Huntsburg, the town's name was later changed to honor Statesman Benjamin Franklin.

•**GEORGIA,** Town; Frnaklin County; Pop. 2,818; Granted in 1763 and named for England's King George III.

•**GLASTENBURY,** Town; Bennington County; Pop. 3; The town was named after Glastonbury in Somerset, England.

•**GLOVER,** Town; Orleans County; Pop. 843; Granted to veterans of the Revolutionary War and named for General John Glover.

•**GOSHEN,** Town; Addison County; Pop. 163; Named after Goshen, Connecticut. Goshen was the biblical land in Egypt where the Israelites lived in exile.

•**GRAFTON,** Town; Windham County; Pop. 604; Zip Code 05146; Elev. 841'; Settled in the 1790's and named for Grafton, Massachusetts.

•**GRANBY,** Town; Essex County; Pop. 70; Zip Code 05840; Elev. 1456'; Lat. 44-34-13 N long. 071-45-15 W; Chartered in 1761 and named in honor of John Manners, the Marquis of Granby, who helped defeat the French in 1759 at the Battle of Minden.

•**GRAND ISLE,** Town; Grand Isle County; Pop. 1,238; Zip Code 05458; Elev. 169'; Lat. 44-43-17 N long. 073-17-39 W; Descriptively named as the largest island in Lake Champlain.

•**GRANVILLE,** Town; Addison County; Pop. 288; Zip Code 05747; Elev. 1013'; Lat. 43-59-05 N long. 072-50-43 W; The town is named after John Carteret (1690-1763), the first Earl of Granville.

•**GREENSBORO,** Town; Orleans County; Pop. 677; Zip Code 05841; Lat. 44-34-34 N long. 072-17-50 W; The town was founded in the 1780's and named in honor of printer Timothy Green.

•**GROTON,** Town; Caledonia County; Pop. 667; Zip Code 05046; Chartered in 1789 and named for Groton, Massachusetts, itself named for Groton in Suffolk, England.

•**GUILDHALL,** Town; Essex County Seat; Pop. 202; Zip Code 05905; Elev. 368'; Lat. 44-33-57 N long. 071-33-36 W; Granted in 1761 and named for London's famous Guildhall.

•**GUILFORD,** Town; Windham County; Pop. 1,532; Granted in 1754 just before the outbreak of the French and Indian War, and named by Benning Wentworth in honor of the Earl of Guilford.

•**HALIFAX,** Town; Windham County; Pop. 488; Halifax's name honors George Montagu-Dunk, the second Earl of Halifax, and a prominent colonial administrator.

•**HANCOCK,** Town; Addison County; Pop. 334; Zip Code 05748; Lat. 43-55-34 N long. 072-50-33 W; Hancock's name honors revolutionary patriot John Hancock.

•**HARDWICK,** Town; Caledonia County; Pop. 2,613; Zip Code 05843; Elev. 841'; Lat. 44-30-19 N long. 072-22-06 W; Chartered after the Revolutionary War and named in honor of Philip Yorke, Earl of Hardwicke.

•**HARTFORD,** Town; Windsor County; Pop. 7,963; Zip Code 05047; Granted in 1761 and named for Hartford, Connecticut.

•**HARTLAND,** Town; Windsor County; Pop. 2,396; Zip Code 05048; Elev. 587'; Hartland is named after the city in Connecticut and the Hartland in Devonshire, England.

•**HIGHGATE,** Town; Franklin County; Pop. 2,493; Named by Governor Benning Wentworth for Highgate, a well-known suburb of London.

•**HINESBURG,** Town; Chittenden County; Pop. 2,690; Zip Code 05461; Lat. 44-19-37 N long. 073-06-45 W; Settled in the 1780's and given the Christian name of the first child born there, i.e. Hine.

•**HOLLAND,** Town; Orleans County; Pop. 473; Holland is named for Samuel Holland, who was the King's Surveyor General of all the colonies north of Virginia.

•**HUBBARDTON,** Town; Rutland County; Pop. 490; Site of the battle of Hubbardtown in 1777, the town was named for a prosperous Boston merchant, Thomas Hubbard.

•**HUNTINGTON,** Town; Chittenden County; Pop. 1,161; Zip Code 05462; Lat. 44-19-45 N long. 072-59-04 W; Granted in 1763 and named for the local Hunt family.

•**HYDE PARK,** Town; Lamoille County Seat; Pop. 2,021; Zip Code 05655; Lat. 44-35-50 N long. 072-36-48 W; The town is named after its original grantee, Captain Jedediah Hyde.

•**IRA,** Town; Rutland County; Pop. 354; Granted in 1781 and named for settler Ira Allen.

•**IRASBURG,** Town; Orleans County; Pop. 870; Zip Code 05845; Elev. 814'; Lat. 44-48-06 N long. 072-16-49 W; Settled in the 1780's and named for pioneer Ira Allen.

•**ISLE LA MOTTE,** Town; Grand Isle County; Pop. 393; Zip Code 05463; Elev. 188'; Lat. 44-53-13 N long. 073-20-28 W; Settled by a French army unit in 1666 and named for its Commander Pierre de St. Paul, Sieur de la Motte.

•**JACKSONVILLE,** Village; Windham County; Pop. 252; Zip Code 05342; Elev. 1334'; Lat. 42-47-47 N long. 072-49-15 W; Named in honor of President Andrew Jackson.

•**JAMAICA,** Town; Windham County; Pop. 681; Zip Code 05343; Elev. 732'; Lat. 43-06-00 N long. 072-46-38 W; The town's name is a Natick Indian word meaning "beaver."

•**JAY,** Town; Orleans County; Pop. 302; Chartered in 1792 and named in honor of Statesman John Jay.

•**JEFFERSONVILLE,** Village; Pop. Lamoille County; Pop. 491; Zip Code 05464; Elev. 459'; Lat. 44-38-38 N long. 072-49-45 W; Named in honor of Thomas Jefferson.

•**JERICHO,** Town; Chittenden County; Pop. 3,575; Zip Code 05465; Elev. 550'; Lat. 44-30-24 N long. 072-59-41 W; Founded in 1763 and given the Biblical name of Jericho.

•**JOHNSON,** Town; Lamoille County; Pop. 2,581; Zip Code 05656; Elev. 516'; Lat. 44-38-09 N long. 072-40-47 W; Granted in 1782 and named for the second grantee, William Samuel Johnson.

•**KIRBY,** Town; Caledonia County; Pop. 282; Incorporated in 1807 and named for Kirby, England. The name means "a village with a church."

•**LANDGROVE**, Town; Bennington County; Pop. 121; Descriptively named by its first settlers for the many trees covering the land.

•**LEICESTER**, Town; Addison County; Pop. 803; Zip Code 05752; Elev. 352'; Lat. 43-51-11 N long 073-09-13 W; Named for the town of Leicester in England.

•**LEMINGTON**, Town; Essex County; Pop. 108; Settled in the late 1700's and named for Leamington, England.

•**LEWIS**, Town; Essex County; Founded in 1762 and named for early settlers, Nathan, Sevignior, and Timothy Lewis.

•**LINCOLN**, Town; Addison County; Pop. 870; Lincoln's name honors Revolutionary War General Benjamin Lincoln.

•**LONDONDERRY**, Town; Windham County; Pop. 1,510; Zip Code 05148; Elev. 1151'; Settled in the late 1700's and named after Londonderry, New Hampshire.

•**LOWELL**, Town; Orleans County; Pop. 573; Zip Code 05847; Elev. 996'; Lat. 44-48-04 N long 072-26-55 W; Originally Kellyvale, the town's name was later changed to honor John Lowell, a prominent manufacturer.

•**LUDLOW**, Town; Windsor County; Pop. 2,414; Zip Code 05149; Elev. 1067'; Granted in 1761 and named in honor of Henry Herbert, Viscount Ludlow.

•**LUNENBURG**, Town; Essex County; Pop. 1,138; Zip Code 05906; Elev. 1202'; Lat. 44-25-42 N long. 071-53-21 W; Named in honor of Prince Ferdinand of Brunswick, a relative of England's George III.

•**LYNDON**, Town; Caledonia County; Pop. 4,924; Zip Code 05849; Elev. 1706'; Lat. 44-30-48 N long. 072-01-01 W; Chartered in 1780 and named after Josiah Lyndon Arnold, the son of a town founder.

•**LYNDONVILLE**, Village; Caledonia County; Pop. 1,401; Zip Code 05851; Elev. 714'; Lat. 44-32-13 N long. 072-00-25 W; Chartered to a group of Revolutionary War soldiers and named in honor of Josiah Lyndon Arnold, son of one of the founders.

•**MAIDSTONE**, Town; Essex County; Pop. 100; Granted in 1761 and named for Maidstone, England.

•**MANCHESTER**, Town; Bennington County Seat; Pop. 3,261; Zip Code 05254; Elev. 899'; Lat. 43-09-38 N long. 073-04-25 W; Granted in the 1760's and named after Manchester, England.

•**MARLBORO**, Town; Windham County; Pop. 695; Zip Code 05344; Lat. 42-52-09 N long. 072-43-09 W; A popular colonial name, it honored John Churchill, the great 17th century soldier and Duke of Marlborough.

•**MARSHFIELD**, Town; Washington County; Pop. 1,267; Zip Code 05658; Elev. 857'; Lat. 44-21-10 N long. 072-21-10 W; Named after Colonel Issac Marsh, an early landowner.

•**MENDON**, Town; Rutland County; Pop. 1,056; Mendon is named after Mendon, Massachusetts.

•**MIDDLEBURY**, Town; Addison County Seat; Pop. 7,574; Zip Code 05753; Elev. 366'; Lat. 44-00-52 N long. 073-10-07 W; Three towns were chartered in this area at the same time, one north, one south, and between them Middlebury.

•**MIDDLESEX**, Town; Washington County; Pop. 1,235; Named by Governor Wentworth after Middlesex, England.

•**MIDDLETOWN SPRINGS**, Town; Rutland County; Pop. 603; Zip Code 05757; Elev. 893'; Lat. 43-28-57 N long. 073-07-18 W; Incorporated in 1784 and named after Middletown, Connecticut and a local mineral springs.

•**MILTON**, Town; Chittenden County; Pop. 6,829; Zip Code 05468; Lat. 44-38-12 N long. 073-06-39 W; Named for a relative of Governor Wentworth.

•**MONKTON**, Town; Addison County; Pop. 1,201; Zip Code 05469; Lat. 44-14-12 N long. 073-08-48 W; Granted in 1762 and named in honor of British Soldier, General Robert Monckton.

•**MONTGOMERY**, Town; Franklin County; Pop. 681; Zip Code 05470; Elev. 493'; Lat. 44-54-05 N long. 072-37-40 W; Established in 1789 and named in honor of Revolutionary War hero, General Richard Montgomery.

•**MONTPELIER**, City; Washington County Seat; Pop. 8,241; Zip Code 05602; Elev. 525'; Lat. 44-15-30 N long. 072-34-14 W; Chartered in 1781 and named for Montpelier, France.

•**MORETOWN**, Town; Washington County; Pop. 1,221; Zip Code 05660; Elev. 602'; Lat. 44-15-01 N long. 072-45-42 W; Granted in the 1760's and named after a local family.

•**MORGAN**, Town; Orleans County; Pop. 460; Zip Code 05853; Lat. 44-54-40 N long. 072-00-56 W; First named Caldersburgh, the town's name was changed in 1801 to honor another landowner, John Morgan.

•**MORRISTOWN**, Town; Lamoille County; Pop. 4,448; The town's name honors the prominent Morris family from New York State.

•**MORRISVILLE**, Village, Lamoille , Pop. 2,074; Zip Code 05657; Elev. 682'; Lat. 44-32-30 N long. 072-31-27 W; Settled right after the Revolutionary War and named in honor of the Morris family of New York.

•**MOUNT HOLLY**, Town; Rutland County; Pop. 938; Zip Code 05758; Elev. 1558'; Lat. 43-27-14 N long. 072-49-07 W; Incorporated in 1792 and named after Mount Holly, New Jersey.

•**MOUNT TABOR**, Town; Rutland County; Pop. 211; Granted as Harwich in 1761, but later renamed to honor Revolutionary War veteran Gideon Tabor.

•**NEW HAVEN**, Town; Addison County; Pop. 1,217; Zip Code 05472; Elev. 455'; Lat. 44-07-24 N long. 073-09-23 W; The town is named after New Haven, Connecticut.

•**NEWARK**, Town; Caledonia County; Pop. 280; Named by its settlers in the 1780's "New Ark" and referring to a new settlement, or project.

•**NEWBURY**, Town; Orange County; Pop. 1,699; Zip Code 05051; Granted in 1763 and named after Newbury, Massachusetts.

•**NEWFANE**, Town; Windham County Seat; Pop. 1,129; Zip Code 05345; Elev. 536'; Lat. 42-59-15 N long. 072-39-33 W; Named for John Fane, seventh Earl of Westmorland, and a favored relative of Governor Wentworth.

•**NEWPORT**, City; Orleans County Seat; Pop. 4,756; Zip Code 05855; Elev. 723'; Lat. 44-56-19 N long. 072-12-31 W; Originally Duncansborough the name was later changed after Newport, Rhode Island.

•**NORTH BENNINGTON**, Village, Bennington , Pop. 1,685; Zip Code 05257; Lat. 42-55-44 N long. 073-14-38 W; Granted by Governor Benning Wentworth and given his first name.

•NORTH HERO, Town; Grand Isle County Seat; Pop. 442; Zip Code 05474; Elev. 365'; Lat. 44-49-07 N long. 073-17-33 W; Chartered by Revolutionary War heros Ethan Allen and Samuel Herrick and so descriptively named.

•NORTH TROY, Village, Orleans , Pop. 717; Zip Code 05859; Lat. 44-59-51 N long. 072-24-24 W; Incorporated as Missisquoi the name was later changed after Troy, New York.

•NORTH WESTMINSTER, Village, Windham, Pop. 310; Settled in the 1760's and named after Westminster, England.

•NORTHFIELD, Town; Washington County; Pop. 5,435; Zip Code 05663; Elev. 7341'; Lat. 44-09-01 N long. 072-39-29 W; Named after Northfield, Massachusetts.

•NORTON, Town; Essex County; Pop. 184; Established in 1779 and named for the Norton family, who were large landowners.

•NORWICH, Town; Windsor County; Pop. 2,398; Zip Code 05055; Elev. 537'; The town is named after Norwich, Connecticut, itself named for Norwich, England.

•ORANGE, Town; Orange County; Pop. 752; The town is named after Orange, Connecticut.

•ORLEANS, Village; Orleans County; Pop. 983; Zip Code 05860; Elev. 740'; Lat. 44-48-35 N long. 072-12-06 W; Named in honor of Louis Phillipe Joseph, the Duke of Orleans, a hero in the French Revolution.

•ORWELL, Town; Addison County; Pop. 901; Zip Code 05760; Elev. 379'; Lat. 43-48-15 N long. 073-17-53 W; Founded in 1763 and named for Francis Vernon,the first Baron Orwell.

•PANTON, Town; Addison County; Pop. 537; Panton was named after the English town of Panton in Lincolnshire.

•PAWLET, Town; Rutland County; Pop. 1,244; Zip Code 05761; Elev. 681'; Lat. 43-20-48 N long. 073-10-49 W; Granted in 1761 and named in honor of Charles Paulet, Duke of Bolton.

•PEACHAM, Town; Caledonia County; Pop. 531; Zip Code 05862; Elev. 1310'; Lat. 44-19-42 N long. 072-10-19 W; The town is named for the popular heroine in John Gay's immensely successful 18th century ploy The Beggar's Opera.

•PERU, Town; Bennington County; Pop. 312; Zip Code 05152; Granted in 1761 as Bromley, but changed in 1804 after the gold-rich South American country.

•PITTSFIELD, Town; Rutland County; Pop. 396; Zip Code 05762; Lat. 43-46-14 N long. 072-49-01 W; Chartered in 1781 and named after Pittsfield, Massachusetts.

•PITTSFORD, Town; Rutland County; Pop. 2,590; Zip Code 05763; Elev. 530'; Lat. 43-42-20 N long. 073-01-15 W; Settled in 1769 and named in honor of William Pitt, first Earl of Chatham.

•PLAINFIELD, Town; Washington County; Pop. 1,249; Zip Code 05667; Elev. 803'; Lat. 44-16-43 N long. 072-25-21 W; Incorporated in 1797 by John Chapman and named for his home in Plainfield, Connecticut.

•PLYMOUTH, Town; Windsor County; Pop. 405; Zip Code 05056; The town's name recalls and honors Plymouth, Massachusetts, site of the first Pilgrim colony.

•POMFRET, Town; Windsor County; Pop. 856; Granted in 1761 and named to honor Thomas Fermor, the first Earl of Pomfret.

•POULTNEY, Town; Rutland County; Pop. 3,196; Zip Code 05741; Elev. 432'; Lat. 43-31-32 N long. 073-12-39 W; Granted in the 1760's and named in honor of the first Earl of Bath, William Poultney.

•POWNAL, Town; Bennington County; Pop. 3,269; Zip Code 05261; Elev. 553'; Lat. 42-46-03 N long. 073-14-11 W; John and Thomas Pownal were original charterers of the town. It was named for them.

•PROCTOR, Town; Rutland County; Pop. 1,998; Zip Code 05765; Elev. 484'; Lat. 43-39-44 N long. 073-02-03 W; Famous as a marble quarry area, the town was named in 1882 to honor Redfield Proctor, president of the Vermont Marble Company.

•PROCTORSVILLE, Village; Windsor County; Pop. 481; Zip Code 05153; Named for an early settler.

•PUTNEY, Town; Windham County; Pop. 1,850; Zip Code 05346; Lat. 42-58-36 N long. 072-31-09 W; Named by Benning Wentworth for Putney, England.

•RANDOLPH, Town; Orange County; Pop. 4,689; Zip Code 05060; Elev. 684'; Probably named for political advantage to honor Edmund Randolph, the well-known Virginia statesman.

•READING, Town; Windsor County; Pop. 647; Zip Code 05062; This Vermont town was named after Reading, Massachusetts, itself named after Reading, England.

•READSBORO, Town; Bennington County; Pop. 638; Zip Code 05350; Elev. 1190'; Lat. 42-45-35 N long. 072-56-53 W; Founded in 1770 and named after the first landowner, John Reade.

•RICHFORD, Town; Essex County; Pop. 2,206; Zip Code 05476; Elev. 1477'; Lat. 44-59-40 N long. 072-40-19 W; Granted in 1780 by Vermont who was raising money to pay its soldiers in the Continental Army. A descriptive name for its fertile soil.

•RICHMOND, Town; Chittenden County; Pop. 3,159; Zip Code 05477; Elev. 319'; Lat. 44-24-17 N long. 072-59-40 W; Incorporated in 1794 and named in honor of Charles Lennox, the third Duke of Richmond.

•RIPTON, Town; Addison County; Pop. 327; Ripton is named after Ripton in Huntingdonshire, England.

•ROCHESTER, Town; Windsor County; Pop. 1,054; Zip Code 05767; Lat. 43-52-27 N long. 072-49-06 W; Chartered in 1781 and named after Rochester, Massachusetts.

•ROCKINGHAM, Town; Windham County; Pop. 5,538; The town's name honors Charles Watson-Wentworth, the second Marquis of Rockingham.

•ROXBURY, Town; Washington County; Pop. 452; Zip Code 05669; Elev. 1010'; Lat. 44-05-45 N long. 072-43-53 W; Roxbury is named after Roxbury, Massachusetts.

•ROYALTON, Town; Windsor County; Pop. 2,100; Named in 1769 by acting Governor Cadwallader Colden to honor King George III, i.e. Royal Town.

•RUPERT, Town; Bennington County; Pop. 605; Zip Code 05768; Elev. 839'; Lat. 43-15-33 N long. 073-13-29 W; Granted in 1761 and named in honor of Prince Rupert (1619-82) Count Palatine of Rhine and Duke of Cumberland.

•RUTLAND, City; Rutland County Seat; Pop. 18,436; Zip Code 05701; Elev. 648'; Lat. 43-36-29 N long. 072-58-35 W; Named by Governor Wentworth in honor of John Manners, the third Duke of Rutland.

•**RYEGATE,** Town; Caledonia County; Pop. 1,000; Named after Reigate, England by its settlers in the 1760's and subsequently undergoing a spelling corruption.

•**ST. ALBANS,** City; Franklin County Seat; Pop. 7,308; Zip Code 05478; Elev. 429'; Lat. 44-48-42 N long. 073-05-03 W; Governor Benning Wentworth granted the town in 1763. Named after St. Albans in Hertfordshire, England.

•**ST. GEORGE,** Town; Chittenden County; Pop. 677; St. George was named in honor of England's King George III.

•**ST. JOHNSBURY,** Town; Caledonia County Seat; Pop. 7,938; Zip Code 05819; Elev. 588'; Lat. 44-25-15 N long. 072-01-14 W; Chartered in 1786 and named to honor author Michel Guillaume St. Jean Creveldeur who wrote under the pen name J. Hector St. John.

•**SALISBURY,** Town; Addison County; Pop. 881; Zip Code 05769; Lat. 43-53-50 N long. 073-06-04 W; Settled in 1720 and named after Salisbury in Wiltshire, England.

•**SANDGATE,** Town; Bennington County; Pop. 234; Settled in the late 1700's and named for Sandgate, England.

•**SAXTONS RIVER,** Village; Windham County; Pop. 593; Zip Code 05154; Elev. 528'; Named for an early settler and its location.

•**SEARSBURG,** Town; Bennington County; Pop. 72; Searsburg is probably named for Revolutionary War patriot Issac Sears.

•**SHAFTSBURY,** Town; Bennington County; Pop. 3,001; Zip Code 05262; Lat. 43-07-53 N long. 073-04-24 W; Shaftsbury is named after Shaftesburg, England.

•**SHARON,** Town; Windsor County; Pop. 828; Zip Code 05065; Elev. 501'; The town is named after Sharon, Connecticut.

•**SHEFFIELD,** Town; Caledonia County; Pop. 435; Zip Code 05866; Lat. 44-36-05 N long. 072-06-57 W; The town is named after Sheffield, Massachusetts.

•**SHELBURNE,** Town; Chittenden County; Pop. 5,000; Zip Code 05482; Elev. 148'; Lat. 44-22-46 N long. 073-14-06 W; Granted by Governor Wentworth and named in honor of the Earl of Shelburne.

•**SHELDON,** Town; Franklin County; Pop. 1,618; Zip Code 05483; Elev. 373'; Lat. 44-52-59 N long. 072-56-33 W; Originally named Hungerford, the town's name was changed in 1792 to honor Revolutionary War veteran Colonel Elisha Sheldon.

•**SHERBURNE,** Town; Rutland County; Pop. 891; Originally named Killington, the name was changed in 1800 to honor one of the first grantees, Colonel Benjamin Sherburne.

•**SHOREHAM,** Town; Addison County; Pop. 972; Zip Code 05770; Elev. 333'; Lat. 43-53-36 N long. 073-18-47 W; Founded in 1766 and named for Shoreham-by-the-Sea in England.

•**SHREWSBURY,** Town; Rutland County; Pop. 866; Granted in 1761 and named for the Earldom of Shrewsbury.

•**SOMERSET,** Town; Windham County; Pop. 2; Governor Benning Wentworth named the town for the County of Somerset in England.

•**SOUTH BURLINGTON,** City; Chittenden County; Pop. 10,679; Zip Code 05401; Elev. 113; Lat. 44-29-02 N, long. 073-13-12 W. Incorporated in 1864 and named after the Earl of Burlington.

•**SOUTH HERO,** Town; Grand Isle County; Pop. 1,188; Zip Code 05486; Elev. 152'; Lat. 44-38-43 N long. 073-19-00 W;

Founded by Revolutionary War hero Ethan Allen and Samuel Herrick and so descriptively named.

•**SPRINGFIELD,** Town; Windsor County; Pop. 10,190; Zip Code 05156; Elev. 410'; Chartered in the 1760's and named after Springfield, Massachusetts.

•**STAMFORD,** Town; Bennington County; Pop. 773; Granted in 1753 and named by Governor Benning Wentworth in honor of Harry Grey, Fourth Earl of Stamford.

•**STANNARD,** Town; Caledonia County; Pop. 142; Originally named Goshen, the name was changed in 1867 to honor Vermont's Civil War hero General George Stannard.

•**STARKSBORO,** Town; Addison County; Pop. 1,336; Zip Code 05487; Elev. 615'; Lat. 44-13-41 N long. 073-03-38 W; Starksboro is named for Revolutionary War General John Stark.

•**STOCKBRIDGE,** Town; Windsor County; Pop. 508; Zip Code 05772; Elev. 857'; Lat. 43-47-02 N long. 072-45-16 W; Stockbridge is named after Stockbridge, Massachusetts, itself named after Stockbridge, England.

•**STOWE,** Town; Lamoille County; Pop. 2,991; Zip Code 05672; Elev. 732'; Lat. 44-27-54 N long. 072-41-05 W; Granted in 1763 and named after Stowe, Massachusetts.

•**STRAFFORD,** Town; Orange County; Pop. 731; Zip Code 05072; The town was named by Governor Benning Wentworth for his family in England, who held the Earldom of Strafford.

•**STRATTON,** Town; Windham County; Pop. 122; The town is named after Stratton in Cornwall, England.

•**SUDBURY,** Town; Rutland County; Pop. 380; Granted by Governor Benning Wentworth in 1763 and named for Sudbury in Middlesex, England.

•**SUNDERLAND,** Town; Bennington County; Pop. 768; Sunderland was named in honor of George Spencer, Sixth Earl of Sunderland.

•**SUTTON,** Town; Caledonia County; Pop. 667; Zip Code 05867; Elev. 1152'; Lat. 44-38-00 N long. 072-01-42 W; Chartered in 1782 as Billymead, but renamed in the early 1800's after Sutton, Massachusetts.

•**SWANTON,** Town; Franklin County; Pop. 5,141; Zip Code 05488; Elev. 157'; Lat. 44-55-09 N long. 073-07-13 W; The town's name honors British naval officer William Swanton, who contributed to the victory over the French at Louisbourg in 1760.

•**THETFORD,** Town; Orange County; Pop. 2,188; Zip Code 05074; The town was named in honor of Augustus Henry Fitzroy, Viscount Thetford.

•**TINMOUTH,** Town; Rutland County; Pop. 406; Granted in 1761 and named after Tynemouth, England.

•**TOPSHAM,** Town; Orange County; Pop. 767; Zip Code 05076; The town is named after Topsham, Maine.

•**TOWNSHEND,** Town; Windham County; Pop. 849; Zip Code 05353; Elev. 574'; Lat. 43-02-54 N long. 072-40-04 W; Named by Benning Wentworth to honor the prominent British political family.

•**TROY,** Town; Orleans County; Pop. 1,498; Zip Code 05868; Elev. 752'; Lat. 44-54-13 N long. 072-24-21 W; Incorporated in 1801 and later named after Troy, New York.

•**TUNBRIDGE,** Town; Orange County; Pop. 925; Zip Code 05077; Settled in the late 1700's and named in honor of William Henry Nassau du Zuylestein, Viscount Tunbridge.

•**UNDERHILL,** Town; Chittenden County; Pop. 2,172; Zip Code 05489; Elev. 706'; Lat. 44-31-36 N long. 072-56-42 W; Settled in the late 1700's and named after the local Underhill family.

•**VERGENNES,** City; Addison County; Pop. 2,273; Zip Code 05491; Elev. 205'; Lat. 44-10-08 N long. 073-15-05 W; The third oldest incorporated city in the United States, it is named in honor of Charles Gravier, Comte De Vergennes, who as French foreign affairs minister gave assistance to the colonies in the Revolutionary War.

•**VERNON,** Town; Windham County; Pop. 1,175; Zip Code 05354; Elev. 301'; Lat. 42-45-44 N long. 072-30-51 W; The town's name recalls Washington's estate, Mount Vernon.

•**VERSHIRE,** Town; Orange County; Pop. 442; Zip Code 05079; Elev. 1268'; Chartered in 1791 and given a boundary name, Vermont and New Hampshire.

•**VICTORY,** Town; Essex County; Pop. 56; Founded in 1780 and named for the anticipated victory over the British in the Revolutionary War.

•**WAITSFIELD,** Town; Washington County; Pop. 1,300; Zip Code 05673; Elev. 698'; Lat. 44-11-25 N long. 072-49-31 W; Chartered in 1782 and named for prominent citizen Benjamin Wait.

•**WALDEN,** Town; Caledonia County; Pop. 575; The town's name remembers original chartee Samuel Walden.

•**WALLINGFORD,** Town; Rutland County; Pop. 1,893; Zip Code 05773; Lat. 43-28-19 N long. 072-58-39 W; Settled in the 1770's and named after Wallingford, Connecticut, itself named after Wallingford, England.

•**WALTHAM,** Town; Addison County; Pop. 394; The town's founders named it after Waltham, Massachusetts.

•**WARDSBORO,** Town; Windham County; Pop. 505; Zip Code 05355; Elev. 995'; Lat. 43-02-27 N long. 072-47-29 W; Among the original grantees in 1780 was William Ward. The town is named after him.

•**WARREN,** Town; Washington County; Pop. 956; Zip Code 05674; Lat. 44-06-49 N long. 072-51-29 W; Warren was named in honor of Doctor Joseph Warren, revolutionary hero and patriot who was killed at the battle of Bunker Hill.

•**WASHINGTON,** Town; Orange County; Pop. 855; Zip Code 05675; Lat. 44-06-24 N long. 072-26-10 W; Named like many other places in the United States after George Washington.

•**WATERBURY,** Town; Washington County; Pop. 4,465; Zip Code 05676; Elev. 428'; Lat. 44-17-37 N long. 072-45-20 W; Many early settlers came from Waterbury, Connecticut, so the new town was named after the old.

•**WATERFORD,** Town; Caledonia County; Pop. 882; Waterford is either named descriptively as having a Ford across the Connecticut River within the town, or after Waterford, Ireland.

•**WATERVILLE,** Town; Lamoille County; Pop. 470; Zip Code 05492; Elev. 556'; Lat. 44-41-27 N long. 072-46-17 W; Incorporated in 1824 and descriptive named for the Lamoille River which flows through the area.

•**WELLS,** Town; Rutland County; Pop. 815; Zip Code 05774; Lat. 43-24-56 N long. 073-12-24 W; Wells was named for Wells in Somerset, England.

•**WELLS RIVER,** Village; Orange County; Pop. 396; Zip Code 05081; Descriptively named for its location.

•**WEST FAIRLEE,** Town; Orange County; Pop. 427; Zip Code 05083; Elev. 741'; Created out of the town of Fairlee and so descriptively named.

•**WEST HAVEN,** Town; Rutland County; Pop. 253; Originally part of Fair Haven, it was renamed in 1792.

•**WEST RUTLAND,** Town; Rutland County; Pop. 2,351; Zip Code 05777; Elev. 492'; Lat. 43-35-51 N long. 073-02-50 W; Incorporated in 1886 from the town of Rutland and so descriptively named.

•**WESTFIELD,** Town; Orleans County; Pop. 418; Zip Code 05874; Elev. 825'; Lat. 44-53-30 N long. 072-25-45 W; Chartered in the 1780's and named in honor of William West of Rhode Island.

•**WESTFORD,** Town; Chittenden County; Pop. 1,413; Zip Code 05494; Elev. 467'; Lat. 44-36-38 N long. 073-00-41 W; Granted in 1763 and named as the most westerly of the towns granted at the time.

•**WESTMINSTER,** Town; Windham County; Pop. 2,493; Zip Code 05158; The town was named after Westminister, England.

•**WESTMORE,** Town; Orleans County; Pop. 257; Founded in the 1780's and named for its location on the then western frontier.

•**WEYBRIDGE,** Town; Addison County; Pop. 667; Weybridge is named after the town in Surrey, England.

•**WHEELOCK,** Town; Caledonia County; Pop. 444; Chartered in 1785 and named for the Reverend Eleazar Wherlock, the founder of Dartmouth College.

•**WHITING,** Town; Addison County; Pop. 379; Zip Code 05778; Elev. 395'; Lat. 43-51-47 N long. 073-12-07 W; The original settlers included five men with the last name Whiting, the town is named after them.

•**WHITINGHAM,** Town; Windham County; Pop. 1,043; Zip Code 05361; Elev. 1689'; Lat. 42-47-19 N long. 072-52-52 W; Nathan Whiting was the first grantee. The town is named for him.

•**WILLIAMSTOWN,** Town; Orange County; Pop. 2,284; Zip Code 05679; Lat. 44-07-18 N long. 072-32-34 W; Chartered in 1781 and named after Williamstown, Massachusetts.

•**WILLISTON,** Town; Chittenden County; Pop. 3,843; Zip Code 05495; Elev. 501'; Lat. 44-26-13 N long. 073-04-12 W; The town was granted in 1763 and named for a wealthy Quaker from Long Island, Samuel Willis.

•**WILMINGTON,** Town; Windham County; Pop. 1,808; Zip Code 05363; Lat. 42-52-07 N long. 072-52-07 W; Governor Benning Wentworth named the town for an old friend, Spencer Compton, First Earl of Wilmington.

•**WINDHAM,** Town; Windham County; Pop. 223; Incorporated in 1795 and named in honor of Charles Wyndham, who had been a close friend of Benning Wentworth.

•**WINHALL,** Town; Bennington County; Pop. 327; Settled after the Revolutionary War and possibly named for Winhall, England.

•**WINOOSKI,** City; Chittenden County; Pop. 6,318; Incorporated in 1921 and named after the adjacent Winooski River.

•**WOLCOTT,** Town; Lamoille County; Pop. 986; Zip Code 05680; Lat. 44-32-44 N long. 072-27-26 W; Chartered in 1781 and named in honor of Revolutionary War statesman and soldier, General Oliver Wolcott.

•**WOODBURY,** Town; Washington County; Pop. 573; Zip Code 05681; Elev. 1164'; Lat. 44-26-28 N long. 072-24-55 W; Founded in 1781 and named for Colonel Ebenezer Wood.

•**WOODFORD,** Town; Bennington County; Pop. 314; Granted in 1753 and named after Woodford in Essex, England.

•**WOODSTOCK,** Town; Windsor County Seat; Pop. 3,214; Zip Code 05682; Elev. 779; Lat. 44-22-17 N, long. 072-33-14 W; Governor Benning Wentworth named the town to honor the ancient English city of Woodstock in Oxfordshire, England.

•**WORCESTER,** Town; Washington County; Pop. 727; Zip Code 05682; Elev. 779'; Lat. 44-22-17 N long. 072-33-14 W; Established in 1763 and named for Worcester, Massachusetts.

VIRGINIA

•**ABINGDON,** Town; Washington County Seat; Pop. 4,318; Zip Code 24210; Elev. 2069; Lat. 36-42-57 N long. 081-58-07 W; Settled in the 1760's and named either for Lord Abingoon or Mary Washington's home town.

•**ACCOMAC,** Town; Accomack County Seat; Pop. 522; Zip Code 23301; Lat. 37-43-15 N long. 075-40-06 W; The town is named after the Accomac Indians. The name means "other side of water place."

•**ALBERTA,** Town; Brunswick County; Pop. 394; Zip Code 23821; Lat. 36-52-09 N long. 077-52-49 W; The town is named after the Canadian province.

•**ALEXANDRIA,** City; Pop. 103,217; Zip Code 22300; Lat. 38-47-05 N long. 077-00-51 W; The town is named after colonial settler John Alexander who came to the area in 1669.

•**ALTAVISTA,** Town; Campbell County; Pop. 3,849; Zip Code 24517; Elev. 596; Lat. 37-06-59 N long. 079-17-28 W; The town is named for a farm owned by settler Henry Lane.

•**AMHERST,** Town; Amherst County Seat; Pop. 1,135; Zip Code 24521; Lat. 37-35-09 N long. 079-02-52 N; Established in 1761 and named in honor of French-Indian War commander, Lord Amherst.

•**APPALACHIA,** Town; Wise County; Pop. 2,418; Zip Code 24216; Elev. 1651; Lat. 36-57-52 N long. 082-46-49 W; The town is named after the Appalachia Mountains.

•**APPOMATTOX,** Town; Appomattox County Seat; Pop. 1,345; Zip Code 24522; Lat. 37-21-15 N long. 078-49-37 W; A famous Civil War historical site, the town's name derives from an early Indian tribe which lived in the area.

•**ASHLAND,** Town; Hanover County; Pop. 4,640; Zip Code 23005; Lat. 37-45-28 N long. 077-28-57 W; The town is named for the Kentucky home of statesman Henry Clay.

•**BEDFORD,** City; Pop. 5,991; Zip Code 24523; Lat. 37-20-20 N long. 079-31-15 W; Originally named Liberty, the name was changed in 1896 after the county name. Bedford, itself, comes from the fourth Duke of Bedford of England.

•**BELLE HAVEN,** Town; Accomack & Northampton Counties; Pop. 589; Zip Code 23306; Elev. 36; Lat. 37-31-53 N long. 075-52-04 W; A pioneer named Bell had a large oven in the area, so the place became Bell's Oven. In 1762 this was changed to Bell's Haven.

•**BERRYVILLE,** Town; Clarke County Seat; Pop. 1,752; Zip Code 22611; Elev. 575; Lat. 39-09-04 N long. 077-59-08 W; Settler Benjamin Berry divided the area into town lots around 1800. The general assembly named it Berryville in 1803.

•**BIG STONE GAP,** Town; Wise County; Pop. 4,748; Zip Code 24219; Lat. 36-56-09 N long. 082-46-35 W; Descriptively named for the gap in the mountains nearby throught which the Powell River emerges.

•**BLACKSBURG,** Town; Montgomery County; Pop. 30,638; Zip Code 24060; Elev. 2080; Lat. 37-13-48 N long. 080-24-35 W; The town's name honors William Black who donated land for the town. Incorporated in 1798.

•**BLACKSTONE,** Town; Nottoway County; Pop. 3,624; Zip Code 23824; Elev. 427; Lat. 37-04-44 N long. 077-59-50 W; Incorporated in 1888 and named for the famous English jurist, Sir William Blackstone.

•**BLOXOM,** Town; Accomack County; Pop. 407; Zip Code 23308; Lat. 37-49-50 N long. 075-37-14 W; The town is named for early postmaster, William Bloxom.

•**BLUEFIELD,** Town; Tazewell County; Pop. 5,946; Zip Code 24605; Elev. 2389; Descriptively named for the blue-grass valley it lies in.

•**BOONES MILL,** Town; Franklin County; Pop. 303; Zip Code 24065; Lat. 37-07-00 N long. 079-57-08 W; Named in honor of Jacob Boone, cousin to Daniel Boone, who settled here in 1782 and built a mill.

•**BOWLING GREEN,** Town; Caroline County Seat; Pop. 665; Zip Code 22427; Lat. 38-03-05 N long. 077-20-52 W; Major Thomas Hoomes received a land grant and settled in the area in 1670. The town is named for his family estate in England.

•**BOYCE,** Town; Clarke County; Pop. 401; Zip Code 22620; Lat. 39-05-32 N long. 078-03-35 W; The town's name remembers U. L. Boycewho owned an estate nearby.

•**BOYDTON,** Town; Mecklenburg County Seat; Pop. 486; Zip Code 239+; Lat. 36-39-49 N long. 078-23-29 W; The town was established in 1812 and named in honor of wealthy merchant and Judge, Alexander Boyd.

•**BOYKINS,** Town; Southampton County; Pop. 791; Zip Code 23827; Lat. 36-35-07 N long. 077-11-47 W; Incorporated in 1884 and named for a local resident named Boykins.

•**BRANCHVILLE,** Town; Southampton County; Pop. 174; Zip Code 23828; Elev. 46; Lat. 36-34-31 N long. 077-14-57 W; The town is named after a family of early settlers.

•**BRIDGEWATER,** Town; Rockingham County; Pop. 3,289; Zip Code 22812; Lat. 38-22-59 N long. 078-58-34 W; Once the site of a ferry across the North River, ultimately a bridge was built and the town so named.

•**BRISTOL,** City; Pop. 19,042; Zip Code 242+; Lat. 36-36-25 N long. 082-10-57 W; Once called Goodson, the name was changed in 1890 to Bristol, after Bristol, England.

•**BROADWAY,** Town; Rockingham County; Pop. 1,234; Zip Code 22815; Lat. 38-36-50 N long. 078-47-41 W; A gathering place for rowdy types in the nineteenth century; townspeople warned they were on the "broadway to destruction," the name stuck on the town.

•**BRODNAX,** Town; Brunswick & Mecklenburg Counties; Pop. 492; Zip Code 23920; Elev. 388; Lat. 36-42-12 N long. 078-01-55 W; Incorporated in 1915 and named for a prominent local family.

•**BROOKNEAL,** Town; Campbell County; Pop. 1,454; Zip Code 24528; Elev. 560; Lat. 37-03-01 N long. 078-56-21 W; The town's name stems from the intermarriage of the Brooks and Neal families.

•**BUCHANAN,** Town; Botetourt County; Pop. 1,205; The town is named in honor of the deputy surveyor of Augusta County, John Buchanan.

•**BUENA VISTA,** City; Pop. 6,717; Zip Code 24416; Lat. 37-44-04 N long. 079-21-12 W; A local iron furance supplied cannonballs used in the Battle of Buena Vista in the Mexican-American War. The furnance was dubbed "Buena Vista" and the town's name followed.

•**BURKEVILLE,** Town; Nottoway County; Pop. 606; Zip Code 23922; Elev. 522; Lat. 37-11-19 N long. 078-12-05 W; The town's name remembers Colonel Samuel Burke (1794 - 1880).

•**CAPE CHARLES,** Town; Northampton County; Pop. 1,512; Zip Code 23310; Lat. 37-16-18 N long. 076-00-05 W; The town is named after the Cape. Cape Charles honored Charles, Duke of Yorke.

•**CAPRON,** Town; Southampton County; Pop. 238; Zip Code 23829; Lat. 36-42-39 N long. 077-12-00 W; Originally called Princeton, the name was later changed to Capron, who was a general passenger agent of the railroad.

•**CEDAR BLUFF,** Town; Tazewell County; Pop. 1,550; Zip Code 24609; Descriptively named for the cedar trees covering the bluff.

•**CHARLOTTE COURT HOUSE,** Town; Charlotte County Seat; Pop. 568; Zip Code 23923; Elev. 596; Lat. 37-03-29 N long. 078-38-30 W; The town had a series of names, but was renamed in 1901 after the county. Charlotte was the wife of King George III.

•**CHARLOTTESVILLE,** City; Pop. 45,010; Zip Code 229+; Elev. 594; Lat. 38-02-12 N long. 078-29-06 W; Founded in 1762 and named for Princess Charlotte, wife of King George III.

•**CHASE CITY,** Town; Mecklenburg County; Pop. 2,749; Zip Code 23924; Elev. 546; Lat. 36-47-55 N long. 078-27-34 W; The town's name honors U. S. Supreme Court Justice Chase.

•**CHATHAM,** Town; Pittsylvania County Seat; Pop. 1,390; Zip Code 24531; Lat. 36-49-30 N long. 079-24-03 W; The town was renamed in 1874 to honor William Pitt, Earl of Chatham.

•**CHERITON,** Town; Northampton County; Pop. 695; Zip Code 23316; Lat. 37-17-18 N long. 075-58-13 W; Called at one time Cherry Stones, Dr. William Stockley shortened this to "Cheriton."

•**CHESAPEAKE,** City; Pop. 114,226; Zip Code 23320; Lat. 36-41-47 N long. 076-03-25 W; An Indian word meaning "great salt water."

•**CHILHOWIE,** Town; Smyth County; Pop. 1,269; Zip Code 24319; Elev. 1950; Lat. 36-47-58 N long. 081-41-06 W; Settled in 1750 and named after an Indian phrase meaning "valley of many deer."

•**CHINCOTEAGUE,** Town; Accomack County; Pop. 1,607; Zip Code 233+; Lat. 37-55-59 N long. 075-22-20 W; The town takes its name from the Chinco-Teague Indians. The name means "beautiful land across the water."

•**CHRISTIANSBURG,** Town; Montgomery County Seat; Pop. 10,345; Zip Code 240+; Lat. 37-08-02 N long. 080-24-24 W; Founded in 1792 and later named in honor of colonial Indian fighter, William Christian.

•**CLAREMONT,** Town; Surry County; Pop. 380; Zip Code 23899; Elev. 112; Lat. 37-13-38 N long. 076-57-56 W; The town is named after "Claremont," a royal home in Surrey, England.

•**CLARKSVILLE,** Town; Mecklenburg County; Pop. 1,468; Zip Code 23927; Elev. 91; Lat. 36-37-17 N long. 078-33-44 W; The town takes its name from an early property owner on the Roanoke River.

•**CLEVELAND,** Town; Russell County; Pop. 360; Zip Code 24225; Elev. 1534; Lat. 36-56-36 N long. 082-09-13 W; Established in 1890 and named in honor of President Grover Cleveland.

•**CLIFTON,** Town; Fairfax County; Pop. 170; Zip Code 22024; Lat. 38-46-58 N long. 077-23-09 W; The town is named after the Wyckliffe family of England, who were large property owners in colonial times.

•**CLIFTON FORGE,** City; Pop. 5,046; Zip Code 24422; Lat. 37-49-01 N long. 079-49-30 W; Incorporated in 1884 and named after James Clifton's iron furnace.

•**CLINTWOOD,** Town; Dickenson County Seat; Pop. 1,369; Zip Code 24228; Lat. 37-08-59 N long. 082-27-09 W; The town's name honors Senator Henry Clinton Wood.

•**CLOVER,** Town; Halifax County; Pop. 215; Zip Code 24534; Elev. 502; Lat. 36-50-09 N long. 078-44-07 W; The town is named for clover Creek.

•**COEBURN,** Town; Wise County; Pop. 2,625; Zip Code 24230; Elev. 1992; Lat. 36-59-38 N long. 082-28-03 W; Settled in the 1770's, and later renamed for chief railroad engineer, W. W. Coe.

•**COLONIAL BEACH,** Town; Westmoreland County; Pop. 2,474; Zip Code 22443; Lat. 38-15-12 N long. 076-57-59 W; Called White Beach from colonial days, it was renamed by a developer in the 1880's to Colonial Beach.

•**COLONIAL HEIGHTS,** City; Pop. 16,509; Zip Code 23834; Lat. 37-00-03 N long. 076-40-07 W; Incorporated in 1926 and named for the general heritage of the area.

•**COLUMBIA,** Town; Fluvanna County; Pop. 111; Zip Code 23038; Lat. 37-45-10 N long. 078-09-33 W; Settled in the 18th century andgiven the popular name for America in 1897.

•**COURTLAND,** Town; Southampton County Seat; Pop. 976; Zip Code 23837; Elev. 32; Lat. 36-42-58 N long. 077-03-45 W; Settled in 1750 and renamed Courtland in 1788.

•**COVINGTON,** City; Pop. 9,063; Zip Code 24426; Lat. 37-46-56 N long. 079-59-22 W; Incorporated in 1833 and named for Prince Edward Covingtons.

•**CRAIGSVILLE,** Town; Augusta County; Pop. 845; Zip Code 24430; Elev. 23; Lat. 38-05-02 N long. 079-23-00 W; The town is named for an early settler.

•**CREWE,** Town; Nottoway County; Pop. 2,325; Zip Code 23930; Lat. 37-10-46 N long. 078-07-28 W; Founded in 1886 as a rail center, and named for the English railway town, Crewe.

•**CULPEPER,** Town; Culpeper County Seat; Pop. 6,621; Zip Code 22701; Elev. 430; Lat. 38-28-24 N long. 077-59-39 W; The town is named for the county. Culpeper honors Lord Culpeper, Governor of Virginia 1680-83.

•**DAMASCUS,** Town; Washington County; Pop. 1,330; Zip Code 24236; Elev. 1928; Lat. 36-38-29 N long. 081-46-50 W; The town is named after the ancient Syrian city.

•**DANVILLE,** City; Pop. 45,642; Zip Code 245+; Lat. 36-35-12 N long. 079-23-09 W; Descriptively named for its location on the Dan River.

•**DAYTON,** Town; Rockingham County; Pop. 1,017; Zip Code 22821; Lat. 38-24-51 N long. 078-56-33 W; Dayton may be named in honor of Jonathan Dayton, a ratifier of the Constitution.

•**DENDRON,** Town; Surry County; Pop. 307; Zip Code 23839; Lat. 37-02-21 N long. 076-55-40 W; Founded in the 1880's and given a Greek name meaning tree, referring to the town's lumber industry.

•**DILLWYN,** Town; Buckingham County; Pop. 637; Zip Code 239+; Lat. 37-28-09 N long. 078-33-52 W; Named for an early settler.

•**DRAKES BRANCH,** Town; Charlotte County; Pop. 617; Zip Code 23937; Elev. 383; Lat. 36-59-40 N long. 078-36-12 W; Named for the stream, Drakes Branch, that flows through town.

•**DUBLIN,** Town; Pulaski County; Pop. 2,368; Zip Code 24084; Lat. 37-06-09 N long. 080-41-17 W; The first settler, Irishman William Christian, named the town for Dublin, Ireland.

•**DUFFIELD,** Town; Scott County; Pop. 148; Zip Code 24244; Elev. 1365; Lat. 36-43-11 N long. 082-47-37 W; The town is named for the Duff family who were early settlers.

•**DUMFRIES,** Town; Prince William County; Pop. 3,214; Zip Code 22026; Lat. 38-35-47 N long. 077-19-02 W; An early settler, John Graham, named the town for his home in Scotland.

•**DUNGANNON,** Town; Scott County; Pop. 339; Zip Code 24245; Elev. 1311; Lat. 36-49-52 N long. 082-28-07 W; Pioneer Captain Patrick Hagan named the town for his former home in Ireland.

•**EASTVILLE,** Town; Northampton County Seat; Pop. 238; Zip Code 23347; Lat. 37-21-09 N long. 075-56-17 W; Descriptively named for its relative location east of other nearby towns.

•**EDINBURG,** Town; Shenandoah County; Pop. 752; Zip Code 22824; Lat. 38-49-26 N long. 078-33-48 W; Incorporated in 1852 as Edinburg, even though it was described as a "Garden of Eden" and Edenburg suggested.

•**ELKTON,** Town; Rockingham County; Pop. 1,520; Zip Code 22827; Lat. 38-24-29 N long. 078-37-06 W; The town takes its name for Elk Run stream which flows through the town.

•**EMPORIA,** City; Pop. 4,840; Zip Code 23847; Elev. 119; Lat. 36-41-24 N long. 077-32-27 W; Settled as two villages in the 1780's divided by the Meherrin River, the towns merged in 1887 and took the name Emporia. The name means "center of trade."

•**EXMORE,** Town; Northampton County; Pop. 1,300; Zip Code 23350; Elev. 41; Lat. 37-26-56 N long. 075-54-56 W; So named because it was the tenth (x) railroad station to the south of Delaware.

•**FAIRFAX,** City; Pop. 19,390; Zip Code 22021; Elev. 447; Lat. 38-53-44 N long. 077-25-59 W; The city is named for Lord Fairfax, one of the early great landowners.

•**FALLS CHURCH,** City; Pop. 9,515; Zip Code 22040; Lat. 38-53-03 N long. 077-10-38 W; Descriptively named for the town's location on the falls of the Potomac and an Episcopal Church built in 1734.

•**FARMVILLE,** Town; Cumberland & Prince Edward Counties; Prince Edward County Seat; Pop. 6,067; Zip Code 23901; Lat. 37-18-02 N, long. 078-23-29 W. The town is a distribution point for agricultural produce and so was named Farmville.

•**FINCASTLE,** Town; Botetourt County Seat; Pop. 282; Zip Code 24090; Lat. 37-30-00 N long. 079-52-39 W; The town was founded in 1772 and named for Lord Fincastle.

•**FLOYD,** Town; Floyd County Seat; Pop. 411; Zip Code 24091; Elev. 2496; Lat. 36-54-25 N long. 080-15-30 W; The town was named in honor of a prominent local citizen.

•**FRANKLIN,** City; Pop. 7,308; Zip Code 23851; Lat. 36-40-38 N long. 076-55-46 W; The city's name honors patriot Benjamin Franklin.

•**FREDERICKSBURG,** City; Pop. 15,322; Zip Code 224+; Lat. 38-22-39 N long. 077-27-23 W; Founded in 1727 and named in honor of Frederic, Prince of Wales.

•**FRIES,** Town; Grayson County; Pop. 758; Zip Code 24330; Elev. 2180; Lat. 36-42-59 N long. 080-58-40 W; The town is named for a local resident.

•**FRONT ROYAL,** Town; Warren County Seat; Pop. 11,126; Zip Code 22630; Elev. 567; Lat. 38-55-21 N long. 078-11-37 W; A "royal" oak stood in the village square. During the Revolutionary War a drill sargeant addressed his troops "front the royal oak." The name stuck on the town.

•**GALAX,** City; Pop. 6,524; Zip Code 24333; Elev. 2382; Lat. 36-39-55 N long. 080-54-52 W; The town is named for the decorative mountain evergreen plant.

•**GATE CITY,** Town; Scott County Seat; Pop. 2,494; Zip Code 24251; Elev. 1304; Lat. 36-37-43 N long. 082-34-06 W; Descriptively named for nearby Moccasin Gap, which was a gateway to western coalfields.

•**GLADE SPRING,** Town; Washington County; Pop. 1,722; Zip Code 24340; Elev. 2084; Lat. 36-47-51 N long. 081-46-03 W; The town is descriptively named for the spring found in a glade by the first settlers.

•**GLASGOW,** Town; Rockbridge County; Pop. 1,259; Zip Code 24555; Lat. 37-37-51 N long. 079-26-52 W; The town was developed on the Glasgow homestead and so named.

•**GLEN LYN,** Town; Giles County; Pop. 235; Zip Code 24093; Elev. 1537; Lat. 37-22-18 N long. 080-51-59 W; Settled in 1750 and named Montreal, the name was changed to Glen Lyn, or lovely glen, in 1883.

•**GORDONSVILLE,** Town; Orange County; Pop. 1,175; Zip Code 22942; Elev. 493; Lat. 078-11-21 W; Early settler Nathaniel Gorden purchased 1300 acres here in 1787. The town is named after him.

•**GOSHEN,** Town; Rockbridge County; Pop. 134; Zip Code 24439; Lat. 37-59-28 N long. 079-29-55 W; The town's name is a biblical synonym of fruitfulness and fertility.

•**GRETNA,** Town; Pittsylvania County; Pop. 1,255; Zip Code 24557; Elev. 844; Lat. 36-57-20 N long. 079-21-52 W; Called Franklin Junction until 1916 when the name was changed to Gretna.

•**GROTTOES,** Town; Augusta & Rockingham Counties; Pop. 1,369; Zip Code 24441; Lat. 38-15-43 N long. 078-49-23 W; Descriptively named for the many grottoes, or caves, in the nearby Shenandoah Mountains.

•**GRUNDY,** Town; Buchanan County Seat; Pop. 1,699; Zip Code 24614; Elev. 1050; Founded in the 1850's and named for a U. S. Senator from Texas in that era.

•**HALIFAX,** Town; Halifax County Seat; Pop. 772; Zip Code 24558; Lat. 36-45-50 N long. 078-55-57 W; Founded in 1752 and named for George Dunk, Earl of Halifax.

•**HALLWOOD,** Town; Accomack County; Pop. 243; Zip Code 23359; Lat. 37-52-38 N long. 075-35-16 W; Although not incorporated until1958 the town is named after an old colonial family, the Halls.

•**HAMILTON,** Town; Loudoun County; Pop. 598; Zip Code 22068; Elev. 275; Lat. 39-08-05 N long. 077-39-46 W; Established in 1829 and named after the town's first postmaster, Charles Hamilton.

•**HAMPTON,** City; Pop. 122,617; Zip Code 236+; The city was founded in 1680 and named in honor of the Earl of Southampton.

•**HARRISONBURG,** City; Pop. 19,671; Zip Code 22801; Elev. 1352; Lat. 38-26-46 N long. 078-52-15 W; Founded in 1780 and named for the Harrison family who were among the earliest settlers.

•HAYMARKET, Town; Prince William County; Pop. 230; Zip Code 22069; Lat. 38-40-12 N long. 077-29-26 W; Pioneer William Skinner named the town for the famous race track in London.

•HAYSI, Town; Dickenson County; Pop. 371; Zip Code 24256; Elev. 1266; Lat. 37-12-21 N long. 082-17-40 W; General store merchants Charles Hay and Mr. Sypher had their last names combined for the town's name.

•HERNDON, Town; Fairfax County; Pop. 11,449; Zip Code 22070; Lat. 38-57-56 N long. 077-21-37 W; The town's names commemorates Captain William Herndon who was lost at sea in 1857.

•HILLSBORO, Town; Loudoun County; Pop. 94; The town is descriptively named for its location on Short Hill Mountain.

•HILLSVILLE, Town; Carroll County Seat; Pop. 2,123; Zip Code 24343; Elev. 2557; Lat. 36-45-40 N long. 080-44-03 W; The town was named after the Hill family who were early Quaker settlers.

•HONAKER, Town; Russell County; Pop. 1,475; Zip Code 24260; Elev. 1860; Lat. 37-01-07 N long. 081-58-39 W; The town was named in honor of Squire Harve Honaker, a one-time postmaster.

•HOPEWELL, City; Pop. 23,397; Zip Code 23860; Lat. 37-17-29 N long. 077-18-11 W; The city is named after the Quaker Hopewell meeting established in 1734.

•HURT, Town; Pittsylvania County; Pop. 1,481; Zip Code 24563; Elev. 736; Lat. 37-05-50 N long. 079-18-09 W; The town's name honors John L. Hurt who helped develop the city.

•INDEPENDENCE, Town; Grayson County Seat; Pop. 1,112; Zip Code 24348; Elev. 2698; Lat. 36-37-15 N long. 081-09-06 W; A group of settlers living here in 1849 refused to take sides over where the county seat would be located. As a result the county seat was located here and named Independence.

•IRON GATE, Town; Alleghany County; Pop. 620; Zip Code 24448; Lat. 37-47-51 N long. 079-47-30 W; Named for the "Iron Gate" gap where the Jackson River cuts through the White Mountain.

•IRVINGTON, Town; Lancaster County; Pop. 567; Zip Code 22480; Elev. 1006; Lat. 37-39-48 N long. 076-25-08 W; Incorporated in 1891 and named for an early pioneer family, the Irvings.

•IVOR, Town; Southampton County; Pop. 403; Zip Code 23866; Lat. 36-54-23 N long. 076-53-46 W; The town's name comes from a Walter Scott novel.

•JARRATT, Town; Greensville & Sussex Counties; Pop. 614; Zip Code 23867; Lat. 36-49-56 N long. 077-28-18 W; The Jarratt family settled in the county in 1652. The town was named in their honor.

•JONESVILLE, Town; Lee County Seat; Pop. 874; Zip Code 24263; Elev. 1530; Lat. 36-40-16 N long. 083-06-51 W; The town is named for pioneer Frederick Jones who donated the land for the townsite.

•KELLER, Town; Accomack County; Pop. 236; Zip Code 23401; Elev. 42; Lat. 37-14-06 N long. 075-55-52 W; The town's name honors the contractor who built the local railroad.

•KENBRIDGE, Town; Lunenburg County; Pop. 1,352; Zip Code 23944; Lat. 36-57-38 N long. 078-07-29 W; The town was built on the Kennedy and Bridgeforth family farms. The town's name was coined from the two names.

•KEYSVILLE, Town; Charlotte County; Pop. 704; Zip Code 23947; Elev. 642; Lat. 37-02-20 N long. 078-28-54 W; The town was named after early settler and tavern owner, John Keys.

•KILMARNOCK, Town; Lancaster & Northumberland Counties; Pop. 945; Zip Code 22482; Lat. 37-42-40 N long. 076-23-18 W; Early settlers named the town for the city in Scotland.

•LA CROSSE, Town; Mecklenburg County; Pop. 734; Zip Code 23950; Lat. 36-41-47 N long. 078-05-39 W; The town is named after the game of La Crosse.

•LAWRENCEVILLE, Town; Brunswick County Seat; Pop. 1,484; Zip Code 23868; Lat. 36-45-33 N long. 077-50-55 W; Established in 1783 and named in honor of Captain James Lawrence.

•LEBANON, Town; Russell County Seat; Pop. 3,206; Zip Code 24266; Lat. 36-59-46 N long. 081-58-32 W; Founded in 1819 and named after Biblical Lebanon for the many cedar trees in the area.

•LEESBURG, Town; Loudoun County Seat; Pop. 8,357; Zip Code 22075; Elev. 352; Lat. 39-06-46 N long. 077-33-49 W; The town was founded in 1758 and named after Francis Lightfoot Lee.

•LEXINGTON, City; Pop. 7,292; Zip Code 24450; Elev. 1084; Lat. 37-47-01 N long. 079-26-28 W; The town was named during the Revolutionary War in honor of the Battle of Lexington.

•LOUISA, Town; Louisa County Seat; Pop. 932; Zip Code 23093; Elev. 468; Lat. 38-01-39 N long. 078-00-10 W; Founded in the 18th century and named for a local settler's wife.

•LOVETTSVILLE, Town; Loudoun County; Pop. 613; Zip Code 22080; Lat. 39-16-24 N long. 077-38-22 W; The town was established in 1820 on David Lovett's land. It is named in his honor.

•LURAY, Town; Page County Seat; Pop. 3,584; Zip Code 22835; Elev. 789; Lat. 38-40-02 N long. 078-27-25 W; The town is named either for early Blacksmith Lewis Ray, or after Lorraine (Luray), France.

•LYNCHBURG, City; Pop. 66,743; Zip Code 24501; Elev. 818; Lat. 37-24-25 N long. 079-09-36 W; The town grew up around John Lynch's ferry which he built in 1756. The town is named after him.

•MADISON, Town; Madison County Seat; Pop. 267; Zip Code 22719; Elev. 589; Lat. 38-31-45 N long. 078-15-38 W; Founded in 1801 and named in honor of James Madison.

•MANASSAS, City; Pop. 15,438; Zip Code 22110; Lat. 38-46-37 N long. 077-27-54 W; Early settlers named the town for the Biblical Manasseh.

•MARION, Town; Smyth County Seat; Pop. 7,029; Zip Code 24354; Elev. 2178; Lat. 36-50-26 N long. 081-31-03 W; Founded in the early 1800's and named for Revolutionary War hero, General Francis Marion.

•MARTINSVILLE, City; Pop. 18,149; Zip Code 241+; Lat. 36-40-20 N long. 079-51-58 W; The city was founded in 1791 and namedafter pioneer settler Joseph Martin.

•MCKENNEY, Town; Dinwiddie County; Pop. 473; Zip Code 23872; Lat. 36-59-07 N long. 077-43-17 W; The town's name honors large area landowner William R. McKenney.

•MELFA, Town; Accomack County; Pop. 391; Zip Code 23410; Lat. 37-39-05 N long. 075-44-22 W; The town was named for an official of the Pennsylvania Railroad Company.

•**MIDDLEBURG,** Town; Loudoun County; Pop. 619; Zip Code 22117; Elev. 492; Lat. 38-58-05 N long. 077-44-22 W; Once called Chinn, the name was later changed to reflect its "middle position" between Alexandria and Winchester.

•**MIDDLETOWN,** Town; Frederick County; Pop. 841; Zip Code 22645; Lat. 39-01-38 N long. 078-16-39 W; Founded in 1796 as Senseny, the name was later changed to Middletown for its location between Winchester and Woodstock.

•**MINERAL,** Town; Louisa County; Pop. 399; Zip Code 23117; Lat. 38-00-37 N long. 077-54-02 W; Established around 1800 and descriptively named for the mineral deposits in the area.

•**MONTEREY,** Town; Highland County Seat; Pop. 247; Zip Code 24465; Elev. 2881; Lat. 38-24-42 N long. 079-34-54 W; The name was changed to Monterey to honor President Zachary Taylor's victory during the Mexican-American War.

•**MONTROSS,** Town; Westmoreland County Seat; Pop. 456; Zip Code 22520; Lat. 38-05-36 N long. 076-49-38 W; The town was named for an early settler.

•**MOUNT CRAWFORD,** Town; Rockingham County; Pop. 315; Zip Code 22841; Lat. 38-21-17 N long. 078-56-26 W; The town is named after an early settler.

•**MOUNT JACKSON,** Town; Shenandoah County; Pop. 1,419; Zip Code 22842; Lat. 38-44-54 N long. 078-38-39 W; The town's name honors President Andrew Jackson.

•**NARROWS,** Town; Giles County; Pop. 2,516; Zip Code 24124; Lat. 37-20-08 N long. 080-48-27 W; The New River cuts a deep gorge, or narrows, through the Alleghenigs at this point. The town is named for this feature.

•**NASSAWADOX,** Town; Northampton County; Pop. 630; Zip Code 23413; Elev. 38; Lat. 37-28-35 N long. 075-53-23 W; Settled in 1656 and given an Indian name meaning "a stream between two streams."

•**NEW CASTLE,** Town; Craig County Seat; Pop. 213; Zip Code 24127; Lat. 37-29-45 N long. 080-06-45 W; Founded as New Fincastle in 1756, but later changed as a result of confusion to New Castle.

•**NEW MARKET,** Town; Shenandoah County; Pop. 1,118; Zip Code 22844; Lat. 38-38-54 N long. 078-40-20 W; Founded in 1784 and named for the famous racing town in England.

•**NEWPORT NEWS,** City; Pop. 144,903; Zip Code 23600; Lat. 37-03-15 N long. 076-28-36 W; Founded in 1619 and named for Sir Christopher Newport and Sir William Newce, or gradually Newport News.

•**NEWSOMS,** Town; Southampton County; Pop. 368; Zip Code 23874; Elev. 92; Lat. 36-37-40 N long. 077-07-28 W; The town is named after pioneer merchant, Thomas Newsoms.

•**NICKELSVILLE,** Town; Scott County; Pop. 464; Zip Code 24271; The town is named for an early settler.

•**NORFOLK,** City; Pop. 266,979; Zip Code 23500; Lat. 36-40-40 N long. 075-48-43 W; Established in 1682 and named for county Norfolk in England.

•**NORTON,** City; Pop. 4,757; Zip Code 24273; Elev. 2141; Lat. 36-59-19 N long. 082-37-31 W; The town is named in honor of Eckstein Norton, who was L & N Railroad president from 1886 - 1891.

•**OCCOQUAN,** Town; Fairfax & Prince William Counties; Pop. 512; Zip Code 22125; Lat. 38-40-56 N long. 077-15-39 W; The town's name is an Indian word meaning "at the river's end."

•**ONANCOCK,** Town; Accomack County; Pop. 1,461; Zip Code 23417; Lat. 37-42-41 N long. 075-44-25 W; Founded in 1680 and eventually given an Indian name meaning "foggy place."

•**ONLEY,** Town; Accomack County; Pop. 526; Zip Code 23418; Lat. 37-41-33 N long. 075-42-57 W; The town was named for the estate of Virginia Governor Henry Wise.

•**ORANGE,** Town; Orange County Seat; Pop. 2,631; Zip Code 22960; Elev. 521; Lat. 38-13-19 N long. 078-06-17 W; The town is named for the county. The county is named for the Prince of Orange who married King George II's daughter.

•**PAINTER,** Town; Accomack County; Pop. 321; Zip Code 23420; Elev. 37; Lat. 37-35-19 N long. 075-47-05 W; The town was named for an official of the Pennsylvania Railroad at the time the station was opened.

•**PARKSLEY,** Town; Accomack County; Pop. 979; Zip Code 23421; Lat. 37-47-12 N long. 075-39-07 W; Founded on land owned by Edmund Parkes in 1742. Originally called Matomkin, but later changed to Parksley.

•**PEARISBURG,** Town; Giles County; Pop. 2,128; Zip Code 24134; Elev. 1804; Lat. 37-19-47 N long. 080-43-44 W; The town was founded in 1808 and named in honor of Captain George Pearis.

•**PEMBROKE,** Town; Giles County; Pop. 1,302; Zip Code 24136; Lat. 37-19-30 N long. 080-38-08 W; The town was named after Pembroke in Wales.

•**PENNINGTON GAP,** Town; Lee County; Pop. 1,716; Zip Code 24277; Elev. 1377; Lat. 36-45-35 N long. 083-01-55 W; An early family named Pennington settled near the mountain gap, and gave the town their name.

•**PETERSBURG,** City; Pop. 41,055; Zip Code 23801; Lat. 37-14-40 N long. 077-20-02 W; Founded in 1646 and later named for trader Peter Jones.

•**PHENIX,** Town; Charlotte County; Pop. 250; Zip Code 23959; Elev. 462; Lat. 37-05-03 N long. 078-44-48 W; The town was named after the "phenix" legend, where it arose from its own ashes.

•**POCAHONTAS,** Town; Tazewell County; Pop. 708; Zip Code 24635; Named for the famous Indian princess, the name means "stream between two hills."

•**PORT ROYAL,** Town; Caroline County; Pop. 291; Zip Code 22535; Lat. 38-10-09 N long. 077-11-32 W; Named by Thomas Roy and called Port Roy for its shipping activily. The name evolved to Port Royal.

•**PORTSMOUTH,** City; Pop. 104,577; Zip Code 23700; Lat. 36-49-34 N long. 076-20-33 W; Established in 1752 and named for the city in England.

•**POUND,** Town; Wise County; Pop. 1,086; Zip Code 24279; Lat. 37-08-02 N long. 082-36-13 W; Site of an early pioneer mill, settlers brought grain to be milled or "pounded," and gave the town its name.

•**PULASKI,** Town; Pulaski County Seat; Pop. 10,106; Zip Code 24301; Lat. 37-03-38 N long. 080-46-34 W; The town was founded in 1839 and named in honor of Polish-American Revolutionary War hero Count Casimir Pulaski.

•**PURCELLVILLE,** Town; Loudoun County; Pop. 1,567; Zip Code 22078; Elev. 576; Lat. 39-06-54 N long. 077-41-42 W; The Purcell family opened the first store and post office in 1832. The town is named after them.

•**QUANTICO,** Town; Prince William County; Pop. 621; Zip Code 22134; Lat. 38-31-15 N long. 077-17-43 W; An Indian word meaning "place of dancing."

•**RADFORD,** City; Pop. 13,225; Zip Code 24141; Elev. 1023; Lat. 37-08-04 N long. 080-34-18 W; The city takes its name from the original landowner, Dr. John Bane Radford.

•**REMINGTON,** Town; Fauquier County; Pop. 425; Zip Code 22734; Lat. 38-32-09 N long. 077-48-32 W; Originally called Millview, the name was changed in 1890 to Remington.

•**RICH CREEK,** Town; Giles County; Pop. 746; Zip Code 24147; Lat. 37-23-09 N long. 080-49-15 W; A large, cool set of creeks run through the town. Water is bottled from one stream because of its medicinal effects. This business named the town.

•**RICHLANDS,** Town; Tazewell County; Pop. 5,796; Zip Code 24641; Elev. 1967; The high-quality pastures in the area gave the town its name.

•**RICHMOND,** City; Pop. 219,214; Zip Code 230+; Lat. 37-17-55 N long. 076-50-26 W; Founded in 1742 and named for Richmond on Thames in England.

•**RIDGEWAY,** Town; Henry County; Pop. 858; Zip Code 24148; Elev. 638; Lat. 36-32-55 N long. 079-51-27 W; Early settler Samuel Sheffield descriptively named the town.

•**ROANOKE,** City; Pop. 100,427; Zip Code 24001; Lat. 37-16-36 N long. 079-57-23 W; The city's name is from an Indian word meaning "swell money".

•**ROCKY MOUNT,** Town; Franklin County Seat; Pop. 4,198; Zip Code 24151; Lat. 36-59-58 N long. 079-53-23 W; Settled in 1760 and descriptively named for an abrupt precipice in the area.

•**ROUND HILL,** Town; Loudoun County; Pop. 510; Zip Code 22141; Elev. 97; Lat. 39-08-03 N long. 077-46-09 W; The town was settled in 1735 and named for a prominent "round hill" landmark nearby.

•**RURAL RETREAT,** Town; Wythe County; Pop. 1,083; Zip Code 24368; Elev. 2510; Lat. 36-53-43 N long. 081-16-27 W; Named after an early inn on the stage route which was a "retreat" for weary travelers.

•**ST. CHARLES,** Town; Lee County; Pop. 241; Zip Code 24282; Lat. 36-49-01 N long. 083-03-28 W; The town was named in honor of early coal developer Charles Bondurant.

•**ST. PAUL,** Town; Russell & Wise Counties; Pop. 973; Zip Code 24283; Elev. 1492; Lat. 36-58-04 N long. 082-18-28 W; Originally Estonoa, the town had a wave of development in 1885 by promoters from St. Paul, Minnesota. The name was changed at that time to St. Paul.

•**SALEM,** City; Pop. 23,958; Zip Code 24153; Elev. 1060; Lat. 37-16-49 N long. 080-03-01 W; The town was laid out in 1802 and named for Salem, New Jersey.

•**SALTVILLE,** Town; Smyth & Washington Counties; Pop. 2,376; Zip Code 24370; Elev. 1718; Lat. 36-52-41 N long. 081-46-10 W; Incorporated in 1896 and named for its two centruy old salt production industry.

•**SAXIS,** Town; Accomack County; Pop. 415; Zip Code 23427; Lat. 37-55-35 N long. 075-43-12 W; The name is a corruption of seventeenth century settler Robert Sike's name.

•**SCOTTSBURG,** Town; Halifax County; Pop. 335; Zip Code 24589; Elev. 380; Lat. 36-45-28 N long. 078-47-28 W; The town's name honors John Scott, a Revolutionary War soldier and officer.

•**SCOTTSVILLE,** Town; Albemarle & Fluvana Counties; Pop. 250; Zip Code 24562; Lat. 37-43-53 N long. 078-39-32 W; The town is named after the Scott family, who were prominent early settlers.

•**SHENANDOAH,** Town; Page County; Pop. 1,861; Zip Code 22849; Lat. 38-29-14 N long. 078-37-19 W; Incorporated in 1884 and given an Indian name meaning "beautiful daughter of the stars."

•**SMITHFIELD,** Town; Isle of Wight County; Pop. 3,649; Zip Code 23430; Elev. 45; Lat. 36-59-20 N long. 076-37-49 W; Founded in 1662 on land owned by settler Arthur Smith, and so named.

•**SOUTH BOSTON,** City; Pop. 7,093; Zip Code 24592; Lat. 36-42-30 N long. 078-54-17 W; Originally slated to be called Boston, post office objections forced a name change to South Boston.

•**SOUTH HILL,** Town; Mecklenburg County; Pop. 4,347; Zip Code 23970; Elev. 440; Lat. 36-43-45 N long. 078-07-25 W; The town is south of a large hill, and was so descriptively named.

•**STANARDSVILLE,** Town; Greene County Seat; Pop. 284; Zip Code 22973; Lat. 38-17-53 N long. 078-26-17 W; The name honors Robert Standards who donated the land for the courthouse.

•**STUART,** Town; Patrick County Seat; Pop. 1,131; Zip Code 24171; Lat. 36-38-16 N long. 080-16-00 W; Founded in the 1700's and later named in honor of General J.E.B. Stuart, Confederate War hero.

•**SURRY,** Town; Surry County Seat; Pop. 237; Zip Code 23883; Lat. 37-08-10 N long. 076-49-56 W; Founded in the later 1700's and named after an area in England.

•**TANGIER,** Town; Accomack County; Pop. 771; Zip Code 23440; Lat. 37-49-29 N long. 075-59-34 W; Settled in 1680 and named for small clay bowls, or tanga, which reminded the colonists of similar products of North Africa.

•**TAPPAHANNOCK,** Town; Essex County Seat; Pop. 1,821; Zip Code 22560; Elev. 22; Lat. 37-55-27 N long. 076-51-39 W; An Indian name meaning "on the running water."

•**TAZEWELL,** Town; Tazewell County Seat; Pop. 4,468; Zip Code 246+; Elev. 2519; The town is named for Henry Tazewell, a U. S. Senator from 1794-1799.

•**THE PLAINS,** Town; Fauquier County; Pop. 382; Zip Code 22171; Lat. 38-51-52 N long. 077-46-22 W; Formerly White Plains, the name was shortened to avoid confusion with a similarly named city in New York.

•**TIMBERVILLE,** Town; Rockingham County; Pop. 1,510; Zip Code 22853; Lat. 38-38-09 N long. 078-46-24 W; Established in the late 1700's and named for the abundant timber nearby.

•**TOMS BROOK,** Town; Shenandoah County; Pop. 226; Zip Code 22660; Lat. 38-56-50 N long. 078-26-28 W; An early settler's cabin named a local stream "Tom's Creek"; this was later changed to Tom's Brook and given to the town.

•**TROUTDALE,** Town; Grayson County; Pop. 248; Zip Code 24378; Lat. 36-42-05 N long. 081-26-23 W; Excellent trout fishing in nearby Fox Creek gave the town its name.

•**TROUTVILLE,** Town; Botetourt County; Pop. 496; Zip Code 24175; Lat. 37-24-54 N long. 079-52-46 W; The town was named in honor of the Trout family.

•**URBANNA,** Town; Middlesex County; Pop. 518; Zip Code 23175; Lat. 37-38-28 N long. 076-34-22 W; Founded in 1705 and named in honor of Queen Anne, or Urb-Anna.

•**VICTORIA,** Town; Lunenburg County; Pop. 2,004; Zip Code 23974; Lat. 36-59-28 N long. 078-13-34 W; The town's name honors Great Britan's Queen Victoria.

•**VIENNA,** Town; Fairfax County; Pop. 15,469; Zip Code 22027; Lat. 38-53-26 N long. 077-13-39 W; The town was named after Vienna, New York.

•**VINTON,** Town; Roanoke County; Pop. 8,027; Zip Code 24179; Lat. 37-22-35 N long. 079-48-36 W; Founded in 1794 as Gish's Mill,but later given a coined name combining pioneer names Vineyard and Preston, or Vinton.

•**VIRGILINA,** Town; Halifax County; Pop. 212; Zip Code 24598; Elev. 534; The town is situated on the Virginia-North Carolina boundary. The name is derived from a combination of the two state names.

•**VIRGINIA BEACH,** City; Pop. 262,199; Zip Code 234+; Lat. 36-50-51 N long. 076-05-52 W; Descriptively named for the state and its ocean location.

•**WACHAPREAGUE,** Town; Accomack County; Pop. 404; Zip Code 23480; Lat. 37-36-29 N long. 075-41-18 W; Incorporated in 1902 and given an Indian name meaning "little city by the sea."

•**WAKEFIELD,** Town; Sussex County; Pop. 1,355; Zip Code 23888; Lat. 36-58-12 N long. 076-58-44 W; Incorporated in 1902 and given the name of a place in a Walter Scott novel.

•**WARRENTON,** Town; Fauquier County Seat; Pop. 3,907; Zip Code 22186; Lat. 38-44-02 N long. 077-44-18 W; The town was named in honor of Revolutionary War hero, Dr. Joseph Warren.

•**WARSAW,** Town; Richmond County Seat; Pop. 771; Zip Code 22572; Lat. 37-57-33 N long. 076-45-30 W; Originally Richmond Courthouse, renamed in honor of the Polish capital in 1846.

•**WASHINGTON,** Town; Rappahannock County Seat; Pop. 247; Zip Code 22747; Lat. 38-42-47 N long. 078-09-35 W; Established by George Washington in 1749, and named for him by Lord Fairfax.

•**WAVERLY,** Town; Sussex County; Pop. 2,284; Zip Code 23890; Lat. 37-02-06 N long. 077-06-54 W; Incorporated in 1879 and given the name from a Walter Scott novel.

•**WAYNESBORO,** City; Pop. 15,329; Zip Code 22980; Lat. 38-04-27 N long. 078-53-34 W; The city was named to honor the GreatRevolutionary War General, Anthony Wayne.

•**WEBER CITY,** Town; Scott County; Pop. 1,543; The town's name is copied from radio era show "Amos and Andy" who lived in mythical "Weber City."

•**WEST POINT,** Town; King William County; Pop. 2,726; Zip Code 230+; Lat. 37-31-48 N long. 076-41-19 W; Called "The Point" in the 18th century and later given the additional name west for a pioneer family.

•**WHITE STONE,** Lancaster County; Pop. 409; Zip Code 22578; Elev. 51; Lat. 37-38-42 N long. 076-23-20 W; The town is descriptively named for White Stone Beach.

•**WILLIAMSBURG,** City; Pop. 9,870; Zip Code 23081; Elev. 86; Lat. 37-12-28 N long. 076-46-29 W; Settled in 1632 and named in honor of William III of England.

•**WINCHESTER,** City; Pop. 20,217; Zip Code 22601; Elev. 720; Lat. 39-11-02 N long. 078-09-32 W; The city was settled in 1738 and named for Winchester, England.

•**WINDSOR,** Town; Isle of Wight County; Pop. 985; Zip Code 23487; Lat. 36-48-37 N long. 076-44-46 W; The town is named after the location in one of Walter Scott's novels.

•**WISE,** Town; Wise County Seat; Pop. 3,894; Zip Code 24923; Elev. 2,454; Lat. 37-01-14 N, long. 082-34-42 W. The town was named for former governor of Virginia, Henry A. Wise.

•**WOODSTOCK,** Town; Shenandoah County Seat; Pop. 2,627; Zip Code 22664; Lat. 38-52-49 N, long. 078-30-39 W. Named by founder Jacob Miller in 1761.

•**WYTHEVILLE,** Town; Wythe County Seat; Pop. 7,135; Zip Code 24382; Elev. 2,284; Lat. 36-56-47 N, long. 081-05-04 W. Named for George Wythe, the first professor of law in America, teacher of Thomas Jefferson, John Marshall and James Monroe; and first Virginia signer of Declaration of Independence.

WASHINGTON

•**ABERDEEN,** City; Grays Harbor County; Pop. 18,739; Zip Code Code 98520; Lat. 46-58-21 N long. 123-45-05 W; The city is named after the famous town in Scotland.

•**AIRWAY HEIGHTS,** City; Spokane County; Pop. 1,730; Zip Code 99001; A descriptive name for the community.

•**ALBION,** Town; Whitman County; Pop. 631; Zip Code 99102; Lat. 47-21-07 N long. 117-42-44 W; The town's name honors early English exploration of the region.

•**ALMIRA,** Town; Lincoln County; Pop. 330; Zip Code 99103; Elev. 1915; Lat. 47-53-27 N 117-21-07 W; The town's name honors Almira Davis, wife of the town's first merchant.

•**ANACORTES,** City; Skagit County; Pop. 9,013; Zip Code 98221; Lat. 48-30-08 N long. 122-37-17 W; Civil engineer Amos Bowman plotted the townsite and named it for his wife's maiden name: Anna Curtis. The spelling was later changed to give it a Spanish sound.

•**ARLINGTON,** City; Snohomish County; Pop. 3,282; Zip Code 98223; Lat. 48-11-34 N long. 122-07-16 W; Two railroad contractors purchased the townsite in 1890 and named it for Lord Henry Arlington, a member of the cabinet of Charles II.

•**ASOTIN,** City; Asotin County Seat; Pop. 943; Zip Code 99402; Elev. 770; Lat. 46-20-13 N long. 117-02-10 W; A Nez Perce Indian word meaning "Eel Creek" and descriptively referring to the eels caught there.

•**AUBURN,** City; King County; Pop. 26,417; Zip Code 980+; Originally called Slaughter, the name was later changed to the more euphonious Auburn.

•**BATTLE GROUND,** City; Clark County; Pop. 2,774; Zip Code 98604; Lat. 45-46-54 N long. 122-31-57 W; The town's name commemorates a battle between the U.S. Army and local Indians during pioneer days.

•**BEAUX ARTS VILLAGE,** Town; King County; Pop. 328; A euphonious name given by the town's settlers.

•**BELLEVUE,** City; King County; Pop. 73,903; Zip Code 98004; Lat. 47-35-00 N long. 122-10-29 W; An old English name given by the town's founders.

•**BELLINGHAM,** City; Whatcom County Seat; Pop. 45,794; Zip Code 98225; Lat. 48-44-54 N long. 122-28-52 W; George Vancouver's expedition honored Sir William Bellingham by naming the bay for him. The city gets its name from the bay.

•**BENTON CITY,** City; Benton County; Pop. 1,980; Zip Code 99320; Lat. 46-15-55 N long. 119-29-16 W; The city was named in 1909 by two employees of the North Coast Railroad Co.--possibly for a fellow employee.

•**BINGEN,** City; Klickitat County; Pop. 644; Zip Code 98605; Elev. 1131; Lat. 45-43-00 N long. 121-27-58 W; Founded in 1892 and named for a city on the Rhine River in Germany.

•**BLACK DIAMOND,** City; King County; Pop. 1,170; Zip Code 98010; Lat. 47-18-41 N long. 122-00-08 W; The city is named after the Black River which runs through the county.

•**BLAINE,** City; Whatcom County; Pop. 2,363; Zip Code 98230; Lat. 48-59-21 N long. 122-45-00 W; Blaine takes its name from 1884 Republican presidential nominee James G. Blaine.

•**BOTHELL,** City; King County; Pop. 7,943; Zip Code 980+; Lat. 47-43-21 N long. 122-13-04 W; Named in honor of the Bothell family who were local businessmen and politicians.

•**BREMERTON,** City; Kitsap County; Pop. 36,208; Zip Code 983+; Lat. 47-34-46 N long. 122-39-59 W; The city's name comes from William Bremer, an early pioneer who founded the town.

•**BURLINGTON,** City; Skagit County; Pop. 3,894; Zip Code 98233; Lat. 48-28-12 N long. 122-19-17 W; Founded in 1891 and named by early settlers for a former home.

•**CAMAS,** City; Clark County; Pop. 5,681; Zip Code 98607; Lat. 45-35-13 N long. 122-24-23 W; The city is named the food plant, Camassia Esculenta, a favorite food of the original Indians.

•**CARBONADO,** To Pierce County; Pop. 456; Zip Code 98323; Lat. 47-04-36 N long. 122-03-05 W; The town gets its name from the adjacent Carbon River, so called for the coal deposits on its banks.

•**CARNATION,** City; King County; Pop. 913; Zip Code 98014; Lat. 47-38-56 N long. 121-54-54 W; The city was named for the flower by action of the state legislature in 1917.

•**CASHMERE,** City; Chelan County; Pop. 2,240; Zip Code 98815; Elev. 795; Lat. 47-31-12 N long. 120-28-08 W; The city is named for the Valley of Cashmere in India.

•**CASTLE ROCK,** City; Cowlitz County; Pop. 2,162; Zip Code 98611; Lat. 46-16-25 N long. 122-54-18 W; A descriptive name for a huge 150 foot high rock which resembles a castle.

•**CATHLAMET,** Town; Wahkiakum County Seat; Pop. 635; Zip Code 98612; Elev. 53; Lat. 46-12-37 N long. 123-22-48 W; An Indian word meaning "stone" and referring to the bed of the adjacent Columbia River.

•**CENTRALIA,** City; Lewis County; Pop. 10,809; Zip Code 98531; Elev. 189; Lat. 46-43-42 N long. 122-58-43 W; Originally called Centerville, the name was later changed to Centralia after the city in Illinois.

•**CHEHALIS,** City; Lewis County Seat; Pop. 6,100; Zip Code 98532; Elev. 226; Lat. 46-39-52 N long. 122-57-42 W; An Indian word meaning "sand" which early settlers incorrectly applied to the local Indians.

•**CHELAN,** City; Chelan County; Pop. 2,802; Zip Code 98816; Lat. 47-50-16 N long. 120-00-42 W; An Indian word meaning either "deep water" or "bubbling water."

•**CHENEY,** City; Spokane County; Pop. 7,630; Zip Code 99004; Lat. 47-29-27 N long. 117-34-44 W; The city is named in honor of Benjamin P. Cheney, a founder of the Northern Pacific Railroad.

•**CHEWELAH,** City; Stevens County; Pop. 1,888; Zip Code 99109; Elev. 1671; Lat. 48-16-45 N long. 117-43-01 W; An Indian word meaning "snake" and possibly applied as a description to meandering streams.

•**CLARKSTON,** City; Asotin County; Pop. 6,903; The town is named for Captain William Clark of Lewis and Clark expedition fame.

•**CLE ELUM,** City; Kittitas County; Pop. 1,773; Zip Code 98922; Elev. 1905; Lat. 47-11-34 N long. 120-55-39 W; An Indian word meaning "swift waters."

519

•**COLFAX,** City; Whitman County Seat; Pop. 2,780; Zip Code 99111; Elev. 1962; Lat. 46-52-55 N long. 117-21-57 W; Founded in 1872 and named in honor of U.S. Vice-president Colfax.

•**COLLEGE PLACE,** City; Walla Walla County; Pop. 5,771; Zip Code 99324; Lat. 46-01-48 N long. 118-26-52 W; The town took its name from a local Seventh Day Adventist college.

•**COLTON,** Town; Whitman County; Pop. 307; Zip Code 99113; Elev. 2562; Lat. 46-34-00 N long. 117-07-43 W; The town is named for an early Settler.

•**COLVILLE,** City; Stevens County Seat; Pop. 4,510; Zip Code 99114; Lat. 48-32-42 N long. 117-53-57 W; Colville takes its name from Andrew Colville who was governor of the Hudson Bay Company in the early 1800s.

•**CONCONULLY,** Town; Okanogan County; Pop. 157; Zip Code 98819; Lat. 48-33-22 N long. 119-44-58 W; The town's name is a corrupt rendering of an Indian word meaning "cloudy."

•**CONCRETE,** Town; Skagit County; Pop. 592; Zip Code 98237; Lat. 48-32-19 N long. 121-45-32 W; Settled in 1888d and later named for the cement industry which grew up in the area.

•**CONNELL,** Town; Franklin County; Pop. 1,981; Zip Code 99326; Elev. 840; Lat. 46-39-40 N long. 118-51-32 W; Named after an early settler.

•**COSMOPOLIS,** City; Grays Harbor County; Pop. 1,575; Zip Code 98537; Elev. 12; Lat. 46-57-12 N long. 123-46-22 W; Following a practice common in the 19th century the town was given a classical name.

•**COULEE CITY,** Town; Grant County; Pop. 510; Zip Code 99115; Lat. 47-36-45 N long. 119-17-10 W; The town is situated in the Grand Coulee. A Coulee is a steep-walled trench like valley created by a lava flow.

•**COULEE DAM,** Town; Douglas, Grant & Okanogan Counties; Pop. 1,412; Zip Code 991+; Lat. 47-57-48 N long. 118-58-53 W; The town takes its name from the nearby world famous dam.

•**COUPEVILLE,** Town; Island County Seat; Pop. 1,006; Zip Code 98239; Lat. 48-12-44 N long. 122-40-03 W; Founded in 1853 by Captain Thomas Coupe and named in his honor.

•**CRESTON,** Town; Lincoln County; Pop. 309; Zip Code 99117; Elev. 2436; Lat. 47-45-24 N long. 118-31-12 W; Named by Northern Pacific Railray engineers after a local butte, the highest point in the county.

•**CUSICK,** Town; Pend Oreille County; Pop. 246; Zip Code 99119; Lat. 48-20-10 N long. 117-17-47 W.

•**DARRINGTON,** Town; Snohomish County; Pop. 1,064; Zip Code 98241; Elev. 549; Lat. 48-15-06 N long. 121-36-12 W; The town was named in honor of a man nammed Barrington, but the first letter got changed in the application.

•**DAVENPORT,** City; Lincoln County Seat; Pop. 1,559; Zip Code 99122; Elev. 2369; Lat. 47-39-10 N long. 118-08-59 W; Named after an early settler.

•**DAYTON,** City; Columbia County Seat; Pop. 2,565; Zip Code 99328; Elev. 1613; Lat. 46-52-16 N long. 122-15-47 W; Early settlers, Jesse and Elizabeth Day, founded the town in the 1870s. It is named in their honor.

•**DEER PARK,** City; Spokane County; Pop. 2,140; Zip Code 99006; Lat. 47-57-14 N long. 117-28-11 W; A descriptive name for the good hunting of pioneer days.

•**DES MOINES,** City; King County; Pop. 7,378; The city is named after the city in Iowa.

•**DUPONT,** City; Pierce County; Pop. 559; Zip Code 98327; The town took its name from the DuPont powder company factory nearby.

•**DUVALL,** City; King County; Pop. 729; Zip Code 98019; Lat. 47-44-31 N long. 121-58-56 W; Pioneer James Duval was the first landowner and the town was named in his honor.

•**EATONVILLE,** Town; Pierce County; Pop. 998; Zip Code 98328; The town takes its name from an early pioneer named Eaton.

•**EDMONDS,** City; Snohomish County; Pop. 27,526; Zip Code 98020; Lat. 47-47-09 N long. 122-20-07 W; With a slight name change the town was named in honor of famous Vermont Senator George Edmunds.

•**ELECTRIC CITY,** Town; Grant County; Pop. 927; Zip Code 99123; Elev. 1655; Lat. 47-55-48 N long. 119-02-13 W; So called because of its relation to hydroelectric power.

•**ELLENSBURG,** City; Kittitas County Seat; Pop. 11,752; Zip Code 989+; Lat. 46-59-51 N long. 120-32-24 W; Pioneer John Shoudy named the town in honor of his wife--Mary Ellen.

•**ELMA,** City; Grays Harbor County; Pop. 2,720; Zip Code 98541; Lat. 47-00-11 N long. 123-24-25 W; The city's name honors early Puget Sound pioneer Miss Elma Austin.

•**ELMER CITY,** Town; Okanogan County; Pop. 312; Zip Code 99124; Lat. 47-59-48 N long. 118-57-05 W; Named for an early settler.

•**ENDICOTT,** Town; Whitman County; Pop. 290; Zip Code 99125; Elev. 1706; Lat. 46-55-45 N long. 117-41-10 W; The town is named for an early pioneer.

•**ENTIAT,** Town; Chelan County; Pop. 445; Zip Code 98822; Lat. 47-40-45 N long. 120-12-28 W; An Indian word meaning "rapid water" and referring to the Entiat River.

•**ENUMCLAW,** City; King County; Pop. 5,427; Zip Code 98022; Lat. 47-12-21 N long. 121-59-29 W; An Indian word meaning "home of the evil spirit."

•**EPHRATA,** City; Grant County Seat; Pop. 5,359; Zip Code 98823; Lat. 47-19-06 N long. 119-32-46 W; Great Northern Railway Surveyors gave the town the ancient Biblicl name for Bethlehem.

•**EVERETT,** City; Snohomish County Seat; Pop. 54,413; Zip Code 982+; Lat. 47-58-03 N long. 122-12-19 W; The city is named in honor of Everett Colby, one of the city fathers.

•**EVERSON,** City; Whatcom County; Pop. 898; Zip Code 98247; Elev. 90; Lat. 48-54-47 N long. 122-20-43 W; Named in honor of Ever Everson, the first white settler north of the Nooksack River.

•**FAIRFIELD,** Town; Spokane County; Pop. 582; Zip Code 99012; Elev. 2559; Lat. 47-22-59 N long. 117-10-28 W; Named in 1888 by E.H. Morrison to describe the extensive grain fields surrounding the town.

•**FARMINGTON,** Town; Whitman County; Pop. 176; Zip Code 99104; Elev. 2626; Lat. 47-05-35 N long. 117-09-43 W; Settler G.W. Truax named the town for the city in Minnesota.

•**FERNDALE,** City; Whatcom County; Pop. 3,855; Zip Code 98248; Lat. 48-51-08 N long. 122-35-42 W; The town's first teacher named the future town for the first school location: a fern patch.

•FIFE, City; Pierce County; Pop. 1,823; Named after the musical instrument.

•FORKS, Town; Clallam County; Pop. 3,060; Zip Code 98331; Lat. 47-57-02 N long. 124-22-56 W; A descriptive geographical name.

•FRIDAY HARBOR, Town; San Juan County Seat; Pop. 1,200; Zip Code 98222; Elev. 91; Lat. 48-30-08 N long. 122-37-17 W; A Hudson Bay Company engineer named "Friday" gave the town his name.

•GARFIELD, Town; Whitman County; Pop. 599; Zip Code 99130; Lat. 47-00-35 N long. 117-08-27 W; The town's name honors President James Garfield.

•GEORGE, Town; Grant County; Pop. 261; Named for an early trapper and fur trader, Indian George.

•GIG HARBOR, Town; Pierce County; Pop. 2,429; Zip Code 98335; Lat. 47-19-32 N long. 122-35-01 W; Named by the 1841 Wilkes expedition who noted it "has sufficient depth for small vessels."

•GOLD BAR, Town; Snohomish County; Pop. 794; Zip Code 98251; Lat. 47-51-26 N, long. 121-41-43 W. Descriptively named by gold prospectors here in 1896.

•GOLDENDALE, City; Klickitat County Seat; Pop. 3,414; Zip Code 98620; Elev. 1633; Lat. 45-49-22 N, long. 120-49-09 W. The city is named after homesteader John J. Golden who settled here in 1863.

•GRAND COULEE, City; Grant County; Pop. 1,180; Zip Code 91333; Lat. 47-56-32 N, long. 119-00-04 W. Descriptively named for its location near the gigantic coulee that was the ancient bed of the Columbia River.

•GRANDVIEW, City; Yakima County; Pop. 5,615; Zip Code 98930; Lat. 46-15-09 N, long. 119-54-30 W. The town was founded in 1906 and named for its view of Mt. Adams and Mt. Rainier.

•GRANGER, Town; Yakima County; Pop. 1,182; Zip Code 98932; Elev. 731; Lat. 46-20-25 N, long. 120-11-19 W. Founded in 1902 and named in honor of irrigation canal company president, Walter N. granger.

•GRANITE FALLS, Town; Snohomish County; Pop. 911; Zip Code 08252; Elev. 391; Lat. 48-04-56 N, long. 121-57-58 W. The town is named forthefalls in the granite rock canyon of the Stillaguamish River.

•HARRAH, Town; Yakima County; Pop. 343; Zip Code 98933; Lat. 46-24-14 N, long. 120-33-06 W. Originally called Saluskin after an Yakima Indian chief, the town's name was changed in 1915 to honor prominent rancher J.T. Harrah.

•HARRINGTON, Town; Lincoln County; Pop. 507; Zip Code 99134; Elev. 2140; Lat. 47-28-43 N long. 118-15-19 W; In 1882, W.P. Harrington, a California banker, invested in the town and subsequently had it named in his honor.

•HARTLINE, Town; Grant County; Pop. 165; Zip Code 99135; Lat. 47-41-11 N long. 119-06-09 W; Early settler John Hartline gave the town his name.

•HATTON, Town; Adams County; Pop. 81; A combined name-- for postmaster J.D. Hackett and a local settler named Sutton--or Hatton.

•HOQUIAM, City; Grays Harbor County; Pop. 9,719; Zip Code 98550; Lat. 46-58-47 N long. 123-52-42 W; An Indian word meaning "hungry for wood" and referring to the large amount of driftwood at the river's mouth.

•ILWACO, Town; Pacific County; Pop. 604; Zip Code 98624; Elev. 11; Lat. 46-18-27 N long. 124-02-14 W; Named for a petty Indian Chief, El-wah-ko.

•INDEX, Town; Snohomish County; Pop. 147; Zip Code 98256; Elev. 532; Lat. 47-49-05 N long. 121-33-26 W; A descriptive name referring to Index Mountain which resembles an index finger pointing to the sky.

•ISSOQUAH, City; King County; Pop. 5,536; Zip Code 98027; Lat. 47-33-29 N long. 122-04-15 W; A proper Indian name whose meaning is uncertain.

•KAHLOTUS, Town; Franklin County; Pop. 203; Zip Code 99335; Elev. 901; Lat. 46-38-41 N long. 118-33-03 W; An Indian name meaning "hole-in-the-ground."

•KALAMA, City; Cowlitz County; Pop. 1,216; Zip Code 98625; Lat. 46-00-42 N long. 122-50-46 W; An Indian word meaning "pretty maiden."

•KELSO, City; Cowlitz County Seat; Pop. 11,129; Zip Code 98626; Lat. 46-08-38 N long. 122-54-08 W; Surveyor Peter Crawford named the town for his former home in Scotland.

•KENNEWICK, City; Benton County; Pop. 34,397; Zip Code 993+; Lat. 46-12-17 N long. 119-08-02 W; An Indian word meaning "grassy place."

•KENT, City; King County; Pop. 23,397; Zip Code 980+; Lat. 47-24-09 N long. 122-15-09 W; The city takes its name from the famous county.

•KETTLE FALLS, City; Stevens County; Pop. 1,087; Zip Code 991+; Elev. 1625; A translation of the Salish Indian word for "kettle" or tightly woven basket.

•KIRKLAND, City; King County; Pop. 18,779; Zip Code 980+; Lat. 47-40-34 N long. 122-11-36 W; The city takes its name from millionaire ironmaker Peter Kirk who lived and died nearby.

•KITTITAS, City, Kittitas County; Pop. 782; Zip Code 98934; Elev. 1647; Lat. 46-59-04 N long. 120-25-09 W; An Indian word meaning either "land of bread" or "clay gravel valley."

•LA CENTER, Town; Clark County; Pop. 439; Zip Code 98629; Lat. 45-51-36 N long. 122-40-13 W; A descriptive name referring to the town's geographical position.

•LA CONNER, Town; Skagit County; Pop. 633; Zip Code 98257; Lat. 48-23-23 N long. 122-29-29 W; Early merchant J.J. Conner named the town in honor of wife Louisa Ann.

•LA CROSSE, Town; Whitman County; Pop. 373; Zip Code 99136; Elev. 1481; Lat. 46-40-32 N long. 117-55-18 W; The town takes its name from the well-known sport.

•LAKE STEVENS, City; Stevens County; Pop. 1,660; Zip Code 98258; Lat. 48-00-58 N long. 122-03-36 W; Named for an early settler.

•LAMONT, Town; Whitman County; Pop. 101; Named for Daniel Lamont, Vice President of the Northern Pacific Railway Company.

•LANGLEY, City; Island County; Pop. 650; Zip Code 98260; Lat. 48-02-20 N long. 122-24-14 W; The town is named in honor of Judge J.W. Langley of Seattle--one of the original landowners.

•LATAH, Town; Spokane County; Pop. 155; Zip Code 99018; Lat. 47-16-45 N long. 117-09-14 W; A corruption of an Indian word meaning "place where fish are caught."

•**LEAVENWORTH**, City; Chelan County; Pop. 1,522; Zip Code 98826; Lat. 47-35-52 N long. 120-39-35 W; Named by early settlers for the famous Army post in Kansas.

•**LIND**, Town; Adams County; Pop. 567; Zip Code 99341; Lat. 46-58-09 N long. 118-36-53 W; Named by the Northern Pacific Railway Company around the turn of century.

•**LONG BEACH**, Town; Pacific County; Pop. 1,199; Zip Code 98631; Lat. 46-21-18 N long. 124-03-07 W; A descriptive name for the twenty mile long beach in the area.

•**LONGVIEW**, City; Cowlitz County; Pop. 31,052; Zip Code 98632; Elev. 21; Lat. 46-09-28 N long. 122-56-08 W; A descriptive name referring to the long view of the Columbia River.

•**LYMAN**, Town; Skagit County; Pop. 285; Zip Code 98263; Lat. 48-31-30 N long. 122-03-42 W; The town is named for the first postmaster B.L. Lyman.

•**LYNDEN**, City; Whatcom County; Pop. 4,022; Zip Code 98264; Elev. 103; Lat. 48-56-35 N long. 122-27-26 W; Named in 1870 by Mrs. Phoebe Judson who changed the name from Linden to Lynden.

•**LYNNWOOD**, City; Snoho County; Pop. 21,9397; Zip Code 98036; Lat. 47-50-21 N long. 122-17-13 W; Named by an early settlers for one of their former homes.

•**MABTON**, Town; Yakima County; Pop. 1,248; Zip Code 98935; Lat. 46-12-41 N long. 119-59-48 W; Named in honor of Mrs. Mabel Anderson, daughter of pioneer railroad builder Dorset Boker.

•**MALDEN**, The Whitman County; Pop. 200; Zip Code 99149; Lat. 47-13-48 N long. 117-28-31 W; The town was by a railroad company official for a town in Massachusetts.

•**MANSFIELD**, Town; Douglas County; Pop. 315; Zip Code 98830; Elev. 2262; Lat. 47-48-39 N long. 119-37-56 W; Settler R.E. Darling named the town in honor of his home town in Ohio.

•**MARCUS**, Town; Stevens County; Pop. 174; Zip Code 99151; Lat. 48-39-54 N long. 118-03-49 W; The town's name honors Marcus Oppenheimer one of the two original settlers.

•**MARYSVILLE**, City; Snohomish County; Pop. 5,080; Zip Code 98270; Lat. 48-03-56 N long. 122-09-51 W; Founded in the 1870s and named by early settlers for Marysville, California.

•**MCCLEARY**, Town; Grays Harbor County; Pop. 1,419; Zip Code 98557; Lat. 47-03-22 N long. 123-15-57 W; Named in honor of timber company President Henry McCleary.

•**MEDICAL LAKE**, Town; Spokane County; Pop. 3,600; Zip Code 99022; Lat. 47-34-08 N long. 117-41-04 W; So named by early settlers because the Indians thought bathing in the nearby lake a cure for rheumatism.

•**MEDINA**, City; King County; Pop. 3,220; Zip Code 98039; Lat. 47-37-29 N long. 122-13-24 W; The city is named after Medina, Turkey.

•**MERCER ISLAND**, City; King County; Pop. 21,522; Zip Code 98040; Lat. 47-3-43 N long. 122-11-42 W; The city's name honors Asa Mercer, an early settler of the region.

•**MESA**, Town; Franklin County; Pop. 278; Zip Code 99343; Lat. 46-34-33 N long. 199-00-13 W; Descriptively named, the town's name means "table-land" in Spanish.

•**METALINE**, Town; Pend Oreille County; Pop. 190; Zip Code 99152; Lat. 48-50-56 N long. 117-23-13 W; The town was named by early miners who thought the entire district a storehouse of minerals.

•**METALINE FALLS**, Town; Pend Oreille County; Pop. 296; Zip Code 99153; Lat. 48-52-05 N long. 117-21-35 W; The town is on the Pend Oreille River at the site of a falls. Named by miners during gold rush days.

•**MILLWOOD**, Town; Spokane County; Pop. 1,717; Descriptively named as the site of a sawmill.

•**MILTON**, Town; King & Pierce Counties; Pop. 3,162; Zip Code 983+; Lat. 47-14-21 N long. 122-18-42 W; The town is named after an early settler.

•**MONROE**, City; Snohomish County; Pop. 2,869; Zip Code 98272; Lat. 47-51-17 N long. 121-58-53 W; The city is believed to be named after resident James Monroe.

•**MONTESANO**, City; Grays Harbor County Seat; Pop. 3,247; Zip Code 98563; Elev. 66; Lat. 46-58-56 N long. 123-35-55 W; Named in 1860 by early pioneers and meaning "the promised place."

•**MORTON**, City; Lewis County; Pop. 1,264; Zip Code 98356; Lat. 46-33-27 N long. 122-22-26 W; The town is named in honor of former Vice-president Levi Morton.

•**MOSES LAKE**, City; Grant County; Pop. 10,629; Zip Code 98837; Lat. 47-08-32 N long. 119-17-59 W; It was named from the fact that the tribe of Chief Moses lived near the shores of the lake.

•**MOSSYROCK**, City; Lewis County; Pop. 463; Zip Code 98564; Elev. 698; Lat. 46-31-48 N long. 122-31-34 W; Named in 1852 after a point of moss-covered rock about 200 feet high near the town.

•**MOUNT VERNON**, City; Skagit County Seat; Pop. 13,009; Zip Code 98273; Lat. 48-25-19 N long. 122-19-28 W; Named in 1877 in honor of the Virginia Estate of George Washington.

•**MOUNTLAKE TERRACE**, City; Snohomish County; Pop. 16,534; Zip Code 98043; Lat. 47-47-59 N long. 122-18-07 W; The city is descriptively named.

•**MUKILTEO**, City, Snohomish County; Pop. 1,426; Zip Code 98275; Lat. 47-56-37 N long. 122-16-48 W; An Indian word meaning "good camping ground."

•**NACHES**, Town; Yakima County; Pop. 644; Zip Code 98929; Lat. 46-52-47 N long. 121-16-51 W; An Indian place name whose meaning has been lost.

•**NAPAVINE**, City; Lewis County; Pop. 611; Zip Code 98565; Elev. 444; Lat. 46-34-46 N long. 122-54-35 W; The name is derived from an Indian word "Napavoon" meaning "small prairie."

•**NESPELEM**, Town; Okanogan County; Pop. 284; Zip Code 99155; Lat. 48-09-54 N long. 118-58-19 W; The origin of the town's name is uncertain.

•**NEWPORT**, City; Pend Oreille County Seat; Pop. 1,665; Zip Code 99156; Lat. 48-10-43 N long. 117-01-22 W; In 1890 when the first steamboat placed on the Pend Oreille River, a new landing place was selected and named Newport.

•**NOOKSACK**, City; Whatcom County; Pop. 429; Zip Code 98276; Elev. 84; Lat. 48-55-39 N long. 122-19-23 W; An Indian word meaning "people who live on the root of the fern."

•**NORTH BEND**, City; King County; Pop. 1,701; Zip Code 98045; Elev. 442; Lat. 47-29-44 N long. 121-46-40 W; Its name comes from its location where the South Fork of the Snoqualmie River bends to the north.

•**NORTH BONNEVILLE**, City; Skamania County; Pop. 394; Zip Code 98639; Lat. 45-38-48 N long. 121-55-57 W; Descriptively named--Bonneville means "beautiful city."

•NORTHPORT, Town; Stevens County; Pop. 368; Zip Code 99157; Lat. 48-54-55 N long. 117-47-06 W; So named for its northern position on the Columbia River.

•OAKESDALE, Town; Whitman County; Pop. 444; Zip Code 99158; Elev. 2461; Lat. 47-07-52 N long. 117-14-45 W; Descriptive and euphoniously named after oak groves.

•OAK HARBOR, City; Island County; Pop. 12,271; Zip Code 98278; Lat. 48-19-07 N long. 122-38-46 W; So named because of the large number of oak trees growing in the area.

•OAKVILLE, City; Grays Harbor County; Pop. 537; Zip Code 98568; Elev. 90; Lat. 46-50-20 N long. 123-13-59 W; The city's name reflects the many oak trees in the area at the time of its founding.

•OCEAN SHORES, City; Grays Harbor County; Pop. 1,692; Zip Code 98569; Lat. 47-04-19 N long. 124-09-51 W; The town is descriptively named for its position on the Pacific Ocean.

•ODESSA, Town; Lincoln County; Pop. 1,009; Zip Code 99159; Elev. 1544; Lat. 47-19-48 N long. 118-41-02 W; Named in 1892 by Great Northern Railway officials on account of the Russian settlers living in the area.

•OKANOGAN, City; Okanogan County Seat; Pop. 2,302; Zip Code 98840; Elev. 860; Lat. 48-21-53 N long. 119-34-45 W; An Indian word meaning "rendezvous."

•OLYMPIA, City; Thurston County Seat and Capital of Washington; Pop. 27,447; Zip Code 985+; The name Olympia comes from the Olympia Mountains, and was suggested by Colonel Isaac N. Ebey.

•OMAK, City; Okanogan County; Pop. 4,007; Zip Code 98841; Elev. 837; Lat. 48-24-37 N long. 119-31-22 W; An Indian word meaning "great medicine" and referring to a nearby lake with supposed curative powers.

•OROVILLE, Town; Okanogan County; Pop. 1,483; Zip Code 98844; Lat. 48-56-16 N long. 119-26-07 W; The town was founded by placer miners. Oro in Spanish means gold.

•ORTING, Town; Pierce County; Pop. 1,763; Zip Code 98360; Lat. 47-05-43 N long. 122-12-09 W; The town is named after an early power.

•OTHELLO, City; Adams County; Pop. 4,454; Zip Code 99332; Elev. 1038; Lat. 46-46-35 N long. 118-49-29 W; The town is named after the great Shakespearean tragic hero Othello.

•PALOUSE, City; Whitman County; Pop. 1,005; Zip Code 99161; Elev. 2426; Lat. 46-54-46 N long. 117-04-21 W; Early French-Canadian fur trappers named the grass covered hills north of the Snake River--"pelouse" or grasslands.

•PASCO, City; Franklin County Seat; Pop. 17,944; Zip Code 99301; Lat. 46-14-23 N long. 119-07-22 W; Surveyor Virgil Bogue named the town after a city in Mexico.

•PATEROS, Town; Okanogan County; Pop. 555; Zip Code 98846; Elev. 776; Lat. 48-03-26 N long. 119-53-30 W; The town is named after an early settler.

•PE ELL, Town; Lewis County; Pop. 617; Zip Code 98572; Elev. 412; Lat. 46-34-18 N long. 123-17-50 W; The name is an Indian mispronunciation of the French name Pierre.

•POMEROY, City; Garfield County Seat; Pop. 1,716; Zip Code 99347; Lat. 46-28-19 N long. 117-35-43 W; Original landowner Joseph Pomeroy founded the town in 1878.

•PORT ANGELES, City; Clallam County Seat; Pop. 17,311; Zip Code 98362; Elev. 32; Lat. 48-06-29 N long. 123-24-25 W; Spanish explorers named it Port of our Lady of the Angels, but the British shortened that to Port Angeles.

•PORT ORCHARD, City; Kitsap County Seat; Pop. 4,787; Zip Code 98366; Lat. 47-31-45 N long. 122-38-25 W; Named of Captain Vancouver in 1792 in honor H.M. Orchard, clerk of the ship "Discovery."

•PORT TOWNSEND, City; Jefferson County Seat; Pop. 6,067; Zip Code 98368; Lat. 48-07-09 N long. 122-46-43 W; British explorer George Vancouver named the bay in honor of Marquis Townsend.

•POULSBO, City; Kitsap County; Pop. 3,453; Zip Code 98370; Elev. 15; Lat. 47-44-09 N long. 122-38-19 W; Norwegian settler named the town in honor of their former home Norway.

•PRESCOTT, Town; Walla Walla County; Pop. 341; Zip Code 99348; Elev. 1055; Lat. 46-17-57 N long. 118-18-48 W; Named in 1881 in honor of C.H. Prescott, General Superintendent of the Oregon Railway and Navigation Company.

•PULLMAN, City; Whitman County; Pop. 23,579; Zip Code 9916+; Lat. 46-43-53 N, long. 117-10-32 W. Founded in 1882 and named in honor of railroad sleeping-car manufacturer George Pullman.

•PUYALLUP, City; Pierce County; Pop. 18,251; Zip Code 9837+; Lat. 47-11-36 N, long. 122-20-05 W. The town is named after the Puyallup River Valley. The Puyallup Indians, whose name means "generous people," gave their name to the valley.

•QUINCY, Town; Grant County; Pop. 3,535; Zip Code 98848; Lat. 47-14-04 N long. 119-51-02 W; The town is named after an early settler.

•RAINIER, Town; Thurston County; Pop. 891; Zip Code 98576; Elev. 428; Lat. 46-53-11 N long. 122-41-07 W; Captain George Vancouver discovered and named the mountain for Rear Admiral Peter Rainier of the British Navy.

•RAYMOND, City; Pacific County; Pop. 2,991; Zip Code 98577; Elev. 14; Lat. 46-40-59 N long. 123-43-52 W; The townis named for L.U.Raymond--the original landowner.

•REARDON, Town; Lincoln County; Pop. 498; Zip Code 99029; Elev. 2496; Lat. 47-40-14 N long. 117-52-28 W; The town is named for a civil engineer who worked for the Washington Central Railroad Co.

•REDMOND, City; King County; Pop. 23,318; Zip Code 98052; Lat. 47-38-30 N long. 122-09-07 W; Luke McRedmond arrived in Washington in 1852 and later founded the town and became its first postmaster.

•RENTON, City; King County; Pop. 30,612; Zip Code 98055; Lat. 47-28-55 N long. 122-12-05 W; The town's name honors Captain William Renton of the Port Blakely Mill Company.

•REPUBLIC, Town; Ferry County; Pop. 1,018; Zip Code 99166; Lat. 48-38-46 N long. 118-44-00 W; The town is named for the famous Republic Mine discovered in 1896.

•RICHLAND, City; Benton County; Pop. 33,578; Zip Code 99352; Lat. 46-17-32 N long. 119-18-44 W; A prominent landowner, Nelson Rich, named the town in 1904.

•RIDGEFIELD, Town; Clark County; Pop. 1,062; Zip Code 98642; Lat. 45-48-51 N long. 122-44-41 W; A descriptive name as the town site on a beautiful ridge.

•RITZVILLE, City; Adams County Seat; Pop. 1,800; Zip Code 99169; Lat. 47-07-40 N long. 118-22-27 W; Ritzville honors early pioneer Phillip Ritz who settled in the area in 1878.

•RIVERSIDE, Town; Okanogan County; Pop. 243; Zip Code 98849; Lat. 48-30-31 N long. 119-30-29 W; On the Okanogan River the town is named for its location.

•ROCKFORD, Town; Spokane County; Pop. 442; Zip Code 99030; Elev. 2361; Lat. 47-27-00 N long. 117-07-49 W; Pioneer D.C. Farnsworth named the town for the many fords crossing Rock Creek which ran through the townsite.

•ROCK ISLAND, Town; Douglas County; Pop. 491; Zip Code 98850; Lat. 47-22-15 N long. 120-08-11 W; A descriptive name given by the U.S. Coast Survey in 1854.

•ROSALIA, Town; Whitman County; Pop. 572; Zip Code 99028; Elev. 2232; Lat. 47-19-19 N long. 117-23-06 W; A common Spanish name the town is the site of the Indian battle with Colonel Steptoe.

•ROSLYN, City; Kittitas County; Pop. 938; Zip Code 98941; Lat. 47-13-20 N long. 120-59-33 W; A manager of the Northern Pacific Railroad Company named the town in 1886 as a compliment to his sweetheart who lived in Roslyn, New York.

•ROY, City; Pierce County; Pop. 417; Zip Code 98580; Lat. 47-00-07 N long. 122-32-34 W; Named in honor of an early settler.

•ROYAL CITY, Town; Grant County; Pop. 676; Zip Code 99357; Lat. 46-54-10 N long. 119-37-33 W; A euphonious name given by the town's incorporators.

•RUSTON, Town; Pierce County; Pop. 612; Ruston is named in honor of W.R. Rust, one time president of the Tacoma Smelting Company.

•ST. JOHN, Town; Whitman County; Pop. 529; Zip Code 99171; Lat. 47-05-29 N long. 117-35-02 W; Named after E.T. St. John, an early settler in the area.

•SEATTLE, City; King County Seat; Pop. 493,846; Zip Code 980+; Lat. 47-45-37 N long. 122-14-27 W; The city takes its name from Chief Seattle of the Suquamish Indians.

•SEDRO-WOOLLEY, City; Skagit County; Pop. 6,110; Zip Code 98284; Lat. 48-30-14 N long. 122-13-46 W; The town of Sedro and nearby Woolley merged at the turn of the century to become Sedro-Woolley.

•SELAH, City; Yakima County; Pop. 4,372; Zip Code 98942; Lat. 46-39-15 N long. 120-31-55 W; An Indian word meaning "still water" and referring to a quiet section of the Yakima River.

•SEQUIM, City; Clallam County; Pop. 3,013; Zip Code 98334; Elev. 183; Lat. 48-03-15 N long. 122-55-20 W; A Clallum Indian word meaning "quiet water."

•SHELTON, City; Mason County Seat; Pop. 7,629; Zip Code 98584; Lat. 47-12-45 N long. 123-06-23 W; The city is named after David Shelton--pioneer and later mayor of his namesake city.

•SKYKOMISH, Town; King County; Pop. 289; Zip Code 98288; Elev. 931; Lat. 47-42-47 N long. 121-21-40 W; An Indian word meaning "inland people."

•SNOHOMISH, City; Snohomish County; Pop. 5,294; Zip Code 98290; Lat. 47-55-19 N long. 122-05-16 W; The name of the dominant Indian tribe in the area.

•SNOQUALMIE, City; King County; Pop. 1,370; Zip Code 98065; Lat. 47-31-38 N long. 121-49-22 W; The name of a tribe of Indians. The name refers to a legend the tribe came from the moon.

•SOAP LAKE, City; Grant County; Pop. 1,196; Zip Code 98851; Lat. 47-23-15 N long. 119-29-16 W; A descriptive name as the lake's water was soapy.

•SOUTH BEND, City; Pacific County Seat; Pop. 1,686; Zip Code 98586; Lat. 46-39-53 N long. 123-47-32 W; So named because the Willapa River takes a bend to the south in what is now the city.

•SOUTH CLE ELUM, Town; Kittitas County; Pop. 449; Zip Code 98943; Lat. 47-11-09 N long. 120-56-56 W; An Indian word meaning "swift waters."

•SOUTH PRAIRIE, Town; Pierce County; Pop. 202; Zip Code 98385; Lat. 47-08-22 N long. 122-05-34 W; Descriptively named in 1889 for its geographic location on South Prairie Creek.

•SPANGLE, City; Spokane County; Pop. 276; Zip Code 99031; Lat. 47-25-51 N long. 117-22-43 W; The city's name honors William Spangle, the homesteader who platted the town in 1886.

•SPOKANE, City; Spokane County; Pop. 171,300; Zip Code 990+; Lat. 47-33-23 N long. 117-12-46 W; The name stems from a chief of the Spokane Indians called Illim-Spokane, or "chief of the sun people."

•SPRAGUE, City; Lincoln County; Pop. 473; Zip Code 99017; Elev. 1899; Lat. 47-12-04 N long. 117-54-14 W; Sprague is named in honor of General John W. Sprague, a director of the Northern Pacific Railroad.

•SPRINGDALE, Town; Stevens County; Pop. 281; Zip Code 99173; Elev. 2070; Lat. 48-03-27 N long. 117-44-21 W; Originally called Squire the Town's name was changed to Springdale after nearby Spring Creek.

•STANWOOD, City; Snohomish County; Pop. 2,744; Zip Code 98292; Lat. 48-14-22 N Long. 122-21-06 W; Settled in 1866 and named by Postmaster D.O. Pearson in honor of his wife's maiden name.

•STARBUCK, Town; Columbia County; Pop. 198; Zip Code 99359; Elev. 645; Lat. 46-30-57 N long. 118-07-30 W; New York businessman, General Starbuck, gave the town church its first bell. The town is named in his honor.

•STEILACOOM, Town; Pierce County; Pop. 4,086; Founded in 1851 and given the Indian name "Tchil-ac-cum" or "pink flower."

•STEVENSON, City; Skamania County Seat; Pop. 1,172; Zip Code 98648; Lat. 45-41-29 N long. 121-52-55 W; Founded in 1894 by George Stevenson and named in his honor.

•SULTAN, Town; Snohomish County; Pop. 1,578; Zip Code 98294; Elev. 114; Lat. 47-51-54 N long. 121-48-27 W; The town is named after the Sultan River. The river received its name from Chief Tseul-tud.

•SUMAS, City; Whatcom County; Pop. 712; Zip Code 98295; Lat. 48-59-41 N long. 122-15-49 W; Sumas is an Indian word meaning "big level opening."

•SUMNER, City; Yakima County; Pop. 9,225; Zip Code 98390; Lat. 47-13-04 N long. 122-15-09 W; Founded by John Kincaid and named in honor of U.S. Senator and anti-slavery proponet Charles S. Sumner.

•SUNNYSIDE, City; Yakima County; Pop. 9,225; Zip Code 98944; Lat. 46-19-23 N long. 120-00-36 W; Walter Granger, president of the Sunnyside Canal Co., founded the town in 1893. It is named in his honor.

•**TACOMA**, City; Pierce County Seat; Pop. 158,501; Zip Code 98303; Lat. 47-11-05 N long. 122-42-11 W; The Indian name for Mt. Rainier is Tacoma--hence the city's name.

•**TEKOA**, City; Whitman County; Pop. 854; Zip Code 99033; Elev. 2494; Lat. 47-13-36 N long. 117-04-20 W; Early settlers borrowed the Biblical Hebrew term tekoa or "settlement of tents" for the town's name.

•**TENINO**, Town; Thurston County; Pop. 1,280; Zip Code 98589; Lat. 46-51-29 N long. 122-50-43 W; A Chinook Indian term meaning "fork" or "junction."

•**TIETON**, Town; Yakima County; Pop. 528; Zip Code 98947; Lat. 46-41-56 N long. 120-45-10 W; Named after the Tieton River. The word Tieton is an Indian word meaning "roaring water."

•**TOLEDO**, City; Lewis County; Pop. 637; Zip Code 98591; Lat. 46-26-15 N long. 122-51-22 W; The town took its name from the riverboat Toledo which worked in the area in 1879.

•**TONASKET**, Town; Okanogan County; Pop. 985; Zip Code 98855; Lat. 48-42-22 N long. 119-26-15 W; The town is named in honor of Chief Tonasket of the Colville Indians.

•**TOPPENISH**, City; Yakima County; Pop. 6,517; Zip Code 98948; Lat. 46-22-38 N long. 120-18-18 W; A Yakima Indian word meaning "people from the foot of the hills."

•**TUKWILA**, City; King County; Pop. 3,578; The town was renamed in 1905 after the Indian word "Tuckwilla" meaning "land of the hazelnuts."

•**TUMWATER**, City; Thurston County; Pop. 6,785; On the falls of the Deschutes River and so named in Chinook jargon "Tun-water."

•**TWISP**, Town; Okanogan County; Pop. 911; Zip Code 98856; Elev. 1614; Lat. 48-21-51 N long. 120-07-25 W; Twisp takes its name from the nearby Twisp River. The word twisp derives from the Indian word Twip.

•**UNION GAP**, City; Yakima County; Pop. 3,184; A descriptive name for the town's location near a gap in the Ahtanum Ridge that connects ports of the Yakima Valley.

•**UNIONTOWN**, Town; Whitman County; Pop. 286; Zip Code 99179; Elev. 2572; Lat. 46-32-18 N long. 117-05-11 W; Settled 1879 and descriptively named by the junction of Union Creek and Union Flat.

•**VADER**, City; Lewis; Pop. 406; Zip Code 98593; Lat. 46-24-15 N long. 122-57-10 W; Named by the state legislature in 1913 for an early settler named Vader.

•**VANCOUVER**, City; Clark County Seat; Pop. 42,834; Zip Code 98660; Lat. 45-38-36 N long. 122-39-51 W; The city is named in honor of George Vancouver, the famous British explorer.

•**WAITSBURG**, City; Walla Walla County Seat; Pop. 25,618; Zip Code 99361; Lat. 46-16-02 N long. 118-09-17 W; The town is named in honor of Sylvester M. Wait who built a flour mill in the area in 1864.

•**WALLA WALLA**, City; Walla Walla County Seat; Pop. 25,618; Zip Code 99362; Lat. 46-03-45 N long. 118-19-51 W; The City's name comes from the Nex Perce Indian word "Walatsa," meaning "running water.

•**WAPATO**, City; Yakima County; Pop. 3,3007; Zip Code 98951; Lat. 46-26-44 N long. 120-25-16 W; Named in 1902 with a variation of the Chinook word "wappatoo" or "potatoe."

•**WARDEN**, Town; Grant County; Pop. 1,479; Zip Code 98857; Lat. 46-58-02 N long. 119-02-38 W; The town was named by railroad official H.R. Williams after an eastern investor named Warden.

•**WASHOUGAL**, City; Clark County; Pop. 3,834; Zip Code 98671; Lat. 45-34-47 N long. 122-20-50 W; Both the river and town take their name from an Indian word meaning "rushing water."

•**WASHTUCNA**, Town; Adams County; Pop. 266; Zip Code 99371; Elev. 1024; Lat. 46-45-13 N long. 118-18-41 W; The name of a Palouse Indian Chief was given to the town by its founders.

•**WATERVILLE**, Town; Douglas County Seat; Pop. 908; Zip Code 98858; Elev. 2622; Lat. 47-38-40 N long. 120-04-12 W; Originally called Jumper's Flat the name was changed to Waterville when a 30-foot well produced water.

•**WAVERLY**, Town; Spokane County; Pop. 99; Zip Code 99039; Lat. 47-20-19 N long. 117-13-45 W; Named by early settlers for their former home in Iowa.

•**WENATCHEE**, City; Chelan County Seat; Pop. 17,257; Zip Code 98801; Lat. 47-25-39 N long. 120-18-47 W; Wenatchee is an adaptation of a Yakima Indian word meaning "river flowing from canyon."

•**WEST RICHLAND**, City; Benton County; Pop. 2,938; The town takes its name from the river. The river's name describe the color spawning salmon have.

•**WESTPORT**, City; Grays Harbor County; Pop. 1,954; Zip Code 98595; Elev. 12; Lat. 46-53-11 N long. 124-06-34 W; Formerly called Peterson's Point, the city is descriptively named as it is on the west side of Chehalis Point Spit.

•**WHITE SALMON**, City; Klickitat County; Pop. 1,853; Zip Code 98672; Lat. 45-43-53 N long. 121-29-10 W; The town takes its name from the river. The river's name describe the color spawning salmon have during their fall runs.

•**WILBUR**, Town; Lincoln County; Pop. 1,122; Zip Code 99185; Elev. 2163; Lat. 47-45-19 N long. 118-42-22 W; Wilbur's name honors its founder Samuel Wilbur Condit who founded the town in 1887.

•**WILKESON**, Town; Pierce County; Pop. 321; Zip Code 98396; Lat. 47-06-36 N long. 122-03-01 W; The town's name Samuel Wilkeson who was an official of the Northern Paciailroad. The railroad began a coal mine there in 1879.

•**WILSON CREEK**, Town; Grant County; Pop. 222; Zip Code 98860; Lat. 47-25-21 N long. 119-07-17 W; The town takes its name from an early settler.

•**WINLOCK**, City; Lewis County; Pop. 1,052; Zip Code 98596; Elev. 309; Lat. 46-29-32 N long. 122-56-10 W; The city is named in honor of original landowner, General Winlock E. Miller.

•**WINSLOW**, City; Lewis County; Pop. 1,052; Winslow is named in honor of Winslow Hall, a founder of the Hall Brothers Shipbuilding Company.

•**WINTHROP**, Town; Okanogan County; Pop. 413; Zip Code 98833; Elev. 1760; Lat. 48-35-37 N long. 120-24-15 W; New England author Theodore Winthrop wrote a well known book on the Washington region--"The Canoe and the Saddle." The town is named in his honor.

•**WOODLAND**, City; Clark & Cowlitz Counties; Pop. 2,341; Zip Code 986+; Lat. 45-54-16 N long. 122-44-56 W; A descriptive name given by the first postmaster, Christopher Bozgath, for the site's wooded surrounding.

WASHINGTON

•**YACOLT,** Town; Clark County; Pop. 544; Zip Code 98675; Lat. 45-51-56 N long. 122-24-24 W; An Indian word meaning "haunted place."

•**YAKIMA,** City; Yakima County Seat; Pop. 49,826; Zip Code 989+; Elev. 1066; Lat. 46-36-09 N long. 120-31-39 W; The city is named for the Indian tribe who originally live in the area.

WEST VIRGINIA

•**ALDERSON,** Town; Greenbrier & Monroe Counties; Pop. 1,375; Zip Code 24910; Elev. 1552; Lat. 37-43-36 N long. 080-38-38 W; The town is named in honor of pioneer Baptist preacher, Rev. John Alderson.

•**ANAWALT,** Town; McDowell County; Pop. 652; Zip Code 24808; Elev. 1687; Lat. 37-20-06 N long. 081-26-22 W; The town was incorporated in 1949 and named after local business manager C. Anawalt.

•**ANMOORE,** Town; Harrison County; Pop. 865; Zip Code 26323; Elev. 1010; Lat. 39-15-27 N long. 080-17-27 W; Originally called Steelton, the name was later changed to recall a local woman, Ann Moore.

•**ANSTED,** Town; Fayette County; Pop. 1,952; Zip Code 25812; Elev. 1312; Lat. 38-08-12 N long. 081-06-02 W; Incorporated in 1891 and named after London geologist Professor D. T. Anstead.

•**ATHENS,** Town; Mercer County; Pop. 1,147; The site of a teachers college, the town is named after the ancient center of learning, Athens.

•**AUBURN,** Town; Ritchie County; Pop. 116; Zip Code 26325; Lat. 39-05-45 N long. 080-51-14 W; Named for an early settler.

•**BANCROFT,** Town; Putnam County; Pop. 528; Zip Code 25011; Elev. 587; Lat. 38-30-37 N long. 081-50-28 W; The town is named after local coal mine operator, George Bancroft.

•**BARBOURSVILLE,** Village; Cabell County; Pop. 2,871; Zip Code 25504; Lat. 38-24-31 N long. 082-17-29 W; Founded in 1813 and named in honor of Phillip Barbour.

•**BARRACKVILLE,** Town; Marion County; Pop. 1,815; Zip Code 26559; Lat. 39-30-18 N long. 080-10-01 W; The town's name honors George Barrack, the first settler.

•**BATH (BERKELEY SPRINGS),** Town; Morgan; Pop. 789; Zip Code 25411; Elev. 612; Lat. 39-37-42 N long. 078-13-31 W; Descriptively named for the warm mineral springs in the town.

•**BAYARD,** Town; Grant County; Pop. 540; Zip Code 26707; Lat. 39-16-13 N long. 079-22-02 W; Named in 1882 for President Grover Cleveland's cabinet member, Thomas Bayard.

•**BECKLEY,** City; Raleigh County Seat; Pop. 20,492; Zip Code 258+; Lat. 37-46-57 N long. 081-11-17 W; The town's name honors U. S. soldier and government official John Beckley.

•**BEECH BOTTOM,** Village; Brooke County; Pop. 507; Zip Code 26030; Elev. 689; Lat. 40-13-35 N long. 080-39-05 W; First settled in 1773 and descriptively named for its location along a beech covered river shallow, or bottom.

•**BELINGTON,** Town; Barbour County; Pop. 2,038; Zip Code 26250; Elev. 1704; Lat. 39-01-20 N long. 079-56-13 W; The town's name remembers pre-Civil War merchant John Bealin.

•**BELLE,** Town; Kanawha County; Pop. 1,621; Zip Code 250+; Lat. 38-15-11 N long. 081-33-05 W; Named after the first postmaster, Belle Gardner Reynolds.

•**BELMONT,** City; Pleasants County; Pop. 887; Zip Code 26134; Lat. 39-22-45 N long. 081-15-46 W; Founded in 1853 and named for one of two prominent men whose first name was Benjamin.

•**BENWOOD,** City; Marshall County; Pop. 1,994; Zip Code 26031; Lat. 40-01-34 N long. 080-45-09 W; Founded in 1853 and honoring one of two prominent men whose first name was Benjamin.

•**BETHANY,** Town; Brooke County; Pop. 1,336; Zip Code 26032; Lat. 40-12-21 N long. 080-33-34 W; Settled in 1847 and given a Biblical town name.

•**BETHLEHEM,** Village; Ohio County; Pop. 2,677; Named for the village Christ was born in.

•**BEVERLY,** Town; Randolph County; Pop. 475; Zip Code 26253; Lat. 38-50-34 N long. 079-52-23 W; Founded in 1790 and named in honor of Beverly Randolph, mother of a governor of Virginia during this time.

•**BLACKSVILLE,** Town; Monongalia County; Pop. 248; Zip Code 26521; Lat. 39-43-06 N long. 080-12-42 W; The town was laid out in 1829 by David Black. It is named in his honor.

•**BLUEFIELD,** City; Mercer County; Pop. 16,060; Zip Code 24701; First settled in 1887 and named for the blue flowers growing locally.

•**BOLIVAR,** Town; Jefferson County; Pop. 672; The town's name honors General Simon Bolivar, Democrat-Liberator of South America.

•**BRAMWELL,** Town; Mercer County; Pop. 989; Zip Code 24715; Elev. 2253; The town's name remembers an English engineer who lived in the area.

•**BRANDONVILLE,** Town; Preston County; Pop. 92; Zip Code 26523; Lat. 39-39-57 N long. 079-37-21 W; Founded in 1827 and named in honor of militia captain, Jonathan Brandon.

•**BRIDGEPORT,** City; Harrison County; Pop. 6,604; Zip Code 26330; Elev. 987; Lat. 39-17-28 N long. 080-15-07 W; Descriptively named when the first bridge in the county was built here in 1803.

•**BRUCETON MILLS,** Town; Preston County; Pop. 296; Zip Code 26525; Lat. 39-39-32 N long. 079-38-28 W; Settled in 1853 and named by pioneer John Huffman for his step-father.

•**BUCKHANNON,** City; Upshur County Seat; Pop. 6,820; Zip Code 26201; Elev. 1443; Lat. 38-59-14 N long. 080-13-03 W; The town takes its name from the Buckhannon River.

•**BUFFALO,** Town; Putnam County; Pop. 1,034; Zip Code 25033; Elev. 580; Lat. 38-37-10 N long. 081-58-43 W; Established in the 1840's and named for an old bison trail in the area.

•**BURNSVILLE,** Town; Braxton County; Pop. 531; Zip Code 26335; Lat. 38-51-28 N long. 080-39-31 W; The town's name remembers lumber businessman John Miller Burns.

•**CAIRO,** Town; Ritchie County; Pop. 428; Zip Code 26337; Elev. 678; Lat. 39-12-30 N long. 081-09-23 W; The first settlers named the area after Cario, Egypt because of its fertile river land.

•**CAMDEN-ON-GAULEY,** Town; Webster County; Pop. 236; Zip Code 26208; Elev. 2029; Lat. 38-21-55 N long. 080-35-41 W; Named for Senator John Camden combined with its location on the Gauley River.

•**CAMERON,** City; Marshall County; Pop. 1,474; Zip Code 26033; Elev. 1060; Lat. 39-49-44 N long. 080-34-06 W; Founded in 1861 and named for railroad agent Samuel Cameron.

•**CAPON BRIDGE,** Town; Hampshire County; Pop. 191; Zip Code 26823; Lat. 39-07-30 N long. 078-29-15 W; Descriptively named as a bridge site across the Cacapon River.

•**CASS,** Town; Pocahontas County; Pop. 148; Zip Code 24927; Lat. 38-23-50 N long. 079-54-55 W; The town is named after 1890's era lumber businessman Joseph Cass.

•**CEDAR GROVE,** Town; Kanawha County; Pop. 1,479; Zip Code 25039; Elev. 618; Lat. 38-13-13 N long. 081-25-42 W; First settled in 1774 and descriptively named for a large cedar grove in the area.

•**CEREDO,** City; Wayne County; Pop. 2,255; Zip Code 25507; Elev. 552; Lat. 38-23-54 N long. 082-34-07 W; Settled in 1857 and named for the roman goddess of agriculture, Ceres.

•**CHAPMANVILLE,** Town; Logan County; Pop. 1,164; Zip Code 25508; Elev. 650; Lat. 37-58-26 N long. 082-01-10 W; Established in 1800 and named after early postmaster Ned Chapman.

•**CHARLES TOWN,** City; Jefferson County Seat; Pop. 2,857; Zip Code 25414; Lat. 39-17-14 N long. 077-51-32 W; The town's name honors George Washington's brother, Charles.

•**CHARLESTON,** City; Kanawha County Seat and Capital of West Virginia; Pop. 63,968; Zip Code 253+; Lat. 38-20-53 N long. 081-37-53 W; Settled in 1794 and named in honor of Charles Clendenin.

•**CHESAPEAKE,** Town; Kanawha County; Pop. 2,364; Named after the local Chesapeake and Ohio Railroad.

•**CHESTER,** City; Hancock County; Pop. 3,297; Zip Code 26034; Elev. 703; Lat. 40-36-51 N long. 080-33-58 W; Founded in 1896 and named after the English city.

•**CLARKSBURG,** City; Harrison County Seat; Pop. 22,371; Zip Code 26301; Elev. 1011; Lat. 39-16-29 N long. 080-19-11 W; Clarksburg's name honors Revolutionary War patriot George Rogers Clark.

•**CLAY,** Town; Clay County Seat; Pop. 940; Zip Code 25043; Elev. 708; Lat. 38-28-30 N long. 081-05-00 W; Named in honor of statesman Henry Clay.

•**CLENDENIN,** Town; Kanawha County; Pop. 1,373; Zip Code 25045; Elev. 629; Lat. 38-29-22 N long. 081-20-53 W; First settled in 1877 and named for pioneer Charles Clendenin.

•**COWEN,** Town; Webster County; Pop. 723; Zip Code 26206; Lat. 38-24-35 N long. 080-33-24 W; Founded in 1899 and named in honor of railroad director John Cowen.

•**DANVILLE,** Town; Boone County; Pop. 727; Zip Code 25053; Elev. 692; Lat. 38-04-42 N long. 081-49-57 W; Danville's name remembers Dan Rock, the first postmaster.

•**DAVIS,** Town; Tucker County; Pop. 979; Zip Code 26260; Elev. 3099; Lat. 39-07-52 N long. 079-27-50 W; Named in honor of U. S. Senator from West Virginia, Henry G. Davis.

•**DAVY,** Town; McDowell County; Pop. 882; Zip Code 24828; Elev. 1189; Lat. 37-28-43 N long. 081-39-04 W; Named after Davy Creek which runs through the town.

•**DELBARTON,** Town; Mingo County; Pop. 981; Zip Code 25670; Lat. 37-42-26 N long. 082-11-12 W; The town is named after an official of a local land company.

•**DUNBAR,** City; Kanawha County; Pop. 9,285; Zip Code 25064; Elev. 603; Lat. 38-22-31 N long. 081-44-35 W; Incorporated in the 1920's and named in honor of Charleston banker, Dunbar Baines.

•**DURBIN,** Town; Pocahontas County; Pop. 379; Zip Code 26264; Elev. 2732; Lat. 38-32-51 N long. 079-49-38 W; Founded in the late nineteenth century and named after bank clerk Charles Durbin.

•**EAST BANK,** Town; Kanawha County; Pop. 1,155; Zip Code 25067; Lat. 38-11-11 N long. 081-27-51 W; Descriptively named for its location on the east bank of the Kanawha River.

•**ELEANOR,** Town; Putnam County; Pop. 1,282; Zip Code 25070; Elev. 574; Lat. 38-32-26 N long. 081-56-10 W; Named in honor of Eleanor Roosevelt.

•**ELIZABETH,** Town; Wirt County Seat; Pop. 856; Zip Code 26143; Elev. 646; Lat. 39-03-40 N long. 081-23-54 W; The town's name remembers the daughter-in-law of founded William Beauchamp.

•**ELK GARDEN,** Town; Mineral County; Pop. 291; Zip Code 26717; Elev. 2288; Lat. 39-23-08 N long. 079-09-26 W; Descriptively named by the early settlers for the abundant elk.

•**ELKINS,** City; Randolph County Seat; Pop. 8,536; Zip Code 26241; Elev. 1930; Lat. 38-55-31 N long. 079-51-04 W; Settled in 1889 and named in honor of Senator Stephen Elkins.

•**ELLENBORO,** Town; Ritchie County; Pop. 357; Zip Code 26346; Elev. 807; Lat. 39-15-52 N long. 081-03-24 W; Named after the daughter of the family, the Williamsons, who donated the right-of-way to the railroad.

•**FAIRMONT,** City; Marion County Seat; Pop. 23,863; Zip Code 265+; Elev. 991; Lat. 39-28-12 N long. 080-09-37 W; Descriptively named in 1843 for the town's location on a hill.

•**FAIRVIEW,** Town; Marion County; Pop. 759; Zip Code 26570; Elev. 1000; Lat. 39-35-36 N long. 080-14-45 W; Incorporated in 1891 and named for the clear view of the countryside from the townsite.

•**FALLING SPRING,** Town; Greenbrier County; Pop. 240; Named for the spring which ran through the town.

•**FARMINGTON,** Town; Marion County; Pop. 583; Zip Code 26571; Lat. 39-30-47 N long. 080-14-54 W; Originally Underwood, the railroad renamed the town after the many farmers in the area.

•**FAYETTEVILLE,** Town; Fayette County Seat; Pop. 2,366; Zip Code 25840; Elev. 1821; Lat. 38-03-20 N long. 081-06-07 W; The town's name honors Revolutionary War hero Marquis Lafayette.

•**FLATWOODS,** Town; Braxton County; Pop. 405; Zip Code 26621; Elev. 1071; Lat. 38-43-25 N long. 080-39-10 W; The town is descriptively named for the wooded level land in the area.

•**FLEMINGTON,** Town; Taylor County; Pop. 452; Zip Code 26347; Lat. 39-16-03 N long. 080-07-47 W; Founded in 1860 and named for an early settler.

•**FOLLANSBEE,** City; Brooke County; Pop. 3,994; Zip Code 26037; Lat. 40-06-15 N long. 080-05-38 W; The city takes its name from the Follansbee Brothers Steel Mill Company.

•**FORT GAY,** Town; Wayne County; Pop. 886; Zip Code 25514; Lat. 38-07-17 N long. 082-35-42 W; The site of a Civil War fort combined with a local settlers surname titled the town.

•**FRANKLIN,** Town; Pendleton County Seat; Pop. 780; Zip Code 26807; Elev. 1739; Lat. 38-38-51 N long. 079-19-48 W; Named for the surveyor who mapped the area in 1769.

•**FRIENDLY,** Town; Tyler County; Pop. 242; Zip Code 26146; Lat. 39-30-53 N long. 081-03-41 W; The town is named after friend Williamson, a descendent of the first settler.

•**GARY,** City; McDowell County; Pop. 2,233; Zip Code 24836; Lat. 37-21-47 N long. 081-32-56 W; Named in honor of Elbert Gary, an official of U. S. Steel Corporation.

•**GASSAWAY,** Town; Braxton County; Pop. 1,225; Zip Code 26624; Elev. 841; Lat. 38-40-23 N long. 080-46-22 W; Senator Henry Gassaway Davis is remembered in the town's name.

•**GAULEY BRIDGE,** Town; Fayette County; Pop. 1,177; Zip Code 25085; Lat. 38-09-56 N long. 081-11-02 W; Named after the Gauley River which flows through the town.

•**GILBERT,** Town; Mingo County; Pop. 757; Zip Code 25621; Elev. 829; Lat. 37-37-01 N long. 081-52-02 W; An early traveller named Gilbert was killed near here. Both the creek and town are named after him.

•**GLASGOW,** Town; Kanawha County; Pop. 1,031; Zip Code 25086; Lat. 38-12-47 N long. 081-25-29 W; Founded in 1914 and named after Glasgow, Scotland.

•**GLENDALE,** City; Marshall County; Pop. 1,875; Zip Code 26038; Lat. 40-01-48 N long. 080-43-07 W; The city is named after Glendale, a local farm.

•**GLENVILLE,** Town; Gilmer County Seat; Pop. 2,155; Descriptively named for a sheltered place, or glen, here at the bend of the little Kanawha River.

•**GRAFTON,** City; Taylor County; Pop. 6,845; Zip Code 26354; Lat. 39-20-03 N long. 080-01-06 W; Named in honor of civil engineer John Grafton who brought the Baltimore and Ohio Railroad here in 1856.

•**GRANT TOWN,** Town; Marion County; Pop. 987; Zip Code 26574; Lat. 39-33-25 N long. 080-10-44 W; Robert Grant, a Boston investor, held mining claims in the area. The town is named after him.

•**GRANTSVILLE,** Town; Calhoun County Seat; Pop. 788; Zip Code 26147; Elev. 713; Lat. 38-55-19 N long. 081-05-39 W; Established shortly after the Civil War and named in honor of General U. S. Grant.

•**GRANVILLE,** Town; Monongalia County; Pop. 992; Zip Code 26534; Elev. 833; Lat. 39-38-44 N long. 079-59-25 W; Captain Felix Scott named the town after an island in the nearby river.

•**HAMBLETON,** Town; Tucker County; Pop. 403; Zip Code 26269; Elev. 1685; Lat. 39-04-48 N long. 079-38-37 W; Founded in 1889 and named in honor of Baltimore banker John Hambleton.

•**HAMLIN,** Town; Lincoln County Seat; Pop. 1,219; Zip Code 25523; Elev. 673; Lat. 38-16-45 N long. 082-06-17 W; Named after the Methodist Hamlin Chapel founded here.

•**HANDLEY,** Town; Kanawha County; Pop. 633; Zip Code 25102; Lat. 38-11-19 N long. 081-22-12 W; Named for an official of the Wyoming Manufacturing Company.

•**HARMAN,** Town; Randolph County; Pop. 181; Zip Code 26270; Elev. 2360; Lat. 38-55-16 N long. 079-31-30 W; The Rev. Asa Harman donated the land for the town. It is named in his honor.

•**HARPERS FERRY,** Town; Jefferson County; Pop. 361; Zip Code 25410; Elev. 484; Lat. 39-21-43 N long. 077-45-53 W; Robert Harper built a ferry across the rivers which merge here. The town was named for him.

•**HARRISVILLE,** Town; Ritchie County Seat; Pop. 1,673; Zip Code 26362; Elev. 873; Lat. 39-12-34 N long. 081-03-15 W; Named in honor of the Harris family who settled here in 1808.

•**HENDRICKS,** Town; Tucker County; Pop. 390; Zip Code 26271; Lat. 39-04-32 N long. 079-37-55 W; Founded in 1894 and named in honor of Vice-President, Thomas Hendricks.

•**HILLSBORO,** Village; Pocahontas County; Pop. 276; Zip Code 24946; Elev. 2303; Lat. 38-08-09 N long. 080-12-46 W; John Hill founded the town. It is named in his honor.

•**HINTON,** City; Summers County Seat; Pop. 4,622; Zip Code 25951; Elev. 1449; Lat. 37-40-10 N long. 080-53-03 W; The town's name honors lawyer John Hinton, an early pioneer in the county.

•**HUNDRED,** Town; Wetzel County; Pop. 485; Zip Code 26575; Elev. 1021; Lat. 39-41-04 N long. 080-27-21 W; Pioneer Henry Church died here in 1860 at age 109. The town's name recalls that memorable feat.

•**HUNTINGTON,** City; Cabell & Wayne Counties; Cabell County Seat; Pop. 63,684; Zip Code 257+; Elev. 569; Lat. 38-24-34 N long. 082-26-59 W; Founded in 1871 and named in honor of Collis Huntington, president of the Cheaspeake and Ohio Railroad.

•**HURRICANE,** City; Putnam County; Pop. 3,751; Zip Code 25526; Lat. 38-26-08 N long. 082-01-21 W; The city is named after nearby Hurricane Creek.

•**HUTTONSVILLE,** Town; Randolph County; Pop. 242; Zip Code 26273; Elev. 2053; Lat. 38-42-54 N long. 079-58-34 W; Pioneer Jonathan Hutton settled here in 1795. The town is named after him.

•**IAEGER,** Town; McDowell County; Pop. 833; Zip Code 24844; Elev. 981; Lat. 37-27-49 N long. 081-49-03 W; Colonel William Iager owned 45,000 acres here in the 1880's. The town is named after him.

•**JANE LEW,** Town; Lewis County; Pop. 406; Zip Code 26378; Elev. 1007; Lat. 39-06-40 N long. 080-24-35 W; Settled in 1835 and named in honor of the mother of town founder, Lewis Maxwell.

•**JUNIOR,** Town; Barbour County; Pop. 591; Zip Code 26275; Lat. 38-58-51 N long. 079-57-05 W; Senator Henry Davis named the town for his son, or junior, John Davis.

•**KENOVA,** City; Wayne County; Pop. 4,454; Zip Code 25530; Elev. 561; Lat. 38-24-01 N long. 082-34-51 W; Established in 1889 and named as the meeting place of three states, Kentucky, Ohio, and West Virginia.

•**KERMIT,** Town; Mingo County; Pop. 705; Zip Code 25674; Elev. 625; Lat. 37-50-28 N long. 082-24-11 W; Founded in 1906 and named in honor of President Theodore Roosevelt's son Kermit.

•**KEYSER,** City; Mineral County Seat; Pop. 6,569; Zip Code 26726; Elev. 810; Lat. 39-26-26 N long. 078-59-00 W; Named for railroad official William Keyser in 1874.

•**KEYSTONE,** City; McDowell County; Pop. 902; Zip Code 24852; Lat. 37-25-00 N long. 081-26-52 W; Originally named Cassville, the name was later changed after the Keystone Coal and Coke Company.

•**KIMBALL,** Town; McDowell County; Pop. 871; Zip Code 24853; Elev. 1492; Lat. 37-25-38 N long. 081-30-29 W; Founded in 1911 and named in honor of Frederick Kimball, president of the Norfolk and Western Railroad.

•**KINGWOOD,** City; Preston County Seat; Pop. 2,877; Zip Code 26537; Elev. 1863; Lat. 39-28-15 N long. 079-41-01 W; Named by the Pocahontas Coal Company where they opened a mine here at the beginning of the century.

•**LEON,** Town; Mason County; Pop. 228; Zip Code 25123; Elev. 569; Lat. 38-44-56 N long. 081-57-24 W; Originally Cologne, the name was changed in 1880 to Leon.

•**LESTER,** Town; Raleigh County; Pop. 626; Zip Code 25865; Lat. 37-44-17 N long. 081-18-02 W; The town is named after early settler Champ Lester.

•**LEWISBURG,** City; Greenbrier County Seat; Pop. 3,065; Zip Code 24901; Elev. 2099; Lat. 37-47-59 N long. 080-26-42 W; Named in honor of Revolutionary War hero General Andrew Lewis.

•**LITTLETON,** Town; Wetzel County; Pop. 335; Zip Code 26581; Elev. 946; Lat. 39-41-49 N long. 080-30-42 W; Probably named for an early settler.

•**LOGAN,** City; Logan County Seat; Pop. 3,029; Zip Code 25601; Elev. 680; Lat. 37-52-28 N long. 081-59-08 W; Originally called Lawnsville and later renamed after Chief Logan of the Cayugas.

•**LOST CREEK,** Town; Harrison County; Pop. 604; Zip Code 26385; Lat. 39-09-40 N long. 080-21-04 W; The town is named after Lost Creek which runs nearby.

•**LUMBERPORT,** Town; Harrison County; Pop. 939; Zip Code 26386; Elev. 994; Lat. 39-22-36 N long. 080-20-44 W; Founded in 1838 and named for a lumber trade on the nearby Tenmile Creek.

•**MABSCOTT,** Town; Raleigh County; Pop. 1,668; Zip Code 25871; Lat. 37-46-18 N long. 081-12-30 W; Incorporated in 1906 and named for the wife of a local coal mine owner.

•**MADISON,** City; Boone County Seat; Pop. 3,228; Zip Code 25130; Elev. 716; Lat. 38-03-37 N long. 081-49-28 W; The city is named in honor of President James Madison.

•**MAN,** Town; Logan County; Pop. 1,333; Zip Code 25635; Elev. 733; Lat. 37-44-38 N long. 081-52-34 W; The town is named after the last syllable of representative Ulysses Hinchman who served the state in the 1860's.

•**MANNINGTON,** City; Marion County; Pop. 3,036; Zip Code 26582; Elev. 975; Lat. 39-31-39 N long. 080-20-27 W; Founded in 1856 and named for a railroad official.

•**MARLINTON,** Town; Pocahontas County Seat; Pop. 1,352; Zip Code 24954; Elev. 2130; Lat. 38-13-17 N long. 080-04-56 W; The town's name honors Jacob Marlin who was the first settler in the region in 1749.

•**MARMET,** Town; Kanawha County; Pop. 2,196; The town took the name of the Marmet Coal Company.

•**MARTINSBURG,** City; Berkeley County Seat; Pop. 13,063; Zip Code 25401; Elev. 457; Lat. 39-27-54 N long. 077-58-09 W; Named in honor of Colonel Thomas Martin, a large landowner in the 18th century.

•**MASON,** Town; Mason County; Pop. 1,432; Zip Code 25260; Elev. 581; Lat. 39-01-09 N long. 082-01-55 W; Mason is named after George W. Mason, a Virginia statesman.

•**MASONTOWN,** Town; Preston County; Pop. 1,052; Zip Code 26542; Lat. 39-33-03 N long. 079-47-57 W; Storekeeper William Mason left his name on the town when it was founded in 1856.

•**MATEWAN,** Town; Mingo County; Pop. 822; Zip Code 25678; Elev. 700; Lat. 37-37-18 N long. 082-09-36 W; The town is named after Matteawan, New York.

•**MATOAKA,** Town; Mercer County; Pop. 613; Zip Code 24736; Elev. 2362; A nickname for the famous Indian princess, Pocahontas, given to the town in 1903.

•**MCMECHEN,** City; Marshall County; Pop. 2,402; Zip Code 26040; Elev. 669; Lat. 40-00-23 N long. 080-44-29 W; Named in honor of the McMechen family who first settled here in the 1780's.

•**MEADOW BRIDGE,** Town; Fayette County; Pop. 530; Zip Code 25976; Elev. 2427; Lat. 37-51-42 N long. 080-51-17 W; The area is known for its meadows and is named for a bridge over the nearby Meadow Creek.

•**MIDDLEBOURNE,** Town; Tyler County Seat; Pop. 941; Zip Code 26149; Elev. 745; Lat. 39-29-38 N long. 080-54-29 W; Middlebourne means "middle point." The town is named for its location as a middlepoint to some geographic feature.

•**MILL CREEK,** Town; Randolph County; Pop. 801; Zip Code 26280; Elev. 2067; Lat. 38-43-53 N long. 079-58-16 W; Descriptively named for a large grist mill built on the adjacent creek.

•**MILTON,** Town; Cabell County; Pop. 2,178; Zip Code 25541; Elev. 584; Lat. 38-26-12 N long. 082-07-56 W; Milton Reece owned the land when the town was laid out in 1872. It is named for him.

•**MONONGAH,** Town; Marion County; Pop. 1,132; Founded in 1891 and named after the Monongahela River with the last three letters left off.

•**MONTGOMERY,** City; Fayette & Kanawha Counties; Pop. 3,104; Zip Code 25136; Lat. 38-10-49 N long. 081-21-12 W; Named for James Montgomery, an early settler.

•**MONTROSE,** Village; Randolph County; Pop. 129; Zip Code 26283; Lat. 39-04-02 N long. 079-48-38 W; Wild roses grow profusely in the local mountains and gave the town its name.

•**MOOREFIELD,** Town; Hardy County Seat; Pop. 2,257; Zip Code 26836; Elev. 829; Lat. 39-03-24 N long. 078-58-09 W; Settled in the 1700's and named after the original landowner, Conrad Moore.

•**MORGANTOWN,** City; Monongalia County Seat; Pop. 27,605; Zip Code 265+; Lat. 39-38-39 N long. 079-58-15 W; First settled in 1768 by Zackquill Morgan and named for his family.

•**MOUNDSVILLE,** City; Marshall County Seat; Pop. 12,419; Zip Code 26041; Elev. 692; Lat. 34-55-57 N long. 070-38-37 W; Founded in 1831 and descriptively named for a nearby Indian mound.

•**MOUNT HOPE,** City; Fayette County; Pop. 1,849; Zip Code 25880; Elev. 1661; Lat. 37-53-58 N long. 081-10-17 W; The city is named for nearby Mount Hope School.

•**MULLENS,** City; Wyoming County; Pop. 2,919; Zip Code 25882; Elev. 1426; Lat. 37-34-47 N long. 081-22-47 W; A. J. Mullins donated the land to the Virginia Railroad in exchange for naming the new town for him.

•**NEW CUMBERLAND,** City; Hancock County Seat; Pop. 1,752; Zip Code 26047; Lat. 40-30-05 N long. 080-36-38 W; Founded in 1839 as Vernon and later named after the Cumberland Trail.

•**NEW HAVEN,** Town; Mason County; Pop. 1,723; Zip Code 25265; Lat. 38-59-09 N long. 081-58-20 W; Settled in the 1850's and named after New Haven, Connecticut.

•**NEW MARTINSVILLE,** City; Wetzel County Seat; Pop. 7,109; Zip Code 26155; Elev. 628; Lat. 39-39-14 N long. 080-51-26 W; The city is named after an early settler, Presley Martin.

•**NEWBURG,** Town; Preston County; Pop. 418; Zip Code 26410; Lat. 39-23-15 N long. 079-51-03 W; Settled in the 1850's and named for its being a new town, or burg, on the railroad line.

•NITRO, City; Kanawha & Putnam Counties; Pop. 8,074; Zip Code 25143; Lat. 38-25-14 N long. 081-50-02 W; The U. S. Government founded an explosives factory here during World War I. The town's name reflects this project.

•NORTHFORK, Town; McDowell County; Pop. 660; Zip Code 24868; Elev. 1708; Lat. 37-24-51 N long. 081-26-04 W; Named for its location on the Northfork of the Elkhorn River.

•OAK HILL, City; Fayette County; Pop. 7,120; Zip Code 25901; Elev. 1961; Lat. 37-58-43 N long. 081-08-59 W; Descriptively named as the town's post office was located on a hill near a large oak tree.

•OCEANA, Town; Wyoming County; Pop. 2,143; Zip Code 24870; Elev. 1269; Lat. 37-41-28 N long. 081-38-00 W; Founded in 1853 and given a popular female name, Ocie.

•OSAGE, Town; Monongalia County; Pop. 285; Zip Code 26543; Elev. 907; Lat. 39-39-28 N long. 080-00-23 W; The town's name remembers the Osage Indians who lived in the area in the early 1800's.

•PADEN CITY, City; Tyler & Wetzel Counties; Pop. 3,671; Zip Code 26159; Lat. 39-36-07 N long. 080-56-08 W; Obediah Paden settled here in 1790. The town is named after him.

•PARKERSBURG, City; Wood County Seat; Pop. 39,967; Zip Code 261+; Elev. 649; Lat. 39-16-57 N long. 081-32-27 W; Alexander Parker was a prominent landowner here by 1810. The town is named after him.

•PARSONS, City; Tucker County Seat; Pop. 1,937; Zip Code 26287; Lat. 39-05-41 N long. 079-40-42 W; Ward Parsons owned the land upon which the town arose. It is named in his honor.

•PAW PAW, Town; Morgan County; Pop. 644; Zip Code 25434; Elev. 572; Lat. 39-31-57 N long. 078-27-34 W; Descriptively named for the many paw paw trees in the area.

•PAX, Town; Fayette County; Pop. 274; Zip Code 25904; Lat. 37-54-36 N long. 081-15-51 W; A corrupt spelling of the name of Samuel Pack who settled here in the 1840's.

•PENNSBORO, City; Ritchie County; Pop. 1,652; Zip Code 26415; Elev. 867; Lat. 39-17-06 N long. 080-58-04 W; A surveyor named Penn laid out the town in the early 1800's. It is named for him.

•PETERSBURG, City; Grant County Seat; Pop. 2,084; Zip Code 26847; Lat. 38-59-38 N long. 079-07-13 W; Jacob Peterson built the first store here in pioneer days. It is named for him.

•PETERSTOWN, Town; Monroe County; Pop. 648; Zip Code 24963; Elev. 1624; Lat. 37-24-00 N long. 080-47-49 W; The town's name remembers Christian Peters who settled here in the 1780's.

•PHILIPPI, City; Barbour County Seat; Pop. 3,194; Zip Code 26416; Elev. 1307; Lat. 39-09-19 N long. 080-02-35 W; Founded in 1844 and named in honor of Phillip P. Barbour.

•PIEDMONT, Town; Mineral County; Pop. 1,491; Zip Code 26750; Lat. 39-28-43 N long. 079-02-43 W; A French word meaning "foot of the mountain," and referring to a ridge which divides the Potomac River watershed from the Ohio River watershed.

•PINE GROVE, Town; Wetzel County; Pop. 767; Zip Code 26419; Elev. 1155; Lat. 39-33-49 N long. 080-40-48 W; Descriptively named for a large grove of nearby pines.

•PINEVILLE, Town; Wyoming County Seat; Pop. 1,140; Zip Code 248+; Elev. 1321; Lat. 37-36-16 N long. 081-36-50 W; Named for the many pine trees in the region.

•POCA, Town; Putnam County; Pop. 1,142; Zip Code 25159; Lat. 38-28-26 N long. 081-48-53 W; Named after the Pocatalico River. This is an Indian word meaning "fat dog."

•POINT PLEASANT, City; Mason County Seat; Pop. 5,682; Zip Code 25550; Lat. 38-51-44 N long. 082-07-430 W; The junction of the Kanawha and Ohio Rivers, the place is descriptively name for its location.

•PRATT, Town; Kanawha County; Pop. 821; Zip Code 25162; Lat. 38-12-32 N long. 081-25-27 W; The Charles Pratt Company owned land in the area and gave its name to the town.

•PULLMAN, Town; Ritchie County; Pop. 196; Zip Code 26421; Lat. 39-11-17 N, long. 080-56-51 W. Pullman was named by the Post Office, probably for George M. Pullman, the owner of the Pullman Palace Car Company.

•QUINWOOD, Town; Greenbrier County; Pop. 460; Zip Code 25981; Lat. 38-03-29 N, long. 080-42-24 W. The city was founded in 1919 by Quin Morton and W.S. Wood, settlers from Charleston.

•RAINELLE, Town; Greenbrier County; Pop. 1,983; Zip Code 25962; Lat. 37-58-09 N, long. 080-46-02 W. The town is named after lumber businessmen John and W.T. Raine.

•RANSON, Town, Jefferson County; Pop. 2,471; Zip Code 25438; 25438; Lat. 39-18-01 N, long. 077-51-37 W. The Ransom family owned the land where the town was built. The town was incorporated in 1910 and named for them.

•RAVENSWOOD, City; Jackson County; Pop. 4,126; Zip Code 26164; Lat. 38-57-23 N, long. 081-45-41 W. The town was laid out in 1852. It was originally known as Ravensworth, but the name was misspelled consistently on early maps as Ravenswood. It was probably named for an English family.

•REEDSVILLE, Town, Preston County; Pop. 564; Zip Code 26547; Lat. 39-30-39 N, long. 079-47-55 W. James Reed, owner of the town site, settled here in 1827. The town was named for him.

•REEDY, Town; Roane County; Pop. 338; Zip Code 25270; Lat. 38-53-59 N, long. 081-25-29 W. The town takes its name from Reedy Creek, which flows through the town.

•RHODELL, Town; Raleigh County; Pop. 472; Zip Code 25915; Elev. 1618; Lat. 37-36-24 N long. 081-18-11 W; Founded in 1907 by I. J. Rhodes, among others, it is named in his honor.

•RICHWOOD, City; Nicholas County; Pop. 3,568; Zip Code 26261; Lat. 38-13-30 N long. 080-31-55 W; Named in 1881 to reflect the rich timber stock in the area.

•RIDGELEY, Town; Mineral County; Pop. 994; Zip Code 26753; Lat. 39-38-28 N long. 078-46-21 W; Named after the original landowner of the site.

•RIPLEY, City; Jackson County Seat; Pop. 3,464; Zip Code 25271; Lat. 38-48-58 N long. 081-42-17 W; The town's name remembers preacher Harry Ripley who died here in 1831.

•RIVESVILLE, Town; Marion County; Pop. 1,327; Zip Code 265+; Lat. 39-32-35 N long. 080-08-41 W; Named in honor of William C. Rives, a U. S. Senator from Virginia in the early 1800's.

•ROMNEY, City; Hampshire County Seat; Pop. 2,094; Zip Code 26757; Lat. 39-20-39 N long. 078-45-23 W; Lord Fairfax named the area after an English seaport in 1762.

•RONCEVERTE, City; Greenbrier County; Pop. 2,312; Zip Code 24970; Elev. 1668; Lat. 37-44-57 N long. 080-28-06 W; On the Greenbrier River, the name is French for Greenbrier.

•ROWLESBURG, Town; Preston County; Pop. 966; Zip Code 26425; Elev. 1406; Lat. 39-20-48 N long. 079-40-34 W; Given its name in 1852 for a railroad official named Rowles.

•RUPERT, Town; Greenbrier County; Pop. 1,276; Zip Code 25984; Elev. 2432; Lat. 37-57-47 N long. 080-41-23 W; Dr. Cyrus Rupert practiced here for several decades. The town is named after him.

•ST. ALBANS, City; Kanawha County; Pop. 12,402; Zip Code 25177; Lat. 38-22-45 N long. 081-48-51 W; Founded in 1816 and later named by a railroad engineer after the English city.

•ST. MARYS, City; Pleasants County Seat; Pop. 2,219; Zip Code 26170; Elev. 628; Lat. 39-24-21 N long. 081-11-30 W; Established by Alexander Creel who had a religious vision here in 1849.

•SALEM, City; Harrison County; Pop. 2,706; Zip Code 26426; Elev. 2144; Settlers from New Salem, New Jersey arrived here in 1788 and named the place for their former home.

•SHEPHERDSTOWN, Town; Jefferson County; Pop. 1,791; Zip Code 25443; Elev. 406; Lat. 39-25-57 N long. 077-48-23 W; Named in honor of Thomas Shepard who laid out the town in 1764.

•SHINNSTON, City; Harrison County; Pop. 3,059; Zip Code 26431; Lat. 39-23-40 N long. 080-17-40 W; Quaker Levi Shinn settled here in 1773. The town is named for him.

•SISTERSVILLE, City; Tyler County; Pop. 2,367; Zip Code 26175; Elev. 647; Lat. 39-33-47 N long. 080-59-47 W; Two sisters, Delilah and Sarah Wells, owned the site in 1839 when the town incorporated and so suggested the name.

•SMITHERS, City; Fayette & Kanawha Counties; Pop. 1,482; Zip Code 25186; Elev. 643; Lat. 38-10-53 N long. 081-20-24 W; The city is named after an early pioneer family.

•SMITHFIELD, Town; Wetzel County; Pop. 278; Zip Code 26437; Lat. 39-30-04 N long. 080-33-52 W; Henry Smith, a local merchant, had the town named after him in the 1880's.

•SOPHIA, Town; Raleigh County; Pop. 1,216; Zip Code 25921; Lat. 37-42-40 N long. 081-14-55 W; Named for Sophia McGinnis, a relative of a prominent official, when the town incorporated in 1912.

•SOUTH CHARLESTON, City; Kanawha County; Pop. 15,968; Descriptively named for its location near Charleston.

•SPENCER, City; Roane County Seat; Pop. 2,799; Zip Code 25276; Elev. 749; Lat. 38-48-11 N long. 081-21-11 W; Originally Tanners Crossroads, the name was later changed to honor Judge Spencer Roane.

•STAR CITY, Town; Monongalia County; Pop. 1,464; The site of a glass-making industry, the town was incorporated in 1907 and named for the Star Glass Company.

•STONEWOOD, City; Harrison County; Pop. 2,058; Incorporated in 1947 and given the made-up name of Stonewood, which was chosen as a result of a naming contest for the new community.

•SUMMERSVILLE, Town; Nicholas County; Pop. 2,972; Zip Code 26651; Elev. 1894; Lat. 38-16-52 N long. 080-51-06 W; Founded in 1824 and named in honor of Judge Lewis Summers.

•SUTTON, Town; Braxton County; Pop. 1,192; Zip Code 266+; Lat. 38-39-53 N long. 080-42-39 W; John D. Sutton arrived here in 1808. The town is named in his honor.

•SYLVESTER, Town; Boone County; Pop. 256; Zip Code 25193; Lat. 38-00-37 N long. 081-33-30 W; Named for a local family when incorporated in 1952.

•TERRA ALTA, Town; Preston County; Pop. 1,946; Zip Code 26764; Elev. 2559; Lat. 39-26-38 N long. 079-32-34 W; Originally Green Glades, the name was later changed to Terra Alta, Latin for "high land." The name reflects the communities 2559 ft. altitude.

•THOMAS, City; Tucker County; Pop. 747; Zip Code 26292; Lat. 39-08-55 N long. 079-29-44 W; Named in 1892 for prominent landowner Colonel Thomas Davis.

•THURMOND, Town; Fayette County; Pop. 67; Zip Code 25936; Lat. 37-57-47 N long. 081-04-44 W; The town's name honors Captain W. D. Thurmond, a confederate army officer, who died here in 1910.

•TRIADELPHIA, Town; Ohio County; Pop. 1,461; Zip Code 26059; Lat. 40-06-11 N long. 080-36-18 W; Three brothers donated the land for the townsite in 1829. The name is a Greek word meaning "three brothers."

•TUNNELTON, Town; Preston County; Pop. 510; Zip Code 26444; Elev. 1816; Lat. 39-23-34 N long. 079-44-50 W; Descriptively named for its location near a Baltimore and Ohio Railroad tunnel.

•UNION, Town; Monroe County Seat; Pop. 743; Zip Code 24983; Elev. 2071; Lat. 37-35-26 N long. 080-32-35 W; Founded in 1800 and named for its function as a meeting place for soldiers in the various Indian wars.

•VALLEY GROVE, Village; Ohio County; Pop. 597; Zip Code 26060; Lat. 40-05-26 N long. 080-33-48 W; Named around 1900 for a favored picnic spot, Valley Grove.

•VIENNA, City; Wood County; Pop. 11,618; Dr. Joseph Spencer laid out the town in 1795 and named it after Vienna, Virginia.

•WAR, City; McDowell County; Pop. 2,158; Zip Code 24892; Lat. 37-18-13 N long. 081-41-12 W; Named after War Creek, a name which remembers the various Indian wars which occurred in the region.

•WARDENSVILLE, Town; Hardy County; Pop. 241; Zip Code 26851; Elev. 1011; Lat. 39-04-33 N long. 078-35-33 W; William Warden built a fort here in 1750. The town's name honors its early founder.

•WAYNE, Town; Wayne County Seat; Pop. 1,495; Zip Code 25570; Elev. 708; Lat. 38-13-23 N long. 082-26-32 W; Established in 1842 and named in honor of Revolutionary War General Anthony Wayne.

•WEIRTON, City; Brooke & Hancock Counties; Pop. 24,736; Zip Code 26062; Lat. 40-19-22 N long. 080-25-04 W; The Wier brothers started a tin plate factory here in 1909 and gave their name to the town.

•WELCH, City; McDowell County Seat; Pop. 3,885; Zip Code 24801; Lat. 37-26-12 N long. 081-35-05 W; Former confederate officer, Captain Isiah Welch, founded the town in 1893. It is named after him.

•WELLSBURG, City; Brooke County Seat; Pop. 3,963; Zip Code 26070; Lat. 40-16-46 N long. 080-26-34 W; Founded in 1791 as Charles Town, but later changed after a Mr. Alexander Wells.

•WEST HAMLIN, Town; Lincoln County; Pop. 643; Zip Code 25571; Elev. 590; Lat. 38-17-18 N long. 082-11-43 W; Descriptively named for its location west of Hamlin.

•WEST LIBERTY, Town; Ohio County; Pop. 744; Zip Code 26074; Lat. 40-10-12 N long. 080-35-41 W; Settled in the 1770's and named for its function as a meeting place for Revolutionary War patriots.

•**WEST LOGAN,** Town; Logan County; Pop. 630; Descriptively named for its location west of Logan.

•**WEST MILFORD,** Town; Harrison County; Pop. 510; Zip Code 26451; Lat. 39-12-06 N long. 080-24-03 W; Two settlers built a mill here in 1821 on the West Fork River, and thus named the town.

•**WEST UNION,** Town; Doddridge County Seat; Pop. 1,090; Zip Code 26456; Elev. 828; Lat. 39-17-46 N long. 080-46-38 W; Originally Lewisport, the town grew on both sides of the Middle Island Creek and later had the name changed to West Union.

•**WESTON,** City; Lewis County Seat; Pop. 6,250; Zip Code 26452; Elev. 1017; Lat. 39-02-36 N long. 080-28-06 W; Founded in 1818 on the West River and thus named.

•**WESTOVER,** City; Monongalia County; Pop. 4,884; The town is across the Monongalia River to the west of Morgantown and hence received its name.

•**WHEELING,** City; Marshall & Ohio Counties; Ohio County Seat; Pop. 43,070; Zip Code 26003; Elev. 678; Lat. 40-02-21 N, long. 080-38-14 W. The town was established in 1769 by Ebenezer Zane of Virginia as the site of Fort Henry. It was the scene of the last battle of the Revolutionary War in 1782. It was known as Zanesburg until 1795, when the name was changed to Wheeling. According to local legend, the name refers to an incident in which the Indians killed some white settlers and put the head on a stake as a warning to other would-be settlers. The name Wheeling is derived from an English version of an Indian word "weeling," meaning "place of the head." The city was chartered in 1806 and incorporated in 1836.

•**WHITE SULPHUR SPRINGS,** City; Greenbrier County; Pop. 3,371; Zip Code 24986; Lat. 37-47-50 N, long. 080-17-52 W. Descriptively named for the nearby mineral springs. The heavily-sulphured water leaves deposits of white sulphur on everything over which it flows.

•**WILLIAMSON,** City; Mingo County Seat; Pop. 5,219; Zip Code 25661; Lat. 37-40-31 N, long. 082-16-03 W. Named for prominent businessman Wallace J. Williamson, who once owned the town's site.

•**WILLIAMSTOWN,** City; Wood County; Pop. 3,095; Zip Code 26187; Lat. 39-24-01 N, long. 081-27-07 W. Settled by frontiersman Isaac Williams in 1786 and named after him.

WISCONSIN

•**ABBOTSFORD,** City; Clark County; Pop. 1,901; Zip Code 54405; Lat. 44-57-14 N long. 090-18-34 W; Named for Edwin H. Abbot, an official for the Wisconsin Central Railway.

•**ADAMS,** City; Adams County; Pop. 1,744; Zip Code 53910; Elev. 960; Lat. 43-57-28 N long. 089-48-55 W; Named in honor of President John Quincy Adams. The town was first called South Friendship."

•**ADELL,** Village; Sheboygan County; Pop. 545; Zip Code 53001; First called Sherman's Station, the name was later changed by the post office to Adell.

•**ALBANY,** Village; Green County; Pop. 1,051; Zip Code 53502; Lat. 42-42-45 N long. 089-26-09 W; Settled by former residents of Albany, New York and named for their hometown.

•**ALGOMA,** City; Kewaukee County; Pop. 3,656; Zip Code 54201; Elev. 600; Lat. 44-36-24 N long. 087-26-29 W; The name is either from the Indian words *Algonquin* and *goma* meaning "Algonquin waters," or from *Algoma* meaning "park of flowers" or "snow shoe."

•**ALLOUEZ,** CDP; Brown County; Pop. 14,882; Named for Father Claude Allouez, a French missionary who preached to the Indians around 1650.

•**ALMA,** City; Buffalo County Seat; Pop. 876; Zip Code 54610; Elev. 687; Lat. 44-19-46 N long. 091-54-30 W; The city was named by W.H. Gates for the Alma River in Russia.

•**ALMENA,** Village; Barron County; Pop. 526; Zip Code 54805; Elev. 1187; Lat. 45-24-53 N long. 092-02-38 W; First known as Lightning City or Lightning Creek. In 1887, it was renamed Almena after storekeepers, Albert and Wilhelmena Koehler.

•**ALMOND,** Village; Portage County; Pop. 477; Zip Code 54909; Elev. 479; Lat. 44-17-06 N long. 089-23-09 W; Founded in 1849 and named by settlers for their hometown of Almond, New York.

•**ALTOONA,** City; Eau Claire County; Pop. 4,393; Zip Code 54720; Lat. 44-48-14 N long. 091-26-49 W; Platted in 1881 as East Eau Claire. Upon incorporation in 1887, it was renamed for Mr. Beal's hometown of Altoona, Pennsylvania.

•**AMERY,** City; Polk County; Pop. 2,404; Zip Code 54001; Lat. 45-18-29 N long. 092-21-27 W; Named in 1887 for William Amery, an Englishman who setted in St. Croix, Wisconsin.

•**AMHERST,** Village; Portage County; Pop. 701; Zip Code 54406; Lat. 44-27-00 N long. 089-14-32 W; Named by Judge Gilbert Park and Adam Uline in honor of their hero General Jeffery Amherst.

•**AMHERST JUNCTION,** Village; Portage County; Pop. 225; Zip Code 54407; Elev. 1126; Lat. 44-28-06 N long. 089-16-48 W; First called Groversberg, later Junction, for the railroad crossing here. It eventually became known as Amherst Junction because of its location, two miles from the village of Amherst.

•**ANIWA,** Village; Shawano County; Pop. 273; Zip Code 54408; Lat. 45-00-32 N long. 089-12-37 W; The name is derived from the Indian word *aniwa* or "those," a Chippewa prefix signifying superiority.

•**ANTIGO,** City; Langlade County Seat; Pop. 8,653; Zip Code 54409; Lat. 45-08-37 N long. 089-08-25 W; Antigo comes from a Chippewa Indian name meaning "balsam evergreen river" or "place where evergreens can be found."

•**APPLETON,** City; Outagamie County Seat; Pop. 59,032; Zip Code 54911; Lat. 41-11-34 N long. 082-15-05 W; Named for Samuel Appleton, one of the founders of Lawrence University.

•**ARCADIA,** City; Trempealeau County; Pop. 2,109; Zip Code 54612; Elev. 728; Lat. 44-16-22 N long. 091-29-57 W; Named for the state of Arcadia in ancient Greece.

•**ARGYLE,** Village; Lafayette County; Pop. 720; Zip Code 53504; Elev. 810; Lat. 42-41-56 N long. 089-51-47 W; Named in 1844 by Scotsman Allen Wright, in honor of the Duke of Argyle.

•**ARLINGTON,** Village; Columbia County; Pop. 440; Zip Code 53911; Elev. 1052; Lat. 43-20-15 N long. 089-22-44 W; Settled around 1838. The source of the name is not known.

•**ARPIN,** Village; Wood County; Pop. 361; Zip Code 54410; Lat. 44-32-30 N long. 090-01-59 W; Named for John D. and Antoine Arpin who settled about one mile east of the present village site.

•**ASHLAND,** City; Ashland County Seat; Pop. 9,115; Zip Code 54806; Elev. 671; Lat. 46-34-47 N long. 090-52-50 W; Named in 1885 for Henry Clay's home in Kentucky. Earlier names include Zham-a-wa-mik, Ojibwa for "the long stretched beaver"; and Wittlesey for Adolph Wittlesey, the town's first postmaster.

•**ASHWAUBENON,** Village; Brown County; Pop. 14,486; The village was named for the great Menominee Chief Ashwaubamie, who left this land to his descendants, the Franks and La Rose families.

•**ATHENS,** Village; Marathon County; Pop. 988; Zip Code 54411; Lat. 45-01-17 N long. 090-03-49 W; Probably named for the capital city of Greece.

•**AUBURNDALE,** Village; Wood County; Pop. 641; Zip Code 54412; Elev. 1220; Lat. 44-37-32 N long. 090-00-29 W; Auburndale is probably an English name brought by settlers. Or possibly came from the auburn-haired daughters of W.D. Connors, a prominent resident.

•**AUGUSTA,** City; Eau Claire County; Pop. 1,560; Zip Code 54722; Lat. 44-40-36 N long. 091-07-14 W; First known as Ridge Creek. Later changed to Augusta, either in honor of Charles Buckman's hometown in Maine, or for August Rickard, who was voted the prettiest girl in town.

•**AVOCA,** Village; Iowa County; Pop. 505; Zip Code 53506; Elev. 698; Lat. 42-48-20 N long. 089-51-29 W; Possibly named for the valley of Avoca in Tom Moore's poem, or by an Irishman in 1857, who was homesick for the vale of Avoca in Ireland.

•**BAGLEY,** Village; Grant County; Pop. 317; Zip Code 53801; Lat. 42-54-10 N long. 091-06-01 W; Platted around 1884 and named for Mary Bagley who owned the land on which the village was built.

•**BALDWIN,** Village; St. Croix County; Pop. 1,620; Zip Code 54002; Lat. 44-58-01 N long. 092-22-54 W; Named either for D.A. Baldwin, an early settler, or for D.H. Baldwin of the West Wisconsin Railway Company. The town was earlier known as Clarksville.

•**BALSAM LAKE,** Village; Polk County Seat; Pop. 749; Zip Code 54810; Elev. 1155; Lat. 45-26-47 N long. 092-27-00 W; Chippewa Indians named both the town and the lake, probably after the natural surroundings.

•**BANGOR,** Village; La Crosse County; Pop. 1,012; Zip Code 54614; Lat. 43-53-22 N long. 090-59-22 W; Named by Welsh settlers for the town of Bangor, Wales.

•**BARABOO,** City; Sauk County Seat; Pop. 8,081; Zip Code 53913; Elev. 894; Lat. 43-28-06 N long. 089-44-58 W; Named for any of three Frenchmen called Baribeau: two brothers who had a mill at the mouth of the Baraboo River, or another Baribeau, who later had a trading post there.

•**BARNEVELD,** Village; Iowa County; Pop. 579; Zip Code 53507; Lat. 43-01-07 N long. 089-53-52 W; The name was suggested by a native of Holland who admired the Dutch leader, Jonna Barneveld.

•**BARRON,** City; Barron County Seat; Pop. 2,595; Zip Code 54812; Elev. 1115; Lat. 45-23-51 N long. 091-51-01 W; Named in honor of Henry D. Barron, a judge and state senator. Previously known as Quaderer's Camp for John Quaderer, foreman of the lumber camp here.

•**BAYFIELD,** City; Bayfield County; Pop. 778; Zip Code 54814; Lat. 46-48-42 N long. 090-49-32 W; Established as a Jesuit Mission in 1665 and named La Pointe du Saint Esprit. It was later known as simply La Pointe, and finally Bayfield, for Admiral Henry W. Bayfield of the Royal Navy.

•**BAYSIDE,** Village; Milwaukee County; Pop. 4,724 , Incorporated in 1953, a suburb of Milwaukee, and named for its geographical location on Lake Michigan.

•**BEAR CREEK,** Village; Outagamie County; Pop. 454; Zip Code 54922; Elev. 817; Lat. 44-31-34 N long. 088-43-04 W; Named in 1885 for nearby Bear Creek. After fire destroyed the town in 1902, it was called Welcome, for lumberman Welcome Hyde. The name was later changed back to Bear Creek.

•**BEAVER DAM,** City; Dodge County; Pop. 14,149; Zip Code 53916; Elev. 879; Lat. 43-27-21 N long. 088-50-35 W; Named by James P. Brower for the many beaver that built dams in nearby streams.

•**BELGIUM,** Village; Ozaukee County; Pop. 892; Zip Code 53004; Elev. 736; Established in 1864. Townspeople wanted the name Luxembourg, after their country in Europe, but when application papers came back from Washington the name Belgium had been assigned by mistake.

•**BELLEVILLE,** Village; Dane County; Pop. 1,302; Zip Code 53508; Elev. 870; Lat. 42-51-44 N long. 089-32-47 W; Founded by John Frederick who came to the area in 1845. Named for his former home of Belleville in Canada.

•**BELMONT,** Village; Lafayette County; Pop. 826; Zip Code 53510; Lat. 42-44-16 N long. 090-19-53 W; Named for its location near three mounds. "Belmont" is derived from French words meaning "beautiful mountain."

•**BELOIT,** City; Rock County; Pop. 5,457; Zip Code 53511; Lat. 42-31-28 N long. 089-02-32 W; Earlier known as Turtle Creek and New Albany. Around 1837, settler Major Johnston, suggested calling the city Beloit, because he liked a name similar to Detroit.

•**BENTON,** Village; Lafayette County; Pop. 983; Zip Code 53803; Elev. 932; Lat. 42-34-16 N long. 090-23-01 W; First known as Swindler's Ridge. "Benton" came into use around 1840. Named to honor Senator Thomas Benton of Missouri.

•**BERLIN,** City; Green Lake County; Pop. 5,478; Zip Code 54923; Elev. 764; Lat. 43-58-52 N long. 088-56-25 W; Named in 1851 for Berlin, Germany. The city was previously called Strong's Landing, and later Strongville.

•**BIG BEND,** Village; Waukesha County; Pop. 1,345; Zip Code 53103; Lat. 42-52-57 N long. 088-12-15 W; The Indians named this place for the bend in the Fox River, which flows on the west side of the village.

•**BIG FALLS,** Village; Waupaca County; Pop. 107; Zip Code 54926; Lat. 44-37-15 N long. 089-00-55 W; Founded in 1862 and named for the falls of the Little Wolf River, which runs through the village.

•**BIRCHWOOD,** Village; Washburn County; Pop. 437; Zip Code 54817; Elev. 742; Lat. 45-39-28 N long. 091-32-37 W; Named by George M. Huss, president of the Soo Line Railroad, for the many white birch trees that grew along the lakeshore here.

•**BIRNAMWOOD,** Village; Shawano County; Pop. 688; Zip Code 54414; Lat. 44-55-57 N long. 089-12-21 W; Named by the son of a railroad official, who saw large piles of brush burning near the tracks here. And Indian said "Heap big burn-em-wood" which reminded the young man of "Birnamwood" in a line from *Macbeth.*

•**BLACK CREEK,** Village; Outagamie County; Pop. 1,097; Zip Code 54106; Elev. 790; Lat. 44-28-12 N long. 088-26-45 W; Originally called Middleburg by a settler. It later beccame known as Black Creek, for a dark creek on the edge of town.

•**BLACK EARTH,** Village; Dane County; Pop. 1,145; Zip Code 53515; Elev. 818; Lat. 43-08-38 N long. 089-44-53 W; Incorporated as Berry in 1848. The village was called Black Earth in 1851, after a creek that ran through town. The name changed again to Ray, and then back to Black Earth in 1858.

•**BLACK RIVER FALLS,** City; Jackson County Seat; Pop. 3,434; Zip Code 54615; Elev. 796; Lat. 44-17-21 N long. 090-50-43 W; Called The Falls by white people who set up camp at the falls here in 1819. Later, the full name, Black River Falls, came into use.

•**BLAIR,** City; Trempealeau County; Pop. 1,142; Zip Code 54616; Elev. 859; Lat. 44-19-12 N long. 091-14-04 W; Platted as Porterville, after the Porter family. Renamed Blair, in 1873, for John Insley Blair, a stockholder in the railroad company.

•**BLANCHARDVILLE,** Village; Lafayette County; Pop. 803; Zip Code 53516; Elev. 833; Lat. 42-48-20 N long. 089-51-29 W; Named for Alvin Blanchard who bought a mill here in 1855. An earlier name, given by Latter Day Saints of the area, was Zarahamia.

•**BLOOMER,** City; Chippewa County; Pop. 3,342; Zip Code 54724; Elev. 1011; Lat. 45-05-57 N long. 091-29-12 W; Known as Bloomer Prairie for Mr. Bloomer, an Illinois merchant who came to build a sawmill on the Chippewa River, and hadto scout for hayfrom the nearby prairie. The name was later shortened to Bloomer.

•**BLOOMINGTON,** Village; Grant County; Pop. 743; Zip Code 53804; Lat. 42-53-27 N long. 090-55-25 W; First called Taft, for Mr. Taft, who built a mill here in 1841. When a local blacksmith patented a new device for sowing oats, there was a surge in agriculture, and the town was named Blooming, and eventually Bloomington.

•**BLUE MOUNDS,** Village; Dane County; Pop. 387; Zip Code 53517; Elev. 1261; Lat. 43-01-08 N long. 089-50-58 W; French missionaries named the village for three mounds, and for the bluish color of the earth, caused by the presence of copper.

•**BLUE RIVER,** Village; Grant County; Pop. 412; Zip Code 53518; Elev. 676; Lat. 43-11-09 N long. 090-34-13 W; Called Minnehaha in 1856. Soon afterward the name changed to Blue River, after a stream that ran through a nearby farm belonging to Mr. Blue.

•**BONDUEL,** Village; Shawano County; Pop. 1,160; Zip Code 54107; Lat. 44-44-41 N long. 088-26-18 W; Named for Father Floribrant Bonduel, a Jesuit priest who started a chapel here for the Menominee Indians.

•**BOSCOBEL,** City; Grant County; Pop. 2,662; Zip Code 53805; Elev. 672; Lat. 43-08-10 N long. 090-42-16 W; Possibly named either for the Boscobel Wood in England, or from the Spanish words *bosque bello* meaning "beautiful wood."

•**BOWLER,** Village; Shawano County; Pop. 339; Zip Code 54416; Elev. 1080; Lat. 44-51-54 N long. 088-58-38 W; Named for Mr. Bowler, a lawyer for the Chicago and North Western Railway Company, who helped purchase right-of-way for the railroad here.

•**BOYCEVILLE,** Village; Dunn County; Pop. 862; Zip Code 54725; Elev. 948; Lat. 45-02-51 N long. 092-02-13 W; Named for the Boyce family which owned a mill at the west end of town.

•**BOYD,** Village; Chaippewa County; Pop. 660; Zip Code 54726; Elev. 1105; Lat. 44-57-10 N long. 091-02-18 W; The village takes its name from a Mr. Boyd, who surveyed for the railroad around 1893.

•**BRANDON,** Village; Fond du Lac County; Pop. 862; Zip Code 53919; Elev. 999; Lat. 43-44-11 N long. 088-46-51 W; First called Bungtown. Renamed by settler William Locklin, after the town of Brandon, Vermont.

•**BRILLIAN,** City; Calumet County; Pop. 2,907; Zip Code 54110; Lat. 44-10-23 N long. 088-03-59 W; Originally called Brandon, the name was changed in 1854 to Brillian, becuase there was already another Brandon in the next county.

•**BROADHEAD,** City; Green County; Pop. 3,153; Zip Code 53520; Elev. 798; Lat. 42-37-35 N long. 089-22-19 W; Named for Edward H. Broadhead of the Chicago, Milwaukee and St. Paul Railway.

•**BROOKFIELD,** City; Waukesha County; Pop. 34,035; Zip Code 53005; Elev. 828; Incorporated in 1954 and named after the numerous brooks and fields in the area.

•**BROOKLYN,** Village; Green County; Pop. 627; Zip Code 53521; Lat. 42-51-24 N long. 089-23-00 W; John E. Glunt, engineer in charge of locating the railroad, named this village after the city of Brooklyn, New York.

•**BROWN DEER,** Village; Milwaukee County; Pop. 12,921; First called White Deer after an albino deer was seen in the area. The named was changed because brown deer were more commonto the vicinity.

•**BROWNSVILLE,** Village; Dodge County; Pop. 433; Zip Code 530+; Named in honor of Alfred D. Brown, an English immigrant who settled here about 1850.

•**BROWNTOWN,** Village; Green County; Pop. 284; Zip Code 53522; Lat. 42-34-28 N long. 089-47-43 W; Earlier known by the names Irion, Wood's Mill and Brown. The village was named for William G. Brown, who helped build the mill here.

•**BRUCE,** Village; Rusk County; Pop. 905; Zip Code 54819; Elev. 1106; Lat. 45-27-25 N long. 091-16-54 W; Named for a son of the famous Weyerhauser lumber family.

•**BURLINGTON,** City; Racine County; Pop. 8,385; Zip Code 53105; Lat. 42-39-50 N long. 088-15-51 W; E.D. Putnam proposed the name Burlington, after his favorite city in Vermont.

•**BUTTERNUT,** Village; Ashland County; Pop. 438; Zip Code 54514; Elev. 1503; Lat. 46-00-35 N long. 090-29-52 W; Named for a grove of huge butternut trees that grew here.

•**CABLE,** Village; Bayfield County; Pop. 227; Zip Code 54821; Elev. 1370; Lat. 46-12-23 N long. 091-17-30 W; The village was named for the first engineer to pull a train into this stop, which in 1878, was the end of the line.

•**CADOTT,** Village; Chippewa County; Pop. 1,247; Zip Code 54727; Elev. 979; Lat. 44-57-10 N long. 091-09-06 W; Named for

Jean Baptiste Cadotte, who ran a trading post near here. Known for many years as Cadotte Falls.

•**CAMBRIA,** Village; Columbia County; Pop. 680; Zip Code 53923; Elev. 868; Lat. 43-32-41 N long. 089-06-28 W; Earlier known as Langdon's Saw Mill, Florence, and Bellville. About 1851 Welsh settlers named the village Cambria, from the old Roman name for Wales.

•**CAMBRIDGE,** Village; Dane County; Pop. 844; Zip Code 53523; Lat. 42-59-21 N long. 089-02-09 W; In 1847, landowner Alvin B. Carpenter named this village for Cambridge, New York, the hometown of his sweetheart.

•**CAMERON,** Village; Barron County; Pop. 1,115; Zip Code 54822; Elev. 1097; Lat. 45-24-33 N long. 091-44-34 W; Settled in 1879 and named for Wisconsin State Senator Cameron of La Crosse.

•**CAMPBELLSPORT,** Village; Fond du Lac County; Pop. 1,740; Zip Code 53010; Named Crouchville in 1843, for settler Ludlow Crouch. Later called New Cassel, after Hesse-Cassel, Germany, and finally named Campbellsport for landowner Stuart Campbell.

•**CAMP DOUGLAS,** Village; Juneau County; Pop. 589; Named for a railroad camp that supplied cut wood for locomotives, and was run by James Douglas.

•**CASCADE,** Village; Sheboygan County; Pop. 615; Zip Code 53011; Located near the rapids in the Wisconsin River. First called Nineveh, and later Cascade, after Cascade Falls in Colorado.

•**CASCO,** Village; Kewaunee County; Pop. 484; Zip Code 54205; Lat. 44-33-15 N long. 087-37-04 W; Settler Edward Decker named this place for his hometown of Casco, Maine.

•**CASHTON,** Village; Monroe County; Pop. 827; Zip Code 54619; Lat. 43-46-11 N long. 090-46-38 W; First called Mt. Pisgah, later Hazen's Corner. In 1879, the village was named for Henry Harrison Cash, who built the railroad through town.

•**CASSVILLE,** Village; Grant County; Pop. 1,270; Zip Code 53806; Elev. 621; Lat. 42-42-56 N long. 090-59-36 W; Founded in 1827 and named for Lewis Cass, Governor of the Michigan Territory, which at that time encompassed Wisconsin.

•**CATAWBA,** Village; Price County; Pop. 205; Zip Code 54515; Lat. 45-32-21 N long. 090-31-40 W; The name probably comes from the Choctaw Indian word *katapa* meaning "divided" or "departed."

•**CAZENOVIA,** Village; Richland County; Pop. 259; Zip Code 53924; Elev. 951; Lat. 43-31-29 N long. 090-11-23 W; Named after Cazenovia, New York, which in turn got its name from Theophilus Cazenove, general agent of the Holland Land Company.

•**CECIL,** Village; Shawano County; Pop. 445; Zip Code 54111; Elev. 811; Lat. 44-49-06 N long. 088-26-20 W; Named in 1884 for Cecil Leavitt, a railroad man.

•**CEDAR GROVE,** Village; Sheboygan County; Pop. 1,420; Zip Code 53013; Elev. 711; Lat. 43-33-49 N long. 087-49-08 W; Named for a forty acre tract of cedar trees at the south end of town.

•**CEDARBURG,** City; Ozoukee County; Pop. 9,005; Zip Code 53012; Lat. 43-17-18 N long. 087-58-21 W; Possibly named for the house of Dr. Fred Luening, which stood on a hill surrounded by cedars.

•**CENTURIA,** Village; Polk County; Pop. 711; Zip Code 54824; Lat. 45-26-36 N long. 092-33-03 W; Named for its founding date, in 1900, at the turn of the century.

•**CHASEBURG,** Village; Vernon County; Pop. 279; Zip Code 54621; Elev. 728; Lat. 43-39-34 N long. 091-06-00 W; Named for P.E. Chase who settled here in 1854 and started a mill.

•**CHENEQUA,** Village; Waukesha County; Pop. 532; There are conflicting sources. The name is of Indian origin, possibly Potawatomi for "big tree grove," Winnebago for "village," or Chippewa for "Indian maiden."

•**CHETEK,** City; Barron County; Pop. 1,931; Zip Code 54728; Lat. 45-19-04 N long. 091-39-07 W; The Chippewa Indian word for Chetek is *Jede-Sagaigan* meaning "swan" or "pelican" and "inland lake."

•**CHILTON,** City; Calumet County Seat; Pop. 2,965; Zip Code 53014; Elev. 902; Lat. 44-01-41 N long. 088-09-34 W; Originally named Chillington, after John Marygold's home in England. The name became Chilton due to an error in recording it.

•**CHIPPEWA FALLS,** City; Chippewa County Seat; Pop. 12,270; Zip Code 54729; Lat. 44-54-54 N long. 091-22-41 W; Named by Jean Brunet in 1836 for the falls here on the Chippewa River. The word *Chippewa* is an adaptation of *Ojibwa,* a tribal name meaning "to roast until puckered up."

•**CLAYTON,** Village; Polk County; Pop. 899; Zip Code 54004; Lat. 45-19-31 N long. 092-10-45 W; Named for Clayton Rogers, who was in charge of a mill at the settlement.

•**CLEAR LAKE,** Village; Polk County; Pop. 899; Zip Code 54005; Elev. 1201; Lat. 45-14-47 N long. 092-15-54 W; The proposed name was Clark's Lake, for one of the town's oldest families, but it had to be changed to Clear Lake since there was already a Clark's Lake in the state.

•**CLEVELAND,** Village; Manitowoc County; Pop. 1,270; Zip Code 53015; Elev. 640; Lat. 43-55-04 N long. 087-45-10 W; Founded in 1850 and named Birch for the birch trees in the area. In 1885 it was renamed for President Grover Cleveland.

•**CLINTON,** Village; Rock County; Pop. 1,751; Zip Code 53525; Elev. 949; Lat. 42-33-17 N long. 088-51-43 W; Probably named for DeWitt Clinton, Governor of New York.

•**CLINTONVILLE,** City; Waupaca County; Pop. 4,567; Zip Code 54929; Elev. 825; Lat. 44-37-42 N long. 088-46-04 W; First called Pigeon Lake, later changed to Clintonville for the Norman Clinton family, the first permanent settlers.

•**CLYMAN,** Village; Dodge County; Pop. 317; Zip Code 53016; Lat. 43-18-09 N long. 088-43-11 W; Named for Colonel Clyman, a frontiersman.

•**COBB,** Village; Iowa County; Pop. 409; Zip Code 53526; Elev. 1165; Lat. 42-58-10 N long. 090-19-53 W; First called Cross Plains for the road that crossed the prairie here. Later named for Captain Amasa Cobb, a congressman influential in establishing the post office and railroad.

•**COCHRANE,** Village; Buffalo County; Pop. 512; Zip Code 54622; Lat. 44-13-36 N long. 091-50-41 W; Named for an officer of the railroad.

•**COLBY,** City; Clark County; Pop. 1,496; Zip Code 54421; Elev. 1350; Lat. 44-55-20 N long. 090-18-25 W; Named for Charles L. Cobly, president of the Wisconsin Central Railroad.

•**COLEMAN,** Village; Marinette County; Pop. 852; Zip Code 54112; Lat. 45-04-24 N long. 088-02-05 W; "Probably named for a Mr. Coleman, who owned land in the area.

•**COLFAX,** Village; Dane County; Pop. 1,149; Zip Code 54730; Lat. 44-59-51 N long. 091-44-21 W; Originally called Begga Town

for the rutabeggas raised here. Renamed around 1868 for Senator Schuyler Colfax.

•**COLOMA,** Village; Waushara County; Pop. 367; Zip Code 54930; Elev. 1044; Lat. 44-02-10 N long. 089-31-08 W; Called Coloma Corners, Coloma Station and finally Coloma. The name came from the township in California where gold was discovered.

•**COLUMBUS,** City; Columbia County; Pop. 4,049; Zip Code 53912; Elev. 871; Lat. 43-19-52 N long. 088-56-20 W; Named by Major Dickason, one of the first white men in the area.

•**COMBINED LOCKS,** Village; Outagamie County; Pop. 2,573; Zip Code 54113; Lat. 43-26-18 N long. 086-40-37 W; The canal locks on the Fox River gave this village its name.

•**CONRATH,** Village; Rusk County; Pop. 86; Zip Code 54731; Elev. 1136; Lat. 45-23-05 N long. 091-02-10 W; Named for Frank and Charles Conrath, loggers who settled here.

•**COON VALLEY,** Village; Vernon County; Pop. 758; Zip Code 54623; Elev. 735; Lat. 43-42-15 N long. 091-00-33 W; Settled by Helge Gulbrandson and named Helgedalen, meaning Helge Valley. It was later renamed Coon Valley for the many racoons in the area.

•**CORNELL,** City; Chippewa County; Pop. 1,583; Zip Code 54732; Lat. 45-09-45 N long. 091-09-13 W; First called Brunet's Falls for Jean Brunet who ran a trading post here. Later named for Ezra Cornell, president of Cornell University, which had large land holdings in Wisconsin.

•**COTTAGE GROVE,** Village; Dane County; Pop. 888; Zip Code 53527; Elev. 888; Lat. 43-04-30 N long. 089-12-00 W; Settler William C. Wells named the town for a grove of burr oaks that surrounded his house.

•**COUDERAY,** Village; Sawyer County; Pop. 114; Zip Code 54828; Elev. 1265; Lat. 45-47-52 N long. 091-18-05 W; From the French words meaning "short ears." Radisson and Groseillers, when they first esplored here in 1659, found Ottawa Indians whome they called Short Ears.

•**CRANDON,** City; Forest County Seat; Pop. 1,969; Zip Code 54520; Lat. 45-34-01 N long. 088-54-13 W; Originally named Ayr, from the city in Scotland. In 1885 the town was named for Major Frank P. Crandon of the Chicago nd North Western Railway.

•**CRIVITZ,** Village; Marinette County; Pop. 1,041; Zip Code 54114; Elev. 681; Lat. 45-14-14 N long. 088-01-05 W; "Called Ellis Junction after the Ellis family. The name was later changed to Crivitz, for Judge Bartels' home in Germany.

•**CROSS PLAINS,** Village; Dane County; Pop. 2,156; Zip Code 53528; Elev. 859; Lat. 43-06-43 N long. 089-39-31 W; In 1838, Postmaster Berry Haney named this village after his hometown in Tennessee.

•**CUBA CITY,** City; Grant County; Pop. 2,129; Zip Code 53807; Elev. 1012; Lat. 42-36-22 N long. 090-25-35 W; First called Western. It was platted as Yuba around 1871, but the Y was changed to C because there was another Yuba in the state.

•**CUDAHAY,** City; Milwaukee County; Pop. 19,547; Zip Code 53110; Lat. 42-58-01 N long. 087-53-12 W; Named for Patrick Cudahay, who grew up in the area and, with his brother John, started the firm of Cudahay Brothers.

•**CUMBERLAND,** City; Barron County; Pop. 1,983; Zip Code 54829; Elev. 1251; Lat 45-32-04 N long. 092-01-44 W; Established as Lakeland in 1876. In 1879 John A. Humbird renamed the city after his hometown of Cumberland, Maryland.

•**CURTISS,** Village; Clark County; Pop. 127; Zip Code 54422; Lat. 44-57-04 N long. 090-25-50 W; Named Quar in 1881. The following year the village was renamed for Charles Curtiss, civil engineer for the railroad.

•**DALLAS,** Village; Barron County; Pop. 477; Zip Code 54733; Elev. 1054; Lat. 45-15-27 N long. 091-48-55 W; Named in honor of George Dallas, Vice-President of the U.S. from 1845 to 1849.

•**DANE,** Village; Dane County; Pop. 518; Zip Code 53529; Lat. 43-15-00 N long. 089-30-00 W; Named after Dane County, which was named for Nathan Dane, framer of the Ordinance of 1787 which established the Northwest Territory.

•**DARIEN,** Village; Walworth County; Pop. 1,152; Zip Code 53114; Elev. 948; Lat. 42-36-14 N long. 088-42-31 W; First known as Bruceville, after landowner John Bruce. Renamed around 1838 by settlers from Darien, New York.

•**DARLINGTON,** City; Lafayette County Seat; Pop. 2,300; Zip Code 53530; Elev. 817; Lat. 42-40-39 N long. 090-06-43 W; Purchased in 1850 and named for land agent Joshua Darling of New York.

•**DE FOREST,** Village; Dane County; Pop. 3,367; Zip Code 53532; Elev. 949; Lat. 43-15-00 N long. 089-20-38 W; Named for Isaac DeForest, who purchsed land here in 1854.

•**DE PERE,** City; Brown County; Pop. 14,892; Zip Code 54115; Lat. 44-27-34 N long. 088-01-33 W; Possibly named for a French settler or missionary. In French *pere* means "father."

•**DE SOTO,** Village; Vernon County; Pop. 318; Zip Code 54624; Lat. 43-25-36 N long. 091-11-45 W; First known as Winneshiek's Landing, after the Winnebago Chief. Later named for Hernando de Soto, the Spanish explorer who discovered the Mississippi River.

•**DEER PARK,** Village; St. Croix County; Pop. 232; Zip Code 54007; Lat. 45-11-32 N long. 092-23-17 W; The village got its name from a 160 acre enclosure built by Otto Neitge, as a park for deer.

•**DEERFIELD,** Village; Dane County; Pop. 1,466; Zip Code 53531; Lat. 43-03-29 N long. 089-03-36 W; Settled mainly by Norwegians and named for the many deer that lived in the area.

•**DELAFIELD,** City; Waukesha County; Pop. 4,083; Zip Code 53018; Lat. 43-04-38 N long. 088-23-26 W; First known by the Indian name *Nehamabin* or *Nemahbin.* Settlers called it Hayopolis. The city was later named after Charles Delafield, who started a mulberry grove here in 1843.

•**DELAVAN,** City; Walworth County; Pop. 5,684; Zip Code 53115; Lat. 42-37-23 N long. 088-37-08 W; Named for Edward Cornelius Delavan, a prominenttemperance leader from New York.

•**DENMARK,** Village; Brown County; Pop. 1,475; Zip Code 54208; Lat. 44-20-56 N long. 087-49-38 W; Settled by immigrants from Denmark and maned for their homeland.

•**DICKEYVILLE,** Village; Grant County; Pop. 1,156; Zip Code 53808; Elev. 957; Lat. 42-37-41 N long. 090-35-33 W; Settled around 1849 and named for Mr. Dickey, an early resident.

•**DODGEVILLE,** City; Iowa County Seat; Pop. 3,458; Zip Code 53533; Lat. 42-57-42 N long. 090-07-54 W; First called Minersville. The name was changed to honor Henry Dodge, a settler here, who in 1836 became the first governor of the Wisconsin Territory.

•**DOUSMAN,** Village; Waukesha County; Pop. 1,153; Zip Code 53118; Lat. 43-00-46 N long. 088-28-17 W; First called Bull Frog Station, for the marshy land at the railroad station here. Renamed either for Talbot C. Dousman or for Colonel John Dousman.

•**DOWNING,** Village; Dunn County; Pop. 242; Zip Code 54734; Elev. 983; Lat. 45-03-05 N long. 092-07-16 W; Named for James Downing, a settler.

•**DOYLESTOWN,** Village; Columbia County; Pop. 294; Zip Code 53928; Lat. 43-25-42 N long. 089-08-45 W; First called Ostego by settlers from Ostego, New York. Renamed for Lemuel H. Doyle, who bought land here and platted the town in 1865.

•**DRESSER,** Village; Polk County; Pop. 670; Zip Code 54009; Lat. 45-21-19 N long. 092-37-35 W; Called Dresser Junction and later Dresser, for Samuel Dresser, who donated land for the railroad.

•**DURAND,** City; Pepin County Seat; Pop. 2,047; Zip Code 54736; Elev. 721; Lat. 44-37-35 N long. 091-57-39 W; Named in honor of Miles Durand Prindle, who with Charles Billings, platted the town in 1856.

•**EAGLE,** Village; Waukesha County; Pop. 1,008; Zip Code 53119; Elev. 949; Lat. 42-52-46 N long. 088-28-21 W; Variously called Eagle Prairie, Eagleville and Eagle Center. The place got its name when a group of prospectors saw a bald eagle onthe prairie here in 1836.

•**EAGLE RIVER,** City; Vilas County Seat; Pop. 1,326; Zip Code 54521; Elev. 1647; Lat. 45-55-16 N long. 089-15-01 W; From the Indian name *Mi-gis-iwis-ibi* meaning "eagle." The place was named for the many eagles that nested in the area.

•**EAST TROY,** Village; Walworth County; Pop. 2,385; Zip Code 53120; Lat. 42-47-36 N long. 088-24-28 W; Named by settlers for their hometown of Troy, New York. At first there was a single township called Troy. When it split, this part became East Troy.

•**EASTMAN,** Village; Crawford County; Pop. 371; Zip Code 54626; Elev. 1224; Lat. 43-09-38 N long. 091-01-36 W; First called Batavia. Later renamed Eastman, the surname of several residents.

•**EAU CLAIRE,** City; Eau Claire County Seat; Pop. 51,509; Zip Code 547+; Lat. 44-48-27 N long. 091-28-54 W; Platted and named in 1855 for the nearby Eau Claire River. In French *eau claire* means "clear water."

•**EDEN,** Village; Fond du Lac County; Pop. 534; Zip Code 53019; Lat. 43-41-55 N long. 088-21-30 W; Either named from the Garden of Eden in the bible, or for John Eden, an early settler.

•**EDGAR,** Village; Marathon County; Pop. 1,194; Zip Code 54426; Lat. 44-56-46 N long. 089-57-19 W; Platted in 1891 and named for railroad employee, William Edgar.

•**EDGERTON,** City; Rock County; Pop. 4,335; Zip Code 53534; Lat. 42-50-18 N long. 089-04-00 W; Named for Benjamin Edgerton, chief surveyor for the railroad.

•**EGG HARBOR,** Village; Door County; Pop. 238; Zip Code 54209; Lat. 45-02-45 N long. 087-17-33 W; First called *Che-bah-ye-sho-da-ning,* Potawatomi words meaning "ghost door." The present name may have come when a nest full of duck's eggs was discovered at the harbor here.

•**ELAND,** Village; Shawano County; Pop. 230; Zip Code 54427; Lat. 44-52-01 N long. 089-12-29 W; Named for the eland, an African varietyof antelope. The herds of wild deer in the area may have suggested some similarity.

•**ELDERON,** Village; Marathon County; Pop. 191; Zip Code 54429; Elev. 1199; Lat. 44-51-27 N long. 089-15-37 W; Named for the beauty of the edlerberry bushes that blossomed here.

•**ELEVA,** Village; Trempealeau County; Pop. 593; Zip Code 54738; Lat. 44-37-03 N long. 091-28-32 W; First called New Chicago, then Dogtown. R.P. Goddard is said to have named the village after the French town of Eleva.

•**ELKHART LAKE,** Village; Sheboygan County; Pop. 1,054; Zip Code 53020; Elev. 938; Lat. 43-48-16 N long. 088-00-52 W; Named after the lake which is said to be shaped like the heart of an elk. German settlers to this village first called it Rhine.

•**ELK MOUND,** Village; Dunn County; Pop. 737; Zip Code 54739; Lat. 44-52-29 N long. 091-42-19 W; Named for a 1,220 foot bluff here, from which elk were sometimes seen

•**ELKHORN,** City; Walworth County; Pop. 4,605; Zip Code 53121; Elev. 1033; Lat. 43-28-19 N long. 087-57-09 W; Named by Colonel Samuel F. Phoenix, who while traveling through in 1836, saw the horns of an elk that someone had hung in a tree.

•**ELLSWORTH,** Village; Pierce County Seat; Pop. 2,143; Zip Code 540+; Elev. 1226; Lat. 44-43-39 N long. 092-29-05 W; First called Perry. Later renamed in honor of Colonel E.E. Ellsworth.

•**ELM GROVE,** Village; Waukesha County; Pop. 6,735; Zip Code 53122; Elev. 746; Lat. 42-55-23 N long. 087-49-26 W; Named for the beautiful elm trees in the area.

•**ELMWOOD,** Village; Pierce County; Pop. 885; Zip Code 54740; Lat. 44-46-39 N long. 092-09-13 W; Named for the elm trees that grew here.

•**ELROY,** City; Juneau County; Pop. 1,504; Zip Code 53929; Elev. 959; Lat. 43-43-59 N long. 090-15-53 W; James Madison Brintnall called the city LeRoy, after his hometown of LeRoy, New York. The first two letters of the name were reversed because there was already another LeRoy in Wisconsin.

•**EMBARRASS,** Village; Waupaca County; Pop. 496; Zip Code 54932; Lat. 44-40-20 N long. 088-43-01 W; French for "impede", "obstruct" or "entangle." So named for the river, which lumberjacks, sending logs downstream, often found impassable.

•**ENDEAVOR,** Village; Marquette County; Pop. 335; Zip Code 53930; Elev. 785; Lat. 43-43-07 N long. 089-27-46 W; First called Merritt's Landing. The village got its present name from the Christian Endeavor Academy, established here in 1891, and named for the Christian Endeavor Society

•**EPHRAIM,** Village; Door County; Pop. 319; Zip Code 54211; Lat. 45-09-56 N long. 087-10-04 W; Settled in 1853 and called Ephrain, a biblical named meaning "doubly fruitful."

•**ETTRICK,** Village; Trempealeau County; Pop. 462; Zip Code 54627; Elev. 771; Lat. 44-11-09 N long. 091-16-18 W; John Chance, a Scotsman, named the village for the Ettrick Forest in Sir Walter Scott's *Marmion.*

•**EVANSVILLE,** City; Rock County; Pop. 2,835; Zip Code 53536; Elev. 897; Lat. 42-47-07 N long. 089-18-03 W; Originally called The Grove. Later changed to Evansville in honor of physician, Dr. Calvin (or J.M.) Evans.

•**EXELAND,** Village; Sawyer County; Pop. 219; Zip Code 54835; Lat. 45-40-08 N long. 091-14-28 W; Named for the crossing or X in the tracks of the Wisconsin Central Railroad and an Arpin Lumber Company line.

•**FAIRCHILD,** Village; Eau Claire County; Pop. 577; Zip Code 54741; Lat. 44-36-06 N long. 090-57-36 W; Named in honor of Lucius Fairchild, Governor of Wisconsin from 1866-1872.

•**FAIRWATER,** Village; Fond du Lac County; Pop. 310; Zip Code 53931; Lat. 43-44-29 N long. 088-51-58 W; Apparently named for its favorable location on the Grand River.

•**FALL CREEK,** Village; Eau Claire County; Pop. 1,148; Zip Code 54742; Lat. 44-45-35 N long. 091-16-40 W; Originally called Cousins, for Mr. Henry Cousins. Renamed Fall Creek after the stream that ran by the village.

•**FALL RIVER,** Village; Columbia County; Pop. 850; Zip Code 53932; Elev. 858; Lat. 43-23-12 N long. 089-03-04 W; Alfred Brayton, a settler here, named the village for the hometown of his father's family in Fall River, Massachusetts.

•**FENNIMORE,** City; Grant County; Pop. 2,212; Zip Code 53809; Lat. 42-58-56 N long. 090-39-04 W; Called Fennimore Center, after John Fennimore, who farmed in the area, and disappeared during the Black Hawk War. In 1881, "Center" was dropped from the name.

•**FERRYVILLE,** Village; Crawford County; Pop. 227; Zip Code 54628; Elev. 634; Lat. 43-21-11 N long. 091-05-39 W; First called Big Landing or simply Landing. Since settlers often crossed the Mississippi here, a ferry service began, and the town was named Ferryville.

•**FOND DU LAC,** City; Fond du Lac County Seat; Pop. 35,863; Zip Code 54935;Elev. 760; Lat. 44-17-11 N long. 088-20-44 W; Menominee Indians called this place *Wanikamiu* meaning "end of lake." The French translated this to Fond du Lac.

•**FONTANA-ON-GENEVA LAKE,** Village; Walworth County; Pop. 1,764; Pioneers named this village by the lake, Fontana, a word they thought was French for "a place of many springs."

•**FOOTVILLE,** Village; Rock County; Pop. 794; Zip Code 53537; Lat. 42-40-18 N long. 089-12-46 W; First called Bachelor's Grove for Mr. Watson, a real estate agent who was unmarried. Later named for settler, Ezra A. Foot.

•**FORT ATKINSON,** City; Jefferson County; Pop. 9,785; Zip Code 53538; Elev. 790; Lat. 42-55-02 N long. 088-50-30 W; First established as Fort Koshkonong, a stockade commanded by Brigadier General Henry Atkinson during the Indian uprising of 1832. In 1836, settlers changed the name in honor of Atkinson.

•**FOUNTAIN CITY,** City; Buffalo County; Pop. 963; Zip Code 54629; Elev. 663; Lat. 44-07-11 N long. 091-41-09 W; Originally called *Wha-ma-dee* by Sioux Indians, later Holmes' Landing for pioneer, Thomas A. Holmes. In 1855 it was renamed Fountain City for the many springs along the bluff's near here.

•**FOX LAKE,** City; Dodge County; Pop. 1,373; Zip Code 53933; Elev. 920; Lat. 43-33-44 N long. 088-54-25 W; From *Hos-a-rac-a-tah*, the Indian name for the lake meaning "fox." The village was later platted under the English translation, Fox Lake.

•**FOX POINT,** Village; Milwaukee County; Pop. 7,649; Called Dutch Settlement by immigrants from Holland. The village eventually became Fox Point, a surveyor's name for the point of land at Doctor's Park.

•**FRANCIS CREEK,** Village; Manitowoc County; Pop. 589; Zip Code 54214; Lat. 44-11-56 N long. 087-43-47 W; Named French Creek for French settlers at a nearby stream. The post office renamed the town Francis Creek because there was already a French Creek in the state. A later name was Axelyn, but that was changed back to Francis Creek.

•**FREDERIC,** Village; Polk County; Pop. 1,039; Zip Code 54825; Lat. 45-41-20 N long. 092-17-37 W; Landowner William J. Starr named this village for his son, Frederic.

•**FREDONIA,** Village; Ozaukee County; Pop. 1,437; Zip Code 53021, Originally called Stoney Creek. Renamed for the town of Fredonia, New York.

•**FREMONT,** Village; Waupaca County; Pop. 510; Zip Code 54940; Lat. 44-15-22 N long. 088-52-31 W; Named in honor of Colonel John Fremont, who explored California and fought in the Mexican War.

•**FRIENDSHIP,** Village; Adams County Seat; Pop. 764; Zip Code 53927; Lat. 43-59-03 N long. 089-56-11 W; Settlers named this village for their hometown of Friendship, New York.

•**FRIESLAND,** Village; Columbia County; Pop. 267; Zip Code 53935; Lat. 43-35-25 N long. 089-03-46 W; First called Randolph Center, because it was at the center of Randolph Township. Dutch settlers renamed the village after the province of Friesland in Holland.

•**GALESVILLE,** City; Trempealeau County; Pop. 1,239; Zip Code 54630; Elev. 712; Lat. 44-05-40 N long. 091-21-20 W; Named for Judge George Gale, who purchased land here and founded Gale College.

•**GAYS MILLS,** Village; Crawford County; Pop. 627; Zip Code 54631; lat. 43-18-24 N long. 090-50-16 W; Named for James Gay, a settler from Virginia who built a sawmill here around 1848.

•**GENOA,** Village; Vernon County; Pop. 283; Zip Code 54632; Lat. 43-34-49 N long. 091-13-44 W; First called Bad Ax, after the river. Later renamed by Italian immigrants who thought the region resembled the Genoa Valley.

•**GENOA CITY,** Village; Walworth County; Pop. 1,202; Zip Code 53128; Lat. 42-30-02 N long. 088-19-25 W; Named after the town of Genoa, New York.

•**GERMANTOWN,** Village; Washington County; Pop. 10,729; Zip Code 53022; Elev. 863; Lat. 43-13-22 N long. 088-07-11 W; Named for German settlers who made up the entire village.

•**GILLETT,** City; Oconto County; Pop. 1,356; Zip Code 54124; Elev. 812; Lat. 44-53-19 N long. 088-17-24 W; Named for Rodney and Mary Roblee Gillett, who settled here in 1858. Originally called Gillett Center.

•**GILMAN,** Village; Taylor County; Pop. 436; Zip Code 54433; Lat. 45-09-59 N long. 090-48-12 W; Named after the son of Mr. Moore, who had an interest in the S.M. & P. Railroad, and livedinthe nearby town of Stanley.

•**GLENBEULAH,** Village; Sheboygan County; Pop. 423; Zip Code 53023; Lat. 43-46-18 N long. 088-02-56 W; First called Clark's Mill, for Hazel P. Clark, who owned a sawmill here. Later named by Edward Appleton, "glen" for the location, and "Beulah" after his mother.

•**GLEN FLORA,** Village; Rusk County; Pop. 83; Zip Code 54526; Elev. 1276; Lat. 45-30-00 N long. 090-53-28 W; First called Miller's Spur, for a Mr. Miller. In 1887, he suggested changing it to Glen Flora, the names of his two children.

•**GLENDALE,** City; Milwaukee County; Pop. 13,882; At one time part of the city of Milwaukee. Also called Lake. Townspeople later voted for the name Glendale, descriptive of the surroundings.

•**GLENWOOD CITY,** City; St. Croix County; Pop. 950; Zip Code 54013; Lat. 45-03-49 N long. 092-11-01 W; Named for the Glenwood Manufactureing Company which came to the area in 1885.

•**GRAFTON,** Village; Ozaukee County; Pop. 8,381; Zip Code 53024; Lat. 42-14-02 N long. 085-45-45 W; First known as Hamburg. Renamed Grafton, possibly from Grafton Street in Dublin, or the Grafton in New Hampshire, Massachusetts or West Virginia. The name changed to Manchester in 1857 and back to Grafton in 1862.

•**GRANTON,** Village; Clark County; Pop. 399; Zip Code 54436; Lat. 44-34-57 N long. 090-27-10 W; The mane is adapted form Grant Township, which was named for Ulysses S. Grant.

•**GRANTSBURG,** Village; Burnett County Seat; Pop. 1,153; Zip Code 54840; Lat. 45-46-36 N long. 092-41-16 W; The Indians called this place *Kitchi-Maski-gimi-tika-ning* meaning "at the great cranberry place." Renamed by white settlers in honor of Ulysses S. Grant.

•**GRATIOT,** Village; Lafayette County; Pop. 280; Zip Code 53541; Lat. 42-34-20 N long. 090-01-04 W; Established as Gratiot's Grove after Henry Gratiot who came here in 1824.

•**GREEN BAY,** City; Brown County Seat; Pop. 87,899; Zip Code 54300; Elev. 594; Lat. 44-30-48 N long. 088-01-10 W; Menominee Indians called it *Putci-wikit* or *puji-kit* meaning "a bay in spite of itself." The French named it *La Baie Verte* or Green Bay, for the greenish color of the water.

•**GREEN LAKE,** City; Green Lake County Seat; Pop. 1,208; Zip Code 54941; Lat. 43-50-32 N long. 088-57-12 W; Established as Dartford, for a Mr. Dart who built a dam and a ford across the river here. Renamed Green Lake after the greenish lake at the center of the county.

•**GREENDALE,** Village; Milwaukee County; Pop. 16,928; Zip Code 53129; Lat. 42-54-49 N long. 087-58-58 W; One of the Greenbelt Towns built around 1936 by the Resettlement Administration. This one became Greendale.

•**GREENFIELD,** City; Milwaukee County; Pop. 31,467; Nathan Dennison named this city for his hometown of Greenfield, Massachusetts.

•**GREENWOOD,** City; Clark County; Pop. 1,124; Zip Code 54437; Elev. 1168; Lat. 44-45-34 N long. 090-35-41 W; Named for the numberous pine and hardwood trees in the area.

•**GRESHAM,** Village; Shawano County; Pop. 534; Zip Code 54128; Elev. 9554; Lat. 44-51-09 N long. 088-46-57 W; Named in honor of Postmaster-General Gresham of President Arthur's cabinet.

•**HALES CORNERS,** Village; Milwaukee County; Pop. 7,110; Zip Code 53130; Lat. 42-55-43 N long. 088-02-04 W; The town got its named from William Hale, who built the first log cabin here in 1837.

•**HAMMOND,** Village; St. Croix County; Pop. 991; Zip Code 54015; Lat. 44-58-34 N long. 092-26-30 W; Named for R.B. Hammond who built the first sawmill here.

•**HANCOCK,** Village; Waushara County; Pop. 419; Zip Code 54943; Elev. 1089; Lat. 44-08-11 N long. 089-30-56 W; Settled in 1854 and called Sylvester after a man by that name. When the post office was extablished, the name changed to Hancock.

•**HARTFORD,** City; Washington County; Pop. 7,046; Zip Code 53027; Lat. 43-18-53 N long. 088-22-54 W; First called Wright after a Mr. Wright. The name Hartford may have come from: the ford at heart-shaped Pike Lake nearby; an Indian name for the area meaning "heart"; or from the city of Hartford, Connecticut.

•**HARTLAND,** Village; Waukesha County; Pop. 5,559; Zip Code 53029; Lat. 43-06-54 N long. 088-23-15 W; Early names include: Warren, for settler Steve Warren; Hersheyvill and Hershey's Mills, for Mr. Christ Hershey; and the Indian *Sha-ba-qua-nake* meaning "a growing group." The current name probably descriptive of the area, the heartland.

•**HATLEY,** Village; Marathon County; Pop. 300; Zip Code 54440; Lat. 44-55-34 N long. 089-20-23 W; Matthew LaBarian named this village for his hometown of Hatley, Quebec.

•**HAUGEN,** Village; Barron County; Pop. 251; Zip Code 54841; Elev. 1229; Lat. 45-36-30 N long. 091-46-47 W; Named for Senator Haugen.

•**HAWKINS,** Village; Rusk County; Pop. 407; Zip Code 54530; Elev. 1369; Lat. 45-30-41 N long. 090-42-46 W; First called Main Creek. Renamed for Mr. Hawkins, who was either a lumberjack or a railroad official.

•**HAYWARD,** City; Sawyer County Seat; Pop. 1,698; Zip Code 54843; Elev. 1198; Lat. 46-00-34 N long. 091-28-57 W; Chippewa Indians called this place *Ba-ke-abash-kang* meaning "swamp which is a branch of a bigger swamp." Later named for Judson Hayward, who built a sawmill here.

•**HAZEL GREEN,** Village; Grant County; Pop. 1,282; Zip Code 53811; Lat. 42-32-05 N long. 090-25-56 W; First called Hardy's Scrape, later Hard Scrabble. Renamed either for Captain Charles McCoy's hometown of Hazel Green, Kentucky, or for the hazel bushes in the area.

•**HEWITT,** Village; Wood County; Pop. 470; Zip Code 54441; Lat. 44-38-46 N long. 090-05-54 W; Known by the names Number 28 (from the railroad), Kreuser, and Hewitt Side Track, for a lumberman named Hewitt who had a railroad sidetrack built here. The words "side track" were later dropped.

•**HIGHLAND,** Village; Iowa County; Pop. 860; Zip Code 53543; Lat. 43-02-53 N long. 090-22-44 W; First called Franklin. In 1846, the village plat was registered under the name Highland.

•**HILBERT,** Village; Calumet County; Pop. 1,176; Zip Code 54129; Lat. 44-08-11 N long. 088-09-48 W; The source of the name is unknown. The village was first called Hilbert Junction, later shortened to Hilbert.

•**HILLSBORO,** City; Vernon County; Pop. 1,263; Zip Code 54634; Elev. 1001; Lat. 43-39-13 N long. 090-20-33 W; Named for Vilentia Hill who laid the first claim here in 1850. The original spelling was Hillsborough.

•**HIXTON,** Village; Jackson County; Pop. 364; Zip Code 54635; Lat. 44-22-25 N long. 091-00-46 W; Originally part of the town of Alma. Platted in 1860 as Williamsport. The name was later changed to Hixton (short for Hick's Town) after settler, John L. Hicks.

•**HOLLANDALE,** Village; Iowa County; Pop. 271; Zip Code 53544; Lat. 42-52-37 N long. 089-56-20 W; First called Bennville and later Hollandale. Both names were for Bjorn Holland who ran a small supply store for railroad construction crews.

•**HOLMEN,** Village; La Crosse County; Pop. 2,411; Zip Code 54636; Elev. 718; Lat. 43-57-49 N long. 091-15-10 W; Early names were Frederickstown and Cricken. Later called Holmen, probably for Senator Holmen of Indiana, who once surveyed this territory.

•**HORICON,** City; Dodge County; Pop. 3,584; Zip Code 53032; Elev. 884; Lat. 43-26-35 N long. 088-38-10 W; Originally a Winnebago village called *Maunk-shak-kah* or "White Breast." Later known as Elk Village, Indian Ford, Hubbard's Ford and finally Horicon, from the home of settlers at Lake Horicon (now Lake George) New York.

•**HORTONVILLE,** Village; Outagamie County; Pop. 2,016; Zip Code 54944; Elev. 794; Lat. 44-20-00 N long. 088-37-23 W; Named for Alonzo Erastus Horton who founded the village in 1849.

•**HOWARD,** Village; Brown County; Pop. 8,240; Named in honor of Brigadier General Benjamin Howard, who fought in the War of 1812.

•**HOWARDS GROVE,** Village; Sheboygan County; Pop. 1,838; Originally called Pitchville. Later named for H.B. Howard, who established a trading post here in 1850.

•**HUDSON,** City; St. Croix County Seat; Pop. 5,434; Zip Code 54016; Lat. 44-59-08 N long. 092-45-15 W; First called Willow River. The name was changed to Hudson when travelers remarked on a resemblance between the St. Croix River and the Hudson River in New York.

•**HURLEY,** City; Iron County Seat; Pop. 2,015; Zip Code 54534; Lat. 46-26-36 N long. 090-11-39 W; Platted in 1885 and named for Judge M.A. Hurley, a lawyer and iron ore mine operator.

•**HUSTISFORD,** Village; Dodge County; Pop. 874; Zip Code 53034; Lat. 43-20-16 N long. 088-36-08 W; First called Rock River Rapids for the half mile of rapids here. Renamed Hustis Rapids, and later, Hustisford after John Hustis, the first settler.

•**HUSTLER,** Village; Juneau County; Pop. 170; Zip Code 54637; Elev. 929; Lat. 43-52-25 N long. 090-15-52 W; Probably named for Hustler Street, an important road in the village.

•**INDEPENDENCE,** City; Trempealeau County; Pop. 1,180; Zip Code 54747; Elev. 782; Lat. 44-23-19 N long. 091-25-33 W; So named because the city was platted during the year of the Centennial celebration of American Independence.

•**IOLA,** Village; Waupaca County; Pop. 957; Zip Code 54945; Elev. 955; Lat. 44-30-24 N long. 089-07-24 W; Named for a Potawatomi Indian girl, Iola, who was said to be the daughter of Old Red Bird, brother of Chief Waupaca.

•**IRON RIDGE,** Village; Dodge County; Pop. 766; Zip Code 53035; Lat. 43-23-48 N long. 088-32-08 W; Named for iron ore mines in the vicinity.

•**JACKSON,** Village; Washington County; Pop. 1,817; Zip Code 53037; Elev. 896; Lat. 43-19-26 N long. 088-10-21 W; Named in honor of Stonewall Jackson.

•**JANESVILLE,** City; Rock County Seat; Pop. 51,071; Zip Code 53542; Elev. 858; Lat. 42-38-21 N long. 089-09-45 W; Winnebago Indians had a village here called *E-nee-poro-poro* or "round rock." Later names include Monteray Point, Black Hawk and finally Janesville, for Henry F. Janes, who ran a ferry service here.

•**JEFFERSON,** City; Jefferson County Seat; Pop. 5,647; Zip Code 53549; Lat. 43-00-17 N long. 088-48-18 W; Named in honor of Thomas Jefferson.

•**JOHNSON CREEK,** Village; Jefferson County; Pop. 1,136; Zip Code 53038; Elev. 812; Lat. 43-05-21 N long. 088-46-28 W; First called Belleville. Renamed Johnson Creek after Timothy Johnson, who had an early land claim here.

•**JUNCTION CITY,** Village; Portage County; Pop. 523; Zip Code 54443; Lat. 44-35-36 N long. 089-47-21 W; Named Junction because the tracks of the Wisconsin Valley Railroad and Wisconsin Central Railroad crossed here. Townspeople later added "City" to the name.

•**JUNEAU,** City; Dodge County Seat; Pop. 2,045; Zip Code 53039; Lat. 43-24-06 N long. 088-42-27 W; First called Victory, later Dodge Center. It was renamed Juneau in honor of Solomon Juneau, founder of Milwaukee.

•**KAUKAUNA,** City; Outagamie County; Pop. 11,310; Zip Code 54130; Lat. 44-17-13 N long. 088-16-41 W; Derived from the Menominee Indian name *okakaning* or *kakaning* for rapids in the Fox river. In translation the word means "place where they fish for pike," "long portage" or "crow nesting place."

•KEKOSKEE, Village; Dodge County; Pop. 224; Originally a Winnebago Indian settlement named *Kekoskee*, meaning "friendly village."

•KELLNERSVILLE, Village; Manitowoc County; Pop. 369; Zip Code 54215; Elev. 827; Lat. 44-13-35 N long. 087-48-05 W; Named for John (or Michele) Kellner who built a sawmill here in 1849. Originally called Kellner's Corners.

•KENDALL, Village; Monroe County; Pop. 486; Zip Code 54638; Elev. 1021; Lat. 43-47-18 N long. 090-22-12 W; Named for L.G. Kendall, a contractor who purchased right-of-way for the railroad.

•KENNAN, Village; Price County Seat; Pop. 194; Zip Code 54537; Lat. 45-31-47 N long. 090-35-16 W; First called Ripley. Later named for K.K. Kennan, a railroad tax lawyer who built a log house station here.

•KENOSHA, City; Kenosha County; Pop. 77,685; Zip Code 53140; Lat. 41-50-32 N long. 086-19-11 W; Potawantomi Indians called their villages *kenosha* meaning "pike" or "pickeral." White settlers adopted the name Pike, which was changed to Southport, and finally Kenosha, the Indian name.

•KEWASKUM, Village; Washington County; Pop. 2,381; Zip Code 53040; Lat. 43-30-48 N long. 088-13-54 W; Named for a Potawatomi Indian chief who died here around 1847. The name means "a man able to turn fate whichever way he wants" or "his tracks are toward home."

•KEWAUNEE, City; Kewaunee County Seat; Pop. 2,801; Zip Code 54216; Lat. 44-27-18 N long. 087-30-24 W; An Indian name meaning either "the way around or across a point of land" or "prairie chicken."

•KIEL, City; Manitowoc County; Pop. 3,083; Zip Code 53042; Elev. 933; Lat. 43-54-39 N long. 088-02-16 W; First called Abel, for settler D. Abel, and later Schleswig. The town was renamed for Colonel Belitz's home in Kiel, Germany.

•KIMBERLY, Village; Outagamie County; Pop. 5,881; Zip Code 54136; Elev. 734; Lat. 44-03-27 N long. 087-55-12 W; Known as The Cedars because the Treaty of Cedars was signed here. Renamed for Kimberly Clark and Company, which built a pulp and paper mill here in 1889.

•KINGSTON, Village; Green Lake County; Pop. 328; Zip Code 53939; Lat. 43-41-29 N long. 089-07-42 W; Named for Kingston, Canada, the hometown of the wife of J.E. Millard, who owned a grist mill here.

•KNAPP, Village; Dunn County; Pop. 419; Zip Code 54749; Lat. 44-57-28 N long. 092-04-41 W; Known as Knapp Station and later, Knapp, for John H. Knapp, who with William Wilson, started the Knapp Stout and Company lumbering firm.

•KOHLER, Village; Sheboygan County; Pop. 1,651; Zip Code 53044; Elev. 676; Lat. 43-42-58 N long. 087-47-04 W; First named Riverside. Renamed for the Kohler Manufacturing Company which moved its plant here in 1912.

•LA CROSSE, City; La Crosse County Seat; Pop. 48,347; Zip Code 54601; Elev. 669; Lat. 43-48-34 N long. 091-13-54 W; So named because when French explorers first arrived, they saw Indians playing a ball game that resembled the French game "la crosse."

•LA FARGE, Village; Vernon County; Pop. 746; Zip Code 54639; Lat. 43-34-35 N long. 090-38-18 W; Originally called Corners. The present name was selected at random from a list of United States place names.

•LA VALLE, Village; Sauk County; Pop. 412; Zip Code 53941; Elev. 896; Lat. 43-35-29 N long. 090-07-45 W; Incorporated in 1883 and named for a fur trapped who settled here.

•LADYSMITH, City; Rusk County Seat; Pop. 3,826; Zip Code 54848; Elev. 1144; Lat. 45-27-46 N long. 091-05-47 W; Earlier called Corbett, Flambeau Falls and Warner. Renamed in 1900 for Lady Smith, the wife of a factory manager, as an enticement for him to move his woodenware company to the town.

•LAKE GENEVA, City; Walworth County; Pop. 5,607; Zip Code 53147; Lat. 42-36-11 N long. 088-27-34 W; Originally called *Muck-Suck* or Big Foot, for a Potawatomi chief. The French called it Gros Pied, but settler John Brink renamed it for the village of Geneva on Seneca Lake in New York.

•LAKE MILLS, City; Jefferson County; Pop. 3,670; Zip Code 53551; Lat. 43-05-23 N long. 088-54-33 W; Called Keyes Mills, for Captain Joseph Keyes, who owned mills here. He later changed the name to Lake Mills. In 1870, however, for one year the town was called Tyranena, before changing back to Lake Mills.

•LAKE NEBAGAMON, Village; Douglas County; Pop. 780; Zip Code 54849; Lat. 46-30-51 N long. 091-42-07 W; The name is hippewa from the words *nee-bay-go-mow-win* meaning "place to still hunt deer by water."

•LANCASTER, City; Grant County Seat; Pop. 4,076; Zip Code 53813; Lat. 42-50-55 N long. 090-42-36 W; Plattd in 1837 and named for Lancaster, Pennsylvania, the hometown of one of the settlers.

•LANNON, Village; Waukesha County; Pop. 987; Zip Code 53046; Lat. 43-09-01 N long. 088-09-57 W; Known as Lannon Springs, and then Stone City, for the limestone quarries here. The town was renamed Lannon for Bill Lannon who built a farm and the post office around 1840.

•LENA, Village; Oconto County; Pop. 585; Zip Code 54139; Elev. 714; Lat. 44-57-34 N long. 088-02-36 W; First called Maple Valley. Later changed to Lena, for the wife of postmaster George R. Hall.

•LIME RIDGE, Village; Sauk County; Pop. 191; Zip Code 53942; Lat. 43-27-51 N long. 090-09-23 W; Called Lime Ridge for the location of the town on a ridge with limestone outcroppings.

•LINDEN, Village; Iowa County; Pop. 395; Zip Code 53553; Elev. 1101; Lat. 42-55-08 N long. 090-16-34 W; Originally called Peddler's Creek, after a nearby stream. Renamed Linden in 1855, for a big linden tree that grew outside the general store.

•LITTLE CHUTE, Village; Outagamie County; Pop. 7,907; Zip Code 54140; Elev. 728; Lat. 44-06-56 N long. 087-58-29 W; French explorers called the falls in the Fox River *La Petite Chute*. The name is believed to have been translated by Father Vanden Broek, who built the first church here in 1836.

•LIVINGSTON, Village; Grant County; Pop. 642; Zip Code 53554; Elev. 1164; Lat. 42-54-03 N long. 090-25-54 W; First called Dublin by Irish settlers. Later named for Hugh Livingston who donated his farmland to the railroad.

•LODI, City; Columbia County; Pop. 1,959; Zip Code 53555; Elev. 833; Lat. 43-18-53 N long. 089-31-52 W; Possibly named after Lodi, Italy or Lodi, New York.

•LOGANVILLE, Village; Sauk County; Pop. 239; Zip Code 53943; Lat. 43-25-51 N long. 090-02-14 W; Named for Chauncey P. Logan, an early settler who was instrumental in starting the village.

•LOHRVILLE, Village; Waushara County; Pop. 336; Named for Lohr Granite Company which was a customer of the Rothman Quarry which was located here.

•**LOMIRA,** Village; Dodge County; Pop. 1,446; Zip Code 53048; Elev. 1039; Lat. 43-35-30 N long. 088-27-01 W; First called Springfield. Renamed in 1849, probably for Lomira Schoonover. The name may also refer to the loamy soil here.

•**LONE ROCK,** Village; Richland County; Pop. 577; Zip Code 53556; Elev. 903; Lat. 43-10-52 N long. 090-11-41 W; Laid out in 1856 and named Lone Rock City after a large sandstone landmark that once stood near the river.

•**LOWELL,** Village; Dodge County; Pop. 326; Zip Code 53557; Lat. 43-19-36 N long. 088-48-50 W; Established in the 1830's as Town Ten. Later named after Lowell, Massachusetts, the hometown of Clark Lawton, a mill owner.

•**LOYAL,** City; Clark County; Pop. 1,252; Zip Code 54446; Lat. 44-43-48 N long. 090-29-25 W; The name was a tribute to the townsmen who fought in the Civil War. It is claimed that every eligible man in the township enlisted.

•**LUBLIN,** Village; Taylor County; Pop. 142; Zip Code 54447; Elev. 1289; Lat. 45-04-30 N long. 090-43-11 W; Named after Lublin, Poland, the home of Marvin Durski, a land agent.

•**LUCK,** Village; Polk County; Pop. 997; Zip Code 54853; Lat. 45-33-57 N long. 092-28-21 W; Possibly named by settlers who used this place as a stopover on their trips to Minnesota for supplies. If they arrived at the site by nightfall they were said to be "lucky." Thus the place came to be called Luck.

•**LUXEMBURG,** Village; Kewaukee County; Pop. 1,040; Zip Code 54217; Lat. 44-32-18 N long. 087-42-19 W; Named by settlers from Luxemburg, Belgium.

•**LYNXVILLE,** Village; Crawford County; Pop. 174; So named because surveyors who laid out the village arrived on the steamboat *Lynx.*

•**MADISON,** City; Dane County Seat and Capital of Wisconsin; Pop. 170,616; Zip Code 53562; Elev. 863; Lat. 39-39-06 N long. 082-16-20 W; Winnebago Indians had a village here called *Dejop* or "four lakes." Incorporated in 1846 as the capital of the Wisconsin Territory and named for President James Madison.

•**MAIDEN ROCK,** Village; Pierce County; Pop. 172; Zip Code 54750; Elev. 689; Lat. 44-33-20 N long. 092-18-44 W; Named for a rocky bluff that towers over the river here, where the Dakota Indian maiden, Winona, was siad to have jumped to her death.

•**MANAWA,** City; Waupaca County; Pop. 1,205; Zip Code 54949; Lat. 44-27-35 N long. 088-55-16 W; First called Brickley, then Elberton, after postmaster Elbert Scott. Renamed Manawa after the hero of an Indian legend.

•**MANITOWOC,** City; Manitowoc County Seat; Pop. 32,547; Zip Code 54220; Elev. 606; Lat. 44-05-32 N long. 087-40-43 W; Derived from Indian words meaning "river of bad spirits" or "devil's den."

•**MAPLE BLUFF,** Village; Dane County; Pop. 1,351; Incorporated in 1930 as Lakewood Bluff. Later renamed for the maple trees growing on a bluff near the lake.

•**MARIBEL,** Village; Manitowoc County; Pop. 363; Zip Code 54227; Elev. 861; Lat. 44-16-49 N long. 087-48-33 W; The name is said to be coined from the words "Mary" and "bell." Known as Maribel Caves, for the limestone caves here, Maribel Station, and eventually just Maribel.

•**MARINETTE,** City; Marinette County; Pop. 11,965; Zip Code 54143; Elev. 598; Lat. 45-05-44 N long. 087-37-29 W; Named for Marguerite Chevallier, nicknamed Marinette, who started a fur trading business on the banks of the Menominee River.

•**MARION,** City; Waupaca County; Pop. 1,348; Zip Code 54950; Lat. 44-40-33 N long. 088-53-20 W; First called Perry's Mills for J.W. Perry, who had a sawmill here. Renamed Marion, wither after Marion, Ohio; General Francis Marion of the Revolutionary War; or after Marion Ransdell, a settler.

•**MARKESAN,** City; Green Lake County; Pop. 1,446; Zip Code 53946; Elev. 847; Lat. 43-42-22 N long. 088-58-50 W; Earlier known as Granville. The present name, Markesan, is said to have come from the Marquesas Islands.

•**MARQUETTE,** Village; Green Lake County; Pop. 204; Zip Code 53947; Lat. 43-44-50 N long. 089-08-01 W; Named in honor of Father Jacques Marquette, a French missionary who explored this area around 1673.

•**MARSHALL,** Village; Dane County; Pop. 2,363; Zip Code 53559; Lat. 43-10-48 N long. 089-03-36 W; First called Bird's Ruins, after the settlement started by A.A. Bird and Zenas Bird, burned in a prairie fire. Later named hanchettville, for postmaster Hanchett, then Howard City, for a railroad contractor, and finally Marshall, after property buyers Porter and Marshall.

•**MARSHFIELD,** City; Wood County; Pop. 18,290; Zip Code 544+; Lat. 44-33-11 N long. 089-57-39 W; Either named for J.J. Marsh, or for his uncle, Samuel Marsh, one of the early owners of the land.

•**MAUSTON,** City; Juneau County Seat; Pop. 3,284; Zip Code 53948; Elev. 883; Lat. 43-47-26 N long. 090-04-32 W; There was an Indian village here calle *To-ko-nee.* White settlers named the place Maughs Mills, for M.M. Maughes who managed a mill here. He platted the city in 1854 as Maughstown, which was shortened to Mauston.

•**MAYVILLE,** City; Juneau County; Pop. 2,284; Zip Code 53050; Elev. 776; Lat. 43-30-41 N long. 088-33-37 W; Named for Eli P. May who established a trading post here in 1845.

•**MAZOMONIE,** Village; Dane County; Pop. 1,248; Zip Code 53560; Lat. 43-11-06 N long. 089-48-14 W; Derived from one of several Indian words: *May-Zhee-Mau-nee* or Walking Mat, a Winnebago chief; *Mo-zo-mee-nan* meaning "mooseberries"; or *mo-so-min-um* meaning "moon berries."

•**MCFARLAND,** Village; Dane County; Pop. 3,783; Zip Code 53558; Lat. 40-59-19 N long. 085-02-07 W; Named for William H. McFarland, who bought land here and laid out the village. For a short time the name was spelled MacFarland.

•**MEDFORD,** City; Taylor County Seat; Pop. 4,035; Zip Code 54451; Lat. 45-08-20 N long. 090-20-37 W; Possibly named for Medford, Massachusetts, the hometown of a young man who passed through here in 1873.

•**MELLEN,** City; Ashland County; Pop. 1,046; Zip Code 54546; Lat. 46-19-37 N long. 090-39-31 W; Platted as Iron City. When the railroad depot was built, the town was called Mellen, after Charles Sanger Mellen, a railroad official.

•**MELROSE,** Village; Jackson County; Pop. 507; Zip Code 54642; Lat. 44-07-11 N long. 090-59-58 W; First named Bristol after the city in England. Changed to Melrose in 1860, for Melrose Abbey in Scotland.

•**MENASHA,** City; Winnebago County; Pop. 14,728; Zip Code 54952; Lat. 44-00-41 N long. 088-00-19 W; The name comes from a Menominee Indian word meaning "thorn" or "island."

•**MENOMONEE FALLS,** Village; Waukesha County; Pop. 27,845; Zip Code 53051; Lat. 43-09-39 N long. 088-06-44 W; Named after the Indian tribe that lived here. The word *menomonee* means "wild rice." An early name for the village was Nehsville, for Frederick Nehs, a settler.

•**MENOMONIE,** City; Dunn County Seat; Pop. 12,769; Zip Code 54751; Elev. 877; Lat. 44-52-44 N long. 091-55-30 W; A variation of the Indian tribal name which translates as "wild rice."

•**MEQUON,** City; Ozaukee County; Pop. 16,193; Derived from the Wau-Mequon or White Feather, the name of Chief Waubaka's daughter.

•**MERRILL,** City; Lincoln County Seat; Pop. 9,578; Zip Code 54452; Lat. 45-11-09 N long. 089-41-34 W; First known as Jenny Bull Falls, shortened to Jenny Falls and then Jenny, for the daughter of a Potawatomi chief. In 1881 the city was named for S.S. Merrill, General Manager of the Wisconsin Central Railroad.

•**MERRILLAN,** Village; Jackson County; Pop. 587; Zip Code 54754; Elev. 937; Lat. 44-26-46 N long. 090-49-50 W; Founded by brothers Benjamin H. and Leander G. Merrill and named in their honor.

•**MERRIMAC,** Village; Sauk County; Pop. 365; Zip Code 53561; Lat. 43-21-27 N long. 089-37-51 W; First called Matt's Ferry, for settler Chester Mattson. Later named Colomar, and then Merrimac, either from Merrimack River and County in New Hampshire, or from the Indian word meaning "sturgeon" or "swift water."

•**MERTON,** Village; Waukesha County; Pop. 1,045; Zip Code 53056; Lat. 43-08-34 N long. 088-19-06 W; Called Warren, for Sylvanus Warren and his family. In 1849 the village was named after the English town of Moreton. The spelling later changed to Merton.

•**MILLADORE,** Village; Wood County; Pop. 250; Zip Code 54454; Lat. 44-36-19 N long. 089-51-09 W; First called Mill Creek. The name had to be changed because there was already a Mill Creek in the state. Residents coined the new name retaining the word "mill" at the beginning.

•**MILLTOWN,** Village; Polk County; Pop. 732; Zip Code 54858; Elev. 1246; Lat. 45-31-08 N long. 092-30-11 W; Orignally named Grainfield. In 1839, it was renamed Milton, either for the author of *Paradise Lose* or after Milton, Pennsylvania.

•**MILWAUKEE,** City; Milwaukee County Seat; Pop. 636,212; Zip Code 53200; Elev. 634; Lat. 43-07-21 N long. 088-00-31 W; Derived from an Indian word; possibly from any one of the following: *Millecki* or *Melchi* meaning "good land"; *Millicki* meaning "there is a good point"; *Milwarkik* meaning "great council place"; or *Milwauky* meaning "good earth."

•**MINERAL POINT,** City; Iowa County; Pop. 2,259; Zip Code 53565; Elev. 1135; Lat. 42-51-41 N long. 090-10-56 W; Named for the lead and zinc found at a high rocky point between two streams.

•**MINONG,** Village; Washburn County; Pop. 557; Zip Code 54859; Elev. 1064; Lat. 46-06-01 N long. 091-49-43 W; The name comes from an Indian word meaning either "a good high place," "a place where blueberries grow" or "a pleasant valley."

•**MISHICOT,** Village; Manitowoc County; Pop. 1,503; Zip Code 54228; Lat. 44-14-13 N long. 087-38-44 W; Probably named for Chief Mishicot of the Ottawas. His name means "hairy legs." In 1853, settlers called the town Saxonburgh, but it was later changed back to Mishicot.

•**MONDOVI,** City; Buffalo County; Pop. 2,545; Zip Code 54755; Lat. 44-34-01 N long. 091-40-32 W; First called Pan Cake Valley, later Farringtons, for Harvey Farrington, the first settler. Renamed for Mondavi, Italy where Napoleon won a victory against the Sardinians.

•**MONONA,** City; Dane County; Pop. 8,809; The name is probably of Indian origin, a word meaning "beautiful."

•**MONROE,** City; Green County Seat; Pop. 10,027; Zip Code 53566; Elev. 1099; Lat. 42-35-52 N long. 089-38-14 W; Probably named in honor of President James Monroe.

•**MONTELLO,** City; Marquette County Seat; Pop. 1,273; Zip Code 53949; Elev. 782; Lat. 43-47-45 N long. 089-19-17 W; First called Serairo, later Hill River. The name Montello may have come from the French words *Mont l'eau* or "hill by the water."

•**MONTFORT,** Village; Grant County; Pop. 616; Zip Code 53569; Lat. 42-58-18 N long. 090-25-49 W; Earlier called by the names Wingville and Podunk. Renamed for a small fort minersbuilt here to protect themselves during the Blackhawk War.

•**MONTICELLO,** Village; Green County; Pop. 1,021; Zip Code 53570; Elev. 84; Lat. 42-44-54 N long. 089-35-16 W; Named Monticello or "little mountain" in 1845 because of the mounds or bluffs along the valley.

•**MOSINEE,** City; Marathon County; Pop. 3,015; Zip Code 54455; Elev. 1153; Lat. 44-51-44 N long. 089-42-24 W; First called Little Bull Falls, because the rapids on the river here sounded like a roaring bull. Later renamed in honor of Old Chief Mosinee.

•**MOUNT CALVARY,** Village; Fond du Lac County; Pop. 585; Zip Code 53057; Lat. 43-49-46 N long. 088-14-57 W; Founded by Catholics and first named St. Nicholas Congregation. In 1853, Bishop Henni renamed it Mount Calvary for its location at the foot of a hill on which a cross had been erected.

•**MOUNT HOPE,** Village; Grant County; Pop. 197; Zip Code 53816; Lat. 42-58-10 N long. 090-51-28 W; Situated on a hill and supposedly named for the communitiy's "hope" to attract an institute of higher learning to the town. The Mt. Hope Academy was eventually established here.

•**MOUNT HOREB,** Village; Dane County; Pop. 3,251; Zip Code 53572; Lat. 43-00-30 N long. 089-45-17 W; The name was taken from the Bible by Mr. Wright, a Methodist minister who was also the town's first postmaster.

•**MOUNT STERLING,** Village; Crawford County; Pop. 223; Zip Code 54645; Lat. 43-18-58 N long. 090-55-39 W; Named for William Sterling, a settler, and for the high hill north of the village.

•**MUKWONAGO,** Village; Waukesha County; Pop. 4,014; Zip Code 53149; Elev. 837; Lat. 42-52-02 N long. 088-20-01 W; The name is derived from an Indian word that probably means "place of the bear." An earlier spelling of the name was Mequanigo.

•**MUSCODA,** Village; Grant County; Pop. 1,331; Zip Code 53573; Lat. 43-11-32 N long. 090-26-24 W; Called English Prairie or English Meadow because an English trader and his son were murdered here. The present name, Muscoda, is derived from *Mash-ko-deng,* an Indian word for "meadow" or "prairie."

•**MUSKEGO,** City; Waukesha County; Pop. 15,277; Zip Code 53150; Lat. 42-54-35 N long. 088-07-09 W; Derived from the name for the original Potawatomi Indian settlement here. It meant either "fishing place," "sunfish," "swamp" or "cranberry bog."

•**NASHOTAH,** Village; Waukesha County; Pop. 513; Zip Code 53058; Lat. 43-06-13 N long. 088-24-32 W; Named for the Upper and Lower Nashotah Lakes. The name is of Indian origin and means "twins."

•**NECEDAH,** Village; Juneau County; Pop. 773; Zip Code 54646; Lat. 44-01-44 N long. 090-04-24 W; Necedah is an Indian name which means either "let there be three of us" or "land of the yellow waters," referring to the Yellow River.

•NEENAH, City; Winnebago County; Pop. 22,432; Zip Code 54956; Lat. 41-54-52 N long. 083-55-32 W; First called Winnebago Rapids. Later renamed from the Winnebago Indian word for "running water."

•NEILLSVILLE, City; Clark County Seat; Pop. 2,780; Zip Code 54456; Lat. 44-33-12 N long. 090-35-20 W; First known as O'Neill's Mills, and later Neillsville for James O'Neill, who ran a sawmill here.

•NEKOOSA, City; Wood County; Pop. 2,519; Zip Code 54457; Lat. 44-19-09 N long. 089-54-13 W; Named Whitney's Rapids, and then Point Boss, Point Basse, or just Boss. In 1893, the town was named Nekoosa from an Indian word meaning "running water."

•NELSON, Village; Buffalo County; Pop. 389; Zip Code 54756; Lat. 44-25-16 N long. 092-00-23 W; Called Nelson's Landing and eventually shortened to Nelson, after James Nelson, a settler.

•NELSONVILLE, Village; Portage County; Pop. 199; Zip Code 54458; Lat. 44-29-54 N long. 089-16-12 W; Named for Jerome Nelson who purchased land and built a grist mill here.

•NEOSHO, Village; Dodge County; Pop. 575; Zip Code 53059; Elev. 883; Lat. 43-18-13 N long. 088-31-15 W; Taken from an Indian word meaning "point of land projecting into a lake." White settlers at one time called this place Cotton's Mill.

•NESHKORO, Village; Marquette County; Pop. 386; Zip Code 54960; Elev. 800; Lat. 43-58-00 N long. 089-13-00 W; Named wither from a Winnebago word meaning "salt" or "sweet water," or from a combination of Nash and Kora, the names of two early settlers.

•NEW AUBURN, Village; Chippewa County; Pop. 466; Zip Code 54757; Lat. 45-12-00 N long. 091-34-21 W; First called Cartwright's Mills, later Cartwright. The origin of the present name, New Auburn, is not certain.

•NEW BERLIN, City; Waukesha County; Pop. 30,529; Named Mentor in 1838. In 1840 it was changed to New Berlin, after the hometown in New York of settler, Sidney Evans.

•NEW GLARUS, Village; Green County; Pop. 1,763; Zip Code 53574; Lat. 42-49-07 N long. 089-38-07 W; Named by Swiss settlers, for Canton Glarus, in which authorities in Switzerland decided to send families to the United States to escape the famine and unemployment in their homeland.

•NEW HOLSTEIN, City; Calumet County; Pop. 3,412; Zip Code 53061; Elev. 935; Lat. 43-56-42 N long. 088-05-32 W; Named for the home of settler Ferdinand Ostenfeld in Schleswig-Holstein, Germany.

•NEW LISBON, City; Juneau County; Pop. 1,390; Zip Code 53950; Elev. 891; Lat. 43-52-20 N long. 090-09-52 W; Indians called this site of their winter camps, Wa-du-shuda meaning "we leave canoe here." White settlers named the place Mill Haven, and later New Lisbon, probably after Lisbon, Ohio.

•NEW LONDON, City; Waupaca County; Pop. 6,210; Zip Code 54961; Elev. 789; Lat. 44-23-22 N long. 088-43-54 W; Established in 1852 and named for New London, Connecticut, the birthplace of the father of Reeder Smith, one of the city developers.

•NEW RICHMOND, City; St. Croix County; Pop. 4,306; Zip Code 54017; Elev. 982; Lat. 45-07-10 N long. 092-32-25 W; First called Foster's Crossing. Later named for Richmond Day, the town surveyor.

•NIAGARA, Village; Marinette County; Pop. 2,079; Zip Code 54151; Lat. 45-46-26 N long. 087-59-52 W; Probably derived from the Iroquois Indian word Oh-nia-ga meaning "bisected bottom land."

•NICHOLS, Village; Outagamie County; Pop. 267; Zip Code 54152; Lat. 44-33-54 N long. 088-27-50 W; Named for Albert L. Nichols, who established the town.

•NORTH BAY, Village; Racine County; Pop. 219; Platted in 1926 and probably named for its location on a bay in Lake Michigan.

•NORTH FREEDOM, Village; Sauk County; Pop. 616; Zip Code 53951; Elev. 867; Lat. 43-27-12 N long. 089-51-42 W; First called Hackett's Corners, after the Hackett family. Later named North Freedom, then Bessemer, for Sir Henry Bessemer. Upon incorporation in 1893, the named North Freedom was reinstated, from the village's location at the north side of the town of Freedom.

•NORTH PRAIRIE, Village; Waukesha County; Pop. 938; Zip Code 53153; Lat. 42-56-19 N long. 088-24-08 W; Settled in 1836 and named for the beautiful prairie land here. Because there was another prairie two miles to the south, this one was termed "north."

•NORWALK, Village; Monroe County; Pop. 517; Zip Code 54648; Elev. 1030; Lat. 43-49-43 N long. 090-37-27 W; S. McGary, an early settler, named this village after Norwalk, Ohio.

•OAKFIELD, Village; Fond du Lac County; Pop. 990; Zip Code 53065; Elev. 894; Lat. 43-41-07 N long. 088-32-40 W; Earlier names for this area were Avoca, and Lime, for the limeston quarries. Renamed Oakfield for the oak trees that grew on the edges of fields.

•OCONOMOWOC, City; Waukesha County; Pop. 9,909; Zip Code 53066; Elev. 873; Lat. 43-06-22 N long. 088-28-39 W; An Indian name, from the word Coo-no-mo-wauk meaning "waterfall," "beautiful waters" or "river of lakes," referring to the string of lakes joined by the Oconomowoc River.

•OCONOMOWOC LAKE, Village; Waukesha County; Pop. 524; From the Indian name Coo-no-mo-wauk which can be translated as "beautiful waters."

•OCONTO, City; Oconto County Seat; Pop. 4,505; Zip Code 54153; Elev. 591; Lat. 44-53-57 N long. 087-51-32 W; Named for the river, whose name was probably derived from okato, o-kon-to or oak-a-toe, Menominee Indian word meaning "pike place," "boat paddle," "river of plentiful fishes," or "black bass;" or from the Chippewa word okando meaning "he watches" or "lies in ambush."

•OCONTO FALLS, City; Oconto County; Pop. 2,500; Zip Code 54154; Elev. 735; Lat. 44-52-31 N long. 088-07-57 W; Named for falls on the Oconto River.

•OGDENSBURG, Village; Waupaca County; Pop. 214; Zip Code 54962; Elev. 861; Lat. 44-27-16 N long. 089-01-25 W; Named for Judge Ogden, who founded the village in 1848.

•OMRO, City; Winnebago County; Pop. 2,763; Zip Code 54963; Lat. 44-02-19 N long. 088-44-21 W; First called Smalley's Landing, later Beckwith Town, for settler, Nelson Beckwith. Platted in 1849 as Omro, in honor of Charles Omro, an Indian trader.

•ONALASKA, City; La Crosse County; Pop. 9,249; Zip Code 54650; Elev. 716; Lat. 43-53-01 N long. 091-13-36 W; The name may either come from an Indian word meaning "bright water," or from Campbell's poem "Pleasure of Hope" which has the line "The wolf's long howl from Oonalaska's shore."

•ONTARIO, Village; Vernon County; Pop. 398; Zip Code 54651; Lat. 43-43-25 N long. 090-35-25 W; O.H. Millard suggested this name, after Ontario County in New York.

•OOSTBURG, Village; Sheboygan County; Pop. 1,647; Zip Code 53070; Lat. 43-36-34 N long. 087-47-59 W; Settled by the Dutch and named for a village in Holland.

•OREGON, Village; Dane County; Pop. 3,876; Zip Code 53575; Elev. 949; Lat. 37-37-43 N long. 078-13-41 W; First called Rome Corners. In 1847 it was renamed Oregon, after the state.

•ORFORDVILLE, Village; Rock County; Pop. 1,143; Zip Code 53576; Lat. 42-37-49 N long. 089-15-33 W; Named after the town of Orford, New Hampshire. The "ville" was added later because of confusion with Oxford.

•OSHKOSH, City; Winnebago County Seat; Pop. 49,678; Zip Code 549+; Lat. 43-01-43 N long. 086-33-22 W; Named for Indian Chief Oskosh. Over a period of time the first "H" was added and the emphasis placed on the last syllable.

•PALMYRA, Village; Jefferson County; Pop. 1,515; Zip Code 53156; Elev. 848; Lat. 42-51-36 N long. 088-35-22 W; Named after Palmyra, Syria, the oasis city mentioned in the Bible. The name means "sandy soil" and is appropriate since this village has sandy earth.

•PARDEEVILLE, Village; Columbia County; Pop. 1,594; Zip Code 53954; Elev. 815; Lat. 43-32-19 N long. 089-17-49 W; Named for John S. Pardee, a Milwaukee merchant and the U.S. consul to San Juan del Sur, Nicaragua.

•PARK FALLS, City; Price County; Pop. 3,192; Zip Code 54552; Elev. 1490; Lat. 45-56-09 N long. 090-26-51 W; First called Muskallonge Falls. In 1885 the name was changed to Park Falls, both for the falls on the river and for the parklike landscape in the area.

•PARK RIDGE, Village; Portage County; Pop. 643; Named for its location on a ridge by the Plover River. Originally spelled Parkridge.

•PATCH GROVE, Village; Grant County; Pop. 259; Zip Code 53817; Lat. 42-56-19 N long. 090-58-15 W; First known as Finntown, for Enos Finn, a settler. Later named for Henry Patch, who built a cabin near a grove of trees, and often accomodated travelers.

•PEPIN, Village; Pepin County; Pop. 890; Zip Code 54759; Lat. 44-26-03 N long. 092-08-42 W; Called Pepin after the lake, which was named by early French explorers, either for a companion of Duluth who came here in 1679, or for a French king Pepin le Bref.

•PESHTIGO, City; Marinette County; Pop. 2,807; Zip Code 54157; Lat. 45-03-39 N long. 087-45-05 W; The name is Indian, for either "snapping turtle" or "wild goose."

•PEWAUKEE, Village; Waukesha County; Pop. 4,637; Zip Code 53072; Elev. 591; Lat. 35-54-06 N long. 073-28-23 W; The village took its name from the lake, which Potawatomi Indians called Pewaukeewinick or "snail lake."

•PHILLIPS, City; Price County Seat; Pop. 1,522; Zip Code 54555; Lat. 45-37-06 N long. 090-20-43 W; Platted in 1876 and named for Elijah B. Phillips, general manager of the Wisconsin Central Railroad Company.

•PIGEON FALLS, Village; Trempealeau County; Pop. 338; Zip Code 54760; Elev. 882; Lat. 44-27-29 N long. 091-13-01 W; A descriptive name, for the falls here, and for wild passenger pigeons that lived in the area.

•PITTSVILLE, City; Wood County; Pop. 810; Zip Code 54466; Lat. 44-26-30 N long. 090-07-10 W; First called Pitt's Mill, later Pittsville, for Oliver Wright Pitts, who settled here in 1856 and built a sawmill.

•PLAIN, Village; Sauk County; Pop. 676; Zip Code 53577; Lat. 43-14-37 N long. 090-02-36 W; Named Cramers Corners, for settlers John and Adam Cramer. In 1852 it was named Logtown, for the logging here. Later changed to Plain, from Maria Von Plain in Austria.

•PLAINFIELD, Village; Waushara County; Pop. 813; Zip Code 54966; Lat. 44-12-54 N long. 089-29-24 W; First known as Norwich. Later named for Elijah C. Waterman's former home in Plainfield, Vermont.

•PLATTEVILLE, City; Grant County; Pop. 9,580; Zip Code 53818; Elev. 994; Lat. 42-44-19 N long. 090-28-42 W; Named Platte River Diggings in 1827. Later called Lebanon, and then Platteville, after the Platte River.

•PLOVER, Village; Portage County; Pop. 5,310; Zip Code 54467; Elev. 1075; Lat. 44-27-20 N long. 089-32-34 W; Chippewa Indians called this place a name meaning "prairie." Later renamed for the Plover River.

•PLUM CITY, Village; Pierce County; Pop. 505; Zip Code 54761; Lat. 44-37-340 N long. 092-11-56 W; Named after nearby Plum Creek, which took its name from the many plum trees on its banks.

•PLYMOUTH, City; Sheboygan County; Pop. 6,027; Zip Code 53073; Lat. 43-43-35 N long. 087-58-38 W; Settled in 1845 by Henry Davidson and his son Thomas. The city was named for Plymouth, Massachusetts, the home of Thomas' girlfriend.

•POPLAR, Village; Douglas County; Pop. 569; Zip Code 54864; Lat. 46-35-04 N long. 091-47-12 W; Originally part of the town of Brule. The village was named for the poplar trees that grew up quickly here after the land had been logged.

•PORT EDWARDS, Village; Wood County; Pop. 2,077; Zip Code 54469; Elev. 975; Lat. 44-21-23 N long. 089-51-46 W; First called Frenchtown, for the large French population. Later named for John Edwards, Sr., who built a sawmill here in 1840.

•PORT WASHINGTON, City; Ozaukee County; Pop. 8,612; Zip Code 53074; Elev. 612; Lat. 43-23-18 N long. 087-52-49 W; Originally named Green Bay, then Wisconsin Bay, and later Washington, after George Washington. "Port" was added to the name after a pier was built and the city became a center for commerce.

•PORTAGE, City; Columbia County Seat; Pop. 7,896; Zip Code 53901; Lat. 43-32-39 N long. 089-27-37 W; The French named this place le portage, and throughout Wisconsin history, this portage on the Fox-Wisconsin River has been an important landmark.

•POTOSI, Village; Grant County; Pop. 736; Zip Code 53820; Lat. 42-41-28 N long. 090-42-05 W; Earlier called Snake Hollow. Renamed Potosi, possibly after the famous Potosi Mine in South America.

•POUND, Village; Marinette County; Pop. 407; Zip Code 54161; Lat. 45-05-53 N long. 088-02-03 W; An early name for the area was Beaver Creek. The village was called Pound, after Thaddeus C. Pound, U.S. Representative from the state.

•POYNETTE, Village; Columbia County; Pop. 1,447; Zip Code 53955; Elev. 847; Lat. 43-23-20 N long. 089-24-12 W; Named Pauquette, after Pierre Pauquette, an Indian interpreter and trader. The name was corrupted to Poynette.

•PRAIRIE DU CHIEN, City; Crawford County Seat; Pop. 5,859; Zip Code 53821; Elev. 632; Lat. 43-02-41 N long. 091-08-41 W; The name came from a Fox Indian Chief know as Dog. Prairie du Chien or Dog's Prairie was the name the French gave to this place.

•**PRAIRIE DU SAC,** Village; Sauk County; Pop. 2,145; Zip Code 53578; Lat. 43-15-41 N long. 089-43-14 W; French for Sauk Prairie, for a Sauk Indian village once located here on the prairie.

•**PRAIRIE FARM,** Village; Barron County; Pop. 387; Zip Code 54762; Lat. 45-14-03 N long. 091-58-54 W; Named for farms the Knapp Stout Lumber Company established here on the prairie.

•**PRENTICE,** Village; Price County; Pop. 605; Zip Code 54556; Lat. 45-32-38 N long. 090-17-25 W; Either named for Alexander Prentice, the town's first postmaster, or for Jackson L. Prentice, an early surveyor.

•**PRESCOTT,** City; Pierce County; Pop. 2,654; Zip Code 54021; Lat. 44-44-53 N long. 092-47-08 W; First called Mouth of the St. Croix and Lake Mouth. Later named Eizabeth, for Elizabeth Schasser, and then Prescott, after Philander Prescott, an Indian interpreter.

•**PRINCETON,** City; Green Lake County; Pop. 1,479; Zip Code 54968; Lat. 43-51-14 N long. 089-07-20 W; Originally called Treat's Landing, for settler Royal C. Treat. He and his brother later obtained title to 132 acres and laid out a town they called Princeton. The source of the name is not known.

•**PULASKI,** Village; Brown County; Pop. 1,875; Zip Code 54162; Lat. 44-40-14 N long. 088-14-54 W; Named in honor of Count Casimir Pulaski of Revolutionary War fame.

•**RACINE,** City; Racine County Seat; Pop. 85,725; Zip Code 534+; Lat. 42-43-36 N long. 087-48-21 W; Known as Belle City of the Great Lakes. The name Racine comes from the French translation of the Potawatomi title for the river here: "Roots."

•**RADISSON,** Village; Sawyer County; Pop. 280; Zip Code 54867; Elev. 1245; Lat. 45-46-03 N long. 091-12-56 W; Named in honor of Pierre Esprit Radisson, who explored this area around 1659.

•**RANDOLPH,** Village; Dodge County; Pop. 1,691; Zip Code 539+; Elev. 964; Lat. 43-32-15 N long. 089-00-13 W; Originally called LeRoy, then Conversville, for settler Jon Converse, and later Westford. In 1870, the village was incorporated as Randolph, after Randolph in Vermont.

•**RANDOM LAKE,** Village; Sheboygan County; Pop. 1,287; Zip Code 53075; Elev. 901; Lat. 43-32-50 N long. 087-57-40 W; Known as Greenleaf, for E.D. Greenleaf, a financial agent for the railroad company. Later named for nearby Random Lake.

•**READSTOWN,** Village; Vernon County; Pop. 396; Zip Code 54652; Elev. 760; Lat. 43-26-56 N long. 090-45-56 W; Named for Daniel Read who platted the village in 1855.

•**RED GRANITE,** Village; Waushara County; Pop. 976; Zip Code 54970; Elev. 789; Lat. 44-02-36 N long. 089-06-50 W; Built up around a red granite quarry, and named for the stone.

•**REEDSBURG,** City; Sauk County; Pop. 5,038; Zip Code 53959; Elev. 926; Lat. 43-32-21 N long. 090-00-08 W; Named for David C. Reed, who founded the city in 1850.

•**REEDVILLE,** Village; Manitowoc County; Pop. 1,134; Zip Code 54230; Lat. 44-09-15 N long. 087-57-16 W; First called Mud Creek. Later named in honor of Judge George Reed of Manitowoc.

•**REESEVILLE,** Village; Dodge County; Pop. 649; Zip Code 53579; Elev. 856; Lat. 43-18-01 N long. 088-50-31 W; Platted and surveyed by Adam Reese, who named this town in honor of his father, Samuel Reese.

•**REWEY,** Village; Iowa County; Pop. 233; Zip Code 53580; Elev. 1140; Lat. 42-50-31 N long. 090-24-01 W; Platted in 1880 and named for J.W. Rewey.

•**RHINELANDER,** City; Oneida County Seat; Pop. 7,873; Zip Code 54501; Elev. 1554; Lat. 45-38-22 N long. 089-24-39 W; Originally named Pelican Rapids. Later changed to Rhinlander, after F.W. Rhineland, president of the railroad company.

•**RIB LAKE,** Village; Taylor County; Pop. 945; Zip Code 54470; Lat. 45-19-00 N long. 090-12-28 W; So named because the lake here is said to be shaped like a rib.

•**RICE LAKE,** City; Barron County; Pop. 7,691; Zip Code 54868; Lat. 45-30-07 N long. 091-44-21 W; The area was once a swamp where Indians gathered wild rice. Around 1868, the Knapp Stout Lumber Company built a dam here which turned the swamp into Rice Lake.

•**RICHLAND CENTER,** City; Richland County; Pop. 4,997; Zip Code 53581; Elev. 731; Lat. 43-19-57 N long. 090-27-10 W; So named for its location at the center of Richland County.

•**RIDGELAND,** Village; Dunn County; Pop. 300; Zip Code 54763; Lat. 45-12-36 N long. 091-54-10 W; Named for the ridges on either side of town.

•**RIVER FALLS,** City; Pierce County; Pop. 9,036; Zip Code 54022; Lat. 44-51-21 N long. 092-37-17 W; First called Kinnickinnic, the Indian name for the river. Later named Greenwood, but changed to River Falls, for the falls here, after it was discovered there was already a Greenwood in the state.

•**RIVER HILLS,** Village; Milwaukee County; Pop. 1,642; Edwin B. Bartlett suggested the name River Hills, because he considered river and hills to be pleasant country.

•**ROBERTS,** Village; St. Croix County; Pop. 833; Zip Code 54023; Lat. 44-58-57 N long. 092-33-19 W; Originally located in Warren Township. Later moved south and named Roberts, after a railroad man.

•**ROCHESTER,** Village; Racine County; Pop. 746; Zip Code 53167; Elev. 777; Lat. 42-44-24 N long. 088-13-24 W; Settlers named this village after their former home in Rochester, New York.

•**ROCK SPRINGS,** Village; Sauk County; Pop. 426; Zip Code 53961; Lat. 43-28-33 N long. 089-54-50 W; First called Excelsior, the New York state motto. Renamed Rock Springs, from natural springs in the rocks here. Also called Ableman's Mills and Ableman for a short time.

•**ROCKDALE,** Village; Dane County; Pop. 200; First called Clinton, later Rockdale, a name descriptive of the location, in a valley between two rock ridges.

•**ROCKLAND,** Village; La Crosse County; Pop. 383; Zip Code 54653; Elev. 752; Lat. 43-54-14 N long. 090-55-13 W; Named for a prominent rock ledge found here.

•**ROSENDALE,** Village; Fond du Lac County; Pop. 725; Zip Code 54974; Elev. 875; Lat. 43-48-35 N long. 088-40-18 W; Settlers arriving here saw a beautiful dale with roses, thus the name, Rosendale.

•**ROSHOLT,** Village; Portage County; Pop. 520; Zip Code 54473; Lat. 44-37-59 N long. 089-15-37 W; Named for J.G. Rosholt who platted the village.

•**ROTHSCHILD,** Village; Marathon County; Pop. 3,338; Zip Code 54474; Lat. 44-55-33 N long. 089-36-58 W; Named for a local man who was nicknamed Baron de Rothschild.

•**RUDOLPH,** Village; Wood County; Pop. 392; Zip Code 54475; Elev. 1138; Lat. 44-29-57 N long. 089-48-02 W; Settled around 1840. In 1856 the town was named for Frederick Rudolph Hecox, the first white boy born here.

•**ST. CLOUD,** Village; Fond du Lac County; Pop. 560; Zip Code 53079; Elev. 930; Lat. 43-49-36 N long. 088-09-58 W; Named after St. Cloud, France.

•**ST. CROIX FALLS,** City; Polk County; Pop. 1,497; Zip Code 54024; Lat. 45-24-15 N long. 092-37-53 W; St. Croix is a French name for Holy Cross. When the city was founded, there was a waterfall here on the St. Croix River, now altered by a power company dam.

•**ST. FRANCIS,** City; Milwaukee County; Pop. 10,066; Indians called this place *No-gosh-ing* meaning "snake" or "enemies." The source of the present name is not known.

•**ST. NAZIANZ,** Village; Manitowoc County; Pop. 738; Zip Code 54232; Lat. 44-00-27 N long. 087-55-35 W; Founded by German immigrants who came to escape religious persecution. They named the village for St. Gregory Nazianz.

•**SAUK CITY,** Village; Sauk County; Pop. 2,703; Zip Code 53583; Elev. 757; Lat. 43-14-39 N long. 089-43-36 W; The village was first called Harszthy, after Count Augustine Harszthy. Later changed to Westfield, and then to the traditional name for the area, Sauk Prairie, which eventually became Sauk City.

•**SAUKVILLE,** Village; Ozaukee County; Pop. 3,494; Zip Code 53080; Lat. 43-23-03 N long. 087-56-24 W; The present town encompasses the early settlements of Voelker's Mills, Schmit's Mill, Mechanicsville and St. Finbars. Named for a Sauk Indian village once located here.

•**SCANDINAVIA,** Village; Waupaca County; Pop. 292; Zip Code 54977; Elev. 931; Lat. 44-27-36 N long. 089-08-19 W; So named because most of the settlers were Scandinavian.

•**SCHOFIELD,** City; Marathon County; Pop. 2,226; Zip Code 54476; Elev. 1198; Lat. 44-56-29 N long. 089-35-59 W; Originally called Scholfield Mill, for Dr. William Scholfield, who built a sawmill here. The "l" was later dropped from the name.

•**SEYMOUR,** City; Outagamie County; Pop. 2,530; Zip Code 54165; Lat. 44-30-31 N long. 088-19-50 W; Named in honor of Horatio Seymour, Governor of New York.

•**SHARON,** Village; Walworth County; Pop. 1,280; Zip Code 53585; Elev. 1027; Lat. 42-30-06 N long. 088-43-55 W; Probably named for the former home of settlers, in Sharon, New York.

•**SHAWANO,** City; Shawano County Seat; Pop. 7,013; Zip Code 54166; Elev. 821; Lat. 44-46-48 N long. 088-35-59 W; Named after Shawano Lake, which was called *Sha-wah-no-hah-pay-sa.* the Menominee words for "lake to the south."

•**SHEBOYGAN,** City; Sheboygan County Seat; Pop. 48,085; Zip Code 530+; Lat. 43-43-54 N long. 087-45-34 W; Named from any of several Indian words. The meanings vary from "pipe stem" or "hollow bone" to "underground river" or "underground noise."

•**SHEBOYGAN FALLS,** City; Sheboygan County; Pop. 5,253; Zip Code 53085; Elev. 659; Lat. 43-42-23 N long. 087-48-55 W; First called Rochester after the city in New York. Later named for falls on the Sheboygan River.

•**SHELDON,** Village; Rusk County; Pop. 292; Zip Code 54766; Elev. 1129; Lat. 45-18-58 N long. 090-57-16 W; Named for an official of the Wisconsin Central Railroad.

•**SHELL LAKE,** City; Washburn County Seat; Pop. 1,135; Zip Code 54871; Lat. 45-44-15 N long. 091-55-08 W; Chippewa Indians called the lake *Mokokesese Sahkiagin* or "frog's navel." In 1855, it was named Frog Lake, and in 1881 a town was laid out and called Summit. Both town and lake were renamed Shell Lake in 1883, because the lake was said to resemble the shape of a shell.

•**SHERWOOD,** Village; Calumet County; Pop. 372; Zip Code 54169; Elev. 1065; Lat. 44-10-23 N long. 088-15-30 W; Established as Lima in 1858. Later called Nicolai's Corners for settler, Steven Nicolai, and then Sherwood for a Civil War veteran of that name.

•**SHIOCTON,** Village; Outagamie County; Pop. 805; Zip Code 54170; Lat. 44-26-32 N long. 088-33-58 W; First called Jordan's Landing or Jordanville, for Dominicus Jordan. Later named Schiocton for Chief Shioc of the Mnominees. His name meant "by force of wind."

•**SHOREWOOD,** Village; Milwaukee County; Pop. 14,327; Platted in 1836 as Mechanicsville. In 1900, the village was incorporated under the name East Milwaukee, later changed to Shorewood, for its location on the shore of Lake Michigan.

•**SHULLSBURG,** City; Lafayette County; Pop. 1,484; Zip Code 53586; Elev. 1021; Lat. 42-34-08 N long. 090-13-48 W; Founded around 1827 and named for Jesse W. Shull, who came to the area in 1818 and established a settlement called Old Shullsburg.

•**SILVER LAKE,** Village; Kenosha County; Pop. 1,598; Zip Code 53170; Lat. 42-32-53 N long. 088-10-07 W; Named for the silvery sheen on the water here.

•**SIREN,** Village; Burnett County; Pop. 896; Zip Code 54872; Elev. 996; Lat. 45-46-45 N long. 092-22-34 W; Charles F. Segerstrom, first postmaster, suggested Syren, the Sweedish name for lilacs, because his house was surrounded by the flowers. The spelling was later corrupted to Siren.

•**SISTER BAY,** Village; Door County; Pop. 564; Zip Code 54234; Elev. 587; Lat. 45-11-10 N long. 087-07-57 W; Named for two "sister islands" in the bay. The place was also known as Pebble Beach, because of the round pebbles on the beaches here.

•**SLINGER,** Village; Washington County; Pop. 1,612; Zip Code 53086; Elev. 1069; Lat. 43-19-50 N long. 088-17-34 W; Called Schleisingerville after B. Schleisinger Weil, who purchased land here. The name was shortened to Slinger in 1921.

•**SOLDIERS GROVE,** Village; Crawford County; Pop. 622; Zip Code 54655; Lat. 43-23-34 N long. 090-46-31 W; First known as Pine Grove. Changed because there was already another Pine Grove in the state. Villagers retained the word "Grove" and added Soldier, for an army that camped here during the Black Hawk War.

•**SOLON SPRINGS,** Village; Douglas County; Pop. 590; Zip Code 54873; Lat. 46-21-06 N long. 091-48-49 W; Established in 1888 as White Birch. Later named for Tom Solon, a settler who bottled water from a spring on his land.

•**SOMERSET,** Village; St. Croix County; Pop. 860; Zip Code 54025; Lat. 45-07-29 N long. 092-40-38 W; Founded by General Samuel Harriman, who named the village after his father's home of Somerset County, England.

•**SOUTH MILWAUKEE,** City; Milwaukee County; Pop. 21,069; Zip Code 53172; Lat. 42-55-22 N long. 087-53-41 W; Named for its location, just south of the city of Milwaukee.

•**SOUTH WAYNE,** Village; Lafayette County; Pop. 495; Zip Code 53587; Elev. 803; Lat. 42-33-36 N long. 089-52-40 W; The area was known as Lost Township after an error in survey records. Resurveyed and named Wayne, because settlers here were descendants of men who served with Anthony Wayne.

•**SPARTA,** City; Monroe County Seat; Pop. 6,934; Zip Code 54656; Elev. 793; Lat. 43-56-28 N long. 090-48-37 W; Named after Sparta of ancient Greece.

•**SPENCER,** Village; Marathon County; Pop. 1,754; Zip Code 54479; Lat. 44-49-56 N long. 090-16-40 W; Known by the names Waltham, and then Irene, after the wife of James L. Robinson, who built a sawmill here. Later named for Spencer, Massachusetts.

•**SPOONER,** City; Washburn County; Pop. 2,365; Zip Code 54801; Elev. 1065; Lat. 45-49-37 N long. 091-53-27 W; Named for John C. Spooner, a lawyer for the Chicago, St. Paul, Minneapolis and Omaha Railroad Corporation, who later became a U.S. senator.

•**SPRING GREEN,** Village; Sauk County; Pop. 1,265; Zip Code 53588; Elev. 729; Lat. 43-07-56 N long. 090-04-01 W; Mrs. Turner Williams suggested the name, after hollows nearby which became green earlier in spring than the rest of the surrounding country.

•**SPRING VALLEY,** Village; Pierce County; Pop. 987; Zip Code 54767; Lat. 44-50-37 N long. 092-14-25; Probably named for two principal streams in this valley: Eagle Springs and Berghardt Springs.

•**STANLEY,** City; Chippewa County; Pop. 2,095; Zip Code 54768; Lat. 44-57-50 N long. 090-56-14 W; Platted in 1881 and named for L.C. Stanley of the Northwest Lumber Company.

•**STAR PRAIRIE,** Village; St. Croix County; Pop. 420; Zip Code 54026; Lat. 45-11-48 N long. 092-31-54 W; Major Edmund Otis gave this village its poetic name.

•**STETSONVILLE,** Village; Taylor County; Pop. 487; Zip Code 54480; Lat. 45-04-42 N long. 090-19-03 W; Named for Isaiah F. Stetson, who built the firt sawmill here in 1875.

•**STEUBEN,** Village; Crawford County; Pop. 175; Zip Code 54657; Elev. 675; Lat. 43-10-57 N long. 090-51-27 W; First called Farris' Landing. Renamed in honor of Baron Von Steuben, a German general of the Revolutionary War.

•**STEVENS POINT,** City; Portage County Seat; Pop. 22,970; Zip Code 54481; Elev. 1093; Lat. 44-30-44 N long. 089-33-33 W; The Indians called this a name that meant Hemlock Island. Later it was called First Island, and then Stevens Point, after George Stevens, who started the settlement here.

•**STOCKBRIDGE,** Village; Calumet County; Pop. 567; Zip Code 53088; Lat. 44-04-00 N long. 088-18-48 W; Named for the Stockbridge Indians who migrated from the east coast to this area around 1830.

•**STOCKHOLM,** Village; Pepin County; Pop. 104; Zip Code 54769; Elev. 690; Lat. 44-28-21 N long. 092-15-15 W; Named by settlers from Sweeden, after the capital city of their nation.

•**STODDARD,** Village; Vernon County; Pop. 762; Zip Code 54658; Elev. 646; Lat. 43-40-08 N long. 091-13-00 W; Henry Hewitt White named this village in honor of Colonel S. Stoddard, former mayor of La Crosse.

•**STOUGHTON,** City; Dane County; Pop. 7,589; Zip Code 53589; Lat. 42-55-08 N long. 089-14-32 W; Named for Luke Stoughton, who bought the land in 1847 and platted the village.

•**STRATFORD,** Village; Marathon County; Pop. 1,385; Zip Code 54484; Lat. 44-52-02 N long. 090-03-44 W; The Connors family, who bought land and built a mill here, named this for their original home in Stratford, Ontario.

•**STRUM,** Village; Trempealeau County; Pop. 944; Zip Code 54770; Lat. 44-35-22 N long. 091-23-50 W; First known as Tilden, for statesman Samuel J. Tilden. Renamed in 1890 for Louis (or Peter) Strum, who was latr a state senator from this district.

•**STURGEON BAY,** City; Door County Seat; Pop. 8,847; Zip Code 54235; Elev. 588; Lat. 44-49-54 N long. 0807-22-14 W; Called Graham in 1855, then Ottumba, and then Graham again. In 1860, it was named Sturgeon Bay because the bay here had a lot of sturgeon fish.

•**STURTEVANT,** Village; Racine County; Pop. 4,130; Zip Code 53177; Elev. 727; Lat. 42-44-04 N long. 087-51-47 W; First named Johnson, for postmaster William M. Johnson. Later called Western Union Junction, then Corliss, and finally, Sturtevant, after the B.F. Sturtevant Company.

•**SULLIVAN,** Village; Jefferson County; Pop. 434; Zip Code 53178; Elev. 860; Lat. 43-00-54 N long. 088-35-23 W; Named Winfield in 1879 because a field between the woods here was open to the wind. Renamed Sullivan in 1883, possibly for John Sullivan, a transient workman.

•**SUN PRAIRIE,** City; Dane County; Pop. 12,931; Zip Code 53590; Lat. 43-11-35 N long. 089-13-05 W; So named because, for a group of workmen traveling out of Milwaukee in 1837 and breaking the wilderness, this was the first place they saw sun on their ten day trip.

•**SUPERIOR,** City; Douglas County Seat; Pop. 29,571; Zip Code 54836; Elev. 642; Lat. 46-29-39 N long. 092-16-41 W; Incorporated and named for Lake Superior. Champlain, the explorer, called the lake Grand Lac, and later Father Marquette named it Lac Superieur de Tracy.

•**SURING,** Village; Oconto County; Pop. 581; Zip Code 54174; Elev. 804; Lat. 45-00-14 N long. 088-21-28 W; Named for John Suring and his wife, pioneer settlers who built a sawmill here.

•**SUSSEX,** Village; Waukesha County; Pop. 3,482; Zip Code 53089; Lat. 43-08-04 N long. 088-13-23 W; The village was laid out by the Weaver brothers, to resemble their former home of Sussex, England.

•**TAYLOR,** Village; Jackson County; Pop. 411; Zip Code 54659; Lat. 44-18-40 N long. 091-07-26 W; Settled around 1854 and named for a railroad official.

•**TENNYSON,** Village; Grant County; Pop. 476; First called Dutch Hollow by settlers from Holland. The source of the present name is not known.

•**THERESA,** Village; Dodge County; Pop. 766; Zip Code 53091; Lat. 43-31-05 N long. 088-27-45 W; Founded by Solomon Juneau, who named the village after his mother, Theresa.

•**THIENSVILLE,** Village; Ozaukee County; Pop. 3,341; Zip Code 53092; Lat. 42-47-16 N long. 087-09-53 W; First known as Mequon River. Later namedfor Joachim Heinrich Thein, a German settler who built the first mill and laid out the village.

•**TOMAH,** City; Monroe County; Pop. 7,204; Zip Code 54660; Lat. 43-58-39 N long. 090-30-08 W; Named for Chief Thomas Carron of the Menominees. The French pronounced his name Tomah.

•**TOMAHAWK,** City; Lincoln County; Pop. 3,527; Zip Code 54487; Lat. 45-28-25 N long. 089-43-40 W; Named after the Tomahawk River, which got its name when warring Sioux and Chippewa Indians buried a tomahawk, or Indian hatchet, here as a symbol of peace between the two tribes.

•**TONY,** Village; Rusk County; Pop. 146; Zip Code 54563; Lat. 45-28-39 N long. 090-59-27 W; First called Deer Tail, after a nearby creek. Later named for Tony Hein of the Hein Lumber Company.

•**TREMPEALEAU,** Village; Trempealeau County; Pop. 956; Zip Code 54661; Elev. 691; Lat. 44-00-29 N long. 091-26-21 W; First known as Reed's Landing or Reed's Town, then Montoville or Mountainville. Later changed to Trempealeau after the nearby island mountain which Indians called "mountain soaked in water" and the French named La Montagne qui trempe a l'eau.

•TURTLE LAKE, Village; Barron County; Pop. 762; Zip Code 54889; Elev. 1264; Lat. 45-23-30 N long. 092-08-55 W; Named Skowhagen, after the former home in Maine of settler, Joel Richardson. Later changed to Turtle Lake, after the nearby lake which was named for turtle's eggs on its shore.

•TWIN LAKES, Village; Kenosha County; Pop. 3,474; Zip Code 53181; Lat. 42-31-26 N long. 088-15-24 W; The village took its name from two lakes, known as twin lakes.

•TWO RIVERS, City; Manitowoc County; Pop. 13,354; Zip Code 54241; Lat. 44-09-13 N long. 087-35-08 W; Named for its location between the North and South Twin Rivers.

•UNION GROVE, Village; Racine County; Pop. 3,517; Zip Code 53182; Lat. 42-41-05 N long. 088-03-05 W; Governor Dodge is said to have named this village, for the Union School established here in 1846, and for a grove of burr oak trees nearby.

•UNITY, Village; Marathon County; Pop. 418; Zip Code 54488; Elev. 1338; Lat. 44-52-24 N long. 090-18-17 W; Possibly named by Mrs. Edmund Creed, because the community was very "united."

•VALDERS, Village; Manitowoc County; Pop. 984; Zip Code 54245; Elev. 840; Lat. 44-04-05 N long. 087-53-16 W; Named by settlers from Valders, Norway.

•VERONA, City; Dane County; Pop. 3,336; First called The Corners because two main roads crossed here. Later named Verona Corners, and then Verona, by settlers from Verona, New York.

•VESPER, Village; Wood County; Pop. 554; Zip Code 54489; Elev. 1110; Lat. 44-29-11 N long. 089-57-40 W; An early suggestion for the name was Hardscrabble. Around 1882, the post office was asked to select a better name, and came up with Vesper.

•VIROQUA, City; Vernon County Seat; Pop. 3,716; Zip Code 54665; Lat. 43-33-20 N long. 090-53-17 W; Platted in 1850 and named Farwell, after Governor Farwell. In 1854 the name was changed to Viroqua, said to be the name of an Indian girl.

•WALDO, Village; Sheboygan County; Pop. 416; Zip Code 53093; Elev. 838; Lat. 43-39-28 N long. 087-56-42 W; First called Lora, then Lyndon Station. Later namedfor O.H. Waldo, president of the Milwaukee and Northern Railroad.

•WALES, Village; Waukesha County; Pop. 1,992; Zip Code 53183; Elev. 1002; Lat. 43-00-23 N long. 088-22-45 W; Settled by Welsh immigrants and named for their home country.

•WALWORTH, Village; Walworth County; Pop. 1,607; Zip Code 53184; Elev. 998; Lat. 42-31-59 N long. 088-35-39 W; Named Douglass Corners, for settler, Christopher Douglass. Later changed to Walworth, after the county, which was named in honor of Reuben Hyde Walworth.

•WARRENS, Village; Monroe County; Pop. 300; Zip Code 54666; Lat. 44-07-44 N long. 090-29-56 W; Originally called Warren's Mills, for George Warren who started a sawmill here. The name was leter shortened to Warrens.

•WATERFORD, Village; Racine County; Pop. 2,051; Zip Code 53185; Lat. 42-45-47 N long. 088-12-48 W; The name is said to be from an old Indian ford across the Fox River at this site.

•WATERLOO, City; Jefferson County; Pop. 2,393; Zip Code 53594; Elev. 819; Lat. 43-12-29 N long. 088-59-21 W; Indians called this place Maunesha. Settler, Bradford Hill renamed the spot after the battle of Waterloo.

•WATERTOWN, City; Jefferson County; Pop. 18,113; Zip Code 53094; Elev. 823; Lat. 43-12-17 N long. 088-43-14 W; The Indian name was Ka-Ka-ree or "ox bow," referring to the bend here in the Rock River. White settlers called the place Johnson's Rapids, and later Watertown, after Watertown, New York.

•WAUKESHA, City; Waukesha County Seat; Pop. 50,319; Zip Code 531+; Elev. 821; Lat. 41-25-29 N long. 084-55-28 W; First called Prairieville. When Waukesha County was formed, the town was made county seat, and named Waukesha, the Potawatomi word for "fox."

•WAUNAKEE, Village; Dane County; Pop. 3,866; Zip Code 53597; Elev. 925; Lat. 41-13-19 N long. 085-23-20 W; The village was wither named for a friendly Indian who camped near here, or from an Indian word said to mean "you win," "sharpshooter," "he lies," or "he lives in peace."

•WAUPACA, City; Waupaca County Seat; Pop. 4,472; Zip Code 54981; Lat. 44-20-59 N long. 089-04-41 W; Derived from an Indian word which could mean: "where one waits for deer," "looking on," "white sand bottom," "pale water," or "tomorrow."

•WAUPUN, City; Dodge County; Pop. 8,132; Zip Code 53963; Elev. 904; Lat. 43-37-50 N long. 088-44-08 W; First named Madrid, after Madrid, Vermont. Later renamed from the Indian word Waubun meaning "dawn" or "early light of day."

•WAUSAU, City; Marathon County Seat; Pop. 32,426; Zip Code 54401; Lat. 44-58-05 N long. 089-38-15 W; The name is a Chippewa Indian word meaning "far away."

•WAUSAUKEE, Village; Marinette County; Pop. 648; Zip Code 54177; Elev. 741; Lat. 45-22-35 N long. 087-57-10 W; First named Big Wausaukee, then simply Wausaukee, from the Indian word meaning "river among the hills," "beyond the hill," or "far away land."

•WAUTOMA, City; Waushara County Seat; Pop. 1,629; Zip Code 54982; Elev. 867; Lat. 44-04-21 N long. 089-17-24 W; The name is a combination of the Indian words wau meaning "good," "life," or "earth," and tomah for "land of Tomah," the name of an Indian chief.

•WAUWATOSA, City; Milwaukee County; Pop. 51,308; Settlers called this place Hart's Mills, after mill owner Chrarles Hart. Later named for Wauwautosa, an Indian chief, whose name is said to mean "great walker."

•WAUZEKA, Village; Crawford County; Pop. 580; Zip Code 53826; Elev. 657; Lat. 43-05-07 N long. 090-53-54 W; Probably named for an Indian, Wauzega, who lived in the area. The name means either "white pine" or "wrinkled."

•WEBSTER, Village; Burnett County; Pop. 610; Zip Code 54893; Lat. 45-52-36 N long. 092-21-42 W; First called Clam River. Later named for Noah Webster, the famous lexicographer.

•WEST ALLIS, City; Milwaukee County; Pop. 63,982; Parts of this city formerly were called North Greenfield and Honey Creek. The present name came from Allis-Chalmers, a manufacturing plant established here.

•WEST BEND, City; Washington County; Pop. 21,484; Zip Code 530+; Elev. 893; Lat. 43-25-05 N long. 088-11-25 W; The city combines the early settlements of Salisbury's Mills (later called Barton), and West Bend. West Bend got its name from a curve in the Milwaukee River.

•WEST SALEM, Village; La Crosse County; Pop. 3,276; Zip Code 54669; Elev. 742; Lat. 43-53-44 N long. 091-04-49 W; First called Salem because it means "peace" and was considered a good omen for the town. "West" was added later to distinguish the village from Salem in Kenosha County.

•**WESTBY,** City; Vernon County; Pop. 1,797; Zip Code 54667; Elev. 1298; Lat. 43-39-20 N long. 090-51-29 W; Named for Ole T. Westby, who built a store here in 1867.

•**WESTFIELD,** Village; Marquette County; Pop. 1,033; Zip Code 53964; Elev. 865; Lat. 43-53-09 N long. 089-29-20 W; Founded by Robert Cochrane and named for his former home in Westfield, New York.

•**WEYAUWEGA,** City; Waupaca County; Pop. 1,549; Zip Code 54983; Lat. 44-19-00 N long. 088-55-54 W; Originally an Indian village by this name was located here. The name means "here we rest."

•**WEYERHAUSER,** Village; Rusk County; Pop. 313; Zip Code 54895; Elev. 1203; Lat. 45-25-26 N long. 091-24-42 W; Named for Frederick Weyerhauser, of the Weyerhauser Lumber Company, which located one of its headquarters here.

•**WHEELER,** Village; Dunn County; Pop. 231; Zip Code 54772; Elev. 938; Lat. 45-02-48 N long. 091-54-30 W; Known as Lochiel, and then Welton, after homesteader, Maria L. Welton. Later named for H.D. Wheeler, the first postmaster.

•**WHITEHALL,** City; Tremealeau County Seat; Pop. 1,530; Zip Code 54773; Elev. 820; Lat. 44-23-42 N long. 091-19-19 W; Named after Whitehall, Illinois.

•**WHITE LAKE,** Village; Langlade County; Pop. 309; Zip Code 54491; Elev. 1286; Lat. 45-09-54 N long. 088-46-02 W; The village took its name from the lake, which before the advent of the lumber mills, had a white sand bottom.

•**WHITEFISH BAY,** Village; Milwaukee County; Pop. 14,930; Incorporated in 1892 and named for the many whitefish found in the bay.

•**WHITELAW,** Village; Manitowoc County; Pop. 649; Zip Code 54247; Elev. 857; Lat. 44-08-39 N long. 087-49-28 W; First called Pine Grove Siding. Later named either for Whitelaw Reed, a railroad official, or for a Mr. White, who established the post office here in 1892.

•**WHITEWATER,** City; Walworth County; Pop. 11,520; Zip Code 53190; Lat. 42-49-51 N long. 088-44-42 W; Translated from the Indian name for the river, *Wau-be-gan-naw-po-cat* which means "white water."

•**WILD ROSE,** Village; Waushara County; Pop. 741; Zip Code 54984; Elev. 1170; Lat. 44-10-35 N long. 089-14-40 W; Named by settlers from Rose, New York. "Wild" was added, possibly because there were wild roses growing here.

•**WILLIAMS BAY,** Village; Walworth County; Pop. 1,763; Zip Code 53191; Lat. 42-34-28 N long. 088-32-34 W; Named for Israel Williams, a settler.

•**WILTON,** Village; Monroe County; Pop. 465; Zip Code 54670; Elev. 995; Lat. 43-48-39 N long. 090-31-43 W; Settled around 1842. The source of the name is not known.

•**WINNECONNE,** Village; Winnebago County; Pop. 1,935; Zip Code 54986; Elev. 753; Lat. 44-06-41 N long. 088-42-37 W; The name is an Indian word meaning "place of skulls," which came from a battle here in which Sauks and Foxes fought against the French, Menominees and Chippewas.

•**WINTER,** Village; Sawyer County; Pop. 376; Zip Code 54896; Lat. 45-49-23 N long. 091-00-35 W; First known as LeBoef. Later named for John Winter, an official of the Omaha Railroad.

•**WISCONSIN DELLS,** City; Columbia County; Pop. 2,337; Zip Code 53965; Elev. 912; Lat. 43-38-03 N long. 089-46-34 W; Originally called Kilbourn, after Byron Kilbourne. In 1931 it was changed to Wisconsin Dells, a name descriptive of the location.

•**WISCONSIN RAPIDS,** City; Wood County; Pop. 17,995; Zip Code 54494; Lat. 44-24-45 N long. 089-48-00 W; Indians called this "rabbit's place." It was later named for rapids on the Wisconsin River.

•**WITHEE,** Village; Clark County; Pop. 509; Zip Code 54498; Elev. 1272; Lat. 44-57-06 N long. 090-35-46 W; Named for Niran H. Withee, a school teacher, who was influential in village affairs.

•**WITTENBERG,** Village; Shawano County; Pop. 997; Zip Code 54432; Lat. 44-42-49 N long. 089-15-44 W; First called Carbenero, for charcoal kilns. The name Wittenberg was suggest by Pastor E.J. Homme who came here with the intention of establishing a home for orphans and the aged.

•**WONEWOC,** Village; Juneau County; Pop. 842; Zip Code 53968; Elev. 938; Lat. 43-38-30 N long. 090-13-07 W; The name is taken from a Chippewa Indian word that means "to howl" and probably referred to wolves in the area.

•**WOODMAN,** Village; Grant County; Pop. 116; Zip Code 53827; Lat. 43-05-27 N long. 090-47-58 W; Named for Cyrus Woodman, who laid out the village in 1864.

•**WOODVILLE,** Village; St. Croix County; Pop. 725; Zip Code 54028; Lat. 44-57-17 N long. 092-17-53 W; First known as Kelly's Switch. Later named Woodville, either for an early settler, or for the Woodlands that stood here before the logging companies came.

•**WRIGHTSTOWN,** Village; Brown County; Pop. 1,169; Zip Code 54180; Lat. 44-19-39 N long. 088-10-07 W; Named for Hoel S. Wright, who settled here around 1833. At one time the village was called Wright's Ferry.

•**WYEVILLE,** Village; Monroe County; Pop. 163; Zip Code 54671; Lat. 44-01-30 N long. 090-23-04 W.

•**WYOCENA,** Village; Columbia County; Pop. 548; Zip Code 53969; Elev. 826; Lat. 43-29-41 N long. 089-18-26 W; Major Dickason is said to have named this village after a dream he had about an Indian girl named Wyocena. In Potawatomi, the name means "somebody else."

•**YUBA,** Village; Richland County; Pop. 72; Laid out in 1856 and named Yuba, possibly after the gold mining area in California.

WYOMING

•**AFTON,** Town; Lincoln County; Pop. 1,481; Zip Code 831 +; Lat. 42-43-36 N long. 110-55-44 W; Founded in 1879 and named by a Scotch settler for the line from poet Robert Burns: "Flow gently, sweet Afton."

•**ALBIN,** Town; Laramie County; Pop. 128; Zip Code 82050; Elev. 5340; Lat. 41-24-52 N long. 104-05-55 W; Founded in 1905 by John Albin Anderson, the first postmaster, and named for him.

•**BAGGS,** Town; Carbon County; Pop. 433; Zip Code 82321; Elev. 6247; Lat. 41-02-07 N long. 107-39-26 W; Established in 1876 as Dixon and later renamed Baggs for a nearby prominent ranch family.

•**BASIN,** Town; Big Horn County Seat; Pop. 1,349; Zip Code 82410; Elev. 3873; Lat. 44-22-41 N long. 108-02-14 W; Settled in 1897 and named after the Bighorn Basin.

•**BIG PINEY,** Town; Sublette County; Pop. 530; Zip Code 83113; Lat. 42-32-51 N long. 110-06-35 W; The town is named after nearby Big Piney Creek.

•**BUFFALO,** City; Johnson County Seat; Pop. 3,799; Zip Code 828+; Lat. 44-21-02 N long. 106-41-55 W; First settled in 1879 and descriptively named as the main street was an old buffalo trail.

•**BURNS,** Town; Laramie County; Pop. 268; Zip Code 82053; Lat. 41-11-39 N long. 104-21-34 W; The town was founded in 1907 and named for a railroad engineer.

•**BYRON,** Town; Big Horn County; Pop. 633; Zip Code 82412; Lat. 44-47-47 N long. 108-30-13 W; Byron Sessions, an early Mormom settler, influenced the region's development and had the town named for him.

•**CASPER,** City; Natrona County Seat; Pop. 51,016; Zip Code 82601; Lat. 42-50-29 N long. 106-22-59 W; The city is named after Fort Casper, originally called Camp Platte. Fort Casper honors Lt. Caspar Collins who was killed by the Indians near here.

•**CHEYENNE,** City; Laramie County Seat and Capital of Wyoming; Pop. 47,283; Zip Code 82001; Lat. 41-07-34 N long. 104-48-59 W; The city is named after Cheyenne Pass to the west of the city.

•**CHUGWATER,** Town; Platte County; Pop. 282; Zip Code 82210; Lat. 41-45-29 N long. 104-49-12 W; The town was named after Chugwater Creek.

•**CLEARMONT,** Town; Sheridan County; Pop. 191; Zip Code 82835; Lat. 44-38-33 N long. 106-22-57 W; Named after Clear Creek, the town is a livestock shipping center.

•**CODY,** City; Park County Seat; Pop. 6,790; Zip Code 824+; Lat. 44-31-24 N long. 109-03-31 W; Incorporated in 1901 and named in honor of "Buffalo Bill" Cody.

•**COKEVILLE,** Town; Lincoln County; Pop. 515; Zip Code 83114; Lat. 42-05-02 N long. 110-57-21 W; Settled in 1874 and named for the good coking coal in the area.

•**COWLEY,** Town; Big Horn County; Pop. 455; Zip Code 82420; Lat. 44-53-02 N long. 108-28-14 W; The town was settled in 1901 and named for Mormom apostle Mathias F. Cowley.

•**DAYTON,** Town; Sheridan County; Pop. 701; Zip Code 82836; Lat. 44-52-25 N long. 107-15-52 W; Dayton was founded in 1882 and named for banker Joseph Dayton Thorn.

•**DEAVER,** Town; Big Horn County; Pop. 178; Zip Code 82421; Lat. 44-53-21 N long. 108-35-46 W; The town's name honors D. C. Deaver, a railroad agent for the Burligton Railroad.

•**DIAMONDVILLE,** Town; Lincoln County; Pop. 1,000; Zip Code 83116; Lat. 41-46-41 N long. 110-32-11 W; Settled in the 1890's and named for the diamond-like quality of the coal found here.

•**DIXON,** Town; Carbon County; Pop. 82; Zip Code 82323; Elev. 6359; Lat. 41-02-01 N long. 107-31-59 W; The town's name honors Robert Dixon, an old trapper who lived in the area before the coming of the railroad.

•**DOUGLAS,** Town; Converse County Seat; Pop. 6,030; Zip Code 82633; Lat. 42-45-15 N long. 105-22-48 W; Named in honor of U. S. Senator Stephen A. Douglas.

•**DUBOIS,** Town; Fremont County; Pop. 1,067; Zip Code 82513; Lat. 43-32-07 N long. 109-37-49 W; Founded in the 1880's and named after U. S. Senator from Idaho, a Mr. Dubois.

•**EAST THERMOPOLIS,** Town; Hot Springs County; Pop. 359; Lat. 43-38-47 N long. 108-11-51 W; Named for the natural hot springs in the area.

•**EDGERTON,** Town; Natrona County; Pop. 510; Zip Code 82635; Lat. 43-24-52 N long. 106-14-41 W; Located on the edge of the Salt Creek oil field and so descriptively named.

•**ELK MOUNTAIN,** Town; Carbon County; Pop. 338; Zip Code 82324; Lat. 41-41-13 N long. 106-24-37 W; The town is named after nearby Elk Mountain.

•**ENCAMPMENT,** Town; Carbon County; Pop. 611; Zip Code 82325; Lat. 41-12-46 N long. 106-47-09 W; Founded as a copper town and named after the Encampment River.

•**EVANSTON,** City; Uinta County Seat; Pop. 6,421; Zip Code 82930; Elev. 6749; Lat. 41-16-06 N long. 110-57-52 W; Union Pacific Railroad officials founded the town in 1869. They named it for surveyor James A. Evans.

•**EVANSVILLE,** Town; Natrona County; Pop. 2,652; Zip Code 82636; Lat. 42-51-07 N long. 106-14-55 W; Blacksmith W. T. Evans homesteaded here in the 1800's. The town is named after him.

•**FORT LARAMIE,** Town; Goshen County; Pop. 356; Zip Code 82212; Lat. 42-12-43 N long. 104-31-03 W; The town is named for the Laramie River. Laramie is derived from Jacques La Ramie, a French-Canadian trapper killed by the Indians in 1818.

•**FRANNIE,** Town; Big Horn County; Pop. 121; Zip Code 82423; Lat. 44-58-10 N long. 108-37-18 W; Railroad officials named the town for Frannie Morris, an early pioneer.

•**FRANNIE,** Town; Park County; Pop. 17; Named for Frannie Morris, an early pineer woman.

•**GILLETTE,** City; Campbell County Seat; Pop. 12,134; Zip Code 82716; Elev. 4550; Lat. 44-17-34 N long. 105-29-55 W; Weston Gillette, a surveyor and civil engineer, directed the railroad's construction through the area. It is named in his honor.

•**GLENDO,** Town; Platte County; Pop. 367; Zip Code 82213; Elev. 4714; Lat. 42-30-12 N long. 105-01-28 W; The site of an attractive glen, it was christened when railroad officials arrived in 1887.

•**GLENROCK,** Town; Converse County; Pop. 2,736; Zip Code 82637; Lat. 42-51-27 N long. 105-52-18 W; Originally Mercedes, it was later changed to describe a large rock in a glen nearby.

•**GRANGER,** Town; Sweetwater County; Pop. 177; Zip Code 82934; Elev. 6268; Lat. 41-35-45 N long. 109-57-47 W; Originally a stagecoach stop, the town is named after General Goroon Granger.

552

•**GREEN RIVER,** City; Sweetwater County Seat; Pop. 12,807; Zip Code 82935; Elev. 6109; Lat. 41-31-17 N long. 109-27-59 W; The town is named after the Green River. So called for its deep green color.

•**GREYBULL,** Town; Big Horn County; Pop. 2,277; Zip Code 82426; Elev. 3787; Lat. 44-29-32 N long. 108-03-05 W; Named for the river, itself named after an albino buffalo bull which roamed here in Indian days.

•**GUERNSEY,** Town; Platte County; Pop. 1,512; Zip Code 82214; Lat. 42-16-03 N long. 104-44-21 W; The town's name honors rancher and author Charles A. Guernsey, who said "A dreamer lives forever; a toiler but a day."

•**HANNA,** Town; Carbon County; Pop. 2,288; Zip Code 82327; Lat. 41-52-19 N long. 106-32-59 W; A coal mining town named for financier Mark Hanna in 1886.

•**HARTVILLE,** Town; Platte County; Pop. 149; Zip Code 82215; Lat. 42-19-43 N long. 104-43-27 W; The town is named after Major V. K. Hart who owned a copper mine in the vicinity.

•**HUDSON,** Town; Fremont County; Pop. 514; Zip Code 82515; Lat. 42-54-13 N long. 108-34-49 W; Rancher John G. Hudson was the original landowner. It is named in his honor.

•**HULETT,** Town; Crook County; Pop. 291; Zip Code 82720; Lat. 44-41-05 N long. 104-36-08 W; Hulett is named after its first postmaster, Lewis M. Hulett.

•**JACKSON,** Town; Teton County Seat; Pop. 4,511; Zip Code 830+; Lat. 43-28-43 N long. 110-45-37 W; Jackson takes its name from Jackson's Hole, or protected valley.

•**KAYCEE,** Town; Johnson County; Pop. 271; Zip Code 82639; Lat. 43-42-36 N long. 106-38-13 W; The town is named after the K. C. Ranch which flourished here in the 1880's.

•**KEMMERER,** Town; Lincoln County Seat; Pop. 3,273; Zip Code 83101; Lat. 41-47-42 N long. 110-32-24 W; Founded in 1897 and named after the Kemmerer Coal Company.

•**LA BARGE,** Town; Lincoln County; Pop. 302; Zip Code 83123; Lat. 42-15-41 N long. 110-11-38 W; The town is named for La Barge Creek. The creek's name remembers Capt. Joseph La Barge, a Missouri river pilot.

•**LA GRANGE,** Town; Goshen County; Pop. 232; Zip Code 82221; Lat. 41-38-23 N long. 104-09-51 W; Incorporated in 1889 and named for rancher Kale La Grange.

•**LANDER,** City; Fremont County Seat; Pop. 9,126; Zip Code 82520; Lat. 42-50-09 N long. 108-45-04 W; Once called Push Root, the town iwas renamed after surveyor General F. W. Lander in 1857.

•**LARAMIE,** City; Albany County Seat; Pop. 24,410; Zip Code 82057; Elev. 7163; Lat. 41-04-43 N long. 106-09-13 W; The city is named after the Laramie River.

•**LINGLE,** Town; Goshen County; Pop. 475; Zip Code 82223; Elev. 4171; Lat. 42-08-04 N long. 104-20-33 W; Hiram Lingle was a major promoter of the valley's agriculture. The town is named in his honor.

•**LOST SPRINGS,** Town; Converse County; Pop. 9; Zip Code 82224; Lat. 42-45-53 N long. 104-55-31 W; The town is descriptively named for a spring that sinks out of sight over the course of its run.

•**LOVELL,** Town; Big Horn County; Pop. 2,447; Zip Code 82431; Elev. 3837; Lat. 44-50-01 N long. 108-23-17 W; Founded in 1900 and named for area rancher Henry T. Lovell.

•**LUSK,** Town; Niobrara County Seat; Pop. 1,650; Zip Code 82225; Lat. 42-45-25 N long. 104-27-03 W; Begun as a mining town and named for rancher Frank Luck.

•**LYMAN,** Town; Uinta County; Pop. 2,284; Zip Code 82937; Lat. 41-19-47 N long. 110-17-46 W; Francis Lyman, a Mormon apostle, started the town in 1898.

•**MANDERSON,** Town; Big Horn County; Pop. 174; Zip Code 82432; Lat. 44-16-13 N long. 107-57-28 W; Originally called the Alamo, it was renamed in 1889 after a lawyer for the Burlington Railroad.

•**MANVILLE,** Town; Niobrara County; Pop. 94; Zip Code 82227; Lat. 42-46-32 N long. 104-36-39 W; The town is named after H. S. Manville who organized the Converse Cattle Co. in 1880.

•**MARBLETON,** Town; Sublette County; Pop. 537; Lat. 42-33-13 N long. 110-06-31 W; Founded in 1912 and named for A. H. Marble.

•**MEDICINE BOW,** Town; Carbon County; Pop. 953; Zip Code 82329; Elev. 6563; Lat. 41-53-49 N long. 106-11-36 W; The town is named after the Medicine Bow Mountains. The mountains were a source of ash wood for bows and medicinal compounds.

•**MEETEETSE,** Town; Park County; Pop. 512; Zip Code 82433; Elev. 6795; Lat. 44-09-11 N long. 108-52-13 W; A Shoshong Indian name meaning "meeting place."

•**MIDWEST,** Town; Natrona County; Pop. 638; Zip Code 82643; Lat. 43-24-39 N long. 106-16-24 W; Originally Shannon Camp, it was later renamed after the Midwest Oil Company.

•**MILLS,** Town; Natrona County; Pop. 2,139; Zip Code 82644; Lat. 42-51-00 N long. 106-23-07 W; Named for the Mills brothers who helped found the town in 1919.

•**MOORCROFT,** Town; Crook County; Pop. 1,014; Zip Code 82713; Lat. 44-29-21 N long. 104-48-00 W; Named for the first white settler in the area, Alexander Moorcroft.

•**MOUNTAIN VIEW,** Town; Uinta County; Pop. 628; Zip Code 82939; Lat. 41-16-18 N long. 110-20-27 W; Founded in 1891 and named after a local ranch.

•**NEWCASTLE,** City; Weston County Seat; Pop. 3,596; Zip Code 82701; Elev. 4317; Lat. 43-51-08 N long. 104-12-19 W; Settled in 1889 and named for the English city of Newcastle-upon-Tyne.

•**PAVILLION,** Town; Fremont County; Pop. 287; Zip Code 82523; Lat. 43-14-37 N long. 108-41-26 W; The town is named for a nearby pavillion shaped butte.

•**PINE BLUFFS,** Town; Laramie County; Pop. 1,077; Zip Code 82082; Elev. 5040; Lat. 41-11-07 N long. 104-03-51 W; Descriptively named for the pines on nearby bluffs.

•**PINEDALE,** Town; Sublette County Seat; Pop. 1,066; Zip Code 82941; Lat. 42-52-00 N long. 109-51-31 W; Postmaster Charles Peterson named the town for its location on Pine Creek.

•**POWELL,** City; Park County; Pop. 5,310; Zip Code 82435; Lat. 44-45-15 N long. 108-45-21 W; The town's name honors Major John Wesley Powell, engineer and explorer.

•**RANCHESTER,** Town; Sheridan County; Pop. 655; Zip Code 82839; Lat. 44-54-32 N long. 107-09-47 W; Founded in 1894 by Englishman S. H. Hardin who combined the word ranch with Chester, the name of an English city.

•**RAWLINS,** City; Carbon County Seat; Pop. 11,547; Zip Code 823+; Elev. 6769; Lat. 41-47-14 N long. 107-14-13 W; The town's name honors General John A. Rawlins who helped build the Transcontinental Railroad in 1868.

•**RIVERSIDE,** Town; Carbon County; Pop. 55; Elev. 7136; Lat. 41-13-03 N long. 106-46-42 W; Descriptively named for its location on the Encampment River.

•**RIVERTON,** City; Fremont County; Pop. 9,588; Zip Code 82501; Lat. 43-01-42 N long. 108-23-04 W; Pioneer residents named the town for the nearby convergence of four rivers.

•**ROCK RIVER,** Town; Albany County; Pop. 415; Zip Code 82083; Elev. 6891; Lat. 41-44-13 N long. 105-58-39 W; Descriptively named for a nearby rocky river.

•**ROCK SPRINGS,** City; Sweetwater County; Pop. 19,458; Zip Code 829+; Lat. 41-35-12 N long. 109-12-48 W; A pony express rider discovered springs here in 1861. The good water led to the founding of the town.

•**SARATOGA,** Town; Carbon County; Pop. 2,410; Zip Code 82331; Lat. 41-27-01 N long. 106-48-27 W; Founded in 1878 and named for the Saratoga Hot Springs in New York.

•**SHERIDAN,** City; Sheridan County Seat; Pop. 15,146; Zip Code 82801; Lat. 44-47-50 N long. 106-57-29 W; Settled in 1878 and named in honor of Civil War General, Phillip Sheridan.

•**SHOSHONI,** Town; Fremont County; Pop. 879; Zip Code 82649; Lat. 43-14-21 N long. 108-06-21 W; Shoshoni is the name of an Indian tribe. The name means "grass lodge people."

•**SINCLAIR,** Town; Carbon County; Pop. 586; Zip Code 82334; Elev. 6593; Lat. 41-46-31 N long. 107-06-57 W; Named after the Sinclair Oil Company in 1934.

•**SOUTH SUPERIOR,** Town; Sweetwater County; Pop. 586; The town is named after the Superior Coal Company.

•**SUNDANCE,** Town; Crook County Seat; Pop. 1,087; Zip Code 82710; Elev. 4765; Lat. 44-38-25 N long. 104-10-54 W; Founded in 1879 and named after the Sundance Mountains.

•**TEN SLEEP,** Town; Crook County Seat; Pop. 1,087; Zip Code 82442; Lat. 44-02-06 N long 107-26-50 W; Named for Indian method of telling time. Town was also ten days *sleeps* from Yellowstone Park and Fort Laramie.

•**THAYNE,** Town; Lincoln County; Pop. 256; Zip Code 83127; Lat. 42-55-11 N long 11-00-04 W. Named for Henry Thayne, first postmaster.

•**THERMOPULIS,** Town; Hot Springs County Seat; Pop. 3,852; Zip Code 82443; Lat. 43-38-41 N long 108-12-13 W. Name chosen by Dr. Julius A. Schuelkle -a combination of the latin *therme* (hot baths) and the Greek word *polis* (city).

•**TORRINGTON,** Town; GOSHEN County; Pop. 5,441; Zip Code 82240; Lat. 42-04-00 long 104-10-52 W. Name select by William Albert Curtis after the city in Connecticut.

•**UPTON,** Town; Western County; Pop. 1,193; Lat. 44-05-52 N long 104-37-30 W. First known as Irontown, later named for George S. Upton an early surveyor in the region.

•**WAMSUTTER,** Town; Sweetwater County; Pop. 681; Zip Code 82336; Lat. 41-40-03 N long 107-58-23 W. First known as Washakie, later changed to present name after a bridge-builder on the Union Pacific Railroad,

•**WHEATLAND,** Town; PLATTE County Seat; Pop. 5,816; Zip Code 82201; Lat. 42-03-13 N long 104-57-18 W. First named Gilchrist later to present name descriptive of the local wheat fields.

•**WORLAND,** City; Washkie County Seat; Pop. 6391; Elev. 4748; Lat. 43-48-17 N;long 108-10-49 W. Named for C. R. "Dad Worland who had buidt an early camp in the area.

•**YODER,** Town; Goshen County; Pop. 110; Zip Code 82244; Lat. 41-54-57 N long 104-17-46. Named for Jess and Frank Yoder pioneer residents in the area.

THE

UNITED STATES

DICTIONARY

OF PLACES

MAP SECTION

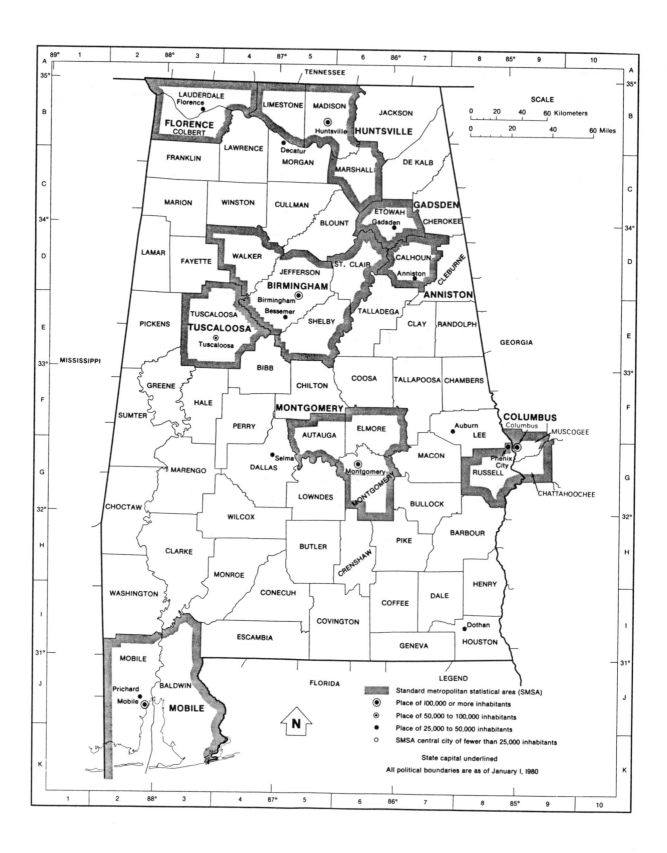

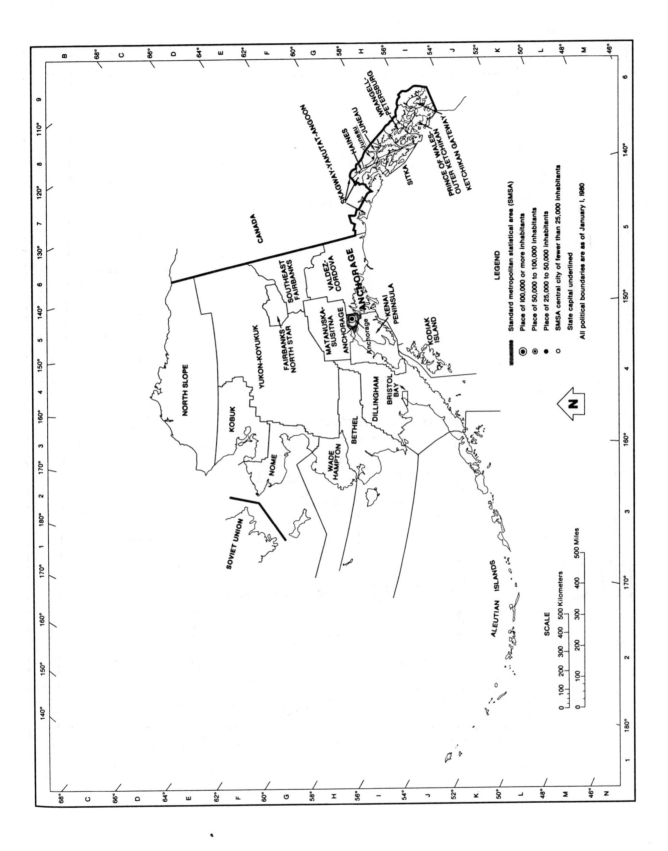

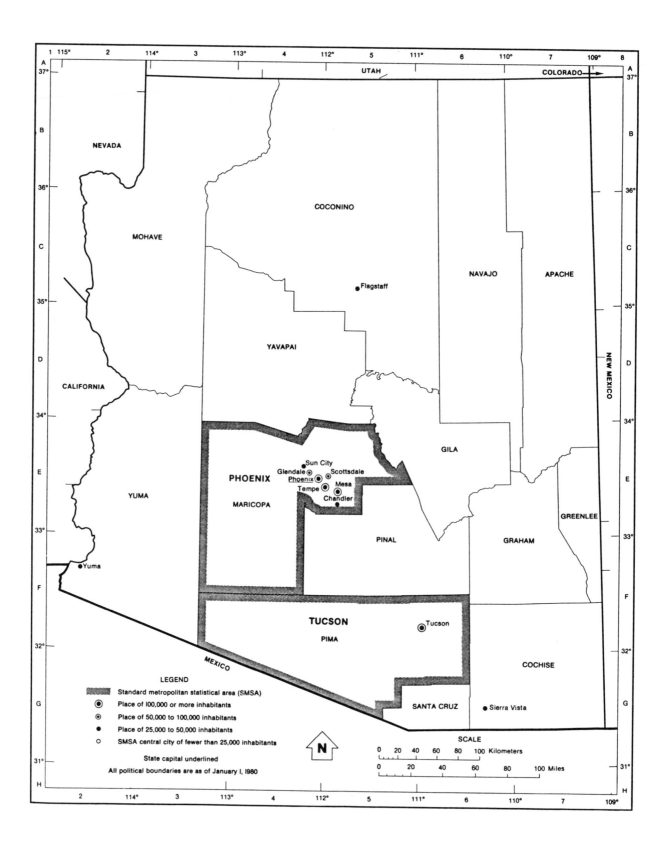

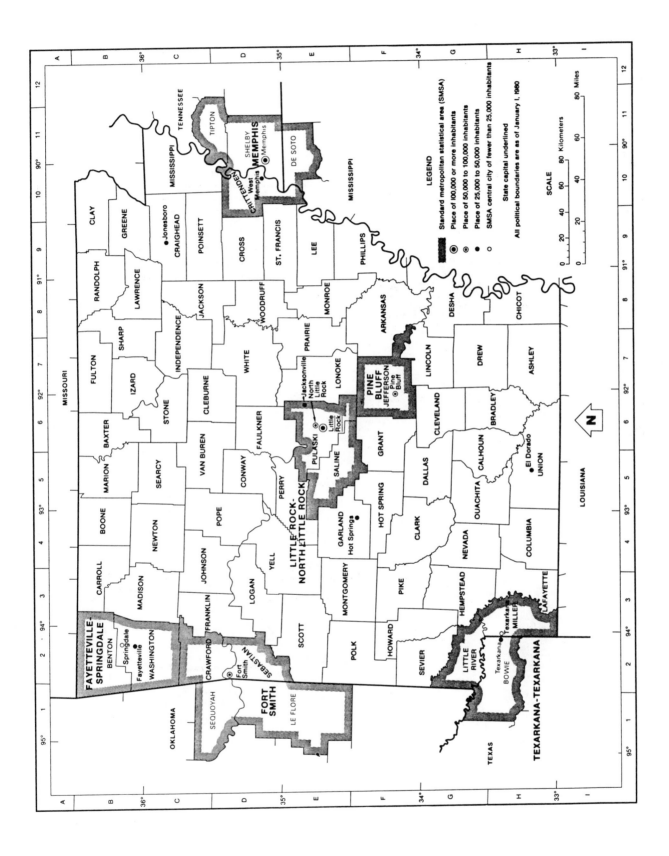

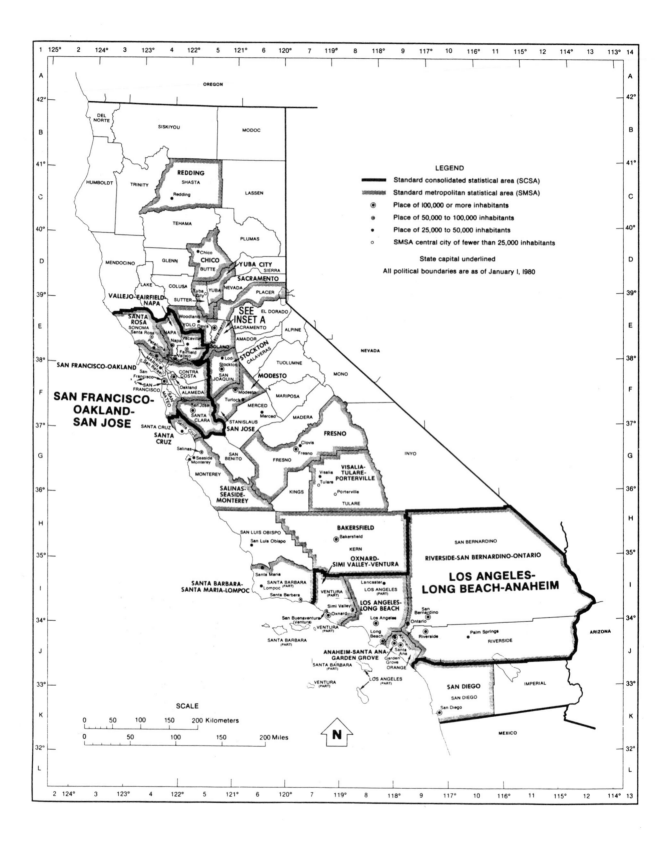

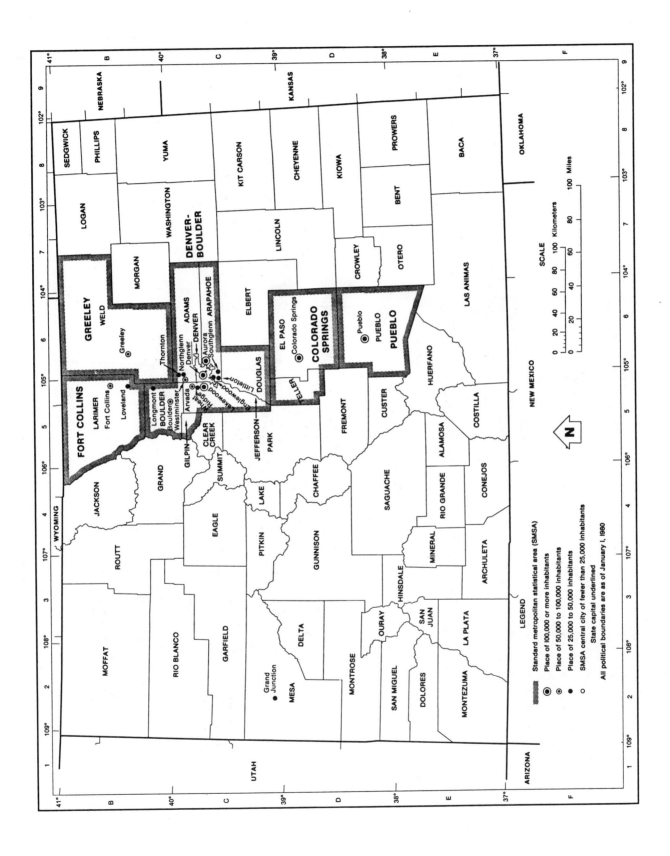

SEDGWICK
PHILLIPS
YUMA
WASHINGTON
LOGAN
MORGAN
GREELEY
WELD
Greeley
Thornton
Northglenn
Denver
ADAMS
ARAPAHOE
Aurora
Southglenn
Littleton
DENVER-
BOULDER
KIT CARSON
CHEYENNE
KIOWA
LINCOLN
ELBERT
DOUGLAS
TELLER
EL PASO
Colorado Springs
COLORADO
SPRINGS
CROWLEY
OTERO
BENT
PROWERS
BACA
OKLAHOMA
NEBRASKA
KANSAS
FORT COLLINS
LARIMER
Fort Collins
Loveland
Longmont
BOULDER
Boulder
Westminster
Arvada
Wheat
Ridge
Lakewood
Englewood
GILPIN
CLEAR
CREEK
JEFFERSON
PARK
SUMMIT
LAKE
CHAFFEE
FREMONT
CUSTER
HUERFANO
PUEBLO
Pueblo
LAS ANIMAS
PUEBLO
JACKSON
GRAND
EAGLE
PITKIN
GUNNISON
SAGUACHE
ALAMOSA
COSTILLA
CONEJOS
RIO GRANDE
MINERAL
HINSDALE
SAN JUAN
OURAY
ROUTT
MOFFAT
RIO BLANCO
GARFIELD
DELTA
MESA
Grand
Junction
MONTROSE
SAN MIGUEL
DOLORES
MONTEZUMA
LA PLATA
ARCHULETA
WYOMING
UTAH
ARIZONA
NEW MEXICO

SCALE
100 Miles
100 Kilometers

LEGEND
Standard metropolitan statistical area (SMSA)
Place of 100,000 or more inhabitants
Place of 50,000 to 100,000 inhabitants
Place of 25,000 to 50,000 inhabitants
SMSA central city of fewer than 25,000 inhabitants
State capital underlined
All political boundaries are as of January 1, 1980

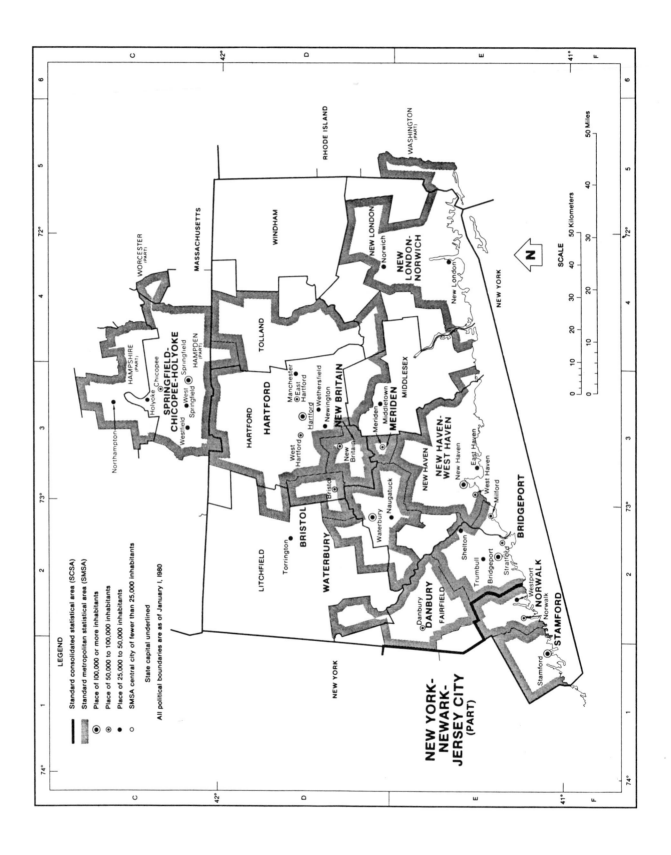

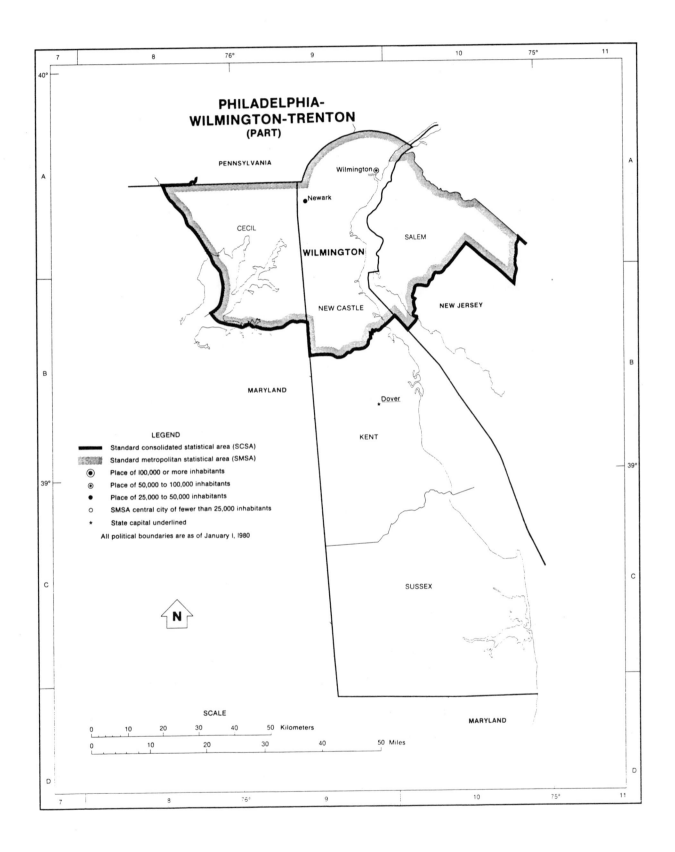

PHILADELPHIA-
WILMINGTON-TRENTON
(PART)

PENNSYLVANIA

Wilmington ◉

● Newark

CECIL

WILMINGTON

SALEM

NEW CASTLE

NEW JERSEY

MARYLAND

Dover
★

KENT

LEGEND

▬▬▬ Standard consolidated statistical area (SCSA)

▓▓▓ Standard metropolitan statistical area (SMSA)

◉ Place of 100,000 or more inhabitants

◎ Place of 50,000 to 100,000 inhabitants

● Place of 25,000 to 50,000 inhabitants

○ SMSA central city of fewer than 25,000 inhabitants

★ State capital underlined

All political boundaries are as of January I, 1980

SUSSEX

N

SCALE

0   10   20   30   40   50 Kilometers

0   10   20   30   40   50 Miles

MARYLAND

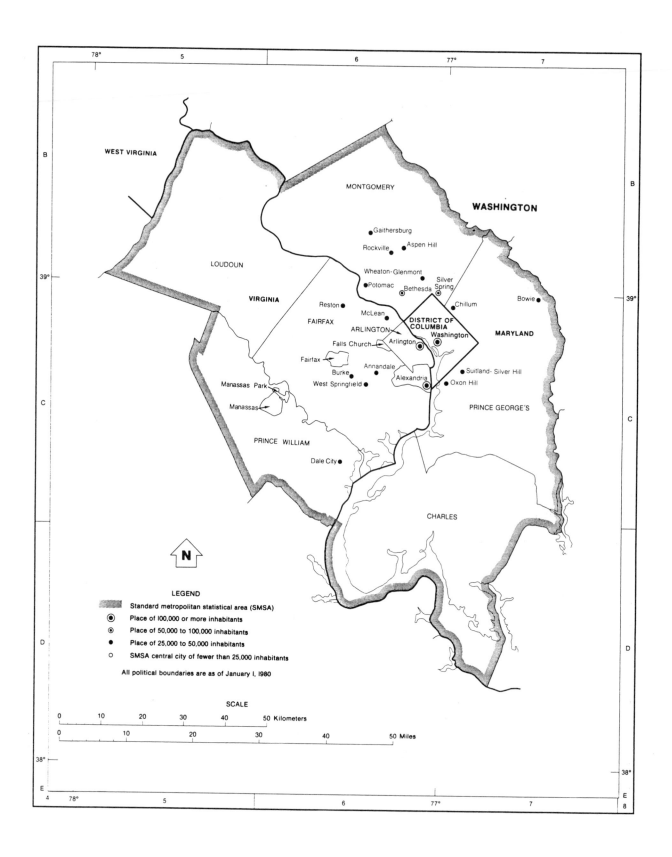

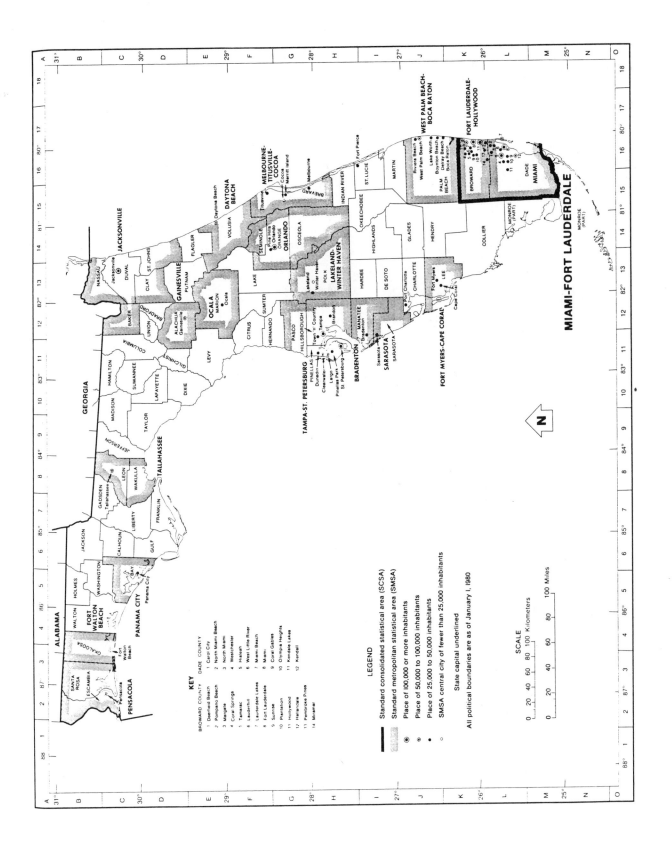

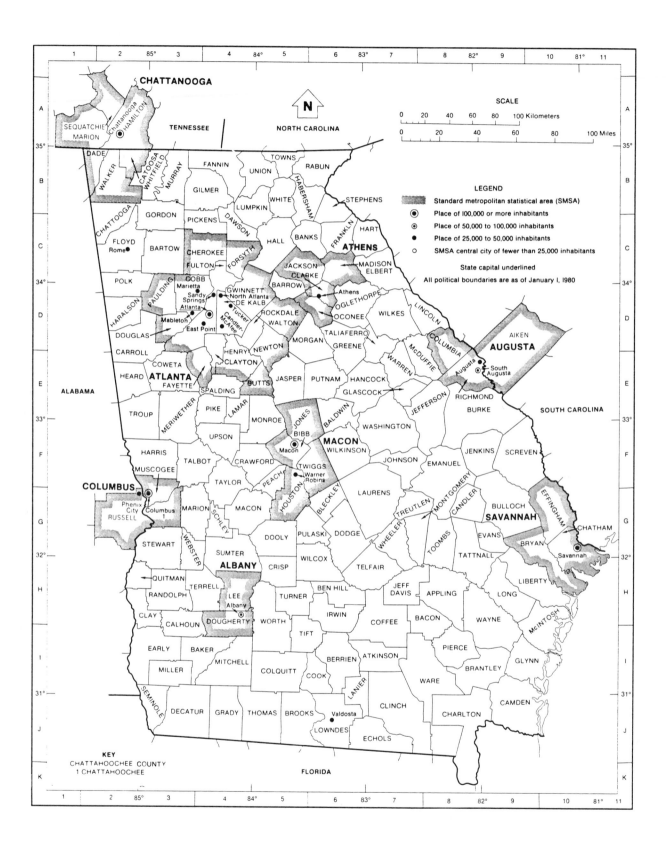

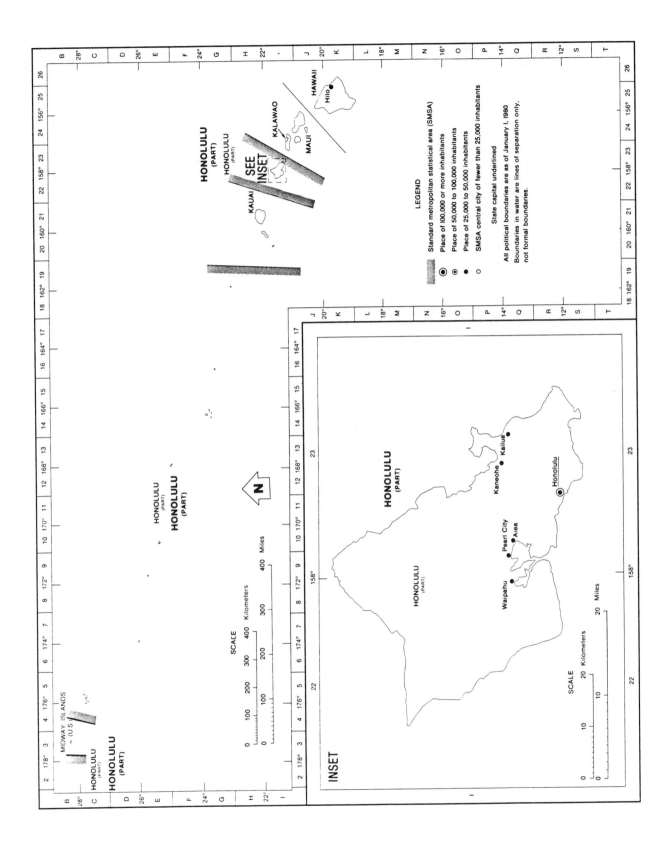

LEGEND

Standard metropolitan statistical area (SMSA)

Place of 100,000 or more inhabitants

Place of 50,000 to 100,000 inhabitants

Place of 25,000 to 50,000 inhabitants

SMSA central city of fewer than 25,000 inhabitants

State capital underlined

All political boundaries are as of January 1, 1980. Boundaries in water are lines of separation only, not formal boundaries.

HONOLULU (PART)

HONOLULU (PART)

KALAWAO

KAUAI

MAUI

SEE INSET

HAWAII

Hilo

MIDWAY ISLANDS (U.S.)

HONOLULU (PART)

HONOLULU (PART)

HONOLULU (PART)

SCALE

Kilometers

Miles

N

INSET

HONOLULU (PART)

HONOLULU (PART)

Kaneohe Kailua

Honolulu

Pearl City
Aiea

Waipahu

SCALE

Kilometers

Miles

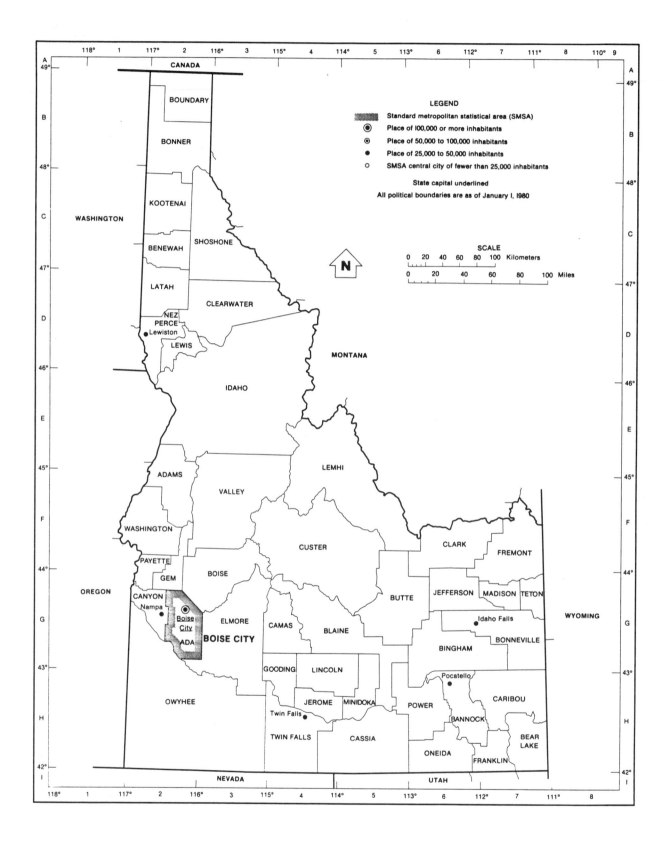

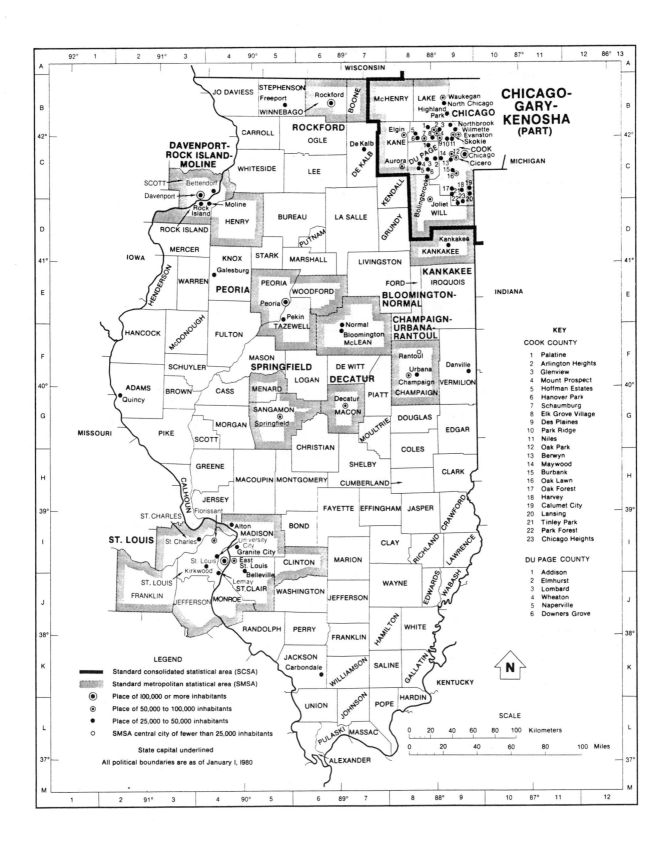

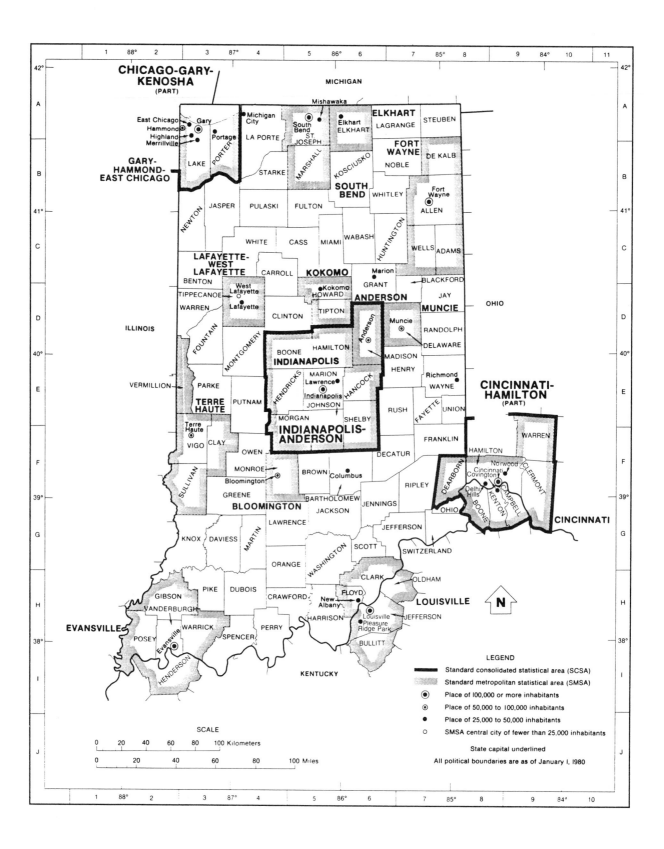

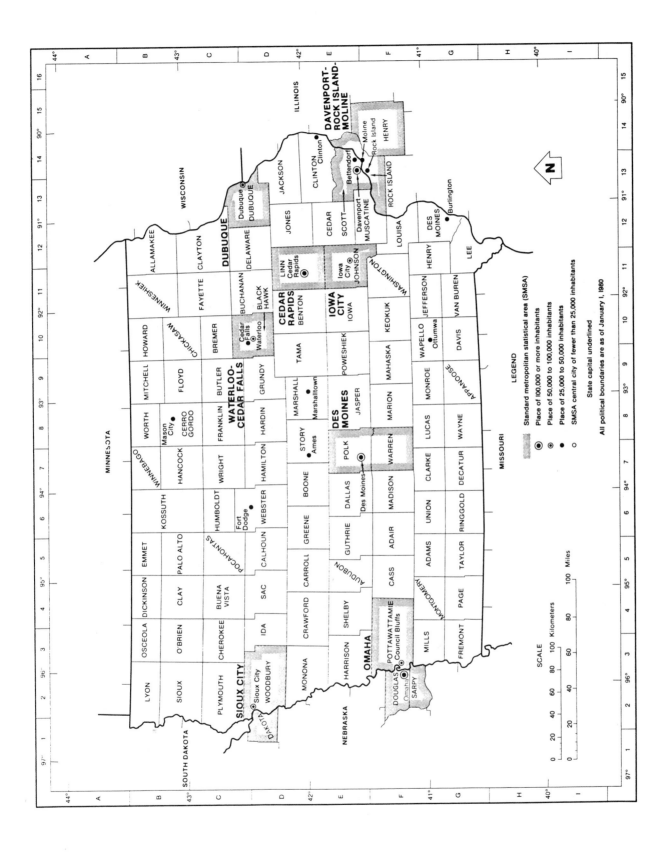

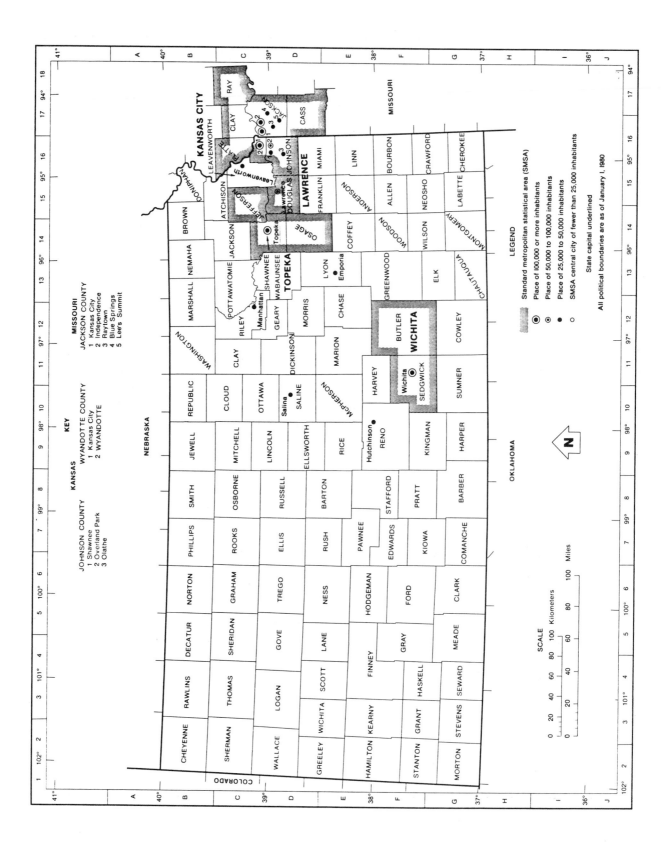

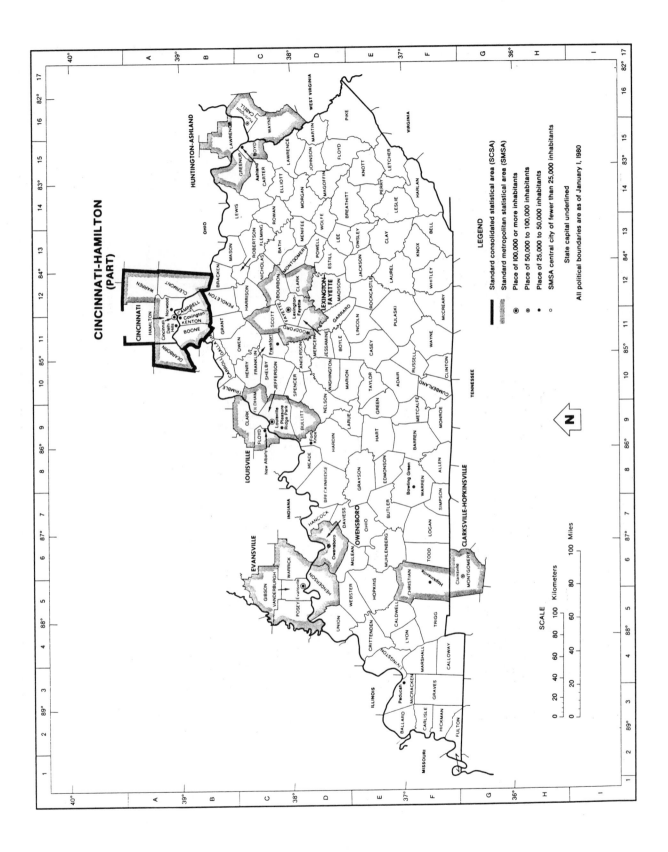

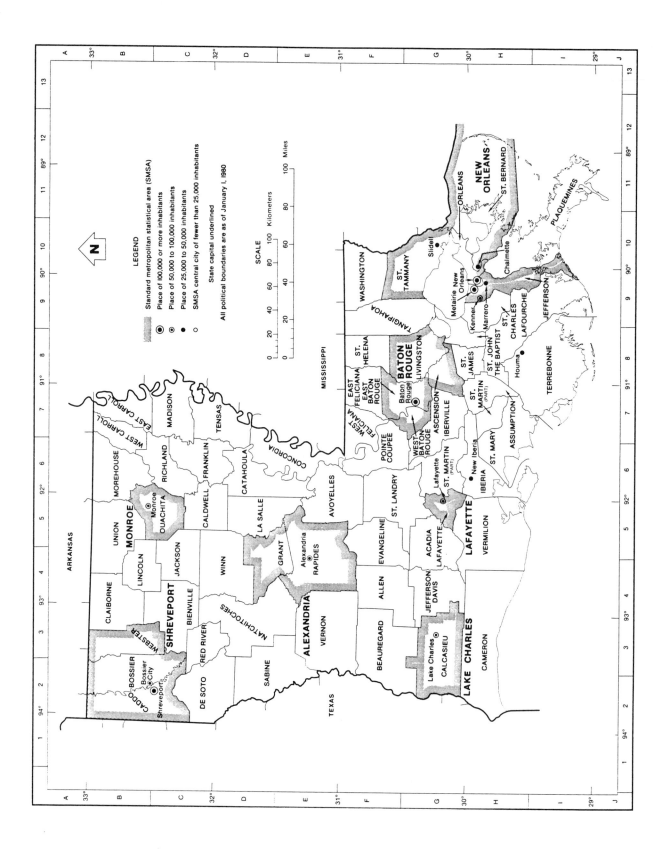

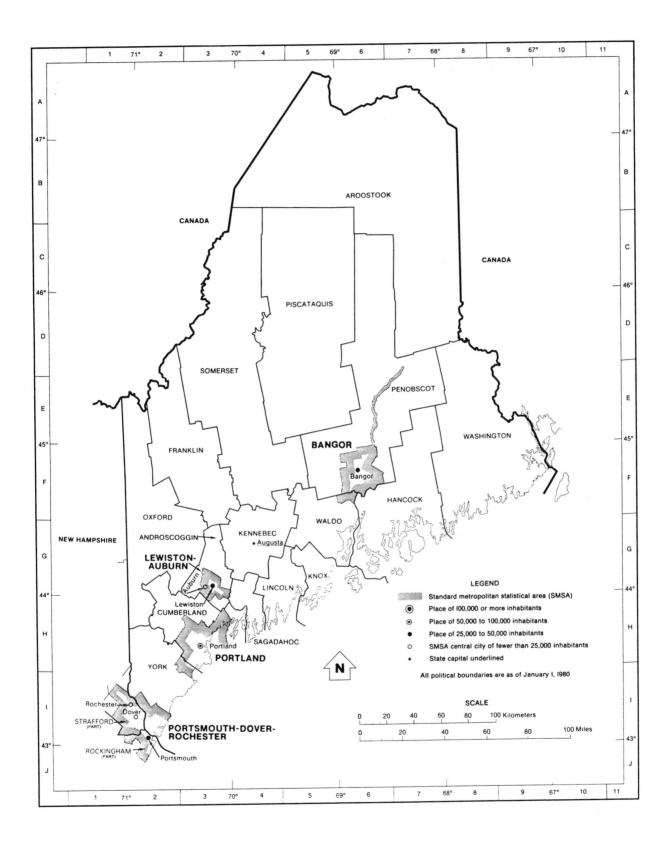

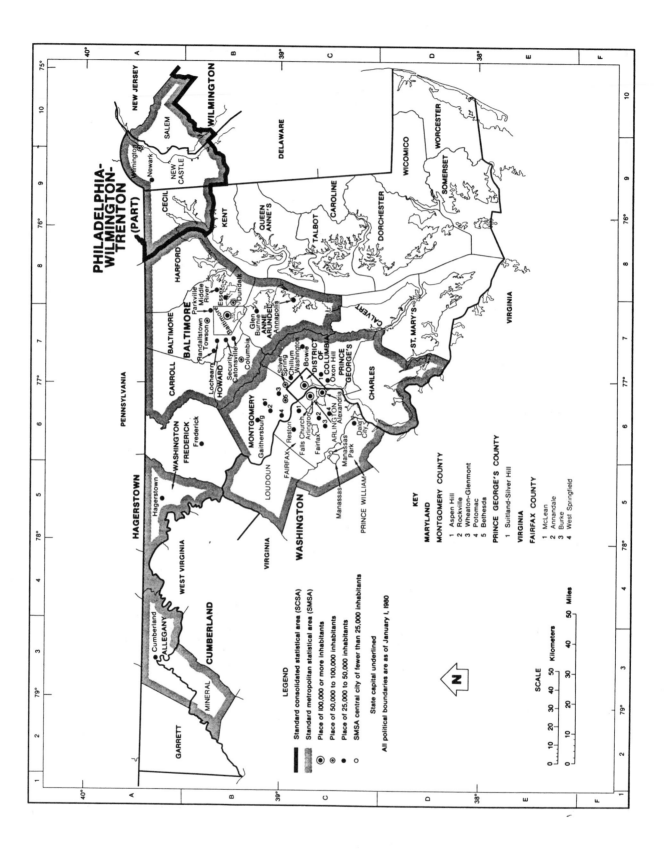

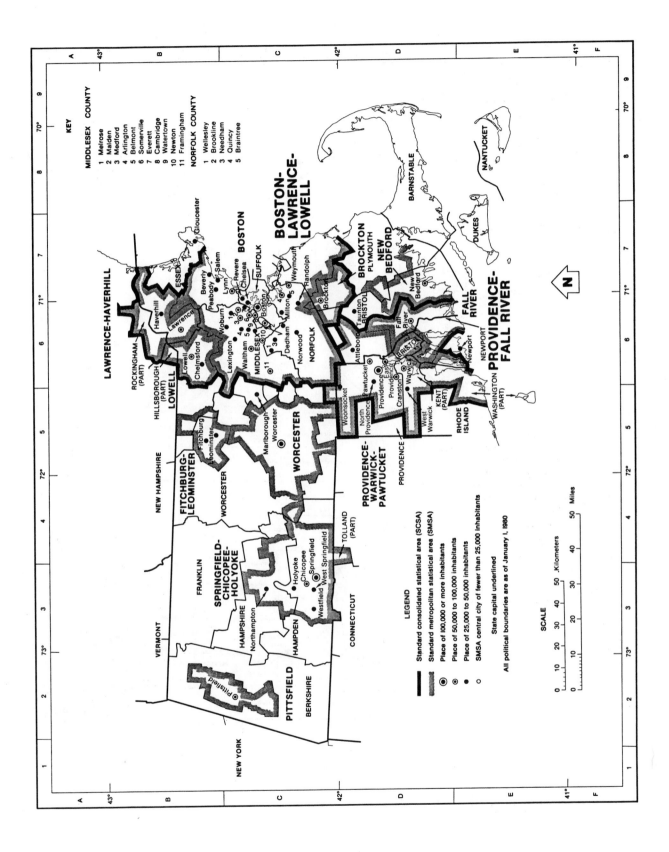

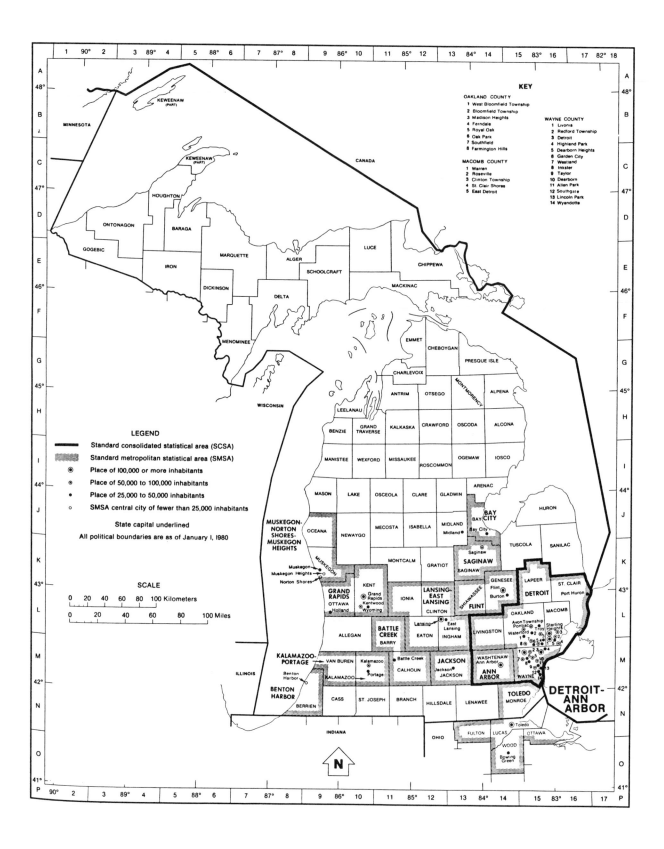

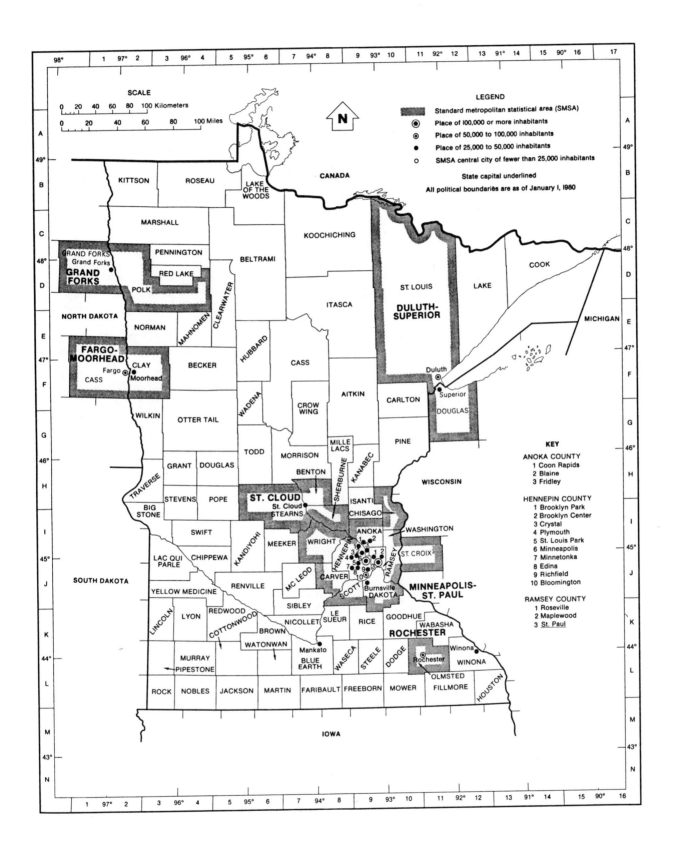

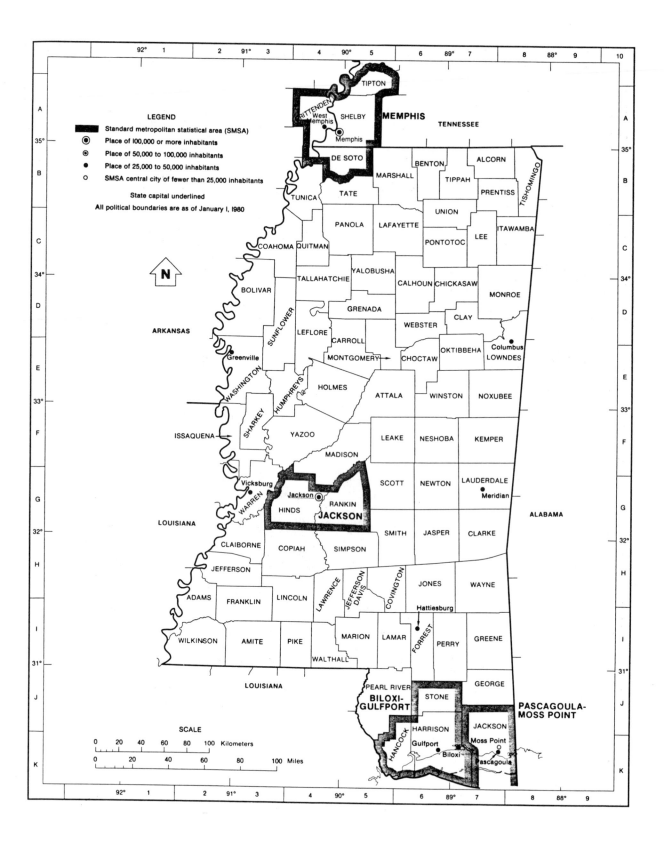

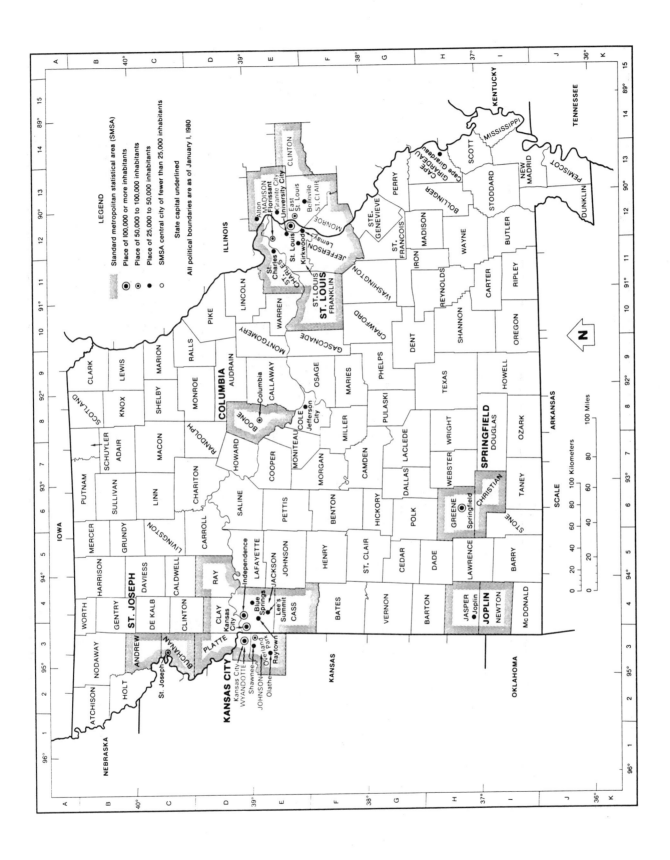

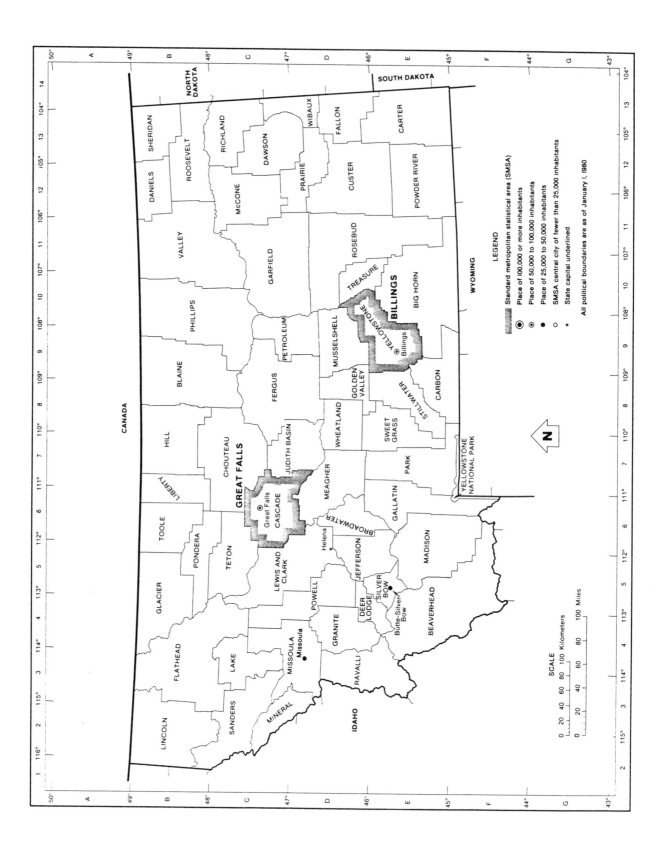

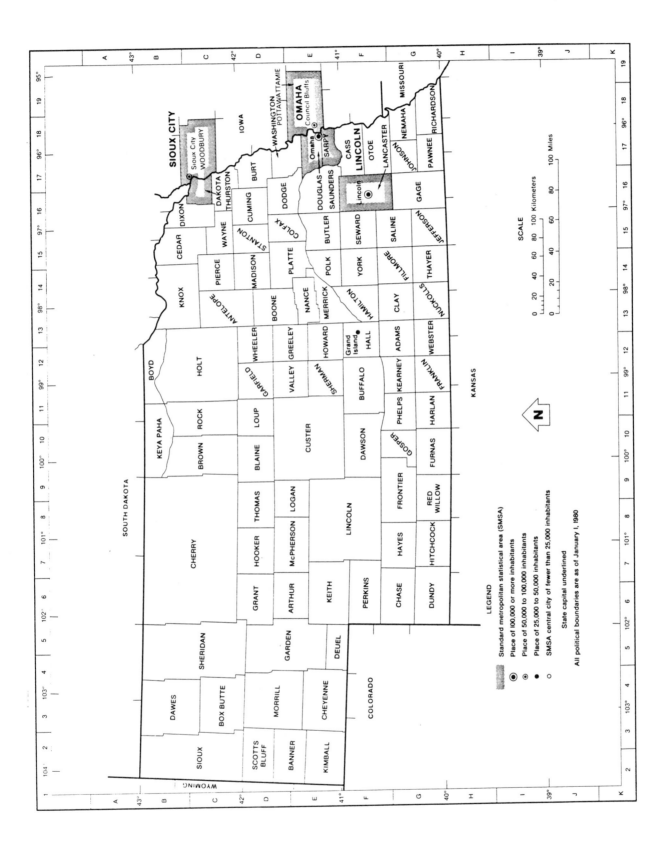

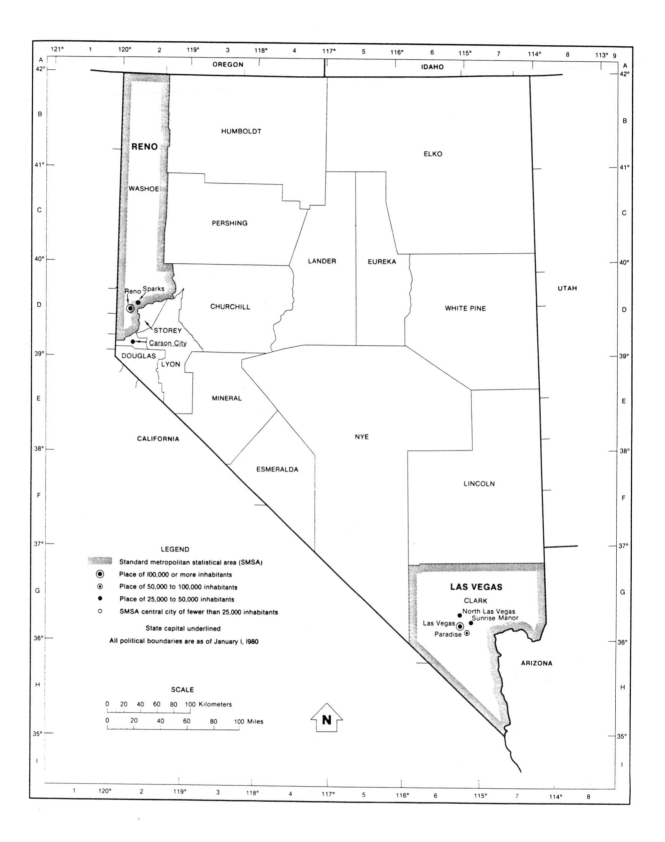

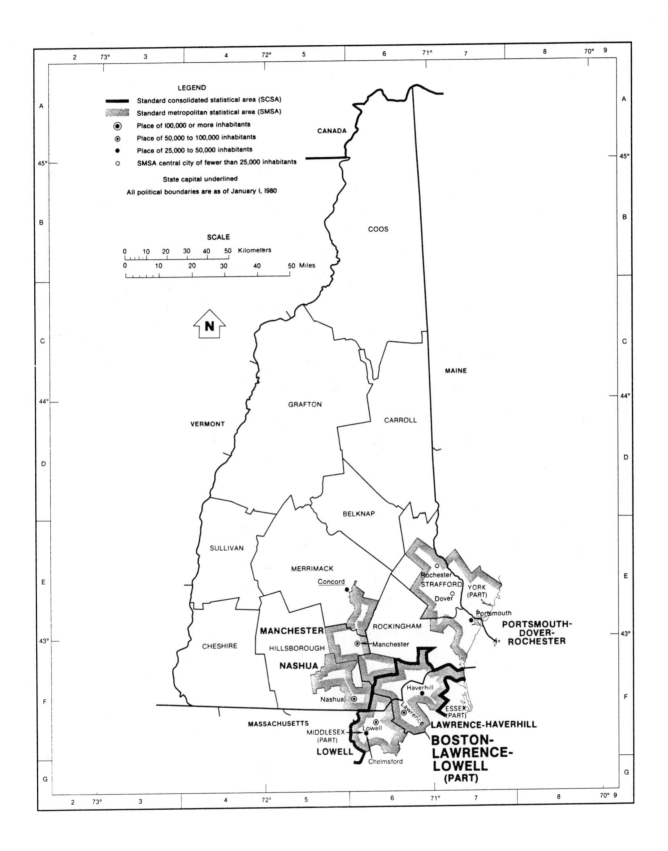

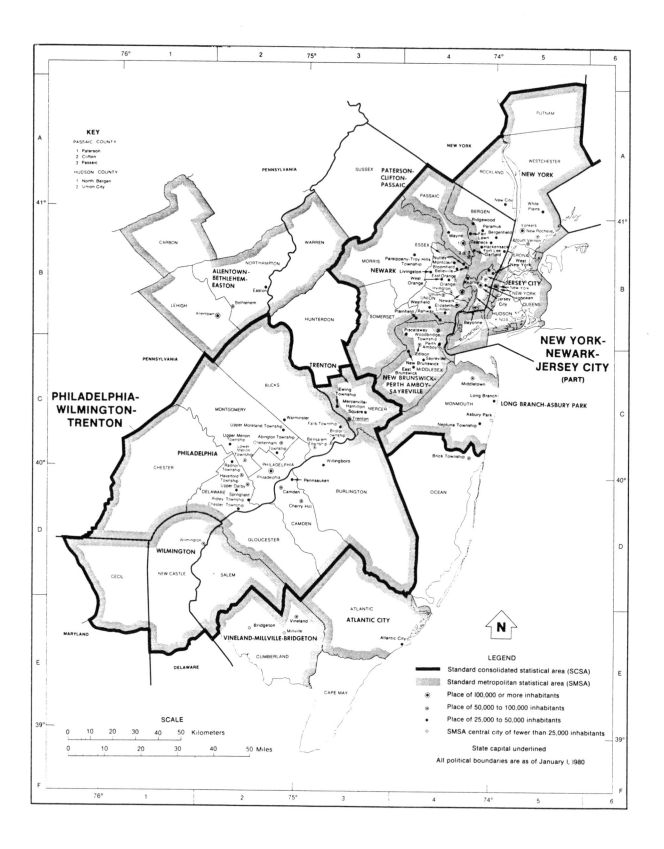

KEY

PASSAIC COUNTY
1 Paterson
2 Clifton
3 Passaic

HUDSON COUNTY
1 North Bergen
2 Union City

PATERSON-
CLIFTON-
PASSAIC

NEW YORK

PENNSYLVANIA

PUTNAM

WESTCHESTER

NEW YORK

SUSSEX

PASSAIC

ROCKLAND

New City

White Plains

BERGEN

Ridgewood

Paramus

Bergenfield

Yonkers

New Rochelle

Mount Vernon

CARBON

NORTHAMPTON

WARREN

ESSEX

Wayne

Fair Lawn

Teaneck

Hackensack

Fort Lee

Garfield

BRONX

West New York

ALLENTOWN-
BETHLEHEM-
EASTON

Easton

MORRIS

Parsippany-Troy Hills Township

Nutley

Montclair

Bloomfield

Belleville

NEW YORK

LEHIGH

Bethlehem

NEWARK

Livingston

West Orange

East Orange

Orange

Irvington

JERSEY CITY

New York

NEW YORK

Hoboken

Jersey City

QUEENS

Allentown

HUNTERDON

SOMERSET

UNION

Union

Westfield

Newark

Elizabeth

Plainfield

Rahway

Linden

HUDSON

Bayonne

KINGS

PENNSYLVANIA

NEW YORK-
NEWARK-
JERSEY CITY
(PART)

RICHMOND

Piscataway

Woodbridge Township

Perth Amboy

TRENTON

Edison

Sayreville

New Brunswick

East Brunswick

MIDDLESEX

Middletown

Long Branch

LONG BRANCH-ASBURY PARK

MONMOUTH

Asbury Park

PHILADELPHIA-
WILMINGTON-
TRENTON

BUCKS

NEW BRUNSWICK-
PERTH AMBOY-
SAYREVILLE

Ewing Township

Mercerville-
Hamilton Square

MERCER

Trenton

Neptune Township

MONTGOMERY

Warminster

Falls Township

Upper Moreland Township

Upper Merion Township

Abington Township

Cheltenham Township

Bensalem Township

Bristol Township

Brick Township

OCEAN

PHILADELPHIA

Lower Merion Township

Radnor Township

PHILADELPHIA

Willingboro

CHESTER

Haverford Township

Upper Darby

Philadelphia

Pennsauken

DELAWARE

Springfield

Ridley Township

Chester Township

Camden

BURLINGTON

Cherry Hill

WILMINGTON

Wilmington

CAMDEN

CECIL

NEW CASTLE

GLOUCESTER

SALEM

ATLANTIC

ATLANTIC CITY

MARYLAND

Bridgeton

Vineland

Millville

VINELAND-MILLVILLE-BRIDGETON

Atlantic City

DELAWARE

CUMBERLAND

CAPE MAY

N

SCALE

0 10 20 30 40 50 Kilometers

0 10 20 30 40 50 Miles

LEGEND

━━━ Standard consolidated statistical area (SCSA)

▨▨▨ Standard metropolitan statistical area (SMSA)

⊙ Place of 100,000 or more inhabitants

⊚ Place of 50,000 to 100,000 inhabitants

• Place of 25,000 to 50,000 inhabitants

○ SMSA central city of fewer than 25,000 inhabitants

State capital underlined

All political boundaries are as of January 1, 1980

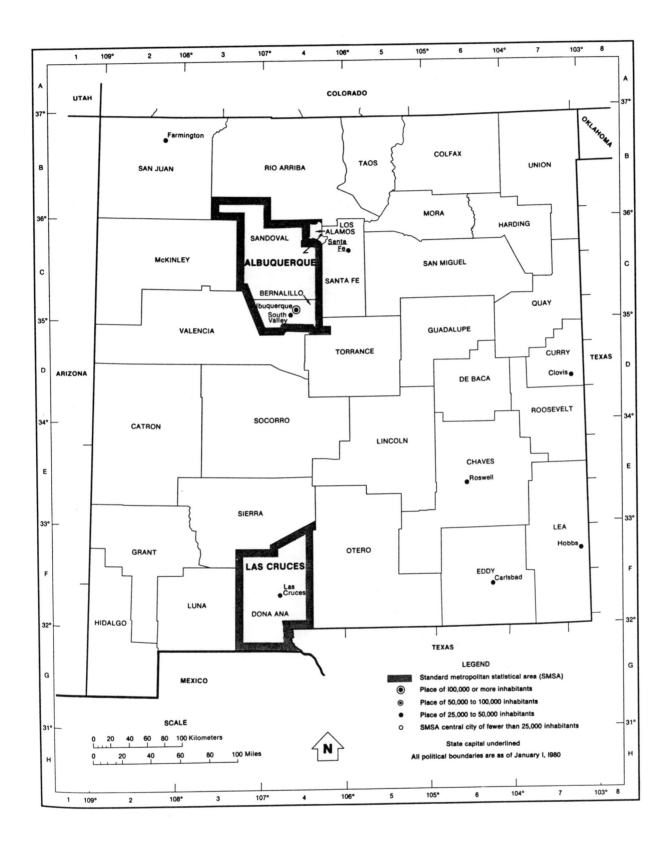

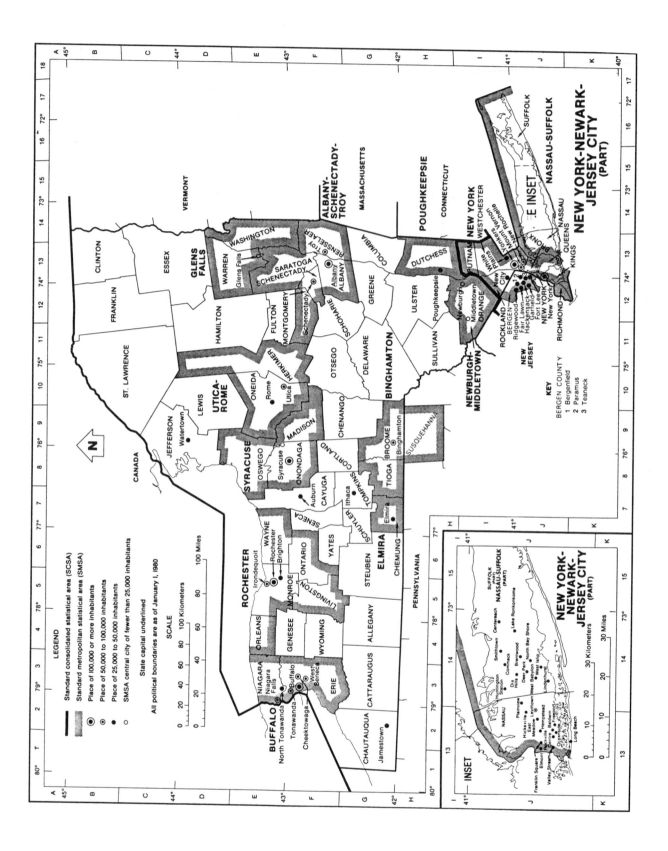

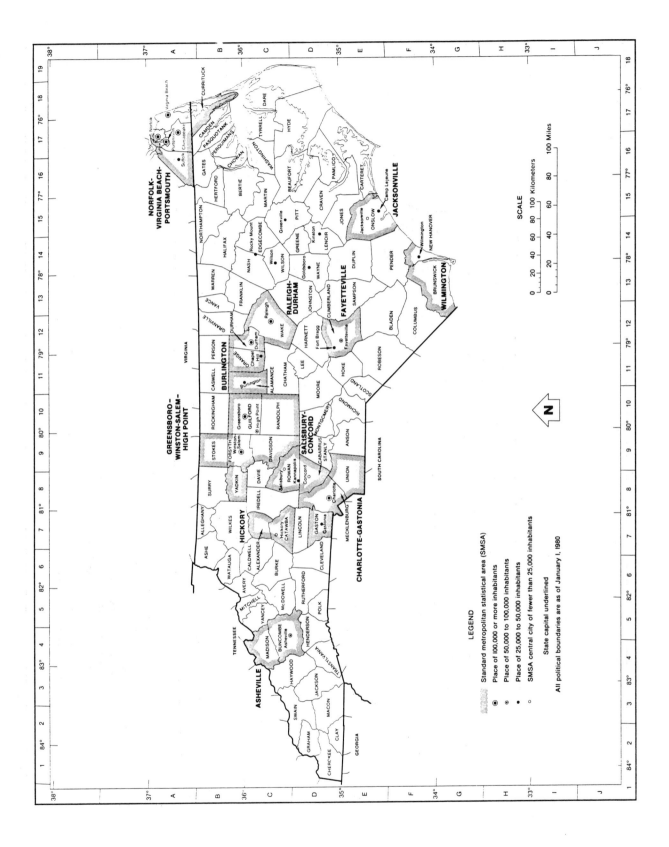

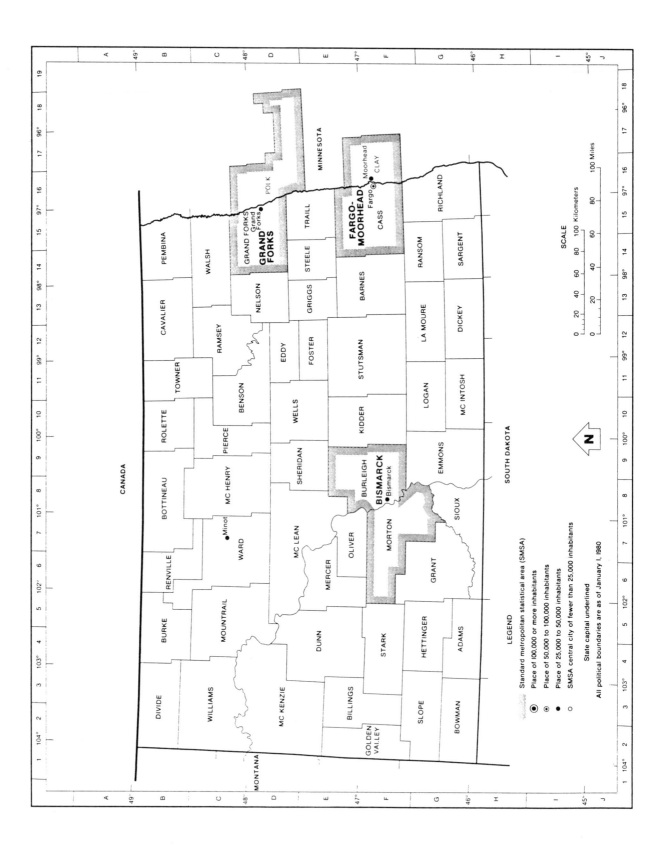

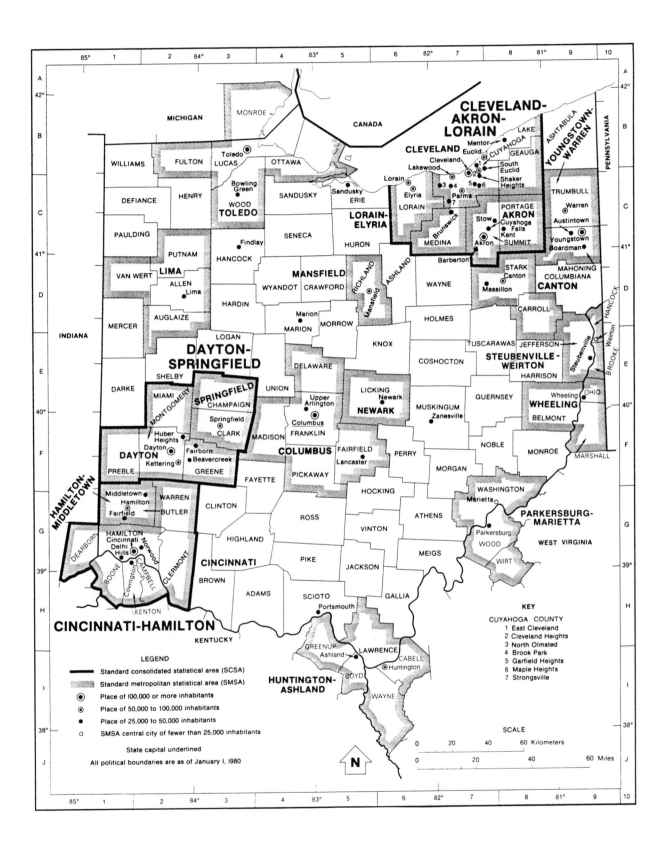

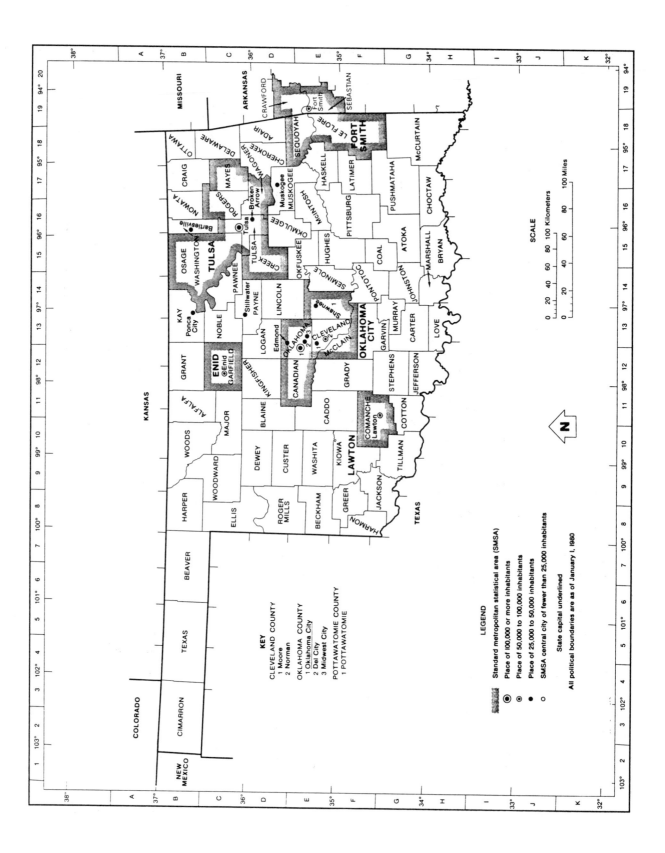

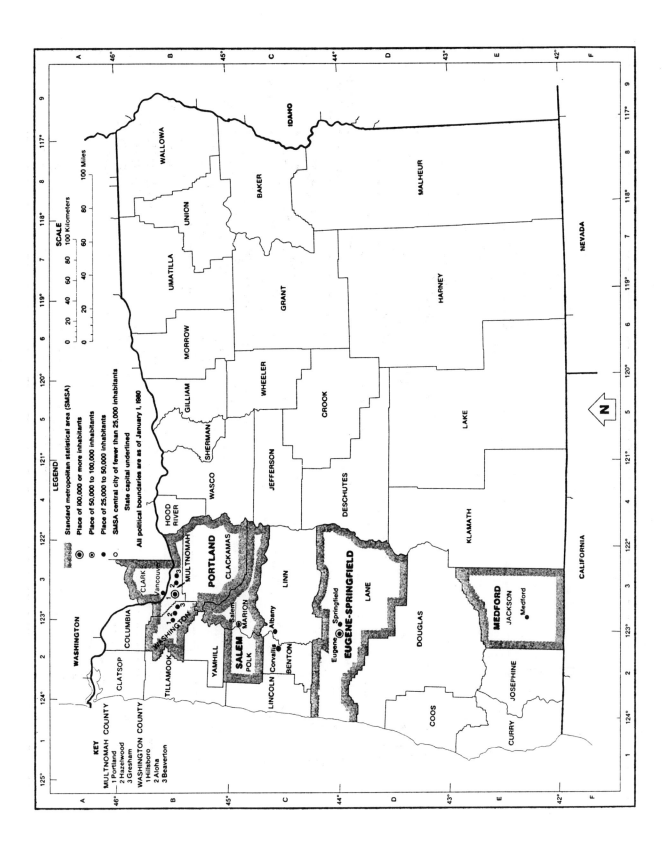

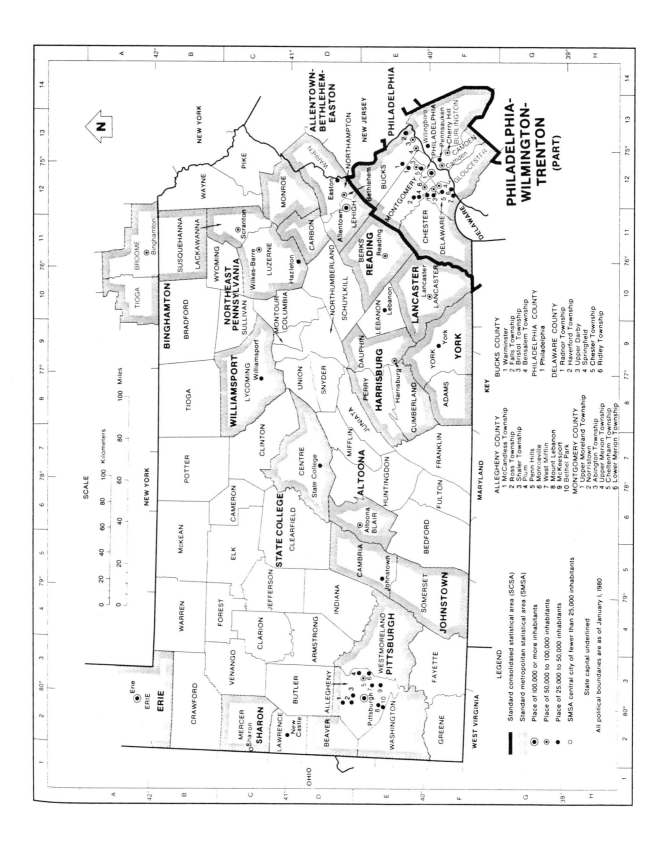

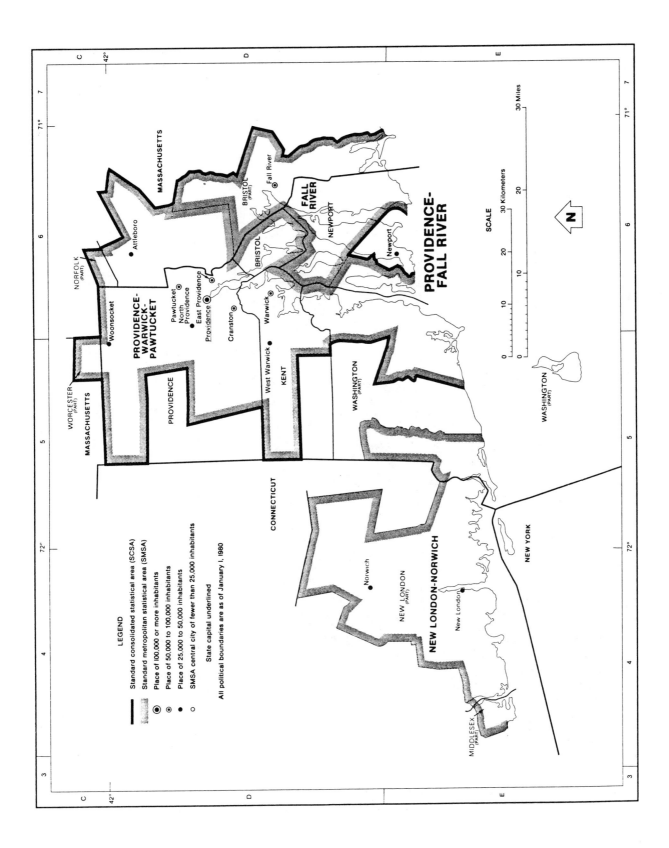

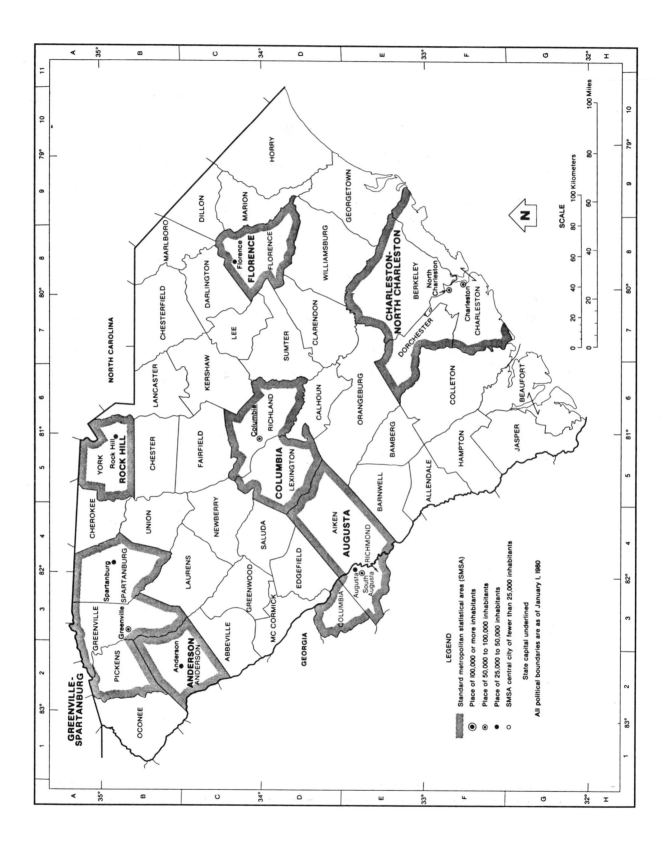

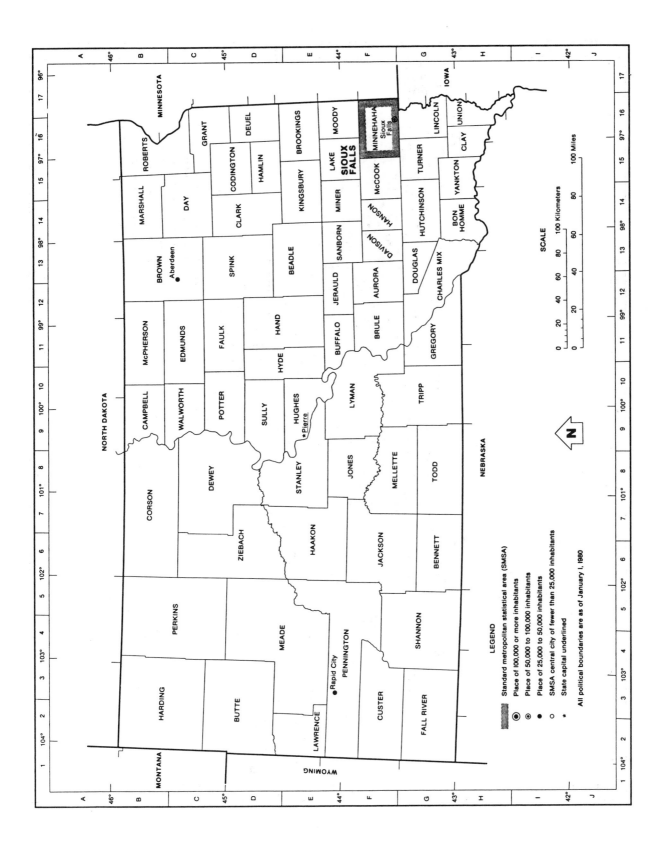

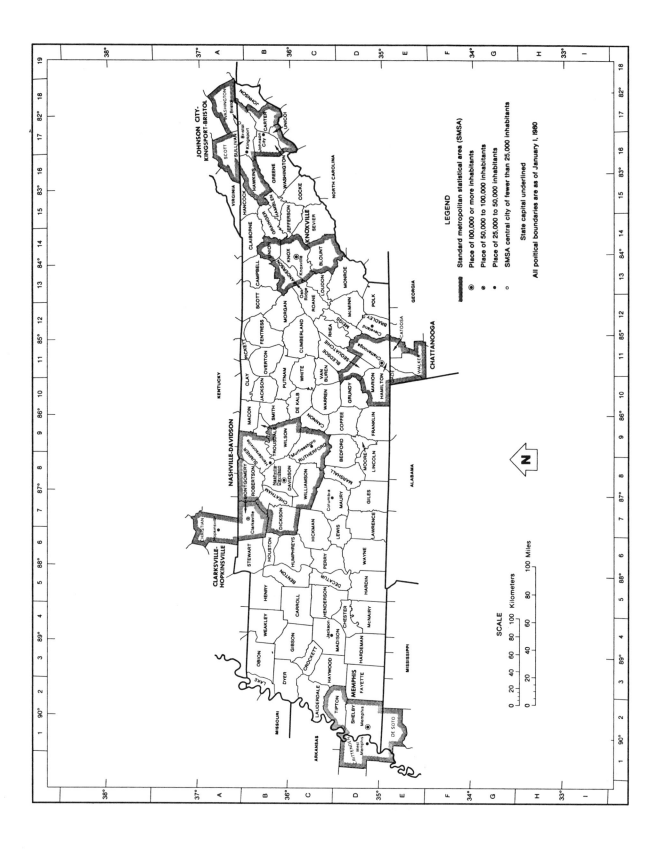

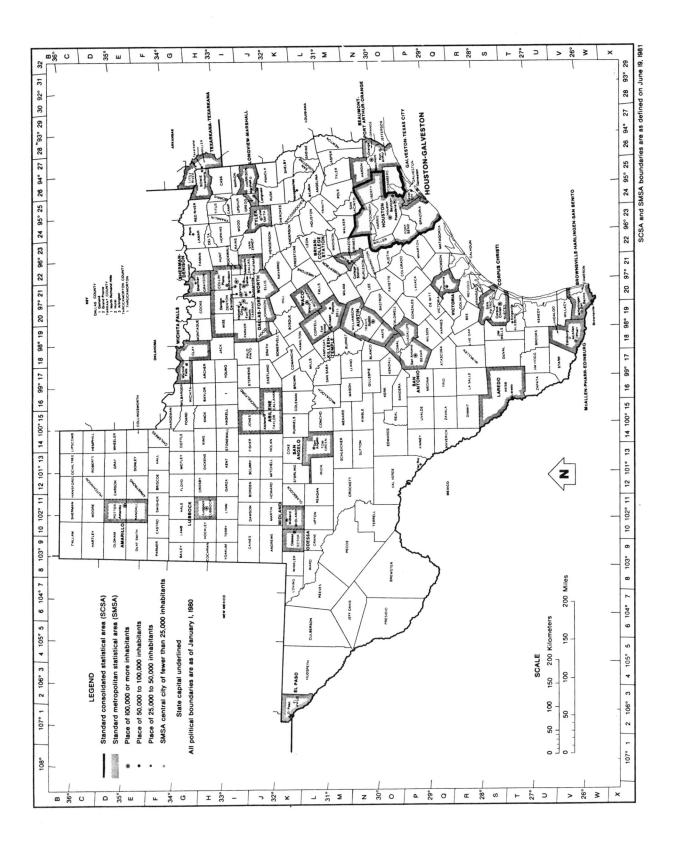

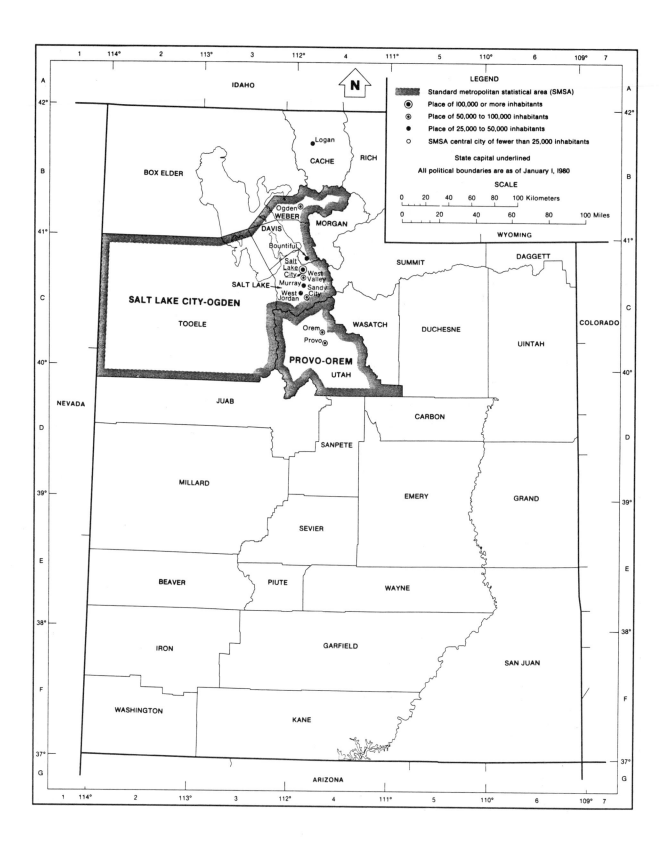

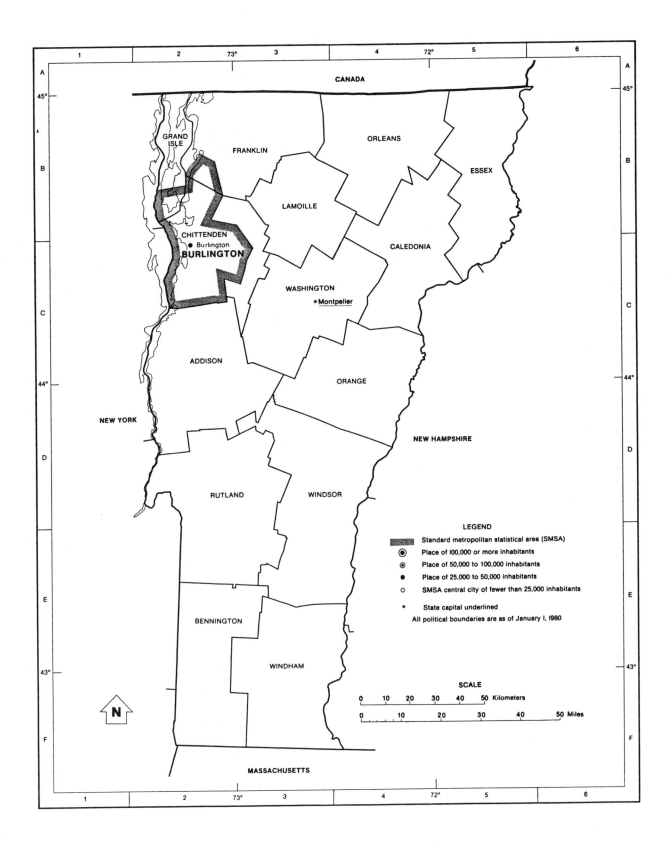

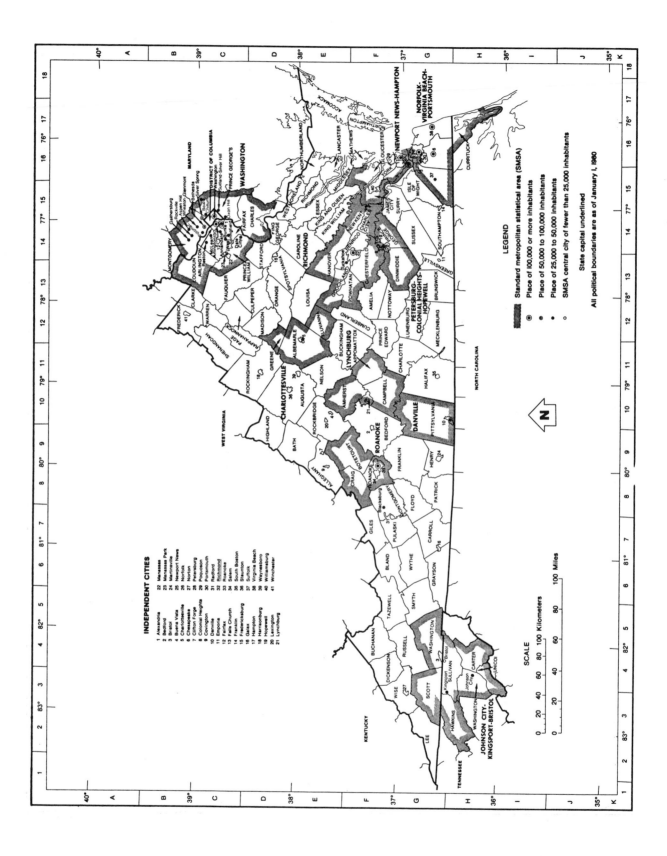

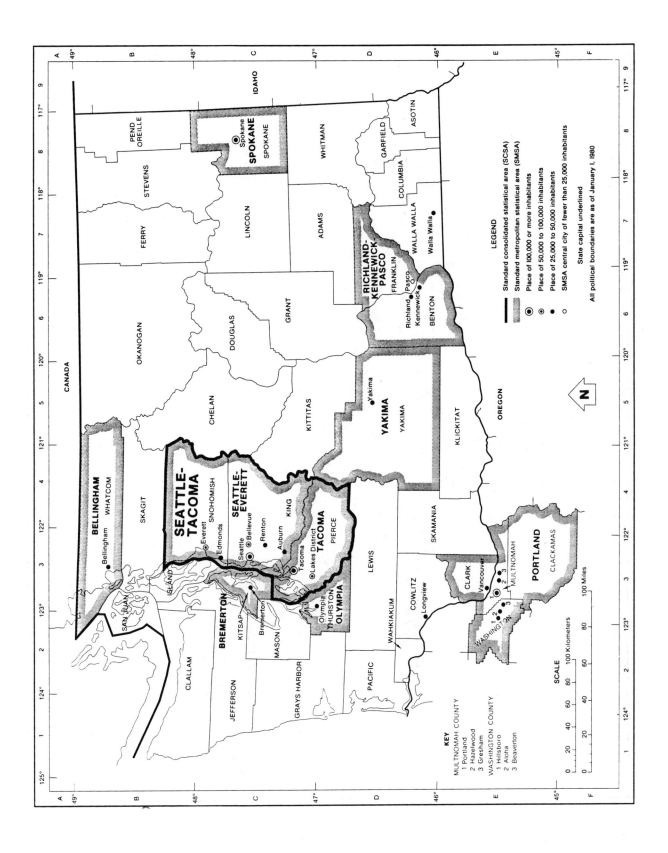

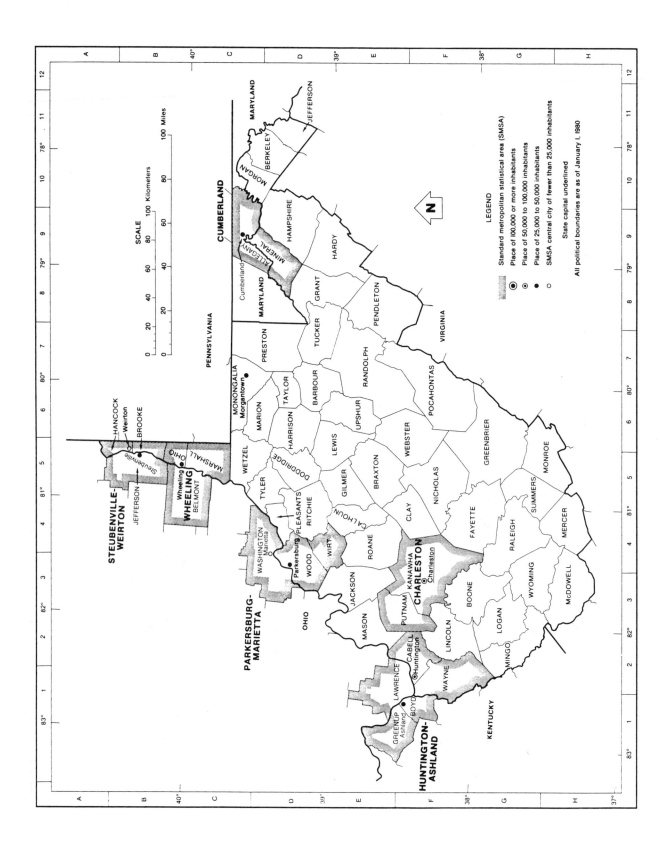

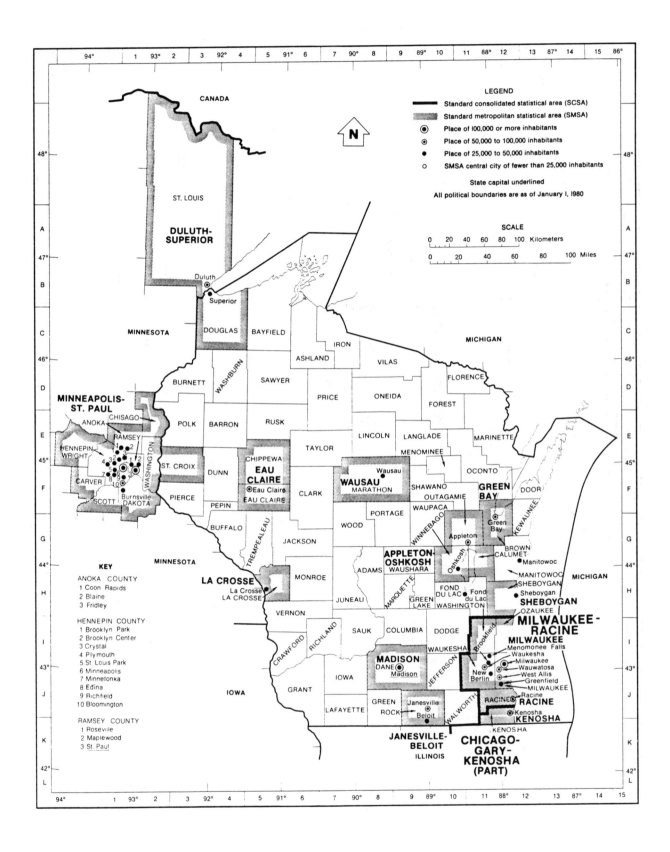

LEGEND

Standard consolidated statistical area (SCSA)
Standard metropolitan statistical area (SMSA)
Place of 100,000 or more inhabitants
Place of 50,000 to 100,000 inhabitants
Place of 25,000 to 50,000 inhabitants
SMSA central city of fewer than 25,000 inhabitants

State capital underlined

All political boundaries are as of January I, 1980

SCALE

0   20   40   60   80   100 Kilometers

0   20   40   60   80   100 Miles

CANADA

ST. LOUIS

DULUTH-
SUPERIOR

MINNESOTA

Duluth

Superior

DOUGLAS   BAYFIELD

MICHIGAN

IRON

ASHLAND   VILAS

BURNETT   FLORENCE

WASHBURN   SAWYER

MINNEAPOLIS-
ST. PAUL

PRICE   ONEIDA   FOREST

CHISAGO

ANOKA

RAMSEY

HENNEPIN
WRIGHT

POLK   BARRON   RUSK

LINCOLN   LANGLADE

MARINETTE

ST. CROIX   TAYLOR   MENOMINEE

CARVER

CHIPPEWA

EAU
CLAIRE

DUNN   Wausau

WAUSAU
MARATHON

GREEN
BAY

SCOTT   Burnsville   DAKOTA

PIERCE   EAU CLAIRE
Eau Claire
EAU CLAIRE

CLARK   SHAWANO

OCONTO   DOOR

PEPIN   WAUPACA

Green
Bay

BUFFALO   WOOD   PORTAGE

BROWN
CALUMET

WINNEBAGO

KEY

ANOKA COUNTY
1 Coon Rapids
2 Blaine
3 Fridley

HENNEPIN COUNTY
1 Brooklyn Park
2 Brooklyn Center
3 Crystal
4 Plymouth
5 St. Louis Park
6 Minneapolis
7 Minnetonka
8 Edina
9 Richfield
10 Bloomington

RAMSEY COUNTY
1 Roseville
2 Maplewood
3 St. Paul

MINNESOTA

JACKSON

APPLETON-
OSHKOSH
WAUSHARA

Appleton

Oshkosh

Manitowoc

MANITOWOC
SHEBOYGAN

MICHIGAN

TREMPEALEAU

LA CROSSE

MONROE

ADAMS

MARQUETTE

GREEN
LAKE

FOND
DU LAC   Fond
du Lac

Sheboygan

SHEBOYGAN

La Crosse
LA CROSSE   WASHINGTON

OZAUKEE

VERNON   JUNEAU

IOWA

CRAWFORD

RICHLAND   SAUK   COLUMBIA   DODGE

MILWAUKEE-
RACINE

WAUKESHA   Brookfield   MILWAUKEE
Menomonee Falls
Waukesha
Milwaukee
Wauwatosa
New   West Allis
Berlin   Greenfield
MILWAUKEE
Racine

MADISON
DANE
Madison

JEFFERSON

IOWA   GRANT

LAFAYETTE

GREEN
ROCK   Janesville
Beloit

RACINE   RACINE

WALWORTH   Kenosha
KENOSHA

ILLINOIS

JANESVILLE-
BELOIT

KENOSHA

CHICAGO-
GARY-
KENOSHA
(PART)

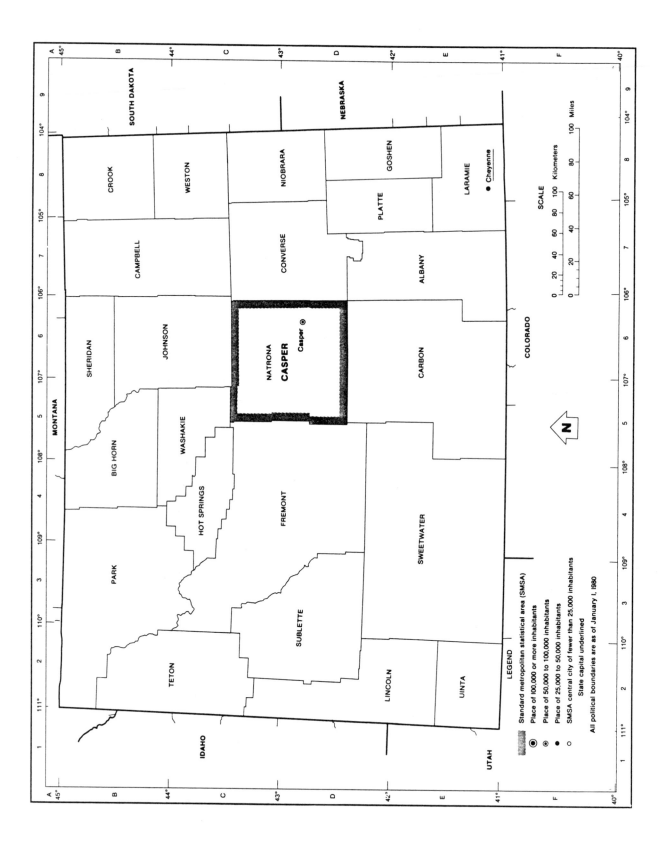

THE

UNITED STATES

DICTIONARY

OF PLACES

PLACE INDEX

STATE ABBREVIATIONS

ALABAMA................AL	KENTUCKY..............KY	OHIO.......................OH
ALASKA...................AK	LOUISIANA..............LA	OKLAHOMA ....OK
ARIZONA ....AZ	MAINE.....................ME	OREGON.................OR
ARKANSAS ....AR	MARYLAND ....MD	PENNSYLVANIA......PA
CALIFORNIA............CA	MASSACHUSETTS...MA	RHODE ISLAND.......RI
COLORADO.............CO	MICHIGAN ....MI	SOUTH CAROLINA.. SC
CONNECTICUT ....CT	MINNESOTA.............MN	SOUTH DAKOTA......SD
DELAWARE..............DE	MISSISSIPPI ....MS	TENNESSEE ....TN
DIST. OF	MISSOURI................MO	TEXAS.....................TX
COLUMBIA ....DC	MONTANA...............MT	UTAH ....UT
FLORIDA.................FL	NEBRASKA.............NB	VERMONT ....VT
GEORGIA................GA	NEVADA..................NV	VIRGINIA.................VA
HAWAII....................HI	NEW HAMPSHIRE ...NH	WASHINGTON.........WA
IDAHO.....................ID	NEW JERSEY..........NJ	WEST VIRGINIA ....WV
ILLINOIS..................IL	NEW MEXICO..........NM	WISCONSIN............WI
INDIANA..................IN	NEW YORK..............NY	WYOMING...............WY
IOWA.......................IA	NORTH CAROLINA.. NC	
KANSAS ....KS	NORTH DAKOTA......ND	

PLACE INDEX

AARONSBURG, PA
ABBEVILLE, AL,GA,LA,MS,SC
ABBOT, ME
ABBOTSFORD, WI
ABBOTTSTOWN, PA
ABBYVILLE, KS
ABE, TX
ABERCROMBIE, ND
ABERDEEN, CA,ID,MD,MS,NC
  OH,PA,SD,TX,WA
ABIE, NB
ABILENE, KS,TX
ABINGDON, IL,VA
ABINGTON, MA,PA
ABITA SPRINGS, LA
ABSECON, NJ
ACADEMY CORNERS, PA
ACALA, TX
ACAMPO, TX
ACCIDENT, MD
ACCOMAC, VA
ACEQUIA, ID
ACHILLE, OK
ACKERLY, TX
ACKERMAN, MS
ACKERMANVILLE, PA
ACKLEY, IA
ACMETONIA, PA
ACME, PA
ACOSTA, PA
ACRA, NY
ACTON, CA,MA,ME,TX
ACUSHNET, MA
ACWORTH, GA,NH
ADA, MN,OH,OK
ADAH, PA
ADAIR, IA,OK
ADAIR VILLAGE, OR
ADAIRSVILLE, GA
ADAMS, MA,MN,NB,ND,NY
  OR,TN,WI
ADAMS DALE, PA
ADAMS HILL, PA
ADAMSBURG, PA
ADAMSTOWN, PA
ADAMSVILLE, AL,PA,TN
ADDINGTON, OK
ADDIS, LA
ADDISON, AL,IL,ME,MI
  PA,TX,VT
ADDRAN, TX
ADDYSTON, OH
ADEL, GA,IA
ADELAIDE, PA
ADELANTO, CA
ADELL, WI
ADIN, CA
ADMIRE, KS,PA
ADONA, AR
ADRIAN, GA,MI,MN,MO,OR
  PA,TX
ADVANCE, IN,MO
AFTON, CA,IA,MN,OK,TX,WY
AGAR, SD
AGAWAM, MA
AGENCY, IA,MO
AGENDA, KS
AGOURA, CA
AGRA, KS,OK
AGUA DULCE, TX
AGUANGA, CA
AGUILAR, CO
AHMEEK, MI
AHOSKIE, NC
AHUIMANU, HI

AHWAHNEE, CA
AIEA, HI
AIKEN, PA,SC
AILEY, GA
AINSWORTH, IA,NB
AIRPORT DRIVE, MO
AIRVILLE, PA
AIRWAY HEIGHTS, WA
AITKIN, MN
AKASKA, SD
AKELEY, MN,PA
AKHIOK, AK
AKIACHAK, AK
AKIAK, AK
AKRON, AL,CO,IA,IN,MI
  NY,OH,PA
AKUTAN, AK
AL TAHOE, CA
ALABAMA, NY
ALABASTER, AL
ALACHUA, FL
ALAKANUK, AK
ALAMANCE, NC
ALAMEDA CITY, CA
ALAMO, CA,GA,IN,ND,NV
  TN,TX
ALAMO HEIGHTS, TX
ALAMOGORDO, NM
ALAMOSA, CO
ALANSON, MI
ALAPAHA, GA
ALBA, MO,PA,TX
ALBANY, CA,GA,IL,IN,KY
  LA,MN,MO,NY,PA,TX,VT,WI
ALBEE, SD
ALBEMARLE, NC
ALBERHILL, CA
ALBERS, IL
ALBERT, KS
ALBERT CITY, IA
ALBERT LEA, MN
ALBERTA, MN,VA
ALBERTON, MT
ALBERTVILLE, AL,MN
ALBIA, IA
ALBIN, WY
ALBION, CA,IA,ID,IL,IN
  ME,MI,NB,NY,OK,PA,WA
ALBRIGHTSVILLE, PA
ALBUQUERQUE, NM
ALBURG, VT
ALBURTIS, PA
ALCESTER, SD
ALCOA, TN
ALDA, NB
ALDAN, PA
ALDEN, IA,MN,NY,PA
ALDENVILLE, PA
ALDERPOINT, CA
ALDERSON, OK,WV
ALDOVIN, PA
ALEDO, IL,TX
ALEKNAGIK, AK
ALEX, OK
ALEXANDER, KS,ME,ND,NY
ALEXANDER CITY, AL
ALEXANDRIA, IN,KY,LA,MN
  MO,NB,NH,PA,SD,TN,VA
ALEXIS, IL
ALFARATA, PA
ALFORD, MA,PA
ALFORDSVILLE, IN
ALFRED, ME,NY
ALGOA, TX
ALGOMA, WI

ALGONA, IA
ALGONAC, MI
ALHAMBRA, CA,IL
ALIANCE, NC
ALICE, TX
ALICIA, AR,PA
ALINDA, PA
ALINE, OK
ALIQUIPPA, PA
ALLAGASH, ME
ALLAKAKET, AK
ALLAMUCHY, NJ
ALLARDT, TN
ALLEGAN, MI
ALLEGANY, NY
ALLEGHANY, CA
ALLEGHENY, PA
ALLEGHENYVILLE, PA
ALLEMANS, PA
ALLEN, KS,KY,MI,NB,OK
  PA,TX
ALLEN PARK, MI
ALLENDALE, NJ,SC
ALLENHURST, GA,NJ
ALLENPORT, PA
ALLENSTOWN, NH
ALLENSVILLE, KY,PA
ALLENTOWN, GA,NJ,PA
ALLEYTON, TX
ALLGOOD, AL
ALLIANCE, NB,OH
ALLIGATOR, MS
ALLISON, IA,PA
ALLISON HEIGHTS, PA
ALLISON PARK, PA
ALLOUEZ, WI
ALLOWAY, NJ
ALLRED, TX
ALMA, AR,CO,GA,IA,IL,KS
  MI,MO,NB,NY,WI
ALMENA, KS,WI
ALMIRA, WA
ALMOND, WI
ALMONT, MI,ND
ALMONTE, CA
ALMYRA, AR
ALNA, ME
ALPENA, AR,MI,SD
ALPHA, IL,MI,MN,NJ
ALPHARETTA, GA
ALPINE, CA,NJ,TX,UT
ALSACE MANOR, PA
ALSIP, IL
ALSTON, GA
ALTA, CA,UT
ALTA LOMA, CA
ALTA VISTA, KS
ALTADENA, CA
ALTAMONT, CA,IL,KS,MO,NY
  PA,SD,TN,UT
ALTAMONTE SPRINGS, FL
ALTAVILLE, CA
ALTAVISTA, VA
ALTENBURG, MO
ALTHEIMER, AR
ALTIAR, TX
ALTO, GA,TX
ALTOGA, TX
ALTON, IA,IL,IN,KS,ME
ALTONA, IL,IN,NY
ALTOONA, IA,KS,PA,WI
ALTURA, MN
ALTURAS, CA
ALTUS, AR,OK
ALUM BANK, PA

ALUM ROCK, CA
ALUTA, PA
ALVA, OK
ALVARADO, MN,TX
ALVERDA, PA
ALVERTON, PA
ALVIN, TX
ALVISO, CA
ALVO, NB
ALVORD, TX
AMADOR CITY, CA
AMAGANSETT, NY
AMAGON, AR
AMANDA, OH
AMARILLO, TX
AMBER, OK
AMBERLEY, OH
AMBIA, IN
AMBLER, AK,PA
AMBOY, CA,IL,IN,MN
AMBRIDGE, PA
AMBRIDGE HEIGHTS, PA
AMBROSE, GA
AMELIA, OH
AMEND, PA
AMENIA, NY
AMERICAN FALLS, ID
AMERICAN FORK, UT
AMERICUS, GA,KS
AMERY, WI
AMES, IA,OK
AMESBURY, MA
AMESVILLE, OH
AMETT, OK
AMHERST, MA,ME,NB,NH
  OH,VA,WI
AMHERST JUNCTION, WI
AMITE CITY, LA
AMITY, AR,ME,MO,OR,PA
AMITYVILLE, NY
AMMON, ID
AMO, IN
AMORITA, OK
AMORY, MS
AMSBRY, PA
AMSTERDAM, MO,NY,OH
ANACOCO, LA
ANACONDA-DEER LODGE, MT
ANACORTES, WA
ANAHEIM, CA
ANAHUAC, TX
ANAKTUVUK PASS, AK
ANALOMINK, PA
ANAMOOSE, ND
ANAMOSA, IA
ANAWALT, WV
ANCHORAGE, AK,KY
ANCIENT OAKS, PA
ANDALE, KS
ANDALUSIA, AL,IL,PA
ANDERSON, AK,AL,CA,IN
  MO,SC,TX
ANDERSONVILLE, GA
ANDOVER, CT,KS,MA,ME,MN
  NH,NJ,NY,OH,SD,VT
ANDRADE, CA
ANDREAS, PA
ANDREWS, IN,NC,SC,TX
ANETA, ND
ANGELS, PA
ANGELS CAMP, CA
ANGIE, LA
ANGIER, NC
ANGLETON, TX
ANGOLA, IN,NY

PLACE INDEX

ANGOON, AK
ANGUILLA, MS
ANGWIN, CA
ANIAK, AK
ANITA, IA,PA
ANIWA, WI
ANKENY, IA
ANMOORE, WV
ANN ARBOR, MI
ANNA, IL
ANNA MARIA, FL
ANNABELLA, UT
ANNANDALE, MN
ANNAPOLIS, MD,MO
ANNAWAN, IL
ANNISTON, AL,MO
ANNONA, TX
ANNVILLE, PA
ANODARKO, OK
ANOKA, MN,NB
ANSELMO, NB
ANSLEY, NB
ANSONIA, CT,OH
ANSONVILLE, NC
ANSTED, WV
ANTELOPE, OR
ANTHONY, KS,TX
ANTIGO, WI
ANTIOCH, CA,IL,OH
ANTLER, ND
ANTLERS, OK
ANTOINE, AR
ANTON, TX
ANTONITO, CO
ANTRIM, NH
ANTWERP, OH
ANVIK, AK
APACHE, OK
APACHE JUNCTION, AZ
APALACHICOLA, FL
APEX, NC
APLINGTON, IA
APOLLO, PA
APOPKA, FL
APPALACHIA, VA
APPLE CREEK, OH
APPLE RIVER, IL
APPLE SPRINGS, TX
APPLE VALLEY, MN
APPLEBY, TX
APPLEGATE, CA,MI
APPLETON, ME,MN,WI
APPLETON CITY, MO
APPOMATTOX, VA
APTOS, CA
AQUILLA, TX
ARAB, AL
ARABI, GA
ARAGON, GA
ARANSAS PASS, TX
ARAPAHO, OK
ARAPAHOE, NB,NC
ARBUCKLE, CA
ARBYRD, MO
ARCADE, NY
ARCADIA, CA,FL,IA,IN,KS
    LA,MO,NB,TX,WI
ARCADIA LAKES, SC
ARCANUM, OH
ARCATA, CA
ARCHBALD, PA
ARCHBOLD, OH
ARCHER, FL
ARCHER CITY, TX
ARCHIE, MO
ARCO, ID,MN
ARCOLA, IL,MS
ARDEN, DE
ARDEN HILLS, MN
ARDENCRAFT, DE
ARDENTOWN, DE
ARDMORE, AL,OK,SD,TN
ARENZVILLE, IL

ARGENTA, NV,IL
ARGONIA, KS
ARGOS, IN
ARGUSVILLE, ND
ARGYLE, GA,ME,MN,MO,WI
ARIMO, ID
ARION, IA
ARITON, AL
ARKADELPHIA, AR
ARKANSAS CITY, AR,KS
ARKOMA, OK
ARLEY, AL
ARLINGTON, GA,IA,KS,KY
    MN,NB,NC,OH,OR,TN
    TX,VA,VT,WA,WI
ARLINGTON HEIGHTS, IL
ARMA, KS
ARMADA, MI
ARMONA, CA
ARMOUR, SD
ARMSTRONG, IA
ARNAUDVILLE, LA
ARNOLD, MO,NB
ARNOLDS PARK, IA
ARNOLDSVILLE, GA
ARNOT, PA
AROMA PARK, IL
ARONA, PA
ARPIN, WI
ARRENDO, FL
ARRIBA, CO
ARROWBEAR LAKE, CA
ARROWHEAD HIGHLANDS, CA
ARROWSIC, ME
ARROYO GRANDE, CA
ARTAS, SD
ARTESIA, CA,MS,NM
ARTESIAN, SD
ARTHUR, IL,NB,ND
ARTHUR CITY, TX
ARVADA, CO
ARVIN, CA
ASBURY PARK, NJ
ASH FLAT, AR
ASH GROVE, MO
ASHBURN, GA
ASHBURNHAM, MA
ASHBY, MA
ASHDOWN, AR
ASHEBORO, NC
ASHEBORO SOUTH, NC
ASHEBORO WEST, NC
ASHER, OK
ASHERTON, TX
ASHEVILLE, NC
ASHFIELD, MA,PA
ASHFORD, AL,CT
ASHLAND, AL,CA,IL,KS,KY
    LA,MA,ME,MO,MS,NB,NH,OH
    OK,OR,PA,VA,WI
ASHLAND CITY, TN
ASHLEY, IL,IN,MI,ND,OH,PA
ASHTON, IA,ID,IL,NB,SD
ASHVILLE, AL,OH,PA
ASHWAUBENON, WI
ASILOMAR, CA
ASKEWVILLE, NC
ASKOV, MN
ASOTIN, WA
ASPEN, CO
ASPERMONT, TX
ASPERS, PA
ASPINWALL, PA
ASSARIA, KS
ASSUMPTION, IL
ASTATULA, FL
ASTI, CA
ASTON, PA
ASTORIA, IL,OR,SD
ASYLUM, PA
ATALISSA, IA
ATASCADERO, CA

ATCHISON, KS
ATGLEN, PA
ATHENA, OR
ATHENS, AL,GA,IL,LA,ME,MI
    NY,OH,PA,TN,TX,VT,WI,WV
ATHERTON, CA
ATHOL, ID,KS,MA,PA
ATKINS, AR,IA
ATKINSON, IL,ME,NB,NC,NH
ATLANTA, GA,IL,IN,KS
    LA,NB,TX
ATLANTIC, IA,PA
ATLANTIC BEACH, FL,NC,NY
ATLANTIC CITY, NJ
ATLANTIC HIGHLANDS, NJ
ATLAS, PA
ATLASBURG, PA
ATMAUTLUAK, AK
ATMORE, AL
ATOKA, OK,TN
ATOMIC CITY, ID
ATTALLA, AL
ATTAPULGUS, GA
ATTELBORO, MA
ATTICA, IN,KS,NY,OH
ATWATER, CA,MN
ATWOOD, CA,IL,KS,PA,TN
AU GRES, MI
AUBREY, AR
AUBURN, AL,CA,GA,IA,IL
    IN,KY,MA,ME,MI,NB,NH
    NY,PA,WA,WV
AUBURNDALE, FL,WI
AUBURNTOWN, TN
AUDENREID, PA
AUDREY, TX
AUDUBON, IA,MN,NJ,PA
AUDUBON PARK, KY
AUGUSTA, AR,GA,IL,KS,KY
    ME,MI,WI
AULANDER, NC
AULT, CO
AULTMAN, PA
AUMSVILLE, OR
AURELIA, IA
AURORA, CO,IA,IL,IN,KS
    ME,MN,MO,NB,NC,OH
    OR,SD,UT
AUSTELL, GA
AUSTERLITZ, NY
AUSTIN, AR,IN,MN,NV,TX
AUSTINBURG, PA
AUSTWELL, TX
AUTAUGAVILLE, AL
AUTRYVILLE, NC
AUXVASSE, MO
AVA, MO
AVALON, CA,NJ,PA
AVANT, OK
AVARD, OK
AVELLA, PA
AVENAL, CA
AVERY, TX
AVILA BEACH, CA
AVILLA, IN
AVINGER, TX
AVIS, PA
AVOCA, AR,IA,MN,NB
    PA,TX,WI
AVON, CO,CT,IL,MA,ME,MN
    NY,OH,PA,SD
AVON BY THE SEA, NJ
AVON LAKE, OH
AVON PARK, FL
AVONDALE, AZ,MO,PA
AVONDALE ESTATES, GA
AVONMORE, PA
AXEMANN, PA
AXTELL, KS,NB
AYDEN, NC
AYER, MA
AYNOR, SC
AYR, NB

AYRSHIRE, IA
AZLE, TX
AZTEC, NM
AZUSA, CA

BABBITT, MN
BABSON PARK, FL
BABYLON, NY
BACHMANVILLE, PA
BACKUS, MN
BACONTON, GA
BAD AXE, MI
BADEN, PA
BADGER, CA,IA,MN,SD
BADIN, NC
BAEDERWOOD, PA
BAGBY, CA
BAGDAD, CA
BAGGALEY, PA
BAGGS, WY
BAGLEY, IA,MN,WI
BAGNELL, MO
BAIDLAND, PA
BAILEY, NC
BAILEYTON, AL
BAILEYVILLE, ME
BAINBRIDGE, GA,IN
    NY,OH,PA
BAINVILLE, MT
BAIR, PA
BAIRD, CA,TX
BAIRDFORD, PA
BAKER, CA,LA,MT,OR
BAKERS SUMMIT, PA
BAKERSFIELD, CA,VT
BAKERSTOWN, PA
BAKERSVILLE, NC,PA
BAL HARBOUR, FL
BALA-CYNWYD, PA
BALANCE ROCK, CA
BALATON, MN
BALBOA, CA
BALCH SPRINGS, TX
BALD EAGLE, PA
BALD KNOB, AR
BALDWIN, FL,GA,LA,ME
    MI,PA,WI
BALDWIN CITY, KS
BALDWIN PARK, CA
BALDWINSVILLE, NY
BALDWYN, MS
BALFOUR, NC
BALL, LA
BALL GROUND, GA
BALLIETTSVILLE, PA
BALLINGER, TX
BALLSTON, NY
BALLWIN, MO
BALLY, PA
BALMORHEA, TX
BALSAM LAKE, WI
BALSINGER, PA
BALTA, ND
BALTIC, SD
BALTIMORE, MD,OH,VT
BAMBERG, SC
BANCROFT, IA,ID,KY,ME
    MI,NB,SD,WV
BANDERA, TX
BANDON, OR
BANGOR, ME,MI,NY,PA,WI
BANGS, TX
BANKERSMITH, TX
BANKS, AL,AR,OR
BANNER, CA
BANNER ELK, NC
BANNING, CA,PA
BANNOCKBURN, IL
BAR HARBOR, ME
BARABOO, WI
BARADA, NB
BARAGA, MI
BARBERS POINT HOUSING, HI
BARBERTON, OH

BARBOURMEADE, KY
BARBOURS, PA
BARBOURSVILLE, WV
BARBOURVILLE, KY
BARCLAY, MD
BARDSTOWN, KY
BARDWELL, KY,TX
BAREVILLE, PA
BARESVILLE, PA
BARGERSVILLE, IN
BARING, ME,MO
BARKER HEIGHTS, NC
BARKHAMSTED, CT
BARKSDALE, TX
BARLING, AR
BARLOW, OR
BARNARD, KS,ME,VT
BARNEGAT, NJ
BARNES, KS,PA
BARNESBORO, PA
BARNESTON, NB
BARNESVILLE, GA,MD
    MN,OH,PA
BARNET, VT
BARNEVELD, WI
BARNEY, GA
BARNSDALL, OK
BARNSLEY, PA
BARNSTABLE, MA
BARNUM, IA,MN
BARNWELL, SC
BARODA, MI
BARRACKVILLE, WV
BARRE, MA,VT
BARREE, PA
BARRETT, MN
BARRETT LAKE, CA
BARRINGTON, IL,NH,NJ,RI
BARRINGTON HILLS, IL
BARRON, WI
BARROW, AK
BARRVILLE, PA
BARRY, IL,MN
BARRYTON, MI
BARSTOW, CA
BART, PA
BARTLE, CA
BARTLETT, CA,IL,KS,NB
BARTLEY, NB
BARTO, PA
BARTON, MD,NY,VT
BARTON HILLS, MI
BARTONVILLE, IL
BARTOW, FL,GA
BARWICK, GA
BASALT, CO,ID
BASCOM, FL
BASEHOR, KS
BASILE, LA
BASIN, WY
BASKIN, LA
BASS LAKE, CA
BASSETT, AR,CA,NB
BASSFIELD, MS
BASTROP, LA,TX
BATAVIA, IA,IL,NY,OH
BATES CITY, MO
BATESLAND, SD
BATESVILLE, AR,IN,IN,MS
BATH, IL,ME,NC,NH,NY,PA
BATH (BERKELEY
    SPRINGS), WV
BATH ADDITION, PA
BATON ROUGE, LA
BATTLE CREEK, IA,MI,NB
BATTLE GROUND, IN,WA
BATTLE LAKE, MN
BATTLEBORO, NC
BATTLEFIELD, MO
BAUDETTE, MN
BAUERSTOWN, PA
BAUMSTOWN, PA
BAUSMAN, PA

BAUXITE, AR
BAXLEY, GA
BAXTER, IA,MN,PA,TN
BAXTER SPRINGS, KS
BAY, AR
BAY CITY, MI,OR,TX
BAY HEAD, NJ
BAY MINETTE, AL
BAY SPRINGS, MS
BAY SAINT LOUIS, MS
BAY VILLAGE, OH
BAYARD, FL,IA,NB,NM,WV
BAYBORO, NC
BAYFIELD, CO,WI
BAYONNE, NJ
BAYOU LA BATRE, AL
BAYPORT, MN
BAYSIDE, TX,WI
BAYTOWN, TX
BAYVILLE, NY
BAZILE MILLS, NB
BAZINE, KS
BEACH, ND
BEACH HAVEN, NJ,PA
BEACH LAKE, PA
BEACHWOOD, NJ,OH
BEACON, IA,NY
BEACON FALLS, CT
BEACONSFIELD, IA
BEALS, ME
BEALSVILLE, PA
BEAR CREEK, AL,PA,WI
BEAR LAKE, MI,PA
BEAR RIVER CITY, UT
BEAR ROCKS, PA
BEAR VALLEY, CA,PA
BEARCREEK, MT
BEARDEN, AR
BEARDSLEY, MN
BEARDSTOWN, IL
BEARGRASS, NC
BEARTOWN, PA
BEATRICE, AL,NB
BEATTIE, KS
BEATTY, NV,PA
BEATTYVILLE, KY
BEAUFORT, NC,SC
BEAUMONT, CA,MS,TX
BEAUX ARTS VILLAGE, WA
BEAVER, IA,OK,PA,UT
BEAVER BAY, MN
BEAVER BROOK, PA
BEAVER CITY, NB
BEAVER COVE, ME
BEAVER CREEK, MN
BEAVER CROSSING, NB
BEAVER DAM, KY,WI
BEAVER FALLS, PA
BEAVER MEADOWS, PA
BEAVERDALE, PA
BEAVERSPRINGS, PA
BEAVERTON, AL,MI,OR
BEAVERTOWN, PA
BECCARIA, PA
BECHTELSVILLE, PA
BECKEMEYER, IL
BECKER, MN
BECKETT, MA
BECKLEY, WV
BECKVILLE, TX
BECKWORTH, CA
BEDDINGTON, ME
BEDFORD, IA,IN,KY,MA,NH
    NY,OH,PA,TX,VA
BEDFORD HEIGHTS, OH
BEDFORD PARK, IL
BEDMINSTER, NJ,PA
BEE, NB
BEEBE, AR
BEECH BOTTOM, WV
BEECH CREEK, PA
BEECH GROVE, IN
BEECHWOOD VILLAGE, KY

BEEDEVILLE, AR
BEEMER, NB
BEERSHEBA SPRINGS, TN
BEERSVILLE, PA
BEEVILLE, TX
BEGGS, OK
BEJOU, MN
BEL AIR, MD
BELCHER, LA
BELCHERTOWN, MA
BELDEN, CA,NB
BELDING, MI
BELEN, NM
BELFAST, ME,NY,PA
BELFAST JUNCTION, PA
BELFIELD, ND
BELGIUM, IL,WI
BELGRADE, ME,MN,MT,NB
BELHAVEN, NC
BELINGTON, WV
BELK, AL
BELL, CA,FL
BELL BUCKLE, TN
BELL CITY, MO
BELL GARDENS, CA
BELLA VILLA, MO
BELLA VISTA, CA,PA
BELLAIR, FL
BELLAIRE, MI,OH,TX
BELLBROOK, OH
BELLE, WV
BELLE FOURCHE, SD
BELLE GLADE, FL
BELLE ISLE, FL
BELLE MEADE, TN
BELLE PLAINE, IA,KS,MN
BELLEAIR BLUFFS, FL
BELLEFONTAINE, OH
BELLEFONTAINE NEIGHBORS, MO
BELLEFONTE, DE,KY,PA
BELLEGROVE, PA
BELLEVIEW, FL
BELLEVILLE, AR,IL,KS
    MI,NJ,WI
BELLEVUE, IA,ID,IL,KY,MI
    NB,OH,PA,TX,WA
BELLFLOWER, CA
BELLINGHAM, MA,MN,WA
BELLMAWR, NJ
BELLOWS FALLS, VT
BELLS, TN,TX
BELLWOOD, IL,NB
BELMAR, NJ
BELMOND, IA
BELMONT, CA,MA,ME,MS,NC
    NY,PA,TX,WI,WV
BELMONT HILLS, PA
BELMONT HOMES, PA
BELMORE, OH
BELOIT, KS,OH,WI
BELPRE, KS,OH
BELSANO, PA
BELT, MT
BELTON, MO,SC,TX
BELTRAMI, MN
BELVEDERE, CA
BELVIDERE, NB,NJ,SD,VT
BELVIEW, MN
BELVUE, KS
BELZONI, MS
BEMENT, IL
BEMIDJI, MN
BEN AVON, PA
BEN AVON HEIGHTS, PA
BEN BOLT, TX
BEN LOMMOND, CA
BEN LOMOND, AR
BENA, MN
BENAVIDES, TX
BENBOW, CA
BEND, OR
BENDERSVILLE, PA
BENEDICT, KS,NB

BENEDICTA, ME
BENEVOLENCE, GA
BENEZETT, PA
BENFER, PA
BENICIA, CA
BENJAMIN, TX
BENKELMAN, NB
BENLD, IL
BENNET, NB
BENNETT, CO,IA
BENNETTSVILLE, SC
BENNINGTON, KS,NB
    NH,OK,VT
BENOIT, MS
BENSENVILLE, IL
BENSON, AZ,MN,NC,VT
BENTLEY, KS
BENTLEYCREEK, PA
BENTLEYVILLE, PA
BENTON, AR,CA,IL,KS,KY
    LA,ME,MO,NH,PA,TN,WI
BENTON CITY, WA
BENTON HARBOR, MI
BENTONIA, MS
BENTONVILLE, AR
BENWOOD, WV
BENZONIA, MI
BEREA, KY,OH
BERENDA, CA
BERESFORD, SD
BERGENFIELD, NJ
BERGMAN, AR
BERKELEY, CA,IL,MO
BERKELEY HEIGHTS, NJ
BERKELEY HILLS, PA
BERKLEY, MI,PA
BERKSHIRE, VT
BERLIN, CT,GA,MA,MD,NH
    NJ,PA,VT,WI
BERLINSVILLE, PA
BERN, KS
BERNALILLO, NM
BERNARDSTON, MA
BERNARDSVILLE, NJ
BERNE, IN,NY,PA
BERNICE, LA,OK
BERNIE, MO
BERRIEN SPRINGS, MI
BERRY, AL
BERRY HILL, TN
BERRYSBURG, PA
BERRYVILLE, AR,VA
BERTHA, MN
BERTHOLD, ND
BERTHOUD, CO
BERTRAM, TX
BERTRAND, NB
BERWICK, LA,ME,PA
BERWINSDALE, PA
BERWYN, IL,NB,PA
BERWYN HEIGHTS, MD
BESCO, PA
BESSEMER, AL,MI,PA
BESSEMER CITY, NC
BESSIE, OK
BESSMAY, TX
BETHALTO, IL
BETHANY, CT,IL,IN,MO
    OK,PA,WV
BETHANY BEACH, DE
BETHEL, AK,CT,DE,ME,MN
    NC,OH,PA,VT
BETHEL ACRES, OK
BETHEL HEIGHTS, AR
BETHEL PARK, PA
BETHEL SPRINGS, TN
BETHESDA, OH
BETHLEHAM, CT,NH
BETHLEHEM, GA,PA,WV
BETHUNE, CO,SC
BETTERAVIA, CA
BETTERTON, MD
BEULAH, MI,MS,ND

BEULAVILLE, NC
BEVERLY, KS,MA,NJ
  OH,TX,WV
BEVERLY ESTATES, PA
BEVERLY HEIGHTS, PA
BEVERLY HILLS, CA,MI,MO
BEVERLY SHORES, IN
BEVIER, MO
BEXLEY, OH
BEYER, PA
BICKNELL, IN,UT
BIDDEFORD, ME
BIEBER, CA
BIENVILLE, LA
BIESECKER GAP, PA
BIG BEAR CITY, CA
BIG BEND, WI
BIG CABIN, OK
BIG FALLS, MN,WI
BIG FLAT, AR
BIG FOOT, TX
BIG LAKE, MN,TX
BIG OAK FLAT, CA
BIG PINE, CA
BIG PINEY, WY
BIG RAPIDS, MI
BIG RUN, PA
BIG SANDY, MT,TN,TX
BIG SPRING, TX
BIG SPRINGS, NB
BIG STONE CITY, SD
BIG STONE GAP, VA
BIG SUR, CA
BIG TIMBER, MT
BIG WELLS, TX
BIGELOW, AR,MN
BIGFORK, MN
BIGGERS, AR
BIGGS, CA
BIGGSVILLE, IL
BIGLERVILLE, PA
BILLERICA, MA
BILLINGSLEY, AL
BILLINGS, MO,MT,OK
BILOXI, MS
BILTMORE FOREST, NC
BINFORD, ND
BINGEN, PA,WA
BINGER, OK
BINGHAM, ME
BINGHAM FARMS, MI
BINGHAM LAKE, MN
BINGHAMTON, NY
BIOLA, CA
BIRCH RUN, MI
BIRCH TREE, MO
BIRCHRUNVILLE, PA
BIRCHWOOD, WI
BIRD ISLAND, MN
BIRD IN HAND, PA
BIRD'S LANDING, CA
BIRDSBORO, PA
BIRDSEYE, IN
BIRMINGHAM, AL,MI
BIRNAMWOOD, WI
BIROME, TX
BISBEE, AZ,ND
BISCAYNE PARK, FL
BISCOE, NC
BISHOP, CA,GA,PA,TX
BISHOP HILL, IL
BISHOPVILLE, SC
BISMARCK, MO,ND
BISON, KS,SD
BIWABIK, MN
BLACK, AL
BLACK CREEK, NC,WI
BLACK DIAMOND, WA
BLACK EARTH, WI
BLACK HAWK, CO
BLACK HORSE, PA
BLACK JACK, MO
BLACK LICK, PA

BLACK MOUNTAIN, NC
BLACK OAK, AR
BLACK POINT, CA
BLACK RIVER FALLS, WI
BLACK ROCK, AR
BLACKBURN, OK
BLACKDUCK, MN
BLACKFOOT, ID
BLACKSBURG, SC,VA
BLACKSHEAR, GA
BLACKSTONE, MA,VA
BLACKSVILLE, WV
BLACKVILLE, SC
BLACKWELL, OK,TX
BLACKWOOD TERRACE, NJ
BLADEN, NB
BLADENSBURG, MD
BLADES, DE
BLAIN, PA
BLAINE, ME,MN,TN,WA
BLAINE HILL, PA
BLAIR, NB,OK,WI
BLAIRSDEN, CA
BLAIRSTOWN, NJ
BLAIRSVILLE, GA,PA
BLAKELY, GA,PA
BLANCA, CO
BLANCHARD, IA,LA,ME,PA
BLANCHARDVILLE, WI
BLANCHESTER, OH
BLANCO, TX
BLAND, MO
BLANDBURG, PA
BLANDENBORO, NC
BLANDFORD, MA
BLANDING, UT
BLANDON, PA
BLANKET, TX
BLENHEIM, SC
BLEVINS, AR
BLISS, ID
BLISSFIELD, MI
BLOCKSBURG, CA
BLOCKTON, IA
BLOMKEST, MN
BLOOMBURG, TX
BLOOMER, WI
BLOOMFIELD, CT,IA,IN,KY
  MO,NB,NJ,NM,PA,VT
BLOOMFIELD HILLS, MI
BLOOMING GROVE, TX
BLOOMING PRAIRIE, MN
BLOOMINGDALE, GA,IN
  MI,NJ,PA
BLOOMINGTON, ID,IL,IN
  MN,NB,WI
BLOOMSBURG, PA
BLOOMSBURY, NJ
BLOOMSDALE, MO
BLOOMVILLE, OH
BLOSSBURG, PA
BLOSSOM, TX
BLOSSOM HILL, PA
BLOUNTSTOWN, FL
BLOUNTSVILLE, AL,IN
BLOXOM, VA
BLUE ASH, OH
BLUE BALL, PA
BLUE BELL, PA
BLUE CANYON, CA
BLUE EARTH, MN
BLUE GRASS, IA
BLUE HILL, ME,NB
BLUE ISLAND, IL
BLUE JAY, CA
BLUE LAKE, CA
BLUE MOUND, IL,KS
BLUE MOUNDS, WI
BLUE MOUNTAIN, AL,AR,MS
BLUE RAPIDS, KS
BLUE RIDGE, GA,TX
BLUE RIVER, WI
BLUE SPRINGS, AL,MO,MS,NB

BLUEFIELD, VA,WV
BLUEJACKET, OK
BLUFFTON, IN,OH,SC
BLUFF CITY, AR,KS,TN
BLUM, TX
BLUNT, SD
BLYTHE, CA
BLYTHEVILLE, AR
BLYTHEWOOD, SC
BOALSBURG, PA
BOARDMAN, OR
BOAZ, AL
BOBTOWN, PA
BOCA RATON, FL
BODEGA, CA
BODIE, CA
BOERNE, TX
BOGATA, TX
BOGER CITY, NC
BOGOTA, NJ
BOGUE, KS
BOGULSA, LA
BOILING SPRING LAKES, NC
BOILING SPRINGS, NC,PA
BOISE CITY, ID,OK
BOKCHITO, OK
BOKOSHE, OK
BOLCKOW, MO
BOLEY, OK
BOLIGEE, AL
BOLINAS, CA
BOLIVAR, MO,NY,OH,TN,WV
BOLIVIA, NC
BOLTON, CT,MS,NC,VT
BOMBAY, NY
BON AIB, AL
BONANZA, OR
BONAPARTE, IA
BONDUEL, WI
BONDURANT, IA
BONESTEEL, SD
BONHAM, TX
BONIFAY, FL
BONITA, CA,LA
BONNE TERRE, MO
BONNEAU, SC
BONNER SPRINGS, KS
BONNERS FERRY, ID
BONO, AR
BONSALL, CA
BOOKER, TX
BOONE, CO,IA,NC
BOONES MILL, VA
BOONEVILLE, AR,MS
BOONSBORO, MD
BOONTOWN, NJ
BOONVILLE, CA,IN,MO,NC
BOOTHBAY, ME
BOOTHBAY HARBOR, ME
BOOTHWYN, PA
BORDENTOWN, NJ
BORGER, TX
BORON, CA
BORREGO SPRINGS, CA
BOSCAWEN, NH
BOSCOBEL, WI
BOSQUE FARMS, NM
BOSSIER CITY, LA
BOSTIC, NC
BOSTON, IN,MA,NY,PA,TX
BOSWELL, IN,OK,PA
BOTHELL, WA
BOTKINS, OH
BOTTINEAU, ND
BOULDER, CO,MT
BOULDER CITY, NV
BOULDER CREEK, CA
BOUNTIFUL, UT
BOUND BROOK, NJ
BOURBON, IN,MO
BOURBONNAIS, IL
BOURNE, MA
BOVEY, MN

BOVILL, ID
BOVINA, TX
BOW MAR, CO
BOWBELLS, ND
BOWDLE, SD
BOWDOIN, ME
BOWDOINHAM, ME
BOWERBANK, ME
BOWERS, DE
BOWIE, MD,TX
BOWLEGS, OK
BOWLER, WI
BOWLING GREEN, FL,KY
  MO,OH,VA
BOWMAN, ND,SC
BOWMANSTOWN, PA
BOX ELDER, SD
BOYCE, LA,VA
BOYCEVILLE, WI
BOYD, MN,TX,WI
BOYDEN, IA
BOYDTON, VA
BOYERS, PA
BOYERTOWN, PA
BOYES HOT SPRINGS, CA
BOYKINS, VA
BOYLE, MS
BOYNE CITY, MI
BOYNE FALLS, MI
BOYNTON, OK
BOYNTON BEACH, FL
BOYS TOWN, NB
BOZEMAN, MT
BOZRAH, CT
BRACKENRIDGE, PA
BRACKETTVILLE, TX
BRADDOCK, PA
BRADEN, TN
BRADENTON, FL
BRADENTON BEACH, FL
BRADENVILLE, PA
BRADFORD, AR,IL,ME,OH
  PA,TN,VT
BRADFORD HILLS, PA
BRADFORDSVILLE, KY
BRADLEY, AR,CA,IL
  ME,OK,SD
BRADLEY BEACH, NJ
BRADNER, OH
BRADSHAW, NB
BRADY, NB,TX
BRAGGS, OK
BRAHAM, MN
BRAIDWOOD, IL
BRAINARD, NB
BRAINERD, MN
BRAINTREE, VT
BRAMAN, OK
BRAMWELL, WV
BRANCH, AR,MN
BRANCHVILLE, AL,NJ,SC,VA
BRANDENBURG, KY
BRANDON, IA,MS,VT,WI
BRANDON CITY, SD
BRANDONVILLE, WV
BRANDT, SD
BRANFORD, CT,FL
BRANSON, CO,MO
BRANTLEY, AL
BRATENAHL, OH
BRATTLEBORO, VT
BRAWLEY, CA
BRAY, CA,OK
BRAYMER, MO
BRAYTON, IA
BRAZIL, IN
BRAZORIA, TX
BREA, CA
BREAUX BRIDGE, LA
BRECKENRIDGE, CO,MI,MN
  MO,OK,TX
BRECKENRIDGE HILLS, MO
BRECKSVILLE, OH

BREDA, IA
BREEDSVILLE, MI
BREESE, IL
BREMEN, GA,IN,ME,OH
BREMERTON, WA
BREMOND, TX
BRENHAM, TX
BRENT, AL
BRENTFORD, SD
BRENTWOOD, CA,MD,MO
  NH,PA,TN
BREVARD, NC
BREVIG MISSION, AK
BREWER, ME
BREWSTER, KS,MN,NB,OH
BREWTON, AL
BRIAN HEAD, UT
BRIAR CREEK, PA
BRICELAND, CA
BRICELYN, MN
BRICK, NJ
BRIDGE CITY, TX
BRIDGEPORT, AL,CA,CT,IL
  NB,OH,OK,PA,TX,WV
BRIDGER, MT
BRIDGETON, MO,NC,NJ
BRIDGEVIEW, IL
BRIDGEVILLE, DE,PA
BRIDGEWATER, CT,IA,ME,NH
  NJ,PA,SD,VA,VT
BRIDGMAN, MI
BRIDGTON, ME
BRIDPORT, VT
BRIELLE, NJ
BRIGANTINE, NJ
BRIGHAM CITY, UT
BRIGHTON, AL,CO,IA
  MI,TN,VT
BRIGHTWATERS, NY
BRILLIANT, AL,OH,WI
BRIMFIELD, IL
BRINKLEY, AR
BRINSON, GA
BRISBANE, CA
BRISTOL, CT,FL,IN,ME,NH
  PA,RI,SD,TN,VA,VT
BRISTOL LAKE, CA
BRISTOW, NB,OK
BRITT, IA
BRITTON, MI,SD
BROADALBIN, NY
BROADDUS, TX
BROADHEAD, WI
BROADLANDS, IL
BROADUS, MT
BROADVIEW, IL,MT
BROADVIEW HEIGHTS, OH
BROADWATER, NB
BROADWAY, NC,VA
BROCK, NB
BROCKPORT, NY
BROCKTON, MA,MT,PA
BROCKWAY, PA
BRODERICK, CA
BRODHEAD, KY
BRODHEADSVILLE, PA
BROGDEN, NC
BROKEN BOW, NB,OK
BROMLEY, KY
BRONAUGH, MO
BRONSON, FL,KS,MI,TX
BRONTE, TX
BRONWOOD, GA
BRONX, NY
BROOK, IN
BROOK PARK, OH
BROOKER, FL
BROOKEVILLE, MD
BROOKFIELD, CT,IL
  MA,MO,VT,WI
BROOKFORD, NC
BROOKHAVEN, MS,NY,PA
BROOKINGS, OR,SD

BROOKLAND, AR
BROOKLET, GA
BROOKLIN, ME
BROOKLINE, MA,MO,NH,VT
BROOKLYN, CT,IA,IN,MI
  NY,OH,WI
BROOKLYN PARK, MN
BROOKNEAL, VA
BROOKPORT, IL
BROOKS, GA,ME,MN
BROOKSBURG, IN
BROOKSHIRE, TX
BROOKSIDE, AL,PA
BROOKSTON, IN
BROOKSVILLE, FL,KY
  ME,MS,OK
BROOKVIEW, MD
BROOKVILLE, IN,KS,OH,PA
BROOKWOOD, AL
BROOMALL, PA
BROOMFIELD, CO
BROOTEN, MN
BROUSSARD, LA
BROWERVILLE, MN
BROWN CITY, MI
BROWN DEER, WI
BROWNDEL, TX,KS
BROWNFIELD, ME,TX
BROWNING, MO,MT
BROWNINGTON, VT
BROWNS VALLEY, MN
BROWNSBORO, TX
BROWNSBORO VILLAGE, KY
BROWNSBURG, IN
BROWNSDALE, MN
BROWNSTOWN, IL,IN,PA
BROWNSVILLE, CA,MN,OR,PA
  TN,TX,WI
BROWNTON, MN
BROWNTOWN, WI
BROWNVILLE, ME,NB
BROWNWOOD, TX
BROXTON, GA
BRUCE, MS,SD,WI
BRUCETON, TN
BRUCETON MILLS, WV
BRUCEVILLE, IN,TX
BRULE, NB
BRUMLEY, MO
BRUNDIDGE, AL
BRUNING, NB
BRUNNERVILLE, PA
BRUNO, NB
BRUNSON, SC
BRUNSWICK, GA,MD,ME,MO
  NB,NC,OH,VT
BRUSH, CO
BRUSLY, LA
BRYAN, OH,TX
BRYANT, AR,IL,IN,SD
BRYCELAND, LA
BRYN GWELED, PA
BRYN MAWR, CA,PA
BRYSON, TX
BRYSON CITY, NC
BUCHANAN, GA,MI,VA
BUCK HILL FALLS, PA
BUCK'S LAKE, CA
BUCKEYE, AZ
BUCKFIELD, ME
BUCKHANNON, WV
BUCKHEAD, GA
BUCKHOLTS, TX
BUCKINGHAM, PA
BUCKLAND, AK,MA
BUCKLEY, IL,MI
BUCKLIN, KS,MO
BUCKMAN, MN
BUCKNER, AR,MO
BUCKSPORT, ME
BUCYRUS, OH
BUDA, IL,TX
BUDD LAKE, NJ

BUDE, MS
BUELLTON, CA
BUENA, NJ
BUENA PARK, CA
BUENA VISTA, CO,GA,VA
BUFFALO, IA,IL,KS,MN,MO
  ND,NY,OK,SD,TX,WV,WY
BUFFALO CENTER, IA
BUFFALO GAP, SD,TX
BUFFALO GROVE, IL
BUFFALO LAKE, MN
BUFORD, GA
BUHL, ID,MN
BUHLER, KS
BUIES CREEK, NC
BULL SHOALS, AR
BULLA, TX
BULLARD, TX
BULLS GAP, TN
BULLY HILL, PA
BUNA, TX
BUNKER HILL, IL,IN,TX,KS
BUNKERVILLE, NV
BUNKIE, LA
BUNN, NC
BUNNELL, FL
BURBANK, CA,OK
BURCHARD, NB
BURDEN, KS
BURDETT, KS
BURDETTE, AR
BURGAW, NC
BURGETTSTOWN, PA
BURGIN, KY
BURKBURNETT, TX
BURKE, SD,TX,VT
BURKESVILLE, KY
BURKET, IN
BURKEVILLE, VA
BURKITTSVILLE, MD
BURLESON, TX
BURLEY, ID
BURLINGAME, CA,KS
BURLINGTON, CO,CT,IA,IL
  IN,KS,MA,ME,MI,NC,ND
  NJ,OK,VT,WA,WI
BURLINGTON JUNCTION, MO
BURLISON, TN
BURNET, TX
BURNETTOWN, SC
BURNETTSVILLE, IN
BURNEY, CA
BURNHAM, IL,ME,PA
BURNS, KS,OR,TN,WY
BURNS FLAT, OK
BURNS HARBOR, IN
BURNSVILLE, MN,MS,NC,WV
BURNT CABINS, PA
BURR, NB
BURR OAK, KS,MI
BURREL, CA
BURRILLVILLE, RI
BURRTON, KS
BURT, IA
BURTON, MI,OH,TX
BURWELL, NB
BUSHKILL, PA
BUSHKILL CENTER, PA
BUSHLAND, TX
BUSHNELL, FL,IL,NB,SD
BUSHTON, KS
BUTLER, AL,GA,IN,MO,NJ
  OK,PA,SD
BUTNER, NC
BUTTE, NB
BUTTE CITY, CA,ID
BUTTE FALLS, OR
BUTTE-SILVER BOW, MT
BUTTERFIELD, MN
BUTTERNUT, WI
BUTTONWILLOW, CA
BUXTON, ME
BYARS, OK

BYERS, TX
BYESVILLE, OH
BYHALIA, MS
BYNG, OK
BYNUM, AL,TX
BYRDSTOWN, TN
BYROMVILLE, GA
BYRON, CA,GA,IL,ME,MI,MN
  NB,NY,OK,WY

CABAZON, CA
CABLE, WI
CABOOL, MO
CABOT, AR,PA,VT
CACTUS, TX
CADDO MILLS, TX
CADDO VALLEY, AR
CADILLAC, MI
CADIZ, IN,KY,OH
CADIZ LAKE, CA
CADOTT, WI
CADWELL, GA
CAHOKIA, IL
CAINSVILLE, MO
CAIRNBROOK, PA
CAIRO, GA,IL,NB,NY,WV
CAJON JUNCTION, CA
CALABASH, NC
CALAIS, ME,VT
CALAMUS, IA
CALAVERAS CITY, CA
CALDEONIA, MI,MS
CALDWELL, AR,ID,KS
  NJ,OH,TX
CALE, AR
CALEDONIA, MN,MO,NY
CALERA, AL
CALEXICO, CA
CALHAN, CO
CALHOUN, GA,KY,TN
CALHOUN CITY, MS
CALHOUN FALLS, SC
CALICO, CA
CALICO ROCK, AR
CALIENTE, CA,NV
CALIFON, NJ
CALIFORNIA, MO,PA
CALIFORNIA CITY, CA
CALIMESA, CA
CALION, AR
CALIPATRIA, CA
CALISTOGA, CA
CALLAHAN, CA,FL
CALLAWAY, FL,MN,NB
CALMAR, IA
CALPELLA, CA
CALPINE, CA
CALPYSO, NC
CALUMET, IA,MI,MN,PA
CALUMET CITY, IL
CALUMET PARK, IL
CALVERT, TX
CALVERT CITY, KY
CALVIN, LA
CALWA, CA
CAMANCHE, IA
CAMARGO, KY
CAMARILLO, CA
CAMAS, WA
CAMBELLTOWN, PA
CAMBRIA, CA,IL,WI
CAMBRIA HEIGHTS, PA
CAMBRIDGE, IA,ID,IL,KS
  MA,MD,ME,MN,NB,NY
  OH,VT,WI
CAMBRIDGE CITY, IN
CAMBRIDGE SPRINGS, PA
CAMDEN, AL,AR,CA,DE,IN
  ME,MI,MO,NJ,NY,OH,SC,TN
CAMDEN-ON-GAULEY, WV
CAMDENTON, MO
CAMERON, MO,NC,OK,PA,SC
  TX,WI,WV

PLACE INDEX

CHEHALIS, WA
CHELAN, WA
CHELMSFORD, MA
CHELSEA, IA,MA,ME
   MI,OK,SD,VT
CHELTENHAM, PA
CHEMUNG, NY
CHENEQUA, WI
CHENEY, KS,WA
CHENEYVILLE, LA
CHENOA, IL
CHERAW, CO,SC
CHERITON, VA
CHEROKEE, AL,CA,IA,KS,OK
CHERRY, IL
CHERRY CITY, PA
CHERRY HILL, NJ
CHERRCY HILLS VILLAGE, CO
CHERRY TREE, PA
CHERRY VALLEY, AR
CHERRYFIELD, ME
CHERRYVALE, KS
CHERRYVILLE, NC
CHESANING, MI
CHESAPEAKE, OH,VA,WV
CHESAPEAKE BEACH, MD
CHESAPEAKE CITY, MD
CHESHIRE, CT,MA
CHESNEE, SC
CHESTER, AR,CA,CT,GA,IL
   MA,ME,MT,NB,NH,NJ,NY,PA
   SC,TX,VT,WV
CHESTER HEIGHTS, PA
CHESTER HILL, PA
CHESTERFIELD, MA,SC
CHESTERTOWN, MD
CHESTERVILLE, ME
CHESWICK, PA
CHESWOLD, DE
CHETEK, WI
CHETOPA, KS
CHEVAK, AK
CHEVERLY, MD
CHEVIOT, OH
CHEVY CHASE SECT.
   FOUR, MD
CHEVY CHASE VILLAGE, MD
CHEWELAH, WA
CHEYENNE, OK,WY
CHEYENNE WELLS, CO
CHICAGO, IL
CHICAGO PARK, CA
CHICAGO RIDGE, IL
CHICHESTER, NH
CHICKAMAUGA, GA
CHICKASAW, AL
CHICKASHA, OK
CHICO, CA,TX
CHICOPEE, MA
CHICORA, PA
CHIDESTER, AR
CHIEFLAND, FL
CHILDERSBURG, AL
CHILDRESS, TX
CHILHOWIE, VA
CHILLICOTHE, IA,IL
   MO,OH,TX
CHILMARK, MA
CHILOQUIN, OR
CHILTON, WI
CHINA, ME,TX
CHINA GROVE, NC
CHINCOTEAGUE, VA
CHINO, CA
CHINO VALLEY, AZ
CHINOOK, MT
CHIPLEY, FL
CHIPPEWA FALLS, WI
CHIRENO, TX
CHISAGO CITY, MN
CHISHOLM, MN
CHITTENANGO, NY
CHITTENDON, VT

CHOCOWINITY, NC
CHOCTAW, OK
CHOKIO, MN
CHOLAME, CA
CHOTEAU, MT
CHOUDRANT. LA
CHOUTEAU, OK
CHOWCHILLA, CA
CHRISMAN, IL
CHRISTIANA, PA
CHRISTIANSBURG, VA
CHRISTINE, TX
CHRISTMAS, FL
CHRISTOPHER, IL
CHRISTOVAL, TX
CHUALAR, CA
CHUATHBALUK, AK
CHUBBUCK, CA,ID
CHUGWATER, WY
CHULA VISTA, CA
CHURCH CREEK, MD
CHURCH HILL, MD,TN
CHURCH POINT, LA
CHURCHILL, PA
CHURCHVILLE, PA
CHURDAN, IA
CIBOLO, TX
CICERO, IL,NY
CIMA, CA
CIMARRON, KS,NM
CINCINNATI, IA,OH
CINCINNATUS, NY
CINNAMINSON, NJ
CIRCLE, MT
CIRCLE PINES, MN
CIRCLEVILLE, KS,OH,UT
CISCO, TX
CISSNA PARK, IL
CITRONELLE, AL
CITRUS HEIGHTS, CA
CITY OF THE DALLES, OR
CLAFLIN, KS
CLAIRE CITY, SD
CLAIRMONT, TX
CLAIRTON, PA
CLANTON, AL
CLARA CITY, MN
CLARE, MI
CLAREDON, NY
CLAREMONT, CA,MN,NC
   NH,SD,VA
CLAREMORE, OK
CLARENCE, IA,LA,MO,NY
CLARENDON, AR,TX,VT
CLARENDON HILLS, IL
CLARINDA, IA
CLARION, IA,PA
CLARISSA, MN
CLARK, MO,NJ,SD
CLARK FORK, ID
CLARKDALE, AZ
CLARKESVILLE, GA
CLARKFIELD, MN
CLARK'S POINT, AK
CLARKS, LA,NB
CLARKS GROVE, MN
CLARKS SUMMIT, PA
CLARKS HILL, IN
CLARKSBURG, CA,MO,TN,WV
CLARKSDALE, MS
CLARKSON, KY,NB
CLARKSTON, GA,MI,UT,WA
CLARKSVILLE, AR,IA,IN
   MI,TN,TX,VA
CLARKTON, MO,NC
CLATONIA, NB
CLATSKANIE, OR
CLAUDE, TX
CLAVERACK, NY
CLAWSON, MI
CLAXTON, GA
CLAY, KY,NY,WV
CLAY CENTER, KS,NB

CLAY CITY, IL,IN,KY
CLAYHATCHEE, AL
CLAYPOOL, IN
CLAYSBURG, PA
CLAYSVILLE, PA
CLAYTON, AL,CA,DE,GA,IA
   ID,IN,KS,LA,MI,MO,NC
   NJ,NM,OK,WI
CLE ELUM, WA
CLEAR CREEK, CA
CLEAR LAKE, IN,SD,WI
CLEAR LAKE CITY, IA
CLEAR SPRING, MD
CLEARBROOK, MN
CLEARFIELD, PA,UT
CLEARLAKE HIGHLANDS, CA
CLEARLAKE OAKS, CA
CLEARMONT, WY
CLEARVIEW, PA
CLEARWATER, FL,KS,MN,NB
CLEBURNE, TX
CLEGHORN, IA
CLEMENTON, NJ
CLEMENTS, MN
CLEMMONS, NC
CLENDENIN, WV
CLEO SPRINGS, OK
CLEONA, PA
CLERMONT, FL,GA,IN
CLEVELAND, AL,GA,MN,MO,MS
   ,NC,OH,OK,TN,TX,UT,VA,WI
CLEVELAND HEIGHTS, OH
CLEVES, OH
CLEWISTON, FL
CLIFFORD, IN,MI,PA
CLIFFSIDE PARK, NJ
CLIFTON, AZ,CA,ID,IL,KS
   ME,NJ,OH,TN,TX,VA
CLIFTON FORGE, VA
CLIFTON HEIGHTS, PA
CLIMAX, GA,KS,MI,MN
CLINT, TX
CLINTON, AR,CT,IL,IN,KY
   LA,MA,ME,MI,MN,MO,MS,NC
   NJ,NY,OH,OK,SC,TN,UT,WI
CLINTONVILLE, WI
CLINTWOOD, VA
CLIO, AL,MI,SC
CLITHERALL, MN
CLONTARF, MN
CLOQUET, MN
CLOSTER, NJ
CLOUDCROFT, NM
CLOVER, SC,VA
CLOVERDALE, CA,IN
CLOVERPORT, KY
CLOVIS, CA,NM
CLYDE, CA,KS,NC,NY,TX
CLYDE PARK, MT
CLYMAN, WI
CLYMER, PA
COACHELLA, CA
COAHOMA, TX
COAL CITY, IL
COAL CREEK, CO
COAL HILL, AR
COALDALE, PA
COALGATE, OK
COALINGA, CA
COALMONT, TN
COALVILLE, UT
COARSEGOLD, CA
COATESVILLE, IN,PA
COATS, KS,NC
COBB, WI
COBBTOWN, GA
COBDEN, IL
COBLESKILL, NY
COBURG, OR
COCHRAN, GA
COCHRANE, WI
COCHRANTON, PA
COCKRELL HILL, TX

COCOA, FL
COCOA BEACH, FL
CODY, NB,WY
CODYVILLE, ME
COEBURN, VA
COEUR D'ALENE, ID
COEYMANS, NY
COFFEE SPRINGS, AL
COFFEEVILLE, AL,MS
COFFEYVILLE, KS
COFIELD, NC
COGSWELL, ND
COHASSET, MA
COHOCTON, NY
COHOES, NY
COHUTTA, GA
COKATO, MN
COKEDALE, CO
COKEVILLE, WY
COLBERT, GA,OK
COLBY, WI
COLCHESTER, CT,IL,VT
COLCORD, OK
COLD SPRING, KY,MN,NY
COLDEN, NY
COLDSPRING, TX
COLDWATER, KS,MI,MS
COLE, OK
COLE CAMP, MO
COLEBROOK, CT
COLEHARBOR, ND
COLEMAN, FL,GA,MI,TX,WI
COLERAIN, NC
COLERAINE, MN
COLERIDGE, NB
COLEVILLE, CA
COLFAX, CA,IA,IN
   LA,WA,WI
COLINSVILLE, OK
COLLBRAN, CO
COLLEGE HEIGHTS, CA
COLLEGE PARK, GA,MD
COLLEGE PLACE, WA
COLLEGE STATION, TX
COLLEGEDALE, TN
COLLEGEVILLE, PA
COLLEYVILLE, TX
COLLIERVILLE, TN
COLLINGSWOOD, NJ
COLLINS, GA,IA,MS
COLLINSTON, LA
COLLINSVILLE, AL
COLLYER, KS
COLMA, CA
COLMAN, SD
COLMESNEIL, TX
COLO, IA
COLOGNE, MN
COLOMA, CA,MI,WI
COLOME, SD
COLON, MI,NB
COLONIA, NJ
COLONIAL BEACH, VA
COLONIAL HEIGHTS, VA
COLONIAL PARK, PA
COLONIE, NY
COLONY, KS,OK
COLORADO CITY, TX
COLORADO SPRINGS, CO
COLQUITT, GA
COLRAIN, MA
COLTON, CA,SD,WA
COLTS NECK, NJ
COLUMBIA, AL,CA,CT,IL,KY
   LA,ME,MN,MO,MS,NC,OR,PA
   SC,SD,TN,VA
COLUMBIA CITY, IN
COLUMBIA FALLS, ME,MT
COLUMBIANA, AL
COLUMBIAVILLE, MI
COLUMBUS, GA,IN,KS,MS,MT
   NB,NC,ND,NM,OH,PA,TX,WI
COLUMBUS JUNCTION, IA

PLACE INDEX

COLUSA, CA
COLVILLE, WA
COLWICH, KS
COLWYN, PA
COMANCHE, OK,TX
COMBES, TX
COMBINED LOCKS, WI
COMER, GA
COMFORT, TX
COMFREY, MN
COMMERCE, CA,GA,OK,TX
COMMERCE CITY, CO
COMO, MS,NC,TX
COMPTON, CA
COMSTOCK, MN,NB
CONCAN, TX
CONCONULLY, WA
CONCORD, AR,CA,GA,MA
   MI,NB,NC,NH,VT
CONCORDIA, KS,MO
CONCRETE, WA
CONDE, SD
CONDON, OR
CONEJO, CA
CONESUS, NY
CONETOE, NC
CONGER, MN
CONNELL, WA
CONNELLSVILLE, PA
CONNERSVILLE, IN
CONNOR, ME
CONOVER, NC
CONRAD, IA,MT
CONRATH, WI
CONROE, TX
CONSHOHOCKEN, PA
CONSTANTINE, MI
CONVENT STATION, NJ
CONVERSE, IN,LA
CONWAY, AR,MA,MO
   NC,PA,SC
CONWAY SPRINGS, KS
CONYERS, GA
CONYNGHAM, PA
COOK, MN,NB
COOKEVILLE, TN
COOKSTOWN, NJ
COOLEEMEE, NC
COOLIDGE, AZ,GA,KS,TX
COON RAPIDS, IA,MN
COON VALLEY, WI
COOPER, ME,TX
COOPER CITY, FL
COOPERSBURG, PA
COOPERSTOWN, ND,NY
COOPERSVILLE, MI
COOPERTON, OK
COOS BAY, OR
COOSADA, AL
COOTER, MO
COPAKE, NY
COPAN, OK
COPCO LAKE, CA
COPE, SC
COPELAND, KS
COPEMISH, MI
COPLAY, PA
COPPELL, TX
COPPER CITY, MI
COPPERAS COVE, TX
COPPERHILL, TN
COQUILLE, OR
CORAL GABLES, FL
CORALVILLE, IA
CORAOPOLIS, PA
CORBIN, KY
CORCORAN, CA,MN
CORDELE, GA
CORDOVA, AK,IL,NB,SC
CORINNA, ME
CORINNE, UT
CORINTH, ME,MS,NY,VT
CORN, OK

CORNELIA, GA
CORNELIUS, NC,OR
CORNELL, IL,WI
CORNERSVILLE, TN
CORNING, AR,CA,IA
   KS,NY,OH
CORNISH, ME,NH,OK,UT
CORNLEA, NB
CORNVILLE, ME
CORNWALL, CT,NY,PA,VT
CORNWELLS HEIGHTS, PA
CORONA, CA,NM,SD
CORONADO, CA
CORPUS CHRISTI, TX
CORRALES, NM
CORRALITOS, CA
CORRECTIONVILLE, IA
CORRELL, MN
CORRY, PA
CORSICA, SD
CORTE MADERA, CA
CORTEZ, CO
CORTLAND, IL,NY,NB,OH
CORUNNA, IN,MI
CORVALLIS, OR
CORWITH, IA
CORYDON, IA,IN
COSBY, MO
COSHOCTON, OH
COSMOPOLIS, WA
COSMOS, MN
COSTA MESA, CA
COTATI, CA
COTESFIELD, NB
COTTAGE CITY, MD
COTTAGE GROVE, MN
   OR,TN,WI
COTTAGEVILLE, SC
COTTER, AR
COTTLEVILLE, MO
COTTON PLANT, AR
COTTON VALLEY, LA
COTTONDALE, FL
COTTONPORT, LA
COTTONWOOD, AZ,CA
   ID,MN,SD
COTTONWOOD FALLS, KS
COTULLA, TX
COUDERAY, WI
COUDERSPORT, PA
COULTERVILLE, CA,IL
COUNCIL, ID
COUNCIL BLUFFS, IA
COUNCIL GROVE, KS
COUNCIL HILL, OK
COUNTRY CLUB, MO
COUNTRY CLUB HILLS, IL
COUNTRY CLUB HEIGHTS, IN
COUNTRYSIDE, IL
COUPEVILLE, WA
COURTLAND, AL,CA
   KS,MN,VA
COUSHATTA, LA
COVE, AR,OR
COVELO, CA
COVENTRY, CT,RI,VT
COVINA, CA
COVINGTON, GA,IN,KY,LA
   OH,OK,TN,TX,VA
COVE CITY, NC
COWAN, TN
COWAN HEIGHTS, CA
COWARD, SC
COWARTS, AL
COWELL, CA
COWEN, WV
COWETA, OK
COWGILL, MO
COWLES, NB
COWLEY, WY
COWLINGTON, OK
COWPENS, SC
COXSACKIE, NY

COY, AR
COYLE, OK
COYVILLE, KS
COZAD, NB
CRAB ORCHARD, NB,TN
CRAFTON, CA,PA
CRAFTSBURY, VT
CRAIG, AK,CO,MO,NB
CRAIG BEACH, OH
CRAIGMONT, ID
CRAIGSVILLE, VA
CRAMERTON, NC
CRANBERRY ISLES, ME
CRANBURY, NJ
CRANDALL, IN,TX
CRANDON, WI
CRANE, IN,MO,TX
CRANFILLS GAP, TX
CRANFORD, NJ
CRANSTON, RI
CRAWFORD, CO,GA,ME
   MS,NB,TX
CRAWFORDSVILLE, AR,IN
CRAWFORDVILLE, FL,GA
CREAL SPRINGS, IL
CREEDE, CO
CREEDMOOR, NC
CREIGHTON, MO,NB,PA
CRENSHAW, MS,MS
CREOLA, AL
CRESBARD, SD
CRESCA, IA
CRESCENT, IA,OK
CRESCENT CITY, CA,FL
CRESCENT SPRINGS, KY
CRESSKILL, NJ
CRESSONA, PA
CREST HILL, IL
CRESTED BUTTE, CO
CRESTLINE, CA,OH
CRESTON, IA,NB,OH,WA
CRESTONE, CO
CRESTVIEW, FL
CRESTWOOD, IL,MO
CRESWELL, NC,OR
CRETE, IL,NB
CREVE COEUR, IL,MO
CREWE, VA
CRICKET, NC
CRIDERSVILLE, OH
CRIEHAVEN, ME
CRIPPLE CREEK, CO
CRISFIELD, MD
CRIVITZ, WI
CROCKETT, CA,TX
CROFTON, NB
CROMWELL, CT,IN,MN,OK
CROOK, CO
CROOKS, SD
CROOKSTON, MN,NB
CROOKSVILLE, OH
CROSBY, MN,ND
CROSBYTON, TX
CROSS CITY, FL
CROSS HILL, SC
CROSS PLAINS, TN,TX,WI
CROSSETT, AR
CROSSLAKE, MN
CROSSNORE, NC
CROSSVILLE, AL,TN
CROSWELL, MI
CROTHERSVILLE, IN
CROUCH, ID
CROWDER, MS,OK
CROWELL, TX
CROWLEY, CO,LA,TX
CROWLEY LAKE, CA
CROWN POINT, IN
CROWS NEST, IN
CROYDON, NH,PA
CRUGER, MS
CRUM LYNNE, PA
CRYSTAL, MN

CRYSTAL CITY, MO,TX
CRYSTAL FALLS, MI
CRYSTAL LAKE, IA,IL
CRYSTAL RIVER, FL
CRYSTAL SPRINGS, MS
CUBA, AL,IL,KS,MO,NM,NY
CUBA CITY, WI
CUCAMONGA, CA
CUDAHAY, WI
CUDAHY, CA
CUDDEBACKVILLE, NY
CUERO, TX
CULBERTSON, MT,NB
CULDESAC, ID
CULLEN, LA
CULLMAN, AL
CULLODEN, GA
CULPEPER, VA
CULVER, IN,KS,OR
CULVER CITY, CA
CUMBERLAND, IA,IN,KY
   MD,ME,RI,WI
CUMBERLAND CITY, TN
CUMBERLAND GAP, TN
CUMMING, GA
CUNNINGHAM, KS
CUPERTINO, CA
CURCHECE, OK
CURRIE, MN
CURRYVILLE, MO
CURTIS, NB
CURTISS, WI
CURWENSVILLE, PA
CUSHING, IA,ME,NB,TX
CUSHMAN, AR
CUSICK, WA
CUSSETA, GA
CUSTAR, OH
CUSTER, MI,SD
CUSTER CITY, OK
CUT AND SHOOT, TX
CUT BANK, MT
CUTHBERT, GA
CUTLER, CA,ME
CUYAHOGA FALLS, OH
CUYUNA, MN
CYGNET, OH
CYLINDER, IA
CYNTHIANA, IN,KY
CYPRESS, CA
CYRIL, OK
CYRUS, MN

DACOMA, OK
DACONO, CO
DACULA, GA
DADE CITY, FL
DADEVILLE, AL,MO
DAGGETT, CA,MI
DAGSBORO, DE
DAHLONEGA, GA
DAILY CITY, CA
DAINGERFIELD, TX
DAISETTA, TX
DAISY, GA
DAKOTA, MN
DAKOTA CITY, IA,NB
DALE, IN,PA
DALEVILLE, AL
DALHART, TX
DALLAS, IA,ME,NC,OR,PA
   SD,TX,WI
DALLAS CENTER, IA
DALLAS CITY, IL
DALLASTOWN, PA
DALTON, MA,MN,NB,OH
DALTON GARDENS, ID
DAMAR, KS
DAMARISCOTTA, ME
DAMASCUS, AR,VA
DANA, IN
DANA POINT, CA
DANBURY, CT,IA,NB
   NC,NH,TX

616

DANBY, VT
DANDRIDGE, TN
DANE, WI
DANEVANG, TX
DANFORTH, IL,ME
DANIA, FL
DANNEBROG, NB
DANNEMORA, NY
DANSVILLE, MI
DANTE, SD
DANUBE, MN
DANVERS, MA,MN
DANVILLE, AR,CA,IA,IL,IN
  KS,KY,NH,OH,VA,VT,WV
DAPHNE, AL
DARBY, MT,PA
DARDANELLE, CA,AR
DARIEN, CT,GA,WI
DARFUR, MN
DARLINGTON, IN,MO,SC,WI
DARMSTADT, IN
DARRINGTON, WA
DARROUZETT, TX
DARTMOUTH, MA
DARWIN, MN
DASSEL, MN
DATTO, AR
DAVENPORT, CA,FL,IA
  NB,ND,OK,WA
DAVEY, NB
DAVID CITY, NB
DAVIDSON, NC,OK
DAVIDSON HEIGHTS, PA
DAVIE, FL
DAVIS, CA,OK,SD,WV
DAVIS CREEK, CA
DAVISBORO, GA
DAVISON, MI
DAVISTON, AL
DAVY, WV
DAWSON, GA,IA,IL
  MN,NB,ND,TX
DAYKIN, NB
DAYTON, AL,IA,ID,IN,KY
  ME,MN,NV,NY,OH,OR,TN
  TX,VA,WA,WY
DAYTONA BEACH, FL
DAYTONA BEACH SHORES, FL
DAYVILLE, OR
DE BEQUE, CO
DE FOREST, WI
DE FUNIAK SPRINGS, FL
DE GRAFF, MN,OH
DE KALB, IL,MO,MS,TX
DE LAND, FL
DE LEON, TX
DE LEON SPRINGS, FL
DE LUZ, CA
DE MOTTE, IN
DE PERE, WI
DE QUEEN, AR
DE QUINCY, LA
DE RIDDER, LA
DE SMET, SD
DE SOTO, GA,IL,KS,MO,WI
DE TOUR, MI
DE VALLS BLUFF, AR
DE WITT, AR,MI,NB
DEADWOOD, SD
DEAL, NJ
DEARBORN, MI,MO
DEARBORN HEIGHTS, MI
DEARING, GA,KS
DEARY, ID
DEAVER, WY
DEBLOIS, ME
DECATUR, AL,AR,GA,IL,IN
  MI,MS,NB,TN,TX
DECATUR CITY, IA
DECATURVILLE, TN
DECHERD, TN
DECKER, IN
DECKERVILLE, MI

DECORAH, IA
DEDA, ID
DEDHAM, IA,MA,ME
DEEP RIVER, CT,IA
DEEPHAVEN, MN
DEER CREEK, IL,MN,OK
DEER RIVER, MN
DEER ISLE, ME
DEER LODGE, MT
DEER PARK, MD,OH
  TX,WA,WI
DEER TRAIL, CO
DEERFIELD, IL,KS,MI
  NH,NJ,WI
DEERFIELD BEACH, FL
DEERING, AK,NH
DEERWOOD, MN
DEFERIET, NY
DEFIANCE, IA,OH
DEL CITY, OK
DEL LOMA, CA
DEL MAR, CA
DEL NORTE, CO
DEL REY, CA
DEL REY OAKS, CA
DEL RIO, TX
DEL ROSA, CA
DELAFIELD, WI
DELANCO, NJ
DELANO, CA,MN
DELAPLAINE, AR
DELAVAN, IL,MN,WI
DELAWARE, IA,OH,OK
DELAWARE CITY, DE
DELBARTON, WV
DELCAMBRE, LA
DELHI, CA,IA,LA,MN,NY
DELIA, KS
DELIGHT, AR
DELL, AR
DELL CITY, TX
DELL RAPIDS, SD
DELLVIEW, NC
DELLWOOD, MN,MO
DELMAR, DE,MD
DELMONT, SD
DELPHI, IN
DELPHOS, KS,OH
DELRAN, NJ
DELRAY BEACH, FL
DELTA, CO,IA,LA,MO,OH,UT
DELTA JUNCTION, AK
DEMAREST, NJ
DEMING, NM
DEMOPOLIS, AL
DEMOREST, GA
DENAIR, CA
DENDRON, VA
DENHAM, MN
DENHAM SPRINGS, LA
DENISON, IA,KS,TX
DENMARK, ME,NY,SC,TN,WI
DENNIS, MA,NJ
DENNISON, MN,OH
DENNISTOWN, ME
DENNYSVILLE, ME
DENT, MN
DENTON, GA,KS,MD
  MT,NB,NC,TX
DENVER, CO,IA,IN,PA
DENVILLE, NJ
DEPAUVILLE, NY
DEPEW, NY,OK
DEPEYSTER, NY
DEPOE BAY, OR
DEPORT, TX
DEPTFORD, NJ
DEPUE, IL
DERBY, CT,KS,VT
DERBY LINE, VT
DERMA, MS
DERMOTT, AR
DERRY, NH,PA

DES ARC, AR,MO
DES LACS, ND
DES MOINES, IA,NM,WA
DES PERES, MO
DES PLAINS, IL
DESCANSO, CA
DESERT CENTER, CA
DESERT HOT SPRINGS, CA
DESHLER, NB
DESLOGE, MO
DESOTO, TX
DETROIT, AL,ME,MI,OR,TX
DETROIT LAKES, MN
DEVAL, OK
DEVILS LAKE, ND
DEVINE, TX
DEVON, PA
DEVORE, CA
DEWAR, OK
DEWEESE, NB
DEWEY, OK
DEWEYVILLE, UT
DEXTER, GA,IA,KS,ME
  MI,MN,MO,NM
DI GIORGIO, CA
DIABLO, CA
DIAMOND, MO
DIAMOND BAR, CA
DIAMOND CITY, AR
DIAMOND SPRINGS, CA
DIAMONDVILLE, WY
DIAZ, AR
DIBBLE, OK
DIBOLL, TX
DICKENS, IA,NB,TX
DICKEYVILLE, WI
DICKINSON, ND,TX
DICKSON, TN
DICKSON CITY, PA
DIERKS, AR
DIETRICH, ID
DIGGINS, MO
DIGHTON, KS,MA
DIKE, IA
DILL CITY, OK
DILLER, NB
DILLEY, TX
DILLINGHAM, AK
DILLON, CO,MT,SC
DILLON BEACH, CA
DILLSBORO, IN,NC
DILLSBURG, PA
DILLWYN, VA
DILWORTH, MN
DIME BOX, TX
DIMMITT, TX
DIMOCK, SD
DIMONDALE, MI
DINOSAUR, CO
DINUBA, CA
DIOMEDE, AK
DISNEY, OK
DISTRICT HEIGHTS, MD
DIVERNON, IL
DIX, NB
DIXFIELD, ME
DIXIE, GA
DIXIELAND, CA
DIXMONT, ME
DIXMOOR, IL
DIXON, CA,IL,MO,NB,WY
DOBBINS, CA
DOBSON, NC
DODGE, NB,TX
DODGE CENTER, MN
DODGE CITY, KS
DODGEVILLE, WI
DODSON, LA,MT
DOERUN, GA
DOLAND, SD
DOLGEVILLE, NY
DOLORES, CO
DOLTON, IL,SD

DOMINGUEZ, CA
DONALD, OR
DONALDS, SC
DONALDSON, MN
DONALDSONVILLE, LA
DONALSONVILLE, GA
DONIE, TX
DONIPHAN, MO,NB
DONNELLSON, IA
DONNELLY, ID,MN
DONORA, PA
DOON, IA
DORA, AL,NM
DORAN, MN
DORAVILLE, GA
DORCHESTER, NB,NH
DORMONT, PA
DORRANCE, KS
DORRIS, CA
DORSET, VT
DORTCHES, NC
DOS PALOS, CA
DOS RIOS, CA
DOTHAN, AL
DOUBLE SPRINGS, AL
DOUGHERTY, IA,OK
DOUGLAS, AL,AZ,GA,MI
  NB,OK,WY
DOUGLAS CITY, CA
DOUGLASS, KS
DOUGLASSVILLE, TX
DOUGLASVILLE, GA
DOUSMAN, WI
DOVE CREEK, CO
DOVER, AR,DE,MA,NC,NH,NJ
  MN,OH,OK,PA,TN,VT
DOVER-FOXCROFT, ME
DOVRAY, MN
DOW CITY, IA
DOWAGIAC, MI
DOWELLTOWN, TN
DOWNERS GROVE, IL
DOWNEY, CA,ID
DOWNIEVILLE, CA
DOWNING, MO,WI
DOWNINGTOWN, PA
DOWNS, KS
DOYLE, CA,TN
DOYLESTOWN, OH,PA,WI
DOYLINE, LA
DOZIER, AL
DRACUT, MA
DRAIN, OR
DRAKE, ND
DRAKES BRANCH, VA
DRAKESBORO, KY
DRAKESVILLE, IA
DRAPER, SD,UT
DRAVOSBURG, PA
DRAYTON, ND
DRESDEN, KS,ME,TN
DRESSER, WI
DREW, ME,MS
DREXEL, MO,NC
DREXEL HILL, PA
DRIFTON, FL
DRIGGS, ID
DRISCOLL, TX
DRUMMOND, ID,MT,OK
DRUMRIGHT, OK
DRY PRONG, LA
DRY RIDGE, KY
DRYDEN, MI,NY
DRYTOWN, CA
DU BOIS, NB
DU PONT, GA
DU QUOIN, IL
DUANESBURG, NY
DUARTE, CA
DUBACH, LA
DUBBERLY, LA
DUBLIN, CA,GA,IN,NC,OH
  PA,TX,VA

PLACE INDEX

DUBOIS, ID,PA,WY
DUBUQUE, IA
DUCHESNE, UT
DUCK HILL, MS
DUCKTOWN, TN
DUCOR, CA
DUDLEY, GA,MA
DUE WEST, SC
DUFFIELD, VA
DUFUR, OR
DUGGER, IN
DULUTH, GA,MN
DULZURA, CA
DUMAS, AR,MS,TX
DUME POINT, CA
DUMFRIES, VA
DUMMERSTON, VT
DUMONT, IA,NJ
DUNBAR, NB,PA,WV
DUNBARTON, NH
DUNCAN, AZ,MS,NB,OK,SC
DUNCANNON, PA
DUNCANS MILL, CA
DUNCANSVILLE, PA
DUNCANVILLE, TX
DUNCOMBE, IA
DUNDEE, FL,IA,IL,MI
 NY,OR,TX
DUNE ACRES, IN
DUNEDIN, FL
DUNELLEN, NJ
DUNGANNON, VA
DUNKIRK, NY
DUNLAP, KS,TN
DUNLAP ACRES, CA
DUNMORE, PA
DUNN, NC
DUNN CENTER, ND
DUNNELLON, FL
DUNNING, NB
DUNREITH, IN
DUNSMUIR, CA
DUPO, IL
DUPONT, IN,PA,WA
DUPREE, SD
DUQUESNE, MO,PA
DURAND, MI,WI
DURANGO, CO
DURANT, MS,OK
DURBIN, WV
DURHAM, CA,CT,KS,ME
 NC,NH,OR
DURYEA, PA
DUSON, LA
DUTCH FLAT, CA
DUTTON, AL,MT
DUVALL, WA
DUXBURY, MA,VT
DWIGHT, IL,KS,NB
DYER, AR,IN,TN
DYER BROOK, ME
DYERSBURG, TN
DYESS, AR

EADS, CO
EAGAN, MN
EAGLE, AK,CO,ID,MI,NB,WI
EAGLE BEND, MN
EAGLE BUTTE, SD
EAGLE GROVE, IA
EAGLE HARBOR, MD
EAGLE LAKE, FL,ME,MN
EAGLE NEST, NM
EAGLE PASS, TX
EAGLE POINT, OR
EAGLE RIVER, WI
EAGLELAKE, CA
EAGLEVILLE, CA
EARL, NC
EARL PARK, IN
EARLE, AR
EARLHAM, IA
EARLIMART, CA

EARLINGTON, KY
EARLVILLE, IA,IL
EARLY, IA,TX
EARP, CA
EARTH, TX
EASLEY, SC
EAST ALTON, IL
EAST ARCADIA, NC
EAST AURORA, NY
EAST BANK, WV
EAST BEND, NC
EAST BERLIN, PA
EAST BETHEL, MN
EAST BRADY, PA
EAST BREWTON, AL
EAST BRIDGEWATER, MA
EAST BROOKFIELD, MA
EAST BRUNSWICK, NJ
EAST CANTON, OH
EAST CARBON, UT
EAST CENTRAL
 WASHINGTON, ME
EAST CHICAGO, IN
EAST CLEVELAND, OH
EAST CONEMAUGH, PA
EAST DETROIT, MI
EAST DUBLIN, GA
EAST DUBUQUE, IL
EAST DUNDEE, IL
EAST FAXON, PA
EAST FLAT ROCK, NC
EAST FORK, NV
EAST FRANKLIN, ME
EAST GERMANTOWN, IN
EAST GRANBY, CT
EAST GRAND FORKS, MN
EAST GRAND RAPIDS, MI
EAST GREENVILLE, PA
EAST GREENWICH, RI
EAST HADDAM, CT
EAST HAMPTON, CT,NY
EAST HANCOCK, ME
EAST HANOVER, NJ
EAST HARTFORD, CT
EAST HAVEN, CT,VT
EAST HELENA, MT
EAST HIGHLANDS, CA
EAST HOPE, ID
EAST JORDAN, MI
EAST KINGSTON, NH
EAST LAKE, MI
EAST LANSDOWNE, PA
EAST LANSING, MI
EAST LAURINBURG, NC
EAST LAWN, PA
EAST LAYTON, UT
EAST LIVERPOOL, OH
EAST LONGMEADOW, MA
EAST LOS ANGELES, CA
EAST LYME, CT
EAST MACHIAS, ME
EAST MARION, NC
EAST MCKEESPORT, PA
EAST MILLINOCKET, ME
EAST MOLINE, IL
EAST MONTPELIER, VT
EAST NEW MARKET, MD
EAST NINNEKAH, OK
EAST NORRITON, PA
EAST ORANGE, NJ
EAST PALESTINE, OH
EAST PALO ALTO, CA
EAST PEORIA, IL
EAST PETERSBURG, PA
EAST PITTSBURGH, PA
EAST POINT, GA
EAST PRAIRIE, MO
EAST PROVIDENCE, RI
EAST ROCKAWAY, NY
EAST ROCKINGHAM, NC
EAST RUTHERFORD, NJ
EAST SAINT LOUIS, IL
EAST SPENCER, NC

EAST STROUDSBURG, PA
EAST THERMOPOLIS, WY
EAST TOWAS, MI
EAST TROY, WI
EAST WASHINGTON, PA
EAST WINDSOR, CT
EASTBROOK, ME
EASTFORD, CT
EASTHAM, MA
EASTHAMPTON, MA
EASTLAKE, OH
EASTLAND, TX
EASTMAN, GA,WI
EASTON, CA,CT,KS,MA,MD
 ME,MN,MO,NH,PA,TX
EASTOVER, NC,SC
EASTPORT, ME
EASTSIDE, OR
EASTVILLE, VA
EATON, CO,IN,NY,OH
EATON RAPIDS, MI
EATONTON, GA
EATONTOWN, NJ
EATONVILLE, FL,WA
EAU CLAIRE, MI,WI
EAU GALLIE, FL
EBENSBURG, PA
EBRO, FL
ECHO, MN,OR,PA
ECLECTIC, AL
ECONOMY, IN,PA
ECORSE, MI
ECRU, MS
EDCOUCH, TX
EDDEY, CO
EDDINGTON, ME
EDDYSTONE, PA
EDDYVILLE, KY,NB
EDEN, ID,NC,NY,TX,VT,WI
EDEN PRAIRIE, MN
EDEN VALLEY, MN
EDENTON, NC
EDGAR, NB,WI
EDGAR SPRINGS, MO
EDGECOMB, ME
EDGEFIELD, SC
EDGEMONT, CA
EDGERTON, KS,MN,MO
 OH,WI,WY
EDGEWATER, CO,FL,NJ
EDGEWOOD, CA,IA,IN,PA,TX
EDGEWORTH, PA
EDINA, MN,MO
EDINBORO, PA
EDINBURG, ME,TX,VA
EDINBURGH, IL
EDISON, CA,GA,NB,NJ
EDISTO BEACH, SC
EDMOND, KS,OK
EDMONDS, WA
EDMONSON, TX
EDMONSTON, MD
EDMONTON, KY
EDMORE, MI
EDNA, KS,TX
EDWARDS, MS
EDWARDSBURG, MI
EDWARDSPORT, IN
EDWARDSVILLE, AL,IL
 KS,PA
EEK, AK
EFFIE, MN
EFFINGHAM, IL,KS
EGAN, SD
EGARTOWN, MA
EGG HARBOR, WI
EGG HARBOR CITY, NJ
EGGAR, AZ
EHRHARDT, SC
EITZEN, MN
EKALAKA, MT
EKWOK, AK
EL CAJON, CA

EL CAMPO, TX
EL CENTRO, CA
EL CERRITO, CA
EL DIOS, CA
EL DORADO, KS
EL DORADO SPRINGS, MO
EL GRANADA, CA
EL MIRAGE, AZ
EL MIRAGE LAKE, CA
EL MODENA, CA
EL MONTE, CA
EL PASO, IL,TX
EL PORTAL, CA
EL RENO, OK
EL SEGUNDO, CA
EL TIO, CA
EL TORO, CA
EL VERANO, CA
ELAND, WI
ELAY, AZ
ELBA, AL,NB,NY
ELBERFELD, IN
ELBERON, IA
ELBERTA, AL,MI
ELBERTON, GA
ELBING, KS
ELBOW LAKE, MN
ELBRIDGE, NY
ELBURN, IL
ELDERON, WI
ELDON, IA,MO
ELDORA, IA
ELDORADO, IL,MD,TX
ELDRIDGE, AL,IA
ELEANOR, WV
ELECTRA, TX
ELECTRIC CITY, WA
ELEVA, WI
ELGIN, IA,IL,MN,NB,ND
 OK,OR,SC,TX
ELIDA, NM,OH
ELIM, AK
ELIOT, ME
ELIZABETH, CO,IL,IN,LA
 MN,NJ,PA,WV
ELIZABETH LAKE, CA
ELIZABETHTOWN, IN
 KY,NC,PA
ELK, CA
ELK CITY, KS,OK
ELK CREEK, CA,NB
ELK FALLS, KS
ELK GARDEN, WV
ELK GROVE, CA
ELK GROVE VILLAGE, IL
ELK HORN, IA
ELK MOUND, WI
ELK MOUNTAIN, WY
ELK PARK, NC
ELK POINT, SD
ELK RAPIDS, MI
ELK RIDGE, UT
ELK RIVER, ID,MN
ELK RUN HEIGHTS, IA
ELKADER, IA
ELKHART, IN,KS,TX
ELKHART LAKE, WI
ELKHORN, NB,WI
ELKHORN CITY, KY
ELKINS, AR,WV
ELKLAND, PA
ELKMONT, AL
ELKO, MN,NV
ELKTON, KY,MD,MI,MN,OR
 SD,TN,VA
ELLAVILLE, FL,GA
ELLENBORO, NC,WV
ELLENDALE, DE,MN,ND
ELLENSBURG, WA
ELLENTON, FL,GA
ELLENVILLE, NY
ELLERBE, NC
ELLETTSVILLE, IN

ELLICOTTVILLE, NY
ELLIJAY, GA
ELLINGTON, CT,MO
ELLINWOOD, KS
ELLIOTT, IA
ELLIOTSVILLE, ME
ELLIS, KS
ELLISVILLE, MO
ELLSWORTH, IA,KS,ME,MI
MN,PA,WI
ELLWOOD CITY, PA
ELM CITY, NC
ELM CREEK, NB
ELM GROVE, WI
ELM SPRINGS, AR
ELMA, IA,NY,WA
ELMATON, TX
ELMDALE, KS
ELMENDORF, TX
ELMER, NJ
ELMER CITY, WA
ELMHURST, IL
ELMIRA, NY
ELMO, UT
ELMORE, MN,OH,VT
ELMORE CITY, OK
ELMSFORD, NY
ELMWOOD, IL,NB,WI
ELMWOOD PARK, IL,NJ
ELMWOOD PLACE, OH
ELNORA, IN
ELON COLLEGE, NC
ELROSA, MN
ELROY, WI
ELSA, TX
ELSAH, IL
ELSBERRY, MO
ELSIE, MI,NB
ELSINORE, CA,UT
ELSMERE, DE,KY
ELSMORE, KS
ELTON, LA
ELVINS, MO
ELWOOD, IL,IN,KS,NB
ELY, MN,NV
ELYRIA, NB,OH
ELYSIAN, MN
EMBARRASS, WI
EMBDEN, ME
EMERADO, ND
EMERALD ISLE, NC
EMERSON, AR,GA,IA,NB,NJ
EMERY, SD,UT
EMHOUSE, TX
EMIGRANT GAP, CA
EMILY, MN
EMINENCE, KY
EMMA, MO
EMMAUS, PA
EMMERYVILLE, CA
EMMET, AR,NB
EMMETSBURG, IA
EMMETT, ID,MI
EMMITSBURG, MD
EMMONAK, AK
EMMONS, MN
EMORY, TX
EMPIRE, CA,CO,MI
EMPORIA, KS,VA
EMPORIUM, PA
ENCAMPMENT, WY
ENCINAL, TX
ENCINITAS, CA
ENCINO, NM,TX
ENDEAVOR, WI
ENDERLIN, ND
ENDICOTT, NB,NY,WA
ENFIELD, CT,IL,ME,NC,NH
ENGLAND, AR
ENGLEWOOD, CO,KS
NJ,OH,TN
ENGLEWOOD CLIFFS, NJ
ENGLISH, IN

ENGLISHTOWN, NJ
ENID, OK
ENIGMA, GA
ENKA, NC
ENNIS, MT,TX
ENOCH, UT
ENOCHVILLE, NC
ENOLA, AR,PA
ENON, OH
ENOSBURG, VT
ENSIGN, KS
ENTERPRISE, AL,KS,OR,UT
ENTIAT, WA
ENUMCLAW, WA
ENVILLE, TN
EOLA, TX
EPES, AL
EPHRAIM, UT,WI
EPHRATA, PA,WA
EPPING, NH
EPPS, LA
EPSOM, NH
EPWORTH, IA
ERATH, LA
ERHARD, MN
ERICK, OK
ERICSON, NB
ERIDU, FL
ERIE, CO,IL,KS,PA
ERIN, TN
EROS, LA
ERSKINE, MN
ERVING, MA
ERWIN, NC,SD,TN
ESCALANTE, UT
ESCALON, CA
ESCANABA, MI
ESCONDIDO, CA
ESKRIDGE, KS
ESMERALDO, NV
ESMOND, ND
ESOPUS, NY
ESPARTO, CA
ESPONOLA, NM
ESSEX, CA,CT,IA,MA,MO,NY
ESSEX FELLS, NJ
ESSEX JUNCTION, VT
ESSEXVILLE, MI
ESTACADA, OR
ESTANCIA, NM
ESTELL MANOR, NJ
ESTELLINE, SD,TX
ESTERO BAY, CA
ESTES PARK, CO
ESTHER, MO
ESTHERVILLE, IA
ESTHERWOOD, LA
ESTILL SPRINGS, TN
ESTO, FL
ESTRAL BEACH, MI
ETHAN, SD
ETHELSVILLE, AL
ETHRIDGE, TN
ETNA, CA,ME,PA
ETNA GREEN, IN
ETOWAH, TN
ETTRICK, WI
EUCALYPTUS HILLS, CA
EUCLID, OH
EUDORA, AR,KS
EUFAULA, AL,OK
EUGENE, OR
EULESS, TX
EUNICE, NM
EUREKA, CA,IL,KS,MO,MT
NC,NV,SD,UT
EUREKA SPRINGS, AR
EUSTACE, TX
EUSTIS, FL,ME,NB
EUTAW, AL
EVA, AL
EVAN, MN
EVANS, CO

EVANS CITY, PA
EVANS MILLS, NY
EVANSDALE, IA
EVANSTON, IL,WY
EVANSVILLE, IN,MN,WI,WY
EVANT, TX
EVART, MI
EVARTS, KY
EVELETH, MN
EVENING SHADE, AR
EVEREST, KS
EVERETT, MA,PA,WA
EVERETTS, NC
EVERGLADES CITY, FL
EVERGREEN, AL,LA
EVERGREEN PARK, IL
EVERMAN, TX
EVERSON, WA
EVERTON, AR
EWA, HI
EWA BEACH, HI
EWING, NB
EXCEL, AL
EXCELSIOR, MN
EXCELSIOR SPRINGS, MO
EXELAND, WI
EXETER, CA,ME,MO
NB,NH,PA,RI
EXIRA, IA
EXMORE, VA
EXTON, PA
EYOTA, MN

FAIR BLUFF, NC
FAIR HAVEN, NJ,VT
FAIR LAWN, NJ
FAIR OAKS, CA
FAIRBANK, IA
FAIRBANKS, AK
FAIRBORN, OH
FAIRBURN, GA,SD
FAIRBURY, IL,NB
FAIRCHANCE, PA
FAIRCHILD, WI
FAIRFAX, CA,IA,MN,MO,OH
OK,SC,SD,VA,VT
FAIRFIELD, AL,CA,CT,IA
ID,IL,ME,MT,NB,OH
PA,TX,VT,WA
FAIRGROVE, MI
FAIRHAVEN, MA
FAIRHOPE, AL,PA
FAIRLAND, OK
FAIRLAWN, OH
FAIRLEE, VT
FAIRLESS HILLS, PA
FAIRMONT, MN,NB,OK,WV
FAIRMONT CITY, IL
FAIRMOUNT, GA,IL,IN,ND
FAIRMOUNT HEIGHTS, MD
FAIRPLAY, CO
FAIRPORT, NY
FAIRVIEW, AL,KS,KY,MO,MT
NJ,OK,OR,SD,TN,TX,UT,WV
FAIRVIEW PARK, IN,OH
FAIRWATER, WI
FAIRWAY, KS
FAITH, SD
FALCONER, NY
FALFURRIAS, TX
FALKVILLE, AL
FALL CREEK, WI
FALL RIVER, KS,MA,WI
FALL RIVER MILLS, CA
FALLBROOK, CA
FALLING SPRING, WV
FALLON, NV
FALLS CHURCH, VA
FALLS CITY, NB,OR,TX
FALLSBURG, NY
FALMOUTH, FL,KY,MA,ME
FAMOSA, CA
FANWOOD, NJ

FARBER, MO
FARGO, ND,OK
FARIBAULT, MN
FARLEY, IA
FARMER, SD
FARMER CITY, IL
FARMERS BRANCH, TX
FARMERSBURG, IN
FARMERSVILLE, CA,TX
FARMERVILLE, LA
FARMINGDALE, ME,NJ,NY
FARMINGTON, AR,CA,CT,DE
IA,ME,MI,MN,MO,NH,NM
UT,WA,WV
FARMINGTON HILLS, MI
FARMLAND, IN
FARMVILLE, NC
FARNAM, NB
FARRAGUT, IA
FARRELL, PA
FARWELL, MI,MN,NB,TX
FATE, TX
FAULKTON, SD
FAUNSDALE, AL
FAXON, OK
FAYETTE, AL,IA,ME,MO,UT
FAYETTEVILLE, AR,GA,NC
PA,TN,TX,WV
FAYSTON, VT
FEATHER FALLS, CA
FEDERAL DAM, MN
FEDERAL HEIGHTS, CO
FEDERALSBURG, MD
FELLSMORE, FL
FELTON, CA,DE,MN
FENNER, CA
FENNIMORE, WI
FENNVILLE, MI
FENTON, IA,LA,MI,MO
FENWICK ISLAND, DE
FERDINAND, ID,IN,VT
FERGUS FALLS, MN
FERGUSON, KY,MO
FERNAN LAKE, ID
FERNANDINA BEACH, FL
FERNBROOK, CA
FERNDALE, CA,MI,PA,WA
FERRIDAY, LA
FERRIS, TX
FERRISBURG, VT
FERRON, UT
FERRYSBURG, MI
FERRYVILLE, WI
FERTILE, IA,MN
FESSENDEN, ND
FESTUS, MO
FIELDING, UT
FIFE, WA
FIFE LAKE, MI
FIFTY LAKES, MN
FIFTY-SIX, AR
FILER, ID
FILLEY, NB
FILLMORE, CA,UT
FINCASTLE, VA
FINDLAY, IL,OH
FINE, NY
FINGER, TN
FINLAYSON, MN
FINLEY, ND
FIREBAUGH, CA
FIRESTONE, CO
FIRTH, ID,NB
FISCHER, TX
FISHER, IL,LA,MN
FISHERS, IN
FISHKILL, NY
FISK, MO
FITCHBURG, MA
FITHIAN, IL
FITZGERALD, GA
FIVE POINTS, AL
FLAGLER, CO

FLAGLER BEACH, FL
FLAGSTAFF, AZ
FLAMINGO, FL
FLANAGAN, IL
FLANDREAU, SD
FLASHER, ND
FLAT RIVER, MO
FLAT ROCK, MI,NC
FLATONIA, TX
FLATWOODS, KY,WV
FLAXVILLE, MT
FLEETWOOD, PA
FLEISCHMANNS, NY
FLEMING, CO
FLEMING-NEON, KY
FLEMINGSBURG, KY
FLEMINGTON, NJ,PA,WV
FLENSBURG, MN
FLETCHER, OK,VT
FLINN SPRINGS, CA
FLINT, MI
FLINTRIDGE, CA
FLIPPIN, AR
FLOMATION, FL
FLOMATON, AL
FLOODWOOD, MN
FLORA, IL,IN,MS
FLORAL CITY, FL,NY
FLORALA, AL
FLORENCE, AL,AZ,CO,KS,KY
  MS,NJ,OR,SC,SD,TX
FLORENCE VILLA, FL
FLORESVILLE, TX
FLORHAM PARK, NJ
FLORIDA, MA,NY
FLORIDA CITY, FL
FLORIEN, LA
FLORIN, CA
FLORISSANT, MO
FLORISTON, CA
FLOSSMOOR, IL
FLOURTOWN, PA
FLOVILLA, GA
FLOWERY BRANCH, GA
FLOYD, IA,NM,VA
FLOYDADA, TX
FLUSHING, MI,OH
FOLCROFT, PA
FOLEY, AL,MN
FOLKSTON, GA
FOLLANSBEE, WV
FOLLETT, TX
FOLLY BEACH, SC
FOLSOM, CA,LA,NM
FOND DU LAC, WI
FONDA, IA,NY
FONTANA, CA,KS
FONTANA-ON-GENEVA
  LAKE, WI
FONTANELLE, IA
FOOTVILLE, WI
FORAKER, OK
FORBESTOWN, CA
FORD, KS
FORD CITY, CA,PA
FORDLAND, MO
FORDVILLE, ND
FORDYCE, AR,NB
FOREMAN, AR
FOREST, LA,MS
FOREST ACRES, SC
FOREST CITY, CA,NC,PA
FOREST GROVE, OR
FOREST HEIGHTS, MD
FOREST HILL, LA
FOREST HILLS, PA
FOREST LAKE, MN
FOREST PARK, GA,IL,OH,OK
FORESTHILL, CA
FORESTON, MN
FORESTPORT, NY
FORESTVILLE, CA,MI
FORGAN, OK

FORKLAND, AL
FORKS, WA
FORKS OF SALMON, CA
FORMAN, ND
FORMOSA, KS
FORNEY, TX
FORREST, IL
FORREST CITY, AR
FORRESTON, IL
FORSAN, TX
FORSYTH, GA,MO,MT
FORT ATKINSON, IA,WI
FORT BENTON, MT
FORT BIDWELL, CA
FORT BRAGG, CA
FORT BRANCH, IN
FORT CALHOUN, NB
FORT COBB, OK
FORT COLLINS, CO
FORT COVINGTON, NY
FORT DAVIS, TX
FORT DEPOSIT, AL
FORT DICK, CA
FORT DODGE, IA
FORT EDWARD, NY
FORT FAIRFIELD, ME
FORT GAINES, GA
FORT GATES, TX
FORT GAY, WV
FORT GIBSON, OK
FORT GRIFFIN, TX
FORT IRWIN, CA
FORT JOHNSON, NY
FORT JONES, CA
FORT KENT, ME
FORT LARAMIE, WY
FORT LAUDERDALE, FL
FORT LAWN, SC
FORT LEE, NJ
FORT LITTLETON, PA
FORT LOUDON, PA
FORT LUPTON, CO
FORT MACCARTHUR, CA
FORT MADISON, IA
FORT MCCLELLAN, AL
FORT MCKAVETT, TX
FORT MEADE, FL
FORT MILL, SC
FORT MITCHELL, KY
FORT MORGAN, CO
FORT MYERS, FL
FORT OGDEN, FL
FORT ORD, CA
FORT PAYNE, AL
FORT PIERCE, FL,SD
FORT PLAIN, NY
FORT RECOVERY, OH
FORT RUCKER, AL
FORT SCOTT, KS
FORT SHAWNEE, OH
FORT SMITH, AR
FORT STOCKTON, TX
FORT SUMNER, NM
FORT SUPPLY, OK
FORT THOMAS, KY
FORT TOWSON, OK
FORT VALLEY, GA
FORT WALTON BEACH, FL
FORT WASHINGTON, PA
FORT WAYNE, IN
FORT WHITE, FL
FORT WORTH, TX
FORT YATES, ND
FORT YUKON, AK
FORTUNA, CA
FORTUNA LEDGE, AK
FORTY FORT, PA
FOSS, OK
FOSSIL, OR
FOSSTON, MN
FOSTER, NB,RI
FOSTER CITY, CA
FOSTORIA, OH

FOUKE, AR
FOUNTAIN, CO,MI,MN,NC
FOUNTAIN CITY, WI
FOUNTAIN GREEN, UT
FOUNTAIN HILL, AR,PA
FOUNTAIN INN, SC
FOUNTAIN VALLEY, CA
FOUR OAKS, NC
FOWLER, CA,CO,KS,MI
FOWLERVILLE, MI
FOX CHAPEL, PA
FOX LAKE, IL,WI
FOX POINT, WI
FOX RIVER GROVE, IL
FOXBOROUGH, MA
FOXFIRE, NC
FOXHOME, MN
FOYIL, OK
FRACKVILLE, PA
FRAMINGHAM, MA
FRANCESTOWN, NH
FRANCIS, OK
FRANCIS CREEK, WI
FRANCONIA, NH
FRANKENMUTH, MI
FRANKFORD, DE
FRANKFORT, IL,KS,KY,ME
  MI,NY,OH,SD
FRANKLIN, AL,AR,CT,GA,IA
  IN,KY,LA,MA,ME,MI,MN,NB
  NC,NH,NJ,NY,PA,TN
  TX,VA,VT,WV
FRANKLIN LAKES, NJ
FRANKLIN PARK, IL,NJ
FRANKLINTON, LA,NC
FRANKLINVILLE, NC,NJ,NY
FRANKSTON, TX
FRANKTON, IN
FRANNIE, WY
FRANNIN, TX
FRASER, CO,MI
FRAZEE, MN
FRAZEYBURG, OH
FRAZIER PARK, CA
FREDERIC, WI
FREDERICK, CO,MD,OK,SD
FREDERICKSBURG, IA,IN
  TX,VA
FREDERICKTOWN, MO,PA
FREDERIKA, IA
FREDONIA, AZ,KS,NY,WI
FREDONIA (Biscoe), AR
FREDRICA, DE
FREE SOIL, MI
FREEBORN, MN
FREEBURG, IL,MO
FREEDOM, CA,ME,NY,OK,PA
FREEHOLD, NJ
FREELAND, PA
FREEMAN, SD
FREEMAN CITY, MO
FREEPORT, FL,IL,ME,MI
  MN,NY,PA,TX
FREER, TX
FREMONT, CA,IA,IN,NB,NC
  NH,OH,WI
FRENCH CAMP, CA,MS
FRENCH CORRAL, CA
FRENCH GULCH, CA
FRENCH LICK, IN
FRENCH SETTLEMEMT, LA
FRENCHBORO, ME
FRENCHTOWN, NJ
FRENCHVILLE, ME
FRESNO, CA
FRIANT, CA
FRIARS POINT, MS
FRIDAY HARBOR, WA
FRIDLEY, MN
FRIEND, NB
FRIENDLY, WV
FRIENDSHIP, AR,ME
  NY,TN,WI

FRIENDSVILLE, MD,TN
FRIENDSWOOD, TX
FRIES, VA
FRIESLAND, WI
FRIJOLE, TX
FRIONA, TX
FRISCO, CO,TX
FRISCO CITY, AL
FRITCH, TX
FROID, MT
FROMBERG, MT
FRONTENAC, KS,MO
FRONT ROYAL, VA
FROST, TX
FROSTBURG, MD
FROSTPROOF, FL
FRUITA, CO
FRUITDALE, SD
FRUITHURST, AL
FRUITLAND, IA,MD
FRUITLAND PARK, FL
FRUITPORT, MI
FRUITVALE, TX
FRYEBURG, ME
FULLERTON, CA,NB,ND
FULSHEAR, TX
FULTON, AL,AR,IL,IN,KS
  MO,MS,NY,SD,TX
FULTONDALE, AL
FUNK, NB
FUNKSTOWN, MD
FUQUAY-VARINA, NC
FURMAN, SC
FURNACE CREEK, CA
FYFFE, AL

GAASTRA, MI
GABBS, NV
GACKLE, ND
GADSDEN, AL,TN
GAFFNEY, SC
GAGE, OK
GAGETOWN, MI
GAIL, TX
GAINES, MI
GAINESBORO, TN
GAINESVILLE, AL,FL
  GA,NY,TX
GAITHERSBURG, MD
GALATIA, IL
GALAX, VA
GALENA, AK,IL,KS
  MD,MO,OH
GALENA PARK, TX
GALESBURG, IL,KS,MI,ND
GALESTOWN, MD
GALESVILLE, WI
GALETON, PA
GALIEN, MI
GALION, OH
GALLATIN, MO,TN,TX
GALLIPOLIS, OH
GALLITZIN, PA
GALLUP, NM
GALT, CA
GALVA, IA,IL,KS
GALVESTON, IN,TX
GALWAY, NY
GAMBELL, AK
GAMBIER, OH
GANADO, TX
GANDY, NB
GANS, OK
GANTT, AL
GARBER, OK
GARBERVILLE, CA
GARDEN, MI
GARDEN CITY, AL,CO,GA,MI
  MO,NY,SD,TX,UT
GARDEN CREEK, NC
GARDEN GROVE, CA,IA
GARDEN PLAIN, KS

GARDENA, CA
GARDENDALE, AL
GARDINER, ME,NY
GARDNER, IL,KS,MA
GAREY, CA
GARFIELD, AR,KS,ME,NJ,WA
GARFIELD HEIGHTS, OH
GARIBALDI, OR
GARLAND, AR,ME,NB,NC
  TN,TX,UT
GARLOCK, CA
GARNAVIELLO, IA
GARNER, AR,IA,NC
GARNETT, KS
GARRETSON, SD
GARRETT, IN
GARRETT PARK, MD
GARRETTSVILLE, OH
GARRISON, IA,NB,ND,TX
GARVIN, OK
GARWIN, IA
GARWOOD, NJ
GARY, IN,SD,WV
GARYSBURG, NC
GAS, KS
GAS CITY, IN
GASQUET, CA
GASSAWAY, WV
GASSVILLE, AR
GASTON, IN,NC,OR,SC
GASTONIA, NC
GATE, OK
GATE CITY, VA
GATES MILLS, OH
GATESVILLE, NC,TX
GATEWAY, AR
GATLINBURG, TN
GAULEY BRIDGE, WV
GAVIOTA, CA
GAYLESVILLE, AL
GAYLORD, KS,MI
GAYS MILLS, WI
GAYVILLE, SD
GAZELLE, CA
GEARHART, OR
GEDDES, SD
GEISTOWN, PA
GEM, KS
GENE AUTRY, OK
GENESCO, KS
GENESEO, IL,NY
GENESSE, ID
GENEVA, AL,GA,IA,IL,IN
  NB,NY,OH
GENEVA-ON-THE-LAKE, OH
GENOA, CO,NB,NY,OH,WI
GENOA CITY, WI
GENTRY, AR,MO
GENTRYVILLE, IN
GEORGE, IA,WA
GEORGE WEST, TX
GEORGETOWN, CA,CO,DE,GA
  ID,IL,IN,KY,LA,MA,ME,MN
  MS,OH,SC,TX
GEORGIA, VT
GEORGIANA, AL
GERALDINE, AL,MT
GERBER, CA
GERING, NB
GERLACH, NV
GERMANTOWN, KY,NY
  OH,TN,WI
GERONIMO, OK,TX
GERRY, NY
GERVAIS, OR
GETTYSBURG, OH,PA,SD
GEUDA SPRINGS, KS
GEYSERVILLE, CA
GHENT, KY,MN,NY
GIBBON, MN,NB
GIBBSBORO, NJ
GIBRALTAR, MI
GIBSLAND, LA

GIBSON, GA,NC,TN
GIBSON CITY, IL
GIBSONBURG, OH
GIBSONTON, FL
GIDDINGS, TX
GIDEON, MO
GIFFORD, FL,IL,SC
GIG HARBOR, WA
GILA BEND, AZ
GILBERT, AR,AZ,IA,LA
  MN,SC,WV
GILBERTOWN, AL
GILBERTVILLE, IA
GILBOA, NY
GILBY, ND
GILCREST, CO
GILEAD, ME,NB
GILLESPIE, IL
GILLETT, AR,WI
GILLETTE, WY
GILLHAM, AR
GILLIAM, LA
GILMAN, IL,MN,WI
GILMAN CITY, MO
GILMER, TX
GILMORE, AR
GILROY, CA
GILTNER, NB
GIRARD, GA,IL,KS,OH,PA
GLADE, KS
GLADE SPRING, VA
GLADEWATER, TX
GLADSTONE, MI,MO,ND,OR
GLADWIN, MI
GLANDORF, OH
GLASFORD, IL
GLASGOW, KS,KY,MO
  MT,VA,WV
GLASSBORO, NJ
GLASSPORT, PA
GLASTENBURY, VT
GLASTONBURY, CT
GLAZIER, TX
GLEASON, TN
GLEN ALLEN, AL
GLEN ALPINE, NC
GLEN AVON HEIGHTS, CA
GLEN COVE, NY
GLEN ECHO, MD
GLEN ELDER, KS
GLEN ELLYN, IL
GLEN FLORA, WI
GLEN LYN, VA
GLEN RAVEN, NC
GLEN RIDGE, NJ
GLEN ROCK, NJ,PA
GLEN ROSE, TX
GLEN SAINT MARY, FL
GLEN ULLIN, ND
GLENARDEN, MD
GLENBEULAH, WI
GLENBURN, ME
GLENCOE, AL,IL,KY,MN,OK
GLENDALE, AZ,CA,CO,MO,OH
  OR,UT,WI,WV
GLENDALE HEIGHTS, IL
GLENDIVE, MT
GLENDO, WY
GLENDORA, CA
GLENHAM, SD
GLENMONT, OH
GLENMORA, LA
GLENN, CA
GLENNS FERRY, ID
GLENNVILLE, GA
GLENOLDEN, PA
GLENPOOL, OK
GLENROCK, WY
GLENS FALLS, NY
GLENSHAW, PA
GLENSIDE, PA
GLENVIEW, CA,IL
GLENVIEW MANOR, KY

GLENVILLE, MN,NB,WV
GLENWOOD, AL,AR,GA
  IL,MN,UT
GLENWOOD CITY, WI
GLENWOOD SPRINGS, CO
GLOBE, AZ
GLOCESTER, RI
GLOSTER, MS
GLOUCESTER, MA
GLOVER, VT
GLOVERSVILLE, NY
GLYNDON, MN
GNADENHUTTEN, OH
GOBLES, MI
GODDARD, KS
GODFREY, IL
GODLEY, TX
GODWIN, NC
GOEHNER, NB
GOESSEL, KS
GOFF, KS
GOFFS, CA
GOFFSTOWN, NH
GOLD BAR, WA
GOLD BEACH, OR
GOLD RUN, CA,NV
GOLDEN, CO,MS
GOLDEN CITY, MO
GOLDEN MEADOW, LA
GOLDEN VALLEY, MN
GOLDENDALE, WA
GOLDONNA, LA
GOLDSBORO, MD,NC
GOLDSBORO NORTHWEST, NC
GOLDSBY, OK
GOLDSMITH, TX
GOLDSTON, NC
GOLDTHWAITE, TX
GOLETA, CA
GOLF MANOR, OH
GOLIAD, TX
GOLOVIN, AK
GOLTRY, OK
GONVICK, MN
GONZALES, CA,LA,TX,FL
GOOD HOPE, GA,IL
GOOD THUNDER, MN
GOODHUE, MN
GOODING, ID
GOODLAND, IN,KS
GOODMAN, MO,MS
GOODNEWS BAY, AK
GOODNO, FL
GOODRICH, MI,TX
GOODSPRINGS, NV
GOODWELL, OK
GOODWIN, SD
GOODYEAR, AZ
GOOSE CREEK, SC
GOOSE LAKE, IA
GORDO, AL
GORDON, AL,GA,NB,OH,TX
GORDONSVILLE, TN,VA
GORDONVILLE, MO
GORE, OK
GOREE, TX
GORHAM, KS,ME,NY
GORMAN, CA,TX
GORMON, NC
GOSHEN, AL,CA,CT,IN,NH
  NY,UT,VA,VT
GOSNELL, AR
GOSPORT, IN
GOTEBO, OK
GOTHENBURG, NB
GOULD, AR,OK
GOULDSBORO, ME
GOUVERNEUR, NY
GOVE CITY, KS
GOWANDA, NY
GOWER, MO
GOWRIE, IA
GRABILL, IN

GRACE, ID
GRACEMONT, OK
GRACEVILLE, FL,MN
GRADY, AR,NM
GRAFORD, TX
GRAFTON, IL,NB,ND,NH,NY
  OH,VT,WI,WV
GRAHAM, NC
GRAIN VALLEY, MO
GRAINFIELD, KS
GRAINOLA, OK
GRAMBLING, LA
GRAMERCY, LA
GRANADA, CO,MN
GRANBURY, TX
GRANBY, CO,CT,MO,VT
GRAND BEACH, MI
GRAND BLANC, MI
GRAND CANE, LA
GRAND COULEE, WA
GRAND COTEAU, LA
GRAND FORKS, ND
GRAND HAVEN, MI
GRAND ISLAND, FL,NB,NY
GRAND ISLE, LA,ME,VT
GRAND JUNCTION, CO,IA,TN
GRAND LAKE, CO
GRAND LAKE STREAM, ME
GRAND LAKE TOWNE, OK
GRAND LEDGE, MI
GRAND MARAIS, MN
GRAND MEADOW, MN
GRAND MOUND, IA
GRAND PRAIRIE, TX
GRAND RAPIDS, MI,MN,OH
GRAND RIDGE, FL,IL
GRAND RIVER, OH
GRAND RIVERS, KY
GRAND SALINE, TX
GRAND TERRACE, CA
GRAND TOWER, IL
GRAND VALLEY, CO
GRAND VIEW, ID
GRANDFALLS, TX
GRANDFIELD, OK
GRANDVIEW, IA,IN
  MO,TX,WA
GRANDVIEW HEIGHTS, OH
GRANDVILLE, MI
GRANGER, IA,TX,WA,WY
GRANGEVILLE, ID
GRANITE, OK,OR
GRANITE CITY, IL
GRANITE FALLS, MN,NC,WA
GRANITE QUARRY, NC
GRANITE SHOALS, TX
GRANITEVILLE, CA
GRANNIS, AR
GRANT, AL,IA,MI,NB
GRANT CITY, MO
GRANT PARK, IL
GRANT TOWN, WV
GRANTHAM, NH
GRANTON, WI
GRANTS, NM
GRANTS PASS, OR
GRANTSBURG, WI
GRANTSVILLE, MD,UT,WV
GRANTVILLE, GA
GRANTWOOD, MO
GRANVILLE, IA,IL,NY
  OH,VT,WV
GRAPELAND, TX
GRAPEVINE, TX
GRASS LAKE, MI
GRASS RANGE, MT
GRASS VALLEY, CA,OR
GRATERFORD, PA
GRATIOT, OH,WI
GRATON, CA
GRAVETTE, AR
GRAVITY, IA
GRAY, GA,ME

GRAY COURT, SC
GRAYLING, AK,MI
GRAYMOOR, KY
GRAYSLAKE, IL
GRAYSON, GA,KY,LA
GRAYSVILLE, AL,OH,TN
GRAYVILLE, IL
GREAT BEND, KS
GREAT FALLS, MT,SC
GREAT NECK, NY
GREAT POND, ME
GREECE, NY
GREELEY, CO,IA,KS,PA
GREELEY CENTER, NB
GREELEYVILLE, SC
GREEN BAY, WI
GREEN CAMP, OH
GREEN CITY, MO
GREEN COVE SPRINGS, FL
GREEN FORREST, AR
GREEN ISLE, MN
GREEN LAKE, WI
GREEN MOUNTAIN FALLS, CO
GREEN OAKS, IL
GREEN RIVER, WY
GREEN ROCK, IL
GREEN SPRINGS, OH
GREEN TREE, PA
GREENBACK, TN
GREENBELT, MD
GREENBRAE, CA
GREENBRIER, AR,TN
GREENBUSH, ME,MN
GREENCASTLE, IN,PA
GREENDALE, IN,WI
GREENE, IA,ME,NY
GREENEVILLE, TN
GREENFIELD, CA,IA,IL,IN
    ME,MO,NH,OH,OK,TN,WI
GREENHILLS, OH
GREENHORN, OR
GREENLAND, AR,NH
GREENLEAF, ID,KS
GREENPORT, NY
GREENS FORK, IN
GREENSBORO, AL,FL,GA
    IN,MD,NC,VT
GREENSBURG, IN,KS
    KY,LA,PA
GREENTOP, MO
GREENTOWN, IN
GREENUP, IL,KY
GREENVIEW, IL
GREENVILLE, AL,CA,FL,GA
    IL,IN,KY,ME,MI,MS,NC,NH
    NY,OH,PA,SC,TX
GREENWALD, MN
GREENWAY, AR
GREENWICH, CT,NJ,NY,OH
GREENWOOD, AR,CA,FL,IN
    LA,ME,MO,MS,NB,SC,WI
GREENWOOD VILLAGE, CO
GREERS FERRY, AR
GREGORY, SD,TX
GREIG, NY
GRENADA, CA,MS
GRENOLA, KS
GRENVILLE, NM,SD
GRESHAM, NB,OR,WI
GRETNA, FL,LA,NB,VA
GREY EAGLE, MN
GREYBULL, WY
GRIDLEY, CA,IL,KS
GRIFFIN, GA,IN
GRIFFITH, IN
GRIFFITHVILLE, AR
GRIGGSVILLE, IL
GRIMES, CA,IA
GRIMESLAND, NC
GRINNELL, IA,KS
GRISWOLD, CT,IA
GROESBECK, TX
GROETTINGER, IA

GROOM, TX
GROSS, NB
GROSSE POINTE, MI
GROSSE POINTE FARMS, MI
GROSSE POINTE PARK, MI
GROSSE POINTE SHORES, MI
GROSSE POINTE WOODS, MI
GROSSE TETE, LA
GROTON, CT,NH,NY,SD,VT
GROTTOES, VA
GROVE, OK
GROVE CITY, MN,OH,PA
GROVE HILL, AL
GROVELAND, CA,FL,NY
GROVEPORT, OH
GROVER, CO,NC
GROVER CITY, CA
GROVER HILL, OH
GROVES, TX
GROVETON, TX
GROVETOWN, GA
GRUBBS, AR
GRUNDY, VA
GRUNDY CENTER, IA
GRUVER, TX
GRYGLA, MN
GUADALUPE, AZ,CA
GUALALA, CA
GUASTI, CA
GUERNEVILLE, CA
GUERNSEY, WY
GUEYDAN, LA
GUIDE ROCK, NB
GUILDERLAND, NY
GUILDHALL, VT
GUILFORD, CT,ME,VT
GUIN, AL
GUINDA, CA
GUION, AR
GULF BREEZE, FL
GULF SHORES, AL
GULFPORT, FL,MS
GULLY, MN
GUNNISON, CO,MS,UT
GUNTERSVILLE, AL
GUNTER, TX
GUNTOWN, MS
GURDON, AR
GURLEY, AL,NB
GURNEE, IL
GUSTINE, CA,TX
GUTHRIE, KY,OK,TX
GUTHRIE CENTER, IA
GUTTENBERG, IA,NJ
GUY, AR
GUYMAN, OK
GUYTON, GA
GWINNER, ND
GYPSUM, CO,KS

HACKENSACK, MN,NJ
HACKETT, AR
HACKETTSTOWN, NJ
HACKLEBURG, AL
HADAR, NB
HADDAM, CT,KS
HADDON HEIGHTS, NJ
HADDONFIELD, NJ
HADLEY, MN,NY
HAGAN, GA
HAGERMAN, NM
HAGERSTOWN, IN,MD
HAGUE, NY
HAHIRA, GA
HAIGLER, NB
HAILEY, ID
HAINES, AK,OR
HAINES CITY, FL
HAINESPORT, NJ
HALE, MO
HALEDON-NORTH HALEDON, NJ
HALEIWA, HI
HALES CORNERS, WI
HALESITE, NY

HALEYVILLE, AL
HALF DOME, CA
HALF MOON, NC
HALF MOON BAY, CA
HALFWAY, OR
HALIFAX, NC,VA,VT
HALL PARK, OK
HALL SUMMIT, LA
HALLAM, NB,PA
HALLANDALE, FL
HALLETT, OK
HALLETTSVILLE, TX
HALLIDAY, ND
HALLOCK, MN
HALLOWELL, ME
HALLS, TN
HALLSTEAD, PA
HALLSVILLE, TX
HALLWOOD, VA
HALMA, MN
HALSEY, NB
HALSTAD, MN
HALSTEAD, KS
HALTOM CITY, TX
HAMBLETON, WV
HAMBURG, AR,CA,IA,IL,MN
    NJ,NY,PA
HAMDEN, CT
HAMER, ID
HAMILTON, AL,GA,IA,IN,KS
    MO,MT,NC,NJ,NY,OH,TX,VA
HAMILTON CITY, CA
HAMLER, OH
HAMLET, IN,NB,NC
HAMLIN, ME,NY,WV
HAMMOND, IL,IN,LA,ME
    MN,OR,WI
HAMMONTON, NJ
HAMPDEN, ME
HAMPSHIRE, IL
HAMPSTEAD, MD,NH
HAMPTON, AR,CT,FL,GA,IA
    MN,NB,NH,NJ,SC,VA
HAMPTON FALLS, NH
HAMPTON SPRINGS, FL
HAMTRAMCK, MI
HANAMAULU, HI
HANAPEPE, HI
HANCEVILLE, AL
HANCOCK, IA,MD,ME,MI,MN
    NH,NY,VT,WI
HANDLEY, WV
HANFORD, CA
HANGING ROCK, OH
HANKINSON, ND
HANLEY FALLS, MN
HANLEY HILLS, MO
HANNA, OK,WY
HANNAWA FALLS, NY
HANNIBAL, MO,NY
HANOVER, IL,IN,KS,ME
    MN,NH,PA
HANOVER PARK, IL
HANSEN, ID
HANSKA, MN
HANSON, MA
HANSTON, KS
HAPPY, TX
HAPPY CAMP, CA
HAPPY VALLEY, OR
HARAHAN, LA
HARALSON, GA
HARBINE, NB
HARBISON CANYON, CA
HARBOR BEACH, MI
HARBOR SPRINGS, MI
HARDEEVILLE, SC
HARDESTY, OK
HARDIN, IL,MO,MT,TX
HARDINSBURG, IN,KY
HARDTNER, KS
HARDWICK, MA,MN,VT
HARDY, AR,NB

HARKER HEIGHTS, TX
HARKERS ISLAND, NC
HARLAN, IA,KY
HARLEM, GA,MT
HARLEYVILLE, SC
HARLINGEN, TX
HARLOWTON, MT
HARMAN, WV
HARMONY, CA,IN,ME,MN,PA
HARPER, KS
HARPER WOODS, MI
HARPERS FERRY, WV
HARPERSFIELD, NY
HARPERSVILLE, AL
HARPSWELL, ME
HARRAH, OK,WA
HARRELL, AR
HARRELLSVILLE, NC
HARRIETTA, MI
HARRIMAN, TN
HARRINGTON, DE,ME,WA
HARRINGTON PARK, NJ
HARRIS, MN,OK
HARRISBURG, AR,IL,NC
    OR,PA,SD
HARRISON, AR,GA,ID,ME,MI
    NB,NJ,NY,OH
HARRISONBURG, LA,VA
HARRISONVILLE, MO
HARRISVILLE, MI,UT,WV
HARROLD, SD
HART, MI,TX
HARTFORD, AL,AR,CT,IL,KS
    KY,ME,MI,NY,OH,SD,VT,WI
HARTFORD CITY, IN
HARTINGTON, NB
HARTLAND, CT,ME,MN,VT,WI
HARTLINE, WA
HARTLY, DE
HARTMAN, AR,CO
HARTSELLE, AL
HARTSHORNE, OK
HARTSVILLE, IN,SC,TN
HARTVILLE, MO,WY
HARTWELL, GA
HARVARD, IL,MA,NB
HARVEY, IL,ND
HARVEY CEDARS, NJ
HARVEYS LAKE, PA
HARVEYSBURG, OH
HARVEYVILLE, KS
HARWICH, MA
HARWINTON, CT
HARWOOD, ND
HARWOOD HEIGHTS, IL
HASBROUCK HEIGHTS, NJ
HASKELL, OK,TX
HASLET, TX
HASSELL, NC
HASTINGS, FL,MI,MN,NB,OK
HASTINGS-ON-HUDSON, NY
HASWELL, CO
HATCH, NM,UT
HATFIELD, AR,MA,MN,PA
HATLEY, WI
HATTIESBURG, MS
HATTON, ND,WA
HAUBSTADT, IN
HAUGEN, WI
HAUGHTON, LA
HAUSER, ID
HAUULA, HI
HAVANA, AR,FL,IL,KS
HAVASU LAKE, CA
HAVELOCK, NC
HAVEN, KS
HAVENSVILLE, KS
HAVERHILL, MA,NH
HAVERSTRAW, NY
HAVERTOWN, PA
HAVILAH, CA
HAVILAND, KS
HAVRE, MT

HAVRE DE GRACE, MD
HAW RIVER, NC
HAWAIIAN GARDENS, CA
HAWARDEN, IA
HAWESVILLE, KY
HAWKEYE, IA
HAWKINS, TX,WI
HAWKINSVILLE, GA
HAWLEY, MN,PA,TX
HAWORTH, NJ,OK
HAWTHORN, PA
HAWTHORNE, CA,FL,NJ,NV
HAXTUN, CO
HAY SPRINGS, NB
HAYDEN, AL,AZ,CO,ID
HAYDEN LAKE, ID
HAYES CENTER, NB
HAYESVILLE, NC,OH
HAYFIELD LAKE, CA
HAYMARKET, VA
HAYNES, AR
HAYNESVILLE, LA,ME
HAYNEVILLE, AL
HAYS, KS
HAYSI, VA
HAYSVILLE, KS
HAYTI, MO,SD
HAYWARD, CA,MN,WI,NC
HAZARD, KY,NB
HAZEL, SD
HAZEL GREEN, AL
HAZEL CREST, IL
HAZEL DELL, IL
HAZEL GREEN, IL,WI
HAZEL PARK, MI
HAZELTON, ID,KS
HAZELWOOD, MO,NC
HAZEN, AR,ND
HAZLEHURST, GA,MS
HAZLET, NJ
HAZLETON, IA,IN,PA
HEADRICK, OK
HEALDSBURG, CA
HEALDTON, OK
HEARNE, TX
HEARTWELL, NB
HEATH, AL,OH
HEATH SPRINGS, SC
HEAVENER, OK
HEBBRONVILLE, TX
HEBER, CA,UT
HEBER SPRINGS, AR
HEBRON, CT,IL,IN,MD,ME
    NB,ND,NH,OH
HECLA, SD
HECTOR, AR,MN,NY
HEDLEY, TX
HEDRICK, IA
HEEIA, HI
HEFLIN, AL,LA
HEIDELBERG, MS,PA
HELEN, GA
HELENA, AL,AR,GA,MT,OK
HELENDALE, CA
HELIX, OR
HELM, CA
HELMETTA, NJ
HELPER, UT
HEMET, CA
HEMINGFORD, NB
HEMINGWAY, SC
HEMPHILL, TX
HEMPSTEAD, NY,TX
HENAGAR, AL
HENDERSON, KY,LA,MD,MN
    NB,NC,NV,TN,TX
HENDERSONVILLE, NC,TN
HENDLEY, NB
HENDRICKS, MN,WV
HENDRIX, OK
HENDRUM, MN
HENEFER, UT
HENLOPEN ACRES, DE

HENNEPIN, IL
HENNESSEY, OK
HENNIKER, NH
HENNING, MN,TN
HENRIETTA, MO,NC,NY,TX
HENRIEVILLE, UT
HENRY, IL,NB,SD,TN
HENRYETTA, OK
HENSHAW LAKE, CA
HEPBURN, IA
HEPHZIBAH, GA
HEPLER, KS
HEPPNER, OR
HERCULANEUM, MO
HERCULES, CA
HEREFORD, TX
HERINGTON, KS
HERKIMER, NY
HERMAN, MN,NB
HERMANDO, MS
HERMANN, MO
HERMISTON, OR
HERMITAGE, AR,MO
HERMLEIGH, TX
HERMON, ME
HERMOSA, SD
HERMOSA BEACH, CA
HERNDON, CA,KS,VA
HERON LAKE, MN
HERREID, SD
HERRICK, SD
HERRIN, IL
HERSEY, ME,MI
HERSHEY, NB,PA
HERTFORD, NC
HESPERIA, CA,MI
HESPERIDES, FL
HESSMER, LA
HESSTON, KS
HETLAND, SD
HETTINGER, ND
HEWITT, NJ,MN,WI
HEYBURN, ID
HEYWORTH, IL
HIALEAH, FL
HIAWASSEE, GA
HIAWATHA, IA,KS,UT
HIBBING, MN
HICKAM HOUSING, HI
HICKMAN, KY,NB
HICKORY, MS,NC,NC
HICKORY FLAT, MS
HICKORY GROVE, SC
HICKORY HILLS, IL
HICKORY NORTH, NC
HICKORY RIDGE, AR
HICKORY VALLEY, TN
HICKSVILLE, OH
HICO, TX
HICORIA, FL
HIDALGO, TX
HIDDEN HILLS, CA
HIGBEE, MO
HIGGINS, TX
HIGGINSON, AR
HIGGINSPORT, OH
HIGGINSVILLE, MO
HIGH BRIDGE, NJ
HIGH SHOALS, NC
HIGH SPRINGS, FL
HIGHGATE, VT
HIGHGROVE, CA
HIGHLAND, CA,IL,IN
    KS,ME,WI
HIGHLAND BEACH, FL,MD
HIGHLAND FALLS, NY
HIGHLAND HEIGHTS, KY
HIGHLAND LAKE, AL
HIGHLAND PARK, IL,NJ,MI
HIGHLANDS, NC,NJ
HIGHMORE, SD
HIGHSPIRE, PA
HIGHTSTOWN, NJ

HIGHWOOD, IL
HILBERT, WI
HILDEBRAN, NC
HILDRETH, NB
HILL, NH
HILL CITY, KS,MN,SD
HILLIARD, FL,OH
HILLMAN, MI
HILLROSE, CO
HILLS, IA,MN
HILLSBORO, AL,IN,KS,MD
    MO,ND,OH,OR,TX,VA,WI,WV
HILLSBOROUGH, CA,NC,NH
HILLSDALE, MI,NJ,NY
HILLSIDE, IL,NJ
HILLSVILLE, VA
HILLTONIA, GA
HILLVIEW, KY
HILMAR, CA
HILO, HI
HILT, CA
HILTON, NY
HINCKLEY, IL,MN,UT
HINES, OR
HINESBURG, VT
HINESVILLE, GA
HINGHAM, MA,MT
HINKLEY, CA
HINSDALE, IL,MA
HINTON, IA,WV
HIRAM, GA,ME
HITCHCOCK, SD,TX
HIXTON, WI
HO HO KUS, NJ
HOBART, IN,OK
HOBART MILLS, CA
HOBBS, NM
HOBE SOUND, FL
HOBGOOD, NC
HOBOKEN, GA,NJ
HOBSON, MT
HOBSON CITY, AL
HODGDON, ME
HODGE, CA,LA
HODGENVILLE, KY
HODGES, AL,SC
HODGKINS, IL
HOFFMAN, MN,NC
HOGANSVILLE, GA
HOHENWALD, TN
HOISINGTON, KS
HOKAH, MN
HOKENDAUQUA, PA
HOKES BLUFF, AL
HOLBROOK, AZ,MA,NB
HOLCOMB, KS,MO
HOLDEN, MA,ME,MO,UT
HOLDEN BEACH, NC
HOLDENVILLE, OK
HOLDERNESS, NH
HOLDINGFORD, MN
HOLDREGE, NB
HOLGATE, OH
HOLLAND, IA,IN,MI
    NY,TX,VT
HOLLANDALE, MN,MS,WI
HOLLENBURG, KS
HOLLEY, NY
HOLLIDAY, MO,TX
HOLLIDAYSBURG, PA
HOLLIS, ME,NH,OK
HOLLISTER, CA,ID,MO
HOLLISTON, MA
HOLLOW ROCK, TN
HOLLOWAY, OH
HOLLY, CO,MI
HOLLY GROVE, AR
HOLLY HILL, FL,SC
HOLLY POND, AL
HOLLY RIDGE, NC
HOLLY SPRINGS, GA,MS,NC
HOLLY VIEW FOREST, NC
HOLLYVILLE, NC

HOLLYWOOD, AL,CA,FL,SC
HOLMDEL, NJ
HOLMEN, WI
HOLMES BEACH, FL
HOLSTEIN, IA,NB
HOLT, MO
HOLTON, IN,KS
HOLTVILLE, CA
HOLUALOA, HI
HOLY CROSS, AK
HOLYOKE, CO,MA
HOLYROOD, KS
HOMECROFT, IN
HOMEDALE, ID
HOMER, AK,GA,LA,MI,NB,NY
HOMER CITY, PA
HOMERVILLE, GA
HOMESTEAD, PA
HOMESTOWN, MO
HOMETOWN, IL
HOMEWOOD, AL,IL
HOMINY, OK
HONAKER, VA
HONCUT, CA
HONDA, CA
HONDO, TX
HONEOYE FALLS, NY
HONESDALE, PA
HONEY GROVE, TX
HONEYVILLE, UT
HONOKAA, HI
HONOLULU, HI
HONOR, MI
HOOD, CA
HOOD RIVER, OR
HOOKER, OK
HOOKERTON, NC
HOOKS, TX
HOOKSETT, NH
HOONAH, AK
HOOPA, CA
HOOPER, CO,NB
HOOPER BAY, AK
HOOPESTON, IL
HOOPPOLE, IL
HOOSICK, NY
HOOT OWL, OK
HOOVER, AL
HOPATCONG, NJ
HOPE, AR,ID,IN,KS
    ME,ND,NJ,NM
HOPE MILLS, NC
HOPEDALE, IL
HOPEWELL, NJ,VA
HOPKINS, MI,MN,MO
HOPKINSVILLE, KY
HOPKINTON, IA,MA,NH,RI
HOPLAND, CA
HOQUIAM, WA
HORATIO, AR
HORDVILLE, NB
HORICON, WI
HORN LAKE, MS
HORNBEAK, TN
HORNBECK, LA
HORNBROOK, CA
HORNELL, NY
HORNITOS, CA
HORNSBY, TN
HORSEHEADS, NY
HORSESHOE BEND, AR,ID
HORTON, KS
HORTONVILLE, WI
HOSCHTON, GA
HOSKINS, NB
HOSMER, SD
HOSPERS, IA
HOSSTON, LA
HOT SPRINGS, AR,MT,NC,SD
HOT SULPHUR SPRINGS, CO
HOTCHKISS, CO
HOUGHTON, MI
HOULTON, ME

PLACE INDEX

HOUMA, LA
HOUSE, NM
HOUSTON, AK,AR,DE,MN,MO
   MS,PA,TX
HOUTZDALE, PA
HOVEN, SD
HOWARD, KS,SD,WI
HOWARD CITY, MI,NB
HOWARD LAKE, MN
HOWARDS GROVE, WI
HOWARDVILLE, MO
HOWE, OK,TX
HOWELL, NJ,MI,UT
HOWELLS, NB
HOWEY IN THE HILLS, FL
HOWLAND, ME
HOXIE, AR,KS
HOYT, KS
HOYT LAKES, MN
HUACHUCA CITY, AZ
HUBBARD, IA,NB,OH,OR
HUBBARDSTON, MI
HUBBARDTON, VT
HUBBELL, NB
HUDSON, CO,IA,IN,KS,MA
   ME,MI,NH,NY,OH,SD,WI,WY
HUDSONVILLE, MI
HUETTER, ID
HUEYTOWN, AL
HUGHES, AK,AR
HUGHES SPRINGS, TX
HUGHESTOWN, PA
HUGHESVILLE, PA
HUGHSON, CA
HUGO, CO,MN,OK
HUGOTON, KS
HULBERT, OK
HULETT, WY
HULL, GA,IA,MA
HULMEVILLE, PA
HUMANSVILLE, MO
HUMAROCK, MA
HUMBLE, TX
HUMBOLDT, IA,KS,MN
   NB,SD,TN
HUME, NY
HUMESTON, IA
HUMMELSTOWN, PA
HUMNOKE, AR
HUMPHREY, AR,NB
HUNDRED, WV
HUNTER, AR,KS,ND,OK
HUNTERTOWN, IN
HUNTINGBURG, IN
HUNTINGDON, PA,TN
HUNTINGTON, AR,IN,MA,NY
   OR,TX,UT,VT,WV
HUNTINGTON BEACH, CA
HUNTINGTON PARK, CA
HUNTINGTON WOODS, MI
HUNTLAND, TN
HUNTLEIGH, MO
HUNTLEY, IL,NB
HUNTSVILLE, AL,AR,MO
   TN,TX,UT
HURLEY, NM,NY,SD,WI
HURLOCK, MD
HURON, CA,KS,OH,SD
HURRICANE, UT,WV
HURST, TX
HURT, VA
HURTSBORO, AL
HUSLIA, AK
HUSTISFORD, WI
HUSTLER, WI
HUTCHINS, TX
HUTCHINSON, KS,MN
HUTTING, AR
HUTTO, TX
HUTTONSVILLE, WV
HYAMPOM, CA
HYANNIS, MA,NB
HYATTSVILLE, MD
HYDABURG, AK

HYDE PARK, NY,UT,VT
HYMERA, IN
HYNDMAN, PA
HYPOLOXO, FL
HYRUM, UT
HYSHAM, MT

IAEGER, WV
IBERIA, MO
IDA, LA
IDA GROVE, IA
IDABEL, OK
IDAHO CITY, ID
IDAHO FALLS, ID
IDAHO SPRINGS, CO
IDEAL, GA
IDALOU, TX
IDER, AL
IDRIA, CA
IDYLLWILD, CA
IGNACIO, CA,CO
IGO, CA
IHLEN, MN
ILA, GA
ILIFF, CO
ILION, NY
ILLIOPOLIS, IL
ILLMO, MO
ILWACO, WA
IMBLER, OR
IMBODEN, AR
IMLAY CITY, MI
IMMOKALEE, FL
IMPACT, TX
IMPERIAL, CA,NB,PA
IMPERIAL BEACH, CA
INDEPENDENCE, CA,IA,KS
   KY,LA,MN,MO,OH,OR
   TX,VA,WI
INDEX, WA
INDIAHOMA, OK
INDIALANTIC, FL
INDIAN CREEK, IL
INDIAN HARBOR BEACH, FL
INDIAN HEAD, MD
INDIAN LAKE, NY
INDIAN MILLS, NJ
INDIAN RIVER CITY, FL
INDIAN RIVER SHORES, FL
INDIAN ROCKS BEACH, FL
INDIAN VILLAGE, IN
INDIANA, PA
INDIANAPOLIS, IN
INDIANOLA, IA,MS,NB,OK
INDIO, CA
INDUSTRIAL CITY, GA
INDUSTRY, IL,ME,PA
INGALLS, IN,KS
INGLESIDE, TX
INGLEWOOD, CA
INGLIS, FL
INGOT, CA
INGRAM, PA,TX
INKOM, ID
INKSTER, MI,ND
INLET, NY
INMAN, KS,NB,SC
INOLA, OK
INTERCESSION CITY, FL
INTERIOR, SD
INTERLACHEN, FL
INTERNATIONAL FALLS, MN
INVERNES, IL
INVERNESS, CA,FL,MS
INVER GROVE HEIGHTS, MN
INWOOD, IA
INYOKERN, CA
IOLA, KS,WI
IONA, ID,MN
IONE, CA,OR
IONIA, MI,MO
IOTA, LA
IOWA, LA

IOWA CITY, IA
IOWA FALLS, IA
IOWA HILL, CA
IOWA PARK, TX
IPSWICH, MA,SD
IRA, VT
IRAAN, TX
IRASBURG, VT
IREDELL, TX
IRENE, SD
IRION COUNTY, TX
IRMO, SC
IRON CITY, GA,TN
IRON GATE, VA
IRON JUNCTION, MN
IRON MOUNTAIN, MI
IRON RIDGE, WI,MI
IRONDALE, AL
IRONDEQUOIT, NY
IRONTON, MN,MO,OH
IRONWOOD, MI
IROQUOIS, IL
IROQUOIS POINT, HI
IRRIGON, OR
IRVINE, CA,KY
IRVING, IL,TX
IRVINGTON, CA,IL
   KY,NJ,NY,VA
IRWIN, IA,ID,PA
IRWINDALE, CA
IRWINTON, GA
ISABEL, KS,SD
ISANTI, MN
ISCHUA, NY
ISELIN, NJ
ISLAMORADA, FL
ISLAND CITY, OR
ISLAND FALLS, ME
ISLAND GROVE, FL
ISLAND HEIGHTS, NJ
ISLAND LAKE, IL
ISLAND PARK, ID,NY
ISLAND VIEW, MN
ISLE, MN
ISLE AU HAUT, ME
ISLE LA MOTTE, VT
ISLE OF PALMS, SC
ISLEBORO, ME
ISLETON, CA
ISLIP, NY
ISMAY, MT
ISOLA, MS
ISSOQUAH, WA
ITALY, TX
ITASCA, IL,TX
ITHACA, MI,NB,NY,OH
ITTA BENA, MS
IUKA, IL,MS
IVA, SC
IVANHOE, CA,MN
IVANPAH, CA
IVOR, VA

JACKSON, AL,CA,GA,KY,LA
   ME,MI,MN,MO,MS,NB,NC,NJ
   OH,SC,TN,WI,WY
JACKSONVILLE, AL,AR,FL
   GA,IL,MO,NC,OH,OR,TX,VT
JACKSONVILLE BEACH, FL
JACKSONVILLE EAST, NC
JACOBUS, PA
JACUMBA, CA
JAKIN, GA
JAL, NM
JAMACHA, CA
JAMAICA, IA,IL,NY,VT
JAMES CITY, NC
JAMESBURG, NJ
JAMESTOWN, CA,CO,IN,KS
   KY,LA,NC,ND,NY,OH
   RI,SC,TN
JAMESVILLE, NC
JAMUL, CA
JANE LEW, WV

JANESVILLE, CA,IA,MN,WI
JANSEN, NB
JARBRIDGE, NV
JARRATT, VA
JASONVILLE, IN
JASPER, AL,AR,FL,GA,IN
   MN,MO,TN,TX
JAVA, SD
JAY, FL,ME,NY,OK,VT
JAYTON, TX
JEAN LAFITTE, LA
JEANERETTE, LA
JEANNETTE, PA
JEFFERS, MN
JEFFERSON, GA,IA,NC,NY
   OH,OR,PA,SD,TX,WI
JEFFERSON CITY, MO,TN
JEFFERSONTOWN, KY
JEFFERSONVILLE, GA,IN,KY
   OH,VT
JELLICO, TN
JEMEZ SPRINGS, NM
JEMISON, AL
JENA, LA
JENKINS, MN
JENKINS HEIGHTS, NC
JENKINSBURG, GA
JENKINTOWN, PA
JENKS, OK
JENNER, CA
JENNINGS, FL,KS,LA,MO,OK
JENSEN BEACH, FL
JERICHO, NY,VT
JERMYN, PA
JEROME, AR,AZ,ID
JERSEY, GA
JERSEY CITY, NJ
JERSEY SHORE, PA
JERSEYVILLE, NJ
JERUSALEM, OH
JESMOND DENE, CA
JESSUP, PA
JESUP, GA,IA
JET, OK
JETMORE, KS
JEWELL, KS
JEWELL JUNCTION, IA
JEWETT, OH,TX
JOHANNESBURG, CA
JOHN DAY, OR
JOHNSBURG, NY
JOHNSON, AR,MN,NB,OR,VT
JOHNSON CITY, KS,NY,TX
JOHNSON CREEK, WI
JOHNSONBURG, NJ,PA
JOHNSONDALE, CA
JOHNSONVILLE, SC
JOHNSTON, RI,SC
JOHNSTON CITY, IL
JOHNSTOWN, CO,NB,NY,OH,PA
JOINER, AR
JOLIET, IL,MT
JOLLYTOWN, PA
JONES, OK
JONESBORO, AR,GA,IL,IN
   LA,ME,TN
JONESBURG, MO
JONESPORT, ME
JONESTOWN, MS
JONESVILLE, IN,MI
   NC,SC,VA
JORDAN, MN,MT,NY
JORDAN VALLEY, OR
JOSEPH, OR
JOSEPHINE, PA
JOSHUA, TX
JOSHUA TREE, CA
JOURDANTON, TX
JUDITH GAP, MT
JUDSON, IN
JUDSONIA, AR
JULESBURG, CO
JULIAETTA, ID
JULIAN, CA,NB

PLACE INDEX

MADISON, AR,CT,FL,IL,IN
KS,ME,MN,MO,MS,NB,NC
NJ,NY,OH,VA,WI,WV
MADISON HEIGHTS, MI
MADISON LAKE, MN
MADISONVILLE, KY,LA,TN,TX
MADRAS, OR
MADRID, AL,IA,ME,NB,NY
MAGALIA, CA
MAGALLOWAY, ME
MAGAZINE, AR
MAGDALENA, NM
MAGEE, MS
MAGGIE VALLEY, NC
MAGNESS, AR
MAGNET, NB
MAGNOLIA, AR,DE,IA,MN,MS
NC,NJ,OH,TX
MAGNOLIA SPRINGS, FL
MAHAFFEY, PA
MAHANOY CITY, PA
MAHASKA, KS
MAHNOMEN, MN
MAHWAH, NJ
MAIDEN ROCK, WI
MAIDSTONE, VT
MAILI, HI
MAINE, NY
MAITLAND, FL
MAIZE, KS
MAKAHA, HI
MAKAKILO CITY, HI
MAKANDA, IL
MAKAPU, HI
MAKAWOO, HI
MALABAR, FL
MALAD CITY, ID
MALAGA, CA
MALAKOFF, TX
MALCOLM, NB
MALCOM, IA
MALDEN, MA,MO,WA
MALIBU, CA
MALIN, OR
MALLARD, IA
MALMO, NB
MALONE, FL,NY,TX
MALTA, ID,MT,OH
MALVERN, AL,AR,IA,OH,PA
MALVERNE, NY
MAMARONECK, NY
MAMASSA, CO
MAMMOTH, AZ
MAMMOTH LAKES, CA
MAMMOTH SPRING, AR
MAMOU, LA
MAN, WV
MANASQUAN, NJ
MANASSAS, VA
MANATEE, FL
MANAWA, WI
MANCELONA, MI
MANCHESTER, CA,CT,IA,IL
KS,KY,MA,MD,ME,MI,MO,NH
NY,OH,OK,PA,TN,VT
MANCOS, CO
MANDAN, ND
MANDERSON, WY
MANDEVILLE, LA
MANGHAM, LA
MANGUM, OK
MANHATTAN, IL,KS,MT,NY
MANHATTAN BEACH, CA
MANHEIM, PA
MANILA, AR,UT
MANILLA, IA
MANISTEE, MI
MANISTIQUE, MI
MANITO, IL
MANITOU, OK
MANITOWOC, WI
MANKATO, KS,MN
MANLEY, NB

MANLY, IA
MANNING, IA,SC
MANNINGTON, WV
MANNSVILLE, OK
MANOKOTAK, AK
MANOR, PA,TX
MANSFIELD, AR,CT,GA,IL
LA,MA,MO,OH,PA,TX,WA
MANSON, IA
MANSURA, LA
MANTACHIE, MS
MANTECA, CA
MANTENO, IL
MANTEO, NC
MANTER, KS
MANTI, UT
MANTOLOKING, NJ
MANTON, CA,MI
MANTORVILLE, MN
MANTUA, NJ,OH,UT
MANVEL, TX
MANVILLE, NJ,WY
MANY, LA
MANZANITA, OR
MAPLE BLUFF, WI
MAPLE GROVE, MN
MAPLE HEIGHTS, OH
MAPLE HILL, KS
MAPLE LAKE, MN
MAPLE PLAIN, MN
MAPLE RAPIDS, MI
MAPLE SHADE, NJ
MAPLESVILLE, AL
MAPLETON, IA,KS,ME
MN,ND,UT
MAPLEWOOD, MO,NJ
MAQUOKETA, IA
MAR-MAC, NC
MARAMEC, OK
MARANA, AZ
MARATHON, FL,IA,TX
MARBLE, MN
MARBLE CITY, OK
MARBLE FALLS, TX
MARBLE ROCK, IA
MARBLEHEAD, MA
MARBLETON, WY
MARCELINE, MO
MARCELLUS, MI,NY
MARCUS, IA,WA
MARCY, NY
MARENGO, IA,IN
MARFA, TX
MARGARET, AL
MARGATE, FL
MARGATE CITY, NJ
MARIANNA, AR,FL
MARIAVILLE, ME
MARIBEL, WI
MARICOPA, CA
MARIEMONT, OH
MARIETTA, GA,MN,MS,OH
OK,PA,TX
MARINA, CA
MARINE, IL
MARINE CITY, MI
MARINE ON SAINT CROIX, MN
MARINETTE, WI
MARINGOUIN, LA
MARION, AL,AR,IA,IN,KS
KY,LA,MA,MI,MS,NC,NY
OH,SC,SD,TX,VA,WI
MARIONVILLE, MO
MARIPOSA, CA
MARISSA, IL
MARKED TREE, AR
MARKESAN, WI
MARKHAM, IL
MARKLEEVILLE, CA
MARKLEVILLE, IN
MARKS, MS
MARKSVILLE, LA
MARLAND, OK

MARLBORO, NJ,VT
MARLBOROUGH, CT,MA,MO
MARLETTE, MI
MARLINTON, WV
MARLOW, OK
MARLTON, NJ
MARMADUKE, AR
MARMET, WV
MARNE, IA
MAROA, IL
MARQUAND, MO
MARQUETTE, IA,KS,MI,NB,WI
MARQUEZ, TX
MARS, PA
MARS HILL, ME,NC
MARSEILLES, IL
MARSHALL, AR,IL,IN,MI,MN
MO,NC,OK,TX,WI
MARSHALLTOWN, IA
MARSHALLVILLE, GA,OH
MARSHFIELD, MA,ME
MO,VT,WI
MARSHVILLE, NC
MARSING, ID
MARSLAND, NB
MARSTON, MO
MART, TX
MARTELL, CA
MARTENSDALE, IA
MARTHA, OK
MARTIN, GA,LA,MI,SD,TN
MARTINEZ, CA
MARTINS FERRY, OH
MARTINSBURG, MO,NB,PA,WV
MARTINSVILLE, IL,IN,MO,VA
MARVELL, AR
MARVEN, NC
MARVIN, SD
MARY ESTHER, FL
MARYLAND, NY
MARYSVALE, UT
MARYSVILLE, CA,KS,MI
OH,PA,WA
MARYVILLE, IL,MO,TN
MASARDIS, ME
MASARYKTOWN, FL
MASCOTTE, FL
MASCOUTAH, IL
MASHPEE, MA
MASKELL, NB
MASON, IL,MI,NH,OH
MASON CITY, IA,IL,NB
MASON VALLEY, NV
MASONBORO, NC
MASONTOWN, PA,WV
TN,TX,WV
MASSAPEQUA PARK, NY
MASSENA, IA,NY
MASSILLON, OH
MASTHOPE, PA
MATADOR, TX
MATAMORAS, PA
MATAWAN, NJ
MATEWAN, WV
MATFIELD GREEN, KS
MATHIS, TX
MATHISTON, MS
MATINICUS ISLE, ME
MATOAKA, WV
MATTAPOISETT, MA
MATTAWAMKEAG, ME
MATTAWAN, MI
MATTESON, IL
MATTHEWS, IN,MO,NC
MATTOON, IL
MAUCKPORT, IN
MAUD, OK,TX
MAULDIN, SC
MAUMEE, OH
MAUNAWILI, HI
MAUPIN, OR
MAURICE, LA
MAURY CITY, TN

MAUSTON, WI
MAXFIELD, ME
MAXWELL, CA,IA,NB,NM
MAYBEE, MI
MAYER, MN
MAYERSVILLE, MS
MAYESVILLE, SC
MAYETTA, KS
MAYFIELD, KS,KY,OH,PA,UT
MAYFIELD HEIGHTS, OH
MAYFLOWER, AR
MAYNARD, AR,IA,MA,MN
MAYNARDVILLE, TN
MAYO, FL
MAYODAN, NC
MAYPEARL, TX
MAYSVILLE, GA,KY,MO,NC
MAYTOWN, AL
MAYVILLE, ND,WI
MAYWOOD, CA,IL,NB,NJ
MAYWOOD PARK, OR
MAZEPPA, MN
MAZOMONIE, WI
MAZON, IL
MCADENVILLE, NC
MCADOO, PA
MCALESTER, OK
MCALLEN, TX
MCARTHUR, CA,OH
MCBAIN, MI
MCBEE, SC
MCBRIDE, MI
MCCALL, ID
MCCAMEY, TX
MCCAMMON, ID
MCCASKILL, AR
MCCAYSVILLE, GA
MCCLEARY, WA
MCCLELLANVILLE, SC
MCCLOUD, CA
MCCLURE, PA
MCCLUSKY, ND
MCCOLL, SC
MCCOMB, MS,OH
MCCONNELLS, SC
MCCONNELLSBURG, PA
MCCOOK, NB
MCCOOL JUNCTION, NB
MCCORMICK, SC
MCCRACKEN, KS
MCCRORY, AR
MCCUNE, KS
MCCURTAIN, OK
MCDERMITT, NV
MCDONALD, KS,NC,OH,PA
MCDOUGAL, AR
MCFARLAN, NC
MCFARLAND, CA,WI
MCGEHEE, AR
MCGRATH, AK,MN
MCGREGOR, IA,MN,TX
MCGREW, NB
MCHENRY, IL,KY
MCINTOSH, AL,FL,MN,SD
MCKEE, KY
MCKEESPORT, PA
MCKENNEY, VA
MCKINLEY, MN
MCKINLEYVILLE, CA
MCKINNEY, TX
MCLAIN, MS
MCLEAN, IL,NB,TX
MCLEANSVILLE, NC
MCLEMORESVILLE, TN
MCLOUD, OK
MCLOUTH, KS
MCMECHEN, WV
MCMINNVILLE, OR,TN
MCNEIL, AR
MCPHERSON, KS
MCRAE, AR
MCSHERRYSTOWN, PA
MEAD, NB,OK

628

MONTREAT, NC
MONTROSE, AR,CO,IA
   MI,SD,WV
MONTROSS, VA
MONTVALE, NJ
MONTVERDE, FL
MONTVILLE, CT,ME,NJ
MONUMENT, CO,OR
MONT BELVIEU, TX
MOODY, TX
MOORCROFT, WY
MOORE, ID,MT,OK
MOORE HAVEN, FL
MOOREFIELD, NB,WV
MOORELAND, IN,OK
MOORES HILL, IN
MOORESBORO, NC
MOORESTOWN, NJ
MOORESVILLE, AL,IN,NC
MOORHEAD, IA,MN,MS
MOORINGSPORT, LA
MOORLAND, IA
MOOSE LAKE, MN
MOOSE RIVER, ME
MOOSIC, PA
MORA, MN
MORAGA, CA
MORAINE, OH
MORAN, KS
MORAVIA, IA,NY
MORAVIAN FALLS, NC
MOREAUVILLE, LA
MOREHEAD, KY
MOREHEAD CITY, NC
MOREHOUSE, MO
MORELAND, GA
MORENCI, MI
MORETOWN, VT
MORGAN, GA,MN,VT
MORGAN CITY, LA,MS,UT
MORGAN HILL, CA
MORGANFIELD, KY
MORGANTON, GA,NC
MORGANTOWN, IN,KY,NC,WV
MORGANVILLE, KS,NJ
MORIAH, NY
MORIARTY, NM
MORLAND, KS
MORLEY, MI,MO
MORNING SUN, IA
MORNINGSIDE, MD
MORO, AR,OR
MOROCCO, IN
MORONI, UT
MORRICE, MI
MORRILL, KS,ME,NB
MORRILTON, AR
MORRIS, AL,CT,IL,MN,OK
MORRIS PLAINS, NJ
MORRISON, CO,IL,OK,TN
MORRISONVILLE, IL
MORRISTOWN, IN,MN
   NJ,SD,TN,VT
MORRISVILLE, MO,NC,NY,VT
MORROW, GA,OH
MORROWVILLE, KS
MORSE, LA
MORSE BLUFF, NB
MORTON, IL,MN,MS,PA,TX,WA
MORTON GROVE, IL
MORTONS GAP, KY
MOSBY, MO
MOSCOW, ID,KS,ME,PA,TN
MOSES LAKE, WA
MOSHEIM, TN
MOSIER, OR
MOSINEE, WI
MOSS POINT, MS
MOSSYROCK, WA
MOTLEY, MN
MOTT, ND
MOULTON, AL,IA,TX
MOULTRIE, FL,GA

MOUND, LA,MN
MOUND BAYOU, MS
MOUND CITY, IL,KS,MO,SD
MOUND VALLEY, KS
MOUNDRIDGE, KS
MOUNDS, IL,OK
MOUNDS VIEW, MN
MOUNDSVILLE, WV
MOUNDVILLE, AL
MOUNT AIRY, GA,NC
MOUNT ANGEL, OR
MOUNT ARLINGTON, NJ
MOUNT AUBURN, IA,IN
MOUNT AYR, IA,IN
MOUNT BALDY, CA
MOUNT CALM, TX
MOUNT CALVARY, WI
MOUNT CARMEL, SC
MOUNT CHASE, ME
MOUNT CLEMENS, MI
MOUNT CRAWFORD, VA
MOUNT CRESTED BUTTE, CO
MOUNT CROGHAN, SC
MOUNT DESERT, ME
MOUNT DORA, FL
MOUNT EDEN, CA
MOUNT ENTERPRISE, TX
MOUNT EPHRAIM, NJ
MOUNT GILEAD, NC,OH
MOUNT HEALTHY, OH
MOUNT HEBRON, CA
MOUNT HOLLY, NJ,NC,VT
MOUNT HOPE, KS,WI,WV
MOUNT HOREB, WI
MOUNT IDA, AR
MOUNT JACKSON, VA
MOUNT LAUREL, NJ
MOUNT LEBANON, LA
MOUNT MORRIS, IL,MI
MOUNT OLIVE, IL,MS
MOUNT OLIVER, PA
MOUNT OLIVET, KY
MOUNT ORAB, OH
MOUNT PLEASANT, IA,MI,NC
   SC,TN,TX,UT
MOUNT PROSPECT, IL
MOUNT PULASKI, IL

MOUNT RAINIER, MD
MOUNT SHASTA, CA
MOUNT STERLING, IL
   KY,OH,WI
MOUNT TABOR, VT
MOUNT VERNON, AL,GA,IA,IL
   KY,ME,MO,NH,NY,OH,OR
   SD,TX,WA
MOUNT WASHINGTON, KY
MOUNT ZION, GA,IL
MOUNTAIN BROOK, AL
MOUNTAIN CITY, GA,NV,TN
MOUNTAIN GROVE, MO
MOUNTAIN HOME, AR
   ID,NC,TX
MOUNTAIN IRON, MN
MOUNTAIN LAKE, MN
MOUNTAIN LAKE PARK, MD
MOUNTAIN LAKES, NJ
MOUNTAIN PARK, OK
MOUNTAIN PINE, AR
MOUNTAIN VIEW, AR
   MO,OK,WY
MOUNTAIN VILLAGE, AK
MOUNTAINAIR, NM
MOUNTAINBURG, AR
MOUNTAINSIDE, NJ
MOUNTLAKE TERRACE, WA
MOUNTVILLE, PA
MOVILLE, IA
MOWEAQUA, IL
MOYIE SPRINGS, ID
MUD LAKE, ID
MUENSTER, TX
MUIR, MI

MUKILTEO, WA
MUKWONAGO, WI
MULBERRY, AR,FL,KS,NC
MULBERRY GROVE, IL
MULDROW, OK
MULESHOE, TX
MULGA, AL
MULHALL, OK
MULLAN, ID
MULLEN, NB
MULLENS, WV
MULLIKEN, MI
MULLIN, TX
MULLINS, SC
MULLINVILLE, KS
MUNCIE, IN MUNCY, PA
MUNDAY, TX
MUNDELEIN, IL
MUNDEN, KS
MUNFORDVILLE, KY
MUNICH, ND
MUNISING, MI
MUNROE FALLS, OH
MURCHISON, TX
MURDO, SD
MURDOCK, NB
MURFREESBORO, AR,NC,TN
MURPHY, NC
MURPHYS, CA
MURPHYSBORO, IL
MURRAY, KY,NB,UT
MURRIETTA HOT SPRINGS, CA
MURTAUGH, ID
MUSCLE SHOALS, AL
MUSCODA, WI
MUSCOTAH, KS
MUSCOY, CA
MUSKEGO, WI
MUSKEGON, MI
MUSKEGON HEIGHTS, MI
MUSKOGEE, OK
MUSTANG, OK
MUTUAL, OK
MYERSTOWN, PA
MYERSVILLE, MD
MYRTLE, MS
MYRTLE BEACH, SC
MYRTLE CREEK, OR
MYRTLE GROVE, NC
MYRTLE POINT, OR
MYRTLEWOOD, AL

NAALEHU, HI
NACHES, WA
NACOGDOCHES, TX
NAGS HEAD, NC
NAHANT, MA
NAHUNTA, GA
NAMPA, ID
NANAKULI, HI
NANTICOKE, PA
NANTUCKET, MA
NAPA, CA
NAPAKIAK, AK
NAPASKIAK, AK
NAPAVINE, WA
NAPER, NB
NAPERVILLE, IL
NAPIER FIELD, AL
NAPILI-HONOKOWAI, HI
NAPLES, FL,ME,NY,TX
NAPOLEAN, MO
NAPOLEON, ND,OH
NAPOLEONVILLE, LA
NAPONEE, NB
NARBETH, PA
NARDIN, OK
NARKA, KS
NARRAGANSETT, RI
NARROWS, VA
NASH, OK
NASHOTAH, WI
NASHUA, IA,MT,NH

NASHVILLE, AR,GA,IL,IN
   KS,MI,NC,TN
NASHWAUK, MN
NASSAU, MN,NY
NASSAWADOX, VA
NATALIA, TX
NATCHEZ, LA,MS
NATCHITOCHES, LA
NATICK, MA
NATIONAL CITY, CA

NATIONAL PARK, NJ
NATOMA, CA,KS
NATURITA, CO
NAUGATUCK, CT
NAUVOO, AL,IL
NAVARRE, OH
NAVASOTA, TX
NAVASSA, NC
NAYLOR, GA,MO
NAZARETH, PA,TX
NEBO, IL,KY
NEBRASKA CITY, NB
NECEDAH, WI
NEDERLAND, CO,TX
NEEDLES, CA
NEEDVILLE, TX
NEELYVILLE, MO
NEENAH, WI
NEESES, SC
NEGAUNEE, MI
NEHALEM, OR
NEHAWKA, NB
NEIHART, MT
NEILLSVILLE, WI
NEKOOSA, WI
NELIGH, NB
NELSON, CA,GA,MN
   NB,NV,WI
NELSONVILLE, OH,WI
NEMAHA, IA,NB
NENANA, AK
NENZEL, NB
NEODESHA, KS
NEOLA, IA
NEOSHA FALLS, KS
NEOSHA RAPIDS, KS
NEOSHO, MO,WI
NEPHI, UT
NEPTUNE BEACH, FL
NEPTUNE CITY, NJ
NESHKORO, WI
NESPELEM, WA
NESQUEHONING, PA
NESS CITY, KS
NETAWAKA, KS
NETTLETON, MS
NEVADA, IA,MO,OH
NEVADA CITY, CA
NEVERSINK, NY
NEVIS, MN
NEW ALBANY, IN,MS,OH
NEW ALBIN, IA
NEW ALLUWE, OK
NEW AMSTERDAM, IN
NEW ATHENS, IL
NEW AUBURN, MN,WI
NEW BADEN, IL,TX
NEW BALTIMORE, MI,NY
NEW BEAVER, PA
NEW BEDFORD, MA
NEW BERLIN, NY,WI
NEW BERN, NC
NEW BETHLEHEM, PA
NEW BLOOMFIELD, MO
NEW BOSTON, IL,NH,OH,TX
NEW BRAUNFELS, TX
NEW BREMEN, NY,OH
NEW BRIGHTON, MN,PA
NEW BRITAIN, CT,PA
NEW BROCKTON, AL
NEW BRUNSWICK, NJ
NEW BUFFALO, MI
NEW CAMBRIA, KS

PLACE INDEX

NOWATA, OK
NOXAPATER, MS
NOYO, CA
NUBIEBER, CA
NUCLA, CO
NUEVO, CA
NUIQSUT, AK
NULATO, AK
NUNDA, NY,SD
NUNEZ, GA
NUNN, CO
NUTLEY, NJ
NYACK, NY
NYSSA, OR

O'BRIEN, TX
O'DONNELL, TX
O'FALLON, MO
O'NEALS, CA
O'NEILL, NB
OACOMA, SD
OAK, NB
OAK BLUFFS, MA
OAK CITY, NC,UT
OAK CREEK, CO
OAK FOREST, IL
OAK GROVE, AR,KY,LA,MO
OAK GROVE HEIGHTS, AR
OAK HARBOR, OH,WA
OAK HILL, AL,FL,KS
  OH,TN,WV
OAK LAWN, IL
OAK PARK, IL,MI
OAK PARK HEIGHTS, MN
OAK RIDGE, LA
OAK VIEW, CA
OAKBORO, NC
OAKBROOK, IL
OAKDALE, CA,LA,MN
  NB,PA,TN
OAKES, ND
OAKESDALE, WA
OAKFIELD, GA,ME,NY,WI
OAKHAM, MA
OAKHURST, NJ
OAKLAND, CA,FL,IA,IL,KY
  MD,ME,MS,NB,NJ,OK,OR,TN
OAKLAND CITY, IN
OAKLAND PARK, FL
OAKLEY, ID,KS,MI,UT
OAKLYN, NJ
OAKMAN, AL,GA
OAKMONT, PA
OAKRIDGE, OR
OAKS, OK
OAKTOWN, IN
OAKVILLE, CA,IA,WA
OAKWOOD, GA,OH,OK,TX
OBERLIN, KS,LA,OH,PA
OBERT, NB
OBETZ, OH
OBION, TN
OBLONG, IL
OCALA, FL
OCCIDENTAL, CA
OCEAN, NJ
OCEAN CITY, MD,NJ
OCEAN GATE, NJ
OCEAN GROVE, NJ
OCEAN ISLE BEACH, NC
OCEAN SHORES, WA
OCEAN SPRINGS, MS
OCEAN VIEW, DE
OCEANA, WV
OCEANO, CA
OCEANPORT, NJ
OCEANSIDE, CA,NY
OCHELATA, OK
OCHEYEDON, IA
OCHLOCKNEE, GA
OCILLA, GA
OCOEE, FL
OCONEE, GA

OCONOMOWOC, WI
OCONOMOWOC LAKE, WI
OCONTO, NB,WI
OCONTO FALLS, WI
OCTAVIA, NB
ODEBOLT, IA
ODELL, NB
ODEM, TX
ODEN, AR
ODENVILLE, AL
ODESSA, DE,MO,MN,TX,WA
ODIN, IL,MN
ODUM, GA
OELRICHS, SD
OELWEIN, IA
OFALLON, IL
OFFERLE, KS
OGALLALA, NB
OGDEN, AR,KS,UT
OGDENSBURG, NJ,NY,WI
OGEMA, MN
OGILVIE, MN
OGLESBY, IL,TX
OGLETHORPE, GA
OGONTZ, PA
OHATCHEE, AL
OHIOVILLE, PA
OHIOWA, NB
OIL CITY, LA,PA
OIL TROUGH, AR
OILTON, OK
OJAI, CA
OKABENA, MN
OKAHUMPKA, FL
OKANOGAN, WA
OKEECHOBEE, FL
OKEENE, OK
OKEMAH, OK
OKETO, KS
OKLAHOMA CITY, OK
OKLEE, MN
OKMULGEE, OK
OKOBOJI, IA
OKOLONA, AR,MS
OKTAHA, OK
OLA, AR
OLANCHA, CA
OLANTA, SC
OLAR, SC
OLATHE, CO,KS
OLD APPLETON, MO
OLD BRIDGE, NJ
OLD FORGE, PA
OLD FORT, NC
OLD HARBOR, AK
OLD LYME, CT
OLD ORCHARD BEACH, ME
OLD SAYBROOK, CT
OLD TAPPAN, NJ
OLD TOWN, FL,ME
OLD WESTBURY, NY
OLDHAM, SD
OLDSMAR, FL
OLDTOWN, ID
OLDWICK, NJ
OLEAN, NY
OLEMA, CA
OLEONA, PA
OLEUM, CA
OLGA, FL
OLIVE BRANCH, MS
OLIVE HILL, KY
OLIVEHURST, CA
OLIVET, MI,SD
OLIVETTE, MO
OLIVIA, MN
OLLA, LA
OLMITZ, KS
OLMSTED FALLS, OH
OLNEY, IL,TX
OLNEY SPRINGS, CO
OLPE, KS
OLSBURG, KS

OLTON, TX
OLYMPIA, WA
OLYMPIC FIELDS, IL
OLYPHANT, PA
OMAHA, AR,GA,NB,TX
OMAK, WA
OMEGA, GA
OMER, MI
OMO RANCH, CA
OMRO, WI
ONAGA, KS
ONAKA, SD
ONALASKA, TX,WI
ONAMIA, MN
ONANCOCK, VA
ONARGA, IL
ONAWA, IA
ONAWAY, ID,MI
ONEIDA, IA,KS,NY,TN
ONEKAMA, MI
ONEONTA, AL,NY
ONG, NB
ONIDA, SD
ONLEY, VA
ONO, CA
ONONDAGA, NY
ONSTED, MI
ONTARIO, CA,NY,OH,OR,WI
ONTONAGON, MI
ONYX, CA
OOLITIC, IN
OOLOGAH, OK
OOSTBURG, WI
OPA-LOCKA, FL
OPELIKA, AL
OPELOUSAS, LA
OPHEIM, MT
OPHIR, CA,CO
OPP, AL
OPTIMA, OK
OQUAWKA, IL
ORADELL, NJ
ORAN, MO
ORANGE, CA,CT,MA,NH,NJ
  OH,TX,VA,VT
ORANGE CITY, FL,IA
ORANGE COVE, CA
ORANGE GROVE, TX
ORANGE PARK, FL
ORANGEBURG, SC
ORANGEVALE, CA
ORANGEVILLE, PA,UT
ORBISONIA, PA
ORCHARD, NB,TX
ORCHARD CITY, CO
ORCHARD LAKE VILLAGE, MI
ORCHARD PARK, NY
ORCUTT, CA
ORD, NB
ORDERVILLE, UT
ORDWAY, CO
ORE CITY, TX
OREGON, IL,MO,OH,OR,PA,WI
OREM, UT
ORESTES, IN
ORFORD, NH
ORFORDVILLE, WI
ORICK, CA
ORIENT, IA,ME,SD
ORIENTAL, NC
ORINDA, CA
ORION, IL
ORISKANY, NY
ORLAND, CA,IN,ME
ORLANDO, FL,OK
ORLEANS, CA,IN,MA,NB,VT
ORLINDA, TN
ORMOND BEACH, FL
ORMSBY, MN
ORO GRANDE, CA
OROFINO, ID
ORONO, ME,MN
ORONOCO, MN

ORONOGO, MO
OROSI, CA
OROVILLE, WA
ORR, MN
ORRICK, MO
ORRINGTON, ME
ORRSTOWN, PA
ORRUM, NC
ORRVILLE, AL,OH
ORTING, WA
ORTLEY, SD
ORTONVILLE, MI,MN
ORWELL, NY,VT
ORWIGSBURG, PA
OSAGE, IA,OK,WV
OSAGE CITY, KS
OSAKIS, MN
OSAWATOMIE, KS
OSBORN, MO
OSBORNE, KS
OSBURN, ID
OSCEOLA, AR,IA,IN,MO,NB
OSGOOD, IN
OSHKOSH, NB,WI
OSKALOOSA, IA,KS
OSLO, MN
OSMOND, NB
OSPREY, FL
OSSEO, MN
OSSIAN, IA,IN
OSSINING, NY
OSTRANDER, MN
OSWEGATCHIE, NY
OSWEGO, KS,NY
OSYKA, MS
OTEGO, NY
OTHELLO, WA
OTIS, CO,KS,MA
OTISFIELD, ME
OTOE, NB
OTSEGO, MI
OTTAWA, IL,KS,OH
OTTAWA HILLS, OH
OTTER CREEK, FL
OTTER LAKE, MI
OTTERBEIN, CA,IN
OTTERTAIL, MN
OTTUMWA, IA
OURAY, CO
OUTLOOK, MT
OUZINKIE, AK
OVERBROOK, KS
OVERLAND, MO
OVERLAND PARK, KS
OVERTON, NB,NV,TX
OVID, CO,MI,NY
OVIEDO, FL
OWASA, IA
OWASCO, NY
OWASSO, OK
OWATONNA, MN
OWEGO, NY
OWENDALE, MI
OWENS CROSSROADS, AL
OWENS LAKE, CA
OWENSBORO, KY
OWENSVILLE, IN,MO
OWENTON, KY
OWINGSVILLE, KY
OWLS HEAD, ME
OWOSSO, MI
OXBOW, ME
OXFORD, AR,CT,IA,ID,IN
  KS,MA,MD,ME,MI,MS,NB
  NC,NJ,NY,OH,PA
OXNARD, CA
OYSTER BAY, NY
OZAN, AR
OZARK, AL,AR,MO
OZAWKIE, KS
OZONA, TX

PACE, MS
PACHECO, CA

PACHUTA, MS
PACIFIC, MO
PACIFIC GROVE, CA
PACIFIC JUNCTION, IA
PACIFICA, CA
PACOLET, SC
PACOLET MILLS, SC
PADEN, OK
PADUCAH, KY,TX
PAGE, AZ,NB,ND
PAGEDALE, MO
PAGELAND, SC
PAGOSA SPRINGS, CO
PAHALA, HI
PAHOKEE, FL
PAHRUMP, NV
PAICINES, CA
PAINESVILLE, OH
PAINT, PA
PAINT ROCK, AL,TX
PAINTED POST, NY
PAINTER, VA
PAINTSVILLE, KY
PAISLEY, OR
PALA, CA
PALACIOS, TX
PALATINE, IL
PALATKA, FL
PALCO, KS
PALERMO, CA,ME
PALESTINE, AR,IL,TX
PALISADE, CO,MN,NB
PALISADES PARK, NJ
PALM BAY, FL
PALM BEACH, FL
PALM DESERT, CA
PALM HARBOR, FL
PALM SPRINGS, CA
PALMDALE, CA
PALMER, AK,IA,KS
    NB,TN,TX
PALMER LAKE, CO
PALMERTON, PA
PALMETTO, FL,LA
PALMYRA, IN,ME,MO,NB,NJ
    NY,PA,WI
PALO, IA
PALO ALTO, CA
PALO PINTO, TX
PALO VERDE, CA
PALOS HEIGHTS, IL
PALOS VERDES ESTATES, CA
PALOUSE, WA
PAMPA, TX
PAMPLICO, SC
PANACA, NV
PANAMA, IA,NB,OK
PANAMA CITY, FL
PANAMA CITY BEACH, FL
PANASOFFKEE, FL
PANDORA, OH
PANGBURN, AR
PANGUITCH, UT
PANHANDLE, TX
PANNA MARIA, TX
PANORA, IA
PANORMA HEIGHTS, CA
PANTEGO, NC,TX
PANTON, VT
PAOLA, KS
PAOLI, CO,IN,OK,PA
PAONIA, CO
PAPAIKOU, HI
PAPILLION, NB
PARADISE, CA,KS,UT
PARADISE HILL, OK
PARADISE VALLEY, AZ,NV
PARAGON, IN
PARAGOULD, AR
PARAMOUNT, CA
PARAMUS, NJ
PARCHMENT, MI
PARDEEVILLE, WI

PARIS, AR,ID,KY,ME,MO
    NY,TN,TX
PARISHVILLE, NY
PARK, KS
PARK CITY, UT
PARK FALLS, WI
PARK HILLS, KY
PARK RAPIDS, MN
PARK RIDGE, NJ,WI
PARK RIVER, ND
PARKDALE, AR
PARKER, AZ,FL,ID,KS,SD
PARKER CITY, IN
PARKERS PRAIRIE, MN
PARKERSBURG, IA,WV
PARKESBURG, PA
PARKFIELD, CA
PARKIN, AR
PARKMAN, ME
PARKSIDE, PA
PARKSLEY, VA
PARKSTON, SD
PARKSVILLE, SC
PARKTON, NC
PARKVILLE, MO
PARKWAY, MO
PARKWOOD, NC
PARLIER, CA
PARMA, MI,MO,OH
PARMELE, NC
PARNELL, IA
PAROWAN, UT
PARRISH, AL
PARROTTSVILLE, TN
PARSHALL, ND
PARSIPPANY, NJ
PARSONS, KS,TN,WV
PARSONSFIELD, ME
PARTRIDGE, KS
PASADENA, CA,TX
PASADENA HILLS, MO
PASADENA PARK, MO
PASCAGOULA, MS
PASCO, WA
PASKENTA, CA
PASO ROBLES, CA
PASS CHRISTIAN, MS
PASS-A-GRILL BEACH, FL
PASSADUMKEAG, ME
PASSAIC, MO,NJ
PASSAMAQUODDY INDIAN
    TOWNSHIP, ME
PASSAMAQUODDY PLEASANT
    POINT, ME
PATAGONIA, AZ
PATASKALA, OH
PATCH GROVE, WI
PATCHOGUE, NY
PATEROS, WA
PATERSON, NJ
PATOKA, IL,IN
PATON, IA
PATRICK, SC
PATRIOT, IN
PATTEN, ME
PATTERSON, AR,CA,LA,NY
PATTERSON SPRINGS, NC
PATTON, PA
PAULDING, OH
PAULINA, IA
PAULS VALLEY, OK
PAULSBORO, NJ
PAUPACK, PA
PAVILION, NY
PAVILLION, WY
PAW PAW, MI,WV
PAWHUSKA, OK
PAWLET, VT
PAWLING, NY
PAWNEE, IL,OK
PAWNEE CITY, NB
PAWNEE ROCK, KS
PAWTUCKET, RI

PAX, WV
PAXICO, KS
PAXTANG, PA
PAXTON, FL,IL,NB
PAYETTE, ID
PAYNE, OH
PAYNESVILLE, MN,MO
PAYSON, AZ,IL,UT
PE ELL, WA
PEA RIDGE, AR
PEABODY, KS,MA
PEACHAM, VT
PEACH ORCHARD, AR
PEACHLAND, NC
PEACHTREE CITY, GA
PEAK, SC
PEAPACK, NJ
PEARBLOSSOM, CA
PEARISBURG, VA
PEARL, MS
PEARL CITY, HI,IL
PEARL RIVER, LA
PEARLAND, TX
PEARSALL, TX
PEARSON, GA
PEASE, MN
PEBBLE BEACH, CA
PECATONICA, IL
PECK, ID,MI
PECOS, NM,TX
PECULIAR, MO
PEDLEY, CA
PEEBLES, OH
PEEKSKILL, NY
PEETZ, CO
PEEVER, SD
PEGRAM, TN
PEKIN, IL
PELAHATCHIE, MS
PELHAM, AL,GA,MA,NH,NY
PELICAN, AK
PELICAN RAPIDS, MN
PELION, SC
PELL CITY, AL
PELLA, IA
PELLSTON, MI
PELZER, SC
PEMBERTON, MN,NJ
PEMBINA, ND
PEMBROKE, GA,MA,ME
    NC,NH,VA
PEMBROKE PINES, FL
PEN ARGYL, PA
PENALOSA, KS
PENBROOK, PA
PENDER, NB
PENDERGRASS, GA
PENDLETON, IN,SC
PENELOPE, NC,TX
PENFIELD, NY
PENN, PA
PENN YAN, NY
PENNDEL, PA
PENNEY FARMS, FL
PENNINGTON, AL,NJ
PENNINGTON GAP, VA
PENNOCK, MN
PENNS GROVE, NJ
PENNSAUKEN, NJ
PENNSBORO, WV
PENNSBURG, PA
PENNSVILLE, NJ
PENNVILLE, IN
PENOBSCOT, ME
PENOBSCOT INDIAN ISLAND, ME
PENRYN, CA
PENSACOLA, FL,OK
PENTWATER, MI
PEORIA, AZ,IL
PEOSTA, IA
PEOTONE, IL
PEPIN, WI
PEPPER PIKE, OH
PEPPERELL, MA

PEQUANNOCK, NJ
PEQUOT LAKES, MN
PERHAM, ME,MN
PERKASIE, PA
PERKINS, CA,ME,OK
PERLEY, MN
PERRINTON, MI
PERRIS, CA
PERRY, AR,FL,GA,IA,KS,ME
    MI,MO,NY,OK,SC,UT
PERRYOPOLIS, PA
PERRYSBURG, OH
PERRYSVILLE, IN
PERRYTON, TX
PERRYTOWN, AR
PERRYVILLE, AR,MD
PERSIA, IA
PERTH AMBOY, NJ
PERU, IL,IN,KS,MA
    ME,NB,NY,VT
PESCADERO, CA
PESHTIGO, WI
PESOTUM, IL
PETAL, MS
PETALUMA, CA
PETERBOROUGH, NH
PETERSBURG, AK,IL,IN,MI
    NB,NY,TX,VA,WV
PETERSHAM, MA
PETERSON, IA,MN
PETERSTOWN, WV
PETOSKEY, MI
PETREY, AL
PETROLIA, CA,TX
PEVELY, MO
PEWAMO, MI
PEWAUKEE, WI
PEWEE VALLEY, KY
PFLUGERVILLE, TX
PHARR, TX
PHELPS, NY
PHENIX, VA
PHENIX CITY, AL
PHIL CAMPBELL, AL
PHILADELPHIA, MS,NY,PA,TN
PHILIP, SD
PHILIPPI, WV
PHILIPSBURG, MT,PA
PHILLIPS, ME,NB,WI
PHILLIPSBURG, KS,NJ
PHILLIPSTON, MA
PHILLIPSVILLE, NC
PHILO, CA,IL
PHIPPSBURG, ME
PHOENIX, AZ,NY
PHOENIXVILLE, PA
PICAYUNE, MS
PICHER, OK
PICKENS, MS,SC
PICKENSVILLE, AL
PICKERING, MO
PICKERINGTON, OH
PICKRELL, NB
PICO RIVERA, CA
PIEDMONT, AL,CA,MO,WV
PIERCE, CO,ID,NB
PIERCE CITY, MO
PIERCETON, IN
PIERCY, CA
PIERMONT, NH,NY
PIERPONT, SD
PIERRE, SD
PIERSON, FL,IA,MI
PIERZ, MN
PIGEON, MI
PIGEON FALLS, WI
PIGEON FORGE, TN
PIGGOTT, AR
PIKETON, OH
PIKEVILLE, KY,NC,TN
PILGER, NB
PILLAGER, MN
PILOT MOUNTAIN, NC

PILOT POINT, TX
PILOT STATION, AK
PIMA, AZ
PINCKARD, AL
PINCKNEY, MI
PINCKNEYVILLE, IL
PINCONNING, MI
PINE APPLE, AL
PINE BLUFF, AR
PINE BLUFFS, WY
PINE CITY, MN
PINE GROVE, CA,PA,WV
PINE HILL, AL,NJ
PINE ISLAND, MN
PINE KNOLL SHORES, NC
PINE KNOT VILLAGE, CA
PINE LAKE, GA
PINE LAWN, MO
PINE LEVEL, NC
PINE MOUNTAIN, GA
PINE PRAIRIE, LA
PINE RIVER, MN
PINE SPRINGS, TX
PINE VALLEY, CA,NC
PINE VILLAGE, IN
PINEBLUFF, NC
PINEDALE, CA,WY
PINEHURST, CA,GA,ID,NC
PINELAND, TX
PINELLAS PARK, FL
PINERIDGE, SC
PINETOPS, NC
PINEVIEW, GA
PINEVILLE, AR,KY,LA
   MO,NC,WV
PINEWOOD, SC
PINEY GREEN-WHITE OAK, NC
PINK HILL, NC
PINOLE, CA
PIOCHE, NV
PIONEER, LA,OH
PIPESTONE, MN
PIQUA, OH
PIRU, CA
PISCATAWAY, NJ
PISGAH, AL,IA
PISGAH FOREST, NC
PISMO BEACH, CA
PITCAIRN, PA
PITKIN, CO
PITMAN, NJ
PITTS, GA
PITTSBORO, IN,NC
PITTSBURG, CA,IL,KS,OK,TX
PITTSBURGH, PA
PITTSFIELD, IL,MA
   ME,NH,VT
PITTSFORD, NY,VT
PITTSTON, ME,PA
PITTSVILLE, MD,WI
PIXLEY, CA
PLACENTIA, CA
PLACERVILLE, CA,ID
PLAIN, WI
PLAIN CITY, OH,UT
PLAIN DEALING, LA
PLAINFIELD, CT,GA,IA,IL
   IN,NH,NJ,VT,WI
PLAINS, GA,MT,TX
PLAINSBORO, NJ
PLAINVIEW, AR,MN,NB,TX
PLAINVILLE, CT,GA
   IN,KS,MA
PLAINWELL, MI
PLAISTOW, NH
PLANADA, CA
PLANKINTON, SD
PLANO, IA,IL,TX
PLANT CITY, FL
PLANTATION, FL
PLANTERSVILLE, MS
PLAQUEMINE, LA

PLATINA, CA
PLATINUM, AK
PLATO, MN
PLATTE, SD
PLATTE CITY, MO
PLATTEKILL, NY
PLATTEVILLE, CO,WI
PLATTSBURG, MO
PLATTSBURGH, NY
PLAZA, ND
PLEASANT GARDEN, NC
PLEASANT GROVE, AL,UT
PLEASANT HILL, CA,IA,IL
   LA,MO,NC,OH,TN
PLEASANT PLAINS, AR
PLEASANT RIDGE, MI
PLEASANT VALLEY, MO
PLEASANT VIEW, UT
PLEASANTO, TX
PLEASANTON, CA,KS
PLEASANTVILLE, IA
   NJ,NY,PA
PLEASUREVILLE, KY
PLENTYWOOD, MT
PLEVNA, KS,MT
PLOVER, WI
PLUM BRANCH, SC
PLUM CITY, WI
PLUMERVILLE, AR
PLUMMER, ID
PLYMOUTH, CA,CT,IL,IN,MA
   ME,MI,MN,NB,NC,NH,NY,OH
   PA,UT,VT,WI
PLYMPTON, MA
POCA, WV
POCAHONTAS, IL,MO,VA
POCATELLO, ID
POCOHONTAS, AR
POCOLA, OK
POCOMOKE CITY, MD
POESTENKILL, NY
POINT, TX
POINT CLEAR, AL
POINT COMFORT, TX
POINT HOPE, AK
POINT MARION, PA
POINT PLEASANT, NJ,WV
POINT PLEASANT BEACH, NJ
POINTBLANK, TX
POLAND, ME
POLK, NB,PA
POLK CITY, FL
POLKTON, NC
POLKVILLE, NC
POLLARD, AR
POLLOCK, LA,SD
POLLOCK PINES, CA
POLLOCKSVILLE, NC
POLO, IL,MO
POMARIA, SC
POMEROY, IA,OH,WA
POMFRET, CT,VT
POMONA, CA,KS,NY
POMONA PARK, FL
POMPANO BEACH, FL
POMPEY, NY
POMPTON PLAINS, NJ
PONCA, NB
PONCA CITY, OK
PONCHA SPRINGS, CO
PONCHATOULA, LA
PONCE DE LEON, FL
POND CREEK, OK
PONDER, TX
PONDEREY, ID
PONDOSA, CA
PONETO, IN
PONTIAC, IL,MI
PONTOTOC, MS
PONTE VEDRA BEACH, FL
POOLER, GA
POOLESVILLE, MD
POPE, MS

POPE VALLEY, CA
POPLAR, WI
POPLAR BLUFF, MO
POPLAR GROVE, IL
POPLAR TENT, NC
POPLARVILLE, MS
PORT ALEXANDER, AK
PORT ALLEGANY, PA
PORT ALLEN, LA
PORT ANGELES, WA
PORT ARANSAS, TX
PORT ARTHUR, TX
PORT BARRE, LA
PORT BYRON, NY
PORT CHARLOTTE, FL
PORT CHESTER, NY
PORT CLINTON, OH
PORT COSTA, CA
PORT DEPOSIT, MD
PORT EDWARDS, WI
PORT ELIZABETH, NJ
PORT GIBSON, MS
PORT HEIDEN, AK
PORT HENRY, NY
PORT HOPE, MI
PORT HUENEME, CA
PORT HURON, MI
PORT ISABEL, TX
PORT JEFFERSON, NY
PORT JERVIS, NY
PORT LAVACA, TX
PORT LIONS, AK
PORT MANSFIELD, TX
PORT NECHES, TX
PORT ORANGE, FL
PORT ORCHARD, WA
PORT REPUBLIC, NJ
PORT RICHEY, FL
PORT ROYAL, SC,VA
PORT SAINT JOE, FL
PORT SAINT LUCIE, FL
PORT SANILAC, MI
PORT TOBACCO VILLAGE, MD
PORT TOWNSEND, WA
PORT VINCENT, LA
PORT WASHINGTON, NY,WI
PORT WENTWORTH, GA
PORTAGE, IN,MI,PA,WI
PORTAGE DES SIOUX, MO
PORTAGE LAKE, ME
PORTAGEVILLE, MO
PORTAL, ND
PORTALES, NM
PORTER, IN,ME,OK
PORTERDALE, GA
PORTERVILLE, CA
PORTIA, AR
PORTIS, KS
PORTLAND, AR,CT,IN,ME,MI
   NY,OR,PA,TX
PORTOLA, CA
PORTOLA VALLEY, CA
PORTSMOUTH, IA,NH
   OH,RI,VA
POSEN, IL,MI
POSEYVILLE, IN
POST, TX
POST FALLS, ID
POSTVILLE, IA
POTEAU, OK
POTEET, TX
POTH, TX
POTLATCH, ID
POTOMAC, IL
POTOSI, MO,WI
POTSDAM, NY
POTTAWATTOMIE PARK, IN
POTTER, NB
POTTER VALLEY, CA
POTTERVILLE, MI
POTTSBORO, TX
POTTSTOWN, PA
POTTSVILLE, AR

POTWIN, KS
POUGHKEEPSIE, NY
POULSBO, WA
POULTNEY, VT
POUND, VA,WI
POUND RIDGE, NY
POWAY, CA
POWDER SPRINGS, GA
POWDERLY, KY
POWELL, OH,TX,WY
POWELLSVILLE, NC
POWERS, MI,OR
POWHATAN, LA
POWHATAN POINT, OH
POWHATTAN, KS
POWNAL, ME,VT
POYEN, AR
POYNETTE, WI
POYNOR, TX
POZO, CA
PRAGUE, NB,OK
PRAIRIE, OR
PRAIRIE CITY, IA,IL
PRAIRIE DU CHIEN, WI
PRAIRIE DU ROCHER, IL
PRAIRIE DU SAC, WI
PRAIRIE FARM, WI
PRAIRIE GROVE, AR
PRAIRIE VIEW, KS,TX
PRAIRIE VILLAGE, KS
PRATHERSVILLE, MO
PRATT, KS,WV
PRATTSBURG, NY
PRATTSVILLE, AR
PRATTVILLE, AL
PREBLE, NY
PREMONT, TX
PRENTICE, WI
PRENTISS, ME,MS
PRESCOTT, AR,AZ,IA,KS,MI
   OR,WA,WI
PRESCOTT VALLEY, AZ
PRESHO, SD
PRESIDIO, TX
PRESQUE ISLE, ME
PRESTON, CT,GA,ID,KS
   MD,MN,NB
PRESTONBURG, KY
PRETTY PRAIRIE, KS
PRICE, UT
PRICEVILLE, AL
PRICHARD, AL
PRIEST RIVER, ID
PRIMGHAR, IA
PRIMROSE, NB
PRINCES LAKES, IN
PRINCETON, CA,IA,IL,IN
   KS,KY,MA,ME,MN,MO,NC
   NJ,WI,WV
PRINCEVILLE, IL,NC
PRINEVILLE, OR
PRINGLE, PA,SD
PRINSBURG, MN
PRIOR LAKE, MN
PRITCHETT, CO
PROBERTA, CA
PROCTOR, MN,VT
PROCTORVILLE, NC
PROMISE CITY, IA
PROPHETSTOWN, IL
PROSPECT, CT,KY,ME,OH,PA
PROSPER, TX
PROSPERITY, SC
PROSSER, NB
PROTECTION, KS
PROVENCAL, LA
PROVIDENCE, AL,KY,RI,UT
PROVINCETOWN, MA
PROVO, UT
PRUE, OK
PRYOR CREEK, OK
PUEBLO, CO
PUKALANI, HI

PUKWANA, SD
PULASKI, GA,IA,NY,VA,WI
PULLMAN, WA,WV
PULTENEY, NY
PUNTA GORDA, FL
PUNTA RASSA, FL
PUNXSUTAWNEY, PA
PURCELL, OK
PURCELLVILLE, VA
PURDIN, MO
PURDY, MO
PURVIS, MS
PUTNAM, CT,OK,TX
PUTNAM VALLEY, NY
PUTNEY, VT
PUXICO, MO
PUYALLUP, WA
PYOTE, TX

QUAKER CITY, OH
QUAKERTOWN, PA
QUAMBA, MN
QUANAH, TX
QUANTICO, VA
QUAPAW, OK
QUASQUETON, IA
QUEEN CITY, MO,TX
QUEENS BOROUGH, NY
QUEENSBURY, NY
QUEENSTOWN, MD
QUEMADO, TX
QUENEMO, KS
QUESTA, NM
QUILIN, MO
QUIMBY, IA
QUINCY, CA,FL,IL,MA,MI,WA
QUINHAGAK, AK
QUINLAN, OK,TX
QUINN, SD
QUINTER, KS
QUINTON, NJ,OK
QUINWOOD, WV
QUITAQUE, TX
QUITMAN, AR,GA,LA,MS,TX
QUOGUE, NY

RACELAND, KY
RACINE, OH,WI
RACKERBY, CA
RADCLIFF, KY
RADCLIFFE, IA
RADFORD, VA
RADISSON, WI
RADIUM, KS
RADNOR, PA
RAEFORD, NC
RAGLAND, AL
RAHWAY, NJ
RAIFORD, FL
RAINBOW CITY, AL
RAINELLE, WV
RAINIER, OR,WA
RAINSVILLE, AL
RAKIN, TX
RALEIGH, MS,NC
RALLS, TX
RALSTON, IA,NB,OK
RAMAH, CO
RAMEY, PA
RAMONA, CA,KS,OK,SD
RAMSEUR, NC
RAMSEY, IL,MN,NJ
RANBURNE, AL
RANCHESTER, WY
RANCHO CORDOVA, CA
RANCHO MIRAGE, CA
RANCHO SANTA FE, CA
RANCHWOOD MANOR, OK
RANDALL, IA,KS,MN
RANDLEMAN, NC
RANDLETT, OK
RANDOLPH, IA,KS,MA,ME,MN
    NB,NH,NJ,NY,UT,VT,WI

RANDOM LAKE, WI
RANDSBURG, CA
RANGELEY, ME
RANGELY, CO
RANGER, GA,TX
RANKIN, IL,PA
RANSOM, KS
RANSON, WV
RANTOUL, IL,KS
RAPID CITY, IL,SD
RARITAN, NJ
RATCLIFF, AR
RATHDRUM, ID
RATLIFF CITY, OK
RATON, NM
RATTAN, OK
RAVENA, NY
RAVENDALE, CA
RAVENDEN, AR
RAVENEL, SC
RAVENNA, MI,NB,OH
RAVENSWOOD, IN,WV
RAVENWOOD, MO
RAVIA, OK
RAWLINS, WY
RAY, ND
RAY CITY, GA
RAYMER, CO
RAYMOND, CA,IA,IL,KS,ME
    MN,MS,NB,NH,WA
RAYMONDVILLE, TX
RAYMORE, MO
RAYNE, LA
RAYNHAM, MA,NC
RAYTOWN, MO
RAYVILLE, LA,MO
REA, MO
READER, AR
READFIELD, ME
READING, KS,MA,MI
    OH,PA,VT
READINGS, MO
READINGTON, NJ
READLYN, IA
READSBORO, VT
READSTOWN, WI
REARDON, WA
REASNOR, IA
REBECCA, GA
RECTOR, AR
RED BANK, NJ
RED BAY, AL
RED BLUFF, CA
RED BUD, IL
RED CLOUD, NB
RED GRANITE, WI
RED HOOK, NY
RED LAKE FALLS, MN
RED LION, PA
RED OAK, IA,NC,OK,TX
RED RIVER, NM
RED ROCK, OK
RED SPRINGS, NC
RED WING, MN
REDBIRD, OK
REDCLIFF, CO
REDDICK, FL
REDDING, CA,CT
REDFIELD, AR,IA,KS,SD
REDINGTON BEACH, FL
REDKEY, IN
REDLANDS, CA
REDMOND, OR,UT,WA
REDONDO BEACH, CA
REDWOOD CITY, CA
REDWOOD FALLS, MN
REDWOOD TERRACE, CA
REDWOOD VALLEY, CA
REE HEIGHTS, SD
REED, AR
REED CITY, MI
REEDER, ND
REEDLEY, CA

REEDSBURG, WI
REEDSPORT, OR
REEDSVILLE, WV
REEDVILLE, WI
REESE, MI
REESEVILLE, WI
REEVES, LA
REEVESVILLE, SC
REFORM, AL
REFUGIO, TX
REHOBOTH, DE,MA
REIDSVILLE, GA
REINBECK, IA
REKLAW, TX
RELIANCE, SD
REMBRANDT, IA
REMER, MN
REMINGTON, IN,VA
REMSEN, IA
RENO, NV
RENOVO, PA
RENSSELAER, IN,NY
RENTIESVILLE, OK
RENTON, WA
RENTZ, GA
RENVILLE, MN
RENWICK, IA
REPTON, AL
REPUBLIC, KS,MO,WA
REPUBLICAN CITY, NB
REQUA, CA
RESERVE, NM
REUBENS, ID
REVERE, MA
REVILLO, SD
REWEY, WI
REXBURG, ID
REXFORD, KS
REYDON, OK
REYNO, AR
REYNOLDS, GA,IN,NB
REYNOLDSBURG, OH
RHAME, ND
RHEEM VALLEY, CA
RHINE, GA
RHINEBECK, NY
RHINELAND, MO
RHINELANDER, WI
RHODELL, WV
RHOME, TX
RIALTO, CA
RIB LAKE, WI
RICE, CA,TX
RICE LAKE, WI
RICEBORO, GA
RICEVILLE, IA
RICH CREEK, VA
RICH HILL, MO
RICH SQUARE, NC
RICHARDS, MO
RICHARDSON, TX
RICHBURG, SC
RICHEY, MT
RICHFIELD, ID,KS,MN
    NC,OH,UT
RICHFIELD SPRINGS, NY
RICHFORD, VT
RICHGROVE, CA
RICHLAND, GA,IA,MI,MO,MS
    NB,NY,OR,PA,TX,WA
RICHLAND CENTER, WI
RICHLAND SPRINGS, TX
RICHLANDS, NC,VA
RICHLANDTOWN, PA
RICHMOND, CA,IL,IN,KS,LA
    MA,ME,MI,MN,MO,RI,TX
    UT,VA,VT
RICHMOND BOROUGH, NY
RICHMOND HEIGHTS, MO,OH
RICHMOND HILL, GA
RICHTON, MS
RICHVALE, CA
RICHWOOD, OH,WV

RICO, CO
RIDDLE, OR
RIDGE FARM, IL
RIDGE SPRING, SC
RIDGECREST, LA
RIDGEFIELD, CT,NJ,WA
RIDGEFIELD PARK, NJ
RIDGELAND, MS,SC,WI
RIDGELEY, WV
RIDGELY, MD,TN
RIDGEVILLE, AL,IN,SC
RIDGEWAY, IA,SC,VA
RIDGEWOOD, NJ
RIDGWAY, CO,IL,PA
RIENZI, MS
RIESEL, TX
RIFLE, CO
RIGBY, ID
RIGGINS, ID
RILEY, IN,KS
RIMERSBURG, PA
RINCON, GA
RINGGOLD, GA,LA
RINGLING, OK
RINGSTED, IA
RINGWOOD, NJ,OK
RIO DELL, CA
RIO GRANDE CITY, TX
RIO HONDO, TX
RIO VISTA, CA,TX
RIPLEY, CA,ME,MS,NY,OH
    OK,TN,WV
RIPON, CA
RIPPEY, IA
RIPTON, VT
RIRIE, ID
RISCO, MO
RISING CITY, NB
RISING STAR, TX
RISING SUN, IN,MD
RISON, AR
RITTMAN, OH
RITZVILLE, WA
RIVER EDGE, NJ
RIVER FALLS, AL,WI
RIVER FOREST, IN
RIVER HEIGHTS, UT
RIVER HILLS, WI
RIVER OAKS, TX
RIVER ROUGE, MI
RIVER VALE, NJ
RIVERBANK, CA
RIVERDALE, CA,GA,MD
    NB,NJ,UT
RIVERGROVE, IL
RIVERHEAD, NY
RIVERMINES, MO
RIVERSIDE, AL,CA,IA,IL
    MO,NJ,OH,PA,WA,WY
RIVERTON, IL,NB,NJ,UT,WY
RIVERVIEW, FL,MI,MO
RIVESVILLE, WV
RIVES, TN
RIVIERA BEACH, FL
ROACHDALE, IN
ROAD'S END, CA
ROANN, IN
ROANOKE, AL,IL,IN,TX,VA
ROANOKE RAPIDS, NC
ROARING SPRINGS, TX
ROBBINS, CA,IL,NC
ROBBINSDALE, MN
ROBBINSTON, ME
ROBBINSVILLE, NC
ROBELINE, LA
ROBERSONVILLE, NC
ROBERT LEE, TX
ROBERTA, GA
ROBERTS, ID,WI
ROBERTSDALE, AL
ROBESONIA, PA
ROBINSON, IL,KS,TX
ROBSTOWN, TX

ROBY, TX
ROCA, NB
ROCHELLE, GA,IL
ROCHELLE PARK, NJ
ROCHESTER, IL,IN,KY,MA
  MI,MN,NH,NY,PA,VT,WI
ROCK CREEK, MN
ROCK FALLS, IL
ROCK HALL, MD
ROCK HILL, MO,SC
ROCK ISLAND, IL,WA
ROCK PORT, MO
ROCK RAPIDS, IA
ROCK RIVER, WY
ROCK SPRINGS, WI,WY
ROCK VALLEY, IA
ROCKAWAY, NJ,OR
ROCKAWAY BEACH, MO
ROCKDALE, TX,WI
ROCKFORD, AL,IA,IL,MI
  MN,TN,WA
ROCKHAM, SD
ROCKINGHAM, NC,VT
ROCKLAND, ID,MA,ME,WI
ROCKLEDGE, FL,PA
ROCKLIN, CA
ROCKMART, GA
ROCKPORT, IN,MA,ME,TX
ROCKSPRINGS, TX
ROCKTON, IL
ROCKVALE, CO
ROCKVILLE, IN,MD,MO,NB
ROCKVILLE CENTRE, NY
ROCKWALL, TX
ROCKWELL, IA,NC
ROCKWELL CITY, IA
ROCKWOOD, MI,TN
ROCKY, OK
ROCKY FORD, CO
ROCKY HILL, CT
ROCKY MOUNT, VA
ROCKY RIVER, OH
RODEO, CA
RODESSA, LA
ROE, AR
ROEBLING, NJ
ROELAND PARK, KS
ROFF, OK
ROGERS, AR,NB
ROGERS CITY, MI
ROGERSVILLE, AL,MO,TN
ROGUE RIVER, OR
ROHNERT PARK, CA
ROHNERVILLE, CA
ROLAND, IA,OK
ROLESVILLE, NC
ROLETTE, ND
ROLFE, IA
ROLINDA, CA
ROLLA, KS,MO,ND
ROLLING FORK, MS
ROLLING HILLS ESTATES, CA
ROLLINGSTONE, MN
ROMA, TX
ROME, GA,IA,ME,NY,PA
ROME CITY, IN
ROMEO, CO,MI
ROMERO, TX
ROMNEY, WV
ROMOLAND, CA
ROMULUS, MI,NY
RONAN, MT
RONCEVERTE, WV
RONDA, NC
RONKONKOMA, NY
ROODHOUS, IL
ROOPVILLE, GA
ROOSEVELT, MN,NJ
  NY,OK,UT
ROOSEVELT CITY, AL
ROOSEVELT PARK, MI
ROPER, NC
ROPESVILLE, TX

ROQUE BLUFFS, ME
ROSALIA, WA
ROSALIE, NB
ROSAMOND, CA
ROSCOE, IL,SD,TX
ROSCOMMON, MI
ROSE, NY
ROSE BUD, AR
ROSE CITY, MI
ROSE CREEK, MN
ROSE HILL, IA,KS,NC
ROSE VALLEY, PA
ROSEAU, MN
ROSEBORO, NC
ROSEBUD, TX
ROSEBURG, OR
ROSEBUSH, MI
ROSEDALE, IN,LA,MS
ROSELAND, IN,LA,NB,NJ
ROSELLE, IL,NJ
ROSELLE PARK, NJ
ROSEMEAD, CA
ROSEMONT, MD
ROSEMOUNT, MN
ROSENBERG, TX
ROSENDALE, NY,WI
ROSEPINE, LA
ROSETO, PA
ROSEVILLE, CA,IL,MI,MN
ROSEWOOD, NC
ROSHARON, TX
ROSHOLT, SD,WI
ROSICLARE, IL
ROSLYN, NY,SD,WA
ROSMAN, NC
ROSS, CA,TX
ROSSFORD, OH
ROSSTON, AR,OK
ROSSVILLE, GA,IL,KS,TN
ROSWELL, GA,NM,SD
ROTAN, TX
ROTHSAY, MN
ROTHSCHILD, WI
ROTTERDAM, NY
ROUND HILL, VA
ROUND LAKE, IL,MN
ROUND MOUNTAIN, NV
ROUND ROCK, TX
ROUND TOP, TX
ROUNDUP, MT
ROUSES POINT, NY
ROWAN, IA
ROWENA, TX
ROWESVILLE, SC
ROWLAND, NC
ROWLESBURG, WV
ROWLETT, TX
ROWLEY, MA
ROXANA, IL
ROXBORO, NC
ROXBURY, CT,ME,NY,VT
ROXIE, MS
ROXOBEL, NC
ROXTON, TX
ROY, NM,UT,WA
ROYAL, IA,NB
ROYAL CITY, WA
ROYAL OAK, MI
ROYALSTON, MA
ROYALTON, IL,MN,PA,VT
ROYERSFORD, PA
ROYSE CITY, TX
ROZEL, KS
RUBIDOUX, CA
RUBONIA, FL
RUBY, AK,SC
RUDD, IA
RUDOLPH, WI
RUFUS, OR
RUGBY, ND
RUIDOSO, NM
RUIDOSO DOWNS, NM
RULE, TX

RULEVILLE, MS
RULO, NB
RUMFORD, ME
RUMNEY, NH
RUMSON, NJ
RUNGE, TX
RUNNEMEDE, NJ
RUPERT, ID,VT,WV
RURAL HALL, NC
RURAL RETREAT, VA
RURAL VALLEY, PA
RUSH, NY
RUSH CENTER, KS
RUSH CITY, MN
RUSH HILL, MO
RUSH SPRINGS, OK
RUSH VALLEY, UT
RUSHFORD, MN,NY
RUSHMORE, MN
RUSHVILLE, IL,NB
RUSK, TX
RUSKIN, FL,NB
RUSSELL, AR,IA,KS,KY,MA
  MN,NY,PA
RUSSELL SPRINGS, KY
RUSSELLS POINT, OH
RUSSELLVILLE, AL,AR,IN,KY
RUSSIAN MISSION, AK
RUSSIAVILLE, IN
RUSTON, LA,WA
RUTH, NC
RUTHERFORD, CA,NJ,TN
RUTHERFORD COLLEGE, NC
RUTHERFORDTON, NC
RUTHVEN, IA
RUTLAND, MA,VT
RUTLEDGE, AL,GA,PA,TN
RYAN, IA,OK
RYDE, CA
RYE, CO,NH,NY
RYEGATE, MT,VT

SABATTUS, ME
SABETHA, KS
SABIN, MN
SABINA, OH
SABINAL, TX
SABINE PASS, TX
SABULA, IA
SAC CITY, IA
SACKETS HARBOR, NY
SACO, ME,MT
SACRAMENTO, CA,KY
SACRED HEART, MN
SADDLE BROOK, NJ
SADDLE RIVER, NJ
SADLER, TX
SAEGERTOWN, PA
SAFETY HARBOR, FL
SAFFORD, AZ
SAG HARBOR, NY
SAGINAW, MI,MO,TX
SAGUACHE, CO
SAINT AGATHA, ME
SAINT ALBANS, ME,VT,WV
SAINT ANN, MO
SAINT ANNE, IL
SAINT ANSGAR, IA
SAINT ANTHONY, ID,MN
SAINT AUGUSTINE, FL
SAINT AUGUSTINE BEACH, FL
SAINT CHARLES, IA,ID,IL
  KY,MI,MN,MO,VA
SAINT CLAIR, MI,MN,MO,PA
SAINT CLAIR SHORES, MI
SAINT CLAIRSVILLE, OH
SAINT CLOUD, FL,MN,WI
SAINT CROIX FALLS, WI
SAINT EDWARD, NB
SAINT FRANCIS, KS,ME
  MN,SD,WI
SAINT FRANCISVILLE, IL,LA
SAINT GEORGE, KS,ME
  SC,UT,VT

SAINT HELENA, NB
SAINT HELENS, OR
SAINT IGNACE, MI
SAINT IGNATIUS, MT
SAINT JAMES, MN,MO,NY
SAINT JO, TX
SAINT JOE, IN
SAINT JOHN, IN,KS
  MO,ND,WA
SAINT JOHNS, AZ,MI
SAINT JOHNSBURY, VT
SAINT JOSEPH, LA,MI
  MN,MO,TN
SAINT LAWRENCE, PA,SD
SAINT LEO, FL
SAINT LEON, IN
SAINT LOUIS, MI,MO,OK
SAINT LOUIS PARK, MN
SAINT MARIES, ID
SAINT MARTINVILLE, LA
SAINT MARY, MO
SAINT MARY'S, AK
SAINT MARYS, IA,KS
  OH,PA,WV
SAINT MATTHEWS, KY,SC
SAINT MICHAEL, AK,MN
SAINT MICHAELS, MD
SAINT MARKS, FL
SAINT NAZIANZ, WI
SAINT PAUL, AK,KS,MN,MO
  NB,OR,VA
SAINT PAUL PARK, MN
SAINT PAULS, NC
SAINT PETER, MN
SAINT PETERS, MO
SAINT PETERSBURG, FL,PA
SAINT PETERSBURG
  BEACH, FL
SAINT ROBERT, MO
SAINT REGIS PARK, KY
SAINT STEPHENS, NC
SAINT THOMAS, MO
SALADO, TX
SALAMANCA, NY
SALAMONIA, IN
SALE CITY, GA
SALEM, AR,CT,IL,IN,KY,MA
  MO,NB,NH,NJ,NY,OH,OR,SC
  SD,UT,VA,WV
SALEMBURG, NC
SALIDA, CA,CO
SALINA, KS,NY,OK,UT
SALINAS, CA
SALINE, LA,MI
SALINEVILLE, OH
SALIS, MS
SALISBURY, CT,MA,MD
  MO,NC,NH,VT
SALLADASBURG, PA
SALLEY, SC
SALLISAW, OK
SALMON, ID
SALT FLAT, TX
SALT LAKE CITY, UT
SALTDALE, CA
SALTILLO, IN,MS,PA,TN
SALTSBURG, PA
SALUDA, NC,SC
SALYER, CA
SALYERSVILLE, KY
SAMBURG, TN
SAMOA, CA
SAMSON, AL
SAN ANDREAS, CA
SAN ANGELO, TX
SAN ANSELMO, CA
SAN ANTONIA, FL
SAN ANTONIO, TX
SAN ARDO, CA
SAN AUGUSTINE, TX
SAN BENITO, TX
SAN BERNARDINO, CA
SAN BRUNO, CA

SAN BUENAVENTURA
  (VENTURA), CA
SAN CARLOS, CA
SAN CLEMENTE, CA
SAN DIEGO, CA,TX
SAN DIMAS, CA
SAN FELIPE, TX
SAN FERNANDO, CA
SAN FRANCISCO, CA
SAN GABRIEL, CA
SAN GREGORIO, CA
SAN JACINTO, CA
SAN JOAQUIN, CA
SAN JON, NM
SAN JOSE, CA
SAN JUAN, TX
SAN JUAN BAUTISTA, CA
SAN JUAN CAPISTRANO, CA
SAN LEANDRO, CA
SAN LORENZO, CA
SAN LUCAS, CA
SAN LUIS, AZ,CO
SAN LUIS OBISPO, CA
SAN LUIS REY, CA
SAN MARCOS, CA,TX
SAN MARINO, CA
SAN MARTIN, CA
SAN MATEO, CA,FL
SAN MIGUEL, CA
SAN PABLO, CA
SAN PASQUAL, CA
SAN PEDRO, CA
SAN RAFAEL, CA
SAN RAMON, CA
SAN REMO, NY
SAN SABA, TX
SAN SIMEON, CA
SAN YSIDRO, CA,NM
SANBORN, MN
SAND LAKE, MI,NY
SAND POINT, AK
SANDBORN, IN
SANDERS, KY
SANDERSON, FL,TX
SANDERSVILLE, GA,MS
SANDGATE, VT
SANDOVAL, IL
SANDOWN, NH
SANDPOINT, ID
SANDSTONE, MN
SANDUSKY, MI
SANDWICH, IL,MA
SANDY, OR
SANDY CITY, UT
SANDY CREEK, NY
SANFORD, CO,FL,ME
  MI,NC,TX
SANGER, CA,TX
SANGERFIELD, NY
SANGERVILLE, ME
SANIBEL, FL
SANTA ANA, CA
SANTA ANNA, TX
SANTA BARBARA, CA
SANTA CLARA, CA,UT
SANTA CLAUS, IN
SANTA CRUZ, CA
SANTA FE, NM
SANTA FE SPRINGS, CA
SANTA MARGARITA, CA
SANTA MARIA, CA
SANTA MONICA, CA
SANTA PAULA, CA
SANTA RITA, CA
SANTA ROSA, CA,NM,TX
SANTA SUSANA, CA
SANTA VENETIA, CA
SANTA YNEZ, CA
SANTA YSABEL, CA
SANTAQUIN, UT
SANTEE, CA,NB,SC
SAPULPA, OK
SARALAND, AL

SARANAC, MI,NY
SARANAC LAKE, NY
SARASOTA, FL
SARATOGA, CA,IN,NC,TX,WY
SARATOGA SPRINGS, NY
SARCOXIE, MO
SARDINIA, NY
SARDIS, AL,GA,MS,TN
SAREPTA, LA
SARGENT, NB
SARITA, TX
SARONVILLE, NB
SARTELL, MN
SASAKWA, OK
SASPAMCO, TX
SASSER, GA
SATANTA, KS
SATELLITE BEACH, FL
SATICOY, CA
SATSUMA, AL,FL
SAUGAS, CA
SAUGATUCK, MI
SAUGERTIES, NY
SAUGUS, MA
SAUK CENTRE, MN
SAUK CITY, WI
SAUK RAPIDS, MN
SAUKVILLE, WI
SAULSBURY, TN
SAULT SAINTE MARIE, MI
SAVAGE, MN
SAVANNA, OK
SAVANNAH, GA,IL,MO,NY,TN
SAVONA, NY
SAVONBURG, KS
SAVOONGA, AK
SAVOY, IL,MA,TX
SAWPIT, CO
SAWYER, KS,ND
SAXIS, VA
SAXMAN, AK
SAXONBURG, PA
SAXTONS RIVER, VT
SAYRE, OK,PA
SAYREVILLE, NJ
SAYVILLE, NY
SCALP LEVEL, PA
SCAMMON, KS
SCAMMON BAY, AK
SCANDIA, KS
SCANDINAVIA, WI
SCAPPOOSE, OR
SCARBOROUGH, ME,NY
SCARSDALE, NY
SCHAGHTICOKE, NY
SCHENECTADY, NY
SCHERERVILLE, IN
SCHERTZ, TX
SCHLATER, MS
SCHNEIDER, IN
SCHOENCHEN, KS
SCHOFIELD, WI
SCHOFIELD BARRACKS, HI
SCHOOLCRAFT, MI
SCHROON LAKE, NY
SCHULENBURG, TX
SCHURZ, NV
SCHUYLER, NB
SCHUYLER FALLS, NY
SCHUYLERVILLE, NY
SCHUYLKILL HAVEN, PA
SCIENCE HILL, KY
SCIO, NY,OR
SCIPIO, UT
SCITUATE, MA,RI
SCOBEY, MT
SCOFIELD, UT
SCOOBA, MS
SCOTCH PLAINS, NJ
SCOTIA, CA,NB,NY
SCOTLAND, CT,GA,SD,TX
SCOTLAND NECK, NC
SCOTT, LA

SCOTT CITY, KS,MO
SCOTTDALE, PA
SCOTTS MILLS, OR
SCOTTS VALLEY, CA
SCOTTSBLUFF, NB
SCOTTSBORO, AL,IN
SCOTTSBURG, VA
SCOTTSDALE, AZ
SCOTTSVILLE, KY,TX,VA
SCOTTVILLE, MI
SCRANTON, AR,ND,PA,SC,KS
SCREVEN, GA
SCRIBNER, NB
SEA BRIGHT, NJ
SEA CLIFF, NY
SEA GIRT, NJ
SEA ISLE CITY, NJ
SEABOARD, NC
SEABROOK, NH,TX
SEADRIFT, TX
SEAFORD, DE
SEAGATE, NC
SEAGOVILLE, TX
SEAGRAVES, TX
SEAGROVE, NC
SEAL BEACH, CA
SEALY, TX
SEARCHLIGHT, NV
SEARCY, AR
SEARSBORO, IA
SEARSBURG, VT
SEARSMONT, ME
SEARSPORT, ME
SEASIDE, CA,OR
SEASIDE HEIGHTS, NJ
SEASIDE PARK, NJ
SEAT PLEASANT, MD
SEATTLE, WA
SEBAGO, ME
SEBASTIAN, FL
SEBASTOPOL, CA,MS
SEBEC, ME
SEBEKA, MN
SEBEWAING, MI
SEBOEIS, ME
SEBOOMOOK LAKE, ME
SEBREE, KY
SEBRING, FL
SECAUCUS, NJ
SECRETARY, MD
SECTION, AL
SEDALIA, MO
SEDAN, KS
SEDGWICK, AR,CO,KS,ME
SEDGEWICKVILLE, MO
SEDRO-WOOLLEY, WA
SEEKONK, MA
SEELEY, CA
SEELYVILLE, IN
SEGUIN, TX
SEIBERT, CO
SEILING, OK
SELAH, WA
SELAWIK, AK
SELBY, SD
SELBYVILLE, DE
SELDEN, KS,NY
SELDOVIA, AK
SELFRIDGE, ND
SELIGMAN, MO
SELINSGROVE, PA
SELLERS, SC
SELLERSBURG, IN
SELLERSVILLE, PA
SELMA, AL,CA,IN,NC,TX
SELMER, TN
SEMINARY, MS
SEMINOLE, FL,OK,TX
SENATH, MO
SENATOBIA, MS
SENECA, IL,KS,MO,NB
  OR,SC,SD
SENECA FALLS, NY

SENNETT, NY
SENOIA, GA
SENTINEL, OK
SEQUIM, WA
SERBIN, TX
SERGEANT BLUFF, IA
SESPE, CA
SESSER, IL
SEVEN SPRINGS, NC,PA
SEVERANCE, CO,KS
SEVERN, NC,KS
SEVIERVILLE, TN
SEVILLE, FL,GA
SEWARD, AK,KS,NB,PA
SEWICKLEY, PA
SEYMOUR, CT,IA,IN
  MO,TX,WI
SHABBONA, IL
SHADY COVE, OR
SHADY FOREST, NC
SHADY GROVE, OK
SHADY POINT, OK
SHAFTER, CA,TX
SHAFTSBURY, VT
SHAGELUK, AK
SHAKOPEE, MN
SHAKTOOLIK, AK
SHALIMAR, FL
SHALLOTE, NC
SHALLOWATER, TX
SHAMOKIN, PA
SHAMROCK, FL,OK,TX
SHANDAKEN, NY
SHANDON, CA
SHANIKO, OR
SHANNON, MS
SHAPLEIGH, ME
SHARON, CT,GA,KS,MA,NH
  OK,PA,SC,TN,VT,WI
SHARON HILL, PA
SHARON SPRINGS, KS
SHARPSBURG, GA,IA,MD,PA
SHARPSVILLE, IN,PA
SHARPTOWN, MD
SHASTA, CA
SHATTUCK, OK
SHAW, MS
SHAWANO, WI
SHAWNEETOWN, IL
SHAWNEE, KS,OK
SHEAKLEYVILLE, PA
SHEBOYGAN, WI
SHEBOYGAN FALLS, WI
SHEFFIELD, AL,IA,MA,PA,VT
SHELBINA, MO
SHELBURN, IN
SHELBURNE, MA,NH,VT
SHELBY, IA,MI,MS,MT,NB,NC
SHELBYVILLE, IN,KY
  MO,TN,TX
SHELDON, IA,IL,VT,WI
SHELDON POINT, AK
SHELL BEACH, CA
SHELL LAKE, WI
SHELL ROCK, IA
SHELLEY, ID
SHELLMAN, GA
SHELLSBURG, IA
SHELOCTA, PA
SHELTER ISLAND, NY
SHELTON, CT,NB,WA
SHENANDOAH, IA,PA,VA
SHEPHERD, MI,TX
SHEPHERDSTOWN, WV
SHEPHERDSVILLE, KY
SHERBURN, MN
SHERBURNE, VT
SHERIDAN, AR,CA,CO,IL,IN
  MI,MO,MT,NY,OR,WY
SHERIDAN LAKE, CO
SHERMAN, CT,ME,SD,TX
SHERRILL, AR
SHERWOOD, AR,MI,ND,OR,WI

PLACE INDEX

TALLASSEE, AL
TALLMADGE, OH
TALLULAH, LA
TALLULAH FALLS, GA
TALMADGE, ME
TALMAGE, NB
TALOGA, OK
TALPA, TX
TAMALPAIS VALLEY, CA
TAMAQUA, PA
TAMARAC, FL
TAMA, IA
TAMORA, NB
TAMPA, FL,KS
TAMPA SHORES, FL
TANANA, AK
TANEYTOWN, MD
TANEYVILLE, MO
TANGENT, OR
TANGIER, VA
TANGIPAHOA, LA
TAOS, MO,NM
TAPPAHANNOCK, VA
TAPPAN, NY
TAPPEN, ND
TAR HEEL, NC
TARBORO, NC
TARENTUM, PA
TARKIO, MO
TARNOV, NB
TARPON SPRINGS, FL
TARRANT CITY, AL
TARRYTOWN, GA,NY
TARZANA, CA
TATUM, NM,SC,TX
TATUMS, OK
TAUNTON, MA,MN
TAVARES, FL
TAVERNIER, FL
TAWAS CITY, MI
TAYLOR, AR,AZ,MI,MS,NB
PA,TX,WI
TAYLOR MILL, KY
TAYLORS FALLS, MN
TAYLORSVILLE, CA,GA,MS,NC
TAZEWELL, TN,VA
TCHULA, MS
TEA, SD
TEACHEY, NC
TEAGUE, TX
TEANECK, NJ
TECATE, CA
TECOMA, NV
TECOPA, CA
TECUMSEH, MI,NB,OK
TEE PEE CITY, TX
TEHACHAPI, CA
TEHAMA, CA
TEHUACANA, TX
TEKAMAH, NB
TEKONSHA, MI
TEKOA, WA
TELFERNER, TX
TELFORD, PA
TELICO PLAINS, TN
TELL CITY, IN
TELLER, AK
TELLURIDE, CO
TEMECULA, CA
TEMPE, AZ
TEMPLE, GA,ME,NH,OK,PA,TX
TEMPLE CITY, CA
TEMPLE TERRACE, FL
TEMPLETON, CA,IA,MA
TEMPLEVILLE, MD
TEN SLEEP, WY
TENAFLY, NJ
TENAHA, TX
TENAKEE SPRINGS, AK
TENINO, WA
TENNILLE, GA
TENNYSON, IN,WI
TENSED, ID

TEQUESTA, FL
TERLTON, OK
TERMINOUS, CA
TERRA ALTA, WV
TERRAL, OK
TERRE HAUTE, IN
TERRELL, TX
TERRIL, IA
TERRY, MS,MT
TERRYVILLE, NY
TESCOTT, KS
TETON, ID
TETONIA, ID
TEUTOPOLIS, IL
TEWKSBURY, MA
TEXARKANA, AR,TX
TEXAS CITY, TX
TEXHOMA, OK,TX
TEXICO, NM
TEXOLA, OK
THACKERVILLE, OK
THATCHER, AZ
THAXTON, MS
THAYER, KS,MO
THAYNE, WY
THE FORKS, ME
THE PLAINS, VA
THEDFORD, NB
THEODORE, AL
THERESA, WI
THERMAL, CA
THERMOPULIS, WY
THETFORD, VT
THIBODAUX, LA
THIENSVILLE, WI
THIEF RIVER FALLS, MN
THOMAS, OK,WV
THOMAS MILLS, PA
THOMASBORO, IL
THOMASTON, AL,CT,GA,ME
THOMASVILLE, AL,GA,NC
THOMPSON, CT,IA,ND,PA
THOMPSON FALLS, MT
THOMPSONS, TX
THOMPSONVILLE, MI
THOMSON, GA
THOR, IA
THORNDALE, TX
THORNDIKE, ME
THORNTON, AR,CA,CO,IA
IL,NH,TX
THORNTOWN, IN
THORSBY, AL
THOUSAND OAKS, CA
THRALL, TX
THREE ARCHES, CA
THREE FORKS, MT
THREE OAKS, MI
THREE RIVERS, CA,MI,TX
THROCKMORTON, TX
THROOP, PA
THURBER, TX
THURMAN, IA
THURMOND, WV
THURMONT, MD
THURSTON, NB
TIBURON, CA
TICKFAW, LA
TICONDEROGA, NY
TIETON, WA
TIFFIN, OH
TIFTON, GA
TIGARD, OR
TIGER, GA
TIGNALL, GA
TIJERAS, NM
TILDEN, NB,TX
TILLAMOOK, OR
TILLAR, AR
TILTONSVILLE, OH
TIMBER LAKE, SD
TIMBERVILLE, VA
TIMKEN, KS

TIMMONSVILLE, SC
TIMNATH, CO
TIMPSON, TX
TINDALL, MO
TINLEY PARK, IL
TINMOUTH, VT
TINTON FALLS, NJ
TIOGA, ND,TX
TIPP CITY, OH
TIPTON, CA,IN,KS,MO,OK
TIPTONVILLE, TN
TISHOMINGO, MS,OK
TITONKA, IA
TITUSVILLE, FL,PA
TIVERTON, RI
TIVOLI, NY
TOAST, NC
TOBIAS, NB
TOBYHANNA, PA
TOCCOA, GA
TOCCOPOLA, MS
TOGIAK, AK
TOKSOOK BAY, AK
TOLAR, TX
TOLEDO, IA,IL,OH,OR,WA
TOLLAND, CT
TOLLESBORO, KY
TOLLESON, AZ
TOLONO, IL
TOLSTOY, SD
TOLUCA, IL
TOM BEAN, TX
TOMAH, WI
TOMAHAWK, WI
TOMBALL, TX
TOMBSTONE, AZ
TOMKINSVILLE, KY
TOMS BROOK, VA
TOMS RIVER, NJ
TONASKET, WA
TONAWANDA, NY
TONGANOXIE, KS
TONKA BAY, MN
TONKAWA, OK
TONOPAH, NV
TONTITOWN, AR
TONY, WI
TOOELE, UT
TOOMSBORO, GA
TOONE, TN
TOPEKA, IN,KS
TOPPENISH, WA
TOPSAIL BEACH, NC
TOPSFIELD, MA,ME
TOPSHAM, ME,VT
TOPTON, PA
TOQUERVILLE, UT
TORONTO, IA,KS,OH,SD
TORRANCE, CA
TORREY, UT
TORRINGTON, CT,WY
TOTOWA, NJ
TOULON, IL
TOWACO, NJ
TOWANDA, IL,KS,PA
TOWER, MN
TOWER CITY, PA
TOWN CREEK, AL
TOWN OF PINES, IN
TOWNER, ND
TOWNSEND, DE,MT
TOWNSHEND, VT
TOXEY, AL
TOYAH, TX
TRACY, CA,MN,MO
TRACY CITY, TN
TRAER, IA
TRAFALGAR, IN
TRAFFORD, PA
TRAIL CREEK, IN
TRAINER, PA
TRANQUILITY, CA
TRAPPE, MD,PA

TRASKWOOD, AR
TRAVELERS REST, SC
TRAVER, CA
TRAVERSE CITY, MI
TREASURE ISLAND, FL
TREECE, KS
TREMONT, IL,ME,MS,PA
TREMONTON, UT
TREMPEALEAU, WI
TRENT, SD,TX
TRENT WOODS, NC
TRENTON, FL,GA,IL,KY,ME
MI,MO,NB,NC,NJ,OH,SC
TN,TX,UT
TRES PINOS, CA
TREYNOR, IA
TREZEVANT, TN
TRIADELPHIA, WV
TRIBUNE, KS
TRICKHAM, TX
TRIMBLE, MO
TRIMMER, CA
TRIMONT, MN
TRINIDAD, CO,TX
TRINITY, AL,NC,TX
TRION, GA
TRIPOLI, IA
TRIPP, SD
TRONA, CA
TROPIC, UT
TROSKY, MN
TROUP, TX
TROUTDALE, OR,VA
TROUTMAN, NC
TROUTVILLE, VA
TROY, AL,ID,IL,IN,KS,ME
MI,MO,MT,NC,NY,OH
SC,TN,TX,VT
TRUCKEE, CA
TRUESDALE, IA
TRUMAN, MN
TRUMANN, AR
TRUMANSBURG, NY
TRUMBULL, CT,NB
TRURO, MA
TRUSSVILLE, AL
TRUTH OR CONSEQUENCES, NM
TRYON, NC,OK
TUCKAHOE, NY
TUCKERMAN, AR
TUCKERTON, NJ
TUCSON, AZ
TUCUMCARI, NM
TUKWILA, WA
TULARE, CA,SD
TULAROSA, NM
TULELAKE, CA
TULIA, TX
TULLAHASEE, OK
TULLY, NY
TULLYTOWN, PA
TULSA, OK
TUMWATER, WA
TUNBRIDGE, VT
TUNICA, MS
TUNITAS, CA
TUNKHANNOCK, PA
TUNNEL HILL, GA
TUNNELTON, WV
TUNUNAK, AK
TUOLUMNE, CA
TUPELO, AR,MS,OK
TUPPER LAKE, NY
TURBEVILLE, SC
TURIN, GA,IA
TURKEY, NC,TX
TURKEY CREEK, LA
TURLOCK, CA
TURNER, ME,MI,OR
TURNEY, MO
TURON, KS
TURTLE CREEK, PA
TURTLE LAKE, ND,WI

TUSCALOOSA, AL
TUSCARAWAS, OH
TUSCOLA, IL,TX
TUSCUMBIA, AL,MO
TUSKEGEE, AL
TUSTIN, CA,MI
TUTTLE, OK
TUTTLETOWN, CA
TUTWILER, MS
TWAIN, CA
TWIN BRIDGES, MT
TWIN CITY, GA
TWIN FALLS, ID
TWIN LAKES, MN,WI
TWIN OAKS, MO
TWIN VALLEY, MN
TWINING, MI
TWINSBURG, OH
TWISP, WA
TWO BUTTES, CO
TWO HARBORS, MN
TWO RIVERS, WI
TY TY, GA
TYBEE ISLAND, GA
TYE, TX
TYLER, MN,TX
TYLERTOWN, MS
TYNDALL, SD
TYNGSBOROUGH, MA
TYRO, KS
TYRONE, GA,NY,OK,PA
TYRONZA, AR

UBLY, MI
UCON, ID
UDALL, KS
UEHLING, NB
UHRICHSVILLE, OH
UINTAH, UT
UKIAH, CA,OR
ULEN, IN,MN
ULLIN, IL
ULM, AR
ULMER, SC
ULSTER, PA
ULYSSES, KS,NB
UMATILLA, FL,OR
UNADILLA, GA,NB,NY
UNALAKLEET, AK
UNALASKA, AK
UNCERTAIN, TX
UNDERHILL, VT
UNDERWOOD, IA,MN,ND
UNION, CT,IA,IL,ME,MO,NB
  NJ,NV,NY,OH,OR,SC,WV
UNION BEACH, NJ
UNION BRIDGE, MD
UNION CITY, CA,GA,IN,MI
  NJ,OK,PA,TN
UNION DALE, PA
UNION GAP, WA
UNION GROVE, AL,TX,WI
UNION PARK, FL
UNION POINT, GA
UNION SPRINGS, AL,NY
UNION STAR, MO
UNIONDALE, IN
UNIONTOWN, AL,KS,KY,PA,WA
UNIONVILLE, MI,MO
UNITY, ME,NH,OR,WI
UNITY VILLAGE, MO
UNIVERSAL, IN
UNIVERSAL CITY, CA,MO,TX
UNIVERSITY HEIGHTS, IA,OH
UNIVERSITY PARK, MD
UPHAM, ND
UPLAND, CA,IN,NB,PA
UPLANDS PARK, MO
UPPER ARLINGTON, OH
UPPER LAKE, CA
UPPER MARLBORO, MD
UPSALA, MN
UPTON, KY,MA,ME,WY
URANIA, LA

URBANA, IA,MO,OH
URBANDALE, IA
URBANNA, VA
URICH, MO
UTE, IA
UTICA, IN,KS,MI,MN,MS,NB
  NY,OH,SD
UTOPIA, TX
UVALDA, GA
UVALDE, TX
UXBRIDGE, MA
VACAVILLE, CA
VADER, WA
VADNAIS HEIGHTS, MN
VAIDEN, MS
VAIL, CO,IA
VALATIE, NY
VALDERS, WI
VALDESE, NC
VALDEZ, AK
VALDOSTA, GA
VALE, OR
VALENTINE, NB,TX
VALHALLA, NY
VALIER, IL,MT
VALLEJO, CA
VALLEY, NB
VALLEY BROOK, OK
VALLEY CENTER, CA,KS
VALLEY CITY, ND
VALLEY FALLS, KS
VALLEY FORD, CA
VALLEY FORGE, PA
VALLEY GROVE, WV
VALLEY HEAD, AL
VALLEY HILL, NC
VALLEY MILLS, TX
VALLEY PARK, MO
VALLEY SPRINGS, AR,SD
VALLEY STREAM, NY
VALLEY VIEW, TX
VALLIANT, OK
VALMEYER, IL
VALPARAISO, FL,IN,NB
VALYERMO, CA
VAN, TX
VAN ALSTYNE, TX
VAN BUREN, AR,IN,ME,MO
VAN HORN, TX
VAN HORNE, IA
VAN METER, IA
VAN ORMY, TX
VAN WERT, OH
VANCE, AL,SC
VANCEBORO, ME,NC
VANCEBURG, KY
VANCOUVER, WA
VANDALIA, IL,MI,MO,OH
VANDEMERE, NC
VANDERBILT, MI,PA,TX
VANDERGRIFT, PA
VANDERPOOL, TX
VANDERVOORT, AR
VANDLING, PA
VANDUSER, MO
VANLEER, TN
VANPORT, PA
VARDAMON, MS
VARNADO, LA
VARNELL, GA
VARNVILLE, SC
VASS, NC
VASSALBOROUGH, ME
VASSAR, MI
VAUGHN, NM
VEBLEN, SD
VEEDERSBURG, IN
VEGA, TX
VELMA, OK
VELVA, ND
VENANGO, NB,PA
VENETA, OR
VENICE, CA,FL,IL

VENTNOR CITY, NJ
VENTURA, CA,IA
VENUS, FL,TX
VERA, OK
VERA CRUZ, IN
VERDEMONT, CA
VERDEN, OK
VERDI, NV
VERDIGRE, NB
VERDON, NB,SD
VERGAS, MN
VERGENNES, VT
VERMILLION, KS,MN,OH,SD
VERMONT, IL
VERMONTVILLE, MI
VERNAL, UT
VERNDALE, MN
VERNON, AL,CT,FL,IN,MI
  NJ,NY,TX,UT,VT
VERNON CENTER, MN
VERNONIA, OR
VERO BEACH, FL
VERONA, ME,MO,MS,NJ
  NY,PA,WI
VERSAILLES, IN,KY
  MO,OH,PA
VERSHIRE, VT
VESPER, WI
VESTA, MN
VESTAL, NY
VESTAVIA HILLS, AL
VEVAY, IN
VIAN, OK
VIBORG, SD
VICCO, KY
VICI, OK
VICKSBURG, MI,MS
VICTOR, CO,IA,ID,NY
VICTORIA, AR,KS,MN,TX,VA
VICTORVILLE, CA
VICTORY, VT
VIDAL JUNCTION, CA
VIDALIA, LA
VIDOR, TX
VIENNA, IL,LA,MD,ME,MO
  NJ,SD,VA,WV
VIKING, MN
VILAS, CO,SD
VILLA HILLS, KY
VILLA PARK, CA,IL
VILLANOVA, PA
VILLARD, MN
VILLE PLATTE, LA
VILLISCA, IA
VILONIA, AR
VINA, AL,CA
VINALHAVEN, ME
VINCENNES, IN
VINCENT, AL,IA
VINCENTOWN, NJ
VINE GROVE, KY
VINE HILL, CA
VINEGARONE, TX
VINELAND, NJ
VINEYARD HAVEN, MA
VINING, IA,MN
VINITA, OK
VINITA PARK, MO
VINTON, CA,IA,LA,VA
VIOLA, AR,CA,DE,IL,KS,TN
VIRDEN, IL
VIRGIL, KS,SD
VIRGILINA, NC,VA
VIRGIN, UT
VIRGINIA, IL,MN,NB,NV
VIRGINIA BEACH, VA
VIRGINIA CITY, MT
VIROQUA, WI
VISALIA, CA
VISTA, CA
VIVIAN, LA
VOLCANO, CA
VOLGA, IA,SD

VOLIN, SD
VOLTA, CA
VOLUNTOWN, CT
VONA, CO
VONORE, TN
VOORHEES, NJ
VOORHEESVILLE, NY
VREDENBURGH, AL

WABASH, IN
WABASHA, MN
WABASSO, FL,MN
WABBASEKA, AR
WACHAPREAGUE, VA
WACO, GA,MO,NB,NC,TX
WACONIA, MN
WADE, NC
WADENA, IA,MN
WADESBORO, NC
WADLEY, AL,GA
WADSWORTH, IL,NV,OH
WAELDER, TX
WAGENER, SC
WAGNER, SD
WAGON MOUND, NM
WAGONER, OK
WAGRAM, NC
WAHIAWA, HI
WAHKON, MN
WAHOO, NB
WAHPETON, IA,ND
WAIALUA, HI
WAIANOE, HI
WAILEA, HI
WAILUA, HI
WAILUKU, HI
WAIMANALO, HI
WAIMANALO BEACH, HI
WAIMEA, HI
WAINWRIGHT, AK,OK
WAITE, ME
WAITE PARK, MN
WAITSBURG, WA
WAITSFIELD, VT
WAKARUSA, IN
WAKE FOREST, NC
WAKE VILLAGE, TX
WAKEENEY, KS
WAKEFIELD, KS,MI,NB,VA
WAKENDA, MO
WAKITA, OK
WAKONDA, SD
WALDEN, CO,NY,VT
WALDO, AR,FL,KS,ME,WI
WALDOBORO, ME
WALDORF, MN
WALDPORT, OR
WALDRON, AR,KS,MI
WALDWICK, NJ
WALES, AK,MA,UT,WI
WALESKA, GA
WALFORD, IA
WALHALLA, ND,SC
WALKER, IA,LA,MI,MN,MO
WALKERSVILLE, MD
WALKERTON, IN
WALKERVILLE, MI,MT
WALL, NJ,SD
WALL SPRINGS, FL
WALLA WALLA, WA
WALLACE, ID,IN,KS,NB,SD
WALLAGRASS, ME
WALLED LAKE, MI
WALLER, TX
WALLINGFORD, CT,IA,PA,VT
WALLINGTON, NJ
WALLINS CREEK, KY
WALLIS, TX
WALLOWA, OR
WALLSBURG, UT
WALNUT, CA,IA,KS,MS
WALNUT COVE, NC
WALNUT CREEK, CA
WALNUT GROVE, CA,MN,MO,MS

PLACE INDEX

WALNUT RIDGE, AR
WALNUT SPRINGS, TX
WALNUTPORT, PA
WALPACK, NJ
WALPOLE, MA
WALSENBURG, CO
WALSH, CO
WALSTONBURG, NC
WALTERBORO, SC
WALTERS, MN,OK
WALTHAM, MA,ME,MN,VT
WALTHILL, NB
WALTHOURVILLE, GA
WALTON, IN,KS,KY,NY
WALWORTH, NY,WI
WAMAC, IL
WAMEGO, KS
WAMPUM, PA
WAMSUTTER, WY
WANAMINGO, MN
WANAQUE, NJ
WANATAH, IN
WANCHESE, NC
WANDA, MN
WANETTE, OK
WANN, OK
WANTAGH, NY
WAPAKONETA, OH
WAPANUCKA, OK
WAPATO, WA
WAPELLO, IA
WAPPINGERS FALLS, NY
WAR, WV
WARBA, MN
WARD, AR,CO,SC,SD
WARDELL, MO
WARDEN, WA
WARDENSVILLE, WV
WARDSBORO, VT
WARE, MA
WAREHAM, MA
WARETOWN, NJ
WARM SPRINGS, GA
WARMINSTER, PA
WARNER, NH,OK,SD
WARNER ROBINS, GA
WARNER SPRINGS, CA
WARR ACRES, OK
WARREN, AR,CT,IL,IN,ME
    MI,MN,NH,OH,PA,RI,VT
WARREN PARK, IN
WARRENS, WI
WARRENSBURG, IL,MO,NY
WARRENTON, GA,MO,NC,OR,VA
WARRENVILLE, IL
WARRINGTON, FL
WARROAD, MN
WARSAW, IL,IN,KY,MO
    NC,NY,VA
WARTBURG, TN
WARTRACE, TN
WARWARSING, NY
WARWICK, GA,NY,OK,RI
WASCO, CA,OR
WASECA, MN
WASHBURN, ME,MO,ND
WASHINGTON, CA,CT,DC,GA
    IA,IL,IN,KS,KY,LA,ME,MO
    NB,NC,NH,NJ,OK,PA
    TX,UT,VA,VT
WASHINGTON COURT HOUSE, OH
WASHINGTON GROVE, MD
WASHINGTONVILLE, NY
WASHOUGAL, WA
WASHTA, IA
WASHTUCNA, WA
WASILLA, AK
WASKOM, TX
WASTA, SD
WATAGA, IL
WATAUGA, TN,TX
WATCHUNG, NJ
WATER VALLEY, KY,MS

WATERBURY, CT,NB,VT
WATERFORD, CA,CT,ME
    NJ,NY,VT,WI
WATERLOO, AL,IA,IL,IN,NB
    NY,OR,SC,WI
WATERPROOF, LA
WATERTOWN, CT,MA,MN,NY
    SD,TN,WI
WATERVILLE, KS,ME
    MN,OH,VT,WA
WATERVLIET, MI,NY
WATFORD CITY, ND
WATHA, NC
WATHENA, KS
WATKINS, MN
WATKINS GLEN, NY
WATKINSVILLE, GA
WATONGA, OK
WATSEKA, IL
WATSON, AR,MN
WATSONTOWN, PA
WATSONVILLE, CA
WATTS, OK
WAUBAY, SD
WAUBUN, MN
WAUCHULA, FL
WAUCOMA, IA
WAUCONDA, IL
WAUKEE, IA
WAUKEGAN, IL
WAUKENA, CA
WAUKESHA, WI
WAUKOMIS, OK
WAUKON, IA
WAUNAKEE, WI
WAUNETA, NB
WAUPACA, WI
WAUPUN, WI
WAURIKA, OK
WAUSA, NB
WAUSAU, FL,WI
WAUSAUKEE, WI
WAUSEON, OH
WAUTOMA, WI
WAUWATOSA, WI
WAUZEKA, WI
WAVELAND, IN,MS
WAVERLY, AL,IA,IL,KS,KY
    MN,MO,NB,NY,TN,VA,WA
WAVERLY CITY, OH
WAVERLY HALL, GA
WAWONA, CA
WAXAHACHIE, TX
WAXHAW, NC
WAYCROSS, GA
WAYLAND, IA,KY,MA
    MI,MO,PA
WAYNE, IL,ME,MI,NB
    NJ,OK,WV
WAYNE CITY, IL
WAYNESBORO, GA,MS
    PA,TN,VA
WAYNESBURG, PA
WAYNESVILLE, MO,NC
WAYNETOWN, IN
WAYNOKA, OK
WAYZATA, MN
WEARE, NH
WEATHERBY LAKE, MO
WEATHERFORD, OK,TX
WEATHERLY, PA
WEAVER, AL
WEAVERVILLE, CA,NC
WEBB, AL,IA,MS
WEBB CITY, MO,OK
WEBBER, KS
WEBBERS FALLS, OK
WEBBERVILLE, MI
WEBER CITY, VA
WEBSTER, FL,IA,MA,NC
    NH,NY,SD,TX,WI
WEBSTER CITY, IA

WEBSTER GROVES, MO
WECHES, TX
WEDOWEE, AL
WEED, CA
WEEHAWKEN, NJ
WEEPING WATER, NB
WEIMAR, CA,TX
WEINER, AR
WEIR, KS,MS
WEIRTON, WV
WELAKA, FL
WELCH, OK,WV
WELCOME, MN,NC
WELD, ME
WELDON, AR,CA,NC
WELDON SPRING HEIGHTS, MO
WELEETKA, OK
WELLEFLEET, MA
WELLESLEY, MA
WELLFLEET, NB
WELLFORD, SC
WELLINGTON, CO,KS,KY,ME
    MO,TX,UT
WELLMAN, IA,TX
WELLS, MN,TX,VT
WELLS RIVER, VT
WELLSBORO, PA
WELLSBURG, IA,WV
WELLSTON, MO,OK
WELLSVILLE, KS,MO,NY,UT
WELSH, LA
WELTON, AZ,IA
WENATCHEE, WA
WENDELL, MA,MN,NC
WENDOVER, UT
WENHAM, MA
WENONA, IL
WENONAH, NJ
WENTWORTH, NH,SD
WENTZVILLE, MO
WEOTT, CA
WESLACO, TX
WESLEY, IA
WESLEYVILLE, PA
WESSINGTON, SD
WESSINGTON SPRINGS, SD
WESSON, MS
WEST, MS,TX
WEST ALLIS, WI
WEST BABYLON, NY
WEST BADEN SPRINGS, IN
WEST BATH, ME
WEST BEND, WI
WEST BLOCTON, AL
WEST BOUNTIFUL, UT
WEST BOYLSTON, MA
WEST BRANCH, IA,MI
WEST BRIDGEWATER, MA
WEST BURLINGTON, IA
WEST CALDWELL, NJ
WEST CENTRAL FRANKLIN, ME
WEST CHESTER, PA
WEST CHICAGO, IL
WEST COLLEGE CORNER, IN
WEST COLUMBIA, SC,TX
WEST CONCORD, MN,NC
WEST COVINA, CA
WEST DEPTFORD, NJ
WEST DES MOINES, IA
WEST END, CA
WEST FAIRLEE, VT
WEST FARGO, ND
WEST FORK, AR
WEST FORKS, ME
WEST FRANKFORT, IL
WEST GARDINER, ME
WEST GROVE, PA
WEST HAMLIN, WV
WEST HARRISON, IN
WEST HARTFORD, CT
WEST HAVEN, CT,VT
WEST HAVERSTRAW, NY
WEST HAZLETON, PA

WEST HOLLYWOOD, CA
WEST HOMESTEAD, PA
WEST JEFFERSON, NC
WEST JORDAN, UT
WEST KINGSTON, RI
WEST KITTANNING, PA
WEST LAFAYETTE, IN
WEST LEBANON, IN
WEST LIBERTY, IA,WV
WEST LINN, OR
WEST LOGAN, WV
WEST LONG BRANCH, NJ
WEST MARION, NC
WEST MEMPHIS, AR
WEST MIFFLIN, PA
WEST MILFORD, NJ,WV
WEST MINERAL, KS
WEST MONROE, LA
WEST NEWBURY, MA
WEST NEW YORK, NJ
WEST ORANGE, NJ
WEST PALM BEACH, FL
WEST PARIS, ME
WEST PATERSON, NJ
WEST PITTSBURG, CA
WEST PLAINS, KS,MO
WEST POINT, AR,CA,GA,IA
    KY,MS,NB,NY,UT,VA
WEST READING, PA
WEST RICHLAND, WA
WEST ROCKINGHAM, NC
WEST RUTLAND, VT
WEST SACRAMENTO, CA
WEST SALEM, OH,WI
WEST SENECA, NY
WEST SPRINGFIELD, MA
WEST STOCKBRIDGE, MA
WEST SAINT PAUL, MN
WEST TERRE HAUTE, IN
WEST TISBURY, MA
WEST UNION, IA,MN
    OH,SC,WV
WEST WARWICK, RI
WEST YELLOWSTONE, MT
WEST YORK, PA
WESTBORO, MO
WESTBOROUGH, MA
WESTBROOK, CT,ME,MN,TX
WESTBURY, NY
WESTBY, MT,WI
WESTCLIFFE, CO
WESTERLY, RI
WESTERN, NB
WESTERN GROVE, AR
WESTERN SPRINGS, IL
WESTFIELD, IA,IN,MA,ME
    NJ,NY,PA,VT,WI
WESTFIR, OR
WESTFORD, MA,VT
WESTGATE, IA
WESTHAMPTON BEACH, NY
WESTLAKE, LA
WESTLAND, MI
WESTMANLAND, ME
WESTMINSTER, CA,CO
    MA,SC,VT
WESTMONT, IL,PA
WESTMORE, VT
WESTMORELAND, CA,KS,NY,TN
WESTON, AL,CT,MA,ME,MO
    NB,OH,OR,WV
WESTOVER, WV
WESTPHALIA, KS,MI,MO
WESTPORT, CA,CT,IN,MA
    MN,SD,WA
WESTSIDE, IA
WESTVILLE, FL,IL,IN,NJ,OK
WESTWEGO, LA
WESTWOOD, CA,KS,MA,NJ
WETHERSFIELD, CT
WETMORE, KS
WETUMKA, OK
WETUMPKA, AL

WEWAHITCHKA, FL
WEWOKA, OK
WEYAUWEGA, WI
WEYBRIDGE, VT
WEYERHAUSER, WI
WEYMOUTH, MA
WHALAN, MN
WHARTON, NJ,TX
WHAT CHEER, IA
WHATELY, MA
WHEAT RIDGE, CO
WHEATCROFT, KY
WHEATFIELD, IN
WHEATLAND, CA,IA,IN
    MO,PA,WY
WHEATON, IL,MN,MO
WHEELER, OR,TX,WI
WHEELER RIDGE, CA
WHEELING, IL,WV
WHEELOCK, VT
WHEELWRIGHT, KY
WHELEN SPRINGS, AR
WHIGHAM, GA
WHIPPANY, NJ
WHISKEYTOWN, CA
WHISPERING PINES, NC
WHITAKERS, NC
WHITE, GA,SD
WHITE BEAR LAKE, MN
WHITE BLUFF, TN
WHITE CASTLE, LA
WHITE CITY, FL,KS
WHITE CLOUD, KS,MI
WHITE DEER, TX
WHITE HALL, AR
WHITE LAKE, NC,SD,WI
WHITE MOUNTAIN, AK
WHITE OAK, PA
WHITE PIGEON, MI
WHITE PINE, TN
WHITE PINES, CA
WHITE PLAINS, GA,KY,NY
WHITE RIVER, SD
WHITE ROCK, SD
WHITE SALMON, WA
WHITE SETTLEMENT, TX
WHITE SPRINGS, FL
WHITE STONE, VA
WHITE SULPHUR
    SPRINGS, MT,WV
WHITE WATER, CA
WHITEFACE, TX
WHITEFIELD, ME,NH,OK
WHITEFISH, MT
WHITEFISH BAY, WI
WHITEHALL, IL,MI,MT,NY
    OH,PA,WI
WHITEHOUSE, OH
WHITELAND, IN
WHITELAW, WI
WHITEMARSH, PA
WHITESBORO, NY,TX
WHITESBURG, KY
WHITESTOWN, IN
WHITESVILLE, KY
WHITEVILLE, NC,TN
WHITEWATER, IN,KS,MO,WI
WHITEWOOD, SD
WHITEWRIGHT, TX
WHITING, IA,IN,KS,ME,VT
WHITINGHAM, VT
WHITINSVILLE, MA
WHITMAN, MA
WHITMIRE, SC
WHITNEY, ME,NB,TX
WHITNEYVILLE, ME
WHITTEMORE, IA,MI
WHITTIER, AK,CA
WHITWELL, TN
WIBAUX, MT
WICHITA, KS
WICHITA FALLS, TX
WICKENBURG, AZ

WICKES, AR
WICKLIFFE, KY,OH
WIGGINS, CO,MS
WILBER, NB
WILBRAHAM, MA
WILBUR, WA
WILBURTON, OK
WILCOX, AZ,NB
WILD ROSE, WI
WILDER, KY,MN
WILDOMAR, CA
WILDWOOD, FL,KY,NJ
WILDWOOD CREST, NJ
WILEY, CO
WILKES-BARRE, PA
WILKESBORO, NC
WILKESON, WA
WILKINSBURG, PA
WILKINSON, IN
WILLACOOCHEE, GA
WILLARD, MO,NM,OH
WILLERNIE, MN
WILLIAMS, AZ,CA,IA,MN,SC
WILLIAMS BAY, WI
WILLIAMS CREEK, IN
WILLIAMSBORO, NC
WILLIAMSBURG, CO,IA,KS
    KY,MA,NM,OH,PA,VA
WILLIAMSON, GA,IA,NY,WV
WILLIAMSPORT, IN,PA
WILLIAMSTON, MI,NC,SC
WILLIAMSTOWN, KY,MA
    NJ,VT,WV
WILLIAMSVILLE, IL,MO
WILLIFORD, AR
WILLIMANTIC, CT,ME
WILLINGBORO, NJ
WILLINTON, CT
WILLIS, KS
WILLISTON, ND,SC,VT
WILLISTON PARK, NY
WILLISVILLE, AR
WILLITS, CA
WILLOUGHBY, OH
WILLOW, OK
WILLOW GROVE, PA
WILLOW LAKE, SD
WILLOW RIVER, MN
WILLOW SPRINGS, MO
WILLOWICK, OH
WILLOWS, CA
WILLOWSPRINGS, IL
WILLS POINT, TX
WILLSBORO, NY
WILMAR, MN
WILMER, AL
WILMERDING, PA
WILMETTE, IL
WILMINGTON, CA,DE,IL
    MA,NC,OH,VT
WILMONT, MN
WILMORE, KS,KY
WILMOT, AR,NH,SD
WILSEY, KS
WILSEYVILLE, CA
WILSON, AR,KS,LA,NC
    OK,PA,TX
WILSON CREEK, WA
WILSONIA, CA
WILSONVILLE, AL,NB,OR
WILTON, AL,AR,CT,ME,MN
    ND,NH,NY,WI
WILTON MANORS, FL
WINAMAC, IN
WINBERLY, TX
WINCHEDON, MA
WINCHESTER, AR,CA,CT,IL
    IN,KS,KY,MA,MO,OH,TN,VA
WIND GAP, PA
WINDBER, PA
WINDEMERE, NC
WINDER, GA
WINDERMERE, FL

WINDFALL CITY, IN
WINDHAM, CT,ME,NH,NY,VT
WINDOM, KS,MN,TX
WINDSOR, CA,CO,CT,MA,ME
    MO,NC,NJ,NY,PA,SC,VA
WINDSOR LOCKS, CT
WINDTHORST, TX
WINFALL, NC
WINFIELD, AL,IA,IL,MO,TX
WINFRED, SD
WINGATE, IN,NC
WINGER, MN
WINHALL, VT
WINIFRED, MT
WINK, TX
WINKELMAN, AZ
WINLOCK, WA
WINN, ME
WINNEBAGO, IL,MN,NB
WINNECONNE, WI
WINNEMUCCA, NV
WINNER, SD
WINNETKA, IL
WINNETOON, NB
WINNFIELD, LA
WINNSBORO, LA,SC,TX
WINONA, KS,MN,MO,MS,TX
WINONA LAKE, IN
WINOOSK, VT
WINSIDE, NB
WINSLOW, AR,AZ,IN,ME
    NB,NJ,WA
WINSTED, MN
WINSTON, MO,OR
WINSTON-SALEM, NC
WINTER, WI
WINTER GARDENS, CA
WINTER GARDEN, FL
WINTER HARBOR, ME
WINTER HAVEN, FL
WINTER PARK, CO,FL,NC
WINTER SPRINGS, FL
WINTERPORT, ME
WINTERS, CA,TX
WINTERSET, IA
WINTERVILLE, GA,ME,NC
WINTHROP, AR,IA,MA
    ME,MN,WA
WINTHROP HARBOR, IL
WINTON, CA,MN,NC
WIOTA, IA
WISCASSET, ME
WISCONSIN DELLS, WI
WISCONSIN RAPIDS, WI
WISE, VA
WISHEK, ND
WISNER, NB
WITHEE, WI
WITT, IL
WITTENBERG, WI
WIXOM, MI
WOBURN, MA
WOLBACH, NB
WOLCOTT, CT,IN,NY,VT
WOLF LAKE, MN
WOLFE CITY, TX
WOLFFORTH, TX
WOLSEY, SD
WOLVERINE, MI
WOLVERINE LAKE, MI
WOLVERTON, MN
WOMELSDORF, PA
WONEWOC, WI
WOOD, SD
WOOD DALE, IL
WOOD LAKE, MN,NB
WOOD RIVER, IL,NB
WOOD-RIDGE, NJ
WOOD VILLAGE, OR
WOODBINE, GA,IA,KS,NJ
WOODBRIDGE, CA,CT,NJ
WOODBURN, IA,IN,OR
WOODBURY, CT,GA,MN
    NJ,TN,VT

WOODCLIFF LAKE, NJ
WOODFIN, NC
WOODFORD, VT
WOODHAVEN, MI
WOODLAKE, CA
WOODLAND, AL,CA,GA
    ME,MI,MN
WOODLAND HILLS, CA,KY
WOODLAND MILLS, TN
WOODLAWN HEIGHTS, IN
WOODLAWN PARK, KY,OK
WOODLYNNE, NJ
WOODMAN, WI
WOODRUFF, SC
WOODS CROSS, UT
WOODSBORO, TX
WOODSFIELD, OH
WOODSIDE, CA,DE
WOODSON, TX
WOODSTOCK, CT,GA,IL,ME
    MN,NH,NY,VA,VT
WOODSTON, KS
WOODSTOWN, NJ
WOODVILLE, ME,MS,OH
    OK,TX,WI
WOODWARD, IA,OK
WOOLWICH, ME
WOONSOCKET, RI,SD
WOOSTER, AR,OH
WORCESTER, MA,VT
WORDEN, IL
WORLAND, WY
WORMLEYSBURG, PA
WORTH, IL,MO
WORTHAM, TX
WORTHINGTON, IA,IN,MN,OH
WORTHINGTON SPRINGS, FL
WRANGELL, AK
WRENSHALL, MN
WRIGHT, MN
WRIGHT CITY, MO,OK
WRIGHTSTOWN, NJ,WI
WRIGHTWOOD, CA
WURTSBORO, NY
WYACONDA, MO
WYANDOTTE, MI,OK
WYANET, IL
WYATT, MO
WYCKOFF, NJ
WYEVILLE, WI
WYKOFF, MN
WYLIE, TX
WYMAN, ME
WYMORE, NB
WYNDMERE, ND
WYNETTEDALE, IN
WYNNE, AR
WYNNEWOOD, OK
WYNOT, NB
WYOCENA, WI
WYOMING, DE,IA,IL,MI
    MN,NY,OH,PA
WYOMISSING, PA
WYTHEVILLE, VA

XENIA, OH

YACOLT, WA
YADKINVILLE, NC
YAKIMA, WA
YAKUTAT, AK
YALE, IA, MI
YAMHILL, OR
YANCEYVILLE, NC
YANKEETOWN, FL
YANKTON, SD
YANTIS, TX
YARD, TX
YARMOUTH, MA,ME
YATES CENTER, KS
YATES CITY, IL
YAZOO, MS
YEADON, PA
YEEHAW, FL
YELLOW SPRINGS, OH

PLACE INDEX

YEOMAN, IN
YERINGTON, NV
YOAKUM, TX
YODER, WY
YOLO, CA
YONCALLA, OR
YONKERS, NY
YORBA LINDA, CA
YORK, NB,NY,PA,SC
YORKSHIRE, NY
YORKTOWN, IA,IN,TX
YORKVILLE, IL,OH,TN
YOUNG AMERICA, MN
YOUNGSTOWN, NY,OH
YOUNGSVILLE, LA,PA
YOUNGTOWN, AZ
YOUNGWOOD, PA
YOUNTVILLE, CA
YPSILANTI, MI
YREKA, CA
YUBA, WI
YUBA CITY, CA
YUCCA VALLEY, CA
YUKON, OK
YULEE, FL

YUMA, AZ
YUTAN, NB

ZACHARY, LA
ZALMA, MO
ZANESVILLE, OH
ZAPATA, TX
ZAVALLA, TX
ZEARING, IA
ZEELAND, MI
ZELIENOPLE, PA
ZENDA, KS
ZENIA, CA
ZEPHYRHILLS, FL
ZILWAUKEE, MI
ZIMMERMAN, MN
ZION, IL
ZIONSVILLE, IN
ZOAR, OH
ZOLFO SPRINGS, FL
ZUMBROTA, MN
ZUMBRO FALLS, MN
ZURICH, KS
ZWINGLE, IA
ZWOLLE, LA